October 19-23, 2015
Melbourne, Australia

AF764911

Association for Computing Machinery

Advancing Computing as a Science & Profession

CIKM'15

Proceedings of the 24th ACM International Conference on Information and Knowledge Management

Sponsored by:

ACM SIGIR and ACM SIGWEB

Supported by:

Microsoft Research, Sportsbet, Google, City of Melbourne, Professor Ram Kumar Memorial Foundation, Yahoo! Labs, Deakin University, RMIT University, and The University of Melbourne

Association for
Computing Machinery

Advancing Computing as a Science & Profession

The Association for Computing Machinery
2 Penn Plaza, Suite 701
New York, New York 10121-0701

Copyright © 2015 by the Association for Computing Machinery, Inc. (ACM). Permission to make digital or hard copies of portions of this work for personal or classroom use is granted without fee provided that copies are not made or distributed for profit or commercial advantage and that copies bear this notice and the full citation on the first page. Copyright for components of this work owned by others than ACM must be honored. Abstracting with credit is permitted. To copy otherwise, to republish, to post on servers or to redistribute to lists, requires prior specific permission and/or a fee. Request permission to republish from: permissions@acm.org or Fax +1 (212) 869-0481.

For other copying of articles that carry a code at the bottom of the first or last page, copying is permitted provided that the per-copy fee indicated in the code is paid through www.copyright.com.

Notice to Past Authors of ACM-Published Articles
ACM intends to create a complete electronic archive of all articles and/or other material previously published by ACM. If you have written a work that has been previously published by ACM in any journal or conference proceedings prior to 1978, or any SIG Newsletter at any time, and you do NOT want this work to appear in the ACM Digital Library, please inform permissions@acm.org, stating the title of the work, the author(s), and where and when published.

ISBN: 978-1-4503-3794-6 (Digital)

ISBN: 978-1-4503-4117-2 (Print)

Additional copies may be ordered prepaid from:

ACM Order Department
PO Box 30777
New York, NY 10087-0777, USA

Phone: 1-800-342-6626 (USA and Canada)
+1-212-626-0500 (Global)
Fax: +1-212-944-1318
E-mail: acmhelp@acm.org
Hours of Operation: 8:30 am – 4:30 pm ET

Printed in the USA

General Chairs' Preface

It is our great pleasure to welcome you to the 24th ACM International Conference on Information and Knowledge Management (CIKM 2015). CIKM is a top-tier ACM conference in the areas of databases, information retrieval, and knowledge management. It has successfully brought together leading researchers and developers from these three communities since 1992, with the purpose of identifying challenging problems facing the development of advanced knowledge and information systems, and shaping future research directions through the publication of high-quality applied and theoretical research findings. The 24th edition of CIKM continues this tradition, placing particular emphasis on the utility of data science across structured and semi-structured data.

We are delighted to present three outstanding keynote speakers: Jaime Teevan, from Microsoft; Andrew Tomkins, from Google; and Xiaofang Zhou, from the University of Queensland. We are also honored to host six distinguished invited speakers for the conference's Industry Track: Hang Li (Huawei Noah's Ark), Wei-Ying Ma (Microsoft Research Asia), Sofus A. Macskassy (Facebook), Igor Perisic (LinkedIn), Amy Shi-Nash (SingTel DataSpark), and Andrew Tomkins (Google).

We are indebted to the many authors who submitted their work to the CIKM technical program, and to the team of people who evaluated them. The Program Committee was expertly led by six PC Chairs: Timos Sellis and Jeffrey Xu Yu (Database Track); Maarten de Rijke and Vanessa Murdock (Information Retrieval Track); and Charu Aggarwal and Ravi Kumar (Knowledge Management Track). The review process was supported by the Microsoft CMT system. A report on the paper selection process appears in the PC Chairs' Preface.

We also thank the other chairs in the organization team: Shonali Krishnaswamy and Marc Najork (Industry Track); Wei Wang and Grace Hui Yang (Tutorials); Shane Culpepper and Chee Yong Chan (Workshops); and Yun Sing Koh (Publicity). CIKM 2015 includes a machine learning competition, sponsored by Sportsbet, with participants tackling the challenge of predicting the outcomes of the Australian Rules Football Finals. A substantial prize will be awarded to the best-performing system on the third day of the conference.

Running a conference the scale of CIKM is a serious undertaking and we are grateful to our local organization team for their effective and efficient handling of logistics. In particular, the Local Arrangements Chairs Tony Wirth and Rui Zhang provided extensive support, as did the team of student volunteers that Tony and Rui helped recruit and manage.

We gratefully acknowledge the support of our sponsors for the conference: Microsoft as Gold Sponsor; Sportsbet as Silver Sponsor; Google, The City of Melbourne, The Professor Ram Kumar Memorial Foundation, and Yahoo Labs, as Bronze sponsors; and The University of Melbourne, RMIT University, and Deakin University, as Academic Sponsors. We also received support from the CIKM Steering Committee, and from the Association for Computing Machinery and their special interest groups SIGIR and SIGWEB.

ICMS Australasia provided expert assistance with the logistics of the event, and we thank them for their professional advice and guidance. We also benefited greatly from the support provided by the Melbourne Convention Bureau during the early stages of our planning; and from the knowledge and skills of the many expert staff at the Melbourne Convention and Exhibition Center, the venue for CIKM 2015.

We trust that you enjoy the conference, and also the other activities you are able to fit in during your visit to Melbourne. Indeed, there are many things to see and enjoy in Victoria and in the whole Australasian region at this time of year, and we hope that you will be able to combine business and pleasure in to a memorable experience while you are here. Finally, CIKM 2016 will be in Indianapolis, in the USA, and we hope to see you again there.

James Bailey and Alistair Moffat
The University of Melbourne

August 2015.

CIKM2015
19–23 October 2015 Melbourne Australia

PC Chairs' Preface

We are delighted to welcome you to the 24th ACM International Conference on Information and Knowledge Management (CIKM 2015), held in Melbourne from October 19–23, 2015. CIKM is now well-established as a leading venue for bringing together researchers from across the Database, Information Retrieval, and Knowledge Management communities.

Continuing the pattern of previous years, we received a large number of high-quality submissions in all three tracks, in both full- and short-paper categories. As a result, we are confident that CIKM 2015 has succeeded in creating an outstanding technical program including research paper presentations; short-paper presentations during the poster session; plenary talks; and an engaging Industry Track arranged by the Industry Track Chairs. In total, we received 646 full-paper (10-page) submissions and 276 short-paper (4-page) submissions, which were reviewed and discussed by 88 area chairs, 471 program committee members, and a further 145 expert external reviewers.

We accepted 165 full papers (26%) and 69 short papers (25%). The acceptance statistics per track were as follows: Databases, 35/129 full papers and 6/37 short papers; Information Retrieval, 43/171 full papers and 27/101 short papers; and Knowledge Management, 87/346 papers and 36/138 short papers. Two of the Knowledge Management short papers were withdrawn by their authors prior to the proceedings being finalized. Our work was greatly eased by the support provided by the Microsoft CMT service, and we thank the CMT team for their assistance.

We are grateful to the many people who helped with the process of bringing this program together. We would in particular like to recognize the immense efforts of the area chairs, program committee members, and external reviewers, who each volunteered many hours of time, and contributed their deep expertise in order to allow the selection of the work that you can see in this volume. Most importantly of all, we thank the authors who submitted contributions for consideration. Without the drive and energy of the several thousand researchers and students who prepared manuscripts and carried out evaluations, the conference would be doomed to failure; but with that drive and energy, we have been able to achieve the success that you see here. We hope that participants in the conference in Melbourne, as well as subsequent readers of the proceedings, will find the technical program of CIKM 2015 to be both inspiring and rewarding.

Charu C. Aggarwal, IBM
Maarten de Rijke, University of Amsterdam
Ravi Kumar, Google
Vanessa Murdock, Microsoft
Timos Sellis, RMIT University
Jeffrey Xu Yu, Chinese University of Hong Kong

August 2015.

CIKM2015
19–23 October 2015 Melbourne Australia

Table of Contents

Session 1D: Text Processing

Session Chair: Tim Baldwin *(The University of Melbourne)*

Session 1E: Applications

Session Chair: Huizhi (Elly) Liang *(The University of Melbourne)*

Session 1F: Social Media 1

Session Chair: Lynda Tamine *(IRIT/CNRS France)*

Session 2A: Graphs

Session Chair: Sourav S. Bhowmick *(Nanyang Technological University)*

Session 2B: Retrieval Algorithms

Session Chair: Guido Zuccon *(Queensland University of Technology)*

Session 2C: Text Analysis

Session Chair: Krisztian Balog *(University Of Stavanger)*

Session 2D: Clustering

Session Chair: Ravi Kumar *(Google)*

Session 2E: Users and Predictions

Session Chair: James Caverlee *(Texas A&M University)*

Session 2F: Heterogeneous Networks

Session Chair: Michael Quan Z. Sheng *(The University of Adelaide)*

Session 3A: Veracity

Session Chair: Laure Berti-Équille *(Qatar Computing Research Institute)*

Keynote Address II

Session Chair: James Bailey *(The University of Melbourne)*

Session 4A: Location-Based Services

Session Chair: Timos Sellis *(RMIT University)*

Session 4B: Query Explanation

Session Chair: Sebastian Link *(The University of Auckland)*

Session 4C: Crowds

Session Chair: Falk Scholer *(RMIT University)*

Session 4D: Optimization

Session Chair: Xuan Vinh Nguyen *(The University of Melbourne)*

Session 4E: Social Networks 2

Session Chair: Hongzhi Yin *(The University of Queensland)*

Session 4F: Matrix Factorization

Session Chair: Jeffrey Chan *(RMIT University)*

Session 5A: Trips and Trajectories

Session Chair: Iadh Ounis *(University of Glasgow)*

Session 5B: Retrieval Enhancements 1

Session Chair: J. Shane Culpepper *(RMIT University)*

Session 5C: Privacy

Session Chair: James Thom *(RMIT University)*

Session 5D: Data Streams

Session Chair: Anthony Wirth *(The University of Melbourne)*

Session 5E: Classification 2

Session Chair: Ping Luo *(Chinese Academy of Sciences)*

Session 5F: Sentiment and Content Analysis

Session Chair: Ke Deng *(RMIT University)*

Session 6A: Time Series and Streams

Session Chair: Jenny Xuizhen Zhang *(RMIT University)*

Session 6B: Adaptive Learning

Session Chair: Damiano Spina *(RMIT University)*

Session 6C: Points-of-Interest

Session Chair: Egemen Tanin *(The University of Melbourne)*

Session 6D: Matrices

Session Chair: Weidong Cai *(The University of Sydney)*

Session 6E: Citation Networks

Session Chair: Zhifeng Bao *(RMIT University)*

Session 6F: Knowledge Bases

Session Chair: Vanessa Murdock *(Microsoft)*

Keynote Address III

Session Chair: Shonali Krishnaswamy *(Institute for Infocomm Research)*

Session 7A: Database Optimization

Session Chair: Sven Helmer *(Free University of Bozen-Bolzano)*

Session 7B: Retrieval Enhancements 2

Session Chair: Mark Sanderson *(RMIT University)*

Session 7C: Search Mechanisms

Session Chair: Justin Zobel *(The University of Melbourne)*

Session 7D: Social Networks 3

Session Chair: Carsten Eickhoff *(ETH Zurich)*

Session 8A: Query Evaluation

Session Chair: Yiqun Liu *(Tsinghua University)*

Session 8B: Web Search

Session Chair: David Hawking *(Microsoft)*

Session 8C: Social Media 2

Session Chair: Karin Verspoor *(The University of Melbourne)*

Session 8D: Recommendation

Session Chair: Gangshan Wu *(Nanjing University)*

Short Papers: Databases

Short Papers: Information Retrieval

Short Papers: Knowledge Management

Workshop Reports

Conference Organization

General Chairs
James Bailey (*The University of Melbourne*)
Alistair Moffat (*The University of Melbourne*)

Program Committee Chairs
Charu C. Aggarwal (*IBM*)
Maarten de Rijke (*University of Amsterdam*)
Ravi Kumar (*Google*)
Vanessa Murdock (*Microsoft*)
Timos Sellis (*RMIT University*)
Jeffrey Xu Yu (*Chinese University of Hong Kong*)

Industry Track Chairs
Shonali Krishnaswamy (*Institute for Infocomm Research*)
Marc Najork (*Google*)

Tutorial Chairs
Wei Wang (*University of New South Wales*)
Grace Hui Yang (*Georgetown University*)

Workshop Chairs
Chee Yong Chan (*National University of Singapore*)
Shane Culpepper (*RMIT University*)

Local Arrangements Chairs
Tony Wirth (*The University of Melbourne*)
Rui Zhang (*The University of Melbourne*)

Publicity Chair
Yin Sing Koh (*The University of Auckland*)

Best Papers Chair
Ramamohanarao Kotagiri (*The University of Melbourne*)

Principal Conference Organizers
ICMS Australasia (`http://icmsaust.com.au`)

Program Committee and Referees

Database Track Senior Program Committee Members

Klaus Berberich (*Max Planck Institut*)
Selcuk Candan (*Arizona State U.*)
Lei Chen (*Hong Kong U. Sc. Tech.*)
Minos Garofalakis (*Tech. U. Crete*)
Wook-Shin Han (*PosTech*)
Nick Koudas (*U. Toronto*)
Laks Lakshmanan (*U. British Columbia*)
Huan Liu (*Arizona State U.*)
Vivek Narasayya (*Microsoft Research*)
Tamer Ozsu (*U. Waterloo*)
Kian-Lee Tan (*National U. Singapore*)
Yufei Tao (*Chinese U. Hong Kong*)
X. Sean Wang (*Fudan U.*)
Jun Yang (*Duke U.*)
Haruo Yokota (*Tokyo Institute Tech.*)
Wenjie Zhang (*U. New South Wales*)
Xiaofang Zhou (*U. Queensland*)

Information Retrieval Track Senior Program Committee Members

Eugene Agichtein (*Emory U.*)
James Allan (*U. Massachusetts Amherst*)
Omar Alonso (*Microsoft*)
Jaime Arguello (*U. North Carolina*)
Javed Aslam (*Northeastern U.*)
Leif Azzopardi (*U. Glasgow*)
Peter Bailey (*Microsoft*)
Krisztian Balog (*U. Stavanger*)
Michael Bendersky (*Google*)
Klaus Berberich (*Max Planck Institut*)
Roi Blanco (*Yahoo Labs*)
Jamie Callan (*Carnegie Mellon U.*)
David Carmel (*Yahoo Labs*)
Ben Carterette (*U. Delaware*)
Carlos Castillo (*QCRI*)
James Caverlee (*Texas A&M U.*)
Charles L.A. Clarke (*U. Waterloo*)
Nick Craswell (*Microsoft*)
Fabio Crestani (*U. Lugano*)
Bruce Croft (*U. Massachusetts Amherst*)
Shane Culpepper (*RMIT U.*)
Brian Davison (*Lehigh U.*)
Franciska de Jong (*U. Twente*)
Gianluca Demartini (*U. Sheffield*)
Fernando Diaz (*Microsoft*)
Debora Donato (*StumbleUpon*)
Shlomo Geva (*Queensland U. Tech.*)
Aristides Gionis (*Aalto U.*)
Claudia Hauff (*TU Delft*)
Ben He (*Chinese Academy Sc.*)
Qi He (*LinkedIn*)
Hideo Joho (*U. Tsukuba*)
Gareth Jones (*Dublin City U.*)
Jaap Kamps (*U. Amsterdam*)
Evangelos Kanoulas (*U. Amsterdam*)
Jussi Karlgren (*Gavagai & KTH*)
Gabriella Kazai (*Lumi*)
Diane Kelly (*U. North Carolina Chapel Hill*)
Oren Kurland (*Technion*)
Mounia Lalmas (*Yahoo Labs*)
Matthew Lease (*U. Texas Austin*)
Yoelle Maarek (*Yahoo Labs*)
Craig Macdonald (*U. Glasgow*)
Donald Metzler (*Google*)
Gonzalo Navarro (*U. Chile*)
Filip Radlinski (*Microsoft*)
Tetsuya Sakai (*Waseda U.*)
Mark Sanderson (*RMIT U.*)
Pavel Serdyukov (*Yandex*)
Ian Soboroff (*NIST*)
Ryen W. White (*Microsoft*)
Emine Yilmaz (*U. College London*)

Knowledge Management Track Senior Program Committee Members

Deepak Agarwal (*LinkedIn*)
Diego Calvanese (*Free U. Bozen-Bolzano*)
Anirban Dasgupta (*IIT Gandhinagar*)
Evgeniy Gabrilovich (*Google*)
Sreenivas Gollapudi (*Google*)
Murat Kantarcioglu (*U. Texas Dallas*)
Yan Liu (*USC*)
Nikos Mamoulis (*U. Hong Kong*)
Qiaozhu Mei (*U. Michigan*)
Wen-Chih Peng (*NTU*)
B. Aditya Prakash (*Virginia Tech.*)
Kunal Punera (*Bento Labs*)
Guojun Qi (*U. Central Florida*)
Sujith Ravi (*Google*)
Chandan Reddy (*Wayne State U.*)
Joerg Sander (*U. Alberta*)
Jimeng Sun (*Georgia Tech*)
Evimaria Terzi (*Boston U.*)
Hanghang Tong (*City U. New York*)
Wei Wang (*UCLA*)

Database Track Program Committee Members

Ashraf Aboulnaga (*QCRI*)
Periklis Andritsos (*U. Toronto*)
Walid Aref (*Purdue U.*)
Spiros Bakiras (*City U. New York*)
Zhifeng Bao (*RMIT U.*)
Spyros Blanas (*Ohio State U.*)
Panagiotis Bouros (*HU-Berlin*)
Bogdan Cautis (*U. Paris-Sud*)
Lijun Chang (*U. New South Wales*)
Muhammad Cheema (*Monash U.*)
Hong Cheng (*Chinese U. Hong Kong*)
Reynold Cheng (*U. Hong Kong*)
Gao Cong (*Nanyang Tech. U.*)
Alfredo Cuzzocrea (*ICAR-CNR & U. Calabria*)
Ke Deng (*RMIT U.*)
Prasad Deshpande (*IBM India*)
Gill Dobbie (*U. Auckland*)
Josep Domingo-Ferrer (*U. Rovira i Virgili*)
Markus Endres (*U. Augsburg*)
Csilla Farkas (*U. South Carolina*)
Ada Fu (*Chinese U. Hong Kong*)
Ariel Fuxman (*Google*)
Floris Geerts (*U. Antwerp*)
Dimitrios Gunopulos (*U. Athens*)
Yeye He (*Microsoft Research*)
Seung-won Hwang (*PosTech*)
Stratos Idreos (*Harvard U.*)
Yoshiharu Ishikawa (*Nagoya U.*)
Mizuho Iwaihara (*Waseda U.*)
Lili Jiang (*Max Planck Institut*)
Anastasios Kementsietsidis (*Google*)
Yannis Kotidis (*AUEB Greece*)
Julien Leblay (*AIST*)
Justin Levandoski (*Microsoft Research*)
Chengkai Li (*U. Texas Arlington*)
Guoliang Li (*Tsinghua U.*)
Chengfei Liu (*Swinburne U. Tech.*)
Mengchi Liu (*Carleton U.*)
Lei Liu (*HP Labs*)
Hua Lu (*Aalborg U.*)
Jiebo Luo (*U. Rochester*)
Balaji Palanisamy (*U. Pittsburgh*)
Ippokratis Pandis (*Cloudera*)
Stavros Papadopoulos (*Intel and MIT*)
Milan Petkovic (*Eindhoven U. Tech.*)
Weining Qian (*East China Normal U.*)
Lu Qin (*UTS*)
Matthias Renz (*U. Munich*)
Senjuti Roy (*U. Washington Tacoma*)
Pierangela Samarati (*U. Milan*)
Rusty Sears (*Pure Storage*)
Mohamed Sharaf (*U. Queensland*)
Fabian Suchanek (*Télécom ParisTech U.*)
Dimitri Theodoratos (*New Jersey Inst. Tech.*)
Yannis Theodoridis (*U. Piraeus*)
Aibo Tian (*LinkedIn*)
Pinar Tozun (*IBM Almaden*)
Goce Trajcevski (*Northwestern U.*)
Stratis Viglas (*U. Edinburgh*)
Chi Wang (*Microsoft*)
Jianyong Wang (*Tsinghua U.*)
Wei Wang (*U. New South Wales*)
Raymond Chi-Wing Wong (*Hong Kong U. Sc. Tech.*)
Yinghui Wu (*UCSB*)
Xiaokui Xiao (*Nanyang Tech. U.*)
Yanghua Xiao (*Fudan U.*)
De-Nian Yang (*Academia Sinica*)

Xiaochun Yang (*Northeastern U.*)
Mi-Yen Yeh (*Academia Sinica*)
Man Lung Yiu (*Hong Kong Polytechnic U.*)
Hwanjo Yu (*Pohang U. Sc. Tech.*)
Ji Zhang (*U. Southern Queensland*)
Ying Zhang (*UTS*)
Kevin Zheng (*U. Queensland*)
Yongluan Zhou (*U. Southern Denmark*)
Lei Zou (*Peking U.*)

Information Retrieval Track Program Committee Members

Pal Aditya (*IBM*)
Dirk Ahlers (*NTNU*)
M-Dyaa Albakour (*U. Glasgow*)
Ismail Altingovde (*Middle East Tech. U.*)
Gianni Amati (*Fondazione Ugo Bordoni*)
Linda Andersson (*Vienna U. Tech.*)
Akash Anil (*IIT Guwahati*)
Avi Arampatzis (*Democritus U. Thrace*)
Ioannis Arapakis (*Yahoo Labs*)
Olga Arkhipova (*Yandex*)
Diego Arroyuelo (*U. Técn. Federico Santa María*)
Paul Baecke (*Microsoft Research Cambridge*)
Niranjan Balasubramanian (*U. Washington*)
Andras Benczur (*Hungarian Acad. Sc.*)
Bodo Billerbeck (*Microsoft*)
Ilaria Bordino (*Yahoo Labs*)
Gloria Bordogna (*CNR Italy*)
Pavel Braslavski (*Ural Federal U.*)
Marc Bron (*Yahoo Labs*)
Eric Brown (*IBM Research*)
Fei Cai (*U. Amsterdam*)
Rui Cai (*Microsoft Research*)
B. Barla Cambazoglu (*Yahoo Labs*)
Bin Cao (*Microsoft Research Asia*)
Mark Carman (*Monash U.*)
Marc-Allen Cartright (*Google*)
Pablo Castells (*U. Autónoma Madrid*)
Suleyman Cetintas (*Yahoo Labs*)
Sunandan Chakraborty (*New York U.*)
Praveen Chandar (*U. Delaware*)
Yi Chang (*Yahoo Labs*)
Francine Chen (*FX Palo Alto Laboratory*)
Lin Chen (*U. Illinois Chicago*)
Wei Chen (*Microsoft Research*)
Aleksandr Chuklin (*U. Amsterdam*)
Francisco Claude (*U. Diego Portales*)
Paul Clough (*U. Sheffield*)
Michael Cole (*Rutgers U.*)
Gordon V. Cormack (*U. Waterloo*)
Peng Cui (*Tsinghua U.*)
Ronan Cummins (*U. Greenwich*)
Sally Jo Cunningham (*U. Waikato*)
Mahashweta Das (*HP Labs*)
Gianmarco De Francisci Morales (*Yahoo Labs*)
Alexey Drutsa (*Yandex*)
Sergio Duarte (*U. Twente*)
Thanh Tran Duc (*San Jose State U.*)
Sourav Dutta (*Max Planck Institut*)
Carsten Eickhoff (*ETH Zurich*)
Andrea Esuli (*ISTI-CNR*)
Henry Feild (*Endicott College*)
Dan Feldman (*MIT*)
Nicola Ferro (*U. Padova*)
Luanne Freund (*U. British Columbia*)
Ingo Frommholz (*U. Bedfordshire*)
Bin Gao (*Microsoft Research Asia*)
Judith Gelernter (*Carnegie Mellon U.*)
Lorraine Goeuriot ()
Simon Gog (*Karlsruhe Inst. Tech.*)
Marcos Goncalves (*UFMG*)
Julio Gonzalo (*UNED*)
David Graus (*U. Amsterdam*)
Artem Grotov (*U. Amsterdam*)
Fan Guo (*Carnegie Mellon U.*)
Qi Guo (*Microsoft*)
Manish Gupta (*Microsoft*)
Gleb Gusev (*Yandex*)
Ido Guy (*Yahoo Labs*)
Martin Halvey (*U. Strathclyde*)
Donna Harman (*NIST*)
Jiyin He (*CWI*)
Bruce Hedin (*H5*)
Tomi Heimonen (*U. Tampere*)
Katja Hofmann (*Microsoft*)
Frank Hopfgartner (*U. Glasgow*)
Winston Hsu (*National Taiwan U.*)
Samuel Huston (*U. Massachusetts Amherst*)
Ichiro Ide (*Nagoya U.*)
Adam Jatowt (*Kyoto U.*)
Jiepu Jiang (*U. Massachussetts*)
Noriko Kando (*National Institute of Informatics*)
Nattiya Kanhabua (*L3S Research Center*)

Sarvnaz Karimi (*CSIRO*)
Mostafa Keikha (*U. Massachusetts Amherst*)
Liadh Kelly (*Trinity College Dublin*)
Tom Kenter (*U. Amsterdam*)
Sadegh Kharazmi (*RMIT U.*)
Eugene Kharitonov (*Yandex*)
Yubin Kim (*Carnegie Mellon U.*)
Akisato Kimura (*NTT Japan*)
Irwin King (*Chinese U. Hong Kong*)
Julia Kiseleva (*Eindhoven U. Tech.*)
Pranam Kolari (*Walmart Labs*)
Bevan Koopman (*CSIRO*)
Yehuda Koren (*Google*)
Udo Kruschwitz (*U. Essex*)
Séamus Lawless (*Trinity College Dublin*)
Chia-Jung Lee (*U. Massachusetts Amherst*)
Kyumin Lee (*Utah State U.*)
Teerapong Leelanupab (*KMITL Thailand*)
Jochen Leidner (*Thomson Reuters*)
Johannes Leveling (*Dublin City U.*)
David D. Lewis (*David D. Lewis Consulting*)
Lei Li (*Florida International U.*)
Shangsong Liang (*U. Amsterdam*)
Daniel Liebling (*Microsoft Research*)
Ee-Peng Lim (*Singapore Management U.*)
Nut Limsopatham (*U. Glasgow*)
Christina Lioma (*U. Copenhagen*)
Suzanne Little (*Dublin City U.*)
Claudio Lucchese (*ISTI-CNR*)
Roger Jie Luo (*Yahoo Labs*)
Yuan Luo (*IBM & MIT*)
Mihai Lupu (*Vienna U. Tech.*)
Yuanhua Lv (*Microsoft*)
Dimitrios Lymberopoulos (*Microsoft Research*)
Andrew MacFarlane (*City U. London*)
Walid Magdy (*QCRI*)
Stephane Marchand-Maillet (*U. Geneva*)
Miguel Martinez Alvarez (*Signal*)
Flavio Martins (*U. Nova de Lisboa*)
Maarten Marx (*U. Amsterdam*)
Yosi Mass (*IBM*)
Richard McCreadie (*U. Glasgow*)
Paul McNamee (*JHU*)
Edgar Meij (*Yahoo Labs*)
Yelena Mejova (*QCRI*)
Marcelo Mendoza (*Yahoo Labs*)
Thomas Mensink (*U. Amsterdam*)
Peter Mika (*Yahoo Labs*)
Natasa Milic-Frayling (*Microsoft Research*)
Bhaskar Mitra (*Microsoft*)
Prasenjit Mitra (*Pennsylvania State U.*)
Marie-Francine Moens (*Katholieke U. Leuven*)
Samaneh Moghaddam (*eBay*)
Yashar Moshfeghi (*U. Glasgow*)
Josiane Mothe (*IRIT U. Toulouse*)
Isabelle Moulinier (*Thomson Reuters*)
Hidetsugu Nanba (*Hiroshima U.*)
Franco Maria Nardini (*ISTI-CNR*)
Wolfgang Nejdl (*L3S Research Center*)
Vincent Ng (*U. Texas Dallas*)
Dong Nguyen (*Twente U.*)
Quoc Viet Hung Nguyen (*EPFL*)
Tu Nguyen (*L3S Research Center*)
Feiping Nie (*UT Arlington*)
Jian-Yun Nie (*U. Montreal*)
Alexandros Ntoulas (*Microsoft Research*)
Neil O'Hare (*Yahoo Labs*)
Daan Odijk (*U. Amsterdam*)
Denis Parra (*PUC Chile*)
Gabriella Pasi (*U. Milano-Bicocca*)
Virgil Pavlu (*Northeastern U.*)
Raffaele Perego (*ISTI-CNR*)
Alvaro Pereira Jr (*Federal U. Ouro Preto*)
Barbara Poblete (*U. Chile*)
John Prager (*IBM Research*)
Mu Qiao (*IBM Research*)
Tao Qin (*Microsoft*)
Edie Rasmussen (*U. British Columbia*)
Mohammad Raza (*Microsoft Cambridge*)
Yongli Ren (*RMIT U.*)
Zhaochun Ren (*U. Amsterdam*)
Haggai Roitman (*IBM Research Haifa*)
Stevan Rudinac (*U. Amsterdam*)
Stefan Rüger (*The Open U.*)
Egor Samosvat (*Yandex*)
Jose San Pedro (*Telefonica Research*)
Rodrygo Santos (*U. Federal de Minas Gerais*)
Shin'ichi Satoh (*NII Japan*)
Klaus Schoeffmann (*Klagenfurt U.*)
Anne Schuth (*U. Amsterdam*)
Satoshi Sekine (*New York U.*)
Jangwon Seo (*Google*)
Jialie Shen (*Singapore Management U.*)
Xiaolin Shi (*Microsoft*)
Milad Shokouhi (*Microsoft*)
Edleno Silva de Moura (*Federal U. Amazonas*)
Fabrizio Silvestri (*Yahoo Labs*)
Marc Sloan (*U. College London*)

Yang Song (*Microsoft Research*)
Hanna Suominen (*NICTA & ANU*)
Idan Szpektor (*Yahoo Labs*)
James Thom (*RMIT U.*)
Paul Thomas (*CSIRO*)
Xinmei Tian (*U. Sc. Tech. China*)
Gabriele Tolomei (*Yahoo Labs*)
Elaine Toms (*U. Sheffield*)
Nicola Tonellotto (*ISTI-CNR*)
Dolf Trieschnigg (*U. Twente*)
Andrew Trotman (*eBay*)
Manos Tsagkias (*904Labs*)
Theodora Tsikrika (*CERTH*)
Julián Urbano (*U. Pompeu Fabra*)
Christophe Van Gysel (*U. Amsterdam*)
Suzan Verberne (*Radboud U. Nijmegen*)
Changhu Wang (*Microsoft Research China*)
Hongning Wang (*U. Virginia*)
Lidan Wang (*U. Maryland College Park*)
Meng Wang (*Hefei U. Tech.*)
Shuaiqiang Wang (*U. Jyväskylä*)
William Webber (*Willaim Webber Consulting*)
Wouter Weerkamp (*904Labs*)
Xing Wei (*Inmobi*)
Jerome White (*New York U.*)
Xiaobing Xue (*Twitter*)
Grace Hui Yang (*Georgetown U.*)
Kuiyuan Yang (*Microsoft Research*)
Liu Yang (*U. Massachusetts Amherst*)
Xuchen Yao (*Johns Hopkins U.*)
Jie Yin (*CSIRO*)
Muhammad Bilal Zafar (*Max Planck Institut*)
Duo Zhang (*Twitter*)
Jianwen Zhang (*Microsoft Research Asia*)
Lanbo Zhang (*Twitter*)
Yongfeng Zhang (*Tsinghua U.*)
Zhiwei Zhang (*Purdue U.*)
Ke Zhou (*Yahoo Labs*)
Imed Zitouni (*Microsoft*)
Guido Zuccon (*Queensland U. Tech.*)

Knowledge Management Track Program Committee Members

Gail-Joon Ahn (*Arizona State U.*)
Mohammad AlHassan (*IUPUI*)
David Anastasiu (*U. Minnesota*)
Azin Ashkan (*Technicolor*)
Bahman Bahmani (*Stanford U.*)
Gustavo Batista (*U. Sao Paulo*)
Srikanta Bedathur (*IBM Research India*)
Kanishka Bhaduri (*Netflix*)
Arnab Bhattacharya (*IIT Kanpur*)
Albert Bifet (*U. Waikato*)
Petko Bogdanov (*SUNY Albany*)
Klemens Böhm (*Karlsruhe Institut Tech.*)
Mohamed Bouguessa (*U. Quebec*)
Christos Boutsidis (*Yahoo Labs*)
Andrea Cali (*Birkbeck College London*)
Ricardo Campello (*U. São Paulo*)
Huiping Cao (*New Mexico State U.*)
Jeffrey Chan (*U. Melbourne*)
Varun Chandola (*U. Buffalo*)
Michael Chau (*U. Hong Kong*)
Nitesh Chawla (*Notre Dame*)
Ye Chen (*Microsoft*)
Zhiyuan Chen (*U. Illinois Chicago*)
Jaegul Choo (*Korea U.*)
Vassilis Christophides (*U. Crete*)
Kun-Ta Chuang (*National Cheng Kung U.*)
James Cook (*Google*)
Bernardo Cuenca-Grau (*U. Oxford*)
Alfredo Cuzzocrea (*U. Calabria*)
Na Dai (*Google*)
Theodore Dalamagas (*Athena Research Greeve*)
Abhimanyu Das (*Google*)
Antonios Deligiannakis (*Tech. U. Crete*)
Christos Doulkeridis (*U. Piraeus*)
Dora Erdos (*Boston U.*)
Alex Fabrikant (*Google*)
Elena Ferrari (*U. Insubria*)
Avrilia Floratou (*IBM Almaden*)
Esther Galbrun (*Boston U.*)
Jing Gao (*SUNY Buffalo*)
Dinesh Garg (*IBM India Research Lab*)
Chiara Ghidini (*FBK Trento*)
Nikos Giatrakos (*Tech. U. Crete*)
Kasneci Gjergji (*Hasso Plattner Institut*)
Aris Gkoulalas-Divanis (*IBM*)
Bart Goethals (*U. Antwerp*)
Manuel Gomez Rodriguez (*MPI*)
Amit Goyal (*Yahoo Labs*)
Francesco Gullo (*Yahoo Labs*)
Stephan Günnemann (*Carnegie Mellon U.*)
Sunil Gupta (*Deakin*)
Maxim Gurevich (*Bento Labs*)

Claudio Gutierrez (*Universidad De Chile*)
Maria Halkidi (*U. Piraeus*)
Jingrui He (*Arizona State U.*)
Raquel Hill (*Indiana U.*)
Thanh Lam Hoang (*IBM Research Dublin*)
Bing Hu (*Samsung*)
Luke Huan (*U. Kansas*)
Ekaterini Ioannou (*Tech. U. Crete*)
Yunliang Jiang (*Thumbtack*)
James Joshi (*U. Pittsburg*)
Panos Kalnis (*KAUST*)
Bhargav Kanagal (*Google*)
Ramakrishnan Kannan (*Georgia Tech*)
Ben Kao (*U. Hong Kong*)
Panagiotis Karras (*Skoltech*)
Daniel Keren (*U. Haifa*)
Arijit Khan (*ETH Zurich*)
Latifur Khan (*U. Texas Dallas*)
Xiangnan Kong (*WPI*)
Ioannis Konstantinou (*NTUA*)
Georgia Koutrika (*HP Labs*)
Zornitsa Kozareva (*Yahoo Labs*)
Tim Kraska (*Brown U.*)
Ashish Kundu (*IBM Research*)
Ni Lao (*Google*)
Theodoros Lappas (*Stevens Inst. Tech.*)
Silvio Lattanzi (*Google*)
Hady Lauw (*Singapore Management U.*)
Wang-Chien Lee (*Pennsylvania State U.*)
Yang Li (*Google*)
Zhenhui Li (*Pennsylvania State U.*)
Lei Liu (*HP Labs*)
Claudio Lucchese (*ISTI-CNR*)
Michael Mathioudakis (*Helsinki U. Tech.*)
Julian McAuley (*UCSD*)
Sebastian Michel (*TU Kaiserslautern*)
Pauli Miettinen (*Max Planck Institut*)
Marco Montali (*Free U. Bozen-Bolzano*)
Abdullah Mueen (*UMN*)
Emmanuel Müller (*Karlsruhe Inst. Tech.*)
Ndapa Nakashole (*Carnegie Mellon U.*)
Xia Ning (*IUPUI*)
Eirini Ntoutsi (*LMU*)
Werner Nutt (*Free U. Bozen-Bolzano*)
Gaurav Pandey (*Mount Sinai School of Medicine*)
Spiros Papadimitriou (*Rutgers U.*)
Apostolos Papadopoulos (*Aristotle U. Thessaloniki*)
Evangelos Papalexakis (*Carnegie Mellon U.*)
Odysseas Papapetrou (*Tech. U. Crete*)
Panagiotis Papapetrou (*Stockholm U.*)
Stott Parker (*UCLA*)
Konstantinos Pelechrinis (*U. Pittsburgh*)
Peter Pietzuch (*Imperial College*)
Ali Pinar (*Sandia National Labs*)
Dimitris Plexousakis (*U. Crete*)
Davood Rafiei (*U. Alberta*)
Santu Rana (*Deakin U.*)
Huzefa Rangwala (*George Mason U.*)
Chotirat Ann Ratanamahatana (*Chulalongkorn U.*)
Chiara Renso (*CNR*)
Matteo Riondato (*Brown U.*)
Dimitris Sacharidis (*Vienna U. Tech.*)
Barna Saha (*U. Massachusetts Amherst*)
Vasilis Samoladas (*Tech. U. Crete*)
Mohamed Sarwat (*U. Minnesota*)
Saket Sathe (*IBM*)
Ralf Schenkel (*U. Passau*)
Erich Schubert (*LMU Munich*)
Matthias Schubert (*LMU Munich*)
Thomas Seidl (*RWTH Aachen U.*)
Nisheeth Shrivastava (*Amazon*)
Alkis Simitsis (*HP Labs*)
Yannis Sismanis (*Google*)
Sucheta Soundarajan (*Rutgers U.*)
Anna Squicciarini (*Pennsylvania State U.*)
Kostas Stefanidis (*FORTH-ICS Greece*)
Karthik Subbian (*Facebook*)
Fabian Suchanek (*Télécom ParisTech U.*)
Yizhou Sun (*NEU*)
Pang-Ning Tan (*Michigan State U.*)
Jiliang Tang (*Yahoo Labs*)
Liang Tang (*LinkedIn*)
Sandeep Tata (*Google*)
Shirish Tatikonda (*IBM Almaden*)
Manolis Terrovitis (*IMIS Athena*)
Brian Thompson (*U.S. Army Research Lab*)
Srikanta Tirthapura (*Iowa State U.*)
Truyen Tran (*Deakin U.*)
Panayiotis Tsaparas (*U. Ioannina*)
Charalampos Tsourakakis (*Brown U.*)
Deepak Turaga (*IBM*)
Leong Hou U (*U. Macau*)
Antti Ukkonen (*Helsinki U. Tech.*)
Aparna Varde (*Montclair State U.*)
Vasilis Vassalos (*AUEB Greece*)
Panos Vassiliadis (*U. Ioannina*)

Akrivi Vlachou (*AUEB Greece*)
Anil Vullikanti (*Virginia Tech*)
Dong Wang (*U. Notre Dame*)
Jason Wang (*New Jersey Inst. Tech.*)
Shengrui Wang (*U. Sherbrooke*)
William Yang Wang (*Carnegie Mellon U.*)
Yue Wang (*U. Michigan*)
Tim Weninger (*Notre Dame*)
Anthony Wirth (*U. Melbourne*)
Dingming Wu (*U. Hong Kong*)
Donghui Wu (*Lexis Nexis*)
Zhaoming Wu (*Georgia Tech*)
Rongjing Xiang (*Google*)
Li Xiong (*Emory U.*)
Shengqi Yang (*Facebook*)
Yuan Yao (*Nanjing U.*)
Ke Yiping (*Nanyang Tech. U.*)
Philip S. Yu (*U. Illinois Chicago*)
Wenchao Yu (*UCLA*)
Reza Zafarani (*Arizona State U.*)
Hessam Zakerzadeh (*U. Calgary*)
Ce Zhang (*U. Wisconsin Madison*)
Jiawei Zhang (*UIC*)
Qin Zhang (*Indiana*)
Ruofei Zhang (*Microsoft*)
Yuchen Zhao (*AppDynamics*)
Zhe Zhao (*U. Michigan*)
Dmitriy Zheleznyakov (*U. Oxford*)
Arthur Zimek (*LMU Munich*)
Andreas Zuefle (*LMU Munich*)

Additional Referees

Karam Abdulahhad (*CNRS Grenoble*)
Tenindra Abeywickrama (*Monash U.*)
Cem Aksoy (*New Jersey Inst. Tech.*)
Daniel Alejandro Garcia Ulloa (*Emory U.*)
Akhil Arora (*Xerox Research Bangalore*)
Besim Avci (*Northwestern U.*)
Alexander Beloborodov (*Ural Federal U.*)
Rafael Berlanga Llavori (*U. Jaume I Castellon*)
Nikos Bikakis (*Athena Research Greece*)
Fei Bi (*U. New South Wales*)
Dritan Bleco (*AUEB Greece*)
Luca Bonomi (*Emory U.*)
Matteo Catena (*ISTI-CNR*)
Kai Ho Chan (*Hong Kong U. Sc. Tech.*)
Anveshi Charuvaka (*George Mason U.*)
Abon Chaudhuri (*Walmart Labs*)
Jiecao Chen (*Indiana U. Bloomington*)
Lisi Chen (*Nanyang Tech. U.*)
Liu Chen (*Wuhan U.*)
Xu Chu (*U. Waterloo*)
David Corney (*Signal*)
Ananya Dass (*New Jersey Inst. Tech.*)
Sabrina De Capitani di Vimercati
(*U. degli Studi di Milano*)
Alberto De Francesco (*ISTI-CNR*)
Amra Delic (*Tech. U. Wien*)
Aggeliki Dimitriou (*National Tech. U. Athens*)
Daniel Ditursi (*SUNY Albany*)
Vasilis Efthymiou (*FORTH-ICS Greece*)
Pavlos Fafalios (*FORTH-ICS Greece*)
Xing Feng (*U. New South Wales*)
Ioanna Filippidou (*AUEB Greece*)
Christian Frey (*Ludwig Maximilians U.*)
Debasis Ganguly (*Dublin City U.*)
Cheng Gao (*U. Kansas*)
Konstantinos Georgoulas (*AUEB Greece*)
Giorgos Giannopoulos (*Athena Research Greece*)
Benoit Groz (*U. Paris Sud*)
Kshiteesh Hegde (*Rensselaer Polytechnic Inst.*)
Zhenying He (*Fudan U.*)
Chuan Hu (*New Mexico State U.*)
Mas-ud Hussain (*Northwestern U.*)
Go Irie (*NTT Japan*)
Saiful Islam (*Swinburne U. Tech.*)
Alankar Jain (*IBM Research India*)
Nandish Jayaram (*U. Texas Austin*)
Meng Jiang (*Tsinghua U.*)
Minhao Jiang (*Hong Kong U. Sc. Tech.*)
Salil Joshi (*IBM Research India*)
Gregor Josse (*Ludwig Maximilians U.*)
Ilias Kanellos (*Athena Research Greece*)
Maria Karanasou (*U. Piraeus*)
Enkelejda Kasneci (*U. Tuebingen*)
Akshar Kaul (*IBM Research India*)
Evgeny Kharlamov (*U. Oxford*)
Roberto Konow (*U. Chile*)
Egor Kostylev (*U. Oxford*)
Jitin Krishnan (*George Mason U.*)
Anastasia Krithara (*IIT Demokritos Greece*)
Alexander Krumpholz (*CSIRO*)
Durgesh Kumar (*IIT Guwahati*)
Christina Lantzaki (*FORTH-ICS Greece*)

Chao Lan (*U. Kansas*)
Léa Laporte (*INSA Lyon*)
Haoran Li (*Emory U.*)
Jianxin Li (*RMIT U.*)
Lei Li (*Hefei U. Tech.*)
Wei Li (*Google*)
Xiaoli Li (*U. Kansas*)
Yuchen Li (*National U. Singapore*)
Zechao Li (*Nanjing U. Sc. Tech.*)
Kewen Liao (*U. Melbourne*)
Aldo Lipani (*Tech. U. Vienna*)
Ruifeng Liu (*Chinese U. Hong Kong*)
Yubao Liu (*Sun Yat Sen U.*)
Cheng Long (*Hong Kong U. Sc. Tech.*)
Xin Lu (*Pennsylvania State U.*)
Nantia Makrynioti (*AUEB Greece*)
Sebastian Mattheis (*BMW Car IT*)
Nianzu Ma (*U. Illinois Chicago*)
Meenakshi Mishra (*U. Kansas*)
Cristina Muntean (*ISTI-CNR*)
Nikhil Muralidhar (*George Mason U.*)
Masaya Murata (*NTT Japan*)
Bin Mu (*City U. New York*)
Azad Naik (*George Mason U.*)
Julia Neidhardt (*Tech. U. Wien*)
Konstantinos Nikolopoulos (*City U. New York*)
Koninika Pal (*Tech. U. Kaiserslautern*)
Panayiotis Papadakos (*FORTH-ICS Greece*)
Theodore Patkos (*FORTH-ICS Greece*)
Kostas Patroumpas (*National Tech. U. Athens*)
Nikos Pelekis (*U. Piraeus*)
Gerardo Pelosi (*Politecnico di Milano*)
Wei Pengfei (*Nanyang Tech. U.*)
Matthias Petri (*U. Melbourne*)
Trang T.M. Pham (*Deakin U.*)
Tuan Anh Nguyen Pham (*Nanyang Tech. U.*)
Layla Pournajaf (*Emory U.*)
Bo Qin (*Hong Kong U. Sc. Tech.*)
Jianbin Qin (*U. New South Wales*)
Ridho Reinanda (*U. Amsterdam*)
Navid Rekabsaz (*Tech. U. Vienna*)
Zhiyun Ren (*George Mason U.*)
Bryan Reynaert (*Akori S.A.*)
Klaus Schmid (*Ludwig Maximilians U.*)
Baoxu Shi (*U. Notre Dame*)
Vasilis Spyropoulos (*AUEB Greece*)
Joseph St.Amand (*U. Kansas*)
Li Su (*U. Southern Denmark*)
Dan Suciu (*U. Washington*)
Yifang Sun (*U. New South Wales*)
Mack Sweeney (*George Mason U.*)
Natasha Tagasovska (*U. Lausanne*)
Aditya Telang (*IBM Research India*)
Camilo Thorne (*U. Mannheim*)
Salvatore Trani (*ISTI-CNR*)
Erald Troja (*City U. New York*)
Yannis Tzitzikas (*FORTH-ICS Greece*)
Utkarsh Upadhyay (*Max Planck Institut*)
Tassos Venetis (*AUEB Greece*)
Thanasis Vergoulis (*Athena Research Greece*)
Hongjian Wang (*Pennsylvania State U.*)
Shuai Wang (*U. Illinois Chicago*)
Xiang Wang (*U. New South Wales*)
Xiaoyang Wang (*U. New South Wales*)
Victor Junqiu Wei (*Hong Kong U. Sc. Tech.*)
Udi Weinsberg (*Facebook*)
Buwen Wu (*U. Southern Denmark*)
Fei Wu (*Pennsylvania State U.*)
Xiaoying Wu (*Wuhan U.*)
Yingjun Wu (*National U. Singapore*)
Xike Xie (*Aalborg U.*)
Xiaofeng Xu (*Emory U.*)
Bin Yang (*Aalborg U.*)
Shiyu Yang (*U. New South Wales*)
Yang Yang (*U. Electronic Sc. Tech. China*)
Zhengwei Yang (*Chinese U. Hong Kong*)
Peifeng Yin (*IBM*)
Quan Yuan (*U. Illinois Urbana-Champaign*)
Ting Yu (*Wuhan U.*)
Shuangfei Zhai (*SUNY Binghamton*)
Bing Zhang (*Northwestern U.*)
Jingyuan Zhang (*U. Illinois Chicago*)
Xu Zhiqiang (*Institute Infocomm Research*)
Rui Zhou (*Victoria U.*)

Sponsors and Supporters

Sponsors

SIGIR
Special Interest Group
on Information Retrieval

sig web

Gold Supporter

Microsoft® Research

Silver Supporter

sportsbet.com.au

Bronze Supporters

Academic Supporters

Large-Scale Analysis of Dynamics of Choice Among Discrete Alternatives

Andrew Tomkins
Google, Inc.
1600 Amphitheatre Parkway
Mountain View, CA
atomkins@gmail.com

ABSTRACT

The online world is rife with scenarios in which a user must select one from a finite set of alternatives: which movie to watch, which song to play, which camera to order, which website to visit. There is a long history of study of these types of questions in economics, machine learning, marketing, and psychology. However, historically the study of choice was limited to relatively modest data scales. Today, we have access to large-scale datasets providing insights into the choices of large populations of users faced with a wide variety of sets of alternatives. From such data, we are beginning to develop more detailed models of how users weigh alternatives and make selections.

I'll begin this talk by covering basic models for choice, along with some standard assumptions made by these models. I'll then cover some more recent work on understanding choice in modern datasets.

First, I'll discuss choice in a geographic setting, in which users make selections of restaurants. Features in this setting provide visibility into the actual time cost to travel to one alternative versus another. In addition to this real cost, we may also tease out the implications on likelihood as the set of alternatives at a particular distance becomes larger or smaller based on the local density of restaurants. The marginals of these factors provide poor quality compared to joint models suggested by choice theory.

From choice of individual restaurants, I'll then move to a setting in which users consume items repeatedly: repeated purchases of a particular brand of product; repeated listens to a song; repeated visits to a favorite coffee shop; and so forth. I'll describe a simple but accurate model for this problem whose behavior moves between two regimes based on parameter choices: in one regime, users settle on particular favorites and maintain them over time; in another regime, even the most favored item will eventually be abandoned after finite reconsumptions.

Finally, I'll move to a more complex scenario of sequential consumption of a range of items, and will show how the theory of discrete choice can be incorporated into the theory of markov processes, requiring a new algorithmic approach to learning the optimal solution.

In all of these instances, the learned models include a per-item quality score that may be viewed as proportional to the residual likelihood of selecting the item after other factors in the choice slate have been accounted for.

The work described in this talk is partly due to other researchers, and partly joint with various colleagues including Ashton Anderson, Ravi Kumar, Mohammad Mahdian, Bo Pang, Sergei Vassilvitskii and Erik Vee.

Categories and Subject Descriptors

G.0 [**Mathematics of Computing**]: General

Keywords

Choice Models

Bio

Andrew joined Google Research in 2009, where he serves as an engineering director working on geo data analysis and machine learning. His earlier research focused on measurement, modelling, and analysis of content, communities, and users on the World Wide Web. Prior to joining Google, he spent four years at Yahoo! serving as chief scientist of search, and eight years at IBM's Almaden Research Center, where he served as chief scientist on the WebFountain project. Andrew has authored over 100 technical papers and 60 issued patents. He received Bachelors degrees in Mathematics and Computer Science from MIT, and a PhD in CS from Carnegie Mellon University.

Permission to make digital or hard copies of part or all of this work for personal or classroom use is granted without fee provided that copies are not made or distributed for profit or commercial advantage and that copies bear this notice and the full citation on the first page. Copyrights for third-party components of this work must be honored. For all other uses, contact the Owner/Author.
Copyright is held by the owner/author(s).
CIKM'15, October 19–23, 2015, Melbourne, Australia.
ACM 978-1-4503-3794-6/15/10.
DOI: http://dx.doi.org/10.1145/2806416.2806419.

On Gapped Set Intersection Size Estimation

Chen Chen Jianbin Qin Wei Wang
University of New South Wales, Australia
{cchen, jqin, weiw}@cse.unsw.edu.au

ABSTRACT

There exists considerable literature on estimating the cardinality of set intersection result. In this paper, we consider a generalized problem for integer sets where, given a gap parameter δ, two elements are deemed as matches if their numeric difference equals δ or is within δ. We call this problem the *gapped set intersection size estimation* (GSISE), and it can be used to model applications in database systems, data mining, and information retrieval. We first distinguish two subtypes of the estimation problem: the *point gap* estimation and *range gap* estimation. We propose optimized sketches to tackle the two problems efficiently and effectively with theoretical guarantees. We demonstrate the usage of our proposed techniques in mining top-K related keywords efficiently, by integrating with an inverted index. Finally, substantial experiments based on a large subset of the ClueWed09 dataset demonstrate the efficiency and effectiveness of the proposed methods.

Categories and Subject Descriptors

H.3.3 [**Information Storage and Retrieval**]: Information Search and Retrieval

Keywords

Indexing; Set Intersection Size Estimation; Top-k

1. INTRODUCTION

Set intersection is a fundamental operation in many fields in computer science. Given two sets S_A and S_B, set intersection $S_A \cap S_B$ is to find all the common elements from two sets. A common case is that all elements in the set are integers (e.g., document IDs or positions in an inverted index). Hence, the common element pair (a, b) satisfies $b - a = \delta$, where $a \in S_A$, $b \in S_B$ and $\delta = 0$.

In this paper, we generalize the set intersection on integer sets to allow for "gaps" (i.e., $\delta > 0$). We define two primitives: the point gap constraint corresponds to a fixed gap of δ, and the range gap constraint corresponds to a gap of size no larger than δ. We are interested in methods to estimate these gapped set intersection size efficiently and accurately. This problem has many applications. For example,

- *Information Retrieval*: In information retrieval, the search engine needs to intersect the positional inverted lists of query keywords to answer a multiple keyword phrase query. A state-of-the-art query processing method, *svs*, performs binary intersection using a heuristic order that is purely based on the length of the inverted lists [11]. This heuristic is not effective when search keywords are not very selective (e.g., "`to be or not to be`"). It is possible that a pair of query keywords with the positional constraint imposed by the phrase query will result in very small intermediate result size (e.g., "`be`" followed immediately by "`or`"). Hence, if we can estimate its cardinality accurately and efficiently, we may find a better inverted list intersection order to process such queries. We can model this as a gapped set intersection size estimation problem with a *point gap constraint* of 1.
- *Sentiment or Event Analyses*: In sentiment analysis, we extract different types of events, including a mention of a product, and an occurrence of sentiment (e.g., the word "`fantastic`"). We are usually interested in events that occur in a close vicinity. For instance, the *positions* of their occurrences in a document are within δ [17] or the timestamps of their occurrences in tweets are within δ [25]. We can model this as a gapped set intersection size estimation problem with a *range gap constraint* of δ.

Motivated by the examples, we define and study the problem of gapped set intersection size estimation (abbreviated as GSISE). For the estimation problem with point gap constraints, we propose a basic method that reduces the problem to the standard set intersection size estimation problem, which can be solved using the state-of-the-art sketch method. However, the index space is linear to the maximum query gap allowed. We improve it by judiciously selecting a subset of sketches to construct, and this reduces our sketch size from $O(N)$ to $O(\sqrt{N})$. The space cost of our approach is proved to be asymptotically optimal, while the time complexity remains the same. For the estimation problem with the range gap constraint, a baseline method is to reduce the problem into multiple estimation problems with different point gap constraints, and this requires estimation time linear in the gap size. We propose an extension of the bottom-k sketch to multiset and an unbiased estimator for inner product, we achieve an accurate and fast estimation method that is independent of the gap size. To demonstrate the use of our estimation methods, we consider the problem of finding highly correlated keywords from a large document collection. We design a new query processing method based

Permission to make digital or hard copies of all or part of this work for personal or classroom use is granted without fee provided that copies are not made or distributed for profit or commercial advantage and that copies bear this notice and the full citation on the first page. Copyrights for components of this work owned by others than ACM must be honored. Abstracting with credit is permitted. To copy otherwise, or republish, to post on servers or to redistribute to lists, requires prior specific permission and/or a fee. Request permissions from Permissions@acm.org.
CIKM'15, October 19–23, 2015, Melbourne, Australia.
© 2015 ACM. ISBN 978-1-4503-3794-6/15/10 ...$15.00.
DOI: http://dx.doi.org/10.1145/2806416.2806438.

on indexing the hash values in our sketches. Finally, we perform large-scale experimental evaluation using 500 million documents from the ClueWeb09 data collection and demonstrate the accuracy and efficiency of our proposed methods.

Contributions. The contributions of this paper are summarized as follows.

- To the best of our knowledge, this is the first work to formally define the point and range gapped set intersection size estimation problems, which can be used as primitive operations in a wide spectrum of applications.
- We design space and time efficient sketch and estimation methods for both types of estimation tasks. Our estimates are unbiased and have theoretical guarantees.
- We demonstrate the application of our technique for approximately mining top-K related keywords from large document collections. Our technique is especially useful in this application scenario where an exact solution requires orders of magnitudes larger space and time.
- Comprehensive experiments on the ClueWed09 dataset demonstrate the efficiency and accuracy of the proposed methods.

Organization of the paper. The rest of the paper is organized as follows. Section 2 briefly surveys the related works. Section 3 defines the problem formally and introduces several useful techniques. Section 4 elaborates the estimation framework for point query and range query, together with their theoretical properties. Section 5 presents algorithm to top-K related keywords mining application. The experimental results are reported and analyzed in Section 6. We conclude the paper in Section 7.

2. RELATED WORKS

Exact set intersection. Set intersection has long been a fundamental problem. There are plenty of literature focusing on set intersection problem [12, 13]. The algorithms working on sorted set are mostly used [24]. By applying linear merge of two sorted set S_A and S_B, the set intersection can be finished in $O(|S_A| + |S_B|)$ time. However, when the set sizes are unbalanced, the method is inefficient. In [18], authors propose a set intersection approach requiring $O(|S_B| + \log \binom{|S_A| + |S_B|}{|S_A|})$ when $|S_A| \ll |S_B|$. There are also works further improving the performance by utilizing hashing, and adaptive methods [3, 2]. Unlike the above literature, we want to *estimate* the gapped set intersection size rather than calculating the exact result.

Set intersection size estimation. The problem of set intersection size estimation is to estimate the cardinality of intersection with a sketch method, which has been extensively studied in [6, 4, 7]. Nevertheless, all existing methods are designed for non-gapped set intersection size estimation. A naïve way to extend existing methods to support the GSISE problem is to build sketch for each possible query gap. However, it will result in the index space linear to the maximum gap. Furthermore, the computational complexity for range query will be linear to the query gap. In this paper, we try to reduce both space and computational complexity in processing GSISE. In addition, there are several works [26, 21] that calculate an upper bound of set intersection size, which is orthogonal to our problem.

Top-K query. One of the most important applications of GSISE is top-K related keyword mining. The problem is well studied in [16, 15]. Afterwards, there are varieties of follow-up works dealing with top-K ranking for different applications, e.g., keyword queries [20], top-K preference ranking queries [23] and semi-structure queries [27].

Most of the works, such as [28], are based on the strategy that gradually scans the inverted index and updates the upper and lower bounds of the ranking terms, in order to achieve early stopping. However, the above strategy is not well suited in our sketch based estimation framework. Since it is non-trivial to obtain a tight bound for the estimation. Instead, a hash table based method is proposed in Section 5 to accelerate the top-K query processing.

3. PRELIMINARIES

In this section, we define two estimation problems, introduce existing work on estimating the size of set intersection using sketch, and finally list important notations used in the paper.

3.1 Problem Definition

Given two sets S_A and S_B, their intersection is defined as $\{ (a, b) \mid \mathtt{eq(a, b)}, a \in S_A, b \in S_B \}$, where the predicate $\mathtt{eq}(a, b)$ checks if a equals b. We can generalize the set intersection by considering other meaningful predicates. Specifically, with a *gap parameter* $\delta \geq 0$, we consider the following two predicates:

- $\mathtt{PointGap}_\delta(a, b)$, which returns **true** if and only if $b - a = \delta$.
- $\mathtt{RangeGap}_\delta(a, b)$, which returns **true** if and only if $0 \leq b - a \leq \delta$.

We call set intersection with these two new predicates collectively *gapped set intersection.* They are denoted as $S_A \cap^{=\delta} S_B$ (named *point gapped set intersection*) and $S_A \cap^{\leq\delta} S_B$ (named *range gapped set intersection*), respectively. Obviously, the standard set intersection is a special case of both types of gapped set intersection where $\delta = 0$.

In this paper, we study space and time-efficient methods to estimate the results size of these two types of gapped set intersection. Motivated by the applications we aim at, we consider sets whose elements are integers.

DEFINITION 1 (GSISE). *Given two sets S_A and S_B, and a gap parameter $\delta \in [0, N]$ where N is a predefined maximum gap value. The* Point *and* Range *Gapped Set Intersection Size Estimation Problem is to estimate $|S_A \cap^{=\delta} S_B|$ and $|S_A \cap^{\leq\delta} S_B|$, respectively. They are abbreviated as* point estimation *and* range estimation *hereafter.*

EXAMPLE 1. *Let $S_A = \{1, 3, 4, 7\}$ and $S_B = \{2, 5, 6, 8\}$, and $\delta = 2$. Under the point gap constraint, $S_A \cap^{=2} S_B = \{(3, 5), (4, 6)\}$. Hence its size is 2. Under the range gap constraint, $S_A \cap^{\leq 2} S_B = \{(1, 2), (3, 5), (4, 5), (4, 6), (7, 8)\}$. Hence its size is 5.*

Discussions. In the above definitions, we only need to consider $\delta \geq 0$. This is because $S_A \cap^{=\delta} S_B = S_B \cap^{=-\delta} S_A$ (this also holds for range gapped set intersection too).

Many other types of interesting gapped set intersections can be defined using our point and range gapped set intersection as primitives. For example, consider the predicate $\mathtt{RangeWithin}_{\delta_1,\delta_2}(\mathtt{a}, \mathtt{b})$ with two range parameters $0 \leq \delta_1 < \delta_2$, which checks if $\delta_1 \leq a - b \leq \delta_2$. It is easy to see that its query result is exactly the difference of two range gapped set intersection, i.e., $(S_A \cap^{\leq\delta_2} S_B) \setminus (S_A \cap^{\leq\delta_1} S_B)$.

In a similar fashion, we can derive point gapped set intersection based on range gapped set intersection, and vice versa. Nevertheless, we still consider them as two separate primitives, as each of them can model different applications respectively, and we will propose related but different estimation methods and optimizations for them.

3.2 Bottom-k Sketch

The state-of-the-art method to estimate the size of set intersections is the bottom-k sketch [7, 8, 9]. It is a lightweight sketch that supports efficient update.

We use $sk(S_A)$ to denote the bottom-k sketch for a set S_A, which is a set of k hash values. To construct the sketch, we apply a random hash function h to every element $a \in S_A$, and keep the k minimum hash values. We also assume the codomain of h is sufficiently large such that we can safely assume that there is no collision.

An important property of the bottom-k sketch is that it is closed under set union operation. Specifically, we can directly compute the bottom-k sketch of the union of two sets from their respective bottom-k sketches. The resulting sketch is called *short combination sketch* [9]: $scs(sk(S_A), sk(S_B)) = \{ v \mid v \in sk(S_A) \cup sk(S_B), v < \min(sk(S_A)^{(k)}, sk(S_B)^{(k)}) \}$, where the notation $S^{(k)}$ denotes the k-th smallest value in the set S.

To estimate the intersection size of two sets S_A and S_B from their respective sketches, we compute

$$t = \frac{|sk(S_A) \cap sk(S_B) \cap scs(sk(S_A), sk(S_B))|}{\min\{ sk(S_A)^{(k)}, sk(S_B)^{(k)} \}}. \quad (1)$$

[9] proved that t is an unbiased estimator of $|S_A \cap S_B|$ that can be computed efficiently. Besides, it is shown to have smaller variance compared with the Minhash [5] method.

3.3 Notations

Table 1 lists notations frequently used in the paper.

Table 1: Summary of Notations

Symbol	Explanation
S_{id}	a set of integers
M_{id}	a multiset; each element has its multiplicity
S_{id}^{+d}	a shifted set by distance d
$\{d_1, d_2, \ldots\}$	the index of a multiset generated by merging the set shifted by $d_1, d_2, \ldots$
$S^{(i)}$ or $M^{(i)}$	i-th smallest value in the set S or the multiset M
N	the maximum gap
δ	the gap parameter; $\delta \in [0, N]$
k	number of hash values in a bottom-k sketch
$sk(S)$	bottom-k sketch of the set S
$msk(M)$	multiset bottom-k sketch of the multiset M
rus	range union sketch of $msk(M_A)$ and $msk(M_B)$

4. ESTIMATION METHODS FOR GAPPED SET INTERSECTION SIZE

In this section, we introduce solutions to point and range estimation problems. The naïve index structure and our intuition are explained in Section 4.1, followed by technique details of GSISE methods in Section 4.2 and 4.3.

4.1 A Baseline Method for Point Estimation

Point estimation is a challenging problem due to the following reasons:

- Almost all the set intersection size estimation methods are based on random hash functions. Therefore, given a gap value δ, and two *different* hash values $h(x+\delta)$ and $h(y)$, it is almost impossible to infer if $x + \delta$ is equal to y.
- While locality sensitive hash functions [19] do preserve locality probabilistically, the intersection size is highly sensitive to the point gap threshold. It is often the case that $|S_A \cap^{=\delta} S_B|$ and $|S_A \cap^{=\delta+1} S_B|$ differ substantially. For instance, in Example 1, $|S_A \cap^{=0} S_B|$ is 0 while $|S_A \cap^{=1} S_B|$ is 3. Therefore, even a small approximation in the gap may result in a large estimation error.

Therefore, we first propose a baseline method, which reduces the point estimation problem to a standard set intersection size estimation problem, which in turn can be solved using the state-of-the-art method, such as the method based on bottom-k sketches.

Our reduction is based on the notion of *shifted sets*. Given a set $S_A = \{ a_1, a_2, \ldots, a_n \}$ and integer parameter d, we define the shifted set with shift d as follows: $S_A^{+d} := \{ a_i + d \mid a_i \in S_A \}$.

Given the maximum gap size N, we compute $N + 1$ bottom-k sketches by shifting S_A: the i-th bottom-k sketch is built for the shifted set S_A^{+i} $(0 \le i \le N)$. To perform the estimation for $S_A \cap^{=\delta} S_B$, we retrieve the sketches of $S_A^{+\delta}$ and S_B^{+0}, and perform the estimation using the bottom-k estimation procedure (i.e., Eq. (1)).

Table 2: The Random Hash Function h

x	0	1	2	3	4	5	6	7	8
$h(x)$	0.47	0.26	0.32	0.84	0.74	0.79	0.22	0.42	0.95
x	9	10	11	12	13	14	15	16	17
$h(x)$	0.48	0.68	0.89	0.16	0.63	0.37	0.53	0.15	0.21

EXAMPLE 2. *Table 3 shows the sketches built by the baseline method for two sets S_A and S_B, where the bottom-k sketch size is* 3 *and maximum gap N is* 9.

To perform the point estimate for $\delta = 5$, we load $sk(S_A^{+5})$ and $sk(S_B^{+0})$, the estimate according to Eq. (1) is $1/\min(0.48, 0.79) = 2.08$. *The actual point gapped intersection size is 2.*

Table 3: $N+1$ bottom-k Sketches Built for $S_A = \{1, 3, 4, 7\}$ and $S_B = \{2, 5, 6, 8\}$ using the Hash Function in Table 2. $N = 9$.

shift	Sketches for S_A	Sketches for S_B
0	$sk(S_A^{+0}) = \{0.26, 0.42, 0.74\}$	$sk(S_B^{+0}) = \{0.22, 0.32, 0.79\}$
⋮	⋮	⋮
5	$sk(S_A^{+5}) = \{0.16, 0.22, 0.48\}$	$sk(S_B^{+5}) = \{0.42, 0.63, 0.68\}$
⋮	⋮	⋮
9	$sk(S_A^{+9}) = \{0.15, 0.16, 0.63\}$	$sk(S_A^{+9}) = \{0.21, 0.37, 0.53\}$

Obviously, this baseline method achieves the same accuracy guarantee as the standard bottom-k sketch [4, 7, 22], and the estimation time is $O(k)$. The main problem is its space complexity of $O(N \cdot k)$ for each set, which is not optimal.

4.2 Improved Point Query Estimation

In this subsection, we seek to improve the space complexity per set from $N \cdot k$ to $\sqrt{N} \cdot k$, while still maintaining the same $O(k)$ estimation time. We also show that this space complexity is asymptotically optimal with an approximation ratio of $\sqrt{2}$.

We observe that we can generate sketches for a *judiciously chosen subset* of all possible shifted sets, to ensure that can still find two appropriate sketches for two sets to perform the point estimation for any $\delta \in [0, N]$.

Let $\lambda := \lceil \sqrt{N} \rceil$. For a set S_A, we generate 2λ sketches for S_A shifted by $i \in I$, where

$$I = \{0, 1, 2, \cdots, \lambda - 1\} \cup \{i \cdot \lambda \mid i \in [1, \lambda]\} \quad (2)$$

Algorithm 1 describes the estimation procedure. Lines 2–5 compute the correct offsets (also called indices) of the sketches of S_A and S_B. Then Line 6 performs the estimation with the corresponding bottom-k sketches.

Algorithm 1: PointQueryOnlineEstimation(S_A, S_B, δ)

Input : δ: query gap. N: maximum gap.
Output: An estimate of $|S_A \cap^{=\delta} S_B|$

1 $\lambda \leftarrow \lceil \sqrt{N} \rceil$;
2 **if** $\delta \pmod{\lambda} = 0$ **and** $\delta \neq N$ **then**
3 | $i_A \leftarrow \lambda + \delta$; $i_B \leftarrow \lambda$;
4 **else**
5 | $i_A \leftarrow \lceil \delta/\lambda \rceil \cdot \lambda$; $i_B \leftarrow \lceil \delta/\lambda \rceil \cdot \lambda - \delta$;
6 **return** Bottom-k-Estimate ($sk(S_A^{+i_A})$, $sk(S_B^{+i_B})$);

EXAMPLE 3. *Continue the previous example.* $\lambda = \lceil \sqrt{N} \rceil = 3$. *In our improved method, the following sketches are generated for every set S*

$$sk(S_i^{+0}), sk(S_i^{+1}), sk(S_i^{+2}), sk(S_i^{+3}), sk(S_i^{+6}), sk(S_i^{+9}).$$

For point estimation with $\delta = 5$, *we compute* $i_A = 6$ *and* $i_B = 1$ *according to Algorithm 1. Then we load* $sk(S_A^{+6})$ *and* $sk(S_B^{+1})$ *and perform the estimation.*

The correctness of Algorithm 1 depends on two facts:

- Gapped set intersection size is shift-invariant as shown in Lemma 1, and
- $\forall \delta \in [0, N]$, we can always locate the i_A and i_B from the index set (Equation (2)) such that $i_A - i_B = \delta$.

LEMMA 1. $\forall d$, $|S_A \cap^{=\delta} S_B| = |S_A^{+d} \cap^{=\delta} S_B^{+d}|$.

The improved method has a $O(\sqrt{N} \cdot k)$ space complexity per set, $O(k)$ estimation time, and the same estimation quality guarantees as the bottom-k sketch.

4.2.1 Asymptotic Space Optimality and Approximation Ratio

We show that our improved method is asymptotically space optimal in this reduction framework. To facilitate the analysis, a computational model is formalized below in Definition 2.

DEFINITION 2. *Given set* $G = \{0, 1, 2, \cdots, N\}$, *where* N *is the maximum gap predefined. We want to find an integer set* P *with minimum cardinality, such that* $\forall g \in G$, *there exist* $i, j \in P$ *satisfying* $i - j = g$.

PROPERTY 1. *The lower bound of* $|P|$ *is* $\Omega(\sqrt{N})$.

PROOF. First there are no duplicate elements in P, otherwise $|P|$ cannot reach the minimum since it is allowed to choose two identical elements from P to get $0 \in G$. Now that all elements in P are different, we can construct a mapping f from $i - j$ to $G \setminus \{0\}$. It is easy to see the lower bound will be achieved when the mapping is bijective. Hence, the number of all possible choices of $i - j$ is $\binom{|P|}{2}$. Since $\binom{|P|}{2} \geq N$, we have $|P| = \Omega(\sqrt{N})$. □

COROLLARY 1. *The number of sketches constructed in our improved method is within a factor of* $\sqrt{2}$ *of the optimal solution.*

4.3 Range Estimation

4.3.1 Basic Method for Range Estimation

Our basic method for range estimation is to reduce a range estimation to multiple point estimations, due to the following equivalence.

THEOREM 1. $S_A \cap^{\leq\delta} S_B = \bigcup_{i=0}^{\delta} (S_A \cap^{=i} S_B)$. *In addition,* $\forall i \neq j, (\{S_A \cap^{=i} S_B\}) \cap (\{S_A \cap^{=j} S_B\}) = \emptyset$.

Theorem 1 reveals that the range gapped set intersection results can be partitioned into disjoint subsets, each is the result of a point gapped set intersection. Taking the cardinality on both sides of the equation and we have the following Corollary.

COROLLARY 2. $|S_A \cap^{\leq\delta} S_B| = \sum_{i=0}^{\delta} |S_A \cap^{=i} S_B|$.

Corollary 2 enables us to sum up $\delta + 1$ point estimation results to answer a range estimation. While this does not increase the space complexity, the estimation time is linear in the range δ. When δ is large, the estimation time grows quickly, which is not desirable.

4.3.2 Merge of Shifted Sets

We introduce several essential concepts, which enable us to present an observation using an example. This relates the range estimation to the problem of estimating the inner product of multisets, each obtained by merging shifted sets in a particular pattern.

We define a multiset M as a set of elements, each associated with its multiplicity, i.e., $M = \{a_1 : m_1, a_2 : m_2, \ldots, a_n : m_n\}$. $\mathsf{elems}(M)$ returns all the elements in the multiset M, i.e., $\{a_1, a_2, \ldots, a_n\}$. The multiplicity of an element e in M is denoted as $\mathsf{cnt}_M(e)$. Note that a set is just a special case of a multiset where all the multiplicities equal 1.

Let U be the universe of all elements. Each multiset can be implicitly cast into a $|U|$-dimensional vector where the dimension values are the multiplicities of the corresponding elements (default to 0). Hence, we can define the *inner product* of two multisets as

$$\langle M_A, M_B \rangle = \sum_{e \in \mathsf{elems}(M_A) \cap \mathsf{elems}(M_B)} \mathsf{cnt}_{M_A}(e) \cdot \mathsf{cnt}_{M_B}(e).$$

Now, we can illustrate an important observation that leads to our improved range estimation in Example 4.

EXAMPLE 4. *Consider the same instance in Example 3 and we want to estimate* $S_A \cap^{\leq\delta} S_B$. *Table 4(a) enumerates for all possible* $\delta \in [0, 8]$ *the shifted* S_A *and* S_B *that will be used for set intersection with point gap* δ. *For example, the*

Table 4: Illustration of Shift Sets Used for Point/Range Estimation for $\delta \in [0, 8]$

(a) Shifted Sets (Illustrating $\delta = 5$)

S_A^{+9}	8	7	6
S_A^{+6}	5	4	3
S_A^{+3}	2	1	0
	S_B^{+1}	S_B^{+2}	S_B^{+3}

(b) Merged Shifted Sets (Illustrating $\delta = 7$)

$\biguplus_{i \in \{3,6,9\}} S_A^{+i}$	8	7	6	S_A^{+9}
$\biguplus_{i \in \{3,6\}} S_A^{+i}$	5	4	3	S_A^{+6}
$\biguplus_{i \in \{3\}} S_A^{+i}$	2	1	0	S_A^{+3}
	$\biguplus_{i \in \{1,2,3\}} S_B^{+i}$	$\biguplus_{i \in \{2,3\}} S_B^{+i}$	$\biguplus_{i \in \{3\}} S_B^{+i}$	

cell with green background is for $\delta = 5$; it is associated with S_A^{+6} and S_B^{+1}. This means $|S_A \cap^{=5} S_B| = |S_A^{+6} \cap S_B^{+1}|$.

Now consider the range gapped set intersection with $\delta = 5$. Corollary 2 shows that the result size $|S_A \cap^{\leq 5} S_B|$ equals the sum of the size of 6 point gapped set intersections, with the gap constraint between 0 and 5. By looking at Table 4(a), we can see the latter is equivalent to $\langle M_A, M_B \rangle$, where

$$M_A = (S_A^{+3} \uplus S_A^{+6}), \qquad M_B = (S_B^{+1} \uplus S_B^{+2} \uplus S_B^{+3})$$

Note that we need to use multiset union (also called ***merge*** *in this paper, denoted as $\uplus$) and the inner product, as there may be potential duplicate elements. Obviously, if we can estimate the inner product of multisets, then we can perform one estimation rather than six point estimations.*

By considering all possible δ values in Example 4, we can observe the pattern where multiple shifted sets are merged. To simplify the notation, we use the set of shift values as an identifier (or index) for the merged multiset, i.e., if $M = S_A^{+i_1} \uplus S_A^{+i_2} \ldots \uplus S_A^{+i_j}$, then we say M's **index** is $\{ i_1, i_2, \ldots, i_j \}$ and it uniquely identifies M.

Let $\lambda = \lceil \sqrt{N} \rceil$, and $i \geq 1$.

- For shift values within $[1, \lambda]$, we need to merge its suffixes, i.e., generating indices $\{ i, i+1, \ldots, \lambda \}$, for $1 \leq i < \lambda$.
- For shift values within $[\lambda, \lambda^2]$, we need to merge its prefixes, i.e., generating indices $\{ \lambda, 2\lambda, \ldots, i \cdot \lambda \}$, for $1 < i \leq \lambda$.

4.3.3 Estimating the Inner Product of Two Multisets

As motivated in Example 4, we need to estimate the inner product of two multisets. While there are many alternative methods (such as Tug-of-War [1] and Count-Min [10] sketches), we observe that the input multisets are always those shifted sets generated for the point estimation task, which means each of them has already its bottom-k sketch built or maintained. Therefore, we develop an estimator by *extending the bottom-k sketch* as follows.

Firstly, we define our **multiset bottom-k sketch** for a multiset obtained by merging multiple shifted sets, each with its own bottom-k sketch. Let $\mathcal{S} = \{ S_1, S_2, \ldots, S_n \}$ denote a set of shifted sets, each with its bottom-k sketch $sk(S_i)$. Let $M = \uplus_{i=1}^{n} S_i$. M's multiset bottom-k sketch, denoted by $msk(M)$, is obtained by a *truncated merge* of the sketches, i.e.,

1. first merging $sk(S_i)$ into a multiset M', and
2. then keeping only the k smallest elements and their multiplicities in M'.

Figure 1 illustrates the relationship between a multiset bottom-k sketch and its constituent bottom-k sketches.

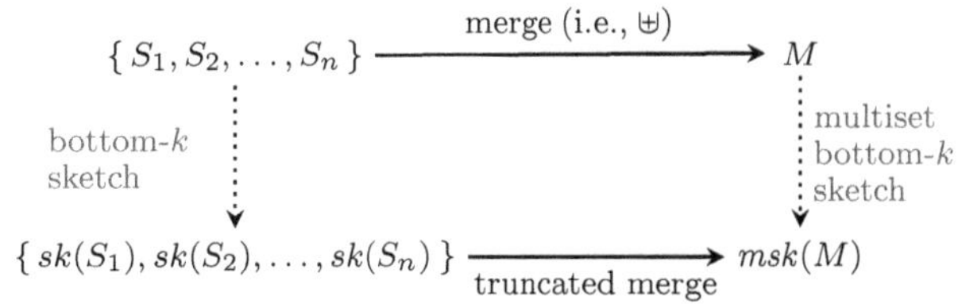

Figure 1: From bottom-k Sketches to a Multiset bottom-k Sketch

Given two multiset bottom-k sketches $msk(M_A)$ and $msk(M_B)$, their *range union sketch*, denoted by $rus(msk(M_A), msk(M_B))$, is a multiset that contains all the hash values in $\mathsf{elems}(msk(M_A)) \uplus \mathsf{elems}(msk(M_B))$ that are smaller than $\min(msk(M_A)^{(k)}, msk(M_B)^{(k)})$, as well as the sum of their multiplicities in $msk(M_A)$ and $msk(M_B)$. Given $msk(M_A)$ and $msk(M_B)$, we propose an unbiased estimator of $\langle M_A, M_B \rangle$, as shown in Theorem 2. Furthermore, it can be shown that, by using the range union sketch, our method takes advantage of all the information available in $msk(M_A)$ and $msk(M_B)$ to arrive at the best possible estimation.

THEOREM 2. *Given two multiset bottom-k sketches $msk(M_A)$ and $msk(M_B)$, let $rus_\cap = \mathsf{elems}(msk(M_A)) \cap \mathsf{elems}(msk(M_B)) \cap \mathsf{elems}(rus(msk(M_A), msk(M_B)))$, then*

$$\hat{t}_r = \frac{\sum_{e \in rus_\cap} (\mathsf{cnt}_{msk(M_A)}(e) \cdot \mathsf{cnt}_{msk(M_B)}(e))}{\min\{ msk(M_A)^{(k)}, msk(M_B)^{(k)} \}}. \quad (3)$$

is an unbiased estimator of $\langle M_A, M_B \rangle$.

PROOF. Define *adjusted multiplicity* for each $e \in \mathsf{elems}(M_A) \cap \mathsf{elems}(M_B)$ to be:

$$a_e = \begin{cases} \frac{\mathsf{cnt}_{msk(M_A)}(e) \cdot \mathsf{cnt}_{msk(M_B)}(e)}{rus^{(l)}} & \text{, if } e \text{ is sampled in } rus_\cap \\ 0 & \text{, otherwise.} \end{cases} \quad (4)$$

where $rus^{(l)} = \min\{ msk(M_A)^{(k)}, msk(M_B)^{(k)} \}$, i.e., it is the l-th smallest hash values in rus. Then we can write $\hat{t}_r$ as $\sum_{e \in rus_\cap} \frac{\mathsf{cnt}_{msk(M_A)}(e) \cdot \mathsf{cnt}_{msk(M_B)}(e)}{rus^{(l)}}$. The expectation is

$$\begin{aligned} \mathbf{E}\left[\hat{t}_r\right] &= \mathbf{E}\left[\sum_{e \in rus_\cap} \frac{\mathsf{cnt}_{msk(M_A)}(e) \cdot \mathsf{cnt}_{msk(M_B)}(e)}{rus^{(l)}} \right] \\ &= \sum_{e \in \mathsf{elems}(M_A) \cap \mathsf{elems}(M_B)} \mathbf{E}\left[a_e\right] \\ &= \sum_{e \in \mathsf{elems}(M_A) \cap \mathsf{elems}(M_B)} \mathsf{cnt}_{msk(M_A)}(e) \cdot \mathsf{cnt}_{msk(M_B)}(e) \\ &= \sum_{e \in \mathsf{elems}(M_A) \cap \mathsf{elems}(M_B)} \mathsf{cnt}_{M_A}(e) \cdot \mathsf{cnt}_{M_B}(e). \end{aligned}$$

The last step is because rus keeps *complete* multiplicity information for each underlying set element included in rus. *Complete* means if element e is sampled in $rus_\cap$, it holds that $\mathsf{cnt}_{msk(M)}(e) = \mathsf{cnt}_M(e)$. Since we are doing consistent uniform sampling in $\mathsf{elems}(M_A) \cup \mathsf{elems}(M_B)$. Therefore, $\mathbf{E}\left[\hat{t}_r\right] = \langle M_A, M_B \rangle$. □

Furthermore, by setting k to an appropriate value, we can achieve a probabilistic guarantee for $\hat{t}_r$, as shown in Theorem 3.

THEOREM 3. *Let $\mu = \langle M_A, M_B \rangle$. For any given ϵ and ρ, by setting $k = \min\{\max\{k_1, k_2\}, \max\{|\mathsf{elems}(M_A)|, |\mathsf{elems}(M_B)|\}\}$, where k_1 satisfies Eq. (5) and $k_2 = \frac{(|\mathsf{elems}(M_A)|+2)N}{\mu} \cdot \frac{2+\epsilon}{\epsilon^2} \ln \frac{4}{\rho}$, we can guarantee that* $\mathbf{Pr}\left[|\hat{t}_r - \mu| \leq \epsilon\mu\right] \geq 1 - \rho$.

PROOF. We first define two propositions (a) and (b). Let $X_i = a_i \cdot \frac{k}{(|\mathsf{elems}(M_A)|+2)N}$ and e_i be the corresponding element, a_i as defined in Eq. (4), and k_1 and k_2 as defined in the Theorem.

- Proposition (a): When $k \geq k_1$, $\mathbf{Pr}[X_i > 1] \leq \frac{\rho}{2}$.
- Proposition (b): When $k \geq k_2$, $\mathbf{Pr}\left[|\hat{t}_r - \mu| \geq \epsilon\mu\right] \leq \frac{\rho}{2}$.

If both of them are proved, then when $k \geq \max\{k_1, k_2\}$, we know that $\mathbf{Pr}\left[|\hat{t}_r - \mu| \geq \epsilon\mu\right] \leq \rho$ based on the Union Bound.

Proof of Proposition (a). Without loss of generality, we assume $|\mathsf{elems}(M_A)| > |\mathsf{elems}(M_B)|$. Given ρ, let k_1 be solution to Eq. (5):

$$\int_0^{\frac{k}{|\mathsf{elems}(M_A)|+2}} \frac{t^{k-1}(1-t)^{|\mathsf{elems}(M_A) \cup \mathsf{elems}(M_B)|-k}}{B(k, |\mathsf{elems}(M_A) \cup \mathsf{elems}(M_B)| - k + 1)} dt \leq \frac{\rho}{2}, \tag{5}$$

where $B(k, |\mathsf{elems}(M_A) \cup \mathsf{elems}(M_B)| - k + 1)$ is the Beta function. It also holds:

$$\begin{aligned} &\mathbf{Pr}[X_i > 1] \\ &= \mathbf{Pr}\left[\frac{\mathsf{cnt}_{msk(M_A)}(e_i) \cdot \mathsf{cnt}_{msk(M_B)}(e_i)}{msk(M_A)^{(k)}} > \frac{(|\mathsf{elems}(M_A)| + 2)N}{k}\right] \\ &\leq \mathbf{Pr}\left[msk(M_A) < \frac{k}{|\mathsf{elems}(M_A)| + 2}\right]. \end{aligned} \tag{6}$$

The last step is because $\mathsf{cnt}_{msk(M_A)}(e_i) \cdot \mathsf{cnt}_{msk(M_B)}(e_i) \leq N$. Besides, when $k > k_1$, Eq. (5) is equivalent to:

$$\mathbf{Pr}\left[msk(M_A)^{(k)} < \frac{k}{|\mathsf{elems}(M_A)| + 2}\right] < \frac{\rho}{2}. \tag{7}$$

Since we are doing uniform random sample in the space of $\mathsf{elems}(M_A) \cup \mathsf{elems}(M_B)$, where $msk(M_A)^{(k)}$ is the k-th order statistics therein.

Thus from Eq. (6) and (7), we know when $k > k_1$, $\mathbf{Pr}[X_i > 1] \leq \frac{\rho}{2}$.

Proof of Proposition (b). Now that we can guarantee $X_i \in [0, 1]$ almost surely by proving Proposition (a), we can define $X = \sum X_i$ and apply the Chernoff bound to X.[1]

Let $k_2 = \frac{(|\mathsf{elems}(M_A)|+2)N}{\mu} \cdot \frac{2+\epsilon}{\epsilon^2} \ln \frac{4}{\rho}$. When $k > k_2$, we have

$$2 \exp\left(-\frac{\epsilon^2}{2+\epsilon} \frac{\mu k}{(|\mathsf{elems}(M_A)| + 2)N}\right) \leq \frac{\rho}{2}.$$

According to the Chernoff bound, we have

$$\begin{aligned} &\mathbf{Pr}\left[|\hat{t}_r - \mu| \geq \epsilon\mu\right] \\ &\leq 2 \exp\left(-\frac{\epsilon^2}{2+\epsilon} \cdot \frac{\mu k}{(|\mathsf{elems}(M_A)| + 2)N}\right) \leq \frac{\rho}{2}. \end{aligned}$$

Then from Union Bound, it guarantees that when $k \geq \max(k_1, k_2)$, $\mathbf{Pr}\left[|\hat{t}_r - \mu| \geq \epsilon\mu\right] \leq \delta$. □

[1]Since bottom-k belongs to sampling without replacement strategy, it will cause negative associations between each sample value [14]. Nevertheless, according to [14], Chernoff bounds are still applicable to sums of random variables with negative associations.

4.3.4 Improved Range Estimator

In our improved methods, given a maximum gap N, let $\lambda = \lceil \sqrt{N} \rceil$. We generate three categories of sketches:

- Category I: $\lambda + 1$ *bottom-k sketches* for shifts $i \in \{ j\lambda \mid 0 \leq j \leq \lambda \}$
- Category II: $\lambda - 1$ *multiset bottom-k sketches* with indices $\{\lambda, 2\lambda\}, \{\lambda, 2\lambda, 3\lambda\}, \cdots, \{\lambda, 2\lambda, \ldots, \lambda^2\}$.
- Category III: $\lambda - 1$ *multiset bottom-k sketches* with indices $\{\lambda, \lambda-1\}, \{\lambda, \lambda-1, \lambda-2\}, \cdots, \{\lambda, \lambda-1, \ldots, 1\}$.

Table 4(b) illustrates Category I sketches on the right-hand side, Category II sketches on the left-hand side, and Category III sketches on the bottom side, for the running example.

For any range $[0, \delta]$, it can always be decomposed to at most two sub-ranges. For example, Table 4(b) illustrates that $[0, 7]$ is decomposed into

- $[0, 5]$. This corresponds to $S_A \cap^{\leq 5} S_B$, and can be answered by estimating the size of $\langle \biguplus_{i \in \{3,6\}} S_A^{+i}, \biguplus_{i \in \{1,2,3\}} S_B^{+i} \rangle$.
- $[6, 7]$. This corresponds to $S_A \cap^{[6,7]} S_B$, and can be answered by estimating the size of $\langle S_A^{+9}, \biguplus_{i \in \{2,3\}} S_B^{+i} \rangle$.[2]

Algorithm 2: DecomposeRange (S_A, S_B, δ)

Input : δ: query gap. N: maximum gap.
Output: An array of indices pairs.

$\lambda \leftarrow \lceil \sqrt{N} \rceil$;
if $\delta < \lambda$ **or** $(\delta + 1) \mod x = 0$ **then**
  $i_A \leftarrow \{ i \cdot \lambda \mid i \in [1, \max(\lceil \delta/\lambda \rceil, 1)] \}$;
  $i_B \leftarrow \{ \lambda - i \mid i \in [0, \delta - \lfloor \delta/\lambda \rfloor \cdot \lambda] \}$;
  return $\{ (i_A, i_B) \}$;
else
  $i_A^l \leftarrow \{ i \cdot \lambda \mid i \in [1, \lfloor (\delta+1)/\lambda \rfloor] \}$;
  $i_B^l \leftarrow \{ i \mid i \in [1, \lambda] \}$;
  if $\delta = N$ **then**
    $i_A^r \leftarrow N$;
    $i_B^r \leftarrow 0$;
  else
    $i_A^r \leftarrow \lambda \cdot \lceil (\delta+1)/\lambda \rceil$;
    $i_B^r \leftarrow \{ \lambda - i \mid i \in [0, \delta \mod \lambda] \}$;
  return $\{ (i_A^l, i_B^l), (i_A^r, i_B^r) \}$;

Algorithm 3: RangeQueryOnlineEstimation (S_A, S_B, δ)

Input : δ: query gap. N: maximum gap.
Output: $\hat{t}_r$: an estimate for $S_A \cap^{\leq \delta} S_B$.

1 $arr \leftarrow$ DecomposeRange(δ) ;
2 $\hat{t}_r \leftarrow 0$;
3 **for each** $(i_A, i_B) \in arr$ **do**
4   Retrieve S_A's sketch based on the index of i_A into $msk(M_A)$ and retrieve S_B's sketch for i_B into $msk(M_B)$;
5   $\hat{t}_r \leftarrow \hat{t}_r +$ Estimate($msk(M_A)$, $msk(M_B)$);
  /* Perform estimation using two multiset bottom-k sketches based on Theorem 2 */;
6 **return** $\hat{t}_r$;

We use Algorithm 3 to perform a range estimation with the gap constraint δ. In Line 1, it calls the DecomposeRange

[2]We deem a bottom-k sketch as a special multiset bottom-k sketch where the multiplicities are all set to 1.

(δ) to decompose the range $[0, \delta]$ into one or two parts, utilizing the multiset bottom-k sketches. The returned results are one or two pairs of indices to these sketches. Lines 3–5 retrieve the corresponding sketches and perform the estimation based on Eq. (3) in Theorem 2.

The space complexity of the sketch for the range estimation is $O(\sqrt{N} \cdot k)$. And the time complexity for the estimate is $O(k)$. Thanks to Theorem 3, by setting the proper k, our estimation has at most ϵ relative error with probability at least $1 - \rho$.

Table 5: Multiset bottom-3 Sketch

indices	$msk(M_A)$	$msk(M_B)$
$\{9\}$	$\{0.15:1, 0.16:1, 0.63:1\}$	$\{0.21:1, 0.37:1, 0.53:1\}$
$\{2,3\}$	$\{0.22:2, 0.42:1, 0.48:1\}$	$\{0.42:1, 0.48:1, 0.68:1\}$
$\vdots$	$\vdots$	$\vdots$
$\{3,6\}$	$\{0.22:1, 0.42:2, 0.48:1\}$	$\{0.16:1, 0.37:1, 0.48:1\}$
$\{1,2,3\}$	$\{0.22:2, 0.32:1, 0.42:1\}$	$\{0.22:1, 0.42:2, 0.48:2\}$

EXAMPLE 5. *We run Algorithm 3 for the same running example given before. Given* $\delta = 7$*, we want to estimate* $|S_A \cap^{\leq 7} S_B|$. *Line 1 decomposes* $[0, 7]$ *into two parts of indices, which is* $arr = \{(\{3,6\},\{1,2,3\}), (\{9\},\{2,3\})\}$. *For* $(\{3,6\},\{1,2,3\})$*, Line 4 retrieves* $msk(S_A^{+3,6}) = \{0.22 : 1, 0.42 : 2, 0.48 : 1\}$ *and* $msk(S_B^{+1,2,3}) = \{0.22 : 1, 0.42 : 2, 0.48 : 2\}$ *from Table 5. Then Line 5 calculates* $\hat{t}_r$ *according to Theorem 2. It returns* $\hat{t}_r$ *to be* $^{(1 \cdot 1 + 2 \cdot 2)}/_{0.48} = 10.42$. *Similar steps go for the second part indexed by* $(\{9\},\{2,3\})$*, while there is no matching for this part. Finally, the algorithm returns* $\hat{t}_r$ *to be* 10.42. *The actual* $|S_A \cap^{\leq 7} S_B|$ *is* 11.

5. APPLICATIONS

The proposed methods have many important applications, e.g. top-K related keywords mining, query optimization for search engine, and system troubleshooting in log analysis. In this section, we present the details of efficient mining top-K related keywords from a document collection.

Let $\mathcal{V}$ be the vocabulary of the document collection. For ease of illustration, we concatenate all documents into one single document D with suitable padding of out-of-vocabulary keywords. For each keyword $v \in \mathcal{V}$, we create a set S_v, which consists of all the positions in D where it occurs. Let query S_Q be a set of positions. For any given keyword v, we can measure its correlation with the query by counting the number of occurrences of v in a δ-vicinity of any position in S_Q. The top-K related keywords problem is to find the K keywords in $\mathcal{V}$ that has the highest correlation.

Solving the problem exactly requires either intersecting all keywords in $\mathcal{V}$ or retrieving the δ-vicinity centered at positions in S_Q. Neither method scales well with large document collections.

To solve the problem approximately, we can apply range estimation to estimate the correlation, then return the K keywords with largest estimated size. Nevertheless, this method is still time consuming, as it is linear to vocabulary size $|\mathcal{V}|$.

We observe that most of the keywords set do not have a significant gapped intersection size with the query, hence it is highly likely that their sketches share *no* common hash value with the sketch of the query. It is thus desirable to consider only those keywords that share at least one hash value in their appropriate multiset bottom-k sketches with the bottom-k sketch of the query.

Therefore, we propose to build an inverted index, which maps $(hashValue, index)$ to a keyword v. Intuitively, by probing the inverted index with every hash value in S_Q's sketch, we can obtain a list of candidate keywords. Due to the range decomposition, we also have the additional constraint that the indices of these shared hash values must agree with those calculated for the current δ (i.e., returned by DecomposeRange).

Algorithm 4: TopKRangeEstimation (S_Q, δ, K, I)

Input : S_Q: sets of query positions; δ: query gap; K: top-K; I: the inverted index that maps hash values (and sketch's indices) to a keyword.
Output: Top-K keywords based on their estimated intersection size with S_Q

```
1 R ← ∅;   Cand ← ∅ ;
2 arr ← DecomposeRange(δ) ;
3 for each (i_A, i_B) ∈ arr do
4     Retrieve S_Q's multiset
      bottom-k sketch whose index value is i_A into M_Q;
5     for each element e ∈ elems(msk(M_q)) do
6         Cand ← Cand ∪ I[(e, i_B)];
          /* A list of keywords will
          be returned by looking up the index I */;
7 for each keyword v ∈ Cand do
8     R ← R ∪ (v, RangeQueryOnlineEstimation(S_Q, S_v, δ));
9 return the K largest
  entries in R in terms of the estimated intersection size;
```

Algorithm 4 gives the pseudocode for the algorithm. Initially the candidate set *Cand* is empty (Line 1). In Line 2, we obtain one or two pairs of indices, indexing into S_Q's and a potential candidate set's multiset bottom-k sketches. We iterate over all the pairs. For each pair of indices, we use i_A to retrieve the sketch of S_Q, and use Line 5–6 to retrieve all keywords such that their sketches with index value i_B share the same hash value (i.e., e in the code). This step is aided by the precomputed inverted index as a simple index lookup. Finally, we perform range estimate between S_Q and the set of each candidate keywords and return the largest K keywords.

The algorithm issues at most $2k - 2$ index lookups, and performs $|Cand|$ number of range estimations, where $|Cand|$ is the size of the candidate set. Finding the top-K entries from R and sorting them take $O(K \log K)$ time. Therefore, the total estimation time is $O(|Cand| \cdot k + K \log K)$.

In our implementation, we also perform the following optimizations. For every keyword returned from the index lookup (Line 6), we can accumulate its partial inner product with the query's sketch (i.e., the numerator of Eq. (3)). It can be shown that the numerator's value will be correctly calculated after the loop of Lines 3–6 ends. Therefore, the RangeQueryOnlineEstimation function only needs to do $O(1)$ computation to get the range estimation for each candidate.

EXAMPLE 6. *Using the same example, we can build the inverted index as shown in Table 6.*

Consider the top-1 related keyword query for A with $\delta = 5$. *DecomposeRange gives us one pair of indices* $(\{3,6\},\{1,2,3\})$. *This means we are concerned with the query's sketch indexed by* $\{3,6\}$ *and the candidate's sketch indexed by* $\{1,2,3\}$. *We load the query sketch* $msk(S_A^{+3,6}) =$

Table 6: Inverted Index for top-K Related Keyword Mining

Key	List of Keywords
$(0.15, \{9\})$	S_A
$(0.16, \{3, 6\})$	S_B
$(0.16, \{9\})$	S_A
$(0.21, \{9\})$	S_B
$(0.22, \{1, 2, 3\})$	S_A, S_B
$(0.22, \{2, 3\})$	S_A
$(0.22, \{3, 6\})$	S_A
...	...

$\{0.22 : 1, 0.42 : 2, 0.48 : 1\}$. *We issue three lookups with keys:* $(0.22, \{1, 2, 3\})$, $(0.42, \{1, 2, 3\})$, *and* $(0.48, \{1, 2, 3\})$. *These lookups find matches* S_B, *which is added to the candidate set. Finally we perform range estimation between the query and the candidates then return the top-1 keyword.*

6. EXPERIMENTAL EVALUATION

In this section, we present the results of a comprehensive performance study to evaluate the efficiency and effectiveness of the proposed techniques.

6.1 Experiment Setup

We use the following algorithms for point and range estimation.

- GSISE-k is our proposed point (range) estimation method and k determines the size of a single bottom-k sketch.
- PointSum-k is our basic range estimation methods by summing up multiple point estimation results.
- Exact calculates the exact answer for point and range estimation, respectively.

We use the following algorithms for the top-K related keyword query.

- TopK is the hash table based top-K range estimation method proposed in Section 5.
- Exact$_{\mathsf{topk}}$ is the exact algorithm for top-K range estimation. The algorithm is conducted by scanning the whole dataset, finding each occurrence of the query keyword, and bookkeeping the count of every other keyword that occurs within the δ neighborhood. Finally, it returns the K keywords with highest number of occurrences.

The dataset we use is a subset of the **ClueWeb** containing 500 million English web pages from the ClueWeb09 collection.[3] We remove infrequent keywords and keep the 100k most frequent keywords. We build the positional inverted index for these keywords, and treat each inverted list as a set. We then build three sets of sketches on these sets, i.e., point sketch, range sketch, and top-K sketch for the respective estimation problems.

The complete original positional index requires more than 2 days to construct using Hadoop on a cluster of 20 PCs, and the final index is stored on the HDFS of the Hadoop cluster. Without compression, the overall index consumes around 1TB space, which is impossible to load into a single commodity PC's memory. The overall size of the sketch is small enough to fit into our testing environment with 96GB RAM. Therefore, the experiments conducted on the sketches are memory-based, while exact algorithms that processes inverted lists or scanning documents have to use disk I/Os.

[3]http://lemurproject.org/clueweb09.php

Estimation Workload. We randomly select 100 pairs of keywords to perform point and range estimation with different parameter settings on their corresponding sets. We set maximum gap $N = 100$. k varies between 1,000 to 100,000 (default). The query gap δ varies between 20 and 100.

We measure the **running time** and **relative error** for point and range estimation methods. We measure **recall** and **extended recall** for TopK methods. Recall is defined as A_K/K, where A_K is the number of exact top-K results returned by an algorithm that outputs K results. The extended recall is defined by $A_{L\times K}/K$, where $A_{L\times K}$ is the number of exact top-K results returned by an algorithm that outputs $L \times K$ results, L is the extension rate. All measurements shown are averaged over 100 queries.

The experiment parameter settings of the evaluated algorithms are listed in Table 7, where the default parameters are highlighted in bold.

Table 7: Parameter Settings

Parameters	Setting (Defaults are in bold)
maximum gap	**100**
top-K	**1**, 10, 100
bottom-k	1000, 5000, 10000, 15000, **20000**
query gaps	20, 40, 60, 80, **100**

6.2 Point Estimation

In Figure 2(a), we show the point estimation time by varying query gaps. Compared with the exact algorithm, the sketch based method is more than 2 order of magnitudes faster. Query gaps do not affect the estimation time and exact time. As both exact and estimation methods rely on intersection algorithm of complexity $O(k)$ to find common elements. GSISE-1k, GSISE-5k, GSISE-10k, GSISE-15k, and GSISE-20k spend 0.38, 1.66, 3.47, 5.03 and 6.92 milliseconds to perform one estimation. The trend is linear. Average length of inverted list size is around 2.5 million, which is 125 times of GSISE-20k's sketch size. Meanwhile, Exact algorithm uses $892ms$ to calculate exact answer, which is $892/6.92 = 128$ times of GSISE-20k's estimation time. When dataset size increases, exact results will need longer time, while the sketch estimation time is immune to the increasing dataset size.

In Figure 2(b) and figure 2(c), we show how the relative error decreases while the bottom-k sketch size is increasing. When gap is 80, the relative error drops from 1 to 0.4 with k changing from 1000 to 20,000. By further increasing k up to 100,000, the relative error reduces to less than 0.19. Based on the analysis in section 3.2, the relative error is inverse proportional to the square root of bottom-k size. Despite the fluctuation, relative error is not affected by the different query gaps, the fluctuation is caused by different intersection sizes at different gaps. In our experiments, gap 40 has slightly more intersections than gap 100, which reflects that gap 40 has slightly less relative error than gap 100.

6.3 Range Estimation

From Figure 2(d) to 2(f), we present range query estimation results.

- **Time.** Figure 2(d) shows that our GSISE range estimation method has the best performance compared to other methods. For example, GSISE-20k is 128 times faster than Exact and 108 times faster than PointSum-20k when gap is 100. Similar to point estimation, GSISE is stable with different gaps. According to Algorithm 2, any range query can be decomposed into at most two estimation queries, and the efficiency of estimation only relies on k. PointSum performs individual point estimations for each gap and uses the summation as the estimation result. Thus the processing time of PointSum is linear to the query gap. When gap is 20, 40, 60, 80 and 100, the processing time of PointSum-20k is 109.0, 213.1, 302.7, 410.6, and 508.0 milliseconds, which is linearly increasing with respect to gap.

- **Relative Error.** As shown in Figure 2(e), when query gap increases, the relative errors of all methods decrease. This is because larger range gap tends to result in larger intersection size. According to Theorem 3, it is equivalent to using a larger k.

It is noted that PointSum achieves slightly lower relative error than range estimation given the same k setting. The reason is that PointSum utilizes all values in the point shifted sketch for estimating, which is equivalent to merging *without* truncating at k-th hash value. As opposed to the truncated merge operation applied to GSISE_r index, PointSum will consume up to more than λ times space.To be more specific, in Figure 2(e), when query gap is 100, the range sketch required for GSISE-20k is $2 \times 20k$, while for PointSum, the cost is $20 \times 20k$. However, the PointSum-20k only decrease the error by less than 0.05. Considering the tremendous performance gain in efficiency and storage, the tiny sacrifice in relative error can be ignored.

Figure 2(f) shows similar trend as Figure 2(c). Larger k will lead to smaller relative error. The relative error decreases rapidly at the initial increasing of k, then flattens after $k > 10,000$. PointSum has smaller relative error than GSISE methods, however, the relative errors are almost the same when k is large. Interestingly, the storage cost of PointSum-1k of gap 100($20 \times 1k = 20k$) and of GSISE-10k of gap 100($2 \times 10k = 20k$) are the same, so are the relative error of PointSum-1k of gap 100 and GSISE-10k, which are 0.267 and 0.266, respectively.

6.4 Top-K Related Keywords Mining

The experiment results of top-K problem are presented in Figures 2(g) to 2(o).

- **Time**. In Figures 2(g), 2(j) and 2(m), we investigate the response time by varying K of top-K from 1 to 100. In general, we can see that the average query processing time is under 25 milliseconds, which is quite small compared to $\mathsf{Exact}_{\mathsf{topk}}$. In fact, as we use large web page corpus, the $\mathsf{Exact}_{\mathsf{topk}}$ algorithm must run on the cluster in a batch mode for the given queries, which takes 6 hours to scan through the original documents in order to output top-K results. In each figure, by increasing the query gaps from 20 to 100, we observe that the query processing time increases slightly. This is due to the processing of top-K range estimation needs to count the number of common sketch values in the hash table. Larger query gap will result in larger intersection size, which means more common sketch values when looking up the hash table. Same reason goes for the increasing query processing time when k increases.
- **Recall**. We show the recall of our algorithms in different top-K settings in Figures 2(h), 2(k) and 2(n). We can observe that the recall grows with the increase of k. Larger k incurs smaller relative error, consequently improves the recall of the top-K algorithms. Furthermore, it is observed that query gap has no influence on the recall, which shows great stability over different query gap settings.
- **Extended Recall**. As shown in Figure 2(g) and Figure 2(m), the processing time of returning top 1 result and top 100 results are similar. This gives us the motivation of measuring extended recall. Figures 2(i), 2(l) and 2(o), present the extended recall. The extension rate is up to 4. In Figure 2(i), when extension rate is larger than 3, the recall of GSISE-15k and GSISE-20k both reach 90%. In other figures, all GSISE-20k experiments can reach more than 80% of recall when extension rate is 4. GSISE-1k performs inadequate even when extension rate reaches 4.

In summary, our top-K estimation algorithm shows substantial performance advantage over exact methods in efficiency. Meanwhile, the recall of our algorithms can reach around 90% with slight extension of returned top-K results.

7. CONCLUSIONS

In this paper, we formally define the GSISE problem, for both point and range gap constraints. We propose space and time efficient estimation methods, based on bottom-k sketches and its extension to multisets. In addition, our estimation methods provide the probabilistic quality guarantees. We also apply our technique to the problem of finding top-K related keyword, by combining our estimation technique with the use of an inverted index. Our experiments using half a billion documents empirically verify the effectiveness and efficiency of the proposed methods.

Acknowledgements. We would like to thank Stefan Böttcher for helpful discussions and comments during our project cooperation. This work has been supported by Go8-DAAD Project RG123842, UNSW ECR/FRG PS35163, and ARC Discovery Projects DP130103401 and DP130103405.

8. REFERENCES

[1] N. Alon, Y. Matias, and M. Szegedy. The space complexity of approximating the frequency moments. In *STOC*, 1996.
[2] J. Barbay, A. López-Ortiz, and T. Lu. Faster adaptive set intersections for text searching. In *WEA*, 2006.
[3] J. Barbay, A. López-Ortiz, T. Lu, and A. Salinger. An experimental investigation of set intersection algorithms for text searching. *Journal of Experimental Algorithmics*, 14, 2009.
[4] K. S. Beyer, P. J. Haas, B. Reinwald, Y. Sismanis, and R. Gemulla. On synopses for distinct-value estimation under multiset operations. In *SIGMOD Conference*, 2007.
[5] A. Z. Broder, M. Charikar, A. M. Frieze, and M. Mitzenmacher. Min-wise independent permutations (extended abstract). In *Symposium on the Theory of Computing*, 1998.
[6] E. Cohen. Size-estimation framework with applications to transitive closure and reachability. *J. Comput. Syst. Sci.*, 55(3), 1997.
[7] E. Cohen and H. Kaplan. Summarizing data using bottom-k sketches. In *PODC*, 2007.
[8] E. Cohen and H. Kaplan. Tighter estimation using bottom k sketches. *PVLDB*, 1(1), 2008.
[9] E. Cohen and H. Kaplan. Leveraging discarded samples for tighter estimation of multiple-set aggregates. In *SIGMETRICS/Performance*, 2009.
[10] G. Cormode and S. Muthukrishnan. An improved data stream summary: The count-min sketch and its applications. In *LATIN*, 2004.
[11] J. S. Culpepper and A. Moffat. Efficient set intersection for inverted indexing. *ACM Trans. Inf. Syst.*, 29(1), 2010.
[12] E. D. Demaine, A. López-Ortiz, and J. I. Munro. Adaptive set intersections, unions, and differences. In *SODA*, 2000.
[13] B. Ding and A. C. König. Fast set intersection in memory. *PVLDB*, 4(4), 2011.

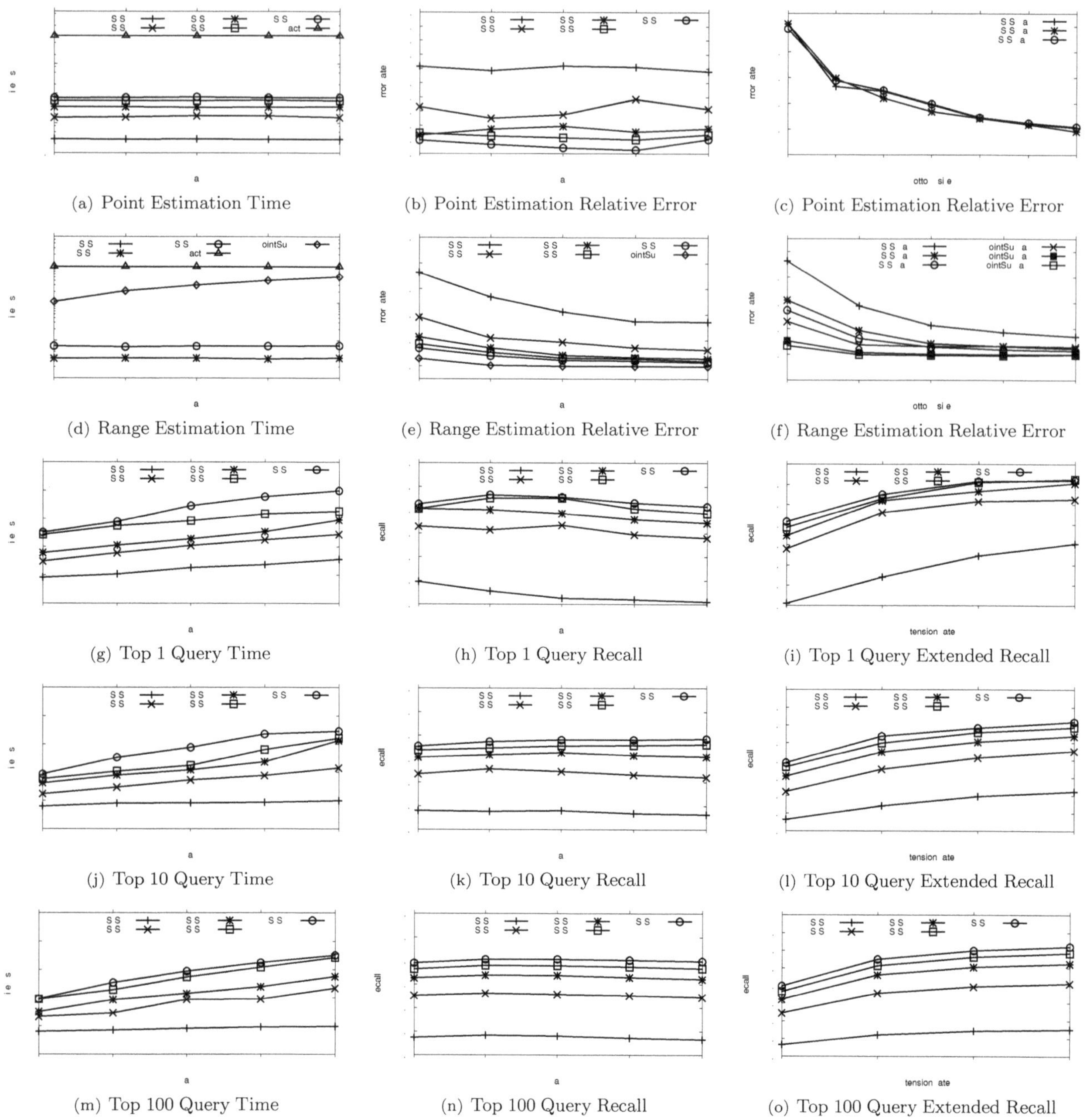

(a) Point Estimation Time (b) Point Estimation Relative Error (c) Point Estimation Relative Error

(d) Range Estimation Time (e) Range Estimation Relative Error (f) Range Estimation Relative Error

(g) Top 1 Query Time (h) Top 1 Query Recall (i) Top 1 Query Extended Recall

(j) Top 10 Query Time (k) Top 10 Query Recall (l) Top 10 Query Extended Recall

(m) Top 100 Query Time (n) Top 100 Query Recall (o) Top 100 Query Extended Recall

Figure 2: Experiment Results

[14] D. Dubhashi and D. Ranjan. Balls and bins: A study in negative dependence. *Random Structures and Algorithms*, 13:99–124, 1996.

[15] R. Fagin. Combining fuzzy information from multiple systems. *J. Comput. Syst. Sci.*, 58(1), 1999.

[16] R. Fagin, A. Lotem, and M. Naor. Optimal aggregation algorithms for middleware. *J. Comput. Syst. Sci.*, 66(4), 2003.

[17] J.-L. Hou and C.-A. Chan. Method for keyword correlation analysis. US Patent 20050071365 A1, 2005.

[18] F. K. Hwang and S. Lin. A simple algorithm for merging two disjoint linearly-ordered sets. *SIAM J. Comput.*, 1(1), 1972.

[19] P. Indyk et al. Approximate nearest neighbors: Towards removing the curse of dimensionality. In *STOC*, 1998.

[20] Y. Luo, W. Wang, X. Lin, X. Zhou, J. Wang, and K. Li. SPARK2: top-k keyword query in relational databases. *IEEE Trans. Knowl. Data Eng.*, 23(12), 2011.

[21] D. Okanohara and Y. Yoshida. Conjunctive filter: Breaking the entropy barrier. In *ALENEX*, 2010.

[22] R. Pagh, M. Stöckel, and D. P. Woodruff. Is min-wise hashing optimal for summarizing set intersection? In *PODS*, 2014.

[23] J. B. Rocha-Junior, A. Vlachou, C. Doulkeridis, and K. Nørvåg. Efficient processing of top-k spatial preference queries. *PVLDB*, 4(2), 2010.

[24] B. Schlegel, T. Willhalm, and W. Lehner. Fast sorted-set intersection using SIMD instructions. In *ADMS*, 2011.

[25] M. Sudhof, A. G. Emilsson, A. L. Maas, and C. Potts. Sentiment expression conditioned by affective transitions and social forces. In *SIGKDD*, 2014.

[26] D. Takuma and H. Yanagisawa. Faster upper bounding of intersection sizes. In *SIGIR*, 2013.

[27] M. Theobald, H. Bast, D. Majumdar, R. Schenkel, and G. Weikum. Topx: efficient and versatile top-k query processing for semistructured data. *VLDB J.*, 17(1), 2008.

[28] C. Xiao, W. Wang, X. Lin, and H. Shang. Top-k set similarity joins. In *ICDE*, 2009.

Inclusion Dependencies Reloaded

Henning Köhler
School of Engineering & Advanced Technology
Massey University, New Zealand
H.Koehler@massey.ac.nz

Sebastian Link
Department of Computer Science
The University of Auckland, New Zealand
S.Link@auckland.ac.nz

ABSTRACT

Inclusion dependencies form one of the most fundamental classes of integrity constraints. Their importance in classical data management is reinforced by modern applications such as data cleaning and profiling, entity resolution and schema matching. Surprisingly, the implication problem of inclusion dependencies has not been investigated in the context of SQL, the de-facto industry standard. Codd's relational model of data represents the idealized special case of SQL in which all attributes are declared NOT NULL. Driven by the SQL standard recommendation, we investigate inclusion dependencies and NOT NULL constraints under simple and partial semantics. Partial semantics is not natively supported by any SQL implementation but we show how classical results on the implication problem carry over into this context. Interestingly, simple semantics is natively supported by every SQL implementation, but we show that the implication problem is not finitely axiomatizable in this context. Resolving this conundrum we establish an optimal solution by identifying the desirable class of not-null inclusion dependencies (NNINDs) that subsumes simple and partial semantics as special cases, and whose associated implication problem has the same computational properties as inclusion dependencies in the relational model. That is, NNIND implication is 2-ary axiomatizable and PSPACE-complete to decide. Our proof techniques bring also forward a chase procedure for deciding NNIND implication, the NP-hard subclass of typed acyclic NNINDs, and the tractable subclasses of NNINDs whose arity is bounded.

Categories and Subject Descriptors

F.4.3 [**Mathematical Logic and Formal Languages**]: Formal Languages—*Decision problems*; H.2.3 [**Database Management**]: Languages—*Data description languages*

General Terms

Management, Theory

Permission to make digital or hard copies of all or part of this work for personal or classroom use is granted without fee provided that copies are not made or distributed for profit or commercial advantage and that copies bear this notice and the full citation on the first page. Copyrights for components of this work owned by others than ACM must be honored. Abstracting with credit is permitted. To copy otherwise, or republish, to post on servers or to redistribute to lists, requires prior specific permission and/or a fee. Request permissions from Permissions@acm.org.
CIKM'15, October 19–23, 2015, Melbourne, VIC, Australia.
© 2015 ACM. ISBN 978-1-4503-3794-6/15/10 ...$15.00.
DOI: http://dx.doi.org/10.1145/2806416.2806539.

Keywords

Axiomatization; Computational complexity; Implication; Inclusion dependency; Null; Semantics; SQL

1. INTRODUCTION

Motivation. Domain, entity and referential integrity form the three most fundamental classes of integrity rules, already proposed by Codd in his seminal paper [14]. Referential integrity is enforced by foreign keys and, more generally, inclusion dependencies (INDs). INDs empower us to specify which data must be duplicated in what relations, they can express referential integrity at the logical level and are an invaluable tool for classical data management tasks, including conceptual data modeling [12], schema design [32], and query answering [25]. Informally, an IND $R[X] \subseteq S[Y]$ with attribute sequences $X = \langle A_1, \ldots, A_n \rangle$ and $Y = \langle B_1, \ldots, B_n \rangle$ on relation schemata R and S, respectively, is satisfied by a relational database with R-relation r and S-relation s, if for every R-tuple t there is some S-tuple t' such that for all $i = 1, \ldots, n$, the value $t(A_i)$ matches the value $t'(B_i)$. An example IND in the TPC-C schema[1] is

$$\text{ORDER}[\text{c\_id, d\_id, w\_id}] \subseteq \text{CUSTOMER}[\text{c\_id, d\_id, w\_id}]$$

which states that every order references some customer c_id who placed the order in a district d_id of a warehouse w_id. As {c_id, d_id, w_id} forms a key over CUSTOMER, this IND is even a foreign key. In the context of the relational model, INDs and their core computational problem of deciding implication have received dedicated interest, see for example [9, 16, 37]. Renewed interest in INDs comes from modern applications such as data cleaning [3], data integration [7], data profiling [13, 40], schema matching [6], the semantic web [8, 38], and query answering [18]. Surprisingly, INDs have only received little attention in the context of the industry standard SQL, which subsumes relations as the idealized special case where all attributes of the schema have been declared NOT NULL, that is, the null marker $\perp$ must not feature in any of the table columns. In fact, the SQL standard proposes a simple and partial semantics for INDs. Both semantics apply the definition from the purely relational case above, but they differ in which tuples t they consider, and the definition of a match between $t(A_i)$ and $t'(B_i)$. For an IND under partial semantics $R[X] \subseteq_p S[Y]$, all tuples t are considered, and $t(A_i)$ matches $t'(B_i)$ if and only if $t(A_i) = \perp$ or $t(A_i) = t'(B_i)$ holds. For an IND under 'simple' semantics $R[X] \subseteq_s S[Y]$ there is a distinction between R-tuples

[1] http://www.tpc.org/tpcc/

t which are total on X, that is, where for all $i = 1, \ldots, n$, the value $t(A_i)$ is different from $\perp$, and R-tuples t which are partial on X, that is, not total on X. Only X-total tuples t are considered, and $t(A_i)$ matches $t'(B_i)$ if and only if $t(A_i) = t'(B_i)$ holds. For an example, consider a database where the only tuple t of the database occurs in the ORDER-relation and has projection $\langle \perp, d_1, w_1 \rangle$ on $\langle c\_id, d\_id, w\_id \rangle$. This database satisfies the simple IND

$$\text{ORDER}[\text{c\_id, d\_id, w\_id}] \subseteq_s \text{CUSTOMER}[\text{c\_id, d\_id, w\_id}] ,$$

but violates the partial IND

$$\text{ORDER}[\text{c\_id, d\_id, w\_id}] \subseteq_p \text{CUSTOMER}[\text{c\_id, d\_id, w\_id}] .$$

It is known that simple semantics for foreign keys is natively supported by all SQL implementations, but partial semantics is not natively supported by any SQL implementation [36]. On the one hand, it is not surprising that the implication problems for INDs under simple and partial semantics are different from one another. For example, the partial IND above implies the partial IND

$$\text{ORDER}[\text{d\_id, w\_id}] \subseteq_p \text{CUSTOMER}[\text{d\_id, w\_id}] ,$$

but the simple IND above does not imply the simple IND

$$\text{ORDER}[\text{d\_id, w\_id}] \subseteq_s \text{CUSTOMER}[\text{d\_id, w\_id}] ,$$

the latter being confirmed by our single-tuple database from before. On the other hand, it is surprising that the implication problem has only been investigated under partial semantics, and only under the assumption that the null marker can occur in every column [29]. In fact, it is a simple observation that the implication problem for INDs under partial semantics and NOT NULL constraints enjoys the same axiomatization as INDs in relational databases. For simple semantics in isolation, the difference to partial semantics is already captured by the example above, that is, we establish an axiomatization for simple INDs that results from the axiomatization for partial INDs by omitting the projection rule. However, things already change dramatically when we consider simple INDs in combination with NOT NULL constraints only. In this case, the associated implication problem is not k-ary axiomatizable for any finite k. This result is rather discouraging for database practice where simple semantics is natively supported, but not partial semantics. We emphasize the importance of the ability to reason about simple and partial INDs under NOT NULL constraints by the following example from database design.

EXAMPLE 1. *Consider the following relation schemata in which NOT NULL attributes A are denoted by $A[NN]$:*
CONFERENCE*(CName[NN],...),*
PARTICIPANT*(PName[NN],...),*
CHAIR*(CName[NN],PName[NN],...),*
BOOKING*(CName,PName,Date[NN],Room[NN]), and*
TALK*(CName,PName,Date,...). The designer has identified the following inclusion dependencies:*
CHAIR*[CName]* ⊆ CONFERENCE*[CName],*
CHAIR*[PName]* ⊆ PARTICIPANT*[PName],*
BOOKING*[CName, PName]* $\subseteq_s$ CHAIR*[CName, PName],*
TALK*[CName, PName]* $\subseteq_p$ TALK*[CName, PName].*
If we were able to reason about simple and partial inclusion dependencies under NOT NULL constraints, this would allow us to detect the following: i) the IND
TALK*[CName, PName]* $\subseteq_s$ CHAIR*[CName, PName]*
is implied by the specified INDs, indicating that (if fully populated) presentations can only be given by conference chairs, which indicates clearly a design flaw, and ii) the IND
TALK*[CName]* $\subseteq_s$ CONFERENCE*[CName]*
is not implied by the specified constraints, but should hold.

The challenge. For these reasons, database research is expected to answer the important practical question how the semantics of INDs should be defined in the context of the industry standard SQL. Ideally, the semantics can be defined such that all of the following targets are met: i) simple and partial semantics are subsumed by the semantics as special cases, and ii) the semantics enjoys similar computational properties to that of its idealized special case in which all attributes are specified NOT NULL. More precisely, condition ii) means that the associated implication problem is finitely axiomatizable and PSPACE-complete to decide. Ideally, there would be some expressive fragments whose implication is easier or even tractable to decide.

Contributions. Strongly motivated by our observations about the simple and partial semantics of SQL inclusion dependencies, we address the challenge as follows.

1. We investigate the implication problem of INDs under both simple and partial semantics, each in combination with that of NOT NULL constraints, as suggested by the SQL standard. The idealized special case where all attributes are declared NOT NULL yields in each case the well-known semantics of INDs over pure relations. Note that finite and unrestricted implication problems coincide for the classes of constraints considered here. Therefore, we commonly speak of the implication problem.

2. In the presence of NOT NULL constraints, we show that partial semantics enjoys the same finite axiomatization as traditional INDs, but simple semantics is not k-ary axiomatizable for any finite k. The latter result already holds when all relation schemata have four or less attributes. Establishing concise axiomatizations aids in human understanding of constraint interaction and forms the foundation for developing (efficient) solutions to decision problems, which are fundamental to applications as critical as schema design, integrity enforcement and query processing.

3. Based on the understanding we gain from showing that the implication of NOT NULL constraints and INDs under simple semantics is not finitely axiomatizable, we propose the class of not null inclusion dependencies (NNINDs). The class of NNINDs exhibits a natural semantics, and subsumes simple and partial semantics as special cases. We show that NNINDs enjoy a finite axiomatization and their implication problem is PSPACE-complete to decide, thereby recovering the positive results about INDs in relational databases.

4. Exploiting our completeness argument of our finite axiomatization, we establish a chase procedure for deciding the implication problem of NNINDs, subsuming the well-known chase for relational INDs as an idealized special case.

5. We show that the arity of NNINDs is a parameter that makes their implication problem fixed parameter-tractable. This also applies to the relational case. For tree-like NNINDs it follows that their implication problem is decidable in linear time. In contrast to the relational case, we show that typed NNINDs are NP-hard and thus unlikely to be decidable in PTIME, already in the acyclic case.

Summary. Our results identify NNINDs as a class of referential integrity rules that accommodates the requirements of the de-facto industry standard and market leader SQL, provides database practitioners with capabilities to express desirable properties of the underlying application domain, and retains the positive computational properties of relational INDs, which the database community has been exploring in classical and modern data management.

Organization. We summarize related work in Section 2 to differentiate our contributions. In Section 3 we formally introduce simple and partial semantics for INDs. The axiomatization and non-axiomatizability, respectively, of partial and simple INDs and NOT NULL constraints is discussed in Section 4. NNINDs are introduced in Section 5, and their implication problem is axiomatized and shown to be PSPACE-complete. The chase and important fragments of NNINDs are identified in Section 6. We conclude in Section 7 and discuss some possible directions of future work.

2. RELATED WORK

INDs form one of the most prolific concepts in database research and practice. We cannot list all the contributions made possible by them. Some insight into their diverse application areas was given in the introduction. Instead, we will focus on the main achievements regarding the implication problem of INDs and to highlight the novelty of our contributions.

INDs generalize the notion of referential integrity, which was known to the broader database community during the 1970s [17]. A seminal paper on INDs is [9], in which inference rules are presented, a Chase procedure is established, and the PSPACE-completeness of the implication problem is shown. Acyclic INDs were introduced in [39], and it was shown in [15] that their implication problem is NP-complete. Typed INDs, i.e. INDs of the form $R[X] \subseteq S[X]$, are decidable in PTIME [10].

The only paper addressing the implication of INDs in the presence of null markers is [29], but it only covers partial semantics and the other extreme case in which all columns can feature nulls. It is shown that the associated implication problem is the same as that for INDs over pure relations. Index design for efficiently enforcing and validating the partial semantics of INDs is discussed in [34, 36].

We conclude that previous research has not investigated the important combined class of inclusion dependencies and NOT NULL constraints, neither under simple nor partial semantics as recommended by the SQL standard. Only the idealized special cases where either all or no attributes are specified NOT NULL have been studied, while the latter has only been studied for partial semantics. Our result that the combined class of simple inclusion dependencies and NOT NULL constraints is not k-ary axiomatizable for any finite k is surprising and discouraging for current database practice. It is surprising since: i) in both idealized special cases inclusion dependencies are axiomatizable, and ii) under the 'no information' semantics of null values, NOT NULL constraints do not increase the difficulty of axiomatizing implication for other classes of equality-generating or tuple-generating constraints that have been studied previously [2, 24]. In [30] it is shown that for functional dependencies under possible world semantics, no k-ary axiomatization exists. Possible world semantics captures only the null marker interpretation 'value exists but unknown' but not 'value does not exist'. For these reasons we apply the popular and SQL-compliant 'no information' interpretation [2, 20, 24, 33].

3. INCLUSION DEPENDENCIES IN SQL

In this section we formalize the notions of partial and simple inclusion dependencies in the context of SQL.

Let $\mathfrak{A} = \{A_1, A_2, \ldots\}$ be a countably infinite set of symbols, called *attributes* or *columns*. A *relation schema* is a finite non-empty sequence $R = \langle A_1, \ldots, A_n \rangle$ of distinct attributes in $\mathfrak{A}$. *Database schemata* are finite sets of relation schemata. Each attribute A of a relation schema R is associated with a countably infinite domain $dom(A)$ of the possible values that can occur in column A. To encompass partial information the domain of every attribute contains a distinguished null marker, denoted by $\perp$.

A *tuple* t over $R = \langle A_1, \ldots, A_n \rangle$ (R-tuple or simply tuple, if R is understood) is an element of the Cartesian product $dom(A_1) \times \cdots \times dom(A_n)$. A *relation* r over R (R-relation or simply relation, if R is understood) is a set of R-tuples. While SQL tables may contain duplicates, these have no impact on whether an IND holds, so it suffices to study relations. Sometimes, we also write *instance* when referring to a relation. We may also refer to a relation with null marker occurrences when we want to emphasize the fact that null markers can be present. When necessary we say that relations are finite. A *database* assigns a relation to each of its relation schemata that are part of the underlying database schema. For $X = \langle A_{i_1}, \ldots, A_{i_m} \rangle$ we use $t[X]$ ($r[X]$) to denote the *projection* of tuple t (relation r) on the attributes $A_{i_1}, \ldots, A_{i_m}$. That is, $r[X] = \{t[X] \mid t \in r\}$. For an R-tuple t (R-relation r) we say that t (r) is X-total if for all $A_{i_j} \in X$, $t[A_{i_j}] \neq \perp$ (all tuples in r are X-total). SQL permits the specification of attributes as NOT NULL. We denote the NOT NULL attributes of a relation schema R by NN(R), and the attributes on which a tuple t is different from $\perp$ by NN(t). For relations with null markers, different extensions of classical inclusion dependencies (INDs) exist. We study the two most prominent extensions, called partial and simple semantics, as defined by the SQL standard.

Definition 1 (less informative tuple).
Consider tuples t_1, t_2 over $R_1 = \langle A_1, \ldots, A_m \rangle$ and $R_2 = \langle B_1, \ldots, B_m \rangle$. We say that t_1 is less informative[2] *than t_2 (or t_2* is more informative *than t_1), written as $t_1 \sqsubseteq t_2$, iff*

$$t_1[A_i] \in \{\perp, t_2[B_i]\} \qquad \forall i = 1 \ldots m$$

If for every tuple in relation r_1 there exists some more informative tuple in relation r_2, we write $r_1 \sqsubseteq r_2$.

Definition 2 (partial/simple IND).
Let neither X nor Y contain duplicate attributes. We call an expression of the form $R[X] \subseteq_p S[Y]$ a partial inclusion dependency, *and an expression of the form $R[X] \subseteq_s S[Y]$ a* simple inclusion dependency.

A partial IND $R[X] \subseteq_p S[Y]$ holds for relations r, s over R, S if $r[X] \sqsubseteq s[Y]$.

A simple IND $R[X] \subseteq_s S[Y]$ holds for relations r, s over R, S if for every X-total tuple $t_r \in r$ there exists a tuple $t_s \in s$ such that $t_r[X] = t_s[Y]$.

While only partial INDs have been considered in the literature [29], both partial and simple semantics are supported in the SQL standard (for foreign keys), and DBMSs support only simple semantics (and again only for foreign keys). This

[2]While "less or equally informative" would be more accurate, "less informative" is predominant in the literature.

motivates a closer investigation of simple INDs, and in particular their relationship to partial INDs.

The core computational problem in the theory of database constraints is the implication problem. The problem is the core problem in logic [4] and has several motivations in practice, inclusive of i) the ability to compute small representation systems (covers) for the sets of constraints that are actively enforced in a database system results in time savings that increase proportionally with the volume of the data that is being updated, and ii) the ability to decide whether a constraint is implied by a given set empowers database systems to decide whether a constraint can be used for optimizing a query on the fly. For a given class $\mathcal{C}$ of constraints, the *(finite) implication problem* for $\mathcal{C}$ is to decide for a given finite set $\Sigma \cup \{\varphi\}$ of constraints in $\mathcal{C}$, whether Σ *(finitely) implies* φ. That is, whether every (finite) database that satisfies all the constraints in Σ also satisfies φ. Two sets of constraints are *semantically equivalent* if either of the sets implies all of the other set's constraints.

When talking about inclusion dependencies, we will need to identify subsets of the left-hand-side that "match" subsets of the right-hand-side. The following concept helps in this.

DEFINITION 3 (INDUCED MAPPING). *Let $X = \langle A_1, \ldots, A_m\rangle$ and $Y = \langle B_1, \ldots, B_m\rangle$ be sequences of equal length, with distinct A_i. The* mapping induced by X and Y, *denoted $(X \mapsto Y)$, is*

$$(X \mapsto Y)(A_i) := B_i$$

When applied to a set of values U, we obtain the images of values in $U \cap X$:

$$(X \mapsto Y)(U) := \{B_i \mid A_i \in U\}$$

We can now express an important relationship between partial and simple INDs precisely.

THEOREM 1. *Every partial IND is semantically equivalent to a set of simple INDs. Specifically:*

$$R[X] \subseteq_p S[Y] \quad \equiv \quad \{\, R[X'] \subseteq_s S[Y'] \mid X' \subseteq X, \; Y' = (X \mapsto Y)(X') \,\}$$

PROOF. It is easy to see that $R[X] \subseteq_p S[Y]$ implies every $R[X'] \subseteq_s S[Y']$ in the set.

To show the reverse, let r, s be instances of R, S so that every $R[X'] \subseteq_s S[Y']$ holds on r, s, and $t \in r$. From $R[X'] \subseteq_s S[Y']$ with $X' = \mathrm{NN}(t) \cap X$, it follows that there exists $t' \in s$ with $t[X'] = t'[Y']$. But this means $t[X] \sqsubseteq t'[Y]$, and since such a t' exists for all $t \in r$, $R[X] \subseteq_p S[Y]$ is satisfied. □

This means that any DBMS which supports simple INDs indirectly supports partial INDs as well. Note that the opposite does not hold:

EXAMPLE 2. *Consider the schemata $R = \langle A\rangle$, $S = \langle B\rangle$ with instances $r = \{\langle\bot\rangle\}$ and $s = \emptyset$. Then the simple IND $R[A] \subseteq_s S[B]$ holds on r, s, but the partial INDs $R[] \subseteq_p S[]$ and $R[A] \subseteq_p S[B]$ are violated.*

Nevertheless, partial INDs are valuable in that they allow constraints to be expressed efficiently, i.e., without resorting to an exponential number of equivalent simple INDs. As users of a database should be encouraged to specify constraints that can enforce quality data, we will investigate both partial and simple INDs.

4. AXIOMATIZATION

Concise axiomatizations aid in human understanding of constraint interaction and form the foundation for developing (efficient) solutions to decision problems. These are fundamental to applications as critical as schema design, integrity enforcement and query processing. In particular, our understanding why simple INDs are not finitely axiomatizable will lead to our proposal of NNINDs in Section 5. While the connection between simple and partial inclusion dependencies as described in Theorem 1 may appear obvious in retrospect, we only discovered it while searching for an axiomatization of NNINDs.

In this section, we will discuss axiomatizations for implication problems of partial and simple INDs, both in isolation and combination with NOT NULL constraints. The notions of inference rules, soundness, completeness and (finite) axiomatization are standard [1].

The following definition falls in the same category as "induced mapping". It formalizes what it means to rearrange the attributes on both sides of an IND "correspondingly".

DEFINITION 4 (INDEX PERMUTATION & PROJECTION). *An* index permutation & projection function of order (k,m), *or (k,m)-IPP, with $k \geq m$, is an injective mapping $\sigma : \{1, \ldots, k\} \to \{1, \ldots, m\}$. We apply a (k,m)-IPP to a list of length m by mapping its indices:*

$$\sigma[A_1, \ldots, A_m] := [A_{\sigma(1)}, \ldots, A_{\sigma(k)}]$$

Where the order (k,m) of an IPP is clear from the context, we will not mention it explicitly.

Given two lists X, Y, the existence of an IPP function mapping X to Y is denoted by $X \subseteq_{IPP} Y$.

An axiomatization for partial INDs has been established by Levene and Loizou in [29, Theorem 3.3]:

THEOREM 2. *The following axioms are sound and complete for partial inclusion dependencies.*

Reflexivity (R):	$\dfrac{}{R[X] \subseteq_p R[X]}$
Transitivity (T):	$\dfrac{R[X] \subseteq_p S[Y] \quad S[Y] \subseteq_p T[Z]}{R[X] \subseteq_p T[Z]}$
Projection & Permutation (P):	$\dfrac{R[X] \subseteq_p S[Y]}{R[\sigma X] \subseteq_p S[\sigma Y]}$ *σ is an IPP*

We remark that although NOT NULL constraints are not considered in [29], the proof of [29, Theorem 3.3] still works, without any modification, when we do consider them.

As long as we do not consider NOT NULL constraints, the axiomatization of simple INDs is even simpler:

THEOREM 3. *The following axioms are sound and complete for simple INDs without NOT NULL constraints.*

Reflexivity (R):	$\dfrac{}{R[X] \subseteq_s R[X]}$
Transitivity (T):	$\dfrac{R[X] \subseteq_s S[Y] \quad S[Y] \subseteq_s T[Z]}{R[X] \subseteq_s T[Z]}$
Permutation (P):	$\dfrac{R[X] \subseteq_s S[Y]}{R[\sigma X] \subseteq_s S[\sigma Y]}$ *σ is an index permutation*

PROOF. As the proof for Lemma 1 in Section 5, except that σ must be a permutation, and the null propagation rule is not needed. □

Next we consider the real-world case in which simple INDs coexist with NOT NULL constraints. Surprisingly, while simple INDs studied in isolation possess an elegant axiomatization (Theorem 3), it turns out that no (finite) axiomatization exists in the presence of NOT NULL constraints.

THEOREM 4. *For the implication of simple inclusion dependencies with NOT NULL constraints, no k-ary axiomatization exists. In particular, no finite axiomatization exists. This holds even if all relation schemata are restricted to contain four (or fewer) attributes.*

PROOF. Consider the database schema $\mathcal{R}$ with relation schemata $R_0 = \ldots = R_{k+1} = ABCD$, with $\mathrm{NN}(R_0) = BC$, $\mathrm{NN}(R_{i>0}) = B$. Let $\Sigma = \{R_i[ABC] \subseteq_s R_{i+1}[ACD] \mid i = 0 \ldots k\}$. One can verify that $\Sigma \models R_0[A] \subseteq_s R_{k+1}[A] =: \varphi_0$. We will show that φ_0 cannot be derived using any k-ary set of (sound) derivation rules. To do so, we first need to establish which intermediate INDs could be derived. In the following we only consider non-trivial INDs with ordered LHS attributes.

Claim (*): If $\Sigma \models R_n[X] \subseteq_s R_m[Y] =: \varphi \notin \Sigma$ with $n \neq 0$ then $\varphi = R_n[AC] \subseteq_s R_{n+1}[AD]$.
To show this, consider an instance over $\mathcal{R}$ with

$$r_i = \emptyset \text{ for } i < n$$
$$r_n = \left\{ \begin{array}{c} (0, 2, 1, *), \\ (\perp, *, *, *), \\ (*, *, \perp, *) \end{array} \right\}$$
$$r_{n+j} = \{(0, j+2, j+1, j)\} \text{ for } j > 0$$

where * donate unique values. One may verify that Σ holds for this instance. If $D \in X$ then φ is violated by the first tuple in r_n. If $AC \nsubseteq X$ then φ is violated by the second or third tuple in r_n. This leaves $X \in \{AC, ABC\}$. As value 1 only occurs in relations r_n and r_{n+1}, and φ is non-trivial, $m = n+1$. Thus either $\varphi = R_n[AC] \subseteq_s R_{n+1}[AD]$ or $\varphi = R_n[ABC] \subseteq_s R_{n+1}[ACD]$. As $\varphi \notin \Sigma$, only the first option remains, showing Claim (*).

Claim (**): If $\Sigma \models R_0[X] \subseteq_s R_m[Y] =: \varphi \notin \Sigma$ then

$$\varphi \in \left\{ \begin{array}{c} R_0[AC] \subseteq_s R_1[AD], \\ R_0[AB] \subseteq_s R_1[AC], \\ R_0[AB] \subseteq_s R_2[AD], \\ R_0[A] \subseteq_s R_m[A] \end{array} \right\}$$

To show this, consider an instance over $\mathcal{R}$ with

$$r_0 = \left\{ \begin{array}{c} (0, 2, 1, *), \\ (\perp, *, *, *) \end{array} \right\}$$
$$r_j = \{(0, j+2, j+1, j)\} \text{ for } j > 0$$

For φ to hold we must have $D \notin X$ (first tuple) and $A \in X$ (second tuple). For $m > 2$, neither 2 nor 1 occurs in r_m, so we must have $X = Y = A$. For $m = 2$ only 2 occurs in r_2, so we must have $X = Y = A$ or $X = AB, Y = AD$. For $m = 1$ the options $X \in \{A, AB, AC, ABC\}$ remain. $X = ABC$ means $Y = ACD$ so $\varphi \in \Sigma$. The remaining cases are all covered in Claim (**).

We can summarize claims (*) and (**) as follows: The set

$$\begin{aligned} \Sigma' := \Sigma &\cup \{R_n[AC] \subseteq_s R_{n+1}[AD] \text{ for } n = 0 \ldots k\} \\ &\cup \{R_0[A] \subseteq_s R_{n+1}[A] \text{ for } n = 0 \ldots k\} \\ &\cup \{R_0[AB] \subseteq_s R_1[AC], R_0[AB] \subseteq_s R_2[AD]\} \end{aligned}$$

contains all (non-trivial) INDs implied by Σ over $\mathcal{R}$.

Finally, let $\Sigma'' \subset \Sigma'$ be any set of at most k INDs implied by Σ such that $\varphi_0 \notin \Sigma''$. Then for some $m \in 1, \ldots, k+1$, Σ'' contains no IND with R_m on its RHS. Consider the instance

$$\begin{aligned} r_i &= \{(0, i+2, i+1, i)\} \text{ for } i < m \\ r_i &= \{(0, i+2, \perp, i)\} \text{ for } m \leq i \leq k \\ r_{k+1} &= \emptyset \end{aligned}$$

It is easy to see that all INDs in Σ' which might lie in Σ'' hold for this instance, while φ_0 is violated. This shows that φ_0 cannot be derived using a rule with k or less premises. Hence no k-ary axiomatization exists. □

We have seen that in the presence of NOT NULL constraints, partial INDs enjoy a finite axiomatization (see the remark after Theorem 2), while simple INDs do not. As a final case, we consider partial and simple INDs together.

COROLLARY 1. *For the implication of partial and simple inclusion dependencies with NOT NULL constraints, no k-ary axiomatization exists. This holds even if all relation schemas are restricted to contain four (or less) attributes.*

PROOF. Assume that such an axiomatization $\mathcal{A}$ existed. Then we can construct an axiomatization $\mathcal{A}'$ by replacing every rule in $\mathcal{A}$ with multiple corresponding rules, in which each partial IND $R[X] \subseteq_p S[Y]$ is replaced by multiple simple INDs, as per Theorem 1, for cardinalities of X up to four. But this would make $\mathcal{A}'$ a k-ary (for some finite k) axiomatization for simple INDs over relation schemata of size four or less, contradicting Theorem 4. □

As simple INDs and NOT NULL constraints are the current reality of database practice, database research must answer the important question whether there is some suitable extension of INDs from relational databases to SQL. In the next section we propose an affirmative answer and establish strong evidence for the suitability of our proposal.

5. NOT NULL INCL. DEPENDENCIES

In this section we propose *not null inclusion dependencies* (NNINDs) as a new class of inclusion dependencies in SQL. The definition of NNINDs is a natural consequence of the non-axiomatizability result for simple INDs and NOT NULL constraints. Both simple and partial INDs are special cases of NNINDs, and we establish a finite axiomatization and the PSPACE-completeness for their implication problem. Therefore, we are able to provide an optimal response to the challenges brought forward by the results of the last section: NNINDs can address the recommendations of the industry standard SQL, and retain the computational properties of its idealized special case of INDs over pure relations.

The central reason why simple inclusion dependencies cannot be axiomatized, is that information about attributes being NOT NULL cannot be propagated. In the following we will define NNINDs, show how they express partial and simple INDs as special cases and how they facilitate the propagation of NOT NULL attributes.

Definition 5 (not null inclusion dependency). *Let R be a relation schema, r a relation over R and $U \subseteq R$. We denote by r^U the set of all U-total tuples in r:*

$$r^U := \{t \in r \mid \forall A \in U.\, t[A] \neq \bot\}$$

A not null inclusion dependency *(NNIND) is an expression of the form*

$$R^U[X] \subseteq S^V[Y]$$

where R, S are schemata, U, V sets and X, Y sequences of equal length with $U, X \subseteq R$ and $V, Y \subseteq S$. We say that such an NNIND holds *on relations r, s over R, S iff*

$$r^U[X] \sqsubseteq s^V[Y]$$

Note that (as for partial/simple INDs) we do not consider repeated attributes in X or Y.

Proposition 1.
Partial and simple INDs are special cases of NNINDs:

$$R[X] \subseteq_p S[Y] \equiv R^{\emptyset}[X] \subseteq S^{\emptyset}[Y]$$
$$R[X] \subseteq_s S[Y] \equiv R^{X}[X] \subseteq S^{\emptyset}[Y]$$

Hence NNINDs generalize partial and simple INDs in a unified framework, which allows more fine-grained control over the handling of null values.

Example 3. *We may now make the following observations for Example 1: i) The attribute CName in* Booking *is NULL and the IND σ_1:*
Booking*[CName, PName]* $\subseteq_s$ Chair*[CName, PName] is simple (and not partial) to allow bookings not related to conferences, ii) the IND σ_2:*
Booking*[CName]* $\subseteq_s$ Chair*[CName]*
also holds, and iii) σ_1 and σ_2 can be replaced by the NNIND Booking^{CName}*[CName,PName]*$\subseteq$Chair*[CName,PName].*

Our central result for this section will be a (finite) axiomatization of NNINDs.

Theorem 5. *The set of axioms from Table 1 is sound and complete for not null inclusion dependencies.*

To establish some results needed to prove Theorem 5, we introduce the auxiliary notion of quasi-simple NNINDs. Quasi-simple NNINDs can be axiomatized without use of the Tertium Non Datur Rule, and completeness of this axiomatization is easier to establish.

Definition 6 (quasi-simple NNIND).
We call NNINDs of the form $R^{UX}[X] \subseteq S^V[Y]$ quasi-simple.

One may note that quasi-simple NNINDs include simple INDs. The relationship between partial and simple INDs extends to NNINDs and quasi-simple INDs (with the difference that NNINDs include quasi-simple NNINDs, whereas partial INDs do not include simple ones):

Theorem 6. *Every NNIND is semantically equivalent to a set of quasi-simple NNINDs. Specifically:*

$$R^U[X] \subseteq S^V[Y] \quad \equiv \quad \{\, R^{UX'}[X'] \subseteq S^V[Y'] \mid X' \subseteq X,\; Y' = (X \mapsto Y)(X') \,\}$$

Proof. It is easy to see that $R^U[X] \subseteq S^V[Y]$ implies every $R^{UX'}[X'] \subseteq S^V[Y']$ in the set.

To show the reverse, let r, s be instances of R, S so that every $R^{UX'}[X'] \subseteq S^V[Y']$ holds on r, s, and $t \in r$ be U-total. From $R^{UX'}[X'] \subseteq S^V[Y']$ with $X' = \mathrm{NN}(t) \cap X$, it follows that there exists a V-total $t' \in s$ with $t[X'] = t'[Y']$. But this means $t[X] \sqsubseteq t'[Y]$, and since such a t' exists for all U-total $t \in r$, $R[X] \subseteq_p S[Y]$ is satisfied. □

We note that carrying not-null sets on the RHS of NNINDs is not a necessary condition for extending partial and simple INDs. However, they are required in order to obtain a finite axiomatization.

Lemma 1. *The first four rules of Theorem 5 are sound, and complete for the derivation of quasi-simple NNINDs.*

Proof. It is easy to verify that the axioms are sounds.

Thus it remains to show that any implied quasi-simple NNIND can be derived.

Let $R_1, \ldots, R_n$ denote our relation schemata. Let Σ be a set of NNINDs, and $\varphi = R^{UX}[X] \subseteq S^V[Y]$ a quasi-simple NNIND with $\Sigma \models \varphi$. We shall create a database $r_1, \ldots, r_n$ by adding tuples, one at a time, and show inductively that for each tuple there exists a matching NNIND which can be derived using our axioms.

Initialize the database with a single tuple $t_0 \in r$ with

$$t_0[X] = [1, \ldots, m] \quad \text{where } m = |X|$$
$$t_0[A \notin X] = \begin{cases} 0 & \text{if } A \in U \cup \mathrm{NN}(R) \\ \bot & \text{otherwise} \end{cases}$$

Further tuples are added by repeated application of the following (*chase*-like) rule:

Rule (*): If Σ contains a dependency $\varphi_i = {R_i}^{U^*}[X^*] \subseteq {R_j}^{V^*}[Y^*]$ and for some U^*-total tuple $t \in r_i$ there does not exist a V^*-total tuple $t' \in r_j$ with $t[X^*] \sqsubseteq t'[Y^*]$, then add the following tuple t' to r_j:

$$t'[B_i \in Y^*] := \begin{cases} 0 & \text{if } t[A_i] = \bot \text{ and } B_i \in V^{**} \\ t[A_i] & \text{otherwise} \end{cases}$$
$$t'[B \notin Y^*] := \begin{cases} 0 & \text{if } B \in V^{**} \\ \bot & \text{otherwise} \end{cases}$$

where we use the abbreviation $V^{**} := V^* \cup \mathrm{NN}(R_j)$ and the notation $A_i := (Y^* \mapsto X^*)(B_i)$ for readability. We say that t' was added as a result of φ_i and t.

The number of different attribute values is finite, so repeated application of Rule (*) terminates. The resulting database $r_1, \ldots, r_n$ satisfies Σ, as otherwise Rule (*) could be applied again. As Σ implies φ by assumption, $r_1, \ldots, r_n$ also satisfies φ. As $t_0 \in r$ is UX-total, this means that there exists a V-total tuple $t_1 \in s$ with $t_0[X] = t_1[Y]$.

Claim (**): If r_j contains a tuple t' with $t_0[X] = t'[E]$, then (with $\vdash$ denoting derivability)

$$\Sigma \vdash R^{UX}[X] \subseteq {R_j}^{\mathrm{NN}(t')}[E]$$

If we prove Claim (**), then since s contains t_1, it follows that $\Sigma \vdash R^{UX}[X] \subseteq S^{\mathrm{NN}(t_1)}[Y]$. From this $\Sigma \vdash \varphi$ follows with another application of reflexivity and transitivity (reducing $\mathrm{NN}(t_1)$ to V).

We proceed by induction on the sequence of tuple additions. For $t' = t_0$ Claim(**) follows by the reflexivity axiom.

$$\frac{}{R^U[X] \subseteq R^V[X]}\ V \subseteq U \cup \mathrm{NN}(R) \qquad \frac{R^U[X] \subseteq S^V[Y] \quad S^V[Y] \subseteq T^W[Z]}{R^U[X] \subseteq T^W[Z]}$$

Reflexivity (R) — *Transitivity (T)*

$$\frac{R^U[X] \subseteq S^V[Y]}{R^U[\sigma X] \subseteq S^V[\sigma Y]}\ \sigma \text{ is an IPP} \qquad \frac{R^U[X] \subseteq S^V[Y]}{R^U[X] \subseteq S^W[Y]}\ W = V \cup (X \mapsto Y)(U)$$

Projection & Permutation (P) — *Not Null Propagation (N)*

$$\frac{R^{UA}[AX] \subseteq S^V[BY] \quad R^U[X] \subseteq S^V[Y]}{R^U[AX] \subseteq S^V[BY]}$$

Tertium Non Datur (D)

Table 1: Axiomatization of NOT NULL Inclusion Dependencies

So let t' be added as a result of φ_i and t from Rule (*). By construction this means

$$\mathrm{NN}(t') = V^* \cup \mathrm{NN}(R_j) \cup (X^* \mapsto Y^*)(\mathrm{NN}(t))$$

From $t_0[X] = t'[E]$ it follows that $E \subseteq Y^*$, as all values in t' outside Y^* are 0 or $\perp$. Hence there exists an IPP σ such that $E = \sigma Y^*$. We thus obtain $t_0[X] = t'[E] = t'[\sigma Y^*] = t[\sigma X^*]$. Thus by induction hypothesis, we have

$$\Sigma \ \vdash\ R^{UX}[X] \subseteq {R_i}^{\mathrm{NN}(t)}[\sigma X^*]$$

Furthermore, as Rule (*) was applicable, we must have $U^* \subseteq \mathrm{NN}(t)$. We can thus derive

$$\cfrac{\cfrac{\vdots}{R^{UX}[X] \subseteq {R_i}^{\mathrm{NN}(t)}[\sigma X^*]} \qquad \cfrac{\cfrac{\cfrac{\cfrac{{R_i}^{U^*}[X^*] \subseteq {R_j}^{V^*}[Y^*]}{{R_i}^{\mathrm{NN}(t)}[X^*] \subseteq {R_j}^{V^*}[Y^*]}\ {\scriptstyle R+T}}{{R_i}^{\mathrm{NN}(t)}[X^*] \subseteq {R_j}^{V^* \cup \mathrm{NN}(R_j)}[Y^*]}\ {\scriptstyle R+T}}{{R_i}^{\mathrm{NN}(t)}[X^*] \subseteq {R_j}^{\mathrm{NN}(t')}[Y^*]}\ {\scriptstyle N}}{{R_i}^{\mathrm{NN}(t)}[\sigma X^*] \subseteq {R_j}^{\mathrm{NN}(t')}[\sigma Y^*]}\ {\scriptstyle P}}{R^{UX}[X] \subseteq {R_j}^{\mathrm{NN}(t')}[\sigma Y^*]}\ {\scriptstyle T}$$

As $E = \sigma Y^*$, this shows Claim (**) and completes the proof. □

We are now ready to show Theorem 5.

Proof (Theorem 5). Soundness of Tertium Non Datur (D) may not be obvious, so we provide a brief proof. Consider any U-total tuple t over R. If $t[A] \neq \perp$ then existence of a V-total t' with $t[AX] \sqsubseteq t'[AX]$ follows from $R^{UA}[AX] \subseteq S^V[BY]$. If $t[A] = \perp$ then by $R^U[X] \subseteq S^V[Y]$ there exists a V-total t' with $t[X] \sqsubseteq t'[X]$. With $t[A] = \perp$ it follows that $t[AX] \sqsubseteq t'[AX]$.

To show completeness, denote again our relation schemata by $R_1, \ldots, R_n$. Let Σ be a set of NNINDs, and

$$\varphi = R^U[X] \subseteq S^V[Y]$$

some NNIND with $\Sigma \models \varphi$. We show that for all IPP σ and $W \subseteq \sigma X$ we have

$$\Sigma \vdash \varphi_\sigma^W := R^{U(\sigma X \setminus W)}[\sigma X] \subseteq S^V[\sigma Y] \qquad (1)$$

We proceed by induction on the cardinality of W.

Let $|W| = 0$. Then $\Sigma \models \varphi \models \varphi_\sigma^\emptyset$, and our claim follows by Lemma 1.

So assume (1) holds for all $|W| \leq n$, and let $|W'| = n+1$ and σ some IPP. Pick $A \in W'$ so that $W' = AW$ with $|W| = n$, and let σ_A be derived from σ by "dropping" A. By (1) we have $\Sigma \vdash \varphi_\sigma^W$ and $\Sigma \vdash \varphi_{\sigma_A}^W$. From

$$\varphi_\sigma^W = R^{U(\sigma X \setminus W')A}[\sigma X] \subseteq S^V[\sigma Y] \quad \text{and}$$
$$\varphi_{\sigma_A}^W = R^{U(\sigma X \setminus W')}[\sigma_A X] \subseteq S^V[\sigma_A Y]$$

we can derive, using Tertium Non Datur (plus Permutation to make A the first attribute):

$$\varphi_\sigma^{W'} = R^{U(\sigma X \setminus W')}[\sigma X] \subseteq S^V[\sigma Y]\ .$$

This shows (1) which includes $\Sigma \vdash \varphi$ as a special case. □

By Lemma 1, the Tertium Non Datur rule is not needed to derive simple INDs. Nor is it required to derive partial INDs from a set of partial INDs, as per Theorem 2. While it is necessary for completeness using our definition of NNINDs, one may thus wonder whether it could be avoided by using a more conservative generalisation of partial and simple INDs. Theorem 1 suggests that this is not possible, and the following example confirms this (it is of course possible to replace it by some other rule, though we suspect that any replacement rule would be very similar and not simpler).

Example 4. *Let $R = AB$, $S = CD$ be relation schemata without NOT NULL constraints, and*

$$\Sigma = \{\ R^A[A] \subseteq S[C],\ R[B] \subseteq S[D]\ \}$$

a set containing only simple and partial INDs. Then Σ implies the partial IND $R[A] \subseteq S[C]$, as shown below:

$$\cfrac{R^A[A] \subseteq S[C] \qquad \cfrac{R[B] \subseteq S[D]}{R[] \subseteq S[]}\ (P)}{R[A] \subseteq S[C]}\ (D)$$

One may verify that $R[A] \subseteq S[C]$ cannot be derived without use of rule (D). Note that $R[] \subseteq S[]$ is non-trivial, and expresses that S is non-empty if R is non-empty.

It has been shown in [9, Theorem 3.3] that implication of standard INDs is PSPACE-complete. As NNINDs extend standard INDs, implication between NNINDs is at least PSPACE-hard. We will show that it lies in PSPACE next.

The following lemma shows PSPACE-computability for quasi-simple NNINDs.

LEMMA 2. *Let Σ be a set of (general) NNINDs and $\varphi = R^{UX}[X] \subseteq S^V[Y]$ a quasi-simple NNIND. Then $\Sigma \models \varphi$ iff there exists a sequence*

$$R^{UX}[X] = S_0^{U_0}[X_0],\ \ldots,\ S_n^{U_n}[X_n] = S^V[Y]$$

where S_i are relation schemata, and $U_i, X_i \subseteq S_i$ such that for each $0 \leq i < n$ the NNIND

$$S_i{}^{U_i}[X_i] \subseteq S_{i+1}{}^{U_{i+1}}[X_{i+1}]$$

is either an instance of the reflexivity axiom (R) or can be derived (non-deterministically in linear space) from a single NNIND in Σ.

PROOF. The "if" direction is obvious. For the "only if" direction, consider the derivation trees constructed in the proof of Lemma 1. Our $S_i^{U_i}[X_i]$ for $i > 1$ are the RHSs

$$\ldots,\ R_i^{\mathrm{NN}(t)}[\sigma X^*],\ R_j^{\mathrm{NN}(t')}[\sigma Y^*],\ \ldots$$

of the NNINDs derived, and each "connecting" NNIND

$$R_i{}^{\mathrm{NN}(t)}[\sigma X^*] \subseteq R_j{}^{\mathrm{NN}(t')}[\sigma Y^*]$$

is derived from the respective $R_i{}^{U^*}[X^*] \subseteq R_j{}^{V^*}[Y^*] \in \Sigma$, in linear space. □

By making use of the relationship between quasi-simple and general NNINDs established in Theorem 6, we can now derive PSPACE-completeness for the latter.

THEOREM 7. *The implication problem for not null inclusion dependencies is PSPACE-complete.*

PROOF. The PSPACE-hardness follows from PSPACE-hardness for relational INDs [9, Theorem 3.3].

It remains to show that it lies in PSPACE. From Lemma 2 it follows that there exists a non-deterministic algorithm that decides derivability of quasi-simple NNINDs in linear space. By Theorem 6 we can check implication of a non-quasi-simple NNIND by sequentially checking quasi-simple NNINDs, again in linear space (while the number of quasi-simple NNINDs is exponential, they can be enumerated in linear space). This provides us with a linear space non-deterministic algorithm. Existence of a deterministic polynomial space algorithm follows from Savitch's Theorem. □

6. NNIND SUBCLASSES

In the case of pure relations, the PSPACE-completeness result for deciding the implication of INDs has motivated researchers to identify expressive fragments whose implication problem is less complex to decide. In this section, we pursue the same goal for NNINDs.

6.1 Chase for NNINDs

To establish tractablility results for NNINDs with bounded arity, we shall require a chase procedure for NNINDs. In any case, the chase is of interest as an algorithm for deciding implication. As implication of an NNIND reduces to implication of a set of quasi-simple NNINDs (of bounded cardinality for NNINDs of bounded arity) by Theorem 6, we will only consider a chase for quasi-simple NNIDs.

ALGORITHM 1 (CHASE FOR QUASI-SIMPLE NNINDS).
Input: *A database schema $(\mathcal{R}, \Sigma)$ with $\mathcal{R} = (R_1, \ldots, R_k)$ and a database $\boldsymbol{r} = (r_1, \ldots, r_k)$ over $\mathcal{R}$.*
Output: *A modified database chase$(\boldsymbol{r}, \Sigma)$.*
Method: *Apply the following rule as long as possible:*

NNIND: If I contains a dependency $R_i{}^U[X] \subseteq R_j{}^V[Y]$ and for some U-total tuple $t \in r_i$ there does not exist a V-total tuple $s \in r_j$ with $t[X] \sqsubseteq s[Y]$, then add the following tuple s to r_j:

$$s[B_i \in Y] := \begin{cases} 0 & \text{if } t[A_i] = \bot \text{ and } B_i \in V^* \\ t[A_i] & \text{otherwise} \end{cases}$$

$$s[B \notin Y] := \begin{cases} 0 & \text{if } B \in V^* \\ \bot & \text{otherwise} \end{cases}$$

where we use the abbreviation $V^* := V \cup \mathrm{NN}(R_j)$ and the notation $A_i := (Y \mapsto X)(B_i)$ for readability.

LEMMA 3. *Let Σ be a set of NNINDs over $\mathcal{R}$, and $\varphi := R_i{}^{UX}[X] \subseteq R_j{}^V[Y]$ be a quasi-simple NNIND over $\mathcal{R}$. Let the initial database $\boldsymbol{r}$ consist of a single tuple $t \in r_i$ with $t[X] = (1, \ldots, |X|)$, $t[A] = 0$ for $A \in (U \cup \mathrm{NN}(R_i)) \setminus X$ and $t[A] = \bot$ elsewhere. Then $\Sigma \models \varphi$ iff relation chase$(\boldsymbol{r}, \Sigma)$ contains a V-total tuple $s \in r_j$ with $t[X] = s[Y]$.*

PROOF. See proof of Lemma 1. □

For classical and partial inclusion dependencies, specialized *chase* algorithms can be found in [1, 29].

6.2 Intractable Subclasses

As a negative result we consider typed NNINDs, which are commonly encountered in database practice. Interestingly, it turns out that the complexity of the implication problem of typed NNINDs differs from that of typed INDs. In [10] it was shown that for typed INDs, implication can be decided in polynomial time. For typed NNINDs the associated implication problem is NP-hard, already in the case where the given set of NNINDs is acyclic.

DEFINITION 7 (TYPED NNINDS).
We call an NNIND $R^U[X] \subseteq S^V[Y]$ typed *if $X = Y$.*

DEFINITION 8 (ACYCLIC NNINDS).
We call a set Σ of NNINDs acyclic *if the directed graph $\mathcal{G}$ with the relation schemata as nodes and an edge $R \to S$ for every NNIND $R^U[X] \subseteq S^U[Y] \in \Sigma$ is acyclic.*

THEOREM 8. *The implication problem for typed acyclic NNINDs is NP-hard.*

PROOF. We will reduce the conjunctive normal form satisfiability problem (CNF-SAT) to it.

Let $\mathcal{V}$ be a set of boolean variables and $\mathcal{C} = \{c_1, \ldots, c_m\}$ a set of clauses over $\mathcal{V} = \{v_1, \ldots, v_n\}$. We construct a schema $\mathcal{R} = \{R_0, \ldots, R_{n+1}\}$ and an acylic set $\Sigma = \{\varphi_{-n}, \ldots, \varphi_n\}$ of typed NNINDs over $\mathcal{R}$ as follows.

- $R_i = X = \{A_1, \ldots, A_m\}$ for $i = 0, \ldots, n+1$
- $\varphi_i = R_{i-1}{}^{\emptyset}[X] \subseteq R_i{}^{V_i}[X]$ for $i = 1, \ldots, n$ with $V_i = \{A_j \mid v_i \in c_j\}$
- $\varphi_{-i} = R_{i-1}{}^{\emptyset}[X] \subseteq R_i{}^{V_{-i}}[X]$ for $i = 1, \ldots, n$ with $V_{-i} = \{A_j \mid \neg v_i \in c_j\}$
- $\varphi_0 = R_n{}^X[X] \subseteq R_{n+1}{}^{\emptyset}[X]$

We claim that Σ implies $\varphi := R_0{}^{\emptyset}[X] \subseteq R_{n+1}{}^{\emptyset}[X]$ iff $\mathcal{C}$ is satisfiable.

Let $\mathcal{S}$ be any derivation sequence that derives φ from Σ. Such a sequence would necessarily consist of exactly one of φ_i, φ_{-i} for $i = 1, \ldots, n$, followed by φ_0. In order for φ_0 to be applicable, a not-null condition must be derived for each A_j. For this to happen, at least one φ_i or φ_{-i} must occur in $\mathcal{S}$ with $A_j \in V_i$ or $A_j \in V_{-i}$, respectively.

Consider now the truth assignment $\mathcal{T}_\mathcal{S}$:

$$\mathcal{T}_\mathcal{S}(v_i) := \begin{cases} true & \text{if } \varphi_i \in \mathcal{S} \\ false & \text{if } \varphi_{-i} \in \mathcal{S} \end{cases}$$

which satisfies a clause $c_j \in \mathcal{C}$ iff $\varphi_i \in \mathcal{S}$ for some $v_i \in c_j$ or $\varphi_{-i} \in \mathcal{S}$ for some $\neg v_i \in c_j$. By definition of V_i and V_{-i} we have $v_i \in c_j$ iff $A_j \in V_i$ and $\neg v_i \in c_j$ iff $A_j \in V_{-i}$.

Thus, if a derivation sequence $\mathcal{S}$ exists showing $\Sigma \models \varphi$, then $\mathcal{T}_\mathcal{S}$ is a truth assignment satisfying $\mathcal{C}$. Conversely, every truth assignment $\mathcal{T}$ satisfying $\mathcal{C}$ gives rise to a derivation sequence $\mathcal{S}$ with $\mathcal{T} = \mathcal{T}_\mathcal{S}$ showing $\Sigma \models \varphi$. $\square$

While the proof of Theorem 8 uses NNINDs with non-empty sets V, this is not strictly necessary. We could easily avoid this by replacing each φ_i with a pair of partial INDs $R_{i-1}[X] \subseteq_p S_i[X]$ and $S_i[X] \subseteq_p R_i[X]$ by adding an additional schema S_i with NOT NULL constraints on V_i, and respectively for φ_{-i}. This gives us the following corollary.

COROLLARY 2. *The implication problem for typed acyclic simple and partial inclusion dependencies with NOT NULL constraints is NP-hard to decide.*

We remark that by Corollary 2 the increased difficulty in deciding implication of typed NNINDs cannot be blamed on our choice in defining NNINDs, but is intrinsic to simple and partial IND in combination with NOT NULL constraints.

6.3 Tractable Subclasses

In [9, 16] it was shown that implication for inclusion dependencies of bounded arity can be decided in polynomial time. As we will show next, this result not only extends to NNINDs, but can actually be strengthened to show fixed-parameter tractability.

DEFINITION 9 (ARITY). *The* arity *of a NNIND $R^U[X] \subseteq S^V[Y]$ is the length of X (equivalently Y). When we talk of implication for bounded arity, we mean implication over subclasses of NNINDs induced by a fixed upper bound on their arity.*

THEOREM 9. *The implication problem for NNINDs is fixed parameter-tractable in their arity.*

PROOF. Let m denote a bound for the arity of all NNINDs in $\Sigma \cup \{\varphi\}$. Consider Algorithm 1 for quasi-simple NNINDs, i.e. where φ is quasi-simple. The number of distinct attribute values that may occur in tuples produced during our chase is bounded by $m + 2$.

For each tuple generated, there exists some NNIND $\varphi' = R_i{}^{U^*}[X^*] \subseteq R_j{}^{V^*}[Y^*] \in \Sigma$ that generates it. Consider now the tuples generated by φ'. By construction they only differ on Y^*, and thus their number is bounded by $(m+2)^{|Y^*|} \leq (m+2)^m$. Hence the total number of tuples generated during our chase is bounded by $|\Sigma| \cdot (m+2)^m$. Since the number of chase steps (successful or not) is limited by $|\Sigma|$ times number of tuples occurring in our chase tables, and each chase step can be implemented to run in polynomial time, this means that running time for our chase is bounded by $P(\text{input size}) \cdot (m+2)^m$ for some polynomial P.

Finally, we can decide implication of a non-quasi-simple NNIND of arity $\leq m$ by checking implication of at most 2^m quasi-simple NNINDs by Theorem 6. This gives us an overall running time bounded by

$$P(\text{input size}) \cdot (2m+4)^m$$

which shows fixed parameter-tractability in m. $\square$

Another tractable class of INDs are *tree-like* INDs, meaning that $\mathcal{G}$ in Definition 8 is a tree (or forest) without duplicate edges. Implication for tree-like INDs can be decided in linear time [31], and the proof generalizes to our setting.

THEOREM 10. *For tree-like NNINDs the implication problem can be decided in linear time.* $\square$

7. CONCLUSION AND FUTURE WORK

SQL will continue to dominate database practice in the foreseeable future. Domain, entity and referential integrity are therefore fundamental rules that real-world data is governed by. We have studied INDs under the SQL requirements of nulls, NOT NULL constraints, simple and partial semantics. We showed the surprising impossibility result that simple INDs and NOT NULL together cannot be finitely axiomatized. This motivated the challenging question whether SQL INDs can be defined such that simple and partial semantics are both covered, and their good computational properties from pure relations are retained. We established that NNINDs provide an affirmative answer: their implication is finitely axiomatizable, PSPACE-complete to decide, and solvable by a chase procedure. We showed the implication of typed acyclic NNINDs to be NP-hard, the implication of general NNINDs to be fixed-parameter tractable in their arity, and the implication of tree-like NNINDs to be decidable in linear time.

The open problems already mentioned and several others warrant future research. Mitchell established an elegant non-k-ary axiomatization for the finite implication of FDs and INDs [37]. Finite and unrestricted implication of FDs and unary INDs and FDs are different but both axiomatizable and PTIME decidable [16]. A seminal paper in query optimization is [25], which exploited a chase for FDs and INDs to characterize containment between conjunctive queries. A seminal paper in schema design is [32] which provides justifications for the IND normal form over relational databases. These results would all be interesting to investigate in the real-world context of SQL.

A fundamental result for relational databases concerns the undecidability of (finite) implication for the combined class of FDs and INDs [11, 37]. Based on this infeasibility, several sufficient conditions on the structure of the given constraint sets have been identified that guarantee no interaction between these fragments of the constraint classes [35]. It is desirable to establish similar conditions in SQL, as these would simplify computation. The combination of NNINDs with different notions of keys [5, 19, 21, 22, 23, 26, 27, 28] appears to be a sensible approach to address entity and referential integrity together.

Acknowledgements

This research is supported by the Marsden Fund Council from New Zealand Government funding, and by the Natural Science Foundation of China (Grant No. 61472263).

8. REFERENCES

[1] S. Abiteboul, R. Hull, and V. Vianu. *Foundations of Databases*. Addison-Wesley, 1995.

[2] P. Atzeni and N. M. Morfuni. Functional dependencies and constraints on null values in database relations. *Information and Control*, 70(1):1–31, 1986.

[3] J. Bauckmann, Z. Abedjan, U. Leser, H. Müller, and F. Naumann. Discovering conditional inclusion dependencies. In *CIKM*, pages 2094–2098, 2012.

[4] E. Börger, E. Grädel, and Y. Gurevich. *The Classical Decision Problem*. Springer, 1997.

[5] P. Brown and S. Link. Probabilistic keys for data quality management. In *CAiSE*, pages 118–132. Springer, 2015.

[6] L. Cabibbo. On keys, foreign keys and nullable attributes in relational mapping systems. In *EDBT*, pages 263–274, 2009.

[7] A. Calì, D. Calvanese, and M. Lenzerini. Data integration under integrity constraints. In *Seminal Contributions to Information Systems Engineering*, pages 335–352. Springer, 2013.

[8] D. Calvanese, W. Fischl, R. Pichler, E. Sallinger, and M. Simkus. Capturing relational schemas and functional dependencies in RDFS. In *AAAI*, pages 1003–1011, 2014.

[9] M. Casanova, R. Fagin, and C. Papadimitriou. Inclusion dependencies and their interaction with functional dependencies. *J. Comput. Syst. Sci.*, 28(1):29–59, 1984.

[10] M. Casanova and V. Vidal. Towards a sound view integration methodology. In *PODS*, pages 36–47, 1983.

[11] A. Chandra and M. Vardi. The implication problem for functional and inclusion dependencies is undecidable. *SIAM J. Comput.*, 14(3):671–677, 1985.

[12] P. Chen. The entity-relationship model - toward a unified view of data. *ACM Trans. Database Syst.*, 1(1):9–36, 1976.

[13] Z. Chen, V. Narasayya, and S. Chaudhuri. Fast foreign-key detection in Microsoft SQL Server PowerPivot for Excel. *PVLDB*, 7(13):1417–1428, 2014.

[14] E. Codd. A relational model of data for large shared data banks. *Commun. ACM*, 13(6):377–387, 1970.

[15] S. Cosmadakis and P. Kanellakis. Functional and inclusion dependencies: A graph theoretic approach. In *PODS*, pages 29–37, 1984.

[16] S. Cosmadakis, P. Kanellakis, and M. Vardi. Polynomial-time implication problems for unary inclusion dependencies. *J. ACM*, 37(1):15–46, 1990.

[17] C. J. Date. Referential integrity. In *VLDB*, pages 2–12, 1981.

[18] J. Gryz. Query folding with inclusion dependencies. In *ICDE*, pages 126–133, 1998.

[19] M. Hannula, J. Kontinen, and S. Link. On independence atoms and keys. In *CIKM*, pages 1229–1238. ACM, 2014.

[20] S. Hartmann, M. Kirchberg, and S. Link. Design by example for SQL table definitions with functional dependencies. *VLDB J.*, 21(1):121–144, 2012.

[21] S. Hartmann, U. Leck, and S. Link. On Codd families of keys over incomplete relations. *Comput. J.*, 54(7):1166–1180, 2011.

[22] S. Hartmann and S. Link. Efficient reasoning about a robust XML key fragment. *ACM Trans. Database Syst.*, 34(2), 2009.

[23] S. Hartmann and S. Link. Expressive, yet tractable XML keys. In *EDBT*, pages 357–367. ACM, 2009.

[24] S. Hartmann and S. Link. The implication problem of data dependencies over SQL table definitions. *ACM Trans. Database Syst.*, 37(2):13, 2012.

[25] D. Johnson and A. Klug. Testing containment of conjunctive queries under functional and inclusion dependencies. *JCSS*, 28(1):167–189, 1984.

[26] H. Köhler, U. Leck, S. Link, and H. Prade. Logical foundations of possibilistic keys. In *JELIA*, pages 181–195. Springer, 2014.

[27] H. Köhler, S. Link, and X. Zhou. Possible and certain SQL key. *PVLDB*, 8(11):1118–1129, 2015.

[28] V. Le, S. Link, and M. Memari. Schema- and data-driven discovery of SQL keys. *JCSE*, 6(3):193–206, 2012.

[29] M. Levene and G. Loizou. Null inclusion dependencies in relational databases. *Inf. Comput.*, 136(2):67–108, 1997.

[30] M. Levene and G. Loizou. Axiomatisation of functional dependencies in incomplete relations. *Theor. Comput. Sci.*, 206(1-2):283–300, 1998.

[31] M. Levene and G. Loizou. Guaranteeing no interaction between functional dependencies and tree-like inclusion dependencies. *Theor. Comput. Sci.*, 254(1-2):683–690, 2001.

[32] M. Levene and M. Vincent. Justification for inclusion dependency normal form. *IEEE Trans. Knowl. Data Eng.*, 12(2):281–291, 2000.

[33] E. Lien. On the equivalence of database models. *J. ACM*, 29(2):333–362, 1982.

[34] S. Link and M. Memari. Static analysis of partial referential integrity for better quality SQL data. In *AMCIS*. Association for Information Systems, 2013.

[35] H. Mannila and K. Räihä. *The Design of Relational Databases*. Addison-Wesley, 1992.

[36] M. Memari and S. Link. Index design for enforcing partial referential integrity efficiently. In *EDBT*, pages 217–228. OpenProceedings.org, 2015.

[37] J. Mitchell. The implication problem for functional and inclusion dependencies. *Information and Control*, 56(3):154–173, 1983.

[38] R. Pichler, A. Polleres, S. Skritek, and S. Woltran. Complexity of redundancy detection on RDF graphs in the presence of rules, constraints, and queries. *Semantic Web*, 4(4):351–393, 2013.

[39] E. Sciore. Inclusion dependencies and the universal instance. In *PODS*, pages 48–57, 1983.

[40] M. Zhang, M. Hadjieleftheriou, B. Ooi, C. Procopiuc, and D. Srivastava. On multi-column foreign key discovery. *PVLDB*, 3(1):805–814, 2010.

Comprehensible Models for Reconfiguring Enterprise Relational Databases to Avoid Incidents

Ioana Giurgiu
IBM Research - Zürich
Rüschlikon, Switzerland
igi@zurich.ibm.com

Mirela Madalina Botezatu
IBM Research - Zürich
Rüschlikon, Switzerland
bot@zurich.ibm.com

Dorothea Wiesmann
IBM Research - Zürich
Rüschlikon, Switzerland
dor@zurich.ibm.com

ABSTRACT

Configuring enterprise database management systems is a notoriously hard problem. The combinatorial parameter space makes it intractable to run and observe the DBMS behavior in all scenarios. Thus, the database administrator has the difficult task of choosing DBMS configurations that potentially lead to critical incidents, thus hindering its availability or performance. We propose using machine learning to understand how configuring a DBMS can lead to such high risk incidents. We collect historical data from three IT environments that run both IBM DB2 and Oracle DBMS. Then, we implement several linear and non-linear multivariate models to identify and learn from high risk configurations. We analyze their performance, in terms of accuracy, cost, generalization and interpretability. Results show that high risk configurations can be identified with extremely high accuracy and that the database administrator can potentially benefit from the rules extracted to reconfigure in order to prevent incidents.

Categories and Subject Descriptors

H.2.7 [**Database Management**]: Database Administration; I.5.2 [**Design Methodology**]: Classifier Design and Evaluation

Keywords

Database configuration; multivariate analysis

1. INTRODUCTION

Configuring enterprise relational databases is a notoriously hard problem [14, 4, 22]. The large number of configuration parameters that come with enterprise DBMS, like IBM DB2[1] [13] or Oracle[2] [21], and their respective widely varying ranges prohibit database administrators to identify and apply the best configurations for specific workloads. Ideally, one would use full factorial design to find the optimal configurations, that is run all possible combinations of configurations. However, as the number of parameters increases linearly, the number of combinations explodes, making this approach intractable in practice. In fact, beyond generating combinations for a handful of parameters [24, 20, 5], the configuration space is rather unknown to us.

Our research is guided by several observations. On the one hand, databases are complex black boxes and applying a top-down approach [25, 15] to reconfigure them on a need basis is difficult. Even the built-in cost-based optimizers, which are actively used by the DBMS advisors, fail to accurately estimate how well a DBMS will perform for specific workloads and configurations [14]. On the other hand, a bottom-up approach requires empirical evidence on the DBMS behavior across various scenarios.

We advocate the idea that instead of employing heuristic algorithms to find approximate solutions for the NP-hard problem at hand, *machine learning – specifically multivariate analysis – can be better suited in the context of DBMS (re)configuration.* Not only it can be successfully used to explore and understand the huge configuration space, but it can generalize beyond specific DBMS scenarios. The techniques we look into vary from linear, such as generalized linear (GLM), to non-linear methods, like additive (GAM) models [11, 29], decision trees or random forests [2].

The goals of this paper are two-fold: (1) to use machine learning techniques for identifying databases with high risk of failure or performance degradation incidents, and (2) to recommend cost effective reconfigurations that can be used by DBMS administrators to mitigate some of the risk, as well as to potentially improve the DBMS availability and performance.

We approach the problem of DBMS (re)configuration in several steps:

1. We gather broad configuration and workload information for over 1700 IBM DB2 and Oracle DBMS belonging to three IT environments, as well as properties of the servers on which they are hosted.
2. We collect and classify vast amounts of incidents spanning 2014 from DBMS line teams and keep only those associated to the instances above.
3. We apply the afore-mentioned models on the collected data to classify the DBMS, and implicitly their configurations, into *problematic* (i.e., associated with high incident risk) and *nonproblematic.*
4. We use the same models to learn what constitutes problematic and nonproblematic configurations and to generalize the findings by extracting rules for specific

Permission to make digital or hard copies of all or part of this work for personal or classroom use is granted without fee provided that copies are not made or distributed for profit or commercial advantage and that copies bear this notice and the full citation on the first page. Copyrights for components of this work owned by others than ACM must be honored. Abstracting with credit is permitted. To copy otherwise, or republish, to post on servers or to redistribute to lists, requires prior specific permission and/or a fee. Request permissions from Permissions@acm.org.
CIKM '15 Melbourne, Australia
© 2015 ACM. ISBN 978-1-4503-3794-6/15/10 ...$15.00.
DOI: http://dx.doi.org/10.1145/2806416.2806448.

configuration parameters. Such rules can be of the type: *If parameter $X \in [x_1, x_2]$ and parameter $Y > y$, then they are highly correlated with a problematic configuration.* Note here that rules can contain an arbitrary number of configuration parameters, and the less parameters are included, the higher is their potential contribution to incidents.

5. We evaluate the linear and non-linear models on the IBM DB2 and Oracle collected data and compare them along several dimensions: (a) *classification accuracy*, (b) *output intelligibility through rule extraction*, (c) *generalization*, and (d) *computational cost.*

Our findings show that high risk configurations can be identified with extremely high accuracy, 91% for IBM DB2 and 96% for Oracle. This is particularly the case for random forest and generalized additive models with interactions, since they have the advantage of exploiting the intricate relationships between the DBMS' configuration parameters. These models also generalize well on new DBMS configurations, achieving 75-80% classification accuracy. However, high accuracy comes at the expense of computational cost and output interpretability. Generalized linear models and decision trees excel at providing rules that can be easily understood and applied by database administrators to reconfigure DBMS. We advocate that some of these models can be used in combination to achieve high accuracy, generalization and interpretability.

The rest of the paper is organized as follows. In Section II we review the state of the art. Section III describes the methodology and provides brief overviews of the models implemented. In Section IV we present the experimental setup, while in Section V we discuss our results and conclude in Section VI.

2. RELATED WORK

Ganek and Corbi [10] were among the first to motivate the push for autonomic computing and devised four important attributes that define it: (1) self-configuring (i.e., systems adapt automatically to dynamic environments), (2) self-healing (i.e., systems discover and react to malfunctions), (3) self-optimizing (i.e., systems monitor their performance and tune automatically), and (4) self-protecting (i.e., systems predict and protect themselves from negative impact events). Substantial work has been done along all these directions for DBMS, with a special focus on providing them with self-optimizing and self-configuring capabilities. The research on self-optimizing/self-configuring DBMS can be divided into two categories, namely the physical or logical tuning of the DBMS, and the tuning of the configuration parameters. The problem of self-optimization and self-configuration is a challenging one. For instance, tuning the buffer pool or the memory allocation for queries is quite disparate from selecting or building the right indexes. Each problem requires different workload abstractions and has different constraints on the optimal solution.

In the context of physical or logical tuning, automatic index tuning has received most of the attention. This is attributed to two reasons: (1) the high impact index selection has on DBMS performance, (2) the difficulty of the optimal index creation problem. Generally, the objective is the performance maximization of the materialized indices given an expected workload, under resource constraints. Various solutions have been proposed in [25, 3, 4, 1, 27].

In configuration parameter analysis, the approaches that account for all parameters are rather few. Instead, attempts have been made in finding optimal values for subsets of configuration parameters [24, 20] or even for only one configuration parameter as in [5], where the authors single out the buffer pool as the most important configuration parameter. However, given our observations on the existence of nontrivial interactions between parameters, there is no clear way to merge the insight obtained through separate models into a comprehensive standalone model that can aid in optimizing the DBMS performance.

Given that DBMS come with tens or hundreds of configuration parameters, whose ranges can vary widely, the exploration space of the problem is combinatorial. Models that account for all parameters have been proposed in [6, 15, 1]. In [6], the authors propose a model to aid in finding configuration settings that deliver best performance for a certain workload. First, they model a response surface of the DBMS performance with respect to the parameter values. Second, they devise a feedback-driven model of a response surface, which they further use to infer the performance expectation of a combination of parameters. The biggest drawbacks of the solution are the large temporal and computational requirements in order to provide a configuration that exhibits a significant margin on performance improvement. IBM DB2's Configuration Advisor [15] recommends parameter settings based on answers given by users to a set of high-level questions (e.g., the approximate number of users who will connect to the DBMS) and information collected automatically. However, if the recommended configuration is still unsatisfactory, the tool does not refine its recommendation. The authors in [1] devise a statistical model that performs parameter ranking based on the workload impact. However, in contrast to our approach in parameter ranking, they conduct a limited set of experiments in which they consider only extreme values (minimum or maximum) for each of the configuration parameters and consider only low-order interactions (maximum two factor interactions).

Given the problem at hand and the other approaches encountered in the literature in solving it (e.g., control theory, Gaussian processes, decision trees), we can conclude that the selection of optimal DBMS configurations is bound to build on mathematical models and their correct integration into the system components [26].

3. METHODOLOGY

Let $\mathcal{D} = \{(X_i, Y_i)\}_1^N$ represent a set of size N, where $X_i = (x_{i1}, ..., x_{in})$ is a feature vector with n features and Y_i is the target parameter. In this paper, X_i consists of a mix of DBMS-specific configuration parameters associated to a particular DBMS instance, $DBMS_i$, and the properties of the server on which it is hosted. We call X_i the *configuration vector.* Let I_i^t denote the set of incidents corresponding to $DBMS_i$ over the period t. This set can either be empty (i.e., if no incidents occurred on $DBMS_i$) or not. Thus, the configuration vector X_i associates to I_i^t. The output, Y_i, represents whether the corresponding configuration X_i is problematic or non-problematic. Any DBMS configuration with no incidents is non-problematic and problematic, otherwise.

We want to be able to establish whether a configuration X_i is problematic or not and model this as a binary classification problem. We want to predict the value of $Y_i \in 0,1$, with $Y_i = 0$ corresponding to non-problematic configurations and $Y_i = 1$ to problematic ones. Given a model M, let $\overline{Y} = F(X_i)$ be the prediction of the model for configuration X_i. Our goal is to minimize the expected value of some loss function $L(\overline{Y}, Y) \in [0,1]$. In our case, the loss function can only take 2 values, 0 if $\overline{Y} = Y$ or 1 if $\overline{Y} \neq Y$.

In the second step, we consider the classified configurations ${X_i}_1^N$ and for each x_i define its set of single rules $\mathcal{R}_i = \{R_{ij}\}_1^J$, where J is its cardinality. Then, we extract general rules r : *Condition* $\rightarrow Y$, where the condition is expressed as a join of rules specific to individual configuration parameters, *Condition* $= R_{1j} \bowtie R_{2j} ... \bowtie R_{kj}$, with $k \in [1, n]$ and $j \in [1, J]$. Note that a generalized rule r can contain an arbitrary number of single rules. In the simplest case, only one rule can determine the output ($r : R_{kj} \rightarrow Y$), whereas in the most complex scenario all input parameters contribute to predict the target ($r : R_{1j} \bowtie R_{2j} ... \bowtie R_{nj}$). Our goal in extracting generalized rules is two-fold. First, we favor simpler rules, as in general predicting the output with fewer input parameters ensures a higher coverage of the data set. Second, we aim for easily generalizable rules, that can achieve high prediction accuracies when applied on unseen data sets.

Next, we briefly review the concepts behind linear, additive and non-linear models used.

3.1 Generalized Linear Models (GLM)

Generalized linear models are defined as:

$$g(E(Y)) = \beta_0 + \beta_1 x_1 + ... + \beta_n x_n + e \tag{1}$$

where ${\beta_i}_1^n$ are the computed coefficients for the individual configuration parameters, β_0 is the intercept, e is the error and g is the link function. The ${\beta_i}_1^n$ coefficients are estimated using maximum likelihood. GLMs are the simplest models to build, since the contribution of each input variable x_i to Y is a linear expression $\beta_i x_i$. One can easily understand the contribution in predicting the output and whether it is positively ($\beta_i > 0$) or negatively ($\beta_i < 0$) correlated to Y. However, they suffer from two major drawbacks which hinder their accuracy. First, they do not capture non-linear relationships between individual parameters and the output. Second, they do not model any interactions between these parameters and assume they are independent. As such, GLMs are not a particularly good fit for classifying DBMS configurations, since incidents mostly occur due to poorly configured combinations of parameters.

To reduce model overfitting, we apply regularization.Thus, instead of minimizing $L(\overline{Y}, Y)$, we minimize $L(\overline{Y}, Y) + \alpha$ ||w||, where ||w|| is the complexity penalty and α is the tuning parameter. We implement and evaluate GLMs with L1 (Lasso), L2 (Ridge) and L1/L2 (ElasticNet) regularization.

3.2 Generalized Additive Models (GAM)

Generalized additive models [11, 29] are defined as:

$$g(E(Y)) = \beta_0 + f_1(x_1) + ... + f_n(x_n) \tag{2}$$

where f_i are the *shape functions* of configuration parameters x_i. GAMs explicitly decompose a complex function into a sum of one-dimensional components, its shape functions. While the expression is simple, these functions can be non-linear, which means they capture non-linear relationships between individual configuration parameters and the output. Thus, GAMs can achieve significantly higher accuracy than GLMs, while retaining much of their comprehensibility. As such, one can visualize the relationship between parameters and the output through plots $f_i(x_i)$ vs. x_i. However, they do not model any interactions between features, as they assume they are all independent. This assumption not only limits the accuracy GAMs can achieve, but it does not apply to the problem of DBMS configuration. For example, increasing *logbufsz* for IBM DB2 implies that *dbheap* has enough space to sustain such a reconfiguration. This can potentially lead to a prerequisite increase in *dbheap*.

In [17], the authors present two methods of modeling shape functions – *regression splines* and *tree ensembles* – and two techniques for fitting – *least squares* and *gradient boosting*, which we use for building several GAMs. We briefly summarize them below for completeness.

3.2.1 Shape Functions

Regression splines – Splines are piecewise-polynomial functions with high degrees of smoothness. The degree of a spline is given by the highest order of the polynomials. We implement spline-based GAMs with 3 well-known spline types, namely *cubic*, *thin plate* [28] and *P* [7].

Tree ensembles – Tree ensembles are sets of binary balanced trees, where the largest variance reduction is used as the split selection method. We use boosted bagged trees [8], since they outperform both boosted and bagged trees, as shown in [17]. The idea behind is that bagged ensembles are used in every step of stochastic gradient boosting, such that each successive tree predicts the overall residual from the preceding trees.

3.2.2 Fitting GAMs

Least squares – The method is used for fitting regression splines. It minimizes the sum of squared residuals, by learning the coefficients of the piecewise polynomials. For classification, this is equivalent to fitting a logistic regression using penalized reweighted least squares.

Gradient boosting – We briefly outline the gradient boosting algorithm presented in [17]. In each iteration ${m}_1^M$, we cycle through all configuration parameters to learn their respective shape functions. First, all functions are set to zero. Second, over the M iterations and all n parameters, the response are computed by

$$\overline{Y}_i = \frac{2Y_i}{1 + exp(2Y_i f(x_i))}, i_1^N \tag{3}$$

Third, in every iteration ${m}_1^M$, for a parameter x_j, the algorithm learns the one-dimensional function to predict $\overline{Y}_i$, as a tree with K leaf nodes using $(X_{ij}, \overline{Y}_i)$ as training set. This function is, then, added to the shape function:

$$f_j = f_j + \sum_{k=1}^{K} \frac{\sum_{x_{ij} \in R_{km}} \overline{Y}_i}{\sum_{x_{ij} \in R_{km}} |\overline{Y}_i|(2 - |\overline{Y}_i|)} \tag{4}$$

3.3 Generalized Additive Models with Pairwise Interactions (GAMx2)

GAMx2 [18] enhance GAMs by adding pairwise interactions. Ideally, improvements of GAMs would consider interactions between any i parameters, where $i \in [2, n]$. Although any interactions beyond pairs quickly diminish the model interpretability, pairwise interactions are still intelligible and can be visualized as heatmaps of $f_{ij}(x_i, x_j)$ in the x_i, x_j space. Therefore, [18] proposes GAMx2 of the form:

$$g(E(Y)) = \sum_{i=1}^{n} f_i(x_i) + \sum_{i,j=1}^{n} f_{ij}(x_i, x_j) \tag{5}$$

The main challenge in building accurate GAMx2s is the large number of parameter pairs to consider. Since not any 2 features truly interact, there is no point to include shape functions for all pairs. Detecting true interactions is a well researched topic. One class of approaches measures the interaction and additive effects [9, 16, 29]. A major drawback of these methods is that false interactions may be reported over low-density regions [12]. Another approach is to measure the performance drop of the model if a particular interaction is left out [23]. Although straightforward, this method is extremely computationally expensive.

Keeping the need for performance in mind, we use the FAST algorithm [18] for quick pairwise interaction detection. The extensive implementation details of FAST are beyond the scope of this paper, but we briefly outline the execution pipeline. First, the standard GAM F is built using only one-dimensional features. Second, x_i, x_j pairs are ranked in ascending order of their interaction strength. To compute the strength, one needs to look only at the residual sum of squares (RSS) for f_{ij}, computed from individual RSS for f_i and f_j. Instead of actually computing f_{ij}, the algorithm prunes the x_i, x_j space to find the interaction predictor T_{ij} with the lowest RSS, which is a measure of the pair's strength of interaction. Finally, the shape functions for the top-k ranked pairs are computed and added to F.

3.4 Decision Trees

In our scenario, the interior nodes of a decision tree correspond to one of the configuration parameters. Each leaf represents one of the two output classes, problematic or nonproblematic, given the values of the parameters composing the path from the root to the leaf. The tree is grown by binary recursive partitioning until the terminal nodes are too small or too few to split.

The biggest advantage of decision trees is the high intelligibility by means of rules. In our scenario, each branch can be formulated as a single conjunctive rule of the form:

$$If\ cond_1(x_1)\ and\ ...\ and\ cond_k(x_j)\ then\ Y = label \tag{6}$$

where ${x_j}_1^n$ are configuration parameters, ${cond_l}_1^k$ are conditions involving single parameters and *label* is either problematic or nonproblematic. However, one major issue with decision trees is the optimal size of the final tree. On the one hand, a tree that is too large risks overfitting the training data and poorly generalizing on unseen sets. On the other hand, a small tree might lose important structural information. We address this problem by first, limiting the minimum number of configurations per node to $0.02 * N$ and second, by pruning the decision tree.

3.5 Random Forests

Random forests [2] are ensembles of decision trees. For every configuration vector X_i, each tree provides a classification into problematic or nonproblematic and votes for that class. The forest, then, chooses the classification having the most votes over all trees. Each tree is grown using bagging. With the training set $\mathcal{D}_{train}$, we randomly sample $|\mathcal{D}_{train}|$ configurations from $\mathcal{D}$, with replacement and use them to grow the tree. The left out configurations are used to get a running unbiased estimate of the classification error as trees are added to the forest. This technique leads to better performance because it decreases the overall variance. This means that while the predictions of a single tree can be highly sensitive to noise in its training set, the average of many trees is not, as long as the trees are not correlated.

The main benefits of using random forests are their high performance, robustness against outliers and the ability to capture nonlinear relations between input and output variables. However, these advantages come at the expense of a small increase in the bias, loss of interpretability and potentially high computational cost.

Table 1: Summary of IBM DB2 and Oracle datasets.

Set	Tkts	DBs	R^+W	RW	RW^+	Params
DB2	11915	914	–	–	–	28
Oracle	10844	802	38%	21%	41%	45

Table 2: Notations for learning models.

Model	CS	TPS	PS	Trees	Interactions
GLM-L1	–	–	–	–	–
GLM-L2	–	–	–	–	–
GLM-L12	–	–	–	–	–
GAM-csNI	√	–	–	–	–
GAM-tpsNI	–	√	–	–	–
GAM-psNI	–	–	√	–	–
GAM-teNI	–	–	–	√	–
GAM-csI	√	–	–	–	√
GAM-tpsI	–	√	–	–	√
GAM-psI	–	–	√	–	√
GAM-teI	–	–	–	√	√
DT	–	–	–	–	√
RF	–	–	–	–	√

4. EXPERIMENTAL SETUP

4.1 Datasets

We collect configuration and workload data for the IBM DB2 and Oracle DBMS from three IT environments over several snapshots in 2014. These snapshots show that the configurations of a DBMS are largely static over time. We use the workload information to cluster configurations in 3 classes: R^+W corresponds to over 80% reads (i.e, DSS), RW^+ to over 80% writes (i.e., OLTP) and RW represents mixed workloads. Table 1 summarizes the 2 datasets, in terms of volume of relevant incidents in 2014, size, number of input configuration parameters, as well as the distribution of configurations across workload types. 41% of the IBM DB2 configurations and 36% of the Oracle ones are problematic. For IBM DB2, we are not able to collect detailed workload information, therefore all models are workload-agnostic. In the case of Oracle, however, 38% of configurations are R^+W, 21% are RW and 41% are RW^+. For each of these subsets, the percentages of problematic configurations are 40%, 24% and 38%, respectively.

To identify the problematic and non-problematic configurations, we collect incident tickets (i.e., description, reso-

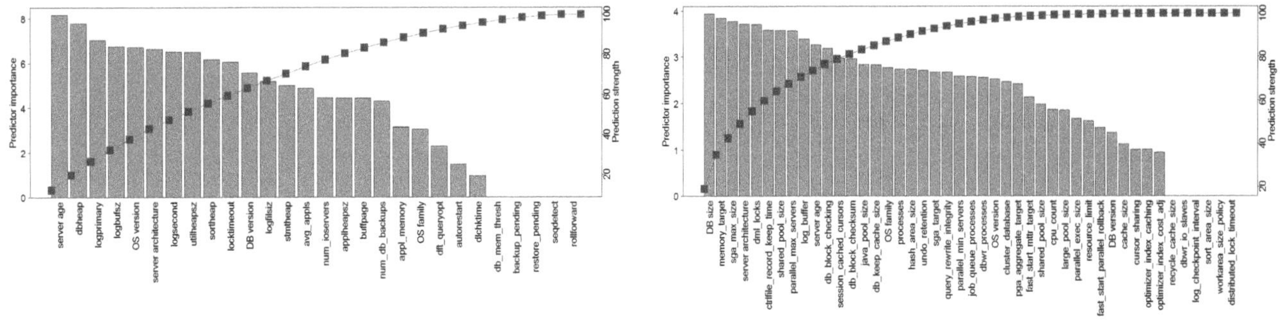

Figure 1: Predictor importance in descending order and cummulative prediction strength for DB2 (left) and Oracle (right).

lution, severity) from database service line teams spanning 2014. We classify them into 5 categories: *backup*, *DB error*, *disk space*, *diagnostics* and *other*. *Backup* incidents refer to backups missing or crashed, backups too old, inconsistent backups, etc. *DB error* refers to database crashes, inability of running transactions, slow performance, too many users connected, deadlocks, etc. We classify incidents as *disk space* only if the low disk space utilization affects the database performance (i.e., otherwise, we exclude them since they can be solved either by removing files to reduce the utilization or increasing the disk capacity). *Diagnostics* refer to transient incidents, that are monitored over extended periods of time, but do not require any action from the service team, and *other* contains any non-database related incidents. Only the *backup*, *DB error* and *disk space* incidents are relevant and are usually associated with high severities, which means they will be resolved first. From all these incidents, we extract the server and database unique identifiers by exact string matching. This step allows us to link incidents to the actual databases on which they occur and classify their configurations into problematic and non-problematic. We consider a configuration as being problematic, if it is associated with at least one incident throughout the time range.

4.2 Feature selection

The number of configuration parameters used in both the Oracle and IBM DB2 models is not extremely large. However, even so, not all of them have high predictive strength and importance. In fact, those with low importance only overcomplicate the models and cause overfitting, without increasing the overall accuracy and should be pruned out. To select the important parameters, we apply feature selection and validate using expert knowledge. We ensure that the importance of each predictor is computed in a model-agnostic fashion, using a filter approach. The output is the list of all configuration parameters for both DB2 and Oracle in decreasing order of their importance.

Figure 1 shows the importance for all parameters and their cumulative prediction strength. For IBM DB2, the top 17 server and database parameters explain over 80% of the dataset variance. The top features in decreasing order of their importance are: *server age*, *dbheap*, *logprimary*, *logbufsz*, *OS version*, *server architecture*, *logsecond*, *util_heap_sz*, *sortheap*, *locktimeout*, *DBMS version*, *logfilsiz*, *stmtheap*, *avg_appls*, *num_ioservers*, *applheapsz* and *buffpage*.

For Oracle, only 15 out of 45 parameters are sufficient to explain over 80% of the data variance. These are in decreasing order: *database size*, *memory_target*, *sga_max_size*, *server architecture*, *dml_locks*, *control_file_record_keep_time*, *shared_pool_size*, *parallel_max_servers*, *log_buffer*, *server age*, *dbblock_checking*, *session_cached_cursors*, *dbblock_checksum*, *java_pool_size* and *db_keep_cache_size*. We use these parameters as input to all models.

Note that configuration parameters like *db_mem_thresh*, *backup_pending*, *restore_pending* or *rollforward* for IBM DB2 have little or no predictive strength for our dataset. This is due to the fact that the same settings are used through the entire dataset, thus presenting no variation from which models can learn. The same observation applies for several Oracle configuration parameters.

4.3 Models and Metrics

Table 2 provides an overview of the models and their denominations, in ascending order of their complexity. GLM-L1, GLM-L2 and GLM-L12 denote GLMs with L1, L2 and L1/L2 regularization, respectively, and are implemented with the `vglm` R package. GAM-csNI, GAM-tpsNI, GAM-psNI and GAM-teNI are GAMs implemented with cubic splines (CS), thin plate splines (TPS), P-splines (PS) (`mgcv` R package) or bagged trees (Java `mltk` library [19]), and model no inter-feature interactions. GAM-csI, GAM-tpsI, GAM-psI and GAM-teI use the same implementations, but also include the top 20 pairwise interactions. For GAM-teNI and GAM-teI, we use 3 leaves for each tree, as indicated in [17]. DT denotes decision tree, while RF stands for the random forest model. We use the `rpart` and `randomForest` R packages, respectively, to implement the models.

In the context of our classification problem, we split both datasets into the train set $\mathcal{D}_{train}$ and the test set $\mathcal{D}_{test}$ by random sampling. 75% of the IBM DB2 and Oracle configurations, respectively, are assigned to $\mathcal{D}_{train}$, and the remaining 25% to $\mathcal{D}_{test}$. We train all models on $\mathcal{D}_{train}$ and evaluate their performance on $\mathcal{D}_{test}$ through several relevant measures: (1) balanced accuracy (ACC), (2) accuracies over the problematic (ACC^{-}) and nonproblematic (ACC^{+}) configurations, respectively, as well as (3) $F1$ score. These metrics are defined as follows:

$$ACC^{-} = \frac{TP}{TP+FN} \qquad ACC^{+} = \frac{TN}{TN+FP}$$

$$ACC = \frac{ACC^{+} * |\mathcal{D}^{+}_{test}| + ACC^{-} * |\mathcal{D}^{-}_{test}|}{|\mathcal{D}_{test}|}$$

$$F1 = \frac{2 * \frac{TP}{TP+FP} * ACC^{+}}{\frac{TP}{TP+FP} + ACC^{+}}$$

where TP = true positives (i.e., correctly classified problematic configurations), TN = true negatives (i.e., correctly classified nonproblematic configurations), FP = false positives and FN = false negatives. $|\mathcal{D}^{-}_{test}|$ and $|\mathcal{D}^{+}_{test}|$represent the number of actual problematic and nonproblematic configurations in the test set, respectively, such that $\mathcal{D}^{-}_{test} \cup \mathcal{D}^{+}_{test} = \mathcal{D}_{test}$. We report averages of the metrics over 10-fold cross validation for all models.

5. RESULTS

5.1 Classification Accuracy

The classification results of all models, when workload is not considered, are shown in Figure 2, for both the IBM DB2 (a-d) and Oracle (e-h) datasets. Each graph is laid out left to right, as follows: The first 3 bars correspond to the generalized linear models, GLM-L1, GLM-L2 and GLM-L12, respectively. The next 4 bars correspond to the generalized additive models modeled with splines, GAM-csNI, GAM-tpsNI and GAM-psNI, as well as with bagged trees, GAM-teNI. The same order is kept for the following 4 bars, that correspond to the generalized additive models with pairwise interactions, GAM-csI, GAM-tpsI, GAM-psI and GAM-teI. Finally, the last 2 bars correspond to the decision tree, DT, and the random forest model, RF.

Several clear patterns emerge for both datasets.

(i) There is a clear gap between linear methods that do not support feature shaping (GLMs) and all other models. This is mostly visible for the IBM DB2 dataset, where all GLMs reach an overall accuracy between 65 and 70%, while the rest exceed 80%. Applying L1/L2 regularization slightly increases the model performance, but only by 1-2%. Even more important is the low accuracy in correctly classifying problematic configurations, around 50%. For Oracle, while still having the lowest performance among all models, GLMs already reach quite high accuracies, over 87%. However, they still suffer from a lower classification accuracy of problematic configurations, between 70 and 78%.

(ii) The tree-based GAM models are in general more accurate than the spline-based ones, by 3-7% for IBM DB2 and 2-4% for Oracle. For IBM DB2, using splines lowers the accuracy of correctly classifying nonproblematic configurations, while the opposite effect is observed for Oracle.

(iii) The GAMx2 models are more accurate than GAMs, which is expected since they model pairwise interactions in addition to feature shaping. For instance, the difference in the overall accuracy and the accuracy in classifying nonproblematic configurations between GAM-teI and GAM-psNI is 11% and 34% for IBM DB2.

(iii) The tree-based GAMs generally perform better than DT. For IBM DB2, GAM-teI is the closest to RF in terms of classification accuracy, with $ACC = 85\%$, $ACC^{-} = 82\%$ and $ACC^{+} = 88\%$. The same observation holds for Oracle as well, where GAM-teI matches RF, with $ACC = 95\%$, $ACC^{-} = 95\%$ and $ACC^{+} = 96\%$. This model is quite robust in providing high accuracies for correctly classifying problematic, as well as nonproblematic configurations, therefore minimizing both false positives and false negatives. While DT also performs excellent, especially for Oracle, we note a lower ACC^{-} than GAM-teI, by 2-6%.

(iv) Full-complexity models, such as RF, perform the best, with 91% overall accuracy for IBM DB2 and 97% for Oracle. RF reaches higher accuracy than GAMs, because it is able to model intricate feature interactions, which linear models of shaped features cannot capture. It also performs better than decision trees, because it trains and fits hundreds of single trees, as compared to a single one.

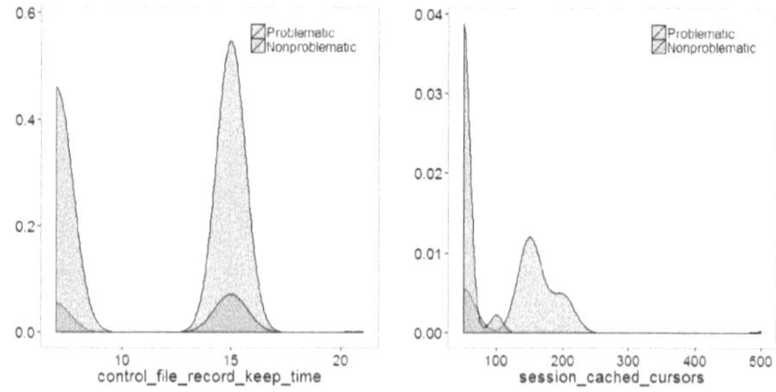

Figure 3: Distributions of selected parameters across problematic and nonproblematic configurations for Oracle.

While the accuracy increase from GLMs to RF is over 25% for DB2, we note only an 8% increase for Oracle. Moreover, for Oracle all GAM models and DT are comparable to RF. This similar performance is caused by the nature of the dataset, more precisely by the strong correlation of particular parameter values or ranges to either problematic or nonproblematic configurations. Examples for selected features – *session_cached_cursors* and *control_file_record_keep_time* – are shown in Figure 3. 98% of configurations where session_cached_cursors < 100 and control_file_record_keep_time < 8 are nonproblematic, whereas all configurations for which these parameters are greater than 150 and 15, respectively, are problematic. These clear trends are easy to detect even for the simple GLMs, therefore explaining the comparable accuracies across all models.

5.2 Computational Cost

Next, we compare all models in terms of their required running time. Since both Oracle and IBM DB2 sets are similar in size, we use them to build several synthetic sets with 30 input features each and 1000, 5000, 10000 or 25000 distinct configurations. Figure 4 summarizes the results for all models, except GLM-L1 and GLM-L2, which we exclude due to their similar performance to GLM-L12. The shortest running time corresponds to GLM-L12 when run on the smallest set. Thus, we use it as the baseline and for the remaining models we report the increase factor in running time as compared to the baseline. This allows us to observe the increase in execution time relative to the set size increase. As expected, the most expensive model is RF by 150x on the 25000 configurations set, although its trend is linear to the set size.

The GAM-csNI, GAM-tpsNI and GAM-psNI are the fastest relative to the baseline, the largest increase factor being 10 for GAM-psNI when run on the largest set. When adding pairwise interactions, all GAM models become significantly slower. In particular, this is noted for the spline models on larger datasets. For instance, GAM-psI is 100x slower than the baseline on the 25000 configurations set, as compared to GAM-teI (64x), whereas for the smallest set GAM-psI is faster than GAM-teI by 50%. This may be attributed to the fact that gradient boosting converges faster since in each iteration it adds a delta to the existing predictor pool.

Finally, DT is the fastest out of the non-linear models, being 58 times slower than the baseline. Although DT is

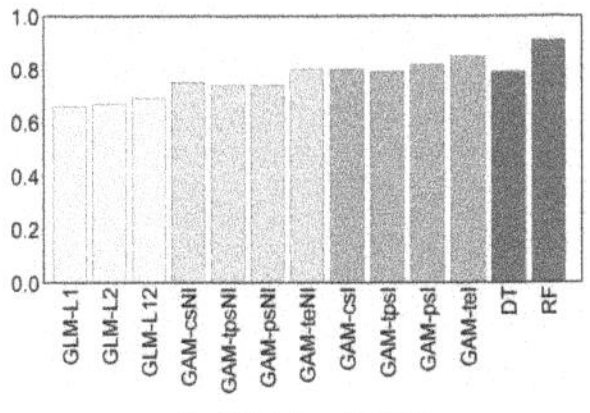

a) DB2 ACC

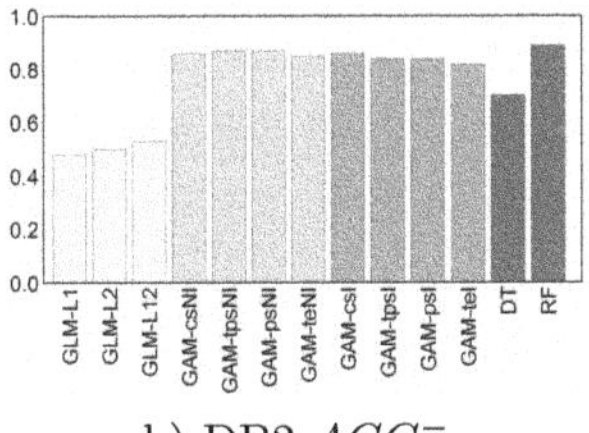

b) DB2 ACC^-

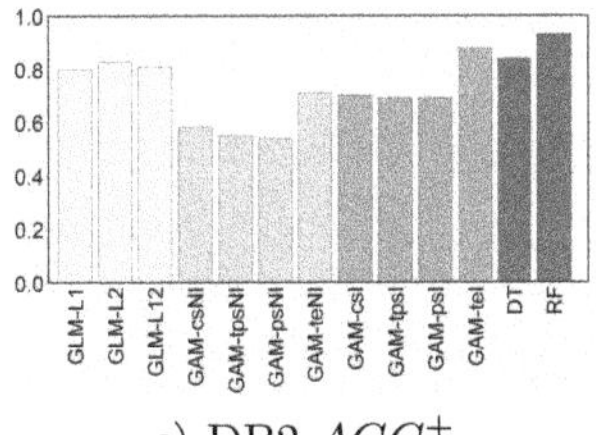

c) DB2 ACC^+

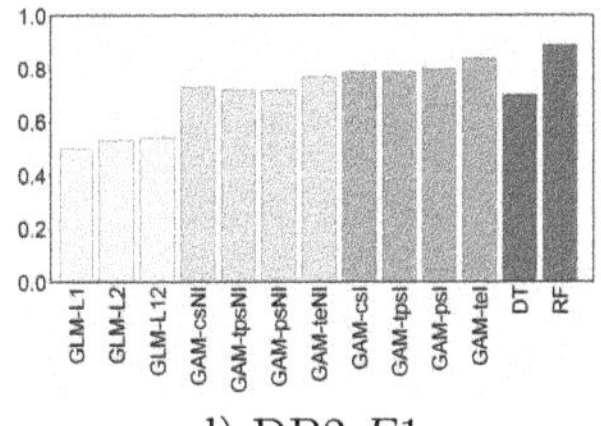

d) DB2 $F1$

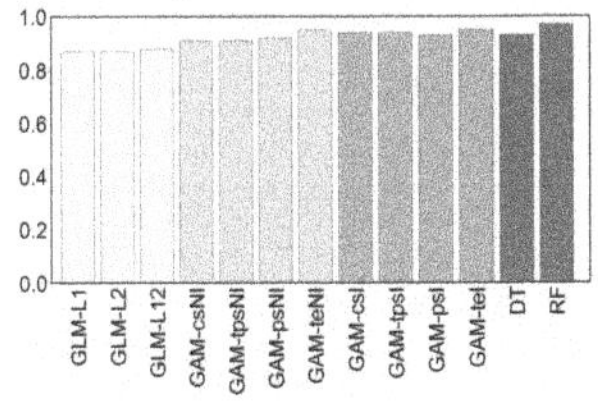

e) Oracle ACC

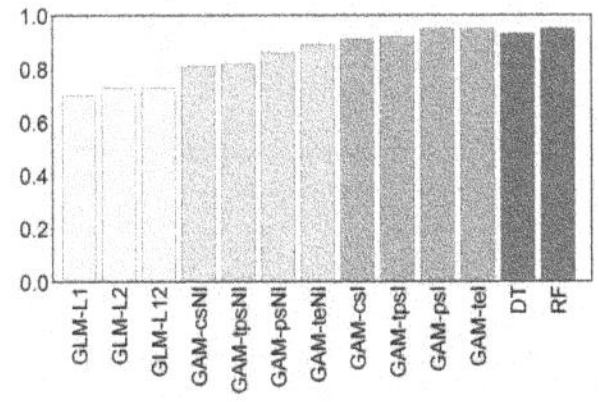

f) Oracle ACC^-

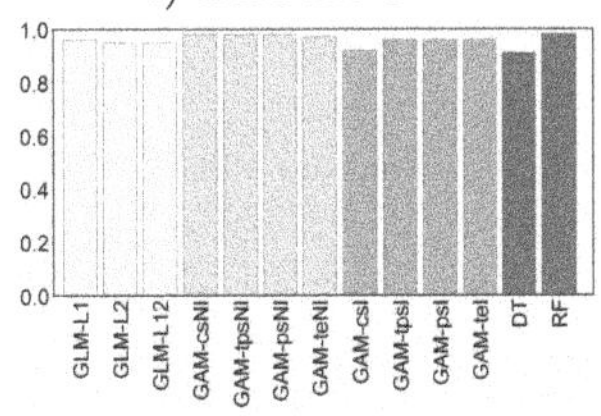

g) Oracle ACC^+

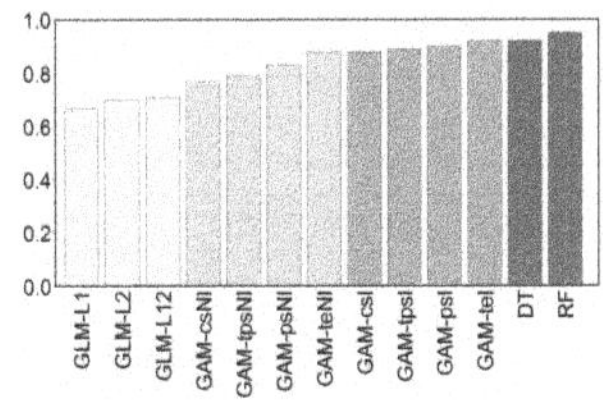

h) Oracle $F1$

Figure 2: Classification accuracy across models for DB2 (a-d) and Oracle (e-h).

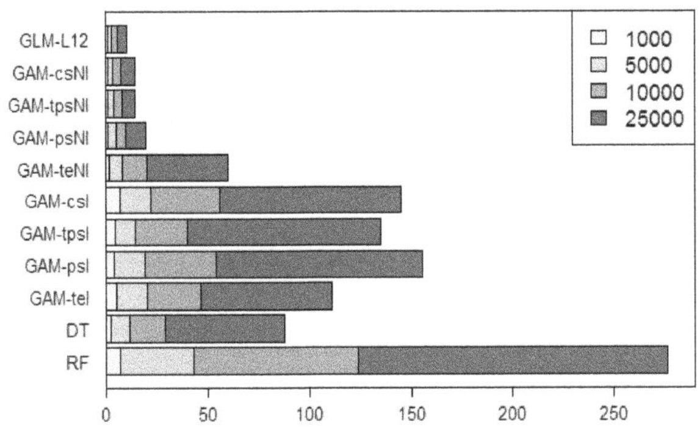

Figure 4: Computational cost of models across datasets consisting of 1000, 5000, 10000 and 25000 configurations.

even faster than GAM-teI, we note a steeper increasing trend with the set size (i.e., polynomial), which leads us to expect slower fitting times already at 50000 configurations.

5.3 Generalization

Next, we evaluate the models' ability to generalize what they learn during fitting on unseen data in three scenarios.

Case #1 – We train the models on two IT environments and use the third ITE's database configurations for testing. Note that this is an extreme scenario, especially since the held-out set contains configurations that are very different from the training configurations, thus making it difficult for the models to reach high accuracies. We can only perform the experiment on the IBM DB2 dataset, as the Oracle dataset has several limitations: (1) either the training set contains only nonproblematic configurations, thus not being able to learn problematic ones, or (2) the train set becomes very small, namely less than 45% of the entire set. For IBM DB2, the test set contains 170 configurations, out of which 47% are problematic. The overall accuracy of the models is shown in Figure 5a. As before, RF has the highest accuracy (72%), although it drops 19% compared to the case when all three IT environments contribute to both the train and test sets. The closest model in performance to RF is GAM-teI, with 67% accuracy. We note two surprising results. First, DT has the lowest accuracy from all models, being outranked even by the GLMs. Second, the GLMs, and especially GLM-L12, is comparable in performance to all GAMs that do not support feature interactions. For brevity, we do not show the models' ACC^- and ACC^+, but we summarize the results next. All models achieve lower accuracies in correctly identifying the problematic configurations and the best performance is reached by RF with 62%. The other models range between 50% and 60%, which means they reach higher ACC^+. Indeed, with the exception of the GLMs and DT, which do not exceed 65% accuracy, all others correctly classify at least 73% of the nonproblematic configurations.

Case #1a – We add 50% of the third IT environment's data to the training set used in Case#1 and leave the remaining 50% for testing. Since the models can learn some of the configurations held-out in Case#1, we expect to obtain higher accuracies. Overall accuracy in Figure 5b shows an increase in performance compared to Case#1 by 4% for GLMs, 3-10% for GAMs, 6-10% for GAMs with interactions, 13% for DT and 11% for RF. GLMs and RF have the lowest, respectively the highest performance, with 64% and 83% accuracy. DT and GAMs are comparable and correctly classify 69-74% of the configurations, with GAM-csI outperforming GAM-teI by 3%.

Case #2 – All three IT environments' configurations are used in both training and testing, but in a temporal manner. More specifically, we train the models on data collected between January and August 2014 and test on the remaining four months. As mentioned before, DBMS are not reconfigured often. However, throughout a year, we note at least 2-3 configuration changes, which means the test data contains configurations that have not been seen before by the models. The overall accuracy for both IBM DB2 and Oracle is shown in Figures 5c and 5d, respectively.

For Oracle, 14% of configurations in the test set are problematic. RF reaches 84% accuracy, and the closest models in performance are GAM-teI, GAM-teNI and GAM-psI with 81%, 80% and 80% correctly classified configurations, respectively. The gap between RF and GLMs is 11-14%, higher than the 8% observed before, which indicates that GLMs do not generalize as well as more complex models. All models obtain high ACC^-, above 80% for GLMs and greater than 95% for the remaining, but perform worse in

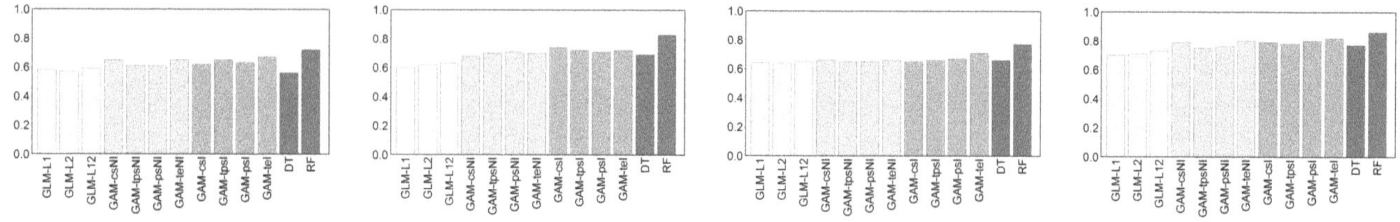

a) DB2 ACC – Case #1 b) DB2 ACC – Case #1a c) DB2 ACC – Case #2 d) Oracle ACC – Case #2

Figure 5: Model accuracy for IBM DB2 in scenarios #1 and #1a (a-b) and for IBM DB2 and Oracle in scenario #2 (c-d).

Table 3: Examples of rules extracted from models for both IBM DB2 and Oracle datasets.

Line	Model	Rule
1	GLMs DB2	$P = 3.9 * 10^{-6} * x_1 + 1.65 * 10^{-4} * x_2 - 4.5 * x_3 - 2.1 * 10^{-2} * x_4 + 2.9 * 10^{-1} * x_5$ $-4 * 10^{-5} * x_6 - 1.85 * 10^{-5} * x_7 + 6.1$
2	GLMs Oracle	$P = 4.5 * 10^{-8} * x_1 + 4.6 * 10^{-3} * x_2 - 1.2 * x_3 + 4.8 * 10^{-4} * x_4 - 2.4 * 10^{-10} * x_5$ $+2.15 * 10^{-10} * x_6 + 1.4 * 10^{-8} * x_7 - 2.7 * 10^{-2} * x_8$
3	DT DB2	If $x_1 < 5488$ pages and $x_2 > 6.1$ and $x_3 > 12$ years, then *problematic*
4	DT DB2	If $x_1 > 5488$ pages and $x_2 \in [6.1, 6.3]$ and $x_4 > 59000$ pages and $x_5 > 13000$ pages and $x_6 > 10$, then *nonproblematic*
5	DT Oracle	If $x_1 \in$ {TRUE, FULL, TYPICAL} and $x_2 > 2.5$ years and $x_3 \geq 15.5$ MB and $x_4 < 50$ GB, then *nonproblematic*
6	RF + DT DB2	If $x_1 > 12$ years and $x_2 < 10$ and $x_3 < 8000$ pages and $x_4 < 5488$ pages and $x_5 < 12$, then *problematic*
7	RF + DT DB2	If $x_1 \leq 4$ years and $x_2 > 20$ and $x_4 > 5488$ pages and $x_6 > 59000$ pages, then *nonproblematic*
8	DT R^+W	If $x_1 \geq 58$ and $x_2 < 0.54$, then *nonproblematic*
9	DT R^+W	If $x_1 \geq 58$ and $x_2 \in [0.54, 3.8 * 10^2]$ and $x_3 \geq 36$, then *problematic*
10	DT RW	If $x_1 = TRUE$ and $x_2 < 0.69$, then *nonproblematic*
11	DT RW	If $x_1 = TRUE$ and $x_2 \geq 0.69$, then *problematic*
12	DT RW^+	If $x_1 \geq 0.54$ and $x_2 < 52$ and $x_4 < 30$ and $x_5 \geq 3$, then *problematic*
13	DT RW^+	If $x_1 \geq 0.54$ and $x_2 \geq 52$ and $x_3 \geq 4644$ and $x_4 \geq 37$, then *nonproblematic*

identifying the nonproblematic configurations (i.e., ACC^+ is in the 70-80% range).

34% of the IBM DB2 configurations in the test set are problematic. RF classifies correctly 77% of configurations, with 14% less than before. Unlike in the initial experiment, all models except GAM-teI have similar performance, between 65% and 67%. As in the previous scenarios, the models achieve lower accuracies in identifying the problematic configurations. Since the same models have an opposite behavior on the Oracle set, we attribute this trend to the IBM DB2 data. In fact, more than 60% of the problematic configurations used in the test phase are significantly different than the training ones, thus explaining the lower performance.

5.4 Intelligibility and Rule Extraction

One of the main reasons to use simpler models, such as GLMs or decision trees, is intelligibility. We discuss this in the context of rule extraction and show examples in Table 3.

GLMs – For each input configuration parameter the model provides a coefficient, which can be either positive or negative. This indicates whether the output correlates positively or negatively to the respective parameter. Generalized equations, rather than rules, can be easily built, as the examples shown in Table 3, lines 1–2. The output of the equation is the classification probability P. If $P < 0.5$, then the configuration is classified as nonproblematic, else it is problematic. For DB2, parameters x_1 to x_7 are *util_heap_sz*, *locktimeout*, normalized *OS version*, *avg_appls*, *server age*, *stmtheap*

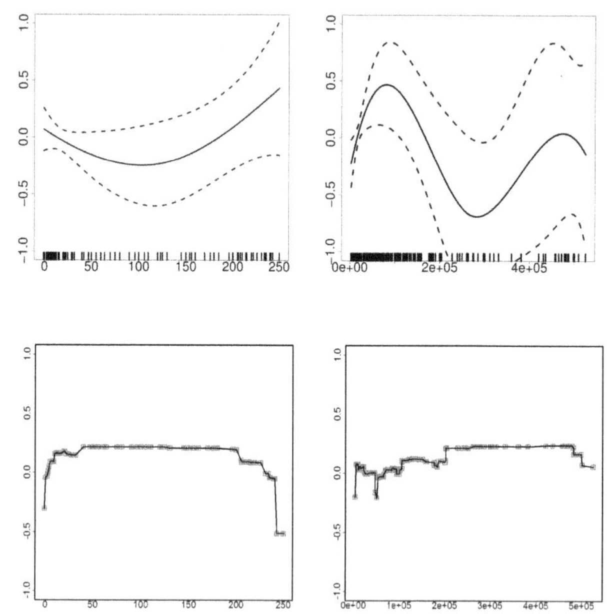

logsecond util_heap_sz

Figure 6: Shapes of selected features for GAM-psI (top) and GAM-teI (bottom) on the IBM DB2 dataset.

and *buffpage*. For Oracle, x_1 to x_8 correspond to *log_size*, *parallel_max_servers*, *server age*, *dml_locks*, *memory_target*, *sga_max_size*, *shared_pool_size* and *session_cached_cursors*. Note that the DB2 equation also includes an intercept value of 6.1, whereas for Oracle its value is negligible.

GAMs – We show shape functions for selected configuration parameters as a result of GAM-psI and GAM-teI in Figure 6. The solid line is the predicted value of the dependent variable as a function of parameter x_i. For brevity, we focus on the IBM DB2 dataset, although similar shape functions are observed for Oracle as well. The selected features are non-linear. The interpretation of the top-left plot, for example, is that a configuration is most likely to be problematic if *logsecond* is on either extreme (e.g., -1 or above 240). Similarly, util_heap_sz > 20000 pages is strongly correlated with nonproblematic configurations. GAM-psI may appear easier to interpret, due to the smoothness of the shape functions. However, there is structure in GAM-teI – captured by sharp turns – which is either less noticeable or missing in the GAM-psI plots, that is important and justifying the higher accuracy of tree-based GAMs. For instance, the models do not agree on a partial slope for *util_heap_sz* and the entire slope for *logsecond*.

DT – Decision trees reveal the basis of the predictive model through the output rules. Examples of such rules are provided in Table 3, lines 3–5. For DB2 (lines 3–4), parameters x_1 to x_6 are *util_heap_sz*, *AIX version*, *server age*, *stmtheap*, *buffpage* and *logsecond*. For Oracle (line 5), x_1 to x_4 correspond to *dbblock_checksum*, *server age*, *log_buffer* and *sga_max_size*. We make several observations. First, most of the parameters captured in the GLM equations are present in the example rules for DT. However, for DB2, *logsecond* is not considered statistically significant in GLMs, which partially explains why these models perform worse in general. Second, typically we observe between 20 and 35 rules. Third, each rule can be constructed from an arbitrary number of parameters, but typically rules with more than 8 to 10 input features are rare. Last, rules are able to capture ranges for continuous parameters and discrete set of values (e.g., *dbblock_checksum* for Oracle), otherwise.

RF – Beyond the classification accuracy, the RF output is extremely difficult to interpret, as it is not expressed as either equations or rules. One alternative is to look at the rules applied by each fitted tree. However, since RF generally uses hundreds of such trees, this can be a tedious task. Other solutions involve either building new learning algorithms on top or using a DT model, which extracts rules from the RF trained set. To illustrate the second approach, we use the RF-trained data in DT to extract rules. For brevity, we only show example rules for DB2 in Table 3, lines 6–7. Parameters x_1 to x_6 correspond to *server age*, *logprimary*, *dbheap*, *util_heap_sz*, *logsecond* and *stmtheap*. On the one hand, by training with RF, the second and third top-ranked parameters (*dbheap* and *logprimary*) appear to significantly contribute in classifying problematic and nonproblematic configurations, whereas with DT they are omitted from the rules. On the other hand, for the configuration parameters where both DT and RF match, the disassociating ranges are either identical or extremely similar.

5.4.1 Rule Extraction from Workload-Driven Models

We split the Oracle dataset by workload type, as show in Table 1. All models perform similarly on the three sets, achieving over 93% accuracy. However, the top-ranked configuration parameters differ from workload to workload.

For R^+W, x_1=*parallel_max_servers*, x_2=*memory_target*, x_3=*log_buffer* and x_4=*DBMS size* are the solely most important features, whereas for RW, x_1=*dbblock_checksum* and x_2=*memory_target* are enough to discriminate between problematic and nonproblematic configurations.

Last, x_1=*memory_target*, x_2=*DBMS size*, x_3=*dml_locks*, x_4=*log_buffer* and x_5=*server age* are ranked highest for the RW^+ type. This difference in the top parameters implies variation in the rules extracted as well. We train DT on the three subsets and build rules as the examples shown in Table 3, lines 8–13. We make several observations. First, the workload type significantly impacts which configuration parameters correlate with incidents. This is expected, since workloads and database behaviors are intrinsically linked. Second, we expect the models to achieve different classification accuracies depending on the ratio of problematic to nonproblematic configurations in the subsets. The fact that all models perform similarly for Oracle is a limitation of our dataset. Finally, we see that *dml_locks* only matters for RW^+ workloads, which is expected since it represents the lock obtained on a table undergoing an insert, update or delete operation.

5.5 Model Selection

Table 4 summarizes our findings on how the models perform relative to classification accuracy, computational cost, intelligibility and generalization. There is no clear front-runner, as all models have pros and cons.

Classification accuracy – For both IBM DB2 and Oracle datasets, the full complexity model, RF, has the highest accuracy in identifying both problematic and nonproblematic configurations, whereas GLMs experience an overall 25% drop in accuracy and 40% decrease in classifying problematic databases. GAMs with pairwise interactions (GAM-I) reach higher performance than the vanilla GAMs and GAMs implemented with bagged boosted trees perform better than the spline-based ones. Moreover, although it does not support interactions beyond pairwise, GAM-teI outperforms DT, placing itself immediately below RF.

Computational cost – High accuracy comes at a high computational cost. When compared to GLMs across different set sizes, the remaining models show relatively stable increase factors within one order of magnitude: (1) RF is 30-32 times slower, (2) DT is more expensive by 6-12x, but follows a polynomial trend, (3) GAM-I are 14 to 20 times slower with GAM-teI being faster than the spline-based models, and (4) GAMs are slower by 2-7x. These results also show that DT and GAM-I models are 50% faster than RF.

Generalization – Models that capture non-linear interactions between features have the potential to generalize better on unseen sets. This is the case for both GAM-I and RF, but not for DT. Not surprisingly, DT overfits on the training data and achieves decreased accuracies on classifying configurations that are significantly different than the ones trained. Across all models, we note a somewhat lower accuracy for problematic configurations and a near 100% accuracy for nonproblematic ones. This is due to the similarities/differences between the train and test configurations, and because we optimize for overall accuracy in all models (i.e., one could optimize for balanced accuracy or F1-score.

Table 4: Summary of models comparison ('+' = worst outcome and '++++' = best outcome for each measure).

Model	Accuracy	Cost	Generalize	Intelligible
GLM	+	++++	++	++++
GAM-NI	++	++++	++	+++
GAM-I	+++	++	+++	++
DT	+++	++	+	++++
RF	++++	+	+++	+

Intelligibility – GLMs and DT are easy to understand, since they automatically output either generalized equations or rules learned. RF models are nearly impossible to interpret, unless another learning algorithm (e.g., DT) is applied after training to facilitate rule extraction. GAMs are somewhat more intelligible than RF, especially since one can plot the shape functions of the input features. However, as interactions are added to increase accuracy, even the visualization of pairwise interactions becomes cumbersome, not to mention if interactions between at least 3 features are modeled.

Finally, workload types influence not only the rankings of configuration parameters, but also the actual rules extracted. Considering the scenario in which a database administrator would need to run a model periodically, as the balance of reads and writes changes, two possible approaches arise. One could use GAM-teI, since it has proven to be highly accurate, and moderately expensive, generalizable and interpretable. Or, to achieve high performance and intelligibility, but at the cost of computation, RF could be used for training, followed by DT for rule extraction.

6. CONCLUSIONS

We propose using machine learning to understand how configuring a DBMS can lead to high risk incidents. We collect historical data from over 1700 DBMS IBM DB2 and Oracle DBMS belonging to three IT environments over 2014. Then, we implement several linear and non-linear multivariate models to identify and learn from high risk configurations. We analyze their performance, in terms of accuracy, computational cost, generalization and interpretability. Results show that random forest and GAMs with pairwise interactions identify high risk configurations with extremely high accuracy, 91% for IBM DB2 and 96% for Oracle, and generalize well on unseen DBMS configurations (i.e., 75-80% accuracy). However, high accuracy comes at the expense of computational cost and output interpretability. All non-linear models are at least an order of magnitude slower than GLMs. In terms of interpretability, GLMs and decision trees excel at providing rules that can be easily understood and applied by database administrators to reconfigure DBMS. We advocate that some of these models, such as random forest and decision trees, can be used in combination to achieve high accuracy, generalization and interpretability.

[1]IBM DB2 is a trademark of International Business Machines Corporation, registered in many jurisdictions worldwide.

[2]Oracle is a registered trademark of the Oracle Corporation in the United States and other countries.

7. REFERENCES

[1] S. Agrawal, S. Chaudhuri, and V. Narasayya. Automated Selection of Materialized Views and Indexes in SQL Databases. *VLDB'00*, pages 496–505.

[2] L. Breiman. Random Forests. *Machine Learning*, 2001.

[3] N. Bruno and S. Chaudhuri. Automatic Physical Database Tuning: A Relaxation-Based Approach. *SIGMOD'05*, pages 227–238.

[4] S. Chaudhuri and V. Narasayya. Self-Tuning Database Systems: A Decade of Progress. *VLDB'07*, pages 3–14.

[5] J. Chung, D. Ferguson, and G. Wang. Goal Oriented Dyanmic Buffer Pool Management for Database Systems. *IBM Research Report RC19807*, pages 191–198.

[6] S. Duan, V. Thummala, and S. Babu. Tuning Database Configuration Parameters with iTuned. *PVLDB'09*, 2(1), 1246–1257.

[7] P. H. C. Eilers and B. D. Marx. Flexible Smoothing with B-splines and Penalties. *Stat. Science*, 11(2):89–121, 1996.

[8] J. Friedman. Stochastic Gradient Boosting. *Computational Statistics and Data Analysis*, 38:367–378, 2002.

[9] J. Friedman and B. Popescu. Predictive Learning via Rule Ensembles. *The Annals of Applied Statistics*, 12(2):916–954, 2008.

[10] A. G. Ganek and T. A. Corbi. The Dawning of the Autonomic Computing Era. *IBM Systems Journal*, 42(1):5–18, 2003.

[11] T. Hastie and R. Tibshirani. Generalized Additive Models. *Chapman and Hall/CRC*, 1990.

[12] G. Hooker. Generalized Functional ANOVA Diagnostics for High-Dimensional Functions of Dependent Variables. *Journal of Computational and Graphical Statistics*, 16(3):709–732, 2007.

[13] IBM DB2. www-01.ibm.com/software/data/db2/.

[14] Y. Ioannidis and S. Christodoulakis. On the Propagation of Errors in the Size of Join Results. *SIGMOD'91*, pages 268–277.

[15] S. Kwan, S. Lightstone, B. Schiefer, A. Storm, and L. Wu. Automatic Configuration for IBM DB2 Universal Database. *IBM Performance Technical Report*, 2002.

[16] W. Loh. Regression Trees with Unbiased Variable Selection and Interaction Detection. *Statistica Sinica*, pages 361–386, 2002.

[17] Y. Lou, R. Caruana, and J. Gehrke. Intelligible Models for Classification and Regression. *KDD'12*, pages 150–158.

[18] Y. Lou, R. Caruana, J. Gehrke, and G. Hooker. Accurate Intelligible Models with Pairwise Interactions. *KDD'13*, pages 623–631.

[19] Machine Learning Tool Kit. github.com/yinlou/mltk.

[20] J. S. Oh and S. H. Lee. Resource Selection for Autonomic Database Tuning. *ICDE'05*, pages 1218–1225.

[21] Oracle. www.oracle.com/us/products/database/.

[22] J. Snoek, H. Larochelle, and R. Adams. Practical Bayesian Optimization of Machine Learning Algorithms. *Advances in Neural Information Processing Systems*, 2012.

[23] D. Sorokina, R. Caruana, M. Riedewald, and D. Fink. Detecting Statistical Interactions with Additive Groves of Trees. *ICML'08*, pages 1000–1007.

[24] A. J. Storm, C. Garcia-Arellano, S. Lightstone, Y. Diao, and M. Surendra. Adaptive Self-tuning Memory in DB2. *VLDB'06*, pages 1081–1092.

[25] G. Valentin, M. Zuliani, D. Zilio, G. Lohman, and A. Skelley. DB2 Advisor: An Optimizer Smart Enough to Recommend Its Own Indexes. *ICDE'00*, pages 101–110.

[26] G. Weikum, A. Moenkeberg, C. Hasse, and P. Zabback. Self-tuning Database Technology and Information Services: From Wishful Thinking to Viable Engineering. *VLDB'02*, pages 20–31.

[27] D. Wiese and G. Rabinovitch. Knowledge Management in Autonomic Database Performance Tuning. *ICAS'09*, pages 129–134.

[28] S. Wood. Thin Plate Regression Splines. *Journal of the Royal Statistical Society*, 65(1):95–114, 2003.

[29] S. Wood. Generalized Additive Models: An Introduction with R. *CRC Press*, 2006.

An Optimal Online Algorithm For Retrieving Heavily Perturbed Statistical Databases In The Low-Dimensional Querying Model

Krzysztof Choromanski
Google Research
76, Ninth Ave
New York, NY 10011, USA
kchoro@google.com

Afshin Rostamizadeh
Google Research
76, Ninth Ave
New York, NY 10011, USA
rostami@google.com

Umar Syed
Google Research
76, Ninth Ave
New York, NY 10011, USA
usyed@google.com

ABSTRACT

We give the first $\tilde{O}(\frac{1}{\sqrt{T}})$-error online algorithm for reconstructing noisy statistical databases, where T is the number of (online) sample queries received. The algorithm is optimal up to the $poly(\log(T))$ factor in terms of the error and requires only $O(\log T)$ memory. It aims to learn a hidden database-vector $w^* \in \mathbb{R}^D$ in order to accurately answer a stream of queries regarding the hidden database, which arrive in an online fashion from some unknown distribution $\mathcal{D}$. We assume the distribution $\mathcal{D}$ is defined on the neighborhood of a low-dimensional manifold. The presented algorithm runs in $O(dD)$-time per query, where d is the dimensionality of the query-space. Contrary to the classical setting, there is no separate training set that is used by the algorithm to learn the database — the stream on which the algorithm will be evaluated must also be used to learn the database-vector. The algorithm only has access to a binary oracle $\mathcal{O}$ that answers whether a particular linear function of the database-vector plus random noise is larger than a threshold, which is specified by the algorithm. We note that we allow for a significant $O(D)$ amount of noise to be added while other works focused on the low noise $o(\sqrt{D})$-setting. For a stream of T queries our algorithm achieves an average error $\tilde{O}(\frac{1}{\sqrt{T}})$ by filtering out random noise, adapting threshold values given to the oracle based on its previous answers and, as a consequence, recovering with high precision a projection of a database-vector w^* onto the manifold defining the query-space. Our algorithm may be also applied in the adversarial machine learning context to compromise machine learning engines by heavily exploiting the vulnerabilities of the systems that output only binary signal and in the presence of significant noise.

Permission to make digital or hard copies of all or part of this work for personal or classroom use is granted without fee provided that copies are not made or distributed for profit or commercial advantage and that copies bear this notice and the full citation on the first page. Copyrights for components of this work owned by others than ACM must be honored. Abstracting with credit is permitted. To copy otherwise, or republish, to post on servers or to redistribute to lists, requires prior specific permission and/or a fee. Request permissions from Permissions@acm.org.
CIKM'15, October 19–23, 2015, Melbourne, VIC, Australia.
© 2015 ACM. ISBN 978-1-4503-3794-6/15/10 ...$15.00.
DOI: http://dx.doi.org/10.1145/2806416.2806421.

Categories and Subject Descriptors

H.2 [**Database management**]: Security, integrity, and protection; H.3 [**Information storage and retrieval**]: Information Search and Retrieval—*Retrieval models*; I.1 [**Symbolic and algebraic manipulation**]: Analysis of algorithms

General Terms

Algorithms, Theory, Security

Keywords

statistical databases, low-dimensional querying model, bisection method, database privacy, online retrieval algorithms, adversarial machine learning

1. INTRODUCTION

1.1 Database setting

Protecting databases that contain sensitive information has become increasingly important due to its crucial practical applications, such as the disclosure of sensitive health data. Privacy preservation plays a key role in this setting since such data is often published in anonymized form so it can be used by analysts and researchers. Several mechanisms have been proposed, such as differential privacy, that allow for learning from a database while preserving privacy guarantees ([1, 2, 3, 4, 5, 6]). At the other extreme are many results showing how database privacy can be compromised by an adversary who is able to collect perturbed answers to a large number of queries regarding the database ([7, 8, 9, 10, 6]). Existing results related to breaking the privacy of a database have several key limitations. For example, most assume that each query is represented by a vector q of D independent entries taken from some fixed distribution (such as the Gaussian distribution or a specific discrete distribution), and that this structure is known to the privacy-breaking algorithm. Also, most methods learn an approximation of the unknown database-vector w^* that has L_2 error ϵD for some small constant $\epsilon > 0$. Such precision is not sufficient to obtain $o(1)$-error on the stream of T queries for $T \gg D$, as is the case in our model. Further, the focus has typically been on the offline setting, where the adversary first collects all the queries, then applies some privacy-breaking algorithm, and finally uses the reconstructed database-vector to compute good approximations of the statistics he needs. From the machine learning point of view this means that the overall protocol for the adversary consists of two distinct phases: a training phase and a testing phase. Finally, the memory resources used by privacy-breaking algorithms are typically not analyzed, even though this is a crucial issue for the setting considered here, where the number of all the queries q coming in the stream may be huge.

The goal of this paper is to present and analyze a database privacy-breaking algorithm for a more realistic setting in which the limitations described above are lifted. The entries of the query-vector are not necessarily independent. The distribution $\mathcal{D}$ of the query-vector is not known to the adversary. The adversary is not able to first learn the database-vector before being evaluated. Our algorithm uses only $O(\log(T))$-size memory to process the entire stream of T queries and therefore is well-suited to the limited resources scenario. To make life of the adversary even more difficult, we assume that the database mechanism provides only a binary oracle $\mathcal{O}$ that answers whether the perturbed value of a dot-product between the database-vector w^* and the query-vector q is greater than a threshold that is specified by the adversary. Thus the algorithm has very limited access to the database even in the noiseless scenario. Dot-products between query-vector and a database-vector are considered in most of the settings analyzing database privacy-breaking algorithms. Considering this more challenging setting, we will show that much less than the noisy answer is needed to carry out an effective attack and compromise data privacy.

In some of the mentioned papers ([5, 6]) an effort is made to learn a good approximation of the database vector with a small number of queries that is only linear in the size of the database D. We use many more queries but our task is more challenging - we need much more accurate approximation, and get the information only about the sign of the perturbed product as opposed to the perturbed product itself. Finally, we are penalized whenever we are making a mistake. Our goal is to minimize the average error of the algorithm over a long sequence of queries so we need to learn this more accurate approximation very fast.

In this paper we present the first online algorithm that an adversary can use to reconstruct a noisy statistical database protected by a binary oracle $\mathcal{O}$ that achieves average error $\tilde{O}(\frac{1}{\sqrt{T}})$ on the stream of T queries and operates in logarithmic memory. The algorithm is optimal, i.e. we show that any other algorithm (not necessarily online and with arbitrary running time) solving this problem achieves error at least $\tilde{O}(\frac{1}{\sqrt{T}})$ in the worst case scenario. From now on we will call this algorithm a *learning algorithm*. The learning algorithm is given a set of queries taken from some unknown distribution $\mathcal{D}$ defined on a neighborhood of the low-dimensional manifold that it needs to answer in the order that they arrive (note that the entries of a fixed query do not have to be independent). The learning algorithm can use the information learned from previously collected queries but cannot wait for other queries to learn a more accurate answer. Every received query can be used only once to communicate with a database. The database mechanism calculates a perturbed answer to the query and passes the result to the binary oracle $\mathcal{O}$. The binary oracle uses the threshold provided by the adversary and passes a "Yes/No"-answer to him. The error made for a single query is defined as: $|z^t - w^* \cdot q^t|$, where q^t and z^t are the query and answer, respectively, provided by the learning algorithm in round t. As a byproduct of our methods, we recover with high precision the projection of the database-vector w^* onto the query-space. Our approximation is within $\tilde{O}(\frac{1}{\sqrt{T}})$ L_2-distance from the exact projection. By comparison, most of the previous papers focused on approximating/recovering all but at most a constant fraction ϵD of all the entries of w^* which is unacceptably inaccurate in our learning setting where $T \gg D$. The assumption that queries are taken from a low-dimensional manifold is in perfect agreement with recent development in machine learning (see: [11], [12], [13]). It leads to the conclusion that, as stated in [11]: "a lot of data which superficially lie in a very high-dimensional space $\mathbb{R}^D$ actually have low *intristic dimensionality*, in the sense of lying close to a manifold of dimension $d \ll D$". Assume that the queries are taken from a truly high-dimensional space. Then as long as the number of all queries is polynomial in D, the average distances between them are substantial. In this scenario any nontrivial noisy setting prevents the adversary from learning anything about the database since a single perturbed answer does not give much information and the probability that a close enough query will be asked in the future is negligible in D. In practice we observe however that noise can be very often filtered out and a significant number of queries can give nontrivial information about a database-vector w^*. In this paper we explain this phenomenon from the theoretical point of view. Our algorithm accurately reconstructs the part of the database that regards the lower-dimensional space used for querying. We show that this suffices to achieve average $\tilde{O}(\frac{1}{\sqrt{T}})$-error on the set of T given queries. In our model, the number of queries significantly exceeds the dimensionality of the database, and therefore we focus on optimizing our algorithm's time complexity and accuracy as a function of T. Having said that, in most of the formulas derived in the paper we will also explicitly give the dependence on other parameters of the model such as the dimensionality of the database D and the dimensionality of the query-space d. We are mainly interested in the setting: $d \ll D \ll T$. If we use the O-notation, where the dependency is not explicitly given then we treat all missing parameters as constants.

It should be also emphasized that, contrary to most previous work on reconstructing databases based on the perturbed statistics, the proposed algorithm does not use linear programming and thus gives better theoretical guarantees regarding running time than most existing methods. The algorithm uses a subroutine whose goal is to solve a linear program, however we show this program has a closed-form solution. Therefore we do not need to use any techniques such as simplex or the ellipsoid method. The algorithm is very fast: it needs only $O(dD)$-time per query. More detailed analysis of the running time of the algorithm as well as memory usage will be given later.

1.2 Connections to adversarial machine learning

One important related setting for our model as well as the algorithm we are going to present comes from adversarial machine learning. In many real world machine learning applications an adversary can use data in order to reveal information about the machine learning classifier and consequently, use this information to trick the classifier. This happens for instance in such domains as fraud, malware and spam detection, biometric recognition, auction allocation/pricing and many more. Thus, the need arises to establish secure learning in the adversarial setting.

Some introduced methods include repeated manual reconstructions of the classifier or randomizing the classifier. For example, an adversary-robust classifier in proposed in [14], where the adversarial learning problem is formally defined. In [15], a randomized approach is analyzed as a tool do defend against the adversary. The paper in fact precisely characterizes all optimal randomization schemes in the presence of both classifier manipulations and adversarial inverse engineering. On the other hand, many practical methods to violate machine learning system security have also been introduced, for example using evasion attacks. In the spam detection framework these may involve, for instance, obfuscating spam emails' content. In general, malicious samples are modified and used to exploit the vulnerabilities of the system. Other techniques take advantage of the frequent retraining phases, where data can be possibly poisoned. In that setting the goal is usually to compromise the process of learning. Most of these aforementioned scenarios fit naturally in the online framework.

The random noise in these settings setup may come from many different sources (noise introduced to protect the machine learning framework, as it is in [15] or noisy channels as is the case for various geophysical signals such as sonar signals that are subject to noise depending on the ocean geometry and weather). The role of noise in machine learning setting was extensively studied (see: [16]) and must be taken into account in many real world settings.

We can think of the database-vector w^* in our model as a linear machine learning classifier. The dot-product given to the oracle has a natural interpretation since it says on which side of the hyperplane the given query is, and consequently determines its classification. The dot-product output has been extensively used in the statistical database setting, however (contrary to many other approaches), the techniques used in our algorithm can be used for various types of outputs, not necessarily linear in the query q (giving rise to applications for nonlinear classifiers). This is due to the generalization of the bisection idea in the presence of noise, that we fully explore in this paper and which constitutes the core of the proposed algorithm, is independent of the particular form of the output. The perturbation added before this dot-product is given to the oracle may be interpreted as a noise introduced to challenge the adversary or an effect of the noisy channel, which was also the case in the database setting described before. The oracle is like the machine learning classification mechanism that outputs the classification of the given query (for instance: spam/no-spam). The answer given by the oracle in our model is binary, however, straightforward extensions of the approach proposed by us lead to models, where the oracle chooses an answer from the larger discrete set.

Finally, let us comment on the interpretation of our algorithm's error in the adversarial classification setting. Note, the goal of our algorithm is to retrieve the vector w^*, which is a stronger goal than what is usually considered in the usual adversarial classification setting, i.e. forcing false classifications. The exact value of the classifier dot-product measures how far a given query is from the boundary of the binary classification, i.e. how confident the system is that a given query should be classified in a particular way. This information is not given explicitly by the engine but is nevertheless of great importance. It is reasonable to assume that the adversary does not have unlimited resources and that issuing queries has a cost. Thus, the goal of the adversary is to minimize the average per-round error during the sequence of queries, which is equivalent to compromising the classifier (within some additive error) with as few queries as possible.

2. MODEL DESCRIPTION AND MAIN RESULT

We will now describe in detail our database access model. We assume that the database can be encoded by the database-vector $w^* \in \mathbb{R}^D$. For definiteness we will consider: $w_i^* \in [0, 1]$ for $i = 1, \ldots, D$. Our method can be however used in the much more general setting, as long as w^* is taken from some fixed ball in L_∞. Each query can be represented as a vector $q = (q_1, \ldots, q_D)$, where: $0 \leq q_i \leq 1$ and $q_1^2 + \cdots + q_D^2 > 0$. Queries are taken independently at random from the unknown distribution $\mathcal{D}$ (notice that entries of a fixed query do not have to be independent). The distribution $\mathcal{D}$ is defined on some d-dimensional linear subspace $\mathcal{U} \in \mathbb{R}^d$ $(d < D)$. The exact answer to the query is given as $a = \sum_{i=1}^{D} w_i^* q_i$. For the tth coming query q^t the learning algorithm $\mathcal{L}$ selects the threshold value θ^t and passes q^t to the database mechanism $\mathcal{M}$ which computes $a^t = w^* \cdot q^t$. The noisy version $\tilde{a}^t$ of a^t as well as θ^t is passed by $\mathcal{M}$ and $\mathcal{L}$ to the binary oracle $\mathcal{O}$:

$$\mathcal{O}(\tilde{a}^t, \theta^t) = \begin{cases} 1 & \text{if } \tilde{a}^t > \theta^t, \\ 0 & \text{otherwise.} \end{cases}$$

The value $\mathcal{O}(\tilde{a}^t, \theta^t)$ is then given to $\mathcal{L}$. The learner records this value and can also use the information obtained from previously received queries to give an answer z^t to the query q^t. However it has only $O(\log(T))$-memory available. Further, for a fixed query the learner only has one-time access to the binary oracle $\mathcal{O}$.

The noise $\epsilon^t = \tilde{a}^t - a^t$ is generated independently at random and is of the form $D\mathcal{E}$, where $\mathcal{E}$ is some known distribution producing values from some bounded range $[-u, u]$. The boundedness assumption is not crucial. Technically speaking, as long as the random variable is not heavy-tailed (which is a standard assumption), our approach works. In fact even this condition is unnecessarily strong. This will become obvious later when we describe and analyze our method.

This setting covers standard scenarios where computing every single product in the sum of d terms for $w^* \cdot q^t$ gives an independent bounded error. We should note here that in most of the previous papers the magnitude of the noise added was of the order $o(\sqrt{D})$ (see: [7, 8, 9, 10, 6]). For instance, in [8] the authors reconstruct a database that agrees with the groundtruth one on all but $(2c\alpha)^2$ entries, where α is a noise magnitude and $c > 0$ is a constant. Thus, even though previous works do not assume that noise was added independently for every query, the average error per single product in the dot-product sum was only of the magnitude $o(\frac{1}{\sqrt{D}})$. This assumption significantly narrows the range of possible applications. This is no longer the case in our setting, where some mild and reasonable assumptions regarding independence of noise added to different queries and low-dimensionality of querying space leads to a model much more robust to noise. We will assume that ϵ^t do not have singularities, i.e. $\mathbb{P}(\epsilon^t = c) = 0$ for any fixed c.

We need a few more definitions.

DEFINITION 2.1. *We say that a vector w computed by the learning algorithm ϵ-approximates database-vector w^* if $|\Pi_{\mathcal{U}}(w) - \Pi_{\mathcal{U}}(w^*)|_\infty \leq \epsilon$, where $\Pi_{\mathcal{U}}(v)$ stands for the projection of v onto d-dimensional querying space $\mathcal{U}$.*

DEFINITION 2.2. *Let $\mathcal{Q}$ be a probability distribution on the unit sphere $\mathcal{S}(0,1)$ in L_2. For a fixed vector $q \in \mathcal{S}(0,1)$ we denote by $p^{\mathcal{Q}}_{q,\theta}$ the probability that a vector x selected according to $\mathcal{Q}$ satisfies: $q \cdot x \geq \cos(\theta)$.*

DEFINITION 2.3. *Take a distribution $\mathcal{D}$ from which queries are taken. Assume that $\mathcal{D}$ is defined on the d-dimensional space $\mathcal{U}$ with orthonormal basis $\mathcal{B}$. Denote by $\mathcal{D}_n$ the normalized version of $\mathcal{D}$ and by $\mathcal{B}_n$ the normalized version of $\mathcal{B}$ (all vectors rescaled to length 1 in the L_2-norm). Then we define: $p_{\mathcal{D},\theta} = \min_{q \in \mathcal{B}_n}(p^{\mathcal{D}_n}_{q,\theta})$.*

The error ϵ_q the algorithm is making on each query q is defined as the absolute value of the difference between the exact answer to the query and the answer that is provided by the algorithm. The average error on the set of queries: $q^1, ..., q^T$ is defined as $\epsilon_{av} = \frac{1}{T}\sum_{i=1}^{T} \epsilon_{q^i}$. Let us state now main result of this paper.

THEOREM 2.1. *Let $q^1, \ldots, q^T$ be a stream of query-vectors coming in an online fashion from some d-dimensional subspace, where: $0 \leq q^t_i \leq 1$ for $i = 1, \ldots, d$ and each q^t is a nonzero vector. Then there exists an algorithm $\mathcal{A}lg$ using $O(\log(T))$-memory, acting according to the protocol defined above, and achieving average error:*

$$e_{av} = O(\frac{1}{\sqrt{T}}(rD^{\frac{7}{2}}d + \sqrt{D}\log(T)))$$

with probability $p_{succ} \geq 1 - O(\frac{\log(dDT)}{T^3} + \frac{d\log(dT)}{T^{30}})$, where $r = \frac{2}{p^2_{\mathcal{D},\phi}}$ and $\phi = 2\arcsin(\frac{1}{64\sqrt{d}})$.

We will give this algorithm, called *OnlineBisection* algorithm, in the next section. Notice that ϕ is well approximated by $\frac{1}{32\sqrt{d}}$. To see what the magnitude of r is in the worst-case scenario it suffices to analyze the setting where q is chosen uniformly at random from the query-space $\mathcal{U}$.

If this is the case then one can notice that $p_{\mathcal{D},\phi}$ is of the order $\Omega(2^{-d\log(d)})$ thus $r = O(2^{d\log(d)})$. If however there exists a basis of $\mathcal{U}$ such that most of the mass of $\mathcal{D}$ is concentrated around vectors from the basis then standard analysis leads to the $\frac{1}{poly(d)}$-lower bound on p, i.e. $poly(d)$-upper bound on r (where $poly(d)$ is a polynomial function of d).

Theorem 2.1 implies a corollary regarding the batch version of the algorithm, where test and training set are clearly separated (the proof of that corollary will be given later):

COROLLARY 2.1. *Let w_T denote the final hypothesis constructed by the OnlineBisection algorithm after consuming T queries drawn from an unknown distribution $\mathcal{D}$. Then the following inequality holds with probability at least $1 - O\left(\frac{\log(dDT)}{T^3} + \frac{d\log(dT)}{T^{30}}\right)$ for any future queries q drawn from $\mathcal{D}$:*

$$\mathrm{E}_{q\sim\mathcal{D}}\left[|w_T \cdot q - w^* \cdot q|\right] \leq \frac{\sqrt{D}\log(T)}{\sqrt{T}}.$$

In the subsequent sections we will prove Theorem 2.1 and conduct further analysis of the algorithm. Unless stated otherwise, log denotes the natural logarithm.

3. THE ALGORITHM

We will now present an algorithm (Algorithm 1) that achieves theoretical guarantees from Theorem 2.1. Our algorithm, called *OnlineBisection*, maintains a tuple of intervals $(\mathcal{I}_1, \ldots, \mathcal{I}_d)$ which encode a hypercube that contains the database-vector w^* (projected onto $\mathcal{U}$) with very high probability.

For each coming query-vector q^t the algorithm outputs an answer $w_{approx} \cdot q^t$, where w_{approx} is an arbitrarily selected vector in the current hypercube. The query-vectors received by the algorithm are used to progressively shrink the hypercube.

Algorithm 1 - *OnlineBisection*
Input: Stream $q^1, \ldots, q^T$ of T queries, database mechanism $\mathcal{M}$ and binary oracle $\mathcal{O}$.
Output: A sequence of answers $(w^1 \cdot q^1, \ldots, w^T \cdot q^t)$, returned online.
begin
  Choose an orthonormal basis $\mathcal{C} = \{e^1, \ldots, e^d\}$ of $\mathcal{U}$.
  Let $\phi = 2\arcsin(\frac{1}{64\sqrt{d}})$.
  Let $\mathcal{I}_i = [-\sqrt{D}, \sqrt{D}]$, $N^+_i = 0$ and $N^-_i = 0$ for $i = 1, \ldots, d$.
  for $t = 1, \ldots, T$ **do**
    Output $w_{approx} \cdot q^t$ for any $w_{approx} = f_1e^1 + \cdots + f_de^d$, where $f_i \in \mathcal{I}_i$, $i = 1, \ldots, d$.
    if $|\mathcal{I}_i| \leq \frac{\log(T)}{\sqrt{Td}}$ for $i = 1, ..., d$ **continue**.
    if $\exists i^* \in \{1, \ldots, d\}$ *such that* $\arccos(e^{i^*}, \frac{q^t}{\|q^t\|_2}) \leq \phi$ **then**
      Let $m = \max_{f_1 \in \mathcal{I}_1, \ldots, f_d \in \mathcal{I}_d} \sum_{i=1}^{d} f_ie^i \cdot (-q^t)$.
      Let $M = \max_{f_1 \in \mathcal{I}_1, \ldots, f_d \in \mathcal{I}_d} \sum_{i=1}^{d} f_ie^i \cdot q^t$.
      Let $b = \mathcal{O}(\mathcal{M}(q^t), \frac{m+M}{2})$.
      If $b > 0$ update $N^+_{i^*} \leftarrow N^+_{i^*} + 1$, otherwise update $N^-_{i^*} \leftarrow N^-_{i^*} + 1$.
    end
    Let $\Delta p = \mathbb{P}(-\frac{|\mathcal{I}_1|}{8D} \leq \mathcal{E} \leq \frac{|\mathcal{I}_1|}{8D})$, $N_i = N^+_i + N^-_i$ and $N_{crit} = \frac{30\log(T)}{\Delta p^2}$.
    if $N_i \geq N_{crit}$ *for* $i = 1, \ldots, d$ **then**
      Run *ShrinkHyperCube*$(\mathcal{I}_1, \ldots, \mathcal{I}_d, N^+_1, \ldots, N^+_d, N^-_1, \ldots, N^-_d)$.
      Update: $N^+_i \leftarrow 0, N^-_i \leftarrow 0$ for $i = 1, \ldots, d$.
    end
  end
end

As the hypercube shrinks, vector w_{approx} ϵ-approximates w^* for smaller values of ϵ. When the hypercube is large the errors made by the algorithm will be large, but on the other hand larger hypercubes are easier to shrink since they require fewer queries to ensure that hypercube continues to contain w^* (with very high probability) after shrinking. This observation plays a crucial role in establishing upper bounds on the average error made by the algorithm on the sequence of T queries.

After outputting an answer for query-vector q^t, the algorithm checks whether q^t has a large inner product with at least one vector in an orthonormal basis $\mathcal{C} = \{e^1, \ldots, e^d\}$ of $\mathcal{U}$. If so, q^t represents an observation for that basis vector; whether it is a positive or negative observation depends on the response of the binary oracle $\mathcal{O}$. The threshold given by the algorithm to $\mathcal{O}$ is chosen by solving the linear program $\max_{y \in \mathcal{HC}} q \cdot y$ for $q = q^t$ and $q = -q^t$, where $\mathcal{HC}$ is the current hypercube. As we will see in Section 5, this linear program is simple enough that there is a closed-form expression for its optimal value. So we do not need to use the simplex method or any other linear programming tools.

Algorithm 2 - ***ShrinkHyperCube***
Input: $\mathcal{I}_1 = [x_1, y_1], \ldots, \mathcal{I}_d = [x_d, y_d]$, $N_1^+, \ldots, N_d^+$, $N_1^-, \ldots, N_d^-$.
Output: Updated hypercube $(\mathcal{I}_1, \ldots, \mathcal{I}_d)$.
begin
  Let $\alpha = \frac{3}{4}$, $\Delta p = \mathbb{P}(-\frac{|\mathcal{I}_1|}{8D} \leq \mathcal{E} \leq \frac{|\mathcal{I}_1|}{8D})$, $p_1 = \mathbb{P}(\mathcal{E} > \frac{|\mathcal{I}_1|}{8D})$ and $N_i = N_i^+ + N_i^-$.
  for $i = 1, \ldots, d$ **do**
    if $N_i^+ > N_i p_1 + \frac{N_i \Delta p}{2}$ **then**
      $\mathcal{I}_i \leftarrow [y_i - \alpha(y_i - x_i), y_i]$;
    else
      $\mathcal{I}_i \leftarrow [x_i, x_i + \alpha(y_i - x_i)]$;
    end
  end
end

The optimal values m and M of the linear programs solved by the *OnlineBisection* algorithm represent the smallest and largest possible value of the inner product of the query-vector and a vector from the current hypercube. The true value lies in the interval $[m, M]$. By choosing the average of these two values as a threshold for the oracle we are able to effectively shrink direction i^*. The intuition is that if the query-vector forms an angle $\alpha = 0$ with this direction and there is no noise added then by choosing the average we basically perform standard binary search for q. Since α is not necessarily 0 but is relatively small (and noise is added that perturbs the output), the search is not exactly binary. Instead of two disjoint subintervals of I_{i^*} we get two intervals whose union is I_{i^*} but that intersect. Still, each of them is only of a fraction of the length of I_{i^*} and that still enables us to significantly shrink each dimension whenever a sufficient number of observations have been collected for each basis vector — specifically, N_{crit} observations — by calling the *ShrinkHyperCube* subroutine (Algorithm 2).

Every shrinking of the hypercube decreases each edge by a factor α for some $0 < \alpha < 1$. A logarithmic number of shrinkings is needed to ensure that any choice of w_{approx} in the hypercube will give an error of the order $\tilde{O}(\frac{1}{\sqrt{T}})$. Notice that N_{crit} grows with T, which reflects the fact that for smaller hypercubes more observations are needed to further shrink the hypercube while preserving the property that it contains the database-vector w^* with very high probability. This is the case since if the hypercube is small we already know a good approximation of the database vector so it is harder to find even more accurate one under the same level of noise. When the hypercube is small enough (condition: $|\mathcal{I}_i| \leq \frac{\log(T)}{\sqrt{Td}}$ for $i = 1, ..., d$) there is no need to shrink it anymore since each vector taken from the hypercube is a precise enough estimate of the database vector.

Note that choosing an orthonormal basis $\mathcal{C} = \{e^1, \ldots, e^d\}$ of $\mathcal{U}$ does not require the knowledge of the distribution $\mathcal{D}$ from which queries are taken. We only assume that queries are from a low-dimensional linear subspace $\mathcal{U}$ of d dimensions. It suffices to have as $\{e^1, \ldots, e^d\}$ some orthonormal basis of that linear subspace. There are many state-of-the-art mechanisms (such as PCA) that are able to extract such a basis, and thus we will not focus on that, but instead assume that such an orthonormal system is already given. Notice that in practice those techniques should be applied before our algorithm can be run. Since such a preprocessing phase requires sampling from $\mathcal{D}$ but does not require an access to the database system, we can think about it as a preliminary period, where evaluation is not being conducted.

4. THEORETICAL ANALYSIS

In this section we prove Theorem 2.1. We start by introducing several technical lemmas. First we will prove all of them and then we will show how those lemmas can be combined to obtain our main result.

We denote: $h_T = \frac{\sqrt{T}}{\log(T)}$. Thus the stopping condition for shrinking the hypercube is of the form: $|\mathcal{I}_i| \leq \frac{1}{\sqrt{d h_T}}$ for $i = 1, ..., d$.

We start with the concentration result regarding binomial random variables.

LEMMA 4.1. *Let $Z^m = Bin(m, p_1)$, $W^m = Bin(m, p_1 + \Delta p)$ and $\mu_1 = mp_1$.*
Then the following is true:

$$\mathbb{P}(Z^m \geq \mu_1 + \frac{m\Delta p}{2}) \leq e^{-\frac{m(\Delta p)^2}{10}}, \tag{1}$$

$$\mathbb{P}(W^m < \mu_1 + \frac{m\Delta p}{2}) \leq e^{-\frac{m(\Delta p)^2}{10}}. \tag{2}$$

Proof. The proof follows from standard concentration inequalities. Let $\delta_1, \delta_2 > 0$. Note that $E(Z^m) \leq mp_1$ and $E(W^m) \geq mp_1 + m\Delta p$. Denote $\mu_2 = E(W^m)$. Note that by Chernoff's inequality we have:

$$\mathbb{P}(Z^m \geq (1+\delta_1)\mu_1) \leq e^{-\frac{\delta_1^2}{2+\delta_1}\mu_1} \tag{3}$$

Similarly,

$$\mathbb{P}(W^m \leq (1-\delta_2)\mu_2) \leq e^{-\frac{\delta_2^2}{2+\delta_2}\mu_2} \tag{4}$$

Take: $\delta_1 = \frac{m\Delta p}{2\mu_1} = \frac{\Delta p}{2p_1}$, $\delta_2 = \frac{m\Delta p}{2\mu_2}$. Using these values of δ_1 and δ_2, we obtain:

$$\mathbb{P}(Z^m \geq \mu_1 + \frac{m\Delta p}{2}) \leq e^{-\frac{1}{1+\frac{2}{\delta_1}}\frac{m\Delta p}{2}} \tag{5}$$

Similarly,

$$\mathbb{P}(W^m < \mu_1 + \frac{m\Delta p}{2}) \leq \mathbb{P}(W^m \leq \mu_2 - \frac{m\Delta p}{2}) \leq e^{-\frac{1}{1+\frac{2}{\delta_2}}\frac{m\Delta p}{2}} \tag{6}$$

Notice that $\delta_1, \delta_2 \geq \frac{\Delta p}{2}$ (the latter inequality holds because obviously: $\mu_2 \leq m$). Thus we get:

$$\mathbb{P}(Z^m \geq \mu_1 + \frac{m\Delta p}{2}) \leq e^{-\frac{m(\Delta p)^2}{2(4+\Delta p)}} \tag{7}$$

and

$$\mathbb{P}(W^m < \mu_1 + \frac{m\Delta p}{2}) \leq e^{-\frac{m(\Delta p)^2}{2(4+\Delta p)}} \tag{8}$$

Since $\Delta p \leq 1$, the proof is completed. ∎

DEFINITION 4.1. *Let $\mathcal{HC}$ be a d-dimensional hypercube in $\mathbb{R}^D$. We denote by $l(\mathcal{HC})$ the length of its side measured according to the L_2-norm (recall that all the sides of a hypercube have the same length).*

Next lemma is central for finding an upper bound on the average error made by the algorithm.

LEMMA 4.2. *Let $(q_1, \ldots, q_T)$ be a sequence of T queries. Let $\mathcal{HC}_0, \ldots, \mathcal{HC}_s$ be a sequence of d-dimensional hypercubes in $\mathbb{R}^D$. Assume that $l(\mathcal{HC}_{i+1}) \leq \alpha l(\mathcal{HC}_i)$ for $i = 0, \ldots, s-1$ and some $0 < \alpha < 1$. Denote $l(\mathcal{HC}_0) = L \leq D$ and assume that $s = \frac{1}{\log_2(\frac{1}{\alpha})} \log_2(L\sqrt{d}h(T))$, where $h(T)$ is some function of T. Assume that $w^* \in \mathcal{HC}_0 \bigcap \cdots \bigcap \mathcal{HC}_s$. Let $\mathcal{E}$ be a random variable defined on the interval $[-u, u]$ for some constant $u > 0$, with density ρ continuous at 0, and such that $\rho(0) > 0$. Define*

$$\phi_\epsilon(i) = \mathbb{P}(-\frac{L\alpha^i(\frac{1}{4} - \epsilon)}{D} < \mathcal{E} \leq \frac{L\alpha^i(\frac{1}{4} - \epsilon))}{D} \quad (9)$$

for some constant $0 < \epsilon \leq \frac{1}{8}$. Let $m_i = \frac{1}{\phi_\epsilon^2(i)} C \log(T)$ for some constant $C > 0$ and let $k_i = m_i r$ for some other constant $r > 0$ and $i = 0, \ldots, s$. Assume that learning algorithm uses a vector $w_{approx} \in \mathcal{HC}_0$ to answer first k_0 queries, a vector $w_{approx} \in \mathcal{HC}_1$ to answer next k_1 queries, etc. Assume also that an algorithm uses a vector $w_{approx} \in \mathcal{HC}_s$ to answer remaining $T - \sum_{i=0}^s k_i$ queries. Then the following is true about the cumulative error ϵ_{cum} made by the algorithm:

$$\epsilon_{cum} = O(L^2 D^{\frac{5}{2}} dr \log(T) h(T) + \frac{\sqrt{D}T}{h(T)}) \quad (10)$$

Proof. Note first that for any d-dimensional hypercube $\mathcal{HC} \in \mathbb{R}^D$ of side length l, two vectors: $w^1, w^2 \in \mathcal{HC}$ and a vector $q = (q_1, \ldots, q_D)$ such that: $q_i = 1$ for $i = 1, \ldots, d$ the following is true: $|w^1 \cdot q - w^2 \cdot q| \leq l\sqrt{dD}$. This comes from the fact that: $\|w^1 - w^2\|_2 \leq l\sqrt{d}$, $\|q\|_2 \leq \sqrt{D}$ and Cauchy-Schwarz inequality. Thus we see that the cumulative error ϵ_{cum}^1 made by the algorithm for the first $\sum_{i=0}^s k_i$ queries satisfies:

$$\epsilon_{cum}^1 \leq \sum_{i=0}^s k_i L\alpha^i \sqrt{dD} \leq L\sqrt{dD} r \sum_{i=1}^s m_i \alpha^i \quad (11)$$

Therefore we have:

$$\epsilon_{cum}^1 \leq CL\sqrt{dD} r \log(T) \sum_{i=0}^s \frac{\alpha^i}{\phi_\epsilon^2(i)} \quad (12)$$

We can write:

$$\epsilon_{cum}^1 \leq CL\sqrt{dD} r \log(T) \sum_{i=0}^t \frac{\alpha^i}{\phi_\epsilon^2(i)} + CL\sqrt{dD} r \log(T) \mathcal{Z},$$

where $\mathcal{Z} = \sum_{i=t+1}^s \frac{\alpha^i}{\phi_\epsilon^2(i)}$ and t is the smallest index such that $\rho(x) \geq \frac{\rho(0)}{\sqrt{2}}$ for $x \in [-\frac{\alpha^t}{8}, \frac{\alpha^t}{8}]$. Since ρ is continuous at 0, t is well-defined. Notice that t does not depend on d, D and T, but only on the random variable $\mathcal{E}$ and constant α. Observe that:

$$CL\sqrt{dD} r \log(T) \sum_{i=0}^t \frac{\alpha^i}{\phi_\epsilon^2(i)} \leq CL\sqrt{dD} r \log(T) \frac{t}{\phi_\epsilon^2(t)} \quad (13)$$

and

$$CL\sqrt{dD} r \log(T) \frac{t}{\phi_\epsilon^2(t)} \leq \frac{2CL\sqrt{d}D^{\frac{5}{2}} r \log(T) t}{\rho^2(0)\alpha^{2t}(\frac{1}{2} - 2\epsilon)^2}, \quad (14)$$

where the last inequality follows immediately from the definition of t (density ρ on the interval considered in the definition of $\phi_\epsilon(t)$ is at least $\frac{\rho(0)}{\sqrt{2}}$ thus the related probability is at least: the length of that interval times $\frac{\rho(0)}{\sqrt{2}}$, i.e.:

$$\phi_\epsilon(t) \geq \frac{\rho(0)}{\sqrt{2}} \frac{L\alpha^i(\frac{1}{2} - 2\epsilon)}{D} \quad (15)$$

Therefore the considered expression is of the order $O(L\sqrt{d}D^{\frac{5}{2}} r \log(T))$. Now let us focus on the expression: $\mathcal{R} = CL\sqrt{dD} r \log(T) \sum_{i=t+1}^s \frac{\alpha^i}{\phi_\epsilon^2(i)}$. From the definition of t we get:

$$\mathcal{R} \leq CL\sqrt{d}D^{\frac{5}{2}} r \log(T) \Pi, \quad (16)$$

where

$$\Pi = \sum_{i=0}^s \frac{2\alpha^i}{\alpha^{2i}(\frac{1}{2} - 2\epsilon)^2 \rho^2(0)} \quad (17)$$

Therefore we have:

$$\mathcal{R} \leq \frac{32CL\sqrt{d}D^{\frac{5}{2}} r \log(T)}{\rho^2(0)} \sum_{i=1}^s \alpha^{-i}. \quad (18)$$

Thus we get:

$$\mathcal{R} \leq \frac{32CL\sqrt{d}D^{\frac{5}{2}} r \log(T)}{\rho^2(0)} \frac{\alpha}{1-\alpha}((\frac{1}{\alpha})^{s+1} - 1), \quad (19)$$

so we also get:

$$\mathcal{R} \leq \frac{32CL\sqrt{d}D^{\frac{5}{2}} r \log(T)}{\rho^2(0)(1-\alpha)\alpha^s} \quad (20)$$

Using the formula on s, we get:

$$\mathcal{R} \leq \frac{32CL^2 D^{\frac{5}{2}} dr \log(T) h(T)}{\rho^2(0)(1-\alpha)} \quad (21)$$

Combining this upper bound on $\mathcal{R}$ with the upper bound on the previous expression, we obtain:

$$\epsilon_{cum}^1 = O(L^2 D^{\frac{5}{2}} dr \log(T) h(T)) \quad (22)$$

Next let us focus on the cumulative error ϵ_{cum}^2 made by the algorithm for the remaining $T - \sum_{i=0}^s k_i$ queries. By the definition of s we know that

$$l(\mathcal{HC}_s) \leq \frac{1}{\sqrt{d}h(T)} \quad (23)$$

This implies that for any $w \in \mathcal{HC}_s$ we have:

$$\|w - w^*\|_2 \leq \frac{1}{h(T)} \quad (24)$$

Thus clearly for any query coming in this phase the learning algorithm makes an error at most $\frac{\sqrt{D}}{h(T)}$ (again, by Cauchy-Schwarz inequality) and we have at most T queries in this phase. Therefore $\epsilon_{cum}^2 = O(\frac{\sqrt{D}}{h(T)} T)$. That completes the entire proof. ∎

In the following lemma we analyze cutting the hypercube according to some linear threshold.

LEMMA 4.3. *Let $w \in \mathbb{R}^D$, let $\{v^1, \ldots, v^d\}$ be a system of pairwise orthogonal vectors such that $v^i \in \mathbb{R}^D$, $\|v^i\|_2 = L$ for $i = 1, .., d$ and let $\mathcal{HC} = \{w + \sum_{i=1}^d f_i v^i : f_1, \ldots, f_d \in [0,1]\}$ be a d-dimensional hypercube. Let e be a unit-length vector in L_2 that is parallel to v^1, i.e. $e = \frac{1}{\sqrt{L}} v^1$. Let z be a unit-length vector satisfying: $z \cdot e \geq \cos(\theta)$ for some $0 < \theta < \frac{\pi}{2}$. Let $0 < \beta < 1$. Define $m = \min_{y \in \mathcal{HC}} y \cdot z$ and $M = \max_{y \in \mathcal{HC}} y \cdot z$. Let $\mathcal{HC}_l = \{y \in \mathcal{HC} : z \cdot y \leq m + \beta(M - m)\}$ and $\mathcal{HC}_r = \{y \in \mathcal{HC} : z \cdot y > m + \beta(M - m)\}$. Then for $\epsilon = 8 \sin(\frac{\theta}{2})\sqrt{d}$:*

$$\max_{y \in \mathcal{HC}_l} e \cdot y - \min_{y \in \mathcal{HC}_l} e \cdot y \leq L(\beta + \epsilon) \quad (25)$$

and

$$\max_{y \in \mathcal{HC}_r} e \cdot y - \min_{y \in \mathcal{HC}_r} e \cdot y \leq L(1 - \beta + \epsilon). \quad (26)$$

Proof. Denote: $\eta = e - z$. Note that

$$\|\eta\|_2 \leq 2 \sin(\frac{\theta}{2}) \quad (27)$$

Take first $y \in \mathcal{HC}_l$. We have:

$$m \leq z \cdot y \leq m + \beta(M - m) \quad (28)$$

Thus we also get:

$$m + \eta \cdot y \leq e \cdot y \leq m + \beta(M - m) + \eta \cdot y \quad (29)$$

Define: $\tilde{m} = \min_{y \in \mathcal{HC}} y \cdot e$ and $\tilde{M} = \max_{y \in \mathcal{HC}} y \cdot e$. Notice that:

$$|\tilde{m} - m| \leq 2 \sin(\frac{\theta}{2}) L\sqrt{d} \quad (30)$$

and besides:

$$|\tilde{M} - M| \leq 2 \sin(\frac{\theta}{2}) L\sqrt{d} \quad (31)$$

This follows directly from:

$$\|y\|_2 \leq L\sqrt{d}, \quad (32)$$

$$\|\eta\|_2 \leq 2 \sin(\frac{\theta}{2}) \quad (33)$$

and Cauchy-Schwarz inequality. Thus we obtain:

$$\tilde{m} - 2 \sin(\frac{\theta}{2}) L\sqrt{d} + \eta \cdot y \leq e \cdot y \quad (34)$$

and

$$e \cdot y \leq \tilde{m} + 2 \sin(\frac{\theta}{2}) L\sqrt{d} + \beta(\tilde{M} - \tilde{m} + 4 \sin(\frac{\theta}{2}) L\sqrt{d}) + \eta \cdot y \quad (35)$$

Since, from the definition of $\tilde{M}, \tilde{m}$ and $\mathcal{HC}$ we have:

$$\tilde{M} - \tilde{m} = L, \quad (36)$$

we obtain:

$$\tilde{m} - 2 \sin(\frac{\theta}{2}) L\sqrt{d} + \eta \cdot y \quad (37)$$

and

$$e \cdot y \leq \tilde{m} + 2 \sin(\frac{\theta}{2}) L\sqrt{d} + \beta(L + 4 \sin(\frac{\theta}{2}) L\sqrt{d}) + \eta \cdot y \quad (38)$$

Therefore

$$\max_{y \in \mathcal{HC}_l} e \cdot y - \min_{y \in \mathcal{HC}_l} e \cdot y \leq L(\beta + 8 \sin(\frac{\theta}{2})\sqrt{d}) \quad (39)$$

This completes the proof of inequality 25. The proof of inequality 26 is completely analogous. ∎

We are ready to prove Theorem 2.1.

Proof. Let $L = 2\sqrt{D}$. Let us notice that the algorithm can be divided into $s + 1$ phases, where in the ith phase ($i = 0, \ldots, s$) all the intervals $\mathcal{I}_i$ are of length $L\alpha^{-i}$ and

$$s = \frac{1}{\log_2(\frac{1}{\alpha})} \log_2(L\sqrt{d}h_T) \quad (40)$$

Indeed, whenever the shrinking is conducted, the length of each side of the hypercube decreases by a factor $\frac{1}{\alpha}$ (see subroutine *ShrinkHyperCube*), the initial lengths are $2\sqrt{D}$ and the shrinking is not performed anymore if the side of each length is at most $\frac{1}{\sqrt{dh_T}}$. We will call those phases: *1st-phase*, *2nd-phase*, etc. Notice also that the value of the parameter N_{crit} is constant across a fixed phase since this number changes only when *ShrinkHyperCube* subroutine is performed. Let us denote the value of N_{crit} during the ith phase of the algorithm as n_i. Notice that

$$n_i = \frac{30 \log(T)}{\Delta p_i^2}, \quad (41)$$

where Δp_i is the value of the parameter Δp of the algorithm used in the ith phase. Denote by k_i the number of queries that need to be processed in the ith phase for $i = 0, \ldots, s-1$. Parameter k_i is a random variable but we will show later that with high probability: $k_i \leq n_i r$ for $i = 0, \ldots, s-1$, where:

$$r = \frac{2}{(p_{\mathcal{D},\phi})^2} \quad (42)$$

Assume now that this is the case. Denote by $\mathcal{HC}_0, \ldots, \mathcal{HC}_s$ the sequence of hypercubes constructed by the algorithm. Assume furthermore that $w^* \in \mathcal{HC}_0 \cap \cdots \cap \mathcal{HC}_s$. Again, we have not proved it yet, we will show that this happens with high probability later. However we will prove now that under these two assumptions we get the average error proposed in the statement of Theorem 2.1. Notice that under these assumptions we can use Lemma 4.2 with $L = 2\sqrt{D}$, $h(T) = h_T$, $\phi_\epsilon(i) = \Delta p_i$, $C = 30$, $m_i = n_i$. We get the following bound on the cumulative error:

$$\epsilon_{cum} = O(D^{\frac{7}{2}} dr \log(T) h(T) + \frac{\sqrt{d}T}{h(T)}). \quad (43)$$

Thus the average error is at most

$$\epsilon_{av} \leq \frac{\epsilon_{cum}}{T} \quad (44)$$

By using the expression $h(T) = \frac{\log(T)}{\sqrt{T}}$ in the above formula, we obtain the bound from the statement of Theorem 2.1.

It remains to prove that our two assumptions are correct with high probability and find a lower bound on this probability that matches the one from the statement of the theorem. We will do it now. Let us focus on the ith phase of the algorithm. First we will find an upper bound on the probability that the number of queries processed in this phase is greater than k_i. Fix a vector e^j from the orthonormal basis $\mathcal{C}$. The probability that a new query q is within angle

ϕ from e^j is at least $p = p_{\mathcal{D},\phi}$, by the definition of $p_{\mathcal{D},\phi}$. Assume that u_i queries were constructed. By standard concentration inequalities, such as Azuma's inequality, we can conclude that with probability at least $1-e^{-2u_i(\frac{p}{2})^2}$ at least $\frac{u_i p}{2}$ of those queries will be within angle ϕ from e^j. If we take:

$$u_i \geq \frac{2n_i}{p}, \tag{45}$$

then we conclude that with probability at least $1-e^{-2u_i(\frac{p}{2})^2}$ at least n_i of those queries will be within angle ϕ from e^j. Denote $u_i = n_i r$, where $r > \frac{2}{p}$. We see that the considered probability is at least $1 - e^{-\frac{p^2}{2}n_i r}$. Using the expression on n_i we get that this probability is at least $1 - e^{-30r\frac{p^2}{2}\log(T)}$. Notice that when n_i queries within angle ϕ from a given vector $e^j \in \mathcal{C}$ are collected, the jth dimension is ready for shrinking. Thus taking union bound over $O(\log(dT))$ phases and all d dimensions we see that if we take $k_i = rn_i$, where: $r = \frac{2}{p^2}$, then with probability at most $\frac{d\log(dT)}{T^{30}}$ some i^{th} phase of the algorithm for $i \in \{0, \ldots, s-1\}$ will require more than k_i queries. Now let us focus again on the fixed i^{th} phase of the algorithm. Assume that *ShrinkHyperCube* subroutine is being run. Fix some dimension $j \in \{1, \ldots, d\}$. We know that, with high probability, at least n_i queries q that were within angle ϕ from the vector $e^j \in \mathcal{C}$ were collected. Denote by w^*_j the jth coordinate of w^*. Let $\mathcal{I}_j = [x_j, y_j]$ and assume that $w^*_j \in [x_j, y_j]$. Let us assume that the *ShrinkHyperCube* subroutine replaced $\mathcal{I}_j = [x_j, y_j]$ by $\tilde{\mathcal{I}}_j$. We want to show that with high probability segment $\tilde{\mathcal{I}}_j$ is constructed in such a way that $w^*_j \in \tilde{\mathcal{I}}_j$. Denote

$$l = y_j - x_j \tag{46}$$

and

$$\delta = (\alpha - \frac{1}{2})l \tag{47}$$

Notice first that if $w^*_j \in [(1-\alpha)l, \alpha l]$ then w^*_j will be in $\tilde{\mathcal{I}}_j$ since no matter how $\tilde{\mathcal{I}}_j$ is constructed, it always contains $[(1-\alpha)l, \alpha l]$. So let us assume that this is not the case. Thus we have either

$$w^*_j \in [x_j, x_j + (1-\alpha)l] \tag{48}$$

or

$$w^*_j \in [y_j - (1-\alpha)l, y_j] \tag{49}$$

Let us assume first the former. Consider a query-vector q within angle ϕ of e^j that contributed to N^+_j. Let us denote by p_+ the probability of the following event $\mathcal{F}_q$: for q the oracle $\mathcal{O}$ gives answer: "greater than 0". Observe that the total error made by the database mechanism $\mathcal{M}$ while computing the dot-product: $w^* \cdot q$ is $D\mathcal{E}$. Now notice, that by Lemma 4.3 and the definition of $\mathcal{E}$, probability p_+ is at most $\mathbb{P}(D\mathcal{E} > \delta - \epsilon l)$, where: $\epsilon = 8\sin(\frac{\phi}{2})\sqrt{d} = \frac{1}{8}$. Thus we get:

$$p_+ \leq \mathbb{P}(\mathcal{E} > \frac{(\alpha - \frac{1}{2} - \epsilon)l}{D}) \tag{50}$$

Notice that in the ith phase the hypercube under consideration has the side of length exactly α^i. Thus, since $\alpha = \frac{3}{4}$, we get:

$$p_+ \leq \mathbb{P}(\mathcal{E} > \frac{(\frac{1}{4} - \epsilon)L\alpha^i}{D}) \tag{51}$$

Let us assume now that $w^*_j \in [y_j - (1-\alpha)l, y_j]$. We proceed with the similar analysis as before. We see that the probability P_+ of an event $\mathcal{F}_q$ is at least $\mathbb{P}(D\mathcal{E} \geq -\delta + \epsilon l)$. Thus we obtain:

$$P_+ \geq \mathbb{P}(\mathcal{E} \geq -\frac{(\frac{1}{4} - \epsilon)L\alpha^i}{D}) \tag{52}$$

But now we see, by Lemma 4.1, using: $m = N_i$, $p_1 = \mathbb{P}(\mathcal{E} > \frac{(\frac{1}{4}-\epsilon)L\alpha^i}{D})$ and

$$\Delta p = \mathbb{P}(\frac{-(\frac{1}{4} - \epsilon)L\alpha^i}{D} \leq \mathcal{E} \leq \frac{(\frac{1}{4} - \epsilon)L\alpha^i}{D}) \tag{53}$$

that $N^+_i > N_i p_1 + \frac{N_i \Delta p}{2}$ is satisfied if $w^*_j \in [x_j, x_j + (1-\alpha)(y_j - x_j)]$ with probability at most $e^{-\frac{n_i(\Delta p)^2}{10}}$. Similarly, $N^+_i \leq N_i p_1 + \frac{N_i \Delta p}{2}$ is satisfied if if $w^*_j \in [y_j, y_j - (1-\alpha)(y_j - x_j)]$ with probability at most $e^{-\frac{n_i(\Delta p)^2}{10}}$. We can use Lemma 4.1 since (as it is easy to notice) in the ith phase Δp is exactly

$$\Delta p_i = \mathbb{P}(-\frac{(\frac{1}{4} - \epsilon)L\alpha^i}{D} \leq \mathcal{E} \leq \frac{(\frac{1}{4} - \epsilon)L\alpha^i}{D}) \tag{54}$$

and p_1 is exactly

$$p_1 = \mathbb{P}(\mathcal{E} > \frac{(\frac{1}{4} - \epsilon)L\alpha^i}{D}) \tag{55}$$

We obtain the following: the probability that there exists i such that $w^* \notin \mathcal{HC}_0 \cap \cdots \cap \mathcal{HC}_i$ is at most: $O(\sum_{i=0}^{s} e^{-\frac{n_i(\Delta p_i)^2}{10}})$. Substituting in that expression the formula on n_i, and noticing that the number of all the phases of the algorithm is logarithmic in T, D and d, we get the bound $O(\frac{\log(dDT)}{T^3})$. Thus, according to our previous remarks, we conclude that with probability at least $1 - O(\frac{\log(dDT)}{T^3} + \frac{d\log(dT)}{T^{30}})$ *OnlineBisection* algorithm makes an average error at most:

$$\epsilon_{av} = O(\frac{1}{T}(D^3 d^{\frac{3}{2}} r \log(T) h_T + \frac{\sqrt{d}T}{h_T})) \tag{56}$$

As mentioned before, we complete the proof by using the formula:

$$h_T = \frac{\sqrt{T}}{\log(T)} \tag{57}$$

∎

5. ANALYSIS OF THE RUNNING TIME OF THE ALGORITHM AND MEMORY USAGE

We start with the analysis of the running time of *OnlineBisection*. First we will show that the linear program used by the algorithm to determine the threshold in each round has a closed form solution.

LEMMA 5.1. *For any query-vector q, $\mathcal{I}_1 = [x_1, y_1], \ldots, \mathcal{I}_d = [x_d, y_d]$ and orthonormal basis $\mathcal{C} = \{e^1, \ldots, e^d\}$ the value*

$$\max_{f_1 \in \mathcal{I}_1, \ldots, f_d \in \mathcal{I}_d} \sum_{i=1}^{d} f_i e^i \cdot q$$

is given by

$$opt = \sum_{j \in \mathcal{J}_+} y_j e^j \cdot q + \sum_{j \in \mathcal{J}_-} x_j e^j \cdot q$$

where $\mathcal{J}_+ = \{i \in \{1, \ldots, d\} : e^i \cdot q \geq 0\}$ *and* $\mathcal{J}_- = \{i \in \{1, \ldots, d\} : e^i \cdot q < 0\}$.

Proof. Take some point: $c_1 e^1 + \cdots + c_d e^d$, where: $x_i \leq c_i \leq y_i$ for $i = 1, \ldots, d$. For $j \in \mathcal{J}_+$ the following is true: $c_j e^j \cdot q \leq y_j e^j \cdot q$, since: $c_j \leq y_j$ and $e^j \cdot q \geq 0$. Similarly, for $j \in \mathcal{J}_-$ we have: $c_j e^j \cdot q \leq x_j e^j \cdot q$, again by the definition of $\mathcal{J}_-$. Combining these inequalities we get that for every point v in the hypercube $\mathcal{HC}$ induced by $\mathcal{I}_1, \ldots, \mathcal{I}_d$ and $\mathcal{C}$ the following is true: $v \cdot q \leq opt$. Besides clearly there exists $v^* \in \mathcal{HC}$ such that: $v^* \cdot q = opt$. ∎

Now let us fix a query q. It is easy to notice that q is being processed by the algorithm in $O(dD)$ time. Indeed, a single query requires updating $O(d)$ variables of the form N_i^+, N_i^- and computing the closed-form solution given in Lemma 5.1 in $O(dD)$ time. Computing dot product of the query with the given approximation of the database vector clearly takes $O(D)$ time. Thus *OnlineBisection* runs in the $O(dD)$-time per query. Notice that *OnlineBisection* algorithm does not store any nontrivial data structures, only segments: $\mathcal{I}_1, \ldots, \mathcal{I}_d$, counts: N_i^+, N_i^- for $i = 1, \ldots, d$ and a constant number of other variables. The counts can be represented by $O(\log(T))$-digit numbers thus we conclude that *OnlineBisection* runs in the $O(\log(T))$-memory.

6. OPTIMALITY OF THE ALGORITHM

In this section we prove a negative result showing that up to the $poly(\log(T))$ factor no algorithm (offline or online) can beat *OnlineBisection* in respect to the achieved error. We prove that this is the case even if the oracle is turned off and the perturbed answer is given directly to the adversary.

THEOREM 6.1. *In the considered database model (but with online mode possibly turned off) any algorithm achieves error at least* $\tilde{O}(\frac{1}{\sqrt{T}})$ *in the worst case scenario.*

Proof. The proof is a direct consequence of the tightness of Azuma's inequality. We will prove that the result holds even for $D = 2$. Our queries q will be of the form $(x, 1)$. Consider a database vector $w = (a, b)$ for some $b > 0$. The perturbed answer that the oracle receives is of the form $ax + b + \epsilon_q$, where ϵ_q is the error added to the exact answer for the query q. Obviously, it suffices to show our result if the oracle is turned off and the adversary receives $ax + b + \epsilon_x$ instead of the binary signal.

Let $\{q_i = (x_i, 1) : i = 1, ..., T\}$ be the set of all the queries. Intuitively, we want to show that for T queries there always exists a vector $w_{near} = (a, b_{near})$, where: $b_{near} - b = \Omega(\frac{1}{\sqrt{T}\log(T)})$ such that with probability almost one the adversary will not be able to distinguish between w and w_{near} based on the outcome for these T queries.

Let us analyze the following expression: $E = \frac{\sum_{i=1}^{T} \epsilon_{q_i}}{T}$. Notice that from Azuma's inequality we know that $\mathbb{P}(E > \frac{f(T)}{\sqrt{T}}) = o(1)$ for any increasing positive function $f(T)$. We heavily used this fact before. However, from the tightness of Azuma's inequality (see: [17]) we also know that there exists a symmetric bounded distribution $\mathcal{Z}$ such that if every ϵ_q is taken from $\mathcal{Z}$ then $\mathbb{P}(E > \frac{1}{\sqrt{T} f(T)}) = 1 - o(1)$, where $f(T) = \log(T)$.

Let us assume that this is the case, i.e. $E > \frac{1}{\sqrt{T}\log(T)}$. But then one can easily check that there exists w_{near} (and related distribution determining the amount of error being added to each answer) that gives the same perturbed answers as w. Thus, given this set of queries the adversary will incur an error of at least $\theta(\frac{1}{\sqrt{T}\log(T)})$ from the exact answer given by at least one of the two database mechanisms determined by vectors: w and w_{near} for each asked query (since the distance between w and w_{near} is of order $\theta(\frac{1}{\sqrt{T}\log(T)})$). Thus, by the Pigeonhole Principle, for at least one of the two mechanisms the adversary will achieve average error at least $\frac{\frac{T}{2} \cdot \theta(\frac{1}{\sqrt{T}\log(T)})}{T} = \theta(\frac{1}{\sqrt{T}\log(T)})$.

That completes the proof since both database mechanisms are legitimate mechanisms that can communicate with the adversary. ∎

7. ONLINE-TO-BATCH CONVERSION

Throughout the paper we have considered the challenging online scenario, where the algorithm both learns and is evaluated on a single set of streaming queries. However, we note that the *OnlineBisection* algorithm also works well in the batch setting, i.e. when there is a separate train and test phase. We prove here Corollary 2.1, that for clarity we state once more:

COROLLARY 7.1. *Let* w_T *denote the final hypothesis constructed by the OnlineBisection algorithm after consuming* T *queries drawn from an unknown distribution* $\mathcal{D}$. *Then the following inequality holds with probability at least* $1 - O\left(\frac{\log(dDT)}{T^3} + \frac{d\log(dT)}{T^{30}}\right)$ *for any future queries* q *drawn from* $\mathcal{D}$:

$$\mathrm{E}_{q \sim \mathcal{D}}\left[|w_T \cdot q - w^* \cdot q|\right] \leq \frac{\sqrt{D}\log(T)}{\sqrt{T}}.$$

PROOF. This simply follows from the fact that, as argued in the proof of Theorem 2.1, $w^* \in \mathcal{HC}_s$ with at least the probability indicated in the statement of this corollary. Furthermore, by definition of the algorithm, we have $w_T \in \mathcal{HC}_s$ and the length of the side of the hypercube $\mathcal{HC}_s \leq \log(T)/\sqrt{T}$. Thus, with at least the probability indicated, $|w_T \cdot q - w^* \cdot q| \leq \|w_t - w^*\|_2 \|q\|_2 \leq \frac{\log(T)}{T}\sqrt{D}$. □

8. CONCLUSIONS AND FUTURE WORK

We presented in this paper the first $\tilde{O}(\frac{1}{\sqrt{T}})$-error algorithm for database reconstruction. It is adapted to the highly challenging, yet very realistic setting, where the answers given by the database are heavily perturbed by a random noise and besides there exists strong privacy mechanism (binary oracle $\mathcal{O}$) that aims to protect the database against an adversary attempting to compromise it. We show that even if the learning algorithm receives only binary answers on the database side and needs to learn database-vector w^* with high precision at the same time it is being evaluated, it can still achieve very small average error. We assume that the query-space is low-dimensional but this fact is needed only to guarantee that the term $r = \frac{2}{p_{\mathcal{D},\phi}^2}$ from the bound on the error is not exponential in D. The low-dimensionality assumption is indispensable here if one wants to achieve average error of the order $o(1)$ and considers nontrivial models with random noise. It is also worth to mention that if no noise is added, the low-dimensionality query-space is not required and a simple modification of our algorithm enables to get rid of the $\frac{2}{p_{\mathcal{D},\phi}^2}$-term. Our algorithm operates in the very limited (logarithmic) memory and is very fast ($O(d)$ processing time per query). By not using linear programming we obtain better theoretical bounds regarding running time of the algorithm than previously considered methods. *OnlineBisection* algorithm adapts next threshold values sent to the binary oracle $\mathcal{O}$ to its previous answers in order to obtain good approximation of the projection of a database-vector w^* onto the low-dimensional query-space $\mathcal{U}$.

It would be interesting to know whether the assumption about the low-dimensional querying model is indeed necessary or may be at least relaxed. Another area that can be explored is the application of the presented method to machine learning settings other than adversarial machine learning. It seems that presented technique provides a general mechanism for efficient online information retrieval. Finally, the authors plan also to extend presented algorithm to work in the setting, where no independence assumption for the mechanism of noise addition is required.

9. REFERENCES

[1] Cynthia Dwork. Differential privacy. In *ICALP (2)*, pages 1–12, 2006.

[2] Cynthia Dwork. Differential privacy in new settings. In Moses Charikar, editor, *SODA*, pages 174–183. SIAM, 2010.

[3] Cynthia Dwork, Moni Naor, Toniann Pitassi, and Guy N. Rothblum. Differential privacy under continual observation. In Leonard J. Schulman, editor, *STOC*, pages 715–724. ACM, 2010.

[4] Cynthia Dwork, Moni Naor, Toniann Pitassi, Guy N. Rothblum, and Sergey Yekhanin. Pan-private streaming algorithms. In Andrew Chi-Chih Yao, editor, *ICS*, pages 66–80. Tsinghua University Press, 2010.

[5] Kobbi Nissim, Rann Smorodinsky, and Moshe Tennenholtz. Approximately optimal mechanism design via differential privacy. *CoRR*, abs/1004.2888, 2010.

[6] Krzysztof Choromanski and Tal Malkin. The power of the dinur-nissim algorithm: breaking privacy of statistical and graph databases. In *PODS*, pages 65–76, 2012.

[7] Sergey Yekhanin. Private information retrieval. *Commun. ACM*, 53(4):68–73, 2010.

[8] Cynthia Dwork, Frank McSherry, and Kunal Talwar. The price of privacy and the limits of LP decoding. In David S. Johnson and Uriel Feige, editors, *STOC*, pages 85–94. ACM, 2007.

[9] Irit Dinur and Kobbi Nissim. Revealing information while preserving privacy. In *PODS*, pages 202–210. ACM, 2003.

[10] Cynthia Dwork and Sergey Yekhanin. New efficient attacks on statistical disclosure control mechanisms. In *CRYPTO*, pages 469–480, 2008.

[11] Sanjoy Dasgupta and Yoav Freund. Random projection trees and low dimensional manifolds. In *STOC*, pages 537–546, 2008.

[12] Mikhail Belkin and Partha Niyogi. Laplacian eigenmaps for dimensionality reduction and data representation. *Neural Computation*, 15(6):1373–1396, 2003.

[13] Richard G. Baraniuk, Volkan Cevher, and Michael B. Wakin. Low-dimensional models for dimensionality reduction and signal recovery: A geometric perspective. pages 959–971, 2010.

[14] Nilesh Dalvi, Pedro Domingos, Mausam, Sumit Sanghai, and Deepak Verma. Adversarial classification. In *Proceedings of the Tenth ACM SIGKDD International Conference on Knowledge Discovery and Data Mining*, KDD '04, pages 99–108, New York, NY, USA, 2004. ACM.

[15] Yevgeniy Vorobeychik and Bo Li. Optimal randomized classification in adversarial settings. In *AAMAS*, pages 485–492, 2014.

[16] Kevin G. Jamieson, Maya R. Gupta, Eric Swanson, and Hyrum S. Anderson. Training a support vector machine to classify signals in a real environment given clean training data. In *Proceedings of the IEEE International Conference on Acoustics, Speech, and Signal Processing, ICASSP 2010, 14-19 March 2010, Sheraton Dallas Hotel, Dallas, Texas, USA*, pages 2214–2217, 2010.

[17] S. Ross. Stochastic processes. *Wiley*, 1996.

Aggregation of Crowdsourced Ordinal Assessments and Integration with Learning to Rank: a Latent Trait Model

Pavel Metrikov Virgil Pavlu Javed A. Aslam*
College of Computer and Information Science
Northeastern University, Boston, MA, USA
{metpavel, vip, jaa}@ccs.neu.edu

ABSTRACT

Existing approaches used for training and evaluating search engines often rely on crowdsourced assessments of document relevance with respect to a user query. To use such assessments for either evaluation or learning, we propose a new framework for the inference of true document relevance from crowdsourced data—one simpler than previous approaches and achieving better performance. For each assessor, we model assessor quality and bias in the form of Gaussian distributed class conditionals of relevance grades. For each document, we model true relevance and difficulty as continuous variables. We estimate all parameters from crowdsourced data, demonstrating better inference of relevance as well as realistic models for both documents and assessors.

A document-pair likelihood model works best, and it is extended to pairwise learning to rank. Utilizing more information directly from the input data, it shows better performance as compared to existing state-of-the-art approaches for learning to rank from crowdsourced assessments. Experimental validation is performed on four TREC datasets.

Categories and Subject Descriptors: H. Information Systems; H.3 Information Storage and Retrieval; H.3.3 Information Search and Retrieval

Keywords: ordinal label aggregation; learning to rank; crowdsourcing; informativeness; assessor modeling

1. INTRODUCTION

To assemble training and testing collections for information retrieval, ground-truth relevance assessments were traditionally obtained from expensive expert assessors, as in numerous TREC efforts. The advent of Amazon Mechanical Turk and other *crowdsourcing* services has given rise to an alternative and far less expensive source of relevance assessments. However, while crowdsourced relevance assessments are far cheaper, they are also less reliable and more difficult to accurately obtain for *graded* relevance assessments, where a common grade scale is $g \in \{0, 1, 2, 3, 4\}$.

*This work supported by NSF grant IIS-1421399.

Permission to make digital or hard copies of all or part of this work for personal or classroom use is granted without fee provided that copies are not made or distributed for profit or commercial advantage and that copies bear this notice and the full citation on the first page. Copyrights for components of this work owned by others than ACM must be honored. Abstracting with credit is permitted. To copy otherwise, or republish, to post on servers or to redistribute to lists, requires prior specific permission and/or a fee. Request permissions from Permissions@acm.org.
CIKM'15, October 19-23, 2015, Melbourne, VIC, Australia
2015 ACM. ISBN 978-1-4503-3794-6/15/10 ...$15.00.
DOI: http://dx.doi.org/10.1145/2806416.2806492

In this paper, we propose a new and simpler framework for the inference of true document relevance from crowdsourced assessments which achieves a performance exceeding state-of-the-art techniques, sometimes markedly so. In our proposed framework, both assessor and document parameters are estimated. Assessor quality is measured as the usefulness for inference, precisely computed as the reduction in uncertainty for relevance inference; thus, assessor quality is closely integrated with how much the assessor's grade counts. Assessor grades are modeled as Gaussian distributed conditionals for each available relevance grade. Each assessor is modeled individually, accounting for: (1) the notion that higher assessor grades, for a good quality worker, correspond on average with higher document true relevance (random and adversarial assessors are modeled within our framework); (2) realistic decomposition into Gaussians of conditional densities; (3) suitability for crowdsourced grades in terms of amount of data collected; (4) the ability to represent grade variance as a function of the assessor, the actual grade, and the document.

For each document, we model its true relevance and difficulty as continuous variables. The true relevance scale (as opposed to an imposed grade scale) allows us to understand and model the perception of each assessor for each grade separately. Naturally, the continuous scale allows for aggregation of crowd-answers on inconsistent scales, for example a NIST assessor with two grades and Mechanical Turkers with five grades. Finally, modeling document difficulty allows for variance in assessor grade due to the documents themselves, as opposed to limiting this variance to be a function of only the assessor and the nominal grade, (e.g., through the use of true-relevance/assessed-grade confusion matrices).

We describe two methods, one based on data likelihood over individual documents and the other based on likelihood over pairs of documents. We estimate all the parameters of our model from crowdsourced data, demonstrating the inference of assessor parameters and quality as well as document difficulty and relevance. Both document-likelihood and document-pair-likelihood optimizations use information directly from the input data and show better performance than existing approaches such as simple averages or majority vote, variants of expectation-maximization aggregation [7, 10, 22], and Polytomous Rasch aggregation [1, 15].

Learning to Rank (LTR). We next consider the use of noisy crowdsourced assessments for training *learning to rank* algorithms. Learning to rank is a common technique in Information Retrieval using labeled documents over a set of training queries in order to obtain a model that can be used to rank documents for new testing queries. For it to work, each document-query datapoint must be represented by a consistent set of features.

We extend the pairwise aggregation model into a relevance scoring model as a function of document features. The training input consists of document features together with crowdsourced assessments ("judgments", "grades" or "labels"). The likelihood is defined on pairs of documents, including all crowdsourced assessments and estimated parameters of user models and document difficulty. A likelihood optimization procedure gives the relevance scoring function, in a form of gradient-boosted ensemble of regression trees.

1.1 Summary contributions

In summary, our contributions are as follows: (1) A new *model for assessors* that includes a novel measure of quality for each assessor, is easier to learn, and is more suitable for crowdworkers (Section 2). (2) A new *model for documents* that incorporates a continuous relevance scale and a document difficulty parameter (Section 2). (3) A new method for the *aggregation of crowdsourced assessments* based on *likelihood of documents*, including the inference of document relevance and difficulty as well as assessor quality. (Section 3.1). (4) A new method for *aggregation of crowdsourced assessments* based on *likelihood of pairs of documents* (section 3.2). (5) A new measure of *assessor quality* ("informativeness") based on a sound information-theoretic measure of reduction in uncertainty due to the assessor (Section 3.7). (6) A novel analysis of aggregation quality as function of number of assessments, by means of confidence intervals for inferred document relevance (Section 3.6). (7) An analysis of *document difficulty vs. crowd disagreement* (Section 3.8). (8) A novel method for *learning to rank* with crowd assessments (Section 4).

We demonstrate significant, at times marked, improvements for all methods proposed on four TREC datasets. Our crowdsource aggregation results are presented in Section 3.5; learning to rank results are presented in Section 4.3.

1.2 Related work

In the literature, there are two main directions of research related to conducting inference about unknown quantities of interest, given human observations about them, that may potentially be biased and inaccurate. The first direction deals with so called *latent class models*, where the unknown quantity is discrete. One of the most popular examples is EM algorithm [7, 10], where a human assessor quality is modeled as a latent confusion matrix with off-diagonal elements representing the probability of mislabeling each item they provide an assessment for. The true labels and the confusion matrices are estimated through an iterative procedure that maximizes the likelihood of observing the assessments given the parameters of the model. As a result, the estimate of the true label is determined mostly by accurate workers, while "bad" workers are weighted out. There are further extensions of this method within Bayesian inference framework aimed to regularize the problem by assuming various prior distributions over confusion matrices and also to improve the quality of inference [20, 14, 26, 12]. An extension modeling item difficulties and solving the problem via minimax entropy principle was proposed in [31], and later further extended to the case of ordinal labels by regularizing the problem with additional ordinality constraints [30]. Another extension of EM by modeling item difficulties was presented in [29], for the case of 2x2 confusion matrices.

For our domain of application (i.e., inferring document relevances), however, the second direction of research dealing with *latent trait models* [25] seems more promising. In these models, each *item* (document in our case) is assumed to have a continuous *latent trait* (true unknown document relevance), while each assessor is assumed to have a set of individual thresholds roughly defining the boundaries, on the scale of latent traits, between adjacent classes (relevance classes in our case). For each item and each assessor, the observed labels are assumed to be generated by a probabilistic model that depends on both item latent trait and assessor thresholds, and additionally may account for variable measurement errors for both assessor (his quality) and item (its difficulty). Polytomous Rasch model [1, 15] can be seen as a special case of a latent trait model when all the assessors have equal measurement errors. Originally, all the items were modeled to have similar measurement errors as well. However, there is known to exist an extension [17] of the basic Polytomous Rasch model for the case of variable difficulties of items (the qualities of workers are, however, modeled to be similar). The methods that we investigate in this paper resemble the one described in [25] which accounts for variable difficulties of assessors and has been shown to work well on medical datasets, the difference is that we choose a more flexible family of functions to model class probability curves, and we also accommodate for item difficulty. Other applications of latent trait models to label aggregation that consider both variability in labeler accuracies and item difficulties [21, 11] are likely limited in scalability due to MCMC simulation they have to rely on to conduct inference. In another recent application [13] a more computationally efficient method (via Approximate Inference) is proposed, however it may be limited by the assumption of same (fixed) thresholds being shared among all the assessors (also authors show no improvement over EM [7] in terms of nDCG).

Other related work includes methods for preference aggregation [27, 6] and ranked lists aggregation [18]. While the problem of ordinal assessment aggregation could be potentially reformulated within either aforementioned framework, it is clear that this transformation would be lossy as the information about degree of confidence with respect to pairwise preferences (encoded with assessor-specific distance between relevance grades) is discarded.

A method for measuring assessor performance in units of information (bits) based on information-theoretic approach was proposed in [28]. Since it was defined within the framework of latent class models, we adapted it to the continuous case, and devised a suitable measure of the informativeness.

Learning to Rank Researchers have shown in the past that the noise (and sometimes the adversarial behavior) of the cheap crowdworkers can be countered with variations of the Expectation Maximization algorithm [10]. For LTR performance we compare against LambdaMART [3], a state-of-the-art learning to rank algorithm that uses gradient boosting to produce an ensemble of weak models (regression trees) that together form a strong model; in the Yahoo! learning to rank challenge [5], the winner used ensembles of LambdaMART models. However LambdaMART takes as training labels a single assessment per document, so we have to make a choice from the multiple crowd-assessments collected; each *label choice* leads to a particular LambdaMART baseline: the *random* crowdsourced label, the *average* crowdsourced label, the *EM-average* crowdsourced label. We also compare with a previously modified LambdaMART [16] that uses as training labels EM-smoothed probabilistic preferences over pairs of documents obtained from crowsourced data.

CROWD AGGREG (crowd assessments)	Trec8	Ent07	CW12	RF10
Queries	10	33	9	100
Rel grades, expert	2	3	4	3
Rel grades, crowd	5	5	4	3
Documents total	18.2K	3.0K	3.2K	20.0K
Doc per query mean	1826	91	359	200
Doc per query med	1798	80	368	199
Crowdworkers	661	132	328	764
Assessments, total	134K	18.5K	56.3K	98.3K
Assess/worker mean	203	140	172	129
Assess/wkr med	39	40	30	18
Assess/wkr/query mean	106	39	47	16
Assess/wkr/query med	39	38	10	5
Assess/doc mean	7.3	6.2	17.4	4.9
Assess/doc med	6	5	15	5
Queries/worker mean	1.9	3.6	3.6	7.9
Queries/worker med	1	1	2	3
TESTING LTR MODEL (expert assessments)	Trec8	Ent07	CW12	MQ09
Queries	40	17	41	584
Documents, total	68.8K	11.3K	11.9K	15.5K

Table 1: Top: datasets for Label Aggregation and training rankers. Bottom: datasets for testing learning to rank models.

1.3 Experiment setup, data, crowd assessments

We run experiments over four datasets with slightly different characteristics: TREC 8, TREC Enterprise 2007, ClueWeb 2012 (subset of it that was used in TREC 2013 Crowdsourcing Track [23]) and ClueWeb 2009 (subset of it that was used in TREC 2010 Relevance Feedback track + Million Query 2009). We perform the label aggregation task and train learning to rank algorithms on a subset of the queries (see Table 1, top for statistics), while using the rest of the queries to test the performance of trained rankers (see Table 1, bottom). In each dataset, the "gold" labels are TREC assessments obtained from expert annotators, present over both training and testing sets. For the former three collections, for each document from the training set we have collected at least 5 additional assessments from crowdworker annotators, such as Amazon Mechanical Turkers; for the latter collection we reused existing crowdsourced judgments collected previously in [4]. The overall goal is both to (1) aggregate these non-expert labels in a meaningful way to estimate the actual relevance, and also (2) train a ranking algorithm with these crowdsourced assessments. For learning to rank, we extract a typical set of features (language models and web-graph properties) for each query-document, on all four collections.

2. ASSESSOR AND DOCUMENT MODELS

Each assessment observation[1] consists of a document d, an assessor a, and the grade observed g, in short (g, d, a). We are assuming a uni-dimensional relevance scale (typical for IR relevance assessments), but *continuous* as opposed to discrete. Each document d is assumed to have "true relevance" r_d on this scale, and a "difficulty" $\epsilon_d > 0$ centered around 1. A fixed relevance prior is used on documents, centering document relevance to a common reference value (arbitrarily chosen to be 0 in our experiments), and having a unit variance. The actual document model $\theta_d = (r_d, \epsilon_d)$ is to be inferred from assessments, starting from this prior and using crowdworkers assessments to optimize the likelihood.

Assessor model. We are modeling each assessor a with a set of sigmoid-like density functions $p(grade|r_d)$, one for each relevance grade (Figure 1). Intuitively, we want the densities to reflect probability of an assessor grade conditional to the true relevance, but we also want them to be decomposable into a set of underlying parametrizable simple functions. The model assumption is that, for any document d, there is an underlying set of grade-gaussians, such that each density corresponds to a normalized gaussian component. The mean of each gaussian is invariant in d (fixed per assessor-grade), while the variance of each gaussian component depends both on assessor variance w_g for the grade g, and on document difficulty ϵ_d : $\sigma^2 = w_g \epsilon_d$. The difficult documents increase the variance already modeled by the assessor grade variance. Depending on the likelihood model, the means and variances will appropriately correspond to either grades (document likelihood, section 3.1) or difference in grades (document-pair likelihood, section 3.2)

The assessor model parameters are thus $\theta_a = (\pi_g^a, \mu_g^a, w_g^a)$ for each grade g available to assessors (for example $g \in \{0..4\}$), where π_g^a are weighting coefficients among the components[2]. These parameters, like the document parameters, are to be inferred from assessments, in our case crowdsourced relevance judgments. The assessor informativeness, not a formal parameter, is calculated as reduction of uncertainty for each likelihood model for each assessor grade (a, g) pair; it is a function of the assessment grade, since an assessor can be differently accurate for different grades.

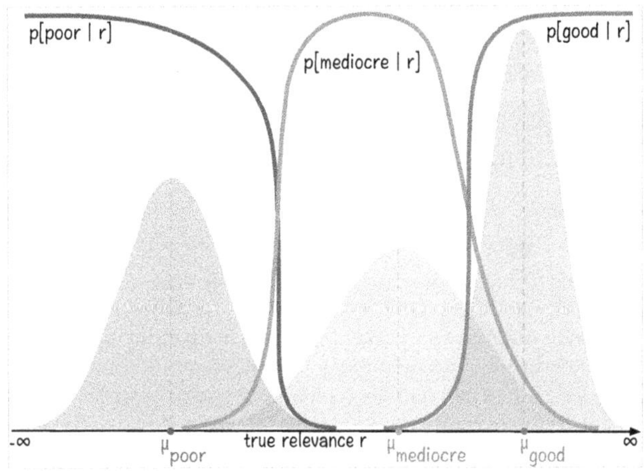

Figure 1: Assessor grade model (conceptual illustration for "GDA" method): given a true relevance scale (continuous real x-axis) and a set of grades (for example "poor", "medicore", "good"), each assessor is modeled by its gaussian parameters.

We can enforce strict ordinality constraints on the assessor grade means, unless we believe there may be adversarial assessors (who intentionally provide out-of-order labels) and we want to use the "reversed" information out of their assessments. If ordinality constraints are enforced, the algorithm will automatically disregard the adversarial judgments – like in the case of random, or uninformative, judgments.

[1]Here we assume all assessments belong to one query. The generalization to multiple queries case is straightforward

[2]In our experiments we restrict the assessor variance to $w_0^a = w_1^a = ... = w_4^a$ to reduce number of free parameters and to enforce unimodality of distributions $p(grade|r_d)$

3. AGGREGATION OF CROWDSOURCED ASSESSMENTS

Given set of assessments set $OBS = \{(g, d, a)\}$, a likelihood objective is defined, followed by an optimization procedure which finds the assessor and document parameters θ_a, θ_d that achieve the maximum likelihood. Generally, the optimization is based on Newton-Raphson procedure [19], often far more efficient than Gradient Descent. We present two likelihood objectives: (1) a likelihood defined on individual documents; (2) a likelihood on pairs of documents.

3.1 Likelihood on documents: "GDA" method

To define a likelihood for observations based on individual documents, the probability of observation (grade g, document d, assessor a) is given by a density of the grade conditional on the assessor and document models[3] :

$$p(g|\theta_d, \theta_a) = \frac{1}{Z_{ad}} \pi_g^a \mathcal{N}(r_d|\mu_g^a, w_g^a \epsilon_d) \quad (1)$$

where $Z_{ad} = \sum_g \pi_g^a \mathcal{N}(r_d|\mu_g^a, w_g^a \epsilon_d)$ is a normalizing sum of gaussian components. Note that variance of each gaussian component is the product of assessor variance and document difficulty: $w_g^a \epsilon_d$. The log likelihood is

$$\log L = \log \prod_{(g,d,a) \in OBS} p(g|\theta_d, \theta_a) \quad (2)$$

Maximizing likelihood with numerical optimization (using analytically derived gradients), we obtain $\theta_a^* = (\pi_g^{a*}, \mu_g^{a*}, w_g^{a*})$ for each assessor and $\theta_d^* = (r_d^*, \epsilon_d^*)$ for each document.

Knowing assessor model θ_a we can reason about the quality of the assessor a in terms of *informativeness* of his judgments. We can compute how much information about the document relevance we gain by obtaining a judgment g from him. To this end, we take the difference between entropy of the prior distribution over relevance and the entropy of posterior distribution given the judgment:

$$I_g(\theta_a) = H[p_0(r)] - H\left[\frac{p_0(r) \cdot p(g|r, \theta_a)}{p_a(g)}\right], \quad (3)$$

where $p_0(r)$ is the prior distribution over relevance for any unjudged document that we choose to be a Gaussian with zero mean and unit variance; $p(g|r, \theta_a)$ is given by our model (eq. 1) assuming the document is of average difficulty ($\epsilon_d = 1$); $p_a(g)$ is the normalizing constant with the meaning of overall frequency of the grade g by assessor a:

$$p_a(g) = \int_{-\infty}^{\infty} p_0(r) \cdot p(g|r, \theta_a) dr \quad (4)$$

Since g is not known in advance, we should take expectation of $I_g(\theta_a)$ over all possible g, with (eq. 3) and (eq. 4):

$$I(\theta_a) = \sum_g p_a(g) \cdot I_g(\theta_a) \quad (5)$$

$I(\theta_a)$ is the expected informativeness of a single judgment of assessor a, it is measured in *nats* (natural units for information entropy, 1 nat $\approx$ 1.44 bits) and depends only on the parameters of the user model θ_a.

3.2 Likelihood on document pairs: "GDA-PW"

For a likelihood of observations on pairs of documents, the probability of two observations (g, d, a) and (g', d', a') is given by density of the grade conditionals of assessors a and a' and the two documents models:

$$p(g|g', \theta_d, \theta_{d'}, \theta_a, \theta_{a'}) = \quad (6)$$

$$= \frac{1}{Z_{aa'dd'}} \pi_g^a \mathcal{N}(r_d - r_{d'}|\mu_g^a - \mu_{g'}^{a'}, \sqrt{w_g^a w_{g'}^{a'} \epsilon_d \epsilon_{d'}}) \quad (7)$$

where $Z_{aa'dd'}$ is the normalization constant. Note that gaussian means are in this model the difference between assessor grade means, and variance of each gaussian component is composed of assessor variance parameters (for both grades) and document difficulty (for both documents): $\sqrt{w_g^a w_{g'}^{a'} \epsilon_d \epsilon_{d'}}$.

Denoting by K the overall number of judgments, we define the log likelihood[4]:

$$\log L = \sum_{(g,d,a),(g',d',a') \in OBS} (K)^{-1} \log p(g|g', \theta_d, \theta_{d'}, \theta_a, \theta_{a'}) \quad (8)$$

For the pairwise model, we can define informativeness of the assessor as well: it becomes the expected reduction of uncertainty of the *relative* relevance for a pair of documents $\Delta_r = r_d - r_{d'}$, given a pair of judgments g and g':

$$I_{gg'}(\theta_a) = H[p_0(\Delta_r)] - H\left[\frac{p_0(\Delta_r) \cdot p(g, g'|\Delta_r, \theta_a)}{p_a(g, g')}\right], \quad (9)$$

where $p_0(\Delta_r)$ is the prior distribution over difference of relevance for any unjudged pair of documents (we choose it to be a Gaussian with zero mean and variance of 2); we model $p(g, g'|\Delta_r, \theta_a) \propto \sqrt{p(g|g', \Delta_r, \theta_a, \theta_a) \cdot p(g'|g, \Delta_r, \theta_a, \theta_a)}$ and compute it using (eq. 7) (again, we assume $\epsilon_d = \epsilon_{d'} = 1$); $p_a(g, g')$ is the normalizing constant:

$$p_a(g, g') = \int_{-\infty}^{\infty} p_0(\Delta_r) \cdot p(g, g'|\Delta_r, \theta_a) d\Delta_r \quad (10)$$

Like before we take the expectation of $I_{gg'}(\theta_a)$ over all possible g and g'. Also, we divide the result by 2, to report the informativeness per judgment, not pair of judgments. With (eq. 9) and (eq. 10):

$$I(\theta_a) = \frac{1}{2} \sum_{g,g'} p_a(g, g') \cdot I_{gg'}(\theta_a) \quad (11)$$

3.3 Baseline comparison: EM algorithm

In the EM algorithm, the observed judgments from crowdsource workers are the input; worker qualities are unknown model parameters to be estimated, the document "true" grades are the latent variables. We take a similar approach as in [10]. Let G be the number of relevance grades and M be the number of workers. We assign each worker a GxG latent confusion matrix: element C_{lg}^j is the probability that worker j labels the document as l, given ground truth relevance g. Let $n_{il}^j = 1$ if the judge j assigns a label l to the document i, otherwise $n_{il}^j = 0$. After computing confusion matrices for all workers, for each document we estimate a relevance grade based on all workers' judgments and matrices. The probability of document i having true grade r:

$$Pr(R_{ir}) = \frac{p_r \cdot \prod_{j=1}^M \prod_{l=1}^G (C_{lr}^j)^{n_{il}^j}}{\sum_{k=1}^G p_k \cdot \prod_{j=1}^M \prod_{l=1}^G (C_{lk}^j)^{n_{il}^j}}$$

While shown to work well on some datasets, in general this method is not very robust to sparse input: it requires

[3]The name "GDA" is due to resemblance of the main expression (eq. 1) to Gaussian Discriminant Analysis

[4]Alternatively, one could consider in (eq. 8) only pairs judged by the same assessor $a = a'$

grades	TREC 8 crowd only			TREC RF 2010 crowd only			TREC Enterprise 2007 crowd only			ClueWeb 2012 crowd only		
Method	MAP	nDCG	Kτ	MAP	nDCG	Kτ	MAP	nDCG	Kτ	MAP	nDCG	Kτ
Random	0.040*	0.432*	0.000*	0.553*	0.669*	0.000*	0.761*	0.815*	0.000*	0.420*	0.618*	0.000*
MV	0.183*	0.615*	0.441*	0.678*	0.751*	0.295*	0.885*	0.902*	0.387*	0.506*	0.660*	0.151*
Average	0.309*	0.724*	0.685*	0.720*	0.777*	0.382*	0.915*	0.923*	0.476*	0.612*	0.708*	0.444
EM	0.368*	0.753*	0.714	0.767*	0.810*	0.446*	0.916*	0.920*	0.475*	0.609	0.697*	0.372
Rasch	0.373*	0.763*	0.713*	0.762*	0.809*	0.449*	0.920*	0.928*	0.501*	0.618*	0.714*	0.420*
GDA	0.448*	0.795	0.748*	0.770	0.815	0.467*	0.928	0.932	0.521	0.652	0.741*	0.480
GDA-PW($\epsilon = 1$)	0.447	0.791	0.753*	0.772	0.819	**0.484**	0.931	0.932	**0.527**	0.660	0.747*	0.479
GDA-PW	**0.463**	**0.802**	**0.756**	**0.776**	**0.821**	**0.484**	**0.932**	**0.936**	**0.527**	**0.664**	**0.769**	**0.484**

Table 2: Performance of various methods for aggregation of crowdsourced assessments, evaluated on 4 different datasets. The highest value in each column is highlighted. Values significantly lower (p < 0.05) than those of GDA-PW are marked with *.

grades	TREC 8 crowd+expert+random			TREC RF 2010 crowd+expert+random			TREC Enterprise 2007 crowd+expert+random			ClueWeb 2012 crowd+expert+random		
Method	MAP	nDCG	Kτ	MAP	nDCG	Kτ	MAP	nDCG	Kτ	MAP	nDCG	Kτ
MV	0.219*	0.647*	0.519*	0.744*	0.804*	0.477*	0.890*	0.899*	0.436*	0.557*	0.676*	0.235*
Average	0.371*	0.771*	0.755*	0.840*	0.872*	0.624*	0.936*	0.942*	0.568*	0.663*	0.733*	0.541*
EM	0.503*	0.814*	0.897*	0.857*	0.877*	0.671*	0.953*	0.946*	0.647*	0.659*	0.708*	0.494*
Rasch	0.415*	0.785*	0.780*	0.865*	0.889*	0.680*	0.945*	0.948*	0.604*	0.670*	0.743*	0.538*
GDA	0.655	0.896	0.941*	0.887*	0.900*	0.732*	**0.976**	0.970	**0.773**	0.763	0.795*	0.668
GDA-PW($\epsilon = 1$)	0.674	0.895	0.955	**0.900**	**0.917**	0.769	0.973	**0.973**	0.768	**0.777**	0.803	0.676
GDA-PW	**0.685**	**0.897**	**0.958**	0.896	**0.917**	**0.770**	0.973	0.972	0.768	0.769	**0.808**	**0.677**

Table 3: Performance of various methods for aggregation of crowdsourced assessments. NIST assessments and random assessments from a virtual assessor are added to the training set. The large jump in performance is no doubt due to NIST assessors (same assessments also used for evaluation), see the red dots in Figure 5.

many judgments per worker to reliably estimate worker parameters (typically, proportional to G^2 or GT when number of "true" classes T is chosen different from G). Also, this EM method was not specifically designed for problems dealing with continuous quantities (like relevance), but rather with discrete classes. So it is not quite clear how many discrete latent classes for relevance we have to pick (with more classes we expect more accurate approximation of continuous relevance, but also increased number of free parameters making the model even more prone to overfitting).

Another shortcoming of EM in the current setup is the lack of guarantee for ordinality: it is not the case that if the latent class $t+1$ corresponds to a higher degree of relevance than the class t, then class $t+2$ should always be expected more relevant than class $t+1$.

3.4 Baseline comparison: Polytomous Rasch

In Polytomous Rasch model, the probability of assessor a assigning a label g to the document d is modeled as follows:

$$p(g|r_d, \tau^a, \epsilon_d) = \frac{\exp\left(\sum_{k=0}^{g} \epsilon_d \left(r_d - \tau_k^a\right)\right)}{\sum_{j=0}^{G-1} \exp\left(\sum_{k=0}^{j} \epsilon_d \left(r_d - \tau_k^a\right)\right)}$$

where r_d is a scalar latent relevance associated with the document d, and τ^a is a vector of latent thresholds associated with assessor a. When $r_d = \tau_g^a$ for some g, the worker is equally likely to assign labels $g-1$ and g (other labels have some likelihood as well). The parameter $\epsilon_d > 0$, supposed to be equal to 1 originally, extends the basic model and represents document difficulty [17]. This model has very few free parameters, as compared to EM, and thus the inference is more robust when the input is sparse. On the downside, it works well only when the assessors are reliable. Notice that an assessor providing random responses (whether uniformly across the grades or not) cannot be accurately modeled within this framework. Therefore, this method (in the current form) is not very appropriate for crowdsourcing, as we expect a massive number of unreliable judgments.

In our experiments, we use the extended version of Polytomous Rasch model (accounting for document difficulty), and estimate all the parameters by maximizing their joint likelihood in a very similar way we perform optimization of the models we propose (GDA and GDA-PW).

3.5 Label Aggregation Results

The task in this experiment was to aggregate crowdsourced labels for datasets from Table 1, rank the documents for each query by estimated relevance based on aggregated labels, and then evaluate these rankings by using expert labels in terms of common IR measures: MAP, nDCG and Kendall τ. We compare the performance of proposed label aggregation methods, namely GDA (eq. 2) and GDA-PW (eq. 8), with performance of several baselines: (a) randomly ordered documents which doesn't rely on training labels at all, (b) majority vote, by ordering documents by the most frequent label (or one of them if there are several), (c) ordering documents by straight average of crowdsourced labels,

(d) expectation-maximization method, see Section 3.3, and (e) Polytomous Rasch model, see Section 3.4. To measure the effect of modeling document difficulty, we run GDA-PW in two modes: with and without it (fixed $\epsilon = 1$). The results are presented in Table 2. First, we observe that our methods, GDA and GDA-PW, outperform the baselines on all datasets by all measures, in many cases by a wide margin[5]. Between these two, the pairwise method (GDA-PW) performs better on all datasets. Modeling document difficulty seems to help, especially in case of TREC 8 and ClueWeb 2012. It should be noted that EM method is not performing very well: it is comparable to Straight Average on two datasets, similar on third and even worse on the fourth, ClueWeb 2012. Perhaps that can be explained by analyzing the dataset statistics (see Table 1): to reliably estimate assessor models (confusion matrices in case of EM) we have too few assessments per worker per query (particularly, on the worst performing dataset, ClueWeb 2012). To partly mitigate this problem, we minimized the number of unknown parameters by assuming each assessor has the same model across all queries (which may not be very realistic), and also by reducing the number of discrete "true" classes of relevance (3 true classes worked best in almost all cases); we report the performance of best working configuration, but nevertheless the algorithm suffers from data sparsity. Polytomous Rasch model is less prone to overfitting on sparse datasets as it has fewer free parameters to optimize, so it tends to perform better than EM.

As an additional experiment, we decided to inject labels of expert assessors along with randomly generated labels of a virtual assessor, into the set of labels to be aggregated, without giving the algorithms a hint about the special properties of these two additional sources. We observe (see Table 3) that the previous conclusions are generally still valid. Our methods do a good job at recognizing the reliable sources, picking up the expert labels to further improve the performance over the rest of the methods.

3.6 Aggregation quality as function of number of assessments

When collecting crowdsourced relevance judgments for a document, we not only can estimate its relevance (assuming we already have some estimates of the qualities of assessors who contributed judgments), but more generally, we also can compute the posterior probability distribution of the true relevance. Having the posterior distribution can be very useful, for instance, to compute confidence intervals for the estimated relevance. If confidence intervals are too wide, then we may want to collect additional assessments for that document in order to obtain more reliable estimates. For our first method (eq. 2) the posterior has a simple expression (assuming we have K independent judgments for that document):

$$p(r_d|\{g_1, g_2..., g_K\}, \theta) \propto p_0(r_d) \cdot \prod_{k=1}^{K} p(g_k|r_d, \epsilon_d, \theta_{a_k}) \quad (12)$$

At the same time, the posterior for the second method (eq. 8) doesn't seem to have a closed form expression. As an alternative, we can readily apply the Laplace approximation for the posterior (refer to [2]), given that we anyway have to compute the second derivatives of likelihood function with respect to the model parameters while performing Newton-

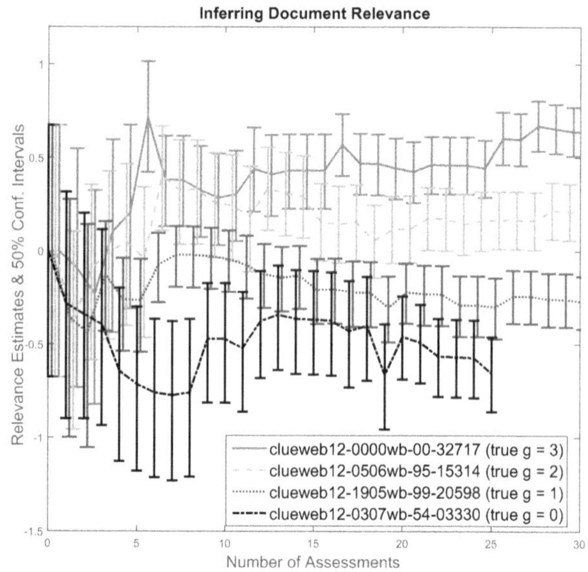

Figure 2: Simulation of online experiment for 4 documents of ClueWeb 2012 collection. Relevance judgments are collected one by one, each time improving the knowledge about true relevance. For each document, the true relevance estimates are plotted along with 50% confidence intervals.

Raphson optimization procedure. A more general and potentially more accurate approach would be to employ the methods of approximate inference [2] to approximate joint posterior distribution for all the parameters of the model.

On Figure 2 we plot the results of simulating online experiment when we collect assessments for a few documents with different relevance (as per expert assessor), one by one, using (eq. 12). One can see how our knowledge about the initially unknown relevance improves over time. The more judgments we collect, the tighter confidence intervals become. We can reason about assessor reliability indirectly, by looking at the reduction of uncertainty caused by each assessment: as a consequence of bayesian inference, high quality assessors will reduce uncertainty more than it will do low quality workers. Abrupt changes in the expected value will also correspond to high-quality assessments.

3.7 Analysis: Assessor Informativeness

On Figure 3 we can observe the user models inferred from the crowdsourced data using document likelihood (eq. 2). These models correspond to several very different assessors. To verify the validity of inference, we analyze the results of experiment when labels of expert TREC assessors, along with randomly generated labels of a virtual "random" assessor, were included into the set of crowdsourced labels. Thus, we can analyze the model for two assessors for which we have *a priori* knowledge about their skills. So, the upper row on the plots corresponds to an expert, then we show models for three real crowdworkers in the decreasing order of their inferred quality, while the bottom row is taken by a random virtual assessor. Starting with the left column where we plot the inferred raw Gaussian for each assessor and each grade, we proceed to the middle column where these Gaussians are combined into category probability curves, for each grade.

[5] We test for significance of improvement using Fisher's two-sided paired randomization test [24].

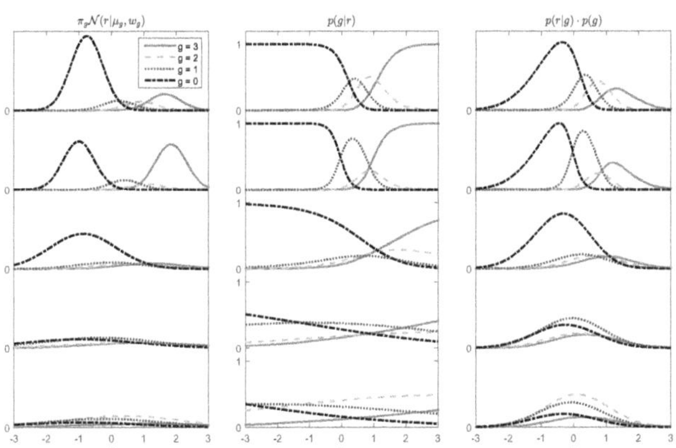

Figure 3: User model parameters inferred from crowdsourced judgments for ClueWeb 2012 dataset query #246: components of Gaussian mixture (left); grade probability curves (middle); joint probability distributions for relevance and grades (right). From top to bottom on each plot: (a) NIST assessors combined; (b) a good quality crowdworker; (c) an average quality crowdworker; (d) a poor quality crowdworker, (e) simulation of an assessor who provides random judgments (not uniform across grades).

On the right plot we can see the joint probability distributions for true relevance and observed grades. The right plot should be interpreted as follows: pick some assessor and look at, let's say, the black curve, corresponding to documents labeled "0". It shows how all the documents labeled "0" by that assessor are expected to be distributed over the true relevance, while the area under that curve is proportional to the overall likelihood of this assessor assigning this grade. Intuitively, the better separated the curves corresponding to different grades, the better is the assessor able to distinguish between these grades, meaning the more informative. The reported results match our intuition: we have well separated curves for expert assessors (top), while we have almost indistinguishable curves (up to normalization constant) for the random one (bottom). Besides, we see that the separability of these curves for the actual crowdworkers vary in a wide range, suggesting we are indeed dealing with assessors of very different quality. We conclude that the family of functions we employ in our aggregation framework is flexible enough to model assessors with a wide range of qualities and biases.

Next, we measure the informativeness of each assessor not just visually, but quantitatively, computing it using (eq. 11). We demonstrate that the inferred informativeness of each assessor makes sense, by plotting it against the measure of how consistent the judgments of that assessor are with the ones of the expert, in terms of Kendall τ coefficient for rank correlation. By looking at Figure 5, we observe that there is indeed high correlation between two plotted quantities (it is particularly true for the cases when we have many judgments made by an assessor). Moreover, we observe almost zero inferred informativeness for random virtual workers and a considerably high informativeness for expert assessors.

An interesting fact: if we rank expert assessors for different collections by their informativeness, the order would be (from lower to higher): TREC 8, TREC 2010 RF, TREC Enterprise 2007 and finally ClueWeb 2012. That can be

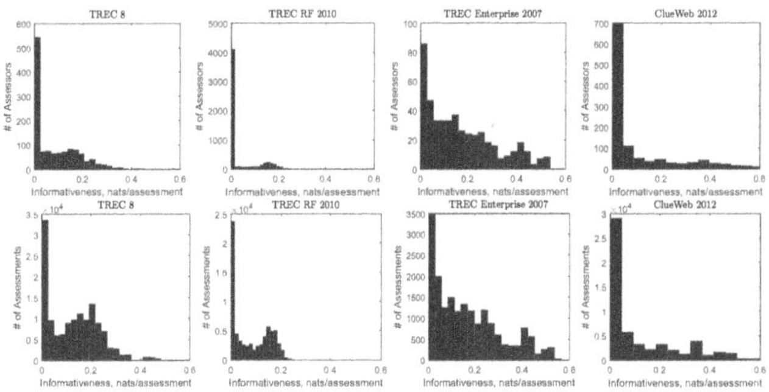

Figure 4: Top plots: the distribution of crowdworkers by their inferred informativeness, for each dataset. Bottom plots: the distribution of collected assessments by their expected informativeness.

explained by the granularity of the judgments provided by these experts: binary judgments, 3, 3 and 4 possible relevance grades for these collections, respectively. While perhaps all these assessors are good in ordering relevant documents vs non-relevant, the judgments on 4 grades scale have, intuitively, much more discriminatory power than binary relevance judgments (moreover, most of the judgments are "0" and only small fraction are "1" for the latter case). Also, note that informativeness of crowdworkers for TREC 2010 RF, on average, is lowest among all the collections: it may be because they were asked to report relevance on 3-grade scale, the least discriminative one.

We conclude the analysis of informativeness by showing macro-level statistics for each dataset (see Figure 4). The main observation is that we have too many poor quality workers bringing in too many poor quality judgments (particularly for ClueWeb 2012 dataset; for TREC 8 and TREC Enterprise 2007 we had a stricter rejection mechanism based on redundant trap questions). This is a good illustration of why measuring the informativeness of the assessors is so important in detecting unconscientious workers as early as possible, and perhaps to incentivize workers by paying for the amount of useful information they bring in to the system [28, 22].

3.8 Analysis: Document Difficulty

The label aggregation models that we propose in this paper include a per-document parameter ϵ_d which captures the degree of inter-assessor disagreement (adjusted for assessor reliability). Previously, we demonstrated empirically that this parameter may help improving the overall quality of aggregation. Now we explore its properties in more details, on the example of aggregating judgments of crowdworkers (not including expert labels) for TREC 8 collection. First, on Figure 6 (left) we explore the pattern of interaction between document difficulty and document relevance, both inferred from judgments (for convenience, the points are colored according to independent NIST labels). One can notice that relevant documents (as per NIST) tend to have a higher spread of difficulty (and several of them being the most difficult); the easy documents tend to be either certainly relevant or certainly non-relevant ones; the in-between documents are more difficult than average (as they cause more disagreement). Secondly, we show that the document difficulty we infer indeed represents an intrinsic property of the document, not just an assessing effect: we split the crowdworkers into two separate groups, so that

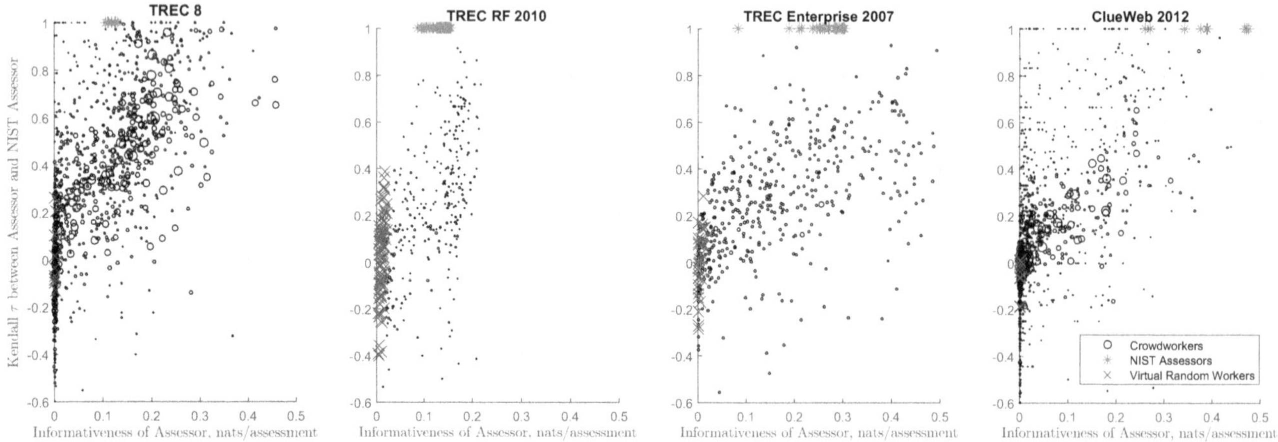

Figure 5: Measured informativeness of assessor vs. Kendall τ coefficient for rank correlation between the assessor and an expert. Each point corresponds to some assessor and some query. Circle size is proportional to the number of judgments made by the assessor for that query.

most of the documents have judgments from both groups. Then we train two separate models, one for each group, each model having independent estimates for each document difficulty. Few of them are plotted on Figure 6 (right): there is a positive correlation between two estimates of difficulty.

Separately, we report a weak correlation between inferred document difficulty and the time it took a crowdworker to complete the judgment (we recorded duration of each judgment while collecting crowdsourced labels).

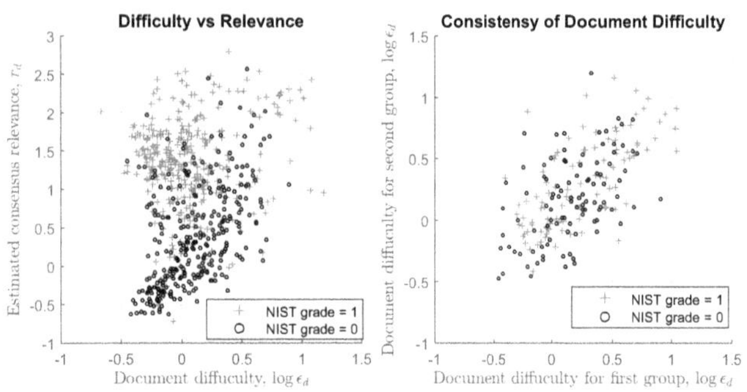

Figure 6: Document difficulties for TREC 8. Left: document difficulties plotted against estimated relevances. Right: document difficulties estimated from labels provided by one group of crowdworkers being consistent with those of another group.

4. LEARNING TO RANK WITH CROWDSOURCED ASSESSMENTS

Most of popular ranking algorithms (e.g. RankBoost, SVMRank, RankNet/LambdaRank/LambdaMART [3]) are designed to train on a collection of documents with reliable, high quality relevance labels. These algorithms internally learn from *pairwise preferences* between documents, usually these preferences being deterministically derived from nominal (ordinal) labels. That is, suppose the document d has nominal label l, and the document d' has nominal label l'; if $l < l'$, d will be considered as being *certainly less relevant* than d'.

We can imagine scenarios when we would like to use such powerful ranking algorithms, but it is not possible to certainly prefer one document to another. This is the case with document assessments in general, when there are multiple judgments for each document available, and these judgments can exhibit some degree of contradiction. It is particularly the case when the judgments are obtained from unreliable sources and therefore noise in the labels have to be processed prior to running the learning algorithm.

In this section we present a new LTR method based on extension of our label aggregation method, GDA-PW (eq. 8). For comparison, an overview is given for adaptation of existing learning to rank method, LambdaMART, to work on pairs of documents.

4.1 Baseline: LambdaMART on prob. pairs

For a given query and for each pair of documents (d, d'), LambdaMART [3, 16] models the probability $P_{dd'}$ that the document d should be ranked higher than document d' via a sigmoid function applied on the difference of the relevance scores, $s_d - s_{d'}$, returned by the model:

$$P_{dd'} \equiv \frac{1}{1 + e^{-(s_d - s_{d'})}}, P_{d'd} = 1 - P_{dd'}$$

Along with these *modeled* probabilities of pairwise preferences $P_{dd'}$, we have the desired or *target* ones: $\bar{P}_{dd'}$ and $\bar{P}_{d'd}$. The cost function of LambdaMART:

$$C = -\sum_{d \prec d'} |\Delta Z_{dd'}| \left(\bar{P}_{dd'} \log P_{dd'} + \bar{P}_{d'd} \log P_{d'd}\right) \quad (13)$$

where $\Delta Z_{dd'}$ is the change in the IR measure of interest (e.g. nDCG) given by swapping the rank positions of documents d and d' in the ranked list sorted by current model scores. In other words, we are interested in minimizing the average cross-entropy between target and modeled probability distributions, weighted by a list-wise component $|\Delta Z_{dd'}|$, which directs the ranking algorithm to focus more on the pairs of documents that are more influential with respect to a particular IR metric.

LambdaMART uses gradient boosting [8] to produce an

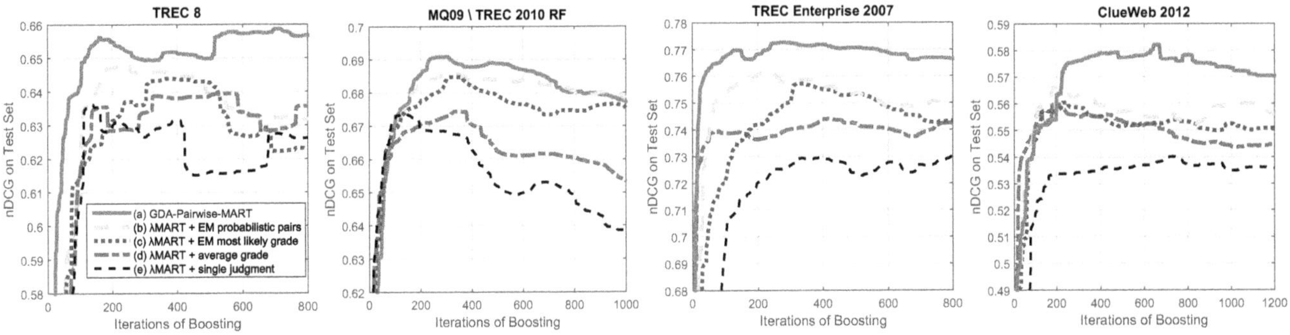

Figure 7: Comparison of various methods for learning to rank from crowdsourced assessments: (a) GDA-PW-MART; (b) modification of LambdaMART trained on probabilistic pairwise preferences from probability distributions returned by EM; (c) LambdaMART trained on the most likely grade returned by EM over multiple crowdsourced judgements; (d) LambdaMART trained on multiple crowdsourced judgments, averaged and rounded to closest integer; (e) LambdaMART trained on single (randomly picked) crowdsourced judgment for each document. Reported is performance (nDCG) on the testing sets of all four TREC collections.

ensemble of weak models (regression trees) that together form a strong model. The ensemble $F(x)$, mapping an input feature vector $x \in \mathbb{R}^n$ to the score s (such that for each document d: $s_d = F(x_d)$), is built in a greedy stage-wise manner by performing gradient descent in functional space (using the first and second derivatives of C with respect to the score of each document d: $\frac{\partial C}{\partial s_d}$ and $\frac{\partial^2 C}{\partial s_d^2}$). At each step m, the ensemble $F_{m-1}(x)$ from previous step is augmented with a new regression tree $h_m(x)$:

$$F_m(x) = F_{m-1}(x) + h_m(x),$$

where $h_m(x)$ is picked greedily so as to minimize cost function (13) which assures better ranking performance on the training set, in terms of a particular IR metric. While LambdaMART has been typically used to train on pairs of documents for which it is known that $\bar{P}_{dd'} = 0$ or $\bar{P}_{dd'} = 1$ (these "hard" preferences being usually based on ordinal judgments of expert assessors), it has been shown in [16] how to train LambdaMART on unreliable crowdsourcing assessments. The trick is to run EM (see section 3.3) to aggregate the assessments and compute the posterior probability distribution over true grades for each document d; then, having these probability distributions separately for documents d and d', one can compute the convolution probability that d is less/more relevant than d' : $p(d \prec d')$, $p(d' \prec d)$, and use them as target probabilities $\bar{P}_{dd'}$ and $\bar{P}_{d'd}$ for LambdaMART.

4.2 Learning to Rank by extending GDA-PW

Here we present how to adapt our label aggregation method GDA-PW (eq. 8) for learning to rank purposes by embedding it into gradient boosting framework [8]. Actually, the new method GDA-PW-MART is very similar to previously described LambdaMART with the difference it uses a cost function similar to GDA-PW:

$$C = -|\Delta Z_{dd'}| \sum_{(g,d,a),(g',d',a')\in OBS} \frac{1}{K} \log p(g|g', s_d, s_{d'}, \epsilon_d^*, \epsilon_{d'}^*, \theta_a^*, \theta_{a'}^*) \quad (14)$$

where ϵ_d^*, $\epsilon_{d'}^*$, θ_a^* and $\theta_{a'}^*$ are the estimates of document difficulty and assessor model parameters obtained as output of GDA-PW (eq. 8). The components of the cost function:

$$p(g|g', s_d, s_{d'}, \epsilon_d, \epsilon_{d'}, \theta_a, \theta'_a) = \quad (15)$$

$$= \frac{1}{Z_{aa'dd'}} \pi_g^a \mathcal{N}(s_d - s_{d'} | \mu_g^a - \mu_{g'}^{a'}, \sqrt{w_g^a w_{g'}^{a'} \epsilon_d \epsilon_{d'}}) \quad (16)$$

where $Z_{aa'dd'}$ is the normalization constant, and $s_d = F(x_d)$ is the scoring function for document d that appears instead of modeled true relevance r_d in (eq. 7). Intuitively, we would like to get, for each document d, a relevance score s_d as close as possible to the estimate of the true relevance r_d^* that we would have gotten by optimizing for (eq. 8). However, the exact equality is rarely achievable, as the relevance scores are constrained by the structure of the scoring function $F(x)$ (namely, by parameters of individual regression trees F is composed of). As such, one can think of minimizing (eq. 14) as a constrained version of (eq. 8), where the volatility of s_d (how much it can deviate from its optimal value, r_d^*) is determined by the confidence we have about r_d^*, being implicitly encoded in (eq. 8). For implementation, we rely on the existing LambdaMART framework (we build upon open source implementation, JForests [9]) to perform optimization for the new cost function (eq. 14).

4.3 Learning to Rank Results

In our experiments we compare the performance of our learning to rank method, GDA-PW-MART, with different LambdaMART models trained on the same training set but with differently aggregated crowdsourced labels. We evaluate the models on the same testing set (see Table 1, bottom) with the same expert judgments, in terms of nDCG. As one can easily see from Figure 7, our method largely outperforms the rest of LambdaMART baselines trained using various label aggregation methods.

The better performance of GDA-PW-MART, as compared to LambdaMART, we explain with the ability to handle uncertainties by the former algorithm. To have more intuition, consider the following example. Suppose we have four documents: d_1, d_2 for some query, and d_3, d_4 for another query, along with multiple assessments of their relevance. Suppose that after label aggregation phase, we obtain estimates of document relevance (along with standard deviations), let's say $r_{d_1} = 0.0 \pm 1.0, r_{d_2} = 0.0 \pm 1.0, r_{d_3} = 0.5 \pm 0.1$ and $r_{d_4} = 0.5 \pm 0.1$. In this example, we are much more confident about relevance of d_3 and d_4, while having a very little information (and high uncertainty) about relevance of d_1 and d_2. Since we can't prefer d_1 to d_2, nor can we prefer d_3 to d_4, all the target probabilities for LambdaMART will be equal: $\bar{P}_{d_1 d_2} = \bar{P}_{d_2 d_1} = \bar{P}_{d_3 d_4} = \bar{P}_{d_4 d_3} = 0.5$. As a result, LambdaMART will "push" equally hard on all four documents with the intention to equate scores $s_{d_1} = s_{d_2}$ and $s_{d_3} = s_{d_4}$, despite a very little evidence of d_1 and d_2 being equally relevant in reality. Unlike LambdaMART, our algorithm GDA-PW-MART will handle this problem by focusing on equating the scores $s_{d_3} = s_{d_4}$, while leaving s_{d_1} and s_{d_2} loose.

5. CONCLUSION AND FUTURE WORK

We have demonstrated a new framework for inference of true document relevance, difficulty, and assessor quality from crowdsourced assessments. It is simpler than previous approaches and with better performance. A document-pair likelihood model works best, via fast Newton-Raphson optimization. Both assessor and documents are realistically modeled. We estimate all the parameters from crowdsourcing data, demonstrating better inference of true relevances and for assessor quality. Our analysis shows that assessor quality can distinguish good crowdworkers, bad crowdworkers, experts, or random assessors.

An extension to pairwise aggregation method to learning to rank is given, and it shows a better performance compared to state of the art learning to rank algorithm LambdaMART on crowdsourced assessments, including a prior modification of the LambdaMART to better use crowdsourced assessments processed by EM algorithm.

Another appealing property of the proposed model with continuous latent relevance is that it could easily be extended to incorporate additional (continuous) signals of relevance, including machine-generated ones (retrieval model scores, output of pre-trained ranking algorithms involving many potentially useful features). The benefit would be in reduction of human efforts needed to achieve the same quality of results.

6. REFERENCES

[1] D. Andrich. A rating formulation for ordered response categories. *Psychometrika*, 43:561–573, 1978.

[2] Christopher M. Bishop. *Pattern Recognition and Machine Learning (Information Science and Statistics)*. 2006.

[3] C.J.C. Burges. From ranknet to lambdarank to lambdamart: An overview, 2010.

[4] M. Lease C. Buckley and M. D. Smucker. Overview of the TREC 2010 Relevance Feedback Track (Notebook). In *TREC*, 2010.

[5] O. Chapelle and Y. Chang. Yahoo! learning to rank challenge overview. *JMLR*, 14:1–24, 2011.

[6] X. Chen, P. N. Bennett, K. Collins-Thompson, and E. Horvitz. Pairwise ranking aggregation in a crowdsourced setting. In *WSDM*, pages 193–202, 2013.

[7] A. P. Dawid and A. M. Skene. Maximum likelihood estimation of observer error-rates using the em algorithm. *Applied Statistics*, 28(1):20–28, 1979.

[8] J. H. Friedman. Greedy function approximation: A gradient boosting machine. *Annals of Statistics*, 2000.

[9] Y. Ganjisaffar, R. Caruana, and C. V. Lopes. Bagging gradient-boosted trees for high precision, low variance ranking models. SIGIR, pages 85–94, 2011.

[10] M. Hosseini, I. J. Cox, N. Milic-Frayling, G. Kazai, and V. Vinay. On aggregating labels from multiple crowd workers to infer relevance of documents. In *ECIR*, 2012.

[11] V. E. Johnson. On bayesian analysis of multirater ordinal data: An application to automated essay grading. *Journal of the American Statistical Association*, 91(433):42–51, 1996.

[12] Chao L. and Y.-M. Wang. Truelabel + confusions: A spectrum of probabilistic models in analyzing multiple ratings. In *ICML*, pages 225–232, 2012.

[13] B. Lakshminarayanan and Y. W. Teh. Inferring ground truth from multi-annotator ordinal data: A probabilistic approach. arXiv:1305.0015, 2013.

[14] Q. Liu, J. Peng, and A. T Ihler. Variational inference for crowdsourcing. In *NIPS*, pages 692–700. 2012.

[15] G. N. Masters. A rasch model for partial credit scoring. *Psychometrika*, 47:149–174, 1982.

[16] P. Metrikov, J. Wu, J. Anderton, V. Pavlu, and J. A. Aslam. A modification of lambdamart to handle noisy crowdsourced assessments. In *ICTIR*, 2013.

[17] Paul Mineiro. Ordered values and mechanical turk. *http://www.machinedlearnings.com*, 2011.

[18] S. Niu, Y. Lan, J. Guo, X. Cheng, L. Yu, and G. Long. Listwise approach for rank aggregation in crowdsourcing. In *WSDM*, pages 253–262, 2015.

[19] W. H. Press, S. A. Teukolsky, W. T. Vetterling, and B. P. Flannery. *Numerical Recipes 3rd Edition: The Art of Scientific Computing*. 3 edition, 2007.

[20] V. C. Raykar, S. Yu, L. H. Zhao, G. H. Valadez, C. Florin, L. Bogoni, and L. Moy. Learning from crowds. *J. Mach. Learn. Res.*, 11:1297–1322, 2010.

[21] S. Rogers, M. Girolami, and T. Polajnar. Semi-parametric analysis of multi-rater data. *Statistics and Computing*, 20(3):317–334, 2010.

[22] V. Sheng, F. Provost, and P. Ipeirotis. Get another label? improving data quality and data mining using multiple, noisy labelers. In *KDD*, 2008.

[23] M. Smucker, G. Kazai, and M. Lease. Overview of the TREC 2013 Crowdsourcing Track. In *TREC*, 2014.

[24] M. D. Smucker, J. Allan, and B. Carterette. A comparison of statistical significance tests for information retrieval evaluation. In *CIKM*, 2007.

[25] J. S. Uebersax and W. M. Grove. A latent trait finite mixture model for the analysis of rating agreement. In *Biometrics*, December 1993.

[26] M. Venanzi, J. Guiver, G. Kazai, P. Kohli, and M. Shokouhi. Community-based bayesian aggregation models for crowdsourcing. In *WWW*, 2014.

[27] Maksims N. Volkovs and Richard S. Zemel. New learning methods for supervised and unsupervised preference aggregation. *JMLR*, 15:1135–1176, 2014.

[28] T. P. Waterhouse. Pay by the bit: An information-theoretic metric for collective human judgment. In *CSCW*, pages 623–638, 2013.

[29] J. Whitehill, P. Ruvolo, T. Wu, J. Bergsma, and J. R. Movellan. Whose vote should count more: Optimal integration of labels from labelers of unknown expertise. In *NIPS*, pages 2035–2043, 2009.

[30] D. Zhou, Q. Liu, J. C. Platt, and C. Meek. Aggregating ordinal labels from crowds by minimax conditional entropy. In *ICML*, 2014.

[31] D. Zhou, J. Platt, S. Basu, and Y. Mao. Learning from the wisdom of crowds by minimax entropy. In *NIPS*, 2012.

Weakly Supervised Natural Language Processing Framework for Abstractive Multi-Document Summarization

Peng Li
Computer Science and Engineering
University of Texas at Arlington
Arlington, TX, 76019
jerryli1981@gmail.com

Weidong Cai
School of Information Technologies
University of Sydney
NSW 2006, Australia
tom.cai@sydney.edu.au

Heng Huang *
Computer Science and Engineering
University of Texas at Arlington
Arlington, TX, 76019
heng@uta.edu

ABSTRACT

In this paper, we propose a new weakly supervised abstractive news summarization framework using pattern based approaches. Our system first generates meaningful patterns from sentences. Then, in order to precisely cluster patterns, we propose a novel semi-supervised pattern learning algorithm that leverages a hand-crafted list of topic-relevant keywords, which are the only weakly supervised information used by our framework to generate aspect-oriented summarization. After that, our system generates new patterns by fusing existing patterns and selecting top ranked new patterns via the recurrent neural network language model. Finally, we introduce a new pattern based surface realization algorithm to generate abstractive summaries. Automatic and manual evaluations demonstrate the effectiveness and advantages of our new methods. Code is available at: https://github.com/jerryli1981

Categories and Subject Descriptors

I.2.7 [**Natural Language Processing**]: Text analysis

General Terms

Algorithms, Experimentation

Keywords

Summarization; Recurrent Neural Network; Capped Norm Semi-Supervised Learning

1. INTRODUCTION

Multi-document summarization (MDS) problem has been mainly solved by the sentence extraction and compression based approaches [12, 4, 8, 13] for decades. However, the top systems so far were only considered as barely acceptable by the human assessment. Moreover, the empirical study [6] found the performance ceiling of pure sentence extraction approaches, which is much lower than human summaries and not much better than the current best automatic systems. Meanwhile, user behavior experiments conducted independently by [6, 20] demonstrated that human always do abstraction instead of simply selecting relevant sentences. More specifically, human tempt to interpret the text to understandable representation in their mind. After that, such representation is transformed to summary representation, also known as content selection. Finally, human generate summary text from summary representation [11]. Therefore, based on human cognitive process, we believe that a fully abstractive approach has the most potential for generating summaries at the level comparable to human summary.

There are some pioneer works towards abstractive summarization (see Section 2). For example, in meeting conversation analysis community, some pattern based approaches first extract patterns from human-authored meeting summaries. Then, their approaches select relevant patterns via clustering and ranking. Finally, the template filling is used to generate summary text. In this paper, we focus on a new and distinct problem – how to generate news events summaries using pattern based abstractive summarization framework. Unlike abstractive meeting conversation summarization, abstractive news summarization faces several unique challenges. First of all, there exist several informative long sentences that have complex syntax structure in each news corpus. Secondly, the approaches of meeting conversation summarization can leverage domain information such as dialogue act or meeting participants to help generate abstractive summaries. However, domain information in news events are not easy to be captured. Thirdly, the standard text generation technologies such as template filling may lead to worse readability in news summarization scenario.

To solve these challenges and achieve the goal of generating high quality abstractive summarization, we propose a new abstractive summarization framework which includes an enhanced pattern extraction module via integrating advanced information extraction technology, a novel robust semi-supervised pattern learning algorithm, and a novel surface realization algorithm for generating abstractive news summaries. More specifically, we first extract tuples by OpenIE [1], recognize argument and predicate's head via Stanford CoreNLP [2], and annotate the type of phrase head via SEMAFOR [3] and wordnet *etc.* Secondly, in order to precisely cluster patterns that better describe user interested information such as what happened, reason, damages and countermeasures, we propose a novel semi-supervised pattern learning algorithm based on a new capped norm based objective function, which can achieve more optimal semi-supervised learning results than existing approaches. Thirdly,

*Corresponding author.

Permission to make digital or hard copies of all or part of this work for personal or classroom use is granted without fee provided that copies are not made or distributed for profit or commercial advantage and that copies bear this notice and the full citation on the first page. Copyrights for components of this work owned by others than ACM must be honored. Abstracting with credit is permitted. To copy otherwise, or republish, to post on servers or to redistribute to lists, requires prior specific permission and/or a fee. Request permissions from Permissions@acm.org.
CIKM'15, October 19–23, 2015, Melbourne, Australia.
© 2015 ACM. ISBN 978-1-4503-3794-6/15/10 ...$15.00.
DOI: http://dx.doi.org/10.1145/2806416.2806494.

[1]http://openie.cs.washington.edu
[2]http://nlp.stanford.edu/software/corenlp.shtml
[3]http://www.ark.cs.cmu.edu/SEMAFOR/

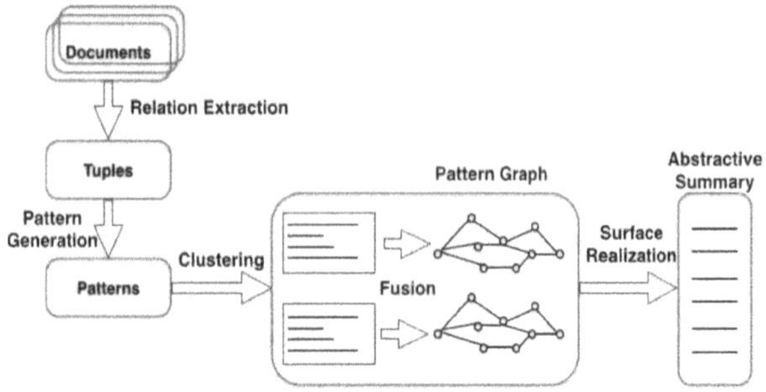

Figure 1: Abstractive news summarization framework flowchart

our system generate new patterns by fusing learned patterns and select top ranked new patterns and sentences via recurrent neural network language model. Finally, we use Integer Linear programming to select top ranked sentences cross clusters. Figure 1 shows the flowchart of our new abstractive summarization framework.

The key contributions in our work are summarized as follows:

1) The first weakly supervised abstractive news summarization system that only leverages a small number of hand-crafted keywords. Note that interpretation and generation phases of our system are purely unsupervised. The reason for us to use keywords for helping clustering patterns is that we hope to generate aspect-oriented summarization [4]. The goal of aspect-oriented summarization is to present the most important content to the user in a condensed form and a well-organized structure to satisfy the user's needs. For example, a summary about "Attacks" event should include aspects about what happened, when/where it happened, reasons, damages, rescue efforts, *etc*. Table 1 shows the aspects and keywords for the "Attacks" event. We use keywords to accomplish domain-specific abstractive summarization.

2) In order to improve pattern clustering purity, we make use of continuous word vectors derived from a recurrent neural network architecture [19]. The vector-space word representations learned from the language models were shown to capture syntactic and semantic regularities. The word relationships are characterized by vector offsets, where in the embedded space, all pairs of words sharing a particular relation are related by the same constant offset. Considering that this distributional semantic theory may benefit our pattern clustering component, we leverage word representations trained from large external data to differentiate patterns.

3) To effectively utilize hand-crafted keywords, we propose a new semi-supervised pattern learning model to group the patterns. Because the number of labeled data is very small, the supervised learning models and many semi-supervised learning (*e.g.* transductive support vector machine) methods cannot get good performance on the pattern labeling. Thus, we use the label propagation based semi-supervised learning model. The previous label propagation based semi-supervise learning models use the ℓ_2-norm loss, which cannot achieve the ideal semi-supervised learning results. Although the ℓ_0-norm based objective is desired in semi-supervised learning, it is an NP-hard problem. To reach the optimal labeling results, we propose a new capped norm based objective, which leads to more optimal results than traditional methods. We also derived a new and concise optimization algorithm to solve the proposed non-smooth and non-convex objective with proved convergence.

4) In order to control wrong facts and generate meaningful sentences given high quality pattern template, our system first filters out noisy templates by estimating the grammaticality with the recurrent neural network language model. After that, in order to generate meaningful sentences, we fuse tuples and select the best paths from the tuple graph that satisfies two ranking criteria. One criteria is the path should best match the most fluent pattern template, and the other criteria is the path should be the most fluent path compared with other paths. Finally, we use Integer Linear programming method to select top ranked facts cross clusters.

2. RELATED WORK

One line of related works focus on the task of news headline abstraction. Alfonseca *et al.* [1] proposed a framework to generate abstractive news headline. They trained a pattern clustering model via Noisy-OR Bayesian network and computed probability distribution of newly extracted patterns from testing news collection via two-step random walk on bayesian network. They selected the pattern with highest ranking score from the most representative pattern cluster as template to generate headline sentence. Pighin *et al.* [25] solved the same problem with the same framework. However, they found that the memory-based pattern extraction method is better than heuristic or sentence compression based pattern extraction.

Another line of research works focus on abstractive meeting conversation summarization. Murray *et al.* [20] followed the framework proposed by Jone [11] for generating abstractive summaries. In interpretation phase, they trained several classifiers to map sentences to domain dependent conversation ontology, then further mapped to predefined message patterns. After that, they utilized integer linear programming to select informative patterns in content selection phase. Finally, ontology based text plan and surface realization was implemented to generate abstractive summarization. Wang *et al.* [26] followed the same generation framework to solve meeting conversation summarization. In interpretation phase, they first clustered human-authored summary sentences and applied a multiple-sequence alignment algorithm to generate templates. In content selection phase, they identified the cluster describing a specific aspect and extracted all summary-worthy relation instances. In generation phase, the templates were filled with these relation instances, then found the top ranked instances to form final summary. Mehdad *et al.* [17] grouped similar sentences with supervised classifier and used the trained entailment graph to select representative sentences. After that, they built a word graph over similar sentences for fusion and selecting highly ranked paths as the final summaries. Oya *et al.* [24] extracted templates from clustered human-authored summaries and further got the generalization via template fusion in interpretation phase. In content selection phase, they borrowed training data to select the best templates. Finally, the templates were filled with matching labels to create summaries. Mehdad *et al.* [16] constructed word graph on human utterances and then selected the top ranked paths corresponding to the queries to generate the final summary.

Genest *et al.* [7] presented a fully abstractive news summarization approach. They pointed out a fully abstractive summarization framework should comprise analysis of the text, content selection and summary generation. However, they created event template manually with linguistic resources. Mausam *et al.* [15] automatically extracted relations from text without requiring a pre-specific vocabulary, by identifying relation phrases and associated arguments in arbitrary sentences. Following their work, Balasubramanian *et al.* [2] generated coherent event schemas. Zhang *et al.* [29] focused on Chinese poetry generation task. Their poetry generator jointly performs content selection and surface realization by learn-

[4] `http://www.nist.gov/tac/2010/Summarization/`

Aspects	Explanations	Hand-crafted keywords
WHAT	what happened	felony, lawlessness, assault, theft, rape, threat, *etc.*
WHEN	date, time, other temporal placement markers	January, Monday, today, yesterday, *etc.*
WHERE	physical location	nearby, street, road, highway, spot, blvd, *etc.*
PERPETRATORS	individuals or groups responsible for the attack	criminal, agent, offender, bomber, terrorist, *etc.*
WHY	reasons for the attack	motive, commit, intent, cause, means, reason, *etc.*
WHO AFFECTED	casualties (death, injury), or individuals otherwise negatively affected	casualty, death, loss, wound, hurt, missing, *etc.*
DAMAGES	damages caused by the attack	ruin, burn, property, possession, loss, *etc.*
COUNTERMEASURES	countermeasures, rescue efforts, prevention efforts, other reactions	prevent,, secure, surveillance, police, *etc.*

Table 1: Aspects for TAC 2010 guided summarization task, category 2: Attacks

ing representations of individual characters via the recurrent neural network.

3. PATTERN GENERATION

We observed that nearly half of the sentences comprise multiple aspects and complicated grammatical structures. In order to better interpret complicated sentences, we expect to extract meaningful relations and split structure-complicated sentences into simple ones. Table 2 illustrates the results of tuple extraction and pattern generation by our system.

In order to generate high quality patterns, we first utilize the sophisticated relation extraction tool such as openIE to generate tuples which have the triple form of {argument1, predicate, argument2}. After that, the head of arguments are replaced with their semantic types. There are two major challenges here. One is how to find argument head precisely if argument contains complicated phrase structure. The other is where to find type ontology and how to design type mapping rules effectively. To solve these challenges, we need linguistic resources and toolkits such as Framenet [5] and Stanford CoreNLP. To leverage Stanford CoreNLP annotation pipeline for pattern quality enhancement, we need map openIE annotation schema to Stanford CoreNLP annotation schema.

3.1 Preprocessing Tuples

Predicate in each relation tuple may share some common grammatical structures such as verb → noun → prep, verb, verb → prep, be→ verb, be→ verb→ prep, adv→ verb→ noun→ prep, be→ prep etc. However, we found OpenIE put prepositional token into argument 2. For example, {"he", "stood two hours", "after killing three of them"}. Therefore, when facing these special cases, we move the preposition into predicate. In order to locate prepositional word, two grammatical relations [6] are used with heuristic rules. One is "pobj" relation, the other is "pcomp" relation. After reassembling, the tuple may become {"he", "stood two hours after", "killing three of them"}.

3.2 Token Mapping

Before argument head extraction via Stanford CoreNLP toolkit, we need map string tokens in each tuple to Stanford IndexedWord objects. The mapping is not easy to implement because openIE and Stanford CoreNLP use different tokenization algorithm that may result in tokenization inconsistence. For example, Stanford CoreNLP treats "Us-led" as one token but openIE just considers "led" as tuple's predicate. We therefore use the token offset as a bridge to conduct token mapping due to tokens in each tuple may not be continuous. More specifically, our system first generates relation tuples and core annotations including pos, lemma, NER, parse tree and semantic dependency graph, and stores token start offset to IndexedWord mappings. If the mapping relation can't be found due to tokenization inconsistence, we use heuristic rules to match correct start offset. If original sentence doesn't contain argument mention due to token order inconsistence, we search begin position in substring via the regular expression and ignore the isolated tokens. After mapping between tuple tokens and IndexedWord objects, we can fully make use of semantic dependencies between tuple tokens to extract phrase head.

3.3 Phrase Head Extraction

Argument and predicate head extraction module is quite important for later head type recognition and pattern clustering. The main challenge here is how to extract head without loosing readability. The arguments and predicate in each relation tuple may have complicated phrase structure. For example, {"The suspect", "apparently called his wife saying", "he was acting out in revenge for something"}, {"Kirchner", "told The Associated Press", "that six people were killed"}. The argument 2 of these two tuples both contain subsentence or clause. Oya *et al.* [24] treated the right most nouns as the head nouns, but this heuristic rule is not always true. Paper [2] used several parts of speech based heuristic rules to conduct argument head extraction. However, we found this approach didn't work very well especially when facing such complicated phrase structures in tuples. We found phrase head extraction on complicated phrases may destroy tuple readability. Therefore, when facing argument mention contains grammatical relation like "nsubj", "nsubjpass" or "ccomp", we just ignore it. This kind of ignorance would make sense due to the fact that openIE will find {"six people", "were", "killed"} relation tuple occasionally.

After the above step, we conduct depth first search on parser tree with the help of CollinHeadFinder rules to locate phrase head. For those heads can't be recognized by CollinHeadFinder, we design heuristic rules on semantic dependency graph to locate potential heads. For example, if grammatical relation is one of {"det", "amod", "poss", "num", "advmod" }, then the governor token is the head. If grammatical relation is one of {"tmod", "nn"}, then the dependent is the head.

3.4 Head Type Tagging

After phrase head extraction, we construct patterns via replacing the heads with their types. Standford NER as the state of

[5] https://framenet.icsi.berkeley.edu/fndrupal/
[6] http://nlp.stanford.edu/software/dependencies_manual.pdf

Aspects	Tuple	Pattern	Simple Sentence
What happened	{"girl", "killed by", "gunman"}	{"PERSON", "killed by", "PROTAGONIST"}	Five girls killed by a gunman inside their one-room, tiny schoolhouse.
Countermeasures	{"buggies", "carried", "mourners"}	{"CONTAINER", "carry", "ACT"}	34 buggies and carriages carried mourners.
Where	{"girls", "inside", "schoolhouse"}	{"PERSION", "inside", "LOCATION"}	five girls inside tiny one-room schoolhouse.

Table 2: An example of splitting structure-complicated sentence into structure-simple sentences via tuples and patterns. Original sentence is "A procession of 34 buggies and carriages carried mourners to a hilltop cemetery Thursday as the Amish community buried the first of five girls killed by a gunman inside their tiny one-room schoolhouse."

the art type tagging tool have good performance on a small number of types. However, we found it can't recognize the tokens like "man", "girl", "chilldren" as person. Also we recognize that the SEMAFOR as the state-of-the-art semantic role labeling tool didn't work well to recognize pronoun. In our case, some argument heads are not name entities, and they are concepts such as "school", "man". Therefore, a combination of several tools to conduct type tagging is a good choice.

Balasubramanian *et al.* [2] used wordnet and Stanford NER combination to conduct head type tagging. They manually selected 29 semantic types from WordNet. Because they built event schema in open domain, their types are too general for our task. Alfonseca *et al.* [1] used Wikipedia and Freebase to annotate head with all its Freebase types and got better results. However, their tagging tool is company private property, not for sharing. Inspired by Chen *et al.* [3] on slot filling, we use SEMAFOR semantic parser based on framenet combined with Stanford NER and wordnet to recognize argument head's type. In our implementation, Stanford NER has priority to find person, location, time and date. For those heads can't be recognized by Stanford NER, we search Framenet and try to match frame elements via SEMAFOR tool. Note that SEMAFOR may produce noisy when labeling. For example, Tuple {"he", "picked up", "milk"} will generate pattern like {"person", "pick up", "food"}, {"a truck", "picked up", "milk"} will generate pattern like {"vehicle", "pick up", "chosen"}. The same "milk" generates two different labels. Therefore, We use wordnet, DBpedia and freebase to filter wrong labeling.

4. PATTERN LABELING

After generating patterns, we use hand-crafted keywords to group aspect relevant patterns for later template generation. In order to precisely group patterns that better describe user interested event aspects such as what happened, reason, damages and countermeasures, we propose a novel semi-supervised pattern labeling algorithm.

4.1 Construct Pattern Feature Vector

We use word2vec [7] as the word embedding resources. It is generated by learning a recurrent neural network [19]. The recurrent neural network language models use the context history to include long-distance information. The word relationships are characterized by vector offsets, where in the embedded space, all pairs of words sharing a particular relation are related by the same constant offset. Considering that this distributional semantic theory may benefit our pattern clustering task, we leverage word representations trained from large external data to generate pattern feature vectors. Word2vec contains pre-trained vectors trained on part of Google News dataset(about 100 billion words). The model contains 300-dimensional vectors for 3 million words and phrases.

Recall that our pattern has the triple form of {arg1Type, predicate, arg2Type}. Therefore, we concatenate the vectors of arg1Type, head of predicate and arg2Type to form pattern feature vector. On the other hand, we use merge strategy to construct labeled feature vectors of hand crafted keywords.

4.2 Capped Norm Based Semi-Supervised Pattern Learning Model

In order to accurately label the patterns via the hand crafted keywords, we propose a novel capped norm based semi-supervised pattern learning model. Given input $\{(\mathbf{x}_1, \mathbf{y}_1), \cdots, (\mathbf{x}_n, \mathbf{y}_n)\}$ where $X = \{\mathbf{x}_1, \ldots, \mathbf{x}_c, \mathbf{x}_{c+1}, \cdots, \mathbf{x}_n\} \subset \Re^d$ is the pattern set, the first c elements are hand crafted keywords with labels as $\{\mathbf{y}_1, \ldots, \mathbf{y}_c\}$ where $\mathbf{y}_i$ is a label indicator vector of size c containing the labels assigned to the pattern $\mathbf{x}_i$: $\mathbf{y}_i(k) = 1$ if $\mathbf{x}_i$ belongs to the k-th class, and 0 otherwise. Our goal is to predict the label sets $\{\mathbf{y}_{c+1}, \cdots, \mathbf{y}_n\}$ for the unlabeled patterns $\{\mathbf{x}_{c+1}, \cdots, \mathbf{x}_n\}$.

Traditional graph based semi-supervised learning model solves the following problem [31, 30]:

$$\min_Q Tr(Q^T L Q) + \gamma Tr(Q - Y)^T (Q - Y), \qquad (1)$$

where L is the Laplacian matrix and $Q \in \Re^{n \times c}$ is the predicted decision values matrix to be solved. Given an affinity matrix W, the Laplacian is defined as $L = D - W$, where $D = \text{diag}(W\mathbf{e})$, $\mathbf{e} = (1, \ldots, 1)^T$. The way to learn affinity matrix will effect the final results, thus in our experiments we test two popularly used methods: heat kernel and cosine similarity.

We can further re-write problem (1) as:

$$\min_Q \sum_{i,j=1}^{n} W_{ij} ||\mathbf{q}^i - \mathbf{q}^j||_2^2 + \gamma Tr(Q - Y)^T (Q - Y). \qquad (2)$$

The ideal solution Q for semi-supervised learning is that $\mathbf{q}^i = \mathbf{q}^j$ if $\mathbf{x}_i$ and $\mathbf{x}_j$ belong to the same class, which means many rows of Q are equal and thus has ideal class indicators. That is to say, it is desired that $||\mathbf{q}^i - \mathbf{q}^j||_0 = 0$ for many pairs (i, j) (the ℓ_0-norm of $\mathbf{w}$ is a count of the nonzero elements in $\mathbf{w}$). However, the ℓ_0-norm minimization problem is an NP-hard problem. Although many recent works used ℓ_1-norm to approximate ℓ_0-norm [23], the gap between them is still large. To solve this problem and obtain a more ideal solution Q, we propose to use the capped norm based loss function [27, 28, 10] and solve the following problem for semi-supervised learning:

$$\min_Q \sum_{i,j=1}^{n} W_{ij} \min\{||\mathbf{q}^i - \mathbf{q}^j||_2, \varepsilon\} + \gamma Tr(Q - Y)^T (Q - Y), \qquad (3)$$

[7] https://code.google.com/p/word2vec

Algorithm 1 The algorithm to solve the proposed capped norm semi-supervised learning model as in (3).

Input The original weight matrix $W \in \Re^{n\times n}$. D is a diagonal matrix with the i-th diagonal element as $\sum_j W_{ij}$. The initial label matrix $Y \in \Re^{n\times c}$.
$t = 1$. Initialize $Q_t \in \Re^{n\times c}$ using standard semi-supervised learning result as in Eq. (1);
while Not Converge **do**

1. Calculate $\widetilde{W}_{ij} = \begin{cases} \frac{W_{ij}}{2\|\mathbf{q}^i-\mathbf{q}^j\|_2}, & \|\mathbf{q}^i - \mathbf{q}^j\|_2 \le \varepsilon \\ 0, & otherwise \end{cases}$;
2. Calculate $\widetilde{L}_t = \widetilde{D}_t - \widetilde{W}_t$, where $\widetilde{D}_t$ is a diagonal matrix with the i-th diagonal element as $\sum_j (\widetilde{W}_t)_{ij}$;
3. Calculate $Q_{t+1} = (\widetilde{L}_t + I)^{-1} Y$;
4. $t = t + 1$;

end while
Output The decision value matrix $Q_t \in \Re^{n\times c}$.

where $\varepsilon > 0$ is a small parameter and can be automatically selected, *e.g.* we can consider 5% of data as noise. In recent work [27, 28], the capped ℓ_1-norm was used to approximate the ℓ_0-norm with better results than ℓ_1-norm. When our new objective is minimized, the capped norm leads $\|\mathbf{q}^i - \mathbf{q}^j\|_2 = 0$ for many pairs (i, j) such that the ideal label assignments are achieved.

The other key challenge is to solve the above non-smooth and non-convex objective. All previous works used tedious algorithms to solve capped norm minimization problem. Based on our previous re-weighted optimization method [21, 22], we propose a novel, concise, and efficient algorithm to solve the proposed new objective.

Taking the derivative of Eq. (3) *w.r.t.* Q, and setting the derivative to zero, we have:

$$\widetilde{L}Q + (Q - Y) = \mathbf{0} \Rightarrow Q = (\widetilde{L} + I)^{-1} Y, \quad (4)$$

where the new Laplacian matrix $\widetilde{L} = \widetilde{D} - \widetilde{W}$ and the re-weighted weight matrix $\widetilde{W}$ is defined by

$$\widetilde{W}_{ij} = \begin{cases} \frac{W_{ij}}{2\|\mathbf{q}^i-\mathbf{q}^j\|_2}, & \|\mathbf{q}^i - \mathbf{q}^j\|_2 \le \varepsilon \\ 0, & otherwise \end{cases} \quad (5)$$

$\widetilde{D}$ is a diagonal matrix with the i-th diagonal element as $\sum_j \widetilde{W}_{ij}$. Note that $(\widetilde{L} + I)^{-1}$ is dependent on Q, we propose an iterative algorithm to obtain the solution Q such that Eq. (4) is satisfied. The algorithm is guaranteed to converge to a local optimum, which will be proved in the next subsection. The algorithm is summarized in Algorithm 1.

4.3 Convergence Analysis

To prove the convergence of the Algorithm 1, we need the following lemma:

LEMMA 1. *For any nonzero vectors $\mathbf{q}, \mathbf{q}_t \in \Re^d$, the following inequality holds:*

$$\|\mathbf{q}\|_2 - \frac{\|\mathbf{q}\|_2^2}{2\|\mathbf{q}_t\|_2} \le \|\mathbf{q}_t\|_2 - \frac{\|\mathbf{q}_t\|_2^2}{2\|\mathbf{q}_t\|_2}. \quad (6)$$

PROOF. Beginning with an obvious inequality $-(\|\mathbf{q}\|_2 - \|\mathbf{q}_t\|_2)^2 \le 0$, we have

$$\begin{aligned} &-(\|\mathbf{q}\|_2 - \|\mathbf{q}_t\|_2)^2 \le 0 \Rightarrow 2\|\mathbf{q}\|_2\|\mathbf{q}_t\|_2 - \|\mathbf{q}\|_2^2 \le \|\mathbf{q}_t\|_2^2 \\ &\Rightarrow \|\mathbf{q}\|_2 - \frac{\|\mathbf{q}\|_2^2}{2\|\mathbf{q}_t\|_2} \le \|\mathbf{q}_t\|_2 - \frac{\|\mathbf{q}_t\|_2^2}{2\|\mathbf{q}_t\|_2} \end{aligned} \quad (7)$$

which completes the proof. □

The following theorem guarantees that the Algorithm 1 will converge to the local optimum of the problem (3):

THEOREM 1. *The Algorithm 1 will monotonically decrease the objective of the problem (3) in each iteration, and converge to the local optimum of the problem.*

PROOF. According to the Step 3 in the algorithm 1, we know that:

$$\begin{aligned} Q_{t+1} = \arg\min_{Q} \sum_{i,j=1}^{n} \widetilde{W}_{ij} \min\{\|\mathbf{q}^i - \mathbf{q}^j\|_2, \varepsilon\} \\ + \gamma Tr(Q - Y)^T (Q - Y). \end{aligned} \quad (8)$$

Because $\widetilde{W}_{ij} = \begin{cases} \frac{W_{ij}}{2\|\mathbf{q}^i-\mathbf{q}^j\|_2}, & \|\mathbf{q}^i - \mathbf{q}^j\|_2 \le \varepsilon \\ 0, & otherwise \end{cases}$, we have:

$$\begin{aligned} &\sum_{k,l\in\mathcal{C}} \frac{W_{lk}\|\mathbf{q}_{t+1}^l - \mathbf{q}_{t+1}^k\|_2^2}{2\|\mathbf{q}_t^l - \mathbf{q}_t^k\|_2} + \gamma Tr(Q_{t+1} - Y)^T (Q_{t+1} - Y) \\ &\le \sum_{l,k\in\mathcal{C}} \frac{W_{lk}\|\mathbf{q}_t^l - \mathbf{q}_t^k\|_2^2}{2\|\mathbf{q}_t^l - \mathbf{q}_t^k\|_2} + \gamma Tr(Q_t - Y)^T (Q_t - Y), \end{aligned} \quad (9)$$

where $\mathcal{C}$ is the set in which $\|\mathbf{q}^l - \mathbf{q}^k\|_2 \le \varepsilon$ for all $k, l \in \mathcal{C}$.

Based on Lemma 1, we have:

$$\|\mathbf{q}_{t+1}^l - \mathbf{q}_{t+1}^k\|_2 - \frac{\|\mathbf{q}_{t+1}^l - \mathbf{q}_{t+1}^k\|_2^2}{2\|\mathbf{q}_t^l - \mathbf{q}_t^k\|_2} \le \|\mathbf{q}_t^l - \mathbf{q}_t^k\|_2 - \frac{\|\mathbf{q}_t^l - \mathbf{q}_t^k\|_2^2}{2\|\mathbf{q}_t^l - \mathbf{q}_t^k\|_2},$$

for any pair (l, k). Thus, for the set $\mathcal{C}$, we have:

$$\begin{aligned} &\sum_{k,l\in\mathcal{C}} W_{lk}(\|\mathbf{q}_{t+1}^l - \mathbf{q}_{t+1}^k\|_2^2 - \frac{\|\mathbf{q}_{t+1}^l - \mathbf{q}_{t+1}^k\|_2^2}{2\|\mathbf{q}_t^l - \mathbf{q}_t^k\|_2}) \\ &\le \sum_{k,l\in\mathcal{C}} W_{lk}(\|\mathbf{q}_t^l - \mathbf{q}_t^k\|_2^2 - \frac{\|\mathbf{q}_t^l - \mathbf{q}_t^k\|_2^2}{2\|\mathbf{q}_t^l - \mathbf{q}_t^k\|_2}). \end{aligned} \quad (10)$$

Summing Eq. (9) and Eq. (10) on both sides, we obtain:

$$\begin{aligned} &\sum_{k,l\in\mathcal{C}} W_{ij}\|\mathbf{q}_{t+1}^l - \mathbf{q}_{t+1}^k\|_2 + \gamma Tr(Q_{t+1} - Y)^T (Q_{t+1} - Y) \\ &\le \sum_{k,l\in\mathcal{C}} W_{ij}\|\mathbf{q}_t^l - \mathbf{q}_t^k\|_2 + \gamma Tr(Q_t - Y)^T (Q_t - Y), \end{aligned} \quad (11)$$

which can be re-written as:

$$\begin{aligned} &\sum_{i,j=1}^{n} \widetilde{W}_{ij} \min\{\|\mathbf{q}_{t+1}^i - \mathbf{q}_{t+1}^j\|_2, \varepsilon\} + \gamma Tr(Q_{t+1} - Y)^T (Q_{t+1} - Y) \\ &\le \sum_{i,j=1}^{n} \widetilde{W}_{ij} \min\{\|\mathbf{q}_t^i - \mathbf{q}_t^j\|_2, \varepsilon\} + \gamma Tr(Q_t - Y)^T (Q_t - Y). \end{aligned} \quad (12)$$

Thus the Algorithm 1 will monotonically decrease the objective of the problem (3) in each iteration t. In the convergence, Q_t and $\widetilde{L}_t$ will satisfy the Eq. (4). As the problem (3) is a non-convex problem, satisfying the Eq. (4) indicates that Q_t is the a local optimum solution to the problem (3). Therefore, the Algorithm 3 will converge to the local optimum of the problem (3). □

5. PATTERN FUSION

In this step, we merge duplicated and complementary patterns to build templates in each cluster. Duplicates may caused by two reasons. One reason is that the same sentence generates duplicated tuples. For example, the two tuples {"they", "refused to divulge", "details"} and {"they", "refused", "to divulge details"} extracted from the same sentence. The other reason is different sentences generate the similar tuples. For example, {"a steady job", "working", "nights"} and {"he", "held", "a steady job working nights"} extracted from different sentences.

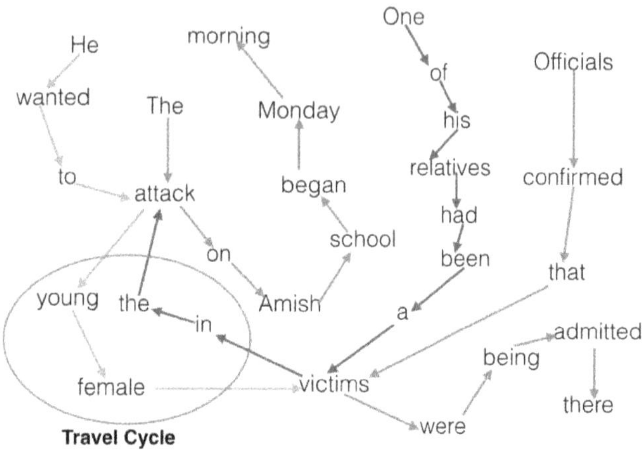

Figure 2: A word graph with cycle generated by tuple fusion

We follow graph-based pattern fusion approach proposed by Oya *et al.* [24]. Instead of using general pattern form of {arg1Type, predicate, arg2Type}, we use specific pattern form in which only replace head of arguments with it's type and keep other parts. Then, a graph is constructed by iteratively adding patterns to it. A node is added to the graph for each word in the pattern, and words adjacent are linked with directed edges. When adding a new pattern, a word from the pattern is merged to an existing node in the graph providing that they have the same POS tag and they share the same lemma. Note that some words such as "he" and "his" have the same POS tag "PRP" and the same lemma, but they should not be merged together. Also some words like "the", "to", "of" and "have" should not be merged together, unless it may lead to produce so many noisy paths. After word graph is constructed, we enumerate all paths from start node to end node. Figure 2 illustrates the word graph generated via tuple fusion instead of pattern fusion for convenience. We can see that the graph may contain cycles. Therefore, when the cycle appears, a backtracking procedure need to be executed.

6. SUMMARY GENERATION

In order to control wrong facts and generate meaningful sentences given pattern template, our system first filters out noisy templates by estimating the grammaticality using the recurrent neural network language model. Then, in order to generate meaningful sentences, we fuse tuples and select the best paths from tuple graph that satisfy two ranking criteria. One criterion is the path should best match the most fluent pattern template, and the other criterion is the path should be the most fluent path compared with other paths. Finally, we use Integer Linear programming to select top ranked facts cross clusters.

In order to filter out noisy templates, we leverage a neural network language model to rank the generated paths and select the top ranked one. We employ a character-based recurrent neural network language model [18] (RLM) interpolated with a Kneser-Ney trigram and find the n-best candidates with a stack decoder.

6.1 Recurrent Neural Network Language Model

A RLM models the probability $P(S)$ that the sequence of words S occurs in a given language. Let $S = w_1, \ldots ,w_m$ be a sequence of m words:

$$P(S) = \prod_{i=1}^{m} P(w_i|w_{1:i-1}) \,. \tag{13}$$

The model explicitly computes without simplifying assumptions the conditional distributions $P(w_i|w_{1:i-1})$. The architecture of an RLM comprises a vocabulary V that contains the words w_i of the language as well as three transformations: an input vocabulary transformation $\mathbf{I} \in \mathcal{R}^{q*|V|}$, a recurrent transformation $\mathbf{R} \in \mathcal{R}^{q*q}$ and an output vocabulary transformation $\mathbf{O} \in \mathcal{R}^{|V|*q}$. For each word $w_k \in V$, we indicate by $i(w_k)$ its index in V and by $v(w_k) \in \mathcal{R}^{|V|*1}$ an all zero vector with only $v(w_k)_{i(w_k)} = 1$.

For a word w_i, the result of $\mathbf{I} \cdot v(w_i) \in \mathcal{R}^{q*1}$ is the input continuous representation of w_i. The parameter q governs the size of the word representation. The prediction proceeds by successively applying the recurrent transformation $\mathbf{R}$ to the word representations and predicting the next word at each step. In detail, the computation of each $P(w_i|w_{1:i-1})$ proceeds recursively. For $1 < i < m$,

$$h_1 = \sigma(\mathbf{I} \cdot v(w_1)) \tag{14}$$

$$h_{i+1} = \sigma(\mathbf{R} \cdot h_i + \mathbf{I} \cdot v(w_{i+1})) \tag{15}$$

$$o_{i+1} = \mathbf{O} \cdot h_i \,. \tag{16}$$

In above equations, σ is a nonlinear function such as $\tanh$. The conditional distribution is given by:

$$P(w_i = v|w_{1:i-1}) = \frac{\exp(o_{i,v})}{\sum_{v=1}^{V} \exp(o_{i,v})} \,. \tag{17}$$

The RLM is trained by back propagation through time [18]. The error in the predicted distribution calculated at the output layer is backpropagated through the recurrent layers and cumulatively added to the errors of the previous predictions for a given number d of steps.

6.2 Sentence Ranking

In order to find the best tuple path on tuple graph, we have devised the following ranking strategy. First, we prune the paths in which a verb does not exist. Then we rank other paths as follows:

Pattern Coverage

To identify the summary sentence with the highest coverage of select pattern, we propose a score to measure the similarity between pattern path and tuple path.

$$C(S) = \sum_{x_a \in Pa, x_b \in Tu} Sim(x_a, x_b) \tag{18}$$

Note that distributional semantics can be captured by continuous space word representation. We transform each token x into its embedding vector $\mathbf{x}$ by pre-trained distributed word representations, and then the similarity between a pair of x_a and x_b can be computed as their cosine similarity.

Fluency

In order to improve the grammaticality of the generated sentence, we estimate the grammaticality of generated paths $F(S)$ using the recurrent neural network language model.

In order to generate an abstractive sentence that combines the scores above, we employ a simple linear ranking model. The purpose of such a model is: 1) to cover the pattern optimally; 2) to generate a more readable and grammatical sentence. Therefore, the final ranking score of the path S is calculated over the normalized scores as:

$$Score(S) = \alpha \cdot C(S) + \beta \cdot F(S)\,, \tag{19}$$

where α and β are the coefficient factors to tune the ranking score and they sum up to 1. In order to rank the tuple graph paths, we select all the paths that contain at least one verb, and re-rank them using our proposed ranking function to find the best path as the summary of the original patterns in each cluster.

6.3 Sentence Selection

After sentence ranking, we prepare for the final abstractive summary generation. In this step, we select one sentence from each cluster. We use Integer Linear Programming to optimize a global objective function for sentence selection. We formulate the optimization problem based on sentence ranking information. More specifically, we would like to select exactly one sentence which receives the highest possible ranking score from each cluster subject to some constraints. We employed lp_solver [8], an efficient mixed integer programming solver using the Branch-and-Bound algorithm to select sentences.

Assume that there are in total K clusters in an event topic. For each cluster j, there are in total R ranked sentences. The variables S_{jl} is a binary indicator of the sentence. That is, S_{jl}= 1 if the sentence is included in the final summary, and S_{jl} = 0 otherwise. l is the ranked position of the sentence in this cluster.

Objective Function

Top ranked sentences are the most relevant corresponding to the related user interested aspects which we want to include in the final summary. Thus we try to minimize the ranks of the sentences to improve the overall responsiveness:

$$\min(\sum_{j=1}^{K}\sum_{l=1}^{R_j} l \cdot S_{jl})\,. \tag{20}$$

Exclusivity Constraints

To prevent redundancy in each aspect, we choose one sentence from each general or specific aspect cluster. The constraint is formulated as follows:

$$\sum_{l=1}^{R_j} S_{jl} = 1 \qquad \forall j \in \{1 \ldots K\}\,. \tag{21}$$

Length Constraints

We add the following constraint to ensure that the length of the final summary is limited to L words. len_{jl} is the length of S_{jl}.

$$\sum_{j=1}^{K}\sum_{l=1}^{R_j} len_{jl} \cdot S_{jl} \leq L \tag{22}$$

7. EXPERIMENTAL RESULTS

7.1 Data Set Description

We use TAC2011 Summarization task [9] data set for the summary content evaluation. This data set provides 44 events. Each event falls into a predefined event topic. Each specific event includes an event statement and 20 relevant newswire articles which have been divided into 2 sets: Document Set A and Document Set B. Each document set has 10 documents, and all the documents in Set A chronologically precede the documents in Set B. We just use document Set A for our task. Assessors wrote model summaries for each event, so we can compare our automatic generated summaries with the model summaries.

7.2 Automatic Evaluation

We use the ROUGE [14] metric for measuring the summarization system performance. Ideally, a summarization criterion should be more recall oriented. So the average recall of ROUGE-1, ROUGE-2, ROUGE-SU4 were computed by running ROUGE-1.5.5 with stemming but no removal of stop words. We compare our method with the following baseline methods.

Baseline 1

In this baseline, we compare our method with traditional ranking and selection extractive summary generation framework [5] to show that the abstractive framework is superior to extractive framework in aspect-oriented summarization scenario. In implementation, we follow LexRank based sentence ranking combined with greedy sentence selection methods. The similarity graph building threshold is 0.2, damping factor is 0.2 and error tolerance for Power Method in LexRank is 0.1. After ranking sentences, we select top ranked sentences as long as the redundancy score (similarity) between a candidate sentence and current summary is under 0.5. This is repeated until the summary reaches a 100 word length limit.

Baseline 2

In this baseline, in order to prove the effectiveness of pattern fusion and surface realization, we replace our pattern fusion and surface realization with natural language generation technology. After grouping patterns via clustering, we choose the pattern that closest to centroid of the cluster. Then realize sentences with these representative patterns via natural language generation technology. More specifically, due to each pattern contains predicate, in order to generate sentence, we need generate noun phrase (See Algorithm 2) to build subject and generate verb phrase(See Algorithm 3) to build object. Then combine subject, predicate and object to become a new sentence. We use Simplenlg[10] which is a simple Java API designed to facilitate the realization of sentences.

Baseline 3

In this baseline, we try to compare our capped norm based semi-supervised learning model with the semi-supervised learning method using gaussian fields and harmonic functions (Har) [31] and the semi-supervised clustering with local and global consistency (LGC) [30].

To construct weight matrix, we use Heat Kernel (HK) [9] and Cosine similarity. Equation 23 illustrates how to construct weight matrix with Heat Kernel.

$$w_{i,j} = \exp(-\sum_{d=1}^{m}\frac{(x_{id}-x_{jd})^2}{\sigma_d^2})\,, \tag{23}$$

where x_{id} is the d-th component of pattern x_i represented as a continuous vector $x_i \in \mathcal{R}^m$ and $\sigma_1, \ldots, \sigma_m$ are length scale hyper parameters for each dimension.

For fair comparison, all the baselines have the summary length no more then 100 words. In Table 3, we show the average ROUGE metrics of 44 summaries generated by our method and three baseline methods. Note that we present the best ROUGE scores after trying different σ settings.

[8]http://lpsolve.sourceforge.net/5.5/

[9]http://www.nist.gov/tac/2011/Summarization/

[10]http://code.google.com/p/simplenlg/

Algorithm 2 Generate Noun Phrase

```
NPPhraseSpec np, tmpNp;
PPPhraseSpec pp;
Stack stack
stack.add(head)
while !stack.isEmpty() do
  children = grpah.adj(head);
  for all td in children do
    GrammaticalRelation gr = td.reln()
    if gr = "prep" then
      pp = generatePrepP(td)
      np.setPostModifier(pp)
    else if gr = "nn" or gr = "conj" then
      tmpNp = generateNP(graph, td.dep())
      np.setPostModifier(tmpNp)
    else if gr = "det" or gr = "num" or gr = "amod" then
      np.setPostModifier(td.dep())
    else
      continue
    end if
  end for
end while
```

Algorithm 3 Generate Verb Phrase

```
VPPhraseSpec vp
NPPhraseSpec dirobjNp, indirObjNp
vp.sertVerb(verb)
if object! = null then
  dirobjNp = generateNP(graph, object)
  vp.setObject(dirobjNp)
  children = grpah.adj(verb);
  for all td in children do
    GrammaticalRelation gr = td.reln()
    if gr = "iobj" then
      indirObjNp = generateNP(graph, td.dep())
      vp.IndirectObject(indirObjNp)
      break
    end if
  end for
else
  for all td in children do
    GrammaticalRelation gr = td.reln()
    if gr = "ccomp" then
      vp.setPostModifier(complement)
      break
    end if
  end for
end if
```

Results and Discussions

We compared our capped norm based semi-supervised learning model to two other popularly used semi-supervised learning methods: Harmonic function (Har) [31] and LGC [30]. In the comparison results, our new model consistently outperforms two other methods. Because we utilize the capped norm based loss, our new objective can achieve better semi-supervised learning label indicator matrix than traditional methods which use the ℓ_2-norm based loss function.

Our abstractive aspect-oriented summarization system shows statistically significant improvements over Baselines 2 and 3 and pure extractive summarization systems for ROUGE. This means our systems can effectively aggregate the extracted patterns and generate abstract sentences based on the relevant keywords. We can also observe that our abstractive summarization system produces the highest ROUGE-1 score among all models, which further confirms the success of our framework that can cover more human-authored words. However, compared with TAC 2011 best system and compression based approaches [12] that use extractive based supervised learning, our system performance is bad. This proved that fully unsupervised abstractive summarization is a very challenge task, however our pattern based approach shows the feasibility and usefulness of this new direction (our framework only uses a small number of hand-crafted keywords for aspect-oriented summarization and all the rest modules are unsupervised).

Methods		Rouge Average Recall R-1	R-2	R-SU4
BL-1	Lexrank	28.93	5.17	9.15
BL-2	Har+HK+NLG	29.64	4.14	8.53
	Har+Cosine+NLG	29.33	4.3	8.59
	LGC+HK+NLG	29.23	4.58	8.68
	LGC+Cosine+NLG	29.5	4.38	8.52
	Capped+HK+NLG	27.58	4.12	8.11
	Capped+Cosine+NLG	28.04	4.26	8.21
BL-3	Har+HK+Fuse	30.54	5.03	9.18
	Har+Cosine+Fuse	30.7	5.42	9.27
	LGC+HK+Fuse	30.6	5.04	9.26
	LGC+Cosine+Fuse	30.94	5.37	9.48
Ours	Capped+HK + Fuse	31.72	5.75	10.03
	Capped+Cosine + Fuse	**31.88**	**5.98**	**10.27**
TAC'11 best	Supervised extractive	n/a	13.44	16.51
Li et al., 2014	Supervised compression	n/a	14.4	16.89

Table 3: ROUGE evaluation results on TAC2011 Summarization data sets, The improvements made by our method over the baselines are all statistically significant at 95% confidence level (p<0.05).

7.3 Manual Evaluation

To judge the quality of generated summaries, we ask three graduate students to score them. The judges will give a grammaticality and coherence scores to each summary. These two scores reflect the fluency and readability of the summary. Also the judges will give a informativeness score to each summary. This score reflects the coverage of all required aspects. The judges follow 5-point Likert scale to score each summary. We then compute the average scores. Note that we use LGC in Baselines 2 and 3 because they can get relative better clustering results. The manual evaluation results are shown in Table 4.

Results and Discussions

As expected, Baseline 1 received the highest rating of grammaticality because it use extractive based approach. Baseline 2 received the lowest rating of grammaticality, this result reflect heuristic summary generation via construct subject and object still need more linguistic knowledge. Referring to coherence rating, Baseline 1 is the lowest due to other methods leverage hand crafted keywords as hints to improve final summary coherence. Referring to informativeness rating, our label propagation clustering can better find semantic similar and complementary patterns that match user interested aspects. Overall, abstractive summary generation via label propagation, tuple/pattern fusion and recurrent neural network language model can improve the fluency, readability and coverage of final summary.

Method		Human judegs Average Score		
		Grammaticality	Coherence	Informativeness
BL-1	Ext	3.4	2.7	3.2
BL-2	NLG	2.9	3.0	3.3
BL-3	Fuse	3.1	3.2	3.4
Our Method		3.3	3.3	3.6

Table 4: Manual evaluation results on TAC2011 Summarization data sets

7.4 Example of Output Summaries

Table 5 presents the output summary of the subject "Amish Shooting" and " China Water Shortage" generated by our method. Comparing against the human-authored summary, our method can capture additional information related to damage of the accident such as "Six people were dead." On the other hand, we realized that n-gram cooccurance based ROUGE metric may not be suitable for abstractive summarization, and the new sentences generated by our approach may not match human-authored golden standard summary well.

Human-Authored Summary: D1101A-A
On October 2, 2006, a gunman, Charles Roberts, entered an Amish school near Lancaster, PA, took the children hostage, killed five girls and wounded seven other children before killing himself. His wife said that Roberts, a truck driver from a nearby town, told her he was acting in revenge for something that happened 20 years ago. He believed that he had molested two relatives. They denied that this ever happened. He also had anguish over his infant daughter's death. Roberts' wife said he was an exceptional father and a loving husband. The Amish community reached out to Roberts' family.

Summary generated by our system: D1101A-A
They were not molested 20 years ago. Two state troopers on horseback and bonnets stood two hours after the shooting. A procession of 34 buggies and graveyard was deserted Monday. Six people were dead. Charles Carl Roberts IV held a steady job working nights driving a truck that collected milk from area dairy farms. State police have said Roberts called her husband an exceptional father who took his children to soccer practice. These families to be left alone.

Human-Authored Summary: D11036G-A
On 3 January, 2007, a report from Beijing stated that global warming is seriously impacting China's ecological, social, and economic systems, and some of this damage will be irreversible. And while concerned about global warming, China says it lacks the money/technology to reduce its greenhouse gas emissions. The most serious of these issues is water shortages. The Yangtze River, the nation's largest, is at its lowest level in 100 years. This shortage is affecting fish and migratory bird survivals, crop productions, availability of drinking water, and numerous maritime shipping problems. China does plan to cut water consumption 20% by 2010.

Summary generated by our system: D1136G-A
Feb. 22, East China is among the driest country as water evaporates more rapidly from river are connected the Yangtze threads its way through 11 regions in Beijing. The floodgates could release an additional 6.1 billion cubic meters per capita income of over 50,000 fishermen around Poyang Lake was less than 600 yuan. The city had 15 million permanent residents and neighboring Sichuan Province in China plans to cut its industrial water per day, only 35 centimeters higher than the record low. Yangtze fishermen are experiencing a record low while its tributaries dropped 30 to 60 percent below average levels

Table 5: A comparison between a human-authored summary and a summary generated by our system

8. CONCLUSIONS AND FUTURE WORK

In this paper, we study the problem of using pattern based approaches to generate abstractive summarization. Our system first generates meaningful patterns from sentences. In order to precisely cluster patterns, we propose a new capped norm based semi-supervised pattern learning algorithm that leverages a hand-crafted list of topic-relevant keywords. Our system generates new patterns by fusing existing patterns and selects top ranked new patterns via the recurrent neural network language model. Finally, we use Integer Linear programming to select top ranked facts cross clusters. Although fully unsupervised abstractive summarization is a challenging task (the performance is still low compared with supervised extractive summarization system), our work shows the feasibility and usefulness of this new direction for summarization research.

There are a number of directions we plan to pursue in the future in order to improve our method. First, we can possibly apply more linguistic knowledge to improve the quality of head type tagging. Currently the tagging pipeline may generate meaningless tags. Second, we may explore more domain knowledge to improve the quality of pattern clustering. For example, we know that the "who-affected" aspect is related to person, and "when, where" are related to time and location, we can leverage these annotated phrases to help group relevant sentences. Third, we want to enhance our semi-supervised clustering model to precisely find similar patterns.

9. ACKNOWLEDGMENTS

This work was supported in part by Australian Research Council (ARC) grants and U.S. NSF-IIS 1117965, NSF-IIS 1302675, NSF-IIS 1344152, NSF-DBI 1356628.

10. REFERENCES

[1] E. Alfonseca, D. Pighin, and G. Garrido. Heady: News headline abstraction through event pattern clustering. In *Proceedings of the 51st Annual Meeting of the Association for Computational Linguistics (Volume 1: Long Papers)*, pages 1243–1253, Sofia, Bulgaria, 2013.

[2] N. Balasubramanian, S. Soderland, Mausam, and O. Etzioni. Generating coherent event schemas at scale. In *Proceedings of the 2013 Conference on Empirical Methods in Natural Language Processing*, pages 1721–1731, Seattle, Washington, USA, 2013.

[3] Y.-N. Chen, W. Y. Wang, and A. I. Rudnicky. Leveraging frame semantics and distributional semantics for unsupervised slot induction for spoken dialogue systems. In

Extened Abstract Presented at The 52nd Annual Meeting of Association for Computational Linguistics 2014 Workshop on Semantic Parsing (ACL-SP 2014), Baltimore, MD, USA, 2014. ACL.

[4] J. M. Conroy, J. D. Schlesinger, P. A. Rankel, and D. P. ÒLeary. Classy 2010: Summarization and metrics. In *Proceedings of the Third Text Analysis Conference, Gaithersburg, Maryland, USA. National Institute of Standards and Technology*, 2010.

[5] G. Erkan and D. R. Radev. Lexrank: Graph-based lexical centrality as salience in text summarization. *Journal of Artificial Intelligence Research*, 2004.

[6] P.-E. Genest and G. Lapalme. Text generation for abstractive summarization. In *Proceedings of the Third Text Analysis Conference, Gaithersburg, Maryland, USA. National Institute of Standards and Technology*, 2010.

[7] P.-E. Genest and G. Lapalme. Fully abstractive approach to guided summarization. In *Proceedings of the 50th Annual Meeting of the Association for Computational Linguistics: Short Papers - Volume 2*, ACL '12, pages 354–358, Stroudsburg, PA, USA, 2012.

[8] D. Gillick, B. Favre, D. Hakkani-Tur, B. Bohnet, Y. Liu, and S. Xie. The icsi/utd summarization system at tac 2009. In *The ICSI/UTD Summarization System at TAC 2009*, 2009.

[9] X. He and P. Niyogi. Locality preserving projections. In *Advances in neural information processing systems*, volume 16, page 153, 2004.

[10] W. Jiang, F. Nie, and H. Huang. Robust dictionary learning with capped l1 norm. *Twenty-Fourth International Joint Conferences on Artificial Intelligence (IJCAI)*, pages 3590–3596, 2015.

[11] K. S. Jones. Automatic summarizing: factors and directions. *Advances in automatic text summarization*, pages 1–12, 1999.

[12] C. Li, Y. Liu, F. Liu, L. Zhao, and F. Weng. Improving multi-documents summarization by sentence compression based on expanded constituent parse trees. *In Proceedings of the 2014 Conference on Empirical Methods in Natural Language Processing (EMNLP)*, 2014.

[13] P. Li, Y. Wang, W. Gao, and J. Jiang. Generating aspect-oriented multi-document summarization with event-aspect model. In *Proceedings of the 2011 Conference on Empirical Methods in Natural Language Processing*, 2011.

[14] C.-Y. Lin and E. Hovy. Automatic evaluation of summaries using n-gram co-occurrence statistics. In *NAACL*, 2003.

[15] Mausam, M. Schmitz, R. Bart, S. Soderland, and O. Etzioni. Open language learning for information extraction. In *Proceedings of the 2012 Joint Conference on Empirical Methods in Natural Language Processing and Computational Natural Language Learning*, EMNLP-CoNLL '12, pages 523–534, Stroudsburg, PA, USA, 2012.

[16] Y. Mehdad, G. Carenini, and R. T. Ng. Abstractive summarization of spoken and written conversations based on phrasal queries. In *Proceedings of the 52nd Annual Meeting of the Association for Computational Linguistics (Volume 1: Long Papers)*, pages 1220–1230, Baltimore, Maryland, 2014.

[17] Y. Mehdad, G. Carenini, F. W. Tompa, and R. Ng. Abstractive meeting summarization with entailment and fusion. In *Proceedings of the 14th European Workshop on Natural Language Generation*, pages 136–146, 2013.

[18] T. Mikolov, M. Karafiát, L. Burget, J. Cernockỳ, and S. Khudanpur. Recurrent neural network based language model. In *INTERSPEECH*, pages 1045–1048, 2010.

[19] T. Mikolov, I. Sutskever, K. Chen, G. S. Corrado, and J. Dean. Distributed representations of words and phrases and their compositionality. In *Advances in Neural Information Processing Systems*, pages 3111–3119, 2013.

[20] G. Murray, G. Carenini, and R. Ng. Generating and validating abstracts of meeting conversations: a user study. In *Proceedings of the 6th International Natural Language Generation Conference*, pages 105–113, 2010.

[21] F. Nie, H. Huang, X. Cai, and C. Ding. Efficient and robust feature selection via joint l2,1-norms minimization. *Neural Information Processing Systems Conference (NIPS)*, pages 1813–1821, 2010.

[22] F. Nie, H. Huang, C. Ding, D. Luo, and H. Wang. Principal component analysis with non-greedy l1-norm maximization. *International Joint Conferences on Artificial Intelligence (IJCAI)*, pages 1433–1438, 2011.

[23] F. Nie, H. Wang, H. Huang, and C. Ding. Unsupervised and semi-supervised learning via l1-norm graph. *IEEE Conference on Computer Vision (ICCV)*, pages 2268–2273, 2011.

[24] T. Oya, Y. Mehdad, G. Carenini, and R. Ng. A template-based abstractive meeting summarization: Leveraging summary and source text relationships. In *Proceedings of the 8th International Natural Language Generation Conference (INLG)*, pages 45–53, Philadelphia, Pennsylvania, U.S.A., 2014.

[25] D. Pighin, M. Cornolti, E. Alfonseca, and K. Filippova. Modelling events through memory-based, open-ie patterns for abstractive summarization. In *Proceedings of the 52nd Annual Meeting of the Association for Computational Linguistics (Volume 1: Long Papers)*, pages 892–901, Baltimore, Maryland, 2014.

[26] L. Wang and C. Cardie. Domain-independent abstract generation for focused meeting summarization. In *Proceedings of the 51st Annual Meeting of the Association for Computational Linguistics (Volume 1: Long Papers)*, pages 1395–1405, Sofia, Bulgaria, 2013.

[27] T. Zhang. Multi-stage convex relaxation for learning with sparse regularization. *NIPS*, 2008.

[28] T. Zhang. Analysis of multi-stage convex relaxation for sparse regularization. *JMLR*, pages 1081–1107, 2010.

[29] X. Zhang and M. Lapata. Chinese poetry generation with recurrent neural networks. In *Proceedings of the 2014 Conference on Empirical Methods in Natural Language Processing (EMNLP)*, pages 670–680, 2014.

[30] D. Zhou, O. Bousquet, T. N. Lal, J. Weston, and B. Schölkopf. Learning with local and global consistency. *Advances in neural information processing systems*, 16(16):321–328, 2004.

[31] X. Zhu, Z. Ghahramani, J. Lafferty, et al. Semi-supervised learning using gaussian fields and harmonic functions. In *ICML*, volume 3, pages 912–919, 2003.

Short Text Similarity with Word Embeddings

Tom Kenter
tom.kenter@uva.nl

Maarten de Rijke
derijke@uva.nl

University of Amsterdam, Amsterdam, The Netherlands

ABSTRACT

Determining semantic similarity between texts is important in many tasks in information retrieval such as search, query suggestion, automatic summarization and image finding. Many approaches have been suggested, based on lexical matching, handcrafted patterns, syntactic parse trees, external sources of structured semantic knowledge and distributional semantics. However, lexical features, like string matching, do not capture semantic similarity beyond a trivial level. Furthermore, handcrafted patterns and external sources of structured semantic knowledge cannot be assumed to be available in all circumstances and for all domains. Lastly, approaches depending on parse trees are restricted to syntactically well-formed texts, typically of one sentence in length.

We investigate whether determining short text similarity is possible using only semantic features—where by *semantic* we mean, pertaining to a representation of meaning—rather than relying on similarity in lexical or syntactic representations. We use word embeddings, vector representations of terms, computed from unlabelled data, that represent terms in a semantic space in which proximity of vectors can be interpreted as semantic similarity.

We propose to go from word-level to text-level semantics by combining insights from methods based on external sources of semantic knowledge with word embeddings. A novel feature of our approach is that an arbitrary number of word embedding sets can be incorporated. We derive multiple types of meta-features from the comparison of the word vectors for short text pairs, and from the vector means of their respective word embeddings. The features representing labelled short text pairs are used to train a supervised learning algorithm. We use the trained model at testing time to predict the semantic similarity of new, unlabelled pairs of short texts.

We show on a publicly available evaluation set commonly used for the task of semantic similarity that our method outperforms baseline methods that work under the same conditions.

Categories and Subject Descriptors

H.3 [**Information Storage and Retrieval**]: H.3.3 Information Search and Retrieval; I.2 Artificial Intelligence [**I.2.7 Natural Language Processing**]: Text analysis

Permission to make digital or hard copies of all or part of this work for personal or classroom use is granted without fee provided that copies are not made or distributed for profit or commercial advantage and that copies bear this notice and the full citation on the first page. Copyrights for components of this work owned by others than the author(s) must be honored. Abstracting with credit is permitted. To copy otherwise, or republish, to post on servers or to redistribute to lists, requires prior specific permission and/or a fee. Request permissions from Permissions@acm.org.
CIKM'15, October 19–23, 2015, Melbourne, Australia.
Copyright is held by the owner/author(s). Publication rights licensed to ACM.
ACM 978-1-4503-3794-6/15/10 ...$15.00.
DOI: http://dx.doi.org/10.1145/2806416.2806475 .

Keywords

Short Text Similarity; Word Embeddings

1. INTRODUCTION

Determining semantic similarity between two texts is to find out if two pieces of text mean the same thing. Being able to do so successfully is beneficial in many settings in information retrieval like search [26], query suggestion [30], automatic summarization [3] and image finding [12].

Many approaches have been proposed for semantic matching that use lexical matching and linguistic analysis, next to semantic features. Methods for lexical matching aim to determine whether the words in two short texts look alike, e.g., in terms of edit distance [31], lexical overlap [23] or largest common substring [21]. While this might work for trivial cases, it is arguably not robust as it allows for simple mistakes. For example, the *US* would be closer to the *UK* this way, than it would be to the *States*. Features based on linguistic analysis, like dependency parses or syntactic trees, are often used for short text similarity [19, 39]. Linguistic tools such as parsers are commonly available these days for many languages, though the quality might vary between languages. However, not all texts are necessarily parseable (e.g., tweets) and high-quality parses might be expensive to compute at run time. More importantly still, relying on parse trees limits an approach to single sentences, while the work presented here, even though it is evaluated on sentences, incorporates no theoretical constraint restricting it to (syntactically well-formed) sentences.

For semantic features, many approaches use external sources of structured semantic knowledge such as Wikipedia [6] or WordNet [6, 17, 18, 31, 37]. Wikipedia is structured around entities and as such is primarily of avail in settings where a focus on rather well-known persons and organisations can be assumed, such as, e.g., news articles. Such an assumption cannot always be made however. A drawback of using dictionaries or WordNet is that high-quality resources like these are not available for all languages, and proper names, domain-specific technical terms and slang tend to be underrepresented [2].

In the present work we aim to make as few assumptions as possible. We aim for a generic model, that requires no prior knowledge of natural language (such as parse trees) and no external resources of structured semantic information.

Recent developments in distributional semantics, in particular neural network-based approaches like [32, 34] only require a large amount of unlabelled text data. This data is used to create a, so-called, semantic space. Terms are represented in this semantic space as vectors that are called *word embeddings*. The geometric properties of this space prove to be semantically and syntactically meaningful [13, 32–34], that is, words that are semantically or syntactically similar tend to be close in the semantic space.

A challenge for applying word embeddings to the task of determining semantic similarity of short texts is going from word-level semantics to short-text-level semantics. This problem has been studied extensively over the past few years [4, 25, 39].

In this work we propose to go from word-level to short-text-level semantics by combining insights from methods based on external sources of semantic knowledge with word embeddings. In particular, we perform semantic matching between words in two short texts and use the matched terms to create a saliency-weighted semantic network. A novel feature of our approach is that an arbitrary number of word embedding sets can be incorporated, regardless of the corpus used for training, the underlying algorithm, its parameter settings or the dimensionality of the word vectors. We derive multiple types of meta-features from the comparison of the word vectors for short text pairs and from the vector means of their respective word embeddings, that have not been used before for the task of short text similarity matching.

We show on a publicly available test collection that our generic method, that does not rely on external sources of structural semantic knowledge, outperforms baseline methods that work under the same conditions and outperforms all methods, to our knowledge, that do use external knowledge bases and that have been evaluated on this dataset.

The rest of the paper is structured as follows. In Section 2 we describe relevant literature. We present our method for short text similarity in Section 3. The experiments and results are detailed in Section 4 and Section 5. In Section 6 we conclude.

2. RELATED WORK

In this section we discuss previous work related to the different aspects of our method.

Distributional semantics.

Distributional semantic approaches are based on the intuition that words appearing in similar contexts tend to have similar meanings. The Latent Semantic Analysis algorithm (LSA) [14] incorporates this intuition by building a word-document co-occurrence matrix and performing singular value decomposition (SVD) on it to get a lower-dimensional representation. Words are represented as vectors in this lower dimensional space. The distance between these word vectors (measured, e.g., with the cosine function) can be used as a proxy for semantic similarity. The full co-occurrence matrix, however, can become quite substantial for a large corpus, in which case the SVD becomes memory-intensive and computationally expensive.

Word vectors—also referred to as word embeddings—have recently seen a surge of interest as new ways of computing them efficiently have become available. In [32, 33] an algorithm called word2vec is proposed. There are two architectures to word2vec, continuous bag-of-words (CBOW) and Skip-gram. Both are a variation on a neural network language model [9, 13], but rather than predicting a word conditioned on its predecessor, as in a traditional bi-gram language model, a word is predicted from its surrounding words (CBOW) or multiple surrounding words are predicted from one input word (Skip-gram). To avoid computing a full softmax over the entire vocabulary, hierarchical softmax can be applied on a Huffman tree representation of the vocabulary, which saves calculations, at the potential loss of some accuracy. An additional strategy to get better embeddings is negative sampling, where, instead of only using the words observed next to one another in the training data as positive examples, random words are sampled from the corpus and presented to the network as negative examples.

An alternative way of getting word embeddings, called GloVe, is proposed in [34]. Rather than being based on language models it is based on global matrix factorisation. As such, it is closer to LSA, only a word-word co-occurrence matrix is used. GloVe avoids the large computational cost of, e.g., LSA by not building the full co-occurrence matrix, but training directly on the non-zero elements in it. As a cost function, the model uses a weighted least squares variant. The weighting function has two parameters, an exponent and a maximum cut-off value that influence the performance.

As both algorithms produce high-quality word embeddings and their implementations are publicly available, we use them in our experiments. In Section 5 we report on the results and analyse the effect of different parameter settings for both methods.

Text-level semantics without external semantic knowledge.

Word embeddings, as described above, provide a way of comparing terms to one another semantically. It is not evident, however, how longer pieces of text should be represented with them. Several approaches have been proposed to go from word-level semantics to phrase-, sentence-, or even document-level semantics.

Le and Mikolov [25] propose a variation on the word2vec algorithm for calculating paragraph vectors, by adding an explicit paragraph feature to the input of the neural network. A convolutional neural network, built on top of word2vec word embeddings, is employed for modelling sentences in [20]. Other corpus-based methods have been proposed, such as [21], in which both semantic and string distance features are employed, and [38] in which a vector space model is used. All four methods, in line with the work presented here, do not rely on external sources of structured semantic knowledge, nor on natural language resources. As such, these methods are natural baselines for our experiments in Section 4. It is problematic to reproduce the work presented in [25], however, as the original source code was not released by the authors and it is not clear, algorithmically, how the second step – the inference for new, unseen texts – should be carried out. Therefore, we omit this method as a baseline.

Many methods rely on natural language resources such as parsers. Socher et al. [39] propose recursive auto-encoders for the task of semantic textual similarity. This method relies on full parse trees for every sentence it processes. Annesi et al. [4] apply a kernel method on dependency parse tree features. Another strong method is presented in [22] where features from dependency parser are used to train a supervised method. The latter method, to our knowledge, yields the highest performance on the MSR Paraphrase Corpus [15, 35], an evaluation set commonly used for textual similarity experiments, and the one we use in our experiments in Section 5.

Sentence representations based on word2vec word embeddings are also the focus in [24], where a convolutional neural network is trained on top of word2vec word embeddings. However, the method is only evaluated on sentence classification tasks (not on semantic similarity).

Text-level semantics with external knowledge.

A large body of research has been directed at using sources of structured semantic knowledge like Wikipedia and WordNet for semantic text similarity tasks. In [17, 18, 28] methods very similar to one another are proposed, using pairings of words and Wordnet-based measures for semantic similarity. Our method of aligning words as described in Section 3 draws on this work. The key difference between these approaches and ours, apart from the fact that WordNet is used, is that parsing/POS tagging is carried out [18, 28], as the WordNet-based measures are limited to comparing words having the same POS tag. Furthermore, no full-scale machine learning step is involved. All methods present one overall score, based on a threshold which is calculated through a simple regression step [18, 28] or set manually [17].

Corpus methods are combined with WordNet-based measures in [27, 31]. In [31] an IDF-weighted alignment approach, based both on WordNet-based and corpus-based similarities, is proposed. Texts are parsed and only similarities within identical part-of-speech categories are considered. Finally, a single score is calculated as an average over the maximum similarities. In [27] a WordNet similarity measure is combined with word order scores. In neither approaches any machine learning step is applied.

SemEval STS.

Recently, the SemEval 2012 Semantic Text Similarity (STS) task [1] and SemEval 2013 STS task [2] (part of *SEM'13) were organised. A full description of the work of all participating teams (over 30 in both years) is beyond the scope of this section. We discuss the approaches of the best-scoring teams.

The best-scoring teams in 2012 both calculate a large number of features based on a wide variety of methods. Additionally, handcrafted rules are applied that deal with currency values, negation, compounds, number overlap [37] and with literal matching [6]. The main difference with our approach, apart from the handcrafted rules, is in the features extracted, and in particular the number of additional resources required (WordNet, a dependency parser, NER tools, lemmatizer, POS tagger, stop word list [37], and WordNet, Wikipedia, Wiktionary, POS tagger, SMT system for three language pairs [6]).

In 2013, we see similar approaches where the best teams extract features from sentence pairs and use regression models (SVRs) to predict a similarity score. The features in [19] are based on LSA, WordNet and additional lists of related words and stopwords. In [29] features are calculated from aggregated similarity measures based on named entity recognition with WordNet and Levenshtein distance, higher order word co-occurrence similarity, the RelEx system, dependency trees and reused features of SemEval 2012 participants. Additionally, handcrafted features like lists of aliases (e.g., *USA* and *United States*) are used. A parallel between our work and both these approaches is the use of word alignment.

Finally, in [5] a method similar to the one we propose here is presented, for a related, but different task of detecting semantic similarity between texts of different lengths. Next to WordNet-based features, a word alignment method is used based on word embeddings, analogous to what we propose. A crucial difference with our approach is that only a single feature is derived from this score, rather than several bins. Moreover, only a single set of word embeddings is used, while we show in our experiments in §5 that it is beneficial to use multiple sets.

Meta-level features.

As described below in Sections 3.1 and 3.2 below, we use bin-based features to capture the characteristics of the differences between vectors and the distribution of word embeddings. This is similar to, e.g., [11] where meta-level features are proposed, in a text classification setting using the kNN algorithm, to exploit the distribution of the nearest neighbour similarities and the within-class cohesion.

Input : List of sentence pairs $((s_{1,1}, s_{1,2}), (s_{2,1}, s_{2,2}), \ldots, (s_{n,1}, s_{n,2}))$
Input : List of associated labels $L = [l_1, l_2, l_3, \ldots, l_n]$
Required: Sets of word embeddings $[WE_1, WE_2, ..., WE_m]$
Required: Multiple feature extractors $[fe_1, fe_2, \ldots, fe_l]$
Output : A trained prediction model M

1 $F =$ empty feature matrix;
2 **for** $i \leftarrow 1$ **to** n **do**
3     $\vec{f} = <>$;
4   **for** $j \leftarrow 1$ **to** m **do**
5   **for** $k \leftarrow 1$ **to** l **do**
6             $\vec{f} = \texttt{concat}(\vec{f}, fe_k((s_{i,1}, s_{i,2}), WE_j))$;
7   **end**
8   **end**
9     $F[i] \leftarrow \vec{f}$;
10 **end**
11 $M = trainModel(F, L)$;

Algorithm 1: Pseudocode of the feature generation step of our method for semantic similarity of short texts

3. SHORT TEXT SIMILARITY WITH SEMANTICS ONLY

To calculate semantic similarity between two short texts we use a supervised machine learning approach. Algorithm 1 shows the pseudocode of the training phase. The training data for the supervised step consists of sentence pairs and associated labels that represent the semantic similarity between the two sentences. Multiple sets of word embeddings can be leveraged, possibly derived from different corpora, with different (hyper)parameter settings or with different algorithms. Every sentence pair in the training data is represented by a set of features. A list of functions that generate features from a set of word embeddings and a sentence pair is required. We detail the different kinds of features below in Section 3.1 and Section 3.2.

At training time, we range over all sentences (Algorithm 1, line 2), all sets of word embeddings (line 4) and feature extraction functions (line 5) to compile a feature vector per sentence pair (line 6). The feature vectors are stored in a matrix (line 9). We train a supervised learning method from the features and the labels of the training examples (line 11). As the labels in the evaluation set that we use are binary, we build a classifier. At testing time, features are generated for the sentence pairs in the test set in a similar fashion as in the training phase, and a final prediction is made with the classifier trained in the training step.

A convenient property of our method of computing semantic textual similarity for short texts, and one which we leverage in our experiments as detailed in Section 4, is that different sets of word embeddings can be combined, regardless of the dimensionality of the word vectors, the parameters that were used at construction time, or the algorithms that were used to generate them.

As we are interested in the performance of different feature types, we carry out experiments per feature type and with various combinations. See Section 4 for further details on the experimental setup.

In the next section we describe the various types of features we derive from the word embeddings. In Section 4.2 we detail how we obtain the word embeddings themselves.

3.1 From word-level semantics to short-text-level semantics

The meaning of longer pieces of text (containing multiple terms) can be captured by taking the mean of the individual term vectors.[1] This approach is taken, next to other approaches, in, e.g., [5, 20, 40]. It works surprisingly well, and we use several features based on vector means, described below. Means, or sums, however, are rather poor ways of describing the distribution of word embeddings across a semantic space. It would be desirable to capture more properties of the two texts, especially with respect to the terms that do or do not match. We will first turn to our algorithm for constructing saliency-weighted semantic networks, which aims to capture this intuition. After that, in Section 3.2, we discuss features based on the mean vectors.

3.1.1 *Saliency-weighted semantic network*

In Figure 1 the word embeddings of two short texts are represented as dots in a two-dimensional space. As can be observed from the picture, the two texts have terms that are close to each other (at the top and bottom in the figure), while the ones at the far left and right have no counterpart in their immediate vicinity. Regardless of this discrepancy, the means of the two are close to one another. The fact that both texts have a term unlike any term in the other text is not well represented by the means. A classifier, however, can benefit from more elaborate information about the distribution of word embeddings across the semantic space.

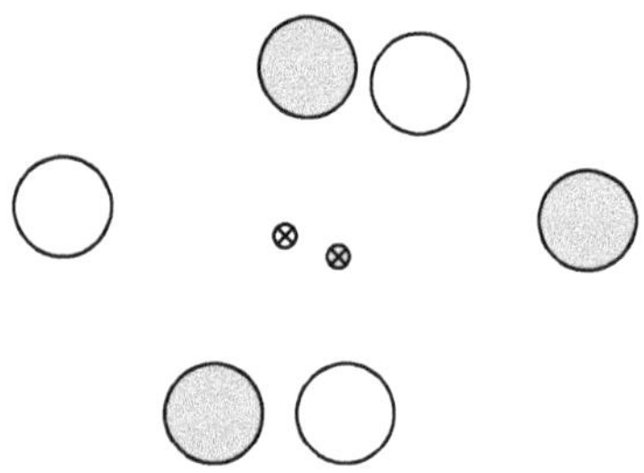

Figure 1: Hypothetical example — two-dimensional representation of the word embeddings for two short texts (each consisting of three terms), represented as transparent and opaque dots respectively. The corresponding means of the two sets of embeddings are depicted as $\otimes$.

We want a way of taking into account the distribution of terms in one short text in the semantic space compared to distribution of terms in another text. Of course, not all terms are equally important. Common terms (like determiners) do not contribute as much to the meaning of a text as less frequent words do. Inverted document frequency (idf) is often used to implement this notion. Idf is usually combined with term frequency, e.g., in the BM25 algorithm. As BM25 has proven to be surprisingly successful [36] we derive our idf weighting scheme from it. Our function for calculating semantic text similarity (sts) is:

$$f_{sts}(s_l, s_s) = \sum_{w \in s_l} \text{IDF}(w) \cdot \frac{sem(w, s_s) \cdot (k_1 + 1)}{sem(w, s_s) + k_1 \cdot (1 - b + b \cdot \frac{|s_s|}{\text{avgsl}})} \quad (1)$$

Here, s_l is the longest text of the two, s_s is the shortest and avgsl is the average sentence length in the training corpus.

The semantic similarity of term w with respect to short text s is represented by $sem(w, s)$:

$$sem(w, s) = \max_{w' \in s} f_{sem}(w, w'). \quad (2)$$

The function f_{sem} returns the semantic similarity between two terms. As terms are represented as vectors in our case, a natural choice for f_{sem}, which we use in our experiments in Section 4, is the cosine similarity between the two vectors.

[1]This is sometimes referred to as vector BOW approach

As is apparent from (1), we always take the longest short text of the two as a reference when calculating f_{sts}. We do so for two reasons. Firstly, we want f_{sts} to be symmetrical. Calculating the semantic similarity between two short texts should yield the same score regardless of their order. Secondly, the reason why the longest of the two short texts is summed over is that we do not want terms to be overlooked. Suppose we have two texts, where one consists of a subset of terms contained in the other. If the shortest text would be taken as a reference this would lead to a perfect score. However, if we take the longest text as a reference, the incongruity between the texts does have its bearing on the score, as desired.

We should note that, although (1) bears a superficial resemblance to the BM25 formula, it in fact models something completely different. We borrow the b and k_1 parameters that have a smoothing effect, together with the length normalisation: the average sentence length, $avgsl$, in our case. The key difference, however, lies in the introduction of semantic similarity term in the formula. Where a tf*idf weighting scheme relies on literal matches between the query and documents it matches, we are, in the present setting, interested in particular in semantic matches. By using (2) for calculating semantic similarity, the maximum similarity of terms in s_s is taken into account for every term in s_l.

One interpretation of f_{sts} is that it allows for non-literal, semantic matching. As noted above, in a tf*idf weighting scheme, terms only contribute to the score if they match perfectly. In f_{sts} all terms contribute, with the semantically most related ones contributing most.

An alternative interpretation of f_{sts} with (2) is as a word alignment method. As a max is being computed in (2) over all words in a sentence, semantically close words are aligned to one another. In this way f_{sts} bears similarity to other alignment approaches such as [5, 19, 29].

Yet another alternative view is that f_{sts} applies saliency weighting to a semantic network. If we interpret the dots in Figure 1 as vertices of a graph, the max in (2) draws edges between the vertices and weights them according to (1). As a result, a mismatch between two terms such as the far left and right ones in Figure 1 is of little consequence if both have a low IDF score (e.g., they are function words). If they are salient however, the mismatch has a larger impact.

As can be seen from (1) the f_{sts} score is a sum over $|s_l|$ terms. However, rather than giving the overall score to the final learning algorithm, we want to capture more information about the way the score is composed. Therefore, we make bins of its summands and normalise by the number of summands, so the value for every bin represents the percentage of summands in (1) between the minimum and maximum values for that bin.

3.1.2 *Unweighted semantic network*

To convey as much information as possible to the final classifier we also construct an unweighted semantic network. For a short text pair (s_1, s_2), we compute the cosine similarities in the semantic space between all terms in short text s_1 and all terms in s_2. This gives us a matrix of similarities between the terms in s_1 and s_2. From this matrix we compute two sets of features.

Firstly, we take all similarities and bin them. If we think of the word embeddings as nodes in a graph this would correspond to an fully connected, unweighted, bipartite graph. In Figure 1 this would be represented by connecting every opaque dot to every transparent dot.

Secondly, the maximum similarity for every word is computed, and bins are made of these maximum values. In this way, small distances between words (such as the top and bottom ones in Figure 1) end up in the same bin, while outliers (the ones at the far left and right) end up in a separate bin.

3.2 Text level features

3.2.1 Distance between vectors means

As noted previously, a standard way of combining word embeddings to capture the meaning of longer pieces of text is to take the mean of the individual term vectors. This aggregation over terms gives us one vector per sentence. We calculate both the cosine similarity and the Euclidean distance between the vectors for every sentence pair in the test set.

3.2.2 Bins of dimensions

The cosine similarity between two vectors can be interpreted as an aggregation over the differences per dimension. As such, it does not capture all information about the similarities or differences between the two vectors. For example, taking the cosine similarity between two vectors that are highly similar in many dimensions and quite different in few, could lead to the same result as taking the cosine similarity between two vectors that differ slightly in all dimensions. Intuitively though, these are two different situations. In order to capture this intuition, we make bins of the number of dimensions in the mean vector of s_1 and the mean vector of s_2 that match within certain limits. See §4.3 for the exact values.

4. EXPERIMENTAL SETUP

The primary focus of our experiments is to determine how our method, which relies solely on semantic features, compares to other methods that work under the same conditions, and to methods that do rely on external sources of structured semantic knowledge, linguistic tools and handcrafted rules. To do so, we perform experiments on the MSR Paraphrase Corpus [15, 35], the evaluation set most commonly used for this purpose.

As described in the previous section, we compute features from word embeddings, which are obtained from large amounts of unlabelled data. A practical feature of word embeddings is that word vectors computed on a large corpus can be made available, without the necessity of disclosing the entire training corpus as well (which can be problematic due to copyright issues). In our experiments we compute features from four publicly available sets of word embeddings (see Section 4.2.1 and Section 4.2.2 for more details). As the word vectors are not trained by ourselves, we refer to them as Out-of-the-Box (OoB).

We distinguish between two feature sets. The *saliency-weighted semantic network* features capture information about the similarity of the distribution of word vectors in the two sentences (Section 3.1.1). The *unweighted* features are calculated from the unweighted semantic network (Section 3.1.2) and the means of the word embeddings of both sentences (Section 3.2). Our hypothesis is that saliency-weighted semantic networks can add valuable features for a classifier that learns to predict semantic similarities between short texts. To verify this hypothesis we perform experiments without the features based on the saliency-weighted semantic networks, and with the saliency-weighted semantic network features added.

Additionally, as there are many parameters that have an impact on the word embeddings we use to construct features, we want to investigate which settings lead to word embeddings best suited for our approach. As it is not possible to do this with out-of-the-box vectors, we construct our own vectors from a publicly available text corpus (see 4.2.3 for details). As we use the features derived from these additional sets of word embeddings supplementary to the OoB features, we refer to them as *auxiliary*.

For the experiments with features derived from the OoB vector sets, the only hyper-parameters of our model are the regularisation parameters of the learning algorithm. We choose their optimal setting by cross validating on the training data with folds of 10 examples. The experiments including the auxiliary vectors are aimed at demonstrating the potential of our method and the effect of the parameter settings. Therefore, we show the best results obtained across all settings and discuss the individual parameter settings in detail.

4.1 Learning algorithm

As discussed in Section 3 we use the features described above to represent sentence pairs in the training material and we train a supervised learning algorithm on these features. As the MSR Paraphrase Corpus is annotated with binary labels (see Section 4.6.1) we use a classifier for prediction. In particular, we use Support Vector Classifier (SVC) with a Radial Basis Function (rbf) kernel because the feature space is not necessarily linear.

4.2 Word embeddings

For ease of comparison with other approaches using word embeddings, we use four sets of vectors that are publicly available (two word2vec sets and two GloVe sets) which we refer to as Out-of-the-Box sets (OoB). Additionally we train our own word vectors, both with word2vec and GloVe, and perform runs with different settings for both algorithms (the auxiliary vectors).

Once word embeddings have been trained on a corpus, there is no way to fold terms that were not observed during training into the semantic space. One way of dealing with these out-of-vocabulary (OOV) words when calculating the features described below is to simply ignore them. However, it is possible that important semantic information is present specifically in these new words. For example, names of persons or organisations occurring in a test set, which are likely to be semantically relevant, might have been absent from the training data. Therefore, following, e.g., [24], we map OOV words to random vectors, while remembering which OOV word maps to which random vector.

The intuition behind this simple scheme is the following. If two texts are being compared in which two different OOV names appear, this incongruity would go unnoticed if the OOV terms would be ignored. Likewise, if the same OOV term is observed in two texts being compared, this contributes to the similarity score between the two (while it would be silently ignored otherwise).

4.2.1 OoB: Word2vec

Mikolov et al. [33] experiment with several settings of the word2vec algorithm to produce the highest quality word embeddings. The resulting vectors have been made publicly available.[2] The vectors are 300-dimensional and were trained on a corpus of about 100 billion words.

Baroni et al. [7] compare word2vec word embeddings to traditional distributional semantics approaches. The best performing vectors were released by the authors.[3] The vectors are 400-dimensional, a 5-word context window was used, with 10 negative samples and subsampling.

---

[2]See `https://code.google.com/p/word2vec/`

[3]See `http://clic.cimec.unitn.it/composes/semantic-vectors.html`

4.2.2 *OoB: GloVe*

In [34] an algorithm is proposed for deriving word embeddings optimised especially for word analogy and similarity tasks. As the GloVe algorithm differs from the word2vec algorithm, it is interesting to see if and how GloVe word embeddings behave differently from word2vec vectors when applied to the task of short text similarity. In our experiments we use two sets of publicly available GloVe vectors. Both sets are 300-dimensional. The word vectors of the first set were trained on a very large corpus of 840 billion tokens while the other set was trained on a 42 billion token corpus.[4]

4.2.3 *Auxiliary word embeddings*

As we are interested in the utility of the vectors and what settings work best for the task of predicting short text similarity, we calculate auxiliary word embeddings both with the word2vec algorithm and with GloVe. We train word embeddings on a publicly available data set released by INEX.[5] The corpus contains 1.2 billion tokens.

The word2vec algorithm has several parameters: the architecture (CBOW or Skip-gram), word sampling threshold, whether or not to apply hierarchical softmax and the number of negative examples. Preliminary experiments indicated that a sampling threshold of 10^{-5} is most robust across settings. We use the default window width of 5 and vector dimensionality of 300.

For the auxiliary GloVe vectors we use the same dimensionality of 300. We set the number of training iterations to 100 as is suggested in [34] for training vectors of dimension 300 and up. There are two parameters in particular to experiment with: (1) the exponent of the weighting function used in the cost function, which we set to any of $[.1, .5, .75, .9]$, and (2) the cut-off in the weighting function, which we set to any of $[10, 50, 100, 500, 1000]$.

Preprocessing of the corpus consists of tokenization with NLTK sentence splitter and token splitter [10] with additional removal of non-ascii quotes and non-word characters. No stemming or stopping is carried out. All text is lowercased.

4.3 Parameter settings

As discussed in Section 3.1 and Section 3.2 a binning approach is used for most features. We use three bins in most cases, where one bin is meant to capture highly similar values, one bin is for the medium values and the third bin is for very dissimilar values. The values were obtained by examining the raw features for the training material. For features calculated from the saliency-weighted semantic network, the values are 0–.15, .15–.4, .4–∞. For the unweighted semantic network features the values are -1–.45, .45–.8, .8–∞ (the same values are used for when all similarities are taken into account, as when only the maximum similarities are considered). For the bins of dimensions, preliminary experiments showed that a four-bin approach, with two bins for similar and highly similar values worked slightly better than a three-bin approach. We use values $-\infty$–.001, .001–.01, .01–.02, .02–∞.

As an extensive tuning of the parameters k_1 and b is beyond the scope of this paper we use the default settings of $k_1 = 1.2$ and $b = 0.75$ when computing f_{sts} in our experiments. The IDF values were calculated from the INEX data set described above.

4.4 Feature sets

All feature sets are calculated per set of word embeddings. Hence, for 3 saliency-weighted semantic network bins, 2×3 unweighted semantic network bins, 2 distances and 4 dimensional bins, we have 15 features per set of word embeddings, and 60 features in total per sentence pair, when, e.g., the 4 OoB sets are used.

4.5 Baselines

As discussed in §2 the systems for detecting short text similarity as described in [20, 21, 38] are natural baselines to our method as they work under the same conditions, i.e., no external sources of structured semantical knowledge are used and no prior knowledge of natural language (such as parse trees) is required.

4.6 Evaluation

We first describe the evaluation set used in our experiments. Then we discuss the associated evaluation metrics.

4.6.1 *Evaluation sets*

We use the Microsoft Research Paraphrase Corpus data set [15, 35] in our primary experiments in Section 5 as it is commonly used for evaluation in short text similarity tasks [4, 17, 20, 21, 31, 38]. The set consists of sentence pairs judged for semantic similarity on a binary scale. The annotator guidelines allowed for an interpretation of semantic similarity that went beyond strict semantic identity, as using the latter notion would yield only trivial examples. The set consists of 5801 sentence pairs in total, divided in a training set of 4076 and a test set of 1725 examples.

Other evaluation sets.

Li et al. [27] present a data set comprising 65 pairs of dictionary glosses extracted from two sources. The set is used for evaluation in, e.g., [18, 21]. We omit this set in our experiment because of its limited size.

The task of semantic textual similarity was part of the SemEval 2012 and SemEval 2013 campaigns [1, 2]. The SemEval data is impractical for evaluation in a supervised learning setting with a substantial number of features, as the training data is limited (maximally 750 training examples per subset in the SemEval 2012 data) which leads to overfitting. Additionally, more recent work in semantic textual similarity is evaluated on the MSR Paraphrase corpus. For these two reasons, we evaluate our methods for calculating semantic text similarity on the latter.

4.6.2 *Evaluation metrics*

As the MSR Paraphrase Corpus has binary annotations, accuracy is the metric most often applied, together usually, with precision, recall and F_1 [4, 17, 20, 31].

5. RESULTS AND ANALYSIS

In this section we show the results of our experiments. We are interested in answering two questions. Firstly, we want to see if our method performs better than the baseline methods that work under the same conditions. Secondly, we want to know if a semantics-only approach, without access to external sources of knowledge, can yield results comparable to the state-of-the-art methods that do use external semantic knowledge bases and/or features based on computationally more involved processes as syntactic parsing.

In Table 1 results of our experiments are listed. For convenience, the results from the baseline methods, as reported in the literature, are displayed in the top three rows.[6] The rows marked 'unwghtd' use all features described above, but for the features based on the saliency-weighted semantic network. The rows marked 'un-

[4]Both sets of vectors can be downloaded from http://nlp.stanford.edu/projects/glove/

[5]The data consists of an English Wikipedia dump from November 2012. It was released as a test collection for the INEX 2013 tweet contextualisation track [8]

[6]No precision and recall numbers were reported in [20].

Table 1: Results on the MSR Paraphrase Corpus set. The rows marked 'unwghtd' display results for runs based on all features, but for the saliency-weighted semantic network features. The rows marked 'unwghtd + swsn' display results for runs that had features based on saliency-weighted semantic network added as well. Results marked† are significantly different from the best performing OoB run (two-tailed paired t-test, p-value < .007)

Baseline methods		Acc.	p	r	F_1
Convolutional NNs [20]		.699	–	–	.809
VSM [38]		.710	.710	.954	.814
Corpus-based PMI [21]		.726	.747	.891	.813
Our method	**Features**	**Acc.**	**p**	**r**	**F_1**
OoB	unwghtd	.746	.768	.882	.822
OoB	unwghtd + swsn	.751	.768	.896	.827
OoB + aux w2v	unwghtd	.754	.770	.897	.829
OoB + aux w2v	unwghtd + swsn	.757	.775	.894	.830
OoB + aux Glv	unwghtd	.756	.774	.894	.830
OoB + aux Glv	unwghtd + swsn	.758	.771	.907	.833
OoB + both aux	unwghtd	.762†	.780†	.893†	.833†
OoB + both aux	unwghtd + swsn	.766†	.781†	.906†	.839†

wghtd + swsn' use the both the 'unwghtd' features and the saliency-weighted semantic network features.

5.1 Using out-of-the-box vectors

For the rows marked 'OoB' only out-of-the-box word embeddings were used of the four sets described in Section 4.2.1 and Section 4.2.2. The settings for the regularisation parameters of the classifier are determined by cross validating on the training set. For the experiment with only unweighted features, the hyper-parameter settings are C $= 10^8$ and gamma $= 10^{-5}$. For the experiment including the saliency-weighted semantic network features we have C $= 10^6$ and gamma $= 10^{-4}$.

Table 1 shows that the result when using only publicly available, out-of-the-box word vectors (the rows marked OoB), surpass all the baselines.[7]

An important observation is that the best scoring approach on this data set using WordNet-based features, to our knowledge, reports an accuracy of .741 and an F_1 score of .824 [17]. As we can see, our generic approach with only publicly available vectors, without any tuning or optimisation, outperforms this method. This is an important finding, as it shows that for computing semantic similarity, the labour-intensive construction of a rich semantic knowledge source such as WordNet is not a necessity. As an aside, our finding supports a claim made in [5] in a different context of matching texts of different lengths, "that traditional knowledge-based features are cornered by novel corpus-based word meaning representations."

5.2 Using auxiliary vectors

To show the potential of our method we report the results when, next to the OoB vectors, the auxiliary vectors—generated from the embeddings trained on the INEX data as described in Section 4.2.3—are used. The bottom rows in Table 1 show the best results obtained with these vectors.

The results of the experiments with the auxiliary vectors are consistently better than the baselines and the results with only OoB vectors, both in terms of accuracy and F_1.

If we compare the results of our method that only uses semantic features, to the current state-of-the-art methods, which rely on linguistic analysis and handcrafted features, we observe that when optimal settings are used, our method can outperform the tree kernel approach described in [4]. This method uses features derived from dependency parses, and yields an accuracy of .753 on this data set (no precision, recall and F_1 score are reported). Furthermore, our top-performing run, the bottom row in Table 1, shows results comparable results presented in [39], based on dynamic pooling and unfolding recursive auto-encoders trained on parse trees—that has an accuracy of .768 and F_1 of .836. Our top-performing run does slightly better in terms of F_1 and slightly worse with respect to the accuracy. It is important to note, however, that the results in [39] are only achieved when, next to the general neural network-based method, several handcrafted features are added, which are designed especially for the evaluation set at hand (the features are primarily dealing with representation of numbers). Interestingly, our method performs better than the neural network-based approach in [39] when the latter is run without the test-set-specific handcrafted features, in which case it yields an accuracy of .726.

The best performance on the MSR Paraphrase Corpus, to our knowledge, is presented in [22]. Matrix decomposition is performed on a co-occurrence matrix, and saliency weighting is applied, where the saliency weight per word or n-gram is optimised on the training data. A dependency parser is used to generate the ngrams. The best performance is obtained by performing matrix decomposition on the training and test data combined. But even if only the training set is used, an accuracy of .786 and .846 F_1 is attained, when no additional hand-crafted features are used. This result is better than ours in terms of accuracy, while in terms of F_1 the scores are comparable.

The word2vec vectors and GloVe vectors, when added separately, yield better performance. This is particularly noteworthy as it shows that high-quality word embeddings can be produced for the present setting by both algorithms, even when the corpus used for training was substantially smaller than what is commonly used (namely ~1B tokens, against 3B and 100B tokens for the OoB word2vec sets and 42B and 840B for the OoB GloVe vectors).

When both the auxiliary word2vec and GloVe vectors are added to the OoB vectors—the rows marked 'OoB + both aux'—we see another increase in performance specifically in terms of precision. These results are significantly different from the OoB run with both feature sets. The results in the 'OoB + both aux' rows also surpass the results in the 'OoB + aux w2v' and 'OoB + aux Glv' separately. This is particularly interesting, as it indicates that, while the performance of both vectors sets on their own is comparable, the two models capture different semantic information.

Finally, an overall observation from Table 1 is that adding the saliency-weighted semantic network features consistently yields better performance. We note that this goes against an observation in [17]: *"Since experiments with document specificity weightings (such as tf-idf) had shown that using these factors actually reduced performance no such weighting factor was used here."*

5.2.1 *Parameter analysis*

Space constraints prevent us from providing an extensive overview of results across all parameter settings. An important observation, however, is that although the settings matter, few consistent

[7]We cannot calculate statistical significance between our results and the baseline results as for the appropriate test—a matched-pairs t-test—we need to compare our output to the outputs of the baseline systems, which are not publicly available (only the aggregate results are).

patterns emerge. To illustrate, for the 'OoB + both aux' setting, the worst performance in terms of accuracy across parameters, with optimal regularisation parameters was .730, which is worse than the performance with only OoB vectors, but above baseline performance. For the auxiliary word2vec vectors, negative sampling seems to be beneficial in general, with a value of 10 being a robust choice. Both the choice of architecture (CBOW or Skip-gram) and applying hierarchical softmax or no seems to be of little consequence.

For the GloVe vectors different values for the exponent of the weighting function and the cut-off in the weighting function were used. The moderate values (.5, .75 for the exponent, and 50 or 100 for the maximum cut-off) yielded the best results.

Lastly, the regularisation parameters (C and gamma) of the classifier are hyper-parameters of our model. We use large values for C (in the range of 10^6–10^9 depending on the number of features) and small values for gamma (10^{-4}, 10^{-5}). Not surprisingly, the setting of these parameters in particular has substantial repercussions on the final performance. To illustrate again, the worst performance with optimal features but across regularisation parameters was .690, which is lower than the lowest baseline. The worst overall performance (worst features and worst regularisation) is roughly equal, at .685, which suggests that the harm is primarily caused by suboptimal regularisation.

These findings indicates that both algorithms for generating word embeddings, word2vec and GloVe, are robust across reasonable parameter settings. While it is important to find the optimal combination of all parameters, the settings for the word embeddings matter less than regularising the learning algorithm.

5.2.2 *Feature importance*

In addition to studying the effect of the different sets of word embeddings as discussed above, it is interesting to see how different sets of features affect the performance. To analyse the effect per feature set we perform an ablation study, where we leave out a set of features for all word embedding sets we calculate features from.[8]

Table 2: Ablation study results

Omitted feature set	Acc.	p	r	F_1
max unweighted sn bins	.739	.766	.874	.817
swsn bins	.741	.768	.874	.818
dimension bins	.746	.767	.886	.822
all unweighted sn bins	.747	.763	.898	.825
distances	.759	.778	.892	.831

In Table 2 the results are shown for leaving out different feature sets, sorted by accuracy. All other settings (the word2vec and GloVe parameters for the auxiliary vectors and the regularisation parameters for the classifier) are identical to the ones used for the top performing run in Table 1 (bottom row).

As can be seen from Table 2 leaving out the word alignment methods, weighted by saliency or not, has the most dramatic effect on performance. This indicates that aligning words is a successful strategy for determining semantic similarity between short texts.

An interesting observation is that leaving out the distance features has the least effect on performance. As noted above, these features measure the distance between the means of the word vectors in both sentences, and are a default method for going from word-level to sentence-level, applied, next to other methods, in e.g., [5, 20, 40]. Table 2 does suggest that binning the differences between dimensions of the mean vectors, as proposed in this paper, increases the gain obtained from them.

[8]Note that it is not possible to use the feature weights as a proxy for feature importance, as this only works for linear kernel functions, and we use a classifier with an RBF kernel.

5.3 Error analysis

To see whether our method of computing semantic textual similarity for short texts is biased we perform an error analysis concerning two important attributes of the test data: sentence length and lexical overlap.

5.3.1 *Performance across sentence length*

Figure 2 shows an overview of the results of our experiments divided by sentence length.

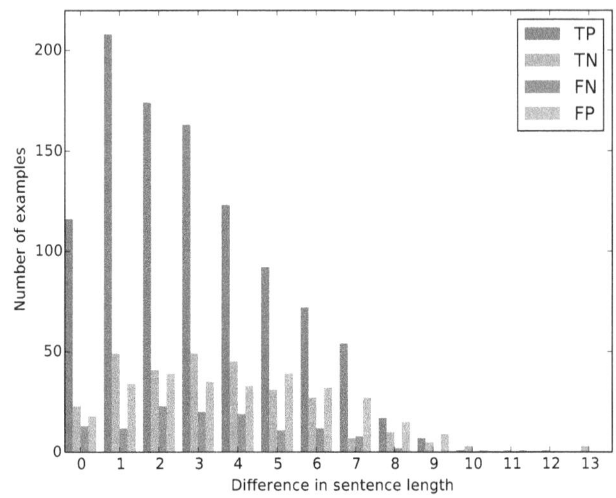

Figure 2: Results 'OoB + both aux – unwghtd + swsn' run divided by difference in sentence length (measured in words). TP: true positives, TN: True negatives, FP: false positives, FN: false negatives. (Best viewed in color.)

As expected, sentences that are alike in in terms of length are easier to perform well on, as reflected in the figure by the large bulge at the left side of the scale for the true positives. The hump for true negatives is less pronounced, which is easily explained by a lower frequency of negative examples in the test set.

One observation from Figure 2 is that the number of false negatives is rather constant in the left half of the figure, which means that it increases relatively with the difference in sentence length, while this is not the case for false positives. This means that the classifier has a tendency to predict semantic dissimilarity when the two input texts differ in length substantially.

Most importantly though, Figure 2 shows that the classifier always predicts the correct label in the majority of cases, regardless of the difference in sentence length.

5.3.2 *Performance across levels of lexical overlap*

As our saliency-weighted semantic network features perform semantic, rather than lexical, word pairings, it is interesting to see how our method performs across different levels of lexical (i.e., *literal*) overlap between the sentence pairs in our test collection.

In Figure 3 we show an overview of the results across different levels of lexical overlap of our best performing run on the MSR Paraphrase Corpus (OoB + both aux – unwghtd + swsn; see bottom row in Table 1).

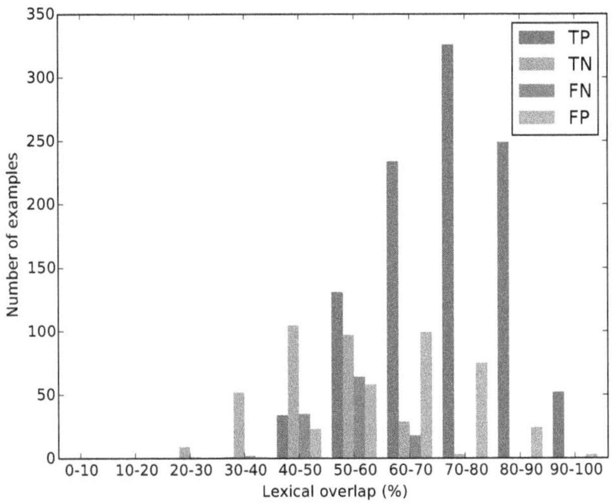

Figure 3: Results for the 'OoB + both aux – unwghtd + swsn' run, grouped by percentage of lexical overlap between test sentences in the MSR Paraphrase Corpus. (Best viewed in color.)

In Figure 3 we can clearly see four different distributions of results, where, e.g., the TP results peak at 70–80% and the TN results peak at 40–50%.

As is to be expected, the 'OoB + both aux – unwghtd + swsn' run is right most times at high levels of lexical overlap. If it is wrong it produced false positives, i.e., it predicts semantic similarity too often, which is easily explained by the high similarity between the sentences. An interesting glitch is the tiny FP bar at the far right of the figure (90%-100% overlap), which denotes 3 cases of high lexical overlap, where the annotators judged the test sentences not to be semantically similar, while our method for predicting short text semantic similarity did. Indeed, the differences are rather subtle, as illustrated by this example pair:

> *Air Canada, the largest airline in Canada and No. 11 in the world, has been under court protection from creditors since April 1*

and

> *The No. 11 airline in the world, Air Canada has been under court protection from creditors since April 1.*

There is a peak in the middle for the FN bars, at 50–60% overlap, where our method cannot make up for the relatively low level of lexical overlap, and mistakenly predicts semantic dissimilarity. Interestingly, though, the bars show that our algorithm, even for these difficult cases, still makes the correct prediction in the majority of cases. An additional noteworthy observation is that even when the majority of words in the sentences that make up the test pairs are different, at 40–50% overlap level, our algorithm still produces true positives, next to true negatives. This clearly shows the benefit of semantic matching over lexical matching. More importantly, it shows a meaningful distinction can be made by the algorithm, even for these non-trivial cases.

The final important observation from Figure 3 is that our method, the 'OoB + both aux – unwghtd + swsn' run, is right in the majority of cases across all levels of lexical overlap.

6. CONCLUSIONS AND FUTURE WORK

We have described a generic and flexible method for semantic matching of short texts, which leverages word embeddings of different dimensionality, obtained by different algorithms and from different sources. The method makes no use of external sources of structured semantic knowledge nor of linguistic tools, such as parsers. Instead it uses a word alignment method, and a saliency-weighted semantic graph, to go from word-level to text-level semantics. We compute features from the word alignment method and from the means of word embeddings, to train a final classifier that predicts a semantic similarity score.

We demonstrate on a large publicly available evaluation set that our generic, semantics-only method of computing semantic similarity between short texts outperforms all baseline approaches working under the same conditions, and that it exceeds all approaches using external sources of structured semantic knowledge that have been evaluated in this dataset, to our knowledge.

An important implication of our results is that distributional semantics has come to a level where it can be employed by itself in a generic approach for producing features that can be used to yield state-of-the-art performance on the short text similarity task, even if no manually tuned features are added that optimise for a specific test set or domain. Furthermore, the word embeddings, when employed as proposed above, substitute external semantic knowledge and make human "feature engineering" unnecessary. As our method does not depend on NLP tools, it can be applied to domains and languages for which these are sparse.

It is interesting to see how other fields of research that deal with large corpora of unstructured text can benefit. For example, in automatically created probabilistic knowledge bases (e.g., [16]) triples are extracted from an input corpus and have a confidence score associated with them based on the number of sentences in the corpus describing the relation in the triple. Short text similarity can be used to improve this confidence score.

An evident limitation of calculating meta-features in the manner we propose, i.e., from averaged word vectors and word alignments, is that the order of words is not taken into account. This goes for any bag-of-words model, of course. The reason the difference between word-order-aware models and bag-of-word models is not apparent from the results on sentence similarity tasks over the years might be that the commonly used evaluation sets do not contain enough sentence pairs (if at all) in which word order is a crucial factor.

Acknowledgments.

We thank our anonymous reviewers for their valuable feedback, which helped to improve the paper. This research was supported by Amsterdam Data Science, the Dutch national program COMMIT, Elsevier, the European Community's Seventh Framework Programme (FP7/2007-2013) under grant agreement nr 312827 (VOX-Pol), the ESF Research Network Program ELIAS, the HPC Fund the Royal Dutch Academy of Sciences (KNAW) under the Elite Network Shifts project, the Netherlands eScience Center under project number 027.012.105, the Microsoft Research Ph.D. program, the Netherlands Institute for Sound and Vision, the Netherlands Organisation for Scientific Research (NWO) under project nrs 727.011.005, 612.001.116, HOR-11-10, 640.006.013, 612.066.930, CI-14-25, SH-322-15, the Yahoo! Faculty Research and Engagement Program, and Yandex.

7. REFERENCES

[1] E. Agirre, M. Diab, D. Cer, and A. Gonzalez-Agirre. Semeval-2012 task 6: A pilot on semantic textual similarity. In *SemEval 2012*, 2012.

[2] E. Agirre, D. Cer, M. Diab, A. Gonzalez-Agirre, and W. Guo. sem 2013 shared task: Semantic textual similarity, including a pilot on typed-similarity. In **SEM 2013*, 2013.

[3] R. M. Aliguliyev. A new sentence similarity measure and sentence based extractive technique for automatic text summarization. *Expert Systems with Applications*, 2009.

[4] P. Annesi, D. Croce, and R. Basili. Semantic compositionality in tree kernels. In *CIKM 2014*, 2014.

[5] C. Banea, D. Chen, R. Mihalcea, C. Cardie, and J. Wiebe. Simcompass: Using deep learning word embeddings to assess cross-level similarity. *SemEval 2014*, 2014.

[6] D. Bär, C. Biemann, I. Gurevych, and T. Zesch. Ukp: Computing semantic textual similarity by combining multiple content similarity measures. In *SemEval 2012*, 2012.

[7] M. Baroni, G. Dinu, and G. Kruszewski. Don't count, predict! a systematic comparison of context-counting vs. context-predicting semantic vectors. In *ACL 2014*, 2014.

[8] P. Bellot, G. Kazai, M. Preminger, M. Trappett, A. Doucet, M. Koolen, E. SanJuan, A. Trotman, S. Geva, A. Mishra, R. Schenkel, M. Sanderson, S. Gurajada, V. Moriceau, X. Tannier, F. Scholer, J. Kamps, J. Mothe, M. Theobald, and Q. Wang. Report on INEX 2013. *SIGIR Forum*, 47(2): 21–32, 2013.

[9] Y. Bengio, H. Schwenk, J.-S. Senécal, F. Morin, and J.-L. Gauvain. Neural probabilistic language models. In *Innovations in Machine Learning*. Springer, 2006.

[10] S. Bird, E. Klein, and E. Loper. *Natural language processing with Python*. O'Reilly Media, Inc., 2009.

[11] S. Canuto, T. Salles, M. A. Gonçalves, L. Rocha, G. Ramos, L. Gonçalves, T. Rosa, and W. Martins. On efficient meta-level features for effective text classification. In *CIKM 2014*, 2014.

[12] T. A. Coelho, P. P. Calado, L. V. Souza, B. Ribeiro-Neto, and R. Muntz. Image retrieval using multiple evidence ranking. *IEEE Transactions on Knowledge and Data Engineering*, 16 (4):408–417, 2004.

[13] R. Collobert and J. Weston. A unified architecture for natural language processing: Deep neural networks with multitask learning. In *ICML 2008*, 2008.

[14] S. C. Deerwester, S. T. Dumais, T. K. Landauer, G. W. Furnas, and R. A. Harshman. Indexing by latent semantic analysis. *Journal of the American Society for Information Science*, 41(6):391–407, 1990.

[15] B. Dolan, C. Quirk, and C. Brockett. Unsupervised construction of large paraphrase corpora: Exploiting massively parallel news sources. In *COLING 2004*, 2004.

[16] X. L. Dong, K. Murphy, E. Gabrilovich, G. Heitz, W. Horn, N. Lao, T. Strohmann, S. Sun, and W. Zhang. Knowledge vault: A web-scale approach to probabilistic knowledge fusion. In *KDD 2014*, 2014.

[17] S. Fernando and M. Stevenson. A semantic similarity approach to paraphrase detection. *CLUK 2008*, 2008.

[18] R. Ferreira, R. D. Lins, F. Freitas, S. J. Simske, and M. Riss. A new sentence similarity assessment measure based on a three-layer sentence representation. In *DocEng 2014*, 2014.

[19] L. Han, A. Kashyap, T. Finin, J. Mayfield, and J. Weese. UMBC EBIQUITY-CORE: Semantic textual similarity systems. In **SEM-2013*, 2013.

[20] B. Hu, Z. Lu, H. Li, and Q. Chen. Convolutional neural network architectures for matching natural language sentences. In *NIPS 2014*, 2014.

[21] A. Islam and D. Inkpen. Semantic text similarity using corpus-based word similarity and string similarity. *TKDD*, 2008.

[22] Y. Ji and J. Eisenstein. Discriminative improvements to distributional sentence similarity. In *EMNLP*, 2013.

[23] V. Jijkoun and M. de Rijke. Recognizing textual entailment using lexical similarity. In *Proceedings Pascal 2005 Textual Entailment Challenge Workshop*, 2005.

[24] Y. Kim. Convolutional neural networks for sentence classification. In *EMNLP 2014*, 2014.

[25] Q. V. Le and T. Mikolov. Distributed representations of sentences and documents. In *Proceedings of the 31st International Conference on Machine Learning*, 2014.

[26] H. Li and J. Xu. Semantic matching in search. *Foundations and Trends in Information Retrieval*, 7(5):343–469, 2014.

[27] Y. Li, D. McLean, Z. A. Bandar, J. D. O'shea, and K. Crockett. Sentence similarity based on semantic nets and corpus statistics. *IEEE Transactions on Knowledge and Data Engineering*, 18(8):1138–1150, 2006.

[28] M. C. Lintean and V. Rus. Measuring semantic similarity in short texts through greedy pairing and word semantics. In *FLAIRS Conference*, 2012.

[29] E. Marsi, H. Moen, L. Bungum, G. Sizov, B. Gambäck, and A. Lynum. Ntnu-core: Combining strong features for semantic similarity. **SEM-2013*, 2013.

[30] D. Metzler, S. Dumais, and C. Meek. Similarity measures for short segments of text. In *ECIR 2007*, 2007.

[31] R. Mihalcea, C. Corley, and C. Strapparava. Corpus-based and knowledge-based measures of text semantic similarity. In *AAAI*, 2006.

[32] T. Mikolov, K. Chen, G. Corrado, and J. Dean. Efficient estimation of word representations in vector space. *arXiv preprint arXiv:1301.3781*, 2013.

[33] T. Mikolov, I. Sutskever, K. Chen, G. S. Corrado, and J. Dean. Distributed representations of words and phrases and their compositionality. In *NIPS 2013*, 2013.

[34] J. Pennington, R. Socher, and C. D. Manning. Glove: Global vectors for word representation. *EMNLP 2014*, 2014.

[35] C. Quirk, C. Brockett, and W. B. Dolan. Monolingual machine translation for paraphrase generation. In *EMNLP 2004*, 2004.

[36] S. Robertson and H. Zaragoza. The probabilistic relevance framework: BM25 and beyond. *Foundations and Trends in Information Retrieval*, 3(4):333–389, 2009.

[37] F. Šarić, G. Glavaš, M. Karan, J. Šnajder, and B. D. Bašić. Takelab: Systems for measuring semantic text similarity. In **SEM-2013*, 2012.

[38] P. Shrestha. Corpus-based methods for short text similarity. *Rencontre des Étudiants Chercheurs en Informatique pour le Traitement automatique des Langues*, 2011.

[39] R. Socher, E. H. Huang, J. Pennin, C. D. Manning, and A. Y. Ng. Dynamic pooling and unfolding recursive autoencoders for paraphrase detection. In *NIPS 2011*, 2011.

[40] R. Socher, D. Chen, C. D. Manning, and A. Ng. Reasoning with neural tensor networks for knowledge base completion. In *NIPS 2013*, 2013.

Building Representative Composite Items

Vincent Leroy, Sihem Amer-Yahia, Eric Gaussier, Hamid Mirisaee
Université Grenoble Alpes - LIG, CNRS
Grenoble, France
Firstname.Lastname@imag.fr

ABSTRACT

The problem of summarizing a large collection of *homogeneous* items has been addressed extensively in particular in the case of geo-tagged datasets (e.g. Flickr photos and tags). In our work, we study the problem of summarizing large collections of *heterogeneous* items. For example, a user planning to spend extended periods of time in a given city would be interested in seeing a map of that city with item summaries in different geographic areas, each containing a theater, a gym, a bakery, a few restaurants and a subway station. We propose to solve that problem by building representative Composite Items (CIs).

To the best of our knowledge, this is the first work that addresses the problem of finding representative CIs for heterogeneous items. Our problem naturally arises when summarizing geo-tagged datasets but also in other datasets such as movie or music summarization. We formalize building representative CIs as an optimization problem and propose KFC, an extended fuzzy clustering algorithm to solve it. We show that KFC converges and run extensive experiments on a variety of real datasets that validate its effectiveness.

Categories and Subject Descriptors

H.3.3 [**Information storage and retrieval**]: Information Search and Retrieval—*Selection process*

Keywords

summarization; fuzzy clustering; composite items

1. INTRODUCTION

The problem of summarizing a large collection of items has received a lot of attention in particular in the case of geo-tagged datasets. For example, in [13], representative tags are used to summarize a large collection of Flickr photos. In the presence of several collections, each representing a different item type (e.g., schools, restaurants, subway stations, and theaters in a city), we are faced with the question of defining an effective summarization. One could summarize one collection at a time and show the results on a map. For example, in the case of a city, each item type such as restaurant and subway station, would be summarized separately and rendered on the same map. This one-type-at-a-time approach does not necessarily guarantee that each area in the map will contain representative items of each type, nor does it ensure that items in the same area will be close to each other, i.e., *cohesive*. In this paper, we propose to explore the applicability of Composite Items (CIs) to this question.

CIs have been shown to be very effective in solving complex information needs such as planning a city tour, selecting books for a reading club, or organizing a movie rating contest [2,3,7,9,10,12,13,15,16]. In those applications, a CI is a set of close items (e.g., geographically close points of interest - POIs, movies rated by the same users) that satisfy *a budget* (e.g., at least two schools and one theater, at least one movie per genre). When summarizing POIs, a CI may correspond to geographically close places that have different types (e.g., theater and museum) and whose total visit time does not exceed 3 hours. When selecting books, a CI may be formed by similar books, i.e., on similar topics, written by different authors and whose total price is less than a maximum amount. When organizing a movie contest, a CI is a set of comparable movies, i.e., having common reviewers, and with different genres or release years. The budget constraint of a CI can therefore be used to *glue together* heterogeneous items, i.e., items with different types. In that case, we say that a CI is *valid*. The problem of summarizing heterogeneous item collections can therefore be formulated as finding K valid, cohesive and representative CIs, i.e., each CI satisfies budget constraints, is formed of "close" items, and the set of CIs "covers" all input items.

Forming valid, cohesive and representative CIs can be naturally expressed as a constrained optimization problem [2]. Existing solutions to solve this problem usually rely on two phases: in one solution, many valid CIs (i.e. satisfying the budget constraint) are built, and then the K farthest are chosen thereby resulting in representative CIs. In the other, a K-clustering is performed in the first stage to address representativity, and then one valid CI, i.e. satisfying constraints, is picked from each cluster in order to produce K CIs overall. This process decouples budget constraint satisfaction (e.g., a CI must contain one museum and 2 restaurants) from the optimization goal (e.g., each CI is a set of closely located POIs). As a result, we can argue that while clustering is a natural solution to finding CIs, existing formulations are not well-adapted to achieve validity, cohesiveness

Permission to make digital or hard copies of all or part of this work for personal or classroom use is granted without fee provided that copies are not made or distributed for profit or commercial advantage and that copies bear this notice and the full citation on the first page. Copyrights for components of this work owned by others than the author(s) must be honored. Abstracting with credit is permitted. To copy otherwise, or republish, to post on servers or to redistribute to lists, requires prior specific permission and/or a fee. Request permissions from Permissions@acm.org.
CIKM'15, October 19–23, 2015, Melbourne, VIC, Australia
Copyright is held by the owner/author(s). Publication rights licensed to ACM.
ACM 978-1-4503-3794-6/15/10 ...$15.00
DOI: http://dx.doi.org/10.1145/2806416.2806465.

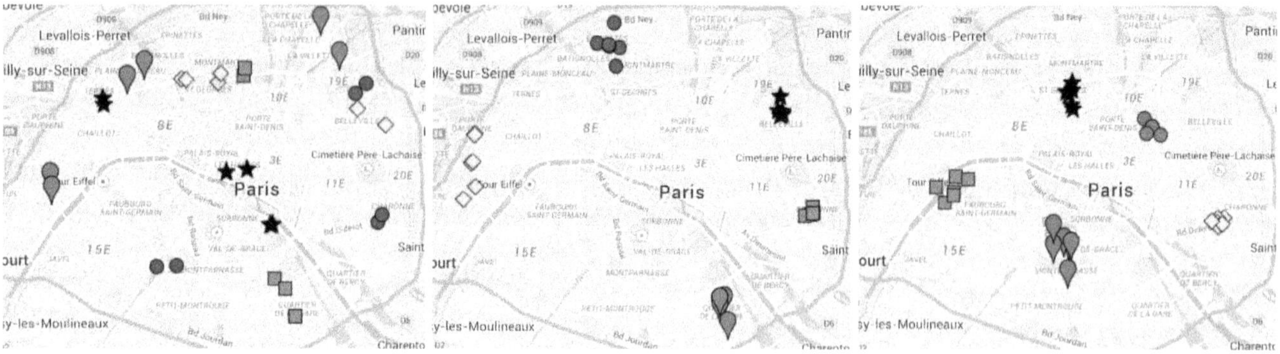

(a) One-at-a-Time Approach (b) Two-Stage Approach (c) Integrated Approach

Figure 1: Alternative approaches to build composite items

and representativity simultaneously. We hence advocate the seamless integration of validity, cohesiveness and representativity when building CIs. We illustrate that on the following example.

EXAMPLE 1. *Consider the case of Mary whose job is to train future users of products developed by a large software company. Mary often travels to different places where she spends extended periods of time, i.e., at least 2 weeks, during which she rents an apartment. In her free time, Mary enjoys going to the theater and dining out wherever she stays. She also practices yoga and likes swimming. Mary would be interested in exploring a map with representative CIs in different areas in the city she is planning to visit. Each CI must be valid, i.e., contain at least one theater, a pharmacy, a gym, two restaurants and a subway station (at least 6 items in total with specific cardinality constraints per item type), and cohesive, i.e., contain closeby items. Figures 1a, 1b and 1c show three sets of CIs for Paris produced using the Tourpedia dataset[1] with three different methods: the one-at-a-time approach that summarizes each homogeneous item collection separately, the two-stage approach that decouples validity, cohesiveness and representativity, and an integrated approach that optimizes validity, cohesiveness and representativity together. The CIs generated using the integrated approach (Figure 1c) offer the best trade-off between validity, cohesiveness and representativity. Indeed, the CIs in Figure 1a tend to favor representativity (coverage of the city) to the expense of cohesiveness (items in each CI are not close to each-other). Those in Figure 1b are located on the edges of the city because this two-stage approach first produces the most cohesive valid CIs, which limits their representativity in the second stage.*

Our example intuitively illustrates that summarizing individual lists of items and decoupling validity and representativity results in finding sub-optimal CIs in case of heterogeneous item collections. In addition, while existing approaches are based on hard clustering techniques imposing that an item must belong to one CI, in the case of a heterogeneous set of items, an item may have multiple types and should be able to belong to more than one CI. Therefore, *we propose to study the applicability of fuzzy clustering [6] to find valid and representative composite items.* In fuzzy clustering, an item may belong to more than one cluster. Our algorithm solves a joint optimization problem where one part aims at identifying item representatives (related here to cluster centroids obtained through fuzzy clustering) whereas the other part ensures that the representatives chosen are "close" to valid CIs (that is CIs satisfying budget constraints) and are cohesive. We consider in fact two problems: a minimization problem involving distance functions, and in particular the Euclidean distance, and a maximization problem involving similarity functions, and in particular cosine similarity.

Our problem naturally arises when summarizing geo-tagged datasets but also in other datasets such as book and movie summarization. That is illustrated in our experiments that make use of real datasets: **Tourpedia**[2], **BookCrossing**[3], and **MovieLens**[4]. We compare our integrated approach with the two-phase approaches proposed in [2] and show that blending validity, cohesiveness and representativity produces higher quality CIs efficiently.

In summary, the paper makes the following contributions:

- We formalize an optimization problem for building valid, cohesive and representative CIs to summarize large collections of heterogeneous items. In particular, we define validity that glues together items of different types into a single CI according to budget constraints such as:

  $$\langle 2\ drama, 2\ action, 1\ comedy, \$5 \rangle$$

  We also define a clustering objective function that captures cohesiveness and representativity. Representativity aims at finding the K CIs that cover best the input set of items. Cohesiveness is ensured by selecting the closest valid CI to each cluster centroid.

- We design `KFC`, a constraint-based fuzzy clustering algorithm that seamlessly integrates validity, cohesiveness and representativity and show that it converges.

- We run an extensive set of experiments on 3 real datasets with different characteristics. Our experiments explore the quality of CIs produced by `KFC` and compares them with state-of-the-art two-stage approaches from the literature [2]. In particular, we show that our CIs are higher quality (validity) and provide a better coverage

[1] *http://datahub.io/dataset/tourpedia*

[2] *http://datahub.io/dataset/tourpedia*

[3] *http://www.bookcrossing.com/*

[4] *https://movielens.org/*

of input items (representativity). We also run performance experiments demonstrating that KFC outperforms two-stage approaches and that it scales linearly with different parameters.

Section 2 contains our formalization and general problem statement. Section 3 describes our integrated algorithm, KFC. Experiments are provided in detail in Section 4. Related work and conclusion are given in Sections 5 and 6 respectively.

2. MODEL AND PROBLEM

In this section, we first define our formal model and discuss the link between clustering, validity, cohesiveness and representativity. We then formalize the problem of *finding a set of K, possibly overlapping, valid, cohesive and representative CIs.*

2.1 Data Model

We are given a set $\mathcal{X}$ of items where $x \in \mathcal{X}$ is uniquely identified. $\mathcal{X}$ is a heterogeneous set of items each of which may have one or several types in $\mathcal{T} = \{t_1, \ldots, t_n\}$. For example, the movie Titanic has two types: romance and drama. A book type could be novel or adventure and the type of a point of interest could be museum, park, etc. We use $x.type$ to refer to the type(s) of x. We furthermore assume that an item x may have a cost, that will be denoted as $x.cost$. For a book, this would typically be its selling price. For a museum, it could either be the cost of an entry ticket or the average time required to visit it.

We define a budget vector $b = \langle \#t_1, \ldots, \#t_n, \#_\$ \rangle$ where each $\#t_i$ specifies a cardinality for an item type $t_i \in \mathcal{T}$ and $\#_\$$ is a total cost (e.g., maximum price a user is willing to pay for a movie or maximum time a user is willing to spend visiting a place). For example, the vector $\langle 1, 2, 1, 90 \rangle$ applied on books would represent 1 novel, 2 art books, and 1 self-help book, assuming those are the only available book types, whose total price does not exceed 90\$. The same vector applied on points of interest in a city would be interpreted very differently and represent 1 gym, 2 subway stops and 1 bakery and a total time not exceeding 90 minutes.

Depending on the context, we will make use of a distance function, noted $d(,)$ or a similarity function, noted $s(,)$, to compare a pair of items $(x, x') \in \mathcal{X} \times \mathcal{X}$. For instance, if x and x' are points of interest in a city, it is natural to use their geographic distance. If items are books, it is more appropriate to compare them according to content similarity, e.g. based on the cosine between their vectors; similarly, if items are movies, their similarity can be computed as the fraction of reviewers who like both x and x'.

2.2 Representativity through fuzzy clustering

We are interested in identifying valid, cohesive and representative sets of items where each item has one or several types. The *validity* of a set of items is expressed in terms of the budget vector $b = \langle \#t_1, \ldots, \#t_n, \#_\$ \rangle$ introduced above. The *cohesiveness* is the ability to identify sets of items relatively close to each other, whereas the *representativity* is the ability to cover the input dataset. The clustering literature contains many proposals for finding representative points of a dataset. Indeed, representative points are typically obtained, in any given dataset, as the centroids of the clusters present in that dataset: The set of clusters "covers" the whole dataset and their centroids represent a summary of the content of each cluster. In *hard* clustering, items are divided into distinct clusters and each item belongs to exactly one cluster, a framework well adapted to homogeneous items [13]. However, in the case of a heterogeneous set of items, an item may have different types and hence belong to more than one cluster. Therefore, we propose to study the applicability of *fuzzy* clustering [6] to the problem of finding valid, cohesive and representative items.

The most popular fuzzy clustering algorithm is Fuzzy C-Means (FCM) [6]. FCM assigns a set of items $\mathcal{X}$ to a collection of K fuzzy clusters represented through their centroids v_j, $1 \leq j \leq K$ (the set of centroids will be denoted V). More precisely, given a set of N items, $\mathcal{X}$, the algorithm returns both the K centroids and a partition matrix $W = w_{i,j} \in [0,1]$, $i \in [1, N]$, $j \in [1, K]$ where each w_{ij} represents the degree to which item x_i belongs to cluster j. Given a distance function $d(,)$, the standard objective function of FCM is as follows:

$$\operatorname*{argmin}_{V,W} \sum_{i=1}^{N} \sum_{j=1}^{K} w_{ij}^{m} d(x_i, v_j)$$

$$s.t.\ \forall i \in [1, N],\ \sum_{j=1}^{K} w_{ij} = 1$$

where m is a weighting exponent, greater than one. A large value of m results in smaller memberships w_{ij} and hence, fuzzier clusters, whereas setting m to 1 leads to hard clustering [6]. The problem above is typically solved through an alternate optimization process in which one fixes v (respectively w) and solves for w (respectively v). The proof that such an approach converges is given in [5]; furthermore, initialization of k-means++ [4] can also be used for the centroids.

Fuzzy clustering thus represents a direct way to identify clusters in a dataset and their representative points defined by their centroids. Furthermore, its fuzzy nature enables each point to be assigned to different clusters (and centroids) through membership values.

2.3 Problem Statement

We seek to find a set of K valid, cohesive and representative items. Intuitively, validity finds sets of items that satisfy a budget constraint (i.e., cardinality and/or cost) b which glues together items of different types into *composite items*, CIs. Cohesion and representativity intuitively try to identify those CIs formed of close items that cover the input dataset (i.e., that are close to cluster centroids). We first define a valid CIs as follows:

DEFINITION 1. *Given a set of items $\mathcal{X}$ and a budget b, a valid CI, denoted $\{x_1, \cdots, x_{le}; x_i \in X, 1 \leq i \leq le\}$, is a set of items such that :*

$$\begin{cases} (i)\ \forall \#t_j \in b,\ \sum_{i=1}^{le} \mathbb{1}(t_j, x_i.type) \geq \#t_j \\ (ii)\ \sum_{i=1}^{le} x_i.cost \leq \#_\$ \end{cases}$$

where $\mathbb{1}$ is an indicator function which is 1 if both arguments are equal and 0 otherwise. le is the number of items in the CI and is such that $le \geq n$, where n is the number of type *values considered. The set of all valid CIs will be denoted as* $\mathcal{V}_{CI}$.

It is easy to check whether for any b and any $\mathcal{X}$ there exists a valid CI or not (one simply gathers the $\#t_j$ cheapest items of each type t_j in b and checks their total cost). We will assume that there exists at least one valid CI for the set of items and budget constraint considered. We also assume that $\mathcal{X} \subseteq \mathbb{R}^p$. This assumption is not restrictive as most data points (or items) can be transformed so as to obtain a vector representation.

We can now formulate our problem as a joint optimization problem where one part aims at identifying good summaries (i.e. cluster centroids that are representative) of the set of items whereas the other part ensures that the representatives chosen are "close" to valid CIs, which are in turn cohesive, i.e., formed of closeby items. The closest cohesive CIs to the obtained centroids are thus valid and representative of the set of items. We in fact face two problems: a minimization problem involving the distance function $d(,)$ and a maximization problem involving the similarity function $s(,)$. Note that the weighting exponent m of the fuzzy clustering part of each problem takes values in $[1, \infty]$ for the maximization problem and in $[0, 1]$ for the minimization problem. This is simply due to the fact that the functions considered should be pseudo-convex in one case and pseudo-concave in the other. This leads to, when considering distances:

$$\begin{cases} \textbf{Distance-based formulation} \\ \underset{V,W}{\operatorname{argmin}} \underbrace{(1-\lambda)\sum_{j=1}^{K}\sum_{i=1}^{N} w_{ij}^{m} d(x_i, v_j)}_{FC} + \\ \qquad \underbrace{\lambda \sum_{j=1}^{K} \min_{C \in \mathcal{V}_{CI}} \left(\sum_{x \in C} d(x, v_j) \right)}_{\texttt{CRCI}} \\ s.t.\ \forall i \in [1, N],\ \sum_{j=1}^{K} w_{ij} = 1 \end{cases} \tag{1}$$

where V denotes a set of K points (centroids) and W a partition matrix of size $N \times K$. The **Similarity-based formulation** is obtained from the above by replacing argmin by argmax, min by max, and $d(,)$ by $s(,)$. λ is a parameter that controls the influence of the two aspects of the problem: identifying cluster centroids that are representative of the complete dataset (*FC - Fuzzy Clustering*) while ensuring that the centroids obtained are close to some valid CI (`CRCI` - *Close Representative CI*). Minimizing the sum of the distances of all the items of the CI to the centroid in `CRCI` additionally ensures the cohesion of the valid CI considered. It is the compromise between these different aspects that allows one to identify valid, cohesive and representative CIs. It is important to note that the above formulation corresponds to an integrated approach that directly yields valid, cohesive and representative CIs. This contrasts with most previous solutions that rely on a two-step approach in which candidate CIs are first generated and then filtered [2].

Note that one could consider a more complex formulation with an explicit term to account for cohesion of items within CIs. Such a problem would however be more difficult to solve and would make us of an additional hyper-parameter. We rely on this study on the simpler form above in which cohesion is implicitly captured through the distance of all items to the centroid, as mentioned above.

Complexity considerations

The minimum sum of squared clustering problem (MSSC) is known to be NP-hard [1] (this problem is the one tackled by the classical k-means heuristic [14]). Setting λ to 0, m to 1 and $d(,)$ to the Euclidean distance in Problem (1) directly corresponds to MSSC (setting m to 1 transforms the fuzzy clustering defined in FC into a hard clustering problem; the fuzzy C-means algorithm becomes standard k-means in that case [6]). Hence, were we able to solve Problem (1) in polynomial time, we would be able to solve MSSC in polynomial time. Problem (1) is thus NP-hard (and so is its maximization version, i.e. its similarity-based counterpart).

Furthermore, the consideration of the cost constraint in the budget may render the minimization problem in `CRCI` NP-hard. We thus introduce below a generalization of the the above optimization problem that allows one to partly circumvent this problem.

3. ALGORITHMIC SOLUTION

We present here an algorithmic solution for the optimization problem above, focusing on the Euclidean distance for $d(,)$ and the cosine similarity for $s(,)$ as these are two widely used measures. Prior to that, we first introduce a slight generalization that partly circumvents the minimization problem in `CRCI`.

Given a set of items $\mathcal{X}$, $\mathcal{X} \subseteq \mathbb{R}^p$, a budget constraint b and the set of valid CIs $\mathcal{V}_{CI}$, let f be a function that associates to a point $v \in \mathbb{R}^p$ a valid CI from $\mathcal{V}_{CI}$: $f : \mathbb{R}^p \to \mathcal{V}_{CI}$. As before, we will denote by V a set of K points (centroids) and by W a partition (weight) matrix of size $N \times K$. We consider the following general minimization problem using the Euclidean distance:

$$\begin{cases} \textbf{Distance-based formulation} \\ \underset{V,W}{\operatorname{argmin}} (1-\lambda)\sum_{j=1}^{K}\sum_{i=1}^{N} w_{ij}^{m} ||x_i - v_j||_2^2 + \\ \qquad \lambda \sum_{j=1}^{K} \sum_{x \in C_j} ||x - v_j||_2^2 \\ with:\ C_j = f(v_j) \\ and\ s.t.\ \forall i \in [1, N],\ \sum_{j=1}^{K} w_{ij} = 1 \end{cases} \tag{2}$$

As before, a **similarity-based formulation** can be obtained by replacing argmin by argmax and the Euclidean distance by the cosine similarity. In the remainder, we will use $\mathcal{G}_{eucl}(V, W, f)$ to denote $(1-\lambda)\sum_{j=1}^{K}\sum_{i=1}^{N} w_{ij}^{m}||x_i - v_j||_2^2 + \lambda \sum_{j=1}^{K} \sum_{x \in C_j} ||x - v_j||_2^2$, with C_j obtained from v_j through f. $\mathcal{G}_{cos}$ is defined in the same way for the cosine similarity.

It is easy to see that Problem 2 is a generalization of Problem 1 as setting f to $f(v_j) = \min_{C \in \mathcal{V}_{CI}} \sum_{x \in C} ||x - v_j||_2^2$ in Problem 2 yields Problem 1. However, as mentioned above, this setting may not be always possible as it relies on a minimization problem that is NP-hard in the worst case. The general formulation provided in Problem 2 allows one to avoid this problem by considering general functions f

that can be computed more easily. We will come back to the choice of f in Section 3.1.

If the set V is fixed and f is given, so that C_j is known for $1 \leq j \leq K$, then $\mathcal{G}_{eucl}(V, W, f)$ is a convex function of W and the W that minimizes it can be obtained by setting the derivative of the Lagrangian of $\mathcal{G}_{eucl}$ (that integrates the constraints on W) with respect to W to 0 and solving for W. This leads to the following update rule for W (equivalent to the standard FCM update rule [6]):

$$w_{ij}^{(l+1)} = \left(\sum_{k=1}^{K} \left(\frac{||x_i - v_j^{(l)}||_2^2}{||x_i - v_k^{(l)}||_2^2} \right)^{\frac{1}{(m-1)}} \right)^{-1} \tag{3}$$

where l serves to indicate that new values are computed from known (old) ones. Similarly, for fixed W and given C_j, the function $\mathcal{G}_{eucl}(V, W, f)$ is convex in V. The values of V minimizing $\mathcal{G}_{eucl}$ are obtained by setting the derivatives of $\mathcal{G}_{eucl}$ with respect to V to 0 and solving for V, leading to:

$$v_j^{(l+1)} = \frac{(1-\lambda)\sum_{i=1}^{N}(w_{ij}^{(l)})^m x_i + \lambda \sum_{x \in C_j^{(l)}} x}{(1-\lambda)\sum_{i=1}^{N}(w_{ij}^{(l)})^m + \lambda |C_j^{(l)}|} \tag{4}$$

where $|C_j^{(l)}|$ represents the number of items in $C_j^{(l)}$.

For the valid composite item C_j associated to the centroid v_j, two cases may arise depending on the function f considered. Either the valid composite item provided by f for the new centroid $v_j^{(l+1)}$ leads to a better solution than the one associated to $v_j^{(l)}$, and it is kept, or it does not lead to a better solution, in which case the previous valid composite item is used. This can be formalized as:

$$C_j^{(l+1)} = \begin{cases} f(v_j^{(l+1)}) \text{ if } \sum_{x \in f(v_j^{(l+1)})} ||x - v_j^{(l+1)}||_2^2 \\ \qquad \leq \sum_{x \in C_j^{(l)}} ||x - v_j^{(l+1)}||_2^2 \\ C_j^{(l)} \text{ otherwise} \end{cases} \tag{5}$$

The above update rules guarantee that, starting with $W^{(l)}$, $V^{(l)}$ and f, one has:

$$\mathcal{G}_{eucl}(V^{(l+1)}, W^{(l+1)}, f) \leq \mathcal{G}_{eucl}(V^{(l)}, W^{(l)}, f)$$

as, for each update of W and V, the function $\mathcal{G}_{eucl}$ is minimized and does not decrease when updating the CIs provided by f. Thus, the algorithm iterating over the update rules defined by Eq. 3, 4 and 5 convergences (as $\mathcal{G}_{eucl}$ is lower bounded by 0) and provides a local minimum for the problem with the Euclidean distance.

The development for the cosine similarity is exactly the same, the convexity condition being replaced by a concavity one. We furthermore consider that all $x \in \mathcal{X}$ are normalized ($||x||_2 = 1$) and add a normalization constraint on v_j ($||v_j||_2 = 1$) so as to rely on a standard dot product ($s(x, x') = x^T x'$, where T denotes the transpose). The update rules obtained in this case are summarized below, where x_r is the rth coordinate of x and m lies in the interval $[0, 1[$:

$$w_{ij}^{(l+1)} = \left(\frac{x_i^T v_j^{(l)}}{\sum_{k=1}^{K} x_i^T v_k^{(l)}} \right)^{\frac{1}{1-m}} \tag{6}$$

Algorithm 1

Input: $\mathcal{X}$, budget constraint b, K, λ, step η, procedure f
Output: Set S of K CIs

1: $S \leftarrow \emptyset$; $\lambda' = \lambda$; $\lambda = 0$
2: Initialize (e.g. through random assignment) V and W $\rightarrow V^{(0)}, W^{(0)}, f^{(0)}(V^{(0)}) = f(V^{(0)})$
3: **repeat**
4:     **repeat**
5:         Update W through Eq. 3 (resp. Eq. 6)
6:         Update V through Eq. 4 (resp. Eq. 7)
7:         Update $f(V)$ through Eq. 5 (resp. Eq. 8)
8:     **until** $\mathcal{G}_{eucl}$ (resp. $\mathcal{G}_{cos}$) does not change
9:     $\lambda = \lambda + \eta$
10: **until** $\lambda \geq \lambda'$
11: $S \leftarrow f(V)$ (with the final f and V obtained)

$$\begin{cases} v_{jr}^{(l+1)} = \dfrac{A_{jr}}{(\sum_{r=1}^{p} A_{jr}^2)^{1/2}} \\ \text{with, for } 1 \leq r \leq p: \\ A_{jr} = (1-\lambda)\sum_{i=1}^{N}(w_{ij}^{(l)})^m x_{ir} + \lambda \sum_{x \in C_j^{(l)}} x_r \end{cases} \tag{7}$$

$$C_j^{(l+1)} = \begin{cases} f(v_j^{(l+1)}) \text{ if } \sum_{x \in f(v_j^{(l+1)})} x^T v_j^{(l+1)} \\ \qquad \geq \sum_{x \in C_j^{(l)}} x^T v_j^{(l+1)} \\ C_j^{(l)} \text{ otherwise} \end{cases} \tag{8}$$

Algorithm 1 summarizes the steps followed. As one can note, we first set λ to 0 and gradually increase its value. By doing so, one first identifies fuzzy centroids that are then moved towards valid, cohesive CIs.

3.1 Choice of f

Because the budget constraints b considered here have two parts, related respectively to type cardinality and cost (see Definition 1), we rely on two scenarios associated to two different choices for f. In the first scenario, we restrict ourselves to budget constraints b that only contain type cardinality constraints: $b = \langle \#t_1, \ldots, \#t_n \rangle$. In that particular case, it is possible to efficiently compute, for any v_j, $\min_{C \in \mathcal{V}_{CI}} \sum_{x \in C} ||x - v_j||_2^2$ through the following process:

1. Set $C \leftarrow \emptyset$
2. For $i = 1$ to n, add to C the $\#t_i$ items of type t_i closest to v_j
3. Return C

The function f defined by the above algorithm, the complexity of which is $\mathcal{O}(KN)$ in the worst case, directly yields the minimizer of CRCI in Problem 1 as there is no other valid CI closer to the given point v_j.

In the second scenario, we consider cost constraints in addition to type cardinality constraints, leading to the general budget constraint: $b = \langle \#t_1, \ldots, \#t_n, \#_\$ \rangle$. In that case one cannot directly use the above approach and we resort in this study to backtracking: we first select the closest item to a given v_j with a type in b, and iteratively add the next closest item to v_j compatible with the constraint in b. If the cost constraint is violated, the process backtracks until all the constraints are satisfied. As mentioned in Section 2.3, for any b, the existence of a solution can be determined efficiently; the search for a valid CI is thus only performed when the existence of a solution is guaranteed. Lastly, the backtracking process may not lead to an optimal solution in the sense of the minimization problem defined in CRCI (Problem 1); it will nevertheless yield a valid CI (close to the centroid considered), which is required to solve Problem 2.

4. EXPERIMENTS

We report the results of an extensive experimental study on a variety of real-world datasets. We first examine the quality of our CIs and compare them to those produced by existing algorithms and then do an in-depth study of our integrated approach.

4.1 Summary of results

Our experiments confirm the superiority of the integrated approach over two-stage approaches using both problem formulations: distance minimization on POIs in a city and similarity maximization on movies. In summary, the CIs produced from POIs using the integrated approach are characterized by a better coverage of the city they belong to, and the CIs produced for movies are representative of a variety of genres and release periods. We also find that the integrated algorithm produces better values for the objective function (distance minimization or similarity maximization) than its competitors. The second half of the experiments studies scalability (in terms of response time) of the integrated algorithm for different parameter values (K and m) and total size of items and shows that it performs very well and can hence be used to build representative CIs on the fly.

4.2 Experimental setup

Our prototype is implemented using JDK 1.8.0. All scalability experiments are conducted on a 2.4 GHz Intel Core i5 with 8 GB of memory on OS X 10.9.5 operating system. Each result is an average of 10 runs with different random seeds.

Datasets.

We use three datasets with different characteristics summarized in Table 1. Section 3.1 defines two scenarios: with and without cost constraint. We apply the former to the first two dataset and the latter to the third dataset.

Tourpedia[5] contains a collection of heterogeneous POIs in various European cities gathered via Facebook and Foursquare. The latitude and longitude of each POI is available allowing us to use Euclidean distance. We collect data for Paris, Berlin, Barcelona and Amsterdam. The heat maps showing the density of POIs in each city are depicted on Figure 2. The budget vector for this use case exploits 4 POI types:

$$\langle 1\ accommodation, 2\ public\ transportation,$$
$$3\ restaurants, 2\ health\ services, \infty\rangle$$

The second dataset is **MovieLens**[6], a movie rating database. We rely on cosine similarity of user vectors to compute the similarity between movies. The budget used for **MovieLens** is defined on movie genres:

$$\langle 2\ drama, 2\ action, 1\ comedy, \infty\rangle$$

The third dataset is **BookCrossing**[7] which contains books and their user ratings, allowing cosine similarity computation. We assign a price to each book uniformly at random between 5\$, 10\$ and 15\$ and define a budget vector on release dates:

$$\langle 3\ 1980s, 2\ 1990s, 3\ 2000s, \$70\rangle$$

Algorithms.

We denote our integrated approach presented in Section 3 as KFC. Our approach competes with two-stage approaches from the literature [2]: BOBO and CAP. BOBO is a produce-and-chose approach that first produces a large number of candidate CIs and then chooses K with the objective to maximize the distance between them. We also designed a variant of BOBO, called RBOBO, that optimizes representativity (i.e. the

Dataset	# items	Obj. function
Tourpedia (POIs)	2 to 3000/city	min geo dist.
MovieLens (movies)	3,952	max review sim.
BookCrossing (books)	270,000	max review sim.

Table 1: Dataset statistics

CI	Year	Genre	Name
CI_1	1996	Drama	Big Night
	1995	Comedy	Welcome to the Dollhouse
	1991	Action	Thelma & Louise
	1997	Drama	Ice Storm, The
	1995	Action	Get Shorty
CI_2	1992	Action	Batman Returns
	1998	Drama	Truman Show, The
	1996	Drama	Jerry Maguire
	1992	Comedy	League of Their Own, A
	1994	Action	True Lies
CI_3	1990	Comedy	Back to the Future Part III
	1997	Drama	Contact
	1990	Action	Total Recall
	1995	Drama	Twelve Monkeys
	1996	Action	Independence Day (ID4)
CI_4	1998	Action	Run Lola Run
	2000	Drama	Erin Brockovich
	2000	Comedy	High Fidelity
	2000	Action	Gladiator
	1999	Drama	Magnolia
CI_5	1967	Drama	Graduate, The
	1969	Drama	Midnight Cowboy
	1973	Comedy	American Graffiti
	1971	Action	French Connection, The
	1969	Action	Butch Cassidy & Sundance Kid

Table 2: Example of results for uKFC with $\lambda = 0.7$ on **MovieLens**

[5] *http://datahub.io/dataset/tourpedia*

[6] *http://movielens.umn.edu*

[7] *http://www.bookcrossing.com/*

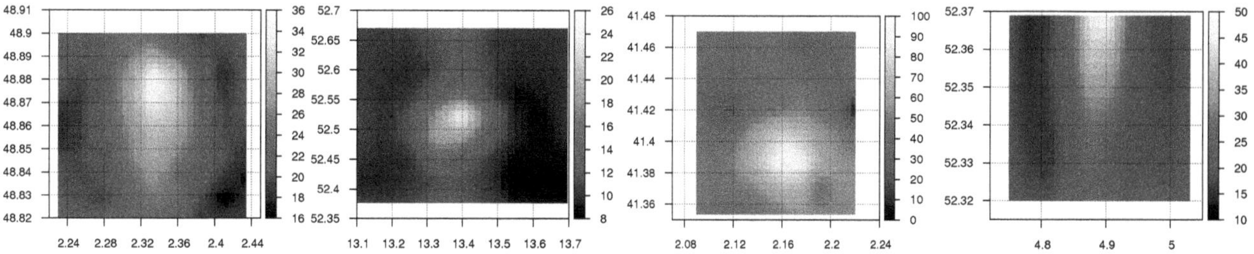

(a) Paris (b) Berlin (c) Barcelona (d) Amsterdam

Figure 2: Heat maps for the **Tourpedia** dataset with respect to latitude and longitude

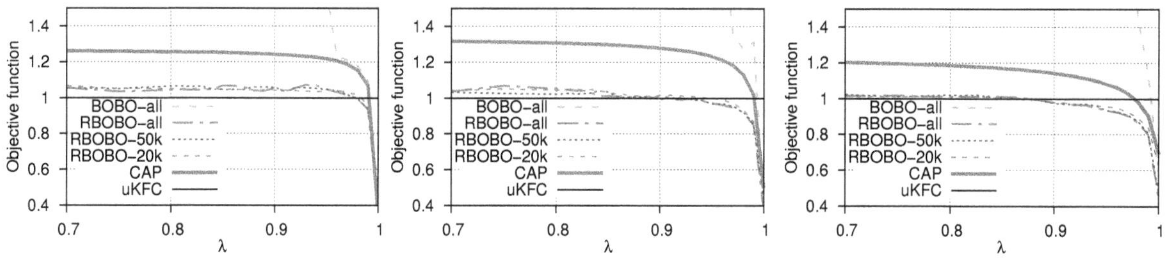

(a) $K = 5$ (b) $K = 10$ (c) $K = 20$

Figure 3: Unweighted objective function with K CIs on **Tourpedia** (Paris)

distance between each item and the closest centroid of a CI) in the second phase. Iteratively, RBOBO removes the candidate that contributes the least to decreasing the distances of data points to their closest CI. Thus RBOBO relies on the same objective function as KFC. CAP is a cluster-and-pick approach that clusters data points into K sets and selects the CI whose items are most similar to each other in each set. Since these approaches do not assign weights between data points and CIs, we only compare them against uKFC, the hard clustering version of KFC (with $m = 1$). Finally, for KFC and uKFC, we set the η parameter to 0.01.

4.3 Qualitative experiment

We first compare the quality of CIs produced with uKFC against those of BOBO, RBOBO, and CAP. Then, we study the quality of CIs produced by KFC in an independent quality evaluation.

4.3.1 Comparative quality evaluation

We use **Tourpedia** (city = Paris) to study the behavior of our objective function with different values of λ and K and for different algorithms (Figure 3). Given our problem definition, this objective function constitutes a proxy to assess the quality of the CIs generated over several executions. We then compare one instance of the CIs produced by KFC against those generated by two-stage approaches (Figure 4).

Figure 3 shows the evolution of the objective function. For better understanding of the results, we normalized each score by the one obtained by uKFC. We observe that, when λ is lower than 0.98, uKFC always produces better values of the objective function, which means that the CIs generated offer a better compromise between cohesiveness and representativity. BOBO selects K CIs by optimizing the distance between them. While it seems as it could indirectly promote representativity, in practice, BOBO tends to select outliers, and thus obtains poor results. This highlights the difference between KFC and existing approaches [2]: the objective function considers all points in the dataset, while BOBO only takes the selected CIs into account. In this evaluation, we varied the number of candidates available to RBOBO, from $20K$ candidates, to CIs formed from all data points. Our experiments show that this only marginally improves the results obtained. Since we adapted RBOBO for representativity, it significantly outperforms BOBO, but remains less efficient than KFC. CAP, while based on clustering, obtains worse results than most algorithms, as CIs selected, while originating from different clusters, can still be close to each other, which is detrimental to representativity. Overall, as K increases, the difference between uKFC and its competitor diminishes. Indeed, as more CIs are selected, each item is on average closer to a CI centroid, and thus the potential difference in the objective function is reduced. When λ nears 1, the objective function almost only takes cohesiveness. In such configurations, algorithms based on generating huge amounts of candidate CIs obtain better results, as they have a higher probability of selecting items very close to each other.

To confirm this analysis of the algorithm's behavior, we present in Figure 4 an instance of the results obtained by each algorithm on the **Tourpedia** (Paris) dataset. As explained previously, to maximize distance between CIs, BOBO selects outliers from the periphery of the city, which is clearly visible on Figure 4a. There are fewer points in the areas around those outliers (Figure 2a), so this achieves bad representativity. RBOBO does significantly better, thanks to the heuristic selecting K CIs among the candidates. The CIs selected are spread on the periphery of dense areas, so representativity is quite good, but not optimal. The results of CAP and uKFC exhibit some similarities. Indeed, they are both based on a clustering approach. However, CAP can still select CIs close to each other, which can be observed on the left of Figure 4c. On the contrary, CIs selected by uKFC are well spread over space and achieve the best representativity. We obtain similar results on the other cities.

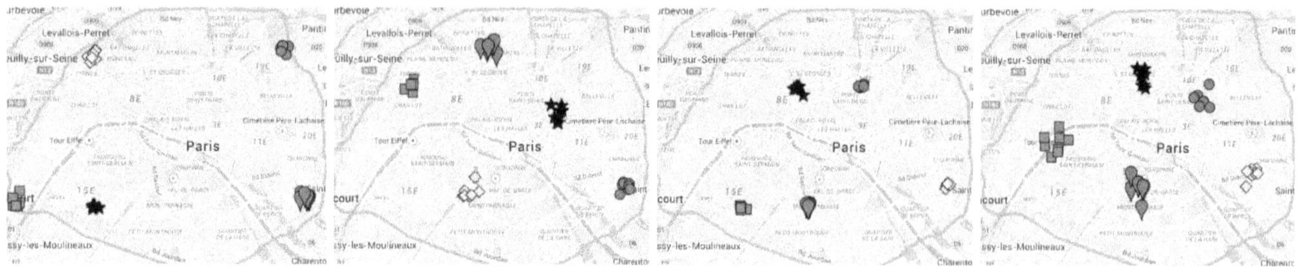

(a) BOBO-all (b) RBOBO-all (c) CAP (d) uKFC ($m = 1$)

Figure 4: CIs selected by each algorithm with $K = 5$ CIs, $\lambda = 0.7$ on **Tourpedia** (Paris)

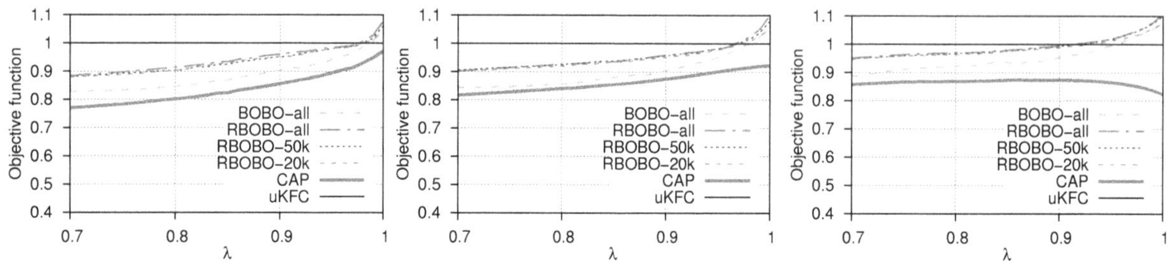

(a) $K = 5$ (b) $K = 10$ (c) $K = 20$

Figure 5: Unweighted objective function for K CIs with **MovieLens**

We conduct a similar experiment on the **Movielens** dataset, and present the results on Figure 5. Note that in this setup (cosine similarity), the goal is to maximize the objective function. We observe a similar trend as in the **Tourpedia** experiment. uKFC achieves a higher score as long as representativity is taken into account. When λ reaches extreme values, cohesiveness becomes the main factor, and produce-and-choose approaches obtain better results. Note that on this dataset CAP performs particularly poorly.

Due to space constraints, we are unable to present examples of the CIs composed by each algorithm. Hence, we will focus on the results of uKFC, presented on Table 2. We can see that these CIs are quite representative of different topics, styles and periods. For example, CI_3 shows mainly science fiction while CI_4 shows movies with good soundtracks.

4.3.2 *Independent quality evaluation*

We first examine the quality of the results obtained by uKFC on the **Tourpedia** Paris dataset (Figure 4d). The CIs generated are clearly localized around some of Paris' most famous attractions: the Eiffel tower, Montmartre, Montparnasse, République and Nation. Indeed, the presence of these attractions affects the distribution of POIs in Paris, and KFC is able to capture this to select representative CIs.

We now consider the results obtained by KFC for Berlin (Figure 6) and Barcelona (Figure 7) for different values of m (the weight exponent that controls the centroid positioning process). The higher m, the fuzzier representativity is. Thus, while CIs are quite spread out for low values of m, they converge towards the most central point of the dataset as m increases. This is particularly true in the case of Berlin, as the dataset contains several POIs located on the outside of the city. In practice, m could be used to control the coverage spread of the resulting CIs, while maintaining representativity.

4.4 Scalability experiment

This last set of experiments report a study of the response time scalability of KFC and RBOBO, its closest competitor, with varying values of K, m and total number of items. **BookCrossing** is the most challenging use case, as it combines a large dataset size and a total cost constraint. Figure 8a shows the execution time of KFC. Overall, we observe that KFC scales linearly with both K and m. This behavior is inherited from the clustering approach underlying KFC, and shows that while the dataset grows, convergence remains rather fast. Despite running on a laptop, KFC generates 20 composite items on a dataset of 250,000 items in less than 7 minutes.

The results for RBOBO are given on Figure 8b. RBOBO computes the distance between each candidate CI and each item. In the case of a large dataset, this can quickly become overwhelming. Furthermore, as the size of the dataset increases, the number of candidate CIs increases in order to preserve results quality. RBOBO iteratively removes candidates until reaching the desired number of K CIs. Hence, its execution time is driven by the number of candidates, and not by K. Consequently, we were unable to execute RBOBO for more than 5000 items, as the execution was lasting over 10 minutes.

5. RELATED WORK

To the best of our knowledge, this is the first study focusing on the identification of "representative" composite items of a heterogeneous set of items. While there is no work that can be directly compared to ours, there are multiple related areas. We provide a brief summary of each area.

Photo Summarization. The problem of summarizing a large collection of homogeneous items has received a lot of attention in particular, for photo summarization. Different metadata was used ranging from location to temporal

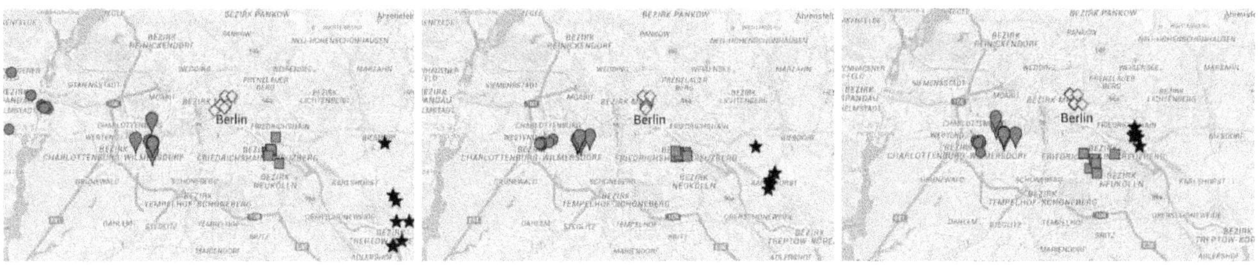

(a) $m = 2$ (b) $m = 3$ (c) $m = 4$

Figure 6: CIs generated by KFC with $\lambda = 0.7$ and $K = 5$ on **Tourpedia** (Berlin)

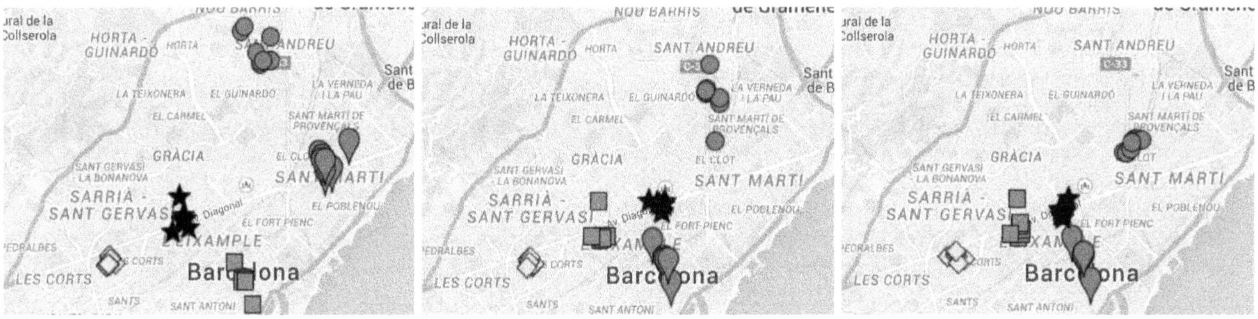

(a) $m = 2$ (b) $m = 3$ (c) $m = 4$

Figure 7: CIs generated by KFC with $\lambda = 0.7$ and $K = 5$ on **Tourpedia** (Barcelona)

data to sharing information. In [13], location information was used to generate photo summaries and visualize them on a map. In [12], representative photos are generated for a given time period using patterns in photo-taking habits (later studied in *http://www.hpl.hp.com/techreports/2003/HPL-2003-165.pdf*). In [11], the authors relied on event detection in personal photo collections (e.g., birthdays) which could be used for collection summarization. In [13], summaries of POIs are generated to aid visualization on a map. All cited approaches provide summaries of homogeneous item collections as opposed to our work where we are able to summarize heterogeneous item collections.

Composite Items. Composite retrieval was studied with different semantics in recent studies [2,3,7,9,10,15,16]. In [2], different algorithms were explored to build composite items. In [8], the authors propose a formalization for composite items (in the case of city tours) that is personalized. Most existing algorithms rely on a two-stage process that decouple constraint satisfaction (e.g., a CI must contain one museum and 2 restaurants) from the optimization goal (e.g., each CI is a set of closely points of interest in a city). In this paper, we show that our integrated approach is more effective than a two-stage approach. The main difference however between our approach and previous ones on composite items lies in the objective functions used for the optimization. To our knowledge, our approach is the first one to fully address the problem of identifying "representative" composite items of a set of heterogeneous items. As discussed before (Section 2), this is achieved by relying on the identification of the centroids of fuzzy clusters that are close to all the items.

Constrained Clustering. We adapt the Fuzzy C-Means (FCM) Algorithm [5] to formalize our problem. More precisely, we extend the standard Fuzzy C-Means formulation with an extra term aiming at "pushing" centroids towards valid CIs. It is that extra term that integrates the budget constraint, that guarantees the identification of valid CIs next to representative centroids, these latter ones being mainly identified as in Fuzzy C-Means. The budget constraint is integrated in this extra term via the procedure f discussed in Section 3 that associates to any given point a "close" and valid CI.

6. CONCLUSION

We explored the use of valid and cohesive composite items (CIs) to represent large collections of heterogeneous items such as POIs in a city or movies with different release dates. Validity is achieved by summarizing items with different types into a single CI. Indeed, CIs can naturally express gluing together items of different types in a budget vector such as $\langle 2\ drama, 2\ action, 1\ comedy, \$5\rangle$ where each entry specifies the minimum number of each item type desired in a CI and an upper-bound of the total cost a user is willing to pay for that CI. Cohesion and representativity are achieved by finding the best K valid CIs according to an objective function. We hence formalized the problem of summarizing large collections of heterogeneous items as that of building the K most valid, cohesive and representative CIs. Our formalization relies on two commonly-used objective functions: distance and similarity. Distance is naturally used for POIs in a city in order to find the K CIs that cover the city best. Similarity is well-adapted to representing movies in order to find the K CIs that are reviewed by similar users.

We designed a new integrated algorithm that builds the K most valid, cohesive and representative CIs of an input dataset. Our algorithm integrates constraint satisfaction into fuzzy clustering in order to simultaneously optimize for validity, cohesion and representativity. Experiments on real datasets showed that the integrated approach outperforms

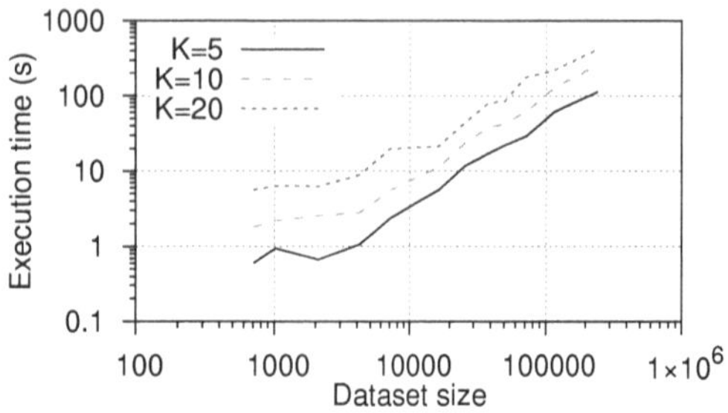

(a) KFC

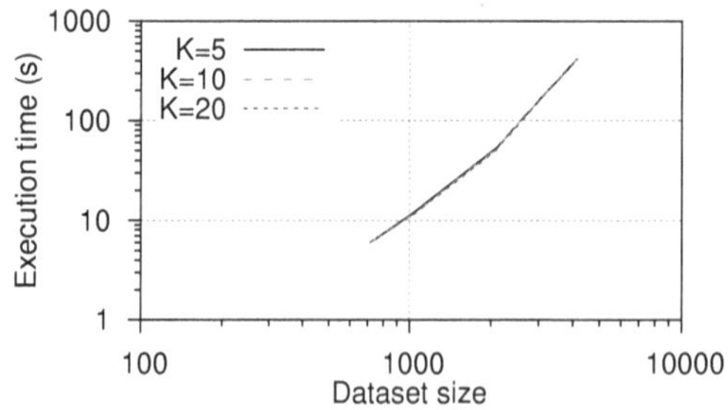

(b) RBOBO-all

Figure 8: Scalability on **BookCrossing**

two-stage ones resulting in CIs that achieve very good representativity of existing items.

Our immediate future plans include running more extensive experiments with user studies in order to refine our notions of validity and representativity in different applications. We are also working on a formalization of our problem that admits adaptive constraints for validity thereby capturing a wide variety of interests in different item types, and on an extension in which cohesion is explicitly modeled.

Acknowledgments

This work was partially funded by ANR-13-CORD-0020.

7. REFERENCES

[1] D. Aloise, A. Deshpande, P. Hansen, and P. Popat. NP-hardness of euclidean sum-of-squares clustering. *Mach. Learn.*, 75(2):245–248, May 2009.

[2] S. Amer-Yahia, F. Bonchi, C. Castillo, E. Feuerstein, I. Méndez-Díaz, and P. Zabala. Composite retrieval of diverse and complementary bundles. *IEEE Trans. Knowl. Data Eng.*, 26(11):2662–2675, 2014.

[3] A. Angel, S. Chaudhuri, G. Das, and N. Koudas. Ranking objects based on relationships and fixed associations. In M. L. Kersten, B. Novikov, J. Teubner, V. Polutin, and S. Manegold, editors, *EDBT*, volume 360 of *ACM International Conference Proceeding Series*, pages 910–921. ACM, 2009.

[4] D. Arthur and S. Vassilvitskii. K-means++: The advantages of careful seeding. In *Proceedings of the Eighteenth Annual ACM-SIAM Symposium on Discrete Algorithms*, SODA '07, pages 1027–1035, Philadelphia, PA, USA, 2007. Society for Industrial and Applied Mathematics.

[5] J. C. Bezdek. A convergence theorem for the fuzzy ISODATA clustering algorithms. *IEEE Trans. Pattern Anal. Mach. Intell.*, 2(1):1–8, 1980.

[6] J. C. Bezdek, R. Ehrlich, and W. Full. FCM: The Fuzzy c-Means Clustering Algorithm. *Computers & Geosciences*, 10(2-3):191–203, 1984.

[7] H. Bota, K. Zhou, J. M. Jose, and M. Lalmas. Composite retrieval of heterogeneous web search. In *23rd International World Wide Web Conference, WWW '14, Seoul, Republic of Korea, April 7-11, 2014*, pages 119–130, 2014.

[8] I. R. Brilhante, J. A. F. de Macêdo, F. M. Nardini, R. Perego, and C. Renso. Where shall we go today?: planning touristic tours with tripbuilder. In *22nd ACM International Conference on Information and Knowledge Management, CIKM'13, San Francisco, CA, USA, October 27 - November 1, 2013*, pages 757–762, 2013.

[9] A. Brodsky, S. M. Henshaw, and J. Whittle. Card: a decision-guidance framework and application for recommending composite alternatives. In P. Pu, D. G. Bridge, B. Mobasher, and F. Ricci, editors, *RecSys*, pages 171–178. ACM, 2008.

[10] M. D. Choudhury, M. Feldman, S. Amer-Yahia, N. Golbandi, R. Lempel, and C. Yu. Automatic construction of travel itineraries using social breadcrumbs. In M. H. Chignell and E. Toms, editors, *HT*, pages 35–44. ACM, 2010.

[11] M. L. Cooper, J. Foote, A. Girgensohn, and L. Wilcox. Temporal event clustering for digital photo collections. In *Proceedings of the Eleventh ACM International Conference on Multimedia, Berkeley, CA, USA, November 2-8, 2003*, pages 364–373, 2003.

[12] A. Graham, H. Garcia-Molina, A. Paepcke, and T. Winograd. Time as essence for photo browsing through personal digital libraries. In *ACM/IEEE Joint Conference on Digital Libraries, JCDL 2002, Portland, Oregon, USA, June 14-18, 2002, Proceedings*, pages 326–335, 2002.

[13] A. Jaffe, M. Naaman, T. Tassa, and M. Davis. Generating summaries and visualization for large collections of geo-referenced photographs. In *Proceedings of the 8th ACM SIGMM International Workshop on Multimedia Information Retrieval, MIR 2006, October 26-27, 2006, Santa Barbara, California, USA*, pages 89–98, 2006.

[14] J. B. MacQueen. Some methods for the classification and analysis of multivariate observations. In *Proceedings of the 5th Berkeley Symposium on Mathematical Statistics and Probability*, pages 281–297, 1967.

[15] S. B. Roy, S. Amer-Yahia, A. Chawla, G. Das, and C. Yu. Constructing and exploring composite items. In A. K. Elmagarmid and D. Agrawal, editors, *SIGMOD Conference*, pages 843–854. ACM, 2010.

[16] M. Xie, L. V. Lakshmanan, and P. T. Wood. Breaking out of the box of recommendations: From items to packages. In *RecSys*, 2010.

More Accurate Question Answering on Freebase

Hannah Bast, Elmar Haussmann
Department of Computer Science
University of Freiburg
79110 Freiburg, Germany
{bast, haussmann}@informatik.uni-freiburg.de

ABSTRACT

Real-world factoid or list questions often have a simple structure, yet are hard to match to facts in a given knowledge base due to high representational and linguistic variability. For example, to answer "who is the ceo of apple" on Freebase requires a match to an abstract "leadership" entity with three relations "role", "organization" and "person", and two other entities "apple inc" and "managing director". Recent years have seen a surge of research activity on learning-based solutions for this method. We further advance the state of the art by adopting learning-to-rank methodology and by fully addressing the inherent entity recognition problem, which was neglected in recent works.

We evaluate our system, called *Aqqu*, on two standard benchmarks, Free917 and WebQuestions, improving the previous best result for each benchmark considerably. These two benchmarks exhibit quite different challenges, and many of the existing approaches were evaluated (and work well) only for one of them. We also consider efficiency aspects and take care that all questions can be answered interactively (that is, within a second). Materials for full reproducibility are available on our website: `http://ad.informatik.uni-freiburg.de/publications` .

1. INTRODUCTION

Knowledge bases like Freebase have reached an impressive coverage of general knowledge. The data is stored in a clean and structured manner, and can be queried unambiguously via structured languages like SPARQL. However, given the enormous amount of information (2.9 billion triples for Freebase), mapping a search desire to the right query can be an extremely hard task even for an expert user. For example, consider the (seemingly) simple question *who is the ceo of apple*. The answer is indeed contained in Freebase, and the corresponding SPARQL query[1] is:

```
select ?name where {
  Managing_Director  job_title.people_with_this_title  ?0 .
  ?0  employment_tenure.company  Apple_Inc .
  ?0  employment_tenure.person  ?name
}
```

It would clearly be preferable, if we could just ask the question in natural language, and the machine automatically computes the corresponding SPARQL query. This is the problem we consider in this paper.

We focus on "structurally simple" questions, like the one above. They involve k entities (typically two or three, in the example above: *ceo* and *apple* and the result entity), which are linked via a single k-ary relation in the knowledge base. For languages like SPARQL, k-ary relations for $k > 2$ can be represented by a special entity (one for each k-tuple in the relation) and $k - 1$ binary relations (in the example above: the three binary relations in the where clause, all connected to the ?0 entity).

The challenge for these questions is to find the matching entities and relations in the given knowledge base. The entity-matching problem is hard, because the question may use a variant of the name used in the knowledge base (synonymy), and the knowledge base may contain many entities with the same name (polysemy). For example, there are 218 entities with the name *apple* in Freebase, but the right match for the question is actually *Apple Inc.* The relation-matching problem has the same problem, which is even more difficult for k-ary relation with $k > 2$. As a further complication, questions like the above do not contain any word that matches the relations from the sought for query.[2] Note how these problems exacerbate for very large knowledge bases. If we restrict to lexical matches, we will often miss the correct query. If we allow weaker matches, the number of possibilities becomes very large. This will become clearer in Section 3.

1.1 Contributions

We consider the following as our main contributions:

- A new end-to-end system that automatically translates a given natural-language question to the matching SPARQL query on a given knowledge base. Several previous systems factor out part of the problem, for example, by assuming the right entities for the query to be given by an oracle. See Section 3 for an overview of our system.
- An evaluation of our system on two standard benchmarks, Free917 and WebQuestions, where it outperforms all pre-

[1] For the sake of readability, prefixes are omitted from the entity and relation names.

[2] This is typical when the verb *to be* is used in the question.

Permission to make digital or hard copies of all or part of this work for personal or classroom use is granted without fee provided that copies are not made or distributed for profit or commercial advantage and that copies bear this notice and the full citation on the first page. Copyrights for components of this work owned by others than ACM must be honored. Abstracting with credit is permitted. To copy otherwise, or republish, to post on servers or to redistribute to lists, requires prior specific permission and/or a fee. Request permissions from Permissions@acm.org.
CIKM'15, October 19–23, 2015, Melbourne, Australia.
© 2015 ACM. ISBN 978-1-4503-3794-6/15/10 ...$15.00.
DOI: http://dx.doi.org/10.1145/2806416.2806472.

vious approaches significantly. These two benchmarks exhibit quite different challenges, and many of the existing approaches were evaluated (and work well) only for one of them. See Section 2 for an overview of the existing approaches, and Section 5 for the details of our evaluation.

- Integration of entity recognition in a learning-based approach. Previous learning-based approaches treated this sub-problem in a simplistic manner, or even factored it out by assuming the right entities to be given as part of the problem.

- Using learning-to-rank techniques to learn pair-wise comparison of query candidates. Previous approaches often use parser-inspired log-linear models for ranking.

- We also consider efficiency aspects and take care that all questions can be answered interactively, that is, within one second. Many of the previous systems do not consider this aspect, and take at least several seconds and longer to answer a single query. Again, see Section 5 for some details.

- We make the code of our system publicly available under `http://ad.informatik.uni-freiburg.de/publications` . In particular, this allows reproducing our results. The website also provides various additional useful materials; in particular, a list of mistakes and inconsistencies in the Free917 and WebQuestions benchmarks.

Throughout this paper, we focus on Freebase as the currently largest general-purpose knowledge base. However, there is nothing in our approach specific to Freebase. It works for any knowledge base with entities and (possibly k-ary) relations between them.

2. RELATED WORK

Much recent work on natural-language queries on knowledge bases has focused on two recent benchmarks, both based on Freebase: *Free917* and *WebQuestions*. Section 2.1 gives an overview over this body of work, introducing the two benchmarks on the way. In Section 5, we compare our new method against *all* methods from this section. Section 2.2 briefly discusses work using other benchmarks.

2.1 Work on Free917 and WebQuestions

We consider the works in chronological order, briefly highlighting the relative innovations to previous works and the corresponding gain in result quality. A more technical description of each of the methods is provided in Section 5.3.

In [7], the Free917 benchmark was first introduced. The benchmark consists of 917 questions along with the correct[3] knowledge-base query. All queries have exactly one (possibly k-ary) relation. The basic approach of [7] is to extend an existing semantic parser with correspondences between natural-language phrases and relation names in the knowledge base. The correspondences are learned using weak supervision techniques and from the training portion of the benchmark (70% = 641 questions).

In [15], query candidates are derived by transforming an underspecified logical form of a CCG [21] parse. This form is grounded to Freebase using a set of collapsing and expansion operators that preserve the type of the expression. This has the advantage that it leverages grammatical structure in the question and can adjust knowledge base mismatches, and the disadvantage that it relies on well-formed questions. A linear model is learned to score derivations, which are built using a dynamic programming based parser.

In [2], the WebQuestions (WQ) benchmark was introduced. This benchmark is much larger (5,810 question) but only provides the result set for each question, not the knowledge-base query. This allows gathering more training data more easily (the results were obtained via crowdsourcing). The WQ questions are also more realistic (they were obtained via the Google Suggest API) and language-wise more diverse than the Free917 questions, and hence also harder (e.g. *who runs china in 2011* asking for the former Chinese Premier). The basic approach of [2] is to generate query candidates by recursively generating logical forms. The generation is guided by a mapping of phrases to knowledge base predicates and a small set of composition rules. Candidate scores are learned with a log-linear model.

In a follow-up work [3], the process from [2] is "turned on its head" by again generating a natural-language question from each query candidate. Scores are then learned (again with a log-linear model) based on the similarity between the question representing the query candidate and the original question. This allows leverage of text-similarity information (paraphrases) from large text corpora (unrelated to the queried knowledge base).

In [25], the authors go another step further by not even generating query candidates. Instead their approach tries to identify the central entity of the question, and then iterates over each entity connected (via a single relation) to that central entity in the knowledge base. It is then decided (via a learned model) separately for each such entity whether it becomes part of the result set. In principle, this allows correct answers even when no single relation from the knowledge base matches the question (e.g., asking for a brother of someone, when the knowledge base only knows about siblings). On the downside, this adds a lot of additional features to the learning process (the attributes of the result entities). Quality-wise, the approach does not improve over [2] and [3].

In [19], the authors go yet a step further by not even using the training data. Instead, weak-supervision is used to generate learning examples from natural language sentences. The parsing step itself is conceptualized as a graph-matching problem between the graph of a CCG parse and graphs grounded in Freebase entities and relations. However, their approach was evaluated only on small (and topically narrow) subsets of the two benchmarks.

In [4], the authors try to solve the problem without any natural-language processing (not even POS-tagging). They match the results from [3] but do not improve them.

2.2 Other benchmarks

Another recent notable effort in open-domain question answering is the QALD (Question Answering over Linked Data) series of evaluation campaigns, which started in 2011. See [22] for the latest report. So far, five benchmarks have been issued, one per year. The challenges behind these benchmarks are somewhat different than those behind the Free917 and WebQuestions benchmarks from Section 2.1:

- The biggest and most diverse knowledge base used is DBpedia, which is more than an order of magnitude smaller than Freebase (about 4M vs. about 40M entities).

[3] Actually, a small portion of the queries are incorrect, but this is not a deliberate feature of the benchmark.

• A significant fraction of the questions involves more than one relation or non-trivial comparatives. For example, *what are the capitals of all countries that the himalayas run through* or *which actor was cast in the most movies.*

• The training sets are relatively small (50-100 queries for QALD 1-3). This is mainly due to the fact, discussed in Section 2.1 above, that the ground truth provides not just the correct result sets but also the corresponding SPARQL queries, which requires expensive human expert work. The benchmarks thus give relatively little opportunity for supervised learning. Indeed, most of the participating systems are unsupervised. It is one of the insights from our evaluation in Section 5 that supervised learning is key for results of the quality we achieve.

• QALD 3 and 4 contain multi-lingual versions of the datasets and questions. For QALD 5, the dataset is a combination of RDF data and free text.

For these reasons, and because there is such a substantial body of very recent work on Free917 and WebQuestions with a series of better and better results, we did not include QALD in our evaluation. We consider it a very worthwhile endeavor for future work though, to extend our approach to the QALD benchmarks.

3. SYSTEM OVERVIEW

We first describe our overall process of answering a natural language question from a knowledge base (KB). In the next sections we describe each of the steps in detail. Assume we are trying to answer the following question (from the WebQuestions benchmark):

what character does ellen play in finding nemo?

Entity identification. We begin by identifying entities from the KB that are mentioned in the question. In our example, *ellen* refers to the tv host *Ellen DeGeneres* and *finding nemo* refers to the movie *Finding Nemo.* However, like for the example in the introduction, this is not obvious: *ellen* could also refer to the actor *Ellen Page* and *finding nemo* to the video game with the same name (besides others). Instead of fixing a decision on which entities are mentioned, we delay this decision and jointly disambiguate the mentioned entities via the next steps. Hence, the result of this step is a set of (possibly overlapping) entity mentions with attached confidence scores.

Template matching. Next, we match a set of query templates to the question. Figure 1 shows our templates. Each template consists of entity and relation placeholders. A matched template corresponds to a *query candidate* which can be executed against the KB to obtain an answer.

Our simplest template consists of a single entity and an answer relation (template 1 in Figure 1). One of the query candidates for our example is generated by matching the entity for the tv host *Ellen DeGeneres* and the relation *parents* [4]:

<Ellen DeGeneres> <parents> <T>

This has the (wrong) interpretation of asking for her parents. A slightly more complex template contains two relations connected to the entity via a *mediator object* (template 2 in Figure 1). In our example, this matches a query candidate connecting *Ellen Page* to abstract *film performance* objects, via a *film performance* relation, and from there to all the films she acted in via a *film* relation:

<Ellen Page> <performance> <M>
<M> <film> <T>

This asks for all films *Ellen Page* acted in. Yet another template combines two entities via relations and a mediator entity (m in template 3 in Figure 1). In our example, *Ellen DeGeneres* and *Finding Nemo* are connected via two relations and a film-performance mediator.

<Ellen DeGeneres> <performance> <M>
<M> <film> <Finding Nemo>
<M> <character> <T>

We find this connection using an efficient inverted index (see Section 4.2) and continue matching from the mediator. In particular, we create query candidates asking for the *character* (Dory) and *performance type* (Voice) of *Ellen DeGeneres* in *Finding Nemo.* The final result of this step is a set of all the matched query candidates.

Relation matching. The query candidates still miss the fundamental information about which relations were actually mentioned and asked for in the question. We distinguish three ways of matching relations of the query candidate to words in the question: 1) via the name or description of the relation in the KB, 2) via words learned for each relation using distant supervision, 3) via supervised learning on a training set. Each match has a confidence score attached.

In our example, a word learned for the relations *performance* and *film* connecting an actor to the film she acted in is *play.* This matches in the query candidates asking for all films of *Ellen Page* and for the performance type or character of *Ellen DeGeneres* in *Finding Nemo.* Furthermore, the word *character* matches the relation with the same name, whereas the relation *performance type* doesn't match. Continuing this way, all relations in all query candidates are enriched with information about what words were matched in which way.

Ranking. We now have a set of query candidates, where each candidate is enriched with information about which of its entities and relations match which parts of the question how well. It remains to rank the candidates in order to find the best matching candidate. Note that performing ranking at this final step has the strong benefit of jointly disambiguating entities and relations. A candidate can have a weak match for an entity, but a strong match for a relation, and vice versa. By deciding this at the final stage we can identify these combinations as correct, even when one of the matches seems unlikely when considered separately.

Intuitively, for our example, the candidate covering most words of the question is best. Matching *ellen* to *Ellen Page* does no longer allow matching *Finding Nemo* because these aren't actually related in the KB. On the other hand, asking for the performance type of *Ellen DeGeneres* in *Finding Nemo* doesn't match the word *character.* This leaves us with the correct interpretation of asking for her character in the movie.

4. SYSTEM DETAILS

In this section, we describe the details of our system, called *Aqqu.* Aqqu works by generating query candidates for each

[4]We use SPARQL-like triple (subject, predicate, object) notation, where uppercase characters indicate variables.

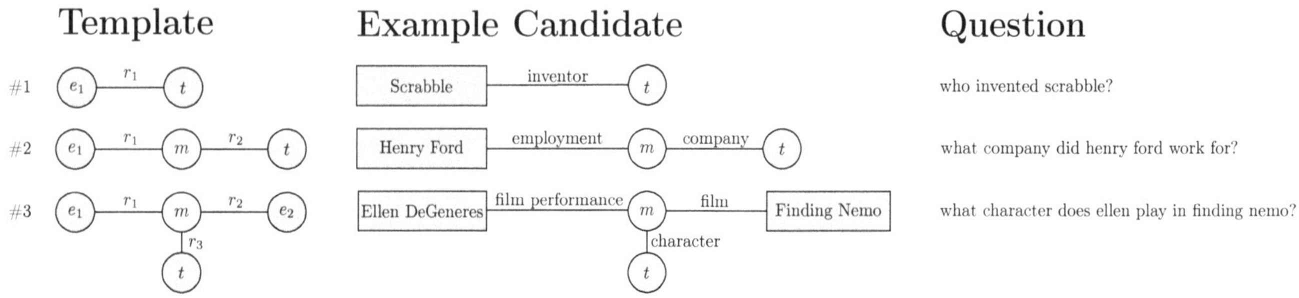

Figure 1: Query templates and example candidates with corresponding questions. A query template can consist of entity placeholders e, relation placeholders r, an intermediate object m and the answer node t.

question. These query candidates are then ranked using a learned model. The top-ranked query is then returned (or "no answer" in case the set of candidates was empty). The following subsections describe the candidate generation and ranking in detail. The previous section explained the process by an example.

4.1 Entity matching

The goal of the entity matching phase is to identify all entities from the knowledge base that match a part of the question. The match can be literal, or via an alias of the entity name.

POS-tagging We POS-tag the question using the Stanford tagger [17]. For entity matching (this subsection), we make use of the tags *NN* (noun) and *NNP* (proper noun). For relation matching (Section 4.3), we also make use of the tags *VB* (verb) and *JJ* (adjective).

Subsequence generation We generate the set S of all subsequences of words from the question, with the following two restrictions. First, a subsequence consisting of a single word must be tagged *NN*. Second, a subsequence must not "split" a sequence of words tagged *NNP*; that is, when it starts (ends) with a word tagged *NNP*, it must not be preceded (succeeded) by a word tagged *NNP*.

Find matching entities For each $s \in S$, we compute the list of all entities from the knowledge base that have s as their name or alias. We use a map from phrases (the aliases) to lists of entities (the entities with the respective alias) obtained from the CrossWikis dataset [20]. CrossWikis was built by mining the anchor text of links to Wikipedia entities (articles) from various large web-crawls. CrossWikis covers around 4 million entities from Wikipedia. Almost all of these entities also exist in Freebase, together with a link to the respective Wikipedia entity. For the remaining Freebase entities, we only consider the literal name match. Overall, we are able to recognize around 44 million entities with about 60 million aliases.

We have also experimented with the aliases provided by Freebase, but they tend to be much more noisy (wrong aliases) and less complete (important aliases missing).

Scores for the entity matches We compute a score for each match s, e computed in the previous step, where s is a subsequence of words from the question and e is an entity from Freebase with alias s. Consider a fixed alias s. CrossWikis also provides us with a probability distribution $p_{cross}(e|s)$ over the Wikipedia entities e with alias s. Let e' be a Freebase entity that is not contained in CrossWikis. Let e_{max} be the CrossWikis entity with the highest $p_{cross}(e|s)$. That is, e_{max} is the most likely Wikipedia entity for alias s. Let $p_{free}(e'|s) = p(e_{max}|s) \cdot pop(e')/pop(e_{max})$, where pop is the (alias-independent) popularity score of an entity, as described in the next subsection. Intuitively, $p_{free}(e'|s)$ estimates the probability that e' has alias s via its relative popularity to the most likely Wikipedia entity for s. We merge $p_{cross}(e|s)$ and $p_{free}(e'|s)$ into one probability distribution by simply normalizing the probabilities to sum 1.

Popularity scores for each entity For each entity, we also compute a (match-independent) popularity score. We simply take the number of times the entity is mentioned in the ClueWeb12 dataset [9], according to the annotations provided by Google [13]. The popularity scores are used for the entity match scores above. They also yield two features used in ranking each candidate; see Section 4.5.

4.2 Candidate generation

Based on the entity matches, we compute a set of query candidates as follows. We generate the query candidates in three (disjoint) subsets, one for each of the three templates shown in Figure 1. Each template stands for a query with a particular kind of structure. These three templates cover almost all of the questions in the Free917 and WebQuestions benchmarks.

Let E be the set of all entities matched to a subsequence of the question, as described in the previous section.

Template 1 For each $e \in E$, find all relations r such that there is some triple $(e, r, \cdot)$ in the knowledge base. We obtain these via a single SPARQL query for each e.

Template 2 For each $e \in E$, find all r_1, r_2, m such that there are two triples (e, r_1, m) and $(m, r_2, \cdot)$ in the knowledge base, where r_1 and r_2 are relations and m is a mediator entity. We obtain these as follows. For each e, we use a single SPARQL query to obtain all matching r_1. For each e, r_1, we then use another SPARQL query to obtain all matching r_2. Note that m remains a variable in the query candidate.

Template 3 For all pairs of entities $e_1, e_2 \in E$ such that the two subsequences matched in the question do not overlap, find all r_1, r_2, r_3 such that there are three triples (e_1, r_1, m), (m, r_2, e_2), and $(m, r_3, \cdot)$ in the knowledge base, where r_1, r_2, r_3 are relations and m is a mediator entity. We obtain these as follows. For each entity e, we precompute the list of all (r, m) such that m is a mediator entity and the triple (e, r, m) exists in the knowledge base. The list is sorted by the ids of the mediator entities. For given e_1, e_2 like above, we then intersect the lists for e_1 and e_2. For each mediator m in the intersection, we then obtain all r_3 via a simple SPARQL query. In the query candidate, m remains a variable.

4.3 Relation matching

Let C be the set of query candidates computed in the previous subsection. For each query candidate $c \in C$, let RW_c be the set of lemmatized[5] words from the relations from c (there can be one, two, or three relations, depending on the template from which c was generated). We compute how well the words from RW_c match the subset QW of lemmatized words from the question that are not already matched by the entities from c.

We consider four kinds of matches, described in the following: literal, derivation, synonym, context. For each of these four kinds of matches, we compute a non-negative score (which is zero, if there is no match at all). It can happen that all four of these scores are zero. In the basis version of our system, we keep such candidates, in a variant we prune them; see Section 4.7.

Literal matches This score is simply the number of pairs w, q, where $w \in RW_c$ and $q \in QW$ and $w = q$. Almost all questions have no repeated words; in that case, this score is just the number of relation words that occur in the question (and are not already matched by an entity).

Derivation matches This score is the number of pairs w, q, where $w \in RW_c$ and $q \in QW$ and w is derivationally related to q. Here we also consider the POS-tag of w in the question. We precompute a map from POS-tagged words to derivations using WordNet [11]. We extract derivation links for verbs and nouns (e.g. *produce.VB* - *producer.NN* and vice versa). We also extract attribute links between adjectives and their describing attribute (e.g., *high.JJ* - *height.NN*). We extend these links with synonyms of the noun in WordNet (e.g. *high.JJ* - *elevation.NN*).

Synonym matches For each $w \in RW_c$ and $q \in QW$, add s to this score if w is a synonym of q with similarity s. We compute the similarity between two words by computing the cosine similarity between the associated *word vectors*. We use 300-dimensional word vectors that were computed with Google's *word2vec* on a news text corpus of size around 100 billion words.[6] We consider only synonyms, where the score is ≥ 0.4. This threshold is based on observation, but chosen very liberally: many word pairs with score above that threshold are not what humans would call "real synonyms", but almost all such "real synonyms" have a score above that threshold.

Context matches For this score, we precompute weighted *indicator* words for each relation from our knowledge base. These are words which are not necessarily synonyms of words in the relation name, but are used in text to express that relation; see below for an example. The score is then the sum of the weights of all words in QW that are indicators for one of the relations from the query candidate. For templates 2 and 3, we consider $r1.r2$ as one relation.

We learn indicator words using distant supervision [18] as follows. First, we identify entity mentions in Wikipedia using Wiki markup and a set of simple heuristics for co-reference resolution, as described in [1]. We also identify dates and values using SUTime [8]. For the 23 million sentences that contain at least two entities (including dates or values), we compute a dependency parse using [17].

For each pair e_1, e_2 of entities occurring in a sentence, we look up all relations r in the knowledge base that connect them. We also treat relations $r1.r2$ that connect the entities via a mediator as a single binary relation r. If the shortest path between e_1 and e_2 in the dependency parse has length at most four, we consider all words along that path as indicator words for r. We also experimented with considering all words in the sentence, or words along longer paths, but these gave considerably worse results.

We find about 4.7 million sentences that match at least one relation this way. For example, we can thus learn that *born* is an indicator word for the relation *place of birth* from the following sentence (assuming that our knowledge base contains the respective fact):

Andy Warhol was born on August 6, 1928 in Pittsburgh.

Note that from the same sentence, we can also learn that *born* is an indicator word for the relation *date of birth*. To distinguish between the two, we need some kind of answer type matching; this is described in Section 4.4.

We compute the weights for the indicator words in the following IR-style fashion. Consider each relation as a document consisting of the words extracted for that relation. Then compute tf.idf scores for all the words in these (relation) documents in the usual way. For each relation, then only consider the top-1000 words and sum up their tf.idf scores. The weight for each word in a (relation) document is then its tf.idf score divided by this sum. This could also be interpreted as a probability distribution $p(w|r)$ over words w given a relation r.

4.4 Answer type matching

For each candidate, we perform a simple but effective binary check based on the relation leading to the answer ($r1$, $r2$, $r3$ for templates 1,2 and 3, respectively). We precompute a list of target types for each relation r by counting the types of objects o in all triples $(\cdot, r, o)$, keeping only the top ten percent of most frequent types. For questions starting with *who*, we check whether the computed target types contain the type person, character, or organization. For questions starting with *where*, we check whether the relation leads to a location or an event. For questions starting with *when* or *since when*, we check whether the type is a date; for all other questions, the check for target objects of type date is negative.

As our evaluation and error analysis shows, these simple heuristics work reasonably well for the Free917 and WebQuestions benchmarks. The reason is that our entity and relation matching already provide ample information for discriminating between candidates. However, as explained in Section 4.3, a question word like *born* alone does not permit discrimination between the two relations *place of birth* and *date of birth*. However, it is exactly those cases that can be easily discriminated with the simple answer-type check from above.

We leave elaborate answer-type detection (which has been addressed by many QA systems) to future work.

4.5 Candidate features

The previous subsections have shown two things. First, how we generate query candidates for a given question. Sec-

[5]For example, *founded* → *found* and *was* → *be*.
[6]`https://code.google.com/p/word2vec/`

ID	Description
1	number of entities in the query candidate
2	number of entities that matched exactly with their name, or with a high probability (> 0.8)
3	number of tokens of all entities that matched literally as per the previous feature
4-5	average (4) and sum (5) of entity match probabilities
6-7	average (6) and sum (7) of entity match popularities
8	number of relations in matched template
9	number of relations that were matched literally via their name
10-13	number of tokens that matched a relation of kind: literal (10), derivation (11), synonym (12), context (13)
14	sum of synonym match scores
15	sum of relation context match scores
16	number of times the answer relation (r_1, r_2, r_3 for templates 1, 2 and 3 respectively) occurs in the KB
17	a value between 0 and 1 indicating how well the relation matches according to n-gram features (Section 4.5)
18	sum of features 3 and 10; that is, the number of tokens matching a relation or entity literally
19	number of tokens that match an entity or relation divided by the total number of tokens in question
20-22	whether the result size is 0 (feature 20), 1-20 (feature 21), or larger than 20 (feature 22); all binary
23	binary result of the answer-type check (Section 4.4)

Table 1: Features used by our ranking approaches. Top/middle/bottom: features for entity matches/features for relation matches/combined or other features.

ond, how we compute various scores for each candidate that measure how well the entities and relations from the candidate match which parts of the question.

In this subsection, we show how we generate a feature vector from each candidate. Most of these features are based on the scores just mentioned. Another important feature, described below, serves to learn the correspondence between n-grams from the question and relations from query candidates. Table 1 provides an overview over all our features. In the description below, we refer to the features by their ID (first column in the table). In Section 4.6, we show how we rank candidates based on these feature vectors.

Entity/Relation matching features Features 1-7 are based on the results from the entity matching described in Section 4.1. Features 8-16 are based on the results from the relation matching step described in Section 4.3. Features 18 and 19 quantify the number of words in the question covered by entity or relation matches (feature 18 = literally, feature 19 = in any way). Features 20-22 quantify the result size. This is important, because some candidates produce huge result sizes or empty results sets, which are both rare. Feature 23 is the binary output of the simple answer-type check from Section 4.4.

N-Gram relation matching feature This feature considers correspondences between words (unigrams) or two-word phrases (bigrams) in the question and the relation in the query candidate. For example, in the WebQuestion benchmark, the question *who is ...* almost always asks for the *profession* of a person. Such a correspondence cannot be learned by any of the mechanisms described in Section 4.3. We learn this feature as follows.

For each query candidate, we generate all unigrams and bigrams of the lemmatized words of the question. The matched entities (Section 4.1) are replaced with a special word *entity*. For each n-gram, we then create an indicator feature by appending the n-gram to the relation names of the candidate. For example, for template 2 from Figure 1, one of the features would be *employment.company+work* for the uni-gram *work* and the relations *employment.company*. We then train an $L2$-regularized logistic regression classifier with all correct candidates as positive examples and all others as negative examples. The value of feature 17 is simply the (probability) output by this classifier.

This feature will be part of a subsequent step to learn a ranking that uses the same training data. To provide realistic feature values (that aren't overfit) we proceed as follows. Split the training data into six folds. In turn, leave out one fold and train the n-gram feature classifier on the remaining folds. Then, for each example in the left-out fold compute the n-gram feature value. Use this computed value as part of the training data for subsequent learning.

4.6 Ranking

For each question, we finally rank the query candidates using the feature vectors described in the previous subsection. The top-ranked query candidate is then used to provide the answer. We say "no answer" only when the set of candidates is emtpy; this is discussed in Section 4.7 below.[7]

We have experimented with state-of-the-art techniques for the learning-to-rank approach from IR [14] [16], including: RankSVM [14], RankBoost [12], LambdaRank [6] and AdaRank [23]. These only lead to moderate results and were outperformed by our approaches described below. We presume that this is because our ranking problem is degenerate. In particular, each query is only associated with a single *relevant* answer. This is different from a typical IR scenario where a query usually has several answers, sometimes with varying degrees of relevance.

We investigate two variants to obtain a ranking: *pointwise ranking* and *pairwise ranking*. These approaches are inspired by the learning-to-rank approaches from IR.

[7]Both benchmarks contain a considerable number of questions starting with *how many ...*, asking for a count. We simply replace *how many* by *what* in these questions, and count the size of the result set (unless the answer already is a count).

Pointwise ranking In the pointwise ranking approach we compute a score for each candidate. Candidates are sorted by this score to infer a ranking. The score is computed by a classifier learned on the candidate features (see Section 4.5) and training data. We create training data by using the correct candidate of each question as positive examples and all other candidates as negative examples.

A drawback of the pointwise approach is that the model "compares" question-independent examples. That is, correct (incorrect) query candidates of questions of different type and difficulty are in the same correct (incorrect) class, when in practice it is not necessary to compare or discriminate between them.

Pairwise ranking In the pairwise ranking approach, we transform the ranking problem into a binary classification problem. The idea is to learn a classifier that can predict for a given pair of candidates, whether one should be ranked before the other.

To infer a ranking, we sort the list of candidates using the learned preference relation. This works very well in practice, although our learning does not guarantee that the learned relation is transitive or anti-symmetric. We have experimented with two alternatives to sorting. Simply computing the maximum turned out to perform badly. This makes sense, because the maximum has to "survive" a larger number of comparisons. Following [10], we have also sorted the candidates by their number of "won" comparisons against all other candidates. The results were identical to those for sorting, but this method requires $\Theta(n^2)$ comparisons for n candidates.

To train the classifiers we create training examples in the following way. For a question with n query candidates, randomly select $n/2$, but at least 200 candidates (or n if $n/2 < 200$) . This is to guarantee that we have enough training examples for questions with few candidates and to avoid putting too much emphasis on questions that have more than 200 candidates.[8] Then, for each randomly selected candidate r_i and the correct candidate c, where $r_i \neq c$, create a positive example pair (c, r_i) and a negative example pair (r_i, c). The feature representation for a pair (a, b) is a tuple of the individual feature vectors and their difference: $\phi_{pair}(a, b) = (\phi(a) - \phi(b), \phi(a), \phi(b))$, where ϕ is a function extracting the features in Table 1.

Both ranking approaches, pointwise and pairwise, require a classifier. Here, we consider two different options.

Linear A logistic regression classifier. In initial experiments, other linear models, such as linear SVMs, have shown similar performance. Logistic regression is also known to output well calibrated probabilities and performs well in high-dimensional feature spaces. We train the model using L-BFGS-B [26]. To avoid over-fitting we apply $L2$-regularization choosing the regularization strength using 6-fold cross-validation on the training set.

Random forest We learn a forest of decision trees [5]. Random forests are able to learn non-linear decision boundaries, require few hyperparameters, are simple to train, and are known to perform very well on a variety of tasks.

[8]Our system generates around 200 candidates on average for a random question, but the exact value had little effect on performance in our evaluation.

4.7 Candidate pruning

Some questions may have no answers in the knowledge base. Our system, as described so far, returns "no answer" only when the set of query candidates is empty. However, as also described, this would rarely happen, since there are matching entities for every question, and we do not require that the relations match any of the words in the question.[9]

We consider two variants of our system to deal with this problem: (1) omitting the n-gram feature, and using hard pruning; and (2) keeping the n-gram feature, and using a pruning-classifier. Note that a nice side-effect of pruning is that it speeds up the ranking process because it needs to consider less candidates.

Without n-grams, with hard pruning When omitting the n-gram feature, there is no reason to keep candidates with the wrong answer type or where features 9-15 are all zero. The natural approach is then to prune such candidates before we do the ranking; this is what we call *hard pruning*. Hard pruning naturally leads to empty candidate sets for some queries. Indeed, on the Free917 benchmark, 10 questions have no answer, and our hard pruning yields an empty candidate set for 7 of them.

With n-grams, with a pruning classifier When keeping the n-gram feature, hard pruning as just described would be counterproductive. As explained in Section 4.5, the answers for the *who is ...* questions from the WebQuestions benchmark are professions. They would be eliminated when hard pruning by answer type. Also, the *profession* relation matches no words from these questions. They would hence also be eliminated when hard pruning if features 9-15 are all zero.

The goal of the pruning classifier is to weed out only the "obviously" bad candidates. For example, candidates that do not match the answer type, have bad relation matches, *and* a weak n-gram feature. We train the pruning classifier in the same way as the pointwise classifiers (see above) with the features from Table 1 using logistic regression. To optimize the classifier for recall we adjust example weights so that positive candidates have twice the weight of negative candidates. Before the ranking step, we apply the classifier to each candidate and only keep candidates classified positively.

5. EVALUATION

We perform an extensive evaluation of our system. In Section 5.1, we provide more details on our two benchmarks. In Section 5.2, we describe the evaluation measures used. In Section 5.3, we describe the systems we evaluate and compare to. In Section 5.4, we provide our main results followed by a detailed analysis in Section 5.5.

5.1 Data

We use all of Freebase as our knowledge base (2.9 billion facts on 44 million entities). Note that our approach is not tailored to Freebase and could easily be adapted to another knowledge base, e.g., WikiData[10].

Datasets We evaluate our system on two established benchmarks: *Free917* and *WebQuestions*. Each benchmark consists of a set of questions and their answers from Freebase.

[9]In that case, features 9-15 are all zero; however, the n-gram features could still be positive.

[10]`http://www.wikidata.org`

The benchmarks differ substantially in the types of questions and their complexity.

Free917 contains 917 manually generated natural language questions [7]. The questions cover a wide range of domains (81 in total). Two examples are *what fuel does an internal combustion engine use* and *how many floors does the white house have*. The most common domains, *film* and *business*, only make up 6% of the questions [7]. All questions are grammatical and tend to be tailored to Freebase. The dataset provides a translation of each question into a SPARQL-equivalent form. We execute the SPARQL queries to obtain a gold answer for each question. [7] also provide an entity lexicon: a mapping from exact text to the mentioned entity for all entities appearing in the questions. This lexicon consists of 1014 different entities. It was used for identifying entities by all systems reporting results on the dataset so far. We only make use of this lexicon where explicitly stated. To report results, we use the original split of the questions by [7] into 70% (641) questions to train and 30% questions (276) to test.

WebQuestions consists of 5,810 questions that were selected by crawling the Google suggest API [2]. Contrary to Free917, questions are not necessarily grammatical and are more colloquial. For example: *where did jackie kennedy go to college* and *what is spoken in czech republic*. Due to how they were selected, the questions are biased towards topics that are frequently asked from Google. According to [19], the *people* domain alone makes up about 7% of questions. Furthermore, the structure of questions tends to be simpler. Most questions only require a single entity with an answer relation [2]. Answers to the questions were obtained by using crowdsourcing. This introduces additional noise; in particular, for some questions only a subset of the correct answer is provided as gold answer. We use the original train-test split of the questions by [2] into 70% (3,778 questions) to train and 30% (2,032 questions) to test.

5.2 Evaluation measures

Given a benchmark and a system, denote the questions by $q_1...q_n$, the gold answers by $g_1...g_n$, and the answers from the system by $a_1...a_n$. Note that an answer can consist of a single value (in particular, a date or a literal) or a list of values. We consider the following two evaluation measures.

Accuracy The fraction of queries answered with the exact gold answer:

$$\text{accuracy} = \frac{1}{n}\sum_{i=1}^{n} I(g_i = a_i)$$

where $I(e)$ is an indicator function returning one if expression e is true and zero else. This is reasonable on Free917 which provides perfect gold answers.

Average F1 The average F1 across all questions:

$$\text{average F1} = \frac{1}{n}\sum_{i=1}^{n} F1(g_i, a_i)$$

where the function $F1$ computes F1 in the regular way. This accounts for partially correct results, which is reasonable for WebQuestions, where gold answers are sometimes incomplete.

In our evaluation we focus on accuracy for Free917 and average F1 for WebQuestions. These are the most reported and most intuitive measures for these datasets. We also performed the evaluation with other measures that were used in previous work, e.g., variants of F1 as defined in [15] and [25]. These provided no new insights and strongly correlated with the measures above.

	Free917		WebQuestions
Method	Accuracy+	Accuracy	Average F1
Cai+Yates	59 %	–	–
Jacana	–	–	35.4 %
Sempre	62 %	52 %	35.7 %
Kwiat. et al	68 %	–	–
Bordes et al	–	–	39.2 %
ParaSempre	68.5 %	46 %	39.9 %
Aqqu	**76.4 %**	**65.9 %**	**49.4 %**

Table 2: Results on the Free917 (267 questions) and WebQuestions (2032 questions) test set. For the results in the second column (Accuracy+) a manually crafted entity lexicon was used.

5.3 Systems evaluated

We evaluate and compare the following systems. See Section 2 for a brief description of the systems from previous work. If we (re-)produced results, we explicitly state so. Otherwise, we report existing results.

Cai+Yates The semantic parser developed by [7].

Kwiat. et al The semantic parser by [15].

Sempre The semantic parser by [2]. We produced results for Free917 without an entity lexicon using the provided code.[11]

ParaSempre The semantic parser suggested by [3]. We used the code provided by the authors[11] to produce results on Free917 without an entity lexicon.

GraphParser The semantic parser developed by [19]. We report results obtained from the code provided by the authors[12]. The results from their code slightly deviates from the results reported in their paper.

Jacana The information extraction based approach by [25]. We report updated results from [24].

Bordes et al The embedding-based model by [4].

Aqqu Our system, as described in Section 4. We want to stress that we use the exact same system on both benchmarks. As shown in Section 5.5 below, results can be further improved by adapting the feature set to the benchmark. However, we consider this overfitting. Note that all of the systems above, except Sempre and ParaSempre, were only evaluated on one of the two benchmarks.

5.4 Main results

Table 2 shows the results on the test sets for Free917 and WebQuestions for all the systems from Section 5.3. GraphParser is discussed separately below, because it was evaluated only on a subset of questions.

On Free917, Aqqu improves in accuracy over the best previous systems by 8% with an entity lexicon, and by 14% without entity lexicon. Performance drops considerably for all systems when not using an entity lexicon. This shows

[11] `http://github.com/percyliang/sempre`
[12] `http://github.com/sivareddyg/graph-parser`

	Top-2	Top-3	Top-5	Top-10
Free917	74.3 %	77.2 %	79.3 %	83.7 %
WebQuestions	67.1 %	72.7 %	77.5 %	82.3 %

Table 3: Top-k results on Free917 (top) and WebQuestions (bottom). Percentage of questions with the best answer in the top-k candidates.

	Free917		WebQuestions
Method	Acc+	Acc	Avg F1
Aqqu-point-lin	73.6 %	63.4 %	46.9 %
Aqqu-point-tree	74.3 %	63.0 %	47.9 %
Aqqu-pair-lin	76.4 %	65.2 %	48.3 %
Aqqu-pair-tree	76.4 %	65.9 %	49.4 %

Table 4: Results for different ranking variants on the test sets for Free917 and WebQuestions. For the results in the second column (Acc+) a manually crafted entity lexicon was used.

that addressing entity recognition is an integral part of the problem that cannot be ignored. Overall, we achieve an oracle accuracy (percentage of questions where at least one produced query candidate is correct) of 89.1% and 85.5%, with and without entity lexicon respectively. This indicates that there is still room for improvement for better matching and ranking.

On WebQuestions our system improves the state of the art by almost 10% in average F1. No system uses an entity lexicon. Note that the WebQuestions benchmark is much harder and contains a considerable amount of imperfect or wrong answers. Out of a random sample of 55 questions we found 9 questions that had a wrong answer, and 10 further question that had only a partially correct answer. This suggests that the upper bound for average F1 is roughly around 80%. Our oracle average F1 is at 68.5%. [2] and [3] report 48% and 63% respectively. Hence, we successfully identify most of the entities and relations. However, there is still much room for improvement in ranking and matching. GraphParser was evaluated only on a subset of Freebase relations. The authors provide a train-test split of questions for WebQuestions. Note that we didn't restrict our system to the specific relations and that GraphParser requires an entity lexicon also on WebQuestions. Our system (without an entity lexicon) scores an average F1 of 66.1 % compared to 40.5 % reported for GraphParser. The selected subset of relations and thus questions seems to be considerably easier to answer for our system.

5.5 Detailed analysis

Top-k results Table 3 shows the top-k results on the two datasets. A large majority of questions can be answered from the top two or three candidates. By providing these interpretations and results (in addition to the top-ranked candidate) to a user, many questions can be answered correctly. Note that on WebQuestions some questions only have an imperfect gold answer with an F1 score smaller than one. Therefore, the percentage of best answers in the top candidates can be slightly larger than the resulting average F1.

Ranking variants As described in Section 4.6, we consider two possible ranking methods: pointwise (*point*) and pairwise (*pair*), each with two different ranking classifiers: logistic regression (*lin*) and random forests (*tree*). This gives a total of four different combinations.

	Free917	WebQuestions
best previous	52.0 %	39.9 %
best now	**69.2 %**	**49.4 %**
no n-grams, all other	69.2 %	39.6 %
no n-grams, no lit-match	65.2 %	39.6 %
no n-grams, no synonyms	61.6 %	28.2 %
n-grams, all other	65.9 %	49.4 %
n-grams, no pruning	64.4 %	49.3 %
n-grams, no synonyms	62.0 %	48.0 %
n-grams, nothing else	18.1 %	43.8 %

Table 5: Feature analysis for Free917 and WebQuestions. No synonyms disables features 11-15 and no lit-match features 2, 3, 9, 10 and 18. When not using the n-gram feature a different type of candidate pruning is performed (see text).

Table 4 shows results of all four ranking variants with the full features of Table 1. On both benchmarks, pairwise ranking is more effective than pointwise ranking. This is consistent with our intuition that learning a pairwise comparator is better (see Section 4.6). Furthermore, random forests are slightly more effective than a weighted linear combination. We therefore use pairwise ranking with random forests as a standard choice.

Feature analysis To gain insight into which features are helpful we evaluate our system with different combinations. Table 5 shows the results. Note that, as described in Section 4.7, without the n-gram feature hard pruning is applied. The following main observations can be made.

The n-gram feature is extremely helpful on WebQuestions but slightly detrimental on Free917. The WebQuestions benchmark contains many questions that are hard to answer without this kind of supervision, e.g., *where is reggie bush from?* (asking for the place of birth) or *what to do downtown san francisco?* (asking for tourist attractions). Our system is able to successfully learn important features for these from the training set. On the other hand, the small Free917 benchmark covers a wide range of domains and relations with only few repetitions. N-gram features aren't helpful on this dataset, which is shown by the low performance when only using the n-gram feature (18.1%). Note that the ranking and learning problem is inherently more difficult when the number of possible candidates increases. This is the case when not using hard pruning which goes along with using the n-gram feature (see Section 4.7). This disadvantage cannot be fully compensated by the weak n-gram feature and leaner pruning and, as a result, the score drops by about 3% for Free917. Still, we consider it more important to have a single approach that performs well on different kinds of datasets than to optimize for a single dataset.

Literal features provide a small benefit for Free917 but no benefit on WebQuestions. This is an artefact of the way Free917 was built. Free917 questions are tailored to Freebase, often using words from the relation name as part of the question. Synonym features are important for both datasets. They give a huge benefit on WebQuestions without the n-gram feature but only a small benefit on top of it.

Finally, the pruning classifier used with the n-gram feature helps on Free917 because it allows to return "no answer" for some questions that have no answer in the knowledge base. The difference on WebQuestions (which always has an answer in the knowledge base) is not significant, and shows that the pruning classifier doesn't negatively affect performance.

Manual error analysis We manually inspected the errors our system makes. Many errors are due to mistakes in the benchmarks (partially or completely wrong gold answers) and inconsistencies in the knowledge base (different relations with contradicting answers on the same piece of information). We provide a list on our website, see the link in Section 1.1.

On that website, we also provide a list of errors due to our system. There is no single large class of errors worth pointing out though.

Efficiency We also evaluated the performance of our system. The average response time for a question is 644 ms for Free917 and 900 ms for WebQuestions.[13] None of the other system from Section 5.3 comes with an efficiency evaluation. For systems that provide code and for which we reproduced results, runtimes are (at least) several seconds per query. Training our system on the large WebQuestions benchmark takes about 90 minutes in total.

6. CONCLUSION

We have presented Aqqu, a new end-to-end system that automatically translates a given natural-language question to the matching SPARQL query on a knowledge base. The system integrates entity recognition and utilizes distant supervision and learning-to-rank techniques. We showed that our system outperforms previous state-of-the-art systems on two very different benchmarks by 8% and more. Aqqu answers questions interactively, that is, within one second.

For around 80% of the queries, the correct answer is among the top-5 candidates. This suggests that a more interactive approach, which asks the user's feedback for critical decisions (e.g., between two relations), could achieve a significantly further improved accuracy.

7. REFERENCES

[1] H. Bast, F. Bäurle, B. Buchhold, and E. Haussmann. Broccoli: Semantic full-text search at your fingertips. *CoRR*, abs/1207.2615, 2012.

[2] J. Berant, A. Chou, R. Frostig, and P. Liang. Semantic Parsing on Freebase from Question-Answer Pairs. In *EMNLP*, pages 1533–1544, 2013.

[3] J. Berant and P. Liang. Semantic Parsing via Paraphrasing. In *ACL*, pages 1415–1425, 2014.

[4] A. Bordes, S. Chopra, and J. Weston. Question Answering with Subgraph Embeddings. *CoRR*, abs/1406.3676, 2014.

[5] L. Breiman. Random forests. *Machine Learning*, 45(1):5–32, 2001.

[13] Answer times are averaged over three runs on a server with Intel E5649 CPUs, 90GB of RAM and warm SPARQL caches.

[6] C. J. C. Burges, R. Ragno, and Q. V. Le. Learning to rank with nonsmooth cost functions. In *NIPS*, pages 193–200, 2006.

[7] Q. Cai and A. Yates. Large-scale Semantic Parsing via Schema Matching and Lexicon Extension. In *ACL*, pages 423–433, 2013.

[8] A. X. Chang and C. D. Manning. Sutime: A library for recognizing and normalizing time expressions. In *LREC*, pages 3735–3740, 2012.

[9] ClueWeb, 2012. The Lemur Projekt.

[10] W. W. Cohen, R. E. Schapire, and Y. Singer. Learning to order things. *JAIR*, 10:243–270, 1999.

[11] C. Fellbaum. *WordNet*. Wiley Online Library, 1998.

[12] Y. Freund, R. D. Iyer, R. E. Schapire, and Y. Singer. An efficient boosting algorithm for combining preferences. *JMLR*, 4:933–969, 2003.

[13] E. Gabrilovich, M. Ringgaard, and A. Subramanya. FACC1: Freebase annotation of ClueWeb corpora, Version 1.

[14] T. Joachims. Optimizing search engines using clickthrough data. In *KDD*, pages 133–142, 2002.

[15] T. Kwiatkowski, E. Choi, Y. Artzi, and L. S. Zettlemoyer. Scaling Semantic Parsers with On-the-Fly Ontology Matching. In *EMNLP*, pages 1545–1556, 2013.

[16] T. Liu. Learning to rank for information retrieval. *Foundations and Trends in Information Retrieval*, 3(3):225–331, 2009.

[17] C. D. Manning, M. Surdeanu, J. Bauer, J. R. Finkel, S. Bethard, and D. McClosky. The stanford corenlp natural language processing toolkit. In *ACL*, pages 55–60, 2014.

[18] M. Mintz, S. Bills, R. Snow, and D. Jurafsky. Distant supervision for relation extraction without labeled data. In *ACL*, pages 1003–1011, 2009.

[19] S. Reddy, M. Lapata, and M. Steedman. Large-scale Semantic Parsing without Question-Answer Pairs. *TACL*, 2:377–392, 2014.

[20] V. I. Spitkovsky and A. X. Chang. A Cross-Lingual Dictionary for English Wikipedia Concepts. In *LREC*, pages 3168–3175, 2012.

[21] M. Steedman. *The syntactic process*, volume 35. MIT Press, 2000.

[22] C. Unger, C. Forascu, V. Lopez, A. N. Ngomo, E. Cabrio, P. Cimiano, and S. Walter. Question answering over linked data (QALD-4). In *CLEF 2014*, pages 1172–1180, 2014.

[23] J. Xu and H. Li. Adarank: a boosting algorithm for information retrieval. In *SIGIR*, pages 391–398, 2007.

[24] X. Yao, J. Berant, and B. V. Durme. Freebase QA: Information Extraction or Semantic Parsing? In *ACL, Workshop on Semantic Parsing*, 2014.

[25] X. Yao and B. V. Durme. Information Extraction over Structured Data: Question Answering with Freebase. In *ACL*, pages 956–966, 2014.

[26] C. Zhu, R. H. Byrd, P. Lu, and J. Nocedal. Algorithm 778: L-BFGS-B: Fortran subroutines for large-scale bound-constrained optimization. *ACM Trans. Math. Softw.*, 23(4):550–560, 1997.

Improving Ranking Consistency for Web Search by Leveraging a Knowledge Base and Search Logs

Jyun-Yu Jiang†, Jing Liu‡, Chin-Yew Lin‡ and Pu-Jen Cheng†
†Department of Computer Science and Information Engineering, National Taiwan University
‡Microsoft Research
jyunyu.jiang@gmail.com, liudani@microsoft.com, cyl@microsoft.com, pjcheng@csie.ntu.edu.tw

ABSTRACT

In this paper, we propose a new idea called ranking consistency in web search. Relevance ranking is one of the biggest problems in creating an effective web search system. Given some queries with similar search intents, conventional approaches typically only optimize ranking models by each query separately. Hence, there are inconsistent rankings in modern search engines. It is expected that the search results of different queries with similar search intents should preserve ranking consistency. The aim of this paper is to learn consistent rankings in search results for improving the relevance ranking in web search. We then propose a re-ranking model aiming to simultaneously improve relevance ranking and ranking consistency by leveraging knowledge bases and search logs. To the best of our knowledge, our work offers the first solution to improving relevance rankings with ranking consistency. Extensive experiments have been conducted using the Freebase knowledge base and the large-scale query-log of a commercial search engine. The experimental results show that our approach significantly improves relevance ranking and ranking consistency. Two user surveys on Amazon Mechanical Turk also show that users are sensitive and prefer the consistent ranking results generated by our model.

Categories and Subject Descriptors

H.3.3 [**Information Storage and Retrieval**]: Information Search and Retrieval

Keywords

Web search; Ranking consistency; Re-ranking

1. INTRODUCTION

Relevance ranking is a critical task aiming to order search results by their relevance to a user's information needs. Previous works make great efforts to improve relevance rankings from different aspects such as the modeling of learning to rank [5,8,26], incorporating personalization [2,4,28] and the accurate evaluation of search results [12,18,29]. However, the ranking consistency[1] of search results for queries with similar search intents has not been carefully investigated. Suppose web pages about a certain topic on a website are treated as a topical cluster. Ranking consistency refers to the relevance of web pages in the same clusters that would be generally consistent in the search results for similar search intents.

Figure 1 shows some ordered search results for three queries about basketball players ("Kobe Bryant," "Tim Duncan," and "Kevin Durant") from a commercial search engine. In general, the ranking results of the first two queries ("Bryant" and "Duncan") are quite consistent by arranging `Wikipedia` at the top and ranking sports-related websites (e.g., `ESPN.com` and `NBA.com`) higher than others like movie-related ones (e.g., `IMDb`). According to our observation, most NBA players follow such consistency. Potentially, if one website focuses mainly on certain topics, the quality of their web pages is more likely to be close to each other. `ESPN.com` collects much personal information about sports-related players while `IMDb` focuses on movie promotion. For those queries with similar search intents, the relevance of these web pages about a certain topic (i.e., athletes) is likely to be consistent. In other words, `ESPN.com` is more relevant than `IMDb`. Unfortunately, the ranking of the third query ("Kevin Durant") is inconsistent in Figure 1. "Kevin Durant" is famous for basketball, rather than movies. Giving `IMDb` a higher ranking than `ESPN.com` does not make sense. The inconsistency represents a flaw in determining relevance ranking: each query is optimized separately so that the potential consistency among queries is totally ignored.

To learn the ranking consistency in web search, there are two challenges: (1) The first one is how to consistently rank topical clusters (i.e., web pages about a certain topic in each website) based on their relevance to those queries with similar search intents. For example, in Figure 1, we would like to discover that, for queries about basketball players, web pages in `ESPN.com` should be ranked higher than ones in `IMDb`. Then the web pages in topical clusters can be consistently ranked in the ranking results according to shared relevance. (2) The second challenge is how to generally rank all web pages for each query because some web pages (e.g., personal websites) may not share the topical cluster with web pages of other queries. Even though they cannot be ranked by the shared relevance with other web pages, they

[1] Although traditional approaches to learning to rank [8] also mention "consistency," their consistency is how the ranking results are consistent with the training orders. Different from their consistency, the ranking consistency in this paper is how the ranking results are consistent with the results of queries with similar search intents.

Permission to make digital or hard copies of all or part of this work for personal or classroom use is granted without fee provided that copies are not made or distributed for profit or commercial advantage and that copies bear this notice and the full citation on the first page. Copyrights for components of this work owned by others than ACM must be honored. Abstracting with credit is permitted. To copy otherwise, or republish, to post on servers or to redistribute to lists, requires prior specific permission and/or a fee. Request permissions from Permissions@acm.org.
CIKM'15, October 19–23, 2015, Melbourne, Australia.
© 2015 ACM. ISBN 978-1-4503-3794-6/15/10 ...$15.00.
DOI: http://dx.doi.org/10.1145/2806416.2806479.

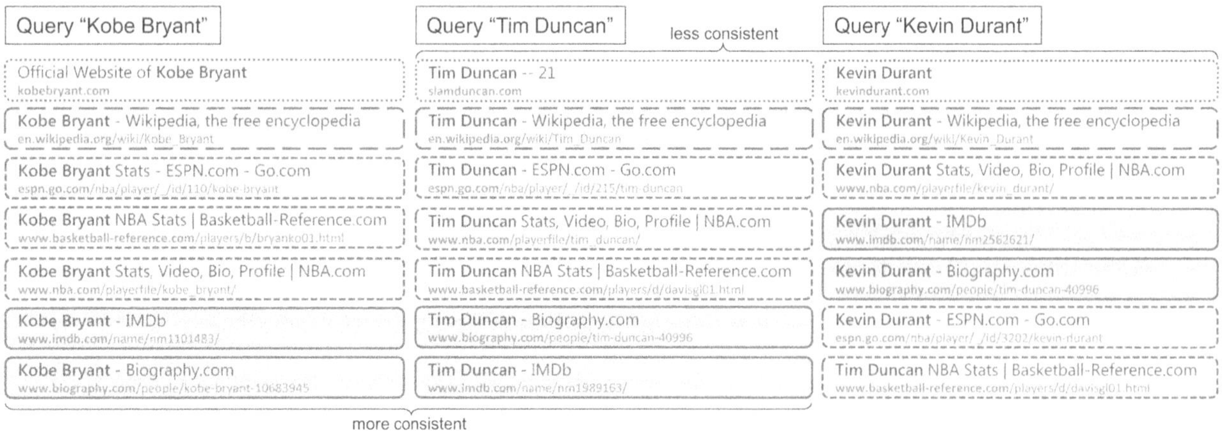

Figure 1: Search results of three queries about NBA basketball player ("Kobe Bryant," "Tim Duncan" and "Kevin Durant") from a commercial search engine captured in April 2015.

are still relevant to specific queries. In Figure 1, three people all have personal websites with the highest relevance. Although these websites do not belong to any shared topical cluster[2], they should still be well ranked in proper positions. Even though sports-related websites are ranked higher than others, the order of different sports-related websites might be different for different queries. In Figure 1, the order of `NBA.com` and `Basketball-Reference.com` are reverse in the rankings of the first two queries. A possible reason is that the quality of contents in the two websites are different for the two queries. The second challenge also includes this issue.

In this paper, we propose a two-stage re-ranking model to conquer the above two challenges and to improve the relevance rankings of existing ranking models. In the first stage, we start with query type extraction for understanding the search intents of queries and URL pattern extraction for exploring topical clusters in each website. By exploiting click-through data in search logs as implicit feedback, numerous pairwise preferences of URL patterns are extracted for each query type, and then optimized as the complete relevance distribution by pairwise ranking aggregation. The rationality of this stage is also proven by an intuitive lemma. In the second stage, an ensemble-based re-ranking model is proposed to generally rank web pages by the results from the previous stage and the original ranker of an existing search engine. By applying click-through data as training data and incorporating eight useful features, the model finds an appropriate way to re-rank each web page from original results.

Extensive experiments have been conducted on the large-scale real-world search log from a commercial search engine. As this is the first study on the ranking consistency in web search, we propose a new metric to evaluate the consistency. The experimental results show that our model significantly improves not only the ranking consistency but also the relevance rankings from the original ranker across various subsets of testing data with different distribution and query types. Moreover, two user surveys on Amazon Mechanical Turk further show the effectiveness of the ranking consistency generated by our approach.

[2]In `ESPN.com`, the web pages share the same topic for various queries (e.g., basketball players). But the web pages in `kobebryant.com` are all about the same query (i.e., "Kobe Bryant").

The rest of this paper is organized as follows. After covering related work in Section 2, we give a brief overview of the two-stage re-ranking model in Section 3. The details of our model are presented in Sections 4 and 5. Section 6 reports the experimental results of our model and two user surveys on Amazon Mechanical Turk. Finally, Section 7 gives our discussions and conclusions.

2. RELATED WORK

In this section, we review substantial previous work related to this paper in a number of topics.

Ranking Consistency. Although ranking consistency has never been discussed in relation to web search, the term ranking consistency is used in other other fields. In image matching and object retrieval, previous works have evaluated ranking consistency by measuring the similarity between image contents [10]. However, such ranking consistency is only about the image search results of the same query. Moreover, this is adopted to estimate similarities between two ranking results of different methods for the same ranked items by Nguyen and Szymanski [25]. Nevertheless, they calculate similarities between the same objects and ranked items, but not between the search results of different queries representing similar topics. Our ranking consistency is calculated at a higher level and is able to have more general applications.

URL Patterns of Webpages. A URL pattern summarizes websites with similar URL strings and properties. This feature is an important characteristic for representing web pages in the deep web. Previous works [16, 20, 31] represent URL patterns as regular expression patterns so that URLs can be matched conveniently. Jiang *et al.* [16] and Li *et al.* [20] learn URL patterns from training URL collections for crawling web forums. Yin *et al.* [31] extract URL patterns from click-through data for information extraction. In our work, we collect URL collections from click-through data and learn URL regular expressions patterns as in [16]. By leveraging click-through data, we derive the user preferences for URL patterns. Therefore, web search performance and ranking consistency can improve if we rank websites consistent with preferences.

Search Intents behind Queries. Understanding users' search intents is an important task for search engines. Some previous work represent the intents with click-through data [21]. Hu *et al.* [15] use Wikipedia concepts to represent user search intents. Guo *et al.* [14] propose a new task called named entity recognition in query (NERQ). They find that more than 70% of queries contain entities [14]. Based on this analysis, in our work, we assume that the search intents of queries can be clustered into many types in a knowledge base, i.e. Freebase, according to entities contained in queries. Moreover, understanding search intents behind queries can also improve relevance ranking. Gao *et al.* [13] extract features from click graphs as additional features. Bennett *et al.* [3] adopt predefined classes and try to estimate class distribution as search intents. However, they do not consider the ranking consistency of search results for multiple queries. Gao *et al.* [13] only treat click-through information as search intents of queries. Bennett *et al.* [3] optimize ranking models with query and document class distribution for each query independently.

Click-through Data in Web Search For a search engine, click-through data is an informative relevance signal from users about relevance ranking quality [18]. Clicks in search engine logs have been used as implicit measures such as satisfied clicks (SAT-Clicks) for evaluation [12]. Learning from click-through data also helps improve the relevance ranking of search engines. Joachims [17] optimizes the search quality with implicit feedback extracted from click-through data. Radlinski and Joachims [26] generate user preferences from search logs with connected query chains. However, they consider only preferences between web pages in the search results of a single query, not between the URL patterns for different queries. If user preferences between URL patterns are also considered, the relevance of rare web pages can be better estimated by leveraging information from popular ones with similar topics.

Pairwise Ranking Aggregation. Our approach deriving consistent rankings of URL patterns is relevant to pairwise ranking aggregation. In web search, Carterette *et al.* [9] and Farah *et al.* [11] aggregate search results of a single query from multiple search engines. In other fields, Bennett *et al.* [1] improve image search quality by aggregating crowdsourcing pairwise annotations. Liu *et al.* [22] aggregate generated pairwise competitions to estimate user expertise in community question answering services. However, they apply ranking aggregation for a single query or only one problem. In this paper, we derive consistent rankings of URL patterns, and then apply to multiple queries.

To summarize the relationship to previous approaches, our approach (1) considers the search results of multiple queries at the same time for ranking consistency; (2) utilizes click-through data to learn URL patterns and represent websites in the deep web; (3) discovers queries with similar intents by leveraging type information in knowledge bases; and (4) exploits click-through data to find out users' preferences between URL patterns for each query type. To the best of our knowledge, this is the first study on ranking consistency in web search.

3. TWO-STAGE RE-RANKING MODEL

In this section, we first give a brief overview of the proposed approach, and then describe the details in the following sections. Based on the concept of the ranking consistency mentioned in Section 1, to simultaneously improve the ranking consistency and relevance rankings, we propose a re-ranking model consisting of two stages: (1) consistent ranking model and (2) ensemble-based re-ranking.

The first stage, i.e., consistent ranking model, is to consistently rank web pages in topical clusters by the relevance of clusters to queries with same types, which are defined as the groups of similar search intents. Hence, to develop the ranking consistency, there are two challenges before ranking web pages: (1) how to discover same-type queries (in other words, how to identify the query types); and (2) how to discover the topical clusters (i.e., web pages with similar topics) in each website.

To recognize the search intents behind queries, a possible solution is named entity recognition in queries (NERQ) [14]. It has been shown that the types of mentioned entities within a query can be used to represent query intents, and more than 70% of queries cover entities [14]. Moreover, many existing knowledge bases (e.g., Freebase [6] and Probase [30]) summarize the types of entities. For example, in Figure 1, the first query will lead to the entity "Kobe Bryant" with the types `people/person`, `basketball_player` and `film/actor`. Hence, the knowledge base can be leveraged to identify the types of the entities as the query types.

As some websites have specific contents (e.g., `ESPN.com` contains web pages about different sports), we need to discover the topical clusters of web pages in each website, where the web pages in each cluster share the same topic. The URL patterns can be utilized to represent the topical clusters because web pages with the same topic usually share the same URL pattern. For instance, in Figure 1, web pages of `ESPN.com` for three queries can be summarized as the URL pattern `espn.go.com/nba/player/_/id/*/*/`. Moreover, the utilization of URL patterns is helpful in determining the ranking consistency. Particularly, the ranking consistency of search results can be decided by the consistency of matched URL patterns. Note that personal websites such as `kobebryant.com` and `slamduncan.com` may not be matched by any URL pattern because their URLs are usually unique and dissimilar to other URLs.

To estimate the relevance of URL patterns (i.e., topical clusters) to query types, we apply the click-through data in search logs because clicks can represent, to some extent, users' satisfaction. By exploring implicit feedback from user clicks [17], numerous pairwise preferences of URL patterns are collected for each query type, and then aggregated into weighted preferences to avoid the bias of too popular queries and contradictions. With the preferences of URL patterns, the cost function of Rank-Net [8] is applied to combine such preferences and optimize the relevance of patterns as probability-like scores by stochastic gradient descent (SGD). In the example of Figure 1, if most users click web pages in `ESPN.com` but not the ones in `IMDb`, the URL pattern of `ESPN.com` will have a higher score than the pattern of `IMDb`.

The second stage, i.e., ensemble-based re-ranking, is to re-rank the ranking results of an original ranker based on the results from the consistent ranking model (Stage 1). The re-ranking model shapes a parameter to decide the weights of the original ranker and the consistent ranking model, and then makes an ensemble of two approaches. However, such parameters should be different for each query and each web page under various situations. For example, in Figure 1, personal websites like `kobebryant.com` are not matched by any URL pattern, so the weight of the original ranker would be larger to make them be ranked in higher positions. Conversely, web pages in `ESPN.com` are matched by a URL pattern, such that the weight would be smaller to gain relevance from the ranking consistency over the queries of the same type. To model various situations, eight features within three categories are proposed, and the parameter can be optimized as a logistic function whose inputs are the features. Finally, the re-ranking model can generally re-rank not only web pages in topical clusters but other web pages, and then well optimize the relevance rankings.

4. CONSISTENT RANKING MODEL

In this section, we discuss the details of the first stage of the proposed approach, which aims to rank web pages in topical clusters according their relevance to query types.

4.1 Model Formalities

Recall that in Section 3 we discuss ranking consistency according to queries of the same types and web pages matched by URL patterns. To apply URL patterns to relevance rankings, we first make an assumption as follows:

Assumption 1 *For the URL patterns that are more relevant to query types, web pages matched by such URL patterns may be also more relevant to the queries.*

With the above assumption, for those queries with only single type, a simple approach is to rank the web pages that are matched with more relevant patterns to higher positions and ignore those web pages without any matched pattern. It ensures consistent rankings because more relevant patterns must be ranked higher than less relevant patterns.

However, a query may have multiple types due to its ambiguity. Moreover, URL patterns may have different levels of relevance for each type. Based on the above approach, we start our model from the following assumption:

Assumption 2 *When a query belongs to multiple types, the relevance distribution is an aggregation over types.*

That is, under the assumption, the relevance distribution of a query can be computed by the distribution of its corresponding types. To model the problem more easily, we use a probability distribution to represent the relevance score. This assumption is natural for a type-based consistent ranking model. Considering all types of a query, the model is able to cover potentially esoteric search intents. Moreover, the problems can be decomposed into type-related tasks, which are simpler and more reliable.

Query Type Extraction. To extract the types of a query, we need to link the query to the corresponding entity in the knowledge base, then the types of the linked entity will be the query types. Although there has been some previous work about named entity recognition in query [14], as a pioneer study of the ranking consistency, we simply exploit the click-through data and make connections between queries and Wikipedia pages of entities. Note that the Wikipedia pages of entities can be found in most of knowledge bases such as Freebase [6]. If an entity's Wikipedia page has been clicked many times after users have submitted a query, the query will likely contain such an entity. Here an entity is treated as the intended entity of a query if the click-through rate of its Wikipedia page is more than 10%. After mapping queries to entities, we transfer types of entities in Freebase [6] to queries as their types.

URL Pattern Extraction. Previous works preset many methods for extracting URL patterns from click-through data [31] or URL collections [16]. In our work, we adopt the method mentioned in [16] because some URL patterns are so complex that we have to use regular expressions to represent them. All URLs clicked in the training logs are collected as a URL collection. We then generalize the URL collection into many regular expressions as URL patterns.

1. Kobe Bryant - Wikipedia, the free encyclopedia
   en.wikipedia.org/wiki/Kobe_Bryant
   p_1 = `en.wikipedia.org/wiki/*`
2. **(Clicked) KB24 - Official Website of Kobe Bryant**
   kobebryant.com, $p_2 = \emptyset$
3. **(Clicked) Kobe Bryant Stats, Video, Bio, Profile**
   www.nba.com/playerfile/kobe_bryant/
   p_3 = `www.nba.com/playerfile/*/`
4. Kobe Bryant Stats, News, Videos, Highlights ...
   espn.go.com/nba/player/_/id/110/kobe-bryant
   p_4 = `espn.go.com/nba/player/_/id/*/*/`
5. Kobe Bryant Biography
   www.biography.com/people/kobe-bryant-10683945
   p_5 = `www.biography.com/people/*`
6. **(Clicked) Kobe Bryant | Los Angeles Lakers**
   sports.yahoo.com/nba/players/3118
   p_6 = `sports.yahoo.com/nba/players/*`

Figure 2: Ranking presented for the query "Kobe Bryant" about a famous basketball player. Five URLs are matched by URL patterns, and the user clicked on URLs 2, 3 and 6.

4.2 Model Formulation

Here our model is formulated formally. In this model, URLs are used to represent web pages. For a query q, we would like to estimate the relevance distribution $P(u \mid q)$, where u is a web page. In order to rank consistently, we only focus on URLs, which can be matched by URL patterns. So we have:

$$P(u \mid q) = \begin{cases} P(p \mid q) & \text{, if } u \text{ is matched by pattern } p \\ 0 & \text{, otherwise} \end{cases},$$

where $P(p \mid q)$ is the relevance distribution of pattern p given the query q. We ignore other URLs without any pattern-match and treat them as irrelevant in this stage. Furthermore, they will be well re-ranked in the second stage with several robust features.

Following Assumption 2, the model ranks a pattern p according to the probabilities that p is relevant to q's types $T(q)$ in the knowledge base. On the other hand, queries are independent to the relevance distribution of URL patterns. Hence, the relevance distribution $P(p \mid q)$ can be re-written by marginalization as follows:

$$\begin{aligned} P(p \mid q) &= \sum_{t \in T(q)} P(p \mid t, q) \cdot P(t \mid q) \\ &= \sum_{t \in T(q)} P(p \mid t) \cdot P(t \mid q) \end{aligned}$$

Therefore, the task can be decomposed into two problems with better reliability: (1) how to estimate the pattern-type relevance $P(p \mid t)$, and (2) how to estimate the type distribution $P(t \mid q)$.

4.3 Pattern-Type Relevance

To estimate the pattern-type relevance $P(p \mid t)$ in the real-world, we adopt a data-driven approach with click-through data from search engine logs. We extract pairwise preferences from original search results and user preference feedback from their behaviors in authentic web search scenarios.

Implicit Feedback from Clicks. As defined in [17], click-through data in search engines can be thought of as

Algorithm 1 Preference Extraction

Input: Given entity: e; Queries of e in the training logs: $Q_e = \{(q, C)\}$, where q is an entity query of e, and C is the set of SAT-clicked URLs in click-through data; Pattern set: S.

Output: Initial preference list for e: D_e.

$D_e \leftarrow [\,]$
for $(q, C) \in Q_e$ **do**
  $clickP \leftarrow \emptyset$
  for $(u, p) \in C \times S$ **do**
    if u is matched by p **then**
      $clickP \leftarrow clickP \cup \{p\}$
    end if
  end for
  for $(p_i, p_j) \in clickP \times (S - clickP)$ **do**
    Add (p_i, p_j) into D_e
  end for
end for
return D_e

Algorithm 2 Preference Aggregation

Input: Given entity: e; Initial preference list of e: D_e.

Output: Weighted preference list for the entity e: R_e.

$cnt \leftarrow$ new RB-Tree (or any key-value data structure)
for $(p_i, p_j) \in D_e$ **do**
  if $(p_i, p_j) \notin cnt$ **then**
    $cnt\left[(p_i, p_j)\right] \leftarrow 0$
    $cnt\left[(p_j, p_i)\right] \leftarrow 0$
  end if
  $cnt\left[(p_i, p_j)\right] \leftarrow cnt\left[(p_i, p_j)\right] + 1$
end for
$R_e \leftarrow [\,]$
for $(p_i, p_j) \in S \times S$ **do**
  if $(p_i, p_j) \in cnt$ **and** $cnt\left[(p_i, p_j)\right] > 0$ **then**
    $w_{ij} \leftarrow cnt\left[(p_i, p_j)\right] / \left(cnt\left[(p_i, p_j)\right] + cnt\left[(p_j, p_i)\right]\right)$
    Add (p_i, p_j, w_{ij}) into R_e
  end if
end for
return R_e

triplets (q, r, c) consisting of the query q, the ranking r presented to the user and the set c of clicked URLs. Figure 2 presents an example of click-through data: the user enters a query, receives the ranking from the search engine, and then clicks on several URLs with his or her opinions. Figure 2 also shows that some URLs can be matched by URL patterns. Here we only focus on these matched URLs.

Using click-through data, many previous works extract user preference feedback by assuming that a user is more likely to click on a URL which is more relevant to the query for her [17]. Here we make a similar assumption: a user is more likely to click a URL matched by a pattern if the pattern is more relevant to types of queries. Different from previous works which only considering the unclicked URLs ranked higher than clicked ones, we assume users observe the top k URLs and extract preferences from unclicked patterns, this is because: (1) we would also like to leverage information from the original rankers, not only users' preference feedback; and (2) if we do not generate preferences between patterns in lower ranks, there will be a bias to such patterns. Consider the example in Figure 2, the user enters a query about a basketball player and clicks the patterns p_3 and p_6. We can extract pairwise preferences as follows:

$$(p_3, p_1), (p_3, p_4), (p_3, p_5), (p_6, p_1), (p_6, p_4), (p_6, p_5).$$

Note that we do not consider p_2 because the URL is not matched by any URL pattern. For each preference (p_i, p_j), it shows that the pattern p_i is more relevant to the type `basketball_player` than p_j in this click-through data. In addition to patterns in the search results, we also assume clicked patterns are more satisfactory than patterns which do not appear in top k URLs in search results. This is because these patterns might have lower relevance to entities' types such that they cannot be ranked higher. In our work, we focus on top k URLs, which are contents of the first page in search results. Moreover, the queries might have no matched URLs. As in previous works [2,4], to ensure the reliability of clicks, we consider only URLs with satisfied clicks (SAT-Clicks) as relevant and treat the other results as irrelevant. To define a SAT-Click, we adopt the definition used in previous work [29] and consider clicks with at least 30 seconds dwell time as SAT-Clicks.

Based on the above strategies, Algorithm 1 extracts the initial preference list D_e. Therefore, we can collect the click-through data of queries with each type and extract preferences. However, there is a drawback. The results might be biased by queries of popular entities because we extract preferences from click-through data respectively. To avoid popularity bias, we aggregate preferences by entities of queries. It is more natural for estimating pattern-type relevance. If a pattern is actually more relevant to a type than the other, we expect that most entities with such a type might make corresponding preferences. Hence, Algorithm 2 aggregates the initial preferences D_e from Algorithm 1 as a weighted preference list R_e for each entity e. Note that we apply the red-black tree (RB-Tree) as the data structure to aggregate occurrences of preferences. More precisely, the physical meaning of weights w_{ij} in the weighted preference list is to estimate the probability of observing the preference for the two patterns. Finally, we have many weighted preferences for each type with better rationalities by aggregating original preferences.

Relevance Optimization. A pairwise preference can be thought of as a partial constraint of two patterns because it represents a pairwise comparison of them. With these preferences, we optimize the pattern-type relevance such that constraints can be satisfied.

First, we assume the distribution of the pattern-type relevance for the pattern p_i can be represented by a logistic function as follows:

$$P(p_i \mid t) = \frac{1}{1 + \exp(-\theta_{i,t})},$$

where $\theta_{i,t}$ is a parameter for p_i and the type t. Therefore, we can optimize $\theta_{i,t}$ to fit constraints from preferences. Specifically, we adopt a gradient descent method with the RankNet cost function [8] to optimize pairwise preference. For each type t, given the set of entities with such type $E(t)$, the RankNet cost function can be computed as follows:

$$\sum_{e \in E(t)} \sum_{(p_1, p_2, w) \in R_e} w \cdot \log\left(1 + \exp\left(P(p_2 \mid t) - P(p_1 \mid t)\right)\right),$$

where R_e is the list of weighted preferences for the entity e, and $P(p_i \mid t)$ is the relevance using current parameters $\theta_{i,t}$. We can then compute gradients for each parameter $\theta_{i,t}$ and minimize the cost function.

Hence, we obtain the pattern-type relevance $P(p_i \mid t)$ of pattern p_i for each type t from optimized parameters $\theta_{i,t}$.

4.4 Type Distribution

The type distribution of a query shows how much users treat it as a query of such a type. For example, although Kobe Bryant types "basketball player" and "actor" at the same time, people are much more concerned about the identity of basketball player. Accordingly, the URL pattern `www.nba.com/playerfile/*/` should be more relevant to Kobe Bryant than the pattern `www.imdb.com/name/*/`.

To estimate type distribution, we use click-through data again. During a search for the query, we assume that users are more likely to click URLs matched by patterns of types with which users are more concerned. Following the above assumption, we can estimate type distribution for a query q by a simple Bayesian m-estimate smoothing [24] as follows:

$$P(t \mid q) = \frac{\sum_{p \in S} P(t \mid p) \cdot Click\,(p, q) + m \cdot P(t)}{m + \sum_{t \in T(q)} \sum_{p \in S} P(t \mid p) \cdot Click\,(p, q)},$$

where S is the set containing all patterns. Here $Click\,(p, q)$ calculates the times users are clicking URLs matched by pattern p during searches for the query q. The prior distribution $P(t)$ can be computed by normalizing the number of entities for each type. The type distribution of patterns $P(t \mid p)$ can be calculated with the Bayes' theorem as follows:

$$P(t \mid p) = \frac{P(p \mid t) \cdot P(t)}{P(p)},$$

where $P(p \mid t)$ is pattern-type relevance estimated in Section 4.3. The pattern distribution $P(p)$ can be computed by normalizing the number of SAT-Clicks for each URL pattern in the pattern set S.

4.5 Theoretical Analysis

To verify the rationality of the consistent ranking model, we conduct a theoretical analysis. Recall that the model follows Assumption 1 and ranks pattern-matched URLs by pattern relevance. Here we consider only the URLs matched by patterns (i.e., non-matched URLs like personal sites are not analyzed here because they will be re-ranked in the second stage by appropriate features as shown in Section 5). Before the analysis, note that the effectiveness of a ranking pair (r_1, r_2) can be computed as the average of the effectiveness of two rankings (i.e., $F(r_1, r_2) = (F(r_1) + F(r_2))/2$). It is consistent with most traditional evaluation measures in information retrieval such as NDCG and MAP.

Consider the ideal case of Assumption 1 (i.e., the relevance of matched URL patterns perfectly leading to the relevance of web pages), we have the following lemma:

Lemma 1 *If the relevance of the web pages is exactly consistent with the relevance of matched URL patterns, for any pair of inconsistent rankings (r_1, r_2) of web pages matched by the identical set of URL patterns for two same-type queries, there must be a consistent pair (r'_1, r'_2) such that the consistent one is at least as effective as the inconsistent one.*

PROOF. Let the effectiveness of a ranking r be $F(r)$, e.g., reciprocal rank or average precision. We prove the theorem with a proof by contradiction. First, we start by assuming there is no ranking pair (r'_1, r'_2) such that:

$$F(r'_1) + F(r'_2) \geq F(r_1) + F(r_2),$$

where r'_1 and r'_2 are consistent.

However, we can construct the counterexample with a structured approach as follows. If $F(r_1) \geq F(r_2)$, let $r'_1 = r_1$, and re-rank r_2 as r'_2 such that the order of matched URL patterns is identical to r_1. Note that (r'_1, r'_2) must be consistent because both of them rank web pages identically with r_1. So we have:

$$F(r'_1) + F(r'_2) = F(r_1) + F(r_1) \geq F(r_1) + F(r_2),$$

which contradicts the initial assumption, then proving the theorem. If $F(r_1) < F(r_2)$, we can still find such a pair with similar methods. Hence, we are guaranteed to find a consistent ranking pair which is at least as effective as the inconsistent pair. □

Hence, the consistent ranking model is rational because, for pattern-matched web pages, the above lemma shows that to improve consistency with pattern relevance may benefit relevance rankings under Assumption 1.

5. ENSEMBLE-BASED RE-RANKING

In Section 4, we propose a method to rank pattern-matched URLs consistently. However, in real situations, there are many URLs without any matched patterns such as personal sites and official websites of entities. These URLs might be as relevant as or more relevant than pattern-matched URLs. Here we propose an ensemble-based re-ranking model to leverage information from both the original ranker and the proposed consistent ranking model.

5.1 Model Formulation

We start by presenting an ensemble-based model that assumes uniform contributions from the consistent ranking model and the original ranker. For a query q, we compute the relevance of a URL ranked in the position i by the original ranker as follows:

$$P(u \mid q, i) = \lambda \cdot P(u \mid q) + (1 - \lambda) \cdot P(u \mid i),$$

where $P(u \mid q)$ and $P(u \mid i)$ are relevance given by the consistent ranking model and the original ranker, λ is a parameter that controls the impact of the former model. In our work, we simply let $P(u \mid i)$ be a linear decay function $(k - i + 1)/k$, where k is the number of URLs in each page of search results.

5.2 Multiple Parameters

Using a single parameter is not always reasonable. In different cases, the most suitable parameter might be different. For example, when the URL is a personal site without any matched pattern, λ should be lower because it may be so relevant, and the consistent ranking model gives zero relevance. As in [27], we replace the parameter λ with a logistic function, which allows some features as the input, whereas the output is bounded to values between 0 and 1.

More formally, the input of a logistic function is a set of features X, whereas the output is the probability-like value predicted by fitting X to a logistic curve. Accordingly, the parameter λ is replaced as follows:

$$\lambda(X) = \frac{1}{1 + \exp(-f(X))}, \quad f(X) = \beta_0 + \sum_{i=1}^{|X|} \beta_i \cdot x_i,$$

where x_i is the i-th feature in X, β_i is the coefficient parameter of x_i, and β_0 is the bias parameter. Note that $|X| = 0$ is a special case of single parameter.

5.3 Parameter Optimization

In the proposed re-ranking model, we would like to learn β parameters for receiving better retrieval performance. As in

[23,27], we use a gradient descent method with the RankNet cost function [8] again to perform an effective parameter optimization. With the assumption mentioned in Section 4.3, we assume that clicked URLs are more relevant than unclicked ones. Therefore, we can extract many pairwise preferences of URLs for optimization. Given a set of queries Q, the cost function can be computed as follows:

$$\sum_{q_e \in Q} \sum_{(u_1,u_2) \in R(q)} \log\left(1 + \exp\left(P\left(u_2 \mid q, i_{u_2}\right) - P\left(u_1 \mid q, i_{u_1}\right)\right)\right),$$

where $R(q)$ is a set of preferences for URLs from q's click-though data, i_u is the ranked position of u in the original search result.

5.4 Re-ranking Features

In our experiments, we adopt various features in different levels, including entity features, query features and URL features. These features are helpful in recognizing different situations and adjusting distribution into a better status. Note that these features are utilized as the feature set X in our model (See Sec. 5.2).

5.4.1 *Entity Features*

The entities of queries are treated as the search intents of queries. It is intuitive that entities with different properties might use different parameters. Therefore, we extract entity features from the information of entities.

Number of types. Entities might have different numbers of types in the knowledge base system. Because the consistent ranking model treats relevance distribution as aggregation over all types, different numbers of types might have different performances in the model.

Type Entropy. We then consider not only the number of types. Some types such as "person" and "location" are too general such that too many entities belong to such types. In other words, patterns of these types might not match URLs which are relevant to users. If most of an entity's types are general, the impact of the consistent ranking model should be lower. To verify that, we calculate the type entropy for an entity e as follows:

$$\sum_{t \in T(e)} -P\left(e \mid t\right) \cdot \log P\left(e \mid t\right).$$

Here we treat all entities have equal importance and compute entity distribution $P(e \mid t)$ by a uniform distribution.

Entity Frequency. Different entities might have different levels of popularity. More popular entities will lead to more queries about them shown in search engines. To improve overall performance, search engines will optimize for them more than other queries. For these queries, the impact of original results should be higher than the consistent model. On the other hand, less popular entities will gain less optimization from search engines. We hope that re-ranking can leverage information from entities of the same type and improve their performance. Here the frequency of an entity query is utilized as the entity frequency.

5.4.2 *Query Features*

A user types characters into a query and asks the search engine with his/her information needs. Such query strings might contain some information of user's search intents.

Query Length. Consider that each term in a query has its meaning in user's search intents, we assume that longer queries contain more information. Following this assumption, the original search engine might have better performance for longer queries.

Query Frequency. Similar to entity frequency, we assume that queries also have different levels of popularity. Generally, search engines optimize for head queries but tail queries. Accordingly, the parameters should be different for queries with different popularity.

5.4.3 *URL Features*

With many properties of URLs, URL features are extracted from each ranked URL respectively. Different URLs might also have different parameters while re-ranking. These URLs might contain more information.

Pattern Matching. In the consistent ranking model, URLs without any pattern-match will be ignored and receive zero relevance. In this case, original results should have a higher impact. We use a binary variable to represent whether a URL is matched by a pattern.

Original Position. Original position represents the relevance score given by the original ranker of search engine. A URL with a high position might be relevant enough and does not need an ensemble with the consistent ranking model.

Consistent Relevance. Similar to the feature of original position, relevance generated by the consistent ranking model might also affect parameter selection.

N-gram Similarity. URLs like personal and official sites might have higher relevance, although they might not be matched by any pattern. To verify this point, we calculate the n-gram similarity between the hosts of URLs and queries. It is highly possible that a URL is the official site of an entity if the host of URL is similar to the query. To cover official sites under public publishing services, we also calculate the n-gram similarity of whole URL strings to queries.

6. EXPERIMENTS

We conduct extensive experiments on large-scale datasets to evaluate the performance of our re-ranking model and to verify the effectiveness of the co-cluster hypothesis.

6.1 Datasets and Experimental Settings

Knowledge Base. We use Freebase [6] dumped in January 2014 as our knowledge base. Freebase classifies entities into types under various domains such as `people/person` and `book/author`. An entity might belong to multiple types in Freebase. Each type under a domain is treated as a query type in our work. We then remove very sparse types such that each type has at least five entities. Finally, there are 444 query types in our type set.

Datasets. Our experimental data is comprised of click-through data submitted to a commercial search engine in November 2013. After extracting entity queries, in total there are 56,466,534 queries for 847,682 distinct entities. By generalizing URL collections, there are 30,765 unique URL patterns utilized in our experiments. We use the queries submitted before 22 November, 2013 as the training data to train models. The remaining data is used as the testing data to evaluate performance. For the ground-truth, we adopt click-through data in search engine logs. We treat URLs with SAT-Clicks as the ground-truth. To evaluate performance in different situations, we divide the testing data into seven testing datasets with different conditions as shown in Table 1. The overall testing dataset consists of all queries for representing the general case. We also evaluate performance for queries with different levels of popularity. For

Table 1: **The description of each testing dataset.**

Dataset	Description
All	All queries in testing data.
Head	Queries with top 10% entity frequency.
Tail	Queries with bottom 10% entity frequency.
New	Queries which do not appear in training data.
Peo.	Queries with type `people/person`.
Loc.	Queries with type `location/location`.
Org.	Queries with type `organization/organization`.

Table 2: Performance of ranking consistency. All improvements of our method against the default ranking are significantly different at 99% level in a paired t-test.

Type	Default	Our Approach
Overall types	0.5671	0.5943 (+4.78%)
`people/person`	0.6410	0.6517 (+1.67%)
`location/location`	0.6327	0.6455 (+2.02%)
`organization/organization`	0.7533	0.7588 (+0.73%)
`celebrities/celebrity`	0.6306	0.6697 (+6.21%)
`music/album`	0.4589	0.4842 (+5.51%)
`book/book`	0.5367	0.5544 (+3.31%)

entities without appearance in the training data, we would like to verify if our model can still make improvements. Finally, we evaluate the performance of queries with different types. Note that we choose those three types because they are the types with the most entities.

6.2 Experimental Results

6.2.1 Evaluation of Ranking Consistency

Because our work is the first study on ranking consistency among same-type queries in web search, there is no standard metric to evaluate that. Here we propose a new metric based on Kendall's tau [19], which is a rank correlation coefficient, to evaluate ranking consistency. For a type t and a set of queries $Q(t)$ with the type t, we define the ranking consistency with ranking correlations of all query pairs as follows:

$$\frac{1}{\binom{|Q(t)|}{2}} \sum_{q_1 \in Q(t)} \sum_{q_2 \in Q(t) \setminus q_1} \boldsymbol{\tau}\left(r\left(q_1, t\right), r\left(q_2, t\right)\right),$$

which $r(q, t)$ denotes the ranking result of t's URL patterns with query q, and $\boldsymbol{\tau}(r_1, r_2)$ is the standard Kendall's tau rank correlation coefficient [19]. To evaluate consistency for all patterns, we give zero rank scores to pattern without appearance in search results while calculating Kendall's tau.

Table 2 shows ranking consistencies of the default ranking and our method for overall types and some sampled types. Generally, our method can significantly improve the ranking consistencies over the original ranking results. Then we attempt to analyze improvements for each type. Regarding the first two types, it is obvious that their improvements are less than the overall cases. This is because they are too general such that their queries have many dissimilar search intents. For example, both queries with the types `basketball/player` and `film/actor` are used to hold the type `people/person`. They might originally have much different ranking results. The type `organization/organization` has the smallest improvement. A reason might be that it has much higher consistency in the default ranking results. The other reason is that the useful patterns of the type are too few to make a significant improvement. For the last three types, their improvements are more than the above ones. We explain that these types are more specific to groups of queries. It means that the queries have more similar URLs for these types. Also, they have larger weights in type distribution to queries such that the consistent ranking model ranks patterns of these types more consistently.

Table 3: Performance of pattern-type relevance estimation. All improvements against the baseline are significantly different at 95% level in a paired t-test.

Measure	Frequency	Our Approach
NDCG@1	0.9607	0.9821 (+2.23%)
NDCG@2	0.7655	0.8145 (+5.87%)
NDCG@3	0.6748	0.7363 (+8.61%)
NDCG@4	0.6267	0.6800 (+8.07%)
NDCG@5	0.5857	0.6450 (+9.69%)

6.2.2 Evaluation of Pattern-Type Relevance

Because the key of the consistent ranking model is to estimate the pattern-type relevance, we first evaluate performance of such relevance. For each type, we collect the five relevant URL patterns with highest estimated pattern-type relevance to be evaluated. For the baseline, we adopt a frequency-based model ranking each URL pattern by its clicked counts in the search engine logs.

In order to evaluate performance, we hire two assessors to manually judge collected URL patterns. For each collected pattern for a type, two assessors annotate it carefully and assign a three-level relevance score as follows: relevant and important (Score 5), generally relevant (Score 1) and irrelevant (Score 0). Note that all collected patterns are annotated by these assessors. With annotated results, we evaluate the quality of collected patterns with the metric NDCG@k as follows:

$$NDCG@k = \frac{DCG@k}{IDCG@k}, \quad DCG@k = \sum_{i=1}^{k} \frac{2^{rel_i} - 1}{\log_2(i+1)},$$

where rel_i is the relevance score of the i-th pattern, $IDCG@k$ is the ideal $DCG@k$. Note that we calculate $IDCG@k$ with k highest relevance scores (Score 5). In the annotation process, the agreement on annotated results by two assessors is 80.76%, with 0.65 unweighted kappa coefficient [7]. The final $NDCG$ is calculated as the average of $NDCG$ by results annotated by two assessors.

Table 3 represents the performance of pattern-type relevance estimation. Our approach significantly outperforms the frequency-based baseline. It shows that our method can rank relevant pattern-matched URLs higher in the consistent ranking model. The baseline's lower performance is caused by the biases from popular entities such that irrelevant patterns are ranked higher. On the other hand, our model considers such a problem and aggregates preferences by entities to achieve a better performance.

Table 4: Performance of re-ranking models and default ranking. All improvements of our methods against the default ranking are significantly different at 99% level in a paired t-test.

		Default	Our Approach (single params)	Our Approach (multiple params)
All	MAP	0.7272	0.7454 (+2.49%)	**0.7571 (+4.12%)**
	MRR	0.7288	0.7469 (+2.49%)	**0.7589 (+4.13%)**
Head	MAP	0.7294	0.7491 (+2.70%)	**0.7611 (+4.34%)**
	MRR	0.7309	0.7505 (+2.68%)	**0.7627 (+4.35%)**
Tail	MAP	0.7116	0.7228 (+1.57%)	**0.7384 (+3.76%)**
	MRR	0.7138	0.7251 (+1.58%)	**0.7408 (+3.78%)**
New	MAP	0.7272	0.7453 (+2.49%)	**0.7572 (+3.83%)**
	MRR	0.7287	0.7468 (+2.48%)	**0.7589 (+3.83%)**
Peo.	MAP	0.7468	0.7756 (+3.86%)	**0.7834 (+4.89%)**
	MRR	0.7483	0.7772 (+3.86%)	**0.7851 (+4.92%)**
Loc.	MAP	0.7268	0.7465 (+2.72%)	**0.7573 (+4.20%)**
	MRR	0.7283	0.7481 (+2.71%)	**0.7588 (+4.19%)**
Org.	MAP	0.8422	0.8615 (+2.28%)	**0.8674 (+2.99%)**
	MRR	0.8432	0.8624 (+2.28%)	**0.8684 (+3.00%)**

6.2.3 Evaluation of Re-ranking Models

Table 4 shows the experimental results of our re-ranking models and the default ranking on different testing datasets. As our evaluation metrics, we adopt the *mean reciprocal rank* (MRR) and *mean average precision* (MAP).

For the results of default ranking, the testing dataset of head queries is better than the overall performance. The reason is that search engines focus on optimizing such queries. On the other hand, tail queries have lower performance. Regarding testing datasets of specific types, although location queries have similar performance to overall cases, people and organizations queries have higher performance. One reason is that people and organization might have their own official sites. To some extent, these official sites are the most relevant to such queries, especially to organization queries. Search engines might notice that and optimize search results. With the above observations and analyses, the performance of default ranking seems reasonable.

For all testing datasets, our methods have significant improvements over the default ranking with both single parameter and multiple parameters at 99% level in a paired t-test. Generally, the model using multiple parameters achieves better performance than using a single parameter. It shows that our proposed features are also valuable in helping the model optimize parameters. Similar to the default ranking, our methods perform better on head entities than tail entities. This is because our model also optimizes parameters by each query although we generate pattern relevance by types. However, there are still great improvements in the queries of tail entities. It demonstrates that our approach can help improve the relevance ranking performance of the low-frequency queries. For queries without appearance in training data, our methods have similar improvements to the overall cases. This is the advantage of our methods which can cover new queries with the same types as training entities. Regarding testing datasets with specific types, the location queries have similar performance to the overall cases. Recall that we conclude that better performance of people queries in default rankings is caused by their own official sites. It is interesting that their improvements are still larger than the overall cases. We explain that there are many sites with URL patterns for people entities such as `www.biography.com`. For some specific groups of people, there are also special sites with URL patterns such as `www.imdb.com` for celebrities and `espn.go.com` for athletes. Learning to rank such patterns well helps the models achieve strong improvements. The other point is that the improvements of organization queries are less than overall cases. Our explanation is that there are few structured websites for multiple organization, so there are also few useful URL patterns to improve the performance.

Based on the experimental results and above analyses, we verify the effectiveness of our approach and its assistance in improving the relevance rankings with the original search results.

6.3 User Surveys

In this section, we would like to understand whether users favor consistent ranking results produced by our consistent ranking model (Stage 1). In order to conduct user surveys, we sample five types as search intents and five pairs of queries for each type. The sampled types consist of two human types (`basketball_player` and `film/actor`), two item types (`film.film` and `music/album`) and one location type (`location/location`). For each pair of queries, we extract their search results from a commercial search engine and keep web pages matched by URL patterns appearing in both search results. With these queries and results, we conduct two user surveys via Amazon Mechanical Turk[3]. In the first survey, we want to understand whether users favor consistent results when they observe two search results at the same time. For each query pair, we re-rank two original results by the consistent ranking model, and then ask all participants to decide whether the consistent results are more likely to rank relevant web pages higher. To avoid the description biases, we ensure that workers do not know which results are re-ranked ones and randomly arrange two kinds of results. The workers decide which kind of rankings is more relevant by their own observation and personal opinion. In the second survey, we show results of only one query in a question. We want to know whether users still favor consistent results when they do not have results of the other query for reference. Finally, there are 25 questions in the first survey and 50 questions in the second one. For each survey, we ask ten Mechanical Turk workers to answer all questions.

Figure 3 shows the results of two user surveys. When users observe two queries and their search results at the same time, it is obvious that users tend to prefer consistent results. It shows that users realize the differences and consider the consistent results are more relevant. In the second survey, the percentage selecting the original results increases when these queries appear separately. The reason is that users cannot directly observe the consistency between two ranking results. However, there are still more questions with more users selecting the results of consistent rankings. It indicates that users really care about the consistency of ranking results whether the results of queries appear at the same time or not. In other words, if we improve the consistency of current search engines, the overall relevance ranking performance may also improve.

7. CONCLUSIONS AND FUTURE WORK

In this paper, we propose a new idea called ranking consistency in web search. The actual observations show that

[3]Amazon Mechanical Turk: `https://www.mturk.com/`

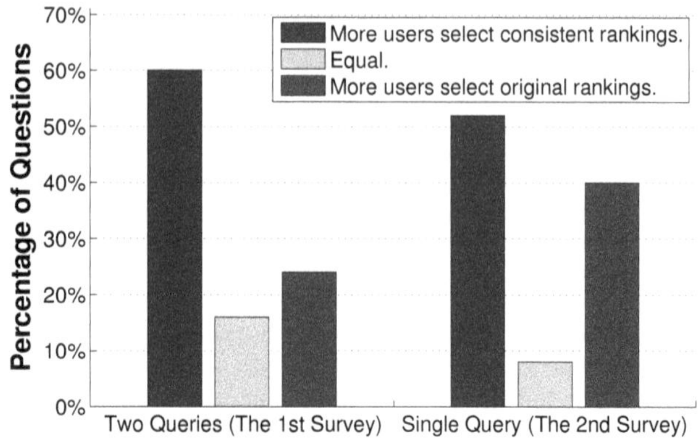

Figure 3: The results of two user surveys.

the search results of different queries with similar search intents should be consistent. However, conventional search engines optimize each query separately so that some queries may have inconsistent and less relevant search results. By leveraging knowledge base and click-through data, we propose a two-stage re-ranking model. The results of the extensive experiments demonstrate that our approach can indeed improve the ranking consistency of search results. In the meanwhile, the results show that our approach significantly improves the performance of both ranking consistency and relevance ranking. Such improvement is consistent across different datasets with different types of queries under different conditions. The reasons are as follows: (1) Our model considers queries with similar queries at the same time by leveraging a knowledge base to identify the types of queries; (2) Our approach precisely discovers the user preferences of URL patterns for each query type from query logs. Additionally, by leveraging the knowledge base and URL patterns , our model can effectively learn the ranking consistency for rare queries from the massive search logs of top queries with similar search intents. Moreover, two user surveys on Amazon Mechanical Turk also show that users are sensitive and prefer consistent search results. Overall, all experimental results demonstrate that the ranking consistency is an important factor in web search.

In future work, the performance may be much improved if it can be applied to modern state-of-the-art ranking models. Future work will consider applying the idea of the ranking consistency into state-of-the-art models for learning to rank.

8. REFERENCES

[1] P. N. Bennett, D. M. Chickering, and A. Mityagin. Learning consensus opinion: mining data from a labeling game. In *Proc. of WWW*, pages 121–130. ACM, 2009.

[2] P. N. Bennett, F. Radlinski, R. W. White, and E. Yilmaz. Inferring and using location metadata to personalize web search. In *Proc. of SIGIR*, pages 135–144. ACM, 2011.

[3] P. N. Bennett, K. Svore, and S. T. Dumais. Classification-enhanced ranking. In *Proc. of WWW*, pages 111–120. ACM, 2010.

[4] P. N. Bennett, R. W. White, W. Chu, S. T. Dumais, P. Bailey, F. Borisyuk, and X. Cui. Modeling the impact of short-and long-term behavior on search personalization. In *Proc. of SIGIR*, pages 185–194. ACM, 2012.

[5] J. Bian, T.-Y. Liu, T. Qin, and H. Zha. Ranking with query-dependent loss for web search. In *Proc. of WSDM*, pages 141–150. ACM, 2010.

[6] K. Bollacker, C. Evans, P. Paritosh, T. Sturge, and J. Taylor. Freebase: a collaboratively created graph database for structuring human knowledge. In *Proc. of SIGMOD*, pages 1247–1250. ACM, 2008.

[7] R. L. Brennan and D. J. Prediger. Coefficient kappa: Some uses, misuses, and alternatives. *Educational and psychological measurement*, 41(3):687–699, 1981.

[8] C. Burges, T. Shaked, E. Renshaw, A. Lazier, M. Deeds, N. Hamilton, and G. Hullender. Learning to rank using gradient descent. In *Proc. of ICML*, pages 89–96. ACM, 2005.

[9] B. Carterette and D. Petkova. Learning a ranking from pairwise preferences. In *Proc. of SIGIR*, pages 629–630. ACM, 2006.

[10] Y. Chen, X. Li, A. Dick, and R. Hill. Ranking consistency for image matching and object retrieval. *Pattern Recognition*, 47(3):1349–1360, 2014.

[11] M. Farah and D. Vanderpooten. An outranking approach for rank aggregation in information retrieval. In *Proc. of SIGIR*, pages 591–598. ACM, 2007.

[12] S. Fox, K. Karnawat, M. Mydland, S. Dumais, and T. White. Evaluating implicit measures to improve web search. *ACM Transactions on Information Systems (TOIS)*, 23(2):147–168, 2005.

[13] J. Gao, W. Yuan, X. Li, K. Deng, and J.-Y. Nie. Smoothing clickthrough data for web search ranking. In *Proc. of SIGIR*, pages 355–362. ACM, 2009.

[14] J. Guo, G. Xu, X. Cheng, and H. Li. Named entity recognition in query. In *Proc. of SIGIR*, pages 267–274. ACM, 2009.

[15] J. Hu, G. Wang, F. Lochovsky, J.-t. Sun, and Z. Chen. Understanding user's query intent with wikipedia. In *Proc. of WWW*, pages 471–480. ACM, 2009.

[16] J. Jiang, N. Yu, and C.-Y. Lin. Focus: learning to crawl web forums. In *Proc. of WWW*, pages 33–42. ACM, 2012.

[17] T. Joachims. Optimizing search engines using clickthrough data. In *Proc. of SIGKDD*, pages 133–142. ACM, 2002.

[18] T. Joachims, L. Granka, B. Pan, H. Hembrooke, F. Radlinski, and G. Gay. Evaluating the accuracy of implicit feedback from clicks and query reformulations in web search. *ACM Transactions on Information Systems (TOIS)*, 25(2):7, 2007.

[19] M. G. Kendall. A new measure of rank correlation. *Biometrika*, 30(1/2):81–93, 1938.

[20] K. Li, X. Cheng, Y. Guo, and K. Zhang. Crawling dynamic web pages in www forums. *Jisuanji Gongcheng/ Computer Engineering*, 33(6):80–82, 2007.

[21] X. Li, Y.-Y. Wang, D. Shen, and A. Acero. Learning with click graph for query intent classification. *ACM Transactions on Information Systems (TOIS)*, 28(3):12, 2010.

[22] J. Liu, Y.-I. Song, and C.-Y. Lin. Competition-based user expertise score estimation. In *Proc. of SIGIR*, pages 425–434. ACM, 2011.

[23] D. Metzler. Using gradient descent to optimize language modeling smoothing parameters. In *Proc. of SIGIR*, pages 687–688. ACM, 2007.

[24] T. M. Mitchell. *Machine Learning*. McGraw-Hill, Inc., 1997.

[25] T. H. Nguyen and B. K. Szymanski. Social ranking techniques for the web. In *Proc. of ASONAM*, pages 49–55. ACM, 2013.

[26] F. Radlinski and T. Joachims. Query chains: learning to rank from implicit feedback. In *Proc. of SIGKDD*, pages 239–248. ACM, 2005.

[27] Y.-I. Song, J.-T. Lee, and H.-C. Rim. Word or phrase?: learning which unit to stress for information retrieval. In *Proc. of ACL*, pages 1048–1056. ACL, 2009.

[28] H. Wang, X. He, M.-W. Chang, Y. Song, R. W. White, and W. Chu. Personalized ranking model adaptation for web search. In *Proc. of SIGIR*, pages 323–332. ACM, 2013.

[29] K. Wang, T. Walker, and Z. Zheng. Pskip: estimating relevance ranking quality from web search clickthrough data. In *Proc. of SIGKDD*, pages 1355–1364. ACM, 2009.

[30] W. Wu, H. Li, H. Wang, and K. Q. Zhu. Probase: A probabilistic taxonomy for text understanding. In *Proc. of SIGMOD*, pages 481–492. ACM, 2012.

[31] X. Yin, W. Tan, X. Li, and Y.-C. Tu. Automatic extraction of clickable structured web contents for name entity queries. In *Proc. of WWW*, pages 991–1000, 2010.

Assessing the Impact of Syntactic and Semantic Structures for Answer Passages Reranking

Kateryna Tymoshenko
University of Trento
Povo (Trento), Italy
k.tymoshenko@gmail.com

Alessandro Moschitti*
Qatar Computing Research Institute
Doha, Qatar
amoschitti@qf.org.qa

ABSTRACT

In this paper, we extensively study the use of syntactic and semantic structures obtained with shallow and deeper syntactic parsers in the answer passage reranking task. We propose several dependency-based structures enriched with Linked Open Data (LD) knowledge for representing pairs of questions and answer passages. We use such tree structures in learning to rank (L2R) algorithms based on tree kernel. The latter can represent questions and passages in a tree fragment space, where each substructure represents a powerful syntactic/semantic feature. Additionally since we define links between structures, tree kernels also generate relational features spanning question and passage structures. We derive very important findings, which can be useful to build state-of-the-art systems: (i) full syntactic dependencies can outperform shallow models also using external knowledge and (ii) the semantic information should be derived by effective and high-coverage resources, e.g., LD, and incorporated in syntactic structures to be effective. We demonstrate our findings by carrying out an extensive comparative experimentation on two different TREC QA corpora and one community question answer dataset, namely Answerbag. Our comparative analysis on well-defined answer selection benchmarks consistently demonstrates that our structural semantic models largely outperform the state of the art in passage reranking.

Categories and Subject Descriptors

I.2.7 [**Artificial Intelligence**]: Natural Language Processing—*Text analysis; Language parsing and understanding*; H.3.3 [**Information Storage and Retrieval**]: Information Search and Retrieval—*Retrieval models*

General Terms

Algorithms, Experimentation

Keywords

Question Answering; Learning to Rank; Kernel Methods; Structural Kernels; Linked Data

*Professor at University of Trento, DISI.

Permission to make digital or hard copies of all or part of this work for personal or classroom use is granted without fee provided that copies are not made or distributed for profit or commercial advantage and that copies bear this notice and the full citation on the first page. Copyrights for components of this work owned by others than the author(s) must be honored. Abstracting with credit is permitted. To copy otherwise, or republish, to post on servers or to redistribute to lists, requires prior specific permission and/or a fee. Request permissions from Permissions@acm.org.
CIKM'15, October 19–23, 2015, Melbourne, VIC, Australia.
Copyright is held by the owner/author(s). Publication rights licensed to ACM.
ACM 978-1-4503-3794-6/15/10 ...$15.00.
DOI: http://dx.doi.org/10.1145/2806416.2806490 .

1. INTRODUCTION

Previous work has shown that advanced natural language processing can positively impact the accuracy of Question Answering (QA) systems. As shown by the experience in the TREC QA task, e.g., [38], the selection of the right passage expressing the answer requires to consider the relation between the question and the passage text. In other words, it is not enough measuring the similarity between question and passage, but it is also important analyzing how some concepts in the questions, e.g., constituting the focus, are structured along with other concepts in the answer passage. For instance, in the following question/answer passage (Q/AP) pair[1]:

Q: *What sports stadium has been billed as "the eighth wonder of the world"?*

AP: *The Titans used to be called the Oilers and played in the dilapidated Astrodome; if this was the eighth wonder of the world, we live on a shabby little planet indeed.*

the question focus, *sports stadium* is linked to the property *the eighth wonder of the world*. Since in the AP the property above is also stated for *Astrodome*, we infer that the latter is the correct answer. The inference is about finding two related statements in Q and in AP regarding the Q focus, where the entities in the statements may not necessarily match. Automatically selecting the right properties to be considered is a difficult task that must exploit the relationship between Q and AP. For example, the property *Titans used to be called the Oilers* can be important but it is not useful for answering the question. It follows that the relation between Q and AP for property selection is necessary.

Since manually selecting properties, i.e., generating rules for any pairs of Q and AP is rather difficult or even impossible, automatic feature engineering approaches based on kernel methods, e.g., [31], have been developed, where syntactic and semantic tree representations of the Q/AP pairs are used in kernel-based L2R algorithms, e.g., SVMs [33]. The role of kernels was to implicitly generate syntactic patterns (i.e., tree fragments) to be used as features in SVMs.

However, this approach would not be able to solve the example above since, to answer the question, *Astrodome* has to be identified as a stadium. This is essential to derive that the focus of Q, *stadium*, and *Astrodome* in AP both own the same property, i.e., to be "*the eighth wonder of the world*". Without this link many incorrect entities may be selected as many entities enjoy the property above[2].

The solution (provided in [13]) for solving this case is the use of semantic resources: the lexical answer type (LAT) of the ques-

[1]This example from TREC QA corpus will be our a running example for the rest of the paper.
[2]For example see `http://en.wikipedia.org/wiki/Eighth_Wonder_of_the_World#Things_labeled_as_the_Eighth_Wonder_of_the_World`

tions, e.g., as provided by Wikipedia[3] category, can be matched against the one of the answers for improving candidate selection, e.g., for *Astrodome* the LAT is *stadium*. More in general, semantic resources help to reduce data sparseness and thus they enable matches between question and answer passages. However, finding the focus word and its category may be difficult and error prone and most importantly does not allow for solving non-factoid questions.

In this paper, we carried out an extensive study on the use of syntactic and semantic structures enriched with LD semantics for answer passage reranking. To make the feature design step easier, we adopt L2R models based on SVMs and structural kernels, which provide SVMs with structural patterns, automatically generated from Q/AP syntactic structures. The latter are enriched with relational semantic knowledge of LD by adding links between the entities in the Q and AP. In particular, we followed the steps below:

First, we design a representation for the Q/AP pair by engineering a pair of shallow syntactic trees connected with relational nodes (i.e., those matching the same words in the question and in the answer passages). This approach capitalizes on our successful models proposed in [31, 32, 29, 37] but we also explore deeper linguistic structure such as dependency trees.

Secondly, we use YAGO [16], DBpedia [4] and WordNet [12] to match constituents from QA pairs and use their generalizations in our semantic structures. Following our previous work in [37], we employ word sense disambiguation to match the right entities in YAGO and DBpedia, and consider all senses of an ambiguous word from WordNet. For example, our system automatically derives that *Astrodome* is a stadium and thus such concept is connected to the question structure: *stadium has been billed as "the eighth wonder of the world"*, through the word *stadium*. This way, we obtain connected structures of pairs of texts, which potentially contain patterns useful for capturing the relatedness of question and answer passage.

Thirdly, we apply structural kernels to the above structures by exploiting SVMs for automatically learning classification and ranking functions. In particular, we apply the Partial Tree Kernel (PTK) [24], which can generate the richest space of tree fragments.

Next, we experiment with three different corpora, (i) the standard TREC QA corpus for passage reranking, (ii) a QA benchmark built for testing sentence reranking [42], and (iii) a community QA dataset based on Answerbag[4]. We tested several models combining (i) traditional feature vectors, (ii) automatic semantic labels derived by statistical classifiers, e.g., question classifiers, and (iii) relational structures enriched with LD relations. The results show that our methods greatly improve on strong IR baseline, e.g., BM25, up to 101%, and on state-of-the-art reranking models, up to 16.0% (relative improvement), e.g., in MAP.

In the remainder of this paper, Sec. 2 reports on related work, Sec. 3 describes our proposed classification and reranking framework, Sec. 4 illustrates our basic representation approach. Sec. 5 describes our new algorithms to carry out semantic matching using LD, Sec. 6 shows how we use LD matches for defining relational structures, Sec. 7 presents our learning to rank models based on tree kernels, Sec. 8 illustrates our experiments and finally, Sec. 9 derives the conclusions.

2. RELATED WORK

A referring work for our research is the IBM Watson system [13] (hereafter referred as Watson). This is an advanced QA pipeline based on deep linguistic processing and semantic resources. Watson uses deep syntactic parsing components and a predicate-argument structure (PAS) builder [22]. Additionally, it uses several semantic resources, e.g., Wikipedia and PRISMATIC [11] combined in a machine learning-based reranker. The Watson system is very accurate and effective but it requires to hand-craft rules, which is typically very costly. Our approach instead can automatically build syntactic/semantic patterns also exploiting LD, which can be used both for matching and generalizing words.

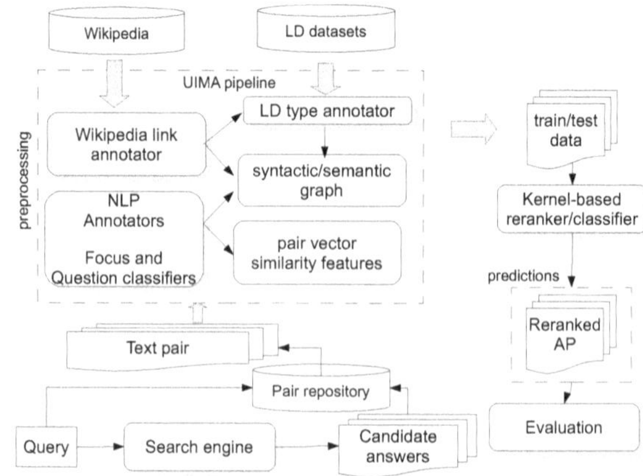

Figure 1: Kernel-based pair classification/reranking framework

Our baseline model is an updated version of our previous system developed in [31]. However, as pointed out in the introduction, such model does not encode dependency structure and the semantic information from LD. Moreover, our previous several attempts of using semantic information, e.g., Latent Dirichlet Allocation, WordNet, Latent Semantic Analysis, failed to improve the structural model. In contrast, we show that our LD approach can effectively encode knowledge improving on passage reranking.

More traditional work in QA using semantics and syntax can be observed in [15, 35]. However, the complexity of the method in [15] along with an obscure fine manual tuning, have made adaption or just replication of such systems rather complex. Recent studies on passage reranking, exploiting structural information, were carried out in [19], whereas other methods explored soft matching (i.e., lexical similarity) based on NE types [1]. [28, 17] applied question and answer classifiers for passage reranking. In this context, several approaches focused on reranking the answers to definition/description questions, e.g., [34, 36].

Next, the models developed in [2, 3] demonstrate that linguistic structures improve QA but the proposed approaches again are based on handcrafted features and rules. In contrast, our method is based on automatic feature engineering, resulting rather adaptable to different application domains.

Regarding answer sentence rerankers, [42] proposed a probabilistic quasi-synchronous grammar, inspired by machine translation, which allows to model Q/AP relations by means of syntactic transformations. [41] designed a probabilistic model to learn tree-edit operations on dependency parse trees. [14] employed a computationally expensive tree kernel-based heuristic to identify tree edit sequences which could serve as good features for a logistic regression model. [43] further improved the [14] approach by proposing a faster dynamic-programming based algorithm for feature extraction and extending the feature set with WordNet features. [45] proposed a model which, in addition to syntax, incorporates features based on rich lexical semantic knowledge, including synonymy, antonymy, hypernymy and semantic similarity, obtained from a number of external systems and resources. In our work, we encode semantic knowledge directly into syntactic tree representations of Q/AP and use PTK to learn the syntactico-semantic

[3]http://www.wikipedia.org

[4]`http://www.answerbag.com/`

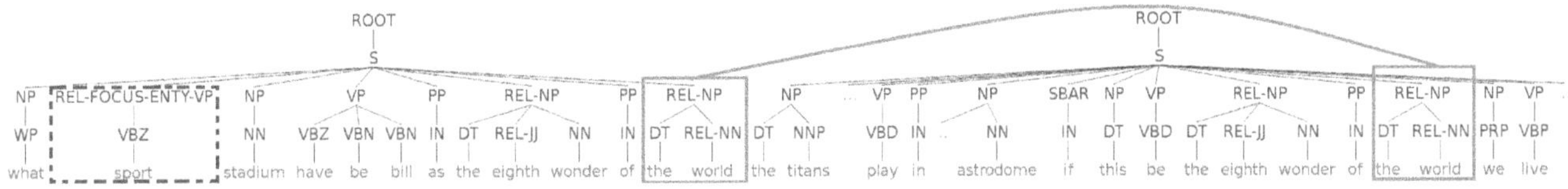

Figure 2: Shallow chunk-based tree (CH) for the Q and AP of the running example

patterns. More recently, the answer selection task was tackled with deep learning, e.g. convolutional deep neural networks [30] and stacked bidirectional Long Short-Term Memory model [40].

3. PASSAGE RERANKING FRAMEWORK

Our framework uses the relations between a question (Q) and its answer passage (AP) to rerank passages. The basic schema is displayed in Figure 1: given a Q we submit it as a query to a search engine, which retrieves a set of candidate AP. Each Q/AP text pair is processed by an NLP pipeline which performs basic tokenization, sentence splitting, lemmatization, stopword removal. Various NLP components, embedded in the pipeline as UIMA[5] annotators, perform more involved linguistic analysis, e.g., part-of-speech (POS) tagging, chunking, Named Entity (NE) recognition, constituency and dependency parsing, etc.

The Q/AP text pair is processed by a Wikipedia link annotator. It automatically recognizes n-grams in plain text, which may be linked to Wikipedia and disambiguates them to Wikipedia URLs. The input text is supposed to be short thus we concatenate the pair members together to provide a larger disambiguation context to the annotator. These annotations are then used to produce computational structures (see Sec. 4) input to pair classifiers. The semantics of such relational structures can be further enriched by adding links between the constituents of the two pieces of text. The relational links can be generated by: (i) matching lemmas as in [31]; (ii) matching the constituent types based on LD as in [37]; (iii) matching the question focus type derived by the question classifiers with the type of the target NE as in [31, 32, 29]. The resulting pairs of trees connected by semantic links are then used to train a kernel-based classifier Sec. 7.

4. TREES FOR Q/AP PAIRS

In our study, we design and compare several syntactic and semantic structural representations of pairs of short texts, including dependency- and shallow chunk-based tree representations.

Shallow chunk-based tree (CH). Similarly to [31, 32, 29], we represent a pair of short texts as two trees with lemmas at leaf level and their part-of-speech (POS) tags at the preterminal level. Preterminal POS-tags are grouped into the chunk nodes and the chunks are further grouped into sentences. For example, Figure 2 shows the shallow tree representation of the two Q and AP reported in the introduction.

Dependency-based tree (DT1) [32]. We structure the output of dependency parsers to design a new grammatical relation centered tree. This is a dependency tree altered so that grammatical relations become nodes. Lemmas and their POS tags are allocated at the leaf and the preterminal levels, respectively. Finally, we add '::' and the first letter of the respective POS tags to the leaves, e.g., "world::n". Figure 3 illustrates a DT1 representation of the question from the running example.

Dependency-phrase based tree (DT2). We further generalize DT1 with an additional layer of chunk label nodes between the POS and the grammatical relation node layers. Lemmas in the same chunk or in the "object of preposition" (**pobj**) or the "possession modifier"(**poss**) relations are grouped under the same chunk node. Figure 4 provides an example of a DT2 structure.

Lexical-centered dependency tree (DT3) [8]. Finally, we engineer DT3 in which dependency relations *rel(head,child)* are represented by a parent and a child node labeled *head::pos* and *child::pos*, respectively (lemmas are specialized with the first letter of their POS tags, i.e.,*::pos*). We add the information about the name of the relation, rel, and POS of its child as the rightmost children, with $GR-$ and $POS-$ tags prepended, respectively. For example, we encode the relation *nsubjpass(bill,stadium)* by creating a parent-child pair of nodes labeled *bill::v* and *stadium::n* and adding children labeled as *GR-nsubjpass* and *POS-NN* to the latter. Figure 5 provides an example of an DT3 structure.

4.1 Encoding Relations in the Tree Pairs

Previous work has shown the importance of encoding information about relations between question and answer passage into their structural representations, e.g., [2, 31]. Two basic methods to enrich our proposed structures with relational information are described hereafter.

Lexical relations (REL). Structural relations in both kinds of trees are encoded using the REL tag, which links the related structures in the two texts. Our previous work [31] used hard string match and soft-matching methods such as WordNet-based or Latent Dirichlet Allocation-based semantic relatedness metrics to find related lemmas. However, soft matching did not improve the models simply using hard-matching. The POS tag and the chunk pos tags in all representations are marked with REL label. In DT3 we mark the POS and grammar relation nodes. For example, Figure 2 shows that the lemma "world" occurs in both Q and AP, (we highlighted this with the solid line box), thus the related POS and chunk nodes are marked with REL.

Question Focus-based relations (FREL). Semantic relations specific to QA can be derived from the question focus and category. These are encoded using the REL-FOCUS-<QC> tag, where <QC> is substituted with a question class in the specific examples. As in [31], we use statistical classifiers to derive focus and categories of the question and of the NEs in the AP. We consider HUM, LOC, ENTY, NUM, ABBR and DESC question classes [20]. Question focus and AP chunks, which contain NEs of type compatible with the question class[6], are marked by prepending the above tags to their label. Figure 2 shows an example of such label in the dotted box, however, note that in this case the statistical classifier has determined the focus incorrectly, as it should be *stadium*, instead of *sport*. No named entities (NEs) of classes compatible with the question class ENTY are in AP, therefore there are no REL-FOCUS-ENTY tags in it.

5. SEMANTIC MATCH USING LD

Encoding relational information between Q and AP, i.e., links between words or constituents, is essential for improving passage reranking. Our previous work [32, 31, 29] has only defined two

[5]http://uima.apache.org/

[6]Compatibility is checked by means of a predefined compatibility table. We use the following mappings: **Person, Organization → HUM ,ENTY; Misc → ENTY; Location →LOC; Date, Time, Money, Percentage, Set, Duration →NUM**

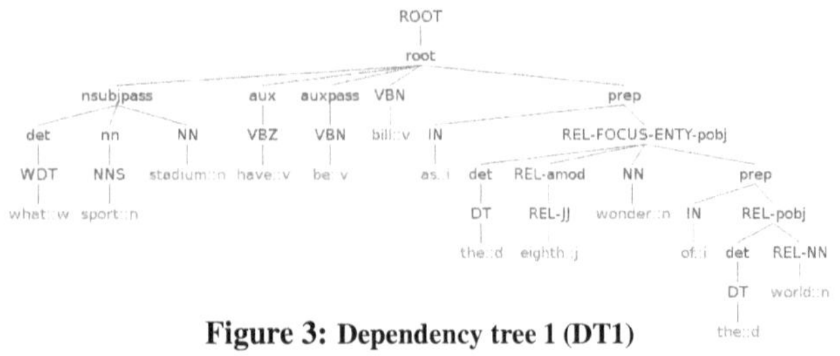

Figure 3: Dependency tree 1 (DT1)

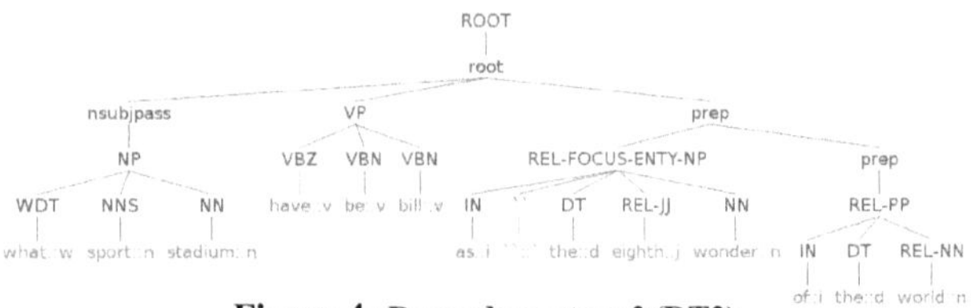

Figure 4: Dependency tree 2 (DT2)

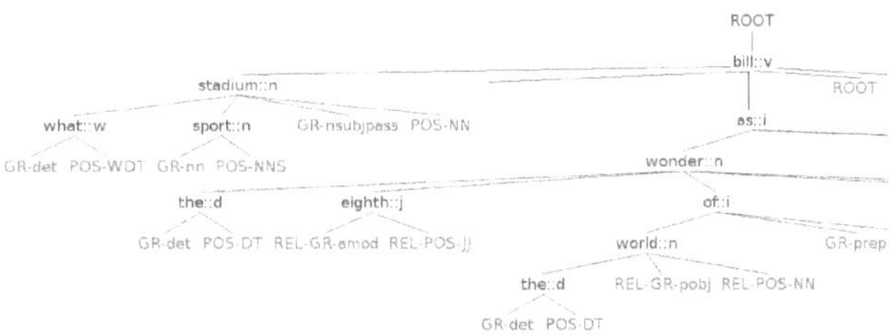

Figure 5: Dependency Tree 3 (DT3)

basic approaches based on string matching or question classifiers. The methods clearly suffer from (i) coverage problems, i.e., due to word mismatch and (ii) the non-perfect coverage and accuracy of classifiers and named entity recognizers (NER). Additionally, other attempts to use semantic matching, e.g., based on WordNet, have failed. Our approach targets entities defined in LD, it highly increases coverage and at the same time avoids errors of classifiers. In this work, we employ robust and accurate entity match algorithms we defined in [37].

More specifically, we detect semantic relations between word sequences in two texts, T_{ent} and T_{gen}. We look for word sequences, e.g., noun phrases, in T_{ent} and T_{gen}, which denote two classes or a class and an entity, which are in a *isSubclassOf* or *isa* relation. Here, class is a set of entities, where two classes, C_1 and C_2, are in a *subClassOf* relation if $C_1 \subseteq C_2$. Similarly, an entity e and class C are in *isa* relation if $e \in C$. We call such relation between word sequences a Type Match (TM). For instance, the word sequences *stadium* and *Astrodome* in the running Q/AP example are in the TM relation, since *stadium* denotes a class of all the stadiums, and *Astrodome* is one particular stadium. We extract knowledge about entities, classes and their relations from the DBpedia, YAGO and WordNet datasets available as LD.

5.1 Linked Data (LD)

LD is structured data published according to defined guidelines[7]. They suggest using HTTP Unique Resources Identifiers (URIs) for naming "things", i.e. *classes*, *entities*, *relationships*, and using standards such as Resource Description Framework (RDF)[8] and SPARQL query language for representing and querying knowledge. In RDF, knowledge is represented as a set of *(subject, predicate, object)* triples forming a directed graph, where subjects/objects are vertices and predicates are edges.

LD publishers reuse a number of vocabularies and ontologies when modeling their data. RDF Schema (RDFS)[9] is the core vocabulary, which contains basic elements for knowledge description. For example, its predicates `rdf:type` and `rdfs:SubClassOf`, denote the *isa* and *subClassOf* relationships that we described above. `rdf:label` predicate is utilized to describe human-readable names of the things uniquely identified by the URIs. For instance, in YAGO, the URIs for the *stadium* class and the *Astrodome* entity are `yago:wordnet_stadium_104295881`[10] and `yago:Reliant_Astrodome`, respectively, and the triple expressing their relationship is *(yago:Reliant_Astrodome, rdf:type, yago:wordnet_ stadium_ 104295881)*.

LD published under an open license is called Linked Open Data (LOD). In this work we use three large cross-domain datasets, namely WordNet, DBpedia and YAGO. WordNet is a manually created lexical database which groups synonymous words into synsets, and stores information about their relationships, e.g., hyponymy, hypernymy or meronymy. Since WordNet was created and is maintained manually, its coverage of NEs and domain-specific classes is limited.

YAGO was automatically created by combining WordNet and Wikipedia. YAGO construction algorithm converts WordNet synset hypernymy/hyponymy hierarchy into a class hierarchy and adds leaf Wikipedia categories as leaf classes to it using a heuristic category-to-synset mapping algorithm. The Wikipedia pages which belong to these categories become individuals of the resulting YAGO classes. A set of heuristics is employed to obtain facts about them from Wikipedia pages.

DBpedia was also automatically created using Wikipedia as a primary source of knowledge, and similarly to YAGO, Wikipedia pages are converted to individuals, and a set of heuristics is used to extract knowledge about them from Wikipedia infoboxes and categories. Hierarchy of classes in DBpedia was manually constructed. The classes are populated with individuals using infobox-class mappings.

Algorithm 1 Type Match algorithm

Require: T_{ent}, T_{gen} - short texts; LD_d - LD knowledge source
1: $TM \leftarrow \emptyset$
2: **for all** $a_{ent} \in$ getAnchors(T_{ent},LD_d) **do**
3: **for all** uri $\in$ getURIs($anchor$,T_{ent},T_{gen}, LD_d) **do**
4: **for all** $type \in$ getTypes(uri,LD_d) **do**
5: **for all** ch $\in$ getChunks(T_{gen}) **do**
6: $a_{gen} \leftarrow$ checkMatch(ch, type.label)
7: **if** $a_{gen} \neq \emptyset$ **then**
8: $TM \leftarrow TM \cup \{(a_{ent}, a_{gen})\}$

5.2 Type Match Detection Algorithm

In this work, we employ Algorithm 1 to detect token sequences (hereafter denoted as *anchors*) in TM relation. The algorithm takes two short texts, T_{ent} and T_{gen}, an LD dataset, LD_d, and an empty set, TM, as input. It (i) scans T_{ent} for the *anchors* that refer to classes or entities in LD_d (line 2); (ii) for each anchor, a_{ent} in T_{ent}, it detects the URIs of the corresponding entities in LD_d (line 3); (iii) for each uri the algorithm extracts a list of types that generalize[11] it along with their human-readable labels (line 4); (iv) finally, it iterates through chunks in T_{gen} and human-readable labels

[7] `http://www.w3.org/DesignIssues/LinkedData.html`

[8] `http://www.w3.org/TR/rdf-concepts/`

[9] `http://www.w3.org/TR/rdf-schema/`

[10] `yago:` is a shorthand for `http://yago-knowledge.org/resource/`

[11] Contain the entity or subsume the class denoted by uri

of types extracted in the previous step and checks them for string match (line 5-6). If the last tokens[12] in the chunk *ch*, a_{gen}, match the last tokens of the human-readable label of a type, $type.label$, extracted for a_{ent} from T_{ent}, we set a_{ent} and a_{gen} to be in TM relation, and add a tuple $\{(a_{ent}, a_{gen})\}$ to the TM set.

For instance, if $T_{ent} = AP$ and $T_{gen} = Q$ from our running example and $LD_d = YAGO$, we: (i) scan AP for all the anchors, which may denote YAGO classes or entities and extract their URIs. In our example, the *Astrodome* token in AP is an anchor with the respective YAGO URI `yago:Reliant_Astrodome`. (ii) We extract the URIs and human-readable names of the classes with which the URIs extracted in step (i) are in `rdf:type` or `rdfs:subClassOf` relation. For example, `yago:Reliant_Astrodome` is in `rdf:type` relation with the `yago:wordnet_stadium_104295881` class with the humane-readable label *stadium*. (iii) We look for the occurrences of the human-readable names of the classes extracted in step (ii) in the Q text. In our example, the human-readable label *stadium* occurs in the question. Therefore, we detect a TM relation between the *Astrodome* anchor from AP and the *stadium* anchor from Q, i.e., in line 8 of Algorithm 1 $(a_{ent}, a_{gen}) =$ ("*Astrodome*", "*stadium*"). We describe the details of the implementations of $getAnchors$, $getURIs$, $getTypes$ procedures in the subsection below.

Detecting anchors and referent entities/classes. We detect the sequences of tokens in text, a_{ent}, which constitute entities and classes in an external knowledge source, i.e., YAGO, DBpedia and WordNet. This is not as simple as a dictionary look-up as the a_{ent} are ambiguous. However, we benefit from the fact that (i) YAGO and DBpedia are aligned with Wikipedia pages on entity-level by construction; and (ii) there are several so-called *wikification* algorithms, which find references to Wikipedia pages in plain text, and disambiguate them to correct Wikipedia pages [9, 23]. Thus, we wikify text to both detect about anchors in T_{ent} and extract URLs of the Wikipedia pages they refer to. In order to have a richer disambiguation context, we concatenate T_{ent} with T_{gen} before passing it to the Wikification tool. We convert the Wikipedia page names to YAGO entities URIs by using YAGO `yago:hasWikipediaUrl` property. We obtain DBpedia URIs by the Wikipedia page prefix, `http://en.wikipedia.org/wiki/`, with `http://dbpedia.org/resource/`. For instance, in our running example the wikification tool maps the *astrodome* token from AP to the `http://en.wikipedia.org/wiki/Reliant_Astrodome` page and YAGO contains a triple *(yago:Reliant_Astrodome, yago:hasWikipediaURL, "http://en. wikipedia. org/ wiki/ Reliant_Astrodome")*.

In case of WordNet, we consider all noun phrases in T_{ent} to be the anchors and all the WordNet synsets containing them to be their references, i.e., we have more than one reference for an anchor.

Extracting generalization classes and their names. In case of YAGO and DBpedia, we employ RDFS predicates `rdf:type` and `rdfs:subClassOf` to extract URIs of classes which generalize the entities/classes returned by the $getURIs$ procedure directly or transitively. The URIs are HTTP unique identifiers. We extract their human-readable names by exploiting the `rdfs:label` property. For example, the output of $getTypes(uri$ =`yago:Reliant_Astrodome`, $LD_d = YAGO)$ includes `yago:wordnet_stadium_104295881` with the human-readable labels such as *bowl*, *stadium* and *arena*.

In case of WordNet, generalizations are all the hypernyms of the uri-s output by the *getURIs* procedure, and their human-readable names are all words belonging to the hypernym synsets.

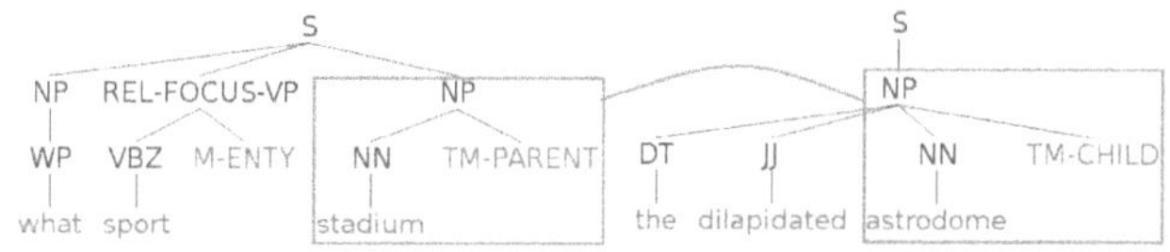

Figure 6: Fragments of a CH tree annotated in TM$_{ND}$ mode.

6. ENCODING RELATIONAL KNOWLEDGE

Encoding relational information in Q/AP is about establishing links between the Q and AP structures, in turn, this is about finding and characterizing matching between text constituents. The previous section has shown powerful methods using LD to establish a match between entities, possibly coming from two different pieces of text, e.g., Q and AP. Considering that in LD instances and classes are defined, we can also define different types of the match occurring between entities.

6.1 REL Based on LD Match Types

We start from the basic structures in Fig. 2 and we enrich them by adding TM[13] labels to their nodes. Let us define L_{ent} and L_{gen} as the sets of nodes corresponding to the tokens composing two anchors, a_{ent} and a_{gen} (from two texts T_{ent} and T_{gen}), respectively. We define the following different types of relational information:

(i) **Untyped (TM$_N$)**. We add a leaf sibling node labeled *TM* to the parent of each node in L_{ent} and L_{gen}.

(ii) **Direction-typed (TM$_{ND}$)**. By construction, one of the anchors in TM relation, a_{gen}, refers to a class in the LD dataset that contains an entity or generalizes a class to which the other anchor, i.e., a_{ent} refers to. We reflect this fact by adding sibling nodes labeled TM-PARENT to the parents of all nodes in L_{gen}, and sibling nodes labeled TM-CHILD to the parents of nodes in L_{ent}. In our running Q/AP example, *stadium* is the generalization of the anchor $Astrodome$. Therefore, as Figure 6 shows, we mark *stadium* as TM-PARENT and *Astrodome* as TM-CHILD.

(iii) **Focus-typed (TM$_{NF}$)**. If one of the anchors is also the question focus, we add sibling nodes, TM-FOCUS, to the parents of nodes in L_{ent} and L_{gen}. Otherwise, we use TM_N.

(iv) **Combo (TM$_{NDF}$)**. We apply both TM$_{ND}$ and TM$_{NF}$ strategies thus adding two different types of nodes.

TM$_{ND}$, TM$_{NF}$, TM$_{NDF}$ are more specific than TM$_N$, therefore we expect them to provide more discriminative patterns. We use the techniques described above for encoding the TM relations into CH, DT1 and DT2 structures, while in DT3 we add a TM node to matched lexicals as a child. Figure 6 illustrates the TM$_{ND}$ strategy applied to CH.

6.2 Wikipedia-based REL (wikiREL)

Section 3 has shown the importance of using REL tags. In our early work [31], these were generated using hard lemma matching. This may result in low coverage as, e.g., it does not capture synonyms or different variants of the same name. Wikification tools handle this problem, as typically they have precomputed sets of different variants of names for the same page, extracted from internal Wikipedia links and redirection pages. Therefore, if a pair of anchors in T_{ent} and T_{gen} are annotated with the link to the same

[12]Matching last tokens helps to increase the number of TM relations. For example, the human-readable name of one of the YAGO classes of *Astrodome* in the running example AP is "covered stadium". We would miss the match with the "stadium" in Q, if we only looked for the entire class name in it.

[13]It is important to use different tags than REL to convey a different type of information.

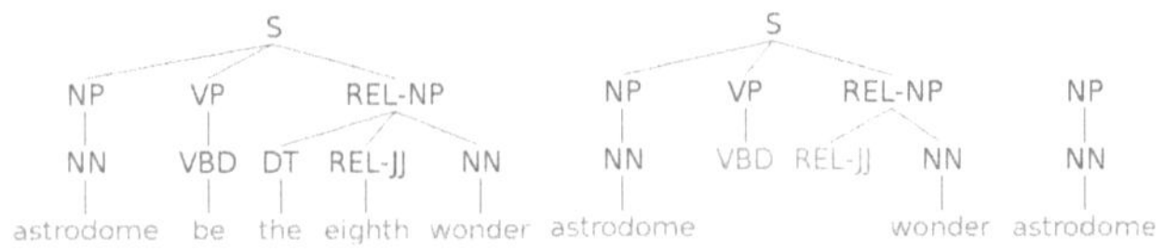

Figure 7: Some fragments generated by PTK or equivalently by SHTK (in faster time) when applied to the question tree of Fig. 2

page by a wikification tool, we consider them to be matching and we mark them with REL tags in the structural representations of T_{ent} and T_{gen} as described in Sec. 4.1.

7. L2R WITH TREE KERNELS

The above structures can be used by a domain expert to design machine learning features for training relational classifiers. Given the complexity of this task, we can rely on kernel machines, e.g., SVMs, for automatic feature generation. These classify a test input $\boldsymbol{x}$ using the function: $h(\boldsymbol{x}) = \sum_i \alpha_i y_i K(\boldsymbol{x}, \boldsymbol{x}_i)$, where α_i are the model parameters estimated from the training data, y_i are target variables, $\boldsymbol{x}_i$ are support vectors, and $K(\cdot,\cdot)$ is a kernel function. The latter computes the *similarity* between two objects. If we use kernel functions, we do not need to represent objects with features and thus we do not need to design features at all. In case of the convolution tree kernels, K counts the number of common subtrees between two trees T_1 and T_2 without explicitly considering the whole fragment space. The general equations for convolution tree kernels is: $TK(T_1, T_2) = \sum_{n_1 \in N_{T_1}} \sum_{n_2 \in N_{T_2}} \Delta(n_1, n_2)$, where N_{T_1} and N_{T_2} are the sets of the T_1's and T_2's nodes, respectively and $\Delta(n_1, n_2)$ is equal to the number of common fragments rooted in the n_1 and n_2 nodes, according to several possible definitions of the atomic fragments. We use the Δ constituting PTK [24], which defines any possible set of connected nodes as features. These capture dependencies between structure elements, e.g., Fig. 7 shows fragments generated for the question tree of Fig. 2.

7.1 Reranking with Kernels

The above section has shown how we can build classifiers based on kernels. However, the same framework can be easily adapted for learning to rank problems. In particular, we can design a function deciding which Q/AP pair is more probably correct than the others, where correct Q/AP pairs are formed by an AP containing a correct answer to Q and a supporting justification. For this purpose, we adopt the following kernel for (preference) reranking: $P_K(\langle o_1, o_2\rangle, \langle o_1', o_2'\rangle) = K(o_1, o_1') + K(o_2, o_2') - K(o_1, o_2') - K(o_2, o_1')$. In our case, $o_i = \langle Q_i, AP_i\rangle$ and $o_j' = \langle Q_j', AP_j'\rangle$, where Q and AP are the trees defined in the previous section, and $K(o_i, o_j') = TK(Q_i, Q_j') + TK(AP_i, AP_j')$. TK can be any tree kernel function, e.g., PTK. Finally, we also add $(\vec{FV}(o_1) - \vec{FV}(o_2)) \cdot (\vec{FV}(o_1') - \vec{FV}(o_2'))$ to P_K, where $\vec{FV}(o_i)$ is a traditional feature vector representing Q/AP pairs. This enables the use of standard features.

8. EXPERIMENTS

We evaluated our structural representations on the passage and sentence retrieval subtasks. We investigated the impact of the different structures described in this paper on several datasets of different nature. Moreover, we compared the impact of various preprocessing annotation pipelines on the final system accuracy.

8.1 Experimental Setup

We utilized three different datasets for testing our models:

TREC QA 2002/2003. TREC QA tasks provide questions along with the answer keys, which can be used to select the passages containing correct answers where the passages are extracted from a given text corpus. We used a total of 824 questions from years 2002 and 2003[14]. The AQUAINT[15] corpus is used for searching the supporting answer passages.

TREC13. Factoid open-domain TREC QA corpus prepared by [42]. The training data was assembled from the 1,229 TREC8-12 questions. The answers for the training questions were automatically marked in sentences by applying regular expressions, therefore the dataset can be noisy. The test data contains 100 questions, whose answers were manually annotated.[16] Consistently with the previous work, we remove the questions that have only correct/only incorrect candidate APs, thus reducing the dataset to 68 questions. We used 10 answer passages for each question for training our classifiers and all the available answer passages for testing.[17]

Answerbag. It is a collaboratively constructed question-answer resource. Some of the answers are marked as "professionally researched" meaning that they have been professionally edited and fact-checked thus making them high-quality QA training data. We used 2,000 questions for training and 1,000 for testing, using 10 and 50 passages, respectively.

LD datasets. We used the core RDF distribution of YAGO2[18], WordNet 3.0 in RDF,[19] and the datasets from the DBpedia 3.9[20].

Feature Vectors. We used several similarity functions between the pairs of texts, computed over various input representations to form a feature vector, as described hereafter: *Term-overlap features:* a cosine similarity over the text pair: $sim_{COS}(T_1, T_2)$. Input vectors are composed of word lemmas, bi-, three- an four-grams, POS-tags. *PTK over tree representations:* similarity based on the PTK score computed for the structural representations of T_1 and T_2: $sim_{PTK}(T_1, T_2) = PTK(T_1, T_2)$, where the input trees can be both the dependency trees and/or the shallow chunk trees. *Search engine ranking score:* when experimenting with TREC QA and Answerbag, we also use a ranking score of our search engine assigned to AP.

Learning Models. We used SVM-Light-TK[21] to train our models. The toolkit enables the use of structural kernels [24] in SVM-Light [18]. We used default PTK parameters as described in [31] and the polynomial kernel of degree 3 on standard features.

Pipeline. We built the entire processing pipeline on top of the UIMA framework.We included many off-the-shelf NLP tools wrapping them as UIMA annotators. We use the Apache OpenNLP[22] and Stanford CoreNLP [21] tools for sentence detection, tokenization, POS-tagging and NE recognition; Illinois chunker [27], Stanford CoreNLP Lemmatizer, and question class and focus classifiers trained as in [31]. For dependency parsing we used Stanford dependency parser (version 2.0.3) and UIMA wrappers provided by the DKPro toolset [10] for the Mate [6] (v3.5), ClearNLP [7] (v2.0.2,

[14] `http://trec.nist.gov/data/qamain.html`

[15] `https://catalog.ldc.upenn.edu/LDC2002T31`

[16] We downloaded the distribution made available by [44] in `https://code.google.com/p/jacana/`.

[17] In order to obtain results comparable to those in the previous works experimeting on TREC13 [45, 40, 42], we used the same evaluation setting as described in footnote 7 in [45]. In this setting the gold judgment file contains 4 extra questions not covered by the test set, thus resulting in lowering the upper bound of MAP and MRR to 94.44 instead of 100

[18] `http://www.mpi-inf.mpg.de/yago-naga/yago1_yago2/download/yago2/yago2core_20120109.rdfs.7z`

[19] `http://semanticweb.cs.vu.nl/lod/wn30/`

[20] `http://dbpedia.org/Downloads39`

[21] `http://disi.unitn.it/moschitti/Tree-Kernel.htm`

[22] `https://opennlp.apache.org/index.html`

Table 1: Comparison of different syntactic structures combined with vectors and basic relations

	TREC QA 2002/2003			Trec13		Answerbag		
	MRR	MAP	P@1	MRR	MAP	MRR	MAP	P@1
BM25	28.02±2.94	21.90±1.67	18.17±3.79	n/a	n/a	65.96	66.24	55.60
V	32.70±2.25	25.76±1.08	23.05±2.91	74.06	64.32	67.94	68.22	58.60
CH+V+FREL [31]	39.49	32.00	30.00	73.58	67.81	n/a	n/a	n/a
DT1+V+FREL [31]	38.05	31.00	28.39	n/a	n/a	n/a	n/a	n/a
CH+FREL	38.85±1.07	31.87±1.29	28.41±0.92	82.29	73.34	63.20	63.53	53.10
CH+V+FREL	41.51±1.65	33.54±1.35	32.20±1.90	81.30	72.65	69.90	70.07	60.80
DT1+V+FREL	41.73±1.71	33.55±1.60	32.44±1.99	78.47	70.56	69.33	69.52	60.20
DT2+V+FREL	42.75±2.43	34.05±2.18	33.66±2.97	78.45*	71.21*	68.97	69.17	59.50
$DT3_Q$+$DT2_A$+FREL	39.80±2.67	31.75±1.66	29.63±2.94	79.98	72.19	62.91	63.26	53.20
$DT3_Q$+$DT2_A$+V+FREL	43.22±2.57	34.37±1.78	34.39±2.91	80.57	73.40	69.51	69.70	60.20

Table 2: Comparing the impact of the preprocessing pipelines in building structures on TREC QA 2002/2003 data.

	Config	MRR	MAP	P@1
CH+V+REL FREL	$OpenNLP_{pos}$	40.75±2.35	32.75±1.79	31.46±2.81
	$Stanford_{pos}$	41.51±1.65	33.54±1.35	32.20±1.90
CH_{pr}+ V+REL+FREL	$OpenNLP_{pos}$	39.81±1.80	32.28±0.98	29.51±2.22
	$Stanford_{pos}$	41.21±1.36	33.40±1.84	32.32±1.93
$DT3_Q$+ $DT2_A$ +V+FREL	Stanford	43.22±2.57	34.37±1.78	34.39±2.91
	Mate	41.31±2.22	33.38±1.30	31.46±3.44
	ClearNLP	40.72±1.64	32.05±1.54	30.98±2.71
	Malt	41.78±1.67	33.25±2.03	32.68±1.40

ontonotes model) and Malt [25] (v1.7.2, linear model) dependency parsers. Moreover, we used annotators for building new sentence representations starting from tools' annotations. For example, we generated annotations with shallow chunk-based structural presentations using POS-tag and chunk annotation output by the previous annotators in the pipeline.

Search engines. We retrieved answer passages for TREC QA 2002/2003 from the AQUAINT corpus and Answerbag answer collection, respectively. We used Terrier[23] along with the accurate BM25 scoring model. We retrieved 50 passages for each question.

Wikification tools. We used the Wikipedia Miner [24] (WM) [23] and the Machine Linking (ML)[25] tools. These return links along with their confidences ranging from 0 to 1. To have high coverage with Wikipedia links, we used all the links with confidence exceeding 0.2 and 0.05 for WM and ML, respectively.

QA metrics. We used common QA metrics: Precision at rank 1 (P@1) i.e., the percentage of questions with a correct answer ranked at the first position, and Mean Reciprocal Rank (MRR). We also report the Mean Average Precision (MAP).

Significance tests. We used paired two-tailed t-test for evaluating the statistical significance of the cross-validation experiments. ‡ and † indicates the significance levels of 0.05 and 0.1, respectively.

8.2 Comparing Shallow and Deep Structures

Table 1[26] reports the performance of the relational syntactic representations enriched with question class, NE and question focus information provided by the statistical classifiers.

Here, BM25 refers to the performance of the Terrier search engine, **V** is a baseline reranker only employing the feature vectors described in Section 8.1. In the following lines, CH, DT1, DT2, DT3 correspond to the eponymous structures described in Section 4. **CH+V+REL+FREL** and **DT1+V+REL+FREL** indicate the systems employing, **CH** and **DT1** representations, respectively whereas **+REL**, **+FREL** indicate that the structures are linked with the REL and FREL approaches (Sec. 4.1). **$DT3_Q$+$DT2_A$** means that question and answer passage are represented by DT3 and DT2, respectively. **+V** indicates that a feature vector is added to the tree representation.

In our experiments on TREC 2002/2003, CH+V+FREL performs comparably to DT1+V+FREL and is outperformed by the other dependency structures. In our intuition, this new outcome may be due to the performance of the dependency parser employed for preprocessing [26].

This intuition motivated us to evaluate the impact of four different parsers for building $DT3_Q$+$DT2_A$. The results in Table 2 show that ClearNLP parser is outperformed by Mate, Malt and Stanford, where the latter always obtains the best result. Additionally, we compared the impact of using sentence splitters, tokenizers and POS-taggers from two basic preprocessing pipelines, Stanford CoreNLP ($Stanford_{pos}$) and OpenNLP ($OpenNLP_{pos}$), on the final performance of the simpler CH structure. The results show that $Stanford_{pos}$ outperforms $OpenNLP_{pos}$.

8.3 Measuring the Impact of LD Semantics

In these experiments, we evaluated the accuracy achieved by the baseline systems enriched with wikiREL (Section 6.2), and TM-relations. First, we ran an evaluation of all possible LD sources combinations with different TM-match knowledge techniques in cross-validation on TREC 2002/2003 and then we ran the resulting best systems on TREC13 and Answerbag.

8.3.1 TREC QA Answer Passage Reranking

We tested the impact of LD relations in structures using (i) basic lexical relations, i.e., CH+V+REL, and (ii) the lexical and semantic relations, i.e., CH+V+REL+FREL, described in Section 4.1. For these experiments, we (i) performed 5-fold cross-validation on TREC 2002/2003 and (ii) employed the preprocessing pipeline based on OpenNLP sentence splitter, tokenizer, POS tagger and Illinois chunker.

Tables 3 and 4 report the results using CH+V+REL and CH+V+REL+FREL, respectively. Since wikiREL improves coverage, we preferred to add it to all TM types of relations. Thus, after the double line, the tables display the baselines (in bold) enriched ("+") with different models based on TM_N, TM_{ND}, TM_{NF}, TM_{NDF}, i.e., different TM-encoding strategies (see Section 6). Additionally, **D**, **Y**, **W** denote that DBpedia, YAGO and WordNet, respectively, were used as the LD dataset, when detecting TM matches. We use **+** to indicate a combination of several LD datasets. We will reuse such notation in all the following tables. We evaluate statistical significance of the results obtained when using TM as compared to the results reported in the CH+V+REL+wikiREL and CH+V+REL+FREL+wikiREL lines for tables 3 and 4.

The tables show that all the systems exploiting LD knowledge, excluding those using DBpedia only, outperform the strong CH+V+REL and CH+V+REL+FREL baselines. Note that CH+V+REL+

[23] `http://terrier.org/`

[24] `http://sourceforge.net/projects/wikipedia-miner/files/wikipedia-miner/wikipedia-miner_1.1`

[25] `http://www.machinelinking.com/wp`

[26] In [31], we reported MAP values rounded to decimals as 0.xx. As we do not have more decimal digits for such results, we converted them to xx.00.

Table 3: Results in 5-fold cross-validation on TREC QA corpus, each TM model is added to CH+V+REL+wikiREL

System	MRR	MAP	P@1
CH+V+REL	36.82±2.68	30.08±1.63	26.34±2.17
CH+V+REL+wikiREL	39.17±1.29‡	31.34±1.34‡	28.66±1.43 ‡
+TM$_{N}$:D	40.60±1.88	33.28±1.11‡	31.10±2.99 †
+TM$_{N}$:W	41.39±1.96 ‡	33.43±1.15‡	31.34±2.94
+TM$_{N}$:W+D	40.85±1.52 ‡	33.41±1.21‡	30.37±2.34
+TM$_{N}$:Y	40.71±2.07	33.27±2.53†	30.24±2.09‡
+TM$_{N}$:Y+D	41.25±1.57‡	33.78±1.92‡	31.10±1.88 ‡
+TM$_{N}$:Y+W	42.01±2.26 ‡	34.38±2.39 ‡	32.07±3.04 ‡
+TM$_{N}$:Y+W+D	41.52±1.85‡	33.78±1.80 ‡	30.98±2.71‡
+TM$_{NF}$:D	40.67±1.94†	33.46±1.28‡	30.85±2.22 †
+TM$_{NF}$:W	40.95±2.27 ‡	33.27±1.37‡	30.98±3.74
+TM$_{NF}$:W+D	40.84±2.18 †	33.73±1.36‡	30.73±3.04
+TM$_{NF}$:Y	42.01±2.44 ‡	34.38±2.39‡	32.07±3.01 ‡
+TM$_{NF}$:Y+D	41.32±1.70 †	34.32±1.79 ‡	31.10±2.48 ‡
+TM$_{NF}$:Y+W	41.69±1.66 ‡	33.95±1.96 ‡	31.10±2.44 ‡
+TM$_{NF}$:Y+W+D	41.56±1.41‡	34.41±1.80‡	30.85±2.22 †
+TM$_{ND}$:D	40.37±1.87	33.36±0.94‡	30.37±2.17
+TM$_{ND}$:W	41.13±2.14‡	33.34±0.77‡	30.73±2.75
+TM$_{ND}$:W+D	41.28±1.03‡	33.80±0.88‡	30.73±0.82 ‡
+TM$_{ND}$:Y	42.11±3.24 ‡	34.41±2.19‡	32.07±4.06 ‡
+TM$_{ND}$:Y+D	42.28±2.01‡	34.76±1.18‡	32.44±1.99‡
+TM$_{ND}$:Y+W	42.96±1.45‡	34.68±1.49	33.05±2.04 ‡
+TM$_{ND}$:Y+W+D	42.56±1.25 ‡	34.78±1.11 ‡	32.56±1.91‡
+TM$_{NDF}$:D	40.35±1.72 †	33.42±1.06‡	30.49±1.78 ‡
+TM$_{NDF}$:W	40.98±1.96	33.25±0.58†	30.85±2.05
+TM$_{NDF}$:W+D	41.37±1.05‡	34.14±0.78‡	31.34±1.40‡
+TM$_{NDF}$:Y	42.02±2.38‡	34.77±2.23‡	32.07±2.78‡
+TM$_{NDF}$:Y+D	42.07±2.40 ‡	35.10±1.70 ‡	32.44±2.91 ‡
+TM$_{NDF}$:Y+W	43.12±1.44 ‡	34.71±2.30 †	33.78±2.88 ‡
+TM$_{NDF}$:Y+W+D	**43.38±1.58**‡	**35.27±1.61**‡	**34.02±2.81**‡
Severyn et al. [31]	39.49	32.00	30.00

wikiREL systems enriched with TM tags perform comparably to CH+V+REL+FREL, i.e., using question and focus classifiers, and in some cases even outperform it. Thus LD models can avoid the use of training data and language/domain specific classifiers.

Additionally, the tables show that we typically obtain better results when using YAGO2 and/or WordNet. In our intuition this is due to the fact that these resources are large-scale, have fine-grained class taxonomy and contain many synonymous labels per class/entity thus allowing us to have a good coverage with TM-links. The DBpedia ontology that we employed in the **D** experiments is more shallow and contains fewer labels for classes, therefore the amount of discovered TM matches is not always sufficient for increasing performance. YAGO2 provides better coverage for TM relations between entities and their classes, while WordNet contains more relations between classes.[27] Note that, we also used WordNet in our experiments in [31] but we employed supersenses whereas in this paper we use hypernymy relations. Moreover, we used a different technique to incorporate semantic match into the tree structures. This allowed our new models to relatively improve the old ones by about 16%, e.g., 37.16 vs. 32.0 in MAP.

Next, using different TM-knowledge encoding strategies, i.e., TM$_{N}$, TM$_{ND}$, TM$_{NF}$, TM$_{NDF}$, results in small performance variations. This means that encoding LD information is basically simpler than what we thought. We further tested the impact of the different encoding strategies when using the Stanford parser. Table 5 reports results of the structures built by such parser and enriched with LD, according to different TM encoding techniques.

Finally, the last three lines of Tab. 4 show our attempt to encode LD information in a feature vector, i.e., VL. This refers to the number of TM matches between the Q and AP, for different types of TM. It is basically the unstructured version of our LD models. As it can be seen, V+VL only slightly improves V and

[27] We consider the WordNet synsets to be classes in the scope of our experiments

Table 4: Results in 5-fold cross-validation on TREC QA corpus, all models are build on top of CH+V+REL+FREL system

System	MRR	MAP	P@1
CH+V+REL+FREL	40.50±2.35	33.07±1.75	31.46±2.42
CH+V+REL+ FREL+wikiREL	41.33±1.17	34.23±1.10	31.46±1.40
+TM$_{N}$:D	40.80±1.01	34.43±1.04	30.37±1.90
+TM$_{N}$:W	42.43±0.56	35.07±0.61	32.80±0.67
+TM$_{N}$:W+D	42.37±1.12	35.46±1.15	32.44±2.64
+TM$_{N}$:Y	43.28±1.91†	36.01±1.33†	33.90±2.75
+TM$_{N}$:Y+D	42.39±1.83	35.21±1.42	32.93±3.14
+TM$_{N}$:Y+W	43.98±1.08 ‡	36.33±0.57‡	35.24±1.46‡
+TM$_{N}$:Y+W+D	43.13±1.38	35.62±0.98	33.66±2.77
+TM$_{NF}$:D	41.43±0.70	35.08±0.85	31.22±1.09
+TM$_{NF}$:W	42.37±0.98	35.10±0.95	32.56±1.76
+TM$_{NF}$:W+D	43.08±0.83	36.24±1.36	33.54±1.29
+TM$_{NF}$:Y	43.82±2.36 †	36.32±1.54‡	34.88±3.35
+TM$_{NF}$:Y+D	43.19±1.17 †	36.30±1.16†	33.90±1.86
+TM$_{NF}$:Y+W	44.32±0.70‡	36.49±0.82‡	35.61±1.11‡
+TM$_{NF}$:Y+W+D	43.79±0.73 ‡	36.56±1.18†	34.88±1.69‡
+TM$_{ND}$:D	41.58±1.02	35.23±0.95 †	31.46±1.59
+TM$_{ND}$:W	42.19±1.39	34.94±0.65	32.32±1.36
+TM$_{ND}$:W+D	42.37±1.16†	35.90±1.11†	32.44±2.71 †
+TM$_{ND}$:Y	44.04±2.05 ‡	36.47±1.18‡	34.63±2.17‡
+TM$_{ND}$:Y+D	43.77±2.02 †	36.55±1.35 †	34.27±2.42
+TM$_{ND}$:Y+W	44.25±1.32 ‡	36.71±0.37 ‡	34.76±1.61 ‡
+TM$_{ND}$:Y+W+D	43.91±1.01‡	36.51±0.84 †	34.63±1.32 ‡
+TM$_{NDF}$:D	41.56±1.10	35.12±1.05†	31.59±1.46
+TM$_{NDF}$:W	41.97±0.96	34.75±0.73	31.71±1.14
+TM$_{NDF}$:W+D	42.12±1.08	35.74±1.46	32.20±2.09
+TM$_{NDF}$:Y	**44.99±2.45** ‡	**37.16±1.69** ‡	**36.59±3.02** ‡
+TM$_{NDF}$:Y+D	44.14±1.85	36.66±1.22	35.00±2.05
+TM$_{NDF}$:Y+W	44.55±1.42 ‡	37.01±1.21 ‡	35.73±2.22 ‡
+TM$_{NDF}$:Y+W+D	43.83±0.95 ‡	36.73±1.29 †	34.51±1.96 †
V	32.67±1.74	26.08±0.83	22.68±2.67
V+VL	35.39±2.49	28.34±1.81	25.73±3.54
CH+V+VL+REL+FREL	41.36±2.17	34.04±1.19	31.46±2.81

CH+V+VL+REL+FREL is about 4 points absolute less than the best model using LD in structures, i.e., +TM$_{NDF}$. This confirms that semantic knowledge requires to be used in syntactic structures.

Comparison with TREC challenge. An approximate (as we used five-fold cross-validation) comparison can be attempted with the results from TREC 2003 for the "best passages tasks" described in TREC-overview [39]. Thanks to LD our system achieves an accuracy (Precision@1) of 36.59, which would allow it to be ranked 3rd in the official evaluation, i.e., higher than MultiText-system (accuracy=35.1) and below the systems of LCC and Singapore (68.5 and 41.9, respectively). However, such top two systems used many handcrafted rules, resources and heuristics, which also prevent researchers to replicate them. In contrast, we generated features automatically, we do not design rules, and all our technology is already off-the-shelf, except for some missing components that we will make freely available to facilitate replicability of our results.

8.3.2 Answerbag

The first two lines of Table 6 report our chosen baselines whereas the last six lines show the accuracy of the systems that typically exhibited the best accuracy on our experiments on TREC QA 2002/2003 corpus. The relative improvement when using LD and Wikipedia is lower. This is likely due to the fact that the textual overlap between questions and answers on Answerbag is higher than that on TREC QA 2002/2003, thus the generalization provided by our structures is less important. Note, that we also experiment with DT1 structure built with OpenNLP pipeline and it is outperformed by the one constructed using Stanford preprocessing tools (see Table 1).

8.3.3 TREC13: Sentence Reranking

Table 7 reports the accuracy of the baseline CH+V+REL+FREL, along with the combinations with wikiREL and TM knowledge. The results on the TREC13 data further confirm the usefulness of LD-based TM knowledge, which allows us to obtain a statistically

Table 5: Syntactic structures using Stanford parser and LD

Model	LD	MRR	MAP	P@1
CH+V+REL+FREL	+ TM_N:Y+W	43.12±2.70	35.56±2.12	33.05±4.08
	+TM_{ND}:Y+W	43.55±1.81	35.72±1.52	33.90±2.64
	+TM_{NF}:Y+W	43.54±1.74	36.22±1.16	33.78±2.31
	+TM_{NDF}:Y	42.57±1.67	35.91±1.94	32.20±2.45
DT1+V+REL+FREL	+TM_{NDF}:Y	42.98±1.32	35.47±0.62	32.68±2.09
DT2+V+REL+FREL	+TM_{NDF}:Y	43.32±2.24	35.96±1.94	33.17±3.49
$DT3_Q$+$DT2_A$ +V+REL+FREL	+TM_{NDF}:Y	43.77±1.79	36.14±1.40	34.15±1.83

Table 6: Experiments of LD on Answerbag data

Model	MRR	MAP	P@1
CH+V+REL+FREL	69.29	69.50	60.00
DT1+V+REL+FREL	62.76	63.08	52.50
CH+V+REL+FREL+wikiREL	70.17	70.31	60.80
$+TM_N$:Y+W	70.66	70.77	61.10
$+TM_N$:Y	70.35	70.46	60.60
$+TM_{ND}$:Y+W	70.62	70.76	61.10
$+TM_{NF}$:Y+W	70.44	70.58	60.50
$+TM_{NDF}$:Y	70.64	70.75	60.80

significant improvement of around 3.5 points in terms of MRR as compared to the baseline CH+V+REL+FREL. The comparison of our models with the state-of-the-art results, reported by Tab. 8, shows that our kernel-based rerankers outperforms the very recent best model, i.e., Wang and Nyberg (2015), by 2.17% absolute in MRR and 1.31% in MAP. Moreover, when we add LD information, the improvement in MAP increases to 2.73% absolute.

8.4 Efficiency

Computational complexity. The complexity of the type match procedure for a short text pair, T_{ent} and T_{gen}, described in Section 5.2 is $O(k \times |T_{gen}| \times |T_{ent}|)$. $|T|$ is the length of text T in terms of words. k is a LD-dataset specific constant denoting the maximal amount of generalizations per all *uri*-s corresponding to a word. For example, in case of WordNet this would be the maximal amount of hypernyms for all the senses of a given word.

Wikipedia annotation time. Wikipedia annotation time depends on the algorithms used to perform wikification, tools and techniques for Wikipedia data storage and retrieval, and hardware capacity. In our experiments we used (i) a local installation of Wikipedia Miner (WM) on a DELL N5110 machine[28] and a (ii) commercial web-service optimized for fast text processing, ML, which we access using REST API. We store preprocessed version of Wikipedia to be used by WM 1.0 in a 5.5.17 MySQL database.

Table 9 provides information about the running time of Wikipedia annotation on two randomly selected subsets of text pairs with different length. *Size* column reports number of Q/AP pairs processed, *Avg length* reports their average length in words, and the two last columns report the average time required to process one pair in seconds (and total time required to process the full corpus in minutes in parentheses). The speed exhibited by the ML service shows that the methods relying on linking to Wikipedia are scalable for large amounts of data given the efficient implementation of the wikification tool.

Type data extraction time. We use Jena TDB 0.9.0[29] RDF triple store to store local YAGO, WordNet and DBpedia data. Jena TDB efficiency[30] was evaluated on a number of benchmarks with results reported, for example, in [5]. We store YAGO2 and WordNet+DBpedia data in separate triple stores.

In our case, extracting all the generalizations of the URI, i.e. sending a set of SPARQL queries to a triple store, took 18.22, 36.28 and 68.59 milliseconds for WordNet, YAGO and DBpedia, respectively. In average, we extracted 32 *type-type label* pairs per anchor from WordNet, 49 from YAGO and 26 from DBpedia.

Table 7: Results of CH+FREL plus the best LD models on TREC13

Model	MAP	MRR
CH+REL+FREL	72.65	81.30
CH+REL+FREL+wikiREL	72.99	80.37
+TM_N:Y	**74.07**	81.10
+TM_{NF} :Y	73.73	79.52
+TM_{ND}:Y	**74.05**	80.19
+TM_{NDF}:Y	72.94	79.78

Table 8: Previous work results on the TREC13.

Model	MRR	MAP
Wang et al. (2007)[42]	68.52	60.29
Heilman and Smith (2010)[14]	69.17	60.91
Wang and Manning (2010)[41]	69.51	59.51
Yao et al. (2013)[43]	74.77	63.07
Severyn and Moschitti (2013)[31]	75.20	68.29
Yih et al. (2013)[45]	77.00	70.92
Wang and Nyberg (2015) [40]	79.13	71.34
CH+FREL (this work)	**81.30**	72.65
CH+FREL+wikiREL+TM_N:Y	81.10	**74.07**

Table 9: Wikipedia annotation time

Dataset	Size	Average length	Average (total) time ML	Average (total) time MW
Sample1	1599	36.78	0.14s (3.6m)	2.84s (75.7m)
Sample2	1146	107.30	0.23s (4.3m)	9.02s (172.7m)

9. CONCLUSIONS

This paper proposes a study on syntactic structures enriched with semantic information from statistical classifiers and knowledge from LD for passage reranking. In particular, YAGO, DBpedia and WordNet are used to match constituents from QA pairs. Such matches are used to enrich semantic structures. The experiments with TREC QA and the above models also combining traditional feature vectors and the improved relational structures greatly outperform a strong IR baseline, i.e., BM25, by 101%, and previous state-of-the-art reranking models, e.g., up to 16% in MAP. Differently from previous work, our models can effectively use semantic knowledge in statistical learning to rank methods. It should be stressed that our experiments have shown that simply using semantic information as features (even if extracted from a powerful resource as LD) does not significantly improve BM25. It is really necessary to encode semantic features in syntactic structures and then generate syntactic/semantic relational patterns between question and answer passage (to be used as features in the reranker).

Our promising results open interesting future directions in designing novel semantic structures and using innovative semantic representations in learning algorithms for IR applications. Additionally, jointly using deep neural networks with our approach is an interesting and promising research direction.

Acknowledgements

This work has been partially supported by the EC project CogNet, 671625 (H2020-ICT-2014-2, Research and Innovation action) and by an IBM Faculty Award. Many thanks to the Center for Advanced Studies of Trento of IBM Italia for the fruitful discussions on the early draft of this manuscript.

[28]6GB RAM, four core Intel(R) Core(TM) i7-2630M CPU @ 2.00GHz processor, 64-bit operating system, 640gb 2.5" Sata II Hard Drive with 5400 RPM

[29]`http://jena.apache.org/documentation/tdb/index.html`

[30]We installed Jena TDB on a server machine with 12*Intel®Xeon®Processor X5670* processors, with 94GB RAM under Linux, with 64-bit *jdk1.7.0_02* and 1TB SATA 6.0Gb/s 2.5" hard drive with 7200 RPM.

10. REFERENCES

[1] E. Aktolga, J. Allan, and D. A. Smith. Passage reranking for question answering using syntactic structures and answer types. In *ECIR*, 2011.

[2] M. W. Bilotti, J. L. Elsas, J. Carbonell, and E. Nyberg. Rank learning for factoid question answering with linguistic and semantic constraints. In *CIKM*, 2010.

[3] M. W. Bilotti and E. Nyberg. Improving text retrieval precision and answer accuracy in question answering systems. In *(IR4QA) Workshop at COLING*, 2008.

[4] C. Bizer, J. Lehmann, G. Kobilarov, S. Auer, C. Becker, R. Cyganiak, and S. Hellmann. Dbpedia - a crystallization point for the web of data. *Web Semantics*, 7(3), 2009.

[5] C. Bizer and A. Schultz. The berlin sparql benchmark. *IJSWIS*, 5(2):1–24, 2009.

[6] B. Bohnet. Top accuracy and fast dependency parsing is not a contradiction. In *COLING*, 2010.

[7] J. D. Choi and M. Palmer. Getting the most out of transition-based dependency parsing. In *ACL*, 2011.

[8] D. Croce, A. Moschitti, and R. Basili. Structured lexical similarity via convolution kernels on dependency trees. In *Proceedings of EMNLP*, 2011.

[9] A. Csomai and R. Mihalcea. Linking documents to encyclopedic knowledge. *IEEE Intelligent Systems*, 23(5):34–41, 2008.

[10] R. E. de Castilho and I. Gurevych. A broad-coverage collection of portable NLP components for building shareable analysis pipelines. In *OIAF4HLT Workshop (COLING)*, 2014.

[11] J. Fan, D. Ferrucci, D. Gondek, and A. Kalyanpur. Prismatic: Inducing knowledge from a large scale lexicalized relation resource. In *NAACL HLT*, 2010.

[12] C. Fellbaum, editor. *WordNet: An Electronic Lexical Database*. MIT Press, 1998.

[13] D. Ferrucci, E. Brown, J. Chu-Carroll, J. Fan, D. Gondek, A. Kalyanpur, A. Lally, J. W. Murdock, E. Nyberg, J. Prager, N. Schlaefer, and C. Welty. Building Watson: An Overview of the DeepQA Project. *AI Magazine*, 31(3), 2010.

[14] M. Heilman and N. A. Smith. Tree edit models for recognizing textual entailments, paraphrases, and answers to questions. In *NAACL*, 2010.

[15] A. Hickl, J. Williams, J. Bensley, K. Roberts, Y. Shi, and B. Rink. Question answering with lcc chaucer at trec 2006. In *TREC*, 2006.

[16] J. Hoffart, F. Suchanek, K. Berberich, and G. Weikum. Yago2: a spatially and temporally enhanced knowledge base from wikipedia. *Artificial Intelligence*, 2012.

[17] J. Jeon, W. B. Croft, and J. H. Lee. Finding similar questions in large question and answer archives. In *CIKM*, 2005.

[18] T. Joachims. Optimizing search engines using clickthrough data. In *ACM SIGKDD KDD*, 2002.

[19] B. Katz and J. Lin. Selectively using relations to improve precision in question answering. In *Workshop on NLP for QA (EACL)*, 2003.

[20] X. Li and D. Roth. Learning question classifiers. In *Proceedings of ACL*, 2002.

[21] C. D. Manning, M. Surdeanu, J. Bauer, J. Finkel, S. J. Bethard, and D. McClosky. The Stanford CoreNLP natural language processing toolkit. In *ACL*, 2014.

[22] M. C. McCord, J. W. Murdock, and B. Boguraev. Deep parsing in Watson. *IBM Journal*, 56(3), 2012.

[23] D. Milne and I. Witten. An open-source toolkit for mining wikipedia. In *NZCSRSC*, volume 9, 2009.

[24] A. Moschitti. Efficient convolution kernels for dependency and constituent syntactic trees. In *ECML*, 2006.

[25] J. Nivre, J. Hall, J. Nilsson, A. Chanev, G. Eryigit, S. Kübler, S. Marinov, and E. Marsi. Maltparser: A language-independent system for data-driven dependency parsing. *Natural Language Engineering*, 2007.

[26] M. Pasca. Open-Domain Question Answering from Large Text Collections. CSLI Publications, 2003.

[27] V. Punyakanok and D. Roth. The use of classifiers in sequential inference. In *NIPS*, pages 995–1001, 2001.

[28] F. Radlinski and T. Joachims. Query chains: Learning to rank from implicit feedback. *CoRR*, 2006.

[29] A. Severyn and A. Moschitti. Automatic feature engineering for answer selection and extraction. In *EMNLP*, 2013.

[30] A. Severyn and A. Moschitti. Learning to rank short text pairs with convolutional deep neural networks. In *SIGIR*, 2015.

[31] A. Severyn, M. Nicosia, and A. Moschitti. Building structures from classifiers for passage reranking. In *CIKM*, 2013.

[32] A. Severyn, M. Nicosia, and A. Moschitti. Learning adaptable patterns for passage reranking. *CoNLL-2013*, page 75, 2013.

[33] J. Shawe-Taylor and N. Cristianini. *Kernel Methods for Pattern Analysis*. Cambridge University Press, 2004.

[34] D. Shen and M. Lapata. Using semantic roles to improve question answering. In *EMNLP-CoNLL*, 2007.

[35] S. Small, T. Strzalkowski, T. Liu, S. Ryan, R. Salkin, N. Shimizu, P. Kantor, D. Kelly, and N. Wacholder. Hitiqa: Towards analytical question answering. In *COLING*, 2004.

[36] M. Surdeanu, M. Ciaramita, and H. Zaragoza. Learning to rank answers on large online QA collections. In *ACL*, 2008.

[37] K. Tymoshenko, A. Moschitti, and A. Severyn. Encoding semantic resources in syntactic structures for passage reranking. In *Proceedings of EACL*, 2014.

[38] E. M. Voorhees. Overview of the TREC 2001 Question Answering Track. In *Proceedings of TREC*, 2001.

[39] E. M. Voorhees. Overview of the trec 2003 question answering track. In *TREC 2003*, 2003.

[40] D. Wang and E. Nyberg. A long short-term memory model for answer sentence selection in question answering. In *ACL*, July 2015.

[41] M. Wang and C. D. Manning. Probabilistic tree-edit models with structured latent variables for textual entailment and question answer- ing. In *ACL*, 2010.

[42] M. Wang, N. A. Smith, and T. Mitamura. What is the jeopardy model? a quasi-synchronous grammar for qa. In *EMNLP-CoNLL*, 2007.

[43] P. C. Xuchen Yao, Benjamin Van Durme and C. Callison-Burch. Answer extraction as sequence tagging with tree edit distance. In *NAACL*, 2013.

[44] X. Yao, B. Van Durme, and P. Clark. Answer extraction as sequence tagging with tree edit distance. In *Proceedings of NAACL-HLT*, pages 858–867, 2013.

[45] W.-t. Yih, M.-W. Chang, C. Meek, and A. Pastusiak. Question answering using enhanced lexical semantic models. In *ACL*, 2013.

Ranking Entities for Web Queries Through Text and Knowledge

Michael Schuhmacher, Laura Dietz and Simone Paolo Ponzetto
Data and Web Science Research Group
University of Mannheim, Germany
{michael,dietz,simone}@informatik.uni-mannheim.de

ABSTRACT

When humans explain complex topics, they naturally talk about involved entities, such as people, locations, or events. In this paper, we aim at automating this process by retrieving and ranking entities that are relevant to understand free-text web-style queries like Argentine British relations, which typically demand a set of heterogeneous entities with no specific target type like, for instance, Falklands_War or Margaret_Thatcher, as answer. Standard approaches to entity retrieval rely purely on features from the knowledge base. We approach the problem from the opposite direction, namely by analyzing web documents that are found to be query-relevant. Our approach hinges on entity linking technology that identifies entity mentions and links them to a knowledge base like Wikipedia. We use a learning-to-rank approach and study different features that use documents, entity mentions, and knowledge base entities – thus bridging document and entity retrieval. Since established benchmarks for this problem do not exist, we use TREC test collections for document ranking and collect custom relevance judgments for entities. Experiments on TREC Robust04 and TREC Web13/14 data show that: i) single entity features, like the frequency of occurrence within the top-ranked documents, or the query retrieval score against a knowledge base, perform generally well; ii) the best overall performance is achieved when combining different features that relate an entity to the query, its document mentions, and its knowledge base representation.

Categories and Subject Descriptors

H.3.3 [**Information Storage and Retrieval**]: Information Search and Retrieval; I.2.4 [**Artificial Intelligence**]: Semantic Networks

Keywords

Entities; Knowledge Bases; Information Retrieval

1. INTRODUCTION

Web search engine research shows an increasing interest in going beyond words, in particular by integrating structured knowledge into the retrieval process, which has recently led to large efforts aimed at building very large entity-centric knowledge bases of ever increasing coverage and complexity [42, 18]. These can be leveraged either as sources of information to be presented directly to the user or as background knowledge sources to be used by retrieval systems to improve the retrieval process itself [8, 14]. But despite the sophistication of existing search engines, the former task of satisfying the user information need by presenting an entity and its related description is still tackled in a very basic way. Common search engines display entity information only for entity-centric queries. For example a query for Falkland islands[1] returns a short description of this British overseas territory, together with information about its capital, currency, etc. However, entity information is missing for more complex queries like Falklands war or broad queries such as Argentine British relations. Consequently, in this work we develop a framework to satisfy the user's information need on any topic from an entity-centric viewpoint by accompanying the document result set with a ranked list of entities that are deemed as relevant for the query.

Entity ranking has recently attracted a lot of attention from researchers, especially in the context of the INEX and TREC initiatives [11, 2, 19]. This line of work is primarily aimed at retrieving entities from a structured knowledge repository based on keyword queries. As a result, the output of these entity ranking systems typically consist of a handful of homogeneous entities of the same type like, for instance, Royal Navy personnel who took part in the Falklands War in response to the query British Navy officer Falklands war. But while this can be adapted to cover many practical search scenarios, it still does not address a large amount of user queries issued as general-purpose search intent, namely those corresponding to complex information needs that could only be satisfied by a list of heterogeneous entities of arbitrary types, covering different aspects of the query. Consider, for instance, the query Argentine British relations. For this query, it is difficult to satisfy the user information need by means of a single entity. Instead, in this case the user probably would like to see a wide spectrum of entities of different types including events (Falklands_War), persons (Margaret_Thatcher) or even songs (March_of_the_Malvinas). Complex queries of this kind are far from being seldom issued. In previous work, Pound et al. [34] classified web-search query types in the context of entity retrieval using real-world querylog data, and showed that 40.6% of sampled queries are entity queries (CJ5 Jeep), 12.1% are type queries (cold medication), and 4.6% are attribute queries (zip code waterville maine). Accordingly, we can conclude that more than 40% of all remaining queries are open domain ones – namely, they are not limited to specific types of entities – which cannot be assigned to any of the previous classes.

Permission to make digital or hard copies of all or part of this work for personal or classroom use is granted without fee provided that copies are not made or distributed for profit or commercial advantage and that copies bear this notice and the full citation on the first page. Copyrights for components of this work owned by others than the author(s) must be honored. Abstracting with credit is permitted. To copy otherwise, or republish, to post on servers or to redistribute to lists, requires prior specific permission and/or a fee. Request permissions from Permissions@acm.org.
CIKM'15 October 19 - 23, 2015, Melbourne, VIC, Australia
Copyright is held by the owner/author(s). Publication rights licensed to ACM.
ACM 978-1-4503-3794-6/15/10 ...$15.00.
http://dx.doi.org/10.1145/2806416.2806480.

[1]In this paper, we use Sans Serif for words and terms, and Monospace for entities.

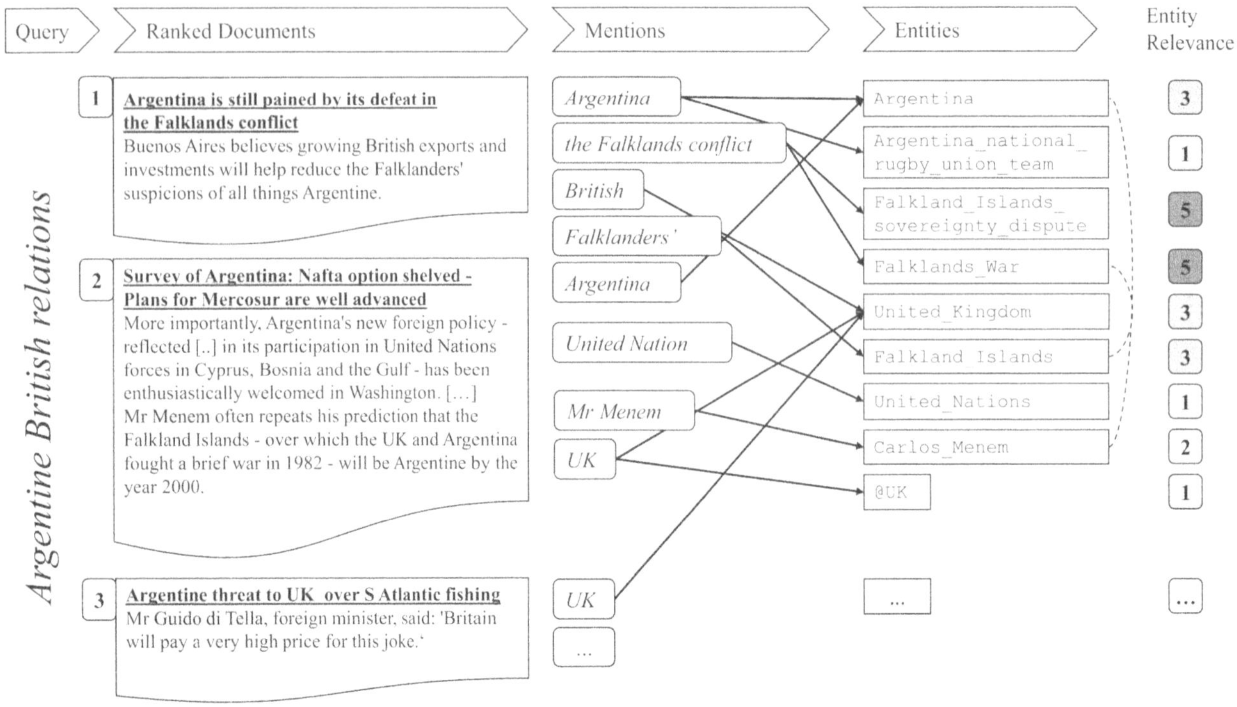

Figure 1: An example of ranking entities for a Web query. Solid arrows represent entity links, dotted lines knowledge base relations.

With this work we aim to fill this gap and specifically address open domain web queries with entity rankings. To this end, we build on a state-of-the-art document retrieval system and an entity linking tool. Entity-linked documents provide us with an initial pool of entity mentions in context. These entities are re-ranked with the goal of providing a ranking of entities according to their relevance for the user query. Key to our approach is the usage of entities that originate from the output of a document retrieval system, as opposed, for instance, to directly rank the entity-centric information stored within an underlying knowledge base. This provides us with a combination of documents and entities as a unified result to the search queries, which can be used later for a variety of higher-level applications like advanced entity-rich search engines [21]: that is, while we focus in this paper on entity ranking only, our method potentially enables the broader vision of a general-purpose search system displaying relevant entities alongside relevant documents or passages as the result to a user query [12], a feature that fits well with and extends existing search interface paradigms (we leave this exploration for future work).

The contributions of this paper are the following ones:

- New task: We formulate a new variant of ad-hoc entity search which is close in spirit to ad-hoc document search and complements existing entity retrieval challenges (e.g, INEX).
- New evaluation dataset: In order to foster a community around joint entity and document retrieval, we create an entity gold standard from queries of established test collections for ad-hoc document retrieval.
- Experimental study: We use ground truth judgments from our dataset to investigate and experiment with different approaches and features arising from the knowledge base and the document collection to evaluate initial solutions for this ranking problem.

To the best of our knowledge, none of the existing entity ranking benchmarks is designed for inter-operation with document retrieval. Therefore, we create a new evaluation set, which we make publicly available and whose details we present in Section 4. Thanks to our dataset, we are able to perform extensive experiments and show that high performance on this task can be achieved, by combining information from heterogeneous knowledge sources – e.g., co-occurrence statistics from large text corpora like ClueWeb, as well as structured knowledge bases such as DBpedia [4] – into a learning-to-rank framework. Our study includes two test sets with different corpus characteristics (news versus web), two document retrieval systems, namely the keyword-based Sequential Dependency Model (SDM, [31]) and the entity-aware EQFE [8], and entity links from the system KBBridge [7] and the FACC1 collection [17].

2. TASK DEFINITION

We tackle the problem of retrieving a ranking of entities in response to a web query. We do not restrict ourselves to address only a limited class of queries. In particular, we aim to retrieve lists of entities for *any* typical web query – even queries that are not posed with entity retrieval in mind. We define an entity as being relevant for a query if a human would mention this entity when providing an answer. Accordingly, the task is to rank entities based on their degree of usefulness for a user to understand what the query is about (i.e., its topic, main themes and involved actors). Ultimately, we aim for an approach that helps to understand queries about complicated topics, such as the Robust04 query Argentine British relations or the TREC Web 2014 query Pink Slime in Ground Beef. Therefore, we focus on informational queries about a general topic – i.e., we do not expect the query to ask for a particular fact or a specific answer [37]. We define our entity ranking task as follows:

- Given: a user-provided textual query (such as Argentine British relations).
- Provided: a background corpus with query-relevant documents that includes entity link annotations from mentions (e.g., the conflict of the Falklands) to entities (e.g., `Falklands_War`) in a background knowledge base.
- Goal: Rank the entities by relevance w.r.t. the query.

Example. We illustrate our problem by means of an example (Figure 1). Initially, we are given the query Argentine British relations and the retrieved query-relevant documents D_q from the document collection (in our experiments we used the TREC Robust04 corpus and the ClueWeb12 corpus, cf. Section 5). Text of these documents is processed by an entity linking system that connects entity mentions from the documents to their equivalent entity in the knowledge base (this work uses entities from DBpedia). The retrieved documents contain a wide spectrum of entities of different kinds such as countries, persons, organizations, and many others. The mentioned entities exhibit different degrees of relevance when compared against the input query. For instance, the `Falklands_War` is a defining event for the diplomatic relations between the United Kingdom and Argentina. However, the entity `United_Nations` does not provide us with very specific information related to the relations between these two countries – i.e., both countries belong to the UN, just like many other countries do. Consequently, our task is to automatically produce a ranking which best correlates with the gold-standard ranking obtained from a set of human judgments: in our case, a ranking which prefers the entities `Falklands_War`, `Argentina`, and `United_Kingdom`, which have been labeled as important for the given query. Note that, in this setting, the notion of 'importance' is not necessarily symmetric: While the `United_Kingdom` is important to understand the topic Argentine British relations, for the entity `United_Kingdom` itself the diplomatic relationships to Argentina are only a minor aspect.

3. ENTITY RANKING FOR WEB QUERIES

We develop a first solution for our entity ranking task that: i) combines heterogeneous knowledge from unstructured document text and structured entity-centric knowledge sources; ii) within a supervised learning approach. Our hunch is that complementary sources of query-relevance for entities can be extracted through entity mentions, their context, and explicit semantic information from a wide-coverage knowledge base through inspecting link structure and article text.

3.1 Learning to Rank Entities for Web Queries

Our study on entity-relevance indicators is performed within a learning-to-rank framework. For that we train different supervised feature-based models on labeled data, an approach that repeatedly demonstrated competitive performance for retrieval tasks [29]. There is a wide range of different learning-to-rank algorithms available, each with their own strengths and weaknesses. In order to reduce the influence of the learning algorithm on our conclusions, we employ different learning-to-rank algorithms in our study. This includes the Ranking Support Vector Machine (SVM, [24]), and an algorithm to optimize an underlying retrieval metric directly, as implemented in the RankLib package[2].

The Ranking Support Vector Machine views the ranking problem as a pairwise classification task and minimizes the number of discordant pairs in Kendall's τ. Therefore, it learns a ranking function that can always be represented as a linear combination of feature vectors, thus making it possible to use also non-linear kernels [24]. We use this to leverage a semantic kernel function that uses relations between entities as a similarity measure (Section 3.6) and also study an alternative linear kernel. In addition, we use a list-wise learning algorithm, here an implementation from RankLib to directly optimize Mean-Average Precision (MAP) and alternatively Normalized Discounted Cumulative Gain (NDCG), thus addressing the so-called metric divergence problem [30]. We use coordinate ascent as an optimization algorithm, since it has demonstrated good performance on low-dimensional feature spaces with limited training data.

This supervised learning setting allows us to study the effect of different document-based and knowledge-based relevance indicators for entity ranking.

3.2 Document Retrieval and Candidate Pool

We start by issuing the query to a document retrieval system and collect the top results. To analyze the impact of this step on the remainder of our approach, we study two retrieval models for two data sets: Robust04 and ClueWeb12.

For the Robust04 dataset, we use the document retrieval method EQFE, which is an entity-aware document retrieval method [8]. This system uses entity links within documents to produce its document ranking. These entity links are created with KBBridge [7], which we also use in our method. In the second experiment on ClueWeb12, we verify our findings by using a different, keyword-based retrieval method, the Sequential Dependency Model (SDM) [31], and a different, existing set of entity links, the FACC1 dataset [17].

In both cases, entity links in high ranked documents are used to build a pool of candidate entities. Consequently, our ranking problem is formulated as the task of comparing the query with the document mentions and associated entities.

3.3 Mention Features

The first feature is based on the number of entity mentions in retrieved query-relevant documents. To this end, count statistics over all the targets of all entity links are collected (notice, that some entity linkers retain multiple targets per link). While we study raw counts (MenFrq) for comparison, we use TF-IDF to weight mention counts across the document collection.

Mention Frequency (MenFrqIdf): The number of occurrences of each entity over all retrieved documents per query, weighted using TF-IDF as follows:

$$\text{MenFrqIdf}(e) = \text{tf}_q(e) \log \frac{N}{\text{df}(e)}$$

This feature is already a strong ranking method by itself (cf. Section 5), since query-relevant documents are likely to contain relevant entities. The downside of this method is that the connection between the query and the entity is only indirectly established – namely through the documents only.

3.4 Query–Mention Features

The second set of features compares entity links more directly with the query. We distinguish between the mention text, i.e. the surface form of the entity links (denoted "M"), and the context of up to ten terms surrounding the entity link (denoted "C").

We define an entity mention as the sequence of words that the entity linking system links to a target entity in the knowledge base. The entity mention is compared to any word in the query. In our example, this means that occurrences of the query term British within entity mentions are an indicator that the target of the links, i.e., entity `United_Kingdom`, is relevant. Likewise, if query terms

[2] http://people.cs.umass.edu/~vdang/ranklib.html

such as Relationship occur near entity links, this is also an indicator that the target of the entity link is relevant. We limit the search terms within a ten-term window surrounding the entity link.

We apply different word similarity methods to compare the surface forms or contexts to all query-terms. These similarities are averaged across all mentions for each entity.

String Edit Distance (SED): We compute the normalized Levenshtein String Edit Distance [28] between the query and the mention (context, respectively) as one string, in order to cover basic morpho-syntactic similarity. This is able to capture exact string matches, as well as approximate ones (e.g., due to spelling mistakes within queries and documents).

GloVe (Glo) / JoBimText (Jo): To generalize across different synonyms and word senses, we study the utility of distributional representations of words. The general idea of these distributional thesauri is to model word meanings based on their global frequency of co-occurrences in large text corpora. They can thus identify general semantic similarity between words, without the explicit need for exhaustive context. Here, we focus on two existing distributional semantics models, namely GloVe [33] and JoBimText [3]. As both frameworks associate single words with vectors, we aggregate all word-wise similarities for multi-word mentions and queries. As aggregation functions we study taking the average and the sum. In our setting, using the JoBimText framework can help us to identify, for instance, the high similarity between the query-term relationship and a contextual term like tension.

3.5 Query–Entity Features

The next set of features compares the knowledge base entities directly with those in the query. We achieve this in two ways: (a) we apply entity linking to query keywords and compare the set of linked query entities with the document entities; (b) we perform retrieval on text associated with an entity in the knowledge base with the query terms. For the first option, we leverage a structured knowledge base (DBpedia, Section 3.5.1), and for the second option a semi-structured textual knowledge resource (Wikipedia, Section 3.5.2).

3.5.1 Entity-set Comparison Using DBpedia

We first run the queries through an off-the-shelf entity linker (TagMe, [16]) to collect entities found within the query. This allows us to compare query entities to candidate entities. We incorporate direct matches and short paths between both sets.

a) **Direct Match (QEnt)**: Boolean feature indicating whether the candidate entity is contained in the query entities.

b) **Path (QEntEntSim)**: Whether the query and document entities are connected by some path along the DBpedia graph.

In our example from Figure 1, a direct match is the entity `United_Kingdom`, which is linked from the query term British and the document mention UK.

Besides, we tap into the structure of the background knowledge base by identifying relations between different, albeit related entities. For example `Carlos_Menem` is not mentioned in the query. However, he is related to Argentina, as he used to be its president. To this end, we build upon the work from [36], who extract weighted paths between entity pairs in DBpedia. Here, we consider entities that are involved in the same relation instance or share the same Wikipedia category. We consider all relations from the DBpedia Ontology (prefix `dbo:`), thereby staying agnostic towards particular predicates.

3.5.2 Knowledge Base Retrieval Using Wikipedia

Arbitrary queries can be rather ambiguous and hard to interpret for an entity linking system. Thus, as an alternative we compare the query keywords directly with text associated with entities in the knowledge base. Given the query keywords, we apply two types of information retrieval models on the English Wikipedia, and accordingly build two different kinds of features.

WikiBoolean: All entities returned by a basic standard Boolean retrieval model, based on a full text index over all Wikipedia articles. We bind query keywords with disjunctive operators. This approach tests if at least one query keyword is found within the Wikipedia article of the candidate entity.

WikiSDM: We further use a Galago[3] search index of an English Wikipedia dump. Using the Sequential Dependency Model (SDM, [31]) with collection-level Dirichlet Smoothing, we use the query to retrieve 1,000 Wikipedia articles. The retrieval score is used as a feature as a measure of relevance for the entity. While the WikiSDM feature is computed on the knowledge base only, it is used to re-rank entities that have a high mention frequency in retrieved, query-relevant documents. The effect of WikiSDM therefore includes both knowledge base and document information.

3.6 Entity–Entity Features

Finally, we leverage the relations between entities from the documents themselves. This is in contrast to Section 3.5.1, where we use direct relations and shared categories as a feature to capture similarity between entities from the query and the document.

At the heart of these features lies the idea that a ranking decision between two candidate entities should be influenced by how similar these two entities are to each other. This is a helpful signal for entity ranking, especially in the case of entities having very different features (as computed w.r.t. the query), but nevertheless being related to each other. Consider, for instance, the two document entities `Falkland_Islands` and `Falklands_War` in Figure 1. Both entities are strongly related due to the fact that the Falklands war took place on the Falkland Islands. This information is available from DBpedia through the relation `dbo:place`.

To capture the similarity between candidate entities, we use the same algorithm that gives rise to the feature QEntEntSim to compute a similarity matrix between all candidate entities. Since the value of the feature depends on the pair of entities that are ranked with respect to each other, we cannot derive a static feature for this. To include this feature into our learning problem, we consequently extend the ranking SVM and replace the linear kernel with a custom mixed kernel. This mixed kernel consists of a linear kernel for the standard features, combined with a semantic smoothing kernel [5] for entity–entity similarity.

The semantic kernel was originally proposed to cover semantic similarity between words: in this work, we use it instead to include the similarity between entities. Hence, with this kernel we can incorporate the information that `Falklands_War` has a strong relation to the islands it took place in, namely the `Falkland_Islands`, without changing any of the query-related features directly.

4. REWQ DATASETS

To the best of our knowledge, there exists no dataset for evaluating entity ranking for web queries; therefore we decided to create our own, the Ranking Entities for Web Queries dataset (REWQ, pronounced "rookie"). We study queries from well-known document

[3]`http://lemurproject.org/galago.php`

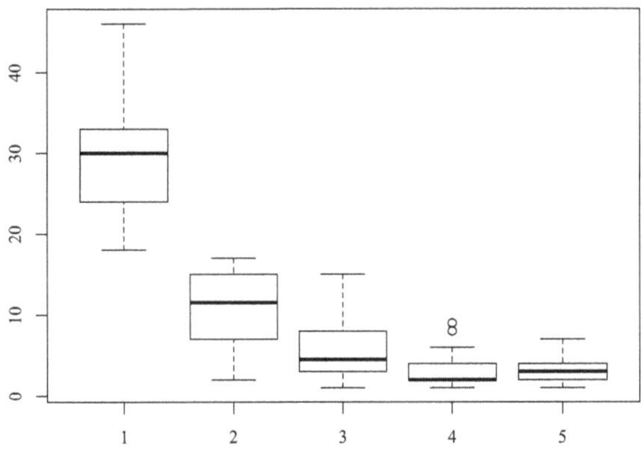

Figure 2: Boxplot for ground truth labels of REWQ-Robust (rounded to a 5-level scale) for 25 query with 50 entities each.

retrieval benchmarks, namely the TREC Robust04 data set [40] and the TREC Web 13/14 data[4], and use the respective corpora as a background corpus to provide a benchmark in two complementary experimental settings. Gold annotations for both datasets are available in the online appendix of this paper.[5]

REWQ-Robust: We aim at covering complex web queries, and accordingly build on the TREC Robust 2004 data set [40] as starting point. In order to study the interplay between document and entity retrieval, we start with a document set that has a high chance of including query relevant entities. Accordingly, we select the 25 top-performing queries of the EQFE system on the dataset (as measured by mean average precision) and collect for each of these the top 19 documents. The final dataset consist of the 50 entities with the highest mention frequency per query.

Entity relevance, defined as the degree of importance that entities play to explain the query (Section 2), was annotated separately by a pool of four different annotators, with each query being annotated by at least two annotators on a 5-level Likert scale ranging from 1 (non-relevant) to 5 (highly relevant). Annotation disagreement were resolved by a standard adjudication process. The final relevance score is obtained by taking the arithmetic mean across all annotations, leading to the final relevance metric $rel \in [1-5]_{\mathbb{R}}$.

We depict the distribution of the annotation scores in the box-plot in Figure 2. The relevance scores indicate that the absolute majority of entities is not relevant. Furthermore, there are only a few highly relevant entities in our dataset. This is a result of our annotation guidelines, which require entities to be marked as highly relevant only if they clearly satisfy the information need expressed in the query. As a result of this, the relevance judgments provided by humans annotators are rather strict. In the case of the query Argentine British relations, for instance, the entity `Falklands_War` receives a high relevance score (5). `Argentina`, instead is annotated only with a mildly relevant score (3.3) because, while being relevant w.r.t. query, it does not actually answer the question about the relationship between both countries.

REWQ-ClueWeb: We use a second dataset to benchmark our ranking problem from a different, yet complementary perspective. We build upon TREC Web 2013/2014 with the ClueWeb12 corpus, since it is an established dataset. It furthermore comes with a set of publicly available entity annotations, namely the FACC1 dataset [17], which allows us to evaluate our approach in another setting by using a entity linker other than KBBridge [7]. Instead of focusing, as in REWQ-Robust, on some specific subset of queries like the top-performing ones from EQFE [8], it is based on a random subset of 22 queries from TREC Web2013/2014. For each query the (entity-agnostic) Sequential Dependency Model [31], implemented in the Galago search toolkit, is used to retrieve the top 20 documents, thus leaving out the effects and potential gains given by EQFE's entity-linked documents. The final dataset consists of all entities per query – we heuristically filter out those entities occurring less than three times to remove many spurious entities from the data. This way we relax the REWQ-Robust's assumption of using only the top-*k* entities per query. Entity relevance is finally annotated in a standard (e.g, TREC-style) way using binary relevance judgments (again, we use the definition of relevance as in Section 2).

[4]`http://lemurproject.org/clueweb12/`

[5]`http://rewq.dswlab.de`

5. EXPERIMENTS

5.1 Evaluation Metrics

We use normalized discounted cumulative gain (NDCG) [23] as evaluation metric for both datasets, so as to capture the intuition that a higher relevance should be honored by higher rank. We additionally report Mean Average Precision (MAP) [41] when evaluating against binary relevance judgments using the REWQ-ClueWeb data. The values are computed with the TREC Evaluation tool[6] and reported in the following as the arithmetic mean over all queries.

5.2 Experimental Settings

We evaluate our approach using all features from Section 3 within two learning-to-rank methods: (a) the SVM^{rank} implementation from Joachims [25] and (b) the coordinate ascent methods as implemented in RankLib. Evaluation for both methods and datasets is performed with a linear 5-fold cross-validation. Parameter tuning for the SVM is done with an additional, random train-validation split, i.e. 3/5 training data, 1/5 parameter validation data, and 1/5 test data. For each fold, features are individually normalized with $x_{norm} = (x - \mu)/\sigma$, where mean μ and standard deviation σ are computed using only the training data folds. We compare the learned feature combinations against the following methods:

Mention Frequency (*MenFreqIdf*): A ranking consisting only of the idf-weighted mention frequency feature. This feature's individual performance comes primarily from the quality of the initial document retrieval: Relevant documents should contain relevant entities. In case the entity linker provides more than one entity per mention (as for the REWQ Robust04 dataset with KBBridge), we take this ranked list of candidate entities into account by replacing the mention frequency ($\mathrm{tf}_q(e)$) with the total reciprocal rank (TRR):

$$\mathrm{tf}_q(e) = \mathrm{TRR}_q(e) = \sum_{d \in D(q)} \sum_{m} \frac{1}{rank_{e,m,d}}$$

Ranking by TRR combines the frequency of occurrence of the mentions with the entity linker's confidence scores on the linking of the mentions to their entities.

Wikipedia Fulltext Index (*WikiSDM*): A ranking based on the scores from a Sequential Dependency Model [31] retrieved from a retrieval index of Wikipedia text (using weight parameters from Dalton et al [8]). This baseline is closest in spirit to INEX-like entity retrieval from Wikipedia [26] and is the alternative to our approach of issuing the query against a document retrieval system and then

[6]Version 9.0; `http://trec.nist.gov/trec_eval/`

Table 1: Evaluation results for REWQ Robust dataset. We report differences w.r.t. the best performing reference method (here WikiSDM), statistically significant improvements are denoted with † (paired t-test p-value ≤ 0.05).

Method	ndcg	Δ%	ndcg10	Δ%
RankLib	0.936	†3.7	0.817	†11.6
SVM (w/ SK)	0.926	†2.6	0.804	†9.7
SVM (w/o SK)	0.923	2.2	0.796	†8.7
WikiSDM	0.903	0.0	0.733	0.0
MenFrqIdf	0.885	-2.0	0.694	-5.3
WikiPR	0.778	-13.8	0.440	-40.0

link the document to the knowledge base instead of querying the knowledge base directly.

Wikipedia PageRank (*WikiPR*): A ranking obtained by applying the (unpersonalized) PageRank algorithm to the link structure of Wikipedia, thus ranking entities by their global authoritativeness.

5.3 Results on the REWQ-Robust Dataset

We present our results in Table 1, where we compare three learning-to-rank models – namely, SVM-rank with (w/ SK) and without the Semantic Kernel (w/o SK) from Section 3.6, as well as the coordinate ascent model from RankLib. All reference methods (MenFrqIdf, WikiSDM, and WikiPR) achieve high NDCG scores, with WikiSDM performing best with slightly above 0.9. This indicates that they all provide hard-to-beat methods to benchmark our learning-to-rank approach against. The low performance of WikiPR, in contrast, suggests that authoritativeness correlates, in our setting, only marginally with entity relevance (0.096 Spearman's rank correlation coefficient). Error analysis reveals that entities ranked high by PageRank were very general ones linked to by many other entities, e.g. `Earth`, `United_States`, etc.. When comparing the reference methods, we observe that the best results are obtained when ranking using the Sequential Dependency Model (WikiSDM), an approach that has been shown to perform well in the context of the INEX competitions.

Finally, we observe that our learning-to-rank methods outperform all reference methods, thus reaching an overall NDCG score of 0.936 – the difference is statistically significant (according to a paired t-test, p-value $\leq \alpha = 0.05$). By re-ranking the entities with our method, we gain up to 3.7% in NDCG over the input ordering (MenFrqIdf), even though we have 'only' 50 entities per query. Among the different rankers, RankLib performs better than SVM-rank, with the semantic kernel (w/ SK) improving the SVM-rank results slightly (+.003 in NDCG).

When looking at the NDCG@10 scores, we observe the same trends on larger scale. That is, i) our supervised rankers beat all reference methods, which nevertheless achieve a very competitive performance, with WikiSDM ranking highest among them; ii) RankLib outperforms SVM-rank, which achieves better scores when using a semantic kernel. The larger relative improvements between baselines and supervised rankers suggests that our feature-based approach makes a difference in particular to move the relevant entities from the long tail into the top ten.

Narrative evaluation. To provide more insights into the actual method output, Table 3 shows the results obtained from RankLib for queries from REWQ-Robust. Queries are sorted by the average ground truth values (*gt*) for the top 3 entities, thus showing queries with meaningful entities at the top. Among the top queries we find e.g poliomyelitis and post polio, for which we are able to retrieve expected and relevant, but not surprising entities like `Poliomyelitis`, `Polio_vaccine` or `Jonas Salk`, resulting in an NDCG@10 score of 0.879. Another interesting query with a very high NDCG@10 of 0.931 is territorial waters dispute, for which not so well-known, yet relevant entities like `United_Nations_Convention_on_the_Law_of_the_Sea` are ranked high, as well as examples of specific water disputes taking place in the Mediterranean Sea (`Aegean_dispute`) and the Pacific Ocean (`Kuril_Islands_dispute`). The query on the bottom, agoraphobia, has a low *gt* value because the initial document retrieval in combination with the entity linking could not obtain any really useful entities besides `Charles_M._Schulz`.

Error analysis on the low-performing queries reveals that our method suffers from errors in the entity links. For the query Argentine British relations, for instance, the top retrieved entity is `Argentina_rugby_union_team`, which is actually an artifact of systematic errors from the entity linking system, which incorrectly links mentions like Argentine or Argentina to the national rugby team, and not to the country (`Argentina`). This suggests that a better entity linking could further boost our performance. Another source of errors comes from the retrieval system itself – e.g., low performance on the query agoraphobia comes from the rather noisy pool of documents we start with to collect potentially relevant entities. Finally, low performance on some queries are due to their degree of difficulty, as highlighted by fine-grained queries for very specific domains (e.g., hydroponics), where additional knowledge could potentially help.

Table 2: Evaluation results for REWQ ClueWeb12 dataset. We report differences w.r.t. the best performing reference method (here MenFrqIdf), statistically significant improvements are denoted with † (paired t-test p-value ≤ 0.05).

	map	Δ%	ndcg	Δ%	ndcg10	Δ%
RankLib	0.328	†9.0	0.572	†3.4	0.710	†10.0
SVM (w/ SK)	0.278	-7.8	0.545	-1.6	0.646	0.1
SVM (w/o SK)	0.308	2.2	0.563	1.6	0.675	4.4
MenFrqIdf	0.301	0.0	0.554	0.0	0.646	0.0
WikiSDM	0.234	-22.3	0.515	-7.0	0.613	-5.1
WikiPR	0.075	-75.1	0.328	-40.8	0.126	-80.5

5.4 Results on REWQ-ClueWeb Dataset

In Table 2 we report our results on the ClueWeb12 portion of the REWQ dataset. Similar to the Robust04 results, the single features perform quite well on their own. In contrast to the Robust dataset, the best single feature is the MenFrqIdf features. Again, our learning-to-rank approach outperforms all reference methods consistently across all measures, both when using RankLib and SVM-rank (up to +9.0% MAP, +3.4% NDCG, +10.0% NDCG@10).

Also in line with the Robust04 findings, the greater relative improvements of our method for the NDCG@10 value suggest that our features make a difference in particular for the top ranked entities. The performance of the SVM with Semantic Kernel (w/ SK) is worse in contrast, the MAP and NDCG scores are even below the MenFrqIdf feature. Because the NDCG@10 value is at par with the MenFrqIdf, we suspect that the knowledge base links between entities used by the Semantic Kernel are only helpful for the top entities - but fail when ranking within the long tail. Another factor is most likely the fact that this dataset has only binary annotations, and is thus not as fine grained as the 1-5 Likert scale of the REWQ Robust04 ground truth. All in all, we take these results to be additional evidence for our previous findings.

Table 3: List of all REWQ Robust04 queries sorted by average ground truth scores for top 3 entities (*gt*). Also showing the NDCG@10 score (*ndcg*) and the top-3 entities as retrieved by the RankLib coordinate ascent method (using the complete set of features). Ground truth values in brackets; abbreviated entities are denoted with *.

gt	ndcg	query	top-1 entity	top-2 entity	top-3 entity
5.0	.895	schengen agreement	Schengen_Agreement (5)	Schengen_Area (5)	Schengen_Inform._Sys. (5)
5.0	.894	magnetic levitation maglev	Maglev (5)	Shanghai_Maglev_Train (5)	Transrapid (5)
4.8	.931	territorial waters dispute	UN_Law_of_Sea* (4.3)	Aegean_dispute (5)	Kuril_Islands_dispute (5)
4.7	.865	el nino	El_Nino-Southern_Oscillation (5)	Pacific_Ocean (4)	La_Nina (5)
4.3	.942	ferry sinkings	MS_Estonia (5)	MS_Herald_of_Free_Enterprise (5)	Silja_Line (3)
4.3	.927	in vitro fertilization	In_vitro_fertilisation (5)	Fertility_clinic (5)	Shan_Ratnam (3)
4.3	.879	poliomyelitis and post polio	Poliomyelitis (4.5)	Polio_vaccine (4.5)	Jonas_Salk (4)
4.3	.787	osteoporosis	Hormone_therapy* (5)	Estrogen (5)	Nutrition (3)
4.0	.803	industrial espionage	Volkswagen (4)	General_Motors (4)	Opel (4)
3.8	.863	polygamy polyandry polygyny	Al-Arqam (4.5)	Code_of_Personal_Status_(Tunisia) (4.5)	Tunisia (2.5)
3.3	.769	amazon rain forest	Amazon_rainforest (5)	Manaus (2)	Amazon_Basin (3)
3.3	.748	argentine british relations	Foreign_relations_of_Argent. (4)	Argentina_national_rugby_team* (1)	Falklands_War (5)
3.2	.751	antarctica exploration	South_Pole (3.3)	Antarctica (4)	Antarctic_ecozone (2.3)
2.8	.860	supercritical fluids	Supercritical_fluid (5)	Euler_equations_(fluid_dyn)* (2.5)	Biodegradation (1)
2.8	.760	computer viruses	Michelangelo_(cmpt_virus)* (5)	Personal_computer (2)	Computer_industry (1.5)
2.7	.836	lyme disease	Lyme_disease (5)	Centers_for_Disease_Control* (2)	Old_Lyme,_Connecticut (1)
2.7	.669	falkland petroleum exploration	Falkland_Islands (4.3)	Falklands_War (2.7)	Stanley,_Falkland_Islands (1)
2.5	.739	hydroponics	NASA (4)	Jordan (1)	Mars (2.5)
2.3	.868	killer bee attacks	Africanized_bee (3)	Ceratitis_capitata (2)	San_Diego (2)
2.3	.831	implant dentistry	Dentistry (4)	Cochlear_implant (1)	Uni_of_Med_&_Dent_NJ* (2)
2.3	.749	agent orange exposure	Agent_Orange (5)	Agent_Orange_(band) (1)	Agent_Orange_(album) (1)
2.3	.718	king hussein peace	Hussein_of_Jordan (4.5)	Abdullah_II_of_Jordan (1)	Black_Septmbr_Jordan* (1.5)
2.0	.672	counterfeiting money	Counterfeit (3)	Los_Angeles (1)	Novosibirsk (2)
2.0	.582	unsolicited faxes	Fax (4)	Personal_computer (1)	ISDN* (1)
1.9	.966	agoraphobia	Charles_M._Schulz (3.3)	Snoopy (1.3)	UGM-27_Polaris (1)

5.5 Feature analysis

To better understand the importance of the different features within our model, we study the individual ranking performance of each feature, and perform a feature ablation study.

Single features as rankers. Analyzing the individual features in isolation, Figure 3 shows the NDCG@10 performance achieved by each feature individually. We find that the mention frequency (MenFrqIdf) and the Wikipedia fulltext search (WikiSDM) both perform individually well as ranking metric for both datasets. For the REWQ-Robust dataset, WikiSDM is the highest performing feature. Since we are only re-ranking the most frequent entity mentions in high-ranked documents, the WikiSDM method is filtered by a very effective whitelist. This confirms our intuition that entities which occur often in relevant documents are themselves relevant, but also that ranking entities based on their Wikipedia article according to WikiSDM is a non-negligible indicator. All context-based query-mention-features (indicated by prefix *C_*) perform worse than their no-context counterparts (indicated by prefix *M_*), e.g. C_GloSum vs. M_GloSum, thus letting us question their value for entity ranking.

The contribution of the other query-entity features, which are based on DBpedia, namely Qent and QEntEntSim, are in between – they perform worse than the strong WikiSDM, but better compared to some of the mention-based approaches. On both dataset, QEntEntSim as single feature performs better than the QEnt feature. Since QEntEntSim is leveraging knowledge base paths and ontological types between entities in the query and the documents, these provide a meaningful way to connect otherwise missing entities.

In summary, the high performance of the MenFrIdf features highlights that the candidate generation strategy already provides a useful approach on its own: this finding holds for both datasets despite using different document retrieval and entity linking methods.

Ablation study on Robust04. To further analyze the individual features, we perform a features ablation study: For each single feature, or set of features, we remove it from the set of features available to RankLib, re-train it with the same parameters and compare its performance against the full-feature setting. Results for the Robust04 are reported in Table 4 which is sorted by relative loss caused by removing a feature (group).

Surprisingly, we find that removing all mention-based features (i.e. SED, Jo, Glo for mention and mention context) actually improves the overall performance by 0.1% in NDCG (0.7% in NDCG@10) – however, the differences are small and not statistically significant. This finding might also results from the fact that the MenContext group combines features of different quality: While the string edit distance (SED) is helpful (-1.3% NDCG, -2.8% NDCG@10), we cannot confirm this for the JoBim text features (-0.2% and +0.3%).

The DBpedia-based features (DBpedia) seem to have a positive influence on the overall performance (-1.0% and -1.9%), even though not being statistically significant. Interestingly, removing any of the two DBpedia features QEntEntSim or Qent individually would let to a different conclusion.

The Wikipedia-based features show a strong and significant influence on the overall performance, removing them leads to a drop of -2.3% for NDCG and -5.1% for NDCG@10. The single most important feature is the mention frequency features (MenFrqIdf), thus supporting our assumption that a good initial document retrieval helps to obtain a good pool of relevant candidate entities.

Ablation study on ClueWeb12. The findings for the ClueWeb12 dataset in Table 5 confirm the findings from the Robust04 dataset. Again, leaving out all mention-based features actually improves the performances – but as above, the difference is not statistically significant. On the other end of the table, and also in line with above findings, the mention frequency is the single most important features with rather large differences between 19.7% (MAP) and 6.5% (NDCG).

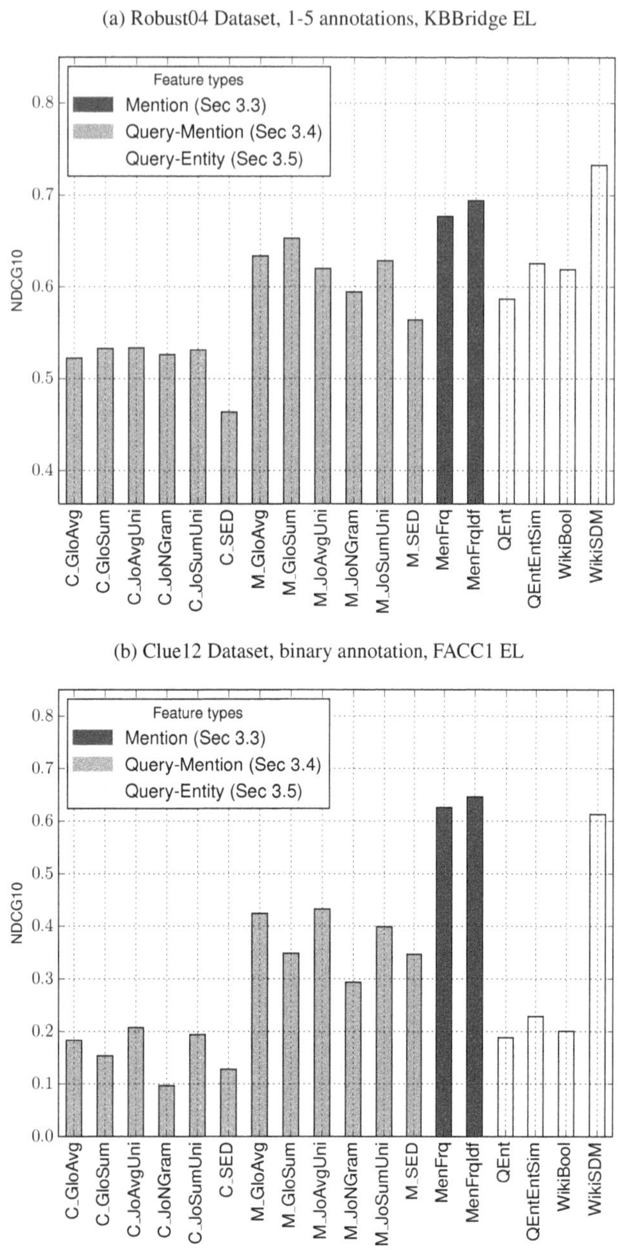

Figure 3: Feature-by-feature analysis for (a) the REWQ-Robust04 and (b) the REWQ ClueWeb12 dataset.

We can also confirm our finding that the simple SED is more effective than the Glove and Jo features. The role of the DBpedia features is slightly different, they seem to be even less helpful for the ClueWeb dataset than for the Robust04 dataset. A possible explanation is the the difference in the annotation method: The binary ClueWeb12 annotations are likely to not capture fine-grained differences between entity relevance levels, which might be expressed by knowledge-base links.

In summary, all findings for this dataset are in line with the findings for the Robust04 data, which is interesting because both datasets are rather different in nature, i.e., different ground truth labels (binary vs. 1-5 scale), different document retrieval (SDM vs. EQFE), and different entity linkers (FACC1 vs. KBBridge).

Table 4: Feature ablation study REWQ Robust04 dataset. Sorted by difference in NDCG value. P-values (p) from two-sided paired t-test ≤ 0.05 are denoted with †.

w/o	ndcg	Δ%	p	ndcg10	Δ%	p
RankLib All	0.936	-	-	0.817	-	-
MenContext	0.937	0.1	0.68	0.823	0.7	0.56
QEntEnt	0.935	-0.1	0.73	0.824	0.8	0.58
Qent	0.934	-0.2	0.58	0.825	0.9	0.44
Jo	0.934	-0.2	0.53	0.819	0.3	0.85
Context	0.933	-0.3	0.28	0.816	-0.1	0.89
Glo	0.928	-0.8	0.10	0.803	-1.7	0.26
DBpedia	0.927	-1.0	0.06	0.802	-1.9	0.21
WikiBool	0.926	-1.1	0.11	0.809	-1.0	0.56
SED	0.924	†-1.3	0.05	0.794	-2.8	0.09
WikiSdm	0.921	†-1.7	0.03	0.781	†-4.4	0.04
MenFrqIdf	0.917	†-2.1	0.04	0.774	†-5.4	0.05
Wikipedia	0.914	†-2.3	0.01	0.776	†-5.1	0.03

Table 5: Feature ablation study on REWQ ClueWeb12 dataset. Sorted by relative difference (Δ) in MAP value. P-values (p) from two-sided paired t-test ≤ 0.05 are denoted with †.

w/o	map	Δ%	p	ndcg	Δ%	p	ndcg10	Δ%	p
RankLib All	.328	-	-	.572	-	-	.711	-	-
MenContext	.333	1.4	.41	.574	0.3	.55	.714	0.5	.70
Jo	.332	1.0	.55	.573	0.2	.69	.716	0.8	.50
DBpedia	.329	0.1	.92	.572	0.0	.90	.701	-1.4	.26
QEntEnt	.327	-0.4	.48	.572	-0.1	.68	.708	-0.4	.64
Context	.326	-0.6	.49	.570	-0.3	.34	.698	-1.7	.06
Glo	.326	-0.7	.51	.571	-0.3	.46	.698	†-1.7	.05
Qent	.326	-0.8	.63	.571	-0.2	.75	.701	-1.4	.32
SED	.326	-0.8	.35	.571	-0.3	.46	.698	-1.8	.15
WikiSdm	.320	-2.6	.25	.566	-1.1	.26	.693	-2.5	.28
WikiBool	.313	†-4.6	.05	.565	-1.3	.08	.670	†-5.7	.01
Wikipedia	.303	†-7.7	.02	.556	†-2.9	.02	.650	†-8.5	.02
MenFrqIdf	.264	†-19.7	.00	.535	†-6.5	.01	.630	†-11.4	.03

6. RELATED WORK

In recent years, there has been a growing interest in research aimed at developing methods to search and rank entities on the web. Starting with the Initiative for the Evaluation of XML Retrieval (INEX) [11] and TREC initiatives [2], the task of entity ranking has gained momentum, and a variety of different approaches have been developed, ranging from natural language interface for XML retrieval and Question Answering over Linked Data ([15, 39, 43], *inter alia*) all the way through open-domain, document-based entity search [13].

Evaluation exercises on entity ranking systems within the INEX evaluation forum have taken place since 2006. Most tracks build upon a definition of entities based on Wikipedia, i.e., every Wikipedia article is a valid entity, which we also use. However, alternative or broader definitions are possible (see, e.g., [2, 13]). The focus on type queries led to the development of systems that leveraged Wikipedia category system – e.g., category overlap [32], or measures capturing the strength of association between terms and category labels [27]. Broadly similar in spirit to our WikiSDM approach, additional structured content from Wikipedia such as links can be also used to perform document retrieval [32, 10]. Wikipedia entities and their categories, in turn, can be used to improve INEX-style entity retrieval [26]. In our work, we also use Wikipedia to define our vocabulary of entities and develop models to rank these entities for keyword queries. However, we also aim to expand the pool of features from a fully-structured knowledge source, and accordingly use facts from DBpedia. Our results indicate that, similarly to the case of a wide range of NLP and IR applications [22] further gains can be obtained by complementing knowledge from text with that from structured knowledge bases like Wikipedia and DBpedia. Knowledge of this kind has been recently exploited also within a feature-based approach to INEX entity ranking [35] and a hybrid approach that combines IR and structured search for Ad-hoc Object Retrieval (AOR) [38].

One of the methods closest to ours is the work of Kaptein and Kamps [26], who also address the problem of retrieving entities for web queries. They assume the availability of type information, either as an explicit category (given by the user) or a latent one that needs to be extracted from the query. Their method accordingly performs a latent estimation of the category, which in a second step is used to select and rank the entities before presentation to the user. In contrast, our goal is to retrieve entities for any (reasonable) web query, including those not posed with the goal of retrieving entities. That is, we crucially depart from the type-centric tasks formulated in the context of INEX and AOR, and embrace a notion of entity relevance which is based on whether a human would talk about this entity when explaining the topic.

The SemSets model [6] also addresses the problem of ranking entities w.r.t. a given keyword query. This approach focuses on type queries, following the entity query classification schema from Pound et al. [34]: in contrast, in this work we look primarily at web queries, which can also, and do in fact often cover one of the "remaining" query types, i.e. untyped relations and keyword queries. Arguably, entity retrieval for type queries has to put more emphasis on the correct interpretation of the query, since the answer crucially requires the intended target type to be correctly recognized. In contrast, we do not limit our approach to queries of specific types, and accordingly leverage instead type-agnostic methods such as, for instance, our DBpedia graph exploration method. Perhaps interestingly, Ciglan et al. mention in their work that for a type query, a "human user would probably enter such a query to a web search engine and inspect several top-k results and [...] search the text of the inspected documents to find the desired set of entities" [6, p. 131]. This is exactly the pipeline we created in this work to solve our entity ranking problem.

The question of ranking entities from documents, which we implicitly touch by ranking entities from the search result documents, is addressed in recent work from Dunietz and Gillick, who define the task of "entity salience [as] assigning a relevance score to each entity in a document" [13]. However, even though our method could also be used for entity ranking at the document level, we take here a query-centric view of the problem. That is, we rank entities from the whole collection of retrieved documents because we aim at ranking entities w.r.t. the query, and not w.r.t. the individual documents. In doing this, we follow the 'traditional' INEX-style Wikipedia-based definition of entities. This makes it possible for us to leverage a Wikipedia-based resource such as DBpedia in a straightforward way, and evaluate the contribution of a wide-coverage knowledge base for our problem. An 'open' definition of entities, like the one found in [13], instead, opens up new problems such as how to detect and include new entities into the background knowledge base: although recently there have been attempts to address this problem at web scale [20], we leave this issue for future work.

7. CONCLUSIONS

In this work, we addressed the problem of ranking entities for open-domain web queries, starting with the query-relevant documents retrieved by a state of-the-art document retrieval system. We investigated the performance of a variety of heterogeneous features, which were combined by two learning-to-rank methods. Our results indicate that query-relevant documents with entity links provide a complementary source of information to direct knowledge base (e.g., Wikipedia) retrieval, yielding an NDCG@10 score on Robust04 of over 0.82, compared to 0.73 for Wikipedia retrieval. Together with the frequency of entity links within the retrieved documents (0.68 NDCG@10), Wikipedia retrieval is one of the strongest individual features. For most other results of the ablation study we cannot find significant differences. For example, we cannot find a unique significant contribution of features based on distributional similarity for this task (JoBimText and GloVE). Likewise, incorporating relations between entities does not yield a measurable benefit (QEntEnt and Semantic Kernel). This finding is in spite of the benefit of directly matched query entities (QEnt), which is another strong signal. Nevertheless, combining all these signals together within a supervised learning framework is able to yield statistically significant improvements over ranking by single features, so as to yield competitive NDCG scores.

Our method relies on the performance of the underlying document retrieval and entity linking systems. While error analysis revealed that our ranking suffers from systematic errors from these two components, our NDCG scores on both datasets – which use different document retrieval and entity linking systems – indicate that our supervised approach is nevertheless able to cope with the noise in the input data.

We view our work as a first step that opens up new opportunities for the development of advanced entity-rich search engines. This is because, arguably, humans tend to think in terms of entities, like persons, places, or organizations when it comes to complex topics. Consequently, entity ranking for Web queries could play a key role in many high-end applications, including entity-centric search [9], topic page generation [1], as well as new approaches to browsable search interfaces [12] that aim at including relevant documents, entities and ontological types, together with textual evidence for how entities are connected to the query, in the search results.

Acknowledgments

This work was partially funded by the Deutsche Forschungsgemeinschaft within the JOIN-T project (research grant PO 1900/1-1). Part of the computational resources used for this work were provided by an Amazon AWS in Education Grant award and the bwUniCluster (funded by the bwHPC program of the state of Baden-Württemberg, Germany). We thank Christian Meilicke for his contributions and the anonymous reviewers for their helpful comments.

Downloads

In order to encourage further research on the topic of retrieving entities for open-domain queries, we make our gold standard annotation for the Robust04 and the TREC Web (ClueWeb12) datasets freely available at `http://rewq.dwslab.de` under a Creative Commons (by-nc-sa, 4.0) license.

8. REFERENCES

[1] N. Balasubramanian and S. Cucerzan. Beyond ranked lists in web search: Aggregating web content into topic pages. *International Journal of Semantic Computing*, 4(4):509–534, 2010.

[2] K. Balog, A. P. de Vries, P. Serdyukov, P. Thomas, and T. Westerveld. Overview of the TREC 2009 entity track. In *Proc. of TREC-09*, 2010.

[3] C. Biemann and M. Riedl. Text: Now in 2D! A framework for lexical expansion with contextual similarity. *Journal of Language Modelling*, 1:55–95, 2013.

[4] C. Bizer, J. Lehmann, G. Kobilarov, S. Auer, C. Becker, R. Cyganiak, and S. Hellmann. DBpedia – A Crystallization Point for the Web of Data. *Journal of Web Semantics*, 7(3), 2009.

[5] S. Bloehdorn, R. Basili, M. Cammisa, and A. Moschitti. Semantic kernels for text classification based on topological measures of feature similarity. In *Proc. of ICDM'06*, pages 808–812, 2006.

[6] M. Ciglan, K. Nørvåg, and L. Hluchý. The SemSets model for ad-hoc semantic list search. In *Proc. of WWW'12*, pages 131–140, 2012.

[7] J. Dalton and L. Dietz. A neighborhood relevance model for entity linking. In *Proc. of OAIR-13*, pages 149–156, 2013.

[8] J. Dalton, L. Dietz, and J. Allan. Entity query feature expansion using knowledge base links. In *Proc. of SIGIR-14*, pages 365–374, 2014.

[9] N. Dalvi, R. Kumar, B. Pang, R. Ramakrishnan, A. Tomkins, P. Bohannon, S. Keerthi, and S. Merugu. A web of concepts. In *Proc. of PODS '09*, pages 1–12, 2009.

[10] G. Demartini, C. S. Firan, T. Iofciu, R. Krestel, and W. Nejdl. Why finding entities in Wikipedia is difficult, sometimes. *Information Retrieval*, 13(5):534–567, 2010.

[11] G. Demartini, T. Iofciu, and A. P. de Vries. Overview of the INEX 2009 entity ranking track. In *Proc. of INEX*, pages 254–264, 2009.

[12] L. Dietz, M. Schuhmacher, and S. Ponzetto. Queripidia: Query-specific Wikipedia construction. In *Proc. of AKBC-14*, 2014.

[13] J. Dunietz and D. Gillick. A new entity salience task with millions of training examples. In *Proc. of EACL-14*, pages 205–209, 2014.

[14] O. Egozi, S. Markovitch, and E. Gabrilovich. Concept-based information retrieval using Explicit Semantic Analysis. *ACM Transactions on Information Systems*, 29(2):8:1–8:34, 2011.

[15] S. Elbassuoni, M. Ramanath, R. Schenkel, M. Sydow, and G. Weikum. Language-model-based ranking for queries on RDF-graphs. In *Proc. of CIKM-09*, pages 977–986, 2009.

[16] P. Ferragina and U. Scaiella. Fast and accurate annotation of short texts with Wikipedia pages. *IEEE Software*, 29(1):70–75, 2012.

[17] E. Gabrilovich, M. Ringgaard, and A. Subramanya. Facc1: Freebase annotation of ClueWeb corpora, version 1, 2013.

[18] R. Gupta, A. Halevy, X. Wang, S. Whang, and F. Wu. Biperpedia: An ontology for search applications. In *Proc. of PVLDB-14*, pages 505–516, 2014.

[19] S. Gurajada, J. Kamps, A. Mishra, R. Schenkel, M. Theobald, and Q. Wang. Overview of the INEX 2013 linked data track. In *Working Notes for CLEF 2013*, 2013.

[20] J. Hoffart, Y. Altun, and G. Weikum. Discovering emerging entities with ambiguous names. In *Proc. of WWW-14*, pages 385–396, 2014.

[21] J. Hoffart, D. Milchevski, and G. Weikum. STICS: Searching with Strings, Things, and Cats. In *Proc. of SIGIR-14*, pages 1247–1248, 2014.

[22] E. Hovy, R. Navigli, and S. P. Ponzetto. Collaboratively built semi-structured content and Artificial Intelligence: The story so far. *Artificial Intelligence*, 194:2–27, 2013.

[23] K. Järvelin and J. Kekäläinen. IR evaluation methods for retrieving highly relevant documents. In *Proc. of SIGIR-00*, pages 41–48, 2000.

[24] T. Joachims. Optimizing search engines using clickthrough data. In *Proc. of SIGKDD-02*, pages 133–142, 2002.

[25] T. Joachims. Training linear SVMs in linear time. In *Proc. of SIGKDD-06*, pages 217–226, 2006.

[26] R. Kaptein and J. Kamps. Exploiting the category structure of Wikipedia for entity ranking. *Artificial Intelligence*, 194:111–129, 2013.

[27] R. Kaptein, P. Serdyukov, A. P. de Vries, and J. Kamps. Entity ranking using Wikipedia as a pivot. In *Proc. of CIKM-10*, pages 69–78, 2010.

[28] V. I. Levenshtein. Binary codes capable of correcting spurious insertions and deletions of ones. *Problems of Information Transmission*, 1:8–17, 1965.

[29] T.-Y. Liu. *Learning to rank for information retrieval.* Springer-Verlag, Berlin, 2011.

[30] D. Metzler and W. Bruce Croft. Linear feature-based models for information retrieval. *Information Retrieval*, 10(3):257–274, 2007.

[31] D. Metzler and W. B. Croft. A markov random field model for term dependencies. In *Proc. of SIGIR-05*, pages 472–479, 2005.

[32] J. Pehcevski, A.-M. Vercoustre, and J. A. Thom. Exploiting locality of Wikipedia links in entity ranking. In *Proc. of ECIR-08*, pages 258–269, 2008.

[33] J. Pennington, R. Socher, and C. D. Manning. GloVe: Global vectors for word representation. In *Proc. of EMNLP-2014*, pages 1532–1543, 2014.

[34] J. Pound, P. Mika, and H. Zaragoza. Ad-hoc object retrieval in the web of data. In *Proc. of WWW-10*, pages 771–780, 2010.

[35] H. Raviv, D. Carmel, and O. Kurland. A ranking framework for entity oriented search using markov random fields. In *Proc. of JIWES '12*, pages 1–6, 2012.

[36] M. Schuhmacher and S. P. Ponzetto. Knowledge-based graph document modeling. In *Proc. of WSDM-14*, pages 543–552, 2014.

[37] M. Surdeanu, M. Ciaramita, and H. Zaragoza. Learning to rank answers to non-factoid questions from web collections. *Computational Linguistics*, 37(2):351–383, 2011.

[38] A. Tonon, G. Demartini, and P. Cudré-Mauroux. Combining inverted indices and structured search for ad-hoc object retrieval. In *Proc. of SIGIR-12*, pages 125–134. ACM, 2012.

[39] C. Unger, L. Bühmann, J. Lehmann, A.-C. Ngonga Ngomo, D. Gerber, and P. Cimiano. Template-based question answering over RDF data. In *Proc. of WWW-12*, pages 639–648, 2012.

[40] E. M. Voorhees. The TREC robust retrieval track. In *ACM SIGIR Forum*, volume 39, pages 11–20, 2005.

[41] E. M. Voorhees and D. K. Harman. *TREC: Experiment and Evaluation in Information Retrieval.* The MIT Press, 2005.

[42] W. Wu, H. Li, H. Wang, and K. Zhu. Probase: A probabilistic taxonomy for text understanding. In *Proc. of SIGMOD-12*, pages 481–492, 2012.

[43] N. Zhiltsov and E. Agichtein. Improving entity search over linked data by modeling latent semantics. In *Proc. of CIKM-13*, pages 1253–1256, 2013.

What Is a Network Community? A Novel Quality Function and Detection Algorithms

Atsushi Miyauchi
Tokyo Institute of Technology
Tokyo, Japan
miyauchi.a.aa@m.titech.ac.jp

Yasushi Kawase
Tokyo Institute of Technology
Tokyo, Japan
kawase.y.ab@m.titech.ac.jp

ABSTRACT

In this study, we introduce a novel quality function for a network community, which we refer to as the *communitude*. The communitude has a strong statistical background. Specifically, it measures the Z-score of a subset of vertices S with respect to the fraction of the number of edges within the subgraph induced by S. Due to the null model of a random graph used in the definition, our quality function focuses not only on the inside of the subgraph but also on the cut edges, unlike some quality functions for extracting dense subgraphs. To evaluate the detection ability of our quality function, we address the communitude maximization problem and its variants for realistic scenarios. For the problems, we propose a two-phase heuristic algorithm together with some modified versions. In the first phase, it repeatedly removes the vertex with the smallest degree, and then obtains the subgraph with maximum communitude over the iterations. In the second phase, the algorithm improves the obtained solution using a simple local search heuristic. This algorithm runs in linear time when the number of iterations is fixed to a constant; thus, it is applicable to massive graphs. Computational experiments using both synthetic graphs and real-world networks demonstrate the validity and reliability of the proposed quality function and algorithms.

Categories and Subject Descriptors

H.2.8 [**Database Management**]: Database Applications—*Data Mining*; I.5.3 [**Pattern Recognition**]: Clustering—*Algorithms*; G.2.2 [**Discrete Mathematics**]: Graph Theory—*Graph Algorithms*

General Terms

Algorithms, Experimentation, Theory

Keywords

Networks; Community Structure; Quality Function

Permission to make digital or hard copies of all or part of this work for personal or classroom use is granted without fee provided that copies are not made or distributed for profit or commercial advantage and that copies bear this notice and the full citation on the first page. Copyrights for components of this work owned by others than ACM must be honored. Abstracting with credit is permitted. To copy otherwise, or republish, to post on servers or to redistribute to lists, requires prior specific permission and/or a fee. Request permissions from Permissions@acm.org.
CIKM'15, October 19–23, 2015, Melbourne, Australia.
© 2015 ACM. ISBN 978-1-4503-3794-6/15/10 ...$15.00.
DOI: http://dx.doi.org/10.1145/2806416.2806555.

1. INTRODUCTION

Identifying community structure is a fundamental primitive in network analysis [14]. Roughly speaking, a *community* (also referred to as a *module* or *cluster*) in a network is a subset of vertices more densely connected with each other than with nodes in the rest of the network. Communities often appear in networked systems from a wide variety of fields such as physics, chemistry, biology, and sociology. Detecting communities is a powerful way to discover components that have some special roles or possess important functions. For example, let us consider the network representing the World Wide Web, where vertices correspond to web pages and edges represent the hyperlinks between pages. As mentioned in Gibson et al. [16], communities in this network are likely to be the sets of web pages dealing with the same or similar topics, or sometimes link spam. As another example, consider the protein–protein interaction networks, where vertices correspond to proteins within a cell and edges represent the interactions between proteins. Communities in this network are likely to be the grouped proteins that have the same or similar functions within the cell [39].

A large body of work has been devoted to developing community detection algorithms, which can be roughly divided into two categories. First, there are methods that divide a network, most of which maximize a globally-defined quality function. The best known and widely used quality function is *modularity*, which was introduced by Newman and Girvan [34]. Here let $G = (V, E)$ be an undirected graph consisting of $n = |V|$ vertices and $m = |E|$ edges. For a subset of vertices $S \subseteq V$, let $D[S]$ denote the sum of degrees of the vertices in S. Also, let $G[S]$ be the subgraph induced by $S \subseteq V$, i.e., $G[S] = (S, E(S))$, where $E(S) = \{\{i,j\} \in E \mid i,j \in S\}$. For simplicity, we denote $e[S] = |E(S)|$. The modularity, a quality function for a division $\mathcal{C} = \{C_1, \ldots, C_k\}$ of V (i.e., $\bigcup_{i=1}^{k} C_i = V$ and $C_i \cap C_j = \emptyset$ for $i \neq j$), can be written as

$$Q(\mathcal{C}) = \sum_{C \in \mathcal{C}} \left(\frac{e[C]}{m} - \left(\frac{D[C]}{2m} \right)^2 \right). \qquad (1)$$

This quantity represents the sum, over all communities, of the fraction of the number of edges within the communities minus the expected fraction of such edges assuming that they are placed at random with the same degree distribution. There are a wide variety of modularity maximization algorithms based on greedy techniques [8, 34], spectral optimization [33], mathematical programming [2, 4, 31], and other techniques.

Second, there are methods that extract one community (a subset of vertices) from a network. We focus on this category in the present study. Most of these methods also maximize a quality function for a subset of vertices $S \subseteq V$ that *well* captures the intuition of a network community. Here define the *edge density* of $S \subseteq V$ as $\delta[S] = e[S]/\binom{|S|}{2}$. On the other hand, define the cut edges of $S \subseteq V$ as the subset of edges whose one endpoint is in S and the other is in $V \setminus S$, and let $\mathrm{cut}(S)$ denote the number of cut edges of S. Intuitively, quality functions for a network community should prefer a subset of vertices that maximizes the edge density but minimizes the number of cut edges *at a time*. To date, a large body of work has examined preferable concepts of a network community. Below we briefly review the traditional and state-of-the-art ones (and their corresponding optimization problems) from various research fields such as discrete mathematics, computer science, and physics.

Cliques. The most fundamental and well-known concept is a clique. A *clique* is a subset of vertices in which every pair of vertices is connected by an edge. As even a singleton or an edge is a clique, we are usually interested in finding a *maximum clique* or a *maximal clique*, i.e., cliques with the maximum size in a graph and cliques not contained in any other clique in a graph, respectively. Finding a maximum clique is one of the most classical optimization problems in the field of theoretical computer science, which is known to be NP-hard and also hard to approximate. In fact, it is known that under some reasonable computational complexity assumption, there exists no polynomial-time algorithm that achieves an approximation ratio of $O(n^{1-\varepsilon})$ for any $\varepsilon > 0$ [19]. As for maximal cliques, Makino and Uno [28] proposed efficient enumerative algorithms.

Quasi-Cliques. Although the definition of a clique is quite intuitive, it is too strong and restrictive to use practically. In fact, if an input graph is incorrect so that some edges are missing, it might happen that the subset of vertices that should be a clique is not a clique. If it is the case, we could no longer recover the subset of vertices by detecting a clique. On the other hand, the concept of quasi-cliques is more robust. A subset of vertices $S \subseteq V$ is called an *α-quasi-clique* if $e[S] \geq \alpha\binom{|S|}{2}$. There are many algorithms for computing quasi-cliques. For example, Abello et al. [1] proposed an algorithm for finding a maximal quasi-clique in massive sparse graphs. Moreover, Uno [42] designed a fast algorithm for enumerating all α-quasi-cliques.

Densest Subgraphs. Let us define the *average degree* of $S \subseteq V$ as $2e[S]/|S|$. The *densest subgraph* is a subset of vertices with the maximum average degree in a graph. The densest subgraph has attracted significant attention because it can be computed in time polynomial in n and m using flow-based algorithm [18] or a linear-programming-based algorithm [10]. Furthermore, Charikar [10] proved that the linear-time greedy algorithm proposed by Asahiro et al. [6] finds a 1/2-approximate solution.

The densest subgraph problem does not have any constraint on the number of vertices of the output subgraph. The densest k-subgraph problem (DkS) can be viewed as a size-constrained variant [13]. In this problem, given an additional input k being a positive integer, we are asked to find $S \subseteq V$ that maximizes average degree $2e[S]/|S|$ under the restriction $|S| = k$. Unfortunately, it is known that such size restriction makes the problem much harder to solve. In

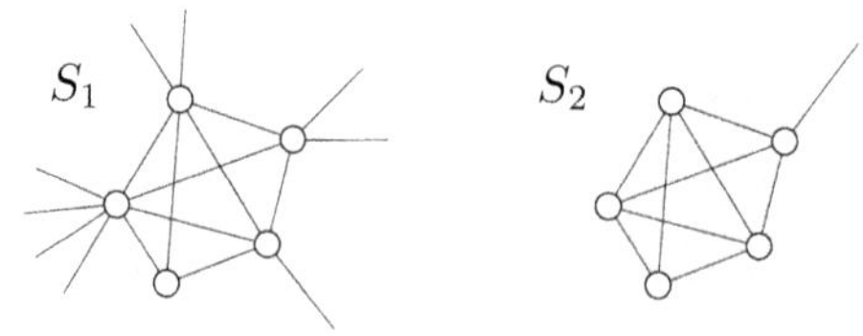

Figure 1: Two subgraphs in a network. Which one is more community-like?

fact, Khot [20] demonstrated that no PTAS exists for DkS under some reasonable computational complexity assumption. The current best approximation ratio is $O(n^{1/4+\varepsilon})$ for any $\varepsilon > 0$ [7]. Recently, Papailiopoulos et al. [35] proposed an almost linear-time approximation algorithm whose approximation ratio depends on the spectrum of the adjacency matrix of the input graph. They experimentally confirmed that the ratio is usually tight for real-world networks.

Furthermore, Andersen and Chellapilla [5] introduced two relaxed versions of DkS: the densest at-least-k subgraph problem (Dal$k$S) and the densest at-most-k subgraph problem (Dam$k$S). They proposed a greedy 1/3-approximation algorithm for Dal$k$S. Note that the NP-hardness of Dam$k$S is immediate because finding a maximum clique can be reduced to it. Later, Khuller and Saha [21] demonstrated that Dal$k$S is also NP-hard and improved the above approximation ratio to 1/2 using a linear-programming-based algorithm.

Optimal Quasi-Cliques. As mentioned above, the densest subgraph problem is attractive because it can be solved in polynomial time and can be approximated within a factor of 1/2 in linear time. In fact, it has been one of the most popular optimization problems for finding communities (or dense subgraphs) in practical applications. However, as reported in Tsourakakis et al. [41], the densest subgraph problem often leads to a large subgraph without high edge density. This should not be surprising since the densest subgraph problem just maximizes the average degree rather than the edge density.

Motivated by this issue, Tsourakakis et al. [41] proposed a general framework for finding subgraphs with very high edge density. As a special case of the framework, they introduced an optimization problem called the OQC-Problem. In this problem, given an undirected graph $G = (V, E)$, we are asked to find $S \subseteq V$ that maximizes

$$\mathrm{OQC}(S) = e[S] - \alpha\binom{|S|}{2},$$

where α is a parameter in the interval $(0, 1)$. The optimal solution to this problem is referred to as the *optimal quasi-clique*. Note that the OQC-Problem turns the α-quasi-clique condition into its objective function. Their computational experiments show that the OQC-Problem with $\alpha = 1/3$ leads to subgraphs with very high edge density and small diameter, unlike the densest subgraph problem.

Ratio Cut. All the above definitions and quality functions focus only on the inside of the subgraph. Thus, they could not distinguish two subgraphs in Figure 1. From now on, we review the definitions and quality functions that take into account the cut edges. The first example is the *ratio cut*, which is defined as

$$\phi_{\mathrm{R}}(S) = \frac{\mathrm{cut}(S)}{|S| \cdot |V \setminus S|}$$

for $S \subset V$. The ratio cut was introduced for circuit partitioning [43], and its minimization is known to be NP-hard [29].

Normalized Cut. The *normalized cut* of $S \subseteq V$ is defined as

$$\phi_{\mathrm{N}}(S) = \frac{\mathrm{cut}(S)}{D[S]}.$$

The normalized cut was proposed for image segmentation [37], and its minimization is also NP-hard [37]. Note that the normalized cut takes into account the number of edges within the subgraph $G[S]$, whereas the ratio cut does not.

Conductance. The *conductance* of $S \subset V$ is defined as

$$\phi(S) = \frac{\mathrm{cut}(S)}{\min\{D[S], D[V \setminus S]\}}.$$

Note that S is usually assumed to contain no more than half of the vertices in V. In the context of community detection, the conductance has been used much more widely than the ratio cut and the normalized cut. Indeed, Leskovec et al. [26] employed the conductance for introducing the *network community profile plot* (NCP plot), which describes the quality of network communities at different size scales. Specifically, the NCP plot is defined as the conductance value of the best subset of vertices with cardinality k in the entire network, as a function of k. That is, they plot the following function value for each k:

$$\Phi(k) = \min_{S \subset V : |S| = k} \phi(S). \tag{2}$$

From the resulting plots, they deduced that in many real-world networks, there are significant communities at very small size scales, and at larger size scales, the best possible communities blend in gradually with the rest of the network. Since the above quantity (2) is intractable to compute, they employed well-studied heuristics to approximate it.

Community in a Strong Sense and a Weak Sense. Radicchi et al. [36] introduced some definitions of a community called a community in a strong sense and a community in a weak sense. A subset of vertices $S \subseteq V$ is called a *community in a strong sense* if for every vertex in S, the number of neighbors in S is strictly greater than the number of neighbors outside S. On the other hand, $S \subseteq V$ is called a *community in a weak sense* if the sum, over all vertices in S, of the number of neighbors in S is strictly greater than the number of cut edges of S. Thus, if $S \subseteq V$ is a community in a strong sense, then it is also a community in a weak sense.

1.1 Our Contributions

In this study, we introduce a novel quality function for a network community, which we refer to as the *communitude*. The advantage of our quality function can be summarized as follows.

- The communitude has a strong statistical background. In fact, it measures the Z-score of a subset of vertices $S \subseteq V$ with respect to the fraction of the number of edges within the subgraph $G[S]$.
- The communitude is parameter-free. Several state-of-the-art quality functions for extracting communities (or dense subgraphs) are parameter-dependent. Those parameters are sometimes useful because we could find a community with some condition (e.g., desired edge density) by tuning the parameters. However, it is rarely the case that an appropriate parameter setting is known in advance.
- Due to the null model of a random graph used in the definition, the communitude focuses not only on the inside of the subgraph but also on the cut edges, unlike the quality functions for extracting dense subgraphs.
- The communitude maximization accurately detects communities in practice. The results of computational experiments for synthetic graphs show that the communitude maximization algorithms more accurately identify the ground-truth communities than the algorithms based on the other quality functions. Furthermore, the results for real-world networks demonstrate that the communitude detects natural and reasonable communities in practical use.
- The definition of the communitude can be naturally extended to edge-weighted graphs. Many real-world networks have edge weights; thus, the weighted version of the communitude is useful in practical applications.

To evaluate the detection ability of our quality function, we address the communitude maximization problem. For realistic scenarios, we also introduce three variants of the problem, and investigate the computational complexity of them. For the problems, we propose a two-phase heuristic algorithm together with some modified versions. In the first phase, it repeatedly removes the vertex with the smallest degree, and then obtains the subgraph with maximum communitude over the iterations. In the second phase, the algorithm improves the obtained solution using a simple local search heuristic. This algorithm runs in linear time when the number of iterations is fixed to a constant; thus, it is applicable to massive graphs. Computational experiments using both synthetic graphs and real-world networks demonstrate the validity and reliability of the proposed quality function and algorithms.

1.2 Related Work

Leskovec et al. [27] have thoroughly examined several community detection algorithms in order to compare them and to understand their relative performance and systematic biases of extracted communities. In their study, as a possible quality function of a community $S \subseteq V$, the following one was considered:

$$Q(S) = \frac{e[S]}{m} - \left(\frac{D[S]}{2m}\right)^2. \tag{3}$$

This is based on the modularity function (1) by Newman and Girvan [34], that is, it computes the fraction of the number of edges within the subgraph $G[S]$ minus the expected fraction of such edges assuming that they are placed at random with the same degree distribution.

Although Leskovec et al. [27] categorized this quality function as a *single criterion score* (i.e., functions that consider only one criteria such as the inside of the subgraph and the cut edges), we wish to point out here that the function takes into account both the inside of the subgraph and the cut edges. To see this, consider two subsets of vertices S_1 and S_2 such that $G[S_1]$ and $G[S_2]$ are isomorphic. Then, we see that $e[S_1] = e[S_2]$. If $\mathrm{cut}(S_1) > \mathrm{cut}(S_2)$, then $D[S_1] > D[S_2]$ follows; thus, we have $Q(S_1) < Q(S_2)$. From this point of view, the function seems to have some potential as a quality function of a network community. However, Leskovec et al. [27] experimentally demonstrate that the function value tends to increase roughly monotonically towards the bisection of the network. They mentioned that this trend should not be surprising since the function measures the *volume* of a community in terms of the number of edges, and the volume clearly increases with community size. In fact, as shown in Section 5, maximizing the function (3) produces poor solutions in benchmark graphs. Our quality function can be viewed as the appropriately normalized version of this function. For details on the normalization, see Section 2.

There is another way to view our quality function. Recently, Miyauchi and Kawase [30] introduced a quality function called *Z-modularity* for community detection in networks. It measures the Z-score of a given division of V with respect to the fraction of the number of edges within communities. Their computational experiments demonstrate that Z-modularity maximization leads to reasonable community structure in practical use. Our proposed quality function can be viewed as the counterpart of their quality function, which is specialized to the case of evaluating a single network community.

1.3 Paper Organization

This paper is structured as follows. In Section 2, our quality function communitude is introduced. In Section 3, the communitude maximization problem and its variants are presented. In Section 4, our algorithms for the problems are described. The experimental evaluation of our proposed quality function and algorithms is conducted in Section 5. Finally, conclusions and suggestions for future work are given in Section 6.

2. DEFINITION OF COMMUNITUDE

In this section, we first describe the concept that leads to our quality function, followed by its formal definition.

2.1 Our Concept

As mentioned above, the modularity-based quality function (3) seems to have some potential as a quality function of a network community. However, the function value tends to increase nearly monotonically towards the bisection of the network, which means that the optimal solution in terms of the quality function might be too large. Roughly speaking, our quality function is the appropriately normalized version of the function, which resolves the above problem.

2.2 Formal Definition

Given an undirected graph $G = (V, E)$ consisting of $n = |V|$ vertices and $m = |E|$ edges, and a subset of vertices $S \subseteq V$, we aim to quantify the *community degree* of $S \subseteq V$ in terms of the fraction of the number of edges within the subgraph induced by S. To this end, we consider some random edge generation process over V, and estimate the probability distribution of the fraction of the number of edges within the subgraph $G[S]$. Specifically, we consider the following edge generation process. Place N edges over V at random with the same degree distribution of the graph G. Then, when we place an edge, the probability that the edge is placed within S is given by

$$p = \left(\frac{D[S]}{2m}\right)^2.$$

Note that this edge generation process is the same as the null-model (known as the *configuration model* [32]) used in the definition of the modularity function (1), with the exception of the sample size. We simply wish to estimate the probability distribution of the fraction of the number of edges within the subgraph $G[S]$. Thus, unlike the null-model, the sample size N is not necessarily equal to the number of edges m.

Let X be a random variable denoting the number of edges generated by the process within S. Then, X follows the binomial distribution $B(N, p)$. By the central limit theorem, when the sample size N is sufficiently large, the distribution of X/N can be approximated by the normal distribution $\mathcal{N}(p, p(1-p)/N)$. Thus, we can quantify the community degree of S in terms of the fraction of the number of edges within the subgraph $G[S]$ using the Z-score as follows:

$$\mathrm{com}(S) = \frac{\frac{e[S]}{m} - \left(\frac{D[S]}{2m}\right)^2}{\sqrt{\left(\frac{D[S]}{2m}\right)^2\left(1 - \left(\frac{D[S]}{2m}\right)^2\right)}}.$$

We omitted the sample size N in the denominator because it never depends on a given subset of vertices. If $S = \emptyset$ or V, we define $\mathrm{com}(S) = 0$. We refer to this quality function as the *communitude*. Note that the numerator is none other than the modularity-based quality function (3), which was presented in Leskovec et al. [27]. Our quality function can be viewed as a modified version of the function (3), which is normalized by the standard deviation of the fraction of the number of edges within the subgraph.

It should be noted that the communitude value has a trivial upper bound. Specifically, for any undirected graph $G = (V, E)$ and any subset of vertices $S \subseteq V$, we see that $\mathrm{com}(S)$ is at most 1. Here we put $t = \sqrt{p}$. Indeed, since $e[S] \leq D[S]/2$, we have

$$\mathrm{com}(S) \leq \frac{t - t^2}{\sqrt{t^2(1-t^2)}} = \sqrt{\frac{1-t}{1+t}} \leq 1.$$

Note also that the communitude can be defined on edge-weighted graphs in a similar manner. In fact, the above edge generation process can be naturally extended by considering the weighted degree distribution. Many real-world networks have edge weights; thus, the weighted version of the communitude is useful in practical applications. It is easy to see that the above upper bound remains valid for this edge-weighted version.

3. PROBLEM DEFINITION

In the previous section, we introduced a new quality function communitude. We are now ready to formally define the *communitude maximization problem*, which is the central problem in the present study.

Problem 1 (Communitude maximization) *Given an undirected graph $G = (V, E)$, we are asked to find $S \subseteq V$ that maximizes $\mathrm{com}(S)$.*

3.1 Problem Variants

In this subsection, we present three variants of the communitude maximization problem for realistic scenarios.

Size-constrained variant. In practical applications, it is often the case that we wish to obtain a community that satisfies specified size constraints. In fact, as for the densest subgraph problem, size-constrained variants (i.e., DkS, Dal$k$S, and Dam$k$S) have been extensively studied [5,13,21]. We define the size-constrained variant of the communitude maximization problem as follows.

Problem 2 *Given an undirected graph $G = (V, E)$ and positive integers $k_{\min}$ and $k_{\max}$ ($k_{\min} \leq k_{\max}$), we are asked to find $S \subseteq V$ that maximizes $\mathrm{com}(S)$ under the restriction $k_{\min} \leq |S| \leq k_{\max}$.*

Query-dependent variant. In many real-world applications, we are interested in detecting a community that contains a given subset of vertices (called *query nodes*). In fact, Sozio and Gionis [38] extensively studied an optimization problem called the *community-search problem* that models this situation. The query-dependent variant of the communitude maximization problem can be defined as follows.

Problem 3 *Given an undirected graph $G = (V, E)$ and a set of query nodes $F \subseteq V$, we are asked to find $S \subseteq V$ that maximizes $\mathrm{com}(S)$ under the restriction $F \subseteq S$.*

Top-k variant. In practical applications, it is often the case that we wish to detect $k > 1$ communities rather than a single one. The top-k variant models this situation, which was studied in Tsourakakis et al. [41] in the context of dense subgraph extraction. We define the top-k variant of the communitude maximization problem as follows, although it may be possible to use other forms of the objective function.

Problem 4 *Given an undirected graph $G = (V, E)$ and a positive integer k, we are asked to find disjoint subsets of vertices $S_1, \dots, S_k \subseteq V$ that maximize $\sum_{i=1}^{k} \mathrm{com}(S_i)$.*

3.2 Computational Complexity Analysis

Here we investigate the computational complexity of the problems. As for Problem 1, although we believe that it is NP-hard, a formal proof of the hardness is still lacking, which we leave as an open problem for future research. On the other hand, we show the complexity of Problem 2 as the following theorem.

Theorem 1 *Problem 2 is NP-hard.*

PROOF. We reduce the problem of finding a clique of size k in an undirected graph wherein every vertex has the same degree. This problem is known to be NP-hard [3,15]. Suppose that we are given an instance of this problem: an undirected graph $G = (V, E)$ consisting of $n = |V|$ vertices and $m = |E|$ edges in which each vertex has degree d, and a positive integer $k < n$.

We claim that the optimal value of Problem 2 for $G = (V, E)$ and $k_{\min} = k_{\max} = k$ attains

$$c^* = \frac{\frac{k-1}{d} - \frac{k}{n}}{\sqrt{1 - \left(\frac{k}{n}\right)^2}}$$

if and only if G contains a clique of size k. The communitude value for $S \subset V$ with $|S| = k$ is

$$\mathrm{com}(S) = \frac{\frac{2e[S]}{n \cdot d} - \left(\frac{k}{n}\right)^2}{\sqrt{\left(\frac{k}{n}\right)^2 \left(1 - \left(\frac{k}{n}\right)^2\right)}} = \frac{\frac{2e[S]}{k \cdot d} - \frac{k}{n}}{\sqrt{1 - \left(\frac{k}{n}\right)^2}},$$

since $m = (n \cdot d)/2$ and $D[S] = k \cdot d$. Here $e[S]$ is at most $\binom{k}{2} = k(k-1)/2$ and achieves this upper bound if and only if $G[S]$ is a clique. Therefore, Problem 2 is NP-hard. □

Note that from the strict monotonic increase of c^* with respect to k, it follows that Problem 2 is NP-hard even without the lower bound $k_{\min}$ on the output community.

Algorithm 1 GREEDYPEELING

Input: Graph $G = (V, E)$
Output: Subset of vertices $S \subseteq V$

```
U ← V, 𝒮 ← ∅
while U is not empty
    𝒮 ← 𝒮 ∪ {U}
    Pick v ∈ U with the smallest degree in G[U]
    U ← U \ {v}
return argmax_{S∈𝒮} f(S)
```

4. ALGORITHMS

In this section, we present algorithms to solve the problems described in Section 3.

4.1 Basic Algorithm

First, we describe an algorithm for Problem 1. We use a greedy algorithm to obtain an initial solution, and then apply a simple local search heuristic to improve it. Let f denote an arbitrary quality function of a network community.

Greedy algorithm. Our algorithm employs the *greedy peeling strategy*, which iteratively removes the vertex with the smallest degree in the currently remaining graph, and then returns $S \subseteq V$ with maximum $f(S)$ over the iterations, where f represents the objective function of the problem at hand. This strategy is shown to be a 1/2-approximation algorithm for the densest subgraph problem [10] and to be an additive approximation algorithm for the OQC-Problem [41]. For convenience, the procedure is described in Algorithm 1. As mentioned in previous works [21,41], the algorithm can be implemented to run in $O(m+n)$ time for both the densest subgraph problem and the OQC-Problem using a doubly-linked list of vertices for each degree. Since we can evaluate the communitude value for $S \subseteq V$ in constant time by keeping the values of $e[S]$ and $D[S]$, the algorithm also runs in $O(m+n)$ time for the communitude maximization problem.

Local search heuristic. We design a simple local search heuristic to improve a given initial solution $S_{\text{init}} \subseteq V$. This algorithm visits all the vertices in a random order. For each $v \in V$, it adds v to S_{init} or removes v from S_{init} appropriately if the objective value is strictly improved. The process continues until a locally optimal solution is obtained or the number of iterations exceeds the specified threshold $T_{\max}$. Furthermore, we repeat the whole process $R_{\max}$ times, and then return the best solution. The detailed procedure is shown in Algorithm 2, where the operator Δ represents the

Algorithm 2 LocalSearch

Input: Graph $G = (V, E)$; Initial solution $S_{\text{init}} \subseteq V$
Output: Subset of vertices $S \subseteq V$

$S \leftarrow \emptyset$
for $r \leftarrow 1, \ldots, R_{\max}$
  $S' \leftarrow S_{\text{init}}$
  for $t \leftarrow 1, \ldots, T_{\max}$
    for $v \in V$ in a random order
      if $f(S'\Delta\{v\}) > f(S')$ **then** $S' \leftarrow S'\Delta\{v\}$
    if there exists no update of S' in the last for-loop
      then break
  if $f(S') > f(S)$ **then** $S \leftarrow S'$
return S

symmetric difference. The time complexity of Algorithm 2 is $O((m + n) \cdot R_{\max} \cdot T_{\max})$. In the later experiments, we set $R_{\max} = 10$ and $T_{\max} = \infty$ since the number of iterations until convergence is small in practice, as mentioned in Section 5.2. Thus, we only take locally optimal solutions in the experiments.

Algorithm for Problem 1. We are now ready to describe our algorithm for Problem 1: it obtains an initial solution S_{init} by Algorithm 1, and then runs Algorithm 2 for S_{init} to improve it.

4.2 Modifications

Here we present algorithms to solve the variants of the communitude maximization problem by modifying the above algorithm.

Algorithm for Problem 2. Let $k_{\min}$ and $k_{\max}$ ($k_{\min} \leq k_{\max}$) be positive integers denoting the lower bound and the upper bound, respectively, on the output community. We use the algorithm for Problem 1 with some modifications. In the greedy peeling phase, the modified algorithm obtains the best community $S \subseteq V$ with $k_{\min} \leq |S| \leq k_{\max}$ over the iterations. In the local search phase, the algorithm skips the changes that violate the size constraint.

Algorithm for Problem 3. Let $F \subseteq V$ be a set of query nodes. We use Algorithm 2, with some modification, by setting F to the initial solution. In the modified algorithm, we skip the updates corresponding to the vertices in F because they must be contained in the output community.

Algorithm for Problem 4. Let k be a positive integer denoting the number of output communities required. We find a single community at a time by the algorithm for Problem 1, and then remove the vertices in the community from the graph. We continue this process until k communities are found or we are left with an empty graph. It should be noted that the values in the algorithm, such as the degree of a vertex and the communitude value for a subset of vertices, are always computed on the input graph. In particular, this operation is critical for the communitude because we wish to obtain a community with maximum communitude on the original graph rather than the remaining graph.

5. EXPERIMENTAL EVALUATION

The purpose of our computational experiments is to evaluate the validity and reliability of the proposed quality function and algorithms. Our experiments are conducted on various synthetic graphs and well-known real-world networks.

5.1 Synthetic Graphs

First, we report the results of computational experiments with synthetic graphs. We deal with three types of synthetic graphs: the single community model, the planted l-partition model, and the Lancichinetti–Fortunato–Radicchi (LFR) benchmark. In these models, once their parameters are set (and some query nodes are chosen in the latter two models), the ground-truth community is fixed. Thus, we can evaluate the quality of the obtained community by comparison with the ground-truth using some similarity measure. To this end, we adopt the Jaccard index. The *Jaccard index* for two sets A and B is defined as

$$J(A, B) = \frac{|A \cap B|}{|A \cup B|},$$

which ranges from 0 to 1. For two sets A and B, the higher the Jaccard index is, the more similar they are (and vice versa). In fact, $J(A, B) = 1$ if A and B are identical, and $J(A, B) = 0$ if they are disjoint.

For each of the above models, we use one of the algorithms presented in Section 4. We compare the following five quality functions as an objective function f in the algorithms: the communitude, the modularity-based function (3), the average degree (i.e., the quality function of the densest subgraph problem), the quality function of the OQC-Problem (with $\alpha = 1/3$), and the conductance. When the algorithm used is clear from the context, we simply denote the algorithms by COM, Q, DS, OQC, and COND, respectively.

Single community model. First, we consider the single community model, where exactly one community is planted in a sparse graph. More specifically, the Erdős–Rényi random graph [12] with c vertices and edge probability p_{in} is planted in the Erdős–Rényi random graph with n ($> c$) vertices and edge probability p_{out} ($< p_{\text{in}}$). Here we set $n = 1000$. We construct four networks corresponding to combinations of two different community sizes ($c = 50$ or 100) and two different edge probabilities inside the community ($p_{\text{in}} = 0.2$ or 0.4). The parameter p_{out} starts with 0.01 and then increases in stages. We use the algorithm for Problem 1 to maximize the quality functions.

The results are shown in Figure 2. As can be seen, COM most accurately detects the planted community for many cases. Consistent with Tsourakakis et al. [41], DS returns the entire set of vertices for almost all cases. OQC seems not to be robust because its performance depends heavily on the edge probability p_{in} of the planted community (which is not known in advance). In fact, although it accurately detects the community when $\alpha < p_{\text{in}}$, whereas it detects too small subgraph when $\alpha > p_{\text{in}}$. The algorithms Q and COND produce poor solutions for all settings. Note finally that DS is a 1/2-approximation algorithm for the densest subgraph problem [10], and OQC is an additive approximation algorithm for the OQC-Problem [41], because the local search heuristic just improves the greedy solution.

Planted l-partition model. The planted l-partition model was introduced by Condon and Karp [11]. In this model, n vertices are divided into l equally sized groups (consisting of $c = n/l$ vertices each). Two vertices in the same group are connected by probability p_{in}, whereas two vertices in different groups are connected by probability p_{out} ($< p_{\text{in}}$). Throughout the experiments, we set $n = 1000$. We construct four networks corresponding to combinations of two

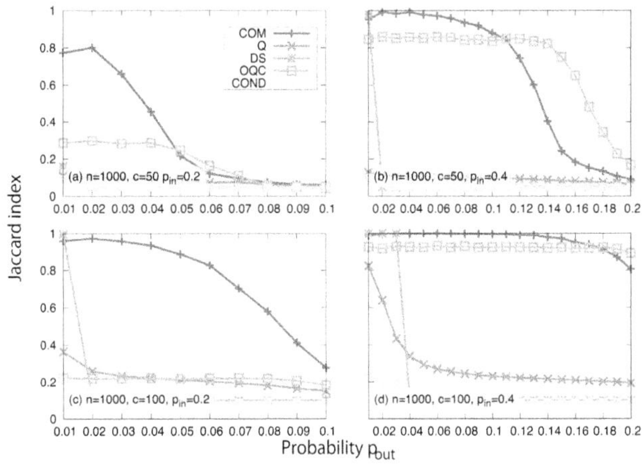

Figure 2: Results for the single community model. Each point corresponds to an average over 100 graph realizations.

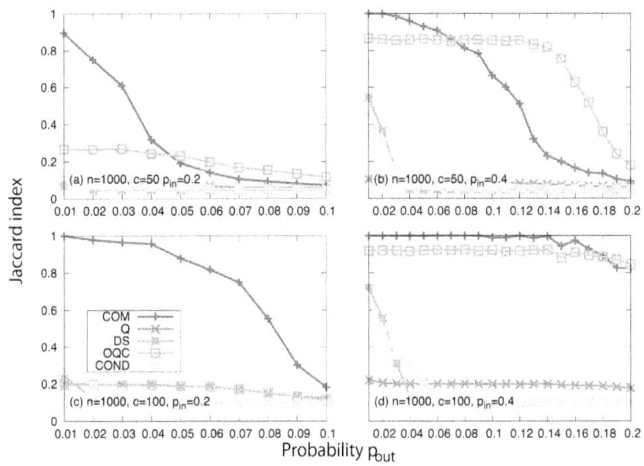

Figure 3: Results for the planted l-partition model. Each point corresponds to an average over 100 graph realizations.

different edge probabilities inside the groups ($p_{\rm in} = 0.2$ or 0.4) and two different community sizes ($c = 50$ or 100). The parameter $p_{\rm out}$ starts with 0.01 and then increases in stages. We randomly choose a group and select five vertices in it as query nodes. We maximize the quality functions by Algorithm 2 for the query nodes.

The results are illustrated in Figure 3. The trend of the results is similar to that of the single community model. It should be noted that this is not a trivial outcome because there are a large number of neighboring communities in a graph generated by this model, unlike the single community model.

LFR benchmark. In the planted l-partition model, each group in a generated graph forms the Erdős–Rényi random graph. Thus, all vertices have approximately the same degree. Moreover, all groups have exactly the same size. These phenomena are rarely observed in networks in real-world systems. As a more realistic model, the LFR benchmark was proposed by Lancichinetti et al. [25] for the case of unweighted and undirected graphs. The LFR benchmark was

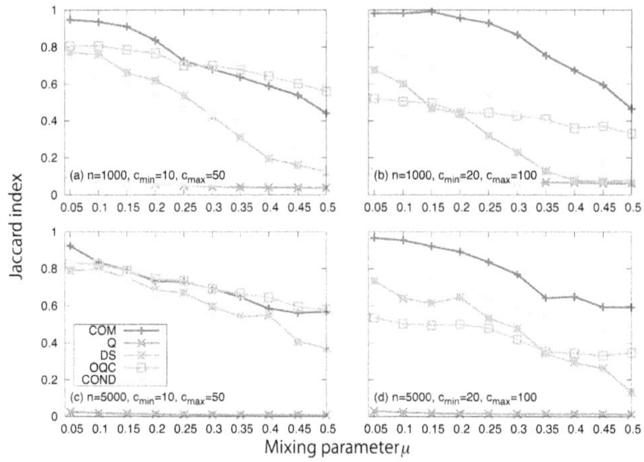

Figure 4: Results for the LFR benchmark. Each point corresponds to an average over 100 graph realizations.

then extended to the case of directed and weighted graphs with overlapping communities [23]. The LFR benchmark has often been used to evaluate community detection algorithms in the data mining community [9, 40]. We now use the original unweighted and undirected case without overlapping communities.

In the model, degree distribution and community size distribution follow the power law with exponents γ and β, respectively. Furthermore, we can specify the number of vertices n, average degree d, maximum degree $d_{\rm max}$, minimum community size $c_{\rm min}$, maximum community size $c_{\rm max}$, and mixing parameter μ. In particular, mixing parameter μ indicates the mixing ratio of communities, that is, the higher μ is, the more densely connected the communities are. The model constructs a network consistent with the specified parameters. For more details, see Lancichinetti et al. [25]. In our experiments, we set the parameters the same as used in Lancichinetti and Fortunato [24] as follows: $\gamma = -2$, $\beta = -1$, $d = 20$, and $d_{\rm max} = 50$. We construct four networks corresponding to combinations of two different network sizes ($n = 1000$ or 5000) and two different ranges of community size ($(c_{\rm min}, c_{\rm max}) = (10, 50)$ or $(20, 100)$). We randomly choose a community and select five vertices in it as query nodes. We maximize the quality functions by Algorithm 2 for the query nodes.

The results are shown in Figure 4. For the smaller community size settings ($(c_{\rm min}, c_{\rm max}) = (10, 50)$), COM and OQC returns nearly the same (and the best) quality solutions. On the other hand, when the network consists of relatively large communities ($(c_{\rm min}, c_{\rm max}) = (20, 100)$), COM outperforms the algorithms based on the other quality functions. From the above, we see that COM is the most robust algorithm. The algorithm Q again produces poor solutions for all cases, whereas COND is of relatively good quality for this model.

5.2 Real-World Networks

Here we report the results of computational experiments with real-world networks. First, we describe the results of well-known networks: the Zachary's karate club network, the Les Misérables network, and the American college foot-

Table 1: Real-world graphs used in the experiments.

Network	n	m	Description
Karate	34	78	Social network
Mexican	35	117	Social network
Dolphins	62	159	Animal social
Lesmis	77	254	Co-appearance
Polbooks	105	441	Co-purchased
Football	115	613	Games network
Jazz	198	2,742	Social network
USAir97	332	2,126	Airport network
Email	1,133	5,451	Email network
Polblogs	1,490	16,715	Blog network
Wiki-Vote	7,155	100,762	Wikipedia
AS-22july06	22,963	48,436	Internet topology
soc-Epinions1	75,879	405,740	Online social
web-Stanford	281,903	1,992,636	Web graph
com-DBLP	317,080	1,049,866	Co-authorship
web-Google	875,713	4,322,051	Web graph
AS-Skitter	1,696,415	11,095,298	Internet topology
com-LiveJournal	3,997,962	34,681,189	Online social

ball network. Specifically, we use the algorithm for Problem 4 with $k = 2$ for these networks. Then, we present the numerical results for the networks listed in Table 1, including large-scale networks such as AS-Skitter (1,696,415 vertices) and com-LiveJournal (3,997,962 vertices).

Zachary's karate club network. The first example is the famous karate club network analyzed by Zachary [44], which is often used as a benchmark to evaluate community detection algorithms. It consists of 34 vertices representing the members in a karate club in an American university, in addition to 78 edges representing friendship relations among individuals. Due to a conflict between the club administrator and the instructor, the club members split into two groups, one supporting the administrator and the other supporting the instructor.

The communities extracted by the algorithm are shown in Figure 5. The label of each vertex represents an identification number of the member. For example, the numbers 1 and 34 represent the administrator and the instructor, respectively. The dashed line gives the division of the network into the above two groups. As can be seen, the extracted communities never straddle two groups. In fact, S_1 is contained in the group supporting the administrator, whereas S_2 is contained in the group supporting the instructor. Furthermore, it should be noted that S_1 and S_2 are communities in a strong sense.

Les Misérables network. The second example is the network of the characters in the novel *Les Misérables* by Victor Hugo, compiled by Knuth [22]. It consists of 77 vertices representing the characters and 254 edges indicating the co-appearance of characters.

The communities extracted by the algorithm are presented in Figure 6. The label of each vertex represents the name of the character. Interestingly, the extracted communities are likely to correspond to specific groups within the story. In fact, S_1 contains major characters belonging to the revolutionary student club *Friends of the ABC*. Moreover, S_2 identifies the characters who appear in Chapter 1 of the book. Both S_1 and S_2 satisfy the condition of a community in a strong sense.

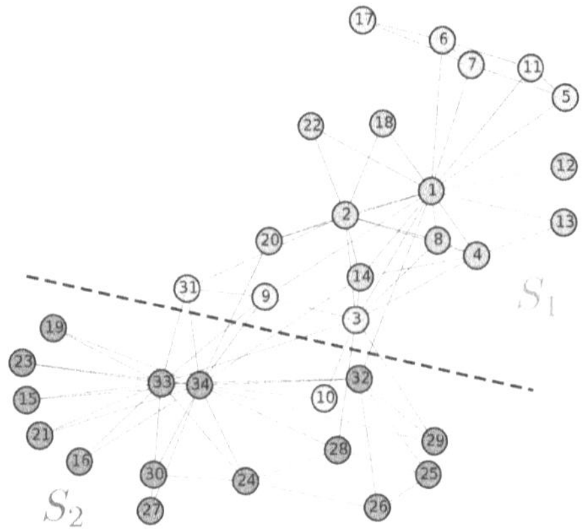

Figure 5: Communities obtained in Zachary's karate club network: S_1 ($|S_1| = 10$ **and** $\mathrm{com}(S_1) = 0.4254$) **and** S_2 ($|S_2| = 15$ **and** $\mathrm{com}(S_2) = 0.4489$).

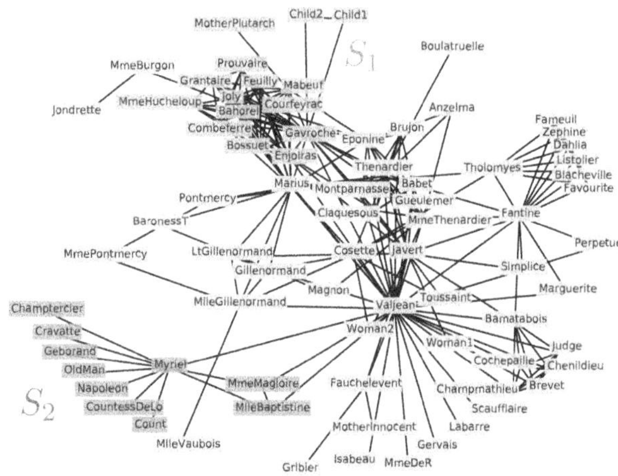

Figure 6: Communities obtained in Les Misérables network: S_1 ($|S_1| = 15$ **and** $\mathrm{com}(S_1) = 0.5775$) **and** S_2 ($|S_2| = 10$ **and** $\mathrm{com}(S_2) = 0.7425$).

American college football network. The third example is a network of college football teams in the United States, which was derived by Girvan and Newman [17]. There are 115 vertices representing the football teams, in addition to 654 edges connecting teams that played each other in a regular season. The teams are divided into 12 groups called *conferences* containing approximately 10 teams each. More games are played between teams in the same conference than between teams in different conferences.

The communities extracted by the algorithm are shown in Figure 7. Each group of circularly-arranged vertices represents a conference. The community S_1 completely recovers a conference consisting of 9 teams. On the other hand, S_2 extracts a conference consisting of 13 teams together with one team from another conference. As can be seen, the additional team has a few edges to the detected conference, whereas it has no edges to the teams in the original conference. Thus, the community S_2 seems to suggest a more reasonable conference than the original one. Both S_1 and S_2 are again communities in a strong sense.

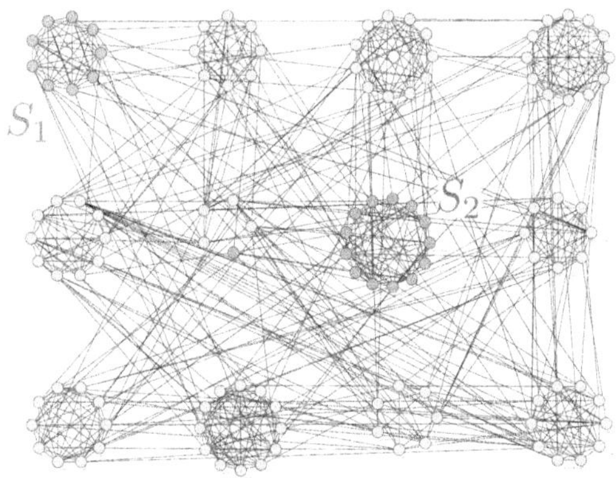

Figure 7: Communities obtained in American college football network: S_1 ($|S_1| = 9$ and $\text{com}(S_1) = 0.6654$) and S_2 ($|S_2| = 14$ and $\text{com}(S_2) = 0.6493$).

Table 2: Numerical results for real-world graphs.

Network	com(S)	$\|S\|$	$e[S]$	cut(S)
Karate	0.4254	10	18	14
Mexican	0.3634	13	36	25
Dolphins	0.5613	12	24	16
Lesmis	0.5775	15	64	23
Polbooks	0.5792	41	176	20
Football	0.6654	9	36	25
Jazz	0.4520	46	510	435
USAir97	0.3478	78	456	479
Email	0.5969	25	113	133
Polblogs	0.5149	500	6,904	1,333
Wiki-Vote	0.4046	1,378	12,436	16,496
AS-22july06	0.5691	7,277	12,572	4,510
soc-Epinions1	0.4595	13,474	71,553	62,096
web-Stanford	0.8651	5,749	227,449	11,142
com-DBLP	0.9017	494	15,389	2,765
web-Google	0.9388	184	3,172	408
AS-Skitter	0.7293	157,216	2,570,493	265,258
com-LiveJournal	0.9574	9,323	1,003,448	27,817

Numerical results. For each real-world network listed in Table 1, we extracted a community by the algorithm for Problem 1. The numerical results are shown in Table 2. As can be seen, each community has a small number of cut edges in comparison with the number of edges within the community. In particular, this trend is significant for the communities with relatively large communitude values. It should be noted that all the obtained communities satisfy the condition of a community in a weak sense.

We conclude this section by reporting the running time of the algorithms. Consistent with the time complexity analysis in Section 4, all the implemented algorithms are sufficiently fast. In fact, even for the largest network com-LiveJournal, the algorithm for Problem 1 runs in a few tens of minutes on a MacBook Pro (with 2.8 GHz CPU and 16 GB RAM). Although the number of iterations corresponding to $T_{\max}$ (in Algorithm 2) depends on the input graph and the randomness of the vertex order, it is usually small enough to accept. For example, we observed that it is always at most 100 for com-LiveJournal network.

6. CONCLUSIONS

In this study, we have introduced a novel quality function for a network community, which we named the *communitude*. The communitude has a strong statistical background, that is, it measures the Z-score of a subset of vertices $S \subseteq V$ with respect to the fraction of the number of edges within the subgraph $G[S]$. Due to the null model of a random graph used in the definition, our quality function focuses not only on the inside of the subgraph but also on the cut edges, unlike the quality functions for extracting dense subgraphs. To evaluate the detection ability of our quality function, we have addressed the communitude maximization problem and its variants for realistic scenarios. For the problems, we have proposed a two-phase heuristic algorithm together with some modified versions. The algorithm runs in linear time when the number of iterations is fixed to a constant; thus, it is applicable to massive graphs. Computational experiments using both synthetic graphs and real-world networks demonstrate the validity and reliability of the proposed quality function and algorithms. Therefore, we conclude that the communitude could be a potential option for the quality function of a network community.

There are several directions for future research. As mentioned in Section 3, the computational complexity of Problem 1 should be investigated, although we believe that it is NP-hard. As another direction, it may be interesting to analyze statistical properties of community structure in real-world networks using our quality function. For instance, the NCP plot can be described using the communitude rather than the conductance. That is, for each positive integer $k \leq n$, we plot the communitude value of the best subset of vertices $S \subseteq V$ with $|S| = k$. To this end, effective algorithms for the size-constrained variant (Problem 2) should be examined more deeply.

7. ACKNOWLEDGMENTS

The authors would like to thank the anonymous reviewers for their valuable suggestions. The first author is supported by a Grant-in-Aid for JSPS Fellows (No. 26-11908). The second author is supported by a Grant-in-Aid for Research Activity Start-up (No. 26887014). This work was partially supported by JST, ERATO, Kawarabayashi Large Graph Project.

8. REFERENCES

[1] J. Abello, M. G. C. Resende, and S. Sudarsky. Massive quasi-clique detection. In *LATIN '02*, pages 598–612, 2002.

[2] G. Agarwal and D. Kempe. Modularity-maximizing graph communities via mathematical programming. *Eur. Phys. J. B*, 66(3):409–418, 2008.

[3] C. C. Aggarwal, R. K. Ahuja, J. Hao, and J. B. Orlin. Diagnosing infeasibilities in network flow problems. *Math. Program.*, 81:263–280, 1998.

[4] D. Aloise, S. Cafieri, G. Caporossi, P. Hansen, S. Perron, and L. Liberti. Column generation algorithms for exact modularity maximization in networks. *Phys. Rev. E*, 82:046112, 2010.

[5] R. Andersen and K. Chellapilla. Finding dense subgraphs with size bounds. In *WAW '09*, pages 25–37, 2009.

[6] Y. Asahiro, K. Iwama, H. Tamaki, and T. Tokuyama. Greedily Finding a Dense Subgraph. *J. Algorithms*, 34(2):203–221, 2000.
[7] A. Bhaskara, M. Charikar, E. Chlamtac, U. Feige, and A. Vijayaraghavan. Detecting high log-densities: An $O(n^{1/4})$ approximation for densest k-subgraph. In *STOC '10*, pages 201–210, 2010.
[8] V. D. Blondel, J.-L. Guillaume, R. Lambiotte, and E. Lefebvre. Fast unfolding of communities in large networks. *J. Stat. Mech.: Theory Exp.*, 2008(10):P10008, 2008.
[9] T. Chakraborty, S. Srinivasan, N. Ganguly, A. Mukherjee, and S. Bhowmick. On the permanence of vertices in network communities. In *KDD '14*, pages 1396–1405, 2014.
[10] M. Charikar. Greedy approximation algorithms for finding dense components in a graph. In *APPROX '00*, pages 84–95, 2000.
[11] A. Condon and R. M. Karp. Algorithms for graph partitioning on the planted partition model. *Random Struct. Algorithms*, 18:116–140, 2001.
[12] P. Erdős and A. Rényi. On random graphs I. *Publ. Math. Debrecen*, 6:290–297, 1959.
[13] U. Feige, D. Peleg, and G. Kortsarz. The dense k-subgraph problem. *Algorithmica*, 29(3):410–421, 2001.
[14] S. Fortunato. Community detection in graphs. *Phys. Rep.*, 486(3):75–174, 2010.
[15] M. R. Garey and D. S. Johnson. *Computers and Intractability: A Guide to the Theory of NP-Completeness*. W. H. Freeman & Co., NY, 1979.
[16] D. Gibson, R. Kumar, and A. Tomkins. Discovering large dense subgraphs in massive graphs. In *VLDB '05*, pages 721–732, 2005.
[17] M. Girvan and M. E. J. Newman. Community structure in social and biological networks. *Proc. Natl. Acad. Sci. U.S.A.*, 99(12):7821–7826, 2002.
[18] A. V. Goldberg. Finding a maximum density subgraph. Technical report, University of California Berkeley, 1984.
[19] J. Håstad. Clique is hard to approximate within $n^{1-\epsilon}$. In *FOCS '96*, pages 627–636, 1996.
[20] S. Khot. Ruling out PTAS for graph min-bisection, dense k-subgraph, and bipartite clique. *SIAM J. Comput.*, 36(4):1025–1071, 2006.
[21] S. Khuller and B. Saha. On finding dense subgraphs. In *ICALP '09*, pages 597–608, 2009.
[22] D. E. Knuth. *The Stanford GraphBase: A Platform for Combinatorial Computing*. Addison-Wesley, MA, 1993.
[23] A. Lancichinetti and S. Fortunato. Benchmarks for testing community detection algorithms on directed and weighted graphs with overlapping communities. *Phys. Rev. E*, 80:016118, 2009.
[24] A. Lancichinetti and S. Fortunato. Community detection algorithms: A comparative analysis. *Phys. Rev. E*, 80:056117, 2009.
[25] A. Lancichinetti, S. Fortunato, and F. Radicchi. Benchmark graphs for testing community detection algorithms. *Phys. Rev. E*, 78:046110, 2008.
[26] J. Leskovec, K. J. Lang, A. Dasgupta, and M. W. Mahoney. Statistical properties of community structure in large social and information networks. In *WWW '08*, pages 695–704, 2008.
[27] J. Leskovec, K. J. Lang, and M. Mahoney. Empirical comparison of algorithms for network community detection. In *WWW '10*, pages 631–640, 2010.
[28] K. Makino and T. Uno. New algorithms for enumerating all maximal cliques. In *SWAT '04*, pages 260–272, 2004.
[29] D. W. Matula and F. Shahrokhi. Sparsest cuts and bottlenecks in graphs. *Discrete Appl. Math.*, 27(1–2):113–123, 1990.
[30] A. Miyauchi and Y. Kawase. Z-score-based modularity for community detection in networks. *arXiv:1501.01909*, 2015.
[31] A. Miyauchi and Y. Miyamoto. Computing an upper bound of modularity. *Eur. Phys. J. B*, 86:302, 2013.
[32] M. Molloy and B. Reed. A critical point for random graphs with a given degree sequence. *Random Struct. Algorithms*, 6(2-3):161–180, 1995.
[33] M. E. J. Newman. Modularity and community structure in networks. *Proc. Natl. Acad. Sci. U.S.A.*, 103(23):8577–8582, 2006.
[34] M. E. J. Newman and M. Girvan. Finding and evaluating community structure in networks. *Phys. Rev. E*, 69:026113, 2004.
[35] D. S. Papailiopoulos, I. Mitliagkas, A. G. Dimakis, and C. Caramanis. Finding dense subgraphs via low-rank bilinear optimization. In *ICML '14*, pages 1890–1898, 2014.
[36] F. Radicchi, C. Castellano, F. Cecconi, V. Loreto, and D. Parisi. Defining and identifying communities in networks. *Proc. Natl. Acad. Sci. U.S.A.*, 101(9):2658–2663, 2004.
[37] J. Shi and J. Malik. Normalized cuts and image segmentation. *IEEE Trans. Pattern Anal. Mach. Intell.*, 22(8):888–905, 2000.
[38] M. Sozio and A. Gionis. The community-search problem and how to plan a successful cocktail party. In *KDD '10*, pages 939–948, 2010.
[39] V. Spirin and L. A. Mirny. Protein complexes and functional modules in molecular networks. *Proc. Natl. Acad. Sci. U.S.A.*, 100(21):12123–12128, 2003.
[40] H. Sun, J. Huang, J. Han, H. Deng, P. Zhao, and B. Feng. gSkeletonClu: Density-based network clustering via structure-connected tree division or agglomeration. In *ICDM '10*, pages 481–490, 2010.
[41] C. E. Tsourakakis, F. Bonchi, A. Gionis, F. Gullo, and M. Tsiarli. Denser than the densest subgraph: Extracting optimal quasi-cliques with quality guarantees. In *KDD '13*, pages 104–112, 2013.
[42] T. Uno. An efficient algorithm for solving pseudo clique enumeration problem. *Algorithmica*, 56(1):3–16, 2010.
[43] Y.-C. Wei and C.-K. Cheng. Towards efficient hierarchical designs by ratio cut partitioning. In *ICCAD '89*, pages 298–301, 1989.
[44] W. W. Zachary. An information flow model for conflict and fission in small groups. *J. Anthropol. Res.*, 33(4):452–473, 1977.

DifRec: a Social-Diffusion-aware Recommender System

Hossein Vahabi
Yahoo Labs, Spain
puya@yahoo-inc.com

Iordanis Koutsopoulos
AUEB and CERTH, Greece
jordan@aueb.gr

Francesco Gullo
Yahoo Labs, Spain
gullo@yahoo-inc.com

Maria Halkidi
Univ. of Piraeus, Greece
mhalk@unipi.gr

ABSTRACT

Recommender systems used in current online social platforms make recommendations by only considering how relevant an item is to a specific user but they ignore the fact that, thanks to mechanisms like sharing or re-posting across the underlying social network, an item recommended to a user i propagates through the network and can reach another user j without needing to be explicitly recommended to j too. Overlooking this fact may lead to an inefficient use of the limited recommendation slots. These slots can instead be exploited more profitably by avoiding unnecessary duplicates and recommending other equally relevant items.

In this work we take a step towards rethinking recommender systems by exploiting the anticipated social-network information diffusion and withholding recommendation of items that are expected to reach a user through sharing/re-posting. We devise a novel recommender system, DifRec, by formulating the problem of maximizing the total user engagement as an allocation problem in a properly-defined neighborhoodness graph, i.e., a graph that models the conflicts of recommending an item to a user who will receive it anyway by social diffusion. We show that the problem is NP-hard and propose efficient heuristics to solve it.

We assess the performance of our DifRec by involving real data from Tumblr platform. We obtain substantial improvements in overall user engagement (130–190%) over the real recommender system embedded in Tumblr and over various existing recommender systems

Categories and Subject Descriptors

H.4 [**Information Systems Applications**]: Miscellaneous

General Terms

Algorithms, Optimization, Experimentation

Keywords

Social diffusion aware recommendation, User engagement

Permission to make digital or hard copies of all or part of this work for personal or classroom use is granted without fee provided that copies are not made or distributed for profit or commercial advantage and that copies bear this notice and the full citation on the first page. Copyrights for components of this work owned by others than ACM must be honored. Abstracting with credit is permitted. To copy otherwise, or republish, to post on servers or to redistribute to lists, requires prior specific permission and/or a fee. Request permissions from Permissions@acm.org.
CIKM'15, October 19–23, 2015, Melbourne, VIC, Australia.
© 2015 ACM. ISBN 978-1-4503-3794-6/15/10 ...$15.00.
DOI: http://dx.doi.org/10.1145/2806416.2806559 .

1. INTRODUCTION

Online social platforms like Twitter, Tumblr, Facebook, Google+, Weibo, where users post multimedia content and create (virtual) social relationships have proliferated a lot in the last few years. The amount of posted information keeps increasing to unimaginable levels. Twitter, for instance, has 271 million active users who generate more than 6,000 tweets per second. Tumblr has a user base of 50 millions and hosts about 200 million blogs and 90 billion posts.

These platforms have even created a new lifestyle and keeping users highly engaged is of utmost importance for their owners. Indeed, increased user engagement is strongly correlated to higher revenue, as the user is more likely to view or click on ads or other items that the platform owner monetizes on. Moreover, when users are engaged with the platform, they contribute in generating content that can be exploited for crucial tasks like profiling or personalization.

Recommender systems constitute a primary component for improving online user experience, and, as such, increase user engagement. Depending on the specific online platform, recommendations concern different types of items. For instance, Twitter uses a recommendation service for accounts or tweets, Facebook recommends friends and news, while Tumblr recommends posts. Regardless of the type of recommended item, the primary goal of a recommender system is to facilitate access to content that is of interest to users, without making them waste time in manually inspecting tons of irrelevant information.

A major feature of existing recommender systems is that they make recommendations by focusing only on the specific user to whom the recommendation is directed [22, 15]: an item is recommended to a specific user if it has been recognized as "relevant" to that user according to a certain measure of relevance. However, in such platforms a user is not an isolated entity, rather she is part of a social network that abstracts relationships among users. The social network underlying these online platforms can be represented as a directed graph where the semantics of each edge (i, j) is that user j "follows" user i, that is, user j has visibility on all content generated or shared/re-posted by user i.

The availability of a social network constitutes a unique opportunity to empower the quality of a recommender system and get higher overall user engagement. Indeed, when an item (e.g., a news, a post, a URL, a multimedia file) is recommended to user i, it directly contributes to an increase in the user i engagement with the platform. However, if this item is spread further by mechanisms like sharing or re-posting, it will also indirectly contribute to the engagement of users that are connected to i through the underlying social network. If in turn these users share/re-post the item, other users connected to them will also receive it, and so on.

As a more concrete example, consider an item that has been recognized as relevant to user i of a certain social platform, and, as such, it has been recommended to her. Assume also that the same item is relevant to i's followers and, as such, has been recommended to them too. If user i re-posts the item, their followers will receive it twice, both via re-posting and from the recommender system. Since the maximum number of items to be recommended to a user is limited to a few at a time (to avoid overloading the user with too much information), the scenario above leads to an undesirable situation where a significant amount of slots available for recommendation is wasted for recommending duplicate items that are expected to reach some users (i.e., i's followers) via re-posting. Instead, a more sophisticated recommender system could take into account anticipated re-posting and recommend other equally relevant items to the followers of i, thus further increasing their engagement.

In this work we aim at incorporating social-network information diffusion in the recommendation strategy of recommender systems underlying online social platforms. To the best of our knowledge, this aspect is overlooked by all existing recommender systems. Even the so-called *social recommender systems* [14, 25, 7] do not consider it. Indeed, they aim at exploiting the social network only for better assessing how relevant an item is to a user, that is, for measuring the relevance of an item to a user by incorporating social contextual information such as the relevance of an item to the social neighborhood of that user.

1.1 Motivating example

Consider the simple example reported in Figure 1, where $N = 5$ users are organized in the social network depicted in the figure. Let $\mathcal{S} = \{t1, t2, t3, t4, t5\}$ be the set of possible items to be recommended to each user, and let the relevance scores of items in $\mathcal{S}$ to a user i be defined by the following vectors: $\vec{r}_1 = [0.9, 0.1, 0.3, 0.7, 0.4]$ (user 1), $\vec{r}_2 = [0.8, 0.6, 0.4, 0.3, 0.5]$ (user 2), $\vec{r}_3 = [0.5, 0.7, 0.2, 0.1, 0.9]$ (user 3), $\vec{r}_4 = [0.4, 0.8, 0.7, 0.1, 0.3]$ (user 4), $[0.7, 0.1, 0.5, 0.7, 0.4]$ (user 5). Moreover, assume that each user can be recommended only $K = 1$ items, and that re-posting always happens, i.e., every item recommended to user i is always re-posted and becomes available to all i's followers.[1]

A traditional recommender system would recommend items to a user based only on the relevance scores to that specific user, thus leading to the recommendations illustrated in Figure 1(a), where each user receives the item that is most relevant to her. Hence, users 1,2,3,4,5 are recommended items $t1$, $t1$, $t5$, $t2$, $t1$, respectively, and the total relevance of the items viewed by users, which include both the recommended items and the ones reaching a user via re-posting, is computed as follows. For user 1, the total relevance is 0.9, due to $t1$ only (she is not follower of anyone). For user 2, the total relevance is 0.8: user 2 receives $t1$ through both recommendation *and* re-posting (from user 1), but it clearly counts only once, as duplicates do not contribute to increase relevance. User 3 receives $t5$ through recommendation and

[1]In the proposed recommendation method we actually include a probability of re-posting so as to maintain as much generality as possible. In this example we assume probability equal to one for simplicity.

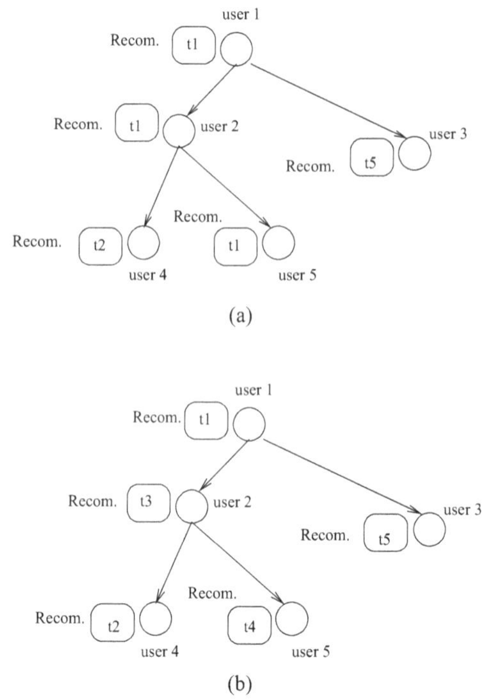

Figure 1: Example showing how more accurate a social-diffusion-aware recommender system can be with respect to traditional recommender systems. *(a)* Recommendations provided by traditional recommender systems lead to overall relevance of 5. *(b)* Social-diffusion-aware recommendations lead to overall relevance equal to 7.3.

$t1$ through re-posting from user 1, therefore her total relevance is 1.4. Similarly, the total relevance of users 4 and 5 are equal to 1.2 and 0.7, respectively. Summing all these individual total relevance scores leads to a relevance of the overall recommendation equal to 5.

Consider now a recommender system that takes into account social-network information diffusion, i.e., it recommends items not only based on the relevance scores but also considering the relevance of the item to the users who will receive that item via re-posting (Figure 1(b)). As shown later on, finding the optimal recommendations according to such a rule is an NP-hard problem. However, even solving the problem heuristically may lead to much higher overall relevance than in the case where social-network diffusion is discarded. Indeed, assume that we process the users in sequence, starting from user 1. Any item recommended to user 1 will reach every other user in the network, thus the item to be recommended to user 1 should correspond to the item that maximizes the sum of the relevance scores among all users; this is item $t1$, which leads to a (maximum) total relevance of $0.9 + 0.8 + 0.5 + 0.4 + 0.7 = 3.3$. For user 2, we exclude $t1$ that will be received anyway via re-posting from user 1, and we pick the item that maximizes the total relevance of nodes 2, 4, 5, which are the nodes that are reached by re-posting originated in user 2; this corresponds to item $t3$, which leads to total relevance of $0.4 + 0.7 + 0.5 = 1.6$. With similar arguments, one can observe that the items recommended to users 3, 4, and 5 are $t5$, $t2$, and $t4$, respectively, and the relevance of the overall recommendation by summing all individual total relevance scores is 7.3, which is 46% more than the previous case.

1.2 Contributions

In this work we aim at rethinking recommender systems underlying online social platforms by incorporating the anticipated social-network information diffusion in the recommendation strategy. The main goal is to withhold recommendations of items that will anyway reach a user via sharing/re-posting mechanisms and utilize the limited slots available for recommendations in a more profitable way. To the best of our knowledge, this dimension is hitherto unexplored in the current recommender-systems literature. Specifically, the contributions of our work are as follows.

- We devise a model of social-network diffusion that captures diffusion and user behavior aspects, such as reposting probability, number of re-posts, and probability that information propagates from one user to another. The proposed diffusion model is exploited to define a neighborhoodness graph that models the redundancy of recommending the same item to two users if this will be received anyway through social-network diffusion.
- We formulate the problem of maximizing total user engagement through social-diffusion-aware recommendations as an allocation problem in the neighborhoodness graph.
- We show that the problem is NP-hard, and propose efficient heuristics that stem from the Max-Weight Independent Set (MWIS) problem.
- We incorporate all these ingredients (i.e., social diffusion models, neighboorhoodness graph, heuristics to solve the social-diffusion-aware recommendation problem) in a novel recommender system that we call DifRec. A major feature of the proposed DifRec is that, thanks to its very general design principles, it can be used in every existing online social platform.
- We assess the performance of the proposed social-diffusion-aware DifRec recommender system in a real-world scenario involving *real* users and posts coming from the Tumblr platform. Our evaluation shows that our method achieves substantial improvement—in most cases 130–190%—in user engagement with respect to the real recommender system currently embedded in that platform and over various existing recommender systems.

The rest of the paper is organized as follows. Section 2 discusses related work. In Section 3 we report the main concepts and notations used in the paper. In Section 4 we describe the proposed DifRec recommender system in detail. Section 5 presents an experimental evaluation on a dataset coming from a real online social platform, while Section 6 concludes the paper.

2. RELATED WORK

To the best of our knowledge, the proposed DifRec recommender systems has unique features that do not appear in any other existing recommender system defined in the literature. Even the so-called *social recommender systems* (that we discuss next) do not consider it. Indeed, they aim at exploiting the social network only for better assessing how relevant an item is to a user, that is, for measuring the relevance of an item to a user by incorporating social contextual information such as the relevance of an item to the social neighborhood of that user.

In the following we however provide an overview of the most prominent works in some neighborhood areas.

Information propagation. Kempe *et al.* [16] formulate the problem information propagation (or influence maximization) as follows: given a graph and a weight w_{ij} for edge (i, j) denoting influence probability, find a set S of seed users such that the largest number of users in the graph are influenced. Kempe *et al.* show that the problem is NP-hard and propose a greedy algorithm with constant-factor approximation guarantees.

Subsequent works on the same problem attempt to improve performance and reduce complexity of seed selection [18], or study different ways of quantifying influence spread that are reasonably close to that of the greedy algorithm [6, 17]. The same problem is also tackled from different perspectives, such as a data-driven approach that learns how influence flows in the network [4], a statistical-physics approach [3], and a mechanism-design approach that elicits influence probabilities [20]. The problem of maximizing diffusion speed under strategic users that make selfish adoption decisions is studied in [21]. There also exists a body of research which focuses on extracting graph and propagation features (e.g., propagation speed) out of observed cascade data through convex maximum-likelihood problem formulations [9, 10, 24], or applying diffusion models in the context of Twitter, e.g., to predict diffusion of URLs, given a training set of URL mentions [8].

In [11] the authors consider the problem of campaign design under an opinion-formation model in social networks. The recent work [19] studies the relation between user (re)posting and social graph evolution in Twitter. The works [12, 13] present models for predicting information diffusion. The former model combines social, semantic and temporal node features to make predictions about information propagation and takes into account local behaviour of users. The latter work presents a survey on information diffusion models and methods for social networks.

Recommender systems for social networks. The work [14] uses Bayesian inference on a social network to measure rating similarity between friends and calculates the most probable recommendation through a Bayesian network inference framework. Pennacchiotti *et al.* [25] introduce the problem of tweet recommendation for one user with the objective to maximize overall interestingness of recommended tweets. Two metrics use textual content of tweets to quantify interestingness of a tweet to a user. Chen *et al.* [7] propose an approach for recommending tweets based on a collaborative ranking model. The method relies on latent factors to unveil common user interests over tweet content and user social relations. Also [2] presents an approach for analyzing social media streams to provide personalized topic recommendation to users using matrix factorization to optimize the personalized ranking of topics.

Another line of works are implicitly connected to recommender systems. In [26], the authors introduce tweet entity linking to model user interests. They identify and link named entities that users mention in their tweets and construct a graph that shows interdependence between named entities for each user. A user interest propagation algorithm similar to PageRank is proposed to propagate interest scores.

In [27], the authors present the use of Co-Factorization Machines to build predictive models in Twitter.

In [28], an online version of collaborative-filtering-based recommender system is presented, that caters for new recommendation requests and item ratings. The work [29] demonstrates an online tweet recommender system based on matrix factorization to recommend topics (hashtags) according to real-time user interests. In [30], the authors propose a tweet summarization approach to select tweets that best represent user interests. The time dimension is integrated with an iterative optimization algorithm to select tweets based on novelty, coverage and diversity. All the works above on recommender systems for social networks deal with the tweet or post recommendation problem without consideration of diffusion of information in the network.

Recommender systems and social-network diffusion. In a recent work Pan *et al.* [31] integrate collaborative filtering and information diffusion to design recommender systems so as to deal with social-update information overload. The diffusion subgraph is used so as to identify similar users to a certain user. However in our work, the diffusion of re-posts is used in a different way that aims at increasing the number of tweets that reach the user through recommendation and re-posts. We *model the anticipated diffusion* of a recommended item and use it to guide recommendation by recommending posts other than the ones that are likely to reach users via re-posts of others.

Another recommendation approach for increasing diffusion of a tweet, that of mentioning users in tweet, is presented in [32]. Users that are recommended (mentioned) in a tweet receive notification about the tweet and may re-tweet it, thus contributing to its diffusion. The problem of selecting users to mention is formulated as a ranking problem. Contrary to that, we exploit the anticipated social-network diffusion so as to optimize the recommendation of posts to users and thus increase user engagement.

Finally it is worth mentioning that avoiding duplicate (or highly similar) items has been a long-studied problem in information retrieval [1, 5, 23]. Our diffusion-aware recommender system can interestingly be viewed as an alternative way to augment the diversity of items seen by users, where the diversity is considered from a new angle, i.e., from a social-network-diffusion perspective.

3. PRELIMINARIES

We consider a set $\mathcal{U}$ of N users that are organized in a directed social graph $G = (V, E)$, where $V = \mathcal{U}$ and E is the set of edges. When a directed edge $(i, j) \in E$ exists between users i and j we say that user j "follows" i, with the implicit meaning that j has visibility on all the content generated/shared/re-posted by i. We also denote by $\mathcal{F}_i$ the set of users who follow user i, i.e., $\mathcal{F}_i = \{j \in V \mid (i, j) \in E\}$, and by $\mathcal{G}_i$ the set of users who are followed by i, i.e., $\mathcal{G}_i = \{j \in V \mid (j, i) \in E\}$.

In the remainder, we use the generic term "post" to refer to any piece of information (e.g., a news, a multimedia file, a URL, a tweet) that circulates through the social network. Thus, the term "post" may refer to either content generated by a user or an item provided to a user as a recommendation. We also use the term "re-post" to denote the action of sharing a piece of information from a user to all her followers. A user i may generate new posts, as well as re-post other posts that she has generated by herself, or have come to her by other users or through a recommender system.

Table 1: List of symbols used in the paper.

$\mathcal{S}$	Set of posts
$\mathcal{U}$	Set of users
N	Number of users
t	Post index
i, j, k	User indexes
$G = (V, E)$	Social-network graph with node (user) set V and edge set E
$G = (V_n, E_n)$	Neighborhoodness graph with node set V_n and edge set E_n
$\mathcal{L}_i$	Set of posts recommended to user i
K	Max number of posts recommended to each user
$\mathcal{F}_i$	Set of users who follow user i
$\mathcal{G}_i$	Set of users who user i follows
r_{it}	Relevance factor of post t to user i
e_{it}	Engagement factor of post t for user i
w_i	Re-post probability of user i
d_i	Out-degree of node i
$\mathcal{I}_t, W(\mathcal{I}_t)$	Independent set corresponding to post t as output of Algorithm 2
$W(\mathcal{I}_t)$	cost of independent set $\mathcal{I}_t$
E_{it}	Global engagement potential for post t when recommended to user i according to the proposed diffusion model
G_i	Diffusion subgraph with source i
$\mathcal{R}_i$	Reliable node set of user i
η	Threshold to compute reliable node sets
$\mathcal{D}$	Set of deterministic graphs sampled to generate reliable node sets
x_{it}	Control variable, equal to 1 if post t is recommended to user i, and 0 otherwise

A user i may therefore receive posts in two different ways: (i) via re-posting from users followed by her, (ii) through recommendations provided by some recommender system. In this work we focus on the impact of the recommended posts on the overall user engagement, i.e., the engagement of all the users in the network. Particularly, we fix the attention to a specific time point and study a static scenario where a set $\mathcal{S}$ of posts is available for recommendation, and the system has to recommend to each user $i \in \mathcal{U}$ a set $\mathcal{L}_i \subset \mathcal{S}$ of up to $K \ll |\mathcal{S}|$ posts from $\mathcal{S}$. K denotes the maximum number of recommendation slots available for each user ($|\mathcal{L}_i| \leq K, \forall i \in \mathcal{U}$). In real online platforms, in order to prevent users from information overload, K is typically in the order of a few tens (in some cases, it can even be equal to one). The dynamic scenario can easily be addressed by periodically updating G and $\mathcal{S}$ and running the recommendation method on the updated data. At the same time, however, a dynamic scenario clearly comes with additional problems and offers further research directions (e.g., incremental computation of the recommendations, changes in the relevance of a post, and so on), which are beyond the scope of this paper and are deferred to future work.

For each post $t \in \mathcal{S}$ and user $i \in \mathcal{U}$, we denote by r_{it} the *relevance* factor (or simply *relevance*) of t to i. Factor r_{it} quantifies how interesting post t is to user i, and, in general, it is estimated from the history of posts that user i has generated, viewed, or re-posted. Here we assume the relevance factors are computed somehow (many methods exist in the literature [25]); we provide further details on the specific method used in this work in Section 5.

The main symbols and notations used in this paper are summarized in Table 1.

4. THE DifRec RECOMMENDER SYSTEM

In this section we describe the proposed social-diffusion-aware DifRec recommender system. A major feature of our DifRec is that its general design principles make it suitable to work on any existing online social platform.

We start by introducing the diffusion model that is used to define the set of users who receive posts re-posted by a user (Section 4.1). Based on this model, we define the concept of *neighborhoodness graph* and formulate the diffusion-aware recommendation problem as an allocation problem on this neighborhoodness graph (Section 4.2). We show that the problem is NP-hard and propose a heuristic aimed at returning suboptimal solutions efficiently (Section 4.3).

4.1 Diffusion Model

We assume each user i is assigned a probability of re-posting w_i. This probability depends on how often a user tends to re-post and can be estimated from past interaction with the social platform. In Section 5 we describe how we specifically compute these probabilities for the platform considered in our experiments.

As said above, when a post is recommended to user i, it directly contributes to the engagement of that user, but it also indirectly contributes to the engagement of users $j \in \mathcal{F}_i$ that follow i. This is because if a post is of interest to user i, she may re-post it, and thus the post will be viewed by her followers as well. In turn, the followers j may re-post that post so that it will reach users that follow them, and so on. It can be seen that the initial direct recommendation of a certain post t to user i results in an *information diffusion process* in the social graph.

In the following we describe the model of diffusion considered in this work. The ultimate goal of using a diffusion model is to define the set of users who are reached by any re-posting initiated by user i. This is exploited later on (Sections 4.2–4.3) to prevent the proposed recommender system to recommend a post that will be received anyway via re-posting. We point out that our overall recommendation method is however independent of the specific diffusion model used. Any other model can be easily plugged in.

Diffusion model: Reliable node set of source i. The proposed diffusion model exploits re-posting probabilities assigned to each user to create a probabilistic graph $\widetilde{G}$ that has the same structure as the input graph G and whose edges are assigned an existence probability. More specifically, the probabilistic graph $\widetilde{G}$ is defined as a triple (V, E, p), where V and E are the node set and edge set of the input graph G, respectively, and $p : E \to (0, 1]$ is a function that assigns a probability of existence to each edge in such a way that $p(i, j) = w_i$, for all $(i, j) \in E$.

Given the probabilistic graph $\widetilde{G}$, the goal is to identify, for each user $i \in V$, a set of nodes that are reachable from i with high probability. This corresponds to finding the so-called *reliable node set* of user i [36]: given a probabilistic graph $\widetilde{G}$, a source node i, and a probability threshold $\eta \in [0, 1]$, find the set $\mathcal{R}_i$ of all nodes that are reachable from i with probability larger that η.

Computing the exact reliable node set is a hard problem, as it intrinsically relies on the problem known as *two-terminal reliability*, which consists in computing the probability that a node is reachable from another in a probabilistic graph and is known to be #P-complete [33, 34]. However, the reliable set $\mathcal{R}_i$ of node i can be accurately yet efficiently estimated via Monte Carlo sampling. The idea is to sample a set $\mathcal{D}$ of deterministic graphs from the probabilistic graph $\widetilde{G}$ according to edge probabilities and, for each of these deterministic graphs, computes the nodes reachable from i. The reliable set $\mathcal{R}_i$ is eventually computed as the set of all nodes that are reachable from i in the majority of the sampled graphs. A pseudocode of the method is reported as Algorithm 1. As the method basically performs a visit of each deterministic graph in $\mathcal{D}$, its time complexity is $\mathcal{O}(|\mathcal{D}| \times |E|)$. As a result, computing the reliable node set of all nodes in the input graph takes $\mathcal{O}(|\mathcal{D}| \times |V| \times |E|))$. Even though this time complexity may seem prohibitive for large graphs, this is not really the case as (*i*) due to the sampling strategy that relies on edge probabilities, deterministic graphs in $\mathcal{D}$ have in practice size much smaller than the input probabilistic graph $\widetilde{G}$, and (*ii*) the overall computation can easily be parallelized since reliable node sets are independent from a node to another.

Algorithm 1 Algorithm *ReliableSet*: Estimate via Monte Carlo sampling the set $\mathcal{R}_i$ of all nodes reachable from node i with probability larger than η in a probabilistic graph.

input: Probabilistic graph $\widetilde{G} = (\widetilde{V}, \widetilde{E}, p)$, node $i \in \widetilde{V}$, probability threshold $\eta \in [0, 1]$, number of samples $T \in \mathbb{N}$.
output: A set of nodes $\mathcal{R}_i \subseteq \widetilde{V}$.

$c(j) \leftarrow 0, \forall j \in V$
for $h = 1, \ldots, T$ **do**
  $E_h \leftarrow \emptyset$
  for all $e \in \widetilde{E}$ **do**
    $rnd \leftarrow$ a random number $\in [0, 1]$
    if $rnd \leq p(e)$ **then**
      $E_h \leftarrow E_h \cup \{e\}$
    end if
  end for
  $\mathcal{R}_i^{(h)} \leftarrow$ all nodes reachable from i in the graph $G_h = (V, E_h)$
  $c(j) \leftarrow c(j) + 1, \forall j \in \mathcal{R}_i^{(h)}$
end for
$\mathcal{R}_i \leftarrow \{j \in V \mid c(j) \geq T/2\}$

The reliable node set $\mathcal{R}_i$ of a node i identifies the set of users that will receive (with high probability) any post re-posted by user i. Thus, it can be safely exploited to compute the *global engagement potential* for post t when recommended to user i. This is defined as the sum of of relevance factors r_{jt} over all nodes j belonging to $\mathcal{R}_i$:

$$E_{it} = \sum_{j \in \mathcal{R}_i} r_{jt} \,. \tag{1}$$

4.2 The diffusion-aware recommendation problem

The ultimate goal of the proposed DifRec recommender system is to optimize the targeted recommendation list of posts $\mathcal{L}_i$ for each user i through exploiting the *anticipated diffusion* of posts through the social-network graph, where the social diffusion is assumed to take place according to the diffusion model presented in the previous subsection. In the following we devise an optimization problem that captures this aspect and whose solution can give the desired diffusion-aware recommendations.

Neighborhoodness graph. Given a social-network graph $G = (V, E)$ and the reliable node sets $\mathcal{R}_i$ for every node $i \in V$, we define the (directed) *neighborhoodness graph* $G_n = (V_n, E_n)$ as follows. The node set of G_n corresponds to the node set of G, i.e., $V_n = V$, while a directed edge $(i, j) \in V_n$ exists between users $i, j \in V$ if and only if node j belongs to the reliable set $\mathcal{R}_i$ of node i.

The neighborhoodness graph is aimed at modeling the conflicts of assigning a post to a user if she will receive it anyway via re-posting according to the diffusion model at hand. In other words, if an edge (i, j) exists in the neighborhoodness graph, then all posts generated/re-posted by i will reach j via re-posting, thus meaning that a post t recommended to i should not be recommended to j too as it will get to j anyway. As it will become clear in the sequel, this is exactly the rule that our DifRec follows to make recommendations: the same post is never recommended to two nodes that are adjacent in the neighborhoodness graph.

Problem statement. The recommendation of post t to user i is denoted by a variable x_{it} that is defined as follows:

$$x_{it} = \begin{cases} 1, & \text{if post } t \text{ is recommended to user } i \\ 0, & \text{otherwise}. \end{cases}$$

Let $\mathbf{x} = (x_{it} : i \in \mathcal{U}, t \in \mathcal{S})$ denote the $(N \times |\mathcal{S}|)$-dimensional vector of zeros and ones denoting the assignment of posts to users. Under the assumptions above, the problem of maximizing total user engagement is formulated as follows.

PROBLEM 1. *Given a social-network graph $G = (V, E)$, a neighborhoodness graph $G_n = (V_n, E_n)$, and a set of posts $\mathcal{S}$, find*

$$\mathbf{x}^* = \arg\max_{\mathbf{x}} \sum_{i=1}^{N} \sum_{t \in S} E_{it} x_{it} \tag{2}$$

subject to:

$$\sum_{t \in S} x_{it} = K, \tag{3}$$

$$x_{it} + x_{jt} \leq 1, \forall (i, j) \in E_n, \forall t. \tag{4}$$

Constraint (3) captures the recommendation space limit of K posts to be assigned to each user. Constraint (4) ensures that the same post is not assigned to any two nodes that are linked with an edge in the neighborhoodness graph.

We next prove that the problem is NP-hard.

THEOREM 1. *Problem 1 is NP-hard.*

PROOF. Given a neighborhoodness graph G_n, an independent set $\mathcal{I}$ on G_n is a subset of vertices so that no two vertices in $\mathcal{I}$ are adjacent in G_n. If nodes are assigned weights (for a given post t, Problem 1 assigns weight E_{it} to each vertex $i \in V_n$), a *Maximum-Weighted Independent Set* $\mathcal{I}_t$ is an independent set exhibiting maximum sum of node weights, and no pair of vertices i, j in $\mathcal{I}_t$ are adjacent in G_n.

Consider Problem 1 for just one post t. The objective is to find the subset $\mathcal{I}_t \subseteq V_n$ of users i in the neighborhoodness graph G_n to assign the post to (i.e., $x_{it} = 1$), so that the total weight $\sum_{i \in \mathcal{I}_t} E_{it} x_{it}$ is maximized, and no pair of nodes in $\mathcal{I}_t$ are linked with an edge. This exactly corresponds to the Maximum-Weighted Independent Set problem (MWIS). The MWIS problem is an extension of the Maximum-Independent-Set (MIS) problem in the sense of relaxing the assumption that all edge weights are equal to one. The MIS problem in a graph G is NP-Hard through its equivalence with the Maximum-Clique problem in the complementary graph of G [35]. As a result, Problem 1 is NP-Hard as well. □

Algorithm 2 Algorithm $IS(G_n, t)$: Heuristic for generating a weighted Independent Set of users from neighborhoodness graph $G_n = (V_n, E_n)$ for a post t.

input: Neighborhoodness graph G_n, post t, engagement weight E_{it} $\forall i \in V_n$.
output: An Independent Set $\mathcal{I}_t$ for post t of weight $W(\mathcal{I}_t)$. Post t is recommended to users $i \in \mathcal{I}_t$.

Initialization: $\mathcal{I}_t \leftarrow \emptyset$; $W(\mathcal{I}_t) = 0$; $V'_n \leftarrow V_n$; $E'_n \leftarrow E_n$.
Sort nodes i in decreasing order of $E_{it}/(1 + d_i)$.

while $V'_n \neq \emptyset$ **do**
  Examine nodes $i \in V'_n$ in the order they are sorted above.
  if $\mathcal{I}_t \cup \{i\}$ is an independent set for graph $G_n(V'_n, E'_n)$ **then**
    $\mathcal{I}_t \leftarrow \mathcal{I}_t \cup \{i\}$
    $W(\mathcal{I}_t) \leftarrow W(\mathcal{I}_t) + E_{it}$
    $V'_n \leftarrow V'_n \setminus \{i\} \setminus \mathcal{F}_i$
    $E'_n \leftarrow E'_n \setminus \{(i, j) \in E_n : j \in \mathcal{F}_i\}$
  end if
end while

4.3 Heuristic algorithm

Given that Problem 1 is NP-hard, we aim at finding a suboptimum by designing efficient yet accurate heuristics. In particular, we propose a two-step algorithm that works as follows. We consider posts to be recommended one at a time and, for each post t, we first employ a classic greedy algorithm (Algorithm 2) so as to find an independent set of users in the neighborhoodness graph. This set represents the users to whom post t can be recommended without violating constraint 4 in Problem 1. In the second step, a further greedy algorithm (Algorithm 3) takes the output of Algorithm 2 and fill the recommendation lists $\mathcal{L}_i$ of the various users accordingly.

The algorithm we employ to find an independent set $IS(G_n, t)$ in the neighborhoodness graph G_n for a given post t is a classic greedy algorithm that works as follows. Nodes i are ordered in decreasing order of $E_{it}/(1+d_i)$, where d_i is the out-degree of node i, and they are included in the independent set in that order. When a node i is included in the independent set, we remove from the graph the outgoing links from node i as well as nodes in $\mathcal{F}_i$, i.e., i's out-neighbors. The rationale is that this way priority is given to: (i) nodes exhibiting large weight, that is, users for which recommendation of post t would lead to large diffusion effect, i.e., large total relevance for users that receive the post through re-post diffusion, and (ii) nodes with small out-degree, which do not incur a large set of conflicting neighbor nodes to which the

Algorithm 3 Algorithm *Recommend*: Heuristic algorithm for post recommendation to users.

```
input: Set U(= V_n) of users, set S of posts, neighborhoodness graph G_n, Engagement metric E_it ∀i ∈ V_n, ∀t ∈ S.
output: Recommendation of a set L_i of K posts to each user i.

Initialization:
for i ∈ V_n do
    L_i ← ∅
end for
V'_n ← V_n ; S' ← S
for t ∈ S do
    IS(G_n, t)
end for

Sort posts t in decreasing order of IS weight W(I_t)
while V'_n ≠ ∅ and S' ≠ ∅ do
    Consider posts t in the order they are sorted above
    for i ∈ I_t do
        L_i ← L_i ∪ {t}
        if |L_i| = K then
            V'_n ← V'_n \ {i}
        end if
    end for
    S' ← S' \ {t}
end while
```

same post cannot be assigned. Nodes with small out-degree would therefore lead to high post reuse, i.e., recommendation of the same post in the graph. The algorithm above is referred to as Algorithm $IS(G_n, t)$ and its pseudocode is reported as Algorithm 2.

In the second stage, we need to find a set of K posts, $\mathcal{L}_i$, to be recommended to each user i. After running the $IS(G_n, t)$ algorithm we obtain an independent set $\mathcal{I}_t$ for each post $t \in \mathcal{S}$. Next, we sort posts in decreasing order of their weight $w(\mathcal{I}_t)$, and we assign posts to users in that order. Whenever for some user j we reach $|\mathcal{L}_j| = K$ assigned posts, we do not further consider this user for recommending posts. The procedure stops when each user has K recommended posts or when all posts (independent sets) are parsed. The outline of the overall recommendation algorithm is reported as Algorithm 3.

The overall time complexity is $\mathcal{O}(|\mathcal{S}|(|V_n|+|E_n|+\log|\mathcal{S}|))$, which is determined by, (i) running the IS procedure for each post $t \in \mathcal{S}$, which takes time linear in the size of the neighborhoodness graph, and (ii) sorting the posts in $\mathcal{S}$.

5. EXPERIMENTS

In this section we present the experiments we conducted in order to evaluate the performance of the proposed DifRec recommender system.

5.1 Dataset

We use real data coming from Tumblr, where users can generate content, can get connected to other users, and have the possibility to see the most recent posts of the users connected to them.[2] Particularly, the dataset consists of (i) a social-network graph that models the follower relationship among users, and (ii) posts and re-posts of the various users. Table 2 reports some public statistics.We refer the interested reader to [37] for more in deep statistics about the Tumblr social network, posts, the diffusion behavior and the similarity with other similar services such as Twitter or Facebook.

Table 2: Main characteristics of the dataset used in our evaluation.

Number of posts per user	26.17
Mean post length	421.01 Bytes
Median post length	84.28 Bytes
Number of unique users in induced graph	1.5 M
Mean indegree neighboorhoodness graph	8.70
Mean outdegree neighboorhoodness graph	10.82

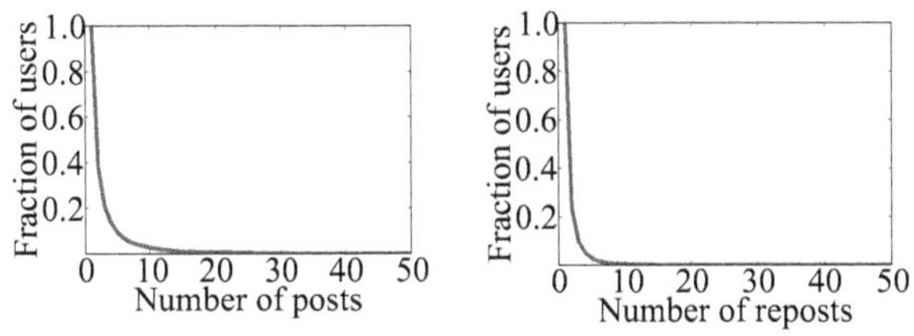

Figure 2: Post and re-post normalized distribution in our dataset.

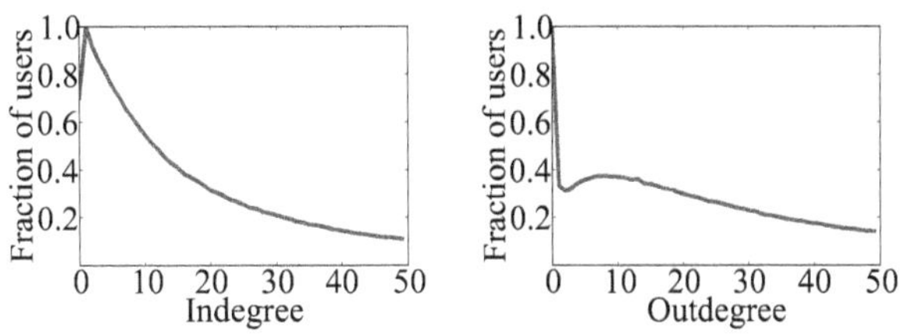

Figure 3: Normalized in-degree and out-degree distribution of our induced social graph.

We randomly sample a set of 1.5M users among users that have made at least one post/re-post during the time period from October 1st, 2013 until November 8th, 2013. As a social network, we therefore consider the subnetwork induced by this sample of users. For each user in our sample, we also extract all her public posts made during that time period. For each post, we focus on these fields: author, content, and reference to the original post (the latter clearly only if the post has been re-posted). We use the posts from October 2013 to build user profiles, posts from November 1–7 2013 to construct the neighborhoodness graph, and posts generated on November 8th for evaluation purpose (i.e., as posts to be recommended).

Figure 2 shows the normalized distribution of posts and re-posts activity in our dataset, while Figure 3 depicts the in-degree and out-degree distribution of the induced social network.

[2]The term "post" refers here to a generic piece of information.

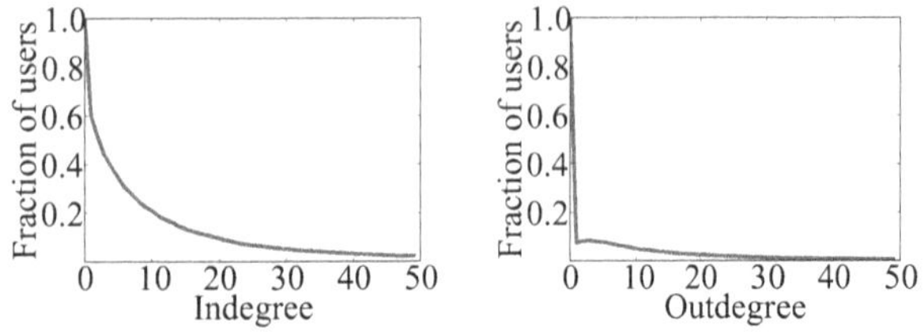

Figure 4: Normalized in-degree and out-degree distribution of our neighboorhoodness graph.

5.2 Setup

Relevance factor. We compute the relevance factor r_{it} of a post t to user i (Section 3) based on the well-established *set similarity measure* [25], which is define as a convex combination between a single-term-based score and a bi-gram-based score derived from the set of all posts that constitute the "profile" of a user. As shown in [25], the similarity set measure is strongly correlated to the actual interests of a specific user, thus making it an effective way of assessing how relevant a post is to that user.

Diffusion model. We experiment with the diffusion model described in Section 4.1. The probability w_i of re-posting of user i is computed as the percentage of re-posts of user i among all the posts she has seen in the time-window considered, that is, all the posts that have been posted or re-posted by any of the users followed by i. After analyzing the distribution of values of w_i, we set the threshold η that defines the reliable set $\mathcal{R}_i$ of user i to 0.02, as a good trade-off between stability of the model and size of the resulting neighborhoodness graph.

With this setting, the neighborhoodness graph that we get has 1.5M nodes (users), average in-degree 10.8, and average out-degree 8.7. Figure 4 depicts the normalized in-degree and out-degree distribution of the resulting neighborhoodness graph.

Baselines. We compare the proposed DifRec to the following baselines:

- *Real recommender system* (Real): this is the real recommender system embedded in the online social/micro-blogging platform we consider in our evaluation.[3]
- *Content-based recommender system* (Content): this approach is based on the estimation of the relevance factor of a post t to user i by considering only the profile of i [25]. In particular, as suggested in [25], for each user we define her profile by selecting the posts that are most relevant to her interests.
- *Social-aware recommender system* (Social): this is an extension of the Content recommender system where also the interests of i's friends are considered to construct her profile [25].

Metrics of performance assessment. We evaluate the performance of our method and the competitors in terms of the average *overall user engagement*, which is defined based on the relevance factor discussed in Section 3 and the reliable sets $\mathcal{R}_i$ used in the diffusion model described in Section 4.1.

[3]The real recommender system combines techniques from content-based and social-based recommender systems. The exact implementation details constitute sensitive information that cannot be disclosed.

As explained in the previous sections, the overall user engagement metric gives direct evidence of the quality of the recommendation.

The idea is to compute, for each user i, the sum of the relevance factors r_{it} for all the posts t that are explicitly recommended to i by the recommendation method at hand, plus the sum of the relevance factors $r_{it'}$ for all the posts t' that reach user i through diffusion according to the aforementioned diffusion model. As the number of posts ultimately recommended to any user can vary from a user to another and from a recommendation method to another (K may be only an upper bound to the number of recommended posts), we average these two sums over the number of posts recommended. The ultimate metric we consider is the average of such a quantity over all users in the network.

Formally, for a user i, let $\mathbf{R}_i$ denote the set of users whose corresponding reliable set contains user i (excluding i herself), i.e., $\mathbf{R}_i = \bigcup_{j\in V} \mathrm{I}[i \in \mathcal{R}_j] \setminus \{i\}$ (where $\mathrm{I}[\cdot]$ denotes the indicator function, which is equal to one if the argument is true, zero otherwise). The (average) user engagement $E(\mathbf{L}, i)$ of a user i given a recommendation $\mathbf{L} = \{\mathcal{L}_i\}_{i\in V}$ is defined as the sum of two terms: the relevance factor of the posts explicitly recommended to her (i.e., the posts in her recommendation list $\mathcal{L}_i$), and the relevance factor of the posts coming to her through diffusion (i.e., the posts present in the recommendation lists of all the users in $\mathbf{R}_i$); the sum of these two terms is then averaged by the size of the i's recommendation list, so as to take into account that recommendation lists may in general have variable size. Formally:

$$E(\mathbf{L}, i) = \frac{1}{|\mathcal{L}_i|}\left(\sum_{t\in\mathcal{L}_i} r_{it} \quad + \sum_{t'\in\bigcup_{j\in\mathbf{R}_i}\mathcal{L}_j} r_{it'}\right),$$

The (average) overall user engagement of a recommendation $\mathbf{L}$ is eventually computed as:

$$E(\mathbf{L}) = \frac{1}{|V|}\sum_{i\in V} E(\mathbf{L}, i). \tag{5}$$

5.3 Results

Here we present the results of our evaluation. We provide two different evaluations:

- First, we test our method along with the aforementioned baselines, on the posts that have been recommended to the selected users by the *real recommender system*. This gives us the opportunity to verify that, by reassigning those posts according to our method, we are able to increase overall user engagement with respect to recommendations provided in reality. Specifically, we select the set of posts for this experiment as follows. Among all posts recommended to the selected users by the real recommender system, we take the ones that have been re-posted by the user to which the post has been recommended; this way, we are sure that the recommendation was really effective for that user. Among all these posts, we finally select a random sample of 5K posts.
- In order to avoid being biased by the set of posts selected by the real recommender system, we also repeat the evaluation on a different set of posts, i.e. a set of 5K posts randomly selected from the most recent ones (re-)posted by the selected users. In this case, we clearly cannot compare to the real recommender

Table 3: Comparison to the reality: (average) overall user engagement results of our method, the real recommender system, and the baselines on the set of posts recommended by the real recommender system, with varying the number K of posts recommended to each user. Engagement values are shown averaged by number of posts recommended and by the number of users who received a recommendation. The last line shows the % gain of our method with respect to the best one of the other competing methods.

K	1	5	10	15	20	25
Content	2 444	2 368	2 298	2 242	2 196	2 156
Social	4 395	4 117	3 912	3 753	3 619	3 498
Real	3 385	3 395	3 404	3 399	3 398	3 398
DifRec	10 080	11 414	10 831	10 504	10 421	10 185
	+129%	+177%	+177%	+180%	+188%	+191%

Table 4: Comparison on general posts: (average) overall user engagement results of our method and the baselines on the set of most recent posts, with varying the number K of posts recommended to each user. Engagement values are shown averaged by number of posts recommended and by the number of users who received a recommendation. The last line shows the % gain of our method with respect to the best one of the other competing methods.

K	1	5	10	15	20	25
Content	13 532	11 356	10 569	10 112	9 777	9 520
Social	11 012	9 077	8 267	7 732	7 310	6 971
DifRec	18 711	20 947	23 328	23 436	23 771	24 643
	+38%	+84%	+121%	+132%	+143%	+159%

system (as the set of posts is different from the ones selected by that system); we therefore only compare with the other baselines Content and Social.

We report the details of both the evaluations next.

Table 3 reports the average overall user engagement of our DifRec compared to the real recommender system and the two other baseline recommender system described above. The set of posts considered correspond to the posts recommended by the real recommender system.

Our method turns out to outperform all competitors at least by a factor that ranges from 129% to 191% for different values of K. This implies that DifRec recommends K posts that are most relevant and interesting to the user on average. These K recommended posts are most often different from the ones that will anyway reach the user through re-posts diffusion. Another observation is that the average overall user engagement for all methods is increasing as K gets larger, but only for small/moderate values of K, i.e., up to $K = 5$ or $K = 10$. For larger values of K ($K = 10, 15, 20, 25$), the average engagement decreases. This can be explained by the fact that, as K increases, the relevance factors of recommended posts decrease (cf. Equation (5)).

The average overall user engagement of our method increases up to $K = 5$ and slightly decreases by $5 - 10\%$ for larger values of K. However, despite that slight decrease in average engagement, the percentage benefit of DifRec compared to other methods increases from 129% or 177% up to 191% as K increases. This implies that our method tends to efficiently exploit the recommendation space better by recommending posts other than the ones that will reach the user through repost diffusion.

Similar performance benefits can be observed when comparing with two baselines over a more general, randomly drawn dataset in Table 4.

More details about both comparisons are shown in Tables 5 and 6, where we report cumulative distributions about percentage of users having (average) overall user engagement larger than various values. It can be observed that the distribution exhibited by the proposed DifRec is above the ones of the other competitors: for every value of user engagement, the proposed DifRec exhibits percentage values larger than all the competitors, thus further attesting its superiority.

6. CONCLUSIONS

In this work we propose DifRec, a novel recommender system that aims at increasing the overall user engagement in online social platforms by taking into account the social-network diffusion process. In particular, we take into account the fact that, when a user shares or re-posts a recommended item, her followers indirectly receive the post. Considering this aspect, that, to the best of our knowledge, has never been considered by any existing recommender systems, may allow for better selecting the items to be recommended to a user, by avoiding for instance to recommend to her an item that would have reached her anyway via re-posting.

We evaluate the proposed DifRec recommender systems by using real data coming from the Tumblr platform. We show that our DifRec improves upon the overall user engagement of the real recommender system embedded in that platform and various other existing recommender systems up to a factor of 130–190%.

Acknowledgement

This work was supported by the LEADS project (ICT-318809) funded by the European Community.

7. REFERENCES

[1] R. Agrawal, S. Gollapudi, A. Halverson and S. Ieong "Diversifying Search Results". In *WSDM*, 2009.

[2] E. Diaz-Aviles, L. Drumond, L. Schmidt-Thieme and W. Nejdl "Real-Time Top-N Recommendation in Social Streams". In *RecSys*, 2012.

[3] F. Altarelli, A. Braunsten, L. Dall' Asta and R. Zecchina, "Optimizing spread dynamics on graphs by message passing". In *Journal of Statistical Mechanics: Theory and Experiment*, 2013.

[4] A. Goyal, F. Bonchi, L. V. S. Lakshmanan, "A Data-Based Approach to Social Influence Maximization". In *PVLDB*, 2011.

Table 5: Percentage of users having (average) overall user engagement larger than a certain value: results of our method, the real recommender system, and the baselines, on the set of posts recommended by the real recommender system ($K = 10$ and $K = 20$).

engagement	$K = 10$				$K = 20$			
(Equation (5))	Content	Social	Real	DifRec	Content	Social	Real	DifRec
> 4000	69.80%	78.27%	69.61%	**78.56%**	69.54%	78.11%	69.73%	**78.67%**
> 6000	67.49%	76.06%	66.77%	**76.47%**	67.22%	75.89%	66.88%	**76.57%**
> 8000	65.95%	74.60%	65.00%	**74.98%**	65.68%	74.42%	65.10%	**75.07%**
> 10000	64.84%	73.51%	63.78%	**73.89%**	64.56%	73.33%	63.85%	**73.97%**

Table 6: Percentage of users having (average) overall user engagement larger than a certain value: results of our method, and the baselines, on the set of most recent posts ($K = 10$ and $K = 20$).

engagement	$K = 10$			$K = 20$		
(Equation (5))	Content	Social	DifRec	Content	Social	DifRec
> 4000	64.23%	72.87%	**73.58%**	63.96%	72.75%	**73.39%**
> 6000	59.92%	68.77%	**69.73%**	59.65%	68.65%	**69.54%**
> 8000	56.91%	65.91%	**67.02%**	56.65%	65.78%	**66.86%**
> 10000	54.66%	63.75%	**64.99%**	54.41%	63.62%	**64.85%**

[5] G. Capannini, F. M. Nardini, R. Perego and F. Silvestri "Efficient diversification of web search results". In *PVLDB*, 2011.

[6] W. Chen, C. Wang, and Y. Wang, "Scalable influence maximization for prevalent viral marketing in large-scale social networks". In *KDD*, 2010.

[7] K. Chen, T. Chen, G. Zheng, Ou Jin, E. Yao, and Y. Yu, "Collaborative personalized tweet recommendation". In *SIGIR*, 2012.

[8] W. Galuba, K. Aberer, D. Chakraborty, Z. Despotovic, W. Kellerer, "Outtweeting the twitterers-predicting information cascades in microblogs". In *WOSN*, 2010.

[9] M. Gomez-Rodriguez, D. Balduzzi, B. Schoelkopf, "Uncovering the temporal dynamics of diffusion networks". In *ICML*, 2011.

[10] M. Gomez-Rodriguez, J. Leskovec, and A. Krause, "Inferring networks of diffusion and influence". In *KDD*, 2010.

[11] A. Gionis, E. Terzi and P. Tsaparas "Opinion maximization in social networks". In *SDM*, 2013.

[12] A. Guille, H. Hacid, "A predictive model for the temporal dynamics of information diffusion in online social networks". In *WWW Companion*, 2012.

[13] A. Guille, H. Hacid, C. Favre, D. Zighed, "Information Diffusion in Online Social Networks: A Survey". In *SIGMOD Record*, 2013.

[14] X. Yang, Y. Guo and Y. Liu, "Bayesian-inference based recommendation in online social networks". In *IEEE Trans. on Parallel and Distr. Systems*, 2013.

[15] Y. Koren, R. Bell and C. Volinsky, "Matrix factorization techniques for recommender systems". In *IEEE Computer*, 2009.

[16] D. Kempe, J. M. Kleinberg, and E. Tardos, "Maximizing the spread of influence through a social network". In *KDD*, 2003.

[17] M. Kimura and K. Saito, "Tractable models for information diffusion in social networks". In *PKDD*, 2006.

[18] J. Leskovec, A. Krause, C. Guestrin, C. Faloutsos, J. VanBriesen, and N. Glance, "Cost-effective outbreak detection in networks". In *KDD*, 2007.

[19] S. Myers and J. Leskovec, "The Bursty Dynamics of the Twitter Information Network". In *WWW*, 2014.

[20] M. Mohite and Y. Narahari "Incentive Compatible Influence Maximization in Social Networks and Application to Viral Marketing". In *AAMAS*, 2011.

[21] J. Ok, Y. Jin, J. Shin and Y. Yi, "On Maximizing diffusion speed in social networks: Impact of random seeding and clustering". In *Sigmetrics*, 2014.

[22] A. Rajaraman and A.D. Ullman, "Mining of Massive Datasets". *Cambridge University Press, 2012.*

[23] Y. Shia, X. Zhaob, J. Wangb, M. Larsona and A. Hanjalic "Adaptive Diversification of Recommendation Results via Latent Factor Portfolio". In *SIGIR*, 2012.

[24] K. Saito, K. Ohara, Y. Yamagishi, M. Kimura, H. Motoda, "Learning diffusion probability based on node attributes in social networks". In *ISMIS*, 2011.

[25] M. Pennacchiotti, F. Silvestri, H. Vahabi, R. Venturini, "Making your interests follow you on Twitter". In *CIKM*, 2012.

[26] W. Shen, J. Wang, P. Luo, M. Wang, "Linking Named Entities in Tweets with Knowledge Base via User Interest Modeling". In *KDD*, 2013.

[27] L. Hong, A. Doumith, B. Davison, "Co-Factorization Machines: Modeling User Interests and Predictiong Individual Decisions in Twitter". In *WSDM*, 2013.

[28] B. Chandramouli, J.J. Levandovski, A. Elwady and M.F. Mokbel, "StreamRec: A real-time recommender system". In *SIGMOD*, 2011.

[29] C. Chen, H. Yin, J. Yao, B. Cui, "TeRec: A Temporal Recommender System Over Tweet Stream", In *Proceedings of the VLDB Endowment*, 2013.

[30] Z. Ren, S. Liang, E. Meij, M. de Rijke, "Personalized Time-Aware Tweets Summarization". In *SIGIR*,2013.

[31] Y. Pan, F. Cong, K. Chen, Y. Yu, "Diffusion-aware Personalized Social Update Recommendation". In *RecSys*, 2013.

[32] B. Wang, C. Wang, J. Bu, C. Chen, W. V. Azhang, D. Cai, X. He, "Whom to Mention: Expand the Diffusin of Tweets by @ recommendation on Micro-blogging Systems". In *WWW*, 2013.

[33] C. J. Colbourn, The combinatorics of network reliability. *Oxford University Press*, 1987.

[34] J.S. Provan and M.O. Ball, "The complexity of counting cuts and of computing the probability that a graph is connected". In *SIAM J. Comput.*, 1983.

[35] M.R. Garey and D.S. Johnson, Computers and intractability: A guide to the theory of NP-Completeness. *Freeman, New York*, 1979.

[36] A. Khan, F. Bonchi, A. Gionis, F. Gullo, "Fast Reliability Search in Uncertain Graphs". In *EDBT*, 2014.

[37] Y. Chang, L. Tang, Y. Inagaki, Y. Liu, "What is Tumblr: a statistical overview and comparison.", In *SIGKDD Explor. Newsl.*, 2014.

Who With Whom And How? - Extracting Large Social Networks Using Search Engines

Stefan Siersdorfer, Philipp Kemkes, Hanno Ackermann, Sergej Zerr
L3S Research Center, Hannover, Germany
{siersdorfer,kemkes,zerr}@L3S.de
ackermann@tnt.uni-hannover.de

ABSTRACT

Social network analysis is leveraged in a variety of applications such as identifying influential entities, detecting communities with special interests, and determining the flow of information and innovations. However, existing approaches for extracting social networks from unstructured Web content do not scale well and are only feasible for small graphs. In this paper, we introduce novel methodologies for query-based search engine mining, enabling efficient extraction of social networks from large amounts of Web data. To this end, we use patterns in phrase queries for retrieving entity connections, and employ a bootstrapping approach for iteratively expanding the pattern set. Our experimental evaluation in different domains demonstrates that our algorithms provide high quality results and allow for scalable and efficient construction of social graphs.

Categories and Subject Descriptors

H.3.3 [**Information Systems**]: Information storage and retrieval; E.1 [**Data Structures**]: Graphs and networks

Keywords

pattern based queries, social network extraction

1. INTRODUCTION

Networking and communication are natural human activities that are massively supported through modern information technologies, most prominently the internet. Large networks of people are present in many parts of the Web, for instance, in form of contacts and friends in Social Web platforms, co-occurring named entities in web pages, or co-authors of articles in scientific portals. Social networks extracted from these information sources are exploited for various purposes: Node centrality measures in networks can help to identify important and influential persons or communities in areas such as entertainment, science, or politics. Information on social connections in customer networks can be leveraged as part of recommender systems that suggest items and new contacts to their users. Furthermore, knowing the topology of social graphs can shed light on the propagation of ideas and trust in social networks [36, 1, 12], and can enhance various IR applications such as personalized query expansion and media recommendation [4, 13].

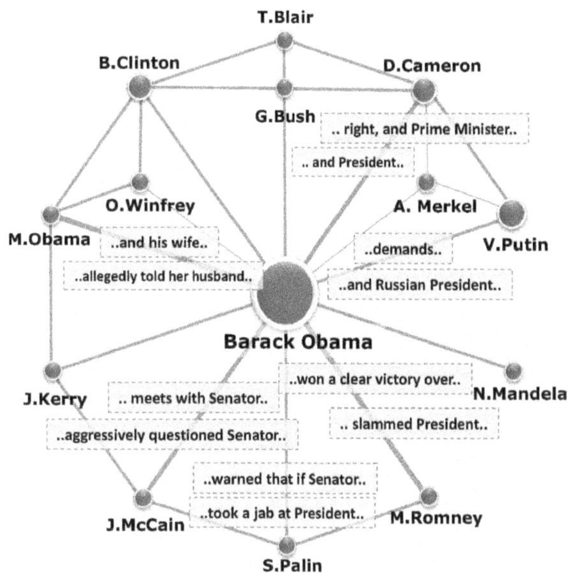

Figure 1: Subgraph of a network extracted using our approach along with examples for connecting phrase patterns.

In order to enable the analysis of social networks they have to be extracted from underlying data in the first place. Some sources already provide explicit and easy to extract information about user relations. This includes online platforms such as Facebook, Twitter, or LinkedIn that maintain user databases and offer software interfaces for accessing contacts, friends, or followers. Other sources - for instance, email corpora revealing communication links between persons, or scientific portals comprising information on co-authorship - contain more implicit, yet easy to extract network information. However, in many cases information about social connections is hidden within unstructured data such as Web pages, archives, and multimedia repositories.

Search engines constitute our main access points to the Web, and there exists a number of works that employ search queries for detecting co-occurrences of entities and leverage these connections for extracting social networks [20, 25, 30]. However, the suggested algorithmic approaches do not scale well and are only suitable for rather small datasets comprising just a few hundred or a few thousand nodes.

Permission to make digital or hard copies of all or part of this work for personal or classroom use is granted without fee provided that copies are not made or distributed for profit or commercial advantage and that copies bear this notice and the full citation on the first page. Copyrights for components of this work owned by others than ACM must be honored. Abstracting with credit is permitted. To copy otherwise, or republish, to post on servers or to redistribute to lists, requires prior specific permission and/or a fee. Request permissions from Permissions@acm.org.
CIKM'15, October 19–23, 2015, Melbourne, Australia.
© 2015 ACM. ISBN 978-1-4503-3794-6/15/10 ...$15.00.
DOI: http://dx.doi.org/10.1145/2806416.2806582.

In this paper, we exploit pattern-based search engine queries for efficient acquisition of large scale networks from unstructured Web data. These queries consist of entities (e.g. "Barack Obama") and connecting patterns (e.g. "meets with", "and his wife") leveraged for mining links between persons. Using such search patterns we can simultaneously explore a large number of connections with a single query. Starting with an initial set of entities, we iteratively expand both entity pair and pattern sets. We identify connections which are likely to be important and use this information to formulate subsequent queries, thereby greatly reducing the number of search engine requests. For illustration, a small excerpt of a constructed graph is shown in Figure 1.

The main contributions of this work can be summarized as follows:

- We introduce intelligent prioritization approaches for efficiently expanding social networks using pattern based search engine queries.
- We employ a bootstrapping approach for covering multiple aspects of social relations by iteratively extending search pattern and entity sets for discovering domain specific social connections.
- We conduct an extensive experimental evaluation demonstrating the high efficiency and accuracy of our methods clearly outperforming the baseline. Furthermore, we analyze various aspects of the extracted social graphs, such as their structural properties, connecting patterns, and strength of social relations.

The remainder of this paper is organized as follows: Section 2 discusses related work on social network construction from semi-structured data sources, search engine based network mining, and extraction of semantic relationships. In Section 3 we describe our methods for network extraction including search patterns and their expansion based on bootstrapping as well as different search prioritization criteria. The evaluation presented in Section 4 studies the cost efficiency and accuracy of our methods, and provides further insights about the structure of the extracted networks. Finally, in Section 5 we conclude and describe directions of our future work.

2. RELATED WORK

There is a plethora of work on social network extraction from text and visual data. In [9], for instance, social connections between fictional characters are inferred from dialogs in books, and, similarly, in [19] a social network is extracted from the narrative of an Ottoman scholar and world traveler. In [10] social connections are constructed from a historical multimedia repository by leveraging co-occurrences of faces in images. Bird et al. [3] extract social networks using information about senders and recipients obtained from headers in email corpora. Social networks extracted from other (semi-)structured sources include academic networks or co-citation graphs in publication databases [28, 34].

Information extraction tackles the problem of deriving structured information from unstructured data. There is a body of work on semantic relationship mining based on textual patterns [2, 22]. In [32] a bootstrapping algorithm is employed for iteratively discovering new patterns and semantic connections. In [33] and [5] categorical facts and concept hierarchies are extracted from web and news corpora as entity-pattern-entity triples. Cimiano et al. [7, 8] leverage pattern-based search engine queries for building ontologies. In [16] comparable entities such as consumer items are extracted using an expandable set of contrasting expressions (e.g. "vs." and "instead of"); Jiang et al. [17] use similar relations for constructing entity graphs and product recommendations in web search. The KnowItAll system [11] employs a supervised learning approach for validating facts extracted using search engine queries based on manually provided pattern templates. Open information extraction systems such as TextRunner [35] employ shallow parsing, and, as patterns, employ normalized expressions between noun phrases in an unsupervised manner. The output of these systems are databases that contain fact tuples such as "*(Berkley, located in, Bay Area)*" or "*(Oppenheimer, professor of, theoretical physics)*". In contrast to works focusing on general fact mining, we provide a novel methodology for extracting social networks. Our contributions include the systematic construction of connected social graphs, their efficient and intelligent expansion, as well as the analysis of their structural properties.

The first approach employing search engines for network mining is probably the work by Kautz et al. [20]. The authors exploit co-occurrences of names on result pages to identify connections between persons; the resulting networks are relatively small and just centered around a single person. The POLYPHONET system [25, 26] determines co-occurrence counts in Google queries to identify pairwise connections. In addition, different types of relationships and correlations with topic-related keywords are taken into account to disambiguate entities. In [6] search engines are used to retrieve connected email addresses. The Flink system [27] focuses on the mining of author networks and combines web search with information from emails and publications. In [29] co-occurrences of persons in search result snippets are leveraged. There are a few attempts to increase efficiency in discovering entity relations on the web [15, 30]; they focus on snippet clustering and entity disambiguation to reduce the number of search requests. However, all of the current methods are based on pair-wise entity queries, making them infeasible for mining larger graphs.

To the best of our knowledge, our methods are the first to go beyond pair-wise querying for social connections and use intelligent query pattern construction and prioritization approaches for graph expansion that allow for tunable and larger scale network construction.

3. SOCIAL GRAPH MINING

In this section we describe our methodology for mining social graphs using search engines. To this end, we first introduce an efficient basic algorithm using web search with a fixed pattern set for identifying connections between persons. We then extend this method by an iterative approach for automatically collecting new patterns. Finally, in order to further improve the cost efficiency of network construction, we introduce methods for prioritizing nodes for graph expansion.

3.1 Mining Graphs with a Static Set of Query Patterns

Given an initial seed set of entities I and a set of patterns P, we use connectivity search queries of the form <*entity*> <*p*> (where <*p*> is a connecting pattern as e.g. in "Barack Obama meets") in order to identify links to other entities. We iteratively issue these queries over an initial seed set of entities (e.g. a list of a politicians). In this way we obtain links between entities in the seed set as well as new entities. This is repeated for all patterns in our pattern set (in our experiments we used a small initial set consisting of the single term "and"). For snippets of the top-k search results in Bing we check for exact strings of the form <*entity*> <*p*> <*entity*> where both entities match a person name in a database (we were using entities from DBpedia and IMDb in our experiments).[1] The process of querying entities is repeated for the newly discovered entities in a "breadth-first" manner. The resulting (undirected) edges between two entities are weighted by the overall occurrence count in the snippets across all patterns, omitting edges whose weight is below a threshold τ.

Algorithm 2 shows the details of the algorithm. The network and a priority queue of nodes are initialized based on the entity seed set (lines 2–4). Here the priority queue is a simple "first-in-first-out" queue; in Section 3.3 we will introduce more enhanced mechanisms for prioritization. The nodes in the queue serve as input for pattern-based queries (line 8), and query results are used for expanding the social network and updating the queue (lines 9–17). The network expansion continues until the query budget is spent or until there are no unvisited nodes left (line 19). The running time of the algorithm is linear in the sum of nodes and edges visited and found.

3.2 Iterative Pattern Mining

We extend the Graph Mining method described above through an approach for iteratively discovering new patterns. To this end, we start with an initial set of seed patterns and extend it in each round of the algorithm, taking into account the weights of edges extracted in that round.

We then iterate over the top-h resulting edges with the highest weight and use them to issue queries of the form "<*entity*>" "<*entity*>". Snippets of the search results are then checked for strings of the form <*entity*> <*c*> <*entity*>, where <*c*> is an arbitrary string between two different entities; <*c*> becomes a candidate for a new pattern. Among the candidates we want to identify patterns with high coverage in the result snippets. To this end, let n be number of occurrences of candidate pattern <*c*> (support), m be the number of distinct entity pairs (diversity) and d be the number of distinct domains (spam resistance) comprising the pattern. We include <*c*> into the pattern set if $n \cdot m \cdot d^2$ is above a threshold σ. Extracting top-k patterns can be managed effectively using a priority queue with $log(n)$ running time for operations like insertion and updating. This pattern mining method is employed after each complete iteration of the algorithm described in the previous paragraph.

[1] We decided to keep the entity recognition sub-component simple and lightweight. More enhanced NLP and disambiguation techniques are out of the scope of this work, but could help to further improve our already very good results.

Algorithm 1: Graph Construction with Pattern Set Expansion

```
Input: I: initial set of entities
IP: initial set of patterns
τ: threshold for edge weights
σ: threshold for pattern weights
maxIter: maximum number of iterations
Output: social graph G = (V, E)
1  begin
2    E ← ∅
3    V ← I
4    Cand ← I // graph extension candidates
5    P ← IP // pattern set
6    iter ← 0
7    repeat
8      NewCand ← ∅
9      NewPatterns ← ∅
10     for e ∈ Cand do
11       edges ← search(e, P, τ) // web search for
           edges with node e, using query patterns
           P and weight threshold τ
12       for ({e, e_i}, w) ∈ edges do
13         if {e, e_i} ∉ E then
14           V ← V ∪ {e_i}
15           NewCand ← NewCand ∪ {e_i}
16           E ← E ∪ {({e, e_i}, w)}
17         else
18           E ← E \ {({e, e_i}, x)}
19           E ← E ∪ {({e, e_i}, x + w)}
20     Cand ← Cand ∪ NewCand
21     NewPatterns ← pSearch(E, σ) // web search
         for patterns, using edges from E, and
         weight threshold σ
22     P ← P ∪ NewPatterns; iter ← iter + 1
23   until iter = maxIter;
24   return (V, E)
```

The details of the algorithm are shown in Algorithm 1. Seed patterns and entities are first used to initialize the bootstrapping approach (lines 2–5). Then, for a fixed number of iterations, the social network is expanded based on the current query patterns (lines 11–19), and, conversely, the pattern set is expanded using the current edges in the network (lines 21–22). The running time of the algorithm is linear in the sum of nodes and edges visited, multiplied by the number of patterns found.

3.3 Prioritization of Nodes for Network Expansion

The algorithms described so far expand the social graph in a "breath-first-search" manner. The advantage of this approach is its good coverage: Seedset and subsequentially found nodes are systematically visited and expanded until our budget of connectivity queries is exhausted. However, in order to further optimize budget usage we might want to put higher priority on more "essential" nodes during the network expansion process. In the following we focus on two criteria for prioritizing nodes: popularity and novelty.

Algorithm 2: Graph Construction with Static Pattern Set

```
Input: I: initial set of entities
       P: set of patterns
       τ: threshold for edge weights
       maxReq: maximum number of requests
       pQueue: A container which sorts the candidates
       according to the employed algorithm
Output: social graph G = (V, E)
begin
    E ← ∅ // Edges
    V ← I // Vertices
    pQueue.addAll(I) // graph extension candidates
    requestCnt ← 0
    repeat
        e ← pQueue.pop()
        (edges, requests) ← search(e, P, τ) // web
            search for edges with node e, using query
            patterns P and weight threshold τ
        for ({e, e_i}, w) ∈ edges do
            if {e, e_i} ∉ E then
                V ← V ∪ {e_i}
                E ← E ∪ {({e, e_i}, w)}
                if e_i ∉ pQueue then
                    pQueue.push(e_i)
            else
                E ← E \ {({e, e_i}, x)}
                E ← E ∪ {({e, e_i}, x + w)}
        requestCnt ← requestCnt + requests
    until requestCnt ≥ maxReq or pQueue.empty();
    return (V, E)
```

Popularity in this context intuitively corresponds to the importance of nodes within the network. We employ the number of inlinks ρ in the current version of the social graph during the extraction process as popularity measure. Although very effective in our experiments, one could easily imagine using alternative node centrality measures such as PageRank [31], hub scores in HITS [21], or one of their various variants (e.g. [23, 18]).

Novelty, on the other hand, corresponds to how recently a node was added in the course of our network construction process. Intuitively, exploring more recent nodes can help to reach out more quickly to new communities within the network. We combine popularity and novelty into a priority measure Φ for a node v using exponential temporal decay as follows: $\Phi(v) = \rho \cdot e^{-\alpha \cdot t}$, where our time measure t corresponds to the number of expansion node steps conducted since the node was added to the queue, and α is a parameter for balancing the influence of popularity and novelty. Exponential decay is often used for time dependent ranking of items in the context of IR (see e.g. TempPageRank [37]). This approach can be directly integrated in the framework provided in Algorithm 2 using a priority queue based on the Φ score, and could, in principle, also be integrated into the dynamic pattern mining process (Algorithm 1).

4. EVALUATION

In this section we evaluate the network extraction methods described in Section 3, starting with entities from two domains: politics and movies. The objective of our evaluation was to study (1) the cost efficiency of different strategies in terms of network size obtained with a given budget of search engine requests, (2) the accuracy of the extracted networks, and (3) the structure of the social graphs as well as properties of discovered social relations. In our experiments, more than 300,000 persons and 1.4 million social connections were retrieved using two seed sets containing just 342 politicians and 100 actors. The resulting networks are coined WikiNet and IMDbNet.

4.1 Setup

Domains and Seed Sets. For initializing our algorithms we used two entity seed sets from political and movie domains as follows:

- *WikiNet seed*: We extracted 342 politician names from the Wikipedia list of the current heads of state and government from all over the world[2].
- *IMDbNet seed*: We considered the 100 current and former leading actors as listed in IMDB[3].

In order to simplify named entity recognition in search engine snippets, we restricted the set of possible persons in our WikiNet to those listed in *DBpedia Version 2014* (containing about 1 million distinct person names) and in the IMDbNet to names from the IMDb directory (about 2 million distinct names).

Implementation Details. We employed the Bing Search Engine API for issuing our network expansion queries. Preliminary tests showed that in most cases the overall result list returned per query did not exceed $k = 200$ entries, although the estimated number of results often went beyond thousands. Therefore, we issued 4 requests per query as Bing provides 50 results per request (if available). In order to avoid recurring API requests we simultaneously cached results from previous queries. The search API has some technical limitations, including the fact that a few (special) characters, like "&", ",", "+" cannot be used as search query. Furthermore, most of the snippets returned for disjunctive queries do not contain query terms, and, thus, cannot be used for relation extraction.

Tested Strategies. We evaluated the following methods:

- The breadth-first graph mining approach with fixed pattern set described in Section 3.1 (**BF**).
- The prioritization approach from Section 3.3, with different values for the tunable decay parameter α (0, 0.005, and 0.01) (**Prio**).
- The iterative pattern mining approach described in Section 3.2 (**PatternIter**).

[2] http://en.wikipedia.org/wiki/List_of_current_heads_of_state_and_government

[3] http://www.imdb.com/list/ls050274118/

	Algorithm	Nodes	Edges
WikiNet	baseline t=0.1	6,956	13,571
	baseline t=0.4	2,925	3,838
	BF	113,988	368,806
	decay α=0	98,479	456,223
	decay α=0.005	110,260	346,663
	decay α=0.01	116,081	323,372
IMDbNet	baseline t=0.1	7,159	34,903
	baseline t=0.4	2,192	6,666
	BF	109,453	376,429
	decay α=0	107,085	425,830
	decay α=0.005	112,736	264,679
	decay α=0.01	112,782	242,184

Table 1: Number of nodes and edges obtained for different strategies.

We set the edge weight threshold τ to 2 for all algorithms. For *PatternIter* we set the cut-off value σ for pattern selection to 5, and used value $h = 100$ for top connections employed for discovering new patterns. The initial query pattern sets used in our experiments consisted only of the general pattern "and"; for extracting connections from snippets we employed an additional small set of manually selected patterns[4].

Baseline. All of the current works on social graph construction using search engines are based on pairwise entity queries. As **baseline** we tested the method described in [25] (POLYPHONET) which tries to reduce the number of pairwise queries by identifying subsets of promising query pairs. More specifically, starting with a seed set of entities, for each entity a list of candidate entities (contained in the entity set) is extracted from Web pages obtained by querying for the entity. Then queries for the pairs of seed entities and the candidates for associated entities are issued in order to obtain co-occurrence values based on search result counts, and edges with a value above a threshold t are included in the graph. In order to allow for network expansion beyond the seed set, we included further entities found in the Web pages for identifying additional query candidates.

4.2 Cost Efficiency

Table 1 shows the number of nodes and edges in the expanded networks computed by our methods using the same seed sets and exhausting a fixed budget of 200k queries per run. The main observations are the following:

- Starting with the small seed sets consisting of just a few hundred entities described in the setup, our methods are able to extract networks containing around 100,000 entities, and between 200,000 and 450,000 edges for both domains. Our quality oriented evaluation in Section 4 will demonstrate the high accuracy of edges generated by our methods.
- The tunable decay parameter α in the prioritization approach *Prio* is applicable for trading novelty against popularity. This is reflected in both domains by the larger number of social relations extracted for lower values of α and the larger number of nodes found for higher values of α.
- Our new methods clearly outperform the *baseline* which does not scale well for expanding entity sets and produces much smaller networks for the given budget. Even for a small co-occurrence threshold $t = 0.1$ the networks obtained by the baseline method are already between one and two orders of magnitude smaller. For $t = 0.4$ (suggested in POLYPHONET for extracting relations of acceptable quality) the reduction in network growth becomes even more apparent.

[4]The following patterns were used: "meets", "␣", "&", ",", "speaks with", "und", "et", "y", "-"

Note, that in addition to the number of search engine requests taken into account for this evaluation, the baseline also introduces a substantial overhead by requiring the download and processing of a large set of Web pages (about 85,000 pages in our experiments). In contrast, our methods avoid these extra costs by working directly on search result snippets.

Figure 2 provides additional details about the network size development with respect to the amount of search engine requests spent. The effect of a stronger emphasis on novelty (corresponding to higher α) is reflected in a slight increase in the number of new nodes, starting from around 50k – 100k requests. On the other hand, prioritization of popular nodes with high in-degree (lower α) leads to a high increase in the number of edges (starting from around 10k requests for both datasets).

4.3 Network Properties

In the following we describe structural properties of the extracted networks as well as the development of the networks during the execution of our algorithms.

Node Degree and Edge Weight Distributions. Table 2 provides summary statistics for the distribution of nodes and edges in the extracted networks. For all experiments we observe a right-skewed distribution of nodes and edges with median node degree of 1 or 2 and median edge weight of 3. (The edge weights in all the experiments follow a power law distribution as exemplarily depicted in Figure 5 for the *BF*-constructed WikiNet.) The decay parameter α for the *Prio* strategy has a clear impact on the distributions: Decreasing the value of α results in an increase of the means for both node degree and edge weights due to the higher prioritization of nodes with already high degree, and also results in a wider "spread" of the values as reflected by a higher standard deviation.

Figure 3 shows the degree distributions of the nodes in the constructed networks. The distribution for the breadth-first (*BF*) strategy is close to a power law distribution. For the *Prio* strategies the described effect for the decay parameter α interferes with the power law, resulting in two local extrema: a minimum for nodes with lower in-degree followed by a maximum for nodes with higher in-degree.

Graph Structures. Figure 4 visualizes the social networks obtained for different methods and seed sets. For the prioritization strategy *Prio* the decay parameter α has a strong influence on the network structure: For a stronger focus on popularity ($\alpha = 0$) the larger number of edges results in higher graph density; putting more emphasis on novelty ($\alpha = 0.01$) leads to a wider spread of the graph, providing a bird's eye view of the discovered space. A more in-depth exploration of community structures is subject to our future work.

		Node Degree			Edge Weight		
	Algorithm	Mean	SD	Median	Mean	SD	Median
WikiNet	BF	6.47	12.53	2	8.53	23.62	3
	decay α=0	9.27	16.24	2	8.84	23.93	3
	decay α=0.005	6.29	9.46	2	7.65	18.43	3
	decay α=0.01	5.57	8.39	2	7.65	17.95	3
IMDbNet	BF	6.88	14.03	1	8.69	24.11	3
	decay α=0	7.95	15.43	1	8.97	25.04	3
	decay α=0.005	4.70	7.60	2	7.43	19.14	3
	decay α=0.01	4.29	6.74	2	7.35	18.67	3

Table 2: Summary statistics for node degrees and edge weights in the extracted networks.

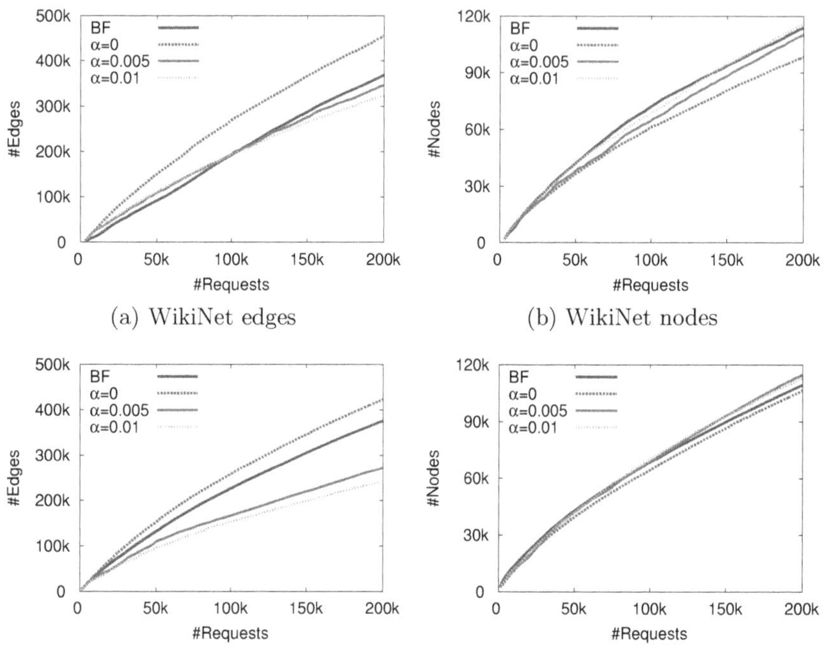

(a) WikiNet edges (b) WikiNet nodes

(c) IMDbNet edges (d) IMDbNet nodes

Figure 2: Nodes and edges versus requests spent for WikiNet and IMDbNet.

Example Connections. Finally, Table 3 lists the top-15 connections in the IMDbNet found by the *BF* method. Among those connections are famous co-actors ("Terence Hill" and "Bud Spencer"), romantic couples ("Ryan Gosling" and "Eva Mendes"), or a combination of both ("Brad Pitt" and "Angelina Jolie" - the strongest connection obtained). In addition, we observe that our methods are also capable of discovering connections from other domains ("Sergey Brin" and "Larry Page").

4.4 Quality of Extracted Networks

We conducted a large user study to evaluate the quality of the constructed networks with overall 5,600 evaluated edges. The goal of our evaluation was two-fold: First to check the correctness of the extracted social connections; second to evaluate strength of the connections in more detail.

Pairwise assessment. Determining the correctness of a connection between two persons is a difficult task for human assessors. Therefore, instead of letting assessors directly assign a relevance value, we first asked them to choose between two reference connections. One of the connected pairs was obtained using our method and the other consisted of persons uniformly sampled from the entity set (the order of these two options was randomized). Users were asked the following question: "Which of the given pairs has the stronger relation?", and were encouraged to use any source including search engines to answer this question (as an aid we provided links to a Google search page). The assessors consisted of 15 undergraduate students of Computer Science and other disciplines, and 5 graduate students of Computer Science.

Table 4 shows that all of our methods achieved accuracy values between 95% and 99%, demonstrating the correct extraction of almost all tested edges. Overall, for 4694 out of 4800 edge pairs the users preferred the connections discovered by our algorithms. We measured inter-rater agreement with 5 users for a subset of 200 edges from each of the constructed networks and obtained an average pairwise percent agreement of 93.7% and 96.5% for WikiNet and IMDbNet, respectively, also reflected by high Fleiss' Kappa [14] values of 0.83 for WikiNet and 0.97 for IMDbNet.

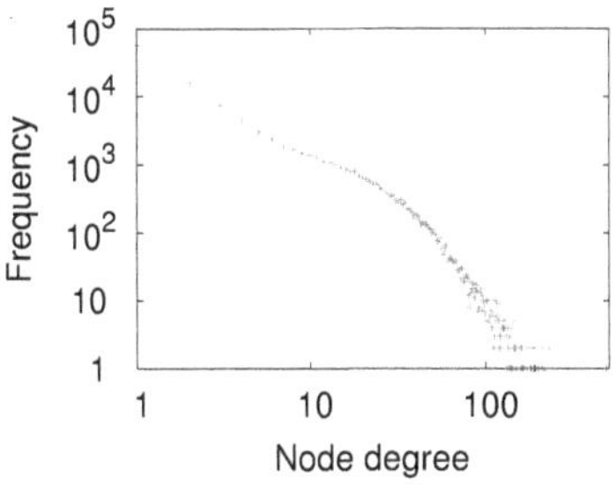

(a) WikiNet BF

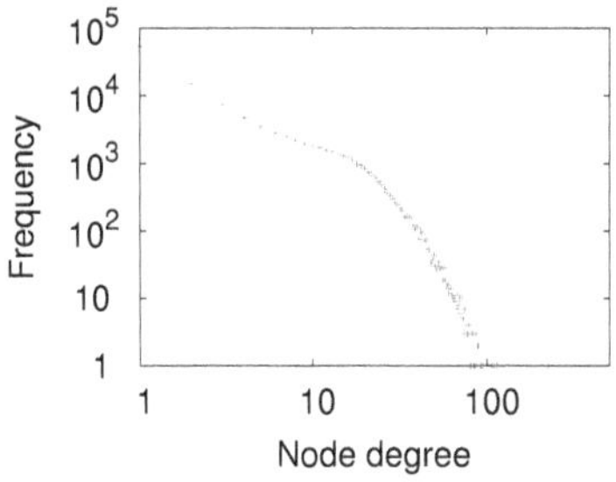

(b) WikiNet α=0.01

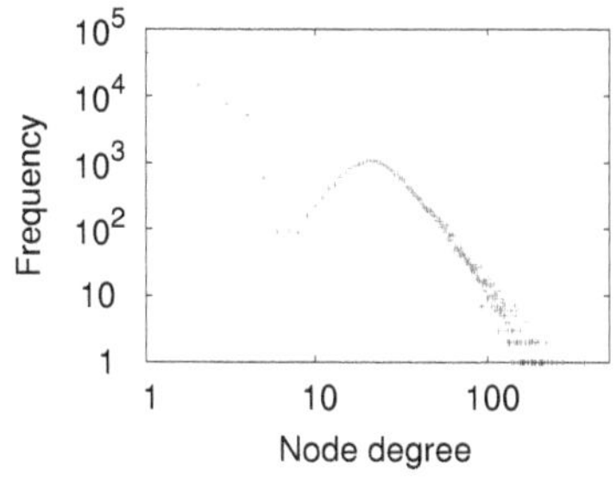

(c) WikiNet α=0.0

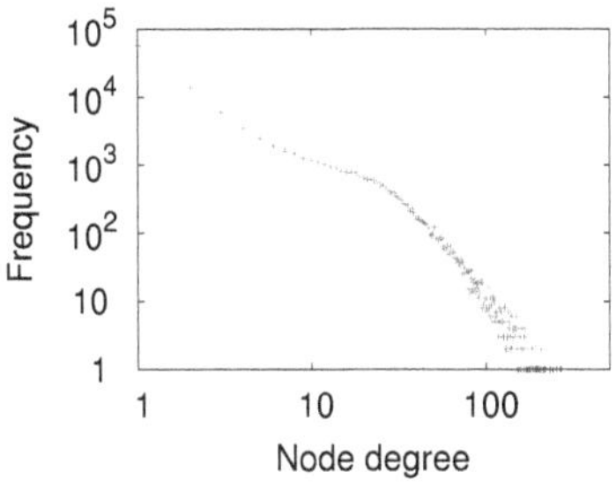

(d) IMDbNet BF

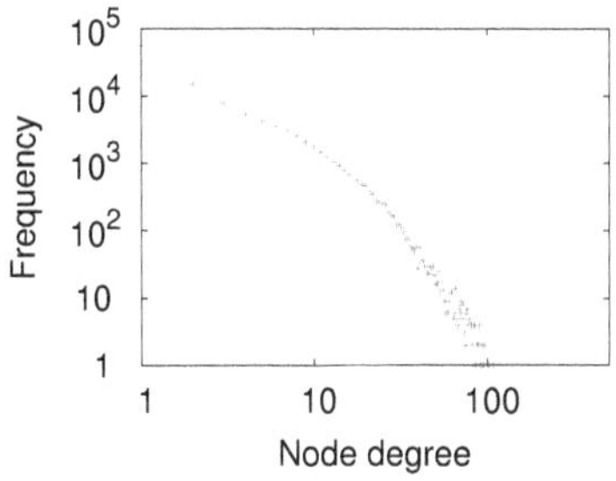

(e) IMDbNet α=0.01

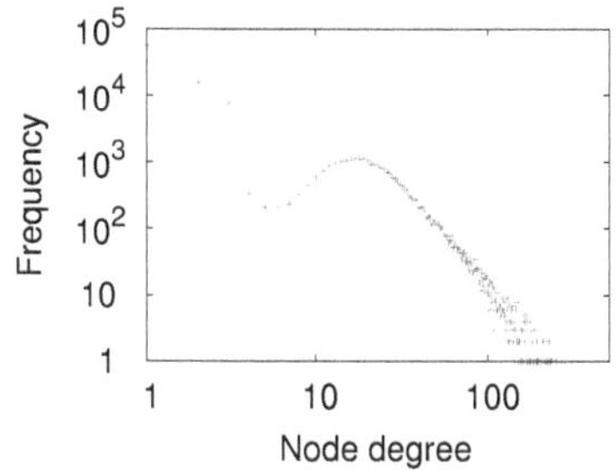

(f) IMDbNet α=0.0

Figure 3: Node degree distribution for different algorithms and the WikiNet/IMDbNet seed sets.

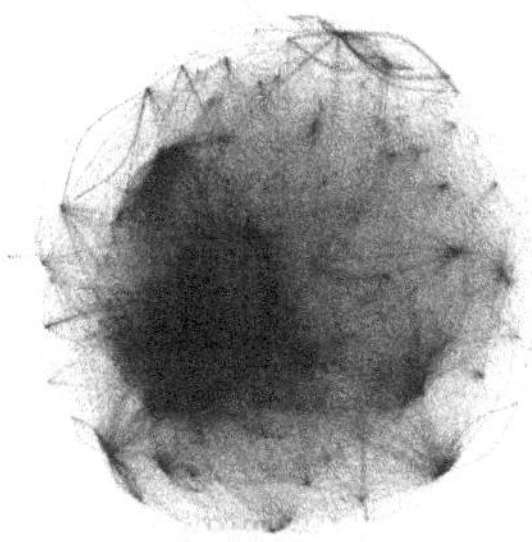

(a) WikiNet BF

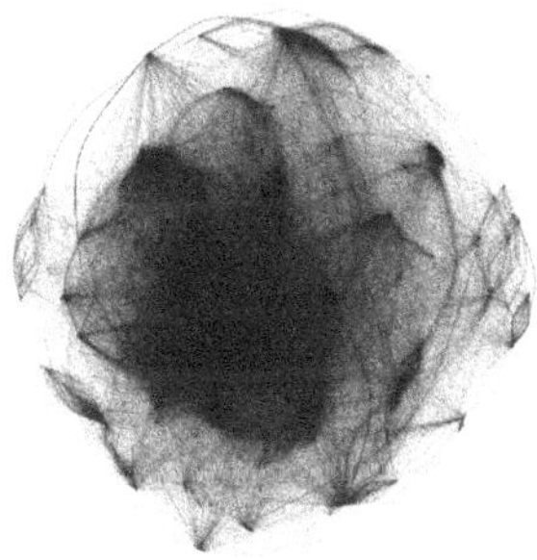

(b) WikiNet α=0.0

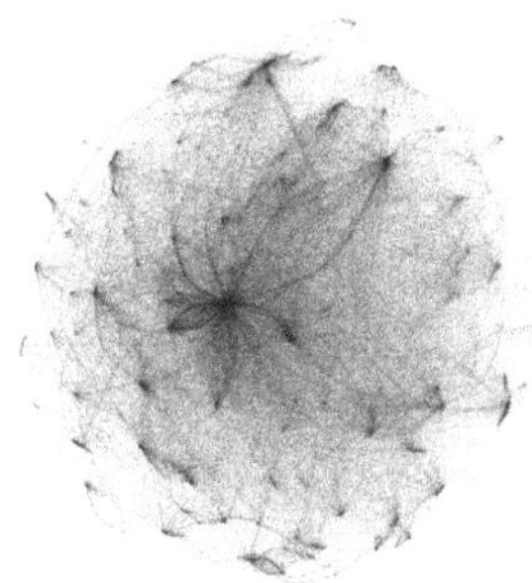

(c) WikiNet α=0.01

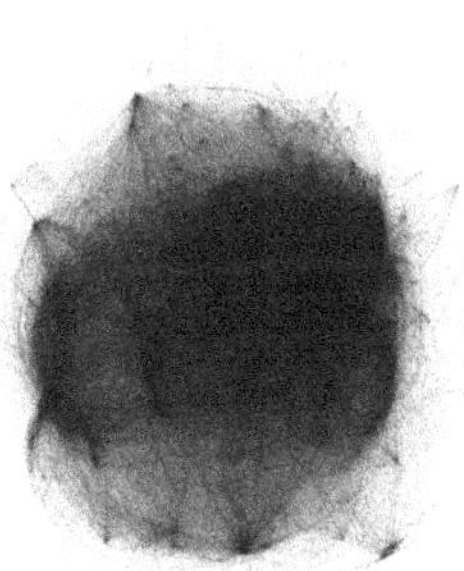

(d) IMDbNet BF

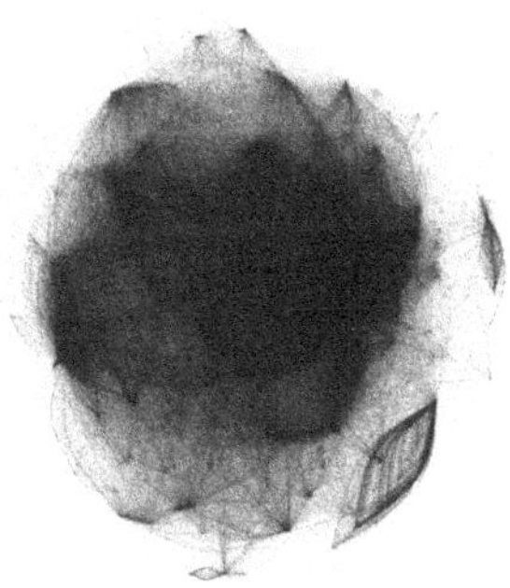

(e) IMDbNet α=0.0

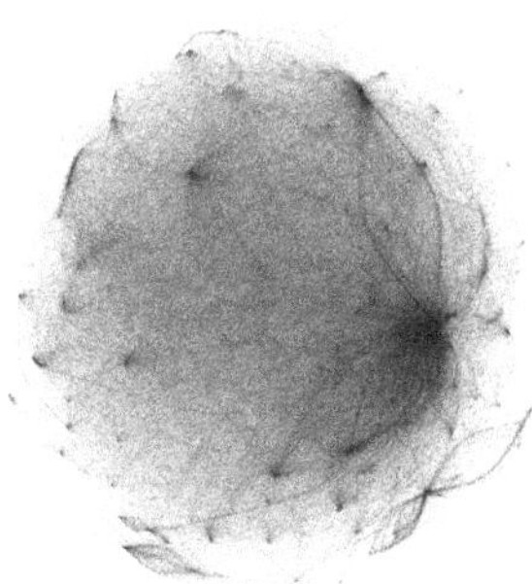

(f) IMDbNet α=0.01

Figure 4: Resulting WikiNet and IMDbNet graphs for different strategies and decay parameters.

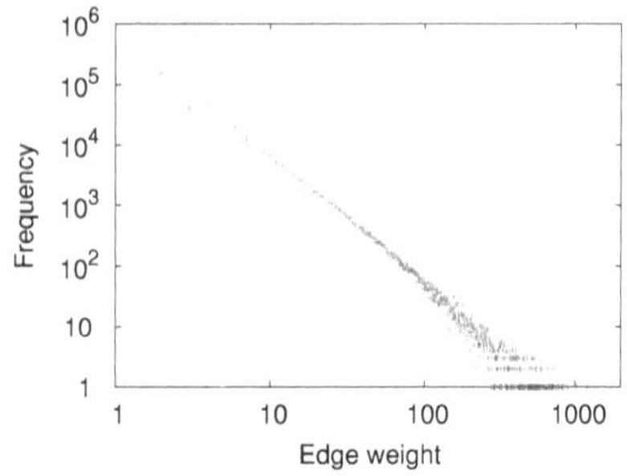

Figure 5: Edge weight distribution for the *BF* algorithm applied on WikiNet seed set

PERSON 1		PERSON 2
Brad Pitt	–	Angelina Jolie
Trey Parker	–	Matt Stone
Spencer Pratt	–	Heidi Montag
Stephen Moyer	–	Anna Paquin
Bud Abbott	–	Lou Costello
Robert Pattinson	–	Kristen Stewart
Bruce Robison	–	Kelly Willis
Ryan Gosling	–	Eva Mendes
Dev Patel	–	Freida Pinto
Terence Hill	–	Bud Spencer
Sergey Brin	–	Larry Page
Nick Cannon	–	Mariah Carey
Tod Williams	–	Billie Tsien
Josh Dallas	–	Ginnifer Goodwin
Eric Dane	–	Rebecca Gayheart

Table 3: Top-15 social relations found for IMDbNet using the BF extraction method.

	Algorithm	Votes	Accuracy
WikiNet	BF	800	0.969 ± 0.008
	decay a=0.0	800	0.990 ± 0.007
	decay a=0.01	800	0.983 ± 0.009
IMDbNet	BF	800	0.958 ± 0.014
	decay a=0.0	800	0.983 ± 0.009
	decay a=0.01	800	0.986 ± 0.008
Overall		4800	0.978 ± 0.004

Table 4: User evaluation results: accuracy of different methods

We also tested how many of the edges in our graphs corresponded to co-workers in movies as listed in IMDb. A large percentage of edges found by our algorithms (e.g. 33.8% for method *BF*, and 32.7% for method *Prio* with $\alpha = 0$) were co-acting in the same movies. However, our algorithms are capable to additionally reveal many relationships between actors not appearing in the same movie as captured by IMDb (for instance, "Tom Cruise" and "Katie Holmes").

Assessment of individual edges. In addition to the pairwise checks described above we also directly assessed strength and correctness of individual connections using a 5 point Likert scale. Levels 1 to 5 corresponded to the following answers to the question "Are these people connected?": 1 - "strongly disagree - Persons are not connected", 2 - "disagree - Persons do not likely know each other in person", 3 - "not known - it is not clear whether the persons know each

Pattern	Edges	Pairs	Domains
and	4,230	94	91
,	1,656	93	87
&	828	90	95
␣	806	91	89
und	1,124	79	71
;	54	33	25
:	36	27	24
-	36	23	20
or	33	19	14
/	28	22	11
with	20	15	15
on	23	15	14
y	16	14	13
and his wife	32	11	10
et	16	11	9
|	18	13	7
mit	14	12	9
e	14	10	9
vs.	13	10	9
and wife	25	7	7
+	9	8	7
left and	13	7	6
and actor	12	7	7
hat	8	7	8
Pictures Photo of	31	28	1

Table 5: Top-25 patterns after 1st iteration of pattern mining algorithm *PatternIter* applied to IMDbNet

other in person or not", 4 - "agree - Persons most probably know each other in person", 5 - "strongly agree - Persons are strongly related or know each other well (in person)". We assessed 600 edges (100 edges per dataset for each of our methods) sampled from the generated social networks and mixed in random order with 200 uniformly sampled pairs of unconnected nodes. Pairs of nodes generated using our approaches obtained an average rating of 4.55 (stdv 0.87), in contrast to an average of 1.81 (stdv 0.99) for unconnected nodes. We also found that just 10.2% of the social connections found in our networks obtained a rating of 3 or lower. These results further confirm the high accuracy of our graph construction methods.

4.5 Pattern Expansion and Analysis

In this subsection we show results for the cost efficiency and accuracy of the iterative pattern mining algorithm described in Section 3.2, and analyze the phrase patterns obtained for social connections.

Cost Efficiency and Accuracy. We conducted two iterations of the pattern mining algorithm leading to 100,319 requests for IMDbNet and 44,089 for WikiNet and obtained over 2,100 and over 5,000 distinct patterns (occurring with frequency of at least 10) for WikiNet and IMDbNet, respectively. The extracted patterns provide additional information about type and topical focus of the extracted social connections. Overall the resulting WikiNet contained 20,622 nodes and 40,342 edges, and the resulting IMDbNet 35,649 nodes and 129,326 edges.

A human assessment of edges extracted by the algorithm, which was conducted in the same way as described in Section 4.4, resulted in accuracy values of more than 0.96 and 0.97 for the graph expansions of the WikiNet and IMDbNet seed sets, respectively - with 95% confidence intervals of 0.01. This demonstrates the viability of our approach for constructing high-quality networks.

Pattern terms in WikiNet (politician seed)				
meet	minist	presid	coach	prime
forward	former	senat	rep	leader
center	beat	back	guard	defens
king	gener	sai	manag	mayor
right	defend	sen	defeat	chief
midfield	lineback	score	receiv	captain
left	governor	secretari	foreign	tackl
replac	khan	player	against	face
assist	deputi	premier	state	while
head	u.	professor	republican	talk

Pattern terms in IMDbNet (actor seed)				
star	direct	photo	produc	actor
director	pictur	wife	written	actress
galleri	husband	latest	daughter	pic
plai	date	welcom	film	cast
girlfriend	join	alongsid	marri	boyfriend
featur	video	screenwrit	attend	movi
imag	danc	perform	show	sister
camilla	frontman	screenplai	dure	skarsgard
mother	born	parker	writer	comedi
fan	also	stellan	best	kiss

Table 6: Top-50 stemmed terms extracted from patterns according to their Mutual Information values with seed sets of politicians in Wikipedia and actors in IMDb.

Extracted Phrase Patterns. Table 5 shows the 25 best patterns extracted by searching for the 100 most highly weighted edges after the first iteration of actor seeded graph construction, and computing pattern ratings as described in Section 3.2. Apart from obvious - yet useful - relationship patterns like *"with"*, *"or"*, and *"on"*, many of the mined patterns consist of special characters such as ",", "&", and "␣" which often serve to connect persons linked to each other. Although English patterns are prevalent, our method found also useful patterns in other languages allowing for more general, multilingual retrieval of social connections, and widening the scope of the mined networks. One such pattern was, for instance, the conjunction term *"and"* in Spanish, French, and German (*"y"*, *"et"*, and *"und"*). Just a small number of patterns do not describe relations between persons. This holds for instance the phrase *"Pictures Photos of"* which occurred in a large spam site containing many person names. However, this pattern obtained a comparably low rating because it appeared in just a single domain. Finally, we observe a few more specific patterns such as *"and US president"*, *"and actors"*, *"and his wife"* that can help to reveal interesting information about the type of detected relationships and contexts.

Term Analysis of Patterns. Patterns can provide useful clues on domains and topical foci of extracted (sub)networks. Although general patterns like *"and"* and *"with"* occurred, for instance, very frequently both in the context of movies and politics we also found various domain specific differences: Patterns such as *"meets"*, *"in conversation with"*, and *"is joined by"* were more dominant in the politician seed based networks, while patterns like *"and director"*, *"and actress"*, *"is starring alongside"* were more prominent in the movie domain.

In order to obtain the most discriminative terms from the patterns, we computed the Mutual Information (MI) measure [24] from information theory, which measures how much the joint distribution of features (terms from patterns in our case) and categories deviates from a hypothetical distribution in which features and categories ("politics" and "movies") are independent of each other. Table 6 shows the top-50 representative *stemmed* words automatically extracted from our query patterns for the politician and actor seeded networks described in Section 4.1. Many of the terms in the patterns falling into the politics category describe personal roles like leadership (*"minist"*, *"presid"*, *"senat"*) and peripheral or assisting positions (*"guard"*, *"assist"*, *"secretari"*), as well as concepts related to competition (*"defend"*, *"score"*, *"beat"*). In contrast, terms from patterns in the movie domain mostly refer to actors (*"star"*, *"actor"*, *"actress"*), film shooting (*"cast"*, *"screenwrit"*, *"plai"*), and family relations (*"husband"*, *"sister"*, *"boyfriend"*). This result indicates that terms found in patterns are often strongly correlated with social communities, and illustrates the potential merit of using machine learning techniques for domain specific selection of pattern candidates. This opens promising directions for focused, topic-oriented network expansion.

5. CONCLUSIONS AND FUTURE WORK

We have introduced efficient methods for extracting social networks from unstructured Web data using connectivity search queries. Our graph expansion algorithms leverage pattern based query mining enhanced by a bootstrapping approach for finding new query phrase patterns and by methods for intelligently prioritizing nodes. Our evaluation shows the applicability of our methods for extracting large scale social networks, and demonstrates the high accuracy of our approach. We also found that popularity and novelty of nodes are important criteria for controlling the network construction process: Popularity of nodes can be leveraged for efficiently extracting networks with more connections and higher density, while exploiting novelty is useful for faster exploration of more entities. An in-depth analysis of the characteristics of the extracted networks sheds additional light on information obtained though connectivity queries and on properties of our algorithms.

In our future work we aim to analyze pattern to reveal sentiment and other information about the social connections found: Are the linked individuals friends or foes? Do they have a personal or private connection? Are the relationships bidirectional or rather unidirectional? Furthermore, we plan to improve the efficiency of our algorithms by prioritizing search patterns based on the context of an entity using observed structures in graphs as training data for machine learning approaches. Finally, we aim to study strategies for extracting social graphs in a way that allows for simultaneously detecting communities in an efficient way. We think that this work has direct applications to social graph exploration and people search and provides a foundation for interesting analyses and findings about social networks and communities.

6. ACKNOWLEDGMENTS

This work is partly funded by the European Research Council under ALEXANDRIA (ERC 339233) and by the European Commission FP7 under QualiMaster (grant agreement No. 619525).

7. REFERENCES

[1] A. Anagnostopoulos, R. Kumar, and M. Mahdian. Influence and correlation in social networks. KDD '08, pages 7–15. ACM, 2008.

[2] N. Bach and S. Badaskar. A Review of Relation Extraction. 2007.

[3] C. Bird, A. Gourley, P. Devanbu, M. Gertz, and A. Swaminathan. Mining email social networks. In *Proceedings of the 2006 International Workshop on Mining Software Repositories*, MSR '06, pages 137–143. ACM, 2006.

[4] M. R. Bouadjenek, H. Hacid, and M. Bouzeghoub. Sopra: A new social personalized ranking function for improving web search. SIGIR '13, pages 861–864. ACM, 2013.

[5] M. J. Cafarella, J. Madhavan, and A. Halevy. Web-scale extraction of structured data. *SIGMOD Rec.*, 37(4):55–61, mar 2009.

[6] X. Canaleta, P. Ros, A. Vallejo, D. Vernet, and A. Zaballos. A system to extract social networks based on the processing of information obtained from internet. In *Proceedings of the 11th International Conference of the Catalan Association for Artificial Intelligence*, pages 283–292. IOS Press, 2008.

[7] P. Cimiano, S. Handschuh, and S. Staab. Towards the self-annotating web. WWW '04, pages 462–471. ACM, 2004.

[8] P. Cimiano, G. Ladwig, and S. Staab. Gimme' the context: Context-driven automatic semantic annotation with c-pankow. WWW '05, pages 332–341. ACM, 2005.

[9] D. K. Elson, N. Dames, and K. R. McKeown. Extracting social networks from literary fiction. In *ACL'10*.

[10] L. W. et al. Building the social graph of the history of european integration - A pipeline for humanist-machine interaction in the digital humanities. In *HISTOINFORMATICS*, 2013.

[11] O. Etzioni, M. Cafarella, D. Downey, S. Kok, A.-M. Popescu, T. Shaked, S. Soderland, D. S. Weld, and A. Yates. Web-scale information extraction in knowitall: (preliminary results). In *WWW'09*.

[12] A. Goyal, F. Bonchi, and L. V. Lakshmanan. Learning influence probabilities in social networks. WSDM '10, pages 241–250. ACM, 2010.

[13] I. Guy, N. Zwerdling, I. Ronen, D. Carmel, and E. Uziel. Social media recommendation based on people and tags. SIGIR '10, pages 194–201. ACM, 2010.

[14] K. Gwet. *Handbook of Inter-rater Reliability: The Definitive Guide to Measuring the Extent of Agreement Among Raters.* Advanced Analytics, LLC, 2010.

[15] J. He, Y. Liu, Q. Tu, C. Yao, and N. Di. Efficient entity relation discovery on web. *JCIS*, 2007.

[16] A. Jain and P. Pantel. Identifying comparable entities on the web. CIKM '09, pages 1661–1664. ACM, 2009.

[17] Z. Jiang, L. Ji, J. Zhang, J. Yan, P. Guo, and N. Liu. Learning open-domain comparable entity graphs from user search queries. CIKM, 2013.

[18] X. Jin, S. Spangler, R. Ma, and J. Han. Topic initiator detection on the world wide web. WWW '10, pages 481–490. ACM, 2010.

[19] C. Karbeyaz, E. Can, F. Can, and M. Kalpakli. A content-based social network study of evliya celebi's seyahatname-bitlis section. In *Computer and Information Sciences II.* Springer, 2012.

[20] H. A. Kautz, B. Selman, and M. A. Shah. The hidden web. *AI Magazine*, 18(2):27–36, 1997.

[21] J. M. Kleinberg. Hubs, authorities, and communities. *ACM Comput. Surv.*, 31(4es), dec 1999.

[22] N. Konstantinova. Review of relation extraction methods: What is new out there? Springer, 2014.

[23] A. N. Langville and C. D. Meyer. *Google's PageRank and Beyond: The Science of Search Engine Rankings.* Princeton University Press, 2006.

[24] C. Manning, P. Raghavan, H. Schutze, and E. Corporation. *Introduction to information retrieval.* Cambridge University Press, 2008.

[25] Y. Matsuo, J. Mori, M. Hamasaki, K. Ishida, T. Nishimura, H. Takeda, K. Hasida, and M. Ishizuka. Polyphonet: An advanced social network extraction system from the web. WWW, 2006.

[26] Y. Matsuo, H. Tomobe, and T. Nishimura. Robust estimation of google counts for social network extraction. In *AAAI*, 2007.

[27] P. Mika. Flink: Semantic web technology for the extraction and analysis of social networks. *Web Semant.*, 3(2-3):211–223, oct 2005.

[28] A. Mohaisen, A. Yun, and Y. Kim. Measuring the mixing time of social graphs. In *SIGCOMM*, 2010.

[29] M. K. M. Nasution and S. A. Noah. Superficial method for extracting social network for academics using web snippets. In *RSKT*, 2010.

[30] R. Nuray-Turan, Z. Chen, D. V. Kalashnikov, and S. Mehrotra. Exploiting web querying for web people search in weps2. In *Web People Search Evaluation Workshop (WePS), 18th WWW Conference*, 2009.

[31] L. Page, S. Brin, R. Motwani, and T. Winograd. The pagerank citation ranking: Bringing order to the web. Technical report, 1999.

[32] P. Pantel and M. Pennacchiotti. Espresso: Leveraging generic patterns for automatically harvesting semantic relations. In *ACL 2006, Sydney, Australia*, 2006.

[33] M. Pasca. Acquisition of categorized named entities for web search. In *CIKM'04*.

[34] J. Tang, J. Zhang, L. Yao, J. Li, L. Zhang, and Z. Su. Arnetminer: Extraction and mining of academic social networks. KDD '08, pages 990–998. ACM, 2008.

[35] A. Yates, M. Cafarella, M. Banko, O. Etzioni, M. Broadhead, and S. Soderland. Textrunner: Open information extraction on the web. In *ACL*, 2007.

[36] S. Ye and S. Wu. Measuring message propagation and social influence on twitter.com. In *LNCS*. 2010.

[37] P. S. Yu, X. Li, and B. Liu. On the temporal dimension of search. WWW, 2004.

Modeling Individual-Level Infection Dynamics Using Social Network Information

Suppawong Tuarob[1], Conrad S Tucker[2], Marcel Salathe[3], Nilam Ram[4]
[1]Faculty of Information and Communication Technology, Mahidol University, Thailand
[2]Industrial Engineering,[3]Department of Biology, [4]Human Development and Family Studies
The Pennsylvania State University, University Park, PA 16802
suppawong.tuarob@gmail.com, {ctucker4, salathe, nur5}@psu.edu

ABSTRACT

Epidemic monitoring systems engaged in accurate discovery of infected individuals enable better understanding of the dynamics of epidemics and thus may promote effective disease mitigation or prevention. Currently, infection discovery systems require either physical participation of potential patients or provision of information from hospitals and health-care services. While social media has emerged as an increasingly important knowledge source that reflects multiple real world events, there is only a small literature examining how social media information can be incorporated into computational epidemic models. In this paper, we demonstrate how social media information can be incorporated into and improve upon traditional techniques used to model the dynamics of infectious diseases. Using flu infection histories and social network data collected from 264 students in a college community, we identify social network signals that can aid identification of infected individuals. Extending the traditional SIRS model, we introduce and illustrate the efficacy of an Online-Interaction-Aware Susceptible-Infected-Recovered-Susceptible (OIA-SIRS) model based on four social network signals for modeling infection dynamics. Empirical evaluations of our case study, flu infection within a college community, reveal that the OIA-SIRS model is more accurate than the traditional model, and also closely tracks the real-world infection rates as reported by CDC ILINet and Google Flu Trend.

Categories and Subject Descriptors

J.3 [**Computer Applications**]: Medical information systems; Health

Keywords

Social Networks; Disease Epidemics; Simulation

1. INTRODUCTION

The unified goal of epidemiology is to mitigate and prevent infectious diseases from governing the population [24]. Having a system that accurately locates infected individuals when they are actually sick would tremendously aid in such an objective. For example, targeted care and treatment could be immediately implemented to students in a class, upon learning that one of the students is being contagious. Reversely, such a system could be used to validate the efficacy of vaccination and other disease control policies.

A brute-force solution for discovering sick individuals involves physically screening everyone for infection. Though such a method sounds promisingly accurate, it is not only diagnosis based, but also only applicable to small communities such as people inside a hospital. Diagnosis based methods would discourage sick individuals from participating, resulting in an underestimation of the real-world infection [2]. In larger communities where frequent mutual physical activities allow the infectious diseases to spread such as schools or colleges, the costs incurred (both financial and time resources) by such a brute-force method would outweigh the benefits.

Online communities generate more than 2.5 quintillion (10^{18}) bytes of data each day [42, 5]. A large portion of this data is generated through social media services such as *Twitter*, *Facebook*, and *Google Plus* that process anywhere between 12 terabytes (10^{12}) to 20 petabytes (10^{15}) of data each day [1]. These social media platforms allow their users to exchange information in a dynamic, seamless manner almost anywhere and anytime. Social media not only acts as a means of communication, but knowledge extracted from such large scale social media data has also proven valuable in a wide variety of applications. For example, real time analysis of Twitter data has been used to implement earthquake warning detection systems [31], identify medical and emergency needs during recovery from natural disasters (such as the Haiti Earthquake) [8], predict the financial market movement [7], identify notable product features [37, 39, 38, 36, 35], etc.

While social media information has been successfully used to predict real-world events, the uses of such information in disease epidemic purposes are limited. Though real-time disease tracking systems that extract disease-related information from social media have been proposed, all such systems track infection in a collective manner that only illustrates coarse-grain comparison of infections among different geographical regions and times [17, 11, 9, 21, 40, 20]. Employing social media signals to predict individual infections is a new area of possibility that we aim to explore.

In communities such as schools and colleges, social networks not only bridge together individuals when face-to-face communication is impossible, but also become a major means of communication that is incorporated into daily routines. Multiple studies have found close ties between offline and online worlds, allowing interactions in the social networks to reflect those of the real world [23, 43]. If such an assumption holds, one could predict whether a person is being sick just by observing his/her social network activities.

For example, Jack who is sick may stay home and post on his *Facebook Timeline* to let his friends know about his condition. Know-

Permission to make digital or hard copies of all or part of this work for personal or classroom use is granted without fee provided that copies are not made or distributed for profit or commercial advantage and that copies bear this notice and the full citation on the first page. Copyrights for components of this work owned by others than ACM must be honored. Abstracting with credit is permitted. To copy otherwise, or republish, to post on servers or to redistribute to lists, requires prior specific permission and/or a fee. Request permissions from Permissions@acm.org.
CIKM'15, October 19–23, 2015, Melbourne, Australia.
© 2015 ACM. ISBN 978-1-4503-3794-6/15/10 ...$15.00.
DOI: http://dx.doi.org/10.1145/2806416.2806575.

ing such, Jill sends a message to Jack offering her sympathy and her lecture notes when Jack is able to return to school. A few days later, when Jack gets better, he returns to school unknowingly that he is still contagious. Jill, who comes to contact with Jack in a class, is then infected and posts messages relating her symptoms on her Facebook. From this example, if we could build a system capable of predicting that Jack were still sick and Jill had a high risk of getting infected from him, then health specialists would be able to take actions to prevent Jack from spreading the disease and Jill would still be healthy.

Our research goal is to build a disease monitoring system that accurately and seamlessly identifies infected individuals. Though previous literature shows successes in using online content such as Google search logs [17], Twitter data [11], and Facebook data [41] to monitor real-world disease spreads, these systems report the infection in a collective manner (i.e. trends). Here, we analyze survey responses from 264 Pennsylvania State University (Penn State) students regarding their history of having flu and their social media usages, and investigate four types of social media signals that can be potentially useful for infection detection. These signals include physical locations, disease-related content emission (e.g. status updates), disease-related content transmission (e.g., comments and messages), and changes in social network behaviors. We propose the Online-Interaction-Aware SIRS (OIA-SIRS) that incorporates these social network signals into a traditional Susceptible-Infected-Recovered-Susceptible (SIRS) model [18], which simulates dynamics of an infectious disease in a contact network. A case study is conducted on a real-world Facebook social network to simulate the flu spread among Penn State students reveals that our proposed OIA-SIRS model is 56.78% more accurate than the traditional SIRS model at predicting individual infections. Finally, our model is able to resemble real-world flu infection as reported by the CDC ILINet[1] and Google Flu Trend[2], which reaffirms that social network signals could be useful for our task.

This paper has the following key contributions:

1. We conducted a survey on 264 Penn State students to obtain their background, histories of the flu infection, and permissions to scrape their Facebook data. The collected flu infection information is used as the ground-truth to validate our models.

2. We investigate the possibility of using only information available on social networks to build a disease monitoring system.

3. We propose to model disease dynamics using social network information. Specifically, we propose the OIA-SIRS model, an extension of the traditional SIRS model, to investigate the feasibility of using these social media signals to accurately locate sick individuals.

4. We evaluate the proposed model using empirical evaluations. Furthermore, we investigate the impact that each social network signal contributes to the prediction.

2. BACKGROUND AND RELATED WORKS

Vast research in computer and information sciences has devoted to collecting and interpreting informative signals from social networks in order to predict real-world events. Literature on computational epidemiology that relies on online data is extensive. Hence, only literature closely relevant to the problem at hand is discussed.

2.1 Offline-Online Interactions

Limited literature has been investigated on the relationship between real- and virtual-world interactions. Liu et al. formally defined a new social network paradigm, event-based social network (EBSN), that captures the offline-online interactions in event-based social media services such as Meetup[3][23]. Yin et al. later extended the work by investigating the tie between offline and online interactions, and found that the collective level of online interaction is independent with offline interaction. However, mutual friends' activities (that can be observed online) may play a significant role in inducing offline activities [43]. These works illustrate initial steps towards studying offline-online interactions in event-based social media networks. However, their analysis is different from our problem in two aspects: 1) Their works aim at predictions in the aggregate level, while our model would make individual-level predictions. 2) Meetup explicitly advocates offline-online interactions by nature. The social media service used in our case study (i.e. Facebook) is not entirely event-based, but acts as an alternative for face-to-face communication. Hence, their models may not directly be applicable to our work due to the differences in the nature of these two social media services.

2.2 Cutting-Edge Solutions for Disease Detection

Diagnosis based disease detection involves physical diagnosing test subjects, and determining whether the subject has the disease. Multiple works have devoted on building predictive models that help physicians to determine the disease progression. Liu et al. proposed a Symptom-Diagnosis-Treatment system that collects heterogeneous medical records to aid the clinical treatments of diabetes mellitus [22]. The diabetes complication patterns are mined to build a prediction model that helps physicians to determine the diabetes progression given the patient's symptoms. Boivin et al. built a prediction model for flu infection using a stepwise logistic regression, and revealed that cough and fever are the only symptoms significantly associated with a positive PCR test for the flu [6]. Furthermore, Franklin et al. discovered that pulse pressure could be used to predict the risk of coronary heart disease [14]. Their method was shown superior than the traditional ones using systolic blood pressure and diastolic blood pressure.

Such diagnosis based methods, though accurate, could be ineffective not only because sick individuals are discouraged from participating [2], but also due to financial and time constraints that make them only applicable on a small group of subjects. To mitigate such issues, monitoring based alternatives exist that collect disease-related information without the awareness of test subjects. Davis et al. proposed the *Collaborative Assessment and Recommendation Engine (CARE)* which mines a patient's medical history using ICD-9-CM[4] codes to predict the risk of future diseases. The method employs collaborative filtering to identify each patient's greatest disease risks based on their own medical history and that of similar patients [12]. The U.S. Outpatient Influenza-like Illness Surveillance Network (*ILINet*) collects information on patient visits to health care providers for influenza-like illness in all 50 states, Puerto Rico, the District of Columbia and the U.S. Virgin Islands, reporting more than 30 million patient visits each year [27]. ILINet provides information through the Centers for Disease Control and Prevention (CDC)[5], in the form of weekly influenza infection rates across all the geographical regions in the United States.

[1] http://www.cdc.gov/flu/weekly/overview.htm

[2] http://www.google.org/flutrends

[3] http://www.meetup.com/

[4] http://www.cdc.gov/nchs/icd/icd9cm.htm

[5] http://www.cdc.gov/

Aside from obtaining disease-related information from healthcare providers, a number of studies have devoted to building non-invasive sensors to predict disease onsets. Galna et al. used the Microsoft Kinect to detect the Parkinson's disease patients from their movement patterns [16]. Semmlow and Rahalkar comprehensively reviewed the theoretical foundations and practical uses of acoustic (sound) signals to detect chronic heart diseases [34]. Though these sensor based disease detection systems may seem ideal to our problem, the applicability to a larger community is still limited since such methods would require hardware installation that would make them bounded to be applicable in tight space (such as in a building, street, or hallway). On the contrary, the system the we aim to implement does not require additional hardware, but only uses already-available social network information to track disease spawns in a mass pool of social network users.

2.3 Disease Monitoring Using Online Data

Literature has illustrated successful usage of large scale online data to predict corresponding real-world events, including epidemic and disease monitoring.

Google Flu Trend[6] successfully demonstrated the volume of flu-related search terms in Google search engine queries could be used to accurately detect the trends of flu infection [34]. Collier and Doan developed an automated text mining system that classifies Twitter messages into six syndromic categories in real time [11]. The classifiers are integrated into a disease surveillance system, DIZIE[7], that shows a series of radial charts for each major world city with each band of the chart indicating the current level of alert for one of the six syndromes. Freifeld et al. developed *HealthMap*[8], a global infectious disease monitoring through automated classification and visualization of internet media reports [15]. HealthMap harvests outbreak data from a variety of sources, including news media (e.g., Google News) and expert-curated accounts (e.g., ProMED Mail). Locations and disease types are detected from pieces of information which are collectively visualized in a map-like interface. All such methods described above monitor disease spreads in a collective, coarse-grain manner; whereas our model aims to track disease spreads in a fine-grain, person-to-person, manner.

The closest work to ours would be the fine-grain epidemic modeling work by Sadilek et al., which models individual flu infection in Manhattan based on sickness-related Twitter messages [30]. Drawbacks of their work come in twofold. 1.) They assumed that a person who posts a sickness-related message would actually be sick. 2.) Even though their model aims to track disease passing from one individual to others, the evaluation was done in a collective manner against Google Flu Trend. In our work, we show that sick individuals do not always announce their sickness in social networks. On the contrary, a majority of users may post sickness-related messages to send their concerns to their sick friends. In fact, all of our test subjects that indicated previous infection did not post anything regarding their sickness in their social networks. Such a previous model would miss sick individuals who do not express their sickness in social networks, and would mistake healthy individuals who post sickness-related messages as being sick.

3. SURVEY STATISTICS

To better understand the nature of flu infection and social network behavior of a sample community, 264 Penn State students (ages range from 16-43) volunteered to participate in an online survey that inquires the information about their history of flu infection and their permissions to access and collect their social network information. The survey was conducted from February 2013 to July 2013.

Questions in the survey can be divided into 3 sets. The first set asks about background information such as gender, ages, and locations. The second set of questions is intended to learn their flu infection history in the past year, including whether they had flu vaccines, what flu symptoms they have experienced, and when (in which months) they had flu infection. The final set of questions asks about their active social networks, including the permission to access and scrape their Facebook personal information in an anynomized manner.

The 264 participants include 95 male (35.98%), 134 female (50.76%), and 35 gender-undefined students (13.26%). 97.78% of the participants have indicated to be active on social networks. Out of these social network active participants, 92% and 58.67% of them have Facebook and Twitter accounts respectively.

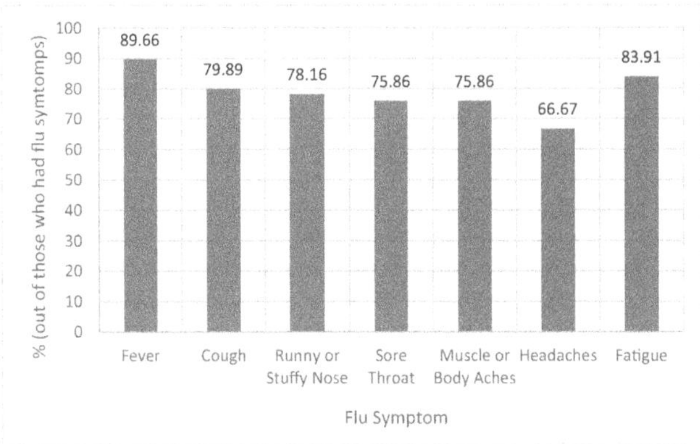

Figure 1: Distribution of flu symptoms that the participants who had the flu experienced.

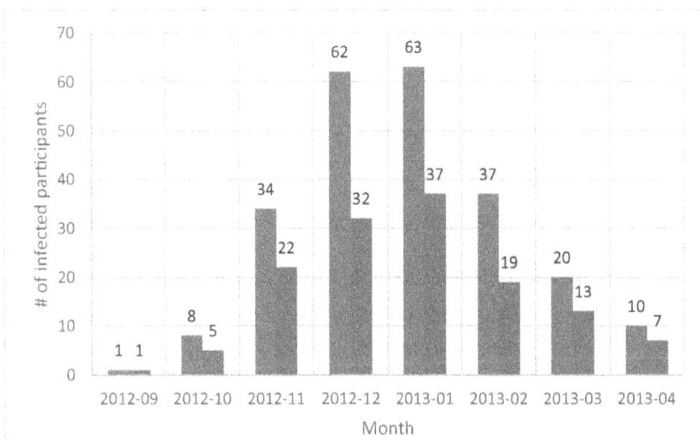

Figure 2: Distribution of monthly flu infections of the participants who had the flu: all participants (Blue) and those with Facebook information (Red).

36.64% of the participants indicate that they had a flu vaccine in the past year; while the other 63.36% did not. 75.32% of the participants indicated that they have experienced flu symptoms in the past year, 22.08% did not, and 2.60% were not sure if the anomalies they experienced were flu-related. Figure 1 illustrates the distribution of flu symptoms that the participants who indicated that they had the flu have experienced in the past year. The predefined flu

[6]http://www.google.org/flutrends
[7]http://born.nii.ac.jp/dizie
[8]http://www.healthmap.org/en/

symptoms include fever, cough, runny or stuffy nose, sore throat, muscle or body aches, headaches, and fatigue. Figure 2 shows the distribution of flu infections during September 2012 to April 2013. The blue bars represent the numbers from all the participants, while the red bars represent only the participants who agreed to provide their social network (Facebook) information (which will be used as ground truth to validate our models). Note that, though it might be a natural intuition that high infection rate should occur around January - March due to being the winter season where flu tends to spread, the distribution shown here does not resemble the natural flu infections. This is because the majority of participants (84.09%) took the survey during January - March 2013; hence, a high volume of infection responses are expected to be inflated during these months.

This survey study not only provides us with flu-related information to be used as the ground truth validation data, but also urges the urgent needs for a better disease surveillance system that accurately locates sick population so that infection can be timely prevented. As the survey data illustrates, 75.32% of a random college population have experienced the influenza-like illness (ILI) symptoms in the past year. This is a very high percentage that behooves disease control policies that should be adopted in such a community.

4. METHODOLOGY

We propose to model the dynamics of infectious diseases using only signals available in social networks. Such signals include actual geographic proximity between two persons, messages that convey sickness, and changes in online activities. These factors are incorporated into the traditional Susceptible-Infected-Recovered-Susceptible (SIRS) model that simulates disease spreads in a contact network. This would allow us not only to investigate the possibility of building a fine-grain disease surveillance system on social networks, but also to illustrate whether these social network signals could be useful for predicting individual infections.

Since both the SIRS and OIA-SIRS models operate on a graph structure, from here on, graph notations will be used. A contact network $\langle N, E\rangle$ is a graph where each node $n \in N$ is a person, and each undirected edge $e \in E$ represents that the two persons come in physical contact. Let $N'(n)$ be the neighbor nodes of the node n, and $e(n_1, n_2)$ represents the edge linking the nodes n_1 and n_2 respectively.

The next subsections will introduce the sickness-related message classification algorithm used in this research, describe the traditional SIRS model, and discuss the proposed OIA-SIRS model.

4.1 Sick-Related Message Classification

Our model is built upon the ability to automatically identify sickness-relates content in user-generated textual messages in social networks. Since we are dealing with millions of social media messages, automated classification of sickness-related messages must be performed. Natural language processing techniques have been proposed to discover sickness-related content using both rule-based (i.e. keyword detection) [17, 4, 32] and learning-based methods [28, 40, 41]. In this work, we replicate and extend the ensemble health-related classification method proposed by Tuarob et al. [40, 41]. Their method is chosen due to being relatively easier to replicate and shown to work on Facebook data (which is our dataset).

In summary, the method extracts 5 feature sets from a short text message, including:

- **N-Gram (NG)** features learn word patterns in the training data, and treat each unigram and bigram as a feature with TF-IDF weights.
- **Dictionary Based Compound (DC)** features address the word disambiguation problem posted by the N-Gram features, since they can identify different sets of terms used in different scenarios. Moreover, higher weights can be given to sickness-related keywords.
- **Topic Distribution (TD)** features summarize the dimension of the data into 200 topics using the Latent Dirichlet Allocation [3] algorithm.
- **Sentiment (ST)** features quantify the explicit illness by measuring emotional levels and frequency of sickness-related keywords in the message.
- **Combined (CB)** features put all the four feature sets above into a single feature pool.

Each feature set is used to train a base classier (i.e. SVM for NG, DC, and CB features. Random Forest for TD. RIPPER for the ST features). These base classifiers are then combined using weighted average probability method with the weight vector $\langle NG = 0.1, DC = 0.2, TD = 0.1, ST = 0.1, CB = 0.5\rangle$ as suggested by [41], to make an ensemble decision.

Each base classifier is trained with 8,129 social media short text messages that are labelled either *SICK* (i.e. positive) and *OTHER* (i.e. negative), and uses 10 fold cross validation to fine-tune the probability threshold to maximize F1. A 10-fold cross evaluation was performed, yielding a precision of 83.65%, recall of 77.52%, and F1 of 80.45%. In this work, since we aim to find disease-specific messages, we add another layer of disease-specific keywords to filter in relevant messages. For example, to collect flu-related messages, general health-concern messages such as "`Healthy food is expensive!! Guess that's why most of americas poverty stricken are overweight`" and non-flu symptoms such as "`stuck home post wrist surgery`" are discarded (even though they would be classified as positive by the classifier); while sick-related messages that contain flu-specific keywords (e.g. "`530am been up all night coughing this is ridiculous`" and "`My body is so hot and glowing..Fever fever fever is killin me!I need a doc..`") would be kept.

4.2 Traditional SIRS Model

The traditional Susceptible-Infected-Recovered-Susceptible (SIRS) has been widely used to study the spread of infectious disease in contact networks that can reoccur after the immunization wear off or a new species of the same disease is introduced. This assumption is valid for most virus-based diseases such as influenza [19]. The model assumes that a person in the network is in one of the three states at a given time: (S)usceptible, (I)nfected, and (R)ecovered.

At a given time period, a susceptible (S) node will become infected (I) with an infection probability of $\alpha = 1-e^{-\beta I}$ [33], where β is the disease transfer rate due to contact, and I is the number of immediate infected neighbor nodes. Once a node is infected, it will become recovered (R) with the probability γ, also called the *recovery rate*. A recovered node will stay immune to the disease for the next T_R periods of time before it becomes susceptible again.

4.3 Online-Interaction-Aware SIRS (OIA-SIRS)

We propose the OIA-SIRS model to show how diseases spread from one node to others using information available in social networks only. In particular, we would like to investigate whether disease infection can be traced using social network structures, along with observable social network information. The traditional SIRS model, described in Section 4.2, is modified to incorporate these signals. In particular, we modify the infection probability (i.e. α) to also incorporate the proximity, sickness-related user-generated content, and changes in online activities into account.

4.3.1 *Proximity Signal*

The proximity signal concerns the actual distance between two nodes. Simply speaking, a susceptible node has a higher chance to get infected if it is located closer to an infected node. This is the case for most respiratory infectious diseases (especially the flu), where the disease carriers can travel through air [10]. Most social network providers such as Twitter and Facebook enable geolocation tags when users post or comment, allowing the proximity signals to be observed and incorporated into our model.

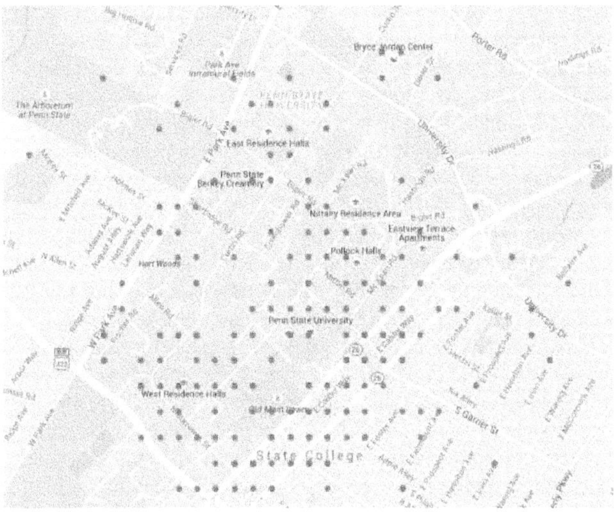

Figure 3: Example of geographical locations (red dots) of Penn State students, tracked by their Facebook Timeline posts during the week of December 10, 2012.

Social networks capture *friend* relationship which does not necessarily infer their physical contacts. Though it may be intuitive that friends have higher tendency to co-join activities (clubs, classrooms, meals, etc.) which allow them to exchange diseases, such an assumption is still too generous to be conclusive. The proximity signals can mitigate this issue by allowing our model to pin point which nodes are actually physically together at a given time. Figure 3 illustrates an example of geolocations of Penn State students that can be tracked from their social network activities. Note that the dots are aligned on the square grids due to accuracy truncating of the display software.

Incorporating the proximity signals, we define the *proximity based infection probability* ($PIP(t)$) at a given time t with the rate of β as:

$$PIP(t) = \left(1 - e^{-\beta I_P(t)}\right) \tag{1}$$

$I_P(t)$ is the number of proximate infected neighbor nodes, and is defined as:

$$I_P(t) = \sum_{i \in N'(n)} isInfected(i,t) \cdot \left(1 + max\left(0, 1 - \frac{distance(n,i)}{CRIT\_DIST}\right)\right) \tag{2}$$

$isInfected(i,t)$ is a binary function that returns 1 if the node i is currently infected at time t, and 0 otherwise. $distance(n,i)$ returns the physical distance between nodes n and i. $CRIT\_DIST$ is the critical distance beyond which the proximity no longer takes effect. Generally speaking, $PIP(t)$ quantifies the chance of getting infected based on how closed a node is to other infected nodes. In this work, $CRIT\_DIST$ is set to be the diagonal of the place of interest (e.g. college campuses, villages, etc.).

4.3.2 *Disease-Related Emission Signal*

Figure 4: Examples of social network emission messages include status updates and Timeline posts.

Messages in social networks can be divided into two groups based on their purposes: *emission* and *transmission*. An emitted message is intended to broadcast information and does not require a designated recipient. Such messages include status updates and Timeline posts (Facebook).

From an observation, in a community where social networks become a prevalent means for communication (such as schools, colleges, etc.), a majority of users tend to disseminate information on social networks when they cannot physically communicate face-to-face with others. Intuitively, infected individuals may not be able to be present at schools/work places, tempting them to emit such information on social networks (e.g., Figure 4). Such sickness-related emission could be a useful signal that indicates that the poster is being sick. We define the *emission based infection probability* ($EIP(t)$), with the emission inference rate λ, at a given time t as follows:

$$EIP(t) = \left(1 - e^{-\lambda M_E(t)}\right) \tag{3}$$

$M_E(t)$ is the number of sickness-related social media emissions that this node produces at time t.

4.3.3 *Disease-Related Transmission Signal*

While an emission message does not require a recipient, a transmission message is intended to transmit information from the sender to at least one receiver. Examples of such messages include comments on a post and tweets with designated recipients. A friend who has heard the news of sickness may be concerned and transmit a message to his/her sick friend (e.g., Figure 5). Such messages can be observed and are mostly available immediately. Hence, even

Figure 5: Examples of social network transmission messages include comments to a status update.

though a person does not announce in the social network that he/she is sick, his/her friends may transmit concern messages that convey their friend's sickness, which could potentially be used as a disease infection indicator. We define the *transmission based infection probability* ($TIP(t)$) at a given time t as follows:

$$TIP(t) = \left(1 - e^{-\mu M_T(t)}\right) \tag{4}$$

Where μ is the emission inference rate. $M_T(t)$ is the number of sickness-related social media transmissions that this node *receives* at time t.

4.3.4 *Online Activity Drift Signal*

In communities where the use of social media is prevalent, engagement in social network activities is typically incorporated into daily, weekly, or even hour routines [29]. Oftentimes, sickness prevents infected individuals from performing such routines. For example, Jack who normally updates his status before his Tuesday and Thursday classes, suddenly stops doing so this week because he is sick at home. Similarly, Jill who is active in her social network suddenly decreases her engagement in online activities due to being occupied by sickness. The changes or irregularity in the usual patterns of social network engagement at time t is referred to as an *online activity drift* ($\triangle U(t)$), and is defined as:

$$\triangle U(t) = 0.5 \cdot \frac{|M(t) - M(t-7)|}{|M(t) + M(t-7)|} + 0.5 \cdot \frac{|M(t) - \bar{M}(t)|}{|M(t) + \bar{M}(t)|} \tag{5}$$

$\triangle U(t)$ is the equal weighted average of two drift components. The first drift component quantifies the deviation of social network activities with respect to the corresponding day of week in the previous week. The second component compares the current online activity at time t with the average activity of the previous week. $M(t)$ is the total number of user-produced messages (all the messages emitted by or sent by this user) within the time period t, and $\bar{M}(t) = \frac{1}{7} \cdot \sum_{i=t-7}^{t-1} M(i)$.

4.3.5 *OIA-SIRS Model*

Our proposed OIA-SIRS model incorporates the four components described above into the traditional SIRS model by modifying the infection probability α to:

$$\begin{aligned} \alpha^*(t) &= \kappa PIP(t) + \rho EIP(t) + \sigma TIP(t) + \phi \triangle U(t) \\ &= \kappa \left(1 - e^{-\beta I_P(t)}\right) + \rho \left(1 - e^{-\lambda M_E(t)}\right) \\ &\quad + \sigma \left(1 - e^{-\mu M_T(t)}\right) + \phi \triangle U(t) \end{aligned} \tag{6}$$

Where $\kappa + \rho + \sigma + \phi = 1$, representing the weights of the individual components. β, λ, and μ are computed so that $R_0 \approx d \cdot \frac{\beta}{\gamma} = 1$, $R_0 \approx d \cdot \frac{\lambda}{\gamma} \approx 1$, and $R_0 \approx d \cdot \frac{\mu}{\gamma} = 1$ respectively as suggested by [33]. d is the average network degree, and R_0 is the basic reproduction number. $R_0 < 1$ means that the infection will eventually fade away; while $R_0 > 1$ indicates that the infection will be able to spread in the population. Though a previous study [33], that simulates a variant of SIRS model on social networks, used $R_0 = 3$ in their research to allow infection to amplify over time, so that effective targeted vaccination policies can be studied, here we use $R_0 = 1$ to allow long term steady rate of infection. In this work, an external activation factor is also added to the infection rate to allow 1% chance of getting infected from external infection sources outside the community. This factor is added to avoid the infections to die out, which is generally not true in real world.

It is important to note that we are simulating the spread of a generic ILI. While R_0 values for influenza are typically in the range of 2-3, we use a lower value with multiple reintroduction, which is arguably closer to the real ILI situation in a college town setting. Furthermore, while the assumption about moving to the susceptible state after recovery is not generally accurate for influenza, it is a good approximation when simulating ILIs, which can be caused by hundreds of different viruses that generally do not confer cross-immunity.

5. CASE STUDY

Influenza, commonly known as "the flu", is an infectious disease caused by the influenza virus. The most common symptoms include: a high fever, runny nose, sore throat, muscle pains, headache, coughing, and feeling tired. Though common flu would only cause temporary malfunction of body systems, it can be fatal in some extreme cases. In 2009-2010, 105,700-395,600 deaths were reported to be caused by the flu [13]. Hence, the ability to automatically discover potential infected individuals could prove to aid health practitioners to issue warnings to those who are in great risk of getting infected or quarantine those who are suspiciously infected. A case study of real-world Facebook network, comprising Penn State students, is used to demonstrate the efficacy of our models against the established baseline on modeling influenza spreads in social networks.

In particular, we explore our research in college settings using the Facebook network for the following reasons:

1. **Rich Social Media Engagement.** College students are actively engaged in social network activities. According to our survey results in Section 3, 97.78% of the test subjects are active social media users, with 92% having active Facebook accounts. Furthermore, Pempek et al. also reported in their study of 92 young adults that Facebook has become part of their everyday routines, with 85% of the social activities on Facebook are devoted to communication with friends [29]. This rich and frequent online engagement allows social net-

work activities to act as a mirror reflecting the users' real-life events.

2. **Facebook College Network Resembles Community Structures.** Salathe and Jones who studied effective targeted vaccination networks with community structure have used Facebook college networks to study their models [33]. This is because friends in social networks are inclined to have frequent face-to-face contacts [26].

5.1 Social Network Data

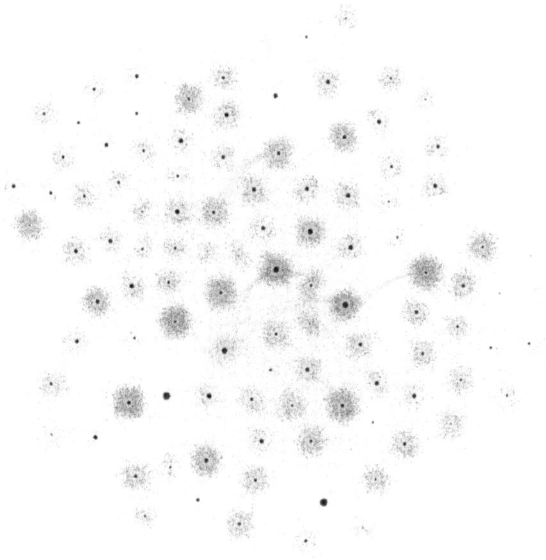

Figure 6: An illustration of the collected Facebook network.

113 survey participants (See Section 3) gave the permissions to collect their Facebook information, including their and their friends' background information, friend lists, Timeline updates, and comments to those updates. We implemented a Facebook data crawler that automatically scrapes this information from each participant who gave an explicit permission. The crawler updates and collects new information everyday until the Access Token[9] expires (60 days). The resulting Facebook dataset comprises 1,348,800 Timeline statuses and 3,541,772 associated comments of 60,776 Facebook users. All identification was removed prior to storage. All the Facebook data will be destroyed upon acceptable progress of our research.

Figure 6 illustrates the Facebook network structure using the large-scale graph layout generation algorithm *OpenORD* [25].

5.2 Experiments

The experiments are conducted against the baseline (traditional SIRS), to investigate whether the proposed online signals could be useful for identifying sick individuals in social networks. The goal of each simulation is to predict infected nodes at a given time period. The simulation is performed daily, and monthly predicted infected nodes are collected to compare with the ground-truth sick individuals from the survey. The simulation starts from May 1, 2011 and finishes on May 31, 2013. The statistics are collected during the months of September 2012 to April 2013. Note that the simulation starts much sooner before we start collecting the statistics to allow the infection to stabilize. Each model is simulated 10 times, and the results are averaged. The simulations were conducted on a Linux machine with 16-core Intel Xenon E5630 (2.5 GHz) processer and 32 GB available RAM. Each simulation is driven by 15 threads that concurrently update equal subsets of the nodes.

5.2.1 Evaluation Metrics

Since the available ground truth data reports actually sick individuals in each month, all the daily predicted infections are accumulated and compared with the ground truth data at the end of each month. Let N be the set of all the nodes, $I(m)$ and $I_G(m)$ be the sets of infected nodes and ground truth infected nodes during the month m. During the simulation, the following statistics are collected at the end of each month.

- **Number of infected nodes ($I(m)$)** is the number of infected nodes accumulated everyday in the month m.
- **Infection Ratio (InfRatio)** quantifies the proportion of infected population over all the population, defined as $|I(m)|/|N|$.
- **Accuracy** quantifies how well the ground truth infected nodes are captured, defined as $|I(m) \bigcap I_G(m)|/|I_G(m)|$.
- **Adjusted Accuracy**. A model can produce high infection ratio which allows more nodes to be infected (e.g., infection ratio of 1.0 means everyone is infected), resulting in an inflated accuracy. In order to fairly compare between the SIRS and OIA-SIRS models, the accuracy produced by the OIA-SIRS model are adjusted so that the monthly infection ratios are the same as the SIRS model, using the following equation:

$$Adjusted\ Accuracy = \frac{Accuracy * InfRatio_{SIRS}}{InfRatio} \quad (7)$$

- **Simulation Time** in milliseconds.

Since the number of available ground truth infected nodes vary month by month, weighted average scores of accuracy are computed that give more weight to the result of the month that has higher number of ground truth infected nodes. Let $acc(m)$ and $I_G(m)$ be the accuracy and the set of ground truth infected nodes associated with the month $m \in M$, and M is the set of months where ground truth data is available (i.e. September 2012 - April 2013). The weighted average accuracy acc^* is defined as:

$$acc^* = \frac{1}{\sum_{m \in M} |I_G(m)|} \cdot \sum_{m \in M} |I_G(m)| \cdot acc(m) \quad (8)$$

5.2.2 Parameter Initialization

In our OIA-SIRS model, β, λ, and μ are computed to be 0.09899 ($R_0 = 1$ and $d = 2.02$). The weight parameters κ, ρ, σ, and ϕ are tuned to achieve maximum accuracy by comparing the results from multiple values of κ, ρ, σ, and ϕ. T_R is drawn from a Gaussian distribution with mean of 120 days and standard deviation of 1, and with minimum 30 days, unless indicated otherwise. $CRIT\_DIST$ is set to 1.60934 km, which is the diagonal length of the Penn State campus. A set of 60 nodes are randomly set to initially infected. Each configuration is run 10 times, and the average accuracy is computed. The best performance in terms of accuracy is yielded by the configuration $\kappa = 0.2$, $\rho = 0.2$, $\sigma = 0.1$, and $\phi = 0.5$.

[9]https://developers.facebook.com/docs/facebook-login/access-tokens

5.3 Results and Discussion

Table 1 lists the averaged monthly results produced by 10 replications of the SIRS and OIA-SIRS models. According to the results, our OIA-SIRS models are able to capture 35.66% of actual infected social network users; while the traditional SIRS model can only capture 24%. The weighted averaged adjusted accuracy of our OIA-SIRS model is 38.04%, which is 56.78% more accurate than the SIRS model which utilizes only network structure information. The standard deviations of the accuracy produced by the OIA-SIRS and SIRS models are on par (0.1602 vs. 0.1486), suggesting equal degrees of randomness during the simulations. The t-statistics computed by a 2-tail paired t-test between the adjusted accuracy of the two models is 0.026, suggesting that these two models are statistically significantly different (with significance level 0.05).

The monthly infection ratios of the SIRS tend to be steady every month (0.12 ± 1, std. dev. = 0.006), this is because we set $R_0 = 1$ to maintain the steady infection rate in the long run. Hence, without external temporal knowledge, it is expected that the infection ratio would remain the same in every time period. Despite such, the monthly infection ratios of the OIA-SIRS model fluctuate with standard deviation of 0.03. This is because the OIA-SIRS model takes temporal social network signals into account, and hence would produce different rates of infections as reflected by sickness-related online activities during each time period. However, the average infection ratios between the two models are the same (0.1215 vs. 0.1134), suggesting that the infection rates of the OIA-SIRS model are steady (i.e. do not explode nor fade away) in the long run.

The average simulation time (monthly) of the OIA-SIRS model (2,848 milliseconds) is larger than that of the SIRS model (595 milliseconds). This is because, the SIRS model only uses the network structure; while our OIA-SIRS model has to compute the distances and process messages when a node is updated.

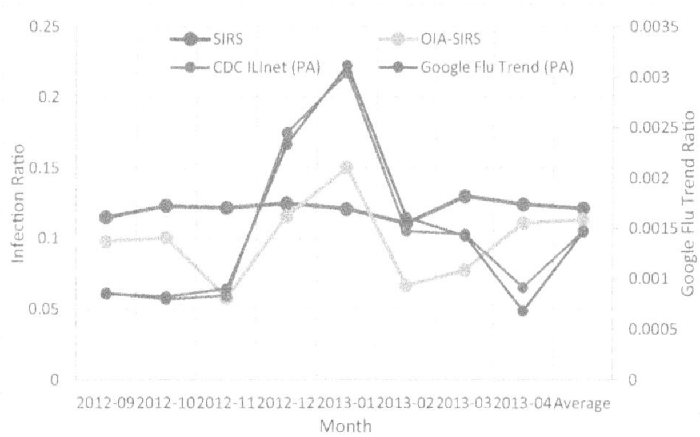

Figure 7: Comparisons of the infection ratios produced by the SIRS and OIA-SIRS models, against the actual monthly infection ratios reported by CDC and Google Flu Trend.

Figure 7 compares the infection ratios produced by our OIA-SIRS model against the baseline SIRS model, the actual monthly ratios reported by CDC, and Google Flu Trend (secondary Y axis) during September 2012 - April 2013. Not surprisingly, Google Flu Trend exhibits very closely to the CDC rates. Since the SIRS model does not take temporal features into account (it only has the network structure which remains the same over time), the infection ratios produced by such a model tend to be steady both in the short run and long run. Our proposed OIA-SIRS model, on the other hands, takes temporal social network information into account, hence it is able to capture real-world flu infection as long as the users exhibit disease-related signals or anomalies in online activities. A notable correlated events occur during the month of December 2012 - March 2013, during which the winter season took place (hence higher infection rates due to the cold whether). The infection rates reported by our OIA-SIRS resemble closer to the actual real-world infection ratios reported by CDC ILINet and Google Flu Trend, as evident from the correlation efficient of 0.65, compared to correlation of 0.08 of the SIRS model.

5.4 Impact of Each Information Type

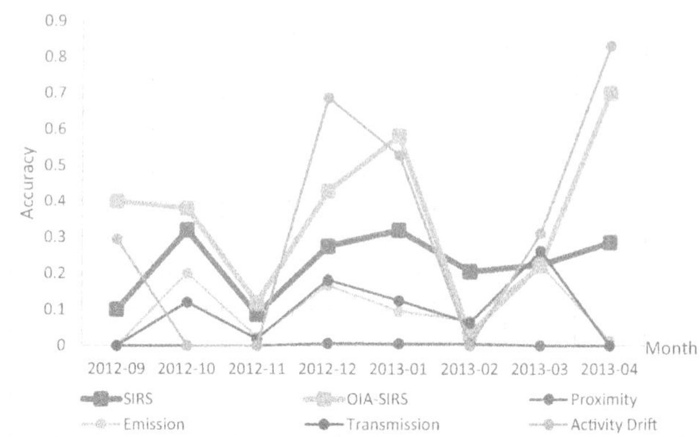

Figure 8: Comparison of the accuracy achieved by the baseline SIRS, the OIA-SIRS, the proximity-only OIA-SIRS ($\kappa = 1$), the emission-only OIA-SIRS ($\rho = 1$), the transmission-only OIA-SIRS ($\sigma = 1$), and the activity drift only OIA-SIRS ($\phi = 1$).

Table 2: Comparison of numbers of infections, accuracy, infection ratios, and simulation times achieved by the baseline SIRS, the OIA-SIRS, the proximity-only OIA-SIRS ($\kappa = 1$), the emission-only OIA-SIRS ($\rho = 1$), the transmission-only OIA-SIRS ($\sigma = 1$), and the activity drift only OIA-SIRS ($\phi = 1$).

Model	# Infected	Accuracy*	Infection Ratio	Simulation Time (Milliseconds)
SIRS	7381.82	0.2268	0.1215	595.30
OIA-SIRS	6890.59	0.3566	0.1134	2848.24
Proximity-Only	356.33	0.0021	0.0059	3048.03
Emission-Only	1262.21	0.0986	0.0208	2976.10
Transmission-Only	1269.19	0.0961	0.0209	2992.84
Activity Drift-Only	6457.74	0.2945	0.1063	2908.91

In order to further investigate which social network signals play bigger roles than others in predicting individual infections, we generate and run another 4 variants of OIA-SIRS models, each of which only uses one signal type. Figure 8 compares the monthly accuracy among these 4 models against the SIRS and the best OIA-SIRS models. Table 2 lists the average statistics. Recall that the best configuration for our dataset is $\kappa = 0.2$, $\rho = 0.2$, $\sigma = 0.1$, and $\phi = 0.5$. Agreeing with Figure 8, the accuracy of the OIA-SIRS is closely correlated with that produced by the Activity Drift Only OIA-SIRS, suggesting that changes in social network activity patterns could be the most important indicator for disease infection. Surprisingly, the accuracy produced by the proximity signals alone is very poor in all months, against the intuition that individuals who are in the same proximity are more likely to get infected. After investigating further, such poor accuracy may be caused by the

Table 1: Comparison of the simulation results produced by SIRS and OIA-SIRS models. Numbers with * are weighted averaged (See Equation 8). The standard deviations shown in the table are computed from the same scores of 10 replications.

Model	Month	# Infected	Accuracy	Accuracy StdDev	Adjusted Accuracy	Δ Adjusted Accuracy (%)	InfRatio	InfRatio StdDev	Simulation Time (millisec)
	2012-09	7001.92	0.1000	0.4899	0.1000	-	0.1152	0.0128	597.90
	2012-10	7497.76	0.3200	0.2272	0.3200	-	0.1234	0.0211	609.70
	2012-11	7407.60	0.0864	0.0649	0.0864	-	0.1219	0.0128	575.60
	2012-12	7595.36	0.2750	0.0576	0.2750	-	0.1250	0.0112	605.00
SIRS	2013-01	7353.95	0.3189	0.0455	0.3189	-	0.1210	0.0199	618.20
	2013-02	6734.47	0.2053	0.0817	0.2053	-	0.1108	0.0266	550.10
	2013-03	7908.92	0.2231	0.1584	0.2231	-	0.1301	0.0243	606.90
	2013-04	7554.54	0.2857	0.1565	0.2857	-	0.1243	0.0158	599.00
	Average	**7381.82**	**0.2426***	**0.1602**	**0.2426***	**-**	**0.1215**	**0.0181**	**595.30**
	2012-09	5934.43	0.4000	0.4000	0.4720	371.95	0.0976	0.0089	1906.10
	2012-10	6097.68	0.3800	0.1744	0.4673	46.02	0.1003	0.0085	2188.20
	2012-11	3525.19	0.1182	0.0897	0.2483	187.55	0.0580	0.0083	2356.50
	2012-12	7042.94	0.4281	0.0622	0.4617	67.89	0.1159	0.0081	2663.80
OIA-SIRS	2013-01	9122.13	0.5811	0.0806	0.4684	46.89	0.1501	0.0103	2773.80
	2013-02	4050.30	0.0316	0.1115	0.0525	-74.42	0.0666	0.0098	2931.80
	2013-03	4704.14	0.2231	0.1112	0.3751	68.13	0.0774	0.0094	3960.20
	2013-04	6747.05	0.7000	0.1591	0.7838	174.32	0.1110	0.0083	4005.50
	Average	**6890.59**	**0.3566***	**0.1486**	**0.3804***	**56.78**	**0.1134**	**0.0089**	**2848.24**

limited geolocation information available in the dataset. Though Facebook enables geo-tag features, one has to explicitly attach a location every time a status is updated. This process can be cumbersome, and encouraging Facebook users to skip this step and proceed with a simple update. Furthermore, a majority of students engage in Facebook activities using the website interface that does not track geolocations.

5.5 Limitations

The Facebook friend network was sampled from the 113 seed participants who gave the permissions to scrape their data. Though, surprisingly, the resulting network is all connected, it still exhibits a cluster-like structure (see Figure 6), where a cluster center is a survey participant. This cluster-like network would be bias because the center of a cluster tends to have higher chance of infection than their neighbor nodes (due to having a higher degree than its neighbors). Furthermore, even though we are able to obtain the ground truth data that describes who actually were sick during September 2012 - April 2013, the data is specific to the monthly level (while the simulation is performed on daily basis). This could result in a biased, inflated accuracy. In order to strengthen the evaluation, we would need to know specific duration of illness of each participant. Regardless, the promising results of this research encourage us to start another data collection campaign where a participant would be asked to report their sickness in more precision in terms of both time of infection and detail.

6. CONCLUSIONS AND FUTURE WORK

The overarching goal of this research is to build a non-invasive disease monitoring system that accurately identifies the specific people who are sick, without explicitly diagnosing them. A successful system would not only enable targeted vaccination, but also serve as a building block towards multiple applications in epidemiology, such as disease discovery and studies of how diseases evolve from time to time. In this paper, we explored the use of social network to achieve such a task. We analyzed the survey results collected from 264 students and determined different signals that can be monitored through social networks that could help identifying sick individuals. We proposed OIA-SIRS, a modification of the traditional SIRS model, to illustrate the performance impacts from introducing such social network factors. As the results illustrated, by introducing such online-observable signals into the traditional SIRS model, we were able increase the performance in terms of accuracy by 56.78%. However, we are aware that the ground truth data may not be enough to be absolutely conclusive; yet the promising results of our current work urge us to collect a larger set of samples that provides more precision and detail about sickness.

7. ACKNOWLEDGMENTS

We gratefully acknowledge financial support from the Penn State's Center for Integrated Healthcare Delivery Systems (CIHDS), the National Center for Research Resources and the National Center for Advancing Translational Sciences, National Institutes of Health, through Grant UL1 TR000127.

8. REFERENCES

[1] What is big data?–Bringing big data to the enterprise. `http://www-01.ibm.com/software/ph/data/bigdata/`, 2013. [Online; accessed 16 August 2013].

[2] C. Beaumont, M. Simon, R. Fauchet, J.-P. Hespel, P. Brissot, B. Genetet, and M. Bourel. Serum ferritin as a possible marker of the hemochromatosis allele. *New England Journal of Medicine*, 301(4):169–174, 1979.

[3] D. M. Blei, A. Y. Ng, and M. I. Jordan. Latent dirichlet allocation. *the Journal of machine Learning research*, 3:993–1022, 2003.

[4] T. Bodnar, V. C. Barclay, N. Ram, C. S. Tucker, and M. Salathé. On the ground validation of online diagnosis with twitter and medical records. WWW Companion '14, pages 651–656, 2014.

[5] T. Bodnar, C. Tucker, K. Hopkinson, and S. G. Bilen. Increasing the veracity of event detection on social media networks through user trust modeling. In *Big Data (Big Data), 2014 IEEE International Conference on*, pages 636–643. IEEE, 2014.

[6] G. Boivin, I. Hardy, G. Tellier, and J. Maziade. Predicting influenza infections during epidemics with use of a clinical case definition. *Clinical infectious diseases*, 31(5):1166–1169, 2000.

[7] J. Bollen, H. Mao, and X. Zeng. Twitter mood predicts the stock market. *Journal of Computational Science*, 2(1):1–8, 2011.

[8] C. Caragea, N. McNeese, A. Jaiswal, G. Traylor, H. Kim, P. Mitra, D. Wu, A. Tapia, L. Giles, B. Jansen, et al. Classifying text messages for the haiti earthquake. In *Proceedings of the 8th International Conference on Information Systems for Crisis Response and Management (ISCRAM2011)*, 2011.

[9] V. W. Chu, R. K. K. Wong, F. Chen, and C.-H. Chi. Microblog topic contagiousness measurement and emerging outbreak monitoring. In *Proceedings of the 23rd ACM International Conference on Conference on Information and Knowledge Management*, CIKM '14, pages 1099–1108, New York, NY, USA, 2014. ACM.

[10] D. Clayton, M. Hills, and A. Pickles. *Statistical models in epidemiology*, volume 161. IEA, 1993.

[11] N. Collier and S. Doan. Syndromic classification of twitter messages. In P. Kostkova, M. Szomszor, and D. Fowler, editors, *Electronic Healthcare*, volume 91 of *Lecture Notes of the Institute for Computer Sciences, Social Informatics and Telecommunications Engineering*, pages 186–195. Springer Berlin Heidelberg, 2012.

[12] D. A. Davis, N. V. Chawla, N. Blumm, N. Christakis, and A.-L. Barabasi. Predicting individual disease risk based on medical history. In *Proceedings of the 17th ACM Conference on Information and Knowledge Management*, CIKM '08, pages 769–778, New York, NY, USA, 2008. ACM.

[13] F. S. Dawood, A. D. Iuliano, C. Reed, M. I. Meltzer, D. K. Shay, P.-Y. Cheng, D. Bandaranayake, R. F. Breiman, W. A. Brooks, P. Buchy, et al. Estimated global mortality associated with the first 12 months of 2009 pandemic influenza a h1n1 virus circulation: a modelling study. *The Lancet infectious diseases*, 12(9):687–695, 2012.

[14] S. S. Franklin, S. A. Khan, N. D. Wong, M. G. Larson, and D. Levy. Is pulse pressure useful in predicting risk for coronary heart disease? the framingham heart study. *Circulation*, 100(4):354–360, 1999.

[15] C. C. Freifeld, K. D. Mandl, B. Y. Reis, and J. S. Brownstein. Healthmap: global infectious disease monitoring through automated classification and visualization of internet media reports. *Journal of the American Medical Informatics Association*, 15(2):150–157, 2008.

[16] B. Galna, G. Barry, D. Jackson, D. Mhiripiri, P. Olivier, and L. Rochester. Accuracy of the microsoft kinect sensor for measuring movement in people with parkinson's disease. *Gait & posture*, 39(4):1062–1068, 2014.

[17] J. Ginsberg, M. H. Mohebbi, R. S. Patel, L. Brammer, M. S. Smolinski, and L. Brilliant. Detecting influenza epidemics using search engine query data. *Nature*, 457(7232):1012–1014, 2009.

[18] H. W. Hethcote. The mathematics of infectious diseases. *SIAM review*, 42(4):599–653, 2000.

[19] M. B. Hooten, J. Anderson, and L. A. Waller. Assessing north american influenza dynamics with a statistical sirs model. *Spatial and spatio-temporal epidemiology*, 1(2):177–185, 2010.

[20] S. Huang, M. Chen, B. Luo, and D. Lee. Predicting aggregate social activities using continuous-time stochastic process. In *Proceedings of the 21st ACM International Conference on Information and Knowledge Management*, CIKM '12, pages 982–991, New York, NY, USA, 2012. ACM.

[21] N. Kanhabua, S. Romano, A. Stewart, and W. Nejdl. Supporting temporal analytics for health-related events in microblogs. In *Proceedings of the 21st ACM International Conference on Information and Knowledge Management*, CIKM '12, pages 2686–2688, New York, NY, USA, 2012.

[22] L. Liu, J. Tang, Y. Cheng, A. Agrawal, W.-k. Liao, and A. Choudhary. Mining diabetes complication and treatment patterns for clinical decision support. In *Proceedings of the 22Nd ACM International Conference on Conference on Information & Knowledge Management*, CIKM '13, pages 279–288, New York, NY, USA, 2013. ACM.

[23] X. Liu, Q. He, Y. Tian, W.-C. Lee, J. McPherson, and J. Han. In *Proceedings of the 18th ACM SIGKDD International Conference on Knowledge Discovery and Data Mining*, KDD '12, pages 1032–1040, New York, NY, USA, 2012. ACM.

[24] P. Lynch, M. Jackson, and S. Saint. Research priorities project, year 2000: establishing a direction for infection control and hospital epidemiology. *American journal of infection control*, 29(2):73–78, 2001.

[25] S. Martin, W. M. Brown, R. Klavans, and K. W. Boyack. Openord: An open-source toolbox for large graph layout. In *IS&T/SPIE Electronic Imaging*, pages 786806–786806. International Society for Optics and Photonics, 2011.

[26] M. R. Parks and K. Floyd. Making friends in cyberspace. *Journal of Computer-Mediated Communication*, 1(4):0–0, 1996.

[27] A. Patwardhan and R. Bilkovski. Comparison: Flu prescription sales data from a retail pharmacy in the us with google flu trends and us ilinet (cdc) data as flu activity indicator. *PloS one*, 7(8):e43611, 2012.

[28] M. J. Paul and M. Dredze. You are what you tweet: Analyzing twitter for public health. In *ICWSM*, pages 265–272, 2011.

[29] T. A. Pempek, Y. A. Yermolayeva, and S. L. Calvert. College students' social networking experiences on facebook. *Journal of Applied Developmental Psychology*, 30(3):227 – 238, 2009.

[30] A. Sadilek, H. A. Kautz, and V. Silenzio. Modeling spread of disease from social interactions. In *ICWSM*, 2012.

[31] T. Sakaki, M. Okazaki, and Y. Matsuo. Earthquake shakes twitter users: real-time event detection by social sensors. WWW '10, pages 851–860. ACM, 2010.

[32] M. Salathe, L. Bengtsson, T. J. Bodnar, D. D. Brewer, J. S. Brownstein, C. Buckee, E. M. Campbell, C. Cattuto, S. Khandelwal, P. L. Mabry, et al. Digital epidemiology. *PLoS computational biology*, 8(7):e1002616, 2012.

[33] M. Salathé and J. H. Jones. Dynamics and control of diseases in networks with community structure. *PLoS computational biology*, 6(4):e1000736, 2010.

[34] J. Semmlow and K. Rahalkar. Acoustic detection of coronary artery disease. *Annu. Rev. Biomed. Eng.*, 9:449–469, 2007.

[35] S. Tuarob and C. S. Tucker. Fad or here to stay: Predicting product market adoption and longevity using large scale, social media data. In *ASME 2013 International Design Engineering Technical Conferences and Computers and Information in Engineering Conference*, pages V02BT02A012–V02BT02A012. American Society of Mechanical Engineers, 2013.

[36] S. Tuarob and C. S. Tucker. Discovering next generation product innovations by identifying lead user preferences expressed through large scale social media data. In *ASME 2014 International Design Engineering Technical Conferences and Computers and Information in Engineering Conference*, pages V01BT02A008–V01BT02A008. American Society of Mechanical Engineers, 2014.

[37] S. Tuarob and C. S. Tucker. Automated discovery of lead users and latent product features by mining large scale social media networks. *Journal of Mechanical Design*, 137(7):071402, 2015.

[38] S. Tuarob and C. S. Tucker. A product feature inference model for mining implicit customer preferences within large scale social media networks. In *ASME 2015 International Design Engineering Technical Conferences and Computers and Information in Engineering Conference*. American Society of Mechanical Engineers, 2015.

[39] S. Tuarob and C. S. Tucker. Quantifying product favorability and extracting notable product features using large scale social media data. *Journal of Computing and Information Science in Engineering*, 15(3):031003, 2015.

[40] S. Tuarob, C. S. Tucker, M. Salathe, and N. Ram. Discovering health-related knowledge in social media using ensembles of heterogeneous features. In *Proceedings of the 22Nd ACM International Conference on Conference on Information & Knowledge Management*, CIKM '13, pages 1685–1690. ACM, 2013.

[41] S. Tuarob, C. S. Tucker, M. Salathe, and N. Ram. An ensemble heterogeneous classification methodology for discovering health-related knowledge in social media messages. *Journal of Biomedical Informatics*, 49(0):255 – 268, 2014.

[42] X. Wu, X. Zhu, G.-Q. Wu, and W. Ding. Data mining with big data. *Knowledge and Data Engineering, IEEE Transactions on*, 26(1):97–107, 2014.

[43] P. Yin, Q. He, X. Liu, and W.-C. Lee. *It Takes Two to Tango: Exploring Social Tie Development with Both Online and Offline Interactions*, chapter 38, pages 334–342.

Finding Probabilistic k-Skyline Sets on Uncertain Data

Jinfei Liu
Emory University
jinfei.liu@emory.edu

Haoyu Zhang
Emory University
haoyu.zhang@emory.edu

Li Xiong
Emory University
lxiong@emory.edu

Haoran Li
Emory University
haoran.li@emory.edu

Jun Luo
Lenovo; CAS
jun.luo@siat.ac.cn

ABSTRACT

Skyline is a set of points that are not dominated by any other point. Given uncertain objects, probabilistic skyline has been studied which computes objects with high probability of being skyline. While useful for selecting individual objects, it is not sufficient for scenarios where we wish to compute a *subset* of skyline objects, i.e., a skyline set. In this paper, we generalize the notion of probabilistic skyline to probabilistic k-skyline sets (Pk-SkylineSets) which computes k-object sets with high probability of being skyline set. We present an efficient algorithm for computing probabilistic k-skyline sets. It uses two heuristic pruning strategies and a novel data structure based on the classic layered range tree to compute the skyline set probability for each instance set with a worst-case time bound. The experimental results on the real NBA dataset and the synthetic datasets show that Pk-SkylineSets is interesting and useful, and our algorithms are efficient and scalable.

1. INTRODUCTION

The skyline of a set of multi-dimensional points consists of the points for which no other point exists that is better in at least one dimension and at least as good along every dimension. It is important for many applications involving multi-criteria decision making.

Assume that we have a dataset of n points, referred to as P. Each point p of d real-valued attributes can be represented as a d-dimensional point $(p[1], p[2], ..., p[d]) \in \mathbb{R}^d$ where $p[i]$ is the ith attribute of p. Figure 1(a) illustrates a dataset of eight points $P = \{p_1, p_2, ..., p_8\}$, each representing an NBA player with two attributes: rank of points and rank of assists. Without loss of generality, we assume that small values are more preferable in this paper. Figure 1(b) shows the corresponding points in the two dimensional space where x and y coordinates correspond to the value of attributes for rank of points and rank of assists, respectively. Given two points $p = (p[1], p[2], ..., p[d])$ and $p' = (p'[1], p'[2], ..., p'[d])$ in $\mathbb{R}^d$, p dominates p' if for every i, $p[i] \leq p'[i]$ and for at least one i, $p[i] < p'[i]$ $(1 \leq i \leq d)$. We can see that point $p_3(4, 2)$ dominates point $p_6(7, 3)$ as an example of dominance. Given a set of points P, the *skyline* of P is the set of points in P that are not dominated by any other point in P. For an NBA coach who is interested in choosing an NBA player considering both rank of points and rank of assists, the skyline of Figure 1(b) includes p_1, p_3, and p_7, which offer Pareto optimal solutions with various tradeoffs between rank of points and rank of assists: p_1 is the player with best rank of points, p_7 is the player with best rank of assists, and p_3 may be a good compromise of the two factors.

player	rank of Ps	rank of As
p_1	1	5
p_2	3	8
p_3	4	2
p_4	5	9
p_5	6	7
p_6	7	3
p_7	8	1
p_8	9	4

(a)

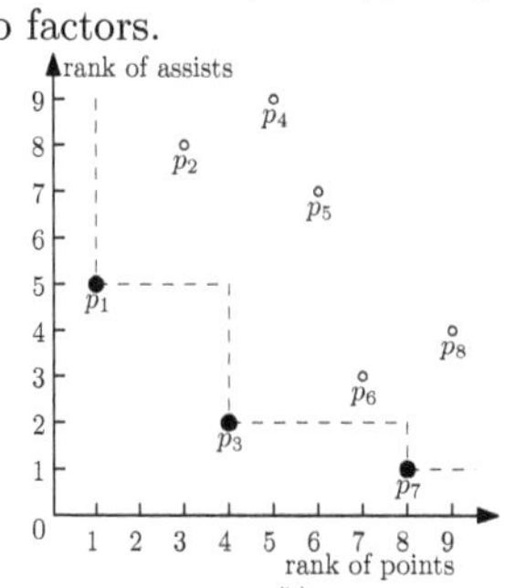

(b)

Figure 1: A skyline example of NBA players.

Motivation. Skyline is also meaningful on uncertain data. For example, NBA players may have different performances in different games. Assume that we have four NBA players $(O_i, 1 \leq i \leq 4)$, each player O_i has two game records or instances $(I_{i,j}, j = 1, 2)$ with different probabilities as shown in Figure 2 (the eight points have the same coordinates as the points in Figure 1). There are 2^4 possible worlds that correspond to the possible states of the four uncertain objects which are shown in Table 1, each with their associated probability. For each possible world, we can compute a set of skyline instances, also shown in Table 1.

The first study on skyline queries on uncertain data by Pei et al. [23] defines the probability of an uncertain object being a skyline as the aggregated (sum) probability of the possible worlds in which any of its instances is a skyline point. It studied p-skyline problem which returns the objects with skyline probability greater than a threshold p. Zhang et al. [29] studied a similar problem, top$k$-skyline, which returns k uncertain objects with the highest skyline probabilities. For example, as shown in Figure 2, the probability of NBA player O_1 being a skyline, denoted as $P_{sky}\{O_1\}$, equals to the aggregated probability of possible worlds that $I_{1,1}$ or $I_{1,2}$ is skyline. $I_{1,1}$ is skyline in $PW_1, ..., PW_8$ and $I_{1,2}$ is skyline in PW_{15}, PW_{16}. Hence, $P_{sky}\{O_1\} = \sum_{i=1}^{8} p(PW_i) + \sum_{i=15}^{16} p(PW_i) = 0.775$, where

Permission to make digital or hard copies of all or part of this work for personal or classroom use is granted without fee provided that copies are not made or distributed for profit or commercial advantage and that copies bear this notice and the full citation on the first page. Copyrights for components of this work owned by others than ACM must be honored. Abstracting with credit is permitted. To copy otherwise, or republish, to post on servers or to redistribute to lists, requires prior specific permission and/or a fee. Request permissions from Permissions@acm.org.

CIKM'15, October 19-23, 2015, Melbourne, VIC, Australia.

© 2015 ACM. ISBN 978-1-4503-3794-6/15/10...$15.00.

DOI: http://dx.doi.org/10.1145/2806416.2806452.

$p(PW_i)$ is the probability of possible world PW_i. Similarly, $P_{sky}\{O_2\} = 0.65, P_{sky}\{O_3\} = 0.625, P_{sky}\{O_4\} = 0.325$. If we set the threshold $p = 0.6$, p-skyline returns O_1, O_2, O_3. If we set $k = 2$, top$k$-skyline returns O_1, O_2.

O_i	$I_{i,j}$	$p(I_{i,j})$
O_1	$I_{1,1}$	0.7
	$I_{1,2}$	0.3
O_2	$I_{2,1}$	0.5
	$I_{2,2}$	0.5
O_3	$I_{3,1}$	0.5
	$I_{3,2}$	0.5
O_4	$I_{4,1}$	0.5
	$I_{4,2}$	0.5

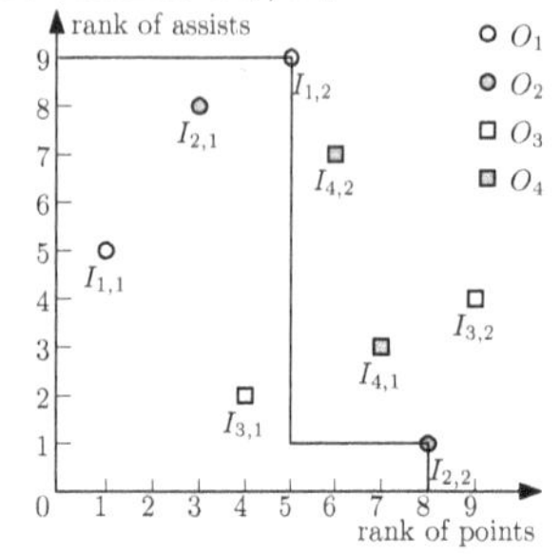

Figure 2: An example with uncertain objects.

While the above definitions compute *individual* skyline objects on uncertain data, there are scenarios where we wish to compute a *subset* of skyline objects, i.e., a skyline set. For example, an NBA coach may wish to choose a set of k best players to compose a team. Without considering uncertain case, a k-skyline set can be simply defined as any subset of k skyline points (assuming k is smaller than the number of skyline points). For uncertain data, existing works do not consider this set notion explicitly. Intuitively, we can use p-skyline or top$k$-skyline notion to choose those k objects with highest skyline probability. However, this is not suitable as each individual object is considered independently while we are more interested in the set of objects with their instances being skyline points simultaneously.

Table 1: Possible worlds semantic.

$Poss.W.$	O_1	O_2	O_3	O_4	Prob.	Skyline
PW_1	$I_{1,1}$	$I_{2,1}$	$I_{3,1}$	$I_{4,1}$	0.0875	$I_{1,1}, I_{3,1}$
PW_2	$I_{1,1}$	$I_{2,1}$	$I_{3,1}$	$I_{4,2}$	0.0875	$I_{1,1}, I_{3,1}$
PW_3	$I_{1,1}$	$I_{2,1}$	$I_{3,2}$	$I_{4,1}$	0.0875	$I_{1,1}, I_{4,1}$
PW_4	$I_{1,1}$	$I_{2,1}$	$I_{3,2}$	$I_{4,2}$	0.0875	$I_{1,1}, I_{3,2}$
PW_5	$I_{1,1}$	$I_{2,2}$	$I_{3,1}$	$I_{4,1}$	0.0875	$I_{1,1}, I_{2,2}, I_{3,1}$
PW_6	$I_{1,1}$	$I_{2,2}$	$I_{3,1}$	$I_{4,2}$	0.0875	$I_{1,1}, I_{2,2}, I_{3,1}$
PW_7	$I_{1,1}$	$I_{2,2}$	$I_{3,2}$	$I_{4,1}$	0.0875	$I_{1,1}, I_{2,2}, I_{4,1}$
PW_8	$I_{1,1}$	$I_{2,2}$	$I_{3,2}$	$I_{4,2}$	0.0875	$I_{1,1}, I_{2,2}$
PW_9	$I_{1,2}$	$I_{2,1}$	$I_{3,1}$	$I_{4,1}$	0.0375	$I_{2,1}, I_{3,1}$
PW_{10}	$I_{1,2}$	$I_{2,1}$	$I_{3,1}$	$I_{4,2}$	0.0375	$I_{2,1}, I_{3,1}$
PW_{11}	$I_{1,2}$	$I_{2,1}$	$I_{3,2}$	$I_{4,1}$	0.0375	$I_{2,1}, I_{4,1}$
PW_{12}	$I_{1,2}$	$I_{2,1}$	$I_{3,2}$	$I_{4,2}$	0.0375	$I_{2,1}, I_{3,2}, I_{4,2}$
PW_{13}	$I_{1,2}$	$I_{2,2}$	$I_{3,1}$	$I_{4,1}$	0.0375	$I_{2,2}, I_{3,1}$
PW_{14}	$I_{1,2}$	$I_{2,2}$	$I_{3,1}$	$I_{4,2}$	0.0375	$I_{2,2}, I_{3,1}$
PW_{15}	$I_{1,2}$	$I_{2,2}$	$I_{3,2}$	$I_{4,1}$	0.0375	$I_{1,2}, I_{2,2}, I_{4,1}$
PW_{16}	$I_{1,2}$	$I_{2,2}$	$I_{3,2}$	$I_{4,2}$	0.0375	$I_{1,2}, I_{2,2}, I_{4,2}$

In this paper, we extend and generalize the notion of p-skyline which computes *individual* skyline objects to probabilistic k-skyline sets (Pk-SkylineSets) which computes *sets* of skyline objects on uncertain data. Similar to p-skyline, we can define the probability of a set of objects being a skyline set as the aggregated probability of the possible worlds in which the instances of the set of objects are skyline points. We can then compute k-skyline sets with skyline set probabilities greater than a certain threshold p. Intuitively, this gives us a set of uncertain objects that have high probabilities of being skyline points simultaneously in the possible worlds. This is semantically different from choosing top$k$-skyline which consider the objects independently. For example, If we set $k = 2$, top$k$-skyline returns O_1, O_2. However, while O_1, O_2 have the highest probability of being a skyline object independently, $P_{sky}\{O_1\} > P_{sky}\{O_2\} > P_{sky}\{O_3\} > P_{sky}\{O_4\}$, the set of O_1, O_2 may not have a high probability of being a skyline set, i.e., being skyline points simultaneously in the possible worlds. In fact, if we compute the skyline set probability, $P_{sky}\{O_1, O_3\} > P_{sky}\{O_1, O_2\}$ ($0.4375 > 0.425$).

Another related notion on uncertain skyline by Liu et al. [22] is named *U-Skyline* query. U-Skyline searches for a set of objects that has the highest probability (aggregated from all possible worlds) as the answer. Back to Table 1, Set $\{I_{1,1}, I_{3,1}\}$ is the answer in PW_1 and PW_2, Set $\{I_{1,1}, I_{2,2}, I_{3,1}\}$ is the answer in PW_5 and PW_6. Those two subsets are returned as U-Skyline because they have the highest probability (0.175) aggregated from all possible worlds. Obviously, U-Skyline is not suitable for choosing a skyline set with fixed size because the results of U-Skyline can have various sizes.

In summary, if we treat the skyline in each possible world as a transaction and each skyline instance as an item, p-skyline and top$k$-skyline essentially compute the most frequent items, while U-skyline computes the most frequent transactions. In this paper, we generalize the notion of p-skyline to Pk-SkylineSets which can be considered as computing frequent itemsets of size k. Obviously, p-skyline and top$k$-skyline are special cases of our problem for $k = 1$.

Given the generalized Pk-SkylineSets problem, how can we compute the skyline sets efficiently? Assume that we have n objects, each object has m instances, we have $N = nm$ total number of instances. With the possible world semantic, a direct approach is to compute the skyline for each possible world and aggregate the results to obtain the answers. Unfortunately, we have $O(m^n)$ possible worlds, each possible world requires $O(nlogn)$ time to compute its skyline points. Then the problem is converted to finding most frequent itemsets with fixed size k from $O(m^n)$ transactions which requires $O(m^n C_n^k)$. Therefore, the total time complexity is $O(m^n nlogn + m^n C_n^k)$ which is prohibitively costly as n is an exponential term.

This motivates us to search for more efficient algorithms. Alternatively, we can enumerate all k-object set from the n objects, and compute their probability to be a skyline set. Since each object has m instances, each object set has m^k possible worlds (instance sets). In total, we need to enumerate $C_n^k m^k$ instance sets. For each instance set, we can scan all possible N instances to compute its probability to be a skyline set. Thus, a baseline implementation of this method leads to $O(C_n^k m^k kN)$ time complexity. Because $k \ll n$ in practical applications, this is much faster than the previous approach. In this paper, we investigate two efficient pruning strategies: object pruning and instance pruning, to further improve this method by reducing the search space. In addition, we propose a novel algorithm to compute the skyline set probability for each candidate instance set based on the layered range tree which achieves a worst-case time bound $O(C_n^k m^k knlog^{d-1}N)$ for the entire algorithm. This improvement is significant because N is required in baseline algorithm while $nlog^{d-1}N$ is only required in the worst-case.

Contributions. We briefly summarize our contributions as follows.

- We propose a new probabilistic k-Skyline Sets notion on uncertain data, called pk-SkylineSets. It generalizes existing work for choosing individual skyline points to choosing sets of skyline points on uncertain data and is useful in finding Pareto solutions of subsets in practical applications. This is the first work to study how to choose skyline sets with fixed size on uncertain data.
- We present an efficient algorithm for computing probabilistic k-skyline sets. It includes two heuristic pruning strategies, object pruning and instance pruning,

which efficiently reduce the search space by reducing the number of candidate object sets and their instances.

- Our algorithm computes the skyline set probability for each instance set using a novel data structure based on the classic layered range tree which achieves a worst-case time bound $O(C_n^k m^k knlog^{d-1}N)$ for the entire algorithm.
- We conduct comprehensive experiments on real and synthetic datasets. Our experimental results demonstrate that the proposed algorithms are much faster than the baseline methods.

The rest of the paper is organized as follows. Section 2 presents the related work to probabilistic skyline. Section 3 formalizes the problem. Section 4 provides an overview of our proposed algorithm and the two pruning strategies. Section 5 presents the algorithm for computing skyline set probability of candidate sets. We report the experimental results and findings for performance evaluation in Section 6. Section 7 concludes the paper.

2. RELATED WORK

The problem of computing skyline (Maxima) is a fundamental problem in computational geometry field [7, 8, 17, 16, 21] because the skyline is an interesting characterization of the boundary of a set of points.

Since the introduction of the skyline operator by Börzsönyi et al. [9], skyline has been extensively studied in the database field [24, 20]. With regard to the concept of "uncertain", there are two series of works: *uncertain preferences* [26, 25, 5, 6] and *uncertain objects* [23, 18, 3, 28, 19, 1, 27, 4, 22, 15]. Our work belongs to the latter. Among these works, Pei et al. [23] introduced the first probabilistic skyline problem, *p*-skyline. They presented bottom-up and top-down algorithms to return those objects with skyline probability larger than the given threshold *p*. Lian and Chen [18] studied the monochromatic and bichromatic reverse skyline search problem over uncertain databases. Atallah and Qi [3] focused on the worst-case time complexity to compute all skyline probabilities for uncertain data, they presented an algorithm with the worst time bound of $O(N^{2-\frac{1}{d+1}} log^{\frac{d(d-1)}{d+1}} N)$ where N is the number of instances. In their journal version [4], they improved the worst-case time bound to $O(N^{2-\frac{1}{d}} log^{d-1}N)$. Independently, Afshani et al. [1] presented the algorithm with worst-case time complexity $O(N^{2-\frac{1}{d}})$. Zhang et al. [28] studied the probabilistic skyline operator over sliding windows. [19, 27] studied the problem of finding an uncertain object with the maximum expected utility. Liu et al. [22] studied the problem of searching a set of tuples that has the highest probability (aggregated from all possible worlds) as the skyline answer. Khalefa et al. [15] focused on the continuous datasets.

Our work focuses on uncertain data and is the first to study how to choose skyline sets with fixed size on uncertain data.

3. PROBLEM DEFINITIONS

In this section, we introduce some preliminary knowledge and formally define the probabilistic *k*-skyline sets (P*k*-SkylineSets) problem.

Skyline and Skyline Sets. We start with the original skyline definition as follows.

Definition 1. (**Skyline**). Given a dataset P of n points in d-dimensional space. Let p and p' be two different points in P, we say p dominates p', denoted by $p \prec p'$, if for all i, $p[i] \leq p'[i]$, and for at least one i, $p[i] < p'[i]$, where $p[i]$ is the ith dimension of p and $1 \leq i \leq d$. The skyline points are those points in P that are not dominated by any other point in P.

We extend the original skyline definition to k-skyline sets as follows.

Definition 2. (**k-SkylineSets**) A k-point set is a k-Skyline Sets (k-SkylineSets) if those k points are all skyline points.

EXAMPLE 1. *In Figure 1, $\{p_1\}$, $\{p_3\}$, and $\{p_7\}$ are 1-SkylineSets, $\{p_1, p_3\}$, $\{p_1, p_7\}$, and $\{p_3, p_7\}$ are 2-SkylineSets, and $\{p_1, p_3, p_7\}$ is a 3-SkylineSets.*

Probabilistic Data Model. Given a dataset P of n uncertain objects in d-dimensional space. Without loss of generality, we assume each object has m possible instances. If one object has m' possible instances where $m' < m$, we can assume that there are $m - m'$ instances with probability 0. We denote the ith object as O_i, and the jth instance of the ith object as $I_{i,j}$, where $1 \leq i \leq n$ and $1 \leq j \leq m$. We use $p(I_{i,j})$ to denote the probability of instance $I_{i,j}$. We assume $\sum_{j=1}^{m} p(I_{i,j}) = 1$.

EXAMPLE 2. *Figure 2 shows a set of uncertain objects where $n = 4, m = 2, d = 2$. For example, O_1 has two possible instances $I_{1,1}$ and $I_{1,2}$ with probabilities of 0.7 and 0.3, respectively.*

Probabilistic Skyline. For uncertain data, we need to reason about the probability of an uncertain object to be a skyline object. This can be computed as the aggregated probability of each of its instances being a skyline point, since the instances are exclusive of each other. The probability of an object O_a being a skyline is,

$$P_{sky}\{O_a\} = \sum_{b=1}^{m} P_{sky}\{I_{a,b}\}.$$

where $P_{sky}\{I_{a,b}\}$ is the probability of $I_{a,b}$ being a skyline.

To compute the probability of $I_{a,b}$ being a skyline, $P_{sky}\{I_{a,b}\}$, we first define the *dominating set* which contains all instances that can dominate $I_{a,b}$, denoted as $\mathcal{DS}\{I_{a,b}\}$,

$$\mathcal{DS}\{I_{a,b}\} = \{I_{i,j(i \neq a)} \mid I_{i,j} \prec I_{a,b}; i = 1, ..., n; j = 1, ..., m\}.$$

The instances of O_l $(l \neq a)$ in the dominating set of $I_{a,b}$ is denoted as $\mathcal{DS}_l\{I_{a,b}\}$,

$$\mathcal{DS}_l\{I_{a,b}\} = \{I_{l,j} \mid I_{l,j} \in \mathcal{DS}\{I_{a,b}\}; j = 1, ..., m\}.$$

Thus, we have $\mathcal{DS}\{I_{a,b}\} = \bigcup_{l=1, l \neq a}^{n} \mathcal{DS}_l\{I_{a,b}\}$. We use $Ps(S)$ to denote the aggregated probability of the instances of the same object in a set S. Therefore, the probability of $I_{a,b}$ to be skyline can be represented as follows.

$$P_{sky}\{I_{a,b}\} = p(I_{a,b}) \times \prod_{l=1, l \neq a}^{n} (1 - Ps(\mathcal{DS}_l\{I_{a,b}\})).$$

where $p(I_{a,b})$ is the probability that $I_{a,b}$ appears, $\prod_{l=1, l \neq a}^{n}(1 - Ps(\mathcal{DS}_l\{I_{a,b}\}))$ is the probability that all those instances dominate $I_{a,b}$ do not appear.

Definition 3. (**p-skyline** [23]) p-skyline are those objects $O_a, 1 \leq a \leq n$ with $P_{sky}\{O_a\} \geq p$.

EXAMPLE 3. *As shown in Figure 2, O_1 has two instances $I_{1,2}$ and $I_{1,1}$. The dominating set of $I_{1,2}$ is $\mathcal{DS}\{I_{1,2}\} = \{I_{2,1}, I_{3,1}\}$, which consists of the instance(s) of O_2, $\mathcal{DS}_2\{I_{1,2}\} = \{I_{2,1}\}$, and instance(s) of O_3, $\mathcal{DS}_3\{I_{1,2}\} = \{I_{3,1}\}$. Therefore, $I_{1,2}$ is a skyline only when $I_{1,2}$ appears and the points in $\mathcal{DS}\{I_{1,2}\}$ do not appear, with probability $P_{sky}\{I_{1,2}\} = p(I_{1,2}) \times (1-p(I_{2,1})) \times (1-p(I_{3,1})) = 0.3 \times 0.5 \times 0.5 = 0.075$. Similarly, $P_{sky}\{I_{1,1}\} = 0.7$. Therefore, the probability of O_1 being a skyline is $P_{sky}\{O_1\} = P_{sky}\{I_{1,1}\} + P_{sky}\{I_{1,2}\} = 0.775$.*

Probabilistic k-Skyline Sets. Now we generalize the notion of probabilistic skyline to probabilistic skyline sets. Let $\{O_{a_1}, ..., O_{a_k}\}$ be a set of k uncertain objects, the probability of the set being a k-SkylineSets is the aggregated probability of each of its possible instance set being a k-SkylineSets.

$$P_{sky}\{O_{a_1}, ..., O_{a_k}\} = \sum_{b_1=1}^{m} ... \sum_{b_k=1}^{m} P_{sky}\{I_{a_1,b_1}, ..., I_{a_k,b_k}\}. \tag{1}$$

Given an instance set $\{I_{a_1,b_1}, ..., I_{a_k,b_k}\}$, we can find its dominating set as follows, which is the union of the points dominating each instance in the set.

$$\mathcal{DS}\{I_{a_1,b_1}, ..., I_{a_k,b_k}\} = \{I_{i,j(i \neq a_1,...,i \neq a_k)} \mid I_{i,j} \in \mathcal{DS}\{I_{a_1,b_1}\}$$

$$\cup ... \cup \mathcal{DS}\{I_{a_k,b_k}\}; i = 1, ..., n; j = 1, ..., m\}.$$

The instance set $\{I_{a_1,b_1}, ..., I_{a_k,b_k}\}$ is a skyline set, i.e., all the instances are skyline points, only when each of the instances appears and all of the points in its dominating set do not appear. The probability can be represented as follows.

$$P_{sky}\{I_{a_1,b_1}, ..., I_{a_k,b_k}\} = p(I_{a_1,b_1}) \times ... \times p(I_{a_k,b_k}) \times$$

$$\prod_{l=1, l \neq a_1, ..., l \neq a_k}^{n} (1 - Ps(\mathcal{DS}_l\{I_{a_1,b_1}, ..., I_{a_k,b_k}\})). \tag{2}$$

We note that if one instance dominates another instance within the same instance set $\{I_{a_1,b_1}, ..., I_{a_k,b_k}\}$, e.g., $I_{a_1,b_1} \prec I_{a_k,b_k}$, then $P_{sky}\{I_{a_1,b_1}, ..., I_{a_k,b_k}\} = 0$ because I_{a_1,b_1}, I_{a_k,b_k} cannot be skyline points simultaneously.

EXAMPLE 4. *Recall Figure 2, assume $k = 2$, we show how to compute $P_{sky}\{O_1, O_2\}$. We have $P_{sky}\{I_{1,1}, I_{2,1}\} = 0$ because $I_{1,1} \prec I_{2,1}$ and $P_{sky}\{I_{2,1}, I_{1,2}\} = 0$ because $I_{2,1} \prec I_{1,2}$. For the instance set $\{I_{1,2}, I_{2,2}\}$, we have its dominating set, $\mathcal{DS}\{I_{1,2}, I_{2,2}\} = \{I_{3,1}\}$ which consists of $\mathcal{DS}_3\{I_{1,2}, I_{2,2}\} = \{I_{3,1}\}$. Therefore, $P_{sky}\{I_{1,2}, I_{2,2}\} = p(I_{1,2}) \times p(I_{2,2}) \times (1 - Ps(\mathcal{DS}_3\{I_{1,1}, I_{2,2}\})) = 0.3 \times 0.5 \times 0.5 = 0.075$. Similarly, $P_{sky}\{I_{1,1}, I_{2,2}\} = 0.35$. Hence, $P_{sky}\{O_1, O_2\} = P_{sky}\{I_{1,1}, I_{2,1}\} + P_{sky}\{I_{1,1}, I_{2,2}\} + P_{sky}\{I_{1,2}, I_{2,1}\} + P_{sky}\{I_{1,2}, I_{2,2}\} = 0 + 0.35 + 0 + 0.075 = 0.425$.*

Problem Statement. We now define our problem that aims to find Pk-SkylineSets which is the k-skyline set with the highest probability of being a skyline set.

Definition 4. (**Pk-SkylineSets**) Pk-SkylineSets is the k-skyline set $\{O_{a_1}, ..., O_{a_k}\}$ with the highest probability of $P_{sky}\{O_{a_1}, ..., O_{a_k}\}$.

4. ALGORITHM OVERVIEW

To solve the probabilistic k-Skyline Sets problem, intuitively, we can enumerate C_n^k candidate k-object sets, and compute their skyline probability as defined in Equation 1. In order to compute the skyline probability for each k-object set, we need to enumerate m^k instance sets since each object has k possible instances. For each instance set, we can scan all possible N instances to compute its probability to be a skyline set as in Equation 2. Thus, a baseline implementation of this method leads to $O(C_n^k m^k kN)$ time complexity.

Algorithm 1 Computation Pk-SkylineSets

```
1: object pruning (see Section 4.1).
2: instance pruning (see Section 4.2).
3: for each k-object set {O_a1, ..., O_ak} chosen from remaining objects do
4:   for each possible instance set {I_a1,b1, ..., I_ak,bk} of the k-object set do
5:     compute P_sky{I_a1,b1, ..., I_ak,bk} (see Section 5).
6:   end for
7:   compute P_sky{O_a1, ..., O_ak} as in Equation 1.
8: end for
9: return the k-object set with highest probability P_sky.
```

We propose an efficient algorithm for computing probabilistic k-skyline sets. It includes two heuristic pruning strategies, object pruning and instance pruning, which efficiently reduce the search space for candidate object sets (C_n^k) and possible instance sets of each object set (m^k). The algorithm then iterate through all candidate object sets from the remaining objects, and compute its skyline probability by enumerating the possible instance sets from remaining instances and computing its skyline probability. It uses a novel algorithm for computing the skyline set probability for each instance set based on the layered range tree with worst-case time bound $O(knlog^{d-1}N)$. The sketch of the algorithm is shown in Algorithm 1. Overall, our algorithm achieves a worst-case time bound $O(C_n^k m^k knlog^{d-1}N)$ while practically it can be much more efficient.

Next we present the pruning strategies in detail. In the remainder of this section, we assume that no two points in P have the same coordinates. This restriction is not very realistic, but it can be overcome with a nice trick [12].

4.1 Object Pruning

We first observe an important property of the skyline probability. Similar to the apriori property in frequent itemset mining [2], the skyline probability of an object set never exceeds the skyline probability of its subsets. We present it as a theorem below.

THEOREM 1. ***(Monotone Property)*** *Given any two object (instance) subsets $\mathcal{S}_1$ and $\mathcal{S}_2$ of P, and $\mathcal{S}_1 \subseteq \mathcal{S}_2$, we have $P_{sky}\{\mathcal{S}_1\} \geq P_{sky}\{\mathcal{S}_2\}$.*

PROOF. We prove this theorem from possible worlds semantic. For each possible world i, $P_{sky}\{\mathcal{S}_1\}_i \geq P_{sky}\{\mathcal{S}_2\}_i$, where $P_{sky}\{\mathcal{S}\}_i$ is the probability of $\mathcal{S}$ being a SkylineSets in possible world i. Therefore, we can obtain $P_{sky}\{\mathcal{S}_1\} \geq P_{sky}\{\mathcal{S}_2\}$ by aggregating all possible worlds. □

Based on this property, the basic idea of our pruning strategy is to find an object set $\{O_{i1}, O_{i2}, ..., O_{ik}\}$ and use it to prune object O_i if $P_{sky}\{O_i\} < P_{sky}\{O_{i1}, O_{i2}, ..., O_{ik}\}$. The reason is that any superset of O_i will have skyline probability $\leq P_{sky}\{O_i\}$, hence cannot exceed $P_{sky}\{O_{i1}, O_{i2}, ..., O_{ik}\}$. The next question is how to choose the set $\{O_{i1}, O_{i2}, ..., O_{ik}\}$.

The higher $P_{sky}\{O_{i1}, O_{i2}, ..., O_{ik}\}$, the more objects can be pruned. To this end, our idea is to compute the skyline probability for each single object O_i and select the k objects with highest $P_{sky}\{O_i\}$. The intuition is that this set will likely have a high skyline set probability, although by no means it is guaranteed to have the highest probability. We summarize the pruning process in Algorithm 2. This pruning strategy proves to be very beneficial in practice as we show later in our experiments. As we recall the overall time complexity $O(C_n^k m^k nlogN)$, it is easy to see the factor C_n^k has a large impact because $O(C_n^k) \approx O(n^k)$. By reducing the number of objects (n), although without worst-case guarantee, it can improve the time efficiency significantly in practice.

Algorithm 2 Object pruning

```
for i=1 to n do
    compute P_sky{O_i}.
end for
choose k objects, {O_i1, ..., O_ik}, with highest P_sky{O_i}, compute
    P_sky{O_i1, ..., O_ik}.
for i=1 to n do
    if P_sky{O_i} < P_sky{O_i1, ..., O_ik} then
        delete O_i directly.
    end if
end for
```

EXAMPLE 5. *Recall the example in Figure 2, we can compute* $P_{sky}\{O_4\} = 0.325$ *and* $P_{sky}\{O_1, O_2\} = 0.425$. *Hence,* O_4 *can be pruned directly.*

4.2 Instance Pruning

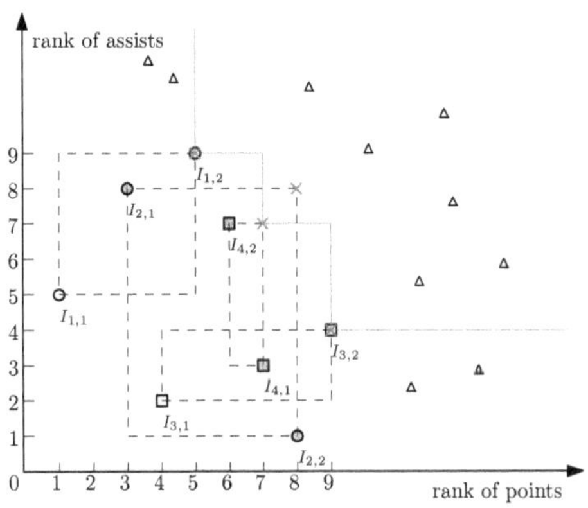

Figure 3: Instance pruning example.

The intuition of the instance pruning strategy is that if an instance is dominated by all possible instances of another object, then we can prune it directly. The reason is that the probability of it being a skyline point is 0, and hence the probability of any of its superset being a skyline set is also 0 based on the monotone property. The challenge is that it is time consuming to check whether an instance is dominated by all possible instances of each object. Hence, our idea is to compute a minimum bounding rectangle for all possible instances of each object. Then if an instance is dominated by its maximum corner, it is dominated by all the instances in the box. Formally, given an uncertain object O_l and let $I_{l_{max}} = (max_{j=1}^m\{I_{l,j}[1]\}, ..., max_{j=1}^m\{I_{l,j}[d]\})$ be the maximum corner of the minimum bounding rectangle of O_l. Note that $I_{l_{max}}$ is not necessarily an actual instance of O_l. In this case, we treat it as a virtual instance.

THEOREM 2. *For any instance* $I_{i,j}, 1 \leq i \leq n, 1 \leq j \leq m$, *if it can be dominated by any of* $I_{l_{max}}, l \neq i, 1 \leq l \leq n$, *then* $P_{sky}\{I_{i,j}\} = 0$.

PROOF. $P_{sky}\{I_{i,j}\} = p(I_{i,j}) \times \prod_{l \neq i, l=1}^n (1 - Ps(\mathcal{DS}_l\{I_{i,j}\}))$. Because $I_{l_{max}} \prec I_{i,j}$, i.e., $I_{l,1} \prec I_{i,j}$, $I_{l,2} \prec I_{i,j}$, ..., $I_{l,m} \prec I_{i,j}$. Thus, $Ps(\mathcal{DS}_l\{I_{i,j}\}) = 1$. Therefore, $P_{sky}\{I_{i,j}\} = 0$. □

Together with Theorem 1, the probability of any instance set containing $I_{i,j}$ being a skyline set is also 0. Hence, we can prune $I_{i,j}$ directly. For example, in Figure 3, we compute the maximum corners of the minimum bounding box of O_1, O_2, O_3, O_4, which are shown as crosses. Those instances on the upper right of the four crosses can be deleted directly.

5. COMPUTING SKYLINE SET PROBABILITY FOR INSTANCE SET

The key step of Algorithm 1 is to compute the skyline set probability $P_{sky}\{I_{a_1,b_1}, ..., I_{a_k,b_k}\}$ given an instance set $\{I_{a_1,b_1}, ..., I_{a_k,b_k}\}$. A naive way is to scan all remaining $O(N)$ instances after pruning to find the dominating set of the instance set which takes $O(kN)$ time. In this section, we present a novel algorithm based on the layered range tree which achieves $O(knlog^{d-1}N)$ worst-case time bound.

It is easy to see that the key to the probability computation is Equation 2, i.e., to find those instances in the range that can dominate any of the instances in $\{I_{a_1,b_1}, ..., I_{a_k,b_k}\}$. Going back to Figure 2, and take $\{I_{1,2}, I_{2,2}\}$ as an example. There are three instances $I_{1,1}, I_{2,1}, I_{3,1}$ that can dominate $\{I_{1,2}, I_{2,2}\}$. Since $I_{1,2}$ and $I_{2,2}$ exclude $I_{1,1}$ and $I_{2,1}$ respectively, we have the dominating set $\mathcal{DS}\{I_{1,2}, I_{2,2}\} = I_{3,1}$. To summarize, the key operation here is to retrieve all instances from the range shown with bold line. In order to find the dominating instances efficiently, we use a range query data structure, layered range tree, as an index to enhance the search process. In addition, we augment the layered range tree with cumulative information in order to compute the skyline set probability efficiently.

We first provide a brief description of the layered range tree in Section 5.1. We show how to build an augmented cumulative layered range tree in two dimensional space with time complexity $O(NlogN)$ in Section 5.2. We then show how to compute the skyline set probability for each instance set in $O(knlogN)$ in Section 5.3. Finally, we show how to extend it to higher dimensional space in Section 5.4. The reasons why we employ layered range tree rather than R-tree [14] are: i) R-tree cannot provide good worst-case guarantee, ii) it is not easy to adapt R-tree to report the cumulative information which is required for the probability computation due to the irregularity of MBRs.

5.1 Layered Range Tree

Layered Range Tree [12]. Let P be a set of N points in d-dimensional space. A layered range tree for P can be constructed in $O(Nlog^{d-1}N)$ time. With this layered range tree one can report the points in P that lie in a rectangular query range in $O(log^{d-1}N + v)$ time, where v is the number of reported points.

The layered range tree of Figure 1 is shown in Figure 4. The main tree is essentially a binary search tree based on the x-coordinate of the points. Each node n_i has an associated structure a_i. The detailed associated structure of Figure 4 implemented by the **fractional cascading** technique

[11, 10] is shown in Figure 5. Each subset of P associated with a node is stored in an array which is sorted on the y-coordinate of the points. Each element in the associated structure $a(v)$ of node v stores a point and two pointers: a pointer to the associated structure of the left child of node v, denoted by $a(lc(v))$, and a pointer to the associated structure of the right child of node v, $a(rc(v))$. In more detail, assume that the $(i+1)^{th}$ element of $a(v)$, $a(v)[i]$, stores a point $p(p_x, p_y)$. Then we store a pointer from $a(v)[i]$ to the element of $a(lc(v))$ storing $p'(p'_x, p'_y)$ such that p'_y is the smallest one that is larger than or equal to p_y. The pointer to $a(rc(v))$ is defined in the same way: it points to the element of $a(rc(v))$ storing $p''(p''_x, p''_y)$ such that p''_y is the smallest one that is larger than or equal to p_y.

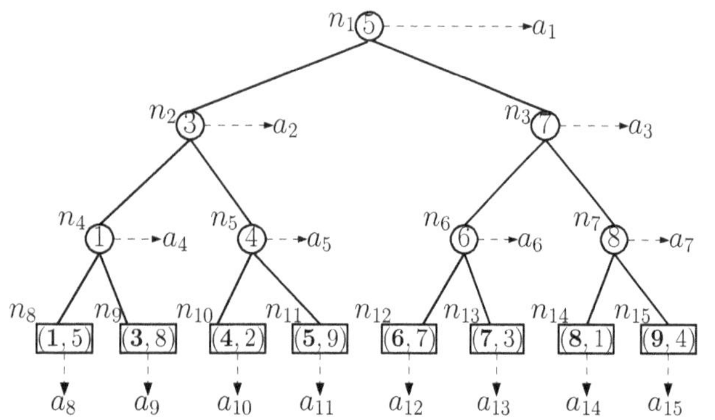

Figure 4: A layered range tree example.

EXAMPLE 6. *The fractional cascading technique is shown in Figure 5. The 5th element of the associated structure a_1 of node n_1, denoted by $a_1[4]$, has two pointers. Its left pointer points to element $a_2[1]$ in the associated structure a_2 of node n_2 (the left child of n_1) because the y-coordinate of the point p stored in $a_2[0]$, denoted by $a_2[0].p_y$, we have $a_2[0].p_y < a_1[4].p_y$ $(2 < 5)$ and $a_2[1].p_y = a_1[4].p_y$ $(5 = 5)$. Its right pointer points to element $a_3[3]$ in the associated structure a_3 of node n_3 (the right child of n_1) because $a_3[2].p_y < a_1[4].p_y$ $(4 < 5)$ and $a_3[3].p_y > a_1[4].p_y$ $(7 > 5)$.*

Given a range query on layered range tree, we go through the main tree to find all the nodes that are associated with the range on the x-coordinate. And then, for the corresponding associated structures of those nodes, we find those points in the range by the pointers of fractional cascading technique based on the y-coordinate.

5.2 Building Cumulative Layered Range Tree

Given an instance $I_{i,j}$, we know that with layered range tree, we can retrieve the points (instances) in P that lies in a rectangular query range, i.e., the dominating instances of $I_{i,j}$, in $O(logN+v)$ time, where N is the number of instances and v is the number of reported instances. Unfortunately, v can be as large as N which leads to $O(N)$ time complexity, i.e., no improvement for the worst-case time complexity because we can achieve $O(N)$ by scanning all the N instances. Analyzing the expression of $O(logN+v)$, part $logN$ is required because we need to scan $O(logN)$ nodes on the tree, part v is required if we need to report all the points in the rectangular range individually. Fortunately, we do not need to retrieve those v points individually, we just need to know the cumulative probability information of those v points, in order to compute the skyline set probability. This is similar to range count, in which case, we do not need to report all v points individually, we only need to know the cumulative count, i.e., how many points there are. If we could build an index structure that can report those cumulative information in $O(logN)$ time, then the range query can be finished in $O(logN)$ time. And our goal is to build such an index structure in $O(NlogN)$ time. In the follows, we show how the accumulative information is defined and then show how to build the accumulative layered range tree with such accumulative information.

Recall the query processing of layered range tree. For any query range $[x, x'], [y, y']$, we need to search those nodes in $[x, x']$ based on the main tree in $O(logN)$ time. Then we need to search $[y, y']$ in those $O(logN)$ associated structures. Hence, if those associated structures record some cumulative information and it can be obtained in constant time, then we can finish the entire search in $O(logN)$ time. Unfortunately, for each associated structure with N' elements and a random range $[y, y']$, there are $O(N'^2)$ different combinations of elements corresponding to different combinations of y and y' for which we need to store the cumulative information. It is both time and space consuming to compute and store such information. Fortunately, in our problem as we will show later, we can always decompose the query range into several $[x, x'], [0, y']$ ranges. Given a $[0, y']$ range, there are only $O(N')$ different combinations of the elements corresponding to different y' for which we need to store the cumulative information. We formally define the *cumulative information* of each element as follows.

Definition 5. (**Cumulative Information**). For the $(j+1)^{th}$ element of ith associated structure a_i, denoted by $a_i[j]$, its corresponding cumulative information $C(a_i[j])$ is an array of n elements (recall n is the number of uncertain objects) recording the aggregated probability of the points (instances) stored at $a_i[0], a_i[1], ..., a_i[j]$. The lth element of the accumulative information array records the aggregated probability of those instances corresponding to object O_l.

EXAMPLE 7. *The associated structure of the cumulative layered range tree of Figure 2 is shown in Figure 5. Each element in the associated structure stores an accumulative information array. In the root associated structure a_1, for the element of $I_{2,2}$, i.e., $a_1[0]$, we store $[0, 0.5, 0, 0]$ because probability of $I_{2,2}$, $p(I_{2,2}) = 0.5$. For the element of $I_{3,1}$, i.e., $a_1[1]$, we store $[0, 0.5, 0.5, 0]$ because it records the aggregated probability of two instances $I_{2,2}$ and $I_{3,1}$.*

In our accumulated layered range tree, in addition to storing the point and the pointers in each element of the associated structure, we store the accumulative information array in this element.

We now show how to build the accumulative layered range tree. The detailed algorithm is shown in Algorithm 3. Line 1-10 is similar to constructing layered range tree which can be finished in $O(NlogN)$ time. Line 1 constructs the associated structure, such as a_1 in Figure 5. Line 2 determines the terminal condition. P is split into two subsets P_{left} and P_{right} by x_{mid} in Line 5. Line 6 and 7 recursively compute the cumulative layered range tree of P_{left} and P_{right}. Line 8 creates the main tree by x_{min}, such as n_1 in Figure 4. Fractional cascading technique is used in Line 9. The cumulative information of each element is computed in Line 11-15. For the cumulative information of each element $a_i[j]$, we need to add the probability of the instance $I_{l,k}$ stored in

Algorithm 3 Build 2D Cumulative Layered Range Tree(P)

1: construct the associated structure: build an array $a(v)$ which is sorted on the y-coordinates of the points in P.
2: **if** P contains only one point **then**
3: create a leaf v storing this point, and make $a(v)$ the associated structure of v;
4: **else**
5: split P into two subsets; one subset P_{left} contains the points with x-coordinate less than or equal to x_{mid}, the median x-coordinate, and the other subset P_{right} contains the points with x-coordinate larger than x_{mid};
6: $v_{left} \leftarrow$ Build2DCumulativeLayeredRangeTree(P_{left});
7: $v_{right} \leftarrow$ Build2DCumulativeLayeredRangeTree(P_{right});
8: create a node v storing x_{mid}, make v_{left} the left child of v, make v_{right} the right child of v, and make $a(v)$ the associated structure of v;
9: add pointers from $a(v)$ to $a(v_{left(right)})$ by fractional cascading technique as we described in Section 5.1;
10: **end if**
11: **for** each associated structure **do**
12: **for** each element of associated structure **do**
13: compute cumulative information;
14: **end for**
15: **end for**

element $a_i[j]$ to the lth element (corresponding to object O_l) of the cumulative information of $a_i[j-1]$. There are in total $O(NlogN)$ elements in the associated structures. Therefore, we can compute the cumulative information in $O(NlogN)$ time. Because Line 1-10 can be finished in $O(NlogN)$, we obtain a theorem as follows.

THEOREM 3. *Algorithm 3 can be finished in $O(NlogN)$ time.*

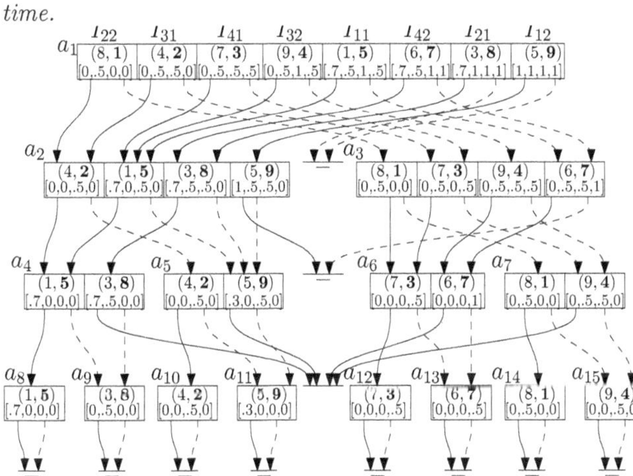

Figure 5: A cumulative layered range tree example.

5.3 Cumulative Layered Range Tree Queries

Given the cumulative layered range tree built in Section 5.2, we illustrate how to compute the skyline set probability $P_{sky}\{I_{a_1,b_1},...,I_{a_k,b_k}\}$ in $O(knlogN)$ time. We first show how to query the cumulative information of a range $[x,x'],[0,y']$ in $O(logN)$ time in Algorithm 4. It works by finding the nodes in the main tree corresponding to the range $[x,x']$, and then reporting the accumulative information in the associated structures corresponding to the range $[0,y']$. We search the first node v_{split} such that $x \leq v_{split} < x'$ in Line 1. If v_{split} is a leaf node, we report its cumulative information. Otherwise, we follow the path from $lc(v_{split})$ to x and report the cumulative information associated with its right subtrees ($\geq x$). For each node v on the path, if $x \leq x_v$, we report the cumulative information of right child of v and make left child of v be the new v. Otherwise, we make right child of v be the new v. If v is a leaf, we just report the cumulative information. Then similarly, we follow the path from $rc(v_{split})$ to x' and report the cumulative information associated with its left subtrees ($< x'$).

Algorithm 4 2D Cumulative Layered Range Query

1: from root, find the first node v_{split} that $x \leq v_{split} < x'$.
2: **if** v_{split} is a leaf **then**
3: report the cumulative information;
4: **else**
5: //follow the path to x and report the cumulative information in right subtrees;
6: $v \leftarrow lc(v_{split})$;
7: **while** v is not a leaf **do**
8: **if** $x \leq x_v$ **then**
9: report the cumulative information of $rc(v)$;
10: $v \leftarrow lc(v)$;
11: **else**
12: $v \leftarrow rc(v)$;
13: **end if**
14: **end while**
15: check if the cumulative information stored at v must be reported;
16: similarly, follow the path from $rc(v_{split})$ to x', report the cumulative information in left subtrees, and check if the cumulative information stored at the leaf where the path ends must be reported.
17: **end if**

From the root to leaves, we need to scan $O(logN)$ nodes: $O(logN)$ to x and $O(logN)$ to x'. To report the cumulative information corresponding to $[0,y']$, we need to be a bit careful. If we report cumulative information of each node by binary search to determine y' individually, it requires $O(logN)$ for each node. However, by the technique of fractional cascading, we can use binary search to find the cumulative information in root node, and use the pointers to find the cumulative information in its children and grandchildren in constant time. Therefore, we obtain a theorem as follows.

THEOREM 4. *Algorithm 4 can be finished in $O(logN)$ time.*

Given an instance $I_{a,b}$, we can query the cumulative information of those instances in a rectangular range that dominates $I_{a,b}$ using the cumulative layered range tree as above. After obtaining those $O(logN)$ cumulative information arrays each with n elements, we sum those $O(logN)$ arrays, the lth element is the sum of all l^{th} elements of the $O(logN)$ arrays, which is equal to $Ps(\mathcal{DS}_l\{I_{a,b}\})$ used in Equation 2, the aggregated probability of all instances corresponding to object O_l that dominate $I_{a,b}$. We can then use Equation 2 to compute the skyline set probability $P_{sky}\{I_{a,b}\}$. Therefore, we can obtain the theorem as follows.

THEOREM 5. *Given any instance $I_{a,b}$, $P_{sky}\{I_{a,b}\}$ can be computed in $O(nlogN)$ time.*

EXAMPLE 8. *We show how to compute $P_{sky}\{I_{1,2}\}$. Because the coordinate of $I_{1,2}$ is $(5,9)$, we set the query range as $[0,5),[0,9)$. First, we need to query $[0,5)$ in the main tree of Figure 4. We determine v_{split} by a binary search algorithm, which is node n_2. Because 0 is smaller than the x-coordinate of node $lc(n_2)$, i.e., 1. We report the cumulative information of the associated structure of rc(n2) which is a_9. Follow the algorithm, we need to report the cumulative information of associated structure a_9, a_8, a_{10}.*

Follow the pointers from element of a_1 to associated structure a_9, a_8, a_{10}, we determine the cumulative information, $[0, 0.5, 0, 0]$, $[0.7, 0, 0, 0]$, and $[0, 0, 0.5, 0]$, respectively. The sum is $[0.7, 0.5, 0.5, 0]$. Therefore, $P_{sky}\{I_{1,2}\} = p(I_{1,2}) \times (1 - 0.5) \times (1 - 0.5) \times (1 - 0) = 0.075$.

Given an instance set, we need to decompose the dominating range into multiple rectangular ranges with the requirement that the range of y coordinates in each rectangle begins with 0. For k instances $I_{a_1,b_1}, ..., I_{a_k,b_k}$, without lose of generality, assume $a_1 < ... < a_k$, then it is easy to see $b_1 > ... > b_k$, otherwise, some point of those k points will dominate another one. We decompose the dominating range into k query ranges as $[0, a_1), [0, b_1)$ then $(a_1, a_2), [0, b_2)$ and so on. Therefore, we can query the cumulative information associated with each range to compute the skyline set probability. We can obtain a theorem as follows.

THEOREM 6. *Given any instance set $\{I_{a_1,b_1}, ..., I_{a_k,b_k}\}$, $P_{sky}\{I_{a_1,b_1}, ..., I_{a_k,b_k}\}$ can be computed in $O(knlogN)$ time.*

EXAMPLE 9. *We show how to compute $P_{sky}\{I_{2,1}, I_{4,1}\}$. Because the coordinates of $I_{2,1}$, $I_{4,1}$ are (3,8), (7,3), respectively. We decompose the query range as [0,3), [0,8) and (3,7), [0,3). For [0,3), [0,8) and (3,7), [0,3), we obtain the cumulative information [0.7,0,0,0], [0,0,0.5,0], respectively. Therefore, $P_{sky}\{I_{2,1}, I_{4,1}\} = (1 - 0.7) \times p(I_{2,1}) \times (1 - 0.5) \times p(I_{4,1}) = 0.0375$.*

5.4 Higher Dimensional Space

It is fairly straightforward to generalize two dimensional cumulative layered range tree to higher dimensional space. Let P be a set of N points in d-dimensional space. The first $d-2$ dimensions can be processed by traditional layered range tree and the last two dimensions can be handled by the algorithms shown in Section 5.2 and 5.3. Detailed discussion is omitted due to the limited space.

6. EXPERIMENTS

In this section, we first study the effectiveness of Pk-SkylineSets on real NBA dataset and then perform an extensive empirical study to examine the heuristic pruning strategies and the skyline set probability computation algorithm based on layered range tree on synthetic and real datasets. Since this is the first work for k-skyline sets on uncertain data, our performance evaluation was conducted against baseline only. We implemented the following algorithms.

- **BL**: **B**ase**L**ine algorithm with worst-case time complexity $O(C_n^k m^k kN)$.
- **RT**: The algorithm based on cumulative layered **R**ange **T**ree index structure with worst-case time complexity $O(C_n^k m^k knlog^{d-1}N)$ without pruning.
- **HBL**: We first use the two **H**euristic pruning strategies and then use **B**ase**L**ine algorithm.
- **HRT**: This is our complete algorithm. We first use the two **H**euristic pruning strategies and then use our algorithm based on cumulative layered **R**ange **T**ree index structure.

6.1 Experiment Setup

We implemented all algorithms in C++ and ran experiments on a machine with Intel Core i7 running Ubuntu with 8GB memory. For the layered range tree index structure, we adapted the implementation of [13]. We used both real NBA dateset and synthetic datasets in our experiments.

6.2 Effectiveness of Pk-SkylineSets

We first demonstrate the effectiveness of Pk-SkylineSets through a small real NBA dataset. We chose 42 players with the highest skyline probability in Table 2 of Pei et al. [23]. We downloaded their recent ten years' statistics from http://www.basketball-reference.com. Please note that the career years of some players are less than ten years and some players stopped their career several years ago. We treat each player as an uncertain object and the annual records of each player as the instances of the object. Three attributes are selected in our experiment: points (PTS), assists (AST), and rebounds (REB). The larger those attribute values, the better. We show how to choose five players to compose a "gold team". Therefore, in this NBA dataset, $n = 42, m = 10, d = 3, k = 5$.

Table 3: Skyline probability of sets.

ID	Set	Prob.	ID	Set	Prob.
0	{0,1,3,9,21}	0.597696	4	{0,3,9,10,21}	0.431482
1	{0,1,3,10,21}	0.488009	5	{0,3,7,9,21}	0.431089
2	{0,1,3,7,21}	0.479059	6	{0,1,7,9,21}	0.426672
3	{0,1,9,10,21}	0.437064	7	{1,3,7,9,21}	0.42394

The skyline probabilities of the individuals and the sets are shown in Table 2 and 3, respectively. Table 2 shows the skyline probabilities of those 42 players. Because we only consider 42 players while [23] considered 1313 players, the skyline probabilities as well as the resulting p-skyline players in our experiment are much higher than and different from those in Table 2 of [23]. For example, Magic Johnson has the highest probability in our example because he did very well in his last ten years career while not so good between 1991 and 2005 (stopped in 1996). The probabilities of the sets being a skyline set are shown in Table 3. Since there are $C_{42}^5 = 850668$ candidate sets from the 42 players, we only show the first 8 sets with highest probabilities. We can see that the first five players ({0,1,3,9,21}) with highest skyline probability in Table 2 compose the Pk-SkylineSets with highest skyline set probability. However, $P_{sky}\{0, 1, 3, 10, 21\}$ is higher than $P_{sky}\{0, 1, 3, 7, 21\}$ while the only differing player Michael Jordan (ID=7) has higher skyline probability than Chris Webber (ID=10). The results verify that the set of objects with higher individual skyline probabilities does not necessarily lead to higher skyline set probability.

6.3 Efficiency and Scalability

We use both real NBA dataset and synthetic datasets to study the efficiency and scalability of our methods. We downloaded recent ten years' statistics of 1000 players from http://www.basketball-reference.com/ with two more attributes (steals (STL) and blocks (BLK)) than Section 6.2, which composes the NBA dataset. We also generated independent (INDE), correlated (CORR), and anti-correlated (ANTI) datasets following the seminal work of [9]. For the uncertain case, we generalized uncertain instances following the method of [23].

We first study the efficiency of the four algorithms on INDE dataset (m=10,k=5,d=5). In Figure 6, we show the time cost for BL, RT, HBL, and HRT on different number of objects n. Although both RT and BL are fairly slow, RT is significantly faster than BL, which validates the efficiency of our probability computation algorithm based on layered range tree. HBL and HRT are much faster than BL and RT, which validates the benefit of our pruning strategies. In the

Table 2: Skyline probability of individuals.

ID	Name	Probability	ID	Name	Probability	ID	Name	Probability
0	LeBron James	0.905062	14	Dwyane Wade	0.358879	28	Steve Francis	0.10701
1	Dennis Rodman	0.839869	15	Tracy Mcgrady	0.265222	29	Dirk Nowitzki	0.063802
2	Shaquille O'Neal	0.453626	16	Grant Hill	0.027655	30	Paul Pierce	0.012171
3	Charles Barkley	0.693831	17	John Stockton	0.108985	31	Gary Payton	0.390831
4	Kevin Garnett	0.400346	18	David Robinson	0.307053	32	Baron Davis	0.150622
5	Jason Kidd	0.393144	19	Stephon Marbury	0.202866	33	Vince Carter	0.002854
6	Allen Iverson	0.440725	20	Tim Hardaway	0.291563	34	Antoine Walker	0.187002
7	Michael Jordan	0.609803	21	Magic Johnson	0.928804	35	Steve Nash	0.118144
8	Tim Duncan	0.049988	22	Chris Paul	0.327774	36	Andre Miller	0.003283
9	Karl Malone	0.664875	23	Gilbert Arenas	0.120904	37	Isiah Thomas	0.219151
10	Chris Webber	0.567586	24	Clyde Drexler	0.188748	38	Elton Brand	0.011283
11	Kevin Johnson	0.328127	25	Patrick Ewing	0.136455	39	Scottie Pippen	0.081097
12	Hakeem Olajuwon	0.357442	26	Rod Strickland	0.073434	40	Dominique Wilkins	0.209298
13	Kobe Bryant	0.345385	27	Brad Daugherty	0.098185	41	Lamar Odom	0.157486

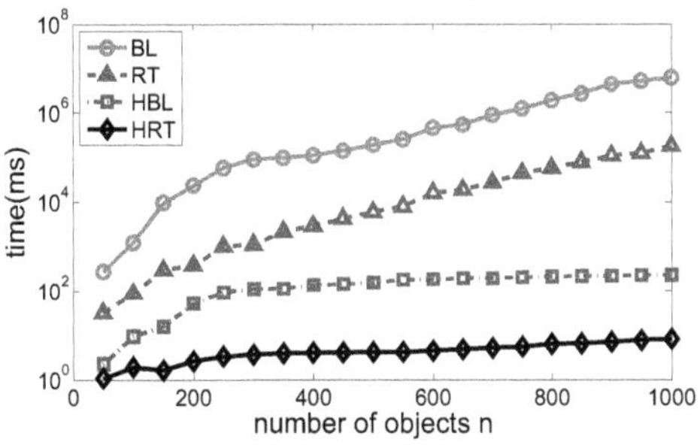

Figure 6: The impacts of RT and BL on different n.

following experiments, because the time cost of RT and BT are prohibitively high, we only compare HRT and HBL.

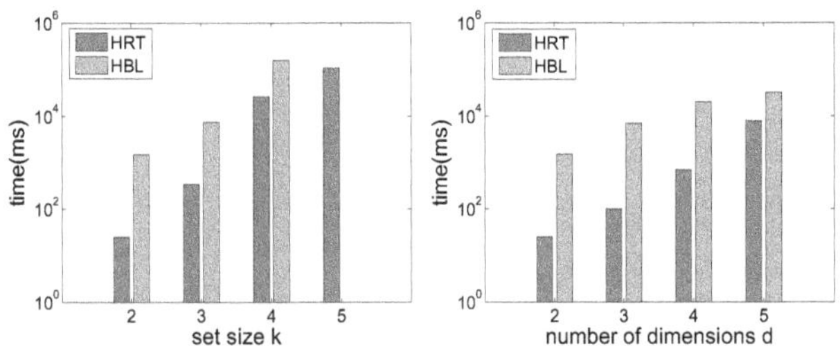

(a) different k (b) different d

Figure 7: The impacts of different k, d on NBA dataset.

Study on NBA dataset. Figure 7 shows the results on different k and d. The time cost grows exponentially with k and HRT significantly outperforms HBL. We did not report the result of HBL algorithm for some figures due to the high cost when k is big. The time cost also grows exponentially with d, HRT significantly outperforms HBL when d is small. However, when d is big, the difference is small due to the effect of "curse of dimensionality".

Study on Synthetic datasets. The results for the synthetic datasets are shown in Figure 8, 9, and 10. Generally speaking, the time cost for ANTI dataset is higher than INDE, and the time cost for INDE is higher than CORR. This is easy to understand because more instances are pruned in CORR dataset by our heuristic pruning strategies. On the other hand, it is harder to prune instances in ANTI dataset. From the global perspective, our algorithms are shown to be efficient and scalable, most of our experiments can be finished in 10^6 ms.

The impacts of different n are shown in (a) of Figure 8, 9, and 10 (m=10, k=5, d=5). Although the time complexity $C_n^k m^k knm < C_n^k m^k knlognm$ when m is small, HRT is much faster than HBL. There are two reasons: 1) the number of objects is much smaller than n after using heuristic pruning strategies, 2) the factor $nlognm$ of HRT is the worst-case while the factor nm is required. Comparing HRT to RT in Figure 6, HRT is almost 10^4 times faster than RT. Similar improvement can be observed for HBL and BL.

The impacts of different m are shown in (b) of Figure 8, 9, and 10 (n=1k, k=5, d=5). When $m = 10$ and $m = 100$, the time cost is fairly small because we can prune most of the instances in the heuristic pruning phase. However, when $m = 1k$, HRT can finish in 10^6 ms but HBL requires too much time which was not reported. The reason is that when m is big, although we can prune some instances, those objects with highest probability to be a skyline cannot be pruned and each object has m instances. For example, even when $n = 10, m = 1k$, $C_n^k m^k N = 4.5 \times 10^{11}$ while $C_n^k m^k nlogN = 6 \times 10^9$ and as we discussed before, $C_n^k m^k nlogN$ is the worst-case.

The impacts of different k are shown in (c) of Figure 8, 9, and 10 (n=1k, m=10, d=5). The set size k has significant effect on both HBL and HRT because k is the exponential term. Again, HRT outperforms HBL significantly.

The impacts of different d are shown in (d) of Figure 8, 9, and 10 (n=1k, m=10, k=5). They show that HRT is much faster than HBL when d is small. But the time cost of HRT grows exponentially because d is the exponential term. The time cost of HBL should increase linearly. However, in the experiment, Figure 10(d) shows that the time cost of HBL grows exponentially, the reason is when d increases, it is hard to prune instances by heuristic pruning strategies on ANTI datasets. Because most of the instances are pruned on CORR datasets, Figure 9(d) shows the time cost of HBL almost does not change for different d.

7. CONCLUSIONS

In this paper, for the first time, we studied probabilistic k-skyline sets problem on uncertain data. We show two significant heuristic pruning strategies which are efficient and simple. We adapted the classic layered range tree index structure to enhance the baseline algorithm from worst-case time bound aspect. The idea should be of independent interest for other problems. The experimental results on the

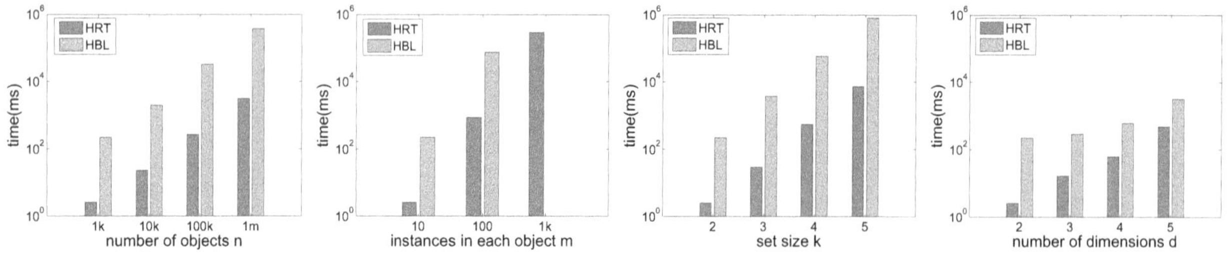

(a) different n (b) different m (c) different k (d) different d

Figure 8: The impacts of different n, m, k, d on INDE dataset.

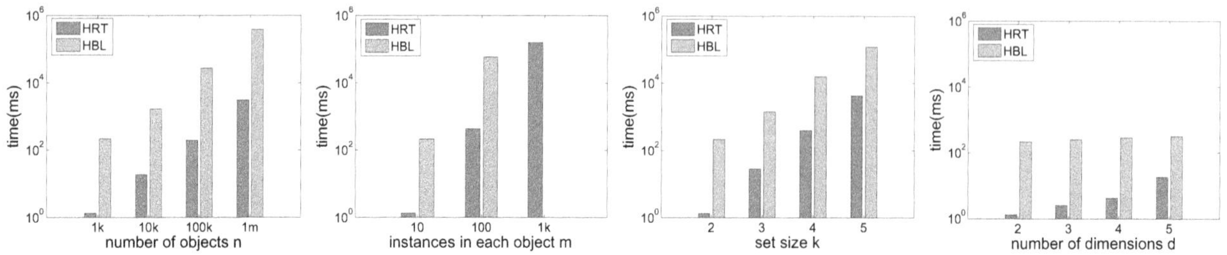

(a) different n (b) different m (c) different k (d) different d

Figure 9: The impacts of different n, m, k, d on CORR dataset.

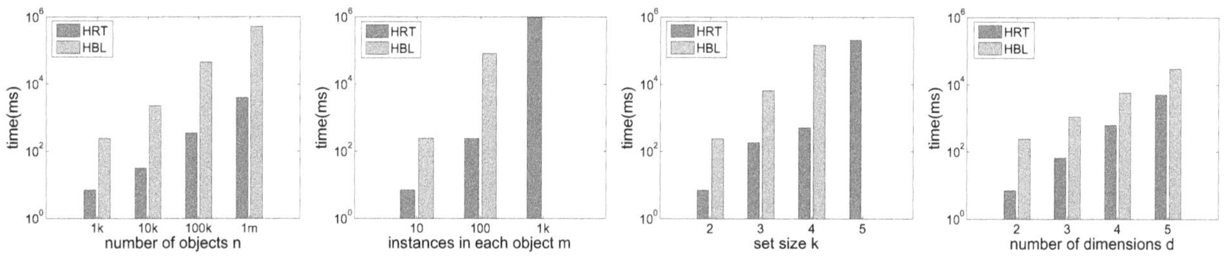

(a) different n (b) different m (c) different k (d) different d

Figure 10: The impacts of different n, m, k, d on ANTI dataset.

real NBA dataset and the synthetic datasets show that Pk-SkylineSets is interesting and useful, and our algorithms are efficient and scalable.

Acknowledgement

This research is partially supported by the Air Force Office of Scientific Research (AFOSR) DDDAS Program under award number FA9550-12-1-0240, the National Natural Science Foundation of China (Grant No. 11271351) and Guangdong Science and Technology Program Fund 2013B091300019.

8. REFERENCES

[1] P. Afshani, P. K. Agarwal, L. Arge, K. G. Larsen, and J. M. Phillips. (approximate) uncertain skylines. In *ICDT*, pages 186–196, 2011.
[2] R. Agrawal and R. Srikant. Fast algorithms for mining association rules in large databases. In *VLDB*, 1994.
[3] M. J. Atallah and Y. Qi. Computing all skyline probabilities for uncertain data. In *PODS*, pages 279–287, 2009.
[4] M. J. Atallah, Y. Qi, and H. Yuan. Asymptotically efficient algorithms for skyline probabilities of uncertain data. *ACM Trans. Database Syst.*, 36(2):12, 2011.
[5] I. Bartolini, P. Ciaccia, and M. Patella. The skyline of a probabilistic relation. *IEEE Trans. Knowl. Data Eng.*, 25(7):1656–1669, 2013.
[6] I. Bartolini, P. Ciaccia, and M. Patella. Domination in the probabilistic world: Computing skylines for arbitrary correlations and ranking semantics. *ACM Trans. Database Syst.*, 39(2):14, 2014.
[7] J. L. Bentley. Multidimensional divide-and-conquer. *Commun. ACM*, 23(4):214–229, 1980.
[8] J. L. Bentley, H. T. Kung, M. Schkolnick, and C. D. Thompson. On the average number of maxima in a set of vectors and applications. *J. ACM*, 25(4):536–543, 1978.
[9] S. Börzsönyi, D. Kossmann, and K. Stocker. The skyline operator. In *ICDE*, pages 421–430, 2001.
[10] B. Chazelle and L. J. Guibas. Fractional cascading: I. A data structuring technique. *Algorithmica*, 1(2):133–162, 1986.
[11] B. Chazelle and L. J. Guibas. Fractional cascading: II. applications. *Algorithmica*, 1(2):163–191, 1986.
[12] M. De Berg, M. Van Kreveld, M. Overmars, and O. C. Schwarzkopf. *Computational geometry*. Springer, 2000.
[13] V. Fisikopoulos. An implementation of range trees with fractional cascading in c++. *CoRR*, abs/1103.4521, 2011.
[14] A. Guttman. R-trees: A dynamic index structure for spatial searching. In *SIGMOD*, pages 47–57, 1984.
[15] M. E. Khalefa, M. F. Mokbel, and J. J. Levandoski. Skyline query processing for uncertain data. In *CIKM*, pages 1293–1296, 2010.
[16] D. G. Kirkpatrick and R. Seidel. Output-size sensitive algorithms for finding maximal vectors. In *Symposium on Computational Geometry*, pages 89–96, 1985.
[17] H. T. Kung, F. Luccio, and F. P. Preparata. On finding the maxima of a set of vectors. *J. ACM*, 22(4):469–476, 1975.
[18] X. Lian and L. Chen. Monochromatic and bichromatic reverse skyline search over uncertain databases. In *SIGMOD Conference*, 2008.
[19] X. Lin, Y. Zhang, W. Zhang, and M. A. Cheema. Stochastic skyline operator. In *ICDE*, pages 721–732, 2011.
[20] J. Liu, L. Xiong, J. Pei, J. Luo, and H. Zhang. Finding pareto optimal groups: group-based skyline. *PVLDB*, 2015.
[21] J. Liu, L. Xiong, and X. Xu. Faster output-sensitive skyline computation algorithm. *Inf. Process. Lett.*, 114(12):710–713, 2014.
[22] X. Liu, D.-N. Yang, M. Ye, and W.-C. Lee. U-skyline: A new skyline query for uncertain databases. *IEEE Trans. Knowl. Data Eng.*, 25(4):945–960, 2013.
[23] J. Pei, B. Jiang, X. Lin, and Y. Yuan. Probabilistic skylines on uncertain data. In *VLDB*, pages 15–26, 2007.
[24] J. Pei, W. Jin, M. Ester, and Y. Tao. Catching the best views of skyline: A semantic approach based on decisive subspaces. In *VLDB*, 2005.
[25] D. Sacharidis, A. Arvanitis, and T. K. Sellis. Probabilistic contextual skylines. In *ICDE*, pages 273–284, 2010.
[26] Q. Zhang, P. Ye, X. Lin, and Y. Zhang. Skyline probability over uncertain preferences. In *EDBT*, pages 395–405, 2013.
[27] W. Zhang, X. Lin, Y. Zhang, M. A. Cheema, and Q. Zhang. Stochastic skylines. *ACM Trans. Database Syst.*, 37(2):14, 2012.
[28] W. Zhang, X. Lin, Y. Zhang, W. Wang, and J. X. Yu. Probabilistic skyline operator over sliding windows. In *ICDE 2009*, pages 1060–1071, 2009.
[29] Y. Zhang, W. Zhang, X. Lin, B. Jiang, and J. Pei. Ranking uncertain sky: The probabilistic top-k skyline operator. *Inf. Syst.*, 36(5):898–915, 2011.

Ordering Selection Operators Under Partial Ignorance

Khaled H. Alyoubi *
Dept. of Computer Science
and Information Systems
Birkbeck, University of London
London WC1E 7HX, UK
khaled@dcs.bbk.ac.uk

Sven Helmer
Faculty of Computer Science
Free University of
Bozen-Bolzano
39100 Bolzano BZ, Italy
shelmer@inf.unibz.it

Peter T. Wood
Dept. of Computer Science
and Information Systems
Birkbeck, University of London
London WC1E 7HX, UK
ptw@dcs.bbk.ac.uk

ABSTRACT

Optimising queries in real-world situations under imperfect conditions is still a problem that has not been fully solved. We consider finding the optimal order in which to execute a given set of selection operators under partial ignorance of their selectivities. The selectivities are modelled as intervals rather than exact values and we apply a concept from decision theory, the minimisation of the maximum regret, as a measure of optimality. The associated decision problem turns out to be NP-hard, which renders a brute-force approach to solving it impractical. Nevertheless, by investigating properties of the problem and identifying special cases which can be solved in polynomial time, we gain insight that we use to develop a novel heuristic for solving the general problem. We also evaluate minmax regret query optimisation experimentally, showing that it outperforms a currently employed strategy of optimisers that uses mean values for uncertain parameters.

Categories and Subject Descriptors

H.2.4 [**Information Systems**]: Database Management—*Systems*

Keywords

query optimisation, decision theory, minmax regret

1. INTRODUCTION

Although query optimisation in database management systems (DBMSs) has been a topic of research for decades, there are still important unresolved issues. In his recent blog post [20], Guy Lohman highlights errors made in estimating cardinalities as a crucial factor. These kinds of errors cause optimisers to generate query execution plans that are way off the target in terms of efficiency. Consequently, an optimiser should try to avoid potentially bad plans rather than strive for an optimal plan based on unreliable information.

For typical workloads, a DBMS can compile statistical data over time to obtain a fairly accurate picture. For instance, estimating the selectivities of simple predicates on base relations in a relational database is fairly well understood and can be done quite accurately [12, 14]. However, the situation changes once systems are confronted with very unevenly distributed data values or predicates that are complex.

Trying to estimate selectivities in dynamic settings, such as data streams [28], or in non-relational contexts, such as XML databases [26, 30], also poses challenges. It may even be impossible to obtain any statistical data, because the query is running on remote servers [29]. Detailed information may also not be available because a user issues an atypical ad-hoc query or utilises parameter markers in a query. We propose to use techniques from decision theory for making decisions under ignorance[1], meaning that we know what the alternatives and their outcomes are, but we are unable to assign concrete probabilities to them [25].

In our approach we propose to build a robust query optimiser that is aware of the unreliability of database statistics and considers this during optimisation. When executing a query, the DBMS encounters a particular instance of concrete parameter values: we call this a *scenario*. The problem is that, during the prior optimisation step, the optimiser does not know which scenario the DBMS will face during plan execution. Additionally, it is highly unlikely that there is a single execution plan that will yield the optimal cost for every potential scenario. Consequently, our goal is to choose a query execution plan that performs reasonably well regardless of the scenario it encounters. More specifically, we try to minimise the difference between the cost of a plan p and the cost of the optimal plan when p is executed under its worst-case scenario. This is called *minmax regret optimisation* (MRO), which is a well-known technique for making decisions under ignorance. Previous work on query optimisation has considered measures of robustness for query plans [3, 4, 21], but not in terms of MRO.

In this paper, we focus on the selection operator σ, an operator common to many data querying languages. Selection is sometimes called a filter operator in contexts such as data stream processing [2, 5] and sensor networks [10], where there is renewed interest in improving the efficiency of processing these operators. A very common setting is determining the order in which to apply a set of commutative filters to a stream or a set of data items, e.g. tuples of a relation, so as to keep the processing costs to a minimum.

There are well-known techniques for ordering selection operators to filter out as many tuples as possible as early as possible at the lowest possible cost [13]. However, these techniques rely on having accurate values for the operators' selectivities, i.e., the percentage of tuples passing a filter, and their processing costs (per tuple). Getting

*Khaled H. Alyoubi was supported by a grant from King Abdulaziz University, Jeddah, Saudi Arabia.

Permission to make digital or hard copies of all or part of this work for personal or classroom use is granted without fee provided that copies are not made or distributed for profit or commercial advantage and that copies bear this notice and the full citation on the first page. Copyrights for components of this work owned by others than the author(s) must be honored. Abstracting with credit is permitted. To copy otherwise, or republish, to post on servers or to redistribute to lists, requires prior specific permission and/or a fee. Request permissions from Permissions@acm.org.

CIKM'15, October 19–23, 2015, Melbourne, Australia.
Copyright is held by the owner/author(s). Publication rights licensed to ACM.
ACM 978-1-4503-3794-6/15/10 ...$15.00.
DOI: http://dx.doi.org/10.1145/2806416.2806446 .

[1]Sometimes these are also called decisions under uncertainty. We refer to them as decisions under ignorance to distinguish them from probability-based methods.

the estimation of selectivities (and/or costs) wrong can lead to high overall costs for the pipelined execution.

Our technique is based on using *intervals* rather than exact values for describing selectivities, aiming at generating query plans that are minmax regret optimal. However, identifying such plans, even for selection ordering, turns out to be NP-hard. As a result, we leave the investigation of further operators for future work and focus first on finding a good heuristic for MRO selection ordering.

Intervals can provide a useful way to model selectivities when exact values are unknown or hard to compute. For example, Babu et al. [4] compute intervals from single-point estimates in order to model levels of uncertainty regarding the accuracy of estimates, based on how such estimates were derived. Moerkotte et al. [23] consider histograms which guarantee a maximum multiplicative error (called the q-error) for cardinality estimates. Given such an estimate, the true cardinality (selectivity) can easily be modelled by an interval, as we show in Section 2.

For another situation in which interval selectivities arise, consider estimating the selectivities of string predicates which perform substring matching using SQL `like`, a problem known to be difficult [6]. As an example, let us consider a database in which email messages are stored in a relation `emails`, with attributes such as `sender`, `subject` and `body` (the textual contents of the email). Assume that many queries use selection predicates such as `subject like '%invest%'`, so the database maintains indexes on words and on 2-grams (say) of words which allow it also to provide selectivities for these.

Although the database maintains an index on words, the selectivity for the word 'invest' will be an underestimate for the selectivity of `subject like '%invest%'` since the strings 'reinvest' and 'investigation' (and many others) also match this predicate. Even if we are able to enumerate all words containing the string 'invest', we do not know how to combine their individual selectivities into a single selectivity. Instead we can use an interval selectivity with the exact match as a lower estimate. As the upper estimate, we can use the minimum selectivity of all the 2-grams of 'invest' since any string containing 'invest' must contain all of its 2-grams as well.

EXAMPLE 1. *As a concrete example, consider the following query on the Enron email data*[2]*:*

```
select sender
from   emails
where  body like '%action%' and
       body like '%like%' and
       subject like '%use%';
```

Let us denote the three predicates by A, L and U (for 'action', 'like' and 'use'). The interval selectivities for the three predicates, as computed using the method proposed above and explained in more detail in Section 7, are $[0.03, 0.68]$ *for A,* $[0.17, 0.27]$ *for L and* $[0.0008, 0.06]$ *for U. Even if we consider only the upper and lower bounds of these intervals, they give rise to 8 possible scenarios. No single plan (order) is optimal for all 8 scenarios, so the best we can do is find the plan which minimises the maximum regret. This plan corresponds to the order* UAL*. The maximum regret for this plan arises in the scenario when U has its maximum selectivity, while A and L have their minimum selectivities (in this case, the predicates U and A should be swapped to get the optimal order).*

In the case of the above query, our heuristic finds the minmax regret optimal solution. By way of contrast, an alternative heuristic such as that which takes the midpoints of the intervals and produces an optimal ordering based on those, produces the plan ULA*. This plan has a maximum regret which is 44% worse than the minmax regret optimal plan.* ◇

We should mention that the technique of using intervals can be applied to other approximate or error-tolerant queries as well. All we need is the selectivity for an exact query as the lower bound and the selectivity for a query that determines a candidate set with false positives as the upper bound.

Our contributions in this paper are as follows:

- We formalise the problem of optimal selection ordering under partial ignorance, i.e., when selectivities are given as intervals.
- We identify a number of properties of the problem, including that (i) only *extreme* scenarios (i.e., in which each operator takes on its minimum or maximum selectivity) need to be considered, (ii) operators which *dominate* others (i.e., both their maximum and minimum selectivities are smaller) must appear before the dominated ones in any optimal plan, and (iii) the decision version of the problem is NP-hard.
- We investigate a number of special cases in which selection ordering under partial ignorance can be solved in polynomial time. Along the way, we also identify other important properties of scenarios in MRO selection ordering.
- Based on our findings we develop efficient optimisation heuristics, which we evaluate experimentally, using synthetic data, the Enron email data, and the Star Schema Benchmark (SSB) [27]. The experiments demonstrate the benefit of using minmax regret optimisation, in some cases halving the deviation from the optimal plan compared to conventional techniques.

The remainder of this paper is organised as follows. We start by reviewing related work on selection ordering and optimisation techniques in the next section. In Section 3, we formalise the problem of selection ordering under partial ignorance, using minmax regret optimisation as the criterion for optimality. Various properties of the problem, including NP-hardness, are identified in Section 4. Section 5 presents some special cases of the problem which can be solved in polynomial time. Our heuristic algorithm is given in Section 6, with its experimental evaluation presented in Section 7. Finally, we conclude in Section 8.

2. BACKGROUND AND RELATED WORK

We assume we are given a set $S = \{\sigma_1, \sigma_2, \ldots, \sigma_n\}$ of selection operators, or equivalently a conjunctive predicate $p_1 \wedge p_2 \wedge \cdots p_n$. The *selectivity* s_i of operator σ_i or predicate p_i is the fraction of tuples that satisfy the operator or predicate. Associated with each operator s_i is also a cost c_i, which is the cost per tuple of evaluating the operator.

Most database systems keep statistics allowing them to estimate the selectivity for single attributes fairly accurately. For the joint selectivity of multiple attributes, much early work and many systems make the *attribute value independence* (AVI) assumption. This assumes that the selectivity of a set of operators $\{\sigma_{i_1}, \sigma_{i_2} \ldots \sigma_{i_m}\}$ is equal to $s_{i_1} \times s_{i_2} \times \cdots \times s_{i_m}$. If instead a system stores (some) joint selectivities (it is infeasible for it to store all of them), we can use the AVI assumption to "fill in the gaps" or use the estimation approach advocated in [22].

2.1 Selection Ordering

Assuming we have accurate values for the selectivity s_i and cost c_i of selection operator σ_i, we can calculate the *rank* r_i of σ_i:

$$r_i = (s_i - 1)/c_i \qquad (1)$$

[2]http://www.cs.cmu.edu/~./enron/

Given a set of selection operators, sorting and executing them in non-decreasing order of their ranks results in the minimal expected pipelined processing cost [18] under the AVI assumption. Clearly, the computation of the ranks and the sorting can be done in polynomial time. A similar argument applies if a query uses a conjunction of predicates on the same relation, and query evaluation uses a simple table scan. In such a case, the optimiser should test the predicates in the order which minimises the total number of tests. Basically, ordering selection operators optimally is a solved problem, but only when given exact values for the s_i and c_i.

Similar optimisation problems have been studied in the context of sequential testing. Here the goal is to find faulty components as quickly as possible by testing them one by one. Each component has a probability of working correctly and a cost for testing it. One of the earliest proposed solutions [15] relies on ranking the components and then ordering them by their ranks, very similar to the selection ordering described above.

2.2 Optimising under Uncertainty

In the following, we review different approaches for dealing with uncertain parameters during query optimisation. A common approach of many optimisers is to use the mean or modal value of the parameters and then find the plan with least cost under the assumption that this value remains constant during query execution, an approach called Least Specific Cost (LSC) in [7]. As Chu et al. point out in [7], if the parameters vary significantly, this does not guarantee finding the plan of least expected cost.

An alternative is to use probabilistic information about the parameters fed into the database optimiser, an approach known as Least Expected Cost (LEC) [7]. (A discussion regarding the circumstances under which LEC or LSC is best appears in [8].) In decision-theoretic terms, we are making decisions under risk, maximising the expected utility. However, probability distributions for the possible parameter values are needed to make this approach work, whereas in our case we do not have these prerequisites.

In parametric query optimisation several plans can be precompiled and then, depending on the query parameters, be selected for execution [11]. However, if there is a large number of optimal plans, each covering a small region of the parameter space, this becomes problematic. First of all, we have to store all these plans. In addition, constantly switching from one plan to another in a dynamic environment (such as stream processing) just because we have small changes in the parameters introduces a considerable overhead. In order to amend this, researchers have proposed reducing the number of plans at the cost of slightly decreasing the quality of the query execution [9]. Our approach can be seen as an extreme form of parametric query optimisation by finding a single plan that covers the whole parameter space.

Another approach to deal with the lack of reliable statistics is adaptive query processing, in which an execution plan is re-optimised while it is running [2, 4, 16, 21]. It is far from trivial to determine at which point to re-optimise and adaptive query processing may also involve materialising large intermediate results. More importantly, this means modifying the whole query engine; in our approach no modifications of the actual query processing are needed. A gentler approach is the incremental execution of a query plan [24]. Deciding on how to decompose a plan into fragments and putting them together is still a complex task, though.

Estimates based on intervals arise explicitly in [4] and implicitly in [23]. As mentioned in the Introduction, Babu et al. [4] use intervals to model uncertainty in the accuracy of a single-point estimate. Uncertainty is represented by a value from 0 (none) to 6 (very high). Upper and lower bounds for the single-point estimate are then calculated using the estimate and the uncertainty value. During optimisation, only three scenarios, those using the low estimates, the exact estimates and the high estimates, are considered, rather than all scenarios as in our approach. Moerkotte et al. [23] study histograms which provide so-called q-error guarantees. Given an estimate $\hat{s}$ for s, the q-error of $\hat{s}$ is $\max(s/\hat{s}, \hat{s}/s)$. An estimate is q-acceptable if its q-error is at most q. So if an estimate $\hat{s}$ is q-acceptable, the true value s lies in the interval $1/q \times \hat{s} \leq s \leq q \times \hat{s}$, but there is no knowledge about any distribution within the interval. The authors of [23] show that these histograms can be implemented efficiently in real-world systems such as SAP HANA.

Notions of robustness in query optimisation have been considered in [3, 4, 21]. Babcock and Chaudhuri [3] use probability distributions derived from sampling as well as user preferences in order to tune the predictability (or robustness) of query plans versus their performance. For Markl et al. [21], robustness means not continuing to execute to completion a query plan which is found to be suboptimal during evaluation; instead re-optimisation is performed. On the other hand, Babu et al. [4] consider a plan to be robust only if its cost is within e.g. 20% of the cost of the optimal plan. None of these papers consider robustness in the sense of MRO. Moreover, these techniques need additional statistical information to work.

2.3 Optimising under Ignorance

Minmax regret optimisation (MRO) has been applied to a number of optimisation problems where some of the parameters are (partially) unknown [1]. The complexity of the MRO version of a problem is often higher than that of the original problem. Many optimisation problems with polynomial-time solutions turn out to be NP-hard in their MRO versions [1].

One example is minimising the *total flow time* (TFT), in which n jobs are scheduled on a single machine [17]. The *flow time* of a job is the sum of its processing time and the time it has had to wait before starting execution. The total flow time is the sum of the flow times of all n jobs. This scheduling problem can be solved in polynomial time given exact job lengths (by sorting the jobs in non-decreasing order of their processing times [19]), but becomes NP-hard in its MRO variant [19]. Researchers have developed approximation algorithms for the problem; for example, a 2-approximation algorithm, bounding the approximate solution to be no more than twice the optimal solution, is proposed in [17].

Among all MRO problems, TFT is the one closest to the problem we are investigating. However, there are substantial differences: the formula for computing the cost of a schedule is much simpler for TFT, and the approach chosen to obtain a 2-approximation does not guarantee a bound for MRO selection ordering, as we show in Section 4.

3. SELECTION ORDERING MRO

In this section we give a formal definition of the generalised selection ordering problem with partially defined selectivities. The exact costs of selection operators can also be unknown, but for the moment we restrict ourselves to partially defined selectivities.

3.1 Basic Definitions

We start out with definitions for selection operators with interval selectivities and basic properties.

DEFINITION 1. *Given a set $S = \{\sigma_1, \sigma_2, \ldots, \sigma_n\}$ of selection operators, each has a selectivity s_i and a cost c_i. Each selectivity is defined by a closed interval: for $1 \leq i \leq n$, $s_i = [\underline{s}_i, \overline{s}_i]$ with $\underline{s}_i, \overline{s}_i \in [0, 1]$ and $\underline{s}_i \leq \overline{s}_i$. For $1 \leq i \leq n$, $c_i \in \mathbf{R}^+$ represents the cost of σ_i for processing an input tuple.*

Depending on their selectivity intervals selection operators may relate to each other in a special way. Later on we exploit this property in order to optimise selection orders.

DEFINITION 2. *Given two selection operators $\sigma_i, \sigma_j \in S$, we say that σ_i* dominates *σ_j if $\underline{s}_i \leq \underline{s}_j$ and $\overline{s}_i \leq \overline{s}_j$. The set S of operators is called* dominant *if for each pair $\sigma_i, \sigma_j \in S$ it is the case that either σ_i dominates σ_j or σ_j dominates σ_i.*

Later on, it will be helpful to consider a special case of dominant sets of operators.

DEFINITION 3. *Given two selection operators $\sigma_i, \sigma_j \in S$, we say that σ_i* strictly dominates *σ_j if $\overline{s}_i \leq \underline{s}_j$. A* strictly dominant *set is defined analogously to a dominant set.*

If for two selection operators $\sigma_i, \sigma_j \in S$, neither σ_i dominates σ_j nor σ_j dominates σ_i, then σ_i and σ_j form a *nested* pair of operators. So, operator σ_i is *nested* in σ_j if $\underline{s}_j < \underline{s}_i$ and $\overline{s}_i < \overline{s}_j$.

EXAMPLE 2. *Let $S = \{\sigma_1, \sigma_2, \sigma_3\}$ be a set of selection operators, with selectivities $s_1 = [.2, .8]$, $s_2 = [.3, .5]$ and $s_3 = [.1, .4]$. Operator σ_3 dominates both σ_1 and σ_2, but does not strictly dominate either of them. Because σ_2 is nested in σ_1, the set S is not dominant.* ◇

DEFINITION 4. *An assignment of a concrete value to each of the n selectivities is called a* scenario *and is defined by a vector $x = (s_1, s_2, \ldots, s_n)$, with $s_i \in [\underline{s}_i, \overline{s}_i]$.*

Every time we actually run a query, we encounter one scenario. However, during the optimisation step we are unaware of which scenario we will face. The set of all possible scenarios can be described by $X = \{x \mid x \in [\underline{s}_1, \overline{s}_1] \times [\underline{s}_2, \overline{s}_2] \times \cdots \times [\underline{s}_n, \overline{s}_n]\}$. There are certain scenarios we are particularly interested in:

DEFINITION 5. *A scenario $x_{ext} = (s_1, s_2, \ldots, s_n)$ is called an* extreme scenario *if, for each $1 \leq i \leq n$, s_i is equal to either $\underline{s}_i$ or $\overline{s}_i$.*

Let π^n be the set of all possible permutations over $1, 2, \ldots, n$. For $\pi_j \in \pi^n$, $\pi_j(i)$ denotes the i-th element of π_j.

DEFINITION 6. *A query execution plan p_j is a permutation $\sigma_{\pi_j(1)}, \sigma_{\pi_j(2)}, \ldots, \sigma_{\pi_j(n)}$ of the n selection operators. The set of all possible query execution plans is given by*

$$P = \{p \mid p = \sigma_{\pi(1)}, \sigma_{\pi(2)}, \ldots, \sigma_{\pi(n)} \text{ such that } \pi \in \pi^n\}.$$

The cost of evaluating plan p_j under a given scenario x is

$$\begin{aligned} \text{Cost}(p_j, x) &= \Omega(c_{\pi(1)} + s_{\pi(1)}c_{\pi(2)} + s_{\pi(1)}s_{\pi(2)}c_{\pi(3)} \\ &\quad + \cdots + \prod_{i=1}^{n-1} s_{\pi(i)}c_{\pi(n)}) \\ &= \Omega\left(\sum_{i=1}^{n}\left(\prod_{j=1}^{i-1} s_{\pi(j)}\right) c_{\pi(i)}\right) \end{aligned} \tag{2}$$

Ω is the cardinality of the relation on which we execute the selection operators. Currently we make the AVI assumption that the selection predicates are stochastically independent. Extending our approach to situations in which (some) joint selectivities are known is a topic for future work.

EXAMPLE 3. *Recall the set $S = \{\sigma_1, \sigma_2, \sigma_3\}$ of selection operators from Example 2, with selectivities $s_1 = [.2, .8]$, $s_2 = [.3, .5]$ and $s_3 = [.1, .4]$. There are 8 extreme scenarios for this example, one being given by scenario $x_1 = (\underline{s}_1, \underline{s}_2, \underline{s}_3) = (.2, .3, .1)$. One the the 6 possible plans for S is given by plan $p_1 = \sigma_1\sigma_2\sigma_3$. Assuming that Ω and each cost c_i is set to 1, we can calculate the cost of plan p_1 under scenario x_1, Cost(p_1, x_1), using Equation (2) as follows:*

$$\textit{Cost}(p_1, x_1) = (1 + .2 + .2 \times .3) = 1.26$$

◇

Let $p_{opt(x)}$ stand for the query execution plan having the minimal cost for scenario x, and let $\pi_{opt(x)}$ be the permutation of the selection operators for this plan. Since we are facing multiple scenarios, the criterion for evaluating the optimality of a plan p_j is different to the one used in the classical selection ordering problem. We utilise minmax regret optimisation to determine the quality of a plan.

3.2 Minmax Regret Optimisation

Below we define the regret for a plan given a scenario, the maximal regret for a plan, and finally the problem of finding a plan that minimises the maximal regret.

DEFINITION 7. *Given a plan p and a scenario x, the absolute* regret *$\gamma(p, x)$ of p for x is:*

$$\gamma(p, x) = \textit{Cost}(p, x) - \textit{Cost}(p_{opt(x)}, x) \tag{3}$$

where $p_{opt(x)}$ is the optimal plan for scenario x. The maximal regret of a plan is the regret for its worst-case scenario and is simply defined as $\max_{x \in X}(\gamma(p, x))$.

DEFINITION 8. *Given the set P of all possible execution plans and the set X of all possible scenarios, minimising the maximal regret is done as follows (where $R(P, X)$ is the optimal regret):*

$$R(P, X) = \min_{p \in P}(\max_{x \in X}(\gamma(p, x)))$$

Given a set S of selection operators, let $P(S)$ denote the set of possible plans for S and $X(S)$ denote the set of possible scenarios for S. Then the minmax regret optimisation *problem for S, which we denote $MRO(S)$, is to find a plan whose maximum regret matches $R(P(S), X(S))$. For simplicity and when there is no confusion, we also use $MRO(S)$ to denote a plan which minimises $R(P(S), X(S))$.*

EXAMPLE 4. *Recall once again the set $S = \{\sigma_1, \sigma_2, \sigma_3\}$ of selection operators from Examples 2 and 3, with selectivities $s_1 = [.2, .8]$, $s_2 = [.3, .5]$ and $s_3 = [.1, .4]$. For simplicity, assume that all operators have the same cost 1 and that the relation has cardinality $\Omega = 1$ (so to get the real costs, the numbers in Table 1 just have to be multiplied by the true cardinality). To find the plan which minimises the maximum regret, we can perform an exhaustive enumeration of all possible execution plans under every possible scenario. We show later in Theorem 1 that it is sufficient to consider only the extreme scenarios since the worst case scenario for any plan is always an extreme one. Hence, if there are n operators, we need to consider $n!$ different execution plans under each of 2^n extreme scenarios. For our example, Table 1 shows the 48 regret values for the 6 possible plans under each of 8 extreme scenarios.*

For example, recall from Example 3 that the cost of the first plan $p_1 = \sigma_1\sigma_2\sigma_3$ under scenario $x_1 = (\underline{s}_1, \underline{s}_2, \underline{s}_3) = (.2, .3, .1)$ is 1.26. The optimal plan $p_{opt(x)}$ for any scenario x is one in which the operators are in non-decreasing order of their selectivities.

	$\underline{s_1}$ $\underline{s_2}$ $\underline{s_3}$	$\underline{s_1}$ $\underline{s_2}$ $\overline{s_3}$	$\underline{s_1}$ $\overline{s_2}$ $\underline{s_3}$	$\underline{s_1}$ $\overline{s_2}$ $\overline{s_3}$	$\overline{s_1}$ $\underline{s_2}$ $\underline{s_3}$	$\overline{s_1}$ $\underline{s_2}$ $\overline{s_3}$	$\overline{s_1}$ $\overline{s_2}$ $\underline{s_3}$	$\overline{s_1}$ $\overline{s_2}$ $\overline{s_3}$	Max Regret
$\sigma_1\sigma_2\sigma_3$	0.14	0	0.18	0.02	0.91	0.62	**1.05**	0.6	1.05
$\sigma_1\sigma_3\sigma_2$	0.1	0.02	0.1	0	**0.75**	0.7	0.73	0.52	0.75
$\sigma_2\sigma_1\sigma_3$	0.24	0.1	0.48	0.32	0.41	0.12	**0.75**	0.3	0.75
$\sigma_2\sigma_3\sigma_1$	0.21	0.16	**0.43**	0.42	0.2	0	0.4	0.1	0.43
$\sigma_3\sigma_1\sigma_2$	0	0.22	0	0.2	0.05	**0.3**	0.03	0.12	**0.3**
$\sigma_3\sigma_2\sigma_1$	0.01	0.26	0.03	**0.32**	0	0.1	0	0	0.32

Table 1: The regret for each plan under each scenario in Example 4.

Therefore, the optimal plan for scenario x_1 *is* $p_{opt(x_1)} = \sigma_3\sigma_1\sigma_2$ *and its cost is:*

$$Cost(p_{opt(x_1)}, x_1) = (1 + .1 + .1 \times .2) = 1.12$$

The regret of plan p_1 *under scenario* x_1 *using Equation (3) is:*

$$\begin{aligned}\gamma(p_1, x_1) &= Cost(p_1, x_1) - Cost(p_{opt(x_1)}, x_1) \\ &= 1.26 - 1.12 = 0.14\end{aligned}$$

In order to find the minmax regret solution, the maximum regret of each plan needs to be found. For plan p_1*, the maximum regret is* 1.05 *which occurs in scenario* $(\overline{s_1}, \overline{s_2}, \underline{s_3})$*, its worst-case scenario. The maximum regret for each plan is shown in bold face in Table 1.*

Finally, we are looking for the plan with the smallest maximum regret (i.e., the smallest value in the last column of Table 1). As a result the minmax regret solution, $MRO(S)$*, is plan* $\sigma_3\sigma_1\sigma_2$*, which has the best performance among all plans when confronted with their worst-case scenarios.* ◇

In the above example, it is interesting to consider which scenario gives rise to the maximum regret for each plan. Note that for each plan its worst-case scenario is one in which the operators in some initial sequence in the plan each take on their maximum selectivity followed by the remaining operators taking on their minimum selectivity. We call such a scenario a *max-min* scenario.

DEFINITION 9. *Let* p *be the plan* $\sigma_{\pi(1)}, \sigma_{\pi(2)}, \ldots, \sigma_{\pi(n)}$*. A scenario for* p *is called a* max-min *scenario if there is a* $0 \leq k \leq n$ *such that for all* $1 \leq i \leq k$*,* $s_{\pi(i)} = \overline{s_{\pi(i)}}$*, and for all* $k+1 < i \leq n$*,* $s_{\pi(i)} = \underline{s_{\pi(i)}}$*.*

So the first k operators in p take on their maximum selectivity, while the rest take on the minimum. Note that for a plan p with n operators, there are $n+1$ max-min scenarios. Max-min scenarios are the only scenarios considered by the max-min heuristic we develop in this paper. However, it is important to state that, in general, the worst-case scenario for a plan may not be a max-min scenario.

4. PROPERTIES OF MRO

Before presenting algorithms for solving the MRO selection ordering problem, we identify some of its important properties[3].

In order to determine the worst-case scenario of a plan, i.e., the scenario for which a plan exhibits its largest regret, we only have to check extreme scenarios.

THEOREM 1. *The worst-case scenario for any query plan* p *is always an extreme scenario.*

[3]The proofs of results in this section and the next are published in a technical report available at `http://arxiv.org/abs/1507.08257`.

We can determine the relative order two operators have to be in to minimise the maximal regret if one operator dominates the other.

THEOREM 2. *If* σ_a *dominates* σ_b*, then there exists a plan* p *minimising the maximal regret in which* σ_a *precedes* σ_b*.*

EXAMPLE 5. *Recall from Example 4 the set* $S = \{\sigma_1, \sigma_2, \sigma_3\}$ *of selection operators, with selectivities* $s_1 = [.2, .8]$*,* $s_2 = [.3, .5]$ *and* $s_3 = [.1, .4]$*. Because* σ_3 *dominates* σ_1 *and* σ_2*, in the minmax regret solution, i.e. plan* $\sigma_3\sigma_1\sigma_2$*,* σ_3 *precedes* σ_1 *and* σ_2*. As a result of domination, in this example we would only have to consider two plans when searching for the minmax regret solution.* ◇

For the TFT problem, Kasperski used the simple heuristic of sorting jobs in non-decreasing order according to the midpoints of their intervals, yielding a 2-approximation [17]. This approach does not guarantee a bound for MRO selection ordering; as shown below, the quality of the solution can become arbitrarily bad.

Given $2n+1$ operators, the first n operators have the selectivities $\underline{s_i} = 0$ and $\overline{s_i} = 1$ $(1 \leq i \leq n)$, while the next n operators have the selectivities $\underline{s_i} = \overline{s_i} = 0.5 + \epsilon$ $(n+1 \leq i \leq 2n)$ for some small ϵ. The final operator has a constant selectivity of 1 to guarantee that it will always be in last position, meaning that its selectivity will not impact any further steps.

The midpoint heuristic will order the operators in exactly this way, from 1 to $2n+1$. Clearly, the worst-case scenario for this plan is when s_i is set to 1 for $1 \leq s_i \leq n$. In the optimal plan for this scenario, the operators σ_i with $n+1 \leq i \leq 2n$ will be executed first.

The regret of this plan is computed as follows:

$$\begin{array}{ccccccccc} & 1 & + & 1^2 & \ldots & + & 1^n & + & f(n) \\ - & (0.5+\epsilon) & - & (0.5+\epsilon)^2 & \ldots & - & (0.5+\epsilon)^n & - & g(n) \end{array}$$

where $f(n)$ and $g(n)$ stand for the cost of the remaining operators in the plan. A lower bound for this expression is the following, since $f(n) \geq g(n)$ (see Lemma 3 below):

$$n - n(0.5 + \epsilon)$$

With increasing n and small values for ϵ, this expression can get arbitrarily large.

LEMMA 3. *Given a query plan* p *and a scenario* x*, we have the following relationship between the summands in* $Cost(p, x)$ *and* $Cost(p_{opt(x)}, x)$*, where* $p_{opt(x)}$ *is the optimal plan for scenario* x*:*

$$\prod_{j=1}^{k} s_{\pi(j)} \geq \prod_{j=1}^{k} s_{\pi_{opt(x)}(j)} \text{ for all } k \text{ with } 1 \leq k \leq n-1$$

In common with other MRO problems, we can show that the decision problem for general $MRO(S)$, which we call MINMAX REGRET, is NP-hard. In this version, we are given a set $S = \{\sigma_1, \sigma_2, \ldots, \sigma_n\}$ of selection operators each having unit cost, as well as a set $X = \{X_1, X_2, \ldots, X_m\}$ of scenarios, where each scenario X_j specifies a selectivity s_{ij} for each operator σ_i, $1 \leq j \leq m$ and $1 \leq i \leq n$.

MINMAX REGRET: given a set S of n selection operators, a set X of m scenarios, and a real number R, is there a plan whose maximum regret is less than R?

We can show that MINMAX REGRET is NP-hard by reducing a version of SET COVER to it.

THEOREM 4. MINMAX REGRET *is NP-hard.*

5. SOME POLYNOMIAL-TIME CASES

In this section we show that, for sets of selection operators S satisfying certain properties, $MRO(S)$ can be found in polynomial time. In particular, we look at dominant operators, which can easily be ordered correctly, and their combination with constant operators, i.e., operators for which we can obtain exact selectivity values. As before, we assume that the cost of each operator is one.

Let S be a set of selection operators such that the selectivity of each operator can be estimated accurately (i.e., each selectivity is constant). Then, as mentioned in Section 2.1, $MRO(S)$ can be found by sorting the operators in non-decreasing order of their rank given by Equation (1). Given our assumption that each operator has cost one, finding $MRO(S)$ reduces to sorting the operators in non-decreasing order of their selectivity alone.

Recall from Section 3.1 the definition of a dominant set S of operators. Given a dominant set S of operators, it follows from Theorem 2 that the minmax regret solution is one where the operators are sorted in non-decreasing order according to their minimum (or maximum) selectivity value. (Note that a set of constant operators is a special case of a dominant set of operators.) We therefore have:

COROLLARY 1. *If S is a dominant set of n operators, then $MRO(S)$ can be solved in $O(n \log n)$ time.*

When we include nested operators (recall the definition from Section 3.1), the problem becomes much more difficult. As a step in the direction of solving the general problem, we consider below the simple case of a strictly dominant set of operators (also defined in Section 3.1) along with a single constant operator nested within one of the non-constant operators. If S is a strictly dominant set of operators, then the plan $MRO(S)$ has zero regret under all scenarios. This is because all operators in $MRO(S)$ will be in the same position as in the corresponding optimal plan under all scenarios.

Let S be a strictly dominant set which includes a constant operator σ_c nested within one of the non-constant operators, say σ_i. In this case, we know how to place the dominant operators relative to each other in $MRO(S)$ but we need to determine the position of σ_c in $MRO(S)$. Since $\underline{s}_i \leq s_c \leq \overline{s}_i$, the constant operator σ_c should be either immediately before or immediately after σ_i in $MRO(S)$. Interestingly, the correct position for σ_c depends only on the midpoint of the selectivity s_i of σ_i.

PROPOSITION 1. *Let S be a strictly dominant set of n operators such that $MRO(S) = (\sigma_1, \ldots, \sigma_n)$. Let σ_c be an operator with constant selectivity s_c such that $\underline{s}_i \leq s_c \leq \overline{s}_i$, for some $1 \leq i \leq n$, and $S' = S \cup \{s_c\}$. In $MRO(S')$, σ_c is placed between (1) σ_{i-1} and σ_i if $s_c \leq (\underline{s}_i + \overline{s}_i)/2$, or (2) σ_i and σ_{i+1} if $s_c \geq (\underline{s}_i + \overline{s}_i)/2$.*

Note that if $s_c = (\underline{s}_i + \overline{s}_i)/2$, then σ_c can be placed either between σ_{i-1} and σ_i or between σ_i and σ_{i+1} in $MRO(S')$.

Proposition 1 can be generalised to the case in which each non-constant operator has at most one constant operator nested within it. An interesting observation about the situation described in Proposition 1 is that the worst-case scenario is a max-min scenario.

PROPOSITION 2. *Let S be a strictly dominant set of n operators such that $MRO(S) = (\sigma_1, \ldots, \sigma_n)$. Let σ_c be an operator with constant selectivity s_c such that $\underline{s}_i \leq s_c \leq \overline{s}_i$, for some $1 \leq i \leq n$, and $S' = S \cup \{s_c\}$. The scenario $(\overline{s}_1, \ldots, \overline{s}_{j-1}, s_c, \underline{s}_j, \ldots, \underline{s}_n)$, in which either σ_{j-1} or σ_j is equal to σ_i, is a worst-case scenario for $MRO(S')$.*

6. MAX-MIN HEURISTIC

Computing the regret of every selection ordering for every possible scenario makes the brute-force algorithm infeasible, since there are $n!$ different orderings and 2^n scenarios, given n operators. So in order to find an efficient heuristic, we have to significantly reduce the number of orderings and scenarios. While doing so, we want to leverage the insights gained from our theoretical investigation.

Let us first look at the number of possible scenarios. As we have seen in the previous section, max-min scenarios seem to play a special role when it comes to the maximum regret of a given plan p. Intuitively this makes sense, as in an optimal plan many of the operators σ_i located towards the beginning of p with selectivities $\overline{s_i}$ will trade places with operators σ_j located towards the end of p with selectivities $\underline{s_j}$. Consequently, there tends to be a large difference between the plan p and an optimal plan for a max-min scenario, leading to a substantial (if not maximal) regret for p. So in our heuristic we aim to generate plans that perform well for max-min scenarios. This reduces the number of scenarios we have to consider from 2^n to $n + 1$.

We now turn to determining the order of the selection operators. There are two well-known basic methods for doing this (efficiently). The first one is constructing a plan by combining partial plans in a way that leads to an optimised execution order. Very often putting the partial plans together requires using a heuristic to solve a combinatorial problem. The second method is to quickly create a complete plan (e.g., by using a simple heuristic) and then try to improve the plan by rewriting it (e.g., by swapping or removing and re-inserting operators). In our approach we wanted to have both options available, so we decided to develop different variants. The complexity of our heuristic shows slight differences depending on the variant we use; however, the algorithms we apply all have polynomial complexity.

Our max-min heuristic algorithm, $H(p, q)$, which is in fact a template for a number of algorithms, is shown as Algorithm 1. It is parameterised by two inputs: p, a (possibly empty) starting plan, and q, an order in which to process operators. Clearly, to generate a complete plan the union of p and q has to contain all the operators. If the intersection of p and q is empty, our algorithm is similar to insertion sort: in turn, we consider each operator in q and place it into p at the position that minimises the regret over all max-min scenarios. If an operator in q is already present in p, then we remove it from p before re-inserting it. This is equivalent to moving an operator to a different position. Again we determine the position minimising the regret over all max-min scenarios.

Algorithm 1: $H(p, q)$

```
foreach operator t from the sequence q do
    if t is in p then remove t from pAssume p currently
    comprises i operators;
    foreach position j, 1 ≤ j ≤ i + 1, in p do
        Temporarily insert t in position j in p;
        foreach max-min scenario for p do
            Calculate the regret of plan p;
            Store the maximum regret for position j;
    Choose as the final position for t in p that which minimises
    the maximum regret;
Return p;
```

It is clear that the max-min heuristic runs in polynomial-time. For each partial plan comprising i operators, we consider $i + 1$ possible positions for the next operator. In each of these positions, we consider $i + 2$ max-min scenarios. Calculating the regret of a plan with n operators can be done in time $O(n \log n)$. Hence the algorithm described above has an overall complexity of $O(n^4 \log n)$ (in the worst case $i = n$ for every execution of the outer loop). However, by computing costs incrementally when an operator moves position and one max-min scenario moves to the next, we can implement the heuristic to run in time $O(n^3)$.

EXAMPLE 6. *Recall from Example 5 the set $S = \{\sigma_1, \sigma_2, \sigma_3\}$ of selection operators, with selectivities $s_1 = [.2, .8]$, $s_2 = [.3, .5]$ and $s_3 = [.1, .4]$. Consider our max-min heuristic algorithm, $H(p, q)$, with initial plan $p = \sigma_3\sigma_1$ and remaining operator $q = \sigma_2$. Since p consists of two operators, σ_2 should be checked in three positions: before σ_3, after σ_1 and between them. For each position and resulting plan, the regret is calculated under all max-min scenarios, of which there are four in this example.*

As an example, consider the plan in which σ_2 is placed between σ_3 and σ_1. The regret will be calculated for the scenarios $(\underline{s}_3, \underline{s}_2, \underline{s}_1)$, $(\overline{s}_3, \underline{s}_2, \underline{s}_1)$, $(\overline{s}_3, \overline{s}_2, \underline{s}_1)$ and $(\overline{s}_3, \overline{s}_2, \overline{s}_1)$. The maximum regret for this plan is 0.3 which occurs in scenario $(\overline{s}_3, \overline{s}_2, \underline{s}_1)$.

Finally, the solution will be the plan with the smallest maximum regret, which happens to be $\sigma_3\sigma_2\sigma_1$. As a matter of fact, the solution returned by the max-min heuristic is the same as the actual minmax regret solution, as was shown in Example 4. ◇

In the following two subsections, we consider various criteria for choosing an initial plan and for ordering the remaining operators.

6.1 Choosing an Initial Plan

Even though we can run our heuristic with an empty initial plan p, i.e., building a solution by inserting all operators one by one, often it makes sense to start with a prebuilt partial plan.

One particular and important case is that of dominant operators. Given a set S of operators, if we can identify a subset $S' \subseteq S$ of dominant operators, we know that we can find an optimal solution p' for S' quickly and that the relative order of the operators in p' will not change in any optimal plan for S (see Theorem 2). Thus, taking p' as the initial plan when calling $H(p, q)$ makes good sense. However, there may be different ways to choose S', as in general there may be more than one such dominant set. If we have more than one option, we can use the following criteria to make a decision: choose the subset S' (1) with the maximum cardinality or (2) whose operators have the largest total width. While the intuition in choosing the largest subset is clear, the motivation for maximising the width may not be so evident: the wider an interval, the more impact it has on the solution, so it is more important to slot wide intervals into the correct positions. As we often encountered several subsets sharing the same maximum cardinality, we introduced a tie-breaker: choose the subset S' (3) with the maximum cardinality whose total width is greatest. In our experiments, we found that this third approach gave the best overall results.

EXAMPLE 7. *Recall from Example 6 the set $S = \{\sigma_1, \sigma_2, \sigma_3\}$ of selection operators, with selectivities $s_1 = [.2, .8]$, $s_2 = [.3, .5]$ and $s_3 = [.1, .4]$. Set S has two dominant subsets: $S_1 = \{\sigma_1, \sigma_3\}$ and $S_2 = \{\sigma_2, \sigma_3\}$. Both obviously satisfy criterion (1) above, being of maximum cardinality. However, if we use criterion (2), namely the set which has operators with the largest total selectivity width, then we will choose S_1 since its total width is 0.9 while that of S_2 is 0.5. S_1 would also be chosen according to criterion (3).*

After choosing the preferable subset, we need to produce initial plan p by sorting the operators in nondecreasing order of their minimum (or maximum) selectivities. Therefore, $p = \sigma_3\sigma_1$ when S_1 is chosen, while $p = \sigma_3\sigma_2$ if S_2 is chosen. ◇

Having an initial plan allows us to combine our algorithm with other heuristics. We can take the output of another algorithm as our initial plan p and then refine this result by running $H(p, q)$ on it. Moreover, we can use the output of $H(p, q)$ as input for another iteration of our own heuristic.

6.2 Ordering Criteria

Since our algorithm makes only a single pass over all the operators when (re-)inserting them into the plan, the order in which operators are considered may have a significant impact on the final outcome. For example, when inserting selections into an empty initial plan, operators considered earlier are tested in fewer positions relative to each other compared to those considered later.

We have considered two different ordering criteria in our experiments: interval *midpoint* (denoted by M) and interval *width* (denoted by W). Given a selectivity interval $s = [\underline{s}, \overline{s}]$, the midpoint of s is $(\underline{s} + \overline{s})/2$ while the width of s is $\overline{s} - \underline{s}$. In each case, operators can be ordered by non-decreasing (denoted $+$) or non-increasing (denoted $-$) values. Overall, the ordering criteria are denoted by $M+$, $M-$, $W+$ and $W-$. So, for example, $W+$ stands for operators being considered in non-decreasing order of their selectivity interval width.

7. EXPERIMENTAL RESULTS

We evaluated the max-min heuristic experimentally, measuring the impact of different parameters on its performance. We also implemented the brute-force algorithm for finding optimal solutions in order to evaluate how well the heuristic performs.

A commodity PC, with 8 GB RAM, Intel Core i5 processor running at 3.19 GHz and Windows 7 Enterprise (64-bit), was used to perform the experiments. The minmax regret brute-force algorithm and max-min heuristic were implemented in Java and compiled with the Eclipse IDE (Juno release), which is JDK compliant and uses the JavaSE-1.7 execution environment. The Star Schema Benchmark (SSB) queries were run on a simulation platform written in Ruby 1.9.3.

7.1 Generating Test Data

We first generated a synthetic data set to investigate the performance of our heuristic. Each test case corresponded to a set of k selection operators, with k ranging from 2 to 10, and for each k we generated a hundred different sets. While $k = 2$ is not hard to solve, it was included for verification purposes (any heuristic has to be able to find the optimal plan for this simple case). Ten operators was the upper limit we were able to solve optimally, checking $10! \cdot 2^{10}$ ($\approx$ 3.7 billion) different costs for each test case. For each set of selection operators we determined the lower and upper bounds of their selectivity intervals by generating $2k$ uniformly distributed random numbers between 0 and 1.

For real-world data, we used the Enron email data set, as introduced in Example 1. Once again, test queries used from 2 to 10 operators/predicates. For each $n \in [2, 10]$, 20 queries were generated, each with one predicate on `subject` and $n - 1$ predicates on `body`. The 20 queries were generated by randomly selecting from 40 keywords for `subject` and 45 keywords for `body`, and were checked to ensure that each returned a nonempty answer.

We also evaluated minmax regret optimisation using a version of SSB with data skew [27] (SSB itself is a variation of the TPC-H benchmark). We generated benchmark data with a scaling factor of 1, meaning that the central facts table, *lineorder*, contains 6,000,197 tuples, and joined all dimensional tables to the *lineorder* table. We then randomly picked from two to ten attributes from a subset of all available attributes to generate queries. Queries basically consist of

a conjunctive predicate whose clauses are made up of the selected attributes compared to a random value taken from the attribute's domain, using a less-than or greater-than operator. The following predicate is an example generated in our experiments:
`orderKey < 2964443 and linenumber > 5 and quantity < 29.`

7.2 Parameters

For the synthetic and Enron data sets, we looked at the effects of the ordering criteria and the choice of initial plan on the quality of our heuristic. Additionally, we investigated the impact of running our heuristic multiple times, using the output of one phase as the initial plan of the next phase.

We measure the performance of our heuristic by defining the *regret ratio* $\lambda(S)$, which is the regret computed by $H(p,q)$ divided by the optimal regret. More formally, given a set S of selection operators, let us denote the set of possible plans by $P(S)$ and the set of possible scenarios by $X(S)$. Recall from Section 3.1 that $R(P(S), X(S))$ then denotes the optimal regret. Then

$$\lambda(S) = \frac{R(H(p,q), X(S))}{R(P(S), X(S))}$$

We only calculate $\lambda(S)$ using the above formula when the optimal minmax regret is non-zero. As mentioned in Section 5, the optimal minmax regret is zero only when S forms a strictly dominating set. For such cases, our max-min heuristic always finds the optimal minmax regret solution, so we define $\lambda(S)$ to be one.

In view of having multiple test cases per number of selection operators, we calculate the *average regret ratio* and the *worst regret ratio* (simply the maximum value of $\lambda(S)$).

For the Enron data, we calculated selectivity intervals for the `like` predicates as described in the Introduction. For each selected keyword, we ran queries to find the minimum selectivity (given by exact matches of the keyword) and the maximum selectivity (given by the minimum selectivity of all 2-grams of the keyword). This gave rise to a range of intervals: those with small values such as $[0.0004, 0.01]$ for keyword 'progress' in the `subject`, those with larger values such as $[0.6, 0.7]$ for 'you' in the `body`, and those with a big range such as $[0.07, 0.6]$ for 'price' in the `body`.

For the Star Schema Benchmark we created some very rudimentary histograms by dividing the domain of an attribute into equal-sized ranges, counting the number of tuples that fall into each range. We do not keep any further information on the distribution of tuples within each range of a histogram. For example, Figure 1 shows the histogram for the attribute ordtotalprice, consisting of 20 ranges each covering roughly 18,000 different values, e.g., bucket #1 covers the range from 1 to 17,673.

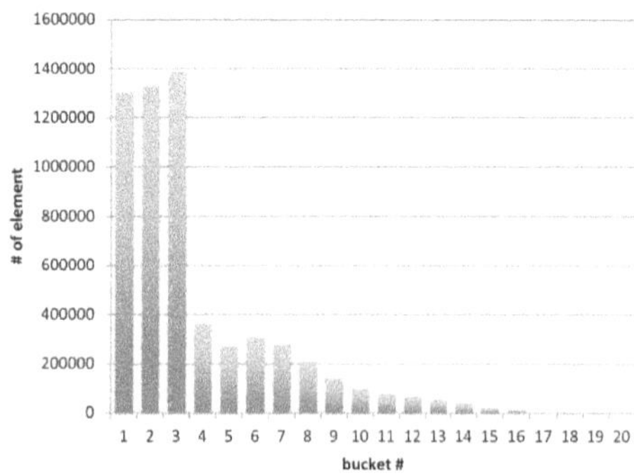

Figure 1: Histogram for attribute ordtotalprice.

This basic information allows us to determine intervals for the selectivities of selection operators. For a "less than" / "greater than" operator, we know that all histogram ranges exclusively covering smaller/larger values have to be included fully. However, for the range the predicate value falls into, we do not know precisely how many elements will be selected. In extreme cases, none or all of the elements satisfy the predicate, giving us the lower and upper bound for the selectivity. Example 8 illustrates this with concrete values.

EXAMPLE 8. *Given the histogram for attribute X below and the predicate $X < 126$, we can compute the lower bound and upper bound for the selectivity as follows: lower bound =* $\frac{200}{1000} = 0.2$, *upper bound =* $\frac{200+100}{1000} = 0.3$. ◇

Range	# of elements
1-100	200
101-200	100
201-300	400
301-400	300

Many sophisticated query optimisation techniques, such as least expected cost (LEC), assume that they have access to probability distributions of parameter values. LEC needs this to be able to compute utilities [7]. However, in our case we only have very rudimentary statistics, since we do not know anything about the distribution of attribute values within a range. The best we can do is to fall back on the assumption of uniform distribution, approximating the distribution using a mean value (this is also what least specific cost (LSC) optimisation would do in this case). For example, applying this method to the numbers given in Example 8 would yield a selectivity of 0.225 for the predicate $X < 126$. We compare our minmax regret optimisation technique to a mean-value-based approach using SSB data. Additionally, we do a comparison with a simple midpoint heuristic, i.e., sorting the intervals in non-decreasing order of their midpoint.

7.3 Results

First we present the results obtained studying the different variants of the max-min heuristic on the synthetic and Enron data, and then move on to the Star Schema Benchmark results.

7.3.1 Synthetic and Enron Data Sets

We experimented with a number of operator ordering criteria and initial plans for the max-min heuristic. These included starting with an empty initial plan (∅), considering random operator ordering (U), ordering by midpoint (M- and M+) and ordering by width (W- and W+). We briefly summarise the findings of our experiments here. Overall, the W+ ordering (non-decreasing width) performed best with an overall average regret ratio of 1.03 and an overall worst regret ratio of 1.94. W- was often even worse than a random order, while M+ and M- sometimes generated plans whose regret ratio was above 3. We also ran a midpoint heuristic that simply ordered the intervals in non-decreasing order of their midpoints (not going through all max-min scenarios). The midpoint heuristic was often worse than running the max-min heuristic with a random order.

While W+ ordering performs better than the M+, M-, and W- max-min heuristics and the midpoint heuristic, it is still not significantly better than the random ordering. In a second phase of our evaluation we seeded our heuristic with an initial plan. The results for initial plan D:CW with operator ordering W+ were best (D:CW stands for the largest subset of dominant operators, and, in case of a tie, the one with the greatest total width of the operators) in terms of the percentage of exact solutions and the average regret ratio. The

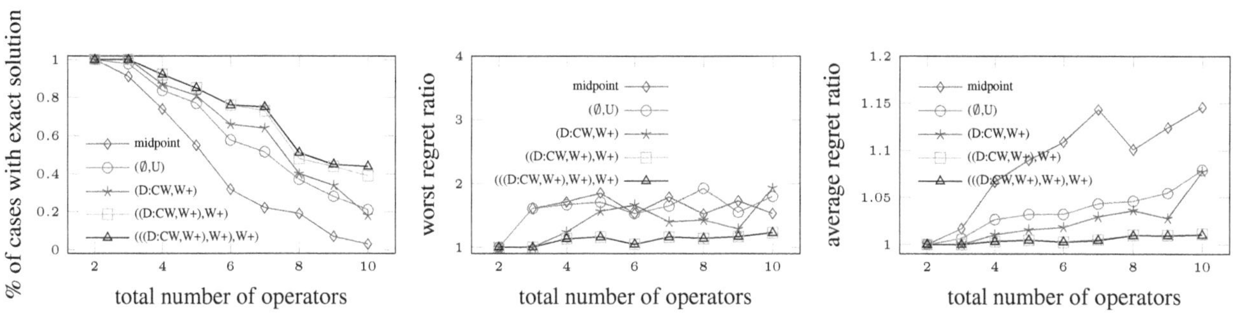

(a) Percentage of exact solutions (b) Worst regret ratio (c) Average regret ratio

Figure 2: Results for synthetic data set.

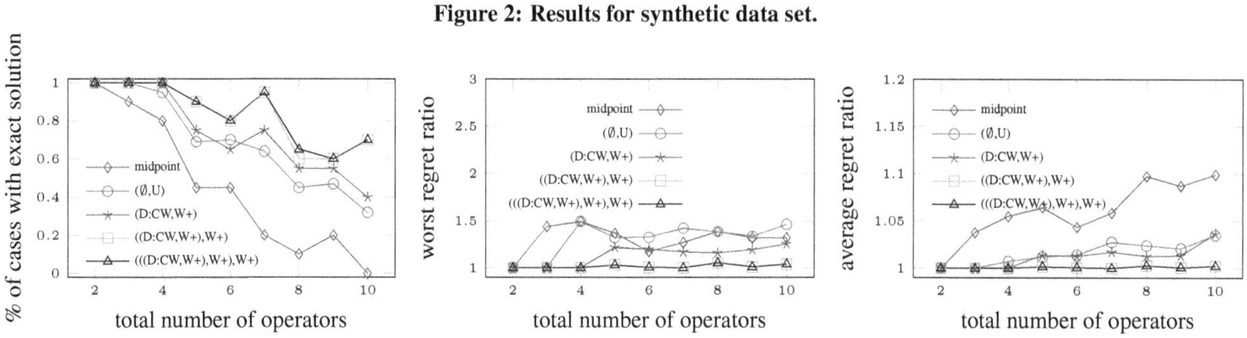

(a) Percentage of exact solutions (b) Worst regret ratio (c) Average regret ratio

Figure 3: Results for Enron data set.

results for the worst case regret ratio were rather inconclusive, so we tried to improve on this by running multiple phases of our heuristic.

Figures 2(a), (b) and (c) show the results for running our heuristic multiple times. This means that we take the output of running one phase of our heuristic and use it as the initial plan for the next phase. The figures show the results for starting off by running (D:CW, W+) first and then executing two more phases.

As can be seen, this variant clearly outperforms the baseline algorithm (∅,U), the midpoint heuristic, and the other variants in all respects. For example, for 10 operators, the worst regret ratio is less than 1.23 and the average ratio is approximately 1.01, compared to approximately 1.94 and 1.08, respectively, for running only a single phase of the heuristic. Moreover, running one additional phase improves the quality of the generated plan significantly, but running another phase makes almost no difference.

The results on the Enron data set (Figure 3) showed similar trends, but were more impressive in every respect. The two- and three-phase variants of the max-min heuristic found the minmax optimal solution in 84% of cases, had a worst regret ratio of only 1.05, and an average regret ratio of less than 1.001. By contrast, the midpoint heuristic had a worst regret ratio of over 1.49, an average of 1.06, and did not find single minmax optimal solution with 10 operators.

To highlight how bad a poor choice of selectivity can be, we also tested using the minimum selectivity values of the intervals (as would be done if estimates were based simply on the selectivity of the keywords themselves). This produced a worst case regret ratio of *almost 30 for only 5 operators*.

Figure 4(a) shows the run time of the W+ ordering variant (single and multiple phases) together with the baseline algorithm (∅,U) when generating plans for up to 200 operators using the synthetic data set (the run times on the Enron data set were similar). Unsurprisingly, the variants midpoint, (∅,U), and (D:CW,W+) have the fastest run times, as they only sort a set of operators or execute a single operator insertion phase. Furthermore, it can be clearly seen that the additional run time of (((D:CW,W+),W+),W+) does not pay off, since it produces plans that are only marginally better than those of ((D:CW,W+),W+).

7.3.2 *Star Schema Benchmark*

We optimised the generated SSB queries using minmax regret optimisation, a mean-value-based approach, and also computed the optimal execution plan using exact selectivities, which means that we are comparing actual query plan costs rather than regret ratios.

Figure 4(b) shows the results for the average difference in costs between the query execution plans generated by different methods and the optimal plan (every data point in the diagram averages the measurement obtained by running 100 different queries). We only include two variants of minmax regret optimisation, (D:CW,W+) and the simple midpoint heuristic, as for SSB no major differences were discernible between the different variants in terms of the quality of the query plans. Surprisingly, the midpoint heuristic, although not very good at optimising the regret ratio, seems to produce efficient query execution plans. Considering the fact that all queries had an average run time between 60 and 80 seconds, the numbers shown in Figure 4(b) may not seem like a big difference. However, this shows that minmax regret optimisation delivers better plans than a mean-value-based approach.

More important is the robustness of the approaches, i.e., how good are they in avoiding bad plans? Figure 4(c) shows the standard deviation of the cost difference to the optimal plan, illustrating that the mean-value-based approach is more erratic than minmax regret optimisation. The most extreme case for all SSB queries was a mean-value-optimised plan more than doubling the run time of the optimal plan (from 60s to 135s), while for minmax regret optimisation the very worst plan added roughly 50% more to the cost of the optimal plan (from 60s to 92s).

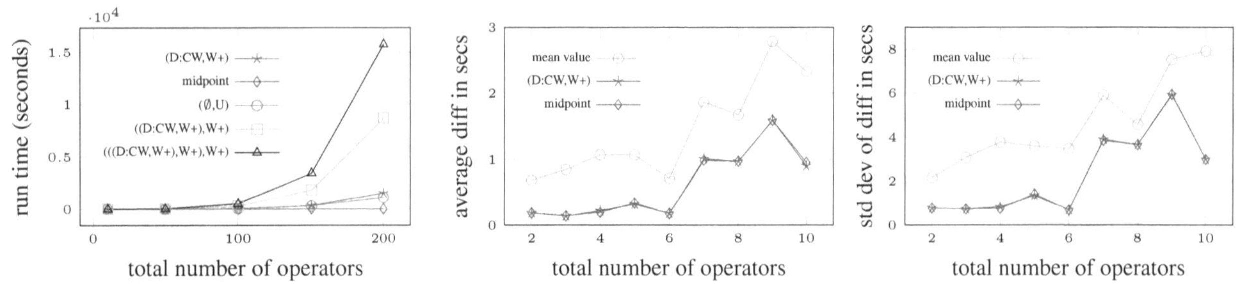

(a) Run time of the heuristic (synthetic data set) (b) Average difference in cost to opt (c) Std dev of difference in cost to opt

Figure 4: Results on run time (synthetic data set) and difference in cost to optimal (SSB).

8. CONCLUSION

We have investigated query optimisation under partial ignorance, in particular ordering selection operators optimally if their selectivities are defined by an interval rather than an exact value. The strategy we employed, minmax regret optimisation (MRO), is considered to be a pessimistic approach compared to other techniques from decision theory. In our opinion this makes it well-suited to query optimisation in database systems, which should be about avoiding bad plans rather than finding the best one. There is one major drawback, though: selection ordering under MRO becomes NP-hard. However, we have shown that special cases can be solved efficiently and that heuristics can quickly find good solutions.

For future work we plan to extend our approach to costs described by intervals and relative regret, i.e., considering the ratio of the cost of a plan to the optimal plan for a scenario rather than the difference. Also interesting are other operators, such as joins, whose ordering is heavily influenced by selectivities as well and suffers from similar issues: it is hard to obtain exact values. Further topics we would like to tackle are finding approximation algorithms with proven bounds and modelling correlation of query predicates. Nevertheless, we think this is an important first step in discovering new approaches for making query optimisers more robust and one of our medium term goals is to build a general framework for query optimisation under partial ignorance.

9. REFERENCES

[1] H. Aissi et al. Min-max and min-max regret versions of combinatorial optimization problems: A survey. *European J. of Operational Research*, 197(2):427–438, 2009.

[2] R. Avnur and J. M. Hellerstein. Eddies: continuously adaptive query processing. In *SIGMOD*, pages 261–272, 2000.

[3] B. Babcock and S. Chaudhuri. Towards a robust query optimizer: a principled and practical approach. In *SIGMOD*, pages 119–130, 2005.

[4] S. Babu, P. Bizarro, and D. DeWitt. Proactive re-optimization. In *SIGMOD*, pages 107–118, 2005.

[5] S. Babu et al. Adaptive ordering of pipelined stream filters. In *SIGMOD*, pages 407–418, 2004.

[6] S. Chaudhuri et al. Selectivity estimation for string predicates: Overcoming the underestimation problem. In *ICDE*, pages 227–238, 2004.

[7] F. Chu et al. Least expected cost query optimization: an exercise in utility. In *PODS*, pages 138–147, 1999.

[8] F. Chu et al. Least expected cost query optimization: what can we expect? In *PODS*, pages 293–302, 2002.

[9] H. D, P. N. Darera, and J. R. Haritsa. On the production of anorexic plan diagrams. In *VLDB*, pages 1081–1092, 2007.

[10] A. Deshpande et al. Exploiting correlated attributes in acquisitional query processing. In *ICDE*, pages 143–154, 2005.

[11] S. Ganguly. Design and analysis of parametric query optimization algorithms. In *VLDB*, pages 228–238, 1998.

[12] M. Garofalakis and P. B. Gibbons. Wavelet synopses with error guarantees. In *SIGMOD*, pages 476–487, 2002.

[13] J. M. Hellerstein and M. Stonebraker. Predicate migration: optimizing queries with expensive predicates. In *SIGMOD*, pages 267–276, 1993.

[14] Y. Ioannidis. The history of histograms (abridged). In *VLDB*, pages 19–30, 2003.

[15] S. M. Johnson. Optimal sequential testing. RAND Research Memorandum RM1652, RAND Corporation, 1956.

[16] N. Kabra and D. J. DeWitt. Efficient mid-query re-optimization of sub-optimal query execution plans. In *SIGMOD*, pages 106–117, 1998.

[17] A. Kasperski. *Discrete Optimization with Interval Data - Minmax Regret and Fuzzy Approach*. Springer, 2008.

[18] R. Krishnamurthy, H. Boral, and C. Zaniolo. Optimization of nonrecursive queries. In *VLDB*, pages 128–137, 1986.

[19] V. Lebedev and I. Averbakh. Complexity of minimizing the total flow time with interval data and minmax regret criterion. *Discrete Appl. Math.*, 154(15):2167–2177, Oct. 2006.

[20] G. Lohman. Is query optimization a "solved" problem? `http://wp.sigmod.org/?p=1075`, 2014.

[21] V. Markl et al. Robust query processing through progressive optimization. In *SIGMOD*, pages 659–670, 2004.

[22] V. Markl et al. Consistent selectivity estimation via maximum entropy. *The VLDB Journal*, 16(1):55–76, Jan. 2007.

[23] G. Moerkotte et al. Exploiting ordered dictionaries to efficiently construct histograms with q-error guarantees in SAP HANA. In *SIGMOD*, pages 361–372, 2014.

[24] T. Neumann and C. A. Galindo-Legaria. Taking the edge off cardinality estimation errors using incremental execution. In *BTW*, pages 73–92, 2013.

[25] M. Peterson. *An Introduction to Decision Theory*. Cambridge University Press, 2009.

[26] N. Polyzotis and M. Garofalakis. Statistical synopses for graph-structured XML databases. In *SIGMOD*, pages 358–369, 2002.

[27] T. Rabl et al. Variations of the star schema benchmark to test the effects of data skew on query performance. In *ICPE*, pages 361–372, 2013.

[28] U. Srivastava et al. Operator placement for in-network stream query processing. In *PODS*, pages 250–258, 2005.

[29] V. Zadorozhny et al. Efficient evaluation of queries in a mediator for websources. In *SIGMOD*, pages 85–96, 2002.

[30] N. Zhang et al. Statistical learning techniques for costing XML queries. In *VLDB*, pages 289–300, 2005.

Querying Temporal Drifts at Multiple Granularities

Sofia Kleisarchaki
LIG, Grenoble, France
Sofia.Kleisarchaki@imag.fr

Sihem Amer-Yahia
CNRS, LIG, Grenoble, France
Sihem.Amer-Yahia@imag.fr

Ahlame Douzal-Chouakria
LIG, Grenoble, France
Ahlame.Douzal@imag.fr

Vassilis Christophides
CSD, UoC, Greece & INRIA, Paris-Rocquencourt, France
christop@csd.uoc.gr

ABSTRACT

There exists a large body of work on online drift detection with the goal of dynamically finding and maintaining changes in data streams. In this paper, we adopt a query-based approach to drift detection. Our approach relies on *a drift index*, a structure that captures drift at different time granularities and enables flexible *drift queries*. We formalize different drift queries that represent real-world scenarios and develop query evaluation algorithms that use different materializations of the drift index as well as strategies for online index maintenance. We describe a thorough study of the performance of our algorithms on real-world and synthetic datasets with varying change rates.

1. INTRODUCTION

Monitoring streaming content is a challenging big data analytics problem, given that very large datasets are rarely (if ever) stationary. In several real world monitoring applications (e.g., newsgroup discussions, network connections, etc.) we need to detect significant change points in the underlying data distribution (e.g., frequency of words, sessions, etc.) and track the evolution of those changes over time. These change points, depending on the research community, are referred to as *temporal evolution*, *non stationarity*, or *concept drift* and provide valuable insights on real world events (e.g. a discussion topic, an intrusion) to take a timely action. In this paper, we adopt *a query-based approach to drift detection* and address the question of processing *drift queries* over very large datasets. To the best of our knowledge, our work is the first to formalize flexible drift queries on streaming datasets with varying change rates.

In the problem of drift detection, given a number of m drifts ordered in time, we need no less than $m + 1$ intervals to detect them. Thus, without any assumption on the underlying distribution, we are interested in exploring how to segment the input stream in order to find a reasonable tradeoff between true positives and false negatives. Existing methods rely on segmenting the input stream, mostly into smaller fixed length intervals [4, 6, 11, 13, 18]. Although some works exist on partitioning the same stream into intervals of different granularities [2, 9, 19], they either adopt an offline analysis or they lack the ability of querying historical drifts in streams.

A granularity in this case is an interval of time (e.g., every hour) or a number of observed data points (e.g., every 200 points). A drift is then defined as a significant difference in data distributions between two consecutive intervals at the same granularity. To detect drifts either statistical tests are directly applied on the data of two intervals [7, 13] or on their summaries, as for instance provided by a clustering algorithm [1, 4, 5]. To this end, two parameters impact the accuracy and efficiency of drift detection: the granularity of the intervals at which the original data items are clustered and the drift significance threshold used to assess whether or not there is a drift between two consecutive clusterings. In fact, fine-grained intervals can be used to capture the evolution of frequently changing streams. However, they may induce computation overhead for slowly changing ones. In addition, they may cause false positives, i.e., detecting drifts that are too sudden and noisy, hence hurting precision. While a coarser granularity will improve precision, since more data is clustered in each interval, it may incur missing a drift that occurred at a finer granularity. Those misses will negatively affect recall. Moreover, the rate of change of a given dataset may vary over time thereby requiring to consider different clustering granularities and drift thresholds for the same dataset.

Understanding the tradeoff between precision (at higher segmentation granularities) and recall (at lower segmentation granularities), and the choice of thresholds to determine what constitutes a drift between two consecutive intervals of the same granularity, are the main objectives of this work. In this paper, we adopt an analytics approach in which we formalize drift queries over both fresh and historical data of arbitrary time granularities, in order to provide flexibility in tracking and analyzing drifts in evolving datasets. For this reason, we propose a flexible drift index to organize past data (or more precisely their summaries) at several granularities. Furthermore. we explore different creation strategies for this index relying on two common clustering approaches, namely independent [8, 15, 20] and cumulative [1, 5]. In independent clustering, data points belonging to a given interval are considered equally important and clustered independently.

Permission to make digital or hard copies of all or part of this work for personal or classroom use is granted without fee provided that copies are not made or distributed for profit or commercial advantage and that copies bear this notice and the full citation on the first page. Copyrights for components of this work owned by others than the author(s) must be honored. Abstracting with credit is permitted. To copy otherwise, or republish, to post on servers or to redistribute to lists, requires prior specific permission and/or a fee. Request permissions from Permissions@acm.org.

CIKM'15, October 19–23, 2015, Melbourne, Australia.

Copyright is held by the owner/author(s). Publication rights licensed to ACM.

ACM 978-1-4503-3794-6/15/10 ...$15.00.
DOI: http://dx.doi.org/10.1145/2806416.2806436.

In cumulative clustering, data points in a given interval are clustered with all previously occurring points and fresher data is more important than older data. Moreover, we propose different materialization strategies in order to explore the tradeoff between index storage and query response time.

Unlike existing approaches [4, 6, 11, 13, 18] comparing only the last most recent intervals, we exploit this index in order to identify drifts at different granularities. In particular, we formalize three kinds of queries: unary, refinement and synthesis aiming to detect drifts against historical data. A unary query is used to extract all drifts detected at a given granularity. A refinement query explores drifts from a source granularity (e.g., 5,000 points) to a finer target granularity (e.g., 500 points), iteratively. Such a query is useful to provide a more detailed description of drifts that have been detected in a high granularity, resulting in better recall. Synthesis queries, on the other hand, start from a relatively low granularity and summarize them into coarser ones. In this case, some of the particular details might be missed (low recall) in order to get drifts with higher precision. This flexibility in querying drifts allows us to explore, in a declarative fashion, precision and recall tradeoffs at different granularities. Also, it addresses a long standing concern in detecting and tracking drifts in streaming content, namely adaptability of drift detection to different drift arrival rates and types.

The evaluation of declarative drift queries relies on traversing the index of historical data summaries and, at each granularity, comparing its nodes pairwise to identify points where clusterings dissimilarity exceeds a threshold θ. Rather than setting drift thresholds a-priori [6, 17], we learn a θ-value for each dataset and at each granularity level in the index.

In summary, this paper makes the following contributions:

1. We introduce and formalize drift queries that provide high flexibility in analyzing precision and recall of drift detection for different time granularities.
2. We propose a drift index, a graph structure that captures change at different granularities and explore different materializations of the index that lead to the design of various index maintenance and query evaluation algorithms.
3. We propose learning algorithms for learning drift and clustering thresholds adaptively for different granularities and rates of change.
4. We perform a thorough study of proposed queries and indices using two real datasets, KDD Cup'99 [1] and Usenet [12], and a synthetically generated dataset. On the effectiveness front, our study confirms the need for our refinement and synthesis queries, as demonstrated by the very good precision/recall results they attain. On the scalability front, it validates the need for different materializations of the drift index in order to achieve a tradeoff between storage and query response time for datasets of varying change rates.

The paper is organized as follows. Section 2 defines our data model and queries. Section 3 describes the drift index, the online index maintenance algorithms and threshold learning. Section 4 is dedicated to query evaluation algorithms. Section 5 contains a description of our experiments and findings. The related work is summarized in Section 6. We conclude in Section 7.

[1] *https://archive.ics.uci.edu/ml/datasets/KDD+Cup+1999+Data*

2. DATA MODEL AND QUERIES

We are given a stream of data points $D = \{d_1, \ldots, d_i, \ldots\}$, $d_i = (tc_i, ts_i)$ where tc_i is an r-dimensional vector of attributes describing d_i and ts_i is the timestamp at which tc_i arrived. For example, on Usenet each attribute represents a term appearing in news feeds, while on KDD Cup'99 an attribute can be any feature (e.g., transmitted bytes, duration of connection) describing a connection record.

2.1 Clustering and Drifts

Definition 1. **Time-Based and Point-Based Granularities.** A time-based granularity g is an interval of time. For example, g could be hourly, daily, bi-daily, or weekly. A point-based granularity g is an interval containing a fixed number of consecutive data points. For example, g could be 500 points or 1000 points. We assume a total order between granularities and use $g \prec\prec g'$ to denote that g' follows g. We also say that g' is coarser than g (and g is finer than g'). We write $g \prec g'$ to denote that g' immediately follows g when there does not exist a granularity between g and g'. In both cases, $g <> g'$.

Definition 2. **Time-Based and Point-Based Intervals.** Granularities are used to segment data points in D. A segmentation of a dataset D using a time-based or a point-based granularity g, results in a list of consecutives intervals denoted I_1^g, I_2^g, ... where I_i^g is the i−th interval (time-based or point-based) of granularity g.

For a daily granularity g applied to segment a week starting on Sunday, I_1^g corresponds to the time interval of Sunday. Respectively, I_1^g corresponds to the interval containing the first 500 data points when a point granularity $g = 500$ is used to segment incoming data.

The choice of point-based or time-based intervals to segment a dataset depends on the rate of arrival of data points. The main advantage of point-based intervals is the processing of data in fixed-size batches (in terms of number of points) although resulting intervals may have different lengths (in terms of time). Time-based intervals on the other hand, give the ability to tune the time granularity of the analysis (e.g., hour, day) resulting in fixed-length intervals (in terms of time) and varying in size (in terms of number of data points). Consequently, in order to generate intervals of comparable size, datasets that exhibit a high changing rate should be segmented with point-based intervals while more stable datasets can be segmented using time-based intervals.

Definition 3. **Granularity Clustering.** A granularity clustering $C^g(D)$ is a partitioning of all data points $d_i \in D$ into a set of clusterings $\{C_i^g, C_{i+1}^g, \ldots\}$ corresponding to consecutive, non-overlapping time intervals $\{I_i^g, I_{i+1}^g, \ldots\}$ at granularity g. A data point $d_i = (tc_i, ts_i)$ will belong to one interval I_j^g s.t. $ts_i \in I_j^g$. Here, tc_i is a vector of r-entries with the j-th entry corresponding to the weight of the j-th attribute (e.g., word). Each cluster $c \in C_i^g$ has a centroid, $center(c)$ which is itself an r-dimensional vector, where the j-th entry is the mean over the j-th entries of all data points in the cluster.

Definition 4. **Clustering Dissimilarity.** Given two clusterings C_i^g and C_j^g, we define, $d^2(c, c')$, the dissimilarity between a cluster $c \in C_i^g$ and a cluster $c' \in C_j^g$ as the Euclidean distance between their centroids:

$$\|center(c) - center(c')\|_2 \quad (1)$$

The dissimilarity between cluster $c \in C_i^g$ and a clustering C_j^g, $cdis(c, C_j^g)$, is defined as the closest cluster to c in C_j^g:

$$\arg\min_{c' \in C_j^g} d^2(c, c') \quad (2)$$

The dissimilarity between two clusterings, $dis(C_i^g, C_j^g)$, is defined as:

$$\frac{1}{|C_i^g|}\sum_{c \in C_i^g} cdis(c, C_j^g) + \frac{1}{|C_j^g|}\sum_{c' \in C_j^g} cdis(c', C_i^g) \quad (3)$$

where $|C_i^g|$ is the number of data points belonging to C_i^g.

Definition 5. **Drift.** For a dataset D, a granularity g, a threshold θ, we say that there is a drift between two consecutive intervals I_i^g and I_{i+1}^g, iff their associated clusterings C_i^g and C_{i+1}^g, satisfy $dis(C_i^g, C_{i+1}^g) \geq \theta$. We use $x_i^g = (I_i^g, I_{i+1}^g)$ to denote the pair of consecutive intervals for which there exists a drift and $X^g = \{x_1^g, x_2^g, \ldots\}$ for the set of all drifts detected at granularity g.

2.2 Drift Queries

The goal of drift queries is to compare drifts at different granularities and provide analysts with the ability to explore drift precison and recall across granularities. We study two kinds of queries, *refinement* and *synthesis*. Both kinds rely on a simpler *unary query* defined as follows.

Definition 6. **Unary Query.** A unary query $UQ(D, g)$ returns the set of all drifts X^g detected at granularity g for a dataset D.

Definition 7. **Refinement Query.** A refinement query $RQ(D, g_s, g_t)$ admits a source granularity g_s and a target one g_t s.t. $g_t \prec\prec g_s$, and returns a set of pairs $(x_i^{g_s}, x_j^g)$ where each drift $x_i^{g_s} \in X^{g_s}$ at g_s is associated to the finest corresponding drift $x_j^g \in X^g$ at a granularity g no finer than g_t as follows:

$$\{x_j^g \in X^g, g_t \prec\prec g \prec\prec g_s \vee g = g_t \mid$$
$$\exists x_i^{g_s} \in X^{g_s}, I_j^g \subseteq (I_i^{g_s} \cup I_{i+1}^{g_s}),$$
$$\nexists x_k^{g'} \in X^{g'}, g_t \prec\prec g' \prec\prec g \vee g' = g_t, I_k^{g'} \subseteq (I_i^{g_s} \cup I_{i+1}^{g_s})\}$$

where $I_i^{g_s} \cup I_{i+1}^{g_s} = [\min_{ts_j \in I_i^{g_s}}(ts_j), \max_{ts_k \in I_{i+1}^{g_s}}(ts_k)]$ and $I_j^g \subseteq (I_i^{g_s} \cup I_{i+1}^{g_s})$ if $\min_{ts_j \in (I_i^{g_s} \cup I_{i+1}^{g_s})}(ts_j) \leq \min_{ts_k \in I_i^{g_s}}(ts_k)$ and $\max_{ts_k \in I_i^{g_s}}(ts_k) \leq \max_{ts_j \in (I_i^{g_s} \cup I_{i+1}^{g_s})}(ts_j)$

Refinement queries provide a detailed analysis of drifts iteratively. For instance, for a source granularity $g_s = 1000$ connections on KDD Cup'99, selecting a granularity $g_t = 500$ might result in missing a more insightful analysis occurring at granularity $g_t = 100$. On the other hand, selecting $g_t = 100$ may result in retrieving false positives which could be avoided at $g_t = 500$. Therefore, the analyst will use the refinement query $RQ(D, 1000, 100)$ to obtain details of each drift at $g_s = 1000$ with a tradeoff between false negatives and false positives.

Definition 8. **Synthesis Query.** A synthesis query $SQ(D, g_s, g_t)$ admits a source granularity g_s and a target one g_t s.t. $g_s \prec\prec g_t$, and returns a set of pairs $(x_i^{g_s}, x_j^g)$ where each drift $x_i^{g_s} \in X^{g_s}$ at granularity g_s is associated to the coarsest corresponding drift $x_j^g \in X^g$ at a granularity g no coarser than g_t as follows:

$$\{x_j^g \in X^g, g_s \prec\prec g \prec\prec g_t \vee g = g_s \mid$$
$$\exists x_i^{g_s} \in X^{g_s}, I_i^{g_s} \subseteq (I_j^g \cup I_{j+1}^g),$$
$$\nexists x_k^{g'} \in X^{g'}, g \prec\prec g' \prec\prec g_t \vee g' = g_t, I_i^{g_s} \subseteq (I_k^{g'} \cup I_{k+1}^{g'})\}$$

Synthesis queries provide a summary analysis of drifts iteratively. For instance, for a source granularity $g_s = 100$ connections on KDD Cup'99, selecting a granularity $g_t = 1000$ might result in missing a more precise synthesis occurring at $g_t = 2000$. On the other hand, selecting $g_t = 2000$ can result in missing a summary of a drift, which could be obtained at $g_t = 1000$. Therefore, the analyst can use the synthesis query $SQ(D, 100, 2000)$ to obtain a summary of each drift at $g_s = 100$ with a tradeoff between false negatives and false positives.

3. DRIFT INDEX

The flexibility of querying drift at different granularities requires the design of appropriate data structures able to capture clusterings at different granularities in such a way that queries are evaluated efficiently. In this section, we describe the *drift index*, an efficient graph data structure that is used to store and compute clusterings at different granularities. We first formalize the index and then study several materializations and develop algorithms for incremental index maintenance as data points continue to arrive.

Definition 9. **Drift Index.** The drift index is an undirected graph $G = (V, E)$ where each node contains a clustering C_i^g of points in D during interval I_i^g of granularity g. Given two different granularities g and g' s.t. $g \prec g'$, and two intervals I_i^g of granularity g and $I_j^{g'}$ of granularity g', there exists an edge in G between nodes C_i^g and $C_j^{g'}$ if $I_i^g \subseteq I_j^{g'}$.

Definition 9 does not necessarily impose an edge between nodes C_i^g and $C_j^{g'}$ every time $I_i^g \subseteq I_j^{g'}$ is satisfied. Indeed, different *materializations* of the index may be explored. The choice of which nodes to materialize affects three parameters: (i) the index size and hence the time it takes to build and maintain it as new data points arrive, (ii) the query response time, and (iii) the accuracy of query results. Since our approach is to serve queries for any time period, and not only the latest period at which data points arrived, the index continuously grows in size. Therefore, the key question we address in designing the index is: what are possible index materialization strategies, how much space they consume and how do they affect query evaluation (response time and accuracy)? In this section, we study index materialization alternatives. The impact of each index on query evaluation will be discussed in Section 4. In all our indices, the smallest granularity, g_{min}, is used to generate leaf-level nodes. In Section 5, we experiment with different values of g_{min}.

3.1 Full Index Materialization

When fully materialized, the drift index is a hierarchical structure where each level contains clusterings of data points

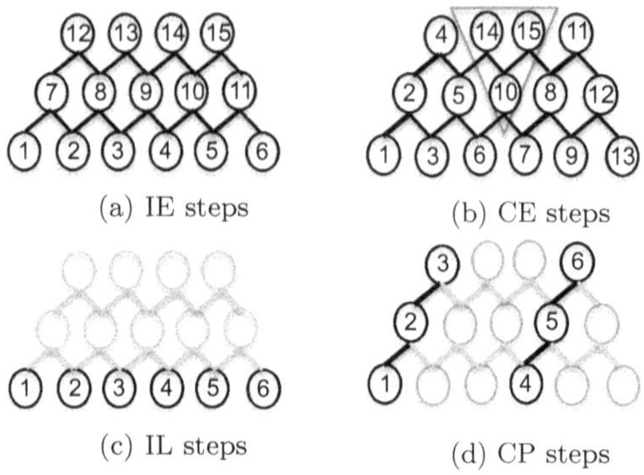

Figure 1: Drift Index Variants

inside intervals of the same granularity. Nodes corresponding to the finest granularity are leaves in the graph and each node, except nodes at the coarsest granularity, has one or two parents. For example, a node containing a clustering of data points for a 1-day granularity, e.g., Monday, will have two parent nodes each of which corresponds to a two-day granularity, in this case, Sun-Mon and Mon-Tue. Similarly, a node containing 1000 data points will have two parents, one containing it with the previous 1000 points and another containing it with the following 1000 points. More formally, given two granularities g and g' s.t. $g \prec g'$, and two intervals I_i^g and $I_j^{g'}$, there exists an edge from node C_i^g to node $C_j^{g'}$ iff $I_i^g \subseteq I_j^{g'}$.

Each node of the index contains a clustering of data points of a given granularity. Thus, an important aspect of index materialization is the selection of a clustering strategy and algorithm to generate the nodes. According to the clustering literature, timestamped datasets can be clustered in one of two ways. The first one, referred to as *the independent strategy*, encompasses a family of algorithms built upon the idea of visiting consecutive batches of data points by considering them as independent (e.g., one batch for Mon and another for Tue) and equally important in terms of arrival time (e.g., older data points are not penalized against fresher ones) [15, 8, 20]. The second approach, referred to as *the cumulative strategy*, parses data in a cumulative, single-pass fashion (e.g., data of Tue are clustered with those of Mon), aging older data points in a such a way that fresher data points are given more importance [1, 5]. Our exhaustive index is designed to work with any of the two clustering strategies which gives rise to two indices: Independent-Exhaustive (IE) and Cumulative-Exhaustive (CE).

3.1.1 Independent Exhaustive Index

IE is generated using the independent strategy where nodes of the same granularity, e.g., Sun, Mon, Tue, are produced using data points of consecutive, non-overlapping intervals. Nodes at the finest granularity level are produced by clustering the arriving data points, while nodes at coarser granularities are produced by summarizing the centroids of clusterings associated with lower granularities.

Figure 1a illustrates an instance of IE with nodes numbered in the order they are created. Algorithm 1 summarizes the different steps for building and maintaining the index. The algorithm takes as input the drift index G (empty at the beginning, non-empty in the case of index maintenance), a data stream D, a maximum granularity g_{max}, and an interval $I^{g_{min}}$ of minimum granularity g_{min}. For each batch of data point inside $I^{g_{min}}$, a clustering is produced (lines 3-6) using an independent clustering algorithm (e.g., DBScan [8] or k-means [10]). Nodes 1 to 6 of Figure 1a are produced by this step. Then, nodes at coarser granularities (e.g., nodes 7-15) are generated by applying the same algorithm over the centroids of clusters at lower granularity (lines 7-12).

Algorithm 1 IE Creation & Maintenance

Input: Drift index G, Stream of data points D, Max granularity g_{max}, Interval $I^{g_{min}}$ of min granularity g_{min}
Output: Updated drift index G'
1: $G' \leftarrow G$
2: $\{I_1^{g_{min}}, I_2^{g_{min}}, ...\} \leftarrow$ consecutive intervals at g_{min}
3: **for all** $I_i^{g_{min}}$ **do**
4: $C_i^{g_{min}} \leftarrow$ clustering in $I_i^{g_{min}}$ (e.g., DBScan, k-means)
5: Store $C_i^{g_{min}}$ in G' at granularity g_{min}
6: **end for**
7: **for all** $g_{min} \prec g \prec\prec g_{max}$ **do**
8: **for all** $C_i^g \in C^g$ **do**
9: $C \leftarrow$ clustering of the centroids of C_i^g and C_{i+1}^g
10: Store C in G' as the right parent of C_i^g
11: **end for**
12: **end for**
13: return G'

3.1.2 Cumulative Exhaustive Index

CE is generated using the cumulative strategy where nodes of the same granularity, e.g., Sun-Mon and Mon-Tue, are produced using data points from overlapping intervals. As a result, data points belonging to a given interval are clustered with previously occurring data points.

Figure 1b shows an instance of CE with its nodes numbered in the order they appear. Algorithm 2 summarizes steps of building and maintaining CE. The algorithm takes as input a drift index G (empty at the beginning, non-empty in the case of index maintenance), a data stream D, as well as the maximum granularity g_{max}, and the minimum granularity interval $I^{g_{min}}$ at g_{min}. After the initialization steps (lines 2-5), each data point is assigned to a cluster (line 7-8). Then every $I^{g_{min}}$ number of points (line 9), a corresponding clustering is generated and its centroid is stored in the index (line 11) at granularity g, which is incremented until g_{max}. Nodes 1, 2 and 4 of Figure 1b are generated by this step. When the maximum granularity g_{max} is reached a new path is initialized starting from the smallest granularity (line 16-21) and the process is repeated. Node 7 initializes this new path. In addition, for every node added in the index, its right sub-path to g_{min} is also produced (line 21). For instance, after the addition of node 4 in Figure 1b, its right sub-path consisting of nodes 5 and 6 is also added. These nodes are produced by applying the subtractive property [1] of clusters (i.e., subtracting clusters centroids). Finally, there is a set of nodes that do not belong to any right sub-path (e.g., nodes 10, 14, 15), forming the inverse triangle of Figure 1b. Each one of these nodes is generated after the addition of its right sibling and its sibling's sub-path. Lines 12-14 of Algorithm 2 illustrate this process using the additive property [1] of clusters (i.e., adding clusters centroids).

To handle infinite streams, several deletion strategies can be provided. A naive approach is to remove x intervals every X data points, including all corresponding nodes. However,

Algorithm 2 CE Creation & Maintenance

Input: Drift index G, Stream of data points D, Max granularity g_{max}, Interval $I^{g_{min}}$ of min granularity g_{min}
Output: Updated drift index G'

1: $G' \leftarrow G$
2: **if** G' is empty **then**
3: $C \leftarrow$ clustering of D (e.g., DBScan, k-means)
4: store C in G'
5: **end if**
6: $g \leftarrow g_{min}$
7: **for all** $d_i \in D$ **do**
8: $C \leftarrow$ clustering of d_i (e.g., CluStream)
9: **if** $(ts_i - ts_1)$ % $I^{g_{min}} == 0$ **then**
10: **if** $g \prec\prec g_{max}$ **then**
11: store C in G' at g-th granularity
12: **if** $\cup_{i=1,2..} I_i^g > g_{max}$ **then**
13: Build inverse triangle at g, by merging each node's left child with right-most child at g_{min}
14: **end if**
15: Move g to immediately following granularity
16: **else**
17: $C' \leftarrow C - C_j^{g_{max}}$ %Initializes path by subtracting the last stored $C_j^{g_{max}}$ from current clustering C
18: Store C' in G' at granularity g_{min}
19: Move g to granularity immediately following g_{min}
20: **end if**
21: Create right sub-path of node C
22: **end if**
23: **end for**
24: return G'

this approach misses valuable historical data. For this reason, we consider an alternative deletion policy in which for every X data points, the oldest x intervals are deleted and only their highest available node in the index is kept.

3.2 Partial Index Materialization

Since fully materialized versions of the drift index are expected to consume a lot of space, we propose Independent-Leaf (IL) and Cumulative-Path (CP) two partial index materializations, where fewer nodes are materialized thereby resulting in indices that are smaller in size.

The main idea in IL is to build nodes at the lowest granularity only (black nodes in Figure 1c), corresponding to lines 3-6 of Algorithm 1. All other nodes of higher granularities can be extracted from the leaf nodes at query time, if necessary. Respectively, the main idea in CP is to build paths containing all the nodes at higher granularities that include a given leaf node (black nodes in Figure 1d). The algorithm that builds and maintains CP is a modification of Algorithm 2, by ignoring lines 12-14 that build nodes of the inverse triangle and line 21 that builds the right sub-paths. From these nodes, built in partial materialization, all the remaining nodes (gray nodes in Figure 1d) may be generated at query time, if necessary (more details in Section 4).

3.3 Time & Space Complexity

The worst-case time complexity of IE and IL is dictated by DBScan, which needs $O(logn)$ time to find the neighbors for each of the n data points within an interval. Thus, the time complexity is $O(m * n * logn)$, where m is the number of nodes in the index. Furthermore, each cluster is represented by the statistics $(CF1; CF2; n)$ where $CF1$ and $CF2$ are r-dimensional vectors. Particularly, $CF1$ (resp, $CF2$) maintains, for each dimension, the sum of data values (resp, sum of the squares of data values). Thus, each cluster maintains $2r+1$ values and the space complexity is $O(K*(2r+1))$, where K is the number of clusters for all nodes.

The worst-case time complexity of CE and CP is specified by k-means, $O(n * k * d * i)$, where n is the number of r-dimensional data points forming k clusters at each interval and i the number of iterations. Furthermore, the space complexity is $O(m * k * (2 * r + 3))$, where $2r + 3$ values are maintained for each of the k-clusters of all m clustering nodes. These values contain the statistics described for IE and two extra values (details in [1]); the sum and the sum of the squares of the timestamps of input data.

Finally, the total number of nodes maintained in IE and CE is $m = \frac{1}{2} * L * (2 * |C^{g_{min}}| - L + 1)$, where $|C^{g_{min}}|$ is the number of clustering nodes at g_{min} and L is the number of index levels. The total number of nodes maintained in IL and CP is $m = \frac{N}{g_{min}}$, where N the total number of points.

3.4 θ and ϵ Learning

According to Definition 5, when the dissimilarity between two clusterings exceeds a threshold θ, a drift is detected. Since fixed threshold values are not always appropriate for data with varying drift rates, we are interested in learning θ experimentally and do so for each granularity of our index.

During the learning phase, a training dataset is used in order to estimate the drift parameter, θ. The training region is independent from the testing dataset over which queries are to be evaluated. Furthermore, the estimation of θ is automated and without any a-priori knowledge of the arrival rates of drifts. However, in order to be well-estimated, it should be learned on a long-enough time period to ensure capturing the occurrence of several drifts.

Algorithm 3 summarizes the learning process of θ_g values per granularity level g. The algorithm takes as input a drift index G, as well as minimum g_{min} and maximum g_{max} granularities for which θ_g values need to be estimated. For each granularity g within g_{min} and g_{max}, it extracts the distribution of dissimilarities X, based on Definition 4, between each pair of consecutive clusterings at g (line 3). Then, it performs DBScan (i.e., any other algorithm could be used, like k-means) over X, given as ϵ the average pairwise similarity of the 3-nearest neighbors in X. DBScan is performed 10 times, in order to select the clustering C that optimizes the *DunnIndex* criterion. The Dunn index aims to identify dense and well-separated clusters. It is defined as the ratio between the minimal inter-cluster to maximal intra-cluster distance. The inter-cluster distance is defined as the average distance between the centroids of the clusters. Similarly, the intra-cluster distance is defined as the average distance of any pair of points inside each cluster. Finally, the value of θ_g is extracted by calculating the average Euclidean distances between clusters in C (line 10).

The precision of θ estimation could be challenged when the similarity between two consecutive clusterings (see line 3) varies significantly (i.e., bimodal distribution). This is due to the fact that the clustering distance is estimated (see line 10) by using the mean of clusters distribution and assuming a low and constant standard deviation over time. Applying a Z-Score statistical test over all training and testing intervals we observed that the variation of the majority of intervals

Algorithm 3 Learning of θ-parameter

Input: Drift index G, Minimum granularity g_{min}, Maximum granularity g_{max}
Output: Parameter θ_g for each $g_{min} \prec\prec g \prec\prec g_{max}$

$minPts \leftarrow$ number of data dimensions
for all $g_{min} \prec\prec g \prec\prec g_{max}$ **do**
  $X \leftarrow$ dissimilarities distribution between consecutive clusterings of g
  $\epsilon \leftarrow$ avg pairwise similarity of 3 NN in X
  for all $i \in [1, 10]$ **do**
    $C \leftarrow DBScan(X, \epsilon, minPts)$
    $dunnIndex \leftarrow DunnIndex(C)$
    Pick C that maximizes $dunnIndex$
  end for
  $\theta_g \leftarrow$ average between clusters similarity of C
end for

(at least 95%) are less than two times the standard deviation from the mean for all granularities and real datasets.

We also propose a training phase to learn the ϵ parameter used by DBScan for building IE. Parameter ϵ defines a maximum ϵ-neighborhood for each cluster. In literature, a common way to choose its value is by plotting all distances to the nearest neighbors and selecting the value where the plot shows a strong bend. A similar approach is followed by our learning process, adapted to each granularity level. For brevity, we omit the algorithm for learning ϵ. The ϵ parameter can be estimated without any condition on the period's length. Thus, we propose to estimate both parameters (θ, ϵ) within the same wide-enough period.

It is worth noticing that the estimation of clustering parameters can quickly become outdated, particularly when dealing with rapidly evolving data distributions. In such cases, parameters re-estimation (e.g., every X intervals) may be useful to periodically adapt their values to data changes.

4. QUERY EVALUATION ALGORITHMS

This section presents our query evaluation algorithms using our proposed indices. Refinement and synthesis queries rely on unary queries that return a set of drifts X^g for any g. This is done by comparing the statistics between each pair of consecutive, non-overlapping clusterings at g using threshold θ_g. When a partial index is used (IL or CP), some index nodes (depicted in gray in Figures 1c, 1d) need to be generated on the fly possibly incurring computation overhead. The unary query algorithm is straightforward and is omitted for brevity. The performance of unary queries will be studied in detail in Section 5.

Algorithm 4 illustrates the steps for evaluating a refinement query. It takes as input any of the four materialized drift indices G and a range of granularities between g_s and g_t. Initially, it applies a unary query to detect all drifts $x_i^{g_s} \in X^{g_s}$ at g_s (line 2). Then, for each of these drifts, it detects all corresponding drifts $x_j^g \in X^g$ at finer granularities g, that are no finer than g_t (lines 3-11) using the condition $I_j^g \subseteq (I_i^{g_s} \cup I_{i+1}^{g_s})$ (line 8) for all drifts at g.

A synthesis query is evaluated over a drift index G and a granularity range between g_s and g_t, where $g_s \prec\prec g_t$. The steps of the algorithm are equivalent to Algorithm 4, by simply replacing the condition in line 8 with $I_i^{g_s} \subseteq (I_j^g \cup I_{j+1}^g)$. Thus, for any observed drift $x_i^{g_s}$ at g_s, a corresponding drift

Algorithm 4 RefinementQuery

Input: Drift index G, Granularity range $[g_s, g_t]$ ($g_t \prec\prec g_s$)
Output: A set S of drift pairs $(x_i^{g_s}, x_j^g)$, $g \prec\prec g_s$

1: $S, prev, curr \leftarrow \emptyset$
2: $X^{g_s} \leftarrow UQ(D, g_s)$
3: **for all** $x_i^{g_s} \in X^{g_s}$ **do**
4:   **for all** $g_s \prec\prec g \prec\prec g_t$ **do**
5:     $prev \leftarrow curr$; $curr \leftarrow \emptyset$
6:     $X^g \leftarrow UQ(D, g)$
7:     **for all** $x_j^g \in X^g$ **do**
8:       **if** $I_j^g \subseteq (I_i^{g_s} \cup I_{i+1}^{g_s}) \wedge I_{j+1}^g \subseteq (I_i^{g_s} \cup I_{i+1}^{g_s})$ **then**
9:         $curr += x_j^g$
10:       **end if**
11:     **end for**
12:     **if** $curr == \emptyset$ **then**
13:       $S += (x_i^{g_s}, prev)$
14:       break
15:     **end if**
16:     **if** $g == g_t$ **then**
17:       $S += (x_i^{g_s}, curr)$
18:     **end if**
19:   **end for**
20: **end for**
21: return S

x_j^g at a coarser granularity g, no coarser than g_t is returned. The time interval $I_j^g \cup I_{j+1}^g$ of the corresponding drift x_j^g should take place during $I_i^{g_s}$ where $x_i^{g_s}$ was observed.

5. EXPERIMENTS

In this section, we provide a thorough investigation of our queries, both from the accuracy and the scalability perspectives. All experiments were conducted on a 2 GHz Intel Core i7 processor with 8 GB memory, which runs MAC operating system. Our accuracy results are the average of 5 consecutive runs. We learn ϵ and θ on a training dataset covering approximately 30% of the input data. Also, unless mentioned otherwise, we set the k parameter of CE to the average number of clusters produced by IE. Finally, we refer to each granularity level using incremental numbers (e.g., level 1 for the lowest granularity, then 2 etc). For both clustering algorithms (Clustream [1] and DBScan [8]), the implementations provided in MOA [3] are used. Some necessary extensions are applied in the implementation of CluStream, in order to provide additive and subtractive properties [1].

5.1 Dataset Preparation

5.1.1 Synthetic Datasets

We developed a synthetic data generator that provides the flexibility to produce datasets deriving from different distributions (i.e., well-separated, overlapping) and rates of change (i.e., sudden, incremental). Furthermore, the parameters of clustering are also tuned, including the number and size of clusters, as well as their density.

Specifically, synthetic datasets are produced with data points deriving from two distributions in a low and a high region. Each distribution consists of a number of close clusterings, that derive from the same region (i.e., low, high). Furthermore, each distribution contains a given number of data points and each clustering is described by k clusters.

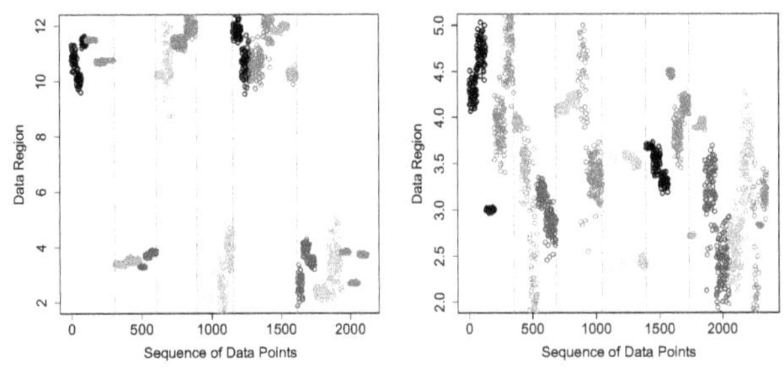

(a) Well-separated regions (b) Overlapping regions

Figure 2: Different Data Distributions

The total size of synthetic data is generated randomly and the number of drifts is also parameterized.

Three data sets are generated, in order to simulate different types of drifts. Figure 2 illustrates two examples. Specifically, Figure 2a depicts sudden drifts, marked with vertical lines, that occur each time the distribution of data oscillates between low and high region. The distribution of data in low region has values within [2, 4], while the distribution of high within [10, 12] forming well-separated regions. On the contrary, Figure 2b illustrates incremental drifts, occurring between low [2,4] and high [3, 5] regions of overlapping values. Finally, a third dataset is generated containing incremental drifts of consecutive regions, with values of low region within [2,4] and high within [4, 6].

For the purpose of building the index, the dataset is split into intervals of 200 data points each forming a leaf node at g_{min}. The next granularity consists of 400 points, the third of 600 and the 10th contains intervals of 2000 data points.

5.1.2 Real Datasets

Query accuracy was evaluated over two datasets derived from two different application domains. The first collection consists of 5,931 Usenet articles from the 20 Newsgroup collection where each article belongs to one of 6 news feeds (e.g., sports, science). A user can subscribe to any of these feeds, showing his interest in receiving relevant articles, or unsubscribe at any time. Each article is represented with a binary vector of 658 attributes, where each attribute indicates the absence or presence of a word. Another attribute indicates whether the user is interested in an article or not. Thus, the clustering procedure will result in clusters containing articles that are likely to derive from the same feed (e.g., sports) and interest the user. A drift is the moment where a user decides to unsubscribe from some feeds and subscribe to others and can be computed on the whole data. The ground truth hence is known and encompasses five drifts. Experiments on Usenet are performed using a small point-based interval of 100 data points, a maximum index depth of 6 and the number of clusters for CE is $k = 3$. The training set consists of 2,400 data points, containing 2 drifts.

The second dataset of KDD Cup'99 is a Network Intrusion detection stream of 494,020 normal TCP connections and cyber attacks. It contains a variety of intrusions that fall into 4 categories: DOS, R2L, U2R and PROBING. Most of the connections in the dataset are normal but occasionally bursts of attacks appear. Thus, we are interested in detecting drifts where realtime attacks occur. Each connection is described by 42 categorical (e.g., type of protocol) or continuous (e.g., bytes transmitted) attributes. For our analysis, we use the 34 continuous attributes. In order to create a ground truth for evaluating query accuracy, we consider as drifts the time moments where at least $minAttacks = 30$ consecutive malicious connections appear. The ground truth hence encompasses 45 drifts on the whole dataset. We set the smallest granularity to 500 points, the index depth to 10, corresponding to an interval length of 5,000 points and $k = 4$. The training dataset contains 20,500 points.

The smallest granularity is a critical parameter, indicated by the magnitude and arrival rate of drifts. To this end, the parameter settings used in [12] are applied for our experiments in Usenet, where 5 drifts exist within 5,931 points. On the contrary, wider intervals are selected for KDD Cup'99 of lower arrival rate with 45 drifts within 494,020 points.

5.2 Summary of Results

Our experiments show that unary queries can reach a 79% accuracy on real datasets. They also show that independent clustering attains a significantly better accuracy than cumulative for incremental changes of overlapping data distributions. They also confirm the usefulness of refinement and synthesis queries, by demonstrating their ability to explore the tradeoff between precision/recall. For instance, using CE, while $UQ(\text{KDD}, 1)$ and $UQ(\text{KDD}, 10)$ attain 52% and 13% accuracy respectively, $SQ(\text{KDD}, 1, 10)$ attains 74%. Moreover, the scalability evaluation of our indices show a tradeoff between full and partial materializations, in terms of index size and query response time. Fully materialized indices are at least an order of magnitude faster in query response time than partial. On the contrary, fully materialized indices require at least 4 times more space than partial.

5.3 Accuracy of Drift Detection

Query accuracy varies between full and partial index materializations. This variation is caused by the random partitioning of data points during DBScan and k-means clustering. However, this variation is minimized with multiple executions and is not statistically significant. Hence we provide accuracy results for exhaustive indices only (IE, CE), assuming a not significantly different performance of partial indices (IL, CP). The accuracy is evaluated by using the traditional F-measure, which is the harmonic mean of precision and recall. A detected drift is considered a true positive if the corresponding real drift is within the compared intervals in the ground truth. This evaluation strategy is also used in [13]. For instance, a detected drift at point 800 extracted by comparing the point-based intervals [400, 800) and [800, 1200) will correspond to a real drift within the region [400, 1200). This drift can, for example, take place at point 1000. However, a drift at point 1000 might also be detected by comparing intervals [800, 1200) and [1200, 1600). Thus, in case of multiple detections of the same drift at a given granularity, we ignore its subsequent detections.

5.3.1 Unary Queries

Synthetic Data. The goal of synthetic data evaluation is to understand how different time granularities, as well as clustering strategies (independent, cumulative) affect query accuracy. To this end, we perform unary queries over different granularity levels and for both CE and IE.

Figure 3a illustrates the accuracy (y-axis) of unary queries for different granularities (x-axis) over the synthetic dataset

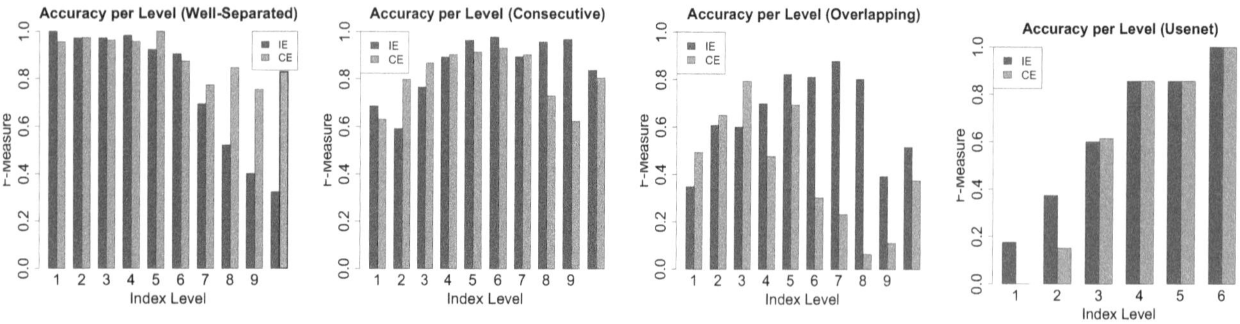

(a) Sudden drifts (b) Incremental (Consecutive) (c) Incremental (Overlapping) (d) Usenet dataset

Figure 3: Unary Queries Accuracy. A tradeoff between precision and recall is observed over different granularity levels.

with sudden drifts (Figure 2a). It shows that accuracy is very good for low granularities. However, recall worsens at higher granularities. Consequently, increasing the resolution of analysis decreases the ability of the algorithm to observe drifts occurring at finer granularities. However, precision remains greater than 0.9 at all levels.

Figure 3b depicts the unary queries behavior when applied on incremental drifts of consecutive data regions. We observe that the algorithm performs badly for very small or very large intervals. Very small intervals are sensitive to subtle changes causing a large number of false positives. Thus, those granularities suffer from low precision but exhibit high recall. Similarly, very wide intervals are susceptible to false negatives as they may miss drifts existing within them. On the contrary, intermediate granularities provide intervals that fit data better and improve accuracy.

The last dataset containing incremental drifts of overlapping regions (Figure 2b) reveals a statistically significant difference in accuracy (Figure 3c) between IE and CE for all levels greater than 2. The observed difference is due to the design of each index. For instance, CE tends to add input data into existing clusters. This addition causes cluster centroids to shift over time and absorb any change, considering it as non-significant. To alleviate that, we ran an experiment varying the number of clusters, k. Although not shown here, we observed no significant improvement in performance. Thus, the online and one-pass design of the algorithm causes the absorption of incremental changes. On the contrary, IE forms clusters by independently visiting data points in different intervals. The algorithm detects data regions of high density and is independent from previously computed clusters. Therefore, IE outperforms CE for overlapping data regions.

Although accuracy tends to decrease at higher index levels, there are some oscillations between levels. These fluctuations can be explained if we consider the statistical error introduced by adding and subtracting clusters' statistics as in [1]. A typical example of this error is illustrated in Figures 3a to 3c regarding the accuracy of CE at levels 9 and 10. Several nodes at level 9 are produced by the additive and subtractive property. On the contrary, none of the nodes at level 10 are generated by these properties. Thus, level 10 has a lower statistical error than level 9 and shows better accuracy despite its wider intervals.

Finally, we provide a comparison of our drift index accuracy with a state-of-the-art drift detection algorithm, named CUSUM [16]. CUSUM calculates the cumulative sum which detects a drift when the mean of the input data is significantly different from zero. Results show that our drift index outperforms CUSUM for each granularity and dataset. Specifically, CUSUM reaches a 98% of accuracy for the dataset of sudden drifts, while the accuracy drops in 24% and 16% for consecutive and overlapping datasets respectively.

Real Data. Figure 3d shows the F-Measure results of unary queries (y-axis) on Usenet for each level in the index (x-axis). The main trend observed is an increase in accuracy as the granularity increases. This is not surprising, as the frequency of drifts in this dataset occurs at least every 700 data points. Thus, when the interval length increases (especially to 600 points at g_{max}) the algorithm performs very well, as there are enough available points to detect the drift. In fact, the unary query at g_{max} reports three different drifts. A user who initially subscribed to electronics and crypt news changed her interests into hockey and sales and then subscribed to motorcycles and space news. It is worth mentioning that the inappropriateness of interval length at the leaf level induces CE to report no drifts.

Tables 1 and 2 illustrate the accuracy (last line) of unary queries for KDD Cup'99 for each granularity level of IE and CE respectively. Similarly to synthetic data, we observe that the finest and coarsest granularities cause a decrease in accuracy for both indices. Indeed, a low precision and a high recall characterize the leaf level and the inverse is observed at the coarsest granularity.

5.3.2 Refinement & Synthesis Queries

We designed refinement and synthesis queries to explore precision and recall tradeoffs. For brevity, in Tables 1 and 2 we present only the accuracy results for KDD Cup'99. Each row (resp. column) corresponds to g_s (resp. g_t) which are given as input to the queries. The tables contain every possible combination of levels in an attempt to discuss the impact of each query on accuracy. For example, a refinement query is evaluated over a small range of levels (e.g., $RQ(D,2,1)$), as well as on the entire index (e.g., $RQ(D,10,1)$). The upper-half of the tables contains the F-Measure of synthesis queries and the lower-half concerns refinement queries. The best accuracy results for each table are mentioned in circles, along with the corresponding unary queries results.

The question we attempt to answer is whether refinement and synthesis queries can attain a tradeoff between accuracy of unary queries at g_s or g_t. All values mentioned in bold indicate those cases. Thus, in the majority of the queries, the analyst will get a summary of drifts that exploits the tradeoff of precision and recall between g_s and g_t. However,

		g_t										
		Unary	1	2	3	4	5	6	7	8	9	10
g_s	1	0.50	-	**0.65**	**0.76**	**0.75**	**0.79**	**0.79**	**0.77**	**0.80**	**0.80**	**0.78**
	2	0.62	0.49	-	**0.74**	**0.74**	**0.78**	**0.76**	**0.76**	**0.78**	**0.78**	**0.75**
	3	0.73	0.48	0.60	-	**0.73**	**0.78**	**0.76**	**0.75**	**0.77**	**0.76**	**0.73**
	4	0.73	0.49	0.61	**0.73**	-	**0.79**	**0.77**	**0.75**	**0.77**	**0.76**	**0.73**
	5	0.79	**0.50**	**0.62**	**0.74**	**0.73**	-	**0.77**	**0.75**	**0.76**	**0.75**	**0.70**
	6	0.77	0.49	**0.62**	**0.73**	**0.73**	**0.79**	-	**0.75**	**0.77**	**0.76**	**0.71**
	7	0.75	**0.50**	**0.63**	**0.74**	**0.74**	**0.79**	**0.77**	-	**0.76**	**0.75**	**0.72**
	8	0.76	**0.50**	**0.63**	**0.74**	**0.74**	**0.79**	**0.77**	**0.75**	-	**0.75**	**0.68**
	9	0.75	**0.51**	**0.63**	**0.74**	**0.74**	**0.79**	**0.77**	**0.75**	**0.76**	-	**0.66**
	10	0.44	0.36	0.41	**0.44**	**0.46**	**0.49**	**0.47**	**0.48**	**0.52**	**0.51**	-
Unary			0.50	0.62	0.73	0.73	0.79	0.77	0.75	0.76	0.75	0.44

Table 1: F-Measure for refinement (lower matrix) and synthesis (upper matrix) queries over **IE**, KDD Cup'99

		g_t										
		Unary	1	2	3	4	5	6	7	8	9	10
g_s	1	0.52	-	**0.63**	**0.72**	**0.73**	**0.69**	**0.68**	**0.68**	**0.68**	**0.71**	**0.74**
	2	0.61	0.50	-	**0.73**	**0.72**	**0.70**	**0.71**	**0.70**	**0.74**	**0.75**	**0.78**
	3	0.73	**0.52**	**0.61**	-	**0.73**	**0.71**	**0.73**	**0.74**	**0.72**	**0.73**	**0.77**
	4	0.70	0.50	0.60	**0.70**	-	0.68	**0.68**	**0.68**	**0.72**	**0.72**	**0.75**
	5	0.69	0.51	0.60	**0.71**	**0.72**	-	**0.66**	**0.68**	**0.66**	**0.68**	**0.76**
	6	0.62	0.50	0.57	**0.68**	**0.67**	**0.63**	-	0.57	**0.63**	**0.58**	**0.65**
	7	0.61	0.49	0.53	**0.65**	**0.62**	**0.64**	0.58	-	**0.56**	**0.58**	**0.67**
	8	0.56	0.48	0.54	**0.65**	**0.64**	**0.62**	**0.56**	0.55	-	**0.48**	**0.56**
	9	0.39	**0.44**	**0.48**	**0.55**	**0.49**	**0.48**	**0.45**	**0.43**	0.36	-	**0.37**
	10	0.13	0.25	**0.20**	**0.25**	**0.19**	**0.22**	0.12	0.12	**0.16**	0.09	-
Unary			0.52	0.61	0.73	0.70	0.69	0.62	0.61	0.56	0.39	0.13

Table 2: F-Measure for refinement (lower matrix) and synthesis (upper matrix) queries over **CE**, KDD Cup'99

note that there are few cases where the F-Measure is worse than any of the two levels. These cases are observed especially when refining queries at very low granularities (i.e., first two columns of tables). Low levels have a high rate of false positives, which negatively affects accuracy even when refining only the most precise drifts of higher levels.

5.4 Scalability Study of All Indices

We perform an index scalability experiment to study index size and build time and query response time. For this purpose, synthetic datasets of different sizes are produced.

5.4.1 *Index Size*

Index size depends exclusively on the number and size of maintained nodes. Therefore, increasing the number of index nodes, for instance by increasing the index depth or the volume of input data or by decreasing the interval length, will inevitably lead to an increase of the index size. Moreover, increasing the size of each node, for instance by increasing the number of clusters (k), will negatively impact index size. We fix the depth to 5 and we test the impact of the other parameters on the scalability of our indices.

Varying Dataset Size. Figure 4a illustrates the drift index size calculated in MBs (y-axis) as a function of input data size calculated in number of points (x-axis). We set the minimum interval size at g_{min} to 100 points for all datasets. The chart is in a log-log scale and we observe a linear trend of all indices as data size increases. We also observe that the lines of cumulative indices have a steeper slope. This is explained by the extra overhead paid for maintaining information about a cluster's origin. This information describes if a cluster is derived from others and is more likely to increase as the dataset increases. Finally, as expected, partially materialized indices consume at least 5 times less space.

Varying Interval Length. The interval length selected for each granularity has also a critical impact on index scalability. Figure 4b shows the result of varying the interval length within [100, 1000] for a fixed dataset size of 225,000 points. Figure 4b reports a decreasing index size trend for all indices with wider intervals. When the size of an interval increases, the size of the clustering inside that interval is not affected. That is because the same clustering statistics are maintained. Thus, wider intervals reduce the number of nodes maintained by the index without affecting the size of each node. This explains the decreasing trend observed.

5.4.2 *Time Results*

The most frequent and time consuming operation of drift detection is the computation of clustering dissimilarities for every pair of nodes at each granularity. The cost of this operation naturally increases with the number of index nodes as shown in Figure 5a. Figure 5a illustrates the response time of all unary queries applied at each granularity for different dataset sizes. It is evident that IL and CP need at least an order of magnitude more time to detect drifts, as they produce missing nodes at query time.

Figure 5b illustrates the build time of each index, providing evidence for the trade-off between index building time and query response time. Figures 5b and 5a indeed show that the more time we spend building the index, the less time we need during query evaluation. Furthermore, Figure 5b illustrates that both independent indices, IE and IL, need more build time than cumulative ones, CE and CP. Despite the fact that IL is a partial index, it needs a higher build time than CE. This could be explained by the fact that IL iteratively visits data points in order to form clusters.

Figure 6a depicts unary query response time (y-axis) per granularity (x-axis) for a synthetic dataset of almost 225K data points. IL shows a sharp increase in drift detection as levels increase, due to generating missing nodes on the fly. On the contrary, IE's response time decreases at higher levels, due to fewer nodes. Thanks to the hierarchical structure of our indices less nodes exist at higher granularities, explaining the almost constant response time after level one for both indices. That also explains the sudden drop in response time for CP.

The performance of refinement queries is measured starting from level $g_s = 5$ until all finer levels of g_t, shown in the x-axis of Figure 6b. We notice that the longer the path from g_s to g_t, the more time it takes for the query to respond (for all indices). The same behavior is observed on synthesis queries, as shown in Figure 6c, where $g_s = 1$.

6. RELATED WORK

Most of the existing drift detection methods rely on segmenting the input stream into smaller fixed length intervals [4, 6, 11, 13, 18]. The comparison of intervals is then based either on statistical tests or on probabilistic measures. In the former case, a null hypothesis of equal distributions is formed [7, 13], while in the latter a user-defined threshold is utilized to detect drifts [6, 18]. However, a drawback of these works derive from the lack of dynamically adapting thresholds to the varying change rates. Furthermore, they suffer from the problem of single granularity, due to fixed length intervals, resulting in low precision/recall.

An attempt to solve the problem of single granularity is made in [14] by providing multi-partition techniques, but it also remains in an offline context. On the contrary, an online drift detection approach that aims to detect the most recent drifts, by comparing the last two intervals, is presented by FLORA2 [19]. FLORA2 dynamically learns interval length.

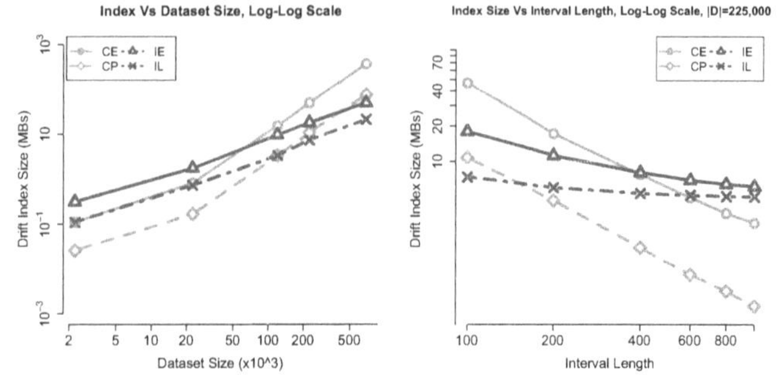

(a) Index size Vs dataset size (b) Index size Vs interval length

Figure 4: Index Size

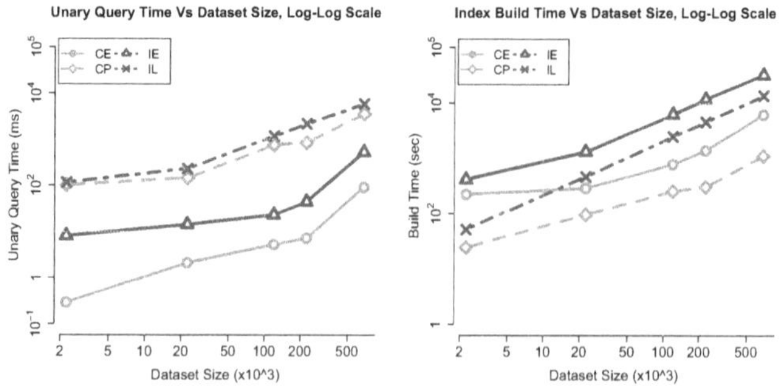

(a) Unary time Vs dataset size (b) Index build time

Figure 5: Unary Query Response and Index Build Time

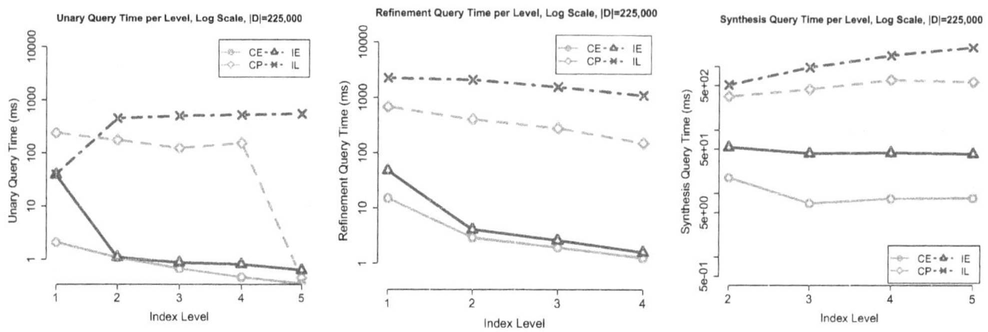

(a) Unary query time response (b) Refinement query time response (c) Synthesis query time response

Figure 6: Query Time. Less nodes at higher levels of hierarchical index reduce the corresponding query time response.

A heuristic method shrinks the interval, by forgetting old data points, each time a drift occurs; otherwise, the interval grows. Also, some other approaches exist [2, 9] calculating statistics over sliding and growing intervals in order to detect a drift. However, all these works lack the flexibility of querying historical and fresh data for detecting drifts at different granularities.

7. CONCLUSION

Our work introduces a novel form of analytical queries for detecting drifts in streaming content. Their evaluation relies on drift indices allowing us to explore, in a declarative fashion, precision and recall tradeoffs introduced by data segmentation at different granularities. We believe that our work lays the foundation for a series of new contributions addressing a long standing concern, namely adaptability of drift detection to different drift arrival rates and types. For fast arrival rates of drifts the detection accuracy could be excelled utilizing fine-grained intervals maintained in the index. On the contrary, for slow rates, coarse-grained intervals are preferred, compromising the computation overhead. Furthermore, sudden drifts can be easily detected by several state-of-the-art clustering techniques, while incremental drift detection is favoured by independent clustering.

One direction we are pursuing is the applicability of our approach to the detection of sales drifts in the retail industry and the ability to compare drifts over time across multiple products and stores.

8. REFERENCES

[1] C. C. Aggarwal, J. Han, J. Wang, and P. S. Yu. A framework for clustering evolving data streams. In *Proc. of VLDB'03 - Volume 29*, pages 81–92.

[2] A. Bifet. Adaptive stream mining: Pattern learning and mining from evolving data streams. In *Proc. of the 2010 Conference on Adaptive Stream Mining: Pattern Learning and Mining from Evolving Data Streams*, pages 1–212, Amsterdam, The Netherlands, 2010. IOS Press.

[3] A. Bifet, G. Holmes, R. Kirkby, and B. Pfahringer. Moa: Massive online analysis. *J. Mach. Learn. Res.*, 11:1601–1604, Aug. 2010.

[4] A. Bondu, B. Grossin, and M.-L. Picard. Density estimation on data streams : an application to change detection. In *EGC'10*, pages 229–240.

[5] F. Cao, M. Ester, W. Qian, and A. Zhou. Density-based clustering over an evolving data stream with noise. In *SIAM CDM'06*, pages 328–339.

[6] T. Dasu, S. Krishnan, S. Venkatasubramanian, and K. Yi. An information-theoretic approach to detecting changes in multi-dimensional data streams. In *Proc. Symp. on the Interface of Statistics, Computing Science, and Applications*, 2006.

[7] A. Dries and U. RÃijckert. Adaptive concept drift detection. *Statistical Analysis and Data Mining*, 2(5-6):311–327, 2009.

[8] M. Ester, H.-P. Kriegel, J. S, and X. Xu. A density-based algorithm for discovering clusters in large spatial databases with noise. pages 226–231. AAAI Press, 1996.

[9] J. Gama, P. Medas, G. Castillo, and P. Rodrigues. Learning with drift detection. In *Advances in AI – SBIA'04*, volume 3171 of *Lecture Notes in Computer Science*, pages 286–295. Springer Berlin Heidelberg.

[10] J. A. Hartigan and M. A. Wong. A K-means clustering algorithm. *Applied Statistics*, 28:100–108, 1979.

[11] N. Japkowicz, C. Myers, and M. Gluck. A novelty detection approach to classification. In *Proc. of AI*, pages 518–523, 1995.

[12] I. Katakis, G. Tsoumakas, and I. Vlahavas. Dynamic feature space and incremental feature selection for the classification of textual data streams. In *in ECML/PKDD-2006*, page 107. Springer Verlag.

[13] D. Kifer, S. Ben-David, and J. Gehrke. Detecting change in data streams. In *Proc. of VLDB'04 - Volume 30*, pages 180–191.

[14] M. Masud, L. Khan, and B. Thuraisingham. A multi-partition multi-chunk ensemble technique to classify concept-drifting data streams. In *KDD'09*. Springer.

[15] L. O'Callaghan, N. Mishra, M. A., S. Guha, and R. Motwani. Streaming-data algorithms for high-quality clustering, 2001.

[16] E. S. Page. Continuous inspection schemes. *Biometrika*, 41(1/2):pp. 100–115, 1954.

[17] R. Sebastião and J. a. Gama. Change detection in learning histograms from data streams.

[18] P. Vorburger and A. Bernstein. Entropy-based concept shift detection. In *ICDM'06*, pages 1113–1118. IEEE Computer Society.

[19] G. Widmer and M. Kubat. Learning in the presence of concept drift and hidden contexts. In *ML*, pages 69–101, 1996.

[20] T. Zhang, R. Ramakrishnan, and M. Livny. Birch: an efficient data clustering method for very large databases. *SIGMOD Rec.*, 25:103–114, 1996.

Efficient Incremental Evaluation of Succinct Regular Expressions

Henrik Björklund
Umeå University

Wim Martens *
Universität Bayreuth

Thomas Timm
Universität Bayreuth

ABSTRACT

Regular expressions are omnipresent in database applications. They form the structural core of schema languages for XML, they are a fundamental ingredient for navigational queries in graph databases, and are being considered in languages for upcoming technologies such as schema- and transformation languages for tabular data on the Web. In this paper we study the usage and effectiveness of the counting operator (or: limited repetition) in regular expressions. The counting operator is a popular extension which is part of the POSIX standard and therefore also present in regular expressions in grep, Java, Python, Perl, and Ruby. In a database context, expressions with counting appear in XML Schema and languages for querying graphs such as SPARQL 1.1 and Cypher.

We first present a practical study that suggests that counters are extensively used in practice. We then investigate evaluation methods for such expressions and develop a new algorithm for efficient incremental evaluation. Finally, we conduct an extensive benchmark study that shows that exploiting counting operators can lead to speed-ups of several orders of magnitude in a wide range of settings: normal and incremental evaluation on synthetic and real expressions.

Categories and Subject Descriptors

H.2.3 [**Database Management**]: Languages—*Data Description Languages (DDL)*; H.2.3 [**Database Management**]: Languages—*Query Languages)*

General Terms

Languages, Algorithms

Keywords

XML; Schema; Regular Expressions

*Supported by grant number MA 4938/2–1 from the Deutsche Forschungsgemeinschaft (Emmy Noether Nachwuchsgruppe).

Permission to make digital or hard copies of all or part of this work for personal or classroom use is granted without fee provided that copies are not made or distributed for profit or commercial advantage and that copies bear this notice and the full citation on the first page. Copyrights for components of this work owned by others than the author(s) must be honored. Abstracting with credit is permitted. To copy otherwise, or republish, to post on servers or to redistribute to lists, requires prior specific permission and/or a fee. Request permissions from Permissions@acm.org.
CIKM'15, October 19 - 23, 2015, Melbourne, VIC, Australia.
Copyright is held by the owner/author(s). Publication rights licensed to ACM.
ACM 978-1-4503-3794-6/15/10 ...$15.00.
DOI: http://dx.doi.org/10.1145/2806416.2806434 .

1. INTRODUCTION

Regular expressions are omnipresent in programming languages, shell tools, and database query- and schema languages. In the context of XML, DTDs and XML Schema definitions use regular expressions for defining content models and XPath uses regular-expression-like constructs for navigation in trees. In the context of graph-structured data and RDF, regular expressions have been studied under the name *regular path queries (RPQs)* for decades and have recently been integrated in popular graph query languages such as SPARQL [16] and Cypher [24]. Currently, they are being considered as a basic building block for processing tabular data on the Web [22].

We investigate the usage and effectiveness of regular expressions with the counter operator, also known as the limited repetition operator. This operator makes some expressions exponentially more succinct and permits a subexpression to be matched anywhere between a given *minimum* and *maximum* number of times. For example, the expression `(ab){9,20}` (in POSIX syntax) matches all words that consist of at least nine and at most twenty repetitions of `ab`. Expressions with counting are relevant to several authoritative languages for processing XML and RDF. In particular, they form the structural core of XML Schema Definitions,[1] where they are used to define content models [10]. In the context of RDF and graph query languages, counting operators are used in Cypher's *path patterns* [24] and they have been considered in SPARQL 1.1 *property paths* [16]. However, the effect of counters in regular expressions is not yet fully understood, which is why they were removed from SPARQL 1.1. For this reason we want to contribute to the understanding of such succinct regular expressions and show that (1) counting operators are widely used in practice and therefore seem desirable to practitioners and (2) can be exploited to develop highly efficient evaluation algorithms.

We start with a practical study that investigates how counters are used in regular expressions in practice. We investigate *RegExLib*, the main regular expression repository available on the Web [26]; *Snort*, a system for detecting network intrusion [28], and a large corpus of XML Schema definitions which we harvested from the Web. The data suggests that counters are used often and that counter values can become rather large. For example, in XML Schema we found values up to ten million. We also discovered that schemas of companies such as Amazon, Ebay, Microsoft, Oracle, and Paypal use expressions with counting.

[1]The counting operators are called minOccurs/maxOccurs in XML Schema.

We then turn to efficient evaluation of expressions. The "standard" evaluation problem for expressions is defined as: Given an expression e and a word w, can e be matched onto w? However, many settings in databases call for a more refined version of evaluation. For example, the word w is usually not static and is subject to updates. Examples of such settings are (a) schema constraints and integrity constraints that safeguard the validity of the data, and (b) trigger conditions that continuously monitor whether some action needs to be performed. In settings like these, one would like to perform *incremental evaluation*. Here, we start with a word w and an expression e that matches w, and then the word w is updated (see, e.g., [2, 3, 7]). We want to find out quickly if the expression still matches the updated word $u(w)$. In order to do so, incremental evaluation algorithms may store *auxiliary data*. Naturally, we are interested in striking a good balance between the speed of handling the update and the size of the auxiliary data.

We develop an incremental evaluation algorithm for regular expressions with counting and show that it is possible to avoid the usual exponential translation of such expressions to (standard) finite automata which is used by e.g., current implementations of tools like grep.

We then perform an extensive experimental study that evaluates the efficiency of our evaluation algorithms on synthetic and real-world expressions. As expected, avoiding the exponential blow-up to automata leads to significant speed-ups. When expressions have large counter values, we see speed-ups of several orders of magnitude in every setting we investigate. We look into both normal and incremental evaluation, on both synthetic and real-world expressions.

Related work. Although incremental evaluation of queries and automata has attracted much attention, this is the first work on incremental evaluation of regular expressions with counters, to the best of our knowledge. In the context of databases, the most well studied problem in this context is *incremental view maintenance*. However, in contrast to that problem, where one aims at maintaining the (possibly large) output of a query, we only want to decide whether a query or a pattern can be matched or not. In this sense, the present work is much closer to incremental evaluation of XML schemas [2, 3] and the matching of XPath patterns [7]; a line of work going back to [25].

Efficient evaluation of regular expressions is also heavily investigated in deep packet inspection in networking (see, e.g., [4, 5]). In this context, fast evaluation of regular expressions with counting has been investigated by Smith et al. [27]. While this line of work bears similarities to ours, the focus is quite different. Most prominently, the focus is on evaluating the expressions on a *data stream*. Our setting is more general because we allow insertions and deletions in arbitrary positions of the word, while a data stream is essentially a word which only receives insertions at the back.

Ghelli et al. [13] study fast evaluation for a class of regular expression with counting and interleaving. In the expressions in their study, each alphabet symbol can appear at most once and iteration (counters and Kleene star) can only be applied directly to alphabet symbols. They develop a linear-time algorithm but it does not work for all regular languages, whereas ours does. It would be interesting to investigate if the advantages of both settings can be combined. Another setting where regular expressions are augmented with intervals was studied by Nakayama et al. [23], who also provide an efficient evaluation algorithm. There, however, the intervals do not signify repetition, but rather duration and the strings considered are ones where each letter has an assigned duration. Our incremental evaluation algorithm is designed for *automata with counters*, see, e.g., [18, 9].

2. EXPRESSIONS WITH COUNTING

The *regular expressions* over a set of symbols Σ, denoted by RE, are defined as follows: ε, $\emptyset$, and every Σ-symbol is in RE; and whenever r and s are in RE, then so are (rs), $(r+s)$, and (r^*). For readability, we omit parentheses where appropriate. The language defined by an expression r is denoted by $L(r)$ and defined as usual. We denote the regular expressions with counters as $\mathrm{RE}^{\#}$ and define them as follows. Every RE-expression is an $\mathrm{RE}^{\#}$-expression. Furthermore, when r is an $\mathrm{RE}^{\#}$-expression then so is $r^{k,\ell}$ for $k \in \mathbb{N}$ and $\ell \in \mathbb{N}^+ \cup \{\infty\}$ with $k \leq \ell$. Here, $\mathbb{N}^+$ denotes $\mathbb{N} \setminus \{0\}$. Furthermore, $L(r^{k,\ell}) = \bigcup_{i=k}^{\ell}(L(r))^i$, where $(L(r))^i$ denotes the i-fold concatenation (or repetition) of $L(r)$. Notice that counters are just syntactic sugar. An expression $r \in \mathrm{RE}^{\#}$ can always be converted to an equivalent RE by "unfolding" the counters. The blow-up is worst-case exponential.

3. A PRACTICAL STUDY

We conducted an extensive practical study to get an idea of how counters are used in regular expressions. We investigated expressions in the RegExLib repository [26], in Snort rules [28], and conducted a thorough search for expressions with counters in XML Schemas on the Web.

In the remainder of this section, we say that an expression uses *non-trivial counters* if it has a subexpression of the form $r^{k,\ell}$ in which one of k or ℓ is at least two, i.e., in $\mathbb{N} - \{0, 1\}$.

In a nutshell, we discovered that RegExLib and Snort rules have a surprisingly large fraction (>50%) of expressions with non-trivial counters. RegExLib and Snort have expressions with fairly large counter values (between 1K and 10K), but the largest counters we found occurred in XML Schemas and were up to ten million.

3.1 RegExLib

The RegExLib.com library describes itself as the Internet's first Regular Expression Library [26]. It has a corpus of expressions for recognising URIs, markup code, pieces of Java code, SQL queries, spam, etc. We crawled the expressions of the library and obtained a set of 3024 expressions after removing duplicates and expressions that could not be parsed by Bart Kiers' PCREParser available at Github.[2]

Of these 3024 expressions, 1705 (about 56.3%) use non-trivial counters. This seems to indicate that counters are widely used in practice. We investigated the size of the counters and the nesting of non-trivial counters so that we could get an idea of how large equivalent expressions *without* counters would become. This estimates the internal blow-up that happens in tools like grep. For subexpressions of the form $r^{k,\ell}$ in the library, we found values of k ranging from 0 to 255 and values of ℓ ranging from 1 to 1500.

However, some expressions use nesting of counters, which lead to even larger minimal equivalent REs. We discovered that 86 expressions in the corpus use nesting of non-trivial counters. Several expressions in the corpus contain nested

[2]https://github.com/bkiers/PCREParser

counters of the form $(r_3(r_2(r_1^{k_1,\ell_1}))^{k_2,\ell_2})^{k_3,\ell_3}$ where $\ell_1 = 12$, $\ell_2 = 255$, and $\ell_3 = 255$. The smallest equivalent RE would require at least 780,000 symbols. Another example uses a four-fold nesting of a counter 9, leading to equivalent REs of at least 10,000 symbols.

In this corpus, we see that expressions with non-trivial counters are used quite often, but often the values of the counters are also rather small. It is unclear whether this is because users do not need large counters or because there are no adequate tools for dealing with expressions involving large counters. (On our own computers, tools such as grep complain quickly when counters grow beyond 1000.)

The majority of the expressions in the corpus have simple parse trees. Most expressions are of the form $\alpha_1 \cdots \alpha_m$, where each α_i is of the form $(a_1 + \cdots + a_n)^{k,\ell}$ — possibly with $n = 1$, $(k, \ell) = (1, 1)$ or $(k, \ell) = (0, \infty)$. We refer to such expressions as *CHAINs*. Therefore, *abc* is a CHAIN and so is $(A + B + C)^{3,4}(0 + 1)^*$. However, $(abc)^{1,2}$ is not, because it has a concatenation nested within the counter.[3]

We classify 2217 expressions (73.3%) from this corpus as CHAINs. Notice that the remaining expressions also contain those that use regex-specific features (e.g., lookahead) or tests beyond regular languages (e.g., backreferences), etc.

3.2 Snort

Snort [28] is an open source system for preventing network intrusion and, according to its web site, the most widely deployed IDS/IPS technology worldwide. It has a set of freely available *community rules*, some of which contain regular expressions. After distilling the expressions from the rules and removing duplicates, we obtained a set of 458 expressions, of which 270 (about 58.9%) use non-trivial counters. For subexpressions of the form $r^{k,\ell}$ we found values for k ranging from 0 to 1024 and values for ℓ ranging from 1 to 1075. We found only two expressions with nesting of non-trivial counters.

Equivalent REs for freely available Snort rules therefore do not become as large as for RegExLib expressions, but Snort has a larger fraction of expressions with non-trivial counters. For example, we found 100 expressions with a three-digit number and 4 with a four-digit number for k. For ℓ, 102 expressions have a three-digit value and 62 have a four-digit number. From a structural point of view, the expressions for Snort seemed to be similar to the ones from RegExLib. A quick analysis showed that at least 85.1% are CHAINs. Those that weren't CHAINs typically used a feature that we don't consider here (lookahead in regexes, for example) or a disjunction of words such as (http+ftp).

3.3 XML Schemas

We conducted a deep and labour-intense search for XML Schema Definitions (XSDs) on the Web. There have been studies of regular expressions in schema definitions in the past [6] but, as far as we know, this is the first study that looks at counters. We harvested XSDs from the Web by crawling the maven.org Central Repository and by using the API of Google's Custom Search Engine (CSE) [15]. We chose the Maven Central Repository because it contains high-quality source code and meta-data for many open source projects[4] and because it showed up very often when we were manually googling for XSDs. We obtained XSDs from Maven by recursively crawling its entire directory, downloading all .jar files from projects, and extracting the XSDs from those.

We used Google's CSE to find results on the entire Web. We experimented with several search engines (Bing and Yahoo) but Google returned a superset of the results we found using the alternatives and allowed us to search more precisely. We used queries of the form

`filetype:xsd "maxoccurs=X"` (1)

(and variations thereof) to explicitly search for schemas with a maxoccurs value of X and

`filetype:xsd "maxoccurs=X..Y"` (2)

to search for schemas with a maxoccurs value Z such that $X \leq Z \leq Y$. (Similarly for minoccurs.) Since Google CSE only allows to process around 100 queries per day, it was infeasible within our time constraints to conduct a query of type (1) for each possible counter value. Furthermore, a single query to Google's CSE only returns at most 100 links. We therefore used queries of type (2) mainly for discovering new values of X that return non-empty results and then use type (1) to find all results with this new value.

Data Cleaning. We extracted 4808 XSDs from the Maven Central Repository. Among them, 285 (about 6%) use a non-trivial counter value. Additionally, through Google we found 12,211 unique URLs outside Maven Central that match at least one of the queries of type (1) or (2) above. About 1400 of these URLs did not directly point to an XSD but to an HTML file that, somewhere, contains a link or path of links to an XSD. By resolving these links recursively and by also downloading XSDs that are referenced in other XSDs, we found 8944 more URLs claiming to point to a file with .xsd extension. From this data set, we removed everything that is not a valid XSD. This operation resulted in a total of 3259 unique URLs containing XSDs with non-trivial counter values that we obtained through Google.

We then removed duplicate files. More precisely, we parsed all XSDs we found, normalized the whitespace, and removed files that occurred more than once after this operation. In total, we obtained 1191 unique, well formed XSD files that contain non-trivial counter values; 906 through Google and 285 from the Maven Central Repository. This set of XSDs forms the input of the study that follows.

Description of the Corpus. The 1191 schemas from our repository contain 9389 regular expressions with non-trivial counter values. Our repository (raw data and the clean corpus) can be found at http://regx.github.io/.

The distribution of counter values in our corpus is summarized in Fig. 1. Here we present, per possible finite maxoccurs value (Fig. 1a) and minoccurs value (Fig. 1b), the number of regular expressions in which it was found. The largest value we found was 9,999,999 and occurred in two different versions of an XSD from IBM, related to electronic data interchange for administration, commerce, and transport (EDIFACT).[5]

Notice that the total sum of count values in Fig. 1 is larger than 9389, because a single expression can contain multiple occurrences of counters. One example is the expression

[3]Chain regular expressions were also studied in [13, 21].

[4]See http://search.maven.org/#browse

[5]https://github.com/DFDLSchemas/EDIFACT/raw/master/EDIFACT-SupplyChain-D03B/EDIFACT-SupplyChain-Messages-D.03B.xsd. This schema contains other large values too.

val	#exp	val	#exp	val	#exp	val	#exp
2	2893	26	26	80	3	363	3
3	1609	27	5	85	3	365	4
4	433	29	3	87	4	500	9
5	3709	30	65	90	19	768	1
6	115	31	14	96	5	990	9
7	99	32	25	98	5	999	214
8	171	35	21	99	2020	1000	39
9	844	36	3	100	192	1024	1
10	995	38	1	120	6	1536	3
11	27	39	6	127	14	2000	10
12	79	40	16	128	23	3000	1
13	31	45	5	136	2	5000	16
14	15	48	2	146	1	9999	87
15	162	50	101	150	1	20000	3
16	83	51	2	176	1	65025	5
17	9	52	3	192	1	65535	25
18	15	54	3	198	2	65536	17
19	17	59	1	200	26	99999	14
20	303	60	20	250	2	200000	6
21	7	62	6	255	3	999999	24
22	4	63	2	256	19	9999999	2
23	4	64	13	299	15		
24	11	66	1	300	4		
25	125	67	1	350	6		

(a) Non-trivial maxoccurs values in our corpus. Column "val" states the maxoccurs value; column "#exp" the number of expressions in which we found the value.

val	#exp	val	#exp	val	#exp	val	#exp
2	1099	9	3	19	1	54	3
3	284	10	4	20	24	60	4
4	73	11	9	22	1	85	3
5	24	12	10	23	2	93	1
6	11	13	1	24	3	127	1
7	11	15	8	31	2	365	4
8	9	16	8	51	1		

(b) Non-trivial minoccurs values in our corpus. Column "val" states the minoccurs value; column "#exp" the number of expressions in which we found the value.

Figure 1: Non-trivial counter values occurring in our corpus.

$(ab^{2,12})^{0,65535}$, which we found in a schema that seems to be related to the MPEG-7 standard. A brief inspection of our corpus exposes that several major companies use regular expressions with non-trivial counters, for example: the Amazon Simple Storage Service (S3) schema[6] (maxoccurs 100), FedEx's web services[7] (maxoccurs 12, 99, 999), Paypal's WSDL interface[8] (maxoccurs 100, 1000), and several schemas for the MPEG-7 standard[9] use maxoccurs values up to 65636. We note that our corpus by no means contains all available XSDs on the Web with non-trivial counter values. Some prominent examples that we did not find automatically can be found in Microsoft's MSDN library, which contains schemas with maxoccurs values of, e.g., 50, 100, 256, 1000, and 100,000.[10]

depth	star	counter	iteration
0	7333		
1	2036	9361	9313
2	19	27	73
3	1	1	3

Figure 2: Star-, counter-, and iteration depth for expressions in our corpus.

Structural Analysis. We analyzed the structure of regular expressions in our corpus, in the same spirit as was done by Bex et al. [6]. This allows us to compare results with [6], which was performed a decade ago. Bex et al. observed that a very large percentage of expressions in practice only use each alphabet symbol at most once. This observation still holds: in our corpus, 98% of all regular expressions use alphabet symbols at most once. A little bit of care is needed when comparing this number to [6]: In the latter study, non-trivial counter values in expressions were first rewritten to trivial ones, e.g., $b^{4,5}$ was rewritten to $bbbbb?$. As such, the expression $b^{4,5}$ would not be counted as having a single b. The highest numbers of occurrences for the same symbol in one expression we found was 200.

When looking at the structural complexity of the expressions in our corpus, we see that they have shallow parse trees. For computing parse tree depth, we first normalize expressions by exploiting associativity of disjunction and concatenation. That is, when we see an expression of the form $((a+b)+c)+d$, we normalize it to $a+b+c+d$ and say that its parse tree has depth two, rather than four. After this preprocessing step, 8132 expressions have depth 3; 620 have depth 4; 542 have depth 5; 36 have depth 6; and 59 have depth ranging from 7 to 9.

Next, we looked at the nesting of repetition operators. Fig. 2 contains the *star depth* of the expressions in our corpus, i.e., the number of nestings of operators that allow an unbounded number of repetitions of their associated subexpression, i.e., operators of the form ${}^{k,\infty}$ for some $k \in \mathbb{N}$. (So, both expressions $(a^{0,\infty})^{2,100}$ and $a^{2,\infty}$ have star depth one.) Not surprisingly, most expressions do not use any nesting of such expressions at all. Only nine expressions in our entire corpus use nesting depth 2 or 3.

Also contained in Fig. 2 is the *counter depth* of regular expressions, which is the nesting depth of counters of the form (k, ℓ) where at least one of k or ℓ is a natural number larger than 1. (So, both expressions $(a^{0,\infty})^{2,100}$ and $a^{2,\infty}$ have counter depth one.)

Finally, we define the *iteration depth* to be the nesting depth of any form of iteration, that is stars and counters. The former of the two aforementioned expressions has iteration depth two and the latter has one. Fig. 2 suggests that expressions with non-trivial counters in XSDs are structurally rather simple. We suspect that this is because highly complex regular expression in an XSD may indicate that the design of the underlying XML database is not very elegant. A closer look at the expressions showed that 8330 expressions from our corpus with non-trivial counter values are

[6]http://doc.s3.amazonaws.com/2006-03-01/AmazonS3.xsd
[7]http://www.fedex.com/templates/components/apps/wpor/secure/downloads/xml/Aug09/Advanced/ShipService_v7.xsd
[8]http://www.paypalobjects.com/wsdl/eBLBaseComponents.xsd
[9]http://standards.iso.org/ittf/PubliclyAvailableStandards/MPEG-7_schema_files/mpeg7-v2.xsd
[10]http://msdn.microsoft.com/en-us/library/cc233001.aspx, http://msdn.microsoft.com/en-us/library/jj583348.aspx, http://msdn.microsoft.com/en-us/library/gg309601.aspx

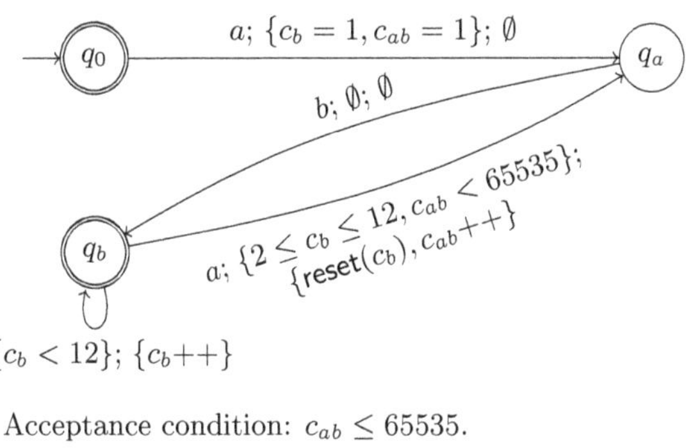

Figure 3: A Counter Automaton for $(ab^{2,12})^{0,65535}$.

CHAINs, which is about 88.7%. (Within the pool of all regular expressions we found in schemas, about 86% were CHAINs.)

4. MEMORY-EFFICIENT AUTOMATA

Most algorithms that process regular expressions with counting (notably, grep and all XML Schema validation tools that we are aware of) first convert them to ordinary regular expressions by expanding the counters. Subsequently, these (already exponentially large) expressions are converted to finite automata. This exponential blow-up can be avoided by directly converting the expressions into a much more memory-efficient representation: finite automata with counters. Such automata have been used and implemented before, for example in the context of deep packet inspection in networks [27], where significant improvements in speed and memory consumption were reported.

We provide a gentle introduction to such automata here and we compare them to other evaluation algorithms in Section 6.1. The performance gain is clear: compared to the above mentioned naive method for evaluation, we see improvements of several orders of magnitude. The differences for incremental evaluation become even more drastic.

Counter Automata by Example. *Counter automata* are a natural representation of expressions with counters that is easier to deal with in algorithms. We first discuss a counter automaton by example and explain them more formally next. Figure 3 depicts a counter automaton for the expression $(ab^{2,12})^{0,65535}$, which we found in our practical study in a schema related to the MPEG-7 standard. An ordinary non-deterministic finite state automaton for this expression would require 851955 states. The counter automaton only has three: a start state q_0 and states for each occurrence of a symbol in the expression – q_a for a and q_b for b. (Given a regular expression with counters that has n occurrences of symbols, we can always construct an equivalent counter automaton with $n+1$ states.)

The automaton has two *counters*: c_b, for counting the number of b's and c_{ab} for counting how many times it has seen a word that matches $ab^{2,12}$. Initially, all counters are set to 1.

The state transitions in the automaton consist of three ingredients: a *symbol*, a set of *guards*, and a set of *counter updates*. For example, the transition from q_0 to q_a reads symbol a, has guards $c_b = 1$ and $c_{ab} = 1$, and an empty set of counter updates. So, the transition reads an a-symbol and can be made when $c_b = c_{ab} = 1$. The next interesting transition is the b-loop on q_b. It allows to read a b when $c_b < 12$, and it increases c_b by one. Finally, the transition from q_b to q_a reads an a, can be performed if c_b is between 2 and 12 and $c_{ab} < 65535$. It increases c_{ab} by one and overwrites c_b with 1.

The automaton accepts if it is in an accepting state (double circles) and if the *acceptance condition* holds, that is, c_{ab} is at most 65535. It is easy to see that the automaton accepts precisely the words that match $(ab^{2,12})^{0,65535}$.

Formal Definition. We now define counter automata formally. Their definition is rather technical but essentially follow the lines of the example above. Readers who already understand the main idea can safely skip this definition.

Formally, counter automata are an extension of non-deterministic finite automata, which we briefly recall here for the sake of clarifying notation. A *non-deterministic finite automaton (NFA)* is a tuple $N = (Q, \Sigma, \delta, I, F)$, where Q denotes its set of states, Σ its alphabet, I its set of initial states, and F its set of final or accepting states. The transition rules δ are of the form $q_1 \xrightarrow{a} q_2$, indicating that reading an $a \in \Sigma$ in state q_1 can bring the automaton to state q_2. Acceptance is defined in the standard manner. We denote by $L(N)$ the set of words accepted by N.

Counter automata extend NFAs with *counter variables* or *counters*. We follow [11] in their definition. Let C be a finite set of *counter variables* and $\alpha : C \to \mathbb{N}$ be a function assigning a value to each counter variable. A *guard over* C is a function $\phi : C \to (\mathbb{N} \times \mathbb{N}_\infty)$, where $\mathbb{N}_\infty$ denotes $\mathbb{N} \cup \{\infty\}$. Furthermore, we will require that, if $\phi(c) = (k, \ell)$, then $k \leq \ell$. The semantics of a guard is defined as follows. We say that a counter assignment α *satisfies* guard ϕ if, for every $c \in C$, whenever $\phi(c) = (k, \ell)$, then $k \leq \alpha(c) \leq \ell$. Intuitively, this means that a guard defines, for each counter c, a minimum allowed value k and a maximum allowed value ℓ. As such, guards are used in counter automata to model the upper and lower bounds of counters in regular expressions. By $\alpha \models \phi$ we denote that the counter assignment α satisfies guard ϕ. By Guards(C) we denote the set of guards over C.

A *basic update over* C is a partial function $\pi : C \to \{\mathsf{reset}, \mathsf{increment}\}$. When $\pi(c) = \mathsf{reset}$, this means that c should be reset to one and when $\pi(c) = \mathsf{increment}$ it means that c should be incremented by one. (If π is undefined on c, we leave c unchanged.) By Basic-Up(C) we denote the set of all basic updates over C.

Definition 4.1. *A (non-deterministic)* automaton with counters *(NFA$^\#$) is a 6-tuple $A = (Q, q_0, C, \delta, F, \tau)$ where*

- *Q is the finite set of states;*
- *$q_0 \in Q$ is the initial state;*
- *C is the finite set of counter variables;*
- *$\delta \subseteq Q \times \Sigma \times$ Guards(C) $\times$ Basic-Up(C) $\times Q$ is the transition relation;*
- *$F : Q \to$ Guards(C) is the acceptance function; and*
- *$\tau : C \to \mathbb{N}$ assigns a maximum value to every counter variable.*

Intuitively, an NFA$^\#$ A can make a transition $(q, a, \phi, \pi, q') \in \delta$ whenever it is in state q, reads label a, and the guard ϕ is satisfied by the current values of the counter variables. It then updates the counter variables according to the update π (in a way which we explain next) and moves into state q'. To explain the update mechanism formally, we use *configurations*. A *configuration* is a pair (q, α) where $q \in Q$ is the current state and $\alpha : C \to \mathbb{N}$ is the function mapping counter variables to their current value. An update π

transforms α into α' by setting $\alpha'(c) := 1$ whenever $\pi(c) =$ reset and $\alpha'(c) := \alpha(c) + 1$ whenever $\pi(c) =$ increment. We sometimes abuse notation and denote α' by $\pi(\alpha)$.

Let α_{init} be the function mapping every counter variable to 1. The *initial configuration* γ_0 is $(q_0, \alpha_{\text{init}})$. A configuration (q, α) is *final* if $\alpha \models F(q)$. A configuration $\gamma' = (q', \alpha')$ *immediately follows* a configuration $\gamma = (q, \alpha)$ by reading $a \in \Sigma$, denoted $\gamma \to_a \gamma'$, if there exists $(q, a, \phi, \pi, q') \in \delta$ with $\alpha \models \phi$ and $\alpha' = \pi(\alpha)$.

For a word $w = a_1 \cdots a_n$ and two configurations γ and γ', we denote by $\gamma \Rightarrow_w \gamma'$ that $\gamma \to_{a_1} \cdots \to_{a_n} \gamma'$. A configuration γ is *reachable* if there exists a word w such that $\gamma_0 \Rightarrow_w \gamma$. A word w is *accepted* by A if $\gamma_0 \Rightarrow_w \gamma_f$ where γ_f is a final configuration. We denote by $L(A)$ the set of words accepted by A.

The *size* of a transition θ or acceptance condition $F(q)$ is the total number of occurrences of alphabet symbols, states, counter variables, and Boolean connectives which occur in it, plus the size of the binary representation of each integer occcurring in it. In the same spirit, the size of A, denoted by $|A|$, is $|Q| + \sum_{q \in Q} \log \tau(q) + |F(q)| + \sum_{\theta \in \delta} |\theta|$.

It is known that RE$^{\#}$ expressions can be efficiently translated into equivalent NFA$^{\#}$s by applying a natural extension of the known Glushkov construction [11, 29].

5. INCREMENTAL EVALUATION

We present a new incremental evaluation algorithm for regular expressions with counters. To the best of our knowledge, this is the first such algorithm that avoids an exponential translation of the expressions. In Section 6 we see that incremental evaluation outperforms evaluation from scratch by factors up to three orders of magnitude and, shifting to automata with counters improves up to another three orders of magnitude. In fact, such speed-ups can be expected: incremental evaluation is an exponential improvement over evaluation from scratch; and doing it with counter automata is an yet another exponential improvement over doing it with ordinary automata.

As a warm-up, we recall how to incrementally evaluate ordinary regular expressions on words. The technique was first described by Patnaik and Immerman [25] and was studied in more detail and implemented by Balmin et al. [2].

Incremental Evaluation of REs and NFAs. Assume that we have a word $w = a_1 \cdots a_n \in \Sigma^*$ and a regular expression r and we want to incrementally maintain whether $w \in L(r)$. The incremental evaluation problem consists of two phases: a one-time *preprocessing phase* in which we construct an auxiliary data structure that we will maintain during updates; and an *evaluation phase* in which updates of the form relabel(i, a), delete(i), or insert(i, a) arrive, where $i \in \{1, \ldots, n\}$ is a position in the word and $a \in \Sigma$ is a symbol. The updates do the obvious: relabel changes a_i to a, delete deletes the symbol a_i and results in a word of length $n-1$, and insert(i, a) inserts an a before position i, resulting in a word of length $n+1$. We denote the newly obtained word by w'. In the evaluation phase, the task is to be able to say whether $w' \in L(N)$ quickly after the update arrives. So, after a one-time preprocessing phase, we want to be able to deal with (multiple) updates quickly. Here, we describe a method for incremental evaluation that uses $\mathcal{O}(n \cdot |r|^2)$ time for preprocessing and then, in the update phase, can answer in time $\mathcal{O}(|r|^3 \cdot \log n)$ per update whether the new word w' is still in $L(r)$ or not. Therefore, when n is large, the procedure is much faster than re-evaluating the expression from scratch, which would require at least linear time in n.

The incremental update algorithm works on the NFA for r, which can be constructed in linear time and which we denote by $N = (Q, \Sigma, \delta, I, F)$. We first describe the auxiliary data structure we will maintain during the updates. For each i, j, $1 \le i < j \le n$, let T_{ij} be the transition relation $\{(p, q) \mid p, q \in Q, p \xrightarrow{a_i \cdots a_j} q\}$, where $p \xrightarrow{a_i \cdots a_j} q$ denotes that N can reach state q when it starts in state p and reads $a_i \cdots a_j$. Note that $T_{ij} = T_{ik} \bowtie T_{(k+1)j}$, (with $i < k < j$), where $\bowtie$ denotes the natural join on binary relations, that is, T_{ij} contains all (x, z) such that there is a y with $(x, y) \in T_{ik}$ and $(y, z) \in T_{(k+1)j}$.

For simplicity, assume first that n is a power of 2, say $n = 2^k$. The main idea is to keep as auxiliary information just the T_{ij} for intervals $[i, j]$ obtained by recursively splitting $[1, n]$ into halves, until $i = j$. More precisely, consider the transition relation tree $\mathcal{T}_n$ whose nodes are sets T_{ij}, defined inductively as follows:

- the root is T_{1n};
- each node T_{ij} for which $j - i > 0$ has children T_{ik} and $T_{(k+1)j}$ where $k = i - 1 + \frac{j-i+1}{2}$; and
- the T_{ii} are the leaves, for all $1 \le i \le n$.

Note that $\mathcal{T}_n$ has $n + (n/2) + \cdots + 2 + 1 = 2n - 1$ nodes and has depth $\log n$. Thus, the size of the auxiliary structure is $\mathcal{O}(n \cdot |Q|^2)$.

The *preprocessing phase* consists of building this auxiliary data structure. Notice that, once we have $\mathcal{T}_n$, it is easy to decide whether $w \in L(N)$. Indeed, $w \in L(N)$ if and only if $(q, f) \in T_{1n}$ for some $q \in I$ and $f \in F$. Therefore, we only have to show that this auxiliary data structure can be updated efficiently.

We now describe the *evaluation phase*. For simplicity, consider the case when one update occurs, changing the label of the symbol in w at position k to b. That is, the new word is $w' = a_1 \cdots a_{k-1} b a_{k+1} \cdots a_n$. The relations $T_{ij} \in \mathcal{T}_n$ that are affected by the updates are those lying on the path from the leaf T_{kk} to the root of $\mathcal{T}_n$. Denote this set of relations by I and notice that it contains at most $\log n$ relations. The tree $\mathcal{T}_n$ is updated by recomputing the relations in I bottom-up as follows: First, the leaf relation T_{kk} is set according to δ and b. Then each $T_{ij} \in I$ with children T' and T'', of which one has been recomputed, is replaced by $T' \bowtie T''$. Thus, at most $\log n$ relations have been recomputed, each in time $\mathcal{O}(|Q|^3)$, yielding a total time of $\mathcal{O}(|Q|^3 \cdot \log n)$.[11] If we arrive at the root, we know that $w' \in L(N)$ if and only if $(q, f) \in T_{1n}$ for some $q \in I$ and $f \in F$.

The above approach can easily be adapted to words whose length is not a power of 2. Further, the auxiliary data structure has size $\mathcal{O}(n \cdot |Q|^2)$. Finally, handling updates in which elements are inserted or deleted is also done in [2], but then some precautions have to be taken in order to make sure that the tree $\mathcal{T}_n$ remains properly balanced.

THEOREM 5.1 ([25]). *Incremental evaluation of an RE r on a word w is possible with preprocessing time $\mathcal{O}(n \cdot |r|^3)$, an auxiliary data structure of size $\mathcal{O}(n \cdot |r|^2)$, and time $\mathcal{O}(\log n \cdot |r|^3)$ per update.*

[11]Using fast matrix multiplication algorithms, this time can be improved to $\mathcal{O}(|Q|^{\omega} \cdot \log n)$ (where ω denotes the best known bound for matrix multiplication).

The Incremental Evaluation Algorithm for RE#s. The incremental evaluation algorithm for RE#s extends the one for REs. It is based on NFA#s rather than NFAs and it does not translate RE#s to exponentially larger automata.

Intuitively, the algorithm for RE#s follows the same lines as the algoritm for REs, but it (1) stores different information at the nodes of the auxiliary tree and, subsequently also (2) uses a different algorithm for joining the information in neighboring nodes. We now describe these two changes.

New information in the auxiliary tree. In the algorithm for REs, a tuple (p, q) is in T_{ij} if and only if the automaton N can read $a_i \cdots a_j$ when going from state p to state q. When we want to do something similar for NFA#s, we need to take the counters in account. To this end, a *(general) update over* C is a function $\pi : C \to (\{\mathsf{inc}, \mathsf{assign}\} \times \mathbb{N})$. For readability we often consider π as a set of statements of the form $\mathsf{inc}(c, k)$ or $\mathsf{assign}(c, k)$. (Hence, π only contains one of $\mathsf{inc}(c, k)$ or $\mathsf{assign}(c, k)$ for each counter c.) Intuitively, when π contains $\mathsf{inc}(c, k)$, then counter c should be incremented with k. If it contains $\mathsf{assign}(c, k)$, then c is assigned the value k, so it is overwritten. We need assign because if we perform some sequence of transitions in which a counter c is reset, then c should be assigned a value k, which will be the number of increments that were done to c *after the last reset* plus 1.[12] To this end, we use a rule $\mathsf{assign}(c, k)$. If we model a sequence of updates without a reset, then we use a rule $\mathsf{inc}(c, k)$, where k is the number of increments to c in the sequence. We write Updates(C) for the set of all general updates over C.

Formally, an update $\pi \in \text{Updates}(C)$ transforms counter assignment α into α' by setting $\alpha'(c) = k$ if π contains $\mathsf{assign}(c, k)$ and setting $\alpha'(c) = \alpha(c) + k$ if π contains $\mathsf{inc}(c, k)$. We sometimes denote α' by $\pi(\alpha)$. Thus, if α is transformed into α' by π, then $\pi(\alpha)(c) = \alpha'(c)$. For the remaining definitions of this section, we fix a NFA# $A = (Q, q_0, C, \delta, F, \tau)$.

In the incremental evaluation algorithm for RE#s, the sets T_{ij} contain *transformation tuples*:

DEFINITION 5.2. A *transformation tuple* of A is a quadruple $t \in Q \times \text{Guards}(C) \times \text{Updates}(C) \times Q$. Tuple $t = (p, \phi, \pi, q)$ is *consistent* with a string w if, for every configuration $\gamma = (p, \alpha)$ such that $\alpha \models \phi$, there is a configuration $\gamma' = (q, \alpha')$ such that $\gamma \Rightarrow_w \gamma'$ in A and $\alpha' = \pi(\alpha)$.

That is, a transformation tuple is consistent with w if it captures the effect of w on the NFA#, i.e., if it describes how configurations that match it change by reading w.

EXAMPLE 5.3. Consider the NFA# $(Q, q_0, C, \delta, F, \tau)$ from Figure 3. The tuple $t_1 = (q_0, \phi_1, \pi_1, q_b)$ where ϕ_1 expresses

$$c_b = 1 \quad \text{and} \quad c_{ab} = 1$$

and π_1 contains $\mathsf{inc}(c_b, 2)$ and $\mathsf{inc}(c_{ab}, 0)$ is consistent with $w = abbb$. (Intuitively, if the NFA# starts in q_0 and reads w, it ends up in state q_b and increases c_b by two.) If ϕ_1 would only require $1 \leq c_b \leq 2$, the tuple would *not* be consistent with w, because we can only read a in q_0 if $c_b = 1$.

The tuple $t_2 = (q_b, \phi_2, \pi_2, q_b)$ where ϕ_2 expresses

$$1 \leq c_b \leq 9 \quad \text{and} \quad 1 \leq c_{ab} \leq 65534$$

and π_2 contains $\mathsf{assign}(c_b, 3)$ and $\mathsf{inc}(c_{ab}, 1)$ is consistent with *babbb* and also with *bbbabbb*. It is not consistent with *abbb* (because we cannot go from q_b to q_a if $c_b = 1$) or with *bbbbabbb* (because we cannot read b in q_b if $c_b = 12$). □

[12]The plus one term comes from the fact that the counters are reset to 1.

So, the auxiliary data structure for incremental evaluation of RE#s is a binary tree $\mathcal{T}_n$ whose nodes are sets T_{ij} that contain precisely the transformation tuples that are consistent with $a_i \cdots a_j$.

Joining of transformation tuples. It remains to explain how the transformation tuples can be computed and updated. To this end, we merely have to redefine the *join* operation $\bowtie$ we used in the algorithm for REs. In other words, we must define when transformation tuples $t_1 = (p_1, \phi_1, \pi_1, q_1)$ and $t_2 = (p_2, \phi_2, \pi_2, q_2)$ can be joined. To this end, we say that t_1 is *compatible with* t_2 if $q_1 = p_2$ and there is a counter assignment α such that $\alpha \models \phi_1$ and $\pi_1(\alpha) \models \phi_2$. Intuitively, if t_1 is consistent with word w_1, t_2 is consistent with word w_2, and t_1 is compatible with t_2, then there is a counter assignment α such that $(p_1, \alpha) \Rightarrow_{w_1 w_2} (q_2, \alpha')$ with $\alpha' = \pi_2(\pi_1(\alpha))$.

EXAMPLE 5.4. For the NFA# of Figure 3, the tuple t_1 from Example 5.3 is compatible with t_2. For example, for the assignment α_0 with $c_b = 1$ and $c_{ab} = 1$ we have that $\alpha_1 := \pi_1(\alpha_0)$ maps c_b to 3 and c_{ab} to 1. Therefore, $\alpha_1 \models \phi_2$. As such, when in configuration (q_0, α_0) the NFA# can read strings *abbbbabbb* or *abbbbbbabbb*.

We now define how transformation tuples are joined.

DEFINITION 5.5. Let $t_1 = (p, \phi_1, \pi_1, r)$ be compatible to $t_2 = (r, \phi_2, \pi_2, q)$. Then the *join of* t_1 *with* t_2, denoted $t_1 \bowtie_c t_2$, is the tuple (p, ϕ, π, q) such that, for every counter assignment α, we have *(i)* $\alpha \models \phi \Leftrightarrow (\alpha \models \phi_1 \wedge \pi_1(\alpha) \models \phi_2)$, and *(ii)* $\pi(\alpha) = \pi_2(\pi_1(\alpha))$.

EXAMPLE 5.6. The join of t_1 with t_2 from Example 5.3 is (q_0, ϕ, π, q_b), where ϕ expresses

$$c_b = 1 \quad \text{and} \quad c_{ab} = 1$$

and π contains $\mathsf{assign}(c_b, 3)$ and $\mathsf{inc}(c_{ab}, 1)$. Consider tuple $t_1' = (q_b, \phi_1', \pi_1', q_b)$ where ϕ_1' expresses

$$3 \leq c_b \leq 9 \quad \text{and} \quad 1 \leq c_{ab} \leq 65535$$

and π_1' contains $\mathsf{inc}(c_b, 2)$ and $\mathsf{inc}(c_{ab}, 0)$, then t_1' is compatible with t_2 and $t_1' \bowtie_c t_2$ is (q_b, ϕ', π', q_b), where ϕ' expresses

$$3 \leq c_b \leq 7 \quad \text{and} \quad 1 \leq c_{ab} \leq 65534$$

and π' contains $\mathsf{assign}(c_b, 3)$ and $\mathsf{inc}(c_{ab}, 1)$. Intuitively, we have $3 \leq c_b \leq 7$ in the result because ϕ_1' requires $3 \leq c_b$ and ϕ_2 requires $\pi_1'(c_b) \leq 9$. □

When regular expressions contain few alphabet symbols and large counter values, as is typically the case in the CHAINs we found in the practical study (Section 3), the new algorithm performs much better. This is seen most clearly when considering RE#s of the form $r = a^{k,k}$. Assuming unit cost for basic arithmetic on numbers up to k, incremental evaluation for their NFA#s on a word of length n costs preprocessing time $\mathcal{O}(n)$ and update time $\mathcal{O}(\log n)$, whereas the algorithm of Section 5 would cost preprocessing time $\mathcal{O}(n \cdot 2^{3|r|})$ and update time $\mathcal{O}(2^{3|r|} \cdot \log n)$. The large speed-ups we obtain in Section 6 are therefore due to the fact that expressions with large counters we found in practice seem to have a rather simple structure, which exploits the potential of NFA#s close to optimal.

6. EXPERIMENTS

We performed an extensive experimental study on regular expression evaluation algorithms; incremental or otherwise. We implemented all algorithms and benchmarks in

Java, mainly because it is very portable and wide-spread. To ensure comparability between measurements, we also reimplemented all other algorithms in Java (and on the same underlying data structures). Since Java uses garbage collection, there are several caveats (which we'll discuss later) for measuring memory consumption as well as execution time. All our experiments are conducted on a machine with an Intel Core i7-2600K. We allocated a heap of at least 3 GiB for all JVM instances during our tests. All tests were executed on a 64-bit JVM.

We perform two kinds of experiments: *evaluation from scratch* (i.e., not dealing with updates) and *incremental evaluation* (dealing with updates). In both settings, we compare algorithms based on NFAs to algorithms based on NFA$^{\#}$s. The NFA$^{\#}$ variants are several orders of magnitude faster than the algorithms based on NFAs, scale much better, and consume much less memory.

6.1 Evaluation from Scratch

The experimental task in this section is the following:

PROBLEM	:	Evaluation
INPUT	:	A regular expression with counting r and a word w.
QUESTION	:	Is $w \in L(r)$?

We compare the following algorithms:

(RE#): Fast squaring algoritm for RE$^{\#}$
(NFAsim): Building and simulating an NFA
(NFA$^{\#}$sim): Building and simulating a NFA$^{\#}$
(NFApre): Preprocessing for incremental NFA evaluation
(NFA$^{\#}$pre): Preprocessing for incremental NFA$^{\#}$ eval

We discuss the five algorithms next. The benchmark (RE#) is an optimization of an algorithm by Kilpeläinen and Tuhkanen [18] which is the only polynomial time algorithm for evaluating RE$^{\#}$ we are aware of that does not translate to automata.[13] It considers the parse tree of the expression r and computes bottom-up, for each node u in the parse tree, all pairs (i, j) of positions in $w = a_1 \cdots a_n$ such that the subexpression rooted at u matches the subword $a_i \cdots a_j$. For example, when node u is labeled by a disjunction, its corresponding relation can be obtained by taking the union of the relations of u's children. If u is a concatenation, its relation is the composition (or natural join) of the relation of its children. If u is a $*$, we need to take the transitive-reflexive closure of the relation of its child. Lastly, if u is a counting operator (say, a k-fold iteration), its relation is the k-fold composition of the relation of its child. In this latter case lies the optimization. Instead of performing $O(k)$ compositions as in [18], we comput the k-fold composition by fast squaring, which only costs $O(\log k)$ compositions. This algorithm is known to have worst-case complexity $O(|w|^m \cdot |r|)$, where m is the best bound for multiplying two $|w| \times |w|$ zero-one matrices. We refer the reader to [18, 20] for further details of the algorithms and their complexity.

The (NFAsim) algorithm translates r into an NFA, which is then evaluated on w. The bottleneck of this approach lies at dealing with the counters of r. A counter value of k typically results in $\Omega(k)$ states in the NFA. Since the counter value is represented by $\log k$ bits in r, this constitutes exponential cost in $|r|$.

In (NFA$^{\#}$sim), we avoid this blow-up by compiling r into a NFA$^{\#}$ of size only $O(|r|)$, which we then evaluate on w.

The algorithms (NFApre) and (NFA$^{\#}$pre) are the preprocessing phases of the incremental evaluation algorithms of Section 5. Once these preprocessing phases are finished, one can decide in constant time whether $w \in L(r)$ by inspecting the root of the auxiliary data structure. By comparing the cost of the (—pre) with the (—sim) variants we can therefore gauge the cost of the one-time overhead for building an auxiliary data structure that allows incremental evaluation for future updates.

We present three benchmarks: a *sanity check*, a *worst-case synthetic* benchmark with much non-determinism in expressions, and a benchmark that shows how *large counter values* behave in real-world and synthetic expressions. The benchmarks use expressions that are structurally very simple, because (1) simplicity in the setup allows for a better understanding of the results and (2) we did not see different results on more complex setups; all behaviour we saw in more complex (real-world or synthetic) settings could be explained by these three experiments.

In order to get reliable measurements in Java we repeated each experiment about five hundred times, discarded the best and worst 10% to get rid of garbage cleaning artefacts, and took the average of the remaining ones. (We observed that this way we consistently obtained the same measurements when experiments were repeated.) Since this procedure makes experiments lengthy, we only measured up to 30 seconds. The charts we present are optimized for readability and drastically summarise the data points we measured.

Sanity Check Benchmark. First we compared the five candidates for $r = a^*$ and w being words containing only a's (Fig. 4, left). The rationale behind this test is to see how the five methods compare *if the NFA$^{\#}$ has no advantage* over the other methods and to *gauge the overhead of NFA$^{\#}$s versus NFAs* in our implementation. Since a^* can be converted to an NFA or NFA$^{\#}$ within microseconds, we only see the time required to process the word. Here, fast squaring (RE#) is by far the slowest of all. The reason is its high complexity in terms of $|w|$. The incremental variants are about an order of magnitude slower than the non-incremental variants. This factor can be explained by the extra cost of building the external data structure for the incremental algorithms. In this setting where the NFA$^{\#}$-based algorithms do not have any advantage over the NFA-based algorithms, the NFA$^{\#}$-based algorithms are marginally slower.

Real-world and large counters. Next we compared the candidates on real-world and synthetic expressions that use very large counter values. The underlying idea of this test is to see how the candidates compare if the NFA$^{\#}$s can exploit counters to their maximum advantage. In this experiment we noticed that the behavior for real-world expressions was the exactly same than on synthetic ones. In Fig. 4, middle, we present for increasing values of n, the expression $r = a^{(n-n/4),(n+n/4)}$, so the range of allowed lengths is about $n/2$. We then perform membership tests of words of length n, $n-n/4$, $n-n/4-1$, $n+n/4$, and $n+n/4+1$ and take the average of the evaluation times we measured. It is striking that, throughout this experiment, the preprocessing phase for incremental NFA$^{\#}$ evaluation is faster than conversion to an NFA and evaluating it.

[13]Notice that rewriting an RE$^{\#}$ into an equivalent RE already costs exponential time.

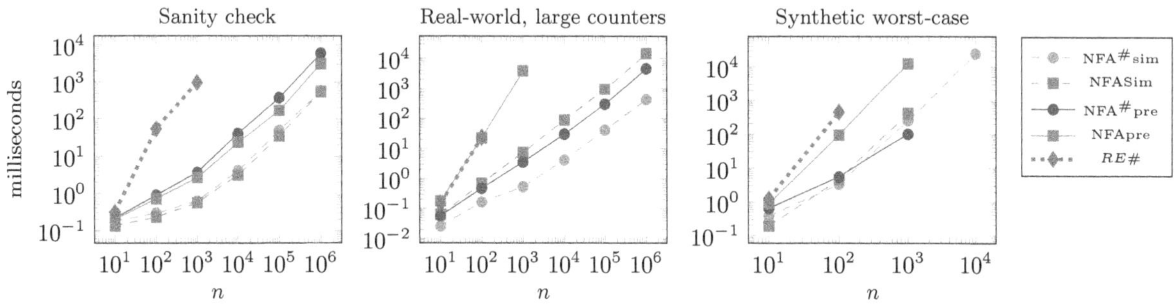

Figure 4: Evaluation from scratch (log-log scale).

Synthetic worst-case. Finally we investigated synthetic expressions with counting, but with a high amount of non-determinism (Fig. 4, right). We consider expressions r for which the minimal deterministic finite automaton is *double* exponentially larger than r. We perform this test because the two previous experiments concerned very simple deterministic expressions and it is well-known that non-determinism complicates fast evaluation.

The most striking and perhaps counter-intuitive fact about this experiment is that (NFA$^{\#}$pre) is the fastest evaluation algorithm in this case. We believe that this is so because the evaluation algorithms for NFAs (resp., NFA$^{\#}$s) need to store and maintain a large number of possible states (resp., configurations) while reading the word. Since (NFA$^{\#}$pre) works completely differently and can summarize configurations, it even outperforms the standard evaluation algorithms.

A second striking fact is that non-determinism combined with large counter values can bring most evaluation algorithms to their knees quickly. This may be the reason why the XML Schema specification only allows very limited non-determinism in regular expressions (cfr. [11]).

6.2 Incremental evaluation

We compare the two variants of incremental evaluation:

(incNFA) Incremental NFA evaluation

(incNFA$^{\#}$) Incremental NFA$^{\#}$ evaluation

For the other evaluation algorithms of Section 6.1, the cost of incremental evaluation will be the same as for evaluation from scratch so we don't include them again here. Our implementations of (incNFA) and (incNFA$^{\#}$) closely follows Section 5. Auxiliary data is stored as AA trees [1].

We use the following methodology to produce our measurements (and to compensate for the side-effects of garbage collection). Given a regular expression and a word, we first construct the auxiliary data structures to prepare for incremental evaluation. We then perform a large (and equal) number of insertions and deletions in the word; equally distributed at the beginning, middle, and end of the word. We then discard the 10% largest and 10% smallest measurements and take the average of the remaining ones.

We perform experiments of two kinds for increasing values of n: one lets the expression and the word grow simultaneously with n and the other keeps the expression constant and only lets the word grow. As such we obtain a detailed insight in how the scalability depends on the word and on the expression.

Expressions with Large Counter Values. The leftmost graph in Fig. 5 contains our measurements for (incNFA) and (incNFA$^{\#}$) for expressions with large counter values as already described in Section 6.1: For a given value of n, we consider the expression $r = a^{(n-n/4),(n+n/4)}$ and we start with the word $w = a^n$. We then perform a large number of insertions and deletions and measure the average time of such an operation (as described before). Throughout the experiment, (incNFA$^{\#}$) outperforms (incNFA) and scales much better. Even for $n = 1{,}000{,}000$, (incNFA$^{\#}$) is faster than (incNFA) for $n = 50$; so, here, (incNFA$^{\#}$) is dealing with a word about five orders of magnitude larger than (incNFA). Lastly, recall that we do not have time measurements for (incNFA) for $n > 1000$ since preprocessing timed out. We also measured memory consumption (not in a separate chart for reasons of space) and noticed that, even for $n = 100$K, (incNFA$^{\#}$) consumes less memory than (incNFA) with $n = 1$K.

Synthetic worst-case. The second graph in Fig 5 depicts the incremental version of the corresponding experiment in Section 6.1. This test is designed to be hard on (incNFA$^{\#}$) even though expressions have large counter values. In this experiment the transformation tuples cannot summarize large sets of configurations of NFA$^{\#}$s as well as in the previous experiment, due to the non-determinism in the expressions. In terms of time, (incNFA$^{\#}$) consistently outperforms (incNFA) about one order of magnitude. In terms of space, (incNFA$^{\#}$) still scales much better than (incNFA); about two orders of magnitude.

Real-world, MPEG7 Expression. In this experiment and the next we consider a (fixed) expression that we found in our practical study and only let the length of the word grow as n increases. This gives a clearer picture of the scalability of both evaluation methods when only the size of the data becomes very large. Here, we consider the expression $(ab^{2,12})^{0,65535}$ that we found in XML Schemas related to the MPEG-7 standard[14] and refer to as *MPEG7 expression.* From all the expressions we found in practice, this one seemed to be among the more challenging ones for state-of-the-art evaluation algorithms because it contains both nested counters and large counter values.

The MPEG7 expression is extremely challenging for (incNFA) because it translates into an NFA with about 850K states. As we can see from the third graph in Fig 5, incremental NFA evaluation for very short words (10 symbols) is already extremely slow. This is strongly contrasted by incremental NFA$^{\#}$ evaluation, which still evaluates incrementally in 0.08 milliseconds for words of length one million. We also say a huge difference in memory consumption: 5 orders of magnitude already for words of length 50.

Real-world, CHAIN Expressions. This final experiment is designed to capture the behavior of CHAIN-like ex-

[14]http://standards.iso.org/ittf/PubliclyAvailableStandards/MPEG-7_schema_files/mpeg7-v2.xsd

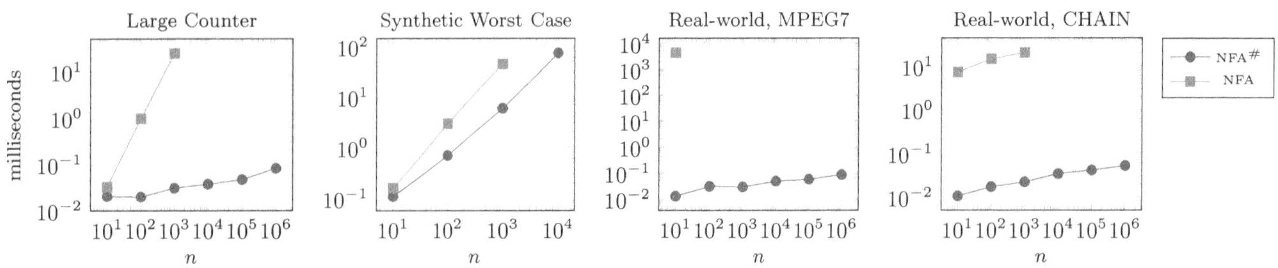

Figure 5: Incremental evaluation (Log-log scale).

pressions which we abundantly found in our practical study (Section 3). The experiment is extremely simple: we consider a fixed regular expression $a^{0,1000}$ (which we also found in our practical study) and incrementally evaluate with respect to words of increasing length n. We experimented with various and more complex forms of CHAIN expressions from our corpus, containing more disjunctions, more concatenations of disjunctions, larger alphabets, but we observed the same behavior in all cases. All experiments for CHAIN-like expressions boil down to this case. Again, as we can see the rightmost graph in Fig. 5, the evaluation algorithms based on NFA$^{\#}$s scale much better than those based on NFAs.

7. CONCLUSION

This paper shows that large counter values in regular expressions do not necessarily imply slow processing. Indeed, while regular expressions with counting often imply high complexity for static analysis problems due to their succinctness [12], it seems that the same succinctness can be exploited for designing highly efficient evaluation algorithms.

In the future, we want to extend the algorithm so that it works for full-fledged XML Schemas, make a more extensive study of regular expressions in Schemas and perhaps even in more general contexts, and look more closely at how to adapt the algorithms towards path expressions on graphs.

8. REFERENCES

[1] A. Andersson. Balanced search trees made simple. In *WADS*, pages 60–71, 1993.

[2] A. Balmin, Y. Papakonstantinou, and V. Vianu. Incremental validation of XML documents. *ACM TODS*, 29(4):710–751, 2004.

[3] D. Barbosa, A.O. Mendelzon, L. Libkin, L. Mignet, and M. Arenas. Efficient incremental validation of XML documents. In *ICDE*, pages 671–682, 2004.

[4] M. Becchi and P. Crowley. Efficient regular expression evaluation: theory to practice. In *ANCS*, pages 50–59, 2008.

[5] M. Becchi and P. Crowley. A-DFA: A time- and space-efficient DFA compression algorithm for fast regular expression evaluation. *ACM TACO*, 10(1), 2013.

[6] G.J. Bex, F. Neven, and J. Van den Bussche. DTDs versus XML schema: a practical study. In *WebDB*, pages 79–84, 2004.

[7] H. Björklund, W. Gelade, and W. Martens. Incremental XPath evaluation. *ACM TODS*, 35(4):29, 2010.

[8] R. Book, S. Even, S. Greibach, and G. Ott. Ambiguity in graphs and expressions. *IEEE Trans. Comput*, C-20(2):149–153, 1971.

[9] S. Dal-Zilio and D. Lugiez. XML schema, tree logic and sheaves automata. In *RTA*, pages 246–263, 2003.

[10] S. Gao, C.M. Sperberg-McQueen, and H. S. Thompson. W3C XML schema definition language (XSD) 1.1 part 1: Structures. Technical report, World Wide Web Consortium, April 2012.

[11] W. Gelade, M. Gyssens, and W. Martens. Regular expressions with counting: Weak versus strong determinism. *SIAM J. Comput.*, 41(1):160–190, 2012.

[12] W. Gelade, W. Martens, and F. Neven. Optimizing schema languages for XML: Numerical constraints and interleaving. *SIAM J. Comput.*, 38(5):2021–2043, 2009.

[13] G. Ghelli, D. Colazzo, and C. Sartiani. Linear Time Membership in a Class of Regular Expressions with Interleaving and Counting. In *CIKM*, 2008.

[14] V.M. Glushkov. The abstract theory of automata. *Russian Math. Surveys*, 16:1–53, 1961.

[15] Google custom search. www.google.com/cse.

[16] S. Harris and A. Seaborne. SPARQL 1.1 query language. Technical report, World Wide Web Consortium, January 2012. http://www.w3.org/TR/2012/WD-sparql11-query-20120105.

[17] D. Hovland. Regular expressions with numerical constraints and automata with counters. In *ICTAC*, pages 231–245, 2009.

[18] P. Kilpeläinen and R. Tuhkanen. Regular expressions with numerical occurrence indicators — preliminary results. In *SPLST*, pages 163–173, 2003.

[19] P. Kilpeläinen and R. Tuhkanen. Towards efficient implementation of XML schema content models. In *ACM DOCENG*, pages 239–241, 2004.

[20] K. Losemann and W. Martens. The complexity of regular expressions and property paths in SPARQL. *ACM TODS*, 2013.

[21] W. Martens, F. Neven, and T. Schwentick. Complexity of decision problems for XML schemas and chain regular expressions. *Siam J. Comp.*, 39(4):1486–1530, 2009.

[22] W. Martens, F. Neven, and S. Vansummeren. SCULPT: A schema language for tabular data on the Web. In *WWW Conference*, pages 702–712, 2015.

[23] K. Nakayama, K. Yamaguchi, and S. Kawai. $\mathcal{I}$-regular Expression: Regular Expressions with continuous interval constraints. In *CIKM*, 1997.

[24] Neo4J. Cypher patterns. http://docs.neo4j.org/chunked/stable/introduction-pattern.html, 2014. Cypher Query Language, Section 8.8.

[25] S. Patnaik and N. Immerman. Dyn-FO: A parallel, dynamic complexity class. *JCSS*, 55(2):199–209, 1997.

[26] Regexlib. www.regexlib.com.

[27] R. Smith, C. Estan, S. Jha, and S. Kong. Deflating the big bang: Fast and scalable deep packet inspection with extended finite automata. In *SIGCOMM*, pages 207–218, 2008.

[28] Snort. www.snort.org.

[29] C.M. Sperberg-McQueen. Notes on finite state automata with counters. http://www.w3.org/XML/2004/05/msm-cfa.html, 2004.

Struggling and Success in Web Search

Daan Odijk
University of Amsterdam
Amsterdam, The Netherlands
d.odijk@uva.nl

Ryen W. White,
Ahmed Hassan Awadallah,
Susan T. Dumais
Microsoft Research, Redmond, WA, USA
{ryenw,hassanam,sdumais}@microsoft.com

ABSTRACT

Web searchers sometimes struggle to find relevant information. Struggling leads to frustrating and dissatisfying search experiences, even if searchers ultimately meet their search objectives. Better understanding of search tasks where people struggle is important in improving search systems. We address this important issue using a mixed methods study using large-scale logs, crowd-sourced labeling, and predictive modeling. We analyze anonymized search logs from the Microsoft Bing Web search engine to characterize aspects of struggling searches and better explain the relationship between struggling and search success. To broaden our understanding of the struggling process beyond the behavioral signals in log data, we develop and utilize a crowd-sourced labeling methodology. We collect third-party judgments about why searchers appear to struggle and, if appropriate, where in the search task it became clear to the judges that searches would succeed (i.e., the pivotal query). We use our findings to propose ways in which systems can help searchers reduce struggling. Key components of such support are algorithms that accurately predict the nature of future actions and their anticipated impact on search outcomes. Our findings have implications for the design of search systems that help searchers struggle less and succeed more.

Categories and Subject Descriptors

H.3.3 [**Information Search and Retrieval**]: Information Storage and Retrieval: *search process, selection process.*

Keywords

Information retrieval; Struggling

1. INTRODUCTION

When searchers experience difficulty in finding information, their struggle may be apparent in search behaviors such as issuing numerous search queries or visiting many results within a search session [5]. Such long sessions are prevalent and time consuming (e.g., around half of Web search sessions contain multiple queries [37]). Long sessions occur when searchers are exploring or learning a new area, or when they are struggling to find relevant information [31, 43]. Methods have recently been developed to distinguish between struggling and exploring in long sessions using only behavioral signals [20]. However, little attention has been paid to *how* and *why* searchers struggle. This is particularly important since struggling is prevalent in long tasks, e.g., Hassan et al. [20] found that in 60% of long sessions, searchers' actions suggested that they were struggling.

Permission to make digital or hard copies of all or part of this work for personal or classroom use is granted without fee provided that copies are not made or distributed for profit or commercial advantage and that copies bear this notice and the full citation on the first page. Copyrights for components of this work owned by others than the author(s) must be honored. Abstracting with credit is permitted. To copy otherwise, or republish, to post on servers or to redistribute to lists, requires prior specific permission and/or a fee. Request permissions from Permissions@acm.org.
CIKM'15, October 19–23, 2015, Melbourne, Australia.
Copyright is held by the owner/author(s). Publication rights licensed to ACM.
ACM 978-1-4503-3794-6/15/10 ...$15.00.
DOI: http://dx.doi.org/10.1145/2806416.2806488.

Before proceeding, let us present an example of a struggling task. Figure 1 presents a session in which a searcher is interested in watching live streaming video of the U.S. Open golf tournament.

9:13:11 AM	**Query**	us open
9:13:24 AM	**Query**	us open golf
9:13:36 AM	**Query**	us open golf 2013 live
9:13:59 AM	**Query**	watch us open live streaming
9:14:02 AM	**Click**	http://inquisitr.com/1300340/watch-2014-u-s-open-live-online-final-round-free-streaming-video
9:31:55 AM	**END**	

Figure 1: Example of a *struggling* task from June 2014.

The first two queries yield generic results about U.S. Open sporting events and the specific tournament. The third query might have provided the correct results but it included the previous year rather than the current year. At this stage, the searcher appears to be struggling. The fourth query is the so-called *pivotal query* where the searcher drops the year and adds the terms "watch" and "streaming". This decision to add these terms alters the course of the search task and leads to a seemingly successful outcome (a click on a page that serves the streaming content sought). Understanding transitions between queries in a struggling session (e.g., the addition of "golf" and the wrong year), and transitions between struggling and successful queries (e.g., the addition of terminology pertaining to the desired action and content), can inform the development of strategies and algorithms to help reduce struggling.

Related research has targeted key aspects of the search process such as satisfaction, frustration, and search success, using a variety of experimental methods, including laboratory studies [5, 12], search log analysis [17], in-situ explicit feedback from searchers [13], and crowd-sourced games [2]. Such studies are valuable in understanding these important concepts, and yield insights that can directly improve search systems and their evaluation. However, they do not offer insights into how people who initially struggle, in some cases, ultimately succeed. Such insights can have value to both searchers and search providers in detecting problems and designing systems that mitigate them. We address these shortcomings with the search described in this paper.

We make the following specific contributions:

- We use large-scale search log analysis to characterize aspects of struggling search tasks and to understand how some tasks result in success, while others result in failure.
- We propose and apply a crowd-sourced labeling methodology to better understand the nature of the struggling process (beyond the behavioral signals present in log data), focusing on why searchers struggled and where it became clear that their search task would succeed (i.e., the pivotal query).
- We develop a classifier to predict query reformulation strategies during struggling search tasks. We show that we can accurately classify query reformulations according to an intent-based schema that can help select among different system actions. We also show that we can accurately identify pivotal (turning point) queries within search tasks in which searchers are struggling.
- We propose some application scenarios in which such a classifier, and insights from our characterization of struggling more broadly, could help searchers struggle less.

The remainder of this paper is structured as follows. Section 2 describes related work in areas such as satisfaction, success, and query reformulation. Section 3 characterizes struggling based on our analysis of large-scale search log data. In Section 4, we describe our crowd-sourced annotation experiment and the results of the analysis. Section 5 describes predictive models and associated experiments (namely, predicting query transitions and identifying the pivotal query), and the evaluation results. In Section 6 we discuss our findings, their implications and limitations, and conclude.

2. RELATED WORK

Characterizing the behavior of searchers has been subject of study from different perspectives using a range experimental methods. Of particular interest to our research is the extensive body of work on (i) satisfaction and search success, (ii) searcher frustration and difficulty, and (iii) query reformulation and refinement.

Satisfaction and Success. The concepts of satisfaction and search success are related, but they are not equivalent. Success is a measure of goal completion and searchers can complete their goals even when they are struggling to meet them [17]. Satisfaction is a more general term that not only takes goal completion into consideration, but also effort and more subjective aspects of the search experience such as searcher's prior expectation [23]. Satisfaction has been studied extensively in a number of areas such as psychology [30] and commerce [33]. Within search, satisfaction and success can be framed in terms of search system evaluation, essential in developing better search technologies. Kelly [25] comprehensively summarizes different methods for evaluating search systems with searchers.

On a session level, Huffman and Hochster [22] found a strong correlation between session satisfaction and the relevance of the first three results for the first query, the number of events and whether the information need was navigational. Hassan et al. [17] showed that it is possible to predict session success in a model that is independent of result relevance. Jiang et al. [23] found that it is necessary and possible to predict subtle changes in session satisfaction using graded search satisfaction. Most prior studies regard search tasks or sessions as the basic modeling unit, from which holistic measures (e.g., total dwell time [44]) can be computed. Beyond tasks and sessions, interest has also grown in modeling satisfaction associated with specific searcher actions [26, 39]. These estimates can then be applied to improve rankings for future searchers [19]. Insights into satisfaction and success are used to predict satisfaction for individual queries [13, 18] and for sessions [17, 22, 23].

Frustration and Difficulty. Related to satisfaction are other key aspects of the search process such as task difficulty and searcher frustration. These have been studied using a variety of experimental methods, including log analysis [20], laboratory studies [5, 12], and crowd-sourced games [2]. Feild et al. [12] found that when given difficult information seeking tasks, half of all queries submitted by searchers resulted in self-reported frustration. Ageev et al. [2] provided crowd-workers with tasks of different levels of difficulty and found that more successful searchers issue more queries, view more pages, and browse deeper in the result pages. When searchers experience difficulty in finding information, their struggle may be apparent in search behaviors such as issuing numerous search queries, more diverse queries or visiting many results within a search session [5]. However, rather than struggling, these longer sessions can be indicative of searchers exploring and learning [10, 43]. Hassan et al. [20] have recently developed methods to distinguish between struggling and exploring in long sessions using only behavioral signals. They found that searchers struggled in 60% of long sessions. Scaria et al. [36] examined differences between successful and abandoned navigational paths using data from a Wikipedia-based human computation game. They compared successful and abandoned navigation paths, to understand the types of behavior that suggest people will abandon their navigation task. They also constructed predictive models to determine whether people will complete their task successfully and whether the next click will be a back click (suggesting a lack of progress on the current path). The terminal click has also been used in other studies of search to better understand searchers' information goals [9] or point people to resources that may be useful to other searchers [40]. In this paper, we focus on struggling tasks (that are thus likely to be unsatisfactory) to understand how some of them end up successful while others end up unsuccessful. We target traditional Web search in this study given its prevalence. Recently, others have studied struggling and success in the context of engagement with intelligent assistants [23].

These studies and those on searcher satisfaction are valuable in understanding these important concepts, and yield insights and signals that can directly improve search systems and their evaluation [19]. They provide important clues on what searchers might do next, such as switching to a different search engine [15, 41] or turning to a community question answering service [29]. Ideally, a search engine would interpret these signals of struggling and frustration to provide personalized hints to help the searcher succeed. These hints can be learned from more successful and advanced users [2, 42] or provide examples that are may work generically for some search intents, such as leading searchers to longer queries [1]. Moraveji et al. [32] showed that the presentation of optimal search tips, where they are presented for a task where they are known to have benefit, can have a lasting impact on searcher efficiency. Savenkov and Agichtein [35] showed that providing a searcher with task-specific hints improves both success and satisfaction. Conversely, generic hints decrease both success and satisfaction, indicating that it is paramount to understand what a searcher is struggling with before providing hints.

Query Reformulation and Refinement. More detailed insight on searcher behavior can be found by analyzing query reformulations. Query reformulation is the act of modifying the previous query in a session (adding, removing, or replacing search terms) with the objective of obtaining a new set of results [18]. For this, a number of related taxonomies have been proposed [3, 14, 21, 27, 38]. Huang and Efthimiadis [21] surveyed query reformulation taxonomies and provided a mapping between these and their own approach. While they provide interesting insight into searchers trying to articulate their information needs, these approaches all focus on superficial lexical aspects of reformulation. Anick [3] examined usage and effectiveness of terminological feedback in the AltaVista search engine. No difference in session success was found between those using the feedback and those not using it, but those using it did continue to employ it effectively on an ongoing basis. A number of recent studies have shown that search tasks provide rich context for performing log-based query suggestion [11, 24, 28], underscoring the importance of studying query reformulation in search tasks.

Contributions over previous work. No previous study examines how searchers struggle and what makes them ultimately succeed. We employ large-scale log analysis and a crowd-sourced labeling methodology to provide new insight into the nature of struggling and what contributes to their success. Based on this, we propose a new taxonomy for intent-based query reformulation that goes beyond the superficial lexical analysis commonly applied in the analysis of query transitions (see [21]). Building on our characterization, we propose predictive models of key aspects of the struggling process, such as the nature of observed query reformulations and the prediction of the pivotal query. Based on insights gleaned from our data analysis, we also provide some examples of the types of support that search systems could offer to help reduce struggling.

3. CHARACTERIZING STRUGGLING

We apply large-scale search behavioral analysis to characterize aspects of struggling search tasks and to understand how some of these searches end up successful while others end up unsuccessful.

3.1 Definitions

We focus on a particular type of search task that exhibits search behavior suggestive of struggling. We assume a broad view of struggling behavior and apply the following definitions:

Struggling describes a situation whereby a searcher experiences difficulty in finding the information that they seek. Note that in this definition they may or may not eventually locate the target of their search [20].

Sessions are a sequence of search interactions demarcated based on a 30-minute user inactivity timeout [9, 42].

Tasks are defined as topically-coherent sub-sessions, i.e., sequences of search activity within sessions that share a common subject area [20]. We follow the approach of [20] and assume that two queries belong to the same task if they are less than ten minutes apart and the queries match one of the following conditions: (i) share at least one non-stop word term, or (ii) share at least one top ten search result or domain name (where popular domains such as wikipedia.org are excluded).

Struggling tasks describe topically coherent sub-sessions in which searchers cannot immediately find sought information.

Quick-back clicks describe result clicks with a dwell time of less than ten seconds [26].

Since we cannot infer that searchers experience difficulty from a single query, we consider only longer struggling tasks in our analysis. Our aim is to obtain a broad understanding of struggling search behavior in natural settings. To do this, we study search tasks where struggling is very apparent. Intuitively, when a searcher cannot locate the information they are seeking, they are much less likely to click search results and examine landing pages. We focus on tasks where a searcher does not examine any of the search results for the first two queries in detail. This includes queries that do not receive any clicks as well as queries with clicks that result in only very short dwell time on the landing page. We use a dwell time of less than 10 seconds to identify these quick-back clicks.

3.2 Mining Struggling Tasks

To better understand struggling search behavior in a natural setting, we analyze millions of search sessions from the Microsoft Bing Web search engine. We select these sessions from the interaction log of Bing for the first seven days of June 2014. All logged interaction data (i.e., queries and clicked search results) are grouped based on a unique user identifier and segmented into sessions. We mine struggling tasks from all sessions using the following steps:

1. **Filter sessions:** We included only search sessions originating from the United States English language locale (en-US), and excluded internal traffic and secure traffic (https). Furthermore, we only considered sessions that started with a typed query (and not with a click on a query suggestion).
2. **Segment sessions into tasks:** Using a time-based segmentation can lead to combining multiple unrelated tasks into a single session. We therefore further refine sessions into topically coherent sub-sessions that cover a single task.
3. **Filter struggling tasks:** From these tasks, we select those with at least three queries where the first two lead to either no clicks or only quick-back clicks.
4. **Partition based on final click:** Lastly, we partition the struggling tasks based on searcher interaction for the last query in the task. Although we cannot directly infer whether the searcher successfully fulfilled their information need, search activity for terminal queries has been shown to be a reasonable proxy for success [13, 17]. We validate this predictor using crowd-sourced annotations in Section 4. More specifically, we partition the tasks into three sets:
   (a) **Unsuccessful:** If a searcher does not click on any result for the final query or when their only clicks are quick-back clicks (less than 10 seconds), we assume the searcher was unsuccessful and abandoned their search task without satisfying their need.
   (b) **Successful:** If a searcher clicks on a search results and we observe no interaction for at least 30 seconds, we assume the searcher was successful. Note that this includes tasks in which the searcher does not return at all to the result page before the session times out.
   (c) **Other:** All other tasks have clicks where searchers examine landing pages between 10 and 30 seconds. Based on previous research [13], we consider these task outcomes to be ambiguous and exclude them.

Following these steps, we obtain two sets of tasks that differ only based on the interaction with the terminal query. The combined dataset contains nearly 7.5 million struggling tasks. We now describe characteristics of these tasks to provide insight into struggling behavior, seeking to understand how some searches result in success, while others are unsuccessful. We begin with struggling tasks, and then consider queries and query reformulations.

3.3 Task Characteristics

Of the struggling tasks in our set, approximately 40% are successful per our definition. Around half of the tasks comprised three queries and successful tasks were slightly shorter than their unsuccessful counterparts. Focusing on the relationship between task duration and task outcome, Figure 2 shows the percentage of struggling tasks that were continued after a specified number of queries. We observe from the figure that the percentage of tasks that are continued increases with the number of queries already issued (i.e., the likelihood of a re-query increases with each successive query). Unsuccessful tasks are continued more frequently than successful tasks. There are many

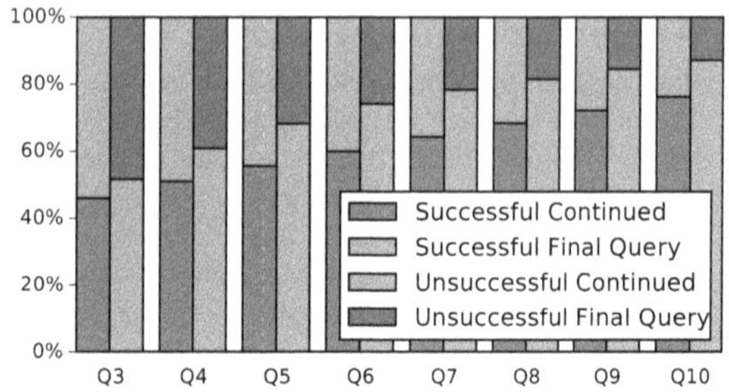

Figure 2: Percentage of successful and unsuccessful struggling tasks continued (onto another query) or completed (task terminates) after the third query (Q3) until the tenth query (Q10).

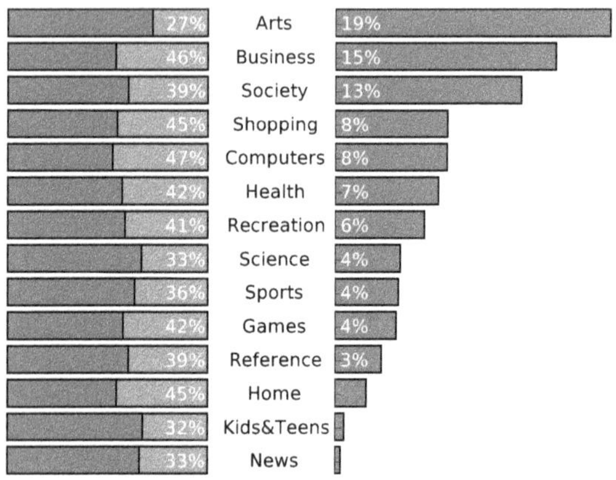

Figure 3: Prevalence of top-level ODP categories in all analyzed tasks (right) and proportion of successful and unsuccessful struggling tasks for that category (left).

important factors, such as searcher tenacity and sunk cost, that may explain more of a reluctance to abandon unsuccessful tasks.

For some topics, searchers experience more difficulty in finding what they are looking for than for others. For example, Hassan et al. [20] reported that exploratory behavior is more than twice as likely as struggling behavior when shopping for clothing compared to downloading software. To obtain greater insight on the relationship between search topics on struggling behavior, we analyze the top 10 search results returned to searchers. We classify each document in the search results using the top-level categories of the Open Directory Project (ODP). For this we use an automatic content-based classifier [6]. We assign the most frequently-occurring topic across all queries in a task as the topic of that task. Figure 3 shows the prevalence of topics in struggling tasks. The proportion of successful tasks ranges from 47% in Computers to 27% in Arts, which is also the most prevalent topic. Next, we analyze the changes within a task by considering characteristics at different stages.

3.4 Query Characteristics

Since we have tasks of different length, we can only directly compare tasks of the same length or align queries in tasks of different length. To analyze the development over the broadest set of tasks, we consider the first and last query in the search task, and collapse all intermediate queries.

Query Length: We observe that the first query in both successful and unsuccessful tasks is typically short (3.35 and 3.23 terms respectively on average). Intermediate queries are typically longer, averaging 4.29 and 4.04 terms respectively. The final queries are also longer, averaging 4.29 and 3.93 terms respectively. Increased success associated with longer queries has motivated methods to encourage searchers to issue queries with more terms [1].

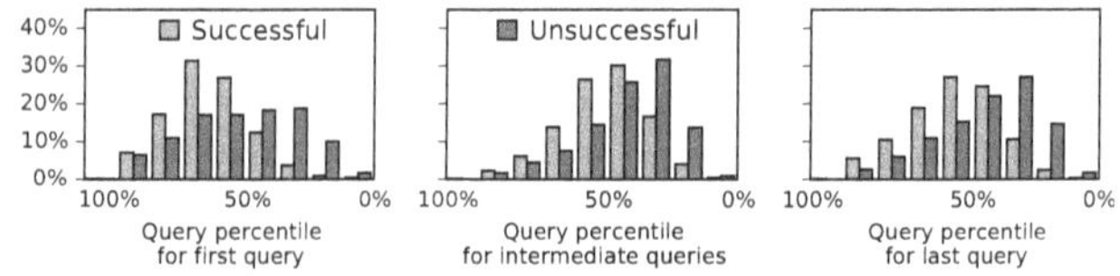

Figure 4: Query percentile. Larger percentile = more frequent.

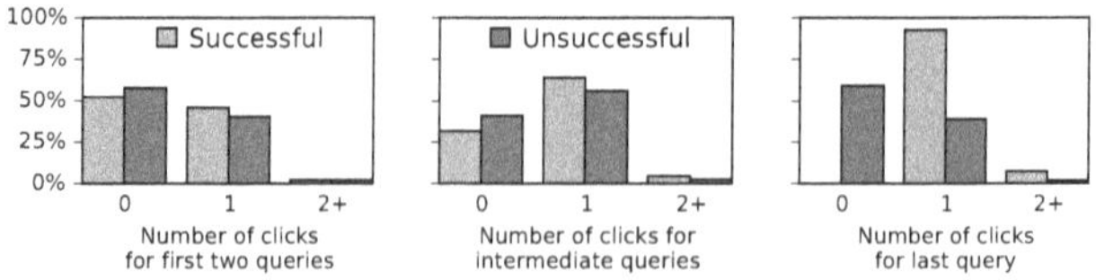

Figure 5: Number of result clicks at different queries.

Query Frequency: For all queries in our dataset we compute the frequency of that query during the previous month. Figure 4 shows the percentile of a query, based on how often the query was issued in the previous month. Queries tend to become less common as the task progresses (distributions shift to the right in each plot). The first query is different than the ones that follow. For successful outcomes, the first query is more common than the successive queries, and more common than the first query for unsuccessful outcomes. This could suggest two different causes for struggling on the first query: (i) if it is common, it may be general and ambiguous, and (ii) if it is uncommon, it might be overly specified.

3.5 Interaction Characteristics

Next, we turn to the interaction within a task. We follow a similar query grouping approach as in Section 3.4, using the position in the task. Since we select struggling tasks based on limited interaction on the first two queries, we separate those from the others. We now have three groups: first and second query, last query and all other intermediate queries. Note that we have no intermediate queries for tasks of only three queries (about half of the tasks). Figure 5 shows the change in the number of clicks in successful and unsuccessful tasks. We observe that for the first and second query, just over 40% of the tasks have a quick-back click. By our definition of struggling task, all clicks for the first two queries were quick-back clicks.

As described in Section 3, we used the clicks on the search results of the final query to partition our dataset into successful and unsuccessful tasks. We observe in Figure 5 that indeed the final query for all successful tasks has at least one click. The characteristics for the final query in the unsuccessful tasks is very similar to the first two queries (that are selected in the same way). When comparing the successful and unsuccessful tasks up to the final query, we observe that queries without clicks are more common in unsuccessful tasks.

Figure 6a shows the time between queries and Figure 6b shows the dwell time (i.e., the time spent on a landing page after a click). Considering the successful tasks, we see the time between queries increases as the task progresses, mostly due to an increase in dwell time. Interestingly, the pattern for unsuccessful struggling tasks is different. We observe less time between queries mid-task perhaps due to fewer clicks (Figure 5) and more quick-back clicks.

3.6 Query Reformulation

To better understand the change in queries within a task, we analyze how the text of a query is refined over time. We classify each query reformulation into one of six types, described in Table 1. We use the algorithm presented in [16] which builds an automatic classifier for a subset of the query reformulation types presented in [21].

Figure 7 shows the distribution over query reformulation types. The most common type of query reformulation is specialization, i.e., adding a term. This is most likely to occur directly after the first query, when it accounts for almost half of all query reformulations

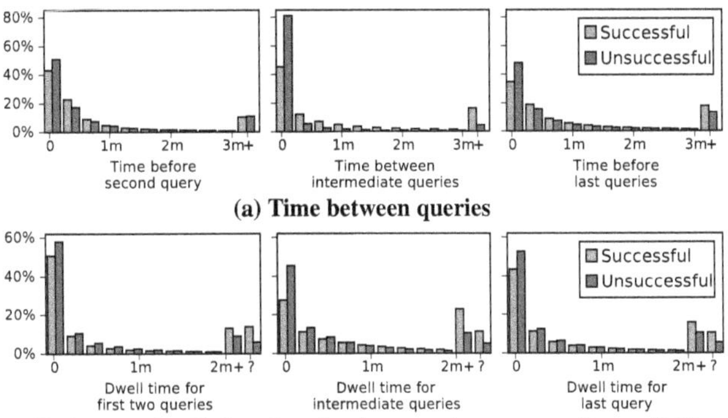

(a) Time between queries

(b) Average dwell time (i.e., the time spent on a page after a click)

Figure 6: Time between queries and spent on a clicked page.

Table 1: Lexical-based query reformulation types.

Type	Description
New	Shares no terms with previous queries.
Back	Exact repeat of a previous query in the task.
Spelling	Changed the spelling, e.g. fixing a typo.
Substitution	Replaced a single term with another term.
Generalization	Removed a term from the query.
Specialization	Added a term to the query.

in successful tasks and a bit less in unsuccessful tasks. Substitutions and generalizations (removing a term) are the next most common reformulations. These query reformulation types are substantially less likely for the first query reformulation and more likely in the middle. Around 10% of the query reformulations are spelling corrections and an equal percentage entirely new queries. Spelling reformulations are most likely directly after the first query. New queries are most likely as second query and, surprisingly, as the last query. Others have observed similar patterns, e.g., Aula et al. [5] showed that searchers try many distinct queries toward the end of difficult search tasks. Lastly, revisiting a prior query is rare and is more likely in the middle of the task than at the final query.

One could argue that of these query reformulation types a specialization is most informative, since it defines an information need in greater detail. This is the most common type and substantially more common in successful tasks (39% of reformulations) than in unsuccessful tasks (30%). For these unsuccessful tasks, almost all other query reformulation types are more common. With more substitutions, spelling corrections, completely new queries and returning to previous queries, it appears that searchers in the unsuccessful tasks experience more difficulty selecting the correct query vocabulary.

Inspired by Lau and Horvitz [27], we examined the temporal dynamics of the query reformulations in addition to their nature. Figure 8 shows the likelihood of observing a particular reformulation type given the time that has elapsed since the previous query. If a new query is issued within seconds after the previous, it is most likely to be a substitution or a spelling change. In fact, a spelling change is unlikely to occur after more than about fifteen seconds.

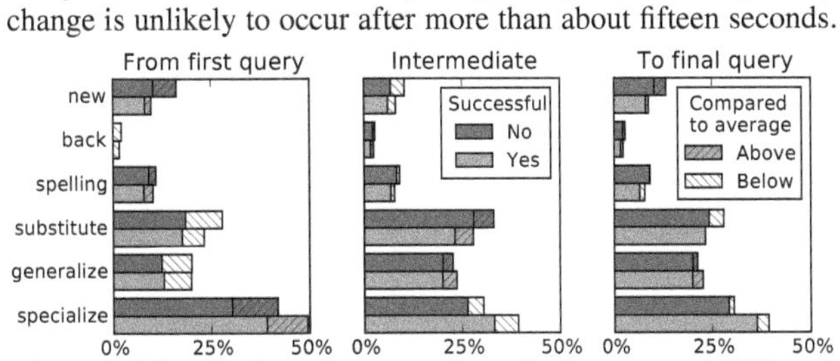

Figure 7: Distribution of query reformulation types at different stages of the search task for successful/unsuccessful tasks.

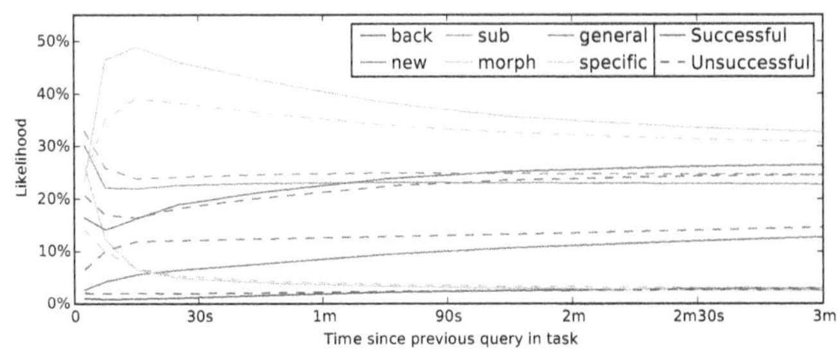

Figure 8: Likelihood of observing a query reformulation type in successful/unsuccessful tasks, given time since last query.

After a few seconds, the most likely type of reformulation is a specialization, with a peak at around fifteen seconds, where nearly half of the queries are expected to be reformulations. After this, some of the likelihood mass is taken over by generalizations and completely new queries. The likelihood per query reformulation type for successful vs. unsuccessful tasks appears similar, except for an increased likelihood of new queries for unsuccessful tasks, accompanied by a decreased likelihood of specialization. Anchoring on previous queries can harm retrieval performance [7]. The increase in new queries may represent an attempt to reset the query stream for the current task. Temporal dynamics such as these are interesting and may prove to be useful signals for the reformulation strategy prediction task described later in the paper.

3.7 Summary

In the analysis in this section, we have shown there are significant differences in how struggling searchers behave given different outcomes. These differences encompass many aspects of the search process, including queries, query reformulations, result click behavior, landing page dwell time, and the nature of the search topic. Given these intriguing differences, we employ a crowd-sourcing methodology to better understand struggling search tasks and the connection between struggling and task outcomes.

4. CROWD-SOURCED ANNOTATIONS

We performed a series of detailed crowd-sourced annotations to obtain a better understanding of what struggling searchers experience. This is also important in validating the assumptions made in the log-based estimation of search success from the previous section. Informed by an initial exploratory pilot with open ended questions on a task level, we annotate tasks on a per-query basis.

To obtain a representative and interesting sample of tasks (and importantly, to also control for task effects), we group the tasks described in Section 3 based on the first query in the task. Recall that these tasks are all struggling tasks, either successful or unsuccessful. For each initial query, we count the number of successful and unsuccessful tasks. We then filter these queries to have an approximately equal number of successful and unsuccessful tasks (between 45% and 55%).

Upon inspection of the selected tasks, we noticed a small set were unsuitable for annotation. To this end, we exclude initial queries that were deemed too ambiguous, are navigational in nature, or show many off-topic follow up queries. We randomly sample from these initial queries and verify whether they meet our criteria until we manually selected 35 initial queries for deeper analysis in an exploratory pilot study.

4.1 Exploratory Pilot

For each of the 35 initial queries, we generate five task pairs, by randomly sampling a successful task and an unsuccessful task that both start with that initial query. These 175 task pairs are annotated

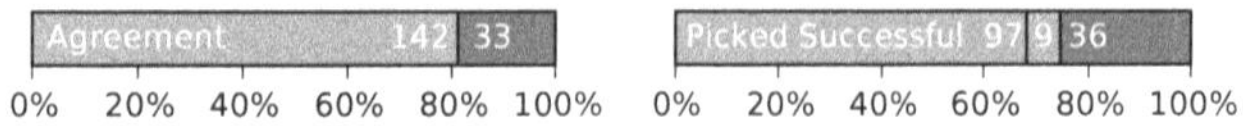

(a) Agreement (b) Distinguishable

Figure 9: (a) Agreement and (b) Distribution of task outcomes of the distinguishable (majority agreement) tasks.

for struggling and success by three judges. We recruited a total of 88 judges from Clickworker.com, a crowd-sourcing service providing access to human annotators under contract to Microsoft and others. We created an interactive judgment interface that displays the search activity (queries and clicks) associated with two paired tasks side-by-side, in random order. To validate whether the activity on the terminal query is a reasonable proxy for success, we asked judges in which of the two tasks they believe the searcher was more successful using three options (one of the two sessions was more successful or they where indistinguishable). We have agreement by majority vote (i.e., at least two of the three judges agreed) for 81% of the pairs (Figure 9a). If there is a majority, the successful task is picked for 68.4% of the pairs and the unsuccessful struggling task for 25.4% of the pairs, while in 6.3% of the cases it is agreed that the tasks are indistinguishable (Figure 9b). These findings suggest that the judgment task is tractable and that tasks we labeled as successful automatically are indeed more often deemed successful by our judges.

We first considered on the search activity connected to the task in which the judge believed the searcher was more successful in more detail. We informed the judge that we believed that the searcher started off struggling with their search, and asked them to look in detail at the task and answer a number of open-ended questions, starting with:

- Could you describe how the user in this session eventually succeeded in becoming successful? *Describe what made the user pull through. Note that this could be multiple things, for example: both fixing a typo and adding a specific location.*

We then considered the task in which the searcher was less successful and asked the judge to look in detail at that task and answer:

- Why was the user in this session struggling to find the information they were looking for? *Describe what you think made the user have trouble locating the information they were looking for. Note that this could be multiple things, for example: looking for a hard to find piece of information and not knowing the right words to describe what they are looking for.*
- What might you do differently if you were the user in this session? *Describe how you would have proceeded to locate the information they were looking for. Note that this could be multiple things, for example: using different terms (please specify) and eventually ask a friend for help.*

The answers to the questions provided diverse explanations for why searchers were struggling and what (could have) made them pull through. The answer typically described specific changes from one query to the other. Some of the explanations were topic-specific (e.g., suggesting a particular synonym for a query term) and some were quite generic (e.g., a suggestion to expand an acronym). We observed from these answers that the main reasons and remedies for struggling are not very well captured by the query reformulation types that are typically used, including the ones we described in Table 1. We adapted our main annotation efforts accordingly.

4.2 Annotations

The exploratory pilot suggested that third-party judges agree on labeling the success or failure of search tasks (especially in the positive case, where it may be more clear that searchers have met their information goals), and provided diverse clues on how and why searchers are struggling in a task. We now dive deeper into specific queries and what searchers did to remedy struggling.

Table 2: Intent-based taxonomy presented to judges for each query transition, multiple response options could be selected.

Added, removed or substituted	☐ an **action** (e.g., download, contact) ☐ an **attribute** (e.g., printable, free,), specifically (if applicable): ☐ a **location** (or destination or route) ☐ a **time** (e.g., today, 2014, recent) ☐ **demographics** (e.g., male, toddlers)
Specified	☐ a **particular instance** (e.g. added a brand name or version number)
Rephrased	☐ Corrected a spelling error or **typo** ☐ Used a **synonym** or related term
Switched	☐ to a **related** task (changed main focus) ☐ to a **new** task

In our main annotation efforts, we consider how a searcher reformulates queries within a task. Based on the open question answers of the exploratory annotation pilot, we propose a new taxonomy of query reformulation strategies (depicted in Table 2). In contrast to the lexical reformulation taxonomy in Table 1, this new taxonomy captures the intent of a query reformulation. Rather than simply observing that a term was substituted, we want to know if this is a related term to the one replaced or if it is a specification of an instance (e.g., refining [microsoft windows] to [windows 8]).

We hypothesize that there is a point during a struggling search task where searchers switch from struggling with little progress to making progress toward task completion (i.e., the so-called *pivotal* query). This could be associated with many factors, including the receipt of new information from an external source such as a search result or snippet. Understanding the pivotal query can provide valuable insight into what enabled the searcher pull through and is an important starting point when finding means to support searchers who are struggling. We ask judges to select the point in the task where they believe the searcher switched from struggling to being successful in finding what they were looking for. Judges could select either a query or a clicked URL in a task presented as shown in Figure 1. Judges could reissue the query to Bing and inspect the clicked pages that the original (logged) searcher selected. Furthermore, the crowd-workers were asked to judge how successful they think the searcher was in the task on a four-point scale: *not at all, somewhat, mostly, completely*. For annotation, we selected two separate, but closely-related sets of tasks. The first is based on the dataset from the exploratory pilot. We exclude six initial queries from the set that showed low agreement on picking the most successful task. For each of the 29 remaining initial queries, we sampled ten new successful tasks that started with that query. In a second set, we sampled 369 successful tasks with any initial query (as a control). This results in a total of 659 tasks.

4.3 Annotation Results

Each task was judged by three human annotators via an interactive interface. This results in a total of 1,977 annotations for 659 tasks. We removed the annotations of three of the 111 judges (80 annotations in total), because their responses were unrealistically quick. On average, judges spent 37 seconds to familiarize with a task and to judge the success and pick the pivotal query. Subsequently, they spent twelve seconds on average to judge each query transitions (at least two per task, depending on the number of queries).

Figure 10: Judgments for the success of tasks.

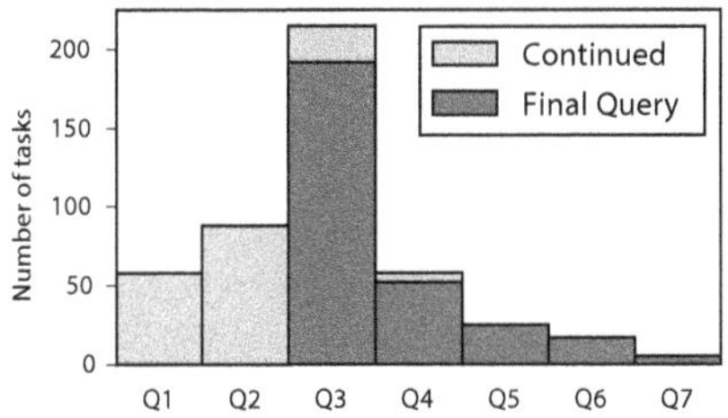

Figure 11: Pivotal query within a task, i.e. where the searcher appeared to switch from struggling to making progress.

Judges show 67% majority agreement on the task of judging the success of a searcher on a four-point scale. Krippendorff's α measures 0.33, signaling fair agreement [4] between three judges. For judging what query is the pivotal query, we observe a 71% majority agreement for choosing one out of three or more queries ($\alpha = 0.44$, signaling moderate agreement between three judges). This demonstrate that third-party labeling is feasible but also challenging given the subjectivity of the labeling task. We deem this satisfactory for our purposes and consider only annotations with majority agreement in the remainder of this section.

Figure 10 illustrates the distribution of success judgments. We selected these tasks assuming that the searcher was struggling, but somewhat successful. We observe that in these tasks searchers are deemed to be at least mostly successful (79%), with only eight tasks (1.8%) not successful at all. This suggests that almost all studied searchers make at least some progress toward completing the task, even though they struggled along the way. We asked judges to consider the tasks carefully and select the pivotal query where searchers appeared to switch from struggling to succeeding. Figure 11 shows the distribution of positions of this pivotal query across the search task. In 62% of tasks, the pivotal query represents the final query in the task.

Query transitions. Judges were asked to examine each sequential pair of queries, while added and removed terms were highlighted. We asked judges to characterize the transition between these two queries by selecting one or more applicable options from the taxonomy. Figure 12 shows the distribution of query reformulation types. The most common are adding, substituting or removing an attribute and specifying an instance. The most common subtype of attribute modified is location with 17.8%, whereas time is only 5% of the attributes and demographic information (e.g., gender, age) occurs in only nine transitions (1.2%). None of the more fine-grained attribute subtypes show qualitatively different characteristics, so we will discuss only the attribute category, without the subtypes. Turning our attention to the different stages within tasks, we observe that adding attributes or actions and specifying an instance is relatively common from the first to the second query. For the transition towards the final query in a task, substituting or removing an attribute, rephrasing with a synonym and switching task are relatively common. This suggests more emphasis on broadly specifying information needs at the outset of tasks and more emphasis on refining it by adding specific details towards the end.

Transitions and task outcomes. Figure 13 shows the relationship between query transitions and success. It is worth noting that switching to a new task occurs substantially more often in less successful tasks. Specifying an instance also occurs relatively often in the less successful tasks. Addition, substitution, and deletion actions or attributions typically occurs in more successful tasks.

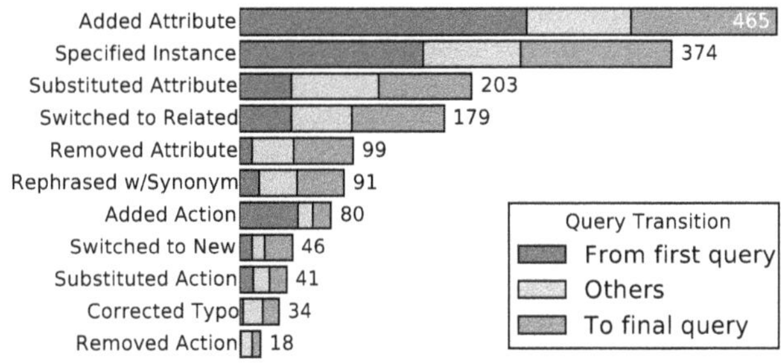

Figure 12: Distribution of query reformulation types.

Figure 13 also shows how often a query transition is deemed pivotal if it occurs. Interestingly, both switching tasks and specifying an instance are more common in less successful tasks, but are relatively frequently considered to be pivotal. Substituting an action is most often seen as pivotal, whereas substituting an attribute and correcting a typo are least frequently pivotal. The differences in the prevalence of pivotal queries as a function of the reformulation type suggests that some actions may be more effective than others and that accurately predicting the next action presents the opportunity for early corrective intervention by search systems. We will discuss this and similar implications toward the end of the paper.

4.4 Summary

Through a crowd-sourcing methodology we have shown that there are substantial differences in how searchers refine their queries in different stages in a struggling task. These differences have strong connections with task outcomes, and there are particular pivotal queries that play an important role in task completion.

5. PREDICT REFORMULATION STRATEGY

Given the differences in query reformulation strategies and to help operationalize successful reformulations in practice, we develop classifiers to (i) predict inter-query transitions during struggling searches according to our intent-based schema (Table 2), and (ii) identify pivotal queries within search tasks. This facilitates the development of anticipatory support to help searchers complete tasks. For example, if we predict a searcher wants to add an action to the query, we can provide query suggestions and auto-completions with actions. Our classifiers can also be applied retrospectively, e.g., to identify frequent transitions between queries and pivotal queries that form useful query suggestions or alterations.

Features. We include five sets of features, described in detail in Table 3. Some of the features relate to the characterizations that have been described in previous sections of the paper.

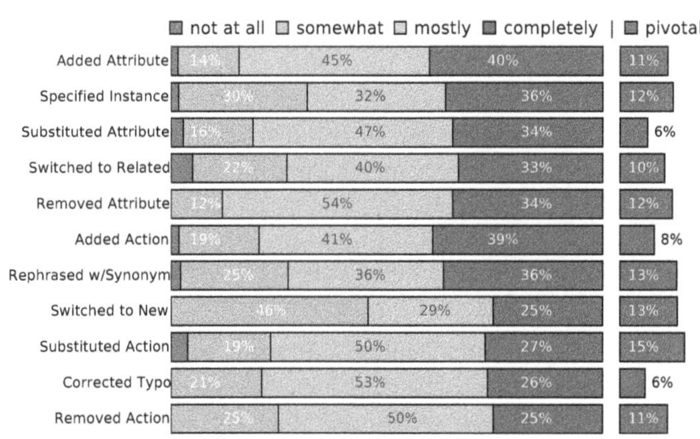

Figure 13: Task-level success on a four-point scale per reformulation type and % of reformulations considered pivotal.

Table 3: Features to predict reformulation strategy. The features marked with * are included for five similarity functions.

Name	Description
Query Features	
NumQueries	Number of queries in task
QueryCharLength	Query length in number of characters
QueryTermLength	Query length in number of terms
Interaction Features	
TimeElapsed	Time elapsed since query issued
ClickCount	Number of clicks observed since query
ClickDwelltime	Dwell time on clicked pages
QueryDwellTime	Dwell time on result page
Query Transition Features	
NewCharLength	New query length in number of characters
NewTermLength	New query length in number of terms
Levenshtein	Levenshtein edit distance in characters
normLevenshtein	Levenshtein edit distance as proportion
commonCharLeft	Number of characters in common from left
commonCharRight	Number of characters in common from right
diffPOS:<type>	Difference in the number of terms that are identified in WordNet as belonging to a specific part of speech type: noun, verb, adjective, adverb
Query Similarity Features	
ExactMatch*	Number of terms that match exactly
AddTerms*	Number of terms not in previous query
DelTerms*	Number of terms not in new query
SubsTerms*	Number of terms substituted
QuerySim*	Proportion of terms exactly match
commonTermLeft*	Number of terms in common from left
commonTermRight*	Number of terms in common from right
Query Reformulation Features	
LexicalType	Lexical query reformulation type (Table 1): new, back, morph, sub, general, specific
RuleBasedType	Lexical reformulation type using rule-based classifier of Huang and Efthimiadis [21]

Query features are used to represent the query before a reformulation. Interaction features describe how a searcher interacted with the search engine results page (SERP). We saw in Figure 8 that the type of reformulation is dependent on the time elapsed since the previous query. After observing a new query, we can compute three new sets of features. First, the query transition features describe characteristics of the new query and low-level lexical measures of how the query has changed. Query similarity features describe the terms in a query have changed. For these features, similarity is measured using five different similarity functions, described in Table 4. Terms can match exactly, approximately, on their root form or semantically. Lastly, we include features that analyze the lexical reformulation of queries. For this, we used the procedure as described in Section 3.6 and a recent rule-based approach [21].

Experimental Setup. We frame this as a multi-class classification problem; one for each of the 11 query reformulation types. We use the 659 labeled tasks with a total of 1802 query transitions (Section 4). We perform ten-fold cross-validation over the tasks and use a RandomForest classifier, since it is robust, efficient and easily parallelizable. We experimented with other classifiers (including logistic regression and SVM), and none yielded better performance. We therefore only report the results of the RandomForest classifier.

Table 4: Similarity matching functions used to compare terms for query similarity features.

Name	Description
Exact	All characters match exactly
Approximate	Levenshtein edit distance is less than two
Lemma	Terms match on their lexical root or lemma form
Semantic	WordNet Wu and Palmer measure greater than 0.5 (measures relatedness using the depth of two synsets and the least common subsumer in Wordnet)
Any	Any of the above functions match

Table 5: Groups of features available at different stages.

Feature group	First Query	First+Interaction	Second Query
Query	✓	✓	✓
Interaction		✓	✓
Transition including Similarity & Reformulation			✓

We evaluate our approach at different stages between two queries:

First query: We only observed the first query and try to predict the next reformulation strategy. At this stage, search systems can tailor the query suggestions on the SERP.

First+Interaction: We observed the first query and interactions (clicks, dwell time). The searcher is about to type in a new query. At this stage, systems can tailor auto-completions for the next query.

Second query: We observed both the first and second query and infer the reformulation strategy that the searcher applied. At this stage, search systems could re-rank results (or blend the results with those from other queries), and suggestions for the next query.

Concretely, the different stages mean that different groups of features become available (see Table 5 for the feature groups available at each stage). Finally, after the first query transition we add history features that represent the reformulation type and previous transition strategy. We report accuracy, area under the ROC curve (AUC) and F1 for our classifiers. F1 is computed as the harmonic mean of precision and recall per class. As a baseline we use the marginal (i.e., always predict the dominant class).

5.1 Prediction Results

Table 6 shows the results of our prediction experiments. The results are grouped by the transition and stage within a struggling search task. A task starts with observing the first query (Q1) and our prediction experiments end with observing the third query (Q3). We observe from the baseline results in Table 6 (lines 1 and 5) that this multi-class prediction task is a difficult problem. Apart from the first transition (where adding attributes is overrepresented, see Figure 12), the baseline approach of always predicting the dominant class is only about 25% correct, and obviously not very informative to support a struggling searcher.

For the first query reformulation (Q1 to Q2, lines 1–4 in Table 6), our classifiers already improve the reformulation strategy prediction before the second query. While just observing the first query does not provide significant improvements on all metrics (line 2), observing clicks and dwell times increases the F1 score significantly from 20% to 34% (line 3). If a struggling searcher issues a second query, we can infer the applied strategy with a 43% accuracy and significantly better on all metrics (line 4). Turning to the second query reformulation (Q2 to Q3, lines 5–8 in Table 6), the baseline performance (line 5) is substantially lower as the dominant class is less prevalent. Directly after observing the second query and using the task history, we can predict the reformulation strategy with 46% accuracy (line 6). Observing the interactions with the second

Table 6: Results for predicting query reformulation strategy. Significant differences, tested using a two-tailed Fisher randomization test against row 1 for 2–4 and row 5 for 6–8, are indicated with △ ($p < 0.05$) and ▲ ($p < 0.01$).

Transition	Stage	Accuracy	F1	AUC
1. Q1 to Q2	Baseline	0.3736	0.2032	0.5000
2. Q1 to Q2	Q1	0.3679	0.3046▲	0.5322△
3. Q1 to Q2	Q1+Interaction	0.3698	0.3371▲	0.5589▲
4. Q1 to Q2	Q2	0.4302△	0.3916▲	0.6077▲
5. Q2 to Q3	Baseline	0.2095	0.0971	0.4908
6. Q2 to Q3	Q2	0.4644▲	0.4595▲	0.6799▲
7. Q2 to Q3	Q2+Interaction	0.4862▲	0.4826▲	0.6896▲
8. Q2 to Q3	Q3	0.5474▲	0.5321▲	0.7306▲

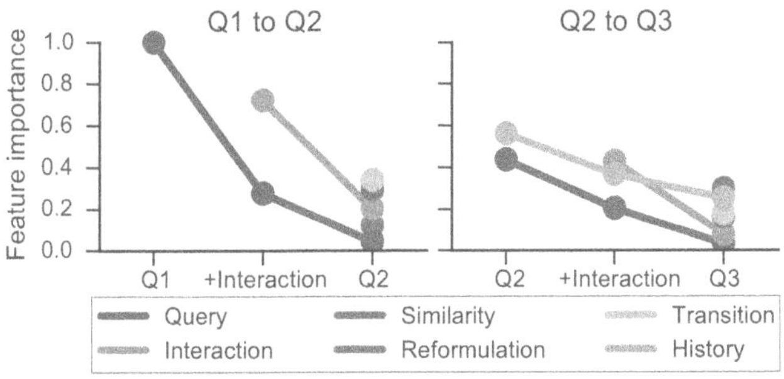

Figure 14: Feature group importance for Q1 to Q2 transition (left) and Q2 to Q3 transition (right).

query does not substantially improve prediction performance (line 7). If we observe the third query, the reformulation strategy can be inferred with 55% accuracy (line 8). All classifiers for the second query transition (lines 6–8) perform substantially better than those for the first transition (lines 2–4). This suggests that knowing what strategy a searcher has used previously helps in predicting the next reformulation strategy that they will use.

Feature Analysis. We measure the feature importance as gini importance [8] averaged over all trees of the ensemble. Figure 14 visualizes the total importance of the six groups of features. For predicting the first transition (Q1 to Q2) directly after the first query, only the query features are available. The interaction features that become available for the first query are substantially more important. If we observe the second query, the similarity and transition features are most important. The query features no longer contribute much to the classifier, as do the reformulation features. For the transition from the second to the third query (Q2 to Q3), the pattern is similar, but the history features contribute more.

Identifying the Pivotal Query. We were also interested in how accurately we can identify the pivotal query. We use a similar set-up as above, using subsets of the described features to identify the pivotal query in the 659 labeled tasks. Table 7 shows the results of this approach. The baseline always predicts the terminal query as the pivotal query (Figure 11). Using only the interaction and query features from Table 3 we significantly outperform this baseline in terms of F1 and AUC. Adding more features does not increase performance on any metric. Although this is promising, our results suggest that identifying the pivotal query is difficult.

6. DISCUSSION AND CONCLUSIONS

Search engines aim to provide their users with the information that they seek with minimal effort. If a searcher is struggling to locate sought information, this can lead to inefficiencies and frustration. Better understanding these struggling sessions is important for designing search systems that help people find information more

Table 7: Results for retrospectively identifying the pivotal query. Significant differences, tested using a two-tailed Fisher randomization test against row 1 are indicated with △ ($p < 0.05$) and ▲ ($p < 0.01$).

	Accuracy	F1	AUC
1. Baseline	0.6245	0.5091	0.7038
2. Query + Interaction	0.6352	0.5817▲	0.7296△

easily. Through log analysis on millions of search tasks, we have characterized aspects of how searchers struggle and (in some cases) ultimately succeed. We found that struggling searchers issue fewer queries in successful tasks than in unsuccessful ones. In addition, queries are shorter, fewer results are clicked and the query reformulations indicate that searchers have more trouble choosing the correct vocabulary.

We have shown quite significant behavioral differences given task success and failure. This informed the development of a crowd-sourced labeling methodology to better understand the nature of struggling searches. We proposed and applied that method to better understand the struggling process and where it became clear the search would succeed. This pivotal query is often the last query and not all strategies are as likely to be pivotal. We developed classifiers to accurately predict key aspects of inter-query transitions for struggling searches, with a view to helping searchers struggle less.

Our research has limitations that we should acknowledge. First, we focused on a very specific and very apparent type of struggling, indicated by limited activity for the first two queries within a task. More forms of struggling exist and might exhibit different search behaviors. Our determinations of search success for the log analysis were based on inferences made regarding observed search activity, especially satisfied clicks based on dwell time. Although these have been used in previous work [13], and were validated by third-party judges as part of a dedicated judgment effort, there are still a number of factors that can influence landing page dwell time [26]. Finally, the crowd-sourced annotations were based on judgments from third-party judges and not the searchers themselves. While this methodology has been used successfully in previous work [20], methods to collect judgments in-situ can also be valuable [13].

Previous work has shown that it is possible to detect struggling automatically from behavior [20, 36]. Our focus has been on better understanding struggling during search and predicting query reformulation strategy. Ideally, a search engine would interpret the behavioural signals that indicate struggling and frustration to provide personalized help to searchers to help them attain task success. The types of support possible include:

Direct application of reformulation strategies: Demonstrating the capability to accurately predict the strategy associated with the next query reformulation (rather than syntactic transformations, as has traditionally been studied) allows us to provide situation-specific search support at a higher (more strategic) level than specific query formulations. For example, if we predict that a searcher is likely to perform an action such as adding an attribute, the system can focus on recommending queries with attributes in query suggestions or query auto-completions depending on when they are applied (and augmented with additional information about popularity and/or success if available from historic data). Sets of (query → pivotal query) pairs can also be mined from log data. Such queries may also be leveraged internally within search engines (e.g., in blending scenarios, where the results from multiple queries are combined [34]) to help generate better quality search result lists, or present them as suggestions to searchers.

Hints and tips on reformulation strategies: As we demonstrated, struggling searchers, especially those destined to be unsuccessful, are highly likely to re-query. Learning the relationship between task success and the nature of the anticipated query reformulation allows search systems to generate human-readable hints about which types of reformulations to leverage (e.g., "add an action" leads to the highest proportion of pivotal queries, per Figure 13), and propose them in real-time as people are searching. Mining these reformulations retrospectively from log data also allows search systems to identify the most successful query transitions in the aggregate—rather than focusing on proxies for success, such as query or resource popularity [24, 42]. These reformulations can be learned from all searchers, or perhaps even more interestingly, from advanced searchers [2, 42] or domain experts [43].

Overall, accurate inferences and predictions about the nature of query reformulations can help searchers and search engines reduce struggling. Although our findings are promising, the nature and volume of our human-labeled data limited the types of the prediction tasks that we attempted. There are others, such as predicting search success given different query reformulation strategies that are interesting avenues for future work. Additional opportunities include working directly with searchers to better understand struggling in-situ, improving our classifiers, and experimenting with the integration of struggling support in search systems.

Acknowledgements. The first author performed this research during an internship at Microsoft Research and is supported by the Dutch national program COMMIT.

REFERENCES

[1] E. Agapie, G. Golovchinsky, and P. Qvarfordt. Leading people to longer queries. In *CHI'13*, pages 3019–3022, 2013.

[2] M. Ageev, Q. Guo, D. Lagun, and E. Agichtein. Find it if you can: A game for modeling different types of web search success using interaction data. In *SIGIR'11*, pages 345–354, 2011.

[3] P. Anick. Using terminological feedback for web search refinement: a log-based study. In *SIGIR'03*, pages 88–95. ACM, 2003.

[4] R. Artstein and M. Poesio. Inter-coder agreement for computational linguistics. *Computational Linguistics*, 34(4):555–596, 2008.

[5] A. Aula, R. M. Khan, and Z. Guan. How does search behavior change as search becomes more difficult? In *CHI'10*, pages 35–44, 2010.

[6] P. Bennett, K. Svore, and S. Dumais. Classification-enhanced ranking. In *WWW'10*, pages 111–120, 2010.

[7] D. C. Blair. Searching biases in large interactive document retrieval systems. *JASIS*, 31(4):271–277, 1980.

[8] L. Breiman, J. Friedman, R. Olshen, and C. Stone. *Classification and regression trees*. Wadsworth, 1984.

[9] D. Downey, S. Dumais, D. Liebling, and E. Horvitz. Understanding the relationship between searchers' queries and information goals. In *CIKM'08*, pages 449–458, 2008.

[10] C. Eickhoff, J. Teevan, R. White, and S. Dumais. Lessons from the journey. In *WSDM'14*, pages 223–232, 2014.

[11] H. Feild and J. Allan. Task-aware query recommendation. In *SIGIR'13*, pages 83–92, 2013.

[12] H. A. Feild, J. Allan, and R. Jones. Predicting searcher frustration. In *SIGIR'10*, pages 34–41, 2010.

[13] S. Fox, K. Karnawat, M. Mydland, S. Dumais, and T. White. Evaluating implicit measures to improve web search. *TOIS*, 23(2): 147–168, 2005.

[14] J. Guo, G. Xu, H. Li, and X. Cheng. A unified and discriminative model for query refinement. In *SIGIR'08*, pages 379–386, 2008.

[15] Q. Guo, R. W. White, Y. Zhang, B. Anderson, and S. T. Dumais. Why searchers switch: understanding and predicting engine switching rationales. In *SIGIR'11*, pages 335–344, 2011.

[16] A. Hassan. Identifying Web search query reformulation using concept based matching. In *EMNLP'13*, pages 1000–1010, 2013.

[17] A. Hassan, R. Jones, and K. L. Klinkner. Beyond DCG: User behavior as a predictor of a successful search. In *WSDM'10*, pages 221–230, 2010.

[18] A. Hassan, X. Shi, N. Craswell, and B. Ramsey. Beyond clicks: Query reformulation as a predictor of search satisfaction. In *CIKM'13*, pages 2019–2028, 2013.

[19] A. Hassan, R. W. White, and Y.-M. Wang. Toward self-correcting search engines: Using underperforming queries to improve search. In *SIGIR'13*, pages 263–272, 2013.

[20] A. Hassan, R. W. White, S. T. Dumais, and Y.-M. Wang. Struggling or exploring? Disambiguating long search sessions. In *WSDM'14*, pages 53–62, 2014.

[21] J. Huang and E. N. Efthimiadis. Analyzing and evaluating query reformulation strategies in web search logs. In *CIKM'09*, pages 77–86, 2009.

[22] S. B. Huffman and M. Hochster. How well does result relevance predict session satisfaction? In *SIGIR'07*, pages 567–574, 2007.

[23] J. Jiang, A. H. Awadallah, X. Shi, and R. W. White. Understanding and predicting graded search satisfaction. In *WSDM'15*, pages 57–66, 2015.

[24] R. Jones, B. Rey, O. Madani, and W. Greiner. Generating query substitutions. In *WWW'06*, pages 387–396, 2006.

[25] D. Kelly. Methods for evaluating interactive information retrieval systems with users. *FnTIR*, 3(1–2):1–224, 2009.

[26] Y. Kim, A. Hassan, R. White, and I. Zitouni. Modeling dwell time to predict click-level satisfaction. In *WSDM'14*, pages 193–202, 2014.

[27] T. Lau and E. Horvitz. *Patterns of Search: Analyzing and Modeling Web Query Refinement*. 1999.

[28] Z. Liao, Y. Song, L.-w. He, and Y. Huang. Evaluating the effectiveness of search task trails. In *WWW'12*, pages 489–498, 2012.

[29] Q. Liu, E. Agichtein, G. Dror, Y. Maarek, and I. Szpektor. When web search fails, searchers become askers: understanding the transition. In *SIGIR'12*, pages 801–801, 2012.

[30] S. Lopez and C. Snyder. *The Oxford Handbook of Positive Psychology*. Oxford University Press, 2011.

[31] G. Marchionini. Exploratory search: from finding to understanding. *CACM*, 49(4):41–46, 2006.

[32] N. Moraveji, D. Russell, J. Bien, and D. Mease. Measuring improvement in user search performance resulting from optimal search tips. In *SIGIR'11*, pages 355–364, 2011.

[33] R. Oliver. *Satisfaction: A Behavioral Perspective on the Consumer*. ME Sharpe, 2011.

[34] K. Raman, P. N. Bennett, and K. Collins-Thompson. Toward whole-session relevance: Exploring intrinsic diversity in web search. In *SIGIR'13*, pages 463–472, 2013.

[35] D. Savenkov and E. Agichtein. To hint or not: exploring the effectiveness of search hints for complex informational tasks. In *SIGIR'14*, pages 1115–1118, 2014.

[36] A. Scaria, R. Philip, R. West, and J. Leskovec. The last click: Why users give up information network navigation. In *WWW'14*, pages 213–222, 2014.

[37] M. Shokouhi, R. W. White, P. Bennett, and F. Radlinski. Fighting search engine amnesia: Reranking repeated results. In *SIGIR'13*, pages 273–282, 2013.

[38] J. Teevan. The re: search engine: simultaneous support for finding and re-finding. In *UIST'07*, pages 23–32, 2007.

[39] H. Wang, Y. Song, M. Chang, X. He, A. Hassan, and R. White. Modeling action-level satisfaction for search task satisfaction prediction. In *SIGIR'13*, pages 123–132, 2013.

[40] R. White, M. Bilenko, and S. Cucerzan. Studying the use of popular destinations to enhance web search interaction. In *SIGIR'07*, pages 159–166, 2007.

[41] R. W. White and S. T. Dumais. Characterizing and predicting search engine switching behavior. In *CIKM'09*, pages 87–96, 2009.

[42] R. W. White and D. Morris. Investigating the querying and browsing behavior of advanced search engine users. In *SIGIR'07*, pages 255–262, 2007.

[43] R. W. White, S. T. Dumais, and J. Teevan. Characterizing the influence of domain expertise on web search behavior. In *WSDM'09*, pages 132–141. ACM Press, 2009.

[44] Y. Xu and D. Mease. Evaluating web search using task completion time. In *SIGIR'09*, pages 676–677, 2009.

Behavioral Dynamics from the SERP's Perspective: What are Failed SERPs and How to Fix Them?

Julia Kiseleva[1] Jaap Kamps[2] Vadim Nikulin[3] Nikita Makarov[3]

[1]Eindhoven University of Technology, Eindhoven, The Netherlands
[2]University of Amsterdam, Amsterdam, The Netherlands
[3]Yandex, Moscow, Russian Federation
[1]j.kiseleva@tue.nl [2]kamps@uva.nl [3]{vnik,nkmakarov}@yandex-team.ru

ABSTRACT

Web search is always in a state of flux: queries, their intent, and the most relevant content are changing over time, in predictable and unpredictable ways. Modern search technology has made great strides in keeping up to pace with these changes, but there remain cases of failure where the organic search results on the search engine result page (SERP) are outdated, and no relevant result is displayed. Failing SERPs due to temporal drift are one of the greatest frustrations of web searchers, leading to search abandonment or even search engine switch. Detecting failed SERPs timely and providing access to the desired out-of-SERP results has huge potential to improve user satisfaction. Our main findings are threefold: First, we refine the conceptual model of behavioral dynamics on the web by including the SERP and defining (un)successful SERPs in terms of observable behavior. Second, we analyse typical patterns of temporal change and propose models to predict query drift beyond the current SERP, and ways to adapt the SERP to include the desired results. Third, we conduct extensive experiments on real world search engine traffic demonstrating the viability of our approach. Our analysis of behavioral dynamics at the SERP level gives new insight in one of the primary causes of search failure due to temporal query intent drifts. Our overall conclusion is that the most detrimental cases in terms of (lack of) user satisfaction lead to the largest changes in information seeking behavior, and hence to observable changes in behavior we can exploit to detect failure, and moreover not only detect them but also resolve them.

Categories and Subject Descriptors: H.3.3 [**Information Storage and Retrieval**]: Information Search and Retrieval—*Query formulation, Relevance feedback, Search process*

Keywords: Query reformulation, Concept drift, Information retrieval.

1. INTRODUCTION

The information seeking behavior of users on the web is inherently sensitive to changes happening in world [25, 28]. As the web reflects the world around us, content is changing in predictable and unpredictable ways, affecting the search intent and queries issued by users. Added to that, searchers express their complex information needs in short queries, causing an inherent ambiguity in their statements of request: the query intent is specific to the context of the user and the point in time. It is a formidable achievement of modern search engines that they manage to keep up to pace with changing content, at equally formidable costs in crawling and updating search engines indexes. In particular, for updating rankers, click through information in interaction logs are crucial [2, 21]

Yet, there remain cases of failure where the organic search results on the search engine result page ($SERP$) are outdated, and no relevant result is displayed. This can be caused by temporal query intent drift, where the desired pages for a query are changing over time, and the historical transaction logs privilege the outdated results. For example, if users were searching for *'Malaysia airlines flight'* in March 2014 they most likely wanted to see news about the *Malaysian flight 370* that disappeared. However, if users issued the same query in July 2014 they mostly likely were searching for information about the *Malaysian flight 17* that is presumed to be shot down. Figure 1 shows daily Wikipedia page views for the MH17 and MH370 pages over 2014, with striking increases from 0 to 100s of thousands of page views when the events happened.

The Malaysian Airlines example can characterized as a "sudden" drift which may cause the $SERP$ to become outdated. Such changes can be associated with the news, and received the most attention in research community [12, 13]. However, changes may happening over a longer period of time and not necessarily bring an increase in the volume of traffic. For instance, if users issued the query *'CIKM conference'* in 2014 they were satisfied with results referring to the page http://cikm2014.fudan.edu.cn/ and this page gets a majority of clicks. However, the conference site has been changed and the same query issued in 2015 should be linked to the different page http://www.cikm-2015.org/. The CIKM example can be characterized as an "incremental" drift where the intent of the original query is changing over a longer period of time.

In this paper, we examine a generic approach to detect $SERPs$ that become out of sync with the query intent. Specifically, users issue a query Q and a search engine returns search result page ($SERP$) that is a ranked list of URLs:

$$SERP = (url_1, \ldots, url_i, \ldots, url_n).$$

Our users are expected to click on some url_i on the $SERP$ that satisfies their information need, and the order of URLs on the $SERP$ is based on various features and optimized to fit a history of user interactions with a pair $\langle Q, SERP\rangle$. As a result, the $\langle Q, SERP\rangle$ shown at a given point in time will reflect the user preferences over an earlier period of time. However, this gives no guarantee on the quality of the current $\langle Q, SERP\rangle$ as user preferences are sensitive to time and events happening in world. We aim to detect cases of $SERP$ failure due to a significant drift in query intent

Permission to make digital or hard copies of all or part of this work for personal or classroom use is granted without fee provided that copies are not made or distributed for profit or commercial advantage and that copies bear this notice and the full citation on the first page. Copyrights for components of this work owned by others than the author(s) must be honored. Abstracting with credit is permitted. To copy otherwise, or republish, to post on servers or to redistribute to lists, requires prior specific permission and/or a fee. Request permissions from Permissions@acm.org.
CIKM'15, October 19–23, 2015, Melbourne, Australia.
Copyright is held by the owner/author(s). Publication rights licensed to ACM.
ACM 978-1-4503-3794-6/15/10 ...$15.00.
DOI: http://dx.doi.org/10.1145/2806416.2806483 .

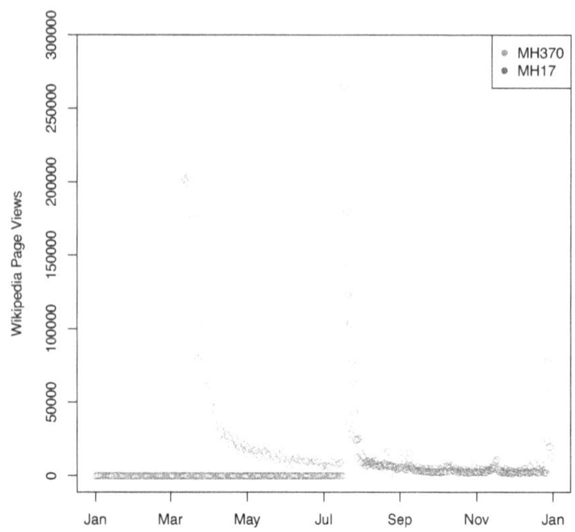

Figure 1: Wikipedia page views per day over 2014 for https://en.wikipedia.org/wiki/Malaysia_Airlines_Flight_17 and https://en.wikipedia.org/wiki/Malaysia_Airlines_Flight_370.

over time. Our aim is to detect failed $SERPs$ due to intent drift in an unsupervised way not relying on signals from other sources than the web traffic, language independent and not relying on rules or templates, independent of volume capturing both head and tail query drift. Hence we use behavioral signals as indicators of user (dis)satisfaction, such as click-through information [2, 22] and in particular query reformulations [1, 17, 24]. Specifically, in this paper, we are trying to answer the following main research question:

By analyzing behavioral dynamics at the SERP level, can we detect an important class of detrimental cases (such as search failure) based on changes in observable behavior caused by low user satisfaction?

We break up the main research problem into three different parts. Our first concrete research question is:

RQ1: *How to include the SERP into the conceptual model of behavioral dynamics on the web? How to identify (un)successful SERPs in terms of drastic changes in observable user behavior?*

We conduct a conceptual analysis of behavioral dynamics from the $SERP$'s perspective, and introduce failure and success at the SERP level, analyzing their behavioral consequences identifying indicators of success and failure. We then analyze success and failure in light of changing query intents over time, and identify an important case of $SERP$ failure due to query intent drift, and suggest an approach to detect a failed $SERP$ due to query intent drift by significant changes in behavioral indicators of failure.

Our second concrete research question is:

RQ2: *Can we distinguish different types of SERP failure due to query intent drift (e.g., sudden, incremental), and when and how should we update the SERP to reflect these changes?*

We study different types of possible query intent drift inspired by the literature on concept drift [15]: sudden, incremental, gradual and reoccurring. It is important to be able to classify the type of changes in user satisfaction because a sequence of actions a search engine should perform to normalize a situation can be different. We identify relevant parameters, such as the window of change, volume or popularity of queries, and relevant behavioral indicators, such as the probability of reformulation, abandonment rates, and click through rates. For the two main categories of intent drift, we define an unsupervised approach to detect failed $SERPs$. We also show how the detected changes can be used to improve a ranking of search results.

Our third concrete research question is:

RQ3: *How effective is our approach on a realistic sample of traffic of a major internet search engine?*

We validate our approach on twelve months of search interaction logs of a major commercial search engine. We run a simplified version of our algorithm on a massive transaction log, and detected pairs of $\langle Q, SERP\rangle$ suspected of failing due to drifting query intents. We investigate the accuracy of drift detection and the accuracy of the clicked URLs of the revision to include on the $SERP$ of the original query. We look at the effectiveness of our approach for both sudden and incremental changes in query intent, by varying the duration of the window to detect failed $SERPs$.

The remainder of this paper is organized as follows. Section 2 introduces earlier work on behavioral dynamics on the web, and behavioral indicators of user satisfaction focusing on the $SERP$ level. Then, Section 3 introduces the concept of $SERP$ success and failure, and outlines behavioral cues for their detecting $SERP$ becoming out of sync over time. Followed by Section 4 zooming in on different types of query drift causing failed $SERPs$, and outlining practical ways of detecting them. Finally, Section 5 reports on extensive experiments demonstrating the real-world utility of our approach.

2. RELATED WORK

In this section we will study related work, focusing on research on topic and concept drift, on the behavioral dynamics of the web, and on user satisfaction signals on the $SERP$ level.

2.1 Topic and Concept Drift

Topic or query drift has been studied for long in IR, usually in the context of evolving information needs as may happen in routing tasks [4], or the opposite negative effect of retrieving off-topic documents lower in the ranking [33]. In particular in adaptive filtering, topic models are continuously updated when new data comes available [5]. The focus is on a general topic or standing profile that monitors a stream of data and selects relevant documents. Our focus is on the SERP, serving results to a population of users with subtle or less subtle variation in query intent, taking into account changes in the query intent over time.

Topic drift is distinct from concept drift [15, 30, 36] which, in a machine learning setting, refers to changes in the conditional distribution of the output (i.e., target variable) given the input (i.e., input features), while the distribution of the input may stay unchanged. We will use a concept drift approach in the next sections, to model changes in features indicating lack of search satisfaction, and for determining thresholds for drift detection.

2.2 Behavioral Dynamics

The changes in query popularity over time have been studied extensively in prior work. Moreover, researchers have also examined the relationship between query behavior and events [27]. There are algorithms for identifying queries that are related to breaking news and for blending relevant news results into core search results [12, 26].

Prior work on behavioral dynamics is based on three factors: (1) on changes in query dynamics and in this case authors are concentrated on the 'head' queries [25, 28, 29, 31]; (2) on changes in web content dynamics and user interaction with dynamic content [25]; and (3) how information about changes can be used:

- to improve the ranking on the $SERP$ [10, 12, 13, 26]; and
- to improve query auto-completion [32].

Additionally, Kulkarni et al. [25] explored how queries, their associated documents, and the intents corresponding to the queries change over time. Radinsky et al. [29] have done an extensive studies how time-series analysis methods can be applied to predict dynamics on the web. Shokouhi [31] proposed using time-series decomposition techniques for identifying seasonal queries.

In summary, the prior studies cited above examine how general changes in content, specific content features, or query volume can be used to improve web search experience. Although much has been done to understand user web search behavior over time, few efforts have sought to construct underlying models to understand changes $\langle Q, SERP\rangle$ and even used to automatically fix the observed problems. We present the construction of models for behaviors over time that can explain observed changes in user satisfaction with $\langle Q, SERP\rangle$.

2.3 User Satisfaction

User satisfaction with the $SERP$ has been researched extensively. It is widely adopted as a subjective measure of search experience. User clicks are reasonably accurate on average to evaluate user satisfaction with pairs $\langle Q, SERP\rangle$ [2, 22], using click-through information. This user satisfaction scenario is successfully applied to navigational queries. It is called *query-level satisfaction*. However, we have to take into account the fact that user clicks are biased:

1. to the page position in the $SERP$ [9, 21];
2. to the quality of the page's snippet [37]; and
3. to the domain of the returned URLs [19].

Al-Maskari et al. [3] claim that the search scenario for informational queries is different. Users can run follow-up queries if they are unsatisfied with the derived results, and reformulations can lead users to the desired information. This scenario is called *task-level satisfaction* [12]. On the one hand, earlier research proposed different methods for identifying successful sessions. Hassan et al. [18] used a Markov model to predict success at the end of a task. Ageev et al. [1] exploited an expertise-dependent difference in search behavior by using a Conditional Random Fields model to predict a search success. On the other hand, separate researches are interested in situations when users are frustrated. Feild et al. [14] proposed a method for understanding user frustration with the pair $\langle Q, SERP\rangle$ based on query log and physical sensor features. Kiseleva et al. [24] showed how to automatically detect changes in user satisfaction using reformulation signal.

Earlier, White and Dumais [35] gave users difficult information seeking assignments and evaluated their level of dissatisfaction via query log features and physical sensors. They demonstrated that the prediction model gets the highest quality when it is built based on query log features. One type of user behavior that can be clearly associated with frustration is search engine switching. Guo et al. [16] showed that one of the primary reasons users switched their search engine was due to dissatisfaction with the results on the $SERP$. A recent study [20] shows a method to predict finer-grained, graded satisfaction levels. This paper significantly extends earlier work [24], analyzing behavioral dynamics at the $SERP$ level, and explaining how and why the changes are happening. In this work we propose a methodology to define a type of changes in user satisfaction and how this information can be used to improve a ranker.

Summarizing, in this section, we presented an overview of prior work on behavioral dynamics and user satisfaction on the web, with a special focus on the $SERP$ level. In the rest of the paper, we will study variations in user satisfaction with $\langle Q, SERP\rangle$ pair over time, starting with a conceptual analysis of success and failure at the $SERP$ level in the next section.

3. SUCCESS AND FAILURE AT THE SERP

In this section we will study RQ1: *How to include the SERP into the conceptual model of behavioral dynamics on the web? How to identify (un)successful SERPs in terms of drastic changes in observable user behavior?*

3.1 (Un)successful SERPs

We first introduce the notions of successful and unsuccessful SERPs as a conceptual model. Recall from the above that we looks at the pair $\langle Q, SERP\rangle$, with a *query* Q and a *search engine result page* ($SERP$) consisting of a ranked list of URLs in response to query Q. That is,

$$SERP_q = (url_1, \ldots, url_i, \ldots, url_n).$$

Let us further assume that queries are issued for a purpose and that the *intent* of query Q can be represented as a non-empty set of desired pages $INTENT_q$. For example, conceptually speaking a navigational query will have a singleton set $INTENT_q$, and an informational query will have a larger set of desired pages. Over a population of users there may be a distribution of intents, each giving rise to a different sets of desired pages, and it is straightforward to incorporate this into the conceptual model, but for simplicity and clarity we use a single set of desired pages here.

We define a successful and unsuccessful $SERPs$ in the following way:

DEFINITION 1. *(a) A $SERP_q$ is a* successful SERP *for query Q if and only if $\exists url_q \in INTENT_q$ such that $url_q \in SERP_q$.*
(b) A $SERP_q$ is a failed SERP *for query Q if and only if $\forall url_q \in INTENT_q$ such that $url_q \notin SERP_q$.*

A user issuing query Q may respond to the $SERP$ in different ways. One of the possible scenario of user interaction with the $SERP$, which is widely studied, is an event when users do not click on presented results. This case is called *search abandonment* that is known as a metrics of how successful a $SERP$ is. Research on search abandonment [7, 8, 11, 34] studied two primary abandonment cases: *bad abandonment* indicating user frustration and dissatisfaction; *good abandonment* suggesting satisfaction without needing to click. Assume we have a successful SERP in the sense of the conceptual definition above, and observe no clicked result, this suggests a case of good abandonment. Good abandonment is quite common in modern search engines because direct answers such as weather and stock quotes are returned for queries with explicit intent. Moreover, snippets can also satisfy users' information needs directly. However, if we assume a failed $SERP$, then a lack of clicked results suggests bad abandonment. Diriye et al. [11] report roughly equal fractions of good and bad abandonment, hence the abandonment rate is a secondary indicator of $SERP$ success or failure.

Table 1: SERP Success and failure

Behavior	Failed $SERP$	Successful $SERP$
No clicks	Bad abandonment	Good abandonment
Clicked result	$DSAT$ clicks	SAT clicks
Revised query	Negative reformulation	Positive reformulation

The other possible scenario is for users to interact with a retrieved $SERP$. Web search users often click on the $SERP$ and/or follow up with other queries. Many researchers have showed that clicks and reformulations can be used for a variety of tasks. However, clicks are usually considered to be as a positive sign [2, 22] to detect user satisfaction with the pair $\langle Q, SERP\rangle$. In the conceptual model, we can distinguish between satisfaction (SAT) and dissatisfaction of clicks based on the desired pages:

DEFINITION 2. *(a) A click on $url_i \in SERP_q$ for query Q is a* SAT click *if and only if $url_i \in INTENT_q$.*

(b) A click on $url_i \in SERP_q$ for query Q is a DSAT click *if and only if $url_i \notin INTENT_q$.*

It is an immediate corollary that there cannot be SAT clicks on a failed $SERP$, and that we can expect SAT clicks, but cannot exclude $DSAT$ clicks, on a successful $SERP$. A practical approximation to detect the difference in satisfaction is the use of dwell time, either with simple thresholds such as 30 seconds, or by advanced classification models [23].

Apart from consulting the results on the $SERP$, users may also decide to revise the query. Query reformulations have been used as indicator of search satisfaction [1, 17, 24]. Query revision may happen both in case of successful and unsuccessful $SERPs$. In case of the a successful $SERP$, for example after interacting with some relevant results, a user may refine her query to explore a further sub-topic or aspect of the query. In want of a better term, we call this type of revisions a *positive reformulation*. In case of an unsuccessful $SERP$, our frustrated user may opt to formulate her query for example by spelling out her information need more explicitly, in the hope to arrive at a successful $SERP$. We call this type of revision a *negative reformulation*.

Table 1 summarizes the relation between the concept of successful and failed $SERP$ and indicators of user satisfaction such as search abandonment, (dis)satisfied clicks, or query revisions. While the detection of failed and successful $SERPs$ in practice is non-trivial, the conceptual analysis allows us to simply assume the existence of abstract concepts like the set of desired pages, and clear up the exact meaning of core concepts and their dependencies and consequences.

3.2 Behavioral Dynamics of SERP Failure

We now look in detail at the impact of changing query intent over time on the $SERP$, and how this affect the pair $\langle Q, SERP\rangle$. Specifically, we look at the transition between the some time point or period t_i and a later time t_{i+1}:

$$\langle Q, SERP_q\rangle_{t_i} \rightarrow \langle Q, SERP_q\rangle_{t_{i+1}}.$$

Assume that at t_i we have a successful $SERP$, hence it contains at least one page satisfying the intent of query Q at that point in time. Due to a satisfaction click on a result, the ranker will reinforce the $SERP$'s content and like present the same organic results at t_{i+1}. Many queries such as navigational requests, are very stable and resulting in a successful $SERP$ at time t_{i+1}. However, there is also an important fraction of queries that has a changing intent due to something happening in the world, which may cause the $SERP_q$ to become unsuccessful at time t_{i+1}.

This requires detecting when a $SERP$ becomes out of sync due to changes in the query intent. There are of course subtle changes in query intent over time, leading to small changes in the click distribution with the $SERP$ for a Q as studied in previous work for updating rankers. But these do not lead to an unsuccessful $SERP$ as defined in the paper. Hence we aim to distinguish cases where the desired page is not part of the $SERP$, at least not part of top n of the organic ranking (e.g., the top 10 results).

There are cases when users are looking for a desired page that does not exist, either no longer exists or was not created or updated yet. For example, a newly created page with a winner or an outcome of an election, users are looking for the next version of iPhone, etc. Although even in these cases, there is usually a surrogate desired page that explains that the page doesn't exist, and may inform or speculate on the time when the information will become available.

3.3 Detecting Failed SERPs

Our analysis leads to the following scenario when user satisfaction at time t_i with $\langle Q, SERP\rangle$ turn into user frustration at t_{i+1} with the same $\langle Q, SERP\rangle$. In other words we aim to detect situations when at time t_i users were satisfied with a pair $\langle Q, SERP\rangle$ and at some moment in time t_{i+1} users are no longer satisfied with the same pair $\langle Q, SERP\rangle$, due to changes in the query intent for example due to some event happening in world.

We consider the following types of behavior BF_j on the $SERP$ as a sign of user frustration (lack of search satisfaction) with the $SERP$:

- BF_1: search abandonment;
- BF_2: query reformulation;
- BF_3: $DSAT$ clicks on a top-10 search results; and
- BF_4: SAT clicks on a low ranked search result (> 10).

The intuition of our approach is that, over a population of users issuing a query, if we see a *sufficient* amount of negative reformulations, $DSAT$ and low-ranked clicks, and bad search abandonment, then we flag the $SERP$ as *failed*, and use information about the ultimately clicked page to update the $SERP$ for the original query —hence avoid failure for future requests.

In order to satisfy a requirement about *sufficient* number we use the phenomenon of *concept drift* [15, 30, 36]. The *real* concept drift refers to changes in the conditional distribution of the output (i.e., target variable) given the input (input features), while the distribution of the input may stay unchanged. For our problem we can formally define *concept drift* between time point t_i and time point t_{i+1} as:

$$\exists BF_j : p_{t_i}(BF_j, \langle Q, SERP\rangle) \neq p_{t_{i+1}}(BF_j, \langle Q, SERP\rangle),$$

where p_{t_i} denotes the joint distribution at time t_i between the set of input variables $\langle Q, SERP\rangle$ and the target variable BF_j. The approach is explained in detail in the next section.

We not only intend to detect failure, but also to find and to inject the missing page to the $SERP$. In case of revisions with following SAT clicks, or low-ranked clicks, we have a clear indication of the "missing" page and boost it's ranking so that it will surface on for the original query's $SERP$ for future users issuing the same query.

Summarizing, in this section, we introduced the concept of a successful and failed $SERP$ and analyzed their behavioral consequences identifying indicators of success and failure. We then analyzed success and failure in light of changing query intents over

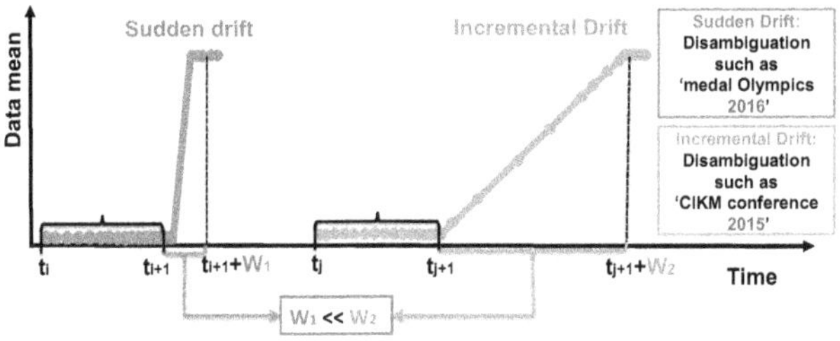

Figure 2: A representation of sudden and incremental types of the drifts.

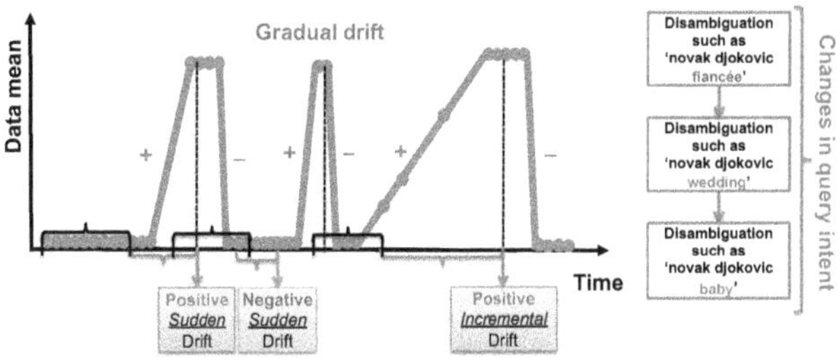

Figure 3: A representation of the gradual drift.

time, and identified an important case of $SERP$ failure due to query intent drift. This suggests an approach to detect a failed $SERP$ due to query intent drift by significant changes in behavioral indicators of failure. Our general conclusion is that more detrimental cases in terms of user satisfaction lead to larger changes in observable user behavior and hence more handles to detect them.

4. TYPES OF DRIFT IN USER SATISFACTION

In this section we will study RQ2: *Can we distinguish different types of SERP failure due to query intent drift (e.g., sudden, incremental), and when and how should we update the SERP to reflect these changes?*

4.1 Classifying Drift Type

This section proposes a method to detect the *types* of changes in user satisfaction. The detection of the type of change is important because it defines a strategy to fix a failed $SERP$ that is a result of changes in user satisfaction. We focus on two main types of the drifts: sudden and incremental, and will argue that the other types (i.e. gradual and reoccurring) can be represented as a combination of sudden and incremental types.

We use an increase in the query reformulations as a sign of user frustration with a shown $SERP$. The main criteria to distinguish between sudden and incremental drifts is the size of the testing window: (1) the sudden drift should be detected during the short period of time and (2) the incremental drift can be characterized by much longer testing period. An example is shown in Figure 2. Moreover, we are proposing a list of *secondary metrics* that can be used to characterize the drifts:

1. if the drift is related to the query popularity (i.e., 'head' or 'tail' queries);
2. if the volume of initial queries is changing a lot;
3. if search abandonment is observed frequently on the initial $SERP$s. In the context of an increasing number of query revisions, we will observe predominantly bad abandonment cases.

Let us characterize in details the types of changes we are studying in this work:

Sudden change. This kind of change gets the most attention in the literature [10, 12, 25, 26, 28] because they bring a most harmful and visible effect to user experience. This drift can be characterized by a growth of query popularity over a short period of time (e.g., 'breaking news queries'), as shown on the left hand side of Figure 2. In order to detect sudden drifts we use a short duration of the testing window (e.g., a couple of hours until a couple of days). Using the secondary metrics the sudden drift can be defined as:

1. the sudden drift is likely concerning more popular or 'head' types of queries;
2. the volume of an initial query Q is changing during the testing period (we also can detect a drift in an increase of Q volume);
3. search abandonment is a frequent behavior on the initial $SERP$ for Q indicating $SERP$ failure, i.e., the required url_q is missing (as presented in Definition 1).

Incremental change. This kind of change is less often studied and can be characterized by a slow change in query intent over a long period of time, as shown on the right hand side of Figure 2. An example it the reformulation of the query *'CIKM conference'* to include the specific year or location. This drift is a more difficult to detect because it does not necessary require an increasing query volume. However, changes in the fraction of query reformulations [24] can be used to detect incremental drift. Using the secondary metrics the incremental drift can be defined as:

1. the incremental drift is likely concerning less popular or 'tail' types of queries;
2. the volume of initial queries is not changing much during the testing period (we hardly can detect changes in an increase of volume);
3. search abandonment is a frequent behavior of initial $SERPs$ that means the initial $SERP$ is failed. Also in case a required URL is present at the $SERP$ but at a low rank, users tend to reformulate their query rather than explore further results on the $SERP$.

We identify two other types of query intent drift that can be represented as a combination of sudden and incremental types.

Gradual change. This is a different type of change that is presented in Figure 3. It can be viewed as a combination of the sudden and (or) incremental types of changes happening over time. For example, we consider the query *'novak djokovic'* (the famous tennis player) that may change its intents over time. For example, it has a drift in September 2013 on the term *'fiancée'* because the tennis player got engaged. Therefore, $SERP$ for the initial query is missing information about his fiancée and users tend to reformulate because they are interested in this topic.

At some moment in time the couple celebrate their wedding and users' interest changes again. Therefore the news about an engagement of famous tennis player becomes outdated and users start to reformulate the query *'novak djokovic'* using the reformulation *'wedding'* (if this information is missing from the $SERP$). As a logical continuation of this story the couple have a baby and users

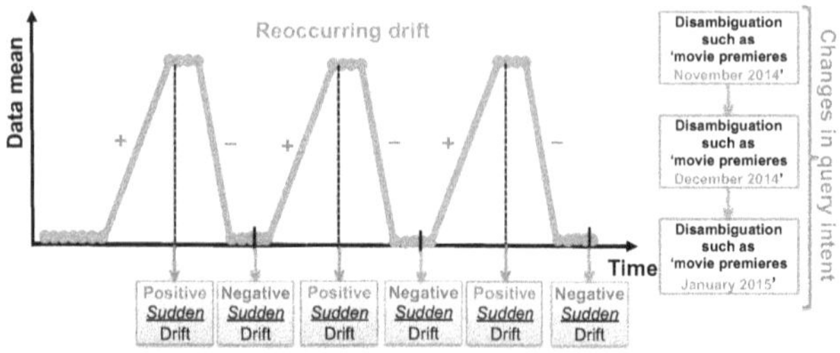

Figure 4: A representation of the reoccurring drift.

are interested to see information about this news, etcetera. It is important to note that the described changes are happening without any pattern, so some of these drifts may be sudden and some may be incremental.

Reoccurring change. The final special case of drifts is presented in Figure 4. A specific characteristic of the the reoccurring change is that it has a regular type of behavior [31]. The example in Figure 4 shows that users reformulate the query *'movies premieres'* regularly according dates. It is important to note that the reoccurring change is a combination of the same type drifts (sudden or incremental).

It is important to track changes for queries over time in order to understand if the $SERP$ is fixed when it is needed. A *positive* drift is typical for those cases where the reformulation signal is growing over time. Basically, the detected positive drift is a sign of a failing $SERP$ (shown as "+" in Figure 3). A *negative* drift is typical for those cases where the probability to reformulate a query is decreasing dramatically (shown as "-" in Figure 3). The *negative* drift may be interpreted in the two following ways:

1. the system has reacted to the positive change first and changed the $SERP$. Therefore a number of query revisions dropped down that means the problem with user satisfaction has been fixed;
2. the system has not reacted to the positive change in the reformulation signal but the moment has passed and users are no longer interested in a revision.

A detailed algorithm how to identify if a detected drift has positive or negative signs is presented in the next section.

4.2 Detecting Sudden and Incremental Drifts

Let us first define formally a set of features $\{F_j\}_{j=1}^4$ we use to detect changes in user satisfaction with the pair $\langle Q, SERP\rangle$: (1) a reformulation signal (RS), (2) a search abandonment signal (AS), (3) a query volume signal (VS), and (4) an average clicked position signal (CS):

- F_1: $RS(Q,Q')_{[t_i,t_{i+1}]}$ for the query Q and its reformulation Q' is a probability to reformulate Q to Q' within a particular time period $[t_i, t_{i+1}]$:
$$RS = P\left(Q \rightarrow Q'\right).$$
- F_2: $AS(Q)_{[t_i,t_{i+1}]}$ for the query Q is a probability to abandon (to give no clicks) $SERP_Q$ within a particular time period $[t_i, t_{i+1}]$.
- F_3: $VS(Q)_{[t_i,t_{i+1}]}$ for the query Q is a frequency of this Q within a particular time period $[t_i, t_{i+1}]$.

Algorithm 1 Algorithm for Detection the Type of Drift in user SATisfaction ($DTDSAT$). We leave out variables, i.e., $drift$ stands for $drift_{Q,Q',w}$, for readability.

Require: the train period $\Delta t = [t_i, t_{i+1}]$;
the test window $w = \{w_1, w_2\}$;
the error thresholds: $e_{RS}, e_{AS}, e_{CS}, e_{VS}$;
Ensure: $drift \leftarrow true, false$;
$drift\_positive \leftarrow true, false$;
$serp\_fail \leftarrow true, false$

for $\{Q, Q'\}_{k=1}^N$ **do**
  $\Delta_{RS} = \mu(RS_{\Delta t+w}(Q,Q')) - \mu(RS_{\Delta t}(Q,Q'))$
  if $|\Delta_{RS}| \geq e_{RS}$ **then**
    $drift \leftarrow true$
    if $\Delta_{RS} > 0$ **then**
      $drift\_positive \leftarrow true$
      $\Delta_{AS} = \mu(AS_{\Delta t+w}(Q)) - \mu(AS_{\Delta t}(Q))$
      $\Delta_{CS} = \mu(CS_{\Delta t+w}(Q)) - \mu(CS_{\Delta t}(Q))$
      $\Delta_{VS} = \mu(VS_{\Delta t+w}(Q)) - \mu(VS_{\Delta t}(Q))$
      if $(|\Delta_{AS}| \geq e_{AS}$ **or** $|\Delta_{CS}| \geq e_{CS})$ **then**
        $serp\_fail \leftarrow true$
        $url_Q \leftarrow getMissingTopURL()$
        $driftType \leftarrow getDriftType(|w|, \Delta_{VS})$
        $fixSerp(url_Q, driftType)$
      else
        $serp\_fail \leftarrow false$
      end if
    else
      $drift\_positive \leftarrow false$
    end if
  else
    $drift \leftarrow false$
  end if
end for
return $drift, drift\_positive, serp\_fail$

- F_4: $CS(Q)_{[t_i,t_{i+1}]}$ for the query Q is an average position clicked on $SERP_Q$ within a particular time period $[t_i, t_{i+1}]$.

We call F_1 as a primary drift metric of drift and $\{F_j\}_{j=2}^4$ as a list of secondary drift metrics. Each of them can be estimated straightforwardly based on observed frequencies in the period: for RS, we calculate the probability of reformulation per day, and for the period use the (observed) average over days (μ).

The proposed algorithm $DTDSAT$ to discover types of changes in user satisfaction is presented in in Algorithm 1. It is a straightforward application of the adaptive windowing algorithm from concept drift detection [6], which calculates a theoretically motivated threshold e for observing a significant drift based on a confidence value δ. We will first explain how $DTDSAT$ works.

DTDSAT Input. We assume that we can detect the *sudden drift* within a short period of time (w_1) such as from three days up to two weeks. In contrast, the *incremental drift* is detected on a larger time slot (w_2) from more than two weeks and up to one month. As the train window (Δt), we use fixed period of time for both considered types of drifts. We calculate an error thresholds: e_{RS}, e_{AS}, e_{CS}, e_{VS} using a standard method described in [6].

DTDSAT Output. The algorithm $DTDSAT$ returns an alarm as an output if the drift happens. Additionally, it produces an extra information about a detected drift: a sign: **(1)** the *'positive sign'* means we need to fix $SERP$; **(2)** the *'negative sign'* means users are no longer reformulating Q, so no action should be taken. A collected sequence of positive and negative drifts for Q can be used to build a dynamics of changes for Q. This dynamics may help to understand if Q has a gradual drift (e.g., Figure 3) or a reoccurring one (e.g., Figure 4) over some longer period of time (e.g., 6 months or 1 year).

The Algorithm 1 includes the following methods:

- a method $getMissingTopURL()$ returns a missing url_Q as defined in Definition 1. It gets url_Q based on a statistics about the most frequently clicked $URLs$ after issuing drifted reformulation Q to Q'.
- a method $getDriftType(\Delta_{AS}, \Delta_{CS}, \Delta_{VS})$ takes into account a statistics about the secondary metrics of drifts in order to estimate a type of drift. There are cases when our system detects a drift on RS but none of the secondary metrics has changed. We called this situation a *'positive reformulation'*. In this case we are not dealing with failed $SERP$.
- a method *fixSerp(url_Q,driftType)* that will produce a list of $URLs$ that users mostly click on after running query revisions. The top $URLs$ from the list a candidates to be included on the $SERP$ served for the original Q, and avoid future user frustration and the need to revise their queries.

Summarizing, in this section, we studied different types of possible query intent drift inspired by the literature on concept drift [15]: sudden, incremental, gradual and reoccurring. We identified relevant parameters, such as the window of change, volume or popularity of queries, and relevant behavioral indicators, such as the probability of reformulation, abandonment rates, and click through rates. For the two main categories of intent drift, we define an unsupervised approach to detect failed SERPs caused by drift. We also showed how the detected changes can be used to improve a ranking of search results.

5. EXPERIMENTS AND RESULTS

In this section we will study RQ3: *How effective is our approach on a realistic sample of traffic of a major internet search engine?*

5.1 Experimental Data

Our experimental data comprises of massive raw and unfiltered search logs of a major commercial search engine that were collected during the whole 2014 year. Our audience consists of about *25 millions users per day*. Our traffic consists of approximately *150 millions of queries per day*. In our experimentation, we are dealing with a multilingual traffic that has at least *five* dominant languages.

5.2 Evaluation Methodology

We now describe our methodology to evaluate the quality of drifts detection algorithm.

Our algorithm is unsupervised, and detects drift in query intent based on a concept drift technique using a simple, theoretically motivated threshold, needing only a single linear pass through the data. To the best of our knowledge, there is no alternative approach to detect failed SERPs that could function as a baseline. We run our algorithm of Section 4 in a simplified form on the logs. First, we choose three fixed windows of 3, 7, and 14 days rather than calculate the optimal window based on the threshold. Second, we use the change in the probability of a revision (Δ_{RS}) as the criterion to select data. Third, we use a single threshold (e_{RS}) based on $\delta = 0.1$, with values in the range of $[0.2, 0.5]$, as we did not observe major differences between the settings.

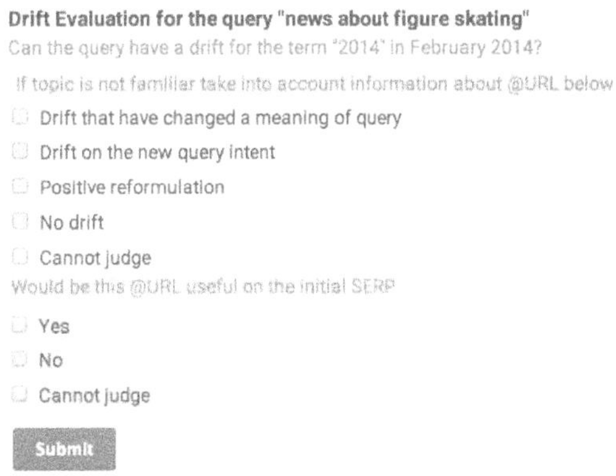

Figure 5: A fragment of an evaluation task for the annotators. We suggest the most clicked *url* after a query revision.

As an approximation, we define the drift type by the size of the test window, so a three days windows size is related to a sudden drift type. However, it is important to note that a fresh intent classifier (based on mostly a query popularity) is already working within the search engine. Let us call it FIC. Therefore, most popular changes in query intents might picked up by FIC and $SERP$ is already fixed for *'head queries'*. As was shown in [26] this can be done within very short period of time.

For evaluation, we selected *randomly* about 150 examples from different batches. Therefore, in total, we selected 450 examples of drifts for test set which we use to report the final results. Each detected drift in our test set was evaluated by three judges and we report overall scores. As a evaluation metrics we use accuracy rates. In the current settings we are more interested to obtain rather precise results.

In order to evaluate the obtained results we set up the following evaluation task. Every judge is supplied with the definition of sudden and incremental types of drift. We gave to judges the following explanation for the drift labels:

1. Drift is detected: *'real' drift* in users intent i.e. new target intent replaces the old target intent: e.g. Q = *'referendum in the Crimea'* has a drift on its revision Q' = *'referendum in the Crimea 16 march'* in March 2014 (due to some events happening in the world); similarly Q = *'Sochi'* has a drift on its revision Q' =*'Sochi **2014**'* in February 2014 (due to Olympics games that took place in the city Sochi in February 2014);
2. Drift is detected: *'new drift'* in users intent i.e. an another/new target intent added to a multifaceted query: e.g. Q = *'Happy New Year wishes'* has a drift on its revision Q' = *'Happy New Year wishes **2015**'* in December 2014 (due to the fact that people are trying to find the next year); similarly Q = *'RoboCop'* has a drift on its revision Q' = *'RoboCop **2014**'* in February 2014 (due to a release of the new movie);
3. Positive reformulation is detected: it signals about a shift in users intent but we suppose that $SERP$ is not broken in this case: e.g. Q = *'schedule of matches of the World Cup 2014'* has a detected positive reformulation Q' = *'schedule of matches of the World Cup 2014 **on tv**'* in June 2014; similarly Q = *'voice 22.11.2014'* has a detected positive re-

Table 2: Accuracy of drift detection (including positive reformulations)

	Window	Drift_Accuracy	URL_Accuracy
1	3 days	0.58	0.87
2	7 days	0.66	0.97
3	14 days	0.91	0.91
4	Combined	0.72	0.92

formulation $Q' =$ *'voice 22.11.2014* ***watch online****'* ('Voice' a a popular TV show);

4. It is not a drift;
5. There is not enough information to judge.

In order to evaluate a quality of our procedure to fix failed $SERPs$ we asked judges to check the suggested $@url$ and answer the question *'Would be this* $@url$ *useful on the initial* $SERP$ *for the query* $@Q$ *at the particular moment in time* $@\Delta t$*?'*. Judges were supplied with the following set of labels:

1. *Yes*, it would be useful to insert the $@url$ to the $SERP$ for the $@Q$ during the time period $@\Delta t$;
2. *No*, it does not make sense to insert the $@url$ to the $SERP$ for the $@Q$ during the time period $@\Delta t$;
3. There is not enough information to judge.

The interface for our labeling procedure is presented in Figure 5. As it turned out, judges were struggling to distinguish between the first two categories of Figure 5, hence we decide to collapse these two categories into a single case of drift due to a failed $SERP$, consistent with the algorithm in Section 4.

5.3 Experimental Results

We detect 100s of thousands of revisions over a whole year, and over 200,000 unique $\langle Q, Q' \rangle$ pairs. This is considerable number, but of course still a small fraction of the overall traffic. The set of revision terms is rather varied, with a revision term occurring in 3-4 unique pairs of $\langle Q, Q' \rangle$. Familiar patterns like 'year' revisions (i.e., '2014' or '2015') account just a around 2-3 percentage of the revisions, and around 17-18 percent contains any number. This suggests we capture a wide variety of revisions, beyond those that could be detected based on rules and templates. For the non-numerical revisions, we also see queries and revisions in many languages, show-casing the general applicability of the unsupervised approach.

Table 2 shows the results of the drift detection approach for three test windows with 3 days, 7 days, and 14 days, where we look at all cases of drift (failed $SERP$ and positive reformulations) versus the 'no drift' judgment, and on the judgment on the utility to include the URL clicked after revisions on the $SERP$ of the original query.

We observe a 72% accuracy for the drift detection and a 92% accuracy for the usefulness of the URL to be included on the original page's $SERP$. While the detection doesn't work flawless, these accuracies are a clear indicator of the value of the approach to detect failed $SERPs$. To put this performance into perspective, these number are based on the simplified algorithm based on the probability of query revisions and the theoretical threshold, rather than optimized tuning. The high levels of accuracy for the picked up $URLs$ confirm that these are of interest to be included on the $SERP$ of the original query.

Table 3: Accuracy of failed SERP and positive reformulation detection

	Window	Drift (Failure)	Pos_Reformulation
1	3 days	0.17	0.41
2	7 days	0.41	0.20
3	14 days	0.80	0.11
4	Combined	0.47	0.25

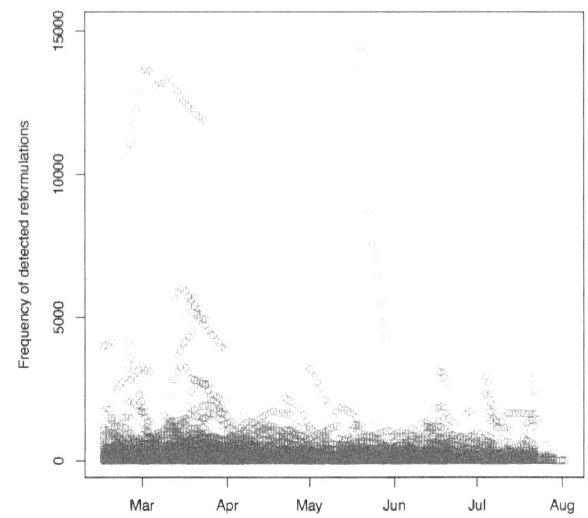

Figure 6: Frequency of detected reformulations over time.

Looking at the breakdown over the duration of the test windows, we see a considerable increase in accuracy for the longer test periods, reaching up to 91% accuracy for the 14 day window. This leads to two observations. First, the approach seems to benefit from more observations to make more reliable judgments, and a revision pattern observed over two weeks is obviously a clearer signal. This also suggests the value of our approach for the detection of incremental change. Second, we expected to obtain high accuracy for popular or head queries in the 3 day window, but observed mostly queries with 1-3 revisions per day. A plausible explanation is that these are picked up and corrected by the $SERP$ already, as recency ranking tools are employed in the search engine that can respond within hours. A possible resolution is to use smaller and adaptive windows, as is done in the concept drift literature, or defining window size in terms of an absolute minimum number of revisions leading to very short window sizes for popular queries.

In Table 3 we break down the two cases of drift: due to a genuine shift in intent toward a new direction, hence indicating a failed SERP, or due to the exploration of another aspect or facet of the original request beyond what's presented on the initial SERP. We observe 47% accuracy for the failed SERP detection relative to all detected $\langle Q, SERP \rangle$ pairs, hence the remaining 25% are positive reformulations. In particular in these 47% of the cases it would be important to consider including the URL clicked after revision into the $SERP$ of the original query. As observed above, the detection accuracy goes significantly up over the larger duration of the detection windows. Over 14 days, no less than 80% of the detected cases indicate a failed $SERP$ due to query intent drift. As observed above, our approach is very effective to detect cases of incremental drift, but less effective to pick up sudden drift over the shortest period.

In this section, we limited ourselves by the varying time windows of detection due to patterns of sudden and incremental drifts. Figure 6 shows the frequencies of detected query reformulations over time. What we observe is that we detect the same drifts on consecutive days, but also that the revisions may disappear after a period of time. Anecdotal evidence suggests that this can be both due to another drift in query intent, for example for revisions specific to events or months of the year, or due to updates of the SERP served for the original query. This supports to importance of detecting both positive and negative drift patterns, and also look at gradual and reoccurring drifts.

Summarizing, in this section, we ran a simplified version of our algorithm on a massive transaction log, and detected over 200,000 pairs of $\langle Q, SERP \rangle$ suspected of failing due to drifting query intents. We observed a reasonable accuracy of drift detection (72%) and a high accuracy of candidate URLs to be included on the $SERP$ of the original query. For incremental change over the longer detection period of 14 days, we detected failed $SERPs$ due to query intent drift with an 80% accuracy. Under the specific conditions of the recency optimized search engine, the performance for detecting sudden change over shorter periods was less effective.

6. CONCLUSIONS

This paper investigated how the dynamic nature of web content and user intents have consequences for the SERP to be displayed for a particular query. In particular, there remain cases of failure where the organic search results on the search engine result page ($SERP$) are outdated, and no relevant result is displayed. This can be caused by temporal query intent drift, where the desired pages for a query are changing over time, and the historical transaction logs privilege the outdated results. Our main research question was: By analyzing behavioral dynamics at the SERP level, can we detect an important class of detrimental cases (such as search failure) based on changes in observable behavior caused by low user satisfaction?

We presented an overview of prior work on topic and concept drift, behavioral dynamics, and user satisfaction on the web, with a special focus on the $SERP$ level. We conducted a conceptual analysis of success and failure at the SERP level in order to answer our first research question: How to include the SERP into the conceptual model of behavioral dynamics on the web? How to identify (un)successful SERPs in terms of drastic changes in observable user behavior? Specifically, we introduced the concept of a successful and failed SERP and analyzed their behavioral consequences identifying indicators of success and failure. By analyzing success and failure in light of changing query intents over time, we identified an important case of SERP failure due to query intent drift. This suggested an approach to detect a failed SERP due to query intent drift by significant changes in behavioral indicators of failure.

We continued our analysis of different types of drifts in query intent over time, answering our second research question: Can we distinguish different types of SERP failure due to query intent drift (e.g., sudden, incremental), and when and how should we update the SERP to reflect these changes? Inspired by the literature on concept drift [15], we studied different changes in query intent: sudden, incremental, gradual and reoccurring, and identified relevant parameters, such as the window of change, volume or popularity of queries, and relevant behavioral indicators, such as the probability of reformulation, abandonment rates, and click through rates. For the two main categories of intent drift, we define an unsupervised approach to detect failed SERPs caused by drift, requiring only a single pass through a transaction log.

Finally, we ran experiments on massive raw search logs, answering our third research question: How effective is our approach on a realistic sample of traffic of a major internet search engine? We ran a simplified version of our algorithm and detected over 200,000 pairs of $\langle Q, SERP \rangle$ suspected of failing due to drifting query intents, observing a reasonable accuracy of drift detection (72%) and a high accuracy of candidate URLs to be included on the SERP of the original query. For incremental change over the longer detection period of 14 days, we detected failed SERPs due to query intent drift with an 80% accuracy, but under the specific conditions of the recency optimized search engine the performance for detecting sudden change over shorter periods was less effective.

As future work, we are further developing the conceptual model, and are running further offline experiments exploring further window sizes, and further features of user dissatisfaction. We are also planning to do online evaluation of how the discovered drifts are useful for fixing SERPs. In addition to the unsupervised methods of this paper, we are also experimenting with tuning the optimal parameters and theshold based on behavioral features and initial results suggest futher improvements.

Real data is messy and has many intricate dependencies, such as continually changing ranking, personalization, customization and localization, and specific tools to update the ranker fast on other signals (i.e., recency ranking). This makes data-driven research a difficult enterprise, and we strongly feel that this should be coupled with theoretical and conceptual analysis. We made a first attempt at this in the current paper, where we conduct conceptual analysis to clarify the meaning of core concepts and their relations and dependencies. And as a conceptual model, work with an idealized model that abstracts away from other factors outside the scope of our interest. For example, we observed in the experimental data relatively few or popular queries as those are tackled within hours by recency ranking methods. We view the experimental part more as initial validation experiments, mostly used to inform the conceptual model as well as identify the most useful features in the context of real world traffic. For this reason we did not "optimize" for the data using supervised methods, but collected a single set of data for three time windows and analyzed this to assess the value of the variables in the conceptual model, and to further develop our model. We strongly belief that conceptual and experimental research should go hand in hand, and without denying the value of "things that work in practice" we should put equal value on experiments that contribute to our conceptual or theoretical understanding.

Acknowledgments

This research has been partly supported by STW and it is the part of the Context Aware Predictive Analytics (CAPA) project.

References

[1] M. Ageev, Q. Guo, D. Lagun, and E. Agichtein. Find it if you can: a game for modeling different types of web search success using interaction data. In *SIGIR*, 2011.

[2] E. Agichtein, E. Brill, and S. T. Dumais. Improving web search ranking by incorporating user behavior information. In *SIGIR*, pages 19–26, 2006.

[3] A. Al-Maskari, M. Sanderson, and P. Clough. The relationship between ir effectiveness measures and user satisfaction. In *SIGIR*, pages 773–774, 2007.

[4] J. Allan. Incremental relevance feedback for information filtering. In *SIGIR*, pages 270–278, 1996.

[5] A. Arampatzis and A. van Hameran. The score-distributional threshold optimization for adaptive binary classification tasks. In *SIGIR*, pages 285–293, 2001.

[6] A. Bifet and R. Gavaldá. Learning from time-changing data with adaptive windowing. In *Proceedings of SIAM International Conference on Data Mining (SDM)*, 2007.

[7] A. Chuklin and P. Serdyukov. How query extensions reflect search result abandonments. In *Proceeding of SIGIR*, pages 1087–1088, 2012.

[8] A. Chuklin and P. Serdyukov. Good abandonments in factoid queries. In *Proceeding of WWW (Companion Volume)*, pages 483–484, 2012.

[9] N. Craswell, O. Zoeter, M. J. Taylor, and B. Ramsey. An experimental comparison of click position-bias models. In *WSDM*, pages 87–94, 2008.

[10] N. Dai, M. Shokouhi, and B. D. Davison. Learning to rank for freshness and relevance. In *Proceeding of SIGIR*, pages 95–104, 2011.

[11] A. Diriye, R. White, G. Buscher, and S. T. Dumais. Leaving so soon?: understanding and predicting web search abandonment rationales. In *Proceeding of CIKM*, pages 1025–1034, 2012.

[12] A. Dong, Y. Chang, Z. Zheng, G. Mishne, J. Bai, R. Zhang, K. Buchner, and C. L. F. Diaz. Towards recency ranking in web search. In *WSDM*, pages 11–20, 2010.

[13] A. Dong, R. Zhang, P. Kolari, J. Bai, F. Diaz, Y. Chang, Z. Zheng, and H. Zha. Time is of the essence: improving recency ranking using twitter data. In *Proceeding of WWW*, pages 331–340, 2010.

[14] H. A. Feild, J. Allan, and R. Jones. Predicting searcher frustration. In *SIGIR*, pages 34–41, 2010.

[15] J. Gama, I. Žliobaitė, A. Bifet, M. Pechenizkiy, and A. Bouchachia. A survey on concept drift adaptation. *ACM Computing Surveys*, 46(4):44:1–44:37, 2014.

[16] Q. Guo, R. W. White, Y. Zhang, B. Anderson, and S. T. Dumais. Why searchers switch: understanding and predicting engine switching rationales. In *SIGIR*, pages 335–344, 2011.

[17] A. Hassan and R. W. White. Personalized models of search satisfaction. In *CIKM*, pages 2009–2018, 2013.

[18] A. Hassan, R. Jones, and K. L. Klinkner. Beyond DCG: user behavior as a predictor of a successful search. In *WSDM*, pages 221–230, 2010.

[19] S. Ieong, N. Mishra, E. Sadikov, and L. Zhang. Domain bias in web search. In *Proceeding of WSDM*, pages 55–64, 2012.

[20] J. Jiang, A. H. Awadallah, X. Shi, and R. W. White. Understanding and predicting graded search satisfaction. In *Proceeding of WSDM*, 2015.

[21] T. Joachims. Optimizing search engines using clickthrough data. In *Proceeding of KDD*, pages 133–142, 2002.

[22] T. Joachims, L. Granka, B. Pan, H. Hembrooke, and G. Gay. Accurately interpreting clickthrough data as implicit feedback. In *SIGIR*, pages 154–161, 2005.

[23] Y. Kim, A. Hassan, R. W. White, and I. Zitouni. Modeling dwell time to predict click-level satisfaction. In *Proceedings of WSDM*, pages 193–202, New York, NY, USA, 2014. ACM.

[24] J. Kiseleva, E. Crestan, R. Brigo, and R. Dittel. Modelling and detecting changes in user satisfaction. In *Proceeding of CIKM*, pages 1449–1458, 2014.

[25] A. Kulkarni, J. Teevan, K. M. Svore, and S. T. Dumais. Understanding temporal query dynamics. In *WSDM*, pages 167–176, 2011.

[26] D. Lefortier, P. Serdyukov, and M. de Rijke. Online exploration for detecting shifts in fresh intent. In *Proceeding of CIKM*, pages 589–598, 2014.

[27] K. Radinsky, S. Davidovich, and S. Markovitch. Predicting the news of tomorrow using patterns in web search queries. In *WI*, 2008.

[28] K. Radinsky, K. Svore, S. T. Dumais, J. Teevan, A. Bocharov, and E. Horvitz. Modeling and predicting behavioral dynamics on the web. In *WWW*, pages 599–608, 2012.

[29] K. Radinsky, K. M. Svore, S. T. Dumais, M. Shokouhi, J. Teevan, A. Bocharov, and E. Horvitz. Behavioral dynamics on the web: Learning, modeling, and prediction. *ACM Transactions on Information Systems (TOIS)*, 31(3):16, 2013.

[30] J. C. Schlimmer and R. H. Granger. Beyond incremental processing: Tracking concept drift. In *AAAI*, 1986.

[31] M. Shokouhi. Detecting seasonal queries by time-series analysis. In *SIGIR*, pages 1171–1172, 2011.

[32] M. Shokouhi and K. Radinsky. Time-sensitive query auto-completion. In *SIGIR*, pages 601–610, 2012.

[33] A. Shtok, O. Kurland, D. Carmel, F. Raiber, and G. Markovits. Predicting query performance by query-drift estimation. *TOIS*, 30:11:1–11:35, 2012.

[34] Y. Song, X. Shi, R. White, and A. H. Awadallah. Context-aware web search abandonment prediction. In *Proceeding of SIGIR*, pages 93–102, 2014.

[35] R. W. White and S. T. Dumais. Characterizing and predicting search engine switching behavior. In *CIKM*, pages 87–96, 2009.

[36] G. Widmer and M. Kubat. Learning in the presence of concept drift and hidden contexts. *Machine Learning (ML)*, 23(1):69–101, 1996.

[37] Y. Yue, R. Patel, and H. Roehrig. Beyond position bias: Examining result attractiveness as a source of presentation bias in clickthrough data. In *WWW*, pages 1011–1018, 2010.

What Users Ask a Search Engine: Analyzing One Billion Russian Question Queries

Michael Völske
Bauhaus-Universität Weimar
michael.voelske@uni-weimar.de

Pavel Braslavski
Ural Federal University
pbras@yandex.ru

Matthias Hagen
Bauhaus-Universität Weimar
matthias.hagen@uni-weimar.de

Galina Lezina
Ural Federal University
galina.lezina@gmail.com

Benno Stein
Bauhaus-Universität Weimar
benno.stein@uni-weimar.de

ABSTRACT

We analyze the question queries submitted to a large commercial web search engine to get insights about what people ask, and to better tailor the search results to the users' needs. Based on a dataset of about one billion question queries submitted during the year 2012, we investigate askers' querying behavior with the support of automatic query categorization. While the importance of question queries is likely to increase, at present they only make up 3–4% of the total search traffic.

Since questions are such a small part of the query stream, and are more likely to be unique than shorter queries, click-through information is typically rather sparse. Thus, query categorization methods based on the categories of clicked web documents do not work well for questions. As an alternative, we propose a robust question query classification method that uses the labeled questions from a large community question answering platform (CQA) as a training set. The resulting classifier is then transferred to the web search questions. Even though questions on CQA platforms tend to be different to web search questions, our categorization method proves competitive with strong baselines with respect to classification accuracy.

To show the scalability of our proposed method we apply the classifiers to about one billion question queries and discuss the trade-offs between performance and accuracy that different classification models offer. Our findings reveal what people ask a search engine and also how this contrasts behavior on a CQA platform.

Categories and Subject Descriptors: H.3.3 [Information Systems]: Information Search and Retrieval

Keywords: Question Queries; Query Log Analysis; Query Classification; Community Question Answering (CQA).

Permission to make digital or hard copies of all or part of this work for personal or classroom use is granted without fee provided that copies are not made or distributed for profit or commercial advantage and that copies bear this notice and the full citation on the first page. Copyrights for components of this work owned by others than the author(s) must be honored. Abstracting with credit is permitted. To copy otherwise, or republish, to post on servers or to redistribute to lists, requires prior specific permission and/or a fee. Request permissions from Permissions@acm.org.

CIKM'15, October 19–23, 2015, Melbourne, Australia.

Copyright is held by the owner/author(s). Publication rights licensed to ACM.

ACM 978-1-4503-3794-6/15/10 ...$15.00.
DOI: http://dx.doi.org/10.1145/2806416.2806457

1. INTRODUCTION

Questions are a natural form of expressing information needs. People ask questions when they seek information, help, or advice. Web search engines have taught users the "telegram style" of keyword search queries such as `[lose weight]`. Nevertheless, the share of natural language questions, for example `[how much exercise should i do to lose 10 pounds]`, in search query logs is increasing [21].

In the late 1990s, queries in question form comprised less than 1% of the query stream of a general-purpose search engine; the most common format was `[where can i find ...]` for general information on a topic [28]. Pang and Kumar report that question queries accounted for about 2% of the entire Yahoo query stream in 2010 [21]. Our analysis shows that question queries already constitute a 3–4% -share of the query log we are using from 2012; questions are thus still on the rise even in keyword-based interfaces.

But why do users formulate search queries as questions? A possible explanation is the general tendency of smoother, more natural human-computer interaction with information retrieval systems, as evidenced by touch, voice, and visual search interfaces. Although voice search queries constitute a marginal share of the entire query log, they support this trend [25]. The spread of community question answering (CQA) services such as Yahoo! Answers provides a parallel setting in which to study question-asking behavior on the web.[1] CQA sites allow users to pose questions to other community members, to answer questions, rate questions and answers, and receive feedback. The services are quite popular and have collected a vast amount of content in the form of questions and answers that is being indexed by major search engines. The odds are high that a question a user has in mind has already been asked by someone before and can be found through search engines.

However, submitting queries in the form of natural language questions does not always yield better search results. As several studies show [7, 1, 21], web search engines perform worse at answering question queries compared to corresponding keyword queries. In view of the growing share of question queries, and the still lagging search quality for them, there is a strong need to improve the processing of such queries. For example, Google's latest major search algorithm update

[1] `https://answers.yahoo.com/`

in the fall of 2013—codenamed Hummingbird—was targeted at answering long natural questions better.[2]

One option to improve the search results for question queries is accounting not only for the query's terms, but also its topic, by means of query classification. The technique has benefited general search [2], query disambiguation and routing to vertical search [16], and search advertising [9].

The main difficulty in query classification is data sparseness: the short query strings. Search queries contain around three words on average [22, 7], and despite the fact that question queries are somewhat longer—around six to seven words, according to different studies [21, 19]—they are still much shorter than web documents.

Our approach exploits CQA data and its categorization scheme as a "bridge classification" for the question query classification problem. CQA services provide a vast amount of questions manually categorized by their users that can inform automatic query categorization. Similarly to [16], our primary goal is to expand the training set, using rather straightforward classification techniques. In our study we employ several million user-generated questions, along with top-level category labels, for building a question-query classifier. To the best of our knowledge, this approach is novel.

Robust topical classification can also boost the identification of users' information needs in contexts different from web search. Mobile voice-activated assistants like Apple's Siri—that suffer from a very limited range of available classification domains [6]—may benefit just as the analysis of short interrogative posts on Twitter [33] or Facebook [20].

Our contributions are two-fold. First, we describe and analyze two large complementary datasets of Russian questions from 2012: (1) a year's worth of questions posted at a popular CQA service, and (2) question queries submitted to a large commercial search engine. To the best of our knowledge, this is the first study dealing with non-English question datasets of this size. Second, we build a question classifier of high quality using CQA data and use it to analyze the information needs of web search question askers.

The paper is organized as follows: In Section 2, we discuss the literature on query classification and question analysis. We then introduce the datasets used in our analyses in Section 3 and explain our classification approach in Section 4. Besides experimental evaluation of the classification approaches, Section 5 also shows the application of our classification approach to one billion web search question queries to shed some light on what people ask their search engine. Finally, Section 6 summarizes the results and suggests interesting directions for future work.

2. RELATED WORK

Question queries have been the subject of dedicated search log studies [28] and have been analyzed in the context of long queries [7]. Pang and Kumar [21] draw attention to the phenomenon of question queries in search engine logs, describe their structural and statistical characteristics, and show that the share of these queries grows. A more recent longitudinal study on the evolution of user behavior shows questions as an important part [17]. The authors also note that the search results for question queries are usually worse than for the corresponding keyword queries expressing the same information need [7, 1, 21].

[2]`http://onforb.es/1bfagwI`

The data sparseness problem is usually addressed by enriching queries with additional information. Queries are categorized based on the category labels of documents returned by a search engine [9] or are enriched by the search results containing document titles and snippets [26]. Bailey and coauthors [2] classify long queries with sparse user interaction data by matching them against shorter and more popular queries categorized based on past users' behavior. Li et al. [16] suggest to substantially expand the set of labeled queries using click-through information: user clicks on the same link returned for different queries are considered as a similarity indicator. Thus, iterative propagation of category labels from seed queries along click edges through co-clicked documents to unlabeled queries allows expanding the initial training set by several orders of magnitude.

Note that, to be practically applicable, all three approaches require the availability of search log information. In case of click-through information this is rather obvious. In case of using returned results or titles and snippets for categorization, the classification can be accounted for in a second retrieval run or performed off-line and then applied on-the-fly if the query appears again. In case of questions, however, the availability of click-through data is a big problem, as questions are typically rather unique, and have little associated log data. This rules out the above classification methods for our use case of question classification and we aim for another approach to analyze our large question query log.

In contrast to classifying isolated queries, topical categorization of a large log should give high-level insights into the spectrum of user interests and their dynamics. Spink et al. [29] manually label several thousand queries from a search log in an attempt to study user interests. Later, Beitzel et al. [4] automatically match queries against manually compiled topical word lists, classifying 13% of a search engine's query stream. A bootstrapping of this method based on word-category distributions yields an improved recall [5] but still low coverage. In a fully automatic large-scale analysis, Bar-Ilan et al. [3] perform a topical classification of the AOL and MSR logs using an SVM classifier over query word uni- and bigrams. Similarly, one of our methods uses query word unigrams for classification.

Besides the large-scale analysis, another important aspect of our study is that we conduct experiments on log data spanning one year. Up to today there are only few studies dealing with query data stretching over such long periods. Richardson [24] explores the long-term dependencies of users' intents and preferences based on a one-year log of millions of users. He concludes that the analysis of user behavior based on such long periods can uncover information not present in shorter logs, and as such be of interest not only for information retrieval, but also for social sciences, psychology, market research, and medical studies. Note that in contrast to Richardson's study, we aim at analyzing question queries in particular, but still the dimensions of the employed log data are comparable. The aforementioned work by Pang and Kumar [21] also draws conclusions based on the analysis of an annual search log, but other studies used much smaller logs. Beitzel et al. [4] explore the topical structure of a six month query log and Liu et al. [17] track user behavior based on log excerpts spanning two weeks in three subsequent years.

There are several studies conducted on the intersection of web search and CQA. Weber et al. [30] aim at finding answers (tips) to web queries with *how-to* intent (not necessarily expressed as well-formed *how-to* questions) in Yahoo! Answers archives. Liu et al. [18] evaluate the utility of existing CQA answers in web search scenarios. In a follow-up study [19] the authors track users, who follow up web searching with asking a question on a CQA platform. In contrast to these studies, our goal is not to develop methods that provide better answers to questions or that recommend CQA items to the users. Instead, we aim at the topical categorization of questions on the scale of a year; the results might then improve retrieval systems, as is proposed in some studies [14, 11].

Topical categorization of questions posted on CQA services is the subject of several studies. For instance, Li et al. [15] suggest to use topic information in a question routing task (i.e., delivering newly posted questions to potential answerers). While this use case is rather different from ours, the study of Qu et al. [23] who investigate the contribution of different components to question classification quality (machine learning methods, n-gram features, data fields, and training sample size) is closer to our setting. We incorporate several of their findings in one of our methods using bag-of-words features. Chan et al. [12] apply a set of kernels corresponding to different aspects of questions to hierarchical question classification. Since we are interested in a rather broad, non-nested category scheme that can be used in the actual retrieval process, we do not aim for any hierarchy. Cai et al. [10] propose to enrich CQA questions with Wikipedia entries as a means to counter the sparseness problem discussed above. However, in contrast to our approach, all these CQA methods do not extend beyond CQA (i.e., they use CQA data for learning and consequently perform classification on the data of the same origin). One of our contributions instead is to show how a classifier trained on CQA questions can be used to classify web search questions as well, affording the opportunity of including on-the-fly class information in the retrieval process for questions submitted to search engines.

Question analysis in other domains, such as questions posted on Twitter [33] or Facebook [20], may also benefit from such an online classification method.

3. DATASETS

The basis for our question query classification are two datasets: a large amount of question-like queries collected from the query log of Yandex[3], a leading Russian search engine, and a year's worth of questions and answers from a popular Russian community question answering (CQA) platform Otvety@Mail.Ru[4]. Both datasets contain Russian queries only, although some of the queries contain words in other languages (mainly named entities such as movie or song titles, video games names, etc.). Below, we outline the data acquisition process and provide further details on the datasets.

3.1 Web Search Questions

The initial dataset comprises of all queries from Yandex logs for the year 2012 containing one of 58 combinations of question word uni- or bigrams (e.g., *what, where, when, why, how, does, should, ..., in which, for what*, etc.). This is similar to previous processes of question extraction from query logs [7] except that the question word set was adapted to Russian. Each entry in the resulting question excerpt is annotated with the query string, a time stamp, and user ID. The nearly 2 billion initially acquired questions form about 3–4% of the actual query log, indicating some further increase in the number of questions submitted to web search engines compared to the 2010 Yahoo figure of about 2% using similar extraction rules [21]. Under the agreement with the search engine, we have access only to the queries containing question words for research purposes; we have no access to the other queries issued by the same users or to the search results. Since it was curated at the end of 2012, the query log contains no entries for the second half of December. Hence, we omit all December entries from our analysis.

[3]`http://yandex.ru`
[4]`http://otvet.mail.ru`

Cleaning step	Unique users	Questions
Raw log	185,700,840	1,980,878,942
Spam & bots	184,630,648	1,903,716,272
Core questions	167,812,003	1,577,657,443
Repeats & prefixes	167,812,003	1,265,433,864
Unoriginal questions	145,688,746	923,482,955
Single-word questions	145,071,912	915,055,325

Table 1: Cleaning the question queries extracted from the web query log.

In an iterative process outlined below, we apply further cleaning steps to keep only queries that represent actual question-asking information needs. Table 1 shows the individual steps of the data cleaning process and their impact.

In a first step, we remove spam and bot queries from the log. After examining user activity statistics, we suggest to characterize a user as a bot when any of the following properties holds: (1) more than 2,000 total interactions over the entire year; (2) more than five questions within the most active one-minute window; (3) a median question length of more than 20 words; or (4) at least 50 questions in total, and the same leading 15 characters in at least 80% of them.

The first two criteria are aimed at the number of questions per time slot, while the latter two are aimed at the type of questions submitted. Users submitting a very large number of questions in one year or in their peak activity minute behave rather "unhuman" and we view them as bots. Users submitting unusually long questions, or questions almost always starting with the same 2–3 words are also behaving rather unnaturally. Extensive spot-check inspections of users matching any of the above four criteria showed that all of them could easily be viewed as bots. The specific numbers might be debatable, especially for the peak activity for some of the affected users, but we decided to rather aggressively remove users to base later examinations only on questions that were very likely submitted as a human information need.

Altogether, the first cleaning step removed about 1 million users and all their 77 million questions. Examples of removed bots include users submitting very many `[how to translate ...]` or `[how is the weather in ...]` questions that probably aim at scraping the search engine's translation or weather service, or for instance bots submitting thousands of long copy-pasted questions from exams. Interestingly, hardly any of the questions containing an actual question mark remain after the first cleaning step; the ones that do remain almost always also seem to be copy-pasted from some exam. Having removed all entries for these suspicious users, we apply subsequent filtering steps to individual questions in the log.

In a second cleaning step, we retain only "core questions" with a question word in the first position, since extensive spot checks of the other queries showed a large number of queries with debatable question intent. Instead of devising sophisticated rules to decide for each such query whether it actually is a question intent or not, we again choose an aggressive removal to reduce the amount of non-question needs in the final dataset. This step removes about 326 million questions, and about 17 million users that would not have any remaining question.

The third cleaning step eliminates repeated questions and collapses prefixes. The goal is to remove bogus query submissions resulting from instant search, accidental submissions of unfinished question strings, or log entries of users paging through search engine results pages (SERPs) (always with the same question string but not really submitting new queries). If a user resubmits the same question within 90 minutes, without a different question in between, we only retain the first occurrence. To catch SERP paging behavior, we again choose to aggressively clean the query log using a long temporal window rather than a 2- or 5-minute gap. To remove "unfinished" questions stemming from instant searches or unintentionally submitted queries, we analyze pairs of questions submitted within 5 seconds. When the first query of such a pair is a prefix of the second, we retain only the latter (e.g., [when was caesar bo] is removed when immediately followed by [when was caesar born]).

In a fourth cleaning step, we remove unoriginal questions, by which we refer to questions not formulated by the user themselves, but probably stemming from some external source. For this, we first remove all questions that match one of 885 titles of Wikipedia articles (e.g., the movie title [what women want]). We then also identify some questions that seek answers to crossword puzzles; we assume a crossword puzzle information need if the query ends with the phrase [n words] for some value of n. In addition, we also remove question queries that contain the phrase [family feud], and variants of that TV show's name in its Russian incarnation.[5] For both the crossword and TV show questions, we include a "bootstrapping" step, in which we also remove all the questions that co-occur ten or more times with one of the characteristic phrases (about 7,600 question strings identified in the bootstrapping). Furthermore, we also remove questions matching a list of 1,764 questions published on fan websites of the Family Feud show. We believe that hardly any of the questions matching a Wikipedia article with the very same title, a crossword puzzle question, or a Family Feud question actually represent an original question intent of the user.

Finally, in a fifth cleaning step, we filter out those question queries that contain only one word after stopword and question word removal. Although this also removes questions like [when is christmas] our spot checks showed many of the single-word questions not to represent real question needs.

The cleaning steps removed more than half of the originally sampled questions; the remaining dataset contains about 915 million question queries from about 145 million users. This represents about 1–2% of the search engine's query stream (cf. Figure 1 for the monthly fraction). Further characteristics and a comparison to our CQA dataset can be found in Section 3.4.

[5]Family Feud is a popular TV show that prominently features questions like [what is a problem most people have in their life] for which the participants have to guess the most popular response of 100 people being asked that question.

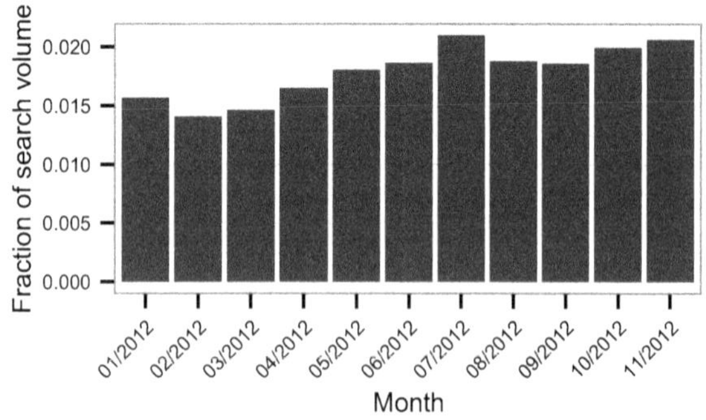

Figure 1: Question queries in the cleaned dataset as a monthly fraction of the total query traffic.

3.2 Community Question Answering Data

The CQA dataset we acquired comprises approximately 11 million questions submitted in Russian by over 2 million unique users to the Russian CQA platform Otvety@Mail.Ru[6] throughout the year 2012. Otvety@Mail.Ru (*otvety* means *answers*) is a Russian counterpart of Yahoo! Answers with similar rules and incentives. Each question is manually categorized by the submitter into one of 28 top-level categories with altogether 189 leaf-level categories forming a two-level hierarchy. In the process of dataset acquisition, we omit several ambiguous categories, and merge closely related categories, leaving the 14 top-level categories shown in the first column of Table 2 as our classification targets.

When using query category labels as additional features for ranking along hundreds of other features, coarse-grained flat categories usually suffice. This is an important difference to query classification for search advertising (advertising-to-query matching is based on category information only), automatic classification of web documents, or category suggestion for questions in the CQA scenario. In both latter cases, the amount of information items under leaf categories must be "digestible" by humans. Hence, hierarchical taxonomies with thousands of categories are used.

We paid special attention to noise in category labels, dissimilarity of the topic distributions in the two datasets, and the alignment of source (CQA) and target categories. Since the user posting a question on the CQA platform manually labels the question with a category—and this seems to be an error-prone task given the number of categories—we decided to further clean the initial dataset. We only keep questions submitted by users that have posted at least three questions that got an answer. This criterion is meant to capture questions with better categorizations. Users posting more than just one or two test questions can be viewed as more experienced with the category scheme and questions that got an answer form a further support of this hypothesis since other users found the query under its category.

The assigned categories in the remaining 6 million questions from the CQA platform are less noisy than the original 11 million questions, making the cleaned CQA data well-suited as a training set for our query classification task. The second column of Table 2 shows the number of instances in

[6]http://otvet.mail.ru/

Category	Number of instances CQA	Test set
Society & Culture	1,267,700	95
Computers & Internet	965,834	131
Family & Relationships	950,180	33
Adult	526,465	13
Games & Recreation	524,533	61
Education	372,600	38
Home & Garden	355,906	117
Entertainment & Music	337,364	64
Cars & Transportation	335,659	89
Health	307,033	70
Consumer Electronics	193,685	43
Beauty & Style	173,825	23
Sports	165,959	16
Business & Finance	99,524	41
Σ	6,576,267	834

Table 2: Class distribution in the CQA dataset and the manually labeled question query test set.

the CQA dataset per category. Further characteristics in comparison to our question queries dataset can be found in Section 3.4.

3.3 Web Search Question Test Data

In order to evaluate the performance of our classification pipeline on the question queries from the search engine log, we randomly sample 1,000 entries from the cleaned dataset. After labeling by three domain experts, no two annotators picked the same category for 166 of the questions. These more ambiguous questions were removed from the test set. The third column of Table 2 shows the class distribution in the remaining test set of 834 questions.

3.4 Descriptive Statistics

We have about 915 million questions from about 145 million users in the web search question query dataset and about 6 million questions from about 0.5 million users in the CQA dataset. The distribution of the number of questions per user per dataset is shown in Figure 2.

Note that we do not have users with less than three questions in the CQA dataset due to our filtering rule. About one third of the CQA users in our cleaned dataset have posted three questions, another half have posted at most ten questions and the remaining 20% have submitted up to 5,000 questions in the year 2012. The average number of questions per user in the CQA data is about 16, with a maximum of 257 questions.

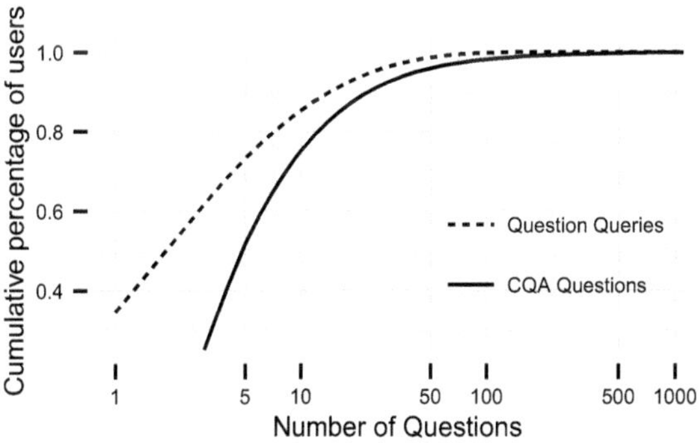

Figure 2: Number of questions per user.

N-gram	English translation	Frequency
CQA Dataset		
можно ли	whether is it possible	113,291
а вы	and you	89,193
у меня	I	68,337
что делать	what to do	66,665
как вы	how you	64,235
что делать если	what to do if	36,990
где можно скачать	where can I download	21,665
как вы думаете	what do you think	20,057
а у вас	and you	16,631
как вы относитесь	what do you think	13,497
Question Queries Dataset		
как сделать	how to make	35,678,293
можно ли	whether is it possible	28,001,988
как правильно	how correctly	23,014,202
сколько стоит	how much costs	19,533,978
где купить	where to buy	11,405,702
как избавиться от	how to get rid of	5,166,515
где можно купить	where to buy	2,804,874
как скачать музыку	how to download music	2,072,003
как доехать до	how to get to	2,028,746
какие документы нужны	what documents are needed	1,818,986

Table 3: The five most frequent initial 2- and 3-grams per dataset.

In the question queries data, the situation is slightly different, with the average user submitting about 6 questions; this is not surprising since we did not remove users with very few questions here. About 40% of the users only submitted a single question in the whole year. However, due to the user identification method on the server side, some questions from the same user might get logged with different user IDs. Similarly to the CQA data, another 40–50% of the users submit at most ten questions while only 10% of the users submit up to 2,000 questions in the whole year. Since 2,000 questions per year was a bot-removal threshold used in our cleaning process, there are no users with more than 2,000 question queries and only a few with more than 1,000 questions; the most interrogative user submitted about 1,500 question queries in the whole year.

The two datasets also differ in the most frequent question prefixes given in Table 3. Not surprisingly, the top prefixes of the question titles in the CQA data show that users often do not explicitly formulate a question but rather ask others for help (e.g., `[I need your help]` or `[can you help me]`). Due to the sampling strategy, the question queries have explicit question words as their initial n-grams. As was already observed in other studies, the most frequent questions are how-to questions that can be formulated using different bi- and trigrams in Russian.

Figure 3 shows the datasets' frequency distributions. In the CQA data, about 98% of queries are unique, as opposed to 88% for the question queries. Not surprising, given that we count title and description as the query, the average question appears just once in the CQA data with the very short most frequent questions appearing five times. In the search engine question queries, the average question appears about two times while the most frequent question, `[how to download music from VK]`, has nearly a million occurrences.[7]

[7]The query refers to the social network site `vk.com`.

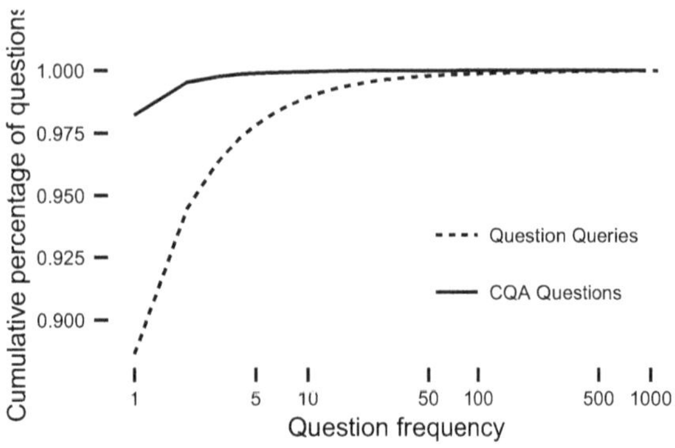

Figure 3: Question frequency in the CQA and question queries datasets.

Figure 4 shows the question length distributions in both datasets. While almost all the question queries have at most ten words, only one third of the CQA questions are that "short." (but note that we combine the question title and description fields). The average question query has a length of about six to seven words (about five to six not counting question words); the longest having 114 words probably copy-pasted from an exam and not reprinted here for space restrictions. The average CQA question is much longer with about 24 words (28 including question words) and the longest CQA question is about 1,000 words including its description.

4. QUESTION QUERY CLASSIFICATION

In order to infer a category assignment for the queries in the question query log, we employ a machine learning approach: Using the CQA questions and their assigned categories as a training set, we train a classifier that predicts the categories of unlabeled search engine question queries with high accuracy. To this end, we first derive different feature representations from the question queries and CQA questions, using the representation strategies outlined below. We compare a bag-of-words representation, which is effective but unwieldy due to its amount of features and only applicable to a subset of the question query data, to a much more compact topic-model-based representation. Since we finally want to classify the question queries, the general process of transferring the trained classifier from CQA data to question queries is as follows: First, we extract features (bag-of-words or topic models) from the question queries, then train a classifier with these features on the CQA questions, and finally apply the classifier to the question queries. The (unsupervised) feature extraction from the target dataset ensures better transferability of the classifier.

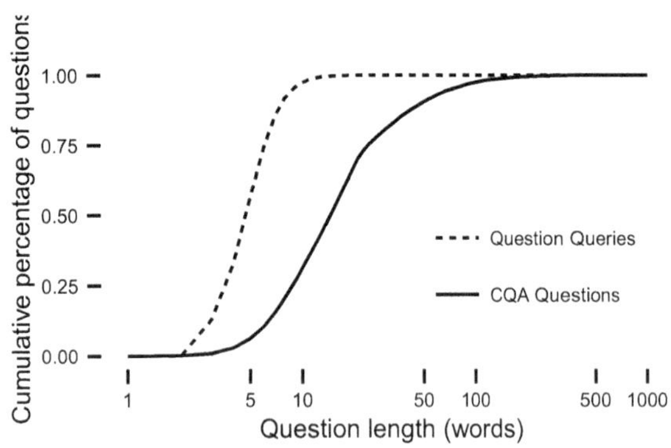

Figure 4: Question length in the CQA and question queries datasets.

4.1 Bag-of-words Features

Our first model is based on a bag-of-words representation, where each question is represented as a term frequency vector of (case-folded and lemmatized) unigrams. A bag-of-words model can be very complex: across the entire question query dataset, there are more than 16 million distinct words. Since we are using the CQA questions as our training set, our classifier can only consider the 1.3 million words that also occur in CQA questions. Out of this number, we retain only those words that occur in at least ten question queries, resulting in 137,032 features for our question query representation.

Besides its complexity, the main drawback of the bag-of-words model is the divergence of the feature sets between the two datasets. Out of our nearly one billion question queries, only 85% contain vocabulary from the bag-of-words model. We employ probabilistic topic modeling in order to reduce the model complexity, as well as to improve the transferability of the classifier. We investigate two different probabilistic topic models: Latent Dirichlet Allocation [8] and the Biterm Topic Model (BTM) proposed by Cheng et al. [13].

4.2 Topic Model Features

Both LDA and BTM are generative Bayesian models that uncover latent topics in a given text corpus by modeling the formation of documents as the result of a probabilistic process. For the purposes of feature derivation for our classification task, they operate in two basic steps, which can be summarized as *inference* and *representation*. The inference step involves finding the model parameters that best fit the observed data (the questions/documents in the corpus) for a given topic number k. Given a topic model thus trained, documents can be represented as k-vectors of topic probabilities. The generative model that is assumed to have generated the observed documents differs significantly between LDA and BTM.

From the LDA perspective, each word in each document is generated by first drawing a topic from a document-specific topic distribution, and then drawing the word from the word distribution for that topic. In order to accurately infer the per-document topic distributions, LDA depends on document-level context, and tends to perform poorly on short texts where word co-occurrence information is sparse [13].

The Biterm Topic Model circumvents the data sparseness problem by modeling term co-occurrence directly: In BTM's generative model, documents are modeled as sets of co-occurring words (biterms). Each biterm in a given document is generated by drawing a topic from a single global topic distribution, and then drawing the biterm from that topic's biterm distribution.

The benefit of representing documents as vectors of latent topic probabilities is two-fold—first, the representation is much more compact than a bag-of-words model of similar performance, and second, it captures high-level semantic structure based on unigram occurrence alone, allowing a larger fraction of the question query log to be classified.

Our topic-model-based classification pipeline operates as follows: we apply stopword removal, case folding and lemmatization to all datasets. We then fit topic models to the question query dataset with the topic count k ranging from 10 to 500. For LDA, we employ the implementation available as part of the *gensim* software package.[8] To fit Biterm Topic Models, we use the implementation maintained by one of the BTM authors.[9] We then represent the CQA questions using the models fitted to the question queries and split the CQA questions into a training and validation set, comprising 70% and 30% of the questions, respectively. We use the validation set to select the best performing topic model, which we then evaluate on the web search question test set.

In the following section, we describe the results of our classification experiments and insights on questioning behavior in the search engine log.

5. EXPERIMENTAL RESULTS

According to the above procedure, we train a multinomial naïve Bayes classifier on the CQA training set for each of our question query models, and compare their performance on the CQA validation set. Having selected the best performing models from this run, we train new classifiers on the entire CQA data and evaluate them using the web search question test set. In order to compare the performance of the different models, we compute the classification performance on each target class, and then average over the classes to arrive at the macro-average precision and recall, as defined by [27]. Finally, we classify all questions in the web search log in order to gain further insights into what users ask search engines. For the classification experiments described below, we employ the multinomial naïve Bayes implementation from the Apache Spark MLlib library.[10]

5.1 Performance on CQA Questions

In order to compare the performance of the different topic models on the CQA data, we first fit a topic model to the question query data for the different numbers of topics. Due to the large amount of input data, this is a time consuming process; fitting the 500-topic BTM model requires approximately 80 hours of wall-clock time on a machine with sixteen 1.6 GHz CPU cores, while the largest LDA model requires about 24 hours. For both topic models, we use an incremental variant of the inference algorithm. Our observations confirm those of [13]— while the processing time for BTM is higher than for LDA, the memory requirements are lower.

Figure 5 shows the classification performance of the topic model-based features on the validation set, with the number of latent topics ranging from ten to 500. The biterm topic model outperforms LDA by a large margin for all topic counts. Considering the sparse word co-occurrence information found in web search queries, this result confirms our expectations. Both topic models' performance increases with growing number of topics, but the effect is more pronounced for LDA. More fine-grained latent topics make more informative features for query categorization in both cases. While the bag-of-words model outperforms both BTM and LDA,

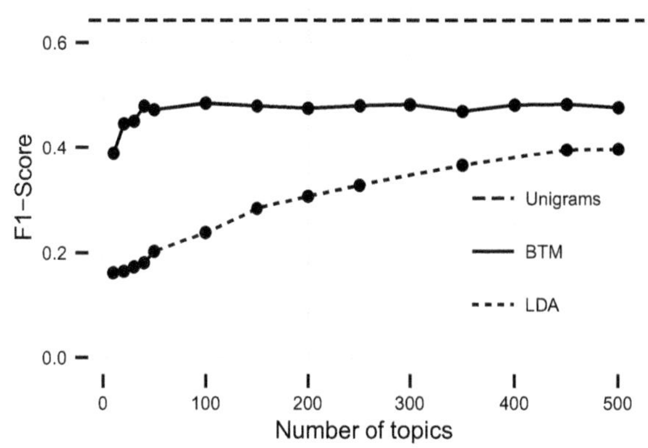

Figure 5: Classification performance of the topic model features on the CQA validation set.

it is at the cost of greater model complexity: the number of dimensions in the feature vector for the bag-of-words model is four orders of magnitude larger.

5.2 Performance on Web Search Test Data

Based on the above results, we conclude that the biterm topic model is better suited than LDA to our application domain. Hence, we compare the performance of the BTM features to the bag-of-words features on the web search query test set. As a simple baseline for comparison, we implement a majority-vote classifier based on CQA retrieval. To this end, we index the CQA dataset using the Okapi BM25 retrieval model, which has served as a baseline in previous studies on CQA retrieval [32]. At classification time, we submit the unlabeled query to this index, and pick the most common category among the ten first search results. In case of ties, we pick the category with the higher aggregate retrieval score.

The results of our comparison are summarized in Table 4, where we show the test set performance of CQA retrieval, the bag-of-words model, and the BTM models which perform best on the validation set. The rightmost column of the

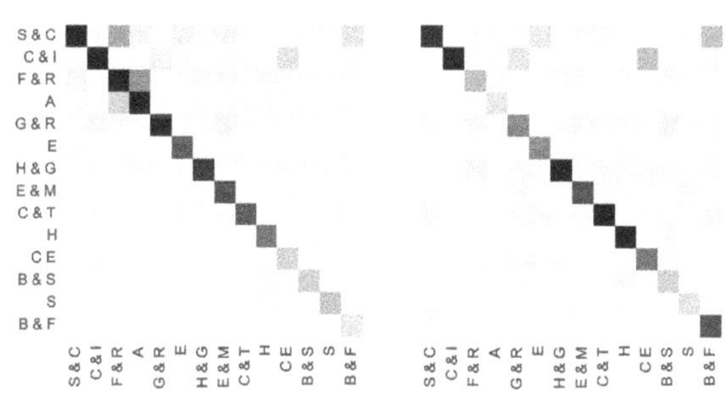

Figure 6: Confusion matrices for the bag-of-words classifier on the CQA validation set (left) and the question queriest test set (right). The rows are the true classes, the columns are the predictions; the ordering of the classes is the same as in Table 2.

[8]`https://github.com/piskvorky/gensim`
[9]`https://github.com/xiaohuiyan/OnlineBTM`
[10]`https://spark.apache.org/mllib/`

Features	Precision	Recall	F_1-Score	Gain
CQA Retrieval Baseline				
—	0.67	0.66	0.66	—
Bag-of-words				
137,032	0.61	0.7	0.65	+2%
Biterm Topics				
100	0.47	0.53	0.50	+1%
200	0.46	0.49	0.47	±0%
300	0.46	0.50	0.48	±0%
400	0.46	0.50	0.48	±0%
450	0.49	0.53	0.51	+4%

Table 4: Performance of the Bag-of-words and BTM models on the web search query test data. The final column shows the change in F_1-score relative to the validation set.

table shows the relative performance gain (or loss) incurred in the transfer from the CQA to the web search data. While bag-of-words features still outperform the topic model on the test set, the difference in F1-score between bag-of-words and the best-performing BTM model is smaller compared to the validation set.

Being the best-performing of our machine learning models, we select the bag-of-words classifier to investigate the topic distribution in the web search question dataset; for the purpose of our post-hoc analysis, classification speed is not a major concern. However, in a live retrieval setting, we argue that one may prefer the BTM classifier despite its lower performance: due to the more compact feature vector, classification with BTM is much faster; on a 100-node Hadoop cluster running many classifications in parallel, the bag-of-words classifier requires on average three milliseconds of CPU time to classify a single question, compared to 1.3 milliseconds for the BTM classifier.

As shown in Figure 6, the classifier succeeds at distinguishing most of the categories rather well. Two exceptions are the "Family & Relationships" and "Adult" categories, which are frequently confused, as well as the "Computers & Internet" and "Consumer Electronics" categories. In both cases, a likely explanation is the natural overlap in vocabulary between these pairs of categories.

While the CQA retrieval classifier achieves a slightly higher F1-score than bag-of-words on the web search question test set, it incurs a much larger computational overhead—an average of 407 milliseconds per query, with the index stored on a solid-state disk. More advanced retrieval models have been shown to outperform BM25 in terms of CQA retrieval performance [32]. However, the overhead of an index lookup for each classification may prove prohibitive in a live retrieval setting.

5.3 Categorizing Web Search Questions

Below, we showcase some of the insights gained from the category distribution of the question queries in our query log. Since even our three human annotators were unable to favor a category assignment by majority in 17% of the cases, and our classifier agrees with them only two thirds of the time, the category of any individual query should be taken with a grain of salt. However, we do consider our model good enough to study general trends in the data.

Figure 7 shows the distribution of question query categories by month over the entire dataset. The shading in the cells

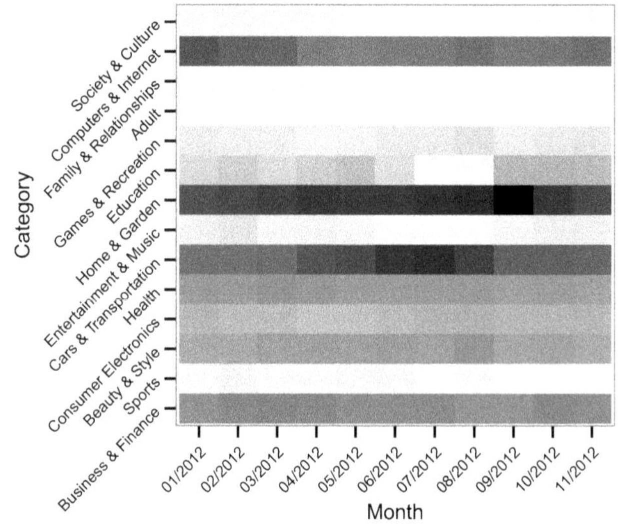

Figure 7: Distribution of monthly question query volume over categories. For each month, the shadings of the grid cells represent the categories' relative contributions to that month's total number of queries.

shows the contribution of each category to the total query volume for the corresponding month. The category axis is ordered by descending frequency in CQA questions, for easy comparison with Table 2. The category distribution our classifier infers for the web search questions is quite different from the distribution of category sizes among the CQA data. For instance, "Home & Garden" is the largest web search question category, covering over 13% of the web search queries, as opposed to 5% of CQA questions. Only 4% of web search queries are assigned to the "Society & Culture" category, compared to 18% of CQA questions.

Beyond this, the development of categories' query volume over time is of interest. While the query volume for some categories, such as "Health" or "Beauty & Style," remains more or less constant throughout the year, others show a pronounced seasonal variation. Most notably, the "Education" category reaches its low point during the months of July and August, while "Cars & Transportation" peaks around the same time. This may reflect askers embarking on their summer vacations, and abandoning education-related inquiries for travel-related ones.

Figure 8 shows the category distribution for some prominent question prefixes and suffixes. For the prefixes, we select a set of *how-to* question prefixes that are the most frequent in the query log, and compute the category proportions for the questions starting with each prefix. Some prefixes are strongly correlated with a single category, such as the `[how to cook ...]` questions with "Home & Garden." Other question prefixes, like `[how to make ...]` or `[how to learn ...]` are more evenly split among categories and occur to some extent in each one. As a side benefit, this analysis provides a sanity check for our classification model: expressions with several plausible contexts are distributed across the appropriate categories. For instance, the `[how to clean ...]` questions, with their corresponding housekeeping-, computer-

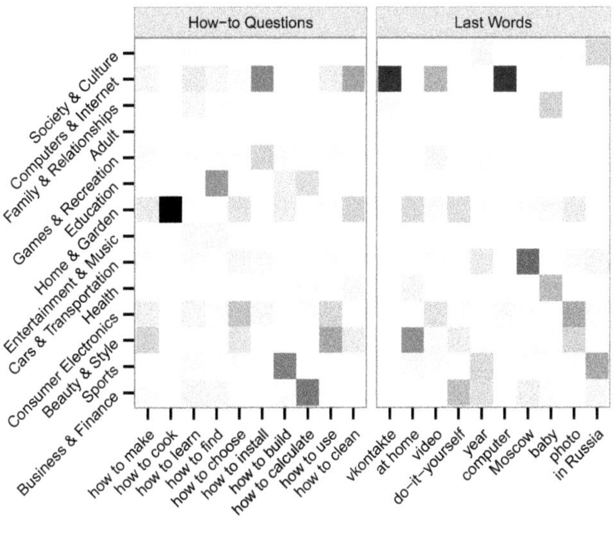

Figure 8: Distribution of common *how-to* questions and last words over categories. The items on the x-axis are ordered by total number of occurrences in the query log, highest at the left. For each item, the shadings of the grid cells represent the categories' relative contributions to that item's occurrences.

maintenance-, and personal-hygiene-related contexts, appear most frequently in the "Home & Garden," the "Computers & Internet," and the "Beauty & Style" categories, respectively.

In the right half of Figure 8, we show the distribution of the ten most common question endings over the categories, which reveals similar patterns to the questions' initial parts.

In an additional avenue of inquiry, we investigate the prevalence of advanced search operators—such as quoting, boolean expressions, or restricting the search to certain domains or file types—among question queries. Studies of general query logs have found a single-digit percentage of queries to use operators. For instance, [31] report 1.12% of queries recorded over a 13-week period containing operators, and 8.7% of users employing operators at least once during that time. We conjecture that among users who formulate queries as natural-language questions, operator use will be even rarer. Indeed, out of the billion question queries in our dataset, only 0.2% contain any search operators; only 1% of the 145 million unique users use operators at all.

In our query log, the quotation operator for phrasal search is by far the most prevalent, accounting for about 96% of all operator occurrences. Well-known operators like quotation and exact word match are equally prevalent across all categories, while the use of more advanced functionality often appears concentrated to a single category. For instance, the word distance operators (for retrieving only documents where the query terms occur within a user-specified distance) occur most often in the "Education" category.

6. CONCLUSION AND OUTLOOK

We have conducted the first large-scale analysis of non-English question querying behavior on a web search engine. Our main goal was to analyze the categories that searchers are interested in over the time of one year. To this end we have based our study on the about 1 billion questions submitted to a large commercial search engine in 2012.

As for the classification of the questions, we could not follow the practice used for classifying general web queries. There, established technologies use the search results to enrich the short query strings and to classify a query based on the results or the documents clicked by a user; however, in the case of questions that are rarely submitted by more than one user, click-through is much sparser. Since we also had in mind to develop a classifier that can be used in an online search engine, the fact that result information is not available for most of the questions ruled out the use of the standard procedure. Contrary to query classification for ad-matching or classification of questions at question answering platforms, that often classify into huge hierarchies with many classes, we aim at a flat set of a few categories only that can be easily integrated as additional features in the retrieval process (e.g., to select appropriate verticals).

Our suggested approach to question query classification is to use features extracted from the question queries to train a classifier on labeled CQA questions (where the asker assigns categories to posted questions) and then transfer this classifier back to the web search question queries. Our experiments show this approach to work very well given the 14 target classes. Hence, even though studies have shown that users tend to submit different questions to search engines than to CQA services, a fact also visible in our analyses, the classification transferability is not harmed. Training the classifiers on all the questions posted to a CQA service in the same year as the search engine questions, an F-measure of about 0.5 shows a decent performance given the 14 classes. Interestingly, the accuracy of the very efficient biterm topic model-based classifier is not much worse than the less efficient bag-of-words-based classifiers that had been proposed in previous studies for question classification.

Our experimental study of the year-long question query log shows some interesting first insights on categorized question asking behavior on a non-English search engine. Not too surprisingly, education questions are hardly observed in the months of summer vacation, while travel questions have their peak appearance in this time. The ratio of questions related to home and garden or health is rather stable over the year, while not too surprisingly "adult" topics are much less present in questions than in general web search queries. Further analyses on how-to questions, the questions' last words, and search operator use, also revealed some interesting insights.

Still, our first analyses should be seen as a starting point to use the question query classification for future work that can help improve retrieval performance on questions by better tailoring the results to the users' needs. This is especially important for questions that cannot directly be answered by showing related CQA questions. The amount of questions not directly answerable from CQA data is still an important direction for future research. Complementing our results with a similar study of question categories on English questions could shed some light on cultural differences in asking behavior and might help search engines to better address the different markets. Since the sheer amount of questions in the total query stream still is increasing, such topics will only get more important in the future. Potential applications abound—for instance in mobile voice search—to enable users to more naturally interact with retrieval systems via questions.

Acknowledgements

We thank Yandex (Alexey Gorodilov, Pavel Serdyukov, and Alexander Sadovskiy) and Mail.Ru (Andrey Oleynik) for preparing the datasets and granting access. The reported study was conceived during Pavel Braslavski's research stay at Bauhaus Universität Weimar supported by DAAD in fall 2013 and advanced during his visit supported by MU-MIA network in October 2014. Pavel Braslasvki's and Galina Lezina's current work is partially supported by RFBR, research project #14-07-00589-a.

References

[1] Anne Aula, Rehan M. Khan, and Zhiwei Guan. How does search behavior change as search becomes more difficult? In *Proceedings of CHI 2010*, pages 35–44.

[2] Peter Bailey, Ryen W. White, Han Liu, and Giridhar Kumaran. Mining historic query trails to label long and rare search engine queries. *ACM Transactions on the Web*, 4(4): 15, 2010.

[3] Judit Bar-Ilan, Zheng Zhu, and Mark Levene. Topic-specific analysis of search queries. In *Proceedings of the WSCD 2009 Workshop*, pages 35–42.

[4] Steven M. Beitzel, Eric C. Jensen, Abdur Chowdhury, Ophir Frieder, and David Grossman. Temporal analysis of a very large topically categorized web query log. *Journal of the American Society for Information Science and Technology*, 58(2):166–178, 2007.

[5] Steven M. Beitzel, Eric C. Jensen, David D. Lewis, Abdur Chowdhury, and Ophir Frieder. Automatic classification of web queries using very large unlabeled query logs. *ACM Transactions on Information Systems*, 25(2):9, 2007.

[6] Jerome R Bellegarda. Spoken language understanding for natural interaction: The Siri experience. In *Natural Interaction with Robots, Knowbots and Smartphones*, pages 3–14. 2014.

[7] Michael Bendersky and W. Bruce Croft. Analysis of long queries in a large scale search log. In *Proceedings of the WSCD 2009 workshop*, pages 8–14.

[8] David M. Blei, Andrew Y. Ng, and Michael I. Jordan. Latent dirichlet allocation. *Journal of Machine Learning Research*, 3:993–1022, 2003.

[9] Andrei Z. Broder, Marcus Fontoura, Evgeniy Gabrilovich, Amruta Joshi, Vanja Josifovski, and Tong Zhang. Robust classification of rare queries using web knowledge. In *Proceedings of SIGIR 2007*, pages 231–238.

[10] Li Cai, Guangyou Zhou, Kang Liu, and Jun Zhao. Large-scale question classification in CQA by leveraging Wikipedia semantic knowledge. In *Proceedings of CIKM 2011*, pages 1321–1330.

[11] Xin Cao, Gao Cong, Bin Cui, and Christian S. Jensen. A generalized framework of exploring category information for question retrieval in community question answer archives. In *Proceedings of WWW 2010*, pages 201–210.

[12] Wen Chan, Weidong Yang, Jinhui Tang, Jintao Du, Xiangdong Zhou, and Wei Wang. Community question topic categorization via hierarchical kernelized classification. In *Proceedings of CIKM 2013*, pages 959–968.

[13] Xueqi Cheng, Yanyan Lan, Jiafeng Guo, and Xiaohui Yan. BTM: Topic modeling over short texts. *IEEE Transactions on Knowledge and Data Engineering*, paper 1, 2014.

[14] Huizhong Duan, Yunbo Cao, Chin-Yew Lin, and Yong Yu. Searching questions by identifying question topic and question focus. In *Proceedings of ACL 2008*, pages 156–164.

[15] Baichuan Li, Irwin King, and Michael R Lyu. Question routing in community question answering: Putting category in its place. In *Proceedings of CIKM 2011*, pages 2041–2044.

[16] Xiao Li, Ye-Yi Wang, and Alex Acero. Learning query intent from regularized click graphs. In *Proceedings of SIGIR 2008*, pages 339–346.

[17] Jian Liu, Yiqun Liu, Min Zhang, and Shaoping Ma. How do users grow up along with search engines?: A study of long-term users' behavior. In *Proceedings of CIKM 2013*, pages 1795–1800.

[18] Qiaoling Liu, Eugene Agichtein, Gideon Dror, Evgeniy Gabrilovich, Yoelle Maarek, Dan Pelleg, and Idan Szpektor. Predicting web searcher satisfaction with existing community-based answers. In *Proceedings of SIGIR 2011*, pages 415–424.

[19] Qiaoling Liu, Eugene Agichtein, Gideon Dror, Yoelle Maarek, and Idan Szpektor. When web search fails, searchers become askers: Understanding the transition. In *Proceedings of SIGIR 2012*, pages 801–810.

[20] Meredith Ringel Morris, Jaime Teevan, and Katrina Panovich. What do people ask their social networks, and why?: A survey study of status message Q&A behavior. In *Proceedings of CHI 2010*, pages 1739–1748.

[21] Bo Pang and Ravi Kumar. Search in the lost sense of query: Question formulation in web search queries and its temporal changes. In *Proceedings of ACL 2011*, pages 135–140.

[22] Greg Pass, Abdur Chowdhury, and Cayley Torgeson. A picture of search. In *Proceedings of Infoscale 2006*, paper 1.

[23] Bo Qu, Gao Cong, Cuiping Li, Aixin Sun, and Hong Chen. An evaluation of classification models for question topic categorization. *Journal of the American Society for Information Science and Technology*, 63(5):889–903, 2012.

[24] Matthew Richardson. Learning about the world through long-term query logs. *ACM Transactions on the Web*, 2(4): 21, 2008.

[25] Johan Schalkwyk, Doug Beeferman, Françoise Beaufays, Bill Byrne, Ciprian Chelba, Mike Cohen, Maryam Kamvar, and Brian Strope. "Your word is my command": Google search by voice: A case study. In *Advances in Speech Recognition*, pages 61–90. 2010.

[26] Dou Shen, Jian-Tao Sun, Qiang Yang, and Zheng Chen. Building bridges for web query classification. In *Proceedings of SIGIR 2006*, pages 131–138.

[27] Marina Sokolova and Guy Lapalme. A systematic analysis of performance measures for classification tasks. *Information Processing & Management*, 45(4):427–437, 2009.

[28] Amanda Spink and H. Cenk Ozmultu. Characteristics of question format web queries: An exploratory study. *Information processing & management*, 38(4):453–471, 2002.

[29] Amanda Spink, Bernard J. Jansen, Dietmar Wolfram, and Tefko Saracevic. From e-sex to e-commerce: Web search changes. *Computer*, 35(3):107–109, 2002.

[30] Ingmar Weber, Antti Ukkonen, and Aris Gionis. Answers, not links: Extracting tips from Yahoo! Answers to address how-to web queries. In *Proceedings of WSDM 2012*, pages 613–622.

[31] Ryen W. White and Dan Morris. Investigating the querying and browsing behavior of advanced search engine users. In *Proceedings of SIGIR 2007*, pages 255–262.

[32] Xiaobing Xue, Jiwoon Jeon, and W. Bruce Croft. Retrieval models for question and answer archives. In *Proceedings of SIGIR 2008*, pages 475–482.

[33] Zhe Zhao and Qiaozhu Mei. Questions about questions: An empirical analysis of information needs on Twitter. In *Proceedings of WWW 2013*, pages 1545–1556.

Does Vertical Bring more Satisfaction? Predicting Search Satisfaction in a Heterogeneous Environment

Ye Chen[†], Yiqun Liu[†], Ke Zhou[‡], Meng Wang[⋆], Min Zhang[†], Shaoping Ma[†]
[†]Tsinghua National Laboratory for Information Science and Technology, Department of Computer Science & Technology, Tsinghua University, Beijing, China
[‡]Yahoo Labs, London, U.K.
[⋆]School of Computer and Information, HeFei University of Technology
yiqunliu@tsinghua.edu.cn

ABSTRACT

The study of search satisfaction is one of the prime concerns in search performance evaluation research. Most existing works on search satisfaction primarily rely on the hypothesis that all results on search engine result pages (SERPs) are homogeneous. However, a variety of heterogeneous vertical results such as videos, images and instant answers are aggregated into SERPs by search engines to improve the diversity and quality of search results. In this paper, we carry out a lab-based user study with specifically designed SERPs to determine how verticals with different qualities and presentation styles affect search satisfaction. Users' satisfaction feedback and external assessors' satisfaction annotations are both collected to make a comparison regarding the perception of search satisfaction. Mouse click-through / movement data and eye movement information are also collected such that we can investigate the influence of vertical results from the perspectives of both benefit and cost. Finally, a vertical-aware learning-based prediction method is proposed to predict search satisfaction on aggregated SERPs. To the best of our knowledge, this paper is the first to analyze the effect of verticals on search satisfaction. The results show that verticals with different qualities, presentation styles and positions have different effects on search satisfaction, among which Encyclopedia verticals, as well as Download verticals, will bring the largest improvement. Furthermore, our proposed vertical-aware prediction method outperforms state of the-art methods that are designed for search satisfaction prediction in homogeneous environment.

Categories and Subject Descriptors

H.3.3 [**Information Storage and Retrieval**]: Information Search and Retrieval

Keywords

search satisfaction; aggregated search; benefit; cost; prediction

Permission to make digital or hard copies of all or part of this work for personal or classroom use is granted without fee provided that copies are not made or distributed for profit or commercial advantage and that copies bear this notice and the full citation on the first page. Copyrights for components of this work owned by others than ACM must be honored. Abstracting with credit is permitted. To copy otherwise, or republish, to post on servers or to redistribute to lists, requires prior specific permission and/or a fee. Request permissions from Permissions@acm.org.
CIKM'15, October 19 - 23, 2015, Melbourne, VIC, Australia
© 2015 ACM. ISBN 978-1-4503-3794-6/15/10 ...$15.00.
DOI: http://dx.doi.org/10.1145/2806416.2806473.

1. INTRODUCTION

Search engine evaluation can be performed using metrics based on result relevance or alternative measures based on users' search experience. Recent studies indicate that relevance-based evaluation metrics, such as MAP and nDCG [20], may not be perfectly correlated with users' search experience (usually considered as the gold standard) [2, 18]. Therefore, search satisfaction has become one of the major concerns in search evaluation studies. Since satisfaction is a relatively subjective concept, several works [18, 36, 21] have tried to quantify users' perceived satisfaction. Furthermore, some works [1, 12, 15, 16] tried to use various types of user interactions (click-through data, mouse/eye movement information) as implicit feedback to predict search satisfaction. These existing works have achieved success on how to model users' judgements on the whole search process and how to improve search engines' ranking strategy. However, most of these works rely on the hypothesis that all results on search engine result pages (SERPs) are homogeneous, which means that all search results in an SERP share similar presentation style (one hyperlink with a short snippet). However, as more and more heterogeneous vertical results (videos, images, instant answers and so on) are aggregated into modern SERPs, a user's examination and clicking behavior can be quite different [35, 38]. Because modern SERPs provide richer content than hyperlinks and short texts, the sense of fulfilling information needs during the search process may be very different from an SERP with "ten blue links." Therefore, we need to investigate users' satisfaction perception process within a heterogeneous search environment. To better describe heterogeneous SERPs, we first give a taxonomy of different search results according to their presentation styles (see Figure 1):

- Non-vertical (organic) result: One blue hyperlink with short snippet contents.
- Textual vertical: Verticals that are composed of a couple of textual snippets and blue hyperlinks. It usually provides more all-around information concerning the query topic.
- Image vertical: Verticals that are usually composed of several images grouped into one or two rows.
- News vertical: Verticals that have an image on the left and provide several hyperlinks lead to the latest news about the query topic.
- Download vertical: Download verticals are a popular type of verticals in SERPs of Chinese commercial search engines. They can provide searchers with a button to directly download the application that the query topic describes.

Figure 1: Different presentation styles of vertical results on SERPs (we use the results of Bing as examples)

- Encyclopedia vertical: Verticals that provide an image as well as some textual information at the same time and thus can provide more comprehensive information to the query topic.

From Figure 1, we can see that the appearances of the vertical results can be rather different from the non-vertical results and may provide information in a completely different way. Previous works [25, 35] showed that such vertical results may have a strong effect on user behavior. These findings inspired us to investigate the effect of verticals on user satisfaction. To shed light on this question, we construct a lab-based search engine system with specifically designed heterogeneous search result pages. We provide SERPs with verticals that vary in qualities, presentation styles and positions to users to study how their satisfaction is affected. Users' explicit satisfaction feedback, as well as mouse click-through / movement data and eye movement data, are collected so that we can make a detailed analysis of how the vertical results affect users' search satisfaction from the perspective of both benefit and cost. To avoid the subjectivity of user satisfaction feedback, we also invite external assessors to annotate the satisfaction scores of the users' search sessions to make a comparison. Finally, we propose a vertical-aware learning-based prediction method to predict search satisfaction on aggregated search result pages. The results show that our proposed method outperforms state-of-the-art methods, which are not specifically designed for heterogeneous search pages.

Our contributions in this paper include:

- To the best of our knowledge, we are among the first to study the effect of vertical search results on search satisfaction.
- With rich information collected by an experimental search engine system, we make a deep analysis of the effect the vertical results have on both users' and external assessors' satisfaction judgements in a benefit-cost framework.
- We propose a vertical-aware learning-based prediction method to predict the search satisfaction of SERPs with heterogeneous vertical results and demonstrate its effectiveness by comparing with state-of-the-art methods.

The rest of this paper is organized as follows: Related works are reviewed in Section 2. Our lab-based search engine system and corresponding data collection process are presented in Section 3. The effect of different verticals on search satisfaction are shown in Section 4 and a deeper analysis in the benefit-cost framework is shown in Section 5. Section 6 introduces our satisfaction prediction framework and discusses its effectiveness. The paper's conclusions are presented in Section 7.

2. RELATED WORK

2.1 Search Satisfaction Prediction

The concept of satisfaction was first proposed by Su et al. [32] and was defined as "the fulfillment of a specified desire or goal" by Kelly [23]. To evaluate a search system, satisfaction can be considered as regarding not only to the whole search experience but also to some specific aspects [33], such as the precision or completeness of search results, response time and so on. Because search satisfaction is a subjective concept that is difficult to measure, some existing works collected explicit feedback directly from users as the ground truth of search satisfaction, such as Guo et al. [15] who predicted user satisfaction with mouse movement information, and Feild et al. [12] who predicted user frustration using query-logs. In addition to explicit search satisfaction feedback, some works [16, 18] have also tried to recruit external assessors to restore the users' search process and make satisfaction annotations according to their own opinions. However, recent research in [34] showed that external annotations may not be a good estimator of users' self-judgements, and a number of works (e.g, [21, 22]) have started using the benefit-cost framework to analyze the satisfaction judgement process of users. In this framework, both the benefit factors (result relevance) and search cost (effort) users spend are used to estimate satisfaction. In this work, we follow the benefit-cost framework to make a deep comparison between search satisfaction from users and external assessors in a heterogeneous environment.

2.2 Behavior Modeling on SERPS with Verticals

Recently, more and more heterogeneous search results have been aggregated into search result pages to promote users' search experiences. There are also a number of existing works which are focused on this kind of federated search. Among them, most prior works focused on predicting which verticals are relevant to a query (vertical selection). Diaz et al. [10] first carried out a system to collect news dynamically and aggregated them into web search results. Arguello et al. [4, 5] showed that query logs will be useful for selecting relevant verticals. Zhou et al. [38] presented an approach that considers both reward and risk within the task of vertical selection.

Because the presentation styles of different verticals may be rather different, a user's browsing behavior may be changed when an SERP becomes more and more heterogeneous. Some existing studies tried to analyze a user's new behavior pattern on a heterogeneous SERP: Wang et al. [35] found that different verticals may create examination biases on users' search behavior. They suggested that images and videos will attract a user's attention more than other search results. Liu et al. [25] further showed three three behavior effect in federated search, namely, the vertical attraction effect, the examination cut-off effect and the examination spill-over effect. Navalpakkam et al. [28] also showed that a knowledge graph will also influence a user's attention distribution on SERPs.

Traditional search result evaluation metrics may also become inappropriate when dealing with federated search pages. Various diversity aware IR metrics have been proposed [7, 8, 30], which may be adjusted to evaluate heterogeneous result pages. Zhou et al. [37] introduced the concept of vertical orientation and instantiated a suite of metrics for evaluating aggregated search pages. Markov et al. [27] proposed two vertical-aware metrics based on user click models for federated search and demonstrated its effectiveness.

Despite of these existing works, how users perceive satisfaction on aggregated search pages still remains uninvestigated. In this paper, we incorporate vertical information into SERPs and follow the benefit-cost framework to analyze the effect of the vertical results on search satisfaction. We also propose a learning-based satisfaction prediction method and demonstrate the effectiveness of vertical information.

3. DATA COLLECTION

In this section, we describe the lab-based search engine system used in our work and show the process of how we collect search satisfaction scores as well as search interaction data, such as mouse and eye movements.

3.1 Experiment Procedure

To investigate the effect of verticals on search satisfaction, we construct a lab-based search engine system to collect user behavior data as well as satisfaction scores from both users and external assessors. The entire experiment procedure is shown in Figure 2, from which we can see that four types of information are collected during the procedure: (1) mouse movements and click-through information, (2) eye movements, (3) users' satisfaction scores and (4) external assessors' satisfaction annotations.

Before the experiment, each participant should first go through a calibration process as required by the eye tracker to make sure that reliable eye movement information is collected. The eye tracker we use in our work is Tobii X2-30. Each participant will be asked to complete 30 search tasks one by one within 1 hour during our

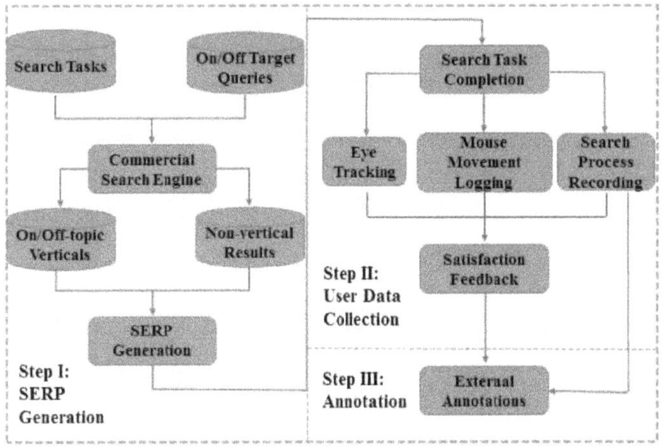

Figure 2: Data Collection Procedure

experiment. The procedure of the experiment is shown in Figure 2. Before each task, they will first go through the search queries and corresponding explanations to make sure they know the task clearly. Then, he/she will be guided to a pre-designed SERP where query and search results are fixed. The participant should examine the search results provided by our system and click a button on the top right corner to end the task either if the search goal is completed or he/she becomes disappointed with the results. During such process, his/her mouse movement information and click-through data were logged by injected JavaScript on the SERPs, and eye movement information is also logged by the eye tracker. Each time the participant finishes a search task, he/she will be required to label a 5-point satisfaction score to the search session, where 5 means the most satisfactory and 1 means the least. Then, they will be guided to continue to the next search task. All participants are required to finish two warm-up search tasks first to become familiar with the experiment process.

3.2 Search Tasks and SERP Generation

To investigate the effect of the vertical results on satisfaction, we sample a large number of search queries based on the search logs from a major commercial search engine. We use such queries to organize our search tasks just to make sure that our experimental SERPs are consistent with the practical scenario. We selected 30 specific search tasks with corresponding on/off-topic verticals and the non-vertical results crawled from the commercial search engine. The queries we use in our experiment are neither long-tailed nor popular ones to avoid unnecessary biases.

The SERPs we present to users vary in three aspects that may have effects on users' search behavior and satisfaction judgements:

- Quality: We investigate whether the quality of a vertical result will affect search satisfaction. We use a subset of the terms from the original query or add a few new items to generate an off-target query and submit it to the search engine to get the off-topic vertical. Because the new query just overlapped a subset of the original one, the vertical results we obtained are usually irrelevant to the original query but appear to be quite similar to the on-topic verticals. This strategy has also been adopted by a number of existing works to generate irrelevant verticals [3, 6, 35]. Table 1 shows some examples of the search tasks and corresponding queries used to crawl on/off-topic verticals in our experiment.

Table 1: Examples of Search Tasks and Manipulated Off-target Queries to Retrieve Verticals

Vertical Presentation Style	Original Query	Off-target Query
Textual	poems describing spring rain	poems describing rain
	ancient Greek architectural style	ancient Greek
Encyclopedia	covering the sky (novel)	covering the sky (game)
	the 9th zone (movie)	the 9th zone (novel)
Image	nike basketball shoes	nike football shoes
	pictures of wine cabinet	pictures of cupboard
Download	iTunes download	iTools download
	Renren desktop app download	Weibo desktop app download
Encyclopedia	ebola virus mutation	news of ebola virus
	Chinese city competitiveness	Chinese enterprise competitiveness

- Position: Existing work show that position bias affects user attention in federated search engine [35], thus may affect search process and satisfaction judgement. So we take this factor into consideration in our experiment. The vertical results will be randomly placed at position 1, 3 and 5 of the result lists, respectively.

- Presentation styles: We further evenly separate out search tasks into five groups according to the vertical's presentation style to see if different types of verticals will have different effect on satisfaction. Thus, the 30 search tasks will contain all 5 types of verticals in Figure 1, namely, textual vertical, image vertical, news vertical, download vertical and encyclopedia vertical results. And for each presentation style, we have 6 search tasks.

To investigate the effect of the above three factors, we generate seven different SERPs for each search task. The first SERP is a non-vertical one, which means that there are only ten non-vertical results shown in the result page. These non-vertical results are crawled from the same commercial search engine, and kept the original orders unchanged. The remaining six SERPs are composed of one vertical result and nine non-vertical results(the last non-veritcal result from the non-vertical SERP is excluded). Two verticals are of the same presentation style but with different quality on these six SERPs, including an on-topic vertical for three of them and an off-topic one for the other three. Each vertical is inserted at three different positions of the non-veritical result list: the first rank, the third rank and the fifth rank. Thus, we obtain seven pages for a search task: 2 quality types $\times$ 3 position ranks (6 pages with vertical results) + 1 non-vertical page (with no verical results). Therefore, we generate 210 (30 search tasks $\times$ 7 pages) SERPs in total.

In our experiment, each participant will go through all 30 search tasks but with different SERP settings. We adopt a Graeco-Latin square design to ensure that each SERP condition has the same opportunity to be shown to users.

3.3 Participants

We recruited 35 participants (aged 18-25) for the data collecting process. All participants are college students and have a variety of self-reported search engine usage experiences. Their majors vary, from biology, economics, social science to engineering. We did not invite computer science or electrical engineering students because they may be too familiar with the use of search engines and cannot represent ordinary search engine users. Each user completed the 30 search tasks and were paid 10 US dollars.

3.4 External Annotation

Considering the fact that the process of satisfaction judgement may be subjective and different users may have different opinions, we recruited several external assessors to label the satisfaction scores of users' search sessions. All these assessors had worked in a commercial search engine company for at least one year and can be regarded as professionals in judging search performance and satisfaction. We exported the video of our participants doing their search tasks from the eye tracker, which had recorded the whole search process as well as eye/mouse movements and click-through information. We split the video into sessions and excluded the part where users labeled satisfaction scores. We showed these videos of search sessions to assessors so that they can fully restore the original searchers' search experience and make a reasonable annotation. The assessors were also asked to give a 5-point satisfaction score so that the satisfaction scores from the two resources will be comparable. They were paid 10 US dollars for annotating every 60 search sessions. Each search session is annotated by two assessors, and the KAPPA coefficient of their annotations is 0.48, which means a moderate agreement according to Cohen [9].

4. EFFECT OF VERTICALS ON SATISFACTION

4.1 Effect of Vertical Quality

We collected 768 search sessions in total because some participants failed to pass the calibration of the eye tracker. With these collected data, we try to compare the difference between the satisfaction scores from actual users and external assessors. Considering that satisfaction judgement may be quite subjective and different users may have different opinions, we regularize the satisfaction scores labelled by each user/assessor to Z-scores according to equation (1), where sat_i is one particular satisfaction score given by one user/assessor and $Avg(Sat)$ is the average of all satisfaction scores he/she labelled. $Var(Sat)$ in this equation refers to the variance of the satisfaction scores of this user/assessor. We should note that in this way, a Z-score may be below zero, which may be difficult to understand. Thus, we add the same δ_1 to all Z-scores of users' satisfaction (and the same δ_2 to all Z-scores of the external assessors) in this section to normalize the minimum value to zero to avoid confusion and to maintain the relative differences at the same time.

$$Z\text{-}score_i = \frac{sat_i - Avg(Sat)}{Var(Sat)} + \delta_{1/2} \quad (1)$$

Figure 3 shows an overview of the effect of vertical qualities on satisfaction scores from two different resources. Different col-

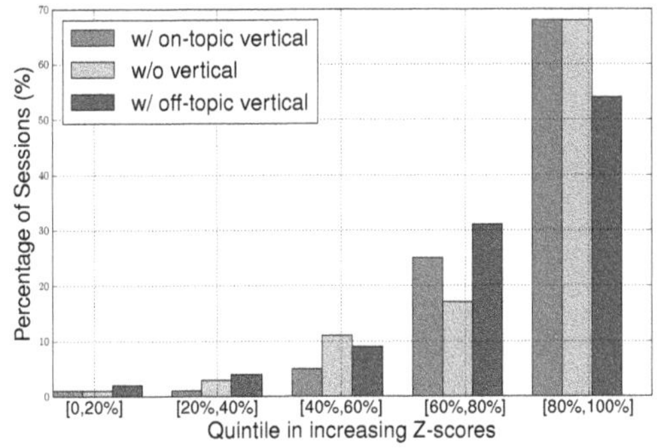

(a) Users' Satisfaction Feedback

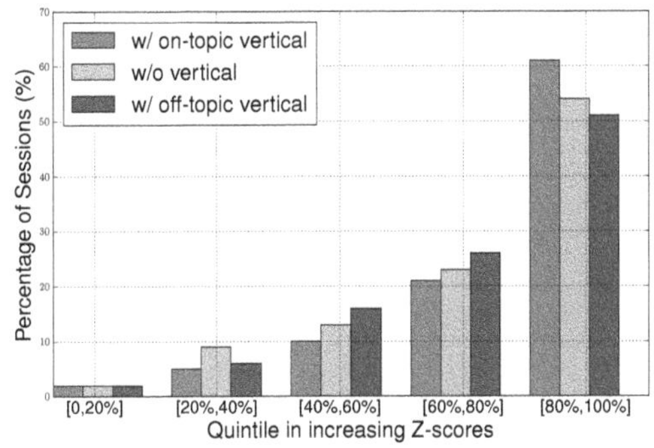

(b) External Assessors' Satisfaction Annotation

Figure 3: Satisfaction Distribution Based on Verticals with Different Qualities

ors show satisfaction scores on pages with on/off-topic verticals or without verticals. We can see that both users and assessors tend to give a high satisfaction score, which indicates that commercial search engines generally provide promising results for these non-long-tailed queries. We can also see from Figure 3 that both users and assessors tend to be less satisfied when the vertical is off-topic because the percentage of sessions with the highest Z-scores (80%-100%) is comparatively lower in the off-topic case, although the difference is not very remarkable (68% for SERPs without verticals, 54% for SERPs with off-topic verticals in user satisfaction and 54%, 51% in assessors' annotations, relatively). Moreover, the percentage of sessions with low Z-scores (0%-60%) is also lower in the on-topic case (6% users and 17% assessors) than that in the non-vertical case (15% users and 24% assessors), which indicates that both users and assessors tend to be more satisfied if there are on-topic verticals on SERPs.

4.2 Effect of Verticals with Different Presentation Styles

Table 2 shows the effect of verticals with different presentation styles on satisfaction scores from both users and external assessors. The values shown in the second, third and fourth columns are the average Z-scores of all the pages' verticals with the corresponding presentation style and quality (non-vertical, on/off-topic vertical). Values shown in parenthesis are the differences compared with that on pages without verticals. Values in the last column shows the improvement in Z-scores from pages with off-topic verticals (in the fourth column) to those with on-topic verticals (in the third column).

Table 2: Effect of Verticals with Different Presentation Styles on Satisfaction (* indicates statistical significance at p < 0.1 level,** indicates statistical significance at p < 0.05 level)

	w/o vertical	w/ on-topic vertical	w/ off-topic vertical	on-off difference
Users' Satisfaction Feedback				
Textual	5.15	5.10 (-0.05)	4.95 **(-0.20**)**	+0.15*
Encyclopedia	4.46	4.99 **(+0.53**)**	4.67 (+0.21)	+0.32**
Image	5.17	5.07 (-0.10)	4.58 **(-0.59**)**	+0.49**
Download	4.75	5.25 **(+0.50**)**	4.60 (-0.15)	+0.65**
News	4.43	4.34 (-0.09)	4.38 (-0.05)	-0.04
External Assessors' Satisfaction Annotation				
Textual	3.75	3.64 (-0.11)	3.45 **(-0.30*)**	+0.19*
Encyclopedia	3.18	3.62 **(+0.44**)**	3.13 (-0.05)	+0.49**
Image	3.34	3.59 **(+0.25*)**	3.18 (-0.16)	+0.41**
Download	2.85	3.58 **(+0.73**)**	3.31 **(+0.46**)**	+0.27**
News	3.10	2.73 **(-0.37*)**	3.02 (-0.08)	-0.29*

A number of interesting findings can be concluded from Table 2: 1) Image verticals do not really bring more satisfaction to users. This is partly because information obtained from image verticals can usually also be easily obtained from the non-vertical results. It is worth noting that off-topic images may result in a remarkable decline because irrelevant images are usually conspicuous and annoying. The fact that images bring more satisfaction to assessors may be because that assessors care more about search effort [24] and on-topic images may sometimes provide an instant answer to the query task, which will save a lot of time. 2) The encyclopedia vertical, as well as the download vertical, will bring more satisfaction for both users and assessors, and there is no significant decline even when the vertical result is irrelevant, which means such two kinds of vertical results are worth inserting into SERPs to improve the page quality. 3) Both on-topic and off-topic news verticals have no significant effect on users' satisfaction. On-topic news verticals will bring a significant drop in satisfaction for assessors, which may be because relevant news verticals may attract users to click them, leading to another search result page (in our experimental environment), which may be considered as a waste of time. 4) It is worth noting that encyclopedia verticals and news verticals have similar appearances (see Figure 1) but have completely different effects on satisfaction scores. This may be because encyclopedia verticals can provide users a more structured information with figures and texts describing the search target. In contrast, the figure provided by news verticals may be not so closely related to the search target and other non-vertical results can also provide as rich information as news vertical results.

Table 2 also shows some subtle differences between users and external assessors. On-topic image verticals will improve satisfaction scores from external assessors but have no significant effect on those from users, which may be because assessors will be more satisfied if the search task is finished in short time periods while users will probably be satisfied as long as their search need is met in not a very long time. Moreover, assessors will be dissatisfied when there are on-topic news verticals on SERPs while users will not, which indicates that assessors may be stricter with the wasted time caused by news verticals than users. All these findings indicate that assessors may care more about search effort, which is in line with the findings in [24].

4.3 Effect of Verticals at Different Positions

We further investigate the effect of verticals at different positions on satisfaction scores from both user's and assessor's perspectives. The results are shown in Table 3.

Table 3: Effect of Ranking Positions of Verticals on Satisfaction (* indicates statistical significance at p < 0.1 level,** indicates statistical significance at p < 0.05 level)

	w/o vertical	w/ on-topic vertical	w/ off-topic vertical	on-off difference
Users' Satisfaction Feedback				
Rank 1	4.79	5.06 **(+0.27**)**	4.43 **(-0.36**)**	+0.63**
Rank 3	4.79	4.93 (+0.14)	4.63 (-0.16)	+0.29**
Rank 5	4.79	4.87 **(+0.08*)**	4.85 (+0.06)	+0.02
External Assessors' Satisfaction Annotation				
Rank 1	3.24	3.48 **(+0.24*)**	3.09 (-0.15)	+0.39**
Rank 3	3.24	3.46 **(+0.22**)**	3.31 (+0.07)	+0.15
Rank 5	3.24	3.37 (+0.13)	3.27 (+0.03)	+0.10

Verticals are placed in three different positions, namely, rank 1, rank 3 and rank 5. Values in Table 3 are organized in a similar form with those in Table 2. Different rows show average Z-scores on pages with verticals at different positions. We can see that on-topic verticals bring significant improvement to satisfaction for both users and assessors when placed at rank 1. The effect is not so significant when verticals are inserted at rank 3 or rank 5. This encourages us to insert on-topic verticals at a very top position so that they may help improve the search experience of users. Meanwhile, an off-topic vertical reduces users' satisfaction the most significantly if inserted at rank 1. Off-topic verticals at rank 3 and 5 do not exert any significant influence.

5. EFFECT OF VERTICALS ON BENEFIT AND COST

According to our experimental results and [21], users' search satisfaction may be greatly affected by the benefit they obtain from the search result page and the cost during the information searching process. In this section, we first discuss some evaluation metrics from the perspective of benefit and cost and then investigate how verticals take effect in these metrics. In this way, we try to obtain a deeper insight into the effect of the vertical results.

5.1 Estimation of Users' Benefit and Cost

5.1.1 Metrics with Cumulative Gain

We use cumulative gain (CG) and normalized discounted cumulative gain (nDCG@N, N=3, 5, 10 in our case) [19] as a measure of search result page outcomes, which is also used in [21].

$$CG = \sum_{r_i \in SERP} Rel(r_i) \quad (2)$$

$$nDCG = \sum_{r_i \in SERP} \frac{Rel(r_i)}{log(i+1)} (n = 3, 5, 10) \quad (3)$$

In Equation (2) and (3), r_i is the ith result on the corresponding SERP and $Rel(r_i)$ is its relevance score. We invite three professional assessors from a commercial search engine company to label a four-point-scaled relevance score for all query-result pairs in our experiment. The KAPPA coefficient of their annotation is 0.73, which can be characterized as a substantial agreement.

5.1.2 Metrics Based on Fixation Data

With the eye movement information we collected during our experiment process, we can exactly figure out users' examined result list and thus measure the search benefit from users' perspective. We use $Rlist$, which represents the examined result list obtained from the eye movement data, to replace the list of all results on SERPs used in equation (2) and (3) to obtain another group of metrics for search benefit. Notice that it is different from metrics in section 5.1.1 as we only sums up the relevance scores of those results which have been exactly examined by users instead of all results on SERPs.

We set the examination threshold to 200 milliseconds, which is recommended in [26, 31]. We also tried a number of other thresholds ranging from 100 ms to 1000 ms, and the results were quite similar. We regard those results with an eye fixation time of more than 200 ms, as examined, and thus we obtain the users' examined result list.

5.1.3 Metrics with Users' Cost

The metrics used to evaluate the cost users spend while examining the search result page can be obtained from two different ways. The first group of metrics, namely, search dwell time, maximum clicked rank and number of clicks, is obtained from users' mouse movement log and click-through data. These three metrics are widely adopted in existing search satisfaction works [16, 21] and are demonstrated to be effective at measuring search cost. The second group of metrics is based on the eye movement data. We can obtain the number of examined results as well as the length of the examined result sequence (note that a user may examine one particular result more than once, and in such case, it will be counted for multiple times). The examination threshold used here is still 200 ms.

5.2 Effect of Verticals on Search Benefit and Cost

In this section, we investigate how verticals affect search satisfaction following the benefit-cost framework. Due to the restriction of space, we only select out some typical metrics discussed in Section 5.1 as an example, including (**CG**) defined by Equation (2), (**nDCG**) defined by Equation (3), length of examined result sequence (**LER**) described in Section 5.1.3, and CG of examined results (**ECG**) described in Section 5.1.2. We take these metrics as examples because they are representative, reflecting the quality of SERP (CG and nDCG) or the examination behavior of users (LER and ECG). The situations of the other metrics are similar with these selected ones in general.

Table 4 shows the correlations between these evaluation metrics and users' satisfaction judgements on SERPs with on/off-topic verticals or without verticals. The results show that satisfaction has

Table 4: Correlation of Measures with User Satisfaction(all correlation values are statistically significant: $p < 0.05$)

		CG (Benefit)	DCG@3 (Benefit)	DCG@5 (Benefit)	DCG@10 (Benefit)	ECG (Benefit)	LER (Cost)	CG / LER (Benefit / Cost)	ECG / LER (Benefit / Cost)
w/o vertical	Pearson	0.27	0.27	0.29	0.29	-0.42	-0.51	0.18	0.31
	Kendall	0.12	0.13	0.13	0.15	-0.17	-0.19	0.20	0.14
w/ on-topic verticals	Pearson	0.16	0.27	0.28	0.21	-0.42	-0.49	0.36	0.30
	Kendall	0.09	0.14	0.14	0.11	-0.26	-0.30	0.28	0.24
w/ off-topic verticals	Pearson	0.21	0.22	0.25	0.25	-0.39	-0.48	0.31	0.28
	Kendall	0.12	0.14	0.13	0.14	-0.22	-0.28	0.28	0.19

a weak positive correlation with CG and nDCG, a weak negative correlation with LER, and a relatively strong positive correlation with and CG/LER. Such findings are similar with that in [21]. It is worth noting that there is a moderate negative correlation between ECG and satisfaction, which is different from that between CG (or nDCG) and satisfaction. This is reasonable because CG and nDCG are metrics which measure the result quality of a certain SERP and has nothing to do with users' examination behavior. Usually, the better the SERP is, the more satisfied the user will feel. However, ECG calculates the information gained from the results examined by the user, and a higher ECG may come from an examination of more search results, which usually means more cost and thus will probably result in less satisfaction. The correlation between satisfaction and ECG per examined result (ECG / LER) is positive, which indicates that a user will be more satisfied if he can get more information with less effort. The results in Table 4 also show that the correlations for different types of verticals share similar trends but there are still some subtle differences. We will provide some insight by showing detailed distributions of these metrics across different types of verticals.

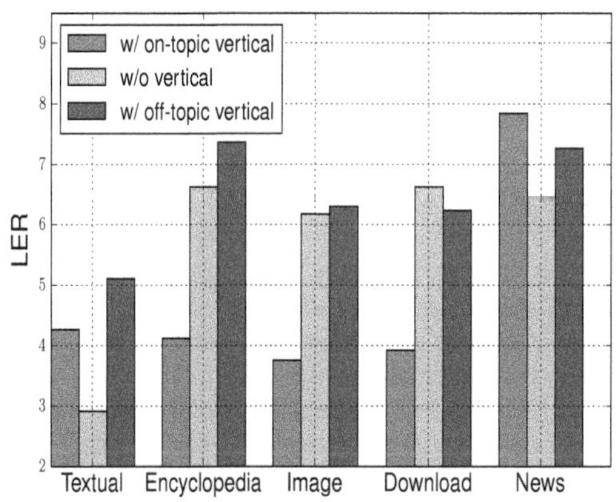

Figure 4: Distribution of LER across verticals with different presentation styles

Figure 4 shows the effect of verticals on LER, which is obtained from the eye movement data and can be a signal of search cost. From this figure, we can see that on-topic image, encyclopedia and download verticals can reduce the number of examined results remarkably, which may be because such vertical results can usually provide instant answers or a direct download link. An on-topic textual vertical or news vertical will not reduce the search cost, which may imply that such type of verticals can hardly improve users' search efficiency. We assume that this is because a textual vertical is usually just a combination of information from several perspectives. Additionally, a news vertical just leads the user to another list of news search results, which may not be satisfying. It is worth noting that nearly all types of off-topic verticals will increase the number of examined results, which indicates that we should be careful not to put low quality verticals on SERPs to reduce users' cost.

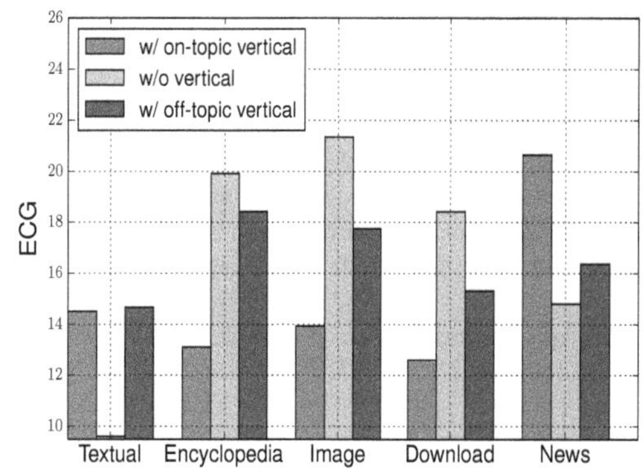

Figure 5: Distribution of ECG across verticals with different presentation styles

Figure 5 shows the effect of verticals on ECG, which is regarded as a metric of search benefit. The results show that ECG is lower when there is an on-topic vertical result of encyclopedia, image and download. This is reasonable because a relevant vertical may be good enough to finish the search task and thus may reduce the number of examined results, which may then lead to a decline in ECG. Relevant textual and news verticals may cause remarkably high CG because they may not be useful to users most of the time and the high relevance of such results may become a waste. The results in Figure 5 indicate that ECG may not be a positive estimator for satisfaction because the it is also affected by search cost. To verify this, we further develop another metric by dividing ECG by LER and the result is shown in Figure 6.

The results in Figure 6 show that for the case of on-topic download verticals, ECG/LER is remarkably higher that on SERPs with off-topic verticals and without verticals, which means on-topic download verticals help improve users' search satisfaction and is in line with the findings in Section 4.2. The differences between ECG/LER on SERPs with other four kind of verticals and without verticals are not significant, which is slightly different from the findings in Section 4.2. This may imply that an evaluation metric defined as benefit divided by cost is still not perfect to model user satisfaction and a more appropriate fitting function is needed. We leave this for future work. Nevertheless, it is easy to find that all types of off-topic

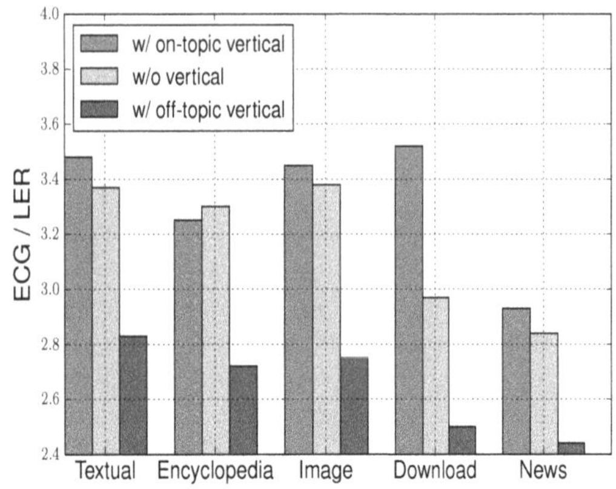

Figure 6: Distribution of ECG / LER across verticals with different presentation styles

verticals will result in a significant reduction in ECG/LER, which implies adding off-topic verticals to SERPs may not be a good idea.

Findings in this section show that user satisfaction can be studied in the benefit-cost framework and that sometimes metrics generated by dividing benefits with costs can better estimate user satisfaction, which is the same with the findings in homogeneous environment [21]. Meanwhile, more suitable metrics are needed in the future to better model search satisfaction. In the next section, we will predict satisfaction scores from both users and external assessors with the collected information and compare the predictive power of features from different resources.

6. SATISFACTION PREDICTION FOR SERPS WITH VERTICALS

Although there are plenty of existing studies [1, 12, 15] in the prediction of search satisfaction, none of them take the existence of the vertical results into consideration. According to the findings in Sections 4 and 5, the vertical results have important impacts on the satisfaction judgements for both users and external assessors. Verticals also affect the cost and benefit of users while completing Web search tasks. Therefore, it is necessary to investigate how we can predict the satisfaction of users while facing SERPs with verticals. Recent studies in [21] and findings in Section 5 encourage us to predict satisfaction with features in a benefit-cost framework. The difference between our proposed method and the existing solutions in [21] is that we mainly focus on the effect of verticals in addition to other interaction behaviors.

Table 5 shows the vertical-aware feature sets adopted in the prediction of search satisfactions. There are two major information sources. One is information related to SERP itself as well as mouse log information, which can both be easily collected at large scale. All these featues we used here are directly related to the vertical results and we denote them as Click-Through features. The other is eye movement information, which is proven to have strong ability in predicting search performance [6, 11, 13, 29] but will be hard and expensive to collect in practice. We denote them as Eye-Tracking features. Recent studies [14] also show that other interaction behaviors, such as mouse movements, can be good substitutes for eye tracking information. We try to compare the predictive power of these two different sources of information to see to what extent we can predict search satisfaction.

Table 5: Vertical-aware Features for Predicting Satisfaction

Feature	Feature Description
Click-Through Features	
v_style	the presentation style of the vertical result, integer variable, ranging from 0 to 5, refers to 6 types of verticals (including pages without verticals)
v_position	the rank position of the vertical result, values can be 1, 3, 5 and 0 (0 is used when there is no vertical result)
arr_time	$(t\_ve - t\_s)/(t\_e - t\_s)$, where t_ve refers to the time when mouse arrives at the vertical result, t_s refers to the time when search session starts and t_e refers to the time when search session ends
if_click	whether the vertical result is clicked
click_time	$(t\_v - t\_s)/(t\_e - t\_s)$, where t_v refers to the time when the vertical result is clicked
aft_time	$(t\_e - t\_fv)/(t\_e - t\_s)$, where t_fv refers to the time when the user finished examining the vertical result. This feature will be assigned as $(t\_e - t\_s)$ if no vertical result is clicked.
hover_time	the mouse hover length (in second) on the vertical result
v_dwell_time	dwell time (in second) on the vertical result landing page
if_other_click	this feature will be $True$ if there is any other result click after the vertical result is clicked, otherwise it will be $False$
Eye-Tracking Features	
exam_num	number of examined results
exam_seq_len	the length of the examined result sequence
fix_arr_time	$(e\_ve - t\_s)/(t\_e - t\_s)$, where e_ve refers to the time when eye fixation arrives at the vertical result
fix_time	eye fixation length (in second) on the vertical result

The data set described in Section 3 is adopted in the prediction with five-fold cross validation. The learning algorithm in the prediction process is ridge regression [17], which is widely used in prediction tasks with continuous values. This prediction model improves the least squares estimation and is usually more reliable in practical use. We implement the satisfaction prediction method in Guo et al. [15] because this prediction method is a state-of-the-art method based on fine-grained mouse behavior data for predicting web search success. The predictive model in [21] is also used here because in this work the features are extracted in a benefit-cost framework and can estimate graded search satisfaction more accurately than most existing works in homogeneous environment. We incorporate vertical-aware features proposed in Table 5 to test if we can achieve significant improvement in satisfaction prediction. Note that in our experiment, there is only one query in a search task. So any feature that is related to multi-queries is not included in the implementation. We use the Normalized Root Mean Square Error (NRMSE, ranging from 0 to 1, smaller values mean better prediction) to evaluate the model performance as in most continuous value regression tasks [21]. The prediction performance of different feature groups is shown in Table 6. We perform a t-test to show the statistical significance on differences between methods with click-through / eye-tracking features and the original method.

Table 6: Comparison of Different Methods for Predicting Search Satisfaction(* indicates statistical significance at $p < 0.1$ level,** indicates statistical significance at $p < 0.05$ level)

Features	NRMSE (Predicting User Satisfaction)		NRMSE (Predicting External Annotation)	
	Guo et al. [15]	Jiang et al. [21]	Guo et al. [15]	Jiang et al. [21]
original	0.259	0.249	0.193	0.223
original + click-through	0.248**	0.243**	0.193	0.219
original + eye-tracking	0.246**	0.242**	0.188	0.201**
original + click-through + eye-tracking	0.242**	0.230**	0.187*	0.193**

The results in Table 6 show a number of interesting findings: 1) The prediction performance for annotations from external assessors is much better than those from users for all types of feature combinations. This probably means that the annotations from the assessors' side are more objective and consistent with each other. 2) The involvement of vertical-aware features significantly improves the prediction performance for both click-through and eye-tracking features. This shows the effectiveness of vertical information in predicting search satisfaction on SERPs with heterogeneous vertical results. 3) Among the two sources of features, we can see that eye-tracking features only perform slightly better than click-through features and the performance of click-through features is quite promising since such type of features can be collected at a low cost and at scale. We achieve the best performance when all feature groups are used for predicting user satisfaction. 4) Finally, we realize that methods based on Guo et al. [15] perform better when predicting external annotations while methods based on Jiang et al. [21] perform better when predicting user satisfaction. This indicates that features in the benefit-cost framework can make better use of users' search information and can estimate user satisfaction more accurately.

We have also conducted a leave-one-out ablation study to explore the contribution of different features in Table 5 on predicting satisfaction. Considering that the number of features is not very big, we leave one feature out each time and test the change in prediction performance to compare the contribution of each individual feature. We find that arr_time contributed the most for the prediction of both user satisfaction and external annotation. This feature measures the time when the user's mouse arrives at the vertical result, which may to some extent measure the time when the user starts to examine the vertical result. Because vertical results usually have a great influence on users' examination behavior [25, 35], arr_time may be important for satisfaction prediction. v_dwell_time contributed the least when predicting user satisfaction, which may reflect the fact that users may care little about the time they spend on result landing page (can be considered as search effort) and is in line with the findings in [24]. When predicting external annotation, the least important feature is $click\_time$. It may because that from the external assessors' point of view, the snippet of a vertical result can usually provide enough information for the user and thus a click may not be necessary. All features in Table 5 are useful when predicting user satisfaction since omitting any one of them will produce a drop in prediction performance.

7. CONCLUSIONS

Satisfaction prediction is an important research issue in the evaluation of search engine performance, and satisfaction studies on federated search pages have not been pursued. In this paper, we carry out a lab-based user study with specifically designed aggregated search result pages to see how verticals affect search satisfaction. We collect satisfaction scores from both users and external assessors to make a comparison because the concept of satisfaction is quite subjective. We find that on-topic Encyclopedia verticals as well as Download verticals will bring significant improvement to search satisfaction and that even off-topic ones will not result in a significant decline. Good Image verticals may not bring too much improvement but irrelevant ones will bring significant dissatisfaction. Most users will not care about News verticals because they only provide another list of search results. Good news verticals sometimes will even bring negative effects because a click leading to another SERP may be considered a waste of time. Verticals will have the largest influence when they are presented at the top of a page. As the position of verticals becomes lower, the effectiveness will decline to a large extent. With the rich information collected in our experimental system, we demonstrate that a benefit-cost framework will be useful when analyzing satisfaction. We find that the vertical results will significantly affect both result benefits and search costs. We also conclude that a metric of dividing benefit by cost will be a more appropriate estimator of user satisfaction. Finally, we propose a vertical-aware method to predict search satisfaction from both users and external assessors. We verify that with features related to verticals, we can achieve significant improvement in predicting search satisfaction based on state-of-the-art methods, which are effective in homogeneous environment. We demonstrate that features extracted from the perspective of both benefit and effort can greatly improve the user satisfaction prediction model. We also conclude that satisfaction scores from external assessors are easier to predict probably because professional assessors are usually more objective while judging satisfaction. Interesting directions for future work include understanding and predicting satisfaction on SERPs with multi-verticals. Moreover, incorporating the effect of verticals into user behavior models will also be a challenge.

8. ACKNOWLEDGMENTS

This work is supported by Tsinghua University Initiative Scientific Research Program (2014Z21032), National Key Basic Research Program (2015CB358700) and Natural Science Foundation (61472206, 61073071) of China. Part of the work has been done at the Tsinghua-NUS NExT Search Centre, which is supported by the Singapore National Search Foundation & Interactive Digital Media R&D Program Office, MDA under research grant (WBS:R-252-300-001-490).

9. REFERENCES

[1] M. Ageev, Q. Guo, D. Lagun, and E. Agichtein. Find it if you can: a game for modeling different types of web search success using interaction data. In *SIGIR'11*, pages 345–354. ACM, 2011.

[2] A. Al-Maskari, M. Sanderson, and P. Clough. The relationship between ir effectiveness measures and user satisfaction. In *SIGIR'07*, pages 773–774. ACM, 2007.

[3] J. Arguello and R. Capra. The effects of vertical rank and border on aggregated search coherence and search behavior. In *CIKM'14*, pages 539–548. ACM, 2014.

[4] J. Arguello, F. Diaz, J. Callan, and J.-F. Crespo. Sources of evidence for vertical selection. In *SIGIR'09*, pages 315–322. ACM, 2009.

[5] J. Arguello, F. Diaz, and J.-F. Paiement. Vertical selection in the presence of unlabeled verticals. In *SIGIR'10*, pages 691–698. ACM, 2010.

[6] G. Buscher, S. T. Dumais, and E. Cutrell. The good, the bad, and the random: an eye-tracking study of ad quality in web search. In *SIGIR'10*, pages 42–49. ACM, 2010.

[7] O. Chapelle, D. Metlzer, Y. Zhang, and P. Grinspan. Expected reciprocal rank for graded relevance. In *CIKM'09*, pages 621–630. ACM, 2009.

[8] C. L. Clarke, M. Kolla, G. V. Cormack, O. Vechtomova, A. Ashkan, S. Büttcher, and I. MacKinnon. Novelty and diversity in information retrieval evaluation. In *SIGIR'08*, pages 659–666. ACM, 2008.

[9] J. Cohen. Weighted kappa: Nominal scale agreement provision for scaled disagreement or partial credit. *Psychological bulletin*, 70(4):213, 1968.

[10] F. Diaz. Integration of news content into web results. In *WSDM'09*, pages 182–191. ACM, 2009.

[11] S. Djamasbi, A. Hall-Phillips, and R. R. Yang. Serps and ads on mobile devices: An eye tracking study for generation y. In *Universal Access in Human-Computer Interaction. User and Context Diversity*, pages 259–268. Springer, 2013.

[12] H. A. Feild, J. Allan, and R. Jones. Predicting searcher frustration. In *SIGIR'10*, pages 34–41. ACM, 2010.

[13] L. A. Granka, T. Joachims, and G. Gay. Eye-tracking analysis of user behavior in www search. In *SIGIR'04*, pages 478–479. ACM, 2004.

[14] Q. Guo and E. Agichtein. Towards predicting web searcher gaze position from mouse movements. In *CHI'10*, pages 3601–3606. ACM, 2010.

[15] Q. Guo, D. Lagun, and E. Agichtein. Predicting web search success with fine-grained interaction data. In *CIKM'12*, pages 2050–2054. ACM, 2012.

[16] Q. Guo, R. W. White, S. T. Dumais, J. Wang, and B. Anderson. Predicting query performance using query, result, and user interaction features. In *Adaptivity, Personalization and Fusion of Heterogeneous Information*, pages 198–201, 2010.

[17] A. E. Hoerl and R. W. Kennard. Ridge regression: Biased estimation for nonorthogonal problems. *Technometrics*, 12(1):55–67, 1970.

[18] S. B. Huffman and M. Hochster. How well does result relevance predict session satisfaction? In *SIGIR'07*, pages 567–574. ACM, 2007.

[19] K. Järvelin and J. Kekäläinen. Cumulated gain-based evaluation of ir techniques. *ACM Transactions on Information Systems (TOIS)*, 20(4):422–446, 2002.

[20] K. Järvelin, S. L. Price, L. M. Delcambre, and M. L. Nielsen. Discounted cumulated gain based evaluation of multiple-query ir sessions. In *Advances in Information Retrieval*, pages 4–15. Springer, 2008.

[21] J. Jiang, A. Hassan Awadallah, X. Shi, and R. W. White. Understanding and predicting graded search satisfaction. In *WSDM'15*, pages 57–66. ACM, 2015.

[22] J. Jiang, D. He, and J. Allan. Searching, browsing, and clicking in a search session: changes in user behavior by task and over time. In *SIGIR'14*, pages 607–616. ACM, 2014.

[23] D. Kelly. Methods for evaluating interactive information retrieval systems with users. *Foundations and Trends in Information Retrieval*, 3(1—2):1–224, 2009.

[24] Y. Liu, Y. Chen, J. Tang, J. Sun, M. Zhang, S. Ma, and X. Zhu. Different users, different opinions: Predicting search satisfaction with mouse movement information. In *SIGIR'15*. ACM, 2015.

[25] Z. Liu, Y. Liu, K. Zhou, M. Zhang, and S. Ma. Influence of vertical result in web search examination. In *SIGIR'15*. ACM, 2015.

[26] L. Lorigo, M. Haridasan, H. Brynjarsdóttir, L. Xia, T. Joachims, G. Gay, L. Granka, F. Pellacini, and B. Pan. Eye tracking and online search: Lessons learned and challenges ahead. *Journal of the American Society for Information Science and Technology*, 59(7):1041–1052, 2008.

[27] I. Markov, E. Kharitonov, V. Nikulin, P. Serdyukov, M. de Rijke, and F. Crestani. Vertical-aware click model-based effectiveness metrics. In *CIKM'14*, pages 1867–1870. ACM, 2014.

[28] V. Navalpakkam, L. Jentzsch, R. Sayres, S. Ravi, A. Ahmed, and A. Smola. Measurement and modeling of eye-mouse behavior in the presence of nonlinear page layouts. In *WWW'13*, pages 953–964. IW3C2, 2013.

[29] M. Richardson, E. Dominowska, and R. Ragno. Predicting clicks: estimating the click-through rate for new ads. In *WWW'07*, pages 521–530. ACM, 2007.

[30] T. Sakai and R. Song. Evaluating diversified search results using per-intent graded relevance. In *SIGIR'11*, pages 1043–1052. ACM, 2011.

[31] D. D. Salvucci and J. H. Goldberg. Identifying fixations and saccades in eye-tracking protocols. In *Proceedings of the 2000 symposium on Eye tracking research & applications*, pages 71–78. ACM, 2000.

[32] L. T. Su. Evaluation measures for interactive information retrieval. *Information Processing & Management*, 28(4):503–516, 1992.

[33] L. T. Su. A comprehensive and systematic model of user evaluation of web search engines: Ii. an evaluation by undergraduates. *Journal of the American Society for Information Science and Technology*, 54(13):1193–1223, 2003.

[34] S. Verberne, M. Heijden, M. Hinne, M. Sappelli, S. Koldijk, E. Hoenkamp, and W. Kraaij. Reliability and validity of query intent assessments. *Journal of the American Society for Information Science and Technology*, 64(11):2224–2237, 2013.

[35] C. Wang, Y. Liu, M. Zhang, S. Ma, M. Zheng, J. Qian, and K. Zhang. Incorporating vertical results into search click models. In *SIGIR'13*, pages 503–512. ACM, 2013.

[36] H. Wang, Y. Song, M.-W. Chang, X. He, A. Hassan, and R. W. White. Modeling action-level satisfaction for search task satisfaction prediction. In *SIGIR'14*, pages 123–132. ACM, 2014.

[37] K. Zhou, R. Cummins, M. Lalmas, and J. M. Jose. Evaluating aggregated search pages. In *SIGIR'12*, pages 115–124. ACM, 2012.

[38] K. Zhou, R. Cummins, M. Lalmas, and J. M. Jose. Evaluating reward and risk for vertical selection. In *CIKM'12*, pages 2631–2634. ACM, 2012.

Characterizing and Predicting Viral-and-Popular Video Content

David Vallet†*, Shlomo Berkovsky‡, Sebastien Ardon†, Anirban Mahanti†, Mohamed Ali Kaafar†
†NICTA, Australia ‡CSIRO, Australia
david.vallet@nicta.com.au, shlomo.berkovsky@csiro.au, sebastien@incoming.tv, anirban.mahanti@nicta.com.au, dali.kafaar@nicta.com.au

ABSTRACT

The proliferation of online video content has triggered numerous works on its evolution and popularity, as well as on the effect of social sharing on content propagation. In this paper, we focus on the observable dependencies between the virality of video content on a micro-blogging social network (in this case, Twitter) and the popularity of such content on a video distribution service (YouTube). To this end, we collected and analysed a corpus of Twitter posts containing links to YouTube clips and the corresponding video metadata from YouTube. Our analysis highlights the unique properties of content that is both popular and viral, i.e., attracts high number of views on YouTube and achieves fast propagation on Twitter. With this in mind, we proceed to the predictions of popular-and-viral clips and propose a framework that can, with high degree of accuracy and low amount of training data, predict videos that are likely to be popular, viral, and both. The key contribution of our work is the focus on cross-system dynamics between YouTube and Twitter. We conjecture and validate that cross-system prediction of both popularity and virality of videos is feasible, and can be performed with a reasonably high degree of accuracy. One of our key findings is that YouTube features capturing user engagement, have strong virality prediction capabilities. This findings allows to solely rely on data extracted from a video sharing service to predict popularity and virality aspects of videos.

Keywords

Popularity; Virality; Video.

1. INTRODUCTION

Over the past decade, video sharing services like YouTube have witnessed exponential traffic growth. In these services, some videos achieve immense popularity and have over a billion views, while others fall into oblivion without attracting any interest. In this corner of the attention economy, views – sometimes called eyeballs – directly impact advertising revenues and are, therefore, of prime importance for content producers, marketing agencies, and service providers. As a result, over the recent years, the dynamics and prediction of user-generated content popularity has captured the attention of service providers, media agencies, and academics alike [26, 6, 9, 3, 22, 17].

In this paper, we study the popularity of content on a video sharing platform (YouTube), while simultaneously observing its propagation in an online social network for micro-blogging (Twitter). Our methodology allows us to evaluate the interplay between a video content *popularity*, i.e., its inherent propensity to attract views on YouTube, and content *virality*, i.e., its potential to elicit Twitter posts from its viewers. Our underlying assumption is that two main types of diffusion channel contribute in combination to a content's popularity: conventional channels and online social networking (OSN) channels. Conventional diffusion channels are essentially mass-media outlets, such as news sites, product reviews, and popular blogs, which can be considered as direct marketing efforts designed to steer traffic and attention towards the videos. OSN channels, in contrast, make use of the crowd to generate traffic toward the videos, as users leverage their social circles to share video links with friends and followers. What drives users to share videos still remains largely under-studied [20], but empirical evidence shows that only some videos (referred to as viral), generate enough interest for a user to share the video.

We use the Twitter service as a proxy for OSN channels. We collect data about tweets and re-tweets containing links to YouTube videos, while simultaneously collecting statistics pertaining to these videos (view counts, number of comments, tags, and so on) from the YouTube service. The data collected simultaneously on both systems allows us to quantify two system-specific metrics for each video: popularity and virality. The popularity reflects the exposure of the video, driven by both the conventional and OSN diffusion channels, whereas virality measures the propagation of the clip on Twitter. Note that the two metrics are measured independently on the two services, although they may be inter-related and fuel each other. Based on those metrics, we define video classes by selecting the set of most popular and most viral videos, and characterize their evolution on the YouTube and Twitter platforms. We then extract a suite of Twitter- and YouTube-specific features, and feed these into a Gradient Boosted Decision Tree classifier [13], trained to predict popularity and/or virality of videos.

*Now with Google.

©2015 Association for Computing Machinery. ACM acknowledges that this contribution was authored or co-authored by an employee, contractor or affiliate of a national government. As such, the Government retains a nonexclusive, royalty-free right to publish or reproduce this article, or to allow others to do so, for Government purposes only.
CIKM'15 October 19-23, 2015, Melbourne, VIC, Australia
©ACM ISBN 978-1-4503-3794-6/15/10 ...$15.00
DOI: http://dx.doi.org/10.1145/2806416.2806556.

Table 1: Overview of example video sub-groups.

popular	5,000 videos with highest view count during the labeling window
viral	5,000 videos with the highest number of mentions during the labeling window
recent	5,000 videos that are less than 2 days old at the time of data collection
random	5,000 videos randomly selected from the seed set of 200,000 videos

We make a number of observations. We demonstrate that we can produce highly accurate predictions of video popularity and virality using only a small amount of training data. For example, our classifier is able to predict with high accuracy the videos in the *viral-and-popular* class up to 7 days in advance, using only 1 day of training data. We find that only the fundamental features, such as past number of views and tweet count, are insufficient to obtain a reasonable classification accuracy for these videos. Using feature importance analysis, we show that the current tweeting rate, along with the volume of original tweets received since upload are the two most important Twitter features to consider for the classification of these videos. Further, an important result presented is on cross-system predictions: we show that YouTube features, and in particular features reflecting the level of user engagement, have a strong prediction capability for the viral-and-popular class, especially for recently uploaded videos. This result in itself motivates the application of our approach for identification of both popular and viral items solely based on data extracted from a video sharing service.

The remainder of the paper is structured as follows. Section 2 presents the datasets used in this work, describes our data collection methodology, and includes a high-level characterization of the collected data. Section 3 presents our results, analyses, and observations in detail. Then, section 4 present related work, before concluding and stating directions for future work in section 5.

2. DATASETS

In this section, we describe our data collection methodology and present a high-level characterization of our datasets. The characterization provides insights into the interplay between popularity and virality, and serves as a prelude to the modeling and analyses presented later in the paper.

2.1 Data collection

We initially selected a set of videos to study by sampling the Twitter stream for 24 hours searching for links to YouTube videos. Specifically, we used the Twitter streaming API with the `expanded_url` keyword matching with the domain names used by YouTube, like youtube.com and youtu.be. Note that the Twitter streaming API is able to resolve shortened URL links, so tweets containing a shortened, e.g., through bit.ly, URL to a YouTube video were also captured by our search. Using this search facility over a 24-hour period, we collected links to a large number of videos from which we randomly selected 200,000 videos to form the seed set for our dataset. Then, for a period of two weeks we collected YouTube and Twitter data for each video included in the seed set. Specifically, we collected statistics from YouTube once per day and concurrently tracked mentions of these videos using the Twitter streaming API. A detailed description of the collected data and extracted features will be presented in Section 3.1.

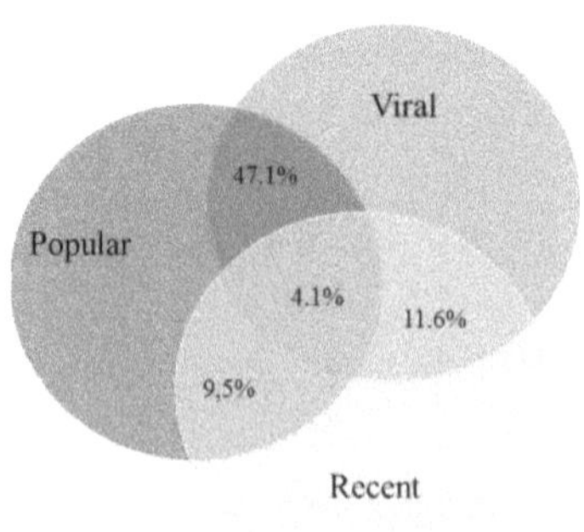

Figure 1: Venn diagram showing the overlaps among the popular, viral, and recent sub-groups.

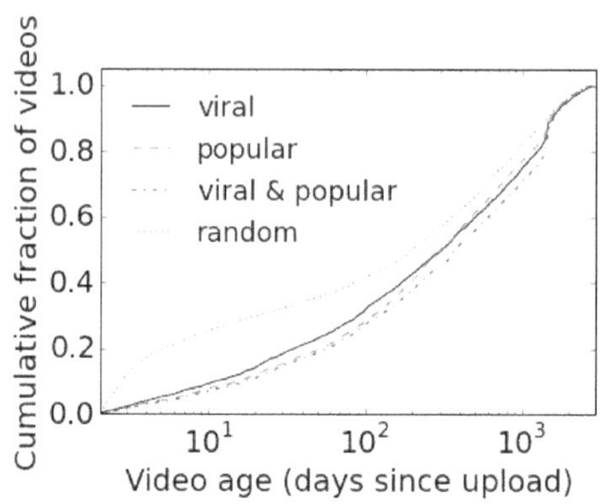

Figure 2: Distribution of video age for different classes.

Out of the 200,000 seed videos, we focus on four sub-groups, described in Table 1, which are then used in the remainder of this paper. The *popular* sub-group contains the 5,000 videos that attracted the largest number of views on YouTube. Specifically, among the 200,000 videos in the seed set, the popular videos account for the most viewed 2.5% of videos. We also define the *viral* sub-group, which consists of the 5,000 videos that were mentioned the most on Twitter[1]. The *recent* sub-group consists of 5,000 randomly selected videos, which are two days old or younger, at the time of data collection. Finally, the *random* sub-group consists of a sample of 5,000 videos selected at random from our initial seed set of 200,000 videos. The relative size of the intersections of these sub-groups is shown in Figure 1.

Given these sub-groups, we define another sub-group, denoted by *viral-and-popular*. As the name suggests, this sub-group includes videos that are both viral and popular, i.e., videos in the intersection of the viral and popular video sets. Note that the cardinality of the viral-and-popular sub-group is close to a half of either sub-group individually.

[1]We define popularity and virality based on YouTube views and Twitter mentions captured during the observation period, referred to as the *labeling* window. More details on the labeling will be given in section 3.1.

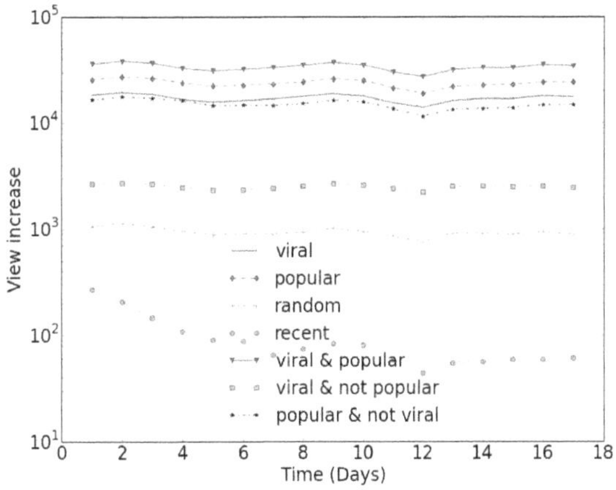

Figure 3: Average daily increase in view count for the various video sub-groups.

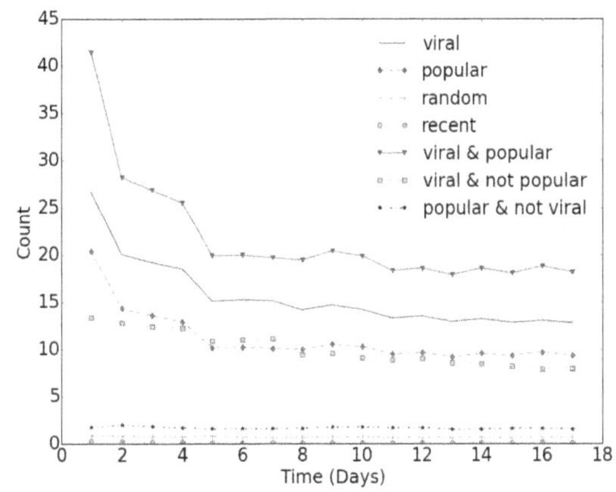

Figure 4: Average number of tweet mentions for the various video sub-groups.

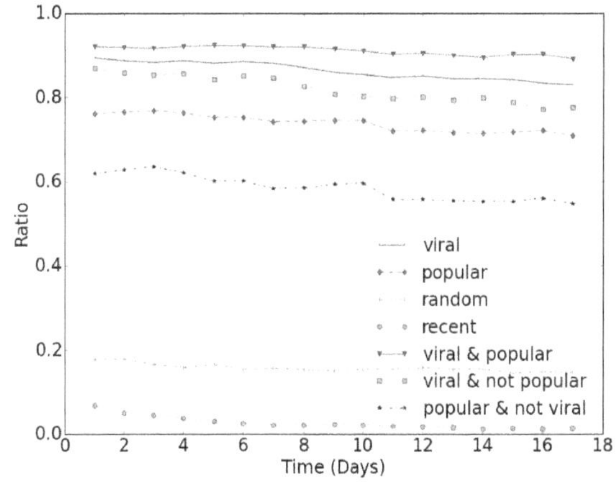

Figure 5: Ratio between the original and overall number of tweets averaged per day and video class.

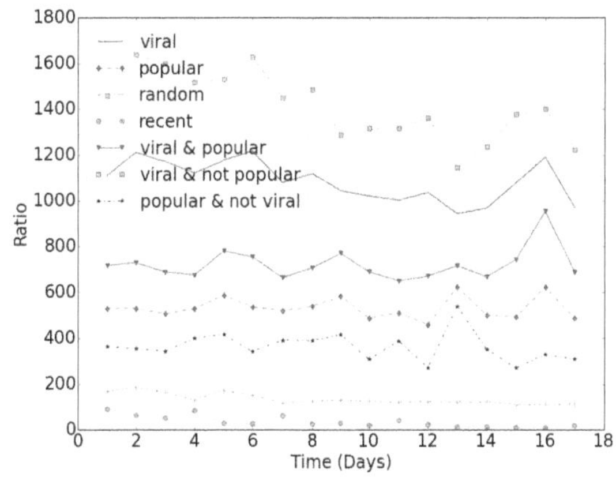

Figure 6: Average number of users reached per day by tweets for videos in the various sub-groups.

2.2 High-Level Characterization

This section presents a high-level characterization of the datasets used in this study. Figure 2 shows the video age distribution, for the random, viral, popular, and viral-and-popular sub-groups. We observe that the video age has a wide range of values, and varies across the three classes, with videos in the random class skewed towards younger videos more than in the other three classes. This shows that, as expected, a random sample of YouTube videos has a higher portion of young videos than the viral and popular sub-groups. Somewhat surprisingly, we find that some very old videos, which are over 7 years old, are amongst the viral-and-popular videos. On investigation, we find that these older videos are music video clips, with a significant number being Michael Jackson's videos that were released in 2009.

Figure 3 shows the average *increase* in the number of YouTube views per day for the video sub-groups introduced above. We notice that with the exception of the videos in the recent sub-group, videos in all other sub-groups add views at a steady rate, showing that the popularity of these sub-groups is not affected during the observation window. Focusing on the standalone viral and popular sub-groups, we notice that, on average, popular videos receive a larger number of additional views per day than those in the viral category. However, it is interesting to note that videos categorized as viral-and-popular add more views per days than any other sub-group, which presumably stems from their definition of being viral and popular at the same time.

Figure 4 shows the average number of Twitter mentions observed, for the various video sub-groups, during our measurement window. As expected, videos in the standalone viral sub-group are the most active ones in Twitter, and are mentioned more often than those that are categorized as popular only. Note that videos in the random and recent sub-groups, on average, are hardly mentioned in Twitter. The important takeaway here, though, is that videos that are both viral-and-popular are mentioned, on average, six times as much as videos that are only popular but not viral, and, on average, twice as much as videos that are only viral but not popular. This observation highlights again our proposition regarding the special attention that needs to be paid to the viral-and-popular sub-group.

Figure 5 further investigates the observed tweeting activity across the video sub-groups, focusing on the level of user engagement. For a given video, we consider the ratio of original tweets to the overall number Twitter mentions, i.e., the ratio between the number of tweets and the sum of the number of tweets and re-tweets. We observe that this ratio is relatively steady across all the video sub-groups. However,

Feature	Description
yt_views_n	Number of views added on day n
yt_likes_n	Number of likes added on day n
$yt\_ratings_n$	Number of ratings added on day n
$yt\_comments_n$	Number of comments added on day n
$yt\_uploaded$	Video upload timestamp
$yt\_category$	Video category
yt_rating	Average rating (0-5)
$yt\_uploader.uploads$	Number of videos uploaded by the uploader
$yt\_uploader.favorites$	Number of times the uploader was favorited
$yt\_uploader.subscribers$	Number of uploader's subscribers

Table 2: YouTube features for a video ($n \geq 1$).

Individual features	Description
tw_tweets_n	Number of tweets on day n
$tw\_orig\_tweets_n$	Number of original tweets on day n
$tw\_retweets_n$	Number of retweets posted on day n
$tw\_replies_n$	Number of tweet-reply posted on day n
$tw\_en\_language$	Number of tweets in English
$tw\_user.en\_language$	Number of users who set English as language
$tw\_user.statuses$	Number of user's status updates
$tw\_user.friends$	Number of user's friends (i.e., 'followees')
$tw\_user.followers$	Total number of followers
$tw\_user.favorites_n$	Number of tweets that were favorited on day n

Table 3: Twitter features for tweets mentioning a video ($n \geq 1$)

we observe also here that a video simply being popular is not sufficient for it to be highly mentioned on Twitter. The viral-and-popular videos not only receive a larger fraction of original tweets than viral and popular sub-groups individually, but also substantially larger than those videos that are only popular but not viral.

Figure 6 depicts how the Twitter OSN facilitates the spread of content. For every day of the observations, we compute the fan-out of the tweets, i.e., the average number of users reached by tweets mentioning videos in various sub-groups. We observe that this number is relatively stable over time in all the sub-groups. Note that the average number of users reached by tweets mentioning viral videos (both popular and not popular) is higher than that of the non-viral videos. Interestingly, the number of users reached by tweets mentioning viral-and-popular videos is inferior to the one reached by tweets mentioning only viral but not popular videos. We posit that this is explained by the large number of short and low-quality videos that are often tweeted by users with many followers. As we show later in the analyses, the number of followers, which is a proxy for a number of users reached by a tweets, is indeed an important feature for detecting content virality.

3. CLASSIFICATION AND PREDICTION RESULTS

In this section, we present performance evaluation of the classifiers trained to predict virality and/or popularity of videos, and analyze cross-system interactions between YouTube and Twitter. We also discuss the results of the feature importance analysis that provide valuable insights on the performance of the classifiers and underpin the observed cross-system interactions. Finally, we present a sensitivity analysis assessing the effect of the training and labeling windows sizes on the classification performance.

3.1 Methodology and Experimental Setting

Our analysis consists of a classification task, where we aim to classify each video, based on a set of input features, as viral and/or popular. For this, we train two binary classifiers capable of separately predicting the virality and popularity label for any given video. Given the outputs of these classifiers, we define the viral-and-popular class as the intersection of the viral and popular video sets. We implement the classifiers using a Gradient Boosted Decision Tree, widely used for general classification problems [13].

Table 2 shows a sample of YouTube features extracted per video. Some features refer to the video characteristics and some to the uploader of the video. It is important to note that the YouTube API returns the cumulative number of video views, likes, ratings, and comments from the upload to the time of query. The value of the desired counters for any given day or period can be derived from the cumulative counts. Table 3 shows a sample of Twitter features extracted for an individual tweet mentioning a YouTube video. Again, some of them refer to the tweet itself and some to the user who posted the tweet.

In addition to the above features, we derive additional features, which we denote using the following modifiers:

- The superscript *ratio* is used to relate a feature value to its magnitude. For example, $yt\_views_n^{ratio}$ is the ratio between the number of views on day n, yt_views_n, and the total number of views since upload.

- The superscript *acc* denotes the acceleration of the feature, i.e., $yt\_views_n^{acc}$ is the ratio between yt_views_n and yt_views_{n-1}.

- The subscript *dif* denotes the difference between the *accumulated* value of a feature at the first and last day of a period, e.g., yt_views_{dif}. For instance, if collecting data over a three-day period, $yt\_views_{dif} = yt\_views_3$ - yt_views_1.

- The superscript *age_ratio* is used to relate a feature value to its age. For example, $yt\_views_n^{age\_ratio}$ is the ratio between the number of views on day n, yt_views_n, and the time since *yt_uploaded.*

The classifiers use these features to predict binary labels of virality and popularity. We define the *training window* as the period used to train the classifier. When the training window is greater than one day, we populate also the above ratio, acceleration, daily, difference, and age ratio features. The ground truth[2] regarding the viral and popular (and the derived viral-and-popular) labels of a video is determined by its uptake during the *labeling window* that comes after the training window. By the uptake we refer to the number of YouTube views as the indicator of popularity and number of tweets mentioning the video as the indicator of virality. The period between the training and labeling windows is referred to as the *offset*. The offset can be set to 0, when predicting the virality and popularity classes of a video immediately after the training period, or to, e.g., 7 days, when predicting these one week after the training period.

We would like to highlight the importance of parameters pertaining to the size of these windows. Clearly, the most

[2]As presented earlier, we label top 2.5% most-viewed videos as popular and top 2.5% most-tweeted videos as viral.

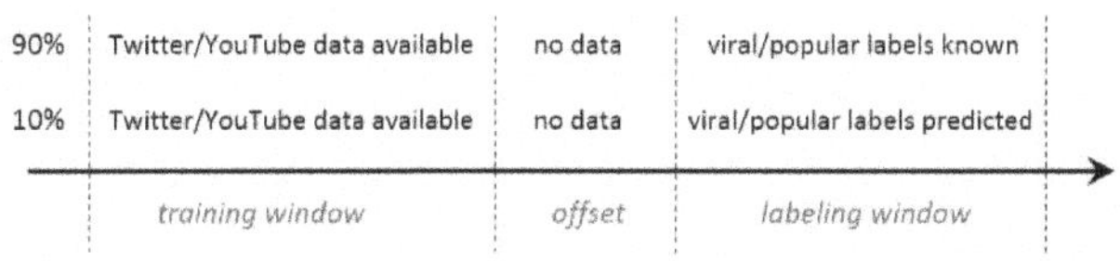

Figure 7: Time line of the experimental methodology and data availability.

challenging predictions are those aiming to predict the virality and/or popularity of new videos as long as possibly in advance, i.e., small to none training window and large offset. This is the use case for predictive analytics in applications like advertisement and content placement. The size of the labeling window is not as important, and generally ranges from days to several weeks. Due to practical limitations, the data collection period was limited in our study to one month. Hence, in the sensitivity analysis we vary the size of the training window, offset, and labeling window from 1 to 7 days. To assess the accuracy of predictions for recently uploaded videos, we break the analysis into two groups: videos that are younger than 2 weeks and older videos.

For the evaluation of the predictive accuracy, we use the 10-fold validation methodology. That is, for 90% of videos we have the data referring both to the training window and the labeling window, such that we know what videos qualified to the viral and popular classes. For the remaining 10% of videos we have the training window data only and predict the the viral and/or popular class labels at the labeling window. The predicted and real labels of these 10% are used to compute the precision and recall scores. Also, the performance of the classifier is quantified using the area under the precision-recall curve (AUC) and the mean F1 score. We then repeat the experiment 10 times for differently chosen 10% chunks and average the obtained accuracy scores across these experiments. Figure 7 visualizes the time line of the windows and the evaluation methodology.

3.2 Prediction Accuracy

We start with examining the accuracy of predicting virality or popularity, or both. Here, we set the training window size to 2 days and the labeling window size to the immediately following 7 days, i.e., no offset. We use all the above mentioned YouTube and Twitter features to train the classifiers. As a comparison baseline, we chose a simple classifier that only uses two features: the number of original tweets and the number of views, i.e., $tw\_orig\_tweets^{cnt}$ as the Twitter feature and yt_views as the YouTube feature. This reflects a simple baseline classifier that uses only the raw statistics on the uptake of the videos in both systems. The analysis splits the videos into two groups, according to their age: those uploaded less than 14 days prior to data collection (referred to as *recent*) and the rest (*others*).

In Figure 8 we show the obtained precision-recall graphs. The rows show the source of features used by the classifiers (Twitter, YouTube, both) and the columns show the video class being predicted (viral, popular, viral-and-popular). In every graph, we depict 4 curves: classifier considering all the features vs. only the baseline counter features $tw\_orig\_tweets^{cnt}$ and yt_views, and accuracy of recent videos' classification vs. older videos.

3.2.1 *Virality or popularity predictions*

First, we focus on predicting the standalone viral and popular class labels. Prior work has shown that high prediction accuracy can be achieved by using simple features [25, 29, 10]. Our results reaffirm this finding, as shown by the high AUC values obtained when predicting virality with Twitter features (top-left graph in Figure 8) and popularity with YouTube features (central graph). The bottom-left and bottom-center graphs in Figure 8 show the performance when features from both systems are used to predict virality and popularity, respectively. In comparison to the previous Twitter- and YouTube-only graphs, we observe that there is little difference in performance. This suggests that, as expected, Twitter features are predominant when predicting virality on Twitter, whereas YouTube features are the most important for YouTube popularity predictions.

Note that very close AUC values are achieved when using only the baseline features from both systems, which suggests that applying regression to the training data is sufficient when predicting viral or popular videos. However, it should be highlighted that the AUC values obtained for predicting recent videos are substantially lower than those obtained when predicting older videos. This is explained by the abundance and reliability of data available for older videos, which allows achieving more accurate predictions. This result indicates that early detection of popularity and/or virality of recent videos, which may be the ultimate goal of content providers, is a rather challenging task that requires mobilizing many predictive features.

3.2.2 *Cross-system predictions*

Next, we proceed to cross-system predictions and assess the feasibility of using YouTube features to predict virality on Twitter, and vice versa, of using Twitter features to predict popularity on YouTube. This scenario investigates the interplay between Twitter and YouTube in terms of similarities between the evolution of content virality and popularity. The results are shown in the top-central and middle-left graphs in Figure 8.

We observe that both cross-system predictions are less accurate than the direct using data from the same system, i.e., virality predictions using Twitter data and popularity predictions using YouTube data. However while the obtained AUC values are lower than previously, we note that a reasonable accuracy is still achieved for all features and not-recent videos. At recall of 0.5, the precision is about 0.75 for both the virality and popularity predictions. For recent videos though, the accuracy deteriorates and the precision drops below 0.5 at a recall of 0.5. Focusing on predictions using all the available features, we observe that virality predictions using YouTube data are more accurate than popularity predictions using Twitter data. We posit that this is due to the fact that some YouTube views can be attributed to Twitter propagation, which is a strong predictive feature of virality. We also note that the baseline features perform considerably worse than all the features, which indicates that features mined from the original data improve the accuracy of cross-system predictions.

3.2.3 *Viral-and-popular predictions*

Videos in this class are usually mentioned and viewed more frequently than those in the standalone viral and popular classes. The accuracy of the classifier, shown in the right column in Figure 8, suggests that the highest accu-

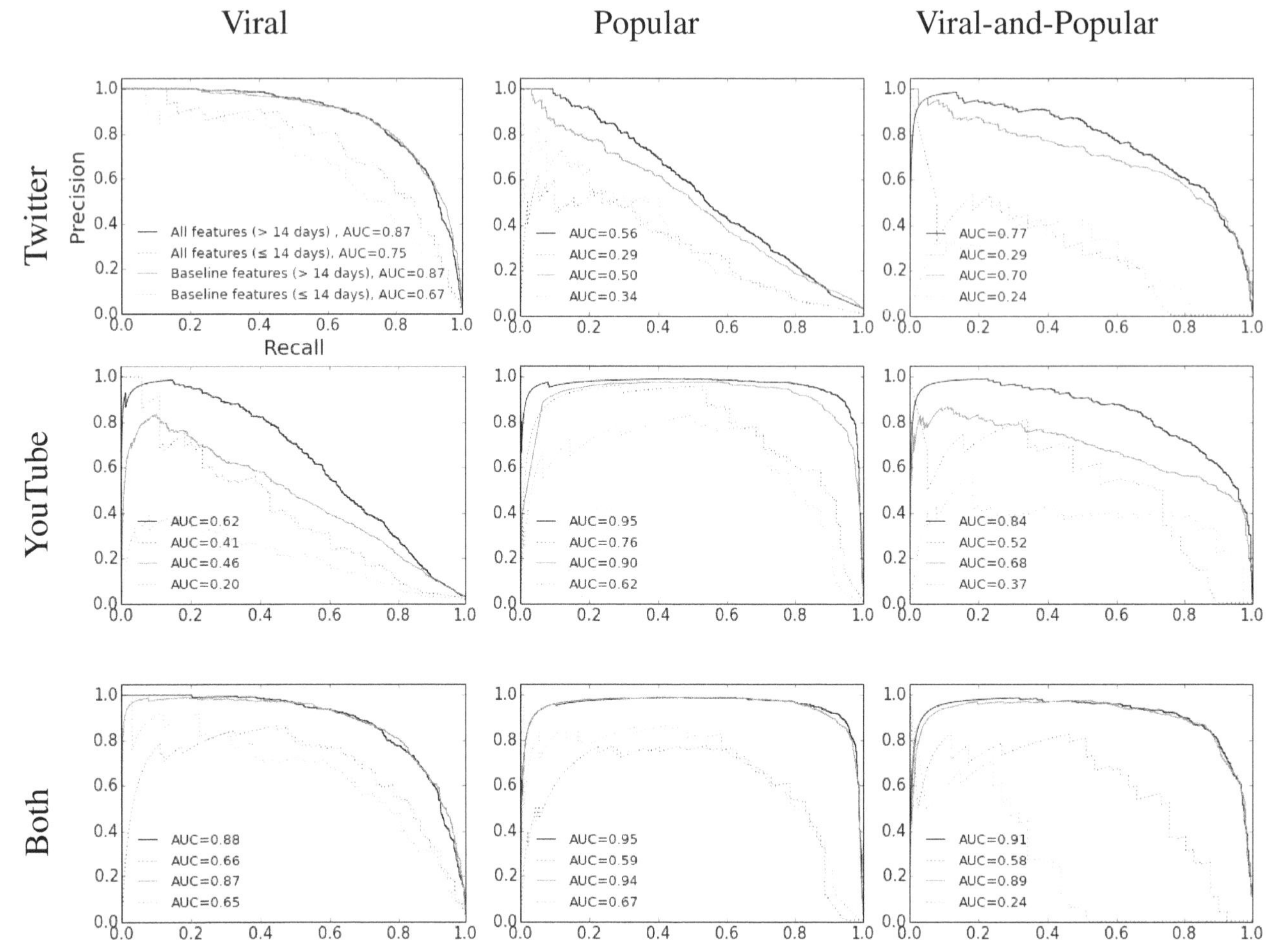

Figure 8: Prediction of top 5,000 (2.5%) most viral and popular videos. Precision-recall graphs and AUC values for all features vs baseline features and recent vs other videos.

racy is achieved when using both Twitter and YouTube features. Comparing the all features and the baseline features classifiers, we observe a substantial difference between the two when only Twitter features (top-right graph) or only YouTube features (middle-right) are used. This indicates that in this scenario, just like in the cross-system prediction task, the mined features substantially improve the accuracy of the classification.

On the contrary, the baseline feature are sufficient when using both YouTube and Twitter features, and the difference observed between the two classifiers is minor. This is also consistent with previous analysis that showed that the baseline features led to reasonably accurate classification. This observation, however, does not hold when focusing on the recent videos, where the gap between the two classifiers is wider. Our analysis reaffirms that early prediction of recently uploaded videos is challenging and, in this case, the baseline features need to be augmented with additional features mined from the original data. Moreover, virality-and-popularity predictions for recent videos achieve lower accuracy than their standalone prediction, showing that this task is hard even with the additional features.

3.3 Feature Importance Analysis

In this section, we focus on the importance of features for the classification task. We infer the feature importance scores[3] from the outputs of the Gradient Boost Decision Tree. They communicate the contribution of features to classifying each instance correctly (readers may refer to [19] for more details). Like in the experiments in section 3.2, the feature importance scores are computed for the setting of 2 training days, 7 labeling days, and no offset between the two. Hence, only simple *dif* and *ratio* features are considered. Since the direct predictions of virality using Twitter data (Figure 8, top-left) and of popularity using YouTube data (Figure 8, central graph) achieved high AUC values, we focus here on the cross-system and viral-and-popular predictions.

3.3.1 Cross-system predictions

Feature importance values when predicting video popularity on YouTube using Twitter features are shown in Table 4. For recently uploaded videos, we find that the current tweet-

[3]Note that the importance scores of the features do not sum up to 100%. Instead, the most important feature is marked as 100% and the importance of other features is computed relatively to the importance of the top feature.

Other (> 14 days)		Recent (≤ 14 days)	
feature	import.	feature	import.
$tw\_orig\_tweets_2$	100%	$tw\_orig\_tweets_2$	100%
$tw\_orig\_tweets_1^{ratio}$	69.6%	$tw\_user.favorites_{dif}$	66.6%
tw_tweets_{dif}	69.6%	$tw\_user.friends_{dif}$	60.9%
$tw\_orig\_tweets_1$	60.5%	$tw\_user.favorites_2$	57.1%
$tw\_orig\_tweets_2^{ratio}$	51.7%	$tw\_user.statuses_{dif}$	47.9%
$tw\_user.statuses_{acc}$	47.2%	$tw\_orig\_tweets_1$	47.3%

Table 4: Popularity predictions using Twitter features.

Other (> 14 days)		Recent (≤ 14 days)	
feature	import.	feature	import.
yt_likes_2	100%	$yt\_ratings_{dif}$	100%
yt_likes_1	61.9%	yt_likes_1	86.1%
yt_views_2	58.6%	$yt\_views_2^{age\_ratio}$	81.0%
yt_views_1	49.5%	yt_likes_2	69.6%
$yt\_user.uploads$	31.5%	yt_views_2	67.8%

Table 5: Virality predictions using YouTube features.

ing rate, captured by $tw\_orig\_tweets_2$ is amongst the most predictive features. (Recall that training window size is 2 days, and, thus, the number of tweets on the second day is the measure of the current tweeting rate.) We also note that the propagation measured by the volume of users reached by tweets over the training period, $tw\_user.friends_{dif}$, is an important feature. Features capturing the user engagement with the Twitter eco-system, such as the number and ratio of tweets that were favorited, also play an important role in the video popularity classification accuracy. When considering predictions for less recent videos, we observe that active user engagement indicated by user's propensity to write original tweets, $tw\_orig\_tweets_2^{ratio}$, is also an important feature. Summarizing, we find that there are three key factors in predicting a future video via Twitter: the current tweeting rate, the propagation effect, and the user's engagement with Twitter content. A combination of these factors communicates the magnitude of audience that can potentially be achieved by a tweet.

When predicting virality of recently uploaded videos using YouTube features (shown in Table 5), we observe that the difference in terms of ratings added to the video, $yt\_ratings_{dif}$, is the most dominant predictive feature. Similarly, the rates capturing the number of likes per day are also important features. It could be argued that rating and liking videos in YouTube is similar in flavor to tweeting activity, which explains their predictive importance. Another relevant feature in the virality classification relates to the ratio between the number of views at the time of classification and the time since the video upload, $yt\_views_2^{age\_ratio}$. In essence, the growth rate of likes, ratings, and likes are the predominant features for predicting the virality of recent videos based solely on YouTube features. Similarly, the number of likes and views seem to be the predominant features when predicting the virality of not-recent videos. In addition, we observed that the number of video uploaded by the uploader plays a role in such predictions.

3.3.2 *Viral-and-popular predictions*

Lastly, Table 6 shows feature importance values obtained when predicting the viral-and-popular class. As can be seen,

Other (> 14 days)		Recent (≤ 14 days)	
feature	import.	feature	import.
yt_views_2	100%	yt_views_2	100%
yt_views_1	29.0%	yt_likes_2	12.7%
$tw\_orig\_tweets_2$	18.8%	$yt\_comments_2$	6.42%
$yt\_views_{ageRate}$	14.3%	$tw\_en\_language_{acc}$	4.98%
$yt\_comments_1$	13.2%	$tw\_user.en\_language_{acc}$	4.45%

Table 6: Virality-and-popularity predictions using all the features.

YouTube features generally dominate Twitter features, with the number of YouTube views in the second training day substantially outweighing other features for predictions of both recent and other videos.

Recall that the viral-and-popular videos are the sub-group that adds, on average, the largest number of views per day, and are also the videos that, on average, receive the highest number of tweets per day. However, for the purposes of prediction, these results indicate that a YouTube video's most recent viewing rate may have sufficient predictive capability for this particular class of videos (as also supported by AUC scores in the right column in Figure 8). Our analysis also indicates that the addition of Twitter features to YouTube features yields a better accuracy of the viral-and-popular classifier. Hence, Twitter features contribute additional knowledge that facilitates more accurate predictions.

All in all, we observe the dominance of the recent features in the predictive mechanism. This is not surprising, considering that recent activity signal are normally reliable indicators for the near future behavior. Hence, we point now to the investigation of the effect ofthe training window size, the labeling window size, and the offset between the two.

3.4 Sensitivity Analysis: Effect of Training and Labeling Window Size

In these section, we vary the size of the training and labeling windows, and the offset between them. We compute the mean F1 score as the performance metric. Again, we focus on the cross-system and viral-and-popular predictions.

3.4.1 *Cross-system predictions*

Table 7 shows the impact of training, labeling, and offset window sizes on the accuracy of virality predictions using YouTube features. As can be seen, wider training window steadily yields higher F1 scores, where using a training window of more than one day produces a noticeable improvement, since the difference between the training window of 3 and 7 days is minor. On top of the mere data availability, training window of more than one day allows for the inclusion of the difference features (subscript *dif*), which were found to be influential in the feature importance analysis.

Turning to the labeling window size (left part of table), we observe that windows of 3 and 7 days allow for more accurate predictions than a 1-day window. We posit that this is explained by the more stable nature of the virality labels based on 3 and 7 days of data. The observed impact of increasing the offset window from 1 day to 7 days (right part of the table) is minor. This finding reaffirms our earlier observation regarding the stability of content virality over reasonably short periods of time, in particular, over a short period closely following the training window.

Training window size	Label window size (offset = 1) 1 day	3 days	7 days	Offset (label window size= 3) 1 day	3 days	7 days
1 day	0.336	0.382	0.407	0.383	0.385	0.400
3 days	0.440	0.496	0.510	0.496	0.494	0.484
7 days	0.447	0.501	0.517	0.506	0.495	0.494

Table 7: Effect of training, labeling, and offset window size on F1 of virality predictions using YouTube data.

Training window size	Label window size (offset = 1) 1 day	3 days	7 days	Offset (label window size= 3) 1 day	3 days	7 days
1 day	0.418	0.426	0.430	0.428	0.412	0.413
3 days	0.464	0.468	0.467	0.469	0.466	0.452
7 days	0.487	0.477	0.480	0.480	0.474	0.479

Table 8: Effect of training, labeling, and offset window size on F1 of popularity predictions using Twitter data.

Table 8 shows a similar analysis conducted for popularity predictions using Twitter data. Again, popularity classification accuracy increases with the training window size, although not to the extent observed for virality predictions. This is in line with our previous observations regarding the greater stability of the popularity scores over time. The main difference with respect to virality predictions refers to the weak impact of the labeling window size (left part of the table), which reaffirms that YouTube popularity is more stable and less susceptible to fluctuations than Twitter virality. Like in the previous case, changes in the offset window size have little impact on the F1 scores.

3.4.2 Viral-and-popular predictions

Finally, Table 9 shows the training and labeling window size analysis when predicting the viral-and-popular class, using features from both YouTube and Twitter. We observe that the impact of the training window size here is weaker than in the previous case of cross-system predictions. We posit that this is explained by the higher ratio of data, which complements and hardly augments previously available data. As such, little new information is introduced over over time and increasing the training window size does not substantially improve the accuracy.

On the contrary, we observe here a stronger impact of the labeling window size and of the offset. The accuracy of the predictions is found to decrease with the offset between the training and test data, indicating that the viral-and-popular class label is more volatile over time than the standalone viral and popular classes, and, therefore, it is more difficult to predict at greater offsets. Since the viral-and-popular class is more volatile, larger labeling window produces a more stable labeling data and leads to a higher predictive accuracy, as we observe in this experiment.

4. RELATED WORK

This section provides an overview of research related to various aspects of our work.

The extensive body of research on *video popularity prediction* spans a number of sub-disciplines. In particular, a number of prior studies analyzed the popularity of YouTube

Training window size	Label window size (offset = 1) 1 day	3 days	7 days	Offset (label window size= 3) 1 day	3 days	7 days
1 day	0.769	0.809	0.825	0.807	0.798	0.788
3 days	0.770	0.823	0.830	0.824	0.817	0.790
7 days	0.778	0.815	0.824	0.816	0.800	0.771

Table 9: Effect of training, labeling, and offset window size on F1 of viral-and-popular predictions.

videos, and interrelation between video popularity and OSN activity. Abisheva et al. combined user data from Twitter with video data from YouTube to discover correlations and temporal dependencies between user features, shares on Twitter, and the number of Twitter views [2]. Wang et al. designed a neural network-based learning framework for predicting the number of video views by exploring patterns of video link propagation in a microblogging system [29]. Several studies exploited the social and contextual activity related to video sharing, aiming at predicting the video view count [25, 11, 26]. Other studies measured the spread of videos within OSNs [10, 16]. Li et al. developed a propagation-based model for predicting peaks and bursts of video views basing on spread patterns [17]. Likewise, by understanding the geographic aspects of video popularity and extracting information from social activity, Scellato et al. proposed various caching strategies for improving the performance of content delivery networks [24].

Furthermore, there have been several efforts towards analyzing the popularity of online video content using early view trends and content meta-data extracted from the video provider data. Pinto et al. proposed a multivariate linear model, configured to capture information about the popularity evolution patterns of videos, which was later on used as an early indicator to predict longer-term popularity [22]. Borghol et al. characterized and modeled video popularity dynamics using a set of measures, such as the video age, churn statistics, the evolution of the viewing rate, and the distribution of view counts over time [9]. Borghol et al. also developed an approach for assessing the impacts of various content-agnostic factors on video popularity, and showed that when controlling for video content strong linear "rich-get-richer" behavior is seen with the total number of previous views as the most important predictor for future views except for very young videos [8]. Ahmed et al. developed an approach that first clustered the temporal data into discretized states, such that transition probabilities between the states were learned and then used to predict future popularity of content [3].

Many previous studies have also examined the *popularity* of social media content. For example, Lee et al. [14] and Lerman et al. [15] proposed somewhat similar models based on endogenous factors, aimed at predicting the popularity of content published in online discussion groups. Their works showed that social activity alone could be a key explanatory factor for accurate popularity predictions. Wang et al. [28] studied the interrelation between the trendiness of content in microblogging systems and its popularity in search queries, and showed that topics of interests in Twitter could serve as reliable early indicator of sudden popularity of related keywords in Google search. Romero et al. [23] focused on the connections between the social graph structure and the topical affiliations, i.e., interests and hashtags, of Twitter users, and concluded that both the hashtags applied by users can predict their social connections and the existing social connections can predict the popularity of hashtags.

Recent studies focused on understanding *how* content spreads and becomes viral on microblogging services [5, 6, 21, 4]. For instance, Bakshy et al. defined influence in the context of Twitter and analyzed the influence of content linked by Tweets with respect to how the content spreads on the network [5]. Their findings showed that both the overall influence of the poster and the characteristics of the content impacted the content's spread range. A related study was done in the context of news sharing behavior by Berger et al. [6], and it was found that emotions evoked by news had a significant effect on their dissemination over the network. Most of the studies into content virality on Twitter assumed little or no external influence on how URLs spread over the network. Myers et al. proposed a model capable of capturing such external influence for breaking news [21]. Somewhat surprisingly, the authors concluded that roughly 30% of the URLs mentions were attributed to external sources, while 70% - exclusively to network effects.

The massive quantity of social content constitutes a gold mine for personalization services and content recommendation engines. Morales et al. [12] exploit Twitter personas to recommend relevant news to users, by studying overall topic popularity in the news and by combining the user profile and the recent interest in the social neighborhood. Twitter diffusion of information, and specifically links, was also successfully leveraged to provide personalized recommendation of trending topics [18]. Content recommendations were achieved by matching highly popular tweets to the recepient's profile, constructed by analyzing their past posts, mentions, URLs, hashtags, and other observable past behaviour [1]. An accurate model for scoring and re-ordering OSN activity feed items through modeling user preferences towards certain actions, users, and content, and matching these preferences to the available network updates, was developed by Berkovsky et al. in [7].

In contrast to the above prior works, our work examines the simultaneous evolution of the popularity and virality of video content, and highlights the inter-relations between the two platforms contributing to these characteristics. We also investigate the compound class of viral-and-popular video content items, as this class is likely to be most attractive for content producers and media agencies alike. We conjecture and verify that cross-system predictions of both popularity and virality of videos is feasible (although not straightforward in certain cases), and can be performed with a reasonably high degree of accuracy. In addition, we analyse the impact of temporal dimension on the predictions and provide insights into the features extracted from both platforms, which contribute to the accuracy of the predictions. This work represents, to the best of our knowledge, the first systematic data-driven study of the predictions of popularity and virality aspects of online video content.

5. CONCLUSIONS

Prediction of content virality on microblogging services and of video popularity on video sharing platforms have been largely investigated so far as two independent tasks. In this work, we propose a new unifying approach for predicting video content virality, popularity, as well as virality-and-popularity at the same time, using a suite of features extracted from Twitter and YouTube logs.

Our experiments indicate that these predictions are feasible, can exhibit very high levels of accuracy, and can be carried out with reasonably low amounts of training data. Specifically, YouTube popularity predictions achieve a remarkably high AUC scores (e.g., 0.95 using all the available data), whereas predictions of rather volatile Twitter virality still achieve reasonably high AUC (e.g., 0.88 using all the available data). Furthermore, we demonstrate that not only direct but also cross-system predictions are possible, although with a lower degree of accuracy. Lastly, the compound predictions of video content virality-and-popularity can also be predicted with high accuracy (e.g., AUC of 0.91, when both Twitter and YouTube features are used for the prediction), highlighting the importance of features mined from the raw data.

We proceed with an analysis of feature importance and highlight what features are predictive of future popularity and virality of content, both for content having solid prior history and for recently uploaded items, where the prediction task is more important and more challenging at the same time. We observe that recent information, and specifically current growth rate, often comes through as a highly predictive feature and that virality-and-popularity of video content is mainly driven by YouTube features. Finally, we analyze the sensitivity of the developed prediction mechanism and its dependence on the availability of reliable training data. While predictions of virality and/or popularity are feasible and accurate for non-recent content having rich prior information, we observe that having training data of only one day allows for the generation of accurate predictions for up to seven days in advance.

In the future, we plan to extend our model and incorporate features mirroring the social facet of the systems, e.g., user influence [6] and external influence [21]. We also intend to capitalize on more sophisticated temporal [3] and graph models [27], and further investigate the evolution of popularity and virality over time. We also intend to apply the developed predictive models to other types of content, like news and music. We believe that our work paves to way to a broad stream of future research investigating the intricacies of cross-system propagation of content, user-to-user influence, and cross-system content discovery.

6. REFERENCES

[1] F. Abel, Q. Gao, G.-J. Houben, and K. Tao. Analyzing user modeling on twitter for personalized news recommendations. In *Proceedings of the International Conference on User Modeling, Adaption, and Personalization*, pages 1–12, 2011.

[2] A. Abisheva, V. R. K. Garimella, D. Garcia, and I. Weber. Who watches (and shares) what on youtube? and when?: Using twitter to understand youtube viewership. In *Proceedings of the international conference on Web search and data mining*, pages 593–602, 2014.

[3] M. Ahmed, S. Spagna, F. Huici, and S. Niccolini. A peek into the future: Predicting the evolution of popularity in user generated content. In *Proceedings of the International Conference on Web Search and Data Mining*, pages 607–616, 2013.

[4] S. Ardon, A. Bagchi, A. Mahanti, A. Ruhela, A. Seth, R. M. Tripathy, and S. Triukose. Spatio-temporal and events based analysis of topic popularity in twitter. In *Proceedings of the International Conference on Information and Knowledge Management*, pages 219–228, 2013.

[5] E. Bakshy, J. M. Hofman, W. A. Mason, and D. J. Watts. Everyone's an influencer: Quantifying influence on twitter. In *Proceedings of the International Conference on Web Search and Data Mining*, pages 65–74, 2011.

[6] J. Berger and K. L. Milkman. What makes online content viral? *Journal of Marketing Research*, pages 1–17, 2011.

[7] S. Berkovsky, J. Freyne, and G. Smith. Personalized network updates: Increasing social interactions and contributions in social networks. In *Proceedings of the International Conference on User Modeling, Adaption, and Personalization*, pages 1–13, 2012.

[8] Y. Borghol, S. Ardon, N. Carlsson, D. Eager, and A. Mahanti. The untold story of the clones: Content-agnostic factors that impact youtube video popularity. In *Proceedings of the International Conference on Knowledge Discovery and Data Mining*, pages 1186–1194, 2012.

[9] Y. Borghol, S. Mitra, S. Ardon, N. Carlsson, D. Eager, and A. Mahanti. Characterizing and modelling popularity of user-generated videos. *Performance Evaluation*, 68(11):1037–1055, 2011.

[10] X. Cheng, H. Li, and J. Liu. Video sharing propagation in social networks: Measurement, modeling, and analysis. In *Proceedings of the International Conference on Computer Communications*, pages 45–49, 2013.

[11] R. Crane and D. Sornette. Robust dynamic classes revealed by measuring the response function of a social system. *Proceedings of the National Academy of Sciences*, 105(41):15649–15653, 2008.

[12] G. De Francisci Morales, A. Gionis, and C. Lucchese. From chatter to headlines: Harnessing the real-time web for personalized news recommendation. In *Proceedings of the International Conference on Web Search and Data Mining*, pages 153–162, 2012.

[13] J. H. Friedman. Greedy function approximation: A gradient boosting machine. *Annals of Statistics*, 29:1189–1232, 2000.

[14] J. G. Lee, S. Moon, and K. Salamatian. An approach to model and predict the popularity of online contents with explanatory factors. In *Proceeedings of the International Conference on Web Intelligence and Intelligent Agent Technology*, pages 623–630, 2010.

[15] K. Lerman and T. Hogg. Using a model of social dynamics to predict popularity of news. In *Proceedings of the International Conference on World Wide Web*, pages 621–630, 2010.

[16] H. Li, J. Liu, K. Xu, and S. Wen. Understanding video propagation in online social networks. In *Proceedings of the Workshop on Quality of Service*, 2012.

[17] H. Li, X. Ma, F. Wang, J. Liu, and K. Xu. On popularity prediction of videos shared in online social networks. In *Proceedings of the International Conference on Information and Knowledge Management*, pages 169–178, 2013.

[18] H. Liang, Y. Xu, D. Tjondronegoro, and P. Christen. Time-aware topic recommendation based on micro-blogs. In *Proceedings of the International Conference on Information and Knowledge Management*, pages 1657–1661, 2012.

[19] Y. Lv, D. Lymberopoulos, and Q. Wu. An exploration of ranking heuristics in mobile local search. In *Proceedings of the International Conference on Research and Development in Information Retrieval*, pages 295–304, 2012.

[20] X. Ma, H. Wang, H. Li, J. Liu, and H. Jiang. Exploring sharing patterns for video recommendation on youtube-like social media. *Multimedia Systems*, 20(6):675–691, 2014.

[21] S. A. Myers, C. Zhu, and J. Leskovec. Information diffusion and external influence in networks. In *Proceedings of the International Conference on Knowledge Discovery and Data Mining*, pages 33–41, 2012.

[22] H. Pinto, J. M. Almeida, and M. A. Gonçalves. Using early view patterns to predict the popularity of youtube videos. In *Proceedings of the International Conference on Web Search and Data Mining*, pages 365–374, 2013.

[23] D. M. Romero, C. Tan, and J. Ugander. On the interplay between social and topical structure. In *Proceedings of the International Conference on Weblogs and Social Media*, 2013.

[24] S. Scellato, C. Mascolo, M. Musolesi, and J. Crowcroft. Track globally, deliver locally: Improving content delivery networks by tracking geographic social cascades. In *Proceedings of the International Conference on World Wide Web*, pages 457–466, 2011.

[25] D. A. Shamma, J. Yew, L. Kennedy, and E. F. Churchill. Viral actions: Predicting video view counts using synchronous sharing behaviors. In *Proceedings of the International Conference on Weblogs and Social Media*, 2011.

[26] G. Szabo and B. A. Huberman. Predicting the popularity of online content. *Communications of the ACM*, 53(8):80–88, 2010.

[27] A. Tiroshi, S. Berkovsky, M. A. Kâafar, D. Vallet, T. Chen, and T. Kuflik. Improving business rating predictions using graph based features. In *Proceedings of the International Conference on Intelligent User Interfaces*, pages 17–26, 2014.

[28] D. Wang, M. A. Kaafar, K. Salamatian, and G. Xie. What's trendy right now? a comparative analysis of web and microblogs trending topics. In *Proceedings of the International Conference on Internet Science*, 2013.

[29] Z. Wang, L. Sun, C. Wu, and S. Yang. Guiding internet-scale video service deployment using microblog-based prediction. In *Proceedings of the International Conference on Computer Communications*, pages 2901–2905, 2012.

Social Spammer and Spam Message Co-Detection in Microblogging with Social Context Regularization

Fangzhao Wu[†], Jinyun Shu[‡], Yongfeng Huang[†], Zhigang Yuan[†]
[†]Tsinghua National Laboratory for Information Science and Technology, Department of Electronic Engineering, Tsinghua University, Beijing, China
[‡]Beijing University of Posts and Telecommunications, Beijing, China
wufangzhao@gmail.com, waityou@bupt.edu.cn, yfhuang@tsinghua.edu.cn, yuanzg14@mails.tsinghua.edu.cn

ABSTRACT

The popularity of microblogging platforms, such as Twitter, makes them important for information dissemination and sharing. However, they are also recognized as ideal places by spammers to conduct social spamming. Massive social spammers and spam messages heavily hurt the user experience and hinder the healthy development of microblogging systems. Thus, effectively detecting the social spammers and spam messages in microblogging is of great value. Existing studies mainly regard social spammer detection and spam message detection as two separate tasks. However, social spammers and spam messages have strong connections, since social spammers tend to post more spam messages and spam messages have high probabilities to be posted by social spammers. Combining social spammer detection with spam message detection has the potential to boost the performance of each task. In this paper, we propose a unified framework for social spammer and spam message co-detection in microblogging. Our framework utilizes the posting relations between users and messages to combine social spammer detection with spam message detection. In addition, we extract the social relations between users as well as the connections between messages, and incorporate them into our framework as regularization terms over the prediction results. Besides, we introduce an efficient optimization method to solve our framework. Extensive experiments on a real-world microblog dataset demonstrate that our framework can significantly and consistently improve the performance of both social spammer detection and spam message detection.

Categories and Subject Descriptors

H.3.3 [**Information Storage and Retrieval**]: Information Search and Retrieval—*Classification*; I.2.7 [**Artificial Intelligence**]: Natural Language Processing

Keywords

Spam Detection; Microblog; Social Context

Permission to make digital or hard copies of all or part of this work for personal or classroom use is granted without fee provided that copies are not made or distributed for profit or commercial advantage and that copies bear this notice and the full citation on the first page. Copyrights for components of this work owned by others than ACM must be honored. Abstracting with credit is permitted. To copy otherwise, or republish, to post on servers or to redistribute to lists, requires prior specific permission and/or a fee. Request permissions from Permissions@acm.org.
CIKM'15, October 19–23, 2015, Melbourne, VIC, Australia.
© 2015 ACM. ISBN 978-1-4503-3794-6/15/10 ...$15.00.
DOI: http://dx.doi.org/10.1145/2806416.2806560.

1. INTRODUCTION

Microbblogging websites, such as Twitter [1] and Sina Weibo [2], have become very popular platforms for information dissemination and sharing [21]. Hundreds of millions of users frequently post short messages on these websites to release latest news and share their opinions on various topics, such as political events, companies and daily life. However, microbblogging websites are also recognized as ideal places to conduct spamming due to their popularity [34, 39, 21]. Massive fake microblogging accounts, which are known as social spammers [37], post masses of spam messages for various purposes, such as conducting social advertising, collecting users' personal information, promoting affiliate websites and so on [5, 23]. These spam messages may contain dangerous content and URLs that are related to scams, malware, phishing [17, 23, 21]. Spam messages are also used to conduct political astroturfing [5, 32]. These massive social spammers and spam messages seriously hurt the user experience and hinder the healthy development of microblogging systems [23]. Thus, effectively detecting the social spammers and spam messages are beneficial to both microblogging websites and users.

Various methods have been proposed for social spammer detection and spam message detection. For example, some researchers suggested to detect social spammers via social network analysis [30, 12]. The basic assumption behind these methods is that social spammers cannot build enough social trust relations compared with legitimate users [21]. However, different from other online social networking platforms, such as Facebook and Youbute, in microblogging websites, a user can follow anyone else without the followee's permission, and it is not too hard for social spammers to gain sufficient social relations with legitimate users [38]. Thus these social network analysis based methods may not work well on social spammer detection in microblogging platforms [21]. Another line of research for social spammer detection is analyzing their attributes, online behaviours, and textual content of the microblog messages they post [4, 34, 36, 24, 20, 19]. These methods are based on the assumption that the online behaviours and textual content of social spammers are different from those of legitimate users. However, social spammers may continue to change their posting behaviours and try to behave like normal users [20]. In addition, besides spam messages, social spammers may also post some normal messages. These strategies may lead to the content and behaviour analysis based methods less accurate. As to spam message detection, existing methods mainly focus on extracting effective features and building a classifier using machine learning techniques [33, 25,

[1]`https://twitter.com/`
[2]`http://www.weibo.com/`

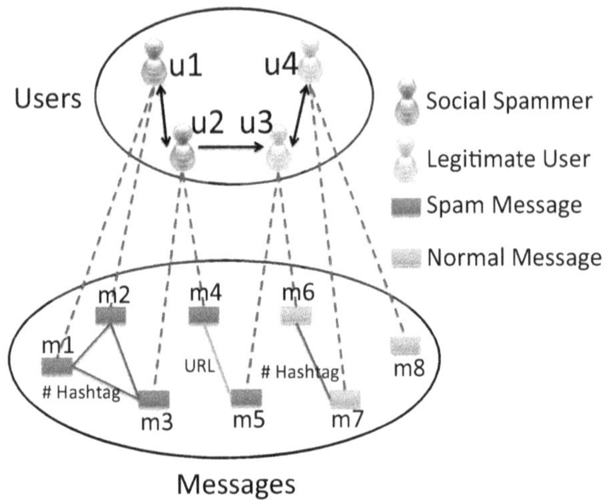

Figure 1: An illustrative example of the social contexts used in our framework. The red and green user figures represent social spammers and legitimate users respectively. The red and green rectangles stand for spam messages and normal messages respectively. The solid black lines with arrows connecting users represent the relations between users. The dashed purple line connecting a message with a user represents the posting relation between the user and the message. The solid blue lines and orange lines represent the connections between messages introduced by hashtags and URLs respectively.

26]. For example, some researchers found that URLs, timestamps are informative features for identifying spam messages [14].

In general, in existing studies social spammer detection and spam message detection are mainly regarded as two separate tasks. However, in microblogging websites, a common phenomenon is that social spammers tend to post more spam messages, and spam messages have high probabilities to be posted by social spammers. Thus there are strong connections between social spammers and spam messages. Detecting social spammers and spam messages simultaneously may achieve better performance than conducting each task in isolation. In addition, the social connections between users and those between messages may also be helpful for social spammer detection and spam message detection. For example, social spammers are often followed by other spammers, because they frequently collaborate in this way to build more social relations and pretend to be normal users. Many spam messages contain the same URLs because they belong to the same promoting campaigns [39]. Some spam messages contain the same hashtags for the purpose of advertising for a brand. An illustrative example of these social contexts is shown in Fig. 1.

Motivated by above observations, in this paper we propose a unified framework for social spammer and spam message co-detection in microblogging with various social contexts. In our framework, social spammer detection and spam message detection are bridged by the posting relations between users and messages. The results of social spammer detection can help refine the results of spam message detection, and vice versa. Both the performance of social spammer detection and that of spam message detection can be boosted. In addition, our framework can incorporate the social contexts of user-user relations and message-message relations by modeling them as regularizations over the prediction results.

The main contributions of this paper are summarized as follows:

- We propose to exploit three kinds of social contexts, i.e., the user-message relations, user-user relations and message-message relations for social spammer detection and spam message detection in microblogging.
- We propose a unified framework to incorporate various social contexts and detect social spammers and spam messages simultaneously.
- We introduce an efficient optimization method based on ADMM [7] to solve our framework .
- We empirically evaluate our framework via extensive experiments on a real-world microblog dataset. The experimental results validate the effectiveness and efficiency of our framework.

The rest of this paper is organized as follows. In Section 2, we briefly introduce several representative works related to social spammer detection and spam text detection. In Section 3, we discuss how to extract various social contexts for detecting social spammers and spam messages in microblogging. In Section 4, we describe our framework for social spammer and spam message co-detection, and the optimization method to solve this framework. In Section 5, we report the experimental results on a real-world microblog dataset. In Section 6 we conclude this paper.

2. RELATED WORK

In this section, we briefly introduce several representative works related to social spammer detection and spam detection.

2.1 Social Spammer Detection

Social spammer detection is an important research topic and has been studied in various social networking websites, such as Twitter [4], Facebook [9], Youtube [29] and Sina Weibo [24]. Existing studies on social spammer detection can be roughly divided into two categories. The first category is using social network analysis to detect social spammers [30, 12, 15]. The assumption behind these methods is that social spammers cannot build a large number of social relations with legitimate users [21]. However, due to the special characteristics of microblogging websites, this assumption may not hold true [38] and these methods cannot be applied to microblog spammer detection directly [21]. The second category of methods is to extract effective features from users' attributes, online behaviours, and the textual contents of the messages they post, and build a classifier using machine learning techniques [4, 34, 24, 20, 19]. For example, McCord and Chuah proposed to extract two kinds of features, i.e., user-based features and content-based features, and use traditional classifiers, such as SVM and Naive Bayes, for detecting the social spammers in Twitter [27]. The user-based features they used include the numbers of friends and followers, and reputation score. The content-based features contain the numbers of URLs, keywords and hashtags in a user's messages. Hu et al. proposed to detect social spammers according to users' textual content, and explored to utilize the resources from email, SMS, and Web spam detection fields to help train the classifier [19]. However, social spammers may continuously change their behaviours and attributes to pretend to be normal users. In addition, they may post some normal messages besides the spam messages. These strategies may make above methods less accurate.

Social contexts have also been explored for social spammer detection. In [21], the authors proposed to incorporate the following relations between users into the classifier learning stage by constraining that the users with social relations are assigned similar scores by the learned classifier. When a new user comes, only the textual content of his/her messages is used to classify this user. Our method is different from their method in two aspects. First, our method models social spammer detection and spam message detection in a unified framework, while their method only focuses on social spammer detection. Second, in our method, the social contexts are used in the prediction stage, while in their method the the social contexts are incorporated into the model learning stage. Even with the help of social contexts, it is still difficult to train an accurate enough social spammer classifer, since spammers' attributes, behaviours and textual content are continuously evolving [20]. However, the social contexts of the unseen users and messages can provide some useful information for classifying them into spam or non-spam. Thus we believe that it is more appropriate to utilize social contexts in prediction stage than in model training stage.

2.2 Spam Detection

Spam detection has been extensively studied on various kinds of texts, such as email [6], webpage [18, 1, 28], SMS [16] and review [22]. There are two main kinds of methods for spam detection, i.e., link-based methods and content-based methods. Link-based methods are widely used for detecting spams in linked texts, such as webpages [18, 1]. These methods are based on the assumption that spam webpages have different link patterns compared with normal webpages and they are seldom linked by high-quality webpages. For example, Becchetti et al. found that degree correlations, number of neighbors, and TrustRank score are effective metrics for Web spam detection [1]. However, since not all the microblog messages contain URLs, and the URLs in microblogs usually point to webpages rather than other microblogs messages, these link-based methods cannot be directly used to detect spam microblog messages.

Content-based methods are extensively studied and popularly used for spam detection [6, 28, 16, 22]. In these methods, effective features are first extracted from the content. Then spam classifiers are trained on labeled data using machine learning techniques. These classifiers are used to classify unseen texts into spam or non-spam according to their content. For example, Ntoulas et al. designed various features for Web spam detection, such as number of words in the page, amount of anchor text, fraction of visible content, and so on [28]. Then they used C4.5 algorithm to train the classifier.

Many microblog spam message detection methods also belong to content-based methods [33, 25, 26]. For example, in order to detect malicious tweets in trending topics, Martinez-Romo and Araujo proposed to extract language model based features, e.g., the K-L Divergence between a tweet and the thread of tweets in this topic. They also incorporated other content-based features, such as the numbers of URL, hashtags, numeric characters and so on [26]. However, since microblog messages are very short and noisy [21], it is quite difficult to detect all the spam messages purely according to their textual content. Different from above methods, our method combines spam message detection with social spammer detection, and exploits various social contexts to refine the spam message detection results.

The benefit of combining spam detection and spammer detection on Web data has been observed by Chen et al. [10]. Given a set of labeled bookmarks and a set of labeled users, they trained a SVM classifier for spam detection and a SVM classifier for spammer detection simultaneously by utilizing the user-user relations and user-bookmark relations. The users with fans relation are constrained to have similar scores during training. Similarly, a user and a bookmark are constrained to be assigned similar scores by the classifiers if the bookmark is created by this user. Different from this method, our method utilizes the social context information in the prediction stage rather than the model learning stage. Since the behaviours and attributes of social spammers are continuously changing and the content of spam messages are evolving, the pre-trained spammer classifier and spam classifier cannot be accurate enough [20]. Meanwhile, social contexts of the messages and users can provide useful information to help make more accurate predictions. Thus we propose to utilize social contexts in the prediction stage.

3. SOCIAL CONTEXT EXTRACTION

In this section, we introduce the social contexts used in our framework for improving social spammer detection and spam message detection in microblogging platforms.

3.1 User-Message Relation

The first kind of social contexts used in our framework is the posting relations between users and messages, i.e., the user-message relations. It has been widely recognized in social spammer detection and spam filtering fields that social spammers tend to post more spam messages than legitimate users, and spam messages have higher probabilities to be posted by social spammers rather than legitimate users [39, 21]. Thus social spammer detection and spam message detection are not independent tasks. In fact, they are closely connected by the social connections between users and messages. Detecting spam messages can help identify more potential social spammers. In turn, if we find that some users are social spammers, we can obtain more candidate spam messages.

Denote $\mathcal{U}$ as the set of users and $\mathcal{M}$ as the set of messages. $U = |\mathcal{U}|$ and $M = |\mathcal{M}|$ are the numbers of all users and messages. We model the user-message relations using matrix $\mathbf{P} \in \mathbb{R}^{U \times M}$. If message j is posted by user i, then $P_{i,j} = 1$. Otherwise, $P_{i,j} = 0$. For example, in Fig. 1, messages m_1 and m_3 are posted by u_1 and u_2 respectively, then $P_{u_1,m_1} = 1$ and $P_{u_2,m_3} = 1$.

3.2 User-User Relation

Microblogging is one kind of Online Social Networks (OSN) and microblog users are networked. If a user wants to receive messages from some other users, he/she can just follow them. However, different from other OSNs such as Facebook, a user in microblogging platforms can follow anyone without the followee's prior permission. Thus, the social relations among microblogging users are directed.

A common observation in social spammer detection is that social spammers usually follow each other, in order to gain more followers and pretend to be normal users [21]. Legitimate users also follow each other frequently, partially because they know each other offline. Thus, if two users follow each other, then they have a high probability to be both social spammers or legitimate users. However, it is also frequently observed in microblogging platforms that some social spammers follow a large number of legitimate users, in order to gain enough social relations with legitimate users and obtain high social influence [38]. Although social spammers can follow legitimate users, it is not very likely that legitimate users will follow them.

Motivated by above observations, in this paper we extract two kinds of user-user relations. The first kind is friend relation, which means that two users follow each other. We use matrix $\mathbf{F} \in \mathbb{R}^{U \times U}$ to denote friend relation. If users i and j follow each other, then $F_{i,j} = 1$ and $F_{j,i} = 1$. Otherwise, $F_{i,j} = 0$ and $F_{j,i} = 0$. The second kind of user-user relation is following relation. Different from friend relation, following relation is directed. We use $\mathbf{D} \in \mathbb{R}^{U \times U}$ to denote this relation. If user i follows user j, but user j

does not follow user i, then $D_{i,j} = 1$ and $D_{j,i} = 0$. Otherwise, $D_{i,j} = 0$.

3.3 Message-Message Relation

Normal messages may be related to various topics. However, masses of spam messages share the same targets. This is because spam messages are usually not used independently. In fact, many of them are used collectively to promote the same products, services or websites. For example, researchers have found that many spam accounts are manipulated by a small group of spammers. They use these accounts to post massive spam messages for some promoting campaigns by adding the same URLs into these messages [39]. In addition, some researchers have found that spam messages share highly similar content and the same hashtags [3, 24].

Motivated by these observations, we propose to extract social connections for microblog messages. We define that the message-message relations are undirected and if two messages are related to the same target, then they are connected. Denote $\mathbf{T} \in \mathbb{R}^{M \times M}$ as the social connections between messages. If message i and message j share the same target, then $T_{i,j} = 1$ and $T_{j,i} = 1$. Otherwise, $T_{i,j} = 0$ and $T_{j,i} = 0$. In this paper, if two messages contain the same URL or hashtag, then we regard they are related to the same target and connected with each other. For example, in Fig. 1, since messages m_4 and m_5 have the same URL, and messages m_6 and m_7 contain the same hastag, then T_{m_4,m_5}, T_{m_5,m_4}, T_{m_6,m_7}, T_{m_7,m_6} all equal to 1.

4. SOCIAL SPAMMER AND SPAM MESSAGE CO-DETECTION IN MICROBLOGGING

In this section we study how to effectively and efficiently incorporate all the three kinds of social contexts into a unified framework and detect social spammers and spam messages simultaneously.

4.1 Problem Formulation

First, we introduce several notations and formally formulize the problem of social spammer and spam message co-detection with various social contexts.

Denote the set of microblog users to be classified as $\mathcal{U}$, and the size of $\mathcal{U}$ as U. Similarly, denote $\mathcal{M}$ as the set of microblog messages to be classified, and the size of $\mathcal{M}$ is M. Following the notations used in previous section, here we denote $\mathbf{P} \in \mathbb{R}^{U \times M}$ as the user-message relation matrix, $\mathbf{F} \in \mathbb{R}^{U \times U}$ as the friend relation between users, $\mathbf{D} \in \mathbb{R}^{U \times U}$ as the following relation between users, $\mathbf{T} \in \mathbb{R}^{M \times M}$ as the message-message relation. Assuming that we already have a social spammer classifier $f_U(\cdot)$ and a spam message classifier $f_M(\cdot)$ which are trained on labeled datasets using machine learning techniques. Denote $\mathbf{u} \in \mathbb{R}^{U \times 1}$ as the classification results of $\mathcal{U}$ using the social spammer classifier f_U, where positive values indicate social spammers and negative values indicate normal users. Similarly, denote $\mathbf{m} \in \mathbb{R}^{M \times 1}$ as the classification results of $\mathcal{M}$ using the spam message classifier f_M, where positive values indicate spam messages and negative values indicate normal messages. Since the features of social spammers and spam messages are continuously evolving, the social spammer classification results $\mathbf{u}$ and spam message classification results $\mathbf{m}$ may not be accurate enough. So we incorporate the social contexts to refine them. Denote $\mathbf{x} \in \mathbb{R}^{U \times 1}$ and $\mathbf{y} \in \mathbb{R}^{M \times 1}$ as the final classification scores of $\mathcal{U}$ and $\mathcal{M}$ outputted by our framework.

Based on above notations, the problem of social spammer and spam message co-detection in microblogging with various social contexts can be formally defined as follows:

Given a set of microblog users $\mathcal{U}$, a set of microblog messages $\mathcal{M}$, and the initial classification results $\mathbf{u}$ and $\mathbf{m}$ generated by an existing social spammer classifier $f_U(\cdot)$ and a spam message classifier $f_M(\cdot)$, as well as three kinds of social contexts of these users and messages, i.e., user-message relations $\mathbf{P}$, user-user relations $\mathbf{F}$ and $\mathbf{D}$, and message-message relations $\mathbf{T}$, we aim to refine the initial social spammer and spam message classification results using these social contexts in a unified framework, and output more accurate social spammer classification results $\mathbf{x}$ and spam message classification results $\mathbf{y}$ simultaneously.

4.2 Model

Our solution to the problem of social spammer and spam message co-detection in microblogging with various social contexts is a unified framework defined as follows:

$$\begin{aligned}\arg\min_{\mathbf{x},\mathbf{y}} \mathcal{L}(\mathbf{x},\mathbf{y}) = &\sum_{i=1}^{U}(x_i - u_i)^2 + \sum_{i=1}^{M}(y_i - m_i)^2 \\ &+ \alpha \sum_{i=1}^{U}\sum_{j \neq i} f_{i,j}|x_i - x_j| + \beta \sum_{i=1}^{U}\sum_{j \neq i} d_{i,j}(x_j - x_i) \\ &- \lambda \sum_{i=1}^{U}\sum_{j=1}^{M} p_{i,j} x_i y_j + \gamma \sum_{i=1}^{M}\sum_{j \neq i} t_{i,j}|y_i - y_j|,\end{aligned} \tag{1}$$

where α, β, λ and γ are non-negative regularization parameters. The terms $\sum_{i=1}^{U}(x_i - u_i)^2$ and $\sum_{i=1}^{M}(y_i - m_i)^2$ mean that we hope the final prediction results do not differ too much from the original classification results. In other words, we take the classification results generated by existing social spammer classifier and spam message classifier as the prior knowledge. The terms $\sum_{i=1}^{U}\sum_{j \neq i} f_{i,j}|x_i - x_j|$ and $\sum_{i=1}^{M}\sum_{j \neq i} t_{i,j}|y_i - y_j|$ are motivated by graph-guided fused lasso [11], which can exploit the graph structure over the output variables for structured regression and classification. $\sum_{i=1}^{U}\sum_{j \neq i} f_{i,j}|x_i - x_j|$ means that if two microblog users follow each other, then their spam scores should be similar, i.e., they tend to be both social spammers or legitimate users. $\sum_{i=1}^{M}\sum_{j \neq i} t_{i,j}|y_i - y_j|$ is introduced to constrain that if two microblog messages contain the same hashtag, or refer to the same URL, then these messages tend to be both spam or non-spam and should be assigned similar spam scores. $\sum_{i=1}^{U}\sum_{j \neq i} d_{i,j}(x_j - x_i)$ incorporates the directed following relations between users. The insight behind this term is that if user i follows user j while user j does not follow user i, then user i has a higher probability to be a social spammer than user j. Thus if the spam score of user j exceeds that of user i, a penalty will occur. The term $\sum_{i=1}^{U}\sum_{j=1}^{M} p_{i,j} x_i y_j$ is introduced to combine the social spammer classification results with spam message classification results. This term constrains that if a message j is posted by user i, then they should have the same spam label, i.e., be both positive (spam) or negative (non-spam). This is motivated by the observation that social spammers tend to post spam messages while legitimate users tend to post more normal messages. If message j is posted by user i, but they are assigned different spam labels, then a penalty will be triggered (note that there is a minus sign before this term in Eq. (1)). Thus our model defined in Eq. (1) can incorporate various social contexts into a unified framework for social spammers and spam messages co-detection.

4.3 Optimization Method

Next, we discuss how to solve our framework in Eq. (1) efficiently. The optimization problem in Eq. (1) is convex with respect to $\mathbf{x}$ and $\mathbf{y}$ respectively. However, it is non-convex with respect to $\mathbf{x}$

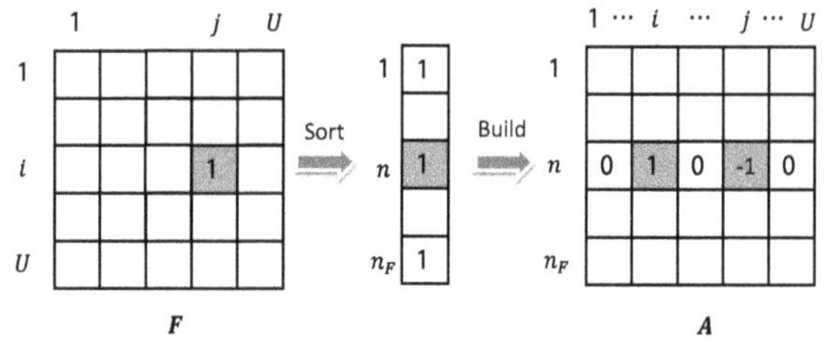

Figure 2: An illustrative example of constructing A from F.

and $\mathbf{y}$ together, due to the term $\sum_{i=1}^{U}\sum_{j=1}^{M} p_{i,j}x_i y_j$, which can be verified using the second-order condition [8]. Thus there is no analytical solution for the optimization problem in Eq. (1). Here we introduce an iterative optimization method to solve our framework.

First, we introduce several new notations. Assuming that there are n_F non-zero elements in $\mathbf{F}$, then we define $\mathbf{A} \in \mathbb{R}^{n_F \times U}$ as a equivalent representation of $\mathbf{F}$. If $F_{i,j}$ is the n_{th} non-zero element in $\mathbf{F}$, then $A_{n,i} = 1$ and $A_{n,j} = -1$. Other elements in the n_{th} row of $\mathbf{A}$ are all zeros. An illustrative example of constructing $\mathbf{A}$ from $\mathbf{F}$ is shown in Fig. 2. Similarly, we define $\mathbf{B} \in \mathbb{R}^{n_D \times U}$ and $\mathbf{C} \in \mathbb{R}^{n_T \times M}$ as the equivalent representations of $\mathbf{D}$ and $\mathbf{T}$ respectively, where n_D and n_T are the numbers of non-zero elements in $\mathbf{D}$ and $\mathbf{T}$. Then the optimization problem in Eq. (1) can be equivalently reformulated as follows:

$$\begin{aligned}\arg\min_{\mathbf{x},\mathbf{y}} \mathcal{L}(\mathbf{x},\mathbf{y}) =& \|\mathbf{x}-\mathbf{u}\|_2^2 + \|\mathbf{y}-\mathbf{m}\|_2^2 + \alpha\|\mathbf{A}\mathbf{x}\|_1 \\ &- \beta\mathbf{1}^T\mathbf{B}\mathbf{x} - \lambda\mathbf{x}^T\mathbf{P}\mathbf{y} + \gamma\|\mathbf{C}\mathbf{y}\|_1.\end{aligned} \tag{2}$$

Inspired by [13], we propose to optimize $\mathbf{x}$ and $\mathbf{y}$ alternatively. When updating $\mathbf{x}$, $\mathbf{y}$ will be fixed. Similarly, $\mathbf{x}$ will be fixed when updating $\mathbf{y}$. The optimization problem in each step of the alternative algorithm is convex and a unique optimal solution exists. The alternative algorithm continues until converges.

Next, we introduce how to update $\mathbf{x}$ and $\mathbf{y}$ respectively.

4.3.1 *Updating* $\mathbf{x}$

When updating $\mathbf{x}$ in the t_{th} iteration, we fix $\mathbf{y}$ as $\mathbf{y}^t$, and optimizing the objective function in Eq. (2) is equivalent to following optimization problem:

$$\arg\min_{\mathbf{x}} \mathcal{L}(\mathbf{x}) = \|\mathbf{x}-\mathbf{u}\|_2^2 + \alpha\|\mathbf{A}\mathbf{x}\|_1 - \beta\mathbf{1}^T\mathbf{B}\mathbf{x} - \lambda\mathbf{x}^T\mathbf{P}\mathbf{y}^t. \tag{3}$$

We can prove that the optimization problem in Eq. (3) is convex [8, 13]. However, the objective function in Eq. (3) is not smooth with respect to $\mathbf{x}$, due to the term $\|\mathbf{A}\mathbf{x}\|_1$. Thus it cannot be solved using standard gradient descent method. Although we can solve Eq. (3) using subgradient descent method, the convergence rate of subgradient descent method is $O(1/\sqrt{k})$ [2], where k is the number of iterations, which is unsatisfactory. In order to solve the optimization problem in Eq. (3) more efficiently, here we introduce an algorithm based on alternating direction method of multipliers (ADMM) [7], which has a convergence rate of $O(1/k)$.

First, we equivalently reformulate Eq. (3) as follows:

$$\begin{aligned}\arg\min_{\mathbf{x},\mathbf{v}} \mathcal{L}(\mathbf{x},\mathbf{v}) =& \|\mathbf{x}-\mathbf{u}\|_2^2 + \alpha\|\mathbf{v}\|_1 - \beta\mathbf{1}^T\mathbf{B}\mathbf{x} - \lambda\mathbf{x}^T\mathbf{P}\mathbf{y}^t, \\ \text{s.t.} \ &: \mathbf{v} = \mathbf{A}\mathbf{x},\end{aligned} \tag{4}$$

where $\mathbf{v} \in \mathbb{R}^{n_F \times 1}$ is introduced as an auxiliary variable.

Since ADMM is a method of multipliers, we further transform Eq. (4) into an augmented Lagrangian problem as follows:

$$\begin{aligned}\mathcal{L}(\mathbf{x},\mathbf{v},\omega) =& \|\mathbf{x}-\mathbf{u}\|_2^2 + \alpha\|\mathbf{v}\|_1 - \beta\mathbf{1}^T\mathbf{B}\mathbf{x} - \lambda\mathbf{x}^T\mathbf{P}\mathbf{y}^t \\ &+ \omega^T(\mathbf{A}\mathbf{x}-\mathbf{v}) + \frac{\rho}{2}\|\mathbf{A}\mathbf{x}-\mathbf{v}\|_2^2,\end{aligned} \tag{5}$$

where $\rho > 0$ is a penalty coefficient and $\omega \in \mathbb{R}^{n_F \times 1}$ is the Lagrangian multipliers vector.

Our ADMM-based method for Eq. (3) is an iterative optimization method. Different from other methods of multipliers, where in each iteration all the variables are updated simultaneously, in our method the variables $\mathbf{x}$, $\mathbf{v}$ and ω are updated in an alternating manner, which breaks the original problem into three easier subproblems. Denote $\mathbf{w} = \omega/\rho$ as the scaled dual variable [7], then in the k_{th} iteration of our method the variables $\mathbf{x}$, $\mathbf{v}$ and $\mathbf{w}$ are updated sequentially as follows:

Updating $\mathbf{x}_{k+1}$**:**

$$\begin{aligned}\mathbf{x}_{k+1} \leftarrow \arg\min_{\mathbf{x}} \ & \|\mathbf{x}-\mathbf{u}\|_2^2 - \beta\mathbf{1}^T\mathbf{B}\mathbf{x} - \lambda\mathbf{x}^T\mathbf{P}\mathbf{y}^t \\ &+ \frac{\rho}{2}\|\mathbf{A}\mathbf{x}-\mathbf{v}_k+\mathbf{w}_k\|_2^2,\end{aligned} \tag{6}$$

Updating $\mathbf{v}_{k+1}$**:**

$$\mathbf{v}_{k+1} \leftarrow \arg\min_{\mathbf{x}} \ \alpha\|\mathbf{v}\|_1 + \frac{\rho}{2}\|\mathbf{A}\mathbf{x}_{k+1}-\mathbf{v}+\mathbf{w}_k\|_2^2, \tag{7}$$

Updating $\mathbf{w}_{k+1}$**:**

$$\mathbf{w}_{k+1} = \mathbf{w}_k + \mathbf{A}\mathbf{x}_{k+1} - \mathbf{v}_{k+1}. \tag{8}$$

According to Eq. (6), $\mathbf{x}_{k+1}$ can be updated by solving a convex optimization problem. We can obtain the analytical solution of $\mathbf{x}_{k+1}$ by setting the first-order derivative of the objective function in Eq. (6) with respect to $\mathbf{x}$ to zero, which is shown in Eq. (9).

$$\mathbf{x}_{k+1} = (\rho\mathbf{A}^T\mathbf{A} + 2\mathbf{I})^{-1}(2\mathbf{u} + \beta\mathbf{B}^T\mathbf{1} + \lambda\mathbf{P}\mathbf{y}^t + \rho\mathbf{A}^T(\mathbf{v}_k - \mathbf{w}_k)). \tag{9}$$

Updating $\mathbf{v}_{k+1}$ also needs solving a convex optimization problem (Eq. (7)), which is non-smooth due to the L_1-norm of $\mathbf{v}$. Luckily, we can have an analytical solution of $\mathbf{v}_{k+1}$ by applying the approximal algorithm [31]:

$$\mathbf{v}_{k+1} = S_{\alpha/\rho}(\mathbf{A}\mathbf{x}_{k+1} + \mathbf{w}_k), \tag{10}$$

where S is the soft thresholding operator which is defined as $S_\kappa(a) = (a-\kappa)_+ - (-a-\kappa)_+$ [31].

$\mathbf{w}_{k+1}$ can be updated directly according to Eq. (8). The complete ADMM-based algorithm for updating $\mathbf{x}$ in Eq. (3) is summarized in Algorithm 1.

Algorithm 1 The optimization algorithm for updating $\mathbf{x}$.

Input: $\mathbf{x}^t$, $\mathbf{y}^t$, $\mathbf{u}$, $\mathbf{A}$, $\mathbf{B}$, $\mathbf{P}$, α, β, λ, ρ.
Output: $\mathbf{x}^{t+1}$.
Initialize $\mathbf{x}_0 = \mathbf{x}^t$, $\mathbf{v}_0 = \mathbf{A}\mathbf{x}^t$, $\mathbf{w}_0 = \mathbf{0}$, $k = 0$.
while the convergence condition is not satisfied **do**
    $\mathbf{x}_{k+1} = (\rho\mathbf{A}^T\mathbf{A} + 2\mathbf{I})^{-1}(2\mathbf{u} + \beta\mathbf{B}^T\mathbf{1} + \lambda\mathbf{P}\mathbf{y}^t + \rho\mathbf{A}^T(\mathbf{v}_k - \mathbf{w}_k))$.
    $\mathbf{v}_{k+1} = S_{\alpha/\rho}(\mathbf{A}\mathbf{x}_{k+1} + \mathbf{w}_k)$.
    $\mathbf{w}_{k+1} = \mathbf{w}_k + \mathbf{A}\mathbf{x}_{k+1} - \mathbf{v}_{k+1}$.
    $k = k + 1$.
end while
$\mathbf{x}^{t+1} = \mathbf{x}_k$.

4.3.2 *Updating* $\mathbf{y}$

Next we discuss how to update $\mathbf{y}$ in Eq. (2). Since $\mathbf{x}$ is fixed to be $\mathbf{x}^{t+1}$ when updating $\mathbf{y}$ in the t_{th} iteration, minimizing the objective function in Eq. (2) is equivalent to following optimization problem:

$$\arg\min_{\mathbf{y}} \mathcal{L}(\mathbf{y}) = \|\mathbf{y} - \mathbf{m}\|_2^2 - \lambda \mathbf{x}^{t+1}\mathbf{P}\mathbf{y} + \gamma\|\mathbf{C}\mathbf{y}\|_1. \quad (11)$$

We can verify that this is a convex optimization problem. It is also non-smooth due to the term $\|\mathbf{C}\mathbf{y}\|_1$. Thus again we can apply ADMM to solve this optimization problem efficiently. We omit the detailed derivations here for the sake of concision since they are similar with those in previous section, and just illustrate the final algorithm for updating $\mathbf{y}$ in Algorithm 2. Interested readers can verify the conclusions in Algorithm 2 following the similar steps in previous section.

Algorithm 2 The optimization algorithm for updating $\mathbf{y}$.

Input: $\mathbf{x}^{t+1}, \mathbf{y}^t, \mathbf{m}, \mathbf{P}, \mathbf{C}, \lambda, \gamma, \rho$.
Output: $\mathbf{y}^{t+1}$.
Initialize $\mathbf{y}_0 = \mathbf{y}^t, \mathbf{n}_0 = \mathbf{C}\mathbf{y}^t, \mathbf{w}_0 = \mathbf{0}, k = 0$.
while the convergence condition is not satisfied **do**
    $\mathbf{y}_{k+1} = (\rho\mathbf{C}^T\mathbf{C} + 2\mathbf{I})^{-1}(2\mathbf{m} + \lambda\mathbf{P}^T\mathbf{x}^{t+1} + \rho\mathbf{C}^T(\mathbf{n}_k - \mathbf{w}_k))$.
    $\mathbf{n}_{k+1} = S_{\gamma/\rho}(\mathbf{C}\mathbf{y}_{k+1} + \mathbf{w}_k)$.
    $\mathbf{w}_{k+1} = \mathbf{w}_k + \mathbf{C}\mathbf{y}_{k+1} - \mathbf{n}_{k+1}$.
    $k = k + 1$.
end while
$\mathbf{y}^{t+1} = \mathbf{y}_k$.

5. EXPERIMENTS

In this section we report the experimental results. We first introduce the real-world dataset used in our experiments. Then we validate the assumptions behind our social spammer and spam message co-detection framework by conducting hypothesis testing on this dataset. After that we evaluate the performance of our framework on both social spammer detection and spam message detection, and compare it with several state-of-the-art methods. We also explore the influence of parameter setting on the performance of our framework. Finally we analyze the time complexity of our framework empirically using experiments on the real-world dataset.

5.1 Dataset

In this section, we introduce the dataset used in our experiments. We first crawled a large microblog dataset using API from Sina Weibo [3], which is the most popular microblogging website in China. The time period of this data crawling process is from January 1st, 2015 to February 1st, 2015. Then we randomly selected 200 users who frequently used some third-party APIs to automatically post microblog messages in our dataset. We found that these users tend to be social spammers. In addition, we randomly selected 200 verified users from our dataset, since verified users have a high probability to be legitimate users. We merged these 400 users together and used them as seed users. Then we crawled followers and followees of these users. Finally we obtained 5,090 users in total including the seed users. Among these users, there are 433 friend relations and 4,748 following relations. We also crawled the profiles and recent microblog messages of these users from their microblogging homepages. We obtained 53,484 messages in total. We used the URLs and hashtags contained in these messages to build connections between them and obtained 234,375 message-message relations. We manually labeled each user and each message into spam or normal. We used $+1$ as the spam label and -1 as the normal label. The detailed statistics of this dataset is illustrated in Table 1.

[3]`http://www.weibo.com/`

Table 1: The statistics of our dataset. *#Friend, #Following* and *#Message-Message* represent the numbers of friend relations, following relations and message-message relations respectively.

#User	# Spammer	#Legitimate	#Friend	#Following
5,090	1,496	3,594	433	4,748
#Message	#Spam	#Normal	#Message-Message	
53,484	25,681	27,803	234,375	

In the preprocessing steps, we extracted feature vector for each user and each message. The features used for user classification include the total number of messages posted by the user, the number of followers of the user, the number of followees, the ratio of followee number to follower number, the self-description of the user, the textual content of the messages posted by the user. As to message, we used the TFIDF vector as feature vector. Stop words as well as the rare words that appeared less than 10 times were removed.

5.2 Hypothesis Testing

Our framework defined in Eq. (1) is mainly based on four assumptions. First, microblog users who follow each other, i.e., users with friend relations, tend to be both social spammers or legitimate users. Second, if two users have directed following relation rather than friend relation, then the follower has a higher probability to be social spammer than the followee. Third, social spammers tend to post more spam messages and legitimate users tend to post more normal messages. In other words, users and their messages tend to share the same spam labels. Fourth, microblog messages connected by the same URL or hashtag tend to be both normal or spam. We verified each of these assumptions by conducting hypothesis testing on our dataset.

In order to verify the first assumption, we built two vectors $\mathbf{h}_1$ and $\mathbf{h}_2$, each with a length of 100. Each element of $\mathbf{h}_1$ is specified by randomly sampling two users with friend relation, and recording the absolute difference of the labels of these two users. Each element of $\mathbf{h}_2$ is specified by randomly sampling two users without friend relation, and computing the absolute difference of the labels of these two users. We used two-sample t-test to compare $\mathbf{h}_1$ with $\mathbf{h}_2$. The null hypothesis is that there is no difference between these two vectors, i.e., $H_0 : \mathbf{h}_1 = \mathbf{h}_2$. The alternative hypothesis is that the difference between users with friend relations is less than that without friend relation, , i.e., $H_1 : \mathbf{h}_1 < \mathbf{h}_2$. The t-test result rejects the null hypothesis with the significance level 0.01, and validates our assumption that users with friend relations tend to have the same spam labels.

We verified the second assumption using following steps. First we built two 1000-dimensional vectors $\mathbf{h}_1$ and $\mathbf{h}_2$. Each element of $\mathbf{h}_1$ is obtained by randomly sampling two users with following relation, and computing the value of the follower's label minus the followee's label. Each element of $\mathbf{h}_2$ is the difference of the labels of two randomly sampled users without following relation. Two-sample t-test was used to compare $\mathbf{h}_1$ with $\mathbf{h}_2$. The null hypothesis is that there is no difference between $\mathbf{h}_1$ with $\mathbf{h}_2$, i.e., $H_0 : \mathbf{h}_1 = \mathbf{h}_2$. The alternative hypothesis is $H_1 : \mathbf{h}_1 > \mathbf{h}_2$, i.e., followers are more likely to be spammers than followees compared with random user pairs. The t-test result shows that we can reject the null hypothesis with significance level 0.01, and validates the second assumption.

The experiments for validating the third assumption and the fourth assumption are similar with that for validating the first assumption. The difference is that when validating the third assumption, each element of $\mathbf{h}_1$ is the absolute difference between the label of a randomly selected user and the label of a randomly selected message posted by this user. Each element of $\mathbf{h}_2$ is the absolute difference between the label of a randomly selected user and the label of a randomly selected message posted by other users. When validating the fourth assumption, the elements of $\mathbf{h}_1$ are the absolute differences of the labels of randomly selected message pairs connected by URLs or hashtags, while the elements of $\mathbf{h}_2$ are the absolute differences of the labels of message pairs without connection. The null hypotheses in these two experiments are both $H_0 : \mathbf{h}_1 = \mathbf{h}_2$, and the alternative hypotheses are $H_1 : \mathbf{h}_1 < \mathbf{h}_2$. The t-test results reject the null hypotheses with strong evidence (significance level 0.01), and validate our third and fourth assumptions.

5.3 Performance Evaluation

In this section, we evaluate the performance of our framework on both social spammer classification and spam message classification by comparing it with several baseline methods. The methods to be compared are listed as follows:

- SVM: Support vector machine, a standard supervised classification method, widely used in social spammer detection and spam message classification [6, 10, 27].
- LR: Logistic Regression, another widely used supervised classification method [6, 25].
- LS_Lasso: Least Squares method with lasso regularization [35]. Some researchers found that since microblog data is noisy and sparse, it is beneficial to use sparse learning techniques such as lasso for social spammer detection and spam message classification [21].
- SSDM: The method proposed in [21], which is designed for social spammer detection. This method is based on LS_Lasso and incorporates the social relations between users into the model learning stage.
- Co-Classify: The method proposed in [10], which trains a social spammer SVM classifier and a spam message SVM classifier simultaneously by incorporating the user-message relations. Note that in this method the social contexts are also used in model learning stage.
- Ours: This is our proposed framework for social spammer and spam message co-detection in microblogging. The initial classification results used in our framework were generated using Logistic Regression.

The experimental results are shown in Table 2. In each experiment, five-fold cross-validation was used. The dataset was randomly partitioned into 5 subsets with equal size, where three for training, one for validation and one for testing. The parameters of our framework and all the baseline methods were tuned on the validation sets, and the results were recorded on the testing sets. Each experiment was repeated 10 times independently, and the average results are reported. In order to explore the influence of dataset size, we conducted another set of experiments. All the experiment settings are the same with previous experiments except that we randomly sampled half of the training data in each experiment. The experimental results are also summarized in Table 2.

Table 2: Accuracies of different methods. *Spammer* represents the accuracy of social spammer detection and *Spam* stands for the accuracy of spam message detection.

Method	Half Training Data		All Training Data	
	Spammer	Spam	Spammer	Spam
SVM	0.8171	0.9023	0.8262	0.9042
LR	0.8353	0.9017	0.8385	0.9068
LS_Lasso	0.8359	0.9067	0.8376	0.9110
SSDM	0.8379	-	0.8396	-
Co-Classify	0.8224	0.9063	0.8288	0.9102
Ours	**0.8637**	**0.9228**	**0.8673**	**0.9297**

By comparing the accuracies of different methods in Table 2, we have following observations:

First, our method achieves the best performance among all the methods compared here on both social spammer detection and spam message classification with difference sizes of training data. We used two-sample one-tail t-tests to compare the results of our method with those of the baseline methods. The hypothesis testing results show that our method performs significantly better than all the baseline methods with the significance level 0.01. Our method can outperform traditional classification methods (such as SVM and Logistic Regression) and the method based on sparse learning (LS_Lasso) because the attributes and content of social spammers and spam messages are various and evolving, and it is quite difficult to build an accurate enough classifier for social spammer detection and spam message detection using traditional classification methods. Our method tries to alleviate this difficulty by exploiting the social contexts of users and messages to refine the classification results, which can provide additional information besides the attributes, behaviours and textual content information. The experimental results show that incorporating social contexts into our framework can improve the classification accuracy significantly. These results validate the usefulness of social contexts in social spammer detection and spam message detection. SSDM and Co-Classify methods also incorporate social contexts for social spammer detection and/or spam message detection. The main difference between these methods and our method is the way of utilizing social contexts. In SSDM and Co-Classify, the social contexts are used in the model learning stage to constrain the user-user pair or user-message pair with social relations to have similar scores. However, in prediction stage, only the textual content and attributes are considered. Due to same reasons mentioned previously, it is still difficult to train an accurate enough classifier even with the help of social contexts. Different from these methods, in our framework, the social contexts are used in the prediction stage. We exploit the graph structure over the output variables extracted from the various kinds of social connections between users and messages to make more accurate predictions. The superior performance of our method compared with those of SSDM and Co-Classify validates the advantage of our framework in utilizing social contexts for social spammer detection and spam message detection.

Second, the accuracies of all the methods with half of the training data are not significantly different from those with all the training data. This result implies that our dataset is big enough for training social spammer classifier and spam message classifer. Thus further increasing the size of training data is not helpful for improving the classification accuracy significantly. The relatively low accuracy is mainly due to the inherent difficulties of these tasks rather than lack of training data. However, our method can improve the classification accuracy consistently and significantly without any additional

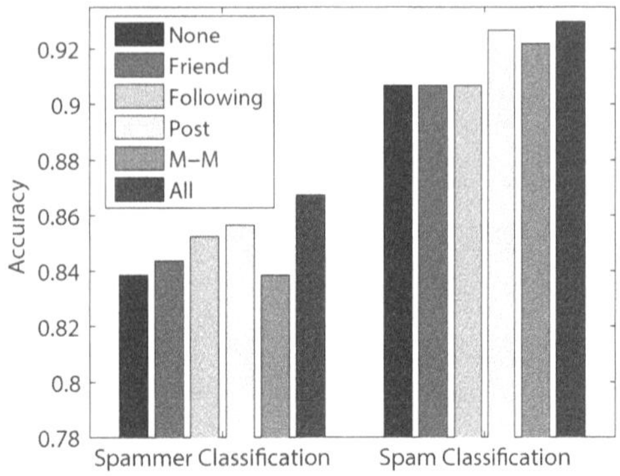

Figure 3: Contributions of different kinds of social contexts to the performance improvement of our framework. *None* represents the performance of the original Logistic Regression. *Friend*, *Following*, *Post* and *M-M* represent the performance of our framework with the friend relations between users, the following relations between users, the user-message relations, and the message-message relations respectively. *All* represents the performance of our framework with all these social contexts.

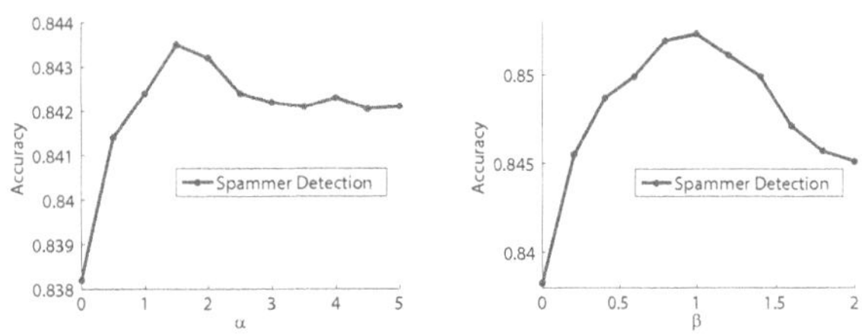

Figure 4: The influences of parameters α and β on social spammer detection.

training data. This is because our method can exploit and incorporate another kind of information in the testing data, i.e., the social contexts, since in social media users and messages are networked.

We also conducted experiments to explore the contributions of different kinds of social contexts to the performance improvement of our framework. We examined the influence of a certain kind of social contexts by setting the coefficients of others to 0 in Eq. (1). The experimental results are shown in Fig. 3.

From the results in Fig. 3, we can draw three conclusions. First, all the user-related social contexts, such as the friend relations, the following relations, and the user-message relations, are helpful for improving the performance of social spammer detection. Similarly, the two kinds of message-related social contexts, i.e., the user-message relations and message-message relations, are both helpful for improving the performance of spam message detection. These results validate that all the social contexts introduced in Section 3 are useful under our framework. Second, among all the social contexts compared here, the user-message relation is the most powerful one on both social spammer detection and spam message classification. This result validates our assumption in the Section 1, i.e., combining social spammer detection and spam message detection together can boost the performance of each task because social spammers and spam messages are closely connected. Third, our framework performs best when all the social contexts are incorporated. This indicates that different kinds of social contexts can collaborate with each other under our framework. Thus our unified framework is effective in incorporating various social contexts.

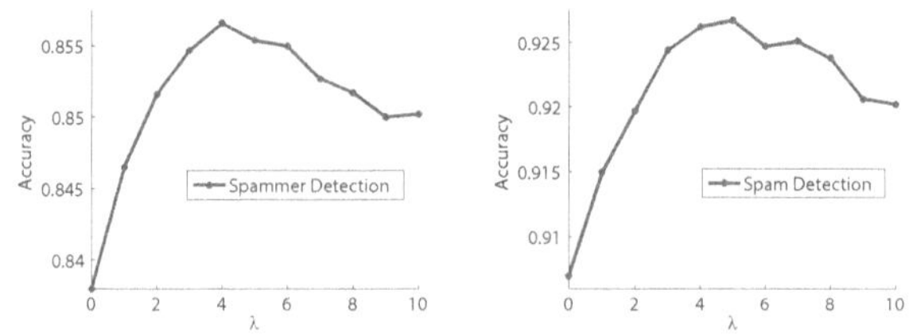

Figure 5: The influence of parameter λ on social spammer detection and spam message detection.

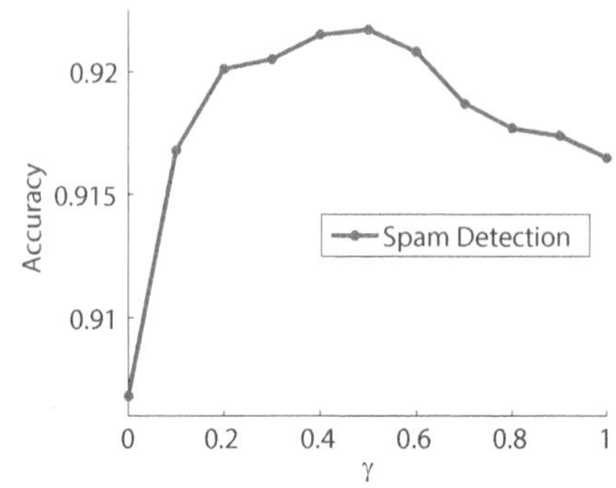

Figure 6: The influence of parameter γ on spam message detection.

5.4 Parameter Analysis

In this section we conducted experiments to explore the influences of parameters on the performance of our framework. There are four important parameters to tune in our framework (Eq. (1)), i.e., α, β, λ and γ. Parameters α and β are used to control the importance of friend relations and following relations between users respectively. Parameter λ is used to control the penalty introduced by user-message relations. Parameter γ represents the importance of message-message relations. We examined the influence of each parameter independently by setting other parameters to zeros. The experimental results are shown in Fig. 4, Fig. 5 and Fig. 6.

From these figures we can see that the influences of parameters α, β, λ and γ on the performance of our framework show similar patterns. When the values of these parameters increase from 0, the performance of our framework first increases quickly, then reaches the peak, and decreases afterwards. This is because when parameter values are too small, the information in these social contexts is not fully used. Thus the performance improves as the parameters increase from a small value. However, when the values of parameters are too large, the information in these social contexts is overemphasized. The prediction results will be overwhelmed by the social contexts. Since social contexts contain some noise inevitably, the performance will be harmed if parameters are too large. An interesting pattern observed in the experiments is that as long as the parameter values are in a moderate range, the performance of our framework is always better than that without social context. This implies that incorporating social contexts is always helpful under our framework, and it is not difficult to select appropriate values for these parameters either by cross validation or empirically.

5.5 Complexity Analysis

In this section we conducted experiments to explore the time complexity of our framework and compare the efficiency of our

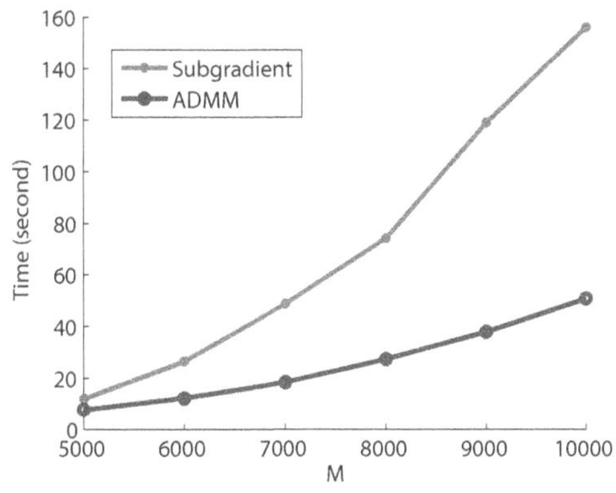

Figure 7: The time complexity of our framework.

ADMM based method with that of subgradient method in solving our framework. In each experiment, we randomly sampled N messages. Then we extracted all the associated users and all the social relations of these messages and users. We varied N from 5,000 to 10,000. Each experiment was conducted 10 times independently and the average results were recorded. The algorithms ware implemented using Matlab R2011b. All the experiments were conducted on a laptop computer running Windows 7 with Core i5 CPU and 8GB RAM. The experimental results are shown in Fig. 7.

From Fig. 7 we can see that the running time of our framework with ADMM-based algorithms is approximately linear with the data size when data size gets large, which is a promising property for analyzing large-scale microblog data. In addition, our framework with ADMM-based algorithms is much faster than that with subgradient algorithm, which validates the usefulness of Algorithm 1 and Algorithm 2 in improving time efficiency.

6. CONCLUSION

This paper presents a unified framework for social spammer and spam message co-detection in microblogging. Our framework can incorporate various social contexts of the microblog users and messages, and refine the results of social spammer classification and spam message classification by exploiting their social connections. Three kinds of social contexts are extracted, i.e., the friend and following relations between users, the posting relations between users and messages, and the connections between messages. In our framework, the social spammer detection and spam message detection are combined using the posting relations between users and messages. The friend and following relations between users and the connections between messages are modeled as the regularization terms over the prediction results in our framework. In addition, we propose an accelerated algorithm based on ADMM to solve our framework efficiently. Extensive experiments on a real-world microblog dataset show that our framework can outperform baseline methods significantly and consistently.

7. ACKNOWLEDGMENTS

We would like to thank Dr. Yangqiu Song for his kind suggestions. We are grateful to the anonymous reviewers for their helpful comments. This research is supported by the Key Program of National Natural Science Foundation of China under Grant No. U1405254, and the National Natural Science Foundation of China under Grant No. 61472092 and 61472092.

8. REFERENCES

[1] L. Becchetti, C. Castillo, D. Donato, S. Leonardi, and R. A. Baeza-Yates. Link-based characterization and detection of web spam. In *AIRWeb*, pages 1–8, 2006.

[2] A. Beck and M. Teboulle. A fast iterative shrinkage-thresholding algorithm for linear inverse problems. *SIAM Journal on Imaging Sciences*, 2(1):183–202, 2009.

[3] K. Beck. Analyzing tweets to identify malicious messages. In *IEEE International Conference on Electro/Information Technology (EIT)*, pages 1–5. IEEE, 2011.

[4] F. Benevenuto, G. Magno, T. Rodrigues, and V. Almeida. Detecting spammers on twitter. In *Collaboration, electronic messaging, anti-abuse and spam conference (CEAS)*, volume 6, page 12, 2010.

[5] L. Bilge, T. Strufe, D. Balzarotti, and E. Kirda. All your contacts are belong to us: automated identity theft attacks on social networks. In *WWW*, pages 551–560. ACM, 2009.

[6] E. Blanzieri and A. Bryl. A survey of learning-based techniques of email spam filtering. *Artificial Intelligence Review*, 29(1):63–92, 2008.

[7] S. Boyd, N. Parikh, E. Chu, B. Peleato, and J. Eckstein. Distributed optimization and statistical learning via the alternating direction method of multipliers. *Foundations and Trends® in Machine Learning*, 3(1):1–122, 2011.

[8] S. Boyd and L. Vandenberghe. *Convex optimization*. Cambridge university press, 2004.

[9] G. Brown, T. Howe, M. Ihbe, A. Prakash, and K. Borders. Social networks and context-aware spam. In *Proceedings of the 2008 ACM conference on Computer supported cooperative work*, pages 403–412. ACM, 2008.

[10] F. Chen, P.-N. Tan, and A. K. Jain. A co-classification framework for detecting web spam and spammers in social media web sites. In *CIKM*, pages 1807–1810. ACM, 2009.

[11] X. Chen, S. Kim, Q. Lin, J. G. Carbonell, and E. P. Xing. Graph-structured multi-task regression and an efficient optimization method for general fused lasso. *arXiv preprint arXiv:1005.3579*, 2010.

[12] G. Danezis and P. Mittal. Sybilinfer: Detecting sybil nodes using social networks. In *NDSS*, 2009.

[13] C. Ding, T. Li, and M. I. Jordan. Convex and semi-nonnegative matrix factorizations. *TPAMI*, 32(1):45–55, 2010.

[14] H. Gao, Y. Chen, K. Lee, D. Palsetia, and A. N. Choudhary. Towards online spam filtering in social networks. In *NDSS*, 2012.

[15] S. Ghosh, B. Viswanath, F. Kooti, N. K. Sharma, G. Korlam, F. Benevenuto, N. Ganguly, and K. P. Gummadi. Understanding and combating link farming in the twitter social network. In *WWW*, pages 61–70. ACM, 2012.

[16] J. M. Gómez Hidalgo, G. C. Bringas, E. P. Sánz, and F. C. García. Content based sms spam filtering. In *Proceedings of the 2006 ACM symposium on Document engineering*, pages 107–114. ACM, 2006.

[17] C. Grier, K. Thomas, V. Paxson, and M. Zhang. @ spam: the underground on 140 characters or less. In *Proceedings of the 17th ACM conference on Computer and communications security*, pages 27–37. ACM, 2010.

[18] Z. Gyöngyi, H. Garcia-Molina, and J. Pedersen. Combating web spam with trustrank. In *VLDB*, pages 576–587. VLDB Endowment, 2004.

[19] X. Hu, J. Tang, and H. Liu. Leveraging knowledge across media for spammer detection in microblogging. In *SIGIR*, pages 547–556. ACM, 2014.

[20] X. Hu, J. Tang, and H. Liu. Online social spammer detection. In *AAAI*, 2014.

[21] X. Hu, J. Tang, Y. Zhang, and H. Liu. Social spammer detection in microblogging. In *IJCAI*, pages 2633–2639. AAAI Press, 2013.

[22] N. Jindal and B. Liu. Review spam detection. In *WWW*, pages 1189–1190. ACM, 2007.

[23] K. Lee, J. Caverlee, and S. Webb. Uncovering social spammers: social honeypots+ machine learning. In *SIGIR*, pages 435–442. ACM, 2010.

[24] C. Lin, J. He, Y. Zhou, X. Yang, K. Chen, and L. Song. Analysis and identification of spamming behaviors in sina weibo microblog. In *Proceedings of the 7th Workshop on Social Network Mining and Analysis*, page 5. ACM, 2013.

[25] L. Liu and K. Jia. Detecting spam in chinese microblogs-a study on sina weibo. In *Eighth International Conference on Computational Intelligence and Security (CIS)*, pages 578–581. IEEE, 2012.

[26] J. Martinez-Romo and L. Araujo. Detecting malicious tweets in trending topics using a statistical analysis of language. *Expert Systems with Applications*, 40(8):2992–3000, 2013.

[27] M. McCord and M. Chuah. Spam detection on twitter using traditional classifiers. In *Autonomic and trusted computing*, pages 175–186. Springer, 2011.

[28] A. Ntoulas, M. Najork, M. Manasse, and D. Fetterly. Detecting spam web pages through content analysis. In *WWW*, pages 83–92. ACM, 2006.

[29] D. O'Callaghan, M. Harrigan, J. Carthy, and P. Cunningham. Network analysis of recurring youtube spam campaigns. In *ICWSM*, 2012.

[30] P. Oscar and V. Roychowdbury. Leveraging social networks to fight spam. *IEEE Computer*, 38(4):61–68, 2005.

[31] N. Parikh and S. Boyd. Proximal algorithms. *Foundations and Trends in Optimization*, 1(3):123–231, 2013.

[32] J. Ratkiewicz, M. Conover, M. Meiss, B. Gonçalves, S. Patil, A. Flammini, and F. Menczer. Truthy: mapping the spread of astroturf in microblog streams. In *WWW*, pages 249–252. ACM, 2011.

[33] J. Song, S. Lee, and J. Kim. Spam filtering in twitter using sender-receiver relationship. In *Recent Advances in Intrusion Detection*, pages 301–317. Springer, 2011.

[34] G. Stringhini, C. Kruegel, and G. Vigna. Detecting spammers on social networks. In *Proceedings of the 26th Annual Computer Security Applications Conference*, pages 1–9. ACM, 2010.

[35] R. Tibshirani. Regression shrinkage and selection via the lasso. *Journal of the Royal Statistical Society. Series B (Methodological)*, pages 267–288, 1996.

[36] A. H. Wang. Don't follow me: Spam detection in twitter. In *Proceedings of the 2010 International Conference on Security and Cryptography*, pages 1–10. IEEE, 2010.

[37] S. Webb, J. Caverlee, and C. Pu. Social honeypots: Making friends with a spammer near you. In *CEAS*, 2008.

[38] J. Weng, E.-P. Lim, J. Jiang, and Q. He. Twitterrank: finding topic-sensitive influential twitterers. In *WSDM*, pages 261–270. ACM, 2010.

[39] X. Zhang, S. Zhu, and W. Liang. Detecting spam and promoting campaigns in the twitter social network. In *ICDM*, pages 1194–1199, 2012.

Central Topic Model for Event-oriented Topics Mining in Microblog Stream

Min Peng[1,2], Jiahui Zhu[1], Xuhui Li[3], Jiajia Huang[2], Hua Wang[4], Yanchun Zhang[4]
[1] State Key Lab of Software Engineering, School of Computer, Wuhan University, Wuhan, China
[2] School of Computer, Wuhan University, Wuhan, China
[3] School of Information Management, Wuhan University, Wuhan, China
[4] Centre for Applied Informatics, Victoria University, Melbourne, Australia
{pengm, zhujiahui, lixuhui, huangjj}@whu.edu.cn,
{hua.wang, yanchun.zhang}@vu.edu.au

ABSTRACT

To date, data generates and arrives in the form of stream to propagate discussions of public events in microblog services. Discovering event-oriented topics from the stream will lead to a better understanding of the change of public concern. However, as the massive scale of the data stream, traditional static topic models, such as LDA, are no longer fit for topic detection and tracking tasks. In this paper, we propose a central topic model (CenTM), where a *Multi-view Clustering* algorithm with *Two-phase Random Walk* (MC-TRW) is devised to aggregate the LDA's latent topics into central topics. Furthermore, we leverage the aggregation of central topics alternately with MC-TRW and sequential topic inference to improve the scalability in the stream fashion, so as to derive the dynamic central topic model (DCenTM). Specifically, our model is able to uncover the intrinsic characteristics of the central topics and predict the trend of their intensity along a life cycle. Experimental results demonstrate that the proposed central topic model is event-oriented and of high generalization, it therefore can dispose the topic trend prediction effectively and precisely in massive data stream.

Categories and Subject Descriptors

H.3.1 [**Information Storage and Retrieval**]: Content Analysis and Indexing

Keywords

Central Topic, Multi-view Clustering, Trend Prediction

1. INTRODUCTION

Microblog systems, such as Twitter and Sina Weibo, have become one of the most popular and influential social media platforms to share the latest news and express user opinions. For example, more than 80% of the Sina Weibo users participate in the topic discussion of the *2014 FIFA World Cup Brazil* and over 76% of the users post feeds (the messages released by users in social networks, also known as user generated contents) on Sina Weibo when they were watching the games[1]. These short messages are created and published in real time from different people to broadcast the latest scores as well as the user reviews. Discovering valuable topics from microblog stream and predicting their evolution is therefore important for a wide variety of applications, such as emergencies detection [22], user interest modeling [23], controversial topics discovering [20], spatio-temporal visualization [16] and so on.

While a massive amount of microblog feeds are generated in every minute, the low value density of information always spoils our research. For example, according to the analysis of 2,000 feeds during the U.S.-Slovenia game[2], only 7.6% of the feeds are meaningful, while 29% are useless observations (most boing 90 minutes), 24% are self-promotions for pundits and companies, and 6% are spams. The characteristics of microblog feeds, such as volume, velocity and low value density are challenging topic mining and trend prediction in microblog stream:

(1) Low value density of microblog feeds makes it difficult for generating a group of topics with meaningful description (coherence) by traditional "bag-of-words" clustering methods or latent topic models, such as K-means and LDA. Table 1 demonstrates two lists of topic terms of the final match *Germany VS Argentina* in *World Cup Brazil*. They are generated by K-Means and Online-LDA [1] respectively, where the data comes from Sina Weibo, including 45,000 feeds. In Table 1, all of the five topics generated by these two methods are about only one certain event *World Cup Brazil*. Besides, some of them also mingle with advertisement words such as "cash". These incoherent or incompact topics may reduce the accuracy of topic trend prediction.

(2) Dynamic change of microblog feeds implies to generate new topics continuously. However, classical topic models, such as Online-LDA, don't perform well in extracting meaningful topics from a large number of rapidly changing feeds (also called as feed stream).

To tackle the first challenge, we consider the generation of a group of more event-oriented topics, which are along with coherence by latent topic clustering based on co-training model [6]. We call these event-oriented topics as *central*

Permission to make digital or hard copies of all or part of this work for personal or classroom use is granted without fee provided that copies are not made or distributed for profit or commercial advantage and that copies bear this notice and the full citation on the first page. Copyrights for components of this work owned by others than ACM must be honored. Abstracting with credit is permitted. To copy otherwise, or republish, to post on servers or to redistribute to lists, requires prior specific permission and/or a fee. Request permissions from Permissions@acm.org.
CIKM'15, October 19–23, 2015, Melbourne, VIC, Australia.
© 2015 ACM. ISBN 978-1-4503-3794-6/15/10 ...$15.00.
DOI: http://dx.doi.org/10.1145/2806416.2806561.

[1] http://www.199it.com/archives/255612.html.
[2] http://www.esquire.com/the-side/feature/world-cup-tweets-062110.

Table 1: Topic terms derived by K-Means and Online-LDA

	K-Means	Online-LDA
Topic terms	world cup + cash + buddy	world cup + Germany + goodbye
	world cup + goodbye + flow	Brazil + Netherlands + Germany
	world cup + Louis Van Gaal + Manchester United	buddy + cash + circusee
	world cup + cash + prize	world cup + transformers + rebirth
	world cup + Germany + German	world cup + Germany + Klose

topics. Then, we design a novel *multi-view clustering* algorithm based on a *two-phrase random walk* (MC-TRW) to obtain a group of central topics. To tackle the second challenge, feeds collection is treated as a stream in temporal order and divided into feed batches at regular time intervals. The central topics of each feed batch can be mined by the MC-TRW algorithm. However, topics in the stream are continuously evolving, which means the central topics of current batch are usually related to those in the prior batch. Therefore, in this paper, the central topics of the feed stream are generated by combining the MC-TRW algorithm with the knowledge of central topics distribution in the prior batch.

To sum up, in this study, we propose a novel topic model, which can extract meaningful topics from feed stream efficiently and also can be updated quickly to capture the evolution history of topics dynamically. The elements of the proposed topic model include: 1) a central topic model (CenT-M): It is a topic model developed from co-training idea to aggregate the latent topics that are trained by Online-LDA. In this model, we propose a two-phrase random walk to construct an intrinsic relevant matrix among different views and design a multi-view clustering algorithm (MC-TRW) based on this matrix. 2) DCenTM: It is a dynamic variant of CenTM that generates a series of central topics for the microblog feed stream by alternately acting the MC-TRW algorithm and topic inference method on the batch sequence. Furthermore, we develop a topic trend prediction task on the DCenTM topic model for exploratory analysis. The contributions of our work are the following:

- We introduce a central topic model in microblog stream to tackle the topic detection and tracking. It focuses on the central topics, which is more event-oriented and meaningful than the LDA's latent topics..
- We design a multi-view clustering algorithm to generate central topics. This algorithm is based on the two-phrase random walk, which is fit for uncovering the relevance of different views in clustering.
- We accommodate the central topic model to the stream mining by before-topic inference, and perform topic trend and intensity prediction on it.

The rest of the paper is structured as follows: Section 2 reviews the related work. Section 3 is the pre-processing. Section 4 presents our central topic model, including CenTM and DCenTM. Section 5 describes the topic trend prediction in detail. Section 6 demonstrates the experimental evaluation. At last, Section 7 concludes our finding.

2. RELATED WORK

Clustering based methods: One line of research is based on the texts or phrases clustering to mine topics. Gong et al. [15] propose a distributed clustering algorithm to dynamically group user generated subscribed topics into topic clusters, which could unify their supporting structures and achieve better utilization of existing platforms. Adam et al. [24] follow the idea of the query model and retrieve user's events by selectively materializing low-rate user's feeds in underlying event streams. Zimmermann et al. [31] also propose a text stream clustering method with two-level hierarchy to detect, track and update global bursty topics and identify local subtopics. Recently, a framework called Twevent [13] has achieved sound performance on event detection. This segment-based strategy can primely retain semantic interpretation by considering both internal and external knowledge.

Topic models: Another line of research is on the basis of latent Dirichlet allocation (LDA) [5], a classical probabilistic topic model. Some of its variants, such as DTM [4] and Online-LDA [1], are widely used in constructing topic models for text collections. These variants of LDA model with temporal consideration are able to extract topics in real time from a massive amount of texts, and usually perform better than the simple LDA in terms of perplexity metrics. Moreover, in order to extract topics that are oriented to events, some models tend to impose semantic coherence on their topics, including the sparsity based SACM [28] and the knowledge based LTM [7].

Topic prediction: The aim of topic prediction is to learn the rules of how topic changes over time and to predict further trend on the basis of these changes. By granting the topics with corresponding life circle states, [29] can monitor the evolution of topics in a more intuitive way. TM-LDA [27] is a model to mine topics and predict how the topics transit over time. It learns the transition parameters among topics by minimizing the prediction error on topic distributions. In view of the real world occasions, spatial information is also incorporated as to figure out the structural aspects of topic transition [3]. [26] stands on the shoulder of the social media reaction to propose a framework to detect the impact and sentiment shifts of events. Assuredly, all of these methods are effective in the prediction tasks, but they need more side information which is not often accessible.

Multi-view clustering: The multi-view clustering algorithm can play to its strengths when the topics generated by K-Means or LDA models are incoherent or incompact. Abhishek et al. [12] propose a co-training approach to mutually update the similarity matrices to generate the discriminative eigenvectors for spectral clustering. [9] performs the subspace projection in multiple mixture models, and exploits the principle of iterated conditional models (ICM) and Bayesian model to optimize for better performance. [18] and [14] try to model a variant of the non-negative matrix factorization to refine the consensus matrix by all the coefficient matrices. Similar to [18] and [14], we try to explore the consensus clustering view, which is a trade-off for all the separate views, while the difference is that our consensus matrix is constructed by a proposed *two-phrase random walk*.

3. PRE-PROCESSING OF FEED STREAM

In this section, we pre-process the microblog stream by selecting high-quality feeds from the whole stream. According to statistics, only 36% of the rated microblog feeds are worth reading [2], while less than 10% in microblog stream are topic keywords relevant feeds [19]. Along with such ideas, the feed's quality can be measured by combining different facets, such as 1) social features, including review number, retweet number, praise number, and reading count, 2) content features, including text length and URL importance, and 3) influence features, which depend on whether the author and his followers play a dominant role in the social networks. In this study, we are mainly interested in the social and textual facets, and select the *review number*, *retweet number*, *text length* and *URL importance* as the attributions for feed quality evaluation.

Microblog feeds are usually ongoing as a stream which is infinite and rapidly changing. Obviously, the global analysis on feed stream is rather difficult. Here, the feed stream S is divided into feed batches $S = \{D^1, D^2, ..., D^t, ...\}$. In order to reduce the impact of spam and redundant tweets on the performance of the central topic model, feed's quality in each batch D^t is evaluated with an EM based algorithm [19] proposed in our previous work and then high-quality feeds HD^t are selected to train the central topic model.

Set four attribution scores of the ith feed in the tth batch D^t as f_i^1, f_i^2, f_i^3, f_i^4 respectively, which are calculated as follows:

$$f_i^j = \frac{f(N_i^j) - \min(N^j) + \delta}{\max(N^j) - \min(N^j) + \delta} \times 100 \tag{1}$$

where δ is a smoothing factor.

Here note that the $f(N_i^j)(j = 1,2,3,4)$ of different attributions are different. According to our statistical analysis [19], the attributions such as the review number and the retweet number satisfy the power-law distribution, so set $f(N_i^j) = log(N_i^j)(j = 1, 2)$, and set the unsatisfied attribution text length as $f(N_i^3) = N_i^3$. As for the URL importance, we first count all the distinct URLs in feed batch D^t to get the URL set $U^t = \{u_1^t, u_2^t, ..., u_r^t\}$ and the corresponding frequency set $UD^t = \{ud_1^t, ud_2^t, ..., ud_r^t\}$, where r is the total number of the distinct URLs. Then, each URL's importance is calculated as $f(N_i^4) = \log(\sum_{u_k^t \in d_i^t} ud_k^t)$, here d_i^t is the ith feed in t^{th} batch.

These four attributions of all feeds form into a score matrix $\mathbf{F}^t = \{f_{ti}^j\} \in \mathbb{R}^{n^t \times 4}$, where n^t denotes the number of feeds in the tth batch. Then, our quality evaluation algorithm is employed to estimate the weights of each attribution to get a weight vector $\mathbf{\Theta}^t = (w_{t1}, w_{t2}, ..., w_{tM})$. Finally, the quality of each feed is:

$$FS_i^t = \sum_{j=1}^{4} w_{tj} f_{ti}^j$$

With the quality evaluation above, the high-quality feeds can be identified from each batch and compose a high-quality feed batch HD^t. In addition, an assumption can be hold that the weight vectors $\mathbf{\Theta}^t$ between the different batches are quite similar. Therefore, in the experimental process, the vector $\mathbf{\Theta}^t$ of the tth batch is taken as the initial value of the $(t+1)^{th}$ batch to accelerate the convergence of the EM algorithm.

4. CENTRAL TOPIC MODEL

In this section, based on multi-view clustering, we propose a central topic model to aggregate latent topics generated by Online-LDA. Preliminary work of this model is introduced in Section 4.1, including multi-view similarity matrices construction and cluster number estimation. Then, Section 4.2 focuses on discussing the two-phase random walk, which is designed to obtain an intrinsic relevant matrix for multi-view clustering. Finally, the central topic model is morphed into a dynamic variant to mine central topics more promptly in feed stream, as discussed in Section 4.3.

4.1 Preliminary

Given a high-quality feed batch HD^t, the Online-LDA is employed to extract K latent topics and gain two matrices: feed-topic distribution matrix $\mathbf{X}^t \in \mathbb{R}^{Q^t \times K}$ and topic-term distribution matrix $\mathbf{Y}^t \in \mathbb{R}^{K \times V}$, where Q^t is the number of high quality feeds in HD^t and V is the number of terms in HD^t. These latent topics are usually incoherent, resulting in poor performance of topic trend prediction. To tackle this problem, central topics with more summarized description terms are further extracted by aggregating these latent topics.

In fact, the matrix of feed-topic $\mathbf{X}^t$ and the matrix of topic-term $\mathbf{Y}^t$ are able to describe the latent topics from two different views: term distribution and feed relevance. In this paper, these two matrices are used for designing a multi-view clustering to aggregate the latent topics.

4.1.1 Multi-view Similarity Matrices

One important preparation point of multi-view clustering is to construct two kinds of similarity matrices for the views.

For the term distribution view, a symmetrical fashion of Kullback-Leibler divergence (KLD) metric is introduced to measure the similarity of every two latent topics $\mathbf{Y}_i^t$ and $\mathbf{Y}_j^t$:

$$\lambda_{ij} = \frac{1}{(KLD(\mathbf{Y}_i^t||\mathbf{Y}_j^t) + KLD(\mathbf{Y}_j^t||\mathbf{Y}_i^t))/2 + 1} \tag{2}$$

Thus, a similarity matrix $\mathbf{W}_1^t \in \mathbb{R}^{K \times K}$ is constructed via Eq.2 to describe the latent topics from the view of term distribution.

For the feed relevance view, we consider to use topic relevant feeds collection to construct the similarity matrix. Each column $\mathbf{X}_i^t(i = 1, 2, ..., K)$ in the feed-topic matrix $\mathbf{X}^t$ reveals the related feeds set of the latent topics $\mathbf{Y}_i^t$ to some extent. For a certain latent topic $\mathbf{Y}_i^t$, if its membership is larger than a given minimum similarity threshold, then the feed HD_i^t is included into its related text set RD_i^t. In this way, each feed can be allocated to different latent topics to form the topic relevant feeds set. At last, the Jaccard metric is implemented to measure the similarity between latent topics $\mathbf{Y}_i^t$ and $\mathbf{Y}_j^t$:

$$\eta_{ij} = Jaccard(\mathbf{Y}_i^t||\mathbf{Y}_j^t) = \frac{|RD_i^t \cap RD_j^t|}{|RD_i^t \cup RD_j^t|} \tag{3}$$

Algorithm 1: Multi-view Clustering based on Two-phrase Random Walk(MC-TRW)

Input: Feed-topic distribution matrix $\mathbf{X}^t$ and topic-term distribution matrix $\mathbf{Y}^t$
Output: Central topics with term distribution matrix $\mathbf{CY}^t$

1 Generate the similarity matrix $\mathbf{W}_1^t$ with Eq.2 for the term distribution view;
2 Generate the similarity matrix $\mathbf{W}_2^t$ with Eq.3 for the feed relevance view;
3 Estimate the number of the central topics r^t according to section 4.1.2;
4 Set $\mathbf{G}_j^t = \mathbf{0}$, $\mathbf{V}_i^t = \mathbf{W}_i^t, i= 1,2$;
5 **for** $i \leftarrow 1, K$ **do**
6 $\quad \mathbf{V}_i^t(k,k) = 0, i = 1,2$;
7 $\quad \mathbf{G}_i^t(k,k) = sum(\mathbf{V}_i^t(k)), i = 1,2$;
8 **end**
9 Set probability transition matrices: $\mathbf{P}_i^t = (\mathbf{G}_i^t)^{-1}\mathbf{V}_i^t, i = 1,2$;
10 Calculate the intrinsic relevant matrix: $\mathbf{IR}^t = (\mathbf{I} - (1-\alpha)(1-\beta)\mathbf{P}_1^t\mathbf{P}_2^t)^{-1}(\alpha(1-\beta)\mathbf{P}_2^t\mathbf{I} + \beta\mathbf{I})$;
11 Normalize the intrinsic relevant matrix: $\mathbf{IR}^t = (\mathbf{IR}^t + (\mathbf{IR}^t)^{\mathrm{T}})/2$;
12 Perform spectral clustering on $\mathbf{IR}^t$ to generate central topics;

Then, another similarity matrix $\mathbf{W}_2^t \in \mathbb{R}^{K\times K}$ is constructed via Eq.3 to describe the latent topics from the view of feed relevance.

4.1.2 Clusters Number

Another key point of the multi-view clustering is how to decide the number of the clusters. The decision of the cluster number is widely discussed in self-adaptive clustering. Here, we just take a simple but effective approach to estimate the cluster number.

In terms of the two views, the term distribution of the latent topic (i.e., $\mathbf{W}_1^t$) is more essential and is treated as the dominant view. Generally, the top-N eigenvalues of the graph Laplacian of $\mathbf{W}_1^t$ have strong discrimination ability for clustering [12]. Based on this, we design a clustering number estimation approach with following steps: 1) rank all eigenvalues of the graph Laplacian in descending order; 2) set a container with capacity $cont = \tau * evsum$, where τ is a ratio and $evsum$ is the sum of all the eigenvalues in the graph Laplacian ; 3) put the eigenvalues into the container in turn until the sum of the eigenvalues in this container is larger than $cont$; 4) the number of the eigenvalues in the container is the estimated value of the clusters number.

4.2 MC-TRW

We propose a *two-phase random walk* based on the restart version of random walk [25] to construct the intrinsic relevant matrix in a heuristically way. In the random work with restart model, the node i jumps to other nodes with transition probabilities $\{p_{ik}\}(k = 1,2,...K, i \neq k)$, and jumps to itself with probability $p_{ii} = \alpha$. Usually, the transition yields to a steady state after several times of jumping. Here, in the multi-view clustering, the intrinsic relevant matrix between the latent topics also changes as the walker goes by and the walker walks crosswise between two views, we call it as *two-phase random walk*.

In order to construct the intrinsic relevant matrix based on the two-phase random walk, the similarity matrix $\mathbf{W}_1^t$ and $\mathbf{W}_2^t$ are regarded as archetypes of the probability transition matrices in random walk model. What calls for our special attention is that the diagonal elements in the probability matrix must be set as zeroes. Thus, the two similarity matrices $\mathbf{W}_i^t(i = 1,2)$ are modified to form the non-self similarity matrix $\mathbf{V}_i(i = 1,2)$ to fit the random walk paradigm as follows:

$$\mathbf{V}_i^t(j,k) = \begin{cases} \mathbf{W}_i^t(j,k), j \neq k \\ 0, j = k \end{cases}, i = 1,2$$

And the probability transition matrices are:

$$\mathbf{P}_i^t = (\mathbf{G}_i^t)^{-1}\mathbf{V}_i^t, i= 1,2 \tag{4}$$

where $\mathbf{G}_i^t$ is the diagonal matrix of $\mathbf{V}_i^t$ and $\mathbf{G}_i^t(k,k)$ is the sum of the kth row of the $\mathbf{V}_i^t$.

We define the intrinsic relevant matrices as $\mathbf{IR}_i^t(i = 1,2)$. Then the deduction of them can be described as a two-phase fashion:

$$\begin{aligned} \mathbf{IR}_2^t(s) &= (1-\alpha)\mathbf{P}_1^t\mathbf{IR}_1^t(s) + \alpha\mathbf{I} \\ \mathbf{IR}_1^t(s+1) &= (1-\beta)\mathbf{P}_2^t\mathbf{IR}_2^t(s) + \beta\mathbf{I} \end{aligned} \tag{5}$$

where α and β are the self-transition probabilities. During the first phase in s^{th} iteration, the intrinsic relevant matrix $\mathbf{IR}_1^t$ is used to update $\mathbf{IR}_2^t$, and vice versa in the second phase. Obviously, Eq.5 can be simplified as a recursive form as:

$$\begin{aligned} &\mathbf{IR}_1^t(s+1) = (1-\alpha)(1-\beta)\mathbf{P}_1^t\mathbf{P}_2^t\mathbf{IR}_1^t(s) \\ &+ \alpha(1-\beta)\mathbf{P}_2^t\mathbf{I} + \beta\mathbf{I} \end{aligned} \tag{6}$$

Set:

$$\begin{aligned} \mathbf{A} &= (1-\alpha)(1-\beta)\mathbf{P}_1^t\mathbf{P}_2^t \\ \mathbf{B} &= \alpha(1-\beta)\mathbf{P}_2^t\mathbf{I} + \beta\mathbf{I} \end{aligned}$$

Then Eq.6 can be rewritten as:

$$\mathbf{IR}_1^t(s+1) = \mathbf{A}(\mathbf{IR}_1^t(s)) + \mathbf{B}$$

Following the convention [25], it can be clear that the intrinsic relevant matrices can converge to a certain matrix, which is irrelevant to the initial value. Then the converged $\mathbf{IR}^t$ can be directly computed as follows:

$$\mathbf{IR}^t = (\mathbf{I} - \mathbf{A})^{-1}\mathbf{B} \tag{7}$$

The converged intrinsic relevant matrix $\mathbf{IR}^t$ of the two views is the key to the latent topic clustering. Usually, the symmetry of the $\mathbf{IR}^t$ cannot be guaranteed, so set $\mathbf{IR}^t = (\mathbf{IR}^t + (\mathbf{IR}^t)^{\mathrm{T}})/2$ as the symmetrical matrix.

Finally, the $\mathbf{IR}^t$ is used as the similarity matrix in spectral clustering [17] to generate central topics. The clustering result lays out the partition of the latent topics, each center of the cluster represents a central topic, which is highly event-oriented and summarized. The whole process of this aggregation algorithm is called as the *Multi-view Clustering* based on *Two-phrase Random Walk*(MC-TRW), which is described in Algorithm 1.

4.3 Dynamic Central Topic Model (DCenTM)

In Section 4.2, the multi-view clustering is used to construct the central topic model. However, as the huge volume of microblog feed stream and with the real-time requirement,

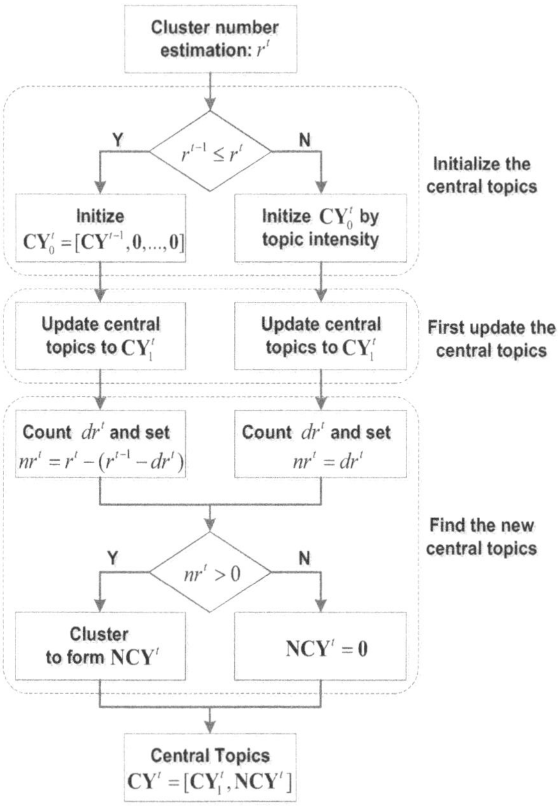

Figure 1: The whole procedure of before-topic inference

applying the multi-view clustering method to mine central topics for every feed batch may not be suitable. Fortunately, rapidly and progressively changed feed stream usually makes two consecutive batches share a certain number of common topics. It means that, if the previous knowledge of the central topics of the $(t-1)^{th}$ batch is acquired, then the central topic of the next stage (i.e., t^{th} batch) can be inferred from it. We name this idea as *before-topic inference*.

Along this line, we propose a dynamic central topic model. In this model, we not only suppose that the two-phase random walk of the multi-view clustering is vital in generating central topics, but also take the before-topic inference idea into consideration to maintain a balance between time consumption and accuracy.

Now, let's discuss how to infer the central topics of the tth batch from that of the $(t-1)^{th}$ batch in detail. Assuming that: 1) central topics of the $(t-1)^{th}$ batch have been obtained by MC-TRW, denoted as $\mathbf{CY}^{t-1}(\in \mathbb{R}^{r^{t-1} \times n^{t-1}})$, where r^{t-1} is the number of the central topics; 2) the latent topics of the tth batch has been obtained by Online-LDA, denoted as the term-topic distribution matrix $\mathbf{Y}^t(\in R^{K \times V})$ and 3) the central topics number of the tth batch has been estimated by its term distribution matrix $\mathbf{Y}^t$, denotes as r^t. This estimation process has been discussed in Section 4.1.2. Then, the central topics $\mathbf{CY}^t$ of the tth batch can be inferred from the $\mathbf{CY}^{t-1}$ and $\mathbf{Y}^t$ with the following steps:

First, initial state of the central topics matrix $\mathbf{CY}_0^t$ is constructed by considering two situations of the relationship between r^{t-1} and r^t:

If $r^{t-1} \le r^t$, select the whole r^{t-1} central topics $\mathbf{CY}^{t-1}$ as a part of initial state of the tth batch's central topics, namely $\mathbf{CY}_0^t = [\mathbf{CY}^{t-1}, \mathbf{0}, ..., \mathbf{0}]$.

If $r^{t-1} > r^t$, select the top-r^t central topics from $\mathbf{CY}^{t-1}$ according to topic cluster size as the initial state of the tth batch's central topics, namely

$$\mathbf{CY}_0^t = [\mathbf{CY}_{1*}^{t-1}, \mathbf{CY}_{2*}^{t-1}, ..., \mathbf{CY}_{r^t*}^{t-1}]$$

where topic cluster size means the included number of the latent topics, and $\mathbf{CY}_i^{t-1}(i = 1*, 2*, ..., r^t*)$ is the row of $\mathbf{CY}^{t-1}$ with the rth largest latent topic cluster.

Second, update the central topics by allocating each latent topic to each existed central topic cluster. By computing the similarity matrix $\mathbf{LC}^t(\in \mathbb{R}^{K \times r^t})$ between each latent topic $\mathbf{Y}_j^t(j = 1, 2, ...K)$ in $\mathbf{Y}^t$ and each initial central topic $\mathbf{CY}_{0j}^t(j = 1, 2, ..., r^t)$ in $\mathbf{CY}_0^t$, each latent topic is allocated to the most similar initial central topic to form the clusters. Thus, each initial central topic is updated by the center of each cluster. The updated central topic matrix is denoted as $\mathbf{CY}_1^t$.

Third, delete the disappeared central topics from the $\mathbf{CY}_1^t$ and add new ones in it. Obviously, not all the central topics inherited from $\mathbf{CY}^{t-1}$ still appear in this batch. That is to say, in matrix $\mathbf{LC}^t$, there may exist columns that all elements are zeroes. Similarly, there may exist some new latent topics that cannot be revealed by the $\mathbf{CY}_1^t$. This situation is manifested as there are some rows in the $\mathbf{LC}^t$ with all elements that are less than a given minimum similarity threshold κ. These elements are the new latent topics, which are not belong to any existed central topics and need to be aggregated as new central topics. As the total central topics number has been estimated, the new central topics numbers nr^t is then inferred from disappeared topics numbers (denoted as dr^t) with the following formula:

$$nr^t = \begin{cases} r^t - (r^{t-1} - dr^t), r^{t-1} \le r^t \\ dr^t, r^{t-1} > r^t \end{cases}$$

With the nr^t and new latent topics, the spectral clustering is then applied to aggregate the new central topics $\mathbf{NCY}^t$. Finally, the central topics $\mathbf{CY}^t$ of the tth batch is the constitution of the new topics $\mathbf{NCY}^t$ and the inherited old topics, namely, $\mathbf{CY}^t = [\mathbf{NCY}^t, \mathbf{CY}_2^t]$, where $\mathbf{CY}_2^t$ is the subset of $\mathbf{CY}_1^t$ in which rows denoting disappeared topics are removed. The whole process is shown in Figure 1.

5. TOPIC PREDICTION

In this section, the focused central topics (called topics for short) are used to predict the trend of the topic intensity in microblog stream. Rather than to track the topic life circle as in [29], we turn to predict the topic trend and intensity, which also reveal the popularity of this topic.

5.1 Topic Trend and Intensity

To put it simply, topic intensity can be measured as the proportion of the topic relevant microblog feeds in a feed batch. A series of intensity values of a certain topic produced by a feed batch sequence compose a time series, which enables the intensity of the topic predicted by regression analysis. However, this way of prediction is far from enough, because some intrinsic characteristics, such as the trend and the fluctuation behind the intensity are more charming. In this study, to model the trend prediction, we assume that the topic intensity consists of two parts: topic trend and topic fluctuation. The former stands for the intrinsic component of the topic intensity, denoted as $\mathbf{TT} = \{TT_i\}(i = 1, 2, ..., T)$, while the latter uncovers the entropy of the topic, denoted as $\mathbf{TF} = \{TF_i\}(i = 1, 2, ..., T)$, T is the time span (i.e., lasting batches number) of topic. Specially, the topic fluctuation in each batch can be evaluated by the inversed entropy of the topic:

$$TF_t = 1/(-\sum_{i=1}^{V_t} p(w_i)\log(p(w_i)))$$

where all the $p(w_i)$ is revealed in the topic term distribution matrix $\mathbf{CY}^t$. In order to integrate $\mathbf{TT}$ and $\mathbf{TF}$ to explain the topic intensity, the two components are normalized to [0, 1] and integrated with Eq.8:

$$TI_t = \mu TT_t + (1-\mu)TF_t \tag{8}$$

where μ is the weight of the trend. Then for a central topic z, the intensity time series can be represented as $\mathbf{TI} = \{TI_i\}(i = 1, 2, ..., T)$. Here, the topic trend is a latent variable, which could not be observed by the present knowledge.

5.2 Kalman Filter-based Prediction

Generally, the Hodrick-Prescott (HP) filter [10] is a reasonable way to extract the trend component in many economic applications. However, as the time series of the topic intensity is not strictly stationary, the HP filter is unaccommodated in this situation. Therefore, we resort this problem to the Kalman filter [11]. Kalman filter is a model for estimating the change of the states recursively in the dynamical system with the help of the relevant observations.

In this paper, the topic life circle can be treated as a stochastic dynamical system, which is mainly composed of topic trend and topic fluctuation. Then the states change along the life circle as:

$$\mathbf{CF}_{t+1} = \mathbf{U}_{t+1,t}\mathbf{CF}_t + \omega_t \tag{9}$$

where $\mathbf{CF}_t = [TT_t, TF_t]^T$ is the combined state, $\mathbf{U}_{t+1,t}$ is a transition matrix from state $\mathbf{CF}_t$ to $\mathbf{CF}_{t+1}$, and ω_t is a Gaussian noise with mean zero and covariance $\mathbf{\Sigma}_{\omega,t}$.

At the same time, the topic intensity formula can be rewritten in matrix style:

$$\mathbf{TI}_t = \mathbf{M}(\mathbf{CF}_t) + \xi_t \tag{10}$$

where $\mathbf{M} = [\mu, (1-\mu)]$ is a measurement matrix, ξ_t is a Gaussian noise with mean zero and covariance $\mathbf{\Sigma}_{\xi,t}$. Eq.9 and Eq.10 altogether define the state space model of the Kalman filter. The former is called as the state equation and the latter is the measurement equation.

In the Kalman filter based topic prediction model, given the topic intensity time series $\{TI_1, TI_2, \cdots, TI_t\}$ and the measurement matrix $\mathbf{M}$, our goal is to predict the topic trend and topic fluctuation factor $\widehat{\mathbf{CF}}_{t+1|t}$ as well as the topic intensity $\widehat{TI}_{t+1|t}$ in time $t+1$, which can be described as follows:

$$\begin{aligned}\widehat{\mathbf{CF}}_{t+1|t} = \mathbf{U}_{t+1,t}(\widehat{\mathbf{CF}}_{t|t-1} + \mathbf{P}_{t|t-1}\mathbf{M}^T(\mathbf{\Sigma}_{\xi,t}\\ +\mathbf{MP}_{t|t-1}\mathbf{M}^T)(TI_t - \mathbf{M}\widehat{\mathbf{CF}}_{t|t-1}))\end{aligned} \tag{11}$$

$$\widehat{TI}_{t+1|t} = \mathbf{M}(\widehat{\mathbf{CF}}_{t+1|t}) + \xi_{t+1} \tag{12}$$

where $\mathbf{P}_{t|t-1} = \mathbb{E}\left[(\mathbf{CF}_t - \widehat{\mathbf{CF}}_{t|t-1})(\mathbf{CF}_t - \widehat{\mathbf{CF}}_{t|t-1})^T\right]$, $\mathbb{E}[.]$ is the expectation operator, and $\widehat{\mathbf{CF}}_{t|t-1}$ is the single step estimation of the state when all the state information is given before t.

By employing the Kalman filter, we can not only predict the topic intensity, but also have an insight into the trend and fluctuation in future step, which uncovers more intrinsic characteristics along the topic life. For multi-step prediction, the topic trend and topic intensity can be calculated iteratively with the computation of Eq.11 and Eq.12.

6. EXPERIMENTAL RESULTS

6.1 Dataset

We evaluate the performance of our approach on two datasets. The first is on the Sina Weibo[3], a popular Chinese microblog service that enables users to post short text messages of up to 140 characters. In this paper, 54 collections of feeds are used as experimental dataset. Each of them is a collection of relevant feeds of a hot event and is crawled by our SNS Hunter[4] by inputting the hashtag and start&end timestamp of the issue. In order to evaluate the performance of the proposed topic models, all of these collections are mixed together in temporal order to form a microblog feed stream. The second is the Twitter user generated contents given by [30].

The Sina Weibo feeds are divided into 102 equal-interval batches (two days per batch), while the Twitter feeds are divided into 462 batches (one day per batch). The detailed information of these two datasets is listed in Table 2.

Table 2: Description of datasets

	Sina Weibo	Twitter
Feeds (after filtering)	6.6 million	2.3 million
Batches	102	462
Time span	2014/01/01 -2014/07/22	2012/10/01 -2014/01/04
Representative events	World Cup Transformers IV CEE	NBA Iphone 5s Game of Thrones

6.2 Topic Model Evaluation

6.2.1 Attribution Weights Estimation

The *review number*, *retweet number*, *text length* and *URL importance* are employed as the attributions to measure the tweets quality. Each feed in the stream gains normalized scores from the four attributions by Eq.1. Ten sequential feed batches are selected for evaluation, and the weights in each batch are presented in Figure 2.

From Figure 2, we can see the weights of these four attributions are approximately the same in every batch, which means our EM based algorithm is an appropriate method to evaluate the weights of different attribution. And this also assures that our initialization in the EM weight scoring is quite reliable. In addition, the review number is a very

[3]http://weibo.com/.
[4]http://sc.whu.edu.cn/.

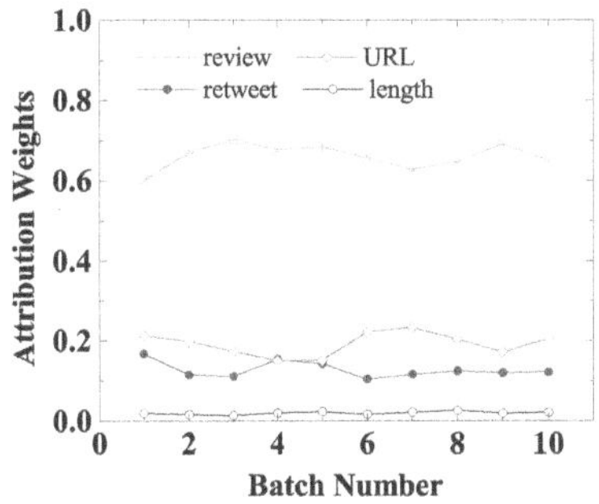

Figure 2: Weights of different attributions

important factor to the contribution of the high quality, which confirms to our cognition of high quality feeds.

6.2.2 Perplexity Evaluation

Generalization ability is a basic indicator for a certain model or a system. Therefore, we use perplexity as a metric to evaluate the topic model's capability of predicting unseen data. Formula of the perplexity is shown as follows:

$$Perp(D_{test}|\mathcal{M}) = \exp\{-\frac{\sum_{d \in D_{test}} \log p(\mathbf{w}_d|\mathcal{M})}{\sum_{d \in D_{test}} V_d}\}$$

where $\mathcal{M}$ is the model learned from training dataset, $p(\mathbf{w}_d|\mathcal{M})$ is the joint probability of all the words in the text d under this model and V_d is the number of words in the text d. A lower perplexity score indicates better generalization ability of the model.

Three baselines are chosen for comparison. The first is called as CenTM-MC, in which the central topics of all batches are generated by MC-TRW. The second is called as CenTM-SP, in which the central topics are generated by spectral clustering of the latent topics. The last is the Online-LDA (O-LDA). All the batches in both two datasets are used to evaluate the perplexity of different models. The latent topic numbers in Sina Weibo dataset are set as 50, 100 and 150 respectively. As for the Twitter dataset, the topic numbers are set as 20, 40 and 60 respectively.

Figure 3(a) and 3(b) show the average perplexity of different topic models with the different latent topic numbers K. In most cases, the perplexity of the DCenTM is the lowest, which demonstrates the considerable generalization ability. At the macroscopic level, with the increasing of K, the perplexity also grows respectively to indicate the lower generalization ability of the numerous topics. Besides, the perplexity among the CenTM-MC, DCenTM and CenTM-SP are quite similar, as they are all based on the theory of LDA and with the clustering of the latent topics. It is also worth noting that the growth of the perplexity of the CenTM-SP behaves sharply in both two datasets, while the CenTM-MC doesn't. This means that the MC-TRW outperforms the spectral clustering in the aggregation of the latent topics. In terms of these two cases, the DCenTM acts the most steadily, while the O-LDA gives an awful result. This enhances our confidence in the robustness of the central topic model in dealing with data streams.

6.2.3 Topic Distinctiveness

The main difference between our central topics and traditional latent topics is the distinctiveness among topics. To evaluate this, the average Kullback-Leibler divergence (KLD) is employed.

As shown in Figure 3(c) and 3(d), the average KL divergence of the central topics (in CenTM-MC, DCenTM and CenTM-SP) are higher than the latent topics (in O-LDA), which indicates that the central topics are more unique than the latent topics. This also has a better accordance with our assumption that the central topics are more event-oriented and share fewer common points.

Apart from the KL divergence, the point-wise mutual information (PMI) is often used to quantitatively measure the coherence of the topics [21]. But in our experiments, we resort to other metrics as the computation of PMI depends on an external corpus. In order to intuitively understand the coherence and distinctiveness of the central topics, we make them correspond to the real world events which are pre-labelled in the dataset. Table 3 depicts the map of the events and the central topics in a certain batch[5]. Here, the central topics in the DCenTM is aggregated by before-topic inference. The symbol "#" represents an event, and each event can be described in different topic terms, e.g., the event "#1 World Cup" comprises of two topic terms, "World Cup" and "Germany". In this feed batch, there exists four true events (#1, #2, #3 and #4), while the estimated central topic number is seven (the sum of the number in the bracket of each topic model). If the number of the central topics is equal to that of the events, then each central topic can be exactly reflected to each event, which lives up to an excellent central topic model, but this can't be always available in real world dataset. The number in the bracket is the occurrence of this central topic. If this number is greater than 1, there must be an overlap between the central topics. In this table, we can see all of the central topics in CenTM-MC and DCenTM are highly consistent with the events, fewer overlaps (Only the World Cup) or fewer vacancies. What's more, they are capable of discovering new topic terms of the events, e.g., the "Graduation" of the event "CEE" (short for College Entrance Examination). Compared with CenTM-MC, DCenTM can uncover the "Germany" from the event "World Cup", which performs the best. However, the central topics of the CenTM-SP are rather poor, as they suffer from overlaps heavily, especially for the central topic "World Cup". Next, we compute the events-topics consistency (ETC) of the CenTM-MC, DCenTM, CenTM-SP and O-LDA with

$$ETC = \frac{|e \cap t|}{|e| + |t| - |e \cap t| + overlap + 1}$$

Here the *overlap* is the number of central topics that occur more than once, e.g., in Table 3, *overlap(CenTM)=3-1=2*, *overlap(CenTM-SP)=6-1=5*. We additionally incorporate the knowledge based topic model LTM[7] as a baseline. As for the latent topics in O-LDA, we compute the ETC in regardless of the overlap to simplify the problem of its looseness. The ETCs of these five methods in ten batches are shown in Figure 3(e) and 3(f). The latent topics number K is set as 50 in Sina Weibo dataset and 20 in Twitter dataset. We can see that the ETC values of the CenTM-MC, DCenTM and CenTM-SP are higher than O-LDA in most cases, which is a powerful evidence for the event-oriented characteristic of the central topics. And because of the simple spectral clustering, the central topics generated by

[5]The map of events and topics is organized manually.

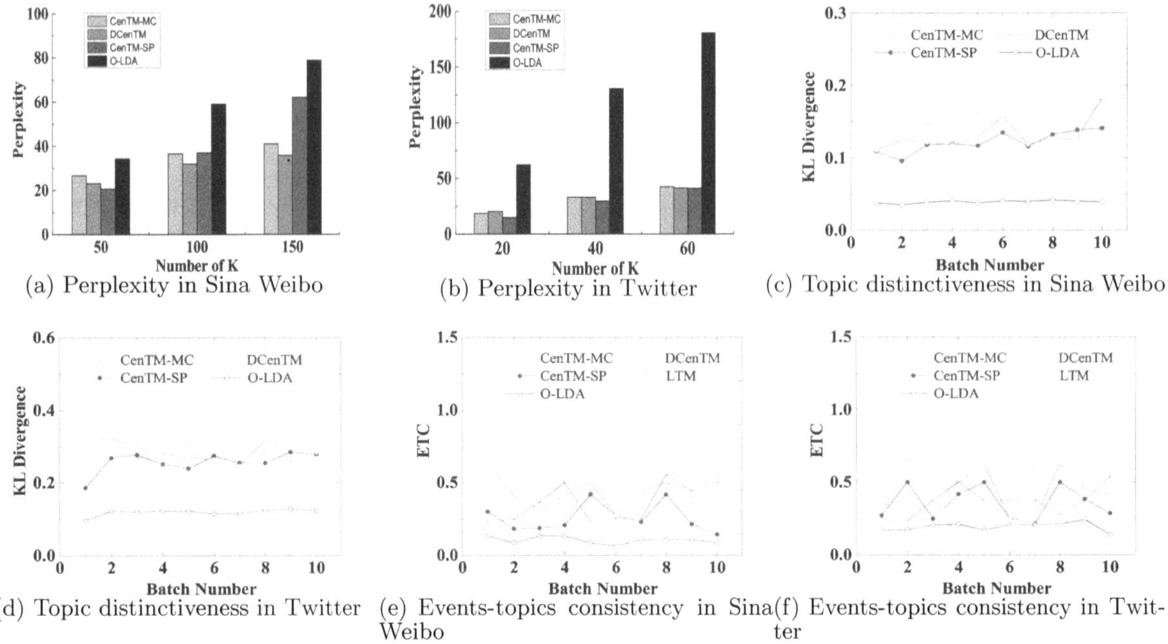

(a) Perplexity in Sina Weibo (b) Perplexity in Twitter (c) Topic distinctiveness in Sina Weibo

(d) Topic distinctiveness in Twitter (e) Events-topics consistency in Sina Weibo (f) Events-topics consistency in Twitter

Figure 3: Topic model evaluation

CenTM-SP are not event-oriented enough, so the ETCs of the CenTM-SP are clearly lower than those of the CenTM-MC and DCenTM. The performance of LTM is quite similar ro DCenTM, because its topics are released according to knowledge. However, as its topic number is fixed, it can not deal with the topic overlap, resulting in slightly lower ETCs compared with DCenTM.

6.2.4 *Scalability*

Based on the model evaluation methods proposed in Section 6.2.3, we compare the running time of CenTM-MC with DCenTM. They are implemented on ten sequential batches in Sina Weibo dataset to obtain central topics respectively and the running time of them is presented in Figure 4(a). Obviously, the running time of CenTM-MC and DCenTM are strictly equal in some batches. In these cases, the central topics are all aggregated by the MC-TRW. As for the other cases, the central topics in DCenTM are generated by before-topic inference, which costs less time in comparison to the MC-TRW. From the results in Figure 4(b) and 4(c), we may also see that, to process a certain number of feeds, the running time of DCenTM grows more slowly than the CenTM-MC and CenTM-SP, indicating a better scalability in data streams. Unlike these three models, the LTM needs to execute LDA and frequent itemset mining as to obtain knowledge in advance, so it seems a little more time-consuming.

6.3 Topic Prediction Evaluation

In this section, we mainly evaluate the accuracy of the topic trend prediction as well as the topic intensity prediction. Obviously, the topics are all referred to the central topics unless with special address.

With Eq.11 and Eq.12, we can compute and update the topic trend and intensity alternately to approach the destination. However, in this case, the state transition matrix $\mathbf{U}$ is not a fixed one, which is different from the standard linear Kalman filter. In our scenario, the states are the trend and the fluctuation (related to topic entropy) with no dependency, thus $\mathbf{U}$ is a two-dimension diagonal matrix. Since the observed topic intensity has a positive correlation with the latent trend factor, so the first diagonal value of $\mathbf{U}_{t,t-1}$ can be estimated by the slope between TI_{t-1} and TI_t while the second diagonal value of $\mathbf{U}_{t,t-1}$ can be estimated by the slope between TF_{t-1} and TF_t. For the $\mathbf{U}_{t+1,t}$, a stepwise Support Vector Regression(SVR) [8] can be taken into the observation of the topic intensity and fluctuation before time $t+1$.

For Sina Weibo dataset, experiments are conducted on the topics between June 2, 2014 and July 21, 2014 with totally 25 time points (two days per time point). Specifically, we choose the *World Cup* as the example to perform the multi-step prediction. We therefore release the topic intensity series from June 2 to July 11 to predict the topic intensity and trend in the next five points. For the Twitter dataset, we choose the event *NBA*. Its selected time span is from November 28, 2013 to December 22, 2013, also with totally 25 time points, and the last 5 points are left out to verify the prediction. We name our prediction method as KFP, meanwhile the SVR is employed as a baseline.

As the trend is a latent intrinsic factor uncovered by the Kalman filter model, there is no such thing as the standard trend value. However, according to Eq.8, once the intensity and the fluctuation are fixed, the trend can also be calculated respectively and this value of trend can be regarded as the standard trend for evaluation. Here, we set the weight of the trend μ to 0.8, and then we use the residual as the measurement to present the results of the prediction.

Figure 5 shows the topic trend, fluctuation and intensity along all the tested time points in Sina Weibo dataset. We can find that the fluctuation changes steadily along the time, and the trend is tightly coherent with the intensity. What's

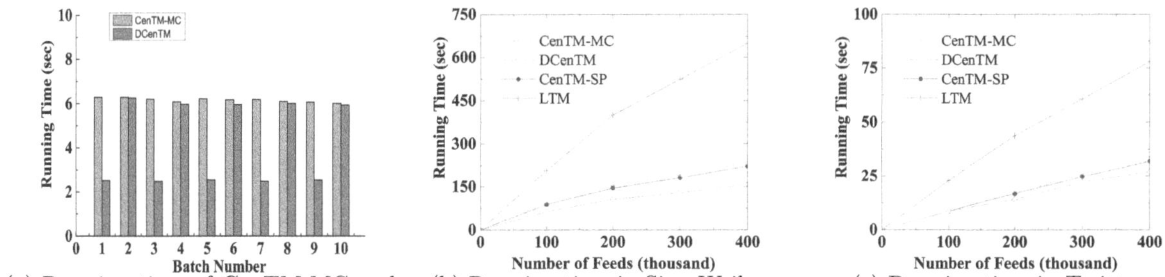

(a) Running time of CenTM-MC and DCenTM on different batches (b) Running time in Sina Weibo (c) Running time in Twitter

Figure 4: Scalability evaluation

Table 3: Map of events and central topics

	CenTM-MC	DCenTM	CenTM-SP
Events	Central Topics	Central Topics	Central Topics
#1 World Cup	#1 World Cup(3)	#1 World Cup(2) #1 Germany(1)	#1 World Cup(6)
#2 Transformers IV	#2 Optimus Prime(1)	#2 Optimus Prime(1)	
#3 CEE(College Entrance Examination)	#3 CEE(1) #3 Graduation(1)	#3 CEE(1) #3 Graduation(1)	#3 Examinee(1)
#4 Dog Meat	#4 Dog Meat(1)	#4 Dog Meat(1)	

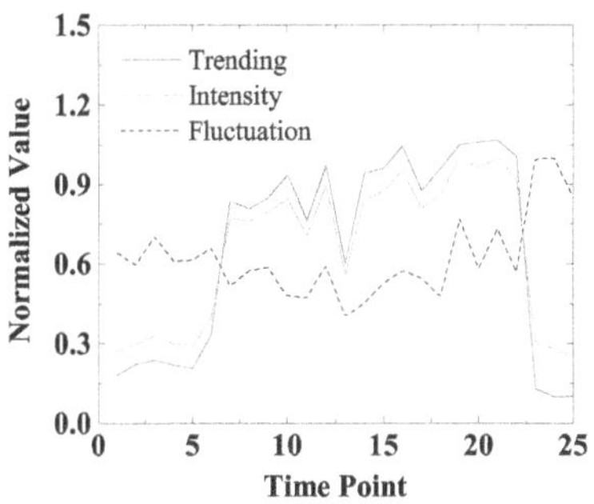

Figure 5: A depiction of topic intensity, trend and fluctuation

more, we get the trend and intensity at a local maximum around the 22nd time point (in July14&15). It is well known that the final of the *World Cup* was held in July 14, thus the discussions explode heavily in this time point. After the world cup, the number of the relevant feeds decreases sharply, which leads to the decline of the topic intensity and trend. Because of this sudden change of the topic, the fluctuation also behaves unnaturally compared with the previous trace.

Table 4 describes the relative residuals of the multi-step prediction in both two datasets. In Table 4, the "I" represents the intensity, "T" represents the trend and the "F" represents the fluctuation. The left list in each column indicates our method KFP, while the right one denotes the baseline SVR. The results in Table 4 demonstrate that our prediction method outperforms the SVR in both the single step and multi-step cases in considering of the relative residual. Furthermore, with the step increasing, the errors of the prediction become much severe in both of the KFP and SVR. We also should note that the residuals for the second step in Twitter dataset are abnormally higher than the rest steps, this is because with the pausity of relevant tweets in that day, the prediction accuracy becomes more impressionable. This will motivate us to establish a more robust prediction framework in the future.

7. CONCLUSIONS

In this study, we address the challenges of mining meaningful topics in microblog feed stream. Based on the multi-view characteristic of the latent topics, we propose a novel central topic model with the combination of multi-view clustering in two-phase random walk and develop it with before-topic inference to better fit the stream. The proposed model is able to generate event-oriented topics for static feed collections as well as the feed stream, and can be reasonably applied in real-time applications. We choose central topics rather than latent topics to fulfill the predefined mining tasks. Experimental results show that our approach can establish topic models with high generalization ability. Meanwhile, these topic models can extract a group of central topics that are event-oriented and more discriminative between each other. In addition, the central topics perform well in the application of the topic trend prediction.

8. ACKNOWLEDGMENTS

This research is supported by the Natural Science Foundation of China(No.61472291, No.61272110, No.71420107026), and the China Postdoctoral Science Foundation under contract No.2014M562070.

9. REFERENCES

[1] L. AlSumait, D. Barbará, and C. Domeniconi. On-line lda: Adaptive topic models for mining text streams with applications to topic detection and tracking. In *ICDM*, pages 3–12, 2008.

Table 4: Relative residual of the multi-step prediction

	Sina Weibo						Twitter					
Step	KFP-I	SVR-I	KFP-T	SVR-T	KFP-F	SVR-F	KFP-I	SVR-I	KFP-T	SVR-T	KFP-F	SVR-F
1	0.093	0.304	0.071	0.339	0.143	0.165	0.129	0.128	0.275	0.196	0.005	0.024
2	0.124	0.244	0.277	0.305	0.001	0.001	0.254	0.267	0.259	0.389	0.035	0.029
3	0.282	0.372	0.382	0.572	0.427	0.429	0.084	0.096	0.104	0.127	0.008	0.012
4	0.338	0.395	0.528	0.602	0.427	0.432	0.096	0.105	0.120	0.134	0.022	0.025
5	0.360	0.424	0.525	0.603	0.277	0.281	0.120	0.151	0.268	0.202	0.010	0.019

[2] P. André, M. S. Bernstein, and K. Luther. Who gives a tweet?: Evaluating microblog content value. In *CSCW*, pages 471–474, 2012.

[3] S. Ardon, A. Bagchi, A. Mahanti, A. Ruhela, A. Seth, R. M. Tripathy, and S. Triukose. Spatio-temporal and events based analysis of topic popularity in twitter. In *CIKM*, pages 219–228, 2013.

[4] D. M. Blei and J. D. Lafferty. Dynamic topic models. In *ICML*, pages 113–120, 2006.

[5] D. M. Blei, A. Y. Ng, and M. I. Jordan. Latent dirichlet allocation. *The Journal of Machine Learning Research*, 3:993–1022, 2003.

[6] A. Blum and T. Mitchell. Combining labeled and unlabeled data with co-training. In *COLT*, pages 92–100, 1998.

[7] Z. Chen and B. Liu. Topic modeling using topics from many domains, lifelong learning and big data. In *ICML*, pages 703–711, 2014.

[8] H. Drucker, C. J. Burges, L. Kaufman, A. Smola, and V. Vapnik. Support vector regression machines. *Advances in neural information processing systems*, 9:155–161, 1997.

[9] S. Günnemann, I. Färber, and T. Seidl. Multi-view clustering using mixture models in subspace projections. In *SIGKDD*, pages 132–140, 2012.

[10] R. J. Hodrick and E. C. Prescott. Postwar us business cycles: An empirical investigation. *Journal of Money, Credit, and Banking*, 29(1):1–16, 1997.

[11] R. E. Kalman. A new approach to linear filtering and prediction problems. *Journal of Fluids Engineering*, 82(1):35–45, 1960.

[12] A. Kumar and H. D. III. A co-training approach for multi-view spectral clustering. In *ICML*, pages 393–400, 2011.

[13] C. Li, A. Sun, and A. Datta. Twevent: segment-based event detection from tweets. In *CIKM*, pages 155–164, 2012.

[14] J. Liu, C. Wang, J. Gao, and J. Han. Multi-view clustering via joint nonnegative matrix factorization. In *SDM*, pages 252–260, 2013.

[15] T. Milo, T. Zur, and E. Verbin. Boosting topic-based publish-subscribe systems with dynamic clustering. In *SIGMOD*, pages 749–760, 2007.

[16] M. Musleh. Spatio-temporal visual analysis for event-specific tweets. In *SIGMOD*, pages 1611–1612, 2014.

[17] A. Y. Ng, M. I. Jordan, and Y. Weiss. On spectral clustering: Analysis and an algorithm. *Advances in neural information processing systems*, 2:849–856, 2002.

[18] F. Pan, X. Zhang, and W. Wang. Crd: Fast co-clustering on large datasets utilizing sampling-based matrix decomposition. In *SIGMOD*, pages 173–184, 2008.

[19] M. Peng, J. Huang, and H. Fu. High quality microblog extraction based on multiple features fusion and time-frequency transformation. In *WISE*, pages 188–201, 2013.

[20] A. Popescu and M. Pennacchiotti. Detecting controverisal events from twitter. In *CIKM*, pages 1873–1876, 2010.

[21] M. Röder, A. Both, and A. Hinneburg. Exploring the space of topic coherence measures. In *WSDM*, pages 399–408, 2015.

[22] T. Sakaki, M. Okazaki, and Y. Matsuo. Earthquake shakes twitter users: real-time event detection by social sensors. In *WWW*, pages 851–860, 2010.

[23] K. Sasaki, T. Yoshikawa, and T. Furuhashi. Online topic model for twitter considering dynamics of user interests and topic trends. In *EMNLP*, pages 1977–1985, 2014.

[24] A. Silberstein, J. Terrace, B. F. Cooper, and R. Ramakrishnan. Feeding frenzy: selectively materializing users' event feeds. In *SIGMOD*, pages 831–842, 2010.

[25] H. Tong, C. Faloutsos, and J.-Y. Pan. Fast random walk with restart and its applications. In *ICDM*, pages 613–622, 2006.

[26] M. Tsytsarau, T. Palpanas, and M. Castellanos. Dynamics of news events and social media reaction. In *SIGKDD*, pages 901–910, 2014.

[27] Y. Wang, E. Agichtein, and M. Benzi. Tm-lda: Efficient online modeling of latent topic transitions in social media. In *SIGKDD*, pages 123–131, 2012.

[28] Y. Xu, T. Lin, W. Lam, Z. Zhou, H. Cheng, and A. M.-C. So. Latent aspect mining via exploring sparsity and intrinsic information. In *CIKM*, pages 879–888, 2014.

[29] X. Yang, A. Ghoting, Y. Ruan, and S. Parthasarathy. A framework for summarizing and analyzing twitter feeds. In *SIGKDD*, pages 370–378, 2012.

[30] X. Zhu, Z.-Y. Ming, and Y. Hao. Customized organization of social media contents using focused topic hierarchy. In *CIKM*, pages 1509–1518, 2014.

[31] M. Zimmermann, I. Ntoutsi, Z. F. Siddiqui, M. Spiliopoulou, and H.-P. Kriegel. Discovering global and local bursts in a stream of news. In *SAC*, pages 807–812, 2012.

Video Popularity Prediction by Sentiment Propagation via Implicit Network

Wanying Ding
College of Computing and Informatics,Drexel University
Philadelphia, PA, 19104, USA
wd78@drexel.edu

Yue Shang
College of Computing and Informatics,Drexel University
Philadelphia, PA, 19104, USA
ys439@drexel.edu

Lifan Guo
TCL Research American
San Jose, CA, 95134, USA
guolifan@tcl.com

Xiaohua Hu
College of Computing and Informatics,Drexel University
Philadelphia, PA, 19104, USA
xh29@drexel.edu

Rui Yan
School of Computer, Central China Normal University
Wuhan, Hubei, 430079, China
yanrui@mail.ccnu.edu.cn

Tingting He
School of Computer, Central China Normal University
Wuhan, Hubei, 430079, China
tthe@mail.ccnu.edu.cn

ABSTRACT

Video popularity prediction plays a foundational role in many aspects of life, such as recommendation systems and investment consulting. Because of its technological and economic importance, this problem has been extensively studied for years. However, four constraints have limited most related works' usability. First, most feature oriented models are inadequate in the social media environment, because many videos are published with no specific content features, such as a strong cast or a famous script. Second, many studies assume that there is a linear correlation existing between view counts from early and later days, but this is not the case in every scenario. Third, numerous works just take view counts into consideration, but discount associated sentiments. Nevertheless, it is the public opinions that directly drive a video's final success/failure. Also, many related approaches rely on a network topology, but such topologies are unavailable in many situations. Here, we propose a Dual Sentimental Hawkes Process (DSHP) to cope with all the problems above. DSHP's innovations are reflected in three ways: (1) it breaks the "Linear Correlation" assumption, and implements Hawkes Process; (2) it reveals deeper factors that affect a video's popularity; and (3) it is topology free. We evaluate DSHP on four types of videos: Movies, TV Episodes, Music Videos, and Online News, and compare its performance against 6 widely used models, including Translation Model, Multiple Linear Regression, KNN Regression, ARMA, Reinforced Poisson Process, and Univariate Hawkes Process. Our model outperforms all of the others, which indicates a promising application prospect.

Permission to make digital or hard copies of all or part of this work for personal or classroom use is granted without fee provided that copies are not made or distributed for profit or commercial advantage and that copies bear this notice and the full citation on the first page. Copyrights for components of this work owned by others than ACM must be honored. Abstracting with credit is permitted. To copy otherwise, or republish, to post on servers or to redistribute to lists, requires prior specific permission and/or a fee. Request permissions from Permissions@acm.org.

CIKM'15, October 19–23, 2015, Melbourne, Australia.

© 2015 ACM.

ISBN 978-1-4503-3794-6/15/10 ...$15.00.
DOI: http://dx.doi.org/10.1145/2806416.2806505.

Categories and Subject Descriptors

I.2.6 [**Artificial Intelligence**]: Learning—*Knowledge acquisition*; H.3.5 [**Information Storage and Retrieval**]: Online Information Service—*Web-based services*

General Terms

Algorithms; Experimentation; Performance

Keywords

Popularity Prediction; Hawkes Process; Sentiment Propagation; Point Process

1. INTRODUCTION

Videos are everywhere. Because they facilitate a complete visual connection and help a strong emotional communication, videos are becoming a preferred carrier for information exchanging online. According to statistics, 75 million U.S. Internet users watch videos online every day, and by 2016, videos will drive 55% of all consumer traffic worldwide[1]. However, users' attention is not symmetrically distributed among all videos. Only a few of them can attract massive attention, and the rest will be left to languish. Thus, an ability to predict the potential popularity of a video may facilitate the design and management of a wide range of systems or services, such as recommendation systems and targeted advertising[23]. Although popularity modeling and predicting has been deeply and extensively explored over decades, several constraints make most of them inefficient for a wide range of applications.

Feature oriented methods are ineffective for many user generated videos. Over the last century, methods, like *Linear Regression* and *Neural Network*, have achieved great success in movies' box office predictions[12, 13], but they could not fit all videos well. Many videos, especially the ones generated by ordinary users, have no significant content features(e.g. strong cast, famous scripts or specific genres) for such methods to work.

[1]http://digitalmunch.tv/importance-of-video-to-promote-your-brand/

Purely count derivation oriented methods could not provide an insight about the mechanisms that drive a video's popularity. In many cases, we want to know not only which videos will be popular, but also why they could be popular. Since Meeyoung-Cha et al.[3] claimed that a YouTube video's popularity is mostly determined by its early view counts, a great number of regression or classification extended approaches[23, 26, 30, 21, 9, 24, 33] have been built. These models aim to simulate the accrual of early views and/or vote counts, and then predict the long-term dynamics. But, such methods fail to reveal the underlying factors that make a video's success. In addition, this "Linear Correlation" assumption on the view counts between early and later days has been challenged by Haito-Li et al.[15], when they explored another social media platform. We also find a noticeable lower correlation between the view counts on early and later days. Figure 1 presents four videos' view evolutions from douban.com[2]. From the views of early days, Video B shows a much more promising potential than Video A, but actually Video A has a more successful outcome than Video B.

Most network-dynamics-oriented studies rely on network topologies[3][15, 14, 6, 2, 27]. Based on a topology, they simulate the "word of mouth" process to predict each video's final popularity. However, there are several challenges in real applications. First, it turns out to be very difficult, if not impossible, to obtain a complete network. Many researchers have to conduct experiments on an incomplete or simulated network; approximation will bring unavoidable inaccuracies. Second, in many scenarios, networks are implicit or even unknown[31]; we can only observe who watches a video, but cannot know from where/whom he/she hears about it. In addition, a video's popularity results not only from the "word of mouth" process, but also from many other influences, such as a video's promotions. A friend's recommendation as well as an attractive billboard could be the reason that makes one watch a video. Obviously, the network-dynamics-oriented methods do not take the latter factor into consideration.

The "Homogeneous Node" assumption is implied in other related research, but it has overlooked the importance of sentiments in the real world. However, it is the public's opinions that often determine a video's success. Intuitively, positive comments will trigger more future views, while negative ones will discourage potential audiences. Taking Figure 1 as an example, although Video B seems to be more appealing at the beginning, its overwhelming negative criticism has already indicated a rapid decline in its view count. On the contrary, despite the initial dissatisfaction, Video A's preponderant positive feedback foresees its future success. Moreover, sentiments will reveal more interesting insights about a video. Video C receives a lot of favorable comments at the beginning, but the devastating negative feedback comes quickly in great numbers later on; Video D seems to be very unpromising at first, but it gains a better reputation over time. The specific reasons how people change their attitude towards a video go beyond the scope of this paper, but this is really inspiring for sociologists and related researchers to explore.

[2]http://www.douban.com/. It is a popular website for users to exchange opinions about videos and books in China

[3]the way in which constituent nodes are interrelated or arranged

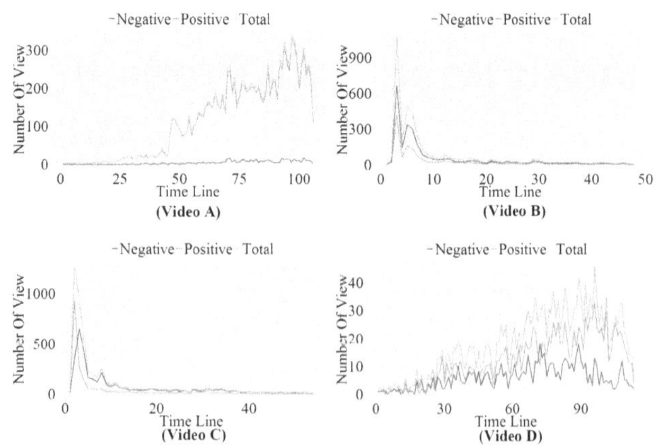

Figure 1: Evolution Patterns of Four Videos from Douban.

In our study, we build a Dual Sentimental Hawkes Process(DSHP) to model videos' watching propagation dynamics. Compared to other related works, DSHP could provide more insightful perspectives and more explanatory results. Generally speaking, this paper has three contributions:

(1) It builds a novel model, DSHP, for video popularity prediction. DSHP has achieved even better performances compared to Multiple Linear Regression, KNN Regression, Autoregressive Moving Average Model, and Reinforced Poisson Process, which are currently the most popular and widely used models.

(2) DSHP reveals more detailed underlying patterns and mechanisms that drive a video's final success. This paper has analyzed various factors(*Exogenous Impact*, *Endogenous Impact*, *Sentiment Impact* and *Sentiment Transfer Pattern Impact*) to conclude their influences on a video's popularity propagation.

(3) We use four important types of videos: Movies, TV Episodes, Music Videos, and Online News, to examine DSHP. We have detected their respective propagation characteristics. In addition, we have constructed four sub-datasets: Elitist Movies, Popcorn Movies, Niche Movies, and Flop Movies from the movie dataset. Based on these sub-datasets, we implement DSHP on each of them, and have found the essential factors which make a movie's popularity.

The rest of this paper is organized as follows. We introduce some related research in Section 2. Section 3 elaborates DSHP's work mechanisms. Section 4 presents our experiment and evaluation details. We conclude in Section 5.

2. RELATED WORK

Popularity prediction is a vast research domain, and has attracted research interests from many fields. Just as mentioned above, even though various theories and models have been proposed [23, 12, 13, 3, 26, 30, 21, 9, 24, 33, 15, 14, 6, 2, 27], improvement is still needed. The most similar studies to our model are the implicit network propagation approaches, which imply the epidemiological process in information diffusion simulation. SIS and SIR are two seminal prototypes in related studies[19, 20]. Both of SIS and SIR classify the nodes into different types, and focus on the evolution of the proportions of nodes in each class[8]. In SIS and SIR, S stands for *Susceptible*, I stands for *Infectious*, and R stands for *Recovered.* In SIR, S class nodes have a fixed probability β to switch to class I, and I class nodes have a fixed probability γ to switch to class R, while in SIS, I class nodes have a fixed probability γ to switch back to class S. However, both of these models have a very strong assumption (fixed value) about the influence parameters, while in a real social network, influence will not be evenly distributed.

Jiqiang-Wu et al.[29] extend SIR to model two hidden processes embedded in a popularity dynamic process, *Information Spreading Process* and *User Reaction Process*, to capture the important underlying factors that drive an individual video's popularity. However, this work still inherits the fixed parameter assumption from SIR. In addition, it only makes a theoretical exploration and is hard to be directly used in a practical scenario.

Yang et al.[31] relaxes the fixed parameter assumption by constructing time-dependent influence functions for each node. They have developed a LIM (Linear Influence Model) to simulate the dynamic information diffusion processes, and the number of activated nodes in each time episode is affected by the sum of influences coming from the previous activated nodes. The influence functions are represented in a non-parametric way, breaking the fixed parameter assumption in SIS and SIR. But the assumption that all nodes are homogeneously activated has undermined the ability of this model.

Hua-Wei Shen et al.[25] proposes a Reinforced Poisson Process to predict popularity. By implementing a temporal relaxation function corresponding to agings in attracting new attention, and a reinforcement mechanism documenting the well-known "rich get richer" phenomenon, their study achieves flexibility and a strong ability to model popularity dynamics. However, it is really a challenge to use a single Poisson process to model a complicated situation.

Riley and Didier[4] first claim that both exogenous and endogenous are two important ingredients that function in social network information propagation. They have introduced a self-excited Hawkes process to model popularity dynamics, and proved that the Hawkes process has a promising predictive power. Inspired by this work, many derivative models have been proposed in recent years to solve various problems in social media[17, 32, 16, 34, 1]. Most models just implement a single self-excited Hawkes process, while the real world is too complicated to be comprehensively represented by a single process

This paper also implements Hawkes process as the fundamental framework to predict videos' popularity. In this paper, we propose a Dual Sentimental Hawkes Process(DSHP) to solve the problems in existing popularity prediction studies. Compared to previous works, the strengths of DSHP are: (1) it enables time-varying infection strength; (2) it models the interaction between inhomogeneous nodes; and (3) it takes various possible influential factors into consideration.

3. PROBLEM DEFINITION AND MODEL DESCRIPTION

In this part, we first define precisely three factors contributing to our model, namely *Exogenous Impact*, *Endogenous Impact*, and *Sentiment.* Then we will formally state our problem definition and model description.

Exogenous Impact or Immigrant Impact denotes the factor that is **not** affected by the "*Word of Mouth*" process, such as the stars' effect or a video's trailers. For example, if one is a big fan of *Beyonce*, he/she will watch everyone of her music videos spontaneously without any previous influences from his/her social network.

Endogenous Impact denotes the factor that is affected by the "*Word of Mouth*" process. For example, it is highly likely for a user to watch a video that is strongly recommended by his/her friends.

Sentiment denotes the factor that reflects users' attitude towards a video. In this paper, we range the sentiment in $\{1, 2\}$, where "1" indicates a *Positive* attitude, and "2" indicates a *Negative* attitude. Clearly, *sentiment* could be either inferred from comments or expressed via thumbs up or down of a video.

Now let us consider a typical scenario where n watchers choose to watch a video v, and these n watchers come in a sequence of $\{t_i\}(t_{i-1} \le t_i$, and $i \in [1, n])$, where t_i indicates the time stamp when watcher i views the video. These n watchers are intrigued by either the exogenous impact or the endogenous impact. After viewing this video, an individual i might have a sentiment $s_i(i \in [1, n]$, and $s_i \in \{1, 2\})$ towards this video.

In this section, we show how we predict video v's popularity based on this $\{(t_i, s_i)\}$ sequence by taking all of the exogenous impact, endogenous impact, and sentiment into consideration. Just as defined by most of similar studies, we use each video's view count as its popularity indication.

3.1 Hawkes Process

Temporal point process has been widely used to describe data that are localized at a finite set of time points[5]. We denote the historical view process as $H_{t-} = \{t_1, t_2, ...t_i : t_i \le t_{i+1}\}$, and the probability of an event occurring at time t can be defined as $\lambda(t|H_{t-})$ according to a point process definition. Thus the expected number of views at time t can be defined as $\Lambda(t|H_{t-}) = \int_0^t \lambda(s|H_{s-})ds = E[N(t)|H_{t-}]$[28]. The question here is how to design a proper $\lambda(t|H_{t-})$ to fit the scenario to be analyzed.

Hawkes Process[11] is an important class of point processes, and has been successfully applied in many areas. The formulation of Hawkes Process is shown as in Equation(1) where μ is called as "Immigrant Function", and $\Phi(t|H_{t-})$ is called as "Response Function". Just as shown in Equation(1),the advantage of Hawkes Process is that it can combine two very different factors, μ and $\Phi(t|H_{t-})$, to simulate reality.

$$\lambda(t|H_{t-}) = \mu + \Phi(t|H_{t-}) \tag{1}$$

where $\Phi(t|H_{t-}) = \sum_{t_j<t} \phi(t - t_j)$.

A Hawkes process should meet the following three assumptions[11]: (1)$\mu \ge 0$, and $\phi(v) \ge 0$, if $v \ge 0$, (2) $\phi(v) = 0$,if $v < 0$,and (3) $\int_0^\infty \phi(v)dv \le 1$ to ensure stationary. These assumptions imply that: $\phi(v) = \eta * f(v; \sigma)$, where $0 \le \eta \le 0$, and $f(v; \sigma)$ is a probability density function with parameter σ. Under this parameterization, η is referred as the *Intensity Parameter*, $f(v; \sigma)$ is the *Response Kernel*, and σ is the *Kernel Parameter.* Thus Equation(1) can be transformed to Equation(2).

$$\lambda(t) = \mu + \eta * \sum_{t_j<t} f(t - t_j; \sigma) \tag{2}$$

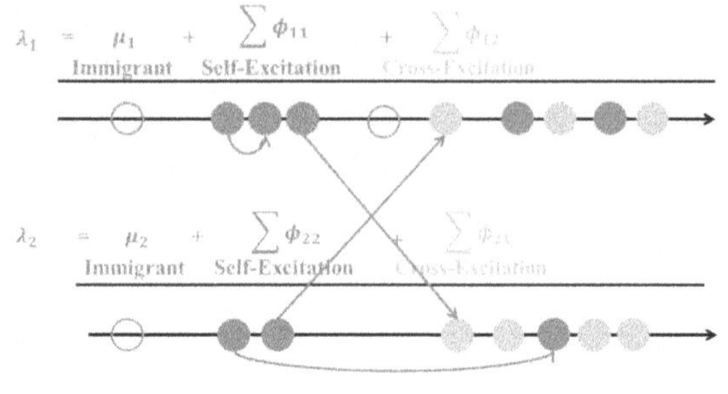

Figure 2: Mechanism of DSHP.

where t is the current time stamp, and s is the time stamp by which event in time t is triggered.

3.2 Dual Sentimental Hawkes Process(DSHP)

Sentiments play essential roles in videos' popularity propagation processes. Generally speaking, we are most concerned with two kinds of sentiments: *Positive* and *Negative*, and they might self-evolve laterally or cross-affect reciprocally.

Commonly, there are three scenarios when a user might choose to watch a video. To make a simple explanation, we take the positive sentiment process as an example.

(1) Exogenous(or Immigrant) Impact. Movies, for instance, usually have fancy trailers before they are released. The trailer might exert a positive impact on viewers, and intrigue a large audience to make their plan to watch. The *Immigrant Function* μ in Hawkes process(shown in Equation(2)) could be used to formulize this influence. However, different from Equation(2), which assumes μ as a constant, we will implement a more flexible function $\mu(t)$ to fit our scenario

(2) Self-Excitation(One Component of Endogenous Impact). Friends' recommendations might intrigue one to watch a video, and after watching it, he/she might also have a positive opinion about it. This positive to positive(PosPos) sentiment transfer describes a self-excitation process, and can be formulized by a *Self Response Function* ϕ_{ii}.

(3) Cross-Excitation(One Component of Endogenous Impact). Friends' complaints could also intrigue one to watch a video, since he/she wants to know how bad it is. However, it often happens that he/she finds the video is not as bad as imagined, and worth a watch. This negative to positive(NegPos) sentiment transfer describes a cross-excitation process, and can be formulized by a *Cross Response Function* ϕ_{ij}.

We use Figure 2 to demonstrate the whole process. In Figure 2, the upper line indicates the positive process and the lower one indicates the negative process. Taking the positive process as an example, a positive individual might be affected by the exogenous influence(the hollow circle), the self-excitation impact(the red solid circle) or the cross-excitation impact(the green solid circle). Equivalently, the mathematical formation of the intensity rate function of DSHP can be represented as Equation(3), where $i, j \in \{1, 2\}$

$$\lambda_i(t) = \mu_i(t) + \sum_{t_{i,k}<t} \phi_{ii}(t - t_{i,k}) + \sum_{t_{j,l}<t} \phi_{ij}(t - t_{j,l}) \quad (3)$$

In a real application, Immigrant Function $\mu_i(t)$ and Response Functions(including $\phi_{ii}(t-t_{i,k})$(Self Response Function) and $\phi_{ij}(t - t_{j,l})$(Cross Response Function)) in Equation(3) need to be instantiated. In the video propagation scenario, we use the kernels mentioned in Section 3.3 to function.

3.3 Kernel Selection

3.3.1 Immigrant Function

In most related studies, μ is treated as a constant[28]. However, in a real situation, it is hard to make such a strong assertion. According to the *Information Cascading Theory*, individuals are inclined to abandon their own private signals in favor of inferences based on earlier people's behavior in the social network. Most hardened fans will be activated at the very beginning, and as time goes on, more and more people will make their viewing decisions according to social signals instead of their private signals. Thus, it is more reasonable to model μ as a decreasing function than as a constant.

The Pareto Distribution is a power law probability distribution that is frequently being used in description of social observable phenomenon, and video watching is exactly a social phenomenon. Thus in this paper, we use the Pareto distribution as the immigrant function. The formulation of the Pareto distribution can be written as Equation(4), where α_i is the immigrant parameter controlling the shape of the this function, and the scale parameter is simplified to be 1 in this paper.

$$\mu_i(t) = \frac{\alpha_i}{t^{(\alpha_i+1)}} \quad (4)$$

3.3.2 Response Function

There are two kinds of response functions: *Self Response Function* and *Cross Response Function*. To make a simple illustration, we use the same function to model both of them. According to Hawkes Process's definition, the response function $\phi(v; \sigma)$ could be detailed as $\eta * f(v; \sigma)$ (Equation(1) and Equation(2)), where η is referred to as the *Intensity Parameter*, $f(t - t_{i,k}, \sigma)$ the *Response Kernel*, and σ is the *Kernel Parameter*.

Exponential, Power-law and Rayleigh distribution are the three most widely used functions in modeling diffusion over networks[7], but exponential and power-law are strict decreasing models. However, a strict decreasing assumption is too strong to apply in a real situation. Just like an infection, the likelihood one responds to a message might rise to a peak and then drop, since he/she needs time to watch the video mentioned by his/her friends, and then give a reaction. Rayleigh distribution, which is previously used in epidemiology, is a non-monotonic parametric model that can fit this situation. Thus, this paper chooses Rayleigh distribution as the response kernel. The Rayleigh distribution can be written as Equation(5)

$$f(x) = \frac{x}{\sigma_2} e^{-\frac{x^2}{2\sigma^2}} \quad (5)$$

Taking cross response function as an example, the whole response function can be illustrated as Equation(6).

$$\phi_{ij}(t - t_k; \sigma_{ij}) = \eta_{ij} * (\sum_{t_k<t} \frac{x}{\sigma_{ij}^2} e^{-\frac{x^2}{2\sigma_{ij}^2}}) \quad (6)$$

and complete intensity rate function can be written as Equation(7). We have 10 parameters,α_i, α_j, η_{ii}, η_{ij}, η_{ji}, η_{jj}, σ_{ii},

σ_{ij}, σ_{ji}, σ_{jj},to optimize. This paper adopts an EM to make parameter inference and optimization.

$$\lambda(t) = \sum_{i,j\in\{1,2\}} (\frac{\alpha_i}{t^{(\alpha_i+1)}} + \sum_{t_{i,k}<t} \eta_{ii} * \frac{(t-t_{i,k})}{\sigma_{ii}^2} e^{-\frac{(t-t_{i,k})^2}{2\sigma_{ii}^2}} + \sum_{t_{j,l}<t} \eta_{ij} * \frac{(t-t_{j,l})}{\sigma_{ij}^2} e^{-\frac{(t-t_{j,l})^2}{2\sigma{ij}^2}}) \quad (7)$$

3.4 Parameter Inference with EM

Equation(3) establishes the equivalence with the following four statistical statements: (1) The number of spontaneous individuals in sentiment i over the interval $[0,T]$ is a Poisson process with rate $\mu_i(t)$. (2) The number of self-excited individuals to event $t_{i,k}$ over the interval $[t_{i,k},T]$ is a Poisson process with rate $\phi_{ii}(t-t_{i,k})$. (3) The number of cross-excited individuals to event $t_{j,l}$ over the interval $[t_{j,l},T]$ is a Poisson process with rate $\phi_{ij}(t-t_{j,l})$. (4) All of the Poisson processes in (1)-(3) are independent.

In this scenario, if we can detect to which Poisson process each individual belongs, the estimation of the whole process is routine. Inspired by Peter Halpin's paper[10], we use an EM to infer the parameters. For each individual k, we use a vector Z_i=($Z_{i,0,0}$, $Z_{i,i,1}$, ..., Z_{i,i,N_i}, $Z_{i,j,1}$, $Z_{i,j,2}$ ..., Z_{i,j,N_j}) to indicate its affiliation. $Z_{i,j,l}=1$ indicates that the associated event happening in the ith process is evoked by the lth event in j^{th} process, and $Z_{i,0,0}=1$ indicates this is an immigrant event in i^{th} process.

In the **E** step, the posterior probability of Z can be obtained from Bayes' rule. The posterior probability of kth event in the ith process is evoked by the lth event in the j^{th}process can be calculated as Equation(8).

$$Prob(Z_{i,j,l}=1|X,\theta) = \frac{\lambda_{z_{j,l}}(t_{i,k})}{\sum_{m\in Z}\lambda_m(t_{i,k})} \quad (8)$$

In the **M** step, the expectation of log-likelihood function can be written as Equation(9).

$$Q_i(\theta) = E_{Z_i|X_i,\theta_i} l_i(\theta_i|X_i,Z_i) = \sum_{z\in Z_i}(\sum_{k=1}^{N_i} ln(\lambda_z(t_{i,k}) * Prob(Z_{i,k}=z|X_i,\theta_i) - \Lambda_Z(T))) \quad (9)$$

According to Olson et al.[22], $\int_0^t \mu(t)dt$ and $\int_0^t f(v,\sigma)dv$ can be treated as 1 when assuming the whole process is stationary. Under the three assumptions (mentioned in Section 3.1), a Hawkes process should be stationary. Thus, Equation(9) can be extended and reformatted as Equation(10).

$$Q_i(\theta) = \sum_{z\in Z_i}\sum_{n=1}^{N_i}(ln(\mu_i(t)) * Prob(Z_{i,0,0}=1) + \sum_{t_{i,k}<t_n} ln(\eta_{ii} * f(t_n - t_{i,k};\sigma)) * Prob(Z_{i,k,n}=1) + \sum_{t_{j,l}<t_n} ln(\eta_{ij} * f(t_n - t_{j,l};\sigma_{ij})) * Prob(Z_{j,l,n}=1)) - (N_i + \eta_{ii} * N_i + \eta_{ij} * N_i) \quad (10)$$

By taking the derivatives of Equation(10), we can get each parameter's optimized value. Taking α_i, η_{ij} and σ_{ij} as examples, the optimized values could be inferred as Equation(11)-(13), and others could be calculated similarly.

$$\alpha_i = \frac{\sum_{n=1}^{N_i} Prob(Z_{i,0,0}=1)}{\sum_{n=1}^{N_i} Prob(Z_{i,0,0}=1) * \ln(t_n)} \quad (11)$$

$$\eta_{ij} = \frac{\sum_{n=1}^{N_i}\sum_{t_{j,l}<t_n} Prob(Z_{i,j,l}=1)}{N_i} \quad (12)$$

$$\sigma_{ij} = \sqrt{\frac{\sum_{n=1}^{N_i}\sum_{t_{j,l}<t_n}(t_{jl}-t_n)^2}{2(\sum_{n=1}^{N_i}\sum_{t_{j,l}<t_n} Prob(Z_{i,j,l}=1))}} \quad (13)$$

According to the point process's definition, the point counts within a period of time $[T,t]$ could be obtained by integrating the rate function over $[T,t]$. Thus, the predicted value could be calculated as Equation(14) with the optimized parameters.

$$C = \int_T^t \lambda(k)dk = \sum_{i,j\in\{1,2\}} (1-(\frac{1}{t-T})^{\alpha_i} + \eta_{ii}(1-e^{-\frac{(t-T)^2}{2\sigma_{ii}^2}}) + \eta_{ij}(1-e^{-\frac{(t-T)^2}{2\sigma_{ij}^2}})) \quad (14)$$

4. EVALUATION AND EXPERIMENT

4.1 Data Set

Because most existing datasets cannot provide sentiment information associated with each view record, we make our own crawlers to get data from websites. In our study, we analyze the four most important types of online videos: Movie, TV Episode(TV), Music Video(MV) and Online News(News). Our data comes from two resources: YouTube and Douban.

(1) YouTube is the largest video website in the world, and it has attracted billions of users to view and comment videos on it. However, because of copyright laws, many movies and TVs are not available from YouTube. Thus, we use YouTube to collect data about MVs and news.

(2) Douban is the largest video community websites in China. Although it does not directly provide videos, Douban provides a friendly platform for users to share their opinions about movies and TVs. Importantly, Douban provides very detailed sentiment information for each view record . Thus, we use Douban to collect data about movies and TVs.

Table 1: Basic Statistics of Dataset

Type	# Video	Time Span	# Comments	Positive
Movies	2638	2188 days	3,333,281	65.1%
TV	1517	1793 days	1,512,773	95.1%
MV	1224	730 days	363,337	66.9%
News	1750	25 days	176,657	9.4%

Table 1 gives general statistics about our four datasets. In Table 1, "# Video" indicates the number of videos included, "Time Span" indicates the average existence periods of videos in the dataset, "# Comments" indicates total comments number in the dataset, and "Positive" indicates the proportion of videos that receive more positive feedbacks. Our four datasets reflect three very different situations: movie and MV have a comparably balance distribution on the positive and negative sentiments, but TV has

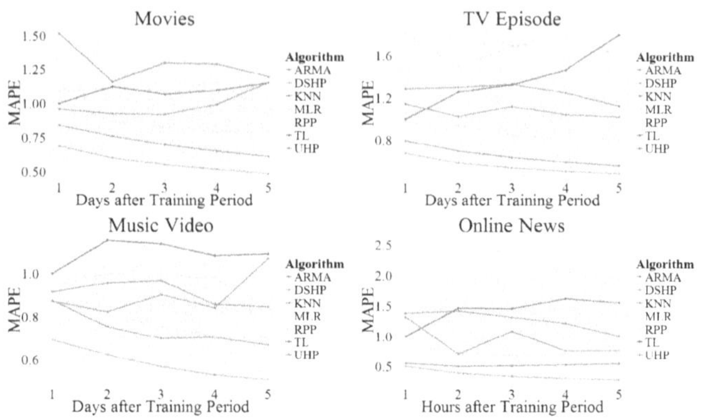

Figure 3: Evaluation by MAPE.

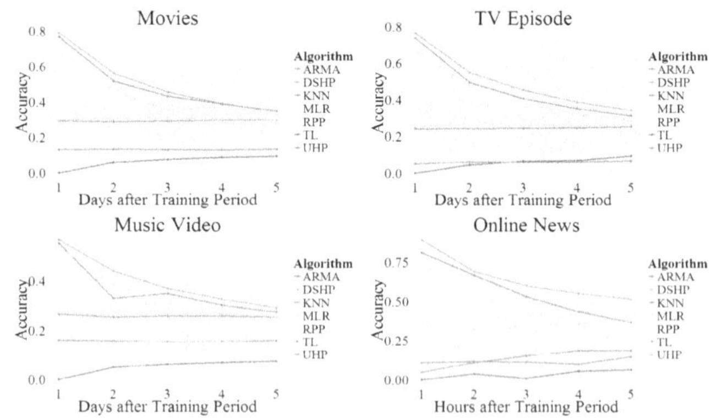

Figure 4: Evaluation by Accuracy.

an extreme positive inclination, while news videos has an extreme negative inclination. This diversity will help us to examine the models from a more reliable way.

Because movie, TV and MV have longer time span, we use *Day* as the time granularity for them, but for news, we take *Hour* as its time granularity. For each video, we use the last half of view records as the test data, and the remaining half as the training data. All the models are run and compared on the same datasets.

Records in movie and TV datasets have been clearly associated with rate information. We tag records whose rate is equal or higher than 7/10 as positive records, and tag the ones whose rate is less than 5/10 as negative records. Records in MV and news datasets have no rate information, so we implement a sentiment tool[4][18]on the comments' contents to get their sentiments.

4.2 Evaluation

Generally speaking, typical solutions for popularity predictions include: *Regression Model*, *Classification Extended Regression Models*, *Time Series Models*, *Poisson Process Models*. To make a complete examination, we compare DSHP with each of the models mentioned above. Six models are constructed as benchmarks to evaluate DSHP's predictive power. Before going to the comparison results, we provide some primary knowledge about these models. In the following models, $Y(t)$ is used to indicate the view count at time point t.

(1) **Baseline Model**: *Translation Model(TL)*. TL simply uses view count from the previous time point as the current view count. It can be defined as Equation(15).

$$Y(t) = Y(t-1) \tag{15}$$

(2) **Regression Model**:*Multiple Linear Regression(MLR)*. In our scenario, early view counts are regarded as independent variables to predict later view counts. The calculation method is shown as Equation(16), where α is the constant, β_i is the weight for time i, and ϵ_i is the residual, n is the number of independent variables taken into consideration. In our experiment, we take n as 5.

$$Y(t) = \alpha + \sum_{i=t-n}^{t-1} \beta_i Y(i) + \epsilon_i \tag{16}$$

[4]http://sentiment.vivekn.com

(3) **Classification Model**:*k-Nearest Neighbors(KNN)*. Traditional KNN is a powerful classification model, and it also could be extended to solve a regression problem. In our scenario, the specific calculation method is shown in Equation(17), where $N(v)$ is the set of k nearest points to video v in the training set with regard to the views in previous 5 days, and $d(\cdot)$ is the distance function. In this paper, we implement the Euclidean distance.

$$Y_v(t) = \sum_{v' \in N(v)} \frac{1/d(v,v')}{\sum_{v'' \in N(v)} 1/d(v,v'')} Y_{v'}(t) \tag{17}$$

(4) **Time Series Model**: *Auto-Regressive Moving Average Model(ARMA)*. ARMA is one of the most popular models in time series analysis. Given the watching counts in the past several days, it can make fine-grained prediction for the video's future popularity, leveraging the trend, periodicity and autocorrelation exhibited in the history information. The function for ARMA is shown in Equation(18), where c is the constant, βs are the parameters for the autoregressive process, θs are the parameters for the moving average process, and ϵs are the white noises.

$$Y(t) = c + \sum_{i=1}^{p} \beta_i Y(t-i) + \sum_{i=1}^{q} \theta_i \epsilon_{t-i} + \epsilon_t \tag{18}$$

(5) **Poisson Process Model**: *Reinforced Poisson Process(RPP)*. Poisson process has long been widely proved to be efficient in dynamic process simulation and prediction. RPP is a recently proposed Poisson process extended model and has been proved to be capable in prediction. The function of RPP is shown in Equation(19), where g_d is the intrinsic attractiveness, $f_d(v, \theta_d)$ is the relaxation function, and $i_d(i)$ is the total view counts received up to time t. $f_d(t, \theta_d)$ is set as log-normal relaxation function as recommended.

$$Y_d(t) = \int_{t-1}^{t} \lambda_d(v)dv = \int_{t-1}^{t} g_d * f_d(v, \theta_d) i_d(v)dv \tag{19}$$

(6) **Hawkes Process Model**: *Univariate Hawkes Process(UHP)*. To test the effects from the dual-sentiment mechanism, we also construct a UHP model for comparison. UHP takes Equation(2) as its framework and implements the kernels described in Section 3.3.

For evaluation purpose, we adopt two standard measurements as metrics: Mean Absolute Percentage Error (MAPE) and Accuracy.

MAPE measures the average deviation between predicted and real data. The lower MAPE values is, the better performance the model has. Denoting with $p_i(t)$ as the predicted view count, and $r_i(t)$ as the real view count, we can obtain the $MAPE$ over N videos as shown in Equation(20).

$$MAPE = \frac{1}{N}\sum_{i=1}^{N} \left|\frac{p_i(t) - r_i(t)}{r_i(t)}\right| \quad (20)$$

Accuracy measures the fraction of videos that are correctly predicted for a given error tolerance ϵ. In this paper, we set ϵ as 1. That is to say, when the count difference between predicted and real view is less than 1, we count it as an accurate result. The Accuracy calculation in this paper is shown as Equation(21).

$$Accuracy = \frac{1}{N}\sum_{i=1}^{N} |\{d : |p_i(t) - r_i(t)| < 1\}| \quad (21)$$

Figure 3 and Figure 4 shows the evaluation results from these two measurements. It is very clear that DSHP, UHP and RPP have better performances than ARMA, MLR,KNN and TL. Strictly speaking, TL has no predictive power; it just takes the previous view count as the current predictive view count, so it is reasonable for TL to have the comparably worst performance. Both MLR and ARMA assume there is a linear relationship between view counts on early and later time points, but this assumption is somehow over strong. Thus, both MLR and ARMA do not perform well. KNN makes prediction from a classification perspective, however, it ignores the historical and trend characteristics along the time line.

In comparison, DSHP, UHP and RPP have better performances. All of these three employ *Poisson Process* as their underlying mechanism. A Poisson process is a stochastic process that directly models events arrival patterns within a system, and it has been widely proved to be suitable for time series modeling.

According to the comparison results, RPP performs a little worse than DSHP and UHP. This is because RPP is designed for paper citation prediction, but not for videos' view counts prediction. The difference is that social media environment is far more complicated than documentation area. Paper citation is a ritual behavior. People cite a paper most result from one simple reason: the cited paper is classical. Thus a single Poisson process may be enough to fit it well. Video watch is a ruleless behavior. People watch a video can result from many different reasons: they like the actors/actresses, they are recommended by friends, they are informed by a billboard, or they just want to kill time. A single Poisson process is insufficient in this scenario. RPP only implements one Poisson process, while DSHP and UHP have exploited Hawkes process, which combines several Poisson processes, to describe various reasons. This is why DSHP and UHP can reach better results than RPP.

DSHP performs a little better than UHP. Basically, DSHP and UHP share the same mechanism, so they have very similar performances. However, UHP implies the "Homogenous Node" assumption and does not distinguish different sentiments, while DSHP has incorporated sentiment information. Compared to UHP, DSHP is closer to reality, and thus get a better result.

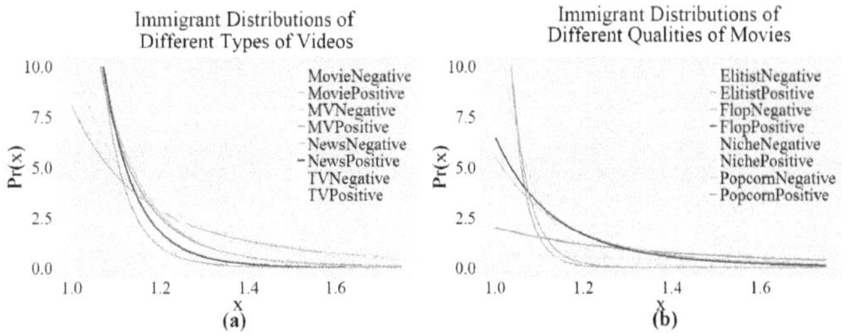

Figure 5: Immigrant Distributions.

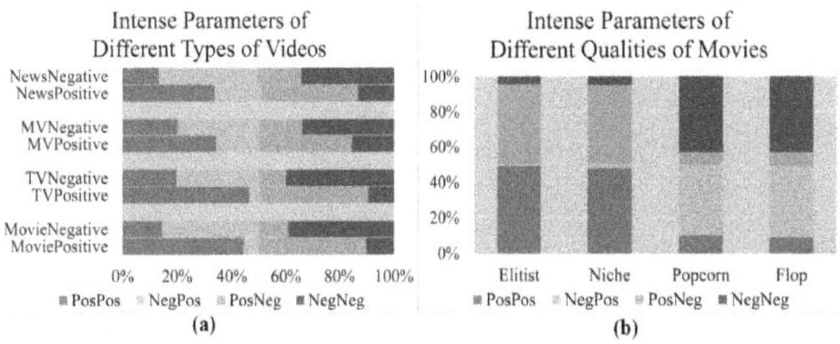

Figure 6: Intense Parameter Proportions.

4.3 Experiments and Results Analysis

In this part, we construct two experiments to reveal the underlying mechanisms that drive videos' dynamics.

(1)Experiment One: Comparison among Different Types of Videos. As shown in Table 1, we have four types of videos at hand, and we will explore different propagation characteristics of different types of videos. In order to make a fair and thorough comparison, we extract two kinds of videos, Positive Video and Negative Video, for further exploration and analysis. *Positive Videos* are the videos that possess more than 60% positive comments, and *Negative Videos* are the videos that possess more than 60% negative comments

(2) Experiment Two: Comparison among Different Qualities of Videos(taking movies as examples). Videos have different qualities even if they are of the same type. Taking movies as examples, some of them gain both fame and wealth, some only obtain good reputations but limited audience, some make money but are widely criticized, and some are total flops. In this experiment, we will get a more detailed view about the propagation differences among videos of different qualities. Due to space limitations, we will only use movies as examples. We have defined four kinds of movies: *Elitist*, with 8/10 or higher rate and more than 10000 comments; *Niche Drama(Niche)* with 8/10 or higher rate but less than 5000 comments, *Popcorn Flick(Popcorn)*, with less than 5/10 rate but more than 10000 comments, and *Flop*, with less than 5/10 rate and less than 5000 comments.

Results are shown in Figure (5)-(7). In these figures, labels like "MoviePositive" represent "Positive Movie" described above, labels like "Elitist" represent "Elitist Movie", and labels like "PosPos" represents the "Positive to Positive" sentiment transfer.

4.3.1 Immigrant Distribution Analysis

Immigrant distribution describes the probability of an individual who spontaneously chooses to watch a video with-

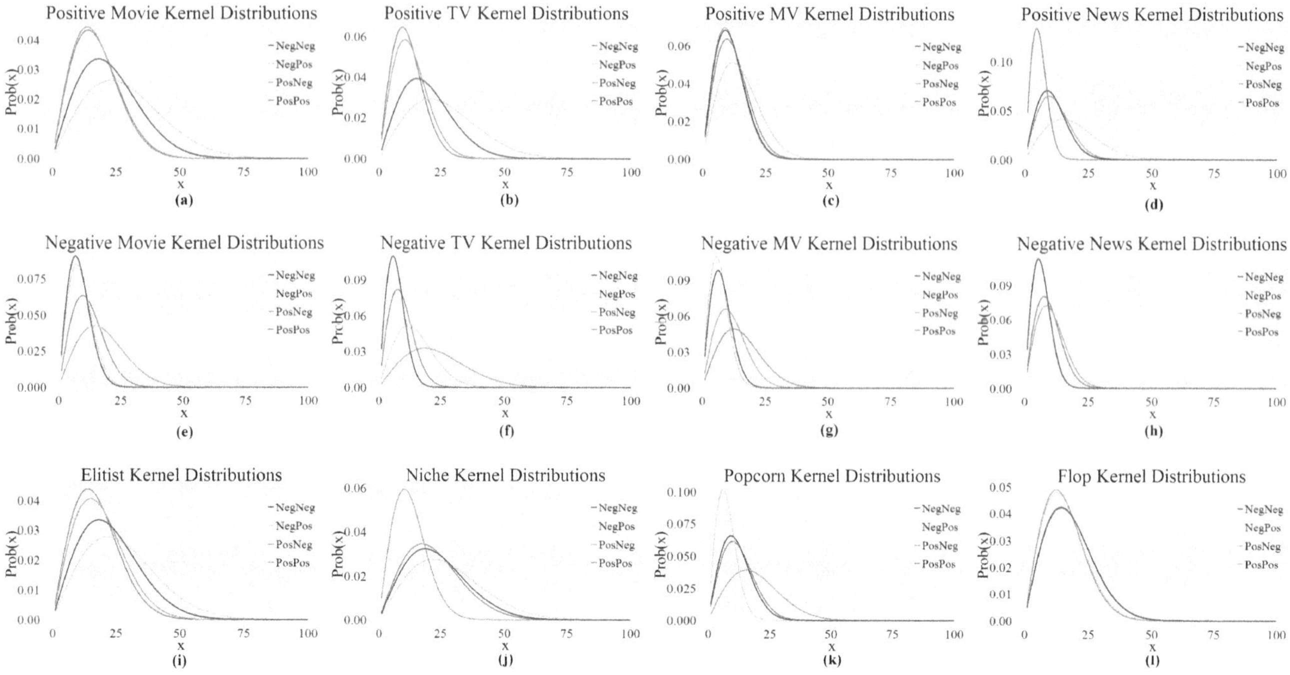

Figure 7: Kernel Distribution Analysis.

out any influence from the "word of mouth" process. Specifically speaking, this distribution is affected by a video's intrinsic attributes, like its cast, scripts, or trailers.

Immigrant Distributions of Different Types of Videos.

Figure 5(a) presents the immigrant distributions of different types of videos. Since there are various types of videos from two different platforms, comparisons among the absolute values of immigrant parameters are meaningless. We pay more attention to the inspiring distribution shapes.

From Figure 5(a) we can see videos are clearly differentiated according to their types. Specifically, the movie's immigrant distributions are gentle and long lasting, while the news' are sharp and soon fading. This result is consistent with reality. The movie always has some significant attributes, such as famous actors/actresses(e.g. Johnny Depp), popular scripts (e.g. Harry Potter), or attractive preview trailers. These features will continuously intrigue potential watchers. On the contrary, social news' timeliness has determined its corresponding videos' short-lasting immigrant influences.

Immigrant Distributions of Different Qualities of Movies.

Figure 5(b) shows the immigrant distributions of movies with different qualities.

Let us start from the good movies, namely Elitist(the popular good movie) and Niche(the unpopular good movie). Both Elitist and Niche open with remarkable positive influences and trivial negative ones. The only difference is that Elitist's first shot is much stronger(Elitist's positive immigrant parameter is 30.44, and Niche's is 13.15). Putting social network propagation processes aside, the intenser initial immigrant influence has already helped accumulate much a larger audience, making a big difference. Thus, even for a good movie, the immigrant impacts, such as star effects or trailer effects, are also essential factors to facilitate a movie's final popularity.

Bad movies, namely Popcorn(the popular bad movie) and Flop(the unpopular bad movie), have very different immigrant distributions from each other. Flop can be detected from the very beginning since it has a noticeable negative start, while Popcorn, although negative sentiment dominates, has comparably gentle and long lasting immigrant distributions, especially the positive one. The intense negative sentiment from the beginning has prevented the public from seeing a bad movie, and makes it a Flop. On the contrary, Popcorn has suppressed the negative impact successfully and gained much more viewers. Thus, a bad movie still a chance to be popular if it can find methods to repress the negative sentiment's explosion and hold a long lasting positive immigrant influence, even insignificant, from the beginning.

4.3.2 Intense Parameter Analysis

The intense parameters reflect the overall intensity of responsiveness of a person to others' opinions[10]. For each Hawkes processes in DSHP, its two intense parameters should meet $\eta_{ii}+\eta_{ij} \approx 1$ indicating the weight proportion of each response kernel. Figure 6 shows the proportions of the intense parameters in our two experiments. The warm color system (red and orange) represents the values from the positive process and the cold color system(blue and green) represents the negative process. *The values are comparable within in one color system, but* ***incomparable*** *across color systems.*

Intense Parameters of Different Types of Videos.

Figure 6(a) shows the proportions of intense parameters among different types of videos. According to the results, all kinds of videos have similar intense distributions. For positive videos, people are more likely to respond to positive comments, while for negative videos, people are more likely to respond to negative comments. This phenomenon might result from the fact that positive/negative comments are dominant, so they have more probability to trigger others.

Intense Parameters of Different Qualities of Movies.

Figure 6(b) shows the intense parameter proportions among different qualities of videos. On one hand, we find the similar patterns which have been emphasized in the previous paragraph: for a good movie, people are more likely to respond to positive comments, and for a bad movie, people are more likely to respond to negative comments. On the other hand, we find that a movie's popularity and its intense parameters are independent. Although Elitist and Popcorn are more popular than Niche and Flop respectively, Elitist and Niche share very similar intense proportions, and Popcorn and Flop also share very similar intense proportions. From this demonstration, we can find that popularity and quality are two independent features of a video. A popular video is not necessary to be good, and similarly, a good video is not necessary to be popular. This result is very instructive for a recommendation system when it needs to decide whether to recommend a "Popular" movie or a "Good" movie.

4.3.3 Kernel Parameter Analysis

The kernel parameters control shapes of kernel distributions, and reflect overall nature of responsiveness between persons. Figure(7) provides a brief view about kernel distributions among different types of videos and different qualities of movies. Figure (7) has high consistency with Figure (6).

Kernel Distributions of Different Types of Videos.

Figures 7(a)-(d) demonstrate the response kernels' distributions of positive videos. It is very clear that positive to positive sentiment transfer(PosPos) is quick and intense among all these videos, especially in news broadcast. PosNeg also easily happens. Interestingly, MV has a very different pattern. Even for positive MV, NegNeg transfer is still considerable. This indicates that although positive dominates, negative comments tend to come densely in a period of time.

Figures 7(e)-(h) demonstrate the response kernels' distributions of negative videos. Similarly, NegNeg transfer is quick and intense in negative videos. NegPos also easily happens in most videos except TV. Figure (7)(f) implies that people have a lower tolerance towards bad TV. For other types of videos, although negatives dominate, positive comments will appear from time to time, but for TV, the positive comments obviously occur much less frequently.

Kernel Distributions of Different Qualities of Movies.

Figures 7(i)-(l) show the kernel distributions for movies of different qualities. It is very understandable that Elitist has an intense and quick PosPos transfer pattern.

Niche has a strong PosNeg transfer pattern, but has a very weak NegPos one. That is why Niche could not be popular. As common sense, positive comments will encourage potential viewers but negative comments will discourage them. However, Niche does not have dramatic PosPos patterns, and most positive comments are disabled by following negative comments. What is worse, Niche could not survive quickly from those negative comments since it has a weak NegPos transfer pattern.

On the contrary, Popcorn enjoys a quick survival since it has a strong NegPos transfer pattern. Although a Popcorn might have many negative comments, these comments could quickly be replaced by the immediately appearing positive ones. Thus Popcorns could continuously encourage future viewers. Moreover, its weak PosNeg pattern indicates once a positive comment appears, it would not be replaced by negative ones instantly.

5. CONCLUSION AND FUTURE WORK

This paper has proposed a novel video popularity prediction model– DSHP. Compared to previous related works, DSHP mainly has two advantages. First, it implements Hawkes process as its framework, modeling the arrival process directly. As shown in our evaluation section, Hawkes process has been proved to have a better performance. Second, DSHP is a sentiment propagation driven model. DSHP not only achieves a better performance by emphasizing sentiments' importance in video's popularity propagation, but also reveals more underlying factors which make a video's popularity.

This paper still has mainly two points that need to be strengthened. First, DSHP is designed for the scenarios where content features, such as cast, descriptions or genre, are unavailable. However, in some situations, these features could be accessed. DSHP could be easily extended by adapting the immigrant function to incorporate content features. In future work, we will explore DSHP's ability by considering content features. Second, we only take two sentiments, positive and negative, into consideration because we assume only these two sentiments will make a difference. However, some viewers might express no obvious sentiment polarities after watching a video. Thus a neutral sentiment inclination should also be taken into consideration. In future work, we plan to add one more Hawkes process, which represent neutral sentiment, to examine an indifferent sentiment's influences on a video's popularity propagation.

6. REFERENCES

[1] P. Bao, H.-W. Shen, X. Jin, and X.-Q. Cheng. Modeling and predicting popularity dynamics of microblogs using self-excited hawkes processes. In *Proceedings of the 24th International Conference on World Wide Web Companion*, pages 9–10. International World Wide Web Conferences Steering Committee, 2015.

[2] M. Cha, H. Haddadi, F. Benevenuto, and P. K. Gummadi. Measuring user influence in twitter: The million follower fallacy. *ICWSM*, 10(10-17):30, 2010.

[3] M. Cha, H. Kwak, P. Rodriguez, Y.-Y. Ahn, and S. Moon. Analyzing the video popularity characteristics of large-scale user generated content systems. *IEEE/ACM Transactions on Networking (TON)*, 17(5):1357–1370, 2009.

[4] R. Crane and D. Sornette. Robust dynamic classes revealed by measuring the response function of a social system. *Proceedings of the National Academy of Sciences*, 105(41):15649–15653, 2008.

[5] D. J. Daley and D. Vere-Jones. *An introduction to the theory of point processes: volume II: general theory*

and structure, volume 2. Springer Science & Business Media, 2007.

[6] M. Goetz, J. Leskovec, M. McGlohon, and C. Faloutsos. Modeling blog dynamics. 2009.

[7] M. Gomez Rodriguez, D. Balduzzi, B. Schölkopf, G. T. Scheffer, et al. Uncovering the temporal dynamics of diffusion networks. pages 561–568, 2011.

[8] A. Guille. Information diffusion in online social networks. pages 31–36, 2013.

[9] G. Gursun, M. Crovella, and I. Matta. Describing and forecasting video access patterns. pages 16–20, 2011.

[10] P. F. Halpin and P. De Boeck. Modelling dyadic interaction with hawkes processes. *Psychometrika*, 78(4):793–814, 2013.

[11] A. G. Hawkes. Spectra of some self-exciting and mutually exciting point processes. *Biometrika*, 58(1):83–90, 1971.

[12] M. Joshi, D. Das, K. Gimpel, and N. A. Smith. Movie reviews and revenues: An experiment in text regression. pages 293–296, 2010.

[13] K. J. Lee and W. Chang. Bayesian belief network for box-office performance: A case study on korean movies. *Expert Systems with Applications*, 36(1):280–291, 2009.

[14] J. Leskovec, L. Backstrom, and J. Kleinberg. Meme-tracking and the dynamics of the news cycle. pages 497–506, 2009.

[15] H. Li, X. Ma, F. Wang, J. Liu, and K. Xu. On popularity prediction of videos shared in online social networks. pages 169–178, 2013.

[16] L. Li, H. Deng, A. Dong, Y. Chang, and H. Zha. Identifying and labeling search tasks via query-based hawkes processes. In *Proceedings of the 20th ACM SIGKDD international conference on Knowledge discovery and data mining*, pages 731–740. ACM, 2014.

[17] L. Li and H. Zha. Dyadic event attribution in social networks with mixtures of hawkes processes. In *Proceedings of the 22nd ACM international conference on Conference on information & knowledge management*, pages 1667–1672. ACM, 2013.

[18] V. Narayanan, I. Arora, and A. Bhatia. Fast and accurate sentiment classification using an enhanced naive bayes model. In *Intelligent Data Engineering and Automated Learning–IDEAL 2013*, pages 194–201. Springer, 2013.

[19] M. E. Newman. Spread of epidemic disease on networks. *Physical review E*, 66(1):016128, 2002.

[20] M. E. Newman. The structure and function of complex networks. *SIAM review*, 45(2):167–256, 2003.

[21] D. Niu, Z. Liu, B. Li, and S. Zhao. Demand forecast and performance prediction in peer-assisted on-demand streaming systems. pages 421–425, 2011.

[22] J. F. Olson and K. M. Carley. Exact and approximate em estimation of mutually exciting hawkes processes. *Statistical Inference for Stochastic Processes*, 16(1):63–80, 2013.

[23] H. Pinto, J. M. Almeida, and M. A. Gonçalves. Using early view patterns to predict the popularity of youtube videos. pages 365–374, 2013.

[24] D. A. Shamma, J. Yew, L. Kennedy, and E. F. Churchill. Viral actions: Predicting video view counts using synchronous sharing behaviors. 2011.

[25] H. Shen, D. Wang, C. Song, and A.-L. Barabási. Modeling and predicting popularity dynamics via reinforced poisson processes. 2014.

[26] G. Szabo and B. A. Huberman. Predicting the popularity of online content. *Communications of the ACM*, 53(8):80–88, 2010.

[27] F. Wang, H. Wang, and K. Xu. Diffusive logistic model towards predicting information diffusion in online social networks. pages 133–139, 2012.

[28] S. Wheatley, V. Filimonov, and D. Sornette. Estimation of the hawkes process with renewal immigration using the em algorithm. *Swiss Finance Institute Research Paper*, (14-53), 2014.

[29] J. Wu, Y. Zhou, D. M. Chiu, Y. Hua, and Z. Zhu. Modeling dynamics of online video popularity. *arXiv preprint arXiv:1412.2326*, 2014.

[30] T. Wu, M. Timmers, D. D. Vleeschauwer, and W. V. Leekwijck. On the use of reservoir computing in popularity prediction. pages 19–24, 2010.

[31] J. Yang and J. Leskovec. Modeling information diffusion in implicit networks. pages 599–608, 2010.

[32] S.-H. Yang and H. Zha. Mixture of mutually exciting processes for viral diffusion. In *Proceedings of the 30th International Conference on Machine Learning (ICML-13)*, pages 1–9, 2013.

[33] P. Yin, P. Luo, M. Wang, and W.-C. Lee. A straw shows which way the wind blows: ranking potentially popular items from early votes. pages 623–632, 2012.

[34] A. H. Zadeh and R. Sharda. Modeling brand post popularity dynamics in online social networks. *Decision Support Systems*, 65:59–68, 2014.

Joint Modeling of User Check-in Behaviors for Point-of-Interest Recommendation

Hongzhi Yin[1] Xiaofang Zhou[1,2] Yingxia Shao[3] Hao Wang[4] Shazia Sadiq[1]
[1]The University of Queensland, School of Information Technology and Electrical Engineering, Qld 4072, Australia
[2]School of Computer Science and Technology, Soochow University, China
[3]Key Lab of High Confidence Software Technologies (MOE), School of EECS, Peking University, China
[4]Science and Technology on Integrated Information System Laboratory & State Key Laboratory of Computer Science, Institute of Software, Chinese Academy of Sciences, Beijing 100190, China
[1]db.hongzhi@gmail.com [1]{zxf,shazia}@itee.uq.edu.au
[3]simon0227@pku.edu.cn [4]wanghao@iscas.ac.cn

ABSTRACT

Point-of-Interest (POI) recommendation has become an important means to help people discover attractive and interesting locations, especially when users travel out of town. However, extreme sparsity of user-POI matrix creates a severe challenge. To cope with this challenge, a growing line of research has exploited the temporal effect, geographical-social influence, content effect and word-of-mouth effect. However, current research lacks an integrated analysis of the joint effect of the above factors to deal with the issue of data-sparsity, especially in the out-of-town recommendation scenario which has been ignored by most existing work.

In light of the above, we propose a joint probabilistic generative model to mimic user check-in behaviors in a process of decision making, which strategically integrates the above factors to effectively overcome the data sparsity, especially for out-of-town users. To demonstrate the applicability and flexibility of our model, we investigate how it supports two recommendation scenarios in a unified way, i.e., home-town recommendation and out-of-town recommendation. We conduct extensive experiments to evaluate the performance of our model on two real large-scale datasets in terms of both recommendation effectiveness and efficiency, and the experimental results show its superiority over other competitors.

Categories and Subject Descriptors

H.3.3 [**Information Search and Retrieval**]: Information Filtering

Keywords

Recommender system; Location-based service; Probabilistic generative model; Joint Modeling

1. INTRODUCTION

The rapid development of Web 2.0, location acquisition and wireless communication technologies have fostered a number of location-based social networks (LBSNs), such as Foursquare and Facebook Places. In these LBSNs, users can post their physical locations or geo-tagged information in the form of "check-in", and share their visiting experiences and tips for points of interest (POI) with friends, such as restaurants, sightseeing sites. In LBSNs, it is crucial to utilize user check-in data to make personalized POI recommendation, which helps users know new POIs and explore new regions, facilitate advertisers to launch mobile advertisements to targeted users, and make LBSNs more attractive to users and advertisers.

Recently, POI recommendation has become a popular research topic due to easy access of large-scale check-in records. One of the most important problems is how to deal with a severe challenge stemming from extreme sparsity of user-POI interaction matrix. There are millions of POIs in LBSNs, but a user can only visit a limited number of them. Moreover, the observation of travel locality exacerbates this problem. The observation of travel locality [15] made on LBSNs shows that most of users' check-ins are limited to their living regions (e.g., home cities) on account of the distance constraint. An investigation demonstrates that the check-in records generated by users in their non-home cities are very scarce and only take up 0.47% of the check-in records left in their home cities, which aggravates the data sparsity problem with POI recommendation for out-of-town users (e.g., if we want to recommend POIs located at Los Angeles to people from New York City) [10, 35].

The most popular approach in recommender systems is that of *collaborative filtering* [1]. There exists a considerable body of research [15, 27, 17, 10, 11] which deposited people's check-in history into user-POI matrix where each row corresponds to a user's POI-visiting history and each column denotes a POI. A collaborative filtering-based method is then employed by [15, 27, 10] to infer the user's preference regarding each unvisited POI. Based on the core idea of collaborative filtering, similar users of the target user (i.e., those who exhibit similar POI visiting behaviors) are chosen to provide clues for making recommendation. Owing to travel locality, most of these similar users are more likely to live in the same region with the target user than other regions. As a recommendation is made by considering POIs visited by the similar users, most of the recommended POIs would be located in the target user's home town. So, these CF-based methods cannot be directly applied to the POI recommendation for out-of-town users [10, 35].

Moreover, unlike the traditional GPS trajectories [42, 41], the time-ordered check-in records of a user are low-sample-rate where the details of movement information are lost. The spatial gap between any two consecutive check-ins is typically in the scale of kilometers while the spatial gap between consecutively logged GPS points in the GPS trajectories is typically 5-10 meters. Besides, the time interval between consecutive check-ins is much larger than

Permission to make digital or hard copies of all or part of this work for personal or classroom use is granted without fee provided that copies are not made or distributed for profit or commercial advantage and that copies bear this notice and the full citation on the first page. Copyrights for components of this work owned by others than ACM must be honored. Abstracting with credit is permitted. To copy otherwise, or republish, to post on servers or to redistribute to lists, requires prior specific permission and/or a fee. Request permissions from Permissions@acm.org.
CIKM'15, October 19–23, 2015, Melbourne, VIC, Australia.
© 2015 ACM. ISBN 978-1-4503-3794-6/15/10 ...$15.00.
DOI: http://dx.doi.org/10.1145/2806416.2806500.

that in the GPS trajectories. Therefore, existing sequential pattern mining methods such as Markov-chain models on GPS trajectories cannot be applied to the sparse users' check-in data in LBSNs.

To deal with the issue of data sparsity, especially for out-of-town recommendation scenario, we explore the following factors which affect users' check-in behaviors.

- Content Effect. Content information on LBSNs related to a user's check-in activity provides a unique opportunity to infer personal interests [35, 20]. For example, by observing a POI's description as "vegetarian restaurant", we infer that users who check-in at this POI might enjoy vegetarian diet.
- Temporal Effect. As observed in [36, 11], users' activity contents exhibit strong temporal cyclic patterns in terms of hour of the day or day of the week. For example, a user is more likely to go to a restaurant rather than a bar at lunch time, and is more likely to go to a bar rather than an office at midnight.
- Geographical Influence. Many recent studies show that people tend to explore POIs near the ones that they have visited before [28]. So, POIs visited by users often form spatial clusters, i.e., people tend to check in around several centers (e.g., "home" and "office") [5, 17].
- Word-of-Mouth Effect. The region-level popularity of POIs also affects user visiting behaviors [35, 19]. In fact, the probability of a user visiting a POI is largely affected by the local word-of-mouth about the POI, especially when users travel in unfamiliar regions.

While there are some studies that exploit one of the above factors to improve POI recommendation effectiveness, they lack an integrated analysis of their joint effect to deal with the issue of data sparsity, especially in the out-of-town recommendation scenario. Specifically, most prior work of POI recommendation focused on exploiting users' mobility patterns by investigating geographical influence [28, 5, 17], temporal effects [36, 11], or social influence [10, 28, 8], but they ignored the potential effect of content information of checked-in POI, thus missing the opportunity to transfer user interests inferred at home town to other out-of-town regions by the medium of POI contents [35]. Although some recent work [35, 12, 20] exploited the content information of POIs to deal with the issue of data sparsity, they did not consider the temporal effect and geographical influence.

In light of this, we propose a Joint probabilistic generative model JIM to simulate the decision-making process of users' check-in behaviors, which strategically integrates the above factors to effectively overcome the issue of data sparsity, especially for out-of-town users. As a POI has both semantic and geographical attributes, two corresponding components are designed in JIM: Time-aware User Interest Component (TIC) and Popularity-aware User Mobility Component (PMC).

TIC aims to exploit both the contents of POIs and their temporal effect to model users' interests. Specifically, we infer individual user's interests according to the contents of his/her checked-in POIs. Thus, TIC alleviates the data sparsity, especially for out-of-town users, as the contents play the role of medium which can transfer users' interests inferred at their home regions to out-of-town regions where they are traveling. Unfortunately, based on recent analysis of LBSNs data [26], about 30% of all POIs are lacking any meaningful textual descriptions. To address this problem, we exploit the temporal effect of users' activity contents, since the check-in time provides important clues to the contents of POIs.

PMC is developed to utilize the geographical influence and word-of-mouth effect to account for users' spatial mobility. Different from user online behaviors in the virtual world, user activities in the physical world are limited by travel distance. In this component, we first infer a user's activity range according to the location distribution of his/her historical visited POIs or his/her current location. Specifically, we divide the geographical space into several regions and compute the probability of each region that an individual user is likely to visit. Then, we infer the POI generating probability from each region according to both the public's check-in behaviors at that region and the distance between the POI and the center of that region, i.e., considering both the region-level popularity of the POI and the geographical influence. By integrating the region-level word-of-mouth effect, i.e., the wisdom of crowds, JIM model can solve the problem of user interest drift across geographical regions which indicates that user interests inferred at one region (e.g., home town) cannot always be applied to recommendation at another region. For example, a user u never goes gambling when he lives in Beijing, China, but when he travels to Macao or Las Vegas he is most likely to visit casinos.

To demonstrate the applicability of JIM, we investigate how it supports two recommendation scenarios in a unified way: 1) home-town recommendation that assumes that the target user is located in his/her home town, i.e., to meet users' information need in their daily life, and 2) out-of-town recommendation that aims to meet users' information need when they travel out of town, especially in unfamiliar regions. It is worth mentioning that both of the recommendation scenarios should be personalized, time-aware [36] and location-based [10], i.e., to recommend different ranked lists of POIs for the same target user at different time and locations.

We conduct extensive experiments to evaluate the performance of our JIM model on two real large-scale datasets in terms of recommendation effectiveness and efficiency, and the results show superiority of JIM model over other competitors. Besides, we study the contribution of each factor to improve the recommendation results in the two respective scenarios under a unified recommendation framework, and find that the *content effect* plays a dominant role in alleviating the data sparsity of out-of-town recommendation, while the *temporal effect* is most important to improve home-town recommendation. To the best of our knowledge, this is the first work to compare the effect of each factor in the two different recommendation scenarios.

The remainder of the paper is organized as follows. Section 2 details JIM model. We present how to effectively and efficiently deploy JIM model to the POI recommendation in Section 3. We report the experimental results in Section 4. Section 5 reviews the related work and we conclude the paper in Section 6.

2. JOINT MODELING OF USER CHECK-IN BEHAVIORS

In this section, we first formulate the problem definition, and then present our proposed JIM model.

2.1 Preliminary

For the ease of presentation, we define the key data structures and notations used in this paper.

ID-Name:	Darling Harbour
Location:	Longitude: 151.200, Latitude: -33.877
Content:	plaza, scenic views, harbour, bar, cafés, entertainment sunsets, harbors, museums, leisure, marina

Table 1: A POI and its associated information

Definition 1. **(POI)** A POI is defined as a uniquely identified specific site (e.g., a restaurant or a cinema). In our model, a POI has three attributes: identifier, location and content. We use v to

Variable	Interpretation
ϑ_u	the activity range of user u, expressed by a multinomial distribution over a set of regions
θ_u	the interests of user u, expressed by a multinomial distribution over a set of topics
ϕ_z	a multinomial distribution over words specific to topic z
ψ_z	a beta distribution over time specific to topic z
φ_r	the region-level popularity distribution of POIs specific to region r
μ_r	the mean location of region r
Σ_r	the location covariance of region r
$\gamma, \alpha, \beta, \tau$	Dirichlet priors to multinomial distributions ϑ_u, θ_u, ϕ_z and φ_r, respectively

Table 2: Notations of parameters

represent a POI identifier and l_v to denote its corresponding geographical attribute in terms of longitude and latitude coordinates. It should be noted that many different POIs can share the same geographical coordinate. Besides, there may be textual semantic information associated with a POI, such as the category and tag words. We use the notation W_v to denote the set of words describing POI v. Table 1 shows an example.

Definition 2. **(User Home Location)** Following the recent work of [16], given a user u, we define the user's home location as the place where the user lives, denoted as l_u.

Note that, we assume a user's home location is "permanent" in our problem. In other words, a home location is a static location instead of a real-time location that is "temporally" related to him (e.g., the places where he/she is traveling). Due to privacy, user home locations are not always available. For a user whose home location is not explicitly given, we adopt the method developed by [22] which discretizes the world into $25km$ by $25km$ cells and defines the home location as the average position of check-ins in the cell with most of his/her check-ins.

Definition 3. **(Check-in Activity)** A user check-in activity is represented by a five tuple $(u,\ v,\ l_v,\ W_v,\ t)$ that means user u visits POI v at time t.

Definition 4. **(User Profile)** For each user u, we create a user profile D_u, which is a set of check-in activities associated with u. The dataset D used in our model consists of user profiles, i.e., $D = \{D_u : u \in U\}$.

Definition 5. **(Topic)** Given a collection of words W, a topic z is defined as a multinomial distribution over W, i.e., $\phi_z = \{\phi_{z,w} : w \in W\}$ where each component $\phi_{z,w}$ denotes the probability of topic z generating word w. Generally, a topic is a semantic-coherent soft cluster of words.

Given a dataset D as the union of a collection of user profiles, we aim to provide POI recommendation for both home-town and out-of-town users. We formulate our problem that takes into account both of the two scenarios in a unified fashion as follows.

PROBLEM 1. ***(POI Recommendation)*** *Given a check-in activity dataset D and a querying user u_q with his/her current location l_q and time t_q (that is, the query is $q = (u_q,\ t_q,\ l_q)$), our goal is to recommend a list of POIs that u_q would be interested in. Given a distance threshold d, the problem becomes an **out-of-town recommendation** if the distance between the target user's current location and his/her home location (that is, $|l_q - l_u|$) is greater than d. Otherwise, the problem is a **home-town recommendation**.*

Following related studies [10, 8], we set $d = 100km$ in our work, since a distance around $100km$ is the typical radius of human "reach" – it takes about 1 to 2 hours to drive such a distance.

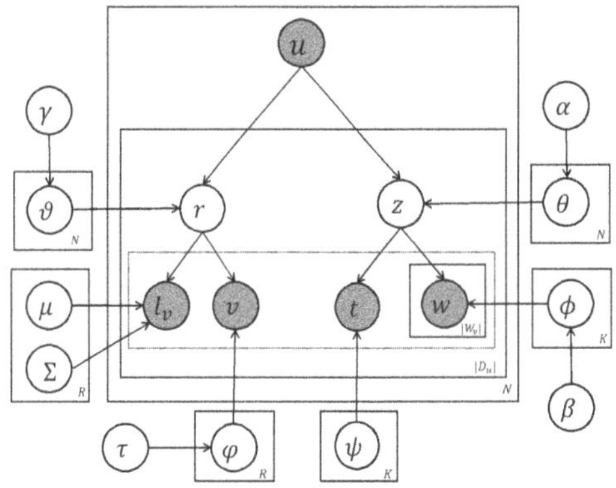

Figure 1: The Graphical Representation of JIM

2.2 Model Description

To mimic users' check-in behaviors in a process of decision making, we propose a joint probabilistic generative model JIM to take various factors into account, including content effect, temporal effect, geographical influences and word-of-mouth effect. Figure 1 shows the graphical representation of JIM. We first introduce the notations of our model and list them in Table 2. Figure 1 shows the graphical representation of JIM where N, K and R denote the number of users, topics and regions, respectively. Our input data, i.e., users' check-in records, is modeled as observed random variables, shown as shaded circles in the figure. The topic and region indexes of check-in records are considered as latent random variables, which are denoted as z and r. Specifically, JIM consists of two components: Time-aware User Interest Component and Popularity-aware User Mobility Component, which will be described in the following.

Time-Aware User Interest Modeling. Intuitively, a user chooses a POI at a given time by matching his/her personal interests with the contents of that POI. Inspired by the early work about user interest modeling [35, 13, 31], JIM adopts latent semantic topics to characterize users' interests to overcome the data sparsity. Specifically, we infer individual user's interest distribution over a set of topics according to the contents (e.g., tags and categories) of his/her checked-in POIs, denoted as θ_u.

Unfortunately, based on the recent analysis of LBSNs data in [26], about 30% of all POIs are lacking any meaningful textual information. To address this problem, we exploit the association between the contents of checked-in POIs and the check-in time by mining the co-occurrence patterns of user activity contents and the activity time, since the check-in time provides important clues to the contents of POIs. Intuitively, the POIs which are checked-in at the same/similar time by most users are more likely to have same/similar functions and categories. So the introduction of check-in time is helpful to infer the topics of POIs, especially whose contents are not available. Technically, each topic z in our JIM model is not only associated with a multinomial distribution over words ϕ_z, but also with a continuous distribution over time ψ_z. This design enables ϕ_z and ψ_z to be mutually influenced and enhanced during the topic discovery process by associating them. Another benefit of this design is that the inferred personal interests are not only semantic-aware, but also time-aware.

To integrate the check-in time information to the topic discovery process, the method of time division is essential. Instead of adopting existing discretization methods to split the time into hourly-based slots [11, 36], we treat time t as continuous real value and normalize the time during a day to a range from 0 to 1, considering that 1) time is intrinsically continuous; 2) discretization of time always begs the question of selecting the proper time interval, and the interval is invariably too small for some periods and too large for others. Following the literature [25], we employ the Beta distribution to describe the time distribution of topic z which can behave versatile shape.

In the standard topic models [3], a document (i.e., a bag of words) contains a mixture of topics, and each word has a hidden topic label. While this is a reasonable assumption for long documents, for short document W_v, it is most likely to be about a single topic since most of POIs belong to a single category. We therefore assign a single topic with the document W_v.

Popularity-Aware User Mobility Modeling. The spatial clustering phenomenon indicates that users are most likely to visit a number of POIs and these POIs are usually limited to some geographical regions [28]. In this component, the geographical space is divided into R regions. We apply a multinomial distribution $\boldsymbol{\vartheta_u}$ over regions to model u's spatial patterns. Following the literatures [19, 18], we assume a Gaussian distribution for each region r, and the location for POI v is characterized by $l_v \sim \mathcal{N}(\boldsymbol{\mu_r}, \boldsymbol{\Sigma_r})$, as follows:

$$P(l_v|\boldsymbol{\mu_r}, \boldsymbol{\Sigma_r}) = \frac{1}{2\pi\sqrt{|\boldsymbol{\Sigma_r}|}} \exp\left(\frac{-(l_v - \boldsymbol{\mu_r})^T \boldsymbol{\Sigma}_r^{-1}(l_v - \boldsymbol{\mu_r})}{2}\right) \quad (1)$$

where $\boldsymbol{\mu_r}$ and $\boldsymbol{\Sigma_r}$ denote the mean vector and covariance matrix.

Popularity can also affect the users' check-in behaviors to a great extent. Especially, when people travel out of town, especially in a new region, their decision-makings are significantly affected by the word-of-mouth opinions, which can be represented as the popularity of the POIs. We use the multinomial distribution $\boldsymbol{\varphi_r}$ to model the normalized popularity of POIs in a region level, i.e., $\varphi_{r,v}$ denotes the normalized popularity of POI v in region r. The local popular POIs represent the local attractions and potentially provide better user experiences. That is why two POIs with the same semantics can be rated differently in the same region.

Note that, to avoid overfitting, we place a Dirichlet prior [30, 34] over the multinomial distribution $\boldsymbol{\theta_u}$, as parameterized by α:

$$P(\boldsymbol{\theta_u}|\alpha) = \frac{\Gamma(\sum_z \alpha)}{\prod_z \Gamma(\alpha)} \prod_z \theta_{u,z}^{\alpha-1}, \quad (2)$$

where $\Gamma(\cdot)$ is the gamma function. Similarly, priors over $\boldsymbol{\vartheta_u}$, $\boldsymbol{\phi_z}$ and $\boldsymbol{\varphi_r}$ are imposed with parameters γ, β, and τ, respectively. We formally describe the probabilistic generative process of the JIM model in Algorithm 1. Finally, we obtain the joint distribution of the observed and hidden variables as described in Equation 3.

2.3 Model Inference

Our goal is to learn parameters that maximize the marginal log-likelihood of the observed random variables $\boldsymbol{v}, \boldsymbol{l_v}, \boldsymbol{W_v}$ and $\boldsymbol{t}$. However, the exact marginalization is intractable due to the coupling between hidden variables. Therefore, we follow the studies [35, 30, 34] to use Markov Chain Monte Carlo method (MCMC) to maximize the complete data likelihood in Equation 3. Note that we adopt conjugate prior (Dirichlet) for multinomial distributions, and thus we can easily integrate out $\boldsymbol{\vartheta}$, $\boldsymbol{\theta}$, $\boldsymbol{\phi}$ and $\boldsymbol{\varphi}$. Due to the space limitation, we omit the derivation details. In this way we facilitate the sampling – that is we need not sample $\boldsymbol{\vartheta}, \boldsymbol{\theta}, \boldsymbol{\phi}$ and $\boldsymbol{\varphi}$ at all. As

Algorithm 1: Probabilistic generative process in JIM

```
for each topic z do
  | Draw φ_z ~ Dirichlet(·|β);
end
for each region r do
  | Draw φ_r ~ Dirichlet(·|τ);
end
for each user u do
  | Draw θ_u ~ Dirichlet(·|α);
  | Draw ϑ_u ~ Dirichlet(·|γ);
end
for each D_u in D do
  for each check-in (u, v, l_v, W_v, t) ∈ D_u do
    | Draw a topic index z ~ Multi(θ_u);
    | Draw a time t ~ Beta(ψ_{z,1}, ψ_{z,2});
    | for each token w ∈ W_v do
    |   | Draw w ~ Multi(φ_z);
    | end
    | Draw a region index r ~ Multi(ϑ_u);
    | Draw a POI index v ~ Multi(φ_r);
    | Draw a location l_v ~ N(μ_r, Σ_r);
  end
end
```

for the hyperparameters α, β, γ and τ, for simplicity, we take a fix value, i.e., $\alpha = 50/K$, $\gamma = 50/R$ and $\beta = \tau = 0.01$, following the studies [35, 30, 34].

In the Gibbs sampling procedure, we need to obtain the posterior probability of sampling latent topic z and latent region r for each user check-in record $(u,\ v,\ l_v,\ W_v,\ t)$. First, we need to compute the conditional probability $P(z|\boldsymbol{z}_{\neg u,v}, \boldsymbol{r}, \boldsymbol{v}, \boldsymbol{l_v}, \boldsymbol{W_v}, \boldsymbol{t}, u, \cdot)$, where $\boldsymbol{z}_{\neg u,v}$ represents topic assignments for all check-in records except the current one. We begin with the joint probability distribution of the latent and observed variables shown in Equation 3, and using the Bayes chain rule, we can obtain the conditional probability conveniently as:

$$\begin{aligned} P(z|\boldsymbol{z}_{\neg u,v}, \boldsymbol{r}, \boldsymbol{v}, \boldsymbol{l_v}, \boldsymbol{W_v}, \boldsymbol{t}, u, \cdot) &\propto \frac{n_{u,z}^{\neg u,v} + \alpha}{\sum_{z'}(n_{u,z'}^{\neg u,v} + \alpha)} \\ \times \frac{(1-t)^{\psi_{z,1}-1} t^{\psi_{z,2}-1}}{B(\psi_{z,1}, \psi_{z,2})} &\prod_{w \in W_v} \frac{n_{z,w}^{\neg u,v} + \beta}{\sum_{w'}(n_{z,w'}^{\neg u,v} + \beta)} \end{aligned} \quad (4)$$

where $n_{u,z}$ is the number of times that latent topic z has been sampled from the interest distribution of user u, and $n_{z,w}$ is the number of times that word w is generated from topic z; the number $n^{\neg u,v}$ with superscript $\neg u, v$ denotes a quantity excluding the current instance. It is worth mentioning that our JIM can handle POIs without any content information. In that case, we will remove the last part related with W_v in the above sampling formula.

Then, we sample region r according to the following posterior probability:

$$\begin{aligned} &P(r|\boldsymbol{r}_{\neg u,v}, \boldsymbol{z}, \boldsymbol{v}, \boldsymbol{l_v}, \boldsymbol{W_v}, \boldsymbol{t}, u, \cdot) \\ &\propto \frac{n_{u,r}^{\neg u,v} + \gamma}{\sum_{r'}(n_{u,r'}^{\neg u,v} + \gamma)} \frac{n_{r,v}^{\neg u,v} + \tau}{\sum_{v'}(n_{r,v'}^{\neg u,v} + \tau)} P(l_v|\boldsymbol{\mu_r}, \boldsymbol{\Sigma_r}) \end{aligned} \quad (5)$$

where $n_{u,r}$ is the number of times that region r has been sampled from the spatial activity distribution of user u, and $n_{r,v}$ is the number of times that POI v is generated by region r.

After each iteration, we employ the method of moments to update the Beta and Gaussian distribution parameters (i.e., $\boldsymbol{\mu}$, $\boldsymbol{\Sigma}$ and $\boldsymbol{\psi}$) according to the assigned latent variables $\boldsymbol{r}$ and $\boldsymbol{z}$ for simplicity

$$\begin{aligned} &P(\boldsymbol{v}, \boldsymbol{l_v}, \boldsymbol{W_v}, \boldsymbol{t}, \boldsymbol{z}, \boldsymbol{r}|\alpha, \beta, \gamma, \tau, \boldsymbol{\psi}, \boldsymbol{\mu}, \boldsymbol{\Sigma}) \\ =&P(\boldsymbol{z}|\alpha)P(\boldsymbol{r}|\gamma)P(\boldsymbol{W_v}|\boldsymbol{z}, \beta)P(\boldsymbol{v}|\boldsymbol{r}, \tau)P(\boldsymbol{t}|\boldsymbol{z}, \boldsymbol{\psi})P(\boldsymbol{l_v}|\boldsymbol{r}, \boldsymbol{\mu}, \boldsymbol{\Sigma}) \\ =&\int P(\boldsymbol{z}|\boldsymbol{\theta})P(\boldsymbol{\theta}|\alpha)d\boldsymbol{\theta} \int P(\boldsymbol{r}|\boldsymbol{\vartheta})P(\boldsymbol{\vartheta}|\gamma)d\boldsymbol{\vartheta} \int P(\boldsymbol{W_v}|\boldsymbol{z}, \boldsymbol{\phi})P(\boldsymbol{\phi}|\beta)d\boldsymbol{\phi} \int P(\boldsymbol{v}|\boldsymbol{r}, \boldsymbol{\varphi})P(\boldsymbol{\varphi}|\tau)d\boldsymbol{\varphi} P(\boldsymbol{t}|\boldsymbol{z}, \boldsymbol{\psi})P(\boldsymbol{l_v}|\boldsymbol{r}, \boldsymbol{\mu}, \boldsymbol{\Sigma}) \end{aligned} \quad (3)$$

and speed. Specifically, parameters $\boldsymbol{\mu_r}$ and $\boldsymbol{\Sigma_r}$ are updated as in Equations (6) and (7).

$$\boldsymbol{\mu_r} = E(r) = \frac{1}{|S_r|}\sum_{v\in S_r} l_v \tag{6}$$

$$\boldsymbol{\Sigma_r} = D(r) = \frac{1}{|S_r|-1}\sum_{v\in S_r}(l_v - \boldsymbol{\mu_r})(l_v - \boldsymbol{\mu_r})^T \tag{7}$$

where S_r denotes the set of POIs assigned with latent region r. The Beta distribution parameters $\boldsymbol{\psi}$ are updated as follows:

$$\psi_{z,1} = \bar{t}_z\left(\frac{\bar{t}_z(1-\bar{t}_z)}{s_z^2} - 1\right) \tag{8}$$

$$\psi_{z,2} = (1-\bar{t}_z)\left(\frac{\bar{t}_z(1-\bar{t}_z)}{s_z^2} - 1\right) \tag{9}$$

where $\bar{t}_z$ and s_z^2 indicate the sample mean and the sample variance of the timestamps assigned with topic z, respectively.

Inference Framework. After a sufficient number of sampling iterations, the approximated posteriors can be used to estimate parameters by examining the counts of $\boldsymbol{z}$ and $\boldsymbol{r}$ assignments to check-in records. The detailed inference framework is shown in Algorithm 2. We first initialize the latent geographical regions by a K-means algorithm (Lines 3-4), and then randomly initialize the topic assignments for the check-in records (Lines 5-9). Afterwards, in each iteration, Equations (4, 5) are utilized to update the region and topic assignments for each check-in record $(u,\ v,\ l_v,\ W_v,\ t)$ (Lines 12-17). After each iteration, we update the Gaussian distribution and Beta distribution parameters (Lines 18-19). The iteration is repeated until convergence (Lines 11-24). In addition, a burn-in process is introduced in the first several hundreds of iterations to remove unreliable sampling results (Lines 20-23). We also introduce the sample lag (i.e., the interval between samples after burn-in) to sample only periodically thereafter to avoid correlations between samples.

Time Complexity. We analyze the time complexity of the above inference framework as follows. Suppose the process needs I iterations to reach convergence. In each iteration, it requires to go through all user check-in records. For each check-in record, it first requires $\mathcal{O}(K)$ operations to compute the posterior distribution for sampling latent topic, and then needs $\mathcal{O}(R)$ operations to compute the posterior distribution for sampling latent region. Thus, the whole time complexity is $\mathcal{O}(I(K+R)\sum_u |D_u|)$.

Algorithm 2: Inference Framework of JIM Model

Input: user check-in collection D, number of iteration I, number of burnin I_b, sample lag I_s, Priors α, γ, β, τ

Output: estimated parameters $\hat{\boldsymbol{\theta}}$, $\hat{\boldsymbol{\vartheta}}$, $\hat{\boldsymbol{\phi}}$, $\hat{\boldsymbol{\varphi}}$, $\hat{\boldsymbol{\psi}}$, $\hat{\boldsymbol{\mu}}$, and $\hat{\boldsymbol{\Sigma}}$

1 Create temporary variables $\boldsymbol{\theta}^{sum}$, $\boldsymbol{\vartheta}^{sum}$, $\boldsymbol{\phi}^{sum}$, $\boldsymbol{\varphi}^{sum}$, $\boldsymbol{\psi}^{sum}$, $\boldsymbol{\mu}^{sum}$ and $\boldsymbol{\Sigma}^{sum}$, and initialize them with zero;
2 Create temporary variables $\boldsymbol{\psi}$, $\boldsymbol{\mu}$ and $\boldsymbol{\Sigma}$;
3 Initialize the clustering of geographical locations using K-Means method.
4 Update $\boldsymbol{\mu}$ and $\boldsymbol{\Sigma}$ according to Equations (6,7), respectively;
5 **for** *each* $D_u \in D$ **do**
6   **for** *each check-in record* $(u,\ v,\ l_v,\ W_v,\ t) \in D_u$ **do**
7   Assign topic randomly;
8   **end**
9 **end**
10 Initialize variable $count$ with zero;
11 **for** $iteration = 1$ *to* I **do**
12   **for** *each* $D_u \in D$ **do**
13   **for** *each check-in record* $(u,\ v,\ l_v,\ W_v,\ t) \in D_u$ **do**
14   Update topic assignment using Equation (4);
15   Update region assignment using Equation (5);
16   **end**
17   **end**
18   Update $\boldsymbol{\mu}$ and $\boldsymbol{\Sigma}$ according to Equations (6, 7), respectively;
19   Update $\boldsymbol{\psi}$ according to Equations (8, 9);
20   **if** *(*$iteration > I_b$*) and (*$iteration$ *mod* $I_s == 0$*)* **then**
21     $count = count + 1$;
22   Update $\boldsymbol{\vartheta}^{sum}$, $\boldsymbol{\theta}^{sum}$, $\boldsymbol{\phi}^{sum}$, $\boldsymbol{\varphi}^{sum}$, $\boldsymbol{\psi}^{sum}$, $\boldsymbol{\mu}^{sum}$ and $\boldsymbol{\Sigma}^{sum}$ as follows:

$$\vartheta^{sum}_{u,r} += \frac{n_{u,r}+\gamma}{\sum_{r'}(n_{u,r'}+\gamma)} \tag{10}$$

$$\theta^{sum}_{u,z} += \frac{n_{u,z}+\alpha}{\sum_{z'}(n_{u,z'}+\alpha)} \tag{11}$$

$$\phi^{sum}_{z,w} += \frac{n_{z,w}+\beta}{\sum_{w'}(n_{z,w'}+\beta)} \tag{12}$$

$$\varphi^{sum}_{r,v} += \frac{n_{r,v}+\tau}{\sum_{v'}(n_{r,v'}+\tau)} \tag{13}$$

$$\boldsymbol{\psi}_{\boldsymbol{z}}^{sum} += \boldsymbol{\psi_z} \tag{14}$$

$$\boldsymbol{\mu}_{\boldsymbol{r}}^{sum} += \boldsymbol{\mu_r} \tag{15}$$

$$\boldsymbol{\Sigma}_{\boldsymbol{r}}^{sum} += \boldsymbol{\Sigma_r} \tag{16}$$

23   **end**
24 **end**
25 **Return** model parameters $\hat{\boldsymbol{\theta}} = \frac{\boldsymbol{\theta}^{sum}}{count}$, $\hat{\boldsymbol{\vartheta}} = \frac{\boldsymbol{\vartheta}^{sum}}{count}$, $\hat{\boldsymbol{\phi}} = \frac{\boldsymbol{\phi}^{sum}}{count}$, $\hat{\boldsymbol{\varphi}} = \frac{\boldsymbol{\varphi}^{sum}}{count}$, $\hat{\boldsymbol{\psi}} = \frac{\boldsymbol{\psi}^{sum}}{count}$, $\hat{\boldsymbol{\mu}} = \frac{\boldsymbol{\mu}^{sum}}{count}$, and $\hat{\boldsymbol{\Sigma}} = \frac{\boldsymbol{\Sigma}^{sum}}{count}$;

---

3. POI RECOMMENDATION USING JIM

Once we have learnt the model parameter set $\hat{\boldsymbol{\Psi}} = \{\hat{\boldsymbol{\theta}}, \hat{\boldsymbol{\vartheta}}, \hat{\boldsymbol{\phi}}, \hat{\boldsymbol{\varphi}}, \hat{\boldsymbol{\psi}}, \hat{\boldsymbol{\mu}}, \hat{\boldsymbol{\Sigma}}\}$, given a query user u_q with the query time t_q and location l_q, i.e., $q = (u_q, t_q, l_q)$, we compute a probability of user u_q checking-in each POI v, and then select top-k POIs with highest probabilities for the query user. Specifically, the probability of user u_q checking-in POI v, given his/her query time t_q and location l_q as well as the learnt model parameters $\hat{\boldsymbol{\Psi}}$, is computed according to Equation 17.

$$\begin{aligned} P(v, l_v, W_v|u_q, t_q, l_q, \hat{\boldsymbol{\Psi}}) &= \frac{P(v, l_v, W_v, t_q|u_q, l_q, \hat{\boldsymbol{\Psi}})}{\sum_{v'} P(v', l_{v'}, W_{v'}, t_q|u_q, l_q, \hat{\boldsymbol{\Psi}})} \\ &\propto P(v, l_v, W_v, t_q|u_q, l_q, \hat{\boldsymbol{\Psi}}) \end{aligned} \tag{17}$$

where $P(v, l_v, W_v, t_q|u_q, l_q, \hat{\boldsymbol{\Psi}})$ is calculated as follows:

$$\begin{aligned} &P(v, l_v, W_v, t_q|u_q, l_q, \hat{\boldsymbol{\Psi}}) \\ &= \sum_r P(r|l_q, \hat{\boldsymbol{\Psi}}) P(v, l_v, W_v, t_q|u_q, r, \hat{\boldsymbol{\Psi}}) \end{aligned} \tag{18}$$

where $P(r|l_q, \hat{\boldsymbol{\Psi}})$ denotes the probability of user u visiting region r given his/her current location l_q, and it is computed as in Equation 19 according to Bayes rule, in which the prior probability of latent region r can be estimated by Equation 20, as follows.

$$P(r|l_q, \hat{\boldsymbol{\Psi}}) = \frac{P(r)P(l_q|r, \hat{\boldsymbol{\Psi}})}{\sum_{r'} P(r')P(l_q|r', \hat{\boldsymbol{\Psi}})} \propto P(r)P(l_q|r, \hat{\boldsymbol{\Psi}}) \tag{19}$$

$$P(r) = \sum_u P(r|u)P(u) = \sum_u \frac{N_u + \kappa}{\sum_{u'}(N_{u'} + \kappa)} \hat{\vartheta}_{u',r} \tag{20}$$

where N_u denotes the number of check-ins generated by user u. In order to avoid overfilling, we introduce the Dirichlet prior parameter κ to play the role of pseudocount. $P(v, l_v, W_v, t_q|u_q, r, \hat{\boldsymbol{\Psi}})$ is defined as in Equation 21 where we adopt geometric mean for the probability of topic z generating word set W_v, i.e., $P(W_v|z, \hat{\boldsymbol{\Psi}}) = \prod_{w\in W_v} P(w|z, \hat{\boldsymbol{\Psi}})$, considering that the number of words associated with different POIs may be different.

Based on Equations (18-21), the original Equation 17 can be reformulated as in Equation 22.

3.1 Efficient Online Recommendation

Our proposed recommendation strategy is to first train JIM offline and obtain a knowledge model containing necessary insights about users' interests, mobility patterns and POIs' properties, and then use the knowledge model to retrieve top-k POIs for the real-time query q. To speed up the process of online recommendation, we propose a ranking framework based on Equation 22, as follows:

$$S(q,v)=\sum_r W(q,r)F(v,r)\sum_z W(q,z)F(v,z) \quad (23)$$

where $S(q,v)$ represents the ranking score of POI v for query q by matching query preference (i.e., $W(q,r)=P(l_q|\hat{\boldsymbol{\mu}}_{\boldsymbol{r}},\hat{\boldsymbol{\Sigma}}_{\boldsymbol{r}})$ and $W(q,z)=\hat{\theta}_{u_q,z}\hat{\psi}_{z,t_q}$) with the attributes of POI v (i.e., $F(v,r)=P(r)P(l_v|\hat{\boldsymbol{\mu}}_{\boldsymbol{r}},\hat{\boldsymbol{\Sigma}}_{\boldsymbol{r}})\hat{\varphi}_{r,v}$ and $F(v,z)=\left(\prod_{w\in W_v}\hat{\phi}_{z,w}\right)^{\frac{1}{|W_v|}}$). Each region/topic can be seen as an attribute (i.e., $a=r\ or\ z$), and $W(q,a)$ represents the weight of query q on attribute a, and $F(v,a)$ represents the score of POI v with respect to attribute a. This ranking framework separates the offline scoring computation from the online scoring computation. Since $F(v,a)$ is independent of queries, it can be computed offline. Although the query weight $W(q,a)$ is computed online, its main time-consuming components (i.e., $\hat{\psi}_{z,t_q}$, $\hat{\theta}_{u_q,z}$ and $(\hat{\boldsymbol{\mu}}_{\boldsymbol{r}},\hat{\boldsymbol{\Sigma}}_{\boldsymbol{r}})$) are also computed offline, the online computation is just a simple combination process. This design enables maximum precomputation for the problem considered, and in turn minimizes the query time.

The straightforward method of generating the top-k POIs needs to compute the ranking scores for all POIs according to Equation (23) and select top-k ones with highest ranking scores, which is, however, computationally inefficient, especially when the number of POIs or the number of POI attributes becomes large. To improve the online recommendation efficiency based on the observation of query preference sparsity that a query q only prefers a small number of attributes (say 3-5 latent dimensions) and the query weights on most attributes are extremely small, we adopt the TA-based query processing technique for top-k recommendation developed in [35, 29]. Since $W(q,a)$ is non-negative, the proposed ranking function in Equation 23 is monotonically increasing given a query q, which meets the requirement of the TA-based query processing technique. This technology has the nice property of finding top-k results correctly by examining the minimum number of POIs without scanning all ones, which enables the JIM model scalable to large-scale datasets.

4. EXPERIMENTS

In this section, we first describe the settings of experiments and then demonstrate the experimental results.

4.1 Experimental Settings

4.1.1 Datasets

Our experiments are conducted on two real datasets: Foursquare and Twitter. Their basic statistics are shown in Table 3.

Foursquare. This dataset contains the check-in history of 4,163 users who live in the California, USA. For each user, it contains his/her social networks, check-in POI IDs, location of each check-in POI in terms of latitude and longitude, check-in time and the contents of each check-in POI. Each check-in is stored as *user-ID, POI-ID, POI-location, POI-content, check-in time*. Each record in social networks is stored as *user-ID, friend-ID* and the total number of social relationship is 32,512. This dataset is publicly available [1].

	Foursquare	Twitter
# of users	4,163	114,508
# of POIs	21,142	62,462
# of check-ins	483,813	1,434,668
time span	Dec 2009-Jul 2013	Sep 2010-Jan 2011

Table 3: Basic statistics of Foursquare and Twitter datasets

Twitter. This dataset is based on the publicly available twitter dataset [7]. Twitter supports third-party location sharing services like Foursquare and Gowalla (where users of these services can share their check-ins on Twitter). But the original dataset does not contain the category and tag information about each POI. So, we crawled the content information associated with each POI from Foursquare with the help of its publicly available API [2]. Each check-in record has the same format with the above Foursquare dataset. But, this dataset does not contain user social network.

4.1.2 Comparative Approaches

We first compare our JIM model with the following four state-of-the-art POI recommendation methods.

SVDFeature. SVDFeature [4] is a machine learning toolkit designed to solve the feature-based matrix factorization. Based on this toolkit, we build a factorization model incorporating more side information beyond the user-POI matrix, including POI content, POI geographical location, temporal dynamics (i.e., check-in time) and popularity of POI, to compare with our model JIM fairly. The limitation of SVDFeature is that it cannot deal with continuous time and location, thus we adopt the discretization methods developed in [36, 30] to segment them into bins and grid squares.

Time-Aware Collaborative Filtering (TACF). TACF is the state-of-the-art time-aware POI recommendation method [36], which is a collaborative filtering model integrating *temporal effect*. Specifically, TACF splits time into hour-based slots and models the temporal preference of a given user in a time slot according to his/her visited POIs in that time slot. Given a query user u at a specific time t, TACF first finds a group of users sharing similar temporal preferences with u.

UPS-CF. UPS-CF, proposed in [10], is a collaborative recommendation framework which is especially designed for out-of-town users. This framework integrates user-based collaborative filtering and social-based collaborative filtering, i.e., recommending POIs to a target user according to the check-in records of both his/her friends and similar users with him/her.

LCA-LDA. LCA-LDA is a location-content-aware recommender model which is developed to support POI recommendation for users traveling in new cities [35]. This model takes into account both personal interests and local preferences of each city by exploiting POI co-visiting patterns and contents of POIs. Compared with JIM, it ignores the temporal effect and geographical influence.

[1] http://www.public.asu.edu/ hgao16/dataset.html
[2] https://developer.foursquare.com/

$$P(v,l_v,W_v,t_q|u_q,r,\hat{\Psi})=P(l_v|r,\hat{\Psi})P(v|r,\hat{\Psi})\sum_z P(z|u_q,\hat{\Psi})P(t_q|z,\hat{\Psi})\Big(\prod_{w\in W_v}P(w|z,\hat{\Psi})\Big)^{\frac{1}{|W_v|}} \quad (21)$$

$$\begin{aligned}P(v,l_v,W_v|u_q,t_q,l_q,\hat{\Psi}) &\propto \sum_r\Big[P(r)P(l_q|r,\hat{\Psi})P(l_v|r,\hat{\Psi})P(v|r,\hat{\Psi})\sum_z P(z|u_q,\hat{\Psi})P(t_q|z,\hat{\Psi})\Big(\prod_{w\in W_v}P(w|z,\hat{\Psi})\Big)^{\frac{1}{|W_v|}}\Big]\\ &=\sum_r\Big[P(r)P(l_v|\hat{\boldsymbol{\mu}}_{\boldsymbol{r}},\hat{\boldsymbol{\Sigma}}_{\boldsymbol{r}})P(l_q|\hat{\boldsymbol{\mu}}_{\boldsymbol{r}},\hat{\boldsymbol{\Sigma}}_{\boldsymbol{r}})\hat{\varphi}_{r,v}\Big]\sum_z\Big[\hat{\theta}_{u_q,z}\hat{\psi}_{z,t_q}\Big(\prod_{w\in W_v}\hat{\phi}_{z,w}\Big)^{\frac{1}{|W_v|}}\Big]\end{aligned} \quad (22)$$

To further validate the benefits brought by exploiting the temporal effect, content effect, word-of-mouth effect and geographical influence, respectively, we design four baselines. **JIM-S1** is the first simplified version of the JIM model where we remove the check-in time information, and the latent variable z only generates the word set W_v for each check-in record. **JIM-S2** is the second simplified version of the JIM model where we remove the content information of POIs, and the latent variable z only generates the check-in time. As the third simplified version of JIM, **JIM-S3** means our model without considering the word-of-mouth effect. So, the latent variable r only generates the location of POI v. As the last simplified version of JIM, **JIM-S4** means our model without considering the geographical influence. So, the latent variable r only generates the ID of POI v, and the popularity-aware user mobility component degenerates into a model-based collaborative filtering method.

4.1.3 *Evaluation methods*

Since our JIM is designed for both home-town and out-of-town recommendation, we evaluate the recommendation effectiveness of our model under the two scenarios respectively. Given a user profile in terms of a collection of user activities, we divide the user's activities into a training set and a test set. For the scenario of home-town recommendation, we randomly select 20% of the activity records occurring at the user's home town as test set, and use the remaining activity records as the training set. Similarly, for the scenario of out-of-town recommendation, we randomly select 20% of the activity records generated by the user when he/she travels out of town as the test set, and use the remaining activity records as training set. To decide whether an activity record occurs at home town or out of town, we measure the distance between the user's home location and the POI (i.e., $|l_u - l_v|$). If the distance is greater than the threshold d, then we assume the activity occurs when the user is out-of-town. Besides, to simulate a more real POI recommendation scenario, we have to choose a location coordinate as the target user's current standing position before visiting v. Specifically, for each test case $(u,\ v,\ l_v,\ W_v,\ t)$, we use a Gaussian function to generate a coordinate l within the circle of radius d centered at l_v, to represent the current standing point of user u. Thus, a query $q = (u,\ l,\ t)$ is formed for the test case.

According to the above dividing strategies, we split the user activity dataset D into the training set D_{train} and the test set D_{test}. To evaluate the recommendation methods, we adopt the evaluation methodology and measurement Accuracy@k proposed in [10, 35, 33, 32]. Specifically, for each activity record $(u,\ v,\ l_v,\ W_v, t)$ in D_{test} as well as its associated query q: First, we compute the ranking score for POI v and all other POIs which are within the circle of radius d centered at l_v and unvisited by u previously. Second, we form a ranked list by ordering all of these POIs according to their ranking scores. Let p denote the position of the POI v within this list. The best result corresponds to the case where v precedes all the unvisited POIs (that is, $p = 1$). Third, we form a top-k recommendation list by picking the k top ranked POIs from the list. If $p \leq k$, we have a hit (i.e., the ground truth v is recommended to the user). Otherwise, we have a miss.

The computation of Accuracy@k proceeds as follows. We define hit@k for a single test case as either the value 1, if the ground truth POI v appears in the top-k results, or the value 0, if otherwise. The overall Accuracy@k is defined by averaging over all test cases:

$$Accuracy@k = \frac{\#hit@k}{|D_{test}|}$$

where $\#hit@k$ denotes the number of hits in the test set, and $|D_{test}|$ is the number of all test cases. The results have been validated by means of a standard 5-fold cross validation.

4.2 Recommendation Effectiveness

In this part, we present the effectiveness of the recommendation methods with well-tuned parameters. Figures 2 and 3 report the performance of the recommendation methods on the Foursquare and Twitter datasets, respectively. We only show the performance where k is set to 1, 5, 10, 15, 20, as a greater value of k is usually ignored for a typical top-k recommendation task.

Out-of-Town Recommendation On Foursquare. Figure 2(a) presents the recommendation accuracy in the scenario of out-of-town recommendation, where the accuracy of JIM is about 0.12 when $k = 10$, and 0.15 when $k = 20$ (i.e., the model has a probability of 12% of placing an appealing POI in the top-10 and 15% of placing it in the top-20). Clearly, our proposed JIM model outperforms other competitor models significantly, and the advantages of JIM over other competitor methods are very obvious in this scenario. Several observations are made from the results: 1) TACF and UPS-CF drop behind JIM, SVDFeature and LCA-LDA, showing the advantages of latent class models incorporating the contents of checked-in POIs. This is because users have few check-in activity records in out-of-town regions (e.g., cities), thus TACF and UPS-CF suffer from the severe data sparsity in this scenario while JIM, SVDFeature and LCA-LDA are latent class models and integrate content information of POIs, which can alleviate the data sparsity problem to a great extent. 2) UPS-CF performs better than TACF, showing the benefits brought by exploiting social influence. The check-in records left by social friends can help alleviate the issue of data sparsity in the out-of-town scenario to a small extent, since we sometimes travel out of town to visit our friends. 3) JIM and SVDFeature perform better than LCA-LDA. This is because LCA-LDA ignores both temporal effect and geographical influence compared with JIM and SVDFeature. 4) JIM achieves much higher recommendation accuracy than SVDFeature although they use the same types of features and information, showing the advantage of probabilistic generative models over feature-based matrix factorization. This may be because some important information is lost when discretizing time and geographical location information.

Home-Town Recommendation On Foursquare. In Figure 2(b), we report the performance of all recommendation models for the home-town scenario. From the results, we observe that the recommendation accuracies of all methods are higher in Figure 2(b) than that in Figure 2(a). Besides, LCA-LDA outperforms TACF in Figure 2(a) while TACF slightly exceeds LCA-LDA in Figure 2(b) due to its incorporation of temporal effect, showing that time-aware collaborative filtering method better suits the setting where the user-POI matrix is not sparse, and the model-based method which integrates content information of POIs is more capable of overcoming the difficulty of data sparsity in the out-of-town scenario. Another observation is that the performance gap between our JIM model and other competitor methods is smaller than that in Figure 2(a), showing that the performance differences among recommendation methods become less obvious when the issue of data sparsity is not serious. The comparison between Figure 2(a) and Figure 2(b) also reveals that the two recommendation scenarios are intrinsically different, and should be separately evaluated.

Recommendation on Twitter. Figure 3 reports the performance of the recommendation models on the Twitter dataset. We do not compare our model with UPS-CF since this dataset does not contain user social network information. From the figure, we can see that the trend of comparison result is similar to that presented in Figure 2, and the main difference is that all recommendation methods achieve lower accuracy. This may be because users in the Foursquare dataset have more check-in records than users in the

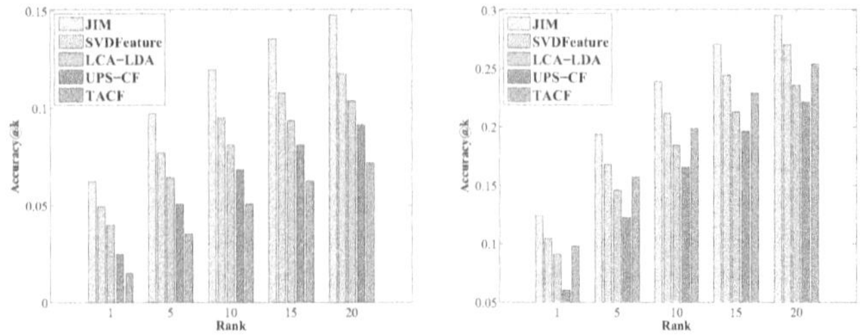

(a) Out-of-town Recommendation (b) Home-town Recommendation

Figure 2: Top-k Performance on Foursquare Dataset

Twitter dataset on average, which enables the models to capture users' interests more accurately.

4.3 Impact of Different Factors

To explore the benefits of integrating the temporal effect, content effect, word-of-mouth effect and geographical influence into JIM model, respectively, we compare our JIM model with four baselines, JIM-S1, JIM-S2, JIM-S3 and JIM-S4. The comparison results are shown in Tables 4 and 5. From the results, we first observe that JIM consistently outperforms the four baselines in both out-of-town recommendation scenario and home-town recommendation scenario, indicating that JIM benefits from simultaneously considering the four factors in a joint way. Second, we find that the contribution of each factor to improving recommendation accuracy is different. Besides, another observation is that the contributions of the same factor are different in the two different recommendation scenarios. Specifically, according to the importance of

Methods	Out-of-Town Scenario			Home-Town Scenario		
	Ac@1	Ac@10	Ac@20	Ac@1	Ac@10	Ac@20
JIM-S1	0.052	0.108	0.134	0.101	0.204	0.253
JIM-S2	0.045	0.096	0.119	0.117	0.226	0.280
JIM-S3	0.049	0.101	0.125	0.112	0.219	0.271
JIM-S4	0.056	0.113	0.140	0.106	0.212	0.262
JIM	**0.062**	**0.121**	**0.149**	**0.124**	**0.241**	**0.298**

Table 4: Recommendation Accuracy on Foursquare Dataset.

Methods	Out-of-Town Scenario			Home-Town Scenario		
	Ac@1	Ac@10	Ac@20	Ac@1	Ac@10	Ac@20
JIM-S1	0.033	0.072	0.089	0.084	0.162	0.199
JIM-S2	0.028	0.064	0.079	0.095	0.179	0.220
JIM-S3	0.031	0.067	0.083	0.091	0.173	0.213
JIM-S4	0.037	0.075	0.093	0.088	0.168	0.206
JIM	**0.041**	**0.080**	**0.099**	**0.100**	**0.191**	**0.235**

Table 5: Recommendation Accuracy on Twitter Dataset.

the four factors in the out-of-town recommendation scenario, they can be ranked as follows: Content Effect > Word-of-Mouth Effect > Temporal Effect > Geographical Influence, while in the home-town recommendation scenario they can be ranked as: Temporal Effect > Geographical Influence > Word-of-Mouth Effect > Content Effect. Obviously, the content information plays a dominant role in overcoming the issue of data sparsity of out-of-town recommendation scenario, while the temporal effect is most important to improve home-town recommendation. This is because the two recommendation scenarios have different characteristics: 1) most of users have enough check-in records in their home towns while few check-in activities are left in out-of-town regions; 2) the limitation of travel distance in the out-of-town scenario does not matter as much as that in home town; and 3) users' daily routines may change when they travel out of town.

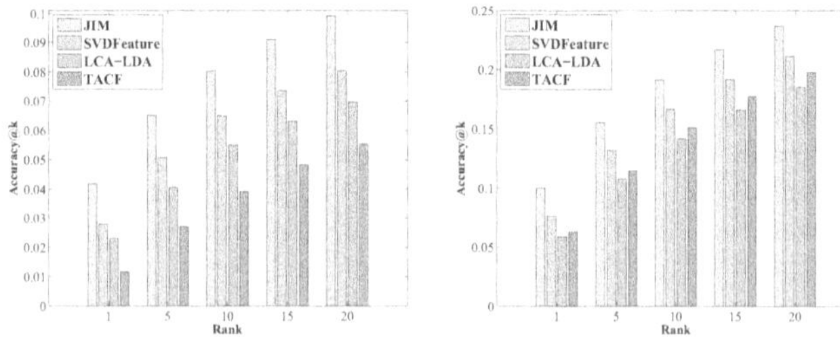

(a) Out-of-town Recommendation (b) Home-town Recommendation

Figure 3: Top-k Performance on Twitter Dataset

4.4 Impact of Model Parameters

Tuning model parameters, such as the number of topics (i.e., K), the number of regions (i.e., R), is critical to the performance of JIM model. We therefore study the impact of model parameters on Foursquare dataset in this section.

As for the hyperparameters α, γ, β and τ, following recent works [23, 35], we empirically set fixed values (i.e., $\alpha = 50/K$, $\gamma = 50/R$, $\beta = \tau = 0.01$). We try different setups and find that the performance of JIM model is not sensitive to these hyperparameters, but the performance of JIM is sensitive to the number of topics and regions. Thus, we test the performance of JIM model by varying the number of topics and regions, and present the results in Tables 6 and 7. From the results, we observe that the recommendation accuracy of JIM first increases with the increasing number of topics, and then it does not change significantly when the number

R \ K	K=20	K=30	K=40	K=50	K=60	K=70
R=20	0.089	0.095	0.099	0.101	0.101	0.101
R=30	0.095	0.102	0.106	0.108	0.108	0.109
R=40	0.101	0.108	0.113	0.115	0.116	0.116
R=50	0.106	0.113	0.118	0.121	0.121	0.121
R=60	0.106	0.113	0.118	0.121	0.121	0.121
R=70	0.106	0.113	0.118	0.121	0.121	0.122

Table 6: Out-of-Town Recommendation Accuracy@10.

R \ K	K=20	K=30	K=40	K=50	K=60	K=70
R=20	0.178	0.190	0.198	0.202	0.203	0.203
R=30	0.191	0.204	0.213	0.217	0.217	0.217
R=40	0.204	0.217	0.227	0.231	0.232	0.232
R=50	0.212	0.227	0.236	0.241	0.241	0.241
R=60	0.212	0.227	0.236	0.241	0.241	0.242
R=70	0.212	0.227	0.237	0.241	0.241	0.242

Table 7: Home-Town Recommendation Accuracy@10.

of topics is larger than 50. Similar observation is made for increasing the number of regions (i.e., R): the recommendation accuracy of JIM increases with the increasing number of regions, and then it does not change much when the number of regions is larger than 50. The reason is that K and R represent the model complexity. Thus, when K and R are too small, the model has limited ability to describe the data. On the other hand, when K and R exceed a threshold, the model is complex enough to handle the data. At this point, it is less helpful to improve the model performance by increasing K and R. It should be noted that the performance reported in Figure 2 is achieved with 50 latent topics (i.e., $K = 50$) and 50 latent regions (i.e., $R = 50$). Similar observations are also made on the Twitter dataset, and the optimal experimental results presented in Figure 3 are obtained with the parameter settings $K = 50$ and $R = 70$.

4.5 Recommendation Efficiency

This experiment is to evaluate the online recommendation efficiency. For the online recommendation of JIM, we adopt two methods. The first one is called JIM-TA which adopts the TA-based query processing technique [35] to produce online recommendation. The second is called JIM-BF which uses a naive brute-force algorithm to produce top-k recommendations by linear scan. As the feature-based matrix factorization model SVDFeature can be seamlessly integrated with the Metric Tree-based retrieval algorithm proposed in [14], we compare JIM-TA with it (SVDFeature-MT). The number of latent factors is set 120 (i.e., $K = 50$ and $R = 70$) for both SVDFeature and JIM. Note that the ranking function in SVDFeature is not monotonic, hence, the TA-based query processing technique cannot be applied to it. All the online recommendation algorithms were implemented in Java (JDK 1.6) and run on a Linux Server with 128G RAM.

Table 8 presents the average online efficiency of three different methods over all queries created for D_{test} on the Twitter dataset. We show the performance where k is set to 1, 5, 10, 15 and 20. For example, on average JIM-TA finds the top-10 recommendations from about 62,000 POIs in 29.67 ms. From the results, we observe that 1) JIM-TA outperforms JIM-BF significantly, justifying the benefits brought by the TA-based query processing technique, and it only needs to access around 16% of all the POIs on average for top-10 recommendations since it takes full advantage of sparsity in query preferences; 2) the time cost of JIM-TA increases with the increasing number of recommendations (i.e., k), but it is still much lower than that of JIM-BF in the recommendation task even when $k = 20$; and 3) the time cost of SVDFeature-MT is higher than that of the naive linear scan method in our task, although Koenigstein et al. [14] reported the good performance of the Metric Tree in the setting with 50 latent factors where it achieved about 1.7 times faster than the linear scan method for $k = 10$. This result shows that the Metric-Tree cannot still overcome the curse of dimensionality when the objects (e.g., POIs) have hundreds of dimensionality or attributes.

Methods	Online Recommendation Time Cost (ms)				
	k=1	k=5	k=10	k=15	k=20
JIM-TA	9.91	18.45	29.67	37.24	44.36
JIM-BF	145.34	145.75	145.89	145.14	145.28
SVDFeature-MT	173.12	223.46	274.78	314.06	349.17

Table 8: Recommendation Efficiency on Twitter Dataset.

5. RELATED WORK

POI recommendation, also called location or place recommendation, has been considered as an essential task in the domain of recommender systems [2]. Recently, with the development of location-based social networks, it is easy for users to check-in at POIs in the physical world, resulting in easy access of large-scale check-in records [9]. Based on the LBSNs data, many recent work has tried to improve POI recommendation by exploiting and integrating geographical and social influence, temporal effect and content information of POIs.

Geo-Social Influence. Many recent studies [7, 10, 28, 8, 37, 21, 39, 40] showed that there is a strong correlation between user check-in activities and geographical distance as well as social connections, so most of current POI recommendation work mainly focuses on leveraging the geographical and social influences to improve recommendation accuracy. For example, Ye et al. [28] delved into POI recommendation by investigating the geographical influences among locations and proposed a system that combines user preferences, social influence and geographical influence. Cheng et al. [5] investigated the geographical influence through combining a multi-center Gaussian model, matrix factorization and social influence together for location recommendation. Lian et al. [17] incorporated spatial clustering phenomenon resulted by geographical influence into a weighted matrix factorization framework to deal with the challenge from matrix sparsity. However, all of them do not consider the current location of the user. Thus, no matter whether the user is located in the home town or traveling out of town, they will recommend the same POIs to the user. In light of this, Ference et al. [10] designed a collaborative recommendation framework which not only investigates the roles of friends and similar users in POI recommendation, but also considers the current location of the user.

Temporal Effect. The temporal effect of user check-in activities in LBSNs has also attracted much attention from researchers. POI recommendation with temporal effect mainly leverage temporal cyclic patterns and temporal chronological patterns on LBSNs. Gao et al. [11] investigated the temporal cyclic patterns of user check-ins in terms of temporal non-uniformness and temporal consecutiveness. Yuan et al. [36] also incorporated the temporal cyclic information into a user-based collaborative filtering framework for time-aware POI recommendation. Cheng et al. [6] introduced the task of successive personalized POI recommendation in LBSNs by embedding the temporal chronological patterns.

Content Information. Most recently, researchers explored the content information of POIs to alleviate the problem of data sparsity. Hu et al. [13] proposed a spatial topic model for POI recommendation considering both spatial aspect and textual aspect of user posts from Twitter. Liu et al. [20] studied the effect of POI-associated tags for POI recommendation with an aggregated LDA and matrix factorization method. Yin et al. [35, 24] exploited both personal interests and local preferences based on the contents associated with spatial items. Gao et al. [12] and Zhao et al. [38] studied both POI-associated contents and user sentiment information (e.g., user comments) into POI recommendation and reported their good performance. However, all of them do not consider the time information associated with the contents of POIs.

As described above, while there are many studies to improve the POI recommendation by exploiting geographical-social influence, temporal effect and content information, they lack an integrated analysis of their joint effect to alleviate the issue of data sparsity, especially in out-of-town recommendation scenario. Most of the above work assumed that users are in home town, thus they ignored that users' interests can vary drastically at different regions (e.g., cities), failing to deal with user interest drift. Our proposed method strategically takes all these factors into consideration and presents a flexible probabilistic generative model for both home-town recommendation and out-of-town recommendation. To deal with the drift of user interests, our method considers the current location of the user and exploits the local word-of-mouth effect. Moreover, we are the first to study the importance of each mentioned factor to overcome the data sparsity in both home-town and out-of-town recommendation scenarios under a unified framework.

6. CONCLUSION AND FUTURE WORK

In this paper, we proposed a joint probabilistic generative model JIM to model users' check-in behaviors in LBSNs, which strategically integrates the factors of temporal effect, content effect, geographical influence and word-of-mouth effect to effectively overcome the issues of data sparsity and user interest drift across geographical regions, especially when users travel out of town. To demonstrate the applicability and flexibility of JIM, we investigated how it supports two recommendation scenarios in a unified way, *home-town recommendation* and *out-of-town recommendation*. We conducted extensive experiments to evaluate the performance of our JIM model in terms of both effectiveness and efficiency. The results showed superiority of JIM model over other competitor methods. Besides, we studied the importance of each factor in improving both home-town and out-of-town recommendation under the same framework, and found that the *content information* plays a dominant role in overcoming the data sparsity in out-of-town recommendation scenario, while the *temporal effect* is most important to improve home-town recommendation.

7. ACKNOWLEDGEMENT

The work described in this paper is partially supported by ARC Discovery Project (DP140103171). It is also partially supported by National Basic Research Program of China (2013CB329305), National Natural Science Foundation of China (Grant No. 61272155, 61232006, 61303164, 61402447), 973 program of China (Grant No. 2014CB340405), Beijing Natural Science Foundation (Grant No. 9144037) and the Scientific Research Foundation for the Returned Overseas Chinese Scholars, State Education Ministry.

8. REFERENCES

[1] G. Adomavicius and A. Tuzhilin. Toward the next generation of recommender systems: a survey of the state-of-the-art and possible extensions. *Knowledge and Data Engineering, IEEE Transactions on*, 17(6):734 – 749, june 2005.

[2] J. Bao, Y. Zheng, D. Wilkie, and M. F. Mokbel. A survey on recommendations in location-based social networks. *GeoInformatica*, 2014.

[3] D. M. Blei, A. Y. Ng, and M. I. Jordan. Latent dirichlet allocation. *J. Mach. Learn. Res.*, 3:993–1022, Mar. 2003.

[4] T. Chen, W. Zhang, Q. Lu, K. Chen, Z. Zheng, and Y. Yu. Svdfeature: A toolkit for feature-based collaborative filtering. *J. Mach. Learn. Res.*, 13(1):3619–3622, Dec. 2012.

[5] C. Cheng, H. Yang, I. King, and M. R. Lyu. Fused matrix factorization with geographical and social influence in location-based social networks. In *AAAI*, 2012.

[6] C. Cheng, H. Yang, M. R. Lyu, and I. King. Where you like to go next: Successive point-of-interest recommendation. In *IJCAI*, pages 2605–2611, 2013.

[7] Z. Cheng, J. Caverlee, K. Lee, and D. Z. Sui. Exploring millions of footprints in location sharing services. In *ICWSM*, 2011.

[8] E. Cho, S. A. Myers, and J. Leskovec. Friendship and mobility: user movement in location-based social networks. In *KDD*, pages 1082–1090, 2011.

[9] B. Cui, H. Mei, and B. C. Ooi. Big data: the driver for innovation in databases. *National Science Review*, 1(1):27–30, 2014.

[10] G. Ference, M. Ye, and W.-C. Lee. Location recommendation for out-of-town users in location-based social networks. In *CIKM*, pages 721–726, 2013.

[11] H. Gao, J. Tang, X. Hu, and H. Liu. Exploring temporal effects for location recommendation on location-based social networks. In *RecSys*, pages 93–100, 2013.

[12] H. Gao, J. Tang, X. Hu, and H. Liu. Content-aware point of interest recommendation on location-based social networks. In *AAAI*, 2015.

[13] B. Hu and M. Ester. Spatial topic modeling in online social media for location recommendation. In *RecSys*, pages 25–32, 2013.

[14] N. Koenigstein, P. Ram, and Y. Shavitt. Efficient retrieval of recommendations in a matrix factorization framework. In *CIKM*, pages 535–544, 2012.

[15] J. J. Levandoski, M. Sarwat, A. Eldawy, and M. F. Mokbel. Lars: A location-aware recommender system. In *ICDE*, pages 450–461, 2012.

[16] R. Li, S. Wang, H. Deng, R. Wang, and K. C.-C. Chang. Towards social user profiling: unified and discriminative influence model for inferring home locations. In *KDD*, pages 1023–1031, 2012.

[17] D. Lian, C. Zhao, X. Xie, G. Sun, E. Chen, and Y. Rui. Geomf: Joint geographical modeling and matrix factorization for point-of-interest recommendation. In *KDD*, pages 831–840, 2014.

[18] M. Lichman and P. Smyth. Modeling human location data with mixtures of kernel densities. In *KDD*, pages 35–44, 2014.

[19] B. Liu, Y. Fu, Z. Yao, and H. Xiong. Learning geographical preferences for point-of-interest recommendation. In *KDD*, pages 1043–1051, 2013.

[20] B. Liu and H. Xiong. Point-of-interest recommendation in location based social networks with topic and location awareness. In *SDM*, pages 396–404, 2013.

[21] A. Noulas, S. Scellato, N. Lathia, and C. Mascolo. A random walk around the city: New venue recommendation in location-based social networks. In *SocialCom*, pages 144–153, 2012.

[22] S. Scellato, A. Noulas, R. Lambiotte, and C. Mascolo. Socio-spatial properties of online location-based social networks. In *ICWSM*, 2011.

[23] J. Tang, S. Wu, J. Sun, and H. Su. Cross-domain collaboration recommendation. In *KDD*, pages 1285–1293, 2012.

[24] W. Wang, H. Yin, L. Chen, Y. Sun, S. Sadiq, and X. Zhou. Geo-sage: A geographical sparse additive generative model for spatial item recommendation. In *KDD*, 2015.

[25] X. Wang and A. McCallum. Topics over time: A non-markov continuous-time model of topical trends. In *KDD*, 2006.

[26] M. Ye, D. Shou, W.-C. Lee, P. Yin, and K. Janowicz. On the semantic annotation of places in location-based social networks. In *KDD*, pages 520–528, 2011.

[27] M. Ye, P. Yin, and W.-C. Lee. Location recommendation for location-based social networks. In *GIS*, pages 458–461, 2010.

[28] M. Ye, P. Yin, W.-C. Lee, and D.-L. Lee. Exploiting geographical influence for collaborative point-of-interest recommendation. In *SIGIR*, pages 325–334, 2011.

[29] H. Yin, B. Cui, L. Chen, Z. Hu, and Z. Huang. A temporal context-aware model for user behavior modeling in social media systems. In *SIGMOD*, pages 1543–1554, 2014.

[30] H. Yin, B. Cui, L. Chen, Z. Hu, and C. Zhang. Modeling location-based user rating profiles for personalized recommendation. *ACM Trans. Knowl. Discov. Data*, 9(3):19:1–19:41, Apr. 2015.

[31] H. Yin, B. Cui, L. Chen, Z. Hu, and X. Zhou. Dynamic user modeling in social media systems. *ACM Trans. Inf. Syst.*, 33(3):10:1–10:44, Mar. 2015.

[32] H. Yin, B. Cui, Z. Huang, W. Wang, X. Wu, and X. Zhou. Joint modeling of users' interests and mobility patterns for point-of-interest recommendation. In *MM*, 2015.

[33] H. Yin, B. Cui, J. Li, J. Yao, and C. Chen. Challenging the long tail recommendation. *Proc. VLDB Endow.*, 5(9):896–907, 2012.

[34] H. Yin, B. Cui, Y. Sun, Z. Hu, and L. Chen. Lcars: A spatial item recommender system. *ACM Trans. Inf. Syst.*, 32(3):11:1–11:37, July 2014.

[35] H. Yin, Y. Sun, B. Cui, Z. Hu, and L. Chen. Lcars: A location-content-aware recommender system. In *KDD*, pages 221–229, 2013.

[36] Q. Yuan, G. Cong, Z. Ma, A. Sun, and N. M. Thalmann. Time-aware point-of-interest recommendation. In *SIGIR*, pages 363–372, 2013.

[37] C. Zhang, L. Shou, K. Chen, G. Chen, and Y. Bei. Evaluating geo-social influence in location-based social networks. In *CIKM*, pages 1442–1451, 2012.

[38] K. Zhao, G. Cong, Q. Yuan, and K. Zhu. Sar: A sentiment-aspect-region model for user preference analysis in geo-tagged reviews. In *ICDE*, 2015.

[39] K. Zheng, S. Shang, N. J. Yuan, and Y. Yang. Towards efficient search for activity trajectories. In *ICDE*, pages 230–241, 2013.

[40] K. Zheng, Y. Zheng, N. J. Yuan, S. Shang, and X. Zhou. Online discovery of gathering patterns over trajectories. *IEEE Transactions on Knowledge and Data Engineering*, 26(8):1974–1988, 2014.

[41] Y. Zheng and X. Xie. Learning travel recommendations from user-generated gps traces. *ACM Trans. Intell. Syst. Technol.*, 2(1):2:1–2:29, Jan. 2011.

[42] Y. Zheng, L. Zhang, X. Xie, and W.-Y. Ma. Mining interesting locations and travel sequences from gps trajectories. In *WWW*, pages 791–800, 2009.

ORec: An Opinion-Based Point-of-Interest Recommendation Framework

Jia-Dong Zhang
Dept. of Computer Science
City University of Hong Kong
jzhang26-c@my.cityu.edu.hk

Chi-Yin Chow
Dept. of Computer Science
City University of Hong Kong
chiychow@cityu.edu.hk

Yu Zheng
Microsoft Research
Beijing, China
yuzheng@microsoft.com

ABSTRACT

As location-based social networks (LBSNs) rapidly grow, it is a timely topic to study how to recommend users with interesting locations, known as *points-of-interest* (POIs). Most existing POI recommendation techniques only employ the check-in data of users in LBSNs to learn their preferences on POIs by assuming a user's check-in frequency to a POI explicitly reflects the level of her preference on the POI. However, in reality users usually visit POIs only once, so the users' check-ins may not be sufficient to derive their preferences using their check-in frequencies only. Actually, the preferences of users are exactly implied in their opinions in text-based tips commenting on POIs. In this paper, we propose an opinion-based POI recommendation framework called ORec to take full advantage of the user opinions on POIs expressed as tips. In ORec, there are two main challenges: (i) detecting the polarities of tips (positive, neutral or negative), and (ii) integrating them with check-in data including social links between users and geographical information of POIs. To address these two challenges, (1) we develop a supervised aspect-dependent approach to detect the polarity of a tip, and (2) we devise a method to fuse *tip polarities* with *social links* and *geographical information* into a unified POI recommendation framework. Finally, we conduct a comprehensive performance evaluation for ORec using two large-scale real data sets collected from Foursquare and Yelp. Experimental results show that ORec achieves significantly superior polarity detection and POI recommendation accuracy compared to other state-of-the-art polarity detection and POI recommendation techniques.

Categories and Subject Descriptors

H.3.3 [**Information Storage and Retrieval**]: Information Search and Retrieval—*Information Filtering*

Keywords

Location-based social networks; point-of-interest recommendations; opinion mining; polarity detection; fusion

Permission to make digital or hard copies of all or part of this work for personal or classroom use is granted without fee provided that copies are not made or distributed for profit or commercial advantage and that copies bear this notice and the full citation on the first page. Copyrights for components of this work owned by others than ACM must be honored. Abstracting with credit is permitted. To copy otherwise, or republish, to post on servers or to redistribute to lists, requires prior specific permission and/or a fee. Request permissions from Permissions@acm.org.
CIKM'15, October 19 - 23, 2015, Melbourne, VIC, Australia
© 2015 ACM. ISBN 978-1-4503-3794-6/15/10 ...$15.00
DOI: http://dx.doi.org/10.1145/2806416.2806516.

1. INTRODUCTION

In location-based social networks (LBSNs) as shown in Figure 1, users establish social links with others, check in some interesting locations, known as *points-of-interest* (POIs), e.g., restaurants, stores and museums, and post tips to express their opinions about various aspects of POIs, e.g., atmosphere, price and service. With the rapid growth of LBSNs, e.g., Foursquare and Yelp, it is prevalent and important to recommend users with their preferred POIs. POI recommendations not only help users explore new places and enrich their life but also enable companies to launch advertisements to potential customers and improve business profits.

Figure 1: A location-based social network (LBSN)

To make POI recommendations, most recent methods [11, 23, 26, 29, 30, 31, 33] only employ users' historical check-in data to learn their preferences for POIs, i.e., these methods assume the check-in frequency of a user to a POI explicitly reflects the user's preference level for the POI. However, the check-in data of users may not be sufficient to indicate their preferences, especially when a user checks in a POI only once, since the user may like the POI very much or conversely. For example, by calculating the distribution of ratings in the five-star scale given by users to POIs from the Yelp Challenge data set [24] as shown in Figure 2(a), it is observed that the attitude of users towards POIs is not always positive (i.e., about 55% ratings > 3) and it is highly possibly negative (i.e., about 30% ratings < 3). One may argue that it is intuitive to assume that a user should have positive preference for a POI with more than one check-in. Unfortunately, in LBSNs users usually check in POIs only once. For instance, Figure 2(b) depicts the distribution of the number of check-ins of a user to a POI in a large-scale check-in data set [3] from Foursquare, in which more than 50% places have been checked in only once by the same user. As a result, merely utilizing check-in data as preference models usually introduces biases to the user preference level.

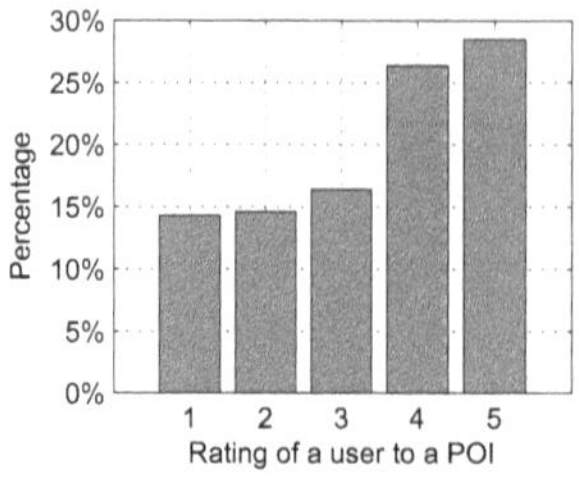

(a) Distribution of user ratings to POIs in Yelp [24]

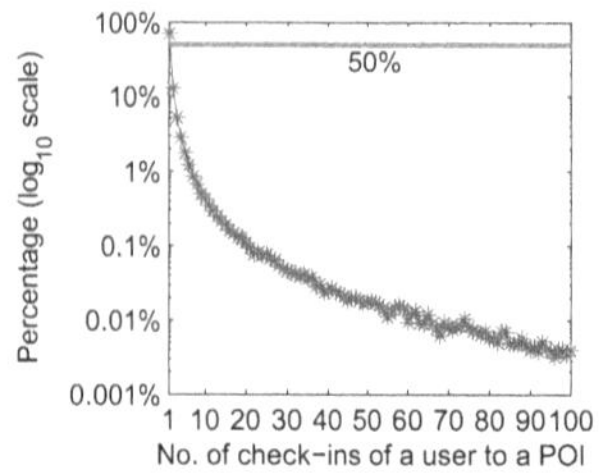

(b) Distribution of check-in times in Foursquare [3]

Figure 2: (a) Only about 55% ratings are positive (> 3); (b) Above 50% places have been checked in only once by the same user.

In fact, users' preferences are exactly reflected in their tips commenting on POIs, in which they express their opinions about various aspects of POIs. For example, consider a typical tip written by a user regarding a restaurant: "I went here last night. I loved the place with good atmosphere. The taste is not bad. The food has high quality but with a little high price." In this tip, the user has expressed different opinions to a variety of aspects of the POI, like "good atmosphere", "not bad taste", "high quality" and "high price". Therefore, the user's actual preference for the POI can be determined by detecting the tip's overall sentiment polarity: positive, neutral or negative, based on the opinions expressed in the tip. To the best of our knowledge, only the study [22] recommends POIs to users through utilizing the polarities of tips determined by a *unsupervised aspect-independent* method, in which the sentiment value of an opinion word is obtained by looking it up in sentiment lexicons (e.g., SentiWordNet) and the polarity of a tip is derived from the sum of sentiment values of all opinion words in the tip. Nevertheless, the unsupervised aspect-independent method cannot accurately detect the polarities of tips because of two main reasons. (1) The method uses *the absolute sentiment value of an opinion word independently of its modifying aspect* instead of using *the sentiment orientation of the opinion word depending on the modifying aspect*. As an example, for the two opinion phrases of "high quality" and "high price" in the aforementioned tip, the opinion word "high" in the two phrases has the same sentiment value by querying a lexicon, but it has completely different sentiment orientations: "high" modifying the aspect "quality" is positive while "high" modifying the aspect "price" is negative. (2) The method utilizes the simple summation function to combine different sentiment values rather than learning a sophisticated combination function from data.

In this paper, we propose a *supervised aspect-dependent* **O**pinion-based POI **Rec**ommendation framework (**ORec**) that derives the sentiment orientations of opinion words depending on aspects in tips and leverages them to predict the polarities of tips for enhancing the quality of POI recommendations. In ORec, there are two main challenges. The first challenge is to accurately detect the polarities of tips. Naturally, the polarity detection problem can be considered as the classical classification problem: training classification models on tips labeled with polarities and using the classification models to predict the polarity of a new tip. A straightforward solution is to apply the text classification methods that view a text as a bag of words and transform the text into a high-dimensional vector, each dimension of which corresponds to a word (e.g., sentiment words or frequent words [12, 17]) in a vocabulary. Unfortunately, these methods result in highly sparse word vectors and low polarity detection accuracy, because the vocabulary is usually very large compared to the text. To this end, we develop an approach that only considers *the aspects of POIs in their tips* rather than *raw words in a large vocabulary* as dimensions of vectors to reduce the number of dimensions for tips. Further, to decrease the dimension of aspect vectors and reduce the ambiguity between aspects, the proposed approach groups the aspects into clusters. Finally, a classification model is trained on the cluster-based vector representations of tips and exploited to predict the polarity of a new tip.

The other challenge is to combine the tip polarities with traditional check-in data (including social links and geographical information) to improve the POI recommendation quality. In terms of the current studies [23, 27], the check-in behaviors of users to POIs are significantly influenced by *others with social links* and *nearby visited POIs*, since users with social links are more likely to share common interests and physical interactions are required for users to check in POIs. For instance, friends often go to some places like restaurants together or a user may visit POIs recommended by friends. Moreover, users tend to visit POIs close to their homes or offices and also may be interested in exploring the nearby places of their visited POIs. How can we effectively fuse tip polarities with social links and geographical information into a unified recommendation framework? This problem is still open. For this purpose, we design a method to integrate *tip polarities of users regarding POIs* with *social links among users* and *geographical information of POIs* into a unified POI recommendation framework.

In general, our contributions can be summarized below.

- To the best of our knowledge, this is the first study to propose a POI recommendation framework based on users' opinions to the aspects of POIs in tips. In this framework, we develop a supervised aspect-dependent approach to accurately detect the polarities of tips. (Section 4)
- To improve the quality of POI recommendations, we design a method to fuse the influences of three different types of information in LBSNs including *tip polarities*, *social links* and *geographical information*. (Section 5)
- We conduct extensive experiments to evaluate the performance of ORec using two large-scale real data sets from Foursquare and Yelp. Experimental results show that: (1) ORec outperforms the classical text classification methods studied in [12, 17] and the unsupervised aspect-independent method [22] in terms of *polarity detection accuracy*. (2) ORec achieves better *recommendation accuracy* than state-of-the-art POI recommendation techniques. (Sections 6 and 7)

Organization of this paper: Section 2 highlights related work. Section 3 defines the research problems and presents an overview of the ORec framework. We present the proposed supervised aspect-dependent polarity detection approach in Section 4 and the developed POI recommendation method in Section 5. In Sections 6 and 7, we describe our experiment settings and analyze the performance of ORec, respectively. Section 8 concludes this paper.

2. RELATED WORK

POI recommendations using check-in data only. Most current studies (e.g., [1, 3, 11, 13, 14, 23, 26, 27, 29, 30, 31, 33]) only utilize the check-in data to learn the preference of users on POIs. Specifically, they employ the social links between users to derive the user similarity as an input of collaborative filtering techniques, based on the fact that friends are more likely to share common interests. They also exploit the geographical information of POIs to estimate the distribution of distances between visited POIs, due to the fact that if a POI is closer to the POIs visited by a user, it is more likely to be visited by the user. For instance, Liu et al. [14] used the instance-level and region-level geographical neighborhood characteristics, other researchers in [13, 23] fitted the distance among visited POIs as a power-law distribution for all users, and the authors of [27, 28, 29, 32] personalized the distance distribution for each user. However, these methods assume that the check-in frequencies of users to POIs directly reflects the preference levels, which may not be true in reality. For example, when a user checks in a POI only once, the user may like the POI very much or conversely.

POI recommendations using textual information. There are a few works that use the textual information of users commenting on POIs for location recommendations. For example, the work [10] employs the tags of POIs to provide interpretable representations for latent topics extracted from check-in data, while the study [35] represents each POI as a vector of words in its tips and utilizes the word vector to derive the similarity between POIs as a regularized term of tensor models over check-in data. More sophisticatedly, the method in [25] applies the well-known latent Dirichlet allocation (LDA) over tags of POIs or posts of users to mine the topic profiles for users and POIs, in which each topic is a distribution over words; then the topic profiles and topic distributions are exploited to determine the preference score of users to POIs. However, these studies do not take into account the opinion or sentiment of users on POIs. To the best of our knowledge, only the study [22] extracts opinion words from tips and employ them to determine the polarity of the tips based on the unsupervised aspect-independent method.

Polarity detection of texts. Existing polarity detection techniques generally fall into two categories: *supervised methods* and *unsupervised methods*. (1) *Supervised methods*. This category learns classification models from labeled texts and uses them to classify a new text into positive or negative based on supervised machine learning methods, such as support vector machines [12, 17], decision trees and naive Bayes [17, 21]. Nevertheless, the supervised methods often regard a feature as a word in a large vocabulary which causes highly sparse word vectors in texts and low polarity detection accuracy. (2) *Unsupervised methods*. The unsupervised methods [17, 22] search sentiment values of opinion words in a text based on sentiment lexicons and aggregate these values to determine the text's polarity. In particular, the works [6, 7] make use of the emoticon sentiment lexicon to increase the accuracy of polarity classification for social media services such as Twitter and Facebook. However, these unsupervised polarity detection methods consider the sentiment values of opinion words independently of their modifying aspects and apply simple aggregation functions to combine different sentiment values. As discussed in Section 1, they cannot accurately detect the polarity of tips, since the actual sentiment orientation of an opinion word strongly relies on its modifying aspect and a more sophisticated combination function should be learned from data.

Aspect-based opinion mining based on aspect extraction and clustering. There are also plenty of studies that mine the opinions from text at aspects. These studies can be classified into two main categories: *topic models* and *language rules*. (1) *Topic models*. A topic model is a generative model for texts: texts are mixtures of topics and each topic is a probability distribution of words. First, topic models (e.g., probabilistic latent semantic analysis and LDA) can be applied to aspect extraction by regarding each topic as an aspect, in which different words expressing the same aspect can be automatically grouped together [15, 34]. Further, to associate aspects with opinions, the topic models can be extended by adding a sentiment layer to detect aspect and opinion words simultaneously from texts [2, 9, 16]. However, topic models leverage *word co-occurrences among texts* rather than *word semantic meanings* to identify topics and word distributions; they are only able to find rough aspects instead of fine-grained aspects. (2) *Language rules*. The language-rule-based methods utilize the grammatical relations between aspects and opinion words to induce extraction rules. Most works [5, 18, 19] employ the modifying relation of opinion words and aspects to extract aspects and associate them with opinion words. Although the language-rule-based methods can discover fine-grained aspects, they need an additional step to group these fine-grained aspects into clusters, usually based on the synonym relation of aspects. In this paper, we utilize not only the synonym relation, but also the hypernymy and meronymy relations among aspects to cluster them into groups.

3. PROBLEM AND OVERVIEW

We first define basic concepts for this paper.

- **Aspect.** An aspect is an attribute or feature of a POI, e.g., "atmosphere", "price" and "quality" for a restaurant.
- **Opinion word.** An opinion word usually indicates a sentiment orientation with a sentiment value from lexicons, e.g., "good", "bad" and "high". Note that the sentiment orientation of "high" is not that intuitive because it depends on the aspect modified by "high".
- **Opinion phrase.** An opinion phrase $\langle a,o\rangle$ is a pair of aspect a and opinion word o, where the opinion word is used to express the sentiment orientation towards the aspect, e.g., $\langle atmosphere, good\rangle$ and $\langle price, high\rangle$. Note that o is also used to indicate the sentiment value of an opinion word in terms of lexicons for simplicity and the specific meaning of o (i.e., "opinion word" or "sentiment value") can be easily determined based on its context.
- **Tip.** A tip is a sequence of words describing a user's opinions on various aspects of a POI and consists of a set of opinion phrases, i.e., $tip = \{\langle a_i, o_i\rangle\}$.
- **Polarity of tip.** The polarity of a user's tip is the overall attitude of the user towards a POI and usually is classified into three cases: positive, neutral and negative. The set of polarities are denoted as $P = \{positive, neutral, negative\}$.

Problem definitions. The two problems addressed in this paper are defined as follows:

- **Problem 1: Polarity detection.** Given a training set of tips $D = \{\langle tip^j, p^j\rangle\}$, where each tip^j is labeled with a class, i.e., polarity $p^j \in P$, the goal is to predict the polarity $p \in P$ of a new *tip*. (Section 4)
- **Problem 2: Opinion-based POI recommendation.** Given all users' *tip polarities* and a certain user u's friends with *social links* $F(u)$ and *geographical information* of check-in POIs $L_u = \{l_1, l_2, \ldots, l_n\}$, the goal is to predict the preference score $s_{u,l}$ of user u regarding a new POI l (i.e., $l \notin L_u$) and then return the top-m POIs with the highest score $s_{u,l}$ for u. (Section 5)

Overview of ORec. Figure 3 demonstrates the overview of ORec, including two major parts: *polarity detection* and *POI recommendations*. (1) The *polarity detection* part generates the polarities of tips for the *POI recommendations* part. This part has three steps: (a) extracting opinion phrases (pairs of aspects and opinions) from tips, (b) grouping aspects into clusters and aggregating opinions of a tip into a sentiment vector in the cluster space,

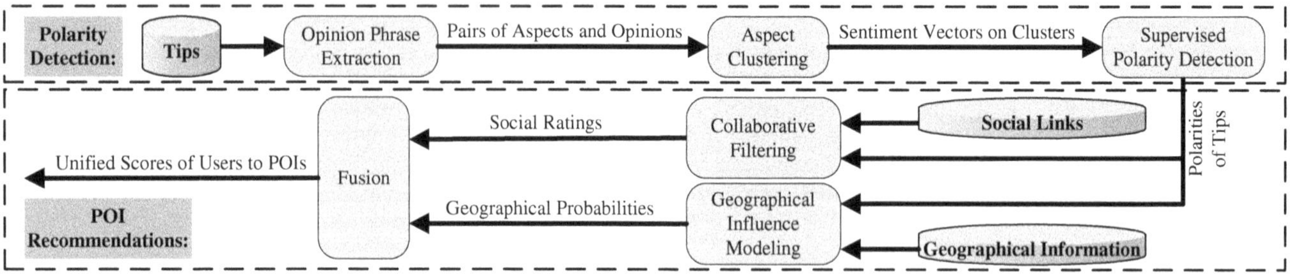

Figure 3: The overview of ORec

and (c) training a classification model in tips labeled with polarities and predicting the polarity of any new tips (without polarity labels). (2) The *POI recommendations* part exploits the tip polarity with social links and geographical information to estimate the score of a user to a new POI in order to recommend POIs for the user. This part also has three steps: (a) using collaborative filtering techniques to combine tip polarities with social links to estimate the social rating of users to new POIs, (b) modeling geographical influence by integrating tip polarities and geographical information of POIs to predict the geographical probability of users visiting new POIs, and (c) fusing the social rating and geographical probability into a unified score for POI recommendations.

4. POLARITY DETECTION

In general, our proposed supervised aspect-dependent approach has **three main phases for polarity detection**: (1) Aspects are extracted through nearby opinion words based on sentiment lexicons; accordingly the aspect vectors store the sentiment values of these opinion words. (2) The obtained aspects are grouped into adaptive K clusters based on the dissimilarities of aspects to decrease the dimension of aspect vectors and reduce the ambiguity between aspects for tips; by this end, each tip can be represented as a K-dimensional vector, each dimension for a cluster. (3) A classification model is trained on the cluster-based vector representations of tips with labeled polarities and employed to predict the polarity of any new tips.

4.1 Phase 1: Opinion Phrase Extraction

We can acquire opinion phrases consisting of pairs of aspects and opinion words through two steps.

Step 1: Tip preprocessing. Using the Stanford natural language parsers [20], a tip is firstly tokenized into words and split into a set of sentences. Then, each word in a sentence is identified with the part-of-speech (e.g., "good" is an adjective, "price" is a noun, "love" is a verb, etc.) and is lemmatized to a base form in order to reduce its inflectional and derivational forms (e.g., "loves", "loving" and "loved" are lemmatized to the same base form "love"). Finally, the grammatical dependencies between words in a sentence are determined by parsing the grammatical structure of the sentence. For example, the sentence of "the taste is not bad" contains a number of grammatical dependencies, such as "nsubj(bad, taste)", "neg(bad, not)", and so on, in which "nsubj" and "neg" are a certain grammatical dependency defined in [20].

Step 2: Opinion phrase extraction. One may consider some kinds of grammatical dependencies as opinion phrases, e.g., "nsubj(bad, taste)" denoting an opinion phrase $\langle taste, bad \rangle$. However, "nsubj" is unnecessary to represent an opinion phrase. For instance, the sentence of "I loved the place with good atmosphere" also contains "nsubj(love, I)" that is not an opinion phrase because of the lack of an aspect. Thus, it is hard to select a set of grammatical dependencies as opinion phrases in advance. To this end, we design a method to discover opinion phrases from grammatical dependencies of a sentence based on sentiment lexicons.

It is observed that an opinion phrase always includes an opinion word with a sentiment value by looking it up in lexicons, e.g., SentiWordNet. Thus, opinion words can be used as the indicators of opinion phrases. Further, given a grammatical dependency with an opinion word, it is regarded as an opinion phrase if the other word in the grammatical dependency is a noun that is required by an aspect. Finally, given an opinion phrase $\langle a, o \rangle$ in a sentence, if the negation dependency "neg(o, not)" exists in the same sentence, the opinion phrase $\langle a, o \rangle$ will be reversed into opinion phrase $\langle a, \text{not } o \rangle$ in order to truly reflect the opinion of a user to an aspect of a POI. As an example, considering the sentence of "the taste is not bad" again, it contains the opinion phrase $\langle taste, bad \rangle$ with the negation dependency "neg(bad, not)"; subsequently $\langle taste, bad \rangle$ is reversed into $\langle taste, \text{not } bad \rangle$.

In sum, a tip can be represented as a set of opinion phrases consisting of aspect a_i and opinion word o_i, i.e., $tip = \{\langle a_i, o_i \rangle\}$, embedded with the negation information if any. Moreover, according to sentiment lexicons, we can obtain a sentiment value for each opinion word o_i. Hereafter, o_i also indicates its corresponding sentiment value for simplicity.

4.2 Phase 2: Aspect Clustering

In tips, users may write different words to represent the same aspect of POIs, e.g., "ambiance", "ambience" or "environment" instead of "atmosphere". Thus, aspects should be grouped into clusters based on their dissimilarities in order to decrease the dimension of vectors of tips represented in the aspect space and increase the correlation among tips that is helpful for training classification models. The grouping process includes three key steps.

Step 1: Aspect distance calculation. To cluster aspects, the dissimilarities between aspects need to be collected in advance. The dissimilarity can be any valid distance metric, most commonly Euclidean distance, Manhattan distance or Minkowski distance. However, these distance metrics are defined over the Cartesian coordinates of clustered data but the aspects of POIs, i.e., linguistic words, do not have the intrinsic Cartesian coordinates. Hence, we define the aspect dissimilarity or distance based on the semantic relationships of words, including synonymy linking words that have similar meanings (e.g., "atmosphere" and "environment"), hypernymy referring to a hierarchical relationship between words (e.g., "food" is a hypernym of "sandwich"), and meronymy referring to a part/whole relationship (e.g., "paper" is a meronym of "book"). Specifically, based on the dictionary WordNet, where words are linked via semantic relationships to form a semantic network, the distance between aspects is considered as the length of the shortest path between corresponding words in the semantic network.

Step 2: Grouping aspects into clusters. Give a set of aspects from all tips and their distance, here we aim to group the aspects into clusters, so that aspects within a cluster have small distance in comparison to one another but are very far from the aspects in other clusters. To achieve this task, one may employ the popular clustering techniques, like K-means or K-medoids. Nonetheless, they are not adaptable to the aspect clustering problem, since the mean of an aspect cluster is not defined for K-means, and normally we cannot group aspects into a small number of clusters due to their large dissimilarities from each other, so K is the same order-of-magnitude with the total number of aspects, which leads to high computation cost for K-medoids.

Therefore, we apply the farthest-point clustering algorithm [4] due to its efficiency and without the requirement of computing mean values for clusters. The primitive farthest-point clustering algorithm discovers a predefined number K of clusters. We utilize this method to find **an adaptive number K of clusters**, in which K is determined by a threshold of distance that is the allowed maximum distance from an aspect to its cluster center. Given a set of aspects $A = \{a_i\}$ from all tips in Section 4.1, distance matrix *distance* between aspects in Step 1, and maximum distance threshold d_{max}, the clustering process is described below:

1. The algorithm initially selects an arbitrary aspect in A as the first cluster center and adds it to the center set C.

2. In the k-th iteration:

   - For each aspect $a_i \in (A - C)$, the algorithm computes the minimum distance from a_i to the center set C:

   $$dist_{min}(a_i, C) = \min_{c \in C} distance(a_i, c). \quad (1)$$

   - The farthest-point a_k^* is determined by:

   $$a_k^* = \arg\max_{a_i \in (A-C)} dist_{min}(a_i, C). \quad (2)$$

   - If $dist_{min}(a_k^*, C) > d_{max}$, the algorithm considers a_k^* as a new cluster center, adds it into C and continues the iteration process; otherwise, it terminates.

3. Aspect $a_i \in A$ is assigned to its nearest cluster $c_k \in C$.

Step 3: Opinion aggregation. After the aspects have been grouped into K clusters, a $tip = \{\langle a_i, o_i \rangle\}$ (i.e., a set of opinion phrases consisting of aspect a_i and sentiment value o_i) can be transformed into a vector $tip\langle o_{c_1}, o_{c_2}, \ldots, o_{c_K} \rangle$ represented in the cluster space C, in which aggregated sentiment value o_{c_k} is the average of o_i for all a_i that are assigned to cluster center $c_k \in C$ $(k = 1, 2, \ldots, K)$, i.e.,

$$o_{c_k} = average_{a_i \text{ assigned to } c_k}(o_i). \quad (3)$$

Note that: for a tip, if there is no aspect a_i assigned to a certain cluster center c_k, the aggregated sentiment value o_{c_k} is missing. Actually, this is the most common case, because the number of aspects described in a short tip is far less than the large number K of clusters generated from all tips.

Example. Figure 4 depicts an example to illustrate the opinion phrase extraction phase and aspect clustering phase. Figure 4(a) gives a set of clusters of aspects from all tips, in which the aspect "atmosphere" has be assigned to cluster c_1, "taste" to c_2, "quality" to c_3, ..., and "price" to c_{100}. Given a new tip shown in Figure 4(b), four opinion phrases are extracted $tip = \{\langle atmosphere, good \rangle$, $\langle taste, not\ bad \rangle$, $\langle quality, high \rangle$, $\langle price, high \rangle\}$. Then, tip is aggregated into a cluster-based vector $tip\langle good, not\ bad, high, ?, \ldots, ?, high \rangle$ in Figure 4(c). **Note that:** The tip's sentiment values on clusters o_{c_1}, o_{c_2}, o_{c_3} and $o_{c_{100}}$ can

c_1	c_2	c_3	...	c_{100}
atmosphere	taste	quality	...	price
ambiance	savor	trait	...	charge
ambience	feel	particularity	...	cost
environment	sense	idiosyncrasy	...	fee

(a) **Clusters of aspects from all tips**

A tip: I went here last night. I loved the place with good atmosphere. The taste is not bad. The food has high quality but with a little high price.
$\Longrightarrow$
$tip = \{\langle atmosphere,\ good \rangle, \langle taste,\ not\ bad \rangle, \langle quality,\ high \rangle, \langle price,\ high \rangle\}$

(b) **Opinion phrases extracted from a tip**

$tip\langle o_{c_1}, o_{c_2}, o_{c_3}, \ldots, o_{c_{100}} \rangle = \langle$good, not bad, high, ?, ..., ?, high$\rangle$

(c) **Cluster-based vector representation of the tip**

Figure 4: Opinion aggregation on clusters

be determined based on opinion words "good", "bad" and "high" in a lexicon, but the sentiment values on clusters o_{c_4}, ..., $o_{c_{99}}$ are missing.

Hereafter, we reduce $tip\langle o_{c_1}, o_{c_2}, \ldots, o_{c_K} \rangle$ to $tip\langle o_1, o_2, \ldots, o_K \rangle$ for the sake of presentation, where each of the subscripts $(1, 2, \ldots, K)$ indicates its corresponding cluster.

4.3 Phase 3: Supervised Polarity Detection

The goal of the supervised polarity detection approach is to predict polarity $p \in P = \{positive, neutral, negative\}$ for a new tip, given a training set of tips $D = \{\langle tip^j, p^j \rangle\}$, where each tip^j is labeled with a class $p^j \in P$. By the opinion phrase extraction and aspect clustering phases described in Sections 4.1 and 4.2, respectively, a tip has been represented as a vector of sentiment values regarding each cluster, i.e., $tip^j\langle o_1^j, o_2^j, \ldots, o_K^j \rangle$ in order to facilitate polarity detection. As aforementioned, $tip^j\langle o_1^j, o_2^j, \ldots, o_K^j \rangle$ contains a large number of missing values since a tip is often short with only a few sentences. Thus, it is required to replace the missing values with the most probable value based on statistics to apply most classification methods, such as decision trees and support vector machines. Nevertheless, filling in a large number of values will result in severely biased classification models. Hence, we employ another important classification approach, i.e., naive Bayes (NB) [8] that can intrinsically handle missing values without any replacement.

The NB classifier is a special form of Bayesian networks and relies on the class conditional independence assumption that the predictive attributes (clusters) are conditionally independent given the class (polarity). Despite the simplifying assumption, experimental results on real-world data have repeatedly shown that the NB classifier is competitive with much more sophisticated classification methods in terms of classification accuracy. Further, the assumption leads to very efficient algorithms for both *predicting* and *training* that are required for processing large-scale Web data. We will discuss the two main steps for the NB classifier.

Step 1: Predicting of naive Bayesian classifier. Specifically, the NB classifier predicts that a new tip belongs to the polarity $p*$ having the highest posterior probability,

$$p^* = \arg\max_{p \in P} \Pr(p|tip), \quad (4)$$

where $P = \{positive, neutral, negative\}$. And we have

$$\Pr(p|tip) = \Pr(p)\Pr(tip|p)/\Pr(tip), \quad (5)$$

in which $\Pr(tip)$ is constant for all polarity $p \in P$, so only $\Pr(p)$ and $\Pr(tip|p)$ need to be computed based on the given training set of tips $D = \{\langle tip^j, p^j \rangle\}$.

Step 2: Training of naive Bayesian classifier. $\Pr(p)$ is the class prior probability and is estimated by

$$\Pr(p) = |\{p^j | p^j = p \wedge p^j \in D\}| / |D|, \tag{6}$$

where the numerator is the number of training tips with polarity $p^j = p$ in D and the denominator is the total number of training tips in D.

$\Pr(tip|p)$ is first factorized based on the class conditional independence assumption that the values of the attributes in $tip\langle o_1, o_2, \ldots, o_K\rangle$ are conditionally independent of one another given the class label p:

$$\Pr(tip|p) = \prod_{k=1}^{K} \Pr(o_k|p). \tag{7}$$

$\Pr(o_k|p)$ is the class conditional probability density function for the k-th cluster and is computed by kernel density estimation with the most general Gaussian kernels using training set $D = \{\langle tip^j, p^j\rangle\} = \{\langle\langle o_1^j, o_2^j, \ldots, o_K^j\rangle, p^j\rangle\}$:

$$\Pr(o_k|p) = \frac{1}{N} \sum_{\{o_k^j | p^j = p\}} \frac{1}{\sqrt{2\pi}\sigma} e^{-\frac{(o_k - o_k^j)^2}{2\sigma^2}}, \tag{8}$$

where o_k^j ranges over the sentiment values of the k-th cluster in training tips with polarity $p^j = p$, N is the number of o_k^j with $p^j = p$, i.e., $N = |\{o_k^j | p^j = p\}|$, and $\sigma = 1/\sqrt{N}$.

5. OPINION-BASED RECOMMENDATION

After the polarity detection part in Section 4, each tip is associated with a polarity, i.e., positive, neutral or negative. In this section, the polarities of tips are integrated with other important information sources of LBSNs (i.e., the social links between users and geographical information of POIs) to make better POI recommendations for users.

5.1 Fusion with Social Links

To use polarities of tips for POI recommendations, they need to be mapped into values that indicate users' ratings to **visited** POIs. As usual, we adopt a five-star rating scale widely used in online e-business Web sites, e.g., Amazon and Yelp. Formally, given a tip with polarity $p_{u,l} \in P = \{positive, neutral, negative\}$ from user u regarding POI l, the rating $r_{u,l}$ of user u to **visited** POI l is defined as follows:

$$r_{u,l} = \begin{cases} 5, & p_{u,l} = positive; \\ 3, & p_{u,l} = neutral; \\ 1, & p_{u,l} = negative. \end{cases} \tag{9}$$

Therefore, we can collect a user-POI rating matrix $R = \{r_{u,l}\}$ for all tips of users to POIs. Note that most entries in R are unknown, since users have only visited a very small proportion of POIs and accordingly tips only contain a little part of interaction between users and POIs.

Here the key task is to estimate the social rating of a user to an **unvisited** POI via existing ratings in R. To achieve this task, we apply the collaborative filtering technique on R. Formally, given a certain entry $r_{u,l} = 0$ (i.e., user u has not visited POI l), the social rating $\hat{r}_{u,l}$ of user u to **unvisited** POI l can be predicted by

$$\hat{r}_{u,l} = \frac{\sum_{u'} sim(u,u') \cdot r_{u',l}}{\sum_{u'} sim(u,u')}, \tag{10}$$

where $r_{u',l}$ denotes the known rating mapped from the tip polarity of user u' concerning POI l using Equation (9), and $sim(u,u')$ is the similarity measure between users u and u'. As friends often share more common interests, $sim(u,u')$ is usually defined by social links, e.g.,

$$sim(u,u') = \begin{cases} 1, & u \text{ and } u' \text{ have the social link;} \\ 0, & \text{Otherwise.} \end{cases} \tag{11}$$

Note that other similarity functions using social links or/and location histories can also be applied here.

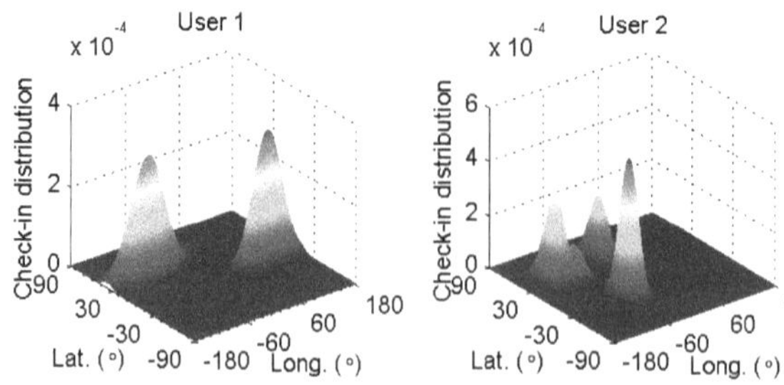

Figure 5: Personal check-in distributions

5.2 Fusion with Geographical Information

The geographical information (geographic coordinates) of spatial POIs included in check-in data plays a significant role in users' check-in behaviors, since POIs are distinct from other non-spatial items, such as books, music and movies in conventional recommendation systems and physical interactions are required for users to visit POIs. For example, users tend to visit POIs close to their homes or offices and also may be interested in exploring the nearby places of their visited POIs. To this end, we exploit the geographical information of POIs to learn a geographical preference model for each user that can be used to predict the geographical probability of the user visiting a new POI.

Concretely, we model the personal check-in distribution for a user using her historical check-in POIs based on kernel density estimation with Gaussian kernels as well, in which however, each check-in of the user to a POI is weighed with the polarity of the tip written by the user to the POI. Formally, given user u's set of visited POIs $L_u = \{l_1, l_2, \ldots, l_n\}$, the probability of u visiting a new POI l is computed by:

$$\Pr(l|L_u) = \frac{\sum_{i=1}^{n} w_{u,l_i} \cdot e^{-\frac{\|l-l_i\|^2}{2\sigma^2}}}{2\pi\sigma^2 \sum_{i=1}^{n} w_{u,l_i}}, \tag{12}$$

where $\sigma = 1/\sqrt{n}$, $l_i = (lat_i, lon_i)$ is a two-dimensional vector with the latitude (lat_i) and longitude (lon_i) coordinates, and $\|\cdot\|$ denotes the Euclidean norm. More importantly, w_{u,l_i} is the normalized weight of u's check-in on POI l_i and is computed in terms of the tip polarity p_{u,l_i} of user u to l_i:

$$w_{u,l_i} = \begin{cases} 1, & p_{u,l_i} = positive; \\ 0.5, & p_{u,l_i} = neutral; \\ 0, & p_{u,l_i} = negative; \end{cases} \tag{13}$$

in which intuitively the check-in with the positive tip ($p_{u,l_i} = positive$) has the positive influence on the user's check-in behavior whereas the check-in with the negative tip ($p_{u,l_i} = negative$) has the negative influence on the user's check-in behavior. Otherwise, the influence is neutral.

Example. Figure 5 depicts two users' check-in distributions over the latitude and longitude coordinates, estimated through Equation (12), which model their geographical preferences on POIs: User 1 usually checks in POIs in two areas while User 2 checks in POIs in three main areas.

Table 1: Statistics of the Foursquare data set

	LA	NYC
Number of users	30,208	47,240
Number of POIs	142,798	203,765
Number of tips	244,861	388,594
Number of social links	349,985	810,672
User-POI matrix density	5.68×10^{-5}	4.04×10^{-5}

5.3 Combining Social-Geographical Influences

Finally, the social rating and geographical probability of user u to POI l in Equations (10) and (12) are combined into a unified score $s_{u,l}$ based on the robust product rule [27]:

$$s_{u,l} = \hat{r}_{u,l} \cdot \Pr(l|L_u). \quad (14)$$

The top-m POIs l having the highest score $s_{u,l}$ are recommended to user u.

6. EVALUATION SETTINGS

This section describes our experiment settings for evaluating the performance of ORec.

6.1 Two Publicly Available Real Data Sets

Yelp Challenge data set [24] for polarity detection. This data set has 113,993 tips labeled by ratings for 15,585 POIs from various categories including Food, Nightlife, etc. We split the tips into different subsets according to their categories and evaluate polarity detection methods on each subset using cross-validation.

Foursquare data set [1] for POI recommendations. The Foursquare data set includes two subsets of POIs in Los Angeles (LA) and New York City (NYC). The statistics of the two data sets are shown in Table 1. The polarity of a tip is determined based on the classification model learned from the Yelp Challenge data set, because the tips in Foursquare and Yelp are essentially the same, i.e., short texts. We also evaluate POI recommendation methods using cross-validation.

6.2 Evaluated Techniques

Polarity detection group. This group includes the widely used polarity detection techniques for tweets and tips: (1) the classical text classification methods such as support vector machines (SVM) [12], decision trees (DT) and naive Bayes (NB) [17]; (2) the unsupervised aspect-independent (UAI) method [22]; and (3) the supervised aspect-dependent approach (ORec) in Section 4.

POI recommendation group. This group incorporates the state-of-the-art POI recommendation techniques that are the most related to our work. Most of them measure the similarity between users by using social links as the input of the collaborative filtering method. **The difference lies in the way they utilize the geographical information of POIs or whether they apply textual information.**

- IRenMF: This technique exploits two levels of geographical neighborhood characteristics by integrating the item-based collaborative filtering with matrix factorization [14].
- PD: This technique estimates a geographical power-law distribution for all users and integrates it with the social user-based collaborative filtering method [23].
- iGSLR: This technique estimates a geographical nonparametric distribution for each user and integrates it with the social user-based collaborative filtering method [27].
- LCARS: This technique builds a location-content-aware recommender system using the check-in data and textual information based on the LDA topic model [25].
- UAI: Besides the social links of users and geographical information of POIs, this technique uses tip polarities from the unsupervised aspect-independent method [22].
- ORec: The proposed method integrates tip polarities with social links and geographical information into a unified recommendation framework, as described in Section 5.

6.3 Performance Metrics

For **polarity detection**, given a class (positive, neutral or negative), the precision and recall are defined as follows:

$$\text{precision} = \frac{\text{No. of tips } \textbf{correctly predicted} \text{ to the class}}{\text{No. of tips } \textbf{predicted} \text{ to the class}}.$$

$$\text{recall} = \frac{\text{No. of tips } \textbf{correctly predicted} \text{ to the class}}{\text{No. of tips } \textbf{actually belonging} \text{ to the class}}.$$

The reported precision and recall are averaged on the three classes.

For **POI recommendations**, a discovered POI is defined as a POI that is recommended to and visited by a target user. Similarly, the precision and recall are defined as follows:

$$\text{precision} = \frac{\text{No. of discovered POIs}}{\text{No. of recommended POIs for the user: } m}.$$

$$\text{recall} = \frac{\text{No. of discovered POIs}}{\text{No. of POIs actually visited by the user}}.$$

6.4 Parameter Settings

Polarity detection. In the aspect clustering step in Section 4.2, the aspect distance is normalized into the range of [0, 1], where 0 indicates two aspects are completely identical, e.g., "ambiance" and "ambience", while 1 denotes two aspect with the largest difference. In the clustering algorithm, the allowed maximum distance from an aspect to its cluster center is set to $d_{max} = 0.2$. **Note that the number K of clusters is adaptive to d_{max}.**

POI recommendations. We examine the effect of various numbers of recommended POIs for users (top-m from 1 to 10) and numbers of visited POIs of users in the training set (n from 1 to 10) on recommendation accuracy. Note that: m and n are set to a relative small number, because a large number m may not be helpful for users and the number n in the training set is small.

7. EXPERIMENTAL RESULTS

This section analyzes the polarity detection accuracy in Section 7.1 and POI recommendation accuracy in Section 7.2.

7.1 Polarity Detection Accuracy

General trends and important findings. Figure 6 compares the polarity detection accuracy of ORec, SVM, DT, NB and UAI on the Yelp challenge data sets from the top-10 active categories, e.g., Food, Nightlife, Restaurants, etc.

SVM, DT and NB. As the classical classification techniques for short texts, e.g., tweets or tips, the three methods still show the low precision and recall around 40%. The reason is that they consider a tip as a bag of words and transform the tip into a highly sparse word vector with a large number of missing values, so the accuracy of polarity detection is deteriorated.

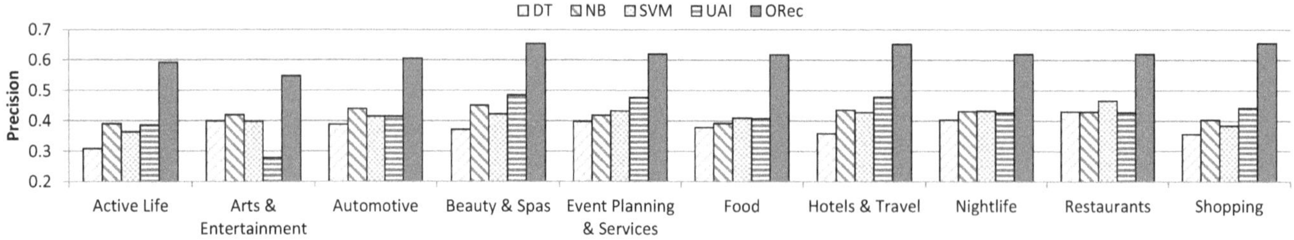

(a) Precision

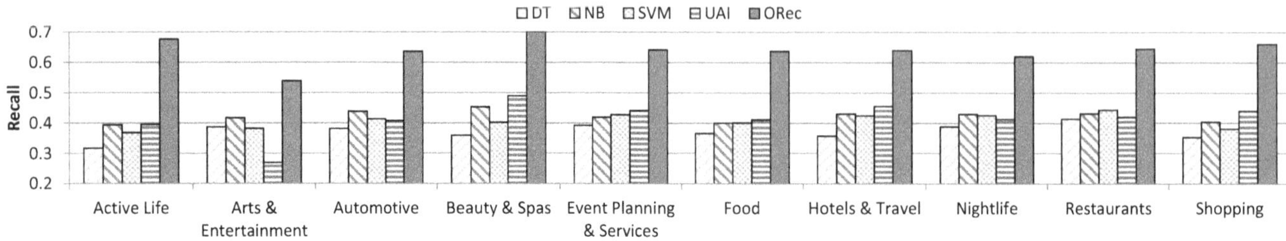

(b) Recall

Figure 6: Polarity detection accuracy of ORec in comparison to SVM, DT, NB and UAI

UAI. By using sentiment values of opinion words in tips in terms of sentiment lexicons, UAI usually records better precision and recall of polarity detection in comparison to SVM, DT and NB, except for the categories of Arts & Entertainment, Automotive, Nightlife and Restaurants. However, the improvement is considerably limited due to its intrinsic limitation: it simply sums up all the sentiment values in a tip as the polarity of the tip. In other words, UAI implicitly assumes that the sentiment orientation of an opinion word is independent of its modifying aspect, which is at variance with objective reality. For example, in opinion phrases of "high quality" and "high price", the opinion word "high" has distinct sentiment orientation: the former "high" modifying the aspect "quality" is positive whereas the latter "high" modifying the aspect "price" is negative.

ORec. Our ORec exhibits the best polarity detection accuracy in terms of precision and recall in all categories and accomplishes 20% absolute improvement and 50% relative improvement on the performance of SVM, DT, NB and UAI. The reason for the promising results is fourfold: (1) ORec associates each opinion word with its modifying aspect by extracting opinion phrases from tips and determining the sentiment orientation of an opinion word depending on the associated aspect, rather than using the implicit independence assumption in UAI. (2) ORec uses the supervised machine learning method to integrate the sentiment orientations of opinion words, instead of using the unsupervised summation function to combine the absolute sentiment values of opinion words in UAI. (3) To reduce the ambiguity and dimension of word vectors representing tips in SVM, DT and NB, ORec only takes aspects as dimensions and groups aspects into clusters according to their dissimilarity, which significantly decreases the sparsity in the cluster-based vector representations of tips. (4) ORec avoids replacing the missing values with default value that will bring severe biases to underlying classification models. Instead, it leverages the important classification approach, i.e., naive Bayes to naturally deal with the missing values without any replacement. These promising results verify the superiority of the proposed supervised aspect-dependent polarity detection approach over the classical classification techniques SVM, DT and NB and the unsupervised aspect-independent method UAI.

7.2 POI Recommendation Accuracy

Low accuracy due to pretty low density. It is worth emphasizing that, unlike the polarity detection accuracy, the accuracy of all POI recommendation techniques for LBSNs is usually not high, because the density of a user-POI interaction matrix is pretty low. For example, the reported maximum precision is 0.06 over a data set with 2.72×10^{-4} density in [23]. Even worse, the two data sets used in our experiments have a lower density, 5.68×10^{-5} in the LA data set and 4.04×10^{-5} in the NYC data set (Table 1), so the relatively low precision and recall values are common and reasonable in the experiments. Thus, we focus on the relative accuracy of ORec compared to the state-of-the-art POI recommendation techniques: IRenMF, PD, iGSLR, LCARS and UAI. We expect that ORec **can improve the accuracy as more tips and check-in activities are recorded**, as shown in Figure 7.

General trends and important findings. Here we compare the POI recommendation accuracy of ORec, IRenMF, PD, iGSLR, LCARS and UAI with various numbers of visited POIs of users in the training set (Figure 7) and numbers of recommended POIs for users (Figure 8).

IRenMF, PD, iGSLR. (1) Based on the combination of item-based collaborative filtering and matrix factorization techniques, IRenMF intensively models the influence of geographical neighborhood characteristics of POIs on users' check-in behaviors in order to learn users' geographical preferences. However, IRenMF does not consider other information, e.g., social links and textual tips. As a result, it performs the worst in most cases in terms of precision and recall. (2) PD models the distance between every pair of POIs visited by the same user as a power-law distribution for all users, and integrates it with the social links based on the user-based collaborative filtering method. Accordingly, PD improves the POI recommendation performance in comparison to IRenMF, but it still suffers from the limitation of the universal distance distribution for all users. (3) iGSLR also utilizes the social links based on the user-based collaborative filtering method, but it personalizes the geographical influence through modeling an individual distance distribution for each user. Consequently, iGSLR further enhances the recommendation precision and recall. (4) Nonetheless, the three methods (IRenMF, PD and iGSLR) only exploit check-

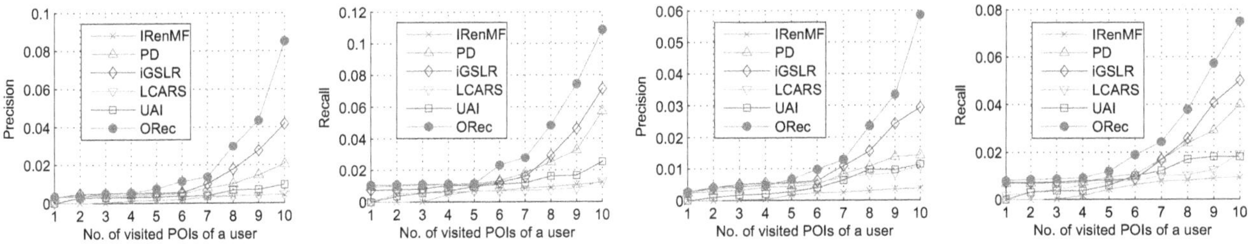

(a) LA (b) LA (c) NYC (d) NYC

Figure 7: Effect of numbers of visited POIs of users in the training set on recommendation accuracy

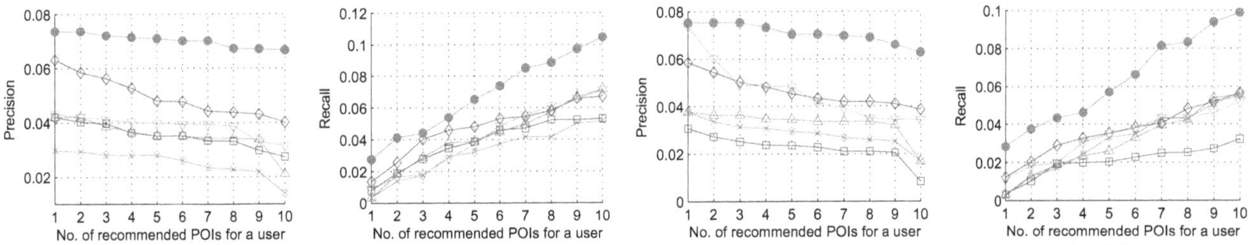

(a) LA (b) LA (c) NYC (d) NYC

Figure 8: Effect of numbers of recommended POIs for users on recommendation accuracy (with the same legend as in Figure 7)

in data **without tips** by supposing that the check-in frequency of a user to a POI directly reflects the preference of the user to the POI, which may not be in accordance with the reality. For example, in most cases that users only check in POIs once, it is hard to deduce the true preference level of users to POIs. Subsequently, merely utilizing check-in data often generates biased user preference models that deteriorate POI recommendation accuracy.

LCARS. By using both check-in data and textual information in tips based on the LDA topic model, LCARS still performs poorly for the cold-start users, i.e., the users who have checked in only a few POIs, as depicted in Figure 7, but it can enhance the overall accuracy (averaged on all users) respecting different numbers of recommended POIs in comparison to IRenMF and PD, as depicted in Figure 8. Our explanation is that LCARS utilizes *topic distributions of users* rather than *polarities of tips* and the accurate topic distributions require much more textual information.

UAI. UAI adopts the unsupervised aspect-independent method to detect the polarity of tips and combines the acquired **tip polarities** with check-in data including **social links** and **geographical information** to make POI recommendations. In general, although UAI has better performance than IRenMF, it shows worse precision and recall than PD, especially iGSLR. The reason is that UAI inherits the intrinsic limitation of the unsupervised aspect-independent polarity detection method, as mentioned in Section 7.1.

ORec. ORec exploits the supervised aspect-dependent approach to predict the polarities of tips and integrates them with social links and geographical information. Accordingly, ORec exhibits the best precision and recall. In particular, ORec achieves the significant improvement compared to the second best technique, i.e., iGSLR. We attribute the promising results to two reasons: (1) The underlying polarity detection method can accurately predict the polarity of a tip as depicted in Figure 6, which guarantees that ORec is able to take full advantage of opinions indicated in tips of users for POI recommendations. (2) ORec seamlessly integrates tip polarities with social links and geographical information. **It is worth emphasizing two important points**: (i) The difference between ORec and iGSLR lies in whether they apply tips or not. ORec with tips greatly enhances the recommendation quality against iGSLR without tips, which shows that the textual information is relevant and useful for POI recommendations. (ii) The only difference between ORec and UAI is how they utilize the tips. ORec using the sophisticated supervised aspect-dependent method is much better than UAI using the simple unsupervised aspect-independent method, which shows the effectiveness and novelty of the proposed method in this paper.

LA vs. NYC. In general, the precision and recall of ORec on the LA data set is a little higher than that in the NYC data set, because the density of the former data set is larger than that of the latter data set, as shown in Table 1. We believe that our ORec will perform better as more data including tips and check-ins are collected.

Effect of the number of visited POIs of users in the training set. Figure 7 depicts the result of the recommendation accuracy as the number of visited POIs of users increases in the training set. As expected, the precision and recall incline accordingly, since ORec can learn users' preferences on POIs more accurately with more check-in data and tips, as they visit more POIs. Interestingly, as for the small number of visited POIs, i.e., less than five, iGSLR is competitive to ORec. However, when the number of visited POIs of users is larger than five, ORec significantly outperforms iGSLR, since the precision and recall of ORec increase dramatically. This fully shows the superiority of exploiting users' opinions implied in tips for POI recommendations.

Effect of the number of recommended POIs for users. Figure 8 depicts the recommendation accuracy by varying the number of recommended POIs for users. The recall gradually gets higher with the raise of the number of recommended POIs, since by returning more POIs for users, it is always able to discover more POIs that users would like to visit. However, the precision generally becomes lower as the number of recommended POIs increases. Our explanation is that some recommended POIs are less possible to be liked by users due to their lower preferences; the recommendation techniques return the top-m POIs based on the estimated visiting score, for example, the second recommended POI has the lower visiting score than the first one.

8. CONCLUSION AND FUTURE WORK

This paper proposes an opinion-based POI recommendation framework ORec to overcome the two challenges: detecting the polarities of tips and integrating them with social links and geographical information. First, ORec exploits the supervised aspect-dependent approach to learn a classification model in the cluster space of aspects to predict polarities of tips. Further, ORec seamlessly fuses *tip polarities* with *social links* and *geographical information*. Finally, experimental results on two large-scale Foursquare and Yelp data sets show that ORec achieves significantly better performance than the state-of-the-art polarity detection and POI recommendation techniques. In the future, we plan to study two directions to extend ORec: (a) how to derive weights for sentiment values of opinion words in tips, and (b) how to build regression models for polarity detection instead of classification models.

9. ACKNOWLEDGEMENTS

The authors were supported by Guangdong Natural Science Foundation of China under Grant S2013010012363.

10. REFERENCES

[1] J. Bao, Y. Zheng, and M. F. Mokbel. Location-based and preference-aware recommendation using sparse geo-social networking data. In *ACM SIGSPATIAL*, 2012.

[2] R. Dong, M. Schaal, M. P. O'Mahony, and B. Smyth. Topic extraction from online reviews for classification and recommendation. In *IJCAI*, 2013.

[3] H. Gao, J. Tang, and H. Liu. gSCorr: Modeling geo-social correlations for new check-ins on location-based social networks. In *ACM CIKM*, 2012.

[4] T. Gonzalez. Clustering to minimize the maximum intercluster distance. *Theoretical Computer Science*, 38:293–306, 1985.

[5] Z. Hai, K. Chang, and G. Cong. One seed to find them all: mining opinion features via association. In *ACM CIKM*, 2012.

[6] A. Hogenboom, D. Bal, F. Frasincar, M. Bal, F. de Jong, and U. Kaymak. Exploiting emoticons in sentiment analysis. In *ACM SAC*, 2013.

[7] X. Hu, J. Tang, H. Gao, and H. Liu. Unsupervised sentiment analysis with emotional signals. In *WWW*, 2013.

[8] G. H. John and P. Langley. Estimating continuous distributions in Bayesian classifiers. In *UAI*, 1995.

[9] S. Kim, J. Zhang, Z. Chen, A. Oh, and S. Liu. A hierarchical aspect-sentiment model for online reviews. In *AAAI*, 2013.

[10] T. Kurashima, T. Iwata, T. Hoshide, N. Takaya, and K. Fujimura. Geo topic model: Joint modeling of user's activity area and interests for location recommendation. In *ACM WSDM*, 2013.

[11] D. Lian, C. Zhao, X. Xie, G. Sun, E. Chen, and Y. Rui. GeoMF: Joint geographical modeling and matrix factorization for point-of-interest recommendation. In *ACM KDD*, 2014.

[12] S. Liu, F. Li, F. Li, X. Cheng, and H. Shen. Adaptive co-training SVM for sentiment classification on tweets. In *ACM CIKM*, 2013.

[13] X. Liu, Y. Liu, K. Aberer, and C. Miao. Personalized point-of-interest recommendation by mining users' preference transition. In *ACM CIKM*, 2013.

[14] Y. Liu, W. Wei, A. Sun, and C. Miao. Exploiting geographical neighborhood characteristics for location recommendation. In *ACM CIKM*, 2014.

[15] J. McAuley and J. Leskovec. Hidden factors and hidden topics: Understanding rating dimensions with review text. In *ACM RecSys*, 2013.

[16] S. Moghaddam and M. Ester. The FLDA model for aspect-based opinion mining: addressing the cold start problem. In *WWW*, 2013.

[17] F. Moraes, M. Vasconcelos, P. Prado, D. Dalip, J. M. Almeida, and M. Gonçalves. Polarity detection of Foursquare tips. In *Social Informatics*. Springer, 2013.

[18] A. Mukherjee and B. Liu. Aspect extraction through semi-supervised modeling. In *ACL*, 2012.

[19] K. Reschke, A. Vogel, and D. Jurafsky. Generating recommendation dialogs by extracting information from user reviews. In *ACL*, 2013.

[20] R. Socher, J. Bauer, C. D. Manning, and A. Y. Ng. Parsing with compositional vector grammars. In *ACL*, 2013.

[21] S. Wang and C. D. Manning. Baselines and bigrams: Simple, good sentiment and topic classification. In *ACL*, 2012.

[22] D. Yang, D. Zhang, Z. Yu, and Z. Wang. A sentiment-enhanced personalized location recommendation system. In *ACM HT*, 2013.

[23] M. Ye, P. Yin, W.-C. Lee, and D.-L. Lee. Exploiting geographical influence for collaborative point-of-interest recommendation. In *ACM SIGIR*, 2011.

[24] Yelp. Challenge Data Set [accessed 25-april-2014]. `http://www.yelp.com/dataset_challenge`, 2014.

[25] H. Yin, B. Cui, Y. Sun, Z. Hu, and L. Chen. LCARS: A spatial item recommender system. *ACM TOIS*, 32(3):11:1–11:37, 2014.

[26] J. J.-C. Ying, W.-N. Kuo, V. S. Tseng, and E. H.-C. Lu. Mining user check-in behavior with a random walk for urban point-of-interest recommendations. *ACM TIST*, 5(3):40:1–40:26, 2014.

[27] J.-D. Zhang and C.-Y. Chow. iGSLR: Personalized geo-social location recommendation - a kernel density estimation approach. In *ACM SIGSPATIAL*, 2013.

[28] J.-D. Zhang and C.-Y. Chow. CoRe: Exploiting the personalized influence of two-dimensional geographic coordinates for location recommendations. *Information Sciences*, 293:163–181, 2015.

[29] J.-D. Zhang and C.-Y. Chow. GeoSoCa: Exploiting geographical, social and categorical correlations for point-of-interest recommendations. In *ACM SIGIR*, 2015.

[30] J.-D. Zhang and C.-Y. Chow. Spatiotemporal sequential influence modeling for location recommendations: A gravity-based approach. *ACM TIST, accepted*, 2015.

[31] J.-D. Zhang and C.-Y. Chow. TICRec: A probabilistic framework to utilize temporal influence correlations for time-aware location recommendations. *IEEE TSC, accepted*, 2015.

[32] J.-D. Zhang, C.-Y. Chow, and Y. Li. iGeoRec: A personalized and efficient geographical location recommendation framework. *IEEE TSC, accepted*, 2014.

[33] J.-D. Zhang, C.-Y. Chow, and Y. Li. LORE: Exploiting sequential influence for location recommendations. In *ACM SIGSPATIAL*, 2014.

[34] X. Zhang, J. Cheng, T. Yuan, B. Niu, and H. Lu. TopRec: Domain-specific recommendation through community topic mining in social network. In *WWW*, 2013.

[35] Y.-L. Zhao, L. Nie, X. Wang, and T.-S. Chua. Personalized recommendations of locally interesting venues to tourists via cross-region community matching. *ACM TIST*, 5(3):50:1–50:26, 2014.

Toward Dual Roles of Users in Recommender Systems

Suhang Wang†, Jiliang Tang‡, and Huan Liu†
†Computer Science & Engineering, Arizona State University, Tempe, AZ, USA
‡Yahoo Labs, Sunnyvalue, CA, USA
†{suhang.wang,huan.liu}@asu.edu, ‡jlt@yahoo-inc.com

ABSTRACT

Users usually play dual roles in real-world recommender systems. One is as a reviewer who writes reviews for items with rating scores, and the other is as a rater who rates the helpfulness scores of reviews. Traditional recommender systems mainly consider the reviewer role while not taking into account the rater role. However, the rater role allows users to express their opinions toward reviews about items; hence it may indirectly indicate their opinions about items, which could be complementary to the reviewer role. Since most real-world recommender systems provide convenient mechanisms for the rater role, recent studies show that typically there are much more *helpfulness ratings* from the rater role than *item ratings* from the reviewer role. Therefore, incorporating the rater role of users may have the potentials to mitigate the data sparsity and cold-start problems in traditional recommender systems. In this paper, we investigate how to exploit dual roles of users in recommender systems. In particular, we provide a principled way to exploit the rater role mathematically and propose a novel recommender system DualRec, which captures both the reviewer role and the rater role of users simultaneously for recommendation. Experimental results on two real world datasets demonstrate the effectiveness of the proposed framework, and further experiments are conducted to understand the importance of the rater role of users in recommendation.

Categories and Subject Descriptors

H.2.8 [**Database applications Subjects**]: Data mining; H.3.3 [**Information Search and Retrieval Subjects**]: Information filtering

General Terms

Algorithms

Keywords

Collaborative filtering; Helpfulness rating; Cold-start

Permission to make digital or hard copies of all or part of this work for personal or classroom use is granted without fee provided that copies are not made or distributed for profit or commercial advantage and that copies bear this notice and the full citation on the first page. Copyrights for components of this work owned by others than ACM must be honored. Abstracting with credit is permitted. To copy otherwise, or republish, to post on servers or to redistribute to lists, requires prior specific permission and/or a fee. Request permissions from Permissions@acm.org.
CIKM'15, October 19–23, 2015, Melbourne, Australia.
© 2015 ACM. ISBN 978-1-4503-3794-6/15/10 ...$15.00.
DOI: http://dx.doi.org/10.1145/2806416.2806520.

1. INTRODUCTION

Recommender systems[22] intend to provide users with information of potential interest based on their demographic profiles and historical data. Collaborative Filtering (CF), which only requires past user ratings to predict unknown ratings, has attracted more and more attention[6, 33, 9]. Collaborative Filtering can be roughly categorized into memory-based[5, 23, 29] and model-based methods[6, 16, 10]. Memory-based methods mainly use the neighborhood information of users or items in the user-item rating matrix while model-based methods usually assume that an underlying model governs the way users rate items, and in general, it has better performance than memory-based methods. Despite the success of various model-based methods [24, 6], matrix factorization (MF) based model has became one of the most popular methods due to its good performance and efficiency in handling large datasets[25, 16, 10, 4, 27, 2].

Users in real-world recommender systems can play as reviewers that write reviews and give ratings for items, and they also can play as raters that rate the helpfulness of reviews. Figure 1 contains two snapshots from a real-world site Ciao[1]. In Figure 1(a)[2] , a user *tara1tomoj*, as a reviewer, writes a review for Apple iPhone 6 16GB, which gives a rating score 4 to iPhone 6. Figure 1(b)[3] shows that other users, as raters, rate the helpfulness of the review in Figure 1(a) - three raters give helpfulness ratings to this review, among which two give somewhat helpful (or score 2) and one gives not helpful (or score 1). However, the vast majority of traditional recommender systems only exploit the reviewer role while overlook the rater role of users. The rater role enables users to conveniently express their personal opinions on reviews about items, which indicates their indirect opinions on items. For example, though we don't know the exact rating scores these three users may give to Apple iPhone 6 16GB, low helpfulness ratings given by these users imply that they don't agree with the review; hence, they are likely to give some ratings different from 4 to Apple iPhone 6. Therefore, the rater role could be complementary to the reviewer role for recommendation. Since real-world recommender systems often provide convenient mechanisms for the rater role, such as clicking helpfulness buttons in Amazon and specifying helpfulness scores in Ciao, recent studies suggest that users usually have more helpfulness ratings produced by their rater role than item ratings

[1] www.ciao.com
[2] http://www.ciao.co.uk/Recent_Reviews/Top100/Smartph-ones_Mobile_Phones_5302356_2/All
[3] http://www.ciao.co.uk/Apple_iPhone_6__Review_6146860

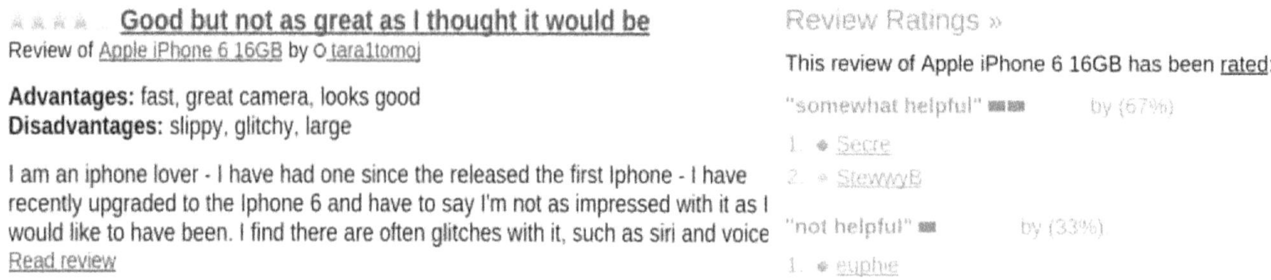

(a) A Product Review Example

(b) Helpfulness Ratings of the Review

Figure 1: An Example of User's Dual Roles in Recommender Systems.

produced by their reviewer role [26]. For example, for those users with few item ratings, they could have many helpfulness ratings. This property of the rater role of users could be useful to mitigate the data sparsity and cold-start problems, which are two major challenges of traditional recommender systems[18]. Therefore, incorporating the rater role of users has potentials to improve the performance of recommender systems.

In this paper, we investigate the dual roles of users, i.e. the reviewer role and the rater role, in recommender systems. In essence, we study two challenges - (1) how to capture the rater role of users mathematically; and (2) how to exploit the dual roles of users simultaneously for recommendation. In an attempt to solve these two challenges, we propose a novel recommendation framework DualRec. The major contributions of this paper are summarized next:

- Providing a principled way to capture the rater role of users mathematically;
- Proposing a novel recommender system DualRec, which exploits the duel roles of users into a coherent model for recommendation; and
- Conducting experiments on real-world datasets to understand the effectiveness of the proposed framework DualRec.

The rest of the paper is organized as follows. In Section 2, we introduce the proposed framework DualRec with the details of how to capture the rater role of users and how to incorporate it with the reviewer role for recommendation. In Section 3, we present a method to solve the optimization problem of DualRec along with the time complexity analysis. In Section 4, we show empirical evaluation with discussion. In Section 5, we present the related work. In Section 6, we give conclusion with future work.

2. A RECOMMENDER SYSTEM WITH DUAL ROLES OF USERS

Before introducing details about the proposed framework, we first introduce notations used in this paper. Throughout this paper, matrices are written as boldface capital letters and vectors are denoted as boldface lowercase letters. For an arbitrary matrix $\mathbf{M} \in \mathbb{R}^{m\times n}$, $\mathbf{M}_{ij}$ denotes the (i,j)-th entry of $\mathbf{M}$ while $\mathbf{m}_i$ and $\mathbf{m}^j$ mean the i-th row and j-th column of $\mathbf{M}$, respectively. $||\mathbf{M}||_F$ is the Frobenius norm of $\mathbf{M}$. Capital letters in calligraphic math font such as $\mathcal{P}$ are used to denote sets. We use $|\cdot|$ to denote the cardinality of a set, for example, $|\mathcal{P}|$ indicates the number of elements in the set $\mathcal{P}$.

Typically there are three types of objects, namely, users, reviews and items. Let $\mathcal{U} = \{u_1, u_2, \dots, u_n\}$ be the set of users, $\mathcal{P} = \{p_1, p_2, \dots, p_m\}$ be the set of items and $\mathcal{R} = \{r_1, r_2, \dots, r_N\}$ be the set of reviews where n, m and N are the numbers of users, items and reviews, respectively. As reviewers, users can write reviews and rate items. For example, (u_i, r_j, p_k) means user u_i writes a review r_j which gives a rating to item p_k. We use the matrix $\mathbf{R} \in \mathbb{R}^{n\times m}$ to denote the user-item rating matrix produced by the reviewer role of users, where $\mathbf{R}_{ik}$ is the rating score if u_i rates p_k otherwise $\mathbf{R}_{ik}$ = "?" for an unknown rating from u_i to p_k. $\mathbf{A} \in \{0,1\}^{N\times m}$ is the review item matrix where $\mathbf{A}_{jk} = 1$ if review r_j is associated with item p_k and $\mathbf{A}_{jk} = 0$ otherwise. As raters, users can rate the helpfulness of reviews and $\mathbf{H} \in \mathbb{R}^{n\times N}$ is employed to represent user review helpfulness rating matrix where $\mathbf{H}_{ij}$ is the helpfulness score if user u_i gives a review r_j a rating and $\mathbf{H}_{ij}$ = "?" denotes an unknown helpfulness score from u_i to r_j. We use $\mathcal{O}(\mathbf{R}) = \{\mathbf{R}_{ij} | \mathbf{R}_{ij} = ?\}$ to denote the set of unknown item ratings. Next we begin the introduction of the proposed framework with the basic model to exploit the reviewer role of users.

2.1 A Basic Model for the Reviewer Role of Users

We choose matrix factorization based collaborative filtering as the basic model to exploit the reviewer role of users since it is a very practical and popular method to build recommender systems [6, 25, 16, 7, 10, 27]. It tries to map both users and items to a joint latent factor space with dimensionality K such that user-item interactions are modeled as inner products in that space[10]. The premise behind a low-dimensional factor model is that there is only a small number of factors that influence the user preferences and a user's preference vector is determined by how each factor applies to the user[25]. Specifically, given the rating matrix $\mathbf{R} \in \mathbb{R}^{n\times m}$, matrix factorization methods try to find two matrices $\mathbf{U} \in \mathbb{R}^{K\times n}$ and $\mathbf{V} \in \mathbb{R}^{K\times m}$ by solving the following optimization problem

$$\min_{\mathbf{U},\mathbf{V}} \sum_{i=1}^{n}\sum_{j=1}^{m} \mathbf{I}_{ij}(\mathbf{u}_i^T\mathbf{v}_j - \mathbf{R}_{ij})^2 + \gamma(\|\mathbf{U}\|_F^2 + \|\mathbf{V}\|_F^2) \quad (1)$$

where $\mathbf{I} \in \{0,1\}^{n\times m}$ is the indicator matrix defined as

$$\mathbf{I}_{ij} = \begin{cases} 1 & \text{if } \mathbf{R}_{ij} \neq \text{"?"} \\ 0 & \text{otherwise} \end{cases} \quad (2)$$

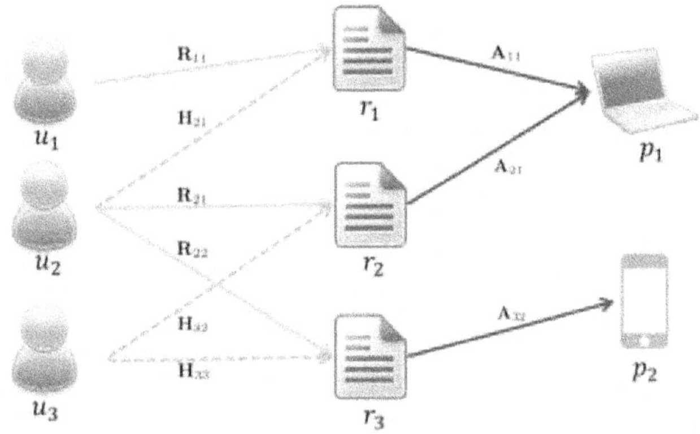

Figure 2: The figure gives an example of user's dual roles in recommender systems. The yellow arrow means that a user, as a reviewer, writes a review and the review assigns a rating score to a product connected by a purple arrow. A green (dashed) arrow denotes that a user, as a rater, gives a helpfulness rating score to a review.

$\mathbf{U}$ is the user latent factor matrix with each column $\mathbf{u}_i$ being u_i's latent factor and $\mathbf{V}$ is the item latent factor matrix with each column $\mathbf{v}_j$ being the latent property of the item p_j. The term $\gamma(\|\mathbf{U}\|_F^2 + \|\mathbf{V}\|_F^2)$ is introduced to avoid overfitting. The rating of u_i to p_j is predicted as $\mathbf{u}_i^T\mathbf{v}_j$. With the basic model for the reviewer role, next we will introduce our solution to capture the rater role and the proposed framework DualRec.

2.2 Capturing the Rater Role of Users

Helpfulness ratings produced by the rater role of users indicate users' opinions toward reviews about items and it could reflect their opinions on items indirectly. Therefore, the key problem to capture the rater role of users for recommendation is how to learn implicit item ratings from helpfulness ratings produced by the rater role. Next we first introduce some definitions and then detail the mathematical model to capture the rater role of users.

Assume that a review r_k is about the item p_j, i.e, $\mathbf{A}_{kj} = 1$. A rater u_i who rates r_k about p_j may or may not be a reviewer of p_j. For example, as shown in Figure 2, user u_2 rates the helpfulness of a review r_1 about item p_1, and he/she also directly writes a review r_2 and gives an item rating to p_1; while u_3 only rates the helpfulness of a review r_2 about p_1. Therefore, for a helpfulness rating from u_i to r_k about p_j, i.e. $\mathbf{H}_{ik}$, according to whether u_i writes reviews about p_j or not, we can assign it as either *Type-I* helpfulness rating or *Type-II* helpfulness rating . The definitions of these two types of helpfulness ratings are given as follows:

DEFINITION 1. *A helpfulness rating $\mathbf{H}_{ik}$ is a Type-I helpfulness rating if the item p_j associated with the review r_k in $\mathbf{H}_{ik}$ is also rated by user u_i. In other words, u_i not only rates the helpfulness of the review r_k about p_j but also directly gives a rating score to p_j . Formally, a Type-I helpfulness rating $\mathbf{H}_{ik}$ satisfies:*

$$\exists p_j \in \mathcal{P}, \quad \mathbf{H}_{ik} > 0 \ \wedge \ \mathbf{A}_{kj} = 1 \ \wedge \ \mathbf{R}_{ij} \neq ? \tag{3}$$

In Figure 2, $\mathbf{H}_{21}$ is a Type-I helpfulness rating since u_2 wrote r_2 which assigns a rating to p_1.

DEFINITION 2. *A helpfulness rating $\mathbf{H}_{ik}$ is a Type-II helpfulness rating if the item p_j associated with the review r_k in $\mathbf{H}_{ik}$ is not rated by user u_i. In other words, u_i only rates the helpfulness of the review r_k about p_j but not the item p_j. Formally, a Type-II helpfulness rating $\mathbf{H}_{ik}$ satisfies:*

$$\nexists p_j \in \mathcal{P}, \quad \mathbf{H}_{ik} > 0 \ \wedge \ \mathbf{A}_{kj} = 1 \ \wedge \ \mathbf{R}_{ij} \neq ? \tag{4}$$

In Figure 2, $\mathbf{H}_{32}$ and $\mathbf{H}_{33}$ are Type-II helpfulness ratings because u_3 doesn't rate any items.

We further use $\mathcal{P}_{ij}$ to represent the set of reviews about p_j that received Type-I helpfulness ratings from u_i. That is, $\forall r_k \in \mathcal{P}_{ij}$, we have that r_k is about p_j, and u_i rates both r_k and also p_j. Formally, $\mathcal{P}_{ij}$ is defined as:

$$\mathcal{P}_{ij} = \{r_k | \mathbf{H}_{ik} \text{ is a Type-I helpfulness rating} \\ \wedge \mathbf{A}_{kj} = 1, 1 \leq k \leq N\} \tag{5}$$

For example, in Figure 2, $\mathcal{P}_{21} = \{r_1\}$ because u_2 rated both p_1 and r_1 of p_1, while $\mathcal{P}_{31} = \emptyset$ because u_3 doesn't give a rating to p_1.

Similarly, we use $\mathcal{Q}_{ij}$ to represent a set of reviews about p_j which received Type-II helpfulness ratings from u_i. That is, $\forall r_k \in \mathcal{P}_{ij}$, we have that r_k is about p_j, and u_i rates r_k but not p_j. Formally, $\mathcal{Q}_{ij}$ is defined as:

$$\mathcal{Q}_{ij} = \{r_k | \mathbf{H}_{ik} \text{ is a Type-II helpfulness rating} \\ \wedge \mathbf{A}_{kj} = 1, 1 \leq k \leq N\}\} \tag{6}$$

For example, in Figure 2, $\mathcal{Q}_{21} = \emptyset$ because while $\mathcal{Q}_{31} = \{r_2\}$.

For a review r_k that is written by u_s and is associated with the item p_j, $\mathbf{R}_{sj}$ is the item rating from u_s to p_j. The helpfulness rating $\mathbf{H}_{ik}$ indicates the opinion of user u_i on the review r_k and the corresponding item rating $\mathbf{R}_{sj}$ from u_s to p_j. Therefore, both the helpfulness rating $\mathbf{H}_{ik}$ and the item rating from the author of r_k to p_j, i.e., $\mathbf{R}_{sj}$, could be useful to learn the implicit item rating from u_i to p_j. Let $\phi(\mathbf{H}_{ik}, \mathbf{R}_{sj}) \in \mathbb{R}^{d\times 1}$ be the feature vector for a helpfulness rating from u_i to r_k[4]. We further assume a linear map matrix $\mathbf{w}$ which predicts the implicit item rating $\hat{\mathbf{R}}_{ij}$ from $\phi(\mathbf{H}_{ik}, \mathbf{R}_{sj})$ as $\hat{\mathbf{R}}_{ij} = \phi(\mathbf{H}_{ik}, \mathbf{R}_{sj})^T\mathbf{w}$. Therefore, we propose the following minimization terms to capture the rater role of users for recommendation as:

$$\min_{\mathbf{w}} \quad \sum_{i=1}^{n}\sum_{j=1}^{m} \mathbf{F}_{ij}\Big(\frac{1}{|\mathcal{P}_{ij}|}\sum_{k\in\mathcal{P}_{ij}} \phi(\mathbf{H}_{ik}, \mathbf{R}_{sj})^T\mathbf{w} - \mathbf{R}_{ij}\Big)^2 \\ + \beta\sum_{i=1}^{n}\sum_{j=1}^{m} \mathbf{G}_{ij}\Big(\frac{1}{|\mathcal{Q}_{ij}|}\sum_{k\in\mathcal{Q}_{ij}} \phi(\mathbf{H}_{ik}, \mathbf{R}_{sj})^T\mathbf{w} - \mathbf{u}_i^T\mathbf{v}_j\Big)^2 \tag{7}$$

Next we give details about the inner working of Eq.(7) as:

- For a user-item pair (u_i, p_j) with $\mathcal{P}_{ij} \neq \emptyset$, u_i not only rates the helpfulness of reviews about p_j but also gives a rating score to p_j; hence the first term in Eq.(7) ensures the consistency between the predicted item ratings from the rater role (or $\frac{1}{|\mathcal{P}_{ij}|}\sum_{k\in\mathcal{P}_{ij}} \phi(\mathbf{H}_{ik}, \mathbf{R}_{sj})^T\mathbf{w}$) and the observed item ratings from the reviewer role (or $\mathbf{R}_{ij}$). Since a user u_i may rate the helpfulness of

[4]The d-dimensional feature vector could encode features from users, reviews and pairs of item and helpfulness ratings. In this paper, we empirically find that some simple features from a pair of item and helpfulness ratings, i.e., $\phi(x, y) = [x; y; xy; x^2; y^2; 1/x; 1/y]$, works well. We would like to investigate other features in the future.

multiple reviews about the same item p_j, we use the average rating $\frac{1}{|\mathcal{P}_{ij}|}\sum_{k\in\mathcal{P}_{ij}}\phi(\mathbf{H}_{ik},\mathbf{R}_{sj})^T\mathbf{w}$ as the final predicted item rating from u_i to p_j. $\mathbf{F}$ is an indicator matrix, which is formally defined as

$$\mathbf{F}_{ij} = \begin{cases} 1 & \text{if } |\mathcal{P}_{ij}| > 0 \\ 0 & \text{if } |\mathcal{P}_{ij}| = 0 \end{cases} \tag{8}$$

- For a user-item pair (u_i, p_j) with $\mathcal{Q}_{ij} \neq \emptyset$, u_i only rates the helpfulness of reviews about p_j and has no rating score to p_j; hence the second term in Eq.(7) ensures the consistency between the predicted item ratings from the rater role (or $\frac{1}{|\mathcal{Q}_{ij}|}\sum_{k\in\mathcal{Q}_{ij}}\phi(\mathbf{H}_{ik},\mathbf{R}_{sj})^T\mathbf{w}$) and the predicted item ratings from the reviewer role (or $\mathbf{u}_i^T\mathbf{v}_j$). Similar to $\mathbf{F}$, $\mathbf{G}$ is an indicator matrix defined as

$$\mathbf{G}_{ij} = \begin{cases} 1 & \text{if } |\mathcal{Q}_{ij}| > 0 \\ 0 & \text{if } |\mathcal{Q}_{ij}| = 0 \end{cases} \tag{9}$$

2.3 The Proposed Framework–DualRec

With model components to capture the reviewer role and the rater role, the proposed recommender system DualRec that exploits the dual roles of users simultaneously is to solve the following optimization problem as:

$$\begin{aligned}\min_{\mathbf{U},\mathbf{V},\mathbf{w}} \quad & \sum_{i=1}^{n}\sum_{j=1}^{m}\mathbf{I}_{ij}(\mathbf{u}_i^T\mathbf{v}_j - \mathbf{R}_{ij})^2 \\ & + \alpha\sum_{i=1}^{n}\sum_{j=1}^{m}\mathbf{F}_{ij}(\frac{1}{|\mathcal{P}_{ij}|}\sum_{k\in\mathcal{P}_{ij}}\phi(\mathbf{H}_{ik},\mathbf{R}_{sj})^T\mathbf{w} - \mathbf{R}_{ij})^2 \\ & + \beta\sum_{i=1}^{n}\sum_{j=1}^{m}\mathbf{G}_{ij}(\frac{1}{|\mathcal{Q}_{ij}|}\sum_{k\in\mathcal{Q}_{ij}}\phi(\mathbf{H}_{ik},\mathbf{R}_{sj})^T\mathbf{w} - \mathbf{u}_i^T\mathbf{v}_j)^2 \\ & + \gamma(\|\mathbf{U}\|_F^2 + \|\mathbf{V}\|_F^2) + \lambda\|\mathbf{w}\|_2^2 \end{aligned} \tag{10}$$

where the first term models the reviewer role of users based on matrix factorization; and the second and third terms incorporate the rater role of users. α and β are introduced to leverage the contribution of reviewer role and rater role. Similar to $\gamma(\|\mathbf{U}\|_F^2 + \|\mathbf{V}\|_F^2)$, the term $\lambda\|\mathbf{w}\|_2^2$ is introduced to avoid overfitting.

If we only consider the reviewer role of users, we cannot learn the user latent factor $\mathbf{u}_i$ for a user u_i without any item rating scores. However, as shown in Eq.(10), we still can learn the user latent factor for u_i if u_i has helpfulness ratings by incorporating the rater role of users. Also both user latent factor matrix $\mathbf{U}$ and the item latent factor matrix $\mathbf{V}$ are learned from the dual roles of users. Therefore, the proposed framework DualRec has potentials to mitigate the cold-start and data sparsity problems in recommendation.

3. AN OPTIMIZATION METHOD FOR DUALREC

The objective function in Eq.(10) is not convex if we update all the variables jointly. To optimize the objective function, we use alternating least squares, which is a popular method for MF based collaborative filtering. Specifically, we optimize one variable by fixing other variables. Next, we give the details to optimize the objective function followed by the complexity analysis of the proposed algorithm.

3.1 Update Rule of U and V

To get the gradients of Eq.(10) w.r.t to $\mathbf{U}$ and $\mathbf{V}$, we first remove terms that are irrelevant to $\mathbf{U}$ and $\mathbf{V}$ and rewrite the objective function as

$$\begin{aligned}\mathcal{L}(\mathbf{U},\mathbf{V}) = & \|\mathbf{I}\odot(\mathbf{U}^T\mathbf{V} - \mathbf{R})\|_F^2 + \gamma(\|\mathbf{U}\|_F^2 + \|\mathbf{V}\|_F^2) \\ & + \beta\|\mathbf{G}\odot(\mathbf{U}^T\mathbf{V} - \mathbf{M})\|_F^2 \end{aligned} \tag{11}$$

where $\odot$ denotes Hadmard product and $\mathbf{M}$ is defined as

$$\mathbf{M}_{ij} = \begin{cases} \frac{1}{|\mathcal{Q}_{ij}|}\sum_{k\in\mathcal{Q}_{ij}}\phi(\mathbf{H}_{ik},\mathbf{R}_{sj})^T\mathbf{w}, & \text{if } \mathbf{G}_{ij} > 0 \\ 0, & \text{o.w.} \end{cases} \tag{12}$$

Then the gradient of $\mathcal{L}(\mathbf{U},\mathbf{V})$ with respect to $\mathbf{U}$ is given as

$$\begin{aligned}\frac{\partial\mathcal{L}(\mathbf{U},\mathbf{V})}{\partial\mathbf{U}} = & 2\mathbf{V}[\mathbf{I}\odot(\mathbf{U}^T\mathbf{V} - \mathbf{R})]^T + 2\gamma\mathbf{U} \\ & + 2\beta\mathbf{V}[\mathbf{G}\odot(\mathbf{U}^T\mathbf{V} - \mathbf{M})]^T \end{aligned} \tag{13}$$

Therefore, $\mathbf{U}$ is updated as

$$\mathbf{U} = \mathbf{U} - \epsilon\frac{\partial\mathcal{L}(\mathbf{U},\mathbf{V})}{\partial\mathbf{U}} \tag{14}$$

where ϵ is the learning rate. Similarly, the gradient of $\mathcal{L}(\mathbf{U},\mathbf{V})$ with respect to $\mathbf{V}$ is given as

$$\begin{aligned}\frac{\partial\mathcal{L}(\mathbf{U},\mathbf{V})}{\partial\mathbf{V}} = & 2\mathbf{U}[\mathbf{I}\odot(\mathbf{U}^T\mathbf{V} - \mathbf{R})] + 2\gamma\mathbf{V} \\ & + 2\beta\mathbf{U}[\mathbf{G}\odot(\mathbf{U}^T\mathbf{V} - \mathbf{M})] \end{aligned} \tag{15}$$

and $\mathbf{V}$ is updated as

$$\mathbf{V} = \mathbf{V} - \epsilon\frac{\partial\mathcal{L}(\mathbf{U},\mathbf{V})}{\partial\mathbf{V}} \tag{16}$$

3.2 Update Rule of w

Similarly, to get the gradient of Eq.(10) w.r.t to $\mathbf{w}$, we first remove terms that are irrelevant to $\mathbf{w}$ and the objective is simplified as

$$\begin{aligned}\mathcal{L}(\mathbf{w}) = & \alpha\sum_{i=1}^{n}\sum_{j=1}^{m}\mathbf{F}_{ij}(\frac{1}{|\mathcal{P}_{ij}|}\sum_{k\in\mathcal{P}_{ij}}\phi(\mathbf{H}_{ik},\mathbf{R}_{sj})^T\mathbf{w} - \mathbf{R}_{ij})^2 \\ & + \beta\sum_{i=1}^{n}\sum_{j=1}^{m}\mathbf{G}_{ij}(\frac{1}{|\mathcal{Q}_{ij}|}\sum_{k\in\mathcal{Q}_{ij}}\phi(\mathbf{H}_{ik},\mathbf{R}_{kj})^T\mathbf{w} - \mathbf{u}_i^T\mathbf{v}_j)^2 \\ & + \lambda\|\mathbf{w}\|_2^2 \end{aligned} \tag{17}$$

For simplicity, let $\mathbf{x}_{ij} = \frac{1}{|\mathcal{P}_{ij}|}\sum_{k\in\mathcal{P}_{ij}}\phi(\mathbf{H}_{ik},\mathbf{R}_{sj})$ and $\mathbf{z}_{ij} = \frac{1}{|\mathcal{Q}_{ij}|}\sum_{k\in\mathcal{Q}_{ij}}\phi(\mathbf{H}_{ik},\mathbf{R}_{sj})$. Then we have

$$\begin{aligned}\mathcal{L}(\mathbf{w}) = & \alpha\sum_{i=1}^{n}\sum_{j=1}^{m}\mathbf{F}_{ij}(\mathbf{x}_{ij}^T\mathbf{w} - \mathbf{R}_{ij})^2 + \lambda\|\mathbf{w}\|_2^2 \\ & + \beta\sum_{i=1}^{n}\sum_{j=1}^{m}\mathbf{G}_{ij}(\mathbf{z}_{ij}^T\mathbf{w} - \mathbf{u}_i^T\mathbf{v}_j)^2 \end{aligned} \tag{18}$$

The derivative of Eq.(18) with respect to $\mathbf{w}$ is given as

$$\begin{aligned}\frac{\partial\mathcal{L}(\mathbf{w})}{\partial\mathbf{w}} = & 2\alpha\sum_{i=1}^{n}\sum_{j=1}^{m}\mathbf{F}_{ij}\mathbf{x}_{ij}(\mathbf{x}_{ij}^T\mathbf{w} - \mathbf{R}_{ij}) \\ & + 2\beta\sum_{i=1}^{n}\sum_{j=1}^{m}\mathbf{G}_{ij}\mathbf{z}_{ij}(\mathbf{z}_{ij}^T\mathbf{w} - \mathbf{u}_i^T\mathbf{v}_j) + 2\lambda\mathbf{w} \end{aligned} \tag{19}$$

By setting the derivative to zero, we have the update rule for $\mathbf{w}$ as

$$\mathbf{w} = (\alpha \sum_{i=1}^{n} \sum_{j=1}^{m} \mathbf{F}_{ij}\mathbf{x}_{ij}\mathbf{x}_{ij}^T + \beta \sum_i \sum_j \mathbf{G}_{ij}\mathbf{z}_{ij}\mathbf{z}_{ij}^T + \lambda\mathbf{I})^{-1}$$
$$(\alpha \sum_{i=1}^{n} \sum_{j=1}^{m} \mathbf{F}_{ij}\mathbf{R}_{ij}\mathbf{x}_{ij} + \beta \sum_i \sum_j \mathbf{G}_{ij}\mathbf{u}_i^T\mathbf{v}_j\mathbf{z}_{ij}) \quad (20)$$

Algorithm 1 DualRec

Input: $\mathbf{R} \in \mathbb{R}^{n\times m}, \mathbf{H} \in \mathbb{R}^{n\times N}, \mathbf{A} \in \{0,1\}^{N\times m}, K, \alpha, \beta, \gamma$
Output: $\hat{\mathbf{R}}$
1: **for** i=1 to n **do**
2:   **for** j=1 to m **do**
3:     Construct $\mathcal{P}_{ij}$ according to Eq.(5)
4:     Construct $\mathcal{Q}_{ij}$ according to Eq.(6)
5:   **end for**
6: **end for**
7: Construct indicator matrix $\mathbf{I}, \mathbf{F}, \mathbf{G}$
8: Initialize $\mathbf{U} \in \mathbb{R}^{K\times n}, \mathbf{V} \in \mathbb{R}^{K\times m}$
9: Initialize $\mathbf{w}$ by solving Eq.(7) with β set to 0
10: **repeat**
11:   Calculate $\mathbf{M}$ using Eq.(12)
12:   Calculate $\frac{\partial \mathcal{L}(\mathbf{U},\mathbf{V})}{\partial \mathbf{U}}$ using Eq.(13)
13:   Update $\mathbf{U}$ as $\mathbf{U} = \mathbf{U} - \epsilon \frac{\partial \mathcal{L}(\mathbf{U},\mathbf{V})}{\partial \mathbf{U}}$
14:   Calculate $\frac{\partial \mathcal{L}(\mathbf{U},\mathbf{V})}{\partial \mathbf{V}}$ using Eq.(15)
15:   Update $\mathbf{V}$ as $\mathbf{V} = \mathbf{V} - \epsilon \frac{\partial \mathcal{L}(\mathbf{U},\mathbf{V})}{\partial \mathbf{V}}$
16:   Update $\mathbf{w}$ using Eq.(20)
17: **until** Convergence
18: Calculate $\hat{\mathbf{R}} = \mathbf{U}^T\mathbf{V}$
19: return $\hat{\mathbf{R}}$

3.3 The Algorithm

With the update rules of $\mathbf{U}, \mathbf{V}$ and $\mathbf{w}$ given above, the optimization algorithm for DualRec is shown in Algorithm 1. Next we briefly review Algorithm 1. For each user-item pair, we first find $\mathbf{P}_{ij}$ and $\mathbf{Q}_{ij}$ from line 1 to line 6. Based on $\mathbf{R}, \mathbf{P}_{ij}$ and $\mathbf{Q}_{ij}$, we can construct the indicator matrix $\mathbf{I}, \mathbf{F}$ and $\mathbf{G}$ in line 7. We randomly initialize $\mathbf{U}$ and $\mathbf{V}$ in line 8. In order to speed up the learning process, $\mathbf{w}$ is initialized by solving Eq.(7) with $\beta = 0$ since it can give a better approximation to $\mathbf{w}$ than randomly guessing in line 9. After initialization, $\mathbf{U}, \mathbf{V}$ and $\mathbf{w}$ are updated sequentially until it converges from line 10 to line 17. Finally, the rating matrix is reconstructed as $\hat{\mathbf{R}} = \mathbf{U}^T\mathbf{V}$. With the reconstructed matrix $\hat{\mathbf{R}}$, an unknown rating from u_i to p_j is predicted as $\hat{\mathbf{R}}_{ij}$

3.4 Complexity Analysis

The algorithm is composed of two parts, i.e., initialization and updating. The most time consuming part is the updating part. The computational cost of $\mathbf{U}^T\mathbf{V}$ in Eq.(13) is $\mathcal{O}(nkm)$. Considering the fact that $\mathbf{I}$ is very sparse, we have that $\mathbf{I} \odot (\mathbf{U}^T\mathbf{V} - \mathbf{R})$ is also very sparse. Thus, the computational cost of $\mathbf{V}[\mathbf{I} \odot (\mathbf{U}^T\mathbf{V} - \mathbf{R})]^T$ is about $\mathcal{O}(nkm)$. Then the computational cost of $\frac{\partial \mathcal{L}(\mathbf{U},\mathbf{V})}{\partial \mathbf{U}}$ using Eq.(15) is $\mathcal{O}(nkm)$. Similarly, the computational cost of $\frac{\partial \mathcal{L}(\mathbf{U},\mathbf{V})}{\partial \mathbf{V}}$ using Eq.(15) is also $\mathcal{O}(nmk)$. To update $\mathbf{w}$ using Eq.(20), we can pre-calculate $(\alpha \sum_{i=1}^{n} \sum_{j=1}^{m} \mathbf{F}_{ij}\mathbf{x}_{ij}\mathbf{x}_{ij}^T + \beta \sum_i \sum_j \mathbf{G}_{ij}\mathbf{z}_{ij}\mathbf{z}_{ij}^T + \lambda\mathbf{I})^{-1}$ and $\alpha \sum_{i=1}^{n} \sum_{j=1}^{m} \mathbf{F}_{ij}\mathbf{R}_{ij}\mathbf{x}_{ij}$ since they are fixed in each iteration. Also, considering the fact that $\mathbf{G}$ is very sparse, the computational cost of $\beta \sum_i \sum_j \mathbf{G}_{ij}\mathbf{u}_i^T\mathbf{v}_j\mathbf{z}_{ij}$ is $\mathcal{O}(ks)$, where s is the number of nonzero elements in $\mathbf{G}$. Thus, the computational cost of $\mathbf{w}$ is $\mathcal{O}(ks)$. Thus the total cost of the algorithm is $\mathcal{O}(t(nkm + ks))$, where t is the number of iterations. From the analysis, we can see that the computational cost of Algorithm 1 in each iteration is actually comparable to that of the matrix factorization based collaborative filtering.

Table 1: Statistics of the Datasets

Dataset	Epinions	Ciao
# of users	2,161	2,368
# of items	2,796	3,046
# of ratings	72,971	69,453
# of H.R.	581,880	1,248,020
# of Type-I H.R.	47,905	177,038
# of Type-II H.R.	533,975	1,070,982

4. EXPERIMENTAL ANALYSIS

In this section, we conduct experiments to evaluate the effectiveness of the proposed framework DualRec. Specifically, we aim to answer the following two questions:

- Can the proposed framework improve the recommendation performance by incorporating the rater role of users? and
- Is the proposed framework able to mitigate the cold-start problem for recommendation by incorporating the rater role of users?

We begin by introducing datasets and experimental settings, then we compare DualRec with the state-of-the-art recommendation systems to answer the first question and we investigate the capability of the proposed framework in handling the cold-start problem to answer the second question. Finally further experiments are conducted to investigate the sensitivity of DualRec to the parameters.

4.1 Datasets and Experimental Settings

We collect two datasets from real-world social media websites, i.e., Epinions[5] and Ciao. From the originally collected datasets, we filter out users who rated few items and also items that received less than 10 ratings. For both datasets, users can rate products and reviews with scores from 1 to 5. The statistics of the resulting datasets are shown in Table 1. In the table, H.R. denotes helpfulness rating, Type-I H.R. denotes Type-I helpfulness ratings and Type-II H.R indicates Type-II helpfulness ratings. It is evident from the statistics in the table that, on average, users have more helpfulness ratings from the rater role than item ratings from the reviewer role of users.

Two widely used evaluation metrics, i.e., mean absolute error (MAE) and root mean square error (RMSE), are adopted to evaluate the rating prediction performance. Specifically, MAE is defined as

$$MAE = \frac{\sum_{(i,j)\in\mathcal{T}} |\mathbf{R}_{ij} - \tilde{\mathbf{R}}_{ij}|}{|\mathcal{T}|} \quad (21)$$

[5]http://www.epinions.com/

Table 2: Performance comparison on Epinions and Ciao in terms of RMSE.

Dataset	Training Size	UCF	WNMF	MF	QMF	DualRec
Epinions	10%	1.3320	1.3581	1.3072	1.3068	1.2338
	20%	1.2642	1.2644	1.2196	1.2137	1.1784
	40%	1.2015	1.1812	1.14 01	1.1415	1.1201
Ciao	10%	1.2644	1.3128	1.2655	1.2551	1.1382
	20%	1.2233	1.2202	1.1652	1.1718	1.0920
	40%	1.1748	1.1378	1.0811	1.0828	1.0497

Table 3: Performance comparison on Epinions and Ciao in terms of MAE.

Dataset	Training Size	UCF	WNMF	MF	QMF	DualRec
Epinions	10%	1.0836	1.0756	1.0514	1.0575	1.0064
	20%	1.0086	0.9927	0.9678	0.9634	0.9403
	40%	1.0104	0.9248	0.8928	0.8901	0.8790
Ciao	10%	0.9385	1.0325	1.0087	1.0015	0.9049
	20%	0.9211	0.9522	0.9149	0.9278	0.8585
	40%	0.8873	0.8914	0.8361	0.8364	0.8187

and RMSE is defined as

$$RMSE = \sqrt{\frac{\sum_{(i,j)\in\mathcal{T}} \left(\mathbf{R}_{ij} - \tilde{\mathbf{R}}_{ij}\right)^2}{|\mathcal{T}|}} \quad (22)$$

where in both metrics, $\mathcal{T}$ denotes the set of ratings we want to predict, $\mathbf{R}_{ij}$ denotes the rating user u_i gives to item p_j and $\tilde{R}_{ij}$ denotes the predicted rating from $\mathbf{u}_i$ and $\mathbf{v}_j$.

For each dataset, we random select $x\%$ as the training set and the remaining $1 - x\%$ as the testing set. To investigate the capability of the proposed framework in handling the data sparsity problem, we vary x as $\{10, 20, 40\}$ in this work. The random selection process is carried out 10 times independently, and the average MAE and RMSE are reported. Note that previous work demonstrated that *small improvement in RMSE or MAE terms can have a significant impact on the quality of the top-few recommendation*[8].

4.2 Performance Comparison of Recommender Systems

To answer the first question, we compare the proposed system with several representative systems. The comparison results are summarized in Tables 2 and 3 for RMSE and MAE, respectively. The representative systems in the table are defined as:

- **UCF**: UCF is the user-oriented collaborative filtering where the rating from u_i to p_j is predicted as an aggregation of ratings of K most similar users of u_i to p_j. We use the cosine similarity to calculate user-user similarity.
- **MF**: matrix factorization based collaborative filtering tries to decompose the user-item rating matrix into two matrices such that the reconstruction error is minimized [10]. In this work, we choose **MF** as the basic model of the proposed framework DualRec.
- **WNMF**: weighted nonnegative matrix factorization tries to decompose the weighted rating matrix into two nonnegative matrices to minimize the reconstruction error [33].
- **QMF**: Review quality aware collaborative filtering [21] uses helpfulness rating as a measure to capture the quality of the rating and then the quality scores $\mathbf{W}$ are incorporated as weights into matrix factorization based CF as

$$\min_{\mathbf{U},\mathbf{V}} \sum_{i=1}^{n}\sum_{j=1}^{m} \mathbf{I}_{ij}(\mathbf{W}_{ij}(\mathbf{R}_{ij} - \mathbf{u}_i^T\mathbf{v}))^2 + \gamma(\|\mathbf{U}\|_F^2 + \|\mathbf{V}\|_F^2) \quad (23)$$

Note that parameters of all baseline methods are determined via cross validation. For DualRec, we set $\alpha = 1$, $\beta = 0.1$, $\gamma = 0.1$ and $\lambda = 1$ throughout the experiments. More details about parameter selection for the proposed framework will be discussed in the following subsections. From results in the Table 2 and 3, we make the following observations:

- In general, matrix factorization based recommender systems outperform the user-oriented CF method and this observation is consistent with that in [10].
- The proposed framework DualRec obtains better performance than baseline methods based on matrix factorization. We perform t-test on these results, which suggests that the improvement is significant. These results indicate that incorporating the rater role of users can improve the recommendation performance.
- The performance gaps between DualRec and MF with respect to the size of the training set are shown in Figure 3. We observe that the improvement of the proposed framework DualRec compared to MF increases as the datasets become sparser, i.e., from 40% to 10%. For example, the relative RMSE improvement of DualRec over MF is 2.90% on Ciao when the training size is 40% and increases to 10.06% when the training size is 10%. Compared to MF, the proposed framework is more robust to the data sparsity problem. These observations suggest that exploiting the rater role of users can mitigate the data sparsity problem for recommendation.

Via aforementioned analysis, we can draw an answer to the first question - incorporating the rater role of users not

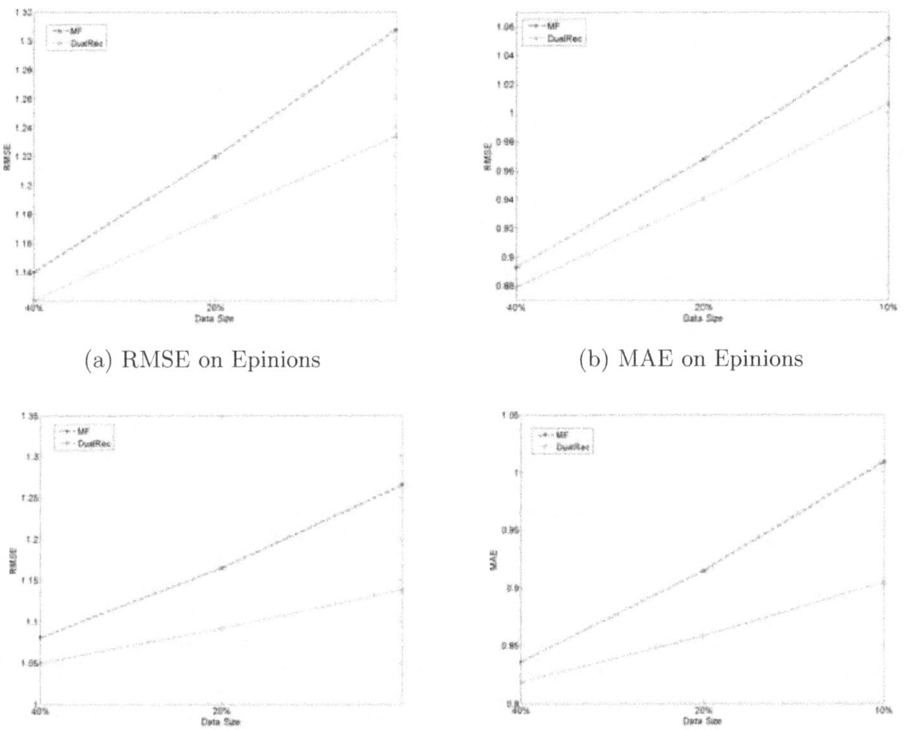

(a) RMSE on Epinions

(b) MAE on Epinions

(c) RMSE on Ciao

(d) MAE on Ciao

Figure 3: The Performance Gaps Between MF and the Proposed Framework DualRec w.r.t. the Size of the Training Set.

only can significantly improve the recommendation performance but also can mitigate the data sparsity problem in recommender systems.

4.3 Capability of Handling Cold-start Users

To answer the second question, we investigate the capability of the proposed framework DualRec in handling cold-start users. In detail, we first randomly select $x\%$ as training set and the remaining $1 - x\%$ as testing set where x is also varied as $\{10, 20, 40\}$. Then, we randomly select 5% users from the training set and remove their item ratings from the training set to the test set. While the helpfulness ratings for these 5% users are kept. In this way, these 5% of users do not have any item ratings but may have helpfulness ratings and we consider these 5% of users as cold-start users. For those baseline methods that cannot handle cold-start users, we randomly guess their item ratings for cold-start users. The results on those training sets with cold-start users are summarized in Table 4 and Table 5 for RMSE and MAE, respectively. Note that numbers inside parentheses in Table 4 and Table 5 denote the performance reductions compared to the performance without cold-start users in Table 2 and Table 3, respectively.

From the tables, we make the following observations

- The performance of all methods degenerates when we introduce cold-start users. For example, the performance for MF decreases up to 5.75% in terms of RMSE and up to 6.35% in terms of MAE.
- Compared to the baseline methods, the performance degeneration of the proposed framework DualRec is much smaller. As aforementioned, the proposed framework can still learn user latent factors for cold-start users by exploiting the rater role of users. These results support that the proposed framework can mitigate cold-start problems for recommendation.

In summary, the introduction of cold-start users could degrade the recommendation performance and the proposed framework is relatively more robust to cold-start users by incorporating the rater role of users.

4.4 Parameter Sensitivity

The proposed framework has two importance parameters α and β, which together control the contributions of incorporating the rater role of users for recommendation. In this section, we investigate the impact of the parameters α and β on the performance of the proposed framework DualRec. We only show results on Epinions and Ciao with 20% and 40% without cold-start users since we have similar observations with other experimental settings. We empirically set the latent dimension $K = 10$, the regularization parameter $\gamma = 0.1$ and $\lambda = 1$. We vary the values of α as $\{0.001, 0.01, 0.1, 1, 10, 100\}$ and β as $\{0.001, 0.01, 0.05, 0.1, 0.5, 1\}$. The results are shown in Figure4.

It can be observed from the figure:

- When we set $\alpha = 0$ and $\beta = 0$, the proposed framework DualRec boils down to MF. When we increase their values to $\alpha = 0.001$ and $\beta = 0.001$, we incorporate

Table 4: **Performance comparison on Epinions and Ciao with 5% cold-start users in terms of RMSE. Note that numbers inside parentheses in the table denote the performance reductions compared to the performance without cold-start users in Table 2.**

Dataset	Training Size	UCF	WNMF	MF	QMF	DualRec
Epinions	10%	1.3915(-4.47)	1.5899(-17.07)	1.3394(-2.46)	1.3296(-1.97)	1.2545(-1.68)
	20%	1.3475(-6.59)	1.5415(-21.91)	1.2459(-2.16)	1.2387(-2.06)	1.1927(-1.01)
	40%	1.3070(-8.78)	1.5347(-29.93)	1.1813(-3.62)	1.1746(-3.07)	1.1388(-1.62)
Ciao	10%	1.3035(-3.09)	1.6109(-22.70)	1.311(-3.60)	1.2879(-3.41)	1.1575(-1.66)
	20%	1.2713(-3.92)	1.5519(-27.18)	1.2125(-4.06)	1.1956(-2.88)	1.1044(-1.14)
	40%	1.2518(-6.55)	1.5404(-35.38)	1.1433(-5.75)	1.1338(-4.71)	1.0629(-1.24)

Table 5: **Performance comparison on Epinion and Ciao with 5% cold-start users in terms of MAE. Note that numbers inside parentheses in the table denote the performance reductions compared to the performance without cold-start users in Table 3.**

Dataset	Training Size	UCF	WNMF	MF	QMF	DualRec
Epinions	10%	1.1237(-3.70)	1.2091(-12.41)	1.0837(-3.07)	1.0754(-2.07)	1.0126(-0.30)
	20%	1.0961(-8.68)	1.1484(-15.68)	0.9917(-2.47)	0.9859(-2.34)	0.9528(-1.21)
	40%	1.0569(-4.60)	1.1123(-20.28)	0.9287(-4.02)	0.9203(-3.84)	0.9043(-2.85)
Ciao	10%	0.9747(-3.86)	1.1967(-15.90)	1.0494(-4.034)	1.0315(-3.69)	0.9238(-1.25)
	20%	0.9658(-4.85)	1.1286(-18.53)	0.9556(-4.45)	0.9383(-2.43)	0.8692(-1.25)
	40%	0.9582(-7.99)	1.1256(-26.27)	0.8892(-6.35)	0.8777(-5.54)	0.8317(-1.53)

the rater role of users for recommendation. In most cases, the proposed framework with $\alpha = 0.001$ and $\beta = 0.001$ obtains much better performance than MF. These results demonstrate the importance of the rater role of users for recommendation.

- In general, with the increment of α (or β), the performance tends to first increases and then decreases. At certain regions, the performance is relatively stable. These patterns ease the parameter selection for the proposed framework in practice.
- Most of the time, better performance is achieved with relatively large values of α and small values of β. The map matrix $\mathbf{w}$ in Eq. (10) is learned from both observed item ratings and predicted item ratings, which are controlled by α and β, respectively. Since observed item ratings should be more reliable than predicted item ratings, relatively large values of α and small values of β can lead to the learned $\mathbf{w}$ more accurate.
- Compared to α, RecDual is more sensitive to β. A larger β tends to make the learned $\mathbf{w}$ overfit to predicted item ratings, which in turn leads to inaccurate estimates of $\mathbf{U}$ and $\mathbf{V}$.
- The parameters α and β have bigger impact on the proposed framework DualRec when the training data is sparse. When the training data is sparse, the proposed framework relies on the rater role of users more to learn $\mathbf{U}$ and $\mathbf{V}$. These observations further suggest the importance of the rater role of users for recommendation.

5. RELATED WORK

In this paper, we investigate the duel roles of users for recommendation; hence our work is related to traditional recommender systems that exploit the reviewer role of users from recommendation, as well as helpfulness rating prediction, which investigates the rater role of users.

5.1 Recommender Systems

Recommender systems can be roughly categorized as content based recommender systems[1, 28, 17, 20] and collaborative filtering[5, 23, 29]. Content based recommender systems recommend items based on user's profile information or similar to the ones the user preferred in the past, while CF only requires past user ratings to predict unknown ratings and has attracted more and more attention. Despite the success of CF based recommender systems, most of them only consider user's role as reviewers but ignore their role as raters[25, 16, 10, 4, 27, 2]. One challenge of traditional recommender system is that the rating matrix is usually very sparse, which degenerates the performance of many recommender systems. To deal with the data sparsity problem, there are some recommender systems relying on extra sources to find similar users or similar items. For example, [15, 14] utilize trust networks by assuming that a user's taste is similar to that of his/her trusted users; [4] incorporates user and item graphs to a matrix factorization framework, which captures user and item similarity; and [13] explores heterogeneous relations for collaborative filtering. Some algorithms also rely on building users profile[34, 19, 32]. For example, [34] uses initial interview process for cold-start users. [19] constructs tensor profiles for user/item pairs from their individual features. The proposed framework differs from aforementioned methods where we consider users' dual roles in real-world recommender systems. Helpfulness ratings encode users' opinions on reviews of items; hence they could be useful to infer users' opinions on items. Therefore, we propose to explicitly learn implicit item ratings from helpfulness ratings, which not only captures the rater role of users in recommendation but also has potentials to mitigate the data sparsity and cold-start problems in recommendation.

5.2 Helpfulness Rating Prediction

The rater role of users allows them to express their opinions on reviews about items via helpfulness ratings, and helpfulness rating prediction has attracted increasing atten-

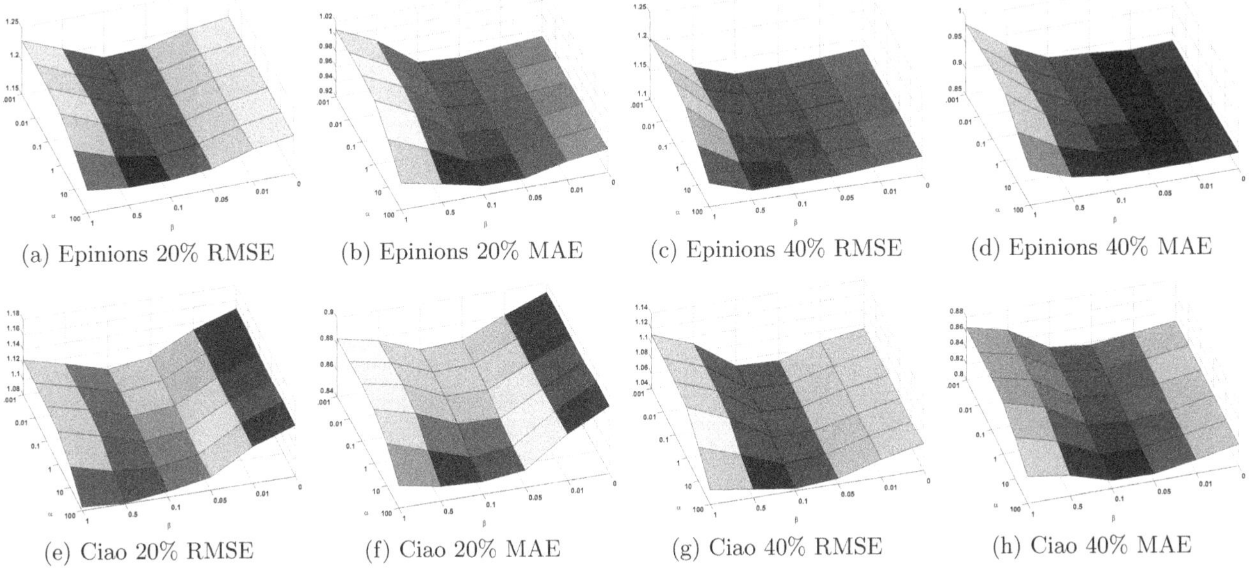

(a) Epinions 20% RMSE (b) Epinions 20% MAE (c) Epinions 40% RMSE (d) Epinions 40% MAE

(e) Ciao 20% RMSE (f) Ciao 20% MAE (g) Ciao 40% RMSE (h) Ciao 40% MAE

Figure 4: Parameter Sensitivity of DualRec w.r.t to α and β

tion recently to understand the rater role of users. [3, 31, 11, 26, 12]. [3] estimates the helpfulness of product reviews by mining text and reviewer characteristics. [26] predicts helpfulness ratings by incorporating the context of reviews and social networks. [12] uses multilayer perceptron neural networks to predict online reviews. Despite various models proposed to predict helpfulness ratings, there's few work about using helpfulness ratings for recommendation. [21] uses helpfulness rating to measure the quality of the review and then uses the quality score as a weight to control the matrix factorization model. In other words, it uses helpfulness ratings of reviews to indicate the reliability about their associated item ratings; while the proposed framework explicitly models how to learn implicit item ratings from helpfulness ratings. Therefore, the proposed framework is substantially different from [21] - (1) the investigation perspectives are different; (2) the proposed formulations are different; and (3) the proposed framework has potentials to mitigate the data sparsity and cold-start problems by incorporating the rater role of users.

6. CONCLUSIONS

In this paper, we investigate users' dual roles, i.e., reviewers that give item ratings and raters that give helpfulness ratings, to advance traditional recommender systems since the vast majority of existing recommender systems only consider the reviewer role of users. To incorporate the rater role of users, we study how to learn implicit item ratings from helpfulness ratings and how to exploit the dual roles simultaneously for recommendation, which lead to a novel recommender system DualRec. Experimental results show that the proposed framework outperforms several state-of-the-art recommender systems. Further experiments are conducted to demonstrate the capability of the proposed framework in mitigating the data sparsity and cold-start problems for recommendation by incorporating the rater role of users.

There are several interesting directions that need further investigation. First, in this work, we choose matrix factorization as our basic model to incorporate the rater role of users, and we would like to investigate other basic models. For example, one new direction in recommender system is to explore implicit hierarchical structures of users and items by using deep non-negative matrix factorization[30]. We would investigate if user duel roles can be incorporated into that model. Second, for effectiveness, we choose linear regression to infer implicit item ratings from helpfulness ratings; we will investigate if other models can improve the performance. Since social networks are pervasively available in social media and provide independent sources for recommendation, we would like to investigate if social networks can be utilized to advance the implicit item rating learning process.

7. ACKNOWLEDGEMENTS

This material is based upon the work supported by, or in part by, Office of Naval Research (ONR) under grant number N000141410095 and Army Research Office (ARO) under grant number 025071.

8. REFERENCES

[1] M. Balabanović and Y. Shoham. Fab: content-based, collaborative recommendation, 1997.

[2] H. Gao, J. Tang, X. Hu, and H. Liu. Exploring temporal effects for location recommendation on location-based social networks. In *Proceedings of the 7th ACM conference on Recommender systems*, pages 93–100. ACM, 2013.

[3] A. Ghose and P. G. Ipeirotis. Estimating the helpfulness and economic impact of product reviews: Mining text and reviewer characteristics. *Knowledge and Data Engineering, IEEE Transactions on*, 23(10):1498–1512, 2011.

[4] Q. Gu, J. Zhou, and C. H. Ding. Collaborative filtering: Weighted nonnegative matrix factorization incorporating user and item graphs. In *SDM*, pages 199–210. SIAM, 2010.

[5] J. L. Herlocker, J. A. Konstan, A. Borchers, and J. Riedl. An algorithmic framework for performing collaborative filtering. In *Proceedings of the 22nd annual international ACM SIGIR conference on Research and development in information retrieval*, pages 230–237. ACM, 1999.

[6] T. Hofmann. Latent semantic models for collaborative filtering. *ACM Transactions on Information Systems (TOIS)*, 22(1):89–115, 2004.

[7] Y. Hu, Y. Koren, and C. Volinsky. Collaborative filtering for implicit feedback datasets. In *Data Mining, 2008. ICDM'08. Eighth IEEE International Conference on*, pages 263–272. IEEE, 2008.

[8] Y. Koren. Factorization meets the neighborhood: a multifaceted collaborative filtering model. In *Proceedings of the 14th ACM SIGKDD international conference on Knowledge discovery and data mining*, pages 426–434. ACM, 2008.

[9] Y. Koren. Collaborative filtering with temporal dynamics. *Communications of the ACM*, 53(4):89–97, 2010.

[10] Y. Koren, R. Bell, and C. Volinsky. Matrix factorization techniques for recommender systems. *Computer*, pages 30–37, 2009.

[11] N. Korfiatis, E. García-Bariocanal, and S. Sánchez-Alonso. Evaluating content quality and helpfulness of online product reviews: The interplay of review helpfulness vs. review content. *Electronic Commerce Research and Applications*, 11(3):205–217, 2012.

[12] S. Lee and J. Y. Choeh. Predicting the helpfulness of online reviews using multilayer perceptron neural networks. *Expert Systems with Applications*, 41(6):3041–3046, 2014.

[13] C. Luo, W. Pang, Z. Wang, and C. Lin. Hete-cf: Social-based collaborative filtering recommendation using heterogeneous relations. In *2014 IEEE International Conference on Data Mining, ICDM*, pages 917–922, 2014.

[14] H. Ma, I. King, and M. R. Lyu. Learning to recommend with social trust ensemble. In *Proceedings of the 32nd international ACM SIGIR conference on Research and development in information retrieval*, pages 203–210. ACM, 2009.

[15] P. Massa and P. Avesani. Trust-aware recommender systems. In *Proceedings of the 2007 ACM conference on Recommender systems*, pages 17–24. ACM, 2007.

[16] A. Mnih and R. Salakhutdinov. Probabilistic matrix factorization. In *Advances in neural information processing systems*, pages 1257–1264, 2007.

[17] R. J. Mooney and L. Roy. Content-based book recommending using learning for text categorization. In *Proceedings of the fifth ACM conference on Digital libraries*, pages 195–204. ACM, 2000.

[18] M. Papagelis, D. Plexousakis, and T. Kutsuras. Alleviating the sparsity problem of collaborative filtering using trust inferences. In *Trust management*, pages 224–239. Springer, 2005.

[19] S.-T. Park and W. Chu. Pairwise preference regression for cold-start recommendation. In *Proceedings of the third ACM conference on Recommender systems*, pages 21–28. ACM, 2009.

[20] M. J. Pazzani and D. Billsus. Content-based recommendation systems. In *The adaptive web*, pages 325–341. Springer, 2007.

[21] S. Raghavan, S. Gunasekar, and J. Ghosh. Review quality aware collaborative filtering. In *Proceedings of the sixth ACM conference on Recommender systems*, pages 123–130. ACM, 2012.

[22] P. Resnick and H. R. Varian. Recommender systems. *Communications of the ACM*, 40(3):56–58, 1997.

[23] B. Sarwar, G. Karypis, J. Konstan, and J. Riedl. Item-based collaborative filtering recommendation algorithms. In *Proceedings of the 10th international conference on World Wide Web*, pages 285–295. ACM, 2001.

[24] L. Si and R. Jin. Flexible mixture model for collaborative filtering. In *ICML*, volume 3, pages 704–711, 2003.

[25] N. Srebro, J. Rennie, and T. S. Jaakkola. Maximum-margin matrix factorization, 2005.

[26] J. Tang, H. Gao, X. Hu, and H. Liu. Context-aware review helpfulness rating prediction. In *Proceedings of the 7th ACM conference on Recommender systems*, pages 1–8. ACM, 2013.

[27] J. Tang, X. Hu, H. Gao, and H. Liu. Exploiting local and global social context for recommendation. In *Proceedings of the Twenty-Third international joint conference on Artificial Intelligence*, pages 2712–2718. AAAI Press, 2013.

[28] R. Van Meteren and M. Van Someren. Using content-based filtering for recommendation, 2000.

[29] J. Wang, A. P. De Vries, and M. J. Reinders. Unifying user-based and item-based collaborative filtering approaches by similarity fusion. In *Proceedings of the 29th annual international ACM SIGIR conference on Research and development in information retrieval*, pages 501–508. ACM, 2006.

[30] S. Wang, J. Tang, and H. Liu. Exploring implicit hierarchical structures for recommender systems. In *Proceedings of 24th International Joint Conference on Artificial Intelligence*, 2015.

[31] W. Xiong and D. Litman. Automatically predicting peer-review helpfulness. In *Proceedings of the 49th Annual Meeting of the Association for Computational Linguistics: Human Language Technologies: short papers-Volume 2*, pages 502–507. Association for Computational Linguistics, 2011.

[32] M. Zhang, J. Tang, X. Zhang, and X. Xue. Addressing cold start in recommender systems: A semi-supervised co-training algorithm. In *Proceedings of the 37th international ACM SIGIR conference on Research and development in information retrieval*, pages 73–82. ACM, 2014.

[33] S. Zhang, W. Wang, J. Ford, and F. Makedon. Learning from incomplete ratings using non-negative matrix factorization. In *SDM*, volume 6, pages 548–552. SIAM, 2006.

[34] K. Zhou, S.-H. Yang, and H. Zha. Functional matrix factorizations for cold-start recommendation. In *Proceedings of the 34th international ACM SIGIR conference on Research and development in Information Retrieval*, pages 315–324. ACM, 2011.

TriRank: Review-aware Explainable Recommendation by Modeling Aspects*

Xiangnan He[1] Tao Chen[1] Min-Yen Kan[1] Xiao Chen[2]
[1]School of Computing, National University of Singapore
[2]Institute of Computing Technology, Chinese Academy of Sciences
{xiangnan, kanmy, taochen}@comp.nus.edu.sg chenxiao3310@ict.ac.cn

ABSTRACT

Most existing collaborative filtering techniques have focused on modeling the binary relation of users to items by extracting from user ratings. Aside from users' ratings, their affiliated reviews often provide the rationale for their ratings and identify what aspects of the item they cared most about. We explore the rich evidence source of aspects in user reviews to improve top-N recommendation. By extracting aspects (*i.e.*, the specific properties of items) from textual reviews, we enrich the user–item binary relation to a user–item–aspect ternary relation. We model the ternary relation as a heterogeneous tripartite graph, casting the recommendation task as one of vertex ranking. We devise a generic algorithm for ranking on tripartite graphs — TriRank — and specialize it for personalized recommendation. Experiments on two public review datasets show that it consistently outperforms state-of-the-art methods. Most importantly, TriRank endows the recommender system with a higher degree of explainability and transparency by modeling aspects in reviews. It allows users to interact with the system through their aspect preferences, assisting users in making informed decisions.

Categories and Subject Descriptors

H.3.3 [**Information Storage and Retrieval**]: Information Search and Retrieval - *information filtering*

Keywords

Reviews, Aspects, Explanable Recommendation, Top-N Recommendation, Tripartite Graph Ranking

1. INTRODUCTION

Recommender systems serve to help users discover choice products to consume, matching users to items of potential interest (*e.g.,* products, businesses, movies, *etc.*). Among the various recommendation techniques, collaborative filtering (CF) is widely used, due to its effectiveness in providing personalized recommendation based on the wisdom of the crowds. By and large, existing CF techniques have focused on modeling user–item relations, such as ratings. As a single rating only indicates a user's overall satisfaction for the item, it is hard to infer the actual rationale of the rating. Different users may care about different aspects of the same item. For example, in the restaurant domain, one user may give a 5-star rating for food quality, while another user may give the same rating, but due to favorable ambiance. Since existing CF techniques largely lack such fine-grained analysis, they can fail to accurately model a target user's interests.

Aside from ratings, most Web 2.0 systems also give users the opportunity to leave reviews on the provided items. These reviews often justify a user's rating, offering the underlying reasons for the rating by discussing the specific properties of the item. Thus they are well-suited as a complementary data source for collaborative filtering. In this work, we leverage on this key observation to address the task of *top-N recommendation*; that is, to produce an ordered list of N items that will be most appealing to a user.

Leveraging user reviews (or interchangably, "comments") is non-trivial for systems, as these reviews are written by users freestyle, exhibiting noise and irrelevant content. Recent research [10, 11, 17, 19] have largely modeled reviews at the word level, distilling them into latent topics to combine with the latent factor model. Although these methods achieve good prediction accuracy, the recommendation process is not transparent and the generated recommendations are not explainable to users, a well-known drawback of the latent factor model [14]. To improve users' experience and trust, transparency and explainability become increasingly important for practical recommender systems [27]. Moreover, improvements in rating prediction (a lower error rate) may not directly translate into improvements in top-N recommendation [3]. As systems usually make only their top suggestions visible, targeting improvement at the top ranks is most beneficial for recommendation in practice.

Instead of modeling reviews at the word level, we propose to model reviews in the level of distilled *aspects*, which are the specific properties of items and expressed in reviews as noun words or phrases [31]. For example, *battery* and *screen* are aspects of digital products, *food quality* and *ambiance* are aspects of restaurants. Given the aspects extracted from reviews, we first model the user–item–aspect relation as a tripartite graph. Then we devise TriRank, a generic al-

*This research is supported by the Singapore National Research Foundation under its International Research Centre @ Singapore Funding Initiative and administered by the IDM Programme Office.

Permission to make digital or hard copies of all or part of this work for personal or classroom use is granted without fee provided that copies are not made or distributed for profit or commercial advantage and that copies bear this notice and the full citation on the first page. Copyrights for components of this work owned by others than ACM must be honored. Abstracting with credit is permitted. To copy otherwise, or republish, to post on servers or to redistribute to lists, requires prior specific permission and/or a fee. Request permissions from Permissions@acm.org.
CIKM'15, October 19–23, 2015, Melbourne, Australia.
Copyright 2015 ACM 978-1-4503-3794-6/15/10 ...$15.00.
http://dx.doi.org/10.1145/2806416.2806504.

gorithm based on the graph regularization framework [9, 36] for ranking in tripartite graphs. TriRank ranks vertices by accounting for both the structural smoothness (encoding collaborative filtering and aspect filtering effects) and fitting constraints (encoding personalized preferences). Besides TriRank's superior performance, there are two key properties making it suitable in practice: first, the recommendation process is transparent by explaining its recommendations with respect to aspects, allowing users to customize their recommendations to fit their preferences (*i.e.*, scrutability [27]). Second, TriRank is tolerant of noisy aspects, common in automated aspect extraction, such that porting to new domains can be done without manual effort.

It is instructive to clarify that this work solely relies on the automatically detected item aspects in user reviews, and not any other additional information, such as sentiment (a separate area of study). We believe regardless of a user's sentiment on a reviewed aspect, its mention at least reflects the user's interest in the aspect. We believe by mining such item aspects latent in reviews, we can infer user preference at a finer granularity, thus providing better personalized recommendation.

This paper is organized as follows. In Section 2, we discuss the process of aspect extraction from reviews. We detail our TriRank method in Section 3, and conduct experiments and empirical studies on aspects in Section 4. We review related work in Section 5, before concluding the paper in Section 6.

2. ASPECT EXTRACTION

Aspect extraction, also termed as feature or attribute extraction, has a long history in review mining (see [31]). Aspects can be seen as the components, attributes, or properties of an item. Early seminal work [12] proposed several language rules to extract product features from reviews. The rules have been widely used and extended by later work, *e.g.*, [32] considered specific phrase patterns and sentence patterns. Aside from the unsupervised rule-based methods, supervised sequence labeling techniques such as the *Conditional Random Field* have been adopted to learn aspects [13].

As our focus is to leverage aspects from user reviews, we do not contribute to aspect extraction, but instead seek to maximally exploit technologies that can perform it. As such, we apply an existing state-of-the-art aspect extraction toolkit [33] that constructs a sentiment lexicon from user reviews. It creates entries that are feature–opinion word pairs with an associated sentiment polarity, represented as (F, O, S). For example, an entry such as (*service, excellent, positive*) might be extracted from a restaurant review. The key feature extraction part of the tool is a rule-based system, mainly adopting and extending the rules proposed by [12]. As each feature is a noun word or phrase, representing the item's property that a user comments on, we can directly use it as an aspect.

We apply the tool with its default settings, extracting $6,025$ and $1,617$ distinct features (*i.e.*, aspects) from our datasets culled from Yelp and Amazon Electronics, respectively (datasets described later in Section 4). Table 1 shows top features extracted from the two datasets, ranked by their $tf \times idf$ score. We notice that the tool produces some features that are good but also many noisy features, such as "ive" ("I've"), "picturesmy", "150", which are quirks of the corpus. Also, some top features are domain-specific stop words (*e.g.*, "food", "restaurant", "product"), which do not represent the specific properties of items. Despite this significant level of noise, we do not perform any post filtering on the extracted aspects to test the robustness of our proposed method to noise.

Table 1: Top automatically extracted aspects.

Yelp	bar, salad, menu, chicken, sauce, restaurant, rice, cheese, fries, bread, sandwich, drinks, patio
Amazon	camera, quality, sound, price, product, battery, pictures, features, screen, size, memory, lens

Table 2: Statistics of aspects extracted from reviews.

		User–Aspect		Item–Aspect	
Dataset	# of Aspects	Avg. # of A / User	Density	Avg. # of A / Item	Density
Yelp	6,025	183.8	3.05%	138.0	2.29%
Amazon	1,617	61.4	3.80%	23.2	1.44%

Note that in terms of manifestation, aspects and tags (in social tagging systems) look alike – they are both usually short noun phrases. However, they differ fundamentally in nature and hence utility. Tags are simple keywords that are directly annotated by users to categorize and manage items. Aspects, on the other hand, describe specific attributes of items, and are implicitly extracted from free-text reviews.

Table 2 summarizes the statistics of extracted aspects on the two datasets. We note that the densities of the user–aspect and item–aspect matrix are much higher than that of the user–item rating matrix (usually less than 1%, see Table 3); a good signal that the aspect matrices contain rich information useful for addressing the sparseness of the original rating matrix.

3. PROPOSED METHOD

We now present our proposed method for review-aware recommendation, by introducing the tripartite graph to model the user–item–aspect ternary relation. We then devise the generic TriRank algorithm for ranking on tripartite graphs. Finally, we detail how to operationalize TriRank for personalized recommendation.

3.1 Data Model and Notation

Let $G = (U \cup P \cup A, E_{UP} \cup E_{UA} \cup E_{PA})$ be a tripartite graph, where U, P and A are vertex sets that represent users, items and aspects, respectively. Let E_{UP}, E_{UA} and E_{PA} be edges that represent user–item, user–aspect, item–aspect relations, respectively. Each input triple $<u_i, p_j, a_k>$ denotes that user u_i has rated item p_j with a review mentioning aspect a_k, is then represented as a triangle with edges e_{ij}, e_{ik} and e_{jk} (as in Figure 1). Each edge carries a weight to denote the strength of two connected vertices; edges with higher weight denote stronger more significant relations between vertices. For example, we can model user u_i's rating on item p_j as an edge with weight of e_{ij}. Without loss of generality, we use the symbol R, Y and X to denote the edge weight matrix of user–item, user–aspect and item–aspect relations, respectively.

3.2 Tripartite Graph Ranking (TriRank)

The goal for item recommendation is to devise a ranking function $f : P \rightarrow \mathbb{R}$, which maps each item in P to a real number such that the value reflects the target user u's (predicted) preference on the item. Then, sorting the resultant items by score yields u's personalized item ranking. Since

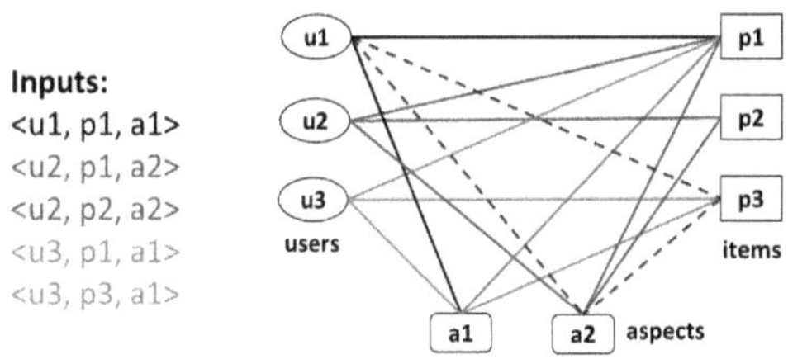

Figure 1: An example tripartite structure of the given inputs (the dashed line illustrates the additional input $<u_1, p_3, a_2>$).

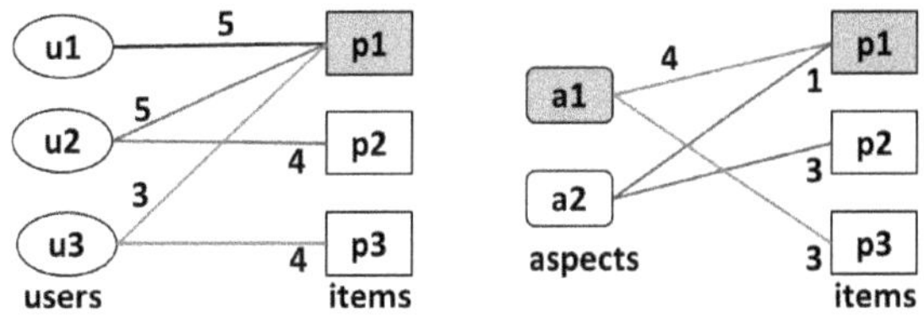

(a) User-Item structure (b) Item-Aspect structure

Figure 2: Smoothness constraints on decomposed graphs from Figure 1. Assume $u1$ previously rated item p_1 with mentioning aspect a_1 (shaded vertices).

TriRank induces scores for all vertices in the graph, it has the important side-affect of assigning scores to the aspect and user vertices: these denote u's interest on aspects and similarity with other users, respectively.

In a nutshell, TriRank assigns the ranking score of vertices by enforcing the structural smoothness and fitting constraints of the graph. By smoothness and fitting constraints, we adopt the same definitions as those common to the graph regularization framework [9, 36]:

· *Smoothness* implies local consistency: that nearby vertices should not vary too much in their scores.

· *Fitting* encodes prior belief: that the ranking function should not cause much deviation from the observations.

TriRank seeks to assign each vertex a score such that *the graph is sufficiently smooth* and *the prior belief is retained.* In the following, we first illustrate how the two constraints in the tripartite graph capture the intuition for recommendation, before describing the TriRank algorithm.

3.2.1 Illustrating Regularization Constraints

Let us first see how the smoothness works by considering the example in Figure 1. We decompose it into two subgraphs in Figure 2 for ease of exposition. The left subfigure gives the user–item structure, where edge weights denote ratings. Assume we want to recommend items to u_1, who has only rated p_1 with a score of 5. As p_1 is connected more strongly to u_2 than u_3, u_2 is given a higher score than u_3. Finally, since the edge weights of $<u_2,p_2>$ and $<u_3,p_3>$ are identical, we infer that p_2 should receive a higher score than p_3. Such smoothness constraints on the user–item relation alone yields the traditional CF effect.

Considering aspects can provide additional evidence that influences the recommendation process. Let us continue to recommend for u_1 but base our decision on item–aspect structure (Figure 2(b)), where edge weight denotes the number of an item's reviews mentioning an aspect. As u_1 only previously mentions aspect a_1, enforcing smoothness would rank p_3 higher than p_2, as p_3 is more strongly connected to a_1, in contrast to p_2. This example also shows that predicting based on CF and aspect filtering yield different results; and that the *smoothness* constraint on the whole graph to combine them may be beneficial.

The fitting constraint serves as a means to personalize the ranking for each user (*cf.* shaded vertices of Figure 2). For a target user u, the past ratings and reviewed aspects indicate u's prior (known) preference on the vertices. It should guide the ranking process such that the resultant ranking function should be consistent with the prior belief.

3.2.2 Regularization on Tripartite Graph

We now define the regularization function to implement the two constraints for ranking vertices.

Smoothness. Similar to the previous work [9] that defines a smoothness regularizer on bipartite graphs, we devise the regularizer on user–item structure as follows:

$$Q_{UP}(f) = \sum_{i=1}^{|U|}\sum_{j=1}^{|P|} r_{ij}\left(\frac{f(u_i)}{\sqrt{d_i^u}} - \frac{f(p_j)}{\sqrt{d_j^p}}\right)^2, \tag{1}$$

where $f(u_i)$ and $f(p_j)$ denote the final ranking scores (*i.e.*, parameters to learn); r_{ij} is the edge weight between u_i and p_j; d_i^u and d_j^p are the weighted degrees (sum of edge weights) of u_i and p_j, respectively, for normalization. The counterpart user–aspect and item–aspect smoothness regularizers for aspect filtering can be obtained similarly.

This smoothness regularizer can be seen as a graph kernel that measures the similarity of vertices. Although there are various kernels [25], we have purposefully chosen this one (originally introduced by [36]) due to its effective encoding of the CF effect in bipartite graph scenarios. To see this, assume we recommend for the target user u. First, minimizing Eq. (1) constrains a vertex's score based on its neighbors – if a user is strongly connected by many high-scoring **items** (*e.g.*, rated items of u), the user will be given a high score (*i.e.*, more similar with the u); likewise, if an item is strongly connected by many high-scoring **users** (*i.e.*, similar users), it will have a high score. Second, the quadratic nature of the normalization suppresses the popularity of highly connected vertices; this property is essential to prevent a ranking from being dominated by popular vertices [1].

Fitting. Let the target user's prior preference on item p_j be p_j^0; then the regularizer to enforce the fitting constraint on items is defined as:

$$Q_P(f) = \sum_{j=1}^{|P|}(f(p_j) - p_j^0)^2. \tag{2}$$

We can similarly achieve such fitting regularizers on users and aspects. This fitting regularizer corresponds to the squared error loss that is commonly used by machine learning models in recommendation. Different with the latent factor model [14, 19] that only optimizes for rated items, Eq. (2) also importantly takes unrated items into account (*cf.* summing over all items). This property is very desirable for the top-N task, as it aims at ranking unrated items [3]. Another option for top-N recommendation is to optimize a ranking-based loss function, such as *AUC* used by *Bayesian Personalized Ranking* [23]. This is an interesting extension to be explored in the future.

Regularization function. To account for the heterogeneous structure of the tripartite graph, we combine the smoothness regularizer on each relation type with the fitting regularizer using different weights for each vertex type:

$$Q(f) = \alpha \sum_{i,j} r_{ij} (\frac{f(u_i)}{\sqrt{d_i^u}} - \frac{f(p_j)}{\sqrt{d_j^p}})^2 + \beta \sum_{j,k} x_{jk} (\frac{f(p_j)}{\sqrt{d_j^p}} - \frac{f(a_k)}{\sqrt{d_k^a}})^2$$
$$+ \gamma \sum_{i,k} y_{ik} (\frac{f(u_i)}{\sqrt{d_i^u}} - \frac{f(a_k)}{\sqrt{d_k^a}})^2 + \eta_U \sum_i (f(u_i) - u_i^0)^2$$
$$+ \eta_P \sum_j (f(p_j) - p_j^0)^2 + \eta_A \sum_k (f(a_k) - a_k^0)^2, \quad (3)$$

where α, β and γ denote the weight of smoothness on user–item, item–aspect and user–aspect relation, respectively; η_U, η_P and η_A denote the weight of fitting constraint on users, items and aspects, respectively (we discuss how to set the prior preference u_i^0, p_j^0 and a_k^0 later in Section 3.3).

3.2.3 Optimizing the Regularization Function

We now minimize Eq. (3) to derive the final ranking scores (*i.e.*, model parameters). As the objective function is strictly convex, standard optimization techniques find a unique solution regardless of initialization. Two widely used techniques are *stochastic gradient descent* (SGD) and *alternating least squares* (ALS). SGD updates all parameters towards the negative gradients for each training instance, while ALS minimizes the objective function per parameter until a joint optimum is found (*i.e.*, coordinate-wise descent). For this scenario, we adopt ALS over SGD as the objective function can be analytically solved for each parameter, and importantly, it does not need to set the learning rate, which is crucial to SGD's effectiveness. Additionally, it usually yields a faster convergence and is easier to parallelize than SGD.

By differentiating $Q(f)$ with respect to $f(u_i)$, $f(p_j)$ and $f(a_k)$, respectively, and letting the derivatives be 0, we obtain the iterative update rules. Let the ranking vector for items be $\vec{p} = [f(p_j)]_{|P|\times 1}$, and the prior preference vector for items be $\vec{p}_0 = [p_j^0]_{|P|\times 1}$. Let similar definitions follow for $\vec{u}, \vec{u}_0$ for users, and $\vec{a}, \vec{a}_0$ for aspects. The equivalent update rules in matrix form are as follows:

$$\vec{u} = \frac{\alpha}{\alpha+\gamma+\eta_U} S_R \cdot \vec{p} + \frac{\gamma}{\alpha+\gamma+\eta_U} S_Y \cdot \vec{a} + \frac{\eta_U}{\alpha+\gamma+\eta_U} \vec{u}_0,$$
$$\vec{p} = \frac{\alpha}{\alpha+\beta+\eta_P} S_R^T \cdot \vec{u} + \frac{\beta}{\alpha+\beta+\eta_P} S_X \cdot \vec{a} + \frac{\eta_P}{\alpha+\beta+\eta_P} \vec{p}_0,$$
$$\vec{a} = \frac{\gamma}{\gamma+\beta+\eta_A} S_Y^T \cdot \vec{u} + \frac{\beta}{\gamma+\beta+\eta_A} S_X^T \cdot \vec{p} + \frac{\eta_A}{\gamma+\beta+\eta_A} \vec{a}_0, \quad (4)$$

where S_R is the symmetric normalized form of matrix R, defined as $[\frac{r_{ij}}{\sqrt{d_i^u}\sqrt{d_j^p}}]_{|U|\times|P|}$; S_X and S_Y are defined similarly. We note that a closed-form solution can be obtained analytically, but omit them due to space limitations.

3.3 Personalized Recommendation

Given the general TriRank algorithm, we need to cover how we obtain the initial graph (specifically, edge weights and the target user's prior preference) to concretize the generic algorithm for our review-based recommendation scenario.

Edge weights. *User–item* edge weights from relation R can be set as in traditional CF: in cases with explicit feedback, it can be the rating score; for implicit feedback, whether the user has interacted with or browsed the item (measured as either a binary yes/no, or an integer view count). Our datasets provide explicit user ratings, so we use these ratings as-is.

For the *user–aspect* relation Y and the *item–aspect* relation X, edge weights connote the degree of user interest (item speciality) with respect to the aspect. Once aspects are identified in reviews, we can use either the actual count (number of mentions) within all a user's (item's) reviews, or the review frequency (number of reviews that mention the aspects). As reviews vary in length, an aspect may occur multiple times in long reviews, but may not imply that the user pays more attention to the aspect[1]. As such, we use review frequency in our experiments. As in general IR, we take the logarithm of the review frequency, to dampen the effect of aspects that appear very frequently.

Prior preference. We need to set the prior preference vectors for the three vertex types, with respect to the target user u_i for personalization.

For *items*, the item prior preference vector $\vec{p}_0$ takes a positive value if the target user has interacted with the item, otherwise, 0. Thus we adopt the ith row vector of R as the $\vec{p}_0$ for the target user u_i. Similarly, for *aspects*, the aspect preference vector $\vec{a}_0$ is set as the row vector of user–aspect matrix Y. As the smoothness part of Eq. (3) normalizes the edge weight by a vertex's degree, we also apply the L_1 norm on $\vec{p}_0$ and $\vec{a}_0$ for meaningful combination.

The user preference vector $\vec{u}_0$ should denote the target user's similarity with other users. We can set $\vec{u}_0$ based on a user's social network when it is available. We can also adopt standard user-based CF, and set $\vec{u}_0$ by measuring user similarity from the rating matrix R. In this work, we adopt the most basic approach, simply setting the target user herself as 1, and all other users as 0. Note that this variable does not directly reflect user's preference on aspects or items, so its design is beyond the scope of this work.

Algorithm 1: TriRank for review-aware top-N item recommendation.

Input: User-Item interactions R and reviews.

Offline Training (for all users):
1. Extract aspects from reviews (Section 2).
2. Build item–aspect matrix X and user–aspect matrix Y.
3. TF term weighting: $X = X.tf(); Y = Y.tf()$.
4. Build symmetric normalized matrices S_R, S_X, S_Y.

Online Recommendation (for target user u_i):

5. Build u_i's prior preference vectors $\vec{p}_0$, $\vec{a}_0$ and $\vec{u}_0$.
6. L_1 norm on $\vec{p}_0$, $\vec{a}_0$ and $\vec{u}_0$.
7. Randomly initialize ranking vectors $\vec{p}$, $\vec{a}$ and $\vec{u}$.
8. Iteratively run update rules Eq. (4), until convergence.
9. Recommend top ranked items to u_i, and explain the recommendation using top ranked aspects.

TriRank works by enforcing the collaborative filtering and aspect filtering effects, and is summarized in Algorithm 1. For convergence, one can monitor $Q(f)$'s value until it stabilizes or set a maximum number of iterations.

The iterative solution Eq. (4) presents a more transparent view on the ranking process. The scores of items, users and aspects mutually reinforce each other – a score increase in an item will increase the score of its connected users and

[1]Note that this is the same argument for the analogous document frequency over collection frequency, in general IR.

Figure 3: Mock user interface for showing the rationale behind recommending *Chick-Fil-A* to a user.

aspects; similarly, for users and aspects. The overall solution can be seen as a semi-supervised learning process [36] on graphs – with the prior preference as labeled data, the algorithm propagates the labels to other unlabeled vertices.

3.4 Discussion

There are three properties of TriRank that merit a more detailed discussion: explainability, insensitivity to noisy aspects, and structural ambiguity.

Explainability. As TriRank ranks items in an easily explainable way, it provides users more transparency in understanding the system behavior. We can attribute recommendations to the top-ranked aspects matching the target user and recommended item. Figure 3 shows a mock-up interface for explaining recommendation based on aspects, inspired by tag-based explanation [28]. Aspects are sorted by item's speciality by default, but a user can sort according to her predicted preference. This property makes the system scrutable [27], allowing a user to control how the system utilizes her reviews. For example, if a user dislikes a recommendation due to inaccurately-captured aspects or she has updated preference not captured in her reviews, she can edit her aspect preference. TriRank can then encode the new aspect query vector (*i.e.*, $\vec{a}_0$) and return the revised recommendations (shown later in Section 4.3).

This is a major advantage over the recent solutions [19, 34] which integrate reviews using a latent factor model (LFM). Such LFM methods only provide single-shot recommendation where the rationale for the recommendation is opaque. In contrast, the scrutability provided by our method easily allows recommendation to become a cyclical process – a user can iteratively interact with the recommender system, where her actions improve the system's recommendations in turn. This iterative and scrutable nature are becoming increasingly important for real-world recommender systems [27].

Insensitivity to noisy aspects. As mentioned in Section 2, extracted aspects are noisy. For noisy aspects which are outliers (*e.g.*, "picturemy", "150"), they usually occur less frequently in reviews as compared with those from normal aspects. As such, they will have smaller edge weights in the tripartite graph, thus exerting less impact on the ranking (see x_{jk} and y_{ik} of Eq. (3)). For noisy aspects which are domain-specific stop words, although they have high frequency in reviews, they actually distribute evenly for all users and items (*i.e.*, column vector of S_X and S_Y of Eq. (4)). As a result, they will contribute evenly across all items' ranking scores, hence not changing the relative ranking among items. As such, TriRank is relatively insensitive to noisy aspects (either outliers or stop words).

Structural ambiguity. Given a list of triples as inputs, we can uniquely represent them as a tripartite graph, but not vice versa. This is because in the tripartite graph, we cannot attribute a specific edge to an input tuple, as the conversion to the tripartite graph does not represent tuple association. More specifically, let the reviewed aspects of user u_i and item p_j be A_i and A_j, respectively. Assume u_i interacts with p_j, then the tripartite structure can not differentiate the aspects in $A_i \cap A_j$ for the interaction r_{ij}. When such ambiguities occur, they can act like unseen additional inputs, which can complement the actual observed data in a manner similar to transitive reasoning.

Table 3: Statistics of datasets in evaluation.

Dataset	Review#	Item#	User#	Avg	Density
Yelp	114,316	4,043	3,835	29.8	0.74%
Amazon	55,677	14,370	2,933	19.0	0.13%

"Avg" denotes the average number of reviews per user.

4. EXPERIMENTS

We first introduce our experimental settings, and then compare its performance with other methods. We then study the utility of aspects in depth. Finally, we perform a few case studies of TriRank's recommendation output.

Datasets. We experiment with two publicly accessible datasets: Yelp[2] and Amazon Electronics [19].

1. Yelp. This is the Yelp Challenge dataset published on April 2013. It includes 11,537 items, 229,907 reviews and 45,981 users. The dataset is very sparse – 49.6% of users only made one review, making it difficult for evaluation.

2. Amazon. This dataset contains user ratings and reviews on Amazon products of Electronics category, published by [19]. The original dataset contains over 800K users, 80K items and 1.3M reviews. It is more sparse than the Yelp dataset – with 77.9% of users making only one review.

Following the common practice by other works [4, 34] in evaluating recommender algorithms, we filter out the items and users having fewer than 10 reviews. Table 3 summarizes the statistics of the filtered datasets. We split each dataset into three parts for training, validation and testing by time. For each user, we sort her reviews in chronological order. The first 80% are used for training, and the remaining most recent 20% are randomly split as validation set (for parameter tuning only) and test set (for evaluation).

Evaluation Metrics. Given a user, each algorithm produces a ranked list of items. To assess the ranked list with the ground-truth item set (GT), we adopt *Hit Ratio* (HR), which has been commonly used in top-N evaluation [15, 29]. If a test item appears in the recommended list, it is deemed a hit. HR is calculated as:

$$HR@K = \frac{Number\ of\ Hits\ @K}{|GT|}. \quad (5)$$

As the HR is recall-based metric, it does not reflect the accuracy of getting top ranks correct, which is crucial in many real-world applications. To address this, we also adopt *Normalized Discounted Cumulative Gain* (NDCG), which assigns higher importance to results at top ranks, scoring successively lower ranks with marginal fractional utility:

$$NDCG@K = Z_K \sum_{i=1}^{K} \frac{2^{r_i} - 1}{log_2(i+1)}, \quad (6)$$

[2]http://www.yelp.com/dataset_challenge

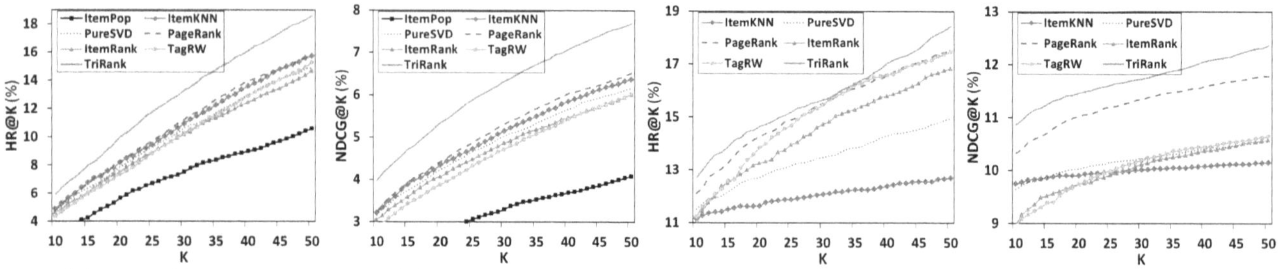

(a) Yelp – Hit Ratio (b) Yelp – NDCG (c) Amazon – Hit Ratio (d) Amazon – NDCG

Figure 4: Performance evaluated by Hit Ratio and NDCG from position 10 to 50 (*i.e.*, K).

where Z_K is the normalizer to ensure the perfect ranking has a value of 1; r_i is the graded relevance of item at position i. We use the simple binary relevance for our work: $r_i = 1$ if the item is in the test set, and 0 otherwise.

For both metrics, larger values indicate better performance. In the evaluation, we calculate both metrics for each user in the test set, and report the average score.

Baselines. We compare TriRank with the following commonly used and competitive methods in top-N evaluation:

1. **Item Popularity (ItemPop)**. Items are ranked by their popularity judged by number of ratings. Although it is not personalized, it is surprisingly competitive in top-N evaluation [3], as users tend to consume popular items.

2. **ItemKNN [24]**. This is standard item-based CF, and has been used commercially by Amazon [16] and MovieLens [28]. We adopt cosine similarity to measure the similarity among items. We test the method with different number of neighbors, finding that using all neighbors works best.

3. **PureSVD [3]**. A state-of-the-art for top-N recommendation, which performs *Singular Value Decomposition* on the whole matrix, thus directly considering all instances. unlike other latent factor methods that optimize against error only on rated instances. This property is important when applying matrix factorization models for top-N evaluation. We follow the implementation in [3], using the package SVDLIBC[3], tuning the number of latent features from 10 to 200, finding the best performance at 30.

4. **Personalized PageRank [8]**. This is a widely used graph method for top-N recommendation, *e.g.*, by [15, 29]. We perform Personalized PageRank on the user–item graph[4], and set the personalized vector same with TriRank's prior item vector $\vec{p}_0$. The damping parameter (*i.e.*, weight of the personalized vector) was respectively optimized to 0.9 and 0.3, for Yelp and Amazon datasets.

5. **ItemRank [6]**. This is another graph based method that recommends based on the item–item correlation graph. Similar to Personalized PageRank, we set the personalized vector identically as $\vec{p}_0$ and tune the damping factor.

6. **TagRW [35]**. This is the state-of-the-art method to model tags for top-N item recommendation. As we have mentioned that aspects are similar with tags in terms of format, we need to compare with such a method to study how tag-aware methods perform on the task of modeling aspects. TagRW enhances ItemRank [6] by incorporating tags into building the item–item graph and performing an additional random walk on user–user graph. We feed aspects (all the same settings with TriRank) as tags into the method, and tune the five parameters of the method in a sequential way, as suggested by their paper.

As the existing review-aware methods [4, 17, 19, 34] are optimized for predicting observed ratings, it is unfair to compare with them for top-N evaluation. We validate this by evaluating the *Hidden Factors and Topics* model [19], which is state-of-the-art for review-aware rating prediction. It achieves poor top-N performance in our settings, worse than Item Popularity. Thus we do not further compare with other methods designed for rating prediction.

TriRank has six regularization parameters to tune – three for the traditional collaborative filtering effect (α, η_U, η_I) and three for the aspect filtering effect (β, γ, η_A). As performing grid-search on all six parameters simultaneously is time-consuming, we separately tune those for CF and those for aspects – first fixing β, γ, η_A as 0, searching for α, η_U, η_I; then performing the reverse with the optimal α, η_U, η_I. Performance was stable across many parameter settings, thus we report results for a selected set.

4.1 Performance Study

Figure 4 plots the performance when K ranges from 10 to 50, and Table 4 shows the concrete scores obtained at position 10 and 50. We first focus on results of the Yelp dataset. From Figure 4(a) and (b), we see that both metrics exhibit the same trend: TriRank performs best, outperforming all other methods with a large margin; followed by PageRank and ItemKNN, where PageRank performs slightly better than ItemKNN. PureSVD, ItemRank and TagRW obtain similar HR scores, while NDCG tells the quality of ranking: PureSVD ranks correct items higher than ItemRank and TagRW. Item Popularity performs the worst, indicating the importance of modeling users' personalized preferences, rather than just recommending popular items.

Surprisingly, TagRW does not always outperform ItemRank, although it utilizes additional aspect information. It shows that their method for integrating tags into recommendation may not be effective for aspects. Analyzing the results, we believe that there are two reasons responsible for TagRW's inferior performance. First, they integrate aspects by transforming to the item–item and user–user similarity graph, which may lead to signal loss. Second, noisy aspects may have an adverse impact on their method, and the impact is highly dependent on the similarity measure they use. Our proposed TriRank mitigates both of these nega-

[3]`http://tedlab.mit.edu/~dr/SVDLIBC`

[4]We also evaluated Personalized PageRank on the user–item–aspect tripartite graph. Even with optimal tuning of each edge and vertex type, performance did not improve; thus we only report Personalized PageRank's performance on the standard user–item graph.

Table 4: Performance of compared methods and TriRank at rank 10 and 50.

Dataset	Yelp				Amazon			
Metric(%)	HR@10	NDCG@10	HR@50	NDCG@50	HR@10	NDCG@10	HR@50	NDCG@50
ItemPop	3.06	1.85	10.61	4.08	2.38	1.36	6.13	2.37
ItemKNN	4.90	3.21	15.72	6.37	11.17	9.75	12.69	10.15
PureSVD	4.79	3.17	14.94	6.16	11.52	9.64	14.94	10.55
PageRank	4.79	3.24	15.90	6.52	12.10	10.33	17.49	11.78
ItemRank	4.64	3.05	14.67	6.01	10.92	8.97	16.84	10.58
TagRW	4.36	2.85	15.25	6.02	11.23	8.96	17.47	10.65
TriRank	**5.92****	**3.97****	**18.58****	**7.69****	**12.71****	**10.86****	**18.44****	**12.36****

"**" denotes the statistical significance for $p < 0.01$.

tive factors by 1) directly modeling aspects into the user–item relation as a tripartite graph, and 2) ranking vertices by regularizing the tripartite graph.

With respect to the Amazon dataset, TriRank again achieves the best performance on both metrics ($p < 0.01$ in most cases). Focusing on Figure 4(c) that shows the HR scores, TriRank is followed by PageRank and TagRW, which significantly outperform other methods. When K is set to 30–40, the HR differences between TriRank and PageRank and TagRW are small, but the NDCG reveals significant gaps among the three methods, indicating that TriRank successfully orders the correct items more effectively than the other two. Meanwhile, TagRW and ItemRank better PureSVD, as evaluated by HR ($K \geq 15$), but not by NDCG, which indicates the matches of TagRW and ItemRank actually occur at lower ranks. This reinforces our point that a good recall score does not necessarily translate to a high-quality ranking, hence the necessity to evaluate by ranking based measures, such as NDCG. ItemKNN performs worst among all the non-trivial personalized methods. ItemPop performed very weak, and as such, was entirely omitted in the figure to better highlight the performance of the other methods.

Looking at the interesting performance variations across the two datasets, we first notice that ItemPop only performs well on the Yelp dataset. We believe this is caused by consumption behavior differences across the two domains – people may visit popular restaurants or businesses rated in Yelp, but only purchase certain products on demand from Amazon. Similarly, ItemKNN performs strongly on the Yelp dataset (better than PureSVD), but poorly on the Amazon. One possible reason comes from data sparsity: as in Table 3, each item of the Amazon dataset only has 3.9 reviews on average. In such cases, the similarity measure fails in neighbor-based CF. An interesting finding is that PageRank consistently outperforms ItemRank, although both rely on Personalized PageRank with the same personalized vector. We believe the explanation is due to the fact that ItemRank ranks based on the transformed item–item correlation graph. Transforming the user–item graph to an item–item correlation graph will lose signal especially when the data is sparse, *e.g.*, when two items have no common users reviewing them. In such cases, it is more beneficial to directly rank from the user–item graph. Finally, TagRW betters ItemRank only on the Amazon dataset, indicating that the tag-based method to integrate aspects does not lead to consistent improvement. Our proposed TriRank achieves the best performance on the two datasets evaluated by both metrics, demonstrating its superiority in providing personalized item ranking to users by mining aspects in reviews.

Table 5: Performance of TriRank with different parameter settings at rank 50.

Dataset	Yelp		Amazon	
Settings	HR	NDCG	HR	NDCG
0. All set	**18.58**	**7.69**	**18.44**	**12.36**
1. $\beta = 0$ (no item–aspect)	17.05	6.91	16.23	11.31
2. $\gamma = 0$ (no user–aspect)	**18.52**	**7.68**	**18.40**	**12.36**
3. $\eta_A = 0$ (no aspect query)	18.21	7.51	17.62	12.10
4. $\beta, \gamma, \eta_A = 0$ (no aspects)	17.00	6.90	15.97	11.16
5. $\alpha = 0$ (no user–item)	11.67	4.84	10.32	5.08

4.2 Utility of Aspects

There are natural issues about aspects that we also wish to address:

1. How do the aspect-related components (*e.g.*, item–aspect and user–aspect) contribute to the performance?
2. How does the quality of aspects impact the performance? Can TriRank handle the inherent noise in automatically extracted aspects well?

4.2.1 Aspect Importance Study

As TriRank is modular, with parameters for each type of vertices and edges, it is easy to answer the first question by varying the aspect-related parameters: β and γ to control the smoothness for the item–aspect and user–aspect relation, respectively, and η_A for the aspect query vector. Setting a parameter to 0 removes the corresponding effect.

Table 5 shows TriRank's performance with different parameter settings, evaluated at rank 50. In both datasets, when item–aspect smoothness is eliminated by setting $\beta = 0$ (Row 1), performance drops significantly. This indicates the importance of item–aspect relation, and validates our motivation that modeling user preference via decomposed aspects can yield more fidelity over modeling user–item ratings only. In contrast, when user–aspect smoothness is removed (Row 2), the performance remains unchanged. This shows that user–aspect smoothness contributes substantially less to TriRank's performance; however, we note that at least the target user's portion of the user–aspect relation can not be removed in recommendation, as the rated aspects of a user form her aspect query vector needed for recommendation. Row 3, which exhibits low performance, validates this point, as here we have removed the aspect query vector by setting η_A as 0. If we remove the modeling of aspects in its entirety (Row 4), TriRank degrades to the *Bipartite User–*

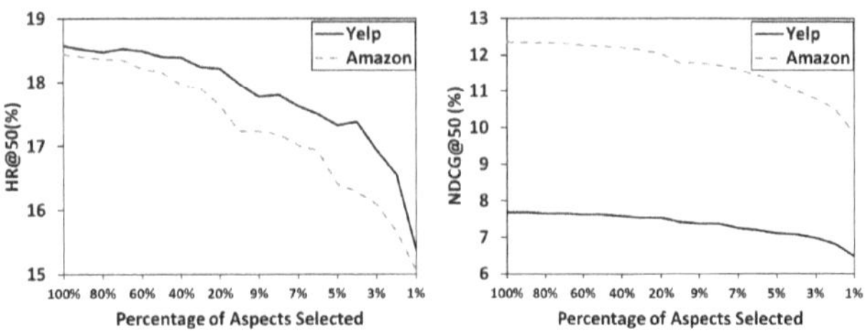

(a) Hit Ratio versus Aspects (b) NDCG versus Aspects

Figure 5: TriRank performance with respect to percentage of top aspects selected.

Figure 6: Training reviews of a sampled Yelp user.

Item Ranking algorithm [9] on the user–item graph, and performs even worse. This further reveals the importance of modeling aspects for quality recommendation.

To round out our study, Row 5 shows the performance of removing user–item smoothness, which encodes standard CF in the terminology of our regularization approach. The resulting performance is worst among all settings. The user–item relation is still fundamental to model and is most important, followed by the importance of the item–aspect smoothness; user–aspect smoothness contributes least and may be removed. However, the reviewed aspects of a particular target user are still critical for capturing her personalized preference.

4.2.2 Aspect Quality Study

For the second question, we first rank aspects by their tf×idf score in the item–aspect matrix, and then select top scoring aspects to build the tripartite graph and inspect TriRank's performance.

Figure 5 shows TriRank's performance with respect to percentage of top aspects selected. As we can see, both datasets show the same trend: when the filtering ratio is moderate, performance remains largely unchanged. The filtering inflection point for both datasets is around 30%. When we filter out aspects beyond this point, performance starts to drop significantly. This indicates that the aspects with $tf \times idf$ play a dominant role in modeling users' preference for quality recommendation. We further validate this conclusion by filtering in the reverse direction (not shown; *i.e.*, dropping the top $x\%$ aspects ranked by $tf \times idf$), finding that even a small amount of filtering (1%) leads to significant degradation. We conclude that one can safely filter out the low $tf \times idf$ scoring aspects for efficiency, as they contribute less to recommendation performance.

Interestingly, TriRank's performance does not improve when only high $tf \times idf$ aspects are utilized. Although slight improvements can be obtained with tuning, they are not statistically significant. We further evaluate TriRank with the 124 high-quality aspects selected in [34]'s work on the same Yelp Challenge dataset. Even after all parameters are re-tuned, test performance is not improved. This validates the nice property of TriRank of being relatively insensitive to noisy aspects, which are also expected to have less impact in the ranking outputs as previously explained (Section 3.4). TriRank can effectively utilize the merits in the automatically extracted aspects, without the need to filter out noisy aspects manually. Compared to the *Explicit Factor Model* [34] that integrates only high-quality aspects into a matrix factorization model and then generates recommendations by optimizing the predicted ratings in an opaque manner, TriRank is more transparent in leveraging aspects and also is more tolerant of low-quality aspects.

4.3 Case Studies

While macro-level empirical analysis are useful, it is also instructive to examine actual results to better understand the outputs of TriRank. To this end, we give two case studies drawn from the Yelp dataset to demonstrate its explainability and scrutability.

4.3.1 Explainability

Figure 6 shows four training reviews of a sampled user[5]. From the first two reviews, we can see the user is interested in "chicken", although she gives low ratings to the two businesses. In the heldout test set, she reviews the business *Chick-Fil-A* with a comment *"I love Chick-Fil-A... the spicy chicken sandwhiches [sic], the lemonade, the soup, the brownies"*, which further validates her preference for "chicken". As expected, TriRank ranks *Chick-Fil-A* highly (6th position), mainly due to chicken being a top aspect of this business (3 of its 7 training reviews mentioned "chicken"). Examining the top items returned by PageRank, none have "chicken" as a top aspect, and most of them are popular items with more than 100 reviews. This is because random walk models are easily biased to popular items, as reported by [1]. Moreover, the third and fourth reviews show that the user is also interested in "shrimp". As a result, TriRank ranks the seafood restaurant *Red Lobster* highly in the 3rd position. Although it is evaluated as a loss as the test set does not contain the item, when we checked her complete history in Yelp.com, we found she actually reviewed this restaurant later (outside of the dates in the Yelp Challenge dataset), mentioning "shrimp". Again, the recommended *Red Lobster* is not a popular item with only 7 training reviews. This case study demonstrates TriRank's capability of recommending more relevant and personalized items (not just popular items) according to a user's reviewed aspects.

4.3.2 Scrutability

Another key property of our TriRank instantiation is the encoding of aspect query vector $\vec{a}_0$, serving as the gateway to edit a target user's preference. We simulate the process on a sampled user[6].

For this user, 9 of the 14 training reviews mentioned "service", which is the top aspect, followed by "beer". However in the test set, he reviews the business "*Total Wine & More*", whose top aspects are "wine" and "liquor". In this case, both

[5]User ID "*8fTTvS499XCz4oP49kxq8A*". Only part of each review is shown as the original is long.

[6]User ID "*omoEjYFKVV7e-DtnezeUOw*".

TriRank and PageRank fail to recommend the correct item, and all top items returned do not have wine as a specialty. We simulate user feedback by editing the aspect query vector to set "wine" to a higher value, and re-run TriRank with all other parameters unchanged. In the updated ranked list, 8 of the top-10 items have "wine" as the top aspect, and the correct item "*Total Wine & More*" is ranked in 2nd position.

5. RELATED WORK

While collaborative filtering systems perform well in general, their performance suffers when the amount of user feedback is insufficient (*i.e.*, in cold-start). Another important shortcoming is that they do not capture the rationale for user's rating, and thus can not accurately capture a target user's preference. To overcome these weaknesses, various forms of side information have been incorporated into CF, including tags [35], geo-location [11] and user reviews [19]. In this section, we first study the area of review-aware methods, and then examine graph-based recommendation techniques as TriRank falls into this category.

5.1 Review-aware Recommendation

User reviews have been utilized to assist recommender systems in many domains, for movies [4], hotels [20], restaurants [5] and e-commerce [19]. Regardless of domain, we can categorize the approaches based on how reviews are integrated into the recommender: 1) word-based, 2) sentiment-based, and 3) aspect-based methods.

Word-based. These approaches directly factorize the review words into CF. [26] used words to measure similarity, whereas [11] modeled each word as a latent vector within the latent factor model. As the original word space is large and sparse, dimension reduction techniques have been adopted. McAuley and Leskovec [19] employed *Latent Dirichlet Allocation* (LDA) [2] to winnow down the word space, and combined with the standard latent factor model. Subsequently, [17, 30] adopted a full Bayesian treatment to combine topics and latent factors for rating prediction.

Sentiment-based. These approaches utilize the user's explicitly mentioned opinions on items. [21] proposed to fill in the missing ratings with a predicted sentiment score before applying neighbor-based CF. [22] built a user–item opinion matrix, where each entry was the aggregated sentiment score of a review, and then applied traditional CF on the opinion matrix. More recently, [4] proposed an integrated graphical model to jointly model the sentiment and ratings for movie recommendation.

Aspect-based. Our work falls into this category. Early work [5] along this line manually annotated six aspects in the restaurant domain (*e.g.*, service, ambiance, *etc.*), and classified sentences with respect to these aspects. Their regression method validated the usefulness of aspects for rating prediction. Musat *et al.* [20] built topical profiles of users and items from reviews, and predicted ratings at the topic level. They tested two ways to extract topics — LDA and opinion word frequency — finding the latter produced higher quality topics. Recently, Zhang *et al.* [34] jointly factorized the user–item rating matrix by inserting aspects, decomposing it into item–aspect and user–aspect matrices, where the aspects were automatically extracted.

Several hybrid methods have also integrated aspect and sentiment [4, 5, 34] as they are closely related. In contrast, our work focuses on integrating aspect into CF for explainable recommendations, thus we forgo incorporating sentiment, to minimize the reliance on sentiment analysis accuracy. Compared to the above review-aware works, our method explores a graph model to integrate aspects, which has not been previously been investigated. Moreover, our proposed TriRank affords the recommender a finer degree of user interaction — aspect preference — allowing for both more accurate and transparent recommendation.

5.2 Graph-based Recommendation

Graphs form a natural representation for modeling the relationship among data objects. In recommender systems, graph models have been used widely and commercially (*e.g.*, by Twitter [7] and YouTube [1]), due to their good interpretability in generating recommendations. A typical workflow is first representing items as vertices of a graph, and then admitting recommendation as a vertex-ranking problem. For example, in YouTube video recommendation, [1] built a user–video co-view graph for video items, adopting label propagation for selecting important videos.

Besides directly working on the heterogeneous user–item graph, another family of approaches [6, 18, 35] projects the user–item graph to an item–item graph (as the ranking target is item), and then applies homogeneous graph ranking techniques, such as personalized PageRank [8]. Specifically, [6] recommended based on an item correlation graph, where entries denoted the likelihood that two items are co-rated. [18] proposed an item preference graph, where entries denoted the strength that users prefer one item over another.

We point out that a key advantage of retaining the user–item structure is that additional information can be easily incorporated by adding new types of vertices. However, existing ranking algorithms do not cater to heterogeneous structures, as they have primarily focused on homogeneous graphs [8, 36] or bipartite graphs [9]. Thus, a corresponding algorithm must be devised to suit the specific heterogeneous graph and ranking purpose. For example, [29] modeled long-term and short-term user preference by introducing session nodes, ranking vertices by propagating user preference via *Breadth-First-Search*; [15] incorporated contexts (*e.g.*, location, time) as vertices in the user's side, and adjusted PageRank for ranking in such a mixed bipartite graph. Similar to above works, our method retains the user–item structure, extending it to a user–item–aspect tripartite graph for modeling aspects. One major difference is that we specifically consider the ternary relationship between user, item and aspect, which has not been studied before.

6. CONCLUSION

We have studied how to utilize item aspects in user reviews for top-N recommendation. We model the user–item–aspect relation as a tripartite graph, and propose TriRank, a generic algorithm for ranking the vertices of tripartite graph by regularizing the smoothness and fitting constraints. We employ TriRank for review-aware recommendation, where the ranking constraints directly model the collaborative and aspect filtering, and also personalization. TriRank achieves state-of-the-art performance over two public review datasets, even with automatically extracted aspects that have significant noise. We validate TriRank as being largely insensitive to low-quality aspects, a desirable property when porting to other domains as it avoids manual efforts in filtering out noisy aspects. Most importantly, TriRank's incorporation of aspects provides users with more transparency into the recommender system behavior and affords user interaction to further improve recommendations.

Our introduction to TriRank is in its basic form, which has already shown significant utility. TriRank can be further extended in many ways, for example by adopting a more suitable loss function, or by extending to more general n-partite graphs. We hope to extend TriRank to such cases, by jointly modeling the additional information latent in user reviews that may be useful for recommendation: temporal factors [9], category taxonomies [10] and sentiment [21]. Another open issue is in optimal parameter settings. Our current work reports results when the regularization parameters are set uniformly for all users; however in some exploratory work, we found that a specific parameter setting for a subset of users improves performance. This reveals the potential for improvement by setting parameters individually or for groups of similar users based on their preference on aspects.

Acknowledgement

We thank Yongfeng Zhang, Haochen Zhang and the Tsinghua Information Retrieval group for developing and sharing their aspect extraction tool. We would also like to thank the anonymous reviewers for their valuable comments.

7. REFERENCES

[1] S. Baluja, R. Seth, and D. Sivakumar. Video suggestion and discovery for Youtube: Taking random walks through the view graph. In *Proc. of WWW '08*, pages 895–904, 2008.

[2] D. M. Blei, A. Y. Ng, and M. I. Jordan. Latent dirichlet allocation. *J. Mach. Learn. Res.*, 3:993–1022, 2003.

[3] P. Cremonesi, Y. Koren, and R. Turrin. Performance of recommender algorithms on top-n recommendation tasks. In *Proc. of RecSys '10*, pages 39–46, 2010.

[4] Q. Diao, M. Qiu, C.-Y. Wu, A. J. Smola, J. Jiang, and C. Wang. Jointly modeling aspects, ratings and sentiments for movie recommendation (jmars). In *Proc. of KDD '14*, pages 193–202, 2014.

[5] G. Ganu, N. Elhadad, and A. Marian. Beyond the stars: Improving rating predictions using review text content. In *Proc. of WebDB '09*, 2009.

[6] M. Gori and A. Pucci. Itemrank: A random-walk based scoring algorithm for recommender engines. In *Proc. of IJCAI '07*, pages 2766–2771, 2007.

[7] P. Gupta, A. Goel, J. Lin, A. Sharma, D. Wang, and R. Zadeh. Wtf: The who to follow service at twitter. In *Proc. of WWW '13*, pages 505–514, 2013.

[8] T. H. Haveliwala. Topic-sensitive PageRank. In *Proc. of WWW '02*, pages 517–526, 2002.

[9] X. He, M. Gao, M.-Y. Kan, Y. Liu, and K. Sugiyama. Predicting the popularity of web 2.0 items based on user comments. In *Proc. SIGIR '14*, pages 233–242, 2014.

[10] X. He, M.-Y. Kan, P. Xie, and X. Chen. Comment-based multi-view clustering of web 2.0 items. In *Proc. of WWW '14*, pages 771–782, 2014.

[11] L. Hu, A. Sun, and Y. Liu. Your neighbors affect your ratings: On geographical neighborhood influence to rating prediction. In *Proc. of SIGIR '14*, pages 345–354, 2014.

[12] M. Hu and B. Liu. Mining and summarizing customer reviews. In *Proc. of KDD '04*, pages 168–177, 2004.

[13] W. Jin and H. H. Ho. A novel lexicalized hmm-based learning framework for web opinion mining. In *Proc. of ICML '09*, pages 465–472, 2009.

[14] Y. Koren and R. Bell. Advances in collaborative filtering. In *Recommender Systems Handbook*, pages 145–186. Springer US, 2011.

[15] S. Lee, S.-i. Song, M. Kahng, D. Lee, and S.-g. Lee. Random walk based entity ranking on graph for multidimensional recommendation. In *Proc. of RecSys '11*, pages 93–100, 2011.

[16] G. Linden, B. Smith, and J. York. Amazon.com recommendations: item-to-item collaborative filtering. *Internet Computing, IEEE*, 7(1):76–80, Jan 2003.

[17] G. Ling, M. R. Lyu, and I. King. Ratings meet reviews, a combined approach to recommend. In *Proc. of RecSys '14*, pages 105–112, 2014.

[18] N. N. Liu and Q. Yang. Eigenrank: A ranking-oriented approach to collaborative filtering. In *Proc. of SIGIR '08*, pages 83–90, 2008.

[19] J. McAuley and J. Leskovec. Hidden factors and hidden topics: Understanding rating dimensions with review text. In *Proc. of RecSys'13*, pages 165–172, 2013.

[20] C.-C. Musat, Y. Liang, and B. Faltings. Recommendation using textual opinions. In *Proc. of IJCAI '13*, pages 2684–2690, 2013.

[21] N. Pappas and A. Popescu-Belis. Sentiment analysis of user comments for one-class collaborative filtering over ted talks. In *Proc. of SIGIR '13*, pages 773–776, 2013.

[22] Š. Pero and T. Horváth. Opinion-driven matrix factorization for rating prediction. In *Proc. of UMAP '13*, pages 1–13. 2013.

[23] S. Rendle, C. Freudenthaler, Z. Gantner, and L. Schmidt. Bpr: Bayesian personalized ranking from implicit feedback. In *Proc. of UAI '09*, pages 452–461, 2009.

[24] B. Sarwar, G. Karypis, J. Konstan, and J. Riedl. Item-based collaborative filtering recommendation algorithms. In *Proc. of WWW '01*, pages 285–295, 2001.

[25] A. Smola and R. Kondor. Kernels and regularization on graphs. In *Learning Theory and Kernel Machines*, volume 2777 of *LNCS*, pages 144–158. Springer, 2003.

[26] M. Terzi, M. Rowe, M.-A. Ferrario, and J. Whittle. Text-based user-knn: Measuring user similarity based on text reviews. In *Proc. of UMAP '14*, pages 195–206. 2014.

[27] N. Tintarev and J. Masthoff. Designing and evaluating explanations for recommender systems. In *Recommender Systems Handbook*, pages 479–510. Springer US, 2011.

[28] J. Vig, S. Sen, and J. Riedl. Tagsplanations: Explaining recommendations using tags. In *Proc. of IUI '09*, pages 47–56, 2009.

[29] L. Xiang, Q. Yuan, S. Zhao, L. Chen, X. Zhang, Q. Yang, and J. Sun. Temporal recommendation on graphs via long- and short-term preference fusion. In *Proc. of KDD '10*, pages 723–732, 2010.

[30] Y. Xu, W. Lam, and T. Lin. Collaborative filtering incorporating review text and co-clusters of hidden user communities and item groups. In *Proc. of CIKM '14*, pages 251–260, 2014.

[31] L. Zhang and B. Liu. Aspect and entity extraction for opinion mining. In *Data Mining and Knowledge Discovery for Big Data*, volume 1, pages 1–40. Springer, 2014.

[32] L. Zhang, B. Liu, S. H. Lim, and E. O'Brien. Extracting and ranking product features in opinion documents. In *Proc. of COLING '10*, pages 1462–1470, 2010.

[33] Y. Zhang, H. Zhang, M. Zhang, Y. Liu, and S. Ma. Do users rate or review?: Boost phrase-level sentiment labeling with review-level sentiment classification. In *Proc. of SIGIR '14*, pages 1027–1030, 2014.

[34] Y. Zhang, M. Zhang, Y. Zhang, Y. Liu, and S. Ma. Explicit factor models for explainable recommendation based on phrase-level sentiment analysis. In *Proc. of SIGIR '14*, pages 83–92, 2014.

[35] Z. Zhang, D. D. Zeng, A. Abbasi, J. Peng, and X. Zheng. A random walk model for item recommendation in social tagging systems. *ACM Transactions on Management Information Systems*, 4(2):1–24, 2013.

[36] D. Zhou, O. Bousquet, T. N. Lal, J. Weston, and B. Schölkopf. Learning with local and global consistency. In *NIPS*, pages 321–328, 2004.

RoadRank: Traffic Diffusion and Influence Estimation in Dynamic Urban Road Networks

Tarique Anwar[*†] Chengfei Liu[*] Hai L. Vu[*] Md. Saiful Islam[*]

[*]Swinburne University of Technology, Melbourne, Australia

[†]NICTA, Melbourne, Australia

{tanwar,cliu,hvu,mdsaifulislam}@swin.edu.au

ABSTRACT

With the rapidly growing population in urban areas, these days the urban road networks are expanding at a faster rate. The frequent movement of people on them leads to traffic congestions. These congestions originate from some crowded road segments, and diffuse towards other parts of the urban road networks creating further congestions. This behavior of road networks motivates the need to understand the influence of individual road segments on others in terms of congestion. In this work, we propose `RoadRank`, an algorithm to compute the influence scores of each road segment in an urban road network, and rank them based on their overall influence. It is an incremental algorithm that keeps on updating the influence scores with time, by feeding with the latest traffic data at each time point. The method starts with constructing a directed graph called *influence graph*, which is then used to iteratively compute the influence scores using probabilistic diffusion theory. We show promising preliminary experimental results on real SCATS traffic data of Melbourne.

Categories and Subject Descriptors

H.2.8 [**Database Management**]: Database Applications—*Spatial databases and GIS, Data mining*

General Terms

Algorithms, Experimentation

Keywords

Influential roads; Road networks; Traffic diffusion

1. INTRODUCTION

Traffic congestion remains a big challenge in the 21st century due to the rapid growth of population and their mobility demand within the urban areas [1]. Congestion often starts in few confined places within the network and propagates through various connected road segments. The propagation of congestion is due to the diffusion (or movement) of traffic from one road segment to another where the amount of traffic on any particular road segment is *influenced by* and *influences* that of others. The level of influence one road segment can have on others in terms of congestion depends on their spatial and temporal attributes and is not the same across the network. Clearly, high influential road segments play a more important role in the building up of congestion and will need to be better managed in order to alleviate or delay the congestion onset.

Identifying important nodes in a network is a problem common to many different kinds of information networks [3]. In the recent years, information propagation and diffusion has been a hot area of research in social networks [6, 8, 4]. Several existing works focus on estimating the user influences [5, 7] and analyzing the influence propagation [2] in different types or platforms of social networks. Though there exists many works on such varied problems, we could not find any research on traffic diffusion in road networks and identifying influential road segments.

In this paper, we propose our novel algorithm named `RoadRank` that computes the influence scores (called *roadrank scores*) of each road segment in an urban road network. To deal with the dynamic nature of traffic on a road network, it also updates the scores incrementally with time, by feeding in the latest traffic measures at each timestamp. The method starts with constructing a directed graph called *influence graph*. It is used to compute the traffic diffusion from one road segment to another, based on the collected traffic measures. Finally the *roadrank* scores are iteratively computed using probabilistic diffusion theory for the starting point of time. At each successive timestamps, they are iteratively updated based on the new traffic measures. We also show preliminary experimental results on real SCATS traffic data of Melbourne.

2. PROBLEM STATEMENT

Traffic data: The developed urban areas these days are well equipped with urban traffic control systems (UTCS) like Sydney coordinated adaptive traffic system (SCATS) and split cycle offset optimisation technique (SCOOT). These traffic management systems log the aggregated traffic movement data on each of the road segments in real-time. This data do not contain individual movement trajectories, rather they are different traffic measures indicating the count of vehicles crossing a road segment during the green time called

Permission to make digital or hard copies of all or part of this work for personal or classroom use is granted without fee provided that copies are not made or distributed for profit or commercial advantage and that copies bear this notice and the full citation on the first page. Copyrights for components of this work owned by others than ACM must be honored. Abstracting with credit is permitted. To copy otherwise, or republish, to post on servers or to redistribute to lists, requires prior specific permission and/or a fee. Request permissions from Permissions@acm.org.

CIKM'15, October 19-23, 2015, Melbourne, VIC, Australia

© 2015 ACM. ISBN 978-1-4503-3794-6/15/10...$15.00

DOI: http://dx.doi.org/10.1145/2806416.2806588.

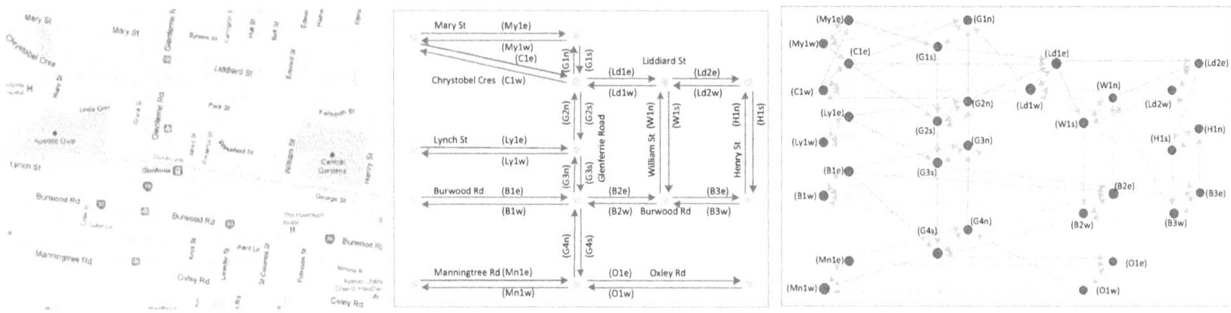

(a) Actual road map (b) Road network (c) Influence graph

Figure 1: Influence graph of road networks

the *traffic volume* and the ratio of the effectively used green time to the total available green time called the *degree of saturation*, at each signal cycle. The proposed RoadRank algorithm uses these traffic measures to compute the influence scores of all road segments in the given road network.

Road networks: Urban roads exist in the form of a physical network spatially spread over a large urban area. A *road* is a generally used term to mean a publicly accessible way for transportation. It has no standard range for its length and can vary from a very short one to a very long. A *road segment* r_i is defined as the smallest unit of a road having its traffic flow in a single direction. Thus a road is composed of one or more road segments, where the two opposite directions of traffic flow form different road segments. A *road intersection point* (or intersection point in short) ι_i is defined as the point connecting two or more road segments.

Definition 1: (**Road Network**) A road network is defined as $\mathcal{N} = (\mathcal{I}, \mathcal{R})$ comprising a set of road intersection points $\mathcal{I} = \{\iota_1, \iota_2, \ldots, \iota_{n_\iota}\}$ as nodes that are connected among themselves by the set of directed road segments $\mathcal{R} = \{r_1, r_2, \ldots, r_{n_r}\}$ as its links, where each road segment r_i associates a set of feature values with itself, including the different traffic measures $r_i.f$. ■

Problem definition: Let us suppose we have a given urban road network $\mathcal{N}$ having all recorded historical traffic data $\mathcal{D}$ corresponding to each of the road segments in the network. Let $\mathcal{T} = \langle t_0, t_1, \ldots, t_{l-1}, t_l \rangle$ be the timestamps of the recorded data, where t_0 is the very first record, and t_l is the latest record that keeps on updating with time. Thus the dataset $\mathcal{D} = \langle d_0, d_1, \ldots, d_{l-1}, d_l \rangle$ becomes an incrementally updating vector, where each d_i is the traffic data recorded at time t_i. The problem of estimating the influence of road segments is to incrementally compute an *influence score* for each road segment r_i in $\mathcal{N}$ corresponding to each d_i (at t_i) and rank them based on this measure. The influence score (also called roadrank score to be defined in Section 3.3) of a road segment r_i gives a measure of how much the traffic on r_i influences that on the global network $\mathcal{N}$ because of the traffic diffusion going on via its linked road segments.

3. ROADRANK ALGORITHM

3.1 Road Influence Graph Construction

Most of the roads exist as two-way roads which are partitioned into two parts from the middle for traffic of the two opposite directions. Each of the two parts undergo different kinds of traffic flow patterns. To accommodate this property, the road network considers the two traffic directions as separate road segments that share common road intersection points in the road network. Thus the road network $\mathcal{N}$ is a directed graph with intersection points as nodes and directed road segments as links, where for the two-way roads there are two different oppositely directed links between the same pair of intersection points.

The method starts with constructing a *road influence graph* $\mathcal{G}^{inf}$ from $\mathcal{N}$, having the road segments as nodes and the directed edges between them represent the *influences* relationship.

Definition 2: (**Road Influence Graph**) Given a road network $\mathcal{N} = (\mathcal{I}, \mathcal{R})$, the corresponding road influence graph $\mathcal{G}^{inf} = (\mathcal{V}, \mathcal{E})$ is constructed by adding each road segment $r_i \in \mathcal{R}$ as a node $v_i \in \mathcal{V}$, and establishing a directed link $e_i \in \mathcal{E}$ from v_j to v_k if these two conditions hold- *i*) there exist at least one intersection point ι_l that is a common intersection for the roads r_j and r_k, and *ii*) the direction of traffic flow leads the movement from r_j to r_k. The directed link e_i shows that the traffic on road segment r_j (or node v_j) influences the traffic on road segment r_k (or node v_k). ■

We assume that the traffic rule allows a moving vehicle to take all the turns including left-, right-, and U-turns at intersection points on all the roads in the network (though in real there exist restrictions). Figure 1 shows an example of the influence graph construction from a real road network segment, showing the map in Figure 1(a). Considering only the yellow major roads to keep the example simple (all the roads including small ones are considered in real), Figure 1(b) shows the equivalent road network, which is then used to construct the influence graph in Figure 1(c). A traversal from one node to another in the influence graph gives the path of the traffic flow as well as the traffic diffusion process. One such example is $(My1e) \xrightarrow{inf} (G1s) \xrightarrow{inf} (G2s) \xrightarrow{inf} (G3s) \xrightarrow{inf} (B2e) \xrightarrow{inf} (B3e) \xrightarrow{inf} (B3w)$.

3.2 Traffic Diffusion Computation

Information diffusion is a widely studied research area in social media, where the information propagates from one sources to another. In road traffic networks, there is a physical movement of the traffic from one road segment to another. We model this movement as a traffic diffusion process, in which the traffic diffuses among differently concentrated road segments through their connectivities. The directed links in the influence graph constructed in Section 3.1 show the direction and order of movement of this traffic. To find the exact amount of traffic that diffuse from one road segment to another in a directed link, we compute a measure based on their real time traffic measures.

Let $Vo = \langle vo_1, vo_2, \ldots, vo_{n_r}\rangle$ and $DS = \langle ds_1, ds_2, \ldots, ds_{n_r}\rangle$ be the vectors having the traffic volume and degree of saturation measures of all the road segments $r_i \in \mathcal{R}$. We compute two similarity matrices S^{vo} and S^{ds} for the Vo and DS vectors respectively such that $S^{vo}_{ij} = GSim(vo_i, vo_j)$ and $S^{ds}_{ij} = GSim(ds_i, ds_j)$. Equation 1 defines the Gaussian similarity measure $GSim(x_i, x_j)$, where $\sigma^2 = \frac{1}{n} \times \sum_{i=1}^{n} (x_i - \mu)^2$ is the variance of all values in the vector.

$$GSim(x_i, x_j) = \exp\left(\frac{-(x_i - x_j)^2}{2 \times \sigma^2}\right) \quad (1)$$

DEFINITION 3: (**Traffic Diffusion**) The *traffic diffusion* $td(r_i \rightarrow r_j)$ is defined as the actual amount of traffic diffused from r_i to r_j. We compute this measure by using Equation 2, where α_{ij} is a balance factor called *traffic condition factor*, whose value is based on the real traffic conditions. ■

$$td(r_i \rightarrow r_j) = \begin{cases} \alpha_{ij} \times S^{vo}_{ij} + (1 - \alpha_{ij}) \times S^{ds}_{ij}, & \text{if } (r_i \rightarrow r_j) \in \mathcal{E} \\ 0, \text{ otherwise} \end{cases} \quad (2)$$

The *traffic condition factor* $\alpha_{ij} \in [0, 1]$ is a measure that quantifies the actual traffic condition on the roads. For example, let r_i and r_j be a narrow and a wide road segment respectively. When a certain number of vehicles move from r_i to r_j, the ds_i will be greater than ds_j. Thus even though all the vehicles from r_i move on to r_j, their similarity in the DS measure becomes low, because of the difference in their width. The traffic condition factor captures this aspect of road segments to balance the Vo and DS similarity measures and aid in accurately computing the traffic diffusion. Setting this value to 1 makes Definition 3 behave as volume diffusion, where as 0 makes it behave as degree of saturation diffusion, and setting an appropriate value[1] in between them makes it behave as the traffic congestion diffusion.

DEFINITION 4: (**Traffic Diffusion Probability**) The *traffic diffusion probability* $tdp(r_i \rightarrow r_j)$ is defined as probability of the traffic that diffuse from r_i to r_j. We compute this measure by using Equation 3, where $r_i \xrightarrow{inf} r_k$ means r_i *influences* r_j in $\mathcal{G}^{inf}$ (in other words, $r_i \rightarrow r_k \in \mathcal{E}$). ■

$$tdp(r_i \rightarrow r_j) = \frac{td(r_i \rightarrow r_j)}{\sum_{\forall k: r_i \xrightarrow{inf} r_k} td(r_i \rightarrow r_k)} \quad (3)$$

3.3 Ranking

In the road traffic network scenario, the top-k influential road segments can be identified by ranking and selecting the top-k of them. Moreover, as the road networks are dynamic in nature because of the frequently changing traffic, the ranking is time-sensitive, and needs to be updated with time based on the real-time traffic measures. Therefore we start with computing the ranking at timestamp t_0, and keep on updating the ranking at each new timestamps $t_1, t_2, \ldots t_l$ to always have the ranking obtained from the latest collected traffic measures.

[1]It can be done based on experimental results and inputs from the experienced traffic management people.

Ranking at t_0**:** Our ranking algorithm borrows some concepts of the well known PageRank algorithm [3]. The PageRank algorithm computes a ranking of webpages to estimate their importance to Web navigators. It initializes each of the pages with a small value as their page rank score (PR(p_i)), and iteratively uses the linkages (L) among them to compute their new page rank score (PR(p_j)) using equation 4, where $d \in [0, 1]$ is the damping factor typically set to 0.85 [3], $\text{prob}(p_j|p_i) = \frac{1}{out\text{-}degree(p_i)}$ is the transition probability from webpage p_i to webpage p_j, and $l_{ij} \in L$ is the hyperlink from page p_i to p_j.

$$\text{PR}(p_j) = (1 - d) + d \times \sum_{\forall p_i : l_{ij} \in L} \text{prob}(p_j|p_i) \times \text{PR}(p_i) \quad (4)$$

The traffic on road networks consists of vehicles moving on its road segments. In the proposed `RoadRank` algorithm, we consider that the traffic moving from one road segment r_i to another road segment r_j as the recommendation made by r_i to r_j. Over a period of time, also new vehicles start and existing vehicles stop randomly on different road segments. Let vpn be the probability that a new random vehicle starts on any road segment in the given road network $\mathcal{N}$ at timestamp t_r, such that $(1 - vpn)$ gives the probability that the vehicle was already there in $\mathcal{N}$. For the new random vehicle that started in $\mathcal{N}$, let $vp(r_j)$ be the probability that the vehicle started on r_j, such that $(1 - vp(r_j))$ gives the probability that the vehicle started on any other road segment $r_k \in \{\mathcal{V} - r_j\}$. Thus $vpn \times vp(r_j)$ gives the probability that a new random vehicle started on r_j, and $(1 - vpn \times vp(r_j))$ gives the probability that the vehicles currently on r_j were there on $\mathcal{N}$ since before. We compute the roadrank score of a road segment r_j by considering and aggregating these two scenarios using Equation 5, where $RR(x)$ denotes the updated score of x and $RR'(x)$ denotes the score of x in the previous iteration. For the new traffic, it simply counts the probability $vpn \times vp(r_j)$, and for the existing traffic it counts the summation of all roadrank scores diffused from the neighboring road segments, multiplied by the probability $(1 - vpn \times vp(r_j))$. The diffused roadrank scores are computed as multiplication of the previous roadrank scores $(RR'(r_i))$ of the roads influencing r_j with their traffic diffusion probability.

$$\begin{aligned} RR(r_j) &= f(\text{new traffic}) + f(\text{existing traffic}) \\ &= vpn \times vp(r_j) + (1 - vpn \times vp(r_j)) \\ &\quad \times \sum_{\forall i: r_i \xrightarrow{inf} r_j} (tdp(r_i \rightarrow r_j) \times RR'(r_i)) \end{aligned} \quad (5)$$

To start with, the roadrank scores $RR(r_i)$ for all the road segments are set to 1. Equation 5 is then used to iteratively update the $RR(r_j)$ scores from the previously available $RR'(r_i)$ scores. Each iteration updates $RR(r_j)$ for all $r_j \in \mathcal{R}$ using $RR'(r_i)$, and the iterations are repeated until convergence is achieved.

Incremental ranking at each new timestamp t_l**:** If we closely monitor the traffic on road networks in very short intervals of time, we will notice that the change in traffic in successive timestamps are very smooth. Therefore we can expect that in these short intervals of time there will be no big change also in the roadrank scores. Let $RR^0(r_j), RR^1(r_j), \ldots, RR^l(r_j)$ denote the roadrank scores at timestamps $t_0, t_1, \ldots, t_l$ respectively, based on the traffic datasets $d_0, d_1, \ldots, d_l$ respectively. Similarly vpn^l, $vp^l(r_j)$, and $tdp^l(r_i \rightarrow r_j)$ denote the values at timestamp t_l based on the dataset d_l. To compute the score at the latest timestamp t_l, the roadrank scores of all r_i are initialized as those computed from the previous timestamp t_{l-1}, i.e., $RR'^l(r_i) = RR^{l-1}(r_i)$. Equation 6 is then used to iteratively compute latest roadrank scores. The iterations are continued until it reaches the convergence.

$$RR^l(r_j) = vpn^l \times vp^l(r_j) + (1 - vpn^l \times vp^l(r_j)) \times \sum_{\forall i: r_i \xrightarrow{inf} r_j} \left(tdp^l(r_i \rightarrow r_j) \times RR'^l(r_i)\right) \quad (6)$$

Thus at each new timestamp, instead of recomputing the roadrank scores by initializing them to 1, we incrementally update them. It significantly improves the performance by requiring comparatively fewer iterations and making the task much faster. In this way, the algorithm is able to maintain the roadrank scores with the real time data.

4. EXPERIMENTAL RESULTS

To show the performance of RoadRank, we conducted experiments on real traffic data collected from the urban Melbourne road network. The considered Melbourne subnetwork consists of 1444 road segments and 581 intersection points, where the traffic measures are logged by 493 SCATS sites. In the dataset, many road segments have their traffic measures missing because of faulty SCATS sensors. We regain those missing data by applying a data repairing technique. The traffic measures are recorded for each signal cycle that differs for the different SCATS sites. To make them consistent, we made slots of 5 minutes each and aggregate the traffic measures during that time slot for all the road segments.

Table 1: Top-5 influential road segments

Rank	Road segment	RR Score
	03-02-2012 08:05 AM	
1.	Hoddle St (Victoria Parade to Elizabeth St)	02.57095
2.	Hoddle St (Elizabeth St to Albert St)	02.00645
3.	Mills St (Canterbury Rd to Danks St)	01.89356
4.	Heidelberg Rd (Hoddle St to The Esplanade)	01.83253
5.	Heidelberg Rd (The Esplanade to Hoddle St)	01.81797
	03-02-2012 10:05 AM	
1.	Hoddle St (Victoria Parade to Elizabeth St)	03.49890
2.	Hoddle St (Elizabeth St to Albert St)	02.50019
3.	Heidelberg Rd (Hoddle St to The Esplanade)	02.38343
4.	Heidelberg Rd (The Esplanade to Hoddle St)	02.35427
5.	Hoddle St (Elizabeth St to Victoria Parade)	02.31045

Table 1 shows the 5 top-ranking influential road segments in the considered network on 03-12-2012 (Monday) at 08:05 AM and 10:05 AM. These results are obtained by setting the traffic condition factor α_{ij} to 0.5, and getting the values of vpn and $vp(r_j)$ from the dataset. A few road segments of Hoddle St and Heidelberg Rd are there in the list which are well known as a congestion hotspot for both the network operators and the commuters during the aforementioned time period. The ranking varies greatly for different values of α. We obtained the rankings at $\alpha = 0.00, 0.25, 0.50, 0.75, 1.00$, and compared the top-100 of them using the Kendal's Tau measure. The measures we obtained are $\text{KT}(RR_{\alpha=0}, RR_{\alpha=0.25}) = 2409$, $\text{KT}(RR_{\alpha=0}, RR_{\alpha=0.5}) = 4516$, $\text{KT}(RR_{\alpha=0}, RR_{\alpha=0.75}) = 6428$, and $\text{KT}(RR_{\alpha=0}, RR_{\alpha=1}) = 7590$. These values show the difference in behavior of Vo diffusion and DS diffusion. A good balance between these two diffusion can be obtained through α_{ij} by incorporating the real traffic conditions to improve the ranking accuracy.

The ranking also keeps on changing with time based on the new traffic measures. Comparing the previous ranking to that obtained at 10:05 AM, we found that while few road segments in the top order remain same, those in the lower order change greatly with $\text{KT}(RR_{08:05AM}, RR_{10:05AM}) = 3794$ for the top 100 segments. Also some small road segments sometimes become influential for a short period of time but quickly goes down in the next time point as the congestion scenario changes. The convergences for t_0 = 08:00 AM and 10:05 AM are achieved[2] in 922 (taking 36 seconds) and 1193 (taking 42 seconds) iterations respectively, which take significantly lesser iterations and time in incrementally computing the ranking at subsequent timestamps t_l. Normally a traffic signal takes one to three minutes to complete a cycle. With this much interval of available time for processing the data, our algorithm is efficient enough to perform the computations in real time.

5. CONCLUSION

In this paper, we devised a probabilistic traffic diffusion model to identify the most influential road segments in an urban road network. We presented RoadRank as a novel algorithm to compute the influence scores (or roadrank scores) of each road segment, which are updated incrementally with time to deal with the dynamic nature of traffic. The method starts with constructing a directed *influence graph* that is used to compute the traffic diffusion from one road segment to another at each timestamp. The *roadrank* scores are iteratively computed using probabilistic diffusion theory. We conducted experiments on historical traffic data collected from the 493 SCATS sites in Melbourne (Australia), and presented insights to the real traffic congestion scenario.

Acknowledgment

This research was supported by the NICTA, ARC Discovery Projects DP120102627 and DP140103499, and Future Fellowship grant FT120100723. NICTA is funded by the Australian Government through the Department of Communications and the Australian Research Council through the ICT Centre of Excellence Program.

6. REFERENCES

[1] T. Anwar, C. Liu, H. L. Vu, and C. Leckie. Spatial partitioning of large urban road networks. In *Proc. EDBT*, 2014.

[2] B. Bi, Y. Tian, Y. Sismanis, A. Balmin, and J. Cho. Scalable topic-specific influence analysis on microblogs. In *Proc. WSDM*, 2014.

[3] S. Brin and L. Page. The anatomy of a large-scale hypertextual web search engine. *Computer Networks and ISDN Systems*, 30(1-7), Apr. 1998.

[4] M. Cha, A. Mislove, and K. P. Gummadi. A measurement-driven analysis of information propagation in the flickr social network. In *Proc. WWW*, 2009.

[5] A. Goyal, F. Bonchi, and L. V. Lakshmanan. Learning influence probabilities in social networks. In *Proc. WSDM*, 2010.

[6] D. Gruhl, R. Guha, D. Liben-Nowell, and A. Tomkins. Information diffusion through blogspace. In *Proc. WWW*, 2004.

[7] J. Herzig, Y. Mass, and H. Roitman. An author-reader influence model for detecting topic-based influencers in social media. In *Proc. HT*, 2014.

[8] D. Kempe, J. Kleinberg, and E. Tardos. Influential nodes in a diffusion model for social networks. In *Proc. ICALP*, 2005.

[2]Performed on a Core i5 computer with 8GB RAM

On Query-Update Independence for SPARQL

Nicola Guido
nicola.guido@inria.fr

Pierre Genevès
pierre.geneves@cnrs.fr

Nabil Layaïda
nabil.layaida@inria.fr

Cécile Roisin
cecile.roisin@inria.fr

Univ. Grenoble Alpes, LIG, F-38000 Grenoble, France
CNRS, LIG, F-38000 Grenoble, France
Inria

ABSTRACT

This paper investigates techniques for detecting independence of SPARQL queries from updates. A query is independent of an update when the execution of the update does not affect the result of the query. Determining independence is especially useful in the context of huge RDF repositories, where it permits to avoid expensive yet useless re-evaluation of queries. While this problem has been intensively studied for fragments of relational calculus, very few works exist for the standard query language for the semantic web. We report on our investigations on how a notion of independence can be defined in the SPARQL context.

1. INTRODUCTION

The Resource Description Framework (RDF) is a graph data format for the representation of information in the Web. An RDF statement is a subject-predicate-object structure, called RDF triple, intended to describe resources and properties of those resources. Due to their homogeneous structure, RDF databases can be considered as labeled directed graphs, where each triple defines an edge from the subject to the object node under label predicate [6].
With SPARQL [7], the W3C has recommended a query language for RDF. SPARQL comes with a powerful graph matching facility, whose basic constructs are called triple patterns. During query evaluation, variables inside these patterns are matched against the RDF input graph. The solution of the evaluation process is then described by a set of mappings, where each mapping associates a set of variables with graph components.
With the introduction of a standard update language for RDF in SPARQL 1.1. Update [7], the query-update independence problem has been introduced.
A query and an update are independent when the query result is not affected by update execution, on any possible input database. Detecting query-update independence is of crucial importance in many contexts, for example to minimize view re-materialization or to ensure isolation, when queries and updates are executed concurrently. Benefits are amplified when query-update independence can be checked by analyzing only the structure of the query against the structure of the update, hence avoiding the costs of (even partial) reevaluation of queries on large datasets. This paper formulates and investigates the problem of SPARQL query-update independence. To the best of our knowledge, it is the first work in this direction.

Permission to make digital or hard copies of all or part of this work for personal or classroom use is granted without fee provided that copies are not made or distributed for profit or commercial advantage and that copies bear this notice and the full citation on the first page. Copyrights for components of this work owned by others than ACM must be honored. Abstracting with credit is permitted. To copy otherwise, or republish, to post on servers or to redistribute to lists, requires prior specific permission and/or a fee. Request permissions from Permissions@acm.org.
CIKM'15, October 19–23, 2015, Melbourne, Australia.
© 2015 ACM. ISBN 978-1-4503-3794-6/15/10 ...$15.00.
DOI: http://dx.doi.org/10.1145/2806416.2806586.

Outline and Contributions

We present some necessary background on RDF and SPARQL in Section 2. We formalize a notion of query-update independence for SPARQL in Section 3. This is the first formalization of the SPARQL query-update independence problem. We discuss characteristics desired for algorithms that effectively check for independence. We introduce a simple condition for detecting independence, which admits an efficient implementation. We discuss the difficulties introduced by SPARQL's open world assumption and draw perspectives for further research in Section 4. Finally we conclude in Section 6.

2. PRELIMINARIES

RDF. RDF is a graph data format for the representation of information in the Web. An RDF statement is a subject-predicate-object structure, called RDF triple, intended to describe resources and properties of those resources. Let U, B, L be three disjoint infinite sets denoting the set of URIs (identifying a resource), blank nodes (denoting an unidentified resource) and literals (a character string or some other type of data) respectively. We abbreviate any union of these sets as for instance, $UBL = U \cup B \cup L$. More formally, an RDF triple t is a tuple $(s, p, o) \in UB \times U \times UBL$, where s is the subject, p the predicate and o the object. A set of RDF triples is often referred to as an RDF graph.

EXAMPLE 1 (RDF GRAPH). *Consider 10 triples about employers and their informations (all identifiers correspond to URIs):*

$\{(A_1,\ name,\ Joe),\quad (A_1,\ email,\ Joe@y.com),$
$(A_2,\ name,\ Martin),\quad (A_2,\ fax,\ 111111),$
$(A_3,\ name,\ Louisa),\quad (A_3,\ phone,\ 222222),$
$(A_4,\ name,\ John),\quad (A_4,\ web,\ www.John.com),$
$(A_4,\ email,\ John@y.com),\quad (A_4,\ phone,\ 333333)\ \}$

The authors are supported in part by ANR TYPEX ANR-11-BS02-00.

SPARQL. SPARQL is a W3C recommended query language for RDF. We restrict ourselves to the core fragment of SPARQL over simple RDF graph, which is sufficient for our purposes.

SYNTAX. SPARQL is based on the notion of query patterns defined inductively from triple patterns. A triple pattern is a tuple $tp \in UBV \times UV \times UBLV$, with V a set of variables disjoint from UBL. Triple patterns grouped together using SPARQL operators (like AND, OPT, UNION) form query patterns (or graph patterns).

DEFINITION 1 (QUERY PATTERN). *The syntax of a query pattern q is inductively defined as follows:*

$$q ::= tp \mid q \text{ AND } q \mid q \text{ OPT } q \mid q \text{ UNION } q$$

SPARQL provide several kind of queries. We focus on `SELECT` queries which are the core of SPARQL queries.

DEFINITION 2 (SELECT QUERY). *A SELECT* QUERY *is a query of the form $q(\overrightarrow{w})$ where $\overrightarrow{w}$ is a tuple of variables in V which are called distinguished variables, and q is a query pattern.*

EXAMPLE 2 (SELECT QUERY). . *Consider the query:*

SELECT ?A ?E ?W
WHERE {(?A *email* ?E) OPT(?A *web* ?W)}

that queries an RDF *graph for an email* ?E *of a person* ?A *and, if available, for a web page* ?P *of* ?A, *where* ?A, ?E, ?W *are distingueshed variables and email and web are* URIs.

SEMANTICS. The standard semantics of SPARQL queries is given by a partial mapping function $\rho : V \rightarrow UBL$, that assigns RDF terms of an RDF graph to variables of a SPARQL query. For a triple pattern t, we denote by $\rho(t)$ the triple obtained by replacing the variables in t according to ρ. For a query pattern q, we denote by $\rho(q)$ the set of ground triples (triples not containing any variables) obtained by replacing the variables in q according to ρ. The set of all possible mapping-sets, each of which represents a SPARQL query solution, is denoted by Ω.

EXAMPLE 3 (QUERY SOLUTION). *Consider the query pattern in Example 2:*

{(?A *email* ?E) OPT (?A *web* ?W}

that queries the RDF *graph in Example 1, the query pattern solution Ω is represented as the set of $\{\rho_1, \rho_2\}$ where:*

- *ρ_1 is the result of successful match of the triple pattern* (?A, *email*, ?E) *against triple* (A_1, *email*, *Joe@y.com*)
- *ρ_2 is the result of successful match of the triple patterns* (?A, *email*, ?E)OPT(?A, *web*, ?W) *against the two triples* (A_4, *email*, *John@y.com*) *and* (A_4, *web*, *www.John.com*)

?A → A_2	?E → *Joe@y.com*	
?A → A_4	?E → *John@y.com*	?W → *www.John.com*

Two mappings ρ_1 and ρ_2 are said to be compatible (written $\rho_1 \sim \rho_2$) when $\forall ?X \in dom(\rho_1) \cap dom(\rho_2)$ we have $\rho_1(?X) = \rho_2(?X)$. Mappings with disjoint domains are always compatible. Let Ω_1 and Ω_2 be sets of mappings, the following operators are defined:

$$\Omega_1 \bowtie \Omega_2 = \{\rho_1 \cup \rho_2 \mid \rho_1 \in \Omega_1, \rho_2 \in \Omega_2, \rho_1 \sim \rho_2\}$$
$$\Omega_1 \cup \Omega_2 = \{\rho \mid \rho \in \Omega_1 \text{ or } \rho \in \Omega_2\}$$
$$\Omega_1 \setminus \Omega_2 = \{\rho \in \Omega_1 \mid \forall \rho' \in \Omega_2 . \rho \not\sim \rho'\}$$
$$\Omega_1 :\bowtie \Omega_2 = \{(\Omega_1 \bowtie \Omega_2) \cup (\Omega_1 \setminus \Omega_2)\}$$

EVALUATION. Now, we can formalize the evaluation of query patterns over an RDF graph G as a function $[\![.]\!]_G$, inductively defined as follows:

$$[\![t]\!]_G = \{\rho \mid dom(\rho) = var(t) \text{ and } \rho(t) \in G\}$$
$$[\![q_1 \text{ AND } q_2]\!]_G = [\![q_1]\!]_G \bowtie [\![q_2]\!]_G$$
$$[\![q_1 \text{ OPT } q_2]\!]_G = [\![q_1]\!]_G :\bowtie [\![q_2]\!]_G$$
$$[\![q_1 \text{ UNION } q_2]\!]_G = [\![q_1]\!]_G \cup [\![q_2]\!]_G$$
$$[\![q\{(\overrightarrow{\omega})\}]\!]_G = \pi_{\overrightarrow{\omega}}([\![q]\!]_G)$$

where $var(t)$ is the set of variables occurring in t, $dom(\rho)$ is the domain of ρ, and the projection operator $\pi_{\overrightarrow{\omega}}$ selects only those part of the mapping relevant to variables in $\overrightarrow{\omega}$.

SPARQL Updates. We now define the syntax and semantics of the SPARQL Update language [7] whose purpose is to modify a RDF database.

SYNTAX. SPARQL Update uses a syntax derived from the SPARQL query language introduced previously. Update operations are performed on a collection of graphs. Possible operations include updating, creating and removing RDF graphs in a collection. In this paper, we consider the operations performed on a single graph such as:

- INSERT DATA - this operation adds some triples, given inlined in the request, into a graph. For example: `INSERT DATA` $\{A_1, phone, 444444\}$
- DELETE DATA - this operation removes some triples, given inlined in the request, if the respective graph contains these triples. For example: `DELETE DATA` $\{A_1, email, Joe@y.com\}$
- INSERT/DELETE - these actions consist of groups of triples to be deleted and groups of triples to be added.

We focus mostly on INSERT/DELETE operations that constitute the fundamental pattern-based actions for graph updates. The specifiation of triples is based on quad patterns.

DEFINITION 3 (QUAD PATTERN). *A quad pattern q_u is inductively defined as follows:*

$$q_u ::= tp \mid q_u \text{ AND } q_u \mid q_u \text{ UNION } q_u \mid q_u \text{ OPT } q_u$$

where $tp \in UV \times UV \times ULV$. A quad pattern is a query pattern that doesn't allow blank nodes.

The INSERT/DELETE operation can be used to remove or add triples from/to a graph based on bindings for a quad pattern specified in a WHERE clause.

DEFINITION 4 (SPARQL UPDATE OPERATION [1]). *Let q_d, q_i, and q_w be quad Patterns, then $u(q_d, q_i, q_w)$, an update operation, has the form*

$$u(q_d, q_i, q_w) = \textit{DELETE } q_d \textit{ INSERT } q_i \textit{ WHERE} q_w$$

SEMANTICS. Intuitively, the semantics of the execution of $u(q_d, q_i, q_w)$ on G, denoted as $G_{u(q_d,q_i,q_w)}$ or simply $u(G)$ is defined interpreting both q_d and q_i as "templates" to be instantiated with the solution $\Omega = [\![q_w]\!]_G$

DEFINITION 5 (NAÏVE UPDATE SEMANTICS [1]). *Let G be a triple store, and $u(q_d, q_i, q_w)$ an update operation, then, a naïve update of G with $u(q_d, q_i, q_w)$, denoted $G_{u(q_d,q_i,q_w)}$ is defined as $(G \setminus A_d) \cup A_i$, where $A_d = \bigcup_{\rho \in [\![q_w]\!]_G} \rho(q_d)$ and $A_i = \bigcup_{\rho \in [\![q_w]\!]_G} \rho(q_i)$*

3. NOTION OF INDEPENDENCE

In this section we introduce and formalize the query-update independence problem for SPARQL. Intuitively, a query q is independent of an update u, if evaluating q after or before u returns the same result. In other terms, independence holds whenever solutions of query patterns remain unchanged during the addition or deletion of triples from the RDF graph. We first recall the closest notion that we have found in the literature:

PROPOSITION 1 (QUERY SOLUTION INVARIANCE[11]). *If Ω is the set of all solutions for the query pattern q, with respect to an RDF graph G and for a triple t, there exists no mapping ρ from query variables to RDF terms such that $t \in \rho(q)$, then Ω is also the set of all solutions for $G_+ = G \cup \{t\}$ and $G_- = G \setminus \{t\}$*

We generalize this proposition below, taking into consideration an update u that defines a set of triples to add or to delete from a graph G.

3.1 Definition

PROPOSITION 2. *Let q be a select query and u be an update. We say that q and u are independent iff*

$$\forall G.\ [\![q]\!]_G = [\![q]\!]_{u(G)}$$

Independence between queries and updates is thus expressed as the equivalence of two evaluations: one evaluation that computes the answer to the query before the update, and a second evaluation that computes the answer after the update.

Detecting independence is important for several reasons. It can be used in view maintenance to identify that some views are independent of certain updates. We can provide greater flexibility by identifying that one query is independent of updates made by another program or person. Finally. We can use independence in query optimization by ignoring parts of the RDF dataset for which updates do not affect a specific query (to ensure isolation).

3.2 Requirements for Independence Analyses

Costs. Obviously, we can verify at runtime whether an update impacts a query: we simply run the update after a first query evaluation, then re-run the query, and finally compare the results. The overall cost c of such a check is dominated by the cost of evaluating the query (twice) on the whole RDF dataset and the update (once). Thus, a method for testing independence makes sense only if its cost is lower than c. A first class of interesting methods regroups all *purely static* analysis methods, whose cost depends only on the size of the query and on the size of the update, and not on the size of the RDF dataset. A second class of interesting methods regroups hybrid static/dynamic methods that might involve evaluation or partial evaluation of the query on a fraction of the RDF dataset, and whose cost lower than c nevertheless depends on the RDF dataset size.

Dealing with the Open-World Assumption. While similar query-update independence problems have been intensively studied for other query languages (in particular for fragments of the relational calculus), very few works exist for SPARQL. We believe that one reason for this is due to SPARQL's underlying open world assumption (a.k.a OWA). We recall that OWA applies to a system that has incomplete information. The web, for instance, is traditionally considered as a system with incomplete information. The absence of some information on the web does not mean that this information is false, but simply that this information has not been made explicit: it is unknown. SPARQL, as a query language for RDF, inherits from this assumption. It thus constitutes an open-world framework that allows anyone to make statements about any resource. Any independence analysis method should thus consider this assumption at its core.

In the next section, we propose a simple condition for testing independence, in the presence of OWA.

3.3 A Condition for Independence

We define a condition for checking query-update independence, as follows:

THEOREM 1 (CONDITION FOR INDEPENDENCE). *Let $\mathcal{Q}$ be the set of all triple patterns that appear in the query pattern of the query q and $\mathcal{U}$ be the set of all quad patterns that appear in the DeleteClause and InsertClause of an update u:*

$$\forall G.\ [\![q]\!]_G = [\![q]\!]_{u(G)} \Leftrightarrow \mathcal{Q} \cap \mathcal{U} = \emptyset$$

where $\mathcal{Q} \cap \mathcal{U} = \emptyset$ is defined as follows:

$$\forall t_q \in \mathcal{Q},\ \forall t_u \in \mathcal{U}, t_q \neq t_u$$

and $\quad t_q \neq t_u \Leftrightarrow \forall \varrho_q \in [\![t_q]\!]_G, \forall \varrho_u \in [\![t_u]\!], \varrho_q(t_q) \neq \varrho_u(t_u).$

PROOF. (Sketch) ($\Rightarrow$) By contradiction.

Suppose $\exists G'.[\![q]\!]_{G'} \neq [\![q]\!]_{u(G')}$, it means that there exists at least a triple t that is added or deleted from G' such that t is a triple in the path or in the solution of the query q. We can easily check that $t \in \mathcal{Q} \cap \mathcal{U} \neq \emptyset$. In fact, $t \in \mathcal{U}$ holds because t is a triple added to or deleted from G', so $\exists t_u \in \mathcal{U}.t = t_u$ and $t \in \mathcal{Q}$ holds because the result of applying q after u changes, so $\exists t_q \in \mathcal{Q}.t = t_q$.

($\Leftarrow$) By contradiction.

Suppose $\mathcal{Q} \cap \mathcal{U} \neq \emptyset$, by definition, $\exists t_u \in \mathcal{U}, t_q \in \mathcal{Q}.t_u = t_q$. Let $t_u = t_q$, there always exists a ground triple t that matches both t_q and t_u (i.e. replacing variables by blank nodes). Starting from t we can easily construct a graph G, such that $[\![q]\!]_G \neq \emptyset$ and $[\![q]\!] \neq [\![q]\!]_{G \setminus \{t\}}$ or $[\![q]\!]_G \neq [\![q]\!]_{G \cup \{t\}}$. □

Our condition above can be checked statically with the query and the update, independently from any particular RDF dataset. Such a test fits in the category of purely static analysis methods. It can easily be implemented in linear time with respect to the size of the query and the update. When independence is detected, it allows to avoid the cost of re-evaluation of queries on large datasets.

4. DISCUSSION

We identify two main research directions for the further development of methods aimed at detecting query-update independence:

Hybrid static/dynamic methods. The condition that we presented above involves reasoning over all graphs, and is thus purely static. It would be very interesting to develop hybrid (static and dynamic) methods that would also take into account a specific dataset as input. Such methods should satisfy our cost requirements in order to remain relevant (c.f. Section 3.2) but would unlock the potential for many more detections of independence cases.

Methods supporting schema constraints. One perspective is the development of methods that analyse the structures of the query and of the update in the presence of constraints on the dataset, when such constraints are available. Typical constraints on RDF datasets include OWL2 constraints that can express, for example, the fact that two classes are disjoint. Such constraints – and more generally constraints expressed with any description logic supporting negation – are game-changers for the independence problem. The potential contradictions that they introduce can be leveraged for detecting more cases of independence.

In order to understand the impact of schema constraints, let us consider the following example.

EXAMPLE 4 (SCHEMA EXAMPLE). *Let q be a query and u be an update defined as follows:*

$$q(\{?\text{X}\}) = \{(?\text{X}, phone,' 222222')$$
$$u\Big(\{(?\text{X}, ?\text{Y}, ?\text{Z})\}, \{\}, \{(A_4, phone, ?\text{X})\}\Big)$$

q and u are dependent under OWA. For example, if we add the triple $t = (\_a, phone, A_3)$ *in the graph of Example1, the resulting graph G is such that* $[\![q]\!]_G \neq [\![q]\!]_{u(G)}$.

However, the situation changes completely if we add schema constraints stating that phone has a domain "Person" and a range "Number" and in addition that "Person" is disjoint from "Number" (which can be easily formulated in OWL2 *for instance). In this case, we can see that the variable ?*X *of q belongs to "Person', while the ?*X *of u belongs to "Number", so the update does not affect the query result. In the presence of such constraints q and u are independent.*

5. RELATED WORK

To the best of our knowledge, our work is the first to formalize and investigate the query-update independence problem for the SPARQL language. Several techniques have been developed for the static analysis of SPARQL, mainly focusing on containment and equivalence of queries [12, 4, 9], possibly in the presence of schemas [4, 5]. Such techniques aim at detecting relations (typically inclusions) between two queries, both evaluated using the same semantics. This common semantics is a key ingredient that these techniques exploit. These techniques hardly extend to the present context where the semantics of an update is significantly different from the semantics of the query. In the presence of schema constraints, as pointed out in [1] several semantics can be provided for SPARQL Update and, there is no "one-size-fits-all" update semantics.

This work is partly inspired by the works on SPARQL query caching [11], where a first notion of query solution invariance for caching is defined. We formalized the notion of query-update independence and made this notion more precise and more general. Outside the SPARQL context, the query-update independence problem has been intensively studied, in particular in the relational context [3, 10] and in the setting of XML structures [2, 8]. However, due to the SPARQL/RDF's open world assumption, these results do not transfer to the SPARQL context.

6. CONCLUSION

We present a first formalization of the SPARQL query-update independence problem. We motivate the interest of searching for methods that solve this problem. We also explain difficulties and discuss characteristics desired for algorithms that effectively check for independence. We introduce a simple condition for detecting independence, which admits an efficient implementation. We identify more general classes of interesting methods and draw perspectives for further research.

7. REFERENCES

[1] A. Ahmeti and A. Polleres. SPARQL update under RDFS entailment in fully materialized and redundancy-free triple stores. In *OrdRing'13, Co-located with ISWC '14*, pages 21–32, 2013.

[2] M. Benedikt and J. Cheney. Destabilizers and independence of XML updates. *Proc. VLDB Endow.*, 3(1-2):906–917, Sep. 2010.

[3] J. A. Blakeley, N. Coburn, and P.-A. Larson. Updating derived relations: Detecting irrelevant and autonomously computable updates. In *VLDB'89*, number 3, pages 369–400.

[4] M. W. Chekol, J. Euzenat, P. Genevès, and N. Layaïda. PSPARQL query containment. In *DBPL'11*.

[5] M. W. Chekol, J. Euzenat, P. Genevès, and N. Layaïda. SPARQL query containment under SHI axioms. In *AAAI'12*.

[6] C. Gutierrez, C. A. Hurtado, and A. O. Mendelzon. Foundations of semantic web databases. In *PODS'04*, pages 95–106.

[7] S. Harris and A. Seaborne. SPARQL 1.1 query language. W3C Recommendation, March 2013.

[8] M. Junedi, P. Genevès, and N. Layaïda. XML query-update independence analysis revisited. In *DocEng'12*, pages 95–98.

[9] A. Letelier, J. Pèrez, R. Pichler, and S. Skritek. Static analysis and optimization of semantic web queries. In *PODS'12*, pages 89–100.

[10] A. Y. Levy and Y. Sagiv. Queries independent of updates. In *PODS'93*, pages 171–181.

[11] M. Martin, J. Unbehauen, and S. Auer. Improving the performance of semantic web applications with SPARQL query caching. In *ESWC'10*, pages 304–318.

[12] G. Serfiotis, I. Koffina, V. Christophides, and V. Tannen. Containment and minimization of RDF/S query patterns. In *ISWC'05*, volume 3729, pages 607–623.

A Structured Query Model for the Deep Relational Web*

Hasan M. Jamil
Department of Computer Science
University of Idaho, USA
jamil@uidaho.edu

H. V. Jagadish
Department of Electrical Engineering and Computer Science
University of Michigan - Ann Arbor, USA
jag@umich.edu

ABSTRACT

The deep web is very large and diverse and queries evaluated against the deep web can provide great value. While there have been attempts at accessing the data in the deep web, these are clever "one-of" systems and techniques. In this paper, we describe an ongoing research of a generic structured query model that can be used against the deep web. Using this query model, the contributions of a community of researchers can be combined freely, leading to a system that can be improved incrementally each time someone develops a specific novel technique to improve a particular operator.

Categories and Subject Descriptors

H.2.3 [**Database Management**]: Languages—*Database semantics; Query languages*

General Terms

Data model; Heterogeneous databases; Data integration

Keywords

Deep web; Schema mapping; Form filling; Recommender systems; Wrappers; Entity resolution; Declarative querying; Query processing; Extended operators

1. INTRODUCTION

Recent research show that the *deep web* [9] is several hundred times larger [23] than the *shallow web* [16] (see [23] for a discussion on the distinction between the shallow and deep web databases). The bulk of recent research on querying structured web contents has focused on exploiting either the exposed tables in the form of indexable documents, or somehow exposing the contents first and then using a traditional method to query them. Among them, the relational web approach [3] aims to locate, extract, and manage a large number of tables contained in already indexed documents in shallow web. In approaches like this, searching [8, 17] and harvesting [1, 7] tables in shallow web are used as key mechanisms. Algebraic query languages were also proposed to manipulate harvested tables in the context of data integration [2]. A complementary approach in querying deep web contents has been devising methods to actively expose the tables (e.g., [25]) based on predicted use, and then querying the exposed contents using conventional techniques.

While such harvesting-based systems can be valuable in specific domains, they suffer from two major drawbacks. First, much deep web content has proprietary value for its owner, who may not be willing to have it harvested and exposed [26]. Second, the sheer scale of the deep web makes a generic harvest of all deep web data a truly daunting venture. For these reasons, we do not consider harvesting-based systems further in this paper.

The alternative is to access the deep web contents that are "relevant" and "permissible" in the context of a query in a dynamic fashion at run time so that we are not required to harvest or index them ahead of time. While there have been notable attempts in this direction (e.g., [10, 15, 18]), these do not establish a reusable general framework with which a community can jointly advance the field. For example, MetaQuerier [10] uses interface clustering to facilitate query mapping for data integration. In contrast, our vision is to have a decomposable deep web querying system framework capable of accepting the most capable implementations for each module. For example, the interface identification task could be performed by a recommender system. To enable such a clean modular approach, we develop a high level abstraction and express it in terms of a declarative language and foundation. Through these means, various independently developed deep web technologies can synergistically come together at the implementation level. While challenges remain, we show that such a model and architecture is entirely feasible today by suitable adaptation of recent research in this area.

2. STRUCTURED DEEP WEB QUERYING

By means of a running example, we establish the main intuitions behind our proposal in this section.

Necessity of Structured Search Over the Deep Web. Search engines today use keyword based querying. This is insufficient for the deep web. To illustrate this, consider Nina, who is searching online for a car. She has a rough idea of what she wants to buy – a fairly new Honda Civic for a price less than $15,000, preferring red trim with aluminium

*Research supported in part by US NSF grants IIS 0612203 (for Hasan Jamil) and IIS 1250880 (for H. V. Jagadish).

Permission to make digital or hard copies of all or part of this work for personal or classroom use is granted without fee provided that copies are not made or distributed for profit or commercial advantage and that copies bear this notice and the full citation on the first page. Copyrights for components of this work owned by others than the author(s) must be honored. Abstracting with credit is permitted. To copy otherwise, or republish, to post on servers or to redistribute to lists, requires prior specific permission and/or a fee. Request permissions from Permissions@acm.org.
CIKM'15, October 19–23, 2015, Melbourne, VIC, Australia.
Copyright is held by the owner/author(s). Publication rights licensed to ACM.
ACM 978-1-4503-3794-6/15/10 ...$15.00.
DOI: http://dx.doi.org/10.1145/2806416.2806589.

alloy wheels. She formulates her query Q_D in an SQL-like language, called <u>d</u>eep web <u>q</u>uery <u>l</u>anguage (DQL), as follows:

> list *Price, Color, Year, DealerName, State*
> where *Price* < *\$15,000* and *Make* = *"Honda"*
> and *Model* = *"Civic"* and *Condition* = *"New"*
> and *Wheel* = *"Alloy Wheel"* and *Year* ≥ *2010*

Notice in this query that although she prefers a red car, she did not mention it as a condition to avoid being overly restrictive. If this query was issued against the view *CarView*

> create view *CarView* as
> select *BasePrice*(1+Margin/100)* as *Price, Make, Model, Color, Options, Year, DealerName, Dealers.State*
> from *Vehicles, Prices, Options, Dealers*
> where *Prices.state* = *Dealers.State* and
> *Prices.Vin* = *Options.Vin* and *Vehicles.Vin* = *Prices.Vin*

defined over a structured database with a scheme as shown in figure 1 as the SQL query Q below,

> select *Price, Color, Year, DealerName, State*
> from *CarView*
> where *Make* = *"Honda"* and *Price* < *\$15,000* and
> and *Model* = *"Civic"* and *Year* ≥ *2010*
> and *Options* = *"Alloy Wheel"*

she would have had a concrete response, i.e., ⟨*\$14,850, blue, 2011, Lone Star, MI*⟩. However, it is well known that had she submitted the DQL query Q_D directly on any contemporary search engine, we would not actually get any meaningful response other than possibly links to a few top ranking car sales web sites including `www.lemonfree.com` for used car sales site and Wikipedia page for Honda Fit as top hits.

Vehicles

Make	Model	Year	VIN	Color
Honda	Civic	2011	123	Blue
Honda	Civic	2010	162	Red

Options

VIN	Options
123	Alloy Wheel
123	Automatic
162	Alloy Wheel

Prices

VIN	State	BasePrice
123	MI	13500
123	CA	15000
162	MI	13750
162	NV	16750

Dealers

Margin	State	DealerName
10	MI	Lone Star
12	CA	Golden Gate
15	MI	Great Lakes

Figure 1: Car information database.

Black-Box abstraction through Deep Web Interfaces. Consider a trivial deep web database comprising a single site, such as cars.com. Nina could issue her query through a web form provided by this web site. This web form would allow her to express various query conditions over the scheme of *CarView*. For many reasons (including security concerns), the form entries and variable names are usually different from the scheme of the view. Upon submission of the form, a well-formed SQL query is created, reflecting user constraints over the view and executed against the back-end database, in this instance the view *CarView*. The response is returned possibly in the form of a table in an HTML document for presentation purposes in which the scheme is transformed and variables renamed. This black-box model essentially helps hide the database structure and details of the view, captures an input-output behavior, and though limiting, obviates the need for a query language.

2.1 Research Challenges

The question we would like address in this paper is: Is it possible for Nina to submit her query Q_D in some system that will scour the web to compute a response that will include the tuple ⟨*\$14,850, blue, 2011, Lone Star, MI*⟩ from the deep web "database" that includes the site cars.com?

Absence of an Explicit Schema for Querying. Nina is using her home computer and is interested in accessing multiple databases across the web. She does not know what schema any web site may have, and is not interested in such information. Instead, she "imagines" a *CarView* table, and expresses her query against this imagined schema. Note that she does not have to express this schema explicitly anywhere. Rather, this schema is implicit in her mind as she writes the query. The query itself is semantically interpreted with respect to this imaginary schema.

In general, this implicit schema could be complex. In this paper, we restrict our attention to single table schema for two reasons. First, joins are very hard for naive users to think through – even if the actual database is decomposed, it is easiest for users to think in terms of a single-table view [14]. Second, the technical challenges in achieving this vision are already significant for single table views, so it is reasonable to leave the more complex cases to future work.

DQL as a subset of SQL. SQL is a powerful language with many valuable features. We model DQL after SQL. Since there is an implicit schema against which DQL queries are written, there is no FROM clause. Therefore, a basic DQL qery would only have a SELECT clause and a WHERE clause. To make DQL easy to distinguish from SQL, we use the keyword LIST rather than SELECT. Nina's query Q_D above, is a LIST-WHERE query. Many important SQL features, such as grouping and aggregation, are easy to add to DQL as are most types of nesting. For lack of space, we do not consider these enhanced features in this paper. Rather we restrict ourselves to a single-block LIST-WHERE query.

Respecting Site Autonomy. Many deep web databases have proprietary value and will only allow limited access through form-based query interfaces. Therefore, the job of the deep web query processing engine is to take the DQL query input (either directly by the user or through some facilitating interface), evaluate the query against multiple sites, using their exposed form-based interface, and then to return results, after suitable composition, back to the user. Figure 2 depicts the overall architecture of our model.

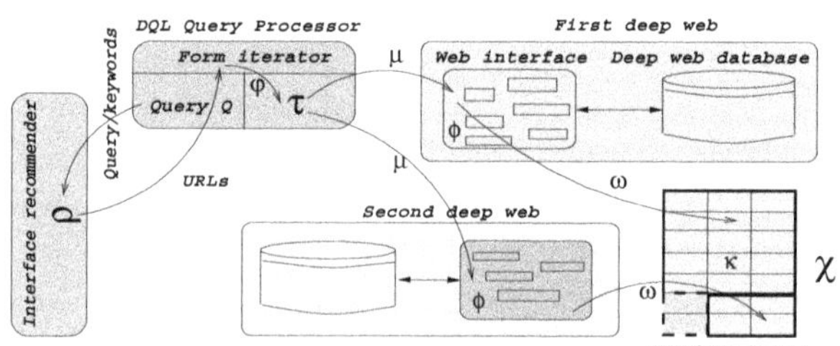

Figure 2: DQL query processor architecture.

3. DEEP WEB ALGEBRAIC OPERATORS

Algebraic operators customarily have defined input-output behavior over a crisp database scheme. The challenge is to define query operators that have defined input-output behaviors but no "explicit" database scheme. Since each site is a black-box, and the only behaviors visible are the input form conditions and scheme of the output table, the visible scheme of a site must at least be the union of all the attributes in the form and the returned table. The implicit database scheme R thus is the union of the set of deep web form schemes. Naturally, the attributes A_θ appearing in the where clause and A_l in the list clause in query Q_D, called the query scheme Q_S, must be a subset of R, i.e, $A_\theta \cup A_l \subseteq R$.

We overcome this challenge by dynamically supplying a tentative scheme to an operator, and the query succeeds if the supplied scheme sufficiently matched the query scheme, i.e., $A_\theta \cup A_l \subseteq R$ is satisfied. In order to define operators we have in mind, we proceed in four intuitive steps.

Site Selection. First, we make an educated guess and choose a set of query forms $\mathfrak{I}$ that we believe adequately captures the conditions in the query Q_D. We capture this process as a function ρ to model our recommender component in figure 2 such that $\rho : 2^{\mathcal{C}} \times 2^{\mathfrak{I}} \rightarrow 2^{\mathfrak{I}}$ where $\mathcal{W}$ is the set of indices of all shallow web pages, $\mathfrak{I} \subseteq \mathcal{W}$ is the set of indices for all web form pages, and $\mathcal{C}$ is a set of terms, tags or key words that can be used to identify a relevant set of web forms that are likely candidates to execute our query. Ideally we would like these forms to have entries corresponding A_θ only and the pages they return to have tables with attributes $A \supseteq A_l$. The research in the area of recommender systems (e.g., [12, 27]) is particularly relevant and we propose to choose ρ as an adaptation of one such system.

Schema Mapping and Form Filling. Second, we map the query condition θ on the form entries using an enhanced schema matching system (e.g., [21]), and if a match is established, we use an automatic form-filling system (e.g., [24]) to submit the query.

Table Extraction. Third, the response table is extracted using a suitable wrapper (e.g., [6]), a match is established with the required fields using a schema matcher and only the needed sub-table is retained. We throw away the response if the combination of the form input and the output scheme does not adequately match the "query semantics."

3.1 Transform Operator

The last two steps above are abstracted in the form of an operator in our language. We adapt the approach of *Data Mapper* [5] and parameterize relational operators with user selectable functions so that operator behavior can be tailored according to the functions supplied. Parameterization also help encapsulate the complex behavior needed for our first deep web operator called *transform* that submits the queries, and extracts responses from supplied web sites as described above. Formally,

DEFINITION 1. Let $\mu \in \Gamma$ be a schema matching function, $\omega \in \Omega$ be a wrapper function, $\phi \in \Phi$ be a form-filling function, $\varphi \in \mathfrak{I}$ be a deep web query form, and Q_D be a DQL query with a query condition θ over the query scheme $A_\theta \cup A_l$. Then, the transform operator τ is defined as $\tau^{\mu,\omega,\phi,\varphi}_{\theta,A_l} = \pi^{\mu}_{A_l}(\omega(A_l, \mu, \phi(\theta, \mu, \varphi)))$.

In the above definition, a query form is treated as a function, which is supplied to a form-filling function ϕ along with a matcher μ. The response of ϕ and the matcher is then piped to the wrapper function ω for the extraction of the target table. The extended projection operator $\pi^{\mu}_{A_l}$ (adapted from [13]) is then applied to generate the query response. Intuitively, θ in τ is the where clause condition, A_l is the list clause attributes, and the scheme of φ is the implicit scheme (say R) of query Q_D which becomes concrete once μ establishes the schema correspondence satisfying $A_\theta \cup A_l \subseteq R$.

Output Processing. Finally, we gather and return all "valid responses" from all the relevant sites in $\rho(\theta \cup A_l, \mathfrak{I})$ in a single table. However, the output scheme may vary from site to site even though the query forms are sufficiently similar, and sites may represent semantically similar objects differently, requiring novel data integration. We use the *combine* operator χ [13], introduced in the context of semantic data integration, discussed next for this purpose.

3.2 Combine Operator

The nature of partial schema matching, and the heterogenous structure of the relations gathered are likely to render a straightforward union of the responses into a single table r impossible. To overcome this hurdle, we propose to adapt the binary operator *combine* ($\chi^{\mu,\kappa}$) [13] that takes two relations with heterogeneous schemes, a schema matcher μ and a key discovery function $\kappa \in \mathcal{K}$ [22] to return a outer union in which duplicates are removed based on object identification in addition to schema matching. Using this operator, we combine the relations iteratively for all the sites $\varphi \in \rho(\theta \cup A_l, \mathfrak{I})$.

The transform and combine operators, in conjunction with the recommender system modeled as the function ρ, are sufficient to assemble a query processing engine to process DQL queries using the high level architecture presented in figure 2. The transform operator (τ) uses functions for schema matching (Γ), wrapping (Ω), and form filling (Ψ); the combine operator (χ) uses the key discovery ($\mathcal{K}$) function.

Intuitively, Nina's query Q_D can now be computed, with the help of an iterator function $\bigotimes$, as the algebraic expression $r \leftarrow \bigotimes_{\forall\varphi,\varphi\in\rho(\theta\cup A_l,\mathfrak{I})}(r\chi^{\mu,\kappa}(\tau^{\mu,\omega,\phi,\varphi}_{\theta,A_l}))$[1].

4. SUMMARY AND FUTURE CHALLENGES

Even though technology exists today to construct a deep web querying system, it can benefit from renewed research on several different fronts, a few of which we suggest below.

Form Recommendation and Query Splitting. When sufficient mapping cannot be established for a DQL query, it can be split to push constraints to the wrapper with the anticipation that the constraint can still be met on the response table. That is, we consider query relaxation where we return a response $r \not\models Q_D$ such that $\exists r', r' \models Q_D, r' \subseteq r$. Additional opportunities exist to model similarity as a function of the user or DQL query context [20]. For these purposes, recommender systems and form filling functions can be enhanced to consider DQL-like structured queries to map query constraints to query forms with a notion of "adequacy" along the line of [10].

Query Subsumption. The black-box model and the privacy concerns of sites requires that we always choose sites

[1]Here, we assume that the iteration starts with an empty table r and combined with each extracted table returned by τ over all $\varphi \in \rho(\theta \cup A_l, \mathfrak{I})$. Also, when the matcher, wrapper, form-filler and key discovery functions are fixed and known, we can write these two operators simply as $\tau^{\varphi}_{\theta,A_l}$ and χ.

to execute our queries whose interface constraints subsume the query constraints in the sense of constraint subsumption [19] and query rewriting. More research is needed to flesh this out.

Table Extraction. While many wrapper systems work fine, they cannot be customized to extract only the required sub-tables. Often the heuristics used miss extracting intended tables. We believe the query scheme and schema matchers together can be used to better identify target tables, even when objects are spread across multiple tables in the response page. Unannotated tables pose another dimension of challenge that needs to be addressed as well.

Schema Expansion. The combine operator has a potential to extend the response scheme when tables from disparate sites are consolidated. Although the query scheme should help guide the pruning, we would prefer to allow a degree of expansion to retain search engines' characteristics of exploration and unknown. Since this is an iterative process, new and more interesting attributes may appear. The challenge is how to prioritize the selection of columns, and prune when needed. Research is needed to study possible ordering of query forms to avoid such pruning so that we monotonically add more interesting columns, rather than take out.

Query Optimization. Optimization of deep web queries is a nascent area of research (e.g., [4]). Having a clean architecture like ours makes this task less daunting, since all the functions in the proposed operators are independent of one another. The query processor can select the matching, wrapping, form-filling and key discovery functions most appropriate for the given query, from among the many possible implementations based on current research. In fact, different implementations can even be used for different parts of the same deep web query.

5. CONCLUSION

We have presented the vision of an ongoing research on the deep web as a virtual database, and proposed a simple query language, DQL, and an algebra for query evaluation. The evaluation algebra divides the task into a set of operators and functions, each of which has a well-specified interface and can be implemented as an independent module. While the black-box model of deep web database content poses significant barriers toward its declarative and structured querying, we proposed a system model with the belief that clever and novel adaptation of existing technologies can overcome this limitation. We have identified ongoing research as well as mature systems that can be leveraged and integrated to form the backbone of the envisioned system. Our hope is that the research community will contribute vigorously toward this larger vision of harvesting the enormous wealth of deep web information using a semantically rich, declarative and convenient query language.

6. REFERENCES

[1] S. Blohm, P. Cimiano, and E. Stemle. Harvesting relations from the web: quantifiying the impact of filtering functions. In *NCAI*, pages 1316–1321, 2007.

[2] M. J. Cafarella, A. Y. Halevy, and N. Khoussainova. Data integration for the relational web. *PVLDB*, 2(1):1090–1101, 2009.

[3] M. J. Cafarella, A. Y. Halevy, D. Z. Wang, E. W. 0002, and Y. Zhang. Webtables: exploring the power of tables on the web. *PVLDB*, 1(1):538–549, 2008.

[4] A. Calì and D. Martinenghi. Querying the deep web. In *EDBT*, pages 724–727, 2010.

[5] P. Carreira, H. Galhardas, A. Lopes, and J. Pereira. One-to-many data transformations through data mappers. *Data Knowl. Eng.*, 62(3):483–503, 2007.

[6] N. N. Dalvi, R. Kumar, and M. A. Soliman. Automatic wrappers for large scale web extraction. *PVLDB*, 4(4):219–230, 2011.

[7] H. Elmeleegy, J. Madhavan, and A. Y. Halevy. Harvesting relational tables from lists on the web. *PVLDB*, 2(1):1078–1089, 2009.

[8] Y. Fang and K. C.-C. Chang. Searching patterns for relation extraction over the web: rediscovering the pattern-relation duality. In *WSDM*, pages 825–834, 2011.

[9] D. Florescu, A. Y. Levy, and A. O. Mendelzon. Database techniques for the world-wide web: A survey. *SIGMOD Record*, 27(3):59–74, 1998.

[10] B. He, Z. Zhang, and K. C.-C. Chang. MetaQuerier: querying structured web sources on-the-fly. In *SIGMOD Conference*, pages 927–929, 2005.

[11] Z. He, J. Hong, and D. A. Bell. Schema matching across query interfaces on the deep web. In *BNCOD*, pages 51–62, 2008.

[12] J. Hong, Z. He, and D. A. Bell. An evidential approach to query interface matching on the deep web. *Inf. Syst.*, 35(2):140–148, 2010.

[13] S. Hosain and H. M. Jamil. An algebraic foundation for semantic data integration on the hidden web. In *IEEE ICSC*, pages 237–244, September 2009.

[14] H. V. Jagadish, A. Chapman, A. Elkiss, M. Jayapandian, Y. Li, A. Nandi, and C. Yu. Making database systems usable. In *SIGMOD Conference*, pages 13–24, 2007.

[15] T. Kabisch, E. C. Dragut, C. T. Yu, and U. Leser. Deep web integration with visqi. *PVLDB*, 3(2):1613–1616, 2010.

[16] S. Lawrence and C. L. Giles. Searching the world wide web. *Science*, 280(5360):98–100, 1998.

[17] G. Limaye, S. Sarawagi, and S. Chakrabarti. Annotating and searching web tables using entities, types and relationships. *PVLDB*, 3(1):1338–1347, 2010.

[18] T. Liu, F. Wang, and G. Agrawal. Instance discovery and schema matching with applications to biological deep web data integration. In *DILS*, pages 148–163, 2010.

[19] J. Maloberti and M. Sebag. Theta-subsumption in a constraint satisfaction perspective. In *ILP*, pages 164–178, 2001.

[20] X. Meng, J. Sun, and C. Liu. Context-sensitive automatic categorization of web database query results. In *FSKD*, pages 1525–1529, 2010.

[21] T. H. Nguyen, H. Nguyen, and J. Freire. PruSM: a prudent schema matching approach for web forms. In *CIKM*, pages 1385–1388, 2010.

[22] G. Papadakis, E. Ioannou, C. Niederée, and P. Fankhauser. Efficient entity resolution for large heterogeneous information spaces. In *WSDM*, pages 535–544, 2011.

[23] S. Raghavan and H. Garcia-Molina. Crawling the hidden web. In *VLDB*, pages 129–138, 2001.

[24] G. A. Toda, E. Cortez, A. S. da Silva, and E. S. de Moura. A probabilistic approach for automatically filling form-based web interfaces. *PVLDB*, 4(3):151–160, 2010.

[25] K. Vieira, L. Barbosa, J. Freire, and A. S. da Silva. Siphon++: a hidden-webcrawler for keyword-based interfaces. In *CIKM*, pages 1361–1362, 2008.

[26] S. Wang, D. Agrawal, and A. El Abbadi. Hengha: data harvesting detection on hidden databases. In *ACM Cloud Computing Security Workshop*, pages 59–64, 2010.

[27] W. Wu, A. Doan, C. T. Yu, and W. Meng. Modeling and extracting deep-web query interfaces. In *Advances in Information and Int. Systs.*, pages 65–90. Springer, 2009.

A Flash-aware Buffering Scheme using On-the-fly Redo

Kyosung Jeong
Dept. of Electronics & Computer Engineering
Hanyang University
Seoul, Korea
Purenim@agape.hanyang.ac.kr

Sang-Wook Kim*
Dept. of Computer & Software
Hanyang University
Seoul, Korea
wook@hanyang.ac.kr

Sungchae Lim
Dept. of Computer Science
Dongduk Women's University
Seoul, Korea
sclim@dongduk.ac.kr

ABSTRACT

In this paper, we address how to reduce the amount of page updates in flash-based DBMS equipped with SSD (solid state drive). We propose a novel buffering scheme that evicts a dirty page *X* without flushing it into SSD, and restores the right image of *X* when *X* is requested for later access. The restoration of *X* having previous flushing-less eviction is performed through our online redo actions on *X*. We call this page-restoring online redo the *on-the-fly redo*. Although our on-the-fly redo mechanism has some overhead of increasing the number of page reads, this can be compensated by infrequent page updates. Additionally, since the proposed buffering scheme with the on-the-fly redo can easily support the *no-steal policy* in buffer management, we can enjoy the advantages of smaller logging overhead and faster recovery. Through the TPC-C benchmarks using a Berkeley DB, we show that our scheme shortens the transaction processing times by up to 53%.

Categories and Subject Descriptors

H.2.4 [**Database Management**]: Systems

Keywords

Flash storage; database recovery; buffer scheme; checkpointing

1. Introduction

Recently, a lot of research efforts have been done to efficiently use flash memory as primary storage media alternative to HDD in DBMS. The popularity of flash memory is mainly due to its faster I/O speeds and lower power consumption, even though it is still more expensive than HDD. However, the update cost in flash memory is much higher than the read cost or the write cost (for writing data into an *empty* page) because of its disability of in-place updating [2][5]. Therefore, it is crucial to reduce the number of page updates for developing high-performance flash-based DBMS [2][3].

Since traditional buffering schemes were mainly targeted at HDD with slow random reads, the hit rate of cached pages acts as a key yardstick for evaluating their efficiency [1][5]. As a result, the LRU (least-recently used) algorithm or its variations are regarded as the most reasonable algorithms for buffer replacement. However, those algorithms may easily yield a lot of flushing of dirty pages to the storage (i.e., incurring page updates), for buffer space reclamation [5]. In addition, traditional buffering schemes often flush out dirty pages into HDD just for faster recovery [1][4]. Because of a relatively cheap update cost in HDD, disk-based DBMS does not require any new buffering scheme whose main goal is to reduce the number of dirty pages flushed to storage media, even with sacrificing performance of other components. However, it is not the case in flash-based DBMS [2-5].

In this light, we propose a novel *flash-aware buffering scheme* that significantly reduces the amount of page updates in SSD (solid state drive). To this end, our scheme evicts a dirty page from the buffer without flushing it to SSD. To identify the pages that lose up-to-date images because of the flushing-less eviction, we keep the information on the history of flushing-less evictions in the *page/frame mapping table* that is managed in a buffer pool. At the same time, we maintain an *online log table* containing a portion of redo log records in order to enable a redo action to restore the correct image of a page experiencing its prior flushing-less eviction. We refer to this redo for online page restoration as the *on-the-fly redo*. Although the on-the-fly redo produces more I/Os for page reads and consumes more CPU time, such extra overheads are sufficiently compensated by the benefit from the considerable reduction of page updates in SSD.

By flushing-less evictions of dirty pages, we can easily support the *no-steal policy* [1] in buffer management, thereby eliminating the need of the undo phase during the system recovery time. In addition, our recovery algorithm does not update data pages for redoing committed updates during the redo phase. Instead, before restarting DBMS, it just rebuilds the before-crash state of the online log table by retrieving the log file in SSD. After system restart, we provide database consistency by applying the on-the-fly redo mechanism in accordance with user's page requests. Thanks to this simple and efficient recovery strategy, we do not need to flush dirty pages constantly to SSD for fast recovery, which is typically required in disk-based DBMS though. The proposed approach significantly reduces the amount of page updates to SSD in normal processing. The advantages of the approach is quantitatively verified through extensive experiments with TPC-C benchmarks conducted on the Berkeley DB that stores its database on SSD.

2. Background

As storage media for DBMS, flash-based SSD, which is composed of multiple flash dices and an embedded H/W

* Corresponding author

Permission to make digital or hard copies of all or part of this work for personal or classroom use is granted without fee provided that copies are not made or distributed for profit or commercial advantage and that copies bear this notice and the full citation on the first page. Copyrights for components of this work owned by others than ACM must be honored. Abstracting with credit is permitted. To copy otherwise, or republish, to post on servers or to redistribute to lists, requires prior specific permission and/or a fee. Request permissions from Permissions@acm.org.

CIKM'15, October 19-23, 2015, Melbourne, VIC, Australia.
© 2015 ACM. ISBN 978-1-4503-3794-6/15/10…$15.00.
DOI: http://dx.doi.org/10.1145/2806416.2806587

controller, has drawn much attention owing to its very fast and uniform speeds of random reads and low power consumption [2-4]. The page write into empty space is also 9~10 times faster, compared with cutting-edge HDD. Recently, the speeds of sequential reads/writes have been remarkably improved due to the use of internal cache memory [2]. To utilize such desirable I/O characteristics, a diversity of research has been done for developing flash-based DBMS [2-5]. For instance, the authors in [4] employ SSD as a kind of *cache storage* deployed between a buffer pool and HDD, thereby obtaining cached pages from SSD rather than HDD. Because of the limited usage of SSD as a cache storage, however, they could not drastically improve the DBMS performance.

Unlike this, the TIPL scheme [3] uses SSD as *primary* storage media and employs the page-granularity recovery mechanism to reduce the number of page updates. In TIPL, an update on any data page is substituted with writing of log data indicating that an update happens. Then, at the time of loading of a page *X*, the TIPL buffer manager performs redo or undo actions on *X*, if *X*'s log data exists. As a result, TIPL replaces a page update with writing of a smaller size of log data to a clean sector in SSD. In order to manage log data sectors within an SSD block, however, TIPL inevitably suffers from a significant degree of storage waste and I/O overhead for block merge operations. Furthermore, since it requires a specific type of SLC (single level cell) SSD, the TIPL scheme appears to be not acceptable in reality these days. To solve those problems, we design a new flash-aware buffering scheme that could run on off-the-shelf SSD without the use of reserved log areas in SSD.

3. Proposed Buffering Scheme

In this section, we present our buffer management scheme. We explain how to maintain an online log table for buffer pool management, how to handle transaction aborts, and how to handle transaction commits.

3.1 Buffer Pool with the Online Log Table

Similarly to the TIPL scheme, we employ a recovery mechanism, which originally aims at restoring a failed system, for the reduction of page updates. However, our buffering scheme does not require extra storage reserved for logging and does not perform undo actions in rolling aborted updates back. To explain this, we use Figure 1 that shows the organization of a buffer pool. The buffer pool has three components: A *set of buffer frames*, a *page/frame mapping table (PFMT)*, and an *online log table*. In this figure, we have five buffer frames for storing users' data, and the mapping information between page *id*'s and its corresponding frame index is maintained in PFMT. The online log table keeps a portion of log records. In Figure 1(a), buffer frames are full with five cached pages, among which pages *B*, *D* and *E* (grayed) are dirty. Log records describing update histories of dirty pages are indexed in the in-memory online log table. Pages *A* and *C* have no log record in the online log table since they are not dirty ones now.

Now, suppose that transaction *T2* wants to read a new page *F* to access a record within page *F*. If page *E* is selected as a victim for buffer replacement, then the cached image of *E* should be flushed into storage and its corresponding PFMT entry is deleted when a traditional buffering scheme is applied. Unlike this, our new buffering scheme simply cleans the frame of page *E* from the buffer pool without flushing it to storage. Correspondingly, the PFMT entry of *E* is updated with (*-1*, *dirty*) as in Figure 1(b) to indicate the flushing-less eviction of *E*. If a page with flushing-less eviction (such as page *E*) is requested later for its access, then our scheme reads the page from SSD and executes a redo action on it using the associated online (redo) log records. Note that only redo log records are required in our scheme since we never execute undo actions. Consequently, the proposed buffering scheme successfully avoids enforced flushing of a victim dirty page in buffer replacement, thereby considerably reducing the amount of page updates to SSD. We refer to such a real-time redo compensating a flushing-less eviction as the *on-the-fly redo*. Due to a big gap between the read cost and the update cost in SSD, the proposed on-the-fly redo mechanism is able to provide a significant performance gain.

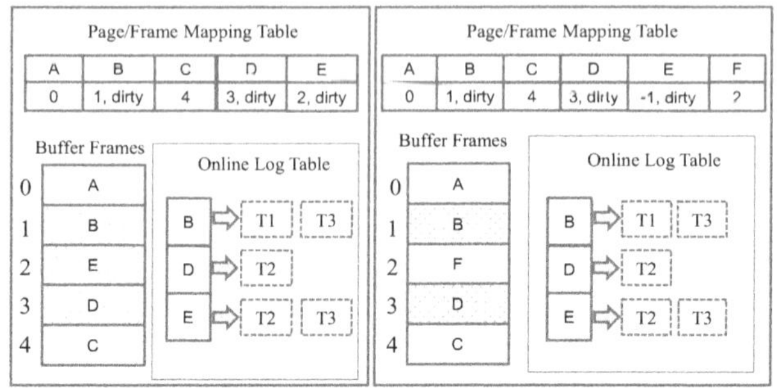

(a) State before the eviction of page *E*. (b) State after buffer replacement with page *F*.

Figure 1. State change in the buffer pool for buffer replacement.

3.2 Handling of Transaction Abort

Besides low update frequency, the on-the-fly redo mechanism provides another advantage of easily supporting the *no-steal policy* in buffer management. If we try to provide the no-steal policy without employing the on-the-fly redo mechanism, the buffer replacement algorithm cannot select a dirty page as a victim when it is owned by any of uncommitted transactions. This restriction is extremely undesirable in victim selections, and thus inevitably aggravates the cache hit rate. In particular, some long-lived transactions may degrade the buffering efficiency seriously [1][5]. For this reason, the steal policy is generally accepted in traditional DBMS. However, our proposed buffering scheme has a way to evict a dirty page from the buffer pool without flushing it into storage, thereby making it possible to delay the update time of a dirty page until its owner transactions commit.

Since the no-steal policy is guaranteed, we do not require the undo phase during recovery from system failure. However, we still need to roll back the updates from the transactions aborted during *normal processing*. In the case of traditional DBMS, compensation log records are stored for persistent cancellation of aborted updates [1][3]. The use of compensation log records, however, requires a complicated recovery algorithm and enlarges I/O overhead to save those compensation log records. However, we can easily handle transaction aborts based on our on-the-fly redo mechanism.

To show this, we use Figure 2, where transaction *T2* has updated two pages of *D* and *F*, and is about to abort at the time of Figure 2(a). In the case of page *D*, there is no update other than *T2*'s and the no-steal policy ensures that transaction *T2* did not affect the in-SSD image of page *D* yet. Therefore, it is sufficient to clean page *D* from the buffer pool to abort *T2*. Meanwhile, page *F* contains other two updates made by transactions *T1* and *T3*. To remove *T2*'s update on *E*, we delete *T2*'s log record from the online log table and set page *F* as required for the on-the-fly redo as in Figure 2(b). Consequently, page *F* is set to include the updates made by *T1* and *T3* only. While the actions for Figure 2(b) are underway, we neither create the compensation log records nor require any page updates to SSD.

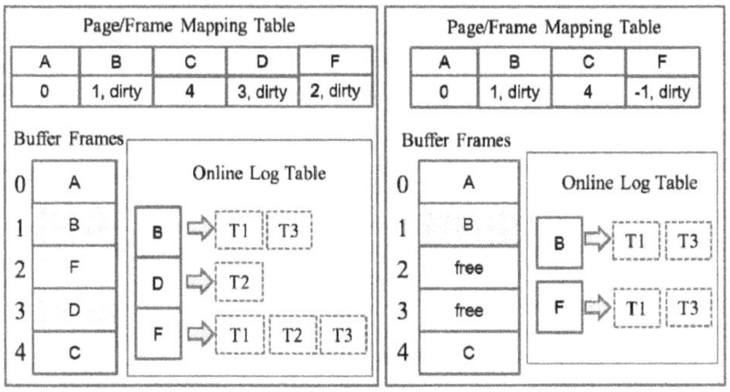

(a) State before transaction *T2* aborts. (b) State after *T2* has been aborted.

Figure 2. State change in the buffer pool due to transaction abort.

3.3 Handling of Transaction Commit

For transaction durability, we write *commit log records* before their owner transaction commits [1][3] as in traditional DBMS. However, while writing committed log records for guaranteeing transaction commit, we do not delete their copies bookkept in the online log table. To explain the idea behind this, let us assume that the online log records owned by *T3* are deleted when transaction *T3* of Figure 2(b) commits. Then, our on-the-fly redo cannot reconstruct page *B* or *F* correctly, if any of them is evicted. For this reason, the deletion of committed log records needs to be carefully conducted by following the checkpointing algorithm given in Section 4. Instead, while flushing dirty pages into storage, we gradually remove online log records for committed transactions.

Since traditional recovery schemes write log records in a *chronological manner*, uncommitted and committed log records are stored together in the same log page via a single I/O call. Since our scheme does not need undo log records, it is sufficient to store only committed log records. Owing to this idea, we save the committed log records only, and adopt the *group commit protocol* [1][3] for making log data written with a single I/O call as large as possible. According to this commit protocol, we defer the commit time of a group of transactions until we gather committed log records large enough to meet a predefined space utilization of the log space. With the group commit protocol, we can reduce a significant number of log writes as well as the waste of storage caused by empty space in the log file. Of course, we need to give a delay limit on the group commit.

4. System Recovery

In this section, we present our schemes of checkpointing and restart processes for system recovery.

4.1 Checkpointing

For faster system recovery, the fuzzy checkpointing scheme is usually accepted. It creates a dirty page table to save the *id*s of dirty pages being snapshot and the log file offset (i.e., log sequence number, LSN in short), from which the redo phase is started for system recovery. Since the scheme does not enforce flushing of dirty pages, the starting offset of the redo phase may go backwards too far in the presence of long-lived dirty pages. To prevent a too long redo phase, a disk-based buffering scheme usually takes a strategy to flush long-lived dirty pages at a proper rate during normal processing [1].

Unlike this, we do another job in checkpointing, i.e., compaction of the online log table. Through this log compaction, we delete online log records for committed transactions while flushing dirty pages into storage. Figure 3 shows our checkpointing algorithm. It is periodically initiated by a background-mode thread that works in collaboration with our buffer manager. To compact the log records of page *P*, the currently cached image of *P* is written into storage, if *P*'s log records are all committed ones (lines 10-11); otherwise, a new image of *P* is generated by applying the *committed* log records to the in-SSD image of *P*. Then, page *P* is updated with the newly generated image (line 15), and *P*'s PFMT entry is modified for demanding the on-the-fly redo on it. To reflect the above update (line 10 or 15), the *committed* log records of *P* are deleted (line 17). If log compaction is not possible with *P*, *P* is recorded as a dirty page (line 19). Note that page *P* having no committed log records is not included in the dirty page table according to our no-steal buffering policy. LSN of the first committed log record of *P* is saved (line 19). In the redo phase, the smallest LSN in all the dirty pages is used as a starting point of a log scan [1]. Finally, the master record in the recovery system is modified to point to the newly created checkpoint record.

```
input: th1 = threshold on No. of removable log records;
       th2 = threshold on the maximum age of log records;
1  SaveLogRec(LogFile, "Beginning of a Checkpoint");
2  Create an empty dirty page table and let it be denoted by DT;
3  foreach page P ∈ Online_Log_Table do // for each dirty page
4      R ← GetPointerToLog(P);  // R contains the list of the
       online log records (LRs) associated with page P
5      N_c ← GetNumCommitedRec(R); // Count committed LRs
6      if N_c ≥ 1 then // Beginning of log compaction
7          I_f = GetFirstIdxCommittedRec(R);
8          if N_c ≥ th1 or (CurrentLSN − R[I_f].LSN) ≥ th2 then
9              if N_c = |R| then // LRs are all committed records
10                 UpdatePage(P, Frame(P)); // Update P with its
                   current cached data
11                 Set the dirty bit of P's PFMT entry to zero;
12             else
13                 POldImage ← ReadPage(P) ; // from the SSD
14                 Image ← RedoWithCommitted(POldImage, R, N_c);
15                 UpdatePage(P, Image); // Actual node update
16                 P's PFMT entry ← (−1, dirty); // free P's frame
17             DeleteCommittedRec(Online_Log_Table, R, N_c);
18         else // P is bookkept as a dirty page in DT
19             DT.SaveDirtyPage(P, R[I_f].LSN);
20 SaveTheCheckpoint(LogFile, DT); ; // Logging of the DT
21 SaveLogRec(LogFile, "End of a New Checkpoint");
22 Update the master log record such that it points to this newly
   created checkpoint record;
```

Figure 3. Algorithm for creating a new checkpoint.

4.2 System Restart

To restart the system after failure, we read the latest checkpoint record by referring to the system master record. Then, we start to restore the crashed buffer pool by following the algorithm of Figure 4. Due to space limitations, we give only a core part of the algorithm. Initially, the log file pointer is set to the starting offset for the redo phase. Recall that, since we store only the log records of committed transactions, the log records in the algorithm are all committed ones. We ignore the log records of *P* (lines 3-4), if their LSNs are earlier than the latest checkpointing time and *P* is not a dirty page. This is because those log records are already reflected on storage. A log record *R* of *P* is inserted into the online log table (lines 7-8), if LSN of *R* is greater than that of the current image of *P*. Lastly, if page *P* has at least one online log record, then *P* becomes a page demanding the on-the-fly redo (line 10). During the recovery process, we reincarnate the online log table without page updates. Then, the database consistency is preserved through the on-the-fly redos on outdated pages. Due to the update-free redo phase and the absence of the undo phase, we can shorten the halting time considerably after an abrupt system failure.

```
SetFilePtrLoc(LogFile, RedoStart); // Rewind the file pointer
while (R_log ← GetNextLR(LogFile)) ≠ NULL do // Log scanning
    P = R_log.PageId; // Actions below will be done for P
    if LSN of R_log < LSN of DT and DT.Exist(P) ≠TRUE then
        continue ; // Ignore this log record
    if Frames.Exist(P) ≠ TRUE then
        ReadThePage(Frames, P); // Data page loading
    if LSN of R_log > Frames.GetPageLSN(P) then
        OnLineLog.AddLogRec(R_log); // Log record insertion
foreach page P having its log records in Online_Log_Table do
    P's PFMT entry ← (-1, dirty);
```

Figure 4. Algorithm for system recovery.

5. Performance Evaluation

For performance evaluation, we incorporated the proposed buffering and logging schemes into the open-sourced Berkeley DB. Then, we executed 100K transactions according to the TPC-C scenarios on both of the original Berkeley DB and that equipped with our buffering and logging schemes. Since our schemes are intended to work well for the off-the-shelf SSD, we have no special H/W assumptions. This is different from other work such as that presented in [3]. Table 1 shows the key H/W specifications for our TPC-C benchmark experiments.

Table 1. H/W Specs for the TPC-C benchmarks

SSD	Samsung 830 Series (128GB)
OS	Solaris 11 (4GB Memory)
Database Size	About 1GB
Data Page Size	8KB
Log Page Size	2KB

Figure 5 gives the comparisons of transaction processing times between *Original* (i.e., the original Berkeley DB) and *OTF* (i.e., that with our schemes). Both of group commit and ordinary immediate-commit protocols are applied to *OTF*. In our experiments, we used three different sizes for the buffer pool, i.e., 20MB, 40MB, and 60MB. Note that, for fair evaluation, we allocated some portion of memory for the online log table in *OTFs* from the total memory. As in the figure, we observe *OTFs* reduce the execution time by 20% to 53% in comparison with *Original*. Particularly, in the case of 60MB, the performance improvement rises up to 53% owing to the page updates greatly reduced. We also see that the group commit protocol reduces the processing time from 15% to 27%, compared with the immediate-commit protocol. It is mainly because the I/O cost for writing log data is decreased with more populated log pages.

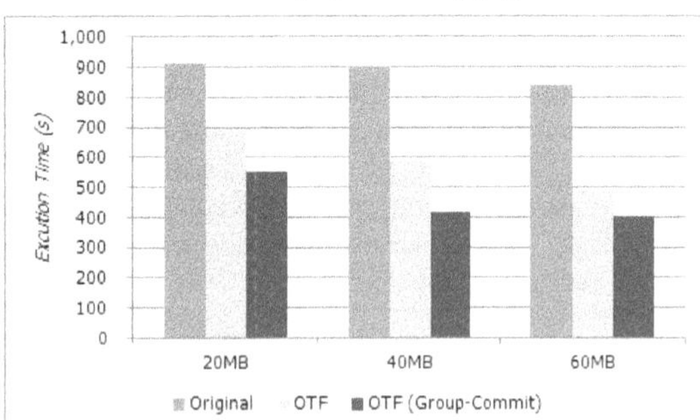

Figure 5. Comparisons on execution times.

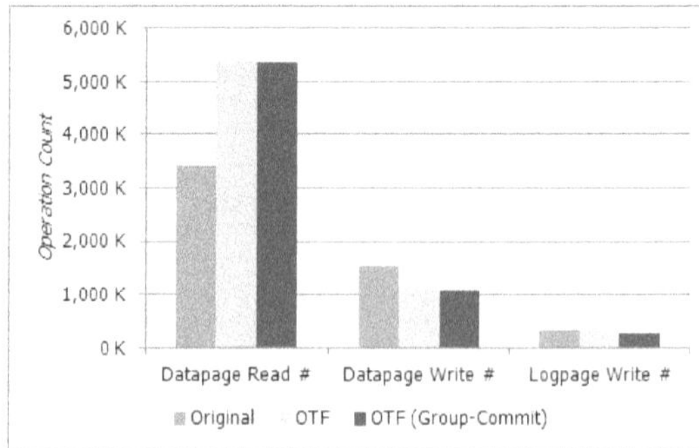

Figure 6. Comparisons on I/Os for transaction processing.

For more detailed analysis on performance improvement, we counted the average numbers of page reads and page writes (including updates) that arise during executing the benchmarks. Figure 6 shows the I/O counting results. We see that OTFs have a larger number of page reads by almost 45% but a less number of page writes by up to 30%. The increasing number of page reads is due to re-caching of the pages for the on-the-fly redos and a relatively low cache hit rate caused by reduced memory space for buffer frames, which is due to our fair evaluation, mentioned before.

6. Conclusions

In this paper, we have proposed a new flash-aware buffering scheme and a recovery mechanism for it. Our buffering scheme employs the page-granularity on-the-fly redo, which nullifies enforced dirty-page flushing at buffer replacement. Owing to our on-the-fly redo, we can substantially reduce the amount of page updates. Additionally, our scheme helps reduce the time for system recovery. Our scheme, however, requires some more memory allocated for the online log table, which could impair the system performance to a degree because of threshing in the buffer pool. Through extensive experiments with TPC-C benchmarks using a modified Berkeley DB running on SSD, we quantitatively verified the merits of our scheme in spite of less buffer space.

7. ACKNOWLEDGMENTS

This work was supported by the National Research Foundation of Korea (NRF) grant funded by the Korea government (MSIP) (No. NRF-2014R1A2A1A10054151).

8. REFERENCES

[1] Ramez Elmasri and Shamkant B. Navathe, Fundamentals of Database Systems, 6/E, Addison-Wesley, 2009.

[2] Yinan Li et al., "Tree Indexing on Solid State Drives," In *Proc.* of VLDB, 2010.

[3] Sang-Won Lee and Bongki Moon, "Transactional In-Page Logging for Multiversion Read Consistency and Recovery," In *Proc.* of ICDE, pp. 876-887, 2011.

[4] Jaeyoung Do, Donghui Zhang, Jignesh M. Patel, and David J. DeWitt, "Fast Peak-to-Peak Restart for SSD Buffer Pool Extension," In *Proc.* of ICDE, 2013.

[5] Jian Hu, Hong Jiang, Lei Tian, and Lei Xu, "PUD-LRU: An Erase-Efficient Write Buffer Management Algorithm for Flash Memory SSD," In *Proc.* of IEEE MASCOTS, 2010.

Defragging Subgraph Features for Graph Classification

Haishuai Wang, Peng Zhang, Ivor Tsang, Ling Chen, Chengqi Zhang
Centre for Quantum Computation & Intelligent Systems (QCIS), FEIT,
University of Technology, Sydney, Ultimo, NSW 2007, Australia
{Haishuai.Wang@student., Peng.Zhang@, Ivor.Tsang@, Ling.Chen@, Chengqi.Zhang@}uts.edu.au

ABSTRACT

Graph classification is an important tool for analysing structured and semi-structured data, where subgraphs are commonly used as the feature representation. However, the number and size of subgraph features crucially depend on the threshold parameters of frequent subgraph mining algorithms. Any improper setting of the parameters will generate many trivial short-pattern subgraph fragments which dominate the feature space, distort graph classifiers and bury interesting long-pattern subgraphs. In this paper, we propose a new *Subgraph Join Feature Selection* (**SJFS**) algorithm. The SJFS algorithm, by forcing graph classifiers to join short-pattern subgraph fragments, can defrag trivial subgraph features and deliver long-pattern interesting subgraphs. Experimental results on both synthetic and real-world social network graph data demonstrate the performance of the proposed method.

Categories and Subject Descriptors

H.2.8 [**Data Management**]: Database Applications—*Data Mining*

Keywords

Graph Classification; Subgraph Join; Feature Selection

1. INTRODUCTION

Graph mining is an important branch of the data mining research. Compared with vectorial data, graph data do not have features readily available to fit into popularly used classifiers such as SVMs and decision trees. Therefore, many research efforts [1, 2, 4] have been focused on selecting discriminative subgraphs as vectorial features for graph classification.

However, generating subgraph features using existing frequent subgraph mining algorithms brings new challenges. The number and size of subgraph features crucially depend on the threshold parameters in frequent pattern mining algorithms. A common situation is that we don't have the prior knowledge of the best threshold parameters and usually set it to be a small number such that many possible candidate subgraph features can be preserved, and we expect the following steps of graph classification and feature selection can remove unnecessary subgraph features. However, an unpleasant situation is that many algorithms will be trapped into short-pattern subgraph fragments, and the interesting long subgraph patterns are buried behind the fragments.

This research is motivated by a recent work on extracting subgraphs from a real-world social network cascade data set for network outbreak prediction. The data set is downloaded from *http://snap.stanford.edu/infopath/*. In the experiments, we observed that the feature space is dominated by subgraph fragments due to the *downward closure property* of the frequent subgraph mining algorithms [3], *i.e.*, the short-pattern subgraph fragments are always more frequent than long-pattern interesting subgraphs. Fig. 1 shows the example that a long-pattern subgraph feature f_3 is buried under two subgraph fragments f_1 and f_2 and a classifier

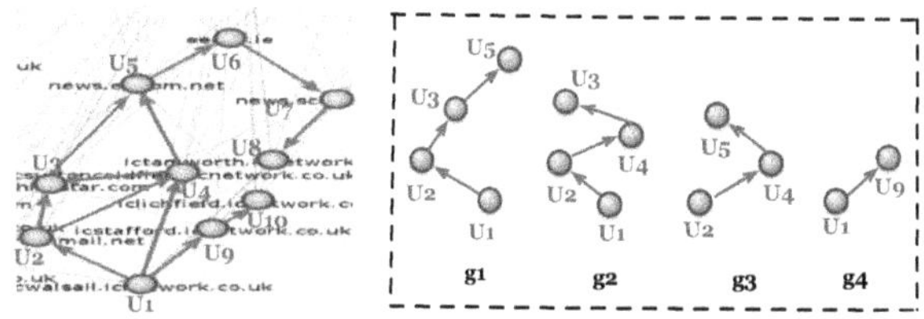

(a) A social network cascade data set from http://snap.stanford.edu/infopath

(b) Four graphs of cascade data (g_1, g_2, g_3, g_4)

	f1: U1→U2	f2: U2→U3	Label
g1	1	1	+1
g2	1	1	+1
g3	0	0	-1
g4	0	0	-1

(c) Subgraph features f1 and f2

	f3: U1→U2→U3	Label
g1	1	+1
g2	1	+1
g3	0	-1
g4	0	-1

(d) Subgraph feature f3

Figure 1: An illustration of a long-pattern subgraph feature buried under two short-pattern subgraph features in the information cascade data. Consider four graphs $g_1, \dots, g_4$. g_1 and g_2 from class "+1" while g_3 and g_4 from "-1". Assume we have two short-pattern subgraphs $f_1 : U_1 \to U_2$ and $f_2 : U_2 \to U_3$, and a long-pattern subgraph $f_3 : U_1 \to U_2 \to U_3$ by joining f_1 and f_2. If one feature is allowed to select for classification, then f_1 or f_2 is likely to be selected, instead of the more interesting f_3.

Permission to make digital or hard copies of all or part of this work for personal or classroom use is granted without fee provided that copies are not made or distributed for profit or commercial advantage and that copies bear this notice and the full citation on the first page. Copyrights for components of this work owned by others than ACM must be honored. Abstracting with credit is permitted. To copy otherwise, or republish, to post on servers or to redistribute to lists, requires prior specific permission and/or a fee. Request permissions from Permissions@acm.org.
CIKM'15, October 19-23, 2015, Melbourne, VIC, Australia.
© 2015 ACM. ISBN 978-1-4503-3794-6/15/10 ...$15.00.
DOI: http://dx.doi.org/10.1145/2806416.2806585.

is likely to choose the two subgraph fragments instead of the more interesting long-pattern subgraph feature which reflects a latent social group.

To discover long-pattern subgraphs buried under a huge number of subgraph fragments, we need to systematically design a new feature selection method. Generally, we set a small value of the frequency support threshold, such that all candidate subgraphs can be preserved in the feature space. However, this method will unavoidably generate an exponential number of short-pattern subgraph fragments which bury interesting long-pattern subgraph features. Therefore, we need to design a new subgraph join approach that can select long-pattern subgraphs. The challenges of designing such a subgraph join approach are as follows:

- *Challenge 1: how to join subgraph fragments.* There are many possible ways to join subgraph fragments. Thus, join rules between subgraph fragments need to be established for efficient computation.
- *Challenge 2: how to design a feature selection model that prefers to select long-pattern subgraph features.* New constraints are required to force traditional max-margin based graph classifiers to select long-pattern subgraph features.
- *Challenge 3: how to evaluate the performance of the proposed method.* Both real-world and synthetic data sets are required to test and compare the proposed method with existing methods.

To solve the challenges, we propose in this paper a new Subgraph Join Feature Selection algorithm (SJFS for short). To solve *Challenge 1*, SJFS uses a correlated subgraph join method to defrag short-pattern subgraph fragments (Definition 3 in Section 2). To solve *Challenge 2*, new constraints of joining subgraphs are added to the max-margin graph classifier (Eq.(1) in Section 3) so that the classifier prefers long-pattern subgraphs. To solve *Challenge 3*, we evaluate the proposed algorithm using both synthetic and real-world social network cascade data (Section 4).

2. PRELIMINARIES

We consider directed and acyclic graphs (DAG). Given a directed acyclic graph $G = (V, E)$, $g_i = (V', E')$ is a subgraph of G, *i.e.*, $g_i \subseteq G$, iff $V' \subseteq V$, and $E' \subseteq E$. If g_i is a subgraph of G, then G is a supergraph of g_i. We use lower-case **bold** letters to represent vectors and upper-case **bold** letters to represent matrices. For example, the symbol $\mathbf{e}$ represents a unit vector with all entries being 1. For a binary classification problem, the purpose is to learn a classification boundary from a training graph set $\{(G_k, y_k)\}$, $1 \leq k \leq n$, where each G_k is a training graph with class label denoted by $y_k \in \{-1, +1\}$.

DEFINITION 1. ***(Subgraph Features)*** *Let $S = \{g_1, \cdots, g_m\}$ be a subgraph feature space. Then, each graph G_k can be encoded as an m-dimensional vector $\boldsymbol{x}_k$ with each element $\boldsymbol{x}_k^u (1 \leq u \leq m)$ denoted by $\boldsymbol{x}_k^u = I(g_u \subseteq G_k)$, $\forall g_u \in S$, where $I(\cdot)$ equals to 1 if the condition satisfies, otherwise, 0.*

Fig. 2 explains the generation of a subgraph feature space. Consider a graph $A \rightarrow B \cdots \rightarrow E$. The graph contains subgraphs $B \rightarrow C$ and $C \rightarrow D \rightarrow E$. Then, the elements in the binary subgraph feature vector are set to 1.

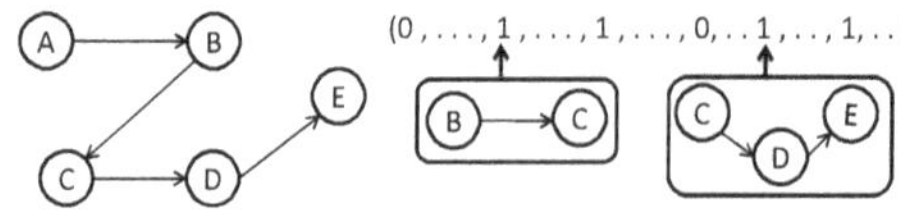

Figure 2: The subgraph feature space. The graph (left) is converted to a binary feature vector (right) by examining the existence of all subgraphs based on Definition 1.

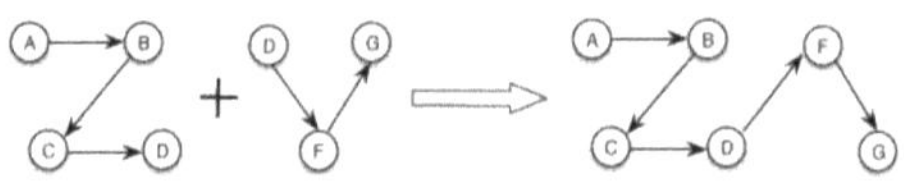

Figure 3: The join of correlated subgraph fragments.

Note the concatenation of two subgraphs is uncertain because of graph isomorphic [5]. In this paper, we only consider to join correlated subgraphs given in Definition 2, because correlated subgraphs have a high probability to generate interesting long-pattern subgraphs. The join result given in Definition 3 is unique, as shown in Fig. 3.

DEFINITION 2. ***(Correlated Subgraphs)*** *Consider two directed acyclic subgraphs $g_i = \{V_\alpha, \cdots, V_\beta\}$ and $g_j = \{V_\alpha', \cdots, V_\beta'\}$, if $V_\beta = V_\alpha'$ or $V_\beta' = V_\alpha$, we regard g_i and g_j as correlated subgraphs.*

DEFINITION 3. ***(Correlated Subgraphs Join (CSJ))*** *If $g_i = \{V_\alpha, \cdots, V_\beta\}$ and $g_j = \{V_\alpha', V_\gamma' \cdots, V_\beta'\}$ are correlated subgraphs, then $g_i \bigotimes g_j = \{V_\alpha, \cdots, V_\beta, V_\gamma', \cdots, V_\beta'\}$ is a new generated subgraph after CSJ, where $\bigotimes$ is a concatenation operation.*

Given a set of graphs, the dimension of subgraph feature space exponentially increases *w.r.t.* graph size. Therefore, it is impractical to use all derived subgraphs as features. Inspired by the frequent substructures popularly used in graph classification, we use frequent subgraphs to prune trivial subgraph patterns.

3. THE PROPOSED METHOD

We present a *Subgraph Join Feature Selection* algorithm (SJFS) based on a max-margin graph classifier and the CSJ definition. The proposed SJFS algorithm can handle extremely high dimensional subgraph features. Subgraph join generates long-pattern subgraphs without actually generating all candidate subgraphs. After subgraph concatenation, discriminative subgraph features can be selected.

We introduce a feature scaling vector $\boldsymbol{\delta} = [\delta_1, \cdots, \delta_m]^T \in \{0, 1\}^m$ with $||\boldsymbol{\delta}||_1 = \sum_{i=1}^m \delta_j \leq B$ to indicate whether the feature is selected ($\delta_j = 1$) or not ($\delta_j = 0$). Thus, at most B subgraphs are selected. Given a graph G_i, we impose $\boldsymbol{\delta} = [\delta_1, \cdots, \delta_m]^T$ to a re-scaled example $\hat{\mathbf{x}_i} = \mathbf{x}_i \bigodot \boldsymbol{\delta}$, where $\mathbf{x}_i \odot \boldsymbol{\delta}$ represents the element-wise product between vectors $\mathbf{x}_i$ and $\boldsymbol{\delta}$. Therefore, the decision function is defined as, $f(\mathbf{x}_i) = \mathbf{w}^T (\mathbf{x}_i \odot \boldsymbol{\delta})$, where $\mathbf{w} = [w_1, \cdots, w_m]^T$ is a weight vector.

Formally, we add extra constraints in the graph classifier to select long-pattern subgraphs by joining short-pattern fragments. The new constrain is stated as: if two short-pattern subgraph fragments p_a and p_b have been selected, denoted by $\delta_{p_a} = 1$ and $\delta_{p_b} = 1$, then the derived pattern $p_a \otimes p_b$ is likely to be selected, denoted by $\delta_{\ p_a \otimes p_b} = 1$. Based on the constraint, we obtain a new long-pattern driven max-margin graph classifier as follows,

$$\min_{\delta \in \Delta} \min_{w,\epsilon,b} \quad \frac{1}{2}||w||^2 + C\sum_{i=1}^{n} \xi_i$$
$$\text{s.t.:} \quad y_i(\mathbf{w}^T(\mathbf{x}_i \odot \boldsymbol{\delta}) + b) \geq 1 - \xi_i \qquad (1)$$
$$\xi_i \geq 0, \ i = 1, \ldots, m.$$
$$\delta_{\ p_a \otimes p_b} = 1, \forall \ \delta_{p_a} = 1 \wedge \delta_{p_b} = 1$$

where $\mathbf{w} \in \mathbb{R}^m$ and b determine the classification boundary, $\xi_i \geq 0$ is the empirical error of example $\mathbf{x}_i$, $\boldsymbol{\Delta} = \{\delta \in \mathbb{R}^m \mid ||\boldsymbol{\delta}||_1 \leq B, \delta_j \in \{0,1\}, j = 1, \cdots, m\}$ be the domain of $\boldsymbol{\delta}$, and C is a trade-off parameter. The problem is non-convex with respect to w and δ simultaneously.

The new constraint shows that if two subgraph fragments can be concatenated according to Definition 3, then the new subgraph will be set to 1. When $\boldsymbol{\delta}$ is fixed, Eq. (1) degenerates to a standard SVM.

By introducing the Lagrangian multiplier $\alpha_i \geq 0$ to each constraint $y_i(\mathbf{w}^T(\mathbf{x}_i \odot \boldsymbol{\delta} + b) \geq 1 - \xi_i$ and setting the derivatives of the Lagrange function to 0 with respect to parameters $\mathbf{w}, \xi$ and b, respectively, we obtain, $\mathbf{w} = \sum_{i=1}^{n} \alpha_i y_i (\mathbf{x}_i \odot \boldsymbol{\delta}), \sum_{i=1}^{n} \alpha_i y_i = 0, \ 0 \leq \alpha_i \leq C, \delta_{\ p_a \otimes p_b} = 1, \forall \ \delta_{p_a} = 1 \wedge \delta_{p_b} = 1$.

Plugging the above results back into Eq.(1), and interchanging the order of $min_{\delta \in \mathbf{D}}$ and $\max_{\boldsymbol{\alpha} \in \mathcal{A}}$ based on the minimax saddle-point theorem, we obtain the dual form of the original problem as follows,

$$\min_{\alpha \in \mathcal{A}} \max_{\delta \in \Delta} \quad \frac{1}{2}||\sum_{i=1}^{n} \alpha_i y_i (\mathbf{x}_i \odot \boldsymbol{\delta})||^2 - \mathbf{e}^T \boldsymbol{\alpha} \qquad (2)$$
$$s.t. \quad \delta_{\ p_a \otimes p_b} = 1, \forall \ \delta_{p_a} = 1 \wedge \delta_{p_b} = 1.$$

where $\mathcal{A} = \{\boldsymbol{\alpha} | \sum_{i=1}^{n} \alpha_i y_i = 0, \boldsymbol{\alpha} \geq 0\}$, $\mathbf{e}$ is unit vector.

Apparently, the primal problem in Eq.(1) can be equivalently formulated as its dual given in Eq.(2). Eq.(2) has only two variables $\boldsymbol{\delta}$ and $\boldsymbol{\alpha}$, and it is linear with respect to $\boldsymbol{\delta}$ and convex *w.r.t.* $\boldsymbol{\alpha}$, which can be solved by a *block coordinate descent approach* that alternates between $\boldsymbol{\delta}$ and $\boldsymbol{\alpha}$.

Given a fixed $\mathbf{d}$, the optimization problem in Eq. (2) is reduced as follows: (**Optimization 1**: fix $\boldsymbol{\delta}$ and solve $\boldsymbol{\alpha}$)

$$\min_{\alpha} \quad \frac{1}{2}||\sum_{i=1}^{n} \alpha_i y_i \hat{\mathbf{x}_i}||^2 - \mathbf{e}^T \boldsymbol{\alpha}$$
$$\text{s.t.} \quad \sum_{i=1}^{n} \alpha_i y_i = 0, \ \alpha_i \geq 0, \ i = 1, \ldots, n, \qquad (3)$$
$$\delta_{\ p_a \otimes p_b} = 1, \forall \ \delta_{p_a} = 1 \wedge \delta_{p_b} = 1.$$

where $\hat{\mathbf{x}_i}$ is re-scaled by the given $\boldsymbol{\delta}$, *i.e.*, $\hat{\mathbf{x}_i} = \mathbf{x}_i \odot \boldsymbol{\delta}$. Due to the sparsity of scaler $\boldsymbol{\delta}$, the above problem can be solved by using the standard quadratic programming with a small set of features $\hat{\mathbf{x}}_i$.

When the variable $\boldsymbol{\alpha}$ is determined, we select at most B features as in Eq. (4). (**Optimization 2**: fix $\boldsymbol{\alpha}$ and solve $\boldsymbol{\delta}$)

$$\max_{\delta} \quad ||\sum_{j=1}^{n} \alpha_j y_j (\mathbf{x}_j \odot \boldsymbol{\delta})||^2$$
$$\text{s.t.} \quad \sum_{j=1}^{m} \delta_j \leq B, \ 0 \leq d_j \leq 1, \ j = 1, \cdots, m, \qquad (4)$$
$$\delta_{\ p_a \otimes p_b} = 1, \forall \ \delta_{p_a} = 1 \wedge \delta_{p_b} = 1.$$

To solve Eq. (4), we define a score function to denote the weight of each feature, i.e., $\mathbf{c}(\boldsymbol{\alpha}) = \sum_{i=1}^{n} \alpha_i y_i \mathbf{x}_i \in \mathbb{R}^m$. Based on the above definition of feature weight, we have $\| \sum_{j=1}^{n} \alpha_j y_j (\mathbf{x}_j \odot \boldsymbol{\delta})\|^2 = \sum_{j=1}^{m} [c_j(\boldsymbol{\alpha})]^2 \delta_j$. Then, the optimization problem in Eq. (4) can be further converted to a linear programming problem with respect to $\boldsymbol{\delta}$ as follows:

$$\max_{\delta} \quad \sum_{j=1}^{m} [c_j(\alpha)]^2 \delta_j$$
$$\text{s.t.} \quad \sum_{j=1}^{m} \delta_j \leq B, \ 0 \leq d_j \leq 1, \ j = 1, \cdots, m, \qquad (5)$$
$$\delta_{\ p_a \otimes p_b} = 1, \forall \ \delta_{p_a} = 1 \wedge \delta_{p_b} = 1.$$

Eq. (5) can be solved analytically. First, we construct a feasible solution by finding the largest scores $[c_j(\alpha)]^2$. Then, we set the scaler δ_j to 1 and the remaining to 0.

Note that Eq. (5) can be solved efficiently by using online linear programming where the constraint matrix is revealed column by column along with the objective function, *i.e.*, the features are processed column by column in a one-scan manner.

Table 1 shows the three different types of results when generating a long-pattern subgraph p_{ab} from two short-pattern subgraph fragments p_a and p_b. For example, consider the four training graphs $g_1, \cdots, g_4$, where g_1 and g_2 belong to the same group while g_3 and g_4 fall into another group. Assume we have obtained two subgraph fragments $P(a) = A \rightarrow B$ and $P(b) = B \rightarrow C$. Then, we can generate a long-pattern subgraph $A \rightarrow B \rightarrow C$ based on Definition 3. The classifier may have three different types of results, Equal, Improve and Reduce. Therefore, we have the following intuitive conclusion.

Table 1: Analysis of the new constraint

X	Equal			Improve			Reduce		
	p_a	p_b	p_{ab}	p_a	p_b	p_{ab}	p_a	p_b	p_{ab}
g_1	1	1	1	1	1	1	1	0	0
g_2	1	1	1	1	1	1	1	0	0
g_3	0	0	0	1	0	0	0	1	0
g_4	0	0	0	0	1	1	0	1	0

OBSERVATION 1. Consider two subgraph fragments $p_a = 1$ and $p_b = 1$, if $p_{ab} = p_a \otimes p_b$, then the generated long-pattern subgraphs p_{ab} can be used to replace the original two patterns p_a and p_b.

4. EXPERIMENTS

To validate the performance, we use four synthetic datasets and one real-world social network information cascade data[1] for testing. The real world data contains about 27.6 million news articles and blog posts from 3.3 million online sources. We select cascades having more than 300 nodes as the positive class (877 cascades in total), and cascades with nodes less than 100 as the negative class (27,515,721 cascades in total). Then, we randomly select 877 negative cascades combined with the 877 positive cascades for experiments. The purpose is to extract interesting long-pattern subgraph features for cascade data classification and prediction.

We compare our algorithm with two methods: 1) subgraph feature selection without subgraph join, denoted by **SFS**, and 2) random subgraph feature selection, denoted by **RSFS**. The accuracy, F1 score, precision and recall are used as measures under support thresholds of 30, 50, 70 and 90. The RSFS algorithm selects B features randomly under the standard SVM classifier.

[1]http://snap.stanford.edu/infopath/

Table 2: F1 score *w.r.t.* support threshold.

Data	*Supp*	SJFS	SFS	RSFS
Albert Barabasi	90	0.651±0.126	**0.682±0.077**	0.611±0.070
	70	**0.791±0.102**	0.770±0.094	0.762±0.027
	50	**0.885±0.037**	0.839±0.094	0.785±0.094
	30	0.903±0.028	**0.903±0.006**	0.667±0.059
Erdos Renyi	90	**0.750±0.125**	0.747±0.178	0.667±0.067
	70	**0.804±0.058**	0.803±0.067	0.787±0.058
	50	0.810±0.122	**0.815±0.100**	0.798±0.044
	30	**0.889±0.114**	0.826±0.114	0.824±0.181
Forest Fire	90	**0.801±0.007**	0.793±0.027	0.710±0.067
	70	**0.880±0.004**	0.799±0.035	0.746±0.001
	50	**0.887±0.002**	0.826±0.044	0.785±0.030
	30	0.899±0.105	**0.916±0.105**	0.889±0.117
Small World	90	0.526±0.005	0.404±0.003	**0.579±0.008**
	70	**0.592±0.009**	0.587±0.009	0.585±0.016
	50	**0.746±0.003**	0.598±0.005	0.595±0.007
	30	0.751±0.021	**0.763±0.006**	0.652±0.107
Real-world Cascade	90	**0.778±0.037**	0.746±0.023	0.611±0.167
	70	0.813±0.101	**0.832±0.035**	0.754±0.117
	50	0.901±0.034	**0.913±0.061**	0.732±0.201
	30	**0.923±0.013**	0.892±0.091	0.867±0.021

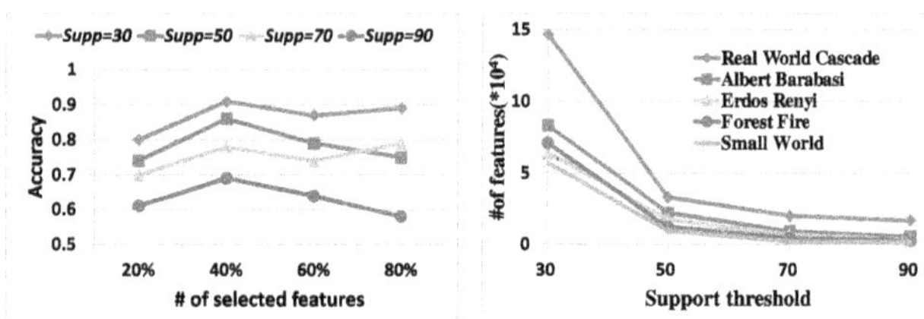

(i) SJFS: accuracy *w.r.t.* # of selected features.

(ii) # of subgraph features *w.r.t.* support threshold.

Figure 4: Parameter study *w.r.t.* the number of selected features and subgraph features.

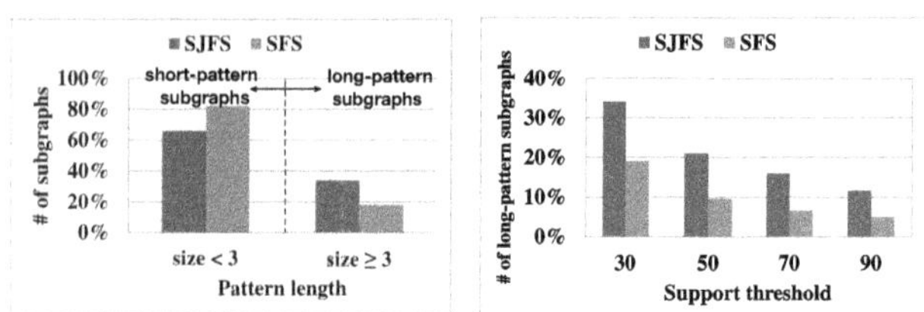

(i) # of subgraph patterns *w.r.t.* pattern length.

(ii) # of long-pattern subgraphs *w.r.t.* support threshold.

Figure 5: Percentage of patterns *w.r.t.* support threshold and pattern length.

Parameter study: We test SJFS *w.r.t.* the number of selected features B and the number of subgraph features. From Fig. 4 (i), we observe that when B equals to 30% of all the generated features, SJFS achieves the best performance. Fig. 4 (ii) shows the number of subgraph features decreases when the support threshold increases.

Experimental results: Fig. 5(i) shows the proportion of short-pattern subgraph features (length < 3) and long-pattern subgraph features (length ≥ 3) when support equals to 30. Fig. 5 (ii) shows the comparisons of long-pattern subgraphs. The performance *w.r.t.* the support thresholds on the real world data is given in Figs. 6 and 7. Table 2 gives the result on the synthetic data set. From these results, we have four interesting observations: 1) SJFS selects more long-pattern subgraphs and has more long-pattern subgraphs under different support thresholds than SFS. 2) The classification

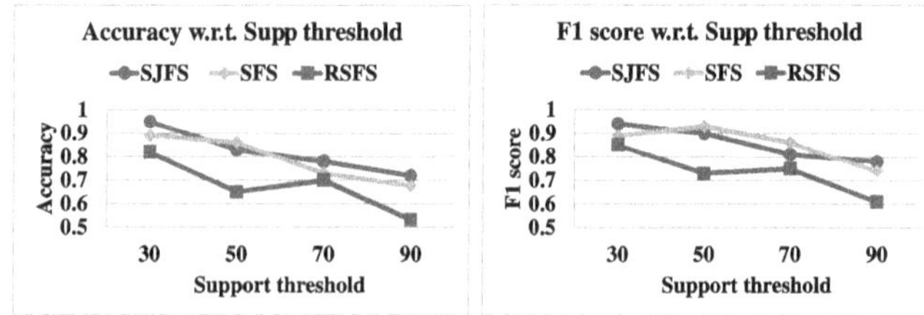

Figure 6: Accuracy and F1 score *w.r.t.* support threshold.

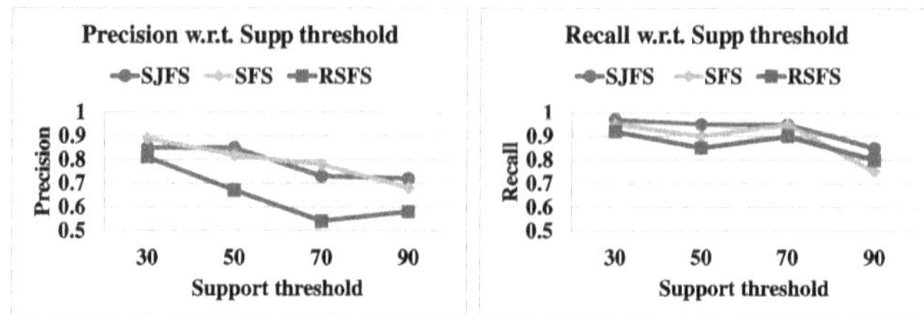

Figure 7: Precision and Recall *w.r.t.* support threshold.

precision, accuracy and F1 score decrease when the support threshold increases. This is because more information will be available when the support threshold increases. 3) The results of precision, accuracy, F1 score and recall show that SJFS and SFS mostly outperform RSFS. SJFS and SFS have similar results. 4) The results in 3) validate our discussion in Table 1. The column "Improve" indicates that SJFS has higher accuracy than SFS, while columns "Equal" and "Reduce" explain why SJFS and SFS have similar results.

5. CONCLUSION

We have studied a new problem of defragging subgraph features for graph classification. The problem is motivated by our recent study on extracting subgraph features from social network cascade data for network outbreak prediction. We have observed that short-pattern subgraph fragments always dominate feature space due to the *downward closure property* of the frequent subgraph mining algorithms [3] and long-pattern interesting subgraphs are often buried under subgraph fragments. In this paper we have proposed a new *Subgraph Join Feature Selection* (**SJFS**) algorithm as the solution. SJFS joins subgraph fragments during graph classification and delivers long-pattern subgraphs. Experiments have validated the performance of the proposed method.

6. ACKNOWLEDGEMENT

This work was supported by the Australian Research Council (ARC) Discovery Project under Grant No. DP140100545 and DP140102206, and ARC Future Fellowship FT130100746.

7. REFERENCES

[1] W. Zheng, L. Zou, et al. Efficient Subgraph Skyline Search Over Large Graphs. *CIKM*, 2014:1529-1538.

[2] X. Kong, P.S. Yu. Semi-Supervised Feature Selection for Graph Classification. *KDD*, pp. 2010: 793-802.

[3] X. Yan, X. Zhou, J. Han, Mining closed relational graphs with connectivity constraints. *KDD*, 2005.

[4] X. Yan, and J. Han. gSpan: graph-based substructure pattern mining. *ICDM*, pp. 721-724, 2002.

[5] Y. Zhu, L. Qin, et al. High efficiency and quality: large graphs matching. *CIKM*, 1755-1764, 2011.

Structural Constraints for Multipartite Entity Resolution with Markov Logic Network

Tengyuan Ye*
College of Computer Science & Technology
Zhejiang University
ytyuan1993@gmail.com

Hady W. Lauw
School of Information Systems
Singapore Management University
hadywlauw@smu.edu.sg

ABSTRACT

Multipartite entity resolution seeks to match entity mentions across several collections. An entity mention is presumed unique within a collection, and thus could match at most one entity mention in each of the other collections. In addition to domain-specific features considered in entity resolution, there are a number of domain-invariant structural contraints that apply in this scenario, including one-to-one assignment as well as cross-collection transitivity. We propose a principled solution to the multipartite entity resolution problem, building on the foundation of Markov Logic Network (MLN) that combines probabilistic graphical model and first-order logic. We describe how the domain-invariant structural constraints could be expressed appropriately in terms of Markov logic, flexibly allowing joint modeling with domain-specific features. Experiments on two real-life datasets, each spanning four collections, show the utility of this approach and validate the contributions of various MLN components.

Categories and Subject Descriptors

H.3.3 [**Information Search and Retrieval**]: Clustering; H.2.8 [**Database Applications**]: Data mining

Keywords

entity resolution; markov logic network; structural constraints;

1. INTRODUCTION

Often the same entity, be it a person, document, or object, is mentioned in several separate collections, and there is a need to identify that several mentions refer to the same entity. For instance, when two health organizations merge, the medical records of patients need to be integrated. While shopping for a camera, one may wish to compare prices on online shops, such as BestBuy, Newegg, or Amazon.

*Work done while at Singapore Management University.

Permission to make digital or hard copies of all or part of this work for personal or classroom use is granted without fee provided that copies are not made or distributed for profit or commercial advantage and that copies bear this notice and the full citation on the first page. Copyrights for components of this work owned by others than the author(s) must be honored. Abstracting with credit is permitted. To copy otherwise, or republish, to post on servers or to redistribute to lists, requires prior specific permission and/or a fee. Request permissions from Permissions@acm.org.

CIKM'15, October 19–23, 2015, Melbourne, Australia.

Copyright is held by the owner/author(s). Publication rights licensed to ACM.

ACM 978-1-4503-3794-6/15/10 ...$15.00.
DOI: http://dx.doi.org/10.1145/2806416.2806590.

This problem, formalized by [3], is known by several terms including entity resolution [2, 9], deduplication, or reference reconciliation. Most works focus on either the similarity measure between two mentions [10, 7, 6], or the algorithmic framework to match the mentions (e.g., graph matching [5]).

This paper focuses on structural constraints facing the entity resolution problem. Real-world scenarios have varying structures. In one scenario (deduplication), a single collection may contain duplicate elements to be resolved. In a different scenario (referred to as multipartite resolution), two or more collections need to be integrated into a unified collection, by resolving which entity from one collection corresponds to which entity from another collection.

Focusing on the multipartite resolution scenario, we assume that each collection is free of duplicates, because each collection belongs to a party (e.g., an online shop, or a hospital) with an interest in maintaining a high-quality collection, or because the collection has been previously cleaned up through deduplication (a related, yet distinct research problem). Thus, when integrating two collections, there is a natural constraint that a mention from one collection could match at most one mention from the other. One possible approach is graph matching [5], whereby a one-to-one assignment may be obtained from maximum weight bipartite matching. However, for three or more collections [15], the 3-dimensional matching problem is NP-hard [1].

Here, we take the approach of incorporating structural constraints into entity resolution with Markov Logic Network (MLN) [12]. An MLN-based formulation has several advantages. First, the proposed domain-invariant structural constraints can be combined with previous MLN predicates for entity resolution based on domain-specific features [14] or constraints [13]. Second, it is "extendable", as MLN is an open framework that allows joining the entity resolution task with other mutually-reinforcing tasks such as segmentation [11]. Third, MLN is probabilistic, whereby the importance of different constraints can be learned from data.

Contributions. *First*, we describe a series of domain-invariant structural constraints for MLN-based bipartite entity resolution (see Section 3), and investigate how the constraints extend to multipartite structures (see Section 4). *Second*, we validate the effectiveness of these constraints on real-life datasets of phones and cameras (see Section 5).

2. OVERVIEW

Problem Statement. As input, we are given a set of N collections $\{X_1, X_2, \ldots, X_N\}$. Each collection X_i consists of M_i entity mentions, where each mention in X_i is associated with some features. Our focus in this work is on structural constraints, and not on the feature set or similarity measure. For simplicity, and without loss of generality, for subsequent discussions we assume there is a single feature, which is the name of the entity, and we use Jaccard similarity [6].

We associate two mentions $x \in X_i$ and $y \in X_j$ from different collections with a binary variable $\texttt{Match}(x, y)$, whose value is 1 if x and y "match", i.e., referring to the same entity, and is 0 otherwise. Our objective is to determine the states of these variables for all pairs of entity mentions. If x and x' belong to the same collection X_i, trivially $\texttt{Match}(x, x') = 0$, i.e., each collection is assumed to be free of duplicates.

Markov Logic Network (MLN). Our approach is to express structural constraints for entity resolution as first-order logic formulae. Each formula may use four types of symbols: constants, variables, functions, and predicates. Constants are objects in the domain of interest, which in this case are the entity mentions. Variables, e.g., x, range over objects in the domain. Predicates represent relations among objects, e.g., $\texttt{Similar}(x, y)$ is a predicate that indicates that x and y are similar in feature, whereas $\texttt{Match}(x, y)$ represents that x and y refer to the same entity. The formulae for the structural constraints are specified in Sections 3 and 4.

Some constraints are *hard* constraints, i.e., they must be satisfied. Others are *probabilistic* constraints, i.e., solutions that satisfy them are more likely to be correct. The first-order logic formulae are weighted, with higher weight indicating higher probabilities. To model these weights in a principled manner, as well as to learn them from data, we employ Markov Logic Network (MLN) [12], which combines probabilistic graphical model and first-order logic. An MLN is a set of weighted first-order logic formulae (each formula f_t is associated with weight w_t). ϕ is a possible solution in the space of possible solutions Φ. The probability $P(\Phi = \phi)$ is expressed in Equation 1, where Z is the partition function and $f_t(\phi)$ is 1 if the formula f_t holds in ϕ and 0 otherwise.

$$P(\Phi = \phi) = \frac{1}{Z} \exp\left(\sum_t w_t f_t(\phi)\right) \tag{1}$$

In the inference stage, we use the learnt weights to estimate the probability of $\texttt{Match}(x, y)$ for every pair of entity mentions from any two different collections.

3. BIPARTITE ENTITY RESOLUTION

In this section, we begin with the first-order logic formulae for constraints in bipartite entity resolution.

Similarity Constraint. There are various features used to match entities in entity resolutions. Some are domain-specific [14], which are not our focus here. Instead, we use a domain-invariant constraint specifying that matching entities share some level of similarity. We introduce the predicate $\texttt{Similar}(x, y)$ when x and y has a similarity above a certain threshold (we try different values based on Jaccard and settle on 0.5 for experiments). The basic formula links Similar (which is observed) to Match (to be determined).

There are several possible instantiations. The first instantiation (Equation 2) indicates that similar pairs should match, which may be too stringent when polysemy is an issue, i.e., many similar entity mentions do not match in real life. The second instantiation (Equation 3) indicates that matching pairs should be similar, which is more appropriate for the electronic products datasets that we experiment with, where different products may share similar features (e.g., iPhone 5 models of different memory sizes).

$$\texttt{Similar}(x, y) \Rightarrow \texttt{Match}(x, y) \tag{2}$$

$$\texttt{Match}(x, y) \Rightarrow \texttt{Similar}(x, y) \tag{3}$$

Cardinality Constraint. Due to the assumption that each collection is duplicate-free, an entity mention $x \in X_i$ cannot match more than one mention within another collection X_j. Otherwise, the two entity mentions $y, y' \in X_j$ matched to x would effectively be themselves matched. This "at most one" rule is expressed in Equation 4, where full stop indicates that it is an inviolable hard rule. In some scenarios, we need an "at least one" rule (Equation 5), if every mention within a collection must match at least one mention in another collection. If there is a bijection or one-to-one match between two collections of the same size, we model it by using both at-most-one and at-least-one rules simultaneously.

$$\texttt{Match}(x, y) \wedge \texttt{Match}(x, y') \wedge (y = y'). \tag{4}$$

$$\forall x \in X_i,\ \exists y \in X_j,\ \texttt{Match}(x, y). \tag{5}$$

Preference Constraint. While the similarity constraint helps to ensure that matching pairs have some level of similarity, it may result in false positives. If a mention x is similar to two different mentions y and y', there should be a way for x to favor a match with the *more* similar mention. We therefore introduce another predicate $\texttt{Prefer}(x, y, y')$, which indicates that x is more similar to y than to y'.

We then link Prefer to Match. The following first-order logic formula is inspired by the Stable Marriage Problem [4], where the objective is to arrive at a matching of "men" and "women", such that no unmatched couple would rather be with each other than with their respective partners. Expressed in first-order logic, Equation 6 makes it more likely that if x is matched to y, and x' to y', we would not have the case where x prefers y' to y, and y' prefers x to x'.

$$\begin{aligned} &\texttt{Match}(x, y) \wedge \texttt{Match}(x', y') \Rightarrow \\ &!(\texttt{Prefer}(x, y', y) \wedge \texttt{Prefer}(y', x, x')) \end{aligned} \tag{6}$$

Global Constraint. The preference constraint above induces a local optimization by preferring one matching pair over another. There is no guarantee that the matching is optimized in a global way for all pairs. Complementarily, this is the strength of graph matching [5]. In graph matching, every mention is a vertex in a bipartite graph. Each edge between two mentions is weighted by the similarity value. Employing maximum weight bipartite matching obtains the matching with the highest sum of similarities. Due to the flexibility of MLN, it is feasible to be informed by this global solution. We introduce another predicate MaxWeight(x, y) that indicates that (x, y) is part of the maximum weight bipartite matching solution. For generality, we also model the greedy version [5], which iteratively constructs the matching solution by selecting the highest-weighted edges first, as the predicate Greedy(x, y). It is feasible to factor these results into the MLN formulation, as shown in Equations 7 and 8.

$$\texttt{MaxWeight}(x, y) \Rightarrow \texttt{Match}(x, y) \tag{7}$$

$$\texttt{Greedy}(x, y) \Rightarrow \texttt{Match}(x, y) \tag{8}$$

4. MULTIPARTITE ENTITY RESOLUTION

When there are $N > 2$ collections to be integrated, the problem turns into multipartite entity resolution. On one hand, the multipartite scenario can be decomposed into its $N(N-1)/2$ constituent bipartite scenarios, which enables the re-use of constraints defined in Section 3. On the other hand, modeling the problem jointly has the benefit of potentially allowing the bipartite matches to correct one another.

Cross-Collection Transitivity. The basic mechanism to join the bipartite matches is through cross-collection transitivity. Suppose $x \in X_i$ matches $y \in X_j$, and in turn y matches $z \in X_k$, it is probable that x also matches z, as expressed in Equation 9. This essentially creates two "pathways" for x to match z. One is direct, through the bipartite constraints defined in Section 3. The other is indirect, through transitivity via y. However, these two pathways may not always agree, which may result in errors.

$$\texttt{Match}(x, y) \wedge \texttt{Match}(y, z) \Rightarrow \texttt{Match}(x, z) \quad (9)$$

To combat this, we accumulate even more evidence from a greater number of collections. For instance, for four collections involving $v \in X_l$, Equation 10 is a more efficient rule that allows accumulation of evidence by combining two cross-collection transitivities. This rule has a notion of "majority". There are now three pathways, the direct pathway to $\texttt{Match}(x, z)$ based on constraints defined in Section 3, and two indirect pathways via y, i.e., $\texttt{Match}(x, y) \wedge \texttt{Match}(y, z)$, as well as via v, i.e., $\texttt{Match}(x, v) \wedge \texttt{Match}(v, z)$. If the direct pathway is incorrect, and the two indirect pathways are correct and in agreement, the latter two (intuitively forming a "majority") could have a corrective effect on the former.

$$\begin{aligned} &\texttt{Match}(x, y) \wedge \texttt{Match}(y, z) \wedge \\ &\texttt{Match}(x, v) \wedge \texttt{Match}(v, z) \Rightarrow \texttt{Match}(x, z) \end{aligned} \quad (10)$$

Label vs. Feature Transitivity. In the above, we rely on the target label $\texttt{Match}(x, y)$ to model cross-collection transitivity. This is not ideal for MLN, because the target label is not grounded, and is to be learned. As a result, it induces too much dependency among the four collections, and may propagate errors. To break these dependencies, we propose to ground the transitivities on observed features. One way is to express these transitivities in terms of global constraints, as shown in Equation 11 (using `MaxWeight` predicate) and Equation 12 (using `Greedy` predicate).

$$\begin{aligned} &\texttt{MaxWeight}(x, y) \wedge \texttt{MaxWeight}(y, z) \wedge \\ &\texttt{MaxWeight}(x, v) \wedge \texttt{MaxWeight}(v, z) \Rightarrow \texttt{Match}(x, z) \end{aligned} \quad (11)$$

$$\begin{aligned} &\texttt{Greedy}(x, y) \wedge \texttt{Greedy}(y, z) \wedge \\ &\texttt{Greedy}(x, v) \wedge \texttt{Greedy}(v, z) \Rightarrow \texttt{Match}(x, z) \end{aligned} \quad (12)$$

5. EXPERIMENTS

The primary objective is to study the effectiveness of the MLN approach, and the contributions of various MLN rules.

Datasets. Existing datasets for entity resolution comprise at most two collections. As our interest is in the multipartite scenario, we construct two new real-life datasets comprising four collections each. *Cameras* consists of the names of 80 cameras that existed on all four Web sites studied (Overstock, Newegg, BestBuy, and Amazon). *Phones* consists of the names of 70 mobile phones obtained from the same four Web sites. We use 30 entities for training, and the rest for testing. The size of the data is restricted by the need to manually label the matching across four collections.

Constraint	MLN								
	#1	#2	#3	#4	#5	#6	#7	#8	#9
Similarity	✓	✓	✓	✓	✓	✓	✓	✓	✓
Cardinality		✓	✓	✓	✓	✓	✓	✓	✓
Preference			✓	✓	✓	✓	✓	✓	✓
Global (MaxWeight)				✓		✓		✓	
Global (Greedy)					✓		✓		✓
Cross-Collection Transitivity (MaxWeight)						✓		✓	
Cross-Collection Transitivity (Greedy)							✓		✓
Domain-Specific (SameModel)								✓	✓

Table 1: MLN's with Various Components

Comparative Methods. Our main focus is on the comparison of various MLN constraints. Table 1 lists the nine MLN's to be studied, indicating the constraints included by each MLN. For learning and inference, we build the MLN solutions on the Alchemy [8] library. In addition, we will compare to two graph matching approaches, namely maximum weight bipartite matching, as well as its greedy version.

Metric. MLN outputs the probability that two mentions match. One possible metric is the likelihood of true matches. However, to put our approach on the same footing as graph matching that outputs binary outcomes, we discretize the probabilities to 1 (matched) or 0 (not matched) by assigning each entity mention to the highest probability match (taking into account any conflict). We then measure the accuracy of the pairs according to the ground truth labels.

Bipartite Entity Resolution. First, we look at the progression of structural constraints in the bipartite scenario (see Section 3). Table 2 shows the accuracies for *Cameras*, while Table 3 shows the accuracies for *Phones*. For four collections, there are six bipartite scenarios. Each row shows accuracies for each bipartite scenario. The last row is the overall accuracies, averaging the first six rows. MLN#1 that only has similarity constraint performs poorly because the one-to-one constraint is not enforced. By adding cardinality constraint, MLN#2 improves in accuracy significantly. The greatest boost in accuracy comes from adding preference constraint as in MLN#3, because the relative ranking of similarities helps to arrive at better pairings. Adding global constraints, through factoring in the MaxWeight (MLN#4) or Greedy (MLN#5), results in only a small increment in accuracies. These show that the progression of structural constraints result in better performances across both datasets.

Multipartite Entity Resolution. In multipartite settings, it is possible to gain further accuracies by modeling all the collections jointly, rather than by decomposing them into the constituent bipartite settings. Table 4 compares accuracy of bipartite versus multipartite modeling. Only the average accuracies are shown due to space limitation. Whether MaxWeight or Greedy is used in the global and cross-collection transitivity constraints, multipartite mod-

	MLN#1	MLN#2	MLN#3	MLN#4	MLN#5
Overstock-Newegg	18.0%	18.0%	90.0%	90.0%	94.0%
Overstock-BestBuy	4.0%	10.0%	88.0%	88.0%	88.0%
Overstock-Amazon	8.0%	30.0%	92.0%	92.0%	94.0%
Newegg-BestBuy	16.0%	26.0%	78.0%	76.0%	96.0%
Newegg-Amazon	6.0%	16.0%	72.0%	72.0%	70.0%
BestBuy-Amazon	12.0%	16.0%	72.0%	72.0%	72.0%
Average	10.7%	19.3%	82.0%	81.7%	85.7%

Table 2: Bipartite Entity Resolution - Cameras

	MLN#1	MLN#2	MLN#3	MLN#4	MLN#5
Overstock-Newegg	2.5%	12.5%	100.0%	100.0%	95.0%
Overstock-BestBuy	10.0%	10.0%	82.5%	85.0%	82.5%
Overstock-Amazon	12.5%	20.0%	85.0%	82.5%	90.0%
Newegg-BestBuy	12.5%	7.5%	95.0%	95.0%	95.0%
Newegg-Amazon	7.5%	35.0%	95.0%	100.0%	100.0%
BestBuy-Amazon	10.0%	12.5%	92.5%	92.5%	100.0%
Average	9.2%	16.3%	91.7%	92.5%	93.8%

Table 3: Bipartite Entity Resolution - Phones

elling helps to improve the accuracies, e.g., from 85.7% to 90.0% for *Cameras* and from 93.8% to 96.7% for *Phones*, in the case of MaxWeight-based constraints.

Comparison to Graph Matching. Our focus is on MLN-based approaches. Previously, when MaxWeight and Greedy are used, they are factored into the MLNs. For completeness, we include a comparison to graph matching on its own. For bipartite matching, we use MaxWeight (MW2) and Greedy (G2) directly. For multipartite matching (MaxWeight is NP-hard), we rely on Greedy for three (G3) and four (G4) sources respectively, as defined in [15]. Table 5 shows that MLN#6 and MLN#7 are quite similar to (in some cases slightly better than) graph matching. Importantly, MLN has not resulted in a drop in accuracy, while providing benefits such as extendability and probabilities.

Extendability via Domain-Specific Feature. Our focus here is on domain-invariant rules. However, to illustrate the potential extendability of MLN, we show how the addition of one new domain-specific rule may improve the accuracies. The rule is $\texttt{SameModel}(x, y) \Rightarrow \texttt{Match}(x, y)$. It uses a new predicate `SameModel`, specific to the domain of consumer electronics (cameras, phones), indicating whether two mentions share similar model and brand. Table 6 shows that by adding this rule, MLN#8 outperforms MLN#6, and similarly MLN#9 outperforms MLN#7. This extendability shows the value of MLN-based approach, which allows additional rules, constraints, or even tasks to be modeled jointly.

6. CONCLUSION

We explore a framework for expressing structural constraints for multipartite entity resolution using MLN. Experiments on real-life datasets indicate the promise of this approach, showing how the various structural constraints contribute to the overall effectiveness. As future work, we plan to investigate further how factoring in domain-specific features and constraints, in addition to the proposed domain-invariant structural constraints, can result in more flexible and yet more accurate entity resolution through MLN.

	with MaxWeight		with Greedy	
	Bipartite MLN#4	Multipartite MLN#6	Bipartite MLN#5	Multipartite MLN#7
Cameras	85.7%	90.0%	81.7%	82.0%
Phones	93.8%	96.7%	92.5%	93.3%

Table 4: Multipartite Entity Resolution

	with MaxWeight		with Greedy			
	MLN#6	MW2	MLN#7	G2	G3	G4
Cameras	90.0%	87.3%	82.0%	81.7%	81.5%	85.0%
Phones	96.7%	95.8%	93.3%	92.5%	91.9%	92.5%

Table 5: Comparison to Graph Matching

	with MaxWeight		with Greedy	
	without MLN#6	with domain-specific MLN#8	without MLN#7	with domain-specific MLN#9
Cameras	90.0%	90.7%	82.0%	83.0%
Phones	96.7%	98.3%	93.3%	93.3%

Table 6: Adding Domain-Specific Feature

7. REFERENCES

[1] Y. Crama, A. G. Oerlemans, and F. C. Spieksma. *Approximation algorithms for three-dimensional assignment problems with triangle inequalities.* Springer, 1996.

[2] A. K. Elmagarmid, P. G. Ipeirotis, and V. S. Verykios. Duplicate record detection: A survey. *TKDE*, 2007.

[3] I. P. Fellegi and A. B. Sunter. A theory for record linkage. *JASA*, 1969.

[4] D. Gale and L. S. Shapley. College admissions and the stability of marriage. *American mathematical monthly*, 1962.

[5] J. Gemmell, B. I. P. Rubinstein, and A. K. Chandra. Improving entity resolution with global constraints. *arXiv preprint arXiv:1108.6016*, 2011.

[6] P. Jaccard. *Etude comparative de la distribution florale dans une portion des Alpes et du Jura.* Impr. Corbaz, 1901.

[7] M.A. Jaro. Probabilistic linkage of large public health data files. *Statistics in Medicine*, 1995.

[8] S. Kok, P. Singla, M. Richardson, P. Domingos, M. Sumner, H. Poon, and D. Lowd. The Alchemy system for statistical relational AI. *University of Washington, Seattle*, 2005.

[9] H. Köpcke and E. Rahm. Frameworks for entity matching: A comparison. *DKE*, 2010.

[10] A. E. Monge and C. Elkan. An efficient domain-independent algorithm for detecting approximately duplicate database records. In *SIGMOD Workshop on Data Mining and Knowledge Discovery*, 1997.

[11] H. Poon and P. Domingos. Joint inference in information extraction. In *AAAI*, 2007.

[12] M. Richardson and P. Domingos. Markov logic networks. *Machine Learning*, 2006.

[13] W. Shen, X. Li, and A. Doan. Constraint-based entity matching. In *AAAI*, 2005.

[14] P. Singla and P. Domingos. Entity resolution with markov logic. In *ICDM*, 2006.

[15] D. Zhang, B. I. P. Rubinstein, and J. Gemmell. Principled graph matching algorithms for integrating multiple data sources. *TKDE*, preprint, 2015.

Know Your Onions: Understanding the User Experience with the Knowledge Module in Web Search

Ioannis Arapakis
Yahoo Labs
Barcelona, Spain
arapakis@yahoo-inc.com

Luis A. Leiva
PRHLT, Universitat Politècnica
de València, Spain
llt@acm.org

B. Barla Cambazoglu
Yahoo Labs
Barcelona, Spain
barla@yahoo-inc.com

ABSTRACT

The increasing availability of large volumes of human-curated content is shifting web search towards a paradigm that introduces seamlessly more semantic information to search engine result pages. This trend has resulted in the design of a new element known as the knowledge module (KM), where certain facts about named entities, obtained from various knowledge bases, are shown to users. So far, little has been done to uncover the role that this module plays on user experience in web search and whether it is perceived by users as a useful aid for their search tasks. Our work is an early attempt to bridge this gap. To this end, we conducted a crowdsourcing study aimed at understanding the effect of the KM on users' search experience and its overall utility. In particular, our study is the first to provide insights about the noticeability and usefulness of the KM in web search, together with comprehensive analyses of usability and workload.

Categories and Subject Descriptors

H.3.3 [**Information Storage and Retrieval**]: Information Search and Retrieval; H.1.2 [**User/Machine Systems**]: Human factors

Keywords

web search engine; knowledge module; user experience

1. INTRODUCTION

In recent years, the knowledge module (KM) has become a standard component on search engine result pages (SERPs) of all major web search engines (Fig. 1). This module provides users with information about the named entities they are searching for as part of their search tasks. The content presented in the KM is typically obtained in a semi-structured format from curated entity databases, such as Freebase or Wikipedia, and often includes both quantitative and qualitative information about the queried entity. This raw information can be further enriched by the search engine; e.g., by showing a ranking of related entities, accompanied with explanations of their relationship. Moreover, the KM is often complemented with additional content, such as multimedia or social media content associated with the entity, typically obtained from third-party data sources.

Permission to make digital or hard copies of all or part of this work for personal or classroom use is granted without fee provided that copies are not made or distributed for profit or commercial advantage and that copies bear this notice and the full citation on the first page. Copyrights for components of this work owned by others than the author(s) must be honored. Abstracting with credit is permitted. To copy otherwise, or republish, to post on servers or to redistribute to lists, requires prior specific permission and/or a fee. Request permissions from Permissions@acm.org.

CIKM'15, October 19–23, 2015, Melbourne, Australia.
Copyright is held by the owner/author(s). Publication rights licensed to ACM.
ACM 978-1-4503-3794-6/15/10 ...$15.00.
DOI: http://dx.doi.org/10.1145/2806416.2806591.

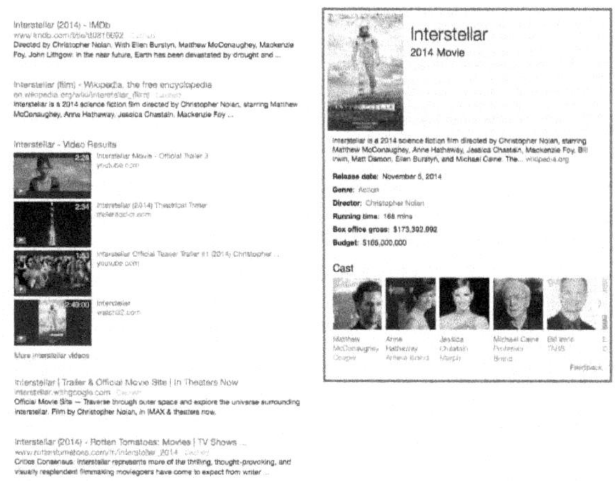

Figure 1: The KM (in red border) displayed on the Yahoo SERP for the query "interstellar".

In this context, most research has focused on general backend system tasks, the most important being knowledge base construction [1, 4, 6, 7, 11], or more specific backend tasks, such as related entity recommendation [2, 3]. With the exception of a recent query log analysis on exploratory search [10], so far little has been done to understand the way web search users interact with the frontend system, i.e., the knowledge component presented as part of the SERP. Our work makes an early attempt to understand the impact of the KM on users' overall search experience in entity-centric search tasks. In particular, we try to answer questions of the following kind: Do users notice the presence of the KM on SERPs? If they notice it, do they find it useful? Does the KM really ease web search? Is it cognitively or physically demanding?

Our contribution can be summarized as follows. To understand the user experience with the KM, we conducted a crowdsourcing study. The study involved questionnaires and self-reported feedback from 533 users about noticeability, usefulness, usability, and workload toward the KM shown on the Yahoo web search engine. We observed that the majority of the participants (about three-fourths) who performed the search tasks noticed the presence of the KM on the SERP, and they felt that, overall, it provided a useful aid to accomplish their search tasks better and faster.

2. CROWDSOURCING STUDY

To understand the impact of the KM in web search, we conducted a crowdsourcing study and collected feedback from users who performed short, entity-centric search tasks using the Yahoo web search engine. With this study, we aimed to determine: (i) what percentage of users notice the KM on the SERP, (ii) to what extent they perceive it as a useful aid to their search tasks, and whether the presence of the KM can affect (iii) the perceived usability and (iv) experienced workload due to web search engine usage.

Crowdsourcing offers several advantages not available in other experimental settings [9], such as access to a large and diverse pool of participants with stable availability, as well as collection and analysis of real usage data at a large scale. Another advantage of crowdsourcing is the low cost of the tasks, which makes it a preferable solution over the more expensive laboratory-based experiments. On the downside, a limited range of parameters can be explored in a controlled manner and experimenters have to account for potential threats to ecological validity, distractions in the physical environment of the user, and privacy issues, to name a few.

In our study, we used the Amazon Mechanical Turk service. All of the aforementioned limitations were taken into consideration and preventive measures were put into practice to discount low-quality responses. Also, strict selection criteria were applied to exclude unsuitable participants (e.g., HIT approval rate $\geq$ 98%, number of HITs approved $\geq$ 1,000).

2.1 Experimental Design

The experiment had a repeated measures design with one independent variable: KM (with two levels: "visible" or "hidden"). The KM visibility was controlled with client-side scripting, removing the KM from the SERP in the "hidden" condition. The dependent variables (Section 2.3) were: (i) KM noticeability, (ii) KM usefulness (ease of use and speed of use), (iii) perceived usability of the search engine (Tables 1 and 2), and (iv) overall workload (Table 3). The experiment consisted of two short search tasks that were completed using the Yahoo search engine, one task displaying the KM on the SERP and one without it. To control for order effects, we counterbalanced task assignments using Latin square design.

Participants accessed the search engine through a custom proxy which did not alter the original look and feel of the SERPs. This allowed us to instrument the browsed pages on the fly and capture user interactions with the SERP without interfering with the actual web search engine interface in production. The proxy had a common entry page for all participants. For each search task, participants were presented with a question and were suggested a search query to begin with. Finally, the suggested queries were all picked from a pool of queries that triggered the KM on the SERP, independent of the KM visibility (Section 2.2).

2.2 Search Query Sample

Our query set consisted of 32 unique query patterns that were selected after a large-scale query log analysis All queries would trigger the KM on the Yahoo SERP, so we could ensure that in all tasks the KM would be displayed on the SERP, thus allowing us to choose between leaving it visible or hiding it, depending on the experimental condition.

The selected query patterns belonged to four different themes (famous people, movies, athletes, sport teams) and required either single or multiple answers. An example of a single-answer query pattern is "Who is the head coach of the team X?" while an example of a multi-answer query is "Who are X's children?". To diversify our search query pool, we produced three questions per query pattern while we introduced some additional multi-answer questions to increase the difficulty of the search tasks. In total, our query set included 144 different queries.[1] In the study, the query set was repeated as many times as needed to accommodate all participants. Each query was answered under each condition by at least two participants and at most six participants.

2.3 Self-Reported Measures

We used three different post-task questionnaires to elicit participants' subjective experience about the search engine and search tasks. More specifically, participants were asked to complete the Computer System Usability Questionnaire (CSUQ), the Perceived Usefulness and Ease of Use questionnaire (PUEU), and the NASA Task Load Index (NASA-TLX), together with custom statements described later.

The CSUQ [8] is a multi-dimensional user satisfaction questionnaire designed for use in scenario-based usability evaluations. Out of the four scales it contains, we considered only the scores from the system usefulness (SYSUSE) subscale (Table 1). The PUEU questionnaire [5] is a psychometric scale with significant empirical relationships with self-reported measures of usage behavior. It focuses on two theoretical constructs, perceived usefulness and ease of use, which are fundamental determinants of system usage. In our study, we considered only the perceived usefulness scale, which consists of the six statements shown in Table 2. The NASA-TLX is a multi-item assessment tool that allows participants to perform subjective workload assessments of human-computer interaction systems. NASA-TLX employs a rating procedure based on the six questions shown in Table 3. Combined together, CSUQ, PUEU, and NASA-TLX gauged key aspects of participants' experience with the search tasks and the search engine. The questions were all forced-choice type and appeared at random to mitigate order effects. A 7-point Likert scale was used in all questionnaires, with high scores representing a stronger agreement with the given statement.

In addition to the above psychometric scales, we also collected demographic information as well as information about participants' agreement to the following statements: (i) "This search engine helped me accomplish my task in a reasonable amount of time", (ii) "I feel satisfied with the retrieved results". Finally, we inquired about the KM through a mini-questionnaire, which only appeared on the SERPs that displayed the KM. The mini-questionnaire was initially hidden, in order not to interfere with regular browsing, and was shown to the user just before unloading the SERP on closing the browser tab. The mini-questionnaire contained three questions: (i) "Did you notice the KM? (yes/no)", (ii) "To what extent did you find the KM useful in answering the question? (1: not useful at all, ..., 5: completely useful)", (iii) "To what extent did the KM help you answer the question faster? (1: not faster at all, ..., 5: extremely faster)".

2.4 Participants

We recruited 612 participants through Amazon Mechanical Turk. From this original sample, we approved assignments

[1] http://personales.upv.es/luileito/kme/queries.tsv

Table 1: CSUQ-SYSUSE subscale items

1. Overall, I am satisfied with how easy it is to use this search site.
2. I feel this search site is simple to use.
3. I can effectively complete my work using this search site.
4. I am able to complete my work quickly using this search site.
5. I am able to efficiently complete my work using this search site.
6. I feel comfortable using this search site.
7. It was easy learning to use this search site.
8. I believe I became productive quickly using this search site.

Table 2: PUEU subscale items

1. Using this search site would allow me to accomplish my search tasks more quickly.
2. Using this search site would improve my performance.
3. Using this search site would increase my productivity.
4. Using this search site would enhance my effectiveness.
5. Using this search site would make it easier to do my search tasks.
6. I would find this search site useful in my search tasks.

Table 3: NASA-TLX factor definitions

Factor	Question
Mental Demand	How mentally demanding was the task?
Physical Demand	How physically demanding was the task?
Temporal Demand	How hurried or rushed was the pace of the task?
Performance	How successful were you in accomplishing what you were asked to do?
Effort	How hard did you have to work to accomplish your level of performance?
Frustration	How insecure, discouraged, irritated, stressed, and annoyed were you?

for 533 participants (female = 226, male = 307), aged from 18 to 66. Participants were of mixed nationality (e.g., Belgian, Finnish, British, American) and had varying educational backgrounds: 29.98% had a high school diploma, 18.98% had a college diploma, 41.56% had a BSc degree, 7.97% had an MSc, and 1.52% had a PhD. All participants were proficient in English, 98.31% being native speakers. When asked about their search engine at home or work, participants reported using primarily Google, followed by Yahoo and Bing.

2.5 Procedure

At the beginning, participants were informed about the terms and conditions of the study, followed by a short description of the SERP. The study had to be done in a single session. The participants could opt out at any moment, in which case they would not be compensated. Participants were asked to "evaluate two different backend systems of Yahoo Search, by performing two search tasks". Therefore, participants were not informed of the actual intent of the study ("understand the impact of KM in web search"), in order to avoid a potential bias. For each task, participants had to answer a question by searching for relevant information on the proxified search engine. They were also presented with a suggested query to begin their search, although participants were free to submit additional queries (e.g., if the suggested query did not lead to the answer) and examine as many results as necessary to complete the search task.

We used informational, entity-centric queries to introduce a common starting point across all participants who tested each particular combination of query and backend system. Upon finishing each task, participants were instructed to submit their answer and complete the post-task questionnaire. The study concluded with a demographics questionnaire. The payment for participation was $1.20 and each participant could take the study only once.

3. RESULTS

In the following, we discuss our findings based on the 1,066 search tasks performed by 533 participants. The results are presented in three sections. The first section discusses the noticeability and the usefulness of the KM. The second section shows the effect of the KM on the web search engine's perceived usability. The third section presents findings of the workload analysis. To quantify the statistical significance of our results, we used the Wilcoxon signed-rank test at an α level of 0.05.

3.1 Noticeability and Usefulness

The first research questions we answered are whether the KM is being noticed by web search users, and to what extent it is considered a useful aid to their search activities. According to the responses from the mini-questionnaire (Section 2.3), out of the 533 participants who were involved in our study, the majority (78.86%) reported noticing the KM on the SERP. Considering that the KM is a relatively new element introduced in SERPs, the high percentage of participants who engaged with it is a first positive indication of its noticeability, even if this was demonstrated for only one of the available commercial search engines. The KM was also found to be very useful in answering the search task questions ($M = 4.03, SD = 1.48$). Moreover, the KM helped the participants who noticed it to answer the search task questions fairly faster ($M = 3.84, SD = 1.60$). These findings suggest that the KM is both noticeable and useful to web search users.

Furthermore, we performed a correlation analysis and computed the point-biserial correlation coefficient (r_{pb}) for the above variables. In the case of r_{pb}, the sign of the correlation depends on the way the coding of the variables was made, therefore we ignore all information about direction. Our findings indicated that noticeability is significantly correlated with both ease of use ($r_{pb} = 0.60, p < .0001$) and speed of use ($r_{pb} = 0.54, p < .0001$). In short, users who noticed the KM felt that they could accomplish their tasks better and faster.

3.2 Perceived Usability

Next, we examined the impact of the KM on perceived system usability. To this end, we looked at the participants' responses to our two custom statements as well as the 8-item CSUQ-SYSUSE and 6-item PUEU scales shown in Table 4. We averaged the responses to obtain the final scores and then contrasted and compared what the participants reported in the experimental conditions (visible or hidden KM).

The Wilcoxon signed-rank test showed that participants found the search engine to be significantly more helpful in accomplishing their search tasks in a reasonable amount of time ($z = 8.13, p < .001, r = 0.35$) when the KM was visible ($Mdn = 7$) compared to when it was hidden ($Mdn = 6$).

Table 4: Usability results for custom statements (CS-1 and CS-2), CSUQ-SYSUSE, and PUEU

	KM status	
Scale	**Visible**	**Hidden**
CS-1: This search site helped me accomplish my task in a reasonable amount of time	6.38 ± 1.10	5.80 ± 1.57
CS-2: I feel satisfied with the retrieved results	6.40 ± 1.04	5.85 ± 1.58
CSUQ-SYSUSE	6.22 ± 1.09	5.66 ± 1.52
PUEU	5.25 ± 1.51	4.73 ± 1.72

Table 5: Workload results: NASA-TLX factors

	KM status	
Factor	**Visible**	**Hidden**
Mental	1.70 ± 1.18	1.93 ± 1.32
Physical	1.33 ± 0.91	1.30 ± 0.82
Temporal	1.78 ± 1.25	1.88 ± 1.29
Performance	6.37 ± 1.42	6.19 ± 1.48
Effort	1.96 ± 1.48	2.29 ± 1.58
Frustration	1.55 ± 1.12	1.86 ± 1.41
Sum	14.70 ± 4.40	15.44 ± 4.73

Moreover, participants felt significantly more satisfied with the retrieved results ($z = 7.36, p < .001, r = 0.32$) when having seen the KM ($Mdn = 7$) rather than not ($Mdn = 6$). Participants also perceived the search engine to be significantly more usable ($z = 9.06, p < .001, r = 0.39$) when the SERP displayed the KM ($Mdn = 6.66$) than when it did not ($Mdn = 6$). Indeed, the CSUQ-SYSUSE scores were higher for the "visible" condition, as observed in Table 4. Moreover, the reported PUEU scores were significantly higher ($z = 8.58, p < .001, r = 0.37$) for the "visible" condition ($Mdn = 5.5$) than the "hidden" condition ($Mdn = 5$).

3.3 Overall Workload

Finally, we looked at the perceived workload experienced by our participants as they performed the search tasks. Table 5 shows the NASA-TLX scores reported for each factor (lower is better). The individual factor scores were summed up to obtain the overall workload scores. Participants who interacted with the SERP that did not display the KM ($Mdn = 14$) experienced a significantly higher workload ($z = 4.40, p < .001, r = 0.19$) than the participants who were shown the KM ($Mdn = 13$). Table 5 also presents the relative contribution of each factor to the overall workload score for both experimental conditions. More specifically, the participants in the "hidden" condition ($Mdn = 1$) reported a significantly higher mental demand ($z = 4.81, p < .001, r = 0.20$) than those in the "visible" condition ($Mdn = 1$). Participants in the "hidden" condition also reported lower physical and temporal demand scores than those in the "visible" condition, although these differences were not statistically significant.

When examining how successful they were in accomplishing the search tasks, participants in the "visible" condition ($Mdn = 7$) reported significantly higher performance ($z = 3.39, p < .001, r = 0.14$) than those in the "hidden" condition ($Mdn = 7$). Furthermore, the search task demanded significantly more effort ($z = 5.25, p < .001, r = 0.22$) in the "hidden" condition ($Mdn = 2$) compared to the "visible" condition ($Mdn = 1$). Lastly, participants in the "hidden" condition ($Mdn = 1$) reported significantly higher levels of frustration ($z = 5.56, p < .001, r = 0.10$) than those in the "visible" condition ($Mdn = 1$).

4. CONCLUSION AND FUTURE WORK

This work entails an early attempt to understand the impact of the KM on users' search experience and provides empirical evidence of its overall utility. To this end, we conducted a crowdsourcing study which revealed the potential benefits of the KM, when dealing with entity-centric search tasks. In particular, we showed that the KM was noticed by most participants and was perceived to be a valuable help in web search. Moreover, the KM was perceived to ease the search process for the users. Our ongoing work is on correlating mouse cursor tracking data and user engagement with the KM. We believe that this is a research avenue worth pursuing given the lack of explicit user feedback about engagement (e.g., clicks or dwell time) in the context of the KM. Finally, we anticipate that further research on the topic may have an impact on future web search interfaces.

Acknowledgments

This work is part of the Valorization and I+D+i Resources program of VLC/CAMPUS and has been funded by the Spanish MECD as part of the International Excellence Campus program.

5. REFERENCES

[1] S. Auer, C. Bizer, G. Kobilarov, J. Lehmann, R. Cyganiak, and Z. Ives. DBpedia: A nucleus for a web of open data. In *Proc. ISWC*, 722–735, 2007.

[2] B. Bi, H. Ma, B.-J. P. Hsu, W. Chu, K. Wang, and J. Cho. Learning to recommend related entities to search users. In *Proc. WSDM*, 139–148, 2015.

[3] R. Blanco, B. B. Cambazoglu, P. Mika, and N. Torzec. Entity recommendations in web search. In *Proc. ISWC*, 33–48. 2013.

[4] K. Bollacker, C. Evans, P. Paritosh, T. Sturge, and J. Taylor. Freebase: A collaboratively created graph database for structuring human knowledge. In *Proc. SIGMOD*, 1247–1250, 2008.

[5] F. D. Davis. Perceived usefulness, perceived ease of use, and user acceptance of information technology. *MIS Quarterly*, 13(3):319–340, 1989.

[6] X. Dong, E. Gabrilovich, G. Heitz, W. Horn, N. Lao, K. Murphy, T. Strohmann, S. Sun, and W. Zhang. Knowledge vault: A web-scale approach to probabilistic knowledge fusion. In *Proc. SIGKDD*, 601–610, 2014.

[7] J. Hoffart, F. M. Suchanek, K. Berberich, and G. Weikum. Yago2: A spatially and temporally enhanced knowledge base from Wikipedia. *Artif. Intell.*, 194:28–61, 2013.

[8] J. R. Lewis. IBM computer usability satisfaction questionnaires: Psychometric evaluation and instructions for use. *Intl. J. Hum.-Comput. Interact.*, 7(1):57–78, 1995.

[9] W. Mason and S. Suri. Conducting behavioral research on Amazon's Mechanical Turk. *Behavior Research Methods*, 1–23, 2010.

[10] I. Miliaraki, R. Blanco, and M. Lalmas. From "Selena Gomez" to "Marlon Brando": Understanding explorative entity search. In *Proc. WWW*, 765–775, 2015.

[11] F. M. Suchanek, G. Kasneci, and G. Weikum. Yago: A core of semantic knowledge. In *Proc. WWW*, 697–706, 2007.

Personalized Federated Search at LinkedIn

Dhruv Arya
darya@linkedin.com

Viet Ha-Thuc
vhathuc@linkedin.com

Shakti Sinha
ssinha@linkedin.com

LinkedIn
2029 Stierlin Ct
Mountain View, CA, USA

ABSTRACT

LinkedIn has grown to become a platform hosting diverse sources of information ranging from member profiles, jobs, professional groups, slideshows etc. Given the existence of multiple sources, when a member issues a query like "software engineer", the member could look for software engineer profiles, jobs or professional groups. To tackle this problem, we exploit a data-driven approach that extracts searcher intents from their profile data and recent activities at a large scale. The intents such as job seeking, hiring, content consuming are used to construct features to personalize federated search experience. We tested the approach on the LinkedIn homepage and A/B tests show significant improvements in member engagement. As of writing this paper, the approach powers all of federated search on LinkedIn homepage.

Categories and Subject Descriptors

H.4 [**Information Systems Applications**]: Miscellaneous

General Terms

Theory

Keywords

Federated search, social network, ranking, machine learning, information retrieval

1. INTRODUCTION

LinkedIn has grown over the years from a professional networking site to becoming a platform containing multiple professional information sources such as member profiles, jobs, professional groups, member posts and slideshows. At the same time, the member base has also increased quickly and currently has more than 350 million members. The members visit the site for various reasons ranging from searching and recruiting candidates to looking for jobs or finding professional content etc. As the number of information verticals and member base increase, the problem of serving the right information to fulfill each individual member's information need becomes more and more critical. This problem contains two subtasks including selecting the right verticals and aggregating the vertical results into a single ranking (See Figure 1) and typically is referred as federated search.

Permission to make digital or hard copies of all or part of this work for personal or classroom use is granted without fee provided that copies are not made or distributed for profit or commercial advantage and that copies bear this notice and the full citation on the first page. Copyrights for components of this work owned by others than the author(s) must be honored. Abstracting with credit is permitted. To copy otherwise, or republish, to post on servers or to redistribute to lists, requires prior specific permission and/or a fee. Request permissions from Permissions@acm.org.
CIKM'15, October 19–23, 2015, Melbourne, Australia.
Copyright is held by the owner/author(s). Publication rights licensed to ACM.
ACM 978-1-4503-3794-6/15/10 ...$15.00.
DOI: http://dx.doi.org/10.1145/2806416.2806615 .

Figure 1: LinkedIn Federated Search Result Page for Query "Software Engineer"

The area of federated search originated from meta search and has been actively researched in the field of information retrieval [5] and particularly in the context of Web search. Diaz [2] addresses the problem of vertical selection, i.e., whether or not to show a specific item above the Web results given a query. Ponnuswami et. al. [4] and Arguello et. al. [1] propose machine learning approaches for aggregating vertical results into single search result pages. They demonstrate effectiveness of the approaches on Bing search. More recently, Lefortier et. al. [3] present a way to blend individual vertical results and individual Web results with a case study on Yandex video search.

However, the problem of federated search on LinkedIn presents unique challenges. First, the level of personalization in a platform like LinkedIn is much deeper than general Web search. For instance, if a member enters a query like "software engineer", depending on if he or she is a recruiter, job seeker or professional content consumer, the member could expect to see software engineers' profiles, jobs or slideshows on the topic. Second, individual results and blocks of results from different verticals are often associated with different features. Moreover, even if a feature is common, it is not equally important to them. This challenge is similar to federated Web search. Nonetheless, unlike Web search which typically blends *either* blocks of results [1][4] or individual results [3] from different verticals, our system aggregates *both* individual results (e.g. jobs as shown in Figure 1) and blocks of vertical results (e.g. people and professional group verticals). Thus, the system has to normalize features and eventually make relevance scores comparable across result verticals and result types (individual vs. block). Third, in Web search, Web results are typically the primary vertical thus they can be used as a "pivot" to normalize scores of the other verticals [4]. In our problem, the primary verticals vary depending on queries and other search context which could includes searcher's data, past activities, location etc.

To overcome these challenges, we propose a data-driven approach to personalize federated search. Specifically, we mine members' data and their recent activities at a large scale to understand whether or not they currently have *intent* of hiring, job seeking or content consuming etc. This insight coupled with other signals are used to select verticals and aggregate vertical results into a single search result page personally relevant to each of our members. To make these signals comparable across different result categories, including verticals and result types (block vs. individual), we construct composite features combining the signals for each of the categories. Then, we let learning algorithms estimate different weights for all of the combinations (i.e., normalize the signals across the result categories) from training data.

A/B tests done on the LinkedIn homepage shows improvements in member engagement and downstream traffic to the verticals. At the time of this writing, the work currently powers all of the federated search on the LinkedIn homepage. We organize the rest of the paper as follows. Section 2 details how we formulate federated search problem and our proposed approach. Section 3 describes searcher intent features and other signals used in the system. We discuss experimental results in Section 4. Finally, concluding remarks can be found in Section 5.

2. OVERALL APPROACH

2.1 Problem Statement and Overall Framework

Given a pair of *(query, searcher)*, our task is to select from a list of all possible verticals including people (members), jobs, companies, professional groups, member posts, slideshows etc. a primary vertical and a set of secondary verticals, then rank the primary individual results and the secondary vertical blocks in a single ranked list as shown in Figure 1, without changing the order in the primary vertical. The reason for this constraint is two fold. First, we believe the base ranker of each vertical is the best one to rank results within its domain. Second, this keeps member experience consistent between federated search and vertical search.

The overall framework is described in Figure 2. When a member issues a query q, the query is passed to verticals and triggers the corresponding vertical search engines to get

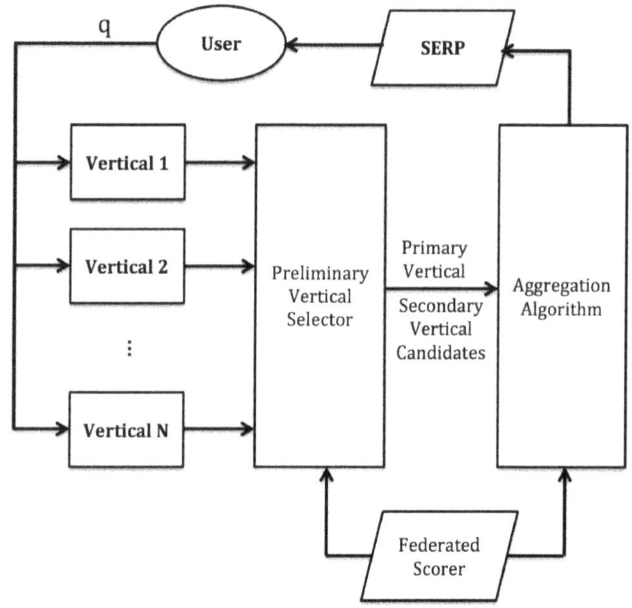

Figure 2: Federated Search Overall Framework

the top K results for each. In preliminary vertical selection phase, the federated scorer extracts features (which are described later in Section 3) and computes a relevance score for each of the verticals. The top vertical is selected as the primary one and the rest are selected as *candidates* for secondary verticals. Then, in aggregation phase, these candidates compete with individual results in the primary vertical to form the final ranking. Note that these candidates are not guaranteed to show up in the ranking. Instead, depending on queries, searchers and vertical results, all, some or none of these candidates could be selected. The aggregation algorithm and the process of training the federated scorer are described in the next subsections.

2.2 Aggregation Algorithm

In this section we discuss how our aggregation algorithm works. Input to the algorithm includes results from the primary vertical P along with all the candidate secondary vertical clusters C and a federated scorer f_s. We go through each of primary vertical result P_i computing the relevance score for this result using the federated scorer (the second loop in Algorithm 1). We compare this score with the relevance scores of all candidate secondary vertical clusters. If the former is higher, we pick the primary vertical result for i^{th} position. If on the other hand there exists a candidate secondary vertical cluster that has a higher relevance score than the primary result, we add the secondary vertical cluster to the aggregated rank list and move on to the next primary result. We repeat this process till we position all the primary results. Any secondary vertical results left are dropped.

2.3 Federated Scorer Training

As presented above, the purpose of federated scorer is to provide a *universal* relevance score for each vertical block as well as each vertical individual result. The scores have to be comparable across verticals (for preliminary vertical

Algorithm 1: Federated Search Aggregation Algorithm

Input : Individual results from primary vertical P
Secondary vertical clusters C
Federated scorer f_s
Output: Aggregated result ranked list

```
sortedSecondaryVerticals → []; rankList → [];
for i=1 to len(C) do
    // data structure sorted based on f_s(C_i)
    sortedSecondaryVerticals.add(C_i)
end
j ← 1;
for i=1 to len(P) do
    if f_s(P_i) > f_s(sortedSecondaryVerticals.get(j)) then
        rankList[i] = P_i
        i ← i + 1
    else
        rankList[i] = sortedSecondaryVerticals.get(j)
        sortedSecondaryVerticals.remove(j)
        j ← j + 1
    end
end
return rankList
```

selection) and between vertical blocks and vertical individual results (for result aggregation). In this work, we train a federated scorer predicting probability that a vertical block or vertical individual result gets clicked if it appears on a search result page (SERP) shown to the member.

Traditionally, ground truth data is labeled by human judges. However, this approach is expensive and not scalable. Moreover, it is very hard for the judges to judge the relevance on behalf of some other member, making it challenging to apply the approach for personalized settings. Thus, in this work the training data is collected from click logs via a randomization experiment exposed to a small random fraction of LinkedIn search traffic. In this experiment, given a query we apply some business rules to come up with a few eligible verticals. We randomly pick one as a primary vertical and leave the others as secondary ones. Then, we randomly insert the secondary verticals (as blocks of results) into the primary ranking without re-ordering the primary individual results. Clicked results (either primary individual results or secondary vertical blocks) are labeled positive and skipped results (unclicked ones ranked above the last clicked result in a ranking) are labeled as negative. The results ranked below the last clicked one are dropped since it is unknown if the member ignored these results or simply did not see them. The benefit of randomization is that it avoids the bias towards the original vertical selection and ranking. Given the training data, we apply logistic regression to train a federated scorer. The features used to train the scorer are described in the next section.

3. FEATURES

3.1 Searcher Intent

A query can be ambiguous in the light of all information that exists in multiple verticals. For example, if a member enters a query like "machine learning", he or she could be interested in recruiting machine learning people, looking for jobs related to machine learning, finding professional groups on the topic to join, discovering content on the topic or some of the use cases. To tackle this issue, we take a data-driven approach to personalize search results. For instance, if we know that the member is currently looking for a job, he or she is likely to be more interested in job results than the other verticals. Similarly, if the member is hiring machine learning scientists, people results should be more important to him or her.

Intents of searchers such as job seeking, hiring, content consuming etc. are inferred from their profiles and past behaviors. At a high level, if a user's title is recruiter, he or she is likely to have hiring intent. Similarly, if a user is a final year student, he or she could have job seeking intent. Another source of data used to infer user intents is their recent activities. For example, if users recently searched or applied for jobs, they tend to have job seeking intent. We train a machine-learned model combining all of the signals to predict intents for all of the member base. The model is run on a daily basic to update members' intents dynamically. It is worth noting that a member could have multiple intents at the same time.

A remaining challenge is that some evidence such as knowing a searcher has job seeking intent might be associated one or a few verticals (e.g. job vertical), but not all of them. Some evidence might be related to multiple verticals but with different levels of importance. To overcome this issue, we construct *composite features*, capturing both searcher intents and result categories including both verticals and result types (individual or block). For instance, the feature below only fires if the searcher has job seeking intent and the result is a block of jobs. Otherwise, it has value of zero. We create all of the combinations of intents and result categories and learn different weights for them. In essence, we let the learning algorithm associate each of the evidence with the categories and normalize them across the categories from training data.

$$f = \begin{cases} 1 & \text{if searcher has job seeking intent} \\ & \quad \text{and the result is job vertical block} \\ 0 & \text{otherwise} \end{cases}$$

3.2 Keyword Intent

The feature category aims to capture the intents (result categories) of queries. Specifically, we mine historical click logs to estimate *p(result category| query)*, for instance the probability that members click on professional group vertical block for the query "leadership". These probabilities are computed offline for every head query and use this insight to construct the features online. One issue of this approach is that the probabilities are biased towards the previous vertical selection and ranking algorithms. Resolving this is a future direction of this work.

3.3 Base Ranking Features

We also exploit information provided by vertical first pass rankers (base rankers) to construct features. One example could be relevance scores from the first pass rankers. These features also have an effect of minimizing the inconsistency between the federated scorer and the first pass rankers (recall that the order in the primary vertical is kept unchanged). One issue with this kind of information is that the relevance scores might not be calibrated well across verticals. To resolve this issue, we again construct composite features like relevance score if result is an individual job or a slideshow vertical block. For the later, we compute relevance score for each block by averaging scores of the top results in the block. Then, we let the learning algorithm normalize the scores across result categories by learning different weights for the features from the training data.

4. EXPERIMENTAL RESULTS

Baseline is a legacy federated search algorithm at LinkedIn. It uses a set of business rules based on past member interaction with verticals associated with keywords and relevance scores returned by vertical ranking functions. It can be viewed as a function on the feature sets described in Sections 3.2 and 3.3. Although the function is manually defined, it has been running on live traffic for a relatively long time and have been iteratively refined. The key difference between the baseline and the new approach is that the later is highly personalized by using searcher intent as a key signal.

We conducted A/B test for sufficient duration of time (6 weeks) to account for any novelty effect. A query is first tagged for existence of entities like *names*, *job titles*, *skills* etc. As we are interested in exploratory search, we only experimented with non-name queries. Based on this condition, a random portion of LinkedIn federated search traffic from our world-wide member base is used for A/B testing. The federated search combines results from all of seven verticals available on LinkedIn including people, job, company, university, group, slideshow and members' posts. The traffic is then randomly split into control and treatment buckets. Each bucket ends up with several hundreds of thousand searches. Searches in the control bucket are processed by the baseline and the treatment bucket uses the proposed approach. We look at three metrics including primary vertical click-throught-rate (CTR), secondary vertical CTR and secondary vertical switches. The difference between the second and the third metrics is that the former is defined on clicks on *individual results* within secondary clusters while the later is based on clicks on *cluster headers* that take users to vertical search pages.

Table 1 shows that the proposed approach is better than the baseline on all of the metrics (all of the improvements are statistically significant). Specifically, the proposed approach is 0.62% better than the baseline on primary vertical CTR. In terms of secondary vertical engagement, the proposed approach largely improves over the baseline: 4.31% and 10.66% improvements on secondary vertical CTR and secondary vertical switches. It is somewhat surprising that the improvement on primary vertical CTR is much lower than on secondary vertical CTR. It is probably because the proposed approach shows more relevant secondary verticals, members are more likely to switch to secondary vertical search result pages (10.66% higher). Thus, they have less chance to engage in the primary results. A deep dive into log data also reveals that the baseline tends to overemphasize primary results and on average ranks secondary vertical clusters lower in result pages. Fully understanding and modeling the trade-off between member engagement on primary and secondary results is another future direction of this work.

Metric	Improvements
Primary Vertical CTR	+0.62%
Secondary Vertical CTR	+4.31%
Secondary Vertical Switches	+10.66%

Table 1: Metrics improvements of treatment over baseline. Due to business sensitivity, we only show relative improvements instead of absolute metric values.

5. CONCLUSIONS

In this paper, we present the problem of personalized federated search at LinkedIn and propose a data-driven approach for this problem. Our approach takes into account members' data and activities to infer their intents such as hiring and job seeking. This insight combined with other signals are used to select primary and candidate secondary verticals and then to aggregate primary individual results and the secondary clusters into a personalized ranking. Though presented in LinkedIn federated search context, the approach is applicable other domains where vertical selection and aggregation are highly personalized. Our A/B tests show that the approach could significantly improve user engagement. The approach is currently serving all of federated search on LinkedIn homepage.

One future direction of this work is to remove the bias towards the previous vertical selection and ranking algorithms in the current keyword intent features. Another direction is to understand and model the trade-off between member engagement on primary verticals and engagement on secondary verticals. Given the insight, we will determine the best balance in terms of member experience.

6. REFERENCES

[1] J. Arguello, F. Diaz, and J. Callan. Learning to aggregate vertical results into web search results. In *Proceedings of the 20th Conference on Information and Knowledge Management*, pages 201–210, 2011.

[2] F. Diaz. Integration of news content into web results. In *Proceedings of the Second International Conference on Web Search and Web Data Mining*, pages 182–191, 2009.

[3] D. Lefortier, P. Serdyukov, F. Romanenko, and M. de Rijke. Blending vertical and web results - A case study using video intent. In *Proceedings of the 36th European Conference on IR Research*, pages 184–196, 2014.

[4] A. K. Ponnuswami, K. Pattabiraman, D. Brand, and T. Kanungo. Model characterization curves for federated search using click-logs: predicting user engagement metrics for the span of feasible operating points. In *Proceedings of the 20th International Conference on World Wide Web*, pages 67–76, 2011.

[5] M. Shokouhi and L. Si. Federated search. *Foundations and Trends in Information Retrieval*, 5(1):1–102, 2011.

Balancing Exploration and Exploitation: Empirical Parameterization of Exploratory Search Systems

Kumaripaba Athukorala° Alan Medlar* Kalle Ilves° Dorota Głowacka°

° Helsinki Institute for Information Technology HIIT, Department of Computer Science, University of Helsinki

* Institute of Biotechnology, University of Helsinki

° first.last@cs.helsinki.fi, * alan.j.medlar@helsinki.fi

ABSTRACT

Exploratory searches are where a user has insufficient knowledge to define exact search criteria or does not otherwise know what they are looking for. Reinforcement learning techniques have demonstrated great potential for supporting exploratory search in information retrieval systems as they allow the system to trade-off exploration (presenting the user with alternatives topics) and exploitation (moving toward more specific topics). Users of such systems, however, often feel that the system is not responsive to user needs. This problem is not an inherent feature of such systems, but is caused by the exploration rate parameter being inappropriately tuned for a given system, dataset or user.

We present a user study to analyze how different exploration rates affect search performance, user satisfaction, and the number of documents selected. We show that the trade-off between exploration and exploitation can be modelled as a direct relationship between the exploration rate parameter from the reinforcement learning algorithm and the number of relevant documents returned to the user over the course of a search session. We define the optimal exploration/exploitation trade-off as where this relationship is maximised and show this point to be broadly concordant with user satisfaction and performance.

Categories and Subject Descriptors

H.4 [**Information Systems Applications**]: Miscellaneous

1. INTRODUCTION

Exploratory search is defined as a class of search activities performed to learn or discover new information [10]. Unlike lookup search, where a discrete set of results achieves a well-defined objective, exploratory search can involve unfamiliar subject areas and uncertainty regarding search goals. For these reasons exploratory search is considered to be challenging for the user and needs additional support from information retrieval (IR) systems. Reinforcement learning (RL) techniques have demonstrated great potential for supporting exploratory search in IR systems [3, 8, 12]. RL allows the system to trade off between exploitation and exploration, allowing the system to gradually build the user model without getting stuck in a local search space [3, 6]. Parameterizing exploratory systems, however, is not trivial. Experimental results from IR systems employing RL techniques demonstrate that users often do not feel that the system is responsive to their information needs [3]. We do not believe this problem is an inherent property of RL-based systems, but is caused by inappropriately tuned exploration rate. In this sense, if the exploration rate is too low, the user may get stuck in a narrow information space. On the other hand, if it is set too high, the user will be presented with too many documents from topics perceived as irrelevant. Our hypothesis is that the trade-off between exploration and exploitation can be modelled as a direct relationship between exploration rate and the number of documents that are perceived by the user as interesting or relevant. Furthermore, we aim to show that this relationship can be maximised and at this point an optimal trade-off between exploration and exploitation will be made.

In order to test this hypothesis, we first built an exploratory search system for scientific literature using LinRel [1] – an RL algorithm that has been used in a number of IR systems [3]. Using simulation, we identify a range of system parameterizations that would expose the user to different numbers of documents resulting from increasing the exploration rate. The level of exploration ranges from 0, where the user is only presented with documents related to their query, to a high level of exploration, where approximately half of the documents would allow the user to steer the search in a different direction. We then conduct a user study to evaluate the different exploration rates and investigate how to infer the optimal exploration rate with a multiple regression model. Furthermore, with qualitative analysis of user interviews and performance data, we confirm that the exploration rate selected by this approach indeed provides the optimal balance between exploration and exploitation. Our investigation provides insights into designing and parameterizing exploratory search systems with appropriate balance between exploration and exploitation.

2. SYSTEM OVERVIEW

The interface of the system is presented in Figure 1. After typing in the search query, the user is presented with 20 documents where seven documents are visible without scrolling. We display more documents than in traditional IR systems

Permission to make digital or hard copies of all or part of this work for personal or classroom use is granted without fee provided that copies are not made or distributed for profit or commercial advantage and that copies bear this notice and the full citation on the first page. Copyrights for components of this work owned by others than the author(s) must be honored. Abstracting with credit is permitted. To copy otherwise, or republish, to post on servers or to redistribute to lists, requires prior specific permission and/or a fee. Request permissions from Permissions@acm.org.
CIKM'15, October 19–23, 2015, Melbourne, Australia.
Copyright is held by the owner/author(s). Publication rights licensed to ACM.
ACM 978-1-4503-3794-6/15/10 ...$15.00.
DOI: http://dx.doi.org/10.1145/2806416.2806609 .

because in exploratory tasks users examine more results [10]. The initial set of documents is ranked based on the Okapi BM25 algorithm [9]. Next, to see more documents the user can indicate which document interests them by clicking on the circle next to it and thus providing relevance score of 1 to that document. After clicking the "next" button in the top right corner of the page, a new set of documents is displayed based on the feedback provided by the user so far. The user can provide feedback to as many or as few documents as she wishes. Documents that do not receive an explicit relevance feedback are assumed to receive relevance score of 0. The current version of the system is based on around 1 million documents obtained from the ArXiv repository.

In order to help the user explore the document space, we use LinRel [1]. Suppose we have a matrix D, where each row d_i is a tf-idf (term frequency-inverse document frequency) feature vector representation of documents presented so far. Let $r = (r_1, r_2 ... r_t)^\top$ be the column vector of relevance scores received from the user up to time t. We estimate the expected relevance r_i of a document d_i as $\mathbb{E}[r_i] = d_i \cdot w$, where the vector w is estimated from user feedback. LinRel estimates $\hat{w}$ by solving $r = D \cdot w$ and estimates relevance score for each d_i as $\hat{r}_i = d_i \cdot \hat{w}$

In order to deal with the exploration-exploitation trade-off, we present documents not with the highest score $\hat{r}_i$, but with the largest upper confidence bound for the relevance score. Thus, if σ_i is an upper bound on standard deviation of relevance estimate $\hat{r}_i$, the upper confidence bound of document d_i is calculated as $r_i + \gamma\sigma_i$, where $\gamma > 0$ is a constant used to adjust the confidence level of the upper confidence bound. In each iteration, LinRel calculates $s_i = d_i \cdot (D^\top \cdot D + \lambda I)^{-1} D^\top$, where λ is the regularization parameter which is set to 1 if each of the feature vectors sums up to 1 (following [1]) and the documents that maximize $s_i \cdot r + \frac{\gamma}{2}\|s_i\|$ are selected for presentation. The first term $s_i \cdot r$ effectively ranks all the documents based on their similarity to the documents the user has selected so far and thus it narrows the area of the search space (exploitation). The second term $\frac{\gamma}{2}\|s_i\|$ ensures that the user is presented with a more diverse set of results. The exploration rate is controlled by the γ parameter. The higher the value of γ, the more diverse, or exploratory, the results are.

2.1 Simulations

To find suitable values of γ to test in our user study, we built a simulator to understand how γ affects how many documents are shown to the user as a result of the exploration term. To simulate searching for a particular target document, we must specify a search query that would ordinarily be provided by the user and a procedure to identify which documents will be given positive feedback.

To generate search queries, we used topic modelling on the 78,131 computer science articles from ArXiv assuming 200 clusters and manually curated the 124 unambiguous clusters with an appropriate label. In order to obtain the topic models, we used MAchine Learning for LanguagE Toolkit (MALLET) [7]. The search query for a given document is the label for the closest cluster.

Given a target document and its initial search query, the simulator proceeds by greedily selecting which documents to give positive feedback to in order to minimise the average euclidean distance between the results in the next iteration and the target. The simulation is performed for $\gamma = 0.0$ and

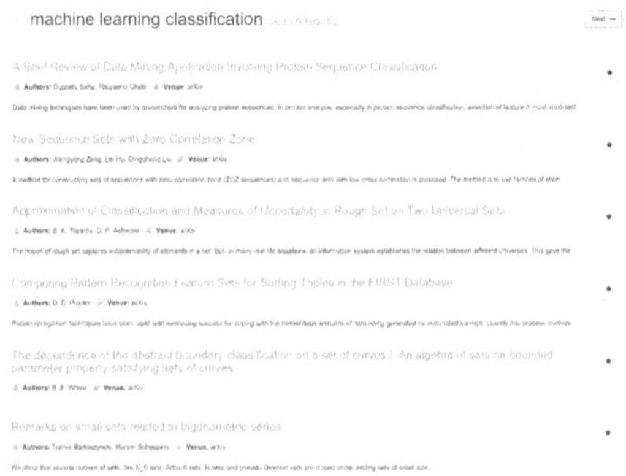

Figure 1: Screen shot of the interface. Search query is displayed on the top. Interesting documents can be selected by clicking the icon next the document and the user can proceed to the next iteration by clicking the next button.

then with different values of γ. For each value of γ we identify which of the 20 documents in the second iteration are present because of using the exploration term. The simulator was run for 200 randomly selected target documents. We identified the exploration rates 0.0, 0.2, 0.5, 1.0 and 2.0 as these resulted in a median number of exploratory documents of 0, 1, 3, 5 and 9, respectively.

3. USER STUDY

The goals of the user study were to investigate how different exploration rates affect 1. the number of documents selected, 2. subjective perception, and 3. overall performance. We recruited ten researchers: 5 finishing MSc students and 5 PhD students. Prior to the study we provided them with a background questionnaire to assess their experience with literature search and knowledge of the search topics. All participants reported experience in scientific literature search. As users engaged in exploratory search tasks aim to acquire new knowledge [11], we specifically selected participants not overly familiar with the search topics.

3.1 Design

An expert researcher from the machine learning domain selected five topics that have sufficient data in the ArXiv dataset: image processing, clustering, classification, natural language processing, and neural networks. The machine learning domain was chosen because it was easier to find both domain experts for creating tasks and assessing performance, and a homogeneous group of participants who had taken at least an introductory machine learning course.We used a within-subject design where every participant performed all five search tasks and every task had a different exploration rate. To avoid order effects, the sequence of performing tasks and assigned exploration rates were counterbalanced using a Latin Square design. We described the tasks using a template that places participants in a scientific essay writing scenario, suitable for exploratory search tasks [11]. To preserve consistency among the tasks, all task descriptions followed the same template.

"Imagine that you are searching scientific literature to write an essay about the topic X. We provide you with

a search engine. Follow your natural literature search process and search for articles that help you to learn about this topic. You have fifteen minutes maximum and prepare an abstract of your essay at the end."

In order to ensure that all the studies were initiated from the same starting point, we provided the initial search query. The first query was always the phrase "machine learning" followed by the the topic of search task – for example "machine learning clustering".

3.2 Measures and Procedure

All the studies were conducted in a controlled laboratory room, with a desktop computer with a 27-inch display. We allocated fifteen minutes per task and automatically terminated the search session at the end of this period. Prior to the study we informed the participants about the maximum duration allowed per task, introduced the search system and gave them one training task. We showed the participants how to select relevant articles and proceed to the next iteration. We explained that by providing feedback they allow the system to learn about their interests and retrieve more suitable results in subsequent iterations. The participants were not aware of the different exploration rates per task. Participants were allowed to take notes using their comfortable technique – using a word processing application or pen and paper. At the end of every task, we provided a web form to write the abstract of their essay as a list of 5-10 bullet points.

We logged details of all the displayed and selected documents. A domain expert performed a blind review of the abstracts and rated them from 0 to 5 (0 = failure and 5 = excellent). In order to assess user satisfaction, after every task we conducted a semi-structured interview. During the interview we asked their opinion on the results and to rate how satisfied they were with the findings. Each study lasted approximately 1.5 hours. We compensated every participant with a movie ticket.

4. RESULTS

Each of the ten participants performed the five tasks using five different exploration rates, resulting in ten observations per exploration rate. During the analysis we decided to exclude two participants from further study. Of the participants that we excluded, one selected no relevant documents and the other selected only a single relevant document per task. Further inspection of their essay abstracts suggested that they did not engage with the tasks and their scores on the abstracts were 0 for two or more tasks according to the external reviewer. We also decided to exclude all observations from the "neural networks" task because six participants failed to complete the task successfully. We hypothesise that these failures were due to neural networks being a more advanced topic and "networks" being a generic term, e.g. social networks, communication networks, etc. The remaining 32 observations were used for further analysis.

4.1 Modelling Document Selection

The raw experimental data was investigated with boxplots to understand what features should be included in the regression model. It was noted that the total number of selected documents was maximised by the middling exploration rate values tested (boxplots not shown), suggesting the necessity of a squared exploration rate term in the model. Analysis was performed using a generalised linear mixed model (GLMM). We used a mixed model to account for repeated measurements on each study participant, explicitly taking into account intra-subject variation by modelling participants as random effects. In our model, we considered the response variable to be the total number of selected documents. As the number of selected documents is count data, it was assumed to be Poisson distributed with a log link function. The fixed effects are the exploration rate, the exploration rate squared and the search query. Participants were treated as random effects, allowing the intercepts to vary. The model was fit using the lme4 R package (ver. 1.1-7) [2]. Confidence intervals were calculated using parametric bootstrapping. P values were calculated by comparison with reduced models using parametric bootstrapping from the pbkrtest package (ver. 0.4-2) [4]. The model was fit with maximum likelihood using the Laplace approximation method and validated by inspection of residual plots. Over-dispersion was tested using the goodness of fit procedure from the aods3 package (ver. 0.4-1) [5] and we found no evidence of over-dispersion (χ^2=12.455, 25 d.f., p=0.983).

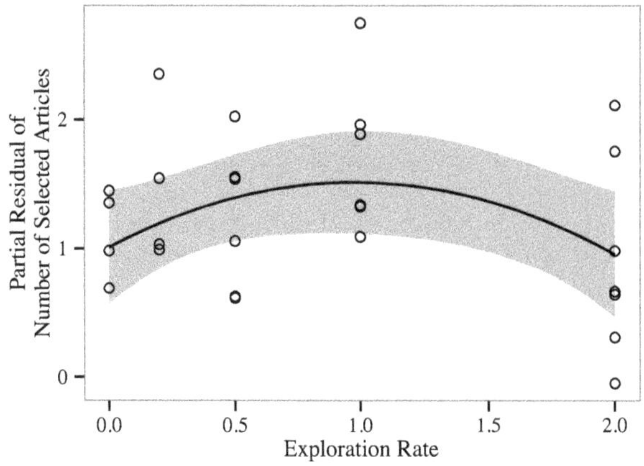

Figure 2: Effect plot of exploration rate on the number of relevant documents selected by the user controlling for all other covariates. Shaded region indicates 95% confidence interval. Circles indicate partial residuals.

There was a significant effect on the square of the exploration rate (95% CI [-2.260, -0.156], p=0.028). The query did not have a statistically significant effect on how many articles the participant selected (p=0.501). The variance of the participant random effect was non-zero (0.114), suggesting that inclusion of the random effect was appropriate. Figure 2 shows an effect plot for exploration rate on the response variable controlling for both query and participant. The number of articles selected as relevant appears to be maximised at an exploration rate of approximately 1.0 (0.97), and corresponds to a 51% increase in the number relevant documents than the baseline exploration rate of 0.0 (95% CI [12%, 91%]). Inspection of partial residuals reveals the presence of several outliers (at exploration rates 0.2 and 1.0) and high variability at exploration rate 2.0. The extent of the influence of these factors is difficult to assess and a larger sample size is required.

4.2 User Satisfaction and Performance

We qualitatively analyzed the user interviews to investigate whether the user satisfaction with search results was affected by different exploration rates. Five participants (out of 8) complained that the search results were too narrow and difficult to interpret for the tasks performed with exploration 0: "Results are not quite satisfactory and about very specific definitions. I did not get [any] understanding of what topics are in this area." [Participant 3], "I selected a paper on semantics, but it took me completely off the way" [Participant 8]. None of the participants made any positive comments about tasks with exploration rate 0. There were mixed comments on tasks performed with exploration rate 0.2 and 0.5. Three participants were satisfied with the search results when exploration rate was set to 0.2, while three gave negative comments: " initially did not show any results that I was expecting [Participant 7]". "At the beginning I had the problem to decide which way I should go. I just selected two different topics for the second iteration and then in the second iteration it gives me mostly [results on] that topic [Participant 2]". We received similar comments for tasks performed with exploration rate 0.5. However, most of the participants were satisfied when the exploration rate was set to 1. Five participants provided very positive comments while none gave any negative comments on exploration rate 1 : "way better than the other tasks. [I] got many different results, but all related [Participant 1]", "I went over several iterations. Results started getting way better [over iterations] and overall I am very satisfied [Participant 5]". Six participants were unhappy with results for the tasks with exploration rate 2. The main reason was that the results are too diverse and not related to the main topic: " [results are] too scattered and many other non-related papers [Participant 5]". Overall, these interviews suggest that users noticed a difference between exploration rates and found exploration rate 1 the most appropriate, which is also the exploration rate that results in the highest number of documents selected by the users according to our regression model.

We analyzed the reviewer rating of the abstracts written by the participants to investigate whether the exploration rate has any effect on their performance. The mean score for – exploration rate 0 is 3 (out of 5) and standard deviation (*std.dev*) is 1.3 , exploration rate 0.2 is 2.6 ($std.dev = 1.4$), exploration rate 0.5 is 2.38 ($std.dev = 1.8$), exploration 1 is 3.2 ($std.dev = 1.2$), and exploration rate 2 is 3.2 ($std.dev = 1.1$). These results confirm that user performance improves with a higher exploration rate, including the exploration rate of 1 which we earlier identified as optimal.

5. DISCUSSION AND CONCLUSIONS

In this paper, we describe a method on how to set the exploration rate in an exploratory IR system. First, we ran a set of simulations to identify a possible set of exploration rates to test in a user study. Our multiple regression analysis of the user studies data showed that exploration rate of 1, which roughly corresponds to a quarter of the presented documents resulting from exploration, corresponds to the highest number of documents to be perceived as relevant by the user. This finding was further confirmed by the qualitative analysis by the user perceived satisfaction with the search results and the task performance results.

The results provide an insight into optimizing RL-based exploratory IR systems and have implications for designing or self-adapting exploratory search systems. For example, by tracking documents selected, the system could automatically set the appropriate level of exploration rate for a given user. Our study was limited to scientific literature search in the machine learning domain with users at similar expertise level – MSc/PhD students. As this is an initial step towards modeling the effect of exploration rate on exploratory search task performance, we purposely controlled several other factors that could also influence search performance, such as the search domain and expertise levels. Currently, we are designing a study involving researchers at different levels of expertise to assess whether users with different expertise level require different exploration rates. Further, we are planning to incorporate more features into our model, such as scroll data or document viewing time. The ultimate goal of our current project is to design an exploratory IR systems that automatically adjust the exploration rate depending on user needs.

6. ACKNOWLEDGEMENTS

This work was partly supported by The Finnish Funding Agency for Innovation (under projects Re:Know and D2I) and by the Academy of Finland (under the Finnish Centre of Excellence in Computational Inference).

7. REFERENCES

[1] P. Auer. Using confidence bounds for exploitation – exploration trade-offs. *JMLR*, 3:397 – 422, 2002.

[2] D. Bates, M. Mächler, B. Bolker, and S. Walker. Fitting linear mixed-effects models using lme4. *arXiv preprint arXiv:1406.5823*, 2014.

[3] D. Głowacka, T. Ruotsalo, K. Konyushkova, K. Athukorala, S. Kaski, and G. Jacucci. Directing exploratory search: Reinforcement learning from user interactions with keywords. In *Proc. IUI*, 2013.

[4] U. Halekoh and S. Højsgaard. A kenward-roger approximation and parametric bootstrap methods for tests in linear mixed models – the R package pbkrtest. *Journal of Statistical Software*, 59(9):1–30, 2014.

[5] M. Lesnoff and R. Lancelot. *aods3: analysis of overdispersed data using S3 methods*, 2013. aods3 package version 0.4-1.

[6] L. Li, W. Chu, J. Langford, and R. Schapire. A contextual-bandit approach to personalized news article recommendation. In *Proc. of WWW*, 2010.

[7] A. K. McCallum. Mallet: A machine learning for language toolkit. http://mallet.cs.umass.edu, 2002.

[8] F. Radlinski, R. Kleinberg, and T. Joachims. Learning diverse rankings with multi-armed bandits. In *Proc. of ICML*, 2008.

[9] K. Sparck Jones, S. Walker, and S. E. Robertson. A probabilistic model of information retrieval: Development and comparative experiments. *Info. Proc. & Manag.*, 36(6):779–840, 2000.

[10] R. W. White and R. A. Roth. Exploratory search: Beyond the query-response paradigm. *Synth. Lec. on Inf. Conc., Retr., and Serv.*, 1(1):1–98, 2009.

[11] B. M. Wildemuth and L. Freund. Assigning search tasks designed to elicit exploratory search behaviors. In *Proc. of the Symposium on HCIIR*. ACM, 2012.

[12] Y. Yue and T. Joachims. Interactively optimizing information retrieval systems as a dueling bandits problem. In *Proc. of ICML*, 2009.

On Predicting Deletions of Microblog Posts

Mossaab Bagdouri
Department of Computer Science
University of Maryland
College Park, MD, USA
mossaab@umd.edu

Douglas W. Oard
iSchool and UMIACS
University of Maryland
College Park, MD, USA
oard@umd.edu

ABSTRACT

Among the many classification tasks on Twitter content, predicting whether a tweet will be deleted has to date received relatively little attention. Deletions occur for a variety of reasons, which can make the classification task challenging. Moreover, deletion prediction might serve different goals, the characteristics of which should be reflected in the evaluation design. This paper addresses the problem of deletion prediction by analyzing the distribution of deleted tweets, presenting a new evaluation framework, exploring tweet-based and user-based features, and reporting prediction scores.

Categories and Subject Descriptors

H.3.3 [**Information Storage and Retrieval**]: Information Search and Retrieval

General Terms: Measurement, Performance

Keywords: Microblogs; Prediction; Deletion

1. INTRODUCTION

Social media platforms have garnered substantial attention from researchers in recent years. The abundance of public content that is available from some services, perhaps most notably Twitter, has inspired a wide range of applications such as characterizing user demographics [7], predicting future events [2] and explaining sociopolitical interactions [10]. Among this work, the thread closest to our focus has explored predicting the reaction of users to specific microblog posts (in Twitter, "tweets"). Work in this thread has included prediction of replies [8], retweeting [5], and deletion[6]. Of these, prediction of deletion has received the least attention to date. A public message on a microblogging service might be deleted for several reasons and in different ways. For instance, some content may be removed by a third party due to a perceived violation of some law, regulation, or norm [1]. In other cases, a person might regret posting an embarrassing comment, later choosing to delete their own tweet [9]. Alternatively, a user might become concerned about privacy and opt to make their profile private, which in Twitter results in deletion of all of their public tweets (these tweets may still be accessible to a restricted number of accounts; they will show as deleted for everybody else). A similar effect can be achieved by Twitter itself, for example when an account is suspended because of spamming or posting inappropriate content. Adding to the complexity, deleting a tweet automatically generates a cascade of deletions for all retweets of that tweet.[1]

Predicting whether a tweet will be deleted might have several applications. Perhaps most obviously, we might help a user avoid posting comments that they may later regret. We might also alert users before they post content that is similar to what has previously been censored. Of greatest importance in our own work, if we can predict which tweets are likely to be deleted, we can act proactively to minimize the "swiss cheese" decay of Twitter test collections in which we have invested annotation effort on tweets that will later be deleted, and thus unusable (by Twitter's terms of service) by future users, including our future selves.

This paper addresses the task of predicting whether a tweet will be deleted. Although we are interested in deletions over many time scales, in this paper we focus on predicting which Tweets will be deleted within 24 hours of being posted. After introducing the datasets and our classifier design in Section 2, we use a simple example to illustrate the importance of reflecting the task characteristics in the evaluation design (Section 3.1). We then propose two new evaluation designs in Sections 3.2 and 3.3, reporting classification results for each. Finally, we summarize our findings and make some remarks on future work in Section 4.

2. METHODS

We present two datasets that we collected to explore the problem of deletion prediction and we describe our classifier design, with particular attention to feature selection.

2.1 Datasets

To conduct our experiments, we collected two datasets in a similar way. We use the first dataset, DS1, to explore the problem and the second, DS2, to validate our results. In our research we are particularly interested in the use of Twitter for Arabic, but the Twitter API does not support language selection alone without specifying some content terms. We therefore started with a list of the most frequent 400 terms

[1]A retweet is a reposting of someone else's tweet.

Permission to make digital or hard copies of all or part of this work for personal or classroom use is granted without fee provided that copies are not made or distributed for profit or commercial advantage and that copies bear this notice and the full citation on the first page. Copyrights for components of this work owned by others than the author(s) must be honored. Abstracting with credit is permitted. To copy otherwise, or republish, to post on servers or to redistribute to lists, requires prior specific permission and/or a fee. Request permissions from Permissions@acm.org.
CIKM'15, October 19–23, 2015, Melbourne, VIC, Australia.
Copyright is held by the owner/author(s). Publication rights licensed to ACM.
ACM 978-1-4503-3794-6/15/10 ...$15.00.
DOI: http://dx.doi.org/10.1145/2806416.2806600 .

Table 1: Summary of the characteristics of the datasets DS1 and DS2.

	DS1	DS2
Seed time	10/24/14 13-14	12/19/14 14-15
Streaming started	10/24/14 14:53	12/21/14 16:58
Streaming ended	11/21/14 01:21	01/22/15 23:59
Users followed	95,000 users	180,000 users
Users who tweeted	91,283	179,425
Number of tweets	80,8239,916	415,582,993
Labeled tweets	78,527,525	406,140,249
Deletion rate	3.64%	2.33%
Mean del rate by user	3.55%	2.88%
S.D. del rate by user	9.15%	7.47%

in a set of 1,050,000 tweets streamed from this API for which Twitter had classified the tweet as Arabic. We then use the API to obtain tweets that contain any of these terms, with a restriction to tweets classified by Twitter as Arabic, for one hour. Using these tweets, we then uniformly sampled a substantial subset of unique users out of those who sent at least one tweet during that hour and we then used the Twitter API to "follow" those users for about a month, tracking both their tweets and any subsequent deletion notifications. Some of the users did not tweet again during the month; we exclude them from the dataset. After sorting all of the tweets chronologically, we used a sliding window of 24 hours to detect which tweets were deleted within one day of being posted. The last tweet we consider is the one received 24 hours before the end of our collection; this allows us to study deletion over a time period of the same duration (one day) regardless of when the tweet arrived. We then labeled each tweet as deleted or not. To comply with Twitter's terms of service, we built our features as soon as the tweet arrived; for deleted tweets we retain the features in order to conduct our study, but we do not retain a readable form of the tweet. Table 1 summarizes the statistics of these datasets.

2.2 Classification

The deletion prediction task exhibits a strong class imbalance, with many fewer positive than negative instances. We prefer an evaluation measure that emphasizes correct decisions on the minority class (deletion), which is the class of interest in this case. We have therefore chosen F_1, the balanced harmonic mean of recall and precision, as our measure of effectiveness. Accuracy is also a commonly reported measure, but on this task accuracy results would be dominated by results on the majority class (not deleted). We would prefer to optimize the classifier directly for F_1 (e.g., using SVM-perf), but this is currently only practical for datasets that are small enough to fit in memory [4]. Given the scale of our datasets, the efficient online classifier Vowpal Wabbit [11] is the better choice. We therefore configured Vowpal Wabbit with logistic regression as the loss function, using default settings for other parameters. We split each dataset into three subsets of 70%, 10% and 20% corresponding respectively to training, development and testing. Vowpal Wabbit assigns a deletion prediction score to every tweet. We use a grid search to find the threshold on that score that maximizes F_1 on the development set. We then classify the testing set using that threshold.

2.3 Feature Selection

Feature selection can have a substantial impact on classifier accuracy. We therefore implement a recursive feature elimination algorithm [3] using DS1. We start with all the features that are available as fields in the JSON object retrieved from Twitter API, which are either tweet-based or user-based. We then derive some synthetic features, such as the word count in the content of a tweet, and the hour of the day when the tweet was created. The features that are provided as a single value (e.g., language of tweet, total number of tweets published by a user) are removed one at a time, whereas those that are provided as a list of values (e.g., bag of words, list of URLs) are removed together at once. Each feature that improves the F_1 value on the DS1 test set when removed during this ablation process is excluded from the feature set. We repeat this process until we settle on a final set of features that each deteriorates the F_1 score on the DS1 test set when (individually) removed. We perform the feature selection process separately for each evaluation condition that we study, but we report DS2 results using the features selected for the same condition using DS1. Our reported DS2 results are thus "fair," in the sense that we believe them to be representative of a classifier that we could actually run on unseen data.

3. PREDICTING DELETIONS

We start the prediction task by observing that a feature as simple as the user ID predicts deletions better than any combination of available features, given the evaluation setup of previous work. We then suggest two alternative evaluation settings and report the corresponding features and scores.

3.1 Naive Features and Evaluation

Petrovic et al. report that the best performance they could achieve was based on training a Support Vector Machine using social and text features in addition to the user IDs [6]. Using their features on our (different) data, we achieve a score of 0.387 on dataset DS1. Surprisingly, however, our feature selection ablation process achieves an even better result with just a single feature, obtaining an F_1 of 0.455 on DS1 just by using the user IDs. Interestingly, Petrovic et al. saw just the opposite, reporting that F_1 fell from 0.270 (for their full feature set), to 0.122 (for user ID alone).

This finding, that on our data (but apparently not on Petrovic et al.'s data) a classifier that learns that some users will often delete their tweets while others will rarely do so does well, suggests a very sharp skew in the data. This led us to investigate the distribution of deletions across all of the users. We do so by first plotting, on a log-log scale, the number of deleted tweets for each user, sorted in a decreasing order, in Figure 1. The resulting plot is piecewise linear, indicating spliced power law distributions that result in a fat head (i.e., an unexpectedly large number of prolific deleters) and thus a thinner tail. The net effect of this is easily seen in the cumulative sum of deletions in Figure 2; this is the area under the (linear scale) deletions-vs.-rank plot. We observe that the first percentile of 912 users is responsible for about a half of all deletions (1,352,043 deletions, 47%), and that 10% of the users (9,127) are responsible for more than four out of every five deletions (i.e., 2,331,268 deletions, 81%). Examining a few new tweets from some of these most prolific deleters suggests to us that many of these prolific deleters may be automated systems that are engaged in advertising

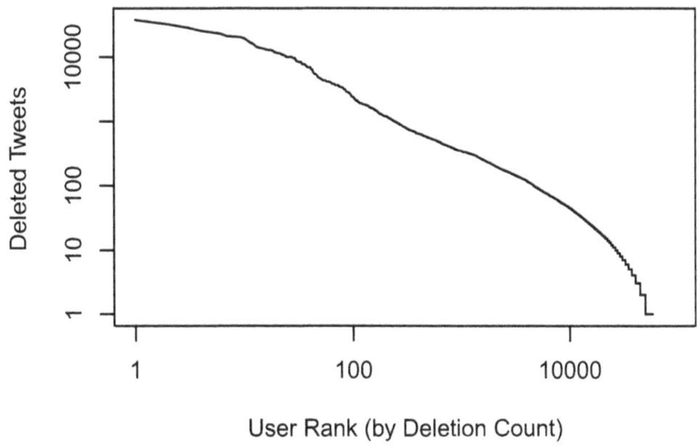

Figure 1: The number of deletions per user for the dataset DS1 in a descendant order. Both axes are in log scale. The deletions appear to follow spliced power-law distributions.

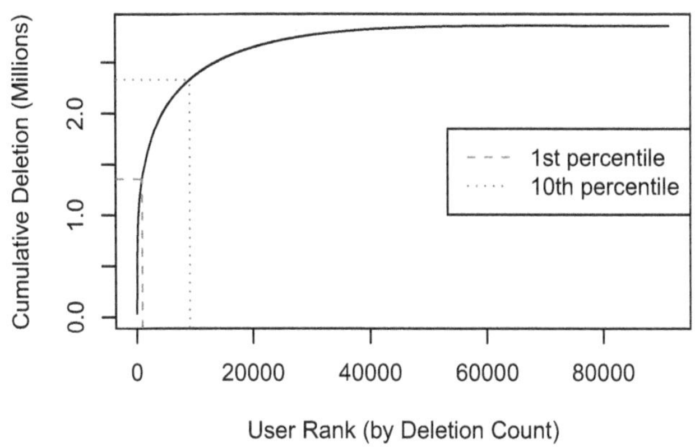

Figure 2: The cumulative count of deletions for the dataset DS1, with a descending sort of users based on their deletes.

activities. Depending on the deletion task, we may, or may not, want to exclude them from our training and prediction. Indeed, for a task such as cleaning a dataset of spam, we would actually want such accounts in the dataset. For a different task such as predicting regret, we might want to focus more on helping real (i.e., human) users and thus we would prefer not to train or test on accounts like these that distort the actual deletion patterns that we wish to learn.

Another aspect of the distribution of the deletions is related to the presence of retweets, since if an original tweet is deleted, then all of its retweets are also automatically deleted.[2] Again, depending on the specifics of the deletion task, we may or may not want to include retweets in the training, prediction and evaluation. For example, we may want to predict that a retweet will be deleted (perhaps because the retweeting user follows several spammers) in a dataset cleaning task. For regret, we may want to restrict our focus to original tweets.

3.2 Separating Users

For this experiment, we want to neutralize the effect of the user ID in the most direct way possible. Simply excluding the user ID from the feature set would not suffice, since a combination of other features (e.g., name, description, number of tweets) might serve as an effective surrogate for the user ID. Even if we were to ignore all user-based features, tweet content might even serve as an effective proxy for the identity of some users (e.g., for users who repeatedly send some distinctive message). For this reason, we opt to split our training, development and test subsets randomly by users rather by tweets, maintaining the respective 70/10/20 ratios. We then use the procedure described in Section 2.3 to select the best features on dataset DS1, which we show in Figure 3. In this plot, the best performance (0.298) is achieved when we include all of the tweet (T) and user (U) features. Excluding all of the features corresponds to predicting all the tweets in the test set to be deleted, which gives a baseline F_1 score of 0.064. An individual or a set of features is either excluded—showing its contribution to the whole combination—while all of the other features are included, or is included—to show its individual contribution compared to the baseline—while the other features are excluded. In combination, the tweet features are stronger predictors than the user features, with the tweet content having the greatest predictive power, both individually, and in combination with other features. The source of the tweet—a field indicating how the tweet was published (e.g., through a smartphone, using a third-party application, or from a desktop browser)—is the second strongest tweet-based feature (by the "Excluded" plot). This is consistent with Sleeper et al.'s qualitative survey in which they report that 45% of regretted tweets were made from a mobile device [9], suggesting a signal might exist from knowing the type of device used. The user-based features add to what can be achieved using the tweet-based features alone, increasing the F_1 score from 0.261 to 0.298.

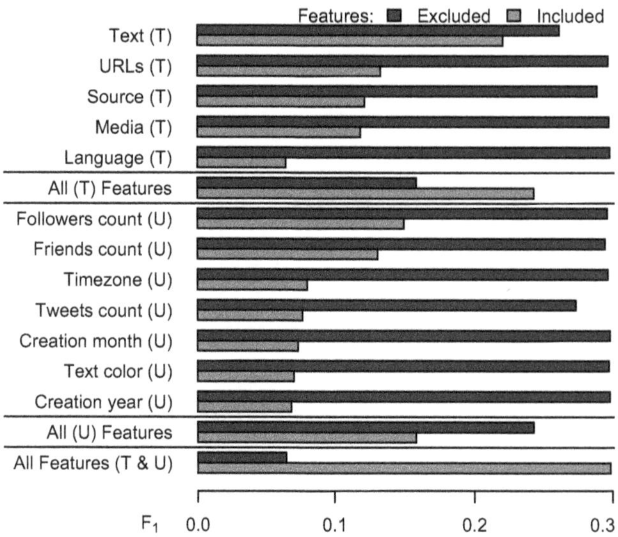

Figure 3: Best features for the dataset DS1 when we split by users. The best performance is achieved when all of the tweet-based (T) and user-based (U) features are included.

We apply these features to dataset DS2 to obtain an F_1 score of 0.375. We also applied Petrovic et al.'s features on this dataset, getting an F_1 score of 0.356. This suggests that on similar unseen data collected as described in Section 2.1 and split by users, we would expect the features we found somewhat to perform better than those of Petrovic et al.

[2]`https://support.twitter.com/entries/18906`

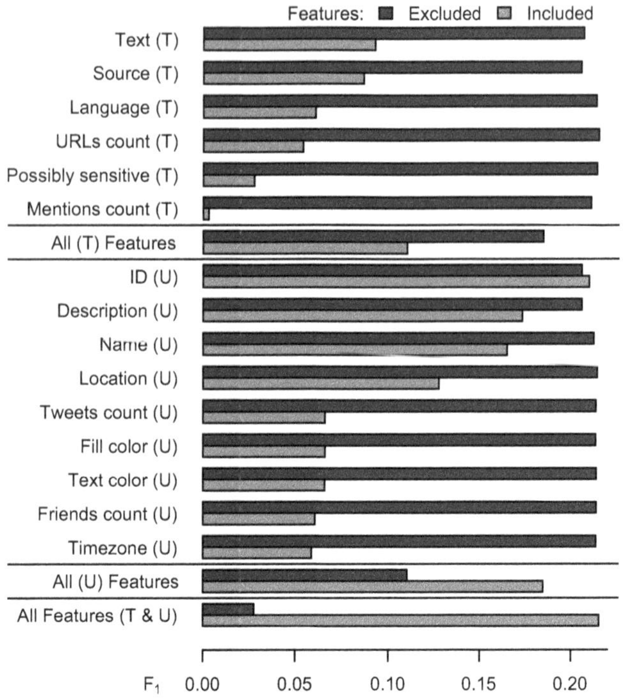

Figure 4: Best features of the dataset DS1 for the chronological split, after excluding the retweets and outliers.

3.3 Excluding Outliers

We now want to maintain the effect of the user information but diminish the noise generated by outlier users. To do so, we first eliminate all of the retweets. This causes the ratio of deleted tweets to go down from 2,861,663 / 78,527,525 = 3.6% to 1,007,760 / 46,233,510 = 2.2%. In other words, the deleted retweets represent 65% of all of the deletions. We are left with 87,469 users (out of 91,274, i.e., 96%) who have posted at least one tweet that is not a retweet. Next we exclude the 2,049 users who have a deletion rate larger than the average deletion rate of these 87,469 users by three standard deviations, because we consider them to be outliers. In fact, these 2% of users are responsible for the deletion of 340,136 tweets that are not retweets, or just above one third of all deletions that are not of retweets. Finally, we have a set of 45,611,445 tweets that are neither retweets nor posted by outliers, containing 667,624 deletions.

Figure 4 shows the best features as found by the process described in Section 2.3. We see that the user ID is still the dominant feature, as it accounts for 0.210 out of the total F_1 score of 0.215. Other user-based identifiers such as the description and the name are good substitutes. Incorporating other user-based features (without any tweet-based features) does actually hurts, reducing the F_1 score to 0.185. Adding tweet-based features slightly improves the F_1 score to 0.215.

We apply these features to dataset DS2 to obtain an F_1 score of 0.188, about the 0.185 that we get with Petrovic et al.'s features. Because user ID is present in both feature sets, we can conclude that removing outliers in the way we have done does little to affect the relative value of the user ID feature (although it does drop the best achievable F_1 by quite a lot, from 0.455 to 0.210, suggesting that user ID is even more useful for the outlier users than for others).

4. CONCLUSION AND FUTURE WORK

We addressed the task of tweet deletion prediction. Among a set of features directly available for a tweet, we found that the user ID is a surprisingly strong feature for both of our datasets, even after removing outliers. From the fact that Petrovic et al. did not see this, we can conclude that our Arabic Twitter datasets have somewhat different characteristics from theirs. Depending on the specifics of the task, we have identified some characteristics that should be considered in the design of evaluation methods, such as the inclusion or exclusion of retweets and the inclusion or exclusion of users with abnormal deletion activity. We have suggested some appropriate feature sets, and reported performance scores for such cases. While we allowed a period of 24 hours to detect deletions in our experiments, we do not know if various deletion types (e.g., regret deletions, cascade of deletions of retweets, spam deletions, etc.) take place at similar or different times. Conducting such a study would require us to build a classifier that differentiates between various types of deletions. In future work, we are also interested in studying the effect of linguistic features on the deletion prediction. Indeed, it is not clear yet whether the behaviors we observed in a dataset where Arabic is the dominant language and the Arab world is the likely originating location will be applicable to datasets of other languages and regions.

ACKNOWLEDGMENT

This work was made possible by NPRP grant# NPRP 6-1377-1-257 from the Qatar National Research Fund (a member of Qatar Foundation). The statements made herein are solely the responsibility of the authors. We thank Maram Hasanain for helping us select the 400 words frequent in Arabic tweets.

5. REFERENCES

[1] D. Bamman et al. Censorship and deletion practices in Chinese social media. *First Monday*, 17(3), 2012.
[2] J. Bollen et al. Twitter mood predicts the stock market. *J. of Comp. Science*, 2(1):1–8, 2011.
[3] I. Guyon, J. Weston, S. Barnhill, and V. Vapnik. Gene selection for cancer classification using support vector machines. *Machine Learning*, 46(1-3):389–422, 2002.
[4] T. Joachims and C.-N. J. Yu. Sparse kernel SVMs via cutting-plane training. In *ECML PKDD'09*.
[5] S. Petrovic, M. Osborne, and V. Lavrenko. RT to win! Predicting message propagation in Twitter. In *ICWSM'11*.
[6] S. Petrovic, M. Osborne, and V. Lavrenko. I wish I didn't say that! Analyzing and predicting deleted messages in Twitter. *CoRR*, abs/1305.3107, 2013.
[7] D. Rao et al. Classifying latent user attributes in Twitter. In *SMUC'10*, pages 37–44.
[8] M. Rowe, S. Angeletou, and H. Alani. Predicting discussions on the social semantic web. In *ESWC'11*.
[9] M. Sleeper et al. "I read my Twitter the next morning and was astonished:" A conversational perspective on Twitter regrets. In *CHI'13*, pages 3277–3286.
[10] K. Starbird and L. Palen. (How) will the revolution be retweeted?: Information diffusion and the 2011 Egyptian uprising. In *CSCW'12*, pages 7–16.
[11] K. Weinberger et al. Feature hashing for large scale multitask learning. In *ICML'09*, pages 1113–1120.

Semi-Automated Text Classification for Sensitivity Identification

Giacomo Berardi[◇], Andrea Esuli[◇], Craig Macdonald[♣],
Iadh Ounis[♣], Fabrizio Sebastiani[♡*]
[◇]Istituto di Scienza e Tecnologie dell'Informazione, Consiglio Nazionale delle Ricerche, Pisa, Italy
[♣]School of Computing Science, University of Glasgow, Glasgow, UK
[♡]Qatar Computing Research Institute, Hamad bin Khalifa University, Doha, Qatar

ABSTRACT

Sensitive documents are those that cannot be made public, e.g., for personal or organizational privacy reasons. For instance, documents requested through Freedom of Information mechanisms must be manually reviewed for the presence of sensitive information before their actual release. Hence, tools that can assist human reviewers in spotting sensitive information are of great value to government organizations subject to Freedom of Information laws. We look at sensitivity identification in terms of semi-automated text classification (SATC), the task of ranking automatically classified documents so as to optimize the cost-effectiveness of human post-checking work. We use a recently proposed utility-theoretic approach to SATC that explicitly optimizes the chosen effectiveness function when ranking the documents by sensitivity; this is especially useful in our case, since sensitivity identification is a recall-oriented task, thus requiring the use of a recall-oriented evaluation measure such as F_2. We show the validity of this approach by running experiments on a multi-label multi-class dataset of government documents manually annotated according to different types of sensitivity.

1. INTRODUCTION

Government documents may be deposited in archives for public viewing after a period of years, or released into the public domain through Freedom of Information mechanisms. However, documents containing *sensitive* information should not be released, as they may reveal personal information, thereby infringing on someone's privacy, or reveal information that may offend other countries.

Classically, for paper documents, the identification of sensitive documents has taken place using human reviewers. However, with limited government budgets, the adoption of text classification techniques that aid in the identification of sensitive documents is attractive, since it can increase the efficiency of human reviewers. The possibility of treating sensitivity review as an automated text classification task has recently been shown in [7], where text classifiers were used in order to automatically detect sensitive documents, and where "sensitive" can have different interpretations (e.g., defence-related issues, or issues related to law enforcement).

The task of sensitivity identification bears strong resemblances with "review for privilege" in e-discovery [8], where expert attorneys must check that "privileged" (i.e., sensitive) information is not accidentally disclosed to a requesting party in the context of a civil litigation process [3, 10]. Another task that bears resemblances with sensitivity identification is record anonymisation, as when e.g., medical records have to be anonymised before they are released for epidemiological studies; in this case, sensitive information such as patients' names and medical doctors' names have to be spotted in order to be redacted [9]. Sensitivity identification and privilege identification are text classification tasks, while record anonymisation is an information extraction task. Notwithstanding the differences, all these cases are characterized by the fact that the costs of accidental disclosure of sensitive information are high.

In this paper we follow in the steps of [7] and investigate automatic techniques for aiding sensitivity review. However, while [7] was concerned with automatically classifying documents by sensitivity, here we are concerned with aiding a human annotator who validates (i.e., inspects and corrects where appropriate) these automatically classified documents, with the goal of maximizing the cost-effectiveness of the annotator's work. In other words, while [7] was concerned with "Step 1" in the workflow, we tackle "Step 2".

We frame the task of aiding our human annotator as a *semi-automatic text classification* (SATC) task. SATC (see [2, 5, 6]) is defined as the task of ranking a set $\mathcal{D}$ of automatically classified textual documents in such a way that, if a human annotator validates the documents in a top-ranked portion of $\mathcal{D}$ with the goal of increasing the overall classification accuracy of $\mathcal{D}$, the expected increase in accuracy is maximized. Therefore, we envisage our annotators as validating documents by sensitivity, starting from the top of the ranked list we generate, and working downwards (until they are confident that the dataset has been cleared up, or until the budget for annotation work has been spent).

We approach SATC by adopting the utility-theoretic approach of [2] (hereafter: U-Theoretic). Essentially, U-Theoretic ranks the automatically labelled documents by taking two factors into consideration, i.e.,

*Fabrizio Sebastiani is currently on leave from Consiglio Nazionale delle Ricerche, Italy.

Permission to make digital or hard copies of all or part of this work for personal or classroom use is granted without fee provided that copies are not made or distributed for profit or commercial advantage and that copies bear this notice and the full citation on the first page. Copyrights for components of this work owned by others than ACM must be honored. Abstracting with credit is permitted. To copy otherwise, or republish, to post on servers or to redistribute to lists, requires prior specific permission and/or a fee. Request permissions from Permissions@acm.org.
CIKM'15, October 19–23, 2015, Melbourne, Australia.
© 2015 ACM. ISBN 978-1-4503-3794-6/15/10 ...$15.00.
DOI: http://dx.doi.org/10.1145/2806416.2806597.

1. the probability that the document has been misclassified by the classifier (documents with high probability of misclassification should be ranked higher, since no benefit will occur from validating a correctly classified document), and

2. the increase (or *gain*) in the overall accuracy of the automatically labelled set that occurs if the document is validated (documents that bring about a higher gain should be ranked higher).

Concerning (2), while the same gain occurs from validating either a true positive (TP) or a true negative (TN) – this gain is 0, since the human annotator will not change their labels – the gain that occurs from validating a false positive (FP) or a false negative (FN) may be, as shown in [2], different. When the two gains are different, the utility-theoretic approach tested in this paper:

- is indeed different from an approach based on (1) only, which we describe as the *purely probabilistic approach* (indeed, the two approaches instead coincide when the two gains are the same), and
- is intuitively superior to the latter, since the goal of SATC is increasing the overall labelling accuracy of $\mathcal{D}$, and this means that we must bring to bear the increase in this overall labelling accuracy that validating a given document brings about.

Note that the gains from validating TPs and TNs are different (as shown in Equations (3) and (4) below) when accuracy is measured via functions such as F_1 (which pays equal importance to precision and to recall). However, this is even more true when using metrics that give more importance to recall than to precision (or vice versa), since the imbalance between the gains deriving from validating a FP or a FN is even higher. This is indeed our case, since sensitivity identification is a recall-oriented task (there is a higher cost involved in missing a sensitive document than in erroneously catching a non-sensitive document), which means that a measure (such as e.g., F_2) that emphasizes recall over precision needs to be adopted.

Hence, in this paper, our application of the utility-theoretic approach for semi-automated text classification to the recall-oriented task of sensitivity identification, brings two contributions: (i) it verifies the utility-theoretic approach on the more difficult task of sensitivity identification, and (ii) it moves the state-of-the-art in sensitivity identification from automatic text classification to an assistive approach that can benefit the efficiency of an annotator examining documents for sensitivities. The rest of the paper is structured as follows. In Section 2 we describe our approach to top-ranking sensitive information via semi-automated text classification. Section 3 describes our experiments carried out on a dataset of documents annotated according to different types of sensitivity. Section 4 provides concluding remarks.

2. SATC SENSITIVITY IDENTIFICATION

The U-Theoretic approach described in [2] tackles SATC in a "multi-label multi-class" context, i.e., there is a set of classes $\mathcal{C} = \{c_1, \ldots, c_{|\mathcal{C}|}\}$ with $|\mathcal{C}| > 1$ (this makes it a "multi-class" problem) and each document d_i may belong to zero, one, or several among the classes in $\mathcal{C}$ (this makes it a "multi-label" problem). The U-Theoretic approach assumes that binary classifiers h_j, one for each $c_j \in \mathcal{C}$, have classified the set of unlabelled documents (which, for the purpose of our experiments, will here be equated with the test set Te), also returning a confidence score for each classification decision; the binary decisions returned by classifier h_j will be collectively denoted as $h_j(Te)$.

U-Theoretic ranks documents in terms of *total utility*, i.e.,

$$U(d_i) = \sum_{c_j \in \mathcal{C}} U_j(d_i) \quad (1)$$

where $U_j(d_i)$ (*class-specific utility*) is defined as:

$$U_j(d_i) = \sum_{\omega_j^i \in \{tp_j^i, fp_j^i, fn_j^i, tn_j^i\}} P(\omega_j^i) G(\omega_j^i) \quad (2)$$

Here, $P(\omega_j^i)$ is the system's estimate of the probability that event ω_j^i occurs, tp_j^i is the event "d_i is a true positive for c_j", and fp_j^i, fn_j^i, tn_j^i are defined similarly. If the classifier is a probabilistic one, the $P(\omega_j^i)$'s are the posterior probabilities directly generated by the classifier (e.g., if d_i is a positive example of c_j, then $P(tp_j^i)$ is $P(c_j|d_i)$, $P(fn_j^i)$ is $(1 - P(c_j|d_i))$, and $P(fp_j^i) = P(tn_j^i) = 0$). If the classifier is not a probabilistic one, these probabilities can be obtained from the confidence scores output by the classifier via the application of a generalized logistic function (see [2, Section 3.3] for details).

In Equation (2), $G(\omega_j^i)$ is the *gain*, defined as the average increase in the value of the evaluation function that derives when an event of type ω_j^i occurs, where the average is computed across all documents of the same type (e.g., if $\omega_j^i \equiv fp_j^i$, the average is computed across all of the false positives for c_j). For instance, we take $G(fp_j^i)$ to be the average increase in the accuracy of Te that derives by correcting a false positive for c_j – i.e. removing from Te a false positive and adding to Te a true negative – calculated as:

$$\begin{aligned} G(fp_j^i) &= \frac{1}{FP_j}(F_1^{FP}(h_j(Te)) - F_1(h_j(Te))) \\ &= \frac{1}{FP_j}(\frac{2TP_j}{2TP_j + FN_j} - \frac{2TP_j}{2TP_j + FP_j + FN_j}) \end{aligned} \quad (3)$$

where by TP_j we indicate the number of true positives for class c_j (and analogously for FP_j, FN_j, TN_j).We assume F_1 to be the chosen evaluation function, where $F_1(h_j(Te))$ denotes the value of F_1 computed on $h_j(Te)$, and where by $F_1^{FP}(h_j(Te))$ we indicate the value of F_1 that would derive by correcting all false positives in $h_j(Te)$ (i.e., turning all of them into true negatives). Similarly, we take $G(fn_j^i)$ to be:

$$\begin{aligned} G(fn_j^i) &= \frac{1}{FN_j}(F_1^{FN}(h_j(Te)) - F_1(h_j(Te))) \\ &= \frac{1}{FN_j}(\frac{2(TP_j + FN_j)}{2(TP_j + FN_j) + FP_j} - \\ &\qquad \frac{2TP_j}{2TP_j + FP_j + FN_j}) \end{aligned} \quad (4)$$

Here, the values of TP_j, FP_j, FN_j, TN_j are unknown (since in a real application the true labels of the examples we have automatically classified are unknown), but may be estimated via k-fold cross-validation (see [2, Sect. 3.4] for details).

Note that the method generates a single ranking (according to the document scores computed via Equation (1)), and not $|\mathcal{C}|$ different ones; this allows the human annotator to scan the document list only once, validating a document for all the classes in $\mathcal{C}$ before moving on to the next document.

3. EXPERIMENTS

In this section we report on experiments that we have conducted in order to test how well U-Theoretic performs on the task of sensitivity identification.

3.1 Experimental setting

For our experiments we have used the same dataset as used in [7]. This dataset contains 1,111 government records sampled from a larger corpus of documents addressing international relations. Unlike the rest of the corpus, which is still unlabelled, these 1,111 records have been manually labelled by government experts according to two types of sensitivity identified in the UK's Freedom of Information Act 2000[1], namely "Section 40", which deals with the occurrence of personal information and "Section 27", which describes material damaging to international relations. Of the 1,111 judged records, 104 were judged to be sensitive for Section 27 and 86 for Section 40 (see [7] for more details on this dataset).

For each of the 1,111 records we use the same features employed in [7] for text classification purposes. In particular, we use the contents of the document represented as a vector of term frequencies, along with four other features, namely the presence of dictionary last names, presence of internationally famous persons as listed in DBpedia (e.g., Royal Family, government leaders, etc.), number of subjective sentences as identified by the OpinionFinder toolkit [11], and a risk score for the record depending on the countries mentioned within the record. Again, see [7] for more details on the feature representations used.

As a measure of classification accuracy we use F_2, an instance of the well-known F_β function defined as:

$$F_\beta = \frac{(\beta^2+1)TP}{(\beta^2+2)TP + (\beta^2+1)FN + FP} \qquad (5)$$
$$F_2 = \frac{5TP}{6TP + 5FN + FP}$$

We adopt F_2 since (as already observed in the introduction) ours is a recall-oriented task, and F_2 is a standard choice for this kind of tasks. Note that, as a consequence, in Equations (3) and (4) we use F_2 (and its definition from Equation (5)) in place of F_1; in other words, for us a gain $G(\omega_j^i)$ is defined in terms of increases in F_2 (and not F_1) obtained from the annotator's validation activity.

As the learning algorithm we use SVMs, c.f. Joachims' SVM-light implementation [4]; in all our experiments we use a linear kernel. Due to the imbalance of the training data, we oversample each training set by generating duplicates of sensitive records until we obtain the same numbers of sensitive and non-sensitive records in the training set. This solution (see e.g., [1]) turns out to be effective in improving the SVM performance despite its simplicity, especially when the number of the minority class examples is small. (Initial experiments we have performed without oversampling have yielded radically worse accuracy results.)

We perform our experiments using repeated random subsampling validation, i.e., (a) we generate multiple (in our case: 10) random training / test splits of the original dataset (in our case: always using 80% of the data for training and 20% for testing), (b) for each such split we train our classifiers on the training set and (c) classify + rank the test data using the trained classifier, and finally (d) we compute the final effectiveness results as the average effectiveness across the different splits.

[1] http://www.legislation.gov.uk/ukpga/2000/36/contents

For each of the 10 splits, as a substep of step (b) we perform parameter optimization on the training data. We do this by first optimizing (via 10-fold cross-validation, and independently for each class) the C parameter of SVMs, which determines the tradeoff between the training error and the margin. Then, using the value of C deemed optimal we optimize the parameter of the generalized logistic function (used for calibrating the $P(\omega_j^i)$ needed in Equation (2) – see Section 2) via a second 10-fold cross-validation phase (in this phase we also obtain the estimates of TP_j, FP_j, FN_j, TN_j which are needed for computing $G(fp_j^i)$ and $G(fn_j^i)$ in Equations (3) and (4)). The test sets are then classified and ranked by employing the parameter values deemed optimal.

In order to evaluate the effectiveness of our approach, we use the $ENER_\rho^M(\xi)$ ("expected normalized error reduction") measure proposed in [2]. $ENER_\rho^M(\xi)$ measures the reduction in classification error (of the automatically labelled document set) obtained when a human annotator validates (i.e., inspects and corrects where appropriate) the top-ranked documents in the ranking generated by ranking method ρ; here, the M superscript stands for "macroaveraging", to indicate that the error is computed for each class separately and the results are then averaged. $ENER_\rho^M(\xi)$ is based on a probabilistic user model, and ξ represents the expected percentage of the ranking that the human annotator inspects; for instance, $ENER_\rho^M(0.10)$ examines a scenario in which the expected number of documents that the user validates is one tenth of the entire automatically labelled set.

In $ENER_\rho^M(\xi)$, "classification error" may be measured according to any desired measure of error; differently from [2], which used $(1 - F_1)$, we obviously use $(1 - F_2)$. The values on which $ENER_\rho^M(\xi)$ ranges are a strict subset of [0,1], with better rankings corresponding to higher values of $ENER_\rho^M(\xi)$. We refer the reader to [2, Section 4] for more details on $ENER_\rho^M(\xi)$.

We follow [2] in using, as the baseline for our experiments, a probabilistic (as opposed to utility-theoretic) system that ranks documents according to the probability of misclassification only, i.e., the documents most likely to be misclassified are top-ranked. This is obtained by using U-Theoretic with both $G(fp_j^i)$ and $G(fn_j^i)$ set to 1. This is a "lower bound" baseline, which we expect the U-Theoretic approach to outperform. Along with [2], we also report two "upper bound", idealised baselines (named Oracle1 and Oracle2), that we expect our system to underperform; both baselines are versions of the U-Theoretic approach endowed with foreknowledge (Oracle1 has foreknowledge of the true values of TP_j, FP_j, FN_j, TN_j and can thus compute $G(fp_j^i)$ and $G(fn_j^i)$ precisely, while Oracle2 even has foreknowledge of the true labels in the test set, and can thus use binary values in place of probabilities in Equation (2)). These two "upper bound" baselines thus indicate how far U-Theoretic is from the ideal performance.

3.2 Results

The results of our experiments are reported in Table 1, for three different values of ξ. As an example, the result $ENER_\rho^M(0.05) = 0.215$ obtained by U-Theoretic can approximately be interpreted as saying that, when using this ranking method, by only validating 5% of the automatically classified documents an annotator is expected to obtain a

Table 1: Results of different ranking methods in terms of $ENER_\rho^M(\xi)$, for $\xi \in \{0.05, 0.10, 0.20\}$, with F_2 as the measure of classification error. Improvements are relative to the baseline.

	$\xi = 0.05$		$\xi = 0.10$		$\xi = 0.20$	
Baseline	0.189		0.263		0.306	
U-Theoretic	0.215	(+14%)	0.283	(+8%)	0.316	(+3%)
Oracle1	0.223	(+18%)	0.289	(+10%)	0.321	(+5%)
Oracle2	0.517	(+174%)	0.629	(+139%)	0.647	(+111%)

reduction in classification error (measured in terms of (1-F_2)) strictly higher than 0.215[2].

The first interesting fact we may observe is that the utility-theoretic method substantially outperforms the baseline, with achieved improvements with respect to it ranging from +3% to +14%. A second interesting fact is that the results of the utility-theoretic method are very close to the results of Oracle1, an idealized method that has foreknowledge of the true values of TP_j, FP_j, FN_j, TN_j; this means that U-Theoretic does a good job in estimating these quantities.

Note that the improvements obtained by U-Theoretic over Baseline are lower than the ones (even exceeding +100%) reported in [2] for training sets of comparable size. The likely reason is that classification by sensitivity is much harder than classification by topic (which is the task [2] tackles), as shown by the fact that the SVM classifiers of [2] obtain (for training sets of comparable size) $F_1 = 0.527$ while our SVM classifiers here obtain (as an average across the 10 test sets) $F_2 = 0.213$. We conjecture that a classifier (such as ours) that obtains lower classification accuracy also generates less reliable confidence scores, which are the key input to U-Theoretic. We can thus expect U-Theoretic to achieve even bigger margins on the probabilistic baseline once training sets are larger and (as a consequence) both the classification accuracy and the quality of the confidence scores are higher.

While the improvements we have obtained are substantial, there are reasons to believe that in realistic applications, characterized by much larger *unlabelled* sets than the one we had access to, the improvements would be even larger; in fact, as [2] shows, the larger the set to be ranked, the more U-Theoretic shines with respect to the baseline.

4. CONCLUSION

The sensitivity review of "digital-born" textual records is an important process for Freedom of Information initiatives at the heart of the open-government agenda. Framing sensitivity identification as an automatic text classification task is challenging, as noted in previous work [7]. For this reason, assistive techniques that can aid a sensitivity reviewer – such as semi-automatic text classification (SATC) – play an important role. In this work, we investigate the applicability of the utility-theoretic approach for SATC, previously proposed in [2]. Our experiments indicate that, when ranking documents in order to maximize the cost-effectiveness of human post-inspection work for sensitivity identification, there are clear benefits to gain from using a utility-theoretic approach instead of the purely probabilistic approach.

[2]We say "strictly higher than 0.215" because $ENER_\rho^M(\xi)$ does not measure the "absolute" reduction in error, but a normalized version of it where we factor out the reduction in error (equal to 5%, i.e., 0.050) we would obtain by using a random ranker. The improvement obtained by U-Theoretic is thus 0.215+0.050=0.265.

5. REFERENCES

[1] G. E. Batista, R. C. Prati, and M. C. Monard. A study of the behavior of several methods for balancing machine learning training data. *ACM SIGKDD Explorations*, 6(1):20–29, 2004.

[2] G. Berardi, A. Esuli, and F. Sebastiani. A utility-theoretic ranking method for semi-automated text classification. In *Proceedings of the 35th Annual International ACM SIGIR Conference on Research and Development in Information Retrieval (SIGIR 2012)*, pages 961–970, Portland OR, US, 2012.

[3] M. Gabriel, C. Paskach, and D. Sharpe. The challenge and promise of predictive coding for privilege. In *Proceedings of the ICAIL 2013 Workshop on Standards for Using Predictive Coding (DESI V)*, Roma, IT, 2013.

[4] T. Joachims. Making large-scale SVM learning practical. In B. Schölkopf, C. J. Burges, and A. J. Smola, editors, *Advances in Kernel Methods – Support Vector Learning*, chapter 11, pages 169–184. The MIT Press, Cambridge, US, 1999.

[5] M. Martinez-Alvarez, A. Bellogin, and T. Roelleke. Document difficulty framework for semi-automatic text classification. In *Proceedings of the 15th International Conference on Data Warehousing and Knowledge Discovery (DaWaK 2013)*, Prague, CZ, 2013.

[6] M. Martinez-Alvarez, S. Yahyaei, and T. Roelleke. Semi-automatic document classification: Exploiting document difficulty. In *Proceedings of the 34th European Conference on Information Retrieval (ECIR 2012)*, Barcelona, ES, 2012.

[7] G. McDonald, C. Macdonald, I. Ounis, and T. Gollins. Towards a classifier for digital sensitivity review. In *Proceedings of the 36th European Conference on Information Retrieval (ECIR 2014)*, pages 500–506, Amsterdam, NL, 2014.

[8] D. W. Oard and W. Webber. Information retrieval for e-discovery. *Foundations and Trends in Information Retrieval*, 7(2/3):99–237, 2013.

[9] G. Szarvas, R. Farkas, and R. Busa-Fekete. State-of-the-art anonymisation of medical data with an iterative machine learning model/framework. *Journal of the American Medical Informatics Association*, 14(5):574–580, 2007.

[10] J. K. Vinjumur, D. W. Oard, , and J. H. Paik. Assessing the reliability and reusability of an e-discovery privilege test collection. In *Proceedings of the 37th ACM Conference on Research and Development in Information Retrieval (SIGIR 2014)*, pages 1047—1050, Gold Coast, AU, 2014.

[11] T. Wilson, P. Hoffmann, S. Somasundaran, J. Kessler, J. Wiebe, Y. Choi, C. Cardie, E. Riloff, and S. Patwardhan. OpinionFinder: A system for subjectivity analysis. In *Proceedings of the HLT/EMNLP 2005 Interactive Demonstrations*, pages 34–35, Vancouver, CA, 2005.

Identification of Microblogs Prominent Users during Events by Learning Temporal Sequences of Features

Imen Bizid
L3i Lab
La Rochelle, France
imen.bizid@univ-lr.fr

Nibal Nayef
L3i Lab
La Rochelle, France
nibal.nayef@univ-lr.fr

Patrice Boursier
IUMW
Kuala Lumpur, Malaysia
patrice@iumw.edu.my

Sami Faiz
LTSIRS Lab
Tunis, Tunisia
sami.faiz@insat.rnu.tn

Antoine Doucet
L3i Lab
La Rochelle, France
antoine.doucet@univ-lr.fr

ABSTRACT

During specific real-world events, some users of microblogging platforms could provide exclusive information about those events. The identification of such prominent users depends on several factors such as the freshness and the relevance of their shared information. This work proposes a probabilistic model for the identification of prominent users in microblogs during specific events. The model is based on learning and classifying user behavior over time using Mixture of Gaussians Hidden Markov Models. A user is characterized by a temporal sequence of feature vectors describing his activities. The features computed at each time-stamp are designed to reflect both the on- and off-topic activities of users. To validate the efficacy of our proposed model, we have conducted experiments on data collected from Twitter during the Herault floods that have occurred in France. The achieved results show that learning the time-series of users' actions is better than learning just those actions without temporal information.

Categories and Subject Descriptors

H.3.3 [**Information Storage and Retrieval**]: Information Search and Retrieval—*selection process, retrieval models*; H.3.1 [**Information Systems**]: User/Machine Systems—*human factors, human information processing*

Keywords

Prominent microblogs users identification, Learning temporal user behavior, MoG-HMM classification

1. INTRODUCTION

Microblogging platforms represent a rich source of information indispensable to manage specific events. These platforms are seen as the perfect ground to mine relevant and exclusive information during such events. Although these microblogs such as Twitter provide many characterizing features about their content – such as the number of retweets or favorites etc. –, such features generally refer to popular users content rather than reflecting the real importance of that content. Therefore, in the context of a specific event – such as a disaster –, it is more logical to associate the relevance and quality of messages with the user's prominence in that specific event [11, 8, 15].

We define *prominent user identification* in microblogging platforms as identifying key users who provide fresh and relevant information during specific events regardless of their popularity in the platform. To the best of our knowledge, this task has never been studied in this context. However, the related problems of finding influencers have been widely explored in the state-of-the-art [10, 4]. Other works have dealt with the identification of topical authorities and domain experts [9, 13, 6]. In these related contexts, key users were identified by analyzing either the network structure using time consuming centrality algorithms such as PageRank [7, 12, 14] and HITS [1], or using the historic topical users activities independently of their temporal characteristics and off-topic activity [10, 13].

These general purpose existing approaches would give a misleading image of users behavior in real scenarios. Users are mainly evaluated according to their on-topic activity while neglecting their off-topic one. Such practice would promote official media channels toggling between several topics and which are not necessarily sharing fresh information. Moreover, users are typically represented in terms of the quantity of their produced and forwarded information independently of the temporal distribution of this information. This would give the same description for users interacting at an early stage of the event by sharing fresh information and other users posting the same information at its end.

This work is thus designed to alleviate these shortcomings. More specifically, we present the following contributions: (1) a novel representation of microblogs user behavior as a temporal sequence of features that characterize both the on- and off-topic user activities, (2) a probabilistic model for the identification of prominent users in microblogs during specific events. This model is based on learning and classifying the mentioned representation using a Mixture of Gaussians Hidden Markov Model (MoG-HMM).

Permission to make digital or hard copies of all or part of this work for personal or classroom use is granted without fee provided that copies are not made or distributed for profit or commercial advantage and that copies bear this notice and the full citation on the first page. To copy otherwise, to republish, to post on servers or to redistribute to lists, requires prior specific permission and/or a fee.

CIKM'15 October 19-23, 2015, Melbourne, VIC, Australia
Copyright 2015 ACM 978-1-4503-3794-6/15/10 ...$15.00
DOI: http://dx.doi.org/10.1145/2806416.2806612.

The rest of this paper is organized as follows. Section 2 presents problem formulation. Section 3 discusses our proposed approach of modeling user behavior. Section 4 describes the used HMM learning model for classifying prominent users. Experimental evaluation is presented in Section 5. Finally, we conclude with directions for future work in Section 6.

2. PROBLEM FORMULATION

We formulate the problem of prominent users identification in the context of specific events as two main sub-problems. The first is representing users so that to reflect their temporal behavior during an event. Each user u has to be represented by a temporal sequence $V_u = (V_u^1, V_u^2, ..., V_u^m)$ where m is the length of the sequence describing the user behavior over m time stamps. $V_u^{(i)}$ represents user description at each time interval i, and can be any set of features characterizing the user. The second sub-problem is learning to classify users' temporal sequences of features as either belonging to prominent c_1 or non-prominent c_2 user classes. Thus we need to learn two probabilistic models H_{c_1} and H_{c_2} by training the continuous temporal sequences describing each class of users. Given these models, we need to estimate the likelihood $L(V|H_{c1})$ and $L(V|H_{c2})$ of each user sequence.

3. MODELING USERS AS TEMPORAL SEQUENCES OF ACTIVITY FEATURES

In order to model users consistently with their realistic behavior in microblogs during events, we propose a temporal sequence representation approach. The behavior of users is represented according to their observed on- and off-topic activities at different temporal stages during an event.

3.1 Temporal Sequence Representation

The time-line of an event is divided into equispaced intervals at m time stamps. During each interval, users activities are characterized by a set of features rather than a single feature as there are several types of activities in microblogs. The user activity is represented by the feature vector $V_u^{t_i}$ calculated based on $t_1, t_2, t_3, ..., t_m$ time stamps. Those features – discussed in the next subsection – describe the user behavior regarding an event (on-topic activity) and also regarding other topics (off-topic activity) during each time interval. Figure 1 illustrates – in its upper part – such a user representation.

Using this user behavior modeling approach, we provide a more enriched representation of microblogs users by considering both on- and off-topic user activeness levels over time. Such representation is capable of characterizing similarities and regularities of users behaviors.

3.2 User Activity Features

We define a set of new features inspired by the features proposed by Pal et al. [9]. For each user u and each time stamp t_m, we compute the following features by taking into account both the on-and off-topic user activities:

Topical Attachment: indicates the involvement rate of the user regarding the analyzed event by referring to the number of his original on-topic tweets ($T1_{on}$) and the number of his on-topic shared links ($T2_{on}$) adjusted by the off-topic metrics ($T1_{off}$) and ($T2_{off}$).

$$F1_u^{(t)} = (T1_{on}^{(t)} + T2_{on}^{(t)}) - (T1_{off}^{(t)} + T2_{off}^{(t)}) \quad (1)$$

Topical Influence: estimates the value (or worthiness) of the user's original tweets regarding the event according to the number of favorites ($T3_{on}$) and the number of retweets ($R2_{on}$) of his produced tweets.

$$F2_u^{(t)} = T1_{on}^{(t)} \times log(T3_{on}^{(t)} + R2_{on}^{(t)} + 1) \quad (2)$$

Retweeting Rate: measures the impact of the shared event-related-tweets on the user retweeting activity. This feature adjusts the number of the user's retweets ($R1_{on}$) by the number of unique users that he has retweeted ($R4_{on}$).

$$F3_u^{(t)} = R1_{on}^{(t)} * log(R4_{on}^{(t)} + 1) \quad (3)$$

Retweeted Rate: calculates the impact of the original tweets produced by the user on the other users. This feature adjusts the number of users who have retweeted the user's on-topic tweets ($R3_{on}$) and the total number of retweets ($R2_{on}$) by the corresponding off-metrics ($R2_{off}$) and ($R3_{off}$).

$$F4_u^{(t)} = R2_{on}^{(t)} * log(R3_{on}^{(t)} + 1) - R2_{off}^{(t)} * log(R3_{off}^{(t)} + 1) \quad (4)$$

Incoming Mention Rate: measures the diversity of mentions related to the user. This feature adjusts the number of received on-topic mentions ($M1_{on}$) by the number of unique users mentioning the user ($M2_{on}$).

$$F5_u^{(t)} = M1_{on}^{(t)} * log(M2_{on}^{(t)} + 1) \quad (5)$$

Outcoming Mention Rate: represents the mentioning activity of the current user by computing the number of his on-topic produced mentions ($M3_{on}$) adjusted by the number of unique mentioned users ($M4_{on}$).

$$F6_u^{(t)} = M3_{on}^{(t)} * log(M4_{on}^{(t)} + 1) \quad (6)$$

Centrality Degree: promotes users having more on-topic followers and followees than off-topic ones. This feature is measured by adjusting the number of on-topic followers ($G1_{on}$) and followees ($G2_{on}$) of each user with the number of his off-topic relations ($G1_{off}$) and ($G2_{off}$).

$$F7_u^{(t)} = log(\frac{G1_{on}^{(t)} + 1}{G1_{off}^{(t)} + 2}) - log(\frac{G2_{on}^{(t)} + 1}{G2_{off}^{(t)} + 2}) \quad (7)$$

Once these features are computed, each user u can be represented by the following feature vector at each time stamp t_m.

$$V_u^{t_i} = (F1_u^{(t)}, F2_u^{(t)}, F3_u^{(t)}, F4_u^{(t)}, F5_u^{(t)}, F6_u^{(t)}, F7_u^{(t)}) \quad (8)$$

The set of concatenated feature vectors computed at all the time stamps represent the temporal sequence of the user behavior.

4. LEARNING TO CLASSIFY USER TEMPORAL SEQUENCES

In order to classify the time-series of feature vectors V describing each microblogs user, we train two models for prominent and non-prominent users classification using MoG HMMs. There are various types of continuous HMM: left-right, parallel left-right and ergodic. To learn our MoG HMMs, we use the ergodic model as the user activity level state at a period of time t_i can change to every other state at the period of time t_{i+1} through a single transition. Figure 1 shows a 3-state ergodic model describing how the sequence of feature vectors representing a given user can be transformed into a sequence of discrete states.

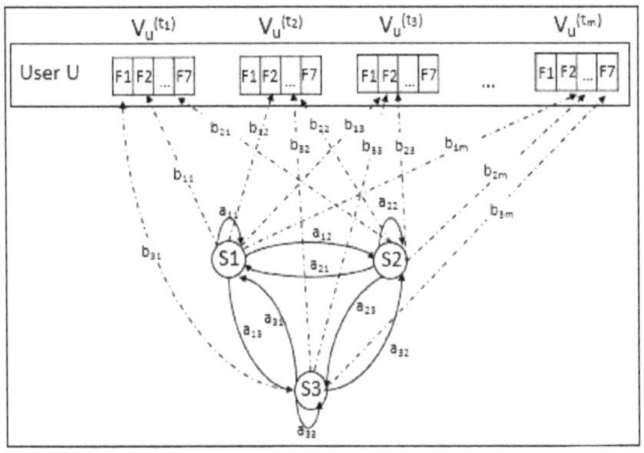

Figure 1: A time-series representation of user activities during an event using a 3-state ergodic HMM

To learn the parameters for our MoG-HMM ergodic models, we use the Baum-Welch algorithm [5]. This algorithm is based on the EM algorithm to search for the maximum probability of the HMM models parameters that better fit the observed temporal users sequences in the training data.

$$H = \arg\max_{H} P(V_{training}|H) \quad (9)$$

A MoG-HMM model H is described by the quadruplet $H = \{S, \pi, A, B\}$, where $S = S_1, S_2, S_3, ..., S_k$ refers to the set of k hidden states describing levels of users activities at each period of time t_i. The state of a user at time t can expressed by $(X_t \in S)_{1 \leq t \leq m}$. π denotes the initial probability of the different states. A is the state transition probability matrix to change from state S_i to S_j, $A = a_{ij}$ where $a_{ij} = P(X_{t+1} = S_j|X_t = S_i)_{1 \leq i,j \leq k}$. B refers to the continuous output probability matrix where the probability $B = b_i(V^t)$ represents the probability of observing a feature vector V^t from a state S_i, where $b_i(t) = P(V^t|X_t) = (S_i)_{1 \leq i \leq k}$.

The transformation of these feature vectors into discrete states is processed by the construction of a continuous observation probability density function (PDF) matrix B. This matrix is represented as a mixture of Gaussians in order to associate the sequence of a user's feature vectors into the different finite states using equation 10.

$$b_i(V^t) = \sum_{k=1}^{M} c_{ik}\mathcal{N}[V^t, \mu_{ik}, W_{ik}] \quad (10)$$

where c_{ik} is the mixture weight, $\mathcal{N}$ is the normal density, μ_{ik} is the mean vector and W_{ik} is the covariance matrix for the kth mixture component in state S_i.

Once the models parameters H_{c1} and H_{c2} are set through training, we can compute the probability of any microblogs user to belong to each class $P(V_u|H_{c1})$ and $P(V_u|H_{c2})$ given the two learned models. These probabilities are obtained using the forward-backward algorithm [2]. If the model H_{c1} gives a higher probability to a represented user compared to $P(V_u|H_{c2})$, then this user is classified as prominent.

5. PERFORMANCE EVALUATION

5.1 Dataset

To conduct experimental performance evaluation on real data, we have tracked the Twitter users who have shared at least one on-topic information about the floods that have occurred from 29th to 30th September 2014 in the Herault area, situated in the south of France using ou multi-agent system MASIR [3]. 3332 users have been tracked during the two days of the disaster.

To create the ground-truth, we conducted a subjective user study in order to label each user in the dataset with **c1** and **c2** indicating respectively whether the user is prominent or not. The tracked users were evaluated according to the relevance and exclusivity of their tweets during the disaster. According to this study, 90 users have been classified as $c1$, and 3242 users have been classified as $c2$.

5.2 Evaluation Set-up and Metrics

For experimental set-up, we randomly sampled 60% of both prominent and non prominent labeled users datasets as training data for building the H_{c1} and H_{c2} classifiers, and the remaining 40% as test data. Features characterizing user behavior were extracted sequentially at each time interval of 90 minutes from the beginning of the event to its end. Thus each user is represented by a sequence of 32 feature vectors. We have also extracted features using different interval lengths.

Following the standard evaluation criteria used in the context of prominent users identification, we use **precision, recall** and **F1-score** measures to evaluate the performance of our approach. In order to choose the coherent parameters for the representation of microblogs users behavior through H_{c1} and H_{c2} models, we have tested different values of "number of states" N_s (from 1 to 6) and "number of multivariate Gaussian" N_G (from 1 to 5) with the training dataset. The experimental results are shown in Table 1. The best results are obtained when N_s = 3 states and N_G = 1, yielding F1-score value to 64%.

Table 1: Prominent users identification performance for different N_s and N_G in terms of F1-score.

N_s/N_G	1	2	3	4	5
1	0.5201	0.5615	0.6035	0.5643	0.6039
2	0.5500	0.5755	0.01	0.01	0.01
3	**0.6455**	0.01	0.01	0.1337	0.2026
4	0.5855	0.01	0.1100	0.01	0.1020
5	0.6156	0.01	0.01	0.01	0.01
6	0.01	0.4700	0.01	0.01	0.01

5.3 Experimental Results

5.3.1 *Importance of Time-series Representation*

To demonstrate the effectiveness of our temporal sequence representation approach for the identification of prominent users, we test the performance of our model by decreasing the length of the feature vectors sequence m(from 32 to 2) (e.g. m=2 users activities features are recorded at each 720 minutes). In other words, users behavior are represented during longer periods of time. Figure 2 shows how the sequence length variation affects the performance of our model. According to these results, we find that larger sequence length characterizing detailed users activities over time works significantly better than smaller ones. Thus, user behavior is better characterized with more time stamps.

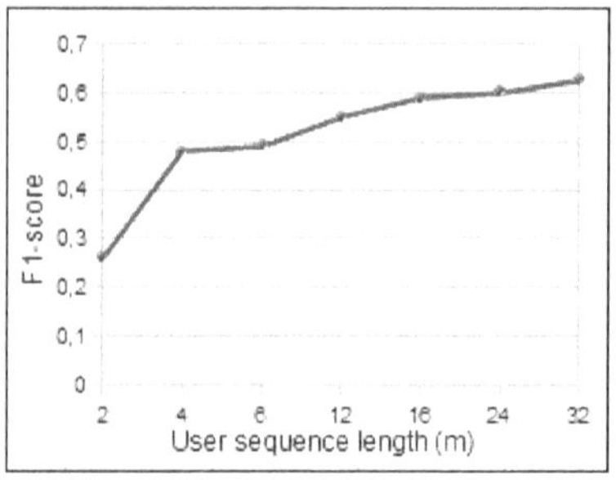

Figure 2: Time-series sequence length effect on the model performance

5.3.2 *Comparison with Different Models*

We compared our HMM temporal sequence classification model with two baseline models:

Baseline 1: refers to an SVM model learned using our proposed features and a classic single vector representation of the user behavior during the event.

Baseline 2: refers to an SVM model learned using Pal et al. features [9] and a single vector user representation.

Figure 3 shows the results of comparing the three different models, where our proposed model significantly outperforms the models which are trained on users activities in the whole event duration (i.e independently of the activity distribution over time). We also note that our features are more effective in the context of prominent users identification in specific events than Pal et al. [9] features which are based on analyzing only the on-topic user activity.

6. CONCLUSION AND FUTURE WORK

This paper has presented a novel microblogs users representation according to their behavior over time in specific events. This representation has been used for building and training a MoG-HMM model to identify prominent users. In our model, users are characterized by a temporal sequence composed of feature vectors recorded in different periods of time during the event. These features characterize the on-topic and off-topic users activities at each time interval. Our experiments show that a longer length of the sequence characterizing the user behavior over time, produces a better identification model. We have additionally compared the performance of our model to traditional machine learning SVM models using our features and state-of-the-art features.

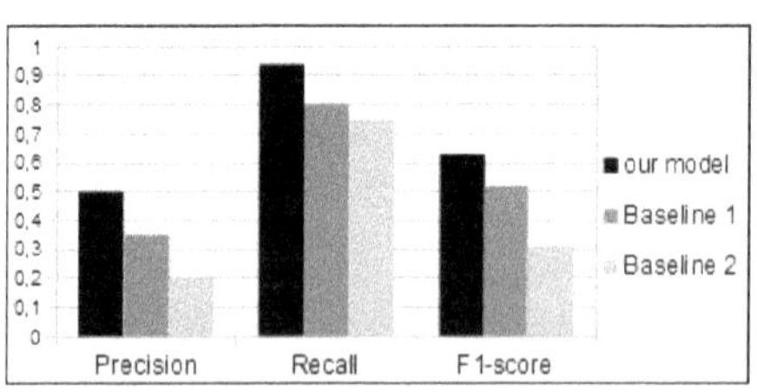

Figure 3: Classification results using different baseline models

The achieved results show the importance of learning time sequences of users activities as compared to learning those activities independently of their temporal characteristics.

For future work, we aim to predict prominent users at different event phases. We would like also to analyze the correlation between temporal activities of prominent users and the time of occurrence of the trending sub-events.

7. REFERENCES

[1] E. Agichtein, C. Castillo, D. Donato, A. Gionis, and G. Mishne. Finding high-quality content in social media. In *WSDM*, pages 183–194, 2008.

[2] L. E. Baum and J. A. Eagon. An inequality with applications to statistical estimation for probabilistic functions of markov processes and to a model for ecology. *Bull. Amer. Math. Soc.*, 73(3):360–363, 1967.

[3] I. Bizid, P. G. Boursier, J. Morcos, and S. Faiz. Masir : A multi-agent system for real-time information retrieval from microblogs during unexpected events. KES-AMSTA-15, pages 1–8, 2015.

[4] W. Chen, Y. Wang, and S. Yang. Efficient influence maximization in social networks. In *Proceedings of the 15th ACM SIGKDD International Conference on Knowledge Discovery and Data Mining*, KDD '09, pages 199–208, 2009.

[5] A. P. Dempster, N. M. Laird, and D. B. Rubin. Maximum likelihood from incomplete data via the em algorithm. *Journal of the Royal Statistical Society*, 39(1):1–38, 1977.

[6] S. Ghosh, N. Sharma, F. Benevenuto, N. Ganguly, and K. Gummadi. Cognos: Crowdsourcing search for topic experts in microblogs. In *SIGIR*, pages 575–590, 2012.

[7] H. Kwak, C. Lee, H. Park, and S. Moon. What is twitter, a social network or a news media? In *WWW*, pages 591–600, 2010.

[8] Q. V. Liao, C. Wagner, P. Pirolli, and W.-T. Fu. Understanding experts' and novices' expertise judgment of twitter users. In *CHI*, pages 2461–2464, New York, NY, USA, 2012.

[9] A. Pal and S. Counts. Identifying topical authorities in microblogs. In *WSDM*, pages 45–54, 2011.

[10] D. M. Romero, W. Galuba, S. Asur, and B. A. Huberman. Influence and passivity in social media. In *WWW*, pages 113–114, 2011.

[11] C. Wagner, V. Liao, P. Pirolli, L. Nelson, and M. Strohmaier. It's not in their tweets: Modeling topical expertise of twitter users. In *SocialCom*, pages 91–100, 2012.

[12] J. Weng, E.-P. Lim, J. Jiang, and Q. He. Twitterrank: Finding topic-sensitive influential twitterers. In *WSDM*, pages 261–270, 2010.

[13] S. Xianlei, Z. Chunhong, and J. Yang. Finding domain experts in microblogs. In *WEBIST*, 2014.

[14] M. Zhang, C. Sun, and W. Liu. Identifying influential users of micro-blogging services: A dynamic action-based network approach. In *PACIS*, page 223, 2011.

[15] G. Zhou, S. Lai, K. Liu, and J. Zhao. Topic-sensitive probabilistic model for expert finding in question answer communities. In *CIKM*, pages 1662–1666, 2012.

A Real-Time Eye Tracking Based Query Expansion Approach via Latent Topic Modeling

Yongqiang Chen[1], Peng Zhang[1], Dawei Song[1,2], Benyou Wang[1],
[1]Tianjin Key Laboratory of Cognitive Computing and Application, Tianjin University, China
[2]Department of Computing and Communications, The Open University, United Kingdom
{cyq, pzhang, waby}@tju.edu.cn, dawei.song2010@gmail.com

ABSTRACT

Formulating and reformulating reliable textual queries have been recognized as a challenging task in Information Retrieval (IR), even for experienced users. Most existing query expansion methods, especially those based on implicit relevance feedback, utilize the user's historical interaction data, such as clicks, scrolling and viewing time on documents, to derive a refined query model. It is further expected that the user's search experience would be largely improved if we could dig out user's latent query intention, in real-time, by capturing the user's current interaction at the term level directly. In this paper, we propose a real-time eye tracking based query expansion method, which is able to: (1) automatically capture the terms that the user is viewing by utilizing eye tracking techniques; (2) derive the user's latent intent based on the eye tracking terms and by using the Latent Dirichlet Allocation (LDA) approach. A systematic user study has been carried out and the experimental results demonstrate the effectiveness of our proposed methods.

Category and Subject Descriptors: H.3.3 [Information Search and Retrieval]

Keywords: Eye Tracking, Query Expansion, Real Time, Implicit Relevance Feedback, LDA

1. INTRODUCTION

Query expansion based on relevance feedback has long been studied for its ability of finding out more relevant documents against ambiguous queries that users might type in. Compared with explicit relevance feedback that often causes the users extra cognitive overhead, implicit relevance feedback (IRF) has the advantage of obtaining the useful feedback information from the user interaction data to better infer users' search intention [6], yet without requiring the users explicit relevance judgments.

Traditional implicit feedback based query expansion methods usually return static results according to the searchers' historical log data, which cannot fully meet searchers' dynamic information needs. Recently various real-time IRF approaches have been proposed [12] [7] [11], to better improve search performance and users' search experience. For example, Singh et al [11] argued that a query expansion framework should expand user's search query dynamically based on user's implicit feedback provided at the time of searching, in order to provide sufficient clues to reflect what the user wants.

Eye Tracking has been used in IR for its ability to record users' eye movement data, which can reveal the users' cognitive process when going through the retrieved documents in a natural way. Gwizdka *et al.* [5] have thoroughly examined the relevance of a document and cognitive effort a user may take using eye movement data. Ajanki *et al.* [1] designed an eye tracking experiment, in which participants were asked to search for relevant documents given a topic, and then the gaze locations were used to find relevant terms to reformulate the queries. However, they had to avoid scrolling the text due to the risk of missing some gaze location to word mappings. Furthermore, this work was not concerned about real-time query expansion.

Buscher *et al.* [3] used eye tracking to extract words based on optical character recognition (OCR) technology, and assign different words with different weights according to the words being read or skipped. They have proved that applying eye tracking as a new data source is feasible for implicit feedback. However, a limitation is that using OCR technique to extract words could not operate in real-time, i.e., the words can not be immediately grabbed when users are reading them. Furthermore, the number of words extracted by using eye trackers may be too small to fully express the users' search intention.

To tackle the problems described above, we propose a real time eye tracking based query expansion model via latent topic modeling. Different from Buscher *et al.* [3], we use a screen word-capturing technique to capture words that the searcher is reading in real-time, from which we could infer what the searcher is currently interested in. In our approach, we will have already refreshed the result list according to the captured words when the searcher clicks on the refresh or the next page button. The words captured by eye tracker are used to expanding the original query. According to [2], documents can be considered as being generated by different latent topics, each of which is a probability distribution of words. Based on this assumption, we apply LDA to further derive the searcher's latent information needs, which naturally relate to the words the user pays attention to. Our experiments show that combining the words captured by

Permission to make digital or hard copies of all or part of this work for personal or classroom use is granted without fee provided that copies are not made or distributed for profit or commercial advantage and that copies bear this notice and the full citation on the first page. Copyrights for components of this work owned by others than the author(s) must be honored. Abstracting with credit is permitted. To copy otherwise, or republish, to post on servers or to redistribute to lists, requires prior specific permission and/or a fee. Request permissions from Permissions@acm.org.
CIKM'15, October 19 - 23, 2015, Melbourne, VIC, Australia
Copyright is held by the owner/author(s). Publication rights licensed to ACM.
ACM 978-1-4503-3794-6/15/10 ... $15.00.
DOI: http://dx.doi.org/10.1145/2806416.2806602.

eye-tracking and the related latent topics can improve the retrieval effectiveness.

2. METHODOLOGY

In this section, we first introduce how we capture a set of terms (or words), denoted as W^{Eye}, from the screen using an eye tracker when the user is viewing the returned documents. The words in W^{Eye} can be considered as words of interest (WoI) and should be properly weighted. We then use LDA to model user's latent topical preferences by extracting another set of terms W^{LDA} from the topics that are ranked according to W^{Eye}. Finally, we combine the weights of the each word in W^{Eye} and W^{LDA} by different strategies to expand the original queries.

2.1 Capturing Words of Interest (WoI) through Eye Tracking

Gwizdka *et al.* [5] have revealed that a user might gaze for a longer time on relevant words than non-relevant ones, and the user's pupil diameter will expand when seeing interesting words during reading. Accordingly, we develop a WoI capture method to capture the words a user is interested in, based on the user's real-time eye-tracking activity.

To begin with, the high accuracy of modern eye trackers allow us to use suitable APIs to obtain the exact set of raw coordinates $\{X_i, Y_i\}$ on the screen in the millimeter level, for the regions where a user gazes on. In addition, there are existing screen word-capturing technologies for capturing words based on mouse cursors, as long as the mouse cursor stay steady over a word for a certain period. Therefore, we could replace the mouse cursor positions with the coordinates set $\{X_i, Y_i\}$ provided by eye tracking. However, the eye tracker's sampling frequency is 300 HZ. Thus the coordinates in $\{X_i, Y_i\}$ may change too fast for the mouse-based screen word-capturing system to capture. To solve the problem, we adopt a real-time fixation filtering method [9] to cluster the raw coordinates in order to generate more stabilized fixation coordinates. Considering the mean minimum time to acquire the full meaning of a word is 151ms [10], we filter out those clustered fixation coordinates that last less than 151 ms. After we get the stabilized fixation coordinates, we can make use of the screen word-capturing technique to capture words with eye tracking in real-time. The captured words (after removing the stopwords but without doing stemming) $W^{Eye} = \{w_1^{Eye}, w_2^{Eye}, \cdots w_s^{Eye}\}$ (s denotes the number of words in W^{Eye}) are written into a temporary file for each user in each search session, which is archived or deleted after the session is completed.

Different from the traditional off-line extracted eye movement features such as regression ratio, which can be only calculated after collecting all eye movement data, we simply record 4 real-time computable features for each captured word w, namely fixation times FT_w, fixation duration FD_w, left eye pupil diameter LEP_w and right eye pupil diameter REP_w.

2.2 Weighting Scheme for WoI

Our weighting scheme for WoIs takes into account the traditional term frequency and the eye tracking features reflecting user's interest.

For each term t in W^{Eye}, we first normalize its term frequency as follows:

$$\mathcal{L}_t = \frac{wf_t^{Eye}}{wf_{max}^{Eye} + \mathcal{C}} \quad (1)$$

where $\mathcal{L}_t$ represents the normalized score for term t. wf_t^{Eye} represents the frequency of each term t and wf_{max}^{Eye} denotes the max frequency of the terms in W^{Eye}. $\mathcal{C}$ is a positive integer constant to guarantee $\mathcal{L}_t$ falls into the range from 0 to 1.

Furthermore, we use eye-tracking information to measure the searcher's degree of interest in the term t, denoted as $\mathcal{I}_t$:

$$\mathcal{I}_t = \mu FT_t + \nu FD_t + (1 - \mu - \nu)\mathcal{G}_t \quad (2)$$

where FT_t and FD_t represent the fixation times and fixation duration for t, respectively. The parameters μ and ν are coefficients for combining different features.

The function $\mathcal{G}_t$ denotes the changing rate of pupil diameters of searcher's both eyes, and it can be calculated by:

$$\mathcal{G}_t = \frac{1}{2}(LEP_t + REP_t) - \frac{1}{s}\sum_{i=1}^{s}(LEP_i + REP_i) \quad (3)$$

where LEP_t and REP_t denote the pupil diameters of the user's left eye and right eye, respectively, and s is the number of words in W^{Eye}.

Finally, the overall weight of each term t in W^{Eye} is computed as:

$$\Omega_t^{Eye}(t|t \in W^{Eye}) = \mathcal{L}_t * \mathcal{I}_t \quad (4)$$

2.3 Deriving and Incorporating Latent Topics

A document may consist of several latent topics, yet users may be just interested in one or two of them. Furthermore, users often tend to check a small number of documents in the search engine result pages (SERP) to find out the information they need. Thus it is likely that the number of captured words of interest W^{Eye} may remain too small to fully model the user's latent intention. To tackle this problem, we adopt LDA, a probabilistic laten topic model to further locate users' latent search intention. LDA assumes that documents are generated by different latent topics which are probabilistic distributions over different words. Practically, we train a topic model by LDA using all the documents in the test collection, and use Gibbs sampling to conduct approximate inference of all the parameters in LDA.

Given a query $Q = \{q_1, q_2, \cdots q_l\}$ (where l denotes the number of terms in the query) and a WoI set W^{Eye}, we first rank the topics according to the probabilities that they generate Q and W^{Eye}, and choose the top $\mathcal{M}$ words ranked in each topic distribution to expand the original query. The formula for ranking topics is given as follows:

$$\begin{aligned} P(z_n) =& \gamma \sum_{j=1}^{l} f_j^Q P(q_j|z_n, \alpha, \beta) + \\ & (1-\gamma) \sum_{j=1}^{s} f_j^{W^{Eye}} P(w_j^{Eye}|z_n, \alpha, \beta) \end{aligned} \quad (5)$$

where $P(z_n)$ is the probability for a topic z_n generating Q and W^{Eye}; f_j^Q and $f_j^{W^{Eye}}$ denote the frequency of term q_j in the query Q and the frequency of w_j^{Eye} in W^{Eye} respectively. γ is a constant parameter to balance the combination between Q and W^{Eye}. In addition, α and β are the hyper-parameters used in LDA.

We then rank all the topics in descending order according to Formula (5). Then we choose top $\mathcal{M}$ words from each of the top ranked $\mathcal{N}$ topics for each query Q. Consequently, a total of $\mathcal{M}$*$\mathcal{N}$ words are selected, forming a new set of WoIs, denoted as W^{LDA}, which can be used for query expansion.

For each term t in W^{LDA}, the weight Ω_t^{LDA} is calculated as below:

$$\Omega_t^{LDA}(t|t \in W^{LDA}) = \sum_{i=1}^{\mathcal{N}} P(t|z_i) \qquad (6)$$

where z_i is one of the top ranked $\mathcal{N}$ topics and $P(t|z_i)$ is the probability that topic z_i generates the term t.

Now we get two sets of WoIs W^{Eye} and W^{LDA}, and all of them contain useful information for inferring users' search intention. Therefore, it is reasonable to integrate them in order to achieve better search performance. We use $W^{Eye+LDA}$ to denote the union of W^{Eye} and W^{LDA}. If a term appears in both W^{Eye} and W^{LDA}, we sum up its weights from the two sets and then normalize the summed weight into the range between 0 and 1.

2.4 Generating Expanded Queries

After we have calculated the weight of each term, we use Lemur toolkit [1] and Indri [2] search engine to implement our algorithm and to generate the expanded queries from W^{Eye} and $W^{Eye+LDA}$:

$$\#weight((1-\lambda)Q + \lambda W^{Eye}) \qquad (7)$$

$$\#weight((1-\lambda)Q + \lambda W^{Eye+LDA}) \qquad (8)$$

where Q represents the original query and λ is the combination coefficient.

3. EXPERIMENTS

To verify whether the proposed eye tracking based query expansion can improve retrieval performance, we have conducted an empirical study consisting of a series of user task-based experiments.

We implemented two proposed approaches for eye-tracking based query expansion. The first method we take only uses the eye-tracking WoIs W^{Eye}, denoted as *Eye-QE*. We use *Eye-LDA-QE* to denote the another one, which combines eye-tracking and latent topic modeling, i.e., $W^{Eye+LDA}$, for query expansion. For comparison, we take two traditional methods as baselines. The first one is a classical language model LM [13], which performs well in most cases without query expansion. The second baseline, $RM3$ [8], is a widely accepted query expansion approach for its power in boosting the search performance.

3.1 Eye Tracker Setup and Participants' Tasks

In our experiment, participants are required to complete a number of ad-hoc retrieval tasks, with queries and documents selected from the TREC AP8890 collection (to be detailed in the next subsection). We recruited 20 postgraduate students from three different departments to diversify the users' background. They are all seated in front of a 23" LCD monitor at a screen resolution of 1920*1080 pixels. The eye tracker we employ is Tobii TX300, which has a sample frequency of 300 HZ and the accuracy is 0.3° of visual angle. Before conducting the experiment, each participant has to make a calibration to ensure the eye movement data captured at high precision. The participants are then instructed to complete several queries in front of the eye tracker, and for each query they have to find at least 5 relevant documents based on the description and narrative of the query.

3.2 Data Selection

Traditional query expansion methods can perform badly upon the so-called "hard" queries. In our experiment, the hard queries are determined by the low average precision of the retrieval results using the RM3 model. We expect our models would perform better especially when dealing with those queries. Considering that reading too many documents may increase the participants' cognitive burden and may even exhaust them, we select 6 queries for all participants, including 4 hard queries and 2 normal queries, from AP8890 data set. During the process of searching for relevant documents, the average number of documents the participants examined is about 10. After all participants have finished all the queries we collected almost 20*6*10=1200 documents in total and each participant was paid 10 $ for about 1 hour of work.

3.3 Results and Discussions

In this section, we present our experiment results of the 4 comparative methods we have described.

We use the Mean Average Precision (MAP) as the main performance indicator, as it has been widely used and have a good discrimination power. We first compare the MAP scores of our proposed methods with the traditional models. For each query, we first calculate the Average Precision (AP) score by averaging all the 20 participants' AP scores. Then, we average all the queries' AP scores to obtain MAP for our proposed model. The results are shown in Table 1, under the manually selected optimal λ. The statistical significance is indicated by * ($p < 0.05$, one-way ANOVA) and ** ($p < 0.01$). The results demonstrate that using the words

Methods	MAP	%↑ over LM	%↑ over RM3
LM	0.1734	-	-
$RM3$	0.2773	59.91%	-
Eye-QE	0.3411	96.71%**	23.01%*
Eye-LDA-QE	0.3508	102.3%**	26.51%*

Table 1: MAP of different methods

of interest captured by eye trackers is feasible and improves search performance dramatically. Further improvement is achieved by combining eye tracking and LDA model, thus verifying that employing LDA model to enrich WoIs can help dig out user's latent search intention to a large extent.

To investigate the impact of WoIs captured by eye-tracking on query expansion, we test different settings of the parameter λ. The dynamic MAP scores along with changing λ are shown in Figure 1. We can see that, when λ is small (meaning more weight is given to the original query), $RM3$ is better than our proposed model. The possible reason is that smaller λ limits our captured WoIs to take an effect.

[1]http://www.lemurproject.org/

[2]http://www.lemurproject.org/indri.php

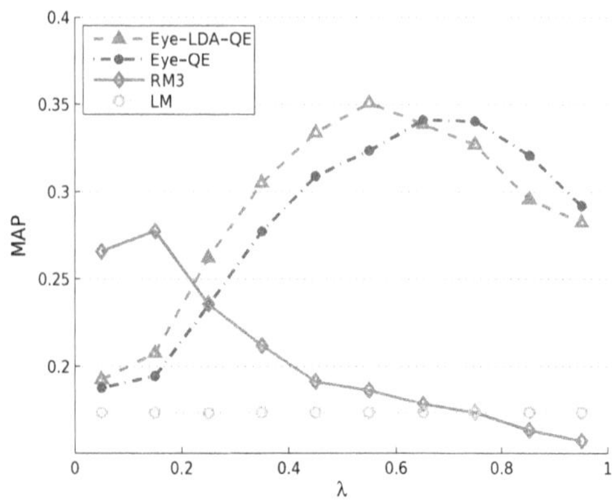

Figure 1: MAP scores along with changing λ

However, with the increase of λ, our models *Eye-QE* and *Eye-LDA-QE* become to outperform *LM* and *RM*3. Both our proposed models achieve the best performance when λ is larger, implying that the captured WoIs contain more resultful information than the original query.

As Granka et al. [4] pointed out, the majority of searchers usually examine the documents that are ranked higher, especially the top two documents. It is essential to rank relevant documents higher in order to improve the users' search experience. Therefore, in addition to MAP, we also averaged the 20 participants' *Precision at K* scores to as another performance indicator. The results (the best performing runs under different λ) are shown in Figure 2. We can find that our proposed models, especially the *Eye-LDA-QE* model, perform much better than the other ones when K is smaller. By taking advantage of latent topic derivation through LDA, we can more precisely locate user's hidden search intention and improve search experience.

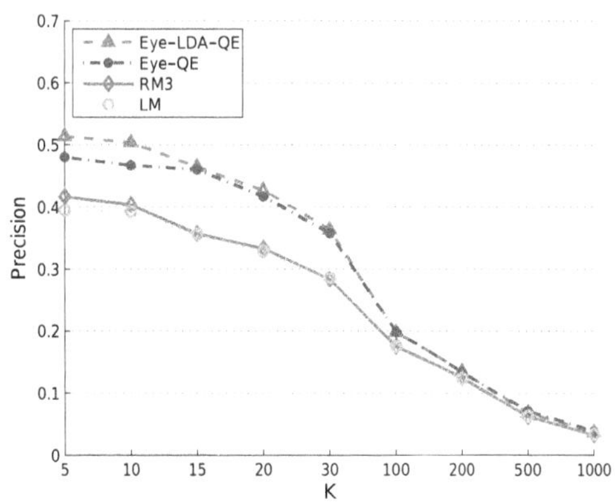

Figure 2: Precision at K for all methods

4. CONCLUSIONS AND FUTURE WORK

In this paper, we have proposed to expand the original query using the words of interest captured by eye tracking in real time. Moreover, considering the words captured by eye tracker are limited due to the insufficient feedback data, the user's latent search intention may not be fully expressed. Therefore, we also train a latent topic model using LDA and then rank the topics, based on which the generated words can be used to further enrich the expansion model. The experimental results have demonstrated that capturing the words of interest based on eye-tracking can considerably improve the retrieval performance. Further, combining the eye-tracked words and the words in topic models can generate further improvement.

In the future, we will test our models on a larger-scale by recruiting more participants on larger datasets. We can further take into account the user's reading sequence or the reading pattern in a feedback-based query expansion model. Moreover, given that the number of mobile searchers is growing rapidly, it will be interesting to explore if and how we could use cameras on mobile devices to track user's gaze to better capture user's preferences.

5. ACKNOWLEDGEMENT

This work is supported in part by them Chinese National Program on Key Basic Research Project (973 Program, grant No.2013CB329304, 2014CB744604), the Chinese 863 Program (grant No. 2015AA015403), the Natural Science Foundation of China (grant No. 61272265, 61402324), and the Research Fund for the Doctoral Program of Higher Education of China (grant No. 20130032120044).

6. REFERENCES

[1] A. Ajanki, D. R. Hardoon, S. Kaski, K. Puolamäki, and J. Shawe-Taylor. Can eyes reveal interest? Implicit queries from gaze patterns. *User Modeling and User-Adapted Interaction*, 19(4):307–339, 2009.

[2] D. M. Blei, A. Y. Ng, and M. I. Jordan. Latent dirichlet allocation. *JMLR*, 3:993–1022, 2003.

[3] G. Buscher, A. Dengel, and L. van Elst. Query expansion using gaze-based feedback on the subdocument level. In *ACM SIGIR*, pages 387–394. ACM, 2008.

[4] L. A. Granka, T. Joachims, and G. Gay. Eye-tracking analysis of user behavior in www search. In *ACM SIGIR*, pages 478–479. ACM, 2004.

[5] J. Gwizdka. Characterizing relevance with eye-tracking measures. In *Proceedings of the 5th Information Interaction in Context Symposium*, pages 58–67. ACM, 2014.

[6] D. Kelly and J. Teevan. Implicit feedback for inferring user preference: a bibliography. In *ACM SIGIR Forum*, volume 37, pages 18–28. ACM, 2003.

[7] J. Y. Kim, M. Cramer, J. Teevan, and D. Lagun. Understanding how people interact with web search results that change in real-time using implicit feedback. In *ACM CIKM*, pages 2321–2326. ACM, 2013.

[8] V. Lavrenko and W. B. Croft. Relevance based language models. In *ACM SIGIR*, pages 120–127. ACM, 2001.

[9] P. Olsson. Real-time and offline filters for eye tracking. 2007.

[10] E. D. Reichle, A. Pollatsek, and K. Rayner. E–z reader: A cognitive-control, serial-attention model of eye-movement behavior during reading. *Cognitive Systems Research*, 7(1):4–22, 2006.

[11] S. R. Singh, H. A. Murthy, and T. A. Gonsalves. Inference based query expansion using user's real time implicit feedback. In *Knowledge Discovery, Knowledge Engineering and Knowledge Management*, pages 158–172. Springer, 2013.

[12] R. W. White and G. Marchionini. Examining the effectiveness of real-time query expansion. *Information Processing & Management*, 43(3):685–704, 2007.

[13] C. Zhai and J. Lafferty. Model-based feedback in the language modeling approach to information retrieval. In *ACM CIKM*, pages 403–410. ACM, 2001.

Clustered Semi-Supervised Relevance Feedback

Kripabandhu Ghosh and Swapan Kumar Parui
Computer Vision and Pattern Recognition Unit
Indian Statistical Institute, Kolkata, West Bengal, India
kripa.ghosh@gmail.com, swapan@isical.ac.in

ABSTRACT

In relevance feedback, first-round search results are used to boost second-round search results. Two forms have been traditionally considered: exhaustively labelled feedback, where all first-round results to depth k are annotated for relevance by the user; and blind feedback, where the top-k results are all assumed to be relevant. In this paper, we consider an intermediate, semi-supervised scheme, in which only a subset of results is selected for annotation, and then their labels are propagated to their nearest neighbours. Specifically, we use clustering to determine the nearest-neighbour groups, and seed selection to choose documents for annotation. We find that the effectiveness of this method is indistinguishable from the exhaustive relevance feedback, and is significantly higher than both blind feedback and the use of the annotated subset alone. We show that this approach works well in environments in which some but limited amounts of human feedback are available, such as early case assessment in e-discovery.

Categories and Subject Descriptors

H.4 [**Information Search and Retrieval**]: Clustering

General Terms

Legal Aspects, Human Factors

Keywords

E-Discovery, Cluster Hypothesis, Relevance Assessment

1. INTRODUCTION

In e-discovery tasks, the judgment of whether a document is relevant (or responsive) to a case is determined by legal experts, either directly or as mediated through the training of a text classification system (known in e-discovery as *predictive coding*) [7]. Legal expertise is expensive, however, and most cases do not proceed to court. Parties therefore have a strong incentive to leverage legal expertise to gain a rapid understanding of the relevant material in their document collections, in order to prepare their case strategies. In the e-discovery field, this process is known as *early case assessment* (ECA).

While relevance feedback and supervised text classification are similar technologies, their goals are somewhat different. We can say that supervised text classification aims at a complete classification of the document collection, while relevance feedback more typically aims at accelerating the discovery of relevant documents. The former goal is that of e-discovery; the latter, that of early case assessment. Whereas in web search domains, it is generally thought that the user's willingness to invest time in improving search recall is insufficient for explicit relevance feedback, in the e-discovery domain, the high costs and stakes of legal proceedings mean that parties are sufficiently incentivized for document relevance assessment to be a feasible proposition. Nevertheless, the expert human legal judgment is still expensive (ranging up to \$1,000 an hour or more), and expending that effort on exhaustive relevance feedback is not an attractive prospect. Moreover, experts want to focus on formulating the case strategy and forming high-level understandings of the document collection. Forcing them to review a large number of repetitive documents hinders these higher-level cognitive goals.

In this paper, we propose a novel approach to relevance feedback. Traditionally, relevance feedback has been performed in one of two modes. On the one hand, *explicit* relevance feedback has been undertaken by asking the user to assess all the top k documents for relevance, and then using these documents and their relevance assessments for feedback. On the other hand, *blind* or *pseudo-* relevance feedback has been performed by assuming that all the top k documents are relevant. In contrast, we propose a *semi-supervised* strategy: ask the user to review a minority $n \ll k$ of the top-ranked documents, and then propagate these relevance assessments to the remaining $k-n$ documents, before performing relevance feedback.

This semi-supervised approach then raises two questions:

1. How to select the *seed* documents for explicit relevance assessment ?
2. How to propagate the relevance assessments from the seeds to the remaining documents ?

We approach these questions in, as it were, the reverse order. We begin by clustering the documents, then picking a seed document that is most representative of each cluster. This

Permission to make digital or hard copies of all or part of this work for personal or classroom use is granted without fee provided that copies are not made or distributed for profit or commercial advantage and that copies bear this notice and the full citation on the first page. Copyrights for components of this work owned by others than ACM must be honored. Abstracting with credit is permitted. To copy otherwise, or republish, to post on servers or to redistribute to lists, requires prior specific permission and/or a fee. Request permissions from Permissions@acm.org.
CIKM'15, October 19-23, 2015, Melbourne, VIC, Australia
© 2015 ACM. ISBN 978-1-4503-3794-6/15/10\$15.00
DOI: http://dx.doi.org/10.1145/2806416.2806596.

seed document is assessed by a human for relevance, and its relevance judgment is propagated to all the documents in the cluster. Finally, we use the full top-k result set for relevance feedback.

The approach to selecting document sets by clusters relies upon the cluster hypothesis that the relevant documents will tend to be more similar ("closer" in the information space) to each other than to non-relevant documents, and vice versa [5]. We therefore begin our study in Section 3 by investigating the cluster hypothesis on a standard test collection for e-discovery research, namely, the Enron collection from the TREC Legal Track [1]. We find that the cluster hypothesis does strongly hold for this data set: documents within one cluster tend to be all relevant or all non-relevant. The next step is to select the seed document to be a representative of a cluster as a whole, which we address in Section 4. We find here that the choosing a centroid document gives a better summarization of the cluster as a whole than picking a document at random. Then, in Section 5 we investigate the relevance feedback performance of our semi-supervised strategy, and compare it with various alternatives, finding that our semi-supervised approach equivalent effectiveness to exhaustive feedback, at a fraction of the cost in human effort, while significantly outperforming blind feedback and equivalent-effort full supervised approaches.

2. METHODOLOGY

2.1 Dataset

We work with the deduplicated EDRM Enron Dataset [2], version 2, prepared by ZL Technologies and used for the TREC Legal Track from 2010 to 2011. This collection has in total 685,592 documents. A total of 14 topics, numbered 200–207, 301–303, and 401–403, were run on this collection, and sampled qrels averaging 5152. For our experiments, we consider the judged documents only.

2.2 Similarity computation

The collection was indexed using Indri toolkit[1], which employed stemming, stopword-removal, case-folding and standard tokenization processing on the documents. Cosine similarity is used to compute similarity between the documents read from the index. The BM25[10] term-weighting formula is used. The topics were converted to query format after standard pre-processing already mentioned. Then, these queries were run and the top retrieved 1,000 documents are considered for our experiments.

3. CLUSTER HYPOTHESIS TEST

We begin by exploring whether the cluster hypothesis holds for this collection. That is, do the documents in a cluster strongly tend to have the same relevance status? We are particulary interested in relevant documents, since these are in the minority class of the collection, and since our assumed task is to find as many highly relevant documents as quickly as possible.

We employ the *nearest neighbour test*, as proposed by Voorhees [11], since this test is relatively agnostic to the clustering technology employed. (See Raiber et al. [9] for an examination of alternative tests.) The n nearest neighbours of a document d are the n documents that are the most similar to d, under a given similarity metric. If the cluster hypothesis holds in a collection, then the nearest neighbours of a relevant document are significantly more likely to be relevant than a randomly selected document.

[1]http://www.lemurproject.org/indri.php

Algorithm	Mean
Complete Linkage	98.1%
Strongest Nbr	97.9%
Average Linkage	97.8%
Single Linkage	97.0%

Table 1: Cluster Purity

Algorithm	Avg. cluster size	Avg. no. of clusters
Complete Linkage	2.31	10.88
Average Linkage	2.69	9.36
Single Linkage	4.1	6.17
Strongest Nbr	2.59	9.72

Table 2: Cluster Statistics

We apply the nearest neighbour test to our dataset by selecting each judged relevant document in turn, and considering the five nearest neighbours to that document (excluding the document itself). We compute the proportion of these documents that are relevant. For topic 207, we compute the number of times a relevant document has 0, 1, 2, 3, 4, or 5 relevant neighbours. The mean number of relevant nearest neighbours for this topic is 4.7; the standard deviation of the number of relevant nearest neighbours is 0.57. This is in contrast to 5.6% percent of the document set (top 1000 docs) as a whole being relevant to the topic.

Figure 1 summarizes these findings for all the topics. It shows the mean and 2 standard-deviations of the proportion of nearest neighbours for each topic, compared to the proportion of relevant documents overall (arranged in the decreasing order of proportion of the relevant documents in the document set). It will be observed that nearest neighbours have a much higher proportion of relevant documents than the document set as a whole. Averaging across all 14 topics, the mean relevant nearest neighbour proportion is 77%, compared to a proportion of 7.3% of relevant documents in the document set as a whole.

3.1 Choice of Clustering Algorithm

In the remaining part of the paper, document clustering will play a pivotal role. In our experiments, the "purity" (i.e., the proportion of documents in the cluster that are in the majority class) is of vital importance. In other words, a cluster which has a higher proportion of relevant documents (if relevant documents is the majority class) has a higher degree of purity. Similarly, purity can be computed for a cluster containing a majority of non-relevant documents.

We consider four clustering algorithms—Complete Linkage, Average Linkage, Single Linkage and Strongest Neighbour. The first three are well known in the literature and the last one has been used by Paik et al. [8] (for term clustering). For the first three algorithms, the cut-off threshold is chosen as 0.6; the fourth method is parameter-free. Table 1 shows the purity values of the EDRM Enron Dataset over all the topics used in this paper. These values are calculated on 25 top retrieved documents. All the four algorithms give similar purity levels. Since complete Linkage is the purest (with 98.1% purity), we use this algorithm for our experi-

Algorithm	Hit%	Assessment accuracy%
Random	91.34	84
Centroid-based	95.14	87

Table 3: Hit Percentage and assessment accuracy : Random vs Centroid-based seed

ments. The cluster statistics of these algorithms over all the queries are shown in Table 2. This shows that Complete linkage (along with Strongest Neighbour and Average Linkage) gives more compact clusters than Single Linkage and hence has higher purity values.

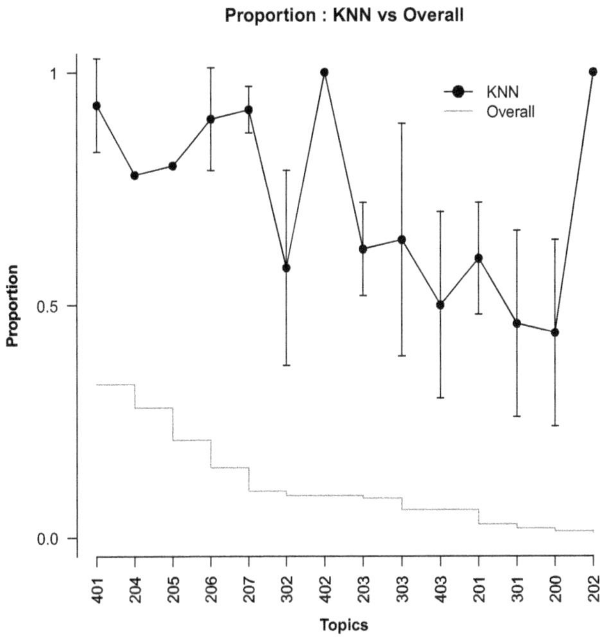

Figure 1: Cluster Hypothesis test

4. SEED SELECTION

Our method, following Ghosh et al. [3], is to select a "representative document" which is called a *seed* for the cluster, and then assume that the remainder of the cluster has the same relevance as the seed document. Clearly, the best seed document is one that is in the majority class of the cluster.

The simplest method is to select a document at random. An alternative is to select the centroid document of the cluster. We define the cluster centroid as follows:

Let d_1, d_2, ..., d_n be the documents in a cluster C. Let $\vec{d_1}$, $\vec{d_2}$, ..., $\vec{d_n}$ be their respective vector representations. Then, the centroid ($\vec{d_C}$) of the cluster C is defined as:

$$\vec{d_C} = \frac{1}{n} \sum_{i=1}^{n} \vec{d_i}$$

Previous studies [4] show that the centroid is the linch-pin of a cluster. The centroid has thus been a stable representative of the documents in the cluster. We suggest that the document (in a cluster) closest to the cluster centroid be chosen as the cluster *seed*. We will now test our hypothesis for each of the topics. Here, we introduce a term "hit" defined as: *We say that a* ***hit*** *has occurred if the document closest to the centroid of a cluster has the relevant status held by a majority of the documents in the cluster.* For example, let a cluster contain 7 relevant and 2 non-relevant documents. We say that a "hit" has occurred if the document closest to the centroid is among the 7 relevant documents. On the other hand, if the *seed* thus chosen turns out to be one of the 2 non-relevant documents, we register a "miss".

Table 3 shows that centroid-based seed choosing is superior to random seed choosing as the former registers more Hit percentage over all queries. Also, the centroid-based method has a higher assessment accuracy through inference from the seed, over random seed choosing.

5. FEEDBACK

The previous sections have shown that (1) the cluster hypothesis holds strongly for our dataset, (2) the complete linkage clustering method has the highest purity among the four clustering methods considered (though all perform well), and (3) the centroid based seed document of a cluster is a good representative of the cluster. We are now ready to test our main hypothesis that the semi-supervised method of inferring document relevance based upon the (human-labelled) relevance of the seed documents provides an effective relevance feedback. We perform Rocchio [6] relevance feedback from the labelled (judged or inferred) relevant documents.

We now consider the following setups:

- *Unexpanded* No relevance feedback is performed; the original retrieval result is evaluated as is.
- *Blind feedback* All the top 25 documents are assumed to be relevant, and are accordingly used in feedback.
- *Seeds only* Only the K labelled seed documents are used for feedback.
- *Random feedback* K documents are selected at random from the top 25 documents for labelling, and these are used for feedback.
- *Expanded feedback* The seed documents are used to infer the relevance of the other documents in their clusters, and all 25 documents (K with true labels, $25-K$ with inferred labels) are used for feedback.
- *Exhaustive judgments* The true labels of all top 25 documents are used, and all 25 documents are used for feedback.

Here K is the number of clusters and its value varies from one query to another. The average value of K is 10.88 as reported in Table 2 for Complete Linkage algorithm. Note that the seeds-only, random, and expanded feedback all require the same number of documents to be labelled by a human expert.

The results of our experiments are shown in Table 4.

We see that blind feedback leads to only a small, and non-significant, improvement over the unexpanded baseline. Random feedback leads to slightly worse MAP but higher recall value than unexpanded. Using only the selected seed documents (*Seeds only*) gives similar effectiveness to blind relevance feedback with all 25 documents and performs better (but not significantly so) than choosing the K documents at random (*Random feedback*) for labelling. None of these methods are significantly different from the others.

Most strikingly, though, our semi-supervised method leads to a numerically large and significant improvement in effectiveness over blind feedback, and over the equal-effort baselines of random and seed-only feedback. Moreover, the performance of the semi-supervised method is indistinguishable from that of having exhaustive judgments of the top 25 documents. This is despite requiring only 43.52% of the human effort. This confirms the effectiveness of our method.

6. CONCLUSION

In this paper, we have proposed a novel semi-supervised feedback method, based on clustering top-retrieved documents, and inferring the relevance of all documents in each cluster based on a representative document. We have demonstrated that (1) the cluster hypothesis performs satisfactorily on our legal dataset, (2) the complete linkage clustering method gives the most relevance-consistent clusters, and (3) the relevance of the cluster seed document is highly representative of that of the cluster as a whole. These findings are encouraging for our proposed method, and indeed our final results do not disappoint. Our semi-supervised feedback method is significantly more effective than blind feedback or equal-effort fully-supervised method. Even more strikingly, our semi-supervised method is indistinguishable in effectiveness from the exhaustive labelling of feedback documents, at a fraction of the human effort. And most importantly, we are capable of reducing assessment effort considerably without hurting the retrieval performance in a significant way.

Method	MAP	Recall@100	Recall@1000
Unexpanded	0.0591	0.0465	0.1655
Blind Feedback	0.0608	0.0511	0.1741
Random Feedback	0.0588	0.0494	0.1699
Seeds only	0.0609	0.0508	0.1737
Expanded feedback	0.0691*	0.0515	0.1909*
Exhaustive judgements	0.0692	0.0513	0.193

Table 4: Relevance Feedback Performance. * sign indicates statistically significant improvement over all 4 previous values at 95% confidence interval ($p < 0.05$).

7. ACKNOWLEDGEMENTS

We are sincerely thankful to William Webber for his support and guidance.

8. REFERENCES

[1] J. Baron, D. Lewis, and D. Oard. Trec-2006 legal track overview. 2006.

[2] G. V. Cormack, M. R. Grossman, B. Hedin, and D. W. Oard. Overview of the trec 2010 legal track. 2010.

[3] K. Ghosh, S. K. Parui, P. Majumder, A. Bandyopadhyay, and S. J. J. R. Singh. Indian statistical institute, kolkata at trec 2010 : Legal interactive. TREC 2010, Nov. 2010.

[4] M. A. Hearst and J. O. Pedersen. Reexamining the cluster hypothesis: Scatter/gather on retrieval results. In *ACM SIGIR*, SIGIR '96, pages 76–84, 1996.

[5] N. Jardine and C. J. van Rijsbergen. The use of hierarchical clustering in information retrieval. *Information Storage and Retrieval*, 7:217–240, 1972.

[6] C. D. Manning, P. Raghavan, and H. Schütze. *Introduction to Information Retrieval.* Cambridge University Press, New York, NY, USA, 2008.

[7] D. W. Oard, J. R. Baron, B. Hedin, D. D. Lewis, and S. Tomlinson. Evaluation of information retrieval for e-discovery. *Artif. Intell. Law*, 18(4):347–386, 2010.

[8] J. H. Paik, D. Pal, and S. K. Parui. A novel corpus-based stemming algorithm using co-occurrence statistics. In *ACM SIGIR*, SIGIR '11, pages 863–872, 2011.

[9] F. Raiber and O. Kurland. The correlation between cluster hypothesis tests and the effectiveness of cluster-based retrieval. In *ACM SIGIR*, SIGIR '14, pages 1155–1158, 2014.

[10] S. E. Robertson and H. Zaragoza. The probabilistic relevance framework: Bm25 and beyond. *Foundations and Trends in Information Retrieval*, 3(4):333–389, 2009.

[11] E. Voorhees. The cluster hypothesis revisited. In *ACM SIGIR*, SIGIR '85, 1985.

On the Effect of "Stupid" Search Components on User Interaction with Search Engines

Lidia Grauer*
Yandex
Saint-Petersburg, Russia
lidia-grauer@yandex.ru

Aleksandra Lomakina
Yandex
Saint-Petersburg, Russia
s-lomakina@yandex-team.ru

ABSTRACT

Using eye-tracking, we investigate how searchers interact with Web search engines which get affected by nonsensical results. We conduct a user survey to choose "stupid" components for our laboratory experiment and explore the most conspicuous ones. This research provides insights about searchers' interactions with different kinds of "stupid" search components, such as organic search results, vertical results, ads and automatic misspell correction. We investigate the influence of each class of "stupid" components on users' attitude to a search engine. We found that sticking in memory of the impression about the "stupidity" of the search engine depended on whether the users were finally satisfied with their searches, or did not find the answer. Experimental results show that classes of "stupid" components can be differentiated by their influence on users' attitude. The most negative impression is caused by word losses, word collocation breaks and inappropriate misspell corrections.

Categories and Subject Descriptors: H.3.3 [Information Storage & Retrieval]: Information Search & Retrieval
Keywords: online evaluation; gaze tracking; user study

1. INTRODUCTION

"Stupids" are search components that appear to be nonsensical (extremely irrelevant) with respect to a given query and make a searcher disoriented and frustrated. A searcher may encounter "stupids" in the scope of different search components such as organic search results, vertical search results, search ads, automatic misspell corrections, automatic query suggestions or related queries. The concept of "stupids" was first introduced in [9]. The authors suggested a way of detecting "stupid" documents in the organic search results. In this paper, we investigate the influence of "stupids" on users' behavior in different search components, not only in organic results, using eye-tracking.

A number of studies used eye-tracking tools to understand how searchers examine search results in detail. Granka et al. [6] provided first insights into how users browse the first page of organic search results. This research was continued in [7]. Buscher et al. investigated how people interact with Web search engine results supplemented with ads and related queries of varying quality [4]. Dumais et al. used the eye-tracking methodology to provide a detailed analysis of the patterns of user attention to search engine result pages consisting of organic results, ads and related searches [5]. Arguello et al. conducted a user study to investigate the "spill-over" effect between vertical and organic results [1, 2]. They show that users are more likely to interact with web results when blended vertical results (images, commercial) are more consistent with the actual query intent. In [10], the presence of following biases is demonstrated: examination bias for multimedia vertical results, trust bias of result lists with vertical results and a higher probability of result revisitation for vertical results. However, no attention has been paid to the problem of the influence of "stupid" results on searchers.

We conducted a qualitative laboratory eye-tracking based research of several classes of "stupids". First, to be sure that chosen "stupids" components are indeed nonsensical according to the majority of users, we organized a user survey to come up with a classification of the most notorious types of "stupids". That enabled us to study some distinct classes in our research and make generalizations not only for any "stupids" on average, but for the components from the same class of "stupids".

Further, by monitoring search behaviour of a user group with eye-tracking, we compared 5 artificial search engines, each of them having "stupids" in only one of the following components: organic search results (2 classes of "stupids"), vertical results, misspell corrections and search ads.

The goals of our research were the following. First, we aimed to investigate how searchers interact with "stupid" components of different classes. Second, we wanted to analyze how different classes of "stupids" affect users' attitude to a search engine.

The remainder of this paper is organized as follows. We describe the classification of "stupid" search components in Section 2. In Section 3 we describe the above-mentioned laboratory eye-tracking experiment and analyze its outcomes. Section 4 concludes the paper with the summary of the major findings.

2. CLASSIFICATION

To set up a controlled eye-tracking experiment with different classes of "stupids" it was necessary to systematize them. As defined in [9], "stupids" are such "extremely" irrelevant results which, in contrast to "moderately" irrelevant documents, do not contain any information on the topic of the

*Now at Saint Petersburg State University

Permission to make digital or hard copies of all or part of this work for personal or classroom use is granted without fee provided that copies are not made or distributed for profit or commercial advantage and that copies bear this notice and the full citation on the first page. Copyrights for components of this work owned by others than ACM must be honored. Abstracting with credit is permitted. To copy otherwise, or republish, to post on servers or to redistribute to lists, requires prior specific permission and/or a fee. Request permissions from Permissions@acm.org.
CIKM'15, October 19–23, 2015, Melbourne, Australia.
© 2015 ACM. ISBN 978-1-4503-3794-6/15/10 ...$15.00.
DOI: http://dx.doi.org/10.1145/2806416.2806601.

Class	%	Experimental system color
Word losses	48.78%	blue
Word collocation breaks	31.71%	garnet
Wrong misspell corrections	29.27%	violet
Inappropriate verticals	24.39%	green
Off the topic advertisement	12.2%	red
Ambiguity of terms	12.2%	—
Wrong regions	9.76%	—
Inconvenient user-prompts	9.76%	—
Wrong language of documents	7.32%	—
Missing misspell corrections	7.32%	—

Table 1: Classes of "stupids" from different search engines, sorted by the percentage of respondents mentioned them and by colors of experimental systems with such "stupid" components ("—" were not in the experiment)

user query and are also completely out of the query's subject area. Meanwhile, "stupids" might mean something different for each user, as the above definition is very subjective.

To determine if there are any distinguishable classes in "stupid" components, we took a poll. Forty-one paid experts (35% females, 65% males) ranging in age from 26 to 66 years old with a diverse range of backgrounds and education levels were asked to respond to some questions. All of them were experienced at Web search and all were familiar with several different search engines.

The survey consisted of three questions:

- Have you ever been faced with any kind of extremely irrelevant ("nonsensical"/"stupid") search components in your search sessions?
- Give some examples of such search components and explain, why you considered them as real "stupids"?
- Describe your attitude to such "stupid" components.

Every of 41 experts noted at least one case when they encountered search components which can be named as "stupid". We systematized all examples and identified several classes of "stupid" components. The classification results are presented in Table 1.

The most noticeable classes of "stupids" are: "word losses" and "word collocation breaks". Almost a half of the experts mentioned cases, which we named "word losses", as an extremely frustrating situation. In this case, "stupidity" of a search engine lies in the fact that some query words can be completely ignored and that is why users get very unexpected results. Often digits, special characters, prepositions and, what is more critical, query specifications are lost. It means that users may get information about entirely different persons, program versions, addresses, organizations, etc. (e.g. a user may receive documents related to books by Stephen Fry in response to the query *"stephen king books"* or iPhone 4s price offers instead of iPhone 6 Plus prices).

"Word collocation breaks" is another class of "stupids" frequently occurring in our survey results. If users get search results with all the query words in each of them but shuffled and scattered over the documents, it is also a "stupid" that one third of experts get easily frustrated with (e.g. one might get a page about both Pamela Anderson and Gillian Flynn in response to the *"gillian anderson"* query). Wrong automatic misspell corrections spoiled interaction with search engines for 29.3% of the experts. For example, there are wrong corrections of queries in other languages, rare words/ names and terms, wrong grammar forms. "Inappropriate verticals" are regarded as "stupids" too: when users get search results blended with unexpected irrelevant videos, images or, for example, weather forecast verticals in response to the query "listen to online radio Monte-Carlo". In this case they cannot explain how and why the search engine could return such nonsensical search result. Some other small classes were mentioned: wrong region in local searches, wrong language of search results, wrong suggestions, missing misspell corrections, duplicated documents.

The experts added ñomments to some answers describing their feelings and further actions they undertook after they had seen "stupid" components on a search engine result page (SERP). Such comments described those feelings as annoyance, indifference or reaction to the situation with humor. The above-mentioned classes of "stupid" results made some experts make more thoroughly formulated queries, whereas others preferred to switch either to specialized search services or just other web search engines. The experts' answers to our questions provided us with information not only about the classes of "stupids" that can be distinguished by users, but also about different possible reactions, which often appeared to be quite emotionally strong. This fact stresses the importance of closely studying the behavior of users facing "stupid" results, what can be done in the scope of a controlled experiment. So, to organize such an experiment, we selected those classes of "stupids" that were mentioned in the majority of the respondents examples. Among them there were two classes that seemed to be very similar at the first glance ("word losses" and "word collocation breaks"). However, many users mentioned both of them separately in their answers. That is why one of the subtasks of this research was to define the difference in users' attitude towards the two classes.

3. EXPERIMENT

We designed a qualitative eye-tracking experiment in which participants were asked to complete a number of given search tasks using a web search engine. We were interested if users pay attention to "stupids" in search results and how it influences their attitude to search engines in general. We used eye-tracking as an instrument to obtain detailed information about the users' visual attention patterns. It is common for eye-tracking studies to take sequences of eye movements as a proxy for visual attention. Thus, eye-tracking and participants' comments during the experiment can provide the data leading us to valuable insights about how users interact with "stupid" components in search results pages.

Next, we describe the experimental setup, the search tasks used, the participants and the experimental procedure in Section 3.1. We describe the observations and experimental results in Section 3.2.

3.1 Experimental Design and Procedure

For each of five selected classes of "stupids" we created an artificial search system. One additional system was used to illustrate the procedure and give participants the opportunity to get used to the systems. All the systems were identical in design and differed only by color. The distribution of classes by systems is presented in Table 1. An example of the start page is presented in Figure 1. All experimental systems were implemented using Yandex Search API.

Tasks.

We prepared 43 search tasks for the experiment. Every system in the experiment had its own set of tasks (from 6 to 11 tasks).

Figure 1: Experiment start page sample

Each task had a description what the participants should be looking for. To be able to compare the participants' behavior on SERPs with and without "stupids", we "spoiled" SERPs only in half of the tasks. In order to make the initial SERPs comparable across participants, we provided them with an initial query for each task. Some examples of task descriptions and the corresponding initial task queries are given in Table 2.

Procedure.

Ten eye-tracking study participants[3] were hired by a recruiting company. None of them were involved in the classification poll from the Section 2. All participants (ranged in age between 22 and 58 years) were familiar with several different search engines.

After a short introduction to the study and eye-tracker calibration, the participants completed a couple of practical tasks in test system to get themselves familiar with search systems. Then they started the experiment. For each task we provided the participants with a written description and the corresponding initial query. After reading a query and its description aloud, the participants typed the query into the search box and pressed the search button to begin searching. The first SERP was always a locally stored, static page containing generated results with "stupid" components for "spoiled" tasks and ordinary ranking for "clean" tasks. Modified search results were prepared for several variations of initial queries in case of the participants' misprints. All the participants were asked to think aloud during browsing and to comment on their actions and their line of reasoning. The participants were free to interact with search results as they wished after getting the initial SERP. They could click links, view the next page of results, or reformulate the query. The combination of an initial fixed SERP and the full search functionality provided good balance between experimental control and search realism for a laboratory study.

To complete the task, the users had to either 1) navigate to a relevant web page and announce the finding of a solution, or 2) decide that an appropriate page cannot be found and stop searching. Then they were assigned with the next task.

We had time limitations for each participant. So each of them performed 20 tasks only in 3 of 5 experimental search systems. Every system was used by 6 participants in a different order (Latin Square design [8] was used) to avoid the perception biases and to ensure there's a better balanced experimental design.

Having found solutions for all the tasks in one system, the participants were to fill in a questionnaire covering their web search experience in completed system and their feelings during the study. The experiment took about one hour per participant.

3.2 Results

Our main goals were to study how searchers interact with "stupid" components of different types and to determine whether such results have any influence on users' attitude to search engines. During the eye-tracking experiment, the participants were asked to comment on their actions aloud, thus making it possible for the observers to summarize the outspoken negative reactions to the search results caused by the presence of "stupids".

It was observed that even "stupids" from the same class can stick in users' minds to a varying degree. It appeared that sticking in memory depends on whether the users were finally satisfied with their searches, or did not find the answer and stopped searching. In case of success, searchers could forget about the "stupids" they had seen. In case of an unsuccessful search, "stupids" reinforced the negative experience and transferred the frustration accumulated during one search session to the whole system.

It was found from eye-tracking results, that if "stupids" were in the components where users do not normally expect to find the answer in the first place (inappropriate verticals/advertisement), the searchers paid no attention and skipped such components. It was particularly noticeable in the system with blended inappropriate vertical results (green system).

For example, the participants tried to find a definition of the word "precedent" in law dictionaries within one of the experiments' tasks. According to eye-tracking data, they skipped unexpected and highly irrelevant image vertical results, just because it was clearly impossible to find appropriate answers there, and then carefully examined other search results.

The similar situation was observed in the red system tracking results. If the participants got a SERP with search ads on the right side, they paid no attention to them. Meanwhile, if such ads were situated at the top of the SERP, searchers had to examine them. However, they perceived that component only as a block of sponsored links and not as a potential source of the information they needed regardless of whether it was "stupid" or not.

In the blue and garnet systems ("word losses" and "word collocation breaks") participants examined results' snippets and titles very carefully, looking for the indications of the presence of the query terms in them. It took a lot of time and caused a negative reaction as they failed to find what they were looking for. However, when "stupids" were blended below relevant documents in search results, the users could not notice that the corresponding SERPS were spoiled.

One of the additional research questions was: do "word losses" differ from "word collocation breaks" in the way they affect user behavior? The participants named different reasons for unsuccessful searches in the system with such "stupids". In case of "word losses", searchers blamed the search engine for poor results and it adversely affected users' feelings about their searches in the blue system. Whereas, when users received search results in the garnet system ("word collocation breaks"), they were upset, but found themselves guilty in those system fails. If searchers saw all query words in the snippets, that made them feel that system "tried to do its best", however something in the query formulation was incorrect. In this case, searchers tried to improve this situation with reformulations and more precise queries. Those eye-tracking results give us an explanation why the experts responded to the "stupids" classification poll, regarded "word losses" and "word collocation breaks" as two different classes.

There were two classes of "stupid" components in the experimental system with inappropriate automatic misspell corrections (violet system). The participants got search re-

Table 2: Example of the search tasks for every system in experiment

Class	initial query	task description
Word losses	nokia c2-01	Find a review of this particular phone model
Word collocation breaks	How I met your mother 3 season 5 episode	Find where you can download the episode from Season 5 of the series
Inappropriate video vertical	movies nokia 5228 download	Find where you can get movies for this model
Inappropriate images vertical	madonna songs online	Find where you can listen to some Madonna songs
Misspell corrections	Betio island	Find where this island is situated
Advertisement	google chrome	Find the most recent version of the browser

Table 3: Participant perceptions of the system used. Ratings ranges for Goodness and Association from 1 to 5 and from 1 to 3 respectively. Higher is more positive.

	garnet	red	blue	violet	green
Goodness	3	4	2.8	3.3	3.8
Association	1.7	2.5	1.5	1.7	2.3

sults with suggestions for corrections or search results affected by automatic misspell correction. In the first case, suggestions were perceived as a part of the search results' binding, so participants did not pay attention to them. In the second case, the results changed by the automatic misspell correction caused increase in negative participants' reaction. Searchers were upset and annoyed as well as in the "word losses" system, because they were forced to spend a lot of time searching for the solution. So, we observed that "stupids" had an influence on the searchers, but it was weaker than in the case of "word losses" and stronger than in the search results in other experimental systems.

Observations made via analyzing the eye-tracking log conform with the results of the survey, filled out by the participants after the experiment completion.

When all the tasks in each search system were complete, the participants filled out a survey covering the following questions about each system they used:
Q1: In your opinion, how good or bad was the search engine? (a five-point scale: very good, somewhat good, neither bad nor good, somewhat bad, very bad) (Goodness).
Q2: Continue the phrase "Users searching in this search engine ..." (open answer) (Association).
Answers to Q2 were transformed into a three-point scale: negative association, neutral association and positive association. Some examples for Q2: "...get first-hand information" (Positive), "...spend too much time to get information they need" (Negative)

Table 3 shows the average answer ratings for each question. The participants perceived the red engine more positively than the blue one. So, the worst "stupid" components were "word losses", "inappropriate misspell corrections" and "word collocation brakes". It coincides with the most conspicuous classes of "stupids" from the survey summarized in Table 1. We also found out that searchers not only noticed stupid components, but also remembered them after the completion of the tasks and transferred that negative attitude to the whole system.

4. CONCLUSIONS

In this paper, we presented the results of a qualitative eye-tracking study to characterize how "stupid" components influence users' visual attention to different components of SERPs and to assess the searchers' attitude to the search engines affected by "stupids". We summarize our observations of "stupids" influence on searchers as follows: the answer whether the impression about the "stupidity" of a search engine will stick in one's memory depends on whether the users were finally satisfied with their searches, or did not find the answer. As consistent with the user survey we found that among such "stupid" components as organic search results, vertical results, ads and automatic misspell correction, "word losses" left the most negative impression, since it induced the most negative attitude towards the whole system. "Inappropriate misspell corrections" and "word collocation breaks" were the next in the list of the most frustrating system failures.

This research represents the first step in understanding how "stupid" components of different types influence search interactions. In future work we plan to analyze the influence of "stupids" in a large-scale experiment on federated searches based on our findings in this paper. We also plan to look at "word losses" more meticulously to find out which missing part of a query has the worst influence on a user.

5. REFERENCES

[1] J. Arguello and R. Capra. The effect of aggregated search coherence on search behavior. In *CIKM 2012*, pages 1293–1302, 2012.

[2] J. Arguello and R. Capra. The effects of vertical rank and border on aggregated search coherence and search behavior. In *CIKM 2014*, pages 539–548, 2014.

[3] A. Aula, R. M. Khan, Z. Guan, P. Fontes, and P. Hong. A comparison of visual and textual page previews in judging the helpfulness of web pages. In *WWW 2010*, pages 51–60, 2010.

[4] G. Buscher, S. T. Dumais, and E. Cutrell. The good, the bad, and the random: An eye-tracking study of ad quality in web search. In *SIGIR 2010*, pages 42–49.

[5] S. T. Dumais, G. Buscher, and E. Cutrell. Individual differences in gaze patterns for web search. In *IIiX 2010*, pages 185–194, 2010.

[6] L. A. Granka, T. Joachims, and G. Gay. Eye-tracking analysis of user behavior in www search. In *SIGIR 2004*, pages 478–479, 2004.

[7] T. Joachims, L. Granka, B. Pan, H. Hembrooke, and G. Gay. Accurately interpreting clickthrough data as implicit feedback. In *SIGIR 2005*, pages 154–161.

[8] D. Kelly. Methods for evaluating interactive information retrieval systems with users. *Found. Trends Inf. Retr.*, pages 1–224, 2009.

[9] A. Lomakina, N. Povarov, and P. Serdyukov. Web search without 'stupid' results. In *SIGIR 2014*, pages 943–946, 2014.

[10] C. Wang, Y. Liu, M. Zhang, S. Ma, M. Zheng, J. Qian, and K. Zhang. Incorporating vertical results into search click models. In *SIGIR 2013*, pages 503–512.

Social-Relational Topic Model for Social Networks

Weiyu Guo[1,2], Shu Wu[1], Liang Wang[1], Tieniu Tan[1]
[1]Center for Research on Intelligent Perception and Computing,
National Laboratory of Pattern Recognition, Institute of Automation,
Chinese Academy of Sciences, Beijing 100190, China.
[2]College of Engineering and Information Technology,
University of Chinese Academy of Sciences, Beijing 100049, China.
weiyu.guo@ia.ac.cn, {shu.wu, wangliang, tnt}@nlpr.ia.ac.cn

ABSTRACT

Social networking services, such as Twitter and Sina Weibo, have tremendous popularity in recent years. Mass of short texts and social links are aggregated into these service platforms. To realize personalized services on social network, topic inference from both short texts and social links plays more and more important role. Most conventional topic modeling methods focus on analyzing formal texts, e.g., papers, news and blogs, and usually assume that the links are only generated by topical factors. As a result, on social network, the learned topics of these methods are usually affected by topic-irrelevant links. Recently, a few approaches use artificial priors to recognize the links generated by the popularity factor in topic modeling. However, employing global priors, these methods can not well capture the distinct properties of each link and still suffer from the effect of topic-irrelevant links. To address the above limitations, we propose a novel Social-Relational Topic Model (SRTM), which can alleviate the effect of topic-irrelevant links by analyzing relational users' topics of each link. SRTM jointly models texts and social links for learning the topic distribution and topical influence of each user. The experimental results show that, our model outperforms the state-of-the-arts in topic modeling and social link prediction.

Keywords

Topic Modeling; Social Networks; Social Link Generation

1. INTRODUCTION

Exploring users' topics on social networks from rich texts and social links is important for marketing activities in real applications. Although a lot of works, e.g., Link-LDA [1], RTM [2] and RankTopic [3], have been proposed for this task, most of them assume that the social links are purely caused by topical factors and are used as the supplement of texts in topic inference. Clearly, this assumption is not suitable for social networks, since many topic-irrelevant factors which can lead to a link generation. For example, on Twitter, President Obama associates with political topics and has a lot of followers. But, as far as we know, many of Obama's followers are not really interested in politics, and these following relationships may be caused by the so-called bandwagon effect [4]. As a result, if we could not recognize such topic-irrelevant links which are not really caused by users' interesting topics, the learned topics tend to be affected by these noise links and are not reliable to reveal personalized interests.

Permission to make digital or hard copies of all or part of this work for personal or classroom use is granted without fee provided that copies are not made or distributed for proŒt or commercial advantage and that copies bear this notice and the full citation on the Œrst page. Copyrights for components of this work owned by others than ACM must be honored. Abstracting with credit is permitted. To copy otherwise, or republish, to post on servers or to redistribute to lists, requires prior speciŒc permission and/or a fee. Request permissions from Permissions@acm.org.
CIKM'15, October 19–23, 2015, Melbourne, Australia.
© 2015 ACM. ISBN 978-1-4503-3794-6/15/10 ...$15.00.
DOI: http://dx.doi.org/10.1145/2806416.2806611.

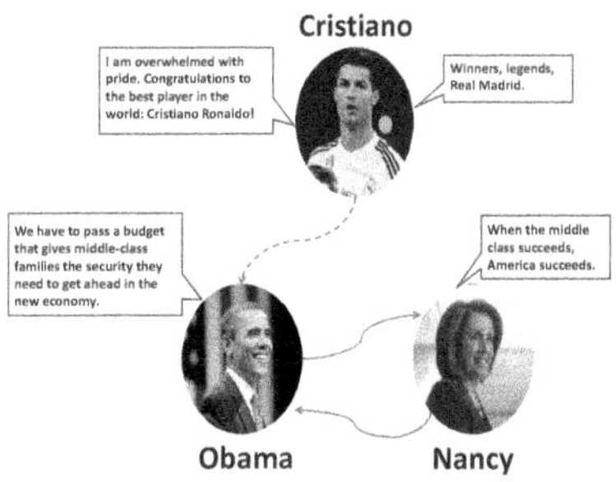

Figure 1: A toy example of Twitter data, which shows several tweets and following relationships among three users. In this example, Obama and Nancy (Minority Leader of the United States House of Representatives) are following each other, and Cristiano (a football star) is following Obama.

Recently, some approaches are proposed for dealing with topic-irrelevant links in topic modeling. For example, FLDA [5] embeds a Bernoulli prior to judge whether following links on Micro-bloging platforms are generated by popularity factors. However, since the factors of link generation on social networks are various, the methods which only rely on prior knowledge and can not well reveal the characteristics of each link. Intuitively, many topic-irrelevant links can be indicated by the texts of their relational users. As shown in Figure 1, Obama and Nancy have published similar political views in their tweets, and they follow each other may because of having similar political topics. While Cristiano mainly publishes tweets about football, he follows Obama may be caused by adoring the political celebrity. Therefore, the topical similarity of users, may be in turn to indicate whether the links between users are caused by topical factors.

In this paper, for alleviating the effect of topic-irrelevant links and obtaining reliable topics, we propose a novel SRTM, which can assess whether a specific link on social networks is caused by topical factors, and jointly model the texts and social links into a unified generative process. Moreover, except for individual topic distribution, our model can learn the individual influence on different topics and the global popularity of each user. To systematically assess our model, we conduct comparisons with several state-of-the-arts in topic modeling using the perplexity metric and social link prediction with ranking metrics.

2. RELATED WORK

Recently, a mass of hybrid data that contain textual information and social information are aggregated into social networking Websites. Topic models, such as Link-LDA [1] and RTM [2], which can discover a given number of topics from data sources, are often used to process such hybrid data. Link-LDA views the citations of a document as a kind of words, and uses LDA [6] to deal with such special words. With a pure topic relational assumption, Chang et al. propose RTM model for document networks, which draws topics for citations according to relational topic distributions of citations. However, the social links on social networks, e.g., Micro-blogs, are more complex than the citations. Many factors may lead to the generation of a social link, such as the bandwagon effect or the marketing advertisement. Thus, FLDA [5] improves Link-LDA by introducing a Multinomial-Bernoulli prior to assess whether a following relationship is caused by topical factors. Different from FLDA using an artificial prior to analyze social links, we leverage the similarity of relational topic distributions of each link to measure whether the link is generated by topic-irrelevant factors.

Ranking based models [3, 7] are another direction for dealing with hybrid data. They usually use topic modeling for analyzing the textual information, and conduct ranking algorithms, e.g., pagerank [8], on the structure information. For example, RankTopic [3] uses basic topic model to explore the topic distribution of each node from its texts, and then conducts Topic Sensitive PageRank [9] on the citation network to obtain more reliable topics. In [7], Yan et al. learn the topic distribution of tweets using LDA, and then compute the topical influence of each tweet on a heterogeneous graph by pagerank. However, since ranking based models often assume that the links are purely generated by topics, their learned topics tend to be effected by the topic-irrelevant effect. Moreover, due to the large scale social networks, these models often suffer from a slow convergence.

3. SOCIAL-RELATIONAL TOPIC MODEL

In this section, we present the Social-Relational Topic Model (SRTM), which jointly models the texts and social links. Through this model, we estimate the topic-irrelevant links, infer the topic distribution for each user, and analyze the users' influence on different topics.

3.1 Definition of SRTM

Our model consists of three major components with each capturing one perspective of our targets. For one following relationship l, the graphical representation of our model is shown in Figure 2. The model embeds two LDA models for processing the texts of relational users on either side of the model. In the middle part, the model estimates whether the link associates with topical factors and analyzes users' influence on different topics. More specifically, in SRTM, each user u is viewed as a mixture of K latent topics, i.e., $\theta_u \in \mathbb{R}^K$, corresponding to the texts and social links. SRTM

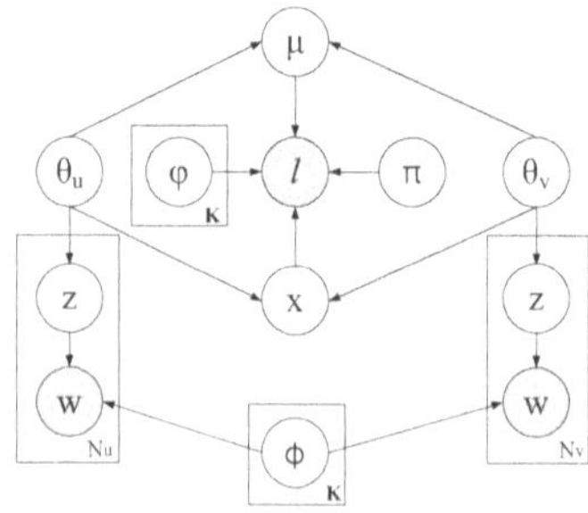

Figure 2: Graphical representation of SRTM. The gray symbols denote the observed variables, i.e., w denotes a word in texts and l is the following link from the user u to the user v. θ_u and θ_v denote the topic distribution of u and v, respectively. z is a topic in texts, and x denotes a topic on following links. ϕ is the topic-word distribution, and ψ is the topic-user distribution. π is the Multinomial distribution over users, which indicates the popularity of users. μ is a switch variable which follows a Bernolli prior and relies on the topic distribution of two related users. N_u and N_v are the number of words in the texts of user u and user v, respectively.

generates a following relationship and estimates whether it is a topic-irrelevant link, by taking relational topic distributions, i.e., θ_u and θ_v into account. In a nutshell, the generative process of SRTM is summarized in Algorithm 1, where σ is a sigmoid function, i.e., $\sigma(x) = 1/(1+exp(-x))$, and $\rho_{u,v} = \theta_u\theta_v + \tau$.

Algorithm 1 Generative process of SRTM

Draw $\pi \sim Dir(\epsilon)$;
for all each topic $k = \{1, 2, ..., K\}$ **do**
  Draw $\phi \sim Dir(\beta)$;
  Draw $\psi \sim Dir(\delta)$;
end for
for all each user $i = \{1, 2, ..., M\}$ **do**
  Draw topic proportions $\theta_i|\alpha \sim Dir(\alpha)$;
  for all each word $w_{i,n}$ in the texts of u **do**
    Draw an assignment $z_{i,n}|\theta_i \sim Mult(\theta_i)$;
    Draw a word $w_{i,n}|z_{i,n}, \phi \sim Mult(\phi_{z_{i,n}})$;
  end for
end for
for all each user $u = \{1, 2, ..., M\}$ **do**
  for all each following relationship $l_{u,v}$ of u **do**
    Draw a switch $\mu_{u,v}|\theta_u, \theta_v, \tau \sim Ber(\sigma(\rho_{u,v}))$;
    if $\mu_{u,v} == 1$ **then**
      Draw an assignment $x_{u,v}|\theta_u, \theta_v \sim Mult(\theta_u \odot \theta_v)$;
      Draw a followed user $e_{u,v}|x_{u,v}, \psi \sim Mult(\psi_{x_{u,v}})$;
    else
      Draw a followed user $e_{u,v} \sim Mult(\pi_v)$;
    end if
  end for
end for

To generate texts of users, each user is treated as a mixture of latent topics from which words are drawn. Similar to LDA, for the u-th user, the model first draws the topic distribution θ_u from a Dirichlet prior with a hyper-parameter α. Then, to generate the n-th word in the texts of the user, a topic assignment $z_{u,n}$ is drawn from θ_u. Finally, the word $w_{u,n}$ is picked from the topic-word distribution $\phi_{z_{u,n}}$.

Clearly, the topic distribution is affected by the social information, and the generative mechanism of following relationships are different from the words in textual contents.

In Algorithm 1, we sculpture a two-stage stochastic process for the generation of following relationships. Specifically, we first assess whether a following relationship is related to users' topics, using a switch variable μ. For a following relationship $l_{u,v}$, there is a switch $\mu_{u,v}$ which is drawn from a Bernoulli prior. If $\mu_{u,v} = 1$, the following relationship is assumed to be associated with the user's topics, then a topic assignment $x_{u,v}$ is drawn according to the relational topic distributions, i.e., θ_u and θ_v. Indicated by $x_{u,v}$, the following relationship $l_{u,v}$ is sampled from the Multinomial distribution $\varphi_{x_{u,v}}$, which corresponds to the topic-specific influence of users. If $\mu_{u,v} = 0$, the following relationship is viewed to be generated by topic-irrelevant factors, and is sampled from another Multinomial distribution π, which mainly indicates the global popularity of users. Moreover, according to the observation in Figure 1, the similarity of textual contents can help us to estimate whether the social link associates with topics. Therefore, for the following relationship $l_{u,v}$, we bring θ_u and θ_v to be the preconditions of $\mu_{u,v}$. More specifically, for drawing the value of $\mu_{u,v}$, we calculate the inner product of θ_u and θ_v and use it as the parameter of Bernoulli prior.

3.2 Model Inference by Gibbs Sampling

Given M users and the hyper-parameters α, β, δ, ϵ and τ, the joint probability distribution for the observed variables of the model can be written as

$$P(W, G \mid \Theta) \propto \prod_{i=1}^{M} P(\theta_i \mid \alpha) \prod_{n=1}^{N_i} P(z_{i,n}|\theta_i) \prod_{k=1}^{K} P(w_{i,n}|z_{i,n}, \beta)$$
$$\times \prod_{u=1}^{M} \prod_{v=1}^{F_u} (P(\mu_{u,v} = 1 \mid \rho_{u,v}) P(x_{u,v}|\theta_u, \theta_v) \prod_{k=1}^{K} P(e_{u,v}|x_{u,v}, \delta)$$
$$+ P(\mu_{u,v} = 0 \mid \rho_{u,v}) \, P(e_{u,v} \mid \epsilon)) \tag{1}$$

where $\Theta = \{\theta, \phi, \psi, \mu, \pi, \alpha, \beta, \delta, \epsilon, \tau\}$ is the set of parameters. F_u is a set which contains all users followed by u-th user, and $G = \{l_{u,v}|u \in M, v \in F_u\}$ is the social graph. W represents the observed word set.

To deal with the coupling of variables in our model, we use collapsed Gibbs sampling to learn variables distributions in Eq.1. Since, in SRTM, the distribution of following relationships is a joint distribution of two-level mixtures and simultaneously associates with two topic mixtures, we need to take both θ_u and θ_v into account when computing the posterior distributions of x, which is the topic distribution on following relationships. More specifically, the posterior distributions for Gibbs sampling in SRTM are given

$$p(z_{u,w} = k \mid z_{-(u,w)}, \alpha, \beta) \propto$$
$$(d_{uk}^{-(u,w)} + s_{uk} + \alpha) \times \frac{(W_{kw}^{-(u,w)} + \beta)}{\sum_{w'}^{N} W_{kw'}^{-(u,w)} + \beta} \tag{2}$$

$$p(\mu_{u,v} = 1 \mid x_{-(u,v)}, \alpha) \propto$$
$$sigmoid(\sum_{k=1}^{K} \frac{d_{uk} + s_{uk}^{-(u,v)} + \alpha}{N_u + L_u + K\alpha} \times \frac{d_{vk} + s_{vk} + \alpha}{N_v + L_v + K\alpha} + \tau) \tag{3}$$

$$p(x_{u,v}, \mu_{u,v} = 0 \mid x_{-(u,v)}, \alpha, \epsilon) \propto$$
$$(1 - p(\mu_{u,v} = 1 \mid \mu_{-(u,v)}, \alpha)) \times \frac{\mu_{*,v,0} - 1 + \epsilon}{\mu_{*,*,0} - 1 + M\epsilon} \tag{4}$$

$$p(x_{u,v} = k, \mu_{u,v} = 1 \mid x_{-(u,v)}, \alpha, \delta) \propto p(\mu_{u,v} = 1 \mid x_{-(u,v)}, \alpha)$$
$$\times (d_{uk} + s_{uk}^{-(u,v)} + \alpha) \times (d_{vk} + s_{vk} + \alpha) \times \frac{V_{ku}^{-(u,v)} + \delta}{\sum_{v'}^{M} V_{kv'}^{-(u,v)} + \delta} \tag{5}$$

where z_{uw} denotes the topic of the w-th word for the u-th user, and $x_{u,v}$ is the topic of the v-th link for the u-th user. Let $z_{-(uw)}$ denote the topics for all words except z_{uw}, and $x_{-(u,v)}$ follow an analogous definition. We use $\mu_{u,v}$ as a factor indicator (topical or non topical) of the v-th link for the u-th user. Moreover, for recording the intermediate process, we bring several counters into the above equations, i.e., W_{kw}, V_{kv}, d_{uk} and s_{uk}. W_{kw} is the number of times that the w-th word is assigned to the k-th topic and V_{kv} is the number of times that the v-th user is assigned to the k-th topic. d_{uk} records the number of times that the u-th user is assigned to the k-th topic from texts. s_{uk} is the number of times that the u-th user is assigned to the k-th topic from following links.

After the sampling algorithm runs for an appropriate number of iterations (until the chain has converged to a stationary distribution), the estimates for the parameters, i.e., θ, ϕ, ψ and π can be obtained via the following equations:

$$\theta_{uk} \propto \frac{d_{uk} + s_{uk} + \alpha}{N_u + L_u + K\alpha} \qquad \pi_v \propto \frac{\mu_{*,v,0} + \epsilon}{\mu_{*,*,0} + M\epsilon} \tag{6}$$

$$\phi_{kw} \propto \frac{W_{kw} + \beta}{\sum_{w'}^{N} W_{kw'} + \beta} \qquad \psi_{kv} \propto \frac{V_{kv} + \delta}{\sum_{v'}^{M} V_{kv'} + \delta} \tag{7}$$

where L_u denotes the number of following links of the u-th user. $\mu_{*,v,0}$ denotes the number of times that the v-th user is followed by other users because of non-topical factors, and $\mu_{*,*,0}$ is the total number of times that the following behaviors are caused by non-topical factors in the dataset.

3.3 Social Link Generation

After the procedure of parameter inference, using the estimated parameters, we can construct a function to describe the generative process of social links in SRTM. In this function, we take the individual topic distribution, individual topic-specific influence and user popularity into account. More specifically, given a user u and a candidate v, we can calculate the value which indicates the likelihood of u following v as below,

$$P(u, v) \propto (1 - \sigma(\rho_{u,v}))\pi_v + \sigma(\rho_{u,v}) \sum_{k=1}^{K} \theta_{uk} \, \theta_{vk} \, \psi_{k,v}. \tag{8}$$

Notice that including proposed SRTM model, the latent space models, e.g., LDA, Link-LDA and FLDA, can easily be embedded in this function. The value computed from this function describes the generation likelihood of the social link from user u to user v.

4. EXPERIMENT

To investigate the performance of SRTM, we perform experiments on two real word datasets, i.e., Sina Weibo and Twitter, which contain a mass of following links and user published short texts. Sina Weibo is a popular Micro-bloging service of China, and the dataset we used contains 1,704,142 users and their related information, i.e., published statuses and social links. The dataset of Twitter is collected from twitter.com, which contains 5,847,699 users, 24,257,080 statuses and 126,964,950 social links. We randomly split training (80%) and testing (20%) data for experiments.

Table 1: Performance comparison on Sina Weibo (K=32, 64) with MAP@3, 10, 20 and AUC.

Method	Sina Weibo (K=32)				Sina Weibo (K=64)			
	MAP@3	MAP@10	MAP@20	AUC	MAP@3	MAP@10	MAP@20	AUC
MF	0.435	0.453	0.436	0.849	0.459	0.468	0.448	0.853
LDA	0.064	0.085	0.091	0.613	0.079	0.102	0.106	0.622
Link-LDA	0.523	0.498	0.460	0.867	0.495	0.477	0.441	0.866
FLDA	0.533	0.506	0.469	0.870	0.496	0.475	0.440	0.868
SRTM	**0.577**	**0.547**	**0.510**	**0.873**	**0.579**	**0.548**	**0.511**	**0.872**

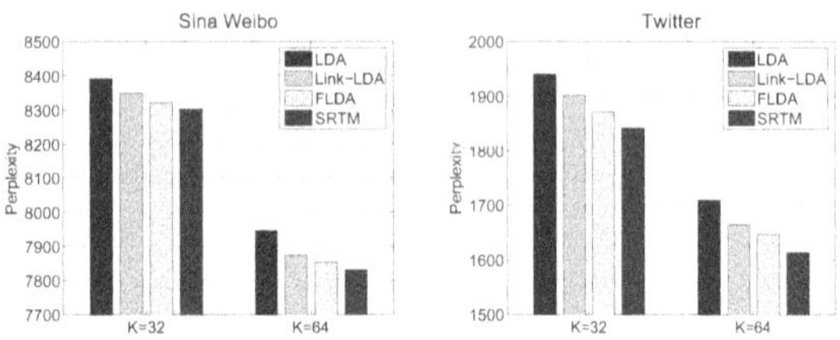

Figure 3: The perplexity of LDA styled models on Sina Weibo and Twitter.

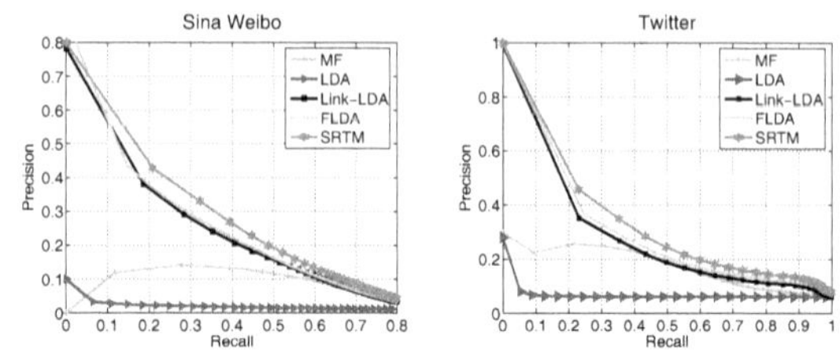

Figure 4: Precision-Recall curves on Sina Weibo (K=32) and Twitter (K=32).

We conduct comparisons with several state-of-the-art methods, including MF [10], LDA [6], Link-LDA [1] and FLDA [5]. Among these compared methods, MF and LDA only take links or texts into account, while Link-LDA and FLDA take both links and texts into account. In order to evaluate the LDA styled models, we use the perplexity which is widely used for topic modeling. To further study our model, we embed it into the TRA framework for social link prediction, and use Area Under the ROC Curve (AUC) and Mean Average Precision (MAP) as metrics.

Figure 3 demonstrates the effectiveness of compared methods on topic modeling, in term of perplexity. Since the training texts usually can not represent all topical information and some topics can be revealed by social links, LDA only taking texts into account can not well model such hybrid data. Since Link-LDA treats links as a kind of words and FLDA introduces a prior for the bandwagon effect of social links, they improve performance of LDA. Owing much to estimating topic-irrelevant links with relational topic distributions, our model yields lower perplexity than both Link-LDA and FLDA on two datasets.

In addition, we show keywords and associated influencers of several topics, which are explored by SRTM from Sina Weibo dataset. Table 2 indicates that our model can not only explain latent properties of users using the keywords extracted from texts, but also find out the users who are the influencers on individual topic. For example, under the topic of Economy, SRTM can not only provide keywords, e.g., investment, market and bank, to describe this topic, but also can discover the influencers, e.g., Xianping Lang who is a famous economist in China.

To evaluate performance of link generation, Table 1 shows the comparison evaluated by ranking metrics on Sina Weibo with two different factor dimensionalities. Owing much to take topic-irrelevant links, popularity of users and topic-specific influence of users into account, our model consistently outperforms the compared methods in terms of MAP@N and AUC. In particular, on MAP@N, improvements of SRTM over compared methods are real significant. This observation indicates that SRTM is very suitable for top-N recommendation, which is the most fundamental problem in practical applications. Figure 4 indicates the precision-recall curves on two datasets. Since short texts on social network contain much noise and lack formal linguistic structures, the performance of LDA is often worse than MF which only takes social links into account. Furthermore, we notice that Link-LDA and FLDA, jointly modeling the texts and links, have great superiority over LDA and MF only considering texts or links. This phenomenon reveals that on social network, the texts and social links can be used to complement each other in topic inference. In all experiments, due to well estimating topic-irrelevant links, SRTM consistently outperforms Link-LDA and FLDA.

Table 2: A sample of topics and their influencers discovered by SRTM from Sina Weibo (K=32). Each topic is shown with top-8 keywords and top-3 influencers.

"Technique"	"Economy"	"Entertainment"	"Sport"
data	investment	movie	game
user	market	director	sport
Internet	company	story	fans
baidu	bank	release	football
problem	dollar	American	basketball
analysis	estate	comedy	champion
retrieval	policy	life	Milan
recommendation	funds	video	player
Yaqin Zhang	Xianping Lang	Kangyong Cai	Jianxiang Huang
Xiaochuan Wang	Shusong Ba	Zhang Wen	Lin Gao.
Hongjiang Zhang	Hongbin Song	Bo Huang.	Jianlian Yi

5. ACKNOWLEDGMENTS

This work is jointly supported by National Basic Research Program of China (2012CB316300), and National Natural Science Foundation of China (61403390, U1435221, 61175003, 61420106015).

6. REFERENCES

[1] Erosheva et al. Mixed-membership models of scientific publications. *PNAS*, 101(suppl 1):5220–5227, 2004.
[2] Chang et al. Relational topic models for document networks. In *ICAIS*, pages 81–88, 2009.
[3] Dongsheng et al. Ranktopic: Ranking based topic modeling. In *ICDM*, pages 211–220, 2012.
[4] Sang-Min et al. A recommendation model using the bandwagon effect for e-marketing purposes in iot. *IJDSN*, 501:475163, 2015.
[5] Bin et al. Scalable topic-specific influence analysis on microblogs. In *WSDM*, pages 513–522, 2014.
[6] David M. Blei et al. Latent dirichlet allocation. *JMLR*, 3(1):993–1022, 2003.
[7] Rui Yan et al. Tweet recommendation with graph co-ranking. In *ACL*, pages 516–525, 2010.
[8] Page et al. The pagerank citation ranking: Bringing order to the web. 1999.
[9] Haveliwala et al. Topic-sensitive pagerank. In *WWW*, pages 517–526, 2002.
[10] Wei-Sheng et al. A learning-rate schedule for stochastic gradient methods to matrix factorization. In *PAKDD*, pages 442–455. 2015.

Building Effective Query Classifiers: A Case Study in Self-harm Intent Detection

Ashiqur R. KhudaBukhsh[1]
Carnegie Mellon University
Pittsburgh, PA 15213
akhudabu@cs.cmu.edu

Paul N. Bennett
Microsoft Research
Redmond, WA 98052
pauben@microsoft.com

Ryen W. White
Microsoft Research
Redmond, WA 98052
ryenw@microsoft.com

ABSTRACT

Query-based triggers play a crucial role in modern search systems, e.g., in deciding when to display direct answers on result pages. We address a common scenario in designing such triggers for real-world settings where positives are rare and search providers possess only a small seed set of positive examples to learn query classification models. We choose the critical domain of self-harm intent detection to demonstrate how such small seed sets can be expanded to create meaningful training data with a sizable fraction of positive examples. Our results show that with our method, substantially more positive queries can be found compared to plain random sampling. Additionally, we explored the effectiveness of traditional active learning approaches on classification performance and found that maximum uncertainty performs the best among several other techniques that we considered.

Categories and Subject Descriptors

H.3.3 [**Information Storage and Retrieval**]: Information Search and Retrieval—*query formulation, search process.*

Keywords

Query classification; Self-harm; Active learning.

1. INTRODUCTION

Query-based triggers play an important role in modern information retrieval (IR) systems. Such triggers can be used to decide when to display rich direct answers (weather or stocks) on search engine result pages (SERPs), target display advertisements to particular queries or query classes, or issue other specific notifications to searchers. While a high-accuracy query classifier can help such systems reach all interested searchers, misclassification has a cost of showing notifications or advertisements in inappropriate contexts which may annoy or frustrate searchers. In the construction of query classifiers, search providers often only possess a small *seed set* of target queries, which can be insufficient for training. Positive queries (examples of queries that should be targeted) are rare in many query classification tasks. A common need is to expand the seed set to identify more positives without adding many negatives.

In this work, we choose one particularly important query classification problem, self-harm intent detection, as a case study to highlight the challenges and approaches to building an effective query classifier for a targeted domain. Currently, the major Web search engines respond to queries such as [how to kill yourself] with an answer-like treatment that provides a telephone number for the National Suicide Prevention Lifeline. The research challenge in this domain is to build classification models that can automatically and accurately detect when a query indicates an intent of the searcher for self-harm. To address that challenge, we make the simplifying assumption that the classifier solely relies on the text of query statements for training and prediction, and does not use additional information such as result clicks, cursor movements, and part of speech tagging—all of which have been used for query classification purposes [6][8][9]. This has the practical benefit that classifying solely based on query features reduces latency which is crucial for Web-scale use.

We make the following contributions with our research. We examine different notions of relatedness in query classification, and whether they provide different benefits when expanding a small set of seed queries to a much larger training and evaluation set. Additionally, this is the first work in IR on self-harm, a critically important topic. Finally, we believe that our work will stimulate discussion in the research community on this important, albeit sensitive, issue with specific questions such as when any intervention should be triggered, how intervention can be best provided, how specific intervention assistance should be, whether query re-writing should occur on such queries and the general question of how search engines should operate in such sensitive areas.

2. RELATED WORK

Query intent classification has been an active research area for many years. Several methods have been proposed to automatically identify three broad classes of intent: navigational, informational and transactional [2][11]. Most of these methods rely on additional information such as result clicks or anchor text [9], part of speech tagging [8] or mouse cursor movements on SERPs [6]. For example, Lee et al. [10] used the observation that the click distribution of navigational queries are usually highly skewed toward a few domains to distinguish navigational and informational search queries.

Jansen et al. [7] proposed a rule-based method that solely relied on queries. This supervised method is similar to ours in that it did not utilize additional information beyond queries. However, general rules such as the presence of terms like "download" indicating a transactional query are not applicable in our context since many queries of opposite labels share terms. Broder et al. [4] proposed methods to find relevant advertisements for tail queries. Our two studies were motivated by a similar goal of building effective classifiers for domains where positives are rare. However, our techniques are different. We propose methods to find positives to build more balanced training sets for classification. In contrast, Broder et al. target offline computation on head and torso queries.

While our focus is not on automatic query expansion (AQE), work in that area is still relevant to the research described herein. A survey of the significant body of literature on AQE can be found in [5]. Broder et al. [3] also targeted rare query classification, proposing a pseudo relevance feedback mechanism for classifying a query by

[1] Work performed at Microsoft Research.

Permission to make digital or hard copies of all or part of this work for personal or classroom use is granted without fee provided that copies are not made or distributed for profit or commercial advantage and that copies bear this notice and the full citation on the first page. Copyrights for components of this work owned by others than ACM must be honored. Abstracting with credit is permitted. To copy otherwise, or republish, to post on servers or to redistribute to lists, requires prior specific permission and/or a fee. Request permissions from Permissions@acm.org.
CIKM'15, October 19-23, 2015, Melbourne, VIC, Australia
© 2015 ACM. ISBN 978-1-4503-3794-6/15/10...$15.00
DOI: http://dx.doi.org/10.1145/2806416.2806594.

first classifying its search results and then using a voting mechanism to determine the label of the query. Their method requires downloading and processing the content of top-ranked results (and of course assumes that these top-ranked results are relevant to the query). Such a method is better suited to query *topic* classification or cases where a document likely satisfies a singular query intent. Topic may help inform query *intent* classification (our task). However, a document (e.g., a page on safe dosing limits for a medicine) can satisfy multiple intents (e.g., a query clearly indicating a user intends to overdose versus checking on how to safely take the medicine), and the query text plays a pivotal role in indicating searcher intentions that is not fulfilled by considering document topic. In contrast to Broder et al. [3], we rely solely on the query text. In these respects, the two methods are quite complementary.

3. TRAINING DATA

We now describe how we collected and manually labeled our query classification data. In particular given a small seed set of positive queries, we broaden this set in a two-step process. First, we automatically expand the query set (denoted as *ThreeHop*) using a three-step graph walk on the set of query suggestions obtained from Bing. In the second step, we further expand this to a set of related queries (denoted as *Related*) that are similar to the queries in *ThreeHop* in some way (specifically in applying bigram matching, trigram matching, or session matching).

3.1 Expansion through Graph Walk

To follow a common paradigm for constructing query classifiers, we assume that we have a small set of positive trigger queries and seek to broaden these to other relevant queries using commonly available resources. We started with a small seed set of queries that unambiguously expressed self-harm intent and expanded it by including the top-ten related query suggestions returned for those queries by Bing. Query suggestions are a convenient way of expanding an initial query set that is also reproducible publicly through search engine APIs. Focusing on query classification, since query suggestions are often largely influenced by session co-occurrence, this step can be viewed as sampling from the head of session co-occurrence. Our initial seed set was constructed manually and contained the following four queries: [how to commit suicide], [how to kill yourself], [I want to kill myself], and [I want to commit suicide]. Our choice of the seed set queries was quite arbitrary; since we lacked knowledge about the query-space for this domain, we selected four queries that we believed unambiguously express self-harm intent. This may also be quite typical: it is unlikely that search engine designers will have domain knowledge in each domain being targeted for specialized query support. With subsequent expansion, we found several positives which were more specific than the four queries that we started with (e.g., [how to od on xanax], [what is the best combination of pills and carbon monoxide in suicide]). Note that mere synonym substitution can help us find queries such as [how to shoot yourself] from [how to kill yourself], but in our process we also find queries which are related in intent but lack common synonyms with other positives (e.g., [final exit], which is a book on assisted suicide). One iteration of expanding our set involves adding all distinct suggestions for each query. We used a standard publicly available API for such expansion with a user account that had no previous search history (to avoid biasing the query suggestions with personalization signals). We repeat to expand our seed set to 662 queries which includes all neighbors within three hops of the seed set in the query suggestion graph. We wanted our set to be diverse enough while keeping the number of queries unrelated to self-harm intent (e.g., queries related to celebrities who attempted self-harm) restricted. For this goal, we found three hops to be a reasonable heuristic.

Table 1: Breakdown of the positives obtained.

Relatedness Category	Number of positives	P(positive)	Pos. Relative to Random
Bigram	15	1.34×10^{-7}	13.4
Trigram	25	1.88×10^{-7}	18.8
Session	128	5.79×10^{-7}	57.9
Random	1	1×10^{-8}	1.0

3.2 Sampling Related Queries

Given the rarity of positive examples, one challenge in building query classifiers is that if we simply sampled randomly, we would likely find no positives. Conversely, building an evaluation set by only leveraging query suggestions would be overly sensitive to head (popular) queries and our initial seed set. To this end, we expanded the set of queries for labeling in a way that would likely either find positive queries or queries that we would likely erroneously trigger on (false positives) without overly-strong assumptions. We sampled queries in one of three ways. First, we sampled from all search sessions with a co-occurring query in *ThreeHop* (denoted *Session*). This expands the set of queries likely covered by the query suggestions to include more tail sessions. We had access to search logs from Microsoft's Bing search engine and employed the commonly-used practice of demarcating session boundaries via 30 minutes of inactivity. All queries were sampled from the logs of the aforementioned search engine from June 1 – December 31, 2013 in the English-speaking U.S. locale. We also sampled queries from the logs that had at least one bigram or trigram (denoted *Bigram* and *Trigram* respectively) overlapping with the queries in *ThreeHop*. We did this since queries with bigram/trigram overlap with this initial set would be more likely to either be predicted positive/negative.

To further ensure diversity and balance across the set of queries we sought a mechanism to help ensure the related query types were distributed across both query frequency and the likely ambiguity of the query. To achieve this, we sampled 600 queries of each related query type. Within each related query type, we sampled evenly between head-queries (20 or more occurrences in a six-month query log) and tail queries (less than 20 occurrences in a six-month query log). Finally, to help ensure that the set covered a likely range from unambiguously negative to unambiguously positive, we trained an initial classifier (see Section 5) on the labeled *ThreeHop* set, and used that classifier's predictions to further stratify the space. From each decile of the classifier's predicted confidence, we sampled 30 head and 30 tail queries for use in our analysis.

We also sampled 600 queries at random stratified similarly (60 from each decile). Sampling yielded 2,400 queries for the related set (in addition to the 662 queries in *ThreeHop*) After manually labeling these 2400 queries, the *Related* query set consists of 169 positive queries (divided between relatedness categories as shown in Table 2), 2212 negative queries, and 19 queries were labeled as indeterminate. Indeterminate queries were discarded from *Related.*

3.3 Labeling

Following the selection of subsets of queries as defined in the previous section, the queries were manually labeled by three labelers. As with any query classification task, deciding how to label a particular query has to be balanced between the specific intent and the likely intent on average across all searchers issuing that query. For example, the query [suicide] is quite general and may express many research intents related to philosophy or ethics courses, medical research, and similar topics. That is, it is not clear that the searcher has a likely intent for self-harm. This is in contrast to the much more specific intentions demonstrated in the seed queries, some of which

Table 2: Classification performance on *Related$_{test}$*.

Measure	Trained on *ThreeHop*	Trained on *ThreeHop* + *Related$_{train}$*
Accuracy	91.06%	93.29%
Precision	68.75%	73.33%
Recall	28.94%	57.89%
F1 score	40.74%	64.70%

include first-person language, e.g., [I want to kill myself]. To help provide consistency in judgments, labeling guidelines instructed labelers to look for a likely clear intent of self-harm which includes, among other things, focused questions on suicide methods and their effectiveness, but does not include queries on suicide demographics, celebrity suicide, and various death-related obsessions. Example queries representing each class were also provided to assist the labelers. Labelers were allowed to inspect the search results for a query but instructed to assume that the searcher may not find any results relevant. Labelers reported that examining results was useful to identify special cases of queries such as lyrics or song titles that were not obvious from the query text alone.

Three annotators labeled all of the queries in the *ThreeHop* set. The Fleiss' kappa measure of the inter-rater agreement between the three labelers was 0.73, indicates substantial agreement between the annotators at this task. Disagreements were examined to help clarify the labeling guidelines with additional examples. After resolving disagreements, the *ThreeHop* set comprised 390 positives, 259 negatives and 13 queries labeled as indeterminate. The fact that some labels could not be resolved, even after discussion among the labelers, reflects the difficulty of this task. These uncertain queries were discarded from the *ThreeHop* set during training.

4. CLASSIFIER DECISION SURFACE

We now briefly consider the types of classification model and representation that are necessary to accurately model both the self-harm domain and more generally the typical interactions seen in query classification problems. Given our focus on classification using only query text, the primary question that we ask is whether a linear classifier employing a bag-of-words representation or even a bag of n-grams is sufficient? Inspection of the labeled data quickly reveals that there are many interactions which are not likely to be additive. For example, there are subtleties of word ordering. The query [painless suicide] is a likely self-harm query but [suicide is painless] is a song for a very popular television series. This latter query is an example of the types of "exceptions" that often occur where a head query has a very specific intent not obvious from the query text alone. A similar example is [kill yourself] which is also a likely self-harm query versus [kill yourself in 5 minutes] which is a popular online game. Finally, while often a single word or phrase can be pivotal as in [painless easy ways to kill yourself] vs. [painless easy ways to kill mold]. The phrase "kill yourself" occurs in both positive and negative examples as seen in the previous example. Alternatively, "kill mold" covers this negative but misses the more general pattern as this same phrase is seen for many related items, e.g., "....kill bugs", "...kill roaches", etc. Thus, more general pattern matching may help with generalization, but a bag-of-words approach is clearly not sufficient given the complexity of the space. As the representation is extended to increasingly longer n-grams, a classifier can learn the general structure while memorizing exceptions. As a compromise between these extremes we target a representation that employs features of unigrams, bigrams, and trigrams.

5. PREDICTING QUERY INTENT

To predict self-harm intent, we first trained an off-the-shelf linear support vector machine (SVM) on the labeled *ThreeHop* set using unigram, bigram, and trigram features. This particular SVM was specifically designed to handle large-scale query classification. This classifier was used to provide the stratified sampling over query class probability for each of the related query methods in Table 1. Since the samples are stratified by posterior, one would expect the number of positives to be similar within each bin across the different methods and the total number of positives to also be the same across the different methods. If the classifier were well-calibrated we would expect the number of positives to match the expected posterior, but even if it did not, a consistent miscalibration would skew each related query method in the same way. If they skew differently, it suggests that building a query classifier by simply sampling suggested queries is subject to bias that can be partially overcome by broadening sampling as described herein.

Table 1 (on the previous page) shows that we obtained far more positives using *Bigram*, *Trigram* and *Session* approaches than via the plain random sampling approach. By using the frequency of bins for stratification, we can estimate the overall probability of positive according to each method. We use the random positive rate as the expected rate of positives for the proportion not matching a related filter. Interestingly, the variance across these estimates demonstrates the difficulty in sampling for rare items. The final column expresses these as a ratio to random to emphasize the magnitude of variation and the greater rate of positive discovery. This result underscores that by plain random sampling we would get very few positives, meaning that the classifier would have limited data for further improvement. Among the three types of relatedness we considered, *Session* obtained the maximum number of positives which follows the intuition that a person with a specific intent will make similar searches within a given session.

We split *Related* for train and test (90:10, *Related$_{train}$* and *Related$_{test}$*) and trained the SVM on *Related$_{train}$* + *ThreeHop*). As a baseline, we compared the performance with a classifier only trained on *ThreeHop*. Table 2 shows that with additional training data, we obtained improvement over all measures of classification performance. Since we have widened the net of different types of self-harm queries through *Related*, our recall performance substantially improves. A classifier that always predicts negative (the marginal) only achieved an accuracy of 89.38%. While our queries are sampled in a manner to help discover positives and likely errors, we should also consider operative performance. Such performance is weighted by query frequency and the most frequent queries are often easily classified. Even in our challenging set, we see better performance when reweighting by query frequency with precision, recall, and F1 of 92.64%, 83.31%, and 91.83% respectively.

On analyzing the misclassified queries, we found that some of them happened as a result of possible typos (e.g., [hbest ways to commit suicide], [how to commit suciside]) and can be accurately classified if the typo is corrected (e.g., by applying automated spelling correction). Some misclassifications can be handled with appropriate domain knowledge. For example, a typical pattern for self-harm queries was found to contain medicines that are used for overdosing (e.g., [lorazepam suicide]). Adding such lists of medicines in the domain knowledge of the classifier and treating them as a wild-card can reduce the number of misclassifications. Some of the misclassified queries were long queries (e.g., [what is the best combination of pills and carbon monoxide in suicide]). Adding higher order n-grams may address these type of queries.

Table 3: Sampling techniques for active learning.

Sampling Technique	Strategy
Batch random	Pick k samples at random
Batch one-sided extreme	Pick k samples with predicted class probability closest to 1, breaking ties arbitrarily
Batch two-sided extreme	Pick k samples with predicted class probability closest to 0 or 1, breaking ties arbitrarily
Batch maximum uncertainty	Pick k samples with predicted class probability closest to 0.5, breaking ties arbitrarily

In various learning scenarios, active learning is found to be useful in reducing the number of training examples required to learn a concept and thus being particularly useful when labeling resources are scarce. Also, in a practical setting, requesting labels in batches is more cost-effective than requesting one at a time. For these reasons, next we analyzed the performance of different sampling strategies for active learning in a batch setting. In doing so, we were interested in whether traditional active learning approaches can succeed in this setting or whether it is primarily the discovery of extreme positive/negative examples that drives classifier improvements. We considered strategies listed in Table 3. We chose random sampling as our baseline and maximum uncertainty since it is a known sampling technique that is useful across many different active learning tasks. We observed that several queries classified as positives with high confidence were actually a negative query with a high degree of n-gram matching with self-harm queries (e.g., [painless easy ways to kill mold]). In order to examine if labeling queries predicted with very high or low confidence can improve performance, we explored two more strategies: one-sided extreme and two-sided extreme. We choose one-sided extreme since it was found to outperform maximum uncertainty sampling in the context of short document classification [1][12]. Figure 1 plots the area under the receiver operating characteristic (AUROC) curve comparison of different sampling strategies. We initially train our SVM on *ThreeHop* and at each step, we add 10 samples from $Related_{train}$. We restrict ourselves to 350 additional samples since the earlier part of the curve is mainly interesting as the performance of each strategy will eventually converge. Since ties are broken randomly, which can create some amount of variability, we repeated the experiment five times for each sampling strategy and report the average performance. Figure 1 shows that maximum uncertainty outperforms other the techniques (in many cases with statistical significance at $p < 0.05$ using t-tests), and there is no clear winner among batch two-sided extreme and random sampling. So we conclude that active learning does help in improving performance, but only identifying one-sided or two-sided extremes do not outperform maximum uncertainty sampling.

6. DISCUSSION AND CONCLUSIONS

We proposed a structured approach to building a classifier when positives are rare and we have a small initial set of positive examples. We showed that our approach finds many more positives than random sampling. We focused on self-harm, an important domain underexplored in IR despite the use of search systems by people interesting in learning about self-harm, and we share valuable insights about our key challenges. We compared the performance in a batch active learning setting and found that maximum uncertainty is the best sampling strategy given limited labeling resources.

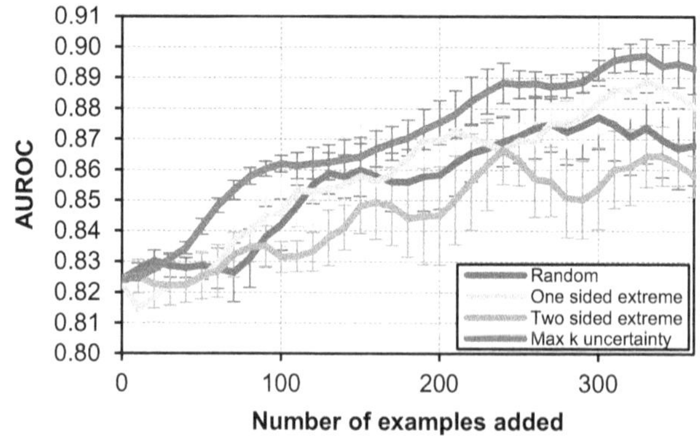

Figure 1: Performance of different query sampling strategies. Lines denote five-point moving average over five runs (±SEM).

Although we focused on self-harm, most of the challenges faced in our work apply to any query classification task with rare positives. We do not address the broader question of when given self-harm queries or the high probability of a self-harm intent, search engines should show an answer or offer other interventions. We hope this research prompts a broader discussion of self-harm intentions within relevant communities, including IR, mental health, and ethics, about if/when/how such interventions should be triggered.

7. REFERENCES

[1] Attenberg, J., Melville, P., and Provost, F. (2010). A unified approach to active dual supervision for labeling features and examples. In *Machine Learning and Knowledge Discovery in Databases*, 40–55.

[2] Broder, A. (2002). A taxonomy of web search. *SIGIR Forum*, 36(2): 3–10.

[3] Broder, A., Fontoura, M., Gabrilovich, E., Joshi, A., Josifovski, V., and Zhang, T. (2007). Robust classification of rare queries using Web knowledge. *SIGIR*, 231–238.

[4] Broder, A., Ciccolo, P., Gabrilovich, E., Josifovski, V., Metzler, D., Riedel, L., and Yuan, J. (2009). Online expansion of rare queries for sponsored search. *WWW*, 511–520.

[5] Carpineto. C. and Romano, G. (2012). A survey of automatic query expansion in information retrieval. *CSUR*, 44(1): 1.

[6] Guo, Q. and Agichtein, E. (2008). Exploring mouse movements for inferring query intent. *SIGIR*, 707–708.

[7] Jansen, B.J., Booth, D.L., and Spink, A. (2008). Determining the informational, navigational, and transactional intent of Web queries. *IP&M*, 44(3): 1251–1266.

[8] Kang, I.H. and Kim, G.C. (2003). Query type classification for web document retrieval. *SIGIR*, 64–71.

[9] Li, Xiao, Wang, Y.-Y., and Acero, A. (2008). Learning query intent from regularized click graphs. *Proc. SIGIR*, 339–346.

[10] Lee, U., Liu, Z., and Cho, J. (2005). Automatic identification of user goals in web search. *WWW*, 391–400.

[11] Rose, D.E. and Levinson, D. (2004). Understanding user goals in web search. *WWW*, 13–19.

[12] Sindhwani, V., Melville, P., and Lawrence, R.D. (2009). Uncertainty sampling and transductive experimental design for active dual supervision. *ICML*, 953–960.

Modelling the Usefulness of Document Collections for Query Expansion in Patient Search

Nut Limsopatham*
University of Cambridge, UK
nl347@cam.ac.uk

Craig Macdonald
University of Glasgow, UK
craig.macdonald@glasgow.ac.uk

Iadh Ounis
University of Glasgow, UK
iadh.ounis@glasgow.ac.uk

ABSTRACT

Dealing with the medical terminology is a challenge when searching for patients based on the relevance of their medical records towards a given query. Existing work used query expansion (QE) to extract expansion terms from different document collections to improve query representation. However, the usefulness of particular document collections for QE was not measured and taken into account during retrieval. In this work, we investigate two automatic approaches that measure and leverage the usefulness of document collections when exploiting multiple document collections to improve query representation. These two approaches are based on resource selection and learning to rank techniques, respectively. We evaluate our approaches using the TREC Medical Records track's test collection. Our results show the potential of the proposed approaches, since they can effectively exploit 14 different document collections, including both domain-specific (e.g. MEDLINE abstracts) and generic (e.g. blogs and webpages) collections, and significantly outperform existing effective baselines, including the best systems participating at the TREC Medical Records track. Our analysis shows that the different collections are not equally useful for QE, while our two approaches can automatically weight the usefulness of expansion terms extracted from different document collections effectively.

Categories and Subject Descriptors: H.3.3 [Information Storage & Retrieval]: Information Search & Retrieval
Keywords: Patient Search, Query Expansion

1. INTRODUCTION

To improve the healthcare service quality, electronic medical records (EMRs) are used to document the medical conditions (e.g. symptom, treatment) of patients visiting a hospital. These EMRs can also be leveraged in medical research. For example, using a patient search system, EMRs can help to identify cohorts of patients suitable for particular clinical trials. In this paper, we tackle the patient search task. In this task, healthcare practitioners describe the medical conditions of patients of interest as a query and the search system retrieves patients based on their relevance towards the stated medical conditions.

Existing work showed that the complexity of medical terminology makes patient search a challenging task [7, 10, 18]. For instance, patients whose medical records state that they are suffering from "deafness" may not be retrieved for a query to find patients with "hearing loss", even though "deafness" and "hearing loss" share the same meaning. Limsopatham et al. [9, 11], as well as Qi and Laquerre [18] dealt with this problem by representing queries and medical records in the forms of medical concepts. As a result, "deafness" and "hearing loss" were represented with the same concept. On the other hand, several approaches exploited various document collections to improve query representation (e.g. [5, 10, 25]). For example, Limsopatham et al. [10] used the relationships between medical concepts found in medical resources, such as UMLS[1] and MeSH[2], to improve the representation of medical conditions in the queries. King et al. [5], whose system achieved the best retrieval performance at the TREC 2011 Medical Records track [21], expanded the queries with terms extracted from the medical record collection itself. Later, Zhu et al. [25] used a query expansion (QE) technique to extract expansion terms from four different document collections, including web documents, medical records and two sets of medical articles. In particular, Zhu et al. [25] suggested that using expansion terms extracted from all of those four collections to expand a query is more effective than using expansion terms from each collection individually. In contrast, we hypothesise that the usefulness of different document collections for QE could be estimated and more effectively exploited when ranking patients based on the relevance of their medical records.

In this work, we investigate two approaches for modelling the likelihood that expansion terms extracted from each document collection are effective for improving query representation. The first approach adapts a resource selection technique [3] to measure the likelihood that a document collection can provide good expansion terms, and then uses the measured likelihood to weight the expansion terms extracted from that collection. On the other hand, the second approach combines the relevance scores computed from the expanded query using each of the document collections by using a learning to rank (LTR) technique (e.g. [15, 23]) to learn an effective combination.

Using the TREC 2011 and 2012 Medical Records track's test collection [20, 21], we evaluate our two proposed approaches when applied with a QE technique to exploit 14 different document collections that are either generic or domain-specific. Our results show that both approaches are effec-

*The work was done at the University of Glasgow.

[1] http://www.nlm.nih.gov/research/umls/
[2] http://www.ncbi.nlm.nih.gov/mesh/

Permission to make digital or hard copies of all or part of this work for personal or classroom use is granted without fee provided that copies are not made or distributed for profit or commercial advantage and that copies bear this notice and the full citation on the first page. Copyrights for components of this work owned by others than ACM must be honored. Abstracting with credit is permitted. To copy otherwise, or republish, to post on servers or to redistribute to lists, requires prior specific permission and/or a fee. Request permissions from Permissions@acm.org.
CIKM'15, October 19–23, 2015, Melbourne, Australia.
© 2015 ACM. ISBN 978-1-4503-3794-6/15/10 ...$15.00.
DOI: http://dx.doi.org/10.1145/2806416.2806614.

tive, as they could significantly outperform existing effective baselines with and without QE. In particular, the resource selection-based approach outperforms the approach of Zhu et al. [25] by up to 32%.

2. RETRIEVAL MODELS

We first describe the retrieval models used for ranking patients based on the relevance of their medical records (Section 2.1), and for extracting expansion terms from a particular document collection (Section 2.2).

2.1 The Patient Ranking Model

Existing work (e.g. [5, 10, 25]) used either *a patient model* or *a two-stage model* to rank patients based on the relevance of their medical records [12]. The patient model ranks patients based on the relevance scores of the concatenations of medical records associated to particular patients, while the two-stage model aggregates the relevance scores of the medical records using an aggregate function (e.g. expCombSUM [14]) to rank their associated patients. In this work, we use the expCombSUM voting technique [14] to rank patients, as it has been shown to be effective in previous works (e.g. [12, 13]). In particular, expCombSUM calculates the relevance score of patient p towards query Q, as follows:

$$score_{patient}(p, Q) = \sum_{d \in R(Q) \cap profile(p)} e^{score(d,Q)} \quad (1)$$

where $R(Q)$ is a ranking of the medical records retrieved using query Q, $R(Q) \cap profile(p)$ is the set of medical records in ranking $R(Q)$ that are also associated to patient p; $score(d, Q)$ is the relevance score of medical record d given the query Q. We follow [13] and use DFR DPH [2] to calculate $score(d, Q)$, and limit the number of voting records ($|R(Q)|$) to 5,000.

2.2 The Query Expansion Model

Query expansion (QE) models (e.g. DFR Bo1 [1] or a relevance model [8]) extract expansion terms from a document collection by firstly retrieving the top N ranked documents, and then extract the top k most informative terms from those documents as expansion terms. Traditional QE uses the targeted collection to extract the expansion terms, while *external QE* (e.g. [4]) extracts the expansion terms from the documents retrieved from an external collection. In this work, we use both the targeted and external collections to expand a query. We deploy the DFR Bo1 model to extract the top k expansion terms from each collection, since it has been shown to be effective for this patient search task [10]. In particular, we follow [10] and extract the 10 most informative terms, as well as their weight, from the top 3 ranked documents in each collection (i.e. $N = 3$ and $k = 10$).

3. THE USEFULNESS OF COLLECTIONS

Sections 3.1 and 3.2 introduce our two proposed approaches to model the usefulness of different document collections when exploiting their extracted expansion terms.

3.1 Resource Selection

Resource selection techniques have been used to select collections that are likely to contain relevant documents, so that a retrieval system can focus on those collections during retrieval [3]. Our first approach adapts a resource selection technique to measure the likelihood that expansion terms extracted from a particular collection are effective for QE. In particular, it is intuitive that expansion terms extracted from collections that are related to the original query are more likely to be useful than those extracted from unrelated collections. When taking into account the likelihood that expansion term t_k extracted from collection c_i is effective for QE, the relevance score of medical record d towards query Q (i.e. $score(d, Q)$) can be calculated as follows:

$$score(d, Q) = \sum_{t_j \in Q} score(d, t_j) + \sum_{c_i \in C} w_c(c_i) \cdot \sum_{t_k \in Qc_i} w_t(t_k) \cdot score(d, t_k) \quad (2)$$

where $score(d, t_j)$ and $score(d, t_k)$ can be calculated using any retrieval function (e.g. DFR DPH [2]), C is the set of used collections, $w_c(c_i)$ is a collection weight, Qc_i is a set of expansion terms extracted from collection c_i, and $w_t(t_k)$ is the weight of expansion term t_k, which can be computed from each document collection using a QE model. Note that in the approach of Zhu et al. [25], $w_c(c_i)$ is equally set to 1 for all collections c_i.

We use the CORI resource selection algorithm [3] to calculate the collection weight $w_c(c_i)$ in Equation (2). Indeed, CORI is calculated as a combination of the score $p(t_j|c_i)$ of each term t_j in query Q, using a probabilistic operator. Using the operator AND, OR or SUM, the CORI score (i.e. $w_c(c_i)$) of collection c_i can be calculated as follows [3]:

$$CORI_{AND}(c_i, Q) = \prod_{t_j \in Q} p(t_j|c_i) \quad (3)$$

$$CORI_{OR}(c_i, Q) = 1 - \prod_{t_j \in Q} (1 - p(t_j|c_i)) \quad (4)$$

$$CORI_{SUM}(c_i, Q) = \frac{\sum_{t_j \in Q} p(t_j|c_i)}{|Q|} \quad (5)$$

where $p(t_j|c_i)$ is calculated as follows [3]:

$$p(t_j|c_i) = b + (1 - b) \cdot T \cdot I \quad (6)$$

$$T = \frac{df}{df + 50 + 150 \cdot \frac{cw}{avg_{cw}}} \quad (7)$$

$$I = \log\left(\frac{|C| + 0.5}{cf}\right) / \log(|C| + 1) \quad (8)$$

df is the number of documents in collection c_i that contain term t_j, cw is the number of terms in collection c_i, avg_{cw} is the average number of terms in each collection, $|C|$ is the number of used collections, cf is the number of collections containing term t_j, and b is the default belief, which is set to 0.4 as recommended in [3].

3.2 Learning to Rank

Our second approach uses an LTR technique to combine rankings produced from the query expanded using each collection separately. In general, the LTR techniques aim to learn an effective ranking model from a set of features using training data. As we aim to leverage QE from multiple collections to improve the patient search performance, our features are the relevance scores computed from the query expanded using each of the used document collections. For a linear LTR technique, such as Automatic Feature Selection (AFS) [15], the weights of these features can be viewed as the usefulness for QE of the associated document collections.

We deploy four existing effective LTR techniques (namely, AdaRank [23], AFS [15], Coordinate Ascent (CA) [16] and LambdaMART [22]) that aim to optimise a targeted evaluation measure (e.g. MAP) during training. Indeed, these four

Table 1: List of document collections used for QE.

Collection	Description[3]
EMRs11	100,710 medical records from the TREC 2011 & 2012 Medical Records track
Genomics04	4,591,008 MEDLINE abstracts from the TREC 2004 & 2005 Genomics track
Genomics06	162,259 full-text medical articles from the TREC 2006 & 2007 Genomics track
eHealth12	~1M documents crawled from health and medicine sites by the CLEF/ShARe eHealth evaluation lab 2012
OHSUMED	348,566 MEDLINE references from TREC-9
ClueWeb09B	~50M English webpages from the TREC 2009 Web track
Wiki09	~21M Wikipedia pages of ClueWeb09B from the TREC 2009 Web track
WT10G	1,692,096 English web documents from the TREC 2000 Web track
WT2G	250,000 English web documents from the TREC 1999 Web track
Blog06	3,215,171 blog posts from the TREC 2006 Blog track
Blog08	28,488,767 blog posts from the TREC 2008 Blog track
CERC	370,715 web documents from the TREC 2008 Enterprise track
W3C	331,037 documents of `w3c.org` sites from the TREC 2005 Enterprise track
Disk45	528,155 documents of Disks 4&5 from TREC-8

techniques deploy different types of algorithms to learn a suitable ranking model from a set of features. AdaRank [23] applies a boosting technique to optimise the targeted evaluation measure by considering each feature as a weak ranker. AFS [15] and CA [16] apply a greedy algorithm to learn an effective linear combination of features by using different underlying optimisation techniques. Our used implementations of AFS and CA deploy simulated annealing [6] and coordinate ascent, respectively, when learning the feature weights. LambdaMART [22] deploys boosted regression trees to find an effective combination of features that optimises a targeted evaluation measure.

4. EXPERIMENTAL SETUP

Test Collection: To evaluate the two proposed approaches, we use the test collection provided by the TREC Medical Records track [20, 21]. The task is to retrieve patient visits relevant to a given query. A patient visit contains medical records related to a particular visit to the hospital by a patient. Due to privacy concerns, a patient visit is used to represent a patient [20, 21]. The topic set includes 34 and 47 queries from TREC 2011 and 2012, respectively. We report the retrieval performance in terms of the track primary measures, which are bpref and infNDCG for TREC 2011 and 2012, respectively.

Expansion Collections: For reproducibility, we leverage 14 widely available document collections for QE, which include both generic and domain-specific collections, as described in Table 1.

Retrieval Toolkits: We conduct experiments using the Terrier platform [17][4], applying Porter's English stemmer and removing stopwords. We use the models discussed in Sections 2.1 and 2.2 to rank patients and to extract expansion terms, respectively. For the LTR techniques, we use the implementation of RankLib[5] with the default setting. In addition, as the LTR techniques require a set of training data to learn a model, we use the queries from TREC 2011 to train an LTR model when testing on TREC 2012, and vice versa. In addition, as the targeted measure of TREC 2011 and 2012 are different, we follow [24] and train the learned model to optimise the MAP measure.

[3] Please consult the TREC/CLEF overview papers for details about each document collection. [4] `http://terrier.org`
[5] `http://www.lemurproject.org/ranklib.php`

5. EXPERIMENTAL RESULTS

We compare the retrieval performances of our proposed approaches with four categories of baselines. The first two categories of baselines are basic baselines that either do not apply QE or use expansion terms from only one of the 14 used collections. The third and the fourth categories of baselines are more advanced. In particular, the third category of baselines uses expansion terms extracted from all 14 collections (as in [25]). The fourth category of baselines firstly retrieves patients for the query that is expanded using each of the 14 collections, and then uses a data fusion technique [19] (i.e. CombSUM, CombMNZ, expCombSUM or expCombMNZ) to combine the relevance scores of the patients. Note that the CombSUM data fusion technique is in some sense similar to the approach of [25] in that the relevance scores of expansion terms extracted from different collections are equally combined to rank patients. However, CombSUM is arguably more robust to topic drift, since the focus of each expanded query is typically still on the original query.

Table 2 shows our experimental results in terms of bpref and infNDCG for TREC 2011 and 2012, respectively. First, we discuss the performance of the baselines that apply QE on each collection individually. From Table 2, we observe that, for TREC 2011, 12 out of 14 collections are useful for improving the query representation, as expansion terms extracted from these collections improve the retrieval performance over the baseline that does not apply QE (i.e. 'No-QE'). Meanwhile, 10 out of 14 collections are effective for TREC 2012. In general, the expansion terms extracted from all medical-related collections (e.g. EMRs11, Genomics04 and Genomics06) effectively improve the retrieval performance for both TREC 2011 and 2012. However, surprisingly ClueWeb09B and WT10G, which are generic collections, are the most effective collections for QE for TREC 2011 and 2012, respectively, and even outperform traditional QE, which expands the queries using the targeted collection (i.e. EMRs11). In particular, leveraging expansion terms from ClueWeb09B is overall the most effective and significantly (paired t-test, $p < 0.05$) outperforms the 'No-QE' baseline for both TREC 2011 and 2012 (bpref 0.5323 vs. 0.4871 and infNDCG 0.4446 vs. 0.4167). Nevertheless, we observe that expanding queries with terms extracted from all collections (i.e. 'All Collections') is not effective. This differs from the conclusion reported in [25]. However, note that our experiments consider more document collections both in number and variety. Meanwhile, the data fusion baselines are more effective than the 'No-QE' and 'All Collections' baselines.

When considering the performance of our two proposed approaches, we observe that they significantly (paired t-test, $p < 0.05$) outperform both the 'No-QE' and 'All Collections' baselines. Indeed, our adaptation of CORI (i.e. $CORI_{SUM}$ and $CORI_{OR}$) to weight the expansion terms from each collection (i.e. Equation (2)) outperforms all of the evaluated approaches, including when applying QE with the ClueWeb09B collection. This shows that expansion terms extracted from different document collections are not equally useful, and our adaptation of CORI could estimate the effectiveness of expansion terms extracted from different collections. However, $CORI_{AND}$ is less effective than $CORI_{SUM}$ and $CORI_{OR}$ since it applies the stronger constraint that a collection should contain all of the query terms. It is of note that both $CORI_{SUM}$ and $CORI_{OR}$ perform better than the best TREC 2011 system [5], and comparably to the top performing systems in TREC 2012 [20], without deploying other well-known performance boosting techniques for pa-

Table 2: Retrieval performances on TREC 2011 and 2012 Medical Records track of different QE approaches. Statistical significance (paired t-test) at $p < 0.05$ over the baseline that does not apply QE and the baseline that uses all expansion terms extracted from the 14 used document collections are denoted $^{\oplus}$ and $^{\odot}$, respectively.

Approaches	2011 (bpref)	2012 (infNDCG)
No-QE	0.4871	0.4167
+ EMRs11	$0.5264^{\oplus}$	$0.4408^{\oplus}$
+ Genomics04	$0.5214^{\oplus}$	$0.4399^{\oplus}$
+ Genomics06	$0.5239^{\oplus}$	0.4399
+ eHealth12	$0.5185^{\oplus}$	0.4372
+ OHSUMED	0.4978	0.4333
+ ClueWeb09B	$\mathbf{0.5323}^{\oplus}$	$0.4446^{\oplus}$
+ Wiki09	$0.5268^{\oplus}$	0.4155
+ WT10G	$0.5215^{\oplus}$	**0.4454**
+ WT2G	$0.5105^{\oplus}$	0.4343
+ Blog06	0.5045	0.4386
+ Blog08	$0.5118^{\oplus}$	0.4159
+ CERC	0.4657	0.4159
+ W3C	0.4671	0.4117
+ Disk45	0.4942	0.4182
+ All Collections [25]	0.4833	0.3551
Data Fusion		
CombSUM	$0.5074^{\oplus}$	$\mathbf{0.4385}^{\oplus\odot}$
CombMNZ	$0.5076^{\oplus}$	$\mathbf{0.4385}^{\oplus\odot}$
expCombSUM	$\mathbf{0.5084}^{\oplus}$	$0.4350^{\oplus\odot}$
expCombMNZ	$0.5080^{\oplus}$	$0.4356^{\oplus\odot}$
Resource Selection		
$CORI_{SUM}$	$\mathbf{0.5597}^{\oplus\odot}$	$0.4603^{\oplus\odot}$
$CORI_{OR}$	$0.5594^{\oplus\odot}$	$\mathbf{0.4689}^{\oplus\odot}$
$CORI_{AND}$	$0.4958^{\oplus}$	$0.4216^{\odot}$
Learning to Rank		
AdaRank	0.4997	$0.4343^{\odot}$
AFS	$0.5212^{\oplus}$	$0.4330^{\odot}$
CA	$\mathbf{0.5289}^{\oplus}$	$\mathbf{0.4475}^{\oplus\odot}$
LambdaMART	0.3590	0.3057

tient search such as negation handling [20, 21]. Meanwhile, our approach that uses LTR techniques could not outperform the ClueWeb09B baseline. In particular, the most effective LTR technique is CA, which achieves bpref 0.5298 and infNDCG 0.4475. The other LTR techniques, e.g. LambdaMART, are less effective. This could be due to the small number of available queries for training the learned models.

When analysing the expansion terms extracted from different collections, we observe that the expansion terms from some collections are not related to the query medical conditions. For instance, for the query "hearing loss", our approach gives low weights to W3C and CERC, from which the extracted expansion terms, such as 'individual', 'argument', 'plan' and 'strategy' were off-topic. Meanwhile, collections such as ClueWeb09B and Wiki09, which obtain high weights, provide expansion terms that are more related to the query e.g. 'earwax', 'sensorineural' and 'deaf'. In contrast, expansion terms extracted from EMRs11, which received a medium weight from our approach, also include an off-topic term (i.e. 'woman'), after a list of related terms (e.g. 'cerumen', 'ear', 'canal'). This might be the reason why QE using ClueWeb09B or Wiki09 is more effective than when applied to EMRs11, since highly ranked documents from the web might contain more effective related terms to "hearing loss" than highly ranked medical records, as the latter could also mention other health information.

6. CONCLUSIONS

We introduced the use of resource selection and learning to rank techniques to weight the expansion terms extracted from particular document collections differently. Our experimental results conducted on the TREC Medical Records track's test collection showed that the two approaches were more effective than an existing approach that used all the expansion terms extracted from all of the used collections equally. Specifically, our approach based on a resource selection technique (i.e. $CORI_{SUM}$ and $CORI_{OR}$) was shown to be the most effective and significantly outperformed the aforementioned baseline by up to 32% (infNDCG 0.4689 vs. 0.3551). This shows that expansion terms extracted from different document collections are not equally useful and that our proposed approaches can automatically and effectively weight these expansion terms during retrieval.

7. REFERENCES

[1] G. Amati. Probabilistic Models for Information Retrieval based on Divergence from Randomness. *PhD thesis*. University of Glasgow, 2003.

[2] G. Amati, E. Ambrosi, M. Bianchi, C. Gaibisso and G. Gambosi. FUB, IASI-CNR and University of Tor Vergata at TREC 2007 Blog Track. *TREC'07*.

[3] J. Callan. Distributed Information Retrieval. *Advances in Information Retrieval*, 2000.

[4] F. Diaz and D. Metzler. Improving the Estimation of Relevance Models Using Large External Corpora. *SIGIR'06*.

[5] B. King, L. Wang, I. Provalov and J. Zhou. Cengage Learning at TREC 2011 Medical Track. *TREC'11*.

[6] S. Kirkpatrick, C. D. Gelatt and M. P. Vecchi. Optimization by simulated annealing. *Science*, 1983.

[7] B. Koopman and G. Zuccon. Why assessing relevance in medical IR is demanding. *MedIR at SIGIR'14*.

[8] V. Lavrenko and W. B. Croft. Relevance Based Language Models. *SIGIR'01*.

[9] N. Limsopatham, C. Macdonald, and I. Ounis. A Task-Specific Query and Document Representation for Medical Records Search. *ECIR'13*.

[10] N. Limsopatham, C. Macdonald and I. Ounis. Inferring Conceptual Relationships to Improve Medical Records Search. *OAIR'13*.

[11] N. Limsopatham, C. Macdonald, and I. Ounis. Learning to Combine Representations for Medical Records Search. *SIGIR'13*.

[12] N. Limsopatham, C. Macdonald and I. Ounis. Learning to Selectively Rank Patients' Medical History. *CIKM'13*.

[13] N. Limsopatham, C. Macdonald, I. Ounis, G. McDonald and M. Bouamrane. University of Glasgow at Medical Records track 2011: Experiments with Terrier. *TREC'11*.

[14] C. Macdonald and I. Ounis. Voting for candidates: adapting data fusion techniques for an expert search task. *CIKM'06*.

[15] D. Metzler. Automatic feature selection in the markov random field model for information retrieval. *CIKM'07*.

[16] D. Metzler and W. B. Croft. Linear feature-based models for information retrieval. *J. of Information Retrieval*, 2007.

[17] I. Ounis, G. Amati, V. Plachouras, B. He, C. Macdonald and C. Lioma. Terrier: A High Performance and Scalable Information Retrieval Platform. *OSIR at SIGIR'06*.

[18] Y. Qi and P.-F. Laquerre. Retrieving Medical Records with "sennamed": NEC Labs America. *TREC'12*.

[19] J. A. Shaw and E. A. Fox. Combination of multiple searches. *TREC'94*.

[20] E. Voorhees and W. Hersh. Overview of the TREC 2012 Medical Records Track. *TREC'12*.

[21] E. Voorhees and R. Tong. Overview of the TREC 2011 Medical Records Track. *TREC'11*.

[22] Q. Wu, C. J. C. Burges, K. Svore and J. Gao. Adapting Boosting for Information Retrieval Measures. *J. of Information Retrieval*, 2007.

[23] J. Xu and H. Li. Adarank: A boosting algorithm for information retrieval. *SIGIR'07*.

[24] D. Zhu and B. Carterette. An adaptive evidence weighting method for medical record search. *SIGIR'13*.

[25] D. Zhu, S. Wu, B. Carterette and H. Liu. Using Large Clinical Corpora for Query Expansion in Text-based Cohort Identification. *J. of Biomedical Informatics*, 2014.

A Convolutional Click Prediction Model

Qiang Liu, Feng Yu*, Shu Wu, Liang Wang
Center for Research on Intelligent Perception and Computing
National Laboratory of Pattern Recognition
Institute of Automation, Chinese Academy of Sciences
{qiang.liu, feng.yu, shu.wu, wangliang}@nlpr.ia.ac.cn

ABSTRACT

The explosion in online advertisement urges to better estimate the click prediction of ads. For click prediction on single ad impression, we have access to pairwise relevance among elements in an impression, but not to global interaction among key features of elements. Moreover, the existing method on sequential click prediction treats propagation unchangeable for different time intervals. In this work, we propose a novel model, Convolutional Click Prediction Model (CCPM), based on convolution neural network. CCPM can extract local-global key features from an input instance with varied elements, which can be implemented for not only single ad impression but also sequential ad impression. Experiment results on two public large-scale datasets indicate that CCPM is effective on click prediction.

Categories and Subject Descriptors

H.3 [**Information Storage and Retrieval**]: Information Filtering

Keywords

Click Prediction, Convolution Neural Network

1. INTRODUCTION

Recently, online advertising has become the most popular approach to do brand promotion and product marketing for the *advertiser*, and contributes the overwhelming majority of income for the commercial web *publisher*.

Nowadays, click prediction on single ad impression [10] has received much attention, and many different approaches have been proposed. For simplicity and effectiveness, Logistic Regression (LR) [7, 9] has been widely used in click prediction. Representing each *element* (e.g. query, ad, user and other contexts) of a single ad impression by a value, LR is not capable enough to describe the latent features of an element or reveal the complicated relation among these elements. As a widely-used technique in recommendation systems, matrix factorization (MF) method [4] in the Collaborative Filtering approach is also employed for click prediction. MF method factorizes and rebuilds the dependency matrix to learn latent semantic representations of pages and ads. Later, Factorization Machines (FM) [5, 6], a extension of MF in multiple element space, obtains latent semantic information of each pairwise elements, which is able to better model relation of various elements. However, MF and FM models capture relevance of pairwise elements in single ad impression and overlook the high-order interaction among these elements.

Different from traditional works taking single ad impression as input instance and overlooking dependency of historical impressions, Recurrent Neural Network (RNN) model [10] is leveraged for click prediction of sequential ad impression. Taking full advantage of historical click sequences, the recurrent structure enhances the accuracy of click prediction further. The model takes each user's browsing history as a sequence and obtains internal sequential dependency of varied impressions. Historical click sequence of a certain user is divided by different time intervals, sequence signals of one time interval can be propagated to next interval by the recurrent connection matrix. Due to the fact that the recurrent connection matrix of a trained RNN model is a constant one, the propagations of sequence signals between every two consecutive time intervals remain all the same. However, in real-world scenarios, since users' attitudes toward ads change over time, RNN models may has its limitation for these scenarios due to using the unchangeable propagations.

In order to mine significant semantic features in complex and dynamic sceneries, deep neural network is a good choice. As stated above, for click prediction on single ad impression, the MF and FM methods only reveal the relevance between pairwise elements, but convolutional neural network (CNN) can treat varied elements in a single ad impression as a whole and obtain complex interaction among them. On the other hand, the unchangeable propagations of RNN models on sequential ad impression has the limitation in effectively modeling dynamic click predictions, while pooling and convolutional layers of a deep CNN architecture can fully extract local-global key features from sequential ad impression. In addition, some recent studies about CNN architecture have successfully model significant semantic features in varieties of fields. CNN approaches to speech recognition [1], image recognition [3], information retrieval [8] have achieved much improvement in respective fields. Moreover, proved

*This author contributed equally as the first author.

Permission to make digital or hard copies of all or part of this work for personal or classroom use is granted without fee provided that copies are not made or distributed for profit or commercial advantage and that copies bear this notice and the full citation on the first page. Copyrights for components of this work owned by others than ACM must be honored. Abstracting with credit is permitted. To copy otherwise, or republish, to post on servers or to redistribute to lists, requires prior specific permission and/or a fee. Request permissions from Permissions@acm.org.
CIKM'15, October 19–23, 2015, Melbourne, Australia.
© 2015 ACM. ISBN 978-1-4503-3794-6/15/10 ...$15.00.
DOI: http://dx.doi.org/10.1145/2806416.2806603.

as a effective sentence model in natural language processing, Dynamic Convolutional Neural Network (DCNN) [2] can analyses semantic content and extracts key features of sentences.

We propose a Convolutional Click Prediction Model (CCPM) for click prediction in sceneries of the single ad impression and sequential ad impression. An input instance of CCPM is composed by elements of an ad impression or elements related to a sequential ad impression. Convolutional layers extract local-global features of input instances, and the dynamic pooling layers can obtain significant features. CCPM investigates significant semantic features of an ad impression and sequential relevance of impression history into enhancing the accuracy of click prediction. Experiments are conducted to validate the CCPM model's effectiveness in modeling different kinds of input instances and reveal that CCPM achieves great improvement on the accuracy of click prediction comparing the state-of-the-art models such as LR, FM and RNN. To the best of our knowledge, CCPM is the first approach that attempts to leverage CNN to improve the accuracy of click prediction.

2. CCPM

In an event of *single ad impression*, there are some noticeable elements like user, query, ad, impression time, site category, device type, etc. On the other hand, sometimes system can collect sequential ad impression of each individual user, where user's behaviors on ads yield high dependency on how the user behaved along with the past time. This *sequential ad impression* is comprised of a series of single ad impressions. The goal of this work is to predict the click probability based on these two kinds of impressions.

We model above input instances using a convolutional architecture that alternates wide convolutional layers with flexible p-max pooling layers. The whole procedure of CCPM is illustrated in Figure 1. In the network the width of an intermediate feature map varies with the length of the input instance. It is remarkable to state that the proposed model can handle input instances with varied length, which make it can be used widely.

2.1 Convolution Layer

Given an input instance with n elements, to obtain the first layer of CCPM, we take an embedding $\mathbf{e}_i \in R^d$ for each element in the instance and construct the instance matrix $\mathbf{s} \in R^{d \times n}$ as

$$\mathbf{s} = \begin{bmatrix} \vdots & \vdots & \vdots \\ \mathbf{e}_1 & \cdots & \mathbf{e}_n \\ \vdots & \vdots & \vdots \end{bmatrix} . \quad (1)$$

The values in the embeddings $\mathbf{e}_i$ are estimated during the training process, which contributes to more suitable representations for input instances. A convolutional layer in the network is obtained by convolving a weight matrix $\mathbf{w} \in R^{d \times \omega}$ with the activation matrix at the layer below in an one-dimensional row-wise way. For example, the second layer is obtained by applying a convolution on the input instance matrix $\mathbf{s}$. Dimension d and filter width ω are hyperparameters of input instances. The resulting matrix $\mathbf{r}$ has dimensions $d \times (n + \omega - 1)$. Given $\mathbf{w}_i \in R^{\omega}$, $\mathbf{s}_i \in R^n$ and $\mathbf{r}_i \in R^{(n+\omega-1)}$ as the i-th row of corresponding matrix, we can obtain one-dimensional convolution as

$$\mathbf{r}_i = \mathbf{w}_i{}^T \mathbf{s}_{i,j-\omega+1:j} , \quad (2)$$

where the index j ranges from 1 to $n + \omega - 1$. Out-of-range values $\mathbf{s}_{i,k}$ (where $k < 1$ or $k > n$) are set to zero.

The optimized weights in the filter $\mathbf{w}$ detects features and recognizes specific ranges of neighborhood in input instances. Applying one-dimensional row-wise convolution on two-dimensional matrix of activations, has the following advantage over simply using two-dimensional convolution. Usually we apply two-dimensional convolution in image identification for the reason that the detectors need to recognize special two-dimensional features, such as edges of an objective. However, in the click prediction model, each dimension of the embedding represents a distinct aspect of an element in an instance. Therefore, each row of the resulting matrix $\mathbf{r}$ obtains distinct features from the activation matrix.

2.2 Flexible p-Max Pooling

Here, we describe the flexible p-max pooling layer. Given a vector $\mathbf{r}_i \in R^n$, p-max pooling selects a sub-vector $\mathbf{s}_i^p \in R^p$, which contains the p biggest values in the original vector $\mathbf{r}_i$. Due to the fact that input instances are of varied length, the vector lengths of intermediate convolutional layer change accordingly, consequently the following pooling layer need to be flexible enough to select prominent features smoothly. Considering all facts mentioned above, we let p be a function of length of the input instance and depth of the network. In spite of many possible functions, we select the following one

$$p_i = \begin{cases} (1 - (i/l)^{l-i})n, & i = 1, \cdots, l-1 \\ 3, & i = l \end{cases} , \quad (3)$$

where l is the total number of convolutional layers of the network, n is the length of the input instance and p_i represents the parameter of the i-th pooling layer. For example, given an input instance of length $n = 18$, in a network of three convolutional layers, whose pooling parameters are as follows: $p_1 = 16$, $p_2 = 6$ and $p_3 = 3$.

This selected function has many advantages. Firstly, the last pooling layer has a fixed parameter, so it is guaranteed that the matrix of the fully connected layer for output has a unified dimensionality, despite varied lengths of different input instances. Secondly, the power-exponential function changes slowly at first compared with linear function, which avoids losing too many important features at the beginning.

The flexible p-max pooling layer can not only select the p most key features, but also preserve the relative order of those features, which plays a critical role in the sequential click prediction.

2.3 Feature Maps

We apply a non-linear function for outputs of pooling layers. The non-linear function is also called as activation function, which obtains activations of threshold values:

$$\tanh(x) = \frac{exp(x) - exp(-x)}{exp(x) + exp(-x)} . \quad (4)$$

So far, convolutional layer, flexible p-max pooling layer and non-linear function have been applied to input instances. In this way, we can obtain a first order feature map. Moreover, the three operations above can be repeated again and again to yield multiple order feature maps and a architecture of

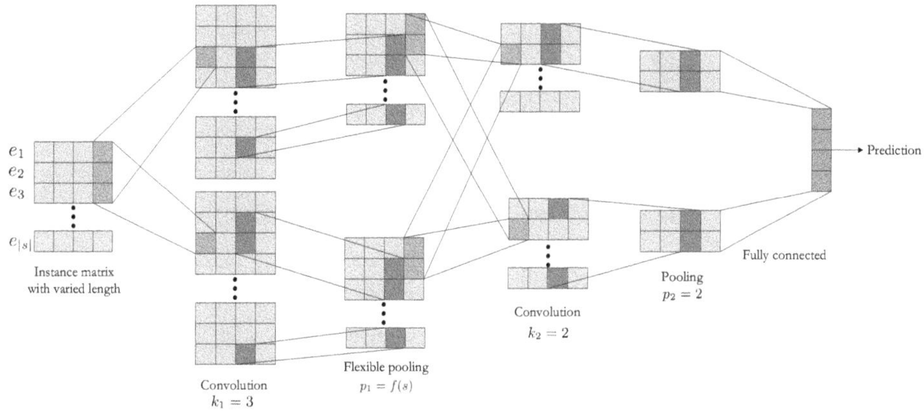

Figure 1: The framework of CCPM. The left part is an input instance (single ad impression or sequential ad impression) with varied elements and the length of element embedding is $d = 4$. The architecture has two convolutional layers with two feature maps each. The widths of filters at two layers are three and two respectively. The flexible pooling layer p_1 changes with length of instance and the last pooling layer $p_2 = 2$.

deeper layers. We denote an i-th order feature map by $\mathbf{F}^i$. At a certain layer, many feature maps can be computed in parallel. For example, $\mathbf{F}_j^i$ represents the j-th feature map of those i-th order feature maps, an is computed by summing the convolutional results of a distinct weight matrix $\mathbf{w}_{j,k}^i$ and each feature map $\mathbf{F}_k^{i-1}$ of the lower order $i-1$,

$$\mathbf{F}_j^i = \sum_{k=1}^{m_i} \mathbf{w}_{j,k}^i * \mathbf{F}_k^{i-1}, \tag{5}$$

where m_i denotes the number of feature map in corresponding i-th order layer, and $*$ refers to the one-dimensional row-wise convolution described in Sec. 2.1. Similarly, flexible p-max pooling and non-linear function can be applied to feature map $\mathbf{F}_j^i$ successively. Finally, there is a fully connected layer, and the prediction is made via softmax.

3. EXPERIMENTS

3.1 Datasets and Baselines

To empirically evaluate the performance of our method on the click prediction with single and sequential impression data, we perform experiments on two public real-world datasets: Avazu[1] and Yoochoose[2]. The Avazu dataset includes several days of ad click-through data, ordered chronologically. In each piece of click data, there are 17 data fields such as ad id, site id, click, etc. These above data fields indicate elements of a single ad impression. We use this dataset to assess the performance of click prediction on the single ad impression. Collected during several months in 2014, the Yoochoose dataset contains many sessions of browse and purchase events from an online retailer, where each session encapsulates the click events of an individual user. Some sessions contain purchase events, which means that the session ends with the user purchasing something. Here, we treat products as ads, then the browse behavior can be viewed as a single ad impression and the purchase behavior as an impression with click. This dataset is employed to evaluate the performance of click prediction on the sequential ad impression.

[1]https://www.kaggle.com/c/avazu-ctr-prediction/data
[2]http://recsys.yoochoose.net

Three state-of-the-art methods are used for empirical comparison, which are LR [7], FM [6] and RNN [10]. (1) As a widely used algorithm for click prediction in industry, LR is easy to understand, quick to train, and efficient enough to be implemented by search engines as an integral part of their advertising system. (2) FM is a general regression model that captures interaction between pairs of elements by using factors. FM has proved to be useful in different tasks and domains. In particular, it can be efficiently used to model the interaction with various elements of ad impressions. (3) RNN models the dependency on user's sequential behaviors into the click prediction process, which depends on not only the current input features, but also the sequential historical information. Since Avazu does not contain sequential ad impression, we only implement RNN model on Yoochoose. In all experiments, we randomly select 90% of dataset as training data and the rest 10% as test data. For CCPM, we apply a CNN architecture of three layers in this work. The parameters of CCPM are set as d=11, m=[4,4,2], w=[6,5,3] for the Avazu dataset, and d=8, m=[3,4,2], w=[6,5,3] for Yoochoose (m, w are the number of feature maps and filter width in three layers).

In the real-world scenarios, the probability of click is extremely low, similar to [7], we adopt logloss as the evaluation metric to measure the accuracy of CTR prediction.

$$\log loss = -\frac{1}{n_{test}} \left[\sum_{i=1}^{n_{test}} y_i \log p_i + (1-y_i)\log(1-p_i) \right], \tag{6}$$

where $p_i = P(y_i = 1|\mathbf{s})$ represents the predicted click probability. and $\mathbf{s}$ donotes an ad impression. y_i is the corresponding observed label, $y_i = 1$ means the user has click the ad impression. m is the total number of input instances.

3.2 Results and Analyses

Left part of Figure 2 illustrates the click prediction performance of CCPM and other competitive compared methods on single ad impression and sequential ad impression. We identify that on both datasets, CCPM outperfom the conventional methods. Since FM can describe the latent features of an element and reveal the relation of pairwise elements, it achieves significant improvement over the that of LR on both datasets. On sequential ad impression, RNN

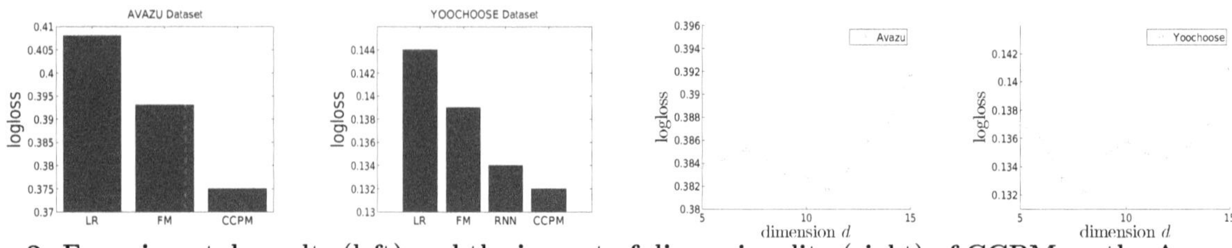

Figure 2: Experimental results (left) and the impact of dimensionality (right) of CCPM on the Avazu dataset and the Yoochoose dataset.

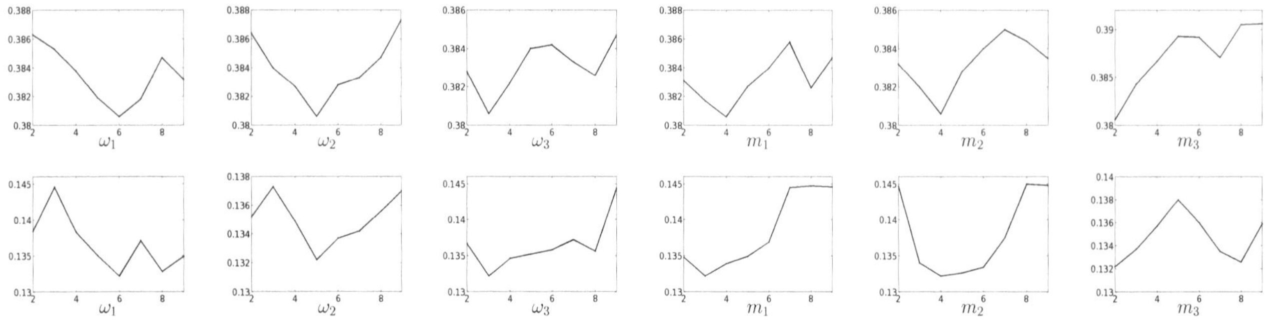

Figure 3: Parameter Study of filter width w and the number of feature maps m in corresponding layer measured by LogLoss. The top part illustrates the results on the Avazu dataset, and the bottom part illustrates the results on the Yoochoose dataset.

leverages sequential dependency of varied impressions, and enhance the effectiveness of click prediction further. Since CCPM obtain underlying semantic information of input instances and extracts local-global features by using convolutional layers, and use k-max pooling to select key features, it can not only reveal the high-order interaction among various elements of a single ad impression but also capture the historical propagation pattern in sequential ad impression.

Furthermore, in the right part of Figure 2, we illustrate the logloss values of CCPM on both datasets with varying dimensionality d of latent vector. On the Avazu dataset, the performance of CCPM achieves the best result at $d = 11$, while on Yoochoose CCPM yields the best performance when the dimensionality $d = 6$. It may be because the Yoochoose dataset is more sparse than the Avazu, latent vector with small dimension can be well estimated. After CCPM obtains the best results on both datasets, the performance decreases gradually with increasing d due to overfitting.

Finally, on both datasets, the parameter impacts of the filter width w and the number of feature map m in corresponding layer are studied. As illustrated in Figure 3, setting smaller corresponding filter width in deeper convolutional layer will contribute to higher accuracy of click prediction. The filters w of convolution layers can learn to recognize specific neighborhoods that have size less or equal to the filter width w. Therefore as reflected in the experiment results, w_1 in the first layer is often set to large enough to grasp all possible neighborhoods. Considering that pooling layers will drop some less significant items, input length of following convolutional layer can decreases. As a result, key features of input instances are further extracted at a deeper layer and kernel size gets smaller. For the sake of enriching the representation of input instances from various angles, there are many parallel feature maps in one layer. Similarly, we can also set smaller number of feature maps in deeper layer to reach better click prediction results. As a layer goes deeper, key features have already been extracted and noise eliminated, deeper layers just need small number of feature maps to extract key features.

4. CONCLUSIONS

In this paper, we have proposed a convolutional click prediction model based on CNN for single and sequential ad impression. Extensive experiments on two public datasets have demonstrated the effectiveness of the proposed model.

5. ACKNOWLEDGMENTS

This work is jointly supported by National Basic Research Program of China(2012CB316300), and National Natural Science Foundation of China (61403390, U1435221, 61175003, 61420106015).

6. REFERENCES

[1] O. Abdel-Hamid, A.-r. Mohamed, H. Jiang, and G. Penn. Applying convolutional neural networks concepts to hybrid nn-hmm model for speech recognition. In *ICASSP*, 2012.

[2] N. Kalchbrenner, E. Grefenstette, and P. Blunsom. A convolutional neural network for modelling sentences. In *ACL*, 2014.

[3] A. Krizhevsky, I. Sutskever, and G. E. Hinton. Imagenet classification with deep convolutional neural networks. In *NIPS*, 2012.

[4] A. K. Menon, K.-P. Chitrapura, S. Garg, D. Agarwal, and N. Kota. Response prediction using collaborative filtering with hierarchies and side-information. In *KDD*, 2011.

[5] S. Rendle. Factorization machines with libfm. *ACM TIST*, 3(3):57, 2012.

[6] S. Rendle. Social network and click-through prediction with factorization machines. In *KDD Cup Workshop*, 2012.

[7] M. Richardson, E. Dominowska, and R. Ragno. Predicting clicks: estimating the click-through rate for new ads. In *WWW*, 2007.

[8] Y. Shen, X. He, J. Gao, L. Deng, and G. Mesnil. A latent semantic model with convolutional-pooling structure for information retrieval. In *CIKM*, 2014.

[9] L. Yan, W.-j. Li, G.-R. Xue, and D. Han. Coupled group lasso for web-scale ctr prediction in display advertising. In *ICML*, 2014.

[10] Y. Zhang, H. Dai, C. Xu, J. Feng, T. Wang, J. Bian, B. Wang, and T.-Y. Liu. Sequential click prediction for sponsored search with recurrent neural networks. In *AAAI*, 2014.

A Study of Query Length Heuristics in Information Retrieval

Yuanhua Lv
Microsoft Research
Redmond, WA 98052
yuanhual@microsoft.com

ABSTRACT

Query length has generally been regarded as a query-specific constant that does not affect document ranking. In this paper, we reveal that query length actually interacts with term frequency (TF) normalization, a key component of all effective retrieval models. Specifically, the longer the query is, the smaller the TF decay speed should be. In order to study the impact of query length, we present a desirable formal constraint to capture the heuristic of query length for retrieval. Our constraint analysis shows that current state-of-the-art retrieval functions, including BM25 and language models, fail to satisfy the constraint, and that, in order to solve this problem, the TF normalization component in a retrieval function should be adapted to query length. As an application, we develop a simple regression algorithm to adapt BM25 to query length, and demonstrate its effectiveness on several representative TREC collections.

Categories and Subject Descriptors

H.3.3 [**Information Search and Retrieval**]: Retrieval models

General Terms

Algorithms, Theory

Keywords

Query length, term frequency normalization, constraints

1. INTRODUCTION

Optimization of retrieval models is a fundamental research problem in information retrieval. Although many studies have attempted to improve retrieval models from various perspectives, e.g., [10, 11, 3, 6], they mainly focused on either document properties (e.g., term frequency and document length) or the estimation of term statistics from the corpus (e.g., IDF and background model), while little attention has been paid to the query length (i.e., the count of terms in a query). In fact, query length has largely been regarded as a query-specific constant that does not affect document ranking.

Permission to make digital or hard copies of all or part of this work for personal or classroom use is granted without fee provided that copies are not made or distributed for profit or commercial advantage and that copies bear this notice and the full citation on the first page. Copyrights for components of this work owned by others than ACM must be honored. Abstracting with credit is permitted. To copy otherwise, or republish, to post on servers or to redistribute to lists, requires prior specific permission and/or a fee. Request permissions from Permissions@acm.org.
CIKM'15, October 19–23, 2015, Melbourne, Australia.
© 2015 ACM. ISBN 978-1-4503-3794-6/15/10 ...$15.00.
DOI: http://dx.doi.org/10.1145/2806416.2806592.

In this paper, we reveal that query length actually plays a role in retrieval models through influencing term frequency (TF) normalization. It is widely recognized that TF should be normalized to properly weaken the contribution of repeated term occurrences (as compared to the first occurrence) of a term, based on the intuition that the first occurrence of the term often brings more relevance evidence. However, we argue that the first occurrence of a term may not be that important when the query is long, as the terms of a longer query generally tends to be more semantically redundant (i.e., one query term may be semantically overlapping with other query terms), and the relative importance of the first occurrence of a new query term (as compared to its repeated occurrences) in a document from a longer query may not be as high as that from a shorter query. We thus hypothesize that the longer the query is, the less penalization the repeated term occurrences should receive. In other words, a document that mis-matches a query term from a longer query should not be penalized as much as that of another document that mis-matches the query term from a shorter query.

We propose a formal constraint to model the interaction between query-length and TF normalization mathematically, so that it is possible to apply it to not only diagnose a retrieval function analytically and but also guide us to fix the problem. We then use constraint analysis to examine BM25 [8, 9] and language models [11], and find that neither of them satisfies the constraint. More specifically, for BM25, the proposed constraint is equivalent to a requirement that its parameter k_1 should increase monotonically with the query length; for the language modeling approach with Dirichlet prior smoothing [11], the constraint requires that the Dirichlet prior μ should increase monotonically with the query length. In other words, the optimal k_1 and μ values for a longer query should generally be larger than that for a shorter query; as a result, a query-independent parameter setting would not be optimal for all queries. This has also been confirmed by the empirical evidences in Section 3.2.

Motivated by this understanding, we propose a simple methodology for adapting retrieval models to query length using a linear regression method, which incurs almost no additional computational cost. As an application, we apply the proposed method to estimate a query-length aware k_1 for BM25. Our experimental results on multiple representative TREC collections demonstrate its effectiveness.

2. RELATED WORK

In our previous works [5, 7], we explored how to adapt TF normalization to the global distribution of individual terms in the whole corpus. Although related, those works are orthogonal to the current work, as they only used global term statistics but did not explore query length. We emphasize that our major contributions in this paper are the query

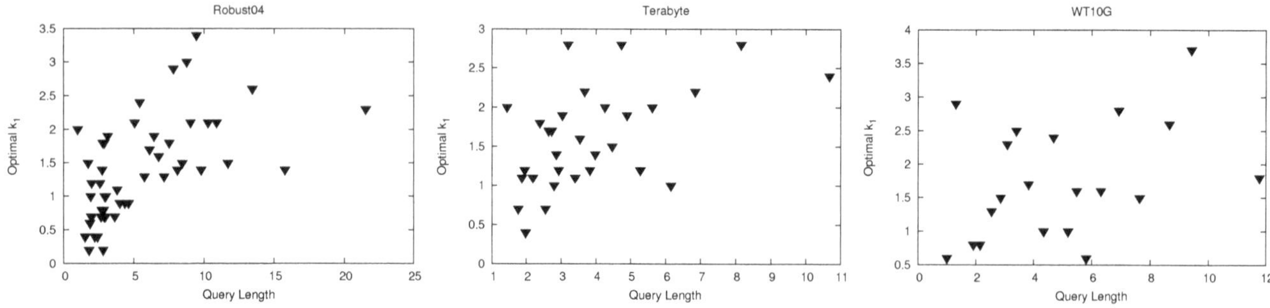

Figure 1: Plots of the optimal k_1 w.r.t. the query length (as described in Section 3.2).

length heuristics and constraints, which are novel. Nevertheless, we have compared the proposed method with our previous work [5] in the experiments.

The interaction between query length and document length normalization has been studied [1, 2]. Chung et al. [1] have incorporated the query length into the pivoted document length normalization in the vector space model (rather than BM25), but they did not reach any conclusive results; Cummins and Riordan's recent work [2] examined a similar heuristic, and formalized a constraint to describe the heuristic, but their method only performs comparably to the baseline retrieval models. Moreover, both works focused only on document length normalization, but did not pay attention to the effect of query length in TF normalization.

Constraint analysis has been explored in information retrieval to diagnostically evaluate existing retrieval models [3], introduce novel retrieval signals into existing retrieval models [6, 2], and guide the development of new retrieval models [4]. Our constraint analysis is inspired by these previous works, but the proposed constraint QLN-TFC is novel.

3. FORMAL QUERY LENGTH CONSTRAINT

How can we regulate the interactions between TF normalization and query length as discussed in Section 1 so that we can adapt a retrieval function to different queries? To answer this question, we first propose a desirable formal constraint, namely QLN-TFC, that any reasonable retrieval function should satisfy.

QLN-TFC: Let $Q = \{q_1, q_2\}$ be a query with two terms q_1 and q_2. Assume D_1 and D_2 are two documents such that $|D_1| = |D_2|$, $c(q_1, D_1) = n > 1$, $c(q_2, D_1) = 0$, $c(q_1, D_2) = c(q_2, D_2) = 1$, and the document relevance scores $S(Q, D_1) = S(Q, D_2)$. If we reformulate the query $Q' = Q \cup \{q_3\}$, by adding another term $q_3 \notin Q$ into the query, where $c(q_3, D_1) = c(q_3, D_2) = 1$, then $S(Q', D_1) > S(Q', D_2)$.

This constraint ensures that the relative importance of the first occurrence of a new query term (as compared to its repeated occurrences) in a longer query should not be as high as that in a shorter query. To illustrate, a document, say D_1, that mis-matches a query term q_2 from a longer query Q' should not be penalized as much as that D_1 mis-matches the query term q_2 from a shorter query Q.

3.1 Analytical Analysis

We now diagnose retrieval models using the proposed constraint QLN-TFC. We use the widely accepted BM25 [8, 9] as an example. The BM25 formula, as presented in [3], scores a document D with respect to query Q as follows:

$$\sum_{q \in Q \cap D} c(q, Q) \cdot dtf(q, D) \cdot \log \frac{N+1}{df(q)} \tag{1}$$

where $c(q, Q)/c(q, D)$ represents the frequency of term q in Q/D, $df(q)$ is the number of documents containing term q, N is the total number of documents in the collection, and $dtf(q, D)$ is the key component of BM25 contributing to its success, i.e., the sub-linear TF normalization formula, which prevents the contribution of repeated occurrences of a term from growing too large:

$$dtf(q, D) = \frac{(k_1 + 1) \cdot c(q, D)}{k_1 \left(1 - b + b\frac{|D|}{avdl}\right) + c(q, D)} = \frac{(k_1 + 1) \cdot c'(q, D)}{k_1 + c'(q, D)}$$

where

$$c'(q, D) = \frac{c(q, D)}{1 - b + b\frac{|D|}{avdl}}$$

is the pivoted normalization method [10] for document length normalization, in which, $|D|$ is the length of document D, and $avdl$ is the average document length. There are two important parameters: (1) k_1 is used to control the shape of this TF normalization component, and a larger k_1 penalizes the repeated term occurrences less; (2) $b \in [0, 1]$ is the slope parameter. Both k_1 and b are usually set independently on query length.

Let's look at the QLN-TFC constraint. Consider the average case when $|D_1| = |D_2| = avdl$. It can be shown that the $S(Q, D_1) = S(Q, D_2)$ implies the following equality:

$$\frac{(k_1 + 1)n}{k_1 + n} \log \frac{N+1}{df(q_1)} \Big|_{|Q|} = \log \frac{N+1}{df(q_1)} + \log \frac{N+1}{df(q_2)} \Big|_{|Q|}$$

And after query reformulation, the constraint $S(Q', D_1) > S(Q', D_2)$ requires

$$\frac{(k_1 + 1)n}{k_1 + n} \log \frac{N+1}{df(q_1)} + \log \frac{N+1}{df(q_3)} \Big|_{|Q'|} > \sum_{i \in \{1,2,3\}} \log \frac{N+1}{df(q_i)} \Big|_{|Q'|}$$

With some basic mathematical derivations, the constraint QLN-TFC is equivalent to the following inequality:

$$\frac{(k_1 + 1)n}{k_1 + n} \Big|_{|Q|} < \frac{(k_1 + 1)n}{k_1 + n} \Big|_{|Q|+1} \tag{2}$$

which clearly cannot be satisfied by the standard BM25, given that k_1 is independent on query length $|Q|$. To satisfy the constraint, *it is required that the parameter k_1 should increase monotonically with the query length $|Q|$*.

Similarly, we also analyze another representative retrieval function, the language modeling approach with Dirichlet prior smoothing method [11], for which the constraint QLN-TFC is equivalent to the following inequality:

$$\frac{1}{\mu \cdot p(q_1|C)p(q_2|C)} \Big|_{|Q|} > \frac{1}{\mu \cdot p(q_1|C)p(q_2|C)} \Big|_{|Q|+1} \tag{3}$$

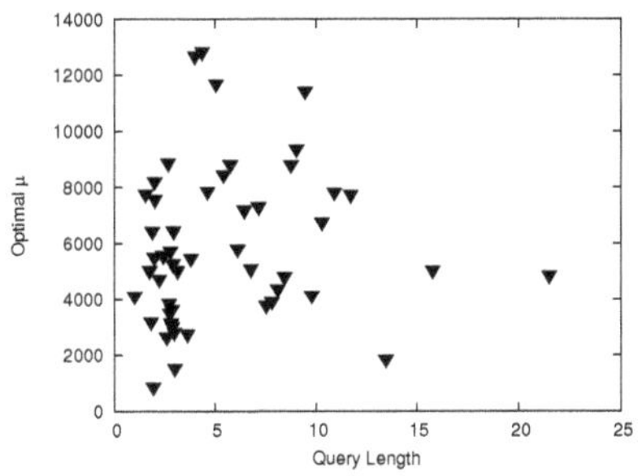

Figure 2: Plots of optimal μ w.r.t. the query length.

where μ is the Dirichlet prior, and $p(q_i|C)$ is the probability of q_i estimated using the whole collection. This shows that *in order for the language modeling approach to satisfy the constraint, an adaptive Dirichlet prior μ that increases monotonically with the query length $|Q|$ is desired.*

3.2 Empirical Analysis

Our above analysis has shown that, analytically, query length interacts with TF normalization. Now we turn to seeking empirical evidence to see if this is a common behavior of modern information retrieval models.

We first plot the optimal k_1 [1] in BM25 for each query w.r.t. the query length on different TREC collections in Figure 1. We do a binning analysis, where we rank all queries according to their lengths and then group every 10 continuous queries into a bin. The "query length" of a bin is the average length of all queries in the bin, and the "k_1" of the bin is the median of all k_1 values in the bin. We can see there is indeed clear correlation between the query length and the optimal k_1 value, especially on Robust04 and Terabyte, probably because Robust04 and Terabyte consist of more query topics (498 and 298 respectively) than WT10G (only 198). Anyway, this confirms our intuition that TF normalization interacts with query length, and thus a query length independent k_1 would not be optimal for all queries.

In addition, we also analyze the optimal Dirichlet prior μ in the language modeling approach w.r.t. the query length in a similar way based on Robust04, as shown in Figure 2, and find μ also has a positive correlation with query length.

4. QUERY-LENGTH AWARE BM25

4.1 Query-Length Aware k_1

In order to improve current retrieval models to satisfy QLN-TFC, we need to make their TF normalization components dependent on query-length. However, we do not want that the addition of this new constraint changes the implementations of other existing retrieval heuristics in these retrieval functions that have been shown to work quite well [3]. We propose a heuristic approach to achieve this goal by making the corresponding parameters in the TF normalization component aware of query-length using a simple regression method. Specifically, $k_1 = f(|Q|)$ in BM25 and the Dirichlet prior $\mu = g(|Q|)$ in the language modeling approach, where $f(\cdot)$ and $g(\cdot)$ are functions to be estimated. In this paper, we focus only on the improvement of BM25 due to the space reason. With $k_1 = f(|Q|)$, the Inequality 2 is equivalent to:

$$f(|Q|) < f(|Q|+1) \tag{4}$$

[1]We do a linear search of the optimal k_1 (that optimizes AP) for each query in range $[0, 5]$ with a step 0.1.

	WT10G	Terabyte	Robust04
queries	451-550	701-850	301-450, 601-700
#qry(with qrel)	198	298	498
mean(ql)	7.93	7.34	9.10
std(ql)	5.44	5.16	8.53
max(ql)	30	24	62
#total_qrel	5,981	28,640	17,412
#documents	$1692k$	$25205k$	$528k$

Table 1: Characteristics of document and query sets

suggesting that a monotonically increasing function $f(\cdot)$ will make BM25 satisfy QLN-TFC unconditionally. And interestingly, this is consistent with the data analysis results in Figure 1, confirming empirically that QLN-TFC is a desirable retrieval constraint. Observing the **sublinear** curves of k_1 w.r.t. the query length in Figure 1, a heuristic approximation of $f(\cdot)$ is thus obtained as follows:

$$k_1 = f(|Q|) = \alpha \cdot \log(|Q|) + \beta \tag{5}$$

where α and β are two free parameters. The logarithm function in $f(\cdot)$ intuitively makes sense: $k_1 = f(|Q|)$ should increase more when the query length increases from 3 to 4 than when the query length increases from 10 to 11.

As we have already collected the optimal k_1 value for each training query, we can use the standard curve-fitting technique and the least square method to fit $f(\cdot)$ to the ground truth to estimate both α and β. Finally, substituting Equation 5 into 1, we get the following retrieval function,

$$\sum_{q \in Q \cap D} c(q, Q) \cdot \frac{(\alpha \cdot \log(|Q|) + \beta + 1) \cdot c'(q, D)}{\alpha \cdot \log(|Q|) + \beta + c'(q, D)} \cdot \log \frac{N+1}{df(q)} \tag{6}$$

4.2 Query-Length Aware b

In addition, we also revisit the heuristic of query length interacting with document length normalization. This heuristic is not entirely novel, as a previous work [1] has reported that a larger b value is often needed for longer queries in the vector space model based on analyzing several small document collections. We revisit this heuristic on BM25 using several larger TREC collections. We first do a similar binning analysis, and plot the optimal b values w.r.t. the corresponding query lengths using BM25, which shows that the optimal b correlates with the query length well (and the optimal b also increases sub-linearly with the query length). We also apply the same linear regression method to compute a query-length aware $b = \alpha' \log |Q| + \beta'$.

5. EXPERIMENTS

5.1 Testing Collections and Evaluation

We use three representative TREC collections: WT10G, Terabyte and Robust04, which represent different sizes and genre of text collections. WT10G and Terabyte are medium and large Web collections respectively. Robust04 is a representative news dataset. Our queries are taken from *both the title and the description fields* of the TREC topics. For all the datasets, the preprocessing of documents and queries is minimum, involving only Porter's stemming. We do not remove any stopwords. An overview of the involved query topics and document collections are shown in Table 1.

The top-ranked 1000 documents for each run are compared in terms of their mean average precisions (MAP), which also serves as the objective function for parameter training. In addition, the precision at top-10 documents (P@10) is also considered.

	WT10G		Terabyte		Robust04	
	MAP	P@10	MAP	P@10	MAP	P@10
BM25	0.1768	0.3051	0.2403	0.5443	0.2352	0.4163
$BM25_Q$	0.1668	0.2904	0.2427	0.5107	0.2335	0.4153
BM25-adpt [5]	0.1765	0.3040	-	-	0.2306	0.4044
BM25QL (b)	0.1800^{2}	0.3045	0.2452^{12}	0.5389	0.2413^{123}	0.4207
BM25QL (k_1)	0.1787^{2}	0.3056	0.2562^{12}	0.5490	0.2371^{13}	0.4155
BM25QL	$\mathbf{0.1817}^{123}$	0.3035	$\mathbf{0.2599}^{12}$	0.5426	$\mathbf{0.2422}^{123}$	0.4211
UpperBound	0.2059	0.3263	0.2723	0.5589	0.2503	0.4295

Table 2: Performance comparison. ^{1}, ^{2} and ^{3} indicate significant MAP improvements over BM25, $BM25_Q$ and BM25-adpt respectively at the 0.01 level using the Wilcoxon non-directional test.

We first employ a two-fold cross-validation for parameter tuning, where the query topics are split into even and odd numbered topics as the two folds. We compare the proposed query-length aware BM25 (labeled as "BM25QL') with two baselines: (1) a standard BM25 for which both b and k_1 are trained (labeled as "BM25"), and (2) a query-length specific BM25 (labeled as "$BM25_Q$") that does a two-fold cross-validation among queries of the same length (if any), and degenerates to "BM25" if there is no other query of the same length. The comparison results are summarized in Table 2. We can see that BM25QL outperforms both BM25 and $BM25_Q$ significantly in terms of MAP. $BM25_Q$ is sometimes even worse than BM25. These observations suggest that a "hard" way to train a query-length specific retrieval model (like $BM25_Q$) may not work well due to the reduction of training data, but a "soft" way, like BM25QL, that uses all the training data to train a query-length aware retrieval function, works effectively. In addition, we can see that although BM25QL improves MAP significantly over the baselines, its P@10 scores are similar to those baselines without any significant differences, probably because BM25QL is trained to optimize MAP rather than P@10.

We also compare BM25QL with our previous work on adaptive BM25, namely BM25-adpt [5], on WT10G and Robust04 in Table 2 [2]. We use an enhanced version of BM25-adpt [5], where we add a free parameter α into the objective function of BM25-adpt to control the range of k_1, formally

$$\arg\min_{k_1} \sum_{i=0}^{T} \left(\alpha \cdot \frac{IG_q^t}{IG_q^1} - \frac{(k_1+1)\cdot t}{k_1+t} \right)^2 \quad (7)$$

Obviously, the new object function takes the original one [5] as its special case when $\alpha = 1$. In our work, α is also optimized using cross validation. We can see that the proposed BM25QL works better. One possible reason is that, although BM25-adpt works well on short keyword queries [5], it does not work effectively on verbose queries that are being used in this work. But the proposed method works better to adapt to different query lengths.

To understand the performance of query-length aware k_1 and query-length aware b separately, we train two retrieval functions "BM25QL (k_1)" and "BM25QL (b)", respectively. We use a query-length aware k_1 and a query-length unaware b [3] in the former, while using a query-length aware b and a query-length unaware k_1 in the latter. We can see that both methods work more effectively than BM25 and $BM25_Q$ in terms of MAP, suggesting that both parts contribute to the performance of BM25QL.

[2]BM25-adpt was implemented based on the Lemur toolkit (http://www.lemurproject.org/lemur.php) that is not scalable to Terabyte data.

[3]From the standard cross validation run "BM25"

6. CONCLUSIONS

In this paper, we revealed that query length affects TF normalization, and explored an idea of query-length aware retrieval models. Specifically, we proposed a desirable formal constraint to capture the heuristic of query length in retrieval functions, diagnosed BM25 and other retrieval functions to show that they cannot satisfy the constraint, and developed a query-length aware TF normalization methodology. We applied the proposed techniques on BM25, which was shown to improve the standard BM25 significantly.

7. ACKNOWLEDGMENTS

I thank Dr. ChengXiang Zhai for his helpful discussions, and three anonymous reviewers for their useful comments.

8. REFERENCES

[1] T. L. Chung, R. W. P. Luk, K. F. Wong, K. L. Kwok, and D. L. Lee. Adapting pivoted document-length normalization for query size: Experiments in chinese and english. *ACM Trans. Asian Lang. Inf. Proc.*, 5(3):245–263, Sept. 2006.

[2] R. Cummins and C. O'Riordan. A constraint to automatically regulate document-length normalisation. In *CIKM '12*, pages 2443–2446, 2012.

[3] H. Fang, T. Tao, and C. Zhai. A formal study of information retrieval heuristics. In *SIGIR '04*, pages 49–56, 2004.

[4] H. Fang and C. Zhai. An exploration of axiomatic approaches to information retrieval. In *SIGIR '05*, pages 480–487, 2005.

[5] Y. Lv and C. Zhai. Adaptive term frequency normalization for bm25. In *CIKM '11*, pages 1985–1988, 2011.

[6] Y. Lv and C. Zhai. Lower-bounding term frequency normalization. In *CIKM '11*, pages 7–16, 2011.

[7] Y. Lv and C. Zhai. A log-logistic model-based interpretation of tf normalization of bm25. In *ECIR'12*, pages 244–255, 2012.

[8] S. E. Robertson and S. Walker. Some simple effective approximations to the 2-poisson model for probabilistic weighted retrieval. In *SIGIR '94*, pages 232–241, 1994.

[9] S. E. Robertson, S. Walker, S. Jones, M. Hancock-Beaulieu, and M. Gatford. Okapi at trec-3. In *TREC '94*, pages 109–126, 1994.

[10] A. Singhal, C. Buckley, and M. Mitra. Pivoted document length normalization. In *SIGIR '96*, pages 21–29, 1996.

[11] C. Zhai and J. D. Lafferty. A study of smoothing methods for language models applied to ad hoc information retrieval. In *SIGIR '01*, pages 334–342, 2001.

Detect Rumors Using Time Series of Social Context Information on Microblogging Websites

Jing Ma[1,3] Wei Gao[2] Zhongyu Wei[4] Yueming Lu[1] Kam-Fai Wong[3,5]

[1]Beijing University of Posts and Telecommunications, Beijing, China
[2]Qatar Computing Research Institute, Hamad Bin Khalifa University, Doha, Qatar
[3]Dept. of SEEM, The Chinese University of Hong Kong, Hong Kong
[4]Computer Science Department, The University of Texas at Dallas, Texas 75080, USA
[5]MoE Key Laboratory of High Confidence Software Technologies, China
{majing,kfwong}@se.cuhk.edu.hk, wgao@qf.org.qa, zywei@hlt.utdallas.edu, ymlu@bupt.edu.cn

ABSTRACT

Automatically identifying rumors from online social media especially microblogging websites is an important research issue. Most of existing work for rumor detection focuses on modeling features related to microblog contents, users and propagation patterns, but ignore the importance of the variation of these social context features during the message propagation over time. In this study, we propose a novel approach to capture the temporal characteristics of these features based on the time series of rumor's lifecycle, for which time series modeling technique is applied to incorporate various social context information. Our experiments using the events in two microblog datasets confirm that the method outperforms state-of-the-art rumor detection approaches by large margins. Moreover, our model demonstrates strong performance on detecting rumors at early stage after their initial broadcast.

Categories and Subject Descriptors

H.4 [**Information Systems Applications**]: Miscellaneous

Keywords

Rumor detection; temporal; time series; social context

1. INTRODUCTION

A rumor is commonly defined as a statement whose truth value is unverifiable or deliberately false [3]. These rumors on microblogging websites, carrying unreal or even malicious information, can bring massive panic and social unrest to our community. For instance, on April 23, 2013, a rumor on Twitter about two explosions in the white house injuring Barack Obama caused the stock market crash in the US[1].

[1]`http://www.bbc.com/news/world-us-canada-21508660`

Permission to make digital or hard copies of all or part of this work for personal or classroom use is granted without fee provided that copies are not made or distributed for profit or commercial advantage and that copies bear this notice and the full citation on the first page. Copyrights for components of this work owned by others than ACM must be honored. Abstracting with credit is permitted. To copy otherwise, or republish, to post on servers or to redistribute to lists, requires prior specific permission and/or a fee. Request permissions from Permissions@acm.org.
CIKM'15, October 19–23, 2015, Melbourne, Australia.
© 2015 ACM. ISBN 978-1-4503-3794-6/15/10 ...$15.00.
DOI: http://dx.doi.org/10.1145/2806416.2806607.

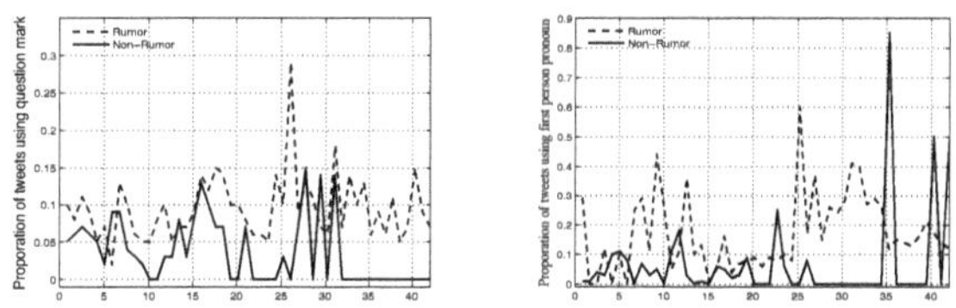

(a) Question mark (b) The first-person pronoun

Figure 1: The two sample features changing over time (in hours) demonstrates different patterns in rumors and non-rumors

Therefore, automatic rumor detection technique that can quickly identify rumor messages and dynamically monitor the propagation of rumors become very useful.

Existing rumor detection methods typically exploit supervised machine learning models based on a wide range of features corresponding to users, contents of messages and their propagation patterns [2, 9, 7, 8, 10, 11]. An obvious limitation of these models is that they just consider the overall statistics on the social context information of messages as features, e.g., the total number of retweets, the time length of propagation, etc., and ignore the variation of these features over time.

To improve the accuracy of detection, we argue that it is of importance not only looking at the overall properties and the properties of individual messages, but also studying the changes or the trends of these properties along the lifecycle of the concerned hypothesis. For example, given two Twitter events, one is about "firing squad" (a rumor) and the other about "Hilton is arrested" (a non-rumor), Figure 1(a) and 1(b) show the variation of proportion of tweets using question marks and first person pronouns using time series, respectively, which are two of the typical features used in previous work. Figure 1(a) implies that the non-rumor tends to use less question marks than the rumor does at the later stage, but according to Figure 1(b), there might be more frequent use of the first person pronoun in the rumor at the early stage. Such variations reflect different characteristics of rumors and non-rumors over time during diffusion.

Kwon et al. [5, 4] recently introduced a time series fitting model that shows better detection result based on the temporal properties regarding a single feature – tweet volume. However, their temporal model focuses on converting the continuous time series of tweet volume into only 3 fitting parameters for capturing the temporal fluctuations of features, which might result in significant information loss given complex time series. Also, it is difficult to extend the number of fitting parameters in their model for further improving the fitting effect.

To overcome these shortcomings, we propose a novel time series model called Dynamic Series-Time Structure (DSTS) to capture the variation of a wide spectrum of social context information over time far more than the tweet volume feature. We will study how well the time series of social context features can capture the variation of these features during the spread of event messages, which is supposed to benefit the differentiation between rumors and non-rumors. We utilize two datasets containing hundreds of events crawled from Twitter and Sina Weibo which are the most popular microblogging websites in English and Chinese, respectively. We build classifiers using the DSTS-based features and the annotated datasets. In our approach, we examine two basic settings: (1) given the complete lifecycle of an event about some specific topic, we decide it is a rumor or not; (2) given the event data at the early stage of propagation, we apply our model for early rumor detection. Experimental results under the two settings demonstrate that our DSTS-based model achieves promising improvements over the state-of-the-art approaches on both datasets.

2. TIME SERIES OF MICROBLOG EVENT

An event is considered as a set of microblogs related to some specific topic, e.g., "Hillary Clinton announces 2016 campaign for president", "MH370 landing in Nanning", etc.. The topics can be compiled manually from Twitter [2] or derived from Sina's community management center [10], which include verified rumors and non-rumor events (Section 4.1).

We model microblog data as a set of events $E = \{E_i\}$, and each event E_i consists of relevant microblogs $\{m_{ij}\}$. We represent each E_i as a D-dimensional vector $\mathbf{F}_i^D$ containing social context features regarding the contents, users and diffusion patterns of the relevant microblogs. To make the number of features tractable, we convert the continuous time stream of microblogs associated with each event into fixed time intervals. For learning our model, we extract a rich set of features sensitive to time, where not only the overall statistics of social context information but also the variation of individual features based on the time intervals can be captured.

In this section, we will first introduce an approach to discretize time stream for generating time stamps, then a method for capturing the variation of features.

2.1 Time Stamps Generation

For an event E_i, let $timeFirst_i$ and $timeLast_i$ be the time when the initial and the last microblog is posted, respectively. We convert the creation time of each microblog m_{ij} to a time interval falling into the range from 0 to N, serving as the time stamp of m_{ij}, where N is the tunable number of time intervals. We determine the length of time interval for E_i and the time stamp (TS) for m_{ij} created at time $t_{m_{ij}}$ as follows:

$$Interval(E_i) = \lceil \frac{timeLast_i - timeFirst_i}{N} \rceil \quad (1)$$

$$TS(m_{ij}) = \lfloor \frac{t_{m_{ij}} - timeFirst_i}{Interval(E_i)} \rfloor \quad (2)$$

where $Interval(.)$ is the length of each time interval in the number of time units like minutes, hours or days, and $TS(.)$ is the index of time stamp which m_{ij} falls into, taking the value of $0, 1, \cdots, N$. We use hour as time unit in this work.

2.2 Dynamic Series-Time Structure (DSTS)

With all the time stamps of E_i, a vector of its social context features $V(E_i)$ can be naturally generated given each time stamp. However, the temporal properties of such information is subject to continuous change over time, which cannot be captured effectively by just modeling features within individual time intervals. A better approach would be to identify the shapes of time series, which are formed by the relative change between the consecutive intervals, as a supplement of the absolute temporal properties.

For this purpose, we propose a Dynamic Series-Time Structure (DSTS), which is used to capture the variation of each feature. In this structure, we not only consider the absolute feature values from the initial time up to each interval, but also incorporate the slopes of features between two consecutive intervals. Therefore, the feature vector based on DSTS is represented as:

$$V(E_i) = (\mathbf{F}_{i,0}^D, \mathbf{F}_{i,1}^D, \ldots, \mathbf{F}_{i,N}^D; \mathbf{S}_{i,1}^D, \ldots \mathbf{S}_{i,N-1}^D) \quad (3)$$

$$\mathbf{F}_{i,t}^D = (\widetilde{f}_{i,t,1}, \widetilde{f}_{i,t,2}, \ldots, \widetilde{f}_{i,t,D}) \quad (4)$$

$$\mathbf{S}_{i,t}^D = \frac{\mathbf{F}_{i,t+1}^D - \mathbf{F}_{i,t}^D}{Interval(E_i)} \quad (5)$$

where $\mathbf{F}_{i,t}^D$ is the feature vector generated from social context features for the microblogs in E_i *from time 0 to the t-th interval*, and $\mathbf{S}_{i,t}^D$ is the slopes of features between the t-th and the $(t+1)$-th intervals.

We use Z-score to normalize feature values along the time series. The Z-score of a feature from 0 to the t-th interval $f_{t,k}$ is defined as[2]:

$$\widetilde{f}_{t,k} = \frac{f_{t,k} - \overline{f}_k}{\sigma(f_k)} \quad (6)$$

where $\overline{f}_k$ is the mean of the k-th feature and $\sigma(f_k)$ is the standard deviation of the k-th feature over all the time intervals, and $f_{t,k}$ is the k-th feature from time 0 to the t-th interval which is obtained by calculating the average or other statistics of the feature over the microblogs falling into that time span (Section 3).

3. FEATURE ENGINEERING

In this section, we will engineer each of the social context features corresponding to $f_{t,k}$ given in Equation 6. Note that $f_{t,k}$ is typically obtained by averaging the original social context feature f_k defined on individual microblogs, but chances are there that some features are defined directly on all microblogs from time 0 to the interval t. We present three types of features: content-based, user-based and propagation-based features, some of which are derived from prior work [2, 10, 11] and several others are newly proposed. Table 1 describes all these features. For clarity, we give more details on some of the following features.

[2]For the simplicity of presentation, we omit the notation of the event index i here

Table 1: Description of features $f_{t,k}$ on microblogs from time 0 to time interval t of an event

Content-based features
LDA-based topic distribution of microblogs with 18 topics [10]
Average length of microblogs [2]
# of positive (negative) words in microblogs [2]
Average sentiment score of microblogs [2, 10]
% of microblogs with URL [2, 10, 11]
% of microblogs with smiling (frowning) emoticons [2]
% of positive (negative) microblogs [2]
% of microblogs with the first-person pronouns [2]
% of microblogs with hashtags [2, 11]
% of microblogs with @ mentions [2]
% of microblogs with question marks [2]
% of microblogs with exclamation marks [2]
% of microblogs with multiple question/exclamation marks [2]
User-based features
% of users that provide personal description [2, 10, 11]
% of users that provide personal picture in profile
% of verified users [2, 10, 11]
% of verified users of each type, e.g., celebrities [10, 11]
% of male (female) users [10, 11]
% of users located in large (small) cities
Average # of friends of users [2, 10, 11]
Average # of followers of users [2, 10, 11]
Average # of posts of users [2, 10, 11]
Average days users' accounts exist since registration [2, 10, 11]
Average reputation score of users (i.e., followers/followees ratio)
Diffusion-based features
Average # of retweets [2, 10, 11]
Average # of comments for Weibo posts [10, 11]
# of microblogs [2]

LDA-based topic distribution: For all the microblogs in E, we use a Latent Dirichlet Allocation (LDA) model [1] to obtain a n-topic distribution for each post. For every post m_{ij} of every event E_i, we have $T(m_{ij}) = (p_{ij}^{(1)}, p_{ij}^{(2)}, \dots, p_{ij}^{(n)})$ where $p_{ij}^{(z)}$ is the probability of m_{ij} belonging to topic z ($z = 1, \cdots, n$). Then the topic distributions of all microblogs in the concerned time span of an event are averaged to obtain the n LDA-based topic distribution features. We set n=18 following previous work [10].

Average sentiment score: Similar feature but not the same was used in [2, 10]. Given a sentiment lexicon and an emoticon lexicon, the average sentiment score of microblogs in a time span of event E_i is calculated as:

$$\frac{1}{|m_i|}\sum_{j=1}^{|m_i|}(|w_{pos}|_{ij} - |w_{neg}|_{ij} + |e_{pos}|_{ij} - |e_{neg}|_{ij})$$

where $|w_{pos}|_{ij}$ and $|w_{neg}|_{ij}$ is the number of positive and negative words, respectively, $|e_{pos}|_{ij}$ and $|e_{neg}|_{ij}$ is the number of smiling and frowning emoticons, respectively, in microblog m_{ij}, and $|m_i|$ is the number of microblogs in the concerned time span of event E_i. For tweets, we use MPQA[3] sentiment lexicon and a set of frequent emoticons collected by ourselves; for Weibo, we used the sentiment lexicon and emoticons described in [10].

4. EXPERIMENTAL EVALUATION

4.1 Datasets and Setup

For tweets, we used the public dataset released by Castillo et al. [2]. They extracted 288 events using Twitter Monitor [6] from tweet feeds in April-September 2010. We filtered out events with less than 10 tweets and left 207 popular events, in which 110 of them are labeled as rumors. We also collected an additional microblog dataset from Sina Weibo, where the verified rumors came from Sina's community management center [10] that accepts reports of various misinformation. We kept those rumor events with at least 100 posts. This left us 422 rumor events. We injected 500 normal (non-rumor) events, each with more than 100 posts. Sina Weibo API[4] provides interfaces to capture the information of original and retweeted posts. Table 2 shows the details for our datasets.

Table 2: Details of the datasets

Statistic	Twitter	Sina Weibo
Users	568,261	585,475
Tweets	1,207,767	473,698
Events	216	922
Rumors	101	500
Non-Rumors	115	422
AVG. time length	35.8 Hours	2,719 Hours

We resorted to *linear* SVM classifier for our model. We made comparison between our DSTS-based SVM model and several strong baselines: (1) DT: The Twitter credibility model using Decision Tree classifier proposed in [2] with the social context features in Table 1 *without considering time series*; (2) RF: The Random Forest classifier proposed in [5] using features consisting of the three parameters fitting tweet volume curve [5] plus all static features in Table 1; (3) RF-ext: Our extension of the RF model [5] with additional features by adding the fitting parameters of time series of all social context features in Table 1; (4) SVM-RBF: The SVM-based model with RBF kernel proposed in [11] using all features in Table 1 without considering time series; (5) SVM_c^{DSTS}, SVM_u^{DSTS}, SVM_d^{DSTS}: Our DSTS model using content-based, user-based and diffusion-based features, respectively; (6) SVM_{all}^{DSTS}: Our fully configured DSTS model. We did not compare with [10] which used specific propagation structure of Sina Weibo platform while our method is much more general.

We implemented DT, RF and RF-ext using Weka[5] and SVM models with LibSVM[6]. We conducted 10-fold cross-validation, and used accuracy, precision, recall and F-measure for evaluation. We fixed N=50 on a development set.

4.2 Experimental Results

Table 3(a) and 3(b) show the performance of different methods. Overall, our system SVM_{all}^{DSTS}, although a linear model, clearly outperforms the baselines that are all based on non-linear models. In terms of accuracy, it improves DT, RF, RF-ext and SVM-RBF by 9.5%, 3.3%, 4.4% and 9.1% respectively on Twitter data, and improves the same by 9.3%, 3.8%, 5.2% and 8.6% respectively on Weibo data. This is because DSTS model could reserve much variation of the rich social context information. DT only uses the static social context features over the entire lifecyle of posts, and RF uses as additional features the three parameters of a model that fits the time series of retweets volume, which may suffer from information loss. Surprisingly, RF-ext performs worse than RF, which implies that representing the variation of each feature with the three parameters cannot

[3]http://mpqa.cs.pitt.edu/lexicons/

[4]http://open.weibo.com/wiki/API

[5]http://www.cs.waikato.ac.nz/ml/weka/

[6]http://www.csie.ntu.edu.tw/~cjlin/libsvm/

Table 3: Results of comparison with different methods (R: Rumor; N: Non-rumor)

(a) Twitter dataset

Method	Class	Accu.	Prec.	Recall	F_1
DT [2]	R	0.818	0.857	0.725	0.785
	N		0.793	0.897	0.842
RF [5]	R	0.867	0.896	0.805	0.848
	N		0.847	0.920	0.882
RF-ext	R	0.858	0.860	0.826	0.842
	N		0.856	0.886	0.871
SVM-RBF [11]	R	0.821	0.96	0.638	0.766
	N		0.760	0.977	0.855
SVM_c^{DSTS}	R	0.858	0.818	0.910	0.861
	N		0.905	0.810	0.855
SVM_u^{DSTS}	R	0.858	0.828	0.894	0.859
	N		0.892	0.825	0.857
SVM_d^{DSTS}	R	0.738	0.756	0.647	0.697
	N		0.725	0.816	0.768
SVM_{all}^{DSTS}	R	0.896	0.880	0.909	0.894
	N		0.912	0.883	0.897

(b) Sina Weibo dataset

Method	Class	Accu.	Prec.	Recall	F_1
DT [2]	R	0.774	0.771	0.830	0.800
	N		0.779	0.709	0.742
RF [5]	R	0.815	0.791	0.894	0.839
	N		0.852	0.720	0.780
RF-ext	R	0.804	0.775	0.898	0.832
	N		0.851	0.692	0.763
SVM-RBF [11]	R	0.779	0.771	0.842	0.805
	N		0.790	0.704	0.744
SVM_c^{DSTS}	R	0.817	0.833	0.828	0.830
	N		0.798	0.803	0.800
SVM_u^{DSTS}	R	0.811	0.815	0.844	0.829
	N		0.807	0.773	0.789
SVM_d^{DSTS}	R	0.760	0.755	0.826	0.789
	N		0.768	0.682	0.723
SVM_{all}^{DSTS}	R	0.846	0.861	0.854	0.857
	N		0.829	0.836	0.833

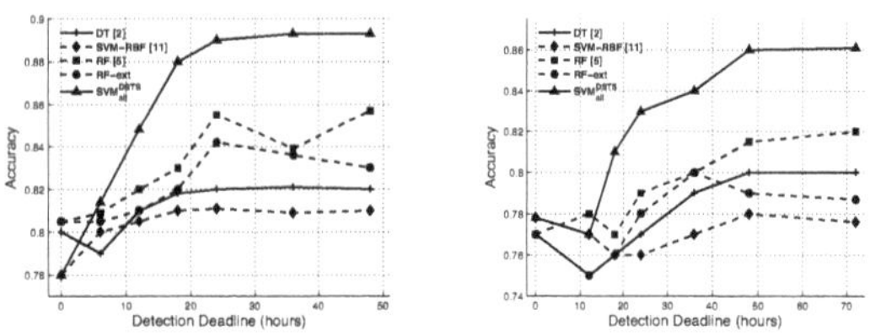

(a) Twitter (b) Sina Weibo

Figure 2: Results of rumor early detection

capture complex propagation patterns and fitting more features may accumulate even more information loss. Extending the three fitting parameters is limited by their original model. SVM-RBF is even worse than our DSTS models just using content-based and user-based subsets of features, indicating that our time series representation is very effective.

We find that using the subsets of features alone except diffusion-based features is already comparably good as the best baselines. Combining all features gives the best performance suggesting that they are complementary.

4.3 Rumor Early Detection

We examine the performance of our model on rumor early detection task that aims to identify rumors in the early stage of propagation. Given a detection deadline, we assume all messages of test events after the deadline are invisible when testing our model. When training the model, the complete lifecyle of training events is assumed observable.

Figure 2 shows the accuracy of our model SVM_{all}^{DSTS} in comparison with the baselines DT, RF, RF-ext and SVM-RBF at different deadlines. At the first few hours, our model does not have obvious advantage because it lacks of sufficient variation of social context. As time goes by, the performance of our model climbs much more rapidly after 5-10 hours while other models do not improve much because DSTS can capture rich variation patterns of features from the time series. Ours model achieves the similar accuracies of baselines at much earlier stage than they need. For example, on Twitter, it takes our model around 15 hours to get the highest accuracy of RF, the second best baseline, while RF needs more than 25 hours; on Weibo, our model needs about 20 hours but RF needs nearly 70 hours to achieve the similar performance. This suggests our model is very effective for early detection.

5. CONCLUSION AND FUTURE WORK

We proposed a novel approach to automatically identify rumors on microblogging websites. We develop a Dynamic Series-Time Structure model which explores the variation of various social context features over time. Experimental results show that our method with the time series of features achieves salient improvement on rumor detection given the complete lifecyle of events as well as at the early stage of diffusion. In future work, we plan to investigate unsupervised models using time series for identifying rumors online.

Acknowledgments

This work is partially supported by General Research Fund of Hong Kong (417112), Shenzhen Fundamental Research Program (JCYJ20130401172046450, JCYJ20120613152557576).

6. REFERENCES

[1] D. M. Blei, A. Y. Ng, and M. I. Jordan. Latent dirichlet allocation. *Journal of Machine Learning Research*, 3:993–1022, 2003.

[2] C. Castillo, M. Mendoza, and B. Poblete. Information credibility on Twitter. In *Proceedings of WWW*, pages 675–684, 2011.

[3] N. DiFonzo and P. Bordia. *Rumor psychology: Social and organizational approaches*. American Psychological Association, 2007.

[4] S. Kwon and M. Cha. Modeling bursty temporal pattern of rumors. In *Proceedings of ICWSM*, 2014.

[5] S. Kwon, M. Cha, K. Jung, W. Chen, and Y. Wang. Prominent features of rumor propagation in online social media. In *Proceedings of ICDM*, pages 1103–1108, 2013.

[6] M. Mathioudakis and N. Koudas. Twittermonitor: trend detection over the Twitter stream. In *Proceedings of SIGMOD*, pages 1155–1158, 2010.

[7] M. Mendoza, B. Poblete, and C. Castillo. Twitter under crisis: Can we trust what we RT? In *Proceedings of the first workshop on social media analytics*, pages 71–79. ACM, 2010.

[8] V. Qazvinian, E. Rosengren, D. R. Radev, and Q. Mei. Rumor has it: Identifying misinformation in microblogs. In *Proceedings of EMNLP*, pages 1589–1599, 2011.

[9] J. Ratkiewicz, M. Conover, M. Meiss, B. Gonçalves, S. Patil, A. Flammini, and F. Menczer. Truthy: Mapping the spread of astroturf in microblog streams. In *Proceedings of WWW (demo)*, pages 249–252, 2011.

[10] K. Wu, S. Yang, and K. Q. Zhu. False rumors detection on Sina Weibo by propagation structures. In *Proceedings of ICDE*, 2015.

[11] F. Yang, Y. Liu, X. Yu, and M. Yang. Automatic detection of rumor on Sina Weibo. In *Proceedings of the ACM SIGKDD Workshop on Mining Data Semantics*. ACM, 2012.

Query Auto-Completion for Rare Prefixes

Bhaskar Mitra
Microsoft
bmitra@microsoft.com

Nick Craswell
Microsoft
nickcr@microsoft.com

ABSTRACT

Query auto-completion (QAC) systems typically suggest queries that have previously been observed in search logs. Given a partial user query, the system looks up this query prefix against a precomputed set of candidates, then orders them using ranking signals such as popularity. Such systems can only recommend queries for prefixes that have been previously seen by the search engine with adequate frequency. They fail to recommend if the prefix is sufficiently rare such that it has no matches in the precomputed candidate set.

We propose a design of a QAC system that can suggest completions for rare query prefixes. In particular, we describe a candidate generation approach using frequently observed query suffixes mined from historical search logs. We then describe a supervised model for ranking these synthetic suggestions alongside the traditional full-query candidates. We further explore ranking signals that are appropriate for both types of candidates based on n-gram statistics and a convolutional latent semantic model (CLSM). Within our supervised framework the new features demonstrate significant improvements in performance over the popularity-based baseline. The synthetic query suggestions complement the existing popularity-based approach, helping users formulate rare queries.

Categories and Subject Descriptors

H.3 [**Information Storage and Retrieval**]: H.3.3 Information Search and Retrieval

Keywords: Query auto-completion; Deep learning

1. INTRODUCTION

As users enter their query into the search box, most modern search engines provide a ranked list of query suggestions based on the current prefix already typed by the user. In a typical approach used by many query auto-completion (QAC) systems, candidate queries are identified by doing an exact prefix lookup against a fixed set of popular queries, using a data structure such as a prefix tree [4]. The candidates are then ranked by their expected likelihood, which is typically computed as a function of its past popularity (commonly referred to as the *MostPopularCompletion* (MPC) model [1]). Such a system can only suggest queries with enough historic popularity to make it into the prefix tree.

We propose an additional candidate generation strategy for QAC by mining popular query *suffixes*. Candidate suffixes are popular n-grams that appear at the ends of queries. By appending such n-grams suffixes to a user's query prefix we can generate synthetic suggestion candidates that have never been observed in the historical query logs. Table 1 contains examples of such suggestions. We further propose a supervised framework for ranking these synthetic queries alongside the traditional full-query suggestion candidates. We also explore new ranking signals in this framework, based on the query n-gram statistics and a deep *convolutional latent semantic model* (CLSM)[15].

Table 1: Synthetic QAC candidates generated by the suffix-based approach and ranked using only the CLSM similarity feature. The CLSM model projects both the prefix and the suffix to a common 128-dimensional space allowing us to rank according to prefix-suffix cosine similarity. One of the lower quality synthetic candidates "cheapest flights from seattle to airport" is ranked seventh in the second list.

what to cook with chicken and broccoli and
what to cook with chicken and broccoli *and bacon*
what to cook with chicken and broccoli *and noodles*
what to cook with chicken and broccoli *and brown sugar*
what to cook with chicken and broccoli *and garlic*
what to cook with chicken and broccoli *and orange juice*
what to cook with chicken and broccoli *and beans*
what to cook with chicken and broccoli *and onions*
what to cook with chicken and broccoli *and ham soup*

cheapest flights from seattle to
cheapest flights from seattle *to dc*
cheapest flights from seattle *to washington dc*
cheapest flights from seattle *to bermuda*
cheapest flights from seattle *to bahamas*
cheapest flights from seattle *to aruba*
cheapest flights from seattle *to punta cana*
cheapest flights from seattle *to airport*
cheapest flights from seattle *to miami*

2. RELATED WORK

Language modelling based approaches for *sentence completion* have been studied in the context of e-mail and document authoring[3, 5, 8, 13]. In Web search, White and Marchionini [17] and Fan et al. [7] proposed models for term recommendations to aid users in their query formulation process. Bhatia et al. [2] extracted frequently

Permission to make digital or hard copies of all or part of this work for personal or classroom use is granted without fee provided that copies are not made or distributed for profit or commercial advantage and that copies bear this notice and the full citation on the first page. Copyrights for components of this work owned by others than ACM must be honored. Abstracting with credit is permitted. To copy otherwise, or republish, to post on servers or to redistribute to lists, requires prior specific permission and/or a fee. Request permissions from Permissions@acm.org.
CIKM'15, October 19–23, 2015, Melbourne, Australia.
© 2015 ACM. ISBN 978-1-4503-3794-6/15/10 ...$15.00.
DOI: http://dx.doi.org//10.1145/2806416.2806599.

Table 2: Most popular query suffixes extracted from the publicly available AOL logs.

Top suffixes	Top 2-word suffixes	Top 3-word suffixes
com	for sale	federal credit union
org	yahoo com	new york city
net	myspace com	in new york
gov	google com	or no deal
pictures	new york	disney channel com
lyrics	real estate	my space com
edu	of america	in new jersey
sale	high school	homes for sale
games	new jersey	department of corrections
florida	space com	chamber of commerce
for sale	aol com	bath and beyond
us	s com	in las vegas

occurring phrases from document corpus and used them to generate suggestion candidates in the absence of a query log. Duan and Hsu [6] have studied the problem of online spelling correction for query auto-completion and Hawking and Griffiths [9] have explored mechanisms for generating query suggestions in the enterprise settings. Our proposed approach generates synthetic query suggestion candidates by combining the input prefix with popular query *suffixes* to augment the regular full-query QAC suggestions.

Within our proposed supervised framework, we explore *convolutional latent semantic model* (CLSM)[10, 15] as a ranking signal. Mitra [11] previously used the CLSM for modelling session context for QAC ranking. Unlike Mitra [11], our focus is on ranking query suffixes and we propose a novel approach for training a CLSM on prefix-suffix pairs for this task.

3. RARE PREFIX AUTO-COMPLETION

We propose two key ideas in this paper. Firstly, we generate synthetic query suggestion candidates for QAC using popular query *suffixes*. We then introduce n-gram and CLSM based features in a supervised learning setting to rank these synthetic suggestions alongside the full-query suggestion candidates.

3.1 Candidate Generation

From every query in the search engine logs we generate all possible n-grams from the end of the query. For example, from the query "bank of america" we generate the suffixes "america", "of america" and "bank of america". By aggregating across all queries we identify the most popular suffixes. Table 2 shows the most frequently observed query suffixes in the publicly available AOL logs [14].

Next, for a given prefix we extract the *end-term* as shown in Figure 1. We match all the suffixes that start with the end-term from our precomputed set. These selected suffixes are appended to the prefix to generate synthetic suggestion candidates. For example, the prefix "cheap flights fro" is matched with the suffix "from seattle" to generate the candidate "cheap flights from seattle". Note that many of these synthetic suggestion candidates are likely to not have been observed by the search engine before.

We merge these synthetic suggestions with the set of candidates selected from the list of historically popular queries. This combined set of candidates is used for ranking as we will describe in Sec 4.

3.2 Ranking Features

For every prefix and suggestion candidate (synthetic or previously observed), we compute a set of common features for the supervised ranking model. We describe these features in this section, focusing on the n-gram and CLSM features that we propose for this setting.

Figure 1: Examples of fully or partially typed end-terms extracted from the input prefixes. The end-term is used for selecting the set of candidate suffixes for the generation of synthetic query suggestions.

N-gram based features. From the set of all n-grams $\mathcal{G}$ in a candidate suggestion we compute the n-gram frequency features $ngramfreq_i$ (for i = 1 to 6).

$$ngramfreq_i = \sum_{g \in \mathcal{G}, len(g)=i} freq(g) \quad (1)$$

Where $len(g)$ and $freq(g)$ are the number of words in the n-gram g and its observed frequency in the historical query logs, respectively. Intuitively, these n-gram features model the likelihood that the candidate suggestion is generated by the same language model as the queries in the search logs.

CLSM based features. For document retrieval, Shen et al. [15] demonstrated that discriminatively training a deep neural network model with a convolutional-pooling structure on clickthrough data can be effective for modelling query-document relevance. We adopt the CLSM by training on a *prefix-suffix* pairs dataset (instead of query-document titles). The training data for the CLSM is generated by sampling queries from the search logs and splitting each query at every possible word boundary. For example, from the query "breaking bad cast" we generate the two pairs ("breaking", "bad cast") and ("breaking bad", "cast"). The architecture shown in Figure 2 is used on both the prefix and the suffix side of the CLSM model.

Now given a prefix $\mathcal{P}$ and a suggestion candidate $\mathcal{C}$, we extract a normalized prefix $\bar{p}$ by removing the *end-term* from the prefix. Then a normalized suffix $\bar{s}$ is extracted by removing $\bar{p}$ from the query $\mathcal{C}$. Then we use the trained CLSM model to project the normalized prefix and the normalized suffix to a common 128-dimensional space and compute a $clsmsim$ feature.

$$clsmsim(\bar{p}, \bar{s}) = cosine(y_1, y_2) = \frac{y_1^{\intercal} y_2}{||y_1|| \, ||y_2||} \quad (2)$$

where y_1 and y_2 are the CLSM vector outputs corresponding to $\bar{p}$ and $\bar{s}$, respectively. Table 1 shows examples of synthetic suggestion candidates ranked by this $clsmsim$ feature alone.

Other features. Other features used in our model includes the frequency of the candidate query in the historical logs, length based features (length of the prefix, the suffix and the full suggestion in both characters and words) and a boolean feature that indicates whether the prefix ends with a space character.

4. EXPERIMENTS

Our experiment setup is based on the *learning to rank* framework proposed by Shokouhi [16]. We generate all possible prefixes[1] from each query impression to use for training, validation and testing. For each prefix we identify the set of candidate suggestions as described

[1]Mitra et al. [12] showed that users use QAC more at word boundaries but for simplicity we sample the prefixes with equal probability.

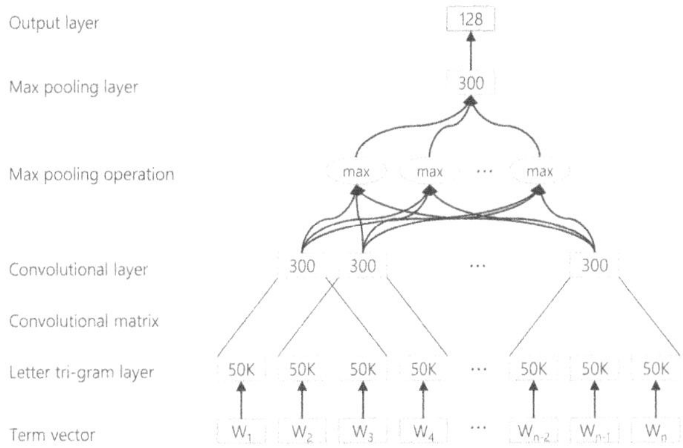

Figure 2: The CLSM model architecture. The model has a convolutional-pooling structure and a 128-dimensional output.

in Section 3.1. We associate a positive relevance judgment with the candidate that matches the original query from which the prefix was extracted. Unlike Mitra [11], to accurately measure the coverage impact of our approach we retain all prefix impressions where the submitted query is not in the list of candidates available for ranking.

We train LambdaMART [18] models for ranking the suggestions using features described in Section 3.2. We limit our ranking task to instances where the prefix contains at least one complete word, since completions with very short prefixes is already well solved by our popularity-based features and we are focusing on rare prefixes. We always train 300 trees (with early stopping using a validation set) and evaluate the model performances on the test set using the *mean reciprocal rank* (MRR) metric.

We conduct all our experiments on the publicly available AOL query logs [14] and reproduce the same results on the large-scale query logs of the Bing search engine. We refer to these two datasets hereafter as the *AOL testbed* and the *Bing testbed*, respectively.

The query impressions on both the testbeds are divided into four temporally separate partitions (background, training, validation and test). On the *AOL testbed* we use all the data from 1 March, 2006 to 30 April, 2006 as the *background* data. We sample queries from the next two weeks for *training*, and from each of the following two weeks for *validation* and *test*, respectively. On the *Bing testbed* we sample data from the logs from April, 2015 and use the first week of data for background, the second week for training, the third for validation and the fourth for testing. We normalize all the queries in each of these datasets by removing any punctuation characters and converting them to lower case.

For candidate generation, both the list of popular queries and suffixes are mined from the *background* portion of the two testbeds. We use 724,340 and 1,040,674 distinct queries on the AOL testbed and the Bing testbed, respectively, as the set of full-query candidates. We evaluate our approach using 10K and 100K most frequent suffixes. We limit the number of full-query candidates per prefix to ten and compute the final reciprocal rank by considering only the top eight ranked suggestions per model. Finally, the CLSM models are trained using 44,558,631 and 212,854,198 prefix-suffix pairs on the AOL and the Bing testbeds, respectively.

5. RESULTS

Table 3 summarizes the experiment results and clearly demonstrates the improvements from the synthetic suggestion over the MPC model. All the LambdaMART models with different feature sets when combined with the suffix-based candidates show an improved MRR over the popularity based baseline. The models however perform no better, and in most cases worse, compared to

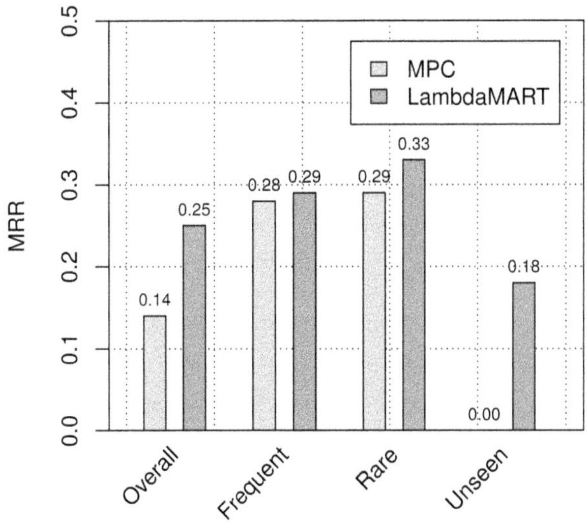

Figure 3: MRR improvements by historical popularity of the input prefix on the AOL testbed. The LambdaMART model uses n-gram and CLSM features and includes suffix-based suggestion candidates. Any prefix in the top 100K most popular prefixes from the background data is considered as *Frequent*. There are 7622, 6917 and 14,135 prefix impressions in the *Frequent*, *Rare* and *Unseen* segments, respectively. All reported differences in MRR with the MPC model are statistically significant by the t-test ($p < 0.01$).

the MPC baseline when only the full-query based candidates are considered. This is expected as the models are trained with the suffix-based candidates in the training data.

Figure 3 analyses the improvements by segmenting the prefixes based on their historical popularity. The improvements from the suffix-based candidates are expectedly higher for the rarer prefixes. Interestingly, the absolute MRR values for both models are higher for rare prefixes than for the frequent ones. One factor in this is that rare prefixes tend to be longer and therefore more specific, giving fewer candidates to rank and making it easier to achieve good MRR.

The models with the *clsmsim* feature perform better than the corresponding models without the feature across all experiments. However, in general the n-gram features seems to be showing higher improvements compared to the CLSM based feature. We hypothesize that the CLSM feature is less precise than the n-gram features. For example, we can see in Table 1 that the CLSM based feature ranks a suffix highly that generates a semantically meaningless query suggestion "cheapest flight from seattle to airport". While "airport" is a location that you can take a flight to, in the context of the given prefix it is clearly an inappropriate suggestion. It is possible that the prefix-suffix pairs based training of the CLSM can be further improved. We believe that this is an important area for future investigations given that the CLSM holds certain other advantages over n-gram models. For example, the CLSM has limited storage requirements[2], and because of the *word hashing* technique the CLSM may be more robust to morphological variations and spelling errors in the input prefix compared to the n-gram based models.

6. CONCLUSION

We proposed a novel candidate generation technique for query auto-completion by mining and ranking popular query *suffixes*. Our empirical study shows that this is an effective strategy for significantly improving MRR for rare and unseen prefixes. The supervised

[2]The CLSM model itself needs to be stored in memory but has no data storage requirements, unlike the n-gram models.

Table 3: Comparison of all models on the AOL and the Bing testbeds. Due to the proprietary nature of the Bing dataset, we only report MRR improvements relative to the MPC model for this testbed. Statistically significant differences by the t-test ($p < 0.01$) are marked with "*". Top three highest MRR values per testbed are bolded.

Models	AOL MRR	AOL % Improv.	Bing % Improv.
Full-query based candidates only			
MostPopularCompletion	0.1446	-	-
LambdaMART Model (n-gram features = no, CLSM feature = no)	0.1445	-0.1	-1.7*
LambdaMART Model (n-gram features = yes, CLSM feature = no)	0.1427	-1.4*	-1.2*
LambdaMART Model (n-gram features = no, CLSM feature = yes)	0.1445	-0.1	-1.2*
LambdaMART Model (n-gram features = yes, CLSM feature = yes)	0.1432	-1.0*	-1.5*
Full-query based candidates + Suffix based candidates (Top 10K suffixes)			
MostPopularCompletion	0.1446	-	-
LambdaMART Model (n-gram features = no, CLSM feature = no)	0.2116	+46.3*	+32.8*
LambdaMART Model (n-gram features = yes, CLSM feature = no)	0.2326	+60.8*	+42.6*
LambdaMART Model (n-gram features = no, CLSM feature = yes)	0.2249	+55.5*	+40.1*
LambdaMART Model (n-gram features = yes, CLSM feature = yes)	0.2339	**+61.7***	+43.8*
Full-query based candidates + Suffix based candidates (Top 100K suffixes)			
MostPopularCompletion	0.1446	-	-
LambdaMART Model (n-gram features = no, CLSM feature = no)	0.2105	+45.5*	+39.9*
LambdaMART Model (n-gram features = yes, CLSM feature = no)	0.2441	**+68.7***	**+54.2***
LambdaMART Model (n-gram features = no, CLSM feature = yes)	0.2248	+55.4*	**+48.9***
LambdaMART Model (n-gram features = yes, CLSM feature = yes)	0.2453	**+69.6***	**+55.3***

ranking framework proposed in this paper is generic and can be employed in any QAC system that combines multiple sources of candidates. We described features based on n-gram language models and convolutional neural networks with demonstrable improvements.

While we have shown significant improvements in MRR using synthetic candidate generation, we have not measured how often this approach generates semantically meaningless synthetic suggestions and have not quantified the effect of showing synthetic suggestions to search users. A user study on this aspect is left as future work. There is also further scope for exploring other language models (such as recurrent neural networks) in the context of this task.

Acknowledgements. The authors are grateful to Piotr Mirowski and Milad Shokouhi for the valuable discussions and their insightful feedback during the early stages of this work.

References

[1] Z. Bar-Yossef and N. Kraus. Context-sensitive query auto-completion. In *Proc. WWW*, pages 107–116, 2011.

[2] S. Bhatia, D. Majumdar, and P. Mitra. Query suggestions in the absence of query logs. In *Proc. SIGIR*, pages 795–804, 2011.

[3] S. Bickel, P. Haider, and T. Scheffer. Learning to complete sentences. In *Proc. ECML*, pages 497–504. Springer, 2005.

[4] S. Chaudhuri and R. Kaushik. Extending autocompletion to tolerate errors. In *Proc. SIGMOD*, pages 707–718, 2009.

[5] J. J. Darragh, I. H. Witten, and M. L. James. The reactive keyboard: A predictive typing aid. *Computer*, 23:41–49, November 1990.

[6] H. Duan and B.-J. P. Hsu. Online spelling correction for query completion. In *WWW '11*, pages 117–126, 2011.

[7] J. Fan, H. Wu, G. Li, and L. Zhou. Suggesting topic-based query terms as you type. In *Proc. APWEB*, pages 61–67, 2010.

[8] K. Grabski and T. Scheffer. Sentence completion. In *Proc. SIGIR*, pages 433–439, 2004.

[9] D. Hawking and K. Griffiths. An enterprise search paradigm based on extended query auto-completion. do we still need search and navigation? In *Proc. ADCS*, pages 18–25, 2013.

[10] P.-S. Huang, X. He, J. Gao, L. Deng, A. Acero, and L. Heck. Learning deep structured semantic models for web search using clickthrough data. In *Proc. CIKM*, pages 2333–2338. ACM, 2013.

[11] B. Mitra. Exploring session context using distributed representations of queries and reformulations. In *Proc. SIGIR*, To appear, 2015.

[12] B. Mitra, M. Shokouhi, F. Radlinski, and K. Hofmann. On user interactions with query auto-completion. In *Proc. SIGIR*, pages 1055–1058, 2014.

[13] A. Nandi and H. V. Jagadish. Effective phrase prediction. In *Proc. VLDB*, pages 219–230, Vienna, Austria, 2007.

[14] G. Pass, A. Chowdhury, and C. Torgeson. A picture of search. In *Proc. InfoScale*. ACM, 2006. ISBN 1-59593-428-6.

[15] Y. Shen, X. He, J. Gao, L. Deng, and G. Mesnil. Learning semantic representations using convolutional neural networks for web search. In *Proc. WWW*, pages 373–374, 2014.

[16] M. Shokouhi. Learning to personalize query auto-completion. In *Proc. SIGIR*, pages 103–112, 2013.

[17] R. W. White and G. Marchionini. Examining the effectiveness of real-time query expansion. *Inf. Process. Manage.*, 43: 685–704, May 2007.

[18] Q. Wu, C. Burges, K. Svore, and J. Gao. Adapting boosting for information retrieval measures. *Journal of Information Retrieval*, 13:254–270, 2009.

Pooled Evaluation Over Query Variations: Users are as Diverse as Systems

Alistair Moffat
The University of Melbourne,
Australia
ammoffat@unimelb.edu.au

Falk Scholer
RMIT University,
Australia
falk.scholer@rmit.edu.au

Paul Thomas
CSIRO,
Australia
paul.thomas@csiro.au

Peter Bailey
Microsoft,
Australia
pbailey@microsoft.com

ABSTRACT

Evaluation of information retrieval systems with test collections makes use of a suite of fixed resources: a document corpus; a set of topics; and associated judgments of the relevance of each document to each topic. With large modern collections, exhaustive judging is not feasible. Therefore an approach called *pooling* is typically used where, for example, the documents to be judged can be determined by taking the union of all documents returned in the top positions of the answer lists returned by a range of systems. Conventionally, pooling uses system variations to provide diverse documents to be judged for a topic; different user queries are not considered. We explore the ramifications of user query variability on pooling, and demonstrate that conventional test collections do not cover this source of variation. The effect of user query variation on the size of the judging pool is just as strong as the effect of retrieval system variation. We conclude that user query variation should be incorporated early in test collection construction, and cannot be considered effectively post hoc.

Categories and Subject Descriptors

H.3.3 [**Information Storage and Retrieval**]: Information Search and Retrieval—*performance evaluation.*

Keywords

User behavior, test collections, relevance measures

1. INTRODUCTION

Batch-mode system evaluation is used extensively in information retrieval system measurement. Compared to user studies in natural or laboratory settings, batch mode experimentation has two key advantages: first, the experiments are easily repeatable; and second, once the initial relevance judgments have been formed (assuming they are reusable), carrying out experiments typically imposes little additional cost, making the methodology cheaper overall. The key outcome of a batch evaluation experiment is a numeric measurement of system effectiveness averaged over the per-topic performance, using some form of effectiveness metric which represents the aggregate relevance of an answer list. They therefore provide a basis for repeatable longitudinal system evaluations.

Measures of system quality, in this approach, are determined from "relevance judgments" which specify, for each query and document, how good that document is for that query. In principle, these judgments cover all possible query–document pairs, but in practice it quickly becomes infeasible to judge all documents in response to a query, even for relatively small collections. To manage this cost, a technique known as *pooling* is used when relevance judgments are being created [9]. In this approach, each of the systems being measured (for example, in a shared evaluation task at an event such as TREC, NTCIR, CLEF, or FIRE) contributes a ranking of d (or more) documents, in decreasing order of predicted relevance. The union of the top-d sets is then identified, and those documents are the ones that are judged for relevance. This ensures that each system has at least its top-d documents judged (and possibly more). Extensive experimentation has shown that this approach tends to lead to an unbiased set of judgments, resulting in the same system ordering as would full evaluation [6, 15].

For the sake of reusability and reliability, pooling should cover possible sources of variation – for example, pools need to cover a large range of present (and anticipated) systems since different retrieval systems act differently and will retrieve different documents. The validity of scoring systems that didn't contribute to the original pool has been explored [4, 15]. For smaller collections, it was found that non-contributing systems are fairly evaluated when test collections are re-used; however, for large collections, where pools are small relative to the full collection, a bias may be introduced towards those documents that directly match query keywords [3].

Differences in the documents that retrieval systems return in response to a query are clearly reflected in batch evaluation. However, most further sources of variation are abstracted out of the process. For example, the usability of an interface is not considered, and a retrieval system is deemed to have completed its role when a ranked list of documents is produced. The interactions between a user and the list of document summaries are also ignored. Nor is user variability considered as a factor in the evaluation process – instead, standard queries are assumed, and a standard user response to the generated rankings is assumed, via the chosen effectiveness

Permission to make digital or hard copies of all or part of this work for personal or classroom use is granted without fee provided that copies are not made or distributed for profit or commercial advantage and that copies bear this notice and the full citation on the first page. Copyrights for components of this work owned by others than the author(s) must be honored. Abstracting with credit is permitted. To copy otherwise, or republish, to post on servers or to redistribute to lists, requires prior specific permission and/or a fee. Request permissions from Permissions@acm.org.
CIKM'15 October 19–23, 2015, Melbourne, VIC, Australia
Copyright is held by the owner/author(s). Publication rights licensed to ACM.
ACM 978-1-4503-3794-6/15/10 ... $15.00.
http://dx.doi.org/10.1145/2806416.2806606.

metric that is employed, as if every user that will ever use an IR system is a genetic and cultural clone of every other user. The only variable that is retained in most experimentation is the system, with the assumption that if a sufficiently representative set of queries is employed, system differences will be reliably identified.

In a recent study, we have explored the way in which users create queries from longer, multi-sentence topic descriptions [1], seeking to identify the role that the users' *a priori* expectations have on the way they react to the result listings that get generated, a project that builds on earlier investigations by Buckley and Walz [2] and Voorhees [11]. We use those variant user queries to investigate the impact of user variability on pool size; the data gathering process is described in Section 2. Our main research question, *"to what extent are query variants adequately covered by existing pooled relevance judgments?"*, is considered in Section 3. As our analysis shows, the answer is *"very little"* – query variants derived in a natural manner from a common information need description lead to markedly different sets of documents being retrieved. This result means that considerable care is required when designing batch-mode IR experiments, and that user variation is at least as important a factor in experimental design as system variability is.

2. TOPICS AND QUERIES

User Variability To analyze the impact of user variability, we constructed English-language information need statements, and asked participants to indicate what search query they would enter into a search engine to fulfill the stated information need. Starting with a selection of 180 TREC topics drawn from the 2002 Question Answering Track [12], the 2003 Robust Track [13], and the 2004 Terabyte Track [5], we created statements that represent scenario-based motivations for the corresponding TREC queries [1]. For example, the TREC topic R03.314 asks about the benefits of eating marine vegetation and is crystallized by the "title" query *"marine vegetation"*. This topic led us to create an information need statement: *"You recently heard a commercial about the health benefits of eating algae, seaweed and kelp. This made you interested in finding out about the positive uses of marine vegetation, both as a source of food, and as a potentially useful drug"*.

Crowd workers were then asked to read a subset of the statements in randomized order, and, for each information need, to indicate what their first query would be. An average of 44 responses were collected for each of 180 information needs, with a very broad range of queries generated. For example, the 47 responses to Topic R03.314 included eight instances of *"positive uses of marine vegetation"*, a phrase extracted directly from the information need statement; but there were also 37 other queries constructed, 35 of which occurred just once, including *"marine vegetation as food or drugs"* and *"edible seaweeds"*. Just one person issued the query *"marine vegetation"* that matched the TREC title query for the topic.

Our goal in this part of the project was to measure the extent to which the different queries that were submitted for the same information need retrieve documents that are not fetched by the canonical TREC title query. To do this, each query variant was executed using two standard retrieval mechanisms (Indri[1] implementations of Okapi BM25 [10] and the Sequential Dependency Model [7] ranking functions) to generate answer rankings. The rankings for each topic were then compared in two different ways, seeking to quantify the extent to which the rankings overlapped. For this investigation on pooling, we omit topics from the Question Answering track, primarily because the judging process was oriented towards identification of facts rather than ad hoc relevance labels.

[1] `www.lemurproject.org/indri`

Pool Size In the first approach, the size of the pool of documents that would need to be judged if all variant user queries were to be evaluated fairly by a depth-d effectiveness metric is computed, regardless of whether or not the TREC topic query is present in the set. For example, if $d = 10$, the set of 38 distinct queries generated for R03.314 places anywhere between 10 and 380 documents in to the judgment pool. In fact, over the 38 queries (from 47 crowd workers), a pool of 153 documents arises at $d = 10$, and 295 at $d = 20$. Full details of pool size as a function of d appear in Section 3.

Ranked List Similarity The second approach takes the canonical TREC topic-only query as a reference point, and computes the average divergence from that document ranking. To give appropriate weighting to the more highly ranked documents, and to allow for the fact that the pairs of lists are not necessarily permutations of each other (which is required to compute Kendall's tau), we employ the *Rank-Biased Overlap* computation (RBO) described by Webber et al. [14]. Rank-Biased Overlap quantifies the expected overlap observed by a probabilistic user who compares the two lists, advancing from depth d' to depth $d'+1$ with probability p. When $p = 0.95$, the value used in our experiments, the expected depth reached is $d' = 20$, but the measure is top weighted, and the greatest single contribution (with weight 0.05) arises at depth $d' = 1$, depending entirely on whether the two lists have the same first element. Hence, a high value of RBO indicates that the two lists are similar, at least to a user with the level of persistence p; conversely, low values of RBO indicate dissimilar or non-overlapping orderings.

Note there is no particular reason to suppose that the TREC topic-only query is more "correct" for the topic than is any of the (other) crowd-generated variants, and we use it as the reference point purely because it represents a default starting position. Any query could have been used as an anchor point for each topic; or all pairwise RBO scores could have been averaged. Our use of the TREC topic-only queries is primarily in deference to more than two decades of TREC-sponsored batch-mode retrieval experimentation; but also because these are the queries that have the most complete coverage in the TREC judgments created in the past.

3. USERS VERSUS SYSTEMS

Pool Size Figure 1 shows how total pool size grows as a function of the number of systems contributing to the pool for each topic (top), and of the number of users contributing to the pool for each topic (bottom), in both cases averaged across 60 topics selected from the TREC 2003 Robust Track (see Bailey et al. [1] for details of the topics). The "systems" are the 78 runs submitted by the TREC participants, taken in alphabetical order of run name, and are identical for each topic. In the lower graph, the horizontal axis represents queries as generated by "users" (crowd workers) based on the information need statements; they are ordered by workers' unique CrowdFlower ID. Repeat queries are included in the count, even though they do not increase the pool size. Note that the pool of users varies across topics, because most of the workers only processed a subset of the 60 selected topics.

The trend in Figure 1 is clear: for each of the pool depths d, the growth in total pool size follows the same trends as it does for systems. Both options give rise (very broadly) to straight lines on log-log graphs, as plotted, but with slightly different exponents: in the case of systems, the four lines are approximated by $v \approx dn^{0.5}$, where v is the volume of judgments, d is the pool depth, and n is the number of systems; in the case of users, the growth rate is higher, with $v \approx dn^{0.7}$. That is, for these users, and these systems, the pools that arise from a given number of users are larger than the pools that arise from the corresponding number of systems.

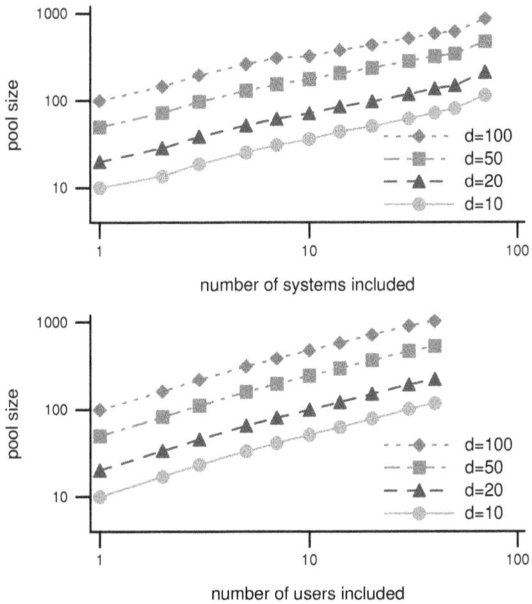

Figure 1: Pool size (average documents per topic) as a function of systems (top) and users (bottom), using 60 topics from the TREC 2003 Robust Track, and a range of pooling depths d. The "systems" are TREC runs, ordered (and included incrementally in the pool) alphabetically; the "users" are crowd workers, ordered (and included incrementally in the pool) by their CrowdFlower ID. The set of workers who created queries differs from topic to topic; in total, 92 workers contributed an average of 28.7 queries each.

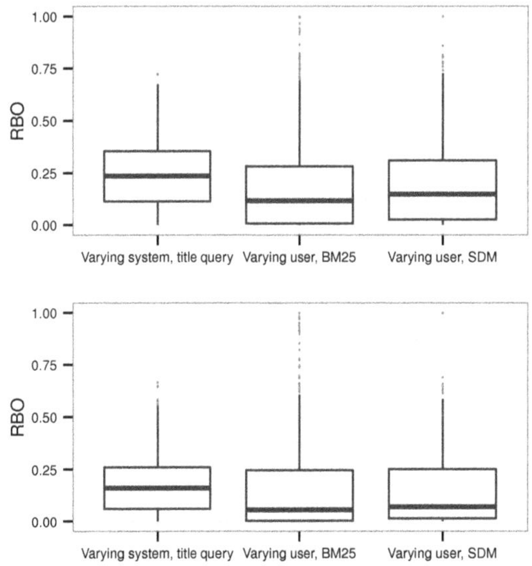

Figure 2: RBO comparisons between ranked lists for the TREC 2003 Robust Track (top), and the TREC 2004 Terabyte Track (bottom).

Ranked List Similarity Figure 2 shows the RBO scores for system-versus-system and user-versus-user comparisons for the TREC 2003 Robust Track and the TREC 2004 Terabyte Track. In this experiment the "systems" are TREC contributed runs that self-identified as having made use of title-only queries. In the case of the 2003 Robust Track, there were 8 runs used, across 60 topics and hence $60 \times 8 \times 7/2 = 1{,}680$ RBO scores computed. In the case of the 2004 Terabyte Track, the eight highest scoring title-only runs as identified by the Track organizers [5, Figure 6] were used, across 50 topics, and hence 1,400 RBO scores were generated. To compare "users", the sets of user queries for each topic were evaluated using the BM25 and SDM computations implemented in Indri, and then those runs compared against the TREC title-only run for that topic using the same computation. In the 2003 Robust Track, this yields 2,649 RBO scores; for the 2004 Terabyte Track, there are 2,222 RBO scores generated. Figure 2 plots the resulting RBO distributions. In both cases a one-sided Mann-Whitney U test indicates that the "varying user" RBO scores (with persistence parameter 0.95) were significantly lower than the "varying system" scores, at $p < 0.001$, further supporting our contention that user variability is at least as high as system variability.

Strategic Pooling Moffat et al. [8] suggest that if a limited judgments budget is available, documents in the pool could be ordered according to how much they reduce the total amount of imprecision in the measurement system as a whole. They do this in the context of weighted-precision effectiveness metrics – Rank-Biased Precision (RBP) in particular – by summing the "votes" for each document, and if J judgments can be carried out, identifying the J documents with the largest sums of weighted votes. The selection can be done on a topic-by-topic basis, or on a global all-topics basis.

Figure 3 shows how the 1,438 TREC relevance judgments for topic R03.314 would sit with this approach. Each of the user query variations was evaluated using Indri's Okapi BM25 computation, and a run of 200 documents created. Each document in each run was then assigned a weight depending on its position in the run, with the document at rank r given a weight of $(1-p)p^{r-1}$, with persistence parameter $p = 0.95$. The total weight of each document was the sum of the weight accorded that document in the 47 runs generated from the query variations, including repeats, or in the 78 system variations. To create the document ordering shown in the horizontal axes in the figure, the pool was then ordered by decreasing total weight, and plotted against minimum rank position, that is, the shallowest depth in any of the corresponding runs at which that document appeared. The correlation that shows is a consequence of the minimum RBP weight associated with each rank. A gray square is plotted for each document. The TREC relevance judgments are then overlaid – red crosses for the 1,394 documents judged as non-relevant, and black plus signs for the 44 documents judged relevant, for the first 1,000 documents in each of the two pools.

Tables 1 and 2 detail the relationship between the system-generated pools for the selected topics, the user-generated pools (using the Indri Okapi similarity rankings), and the existing TREC relevance judgments. In both data sets the user-generated pools have many more unjudged documents than the system-generated pools, further evidence that user variations give rise to quite different sets of documents being retrieved. In the rows labeled "combined", all system runs and all Okapi-based user runs are combined in a single pool. The fact that the combined pools are close in size to the sum of the two separate pools highlights the relatively disjoint nature of the respective sets of documents.

4. CONCLUSION

Our findings can be summarized simply: diversity in the pools of documents for judging arising from user variation is at least as substantial as that from system variation. We have also demonstrated that pools grow in size at a comparable rate in each case. Even when using the same system, different user queries typically produce very

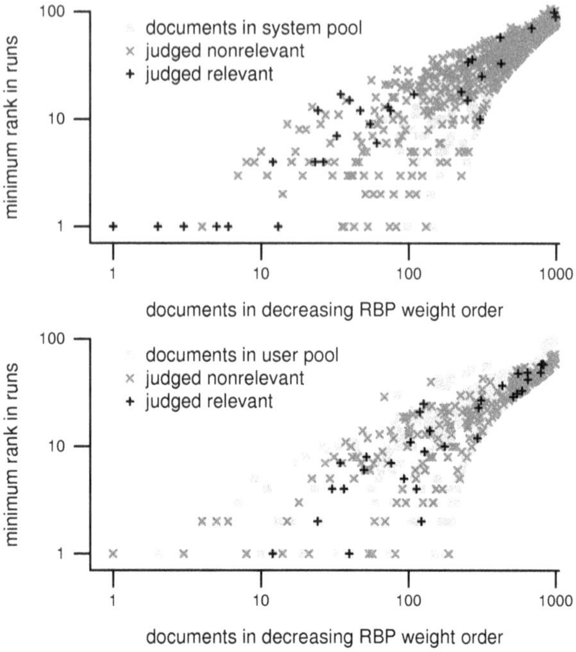

Figure 3: Depth of judged and unjudged documents for TREC 2003 Robust Track topic R03.314, pooled by systems (top), and users (bottom), covering the first 1,000 documents ordered by aggregate RBP weight. The horizontal axis orders documents by their summed RBP-like assessment weights when evaluated using BM25; the vertical axis shows the minimum rank of that document in any of the runs. The $d = 200$ pool for the 47 query variations for this query contains 3,292 documents; the $d = 200$ pool for the 78 system variations contains 2,131 documents.

Source	Depth	Size	Rele.	Irre.	Unjd.
TREC systems	$d = 20$	216.0	11.3%	74.0%	14.7%
(78 runs)	$d = 100$	883.1	5.5%	61.5%	32.9%
Users	$d = 20$	240.5	10.3%	45.8%	43.9%
(44.2 avg.)	$d = 100$	1110.9	4.5%	32.3%	63.3%
Combined	$d = 20$	394.7	8.5%	56.3%	35.2%
(122.2 avg.)	$d = 100$	1701.2	3.6%	39.2%	57.2%

Table 1: Fraction of pool covered by existing judgments, averaged over 60 TREC 2003 Robust Track topics evaluated using BM25. The judgments for these topics were created in 1998, 1999, 2000, and 2003, with the 2003 runs not re-judged against the earlier topics, see Voorhees [13].

different ranked lists. Finally, we have shown that incorporating user variation cannot be a post-hoc exercise, after a collection has been created in a conventional manner using variation solely from systems. There are substantially larger sets of unjudged documents from new "user runs" than existing "system runs", and these can occur high in rankings. Examining combined pools, we found that approximately one third of documents are unjudged at a pool depth of 20, and more than half are unjudged at depth 100.

We conclude that user variation should be designed in when creating test collections, by collecting different query responses to specific information needs, and that this would lead to more representative sets of documents being judged. In future work, we plan to investigate building just such a test collection. The collection will allow us to examine various aspects of relevance evaluation, when using both a diversity of systems and a diversity of users.

Source	Depth	Size	Rele.	Irre.	Unjd.
TREC systems	$d = 20$	445.7	22.4%	63.0%	14.6%
(70 runs)	$d = 100$	1912.9	11.6%	49.0%	39.4%
Users	$d = 20$	236.7	25.4%	28.6%	46.0%
(44.4 avg.)	$d = 100$	974.7	14.3%	22.0%	63.7%
Combined	$d = 20$	607.7	19.3%	51.6%	29.1%
(114.4 avg.)	$d = 100$	2527.8	9.1%	38.3%	52.6%

Table 2: Fraction of available pool covered by existing judgments, averaged over 50 TREC 2004 Terabyte Track topics evaluated using the BM25 retrieval mechanism. The original judging for these topics covered a subset of the 70 runs submitted to the Track, and to a depth of $d = 85$ [5].

Acknowledgment This work was supported by the Australian Research Council's *Discovery Projects* Scheme (projects DP110101934 and DP140102655). We thank Xiaolu Lu, who generated all of the user runs. This work was approved by the CSIRO Human Research Ethics Committee, ref. 077/14.

References

[1] P. Bailey, A. Moffat, F. Scholer, and P. Thomas. User variability and IR system evaluation. In *Proc. SIGIR*, 2015.

[2] C. Buckley and J. Walz. The TREC-8 query track. In *Proc. TREC*, 1999.

[3] C. Buckley, D. Dimmick, I. Soboroff, and E. Voorhees. Bias and the limits of pooling for large collections. *J. Inf. Ret.*, 10(6):491–508, 2007.

[4] S. Büttcher, C. L. Clarke, P. C. Yeung, and I. Soboroff. Reliable information retrieval evaluation with incomplete and biased judgements. In *Proc. SIGIR*, pages 63–70, 2007.

[5] C. L. A. Clarke, N. Craswell, and I. Soboroff. Overview of the TREC 2004 terabyte track. In *Proc. TREC*, 2004.

[6] D. Harman. The TREC test collections. In E. M. Voorhees and D. K. Harman, editors, *TREC: Experiment and Evaluation in Information Retrieval*, chapter 2, pages 21–52. MIT Press, 2005.

[7] D. Metzler and W. B. Croft. A Markov random field model for term dependencies. In *Proc. SIGIR*, pages 472–479, 2005.

[8] A. Moffat, W. Webber, and J. Zobel. Strategic system comparisons via targeted relevance judgments. In *Proc. SIGIR*, pages 375–382, 2007.

[9] K. Sparck Jones and C. J. van Rijsbergen. Report on the need for and the provision of an "ideal" information retrieval test collection. Technical report, Computer Laboratory, University of Cambridge, 1975. British Library Research and Development Report No. 5266.

[10] K. Sparck Jones, S. Walker, and S. E. Robertson. A probabilistic model of information retrieval: development and comparative experiments. Part 1. *Inf. Proc. Man.*, 36(6):779–808, 2000.

[11] E. M. Voorhees. Variations in relevance judgments and the measurement of retrieval effectiveness. *Inf. Proc. Man.*, 36(5):697–716, 2000.

[12] E. M. Voorhees. Overview of the TREC 2002 question answering track. In *Proc. TREC*, 2002.

[13] E. M. Voorhees. Overview of the TREC 2003 robust retrieval track. In *Proc. TREC*, 2003.

[14] W. Webber, A. Moffat, and J. Zobel. A similarity measure for indefinite rankings. *ACM Trans. Inf. Sys.*, 28(4):20.1–20.38, 2010.

[15] J. Zobel. How reliable are the results of large-scale information retrieval experiments? In *Proc. SIGIR*, pages 307–314, 1998.

The Influence of Pre-processing on the Estimation of Readability of Web Documents

João Palotti
Vienna University of Techonlogy
Vienna, Austria
palotti@ifs.tuwien.ac.at

Guido Zuccon
Queensland University of Technology
Brisbane, Australia
g.zuccon@qut.edu.au

Allan Hanbury
Vienna University of Techonlogy
Vienna, Austria
hanbury@ifs.tuwien.ac.at

ABSTRACT

This paper investigates the effect that text pre-processing approaches have on the estimation of the readability of web pages. Readability has been highlighted as an important aspect of web search result personalisation in previous work. The most widely used text readability measures rely on surface level characteristics of text, such as the length of words and sentences. We demonstrate that different tools for extracting text from web pages lead to very different estimations of readability. This has an important implication for search engines because search result personalisation strategies that consider users reading ability may fail if incorrect text readability estimations are computed.

Categories and Subject Descriptors: H.3 [Information Systems]: Information Storage and Retrieval
General Terms: Algorithms, Experimentation.
Keywords: Readability, Text pre-processing

1. INTRODUCTION

Search result personalisation is an area of active research within information retrieval [5]. User location, their search history, time the query is issued and type of device used to query are among the many features that current web search engines use to contextualize and personalise the search, aiming to increase the user's satisfaction with the retrieved results. In this paper we investigate one important contextual aspect: the readability of information as presented to users.

The readability of a document is often referred to as the the minimal required level of knowledge to comprehend the text, often measured using the U.S. grade level system. For example, a text with a score of 1 would be suitable for a 6-7 year old child, while a score of 13 requires the knowledge of a freshman undergrad student. In general, the higher the readability score, the harder it is to understand the text.

Within information retrieval, using readability as a way to personalise search results has received substantial attention [3, 15, 18, 9, 17]. For example, Collins-Thompson et al. [3] have investigated methods for estimating user proficiency and readability of results, as well as for re-ranking results according to this information. In health web search, accounting for the readability of the retrieved information is a core requirement to effectively support users (see for example [16]). Health consumers may have a limited understanding of the medical terminology and processes, and thus they should be shown text that is simple to understand and limits expert terminology. Notwithstanding, if experts were to query, the search engine should instead provide more advanced material and detailed information.

Numerous studies have proposed and analysed methods to accurately measure the level of knowledge required to read a text [4]. While recent research has proposed sophisticated readability estimation methods [3, 7], often tailored to specific domains [17], traditional readability measures such as the Automated Readability Index and the Gunning Fog Index are extensively used for assessing information on the web (see for example [16, 18]). These long-established readability measures consider the surface level of the text contained in web pages, that is, the wording and the syntax of sentences. In this framework, the presence of long sentences, words containing many syllables and unpopular words, are all indicators of difficult text to read.

Because traditional readability measures are based on surface level characteristics of text, the accurate parsing of web pages is fundamental to ensure readability is accurately estimated and taken into account for search result personalisation. For example, text contained in different HTML fields, tables, lists, etc., should be adequately processed so as to determine the wording and the syntax of sentences, including sentence length. This pre-processing step is often omitted or simplified (see for example [18]) and the influence of parsing errors on the readability estimation of web pages is unknown. On the other hand, the cleansing of web pages' text has been recognised as an important issue in linguistics and language technology research [1].

In this work we contribute an understanding of:

- how different pre-processing steps influence the estimation of web pages' readability;
- how pre-processing affects the order relations between documents produced by readability measures.

2. READABILITY MEASURES

In this paper we consider a number of traditional readability measures to study how web page pre-processing affects the corresponding estimations of readability. More recent and sophisticated readability measures are not considered

Permission to make digital or hard copies of all or part of this work for personal or classroom use is granted without fee provided that copies are not made or distributed for profit or commercial advantage and that copies bear this notice and the full citation on the first page. Copyrights for components of this work owned by others than ACM must be honored. Abstracting with credit is permitted. To copy otherwise, or republish, to post on servers or to redistribute to lists, requires prior specific permission and/or a fee. Request permissions from Permissions@acm.org.

CIKM'15, October 19–23, 2015, Melbourne, Australia.

Copyright is held by the owner/author(s). Publication rights licensed to ACM.
© 2015 ACM. ISBN 978-1-4503-3794-6/15/10 ...$15.00.

DOI: http://dx.doi.org/10.1145/2806416.2806613.

here because they usually introduce additional complexity to the estimation process and thus introduce more degrees of variation which are difficult to control for and compare across. For example, Yan's et al. [17] measure requires access to a domain knowledge resource and a method to map text to named entities in such resource.

The readability measures we consider are listed in Table 1; To estimate readability, these measures take into account the surface level of text (i.e., the wording and the syntax of sentences). We do not consider the Dale-Chall and the Flesch Reading Ease (FRE) measures, which share similarities with the measures in Table 1, as their readability score scales widely differ from that of the others, and thus make their comparison more difficult to interpret. An easier way to compare different metrics was also one motivation to update the FRE formula to the FKGL [10].

There are two main factors that have been identified as affecting the user perception of text difficulty and that thus characterise the readability measures of Table 1:

Word Length: short words are commonly used and understood, while long words are usually rare, harder to read, write and remember. This factor is measured by expressions such as $\frac{Sy}{W}$, $\frac{C}{W}$ and $\frac{PW}{W}$.

Sentence Length: while short sentences are usually simple, long ones are usually complex, demanding more cognitive processing and attention. This factor is measured by the average words per sentence, i.e., $\frac{W}{S}$.

Each measure differs from the others in the way these factors are combined, usually via a coefficient that has been tuned through comprehensive readability experiments [4].

Web pages contain text strings that do not belong to the information content of pages, but are instead used to format, structure and layout (e.g., tags) and to embed functionalities (e.g., scripts). The presence of these strings affect both word length and sentence length. While the use of HTML parsers allow to remove all strings not associated with the actual informative content of the pages (and thus reducing the errors in estimating word lengths), the estimation of sentence lengths is heavily affected by how the text is extracted from web pages, as we show with a concrete example in Section 3. This is because web pages are rich in tables, menus, lists, figures, captions, titles and subtitles: these are often part of the information content of the pages, but do not follow the expected structure of a sentence as assumed by the traditional readability measures. For example, often titles, menus and lists do not end with a punctuation mark that delimits the end of the sentence. In this paper we determine the effects that different ways of pre-processing web pages to extract the text associated with their information content have on the estimation of readability scores.

It is interesting to note that, already in the 1960s, the precise identification of sentence boundaries was a topic of concern for evaluating the readability of text. For example, Smith and Senter [14], authors of the Automated Readability Index (ARI), recommend typists to add to the end of each sentence an equal sign, aligned with a full stop, so as to explicitly demarcate sentence boundaries.

Table 1: Five of the most used readability measures. W is the number of words in the text, Sy the number of syllables, S the number of sentences, C the number of characters, PW the number of polysyllables words (words with more than 3 syllables).

Automated Readability Index (ARI) [14]

$$ARI = 4.71 \times \frac{C}{W} + 0.5 \times \frac{W}{S} - 21.43$$

Coleman-Liau Index (CLI) [2]

$$CLI = 5.89 \times \frac{C}{W} - (30.0 \times \frac{S}{W}) - 15.8$$

Flesch-Kincaid Grade Level (FKGL) [10]

$$FKGL = 0.39 \times \frac{W}{S} + 11.8 \times \frac{Sy}{W} - 15.59$$

Gunning Fog Index (GFI) [8]

$$GFI = 0.4 * (\frac{W}{S} + 100.0 \times \frac{PW}{W})$$

Simple Measure of Gobbledygook (SMOG) [12]

$$SMOG = 1.0430 * \sqrt{PW \times \frac{30.0}{S}} + 3.1291$$

3. PRE-PROCESSING OF WEB PAGES

Before it is possible to estimate the readability of web pages, it is required to remove the HTML tags and the boilerplate text, so as to maintain only the text associated with the information content of the web pages. One approach to perform this text cleansing process is to use standard HTML parsing tools such as JSoup[1] for Java or Beautiful Soup[2] for Python. We used Beautiful Soup version 4.3.2, and we term this approach as **Naïve**.

We also consider two open sourced tools developed specifically for removing the boilerplate from HTML pages: **Boilerpipe** [11] and **Justext** [13]. We used the Python version 1.2.0.0 of Boilerpipe[3] and version 2.1.1 of Justext[4].

Figure 1 shows the output of the *Naïve* approach applied to the fist paragraph of a web page from Wikipedia. The extracted text often presents an interesting characteristic: it lacks the punctuation marks to delimit the sentence boundaries. This has a clear effect on the readability measures that consider sentence length as an indication of text difficulty. To better understand the effect of this, we explore two possible approaches:

1. a sentence boundary (full stop) is added at the end of a line if no punctuation mark is found, resulting in **Short** sentences;
2. no sentence boundary is added, possibly resulting in **Long** sentences.

Note that the *Naïve-Short* approach is often used when processing web pages to automatically estimate readability measures, see for example [18].

4. READABILITY EVALUATION

To better understand the impact that parsing methods and approaches to sentence boundaries have when processing web pages, we consider the CLEF 2014 eHealth Task 3 collection, along with the 50 topics used in 2014 [6]. This collection contains web pages related to the medical domain and is used as a resource to evaluate search engines tailored to health consumers. We use this collection because of the importance the readability (and, more generally, the understandability) of web pages presenting medical advice has within consumer health search [16, 18].

[1] `http://jsoup.org`

[2] `https://pypi.python.org/pypi/beautifulsoup4`

[3] `https://pypi.python.org/pypi/boilerpipe`

[4] `https://pypi.python.org/pypi/jusText`

```
<body class="mediawiki page-Readability skin-vector action-view">
        <div id="siteNotice"><!-- CentralNotice --></div>
        <h1 id="firstHeading" class="firstHeading" lang="en">Readability</h1>
        <div id="siteSub">From Wikipedia, the free encyclopedia</div>
        <div id="jump-to-nav" class="mw-jump"> Jump to:  <a href="#mw-head">navigation</a>, <a href="#p-search">search</a> </div>
        <div id="mw-content-text" lang="en" dir="ltr" class="mw-content-ltr">
            <p>Readability</b> is the ease with which a text can be understood.
        </div>
</body>
```

```
CentralNotice
Readability
From Wikipedia, the free encyclopedia
Jump to: navigation, search
Readability is the ease with which a text can be understood.
```

```
CentralNotice.
Readability.
From Wikipedia, the free encyclopedia.
Jump to: navigation, search.
Readability is the ease with which a text can be understood.
```

Figure 1: Simplified Wikipedia entry for Readability (top) and the output of *Naïve* (bottom). In the bottom part, we show the result of the pre-processing approach termed *Long* (left), which does not modify the text extracted by the HTML parser, and that of the alternative pre-processing approach termed *Short* (right), which adds a full stop as sentence boundary at the end of every line. The *Long* approach concatenates all the text till it reaches a sentence boundary, producing longer sentences than the *Short* one.

Table 2: Number of words and sentences (mean and standard deviation) for documents CLEF 2014 eHealth Task 3 collection, as obtained by the three pre-processing tools and the two approaches to sentence boundaries (see Section 3).

Tool	# Words	# Sentences	
		Short	Long
Naïve	1001.5 ± 2062	137.2 ± 443	37.9 ± 93
Boilerpipe	364.2 ± 884	24.4 ± 55	18.6 ± 49
Justext	409.9 ± 1403	24.4 ± 82	19.4 ± 68

Table 2 reports the average number of words and sentences in the CLEF 2014 collection as extracted by the different pre-processing methods. These statistics are at the basis of the readability measures of Table 1. From the table, we can observe that the *Naïve* method produces one order of magnitude more words and sentences (except when using *Long*) than the other two methods. While small, the differences between *Boilerpipe* and *Justext* are still significant in that they can influence the estimations of readability measures. Similarly, the use of the *Short* approach for sentence boundary rather than the *Long* produces significant differences among all text pre-processing approaches.

We use the default vector space retrieval model of Apache Lucene 4.8 to retrieve the top 1,000 documents per query, using the query titles of the topics in the CLEF 2014 collection. For each query, we compute the readability scores of the retrieved documents according to the different settings considered here in terms of pre-processing tools and the approaches to sentence boundaries.

Figure 2 reports the mean values of readability scores averaged over the 50 topics for each combination of pre-processing and sentence boundary approaches. The results suggest that the choice of approach to use for sentence boundary has a significant influence on readability measures: the variance between the readability scores obtained with *Long* and *Short* is large across all methods, apart for CLI that appears to be the most robust readability formula in this aspect. For example, when using the *Naïve* pre-processing method, the mean readability score of ARI can vary more than 100%, from 10.9 ± 0.4, when using *Short* sentences to 22.5 ± 1.8, when using *Long* sentences. This high variability in the estimation of readability measures influences the conclusions one would infer about the difficulty of the retrieved documents: pages that could be readable by high school students (grade 11) – when sentence boundaries are detected with *Short* – become suddenly intractable for people with level of education below that of a PhD student (grade 22) – according to the readability measures computed using the *Long* method. In addition, note that different pre-processing methods (i.e., *Naïve*, *Boilerpipe*, *Justext*) lead to different conclusions about the readability of text. For example, Figure 2 suggests that, when ARI is used as readability measure and the *Long* approach is employed to identify sentence boundaries, *Naïve* and *Justext* provide contrasting results, with the mean readability of text assessed as being 22.5 ± 1.8 according to *Naïve* and 14.1 ± 0.6 according to *Justext*. These results highlight the significance that choices of pre-processing tool and sentence boundary identification approach have on the estimation of readability scores for web pages, when using the commonly adopted readability measures considered in this study.

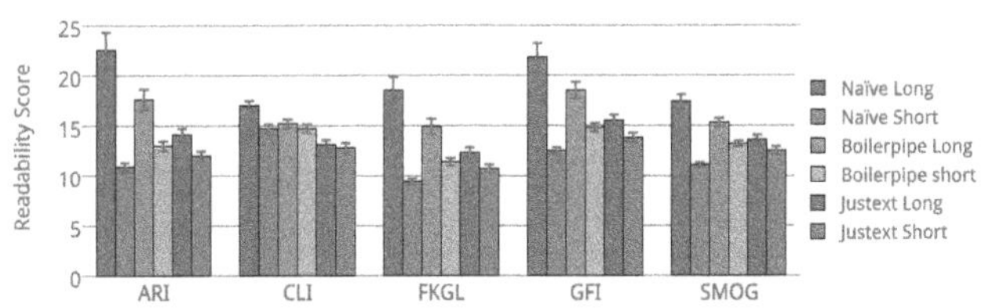

Figure 2: Readability scores for each measure based on different pre-processing and sentence boundary methods. Error bars indicate 95% confidence intervals around the mean.

The results in Figure 2 also suggest that CLI is the most stable readability measure among those considered in this paper. In particular, variations in pre-processing tool and sentence boundary identification have little impact on the estimated readability scores for this measure. The stability of CLI is due to the fact that $W \gg S$ and thus $\frac{S}{W} < 0$, dampening the effect of the relation between the number of words and sentences (in our experiments, $1 < 30.0 \times \frac{S}{W} < 4$), and ensuring stability across different values of S. This is unlike measures such as ARI, where $3 < 0.5 \times \frac{W}{S} < 13$.

Next, we consider how similar document rankings obtained from readability measure estimations are when using different pre-processing and sentence boundary approaches. This is interesting for information retrieval because it is often these differences between rankings, rather than the actual absolute value of the readability estimation, that are used to demote or promote web pages when taking into ac-

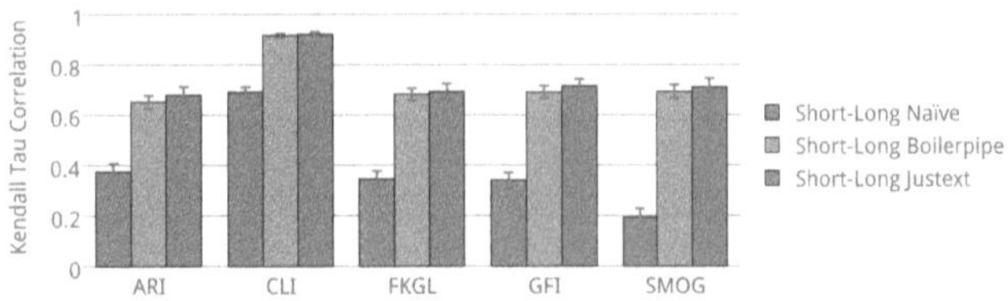

Figure 3: Kendall τ correlation and 95% confidence intervals between the *Short* and *Long* approaches for sentence boundary identification.

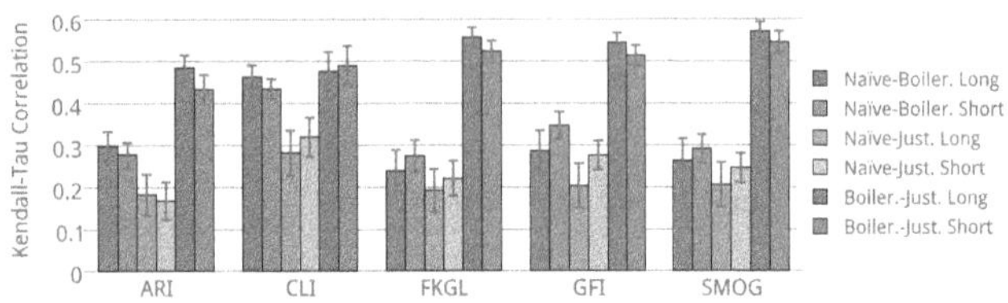

Figure 4: Kendall τ correlation and 95% confidence intervals between the approaches for HTML pre-processing, under different settings for sentence boundary identification.

count reading levels. For example, a high correlation between two different pre-processing settings would suggest that, although the actual readability scores may be very different, the preference ordering obtained by the readability measures (i.e., the ranking according to readability scores) are similar and therefore these two pre-processing settings would lead to little difference in terms of impact on retrieval.

To this aim, we consider the Kendall τ ranking correlation between different settings of sentence boundary identification (Figure 3) and pre-processing tool (Figure 4).

Figure 3 shows that, independently of the pre-processing tool used, the correlation between *Long* and *Short* rankings obtained when using *Boilerpipe* or *Justext* as pre-processing tools is generally high, with the maximum achieved using CLI ($\tau = 0.92 \pm 0.01$). However, if the *Naïve* approach to text pre-processing is used, then correlations deteriorate, with the SMOG measure exhibiting only marginal correlation ($\tau = 0.20 \pm 0.03$). CLI exhibits the least variance in correlation among the three pre-processing approaches (and indeed, the highest correlations) – a stability that was already observed when analysing Figure 2.

The results of Figure 4 suggest that different pre-processing tools produce different document rankings (when using readability to rank). Specifically, the highest correlation between two of these tools is achieved by the *Boilerpipe-Justext* pair – but these exhibit correlations of *only* about 0.5, independently of the readability measure or the sentence boundary approach (the highest correlation is achieved for SMOG by *Boilerpipe-Justext* using *Long*: $\tau = 0.57 \pm 0.02$). When comparing these methods to the *Naïve* approach, correlation sensibly decreases (apart for CLI that once again shows the smallest difference between settings).

5. CONCLUSION

This paper analysed the influence pre-processing and sentence boundary identification choices have on the estimation of readability measures for web pages. The experimental results show that these choices have a large impact on the estimation of readability scores, which in turn can drastically influence the order relations among documents that can be obtained from the readability scores. Our findings suggest that attention should be put on the choice of pre-processing settings when measuring readability for web pages. Advanced HTML cleansing tools such as *Boilerpipe* and *Justext* provide more stable results across settings. In addition, the use of the Coleman-Liau Index (CLI) as readability measure leads to the most stable results across choices of pre-processing tools and sentence boundary identification strategies (although we could not assess the quality of CLI for correctly estimating the readability of documents). In future work, we plan to study which combination of pre-processing settings and readability measure lead to estimations of readability that most agree with user assessments. The data and source code used in this work can be found online at: `https://github.com/joaopalotti/cikm_readability_2015`.

ACKNOWLEDGMENTS.

JP and AH are supported in part by the European Union Seventh Framework Programme (FP7/2007-2013) n°257528 (KHRESMOI), by Horizon 2020 program (H2020-ICT-2014-1) n°644753 (KCONNECT), and by the Austrian Science Fund (FWF) n°I1094-N23 (MUCKE).

6. REFERENCES

[1] M. Baroni, F. Chantree, A. Kilgarriff, and S. Sharoff. Cleaneval: a competition for cleaning web pages. In *LREC*, 2008.

[2] M. Coleman and T. L. Liau. A Computer Readability Formula Designed for Machine Scoring. *JAP*, 1975.

[3] K. Collins-Thompson, P. N. Bennett, R. W. White, S. de la Chica, and D. Sontag. Personalizing Web Search Results by Reading Level. In *CIKM*, 2011.

[4] W. H. Dubay. The principles of readability. *Costa Mesa, CA: Impact Information*, 2004.

[5] S. Dumais. Putting searchers into search. In *SIGIR*, 2014.

[6] L. Goeuriot, L. Kelly, et al. Share/clef ehealth evaluation lab 2014, task 3: User-centred health information retrieval. In *Working Notes of CLEF*, 2014.

[7] A. Graesser, D. McNamara, M. Louwerse, and Z. Cai. Coh-Metrix: Analysis of Text on Cohesion and Language. *Behav Res Meth Instrum Comput*, 2004.

[8] R. Gunning. *The Technique of Clear Writing.* McGraw-Hill, 1952.

[9] A. Jatowt and K. Tanaka. Is wikipedia too difficult?: Comparative analysis of readability of wikipedia, simple wikipedia and britannica. In *CIKM*, 2012.

[10] J. Kincaid, R. Fishburne, R. Rogers, and B. Chissom. Derivation of New Readability Formulas for Navy Enlisted Personnel. Technical report, 1975.

[11] C. Kohlschütter, P. Fankhauser, and W. Nejdl. Boilerplate detection using shallow text features. In *WSDM*, 2010.

[12] G. H. McLaughlin. SMOG Grading - a New Readability Formula. *Journal of Reading*, 1969.

[13] J. Pomikálek. *Removing Boilerplate and Duplicate Content from Web Corpora.* PhD thesis, 2011.

[14] E. A. Smith and R. J. Senter. Automated Readability Index. Technical report, 1967.

[15] C. Tan, E. Gabrilovich, and B. Pang. To Each His Own: Personalized Content Selection based on Text Comprehensibility. In *WSDM*, 2012.

[16] R. C. Wiener and R. Wiener-Pla. Literacy, pregnancy and potential oral health changes: The internet and readability levels. *Maternal and child health journal*, 2013.

[17] X. Yan, D. Song, and X. Li. Concept-based document readability in domain specific information retrieval. In *CIKM'06*, 2006.

[18] G. Zuccon and B. Koopman. Integrating Understandability in the Evaluation of Consumer Health Search Engines. In *MedIR*, 2014.

Atypical Queries in eCommerce

Neeraj Pradhan
Search and Data Mining
Groupon
npradhan@groupon.com

Vinay Deolalikar
Search and Data Mining
Groupon
vdeolalikar@groupon.com

Kang Li
Search and Data Mining
Groupon
kli@groupon.com

ABSTRACT

Understanding how specific, ambiguous, or broad the intent of a search query is, across all users of the system, is important in improving search relevance in eCommerce. There is scant literature on such a structural characterization of queries in eCommerce. In this paper, we use query-click log data to address the problem of identifying "atypical queries": these are queries that are extremal in terms of specificity, ambiguity, or breadth of intent. We isolate three components of atypicality: geometric, statistical, and topological. We demonstrate, using query-click logs at Groupon, that certain *combinations* of these properties render a query atypical, and discuss how search analysts treat such queries differently. Our work is being used to improve search relevance at Groupon.

Categories and Subject Descriptors

H.3.3 [**Information Storage and Retrieval**]: Information Search and Retrieval—*search process; relevance feedback*

Keywords

eCommerce search; atypical queries; query intent disambiguation

1. INTRODUCTION

eCommerce is one of the cornerstones of the internet age. As of 2013, the global eCommerce business-to-consumer market was valued at USD 1.3 Trillion. eCommerce companies devote a large amount of effort in trying to gain structural insights about user intent for high-volume queries. In particular, they are highly interested in the specificity, breadth, and ambiguity associated with a query. Understanding these properties of a query allows them to show an appealing result set to their users. It also enables them to personalize this result set based on user attributes. Finally, such an understanding powers alternative product recommendations made to users who have issued the query.

Although characterizing queries in the manner described above requires intensive effort, often with a significant manual component, there is scant literature on this problem. In contrast, the problem of understanding query ambiguity (and its relationship to query performance) is an active field in text document retrieval.

In this paper, we address this gap. We consider the research question of automatically identifying queries that are extremal in each of the aforementioned aspects: namely, queries that are highly specific, or very broad, or highly ambiguous. We call such queries *atypical queries*. Furthermore, we would like to identify atypical queries with very little manual intervention or inspection, except for an initial configuration of our system.

The hurdle to answering our research questions lies in extracting notions of typicality that are *general* enough to capture aggregate user behavior. Our approach is to *bootstrap out notions of typicality from query-click data, without external knowledge*. This makes our methods completely general. We demonstrate our approach on a dataset of six months of query logs from the Groupon site.

Our contributions are outlined below.

1. We introduce research on a broad structural understanding of queries in eCommerce.
2. We provide a theoretical framework for identifying queries that are atypical in specificity, breadth, or ambiguity.
3. Our framework considers three aspects of a query-click distribution: geometric, statistical, and topological. We show that certain *combinations* of these aspects render a query atypical. We provide examples of atypical queries.
4. The three properties above, being inherent to the query-click distribution, represent structural knowledge that can be used more generally.

2. KEY IDEA

Users interact with eCommerce sites primarily through searches. A specific search is called a *query* and may consist of one or more terms (e.g. "adidas" or "Apple iMac"). Each product in the inventory is placed into one or more *categories* in the product taxonomy (e.g. men's shoes or electronics, for the previous examples). Let us assume that we are studying the set of all queries $\mathscr{Q} = \{Q_1, Q_2, \ldots, Q_m\}$ made over a specific period of time. Let the set of categories in the product taxonomy be $\mathscr{C} = \{C_1, C_2, \ldots, C_n\}$.

When a user makes a query, and then clicks on products in the result set, these clicks are recorded against the categories that the products are in. For each query, we aggregate these user clicks over a certain time period. These aggregated clicks, when normalized, form a distribution over categories. For example, the query "vintage" might result in a bimodal distribution, with peaks over the categories "wine stores" and "auto parts." Some formal definitions are in order.

Definition 1. The *signature* of a query $Q_i \in \mathscr{Q}$, is denoted by $\text{sign}(Q_i)$, and defined as the vector $\mathbf{w}_i = (w_{i1}, \ldots, w_{in})$, where w_{ij} is the ag-

Permission to make digital or hard copies of all or part of this work for personal or classroom use is granted without fee provided that copies are not made or distributed for profit or commercial advantage and that copies bear this notice and the full citation on the first page. Copyrights for components of this work owned by others than the author(s) must be honored. Abstracting with credit is permitted. To copy otherwise, or republish, to post on servers or to redistribute to lists, requires prior specific permission and/or a fee. Request permissions from Permissions@acm.org.
CIKM'15, October 19–23, 2015, Melbourne, Australia.
Copyright is held by the owner/author(s). Publication rights licensed to ACM.
ACM 978-1-4503-3794-6/15/10 ...$15.00.
DOI: http://dx.doi.org/10.1145/2806416.2806605 .

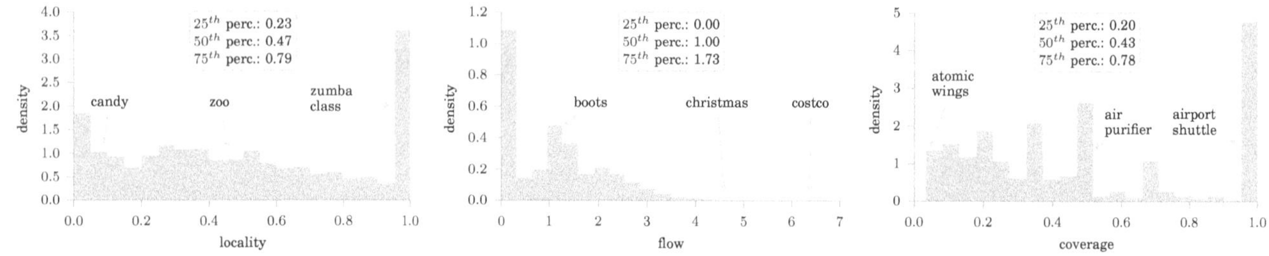

Figure 1: Distributions of locality, flow, and coverage for queries in Groupon_QL. Also shown are quartile values, and examples of some queries and where they lie in the distribution.

gregate number of clicks on (products of) category C_j, generated by query Q_i.

The signature $\text{sign}(Q_i)$ can be converted into a probability distribution over $\mathscr{C}$ by normalizing by $\sum_{j=1}^{j=n} w_{ij}$. We refer to this as the *normalized signature*. To keep notation light, we use the same symbols for the signature and the normalized signature.

Definition 2. The *support of a query* Q_i is defined as

$$\text{supp}(Q_i) = \{C_j \colon w_{ij} \neq 0\}.$$

Namely, it is the set of categories where the query Q_i has a non-zero signature.

Definition 3. The set of signatures for all $Q \in \mathscr{Q}$ is called the *query-category click model.*

The key idea that guides our approach is the following.

> Certain combinations of properties of the query's signature, relative to that of the query-category click model as a whole, mark the query as being atypical.

The question now is: what are these properties of the query's signature? Based on our extensive collaboration with search analysts at Groupon, we have identified three properties that we call *locality, flow, and coverage.* These are formalized in the next section.

3. THEORETICAL FRAMEWORK

In this section, we build a mathematical framework in which the ideas of the previous section can be precisely expressed.

3.1 Signatures, Similarity, and Closure

In order to define the quantities of our interest, it will help to place some preliminary definitions.

Definition 4. Let w_{ij} be the aggregate number of clicks generated by Q_i that go to category C_j in the query-category click model (Def. 3). The *signature of a category* C_j is defined as

$$\text{sign}(C_j) = (w_{1j}, \ldots, w_{mj}).$$

Definition 5. The *similarity* between two categories C_i and C_j is defined as the cosine similarity of their query signatures.

$$\text{sim}(C_i, C_j) = \cos\left(\text{sign}(C_i), \text{sign}(C_j)\right).$$

Definition 6. The *closure* of a category C_i, w.r.t. a threshold T is defined as follows:

$$\text{closure}(C_i) = \{C_j \colon \text{sim}(C_i, C_j) > T\}.$$

The value of T is determined empirically based on the application, and is suppressed in order to keep notation light.

3.2 Locality, Flow, and Coverage

Locality (Geometric).

Definition 7. The *locality of a query* is the average of the pairwise similarities of the categories in its support. Namely,

$$\text{locality}(Q) = \text{avg}\{\text{sim}(C_i, C_j) \colon C_i, C_j \in \text{supp}(Q) \text{ and } C_i \neq C_j\}.$$

If $|\text{supp}(Q)| = 1$, then $\text{locality}(Q) = 1$ by definition.

Locality is a geometric notion: it measures *distances* between the categories in $\text{supp}(Q)$. These distances are, in turn, based on the aggregate query-click log. Namely, two categories are "close" when many queries have clicks that distribute over both categories.

Flow (Statistical).

We refer the reader to [2] for a detailed treatment of entropy.

Definition 8. The (information-theoretic) *entropy* of a discrete probability distribution P, whose masses are $\{p_i\}$, is defined as

$$\text{entropy}(P) = -\sum_i p_i \log_2(p_i).$$

Definition 9. The *flow* for a query is defined as the entropy of its normalized signature.

$$\text{flow}(Q) = \text{entropy}(\text{sign}(Q)).$$

Flow is a statistical notion: it measures how "evenly" the distribution over categories in $\text{supp}(Q)$ is. Namely, what is the uncertainty (in the sense of information theory) in this distribution.

Coverage (Topological).

Definition 10. The *coverage* of a query Q is defined as

$$\text{coverage}(Q) = \frac{|\text{supp}(Q)|}{|\text{closure}(\text{supp}(Q))|}.$$

Coverage is related to the notion of local cover in topology [7]. It examines how closed $\text{supp}(Q)$ is w.r.t. "similar" categories. Namely, if $C_i \in \text{supp}(Q)$, then how many categories similar to C_i are also in $\text{supp}(Q)$.

4. REGIONS OF ATYPICALITY

In this section, we argue that there are certain combinations of locality, flow, and coverage that mark a query as being atypical.

Our framework is general, and the set of atypical combinations can be expanded for specific applications. We provide three such combinations as working examples, explain why they are atypical, and what eCommerce search analysts aim to do in each case. §6.4 gives examples of queries in each of the three regions.

4.1 Region I: Low Locality and High Flow

Locality measures how similar are the categories that appear in the signature of a query. Low locality means that the clicks generated by a query are distributing over dissimilar categories. High flow means that there is a more uniform distribution over several such categories. Due to this, it is more likely that the query is broad, having inventory in multiple categories. For such queries, search analysts aim to **maximize recall** so that all products that could potentially match the broad query be shown.

4.2 Region II: Low Locality and Low Flow

This combination of properties indicates that the query is being made by a small number of different sets of users having different intents. A toy example would be a query such as "apple" which might be made with intents varying between food and computers. Food and computers have a low similarity score since they do not frequently co-occur in query signatures; consequently, such a query would have low locality. Such queries are **candidates for disambiguation** by eCommerce search analysts.[1]

4.3 Region III: High Locality, Low Flow, and Low Coverage

The combination of properties in this case indicate high specificity of the query. Not only does the signature not have a large support, the support is very "selective" in that it has low coverage, and high locality. eCommerce search analysts treat such queries as being highly specific, and aim for **high precision** here in order to satisfy the user. Ensuring high recall is secondary for such queries.

5. RELATED WORK

To our knowledge, this is the first work focused on the question of characterizing atypical queries in the context of eCommerce. There are a few related areas of research in information retrieval that our work touches upon.

The problem of predicting query performance has been studied by many research groups in the context of content-based queries [3, 1, 10] or, more generally, web search queries [11, 6]. The research can broadly be categorized as being focused on pre-retrieval or post-retrieval performance measures. Pre-retrieval measures predict how a query would perform in a search system by using only the properties associated with the query and assuming that the result-set is not available. A survey of pre-retrieval performance predictors can be found in [5]. We focus specifically on post-retrieval measures as the low dimensionality of the query space in eCommerce negates many of the advantages of pre-retrieval performance predictors. Some examples of post-retrieval measures are Jensen-Shannon divergence [1] and weighted information gain [11], which predict the performance of a query in terms of average precision on a retrieval task, using characteristics of the query and the result-set.

A related area of research is the problem of detecting ambiguous queries. In [3], the authors claim that a strong predictor of low performing queries is lack of query ambiguity, namely how much information does the query term contain with regard to specifying user intent. They have quantified this through a measure called clarity score which measures the relative entropy between the query and the retrieved result-set. The variability in user intent, captured by query ambiguity measures, has also been studied in the context of search personalization by [9, 4]. Dou et al. [4] introduce the click entropy measure for a query to judge its suitability for personalization. This is one of the measures that we use in the classification of atypical queries. Song et al. [8] developed a supervised learning model to classify ambiguous queries and recognized that queries that are not ambiguous could either be "broad" or "clear" queries. Their model, however, does not distinguish between these two classes. Our notion of atypicality in the context of eCommerce is broader. Rather than defining a single measure of ambiguity, we focus on measures derived from the implicit query-click data that can be collectively used to categorize queries in terms of the broadness or ambiguity of user intent. Our framework is general and can be adapted to any domain-specific search engine.

[1] A frequently used technique is "search in:" where the user is presented with (for the example of apple) the choice to search in electronics or in food, in order to disambiguate.

6. EMPIRICAL WORK

6.1 Dataset

We demonstrate our approach on a dataset, Groupon_QL, containing roughly 41,000 distinct queries with the highest query volume, aggregated from search logs at Groupon over a six month period beginning October 2014. For each query, the aggregated user clicks are normalized to form a distribution over the set of categories. The number of categories is 986. In order to reduce noise in the computation of locality, we only consider categories having at least 10% contribution in the normalized query signature.

6.2 Distribution of Key Properties

Objective. To examine the distributions of locality, flow, and coverage in Groupon_QL.
Methodology. We computed locality, flow, and coverage for each of the queries in Groupon_QL to obtain the distribution.
Results. The results are shown in Fig. 1.
Discussion. Each of the three distributions displays different characteristics. Locality is roughly evenly distributed in its range of $[0, 1]$. This is surprising, since we might expect the distribution to be significantly concentrated at higher values; however this is not so. This shows that queries are not, in general, significantly more local. Flow peaks around the value of 1. Since flow is an entropy, its unit is "number of bits." One bit of entropy describes a two state even distribution, and this is roughly the mode of the flow distribution. Coverage displays a falling mean-trend with increased values, except for a peak at coverage of one. The pearson correlation between the three quantities is very low, except for locality and flow which are negatively correlated [2].

6.3 Identifying Atypical Queries Accurately

Objective. To identify atypical queries in Groupon_QL, and investigate the accuracy of the proposed techniques.
Methodology. We isolated a set of 3000 previously untagged queries in Groupon_QL which had sufficient query volume (i.e. were queried more than 100 times in 6 months). We computed locality, flow, and coverage for each of these queries, and then used the framework of §4 to identify atypical queries. The thresholds to define the regions were: Region I (locality < 0.05 and flow > 3.5), Region II (locality < 0.05 and flow < 1.4) and Region III (locality > 0.7, flow < 1.4, and coverage < 0.05). This gave us 590 queries, out of which 120 were randomly sampled from each of the three regions to generate the test data set. Then, two experienced search analysts at Groupon were asked to tag each of these 120 queries as "maximize recall," "disambiguate" or "maximize precision," (resp.) depending on which region of atypicality the query lay.

[2] Correlation between coverage and locality is near zero, between locality and flow is -0.47 and between coverage and entropy is 0.11.

Table 1: Examples of atypical queries: causes, individual properties, and notes.

Cause of Atypicality	Query	Flow	Locality	Coverage	Clarifying Comments
low locality, high flow	romantic	5.27	0^a	0.69	broad query
	organic	4.98	0^a	0.50	broad query
	picnic	3.03	0.03	0.12	broad query
	amore	3.07	≈ 0	0.12	restaurant, dance class, spa, salon etc.
low locality, low flow	edison	0.97	≈ 0	0.33	hotel, also lighting goods
	solo	1.00	≈ 0	0.06	headphones, also italian restaurant
	allegria	0.90	≈ 0	0.04	popular restaurant, also hotel
	d-link	1.00	≈ 0	1.00	broadband routers, also surveillance cameras
high locality, low flow, low coverage[b]	squid lips	0.48	0.59	0.08	seafood restaurant
	meal replacement	1.00	0.90	0.28	specific intent
	olaf	1.31	0.55	0.17	stuffed toy for kids
	sound machine	0^c	1^c	0.04	sounds for babies
TYPICAL QUERY	pizza	1.08	0.88	0.82	medium flow, high locality and coverage

[a] Each category in supp(Q) has normalized count less than 0.1 [b] Eight of the top 20 low coverage queries correspond to brands
[c] $|\text{supp}(Q)| = 1$, hence flow$(Q) = 0$ and locality$(Q) = 1$ by definition

Results. Shown in Table 2
Discussion. Region III queries were most easily isolated by the two analysts, due to predominance of easily distinguishable brands, both local and global. The lowest agreement was found on Region II queries, and almost all the differing queries were assigned the label "maximize precision" by the analysts. This is both due to a certain amount of randomness in click activity and the presence of dual intent behind some seemingly specific queries. For instance, when people search for "Serta", the underlying intent is commonly assumed to be a mattress purchase, but it could also refer to a furniture purchase intent. Some Region I queries were assigned the label "maximize precision" due to specific keywords like "Sams Club" but the underlying click activity has very high flow because the intent cannot be localized to a definite category. Despite the shift in labels, the *common consensus amongst the analysts was that all the queries were atypical, and needed to be flagged for special care.*

Table 2: Analysts verdict (proportion of agreement) on top 120 queries tagged as atypical with our approach.

	Region I	Region II	Region III
Total Queries	40	30	50
Analyst A	0.75	0.83	1.00
Analyst B	0.68	0.57	0.86

6.4 Examples of Atypical Queries

Objective. To provide examples of atypical queries in Groupon_QL.
Methodology. From the atypical queries identified in §6.3, we show four of each of the three types.
Results. Twelve examples results are shown in Table. 1. Specifically, queries of type described in §4.1, §4.2, §4.3 are color coded orange, green, and blue, respectively.
Discussion. In table.

7. CONCLUSION

In this paper, we have introduced work on the important problem of structural understanding of queries in eCommerce in terms of specificity, breadth, and ambiguity. We identified three inherent properties of query-click distributions: geometric, statistical, and topological. We studied these properties, and showed that queries that have certain combinations of these properties are atypical in certain senses. By way of example, we showed three regions of atypicality. The framework that we established is flexible, and can be adapted by search analysts for specific applications.

Our work is being used in production to improve relevance of search results at Groupon. We would like to bring research questions from eCommerce retrieval to the attention of the broader retrieval community, and this work is a starting step in that direction.

8. DEDICATION

This work is dedicated to Shiva Kashid (d. July 1660) for his sacrifice in enabling Shivaji to escape from the siege of Panhala.

References

[1] D. Carmel, E. Yom-Tov, A. Darlow, and D. Pelleg. What makes a query difficult? In *Proc. SIGIR '06*, pages 390–397, New York, NY, USA, 2006. ACM.

[2] T. M. Cover and J. A. Thomas. *Elements of Information Theory (Wiley Series in Telecommunications and Signal Processing).* Wiley-Interscience, 2006.

[3] S. Cronen-Townsend, Y. Zhou, and W. B. Croft. Predicting query performance. In *Proc. SIGIR '02*, pages 299–306, New York, NY, USA, 2002. ACM.

[4] Z. Dou, R. Song, and J.-R. Wen. A large-scale evaluation and analysis of personalized search strategies. In *Proc. WWW '07*, pages 581–590, New York, NY, USA, 2007. ACM.

[5] C. Hauff, D. Hiemstra, and F. de Jong. A survey of pre-retrieval query performance predictors. In *Proc. CIKM '08*, pages 1419–1420, New York, NY, USA, 2008. ACM.

[6] C. Hauff, V. Murdock, and R. Baeza-Yates. Improved query difficulty prediction for the web. In *Proc. CIKM '08*, pages 439–448, New York, NY, USA, 2008. ACM.

[7] J. Munkres. *Topology (2nd Edition).* Pearson, 2 edition, 2000.

[8] R. Song, Z. Luo, J.-R. Wen, Y. Yu, and H.-W. Hon. Identifying ambiguous queries in web search. In *Proc. WWW '07*, pages 1169–1170, New York, NY, USA, 2007. ACM.

[9] J. Teevan, S. T. Dumais, and D. J. Liebling. To personalize or not to personalize: Modeling queries with variation in user intent. In *Proc. SIGIR '08*, pages 163–170, New York, NY, USA, 2008. ACM.

[10] V. Vinay, I. J. Cox, N. Milic-Frayling, and K. Wood. On ranking the effectiveness of searches. In *Proc. SIGIR '06*, pages 398–404, New York, NY, USA, 2006. ACM.

[11] Y. Zhou and W. B. Croft. Query performance prediction in web search environments. In *Proc. SIGIR '07*, pages 543–550, New York, NY, USA, 2007. ACM.

Bottom-up Faceted Search: Creating Search Neighbourhoods with Datacube Cells

Mark Sifer
School of Computing and Information Technology
University of Wollongong, Australia
msifer@uow.edu.au

ABSTRACT

Browsing a collection can start with a keyword search. A user visits a library, performs a keyword search to find a few books of interest; finding their location in the library. Then they go to these locations; the corresponding bookshelves, where they do not just retrieve the found books, but rather they start browsing the *nearby* books; the books which have a similar Dewey classification. This paper extends this approach to curated corpora that contain items or documents that have been classified in multiple dimensions (facets), where each dimension classification may be a hierarchy. In particular (i) a technique for determining *near* items based on OLAP datacube cells and (ii) user interfaces that support browsing of *near* items are presented.

Categories and Subject Descriptors

H.3.3 [Information Search and Retrieval]: Selection Process. H.5.2 [User Interfaces]: GUI.

General Terms

Algorithms, Design, Experimentation.

Keywords

Faceted search, user interface, OLAP, similarity.

1. INTRODUCTION

With the advent of large online collections such as the Amazon shop, the various music, video and app stores that can contain millions of items, customer discovery of items can be a challenge. Two major approaches are; keyword search over items descriptions that return ranked lists of items, and top-down directory based search where users make successive category choices that filter the collection down to an item list for browsing. The latter approach includes faceted search over an item collection [3][10]. Faceted search relies on item meta-data that classifies each item into multiple dimensions (the facets) where each dimension is a category tree. An example is a real-estate rental website, where users can in a top-down manner filter on location, number of rooms and price interval to see a list of matching properties that can then be browsed. Keyword and faceted search approaches can be combined, so that keyword search acts as an additional dynamic facet filter that is combined with the other facet filters to produce the list of matching items for browsing.

Providing top level categories for one or more dimensions, then listing items within these categories, ranked in an order such as popularity, is another top-down approach to item discovery. Another bottom-up approach is to use keyword search to find a few initial items of interest, then continue the browsing by providing lists of similar items based on heuristics such as common shopping baskets or similar content [9].

A major difficulty for top-down directory based approaches such as faceted search is the creation of manually defined hierarchies, particularly topic hierarchies. A large effort was made by Yahoo to create such a hierarchy manually, with its directory for the web, but this has closed recently. An ongoing alternative is the Open Directory Project [5]. One of the most import parts of such a classification is the category titles; they must be meaningful to users. Heuristics have a poor record here. There are many heuristics to cluster documents but algorithmically labeling the clusters remains difficult. Solutions include integrating the use of an external resource such as Wikipedia [1], or combining an initial top-level of manually created categories with content based clustering to provide better category labeling [2].

This paper proposes a new approach to searching and browsing a collection that has been classified with predefined hierarchies: bottom-up faceted search. It starts with a keyword search to find a few initial items of interest, but then browsing continues by successively adding nearby items to a browsing list. However, unlike similarity measures which are based on website navigation or content, nearby is determined by an item's position in the space defined by the dimension hierarchies. In the case of one dimension this equates to tree distance. In the multidimensional case, items that have the same category value in each dimension are near. Our approach is based on an application of OnLine Analytical Processing (OLAP) [6], a technique that is normally used for data analysis. Our approach utilises OLAP aggregation (datacube cells) and aggregation control (rollups). Near items share a datacube cell which can be successively expanded through dimension rollups. This will be explained further in section two.

Our three use cases are: (i) a user wishes to find books in a narrow topic. Using keyword search they locate a few books that seems to fit and go to the shelf to find these books. *Then they browse nearby books in the same and adjacent topics to see if any of them are also of interest,* (ii) a user has previously browsed the shelf and remember there was something of interest and wishes to return to find it and (iii) a user has previously browsed the shelf and wish to continue the browsing from where they ended browsing last time. The latter two cases require a 'stable' shelf, where items retain their order and organisation.

The contributions of this paper are: a description of a bottom-up search method that induces a ranking based on nearness in a predefined dimension hierarchy space, and two user interfaces that support bottom-up faceted search: compact and full.

Permission to make digital or hard copies of all or part of this work for personal or classroom use is granted without fee provided that copies are not made or distributed for profit or commercial advantage and that copies bear this notice and the full citation on the first page. Copyrights for components of this work owned by others than ACM must be honored. Abstracting with credit is permitted. To copy otherwise, or republish, to post on servers or to redistribute to lists, requires prior specific permission and/or a fee. Request permissions from Permissions@acm.org.
CIKM'15, October 19-23, 2015, Melbourne, VIC, Australia
© 2015 ACM. ISBN 978-1-4503-3794-6/15/10…$15.00
DOI: http://dx.doi.org/10.1145/2806416.2806593

2. OLAP ORIGINS

In this section the OLAP origins of our approach are described. OLAP is a standard database technique for data analytics. It assumes a table of facts where each fact has a value in multiple dimensions. For example a sale record that includes location-city, product type, date-day and price range. When facts are aggregated with a group-by on all dimensions the resulting table forms a datacube where each row is a non-empty cell in the datacube. A user can then view cross-sections of the datacube as cross-tabulations with pivot tables or charts, where the table or chart axis are a dimension's categories or intervals. This alone is not sufficient, as such axes would be too detailed. Further aggregation is required to support higher levels views such as sales by quarter rather than by individual days.

Dimensions are typically not flat sets of categories, that partition the data, but rather a hierarchy of categories or intervals. In such cases each dimension column in the fact table will contain leaf dimension category values, while the dimension hierarchy itself is stored in separate table that can be joined with the fact table. This organisation of fact and dimension tables is referred to as a star schema.

Further aggregation is supported by summary datacube views, that were created with higher levels of the dimension hierarchies. For each dimension, a user selects the level they wish for the table or chart view. For example they could select date-quarter (rather than date-day), location-state (rather than location-city) only, a two dimension cube. In OLAP terminology we say that date has been rolled-up from day to quarter, and location from city to state, while product type and price interval have been rolled-up to their respective root categories (i.e. all).

OLAP data exploration also includes filtering that restricts data to some slice, by applying constraints to one or more dimensions; such as product type is electrical goods. Filtering is combined with aggregation control; rollup and their inverse drill-down operations to respectively restrict and change the granularity of views. Together these are the two basic operations of OLAP data explorations; slice & dice (filtering) and rollup & drilldown (aggregation).

Faceted search like OLAP relies on pre-defined hierarchies that facilitate top-down filtering. Faceted search interfaces typically provide a view that presents a filtered list of items together with the interactive filter widgets. These widgets can include radio buttons or check-boxes for each facet, where facet categories are decorated with item counts to guide user browsing. Faceted search browsing is a top-down process of iterative filter refinement. Aggregation control or rollups are simply not part of this. This work provides a deeper integration of OLAP and faceted search, in which OLAP aggregation control is also utilised.

3. NEIGHBOURHOODS

In this section item nearness, that is, item neighbourhoods and how they can be successively expanded through OLAP aggregation control (rollups) is defined.

Our collection is a set of items denoted *Items*. Let there be n dimensions denoted as D_1, .. D_n. Denote the location of an item x, as location $(x) = (v_1, v_2, .. v_{an})$ where $v_i \in$ Leaves (D_i), where each D_i is a set of categories equipped with a partial order that is a tree. Denote a set of selected search results as R, where $R \subseteq Items$. The initial set of near items for R is simply those items that have the same location as some $r \in R$. To expand the near-set rollup operations are used. A rollup merges cells into summary cells.

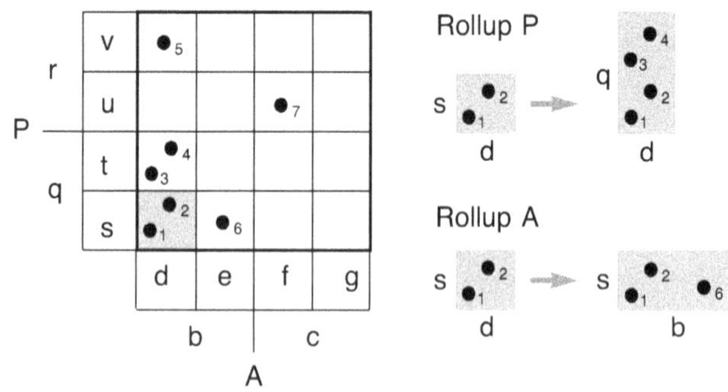

Figure 1. A collection of 7 items distributed over dimensions A and P with the two alternatives rollups of item 1 shown.

The function Rollup (R, k, j) returns a set of locations; summary cells S, where the k'th dimension's categories have been lifted to level j. Denote each cell $c \in$ Location (R) as $(v_1, v_2, .. w_{k.}, .. v_n)$. Then each corresponding cell $c' \in$ Rollup (R, k, j) is given by $c' = (v_1, v_2, ..$ ancestor (v_k, j) , .. $v_n)$ where ancestor (v_k, j) is the ancestor of v_k in D_k at tree level j.

The items located in a summary cell $s = (s_1, s_2, \dots s_n)$ are those items x such that location $(x) = (v_1, v_2, .. v_n)$ where $v_i \leq s_i$ using the D_i ordering. The items that are in S but are not in initial Location (R) are the additional near items added by the rollup.

Figure 1 shows an example rollup of a small collection; of 7 items that are classified by two dimension trees A and P. Both dimensions have two levels. There is one selected result located in cell (d,s): item {1}. The initial near set {(d,s)} contains two items: {1,2}. There are two possible rollups: A or P. A rollup of dimension A, Rollup (R, A, 1) = {(b,s)} which contains 3 items: {1,2,6}, while a rollup of dimension P, Rollup (R, P, 1) = {(d, q)} which contains 4 items: {1,2,3,4}.

When there are n dimensions there can be n alternative rollups to choose from. Our system provides three methods for this. Firstly, a default rollup where the dimension that adds the least number of items is chosen. Secondly, a manual rollup, where a user makes a choice from a list of dimensions that are decorated with counts of the additional items that would be added if the dimension was selected for rollup. Thirdly, a manual rollup, where a user can set any dimension directly to an arbitrary level.

In most cases the first and second rollup methods lift a dimension by one tree level. However, sometimes such a rollup adds no additional items, so a further rollup to a higher tree level is applied. Sometimes lifting a dimension to the root level still does not add any additional items, so a further rollup may applied to another dimension. The next section will show the three rollup methods in action.

4. BOTTOM-UP FACETED SEARCH

In this section compact and full-size user interfaces for bottom-up faceted search via rollups are described and demonstrated. But first, we provide an overview of our system. Figure 4 shows a complete screenshot of our user interface. The RHS panel is the compact interface, while the LHS and RHS panels together form the full interface. The collection shown is a portion of a local file system. The items in this collection are the individual files and the dimensions are their: directory path, file type, modify date and size. The top of the compact interface contains a keyword search field which uses the open source Lucene keyword search library [4]. A scan of the file system created the initial fact table of files

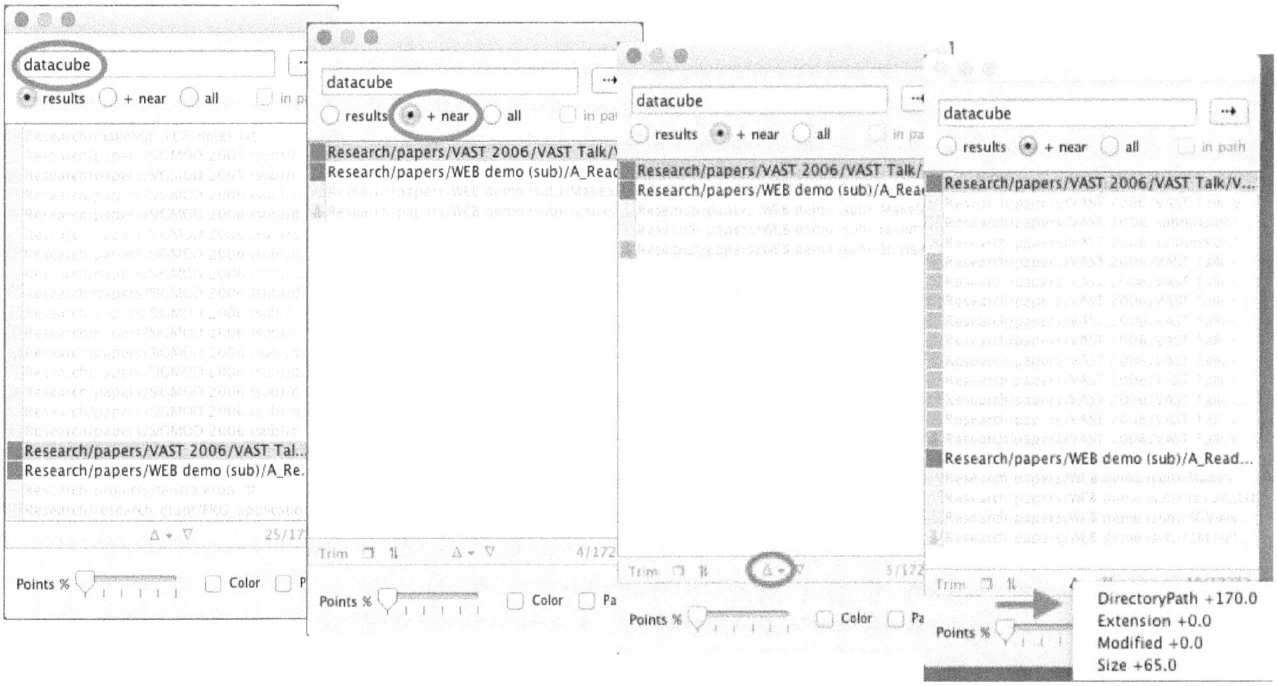

Figure 2. Four screenshots of the compact interface. The first from the left shows a list of 25 results after "datacube" was entered into the keyword search field. Two of these have been selected. They are highlighted with magenta. The second shows the interface after the + near option (circled) was clicked. Two additional near items were added. The third shows another item is added after the default rollup button (circled) was clicked. The fourth shows 14 more items have been added after several more default rollups. It also shows the manual-rollup context-menu for the next rollup.

and their meta-data, while a separate scan by Lucene populated the indexes needed for content based search. The hierarchies for file type and size were manually created, while the hierarchies for file path and modify date were induced.

4.1 Compact Interface

Bottom-up faceted search starts with a keyword search. Figure 2 (left-most screenshot) shows our compact interface after *datacube* was entered. Twenty five matching results were returned, of these two were selected. They are shown as the two highlighted rows. The second screenshot shows the two selected results with their initial near items; that is the other items that are in the same datacube cell. To add more near items a default rollup is done. This is shown in the third screenshot. Only one extra item was added. This extra item is highlighted with a darker gray LHS

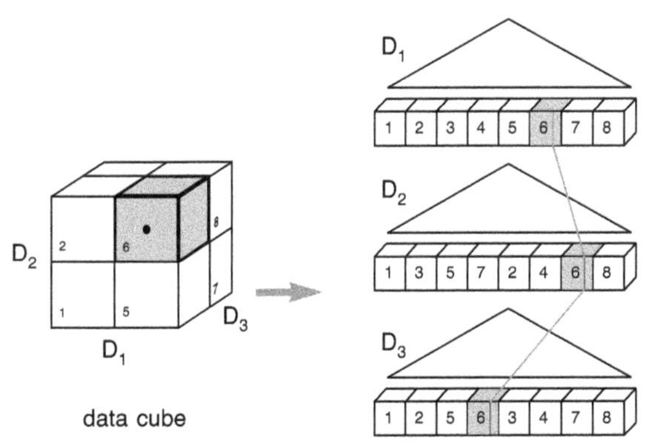

Figure 3. Parallel dimension hierarchies over a cube vector.

box. The rollup dimension choices were: directory Path (+ 3 items), extension (+ 1 item), modified (+ 0 items) and size (+ 2 items). The default rollup chose the dimension that added the least non-zero number if items, so the extension dimension was rolled-up adding that one item. To reverse a rollup the inverted triangle beside the rollup button is clicked.

The last screenshot shows the effect of several more default rollups. The list of the two initially selected results and their near items has grown to 19 items. The last of these rollups added 10 items, those with a gray LHS boxes. Note that as each rollup is done, additional items are added to the end of a list that starts with a selected result, creating a ranking. If sufficient rollups are done these two selected results would end up in the same cell, at that time, they and their list of near items would be merged in a manner that preserves their rollup step order.

A user can manually chose which dimension to rollup. If they apply a right click to the rollup button, a context menu that shows the choice of dimensions decorated with item counts, is shown. For example, if a rollup of dimension size was selected in the last screenshot 65 additional items would be added.

4.2 Full Interface

Our full interface supports arbitrary rollups. That is, the user can select the rollup level of each dimension directly. For example, a user may decide that there should be no constraint on document size, so it can be rolled-up to the root level at the beginning of the search, creating larger cells hence larger neighbourhoods that will contain more near items. Figure 3 shows an overview of the visualisation used in the full interface that places each dimension hierarchy over an appropriately sorted data cube vector. This visualisation extends [7][8]. However, while the earlier system

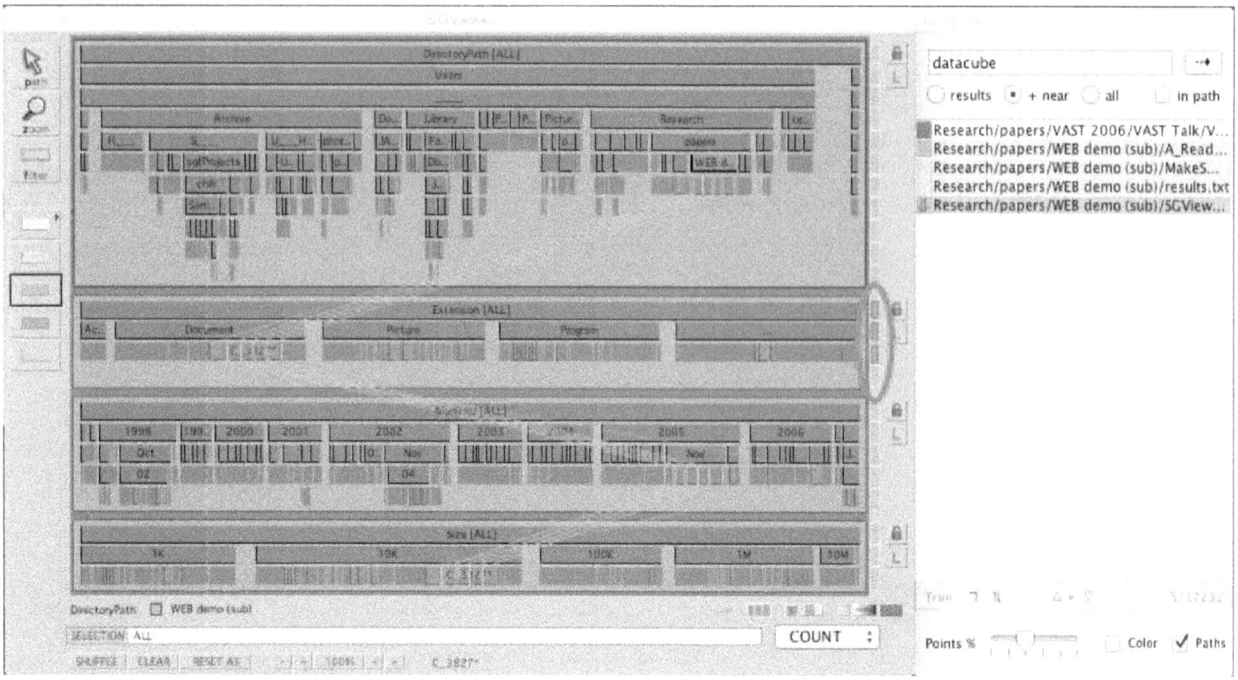

Figure 4. Paths for the five items in the compact view are shown in the full view, passing through each dimension hierarchy.

offered top-down faceted search support, it included no support for OLAP rollup or near item browsing. Returning to figure 3, the dot in cell 6 represents one item. The overall location of such an item is shown by the path it traces across the dimensions. Figure 4 shows a local file system. A key difference with figure 3 is: dimension hierarchies are shown with a proportional layout, where the width of each cell depends on the number of items contained. However, a fixed scale layout that allocates a fixed width to each leaf category is also supported.

Figure 4 shows the same rollup-step as the third screenshot in figure 2; the one that contained two selected results with three near items. Selecting a row in the compact view makes those items' paths visible in the full view. In figure 4 all rows have been selected to make all five paths appear. A distortion slider at the bottom of the compact view make the cells and leaf categories that contain the five points wider and more visible. Colouring can also be applied to one of more categories to make subsets of paths more visible. The first selected result appears as a gray path that joins magenta bars in each dimension. The second selected result and its three near items appear as four green paths; joining the green bars located in cell 3827 in each dimension.

A close look at the extension hierarchy in figure 4 shows it is missing a level. The initial rollup in figure 2 was a rollup of extension that added one item and removed its lowest level, that had included the document sub-categories: doc, html, pdf and txt. The rollup level control for extension is circled. Each dimension has a similar rollup level control. A user simply clicks the desired level for one of more dimensions to change their rollup level. The list of items in the compact view then changes to reflect these new rollup levels.

The discussion so far has assumed the initial search is done over the entire collection. However, the full view also supports top-down faceted search. For example, in filter mode (shown on the LHS) a user can restrict the collection, by selecting one or more categories in several dimensions. For example, research AND (2005 or 2006) could be selected, this would restrict both results and near items to that slice of the collection.

5. CONCLUSION

This paper has presented a new technique for corpus browsing that is directory based rather than content based; one that relies on predefined classifications of corpus items. The technique is an application of OLAP aggregation control; via rollups that create expandable neighbourhoods for search results. It integrates with top-down faceted search filtering; that is with OLAP slice & dice. In summary, a deep integration of OLAP with search that supports the browsing of *near* items has been provided.

6. REFERENCES

[1] Carmel D., Roitman H. and Zwerdling N. Enhancing cluster labeling using wikipedia. In *ACM SIGIR'09*, 139-146, 2009.

[2] Cooper, E. System and method for divisive textual clustering by label selection using variant-weighted TFIDF. *US Patent Application* 20140136542, 2014.

[3] Hearst, M. Clustering versus faceted categories for information exploration. *CACM* 49 (4), 59-61, 2006.

[4] Lucerne. http://lucene.apache.org/.

[5] Open Directory Project. http://www.dmoz.org/.

[6] Pedersen, T. and Jensen, C. Multidimensional Database Technology. *IEEE Computer* 34 (12), 2001.

[7] Sifer, M. and Lin, J. Refining search results with facet landscapes. In Proc. *ACM SGIR'08*, 181, 2008.

[8] Sifer, M., Lin, J., Watanobe, Y. and Bhalla, S. Integrating Keyword Search with Multiple Dimension Tree Views over a Summary Corpus Data Cube. In Proc. *ACM SIGMOD'10*, 1167-1170, 2010.

[9] Singhal, A. Modern information retrieval: A brief overview. *IEEE Data Eng. Bull.* 24 (4), 35-43, 2001.

[10] Tunkelang, D. Faceted search. *Synthesis lectures on information concepts, retrieval, and services* 1 (1), 1-80, 2009.

Personalized Recommendation Meets Your Next Favorite

Qiang Song, Jian Cheng, Ting Yuan, Hanqing Lu
National Laboratory of Pattern Recognition
Institute of Automation, Chinese Academy of Sciences
Beijing, China
{qiang.song, jcheng, tyuan, luhq}@nlpr.ia.ac.cn

ABSTRACT

A comprehensive understanding of user's item selection behavior is not only essential to many scientific disciplines, but also has a profound business impact on online recommendation. Recent researches have discovered that user's favorites can be divided into 2 categories: long-term and short-term. User's item selection behavior is a mixed decision of her long and short-term favorites. In this paper, we propose a unified model, namely **S**tates **T**ransition p**A**ir-wise **R**anking Model (STAR), to address users' favorites mining for sequential-set recommendation. Our method utilizes a transition graph for collaborative filtering that accounts for mining user's short-term favorites, jointed with a generative topic model for expressing user's long-term favorites. Furthermore, a user's specific prior is introduced into our unified model for better modeling personalization. Technically, we develop a pairwise ranking loss function for parameters learning. Empirically, we measure the effectiveness of our method using two real-world datasets and the results show that our method outperforms state-of-the-art methods.

Categories and Subject Descriptors

H.3.3 [**Information Systems**]: Information Search and Retrieval—*Information Filtering*

General Terms

Models

Keywords

Recommender Systems, Sequential Data, Personalized

1. INTRODUCTION

The ability of Recommender Systems (RS) to predict connections between users and items makes them an important tool for web users, e.g., movies (Netflix), products (Amazon), restaurants (Yelp), etc. Overall, user's favorites can be expressed either explicitly, such as by ratings, or implicitly by her clicked or purchased history. Traditional methods [2, 5] in Recommender Systems usually focus on mining global patterns by analyzing the entire history in a chaotic order. However, in real-world applications, items purchased by a user come in a sequence. Sequential data recommendation problem [4, 7] has attracted more and more attention in recent years. In this paper, we deal with top-N recommendation problem under the setting where sequential data with implicit feedback is given per user. Common examples include 1) an online music website where users frequently select songs in their favor; 2) an online shop where users constantly buy books or CDs. In these applications, the target is to mine user's favorites, so as to recommend items that she might want to listen/purchase in her next visit.

In general, user's item purchased sequence can be viewed as a states transition process, in which user's latent favorites are treated as hidden states. The user's next action can be predicted based on her previous actions. Recently, a variety of methods have been proposed, e.g., Yang et.al,[6] proposed a modified sequential Matrix Factorization model for mining user's short-term favorites. Rendle et al.[3] firstly put forward a unified model, embedding both Markov Chains and Matrix Factorization, to provide the next point of interest (POI) recommendation. However, these methods can not fully express a user's item selection behavior, since they merely capture user's sequential dependent favorites (short-term favorites), while ignore user's sequential independent favorites (long-term favorites). More comprehensive analysis and strategies should be carried out. To date, representing user's item selection behavior with good interpretability is still an open problem.

In summary, the major challenges of this work lie in:

1) **How to effectively model and predict user's long and short-term favorites simultaneously:** Basically, user's item selection behavior is a mixed decision of her long and short-term favorites. Some special models should be considered to effectively capture the characteristics of different favorites patterns.

2) **How to properly express user's personalization:** Due to the reason that different users may have different favorites distribution, a personalized item recommendation is an enabling mechanism to overcome information overload occurred and to really meet user's individualized favorites.

In this paper, we propose a unified model, namely **S**tates **T**ransition p**A**ir-wise **R**anking Model (STAR), to address users' favorites mining for sequential-set recommendation. Our method collaboratively combines a transition graph with

Permission to make digital or hard copies of all or part of this work for personal or classroom use is granted without fee provided that copies are not made or distributed for profit or commercial advantage and that copies bear this notice and the full citation on the first page. Copyrights for components of this work owned by others than ACM must be honored. Abstracting with credit is permitted. To copy otherwise, or republish, to post on servers or to redistribute to lists, requires prior specific permission and/or a fee. Request permissions from Permissions@acm.org.
CIKM '15 Oct 19-23, 2015, Melbourne, Australia
© 2015 ACM. ISBN 978-1-4503-3794-6/15/10 ...$15.00.
DOI: http://dx.doi.org/10.1145/2806416.2806598.

a generative semantic model: 1) users' long-term favorites (hobbies) are seized as topics which can be effectively generated by Latent Dirichlet Allocation (LDA); 2) users' short-term favorites (ad-hoc interest) are captured by a transition matrix in Markov Chains (MC). A unified states transition matrix is learnt as a trade-off strategy for effectively modeling the user's item selection behavior. Furthermore, a user's specific prior is introduced into our unified model to distinguish personalized favorites. Technically, we develop a pair-wise ranking loss function for parameters learning and derive inference to obtain better performance. Experimental results show that our proposal outperforms state-of-the-art methods. In a word, our contributions can be summarized as follows:

- We present a transition graph for collaborative filtering that accounts for mining user's short-term favorites, jointed with a generative topic model for expressing user's long-term favorites.
- Users' individual favorites are better modeled by the specific priors which are learnt through our proposed pair-wise ranking loss function.

2. SEQUENTIAL-SET METHOD

Let $U = \{u_1, u_2, ..., u_{|U|}\}$ be a set of users, and $W = \{w_1, w_2, ..., w_{|W|}\}$ denote a set of items. For each user u, the purchased history H^u is known: $H^u := (H_1^u, H_2^u, ..., H_{t-1}^u)$ with $H_t^u \subseteq W$. And the purchased history of all users is $H := \{H^{u_1}, H^{u_2}, ..., H^{u_{|U|}}\}$. Given this history, the task is to recommend items to a user the next time she visits the shop. Note that we deal not with absolute time points, but with relative ones regarding a user, e.g., the first, second, etc. The item recommendation task can be formalized in creating a personal ranking over all pairs of items for user u in her next visit. With this ranking, we recommend top-N items W_{re} to the user.

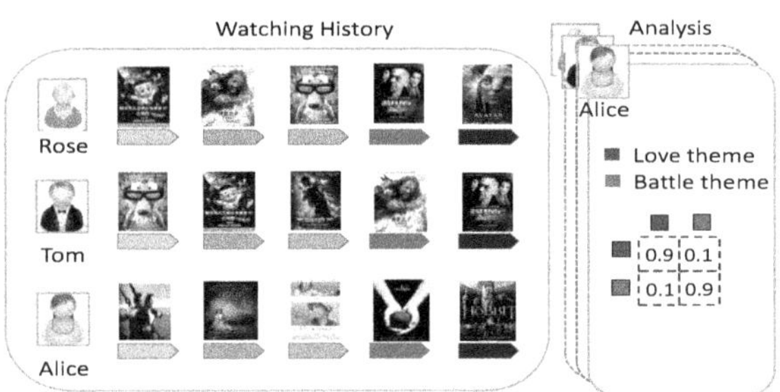

Figure 1: Top-N recommendation will be based on the scores under the candidates.

2.1 Next Favorite Modeling

In this paper, we express a general item selection process through a unified model for sequential set recommendation. According to Figure 1, imagine we have recorded a target user's (e.g., Alice) purchased history $H^u := (H_1^u, ..., H_{t-1}^u)$ with $H_t^u \subseteq W$, we find that she usually purchased love theme movies like 'Titanic' and 'Gone with the Wind'. But recently she bought some tickets of 'The Hobbit: The Desolation of Smaug'. Thus, instead of recommending some movies in her favor, it is also promising to give another style movies such as 'The Lord of the Rings' to her.

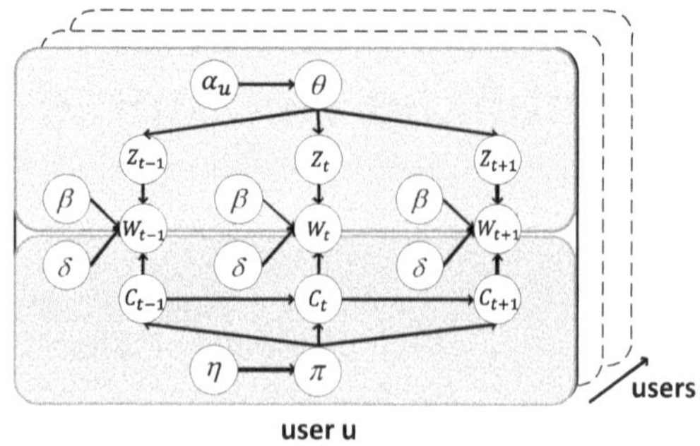

Figure 2: A unified model for recommendation. Where $\alpha_u, \beta, \delta, \eta$ are four hyper-parameters

As shown in Figure 2, we elaborate above case with our unified model. The light blue box represents a generative semantic model, in which user's general taste is expressed by topics. A multinomial distribution θ is over the latent topics to model the prior distribution of a target user u. And each latent topic z has a multinomial distribution ϕ^z over the item set, which represents the relevance of items to the topic. On the other hand, the light green box stands for a hidden Markov model, in which user's purchased record can be viewed as a Markov Chain, and her recent favorites can be captured by the hidden states c. Then the recommended items will be generated based on the probability of the unified model. Similar to the idea of Topics and Syntax Model [1], we treat all the topics in LDA as a special hidden state (e.g., c=1), so that the state transition matrix π can be learned as a trade-off selective strategy for the unified model. Furthermore, due to the reason that different users may have different favorites distribution, a user's specific prior (e.g., α_u) is introduced into our unified model so as to distinguish personalized favorites.

The total likelihood can be represented as a conditional probability of hyper-parameters $\alpha_u, \beta, \delta, \eta$. And here we write the user's event corpus as follows:

$$\begin{aligned} & P(z, c_t, w|\alpha_u, \beta, \delta, \eta) \\ &= \int\int P(w|z, c_t, \phi^z, \phi^c) P(\phi^z|\beta) P(\phi^c|\delta) d\phi^z d\phi^c \cdot \\ & \int P(z|\theta, c_t) P(\theta|\alpha_u) d\theta \cdot \int P(c_t|\pi) P(\pi|\eta) d\pi \end{aligned} \quad (1)$$

We then use the probability as the final score of each item for the ranking measure. The probability is given as follows:

$$\begin{aligned} & P(w_i|H^u, \theta, \pi) \\ & \propto (\mathcal{I}^{c_t=1} P(w_i|z, \theta) + \mathcal{I}^{c_t \neq 1} P(w_i|c_t)) P(c_t|\pi_u^{c_t-1}) \\ &= (\mathcal{I}^{c_t=1} \sum_{z_t=1}^{T} \phi_{w_i z_t}^z \theta_{z_t} + \mathcal{I}^{c_t \neq 1} \phi_{w_i}^{c_t}) \pi_u^{c_t-1} \end{aligned} \quad (2)$$

where $\mathcal{I}$ is an indicator variable which equals to 1 if the argument is true. We introduce a pair-wise log-loss function for parameters adaptation.

$$\varepsilon(f) = -\sum_{u \in U} \sum_{i,j \in W} \Delta r_{ij} \log(1 + e^{\gamma - f}) \quad (3)$$

where r denotes the ranking, $\Delta r_{ij} = r_i - r_j$ denotes the difference of observed ranking (ground-truth) in validation set. Note that smaller ranking means more relevant. The scalar γ is a free parameter which designates a target margin value. $f = P(w_i|H^u) - P(w_j|H^u)$ denotes the difference of the

Algorithm 1 STAR Algorithm

Input: U,W, and the sequential dataset H
Output: top-N recommendation W_{re}

```
Initialize the parameters and set α_u equally for all users.
for outeriter in (0, maxouteriter) do
    for each user u in U do
        Sample θ from a Dirichlet(α_u) prior.
    end for
    for inneriter in (0, maxinneriter) do
        Use MCMC for sampling.
        Calculate the distribution of each z and c.
    end for
    Calculate the item distribution parameters φ^z_{w_i}, φ^c_{w_i}.
    for each user u in U do
        Calculate the transition probability π_u.
        Calculate items' probability for recommendation.
        Random select i ∈ FalsePositive, j ∈ FalseNegative.
        Minimize the loss function and update the hyper parameter α_u based on validation.
    end for
end for
Rerun MCMC on testing set, recommend W_re to target users.
```

prediction scores. Our main process is shown in Algorithm 1.

2.2 Inference

We apply a detailed inference for the proposed algorithm. Based on Algorithm 1, we use Markov Chain Monte Carlo (MCMC) to perform full Bayesian inference in this model. We firstly derive topic assignment z_t. Given items w, the state assignments c, other topic assignments z_{-t}, and the hyper-parameters, each z_t is drawn from:

$$\begin{aligned} P(z_t|z_{-t},c,w) &= \frac{P(z,c,w)}{P(z_{-t},c,w)} \\ &= \frac{P(w_t|z,c,w_{-t})P(z,c,w_{-t})}{P(w_t|z_{-t},c,w_{-t})P(z_{-t},c,w_{-t})} \\ &\propto P(w_t|z,c,w_{-t})P(z_t|z_{-t},c,w_{-t}) \\ &\propto \begin{cases} n_{z_t}^{u_t}+\alpha_{u_t}, & c_t \neq 1 \\ (n_{z_t}^{u_t}+\alpha_{u_t})\cdot \frac{n_{w_t}^{z_t}+\beta_t}{n_\bullet^{z_t}+\sum_{t=1}^{W}\beta_t}, & c_t = 1 \end{cases} \end{aligned} \tag{4}$$

where $n_{w_t}^{z_t}$ denotes the number of items in topic z_t that are the same as w_t, $n_\bullet^{z_t}$ represents the total number of items in topic z_t. We have obtained these conditional distributions by using the conjugate of the Dirichlet and multinomial distributions to integrate out the parameters θ, ϕ. Similarly, each c_t is drawn from:

$$\begin{aligned} P(c_t|c_{-t},z,w) &= \frac{P(c,z,w)}{P(c_{-t},z,w)} \\ &= \frac{P(w_t|c,z,w_{-t})P(c,z,w_{-t})}{P(w_t|c_{-t},z,w_{-t})P(c_{-t},z,w_{-t})} \\ &\propto P(w_t|c,z,w_{-t})P(c_t|c_{-t},z,w_{-t}) \\ &\propto \begin{cases} \frac{(n_{w_t}^{c_t}+\delta_t)}{(n_\bullet^{c_t}+\sum_{t=1}^{W}\delta_t)}\frac{(n_{c_t}^{c_{t-1}}+\eta)(n_{c_{t+1}}^{c_t}+\eta)}{(n_\bullet^{c_t}+C\eta)}, & c_t \neq 1 \\ \frac{(n_{w_t}^{z_t}+\beta_t)}{(n_\bullet^{z_t}+\sum_{t=1}^{W}\beta_t)}\frac{(n_{c_t}^{c_{t-1}}+\eta)(n_{c_{t+1}}^{c_t}+\eta)}{(n_\bullet^{c_t}+C\eta)}, & c_t = 1 \end{cases} \end{aligned} \tag{5}$$

where $n_\bullet^{c_t}$ denotes the total number of items in state c_t. $n_{c_t}^{c_{t-1}}$ is the number of transitions from state c_{t-1} to c_t. C denotes the total number of states. We then calculate the item distribution $\phi_{w_t}^{z}$, $\phi_{w_t}^{c}$ as follows:

$$\phi_{w_t}^{z} = \frac{(n_{w_t}^{z_t}+\beta_t)}{(n_\bullet^{z_t}+\sum_{t=1}^{W}\beta_t)} \tag{6}$$

$$\phi_{w_t}^{c} = \frac{(n_{w_t}^{c_t}+\delta_t)}{(n_\bullet^{c_t}+\sum_{t=1}^{W}\delta_t)} \tag{7}$$

For each user, the transition probability $\pi_u^{c_{t-1}}$ is given by

$$\pi_u^{c_{t-1}} = \frac{(n_{u\,c_t}^{\,c_{t-1}}+\eta)(n_{u\,c_{t+1}}^{\,c_t}+\eta)}{(n_{u\bullet}^{\,c_t}+C\eta)} \tag{8}$$

where n_u stands for a transition counter only for user u. Based on equation (2) and (3), the partial derivative of the parameter α_u on the loss function is given by

$$\frac{\partial\varepsilon(f)}{\partial\alpha_{u_k}} = \frac{\partial\varepsilon(f)}{\partial f}\frac{\partial f}{\partial\alpha_{u_k}} = \sum_{u\in U}\sum_{i,j\in W}\frac{\Delta r_{ij}e^{\gamma-f}}{1+e^{\gamma-f}}\frac{\partial f}{\partial\alpha_{u_k}} \tag{9}$$

$$\frac{\partial f}{\partial\alpha_{u_k}} = \frac{\boldsymbol{\mathcal{I}}^{c_t=1}\sum_{q\neq k}(\alpha_{u_q}+n_{z_q}^{u_q})(\phi_{w_i z_k}^{z}-\phi_{w_j z_k}^{z})}{(\sum_p(\alpha_{u_p}+n_{z_p}^{u_p}))^2}\pi_u^{c_t-1} \tag{10}$$

where α_{u_k} represents the prior for kth topic. Finally, the updating strategy is given by follows through Stochastic Gradient Descent(SGD) algorithm.

$$\alpha_{u_k} = \alpha_{u_k} - l\frac{\partial\varepsilon(f)}{\partial\alpha_{u_k}} \tag{11}$$

where l stands for a learning rate.

3. EXPERIMENTS

3.1 Experimental Setup

Two real-world datasets used here are MovieLens[1] and Douban [2]. MovieLens is widely used in related work. Douban is a real-world dataset crawled from a publicly available website. Both datasets have users' sequential behavior history. For experiments, we obtain 1,000,209 observations from 6040 users and 3900 items in MovieLens, 2,152,962 observations from 6000 users and 14648 items in Douban. For each dataset, we mark of the last 10% items of each user as the test set to evaluate the recommendation accuracy of different methods. And we use the rest as train dataset and 10% of train dataset as validation to fit the models.

We evaluate the accuracy of different methods with four traditional metrics, namely precision(*Pre*), recall(*Rec*), mean average precision(*MAP*) and normalized discounted cumulative gain(*NDCG*). Here we consider top-N(i.e.,10, 15, 20) recommendation.

To validate the effectiveness of our model, we implement the following baselines for comparison, namely User-based kNN(k=50), LDA, FPMC[3], HMM[4], NSTAR('N' is short for Non-personalized, where users share a common prior).

3.2 Experimental Results

Quality: Table 1 shows the quality of evaluation metrics on the two datasets for different methods respectively. We discover that our proposed methods, which take advantage of both the LDA and MC, are superior to any single model of LDA or MC, because the global patterns of items and the first-order markov property have been captured as the transition matrix in our model. Additionally, Both FPMC[3] and our method work pretty well in MAP and $NDCG$ on the two sequential datasets since we all consider designing a ranking loss function directly. Furthermore, STAR also surpasses NSTAR with the fact that learning a personalized

[1]http://grouplens.org/datasets/movielens/
[2]http://www.douban.com

Metric		*Pre*	*Rec*	*MAP*	*NDCG*	*Pre*	*Rec*	*MAP*	*NDCG*	*Pre*	*Rec*	*MAP*	*NDCG*
Data	Method	@10				@15				@20			
MovieLens	User kNN	0.0091	0.0162	0.0103	0.0364	0.0109	0.0302	0.0197	0.0515	0.0122	0.0456	0.0305	0.0638
	LDA	0.0478	0.0395	0.0437	0.1610	0.0453	0.0540	0.0623	0.1726	0.0430	0.0687	0.0798	0.1791
	HMM[4]	0.0500	0.0447	0.0520	0.1611	0.0465	0.0625	0.0735	0.1703	0.0432	0.0764	0.0933	0.1750
	FPMC[3]	0.0473	0.0448	0.0499	0.1808	0.0448	0.0637	0.0716	0.1958	0.0422	0.0794	0.0920	**0.2026**
	NSTAR	0.0514	0.0451	0.0517	0.1746	0.0481	0.0623	0.0731	0.1866	0.0450	0.0775	0.0931	0.1941
	STAR	**0.0566**	**0.0489**	**0.0558**	**0.1872**	**0.0521**	**0.0687**	**0.0793**	**0.1980**	**0.0483**	**0.0837**	**0.1011**	**0.2026**
Douban	User kNN	0.0091	0.0010	0.0010	0.0301	0.0313	0.0055	0.0054	0.1131	0.0316	0.0074	0.0073	0.1217
	LDA	0.0546	0.0062	0.0067	0.1534	0.0505	0.0086	0.0097	0.1629	0.0476	0.0108	0.0124	0.1689
	HMM[4]	0.0528	0.0062	0.0062	0.1709	0.0516	0.0091	0.0093	0.1798	0.0518	0.0120	0.0123	0.1835
	FPMC[3]	0.0528	0.0062	**0.0070**	0.1656	0.0493	0.0086	**0.0103**	0.1797	0.0474	0.0110	0.0127	0.1887
	NSTAR	0.0533	0.0061	0.0068	0.1609	0.0507	0.0088	0.0098	0.1732	0.0477	0.0110	0.0126	0.1814
	STAR	**0.0586**	**0.0067**	**0.0070**	**0.1744**	**0.0564**	**0.0096**	**0.0103**	**0.1867**	**0.0546**	**0.0125**	**0.0134**	**0.1967**

Table 1: Metrics evaluation of different methods on two datasets.

prior for distinct users is beneficial to modeling users' personalized favorites. In a word, our model could give a better explanation for the general item selection process and thus move a step closer to persuasive recommendations.

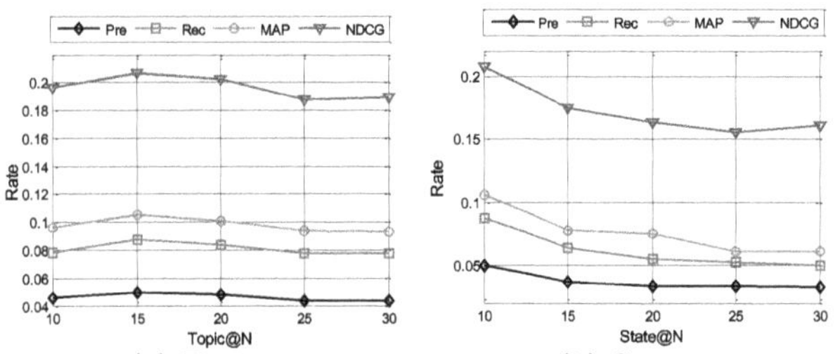

(a) Topics (b) States

Figure 3: The Number of States and Topics Analysis

Topics and States Analysis: We fix the number of states/topics at 10, and vary the number of topics T/states C from 10 to 30 respectively. The evaluation metrics results on the MovieLens are plotted in Figure 3(a) and (b) respectively. We can see in 3(a) that the recommendation performance remains relatively stable when varying the value of T. It can be shown in 3(b) clearly that the performance consistently decreases as the number of states increases. Furthermore, it is shown that both MAP and $NDCG$ have shaken greater than Pre as well as Rec with the mutative number of topics.

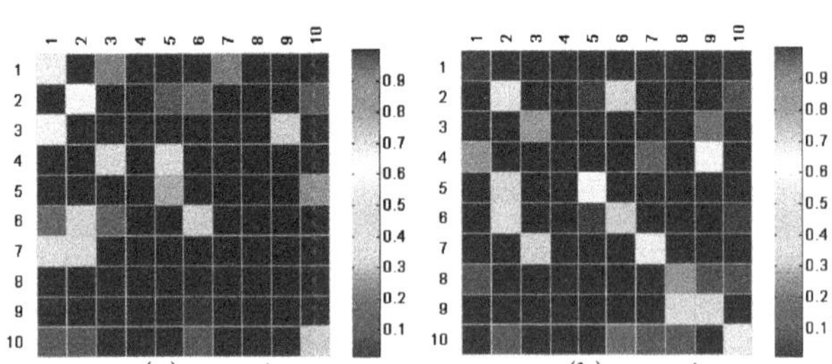

(a) user i (b) user j

Figure 4: User's Personalized Favorites Study

User's Personalized Favorites Study: Figure 4 shows the transition matrices of a pair randomly selected users in MovieLens (we denote as user i, j). Each row/column denotes a hidden state of the unified model. Brighter colors indicate high probability. We can draw that the item selection of user i usually depends on her long-term favorites (e.g., c=1, a special hidden state for topics in LDA, occupies a high percentage.), while user j would also like to follow her short-term favorites (e.g., large values in diagonal elements, indicating that the user probably selects items based on her recent favorites).

4. CONCLUSION

In this paper, we try to model user's item selection behavior and address the recommendation task on sequential data. Specifically, we present a transition graph for collaborative filtering that accounts for mining user's short-term favorites, jointed with a generative topic model for expressing user's long-term favorites. A personalized prior is introduced so as to express users' distinct favorites. The results show that our method outperforms state-of-the-art methods.

5. ACKNOWLEDGMENTS

This work was supported in part by National Natural Science Foundation of China (Grant No. 61170127).

6. REFERENCES

[1] T. L. Griffiths, M. Steyvers, D. M. Blei, and J. B. Tenenbaum. Integrating topics and syntax. In *Advances in neural information processing systems*, pages 537–544, 2004.

[2] R. Krestel, P. Fankhauser, and W. Nejdl. Latent dirichlet allocation for tag recommendation. In *Proceedings of the third ACM conference on Recommender systems*, pages 61–68. ACM, 2009.

[3] S. Rendle, C. Freudenthaler, and L. Schmidt-Thieme. Factorizing personalized markov chains for next-basket recommendation. In *Proceedings of the 19th international conference on World wide web*, pages 811–820. ACM, 2010.

[4] N. Sahoo, P. V. Singh, and T. Mukhopadhyay. A hidden markov model for collaborative filtering. *MIS Quarterly*, 36(4):1329–1356, 2012.

[5] B. Sarwar, G. Karypis, J. Konstan, and J. Riedl. Item-based collaborative filtering recommendation algorithms. In *Proceedings of the 10th international conference on World Wide Web*, pages 285–295. ACM, 2001.

[6] D. Yang, T. Chen, W. Zhang, and Y. Yu. Collaborative filtering with short term preferences mining. In *Proceedings of the 35th international ACM SIGIR conference on Research and development in information retrieval*, pages 1043–1044. ACM, 2012.

[7] F. Zhang, N. J. Yuan, D. Lian, and X. Xie. Mining novelty-seeking trait across heterogeneous domains. In *Proceedings of the 23rd international conference on World wide web*, pages 373–384. International World Wide Web Conferences Steering Committee, 2014.

Recommending Short-lived Dynamic Packages for Golf Booking Services

Robin M. E. Swezey Young-joo Chung
Rakuten Institute of Technology
1-14-1 Tamagawa, Setagaya-ku
Tokyo, Japan
{rswezey, yjchung}@acm.org

ABSTRACT

We introduce an approach to recommending short-lived dynamic packages for golf booking services. Two challenges are addressed in this work. The first is the short life of the items, which puts the system in a state of a permanent cold start. The second is the uninformative nature of the package attributes, which makes clustering or figuring latent packages challenging. Although such settings are fairly pervasive, they have not been studied in traditional recommendation research, and there is thus a call for original approaches for recommender systems. In this paper, we introduce a hybrid method that leverages user analysis and its relation to the packages, as well as package pricing and environmental analysis, and traditional collaborative filtering. The proposed approach achieved appreciable improvement in precision compared with baselines.

Categories and Subject Descriptors

H.3.3 [**Information Search and Retrieval**]: Information Filtering

General Terms

Experimentation, Measurement, Verification

Keywords

Dynamic packages, cold-start, recommendation, field study, user analysis

1. INTRODUCTION

Consider the booking or renting of a particular place on a reservation site. Specifically, we consider booking a round of golf through a golf booking service. Golf courses can be booked by users with a variety of options and prices: party size, a caddie to carry golf clubs, lunch, a guarantee of two-person *pair* parties, a competition option for several parties, and a certain start time, among many other options. We would like to recommend to users not only courses they may like, but also priced packages of options that they may like on top of recommended parent courses.

Such options as described above are wide ranging. Extensive options are provided not only for golf courses on Rakuten GORA, but hotels as well: rooms on Rakuten Travel can be booked with many options ranging from breakfast/lunch/dinner to late checkout, and an outdoor bath. Additionally, coupons can be considered as short-lived dynamic packages that target regular E-commerce products. Car rental services also use such packages. In the present paper, we refer to these packages as *short-lived dynamic booking packages*. Recommendations exist in the form of advertisement for this type of item in golf, but a preliminary survey[1] tells us that non-trivial recommendation systems seem not to exist. Considering the scale of the target industry given its user mass[2] as well as its average order value[3], the recommendation of packages is essential for business success. However, to the best of our knowledge, such recommendations have not been studied in traditional research.

There are two main challenges in recommending such packages. The first relates to their *short-lived* aspect; on a B2B2C site, merchants (e.g., golf course owners or hotel owners) input the packages for their course and set different prices according to options, season, trends, and target customers. We found that most such packages expire in a month after the start of their active period, including very short time-limited special offers (Figure 1). Moreover, the price trends is what makes the packages *dynamic* (Figure 2). This puts the package recommendation system under a regime of a permanent cold start. Ratings, the objective variable most favored by classical collaborative filtering approaches for atomic items, are not available. Co-counting using purchasing/browsing history is also very limited, as customers book an average of 4.5 courses per year, i.e., one package every 2.7 months. This means that they do not book packages fast enough on average for traditional models to be learned and used in the short term.

In recommendation, the straightforward approach under a cold start regime or working on long-tailed items is to turn to content-based methods of information retrieval. This gives rise to the second challenge: uninformative data. Package

Permission to make digital or hard copies of all or part of this work for personal or classroom use is granted without fee provided that copies are not made or distributed for profit or commercial advantage and that copies bear this notice and the full citation on the first page. Copyrights for components of this work owned by others than ACM must be honored. Abstracting with credit is permitted. To copy otherwise, or republish, to post on servers or to redistribute to lists, requires prior specific permission and/or a fee. Request permissions from Permissions@acm.org.
CIKM'15, October 19–23, 2015, Melbourne, Australia.
© 2015 ACM. ISBN 978-1-4503-3794-6/15/10 ...$15.00.
DOI: http://dx.doi.org/10.1145/2806416.2806608.

[1]Survey conducted in 2013 on the following websites: Alba (Japan), GDO (Japan), Golf-Jalan (Japan), GolfDigest (US), TeeOffTimes (UK).
[2]On the order of 3 million users on Rakuten GORA alone, approximately 2.5% of the population of Japan.
[3]The AOV is approximately 90 USD per golf reservation.

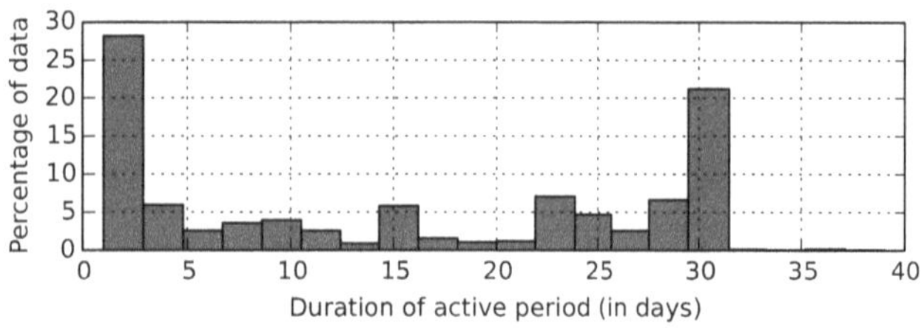

Figure 1: Histogram of package lifespans in the period of June 2012 through May 2013.

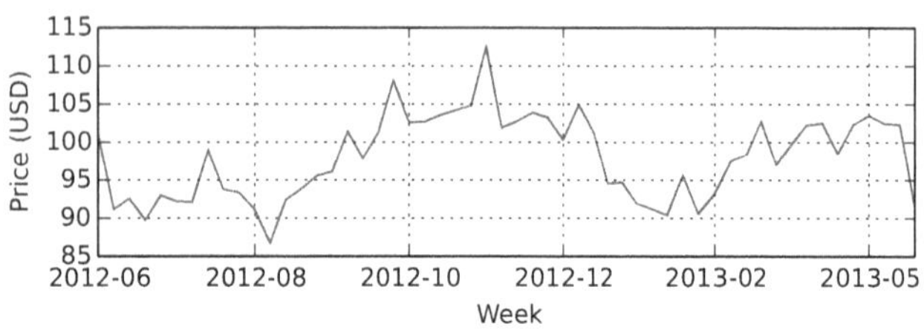

Figure 2: Weekly price trends of packages.

contents comprise flags and categorical variables for various options, but analysis of the items alone based on their content results in poor clusters or latent packages, because options have different importance to the package value from the point of view of the user. Thus, direct application of clustering using similarities such as the Jaccard index, where every attribute is weighed the same, performs poorly.

In addressing the challenges mentioned, we leverage reservation histories enriched with package and course data to assess user behavior, and conduct an analysis of package pricing. This allows us to construct a similarity score that performs well. Our approach is threefold, in that we:

1. extract user behavioral characteristics,
2. conduct collaborative filtering on parent items, and
3. perform content-based information retrieval using user preferences and the package price.

2. RECOMMENDING GOLF PACKAGES

2.1 User-weighed package similarity

Plan data themselves are uninformative for similarity (as shown in Section 3.1 by Jaccard's poor precision). We analyze packages through users, enriching their reservation history with package and course data. The data were aggregated to build user behavior vectors, which we Z-transformed and clustered using Euclidean k-means. Figure 3 shows vastly different behaviors with regard to package options and price (e.g., spending deviation growing with the spending average), and a need to develop adequate similarity metrics. We define the user-weighed option similarity score for a package p with respect to a user u as

$$\tilde{S}_{opt}(p|u) = \sum_{k \in O} P(p_k|u)$$

where k belongs to the subset O of vector indices of p denoting flags or dummy-coded categorical attributes, and P is a logistic factor such as

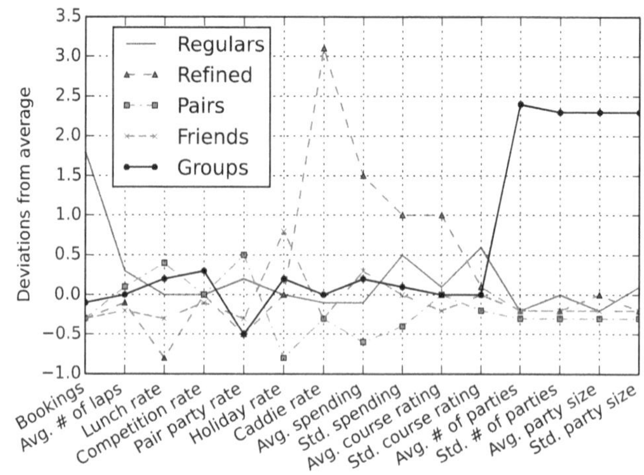

Figure 3: Cluster centroids of users having booked at least two courses. ***Pairs*** **and** ***friends*** **each comprise 35% of users, while the others each comprise 10%.**

Table 1: Weights of logistic models predicting occurrence of options in the next booking. Only weights that are over 10^{-1} for a response (in bold) are shown.

	Options		
User attribute	Caddie	Holiday	Lunch
Lunch rate	**-0.315**	**-0.1829**	**1.4113**
Competition rate	0.0351	-0.0166	**0.1656**
Holiday rate	**-0.351**	**1.6612**	**-0.1516**
Caddie rate	**3.0924**	**-0.6099**	**-0.1776**
Avg. spending	**0.201**	0.092	**-0.103**
Avg. course rating	**0.3673**	**-0.3004**	**0.2138**
Std. course rating	**0.295**	**-0.3063**	0.0637
Avg. # of parties	**-0.9268**	**-0.1061**	**-0.1751**
Std. # of parties	**0.1424**	0.0083	**0.117**
Avg. party size	**0.2164**	0.0064	0.0667
Intercept	**-5.6731**	**-0.6552**	0.0487

$$P(p_k|u) = \frac{1}{1 + e^{-(\beta_{0,S_u} + \beta_{1,S_u}^T u)}},$$

where β_{0,S_u} and β_{1,S_u} are respectively the intercept and coefficient vector for cluster S_u to which u belongs after clustering. This probability corresponds to user u choosing the option p_k for the next booking. $P(P_k|U)$ is learned by leaving the last package $p^{(last)}$ booked by a user and using its $p_{k \in O}^{(last)}$ as dependent variables and the user vector as independent variable for learning. We show example logistic weights for three output probabilities in Table 1, each predicting the future occurrence of an option[4].

2.2 Reference course and package

The reference package is used mainly to compute the price similarity described in Section 2.4. It is also necessary to perform the subsequent experiments of this paper for the

[4]We used Weka version 5.3.001 for computing logistic regression (http://www.cs.waikato.ac.nz/ml/weka/).

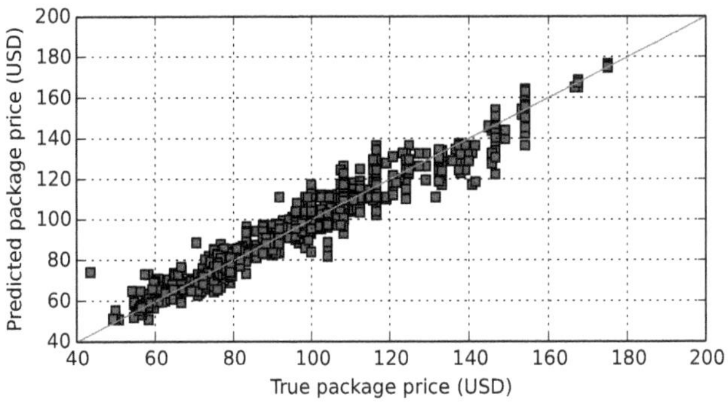

Figure 4: True prices vs. predictions for a course.

Table 2: Sets of features for the linear model of price. The final set is $\{m\} \times \{d\} \times A \times P$.

Set	Features
Temporal	Month of year (m), day of week (d)
Attributes (A)	Lunch, caddie, competition, pair party, min. party size, min. nb. of parties, nb. of laps
Promotional (P)	Promotion type, shortness of package

Jaccard baseline (Section 3.1). We first extract the reference course that was played the most in the season closest to the target season, using a simple scoring function. For example, if we would like to recommend packages in June, a course played twice around June scores higher than one played twice in December. This is based on the assumption that a user likes a course if he has booked it several times, and the observation that users have affinities to courses that are seasonal. Once the reference course is selected, we simply select the last package booked as the reference package.

2.3 Filtering of parent items

Collaborative filtering should be leveraged wherever possible, even if impractical for the granularity of packages. In our case, there are 1,951 courses in our system, each generating packages that we want to recommend on top of them to users. This gives us a parent course item/item co-occurrence matrix for courses of rank 1,951. Because we have at least 100,000 active users in the period to populate the co-occurrence matrix, the matrix is very dense, which works well with collaborative filtering. As the course recommender already performs well on Rakuten GORA, we choose to use it in a collaborative filtering step to filter courses of interest to the user.

2.4 Price similarity

To improve the scoring function, we develop a similarity component based on package price, which should be leveraged because our analyses reveal two important patterns:

1. 90% of users do not deviate by more than 30% from their average spending (the remaining 10% belong to the cluster of *refined* users in Figure 3), and

2. the price itself contains enough information about the package to make it a potent similarity measure.

To demonstrate point (2), we run a regression on a course in the data that has generated many packages. Using the Cartesian feature set of Table 2, we build a linear model that gives prices of packages that are fairly close to the truth (see Figure 4). Note that the plot in Figure 4 is heteroscedastic, which shows that pricing becomes loose at the high end, as consistently does spending (Section 2.1). We define price similarity score for a package p with respect to a user u and a reference plan $p^{(ref)}$ selected from his/her history as

$$\tilde{S}_{price}(p|p^{(ref)}, u) = \frac{1}{1 + \frac{r_{t_p, t_{p^{(ref)}}}}{\omega + \sigma^{(u)}_{price}} \|price_p - price_{p^{(ref)}}\|},$$

where $r_{t_p, t_{p^{(ref)}}}$ is the ratio of seasonal averages between p and $p^{(ref)}$ compensating for seasonal trends, ω is a currency scaling factor, and $\sigma^{(u)}_{price}$ is the user's spending deviation.

2.5 Final score

The final score is defined as

$$\tilde{S}(p|p^{(ref)}, u) = (w_p \tilde{S}_{price} + w_o \tilde{S}_{opt} + w_c \tilde{S}_c)[p|p^{(ref)}, u],$$

where $\tilde{S}_c$ is the parent course score after filtering (Section 2.3), and w_p, w_o and w_c are weights whose optimal values can be found through hill-climbing with respect to EMP@n.

3. EXPERIMENTS

This section details the offline and online evaluation. For offline evaluation, we compared the precision of our approach with that of the basic similarity method, and tested three different options. We then launched an e-mail campaign for online evaluation. None of our data contains personal information such as names or addresses.

3.1 Offline evaluation

We tested our proposed methods on golf booking data collected from June 2012 to May 2013. The number of unique users in this period is 521,442 and the total number of bookings is 2,499,678. We used the booking history from June 2012 to May 2013 to generate the package recommendations. We then checked what packages users actually booked from 1 June 2013 to 15 June 2013. We call this evaluation index the *expected minimum precision* (EMP), because the number of booked packages would increase if users interact with our recommendation results. This setting has been widely used in the evaluation of recommender systems; e.g., [5]. The EMP is defined as

$$P_n = \sum_{u \in U} \frac{|recommendations_{u,n} \cap truth_u|}{|truth_u|}.$$

We test four settings in this experiment:

1. the Jaccard score computed as

$$S_J(p, p^{(ref)}) = \frac{|p \cap p^{(ref)}|}{|p \cup p^{(ref)}|}$$

in place of S_{price} and S_{opt}, where the p values are here used to denote the attribute sets,

2. the user-weighed option similarity S_{opt} without S_{price},

3. the final score incorporating S_{opt} and S_{price} without $r_{t_p, t_{p^{(ref)}}}$ for price adjustment, and

4. the final score incorporating S_{opt} and S_{price} with $r_{t_p, t_{p^{(ref)}}}$ for price adjustment.

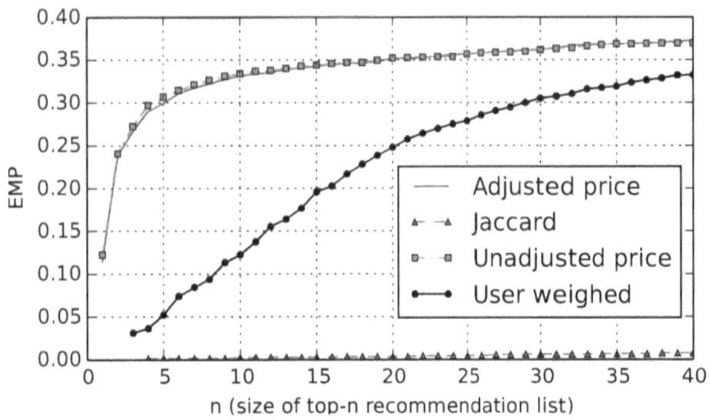

Figure 5: EMP@n curves for each tested method.

Each of these settings incorporate the same reference course and package selection step (Section 2.2) and course filtering step (Section 2.3).

Figure 5 shows that the scores incorporating price similarity perform best, independently of price trend adjustment. User-weighed similarity performs reasonably well but not nearly as well as when price is incorporated. Finally, the Jaccard baseline shows very poor performance. For a top-five returned list, the EMP of the proposed method is 25% more efficient than that of user-weighed similarity, and 30% more than that of the Jaccard baseline.

3.2 Online Evaluation

We performed online evaluation by conducting a personalized e-mail campaign. We sent e-mails that contained six recommended packages on one day in December 2014 and evaluated the click-to-open-rate (CTOR) and conversion-to-open-rate (CVR). Here, the CVR refers to the event that a customer clicked on the recommended package and made a reservation. We compared the performance to that of previous and following e-mail campaigns. E-mails in these two campaigns contained approximately 100 packages selected by specialists based on their contents and target demographics. Our approach achieved the highest CTOR and CVR with the maximum improvement in the CTOR was 200%.

4. RELATED WORK

We briefly describe previous research on dynamic items and a cold start. Schein et al. [4] raised the cold-start problem in recommendation. To overcome the lack of user preference information that is essential for collaborative filtering, they proposed a probabilistic model that combines content and collaborative filtering. Chu and Park [1] combined user and item profiles in a dynamic bilinear model for time-aware recommendation for the Today module on the Yahoo! front page. Matrix factorization techniques that solve a cold-start problem were also proposed in several works [2, 3].

The crucial difference between short-lived dynamic items and the items in the research body on permanent cold-start regimes is their short life-span and non-retrievable aspects. To be more specific, *short-lived* items will expire within a month after the start of their active period, as is shown by our observations (Figure 1). Such items cannot be retrieved (i.e., booked, searched for, browsed, or recommended) by/to users once they expire. They also have generally poor statistical value in a user/item matrix because of their capped counts, especially when this matrix does not embody a notion of time and relevance to the present.

On the other hand, Zhu et al. [5] proposed the bundle recommendation problem in e-commerce. According to the observation that users usually buy more than one item on e-commerce sites and that displaying related items together improves conversion, they proposed a recommender system that maximizes the reward function (conversion rate and revenue/profit of the bundle). This work is different from ours in that it focused on creating bundles, whereas our work focuses on recommending packages that are created by merchants using different values of limited attributes such as lunch, and competition.

5. CONCLUSION AND FUTURE WORKS

In this work, we identified a pervasive subset of items that ought to be the subject of a recommendation research: short-lived dynamic booking packages. We showed that the problem is unique in terms of the short lifespan of items and the uninformative nature of the data, which calls for an original recommendation approach. We performed an experiment over a subset of users that resulted in appreciable improvements in EMP when leveraging user analysis and price analysis of the package to define adequate scoring functions. We also performed an actual A/B test for a mail recommendation and found that the click-to-open rate was twice that achieved with human selection of packages. In further work, we would like to refine the metrics and address a third challenge, namely that booking packages are designed to *book* a parent item, which inherently adds a notion of *schedule* to the problem constraints and makes recommendation challenging when the user schedule is unknown.

Acknowledgements

We would like to thank Satoko Marumoto, Takahiro Kuroda, Yusuke Sasamori, Ryo Yoneda, Yoshiro Matsuda, Yu Hirate, and all contributors to this research for their support.

6. REFERENCES

[1] Chu, W., and Park, S.-T. Personalized recommendation on dynamic content using predictive bilinear models. In *Proceedings of the 18th International Conference on World Wide Web* (New York, NY, USA, 2009), WWW '09, ACM, pp. 691–700.

[2] Koenigstein, N., Dror, G., and Koren, Y. Yahoo! music recommendations: Modeling music ratings with temporal dynamics and item taxonomy. In *Proceedings of the Fifth ACM Conference on Recommender Systems* (New York, NY, USA, 2011), RecSys '11, ACM, pp. 165–172.

[3] Saveski, M., and Mantrach, A. Item cold-start recommendations: Learning local collective embeddings. In *Proceedings of the 8th ACM Conference on Recommender Systems* (New York, NY, USA, 2014), RecSys '14, ACM, pp. 89–96.

[4] Schein, A. I., Popescul, A., Ungar, L. H., and Pennock, D. M. Methods and metrics for cold-start recommendations. In *Proceedings of the 25th Annual International ACM SIGIR Conference on Research and Development in Information Retrieval* (New York, NY, USA, 2002), SIGIR '02, ACM, pp. 253–260.

[5] Zhu, T., Harrington, P., Li, J., and Tang, L. Bundle recommendation in ecommerce. In *Proceedings of the 37th international ACM SIGIR conference on Research & development in information retrieval* (2014), ACM, pp. 657–666.

Large-Scale Question Answering with Joint Embedding and Proof Tree Decoding

Zhenghao Wang, Shengquan Yan, Huaming Wang, Xuedong Huang
Microsoft Corporation
One Microsoft Way
Redmond, WA 98052
{zhwang | shenyan | huawang | xdh}@microsoft.com

ABSTRACT
Question answering (QA) over a large-scale knowledge base (KB) such as Freebase is an important natural language processing application. There are linguistically oriented semantic parsing techniques and machine learning motivated statistical methods. Both of these approaches face a key challenge on how to handle diverse ways natural questions can be expressed about predicates and entities in the KB. This paper is to investigate how to combine these two approaches. We frame the problem from a proof-theoretic perspective, and formulate it as a proof tree search problem that seamlessly unifies semantic parsing, logic reasoning, and answer ranking. We combine our word entity joint embedding learned from web-scale data with other surface-form features to further boost accuracy improvements. Our real-time system on the Freebase QA task achieved a very high F1 score (47.2) on the standard Stanford WebQuestions benchmark test data.

Categories and Subject Descriptors
H.3.3 [**Information Search and Retrieval**]: Selection process; I.2.3 [**Deduction and Theorem Proving**]: Deduction; I.2.6 [**Learning**]: Concept learning; I.2.7 [**Natural Language Processing**]: Language parsing and understanding

General Terms
Algorithms, Experimentation

Keywords
Question answering, Freebase, Joint embedding, Proof tree

1. INTRODUCTION
Question Answering (QA) from an existing knowledge base (KB) has drawn significant interest from both the industry and the academia [12], [8], [10], [3], [4], [2], [16], [19], [7], and [14]. QA on large scale structured KBs are critical to modern web search engines such as Bing and Google, spoken language dialog systems such as Cortana or Siri [11], and integrated search and browsing applications [9]. However, open-domain QA with complex natural language and logic reasoning remains a major scientific and engineering challenge. The scale of the KB and the difficulty for machines to interpret spoken language questions accurately make open-domain QA an unsolved problem.

Permission to make digital or hard copies of all or part of this work for personal or classroom use is granted without fee provided that copies are not made or distributed for profit or commercial advantage and that copies bear this notice and the full citation on the first page. Copyrights for components of this work owned by others than ACM must be honored. Abstracting with credit is permitted. To copy otherwise, or republish, to post on servers or to redistribute to lists, requires prior specific permission and/or a fee. Request permissions from Permissions@acm.org.
CIKM'15, October 19–23, 2015, Melbourne, VIC, Australia.
© 2015 ACM. ISBN 978-1-4503-3794-6/15/10…$15.00.
DOI: http://dx.doi.org/10.1145/2806416.2806616

We focus on our text-based QA system over a well-known large scale knowledge base Freebase [5]. We use a version of Freebase as referenced in http://www-nlp.stanford.edu/software/sempre/, which contains 41m entities, 19k properties, and 596m assertions [4]. The underlying text-based QA technology discussed in this paper can be easily extended for other spoken language or multimodal interactive systems [11][11]. One of the key challenges is how to handle the diverse ways natural language questions are expressed about predicates and entities in the KB. Traditionally, a semantic parser is used to convert questions in natural language utterances into logical forms such as lambda expressions, which are then evaluated against the KB. Such a semantic parser may be learned from pairs of utterances and logical forms, but such labeled training data are typically associated with high development cost and thus limit coverage of the trained semantic parser [21]. Recently, a number of novel approaches have been proposed to loosen the requirement of KB-specific logical forms and to utilize models learned from large amounts of data not covered by the KB [13], [3], [4]. We follow along this path and present a new practical approach that demonstrates a significant improvement over current state-of-the-art systems on the WebQuestions evaluation data set [3]. Our approach is different from ParaSempre in two ways: first we use a domain-independent word-entity embedding system in enhancing the quality of entity linking; second we allow arbitrarily complex logic formula generation to help us search for the best match, while ParaSempre uses predefined templates to generate finite logic formula.

In our approach, ground facts in the KB are used to derive an infinite number of ground logical formulae (i.e., no free variables) in the form of proof trees. An answer to a question is backed by a proof tree that uses ground facts in the KB as input and generates a logical formula that matches the input question. The QA process is thus a logic reasoning process to find a proof that generates a logical formula to best match the input question.

Our KB-based QA system can be viewed as a decoding problem where the search space is composed of proof trees derived from the KB. The objective function of the decoder is our match score between the output of a proof tree and the input question. The former (proof tree output) is a logical formula, while the latter (input question) is a natural language utterance. The physical interpretation of the match score is related to the probability for the natural language utterance to express the corresponding logical formula.

We define our system match score between a logical formula and a question utterance as a log-linear superposition of several features. The features are based on the logical formula, the question utterance, and/or a set of utterances realized from the logical formula.

A layered pruning approach is adopted to significantly improve our decoding efficiency. Our system consists of three layers:

- L0 entity linking,
- L1 proof tree searching, and
- L2 proof tree ranking.

L0 derives anchor entities to form the leaf nodes of our proof trees. L1 further searches for the best N candidate proof trees using only the most efficient match score features. L2 ranks the best N proof trees using a more comprehensive set of match score features.

We demonstrate a competitive QA system in terms of accuracy. In our benchmarking with the Stanford WebQuestions dataset, which contains questions commonly asked by web users, our system achieved F1 measure of 47.2 on the test set using the same dev and test data split and evaluation script as published at http://www-nlp.stanford.edu/software/sempre/. The F1 measure is significantly higher than the best published result of 39.9 achieved by a single system ([4]), or 41.8 from an ensemble of two best systems ([7]).

2. JOINT EMBEDDING

All words and entities can be jointly embedded into a low-dimensional intent space through massive scale statistical learning. The training data are text-entity pairs. There are several means to obtain such training pairs. For example, we can use entity names, aliases, descriptions, etc. contained in Freebase itself. User interaction data such click-through data logged by search engines are also very valuable. We mixed and deduped text-entity pairs from several sources to create a massive training corpus with over 50 billion text-entity pairs to develop our domain-independent language embedding.

Every word (q) and every entity (E) are embedded into a low-dimensional vector space with a joint objective function. The parameters to be learned are the vectors for each word ($\mathbf{x}_q$) and entity ($\mathbf{x}_E$). The training objective is to maximize mutual information (MMI) between word and entity pairs ([15]):

$$\Lambda = \sum_{q,E} P(q,E) \log \frac{\exp(\lambda \mathbf{x}_q \cdot \mathbf{x}_E) P(q)}{\sum_q \exp(\lambda \mathbf{x}_q \cdot \mathbf{x}_E) P(q)},$$

Where $P(q,E)$ are empirical (observed) pair probability and $P(q) = \sum_E P(q,E)$. Informally, $\mathbf{x}_q \cdot \mathbf{x}_E$ is the similarity measure between vector $\mathbf{x}_q$ and $\mathbf{x}_E$, and usually dot product works reasonably well. Formally, the model predicts $P(q|E)$ as:

$$P(q|E; \mathbf{x}_q, \mathbf{x}_E) = \frac{\exp(\lambda \mathbf{x}_q \cdot \mathbf{x}_E) P(q)}{\sum_{q'} \exp(\lambda \mathbf{x}_{q'} \cdot \mathbf{x}_E) P(q')}.$$

The gradient descent algorithm is used to estimate our model, with gradient calculated using the back propagation method.

We use the learned embeddings in two ways: first we use them in L0 entity linking to rank entity candidates for a given question; second we use word-entity embedding similarity as feature to L2 proof tree ranking.

3. PROOF TREE DECODING

3.1 Logical formulae

Every ground fact in the KB is a ground (no free variable) logical formula that is deemed true. Multiple facts can be combined through a reasoning process to achieve a new fact, which is another logical formula that is also true. If the new fact matches the input question, it provides an answer to the input question. The logical reasoning process can be described by a deduction with KB facts as input and the new fact as output.

The logical formulae are formulated after combinators because we would like to match them against natural language utterances. For example, "Barack Obama's spouse is Michelle Obama" is expressed as

$$= (\text{spouse bo})\ \text{mo},$$

where bo and mo means entities for "Barack Obama" and "Michelle Obama".

Existential variables are used for implicit entities (e.g., events) in the sentence. For example, "Barack Obama married Michelle Obama" is expressed as

$$\exists e.\text{all}\ (= (\text{v}\ e)\ \text{marry})\ (= (\text{s}\ e)\ \text{bo})\ (= (\text{o}\ e)\ \text{mo}),$$

i.e., there exists an event e whose verb is marry, subject is bo, and object is mo. Please note event e is a real entity in the KB, but it is not explicitly mentioned in natural language utterances.

The most basic combinators in our logical formulae are the properties in the KB (of type $Value \rightarrow Value$) and the "=" combinator (of type $Value \rightarrow Value \rightarrow Bool$). We also introduce a limited number of additional combinators inspired by natural language, such as "v", "s", and "o" in the above expression.

Inference rules are specified to derive new logical formula. For example, the following inference rule derives "Barack Obama married Michelle Obama" from two facts in the KB:

$$\frac{\begin{array}{c} = (e'\ \text{fb:/people/marriage/spouse})\ x \\ = (e'\ \text{fb:/people/marriage/spouse})\ y \\ x \neq y \end{array}}{\exists e.\text{all}\ (= (\text{v}\ e)\ \text{marry})\ (= (\text{s}\ e)\ x)\ (= (\text{o}\ e)\ y)},$$

And the following rule further derives "Barack Obama's spouse is Michelle Obama:"

$$\frac{\exists e.\text{all}\ (= (\text{v}\ e)\ \text{marry})\ (= (\text{s}\ e)\ x)\ (= (\text{o}\ e)\ y)}{= (\text{spouse}\ x)\ y}.$$

The purpose of inference rules is to enable introducing human knowledge easily into the QA system.

3.2 Surface-form utterances

We specify syntax to generate surface-form utterances from logical formulae in CFG-like production rules. For example:

$$\begin{array}{l} \Sigma(= (p\ x)\ y) \rightarrow \text{what is } \Sigma(x)\text{ 's } \Sigma(p); \\ \Sigma(= (p\ x)\ y) \rightarrow \text{what is } \Sigma(p) \text{ of } \Sigma(x); \\ \Sigma(= (p\ x)\ y) \rightarrow \text{what } \Sigma(T(y)) \text{ is } \Sigma(x)\text{ 's } \Sigma(p); \\ \Sigma(= (p\ x)\ y) \rightarrow \text{what } \Sigma(T(y)) \text{ is } \Sigma(p) \text{ of } \Sigma(x); \\ \Sigma(= (p\ x)\ y) \rightarrow \text{who is } \Sigma(x)\text{ 's } \Sigma(p); \\ \Sigma(= (p\ x)\ y) \rightarrow \text{who is } \Sigma(p) \text{ of } \Sigma(x), \end{array}$$

where $\Sigma(L)$ can be interpreted as the set of utterances L can realize, and $T(y)$ is the type of y.

The realized utterances are used to provide mostly surface-form features to compute a match score of a logical formula to the input question. Specifically, the match score is defined as

$$M(L,Q) = \max_{S \in \Sigma(L)} \log P(L,S|Q),$$

where L is a logical formula, Q is the input question utterance, and S is a realized utterance L produces. $\log P(L, S|Q)$ is defined with a superposition of various log-linear features:

$$\log P(L, S|Q) = \sum_i \lambda_i f_i(L, S, Q),$$

where each feature f_i might depend on only some of L, S, Q. For example, paraphrasing features are only between S and Q.

3.3 Search Problem

The search graph starts with individual ground facts contained in the KB. They derive new logical formulae using inference rules. Every logical formula has a match score against the input question. The goal is to find the logical formula with the highest match score:

$$L^* = \underset{\text{KB} \Downarrow L}{\operatorname{argmax}} M(L, Q),$$

where KB $\Downarrow L$ means that KB can derive L.

3.4 Search Algorithm

We use best-first search algorithm. At every step, an existing logical formula L with the highest heuristic future match score is chosen. All inference rules that take L as one input premise are applied to generate more logical formulae, which are pushed to the priority queue according to their future match scores.

We currently use the following simple heuristics to obtain future match scores. We create a directed graph of terminal symbols, where an edge is added between two terminal symbols when there is an inference rule that mentions the terminal symbols in the premise and in the result respectively. For example, there is an edge from "marry" to "spouse" in the directed graph. Then the syntactic production rules are augmented with descendent terminal symbols up to a certain depth. For example, in addition to producing "Who did Barack Obama marry," the corresponding formula also produces "Who did Barack Obama spouse" as a future utterance. Please note a future utterance is usually not a valid natural language utterance, and is only used to calculate the heuristic future match score. The future utterance is closer to the real utterance, e.g., "Who is Barack Obama's spouse."

The simple heuristic should in most cases generate an underestimate of the true match score. On the other hand, a good paraphrasing model complements the simple heuristic, although a complex paraphrasing model may be impractical to be used in our search due to runtime efficiency concerns.

3.5 Ranking Features

The top candidates from the search are ranked by a paraphrasing model. This is a log-linear model similar to the one used in [4], but is different in the feature sets and training algorithm.

We used the following groups of features in our paraphrasing model:

1. Matching scores from L1 candidate search.
2. 13 features from [17].
3. A subset of association features proposed in [4]. The subset was empirically chosen via cross validation to balance accuracy and computation cost.
4. Cosine similarity score between the vector representations for input question and candidate utterance realization.
5. L0 entity ranking score for the entity appear in the candidate.

The parameters of the log-linear model is learned using L-BFGS, with L1-regularization to avoid over fitting [1].

4. EXPERIMENT

4.1 Datasets

We use WebQuestions [3] dataset for training and evaluation of our system. WebQuestions dataset contains 5,810 question-answer pairs. Following [3], we use the same subset (3,778 question-answer pairs) as the development set (Dev), and use the other part (2,032 question-answer pairs) for evaluation.

We also used the same Freebase KB that was used by [3]. However we don't use off-the-shelf KB query engine, instead we process the KB data file, and load it into memory of our workstation for serving as it is now practical to do so with current hardware spec.

4.2 Search Parameters

We use the following search parameters in L1. At most 50 entities are returned by L0 and all their properties form the initial search nodes. The best-first search is capped at 100k logical formulae (with duplicates). The complexity of logical formulae is limited to 4 levels of composition. Top 10k logical formulae are deduped and passed onto L2 ranker.

With these search parameters, we are able to achieve an average L1 latency of 923ms single-threaded on the test set on a work-station with Intel Xeon E5-2630 CPU @ 2.60GHz and 256GB DDR3 RAM @ 1600MHz

4.3 Evaluation Results

Our system is compared with other systems in terms of F1 score. We use the evaluation script by [4] published at http://www-nlp.stanford.edu/software/sempre/. All other systems were reported by [7], except for the scores marked with *, which are clarified in [20].

Table 1. Results on WebQuestions test set

Method	F1 Score
(Berant et al., 2013)	35.7*
(Bordes et al., 2014a)	29.7
(Yao and Van Durme, 2014a)	35.4*
(Berant and Liang, 2014)	**39.9**
(Bordes et al., 2014b)	39.2
Ensemble of (Berant and Liang, 2014) and (Bordes et al. 2014b)	41.8
Our system	**47.2**

To understand the contribution of the joint word-entity embedding feature, we performed two variant experiments because the feature is used both in L0 entity linking and in L2 ranking: one removes the feature from L2, and the other removes it from both L0 and L2. The results are shown in Table 2, and indeed show that it contributes significant end-to-end accuracy gain when used both in L0 and in L2.

Table 2 Contribution from joint embedding

Variant	F1 Score
Full system	47.2
Without joint embedding in L2	46.4
Without joint embedding in L0+L2	41.3

5. CONCLUSION

Both semantic parsing and representation learning have been applied to the QA problem on a large KB. We attempted to unify the two approaches with a proof-theoretical frame-work. The problem is framed as searching for a proof tree from the KB to answer the natural language question. There are several advantages of our new approach.

Firstly, the logic forms explored by our decoding process are not limited by simple templates and thus we can potentially expand answering arbitrarily compositional questions.

Secondly, instead of approaching the KB from the input question, our approach reaches the input question from the KB. This means semantic parsing is embedded in the whole question answering process, and all facts in the KB can be used as early as possible to guide our improved semantic parsing.

Thirdly, our approach easily takes in representations learned from the KB itself and other domain-independent sources. In particular, we have shown that our maximum mutual information derived word-entity joint embedding can significantly improve accuracy of our QA system albeit these embedding vectors are domain-independent without task specific data adaptation.

Our QA system significantly outperforms the state of the art system on the same Stanford WebQuestions benchmark data. The proposed approach can be easily extended to other spoken language or multimodal interactive systems.

6. REFERENCES

[1] G. Andrew and J. Gao. 2010. Scalable training of L1-regularized log-linear models. In *Proceedings of the 24th International Conference on Machine Learning*, pages 33-40.

[2] J. Bao, N. Duan, M. Zhou, T. Zhao. 2014. Knowledge-Based Question Answering as Machine Translation. In *Proceedings of the 52nd Annual Meeting of the Association for Computational Linguistics*, pages 967-976.

[3] J. Berant, A. Chou, R. Frostig, and P. Liang. 2013. Semantic parsing on Freebase from question-answer pairs. In *Proceedings of the 2013 Conference on Empirical Methods in Natural Language Processing*, pages 1533-1544.

[4] J. Berant and P. Liang. 2014. Semantic Parsing via Paraphrasing. In *Proceedings of the 52nd Annual Meeting of the Association for Computational Linguistics*, pages 1415-1425.

[5] K. Bollacker, C. Evans, P. Paritosh, T. Sturge, and J. Taylor. 2008. Freebase: A Collaboratively Created Graph Database for Structuring Human Knowledge. In *Proceedings of the 2008 ACM SIGMOD International Conference on Management of Data*, pages 1247-1249.

[6] A. Bordes, J. Weston, and N. Usunier. 2014a. Open Question Answering with Weakly Supervised Embedding Models. In *Proceedings of the 7th European Conference on Machine Learning and Principles and Practice of Knowledge Discovery in Databases (ECML-PKDD'14)*, pages 165-180.

[7] A. Bordes, S. Chopra, and J. Weston. 2014b. Question Answering with Subgraph Embeddings. In *Proceedings of the 2014 Conference on Empirical Methods in Natural Language Processing (EMNLP)*, pages 615–620.

[8] Q. Cai. and A. Yates. 2013. Large-Scale Semantic Parsing via Schema Matching and Lexicon Extension. In *Proceedings of the 51st Annual Meeting of the Association for Computational Linguistics*, pages 423–433.

[9] Z. Chen, J. Sun, and X. Huang. 2014. Web Information at Your Fingertips: Paper as an Interaction Metaphor. In *Computer*, pages 62-66.

[10] A. Fader, L. Zettlemoyer, and O. Etzioni. 2013. Paraphrase-driven learning for open question answering. In *Proceedings of the 51st Annual Meeting of the Association for Computational Linguistics*, pages 1608–1618.

[11] X. Huang, J. Baker, and R. Reddy. 2014. A Historical Perspective of Speech Recognition. In *Communications of the ACM,* 57 (1), pages 94-103.

[12] O. Kolomiyets and M.-F. Moens. 2011. A survey on question answering technology from an information retrieval perspective. In *Information Sciences*, 181(24), pages 5412-5434.

[13] T. Kwiatkowski, E. Choi, Y. Artzi, and L. Zettlemoyer. 2013. Scaling semantic parsers with on-the-fly ontology matching. In *Proceedings of the 2013 Conference on Empirical Methods in Natural Language Processing*, pages 1545-1556.

[14] R. Mooney. 2014. Semantic Parsing, Past, Present and Future, In *ACL 2014 Workshop on Semantic Parsing*, Invited Talk.

[15] J. R. Pierce. 1980. An Introduction to Information Theory: Symbols, Signals and Noise, Dover Books on Mathematics, Dover Publications.

[16] M. Steedman. 2014. Robust Semantics of Semantic Parsing, In *ACL 2014 Workshop on Semantic Parsing*, Invited Talk.

[17] S. Wan, M. Dras, R. Dale, and C. Paris. 2006. Using dependency-based features to take the "para-farce" out of paraphrase. In *Australasian Language Technology Workshop.*

[18] Z. Wang, S. Yang, H. Wang, and X. Huang. 2014. An Overview of Microsoft Deep QA System on Stanford WebQuestions Benchmark. *Microsoft Research Technical Report MSR-TR-2014-121*

[19] X. Yao and B. Van Durme. 2014a. Information Extraction over Structured Data: Question Answering with Freebase. In *Proceedings of the 52nd Annual Meeting of the Association for Computational Linguistics*, pages 956-966.

[20] X. Yao, J. Berant, and B. Van Durme. 2014b. Freebase QA: Information Extraction or Semantic Parsing? In *Proceedings of the ACL 2014 Workshop on Semantic Parsing*, pages 82–86.

[21] L. Zettlemoyer and M. Collins. 2005. Learning to map sentences to logical form: structured classification with probabilistic categorial grammars. In *Proceedings of the Twenty First Conference on Uncertainty in Artificial Intelligence*, pages 658-666.

Query Length, Retrievability Bias and Performance

Colin Wilkie
School of Computing Science, University of Glasgow
Glasgow, United Kingdom
Colin.Wilkie@glasgow.ac.uk

Leif Azzopardi
School of Computing Science, University of Glasgow
Glasgow, United Kingdom
Leif.Azzopardi@glasgow.ac.uk

ABSTRACT

Past work has shown that longer queries tend to lead to better retrieval performance. However, this comes at the cost of increased user effort effort and additional system processing. In this paper, we examine whether there are benefits of longer queries beyond performance. We posit that increasing the query length will also lead to a reduction in the retrievability bias. Additionally, we speculate that to minimise retrievability bias as queries become longer, more length normalisation must be applied to account for the increase in the length of documents retrieved. To this end, we perform a retrievability analysis on two TREC collections using three standard retrieval models and various lengths of queries (one to five terms). From this investigation we find that increasing the length of queries reduces the overall retrievability bias but at a decreasing rate. Moreover, once the query length exceeds three terms the bias can begin to increase (and the performance can start to drop). We also observe that more document length normalisation is typically required as query length increases, in order to minimise bias. Finally, we show that there is a strong correlation between performance and retrieval bias. This work raises some interesting questions regarding query length and its affect on performance and bias. Further work will be directed towards examining longer and more verbose queries, including those generated via query expansion methods, to obtain a more comprehensive understanding of the relationship between query length, performance and retrievability bias.

Categories and Subject Descriptors

H.3.4 [**Information Storage and Retrieval**]: Systems and Software:Performance Evaluation

General Terms

Theory, Experimentation

Keywords

Retrievability, Performance, Evaluation, Query Length

Permission to make digital or hard copies of all or part of this work for personal or classroom use is granted without fee provided that copies are not made or distributed for profit or commercial advantage and that copies bear this notice and the full citation on the first page. Copyrights for components of this work owned by others than ACM must be honored. Abstracting with credit is permitted. To copy otherwise, or republish, to post on servers or to redistribute to lists, requires prior specific permission and/or a fee. Request permissions from Permissions@acm.org.
CIKM'15, October 19–23, 2015, Melbourne, Australia.
© 2015 ACM. ISBN 978-1-4503-3794-6/15/10 ...$15.00.
DOI: http://dx.doi.org/10.1145/2806416.2806604.

1. INTRODUCTION

The retrievability of a document is essentially how easily a document can be found given a large set of queries and a retrieval system [3]. Consequently, retrievability is considered a precursor to relevance as it is a measure that predicts the likelihood that a document will be retrieved, and a document must be retrieved before it can be judged relevant. Recently, a number of studies have examined the relationship between retrievability and performance [12, 14]. The working hypothesis is, if a system reduces the retrieval bias (i.e. makes all documents equally retrievable) it will lead to better performance [12]. The intuition being if a system provides some chance to each document in the collection (assuming the document is worthy of retrieval) to be retrieved if that document is relevant to an information need, then there would be a number of queries that would retrieve the document at a rank sufficiently high enough that a user would encounter it. In these papers, they have shown that this hypothesis tends to hold for system ranking, parameter tuning, and document length normalisation Here we investigate the relationship between retrievability bias, query length and retrieval performance. Specifically, we examine whether increasing query length decreases the retrievability bias. The intuition being that as queries become more specific (by increasing their length), they focus on the a smaller set of documents and so provide those documents some level of retrievability. On the other hand, if one term is issued, then a large set of documents will be returned, so the documents at the top will amass retrievability. Consequently, if the system tends to favour certain documents over others then shorter queries are more likely to be subject to the system bias. We further speculate that longer queries will introduce other biases i.e. tend to favour the retrieval of longer documents because they have a higher likelihood of matching more query terms, and so could inadvertently introduce length bias thus may require more document length normalisation. To this end, we perform a comprehensive retrievability analysis to explore the relationship between queries containing one to five terms, on two TREC Test collections, using three standard retrieval model (using a range of parameter settings). The main contribution here is the first investigation into the impact of query length on retrievability bias.

2. BACKGROUND

In this section, we will give a brief overview of query length studies, before formally defining the retrievability measures and how retrievability relates to performance. Past research has shown that query length and retrieval performance is

	Collection	AQ					DG				
	# Terms	One	Two	Three	Four	Five	One	Two	Three	Four	Five
BM25	b	0.70	0.75	0.80	0.85	0.85	0.90†	0.90†	1.00	1.00	1.00
	Min Gini	0.69	0.44	0.38	0.36	0.35	0.76	0.58	0.56	0.56	0.56
	Max S@10	0.06	0.24	0.43	0.56	0.66	0.04	0.16	0.22	0.25	0.26
LM	β	200†	100†	100†	100†	200†	100†	50†	1†	50†	50†
	Min Gini	0.69	0.40	0.35	0.34	0.34	0.76	0.58	0.56	0.57	0.58
	Max S@10	0.06	0.26	0.45	0.58	0.68	0.05	0.15	0.21	0.24	0.25
PL2	c	2.0	3.0	2.0	2.0	1.0	0.1†	1.0†	1.0†	1.0†	1.0†
	Min Gini	0.69	0.46	0.40	0.38	0.37	0.76	0.64	0.63	0.63	0.64
	Max S@10	0.06	0.26	0.44	0.57	0.67	0.05	0.14	0.20	0.22	0.23

Table 1: Shows the parameter setting at which minimum bias occurs (†indicates the parameter setting also achieved maximum Success@10) followed by the value of the minimum Gini and the value of the maximum Success@10 for each model on both collections.

related, such that longer queries tend to result in better performance. In [7], they show that as the length of TREC queries increases the performance also increases. This has lead researchers in interactive IR to try and extract longer queries from users [1, 10]. In a more systematic study, Azzopardi [2], generated queries of length 1 to 30, issued them to three retrieval models and showed that both precision and MAP increased as query length increased. However, once the length exceeded 2-3 terms, smaller and smaller increases in performance were observed (i.e. the law of diminishing returns). The author argues that this is why query lengths tend to be short in practice. Performance does not always increase as the length of a query increases. Invariably, as more terms are added, the relevance of the terms with respect to the information need decreases, and so performance can drop because more noise is being added.

Little work has directly studied the relationship between query length and parameter estimation. When studying document length normalisation in BM25, Cummins [8] found that as the query length increased, more normalisation was required (i.e. b has to increase) to achieve optimal performance. They hypothesised that this is due to longer queries giving longer documents more chances to match terms and thus, score higher. This potentially leads to a bias towards longer documents and so should be regulated. This result was also observed in a study by He and Ounis [9]. They noted that for the divergence from randomness model PL2, more normalisation was required for longer queries (i.e. a decrease in the c parameter) in order to achieve best performance. In [15], Zhai and Lafferty performed a study of smoothing parameters on various language models, they found that longer queries required more smoothing (i.e. an increase in β) to extract the best performance from the model. To explore the notion in more detail, we will be investigating the bias that results from different query lengths across the parameter space of BM25, PL2, and Language Modelling. To estimate the bias stemming from query length, we shall use the novel evaluation measure, retrievability.

Retrievability

In [3], Azzopardi and Vinay introduced the concept of retrievability, a measure that defined how *easily* a document could be retrieved by a particular configuration of an IR system. Formally, retrievability $\mathbf{r}$ of a document $\mathbf{d}$ with respect to an IR system is defined as:

$$\mathbf{r}(\mathbf{d}) \propto \sum_{\mathbf{q}\in\mathbf{Q}} \mathbf{O_q}.\mathbf{f}(\mathbf{k_{dq}}, \mathbf{c})$$

where $\mathbf{q}$ is a query from the very large query set $\mathbf{Q}$, meaning $\mathbf{O_q}$ is the opportunity of the query being chosen from this set. $\mathbf{k_{dq}}$ is the rank at which $\mathbf{d}$ is retrieved given $\mathbf{q}$, and $\mathbf{f}(\mathbf{k_{dq}}, \mathbf{c})$ is a utility function which denotes how retrievable the document $\mathbf{d}$ is for the query $\mathbf{q}$ given the rank cutoff $\mathbf{c}$. Retrievability is then calculated by summing over all queries $\mathbf{q}$ in query set $\mathbf{Q}$. Theoretically, $\mathbf{Q}$ represents the universe of all possible queries, but in practice $\mathbf{Q}$ is very large set of queries [3, 4, 6, 12]. The standard measure of retrievability used is a cumulative based approximation, which employs an utility function $\mathbf{f}(\mathbf{k_{dq}}, \mathbf{c})$, such that if a document, $\mathbf{d}$, is retrieved in the top $\mathbf{c}$ documents given $\mathbf{q}$, then $\mathbf{f}(\mathbf{k_{dq}}, \mathbf{c}) = 1$, otherwise $\mathbf{f}(\mathbf{k_{dq}}, \mathbf{c}) = 0$. This measure provides an intuitive value for each document as it is simply the number of times that the document is retrieved in the top $\mathbf{c}$ documents. Documents falling outside the the top $\mathbf{c}$ are completely ignored, simulating a user who is only willing to pursue the first $\mathbf{c}$ results. Essentially, the more queries that retrieve a document, the more retrievable a document is. Using the $r(d)$ scores of each of the documents, the Gini Coefficient is used to then estimate bias in a single value.

Retrieval Bias and Query Length

The relationship between retrieval bias and performance has been investigated in a number of different ways [3, 4, 5, 11, 12, 14]. In [12] the focus was the relationship between performance and bias in system ranking, while in [11, 14] it was on how retrieval bias correlates to performance and document length normalisation. These studies have shown, that in general, a reduction in retrieval bias correlates to an increase in performance, and that systems that exhibit a lower retrieval bias tend to deliver better performance (with the strongest correlation being with Time-Biased gain and the U-Measure) [11].

However, there has not been any studies that have directly investigated the relationship between bias, performance and query length. Indeed most studies use queries of one length, typically, bigram queries [3, 11, 12, 14]. A few studies, however, do provides some insights into the relationship, as they have explored different length queries [4, 5] though for a different purpose.

In [4], Bashir and Rauber perform a retrievability analysis using query sets with two, three and four terms. There results show that the average retrievability of documents decreased with the length of the queries, suggesting that more bias may be introduced due to query length. However, they did not report the retrieval bias scores (i.e. the Gini Coefficients), so it is not possible to determine if this is the case, or whether this is an artefact of the different number of queries used in each set. In [13], Wilkie and Azzopardi show that the retrieval bias estimate is greatly influenced by the size of the query set used. Therefore in our experiments we control and ensure that the same number of queries per length is used.

In [5], Bashir and Rauber undertake a different retrievability analysis where they examine the influence of query expansion on retrieval bias. They show that for typical query expansion methods retrieval bias increased substantially between the non-expanded (short) queries and the expanded (long) queries. This suggests that longer queries may indeed increase retrieval bias. While they devise an alternative query expansion technique that ameliorates the bias increase, they did not report the corresponding retrieval performances, so it is unclear how the bias stemming from query length relates to performance. In this paper, we specifically probe the relationship between between query length, performance and bias using a methodology designed to compared the differences across lengths.

3. EXPERIMENTAL METHOD

The aim of this study is to investigate how varying the length of queries to estimate retrievability alters how retrievability bias relates to performance. More succinctly, we wish to observe whether using longer queries queries leads to a decrease in the estimation of bias by a system.

Data and Materials

To perform our experiments, we employed 2 standard TREC test collections: AQ (Aquaint) and DG (DotGov). We utilised 3 standard retrieval models: BM25, PL2 and Language Modelling with Bayes Smoothing and varied the document length normalisation parameter. With BM25 we used 11 parameter settings for b between 0.0 and 1.0 increasing in steps of 0.1. We also include b at 0.75 and 0.85 for further granularity. For PL2 we set parameter c to values between 1 and 10 but also included 0.1 and 100 to test extreme cases. For Bayes Smoothing (LM), we set the β to values of: 1, 5, 10, 20, 50, 100, 200, 300, 500, 1000, 2000, 3000, 5000 and 10,000.

Query Generation Method

To perform our experiments we use a novel query generation technique that generates queries from the titles of documents. We generate queries of 1 to 5 terms by extracting terms from the title and when there is not enough terms in the title, we extract terms from the main text. This means we have 5 query sets (a set of single term queries, a set of two term queries, etc.) that contain a query for every document in the collection. A number of issues exist in the domain of query generation that we must address. One such issue that we must mitigate against is the generation of duplicate queries. For example when extracting queries from two unique documents on similar topics, it would be common to extract the same query from both. To reduce the chance of this occurring, we extract terms ordered by their IDF in the hope that more original terms will be picked out for each document that are less likely to have been seen before. Extracting queries strictly from the title was impractical as many titles are very short and many unique documents share the same title. Therefore to avoid this issue, we include the main body of the document to locate additional terms.

Performance Evaluation

Given the query generation method, for each query there is a corresponding relevant document, creating a series of known-item query pairs which result in a relevance judgements file. Using these judgements we computed a number of measures (i.e. P@10, MAP/MRR, Success@10), but report Success@10. Similarly correlations and findings were observed on these other measures.

4. RESULTS AND ANALYSIS

Query Length and Length Normalisation: Table 1 demonstrates the relationship between query length and the length normalisation parameter associated with a model. From this table it is apparent, that to minimise the bias of a system, issuing short queries requires less length normalisation than issuing longer queries. For example, when using BM25 on AQ to minimise bias, b must increase as we issue more terms (0.7, 0.75, 0.8, 0.85 and 0.85 in that order for one to five terms). This trend can also be observed on PL2 although it is not as pronounced. For PL2 on DG c must be set to 0.1 for minimal bias using one term and $c = 1$ for two or more terms. The need for different parameter settings for two to five terms may have been evident if the space between 0.1 and 1 was further explored. The increase in the amount of length normalisation required to minimise bias may be attributed to longer documents being returned when longer queries are issued, as was suggested by Cummins [8]. Interestingly, LM performs very differently from BM25 and PL2 and we see a dip in the amount of length normalisation required. This finding suggests that an ideal length of query for LM may exist but would require further exploration of queries with more than five terms and the β parameter space between 0 and 100.

Query Length and Retrievability Bias: The effect of query length and retrievability bias is shown to be complex as we see conflicting evidence in Table 1. For most models we see that increasing the number of terms results in a decrease in bias but this trend is subject to diminishing returns (particularly evident when using BM25 on AQ). However, when employing some models on DG (LM and PL2) we see that adding more than three terms actually results in an increase in bias. We hypothesise this increase is due to the large differences in average document length in each of the collections. As we previously observed more terms requires more length normalisation, it is plausible that given the much larger average document length present in DG causes the system to be unable to apply enough length normalisation once too many terms are used to continue to reduce bias. We argue this explanation is more probable than that adding more terms adds more noise [5], due to the fact our method of query generation extracts discriminative terms from a single document rather than from a several of documents like typical query expansion techniques.

Query Length, Retrievability Bias and Performance: The plots of Figure 1 in conjunction with Table 2 summarise the relationship between query length, retrievability bias and performance. Table 2 shows that there is strong negative and significant correlations between performance and bias in all but one case. This indicates that decreasing bias tends to improve performance, agreeing with the findings reported in [12, 14]. Tables 1 and 2 also shows that in over half of the cases, minimising bias leads to the

Collection		AQ					DG				
# Terms		One	Two	Three	Four	Five	One	Two	Three	Four	Five
Model	**BM25**	-0.84*	-0.91*	-0.89*	-0.88*	-0.91*	-0.99*	-1.00*	-0.99*	-0.99*	-0.99*
	LM	-0.74*	-1.00*	-0.98*	-0.99*	-1.00*	-0.99*	-1.00*	-1.00*	-1.00*	-1.00*
	PL2	-0.57	-0.99*	-0.91*	-0.80*	-0.71*	-0.99*	-0.97*	-1.00*	-0.99*	-0.98*

Table 2: Correlations between Gini and Success@10. * denotes statistical significance at p<0.05.

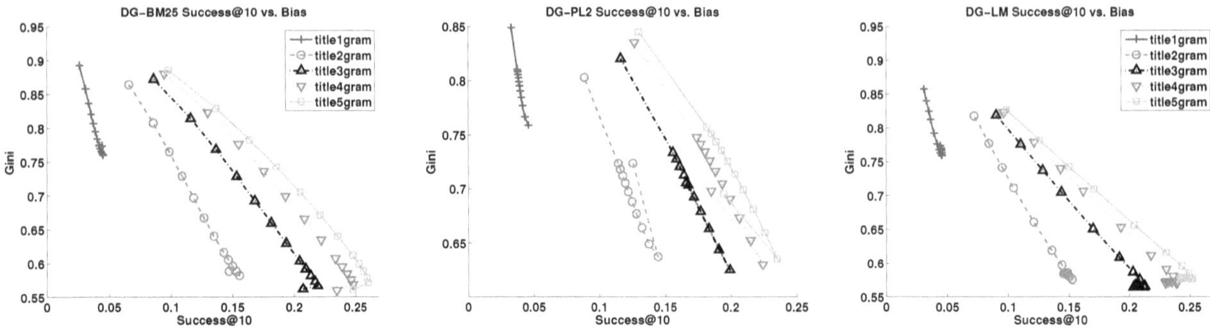

Figure 1: Plots showcasing the relationship between bias, performance and query length. We see a trend that decreasing bias leads to better performance and that increasing the length of queries does not necessarily lower bias.

best performance and the plots of Figure 1 reinforce this. In terms of query length and performance, we see that as query length increases, then the performance increases but with diminishing returns (as was observed in [2]).

5. FUTURE WORK AND CONCLUSIONS

This work has helped further discern the nature of the relationship between bias and performance by investigating the effects of query length, another variable in the retrieval process that impacts on retrieval bias. The findings have highlighted the relationship between performance and bias where reducing bias tends to improve performance, conforming with the findings of previous studies [12, 14]. In addition to this, we have found that increasing the length of queries generally reduces bias, but at a decreasing rate (i.e. diminishing return). However, issuing queries longer than five terms may actually lead to increases in bias due to noise being added which motivates examining queries with more terms. Query expansion techniques often generate very long queries and so is an ideal domain in which to explore the relationship in more detail. Finally, during this study it became evident that the parameter space we explored for certain models (mainly PL2 and LM) was not fine grained enough, so it would be interesting follow up this study probing more deeply into the parameter space.

6. REFERENCES

[1] E. Agapie, G. Golovchinsky, and P. Qvarfordt. Leading people to longer queries. In *Proc. of ACM SIGCHI*, pages 3019–3022, 2013.

[2] L. Azzopardi. Query side evaluation: an empirical analysis of effectiveness and effort. In *Proc. of the 32nd ACM SIGIR*, pages 556–563, 2009.

[3] L. Azzopardi and V. Vinay. Retrievability: An evaluation measure for higher order information access tasks. In *Proc. of the 17th ACM CIKM*, pages 561–570, 2008.

[4] S. Bashir and A. Rauber. Improving retrievability of patents with cluster-based pseudo-relevance feedback documents selection. In *Proc. of the 18th ACM CIKM*, pages 1863–1866, 2009.

[5] S. Bashir and A. Rauber. Improving retrievability & recall by automatic corpus partitioning. In *Trans. on large-scale data & knowledge-centered sys. II*, pages 122–140. 2010.

[6] S. Bashir and A. Rauber. Improving retrievability of patents in prior-art search. In *Proc. of the 32nd ECIR*, pages 457–470, 2010.

[7] N. J. Belkin, D. Kelly, G. Kim, J.-Y. Kim, H.-J. Lee, G. Muresan, M.-C. Tang, X.-J. Yuan, and C. Cool. Query length in interactive information retrieval. In *Proc. of the 26th ACM SIGIR*, pages 205–212, 2003.

[8] R. Cummins and C. O'Riordan. Learning in a pairwise term-term proximity framework for information retrieval. In *Proc of the 32nd ACM SIGIR*, 2009.

[9] B. He and I. Ounis. Parameter sensitivity in the probabilistic model for ad-hoc retrieval. In *Proc. of the 16th ACM CIKM*, pages 263–272, 2007.

[10] D. Kelly, V. D. Dollu, and X. Fu. The loquacious user: A document-independent source of terms for query expansion. In *Proc. of the 28th ACM SIGIR*, pages 457–464, 2005.

[11] C. Wilkie and L. Azzopardi. Relating retrievability, performance and length. In *Proc. of the 36th ACM SIGIR conference*, pages 937–940, 2013.

[12] C. Wilkie and L. Azzopardi. Best and fairest: An empirical analysis of retrieval system bias. *Advances in Information Retrieval*, 2014.

[13] C. Wilkie and L. Azzopardi. Efficiently estimating retrievability bias. In *Advances in Information Retrieval*, pages 720–726, 2014.

[14] C. Wilkie and L. Azzopardi. A retrievability analysis: Exploring the relationship between retrieval bias and retrieval performance. In *Proc. of the 23rd ACM CIKM*, pages 81–90, 2014.

[15] C. Zhai and J. Lafferty. A study of smoothing methods for language models applied to ad hoc information retrieval. In *Proc. of the 24th ACM SIGIR*, pages 334–342, 2001.

Gauging Correct Relative Rankings For Similarity Search

Weiren Yu[†], Julie A. McCann[†]
[†]Imperial College London, United Kingdom
{weiren.yu, j.mccann}@imperial.ac.uk

ABSTRACT

One of the important tasks in link analysis is to quantify the similarity between two objects based on hyperlink structure. SimRank is an attractive similarity measure of this type. Existing work mainly focuses on absolute SimRank scores, and often harnesses an iterative paradigm to compute them. While these iterative scores converge to exact ones with the increasing number of iterations, it is still notoriously difficult to determine how well the relative orders of these iterative scores can be preserved for a given iteration. In this paper, we propose efficient ranking criteria that can secure correct relative orders of node-pairs with respect to SimRank scores when they are computed in an iterative fashion. Moreover, we show the superiority of our criteria in harvesting top-K SimRank scores and bucket orders from a full ranking list. Finally, viable empirical studies verify the usefulness of our techniques for SimRank top-K ranking and bucket ordering.

1. INTRODUCTION

The problem of identifying similar objects based on graph structure is a fundamental primitive in hyperlink analysis, arising in numerous applications, *e.g.*, anomaly detection, recommendation systems, and automated image annotation. It often demands a measure of closeness between two objects. For instance, Shortest distance can be regarded as a simple measure that counts only *one* path with minimum length to evaluate pair-wise similarity. Recently, SimRank has been proposed by Jeh and Widom [1] as a promising measure of affinity between two nodes. It follows the idea that "two nodes are similar if they are referenced by similar nodes". Due to its recursion, SimRank can count *multiple* paths with different lengths between two nodes to evaluate similarity, which is a substantial improvement over shortest distance.

To serve ranking purposes, this paper focuses on SimRank measure due to its two advantages:

1. Unlike PageRank that is query-independent, SimRank scores between all nodes and a given query q can yield a query-specific ranking list of all nodes imposed by q.

Permission to make digital or hard copies of all or part of this work for personal or classroom use is granted without fee provided that copies are not made or distributed for profit or commercial advantage and that copies bear this notice and the full citation on the first page. Copyrights for components of this work owned by others than ACM must be honored. Abstracting with credit is permitted. To copy otherwise, or republish, to post on servers or to redistribute to lists, requires prior specific permission and/or a fee. Request permissions from Permissions@acm.org.
CIKM'15, October 19-23, 2015, Melbourne, VIC, Australia.
© 2015 ACM. ISBN 978-1-4503-3794-6/15/10 ...$15.00.
DOI: http://dx.doi.org/10.1145/2806416.2806610.

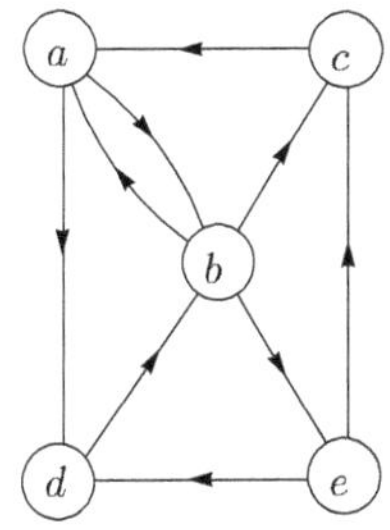

Node-Pairs	Relative Ranking			
	$k=1$	$k=2$	$k=3$	$k=\infty$
(a,e)	1	1	1	1
(c,e)	1	1	2	2
(a,c)	3	4	4	4
(b,d)	3	4	5	5
(c,d)	3	3	3	3
(a,b)	-	6	6	6
(a,d)	-	6	7	7
(b,c)	-	6	8	8
(b,e)	-	9	9	9
(d,e)	-	-	10	10
Accuracy C^{k+1}	0.36	0.216	0.130	-

Figure 1: Relative Ranking *w.r.t.* Iteration k

2. SimRank scores can rank both nodes and node-pairs, in contrast to PageRank only for node ranking.

While most existing work [1–7] focuses on iterative computations of *absolute* SimRank scores, the issue of gauging the correctness of their *relative* ranking has received little attention. To the best of our knowledge, the previous iterative methods to compute SimRank often first empirically set the total number of iterations, k, and then use the k-th iterative SimRank score $s_k(a,b)$ to estimate the exact solution $s(a,b)$. For accuracy guarantee, Lizorkin *et al.* [5] showed an upper bound of the gap between $s_k(a,b)$ and $s(a,b)$:

$$0 \le s(a,b) - s_k(a,b) \le C^{k+1}, \qquad \forall k, \quad \forall a,b \qquad (1)$$

where $0 < C < 1$ is a decay factor. However, from the ranking perspective, it seems hard to use this (*absolute*) gap to determine how well the relative ranking with respect to k-th iterative SimRank scores can be preserved, since even a large gap in Eq.(1) does not necessarily imply incorrect *relative* ranking of objects, as illustrated in Example 1.

EXAMPLE 1. *Figure 1 depicts how the relative ranking of node-pairs in graph G (with respect to their k-th iterative SimRank scores sorted in descending order) is updated when the number of iteration k increases. The last column of the table ($k=\infty$) shows the "true" relative ranking with respect to exact SimRank scores. The (absolute) error bounds of SimRank for every iteration k are depicted in the last line.*

From the table, it can be noticed that the relative ranking tends to the "true" one as k increases. In fact, when $k=3$, the relative ranking with respect to $s_3(\star,\star)$ has become the same as the "true" one, but the (absolute) gap of SimRank scores between $s_3(\star,\star)$ and exact $s(\star,\star)$ is not suitably small, which can be bounded by $C^{k+1} = 0.6^{3+1} = 0.130$. [1] □

Example 1 indicates that the correctness of relative ranking of node-pairs may not be solely judged by the *absolute*

[1]As previously used in [1], we set the decay factor $C = 0.6$ for SimRank computation in Example 1.

gap of SimRank scores in Eq.(1). For ranking purposes, the correct relative orders of node-pairs are more important than their absolute SimRank scores. Thus, it is imperative to identify efficient ranking criteria that can guarantee the correct relative order of node-pairs with respect to their SimRank scores during the iterative computation.

Hence, we consider the following problem, referred to as *Relative Ranking Criterion of SimRank* (RRCS).

Given the number of iterations k, for every two node-pairs (a, b) and (c, d), our goal is to find δ_k *such that*

$$s_k(a,b) - s_k(c,d) \geq \delta_k \text{ implies } s(a,b) \geq s(c,d). \quad (2)$$

The main challenge in RRCS is the determination of δ_k, which can be used as a threshold to check whether the k-th iterative SimRank scores $s_k(\star,\star)$ of any two node-pairs are well separated. If affirmative, we can conclude at iteration k that their final ("true") relative ranking with respect to the exact SimRank scores $s(\star,\star)$ can be consistently preserved. Another direct benefit of RRCS lies in its high effectiveness for top-K ranking and bucket ranking.

Contributions. We make the following contributions:

1. A proposed ranking criterion to gauge the correct relative order of node-pairs with respect to their SimRank scores. (Section 3)
2. Two induced ranking criteria for SimRank top-K ranking and bucket ordering. (Section 4)
3. Viable empirical studies showing the effectiveness of these criteria for ranking objects. (Section 5)

We contend that our techniques for RRCS yield a promising systematic method, which is also applicable to many other metrics, such as PageRank, Random Walk with Restart, ObjectRank, and SimFusion.

Related Work. Ranking nodes or node-pairs based on link structure is an important application of SimRank similarity. Nonetheless, most existing work mainly concerns *absolute* SimRank scores computation [1, 3, 5, 6, 8–10]. As for *relative* ranking, there is only one work by Lizorkin *et al.* who made the first effort in Proposition 2 of [5] to establish the following ranking accuracy estimate:

$$s(a,b) - s(a,d) \geq C^{k+1} \text{ implies } s_k(a,b) \geq s_k(a,d).^2 \quad (3)$$

A striking difference between Eqs.(3) and (2) is the logical order — Eq.(3) infers k-th relative ranking from exact one, whereas Eq.(2) infers exact relative ranking from k-th iterative one. In fact, in an iterative process, exact $s(\star,\star)$ are unknown beforehand. Hence, we can only use k-th iterative information in $s_k(\star,\star)$ to infer exact $s(\star,\star)$. In this sense, Eq.(2) is more useful in practice.

There has been work on other accuracy estimates [3,5] for iterative SimRank computation. Lizorkin *et al.* [5] are the first to propose an (absolute) error estimate for SimRank:

$$0 \leq s(a,b) - s_k(a,b) \leq C^{k+1}, \qquad \forall k, \quad \forall a,b$$

Based on this bound, it is easy to find out the total number of iterations required to guarantee a given accuracy. However, from the ranking perspective, the relative order of node-pairs can be correctly preserved *before* C^{k+1} becomes small.

[2] [5] uses $R_k(\star,\star)$ to denote k-th iterative SimRank scores, in contrast to $s_k(\star,\star)$ in this paper.

Later, Zheng *et al.* [3] showed the gap between two consecutive SimRank iterations:

$$0 \leq s_{k+1}(a,b) - s_k(a,b) \leq C^{k+1}, \qquad \forall k, \quad \forall a,b$$

with the aim to deduce an upper bound for SimRank score of each node-pair. Although the accuracy estimates in [3,5] can be used as stopping criteria in iterative SimRank computation, they may not guarantee correct relative ranking.

Recently, SimRank top-K queries [7, 10] have witnessed growing interests. Lee *et al.* [7] proposed a novel random walk based method to identify top-K nearest neighbors with respect to a given query q based on SimRank scores $s(q,\star)$. If our ranking criteria were incorporated into their method, the speedup for top-K nodes would be more pronounced. Fujiwara *et al.* [10] leveraged a min-heap structure as well as a Cauchy-Schwarz inequality to prune unlikely nodes for top-K SimRank search. However, their approach is based on the matrix decomposition, which is different from ours.

Our RRCS criteria can also applied to iterative PageRank computation. Most existing convergence criteria for PageRank (*e.g.,* [11, 12]) are based on the *absolute* difference between 1) the k-th iterative PageRank values and the ideal ones, or 2) the two consecutive PageRank iterations. Several work has exploited geometric distance [13] and Kendall's τ distance [14] for top-K PageRank rankings. When our RRCS criteria are integrated into these methods, the relative rankings of PageRank can be efficiently obtained as well.

2. PRELIMINARIES

In this section, we briefly revisit the SimRank background. For presentation ease, we use its matrix representation [4].

Notations. The following notations are used in the paper.

$[\mathbf{X}]_{x,y}$	(x,y)-entry of matrix $\mathbf{X} \in \mathbb{R}^{n \times n}$
$\|\mathbf{X}\|_{\max}$	max-norm matrix of $\mathbf{X}$ $(= \max_{i,j=1}^{n} \|x_{i,j}\|)$
$\|\mathbf{X}\|_{\infty}$	∞-norm matrix of $\mathbf{X}$ $(= \max_{i=1}^{n} \sum_{j=1}^{n} \|x_{i,j}\|)$

Consider a graph $G = (V, E)$ with node set V and edge set E. Let $\mathbf{S}$ be the SimRank matrix whose entry $[\mathbf{S}]_{a,b}$ is the similarity $s(a,b)$ between nodes a and b, and let $\mathbf{Q}$ be the backward transition matrix whose entry $[\mathbf{Q}]_{a,b} = 1/(\text{in-degree of } a)$ if there is an edge $b \to a$, and 0 otherwise. Then, $\mathbf{S}$ satisfies the following recursion:

$$\mathbf{S} = \max\{C \cdot (\mathbf{Q} \cdot \mathbf{S} \cdot \mathbf{Q}^T), \mathbf{I}\}, \quad (4)$$

where $0 < C < 1$ is a decay factor, $(\star)^T$ is matrix transpose, and $\mathbf{I}$ is an identity matrix with compatible dimension, and $\max\{\star\}$ is an element-wise maximum operation.

Intuitively, $[\mathbf{S}]_{a,b}$ depends on two terms in Eq.(4):

1) The term $[\mathbf{Q} \cdot \mathbf{S} \cdot \mathbf{Q}^T]_{a,b}$ includes the average similarity of (a,b)'s in-neighbor pairs, which implies that "two nodes are similar if their in-neighbors are similar".

2) $\max\{\star, \mathbf{I}\}$ guarantees that the diagonals of $\mathbf{S}$ are all 1s, corresponding to "every node is maximally similar to itself".

Let $\mathbf{S}_k$ be the k-th iterative SimRank matrix. Then, the exact $\mathbf{S}$ in Eq.(4) can be iteratively computed as

$$\mathbf{S}_{k+1} = \max\{C \cdot (\mathbf{Q} \cdot \mathbf{S}_k \cdot \mathbf{Q}^T), \mathbf{I}\} \text{ with } \mathbf{S}_0 = \mathbf{I}. \quad (5)$$

3. RELATIVE RANKING OF SIMRANK

We provide a ranking criterion to gauge the correct relative order of node-pairs with respect to the SimRank scores. The main result in this section is as follows.

THEOREM 1. *For every two node-pairs* (a, b) *and* (c, d), *if*

$$[\mathbf{S}_k]_{c,d} - [\mathbf{S}_k]_{a,b} \geq \frac{C^k}{1-C^k} \cdot \max_{i \neq j}\{[\mathbf{S}_k]_{i,j}\}, \quad \forall k = 1, 2, \cdots$$

then it necessarily follows that $[\mathbf{S}]_{c,d} \geq [\mathbf{S}]_{a,b}$. $\square$

(The proof will be given later after some discussion.)

Intuitively, Theorem 1 provides an efficient criterion for SimRank relative order preservation, by finding a suitable δ_k in Eq.(2), which is practically small and easy-to-compute. It suggests that, when SimRank is iteratively computed from Eq.(5), for any two node-pairs, if the gap of their k-th iterative scores is no less than $\delta_k := \frac{C^k}{1-C^k} \cdot \max_{x \neq y}\{[\mathbf{S}_k]_{x,y}\}$, then we can determine, at iteration k, their correct ("true") relative rankings with respect to the exact SimRank scores.

Other important applications of Theorem 1 are top-K ranking and bucket ordering, as will be seen in Section 4.

To prove Theorem 1, the following lemmas are needed.

LEMMA 1. *For every* $k = 0, 1, \cdots$, *and each* $j = 0, 1, \cdots, k$,

$$\|\mathbf{S}_k - \mathbf{S}_{k+j}\|_{\max} \leq C^j \cdot \|\mathbf{S}_{k-j} - \mathbf{S}_k\|_{\max}. \quad \square$$

PROOF. One can readily derive from Eq.(5) that

$$\mathbf{S}_k - \mathbf{S}_{k+j} = C \cdot \mathbf{Q} \cdot (\mathbf{S}_{k-1} - \mathbf{S}_{k+j-1}) \cdot \mathbf{Q}^T,$$

from which it follows inductively that

$$\mathbf{S}_k - \mathbf{S}_{k+j} = C^j \cdot \mathbf{Q}^j \cdot (\mathbf{S}_{k-j} - \mathbf{S}_k) \cdot (\mathbf{Q}^T)^j.$$

Take $\|\star\|_{\max}$ norm on both sides, and apply the fact that

$$\|[\mathbf{Q}]_{a,\star} \cdot \mathbf{X} \cdot [\mathbf{Q}^T]_{\star,b}\|_{\max} \leq \|\mathbf{X}\|_{\max} \text{ with } \mathbf{X} = \mathbf{S}_{k-j} - \mathbf{S}_k,$$

to the above equation, it follows that

$$\begin{aligned}\|\mathbf{S}_k - \mathbf{S}_{k+j}\|_{\max} &\leq C^j \cdot \|\mathbf{Q}^j \cdot (\mathbf{S}_{k-j} - \mathbf{S}_k) \cdot (\mathbf{Q}^T)^j\|_{\max} \\ &\leq C^j \cdot \|\mathbf{Q}^{j-1} \cdot (\mathbf{S}_{k-j} - \mathbf{S}_k) \cdot (\mathbf{Q}^T)^{j-1}\|_{\max} \\ &\leq \cdots \leq C^j \cdot \|\mathbf{S}_{k-j} - \mathbf{S}_k\|_{\max}. \quad \square\end{aligned}$$

Intuitively, for a current iteration k, Lemma 1 provides an accuracy estimate for predicting new SimRank in the future j iterations, by using old SimRank in the past j iterations.

LEMMA 2. *For* $j = 1, 2, \cdots$, *the following estimate holds:*

$$\|(\mathbf{I} - C^j \cdot (\mathbf{Q}^j \otimes \mathbf{Q}^j))^{-1}\|_\infty \leq \frac{1}{1-C^j}. \quad \square$$

PROOF. Since $\|\mathbf{Q}^j \otimes \mathbf{Q}^j\|_\infty \leq 1$, by using the fact that

$$(\mathbf{I} - \mathbf{X})^{-1} = \sum_{k=0}^{\infty} \mathbf{X}^k \text{ with } \mathbf{X} = C^j \cdot (\mathbf{Q}^j \otimes \mathbf{Q}^j),$$

we can obtain

$$\begin{aligned}\|(\mathbf{I} - C^j \cdot (\mathbf{Q}^j \otimes \mathbf{Q}^j))^{-1}\|_\infty &= \|\sum_{k=0}^{\infty} C^{jk} (\mathbf{Q}^j \otimes \mathbf{Q}^j)^k\|_\infty \\ &\leq \sum_{k=0}^{\infty} C^{jk} = \frac{1}{1-C^j}. \quad \square\end{aligned}$$

Lemma 2 gives a neat bound for $\|(\mathbf{I} - C^j \cdot (\mathbf{Q}^j \otimes \mathbf{Q}^j))^{-1}\|_\infty$, which lays the foundation for the proof of Theorem 1. Such an upper bound is tight since it can be readily shown that "=" in Lemma 2 is attainable whenever every node in a graph has at least one incoming edge.

LEMMA 3. *For every* $k = 1, 2, \cdots$, *and each* $j = 1, 2, \cdots, k$,

$$\|\mathbf{S}_k - \mathbf{S}\|_{\max} \leq \frac{C^j}{1-C^j} \cdot \|\mathbf{S}_{k-j} - \mathbf{S}_k\|_{\max}. \quad \square$$

PROOF. We can readily verify by induction that

$$\mathbf{S}_{k+j} - \mathbf{S} = C^j \cdot \mathbf{Q}^j \cdot (\mathbf{S}_k - \mathbf{S}) \cdot (\mathbf{Q}^T)^j.$$

Thus, we have

$$\begin{aligned}\mathbf{S}_k - \mathbf{S}_{k+j} &= (\mathbf{S}_k - \mathbf{S}) - (\mathbf{S}_{k+j} - \mathbf{S}) \\ &= (\mathbf{S}_k - \mathbf{S}) - C^j \cdot \mathbf{Q}^j \cdot (\mathbf{S}_k - \mathbf{S}) \cdot (\mathbf{Q}^T)^j.\end{aligned}$$

Taking $vec(\star)$ operator on both sides, and then applying the tensor product $\otimes$ property, we have

$$vec(\mathbf{S}_k - \mathbf{S}_{k+j}) = (\mathbf{I} - C^j \cdot (\mathbf{Q}^j \otimes \mathbf{Q}^j)) \cdot vec(\mathbf{S}_k - \mathbf{S}).$$

On both sides, we first multiply by $(\mathbf{I} - C^j \cdot (\mathbf{Q}^j \otimes \mathbf{Q}^j))^{-1}$, and then take $\|\star\|_\infty$, which yields

$$\begin{aligned}\|\mathbf{S}_k - \mathbf{S}\|_{\max} &\leq \underbrace{\|(\mathbf{I} - C^j \cdot (\mathbf{Q}^j \otimes \mathbf{Q}^j))^{-1}\|_\infty}_{\text{by Lemma 2}} \cdot \underbrace{\|\mathbf{S}_k - \mathbf{S}_{k+j}\|_{\max}}_{\text{by Lemma 1}} \\ &\leq \frac{C^j}{1-C^j} \cdot \|\mathbf{S}_{k-j} - \mathbf{S}_k\|_{\max}. \quad \square\end{aligned}$$

Lemma 3 suggests that the accuracy of SimRank scores at iteration k can be estimated by utilizing the old SimRank in the past j iterations.

Combining Lemmas 1-3, we can prove Theorem 1.

PROOF OF THEOREM 1. Since the iterative SimRank score monotonically increases to the exact solution with respect to k, it follows that $[\mathbf{S}]_{x,y} \geq [\mathbf{S}_k]_{x,y}$, for every node-pair (x, y).

Setting $j = k$ in Lemma 3, we denote by

$$\delta_k = \frac{C^k}{1-C^k} \cdot \|\mathbf{I} - \mathbf{S}_k\|_{\max} = \frac{C^k}{1-C^k} \cdot \max_{x \neq y}\{[\mathbf{S}_k]_{x,y}\}.$$

Then, Lemma 3 can be rewritten as $\|\mathbf{S}_k - \mathbf{S}\|_{\max} \leq \delta_k$, which implies that, for every two node-pairs (a, b) and (c, d),

$$[\mathbf{S}]_{c,d} - [\mathbf{S}_k]_{c,d} \leq \delta_k \text{ and } [\mathbf{S}]_{a,b} - [\mathbf{S}_k]_{a,b} \geq 0.$$

Subtraction of the above two equations yields

$$[\mathbf{S}_k]_{a,b} - [\mathbf{S}_k]_{c,d} - \delta_k \leq [\mathbf{S}]_{a,b} - [\mathbf{S}]_{c,d}.$$

This implies that

$$\text{if } [\mathbf{S}_k]_{a,b} - [\mathbf{S}_k]_{c,d} - \delta_k \geq 0, \text{ then } [\mathbf{S}]_{a,b} - [\mathbf{S}]_{c,d} \geq 0,$$

which completes the proof. $\square$

4. APPLICATIONS

To appreciate the utility of our relative ranking criteria for SimRank (RRCS), we next illustrate two real applications.

Notations. Let $\mathbf{T}$ be a permutation matrix that arranges all the entries of a vector in decreasing order, *i.e.*,

$$\hat{\mathbf{s}}_k := \mathbf{T} \cdot vec(\mathbf{S}_k) \text{ with } [\hat{\mathbf{s}}_k]_1 \geq [\hat{\mathbf{s}}_k]_2 \geq \cdots \geq [\hat{\mathbf{s}}_k]_{n^2},$$ [3]

Given the above $\mathbf{T}$, we also define $\hat{\mathbf{s}} := \mathbf{T} \cdot vec(\mathbf{S})$. Note that the entries in $\hat{\mathbf{s}}$ are generally not sorted in decreasing order, as opposed to those in $\hat{\mathbf{s}}_k$.

Top-K Ranking. One application of RRCS is to validate top-K node-pairs search, based on the following corollary.

COROLLARY 1. *For every iteration* $p = 1, 2, \cdots$, *if*

$$[\hat{\mathbf{s}}_p]_K - [\hat{\mathbf{s}}_p]_{K+1} \geq \frac{C^p}{1-C^p} \cdot \max_{x \neq y}\{[\mathbf{S}_p]_{x,y}\}, \qquad (6)$$

then $[\hat{\mathbf{s}}]_1, \cdots, [\hat{\mathbf{s}}]_K$ *are the top-K highest SimRank scores.*

[3]Recall that $[\hat{\mathbf{s}}_k]_i$ denotes the i-th element of vector $\hat{\mathbf{s}}_k$, and $vec(\mathbf{S}_k)$ stacks columns of $\mathbf{S}_k$ on top of one another [9].

PROOF. As $[\hat{\mathbf{s}}_p]_1 \geq \cdots \geq [\hat{\mathbf{s}}_p]_K \geq \cdots \geq [\hat{\mathbf{s}}_p]_{n^2}$, it follows from Eq.(6) that, for all $i = 1, \cdots, K$, and $j = K+1, \cdots, n^2$,

$$[\hat{\mathbf{s}}_p]_i - [\hat{\mathbf{s}}_p]_j \geq \tfrac{C^p}{1-C^p} \cdot \max_{x \neq y}\{[\mathbf{S}_p]_{x,y}\}.$$

By Theorem 1, we have $[\hat{\mathbf{s}}]_i \geq [\hat{\mathbf{s}}]_j$, for all $i = 1, \cdots, K$, and $j = K+1, \cdots, n^2$, which implies that $[\hat{\mathbf{s}}]_1, \cdots, [\hat{\mathbf{s}}]_K$ are the top-K highest SimRank scores. □

Corollary 1 tells that the "true" top-K node-pairs *w.r.t.* the exact SimRank scores are the same as the top-K node-pairs *w.r.t.* the p-th iterative SimRank scores if the p-th iterative SimRank ranking scores between positions K and $K+1$ are well separated above a threshold.

Bucket Ordering. Another application is bucket ordering. In this case, we need to assign SimRank scores of $n \times n$ node-pairs to several "bucket" intervals, as shown in Corollary 2.

COROLLARY 2. *Let* $\delta_p := \frac{C^p}{1-C^p} \cdot \max_{x \neq y}\{[\mathbf{S}_p]_{x,y}\}$. *For every iteration* $p = 1, 2, \cdots$, *if for* $u, v = 1, 2, \cdots$,

$$[\hat{\mathbf{s}}_p]_K - [\hat{\mathbf{s}}_p]_{K+u} \geq \delta_p, \quad [\hat{\mathbf{s}}_p]_{K+u} - [\hat{\mathbf{s}}_p]_{K+u+v} \geq \delta_p,$$

then $[\hat{\mathbf{s}}]_{K+u}$ *is ranked between* $(K+1)$ *and* $(K+u+v-1)$.

PROOF. Analogous to the proof of Corollary 1, $[\hat{\mathbf{s}}_p]_K - [\hat{\mathbf{s}}_p]_{K+u} \geq \delta_p$ implies that $[\hat{\mathbf{s}}]_i \geq [\hat{\mathbf{s}}]_{K+u}$, for all $i = 1, \cdots, K$. Thus, the rank position of $[\hat{\mathbf{s}}]_{K+u}$ is after K.

Besides, from $[\hat{\mathbf{s}}_p]_{K+u} - [\hat{\mathbf{s}}_p]_{K+u+v} \geq \delta_p$ and $[\hat{\mathbf{s}}_p]_{K+u+v} \geq \cdots \geq [\hat{\mathbf{s}}_p]_{n^2}$ follows that $[\hat{\mathbf{s}}_p]_{K+u} - [\hat{\mathbf{s}}_p]_j \geq \delta_p$ for all $j = K+u+v, \cdots, n^2$. This implies that

$$[\hat{\mathbf{s}}]_{K+u} \geq [\hat{\mathbf{s}}]_j \text{ for all } j = K+u+v, \cdots, n^2.$$

Hence, the rank position of $[\hat{\mathbf{s}}]_{K+u}$ is before $K+u+v$.

Taking these together, we can obtain that $[\hat{\mathbf{s}}]_{K+u}$ is ranked between $(K+1)$ and $(K+u+v-1)$. □

Corollary 2 assigns SimRank score $[\hat{\mathbf{s}}_p]_{K+u}$ to a "bucket" that represents a rank interval $[K+1, K+u+v-1]$. Indeed, the top-K ranking in Corollary 1 is a special case of bucket ranking with two (interval) "buckets": $[1, K]$ and $[K+1, n^2]$.

5. EXPERIMENTS

We present an empirical study on real networks to evaluate the usefulness of our criteria for ranking node-pairs.

Datasets. Two real networks are used: 1) ENRON, an email communication network from Enron, with 367,662 edges and 36,692 nodes. 2) AMAZON, an Amazon product co-purchasing graph, with 1,234,877 edges and 262,111 nodes.

We implement iterative SimRank algorithm [5] [4] in Visual C++, and use a machine with an Intel Core(TM) 3.10GHz CPU and 8GB RAM, running Windows 7.

Results. By tying our ranking criterion of Corollary 2 to algorithm [5], Figure 2 shows how many distinct ranks can be identified (*i.e.,* the number of buckets) and how many elements per bucket (*i.e.,* bucket sizes) at the last iteration $(k = 10)$[5]. To ensure better visibility for top-ranked buckets, we omit the rightmost bucket (whose size is the largest, yet contains node-pairs with the smallest SimRank scores). The detailed information is depicted in Table 1, where we see that on ENRON, 8.6% of the smallest node-pairs cannot

Dataset	% of pairs in exact ranking	# of pairs in exact top-100	% of pairs in last bucket
ENRON	41.7%	91	8.6%
AMAZON	34.5%	100	58.2%

Table 1: Statistical Information of Bucket Ranking

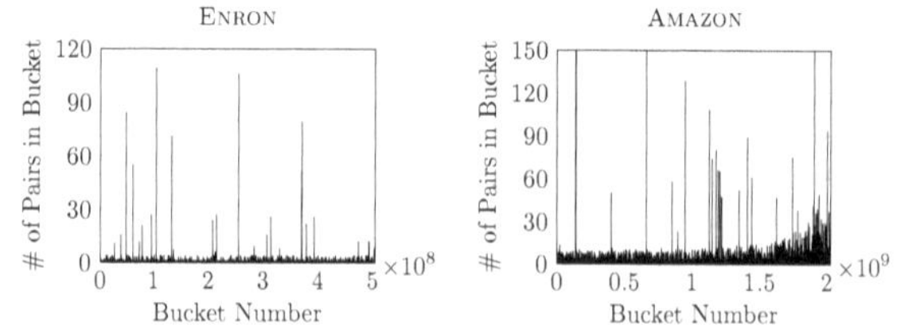

Figure 2: Bucket Ranking on Real Networks ($k = 10$)

be ranked, whereas on AMAZON, this number increases to 58.2%. Among the top-100 ranking results, 91 (*resp.* 100) node-pairs on ENRON (*resp.* AMAZON) are exactly ranked. These indicate the effectiveness of our ranking criterion for identifying SimRanks of the top-ranked node-pairs.

6. CONCLUSIONS

This paper provides several useful relative ranking criteria for SimRank iterations. Important applications of our ranking criteria include top-K ranking and bucket ordering.

As a future avenue, we will incorporate these criteria for K nearest neighbor search and other similarity models [16,17].

Acknowledgements. This research is supported by NEC Smart Water Network research project.

7. REFERENCES

[1] G. Jeh and J. Widom, "SimRank: a measure of structural-context similarity," in *KDD*, 2002.
[2] M. Kusumoto, T. Maehara, and K. Kawarabayashi, "Scalable similarity search for SimRank," in *SIGMOD*, 2014.
[3] W. Zheng, L. Zou, Y. Feng, L. Chen, and D. Zhao, "Efficient SimRank-based similarity join over large graphs," *PVLDB*, vol. 6, no. 7, pp. 493–504, 2013.
[4] W. Yu and J. A. McCann, "Efficient partial-pairs SimRank search for large networks," *PVLDB*, vol. 8, no. 5, pp. 569–580, 2015.
[5] D. Lizorkin, P. Velikhov, M. N. Grinev, and D. Turdakov, "Accuracy estimate and optimization techniques for SimRank computation," *VLDB J.*, vol. 19, no. 1, pp. 45–66, 2010.
[6] W. Yu, X. Lin, W. Zhang, and J. A. McCann, "Fast all-pairs SimRank assessment on large graphs and bipartite domains," *IEEE Trans. Knowl. Data Eng.*, vol. 27, no. 7, pp. 1810–1823, 2015.
[7] P. Lee, L. V. S. Lakshmanan, and J. X. Yu, "On top-*k* structural similarity search," in *ICDE*, 2012.
[8] G. He, H. Feng, C. Li, and H. Chen, "Parallel SimRank computation on large graphs with iterative aggregation," in *KDD*, 2010.
[9] C. Li, J. Han, G. He, X. Jin, Y. Sun, Y. Yu, and T. Wu, "Fast computation of SimRank for static and dynamic information networks," in *EDBT*, 2010.
[10] Y. Fujiwara, M. Nakatsuji, H. Shiokawa, and M. Onizuka, "Efficient search algorithm for SimRank," in *ICDE*, pp. 589–600, 2013.
[11] P. Berkhin, "Survey: a survey on PageRank computing," *Internet Mathematics*, vol. 2, pp. 73–120, 2005.
[12] R. S. Wills and I. C. F. Ipsen, "Ordinal ranking for Google's PageRank," *SIAM J. Matrix Analysis Applications*, vol. 30, no. 4, pp. 1677–1696, 2008.
[13] A. Borodin, G. O. Roberts, J. S. Rosenthal, and P. Tsaparas, "Link analysis ranking: algorithms, theory, and experiments," *ACM Trans. Internet Techn.*, vol. 5, no. 1, pp. 231–297, 2005.
[14] R. Fagin, R. Kumar, and D. Sivakumar, "Comparing top k lists," in *SODA*, pp. 28–36, 2003.
[15] W. Yu, X. Lin, and W. Zhang, "Fast incremental SimRank on link-evolving graphs," in *ICDE*, pp. 304–315, 2014.
[16] W. Yu and X. Lin, "IRWR: Incremental random walk with restart," in *SIGIR*, pp. 1017–1020, 2013.
[17] W. Yu, X. Lin, W. Zhang, Y. Zhang, and J. Le, "SimFusion+: Extending SimFusion towards efficient estimation on large and dynamic networks," in *SIGIR*, pp. 365–374, 2012.

[4] Our ranking criteria can also be applied to other iterative SimRank algorithms [1,6,15], yielding the same results.

[5] As used in [5], the total iteration number k is set to 5–10.

Learning User Preferences for Topically Similar Documents

Mustafa Zengin and Ben Carterette
Department of Computer and Information Sciences
University of Delaware
Newark, DE, USA
[zengin | carteret]@udel.edu

ABSTRACT

Similarity measures have been used widely in information retrieval research. Most research has been done on query-document or document-document similarity without much attention to the user's perception of similarity in the context of the information need. In this study, we collect user preference judgements of web document similarity in order to investigate: (1) the correlation between similarity measures and users' perception of similarity, (2) the correlation between the web document features plus document-query features and users' similarity judgements. We analyze the performance of various similarity methods at predicting user preferences, in both unsupervised and supervised settings. We show that a supervised approach using many features is able to predict user preferences close to the level of agreement between users, and moreover achieve a 15% improvement in AUC over an unsupervised approach.

Categories and Subject Descriptors

H.3.3 [**Information Storage and Retrieval**]: Clustering

Keywords: document similarity, similarity measures, users

1. INTRODUCTION

Measures of similarity between documents are widely used in information retrieval: as scores to rank documents, for clustering, for diversity, and more. Most of these measures are based on simple textual features, primarily term counts, document counts, and document lengths.

Since most uses of such similarity measures are meant to help users with some task, it is worth asking whether they correspond to the notion of similarity that users actually have. The field of IR has always compared query-document similarity measures to human judgements of relevance —this is the foundation of effectiveness evaluation—but there is very little work comparing document-document similarity measures to human opinion.

Permission to make digital or hard copies of all or part of this work for personal or classroom use is granted without fee provided that copies are not made or distributed for profit or commercial advantage and that copies bear this notice and the full citation on the first page. Copyrights for components of this work owned by others than the author(s) must be honored. Abstracting with credit is permitted. To copy otherwise, or republish, to post on servers or to redistribute to lists, requires prior specific permission and/or a fee. Request permissions from Permissions@acm.org.
CIKM'15, October 19–23, 2015, Melbourne, VIC, Australia.
Copyright is held by the owner/author(s). Publication rights licensed to ACM.
ACM 978-1-4503-3794-6/15/10 ...$15.00.
DOI: http://dx.doi.org/10.1145/2806416.2806617 .

In one of the few works on the subject, Lee et al. studied document similarity measures with human subjects [3]. They compared a number of different similarity measures in terms of their correlation to human judgments of similarity, finding that a model based on Latent Semantic Analysis correlated best to human judgments. However, they only looked at very short news articles outside of the context of any search or information seeking task.

In this paper, we describe an experiment to collect human judgments of document-document similarity for web pages with respect to a web information need, and investigate the extent to which similarity measures capture them. Because asking users to express a similarity judgment between two documents is difficult [6], we present a novel *triplet*-based approach that only requires users to say whether one document is more or less similar to a reference document than another. As we will show, this simplifies the problem such that user agreement about similarity is quite high. We then compare published measures of similarity to our user preferences and show that we can train a classifier that predicts user preferences at a level close to agreement between users.

2. USER EXPERIMENT

Preference judgements have been used in the field of IR in order to help assessors make finer distinctions between relevancy levels of documents [2]. Comparison studies between graded absolute judgements and preference judgements show that the latter can be done faster and with about the same level of agreement [1].

We designed a preference-based experiment to collect human judgements about document *similarity*. In this section we describe the experiment setting, experimental data, and the preferences we collected.

2.1 Queries and Documents

We selected 10 queries from the TREC Web Track 2009—2012, specifically queries that we judged to have a clear and unambiguous topic description. For each query we selected 8 highly relevant and easily readable web documents (based on sentence and document lengths, vocabulary and document style) from the first four pages of Google search results for the query.

2.2 Task Design

We present a participant with *three* highly relevant documents (referred to as a *triplet*) along with a query and the primary topic description from the Web track. One of the documents of the triplet is displayed at the top and the two

Table 1: User experiment statistics

# queries	10
# documents per query	8
# documents	80
# triplets per task	14
# tasks completed	160
# distinct triplets	1680
# preference judgements collected	2240
# participants	21
# man-hour	33

others are displayed below it side by side. We use D_t to denote the document at the top, D_l the document to the left, and D_r the document to the right. The participant is asked to choose which of D_l or D_r is *more similar* to D_t in terms of satisfying the given information need.

Since we have 8 documents per query, there are a total of 168 triplets ($= 8 \cdot \binom{7}{2}$) covering all possible placement of 3 documents for each query. For any given D_t there are 21 possible $\langle D_l, D_r \rangle$ pairs. In order to ensure that each pair would be judged at least once, and that some would be judged twice (so that we could evaluate agreement), we assigned 14 of these to one participant and 14 to another in such a way that guaranteed that all 21 preferences would be judged at least once, and exactly 7 would be judged twice for each D_t in each query.

All participants of the experiment were graduate students. They were paid 8 US dollars per hour of work.

Table 1 shows some statistics of the collected data. All tasks were completed, resulting in 1,680 ($= 10 \cdot 8 \cdot \binom{7}{2}$) distinct triplets judged and 560 ($= 10 \cdot 8 \cdot 7$) that were judged twice.

2.3 Agreement

We investigated agreement among participants that worked on the same document triplets. Overall agreement, calculated as the total number of identical preferences over the total number worked on, is about 71% (402/560), which is above previously-reported human agreement about document relevance [1, 4]. We believe agreement is high because we carefully chose topics and documents of a high quality. Also, it seems that it is easier for participants to judge similarity relative to a reference document (in this case our top document D_t) than to judge similarity on an absolute scale. Zengin and Carterette reported much lower agreement for the latter case [6].

3. SIMILARITY METHODS

We will use the data collected from our participants in an experiment to determine the ability of similarity measures and machine-learned classifiers to capture our participants' notion of similarity. Similarity measures like cosine similarity, Jaccard distance, and others have a long history in IR. Recently, Whissell and Clarke proposed that most similarity measures are composed of three components: a term weighting method, a normalization technique, and a distance measure [5]. The term weighting method determines the importance of a term occurring in the document. Normalization is used to adjust the term weights in order to normalize the effect of document length. Distance measures quantify the distance between two document vectors.

Table 2, due to Whissell and Clarke, provides various types of term weighting methods. Combining a term weighting method from that table with a normalization scheme (which could be Manhattan (M), Euclidean (N), or none) and a distance measure (Euclidian (E), Jaccard (J), or Cosine (C)) produces a similarity measure. For example, a measure called TJM corresponds to using tf_{il} for term weighting, Jaccard distance, and Manhattan normalization, while a measure called TE corresponds to using tf_{il} for term weighting, Euclidian distance, and no normalization.

Table 2: Term weighting functions for standard similarity methods.

short name	definition
B	1,if $tf_{it} > 0$,else 0
T	tf_{it}
L	$\log(1+tf_{it})$
TI	$tf_{it} \log(\frac{n}{n_t})$
LI	$\log(1+tf_{it}) \log(\frac{n}{n_t})$
I	$\log(\frac{n}{n_t})$
TF	$tf_{it} \log(\frac{cf_{max}}{cf_t})$
LF	$\log(1+tf_{it}) \log(\frac{cf_{max}}{cf_t})$
F	$\log(\frac{cf_{max}}{cf_t})$

Whissell and Clarke also showed how the BM25 scoring function can be used as a similarity measure:

$$OK(D_j, D_i) = \sum_{t \in D_i \cup D_j}^{m} \frac{tf_{jt}(k_1+1)}{tf_{jt}+k_1 b_j} \frac{tf_{it}(k_1+1)}{tf_{it}+k_1 b_i} log\left(\frac{n}{n_t}\right) \quad (1)$$

Here $b_i = (1-b) + b\frac{dl_i}{avgdl}$, and k_1 and b are free parameters. The idf weight at the end could be dropped as well, producing an alternative measure referred to as OKTF.

3.1 Similarity Based on Features

In addition to computing similarity based on terms in documents, we could compute similarity based on other features of the document, or of the two documents, or of the documents and a query. For example, we could compute the similarity between two documents on the basis of the number of query terms that appear in their URLs; the similarity would simply be the absolute difference between the number of query terms in the URL of D_i and the number in the URL of D_j.

Features we used are derived from those in the LETOR [7] datasets and include text-based features such as document length, query term frequency counts in document title and body, query-document score (using standard retrieval scores like BM25, language modeling and cosine similarity in vector space), term counts normalized by length, and web-specific features such as URL length, URL depth (i.e. how deep in a tree of subfolders the page is, as captured by the number of slashes in the URL), and the number of outlinks from a document. We refer to Tables 3 and 4 in Section 4 below for lists of feature classes and specific features.

4. EXPERIMENTS

In this section we analyze the effectiveness of "standard" similarity measures and document/query-document features as described in Section 3 for predicting the similarity preferences of participants from Section 2. We then present a supervised learning method that can use similarity measures, document features, and document-query features to learn user preferences.

4.1 Classification Effectiveness of Individual Features

Let Sim(Q,D_i,D_j) be the similarity between D_i and D_j with respect to query Q. We will define a simple binary classifier *classify* that predicts only a *left* or *right* user preference. Given a similarity method *sim*, the documents in a triplet D_t,D_l,D_r, and the query Q, if the similarity between the top document D_t and left document D_l is greater than the similarity between the top document D_t and right document D_r (i.e. $sim(Q, D_t, D_l) > sim(Q, D_t, D_r)$), then the output of $classify(sim, Q, D_t, D_l, D_r)$ is *left*. Otherwise it is *right*. Note that no training is necessary: the predicted class is based solely on whether similarity between two documents is greater than the same similarity measure between two other documents. We can then compare these predictions to the actual user preferences obtain as described above.

We first calculated the predictions of *classify* with each of the similarity measures derived from Whissell and Clarke's framework along with the BM25 similarity methods. We evaluated predictions using classification accuracy, area under the ROC curve (AUC), and Pearson correlation between predictions.

4.1.1 Standard similarity measures

Figure 1 summarizes the classification performances of similarity measures by AUC. As the figure shows, AUC is determined primarily by the method used for term weighting. Within any given term weighting scheme, there is only a small amount of variation due to distance measure and normalization. Figures for classification accuracy and correlation show very similar results, so they have been excluded. This suggests that term weighting plays the greatest role in in classification performance, and specifically that the B, L, I, and F weightings giving the best predictions of user preference. Results for classification accuracy and correlation are essentially the same as those for AUC, so we have omitted them for space.

Figure 2 shows AUC results for the OK similarity measure with different values of free parameters k and b. The best classification performance is achieved with higher values of b and lower values of k, though increasing b causes a steeper decrease in AUC as k increases. Overall, though, the measure is fairly robust to parameter values. The other BM25-based similarity measure OKTF is not shown here, but it shows a similar pattern with regards to making changes to k and b. However, it is more resistant to performance decrease when increasing k.

4.1.2 Document and query/document features

The *sim* function used in our classifier does not have to be a standard similarity measure; as suggested in Section 3.1 it could be a feature of the document or the document/query pair. In this section we use such features to predict user preferences, again evaluating by accuracy, AUC, and correlation.

Table 3 and Table 4 summarize the classification performances of document and query-document features respectively. Because we tested a large number of features, we only report a select subset; in particular, when a feature can be computed for different document fields (URL, title, body, or full text), we report only the field that gives maximum performance.

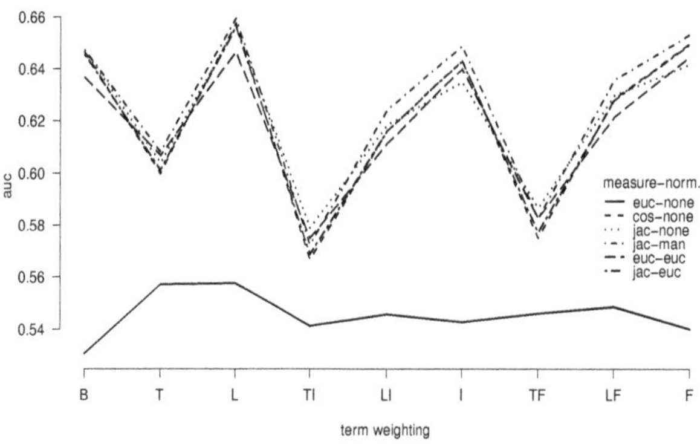

Figure 1: AUC of standard similarity methods

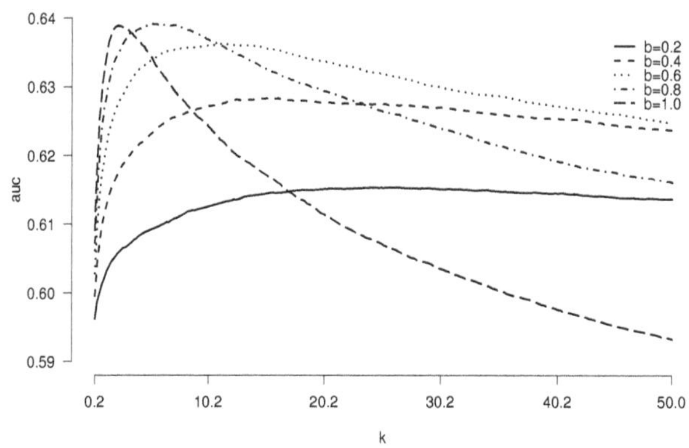

Figure 2: AUC of OK method with k and b values

Table 3: Pearson correlation, accuracy and AUC of document features on document fields. Only document fields with maximum values are reported. † represents URL, ‡ represents title, ⋆ represents body, and ∗ represents full text.

Feature Desc.	Cor.	Acc.	AUC
stream length	0.073∗	0.538∗	0.530∗
number of slash in URL	0.016†	0.512†	0.518†
length of URL	-0.055†	0.477†	0.471†
outlink number	0.075∗	0.536∗	0.523∗

Compared to standard similarity measures in Figures 1 and 2, these features have substantially lower effectiveness for predicting user preferences: AUC ranges between 0.47 and 0.57, only reaching the lower echelons of AUCs shown in those figures. This suggests that overlapping terms in documents make a bigger difference to the user's notion of topical similarity than the overlap of terms between documents and the query.

4.2 Learning User Preference

We next used a supervised method to learn a classifier. We employed a random forest on individual features and combinations of features. For an individual feature such as the OK similarity measure, the feature vector consists of $sim(Q, D_t, D_l)$ and $sim(Q, D_t, D_r)$, and the true class is the user preference for D_l or D_r (relabeled to 0 or 1). For

Table 4: Pearson correlation, accuracy and AUC of query-document features on document fields. Only document fields with maximum values are reported. † represents URL, ‡ represents title, ⋆ represents body, and ∗ represents full text. tn represents term number, tf represents term frequency, tr represents term ratio, sl represents stream length.

Feature Desc.	Cor.	Acc.	AUC
covered query tn	-0.220†	0.504∗	0.503†
covered query tr	-0.025†	0.504∗	0.502†
sum of tf	0.038†	0.524†	0.540†
min of tf	-0.008†	0.508†	0.502†
max of tf	0.057∗	0.528∗	0.538†
mean of tf	0.033†	0.522†	0.538†
var. of tf	0.058‡	0.533‡	0.534†
sum of sl norm.tf	0.098∗	0.546∗	0.543∗
min of sl norm.tf	0.017∗	0.508∗	0.521∗
max of sl norm.tf	0.094∗	0.548∗	0.555∗
mean of sl norm.tf	0.101⋆	0.552⋆	0.537⋆
variance of sl norm.tf	0.145†	0.562†	0.568†
sum of tf*idf	0.043†	0.526†	0.542†
min of tf*idf	0.015†	0.515†	0.514†
max of tf*idf	0.036†	0.519†	0.524∗
mean of tf*idf	0.046†	0.528†	0.543†
variance of tf*idf	0.035†	0.523†	0.540†
boolean model	-0.018†	0.508⋆	0.510†
vector space model	0.044∗	0.522∗	0.534∗
bm25	0.078∗	0.538∗	0.540∗
lm-dir	0.047∗	0.523∗	0.536∗
lm-jm	0.059∗	0.530∗	0.538∗

combinations of features, we use the same idea, with two similarity calculations for each feature in the model.

Table 5 and Figure 3 summarize the performance of models using OK and OKTF as individual features, a model using all document and query/document features, a model using all standard similarity measures as features, and finally a model using all of the above.

The AUC of the OK measure with $k = 8.2$ and $b = 0.6$ is 0.639 in the unsupervised setting (see Fig. 2). Training with OK increases its classification performance by 3.3%. Using all document and query/document features in combination gives an AUC of 0.719, 27% higher than any individual feature in that set and 9% higher than OK on its own. Using all standard similarity measures together gives an AUC of 0.739, 12% higher than OK but only 3% higher than the document + query/document features. Using all of the above features together further increases AUC by a small amount, and produces classifiers which have accuracies close to the agreement between participants reported in Section 2.3 (67.8% vs 71%).

These results suggest that both classes of features do quite a good job of capturing user preferences—almost to the extent that users can predict each others' preferences.

5. CONCLUSIONS

We have presented an experiment on having users judge similarity between documents by expressing a binary preference for one document being more similar to a reference document than another. We compared those preferences

Table 5: Supervised learning with individual and combination of features

Feature Desc.	Cor.	Acc.	AUC
OKTF (k=8.2, b=0.6)	0.205	0.603	0.652
OK (k=8.2, b=0.6)	0.214	0.608	0.660
Document+Query/Doc Features	0.296	0.649	0.719
Standard Sim. Methods	0.344	0.672	0.739
All	0.354	0.678	0.749

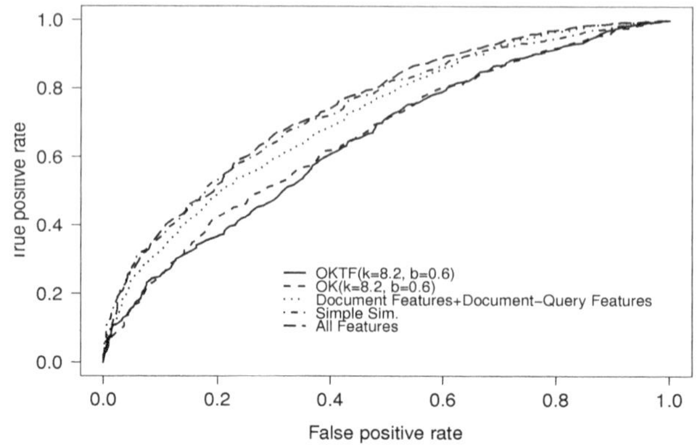

Figure 3: ROC curve of supervised models

to standard tf/idf-based similarity measures, unsupervised feature-based similarity, and a supervised classifier including both. We found that the latter achieves accuracy close to the level of human agreement (which in turn is high for an IR task). We next intend to investigate tasks for which this classifier could be useful—tasks that are helped by clustering is a clear direction for future work.

Acknowledgments

This work was supported in part by the National Science Foundation (NSF) under grant number IIS-1350799. Any opinions, findings and conclusions or recommendations expressed in this material are the authors' and do not necessarily reflect those of the sponsor.

6. REFERENCES

[1] B. Carterette, P. N. Bennett, D. M. Chickering, and S. T. Dumais. Here or there: preference judgments for relevance In *Proceedings of the ECIR*, pages 16-27, 2008

[2] M. E. Rorvig. The simple scalability of documents. *JASIS*, 41(8):590-598, 1990

[3] Michael D. Lee and Matthew Welsh. An empirical evaluation of models of text document similarity. In *CogSci2005*, 2005.

[4] E. Voorhees. Variations in relevance judgments and the measurement of retrieval effectiveness. *Information Processing & Management*, 36(5):697-716, September 2000.

[5] John S. Whissell and Charles L. A. Clarke. Effective measures for inter-document similarity. In *Proceedings of the 22nd ACM international conference on Information and knowledge management*, 2013

[6] M. Zengin and B. Carterette. User judgements of document similarity. *Proceedings of the SIGIR 2013 Workshop on Modeling User Behavior for Information Retrieval Evaluation (MUBE 2013)* ,2013

[7] Qin, Tao, Tie-Yan Liu, Jun Xu, and Hang Li. LETOR: A benchmark collection for research on learning to rank for information retrieval. In *Information Retrieval 13, no. 4* (2010): 346-374.

Modeling Parameter Interactions in Ranking SVM

Yaogong Zhang[†§*] Jun Xu[‡] Yanyan Lan[‡] Jiafeng Guo[‡]
Maoqiang Xie[†§] Yalou Huang[†§] Xueqi Cheng[‡]
[†]College of Computer and Control Engineering ,Nankai University
[‡]CAS Key Lab of Network Data Science and Technology,
Institute of Computing Technology, Chinese Academy of Sciences
[§]College of Software, Nankai University
ygzhang@mail.nankai.edu.cn, {junxu, lanyanyan, guojiafeng}@ict.ac.cn,
{xiemq, huangyl}@nankai.edu.cn, cxq@ict.ac.cn

ABSTRACT

Ranking SVM, which formalizes the problem of learning a ranking model as that of learning a binary SVM on preference pairs of documents, is a state-of-the-art ranking model in information retrieval. The dual form solution of Ranking SVM model can be written as a linear combination of the preference pairs, i.e., $\boldsymbol{w} = \sum_{(i,j)} \alpha_{ij}(\boldsymbol{x}_i - \boldsymbol{x}_j)$, where α_{ij} denotes the Lagrange parameters associated with each pair (i, j). It is obvious that there exist significant interactions over the document pairs because two preference pairs could share a same document as their items. Thus it is natural to ask if there also exist interactions over the model parameters α_{ij}, which we may leverage to propose better ranking model. This paper aims to answer the question. Firstly, we found that there exists a low-rank structure over the Ranking SVM model parameters α_{ij}, which indicates that the interactions do exist. Then, based on the discovery, we made a modification on the original Ranking SVM model by explicitly applying a low-rank constraint to the parameters. Specifically, each parameter α_{ij} is decomposed as a product of two low-dimensional vectors, i.e., $\alpha_{ij} = \langle \boldsymbol{v}_i, \boldsymbol{v}_j \rangle$, where vectors $\boldsymbol{v}_i$ and $\boldsymbol{v}_j$ correspond to document i and j, respectively. The learning process, thus, becomes to optimize the modified dual form objective function with respect to the low-dimensional vectors. Experimental results on three LETOR datasets show that our method, referred to as Factorized Ranking SVM, can outperform state-of-the-art baselines including the conventional Ranking SVM.

Categories and Subject Descriptors: H.3.3 [Information Systems Applications]: Information Search and Retrieval – Retrieval Models

Keywords: Parameter interaction; Ranking SVM

*The work was conducted when Yaogong Zhang was visiting CAS Key Lab of Network Data Science and Technology.

Permission to make digital or hard copies of all or part of this work for personal or classroom use is granted without fee provided that copies are not made or distributed for profit or commercial advantage and that copies bear this notice and the full citation on the first page. Copyrights for components of this work owned by others than ACM must be honored. Abstracting with credit is permitted. To copy otherwise, or republish, to post on servers or to redistribute to lists, requires prior specific permission and/or a fee. Request permissions from Permissions@acm.org.
CIKM'15, October 19–23, 2015, Melbourne, Australia.
© 2015 ACM. ISBN 978-1-4503-3794-6/15/10 ...$15.00.
DOI: http://dx.doi.org/10.1145/2806416.2806595.

1. INTRODUCTION

Learning to rank has been widely used in information retrieval and recommender systems. Among the learning to rank models, Ranking SVM is a representative pairwise ranking model, evolving from the popular support vector machines (SVM) [1] for classification problems. In training, Ranking SVM first constructs the preference pairs of the documents based on their relevance labels (or click-through data [7]). Then, a binary SVM model is learned based on the preference pairs to capture the differences between documents with different relevance labels. In ranking, each document is assigned a relevance score based on the learned ranking model. Usually, the ranking model can be written in its dual form, the solution is a linear combination of the training preference pairs, i.e., $\boldsymbol{w} = \sum_{(i,j)} \alpha_{ij}(\boldsymbol{x}_i - \boldsymbol{x}_j)$, where $\boldsymbol{x}_i$ and $\boldsymbol{x}_j$ are the first and second document in the pair (i, j), and α_{ij} is the corresponding Lagrange multiplier.

It is obvious that the constructed preference pairs have significant interactions, since two preference pairs could share a same document as their items. In the dual form solution of Ranking SVM, each preference pair is associated with a Lagrange multiplier α. Therefore, it is natural to ask *whether there also exist interactions among these Lagrange multipliers*. If the answer is yes, how to utilize the interactions to improve Ranking SVM?

This paper tries to answer the above questions by analyzing the Lagrange multipliers of the trained Ranking SVM models. Specifically, we made an arrangement of the Lagrange multipliers and constructed a block diagonal matrix $\mathbf{A}$, where $A(i, j) = \alpha_{ij}$ if α_{ij} appears in the Ranking SVM model and zero otherwise. Then, we performed singular value decomposition (SVD) on each block of $\mathbf{A}$ and sorted the eigenvalues in descending order. We found that for all the queries, we just need 40% dimensions to capture 90% energy, but if we want to capture 100% energy, almost all the queries need at least 80% dimensions, it means there exists a low-rank structure in the matrix, which indicates strong interactions among the Lagrange multipliers.

Based on the discovery, we propose to improve the original Ranking SVM through explicitly modeling the parameter interactions in the training process. Specifically, we apply a low rank constraint over the Lagrange multipliers in the dual form solution of Ranking SVM. Each Lagrange multiplier α_{ij} in the dual form objective function is factorized as the dot product of two K-dimensional latent vectors, i.e., $\alpha_{ij} = \langle \boldsymbol{v}_i, \boldsymbol{v}_j \rangle$, where $\boldsymbol{v}_i$ and $\boldsymbol{v}_j$ correspond to the first and second document in the preference pair, respectively. In this way, the rank of the matrix $\mathbf{A}$ would not be larger than K. The learning of the ranking model, then, becomes optimizing the factorized dual form objective function with respect to the latent vectors. An effective algorithm based on gradient descent is proposed to conduct the optimization.

The proposed algorithm, referred to as Factorized Ranking SVM, offers several advantages: 1) The interactions among model parameters are explicitly captured when training the ranking model; 2) Compared with original Ranking SVM, the space complexity is dramatically reduced. Experimental results indicate that Factorized Ranking SVM can outperform several state-of-the-art baseline methods including Ranking SVM, on three LETOR benchmark datasets.

2. RANKING SVM

Ranking SVM formalizes the problem of learning a ranking model as the problem of learning a binary classification over preference document pairs. Suppose we are given a set of training label-query-document tuples $\{(y_i, q_i, \boldsymbol{x}_i)\}_{i=1}^{N}$, where N is the number of training tuples, $y_i \in \{r_1, \cdots, r_\ell\}$ is the relevance label for the i-th query-document pair, $q_i \in Q$ is the query, and $\boldsymbol{x}_i \in \mathcal{R}^n$ is the feature vector encoding the i-th query-document pair. There exists a total order between the relevance labels $r_\ell \succ r_{\ell-1}, \cdots, \succ r_1$, where '$\succ$' denotes a preference relationship. The set of preference pairs is defined as $P \equiv \{(i,j) | q_i = q_j, y_i \succ y_j\}$ and the linear Ranking SVM minimizes the loss function

$$\min_{\boldsymbol{w} \in \mathcal{R}^n} \frac{1}{2} ||\boldsymbol{w}||^2 + C \sum_{(i,j) \in P} [1 - \langle \boldsymbol{w}, \boldsymbol{x}_i - \boldsymbol{x}_j \rangle]_+ , \quad (1)$$

where $C > 0$ is a parameter and $[x]_+ = \max(0, x)$. It is common to solve the dual problem of (1):

$$\begin{aligned} \min_{\boldsymbol{\alpha}} \ & \frac{1}{2} \boldsymbol{\alpha}^T M \boldsymbol{\alpha} - \boldsymbol{e}^T \boldsymbol{\alpha}, \\ \text{s.t.} \quad & 0 \leq \alpha_{ij} \leq C, \forall (i,j) \in P \end{aligned} \quad (2)$$

where $\boldsymbol{\alpha} \in \mathcal{R}^{|P|}$ is a vector of Lagrange multipliers indexed by pairs in P, $\boldsymbol{e} \in \mathcal{R}^{|P|}$ is the vector of ones, and $M_{(i,j),(u,v)} = \langle \boldsymbol{x}_i - \boldsymbol{x}_j, \boldsymbol{x}_u - \boldsymbol{x}_v \rangle, \forall (i,j), (u,v) \in P$ is a $|P| \times |P|$ matrix.

In ranking, the learned ranking model $f(\boldsymbol{x}) = \langle \boldsymbol{w}, \boldsymbol{x} \rangle$ assigns a relevance score for any test document $\boldsymbol{x}$. From the prime-dual relationship, optimal $\boldsymbol{w}$ and $\boldsymbol{\alpha}$ satisfy

$$\boldsymbol{w} = \sum_{(i,j) \in P} \alpha_{ij} (\boldsymbol{x}_i - \boldsymbol{x}_j). \quad (3)$$

In machine learning, it is assumed that all of the training instances are independently identically distributed. In Ranking SVM, however, it is obvious that the preference pairs have significant interactions because two pairs (e.g.,(i,j) and (i,k))could share a document(e.g.,document i). Since the model parameters $\boldsymbol{\alpha}$ are associated with each preference pair, it is natural to ask whether these parameters also have interactions each other.

3. ANALYSIS OF PARAMETER INTERACTIONS

In this paper, we propose to analyze the interactions between model parameters based on singular value decomposition (SVD). Specifically, given a learned Ranking SVM model, we rearrange the model parameters $\boldsymbol{\alpha}$ as a matrix

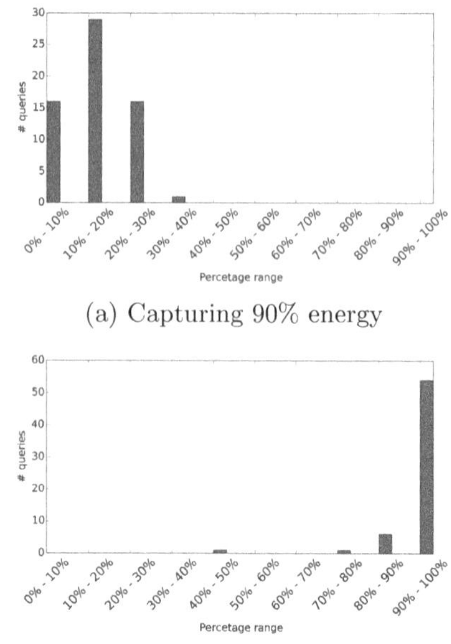

(a) Capturing 90% energy

(b) Capturing 100% energy

Figure 1: Distribution of queries over percentage ranges when capturing 90% and 100% of the energy.

$A \in \mathcal{R}^{N \times N}$ and defined as $A(i,j) = \alpha_{ij}$ if $(i,j) \in P$ and 0 otherwise. Note that A is a block diagonal matrix, which consists of sub-matrices $A_i (i = 1, \cdots, |Q|)$, and each block A_i corresponds to a training query. This is because the preference pairs are constructed within the documents retrieved by one query.

We performed SVD on each submatrix A_i (corresponds to a query) and sorted the eigenvalues in descending order[1]. Figure 1(a) shows the statistics on the percentages of dimensions needed per query for capturing 90% of the energy. The statistics are based on a Ranking SVM model trained on one fold of OHSUMED dataset. The queries are grouped into different categories based on the ranges of the percentages. For example, all the queries in the category 0% $\sim$ 10% should need 0% $\sim$ 10% of the dimensions for capturing the 90% energy. We can see that all of the queries fall into the ranges less than 40%. Figure 1(b) shows the statistics for capturing 100% of the energy on the same data with the same Ranking SVM model,We can see that if we want to capture 100% of the energy, almost all of the queries fall in the ranges of 80% $\sim$ 90% and 90% $\sim$ 100%, which indicates that A is a nearly full rank matrix.

We also conducted the analysis on the Ranking SVM models trained on the datasets of MQ2007 and MQ2008. Similar phenomenons were observed. The results indicate there exist significant interactions between the Ranking SVM model parameters. The interactions can be characterized with a low-rank structure.

4. FACTORIZED RANKING SVM

Based on the analysis above, we propose a new learning to rank model for capturing the parameter interactions. The model, referred to as Factorized Ranking SVM, is based on

[1]SVD can be performed on each submatrix independently because A is block diagonal.

original Ranking SVM and explicitly applies a low-rank constraint over the model parameters. Specifically, each parameter α_{ij} is assumed to be a product of two K-dimensional vectors $\boldsymbol{v}_i$ and $\boldsymbol{v}_j$, i.e., $\alpha_{ij} = \langle \boldsymbol{v}_i, \boldsymbol{v}_j \rangle$, where K is the size of latent dimension.

The ranking model in Equation (3), therefore, becomes

$$\boldsymbol{w} = \sum_{(i,j)\in P} \langle \boldsymbol{v}_i, \boldsymbol{v}_j \rangle (\boldsymbol{x}_i - \boldsymbol{x}_j). \quad (4)$$

Therefore, the loss function (1) can be written as

$$\min_{\boldsymbol{v}_1,\cdots,\boldsymbol{v}_N} \frac{1}{2} \left\| \sum_{(i,j)\in P} \langle \boldsymbol{v}_i, \boldsymbol{v}_j \rangle (\boldsymbol{x}_i - \boldsymbol{x}_j) \right\|^2 + C \sum_{(k,l)\in P} \left[1 - \left\langle \sum_{(i,j)\in P} \langle \boldsymbol{v}_i, \boldsymbol{v}_j \rangle (\boldsymbol{x}_i - \boldsymbol{x}_j), \boldsymbol{x}_k - \boldsymbol{x}_l \right\rangle \right]_+ . \quad (5)$$

Since the size of preference pairs is large, to conduct efficient optimization, we adopt a similar method used in [10, 12] in which the prime form of linear Ranking SVM is optimized. Specifically, It can be shown that the loss function in (5) can be written as

$$L(\boldsymbol{v}_1, \cdots, \boldsymbol{v}_N) = \frac{1}{2} \|\boldsymbol{w}\|^2 + C \left(p_{\boldsymbol{w}} - \left\langle \boldsymbol{w}, \sum_{i=1}^{l} \left(l_i^+(\boldsymbol{w}) - l_i^-(\boldsymbol{w}) \right) \boldsymbol{x}_i \right\rangle \right), \quad (6)$$

where $\boldsymbol{w}$ is defined in Equation (4), $p_{\boldsymbol{w}}, l_i^+(\boldsymbol{w})$, and $l_i^-(\boldsymbol{w})$ are defined as follows:

$$\begin{aligned} SV(\boldsymbol{w}) &\equiv \{(i,j) \in P, 1 - \boldsymbol{w}^T(\boldsymbol{x}_i - \boldsymbol{x}_j) > 0\}, p_{\boldsymbol{w}} = |SV(\boldsymbol{w})|, \\ SV_i^+(\boldsymbol{w}) &\equiv \{j|(j,i) \in SV(\boldsymbol{w})\}, l_i^+(\boldsymbol{w}) = |SV_i^+(\boldsymbol{w})|, \\ SV_i^-(\boldsymbol{w}) &\equiv \{j|(i,j) \in SV(\boldsymbol{w})\}, l_i^-(\boldsymbol{w}) = |SV_i^-(\boldsymbol{w})|. \end{aligned} \quad (7)$$

Please refer to [9] for the derivation details. The gradient of $L(\boldsymbol{v}_1, \cdots, \boldsymbol{v}_N)$ in Equation (6) , then, can be written as $\left(\frac{\partial L}{\partial \boldsymbol{v}_1}, \cdots, \frac{\partial L}{\partial \boldsymbol{v}_N} \right)$, where

$$\begin{aligned} \frac{\partial L}{\partial \boldsymbol{v}_k} = & \sum_{j:(k,j)\in P} \boldsymbol{v}_j \sum_{(i',j')\in P} \langle \boldsymbol{v}_{i'}, \boldsymbol{v}_{j'} \rangle \langle \boldsymbol{\phi}_{i'j'}, \boldsymbol{\phi}_{kj} \rangle \\ & + \sum_{j:(j,k)\in P} \boldsymbol{v}_j \sum_{(i',j')\in P} \langle \boldsymbol{v}_{i'}, \boldsymbol{v}_{j'} \rangle \langle \boldsymbol{\phi}_{i'j'}, \boldsymbol{\phi}_{jk} \rangle \\ & - C \left(\sum_{j:(k,j)\in P)} \boldsymbol{v}_j \cdot \langle \boldsymbol{\phi}_{kj}, \boldsymbol{u} \rangle + \sum_{j:(j,k)\in P} \boldsymbol{v}_j \langle \boldsymbol{\phi}_{jk}, \boldsymbol{u} \rangle \right), \end{aligned} \quad (8)$$

for $k = 1, \cdots, N$. Here $\boldsymbol{u} = \sum_{i=1}^{N} \left(l_i^+(\boldsymbol{w}) - l_i^-(\boldsymbol{w}) \right) \boldsymbol{x}_i$ and $\boldsymbol{\phi}_{ij} = \boldsymbol{x}_i - \boldsymbol{x}_j$. Thus, the updating criteria for gradient descent is $\boldsymbol{v}_k^{(t)} \leftarrow \boldsymbol{v}_k^{(t-1)} - \eta \frac{\partial L}{\partial \boldsymbol{v}_k}$, where t is the iteration number and η is the learning rate. Algorithm 1 shows the pseudo code of the optimization algorithm.

The space complexity of Factorized Ranking SVM is $\mathcal{O}(N \times n + N \times K + N + \frac{N}{|Q|})$, where n is the number of features,|Q| is the number of queries in training data, $N \times n$ is used for storing the original training data, $N \times K$ is used for storing $\boldsymbol{v}_1, \cdots, \boldsymbol{v}_N$, N is used for storing $l^+(\boldsymbol{w})$ and $l^-(\boldsymbol{w})$, and $\frac{N}{|Q|}$ is used for dynamically constructing the order-statistic tree [9]. Compared with the original Ranking SVM whose space complexity is $\mathcal{O}(N \times n + N^2)$ [9], Factorized Ranking SVM needs much less memory because $K \ll N$.

The time complexity of Factorized Ranking SVM is $\mathcal{O}(T \times (N^2 + N \times (\log K + \log N + n) + \frac{N^2}{|Q|} \times n))$, where T is the number of iterations. N^2 is for computing $\boldsymbol{w}$, $N \times (\log K + \log N + n)$ is for computing $p_w, l^+(\boldsymbol{w}), l^-(\boldsymbol{w}), \boldsymbol{u}$ with the trick of order-statistic tree (see [9] for details). $\frac{N^2}{|Q|} \times n$ is for calculating the gradient $\frac{\partial L}{\partial \boldsymbol{v}_k}$ for $k = 1, \cdots, N$.

Algorithm 1 Factorized Ranking SVM

Input: training data $\{y_i, q_i, \boldsymbol{x}_i\}_{i=1}^N$, learning rate $\eta > 0$, number of hidden dimensions K, and parameter C
Output: model parameters $\boldsymbol{v}_1, \cdots, \boldsymbol{v}_N$

```
1: (v_1, ..., v_N) ← random values
2: repeat
3:    w = Σ_{(i,j)∈P} ⟨v_i, v_j⟩(x_i − x_j), where P = {(i,j)|q_i = q_j, y_i ≻ y_j}
4:    Calculate p_w, l_i^+(w), and l_i^-(w) {Equation (7)}
5:    for k = 1 to N do
6:       v_k ← v_k − η ∂L/∂v_k {Equation (8)}
7:    end for
8: until convergence
9: return v_1, ..., v_N
```

Table 1: Statistics on OHSUMED,MQ2007,and MQ2008.

Data Set	#labeled docs	#queries	#preference pairs
OHSUMED	16,140	106	582,588
MQ2007	42,158	1017	246,051
MQ2008	9,360	471	52,325

5. EXPERIMENT

5.1 Experiment settings

We conducted experiments to test the performances of our approach using three LETOR benchmark datasets[14]: OHSUMED, Million Query track of TREC 2007 (MQ2007), and Million Query track of TREC 2008 (MQ2008). Each dataset consists of queries, corresponding retrieved documents, and human judged labels. The possible relevance labels are relevant, partially relevant, and not relevant. Statistics on the datasets are given in Table 1. The number of preference pairs for each dataset is also shown in the table.

Following the LETOR configuration, We conducted 5-fold cross-validation experiments on the three datasets. The results reported were the average over the five folds. In all of the experiments, LETOR standard features were used.

As for evaluation measures, MAP (mean average precision) and NDCG (normalized discounted cumulative gain)[5] at position of 1, 3, and 5 were used in our experiments. We compared the proposed Factorized Ranking SVM (denoted as "Fac-RSVM" in the experiments) with several state-of-the-art baseline methods, including the conventional Ranking SVM model (denoted as "RSVM"), and two representative learning to ranking models of RankNet [2] and ListNet [4]. As for Ranking SVM, we used the implementation released in [6][2] in all of the experiments. For RankNet and ListNet, we used the implementations in RankLib[3].

Factorized Ranking SVM has some parameters to tune. The learning rate parameter η, number of latent dimensions K, and parameter C were tuned based on the validation set

[2]http://svmlight.joachims.org
[3]http://pepple.cs.umass.edu/~vdang/ranklib.html

Table 2: Ranking accuracies on dataset OHSUMED.

Method	MAP	NDCG@1	NDCG@3	NDCG@5
RSVM	0.4427	0.5289	0.4553	0.4392
RankNet	0.404	0.4007	0.3616	0.3388
ListNet	0.4443	0.5134	0.4664	0.4530
Fac-RSVM	**0.4463**	**0.5507**	**0.4798**	**0.4546**

Table 3: Ranking accuracies on dataset MQ2007.

Method	MAP	NDCG@1	NDCG@3	NDCG@5
RSVM	0.4442	0.3821	0.3796	0.3890
RankNet	0.4184	0.3527	0.3599	0.3660
ListNet	0.4466	**0.3897**	0.3897	**0.3956**
Fac-RSVM	**0.4483**	0.3824	**0.3900**	0.3940

during each experiment. For all of the baselines, we also tuned their parameters based on the validation set.

5.2 Experimental results

The experimental results on OHSUMED, MQ2007, and MQ2008 are reported in Table 2, Table 3, and Table 4, respectively. Boldface indicates the highest score among all runs. From the results, we can see that Fac-RSVM outperformed RSVM on all of the three datasets in terms of all of the evaluation measures (except on MQ2008 in terms of NDCG@1). The results indicate that Fac-RSVM effectively captures the parameter interactions and thus improved ranking performances. The results also showed that Fac-RSVM can outperform pair-wise and list-wise learning to rank methods of RankNet and ListNet (except for ListNet on MQ2007 in terms of NDCG@1 and NDCG@5), which further proved that Fac-RSVM is effective in relevance ranking.

In the experiments, Fac-RSVM underperformed RSVM in terms of NDCG@1 on MQ2008. MQ2008 has the most sparse labeled documents and preference pairs (see Table 1), which may make the parameter interactions weak. Note that the performances of Fac-RSVM degrade as the number of preference pairs gets smaller. We will analyze the phenomenon in our future work.

6. RELATED WORK

Learning to rank has become one of the most active research topics in IR [11]. State-of-the-art learning to rank models can be categorized into pointwise methods, pairwise methods, and listwise methods. Ranking SVM [7] is a representative pairwise learning to rank method. To make the algorithm more suitable to real-world IR applications, Joachims et al. [7] proposed to train Ranking SVM with users' click-through data from search engines. Cao et al. [3] adapted Ranking SVM to document retrieval by modifying the loss function so that the training can focus on the top ranked documents. Qiang et al. proposed Ranking FM to rank tweets in microblog retrieval [13]. In Ranking FM, the interactions between features are modeled with factorization machine [15]. In this paper, we also propose to improve Ranking SVM by explicitly capturing the parameter interactions in training.

Improving the scalability of Ranking SVM is another important research direction. Kuo et al. [8] proposed an efficient algorithm for optimizing large scale kernel ranking SVM. Lee and Lin [9] proposed to directly optimize the prime form of linear Ranking SVM and significantly improved the scalability. In this paper, we adopted the method proposed in [9] for conducting the optimization.

Table 4: Ranking accuracies on dataset MQ2008.

Method	MAP	NDCG@1	NDCG@3	NDCG@5
RSVM	0.4713	**0.3686**	0.4277	0.4730
RankNet	0.4522	0.3410	0.3991	0.4500
ListNet	0.4415	0.3244	0.3916	0.4396
Fac-RSVM	**0.4714**	0.3660	**0.4289**	**0.4731**

7. CONCLUSIONS

In this paper we investigated the parameter interactions in Ranking SVM. We empirically found that there exists a low-rank structure among the Lagrange multipliers of Ranking SVM model. Based on the discovery, we proposed a new ranking model in which the low-rank constraint is explicitly applied to the Lagrange multipliers, called Factorized Ranking SVM. In training, Factorized Ranking SVM decomposes each Lagrange multiplier as a dot product of two low-dimensional vectors. An efficient algorithm was developed to conduct the optimization. Advantages of factorized Ranking SVM include explicitly modeling parameter interactions in pairwise ranking and dramatically reduced space complexity of the ranking model. Experimental results based on three LETOR benchmark datasets show that Factorized Ranking SVM outperforms the state-of-the-art methods including Ranking SVM, RankNet, and ListNet.

Acknowledgements

The research work was funded by the 973 Program of China under Grants No. 2014CB340401, No. 2012CB316303, the 863 Program of China under Grants No. 2014AA015204, the National Natural Science Foundation of China under Grant No. 61203298, No. 61232010, No. 61425016, No. 61173064, No. 61472401, No. 61300166 and No. 61105049.

8. REFERENCES

[1] Bernhard E. Boser, I. M. Guyon, and V. N. Vapnik. A training algorithm for optimal margin classifiers. In *Computational Learning Theory*, pages 144–152, 1992.

[2] Chris Burges, Tal Shaked, and et.al. Learning to rank using gradient descent. In *ICML*, pages 89–96, 2005.

[3] Yunbo Cao, Jun Xu, Tie yan Liu, Hang Li, Yalou Huang, and Hsiao wuen Hon. Adapting ranking SVM to document retrieval. In *SIGIR*, pages 186–193, 2006.

[4] Zhe Cao, Tao Qin, Tie yan Liu, Ming feng Tsai, and Hang Li. Learning to rank: from pairwise approach to listwise approach. In *ICML*, pages 129–136, 2007.

[5] Kalervo Järvelin and Jaana Kekäläinen. IR evaluation methods for retrieving highly relevant documents. In *SIGIR*, pages 41–48, 2000.

[6] Thorsten Joachims. Making large-scale SVM learning practical. In *Advances in Kernel Methods*. MIT Press, 1999.

[7] Thorsten Joachims. Optimizing search engines using clickthrough data. In *KDD*, pages 133–142, 2002.

[8] Tzu-Ming Kuo, Ching-Pei Lee, and Chih-Jen Lin. Large-scale kernel rankSVM. In *SDM*, 2014.

[9] Ching-Pei Lee and Chih-Jen Lin. Large-scale linear rankSVM. *Neural Computation*, 26(4):781–817, 2014.

[10] Kuan-Min Lin and Chih-Jen Lin. A study on reduced support vector machines. *IEEE Transactions on Neural Networks*, 14(6):1449–1559, 2003.

[11] Tie-Yan Liu. Learning to rank for information retrieval. *Springer*, 2011.

[12] O.Chapelle. Learning a support vector machine in the primal. In *Neural Computation*, pages 19(5):1155–1178, 2007.

[13] Runwei Qiang, Feng Liang, and Jianwu Yang. Exploiting Ranking Factorization Machines for Microblog Retrieval. In *CIKM*, pages 1783–1788, 2013.

[14] Tao Qin, Tie-Yan Liu, Jun Xu, and Hang Li. LETOR: A Benchmark Collection for Research on Learning to Rank for Information Retrieval. *Information Retrieval*, 2009.

[15] Steffen Rendle. Factorization machines with libFM. *ACM Trans. Intell. Syst. Technol.*, 3(3):57:1–57:22, May 2012.

Best First Over-Sampling for Multilabel Classification

Xusheng Ai
The Institute of Intelligent Information Processing and Application
Soochow University
Suzhou, China 215006

Jian Wu*
The Institute of Intelligent Information Processing and Application
Soochow University
Suzhou, China 215006
jianwu@suda.edu.cn

Victor S. Sheng
Department of Computer Science
University of Central Arkansas

Yufeng Yao
The Institute of Intelligent Information Processing and Application
Soochow University
Suzhou, China 215006

Pengpeng Zhao
The Institute of Intelligent Information Processing and Application
Soochow University
Suzhou, China 215006

Zhiming Cui
The Institute of Intelligent Information Processing and Application
Soochow University
Suzhou, China 215006

ABSTRACT
Learning from imbalanced multilabel data is a challenging task. It has attracted considerable attention recently. In this paper we propose a MultiLabel Best First Over-sampling (ML-BFO) to improve the performance of multilabel classification algorithms, based on imbalance minimization and Wilson's ENN rule. Our experimental results show that ML-BFO not only duplicates fewer samples but also reduces the imbalance level much more than two state-of-the-art multilabel sampling methods, i.e., an over-sampling method LP-ROS and an under-sampling method MLeNN. Besides, ML-BFO significantly improves the performance of multilabel classification algorithms, and performs much better than LP-ROS and MLeNN.

Categories and Subject Descriptors
I.2.6 [**Artificial Intelligence**]: Learning - Induction

Keywords
Resampling, Heuristic, Multilabel learning.

1. INTRODUCTION
Multilabel imbalance is a typical problem of multilabel classification. It occurs when there are many more examples containing one label than those containing other labels in multilabel classification. Under imbalance circumstances, most multilabel classification algorithms fail to learn a proper model to represent the distributive characteristics of a multilabel dataset. Their prediction accuracies across multiple labels are relatively low.

A few existing methods deal with this problem through adapting multilabel classification algorithms. Charte et al. [1] introduced two resampling methods LP-ROS and LP-RUS. LP-ROS is a random over-sampling method, which generates new samples in which minority labels appear. LP-RUS is a random under-sampling method, which deletes some samples associated to majority labels. They further developed a heuristic multilabel under-sampling method MLeNN [2], based on the well-known Wilson's Edited Nearest Neighbor (denoted as ENN) Rule [3]. The main idea behind is to select the most proper samples associated with majority labels to remove. Their experimental results show that MLeNN performs significantly better than LP-RUS.

According to our knowledge, LP-ROS is the only one state-of-the-art over-sampling algorithm for multilabel classification. It randomly selects samples for duplication. Although LP-ROS works well in many cases, it fails to satisfy two key desiderata as follows:

- Consistently reducing the level of imbalance

As we know, LP-ROS is a random over-sampling method. It could not guarantee that the imbalance level of a preprocessed multilabel dataset decreases. Charte et al. [1] mentioned how to measure the imbalance level in a multilabel dataset, but it didn't study the change of the imbalance level after a multilabel dataset is preprocessed by LP-ROS. We would like to know to what extent a preprocessing method reduces the imbalance level of a multilabel dataset.

- Bias Correction

Based on the experimental results in [1], we found that LP-ROS does not improve accuracy, precision, or recall in a consistent manner. Intuitively, we think the overfitting of over-sampling could be one of potential reasons. We would like to minimize the number of samples duplicated in over-sampling to avoid overfitting, so that the prediction performance of a multilabel classification model built from the preprocessed multilabel dataset increases while the imbalance level of a multilabel dataset preprocessed decreases.

Therefore, we propose another multilabel over-sampling method MultiLabel Best First Over-sampling (ML-BFO), which heuristically rather than randomly selects samples for duplication. Its heuristic is founded on imbalance minimization and Wilson's Edited Nearest Neighbor Rule [3], relying on MeanIR measure [1] to assess the imbalance level of a multilabel dataset, as well as on

Permission to make digital or hard copies of all or part of this work for personal or classroom use is granted without fee provided that copies are not made or distributed for profit or commercial advantage and that copies bear this notice and the full citation on the first page. To copy otherwise, or republish, to post on servers or to redistribute to lists, requires prior specific permission and/or a fee. Request permissions from Permissions@acm.org.
CIKM'15, October 19 - 23, 2015, Melbourne, VIC, Australia
Copyright is held by the owner/author(s). Publication rights licensed to ACM.
ACM 978-1-4503-3794-6/15/10…$15.00
DOI: http://dx.doi.org/10.1145/2806416.2806634

a distance metric between the sets of labels (labelsets) appearing in each pair of instances.

2. RELATED WORK

Learning from imbalanced data has been thoroughly studied in the context of traditional binary classification. The measurement of the imbalance level in a dataset is obtained as the ratio of the number of samples belonging to a majority class and the number of sample belonging to a minority class, known as imbalance ratio. The higher the imbalance ratio, the greater the imbalance level is.

However, traditional under-sampling and over-sampling methods for single-label imbalance classification cannot be directly used in multilabel classification, as they are designed to work with only one output class label. Besides, most preprocessing methods were developed for binary classification, assuming only one minority label and one majority label. Thus, an approach to preprocess multilabel datasets, which have a set of labels as their outputs and several of them could be considered minority/majority labels, is needed. Recently, a triad of measures of assessing the imbalance level of multilabel datasets were proposed in [1], along with two sampling algorithms, an over-sampling (LP-ROS) and an under-sampling (LP-RUS). LP-ROS clones random samples with minority labelsets until the size of the rebalanced dataset is 25% larger than its original size of a multilabel dataset. Charte et al. [1] concluded that LP-ROS obtains better experimental results than LP-RUS does, under different performance evaluation measures, such as accuracy, precision and recall. They also claimed that LP-ROS is able to improve classification results when it is applied to multilabel datasets with a very large level of imbalance. Our proposed method ML-BFO is closely related to LP-ROS. However, it introduces a complete new approach, best-first replication, to over-sample heuristically selected samples with minority labelsets.

3. MULTILABEL BEST FIRST OVER-SAMPLING

An instance in a multilabel dataset may have a group of relevant labels. It is difficult to select a sequence of instances to clone so that the imbalance level of a multilabel dataset monotonically decreases, since it is highly possible that over-sampling increases the occurrence of both the minority and majority labels simultaneously. Meanwhile, the instances that only contain minority labels are scarce. Over-sampling these scarce "noisy" instances would impact subconcepts learned from the preprocessed data. As a result, choosing the most proper instances to duplicate is of critical importance. ML-BFO takes three steps to gradually handle its selection. First, ML-BFO ranks the instances that act as candidates using an instance tree. Second, it finds the proper instance according to the measure MeanIR. Finally, it adopts ENN to probe whether candidates are outliers using a distance metric, which measures the difference between any pair of labelsets.

3.1 An Instance Tree

ML-BFO intends to replicate instances with minority labels. The principle behind ML-BFO is: if a label appears less frequently, its related instances should have the higher probability to be cloned. Note that ML-BFO tries to create a higher balanced superset from a multilabel dataset. As we know, any labelset of the multilabel set Y of a multilabel dataset could contain both minority and majority labels. If there are more minority labels and fewer majority labels appearing in this labelset, ML-BFO preferably selects instances belonging to this subset to clone. In order to find these instances, we construct a simple rank tree with three layers: a root, a label node layer, and a leaf node layer. Its root layer has one root node, which contains all instances of a multilabel dataset D. Its label node layer contains |Y| label nodes, where each label node corresponds to a label in Y. The |Y| label nodes are ranked from right to left according to the frequency of each label in D. That is, the most frequent label locates on the rightmost. The details of ranking these label nodes will be discussed in the next subsection. Its leaf node layer contains many leaf nodes, where each leaf node represents an instance whose labelset contains the label represented in its parent label node. Notice that an instance may appear several times in the leaf node layer of the instance tree, since the labelset of the instance is composed of one or many labels.

3.2 Candidate Selection

Candidate selection is an important component of our ML-BFO. In order to choose proper instances to be candidates for replication, a method to tell that which labels are minor is needed. To complete this task successfully, ML-BFO relies on two measures (IRL*bl* and MeanIR) proposed in [1]. IRL*bl* is a measure to assess the imbalance level of each label in Y. The IRL*bl* value of the most frequent label is set as 1. Then, the IRL*bl* values of other labels should be greater than 1. In general, the higher the IRL*bl* value of a label, the greater the imbalance level of this label is. Besides, it is also useful to estimate the global imbalance level of an entire multilabel dataset. MeanIR is such a measure which measures the average of the IRL*bl* values of all labels of a multilabel dataset.

$$\mathrm{IR}Lbl(y) = \frac{\arg\max_{y' \in \mathrm{Y}} \sum_{i=1}^{|D|} h(y', Y_i)}{\sum_{i=1}^{|D|} h(y, Y_i)}, \quad h(y, Y_i) = \begin{cases} 1 & y \in Y_i \\ 0 & y \notin Y_i \end{cases}$$

$$MeanIR(D) = \frac{1}{|Y|} \sum_{y \in Y} IRLbl(y)$$

ML-BFO ranks the label nodes in the instance tree according to their corresponding IRL*bl*s. The label node with the largest IRL*bl* locates at the leftmost, under which the leaf nodes (child instances) are preferably selected. That is, these instances have more odds to be proliferated. They are the candidates. ML-BFO takes two steps to evaluate these candidates one by one to determine which is proper to be cloned. The first step of ML-BFO is to evaluate whether a candidate instance can reduce the MeanIR of the current superset of the multilabel dataset D. Note that the superset of a multilabel dataset is an enlarged multilabel dataset with some already duplicated instances. Only the candidates that can reduce the MeanIR of the current superset are further evaluated in the second step of ML-BFO for duplication.

The second evaluation step of ML-BFO is a heuristic evaluation. It is based on Wilson's ENN rule. As we know, the ENN rule has been extensively used in traditional classification. It is often used to remove an example whose class differs from the class of at least two of its three nearest neighbors. ML-BFO uses ENN in its second evaluation step to exclude suspicious candidates to duplicate, so that it avoids noise proliferation. Specifically, ML-BFO proposes a simple similarity measure to evaluate the similarity of a candidate to each of its neighbors. This simple similarity is proposed based on our investigation. According to our study, we found that only a small proportion of instances share more than one label with their nearest neighbors in a multilabel dataset. Thus, we define a loose criterion to evaluate the similarity between a candidate and its neighbors. If the labelset of the candidate and the labelset of one of its neighbors contain one common label, the candidate is considered to be similar to this neighbor. For a candidate, if there are more than half neighbors similar to it, this candidate will be duplicated.

After the candidates under the first label node are used up, and the size of the superset does not reach the ideal size, which is set at the beginning of this preprocessing method ML-BFO, ML-BFO moves to the next label node. The instances under the next label node become candidates. ML-BFO evaluates each candidate as before and duplicates proper candidates. ML-BFO keeps evaluating each instance under each label node until either the size of the superset reaches or the candidates under the most frequent label node in the instance tree are evaluated. Note that ML-BFO iteratively calculates the MeanIR value of the superset when a candidate is duplicated. Thus, each duplication can reduce the MeanIR value. The pseudo code of our over-sampling algorithm ML-BFO is shown in Algorithm 1.

Algorithm 1. Multilabel Best First Over-sampling.

```
Inputs: <Dataset> D, <LabelSet> Y, <NumNeighbors> NN, Int
sampleToDuplicate
Output: Resampled dataset R
Construct an instance tree from D
while N < sampleToDuplicate do
   candidates = instances whose labelset contains with the largest
unvisited IRLbl
   foreach candidate in candidates
     newMeanIR = MeanIR(D ∪R ∪candidate);
     if newMeanIR < currentMeanIR
        go to next for loop
     end if
     if less than half of the nearest neighbors sharing a common
label
        go to next for loop
     end if
     if newMeanIR > currentMeanIR
        currentMeanIR = newMeanIR
        bestCandiate = candidate
     end if
   end for
   R = R ∪ bestCandiate
   N = N + 1
end while
```

4. Experiments

We conduct experiments on four datasets from MULAN repository, the characteristics of which are shown in Table 2.

Table 1. The characteristics of the four multilabel datasets.

Dataset	#Ex.	#Atts.	#Labels	MaxIR	MeanIR
emotions	593	72	6	1.78	1.48
enron	1702	753	53	913	73.95
yeast	2417	198	14	53.41	7.20
corel5k	5000	499	374	1120	189.57

As we know, the main purpose of preprocessing is to improve the model performance. We investigated the performance of our ML-BFO, comparing with LP-ROS and MLeNN, under the three different multilabel classification algorithms, Binary Relevance (BR) [4], Calibrated Label Ranking (CLR) [5], and Random K-labelsets (RAKEL) [6], respectively. In our ML-BFO, the number of duplications is set as 25% of its original size. Our experimental results obtained through a 5-fold cross-validation are shown in Figures 1-6 respectively. Figures 1-3 show the average accuracy of each approach under each multilabel classification algorithm respectively. Figures 4-6 show the average F-measure value of each approach under each multilabel classification algorithm respectively. These figures show that ML-BFO significantly improves the performance of all three multilabel classification algorithms on all four datasets, in terms of accuracy and F-measure. The performance of LP-ROS is consistent under different multilabel classification algorithms, but varies with the datasets. The performance of MLeNN depends on the underline multilabel classification algorithms and also varies with the datasets. On the dataset emotions, MLeNN improves the performance of Binary Relevance. However, it doesn't improve the performance of both Calibrated Label Ranking and Random K-labelsets. It downgrades the performance of Calibrated Label Ranking. On the dataset Corel5k, MLeNN consistently performs better than LP-ROS, improving the performance of all three multilabel classification algorithms. On the other two datasets, MLeNN performs similarly to LP-ROS. Figures 1-6 show that LP-ROS only consistently improves the performance of all the three multilabel classification algorithms on the dataset emotions, but not on the other three datasets. It even downgrades the performance of all the three multilabel classification algorithms on the two datasets enron and yeast. Among the three sampling methods, it is obvious that our ML-BFO consistently performs the best, under different multilabel classification algorithms and on different datasets, in terms of prediction accuracy and F-measure.

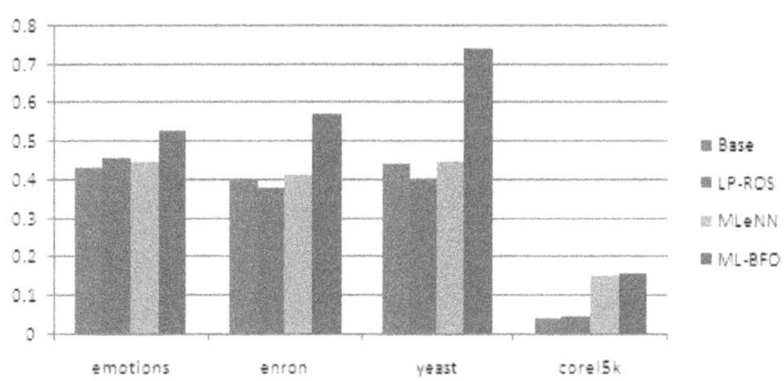

Figure 1. The average accuracy values on the four datasets when BR is used as the base learner.

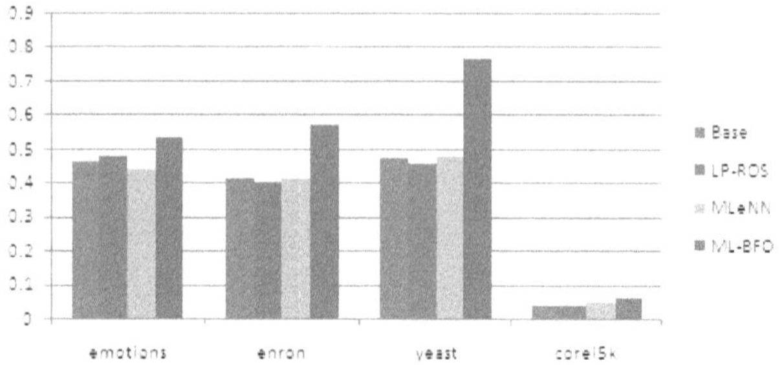

Figure 2. The average accuracy values on the four datasets when CLR is used as the base learner.

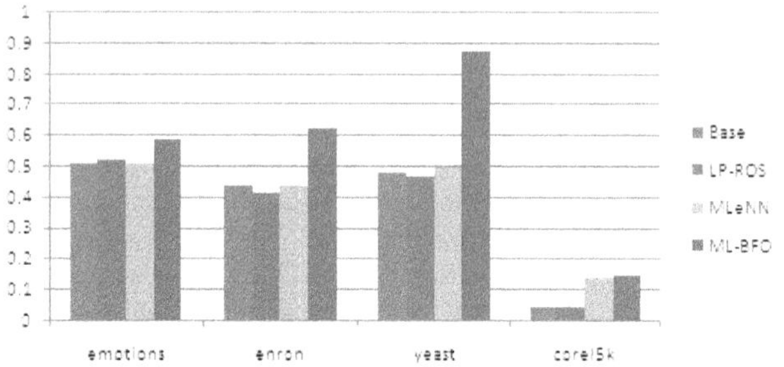

Figure 3. The average accuracy values on the four datasets when RAKEL is used as the base learner.

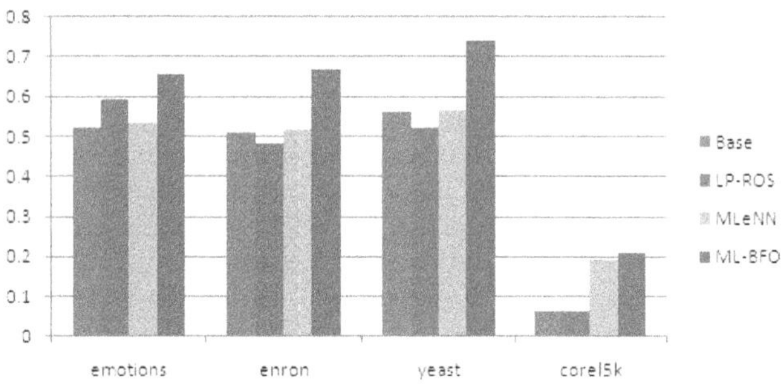

Figure 4. The F-measure values on the four datasets when BR is used as the base learner.

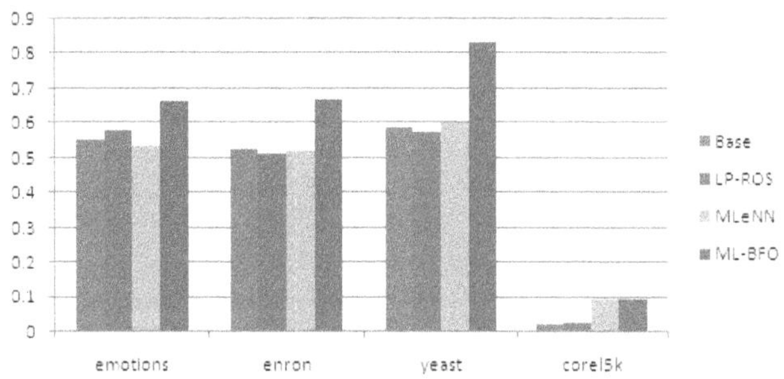

Figure 5. The F-measure values on the four datasets when CLR is used as the base learner.

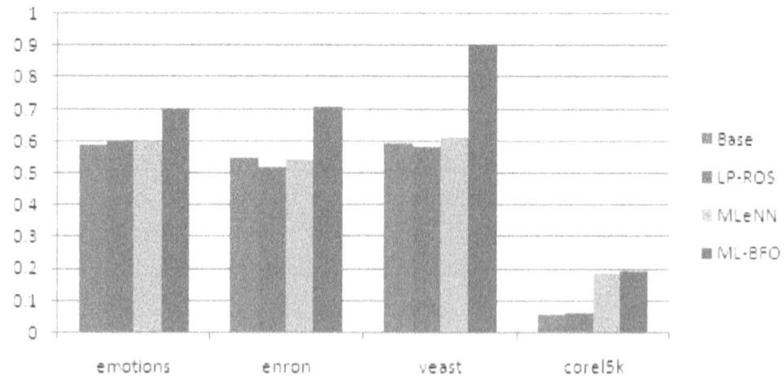

Figure 6. The F-measure values on the four datasets when RAKEL is used as the base learner.

5. CONCLUSIONS

In this paper, we proposed a novel over-sampling method ML-BFO for imbalanced multilabel classification. This method heuristically selects examples to clone to reduce the imbalance level of a multilabel dataset. To avoid the proliferation of potential noises, it further utilizes Wilson's ENN rule to refine its selection. Our experimental results showed that our method ML-BFO not only duplicates fewer examples for a multilabel dataset, but also reduces its imbalance level much more, comparing with the state-of-the-art multilabel over-sampling method LP-ROS. Furthermore, in terms of prediction accuracy and F-measure, ML-BFO not only performs much better than the state-of-the-art over-sampling method LP-ROS, but also performs much better than the state-of-the-art under-sampling method MLeNN on all four datasets under all three multilabel classification algorithms.

6. ACKNOWLEDGMENTS

This research was partially supported by the Natural Science Foundation of China under grant No. 61170020, 61402311 and 61440053, the Jiangsu Province Colleges and Universities Natural Science Research Project under grant No. 13KJB520021, the U.S. National Science Foundation (IIS-1115417), and the Jiangsu Province Postgraduate Cultivation and Innovation Project under grant No. ZY32001814.

7. REFERENCES

[1] Charte, F., Rivera, A.J., Jesus, M.J.D., and Herrera, F. 2013. A first approach to deal with imbalance in multi-label datasets. LNAI 8073 (2013), 150–160.

[2] Charte, F., Rivera, A.J., Jesus, M.J.D. and Herrera, F. 2014. MLeNN: A First Approach to Heuristic Multilabel Undersampling. LNCS 8669 (2014), 1–9.

[3] Wilson, D.L. 1972. Asymptotic Properties of Nearest Neighbor Rules Using Edited Data. IEEE Transactions on Systems, Man, and Communications 2, 3 (1972), 408–421.

[4] Godbole, S. and Sarawagi, S. 2004. Discriminative Methods for Multi-labeled Classification. PAKDD 2004, LNCS (LNAI) 3056 (2004), 22–30, Springer, Heidelberg (2004).

[5] Fürnkranz, J., Hüllermeier, E., Loza Mencía, E. and Brinker, K. 2008. Multilabel classification via calibrated label ranking. Machine Learning 73 (2008), 133–153.

[6] Tsoumakas, G. and Vlahavas, I. 2007. Random k-labelsets: An ensemble method for multilabel classification. LNCS (LNAI) 4701 (2007), 406–417.

Co-clustering Document-term Matrices by Direct Maximization of Graph Modularity

Melissa Ailem François Role Mohamed Nadif

LIPADE, Université Paris Descartes
45, rue des Saints-Pères
75006 Paris, France
{melissa.ailem,francois.role,mohamed.nadif}@parisdescartes.fr

ABSTRACT

We present *Coclus*, a novel diagonal co-clustering algorithm which is able to effectively co-cluster binary or contingency matrices by directly maximizing an adapted version of the modularity measure traditionally used for networks. While some effective co-clustering algorithms already exist that use network-related measures (normalized cut, modularity), they do so by using spectral relaxations of the discrete optimization problems. In contrast, *Coclus* allows to get even better co-clusters by directly maximizing modularity using an iterative alternating optimization procedure. Extensive comparative experiments performed on various document-term datasets demonstrate that our algorithm is very effective, stable and outperforms other co-clustering algorithms.

Categories and Subject Descriptors

H.3.3 [**Information Search and Retrieval**]: Clustering

Keywords

Co-Clustering, Modularity

1. INTRODUCTION

In the era of big data, there is more than ever a need for techniques that simultaneously group words and documents into meaningful clusters, thus making large data sets easier to handle and interpret. Co-clustering techniques just serve this purpose.

Given a data matrix X of size $n \times d$ where I is the set of n rows, and J the set of d columns, a co-cluster k is a submatrix $I_k \times J_k$ ($I_k \subseteq I, J_k \subseteq J$) where rows and columns follow some consistent patterns.

For a survey of the different structures of co-clusters and the different algorithms employed the reader is referred to [6, 8, 2, 3].

Permission to make digital or hard copies of all or part of this work for personal or classroom use is granted without fee provided that copies are not made or distributed for profit or commercial advantage and that copies bear this notice and the full citation on the first page. Copyrights for components of this work owned by others than ACM must be honored. Abstracting with credit is permitted. To copy otherwise, or republish, to post on servers or to redistribute to lists, requires prior specific permission and/or a fee. Request permissions from Permissions@acm.org.
CIKM'15, October 19-23, 2015, Melbourne, VIC, Australia
Copyright 2015 ACM. ISBN 978-1-4503-3794-6/15/10 ...$15.00
DOI: http://dx.doi.org/10.1145/2806416.2806639

In this paper, we are especially concerned with algorithms that seek an optimal block diagonal co-clustering, meaning that data points and features have the same number of clusters and that, after proper permutation of the rows and columns, the algorithm produces as result a block diagonal matrix (see figure 1). In the context of document-term matrices, this co-clustering model has the advantage of directly producing interpretable descriptions of the resulting document clusters. For example, Li [5] has proposed a block diagonal clustering algorithm that, given a binary document-term matrix, produces a block diagonal matrix of ones. This algorithm consists in alternating the clustering

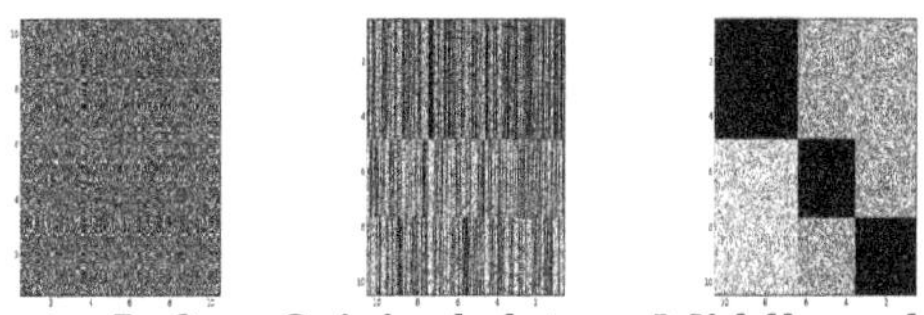

Figure 1: Left : Original data - Middle : data reorganized according to row partition - Right : data reorganized according to row and column partitions.

of rows and columns minimizing the squared error between the original X data and its approximation AB^T where A and B are binary matrices. Another notable co-clustering algorithm is the bipartite spectral graph partitioning algorithm described in [1]. This algorithm finds the optimal minimum cut partitions in a bipartite document-term graph by computing the second left and right singular vector of the normalized document-term matrix, thus using a real relaxation of the discrete optimization problem. More recently, another attempt to use network-related criteria in the field of block diagonal structure is the spectral co-clustering maximizing a generalization of the modularity [4]. Compared to other binary clustering methods based on *nonnegative matrix factorization* or *tri-factorization*, this algorithm appears to perform better in the field of document clustering. The two last-mentioned co-clustering algorithms [1, 4] both try to optimize criteria initially used in the studies of networks (normalized cut, modularity). However they do so by using a spectral relaxation of the discrete optimization problem. In contrast, our algorithm, *Coclus*, is based on a direct maximization of one of these criteria, namely bipartite modularity. We show that this approach outperforms previous block diagonal co-clustering algorithms, as demonstrated by comparative experiments conducted on numerous datasets.

Notation. We will consider the partition of the sets I of n objects and the set J of d attributes into g non overlapping clusters, where g may be greater or equal to 2. Let us define an $n \times g$ index matrix Z and an $d \times g$ index matrix W with one column for each cluster; $Z = (Z_1|Z_2|\dots|Z_g)$ and $W = (W_1|W_2|\dots|W_g)$. Each column Z_k or W_k is defined as follows: $z_{ik} = 1$ if object i belongs to cluster Z_k and $z_{ik} = 0$ otherwise, and in the same manner $w_{jk} = 1$ if attribute j belongs to cluster W_k and $w_{jk} = 0$ otherwise.

2. MODULARITY MEASURE

In this section we first review the standard graph modularity measure and then present the adaptation needed for using modularity in the co-clustering context.

2.1 Standard Modularity

Modularity is a quality criterion for graph clustering, which has received considerable attention in several disciplines since the seminal work presented in [9]. Maximizing the modularity measure can be expressed in the form of an integer linear programming. Given the graph $G = (V, E)$, let A be a binary, symmetric adjacency matrix with (i, i') as entry; and $a_{ii'} = 1$ if there is an edge between the nodes i and i'. If there is no edge between nodes i and i', $a_{ii'}$ is equal to zero. Finding a partition of the set of nodes V into homogeneous subsets leads to the resolution of the following integer linear program: $\max_C Q(A, C)$ where $Q(A, C)$ is the modularity measure $Q(A, C) = \frac{1}{2|E|}\sum_{i,i'=1}^{n}(a_{ii'} - \frac{a_{i.}a_{i'.}}{2|E|})\sum_{k=1}^{g} z_{ik}z_{i'k}$. Taking $c_{ii'} = \sum_{k=1}^{g} z_{ik}z_{i'k}$, the expression of Q becomes

$$Q(A, C) = \frac{1}{2|E|}\sum_{i,i'=1}^{n}(a_{ii'} - \frac{a_{i.}a_{i'.}}{2|E|})c_{ii'}, \quad (1)$$

where $2|E| = \sum_{i,i'} a_{ii'} = a_{..}$ is the total number of edges and $a_{i.} = \sum_{i'} a_{ii'}$ the degree of i. Let $\delta = (\delta_{ii'})$ be the $(n \times n)$ data matrix defined by $\forall i, i' \quad \delta_{ii'} = \frac{a_{i.}a_{i'.}}{2|E|}$, the expression (1) becomes $Q(A, C) = \frac{1}{2|E|}Trace[(A-\delta)C]$. The researched binary matrix C is defined by ZZ^t which models a partition in a relational space and therefore must check the properties of an equivalence relation.

2.2 Modularity for Co-clustering

In a bipartite context, the basic idea is to model the simultaneous row and column partitions using the relation C defined on $I \times J$ and called *block seriation* in [7]. Noting that $C = ZW^t$ and the general term can be expressed as follows: $c_{ij} = 1$ if object i is in the same block as attribute j and $c_{ij} = 0$ otherwise. Then $c_{ij} = \sum_{k=1}^{g} z_{ik}w_{jk}$. Now, given a rectangular matrix A defined on $I \times J$, modularity can be reformulated as follows in the co-clustering context:

$$Q(A, C) = \frac{1}{a_{..}}\sum_{i=1}^{n}\sum_{j=1}^{d}\sum_{k=1}^{g}(a_{ij} - \frac{a_{i.}a_{.j}}{a_{..}})z_{ik}w_{jk}, \quad (2)$$

where $a_{..} = \sum_{i,j} a_{ij} = |E|$ is the total weight of edges and $a_{i.} = \sum_j a_{ij}$ (the degree of i) and $a_{.j} = \sum_i a_{ij}$ (the degree of j). This modularity measure can also take the following form:

$$Q(A, C) = \frac{1}{a_{..}}Trace[(A - \delta)^t ZW^t] = Q(A, ZW^t). \quad (3)$$

Matrix ZW^t represents a block seriation relation respecting the *binary*, *assignment constraints* and triad impossible properties (see [7] for further details). As the objective function (3) is linear with respect to C and as the constraints that C must respect are linear equations, the problem can theoretically be solved using an integer linear programming solver. However, this problem is NP hard, and as a result, in practice, we use heuristics for dealing with large data sets.

3. CO-CLUSTERING ALGORITHM

Hereafter, we propose to tackle the co-clustering problem by maximizing the modularity criterion.

Proposition 1: Let A be a $(n \times d)$ binary or contingency data and C be a $(n \times d)$ defining a block seriation, the modularity measure $Q(A, C)$ can be rewritten as

1. $Q(A, C) = \frac{1}{a_{..}}Trace[(A^W - \delta^W)^t Z] = Q(A^W, Z)$ where $A^W := \{a_{ik} = \sum_{j=1}^{d} w_{jk}a_{ij}; i = 1, \dots, n; k = 1, \dots, g\}$ and $\delta^W := \{\delta^W_{ik} = \frac{a_{i.}a^W_{.k}}{a_{..}}; i = 1, \dots, n; k = 1, \dots, g\}$ with $a^W_{.k} = \sum_{j=1}^{d} w_{jk}a_{.j}$
2. $Q(A, C) = \frac{1}{a_{..}}Trace[(A^Z - \delta^Z)^t W] = Q(A^Z, W)$ where $A^Z := \{a_{jk} = \sum_{i=1}^{n} z_{ik}a_{ij}; k = 1, \dots, g; j = 1, \dots, d\}$ and $\delta^Z := \{\delta^Z_{jk} = \frac{a_{j.}a^Z_{.k}}{a_{..}}; k = 1, \dots, g; j = 1, \dots, d\}$ with $a^Z_{.k} = \sum_{i=1}^{n} z_{ik}a_{i.}$

Proof:

$$\begin{aligned} Q(A, C) &= \frac{1}{a_{..}}\sum_{i=1}^{n}\sum_{j=1}^{d}(a_{ij} - \frac{a_{i.}a_{.j}}{a_{..}})c_{ij} \\ &= \frac{1}{a_{..}}\sum_{i=1}^{n}\sum_{j=1}^{d}\sum_{k=1}^{g}(a_{ij} - \frac{a_{i.}a_{.j}}{a_{..}})z_{ik}w_{jk} \\ &= \frac{1}{a_{..}}\sum_{i=1}^{n}\sum_{k=1}^{g} z_{ik}\sum_{j=1}^{d} w_{jk}(a_{ij} - \frac{a_{i.}a_{.j}}{a_{..}}) \\ &= \frac{1}{a_{..}}\sum_{i=1}^{n}\sum_{k=1}^{g} z_{ik}\left(\sum_{j}^{d} w_{jk}a_{ij} - \frac{a_{i.}}{a_{..}}\sum_{j=1}^{d} w_{jk}a_{.j}\right) \\ &= \frac{1}{a_{..}}\sum_{i=1}^{n}\sum_{k=1}^{g}\left(a^W_{ik} - \frac{a_{i.}a^W_{.k}}{a_{..}}\right)z_{ik} \\ &= \frac{1}{a_{..}}Trace[(A^W - \delta^W)^t Z] = Q(A^W, Z) \end{aligned}$$

In the same manner, we can show that

$$\begin{aligned} Q(A, C) &= \frac{1}{a_{..}}\sum_{j=1}^{d}\sum_{k=1}^{g}(a^Z_{jk} - \frac{a_{j.}a^Z_{.k}}{a_{..}})w_{jk} \\ &= \frac{1}{a_{..}}Trace[(A^Z - \delta^Z)^t W] = Q(A^Z, W) \end{aligned}$$

Using proposition 1, the goal is to maximize modularity by alternatively maximizing $Q(A^W, Z)$ and $Q(A^Z, W)$. The optimal classification binary matrices Z^* and W^* are respectively defined by $Z^* = \arg\max_Z Trace(A^W - \delta^W)^t Z$ and $W^* = \arg\max_W Trace(A^Z - \delta^Z)^t W$. This alternated co-clustering is described in more details in algorithm 1. Hereafter, we illustrate an execution by means of a small example (a binary matrix A of size (5×4) with $g = 2$ co-clusters).

INPUT: Let $A = \begin{pmatrix} 1 & 0 & 1 & 0 \\ 0 & 1 & 0 & 1 \\ 1 & 0 & 1 & 0 \\ 0 & 1 & 0 & 1 \\ 1 & 0 & 1 & 0 \end{pmatrix}$ be a data matrix, $W = \begin{pmatrix} 0 & 1 \\ 1 & 0 \\ 0 & 1 \\ 0 & 1 \end{pmatrix}$, $Z = \begin{pmatrix} 0 & 1 \\ 1 & 0 \\ 0 & 1 \\ 1 & 0 \\ 1 & 0 \end{pmatrix}$ initial indices matrices, then $\mathbf{Q(A, ZW^t) = 0.16}$.

Algorithm 1 *Coclus*

Input: binary or contingency data A, number of co-clusters g
Output: partition matrices Z and W
1. Initialization of W
repeat
  2. Compute A^W
  3. Compute Z maximizing $Q(A^W, Z)$ by

$$z_{ik} = \arg\max_{1 \leq \ell \leq g} \left(a^W_{i\ell} - \frac{a_{i.}a^W_{.\ell}}{a_{..}} \right) \forall i = 1, \ldots, n; k = 1, \ldots, g$$

  4. Compute A^Z
  5. Compute W maximizing $Q(A^Z, W)$ by

$$w_{jk} = \arg\max_{1 \leq \ell \leq g} \left(a^Z_{j\ell} - \frac{a_{j.}a^Z_{.\ell}}{a_{..}} \right) \forall j = 1, \ldots, d; k = 1, \ldots, g$$

  6. Compute $Q(A, ZW^t)$
until *noChange* of $Q(A, ZW^t)$

Compute Z **given** W: To this end, we compute $(A^W - \delta^W)$

$$A^W = \begin{pmatrix} 0 & 2 \\ 1 & 1 \\ 0 & 2 \\ 1 & 1 \\ 0 & 2 \end{pmatrix} \delta^W = \begin{pmatrix} 0.4 & 1.6 \\ 0.4 & 1.6 \\ 0.4 & 1.6 \\ 0.4 & 1.6 \\ 0.4 & 1.6 \end{pmatrix} \Rightarrow (A^W - \delta^W) = \begin{pmatrix} -0.4 & 0.4 \\ 0.6 & -0.6 \\ -0.4 & 0.4 \\ 0.4 & -0.6 \\ -0.4 & 0.4 \end{pmatrix}$$

then $Z = \begin{pmatrix} 0 & 1 \\ 1 & 0 \\ 0 & 1 \\ 1 & 0 \\ 0 & 1 \end{pmatrix}$ and $\mathbf{Q(A^W, Z) = 0.24}$.

Compute W **given** Z: To this end we compute $(A^Z - \delta^Z)$

$$A^Z = \begin{pmatrix} 0 & 3 \\ 2 & 0 \\ 0 & 3 \\ 2 & 0 \end{pmatrix} \delta^Z = \begin{pmatrix} 1.2 & 1.8 \\ 0.8 & 1.2 \\ 1.2 & 1.8 \\ 0.8 & 1.2 \end{pmatrix} \Rightarrow (A^Z - \delta^Z) = \begin{pmatrix} -1.2 & 1.2 \\ 1.2 & -1.2 \\ -1.2 & 1.2 \\ 1.2 & -1.2 \end{pmatrix}$$

then $W = \begin{pmatrix} 0 & 1 \\ 1 & 0 \\ 0 & 1 \\ 1 & 0 \end{pmatrix}$ and $\mathbf{Q(A^Z, W) = 0.48}$.

OUTPUT: $W = \begin{pmatrix} 0 & 1 \\ 1 & 0 \\ 0 & 1 \\ 1 & 0 \end{pmatrix}$ $Z = \begin{pmatrix} 0 & 1 \\ 1 & 0 \\ 0 & 1 \\ 1 & 0 \\ 0 & 1 \end{pmatrix}$ and we obtain a reorganized version of the matrix A according to (Z, W) $\begin{pmatrix} 1 & 1 & 0 & 0 \\ 1 & 1 & 0 & 0 \\ 0 & 0 & 1 & 1 \\ 0 & 0 & 1 & 1 \\ 0 & 0 & 1 & 1 \end{pmatrix}$.

Coclus is computationally efficient for sparse data and its complexity can be shown to be $O(nz.it.(2.g))$ where nz is the number of non-zero values in the input data and it the number of iterations which is small. Empirically, about 15 iterations seemed sufficient for the datasets we used in our experiments.

4. NUMERICAL EXPERIMENTS

To test the clustering performance of *Coclus* against other algorithms, we ran it on 10 real datasets with different sizes and balances[1] coefficient (table 1). In Figure 2, we report the distributions of document sizes[2] defined by $a_{i.} = \sum_j a_{ij}$. We observe that, unlike other datasets, SPORTS and REVIEWS have very different document sizes. We will see how we can exploit this remark.

[1]The balance coefficient is defined as the ratio of the number of documents in the smallest class to the number of documents in the largest class.
[2]Number of terms in a document.

Table 1: Description of Datasets

Datasets	Characteristics				
	documents	words	#clusters	Sparsity (%)	Balance
CSTR	475	1000	4	96.60	0.399
WEBKB4	4199	1000	4	93.90	0.307
WEBACE	2340	1000	20	91.83	0.169
NG2	500	2000	2	96.90	1
CLASSIC3	3891	4303	3	98.0	0.71
CLASSIC4	7095	5896	4	99.41	0.323
NG20	19949	43586	20	99.99	0.991
RCV1	9625	29992	4	99.75	0.766
SPORTS	8580	14870	7	99.99	0.036
REVIEWS	4069	18483	5	99.99	0.098

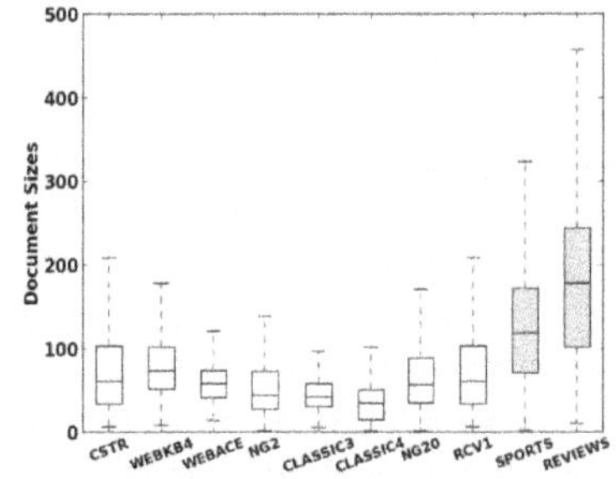

Figure 2: Boxplot of document sizes of each dataset

The competitive algorithms retained for comparison with ours are: the spectral graph partitioning proposed in [1] denoted as *Spec* in the sequel and the spectral co-clustering maximizing a generalized bipartite modularity, normalized by the row and column cluster size [4], denoted as *SpecCo*. We chose these algorithms because they seek a block diagonal co-clustering of terms and documents, just as ours. For *Spec* we used the Scikit-learn implementation of Dhillon's algorithm[3], and we reimplemented the *SpecCo* algorithm.

To evaluate *Coclus*, we consider three situations: original data, binarized data and finally after normalized TF-IDF transformation. The used TF-IDF weighting scheme is the following: $w_{ij} = tf_{ij}(1 + \log(\frac{1+n}{1+d_j}))$, where w_{ij} is the weight of term i in document j, tf_{ij} is the frequency of term i in document j, n is the total number of documents and d_j is the number of documents containing term j. The L_2 normalization was applied on the obtained TF-IDF matrix. When the data sets are binary or original we perform a normalization only when the datasets present high variance in terms of document sizes. In this case, we propose to divide each row by its norm before applying the co-clustering algorithms in order to eliminate the biases induced by the length of a document. For instance, SPORTS and REVIEWS require this normalization. For the other datasets, this normalization does not increase significantly the performance of compared algorithms.

To validate the obtained results, we used the clustering accuracy and normalized mutual information. Clustering accuracy, denoted *Acc*, measures the extent to which each cluster contains data points from the corresponding class and is defined as follows: $Acc = \frac{1}{n} max[\sum_{\mathcal{C}_k, \mathcal{L}_m} T(\mathcal{C}_k, \mathcal{L}_m)]$, where $\mathcal{C}_k$ is the kth cluster in the final results, and $\mathcal{L}_m$ is the true mth class. $T(\mathcal{C}_k, \mathcal{L}_m)$ is the number of entities which belong to class m and are assigned to cluster k. The greater the clustering accuracy, the better the clustering performance. We also used the normalized mutual information (NMI),

[3]http://scikit-learn.org/stable/

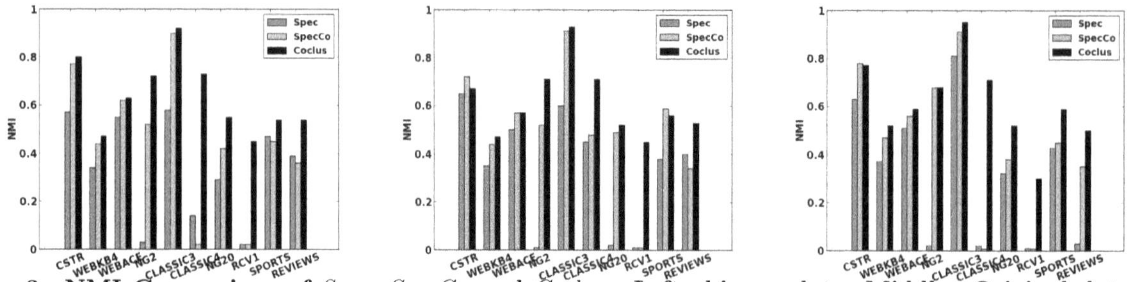

Figure 3: NMI Comparison of *Spec*, *SpecCo* and *Coclus*. Left: binary data, Middle: Original data, Right: TF-IDF data.

Table 2: T-tests results comparing *SpecCo* and *Coclus*

		Binary			Original			TF-IDF		
datasets	per.	SpecCo	Coclus	p-value	SpecCo	Coclus	p-value	SpecCo	Coclus	p-value
CSTR	Acc	0.89±0.0005	**0.90±0.007**	**<0.001**	0.82± 3.3e-16	**0.85±0.007**	**<0.001**	**0.89±0.003**	0.89±0.02	0.43
	NMI	0.77±0.001	**0.78±0.02**	**<0.001**	**0.72± 2.8e-16**	0.65±0.003	**<0.001**	**0.77±0.004**	0.73±0.04	**<0.001**
WEBKB4	Acc	0.69±0.007	**0.72±0.008**	**<0.001**	0.70±0.003	**0.71±0.009**	**<0.001**	0.73±0.0002	**0.77±0.03**	**<0.001**
	NMI	0.44±0.0007	**0.47±0.01**	**<0.001**	0.44±0.001	**0.46±0.01**	**<0.001**	0.51±0.0002	**0.52±0.002**	**<0.001**
WEBACE	Acc	0.52±0.03	**0.58±0.02**	**<0.001**	0.45±0.02	**0.56±0.01**	**<0.001**	0.47±0.04	**0.58±0.01**	**<0.001**
	NMI	**0.61±0.01**	0.60±0.007	**0.045**	0.56±0.009	**0.57±0.003**	**0.01**	0.56± 0.02	**0.59±0.002**	**<0.001**
NG2	Acc	0.89±0.004	**0.93±0.0007**	**<0.001**	0.89±5.6e-16	**0.94±0.02**	**<0.001**	**0.94±0.001**	0.92±0.01	**<0.001**
	NMI	0.53±0.009	**0.65±0.02**	**<0.001**	0.52±1.1e-16	**0.67±0.05**	**<0.001**	**0.68±0.004**	0.61±0.04	**<0.001**
CLASSIC3	Acc	0.98±3.3e-16	**0.98±0.0005**	**<0.001**	0.98±4.6e-05	**0.98±0.002**	**<0.001**	0.98±0.0003	**0.99±0.0006**	**<0.001**
	NMI	0.90±3.46e-16	**0.91±0.003**	**<0.001**	0.91±0.0002	**0.92±0.004**	**<0.001**	0.91±0.0007	**0.94±0.003**	**<0.001**
CLASSIC4	Acc	0.45±2.8e-16	**0.91±0.006**	**<0.001**	0.58±6.8e-05	**0.90±0.01**	**<0.001**	0.45±1.7e-16	**0.85±0.02**	**<0.001**
	NMI	0.02±1.1e-17	**0.73±0.01**	**<0.001**	0.48±0.0003	**0.73±0.02**	**<0.001**	0.01±1.7e-18	**0.67±0.02**	**<0.001**
NG20	Acc	0.19±0.01	**0.39±0.02**	**<0.001**	0.26±0.01	**0.37±0.03**	**<0.001**	0.15±5.7e-05	**0.37±0.05**	**<0.001**
	NMI	0.41±0.01	**0.53±0.02**	**<0.001**	0.46±0.01	**0.50±0.02**	**<0.001**	0.38±0.0002	**0.45±0.02**	**<0.001**
RCV1	Acc	0.3±0.0006	**0.58±0.09**	**<0.001**	0.3±1.6e-17	**0.67±0.06**	**<0.001**	0.30±2.2e-16	**0.56±0.07**	**<0.001**
	NMI	0.02±0.002	**0.40±0.05**	**<0.001**	0.01±1.7e-18	**0.44±0.04**	**<0.001**	0.008±6.1e-18	**0.30±0.05**	**<0.001**
SPORTS	Acc	0.59±0.0001	**0.68±0.02**	**<0.001**	**0.68±0.0002**	0.67±0.02	**<0.001**	0.61±0.0007	**0.65±0.05**	**<0.001**
	NMI	0.45±0.0001	**0.53±0.03**	**<0.001**	**0.59±0.0001**	0.57±0.004	**<0.001**	0.45±0.0008	**0.56±0.03**	**<0.001**
REVIEWS	Acc	0.56±0.003	**0.64±0.03**	**0.006**	0.45±5.6e-17	**0.61±0.05**	**<0.001**	0.46±0.0001	**0.60±0.03**	**<0.001**
	NMI	0.36±0.002	**0.52±0.03**	**<0.001**	0.342.7e-16	**0.51±0.02**	**<0.001**	0.35±0.0001	**0.50±0.02**	**<0.001**

which is estimated by: $NMI = \frac{\sum_{k,\ell} \frac{N_{k,\ell}}{n} \log \frac{nN_{k,\ell}}{N_k \hat{N}_\ell}}{\sqrt{(\sum_k \frac{N_k}{n} \log \frac{N_k}{n})(\sum_\ell \frac{\hat{N}_\ell}{n} \log \frac{\hat{N}_\ell}{n})}}$, where N_k denotes the number of data contained in the cluster $\mathcal{C}_k (1 \leq k \leq g)$, $\hat{N}_\ell$ is the number of data belonging to the class $\mathcal{L}_\ell (1 \leq \ell \leq g)$, and $N_{k,\ell}$ denotes the number of data that are in the intersection between cluster $\mathcal{C}_k$ and class $\mathcal{L}_\ell$. The larger the NMI, the better the quality of clustering. The results presented in figure 3 and table 2, were obtained by running each algorithm 100 times with random initialization. NMI values reported in figure 3 show that our algorithm is very stable and has a good behavior whatever the nature of the data (binary, contingency or TF-IDF). The results show that *Coclus* is better than *SpecCo* which is almost always better than *Spec*. To confirm this, we perform t-tests comparing the two best algorithms *Coclus* and *SpecCo*. In Table 2, we observe that *Coclus* outperfoms significantly *SpecCo* in almost all situations.

5. CONCLUSION

We have presented a novel diagonal co-clustering algorithm which directly maximizes a modularity measure adapted to a bipartite context. In particular, we have shown that this modularity can be maximized using an iterative alternating optimization, which led to a new, effective co-clustering algorithm. Experimental results obtained on several real datasets indeed demonstrated the effectiveness of our algorithm. The experiments also showed its robustness and flexibility since it can achieve very good results both on binary and contingency document-term tables. Paths for future research might include extending the approach to fuzzy co-clustering and assessing the number of co-clusters.

References

[1] I. Dhillon. Co-clustering documents and words using bipartite spectral graph partitioning. KDD'01, pages 269–274, 2001.

[2] G. Govaert and M. Nadif. Block clustering with bernoulli mixture models: Comparison of different approaches. *Computational Statistics & Data Analysis*, 52:3233–3245, 2008.

[3] G. Govaert and M. Nadif. *Co-Clustering: Models, Algorithms and Applications. Wiley.* 2013.

[4] L. Labiod and M. Nadif. Co-clustering for binary and categorical data with maximum modularity. In *ICDM'11*, pages 1140–1145, 2011.

[5] T. Li. A general model for clustering binary data. In *KDD '05*, pages 188–197, 2005.

[6] S. C. Madeira and A. L. Oliveira. Biclustering algorithms for biological data analysis: A survey. *IEEE/ACM Trans. Comput. Biol. Bioinformatics*, 1:24–45, 2004.

[7] F. Marcotorchino. Seriation problems: An overview. *Applied Stochastic Models And Data Analysis*, 7:199–202, 1991.

[8] I. V. Mechelen, H. Bock, and P. De Boeck. Two-mode clustering methods: a structured overview. *Statistical methods in medical research*, 13, (5):363–394, 2004.

[9] M. E. J. Newman and M. Girvan. Finding and evaluating community structure in networks. 2004.

A Data-Driven Approach to Distinguish Cyber-Attacks from Physical Faults in a Smart Grid

Adnan Anwar
UNSW Australia, Canberra
School of Engineering and IT
adnan.anwar@adfa.edu.au

Abdun Naser mahmood
UNSW Australia, Canberra
School of Engineering and IT
A.Mahmood@adfa.edu.au

Zubair Shah
UNSW Australia, Canberra
School of Engineering and IT
Z.shah@unsw.edu.au

ABSTRACT

Recently, there has been significant increase in interest on Smart Grid security. Researchers have proposed various techniques to detect cyber-attacks using sensor data. However, there has been little work to distinguish a cyber-attack from a power system physical fault. A serious operational failure in physical power grid may occur from the mitigation strategies if fault is wrongly classified as a cyber-attack or vice-versa. In this paper, we utilize a data-driven approach to accurately differentiate the physical faults from cyber-attacks. First, we create a realistic dataset by generating different types of faults and cyber-attacks on the IEEE 30 bus benchmark test system. Next, we provide a data-driven approach where labelled data are projected in a new low-dimensional subspace using Principal Component Analysis (PCA). Next, Sequential Minimal Optimization (SMO) based Support Vectors are trained using the new projection of the original dataset. With both simulated and practical datasets, we have observed that the proposed classification method outperforms other existing popular supervised classification approaches considering the cyber-attack and fault datasets.

Categories and Subject Descriptors

[**J.7 Computers in Other Systems**]: Industrial control

Keywords

False Data Injection Attack, Smart Grid, Faults, Anomaly

1. INTRODUCTION

State Estimator (SE), which is a key operational module used in an Energy Management System (EMS) to estimate the system states (e.g., voltage magnitudes and angles) from the sensor measurements by minimizing estimation error. A bad data detector module (BDD) works in conjunction with the SE module to identify anomalies in the measurement data [1, 5]. In recent studies, it has been revealed that the smart grid key operational modules (e.g., SE and BDD) are vulnerable to a class of cyber-attacks [10, 4], known as *False Data Injection* (FDI) Attack.

In [10], Liu et al. shows for the first time, that an attacker can construct an FDI attack which can bypass the traditional anomaly detection modules (BDD) of an EMS and remains hidden. Most of the proposed anomaly detection techniques for EMS as well as existing BDD works based on some threshold derived from normal stable behaviour of the system and detects the existence of attack if the measurement data deviates from that threshold. Interestingly, these approaches may provide a good detection accuracy of the anomalous data but can not differentiate the classes of anomalies. Note, other than cyber-attacks, measurement data will also show anomalous behaviour in the presence of *physical faults* which produce different power flow patterns than that of a normal stable profile. Current approaches for detecting cyber-attack in smart grid ignores the presence of faults. In this paper, we create a realistic dataset by generating different types of faults and cyber-attacks on the IEEE 30 bus benchmark test system. With extensive experiments, we observe that most of the established supervised methods perform poorly for the classification of faults and cyber-attacks. To improve the classification accuracy, we use a Principal Component Analysis (PCA) based technique to enhance the classification accuracy of the Sequential Minimal Optimization (SMO) based Support vector Machines (SVM). We conduct experiments on both simulated and practical datasets using the proposed method, as well other supervised classification methods. For this specific classification problem, we observed that the proposed technique outperforms other existing well performed supervised classification methods.

2. FAULT AND CYBER-ATTACK DATA

Both fault and cyber-attack data for smart grid is simulated considering IEEE benchmark 30 bus test system [16]. Fig. 1 provides a conceptual diagram of data preparation where fault data is prepared using EPRI's smart grid tool-OpenDSS and matlab platform considering sequence-modelling of the benchmark system. All FDI attack is simulated using Matlab for the same test system considering similar operating conditions following state-of-the-art techniques. Simulating attacks or faults, we obtain system states which are voltage angles and magnitudes of all nodes. Finally, all injection attacks and fault data are stored in a database with 2000 instances. A detailed description of the whole procedure is discussed below:

Permission to make digital or hard copies of all or part of this work for personal or classroom use is granted without fee provided that copies are not made or distributed for profit or commercial advantage and that copies bear this notice and the full citation on the first page. Copyrights for components of this work owned by others than ACM must be honored. Abstracting with credit is permitted. To copy otherwise, or republish, to post on servers or to redistribute to lists, requires prior specific permission and/or a fee. Request permissions from Permissions@acm.org.
CIKM'15, October 19–23, 2015, Melbourne, Australia.
© 2015 ACM. ISBN 978-1-4503-3794-6/15/10 ...$15.00.
DOI: http://dx.doi.org/10.1145/2806416.2806648.

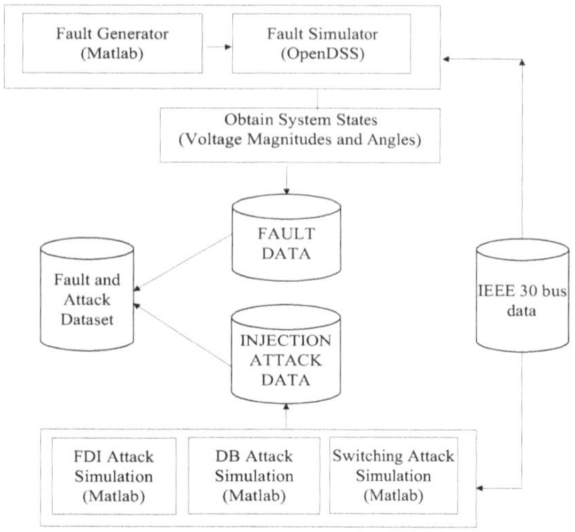

Figure 1: Simulated data preparation

2.1 Preparation of Fault Data

We include both symmetrical and asymmetrical faults. The asymmetrical faults are further classified as Single Line-to-Ground (SLG) fault, Double Line-to-Ground (DLG) fault and Line-to-Line (LL) fault. For a three-phase power system line section with A,B,C phases and ground denoted by G, the SLG fault occurs when any of the three phases of the conductor is shorted with the ground which includes the scenarios A-G, B-G, and C-G. A DLG fault occurs when two of the phases are grounded, such as (A,B)-G, (A,C)-G and (B,C)-G. The LL fault occurs when one phase is shorted with another, such as A-B, B-C and C-A. These faults can happen anywhere in the network, e.g., there are 41 line sections in IEEE 30 bus test system. So, fault can be occurred in any of the phases of the 41 line sections and the magnitude of the fault will depend on the fault resistance. During the data preparation, we used OpenDSS which can handle symmetrical component modelling for fault analysis. First we model 30 bus system considering positive, negative and zero sequence line parameters. Next, we apply faults using a monte carlo simulation of 500 samples by varying *fault locations*, *fault magnitudes* and *fault types*. For each sample, we obtain voltage magnitudes and angles for all nodes of the test system. Since IEEE 30 bus test system has 30 nodes and each node has 3 phases, we obtain 90 voltage magnitudes and 90 phase angles as attributes for each case[1].

2.2 Preparation of Cyber-Attack Data

In this work, we have considered three different types of injection attacks for smart grid. First we review the definition of *injection* attacks and then discuss the attack constructions.

2.2.1 FDI Attacks on measurement sensors

Recently, Yu et al. have that PCA can be used to transform the measurement data matrix into a new subspace, preserving the spatial characteristics as much as possible [18]. Hence, authors construct FDI attacks based on the data of the new projected space. In this paper, similar approach has been adopted to construct blind FDI attacks vector $\mathbf{a}$ following:

$$\mathbf{a}_{pca} = H_{pca}\mathbf{c} \tag{1}$$

where $\mathbf{c}$ is an arbitrary non-zero vector of length $n \times 1$ [18] and H_{pca} is the first n principal components of the measurement matrix where n is the total number of states of the system. Detail procedure of the blind FDI attack construction can be obtained from [18]. In this experiment, we have used Matlab based tool MatPower [19] to generate measurement matrix. 500 different values of $\mathbf{c}$ vectors are considered randomly to create the FDI attack vectors. Adding these attack vectors with the original measurements, we conduct a state estimation which provide us corrupted system states $\mathbf{x}'_a$.

2.2.2 Database Attack

Electric Network Database contain information on the physical properties or a 'blueprint' of the power system information that is critical to the correct operation of many aspects of the power grid; from planning to real-time operation and control. Recently, it has been shown that the Electric Network DB is also vulnerable to cyber attacks [16, 13]. By gaining access to the SCADA network, an attacker can manipulate the database. Based on the manipulated database, SE/OPF will produce incorrect system states that do not represent the actual physical system. Consequently, this will lead to the network operator taking incorrect decisions. Sometimes, these actions may result in the destabilization of the whole system. In this work, we have created the DB manipulation attack by modifying the line resistance and reactance parameters following [16, 13]. Here, we have conducted 500 attack cases where line parameters (resistance and reactance) have been varied between 10% to 190% of its original values.

2.3 Practical Fault and Attack Data

This paper also considers the practical cyber attack and fault dataset obtained from [2, 7]. The measurements of the 2-class dataset includes 37 power system events of a 3-bus 2 generator power system as shown in Fig. 1 (b). Short circuit fault data, and injection attack data (remote tripping command injection, relay setting change, data injection) are considered as two separate classes [2, 7].

3. PROPOSED METHODOLOGY

Most of the well-performed supervised technique for classification performs poorly for the above datasets, specially for the practical dataset. Note, it is important to classify the attack and fault very accurately. Even an operational decision based on a small fraction of miss classification can cause a severe damage in the physical grid. Hence, we focus on enhancing the overall classification performance by adopting a two step procedure. First, we obtain the labelled cyber-attack and fault data. Next, the covariance matrix of attack data and fault data are calculated separately. Next, the coefficients of Principal Components (PC) both for attack and fault data are calculated and stored. Based on the eigenvalues of the PCs, we plot a scree plot and determine the optimal number of PCs we want to consider to make a good approximation of the original datasets obtained separably from fault and attack instances. A new projection of these original data are then obtained by multiplying the

[1]data can be obtained from goo.gl/niINZU

Table 1: **Classification Accuracy in Percentage**

method	Naive Bayes	SMO	OneR	Jrip	Decision Stump	Random Forest	Random Tree	Proposed Method
Dataset1	26.29	77.84	23.76	90.21	77.85	79.54	80.085	**99.99**
Dataset2	33.75	70.073	31.4	86.74	69.54	75.02	75.01	**99.99**
Dataset3	33.77	70.37	30.75	89.76	70.38	76.65	74.94	**99.99**
Dataset4	37.51	65.39	36.23	87.61	67.05	76.98	71.01	**99.99**
Dataset5	31.97	71.3	30.3	89.4	71.3	76.8	77.07	**99.99**
Dataset6	34.24	70.26	30.96	87.23	70.26	71.87	72.58	**99.99**
Dataset7	29.5	74.67	26.5	89.11	74.67	80.71	78.78	**99.99**
Dataset8	59.84	71.28	30.23	90.21	70.93	76.74	72.81	**99.96**
Dataset9	35.37	66.94	34.92	84.88	66.94	71.31	68.83	**99.99**
Dataset10	33.84	70.4	31.33	89.28	70.4	74.87	73.46	**99.99**
Dataset11	26.58	75.5	25.36	89.08	75.58	77.05	77.91	**99.99**
Dataset12	37.74	67.57	36.4	87.98	67.93	73.35	69.91	**99.99**
Dataset13	27.85	78.12	23.16	90.76	78.12	80.06	79.89	**99.96**
Dataset14	29.02	73.54	27.39	89.23	73.58	76.05	75.52	**99.99**
Dataset15	37.75	64.72	35.51	85.29	64.72	77.14	69.23	**99.99**
Simulated	87	81.25	99.95	99.95	94.90	99.97	99.55	**99.99**

fault and attack data with their corresponding PC coefficients. Then, a new transformed dataset is created with the new projection of the fault and attack data along with their labels. Finally, this transformed dataset is used as an input in the SVM module. A step-by-step procedure is discussed below:

1. ***Projecting Data into a new subspace using PCA:*** For a dataset **Z**, we obtain attack (Z_A) and fault data (Z_F) according to the class label. Both the attack and fault data are standardized separately according to $\mathbf{Z}_s = \frac{\mathbf{Z} - mean(\mathbf{Z})}{std(\mathbf{Z})}$, where Z_s is the standardized data. Next, we apply the PCA technique on the standardized data. PCA is a multivariate statistical technique widely used for dimensionality reduction and data transformation. It can transform the correlated observations into uncorrelated variables which is known as principal components. These orthogonal principal components are the linear combinations of the original observations. After a successful PCA transformation, we obtain the PC coefficients, A_A, A_F and the eigenvalues of PCs, λ_A, λ_F, for attack and fault data respectively. Now, the new projection of the original standardized data ($\tilde{\mathbf{Z}}$) can be obtained as $\tilde{\mathbf{Z}} = \mathbf{Z}_s\mathbf{A}$ for both attack data and fault data. Then, these projected fault and attack data are stored with their corresponding labels and fed to SVM for classification.

2. ***Classification using SMO based SVM:*** SVM is a set of supervised learning methods which are built on statistical learning theory. SVM searches for an optimal separating plane which could separate training samples with the least error by finding maximum margin width between the two parallel bounding planes. The data points which are closer to the separating hyper plane are so-called support vectors. The $\mathrm{w}^T\mathrm{x} + \mathrm{b} = 0$ is separating plane in original space and $\mathrm{w}^T\Phi(\mathrm{x}) + \mathrm{b} = 0$ is separating plane in high dimensional space. In both of these cases w is a perpendicular to the classification of surface vector, x is the input vector, and b is a constant. $\Phi(\mathrm{x})$ is a nonlinear function which map the training sample to a high dimensional feature space. In our experiment we used radial basis function (RBF) kernel given by $K(x_i, x_j) = exp(-\frac{1}{2\gamma}\|x_i - x_j\|^2)$. The state of the art in training SVMs performs an iterative decomposition strategy which focuses on working set selection in order to solve QP problems without requiring complex QP solver software. In this work, SMO based decomposition strategy is employed to perform SVM on the new projected datasets of fault and attack instances.

4. RESULTS AND DISCUSSION

We have used a well-established machine learning tool-Weka [8] to evaluate the performance of the proposed method as well other popular techniques. For performance evaluation, we use the following classifiers- probabilistic classifier (e.g., Naive Bayes), non-probabilistic binary classifier (e.g., SVM), rule based (e.g., OneR, JRipper), decision-tree based (e.g., Random forests, Random tree). Description of these techniques can be obtained from [8]. The above mentioned methods and the proposed method is tested using both simulated and practical datasets considering a 10-fold cross validation. Results obtained from the 16 datasets (15 practical datasets and one simulated) are presented in Table 1 and the average accuracy is plotted in Fig 2. We see that the classification accuracy for all methods except existing SMO based SVM and Naive Bayes are satisfactory for simulated data. However, all existing methods perform extremely poor for practical datasets. Among the existing techniques, JRip has the highest accuracy which is around 90% in average and OneR has the lowest accuracy that is below 40%. SVM has an average accuracy of 71.83%. For all test cases, SVM accuracy remains less than 80% considering practical datasets and has just 81% for simulated data. JRip, the best performing among the considered existing algorithms, also shows its weakness for practical datasets. It could never cross the margin of 91% for any of the 15 practical datasets. Considering all of these 16 datasets, the proposed technique outperforms all other techniques for all test setups. The average classification accuracy is 99.986% and it is consistent for both simulated and practical datasets. To evaluate the performance of all methods in a more comprehensive manner, we also consider other measures including, recall, precision and F-measure [8]. For the space limitation, we only discuss the top three performing algorithms- Proposed, JRip and Random Forest. Considering Dataset2, we observe that the Random Forest has recall, precision and F-

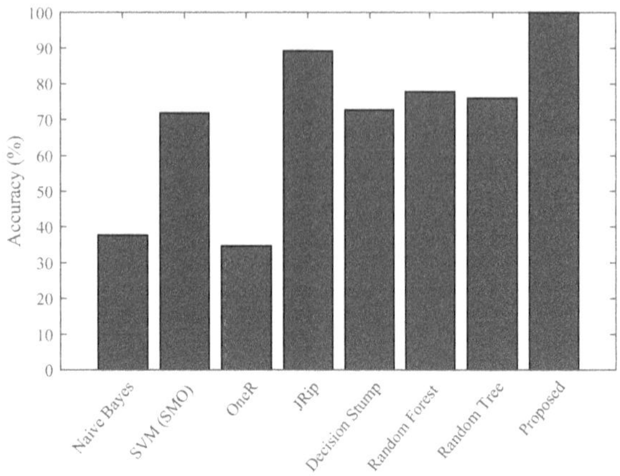

Figure 2: Average Accuracy of all methods

measure as 0.75, 0.798 and 0.687 respectively. For the same indicators, we obtain 0.868,0.866 and 0.864 respectively for JRip algorithm. All three indicators are close to one for our proposed method. Similar observations are made for other test datasets. From these observations, we conclude that the proposed method outperforms all of the above considered benchmark algorithms for these cyber-attack and fault classification datasets.

5. CONCLUSION

In this paper we evaluate the performance of different state-of-the-art supervised machine learning techniques. In this paper, we generate a realistic dataset of faults and injection attacks considering benchmark power test system. We also consider practical dataset that includes the disturbances (faults) as well as cyber-attacks. We observe that our proposed method significantly improves the classification accuracy which is essential for stable smart grid operation. We have validated the results obtained from the proposed method using existing well-performed classification techniques.

6. ACKNOWLEDGEMENT

Author are grateful to Tommy Morris, Uttam Adhikari, Shengyi Pan from Mississippi State University and, Raymond Borges, Justin Beaver of Oak Ridge National Laboratories (ORNL) for sharing their ICS dataset.

7. REFERENCES

[1] A. Abur and A. Expósito. *Power System State Estimation: Theory and Implementation.* Power Engineering (Willis). CRC Press, 2004.

[2] U. Adhikari, T. Morris, and S. Pan. A cyber-physical power system test bed for intrusion detection systems. In *PES General Meeting | Conference Exposition, 2014 IEEE*, pages 1–5, July 2014.

[3] A. Anwar and A. Mahmood. Cyber security of smart grid infrastructure. *The State of the Art in Intrusion Prevention and Detection*, CRC Press, Taylor & Francis Group:139–154, 2014.

[4] A. Anwar and A. Mahmood. Vulnerabilities of smart grid state estimation against false data injection attack. In *Renewable Energy Integration*, pages 411–428. Springer, 2014.

[5] A. Anwar, A. N. Mahmood, and Z. Tari. Identification of vulnerable node clusters against false data injection attack in an AMI based smart grid. *Information Systems*, 53:201 – 212, 2015.

[6] S. Bi and Y. J. Zhang. Graphical methods for defense against false-data injection attacks on power system state estimation. *IEEE Transactions on Smart Grid*, 5(3):1216–1227, May 2014.

[7] R. Borges Hink, J. Beaver, M. Buckner, T. Morris, U. Adhikari, and S. Pan. Machine learning for power system disturbance and cyber-attack discrimination. In *2014 7th International Symposium on Resilient Control Systems (ISRCS)*, Aug 2014.

[8] M. Hall, E. Frank, G. Holmes, B. Pfahringer, P. Reutemann, and I. H. Witten. The weka data mining software: An update. *SIGKDD Explor. Newsl.*, 11(1):10–18, Nov. 2009.

[9] J. Kim, L. Tong, and R. Thomas. Subspace methods for data attack on state estimation: A data driven approach. *IEEE Transactions on Signal Processing*, 63(5):1102–1114, March 2015.

[10] Y. Liu, P. Ning, and M. K. Reiter. False data injection attacks against state estimation in electric power grids. In *Proceedings of the 16th ACM Conference on Computer and Communications Security*, CCS '09, pages 21–32, New York, NY, USA, 2009. ACM.

[11] Y. Liu, P. Ning, and M. K. Reiter. False data injection attacks against state estimation in electric power grids. *ACM Trans. Inf. Syst. Secur.*, 14(1):13:1–13:33, June 2011.

[12] R. McMillan. Siemens: Stuxnet worm hit industrial systems. *COMPUTERWorld*, Sept. 2010.

[13] S. Mousavian, J. Valenzuela, and J. Wang. Real-time data reassurance in electrical power systems based on artificial neural networks. *Electric Power Systems Research*, 96(0):285 – 295, 2013.

[14] S. Pan, T. Morris, and U. Adhikari. Developing a hybrid intrusion detection system using data mining for power systems. *IEEE Transactions on Smart Grid*, 2015.

[15] The Industrial Control Systems Cyber Emergency Response Team (ICS-CERT). Incident response activity (april-june 2013).

[16] J. Valenzuela, J. Wang, and N. Bissinger. Real-time intrusion detection in power system operations. *IEEE Transactions on Power Systems*, 28(2), 2013.

[17] Q. Yang, J. Yang, W. Yu, D. An, N. Zhang, and W. Zhao. On false data-injection attacks against power system state estimation: Modeling and countermeasures. *IEEE Transactions on Parallel and Distributed Systems*, 25(3):717–729, March 2014.

[18] Z.-H. Yu and W.-L. Chin. Blind false data injection attack using pca approximation method in smart grid. *IEEE Transactions on Smart Grid*, PP(99), 2015.

[19] R. Zimmerman, C. Murillo-Sanchez, and R. Thomas. MATPOWER: steady-state operations, planning, and analysis tools for power systems research and education. *IEEE Transactions on Power Systems*, 26(1):12–19, Feb 2011.

Improving Event Detection by Automatically Assessing Validity of Event Occurrence in Text

Andrea Ceroni
L3S Research Center
Hannover, Germany
ceroni@l3s.de

Ujwal Gadiraju
L3S Research Center
Hannover, Germany
gadiraju@l3s.de

Marco Fisichella
L3S Research Center
Hannover, Germany
fisichella@l3s.de

ABSTRACT

Manually inspecting text to assess whether an event occurs in a document collection is an onerous and time consuming task. Although a manual inspection to discard the false events would increase the precision of automatically detected sets of events, it is not a scalable approach. In this paper, we automatize *event validation*, defined as the task of determining whether a given event occurs in a given document or corpus. The introduction of automatic event validation as a post-processing step of event detection can boost the precision of the detected event set, discarding false events and preserving the true ones. We propose a novel automatic method for event validation, which relies on a supervised model to predict the occurrence of events in a non-annotated corpus. The data for training the model is gathered via crowdsourcing. Experiments on real-world events and documents show that our method (i) outperforms the state-of-the-art event validation approach and (ii) increases the precision of event detection while preserving recall.

Categories and Subject Descriptors

H.3.3 [**Information Storage and Retrieval**]: Information Search and Retrieval

Keywords

Event Validation; Event Detection; Precision Boosting

1. INTRODUCTION

Event descriptions are of paramount importance and provide concise summaries of news articles, making the search for information more enjoyable for general readers and more effective for professionals like historians and journalists.

In our work, we do not focus on how events are detected or extracted from text, but we are interested in assessing their occurrence within a given corpus. For this purpose, we model events as a set of participants related within a given time period. This is in line with both, the basic definition of *event* given by the Topic Detection and Tracking (TDT) project ("something that happens at some specific time and place") [1] and with more recent works on event detection, e.g. [4, 6, 10]. For instance, the event {(*Kim Clijsters, Li Na, Australian Open*), *2011-01-18 to 2011-02-07*} would represent the participation of two tennis players in the 2011 Australian Open.

Manually assessing whether an event occurs in a document collection becomes infeasible in scenarios where events are continuously and automatically detected from news streams on a large-scale. In this paper, we propose to automate event validation by learning to assess the occurrence of events in a given unannotated corpus. Given a set of events, our approach can (i) reduce the number of false events with respect to a given corpus, and (ii) find documents to corroborate the occurrence of events and enrich available knowledge bases (e.g. [7]) with such event descriptions. We particularly tackle the former application, introducing event validation as a post processing step of event detection to boost the precision within the detected set of events. This has to be accomplished without affecting recall, i.e. preserving accurately detected events. Since the verity of occurrence of an event depends on the considered documents in a corpus, we distinguish two levels of validation: *document-level validation* validates the occurrence of an event in a given document, while *corpus-level validation* considers the occurrence within the entire corpus. This distinction is compliant with the two aforementioned use cases: a user or application would benefit by either handling a cleaner event set (corpus-level) or having more available information related to the event (document-level).

To validate events, we develop a supervised learning model by extracting different features from events and documents. Given the lack of assumptions on the nature of events and documents, our model for event validation can be applied to a wide range of events and related corpora. Validity annotations for training our model are acquired by exploiting the crowdsourcing paradigm.

Our main contributions are: (i) the introduction of automatic event validation in cascade to event detection; (ii) a novel and effective automatic event validation approach, which outperforms baselines and previous state-of-the-art approaches; (iii) significant boost of precision with a low decrease in recall of event detection, when experimenting with a state-of-the-art event detection method.

2. RELATED WORK

The automatic detection of events from natural language content has been widely studied, e.g. in [1, 4, 5, 6]. However, event detection is different from event validation, since the output of event detection methods (i.e., a set of *events*) constitute the known input for event validation methods. Although the task of event validation with respect to a corpus can be posed as being analogous to an *Information Retrieval* task, we find that checking the mere appearance of event participants in text (e.g. via keyword matching) is insufficient to validate the occurrence of events in documents while establishing mutual relationships and temporal conformation.

A first attempt at automatic event validation has been proposed

Permission to make digital or hard copies of all or part of this work for personal or classroom use is granted without fee provided that copies are not made or distributed for profit or commercial advantage and that copies bear this notice and the full citation on the first page. Copyrights for components of this work owned by others than ACM must be honored. Abstracting with credit is permitted. To copy otherwise, to republish, to post on servers or to redistribute to lists, requires prior specific permission and/or a fee.
CIKM'15, October 19-23, 2015, Melbourne, VIC, Australia
Copyright 2015 ACM ISBN 978-1-4503-3794-6/15/10 ...$15.00
http://dx.doi.org/10.1145/2806416.2806624.

in [3], where the occurrence of events in documents was evaluated based on hand-crafted rules. On the contrary, our proposed method relies on combining a wide set of features extracted from events and documents and developing a supervised model. Araki et al. [2] performed historical fact validation by casting the problem as *Passage Retrieval*. Differing from our approach, they assess event validity in terms of the textual similarity between facts and passages of fixed length, thus assuming the evidence of facts in documents to be restricted to the pieces of adjacent content. Moreover, their approach is focused and evaluated only on historical facts. In [8] events are used as input, albeit with the different goal of attaching temporal references in documents to the events.

3. OVERVIEW

3.1 Data Model

Event. An *event* e is a tuple $e := (K_e, t_e^0, t_e^f)$, where $K_e = \{k_e^1, \dots, k_e^{n_e}\}$ is a set of keywords representing the participants of the event, t_e^0 and t_e^f indicate the timespan within which the event occurred. Although this is in line with event definitions used in previous works [4, 6, 10], other representations like named events, temporal subject-object predicates [7], or sentences in natural language can be adapted to our model by aligning the keyword sets.

Document. A document d is defined by its textual content that is subject to scrutiny in order to assess the validity of an event.

Evidence. An event e is said to have evidence of its occurrence in a document d with a threshold $\tau, 0 < \tau \leq 1$, iff at least $\tau\%$ of the keywords K_e participate together in an event reported in d, strictly within the timespan $\{t_e^0, t_e^f\}$ of the event.

Pair. Given an event e and a document d, we logically couple them within an *(event, document)* pair $p := (e, d)$.

3.2 Event Validation

We distinguish between two levels of event validation: document-level and corpus-level. An (e, d) pair may be judged as *invalid* if the document contains no evidence of the event, although the event might be true with respect to other documents in the corpus. Conversely however, a pair that is judged as being *valid* may sufficiently indicate the validity of an event at the corpus-level. We do not aim at stating whether an event is true or false in general, but whether it occurs in a document or a collection.

Document-level Validation. Given a pair p and an evidence threshold τ, we define the *document–level validation* as a function

$$\gamma_d = V_d(p, \tau) \tag{1}$$

which determines the evidence γ_d of e in d with threshold τ. The codomain of $V_d(\cdot)$ can vary based on the application requirements. In case a binary classification between valid and invalid pairs based on the threshold is required, then $\gamma_d \in \{valid; invalid\}$; otherwise, one can measure evidence as the percentage of conforming event keywords without considering any threshold, and $\gamma_d \in [0, 1]$.

Corpus-level Validation. Given an event e, a set of documents D, and an evidence threshold τ, we define the *corpus–level validation* as a function

$$\gamma_c = V_c(e, D, \tau) \tag{2}$$

which determines the evidence γ_c of e in the corpus D. Just like at the document-level, the codomain of $V_c(\cdot)$ depends on the application requirements. The function depends on which corpus is used as reference to validate occurrence of the given event.

3.3 Precision Boosting

We introduce automatic event validation as a post-processing step of event detection to boost its precision. Given the set of events originally detected, only the ones judged as valid by our validation at corpus-level are retained in the set. In addition to advances introduced within the event detection itself, we believe that automatic event validation can boost the overall performances by processing the detected events in a dedicated way, exploiting information that is unavailable as input to event detection (i.e. participants and timespan of events). Event detection usually identifies events in a document collection based on a vague input, represented by a wide set of entities [4] or terms with high occurrence frequency [5, 6]. In contrast, we do not intend event validation to discover new events, since entity relationships and their durations are already suggested by event detection in form of candidate events. We instead focus on verifying their occurrence in documents.

We call this effect *precision boosting*, because the goal is to increase the precision within the set of detected events by discarding invalid events. However, this has to be accomplished without affecting recall, i.e. the valid events originally detected by the event detection phase should not be discarded during the validation. The benefits of this approach will be shown in Section 5.2.2.

4. AUTOMATIC EVENT VALIDATION

4.1 Features

We build a supervised learning model using features from pairs to predict their validity. Features are extracted from plain text, without requiring any information about structure, publication date, or markup, making our approach potentially applicable to any kind of corpora. We use the term *statistics* to indicate average, standard deviation, minimum, and maximum values of a given feature.

Event Features. Event features describe the event without coupling it with any document. They consist of the number of event keywords, their length statistics, as well as the percentage of keywords representing people, locations, organizations, and artifacts.

Document Features. Document features are extracted from each document, independent of the event to be validated. For each document, we compute the percentage of words representing different parts of speech (nouns, verbs, adjectives) and named entity types (people, locations, organizations, artifacts). For each of the pos and named entity types mentioned above, we also compute statistics about their positions and mutual distances. We derive features from time information in each document, such as number of temporal expressions, statistics of time (in days), statistics of temporal expressions positions and mutual distances in the document. We also consider the length of the document, number of sentences, length statistics of words, and length statistics of sentences.

Pair Features. Pair features are extracted from (e, d) pairs to give information about the extent to which a document contains evidence of the event. First, we compute the percentage of event keywords that have at least one match in the document, statistics about the number of matches of event keywords, and the percentage of event keywords that fully appear in the document. Since matched event keywords that are far apart might have a higher probability of being unrelated, we compute statistics regarding the positions and mutual distances of matching keywords. Despite event keywords being mentioned in a document, they might refer to a different timespan than that of the event. Therefore, we derive features considering the temporal expressions within the event timespan (called matching dates hereafter). We compute statistics about positions and mutual distances of both matching and not matching dates (the proximity of not matching dates to matching dates might be a hindrance to assessing the validity of the timespan). We also consider the position of the first date and whether it belongs to the event timespan, supposing that it might have more impact than other dates. Finally, to estimate the likelihood of event keywords being mutually related while referring to a matching date, we compute features representing distances between them. For each matching date and distinct keyword, we compute statistics about the distances between the date and the nearest matching word.

4.2 Event Validation

Document-level Validation. Once pairs have been described in terms of the features, a Support Vector Machine (SVM) is trained to predict the validity of new unseen pairs. The meaning of the pair labels l_p depends on which of the scenarios discussed in Section 3.2 is considered: in case of binary classification based on a validity threshold, then $l_p \in \{valid; invalid\}$; in case of regression of the percentage of event keywords conforming to the same event in the document and within the event timespan, $l_p \in [0, 1]$.

Given a set of pairs p_i, their corresponding feature vectors $\boldsymbol{f}_{p_i}$, and their validity labels l_{p_i}, an SVM is trained and the learned model V_d is used to predict the validity of unseen pairs p_{new}:

$$\gamma_d = V_d\left(\boldsymbol{f}_{p_{new}}\right) \quad (3)$$

The model was trained via 10-fold cross validation over the pairs.

Corpus-level Validation. We performed corpus-level validation by combining document-level decisions. Given an event e, a set of candidate documents D, a validity threshold τ, and a document-level validation function $V_d(\cdot)$, our corpus-level validation function $V_c(e, D, \tau)$ is designed as follows. In case of classification, it returns *valid* iff $\exists d \in D : V_d(e, d, \tau) = valid$, while in case of regression $V_c(e, D, \tau) = \max_{d \in D} V_d(e, d, \tau)$. This means that the best (e, d) pair evaluated at document-level drives the decisions at corpus-level. We chose this policy, as opposed to others such as averaging the validity values computed at document-level, because we believe that the evidence of event occurrence in a single document is sufficient to indicate event validity in many scenarios.

5. EXPERIMENTS AND RESULTS

5.1 Experimental Setting

Dataset. The dataset that we considered consists of a set of events and candidate documents associated with each one of them. This information is used to construct input pairs.

We used the publicly available event set considered in [3], made of 258 events detected through the algorithm presented in [11]. In this set, event keywords are titles of Wikipedia pages and the considered timespan is from 18th January 2011 to 7th February 2011.

We chose the Web as a source for documents due to its easy accessibility and wide event coverage. However, any document collection could be used in principle to build the ground truth. For each event, queries have been constructed by concatenating the event keywords along with month and year of the event timespan (one distinct query for each month). We used the Bing Search API to perform queries and to retrieve the top-20 webpages for each query in terms of URLs. After removing duplicates and discarding non-crawlable webpages we got 7257 documents. Plain text has been extracted from each html document by using BoilerPipe[1], while the Stanford CoreNLP parser[2] has been used for POS tagging, named entity recognition, and temporal expression extraction.

Ground Truth. We exploit crowdsourcing, deploying the tasks on CrowdFlower[3], in order to manually evaluate the validity of the 7257 (e, d) pairs in our dataset. For each pair, workers were presented with a description of the event keywords and timespan as well as the document URL. The event timespan, specified by a start and end day, was strictly considered during the tasks. The workers were then asked to report the number of event keywords conforming to the same event in the document and within the event timespan. We followed task design guidelines and employed gold standard questions to detect untrustworthy workers.

For each pair, we gathered 5 independent judgments resulting in $36,285$ responses in total (pairwise percent agreement of 0.7). We accumulated these judgments to arrive at the notions of validity of each pair by considering the judgment with the highest pairwise percent agreement between workers to indicate the validity label (in case of a tie, we considered the label that is closest to the average of all judgments). From these real-valued pair labels l_p, we derived binary validity labels $(l_{p,\tau})$ for pairs (i.e. *valid* or *invalid*) by applying a validity threshold τ as discussed in Section 3.2, such that $l_{p,\tau} = valid$ iff $l_p > \tau$ and $l_{p,\tau} = false$ otherwise. These binary labels are used when considering event validation as a classification task (Section 3.2) and allow to have a more intuitive notion of document-level validity. In our experiments, we consider three different values for τ: 0.5, 0.65, and 1.0 (depending on the fraction of the event keywords required to conform to the event within the given timespan). At the corpus-level, following the merging process described in Section 4.2, 70.9% of the events depict a validity greater than '0'. After performing the same binarization as for document-level, the percentage of *valid* events at the corpus-level is 63.2% ($\tau = 0.5$), 62.7% ($\tau = 0.65$), and 60.4% ($\tau = 1.0$).

Evaluation Metrics. We center the evaluation around the Cohen's Kappa between validity labels and the output of our automatic validation, both at document and corpus-level. The Cohen's Kappa (K) determines the level of agreement between two judges by considering the probability that they agree by chance. We also report the accuracy (ACC) of the methods for completeness. We compute ACC and K for each validity threshold previously discussed. For instance, K with $\tau = 0.5$ represents the Cohen's Kappa observed after binarizing the validity labels with a threshold of 0.5. Since the original validity labels are real-valued, we also report the Pearson Correlation Coefficient (r) when predicting them via regression.

Parameter Settings. The classifiers employed to predict validity of pairs, built using the SVM implementation of LibSVM[4], have Gaussian Kernels and were trained via 10–fold cross validation. The parameters were tuned to $C = 6.2, \gamma = 1.0$ in case of classification, and to $\nu = 0.5, \gamma = 0.3$ for regression. The evaluation was done using the predictions generated during the cross validation.

Baselines. The first baseline, *Keyword Matching* (KM), validates pairs by counting the percentage of event keywords present in documents. In case of multi-term keywords, the matching of one term is considered a match for the entire keyword. The second one is the approach described in [3], denoted *CF Validation* (CF). The occurrence of events in documents is assessed by considering the presence of dates within the event timestamps, estimating the regions of text associated to these dates, and returning the percentage of event keywords present in these regions. The validation is based on hand-crafted rules, a big limitation of the work. The thresholds imposed on validity labels are also applied to the baselines.

5.2 Results

5.2.1 Event Validation

Document-level. The results of event validation at the document-level, considering different validity thresholds ($\tau = 0.5, 0.65, 1.0$), are reported in Table 1. We evaluated our method, called *Eventful*, when considering two different models, namely *pairs* and *all*: the former only considers pair features in the learning, while the lat-

[1] http://code.google.com/p/boilerpipe/
[2] http://nlp.stanford.edu/software/corenlp.shtml
[3] http://www.crowdflower.com/
[4] http://www.csie.ntu.edu.tw/~cjlin/libsvm/

	τ = 0.5		τ = 0.65		τ = 1.0		-
	ACC	K	ACC	K	ACC	K	r
Baselines							
KM	0.575	0.091	0.575	0.090	0.668	0.191	0.314
CF	0.867	0.401	0.868	0.400	0.870	0.286	0.540
Eventful							
pairs	0.910	0.659	0.909	0.655	0.916	0.605	0.713
all	0.925	0.728	0.923	0.719	0.926	0.680	0.758

Table 1: Performances of the automatic document-level validation.

	τ = 0.5		τ = 0.65		τ = 1.0		-
	ACC	K	ACC	K	ACC	K	r
Baselines							
KM	0.663	0.022	0.663	0.022	0.743	0.178	0.410
CF	0.823	0.653	0.827	0.647	0.824	0.601	0.701
Eventful							
pairs	0.904	0.799	0.908	0.802	0.904	0.806	0.862
all	0.876	0.740	0.896	0.782	0.901	0.797	0.845

Table 2: Performances of the automatic corpus-level validation.

ter exploits all the available features described in Section 4.1. Our approach outperforms the baselines under all the criteria, showing that combining information from events and documents via machine learning is more effective than (i) considering mere keyword matching (*KM*), or (ii) designing validation rules that cater for relationships between event keywords and temporal conformity to the event timespan (*CF*). In particular, according to [9], the values achieved by our models indicate a *substantial* level of agreement. The improvement of the *all* model over *CF* is of 81% for $\tau = 0.5$ and of 138% for $\tau = 1$. *Pairs* alone sufficiently outperforms the baselines. However, exploiting support information from events and documents (*all* model), we achieve higher agreement.

Considering different validity thresholds, we observe a decreasing trend of performances for increasing validity thresholds (except *KM*, characterized by low and noisy results). We allude this to the fact that the methods face hindrance when validating those pairs where all the event keywords appear in a document, but only a subset of them conform to the same event within the given timespan.

Corpus-level. Table 2 shows the results for corpus-level validation. Our method outperforms the baselines under all the criteria, with *all* achieving the highest performances. Comparing the results of document-level and corpus-level evaluation (Tables 1 and 2), it can be observed that the absolute values in the latter are relatively higher. This is because at the corpus-level a single valid (e, d) pair is sufficient to validate the event, despite the presence of errors in the other pairs corresponding to the event.

Another point of difference is that the values of K at corpus-level increase for increasing values of validity threshold τ, while they decrease at document-level. As mentioned before, increasing the validity threshold at document-level introduces difficulties in correctly evaluating valid pairs. Inspecting the confusion matrices, we found that the learning process adapted by increasing the percentage of negative detections (either true or false) to reduce classification errors. This ensured a lower number of false positives at corpus-level despite being less accurate at document-level. On the contrary, when the validity threshold is low ($\tau = 0.5$), the learning process was more confident in classifying valid pairs and the resulting output rate of positive detections was higher, leading to an increase of false positive pairs as well. This generated more false positive events at corpus-level, since a single false positive pair is sufficient to validate an invalid event as valid.

5.2.2 *Precision Boosting*

The effects on the performances of event detection after applying event validation as post-processing phase are reported in Table 3 for different values of τ. P_{det} refers to the precision values (one for each τ) within the set of detected events, which are coherent with the performances reported in [4]. The precision and recall (with respect to the true events discovered through event detection) in the event set after applying event validation are indicated as P_{val} and R_{val}, respectively. Our method boosts the precision achieved by event detection up to 0.894 for $\tau = 0.5$ and 0.919 for $\tau = 1.0$. Moreover, the high values of recall (0.899 or higher) indicate that most of the true events present in the original set are preserved by the validation. Our method beats *CF* both in precision and especially in recall, showing a better capability of not discarding true events. Regarding *KM*, the low increase in precision and the high recall show that performing validation via keyword matching has no effect on the performances of event detection: most of the events are judged as valid and retained, since the appearance of their keywords in documents is a sufficient condition of event validity.

	τ = 0.5			τ = 0.65			τ = 1.0		
	P_{det}	P_{val}	R_{val}	P_{det}	P_{val}	R_{val}	P_{det}	P_{val}	R_{val}
Baselines									
KM	0.632	0.636	0.993	0.627	0.631	0.995	0.604	0.628	1.000
CF	0.632	0.842	0.773	0.627	0.845	0.771	0.604	0.863	0.618
Eventful									
all	0.632	0.894	0.900	0.627	0.913	0.913	0.604	0.919	0.899

Table 3: Effects of applying event validation after event detection.

6. CONCLUSIONS AND FUTURE WORK

In this paper, we investigated the problem of event validation with respect to a given corpus, proposing an effective method for automatically validating the occurrence of events in documents. We also introduced automatic event validation as a post-processing step of event detection to boost precision. The proposed method outperforms baseline and state-of-the-art methods for event validation and allows to increase the precision of event detection. We plan to extend our work by considering semantic features to predict validity, as well as by incorporating user feedback via active learning.

Acknowledgments This work was partially funded by the European Commission in the context of the FP7 ICT projects ForgetIT (grant no: 600826) and DURAARK (grant No. 600908).

7. REFERENCES

[1] J. Allan, R. Papka, and V. Lavrenko. On-line new event detection and tracking. In *SIGIR*, 1998.

[2] J. Araki and J. Callan. An annotation similarity model in passage ranking for historical fact validation. In *SIGIR*, 2014.

[3] A. Ceroni and M. Fisichella. Towards an entity-based automatic event validation. In *ECIR*, 2014.

[4] A. Das Sarma, A. Jain, and C. Yu. Dynamic relationship and event discovery. In *Proc. of WSDM '11*, 2011.

[5] G. P. C. Fung, J. X. Yu, P. S. Yu, and H. Lu. Parameter free bursty events detection in text streams. In *Proc. of VLDB '05*, 2005.

[6] Q. He, K. Chang, and E.-P. Lim. Analyzing feature trajectories for event detection. In *Proc. of SIGIR '07*, 2007.

[7] J. Hoffart, F. Suchanek, K. Berberich, and G. Weikum. Yago2: A spatially and temporally enhanced knowledge base from Wikipedia. *Artificial Intelligence*, 2012.

[8] D. Hovy, J. Fan, A. Gliozzo, S. Patwardhan, and C. Welty. When did that happen? linking events and relations to timestamps. EACL'12.

[9] J. R. Landis and G. G. Koch. The measurement of observer agreement for categorical data. *Biometrics*, 1977.

[10] A. J. McMinn, Y. Moshfeghi, and J. M. Jose. Building a large-scale corpus for evaluating event detection on twitter. In *CIKM*, 2013.

[11] T. Tran, A. Ceroni, M. Georgescu, K. Djafari Naini, and M. Fisichella. Wikipevent: Leveraging wikipedia edit history for event detection. In *WISE*, 2014.

DAAV: Dynamic API Authority Vectors for Detecting Software Theft

Dong-Kyu Chae
Dept. of Computer and Software
Hanyang University, Korea
kyu899@hanyang.ac.kr

Sang-Wook Kim*
Dept. of Computer and Software
Hanyang University, Korea
wook@hanyang.ac.kr

Seong-Je Cho
Dept. of Computer Science
Dankook University, Korea
sjcho@dankook.ac.kr

Yesol Kim
Dept. of Computer Science
Dankook University, Korea
kys_89@dankook.ac.kr

ABSTRACT

This paper proposes a novel birthmark, a *dynamic API authority vector* (*DAAV*), for detecting software theft. *DAAV* satisfies four essential requirements for good birthmarks—*credibility*, *resiliency*, *scalability*, and *packing-free*—while existing birthmarks fail to satisfy all of them together. In particular, existing static birthmarks are unable to handle the packed programs and existing dynamic birthmarks do not satisfy credibility and resiliency. Our experimental results demonstrate that *DAAV* provides satisfying credibility and resiliency compared with existing dynamic birthmarks and also can cover packed programs.

Categories and Subject Descriptors

H.2.8 [**Database Management**]: Database Applications—*Data Mining*

General Terms

Security

Keywords

Software theft detection, Similarity, Graph, Random walk

1. INTRODUCTION

Along with the blossom of open source projects available on the Internet, such as Sourceforge.net, OSDir.com, and Freshmeat.net, software theft has become easy to commit. Such software codes are easily downloaded and incorporated into a new software product with serious disguises (i.e., ripping off the interface components of the original software and modifying the source codes with some semantics-preserving transformations), which is quite difficult to notice. Detecting such theft is crucial to protect intellectual property right of software developers [10].

Recently, *software birthmarks* (*birthmarks*) have been studied as a way of detecting software theft, even without the source codes of suspicious software products, which never open their source codes. A birthmark of software is defined as its *unique characteristics* and can be used to identify itself. The identification consists of two parts: (1) extracting representative birthmarks from executable codes (*programs*) of two target software and (2) comparing similarity between birthmarks. The similarity can be considered as how much one program is likely to be a copy of the other program [11].

Birthmarks can be categorized in different ways according to criteria: depending on extraction schemes, they are categorized into *static* and *dynamic* birthmarks; depending on the form of birthmarks, they are classified into *frequency-based*, *sequence-based*, and *graph-based* birthmarks.

Regardless of these categories, all birthmarks essentially need to meet the following requirements [11, 12, 3]:

- ***Credibility***: Birthmarks extracted from independently developed programs should be dissimilar even if they may accomplish similar tasks.
- ***Resiliency***: Birthmarks should be robust even if plagiarizers modify the structure of a program or reorder the statements in source codes while preserving the semantics of the program.
- ***Scalability***: Birthmarks should be applicable even to the programs or runtime codes of a large size.
- ***Packing-free***: Birthmarks need to be able to deal with *packed* (i.e., encrypted) programs.

However, existing birthmarks do not satisfy all of the four requirements [12, 13]. Dynamic frequency-based birthmarks have a problem of credibility; dynamic sequence-based birthmarks suffer from poor resiliency; dynamic graph-based birthmarks have a problem in scalability, and thus are not suitable in case a birthmark of a large size is extracted because of a long execution time. Even though static birthmarks provide reasonable performance in credibility and resiliency,

*Corresponding author.

Permission to make digital or hard copies of all or part of this work for personal or classroom use is granted without fee provided that copies are not made or distributed for profit or commercial advantage and that copies bear this notice and the full citation on the first page. Copyrights for components of this work owned by others than ACM must be honored. Abstracting with credit is permitted. To copy otherwise, or republish, to post on servers or to redistribute to lists, requires prior specific permission and/or a fee. Request permissions from Permissions@acm.org.
CIKM'15, October 19-23, 2015, Melbourne, Australia.
© 2015 ACM. ISBN 978-1-4503-3794-6/15/10 ...$15.00.
DOI: http://dx.doi.org/10.1145/2806416.2806646.

they are *not applicable to packed programs*. Dynamic birthmarks should be employed these packed programs [9].

In this paper, we propose a novel dynamic birthmark, named *dynamic API authority vector* (*DAAV*), satisfying all the four requirements above.

2. SYSTEM OVERVIEW

DAAV is a vector whose dimension corresponds to an API used in the program, and the value of each dimension indicates an *authority score*, which represents how *importantly* the corresponding API is called by the program. To measure such importance of each API, (1) we first construct a *dynamic API call graph* (*DACG*), which is a directed graph that represents caller-callee relationships between APIs. (2) Then, we figure out which APIs are in a core position in *DACG* and which are not by the notion of *random walk with restart* (*RWR*) [6, 1]. (3) Finally, the vector of the authority scores over all the APIs becomes *DAAV*.

Our design ensures *DAAV* to satisfy the four essential requirements as follows. Since *RWR* measures the importance of each node in a graph by giving a high score to the nodes receiving a lot of edges and also to the nodes closely connected to those nodes that receive high scores, the characteristics related to both sequence and frequency of APIs are reflected in *DAAV*. For example, frequently called APIs may get a high score because they may be called by a number of other functions, and some other APIs, even though they are rarely called, also may get a high score as long as they are called by those functions that are frequently called. As a result, *DAAV* is affected by *not only the frequency but also the sequence of APIs*. This property remedies deficiencies that the previous sequence-based and frequency-based birthmarks have, making our birthmark *more resilient* and *credible*. Moreover, by generating an n-dimensional vector which inherits the structural characteristics of *DACG*, the problem of comparing the two *DACG*s becomes a quite simple and scalable task even if the size of *DACG* is large. We compute the similarity between *DAAV*s very efficiently by using the *cosine similarity* [5]. Finally, *DAAV* is applicable even when target programs are packed since it is derived by runtime code, which is unpacked at runtime [9]. We note that our goal is to detect *whole-program copy*, where the plagiarizer copies the whole of the plaintiff program and wraps it in a modified interface [8].

3. BIRTHMARK EXTRACTION

3.1 *DACG* Construction

DACG has almost the same concept with a *call graph* [4] which has been widely known in software engineering context. The main difference between them is that *DACG* has both user-defined functions (UDFs) and APIs as nodes, while a call graph has only UDFs. Following is a formal definition of *DACG*.

Definition 3 (*dynamic API call graph*) It is a directed 2-tuple graph (N, E), which represents the caller-callee relationships among a set of APIs and UDFs in a program, where N and E satisfy the following conditions:

- N is a set of nodes, where node $n \in N$ corresponds to an API or a UDF used in running a program.
- $E(\subseteq N \times N)$ is a set of edges, where edge $n_1 \rightarrow n_2 \in E$ denotes that n_1 called n_2 in running a program. The edge has a weight, which is the number of the same function calls.

Figure 1 shows an example of *DACG* consisting of four UDFs described as circles and eight APIs described as rectangules. The number assigned to each edge indicates how many times the corresponding function calls occurred.

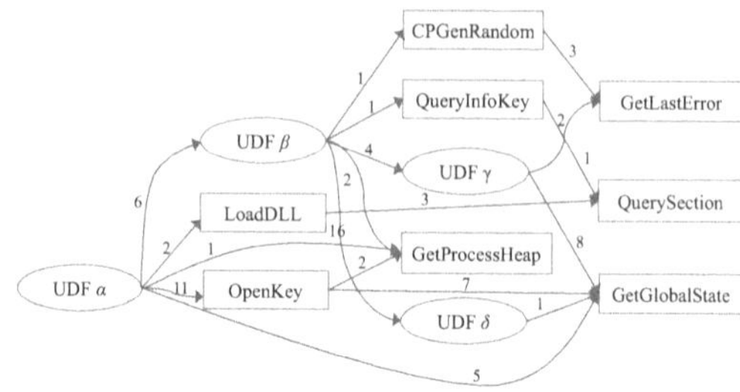

Figure 1: Dynamic API call graph (*DACG*).

To construct *DACG* for a program, dynamic analysis is performed on the program via *PIN*[1], a popular dynamic analyzer recording API call traces and caller-callee relationships among APIs. Specifically, we first execute a program by *pre-defined scenarios*. For example, if the program is an FTP client, we may perform uploadig and downloading some files. At this step, we flag whether each called function is a UDF or an API, and which function is a caller. After the execution is completed, we construct *DACG* based on all the caller-callee information. In the graph, all the APIs appear as nodes with their names as labels and UDFs as unlabeled nodes. All the caller-callee relationships appear as *directed* edges with the number of appearances of the call as weights. The starting weight is 1 and increases as the event of the same function call is repeated.

3.2 *DAAV* Generation

We first define *DAAV* as follows:

Definition 4 (*Dynamic API authority vector*) It is an n-dimensional vector, where:

- n is the number of APIs defined in MSDN[2].
- A dimension corresponds to an API.
- The value of a dimension indicates the authority score of the API, which represents the strength of importance of the API in the program.

For the purpose of computing the *authority score* (i.e., importance) of each API, we utilize the concept of *random walk with restart* (*RWR*). *RWR* is a probabilistic model for a random walker to reach a node after a given number of iterations. It is widely used in ranking to understand the authority of each node in a graph [6, 1]. *RWR* is expressed by the following Eq. (1), where A represents an adjacency matrix column-normalizing the connectedness among nodes, R^t a vector having authority scores of each node, w a restart vector having the value $\frac{1}{n}$ where n indicates the number of nodes, and α the restart probability:

$$R^{t+1} = (1 - \alpha)AR^t + \alpha w \quad (1)$$

[1]https://software.intel.com/en-us/articles/pin-a-dynamic-binary-instrumentation-tool
[2]https://msdn.microsoft.com/en-us/library

Using *RWR* gives our system several benefits. First, the authority score of each API computed by *RWR* reflects not only the frequency but also the sequence information in calling APIs. Along the procedure of computing authority scores, *RWR* gives a high authority score to (1) the nodes that receive a lot of edges and (2) the nodes closely connected to the nodes that have already received high scores [6]. Thus, frequently-called APIs receive a high authority score through *RWR*, since their nodes are pointed by a number of nodes or have some incoming edges with high weights due to iterative calls. Also, some APIs, even though they are rarely called, could get a high authority score if they are closely connected to nodes with a high authority score. In contrast, if APIs are rarely called and their pointing nodes have a low authority score, they are likely to get a low authority score as well. In conclusion, each authority score is strongly affected by both the frequency and the sequence of APIs. This makes our birthmark unique to each program because the frequency and the sequence of API calls are capturing unique program behaviors. Moreover, the manipulation of API call frequencies or API call orders while maintaining a program's original semantics is a difficult task, which indicates that our proposed birthmark is resilient.

Second, by a simple modification of Eq. (1), we can consider the *popularity* of each API. The popularity indicates how much the corresponding API is commonly used among many programs. There are general tasks for most programs, such as exception handling, memory management, and thread creation & termination. The APIs which perform the general tasks may be frequently called in most programs. Thus, these APIs may receive high authority scores regardless of the kind of programs, eventually making different programs look similar [3, 2]. To address this problem, we measure each API's popularity and reflect it to the process of computing authority scores. Specifically, we modify the probability values in restart vector w in Eq. (1) by assigning a modified probability to each API node computed as follows:

$$w(API) = \frac{1}{CF(API) \times PF(API)} \tag{2}$$

In Eq. (2), $w(API)$ denotes a restart probability value corresponding to the API in vector w. $CF(API)$ corresponds to the call frequency of the corresponding API. $PF\ (API)$ indicates the number of programs that call the API. Because popular APIs are used in most programs and also used frequently, Eq. (2) assigns a low probability in inverse proportion to the call frequency and the program frequency. This modification not only gives low authority scores to popular APIs but also gives high authority scores to the APIs that are uniquely used in each program successfully. Thus, we can not only characterize each program but also make different programs look different.

The third advantage is computation efficiency. The stationary authority scores for each node are obtained by iterative computations of Eq. (1) until R^t converges. The complexity of this computation is $O(n+e)$ where n denotes the number of nodes and e the number of edges in the graph; thus our system requires a reasonable time even with a large size of *DACG* [14].

4. SIMILARITY COMPUTATION

Two programs having similar *DAAV*s not only use similar APIs as their major important APIs and some other similar APIs as minor APIs but also have similar caller-callee relationships of those APIs, eventually getting highly suspected of theft. As a similarity measure between two *DAAV*s, we use *cosine similarity*, which is a widely used measure for computing similarity between two vectors [5]. Let p and q be programs or program components, and V_p and V_q be *DAAV*s of p and q, respectively. The cosine similarity is defined as follows.

$$SIM(V_p, V_q) = \frac{\sum_1^n (V_{p,i} \times V_{q,i})}{\sqrt{\sum_1^n {V_{p,i}}^2} \times \sqrt{\sum_1^n {V_{q,i}}^2}} \tag{3}$$

$V_{p,i}$ and $V_{q,i}$ in Eq. (3) denote the i-th elements of V_p and V_q, respectively. The similarity between two birthmarks ranges between 0 and 1. As the similarity approaches 1, one program is regarded as more likely to be a copy of the other.

5. EXPERIMENTAL RESULTS

In this section, we evaluate *DAAV* in terms of credibility and resiliency by comparing it with previous *dynamic* birthmarks. Also, by comparing it with previous *static* birthmarks, we show that *DAAV* is a reasonable substitute for static birthmarks, which have been providing satisfactory credibility and resiliency but have fundamental vulnerability to packing schemes.

Table 1: Benchmark programs and scenarios

Types	Programs (version)	Scenarios
FTP clients	WinSCP (5.3.3)/(5.5.1)	(a) Start→end
	FileZilla (3.7.1)/(3.7.4)	(b) Start→upload file→end
	CoreFTP (2.1)/(2.2)	(c) Start→download file
	SmartFTP(5.0.1)/(6.0.2)	→end
Archivers	7-Zip (9.2.0)/(9.2.2)	(a) Start→end
	FreeARC (0.6.0)/(0.6.6)	(b) Start→compress file→end
	Peazip (5.4.0)/(5.4.1)	(c) Start→decompress file
	Winrar (5.07)/(5.10)	→end
Media Players	Winamp (5.6.0)/(5.6.3)	(a) Start→end
	Mplayerc (1.7.0)/(1.7.6)	(b) Start→play video→end
	RealPlayer (15.6)/(16.3)	(c) Start→play video→open
	VLCPlayer(2.0.5)/(2.1.3)	subtitles→end

We collected 12 benchmark programs and divided them into three categories: FTP clients, archivers, and media players, as shown in Table 1. In each category, there are four different programs, each of which has two different versions.Since there are no available, public samples thought to plagiarize commercial Windows programs, following on previous work, we decided to regard a recent version of a program as a copy of its previous version [3, 7, 2].

For each category, we defined three execution scenarios: the first one is running and then terminating the program without performing any operations, and other two scenarios are performing core tasks of programs in each category. We executed each benchmark program with the three different scenarios to obtain three *DAAV*s. Then, we computed the similarity between *DAAV*s, derived from the identical scenario. Because we defined three scenarios, three similarities are computed between the two programs. Their average is defined as the final similarity of the two programs.

For comparative study, we implemented state-of-the-art birthmarks as follows: dynamic *EXEFREQ* and *EXEFREQ* birthmarks proposed by Tamada [13]; dynamic *Core API* birthmark proposed by Jang [7]; static *API-labeled CFG* birthmark proposed by Chae [2]. We simply call them *SEQ*, *FREQ*, *CA*, and *ACFG*, respectively.

Table 2: Comparisons with previous birthmarks

FTP clients	WinSCP 5.5.1		FileZilla 3.7.4		CoreFTP 2.2		SmartFTP 6.0.2	
WinSCP 5.3.3	97.6 99.1	88.0 99.9 90.8	3.6 11.4	9.9 28.4 54.5	15.9 1.2	2.9 69.7 43.0	10.4 2.6	5.6 57.3 17.5
FileZilla 3.7.1			98.8 96.1	87.1 99.9 99.3	2.5 8.2	6.6 44.5 43.2	12.0 12.5	2.0 46.1 23.5
CoreFTP 2.1					99.9 93.3	81.4 99.9 95.3	2.1 3.2	2.8 84.7 15.3
SmartFTP 5.0.1	DAAV ACFG	SEQ FREQ CA					89.7 97.1	41.2 91.1 91.4
Archivers	7-zip 9.2.2		FreeARC 0.6.6		Peazip 5.4.1		Winrar 5.1	
7-zip 9.2.0	99.9 99.9	96.7 99.9 97.2	17.0 14.2	9.6 62.8 36.5	2.2 2.6	14.2 80.5 41.6	7.1 12.1	15.1 90.6 43.5
FreeARC 0.6.0			99.9 96.3	57.9 99.9 81.7	3.4 11.4	3.6 48.7 35.4	2.1 3.4	5.3 65.8 24.0
Peazip 5.4.0					99.9 97.6	66.4 99.9 94.5	3.5 3.6	11.8 82.0 33.0
Winrar 5.07	DAAV ACFG	SEQ FREQ CA					98.7 98.5	89.5 98.4 81.3
Media Player	Winamp 5.6.3		Mplayerc 1.7.6		RealPlayer 16.3		VLCPlayer 2.1.3	
Winamp 5.6.0	98.3 99.9	66.0 86.4 93.0	7.1 1.2	9.5 52.7 21.5	3.0 4.2	4.1 38.6 9.0	22.5 3.6	7.7 22.3 14.9
Mplayerc 1.7.0			93.2 96.5	70.8 97.4 84.8	31.8 21.2	2.6 44.5 8.7	9.3 12.3	7.4 26.3 17.9
RealPlayer 15.6					99.7 98.3	66.8 99.1 61.4	12.1 16.1	5.2 33.3 11.1
VLCPlayer 2.0.5	DAAV ACFG	SEQ FREQ CA					92.3 97.1	41.3 90.7 68.8

Table 2 shows the results of similarity analysis among programs. Five float numbers in each pair of cells represent similarity values between two programs shown in its column and row. From the upper left one in clockwise order, the numbers indicate the similarity computed by *DAAV*, *SEQ*, *FRQ*, *CA*, and *ACFG*.

Ideally, the similarity between the original program and its copy should be high (*resiliency*). Also, to avoid false alarms, it should be low in the case of two independently developed programs (*credibility*). The sequence-based birthmark (*SEQ*) shows a satisfactory performance in credibility but a poor performance in resiliency. *SEQ* tends to indicate a low similarity between two different programs. However, it also tends to indicate a low similarity even between copied programs. As opposed to *SEQ*, frequency-based birthmarks, i.e., *FRQ* and *CA*, indicate a high similarity between copied programs. However, they mostly provide a high similarity between different programs too, which indicates their poor credibility. Since the frequency-based birthmarks lack the sequence information of APIs, they have difficulty in differentiating two different programs that use some APIs in common. Also, since the sequence-based birthmarks lack the frequency information of APIs, they are vulnerable to semantics-preserving modifications on programs.

In contrast, by considering the sequence and frequency information of APIs together, *DAAV* can have both robustness against evasions and ability to differentiate different programs. Consequently, *DAAV* shows a low similarity between different programs and a high similarity between copied programs. Moreover, *DAAV* shows comparable results to those of the static birthmark (i.e., *ACFG*). Regarding that *DAAV* can cover packed programs that static birthmarks cannot deal with, we can conclude that *DAAV* outperforms all the existing static and dynamic birthmarks in terms of the four requirements.

6. ACKNOWLEDGEMENTS

This research was supported by (1) Ministry of Culture, Sports, and Tourism (MCST) via Korea Copyright Commission in 2014, (2) the National Research Foundation of Korea (NRF) grant funded by the Korea government (MSIP) (No. NRF-2014R1A2A1A10054151), and (3) the Ministry of Science, ICT and Future Planning (MSIP), Korea, under the Information Technology Research Center (ITRC) support program (IITP-2015-H8501-15-1013) supervised by the Institute for Information and communication Technology Promotion (IITP).

7. REFERENCES

[1] D.-H. Bae et al. On constructing seminal paper genealogy. *Cybernetics, IEEE Transactions on*, 44(1):54–65, 2014.

[2] D. Chae et al. Software plagiarism detection: A graph-based approach. In *CIKM*, pages 1577–1580. ACM, 2013.

[3] D. Chae et al. Software plagiarism detection via the static api call frequency birthmark. In *SAC*, pages 1639–1643. ACM, 2013.

[4] D. Grove et al. Call graph construction in object-oriented languages. *ACM SIGPLAN Notices*, 32(10):108–124, 1997.

[5] J. Han et al. *Data Mining: Concepts and Techniques*. Morgan Kaufmann, 2006.

[6] T. H. Haveliwala. Topic-sensitive pagerank. In *WWW*, pages 517–526. ACM, 2002.

[7] M. Jang et al. An efficient similarity comparison based on core api calls. In *SAC*, pages 1634–1638. ACM, 2013.

[8] Y.-C. Jhi et al. Value-based program characterization and its application to software plagiarism detection. In *Proceedings of the 33rd International Conference on Software Engineering*, pages 756–765. ACM, 2011.

[9] D. Lee et al. An efficient categorization of the instructions based on binary excutables for dynamic software birthmark. *International Journal of Information and Education Technology*, 5(8):571, 2015.

[10] C. Liu et al. Gplag: Detection of software plagiarism by program dependence graph analysis. In *KDD*, pages 872–881. ACM, 2006.

[11] G. Myles et al. Detecting software theft via whole program path birthmarks. In *Information Security*, pages 404–415. 2004.

[12] G. Myles et al. k-gram based software birthmarks. In *SAC*, pages 314–318. ACM, 2005.

[13] H. Tamada et al. Dynamic software birthmarks to detect the theft of windows applications. In *ISFST*, 2004.

[14] H. Tong et al. Fast random walk with restart and its applications. In *ICDM*, pages 613–622. IEEE, 2006.

Towards Multi-level Provenance Reconstruction of Information Diffusion on Social Media

Tom De Nies[‡] Io Taxidou[*] Anastasia Dimou[‡] Ruben Verborgh[‡]
Peter M. Fischer[*] Erik Mannens[‡] Rik Van de Walle[‡]
[‡]{tom.denies,anastasia.dimou,ruben.verborgh,erik.mannens,rik.vandewalle}@ugent.be
Ghent University - iMinds - Multimedia Lab, Belgium
[*]{taxidou,peter.fischer}@informatik.uni-freiburg.de
University of Freiburg, Germany

ABSTRACT

In order to assess the trustworthiness of information on social media, a consumer needs to understand where this information comes from, and which processes were involved in its creation. The entities, agents and activities involved in the creation of a piece of information are referred to as its provenance, which was standardized by W3C PROV. However, current social media APIs cannot always capture the full lineage of every message, leaving the consumer with incomplete or missing provenance, which is crucial for judging the trust it carries. Therefore in this paper, we propose an approach to reconstruct the provenance of messages on social media on multiple levels. To obtain a fine-grained level of provenance, we use an approach from prior work to reconstruct information cascades with high certainty, and map them to PROV using the PROV-SAID extension for social media. To obtain a coarse-grained level of provenance, we adapt our similarity-based, fuzzy provenance reconstruction approach – previously applied on news. We illustrate the power of the combination by providing the reconstructed provenance of a limited social media dataset gathered during the 2012 Olympics, for which we were able to reconstruct a significant amount of previously unidentified connections.

1. INTRODUCTION

Nowadays, information from social media is frequently analysed and processed for professional use. Examples include online journalism, rumor detection, and viral marketing [10]. In all these cases, it is important for the consumer to know the level of trust and relevance that the information carries. An important step in the process of determining trust of information is to expose its provenance [4]. To model provenance for information diffusion on social media, we specified PROV-SAID [14], an extension to the W3C PROV model. Using this model, the social and influence graphs can be represented in an interoperable way. However, automatically reconstructing the aforementioned graphs based on the APIs that most social media provide poses a challenge. Most current methods are designed to only model direct, high certainty influence edges, caused by *explicit* re-emission of messages (e.g., retweets) and combined with connections between users (social graph), in order to unveil who was influenced by whom. This approach does not consider the potentially large amount of *inexplicit* influences that are less certain, and thus more difficult to detect automatically (e.g., a user adapting another user's message, without explicitly referring to it). In this case, the provenance must be *reconstructed* somehow, unravelling the unobserved references that users are using but not giving credit to, and revealing their influencers.

In this paper, we combine a fine-grained, high-certainty approach, with a coarse-grained, less certain approach for provenance reconstruction. By doing this, we propose a multi-level approach for provenance reconstruction of information diffusion on social media. Our contributions in this paper are: 1) an approach for creation and integration of multi-level provenance; 2) a real-world application and evaluation of the PROV-SAID model; 3) a mapping in order to convert input data from social media into RDF; 4) a novel application of our previous work on similarity-based provenance reconstruction in the context of social media.

Permission to make digital or hard copies of all or part of this work for personal or classroom use is granted without fee provided that copies are not made or distributed for profit or commercial advantage and that copies bear this notice and the full citation on the first page. Copyrights for components of this work owned by others than the author(s) must be honored. Abstracting with credit is permitted. To copy otherwise, or republish, to post on servers or to redistribute to lists, requires prior specific permission and/or a fee. Request permissions from Permissions@acm.org.
CIKM'15, October 19–23, 2015, Melbourne, Australia.
Copyright is held by the owner/author(s). Publication rights licensed to ACM.
ACM 978-1-4503-3794-6/15/10 ...$15.00.
DOI: http://dx.doi.org/10.1145/2806416.2806642 .

2. RELATED WORK

While *information diffusion* in social media has received a lot of attention, in particular its modeling [7], there is limited work on the reverse procedure, i.e. *information provenance*, which is the focus of this paper. We divide the state-of-the-art in this area in the following categories: (i) provenance through content similarity; (ii) provenance through social graph connections; (iii) provenance through user profile metadata.

(i) The work of [11] focuses on tracing news and quotes (referred to as *memes*) on the Web over time. The focus is on temporal patterns, mutations (alterations) that online phrases undergo and properties of the news' life cycle. A subsequent work using the same datasets and methods [13] shifts the focus on fine-grained content alterations. In [3], we reconstructed provenance of news articles automatically using semantic similarity. In this paper, we adapt this approach for social media and the PROV-SAID model.

(ii) Traditional information diffusion research includes tracing a piece of information back to its sources through social connections, revealing the concepts of influence and trust among the users involved. The work of [6] recovers information recipients sub-graphs given a small fraction of known recipients. In [8] unknown recipients are identified under the assumptions of degree and closeness propensity: nodes with a higher degree and closer to the sources are more likely to propagate information. [2] provides a provenance reconstruction method through social connections based on well established information diffusion models. Finally, in [15], we automatically reconstruct *information cascades* that show which paths information took, given a piece of information that propagates over a social graph. Information cascades are graphs that model how information is being diffused from user to user; in other words, our approach in [15] reconstructs the paths of users who propagate information back to the sources by finding intermediate influencers.

(iii) Lastly, provenance can be derived through user profile metadata, attributing relevance and trust to the information emitted according to the characteristics of the contributor. The work of [9] implements a tool for collecting such user information from different media sites, while not providing any information on the provenance paths and sources.

The work in this paper combines concepts from (i) and (ii) in order to reveal provenance paths, by extending and adapting the solutions proposed in [15] and [3]. Finally, the results are modeled and combined in an interoperable way using the PROV-SAID model [14], which extends the W3C PROV model [12]. PROV-SAID provides a rich description of provenance with regard to information diffusion concepts such as: *direct* and *indirect derivations*, *copied* and *modified messages*, and influence types such as *follow relationships* and *interaction influences*.

3. METHOD

As highlighted in the related work and illustrated in Figure 1, we reveal provenance paths on two levels: (1) *low-level (fine-grained)*, based on structure as in [15] and (2) *high-level (coarse-grained)*, based on content similarity as in [3]. These methods are then combined using *PROV-SAID* [14]. In order to convert the XML-based influence graph of [15] into PROV-SAID, we use the *RML mapping language* [5]. RML is used in combination with a processor to convert proprietary data – such as XML – to RDF. In our case the data is converted to PROV-O, which is the ontology that expresses the PROV Data Model. Note that by using RML, we ensure that any input can be converted to PROV-O, rendering our method interoperable and reusable in many applications.

3.1 Low-level, fine-grained provenance

To obtain low-level provenance, we build upon on our previous work [15], that reconstructs the so-called *information cascades* found in social media. Diffusion paths are reconstructed according to who is influenced by whom given messages that propagate over a social graph, with the assumption that users propagate identical messages (e.g., by retweeting) and identify possible influencers. When applied to the Twitter dataset described in Section 4, the reconstructed information cascades comprise of retweets, where users give credit only to the initial source of a message, not the intermediate source that exposes the message to them. In other words, it remains unclear which paths information took from the sources to the recipients. Therefore, the algorithm as described in [15] leverages the social graph in order to reconstruct the intermediate diffusion paths and find influencers, given the assumptions that information flows over the social graph and users are influenced by their connections in order to propagate a piece of information.

The algorithm outputs *edges*, directed from a *tweet A* to a *tweet B*. For each tweet, we have access to the *tweet-id*, *timestamp* and *userid*. When we map this to PROV-SAID using RML, we obtain the following PROV-O sub-graph for each edge:

```
status:tweetA_id  a  prov-said:Message ;
  prov:wasAttributedTo  user:tweetA_userid ;
  prov:wasGeneratedBy  _:emit-tweetA_id ;
  prov:generatedAtTime  tweetA_time .

status:tweetB_id a prov-said:CopiedMessage;
  prov:wasAttributedTo  user:tweetB_userid ;
  prov:wasQuotedFrom  status:tweetA_id ;
  prov:wasGeneratedBy  _:emit-tweetB_id ;
  prov:generatedAtTime  tweetB_time .

user:tweetA_userid  a  prov:Agent .
user:tweetB_userid  a  prov:Agent ;
  prov:wasInfluencedBy user:tweetA_userid ;
  prov:qualifiedInfluence  [
    a prov-said:FollowRelationship ;
    prov:agent user:tweetA_userid . ] ;
  prov:qualifiedInfluence  [
    a prov-said:InteractionInfluenceRelationship;
    prov:agent user:tweetA_userid . ] ;

_:emit-tweetA_id a prov-said:EmitMessage .
_:emit-tweetB_id a prov-said:EmitMessage ;
  prov:used  status:tweetA_id .
```

Note that the prefixes `status:` and `user:` refer to `https://twitter.com/statuses/` and `https://twitter.com/intent/user?user_id=`, respectively, and that the prefixes `prov:` and `prov-said:` refer to their respective namespaces. This representation of the information cascades as provenance is now suitable to be merged with other interoperable provenance, such as the high-level provenance described in Section 3.2.

3.2 High-level, coarse-grained provenance

To obtain high-level provenance, we consider what is missing from the dataset generated in Section 3.1. Since the approach in [15] only relies on relationships exposed through a social media API, it does not consider all messages that were copied or revised without this being tracked by the social media software (e.g., when a user copy-pastes a message instead of retweeting it). To reconstruct this kind of information diffusion, we adapt our approach introduced in [3] to be usable with social media content. The core assumption of this approach is: *"if two messages are highly similar, there is a high probability that they share some provenance"*. The adapted approach consists of the following steps:

1. remove all tracked copied messages from every information cascade as generated in Section 3.1, keeping only the root messages;
2. index this reduced dataset using a feature model and semantic similarity function (e.g., TF-IDF and the cosine similarity), and compute the full similarity matrix of all messages;
3. apply a similarity-based clustering algorithm such as SimClus [1] to divide the dataset into (possibly overlapping) clusters of messages that all have a similarity to each other higher than a predetermined threshold;
4. for each cluster:
   - identify the oldest message as the root message of that cluster;
   - connect all other messages to the root message:
     - if the message is identical to the root message, using a `prov:wasQuotedFrom` relationship;
     - if the message is not identical to the root message, using a `prov:wasRevisionOf` relationship.

The expected result of this approach is that the vast majority of messages will be clustered as a singleton, meaning that no new relationships are introduced. Nonetheless, for those messages that do get clustered together, we know that they exhibit a high similarity. We use their temporal information to estimate their provenance relationship, thereby enriching the dataset and exposing previously hidden knowledge about the information diffusion.

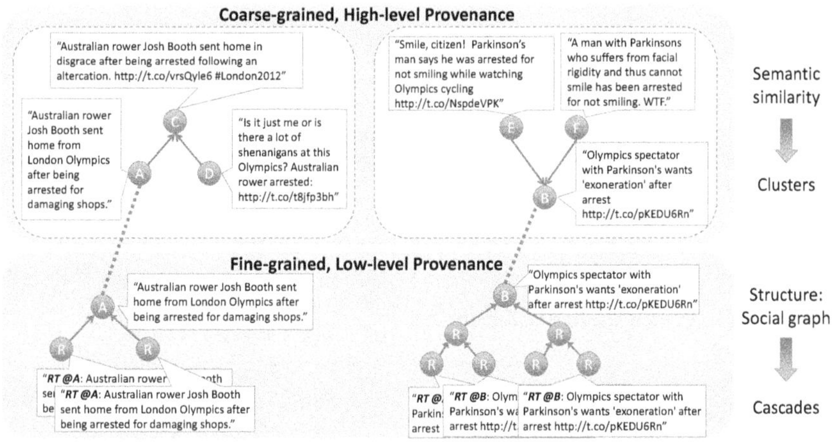

Figure 1: Overview of the integrated, multi-level provenance. The arrows for the low-level refer to `prov:wasQuotedFrom` for all copied messages (retweets); for the high-level they refer to `prov:wasRevisionOf` for all modified messages.

When we integrate this result in the next step, we are effectively reconnecting entire information cascades, whose connection was lost to the social media API. Note that due to the calculation of the full similarity matrix, this approach will have an quadratic complexity w.r.t. the number of messages considered, so it should always be applied on a pre-filtered dataset (e.g., a search result).

3.3 Integration of Multi-level Provenance

Because both algorithms output interoperable PROV, the integration of the two aforementioned levels of provenance consists of simply merging the two sets of RDF statements. However, it is important to understand the new structure this will give to the data. We clarify how the data is enriched by the combination of the two reconstructed provenance sets using Figure 1.

Each level of provenance differs in precision and granularity. The fine-grained, low-level provenance is very detailed, and was constructed with high certainty, since it consists solely of copied messages exposed by a social media API (in our case: the Twitter API). The coarse-grained, high-level provenance, however, was constructed in a much less certain way, relying on semantic similarity to reconstruct connections that were lost to the social media API. The two levels enrich each other, providing previously unidentifiable connections between messages for data consumers (e.g., social media analysts) to explore.

4. EVALUATION AND DISCUSSION

As a preliminary evaluation, we tested our approach on a dataset gathered using the Twitter Streaming API during the 2012 Olympics. We chose Twitter because it provides trace information for copied messages (retweets). The dataset was collected by following the keywords 'Olympics2012' and 'London2012'. We limited the dataset by only considering tweets with a certain keyword, in our case: *'arrest'*. This simulates a realistic scenario where a social media analyst first searches for a broad keyword (e.g., a trending topic), and then investigates the information diffusion paths among the results. Complementary, we desired to avoid messages carrying not important information, for example: "I am watching the Olympics". This way, we include relevant events that attract attention both by individual users and mass media, while yielding information cascades by being retweeted. The final dataset consists of 9047 tweets, of which 5174 are copied messages (retweets), and 3873 are original messages according to the Twitter API.

4.1 Low-level Provenance Reconstruction

We identified 31 cascades using the low-level reconstruction approach from Section 3.1, resulting in a skewed distribution from 5 to 1771 recorded retweets with the root tweet contained in the dataset (out of the total of 5174 retweets). This approach has already been thoroughly evaluated in [15], so we can safely assume that the identified cascades are correct.

4.2 High-level Provenance Reconstruction

Using the approach described in Section 3.2, we clustered the 3873 original messages from the dataset based on their semantic similarity. More specifically, we used the TF-IDF approach from traditional information retrieval to model all messages as vectors, and computed their similarity using the cosine similarity. We then executed the SimClus algorithm described in [1]. Essentially, SimClus divides the set of messages into clusters of messages that all exhibit a similarity higher than a predefined threshold to their respective cluster centre. To use the clusters to reconstruct provenance as described in Section 3.2, the major challenge lies in identifying the optimal similarity threshold. The threshold must be high enough to ensure that only messages that actually share provenance get clustered together, while it must also be low enough to avoid that too many messages are clustered as singletons, which would result in missed connections. Ideally, the optimal threshold would be found empirically by analysing the precision and recall of the provenance reconstruction approach, as it was done for news in [3]. For this paper we do not have access to a ground truth as the authors of [3] did. However, we can investigate the influence of the similarity threshold on the number of clusters and their size, which at least gives us an idea of its behaviour.

As illustrated by Figure 2, the total number of clusters is approximately proportionate to the similarity threshold. This means that if we use a low threshold, we will have a small number of relatively large clusters. On the other hand, if we use a high threshold, we can expect a high number of smaller clusters. When the threshold is set to 1, only identical messages will be clustered together, and therefore only retweets – no modified tweets – missed by the Twitter API will be identified. This is further confirmed by our observations of the number of clusters per cluster size, as illustrated by Figure 3. Here, we see that for the lower thresholds (0.3 and 0.5), the cluster size varies highly, whereas there are less different cluster sizes for the threshold 0.7. These observations are an indication that for the

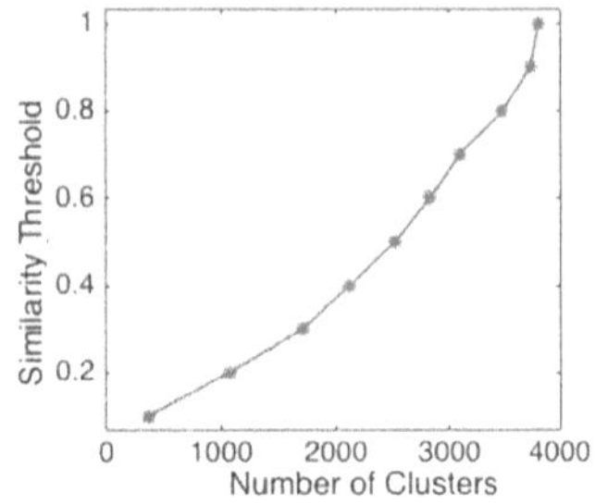

Figure 2: Total number of clusters for each similarity threshold.

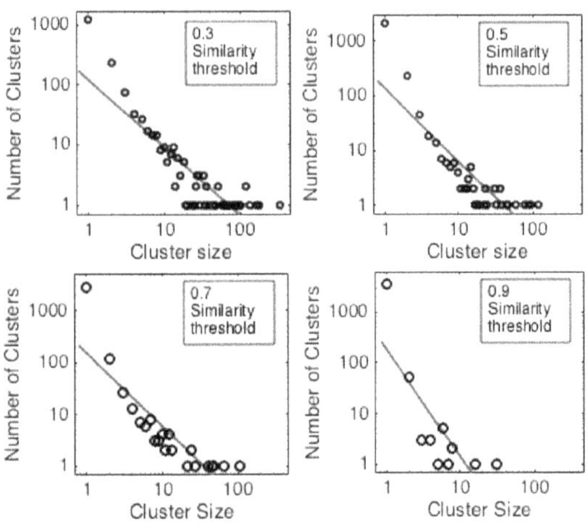

Figure 3: Distribution of the number of clusters per cluster size.

lower thresholds, many clusters are incorrectly merged, which will affect the precision of the reconstruction. On the other hand, we see that if the threshold is set too high (e.g., 0.9), that the larger clusters are split, resulting in missed provenance relationships – and thus affecting the recall. In all cases above 0.3, we see that the number of singletons does not vary significantly, which means that messages that do not belong together will most likely not be clustered together, regardless of the similarity threshold. While it is too early to make a definite decision regarding the optimal threshold without a content-based evaluation, these results lead us to expect that the optimum will be somewhere in the vicinity of 0.7. Using this threshold (0.7), we generated a set of 3094 clusters, and used the 206 non-singletons to reconstruct 879 provenance relationships (32 quotations and 847 revisions).

In other words, when we integrate this high-level provenance with the 31 cascades discovered by the low-level provenance reconstruction, we effectively introduce 879 new connections that were previously unidentified. This creates much larger graphs for the consumers of the provenance data to analyse, and provides an enriched view on the information diffusion process. The entire reconstructed provenance graph can be downloaded at `http://semweb.mmlab.be/ns/prov-said/cikm2015.ttl`

5. CONCLUSION AND FUTURE WORK

We proposed a method to reconstruct and integrate provenance on two levels of granularity: low-level through information cascades, and high-level through similarity-based clustering. This method augments the provenance of messages on social media, especially when there is external influence not deriving from one single source (in our case: Twitter) or for copied messages that do not give credit to their initial contributors. In these cases, an obvious influencer is not exposed by the social media API. Such messages do not produce large cascades resulting in low-level provenance, but are clustered together in the high-level provenance reconstruction of our approach.

For future work, we will extensively evaluate our approach on diverse datasets and combined data from different social media. Additionally, we will improve our method by applying more suitable metrics of message similarity for micropost text.

6. REFERENCES

[1] M. Al Hasan, S. Salem, and M. J. Zaki. Simclus: an effective algorithm for clustering with a lower bound on similarity. *Knowledge and information systems*, 28(3):665–685, 2011.

[2] G. Barbier, Z. Feng, P. Gundecha, and H. Liu. Provenance data in social media. *Synthesis Lectures on Data Mining and Knowledge Discovery*, 4(1):1–84, 2013.

[3] T. De Nies, S. Coppens, D. Van Deursen, E. Mannens, and R. Van de Walle. Automatic discovery of high-level provenance using semantic similarity. In *Provenance and Annotation of Data and Processes*, pages 97–110. Springer, 2012.

[4] T. De Nies, S. Coppens, R. Verborgh, M. Vander Sande, E. Mannens, R. Van de Walle, D. Michaelides, and L. Moreau. Easy access to provenance: an essential step towards trust on the web. In *COMPSACW*, 2013.

[5] A. Dimou, M. Vander Sande, P. Colpaert, R. Verborgh, E. Mannens, and R. Van de Walle. RML: a generic language for integrated RDF mappings of heterogeneous data. In *Proceedings of the 7th Workshop on Linked Data on the Web (LDOW2014), Seoul, Korea*, 2014.

[6] Z. Feng, P. Gundecha, and H. Liu. Recovering information recipients in social media via provenance. In *ASONAM*, pages 706–711, 2013.

[7] A. Guille, H. Hacid, C. Favre, and D. A. Zighed. Information diffusion in online social networks: A survey. *ACM SIGMOD Record*, 42(2):17–28, 2013.

[8] P. Gundecha, Z. Feng, and H. Liu. Seeking provenance of information using social media. In *CIKM*, 2013.

[9] P. Gundecha, S. Ranganath, Z. Feng, and H. Liu. A tool for collecting provenance data in social media. In *KDD*, pages 1462–1465, 2013.

[10] J. Leskovec, L. A. Adamic, and B. A. Huberman. The dynamics of viral marketing. *ACM TWEB*, 1(1):5, 2007.

[11] J. Leskovec, L. Backstrom, and J. Kleinberg. Meme-tracking and the dynamics of the news cycle. In *KDD*, pages 497–506, 2009.

[12] L. Moreau, P. Missier (Eds.), and W3C Provenance Working Group. PROV-DM: The PROV Data Model. W3C, 2013.

[13] M. P. Simmons, L. A. Adamic, and E. Adar. Memes Online: Extracted, subtracted, injected, and recollected. *ICWSM*, 11:17–21, 2011.

[14] I. Taxidou, T. De Nies, R. Verborgh, P. M. Fischer, E. Mannens, and R. Van de Walle. Modeling information diffusion in social media as provenance with W3C PROV. In *Proceedings of the 24th International Conference on WWW Companion*, pages 819–824, 2015.

[15] I. Taxidou and P. M. Fischer. Online analysis of information diffusion in twitter. In *Proceedings of the 23rd International Conference on WWW Companion*, pages 1313–1318, 2014.

Profiling Pedestrian Distribution and Anomaly Detection in a Dynamic Environment

Minh Tuan Doan, Sutharshan Rajasegarar, Mahsa Salehi, Masud Moshtaghi, Christopher Leckie
National ICT Australia, Department of Computing and Information Systems
The University of Melbourne, Australia
Email: {mdoan, m.salehi}@student.unimelb.edu.au
{sraja, masud.moshtaghi, caleckie}@unimelb.edu.au

ABSTRACT

Pedestrians movements have a major impact on the dynamics of cities and provide valuable guidance to city planners. In this paper we model the normal behaviours of pedestrian flows and detect anomalous events from pedestrian counting data of the City of Melbourne. Since the data spans an extended period, and pedestrian activities can change intermittently (e.g., activities in winter vs. summer), we applied an Ensemble Switching Model, which is a dynamic anomaly detection technique that can accommodate systems that switch between different states. The results are compared with those produced by a static clustering model (HyCARCE) and also cross-validated with known events. We found that the results from the Ensemble Switching Model are valid and more accurate than HyCARCE.

Categories and Subject Descriptors

H.4 [**Information Systems Applications**]: Miscellaneous; D.2.8 [**Software Engineering**]: Metrics

General Terms

Application; Anomaly Detection

1. INTRODUCTION

The ease of movement of pedestrians is a major challenge for the operation of cities. Understanding patterns of pedestrian movement provides valuable information to city infrastructure and transportation planning. Advances in sensor technology have enabled new counting systems that operate continuously with high accuracy. While many projects to monitor pedestrian counts have been initiated, there are still limited efforts in modelling the normal behaviour and detecting interesting events from this data.

In this study we aim to characterize normal behaviour of pedestrian flows in terms of correlations in the load profile by time of day across multiple locations. This knowledge can be used by city planners in catering for pedestrian flows, in assisting business to target their services according to demand, or in understanding the dynamics of cities. We also detect anomalous pedestrian activities, which help to characterise and forecast the impact of special events.

Permission to make digital or hard copies of all or part of this work for personal or classroom use is granted without fee provided that copies are not made or distributed for profit or commercial advantage and that copies bear this notice and the full citation on the first page. Copyrights for components of this work owned by others than ACM must be honored. Abstracting with credit is permitted. To copy otherwise, or republish, to post on servers or to redistribute to lists, requires prior specific permission and/or a fee. Request permissions from Permissions@acm.org.
CIKM'15, October 19–23, 2015, Melbourne, VIC, Australia.
© 2015 ACM. ISBN 978-1-4503-3794-6/15/10 ...$15.00.
DOI: http://dx.doi.org/10.1145/2806416.2806645.

This paper presents the use of clustering and anomaly detection techniques on large-scale urban pedestrian counting data. By analysing one year's worth of data we aim to construct a reliable and meaningful model of pedestrian movements. This raises two key research challenges: (1) The data is periodic on daily, weekly and monthly cycles, hence looking only at the sequence of data might hide important patterns. (2) The quality of clusters can decrease when input data is collected over longer time scales, as the models of normal behaviours may vary throughout the year. It is essential to identify these normal states of the system, as well as how the system switches between these different states, in order to accurately detect anomalous conditions.

We examine two approaches in this study. HyCARCE [11][12] is a computationally and memory efficient clustering technique that uses ellipsoids for clustering. It performs clustering on the entire input data in a single pass. In contrast, the Ensemble Switching Model [13] is an anomaly detection technique that can cope with dynamic environments where the system switches between different states intermittently. It learns from the historical states of normal behaviour and accounts for the switching states while detecting anomalies. These two approaches are evaluated and validated against known events. The data used in this study is pedestrian counting data from the City of Melbourne, Australia [1], where sensors collect pedestrian counts over 28 locations around the CBD. The counts are captured continuously at intervals of 1 hour. Our key contribution is that we test whether the accuracy of an Ensemble Switching Model outweighs its complexity compared to the static HyCARCE clustering model for modelling pedestrian movements.

The rest of the paper is organized as follows. Section 2 describes the related work in profiling pedestrian movements. Section 3 defines the analysis problem and explains the techniques of HyCARCE and Ensemble Switching. Section 4 describes the experiment and results.

2. RELATED WORK

Multiple studies have analysed user-centric pedestrian activity by tracking the path of pedestrians using GPS or ubiquitous devices in historic districts or shopping malls, such as [14][9]. However, there are relatively few studies on the crowd behaviour of the city as a whole.

There have been multiple studies using location based social networks, e.g., Facebook, Twitter and Flickr to understand crowd distribution [7][8]. For example, [4] utilized the

Twitter data of Manhattan-based users to model the crowd footprint of particular locations. By associating the crowd footprint to the words used in messages, the authors used Latent Dirichlet Allocation [3] to reveal trends and routine behaviour in the city for each day of the week. However, one limitation of this study is the number of topics, corresponding to different pedestrian load profiles, needs to be predicted in advance. Moreover, the pedestrian load profile was assumed to be constant throughout the one year span of the collected data, which may affect accuracy.

The studies above either use a short period of collected data or assume a constant state of the load profile, which can cause false alarms in anomaly detection. In this study, we consider the pedestrian distribution as a state-switching system, and we examine how such a dynamic model of normal behaviour can improve anomaly detection in comparison to a more static model of pedestrian behaviour.

3. CLUSTER AND ANOMALY DETECTION

We formally define our problem, and then present the clustering and anomaly detection techniques used in this study.

3.1 Problem Statement

Let O denote the set of N observations from time t_1 to t_N: $O = \{o_i : i = 1..N\}$ where $o_i \in \mathbb{R}^d$ is a vector of d dimensions corresponding to the pedestrian counting values of d different locations.

We aim to find (1) the set of K clusters $C = \{c_i : i = 1..K\}$ that partition the dataset O, and (2) the set A_H containing all anomalies that do not belong to any clusters. However, A_H provides a static model of the underlying system, and does not consider how the clusters change over time. Consequently, we need to develop a clustering model that can cope with nonstationarity, or systems that switch between different states over time. To this end, by using an Ensemble Switching Model, we aim to find the set of anomalies A_{ES} while accomodating a dataset O that switches between different states. By evenly dividing O into windows of length w, we identify the different states in the data and select only the relevant states as the basis for anomaly detection.

By analysing and comparing A_H and A_{ES} we seek to evaluate to what extent the dynamic Ensemble Switching Model provides greater accuracy in detecting anomalies in comparison to static clustering, given the extra logic and resources required to model switching data streams.

3.2 Static Clustering HyCARCE

HyCARCE (Hyperellipsoidal Clustering for Resource Constrained Environment) is a grid-based clustering algorithm with low computational complexity of $O(N)$ [11]. The algorithm can be summarized in 4 steps as follows:

Input: dataset of N d-dimensional records $S = \{s_k : k = 1..N\}, s_k \in \mathbb{R}^d$

Ouput: set of K clusters $C = \{c_j : j = 1..K\}$ (K is determined algorithmically)

Step 1: Divide the input space into a set of fixed-size d-dimension cells and prune the cells with low density.

Step 2: Fit a hyperellipsoid into each cell that covers at least 95% of the cell data. The hyperellipsoid is defined by:

$$(X - \mu)^T \Sigma^{-1} (X - \mu) = (\chi_d^2)_{0.95}^{-1}$$

where μ and Σ are respectively the mean and covariance of the data in the cell. Σ^{-1} defines the characteristic matrix of the ellipsoid.

Step 3: Enlarge each ellipsoid by scaling the characteristic matrix to accommodate new data points. After each enlargement the mean μ and covariance matrix Σ are recomputed. Enlargement and re-adjustment are repeated until the change in the number of data points being added to the new hyperellipsoid is smaller than a predefined threshold.

Step 4: Remove redundant ellipsoids. If the distances between the centres of two ellipsoids are smaller than a threshold, the one with a lower number of data points is considered to be redundant and removed.

Studies [11][12] have shown that HyCARCE produces equivalent or better accuracy compared to popular clustering algorithms such as DENCLUE[6], k-means[15] and GK[5].

3.3 Ensemble Switching Model

The Ensemble Switching Model [13] is a dynamic anomaly detection technique that addresses the problem of the underlying system switching between multiple states in the stream of data. By evenly dividing the input data stream into small windows, it constructs a model of the states corresponding to normal behaviours, and uses this dynamic model to detect anomalies, rather than using the static model of HyCARCE.

Step 1 (windowing): The stream of data is divided into windows of size w. The w observations of window k are then clustered using HyCARCE into a set of hyperellipsoids that form the clustering model C_k of that window.

Step 2 (weighting): The distances between the clustering model of the current windows C_k to previous windows $\{C_j : j = 1..k-1\}$ are computed. The distance between two models is defined as the sum of the focal distances [10] between all pairs of corresponding clusters that match between the two models. The relevance between clustering models are then deduced from the distances, which is then used in the final step to score anomalies.

Step 3 (anomaly scoring): The detection of whether an observation is an anomaly is calculated using the clustering models of both the current and previous windows. The relevance weighting computed in **Step 2** ensures only relevant clustering models take part in the scoring.

4. EVALUATION AND RESULT

In this section, we empirically evaluate our two approaches to anomaly detection based on static clustering and ensemble switching for pedestrian modelling.

4.1 Evaluation

Each method was evaluated in terms of its ability to produce consistent and meaningful clusters, as well as its accuracy in detecting anomalous activities, with reference to known events. We also focused on evaluating the advantages of the dynamic models of Ensemble Switching and investigating how these models enable it to detect events not visible to static clustering like HyCARCE.

We focused on two adjacent locations from the pedestrian counting deployment in the City of Melbourne [1] for analysis: Flinders Street Station and Princes Bridge. These two monitoring points are located at the heart of the CBD and are representative of the movement of pedestrians between the CBD and South Melbourne. The time period of the monitored data was from 1st January to 31st December 2014.

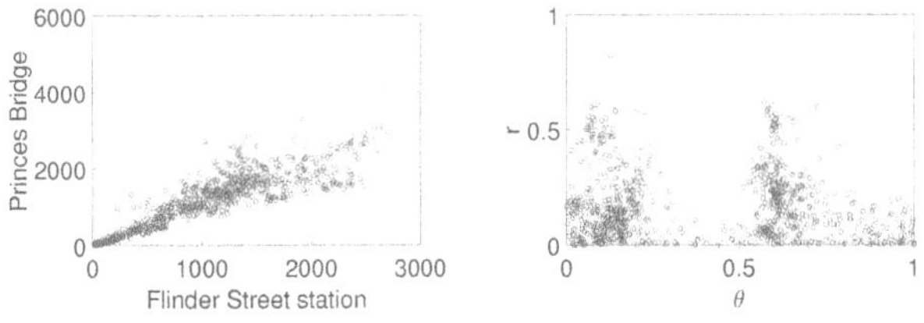

(a) (b)

Figure 1: Data preprocessing steps: (a) raw count values, (b) polar transformation and normalization to range $[0, 1]$ ((θ, r) are the polar coordinates)

Since the counting data is not evenly distributed, with a big portion of the observations being skewed towards the low values, the data was preprocessed to reveal its structure more clearly. The steps are illustrated in Figure 1. First, instead of using the absolute counts of pedestrians, we used the differences between successive counts. These values represent the hourly changes in the number of pedestrians. Second, we apply a polar transformation to separate the values into different segments and to achieve a more even distribution. Finally, the data was normalised to the range $[0, 1]$ and counts during weekends were excluded.

Clustering and anomaly detection were evaluated in different stages. Initially, we applied HyCARCE on a small subset of one week of data. Since HyCARCE is the underlying clustering method of Ensemble Switching, it is necessary to verify its effectiveness. Subsequently, both HyCARCE and Ensemble Switching were applied on the entire range of data. Finally the two sets of anomalies generated by the two approaches were compared with each other. Since it is infeasible to verify each of the anomalies detected due to the lack of ground data labels, to compare the performance between the two methods, we selected 15 major events from the calendar of the City of Melbourne [2]. These events include New Year's Eve, Christmas Eve, etc., when the pedestrian distribution is expected to be different from the norm, i.e., these pedestrian distributions are considered as anomalies. Each method is assessed by its capability to distinguish the anomalies in accordance with this schedule of events.

4.2 Results and Discussion

4.2.1 HyCARCE

HyCARCE successfully modelled the distribution of pedestrians when applied on one week's worth of data. The clusters are presented in Table 1; for example, HyCARCE groups $7am$ of all five days of the week, i.e., $(7, 5)$ into Cluster 4. As illustrated in Figure 2a, it clustered the distribution into visually clear groups of $7am$, $8am$, $11am$, $1pm$, $5pm$, $6pm$, $10 - 11pm$, which can be mapped to morning peaks, lunch breaks, afternoon peaks and midnight.

However, when a longer period of data is analysed using clustering, the quality of clustering results start to degrade. Many values are found to be clustered into the wrong group and the meaningful characteristics of the clusters as found in one week's data are no longer observed. Moreover, the states between different weeks vary intermittently, causing superpositions in the data distribution and reducing the clustering accuracy. As an example, the pedestrian activities in a summer week are different from those in a winter week, hence considering these two weeks using a single, static clustering model might ignore the characteristics of each week.

To test the performance of HyCARCE with a large dataset and also to provide a reference for comparison with Ensemble Switching later, we applied HyCARCE on the entire data of one year's worth of observations. The clusters are illustrated in Figure 2b and presented in Table 1.

Clusters	(Hour of Day, Instance Count)	
	One week's data	One year's data
1	(22, 5), (23, 5), (0, 5), (2, 2), (19, 2)	(18, 225), (9, 239), (19, 108)
2	(2, 2)	(14, 187), (20, 220), (21, 135), (22, 191), (23, 243), (0, 226), (1, 258), (2, 191), (19, 139)
3	(5 ,5)	(16, 180), (6, 229)
4	(7, 5)	(5, 253)
5	(6, 5), (17, 4), (11, 3)	no grouping of hour
6	(8, 4), (12, 4), (16, 5)	(7, 233), (8, 196)
7	(9, 5), (18, 5)	false clustering of values on random days
8	(1, 4)	
9	(13, 4), (20, 2), (21, 3)	

Table 1: HyCARCE clusters of pedestrian counting data

The following issues emerge when analysing the result:

- Clusters are large with less clearly defined characteristics. This can be observed in Cluster 2 in Table 2b, which corresponds to the distribution model spanning from $8pm$ to $2am$ the next day. The cluster also packs the distribution at $2pm$ and $7pm$ into the same group. Although this result is arguably sensible, details are lost. The results shown by clustering one week's data offers more meaningful clusters, which manage to not only distinguish the distributions of the period $8 - 9pm$ from $10pm$-midnight and $1am - 2am$ periods, but also group distributions at $2pm$ and $7pm$ into different groups.
- Clusters can be formed unexpectedly when the counts of random days happen to be near one another. Figure 2b shows a small cluster (on top right) that contains the observations of 5 different hours of 5 different days spread throughout the year. Each of these should be considered as anomalies but instead form an invalid cluster, causing false negatives in anomaly detection.

The evaluation of anomaly detection using static HyCARCE clustering is discussed in greater detail in comparison with Ensemble Switching in the next section.

4.2.2 Ensemble Swiching

When Emsemble Switching is used as the basis of building a model for anomaly detection instead of a static HyCARCE clustering model, the following observations were made:

- The method is more immune to false positives and false negatives because each observation is assessed for being an anomaly using not only its own window of data but also with the support of cluster models of other relevant windows. A good example of a false negative is the pedestrian count at 11pm on 5th Dec 2014. In its window, this observation was grouped in the cluster of 6pm because their values share some proximity. However this erroneous clustering is corrected when the point is assessed with other windows and consequently classified as an anomaly. In the city event calendar, there was a movie screening organized right next to the Princes Bridge until 11pm that day, which can support this decision.

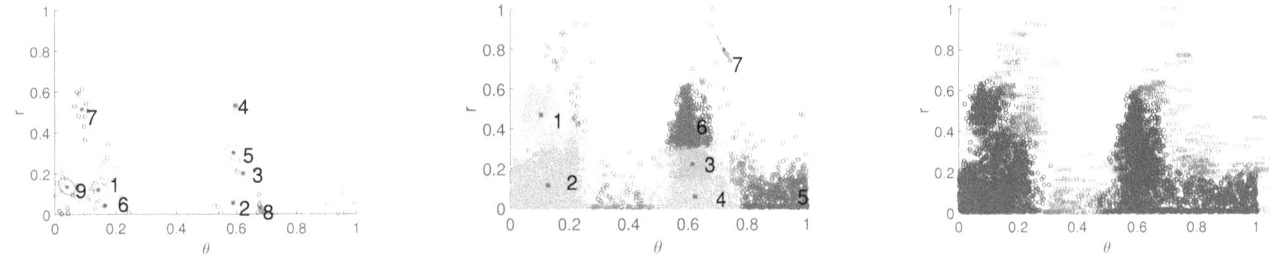

(a) (b) (c)

Figure 2: HyCARCE and Ensemble Switching applied on different datasets of pedestrian counting data. (a) HyCARCE on one week's data, (b) HyCARCE on one year's data, (c) Ensemble Switching on one year's data. (θ, r) are the polar coordinates.

- By splitting the input into multiple windows, the method is capable of handling superpositions of different data distributions. Figure 2c shows all the anomalies in red. A quick examination shows that although these values are in close proximity, they belong to random hours of different days throughout the year, and arguably do not express any trends or repeating patterns in pedestrian activities.

A total of 15 major events and public holidays were selected from the calendar of the City of Melbourne and used as a reference set of anomalous events to evaluate and compare the performance of the two methods. Each method was assessed in terms of whether it can detect the reference set of anomalies, and if so, whether the results match closely with the actual schedule of the events. A portion of the evaluation (Jan to Mar 2014) is presented in Table 2.

Events	Ensemble Switching	HyCARCE
New Year Day	1-3am	1-2am
Australia open	9pm	not detected
Moomba parade	9am-1pm, 9-10pm	12pm, 9-10pm
Formula one	5-8pm	11pm(invalid)

Table 2: Anomalies detected during major events from Jan to Mar 2014

Out of 15 events, Ensemble Switching manages to detect correctly 13 anomalies while HyCARCE detects 10 anomalies. In addition, the output of Ensemble Switching provides better coverage and match the schedule of the events more accurately. For example, the Moomba parade took place at 11am on 10th Mar 2014, and it is likely that a higher than normal number of pedestrians would be observed before, during and after the event; hence the anomalies of 9am to 1pm as returned by the Ensemble Switching method are more accurate compared to the HyCARCE result. Although HyCARCE also detects some of the unusual events, many valid anomalies were not detected.

5. CONCLUSION

In this paper we applied HyCARCE and Ensemble Switching to pedestrian counting data with the aim of modelling the pedestrian load profile across multiple locations and to extract anomalies, which are then cross-examined with known events. The experiments revealed that the Ensemble Switching Model produces more accurate results in terms of false alarms compared to HyCARCE. The results illustrate that pedestrian distributions can be clustered into meaningful profiles characterizing major activities throughout the day.

6. ACKNOWLEDGMENTS

The authors would like to thank the support from National ICT Australia (NICTA).

7. REFERENCES

[1] City Of Melbourne : Pedestrian Counting System. http://www.pedestrian.melbourne.vic.gov.au/.
[2] Events Calendar for 2014 | Victorian Government. http://www.vic.gov.au/calendar/2014/01.html.
[3] D. M. Blei et al. Latent Dirichlet allocation. *the Jnl. of Machine Learning Research*, 3:993–1022, 2003.
[4] L. Ferrari et al. Extracting urban patterns from location-based social networks. In *ACM SIGSPATIAL Intl. Workshop on Location-Based Social Networks*, LBSN '11, pages 9–16, 2011.
[5] D. Gustafson et al. Fuzzy clustering with a fuzzy covariance matrix. In *IEEE Decision and Control including the 17th Symposium on Adaptive Processes*, pages 761–766, 1978.
[6] A. Hinneburg and H.-H. Gabriel. Denclue 2.0: Fast clustering based on kernel density estimation. In *Advances in Intelligent Data Analysis VII*, pages 70–80. Springer, 2007.
[7] L. Hollenstein and R. Purves. Exploring place through user-generated content: Using Flickr tags to describe city cores. *Jnl. of Spatial Information Science*, (1):21–48, 2015.
[8] M. Mamei et al. Automatic analysis of geotagged photos for intelligent tourist services. In *Intelligent Environments*, pages 146–151, 2010.
[9] A. Millonig and G. Gartner. Shadowing, tracking, interviewing: How to explore human spatio-temporal behaviour patterns. In *BMI*, pages 1–14, 2008.
[10] M. Moshtaghi et al. Clustering ellipses for anomaly detection. *Pattern Recognition*, 44(1):55 – 69, 2011.
[11] M. Moshtaghi et al. An efficient hyperellipsoidal clustering algorithm for resource-constrained environments. *Pattern Recognition*, 44(9):2197 – 2209, 2011.
[12] S. Rajasegarar et al. Ellipsoidal neighbourhood outlier factor for distributed anomaly detection in resource constrained networks. *Pattern Recognition*, 47(9):2867 – 2879, 2014.
[13] M. Salehi et al. A relevance weighted ensemble model for anomaly detection in switching data streams. In *PAKDD*, pages 461–473. Springer, 2014.
[14] S. van der Spek. Spatial metro–tracking pedestrians in historic city centres. *Research in Urbanism Series*, 1(1):77–97, 2008.
[15] R. Xu et al. Survey of clustering algorithms. *IEEE Trans. on Neural Networks*, 16(3):645–678, 2005.

A Clustering-based Approach to Detect Probable Outcomes of Lawsuits

Daniel Lemes Gribel
Pontifical Catholic University of Rio de Janeiro
Marquês de São Vicente, 225
Rio de Janeiro, Brazil
dgribel@inf.puc-rio.br

Maira Gatti de Bayser
IBM Research Brazil
Av. Pasteur, 458
Rio de Janeiro, Brazil
mairacg@br.ibm.com

Leonardo Guerreiro Azevedo
IBM Research Brazil
Av. Pasteur, 458
Rio de Janeiro, Brazil
lga@br.ibm.com

ABSTRACT

The numerous lawsuits in progress or already judged by the Brazilian Supreme Court consists of a large amount of non-structured data. This leads to a large number of hidden or unknown information, since some relationships between lawsuits are not explicit in the available data; and contributes to generate non-intuitive influences between variables, which in addition increases the degree of uncertainty on judicial outcomes. This work proposes an approach to identify possible judgment outcomes that considers the use of similarity calculations and clustering mechanisms based on lawsuits patterns. The similarity problem was tackled by analysing metadata manually extracted from lawsuits; and this work also presents an approach to detect clusters and to compile past votes. From the results, it is possible to verify lawsuits most likely outcomes and to detect their degree of uncertainty.

Keywords

Clustering; Similarity; Lawsuit; Prediction

1. INTRODUCTION

At the Brazilian Supreme Court (STF), the large amount of non-structured data and the huge number of parameters coming from the numerous lawsuits leads to non-intuitive influences between variables and to some degree of uncertainty on outcomes. In this context, this work proposes an approach to infer possible results through the use of clustering methods. Much of the analysis involving judicial lawsuits depends on a large cognitive effort, which demands deep domain knowledge and ability to deal with subjective questions. These conditions surely introduce a component of difficulty to available AI technology and methods [4]. For instance, some questions that could arise are: "Which similar lawsuits could be a reference to a new lawsuit?"; "What is the estimated time for taking a decision?"; "What is the likelihood for the possible emergent results?". These issues are examples of information required to understand the dynamics of a judicial decision and may be lost in the large volume of data generated over time. However, many lawsuits can be decided based on certain parameters, as the comparison to lawsuits with similar features and the comparison to outcomes taken by a judge with a history of judging similar cases.

This work developed an approach to recommend possible outcomes for a given lawsuit based on modelling, similarity detection and clustering. It analyses past data to detect similarities and to anticipate judgments results. The solution searches for similar past cases and tests the behaviour of the involved judges through past judgments and the degree of agreement between them.

The remainder of the work is divided as follows: Section 2 describes how lawsuits were modelled; Section 3 describes the solution to infer lawsuits outcomes; Section 4 presents the main results achieved; and finally, Section 5 presents the final remarks and future work.

Permission to make digital or hard copies of all or part of this work for personal or classroom use is granted without fee provided that copies are not made or distributed for profit or commercial advantage and that copies bear this notice and the full citation on the first page. Copyrights for components of this work owned by others than ACM must be honored. Abstracting with credit is permitted. To copy otherwise, or republish, to post on servers or to redistribute to lists, requires prior specific permission and/or a fee. Request permissions from Permissions@acm.org.
CIKM'15, October 19-23, 2015, Melbourne, VIC, Australia
© 2015 ACM. ISBN 978-1-4503-3794-6/15/10$15.00
DOI: http://dx.doi.org/10.1145/2806416.2806640.

2. LAWSUITS MODELLING

2.1 Law classes

In the Brazilian judicial system, there are several lawsuit classes. In this work, only lawsuits belonging to the ***Appeal*** class are considered. This choice was supported by two main reasons: the ***Appeal*** class corresponds to more than 50% of lawsuits judged by the STF, which is important in terms of the heterogeneity of the data, and its lawsuits have similar dynamics in their life cycles, not observed in other classes, which is important in terms of pattern detection. Thus, this class of lawsuits constrains the boundaries of the problem and approximates the solution results to the real outcomes.

In Law, appeal is an instrument to request a change on a lawsuit being judged, *i.e.*, it is the mean to review a judgment in order to get the reform, the invalidation, or the clarification of a lawsuit.

2.2 Mental modelling

Lawsuits information were extracted from public data available on STF website[1]. The following steps were taken to model and add a lawsuit to the dataset:
i) Look for an appeal lawsuit page in the STF website and identify its metadata, such as id, period (start and end date), state of origin, rapporteur, author, defendant, area of Law and subjects associated to the lawsuit.

[1]Available in portuguese only.

ii) Identify the lawsuit summary and claim, which can be found in a PDF document that includes the Court final decision and represents a formal report of the judgment, containing the votes given by each judge.

A lawsuit can have many decisions before a final decision. Hence, a lawsuit is related to many decisions and a decision is related to many judges. A decision may take the value "accepted" or "denied", depending on the majority of votes.

3. INFERENCE OF LAWSUITS OUTCOMES

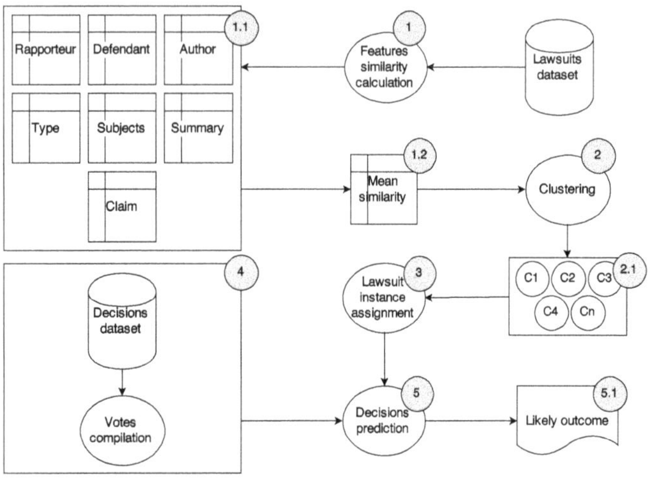

Figure 1: Workflow proposed for lawsuits outcomes

The general workflow of the proposed solution is depicted in Figure 1. Each step (highlighted in numbers) is described below:

1. Features similarity extraction: At this step, each pair of modelled lawsuit receives a similarity coefficient regarding to a property. For this purpose, one adjacency matrix NxN is calculated for each property (rapporteur, defendant, author, area of Law, subjects, summary and claim), where N is the number of lawsuits composing the dataset (see Step 1.1). In order to fill the similarity matrix regarding to a property, Jaccard index is applied for each pair of lawsuits:

$$J_x(a,b) = \frac{|a_x \bigcap b_x|}{|a_x \bigcup b_x|} \tag{1}$$

where a and b are two lawsuits being compared and x is the property. Note that sets involved on Jaccard calculation correspond to the property x observed on lawsuits a and b. Thus, the Jaccard coefficient generates a number between 0 and 1. To meet a normalization that will be required later, we consider the value $1-J_x(a,b)$ for each pair (a,b). So, lawsuits are more similar if the coefficient is closer to zero. For some properties, as defendant and rapporteur, each lawsuit contributes with a single set; so, we have similarity matrices with 0's and 1's, indicating if two lawsuits have the same property. For other properties, as subjects and summary, sets have one or more elements; so, we have similarity matrices with values between 0 and 1. However, in both cases we can apply Jaccard index to calculate similarities.

In order to generate a mean similarity matrix, which is a resultant similarity metric (Step 1.2), the following mean calculation is performed:

$$M(a,b) = \frac{\sum_{x=1}^{n} J_x(a,b) \cdot w_x}{\sum_{x=1}^{n} w_x} \tag{2}$$

Note that x varies from 1 to n, where n represents the number of properties, which in this case is 7. The $J_x(a,b)$ is the Jaccard index computed for lawsuits a and b, considering the x property, as described in equation 1. The w_x is the weight assigned to the property x, where $1 \leq w_x \leq 4$, depending on the degree of influence that each property has in the decision process.

2. Clustering algorithm: In this step, lawsuits are assigned to groups according to their similarities. For this purpose, the mean similarity matrix generated on previous step is used as input for the hierarchical clustering algorithm. To achieve clustering results, it was adopted three agglomerative algorithms to guide the hierarchical clustering: Ward's, Single-linkage and Complete-linkage [1]. The output of this step is a set of lawsuits clusters (Step 2.1).

3. Lawsuit instance assignment: This step checks in which cluster a single test lawsuit t should be assigned, considering the lawsuits clusters computed in Step 2. For this purpose, we use the similarity calculation method described in Step 1. The instance t is compared to each classified lawsuit of each cluster, and then a coefficient from 0 to 1 is generated, indicating how similar the lawsuits are. With established clusters and similarity coefficients, an average is applied by cluster. Then, the instance t is assigned to a cluster δ – the cluster with the smallest average of coefficients and, therefore, the most similar group.

4. Decisions compilation: Considering the decisions dataset, this step collects the past votes given by judges on lawsuits belonging to cluster δ (obtained from Step 3). We consider only the votes given by the judges that would decide the lawsuit t – such information is given as an input of the system – to then apply a filter on cluster votes.

5. Decisions prediction: Finally, the degree of agreement between judges is calculated based on collected past votes, *i.e.*, if judges agreed in past decisions taken on cluster δ. This is important to detect some divergent behaviour in the judgment, and then infer the uncertainty degree of the outcome. The output of this step, which is the output of the whole process, is the likely outcome (Step 5.1) – a number between 0 and 1, with 0 indicating the lawsuit denial and 1 corresponding to its acceptance.

4. RESULTS

This section presents the main results achieved from the proposed approach and the interpretation we can extract from them.

4.1 Datasets

Two datasets were used: one composed by a set of 16 extracted lawsuits, and another one composed by 24 decisions taken on lawsuits. Each lawsuit may have one or more decisions.

Manual extraction of lawsuits features requires time and some cognitive efforts. The document containing important information like the summary and the claim of a lawsuit is extensive and written in a non-trivial language. Thus, the size of the dataset is due to this manual extraction limitation, which makes the phase of data collection an exhaustive task. In the final considerations, we point out a proposal to automate this process.

Each lawsuit composing the lawsuits dataset provides the following information: lawsuit id, start/end date, state of origin, rapporteur, defendant, author, area of Law, subjects, summary and claim. On the other hand, each decision composing the decisions dataset provides the following information: associated lawsuit id, decision id, type of decision, date, votes tuple <judge name, vote (*accepted* or *denied*)> and resultant decision (*accepted* or *denied*). The type of decision may be *Monocratic* (1 judge), *First Panel* (5 judges), *Second Panel* (5 judges) or *Plenary* (11 judges).

For exemplification purpose, the lawsuit below describes an instance composing the dataset:

Lawsuit id: AI769177; **Start/end date:** 07/10/2009 , 28/03/2014; **State of origin:** SP; **Rapporteur:** Toffoli; **Defendant:** Claro Telecom S.A.; **Author:** City of Sao Jose dos Campos; **Area of Law:** Administrative Law; **Subjects:** Administrative acts, Licenses; **Summary:** Municipal Law, Right to build, Legislative power, Irregular construction, Urban planning, Urban land use, Telephony, Antenna; **Claim:** Legislative power.

4.2 Similarity and Clustering analysis

In order to achieve the similarities between lawsuits, all lawsuits are compared in pairs taken into account each of their properties. After all similarity matrices are computed, it is necessary to calculate a resultant matrix, which is obtained through a weighted average of each property similarity matrix. Figure 2 shows the final result for the similarities compilation between lawsuits, where each row (column) represents a lawsuit of the dataset and each cell indicates the similarity degree between two lawsuits. This matrix is the input necessary to perform clustering analysis.

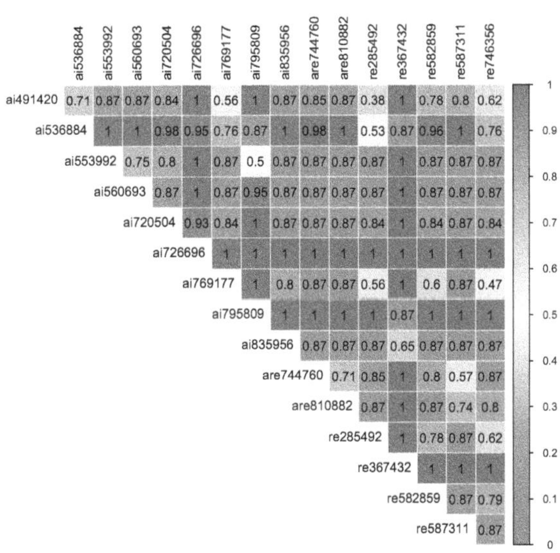

Figure 2: Mean similarity matrix: the closer to zero the coefficient is, more similar the lawsuits are

Figure 3 presents a heat map which displays clusters being formed from the similarity matrix, indicating how hierarchical clustering has performed with Complete-linkage algorithm.

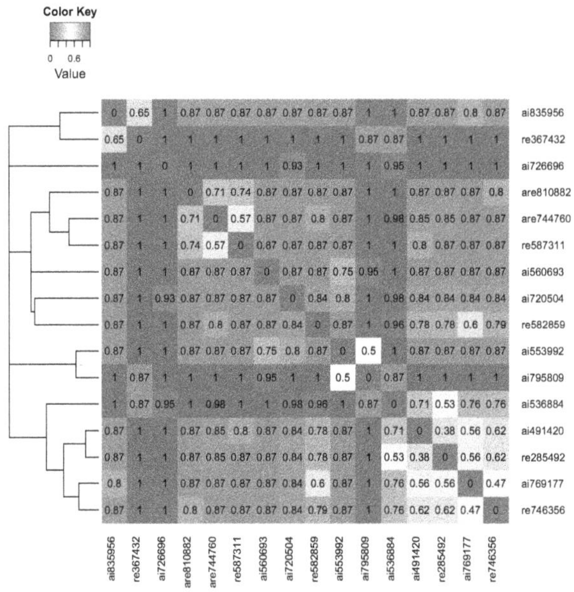

Figure 3: Heatmap illustrating clusters formation from lawsuits similarities

4.3 Input

Once the clustering analysis was made and the dataset is classified, we need to evidence what input structure is used. The input is basically a properties file that can be easily customizable for test purposes, and contains the following information:

- Agglomeration method: Defines the agglomerative algorithm used in hierarchical clustering. In this work, Ward's, Single-linkage and Complete-linkage methods were tested.
- Instance: Describes the lawsuit instance t that will have the outcome predicted. The same properties of a lawsuit belonging to the dataset is used to characterize t.
- Judges: Lists the ministers that would judge the lawsuit – a single, 5 or 11 judges, according to the type of decision.

4.4 Clustering performances

Determining the number k of clusters in a dataset is a common problem in data clustering [2]. Table 1 displays the similarity rate for instance t, considering different agglomerative algorithms and k varying from 2 to $\sqrt{N}$, where N is the number of lawsuits dataset entries.

Table 1 shows that Ward's and Complete-linkage algorithms performed better for the given instance, since Complete-linkage algorithm found the cluster with the smallest distance for $k = 4$ and Ward's found the best one for $k < 4$.

k	Ward's best cluster		Single-linkage best cluster		Complete-linkage best cluster	
k	Distance	Cluster size	Distance	Cluster size	Distance	Cluster size
2	**0.79**	10	0.81	15	0.81	14
3	**0.76**	8	0.79	11	0.80	13
4	0.70	6	0.79	11	**0.68**	6

Table 1: Clustering results obtained for instance t

4.5 Prediction results

The output presented in Table 2 corresponds to the final results achieved for test instance t, once the most similar cluster δ was chosen. The *Votes* vector indicates the degree of acceptance of each judge in the cluster. That is, it corresponds to the ratio $\frac{A_\delta}{A_\delta+D_\delta}$, where A_δ is the number of lawsuits accepted by the judge in the cluster δ and D_δ is the number of denied lawsuits in the same cluster. Thus, 0 means that the judge denied all lawsuits in the cluster and 1 means that all lawsuits were accepted by him/her. It is important to note that each element of the vector represents a judge. In this way, for results shown in Table 2, we have a vector of size 5, which means that this case is a *Collegiate* judgment. In addition, the prediction results for this test instance were achieved considering a configuration with 5 specific judges participating. However, the list of judges can be easily changed, by just editing the properties file, *i.e.*, the solution supports other scenarios.

The *Judges agreement* vector corresponds to the degree of agreement among judges, *i.e.*, for each lawsuit belonging to cluster δ where the judge voted and other judges composing the input also voted, it is computed if they agreed or disagreed (1 or 0 is assigned, respectively). Then, the average is calculated for each judge. As the *Votes* vector, each element of the *Judges agreement* vector represents a judge.

The *Likely outcome* column is the average applied in the *Votes* vector. It can assume a prediction value from 0 to 1, where 0 indicates that the lawsuit would be denied and 1 indicates that it would be accepted. The *Judges agreement* vector is not used for outcome calculation purpose, but is an extra and useful information to reinforce the degree of uncertainty of the outcome and to detect whether a certain judge usually has a discrepant behaviour within the cluster context.

Finally, *Lawsuits mean duration* column is the average duration of lawsuits belonging to cluster δ, which may be a general estimation for the time required to have lawsuit t judged.

k	Best cluster (δ)	Distance	Votes	Judges agreement	Likely outcome	Lawsuits mean duration (days)
2	1	0.81	(0.25, 0, 0.29, 0, 0.38)	(0.93, 1, 0.93, 1, 0.86)	**0.18**	1313
3	1	0.80	(0.14, 0, 0.17, 0, 0.29)	(0.92, 1, 0.92, 1, 0.83)	**0.12**	1299.31
4	2	0.68	(0, 0, 0, 0, 0.33)	(0.83, 1, 0.83, 1, 0.67)	**0.07**	1286.5

Table 2: Outcomes for instance t, considering best solution found (Complete-linkage algorithm)

As pointed by Table 2, the outcome prediction for this instance seems to be well established, since all suggested results are close to 0. Indeed, for this lawsuit being tested, all judges denied it, following the rapporteur vote. That is, the actual outcome of the lawsuit was 0 (once this is an already judged lawsuit). In a scenario with $k = 4$, the prediction result was 0.07, being close to the real outcome.

However, depending on the test instance, it may happen that a large uncertainty appear. In this case, the cluster may have a similar proportion of accepted and denied decisions, which would demand a deep analysis in lawsuits composing the cluster to take more accurate conclusions.

5. CONCLUSIONS AND FUTURE WORK

In this work, the efforts were directed in order to use similarity calculations and clustering algorithms to find the most similar lawsuits when compared to a new lawsuit being tested. By analysing some metadata, it is possible that the test instance has a similar case already judged, since the amount of data provided by the judicial system are quite large. Thus, the challenge is to find the best way to detect such similarities and to evaluate how close the past results are from the lawsuit being tested. To the best of our knowledge, this is the first work that attempts to solve this kind of problem and the main contribution was the proposed workflow described by Figure 1. The results demonstrate that it is possible to verify the most likely outcome and to detect the degree of outcome uncertainty by checking the degree of judges voting agreement.

As future work, some improvements and modifications are already addressed. Firstly, the use of machine learning techniques are required, in order to improve the results accuracy and to detect other relationships that are currently hidden. Secondly, it is important to define a criterion for determining the number of clusters according to the dataset size and the variance of lawsuits features. Thirdly, it is important to extract more data from the STF website in order to increase the dataset. For this purpose, we intend to replace manual extraction of features by automatic extraction through NLP techniques. So far we have only tested this solution with few cases, once this is a on-course work.

Another future direction of this work is the modelling and simulation of lawsuit decision process on which multiple variables are predicted, multiple scenarios are explored and *what-if* analyses could be done. Some approaches, as the one adopted by Gatti *et al.* [3], consider the use of stochastic modelling and simulation to evaluate the emergent behaviour originated from the observed relationships.

6. REFERENCES

[1] M. Ackerman and S. Ben-David. Discerning linkage-based algorithms among hierarchical clustering methods. In T. Walsh, editor, *IJCAI*, pages 1140–1145. IJCAI/AAAI, 2011.

[2] L. Cao, A. Bazzan, A. Symeonidis, V. Gorodetsky, G. Weiss, and P. Yu. *Agents and Data Mining Interaction: 7th International Workshop, ADMI 2011, Taipei, Taiwan, May 2-6, 2011, Revised Selected Papers.* LNCS sublibrary. SL 7, Artificial intelligence. Springer, 2012.

[3] M. Gatti, P. Cavalin, S. Barbosa Neto, C. Pinhanez, C. dos Santos, D. Gribel, and A. Appel. Large-scale multi-agent-based modeling and simulation of microblogging-based online social network. In *Multi-Agent-Based Simulation XIV - International Workshop, MABS 2013, Saint Paul, MN, USA, May 6-7, 2013, Revised Selected Papers*, 2013.

[4] H. Surden. Machine Learning and Law. *Social Science Research Network Working Paper Series*, Mar. 2014.

Detecting Check-worthy Factual Claims in Presidential Debates

Naeemul Hassan
Department of Computer Science and Engineering
University of Texas at Arlington
naeemul.hassan@mavs.uta.edu

Chengkai Li
Department of Computer Science and Engineering
University of Texas at Arlington
cli@uta.edu

Mark Tremayne
Department of Communication
University of Texas at Arlington
tremayne@uta.edu

ABSTRACT

Public figures such as politicians make claims about "facts" all the time. Journalists and citizens spend a good amount of time checking the veracity of such claims. Toward automatic fact checking, we developed tools to find check-worthy factual claims from natural language sentences. Specifically, we prepared a U.S. presidential debate dataset and built classification models to distinguish check-worthy factual claims from non-factual claims and unimportant factual claims. We also identified the most-effective features based on their impact on the classification models' accuracy.

Categories and Subject Descriptors

H.2.8 [**Database Management**]: Database Applications—*Data mining*; H.4.m [**Information Systems Applications**]: Miscellaneous; I.2.7 [**Artificial Intelligence**]: Natural Language Processing—*Text analysis*

General Terms

Algorithms, Design, Experimentation

Keywords

computational journalism; fact checking; text classification

1. INTRODUCTION

Public figures such as politicians make claims about "facts" all the time. Oftentimes there are false, exaggerated and misleading claims on important topics, due to careless mistakes and even deliberate manipulation of information. With technology and modern day media helping spread information to mass audiences through all types of channels, there is a pressing need for checking the veracity of factual claims important to the public. Journalists and citizens spend good amount of time doing that. More and more dedicated platforms and institutes are being created for fact checking. According to a census from the Duke University Reporters' Lab,[1] the number of fact checking platforms such as *PolitiFact.com* and *FactCheckEU.org* has increased from 59 (May 2014) to 89 (January 2015), a *50.8%* increase in eight months. This genre of investigative reporting has become a basic feature of political coverage, especially during elections, and plays an important role in improving political discourse and increasing democratic accountability [8, 5].

The process of fact checking requires many challenging steps—extracting natural language sentences from speeches, interviews, press releases, campaign brochures and social media; separating factual claims from opinions, beliefs, hyperboles, questions, and so on; detecting topics of factual claims and discerning which are "check-worthy"; assessing the veracity of such claims, which itself requires collecting information and data, interviewing experts, and presenting evidence and explanations.[2]

Part of the goal of *computational journalism* [3, 4] is use computing to automate fact checking [11, 9]. A fully automatic fact checking system is not yet within our reach. It calls for breakthroughs in several fronts related to the aforementioned fact checking steps. This paper's focus is on detecting check-worthy factual claims from natural language sentences, specifically transcripts of presidential debates.

We model this problem as a classification task and we follow a supervised learning approach to tackle it. We constructed a labeled dataset of spoken sentences by presidential candidates during 2004, 2008 and 2012 presidential debates. (Data collection for earlier debates is still in progress.) Each sentence is given one of three possible labels—it is not a factual claim; it is an unimportant factual claim; it is an important factual claim. We trained and tested several multi-class classification models using the labeled dataset. Experiment results demonstrated promising accuracy of the models. We further identified and analyzed the most-effective features in the models.

We envision, during presidential debates of U.S. Election 2016, for every sentence spoken by the two candidates and extracted into transcripts, our model will immediately predict whether the sentence has a factual claim and whether checking its truthfulness is important to the public. Furthermore, factual claims will be ranked by their significance, which will help professional and citizen journalists focus on

Permission to make digital or hard copies of all or part of this work for personal or classroom use is granted without fee provided that copies are not made or distributed for profit or commercial advantage and that copies bear this notice and the full citation on the first page. Copyrights for components of this work owned by others than the author(s) must be honored. Abstracting with credit is permitted. To copy otherwise, or republish, to post on servers or to redistribute to lists, requires prior specific permission and/or a fee. Request permissions from Permissions@acm.org.
CIKM'15, October 19–23, 2015, Melbourne, VIC, Australia.
Copyright is held by the owner/author(s). Publication rights licensed to ACM.
ACM 978-1-4503-3794-6/15/10 ...$15.00.
DOI: http://dx.doi.org/10.1145/2806416.2806652.

[1]http://reporterslab.org/fact-checking-census-finds-growth-around-world/

[2]http://www.politifact.com/truth-o-meter/article/2013/nov/01/principles-politifact-punditfact-and-truth-o-meter/

the right target. Although so far we have only collected data related to presidential debates, the studied models can be possibly applied on other types of text, including speeches, radio/TV interviews, and social media.

To the best of our knowledge, no prior study has focused on computational methods for detecting factual claims and discerning their importance. The most relevant line of work is subjectivity analysis of text (e.g., [12, 1, 10]) which classifies sentences into objective and subjective ones. However, not all objective sentences are check-worthy important factual claims. Wu et al. [11] studied how to model the quality of facts and find their supporting arguments and counterarguments. Vlachos and Riedel [9] analyzed the tasks in fact checking and presented a dataset of factual claims collected from *PolitiFact.com* and *Channel4.com*. Another area of related research is checking information credibility in microblog platforms. For instance, [13] finds trending rumors containing disputed factual claims. [2, 6] focus on assigning credibility scores to tweets. The scoring models are highly dependent on Twitter-specific features such as the credibility of twitter users. A tweet with high credibility does not necessarily contain a check-worthy factual claims.

2. PROBLEM FORMULATION

We categorize sentences in presidential debates into three categories. Below, each category is explained with examples.

Non-Factual Sentence (*NFS*): Subjective sentences (opinions, beliefs, declarations) and many questions fall under this category. These sentences do not contain any factual claim. Below are some examples.

- *But I think it's time to talk about the future.*
- *You remember the last time you said that?*

Unimportant Factual Sentence (*UFS*): These are factual claims but not check-worthy. In other words, the general public will not be interested in knowing whether these sentences are true or false. Fact-checkers do not find these sentences as important for checking. Some examples are as follows.

- *Next Tuesday is Election Day.*
- *Two days ago we ate lunch at a restaurant.*

Check-worthy Factual Sentence (*CFS*): These sentences contain factual claims and the general public will be interested in knowing whether the claims are true or false. Journalists look for these type of claims for fact checking. Some examples are:

- *He voted against the first Gulf War.*
- *Over a million and a quarter Americans are HIV-positive.*

Our goal is to automatically detect *CFS*s. We model it as a supervised learning problem. Specifically, we model it as a multi-class classification problem where the classes are *NFS*, *UFS* and *CFS*.

3. DATA COLLECTION

In order to construct a dataset for developing and evaluating approaches to detect check-worthy factual claims, we used presidential debate transcripts. The first general election presidential debate was held in 1960. Since then, there have been 14 elections till 2012. In 1964, 1968 and 1972, no presidential debate was held. There were 2 to 4 debate episodes in each of the remaining 11 elections. A total of 30 debate episodes spanned 1960–2012. We parsed the debate transcripts and identified the speaker for each sentence. There are a total of 123 speakers including 18 presidential candidates, moderators and guests. The whole dataset consists of 28029 sentences. We are interested in sentences spoken by the presidential candidates only. There are 23075 such sentences. We discarded very short sentences (less than 5 words long) and we were remained with 20788 sentences. Figure 1 shows the distribution of sentences among 30 debate episodes. Figure 2 shows the average length of sentences. These figures show that recent candidates used more sentences and shorter ones than earlier candidates.

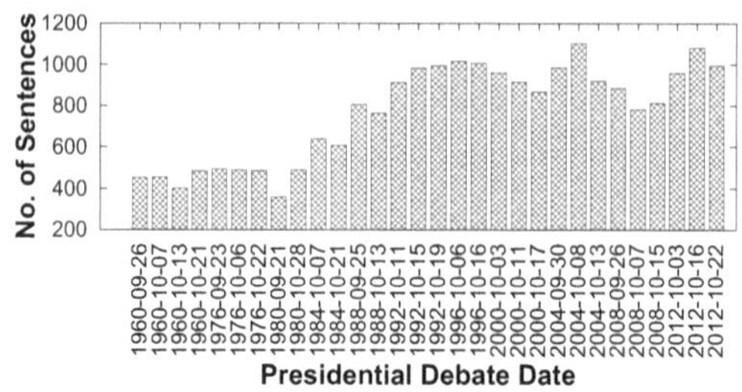

Figure 1: Sentence Distribution

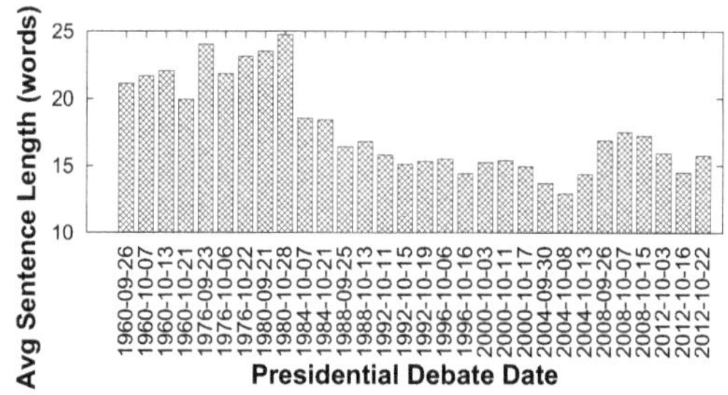

Figure 2: Average Sentence Length in Words

To label the sentences, we developed a data collection website. Journalists, professors and university students were invited to participate in the survey. There was a reward system to encourage high quality answers. A participant was given one sentence at a time and was asked to label it with one of the three possible options as shown in Figure 3. If the participant was not sure about their answer, they could click the "More Context" button to see five preceding sentences of the given sentence. They could also click the "Skip" button to skip the sentence.

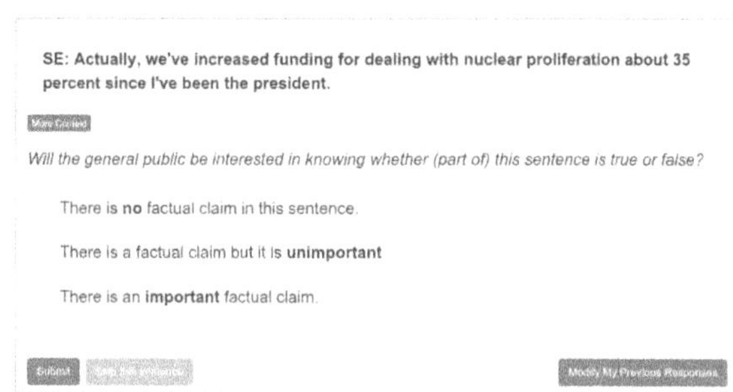

Figure 3: Data Collection Interface

In 15 days, we accumulated 140 participants. To detect spammers and low-quality participants, we used 123 screening sentences (48 *NFS*s, 32 *UFS*s and 43 *CFS*s). These sentences were picked from all debate episodes. Three domain experts agreed upon their labels. On average, one out of every ten sentences given to a participant (without letting the participant know) was randomly chosen to be a screening question and selected from the pool of 123 sentences. The participants were scored in the range of [0.0, 1.0] based on their performance on the screening sentences. Those scored more than 0.85 were considered top-quality participants.

We aimed to get the latest debates labeled first. Sentences from one debate episode were randomly presented to the participants. Once all sentences in an episode were labeled by at least two participants, we moved on to the next episode. The data collection is still in progress. So far, 2012, 2008 and 2004 presidential debates (12 debate episodes) have been labeled. For training and evaluating our classification models, we only used a sentence if its label was agreed upon by two top-quality participants. Thereby we got 1571 sentences (882 *NFS*s, 252 *UFS*s, 437 *CFS*s). Figure 4a shows the distribution of these sentences' class labels. One interesting observation is that recent presidential candidates were making more check-worthy factual claims than earlier candidates.

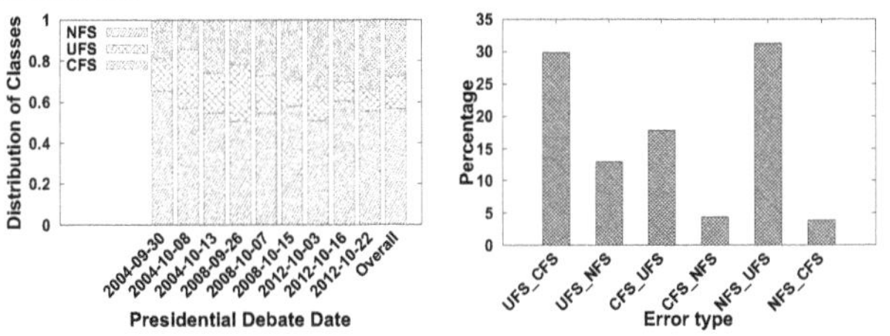

(a) Class Distribution (b) Error Distribution

Figure 4

Category	Type	# of Features	Example
Sentiment	continuous	1	-0.5, 0.0, 0.5
Length	discrete	1	5, 10, 50
Word (W)	continuous	6130	*debt, five*
POS Tag (P)	discrete	43	*VBD, CD*
Entity Type (ET)	discrete	26	*Person*

Table 1: Summary of Feature Categories

4. FEATURE EXTRACTION

We extracted multiple categories of features from the sentences. Table 1 summarizes these features. We use the following sentence to explain the features.

When President Bush came into office, we had a budget surplus and the national debt was a little over five trillion.

Sentiment: We used AlchemyAPI[3] to calculate a sentiment score for each sentence. The score ranges from -1 (most negative sentiment) to 1 (most positive sentiment). The above sentence has a sentiment score -0.846376.

Length: This is the word count of a sentence. Natural language toolkit NLTK[4] was used for tokenizing a sentence into words. The example sentence has length 21.

Word (*W*): We used words in sentences to build *tf-idf* features. After discarding rare words that appear in less than three sentences, we got 6130 words. We did not apply stemming or stopword removal.

Parts of Speech (POS) Tag (*P*): We applied NLTK POS tagger on all sentences. There are 43 POS tags in the corpus. We constructed a feature for each tag. For a sentence, the count of words belonging to a POS tag is the value of the corresponding feature. In the example sentence, there are 3 words (*came, had, was*) with POS tag *VBD (Verb, Past Tense)* and 2 words (*five, trillion*) with POS tag *CD (Cardinal Number)*.

Entity Type (*ET*): We used AlchemyAPI to extract entities from the sentences. There are 2727 entities in the labeled sentences. These entities belong to 26 types. The above sentence has an entity *"Bush"* of type *"Person"*. We constructed a feature for each entity type. For a sentence, its number of entities of a particular type is the value of the corresponding feature.

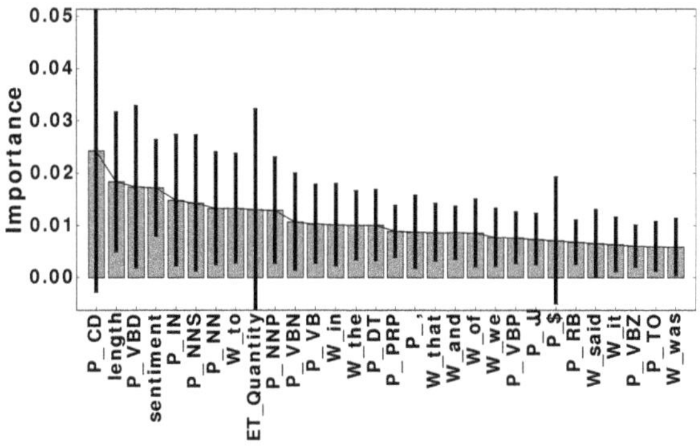

Figure 5: Feature Importance

Feature Selection: There are 6201 features in total. To avoid over-fitting and to attain a simpler model, we performed feature selection. We trained a random forest classifier for which we used GINI index to measure the importance of features in constructing each decision tree. The overall importance of a feature is its average importance over all the trees. Figure 5 shows the importance of the 30 best features in the forest. The black solid lines indicate the standard deviations of importance values. Category types are prefixes to feature names. It is unsurprising that *P_CD* is the top discriminator—check-worthy factual claims are more likely to contain numeric values (*45%* of *CFS* sentences in our dataset contain numeric values) and non-factual sentences are less likely to contain numeric values (*6%* of *NFS* sentences in our dataset contain numeric values). Figure 6 shows the value distributions across all three classes for the four most important features. It depicts the features' discriminative capacities.

5. CLASSIFICATION

We performed 4-fold cross-validation using several supervised learning methods, including Multinomial Naive Bayes Classifier (*NBC*), Support Vector Classifier (*SVM*) and Random Forest Classifier (*RFC*). Table 2 shows these classifiers' performance in terms of precision (p), recall (r), f-measure (f) and Cohen's kappa coefficient (κ). We experimented with four combinations of features—Word (*W*), Word + POS Tag (*W_P*), Word + POS Tag + Entity Type (*W_P_ET*), and the 100 most important features (*best_100*). *Sentiment* and *Length* were included in all the combinations. The *SVM* classifier paired with *W_P* achieved *70%*, *72%* and *70%* weighted average precision, recall and f-measure, respectively. *RFC* and *SVM* outperformed *NBC* in most cases. To understand the level of agreement between classifiers and human participants, we used κ coefficient. According to the guideline set in [7], *RFC* and *SVM* agreed moderately with the participants and *NBC* agreed fairly.

All the classification models had better accuracy on *NFS*s and *CFS*s than *UFS*s. This is not surprising, since *UFS* is

[3]http://www.alchemyapi.com/

[4]http://www.nltk.org/

algorithm	features	p_NFS	p_UFS	p_CFS	p_wavg	r_NFS	r_UFS	r_CFS	r_wavg	f_NFS	f_UFS	f_CFS	f_wavg	κ
NBC	W	0.55	0.00	0.60	0.47	1.00	0.00	0.01	0.55	0.71	0.00	0.02	0.39	0.01
SVM	W	0.75	0.48	0.67	0.69	0.88	0.20	0.64	0.70	0.81	0.27	0.64	0.68	0.45
RFC	W	0.66	0.60	0.85	0.71	0.97	0.03	0.47	0.69	0.78	0.06	0.61	0.62	0.35
NBC	W_P	0.65	0.00	0.79	0.58	0.98	0.00	0.44	0.67	0.78	0.00	0.56	0.59	0.32
SVM	W_P	0.76	0.45	0.69	0.70	0.89	0.22	0.65	0.72	0.82	0.29	0.67	0.70	0.48
RFC	W_P	0.70	0.72	0.73	0.71	0.95	0.04	0.56	0.70	0.81	0.08	0.63	0.64	0.40
NBC	W_P_ET	0.69	0.00	0.77	0.61	0.98	0.00	0.51	0.70	0.81	0.00	0.61	0.63	0.38
SVM	W_P_ET	0.74	0.47	0.70	0.69	0.90	0.23	0.62	0.71	0.81	0.31	0.66	0.69	0.47
RFC	W_P_ET	0.70	0.57	0.77	0.70	0.97	0.04	0.56	0.71	0.81	0.08	0.65	0.65	0.41
NBC	best_100	0.74	0.31	0.67	0.65	0.88	0.21	0.52	0.67	0.80	0.25	0.58	0.66	0.40
SVM	best_100	0.72	0.43	0.76	0.69	0.92	0.13	0.56	0.70	0.80	0.16	0.63	0.66	0.42
RFC	best_100	0.74	0.56	0.68	0.70	0.91	0.14	0.64	0.72	0.82	0.22	0.66	0.68	0.45

Table 2: Comparison of NBC, SVM and RFC coupled with various feature sets, in terms of Precision (p), Recall (r), F-measure (f) and Cohen's kappa coefficient (κ). *wavg* denotes weighted average of corresponding measure across three classes.

between the other two classes and thus the most ambiguous. The top-quality participants faced screening sentences 1395 times and made incorrect judgment 208 times (*14.9%*). Figure 4b shows the percentages of different error types among these 208 cases. For instance, *UFS_CFS* represents the cases in which *UFS*s were incorrectly labeled as *CFS*s by participants. It is evident from this figure that even the top-quality participants made more mistakes when class *UFS* is in question.

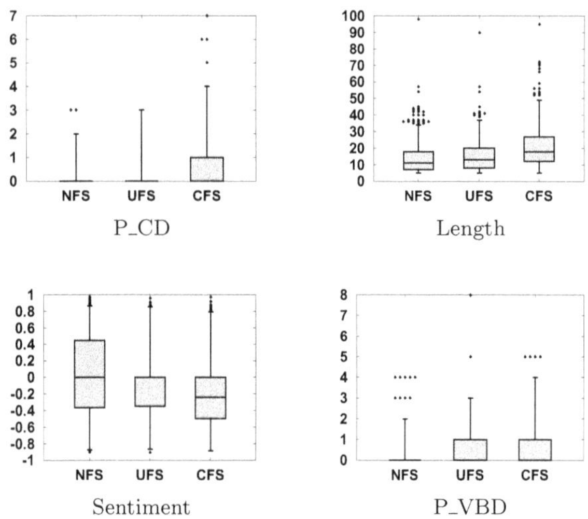

Figure 6: Value Distributions of the Four Most Important Features

6. CONCLUSIONS AND FUTURE WORK

We presented a supervised learning based approach to automatically detect check-worthy factual claims from presidential debate transcripts. We conducted a closely monitored survey to collect labels on sentences from the debates. We performed feature extraction and important feature selection. Preliminary experiment results show that the models achieved *85%* precision and *65%* recall in classifying check-worthy factual claims. We plan to carry on future research along the following directions:

- We will complete label collection for the remaining (1960–2000) debate transcripts. We will analyze how classification performance changes by training data from different years' debates. For the upcoming 2016 U.S. presidential election, we will offer a website that ranks check-worthy factual claims, which can assist journalists and citizens in prioritizing their fact checking endeavor.
- We will extend the study to other types of texts, including interviews, congressional records, and social media.
- We aim at improving feature extraction, feature selection, and classification methods, to obtain better classification accuracy. We also plan to develop methods for tackling claims spanning over multiple sentences.

Acknowledgments The authors have been partially supported by NSF grants IIS-1018865, CCF-1117369 and IIS-1408928. Any opinions, findings, and conclusions in this publication are those of the authors and do not necessarily reflect the views of the funding agencies.

7. REFERENCES

[1] P. Biyani, S. Bhatia, C. Caragea, and P. Mitra. Using non-lexical features for identifying factual and opinionative threads in online forums. *Knowledge-Based Systems*, 69:170–178, 2014.
[2] C. Castillo, M. Mendoza, and B. Poblete. Information credibility on twitter. In *WWW*, pages 675–684, 2011.
[3] S. Cohen, J. T. Hamilton, and F. Turner. Computational journalism. *CACM*, 54(10):66–71, Oct. 2011.
[4] S. Cohen, C. Li, J. Yang, and C. Yu. Computational journalism: A call to arms to database researchers. In *CIDR*, pages 148–151, 2011.
[5] L. Graves. *Deciding What's True: Fact-Checking Journalism and the New Ecology of News*. PhD thesis, COLUMBIA UNIVERSITY, 2013.
[6] A. Gupta, P. Kumaraguru, C. Castillo, and P. Meier. Tweetcred: Real-time credibility assessment of content on twitter. In *Social Informatics*, pages 228–243. 2014.
[7] J. R. Landis and G. G. Koch. The measurement of observer agreement for categorical data. *Biometrics*, pages 159–174, 1977.
[8] B. Nyhan and J. Reifler. The effect of fact-checking on elites: A field experiment on us state legislators. *American Journal of Political Science*, 59(3):628–640, 2015.
[9] A. Vlachos and S. Riedel. Fact checking: Task definition and dataset construction. In *ACL*, pages 18–22, 2014.
[10] J. Wiebe and E. Riloff. Creating subjective and objective sentence classifiers from unannotated texts. In *CICLing*, pages 486–497. 2005.
[11] Y. Wu, P. K. Agarwal, C. Li, J. Yang, and C. Yu. Toward computational fact-checking. In *PVLDB*, pages 589–600, 2014.
[12] H. Yu and V. Hatzivassiloglou. Towards answering opinion questions: Separating facts from opinions and identifying the polarity of opinion sentences. In *EMNLP*, pages 129–136, 2003.
[13] Z. Zhao, P. Resnick, and Q. Mei. Enquiring minds: Early detection of rumors in social media from enquiry posts. In *WWW*, pages 1395–1405, 2015.

Where You Go Reveals Who You Know: Analyzing Social Ties from Millions of Footprints

Hsun-Ping Hsieh
National Taiwan University
Taipei, Taiwan
d98944006@csie.ntu.edu.tw

Rui Yan
Baidu Inc.,
Beijing, China
yanrui02@baidu.com

Cheng-Te Li
Academia Sinica
Taipei, Taiwan
ctli@citi.sinica.edu.tw

ABSTRACT

This paper aims to investigate how the geographical footprints of users correlate to their social ties. While conventional wisdom told us that the more frequently two users colocate in geography, the higher probability they are friends, we find that in real geo-social data, Gowalla and Meetup, almost all of the user pairs with friendships had *never* met geographically. In this sense, can we discover social ties among users *purely* using their geographical footprints even if they never met? To study this question, we develop a two-stage feature engineering framework. The first stage is to characterize the *direct* linkages between users through their spatial co-locations while the second is to capture the *indirect* linkages between them via a *co-location graph.* Experiments conducted on Gowalla check-in data and Meetup meeting events exhibit not only the superiority of our feature model, but also validate the predictability (with 70% accuracy) of detecting social ties solely from user footprints.

1. INTRODUCTION

Location-acquisition techniques and ubiquitous mobile devices, along with the social networking services, foster the emergence of geo-social media, including Facebook Place, Foursquare, Meetup, and Plancast. Geo-social media allows users to not only maintain social connections but also keep track of their geographical footprints that are reflected by either *check-in* records or *social activities* (e.g. dinner gathering, attending conferences, and seeing movies). Both check-in records and social activities consist of latitude-longitude information and time stamps. Such geographical footprints depict where people show up and have face-to-face interactions in the physical world.

In this paper, we aim to uncover the hidden relationship between users' social ties and their geographical footprints. Specifically, we would like to answer the following three questions. First, can we discover social ties *purely* based on the geographical footprints of users? That said, to understand how footprints shape social ties, no social network information can be used. Second, what is the deterministic factor among users' geographical activities that reflect their friendships? Last but not least, is it possible to detect social ties between users even if they do *not* have any geographical footprints, because in real data the fraction that user pairs with friendships had ever met in geography is very low (i.e., only 3%, see Section 2)? We think analyzing geo-social interactions can bring insights for various applications, such as geo-social recommendation, anti-terrorism strategies, and computational advertising.

Table 1: Social & geo-info used to study social ties.

	Social	Direct Linkage							Indirect
	Links	**FoCL**	**CoSL**	**PoCL**	**SoLH**	**PF**	**CF**	**TF**	**Co-location Graph**
[2]	√	√		√				√	
[7]	√	√	√		√			√	
[10]		√			√			√	
[5]	√	√	√	√	√				
[8]	√	√	√	√	√				
[9]		√				√	√	√	
Ours		√	√	√	√	√	√	√	√

Some studies showed how social ties correlate to spatio-temporal co-occurrence [2], group events [7], check-in records [1][9], location history of users [10], and geographical events [11]. Some work leverage geographical information for link prediction [3], such as co-location [5][8]. However, most of them assume a partial social network structure has been observed and used as features when analyzing the geographical properties that affect the formation of social links, or measuring the probability of being acquainted with each other. We think such assumption will prevent us from purely understanding the relationship between footprints and social ties. Therefore, we erase the social effect by setting no social ties are known in prior, and propose a robust set of features to model the direct and indirect linkages between users. To highlight the social and geographical information we consider, comparing to existing work, we create Table 1, in which the abbreviations and the meanings are described in Section 3.

It is very challenging to use solely geographical footprints of users to study social ties. The reason is three-fold. First, assume Alice and Bob do not know each other but they live in the same area and have similar moving behaviors, how to avoid treating them as friends? Second, on the contrary, assume Claire and David are friends but they *never* have interactions in geography, how to reveal their social connection? Third, different individuals have various geographical behaviors due to their personalities. One may be very active on producing her footprints (lead to a rich set records of geographical interactions with others) while another could be very down-to-earth and have very rare encountering infor-

Permission to make digital or hard copies of all or part of this work for personal or classroom use is granted without fee provided that copies are not made or distributed for profit or commercial advantage and that copies bear this notice and the full citation on the first page. Copyrights for components of this work owned by others than ACM must be honored. Abstracting with credit is permitted. To copy otherwise, or republish, to post on servers or to redistribute to lists, requires prior specific permission and/or a fee. Request permissions from Permissions@acm.org.
CIKM '15, Oct 19-23, 2015, Melbourne, Australia
Copyright 2015 ACM 978-1-4503-3794-6/15/10 ...$15.00.
http://dx.doi.org/10.1145/2806416.2806653

mation with friends. How to represent their possible spatial behaviors that characterize social ties?

To answer the three questions, we develop a novel feature engineering framework. We represent the geographical footprints of two users considering various degree of importance on their co-occurrence from the *personal*, *collective*, and *temporal* aspects, which will be validated to deal with some of the aforementioned challenges. Besides the co-location features that depict the possibility of *direct* linkage between nodes, to model the the potential *indirect* friendships among users, we further devise a series of structural features based on a *Co-location Graph* that is constructed from co-location features of users. In the end, we conduct a systematic experiment on two well-known geo-social media datasets, GOWALLA and MEETUP, to evaluate the proposed feature engineering. framework.

2. DEFINITION AND DATASETS

Definition 1: Social Network. A social network is a graph $G = (V, E)$, where V is the set of nodes and E is the set of edges. Each node $v \in V$ is associated with a list of geographical footprints a_v.

Definition 2: Geographical Footprint. The geographical footprint of node v is a sequence of locations and timestamps, $a_v = \langle(l_1^v, t_1^v), (l_2^v, t_2^v), ..., (l_n^v, t_n^v)\rangle$, where each location $l_i \in L_v$ is a geographic coordinate (longitude and latitude), and L_v is the set of locations visited by node v.

Definition 3: Co-location. The geo-footprint $(l_i^u, t_i^u) \in a_u$ and $(l_j^v, t_j^v) \in a_v$ of nodes u and v can form a co-location $c = (l_k, t_k)$ if they satisfy both a spatial condition $dist(l_i^u, l_j^v) < \delta$ and a temporal condition $|t_i^u - t_j^v| < \tau$, where δ and τ are the distance and time thresholds respectively, and l_k is the average geographic position of l_i^u and l_j^v and t_k is the average time of t_i^u and t_j^v. We also denote the set of co-locations of nodes u and v as $C_{uv} = \{c_1, c_2, ...\}$. Note that the settings of δ and τ empirically depends on the various applications, and this study sets $\delta = 20$ (meters) and $\tau = 1$ (hour).

Datasets. We use two datasets in this study, and their statistics are given in Table 2. GOWALLA[1] data, which is crawled from Sep 2011 to Nov 2011, is an online location-based social networking service that allow users to "check-in" their geographical locations and share with their friends. MEETUP[2] is crawled from an event-based social network *meetup.com* from July 2013 to Oct 2013, in which users belong to multiple online social groups, and they can publish and participate geographical events via RSVP ("yes", "no", or "maybe"). Each node represents a user, and two users are connected by an edge if they appear in the same social group at least three times. Note that we have the time of each check-in in Gowalla data, but the Meetup data does not provide event time information. Table 3 reports the numbers of node pairs related to "friends" vs. "non-friends" and "co-location" vs. "no co-location", where "co-location" indicates that two users had ever meet in terms of geography and time. We can find that friends without co-locations take the major fraction, which reflects that users who are friends *nearly never* meet in the physical world (98% for Gowalla and 97% for Meetup).

3. FEATURE ENGINEERING FRAMEWORK

The feature engineering has two stages. We first depict the *direct* linkages between users through their *co-location features*. By first introducing four basic features, which represent the degree of co-location between users. Then by modeling the *personal* importance and the *collective* characteristics of each location and the temporal factor between co-locations, basic features are integrated into personal (PF), collective (CF), and temporal features (TF). The second stage targets at capturing the *indirect* linkages between users who have no co-locations. We construct a *co-location graph* from co-location features of node pairs and develop three categories of structural features: graph-based personal (GPF), collective (GCF), and temporal features (GTF).

[1]https://snap.stanford.edu/data/loc-gowalla.html
[2]http://lsna2012.net76.net/ebsn/

Table 2: Data Statistics.

	Gowalla	Meetup
#Locations	1,280,969	5,183,840 (events)
#GeoActivities	6,442,890 (checkins)	42,733,136 (RSVPs)
#Nodes $\|V\|$	196,591	1,013,453
#Edges $\|E\|$	1,900,654	34,410,754

Table 3: Statistics of node pairs.

	Gowalla	Meetup
Friends & Co-location	40,694	892,117
Friends & No Co-location	1,859,960	33,518,637
Non-Friends & Co-location	482,568	10,173,539
Total	2,342,528	44,584,293

3.1 Co-Location Features

3.1.1 Basic Features

Basic features model the affinity of geographical interactions between users. The idea is two-fold. First, two nodes with higher closeness, frequency, probability, and similarity for their co-locations are expected to have a higher possibility to be acquainted with each other. Second, if the locations of their meetings are more meaningful or important to both nodes, such co-location should be assigned a higher weight which indicates they have higher potential to be friends.

- *Frequency of Co-location.* Two users possess higher meeting frequency tend to have the friendship. We can use the number of their co-locations as the feature value: $FoCL(u, v) = |C_{uv}|$.
- *Closeness of Significant Locations.* If the locations *significantly* visited by two nodes are closer to one another, they have a better likelihood of being friends. We denote the *location significance* of a location l for a node u as $LS(u, l)$, which will be defined under different personal and collective factors in the following. Let the most significant location of node u as $l^\star(u) = \arg\max_{l \in L_u} LS(u, l)$. The feature of closeness of significant locations is defined as: $CoSL(u, v) = \text{dist}(l^\star(u), l^\star(v))$, standing for the geographical distance between their most significant locations.
- *Probability of Co-location.* The co-location probability measures the possibility of two nodes visiting the same location (not necessarily at the same time). We define the co-location probability as: $PoCL(u, v) = \sum_{l \in L_u \cap L_v} LS(u, l) \times LS(v, l)$.
- *Similarity of Location History.* If the location histories of two nodes are more similar to each other, in terms of the locations themselves and the significance, they tend to be friends. We define the similarity as: $SoLH(u, v) = \sum_{l \in L_u \cap L_v} \frac{LS(u,l) \times LS(v,l)}{\|LS(u,l)\| \times \|LS(v,l)\|}$.

3.1.2 Personal Factor

People have different probabilities to visit a particular location. One may prefer to visit a place than another places.

Hence, it is important to consider the personal location history into the measure of location significance $LS(u, l)$. The most intuitive and effective way to model the personal factor is the probability that a node u visits a location l among all of its visits (at any locations), which is defined as $p_{per}(u, l) = \frac{freq(u,l)}{\sum_{l' \in L_u} freq(u,l')}$, where $freq(u, l)$ is the times of visiting of node u at location l.

In addition to the visiting probability at a specific location, a more general way to model the personal factor is consider the probability of traveling around a *region*, because sometimes people prefer to visit a certain district containing multiple locations. For a node u, we use a density function with respect to the geographical distances between a certain location l and all the locations visited by u, given by:

$$d(u, l) = \sum_{l' \in L_u} \frac{\exp(-\rho_d \cdot \text{dist}(l, l'))}{freq(u, l)}, \quad (1)$$

where ρ_d is a parameter that implicitly determines the area of a region. A larger ρ_d may refer to a certain suburb district (e.g. an amusement park or zoo) while a smaller ρ_d may be suitable for an urban district. We choose a small $\rho_d = 1.5$ since the data we use for experiments is an urban area.

We can treat the probability $p_{per}(u, l)$ and the density $d(u, l)$ as the weight of $FoCL$, i.e., $w_{uv}^{p_{per}} = \arg\max_{l \in L_u \cap L_v} - \log(p_{per}(u, l) \cdot p_{per}(v, l))$ and $w_{uv}^{d} = \arg\max_{l \in L_u \cap L_v} - \log(d(u, l) \cdot d(v, l))$, and derive two personal features: $w_{uv}^{p_{per}} \times FoCL(u, v)$ and $w_{uv}^{d} \times FoCL(u, v)$. In addition, both $p_{per}(u, l)$ and $d(u, l)$ are considered as the measure location significance $LS(u, l)$. Therefore, there are 3 basic (i.e., $CoLS$, $PoCL$ and $SoLH$) $\times$ 2 personal (i.e., $p_{per}(u, l)$ and $d(u, l)$) = 6 features. Totally we have 8 personal features.

3.1.3 Collective Factor

The collective factor of a location reflects the visiting behaviors of the general public (i.e., all the users in the data). Some locations are frequently visited by a number of users such as famous landmarks and transportation sites while other locations are more specific to only a few persons, such as a private house. Those people co-locating at a *public* place tends to be strangers who encounter by coincidence. In contrast, co-locating at a *private* place has higher potential to be friends. We take advantage of *location entropy* [4] to model the collective factor of a location. We first define the probability that a node u visits a location l among all the visits by all the nodes in the data as: $p_{col}(u, l) = \frac{freq(u,l)}{\sum_{u \in V} \sum_{l' \in L_u} freq(u,l')}$. Then the entropy of a location l can be defined as:

$$e(l) = - \sum_{\{u : u \in V \text{and} p_{col}(u,l) \neq 0\}} p_{col}(u, l) \cdot \log(p_{col}(u, l)). \quad (2)$$

A high entropy $e(l)$ means location l is a public place at which many people have ever visited while a low $e(l)$ implies l tends to be a private place that is visited by few users.

Similar to the personal features, we can consider the location entropy $e(l)$ as the weight of $FoCL$, and derive a collective feature: $\sum_{l \in L_u \cap L_v} \exp(-e(l))$. In addition, $e(l)$ can be regarded as the location significance $LS(u, l)$, and thus we have three additional collective features (i.e., $CoLS$, $PoCL$ and $SoLH$). Totally we have 4 collective features.

3.1.4 Temporal Factor

Considering consecutive co-locations of two users, the *time gaps* of friends are different from those of strangers who meet occasionally. Strangers have higher possibility (but not absolutely) to co-locate with each other up to several times within a short time period (e.g. several times in a day), such as traveling by the same train or doing daily routines to work there and back. As for friends, on the contrary, the time gaps of their co-locations have much higher potential to be longer (e.g. once after several days or weeks). Therefore, we think the time gap is an indispensable factor to characterize the co-locations between two persons. We define the time gap between two co-locations l_{k-1} and l_k as: $g(l_{k-1}, l_k) = \exp(-\rho_t \cdot (t_{l_k} - t_{l_{k-1}}))$, where ρ_t is a parameter that controls the extent of correlation between time gap and friendship, and should be determined by the types of co-location events. Similar to ρ_d, we empirically choose $\rho_t = 0.3$.

Similar to the personal and collective features, $g(l_{k-1}, l_k)$ is treated as the weight of $FoCL$: $w_{uv}^{t}(l_k) = 1 - g(l_{k-1}, l_k)$. Thus we can have a temporal feature: $\sum_{l_k \leftarrow \text{sort}(L_u \cap L_v)} w_{uv}^{t}(l_k)$, where sort() orders the co-locations by time, "$\leftarrow$" gets the co-location by time, and $k > 1$.

Table 4: The list of graph features computed on $\mathbb{G}$.

GF	Formula
Sum	$\sum_{z \in \Gamma_u} s(u, z) + \sum_{y \in \Gamma_v} s(v, y)$
pref-att	$\sum_{z \in \Gamma_u} s(u, z) \times \sum_{y \in \Gamma_v} s(v, y)$
ComNbr	$\sum_{z \in \Gamma_u \cap \Gamma_v} s(u, z) \times s(v, z)$
Jaccard	$\frac{\sum_{z \in \Gamma_u \cap \Gamma_v} s(u,z) \times s(v,z)}{\sum_{z \in \Gamma_u \cup \Gamma_v} s(u,z) \times s(v,x)}$
Ada-Adar	$\sum_{z \in \Gamma_u \cap \Gamma_v} \frac{1}{\log(\sum_{y \in \Gamma_z} s(z,y))}$
Katz	$\sum_{len=1}^{\infty} \sum_{p \in path_{u,v}^{\langle len \rangle}} \prod_{(y,z) \in p} s(y, z)$
RWR	$\frac{RWR(u,v) + RWR(v,u)}{2}$

3.2 Graph Features

The co-location features aim to characterize the relationships between users using their geographical footprints. However, not all of the users have *rich* and plentiful spatio-temporal footprints. Some may be very enthusiastic to leave their geographical activities in a digital form (e.g. via doing check-in actions or responding to R.S.V.P. of social events) while other people might have the geographical interactions with only few of their friends. In addition, users can have no *direct* co-locations with their friends (as exhibited in Table 2), and thus using purely co-location features might not be able to capture all of their social relationships. Therefore, we propose to construct a *co-location graph* from co-location features, and extract a series of graph features that refine the predictability via *transitivity* of co-location relationships. The idea is similar to link prediction [3]: if two individuals have more common co-locating persons with similar co-location features, they are more likely to be friends. In the following, we define the co-location graph and the graph features that are extended from link prediction [3].

Definition 4: Co-location Graph. A co-location graph is a weighted graph $\mathbb{G} = (V, \mathbb{E})$, where V is the set of nodes (the same as V in the network G), and $\mathbb{E}$ is a set of edges that represent the *co-location relationships* between nodes. Each edge $(u, v) \in \mathbb{E}$ is associated with a weight $s_{uv} = [0, 1]$ that stands for the strength of co-location relationship, which is defined as a normalized feature score of nodes u and v: $s_{uv} = \frac{\log(fs(u,v)+1)}{\log(\arg\max_{u,v \in V} fs(u,v)+1)}$, where $fs(u, v)$ is the feature score of one of the co-location features described above. Note that, to avoid too many edges being constructed, we use a threshold parameter μ to filter out edges with lower s_{uv}. We set $\mu = 0.2$ by default.

By extending link prediction features [3], Table 4 lists the graph features (GF) based on the co-location strength values on edges in the co-location graph $\mathbb{G}$, in which Γ_u is the set of neighbors of node u in $\mathbb{G}$, $path_{u,v}^{\langle len \rangle}$ is the set of paths of length len between nodes u and v, and $RWR(u,v)$ [6] restarts from u. We construct a location graph for each co-location feature, Graph-based Personal/Collective/Temporal Features (GPF/GCF/GTF), and the list of graph features is computed for each $\mathbb{G}$.

4. EXPERIMENTS

The experiment consists of two parts: *feature-based user pair ranking* and *social tie detection*. The former is an unsupervised method to present the effectiveness of various feature sets while the latter uses a supervised learning method to determine whether a given user pair has a friendship.

Feature-based User Pair Ranking. We rank all pairs of nodes in the social network using each feature set, select *top* N node pairs, and compute the ratio of node pairs with social ties (termed Accuracy@N) by varying N. Note that to we simply use geometric mean to combine the feature values of each feature category (i.e., PF, CF, and TF). While the MEETUP data do not have timestamps for user meeting events, we do not report the results of TF and GTF for the MEETUP part. In addition to all user pairs, to understand whether our feature engineering model can identify users who have friendships but no geographical interactions, we also report the results of user pairs who do not have any co-location, termed by "No Co-location (NCL) user pairs." The results are shown in Table 5. We can find that for lower N (= 50, 100), our feature model is able to near perfectly distinguish friends from non-friends user pairs. However, as N increases, the distinguish ability decreases, especially being drastic for conventional features PF, CF, and TF. The accuracy values of our co-location graph-based features GPF, GCF, and GTF are much more stable, and using *all* the features can achieve the best accuracy. Moreover, by looking into the results of "no co-location user pairs," the superiority of GPF, GCF, and GTF is more clear. Since PF, CF, and GTF highly depend on co-locations of users, their accuracy values are generally very low under this case. Such results indicate that the proposed graph-based features are capable of identifying friends who have no geographical meetings. Nevertheless, the accuracy values of $N > 1000$ are still very low. Hence we resort to the supervised learning to detect whether any given user pair has a social tie in the following.

Social Tie Detection. We divide node pairs in the social network into $R\%$ training instances and $1 - R\%$ testing instances (R = 20, 80). The *Area under the ROC Curve* (AUC) are used as evaluation metrics. Node pairs with social ties (ground truth) are treated as *positive* instances. We use Random Forest, Support Vector Machine, and Logistic Regression as the supervised learning methods. Since different learning methods exhibit very similar results, here we report the results of Random Forest due to the page limit. The results are shown in Table 6. We can find three things. First, the GPF, GCG, and GTF still generally outperform PF, CF, and TF, especially on "no co-location user pairs." Second, using only geographical footprints (no social network information are employed) can achieve up to 70% AUC. This result tells us that social ties are able to be successfully detected through indirect linkages in the proposed co-location graph. Third, even using 20% pairs as the training set can lead to AUC around 60%.

Table 5: Results of feature-based user pair ranking.

	Top-N Ranked User Pairs											
	Gowalla							Meetup				
	PF	CF	TF	GPF	GCF	GTF	All	PF	CF	GPF	GCF	All
50	**0.90**	**0.97**	**0.98**	**0.96**	**0.98**	**0.98**	**0.99**	**1.00**	**1.00**	**1.00**	**1.00**	**1.00**
100	**0.95**	**0.88**	**0.96**	**0.97**	**0.93**	**0.95**	**0.98**	**0.98**	**0.98**	**1.00**	**0.99**	**1.00**
500	0.70	0.62	0.71	**0.85**	0.77	0.79	**0.88**	**0.96**	**0.96**	**0.98**	**0.96**	**0.98**
1000	0.43	0.38	0.43	0.64	0.56	0.55	0.68	0.64	0.60	0.78	0.73	**0.81**
5000	0.12	0.11	0.10	0.51	0.47	0.44	0.55	0.31	0.29	0.62	0.59	0.65
10000	0.07	0.06	0.06	0.33	0.28	0.27	0.35	0.26	0.26	0.39	0.33	0.43
	Top-N Ranked "No Co-Location" User Pairs											
	Gowalla							Meetup				
	PF	CF	TF	GPF	GCF	GTF	All	PF	CF	GPF	GCF	All
50	0.000	0.000	0.000	**0.62**	**0.58**	**0.60**	**0.69**	0.000	0.000	0.46	0.44	0.49
100	0.020	0.010	0.010	**0.53**	0.47	**0.51**	**0.61**	0.000	0.000	0.38	0.37	0.41
500	0.008	0.006	0.005	0.44	0.41	0.39	0.46	0.003	0.002	0.32	0.32	0.35
1000	0.007	0.004	0.006	0.23	0.21	0.22	0.29	0.005	0.004	0.18	0.17	0.20
5000	0.005	0.004	0.005	0.16	0.15	0.11	0.19	0.003	0.003	0.11	0.10	0.14
10000	0.007	0.007	0.006	0.13	0.11	0.12	0.15	0.004	0.003	0.09	0.08	0.13

Table 6: Results of AUC for social tie detection.

	80% Training, 20% Testing				**20% Training, 80% Testing**			
	User Pairs		**NCL User Pairs**		User Pairs		**NCL User Pairs**	
	Gowalla	Meetup	Gowalla	Meetup	Gowalla	Meetup	Gowalla	Meetup
PF	0.66	**0.73**	0.20	0.02	0.48	**0.64**	0.16	0.02
CF	0.62	**0.74**	0.16	0.02	0.43	**0.64**	0.15	0.02
TF	0.65	N/A	0.14	N/A	0.47	N/A	0.11	N/A
GPF	**0.73**	**0.75**	0.66	0.68	**0.66**	**0.67**	0.52	**0.60**
GCF	**0.70**	**0.76**	0.67	0.69	**0.64**	**0.68**	0.57	**0.60**
GTF	**0.71**	N/A	0.65	N/A	**0.66**	N/A	0.47	N/A
All	**0.74**	**0.77**	0.68	0.69	**0.68**	**0.68**	0.59	**0.63**

5. CONCLUSIONS

This paper analyzes social ties using solely geographical footprints of users in GOWALLA and MEETUP data, considering the observation that friends are quite rare to meet in the physical world. We develop a novel feature engineering model composed by a robust set of co-location and structural features. We believe our feature model can benefit for both link prediction and recommendation tasks to not only further boost the prediction accuracy but also deal with the link sparsity problem in cold-start scenarios.

6. ACKNOWLEDGEMENT

This work was sponsored by Ministry of Science and Technology of Taiwan under grant 104-2221-E-001-027-MY2. This work is also supported by Multidisciplinary Health Cloud Research Program: Technology Development and Application of Big Health Data, Academia Sinica, Taipei, Taiwan under grant MP10212-0318.

7. REFERENCES

[1] E. Cho, S. A. Myers, and J. Leskovec. Friendship and mobility: User movement in location-based social networks. In *KDD*, 2011.

[2] D. J. Crandall, L. Backstrom, D. Cosley, S. Suri, D. Huttenlocher, and J. Kleinberg. Inferring social ties from geographic coincidences. *PNAS*, 2010.

[3] D. Liben-Nowell and J. Kleinberg. The link prediction problem for social networks. In *CIKM*, 2003.

[4] H. Pham, C. Shahabi, and Y. Liu. Ebm: An entropy-based model to infer social strength from spatiotemporal data. In *SIGMOD*, 2013.

[5] S. Scellato, A. Noulas, and C. Mascolo. Exploiting place features in link prediction on location-based social networks. In *KDD*, 2011.

[6] H. Tong, C. Faloutsos, and J.-Y. Pan. Fast random walk with restart and its applications. In *ICDM*, 2006.

[7] C. Wang, M. Ye, and W.-C. Lee. From face-to-face gathering to social structure. In *CIKM*, 2012.

[8] D. Wang, D. Pedreschi, C. Song, F. Giannotti, and A.-L. Barabasi. Human mobility, social ties, and link prediction. In *KDD*, 2011.

[9] H. Wang, Z. Li, and W.-C. Lee. Pgt: Measuring mobility relationship using personal, global and temporal factors. In *ICDM*, 2014.

[10] X. Xiao, Y. Zheng, Q. Luo, and X. Xie. Inferring social ties between users with human location history. *Journal of Ambient Intelligence and Humanized Computing*, 5(1), 2014.

[11] P. Yin, Q. He, X. Liu, and W.-C. Lee. It takes two to tango: Exploring social tie development with both online and offline interactions. In *SDM*, 2014.

Message Clustering based Matrix Factorization Model for Retweeting Behavior Prediction

Bo Jiang, Jiguang Liang, Ying Sha, Lihong Wang
National Engineering Laboratory for Information Security Technologies
Institute of Information Engineering, Chinese Academy of Sciences
Beijing 100190, China
{jiangbo, liangjiguang, shaying, wanglihong}@iie.ac.cn

ABSTRACT

Retweeting is an important mechanism for information diffusion in social networks. Through retweeting, message is reshared from one user to another user, forming large cascades of message forwarding. Most existing researches of predicting retweeting utilize user social relationships for modeling which leads to vast calculating amount. In this paper, we propose two message clustering based matrix factorization models for retweeting prediction. Unlike previous approaches, our models exploit the clustering relationships of messages instead of social relationships. Our models are quite general because we do not need any auxiliary information except for message content. Several experiments on real datasets show that our models are effective and outperform the state-of-the-art methods.

Categories and Subject Descriptors

H.2.8 [**Database and Management**]: Data Mining; J.4 [**Social and Behavioral Sciences**]: Sociology

General Terms

Theory, Experimentation

Keywords

Retweeting Prediction; Clustering; Matrix Factorization

1. INTRODUCTION

Social media platforms such as Facebook, Twitter and Weibo play an increasingly important role for human interaction and information diffusion, where people can not only follow popular celebrities and experts, but also share interesting information with their peers. In particular, retweeting is one of the most important functions in social networks. Through this feature, message can be rapidly spread to hundreds of thousands of people. This causes messages to forward from user to user, forming large cascades of information [2]. Hence, understanding the mechanisms of retweeting and predicting who will retweet are important tasks to monitor the spread of information. But how do we predict retweeting behavior?

To achieve the task, considerable efforts [1, 4, 5, 6, 7, 8] have been conducted. Luo et al. [4] explored plenty of features, such as retweeting history, followers status, followers active time and followers interests, to find who will retweet a message posted on Twitter. Zhang et al. [8] conducted an investigation to verify the existence of influence locality in microblogging network and proposed an social influence locality based model for retweeting behaviors prediction. Can et al. [1] utilized content, structure and image based features to predict the retweeting count of tweets which link an image. Although these methods have been obtained some significantly performance in users' retweeting behavior prediction, many of them have their own unique purposes and features. This causes that these feature-based approaches are too dependent on manually defined features, and the lack of any important feature may lead to poor performance. Recently, Wang et al. [6] proposed a nonnegative matrix factorization framework with social regularization for retweeting prediction. As well as previous works, they employed strength of social relationships to constrain objective function and obtained a relatively satisfactory prediction result. However, it has to compute the similarity between every pair of users to determine neighborhoods which leads to expensive computation. This is not computationally feasible for rewteeting prediction with millions of users in social networks.

In this paper, aiming at solving the problem mentioned above, we propose two message clustering based matrix factorization models for retweeting behavior prediction. Unlike the previous researches, we utilize the clustering relationships information among messages to improve the prediction accuracy of retweeting. More specifically, we argue that if two messages are similar (or belong to the same cluster) in the observation space, they are also similar in the latent space as shown in Figure 1. We call this phenomenon as "similarity consistency". Then, those similarity consistency information are employed in designing two message regularization terms to constrain the matrix factorization objective function. Our proposed approaches are quite general, and they can be applied to predict retweeting behavior for any social network platforms. The experimental analysis shows that our models outperform the state-of-the-art algorithms.

The rest of the paper is organized as follows: In Section 2, we give a formal definition of our problem. Section 3 presents our models. We describe our experimental study in Section 4 and conclude in Section 5.

Permission to make digital or hard copies of all or part of this work for personal or classroom use is granted without fee provided that copies are not made or distributed for profit or commercial advantage and that copies bear this notice and the full citation on the first page. Copyrights for components of this work owned by others than the author(s) must be honored. Abstracting with credit is permitted. To copy otherwise, or republish, to post on servers or to redistribute to lists, requires prior specific permission and/or a fee. Request permissions from Permissions@acm.org.
CIKM'15, October 19–23, 2015, Melbourne, Australia.
Copyright is held by the owner/author(s). Publication rights licensed to ACM.
ACM 978-1-4503-3794-6/15/10 ...$15.00.
DOI: http://dx.doi.org/10.1145/2806416.2806650 .

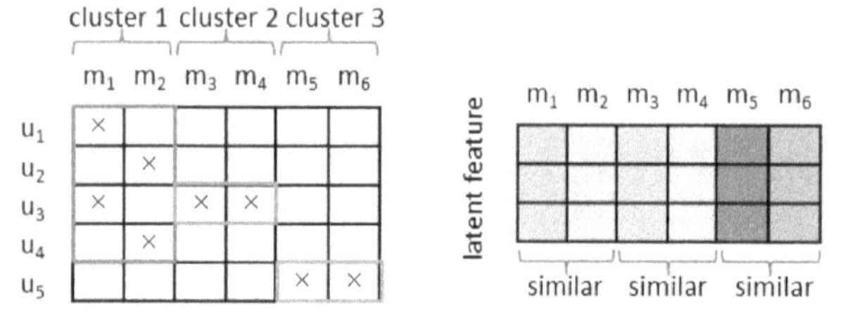

(a) user-message matrix (R) (b) latent feature-message matrix (V)

Figure 1: Similarity consistency in the observed and latent space.

2. PROBLEM STATEMENT

Suppose that we have M users with the i-th user denoted as u_i, and N messages with the j-th message denoted as m_j. These messages can be grouped into K clusters. For the k-th cluster, it could be represented by $C_k = \{c_{k1}, c_{k2}, \cdots, c_{kn}\}$ where each c_{ki} is a message from $\{m_j\}_{j=1}^N$ and n is the size of the cluster.

We denote the user-message retweeting matrix as $R \in \mathbb{R}^{M\times N}$ where $R_{ij} = 1$ if u_i retweets m_j and $R_{ij} = -1$ otherwise. Let $U \in \mathbb{R}^{M\times L}$ be the latent user feature matrix, in which each row corresponds to a user and L ($L \ll M, N$) is the number of the latent features. $V \in \mathbb{R}^{L\times N}$ is the latent message feature matrix where $V_j = [V_{1j}, V_{2j}, \cdots, V_{Lj}]^T$ stands for the representation of m_j in latent feature space.

The problem we study in this paper is how to effectively predict the missing values of R.

3. METHODOLOGY

In this section, the retweeting prediction problem will be converted to matrix factorization problem. More specifically, we propose two message clustering based models exploiting similarity consistency phenomenon.

3.1 Basic Matrix Factorization Model

The standard matrix factorization model maps both users and messages to a joint latent factor space, so that user retweeting behavior can be modeled as inner products in that space, i.e. $R_{ij} \approx U_iV_j$. To learn the latent factors, it minimizes the regularized squared error on the set of known retweeting behaviors

$$\min_{U,V} \mathcal{J}(R,U,V) = \frac{1}{2}\sum_{i=1}^{M}\sum_{j=1}^{N} I_{ij}(R_{ij} - U_iV_j)^2 + \frac{\beta}{2}\|U\|_F^2 + \frac{\gamma}{2}\|V\|_F^2 \tag{1}$$

where $\|\cdot\|_F$ is the Frobenius 2-norm, β and γ are regularization parameters. $I_{ij} \in \{0, 1\}$ indicates whether R_{ij} is observed. The last two regularization terms are added to avoid overfitting. In general, gradient descent techniques are always used to find local optimal solutions.

3.2 Centroid-based Regularization Prediction Model (CRPM)

In this section, we propose a novel message clustering based matrix factorization model, called centroid-based regularization prediction model (CRPM), for retweeting prediction. Unlike the previous works which employ user social relationships, CRPM exploits clustering relationships among messages for constraints. We argue that these clustering information have an impact on user retweeting behavior on account of the assumption that users are more likely to retweet similar content due to their personal interests. More precisely, we firstly group messages into clusters. Messages that are similar to one another within the same cluster and are dissimilar to messages in other clusters. We believe that if message m_j is grouped to cluster C_k in observed spaces, it should be consistent with the latent space. Hence, once the clusters are created, in latent message feature space, an individual message should more close to the centroid of that cluster to which it belongs. Under this scenario, we may arrive at the following cluster centroid regularizer

$$\sum_{j=1}^{N}\sum_{k=1}^{K} T_{jk}\|V_j - \frac{1}{|C_k|}\sum_{m_x\in C_k} V_x\|_F^2 \tag{2}$$

where T_{jk} is a indicator function that is equal to 1 if the j-th message belongs to the k-th cluster and equal to 0 otherwise. The details on how to cluster messages will be explained in Section 3.4. Then, we can obtain the following objective function through imposing the above cluster-based regularization term (2) onto (1):

$$\begin{aligned}\min_{U,V} \mathcal{J}(R,U,V) = &\frac{1}{2}\sum_{i=1}^{M}\sum_{j=1}^{N} I_{ij}(R_{ij} - U_iV_j)^2 \\ &+ \frac{\alpha_1}{2}\sum_{j=1}^{N}\sum_{k=1}^{K} T_{jk}\|V_j - \frac{1}{|C_k|}\sum_{m_x\in C_k} V_x\|_F^2 \\ &+ \frac{\beta}{2}\|U\|_F^2 + \frac{\gamma}{2}\|V\|_F^2\end{aligned} \tag{3}$$

where α_1 is a positive regularization parameter.

In this paper, stochastic gradient descent method is used to solve the problem. Specifically, the gradients of the objective function with respect to U_i and V_j are

$$\frac{\partial\mathcal{J}}{\partial U_i} = \sum_{j=1}^{N} I_{ij}(R_{ij} - U_iV_j)(-V_j) + \beta U_i \tag{4}$$

$$\begin{aligned}\frac{\partial\mathcal{J}}{\partial V_j} = &\sum_{i=1}^{M} I_{ij}(R_{ij} - U_iV_j)(-U_i) + \gamma V_j \\ &+ \alpha_1\sum_{k=1}^{K} T_{jk}(V_j - \frac{1}{|C_k|}\sum_{m_x\in C_k} V_x)(1 - \frac{1}{|C_k|}).\end{aligned} \tag{5}$$

3.3 Individual-based Regularization Prediction Model (IRPM)

CRPM emphatically considers the constraint on an individual message and the cluster to which it belongs. Factually, similar messages within a cluster in observed space are expected to be close to each other in the latent feature space. Therefore, we propose another regularization term to constrain messages in a cluster

$$\sum_{j=1}^{N}\sum_{k=1}^{K} T_{jk}\sum_{m_x\in C_k} S(j,x)\|V_j - V_x\|_F^2 \tag{6}$$

where $S(j,x)$ stands for the similarity between m_j and m_x, and the next section will introduce the details. Hence, it can be formulated as solving the following objective function

$$\min_{U,V} \mathcal{J}(R,U,V) = \frac{1}{2}\sum_{i=1}^{M}\sum_{j=1}^{N} I_{ij}(R_{ij} - U_iV_j)^2 + \frac{\alpha_2}{2}\sum_{j=1}^{N}\sum_{k=1}^{K} T_{jk}\sum_{m_x \in C_k} S(j,x)\|V_j - V_x\|_F^2 + \frac{\beta}{2}\|U\|_F^2 + \frac{\gamma}{2}\|V\|_F^2 \quad (7)$$

where $\alpha_2 > 0$. Similar to CRPM, the gradients of the objective function with respect to the variables are

$$\frac{\partial \mathcal{J}}{\partial U_i} = \sum_{j=1}^{N} I_{ij}(R_{ij} - U_iV_j)(-V_j) + \beta U_i \quad (8)$$

$$\frac{\partial \mathcal{J}}{\partial V_j} = \sum_{i=1}^{M} I_{ij}(R_{ij} - U_iV_j)(-U_i) + \gamma V_j + \alpha_2 \sum_{k=1}^{K} T_{jk}\sum_{m_x \in C_k} S(j,x)(V_j - V_x). \quad (9)$$

3.4 Message Clustering

Clustering is the critical and important step in our approaches because the clusters give the centroid or neighborhoods of the active messages. All the computations following clustering step depends on the clusters. In this section, we are concerned with clustering techniques using messages' structure and content features.

Structure-Based Features: Many works [4, 6, 7] have shown that messages' structure characteristics that whether contains hashtag, URL, media or not, are important factors for affecting users' retweeting behaviors. Hence, we take the number of hashtag, URL, media and mention as prediction features in our framework.

Content-Based Features: There is a consensus among researchers that users prefer to post or retweet a message which he is interested in. Furthermore, users' interests can be reflected in the content of users' messages, and users who retweet similar kinds of messages may have similar interests. Therefore, for better describing and understanding messages in semantic space, we use paragraph vector [3], an unsupervised vector-based approach which can model rich semantic information, to learn the vector representations of messages.

Hence, the vector of message presented to be clustered is a concatenation of two vectors, one from structure-based features and one from content-based features. In this paper, K-means algorithm is used for clustering.

In addition, we also use the vectors mentioned above to calculate the similarities among messages. More specifically, the similarity between m_i and m_j is calculated as

$$S(i,j) = \lambda \times S_{structure}(i,j) + (1-\lambda) \times S_{content}(i,j) \quad (10)$$

where λ is employed to control the contribution of each factor and we set $\lambda = 0.5$ in this paper. $S_{structure}(i,j)$ and $S_{content}(i,j)$ are cosine similarities based on structure-based vectors and content-based vectors, respectively.

Table 1: Retweeting data statistics

Dataset	#Users	#Tweets	#Retweets	Sparseness
D_{100}	15,544	100	15,678	$\frac{1}{100}$
D_{200}	27,117	200	27,649	$\frac{1}{200}$
D_{500}	74,184	500	78,223	$\frac{1}{500}$
D_{1000}	133,620	1,000	147,889	$\frac{1}{1000}$

Table 2: Tradeoff parameters for CRPM on D_{100}. (L = 30)

α_1	β	γ	F_1-value	Accuracy
10^{-4}	10^{-4}	10^{-3}	0.632	0.636
10^{-4}	10^{-4}	10^{-4}	0.780	0.779
10^{-3}	10^{-4}	10^{-4}	0.814	0.813
10^{-3}	10^{-3}	10^{-4}	**0.823**	**0.821**
10^{-3}	10^{-3}	10^{-5}	0.821	0.820

4. EXPERIMENTS

In this section, we conduct several experiments to compare the retweeting prediction qualities of our approaches with other state-of-the-art methods. Impacts brought by parameters, latent feature number and iteration number are further discussed.

4.1 Datasets Description

To evaluate the performance of our models, a publicly available Sina Weibo dataset collected by Zhang et al. [8] is employed. Our models are quite general, and can be utilized to predict retweeting with any sparse matrices. Hence, in this paper, we reconstruct four datasets which are randomly selected from the above dataset. Detailed statistics of the four sub-datasets are summarized in Table 1. However, we observe that positive instances (retweeting) and negative instances (un-retweeting) are much unbalanced. Thus we randomly select a subset of negative instances with the equal number of positive number for experiments.

4.2 Experimental Settings

The training/testing sets are from a random 80% and 20% split of the constructed datasets. The corresponding entries in R of positive and negative instances for training are set to ± 1. The testing entries and the rest entries are set to 0. The cluster number is set to $K = \#Tweets/10$. After training, we use the learned approximate entries as feature for retweeting classification with Liblinear[1] as classifier. Four popular metrics, Precision, Recall, F_1-value and Accuracy, are employed to measure the retweeting prediction qualities of our proposed approaches.

4.3 Parameter Settings

Here we focus on parameter settings. We investigate the performances of our models when the parameters change.

Tradeoff Parameters: The tradeoff parameters α_1, α_2, β and γ in our models play the role of adjusting the strengths of different terms in the objective functions. The impact of α_2 generally shares the same trend as the impact of α_1. Hence we only discuss the influences of α_1 here due to the space limitation. Taking the scales of U and V into account, we scan orders of magnitude and try different combinations

[1]http://www.csie.ntu.edu.tw/ cjlin/liblinear/

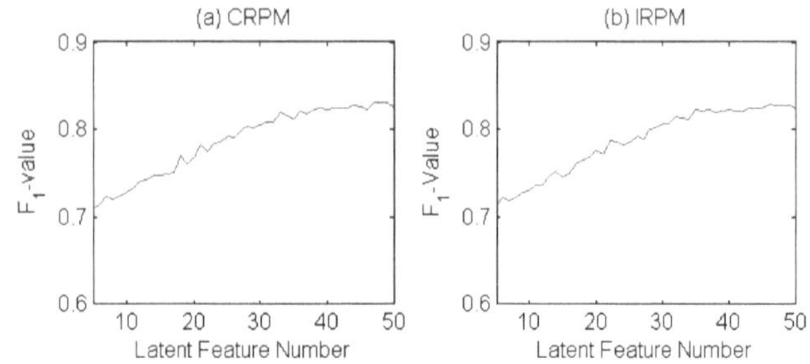

Figure 2: F_1-value vs. Latent Feature Number (L) on D_{100}.

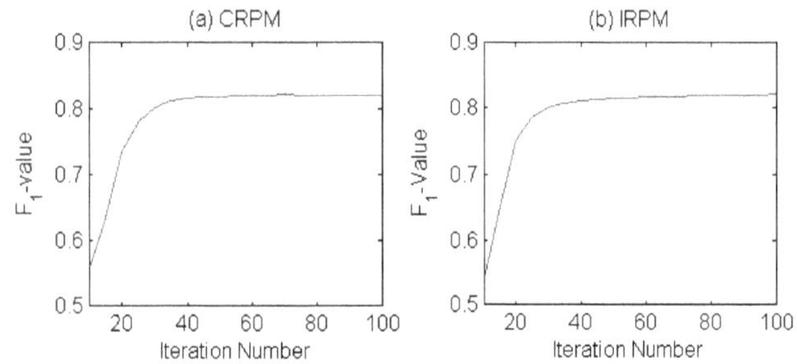

Figure 3: F_1-value vs. Iteration Number on D_{100}.

of parameters as shown in Table 2. We use the fourth row for all datasets. Although they are not the perfect ones, the following experiments demonstrate they are adequate.

Number of Latent Features: We train U and V to find the proper number of latent features L for users and messages. More specifically, we conduct experiments with L from 5 to 50 on D_{100} dataset. The results are shown in Figure 2, from which we can find that with the latent feature number L increasing, F_1-value increases gradually. We can also observe that F_1-value becomes stable when $L > 30$. Therefore, considering the calculation effect and time efficiency, we choose $L = 30$ as the latent space dimension in our experiments.

Number of Iterations: Figure 3 illustrates the impacts of the number of iterations on F_1-value. It is observed that it is better to run 30 iterations in order to reach a converged result with an acceptable time cost.

4.4 Prediction Performance

Table 3 shows the average results of the 5 runs with the 30 dimensions to represent the latent features. It should be noted that [6] and [8] share the same original dataset with us. From the results, we can draw the following observations: (1) Our models consistently obtain good performance in all datasets with different sparseness which shows our models have good robustness; (2) The two proposed models achieve a comparable performance with each other. Both of them could accurate in capturing the clustering relationships between two messages; (3) CRPM and IRPM could generate better results than the social influence locality based models (LRC) and the state-of-the-art matrix factorization based algorithm (MNMFRP) even with less similarity calculation. In general, the results suggest that our proposed models provide a new thought for retweeting behavior prediction in social networks.

Table 3: Performance of retweeting behavior prediction.

Dataset	Method	Pre.	Rec.	F_1	Acc.
D_{100}	CRPM	0.814	0.833	0.823	0.821
	IRPM	0.817	0.833	0.825	0.823
D_{200}	CRPM	0.801	0.833	0.816	0.813
	IRPM	0.803	0.831	0.824	0.813
D_{500}	CRPM	0.809	0.844	0.826	0.822
	IRPM	0.809	0.844	0.826	0.822
D_{1000}	CRPM	0.803	0.839	0.821	0.817
	IRPM	0.801	0.837	0.818	0.814
Zhang [8]	LRC-B	0.681	0.742	0.710	0.697
	LRC-Q	0.668	0.772	0.716	0.694
	LRC-BQ	0.698	0.770	0.733	0.719
Wang [6]	MNMFRP	0.796	0.791	0.793	N/A

5. CONCLUSION

In this study, we put forward two message clustering based matrix factorization models for retweeting behavior prediction. Both of models are constructed on the basis of the clustering of messages with both structure and semantic features. We construct extensive experiments to validate our proposed models. The experimental results reveal that the proposed methods can effectively improve the performance of retweeting behavior prediction only based on message features. In future work, we will explore combining user clustering relationships to our models for further research.

6. ACKNOWLEDGMENT

This work was supported by National Key Technology R&D Program(No.2012BAH46B03), and the Strategic Leading Science and Technology Projects of Chinese Academy of Sciences(No.XDA06030200).

7. REFERENCES

[1] E. F. Can, H. Oktay, and R. Manmatha. Predicting retweet count using visual cues. In *CIKM*, pages 1481–1484, 2013.

[2] J. Cheng, L. Adamic, P. A. Dow, J. M. Kleinberg, and J. Leskovec. Can cascades be predicted? In *WWW*, pages 925–936, 2014.

[3] Q. V. Le and T. Mikolov. Distributed representations of sentences and documents. In *ICML*, 2014.

[4] Z. Luo, M. Osborne, J. Tang, and T. Wang. Who will retweet me? finding retweeters in twitter. In *SIGIR*, pages 869–872, 2013.

[5] B. Suh, L. Hong, P. Pirolli, and E. H. Chi. Want to be retweeted? large scale analytics on factors impacting retweet in twitter network. In *SocialCom*, 2010.

[6] M. Wang, W. Zuo, and Y. Wang. A multidimensional nonnegative matrix factorization model for retweeting behavior prediction. *Mathematical Problems in Engineering*, 2015.

[7] Z. Yang, J. Guo, K. Cai, J. Tang, J. Li, L. Zhang, and Z. Su. Understanding retweeting behaviors in social networks. In *CIKM*, pages 1633–1636, 2010.

[8] J. Zhang, B. Liu, J. Tang, T. Chen, and J. Li. Social influence locality for modeling retweeting behaviors. In *IJCAI*, pages 2761–2767, 2013.

Heterogeneous Multi-task Semantic Feature Learning for Classification

Xin Jin[1,2], Fuzhen Zhuang[1], Sinno Jialin Pan[3], Changying Du[1], Ping Luo[1] and Qing He[1]
[1]Key Lab of Intelligent Information Processing of Chinese Academy of Sciences (CAS), Institute of Computing Technology, CAS, Beijing 100190, jinxin11@huawei.com, {zhuangfz, ducy, heq}@ics.ict.ac.cn, luop@ict.ac.cn
[2]Central Software Institute, Huawei Technologies Co. Ltd., Beijing 100085, China
[3]School of Computer Engineering, Nanyang Technological University, Singapore 639798, sinnopan@ntu.edu.sg

ABSTRACT

Multi-task Learning (MTL) aims to learn multiple related tasks simultaneously instead of separately to improve generalization performance of each task. Most existing MTL methods assumed that the multiple tasks to be learned have the same feature representation. However, this assumption may not hold for many real-world applications. In this paper, we study the problem of MTL with heterogeneous features for each task. To address this problem, we first construct an integrated graph of a set of bipartite graphs to build a connection among different tasks. We then propose a multi-task nonnegative matrix factorization (MTNMF) method to learn a common semantic feature space underlying different heterogeneous feature spaces of each task. Finally, based on the common semantic features and original heterogeneous features, we model the heterogenous MTL problem as a multi-task multi-view learning (MTMVL) problem. In this way, a number of existing MTMVL methods can be applied to solve the problem effectively. Extensive experiments on three real-world problems demonstrate the effectiveness of our proposed method.

1. INTRODUCTION

In many real-world scenarios, one needs to collectively solve a number of related tasks, where little side information (e.g., labels) is available for each task. To solve this kind of problems, multi-task learning (MTL) has been proposed [5].

Most existing MTL methods assumed that all the tasks have the same feature representation as shown in Figure 1(a). Though this assumption holds for some applications, it may not hold for many other applications. For example, given an emergent event in social media, suppose that one task is to predict whether a social post in text is related to the event, and another task is to predict whether a social image is related to the event. On one hand, these two tasks are related as they are to make predictions on the same event. On the other hand, for each of these two tasks, label information is limited as the event is emergent. Therefore, MTL methods are desirable to solve these two tasks. However, most existing MTL methods are not applicable here because the feature representations of these two tasks are totally different (i.e., image pixels v.s. textual words) as shown in Figure 1(b). In this paper, we proposed a new method to solve the problem of MTL with heterogeneous feature spaces.

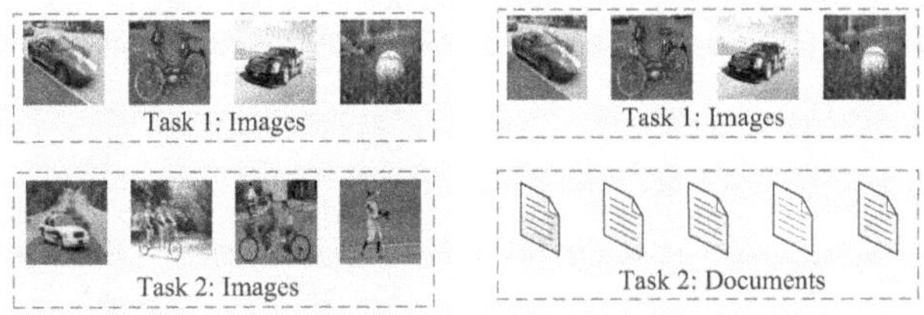

(a) *Homogeneous Features* (b) *Heterogeneous Features*

Figure 1: Two kinds of MTL problems

Our motivation is that though the instances of the different and related tasks are represented in different feature spaces, they may share a same semantic feature space. As in the example on social media event prediction described above, though an event-related image and an event-related post are represented differently, they should share the same semantic meanings because both of them describe the event. Once such a common semantic feature space is discovered, it can be used to share knowledge among multiple heterogeneous tasks, and thus improve their learning performance.

Specifically, in this paper, we assume multiple tasks share the same output space (i.e., the class labels of different tasks are the same or at least overlapping). Firstly, for each task, we build a bipartite graph to model the relationship between the labeled instances and the class labels. Secondly, based on the bipartite graphs of each task, we integrate them (i.e. the corresponding multiple tasks) through the layer of the class labels. After that we further build a correlation matrix between the class labels and the input features for each task based on the integrated graph. Finally, we propose a Multi-Task Nonnegative Matrix Factorization (MTNMF) method on the constructed correlation matrices as well as the original instance-feature matrices, which consists of both labeled and unlabeled data of each task, to learn a common semantic feature space underlying the multiple tasks. Once the semantic feature space is learned, together with the original heterogeneous features for each task, we can apply Multi-Task Multi-View Learning (MTMVL) methods to solve the target heterogenous MTL problem.

In summary, our proposed MTNMF method has several advantages. 1) It solves the problem of heterogeneous multi-task learning without requiring any correspondences between tasks. 2) It fully makes use of both labeled and unlabeled instances to learn the common semantic feature space for multiple tasks. 3) The learned semantic features and the original features can be concatenated to form a MTMVL problem, where a number of existing MTMVL methods can be applied.

Permission to make digital or hard copies of all or part of this work for personal or classroom use is granted without fee provided that copies are not made or distributed for profit or commercial advantage and that copies bear this notice and the full citation on the first page. Copyrights for components of this work owned by others than ACM must be honored. Abstracting with credit is permitted. To copy otherwise, or republish, to post on servers or to redistribute to lists, requires prior specific permission and/or a fee. Request permissions from Permissions@acm.org.
CIKM'15, October 19-23, 2015, Melbourne, VIC, Australia.
Copyright 2015 ACM. ISBN 978-1-4503-3794-6/15/10 ...$15.00.
DOI: http://dx.doi.org/10.1145/2806416.2806644.

2. RELATED WORK

In the past decade, MTL has attracted a lot of attention. Previous work on MTL was focused on learning multiple tasks with homogeneous features. Most methods aim to learn common features among different tasks [5, 2, 15], or common predictive structure underlying different tasks [1, 6], or common prior of model parameters among different tasks [11, 21, 22].

Recently, several heterogeneous MTL methods have been proposed. Zhang and Yeung [24] proposed the Multi-task Discriminant Analysis (MTDA) algorithm, which aims to learn transforms for instances of heterogeneous features such that the transformed instances of the same class from different tasks are closer to each other. However, MTDA is a supervised learning method, which fails to exploit unlabeled instances to learn to the transformation. He *et al.* [14] also proposed the MUSH algorithm for heterogenous MTL. However, in MUSH, some correspondence among inputs of different tasks is assumed to be given in advance.

In transfer learning, there have been some methods proposed for cross- domain/task learning with heterogenous features [25, 10, 20, 8]. However, different from transfer learning, the objective of MTL is not to transfer knowledge from a domain/task to another domain/task, but learn a prediction model for each task simultaneously by exploiting relatedness among the tasks.

Multi-Task Multi-View Learning (MTMVL) is a special setting of MTL, where each task has multiple views rather than a single view. State-of-the-art approaches to MTMVL include IteM^2 [13], which is a transductive learning method, regMVMT [23], CSL-MTMV [16] and MAMUDA [17], which are inductive learning methods.

3. PROBLEM FORMULATION

In this paper, we denote by $X_{(i,j)}$ the element in the i-th row and j-th column of a matrix X, $\|\cdot\|$ the Frobenius norm, and I_l the $l\times l$ identity matrix. In addition, we denote by $[N:M]$ $(N<M)$ a set of integers in the range between N and M inclusively.

Suppose we are given T related classification tasks. For each task $t\in[1:T]$, there are n_t labeled and m_t unlabeled instances. The dimension of an instance of the t-th task is d_t. A nonnegative matrix $X_t\in\mathbb{R}^{n_t\times d_t}\geq 0$ is used to denote the labeled instances of task t, each row of which represents an instance. Accordingly, $P_t\in\mathbb{R}^{m_t\times d_t}\geq 0$ is used to denote the corresponding unlabeled instances of task t. For simplicity, we suppose that the classification tasks are binary, and different tasks have the same set of class labels. Let $Y_t\in[-1,1]^{n_t\times 1}$ be the label vector of the labeled instances of task t.

4. MULTI-TASK SEMANTIC FEATURE LEARNING

4.1 Connection among Multiple Tasks

Recall that, for each task t, we have a set of labeled instances X_t and their corresponding labels Y_t. Based on X_t, we first build a bipartite graph to capture the relationship between the labeled instances and the class labels. To be specific, we use a matrix $U_t\in\mathbb{R}^{n_t\times C}$ to represent the bipartite graph for task t, where C is the number of classes[1], $U_{t(i,j)}=1$ if the i-th instance belongs to the j-th class, otherwise, $U_{t(i,j)}=0$. As the class labels of multiple tasks are assumed to be the same or at least overlapping, the multiple bipartite graphs can be integrated into a unified graph through the layer of the class labels. An example of the integrated graph of a pair of tasks (i.e., a pair of bipartite graphs) is shown in Figure 2.

[1]Note that in general, C can be larger than 2. For simplicity, here we assume the multiple classification tasks be binary.

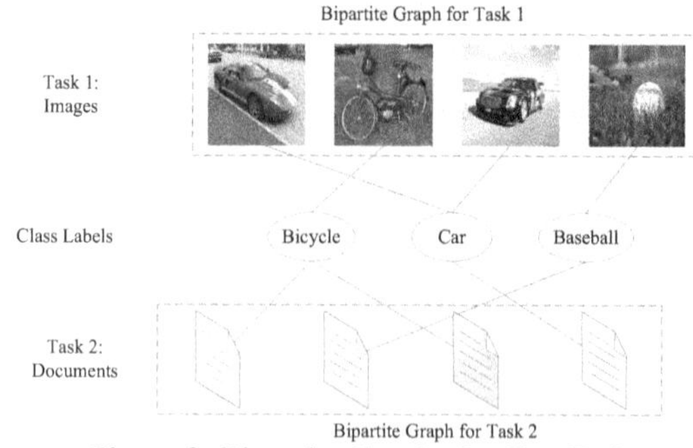

Figure 2: Bipartite Graphs for Two Tasks

Based on the matrix U_t, which is used to represent the relationship between instances and classes, we can further generate a correlation matrix G_t between input features and class labels for task t by setting $G_t=X_t{}^\top U_t\in\mathbb{R}^{d_t\times C}$, where $G_{t(i,j)}=\sum_{k=1}^{n_t}X_{t(k,i)}\times U_{t(k,j)}$, and $X_{t(k,i)}\geq 0$ is the value of the i-th feature of the k-th labeled instance of task t. It can be shown that $G_{t(i,j)}$ is large if there are many instances whose the values of the i-th feature are large and class labels are the j-th class. This implies that $G_{t(i,j)}$ is large if the i-th feature and the j-th class have strong correlation.

4.2 Semantic Feature Learning

For each task, to extract latent semantic features, one can apply NMF to decompose G_t to latent factor matrices,

$$G_t=W_tH_t,\ \text{s.t.}\ W_t\geq 0, H_t\geq 0,\ W_t{}^\top W_t=I. \quad (1)$$

where $W_t\in\mathbb{R}^{d_t\times k}$, $H_t\in\mathbb{R}^{k\times C}$, and k is the dimension of the latent semantic space. Each column in W_t can be referred to as a base vector of the latent space, which is represented by a linear combination of the original task-specific features. The i-th column of H_t can be referred to as the latent semantic representation for i-th class. The constraint $W_t{}^\top W_t=I$ is to ensure the solution to be unique and reduce redundancy [9].

For MTL, because the multiple tasks to be learned are assumed to be related, it is more desirable to learn the semantic features for each task jointly by exploiting their relatedness. In addition, as from the integrated graph, the layer of label classes is shared by all the tasks, intuitively, we can collectively learn W_t for each task by enforcing the class representations $\{H_t\}$'s to be the same. Therefore, we propose to decompose $\{G_t\}$'s jointly as follows:

$$\min_{W_t\geq 0, H\geq 0, W_t{}^\top W_t=I}\sum_{t=1}^{T}\|G_t-W_tH\|^2. \quad (2)$$

Note that the optimization problem (2) can facilitate knowledge transfer among multiple tasks through sharing H in semantic feature learning for different tasks. However, (2) only makes use of labeled data because G_t is constructed based on labeled instance only. However, in MTL, because labeled data for each task are scarce, the semantic features learned from (2) may not be robust and reliable. Therefore, how to exploit unlabeled data in semantic feature learning for different tasks is crucial. Intuitively, besides performing collective NMF on $\{G_t\}$'s to learn W_t jointly, one can also apply NMF on the original data, which include both labeled and unlabeled instances, to learn W_t for each task. To be specific, by defining $X'_t=[X_t;P_t]\in\mathbb{R}^{(n_t+m_t)\times d_t}$, we can learn W_t by solving the following NMF problem:

$$X'_t=V_tW_t{}^\top,\ \text{s.t.}\ W_t\geq 0,\ V_t\geq 0,\ W_t{}^\top W_t=I, \quad (3)$$

where $V_t\in\mathbb{R}^{(n_t+m_t)\times k}$, $W_t\in\mathbb{R}^{d_t\times k}$, and V_t is the new representation of X'_t under the new bases $\{W_t\}$'s. By combining (2) and (3), our proposed Multi-Task NMF method for semantic feature learning can be written as follows:

$$\min_{\substack{W_t{}^\top W_t=I \\ W_t,V_t,H\geq 0}} \sum_{t=1}^{T}\left(\|G_t - W_tH\|^2 + \alpha_t\|X'_t - V_tW_t{}^\top\|^2\right), \quad (4)$$

where $\alpha_t > 0$ is a tradeoff parameter to balance the importance between the labeled and unlabeled data. For simplicity, α_t is set to 1 in this paper, which means that we assume the two terms in (4) be equally important. Note that the optimization problem (4) is not convex for V_t, W_t and H jointly. To solve (4), we use an alternative optimization approach to alteratively optimize one variable while fixing the other variables. The update rules of the alterative optimization approach are summarized as follows:

$$W_{t(i,j)} \leftarrow W_{t(i,j)}\sqrt{\frac{(G_tH^\top + \alpha_tX'^\top_t V_t)_{(i,j)}}{\left(W_tW_t^\top(G_tH^\top+\alpha_tX'^\top_tV_t)\right)_{(i,j)}}}, \quad (5)$$

$$H_{(i,j)} \leftarrow H_{(i,j)}\frac{\left(\sum_{t=1}^{T}(W_t{}^\top G_t)\right)_{(i,j)}}{\left(\sum_{t=1}^{T}(W_t{}^\top W_tH)\right)_{(i,j)}}, \quad (6)$$

$$V_{t(i,j)} \leftarrow V_{t(i,j)}\frac{(X'_tW_t)_{(i,j)}}{(V_tW_t{}^\top W_t)_{(i,j)}}, \quad (7)$$

where $W_{t(i,j)}$, $V_{t(i,j)}$ and $H_{(i,j)}$ denote the (i,j)-th element of the matrices W_t, V_t, and H, respectively. By applying the update rules in (5), (6) and (7), the solution converges to a local optima. Existing approaches to proving the convergence of the NMF algorithm can be adapted to prove the convergence of our proposed algorithm.[2]

4.3 Learning Classifiers

For each task t, one can use the learned matrix W_t to map the original data to the common semantic space underlying all the T tasks via $X_t^{(c)} = X_tW_t$. Combining with the original features, in total, there are $T+1$ views for a heterogeneous MTL problem with T tasks. MTMVL techniques can be applied. In this paper, we adopt the regMVMT algorithm [23][3].

5. EXPERIMENTS

5.1 Datasets and Preprocessing

In Table 1, N_p and N_n are the numbers of positive and negative instances, respectively. On the second and third datasets, different tasks have some overlapping features. Besides comparing with heterogeneous MTL methods on the three datasets, we also compare MTNMF with homogeneous multi-task learning baselines on the second and third datasets.

Table 1: Statistics of Data Sets with Heterogeneous Features

Problem	Task #	N_p	N_n	Feature #
20News & Image	6	986 ~ 1,555	993 ~ 1,427	900 ~ 3000
Email Spam	15	200	200	996 ~ 2583
Sentiment	4	1000	1000	1611 ~ 2793

20Newsgroups & ImageNet Classification: The documents are from the 20 Newsgroups dataset[4], while the images are from the ImageNet dataset[5].

Email Spam Detection [3]: each task has a set of specific features which only include the words appear in the corresponding person's emails. When conducting comparison experiments with homogeneous MTL methods, we use another feature representation for emails that is based on a unified vocabulary for all the tasks.

Sentiment Classification: we use the multi-domain sentiment classification dataset [4]. The features are similarly constructed as for Email Spam dataset.

5.2 Experimental Setting

For each configuration, we perform 10 random trials and report the average classification accuracy.

5.2.1 *The First Group:*

TSVM: Transductive SVM (TSVM) [18] is a semi-supervised learning method, we use the SVM-light[6] implementation for the TSVM classifier.

NMF: we first apply NMF on both the labeled and unlabeled data to learn semantic features for each task separately as shown in Eq.(3), and then train a TSVM classifier for each task with the learned semantic features separately.

MTDA: Multi-task Discriminant Analysis (MTDA) [24] is a multi-task learning algorithm that can deal with heterogeneous features across different tasks.

5.2.2 *The Second Group:*

Four multi-task learning algorithms aim at problems with homogeneous features are tested, they are GMTL [19], rMTFL [12], DirtyMTL [15] and RMTL [7].

5.3 Experimental Results

5.3.1 *MTL Problems with Heterogeneous Features*

Comparison results of MTNMF with the first group of baseline methods on the three datasets are shown in Tables 2, 3, 4 respectively. As shown on the tables, MTNMF performs better than NMF though both of these two methods are based on nonnegative matrix factorization. This is because the semantic features for different tasks extracted by MTNMF are not only based on the factorization on the original data matrix, but also based on the factorization on the integrated bipartite graphs which capture the correlation among different tasks. Moreover, in general, multi-task learning methods, MTNMF and MTDA, outperform the methods that learn different tasks individually, such as TSVM and NMF. This is because for each task, labeled information is too sparse to learn a precise prediction model. Last but not least, the superiority of MTNMF over MTDA suggests that the semantic features learned by MTNMF is more effective for solving multi-task learning problems with heterogeneous features.

Table 3: Experimental Results for 20Newsgroups&Imagenet

Task	1	2	3	4	5	6	mean
TSVM	70.2	81.9	76.5	72.6	78.5	81.3	76.8
NMF	52.1	70.1	63.3	62.7	64.5	65.5	63.0
MTDA	77.3	83.6	77.7	77.2	80.7	83.2	79.9
MTNMF	**78.9**	**84.5**	**78.5**	**78.6**	**82.8**	**86.6**	**81.6**

Table 4: Experimental Results for Sentiment Problem

Task	1	2	3	4	mean
TSVM	62.5	61.8	67.0	74.3	66.4
NMF	58.8	59.4	59.8	57.7	58.9
MTDA	67.4	68.0	71.8	74.0	70.3
MTNMF	**68.6**	**69.2**	**73.8**	**75.6**	**71.8**

In the second series of experiments, we compare performance between different methods under varying numbers of labeled and unlabeled training data. Note that the sizes of labeled and unlabeled data are set to be the same for this series of experiments. The results are shown in Figure 3, where both average results and standard deviation of 10 random runs are reported. As can be seen from the

[2]Due to the limited space, the detailed proof is omitted.
[3]In general, any MTMVL method can be adopted.
[4]http://people.csail.mit.edu/jrennie/20Newsgroups/
[5]http://www.image-net.org/download-features
[6]http://svmlight.joachims.org/

Table 2: Experimental Results for Email Spam Problem (300 instances, 150 labeled and 150 unlabeled)

Task	1	2	3	4	5	6	7	8	9	10	11	12	13	14	15	mean
TSVM	84.9	83.1	78.5	78.4	86.9	65.1	76.3	85.7	86.2	85.4	73.0	76.8	87.2	64.0	73.8	79.0
NMF	83.8	67.7	62.3	65.0	60.7	55.2	65.0	73.1	61.6	80.0	60.0	53.3	63.3	64.3	56.4	64.8
MTDA	91.0	93.0	93.0	93.7	88.2	87.5	85.8	93.4	93.1	**92.8**	87.3	82.6	93.6	**86.8**	89.4	90.1
MTNMF	**94.2**	**95.7**	**96.0**	**95.7**	**91.4**	**89.0**	**91.7**	**95.7**	**95.2**	**92.8**	**90.7**	**85.3**	**94.9**	86.7	**91.5**	**92.4**

figure, MTNMF performs best under different number of training data for these 3 problems, which shows the advantage of learning a shared latent semantic space from multiple tasks.

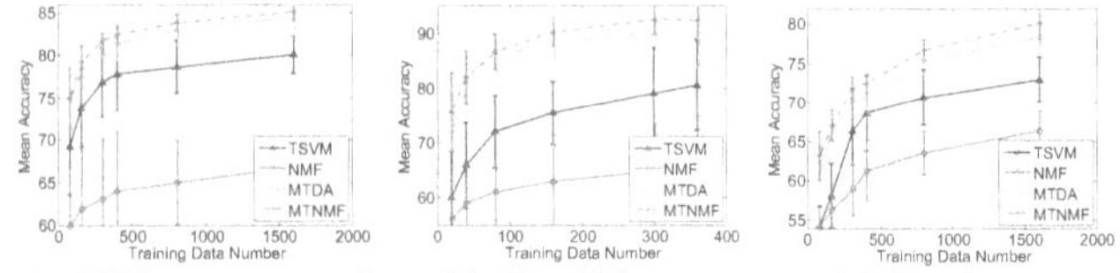

(a) *20Newsgroups & ImageNet* (b) *Email Spam* (c) *Sentiment*

Figure 3: Experimental Results for 3 Problems (Heterogeneous Features)

5.3.2 MTL Problems with Homogeneous Features

To conduct comparison experiments with homogeneous MTL methods, i.e., the second group of baseline methods, we use the **Email Spam Detection** and **Sentiment Classification** dataset with a unified feature representation for different tasks as described in Section 5.1. As the baseline methods are supervised learning approaches, in this series of experiments, we only use labeled training data for all the comparison methods including MTNMF. The comparison results in terms of classification accuracy are shown in Figure 4 under varying sizes of training instances. As can be seen from the figures, by extracting semantic features for each task collectively, MTNMF can also boost the performance of homogeneous MTL.

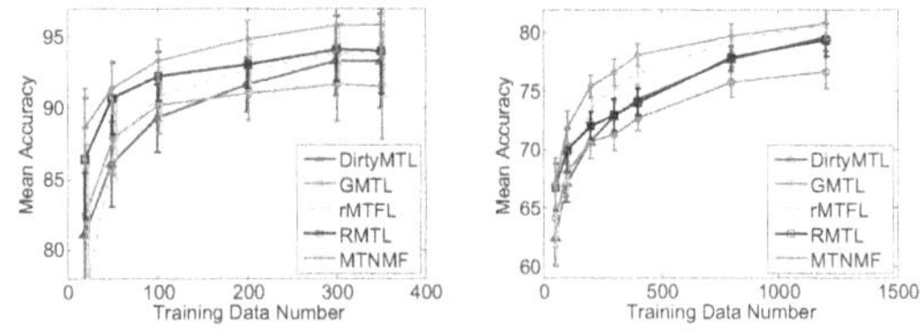

(a) *Email Spam* (b) *Sentiment*

Figure 4: Experimental Results (Homogeneous Features)

6. CONCLUSIONS

In this paper, we propose the Multi-Task Nonnegative Matrix Factorization (MTNMF) method to solve multi-task learning problems with heterogeneous feature spaces. In MTNMF, a set of integrated bipartite graphs are built based on the labeled data to model the relationship between original features and class labels among multiple tasks. A collective NMF method is then proposed to extract common semantic features from the integrated bipartite graphs as well as the unlabeled data for different tasks. Experiments on 3 real-world problems demonstrate the effectiveness of the proposed method.

7. ACKNOWLEDGMENTS

This work is supported by the National Natural Science Foundation of China (No. 61473273, 61473274, 61175052, 61203297), National High-tech R&D Program of China (863 Program) (No. 2014AA015105, 2013AA01A606).

8. REFERENCES

[1] R. K. Ando and T. Zhang. A framework for learning predictive structures from multiple tasks and unlabeled data. *JMLR*, 6:01, 2005.

[2] A. Argyriou, T. Evgeniou, and M. Pontil. Multi-task feature learning. In *NIPS*, pages 41 – 48, Vancouver, BC, Canada, 2007.

[3] S. Bickel. Ecml-pkdd discovery challenge 2006 overview. In *ECML-PKDD Discovery Challenge Workshop*, pages 1–9, 2006.

[4] J. Blitzer, M. Dredze, and F. Pereira. Biographies, bollywood, boom-boxes and blenders: Domain adaptation for sentiment classification. In *ACL*, pages 440 – 447, Prague, Czech republic, 2007.

[5] R. Caruana. Multitask learning. *Machine learning*, 28(1):41–75, 1997.

[6] J. Chen, L. Tang, J. Liu, and J. Ye. A convex formulation for learning shared structures from multiple tasks. In *ICML*, pages 137 – 144, Montreal, QC, Canada, 2009.

[7] J. Chen, J. Zhou, and J. Ye. Integrating low-rank and group-sparse structures for robust multi-task learning. In *ACM SIGKDD*, pages 42 – 50, San Diego, CA, United states, 2011.

[8] W. Dai, Y. Chen, G.-R. Xue, Q. Yang, and Y. Yu. Translated learning: Transfer learning across different feature spaces. In *NIPS*, pages 353–360, 2008.

[9] C. Ding, T. Li, W. Peng, and H. Park. Orthogonal nonnegative matrix t-factorizations for clustering. In *ACM SIGKDD*, pages 126–135. ACM, 2006.

[10] L. Duan, D. Xu, and I. W. Tsang. Learning with augmented features for heterogeneous domain adaptation. In *ICML*, 2012.

[11] T. Evgeniou and M. Pontil. Regularized multi-task learning. In *ACM SIGKDD*, pages 109 – 117, Seattle, WA, United states, 2004.

[12] P. Gong, J. Ye, and C. Zhang. Robust multi-task feature learning. In *ACM SIGKDD*, pages 895–903. ACM, 2012.

[13] J. He and R. Lawrence. A graph-based framework for multi-task multi-view learning. In *ICML*, pages 25 – 32, Bellevue, WA, United states, 2011.

[14] J. He, Y. Liu, and Q. Yang. Linking heterogeneous input spaces with pivots for multi-task learning. In *SDM*, 2014.

[15] A. Jalali, P. Ravikumar, S. Sanghavi, and C. Ruan. A dirty model for multi-task learning. In *NIPS*, Vancouver, BC, Canada, 2010.

[16] X. Jin, F. Zhuang, S. Wang, Q. He, and Z. Shi. Shared structure learning for multiple tasks with multiple views. In *ECML PKDD*, volume 8189 LNAI, pages 353 – 368, Prague, Czech republic, 2013.

[17] X. Jin, F. Zhuang, H. Xiong, C. Du, P. Luo, and Q. He. Multi-task multi-view learning for heterogeneous tasks. In *CIKM*, pages 441–450, New York, NY, USA, 2014. ACM.

[18] T. Joachims. Transductive inference for text classification using support vector machines. In *ICML*, pages 200–209, San Francisco, CA, USA, 1999.

[19] Z. Kang, K. Grauman, and F. Sha. Learning with whom to share in multi-task feature learning. In *ICML*, pages 521–528, 2011.

[20] G.-J. Qi, C. Aggarwal, and T. Huang. Towards semantic knowledge propagation from text corpus to web images. In *WWW*, pages 297–306. ACM, 2011.

[21] G. Skolidis and G. Sanguinetti. Bayesian multitask classification with gaussian process priors. *IEEE Transactions on Neural Networks*, 22(12):2011–2021, 2011.

[22] S. Yu, V. Tresp, and K. Yu. Robust multi-task learning with t-processes. In *ICML*, volume 227, pages 1103 – 1110, Corvalis, OR, United states, 2007.

[23] J. Zhang and J. Huan. Inductive multi-task learning with multiple view data. In *ACM SIGKDD*, pages 543 – 551, Beijing, China, 2012.

[24] Y. Zhang and D.-Y. Yeung. Multi-task learning in heterogeneous feature spaces. In *AAAI*, volume 1, pages 574 – 579, San Francisco, CA, United states, 2011.

[25] Y. Zhu, Y. Chen, Z. Lu, S. J. Pan, G.-R. Xue, Y. Yu, and Q. Yang. Heterogeneous transfer learning for image classification. In *AAAI*, 2011.

Top-k Reliable Edge Colors in Uncertain Graphs

Arijit Khan*, Francesco Gullo#, Thomas Wohler*, Francesco Bonchi#
*Systems Group, ETH Zurich, Switzerland #Yahoo! Labs, Barcelona, Spain
arijit.khan@inf.ethz.ch, {gullo, bonchi}@yahoo-inc.com, twohler@student.ethz.ch

ABSTRACT

We study the fundamental problem of finding the set of top-k edge colors that maximizes the reliability between a source node and a destination node in an uncertain and edge-colored graph. Our top-k reliable color set problem naturally arises in a variety of real-world applications including pathway finding in biological networks, topic-aware influence maximization, and team formation in social networks, among many others. In addition to the $\#\mathbf{P}$-completeness of the classical reliability finding problem between a source and a destination node over an uncertain graph, we prove that our problem is also $\mathbf{NP}$-hard, and neither sub-modular, nor super-modular. To this end, we aim at designing effective and scalable solutions for the top-k reliable color set problem. We first introduce two baselines following the idea of repetitive inclusion of the next best edge colors, and we later develop a more efficient and effective algorithm that directly finds the highly-reliable paths while maintaining the budget on the number of edge-colors. An extensive empirical evaluation on various large-scale and real-world graph datasets illustrates that our proposed techniques are both scalable and highly accurate.

Categories and Subject Descriptors

H.3.3 [**Information Search and Retrieval**]: Search process; H.2.8 [**Database Applications**]: Uncertain networks

General Terms

Algorithms, Performance

Keywords

Uncertain Graphs; Reliability; Edge Colors; Top-K

1. INTRODUCTION

Uncertainty is inherent in graph data due to a variety of reasons, such as noisy measurements, inference and prediction models, or explicit manipulation, e.g., for privacy purposes. In these cases, data is represented as an uncertain graph, that is, a graph whose arcs are accompanied with a probability of existence. A fundamental problem in uncertain graphs is *reliability query*, which asks to estimate the probability that a given destination node is reachable from a given source node. The reliability estimation problem has been widely studied in device networks [1], social networks [9], as well as in biological networks [10].

Permission to make digital or hard copies of all or part of this work for personal or classroom use is granted without fee provided that copies are not made or distributed for profit or commercial advantage and that copies bear this notice and the full citation on the first page. Copyrights for components of this work owned by others than ACM must be honored. Abstracting with credit is permitted. To copy otherwise, or republish, to post on servers or to redistribute to lists, requires prior specific permission and/or a fee. Request permissions from Permissions@acm.org.
CIKM'15, October 19-23, 2015, Melbourne, VIC, Australia
Copyright 2015 ACM 978-1-4503-3794-6/15/10 ...$15.00.
http://dx.doi.org/10.1145/2806416.2806619.

Nevertheless, most of these reliability queries over uncertain graphs are performed without considering any edge attributes, which we simply refer to as edge colors. Since complex networks, such as biological, social, and information networks usually exhibit diverse types of relationships among the entities, it is often meaningful to define reliability via a constrained set of edge colors [3]. To this end, we study the following novel and critical problem: *given a source and a destination node in an edge-colored, uncertain graph and a small positive integer k, find the edge-color-set of size k that maximizes the reliability from the source to the destination.*

Application. The top-k reliable color set problem naturally arises in a variety of real-world scenarios as follows.

Pathway Formation in Biological Networks: In order to understand the metabolic chain reactions in cellular systems, biologists utilize metabolic networks, where each vertex represents a compound, and a directed edge between two compounds indicates that one compound can be transformed into another through a certain chemical reaction [8]. The edge colors record the enzymes which control these reactions. In addition, uncertainty arises in metabolic network edges due to noisy measurements, experimental errors, inference, and prediction models. One of the basic questions on such networks is finding the top-k set of enzymes which create pathways of very high probabilities between two given compounds.

Topic-Aware Information Cascade: Marketing companies are gradually turning to social networks such as Facebook, Twitter, and LinkedIn for campaigning of their products. However, the influence of an individual over another in a social network often changes drastically based on advertisement contents [2]. Therefore, one can formulate the topic-aware information cascade problem with an uncertain graph model, where the probabilities on the edges vary based on advertisement features. In this setting, it is critical for the marketing companies to identify the top-k advertisement features such that the information cascade from an early adopter to a group of target customers could be maximized.

Challenges. Our top-k reliable color set problem is a non-trivial one — in fact, the simplest reliability computation problem over uncertain graphs is a $\#\mathbf{P}$-complete problem [1]. Due to the large size of networks, most work in this regard has resorted to Monte-Carlo (MC) sampling methods [6], as well as other sampling techniques improving upon the efficiency of MC methods (e.g., RHT-sampling [9]). These sampling-based approaches, in reality, estimate the reliability between two nodes very well, and they usually require only polynomial time in the size of the network.

However, even considering polynomial-time sampling techniques to estimate reliability, the top-k reliable color set problem remains **NP**-hard. More importantly, unlike the classical max-k cover problem, our problem is neither sub-modular, nor super-modular. Therefore, an iterative hill-climbing algorithm that maximally increases the marginal gain at every iteration, and which has been widely used for solving the max-k cover problem, can no longer be employed in our case for deriving similar approximation guarantees.

Our contribution. We propose two baselines to solve our top-k reliable color set problem, and we also design a more efficient and effective algorithm that directly finds the highly-reliable paths while maintaining the budget on the number of edge-colors. Our experimental results over three real-world large-scale graph datasets attest the effectiveness and efficiency of our approach.

2. PRELIMINARIES

2.1 Problem Formulation

An edge-labeled, uncertain graph $\mathcal{G}$ is a quadruple (V, E, C, P), where V is a set of n nodes, $E \subseteq V \times V$ is a set of m directed edges, C is the set of all edge-colors in $\mathcal{G}$, whereas $C(e) \subseteq C$ is a set of edge-colors assigned to the edge $e \in E$. Finally, $P : E \times C \to (0, 1)$ assigns a conditional probability on an edge given a specific color, i.e., $P(e|c) \in (0, 1)$.

Edge Existence Probability. In this work, we assume that the conditional probability of an edge $e \in E$ given some color $c \in C(e)$, that is, $P(e|c)$ is independent [3] of the other colors in $C(e)$. Thus, the edge-existence probability of e given the edge-colors $c_1, c_2, \ldots, c_r \in C$ is: $P(e|c_1c_2\ldots c_r) = 1 - \prod_{i=1}^{r}(1 - P(e|c_i))$. Given a predefined edge-color set $C_1 \subseteq C$, one can compute all the edge-existence probabilities in the uncertain graph $\mathcal{G}$. If the edge-color set C_1 is predefined, we simply write the edge-existence probabilities as $P(e|C_1)$.

Possible World Semantics. The bulk of the literature on uncertain graphs and device-network-reliability assumes the existence of the edges in the graph independent from one another and interprets uncertain graphs according to the well-known possible-world semantics [6, 8, 9]. More precisely, given a pre-defined edge-color set C_1, a possible graph $G \sqsubseteq \langle \mathcal{G}, C_1 \rangle$ is a pair (V, E_G), where $E_G \subseteq E$, and its sampling probability is:

$$Pr(G|C_1) = \prod_{e \in E_G} P(e|C_1) \prod_{e \in E \setminus E_G} (1 - P(e|C_1)) \quad (1)$$

For a possible deterministic graph $G \sqsubseteq \langle \mathcal{G}, C_1 \rangle$, we define an indicator function $I_G(s, t)$ to be 1 if there is a path in G from a source node $s \in V$ to a target node $t \in V$, and 0 otherwise. Finally, the probability that t is reachable from s in the uncertain graph $\mathcal{G}$ and via a pre-defined edge-color set C_1 is defined as the *edge-color-constrained reliability* from s to t, and it is denoted by $R_{C_1}(s, t)$. The edge-color-constrained reliability is computed as follows.

$$R_{C_1}(s, t) = \sum_{G \sqsubseteq \langle \mathcal{G}, C_1 \rangle} [I_G(s, t) \times Pr(G|C_1)] \quad (2)$$

The number of possible worlds $G \sqsubseteq \langle \mathcal{G}, C_1 \rangle$ is exponential in the number of edges, which makes the exact reliability computation a #**P**-complete problem; and hence, almost infeasible even for moderately-sized graphs.

Problem Statement. We are now ready to define our problem statement.

PROBLEM 1 (TOP-k RELIABLE COLOR SET). *Given a source node $s \in V$ and a destination node $t \in V$ in an edge-colored, uncertain graph $\mathcal{G} = (V, E, C, P)$, and a small positive integer k, find the edge-color-set C_1 of size k that maximizes the edge-color-constrained reliability $R_{C_1}(s, t)$ from s to t. Formally,*

$$\arg\max_{C_1 \subseteq C} R_{C_1}(s, t)$$
$$\text{such that} \quad |C_1| = k \quad (3)$$

Intuitively, the top-k reliable edge-colors create multiple paths of high probabilities from source to destination node.

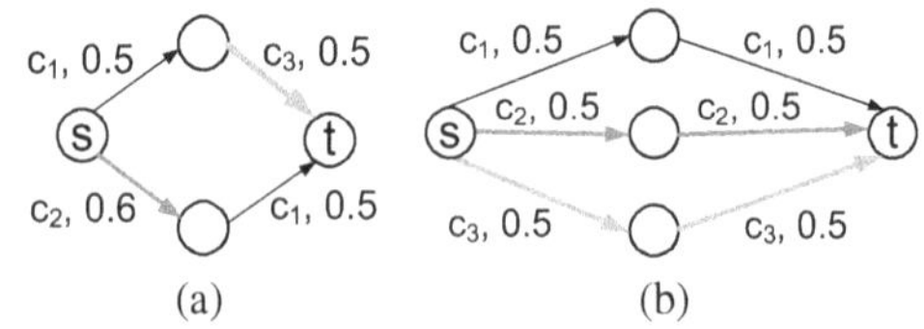

Figure 1: Example for Non-Sub-Modularity and Non-Super-Modularity

2.2 Hardness Results

Our problem, however, is non-trivial. Theorem 1 shows that Problem 1 is **NP**-hard, even when one considers polynomial-time reliability estimation approaches (e.g., MC sampling).

THEOREM 1. *The top-k reliable color set problem is* **NP**-*hard.*

PROOF. We prove **NP**-hardness by a reduction from the max-k cover problem. In max-k cover problem, we are given a universe U, and a set of h subsets of U, i.e., $\mathcal{S} = \{S_1, S_2, \ldots, S_h\}$, where $S_i \subseteq U$ for all $i \in [1 \ldots h]$. The objective is to find a subset $\mathcal{S}^*$ of $\mathcal{S}$ of size k such that the number of elements covered by $\mathcal{S}^*$ is maximized, i.e., so as to maximize $|\cup_{S \in \mathcal{S}^*} S|$. Given an instance of the max-k cover problem, we construct in polynomial time an instance of our top-k reliable color set problem.

We put in our edge-colored, uncertain graph $\mathcal{G}$ a source node s and a destination node t. Next, we include a set of nodes $u_1, u_2, \ldots, u_Z$, one for each element in $U(Z = |U|)$, and connect each of these nodes u to the destination node t with a directed edge (u, t). Each such edge (u, t) has color c, and we assign a probability $P((u, t)|c) = p$, with $p < 1$. We then add a set of nodes $x_1, x_2, \ldots, x_Z$, one for each element in $U(Z = |U|)$, and connect each of these nodes x to the source node t with a directed edge (s, x). Each such edge (s, x) also has color c, and we assign a probability $P((s, x)|c) = p$, with $p < 1$. Finally, if some element $u_i \in U$ is covered by at least one of the subsets in $\mathcal{S}$, we add a directed edge (x_i, u_i) in $\mathcal{G}$. For each of $S_j \in \mathcal{S}$ that covers the item u_i, we assign a color c_j on the edge (x_i, u_i), and then, we also assign a probability $P((x_i, u_i)|c_j) = 1$.

Now, we ask for a solution of our problem on the graph constructed this way by using $k + 1$ colors. One may observe that every solution to our problem necessarily takes color c, because otherwise there would be no way to connect s to t. Also, the reliability is maximized by properly selecting colors that make each of the edges (x_i, u_i) exist with probability 1. However, in order for each edges (x_i, u_i) to exist with a probability 1, it suffices to have selected only one of the colors between such a pair of nodes. Thus, we can see that maximizing reliability with $k + 1$ colors corresponds to maximizing coverage of elements in U with k sets in $\mathcal{S}$. Hence, the theorem. □

In this paper, we leave the following question open whether Problem 1 can be approximately solved within a constant factor in polynomial time or not. However, we show that unlike the max-k cover problem, our top-k reliable color set problem is neither sub-modular, nor super-modular; therefore, making it difficult to design an approximate solution with provable performance guarantees.

CLAIM 1. *The top-k reliable color set problem is not sub-modular.*

A function $f()$ is sub-modular if it satisfies the following property: $f(A \cup x) - f(A) \geq f(B \cup x) - f(B)$, for all elements x and all pairs of sets $A \subseteq B$. We show non-sub-modularity of our problem with an example in Figure 1(a). More specifically, let $C_1 = \{c_2\}$, $C_2 = \{c_1, c_2\}$. It is easy to verify that $R_{C_1}(s,t) = 0$, $R_{C_1 \cup \{c_3\}}(s,t) = 0$, $R_{C_2}(s,t) = 0.3$, and $R_{C_2 \cup \{c_3\}}$=0.475. Clearly, the sub-modularity property does not hold in this example.

CLAIM 2. *The top-k reliable color set problem is not super-modular.*

A function $f()$ is super-modular if it satisfies the following property: $f(A \cup x) - f(A) \leq f(B \cup x) - f(B)$, for all elements x and all pairs of sets $A \subseteq B$. We show non-super-modularity of our problem with an example in Figure 1(b). Let $C_1 = \{c_1\}$, $C_2 = \{c_1, c_3\}$. One may verify that $R_{C_1}(s,t) = 0.25$, $R_{C_1 \cup \{c_2\}}(s,t) = 0.438$, $R_{C_2}(s,t) = 0.438$, and $R_{C_2 \cup \{c_2\}} = 0.578$. Hence, the super-modularity property does not hold in this example.

3. ALGORITHMS FOR TOP-K COLOR RELIABILITY

As the top-k reliable color set problem is **NP**-hard, we develop two greedy baselines, as well as a more effective and efficient heuristic solution that provides a good approximation to our problem.

3.1 Individual Top-k: First Baseline

Our individual top-k algorithm estimates the reliability between the source and the destination nodes attained by each edge-color individually. In other words, we compute $R_{\{c\}}(s,t)$ for every edge-color $c \in L$. We report the top-k edge colors that achieve the highest reliability individually.

Time Complexity. For each color, we can estimate reliability by applying the MC sampling technique. If we require total K iterations of MC sampling in order to get a good estimate, then the time complexity to compute the reliability for each color is given by: $\mathcal{O}(K(n+e))$. Here, n and e are the number of nodes and edges in the uncertain graph, respectively. Therefore, the overall complexity of our individual top-k baseline algorithm is $\mathcal{O}(|C|K(n+e) + |C| \log k)$, the last term is due to finding the top-k colors based on individual reliability values.

Difficulties. The individual top-k algorithm suffers from several shortcomings, which are both accuracy and efficiency-driven.

- This baseline algorithm is unable to capture the contribution of the paths that consist of multiple edge-colors. For example, in Figure 1(a), the individual reliability attained by each of the three colors is 0; and therefore, if we are to select the top-2 color-set, it will be a random selection by our first baseline. However, in reality, the top-2 color set is $\{c_1, c_2\}$.
- For large-scale graph datasets, the MC sampling itself is very inefficient [9]; and performing such sampling for $|C|$ times, that is, one for each edge-color causes scalability bottleneck.

3.2 Iterative Hill-Climbing: Second Baseline

Our iterative hill-climbing baseline approach attempts at solving the accuracy bottleneck of the individual top-k algorithm. At each iteration of our hill-climbing algorithm, we add the color c^* to C_1 that maximizes the marginal gain in terms of reliability given the partial set C_1, which was already computed in the previous iterations. Formally,

$$c^* = \arg\max_{c \in C \setminus C_1} [R_{C_1 \cup \{c\}}(s,t) - R_{C_1}(s,t)] \qquad (4)$$

We perform k iterations to identify the top-k reliable color set.

Time Complexity. The time complexity of each iteration of our hill-climbing algorithm is $\mathcal{O}(|C|K(n+e))$. Since, we require total k iterations, the overall complexity of our second baseline is $\mathcal{O}(|C|kK(n+e))$.

Difficulties. The iterative hill-climbing method also suffers from both accuracy and efficiency issues.

- Our second baseline performs MC sampling over the entire graph for $|C|k$ times. Hence, this is even slower than our first baseline method.
- Although the iterative hill-climbing algorithm partially solves the accuracy issue of our first baseline, the issue is still present in the initial phases of the algorithm. For example, in Figure 1(a), the individual reliability attained by each of the three colors is 0. Therefore, in the first iteration of our hill-climbing method, it will perform a random selection. If our algorithm selects c_3 as the first color in C_1, then the second selected color would be c_1. One may note that the top-2 reliable color set is $\{c_1, c_2\}$, while the iterative hill-climbing may find the set $\{c_1, c_3\}$, which is a sub-optimal choice. We refer to this issue as the *"cold-start"* problem.

3.3 Most-Reliable-Path based Heuristic

We finally introduce our most-reliable-path based heuristic approach that eliminates the efficiency bottleneck of the two baselines. We follow a two-step approach as discussed below.

Most Reliable Paths Selection. Given an uncertain, edge-colored graph $\mathcal{G} = (V, E, L, P)$, a source $s \in V$, and a destination $t \in V$, we first convert $\mathcal{G}$ into an edge-colored, uncertain, multi-graph $\mathcal{G}'$ as follows. For each edge (u,v) in $\mathcal{G}$, if the edge-color set $C(u,v) = \{c_1, c_2, \dots, c_i\}$ has total i colors, we add i edges $\{e_1, e_2, \dots, e_i\}$, with colors $c_1, c_2, \dots, c_i$, respectively, between u and v in the multi-graph $\mathcal{G}'$. Each newly constructed edge e_i is assigned a probability: $P(e_i) = P((u,v)|c_i)$. One may note that $\mathcal{G}$ and $\mathcal{G}'$ are equivalent in terms of our problem. Next, we select the top-r most reliable paths from source s to destination t in $\mathcal{G}'$, where the reliability of a path is defined as the product of the edge-probabilities along that path. The main intuition behind selecting the top-r most reliable paths is that the reliability between two nodes can often be approximated well by a collection of the top-r most-reliable paths between those two nodes [4]. The value of the parameter r is determined empirically, such that the inclusion of the top-$(r+1)$-th reliable path does not significantly increase the reliability from s to t that was already achieved via the subgraph induced by the top-r most reliable paths.

The top-r most reliable paths from s to t can be obtained by first converting the uncertain, multi-graph $\mathcal{G}'$ into an edge-weighted, multi-graph $\mathcal{G}''$ as follows. Each edge e with probability $P(e)$ in $\mathcal{G}'$ is assigned a weight $\{-\log P(e)\}$ in $\mathcal{G}''$. Therefore, the top-r shortest paths in $\mathcal{G}''$ will be the top-r most reliable paths in $\mathcal{G}'$. We next apply the fastest known algorithm by Eppstein et. al. [5] in order to find the top-r shortest paths (with cycles) in $\mathcal{G}'$, which has time complexity $\mathcal{O}(|C|e + nlogn + r)$. Here, $|C|e$ denotes the maximum possible number of edges in the multi-graph G'.

Iterative Path Inclusion. We formally define our iterative path inclusion problem as follows.

PROBLEM 2 (ITERATIVE PATH INCLUSION). *Given a set $\mathcal{P}$ of the top-r most reliable paths from s to t in $\mathcal{G}'$, find the subset $\mathcal{P}_1 \subseteq \mathcal{P}$, such that the reliability $Rel_{\mathcal{P}_1}(s,t)$ from s to t, via the*

Algorithm 1 Iterative Path Inclusion Algorithm

Require: Top-r most-reliable path set $\mathcal{P}$ between s to t in $\mathcal{G}'$, budget k on the number of colors

Ensure: A subset of paths $\mathcal{P}_1 \subseteq \mathcal{P}$ that maximizes $Rel_{\mathcal{P}_1}(s,t)$, while total no. of edge-colors in $\mathcal{P}_1$ less than k

$\mathcal{P}_1 = \phi$

while total no. of edge-colors in $\mathcal{P}_1$ less than k **do**

  $P^* = \arg\max_{P \in \mathcal{P} \setminus \mathcal{P}_1} Rel_{\mathcal{P}_1 \cup \{P\}}(s,t)$,
  such that total no. of edge-colors in $\mathcal{P}_1$ and P^* less than k

  $\mathcal{P}_1 = \mathcal{P}_1 \cup \{P^*\}$

end while

output $\mathcal{P}_1$

Table 1: Graph Dataset Characteristics

Data Set	# Node	# Edge	# Color	Avg. # Color per Edge	Edge Prob: Mean, SD, Quartiles
Freebase	28 483 132	46 708 421	5 428	1	0.50, 0.24, {0.250, 0.500, 0.750}
BioMine	1 045 414	6 742 943	20	1	0.27, 0.17, {0.116, 0.216, 0.363}
Flixter	29 357	280 517	10	4	0.17, 0.26, {0.003, 0.056,0.212}

Table 2: Avg. Reliability and Efficiency over Datasets; Top-k=5

	Reliability			Running Time (Sec)		
Datasets	Base1	Base2	Rel-Path	Base1	Base2	Rel-Path
Freebase	0.21	0.21	**0.22**	104.9	1278.0	**0.6**
BioMine	0.21	**0.38**	0.35	4240.7	341960.5	**27.5**
Flixter	0.29	**0.62**	0.53	1.3	15355.6	**0.99**

subgraph induced by the paths in $\mathcal{P}_1$, is maximized; while the total number of colors on the edges of paths in $\mathcal{P}_1$ does not exceed k.

$$\arg\max_{\mathcal{P}_1 \subseteq \mathcal{P}} Rel_{\mathcal{P}_1}(s,t) \quad \textit{such that} \quad |\cup_{e \in \mathcal{P}_1} C(e)| \leq k \tag{5}$$

Unfortunately, our iterative path inclusion problem is **NP**-hard; and it is neither sub-modular, nor super-modular with respect to the inclusion of paths. We omit the details of the proof due to limitation of space. Next, we design an efficient heuristic algorithm (Algorithm 1) for the iterative path inclusion problem.

Our heuristic procedure works in successive iterations. At each iteration, we add the path P^* to $\mathcal{P}_1$ that maximizes the marginal gain in terms of reliability given the partial set $\mathcal{P}_1$, that was already computed in the previous iterations. While selecting the path P^* in the current iteration, we also ensure that the total number of colors used in the paths $\mathcal{P}_1 \cup \{P^*\}$ is no more than k. Finally, we terminate our algorithm either when there is no path left in the top-r most reliable path set $\mathcal{P}$, or we cannot include any more paths without violating the overall edge-color budget k. We report the edge-colors present in $\mathcal{P}_1$ as our final solution. Also, if the total number of edge-colors present in $\mathcal{P}_1$ is $k' < k$, then we select uniformly at random additional $k - k'$ colors that are not in $\mathcal{P}_1$. We report all of them, along with the edge-colors in $\mathcal{P}_1$, as our output for the top-k reliable color set problem.

Time Complexity. Let us denote by n' and e' the number of nodes and edges in the subgraph induced by the top-r most-reliable path set $\mathcal{P}$. Our iterative path selection algorithm can have at most r iterations. At each iteration, we perform MC sampling for $\mathcal{O}(r)$ times over the subgraph induced by the selected paths. If K is the number of samples used in each MC sampling, the overall time-complexity of our iterative path selection algorithm is $\mathcal{O}(r^2(n' + e')K)$. We here emphasize that the subgraph induced by the top-r most reliable paths is much smaller than the input uncertain graph $\mathcal{G}$. Thus, our iterative path selection technique is more efficient than the two baselines introduced earlier.

4. EXPERIMENTS

Datasets: We summarize our data sets in Table 1. While *BioMine* [10] and *Flixter* [2] have both edge-probabilities and edge-colors, *Freebase* [7] contains only edge-colors. Thus, we assign edge-probabilities in *Freebase* with uniform distribution from $(0, 1)$.

Accuracy and Efficiency: We compare the accuracy and efficiency of our reliable-path based heuristic with two baselines in Tables 2, 3, and 4. Each result is reported as an average over 500 uniformly selected source-destination pairs. The number of top-r paths for our reliable-path based heuristic is set as 20, as increasing it more than that value does not significantly increase the reliability between the source-destination pair. The number of Monte Carlo samples is fixed as 1000 [9]. In all our experiments, we find that the reliable-path based method is several orders of magnitude faster compared to the second baseline, while it still achieves similar reliability from the source to the destination node. Also, the reliability achieved by reliability-path based method and by the second baseline is much higher than that of the first baseline.

Table 3: Avg. Reliability and Efficiency with Varying Top-k, *Freebase*

	Reliability			Running Time (Sec)		
Top-k	Base1	Base2	Rel-Path	Base1	Base2	Rel-Path
5	0.21	0.21	**0.22**	104.9	1278.0	**0.6**
10	0.21	0.21	**0.23**	116.6	2560.2	**0.6**
15	0.21	0.21	**0.23**	120.0	3835.0	**0.6**
20	0.21	0.21	**0.23**	139.9	5112.0	**0.7**

Table 4: Avg. Reliability and Efficiency with Varying Distance from Source to Destination, *BioMine*, Top-k=5

Distance	Reliability			Running Time (Sec)		
(# hop)	Base1	Base2	Rel-Path	Base1	Base2	Rel-Path
2	0.30	**0.53**	0.46	3615.0	283621.0	**19.1**
4	0.12	**0.23**	**0.23**	4865.0	400300.0	**35.8**

5. CONCLUSIONS

We study the novel problem of finding the top-k edge-colors set that maximizes the reliability from a source to a destination node in an uncertain graph. Our proposed reliable-path based heuristic is several orders of magnitude faster than various naïve baselines, while it also achieves comparable accuracy to that of our most effective baseline method. In future work, we shall consider the problem with a set of source and destination nodes.

6. REFERENCES

[1] M. O. Ball. Computational Complexity of Network Reliability Analysis: An Overview. *IEEE Tran. on Reliability*, 1986.

[2] N. Barbieri, F. Bonchi, and G. Manco. Topic-Aware Social Influence Propagation Models. In *ICDM*, 2012.

[3] M. Chen, Y. Gu, Y. Bao, and G. Yu. Label and Distance-Constraint Reachability Queries in Uncertain Graphs. In *DASFAA*, 2014.

[4] W. Chen, C. Wang, and Y. Wang. Scalable Influence Maximization for Prevalent Viral Marketing in Large-Scale Social Networks. In *KDD*, 2010.

[5] D. Eppstein. Finding the k Shortest Paths. *SIAM J. Comput*, 28(2):652–673, 1998.

[6] G. S. Fishman. A Comparison of Four Monte Carlo Methods for Estimating the Probability of s-t Connectedness. *IEEE Tran. Rel.*, 1986.

[7] N. Jayaram, A. Khan, C. Li, X. Yan, and R. Elmasri. Querying Knowledge Graphs by Example Entity Tuples. *TKDE*, 2015.

[8] R. Jin, H. Hong, H. Wang, N. Ruan, and Y. Xiang. Computing Label-Constraint Reachability in Graph Databases. In *SIGMOD*, 2010.

[9] R. Jin, L. Liu, B. Ding, and H. Wang. Distance-Constraint Reachability Computation in Uncertain Graphs. *PVLDB*, 2011.

[10] P. Sevon, L. Eronen, P. Hintsanen, K. Kulovesi, and H. Toivonen. Link Discovery in Graphs Derived from Biological Databases. In *DILS*, 2006.

Probabilistic Non-negative Inconsistent-resolution Matrices Factorization

Masahiro Kohjima, Tatsushi Matsubayashi, and Hiroshi Sawada
NTT Service Evolution Laboratories, NTT Corporation, Japan
{kohjima.masahiro, matsubayashi.tatsushi, sawada.hiroshi}@lab.ntt.co.jp

ABSTRACT

In this paper, we tackle with the problem of analyzing datasets with different resolution such as a pair of user's individual data and user group's data, for example "userA visited shopA 5 times" and "users whose attributes are men purchased itemA 80 times in total". In order to establish a basic approach to this problem, we focus on the simplified scenario and propose a new probabilistic model called probabilistic non-negative inconsistent-resolution matrices factorization (*pNimf*). *pNimf* is rigorously derived from the data generative process using *latent high-resolution data* which underlie low-resolution data. We conduct experiments on real purchase log data and confirm that the proposed model provides superior performance, and that the performance improves as the number of low-resolution data increases. These results imply that our way of modeling using *latent high-resolution data* can become the basic approach to the problem of analyzing dataset with different resolution.

Categories and Subject Descriptors: I.5.1 [Pattern Recognition]: Models
Keywords: Inconsistent Resolution Dataset; Probabilistic Models; Non-negative Matrix Factorization

1. INTRODUCTION

The success of companies that utilize the data analytical approach is driving projects on data collection and analysis in many business fields. Almost every week, there is a press release describing one or more projects by companies to collect customer information, to collaborate with other companies and so on. These trends increase the need to analyze datasets with different resolution such as a pair of user's individual data and user group's data, for example "userA visited shopA 5 times" and "users whose attributes are men purchased itemA 80 times in total". Since the user's individual data represent more precise information than the user group's data, we call these the high-resolution data and the low-resolution data, respectively. Thus, we call this problem the inconsistent resolution dataset analysis problem (IRDAP) in this paper.

There are several examples of the importance of IRDAP. First involves the analysis of retailer data. Recently, many retailers issue membership cards to users and collect purchase data. However, since some customers do not have a card, some part of the retailer's purchase logs do not include a user ID, and instead only the user's sex and age information (estimated by appearance) is recorded by the staff. Thus, collected data consist of user purchase data and user group's data. Second example is the integrated analysis of own company data and that of another company. In social data such as foursquare data[1] and Yelp data[2], the user's individual check-in data is hidden, and only user group's check-in data (e.g. how many women visited a shop) is available to ensure privacy. Thus, when a company wants to use the foursquare data, integrated analysis of their own high-resolution data and foursquare's low-resolution data is needed.

In this paper, we establish a basic approach to IRDAP. Thus, we focus on the simplified scenario that satisfies two assumptions: (A1) *common user population assumption* and (A2) *independent and identically distributed (iid) assumption*. In addition, we consider an extension of non-negative matrix factorization (NMF) [7], whose effectiveness is confirmed in a wide range of research field [4]. Using the above assumptions and the formulation of NMF, we propose a new probabilistic model called probabilistic non-negative inconsistent-resolution matrices factorization (*pNimf*), which can analyze both high-resolution and low-resolution data simultaneously. *pNimf* is rigorously derived from the data generative process using *latent high-resolution data* that underlie the low-resolution data. (A1) allows us to define *latent high-resolution data* and (A2) is the assumption that both latent and observed high-resolution data follow. The scenario which assumptions (A1) and (A2) are satisfied is a limited case in the original IRDAP. However, we consider that our way of modeling using *latent high-resolution data* to IRDAP is a basic approach for solving more general problem.

We conducted experiments on real purchase logs to confirm the effectiveness of the proposed model. Using test set log-likelihood as a performance measure, experiments show that the proposed model provides superior performance to others as it effectively integrates low-resolution data. Moreover, *pNimf* works well even if multiple low-resolution data are available by generalizing the data generative process.

[1]`http://gnip.com/sources/foursquare/`
[2]`http://www.yelp.com/dataset_challenge`

Permission to make digital or hard copies of all or part of this work for personal or classroom use is granted without fee provided that copies are not made or distributed for profit or commercial advantage and that copies bear this notice and the full citation on the first page. Copyrights for components of this work owned by others than ACM must be honored. Abstracting with credit is permitted. To copy otherwise, or republish, to post on servers or to redistribute to lists, requires prior specific permission and/or a fee. Request permissions from Permissions@acm.org.
CIKM'15, October 19–23, 2015, Melbourne, Australia.
© 2015 ACM. ISBN 978-1-4503-3794-6/15/10 ...$15.00.
DOI: http://dx.doi.org/10.1145/2806416.2806636.

These results imply that our model using *latent high-resolution data* can become the basic approach to IRDAP.

2. RELATED WORK

NMF [7] is a method that factorizes a matrix into factor matrices with non-negative values. The result of factorization can be used for missing value completion and soft clustering by considering factor matrices represent cluster assignment. Since NMF has a loss function flexibility, NMF can be applied to various types of data such as ratings, documents, and purchase logs by choosing the appropriate function [4]. More interestingly, Ding et al. proved that NMF using generalized KL divergence is equivalent to probabilistic latent semantic indexing, which is the basis of latent dirichlet allocation [6, 2, 5]. Thus, NMF is a key machine learning algorithm and we choose it as the basis of our model.

For integrated data analysis, collective matrix factorization (CMF) methods, which factorize multiple matrices simultaneously, have become popular tools [9]. NMF has also been extended to the CMF method [8, 10] and is called non-negative multiple matrix factorization (NMMF) in [10]. It is reported that these methods achieve better predictive performance than NMF. However, these methods don't consider the differences in dataset resolution. In a different context of CMF, Aimoto and Kashima proposed a factorization method that uses a kind of low-resolution data (they call it aggregated data) [1]. However, the assumption they made as to the association between datasets with different resolution does not suit our problem.

3. PROPOSED METHOD

3.1 Problem Formulation

In this paper, we focus on the simplified IRDAP that satisfies the two assumptions of (A1) *common user population assumption* and (A2) *iid assumption*. These assumptions are formally defined later, and here we provide an intuitive explanation. Let us consider the example that a supermarket started to issue membership cards from December and all users must use the card at the point of purchase from Dec. Then, since user-ID is not present in the November log, purchase log of Nov. is a low-resolution data while that of Dec. is a high-resolution data as shown in Fig. 1. Note that the reason why user attribute is recorded in the low-resolution data in this example is that user's sex and age information, estimated by appearance, are recorded by the staff at the point of purchase. In this example, (A1) requires that the set of store users in Nov. and Dec. are the same (regardless of whether they purchase anything or not) and (A2) requires that the probability of item purchase by some user in Nov. is equal to that in Dec. Hereafter, we address this purchase log analysis problem, so all notations follow this example. However, our scope of study is not limited to this example and more general scenario is discussed in §3.4.

Notation: Let I, J and K represent the number of users, items, and attributes, respectively. We define the element of $\boldsymbol{X}$, x_{ij}, as the number of purchases of item j by user i in Dec. and the element of $\boldsymbol{Y}$, y_{kj}, is the number of times item j was purchased by users with attribute k in Nov. Each $\boldsymbol{X}$ and $\boldsymbol{Y}$ is regarded as the high-resolution matrix and the low-resolution matrix, respectively. We also assume that user's attribute information is available. This assumption is

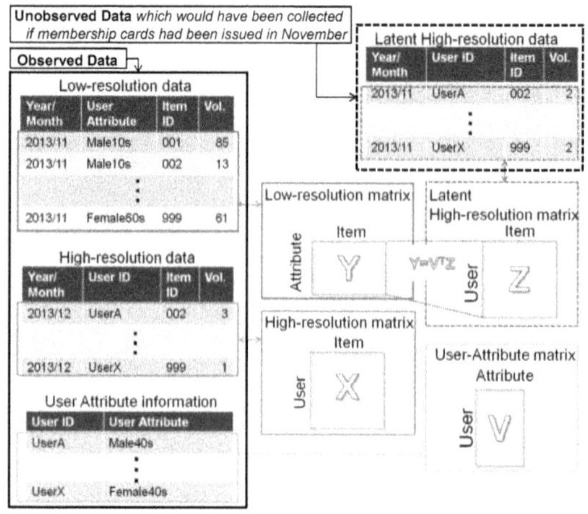

Figure 1: Example of observed data and unobserved *latent high-resolution data*. Relation between *latent high-resolution data* and low-resolution data is also shown.

natural because such data is required, for example, when the user creates the membership card. $\boldsymbol{V} = \{v_{ik}\}_{i,k=1}^{I,K}$, whose element $v_{ik} \in \{0, 1\}$ is set to 1 if the attribute of user i is k, otherwise 0, represents this information.

Latent high-resolution data: Next, we define the *latent high-resolution matrix*, $\boldsymbol{Z}$. This matrix plays an important role in our model. We define $\boldsymbol{Z}$ as the matrix which corresponds to the high-resolution data in Nov., i.e. data which would have collected if membership cards had been issued in Nov. Since only low-resolution data is collected in Nov., $\boldsymbol{Z}$ is the unobserved *latent high-resolution data* which lies under the low-resolution data. Thus, we are usually unable to know the set of users that exist behind $\boldsymbol{Z}$ and the number of rows of $\boldsymbol{Z}$ cannot be defined. To resolve this, we use (A1), which we formally defined as follows: *user population of high-resolution data* $\boldsymbol{X}$ *and that of latent high-resolution data* $\boldsymbol{Z}$ *are identical.* (A1) allows us to define the number of the rows of $\boldsymbol{Z}$ as being identical to $\boldsymbol{X}$, I. Then, we define its element z_{ij} as the number of purchases of item j by user i in Nov. Importantly, this definition yields a relation between $\boldsymbol{Y}$ and $\boldsymbol{Z}$, $\boldsymbol{Y} = \boldsymbol{V}^T\boldsymbol{Z}$. This comes from the fact that y_{kj} is equal to the summation of z_{ij} over user i with attribute k, i.e. $y_{kj} = \sum_i v_{ik} z_{ij}$.

3.2 Model

This subsection presents the proposed model. Let $\boldsymbol{A} := \{a_{ir}\}_{i,r=1}^{I,R}$, $\boldsymbol{B} := \{b_{jr}\}_{j,r=1}^{J,R}$ denote user latent factor matrix and item latent factor matrix, respectively. R is the number of factors. We also define $\hat{\boldsymbol{X}}$, whose element $\hat{x}_{ij} = \sum_r a_{ir} b_{jr}$. For simplicity we focused on the case that Poisson distribution is used to modeling the data generation, which is frequently used for purchase data,

$$\mathcal{PO}(x_{ij}|\hat{x}_{ij}) = \exp\{-\hat{x}_{ij} + x_{ij}\log(\hat{x}_{ij}) - \log\Gamma(x_{ij}+1)\}.$$

In original NMF, the generation of $\boldsymbol{X}$ is modeled as follows:

$$p(\boldsymbol{X}|\boldsymbol{A},\boldsymbol{B}) = \prod_{i,j=1}^{I,J} \mathcal{PO}(x_{ij}|\hat{x}_{ij}). \tag{1}$$

Note that other distribution such as Gaussian is also available in analogous manner.

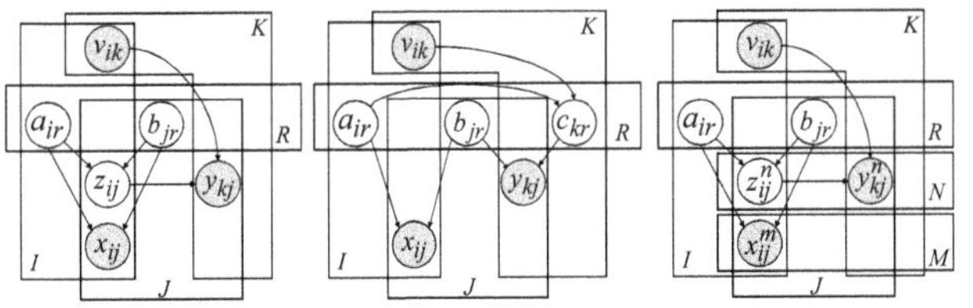

(a) (b) (c)

Figure 2: Graphical models. Shaded nodes indicate observed variables. Figure (a) represents the original definition of proposed model described in Eq.(2). By marginalizing out Z from Eq. (2), Fig. (b) is obtained. Figure (c) represents the generalized model of Fig. (a) stated in §3.4.

We derive the proposed method based on the data generative process summarized as follows: (i) define the probability distribution that generates both $\boldsymbol{X}$ and $\boldsymbol{Z}$. (ii) use (A2) *iid assumption*, which we formally defined as follows: elements of $\boldsymbol{X}$ and $\boldsymbol{Z}$ that have the same indices, x_{ij} and z_{ij}, follow the identical probability distribution (in this case, Poisson dist. with parameter $\hat{x}_{ij}$ as in Eq. (1)) and these are mutually independent. (A2) helps to extract factors which are independent of month. (iii) use the relation between $\boldsymbol{Z}$ and $\boldsymbol{Y}$ ($y_{kj} = \sum_i v_{ik} z_{ij}$) explained in the previous section. Putting all this together, the joint dist. of $\boldsymbol{X}$, $\boldsymbol{Z}$, $\boldsymbol{Y}$ is written as

$$p(\boldsymbol{X}, \boldsymbol{Z}, \boldsymbol{Y} | \boldsymbol{A}, \boldsymbol{B}, \boldsymbol{V}) = \prod_{i,j} \mathcal{PO}(x_{ij}|\hat{x}_{ij}) \mathcal{PO}(z_{ij}|\hat{x}_{ij}) \prod_{k,j} \delta(y_{kj} - \sum_i v_{ik} z_{ij}), \tag{2}$$

where $\delta(\cdot)$ denotes delta function. Figure 2(a) shows graphical model representation. By explicitly modeling the generation of *latent high-resolution matrix* $\boldsymbol{Z}$, we can naturally define the probability distribution of all matrices. However, since the size of $\boldsymbol{Z}$ is $I \times J$, which is considerable, it is desirable to work with more convenient probabilistic models.

The key is a characteristic of Poisson distributions: the sum of Poisson-distributed random variables is also Poisson-distributed random variable. In our model, z_{ij} represents Poisson-distributed random variables and y_{kj} is their summation. Thus, we can marginalize out $\boldsymbol{Z}$ from Eq. (2) which yields the following equation:

$$p(\boldsymbol{X}, \boldsymbol{Y} | \boldsymbol{A}, \boldsymbol{B}, \boldsymbol{V}) = \int p(\boldsymbol{X}, \boldsymbol{Z}, \boldsymbol{Y} | \boldsymbol{A}, \boldsymbol{B}, \boldsymbol{V}) d\boldsymbol{Z} = \prod_{i,j} \mathcal{PO}(x_{ij}|\hat{x}_{ij}) \prod_{k,j} \mathcal{PO}(y_{kj}|\hat{y}_{kj}), \tag{3}$$

$$\text{where} \quad \hat{y}_{kj} = \sum_{r=1}^{R} c_{kr} b_{jr} \quad \text{and} \quad c_{kr} = \sum_{i=1}^{I} v_{ik} a_{ir}. \tag{4}$$

Figure 2(b) shows graphical model representation. Considering that $\boldsymbol{C} := \{c_{kr}\}_{k,r=1}^{K,R}$ is attribute latent factor matrix, Eq. (3) can be interpreted as factorizing the high-resolution matrix and low-resolution matrix simultaneously, while retaining the relation between factor matrices $\boldsymbol{A}$ and $\boldsymbol{C}$ using $\boldsymbol{V}$ ($\boldsymbol{C} = \boldsymbol{V}^T \boldsymbol{A}$ as in Eq. (4)). Thus, we call this proposal probabilistic non-negative inconsistent-resolution matrices factorization (*pNimf*). Note that removing the linear equality relation between factor matrices, $\boldsymbol{C} = \boldsymbol{V}^T \boldsymbol{A}$, *pNimf* reduces to one of CMF method (NMMF) [10]. Thus, *pNimf* can be seen as an extension of NMMF.

3.3 Inference

Parameter estimation procedure of *pNimf* is derived in a similar manner to that of NMF. Let us consider that logarithm of Eq. (3) is the objective function and Eq. (4) is the linear equality constraint. $\boldsymbol{A}, \boldsymbol{B}$ and $\boldsymbol{C}$ are variables. Applying Jensen's inequality yields the following lower bound of the objective function:

$$\mathcal{F} = \sum_{i,j} \Big\{ -\Big(\sum_{r=1}^{R} a_{ir} b_{jr}\Big) + x_{ij} \sum_{r=1}^{R} s_{ijr} \log\Big(\frac{a_{ir} b_{jr}}{s_{ijr}}\Big) \Big\} + \sum_{k,j} \Big\{ -\Big(\sum_{r=1}^{R} c_{kr} b_{jr}\Big) + y_{kj} \sum_{r=1}^{R} t_{kjr} \log\Big(\frac{c_{kr} b_{jr}}{t_{kjr}}\Big) \Big\},$$

where the equality holds if and only if

$$s_{ijr} = \frac{a_{ir} b_{jr}}{\sum_{r'=1}^{R} a_{ir'} b_{jr'}}, \quad t_{kjr} = \frac{c_{kr} b_{jr}}{\sum_{r'=1}^{R} c_{kr'} b_{jr'}}. \tag{5}$$

Setting $\frac{\partial \mathcal{F}}{\partial a_{ir}} = 0$ and substituting the auxiliary variables $\{s_{ijr}\}$ and $\{t_{kjr}\}$ to the value in Eq. (5) yields the update rule of a_{ir}. Update rules of b_{jr} are derived in the same manner and that of c_{kr} is directly derived from the linear equality relation. Update rules are summarized as follows:

$$a_{ir}^{new} \leftarrow a_{ir} \frac{\Big(\sum_j \frac{x_{ij}}{\hat{x}_{ij}} b_{jr} + \sum_k \sum_j v_{ik} \frac{y_{kj}}{\hat{y}_{kj}} b_{jr}\Big)}{\sum_j b_{jr} + \sum_k \sum_j v_{ik} b_{jr}}, \tag{6}$$

$$b_{jr}^{new} \leftarrow b_{jr} \frac{\Big(\sum_i \frac{x_{ij}}{\hat{x}_{ij}} a_{ir} + \sum_k \frac{y_{kj}}{\hat{y}_{kj}} c_{kr}\Big)}{\sum_i a_{ir} + \sum_k c_{kr}}, \tag{7}$$

$$c_{kr}^{new} \leftarrow \sum_i v_{ik} a_{ir}. \tag{8}$$

In this paper, we omit the treatment of missing values for brevity. For details, see [3].

3.4 Generalization

We add the explanation for the more general scenario which *pNimf* can be applied to. In §3.1, we gave the example that both high-resolution data and low-resolution data are one month purchase logs. However, as long as assumptions (A1) and (A2) are satisfied, *pNimf* could be applied to any problem with theoretical support. Moreover, *pNimf* can deal with multiple high-resolution and low-resolution data by generalizing data generative process. Let M be the number of high-resolution data and $\boldsymbol{X}^m = \{x_{ij}^m\}$ is the m-th high-resolution matrix. Similarly, let N be the number of low-resolution data and $\boldsymbol{Y}^n = \{y_{kj}^n\}$ is the n-th low-resolution matrix. Each m(or n) need not to correspond to a period of time, e.g. day, week and month as a previous example and it may be a indicator of a location such as prefecture and country where data is collected. By extending data generative process represented by Fig. 2(a) to Fig. 2(c), the estimation procedure is obtained by slight modification of update rules Eq. (6)(7) as follows:

$$a_{ir}^{new} \leftarrow a_{ir} \frac{\Big(M \sum_j \frac{\bar{x}_{ij}}{\hat{x}_{ij}} b_{jr} + N \sum_k \sum_j v_{ik} \frac{\bar{y}_{kj}}{\hat{y}_{kj}} b_{jr}\Big)}{M \sum_j b_{jr} + N \sum_k \sum_j v_{ik} b_{jr}}, \tag{9}$$

$$b_{jr}^{new} \leftarrow b_{jr} \frac{\Big(M \sum_i \frac{\bar{x}_{ij}}{\hat{x}_{ij}} a_{ir} + N \sum_k \frac{\bar{y}_{kj}}{\hat{y}_{kj}} c_{kr}\Big)}{M \sum_i a_{ir} + N \sum_k c_{kr}}, \tag{10}$$

where $\bar{x}_{ij} = \frac{1}{M} \sum_{m=1}^{M} x_{ij}^m$ and $\bar{y}_{kj} = \frac{1}{N} \sum_{n=1}^{N} y_{kj}^n$.

4. EXPERIMENT

4.1 Setting

Data Description: We evaluate the performance of our methods using real purchase log data: consumer panel research data "SCI" provided by Intage Inc. We use purchase logs of daily necessities (such as milk, coffee and snacks) from 2013.1.1 to 2013.12.31 in Japan. Thus, we can expect that (A2) is satisfied since these items likely to be purchased in each month repeatedly. SCI includes user's attribute information such as age, sex and job. We construct Two-month data and Four-month data as follows. Two-month data is constructed using the log in Nov. and Dec. as in Fig. 1. We use only the logs of active users who have a purchase log in each month to satisfy (A1) and items that appeared more than ten times. The size and sparseness of $\boldsymbol{X}^{\text{Dec}}$ and $\boldsymbol{Y}^{\text{Nov}}$ are $I = 1589, J = 3164, K = 34$, 99.15% and 54.4%, respectively. We repeat this procedure for the logs of Jan. and Feb. Size and sparseness are almost similar to that of Nov. and Dec. Four-month data is also prepared in an analogous manner. For Four-month data, we used the logs of Sep, Oct, Nov and Dec and made high-resolution matrix $\boldsymbol{X}^{\text{Dec}}$ and low-resolution matrices $\boldsymbol{Y}^{\text{Nov}}$, $\boldsymbol{Y}^{\text{Oct}}$ and $\boldsymbol{Y}^{\text{Sep}}$. The resulting size was $I = 1288, J = 4842, K = 34$.

Evaluation Measure: In our experiments, we use a test set log likelihood to evaluate performance. We split the elements of matrix $\boldsymbol{X}$ into a training dataset and a test dataset and compute the log likelihood of the elements in the test. Test data are treated as missing values in the training phase. Log likelihood of the test data set is defined as $\frac{1}{|\mathcal{T}|}\sum_{(i,j)\in\mathcal{T}} \log \mathcal{PO}(x_{ij}|\hat{x}_{ij})$, where $\mathcal{T}$ is the set of element indexes in the test data and $|\cdot|$ indicates the number of elements in the set. We prepared 10 pair of the training and the test data by randomly extracting 5% of non-zero elements as the test data.

Baseline Methods: For comparison, we consider the following methods. (1)NMF [7], traditional method which use only high-resolution matrix $\boldsymbol{X}$. (2)NMMF [10], an NMF based state of the art CMF method that uses both $\boldsymbol{X}$ and $\boldsymbol{Y}$. The weight parameter of NMMF is chosen from the candidates $\alpha = 0.1, 0.5, 1.0$. We report the result for $\alpha = 1.0$ since it shows the best result among the candidates.

4.2 Result

Our first experiment used the Two-month data. Table 1 shows the results. It is confirmed that *pNimf* and NMMF outperform NMF regardless of the number of factors in all datasets. This result indicates that the use of low-resolution data improves the performance. Moreover, the performance of *pNimf* is superior to that of NMMF in all settings. It seems that the linear relation between factor matrices using user's attribute information supports *pNimf* in handling the difference in resolution and thus achieving better factorization results.

Next, we evaluate the performance achieved while varying the number of low-resolution data N using Four-month data. We set the number of factors to ten and compared it to *pNimf* using a different number of low-resolution data N. Fig. 3 shows the results. As the number of low-resolution data N increases, the performance of *pNimf* improves. Since *pNimf* can deal with multiple low-resolution data by generalization of data generative process, it works well even if the amount of high-resolution and low-resolution data differ.

Table 1: Result of two-month data: test set log-likelihood for different numbers of factors, R. Average and standard deviation are presented. Larger values are better.

Data	R	NMF	NMMF	*pNimf*
SCI	10	-13.3±0.63	-7.89±0.38	**-7.84**±0.17
$\boldsymbol{X}^{\text{Feb}}$&	20	-18.7±1.95	-9.14±0.48	**-8.81**±0.20
$\boldsymbol{Y}^{\text{Jan}}$	50	-32.7±2.15	-11.8±0.48	**-10.4**±0.33
SCI	10	-13.9±0.99	-8.24±0.59	**-7.83**±0.23
$\boldsymbol{X}^{\text{Dec}}$&	20	-14.4±0.73	-8.95±0.37	**-8.68**±0.27
$\boldsymbol{Y}^{\text{Nov}}$	50	-32.59±2.17	-12.32±0.50	**-10.45**±0.30

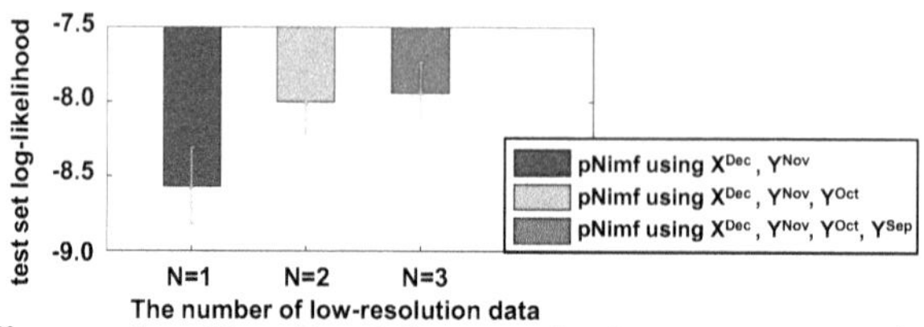

Figure 3: Result of four-month data: test set log-likelihood varying the number of low-resolution data, N. Height of histogram and error-bar shows average and standard deviation. Larger values are better.

5. CONCLUSION

This paper addressed the simplified IRDAP that (A1) *the common user population assumption* and (A2) *the iid assumption* are satisfied. We proposed *pNimf* based on the data generative process using *latent high-resolution data*. Experiments showed that the proposed model provides best performance, and that the performance improves as the number of low-resolution data increases. The results imply that our approach using *latent high-resolution data* can become the basic approach to IRDAP. In order to solve more general IRDAPs, a promising direction is to weaken the assumptions (A1) and (A2). In addition, the degree of improvement using low-resolution data must be related to the size of I and K and clarification of this also remains as future work.

6. REFERENCES

[1] Y. Aimoto and H. Kashima. Matrix factorization with aggregated observations. In *Advances in Knowledge Discovery and Data Mining*, 2013.

[2] D. M. Blei, A. Y. Ng, and M. I. Jordan. Latent dirichlet allocation. In *JMLR*, 2003.

[3] A. T. Cemgil. Bayesian inference in non-negative matrix factorisation models. Technical Report, Univ. of Cambridge, 2008.

[4] A. Cichocki, R. Zdunek, A. H. Phan, and S. I. Amari. Nonnegative matrix and tensor factorizations: applications to exploratory multi-way data analysis and blind source separation. John Wiley & Sons, 2009.

[5] C. Ding, L. Tao, and P. Wei. On the equivalence between non-negative matrix factorization and probabilistic latent semantic indexing. Comp. Statistics & Data Analysis, 2008.

[6] T. Hofmann. Probabilistic latent semantic indexing. In *SIGIR*, 1999.

[7] D. D. Lee and H. S. Seung. Learning the parts of objects by non-negative matrix factorization. In *Nature*, 1999.

[8] H. Lee and S. Choi. Group nonnegative matrix factorization for EEG classification. In *AISTATS*, 2009.

[9] A. P. Singh and G. J. Gordon. Relational learning via collective matrix factorization. In *KDD*, 2008.

[10] K. Takeuchi, K. Ishiguro, A. Kimura, and H. Sawada. Non-negative Multiple Matrix Factorization. In *IJCAI*, 2013.

Identifying Attractive News Headlines for Social Media

Sawa Kourogi,
Hiroyuki Fujishiro
Hosei University, Japan.
fujisiro@hosei.ac.jp

Akisato Kimura
NTT Communication Science
Laboratories, Japan.
akisato@ieee.org

Hitoshi Nishikawa
Tokyo Institute of Technology,
Japan.

ABSTRACT

In the past, leading newspaper companies and broadcasters were the sole distributors of news articles, and thus news consumers simply received news articles from those outlets at regular intervals. However, the growth of social media and smart devices led to a considerable change in this traditional relationship between news providers and consumers. Hundreds of thousands of news articles are now distributed on social media, and consumers can access those articles at any time via smart devices. This has meant that news providers are under pressure to fin ways of engaging the attention of consumers. This paper provides a novel solution to this problem by identifying attractive headlines as a gateway to news articles. We firs perform one of the firs investigations of news headlines on a major viral medium. Using our investigation as a basis, we also propose a learning-to-rank method that suggests promising news headlines. Our experiments with 2,000 news articles demonstrate that our proposed method can accurately identify attractive news headlines from the candidates and reveals several promising factors of making news articles go viral.

Categories and Subject Descriptors

I.2.7 [**Artificia Intelligence**]: Natural Language Processing

Keywords

News headlines; virality; social media; learning to rank

1. INTRODUCTION

In the golden era of mass media, leading news outlets and TV broadcasting stations played a central role in publishing and distributing news articles. News consumers simply received and digested news articles from those outlets at regular pre-define intervals, according to the broadcast schedule of news programs. The emergence of the internet gave news providers a new channel for distributing news articles, and it also generated new opportunities for consumers to access news articles whenever they used their PCs. However, leading news outlets continued to dominate the market, and the relationship between news providers and consumers has remained unilateral.

However, the wide-spread use of hand-held devices such as smartphones and tablets has completely changed the way of accessing news articles. Consumers can check news articles whenever they want through such hand-held devices. At the same time, the resources and platforms for publishing and distributing news articles have also shifted from the officia sites of leading news outlets to social media. Any type of news article published by any news provider has a potential to go viral across social media. This has led to a considerable change in the traditional relationship between news providers and consumers. Consumers have no choice but to select news articles so that they can read within a limited amount of time, and news providers are under pressure to fin ways of engaging consumer attention.

The change in relationship shown above also encouraged the commercial growth of new types of social platforms such as curation, aggregation, and viral media. Those platforms employ various strategies to steer consumers towards their news content. For example, Upworthy, a major viral medium, proposes ten ways to make content go viral [4], including web designs, impressive images, and optimization for target social platforms. Another viral medium, Buzzfeed, introduces A/B testing to fin promising stories and improve the user interface [1]. Of those approaches, headlines are the most significan factor in terms of providing a gateway to news articles, and greatly influenc our impression of news articles. Upworthy recommends us to write 25 headlines and to test the best ones. However, the process of generating and identifying attractive news headlines relies heavily on *seat of the pants* work by highly skilled editors and curators.

Our ultimate goal is the fully automatic generation of attractive headlines for news articles that have the potential to go viral on social media. As the firs step towards this goal, we now focus on the problem of suggesting a promising headline from a given set of hand-crafted candidate headlines. This will contribute to the quantificatio and visualization of the virality of news headlines that might be considered difficul to measure and even to assist the editors and curators working for news providers.

Our contributions can be summarized as follows: (1) We begin by performing one of the firs examinations of viral media data. In particular, we analyze the relationships between (a) news articles published on a major viral medium, (b) tweets as Twitter-focused news headlines posted by the officia Twitter account and (c) retweet/favorite counts as a tractable measure of virality. This investigation reveals promising factors that boost the virality of headlines. (2) Based on the investigation, we propose a learning-to-rank approach to the problem of suggesting attractive news head-

[1] http://www.wired.co.uk/magazine/archive/2014/02/features/buzzfeed

Permission to make digital or hard copies of all or part of this work for personal or classroom use is granted without fee provided that copies are not made or distributed for profi or commercial advantage and that copies bear this notice and the full citation on the firs page. Copyrights for components of this work owned by others than ACM must be honored. Abstracting with credit is permitted. To copy otherwise, or republish, to post on servers or to redistribute to lists, requires prior specifi permission and/or a fee. Request permissions from permissions@acm.org.

CIKM'15, October 19-23, 2015, Melbourne, Australia.

© 2015 ACM. ISBN 978-1-4503-3794-6/15/10 ...$15.00.

DOI: http://dx.doi.org/10.1145/2806416.2806631.

lines. Given a news article ("a query" in the learning-to-rank framework) and headline candidates ("documents"), our method ranks candidates in descending order of estimated virality ("relevance"). We evaluate the performance of the proposed method with a large corpus, and reveal which factors actually helped to boost virality.

2. RELATED WORK

The spread of social media use on news outlets, the emergence of data journalism and the rise of automatic news aggregation imply a new trend for the seamless integration of news media, social media and data mining. Interdisciplinary work across news media, social media and data mining is becoming a hot research topic. Tsagkias et al. [14] developed a method of constructing queries to discover tweets that implicitly refer to a target news article. Moniz et al. [12] used a regression technique to estimate future tweet counts of news events and to re-rank news articles. Castillo et al. [1] presented a study of the life cycle of news articles posted on social media. However, all the above researches focused mainly on social messages posted by news consumers, and research and discussion from the perspective of news providers has been largely neglected. This paper is unique in that we explore ways of distributing news articles on social media via data mining approaches.

Several studies tried to quantify and predict content virality. Suh et al. [13] and Diakopoulos et al. [3] independently investigated which factors contribute to the virality of Twitter messages posted from major news outlets from sociological standpoints. Guerini et al. [5], Deza and Parikh [2] tried to understand the virality of image content. However, all the above studies focused only on the effect of content (Tweets or images) on virality, and relationships between content (Tweets) and hyperlinked destinations (news articles) have yet to be explored. In contrast, this paper tries to reveal the source of virality from headlines themselves and the relationships between headlines and news articles.

3. CORPUS ANALYSIS

We firs investigate a corpus of viral media data. We chose The Huffingto Post (Japan Edition) as the target news outlet. The oficia Twitter account @HuffPostJapan produces tweets an average of 40 tweet posts per day. Every tweet consists of a description and a link to an article, and every article is linked to an average of three officia tweets with different descriptions. We believe The Huffington Post to be one of the best subjects for investigating relationships between news articles, their descriptions and the power of virality, since side effects caused by the accounts can be removed.

We crawled news articles published by The Huffingto Post and tweets posted by their officia account in September and October 2014, and manually investigated the obtained corpus. The number of tweets we used is 858 (almost half of all the tweets posted in this period) and the number of articles contained in those tweets is 276. First, the main text, the time stamp, links to images, the retweet and favorite count are extracted from every tweet. We observe that only 5% (40 tweets) obtain 100 RT+fav counts and 85% (732 tweets) have less than 50RT+fav counts. The maximum RT+fav count is 703, and the minimum is 0. Next, the main text is split into a header noted in brackets and the content. The content is further segmented into morphemes. Then, meaningless parts are removed such as postpositions and symbols.

Of all the tweets, 1/3 (285 tweets) contain links to image contents, and many of them were the firs tweet for a news article. We also found that tweets with images tend to get higher RT+fav count. In fact, all but one of the top 50 tweets of the RT+fav count contain images, and only one tweet with an RT+fav count of less than

Table 1: Extracted features (b: binary, i: integer, r: real value)

Group	Feature	type	dimension
Image	-	b	1
Time	diff	r	1
	period	b	7
	weekday	b	1
Keyword	pre-define	b	24
	publisher	i	1
	paragraph	b	2
Structure	header	b	1
	keyword	b	4
	front	b	5
	distance	i	1
	title	b	1
	length	r	2
User	-	r	4
Distribute	similarity	r	4
	gaps	r	5
Total			64

f ve contains an image. This indicates that the presence of shared images contributes greatly to increased virality.

We also check the firs appearance in an article of words used in a tweet. We found that less than 50% (43.3%) of words firs appeared in the firs paragraph. In most of leading newspapers, headlines are constructed from the content of the firs paragraph of the article. However, this is not in the case with The Huffingto Post. We also found that there are many examples of re-phrasing, paraphrasing and abbreviations (28%, 539 words) in tweets. This implies that it is insufficien simply to extract certain features with low-level keyword matching and we should introduce some sophisticated techniques that take the meaning of the word into account.

We also observed that several tweets with large RT+fav counts include certain surprises or curiosity gaps in relation to the usage of words and phrases. Upworthy also noticed that social headlines require a curiosity gap [4]. We have to understand the meanings of words and phrases in some ways and combine them so as to generate curiosity gaps and surprises.

4. SUGGESTING NEWS HEADLINES

Having analyzed the characteristics of viral media as they operate today, we also hope to build a method that identifie attractive news headlines from candidate hand-crafted sentences.

Our method consists of the following three steps: (1) Feature extraction: This step extracts a feature vector $\boldsymbol{x}_c \in \mathcal{R}^N$ from a given candidate headline h_c, the corresponding news article a_c, and several additional pieces of meta information m_c related to posting time and user statistics. (2) Model training: This step obtains a model $f : \mathcal{R}^N \to \mathcal{R}$ that produces an estimated degree $v_c \in \mathcal{R}$ of virality from a given feature $\boldsymbol{x}_c \in \mathcal{R}^N$. A model can be trained with triads $\{(\boldsymbol{x}_c, a_c, v_c)\}_{c=1,2,\ldots,C_{tr}}$ of a feature vector $\boldsymbol{x}_c$, the corresponding news article a_c and the ground-truth degree v_c of virality. A naive solution to this problem is the regression of the degree v_c of virality from a given feature $\boldsymbol{x}_c$. However, this strategy is not appropriate since virality can be affected by both the candidate and the corresponding article. Instead, we adopt a learning-to-rank approach, which is frequently used for information retrieval. In this framework, we can consider a news article to be "a query" and candidate headlines as "documents" that must be retrieved and ranked. (3) Candidate selection: This step selects the best headline $\hat{h}_{\hat{c}}$ with the high estimated degree of virality from a set of candidate headlines $\{\hat{h}_c\}_{c=1,2,C_{te}}$ with the help of the trained model.

In the following, we describe feature extraction in detail. We assume Twitter as the target social platform, and assume that every candidate headline (hereafter *candidate*) will be posted as a tweet with a link to the corresponding news article. Table 1 outlines the features we propose in this paper. As shown in this table, all the features can be categorized into six feature groups: Image, Time, Keyword, Structure, User and Distribute.

Image: shared images Major viral media have noticed that shared images (images attached to a headline) are essential to gain a high click-through rate [4]. Meanwhile, a previous paper [6] pointed out that we cannot estimate the click-through rates from image contents even with gold-standard features. Thus, we defin a binary feature *Image* representing the presence of image links.

Time: time stamps of headlines and articles Many previous studies have indicated that posting time of candidates highly contributes to virality. We defin the following three types of features related to posting time: (1) *Time-diff*: Negative logarithm of the difference between the time stamp of a candidate and that of the corresponding article. (2) *Time-period*: Time slots, every slot define a single binary feature: Midnight (1-5am), morning (6-8am), AM (9-11am), noon (12am-1pm), PM (2-4pm), evening (5-7pm), night (8-12pm). (3) *Time-weekday*: We defin a binary feature representing weekdays or weekends.

Keyword: specifi / predefine keywords We observed in the investigation that low-level keyword matching might not help to boost virality. To validate the hypothesis, we select the following 24 keywords that were frequently used in the top tweets of the RT+fav count and defin a binary feature *Keyword-predefine* for each keyword [2]: reasons (background, reason, secret, why, behind, truth, dark side, true picture, what is, fact), methods (theory, how to, method, know-how), surprise (awesome, brilliant, amazing, wonderful, surprising, shocked), special (customized, special, reserved, only). We also count the number of publisher-define keywords [3] contained in a headline and defin a single integer feature *Keyword-publisher*. As the last feature, we count the number of common nouns and proper nouns contained in both a candidate and the firs paragraph of the article and defin a single binary feature *Keyword-paragraph* for each count.

Structure: structure of candidate headlines Our investigation indicated that brackets are often utilized at the beginning of tweets to drive the attention of readers and to emphasize the keywords or key phrases noted in the brackets. We here defin a binary feature *Structure-header* representing the presence of leading brackets and four other binary features *Structure-keyword* representing the presence of pre-define keywords (new, updated, picture, breaking) in the brackets. Another type of feature can be define from the order of words. We defin f ve binary features *Structure-front* representing whether the firs word is (1) a common noun, (2) a pronoun or (3) a proper noun and the second word is (4) a common noun or (5) a proper noun. We use Mecab [9] to split Japanese sentences into morphemes and to obtain a word class for every morpheme. We also defin another single binary feature *Structure-title* that represents whether a candidate contains the title of the corresponding article or not, since the title of a news article might not be the most suitable as a viral headline. For the same purpose, we defin another real-valued feature *Structure-distance* as a negative logarithm of Levenshtein distance between a candidate and the article title. In addition, as the net slang "tl;dr" suggests, social media users tend to skip long messages. We thus introduce two real-valued features *Structure-length*, each representing the negative logarithm of the total number of words and characters in a candidate.

User: user statistics We also defin four real-valued features *User* based on user statistics for social platforms: logarithms of (1) the number of followers, (2) the number of following users, (3) the number of lists and (4) the total number of posts.

Distribute: distributed representation of words As mentioned in our investigation, taking the meanings of words into account is essential. For this purpose, we exploit a distributed representation [11], which learns a model for embedding a word w in a multi-dimensional vector $\boldsymbol{y}(w) \in \mathcal{R}^M$ representing certain conceptual relationships. A simple similarity measure $s : \mathcal{R}^M \times \mathcal{R}^M \rightarrow \mathcal{R}$ such as a cosine similarity works well to compute a conceptual similarity, and simple vector operations such as addition and subtraction while also preserving conceptual relationships. We use word2vec [11] to obtain distributed representations and Wikipedia as a corpus. We firs defin the following four types of features *Distribute-similarity* related to the similarity of words or phrases:
(1) Similarity between a pair of most similar nouns.

$$s_1(h_c) = \max_{w_1, w_2 \in g(h_c)} s(\boldsymbol{y}(w_1), \boldsymbol{y}(w_2)),$$

where $g(h_c)$ is a subset of a candidate h_c that contains only nouns.
(2) Similarity between a tweet and the title $t(a_c)$ of the corresponding article a_c.

$$s_2(h_c, a_c) = s(\sum_{w_1 \in h(c)} \boldsymbol{y}(w_1), \sum_{w_2 \in t(a_c)} \boldsymbol{y}(w_2)).$$

(3) Similarity between a tweet and a set $k(a_c)$ of article keywords.

$$s_3(h_c, a_c) = \sum_{w_1 \in k(a_c)} \max_{w_2 \in h(c)} s(\boldsymbol{y}(w_1), \boldsymbol{y}(w_2)),$$

(4) Similarity between a tweet and the firs paragraph of the article. This is computed almost the same way as the second one.

Our investigation also indicates that social headlines might require surprises or curiosity gaps. We try to explore these types of abstract concepts through a distributed representation. We defin the following three types of features *Distribute-gap*:
(1) Negative similarity between an outlier and all the others in a candidate. We firs select an outlier word $o(h_c)$ (resp. noun $o(g(h_c))$) from a candidate h_c, and then compute the similarity between the outlier word (resp. noun) and the others.

$$d_{1,1}(h_c) = -s(\boldsymbol{y}(o(h_c)), \sum_{w \in h_c - \{o(h_c)\}} \boldsymbol{y}(w)),$$
$$d_{1,2}(h_c) = -s(\boldsymbol{y}(o(g(h_c))), \sum_{w \in g(h_c) - \{o(g(h_c))\}} \boldsymbol{y}(w)).$$

(2) Negative similarity between the outlier and the pair of the most similar nouns.

$$d_2(h_c) = -s(\boldsymbol{y}(o(h_c)), \sum_{w \in p(h_c)} \boldsymbol{y}(w)),$$
$$p(h_c) = \arg \max_{w_1, w_2 \in g(h_c)} s(\boldsymbol{y}(w_1), \boldsymbol{y}(w_2)).$$

(3) Negative similarity between the outlier word (resp. noun) and the word (resp. noun) furthest from the outlier.

$$d_{3,1}(h_c) = - \min_{w \in h_c - \{o(h_c)\}} s(\boldsymbol{y}(o(h_c)), \boldsymbol{y}(w)),$$
$$d_{3,2}(h_c) = - \min_{w \in g(h_c) - \{o(g(h_c))\}} s(\boldsymbol{y}(o(h_c)), \boldsymbol{y}(w)).$$

5. EXPERIMENTS

To evaluate our proposed method, we crawled Twitter posts through Twitter Firehose API [4] for 4 months (December 2014 - March

[2]All the keywords are originally Japanese.

[3]Those keywords can be obtained from META elements in the article HTML.

[4]We can obtain almost half of the whole Japanese tweets.

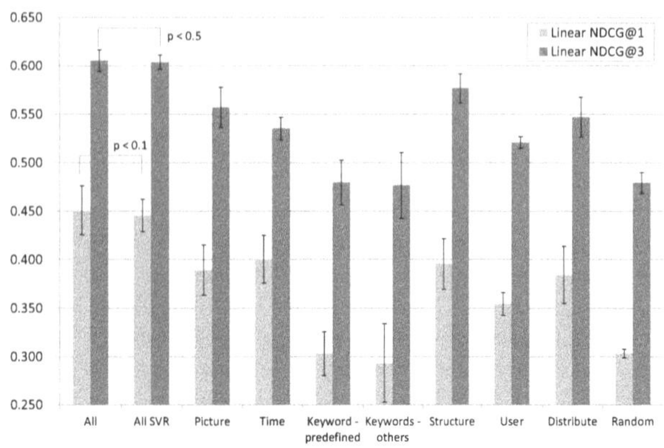

Figure 1: Experimental evaluation results. All: our proposed method, All SVR: direct regression of virality with the same features as our method, Random: random prediction, others: ranking with individual feature groups.

2015). From the tweets, we extracted those that (a) contained a link to an article in The Huffingto Post Japan, (b) were retweeted or favorited by someone, and (c) found other tweets with the link to the same article, resulting in a total of 24,000 tweets. Concurrently, we retrieved articles of The Huffingto Post Japan contained in those tweets, which provided us with 2,900 articles. We adopted the sum of the retweet and favorite counts as a measure of virality. We use the normalized discount cumulative gain (NDCG@k, k is a predefine integer) for evaluating ranked results. We compared the proposed method with (1) random prediction for reference, (2) a learning-to-rank method with individual feature groups, and (3) a regression method with all the features. We used SVMrank [7] with linear kernels to train learning-to-rank models and SVMlight with linear kernels to train regression models. We randomly chose 90% of the tweets as training data and the remaining 10% as test data. We trained models on the training data and tuned the SVM hyper-parameters with 9-fold cross validation, and obtained evaluation results for the test data.

Figure 1 summarizes the result. We observe that our method is the best performer with NDCG@1=0.451 and NDCG@3=0.605. We also fin that the proposed learning-to-rank approach outperformed a regression approach (NDCG@1=0.445, NDCG@3=0.603). Several individual feature groups such as *Picture*, *Structure* and *Distribute* also worked reasonably well, and the feature group *Keyword* yielded poor performance. This supports our hypothesis that low-level keyword matching does not make sense and taking the meanings of words into account is essential.

To explore which factors actually helped to boost virality, we investigated the weight of the features in the leaned linear models. Figure 2 shows the features yielding the top 10 and bottom 10 weights. This result indicates that (1) we should post headlines as early as possible, (2) article titles might not be appropriate as news headlines for social media, (3) headers consisting of brackets and special keywords such as "breaking" and "new" drive the attention of readers, and (4) there should be as few as possible characters in headlines. We also see that the feature group *Distribute* yielded larger weights, which again supports our hypothesis that taking the meanings of words into account is essential. Interestingly, user statistics such as the number of followers, friends and lists had a detrimental effect on virality.

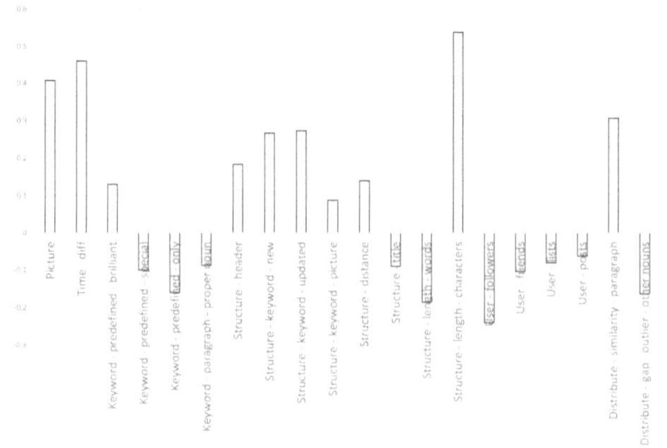

Figure 2: Major coefficient of learned linear SVM rankers.

6. CONCLUDING REMARKS

We have proposed a novel approach for suggesting attractive headlines for news articles for social media. Our investigation of viral media data revealed several promising factors that might boost the virality of news headlines. Based on our investigation, we proposed a novel learning-to-rank approach for the problem of selecting attractive news headlines from a given set of hand-crafted candidate headlines. Experiments with a corpus consisting of Twitter posts and linked news articles showed the effectiveness of our proposed method. The promising result provided by the proposed method is simply the firs step to our ultimate goal, namely fully automatic generation of attractive headlines of news articles. Much future research can be done in this aspect. We are especially interested in developing more effective features, applying our method to other news outlets and generating candidate tweets automatically.

7. REFERENCES

[1] Castillo et al. Characterizing the life cycle of online news stories using social media reactions. In *Proc. CSCW2014*.

[2] Deza and Parikh. Understanding image virality. In *Proc. CVPR2015*.

[3] Diakopoulos and Zubiaga. Newsworthyness and network gatekeeping on Twitter In *Proc. ICWSM2014*.

[4] Gidfar et al. Upworthy's how to make that one thing go viral. RootsCamp 2012, `http://slidesha.re/QA1Tn9`.

[5] Guerini et al. Exploring image virality in Google Plus. In *Proc. SocialCom2013*.

[6] Ishiguro et al. Towards automatic image understanding and mining via social curation. In *Proc. ICDM2012*.

[7] Joachims. Training linear SVMs in linear time. In *Proc. KDD2006*.

[8] Kim et al. Diversity-seeking users and their influenc on social news sites. In *Proc. NewsKDD2014*.

[9] Kudo et al. Applying conditional random field to Japanese morphological analysis. In *Proc. EMNLP2004*.

[10] Mclnerney et al. Discovering newsworthy tweets with a geographical topic model. In *Proc. NewsKDD2014*.

[11] Mikolov et al. Distributed representation of words and phrases and their compositionality. In *Proc. NIPS2013*.

[12] Moniz and Torgo. Improvement of news ranking through importance prediction. In *Proc. NewsKDD2014*.

[13] Nagarajan et al. A qualitative examinztion of topical tweet and retweet practices. In *Proc. ICWSM2010*.

[14] Tsagkias et al. Linking online news and social media. In *Proc. WSDM2011*.

[15] Zhang et al. Which tweets will be headlines? A hierarchical Bayeian model for bridging social media and traditional media. In *Proc. SNAKDD2014*.

A Probabilistic Rating Auto-encoder for Personalized Recommender Systems

Huizhi Liang
The University of Melbourne
VIC 3010, Melbourne
oklianghuizi@gmail.com

Timothy Baldwin
The University of Melbourne
VIC 3010, Melbourne
tb@ldwin.net

ABSTRACT

User profiling is a key component of personalized recommender systems, and is used to generate user profiles that describe individual user interests and preferences. The increasing availability of big data is driving the urgent need for user profiling algorithms that are able to generate accurate user profiles from large-scale user behavior data. In this paper, we propose a probabilistic rating auto-encoder to perform unsupervised feature learning and generate latent user feature profiles from large-scale user rating data. Based on the generated user profiles, *neighborhood* based collaborative filtering approaches have been adopted to make personalized rating predictions. The effectiveness of the proposed approach is demonstrated in experiments conducted on a real-world rating dataset from `yelp.com`.

Categories and Subject Descriptors

H.3.3 [**Information Storage and Retrieval**]: Information Search and Retrieval-Information Filtering

General Terms

Algorithms; Experimentation; Performance

Keywords

User profiling; Recommender Systems; Auto-encoder; Dimensionality Reduction

1. INTRODUCTION

Recommender systems are popular for personalization, and can help to reduce information overload for users in online communities, i.e., making suggestions regarding which information is most relevant to an individual user [1]. User profiling is the foundation of personalized recommender systems, and provides the basis to discover knowledge about users' interests, preferences, and information needs, from user-generated social data including user-generated content and behavioral information [8, 9]. With the rapid growth of social data, methods that support efficient and effective extraction of features from big social data are becoming increasingly important.

Rating (explicit or implicit) is one type of user behaviour information that has been popularly used to profile users' individual preferences and interests. For example, a user may use a rating score ranging from 1 to 5 to express their preferences or sentiment orientation with respect to an item. The typical approach is to profile users directly based on their rating behavior, and based on this, to use *neighborhood* based collaborative filtering approaches [11] to make rating predictions or top-N item recommendations [1]. Learning latent representations of users or items from user rating behavior can find latent or hidden relations between users or items, and reduce data dimensionality, thus contributing to scalable recommender systems. Although some dimensionality reduction approaches such as matrix factorization [5] have been proposed, the development of methods for learning latent representations from large-scale user rating behaviour data remains an open research question.

Deep learning techniques [4] have recently emerged as a promising framework for automatically training models over large-scale unlabeled and labeled datasets. Notably, auto-encoders [12] can learn latent representations for unlabelled data, and have been successfully applied to text, image, and audio information [7]. However, there has been less work on applying auto-encoders to rating data [13]. In this paper, we propose a rating auto-encoder to learn latent features from user rating behavior, for the purpose of constructing more accurate user profiles. The generated latent user representations can then be used in recommender systems to perform personalized recommendation.

2. RELATED WORK

Recommender systems have been an active research area for more than a decade, with the main focus being recommendation approaches based on explicit ratings. Popular recommender systems applications include predicting ratings and recommending items to a user. Rating prediction is the task of predicting the rating a user will give to an item, while item recommendation is the task of recommending a set of unrated or new items to a target user [1]. Root Mean Squared Error (RMSE) and Mean Absolute Error (MAE) are widely used to measure the accuracy of rating predictions, while precision and recall are commonly used to evaluate top-N item recommendation. For explicit ratings, both tasks are applicable, while for implicit ratings, top-N recom-

Permission to make digital or hard copies of all or part of this work for personal or classroom use is granted without fee provided that copies are not made or distributed for profit or commercial advantage and that copies bear this notice and the full citation on the first page. Copyrights for components of this work owned by others than ACM must be honored. Abstracting with credit is permitted. To copy otherwise, or republish, to post on servers or to redistribute to lists, requires prior specific permission and/or a fee. Request permissions from Permissions@acm.org.
CIKM'15, October 19–23, 2015, Melbourne, Australia.
© 2015 ACM. ISBN 978-1-4503-3794-6/15/10 ...$15.00.
DOI: http://dx.doi.org/10.1145/2806416.2806633.

mendation is more applicable [1]. Recommender systems can be broadly classified into three categories: content-based, collaborative filtering ("CF"), and hybrid approaches [1]. *Neighborhood* methods [11] and *latent factor* methods [5] are the two primary collaborative filtering approaches.

Learning latent representations or latent factor models of users and items has generated recent attention, given the rapid growth of rating data in online communities [3]. Matrix factorization [5] is a state-of-the-art *latent factor* method. It jointly learns latent user and item features, and uses the dot product of the latent user and item features to predict ratings. However, there is less discussion about whether the learned latent user features themselves can be used to accurately represent user profiles. The general question of accurately learning latent user representations is still relatively unexplored. Recently, deep learning techniques [4] and neural network models [2] such as auto-encoders have been applied to various application areas to learn latent or abstract representations of words, documents, images, audio, and videos. For example, *word2vec* [10, 6] can be used to efficiently learn latent word representations based on large-scale, unlabelled text corpora. Our contribution in this work is to apply deep learning methods to user rating data, and learn latent user representations.

3. THE PROPOSED PROBABILISTIC RATING AUTO-ENCODER

To describe the proposed approach, we define some key concepts used in this paper:

- **Users:** $U = \{u_1, u_2, ..., u_{|U|}\}$ is the set of all users in an online community.
- **Items** (e.g., Products or Businesses): $P = \{p_1, p_2, ..., p_{|P|}\}$ is the set of all items rated by users in U.
- **Ratings:** $R = \{(u_i, p_j, r_{ij}) | u_i \in U, p_j \in P, r_{ij} \in \mathbb{R}\}$ is the set of all ratings that users have assigned to items, where $\mathbb{R}$ denotes the set of real numbers. Real-valued rating numbers are often binned into ordinal **Rating Categories**, denoted as $C = \{c_1, c_2, ..., c_{|C|}\}$. For example, we can represent ratings using a 5-point scale of 1 to 5, or a more coarse-grained scale such as: `negative`, `neutral`, and `positive`.

A user profile is used to describe an individual user's interests and preferences. Typically, an explicit or implicit item rating vector with numeric or binary values is used to profile the preferences or interests of a user to these items [1]. Let $\vec{u}_i$ denote the rating vector representation of user u_i, for example in the form of a set of items with ratings, $\vec{u}_i = \{(p_1, r_{i1}), (p_2, r_{i2}), ..., (p_{|P|}, r_{i|P|})\}$. For a target user u_i and target item p_j, the rating prediction task is defined as predicting the rating value r_{ij}, given a user u_i's profile.

For a given user u_i, if two items p_i and p_j are assigned the same rating score, then these two items are similar in terms of the sentiment orientation implied in the user rating information from this user's viewpoint. Based on this assumption, we propose a probabilistic auto-encoder [10] to capture the co-occurrence of items with the same rating score for the same user and learn the latent feature representation of items. For a given user and rating score, we can use the items with the same rating score from a given user as context, and use a neural probabilistic model to predict the occurrence of other items given an item in this context. For example, if user u_i rated items p_1, p_2, p_3 with the same rating score of 3, the rating auto-encoder can predict the occurrence of item p_2 or p_3 given item p_1 in this context. If the rating scores are of very fine granularity, it will result in a small context set containing very few items. To avoid data sparsity, we bin the rating scores and map them to rating categories with coarser granularity.

Let $P_{ix} \subseteq P$ denote the items in the context of user u_i and rating category c_x. The objective of the rating auto-encoder is then to maximize the average log probability:

$$\frac{1}{|P_{ix}|} \sum_{p_s \in P_{ix}} \sum_{p_t \in P_{ix} \setminus \{p_s\}} \log \Pr(p_t | p_s) \quad (1)$$

Inspired by the *skip-gram* model of *word2vec* [10], the rating auto-encoder contains two layers: an input and output layer. The input to the rating auto-encoder is the vector representation of an item $p_s \in P_{ix}$ with random initialization, while the output of the rating auto-encoder is every other item in the same context $p_t \in P_{ix} \setminus \{p_s\}$. Let W be the weight matrix between the input layer and output layer; W is randomly initialized and shared across all contexts. Let y denote the un-normalized log-probability for each output item p_l, which can be computed as:

$$y = W \cdot p_s \quad (2)$$

We use a multi-class classifier (e.g., softmax) to conduct the prediction task:

$$\Pr(p_t | p_s) = \frac{e^{y_{p_t}}}{\sum_{l=1}^{|P|} e^{y_{p_l}}} \quad (3)$$

We use the squared difference error as the loss function, stochastic gradient descent to train the auto-encoder model, and back propagation to obtain the gradient to update each input vector of item p_s and weight matrix W. After convergence over the training data, items with similar ratings are mapped to a similar position in the vector space. We generate latent representations of both items and users, as detailed below.

The **item representation** represents each item's latent rating behavior by users. Let $L = \{1, 2, ..., d\}$ denote the latent factor, v_{ja} denote the relevance of item p_j to latent factor $l_a \in L$ (i.e., the value of dimension l_a of the learned or updated vector of item p_j), and $2^{L \times \mathbb{R}}$ denote the power set of $L \times \mathbb{R}$. The relationship between an item and a set of latent factors can then be defined as the mapping $\mathcal{R}^p : P \to 2^{L \times \mathbb{R}}$, such that $\mathcal{R}^p(p_j) = \{(p_j, v_{ja}) | l_a \in L\}$. $\mathcal{R}^p(p_j)$ is called the item representation of item p_j.

Based on the item representation and the rating profile of each user, we can derive the latent representation profile of a given user u_i in a rating category $c_x \in C$. The **user representation** represents the latent rating behavior of each user. Let $w_{ia}^{c_x}$ denote the value of how much user u_i is interested in latent factor $l_a \in L$ in rating category $c_x \in C$. The relationship between a user and a set of latent factors in rating category $c_x \in C$ can then be defined as the mapping $\mathcal{R}^{u,c_x} : U \to 2^{L \times \mathbb{R}}$, such that $\mathcal{R}^{u,c_x}(u_i) = \{(l_a, w_{ia}^{c_x}) | l_a \in L\}$. $\mathcal{R}^{u,c_x}(u_i)$ is the user representation of u_i in rating category $c_x \in C$, and $\mathcal{R}^u = \{\mathcal{R}^{u,c_1}(u_i), \mathcal{R}^{u,c_2}(u_i), ..., \mathcal{R}^{u,c_{|C|}}(u_i)\}$ is the user representation of u_i.

We adopt **mean pooling** [7] to get the summary statistics of the latent features of u_i in category $c_x \in C$. The weight

$w_{ia}^{c_x}$ can be calculated as:

$$w_{ia}^{c_x} = \frac{\sum_{p_j \in P_{ix}} v_{ja}}{|P_{ix}|} \quad (4)$$

Based on user profiles, we use the *neighborhood* based collaborative filtering approach to find a set of similar users, then perform rating prediction based on neighboring users' ratings. This will be discussed in the following section.

4. PERSONALIZED RECOMMENDER SYSTEMS

The *neighborhood* based collaborative filtering approach is a common method for making recommendations. We apply the generated user profiles in *neighborhood* based recommender systems to make rating predictions. Neighborhood formation is the task of generating like-minded peers (i.e., the k nearest neighbors, "k-NN") for a target user $u_i \in U$. The distance or similarity measure can be calculated through various kinds of proximity computing approaches such as cosine similarity or Pearson's correlation. The more accurate a user profile is, the higher quality the user neighborhood.

Typically, the similarity of two users u_i and u_j can be measured by the similarity of their user profiles (i.e., user representations). Cosine is used to measure the similarity of two user latent representation vectors. The similarity of u_i and $u_j \in U$ can be calculated based on the maximum similarity of their representations over all the rating categories:

$$sim(u_i, u_j) = \max_{c_x \in C}\{cosine(\mathcal{R}^{u,c_x}(u_i), \mathcal{R}^{u,c_x}(u_j))\} \quad (5)$$

The neighborhood of user u_i is denoted as $\mathcal{N}(u_i) = \{u_j | u_j \in maxK_{u_j \in U}\{sim(u_i, u_j)\}\}, u_j \in U$, where $maxK\{\}$ returns the top-k most similar users to u_i. For each target user u_i, the prediction score of how much u_i will be interested in item p_j is calculated by considering the similarities between user u_i and those users who are neighbors of u_i and have rated item p_j [11]:

$$\hat{r}_{ij} = b_{ij} + \frac{\sum_{u_z \in \mathcal{N}_{u_i}} sim(u_i, u_z)(r_{zj} - b_{zj})}{\sum_{u_z \in \mathcal{N}_{u_i}} sim(u_i, u_z)} \quad (6)$$

where $b_{ij} = \mu + b_{u_i} + b_{p_j}$, μ is the average rating score of all known ratings, b_{u_i} is the observed rating deviation of user u_i, $b_{u_i} = \bar{r}_{u_i} - \mu$, and $\bar{r}_{u_i}$ denotes the average rating of user u_i. b_{p_j} is the observed rating deviation of item p_j, $b_{p_j} = \bar{r}_{p_j} - \mu$, where $\bar{r}_{p_j}$ denotes the average rating of item p_j. $b_{zj} = \mu + b_{u_z} + b_{p_j}$, where b_{u_z} is the observed rating deviation of user u_z.

5. EXPERIMENTS

To evaluate the effectiveness of the proposed approach, we conducted experiments on a real-world rating dataset from `yelp.com`.

5.1 Dataset

The Yelp dataset is a customer review dataset.[1] Each user rates businesses with a score ranging from 1 to 5. To reduce sparseness in the dataset, we filtered out those users who have rated no more than 3 items, and those items that have been rated by no more than two users. The dataset includes 37,915 users, 40,021 items (i.e., businesses), and 713,291 ratings. For each user, we randomly selected 80% of ratings as training data, and 20% of ratings as test data. The task is to predict ratings for the test set based on the training data. The descriptive statistics of this dataset are shown in Table 1.

Table 1: The composition of the Yelp dataset

	Training Set	Test Set
Users	37,915	37,915
Items	38,977	20,413
Ratings	599,546	113,745

5.2 Experimental Setup

We use root mean squared error ("RMSE") to measure the accuracy of rating prediction:

$$\text{RMSE} = \sqrt{\sum_{r_{ij} \in \text{TestSet}} (r_{ij} - \hat{r}_{ij})^2 / |\text{TestSet}|} \quad (7)$$

We compared the RMSE value of the proposed approaches (i.e, *RA-implicit* and *RA-explicit*) with *neighborhood* methods over the Yelp dataset. To evaluate the effectiveness of user profiles, we compare the following user profile representations using a standard user-based k-NN collaborative filtering approach:

- ***RA-implicit***: latent user profiles generated by the proposed implicit rating auto-encoder. For this approach, the size of the rating space is 1 (i.e., $|C| = 1$). That is, all user ratings in the training set are mapped to one rating category, meaning that $C = \{1\}$. If a rating is greater than 0, then the value of the rating is 1.
- ***RA-explicit***: latent user profiles generated by the proposed explicit rating auto-encoder. For this approach, the size of the rating space is 3 (i.e., $|C| = 3$). That is, all user ratings in the training set are mapped to three rating categories, namely $C = \{1, 2, 3\}$. If the original rating is greater than 0 and smaller than 3, then a category of 1 is assigned; if a rating equals 3, then a category of 2 is assigned; and if a rating is greater than 3, then a category of 3 is assigned.
- ***Random***: latent user profiles generated by assigning random values for each latent factor (based on the same dimensionality d as *RA-implicit* and *RA-explicit*). The purpose of this method is to determine whether any gains to the proposed approaches (*RA-implicit* and *RA-explicit*) are due simply to the expressivity of the representation (in which case *Random* should perform comparably to the other two methods), or the representation learning (in which case *Random* should perform worse than *RA-implicit* and *RA-explicit*).
- ***MF***: latent user profiles generated by the matrix factorization approach [5].
- ***CF***: explicit ratings, in the form of the original ratings.

For all of *RA-implicit*, *RA-explicit*, *Random* and *MF*, we set the dimensionality parameter d to 100.

[1] `http://www.yelp.com.au/dataset_challenge`

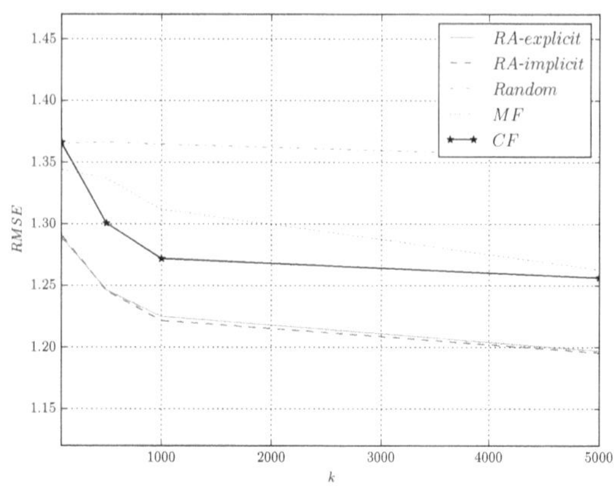

Figure 1: The RMSE of rating predictions for the different approaches over the Yelp dataset

5.3 Results

Figure 1 shows the RMSE results of the different approaches under varying values of k. We can see that *RA-implicit* performs slightly better than *RA-explicit*, while *RA-explicit* and *RA-implicit* achieved better performance (i.e., lower RMSE scores) than the other models. Given that the accuracy of rating prediction relies on the quality of the target user representation, this indicates that *RA-implicit* and *RA-explicit* result in better user representations. Despite having the same dimensionality as *RA-implicit* and *RA-explicit*, *Random* performed the worst, indicating that our results are not simply an artefact of the more expressive representation, but rather due to the quality of the learned representation. The user profiles generated by the proposed rating auto-encoder are also more accurate than the latent factor user profiles generated by *MF*.

Based on a one-tailed paired t-test, both *RA-explicit* and *RA-implicit* are significantly better than the other *neighborhood* baselines ($p < 0.005$), but there is no significant difference between the two *RA* methods ($p > 0.1$). Because the dataset is sparse (81.2% users have provided less than 5 ratings), coarser granularity leads to higher co-occurrence of items in the same context, explaining why *RA-implicit* is slightly better than *RA-explicit*.

6. CONCLUSION

In this paper, we have proposed a probabilistic rating auto-encoder to conduct unsupervised feature learning for learning latent user profiles from large-scale rating data. The rating auto-encoder learns item similarity based on analysis of items which have been given similar ratings by a given user. Based on the generated latent item representations, we generate latent user representations in each rating category. After that, we applied the generated latent user profiles to *neighborhood* based collaborative filtering recommender systems to predict rating scores. The experiments were conducted on real-life rating data from `yelp.com` shows that the latent user profiles generated by the proposed rating auto-encoder are able to find more similar neighboring users without further fine tuning or optimization, and make more accurate rating predictions than traditional rating-based user profiles and latent user profiles generated by state-of-the-art latent factor learning models such as matrix factorization.

In future work, we plan to explore how to learn latent user features from multi-modality social data such as both rating and user-created text information. We are also interested in combining the proposed approach with matrix factorisation for rating prediction, to see whether further gains can be achieved.

Acknowledgements

This research was supported by the Australian Research Council. The authors would like to acknowledge the support of Pitchwise (`www.pitchwi.se`), and valuable feedback from the anonymous reviewers and Joel Nothman.

7. REFERENCES

[1] G. Adomavicius and A. Tuzhilin. Toward the next generation of recommender systems: A survey of the state-of-the-art and possible extensions. *TKDE*, 17(6):734–749, 2005.

[2] Y. Bengio, R. Ducharme, P. Vincent, and C. Janvin. A neural probabilistic language model. *J. Mach. Learn. Res.*, 3:1137–1155, Mar. 2003.

[3] X. Chen and X. Lin. Big data deep learning: Challenges and perspectives. *IEEE Access*, 2:514–525, 2014.

[4] G. Hinton and R. Salakhutdinov. Reducing the dimensionality of data with neural networks. *Science*, 313(5786):504–507, July 2006.

[5] Y. Koren, R. Bell, and C. Volinsky. Matrix Factorization Techniques for Recommender Systems. *Computer*, 42(8):30–37, Aug. 2009.

[6] Q. V. Le and T. Mikolov. Distributed representations of sentences and documents. *CoRR*, abs/1405.4053, 2014.

[7] Y. LeCun, Y. Bengio, and G. Hinton. Deep learning. *Nature*, 521(7553):436–444, May 2015. Insight.

[8] H. Liang, Y. Xu, Y. Li, R. Nayak, and X. Tao. Connecting users and items with weighted tags for personalized item recommendations. In *Proceedings of the 21st ACM Conference on Hypertext and Hypermedia (Hypertext 2010)*, pages 51–60, 2010.

[9] H. Liang, Y. Xu, D. Tjondronegoro, and P. Christen. Time-aware topic recommendation based on micro-blogs. In *Proceedings of the 21st ACM International Conference on Information and Knowledge Management (CIKM 2012)*, pages 1657–1661, Maui, USA, 2012.

[10] T. Mikolov, K. Chen, G. Corrado, and J. Dean. Efficient estimation of word representations in vector space. *CoRR*, abs/1301.3781, 2013.

[11] B. Sarwar, G. Karypis, J. Konstan, and J. Riedl. Item-based collaborative filtering recommendation algorithms. In *Proceedings of the Tenth International World Wide Web Conference (WWW10)*, pages 285–295. ACM, 2001.

[12] J. Schmidhuber. Deep learning in neural networks: An overview. *Neural Networks*, 61:85–117, 2015. Published online 2014; based on TR arXiv:1404.7828 [cs.NE].

[13] H. Wang, N. Wang, and D. Yeung. Collaborative deep learning for recommender systems. *CoRR*, abs/1409.2944, 2014.

Real-time Rumor Debunking on Twitter

Xiaomo Liu, Armineh Nourbakhsh, Quanzhi Li, Rui Fang, Sameena Shah*
Research and Development
Thomson Reuters
3 Times Square, NYC, NY 10036
{xiaomo.liu,armineh.nourbakhsh,quanzhi.li,rui.fang,sameena.shah}@thomsonreuters.com

ABSTRACT

In this paper, we propose the first real time rumor debunking algorithm for Twitter. We use cues from 'wisdom of the crowds', that is, the aggregate 'common sense' and investigative journalism of Twitter users. We concentrate on identification of a rumor as an event that may comprise of one or more conflicting microblogs. We continue monitoring the rumor event and generate real time updates dynamically based on any additional information received. We show using real streaming data that it is possible, using our approach, to debunk rumors accurately and efficiently, often much faster than manual verification by professionals.

Categories and Subject Descriptors

H.3.3 [**Information Storage and Retrieval**]: Information Search and Retrieval

Keywords

Rumor Debunking, Twitter, Social Computing

1. INTRODUCTION

A rumor may be defined as a statement whose truth value is unverified or deliberately false [7]. Rumors spread fear, hate, or even euphoria. They may lead to defamation (of people, brands, governments etc.), protests, destruction of properties, or other undesirable responses. With the permeation of social media in our lives, the amount of rumors has increased remarkably and in significance. Twitter has a plethora of rumors that are spread intentionally or unintentionally. Perhaps, one of the most infamous cases is of the hacked AP account tweeting a rumor that Barack Obama had been injured in an explosion at the White House [5]. The tweet caused the S&P to decline and wipe off $130 Billion in stock value in a matter of seconds.

Traditionally, rumors were debunked by common sense and investigative journalism. Recently, a new line of research has emerged that uses cues from 'wisdom of the crowds', that is, the aggregation of 'common sense' and investigative journalism of Twitter users. In this paper, we consider the problem of rumor debunking using only cues from social media data, specifically Twitter. We propose a systematic methodology to mine language features like people's opinion, find witness accounts, derive underlying belief from messages, use sourcing, network propagation, credibility and other user and meta features to debunk rumors. We show that it is possible, using our approach, to debunk rumors on Twitter accurately and efficiently, often much faster than manual verification by professionals.

*Corresponding author

Permission to make digital or hard copies of all or part of this work for personal or classroom use is granted without fee provided that copies are not made or distributed for profit or commercial advantage and that copies bear this notice and the full citation on the first page. Copyrights for components of this work owned by others than the author(s) must be honored. Abstracting with credit is permitted. To copy otherwise, or republish, to post on servers or to redistribute to lists, requires prior specific permission and/or a fee. Request permissions from Permissions@acm.org.
CIKM'15, October 19–23, 2015, Melbourne, Australia.
Copyright is held by the owner/author(s). Publication rights licensed to ACM.
ACM 978-1-4503-3794-6/15/10 ...$15.00.
DOI: http://dx.doi.org/10.1145/2806416.2806651

Our contributions include: (1) method to automatically debunk rumors on social media using only social media data; (2) an authentic rumor data base constructed on real data, and the process of its creation; (3) real time algorithmic veracity prediction that is potentially faster than human verification. To the best of our knowledge, this is the first such solution based on Twitter platform. Primarily, most research relevant to debunking rumors on social media, has concentrated on 'fitting' data retrospectively and on a static set. Our method allows for a dynamic real time prediction. We show that we are able to beat baseline methods and even professionals by a significant margin even when as less as five tweets about an event are available. We study how performance and top features change when more information is known about rumors.

2. RELATED WORK

Separating newsworthy stories from misinformation on Twitter has been a popular research topic in recent years. Early exploration of this problem started from two special case studies on rumor propagation during natural disasters like earthquakes and hurricanes[6, 3]. So their results are not necessarily generalizable to other types of rumors. Many existing algorithms [11, 10] for debunking rumors followed the work of Castillo et al. in which they studied information credibility and proposed a set of features that are able to retrospectively predict if an event is credible [1]. However, credibility prediction and rumor debunking are related problems but not equivalent. Even trustable news agencies and celebrities can get involved in propagating rumors. Thus, there is a need to invent new features that can capture how journalists verify rumors.

Another distinction is that current research of rumor debunking on Twitter and its equivalent in China, Sina Weibo, mainly focused on identifying rumor microblogs [7, 10, 11]—a tweet level metric. While we concentrate on detection of a rumor as an event comprised of multiple conflicting microblogs. Individual microblog is short in nature and contains quite limited information. Thus, predicting on a single microblog may not be very reliable. In contrast, grouping tweets of the same event is like collecting wisdom from the crowd. Intuitively, the latter approach should be more robust. Also, it is closer to a real life scenario that journalists need go through a set of tweets before verifying a rumor. The work of Sun [9] is similar to our work in this respect, where they studied rumor events in Sina Weibo. It is worth noting that Twitter's API does not let us track the propagation of retweets in as much detail as Sina Weibo. Thus, recent research on rumor detection using propagation networks in Sina Weibo [10] cannot be applied to Twitter. However, understandings how rumor propagates on social media [2] can help inspire more creative rumor debunking algorithms.

3. PROBLEM STATEMENT

We assume our system ingests real time streaming tweets. Our event detector (see section 4 for a more detailed description) organizes the stream into a set of events and identifies fast-evolving news stories dynamically. Our goal is not to compute a static veracity score retrospectively, rather to update the veracity score in real time for an event as it grows with new tweets. Thus, we are constrained to use only the initial meta data associated with incoming tweets. Certain meta data like number of retweets and likes, dynamically updated, are in fact very discriminatory after a significant lapse in time. Since they take time to build, and are all zero valued initially, we cannot use them, although they have been shown to be very useful in previous retrospective studies.

Based on the above requirements, we can articulate our prediction task as follows. We define a set of news events $E = \{e_1, ..., e_n\}$, where each event e_i is associated with a set of tweets $P_i = \{p_{i,1}, ..., p_{i,m_i}\}$. As time elapses, m_i, the number of associated tweets will grow. Thus, we can define a Twitter event at time t as a set of event tweets at that moment $P(t) = \{(p_1, t_1), ..., (p_m, t_m)\}$ with the order $t_1 <, ..., < t_m \leq t$. So, a real-time rumor predictor $M(t)$ is a function $\mathbb{R}^{m \times f} \to \mathbb{R}^f \to \{1, 0\}$ that aggregates a feature matrix for all event tweets $P(t)$ to a f-dimensional feature vector of this event and, then, maps it to a binary veracity class: truth (1) or rumor (0) at time t.

The time component allows us to study the early and subsequent predictions as events propagate. While retweets and other evolving features become meaningful at subsequent stages' time, and it is also possible to issue new API calls to re-obtain those values for each tweet, but considering Twitter rate limitations, it is not a feasible approach. Hence, we continue not to use those even for later stages. Next, we describe how we created a suitable data set to train on.

4. DATA COLLECTION

A critical challenge in creating appropriate training data is access to *confirmed rumors*. Rumors are a tiny portion of the total social media content. Moreover, we need access to rumors that are confirmed to be true or false by trustworthy sources. Fortunately, there exist two rumor tracking websites, namely, `snopes.com` and `emergent.info`. We crawled both sites and collected 2,299 stories posted until March 2015. We eliminated stories that were either not 'newsworthy' or that did not have an explicit confirmation of veracity. The resulting dataset consists of 94 true and 446 false stories.

Table 1: Example of collected rumors and truths

Date	Events	Veracity
01-15	Musician Macklemore joins the ISIS.	rumor
02-14	Nestle recalls hot-pocket products.	truth

Since the prediction is based on event level, we also need to collect all relevant tweets for each story. Following the approaches used in [1, 11], we formulated keyword-based queries that can describe each story. The form of queries is $A \wedge B$, where A is a conjunction of objects and subjects in an event and B is a disjunction of possible action words. For example, query (macklemore $\wedge$ ISIS) $\wedge$ (joins $\vee$ joined $\vee$ participates ...) refers to a rumor as described in Table 1. Instead of using Twitter's search API which limits its results to one week, we submitted each query directly to Twitter's search interface[1] to get full history and used a web scraper to download all matched tweets automatically. Three researchers sampled and cross-checked the results to ensure that the queries were capturing relevant tweets.

To collect additional true stories, we sent Twitter's free data stream[2], i.e. 1% of firehose, to our event detection system which essentially is a clustering algorithm that groups tweets of the same stories or events[3], very close to the outcomes of *Twitter Monitor* [4]. Like rumor data collection, we applied the same approach to go beyond the 1% limit and assemble all relevant tweets of each event. To further ensure those events had truly occurred, we further picked out events containing links to news that could confirm them. We kept running our system with Twitter's streaming data in March 2015 until the same number of true stories as rumors were collected. Thus, the final dataset for evaluation consisted of 421 true and 421 false events. Table 1 shows a few examples of rumors and true events from our dataset.

5. METHODOLOGY

5.1 Feature Hypotheses

Numerous features have been proposed for classifying rumors in social media[9, 10, 11]. They are largely rooted in the seminal paper on credibility [1], and include features based on language, user, propagation, and other meta data. However, investigative journalists consider features like originating source, source diversity, source credibility to be incredibly important [8].

Another observation is that wisdom of the crowd is very helpful for debunking rumors. People often express mixed beliefs such as support, denial and neutrality in response to events[6, 7]. Intuitively, we can conceptualize the crowd's contradictory beliefs as their debates on veracity. For an

[1]https://twitter.com/search-home

[2]https://dev.twitter.com/streaming/public

[3]The details of this system are to be reported in upcoming publications

Table 2: Description of new features

Category	Feature Name
Source Credibility	Is trusted/satirical news account
	Has trusted/satirical news url
	Profile has url from top domains
	Client application name
Source Identity	Profile has person name
	Profile has location
	Profile includes profession information
Source Diversity	Has multiple news/non-news urls after dedup
	Deduped tweets' text is dissimilar
Source Location & Witness	If tweet location matches event location
	If profile location matches event location
	Has witness phrases, i.e. "I see" and "I hear"
Msg. Belief	Is support, negation, question or neutrality
Event Propagation	Event Topic
	Retweet, mention, hashtag h-index
	Max reply/retweet graph[4] size/depth

event, if information from negation/question side is more authentic (represented by other features) than the support side, it is more likely to be confirmed as a rumor later.

Thus, we hypothesize: H_1 - investigative journalism based verification features can improve veracity prediction; H_2 - features involving belief partitions can improve the veracity prediction.

5.2 Classification Features

Verification Features We propose six categories of verification features based on insights from journalists [8], as shown in Table 2. They largely overlap with the features of the baseline algorithms [1, 11]. Due to space limitations, we only summarize new proposed features in each category.

Belief Identification classifies Twitter users into who believe or support that event versus who deny or question the event. We implemented two belief identification algorithms: one is a replication of [7]'s model, the other is a rule-based method using an extensive list of positive (e.g., truth), negative (i.e., rumor) and negation (e.g., not) keywords with a set of language rules such as "negative words not preceded by a negation word imply that the user denies the event". Both algorithms were evaluated on [7]'s dataset and a labeled dataset we got annotated by Amazon Mechanical Turk. The results showed that our rule-based algorithm performed better in the cross dataset evaluation (80.5% in accuracy). Hence, we used it to build the belief features.

Feature Aggregation. A key characteristic of our system is to detect event-level rumors rather than individual tweets. This requires us to aggregate features of a set of event tweets to a single event feature vector. We convert *Boolean* features, for example, "if tweet contains a news url" to "fraction of event tweets that have a news url". *Numeric* features are aggregated to minimum, maximum, and average of values. For *categorical* features, whose values are strings like "Monday", we break them down into an array of *Boolean* features at tweet level. Again, the aggregation for *Boolean* feature is applied to further convert them to "fraction" features. In addition, we partitioned event tweets into different belief groups. All existing features were recomputed for each group and treated as new belief features. They were added to our feature set to test the hypothesis H_2.

[4]Retweet graph was constructed by linking RT @mention in tweet text

Table 3: Performance comparison of prediction models

Method	Castillo	Yang	+H1	+H1+H2
5-tweet-accuracy	0.655	0.666	0.736	**0.780**
100-tweet-accuracy	0.729	0.737	0.812	**0.857**
400-tweet-accuracy	0.745	0.747	0.843	**0.897**
1-hour-accuracy	0.724	0.657	0.789	**0.795**
12-hour-accuracy	0.679	0.673	0.821	**0.834**
72-hour-accuracy	0.781	0.729	0.854	**0.875**

6. EVALUATION

We perform three evaluations: (1) performance comparison with the two baseline algorithms on the dynamic prediction task; (2) timeliness comparison of our automatic method in contrast to human verification; (3) analysis of the most effective features for early and subsequent predictions.

6.1 Comparison of Prediction Models

We compared our proposed method with two state-of-the-art algorithms [1, 11]. Although [1] is for credibility task, the idea here is to compare the predictive power of those features for the verification task. Hence, following the experiment design of [10], we used J48 decision tree and 15 best features reported in [1] to construct the first baseline; Yang's SVM classifier [11] was implemented with all their 19 features except 4 features. The metadata of "gender of user", "avatar type" and "user name type" are not available in Twitter; Twitter stream cannot capture "number of comments" as explained in section 3. We also constructed two classifiers based on our hypotheses. The first classifier followed H_1 to combine the new proposed verification features with all features in [1, 11]. The second classifier included additional belief partition features as designed by H_2. We applied a 'best first' feature selection strategy and experimented with a multitude of algorithms including SVM, random forest and decision tree to select the best classifier for each classification model. Since SVM performed best across the board, we selected it for the comparison.

Table 3 shows the accuracy of 10-fold cross validation for all four classifiers. The result shows that our new verification features can outperform both baseline models. Also, including belief partition can improve the performance even more. This is further evidenced by the t-test, where all comparisons' $p < 0.05$. Thus, both our hypotheses are supported. With regards to early prediction, our method can achieve 78% and 79% accuracy when events initiate with the first 5 tweets and the first 1 hour respectively.

6.2 Timeliness Comparison with Humans Verification

In this subsection, we investigate a more interesting question: can our method effectively debunk rumors faster than

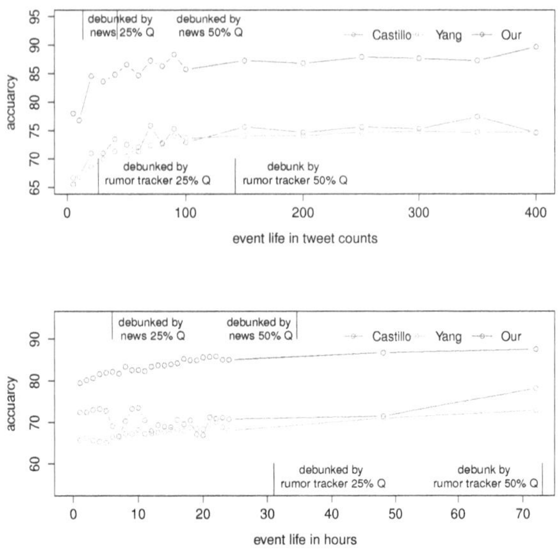

Figure 1: Comparison with human verification

human verification? To conduct this evaluation, we first compare the timeliness of our method with real-time rumor trackers, `snopes.com` and `emergent.info`, where debunking is performed by professionals. The delays between the first tweet in a rumor event and the debunking tweet published by rumor trackers are measured by tweet count and elapsed time. We then compute 25% and 50% quantiles of their delays and compare with our algorithm. Figure 1 shows that our algorithm can detect rumors with 85% accuracy when reaching 25% quantile lines (in the bottom of each subplot). In other words for other 75% of rumors, our method can already attain an 85% accuracy before rumors trackers can verify them. Next, we want to evaluate if our method can also verify rumors before news media. We adopt the same evaluation steps to measure the delays of rumor debunking by news agencies. In this case, we use the first event tweet linking to a debunking news article to measure the delay. However, there are some limitations here. We can only capture url links to news articles from tweets that appear in our data collection. So the earliest debunking time by news media is limited to the scope of our data. Also, we have to manually confirm the debunking time by reading each news article and making sure they are debunking the rumor. By the time of this paper's completion, 86 rumors were checked using this method. Thus, delays we measured for news media are an approximation. Based on the 25% quantile lines (in the top of each subplot) in Figure 1, we can again conclude that our method debunks 75% of rumors earlier than news media with at least 80% accuracy.

6.3 Feature Analysis

In total, 720 features were generated by our method. We examined the best features for early (5 tweets) vs. late (400 tweets) predictions. On comparing the top features in each case, we found that some features are more important for early detection while others begin dominating in later stages; some are consistently important. Actually, half of the consistently important features are based on user characteristics. We also observed that while belief features comprise 21% of best features in early prediction, they rise to 43% for later stage prediction. Thus, adding belief features to our model not only benefits the early prediction, but becomes increasingly important as more information becomes available.

7. CONCLUSIONS

Rumor debunking research has mostly concentrated on 'fitting' data retrospectively. In this paper, we propose the first real time rumor debunking algorithm for Twitter. We concentrate on identification of a rumor as an event that may comprise of one or more conflicting microblogs. We use beliefs of the crowd, along with traditional investigative journalism features on top of language, user, propagation and other meta features. We show that we are able to beat baseline methods and even professionals by a significant margin even when as little as five tweets about an event are available. Our system continues monitoring the rumor event and generates dynamic real time updates based on any additional information received.

8. REFERENCES

[1] C. Castillo, M. Mendoza, and B. Poblete. Information credibility on twitter. In *Proc. International Conference on World Wide Web*, pages 675–684, 2011.

[2] A. Friggeri, L. A. Adamic, D. Eckles, and J. Cheng. Rumor cascades. In *Proceedings of the International AAAI Conference on Weblogs and Social Media*, 2014.

[3] A. Gupta, H. Lamba, P. Kumaraguru, and A. Joshi. Faking sandy: characterizing and identifying fake images on twitter during hurricane sandy. In *Proc. International Conference on World Wide Web Companion*, pages 729–736, 2013.

[4] M. Mathioudakis and N. Koudas. Twittermonitor: trend detection over the twitter stream. In *Proceedings of the 2010 ACM SIGMOD International Conference on Management of data*, pages 1155–1158. ACM, 2010.

[5] C. Matthews. How does one fake tweet cause a stock market crash. *Wall Street & Markets: Time*, 2013.

[6] M. Mendoza, B. Poblete, and C. Castillo. Twitter under crisis: Can we trust what we rt? In *Proc. First Workshop on Social Media Analytics*, pages 71–79, 2010.

[7] V. Qazvinian, E. Rosengren, D. R. Radev, and Q. Mei. Rumor has it: Identifying misinformation in microblogs. In *Proceedings of the Conference on Empirical Methods in Natural Language Processing*, pages 1589–1599. ACL, 2011.

[8] C. Silverman. *Verification handbook*. 2014.

[9] S. Sun, H. Liu, J. He, and X. Du. Detecting event rumors on sina weibo automatically. In *Web Technologies and Applications*, pages 120–131. Springer, 2013.

[10] K. Wu, S. Yang, and K. Q. Zhu. False rumors detection on sina weibo by propagation structures. In *IEEE International Conference of Data Engineering*, 2015.

[11] F. Yang, Y. Liu, X. Yu, and M. Yang. Automatic detection of rumor on sina weibo. In *Proc. of the ACM SIGKDD Workshop on Mining Data Semantics*, page 13, 2012.

Fraud Transaction Recognition: A Money Flow Network Approach

Renxin Mao, Zhao Li, Jinhua Fu
Alibaba Group
969 Wenyi West Road, Hangzhou
Zhejiang, China
{renxin.mrx, lizhao.lz, jinhua.fjh}@alibaba-inc.com

ABSTRACT

In this paper, we provide some insights into analysis of fraud transaction recognition on Alipay's Money Flow Network. We first show that the Money Flow Network follows a power-law distribution on daily, monthly or yearly basis, based on which we propose a new approach of fraud transaction recognition on the Money Flow Network from two perspectives. First, the Collapse Network is identified by the discovery that fraud transaction requires a huge amount of active controlled 'zombie' accounts, which are always intentionally manipulated by fraudulent online sellers, and the collapse of the Money Flow Network emerges due to their economic inactivity; Second, we define the Activation Forest that leads to the recognition of the controlled 'zombies' even no sooner than they enter into Alipay's ecosphere. These two networks are fully explored from the perspective of detecting 'zombies', and several key features have been adopted into anti-fraud recognition. Experimental results show that our strategy is capable of effectively identifying fraud transactions on the Money Flow Network with the accuracy as high as 99.88%.

Categories and Subject Descriptors

H.2.8 [**Database Management**]: Data Applications—*Data Mining*

Keywords

Fraud Transaction; Money Flow Network

1. INTRODUCTION

Online Shopping, providing a convenient means for purchasing items from various sources, is increasingly flourishing and getting more and more popular in our daily life. In China, over 80% online shopping market is mainly facilitated by Taobao, the largest consumer-to-consumer E-commence platform around the world that launched by Alibaba Group in 2003. Taobao serves more than hundreds of million active buyers and tens of million sellers along with an online payment system called Alipay, where nearly tens of million transactions are made on daily basis. The huge amount of money flow addresses the credibility issue of transactions on e-commence.

Fraud transactions [3] do incalculable harm to buyers and platforms while in favor of insincere sellers from two perspectives. On one hand, similar to most of e-commence markets, Taobao also makes use of the number of completed transactions as a ranking index and a reputation factor for sellers. The ever growing number of buyers on Taobao is the major source of online sellers' revenue. More often than not, buyers are biased towards those sellers with high sales volume or reputation. As a result, insincere sellers are motivated to boost their sales by a large margin in a short period of time to gain advantages over other sellers. However, it takes time to achieve this end in a regular lifecycle of sales. Consequently, a few insincere sellers carry out fake purchases to accumulate sales volume in order to attract more legitimate buyers. Therefore, several buyers are misguided into purchasing items seemingly only good on numbers over quality. On the other hand, online sales are always promoted by Taobao and Alipay platforms, for example, buyers are encouraged to do online shopping on holidays by getting rewarded with allowance or gift cards equivalent to the same amount of money they spend on each purchase. In this scenario, insincere sellers misappropriate these rewards by hiring people to make fraud transactions, which would result in a huge loss for the platforms. Although some fraud transactions are often made in a elaborately manner that minor difference of shopping behaviors could be distinguished from legitimate ones, various efforts have been made to detect and intercept fraud transactions in this regard, and follow-up regulations are successfully applied in order to maintain a fair E-commence ecosystem.

In this paper, we investigate fraud transaction recognition from the perspective of the Money Flow Network. Usually, fraudulent online shopping conduct needs a tremendous amount of mendacious buyers referred as 'zombies' that are manipulated by fraudulent online sellers, they demonstrate synchronized economic behavior, e.g. each of 'zombies' receives one transfer from the insincere sellers uniformly both in time and amount; a surge of one single merchandise purchasing by a group of 'zombies'; hibernated uniformly with no deposit. Two different forms of the Money Flow Network are developed for 'zombies' recognition. The first is called 'The Collapse Network' which measures how the economic inactivity 'zombies' behave in the Money Flow Network; The Second one is called 'The Activation Forest' which monitors the tree topology formed by the first-active transfer of each single account.

The rest of the paper is organized as follows. Section 2 uncovers two topologies of the Money Flow Network on Alipay data: the Collapse Network and the Activation Forest. Section 3 illustrates fraud transaction recognition based on feature analysis of two net-

Permission to make digital or hard copies of all or part of this work for personal or classroom use is granted without fee provided that copies are not made or distributed for profit or commercial advantage and that copies bear this notice and the full citation on the first page. Copyrights for components of this work owned by others than ACM must be honored. Abstracting with credit is permitted. To copy otherwise, or republish, to post on servers or to redistribute to lists, requires prior specific permission and/or a fee. Request permissions from Permissions@acm.org.
CIKM'15, October 19 - 23, 2015, Melbourne, Australia.
© 2015 ACM. ISBN 978-1-4503-3794-6/15/10 ..$15.00.
http://dx.doi.org/10.1145/2806416.2806647 .

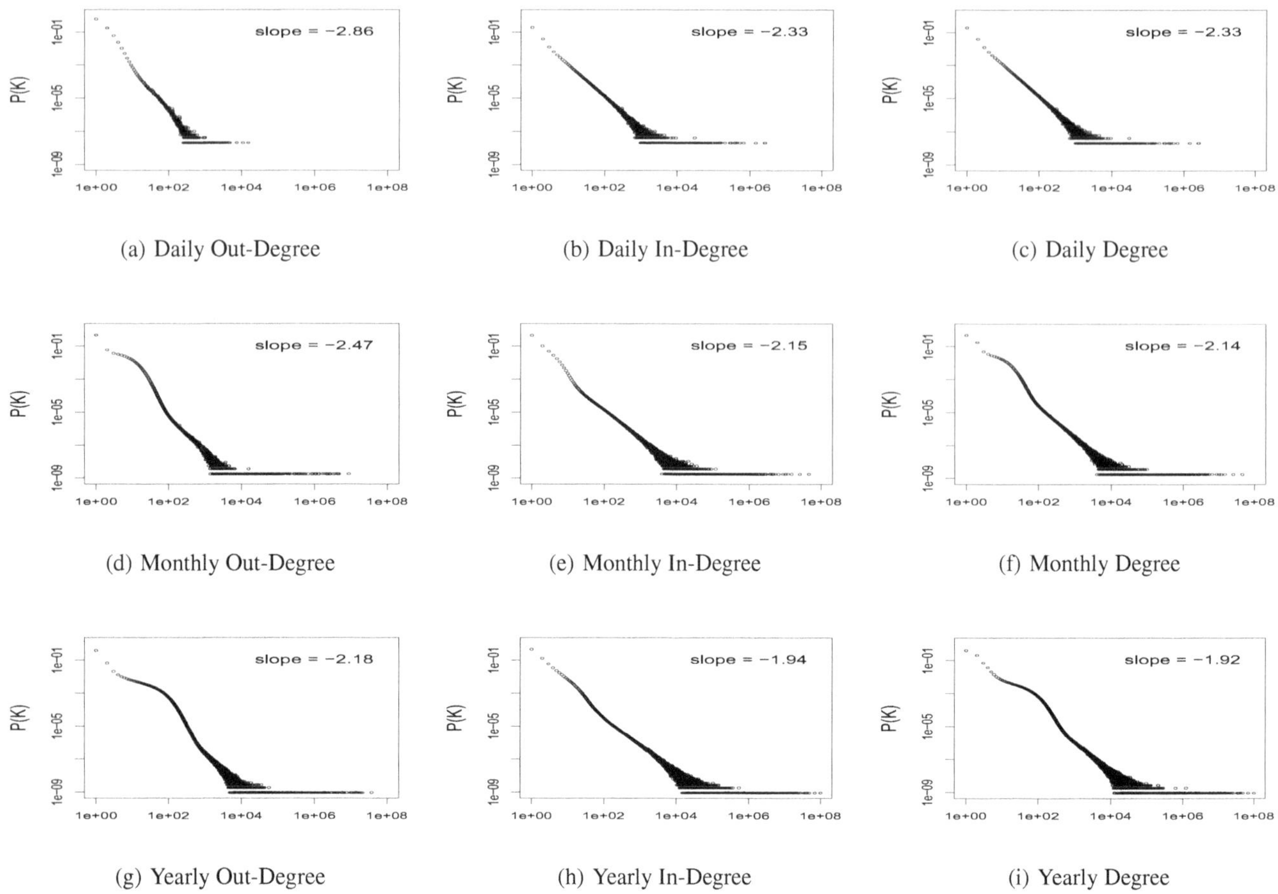

(a) Daily Out-Degree (b) Daily In-Degree (c) Daily Degree

(d) Monthly Out-Degree (e) Monthly In-Degree (f) Monthly Degree

(g) Yearly Out-Degree (h) Yearly In-Degree (i) Yearly Degree

Figure 1: Empirical Out-degree, In-degree and Degree Distribution of the Money Network Work on Daily, Monthly, and Yearly Basis.

works, followed by experimental results in Section 4. Finally, the conclusions are briefly summarized in Section 5.

2. MONEY FLOW NETWORK TOPOLOGY

To the best of our knowledge, the network topology of online shopping markets has so far not been studied empirically. Limited academic studies of the Money Flow Network have been focused on the interbank money market, which has shown a very typical power-law distribution [1] given that Austrian interbank market, Italian segment of the European overnight money market[4],etc. In this paper, degree distributions and density are revisited to reveal Alipay Money Flow Network which is a directed graph G=(V,E), where V is a finite set of nodes representing accounts and E is a set of directed edge representing trade, transfer, withdraw or deposit from one account to another.

Degree Distributions: Similar to many real world networks, the degree distribution of the Money Flow Network (Figure 1) follows scale-free power-law distribution for out-degree, in-degree, and degree. It is worthy noting that degree distribution power law drops as the time window scales up. Moreover, the size of the out-degree exponent is within the range of several other complex networks, e.g. collaboration networks of actors[7]. The size of the in-degree and degree exponent is within the range of 2 and examples are the Web Networks [5] and Mathematician Collaboration Networks [2].

Density: Another intuitive way to observe the evolution of the complex network is the change of density (See Figure 2). We collect a continuously 63 months of the Money Flow Network on Alipay transaction data to see if the density would evolve as more nodes and edges added into the network. For directed graphs, the density is defined as:

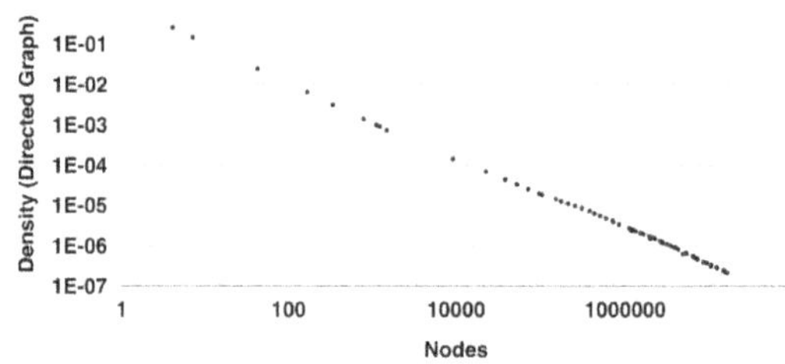

Figure 2: Density evolves as the network grows

$$D = \frac{|E|}{|V|(|V|-1)} \quad (1)$$

It is worthy noting that density decays as the nodes of the network increases and subjects to the equation $lnD = -0.530 - 0.889lnV$, which indicates an exponential decline of the density.

Boom and Collapse Structure: As accounts hold different economic activity in the market, Money Flow Network possess local

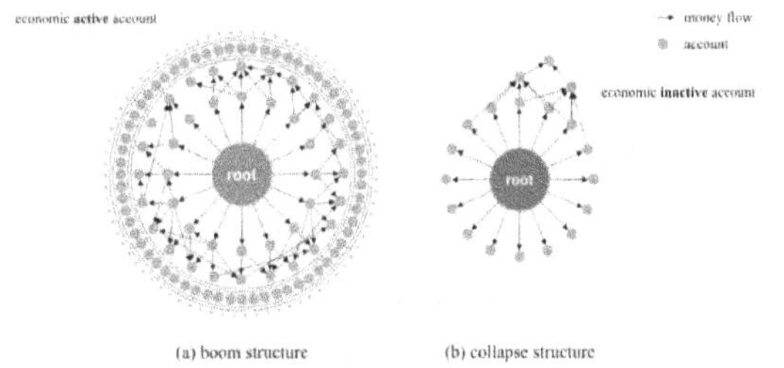

Figure 3: Boom and Collapse Structure Due to Economic Activity

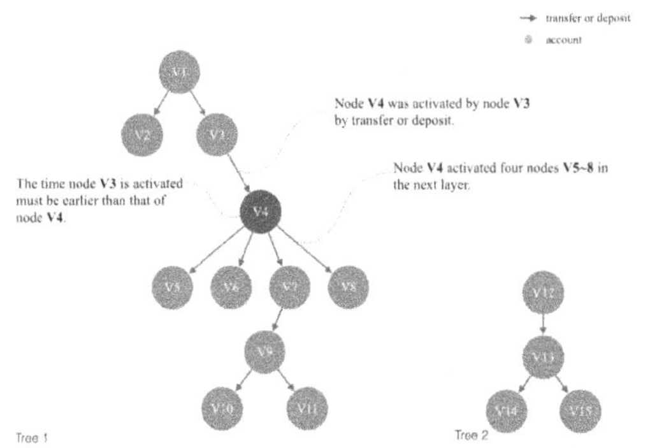

Figure 4: The Topology of Activation Forest

structures of boom and collapse, which are consisted of one root node in the very center that radiates money flows, however the second-order degree increases by several orders of magnitude as a result of normal economic activity and decreases due to economic inactivity (Figure 3). So distinguishable as the local structures are in the network, we observe that 1070 out of 1306 nodes of local network possess collapse structures and the rest exhibits boom structures in one randomly selected Money Flow Network (1306 nodes with out-degree larger than 30 are found in tens of millions of edges and nodes in 48 hours).

Activation Forest: The first entrance of one new account into the money flow network must bring along one directed transfer or deposit money flow which is pointed to this very account from some money source, we defined this transfer or deposit money flow as an activation money flow. Historically, all the accounts in the money flow network should have this very activation money flow and all the activation money flows will form a bunch of trees which is defined as Activation Forest. The Activation Forest is, in fact, characterized as follows: suppose node V_j is activated by node V_i, then (1) V_j can only be activated once; (2) V_i can activate many accounts; (3) V_i must be activated earlier than V_j; (4) V_i can also be activated by another account. This sequence of activation forms a directed acyclic topology illustrated in Figure 4.

3. FRAUD TRANSACTION RECOGNITION ANALYSIS

We build a framework of fraud transaction recognition system based on the phenomena of collapse and activation on the Money Flow Network for the purpose of tracking and intercepting 'zombies' at any time, e.g. the first entry or ongoing money flow, and preventing them from affecting legitimate buyers and platforms.

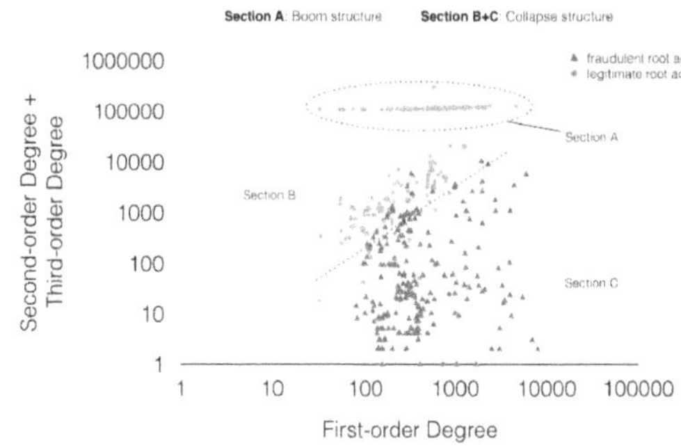

Figure 5: Classification of the Collapse Network via Network Features

3.1 The Collapse Network

Since the registration of many E-Commerce sites require only email or phone number, 'zombies' can be produced numerously in short periods. Focus has been put on the recognition of 'zombies' not only through static registration information but also ongoing economic activities. Most of the time, 'zombie' buyers behave exactly the same as legitimate buyers when performing transactions. But the way that 'zombie' buyers get their fund source leaves us clues to track them down. For example, 'zombie' buyers stampede towards the item after receiving a transfer amount from the insincere sellers, after which their economic activity fades away. Economic inactivity is then used to detect them and be modeled as collapse structure in Money Flow Network: the local network around one fraudulent account will possess collapse structure due to economic inactivity of 'zombies' crowded at the first-order degree.

One attempt is made to demonstrate the relationship between boom and collapse structures in the selected Money Flow Network above. We projected well labeled 1306 root accounts onto two dimensions (log scale) illustrated in Figure 5. We first observe that most of the regular centroid nodes (Section A) hold the property that the second-order or third-order degree booms due to normal economic activities, while the Money Flow Network starts to collapse from other centroid nodes (Section B + Section C) due to abnormally low economic activities. As for Section B, centroid nodes do not boom to Section A because nodes linked to them at the first-order degree behave so much like 'zombie' buyers that they actually are just newly registered users. Section C is full of 'zombie' buyers that they cause the network to collapse because of their synchronous economic inactivity.

3.2 The Activation Forest

Besides the recognition of 'zombies' through the ongoing Money Flow Network, however, it's imperative that we detect 'zombies' from their first entrance into the Money Flow Network so their economic activities could be monitored in a timely manner that further regulations are enforced. Activation Forest extends fraud transaction recognition from an individual account to the entire forest. It allows us to take advantage of global features of trees in the forest, such as tree size, depth, growth rate, activation amount mode, and proportion of activation amount mode, to decide whether trees themselves are abnormal which also provides an intuitive interpretation of the network structures.

It is noted that, in most cases, trees of only two nodes and one edge account for around 73 percent in the forest. While in extreme cases, maximum tree size reaches 240861, maximum tree depth reaches 28, maximum daily growth rate is 38576, and maximum proportion of activation amount mode is 100%. This phenomena explains insincere sellers need to activate a large number of 'zombies' recursively in favor of fraud transactions.

4. EXPERIMENTAL RESULTS

The Collapse Network was constructed on Alipay 48 hours of Money Flow Network consists of tens of millions of edges and nodes, then nodes with out-degree larger than 30 are selected to ensure a second-order degree boom. The Activation Forest was built on Alipay Money Flow Network with historical activation data which also includes tens of millions of edges and nodes. Both networks were implemented on ODPS-GRAPH, a large-scale graph processing framework based on ODPS [1]. As mentioned before, network features play a significant role in fraud transaction recognition. In the Collapse Network, account numbers in the first-order degree, the second-order degree, the third-order degree, and the forth-order degree are considered, while tree size, depth, growth rate, activation amount mode and proportion of activation amount mode in Activation Forest.

Two datasets are extracted to verify our strategies of fraud transaction recognition from the Collapse Network and the Activation Forest individually, where each node represents an account which is manually labelled as fraudulent or legitimate based on cognizance history on Alipay's back-end platform through double-review process by over 100 independent individuals. One dataset was selected with 982 fraudulent accounts and 1018 legitimate ones for testing the Collapse Network, and the other dataset is consisted of 2000 tree nodes with 1031 fraudulent accounts and 969 legitimate ones for testing the Activation Forest. Seven popular classifiers are selected for performance comparisons: Lasso Regression(LR), Naive Bayes(NB), KNN(k=5), SVM(linear kernel), Random Forest(RF), AdaBoost, Neural Network(NN)[8].

All algorithms were implemented with and without network features to demonstrate the difference using 10-fold cross-validation. All classifiers with network features have a higher AUC [6](the area under the receiver operating characteristic curve) than without network features in both scenarios. In the Collapse Network, the AdaBoost classifier without additional network features shows the lowest AUC as equal as 0.8173, and the highest AUC is 0.9988 obtained by the Random Forest classifier with network features by an increase of 22.21%. Top three most important features are d_3/d_1, d_3 and d_4/d_1, where d_i represents the ith-order of degree. In the Activation Forest, the Naive Bayes classifier without additional network features exhibits the lowest AUC of 0.8408, while the Random Forest classifier with network features achieves the highest AUC of 0.9947 by an improvement of 18.30%. Top three most importance features are growth rate, tree size and proportion of edges whose activation amount equals the mode. It is clear that the addition of network features significantly improves the performance of fraud transaction recognition.

Table 1: The AUC Performance of Collapse Network and Activation Forest with or without Features

Classifiers	Collapse Features		Activation Features	
	N	Y	N	Y
LR	0.8755	0.9602	0.8915	0.9782
NB	0.8336	0.9956	0.8408	0.9830
KNN	0.8526	0.9650	0.8756	0.9344
SVM	0.8393	0.9437	0.8847	0.9654
RF	0.9109	**0.9988**	0.9528	**0.9947**
AdaBoost	0.8173	0.9900	0.8713	0.9754
NN	0.8918	0.9890	0.9077	0.9857

5. CONCLUSIONS

In this paper, we have investigated the fraud transaction recognition based on Alipay's Money Flow Network which follows a power-law distribution on daily, monthly and yearly basis. Fraud transaction involves fraudulent buyers referred as 'zombies' who are intentionally collaborated with insincere sellers for making illegimate profit. Two different kind of networks, the Collapse Network and the Activation Forest, are uncovered for identifying 'zombies' in different phases of online transaction. One is the Collapse Network, which measures how economic inactivity of 'zombies' collapses the ongoing Money Flow Network with four key features: the first-order degree, the second-order degree, the third-order degree, and the forth-order degree. The other is the Activation Forest, which monitors the abnormality of tree topology of the Money Flow Network accumulated by the first entry of all accounts from the very beginning with five key features: tree size, depth, growth rate, activation amount mode, and proportion of activation amount mode. The experimental results demonstrate that our approach with key network features significantly outperforms the baseline without network features by an improvement as high as 22.21%. The Money Flow Network based on online shopping markets has a brand new network morphology with little study in literature. At the very first time, we have explored the topology of the Money Flow Network regarding fraud transaction recognition, which has been extensively applied to the anti-fraud system of online transaction.

[1]Open Data Processing Service, a distributed cloud storage and computation system developed by Alibaba for providing data analysis, data mining and business intelligence service on TB or PB scale of data.

6. REFERENCES

[1] L. A. Adamic and B. A. Huberman. Power-law distribution of the world wide web. *Science*, 287(5461):2115–2115, 2000.

[2] A.-L. Barabâsi, H. Jeong, Z. Néda, E. Ravasz, A. Schubert, and T. Vicsek. Evolution of the social network of scientific collaborations. *Physica A: Statistical Mechanics and Its Applications*, 311(3):590–614, 2002.

[3] R. J. Bolton and D. J. Hand. Statistical fraud detection: A review. *Statistical Science*, pages 235–249, 2002.

[4] M. Bossa, H. Elsingerb, M. Summera, and S. Thurner. Network topology of the interbank market. *Quantitative Finance*, 4(6):677–684, August 2006.

[5] L. A. A. E. H. S. F. Liljeros, C. R. Edling and Y. Aaberg. Diameter of the world wide web. *Nature*, 411(6840):907–908, 2001.

[6] J. Huang and C. X. Ling. Using auc and accuracy in evaluating learning algorithms. *Knowledge and Data Engineering, IEEE Transactions on*, 17(3):299–310, 2005.

[7] A. R and B. AL. Topology of evolving networks: Local events and universality. *Physical Review Letters*, 85(24):5234–7, December 2000.

[8] X. Wu, V. Kumar, J. R. Quinlan, J. Ghosh, Q. Yang, H. Motoda, G. J. McLachlan, A. Ng, B. Liu, S. Y. Philip, et al. Top 10 algorithms in data mining. *Knowledge and Information Systems*, 14(1):1–37, 2008.

Identifying Top-k Consistent News-Casters on Twitter

Sahisnu Mazumder†, Sameep Mehta‡ and Dhaval Patel†
†Indian Institute of Technology - Roorkee, Uttarakhand, India.
‡IBM Research Lab - India, New Delhi, India
sahisnumazumder@gmail.com, sameepmehta@in.ibm.com, patelfec@iitr.ac.in

ABSTRACT

News-casters are Twitter users who periodically pick up interesting news from online news media and spread it to their followers' network. Existing works on Twitter user analysis have only analysed a *pre-defined set of users* for user modeling, influence analysis and news recommendation. The problem of identifying *prominent*, *trustworthy* and *consistent* news-casters is unaddressed so far. In this paper, we present a framework, **NCFinder**, to discover top-k consistent news-casters *directly* from Twitter. NCFinder uses news headlines published in online news sources to periodically collect authentic news-tweets and processes them to discover news-casters, news sources and news concepts. Next, NCFinder builds a tripartite graph among news-casters, news source and news concepts and employs HITS algorithm on it to score the news-casters on daily basis. The daily score profiles of the news-casters collected over a time-period are then used to infer top-k consistent news-casters. We run NCFinder from 11th Nov. to 24th Nov., 2014 and discover top-100 consistent news-casters and their profile information.

Categories and Subject Descriptors

H.3.3 [**Information Storage and Retrieval**]: Information Search and Retrieval—*Search process, Information filtering.*

Keywords

News, Twitter, News-Tweet, Tweet Authentication, User Profiling.

1. INTRODUCTION

Twitter is playing a key role in disseminating news among large number of people across globe [4]. Broadly, two types of twitter users, *online new sources* and *news-casters* facilitate the news dissemination process. Online news sources like *@timesofindia*, *@BBCWorld* etc. inject fresh news on Twitter from their webpages as early as possible. Whereas, news-casters acquire news from various news websites *based on their interest* and spread them to their followers' network. Thus, news-casters act as *news curators* as well as *opinion leaders* on Twitter and are good candidates for targeted advertisements [10], news recommendation [1], topic-aware influential user analysis [9] etc. applications.

Permission to make digital or hard copies of all or part of this work for personal or classroom use is granted without fee provided that copies are not made or distributed for profit or commercial advantage and that copies bear this notice and the full citation on the first page. Copyrights for components of this work owned by others than ACM must be honored. Abstracting with credit is permitted. To copy otherwise, or republish, to post on servers or to redistribute to lists, requires prior specific permission and/or a fee. Request permissions from Permissions@acm.org.
CIKM'15, October 19-23, 2015, Melbourne, VIC, Australia.
© 2015 ACM. ISBN 978-1-4503-3794-6/15/10 ...$15.00.
DOI: http://dx.doi.org/10.1145/2806416.2806649.

Spotting of news-casters on Twitter can be done by monitoring and profiling individual Twitter user's activity. The profiling task can be performed using user modeling systems, such as TUMS[1]. But, TUMS takes about 1-2 mins to profile a first-time user and often, the system fails to profile certain users (see Table 2). Thus, profiling millions of Twitter users for news-caster discovery is not a feasible task. Even if we consider the follower lists of prominent news sources on Twitter to form a good candidate set, the lists are huge in general and there may be a news-caster who is not follower of any news source on Twitter. Moreover, if we use a set of pre-defined keywords/hashtags for sampling the Twitter users, it is also not fruitful as the interests of news-casters change over time along with the dynamics of news and it's importance [5]. So, the problem is how can we directly discover the set of Twitter users who have high potential to qualify as news-casters? Further, news-casters may not be consistent in their news advertisement activity and/or have ill-intention of making use of news for advertising non-news sources [2]. Such news-casters are not beneficial for real-world applications and should be separated out from the authentic ones.

In this paper, we present a framework, *NCFinder* that discovers top-k consistent news-casters *directly* from Twitter. NCFinder periodically collects fresh news headlines published in a pre-identified list of popular online news sources, extracts news concepts from the headlines, and uses those concepts to acquire the tweets (news-tweets) that are similar to the headlines. Next, NCFinder evaluates authenticity of the downloaded news-tweets and processes the authentic news-tweets to discover the news-casters and news sources, news concepts referred by them. Finally, NCFinder forms a tripartite graph consisting of news-casters, news sources and news concepts and employs HITS algorithm on it to compute score of each news-caster on daily basis. The daily score profiles of the news-casters collected over a given time-period are then used to output top-k consistent (having k highest average scores) news-casters. Our contributions in developing NCFinder include:

- We present a systematic and effective solution to the problem of *direct discovery* of news-casters on Twitter by leveraging online news source content.
- We design a novel URL validation based news-tweet authentication technique to detect the *trustworthiness* of content published by news-casters on Twitter.
- We extend HITS algorithm to work on a tripartite graph and use it to score the news-casters on daily basis. The scores thus calculated help us to measure *news-awareness* and study *temporal consistency* of the news-casters over a time-span.

We ran NCFinder for two weeks, collected 6,87,740 authenticated news-tweets and obtained top-100 consistent news-casters along with their news interest profile.

[1] `http://wis.ewi.tudelft.nl/tums/`

2. RELATED WORK

A couple of research works have been performed on Twitter user analysis in recent years for influential user discovery [9], news spread analysis [6], user interest modeling and news recommendation [1]. But, these works mainly focus on analysing a *pre-defined set* of Twitter users. Our work leverages news headlines for direct discovery of news casters without using any pre-defined user set. The idea of leveraging online news media is also presented in [8] that analyses implicitly linked social media utterance for a given news article. However, our aim is to perform user centric analysis.

Information credibility is an important problem on Twitter that focuses on identifying the credibility of a tweet content and has mostly been tackled using feature-based learning technique [2]. But, our news-tweet authentication method works in a straight forward way without learning any features. The idea of leveraging news headlines (act as a ground truth) and usage of embedded URL in a news-tweet make it easy to verify the tweet in real-time.

Regarding consistency analysis on Twitter domain, [7] has recently studied the consistency of Twitter user's behavior for measuring topical engagement of the user. However, the work does not concern about top-k consistent user discovery and profiling. Thus considering the existing works, our work can be considered as a new addition that have explored the consistency of the trustworthy news-casters and their news interest profile on Twitter domain.

3. NCFINDER

The working of NCFinder is decomposed into three functional modules: (1) *News-Tweet Corpus Collection*, (2) *News-Tweet Authentication* and (3) *News-Caster Discovery and Ranking*. At present, the first two modules run at an interval of 30 minutes and the third module runs on daily basis.

3.1 News-Tweet Corpus Collection

The News-Tweet Corpus Collection module works by co-operation of two distinct sub-modules: *Headline-Crawler* and *Tweet-Crawler*. The Headline-Crawler module periodically crawls reliable online news sources (selected from various categories like Politics, Sports, Technology, Finance etc.) and captures fresh news headlines. At present, Headline-Crawler crawls 137 news sources and obtains around 200-300 fresh headlines in each execution on an average.

The Tweet-Crawler module periodically downloads the news-tweets using Twitter REST API and the crawled news headlines one by one. As news-tweets are generally posted after the news headlines, Tweet-Crawler selects news headlines that are crawled t hours earlier from the Tweet-Crawler execution time for tweet crawling purpose. In our approach, Tweet-Crawler selects news headlines crawled at 3 hrs. before from its current execution time.

The process of crawling news-tweets using headline H is as follows. First, we process headline H to discover the news concepts. News concepts are basically important terms/keywords in a headline and often used by Twitter users in their tweets to grab the attention of their followers. In our approach, the news concepts are nouns and/or collocation of nouns (noun phrases) and/or collocation of nouns and numbers present in the headline. We use Stanford Part-of-Speech Tagger to tag each word in H with its corresponding parts-of-speech and extract the set of news concepts present in the headline. E.g., considering the headline "*Passenger plane crashes in Taiwan with 58 people aboard 9 killed*", "*Passenger plane crashes*", "*Taiwan*" and "*58 people*" are news concepts.

Let C be the set of news concepts extracted from headline H. Using C, Tweet-Crawler generates a search keyword in the form of a triplet $\langle c_i, c_j,$ "http"$\rangle$ such that $c_i, c_j \in C,\ i < j \ and\ 1 \leq i, j \leq |C|$, and uses the triplet for tweet crawling purpose. E.g., If C = {*Passenger plane crashes, Taiwan, 58 people*}, then ⟨*Passenger plane crashes, Taiwan, http*⟩ is a search keyword. Note that, using *pair of news concepts* to form the search keyword ensures that the downloaded tweets have high probability to be contextually similar with the headline. Compared to this, *use of single news concept* as a search keyword will download many irrelevant tweets and *use of all news concepts* will discard many contextually similar news-tweets. Besides that, we use "*http*" tag in the search keyword to ensure that each downloaded tweet contains at least one URL. Generally, news-casters embed URL in tweet content to emphasize that the news is not fake/remour and let their followers to click the link for getting the news article details.

Now, we identify news-tweets from the set of crawled tweets (say, T) that are contextually similar to headline H. In particular, tweet $t \in T$ is a *news-tweet* if $Sim(H,\, t)$ is greater than or equal to the user-defined similarity threshold. In our approach, $Sim(H,\, t)$ is an average of unigram similarity and bigram similarity of tweet content with the headline. The unigram similarity, given by $UniSim(H,\, t) = \frac{|U_H \bigcap U_t|}{|U_H|}$, is the fraction of headline words that appear in the tweet and bigram similarity, given by $BiSim(H,\, t) = \frac{|B_H \bigcap B_t|}{|B_H|}$, captures the contextual similarity of the tweet with the headline. Here, U_H and U_t (B_H and B_t) are the sets of unigram (bigram) words present in H and t respectively. Before calculating $Sim(H,\, t)$, we remove single letter words and stopwords from the tweet and the headline. Also, the words starting with '@', "RT", "http://" and '#' are removed from the tweet.

3.2 News-Tweet Authentication

Advertising E-commerce websites using news headline content is a common spamming activity on Twitter. E.g., we discover a news-tweet "#usa » `http://t.co/1NKSIAD8iX` *North Korea to send envoy to Russia ...*" posted by user "**@olga_casey**", where the shown embedded URL points to the fashion website "**`BAKMODA.com`**". As news-tweets are leveraged to discover and rank the news-casters, it is important to remove the news-tweets which intentionally use news media content to advertise non-news sources.

The News-Tweet Authentication module uses the embedded URL of tweet t for its verification purpose. First, we obtain long URL from the shortened URL using URL expansion technique. Next, if the domain of the expanded URL is a news source, we declare the news-tweet as authentic. However, it is not feasible to have the exhaustive list of all news sources for news-tweet authentication purpose. Thus, we devise a technique to incrementally learn a list of news sources as well as a list of non-news sources as follows.

Let $AList$ be the list of news source domains and $BList$ be the list of non-news source domains. Initially, $AList$ and $BList$ are empty. Let, $t.url$ be the expanded URL obtained from the shortened URL in a given news-tweet t. We mark tweet t as authentic if domain of $t.url$ is in $AList$ or as not authentic if the domain is in $BList$. However, if the domain of $t.url$ is not contained by both $AList$ and $BList$, we process tweet t further. We check whether the web page pointed by $t.url$ contains the headline H or not, where H has been used for crawling t. If the webpage does not contain H, the domain of $t.url$ becomes a candidate for non-news source. However, we follow a lazy approach and wait for more evidences in order to declare the domain of $t.url$ as news source; as sometimes news sources remove the news headline after a certain period of time. At present, we make a decision about any URL domain, if it is encountered in 100 different news-tweets. We put the URL domain in $AList$ if out of 100 times, we get evidence for the URL domain of being a news source for at least 30 times. Otherwise, we put it into $BList$. In summary, current module uses $AList$ and $BList$ and discovers the authentic news-tweets.

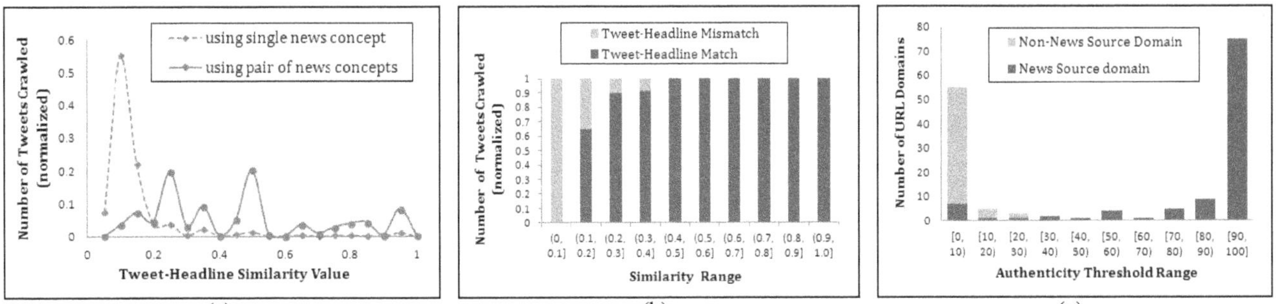

(a) (b) (c)

Figure 1: (a) Histogram of tweets against various similarity ranges obtained in single concept based and concept pair based tweets crawling. (b) Histogram of tweets (with match and mismatch ratio) against various similarity ranges obtained in concept pair based tweets crawling. (c) Distribution of news-sources and non-news source domains of 160 classified URL domains against various authenticity threshold ranges.

3.3 News-Caster Discovery and Ranking

The Twitter users associated with authentic news-tweets are the candidates for news-casters. However, it is possible that some of the users associated with the authentic news-tweets may be online news sources. In order to remove online news sources from the set of *true* news-casters, we obtain user profile information viz., *original user name* and *profile description* of each Twitter user. If the *original user name* or *profile description* of a given user contains "*news*" word in it, the user is declared as *online news source* and discarded from further analysis.

Now, we proceed to score the discovered news-casters on daily basis. We borrow the idea of HITS algorithm which scores a webpage high if it is associated with high authority webpages and many hubs point to it [3]. In our case, we score a news-caster higher if he/she publishes large number of distinct news-tweets where he/she has referred many popular news sources as embedded links and discussed about many popular news concepts. Here, we consider a news source's popularity higher if many news-casters have referred it in their news-tweets and the news source has published news headlines involving many popular news concepts. Similarly, a news concept's popularity can be explained accordingly.

We first build a weighted tripartite graph $G = (V, E)$ consisting of three types of vertices, namely *news-casters*, *news sources* and *news concepts*. The news-casters are already obtained in the previous paragraph and $AList$ is used as the list of news sources. The news concepts are taken as the concepts that co-occur in both news headline and corresponding news-tweet. Let u, c, s are vertices of graph G, where u is a news-caster, c is a news concept, and s is a news source. The weight of an edge between u and s, denoted as $W(u, s)$, is the number of distinct news-tweets where u has referred s. Similarly, $W(u, c)$ is the number of distinct news-tweets where u has talked about c, and $W(s, c)$ is the number of distinct news-tweets where s and c has co-occurred.

Given the graph G, we compute score for each node in G using HITS algorithm. Compared to the existing version of the HITS algorithm [3], the score of each node in our case is iteratively calculated by enforcing two mutual reinforcement relationships. E.g., the score of news source s, denoted as s_{score} is calculated based on the importance of its relationship with the news concepts and news-casters to which it is connected in G (See Equation 1).

$$s_{score} = \sum_{u \in V_U} W(u,s) * u_{score} + \sum_{c \in V_C} W(s,c) * c_{score} \quad (1)$$

where V_U, V_C are the set of news-caster nodes and news concept nodes and u_{score}, c_{score} are the scores of u and c in G respectively.

We initialize score of each node as 1 and then run the score computation process for N iterations. In each iteration, the score of news source nodes are computed, normalized and used in the score computation of other two types of nodes. In a similar way, the scores of the news concepts and news-casters are subsequently used in next iteration. After N iterations, we consider the normalized u_{score} as the final score of news-caster u on day d.

Once we acquire the daily score profiles of the news-casters over a specified time-period, we compute average score of each news-caster over that time-period and rank them based on their average score values. Finally, we infer news-casters with k highest average scores as the top-k consistent news-casters for that time-period.

Table 1: Examples of new news source domains and non-news source domains discovered by NCFinder.

New News Source Domains	Non-news Source Domains
wsj.com	bakmoda.com
engadget.com	ebay.com
reuters.com	brainyquote.com

4. EXPERIMENTAL ANALYSIS

We evaluate NCFinder empirically at different steps of processing and present sample output inferred by our system. Unless specified explicitly, the result reported in this section is obtained by running NCFinder from 11th Nov. to 24th Nov., 2014.

4.1 Evaluation I: News-Tweet Corpus Collection

We evaluate usefulness of our *news-concept pair based tweet crawling* scheme. We randomly select 10 news headlines, download a tweet dataset using the technique discussed in Section 3.1 and discovered 670 distinct tweets. For comparison purpose, we also download another tweet dataset using *single* news concept as a search keyword for the same set of headlines and obtain 4783 distinct tweets. Next, we plot the distribution of the tweets' similarity values for both the samples [see Figure 1(a)]. We observe that single news-concept based tweet crawling scheme downloads majority of the tweets (88.66%) having low similarity value (range of 0.05 to 0.2). Whereas, only 15.97% of the tweets obtained using our scheme, belong to the said low similarity range. On detailed analysis, we identify that news-tweets with low similarity value are not contextually similar to the selected news headlines. To validate this claim, we have sampled a set of 364 news-tweets from the 670 distinct tweets crawled by our approach and manually annotated each (*tweet, headline*) pair in the sample as *match* (contextually similar) or *mismatch* along with corresponding computed similarity value. Figure 1(b) shows the distribution of match and mismatch counts against various similarity ranges. The histogram shows that majority of the tweet-headline mismatches occur in the low similarity value range (0, 0.2] and majority of the tweets downloaded by our method have similarity value higher than 0.2 [see Figure 1(a)] and have high chance of match with headline [see Figure 1(b)]. Thus, our news-tweet corpus collection module is able to

Table 2: **Top-5 consistent news-casters and their profile statistics discovered during 11th Nov. to 24th Nov., 2014.**

NCFinder				TUMS
Sr. No.	Twitter User Handle	Top News Concepts	Top News Sources	Topic Profile
1	TopUp__	australia, uk, france, ebola, roger federer	bbc.co.uk	-
2	krs21da	ukrane, us, putin, obama, g20, ebola, suicide bomber	bbc.co.uk, abcnews.go.com, edition.cnn.com	Entertainment, Culture, Law, Crime, Politics
3	SubrataDhoni	india, australia, england, pakistan, modi	bbc.co.uk, ndtv.com, abplive.in	-
4	guilhermecorde	china, ebola, g20, romania, inquiry	bbc.co.uk	Entertainment, Buisness, Health
5	davidcunha_	china, g20, ebola, romania, growth	bbc.co.uk	-

process many headlines, downloads more relevant news-tweets and meets the Twitter rate limit. E.g., we noted that the said module has crawled 16,212 news-tweets using 211 headlines in 22.41 minutes.

4.2 Evaluation II: News-Tweet Authentication

We evaluate how accurately we have learned $AList$ and $BList$ to infer the authenticity of the crawled news-tweets. We have analysed the URLs accumulated in $AList$ and $BList$ and obtained 160 classified URL domains for one week period, where $AList$ contains 97 URL domains and BList contains 63 URL domains. We have manually verified the webpage of each of the 160 URL domains and observed that out of 97 authenticated URLs, 96 are news sources and 55 URLs in $BList$ are blacklisted (non-news source domains). In summary, F-measure of classifying URL domain as authentic news-source following our technique is 0.956.

Table 1 shows examples of correctly identified 3 new news source domains and 3 non-news source domains discovered by NCFinder. NCFinder has discovered many new news sources that does not belong to our *pre-defined news source set*. In fact, we have discovered 71 new news source domains frequently referred on Twitter.

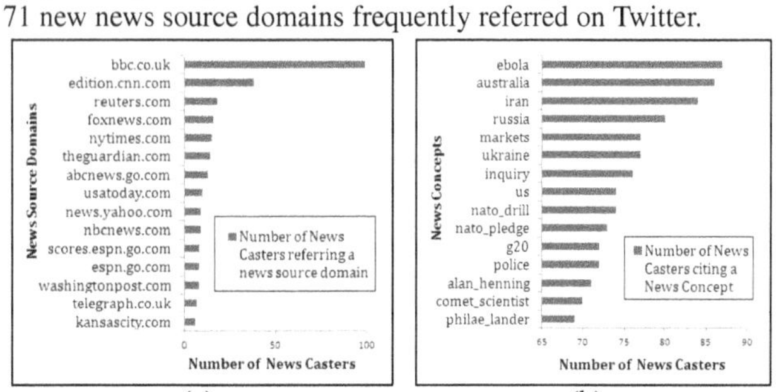

(a) (b)

Figure 2: Distributions of (a) news source domains and (b) news concepts for Top-100 consistent news-casters.

Note that, the content of $AList$ and $BList$ depend on a threshold value which we use for making decision. Figure 1(c) plots a distribution of news-sources and non-news sources against authenticity threshold ranges. Here, an URL domain l belonging to the range [10, 20) signifies that l has been authenticated at least 10 and at max 20 number of times out of 100 trials. The histogram shows that, majority (86.67%) of the URL domains belonging to the range [0, 30) are non-news source domains. In tweet authentication, precision being more important than recall, we have chosen 30 as the threshold and obtained a precision of 0.99 and recall 0.92. In terms of performance, our multi-threaded implementation of the authentication module has validated 16,212 news-tweets in 5.45 minutes.

4.3 Evaluation III: News-Caster Discovery

We evaluate our news-caster discovery step using user verification process. we have randomly collected sets of 100 users, visited their Twitter page and verified whether the user is news source or not and obtained 0.975 precision and 0.927 recall values.

4.4 Analysis of Output of NCFinder

Table 2 shows top news concepts and news sources cited by top-5 consistent news-casters discovered by NCFinder along their topic profile information obtained from TUMS. The results show that the news interest profile (top news concepts and news sources) discovered by NCFinder are more fine grained compared to the topic profile given by TUMS. In fact, the results of NCFinder for a given news-caster are not only complementing the topic profile, but also specifying detailed behavior of the news-caster over a given time-span. E.g., the news-caster "*guilhermecorde*" has posted tweets about "*ebola*" (Health) by acquiring news from "*bbc.co.uk*".

Figure 2 shows the distribution of news sources and news concepts of Top-100 consistent news-casters. In Figure 2(a) and (b), we see that "*bbc.co.uk*", "*edition.cnn.com*" etc. are popular news sources and "*ebola*", "*australia*" etc. are top news concepts that have been referred by majority of the top-100 consistent news-casters. The skewness of the distributions shows that news-casters mostly browse limited number of popular news sources rather than scrolling through different domains and almost talk about a diverse set of popular news concepts rather than a certain one.

5. CONCLUSIONS AND FUTURE WORK

In this paper, we propose a framework NCFinder to directly discover top-k consistent news-casters on Twitter. We have performed experiments to evaluate the effectiveness and efficacy of NCFinder and analyzed the discovered top-100 news-casters' profile. However, at present, NCFinder does not address the issue of Twitter Bots. As a future work, we aim to incorporate a *Bot filtering step* into NCFinder and also, enrich the ranking process of news-casters by considering their popularity aspects and social influence on Twitter.

6. REFERENCES

[1] F. Abel, Q. Gao, G.-J. Houben, and K. Tao. Analyzing user modeling on twitter for personalized news recommendations. In *User Modeling, Adaption and Personalization*, 2011.

[2] C. Castillo, M. Mendoza, and B. Poblete. Information credibility on twitter. In *WWW*, 2011.

[3] J. M. Kleinberg. Authoritative sources in a hyperlinked environment. *JACM*, 1999.

[4] H. Kwak, C. Lee, H. Park, and S. Moon. What is twitter, a social network or a news media? In *WWW*, 2010.

[5] S. Mazumder, B. Bishnoi, and D. Patel. News headlines: What they can tell us? In *IBM I-CARE*, 2014.

[6] J. Sankaranarayanan, H. Samet, B. E. Teitler, M. D. Lieberman, and J. Sperling. Twitterstand: news in tweets. In *SIGSPATIAL*, 2009.

[7] A. Schmidt, C. Fink, and N. Bos. Topical engagement on twitter: Using consistency of activity as a means of user segmentation. In *AAAI*, 2014.

[8] M. Tsagkias, M. de Rijke, and W. Weerkamp. Linking online news and social media. In *WSDM*, 2011.

[9] J. Weng, E.-P. Lim, J. Jiang, and Q. He. Twitterrank: finding topic-sensitive influential twitterers. In *WSDM*, 2010.

[10] W.-S. Yang, J.-B. Dia, H.-C. Cheng, and H.-T. Lin. Mining social networks for targeted advertising. In *HICSS*, 2006.

Mining the Minds of Customers from Online Chat Logs

Kunwoo Park* Jaewoo Kim† Jaram Park† Meeyoung Cha†
Graduate School of Web Science Technology, School of Computing*
Graduate School of Culture Technology†
KAIST, South Korea
{kw.park,jaewoo.kim,jaram.park,meeyoungcha}@kaist.ac.kr

Jiin Nam Seunghyun Yoon Eunhee Rhim
Intelligence Platform Lab, Software R&D Center
Samsung Electronics, South Korea
{jiin.nam,sh001.yoon,eunhee.rhim}@samsung.com

ABSTRACT
This study investigates factors that may determine satisfaction in customer service operations. We utilized more than 170,000 online chat sessions between customers and agents to identify characteristics of chat sessions that incurred dissatisfying experience. Quantitative data analysis suggests that sentiments or moods conveyed in online conversation are the most predictive factor of perceived satisfaction. Conversely, other session related meta data (such as that length, time of day, and response time) has a weaker correlation with user satisfaction. Knowing in advance what can predict satisfaction allows customer service staffs to identify potential weaknesses and improve the quality of service for better customer experience.

1. INTRODUCTION
For businesses, operating Customer Service (CS) to recognize product-related problems and heighten customer satisfaction is a crucial management function [7]. Among the various strategies employed in traditional CS operations, much effort has been paid to efficiency and functionality such as providing prompt and accurate response to customers (e.g., minimize waiting times, optimize agent assignment) [3, 6]. Aspects of customer experience such as their moods and sentiments, on the other hand, have received relatively little attention. As many companies now employ live chats as a means of running their support service, this new method gives clear benefits over traditional phone support in terms of making available the logged chats immediately in text format for further analysis.

Analyzing text logs in live chats can help identify what customers are saying about products and services as well as how well the support staff is performing, which is crucial for improving customer experience. Nonetheless, inferring customer feedback and satisfaction from text is not trivial. Existing methods rely on surveys posted to customers at the each support session, which call for voluntary participation. Another difficulty in customer experience is due to an asymmetric bimodal (J-shaped) distribution of feedback, where the average is a poor proxy of the overall quality. A large majority of customers often marking the service 'very satisfactory' and another large group mark 'very dissatisfying', which leads to divided opinions.

Given the wealth of data in live chat systems, this research proposes a novel data mining approach to evaluate customer experience from unstructured chat dialogs. We explored the opportunity to mind the minds of customers based on a set of features about sessions and sentiments. By analyzing unstructured chat content, we can extract the possible feedbacks buried in chat logs and determine (1) what topics are being discussed in chat logs, (2) what sentiments those chats accompany, and (3) what the overall satisfaction level of customers is.

We utilized data of dyadic chat logs provided by the IT-mediated CS centers of Samsung Electronics, which offer a 24/7 live chat service (http://www.samsung.com/us/support/live-chat.html) [1]. The data are text-based and cover all conversation logs between customers and agents on the topic of mobile products of Samsung Electronics in the United States. The live chat system asks for feedback at the end of each chat session, yet only a marginal portion of customers (16%) participate and a larger majority's experience (84%) remain unknown. In order to infer customer satisfaction for these unevaluated sessions, we examine sentiments in text. This work was motivated by a finding in [5] that says affective aspects of satisfaction are a key to a successful relationship between service providers and consumers.

This work demonstrates how computational methods offer a chance to understand sentiments on conversational data through big data analysis. The key method relied on machine learning techniques and was cross-validated on pre-answered dataset. We make several findings. First, sentiments conveyed in online conversation is the most predictive factor of customer satisfaction. Conversely, other session related meta data (e.g., length, time of day) have a weaker correlation with user satisfaction. Second, this work identifies that not only sentiments of customers but also those from

[1] We plan to make an anonymized version of the chat data available for the wider research community. Please contact Eunhee Rhim for data if interested.

Permission to make digital or hard copies of all or part of this work for personal or classroom use is granted without fee provided that copies are not made or distributed for profit or commercial advantage and that copies bear this notice and the full citation on the first page. Copyrights for components of this work owned by others than ACM must be honored. Abstracting with credit is permitted. To copy otherwise, or republish, to post on servers or to redistribute to lists, requires prior specific permission and/or a fee. Request permissions from Permissions@acm.org.
*CIKM'*15, October 19-23, 2015, Melbourne, VIC, Australia
©2015 ACM. ISBN 978-1-4503-3794-6/15/10...$15.00
DOI: http://dx.doi.org/10.1145/2806416.2806621

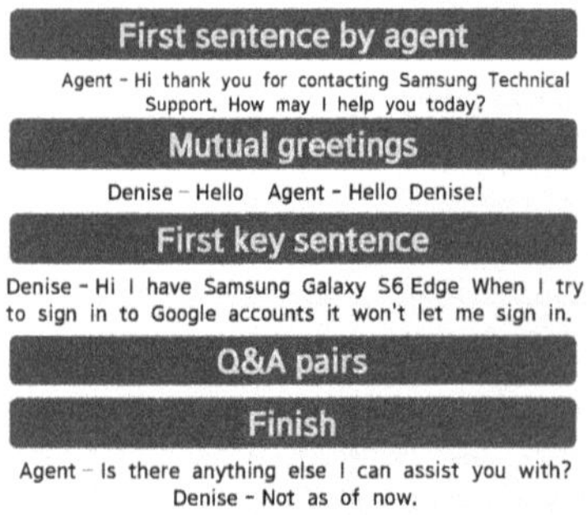

Figure 1: Procedure of the Livechat service

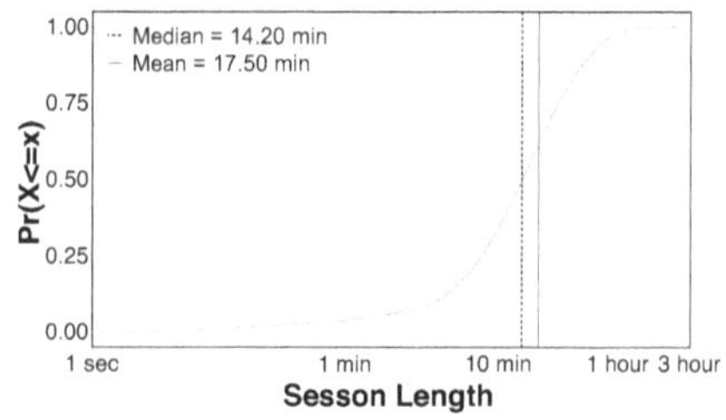

Figure 2: CDF on session lengths

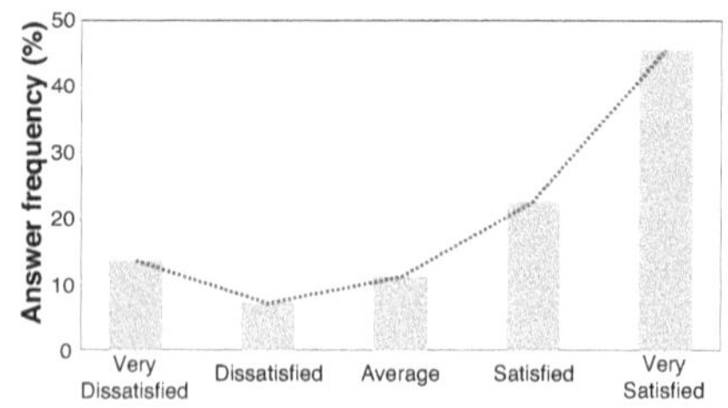

Figure 3: Post-chat survey results

agents play an important role in predicting customer satisfaction. This finding suggests the feasibility of utilizing sentiments in inferring customer satisfaction. Inferring customer satisfaction from conversation could be an essential component for automated CS agent, which is expected to be realized in near future. Sentiments of agents were more stable over time than those of customers. We discuss a possible approach to expand sentiment dictionaries to better handle domain- and context-specific words for the task.

2. DATA METHODOLOGY

2.1 Live Chat Logs

Upon entering Samsung Electronics's live chat system, customers are asked to choose the type of device they need help for (e.g., Galaxy S3). A chat session starts then as soon as an agent is allocated to that customer. Chats are in free text form, yielding varying intensity and length. Nonetheless, we could find a common structure by manual coding 3% of sample sessions as depicted in Figure 1. A chat is initiated by a greeting sentence from an agent (e.g., "Hi, thank you for contacting Samsung Technical Support. How may I help you today?") and is followed by mutual greetings. A customer typically describes a problem immediately after the greeting part, which is then followed by a series of question–and–answer–style conversation. In this work, we refer to each unit of conversation "utterance"(i.e., the smallest unit in chats separated by pressing "enter"), for which the log specifies the timestamp, the speaker, and text content. Often a given utterance is not a full sentence (e.g., "Every time I try to sign into Google accounts"), when a sentence is spread across multiple utterance instances (e.g., "I ran an update" "last week" "and I am not getting picture messages" "now").

We obtained 12-month worth of complete conversation logs between customers and agents on a representative mobile products of Samsung Electronics in the United States. The dataset was given in the XML format and contained 173,886 sessions as well as 5,641,172 utterance instances. For each session, the log contained information about the following: (1) product type, (2) agent ID, (3) customer info (ID, geolocation, timezone), (4) duration info (start time, endtime, disconnecting entity), (5) utterance info (speaker, timestamp, text content), and (6) post-session survey results (4 questions). Figure 2 shows the distribution of session length, where the x-axis represents session length in a log scale. On average, each session lasts 17.50 minutes (Std=13.47), while the median is 14.20 minutes. This plot suggests that many sessions end within 20 minutes, while there exist extremely long sessions that lasted over one hour. 75% of all sessions terminated after exchanging no more than 45 messages.

Once a live chat session ends, customers are provided with survey questionnaires to indicate their satisfaction level as follows:

1. *How would you rate your overall satisfaction with the chat?*
2. *In the future, would you prefer to chat instead of calling?*
3. *How would you rate satisfaction with the representative's overall knowledge?*
4. *Please choose the main reason you were dissatisfied from the following choices.*

Answer for the first question represents the satisfaction score and was logged by 5-point Likert scale (Very Dissatisfied–Dissatisfied–Average–Satisfied–Very Satisfied). This survey helps us infer the quality of each session. Figure 3 shows the distribution of responses, where the vertical axis represents the answer frequency. Note that these statistics are based on only 16% of sessions that had complete survey results, as the survey was voluntary in nature. The overall satisfaction score follows a J-shaped distribution, where a large fraction (45%) found chats to be very satisfactory and another large group (14%) indicated extreme unhappy experience. We later use this result to infer characteristics of sessions when customers were dissatisfied.

2.2 Customer Sentiment Extraction

In order to identify sentiments from unstructured human chat data, we utilize an existing state-of-the-art sentiment tool called VADER (Valence Aware Dictionary and sEntiment Reasoner) [2]. VADER extends several human-validated sentiment lexicons such as LIWC, ANEW, and GL. One of the most popular sentiment analysis tool is LIWC (Linguistic Inquiry and Word Count), which does not perform well for online text containing slangs and short sentences. VADER constructed a gold-standard list of lexical features mainly focused on microblog context and performs well even for short messages. In this research, we analyzed sentiment of each utterance (i.e., the unit of chat dialog) through VADER. Examples chat utterances and their sentiment results are shown below. The score in parenthesis indicates valence (scaled from -1 to 1) a negative score refers to negative sentiment and vice versa.

> *Customer: I purchased phone and then I noticed a terrible scuff on my screen. (-0.389)*

> *Agent: It was a pleasure assisting you, thank you for contacting Samsung Technical Support. (0.348)*

As depicted in Figure 1, chat dialogs usually followed common flow. Based on the flow, we may assume four steps of composition and we divide a conversation into an arbitrary set of four steps

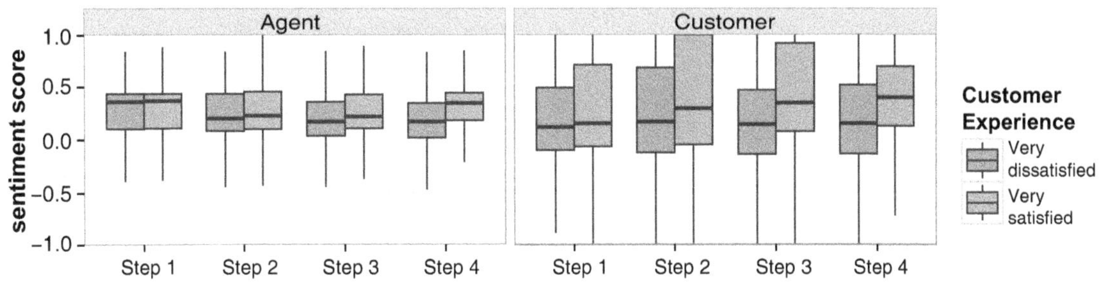

Figure 4: Dynamics of sentiment according to conversation stage

based on the total conversation length of each session as a simple approximation. We conducted sentiment analysis and aggregated the sentiment results for each conversation step.

The resulting sentiment dynamics is shown in Figure 4 for two extreme sets of sessions: Very Satisfied (VS) group and Very Dissatisfied (VD) group. While the VS group exhibits more positive sentiment, the VD group shows more negative sentiment as conversation progresses for both customers and agents. It is interesting to observe that customers typically exhibit a wider variation in sentiments than agents. Both agents and customers start with a similar sentiment score. However, from Step 2 and onward, sentiments start to deviate between the two groups especially for customers. These changes imply customers' moods are dynamic, especially after the Step 1. Agent on the other hand have consistent sentiment in early stages (i.e., Step 1 and Step 2) regardless of customers' sentiment.

3. PREDICTING SATISFACTION

We now seek to predict which sessions mark low satisfaction based on the available quantitative measures. We transformed the 5-point Likert Scale from user survey into a binary label to indicate whether each session is dissatisfactory to a customer or not. We did because identifying a dissatisfying session (rather than the opposite) is crucial for CS operation. Dissatisfied customers may be a minority group in terms of numbers, but meeting their needs is critical in customer management. Therefore we labelled satisfaction of customer as follows: (Very Dissatisfied, Dissatisfied) to TRUE, (Very Satisfied, Satisfied, Average) to FALSE in terms of *dissatisfaction*. This grouping led to 4,649 TRUE and 20,175 FALSE sessions for prediction. To predict dissatisfaction, we extracted a total of 14 features for each chat steps across the following: session-level meta information (e.g., number of utterances, session length of a session), agent's sentiment (e.g., agent's sentiment at each step), and customer's sentiment (e.g., customer's sentiment at each step).

Table 1 shows the performance of algorithms used for predicting dissatisfying sessions. Every measurement is based on 10-fold cross validation. For prediction, we utilize logistic regression, SVM with radial kernel (note as SVM-R), and random forest to classify sessions into binary scheme: TRUE/FALSE for dissatisfaction. As a baseline, we set up the majority voting and found accuracy of 0.8127. We make the following observations. Firstly, random forest outperforms the baseline. SVM-R is the best in terms of prediction accuracy, yet random forest yields the highest F1 score. Secondly, sentiments extracted from sessions can significantly improve the performance of the prediction task. Compared to the random forest model only using session-level meta information that is even beaten by the baseline (termed "w/o sentiments"), incorporating sentiments makes a significant improvement in performance. Because label distribution is biased toward FALSE cases for dissatisfaction, it is naturally difficult to predict dissatsfaction well. However, the above results imply the importance of sentiments for understanding dissatisfying sessions.

Measure	All features			w/o sentiments
	Logistic Regression	SVM-R	Random Forest	Random Forest
Accuracy	0.7941	**0.8378**	0.8372	0.8118
F1 score	0.3154	0.2867	**0.3949**	0.0275

Table 1: Performances of algorithms for predicting customer's satisfaction under 10-fold cross validation

Subsequently, we investigated the importance of individual features in the prediction task. Figure 5 shows the list of features and their mean decrease entropy in random forest. Entropy explains node impurity for a feature. Thus if a decision tree is well separated by a predictor, the measure will have a low value. Since there are multiple number of trees in a random forest, mean decrease entropy indicates the average importance of feature for each tree inside the random forest. The results show that sentiments play an important role in predicting customer's satisfaction for overall sessions. Sentiments of both customers and agents are important in understanding customer satisfaction. Moreover, agent's sentiment from Step 4 of the chat dialog is the most important feature in random forest, followed by the same quantity for customers. Agents, who generally are conservative in revealing their sentiments than customers, could express their sentiments stronger toward the end of chat sessions.

To figure out the context deeper, we conducted N-gram analysis for unigrams and bi-grams (N=1,2), and retrieved discriminative N-grams for dissatisfaction. Table 2 presents the list of N-grams used in Step 4 of agent's conversation. In order to decide the discriminative power of each N-gram, we calculated Cramer's V, which is a normalized variant of Chi-squared value. Every term listed in this table is dominantly used in FALSE sessions (i.e., satisfactory or average). For example, 'button' and 'the blue' are more written in FALSE sessions than TRUE sessions (i.e., dissatisfying). Agents may ask customers to participate in post-survey by clicking a button (e.g., 'please click', 'button'). However in sessions where the customer's problem is not resolved properly, it may be difficult for agents to ask for a survey to customers or even customers may disconnect in the middle, leaving to a sudden end for that session.

4. DISCUSSION

While this work demonstrated the possibility of applying sentiment analysis and machine learning to infer customer satisfaction, more

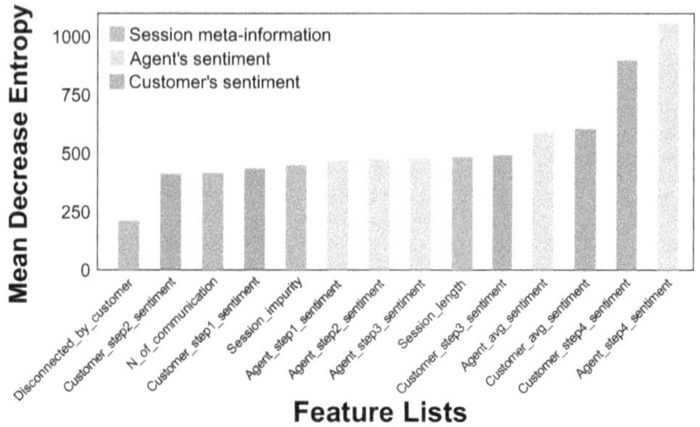

Figure 5: Feature importance for predicting customer's satisfaction

efforts are needed before this idea can be implemented in a real system. Analyzing sentiments in dyadic chats between customers and agents is non-trivial for a number of reasons, because (1) individual variance is large, (2) sentiments tend to change over time, (3) utterances are unstructured and short in length, and (4) human sentiments are further subject to culture of the society they belong to. Chat data did not lend itself well to existing sentiment analysis tools in terms of coverage and biases—only 1.25% of all utterances in chats contained any single word related to sentiments from state-of-the-art tools. Qualitative analysis that we conducted over a small subset of data revealed that automated tools sometimes could not understand sentiments and misjudged the valence. The following sentences contain negative sentiment based on a human coder's judgement, for instance, could not be understood correctly with automated sentiment analysis tools:

> "*I have tried to restart my phone over hundred times but the problem still persists*"
>
> "*My 5-year old can answer the same*"
>
> "*YEAH RIGHT.*"

In order to identify sentiments from unstructured human chat data, we plan to expand existing sentiment dictionaries to handle domain-specific words and expressions. For example, training with the CS chat data would allow us to fine tune the sentiment dictionary with domain- and context- specific words (e.g., 'crack' would indicate problem on screens). Such joint expansion can be made through a variety of approaches including the PMI (Pointwise Mutual Information) approach [1]. The PMI-based framework assumes that when a word A is frequently used with another word B containing positive sentiment, A is likely to represent positive sentiment as well. While omitted due to space limitation, we expended existing state-of-the-art sentiment dictionaries extensively and found potential for better understanding more complex sentences that often appear for the CS chat logs. For instance, a phrase such as 'hundred times' in the above mentioned example becomes associated with negative sentiment in CS chats and hence the particular chat sentence can be better understood automatically. On top of the above approach, we could adopt non-seed approaches [4] to improve the coverage of sentiments in online chats.

5. CONCLUSION

The IT-based Customer Service (CS) is a crucial operation for a number of businesses around the world. In this study we tested the feasibility of utilizing chat text to infer customer satisfaction in CS conversation by utilizing computational sentiment extraction

Rank	Unigram	Frequency		Bigram	Frequency	
		TRUE	FALSE		TRUE	FALSE
1	button	0.294	0.801	the blue	0.280	0.774
2	survey	0.294	0.796	transcript of	0.275	0.758
3	blue	0.282	0.776	please click	0.273	0.755
4	fill	0.280	0.767	to receive	0.282	0.766
5	transcript	0.288	0.791	your chat	0.273	0.751
6	pleasure	0.275	0.775	button to	0.272	0.749
7	click	0.300	0.791	a transcript	0.273	0.749
8	close	0.271	0.747	Have a	0.288	0.811
9	assisting	0.269	0.744	It was	0.275	0.775
10	brief	0.271	0.744	receive a	0.274	0.752

Table 2: Discriminative N-grams (N=1,2) ranked by Cramer's V in the 4th step of session for agents

of conversational data. The main finding suggests that sentiments of both customers and agents play an important role for predicting customers' satisfaction, and consequently this can be used as a source of feedback to improve customer experience. Interestingly, agents tend to exhibit a lower degree of variance in their sentiments than customers, yet show negative sentiment at the last step of a chat particularly in those conversations that were marked as 'very dissatisfying' (see Figure 4). This result could imply that emotional interaction in the CS sessions is one of the key factors for understanding customer experience, so computational sentiment analysis could be a helpful albeit challenging tool.

The sentiment lexicon we utilized is designed for understanding general online messages. For better performance, future studies can use CS domain-specified sentiment lexicons by expanding of existing sentiment dictionaries. In addition, service agents tend to ask customers to answer a post-chat survey when the conversation seems satisfactory to customers. This can cause a bias in answers and lead to a degree of skew to the J-shaped distribution in survey result. Therefore, further investigation on distribution of unsatisfactory and satisfactory conversations could be conducted to identify a clear difference between them and improve prediction performance.

6. REFERENCES

[1] J. Bross and H. Ehrig. Automatic construction of domain and aspect specific sentiment lexicons for customer review mining. In *proc. of the ACM CIKM*, 2013.

[2] C. Hutto and E. Gilbert. Vader: A parsimonious rule-based model for sentiment analysis of social media text. In *proc. of the AAAI ICWSM*, 2014.

[3] M. M. Kazmer, G. Burnett, and M. H. Dickey. Identity in customer service chat interaction: Implications for virtual reference. *Library & Information Science Research*, 2007.

[4] J. Liang, X. Zhou, Y. Hu, L. Guo, and S. Bai. CONR: A Novel Method for Sentiment Word Identification. In *proc. of the ACM CIKM*, 2014.

[5] D. J. Shemwell, U. Yavas, and Z. Bilgin. Customer-service provider relationships: an empirical test of a model of service quality, satisfaction and relationship-oriented outcomes. *Int'l Journal of Service Industry Management*, 1998.

[6] C.-W. Tan, I. Benbasat, and R. T. Cenfetelli. IT-mediated customer service content and delivery in electronic governments: An empirical investigation of the antecedents of service quality. *MIS Quarterly*, 2013.

[7] L. Yan, R. H. Wolniewicz, and R. Dodier. Predicting customer behavior in telecommunications. *IEEE Intelligent Systems*, 2004.

A Fast k-Nearest Neighbor Search Using Query-Specific Signature Selection

Youngki Park
CSE, Seoul National University, Seoul, Korea
ypark@europa.snu.ac.kr

Heasoo Hwang*
CSE, University of Seoul, Seoul, Korea
hwang@uos.ac.kr

Sang-goo Lee
CSE, Seoul National University, Seoul, Korea
sglee@snu.ac.kr

ABSTRACT

k-nearest neighbor (k-NN) search aims at finding k points nearest to a query point in a given dataset. k-NN search is important in various applications, but it becomes extremely expensive in a high-dimensional large dataset. To address this performance issue, *locality-sensitive hashing* (LSH) is suggested as a method of probabilistic dimension reduction while preserving the relative distances between points. However, the performance of existing LSH schemes is still inconsistent, requiring a large amount of search time in some datasets while the k-NN approximation accuracy is low.

In this paper, we target on improving the performance of k-NN search and achieving a consistent k-NN search that performs well in various datasets. In this regard, we propose a novel LSH scheme called *Signature Selection LSH* (S2LSH). First, we generate a highly diversified signature pool containing signature regions of various sizes and shapes. Then, for a given query point, we rank signature regions of the query and select points in the highly ranked signature regions as k-NN candidates of the query. Extensive experiments show that our approach consistently outperforms the state-of-the-art LSH schemes.

Categories and Subject Descriptors

H.3.3 [**Information Storage and Retrieval**]: Information Search and Retrieval—*Search process*

Keywords

k-nearest neighbor search; locality sensitive hashing

1. INTRODUCTION

Multimedia search engines and recommendation systems such as Google image search and YouTube video recommender need to perform k-nearest neighbor (k-NN) search over a large collection of high-dimensional data points [3]. Since they need to adaptively refine k-NN results as soon as each user clicks on an image or a video, the performance of a k-NN search algorithm becomes increasingly important.

Locality sensitive hashing (LSH) is known as one of the most efficient approximation methods for k-NN search [7]. Using locality sensitive hash functions that assign close points to the same hash bucket with high probability, one can pick points sharing buckets with a given query point as candidates for k-NN search. However, recently proposed approaches such as *Collision Counting LSH* (C2LSH) [4], LSB-tree and forest [8], and *Exact Euclidean LSH* (E2LSH) [7, 2] show a poor performance in some datasets while they work well in some others. In fact, our experiments show that their performance is significantly affected by the characteristics of a dataset such as the number of points and the feature extraction method.

In this paper, we propose a consistently efficient LSH scheme for fast k-NN search, called *Signature Selection LSH* (S2LSH), that performs well in various types of datasets. To describe our key intuition more clearly, let us first define two concepts, a *signature* and a *signature region* of a point q. A locality sensitive hash function g projects q onto a lower dimensional space, and the projected coordinate of q is called the *signature* of q by g. Then, g defines a region in the projected space that contains a set of points represented as the same signature. We denote the region containing q defined by g as the *signature region* of q by g. Note that LSH schemes usually define multiple signature regions of q using multiple locality sensitive hash functions in order to capture the neighborhood of q more effectively.

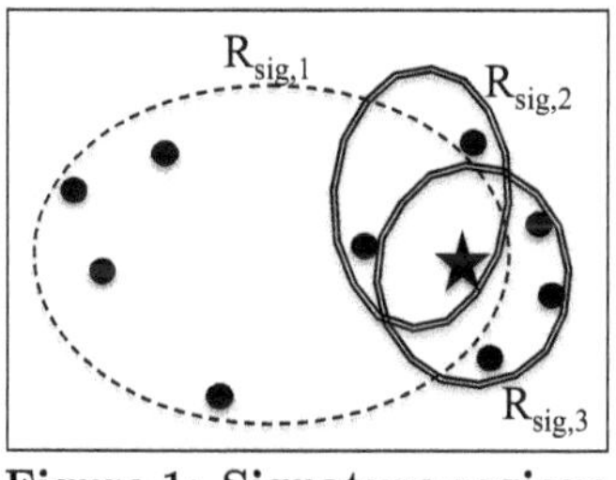

Figure 1: Signature regions and k-NN candidates.

Figure 1 demonstrates our key observation on the relationship between signature regions and the performance of k-NN search. The signature regions of q are not equally important for k-NN search of q. Let us consider that we need to find k-NN points of q (the star node) by selecting 5 candidates from a large collection of points. All of the three signature regions, $R_{sig,1}$, $R_{sig,2}$, and $R_{sig,3}$, cover the neighborhood of q. However, $R_{sig,1}$ contains some points that are far from q. It is because q is near the boundary of the signature region and the size of $R_{sig,1}$ is large. Since $R_{sig,2}$ and $R_{sig,3}$ are relatively small, the points in the union of the two regions become good k-NN candidates of q.

*corresponding author

Permission to make digital or hard copies of all or part of this work for personal or classroom use is granted without fee provided that copies are not made or distributed for profit or commercial advantage and that copies bear this notice and the full citation on the first page. Copyrights for components of this work owned by others than ACM must be honored. Abstracting with credit is permitted. To copy otherwise, or republish, to post on servers or to redistribute to lists, requires prior specific permission and/or a fee. Request permissions from Permissions@acm.org.
CIKM'15, October 19–23, 2015, Melbourne, Australia.
© 2015 ACM. ISBN 978-1-4503-3794-6/15/10 ...$15.00.
DOI: http://dx.doi.org/10.1145/2806416.2806632.

Notice that a point in a small signature region is more likely to be a k-NN point of q than a point in a large signature region is. Therefore, it is usually more effective to pick the points in small signature regions as k-NN candidates of q. A large signature region is not effective in k-NN search of q especially if q is located near the boundary of the region; the points on the other side of the region are actually distant from q, but included as k-NN candidates of q, which is undesirable. Rather, we suggest to pick k-NN candidates of q from the union of small signature regions of q. However, even though we prefer small signature regions, we also need large ones since the distances from q to its actual k-NN points can be large if the density of points around q is low.

Our approach, S2LSH, is composed of two stages, signature pool generation and signature selection. Since the distances from each point to its k-NN points may vary significantly, we generate a highly diversified signature pool that contains signature regions of various sizes and shapes. Once a query point q is given, we measure the effectiveness of each signature region of q. Then, we choose a predefined number of candidates from the signature regions with high effectiveness scores. Experiments show that S2LSH is consistently efficient in generating k-NN results with high approximation accuracy.

2. RELATED WORK

Locality sensitive hashing (LSH) converts high-dimensional points into low-dimensional points called *signatures* while preserving the relative distances between them. We can perform approximate k-NN search based on the distances between signatures of points, instead of using the distances between the original coordinates of points. However, even very effective hypersphere-based hash functions fail in achieving high approximation accuracy if the dimension of signatures is low [6]. k-NN approximation accuracy is improved with high-dimensional signatures, but it takes very long time to calculate distances between signatures.

Instead, state-of-the-art LSH schemes suggest to use signature regions to choose k-NN candidates of q. The followings are three existing LSH schemes that are known as efficient k-NN approximation methods: (1) *Exact Euclidean LSH* (E2LSH) [7, 2] constructs multiple signature regions for q. If a point p is in one of the signature regions of q, p is selected as a k-NN candidate of q. This means that E2LSH selects all the points in the union of the signature regions of q as k-NN candidates of q. (2) *LSB-tree* and *LSB-forest* [8] compress the signatures generated by E2LSH further into one-dimensional values using the z-order curve. Then, they select a point that has a z-order value with the greatest LLCP (length of longest common prefix) as a candidate for q. (3) *Collision Counting LSH* (C2LSH) [4] counts the number of signature regions in which q and a point p co-occur. If the collision count of p is equal to or greater than a given threshold l, it selects p as a candidate for q. However, the collision counting step of C2LSH requires a number of set intersection computations, which is very expensive. C2LSH suggests to use virtual rehashing technique, but its application is limited to random projection [5, 7].

3. SIGNATURE SELECTION LSH

The motivation of our approach is that among multiple signature regions of q, there are some signature regions that are more effective in performing a fast k-NN search of q than the rest. The example in Figure 1 shows that points in smaller signature regions are more likely to be k-NN points of q.

Ideally, the most effective signature region of q for the approximate k-NN search is the signature region containing q and k-NN points of q only, since it does not introduce any false positive or false negative. However, generating such a signature region of q takes as much effort as finding k-NN points of q directly among all the points in a dataset. Instead, we keep merging signature regions of q starting from small ones until the number of points in the merged region reach a fixed threshold. However, notice that since the points in a dataset are not uniformly distributed, the neighborhood regions of points can be very diverse both in size and shape. Therefore, we first construct a large collection of highly diversified signature regions, called a *signature pool*.

3.1 Signature Pool Generation

When a collection of points, D, is given, we construct a highly diversified signature pool in order to improve both k-NN approximation accuracy and the search time in D. To this end, we generate a signature pool of size L by defining L compound hash functions, $\{g_1, g_2, \cdots, g_L\}$. Each g_i needs to be locality-sensitive. The ith compound hash function, g_i, defines the ith signature region of q, $R_{sig,i}(q)$. Then, for a given query point q, our signature pool provides L signature regions of q using the compound hash functions. Notice that $R_{sig,i}(q)$ covers a point p in D along with q if the ith signature of p is $g_i(q)$, i.e., $g_i(p) = g_i(q)$.

Since each g_i is locality-sensitive, the points in $R_{sig,i}(q)$ tend to be close to q. If we pick all the points in the L signature regions of q as k-NN candidates of q, the hashing performance of each g_i directly determines the overall performance of k-NN search. However, in S2LSH, we reduce the dependence on the hashing performance of each g_i and improve the average performance of k-NN search by increasing the diversity of signature regions in a signature pool and using highly effective signature regions only.

We can use various types of compound hash functions in S2LSH such as random hyperplane [1] and Spherical Hashing [6] by considering the characteristics of a given dataset. If the distance between points in D is best measured by the cosine distance, we can use, for instance, random hyperplane to define g_i. The number of hyperplanes defining g_i corresponds to the length of signatures generated by g_i; as we add one more hyperplane, we append $+1$ to the signatures of points on a side of the hyperplane and -1 to those on the other side of it. For a dataset in Euclidean space, we can use a hypersphere-based hash function such as Spherical Hashing. In this case, the number of hyperspheres of g_i determines the length of signatures generated by g_i. Throughout this paper, we mainly use Spherical Hashing to define compound hash functions of S2LSH and baseline approaches since it achieves a high hashing performance by considering the distribution of points in D. In order to generate signature regions of diverse shapes and sizes, each g_i is allowed to be defined using a various number of hyperspheres.

To generate a diversified signature pool based on Spherical Hashing, we need three more parameters: H, m_1, and m_2. m_1 and m_2 define the minimum and the maximum lengths of signatures and H represents the total number of hyperspheres from which we randomly select a subset of hyperspheres and use them to define g_i. For example, let us assume that H, m_1 and m_2 are 300, 5 and 15 respectively. Then, after generating 300 hyperspheres for D, we generate each g_i composed of n_i hyperspheres randomly chosen among them. n_i is a random number between m_1 and m_2, and it corresponds to the length of signatures generated by g_i. Notice that we execute Spherical Hashing just once to generate 300 hyperspheres, instead of executing it whenever we define g_i. Through experiments, we see that this significantly reduces the time for generating a signature pool without affecting k-NN approximation accuracy.

3.2 Signature Selection

For a given query q, we want to select a subset of signature regions from which we can get high-quality k-NN candidates of q. Recall that the state-of-the-art LSH schemes either introduce too many false positives by picking the points in all of the signature regions as k-NN candidates, or spend too much time in selecting the points frequently co-occurring with q in many of the signature regions.

In S2LSH, we define an *effectiveness measure of a signature region* by considering the followings: Firstly, assuming that a point in a smaller signature region of q is more likely to be a k-NN point of q, we assign a higher effectiveness score to a small signature region than to larger ones. Notice that the distance between q and a point in $R_{sig,i}(q)$ is bounded by the size of $R_{sig,i}(q)$. Secondly, if two signature regions of q are of similar size, we assign a higher effectiveness score to the signature region in which q is located closer to the center of the region. Lastly, we should be able to compute the effectiveness scores of signature regions without heavy computation overhead. Otherwise, the execution time of k-NN approximate search will significantly increase.

We identify a set of features of signature regions and measure the correlation between every combination of features and the performance of k-NN approximation. Then, we select four features that are highly correlated with the performance of k-NN approximation. We consider them as strong indicators of the effectiveness of a signature region for k-NN search of q. Let us describe the four selected features by comparing two signature regions of q, $R_{sig,i}(q)$ and $R_{sig,j}(q)$.

(F_1) **Signature Length.** A signature length corresponds to the number of hyperspheres that partition the points in D. Therefore, as it grows, the corresponding signature region tends to shrink to a smaller one. It is also shown that popular LSH schemes achieve high mean average precision by using longer signatures [6].

(F_2) **Cardinality.** If $R_{sig,i}(q)$ contains fewer points than $R_{sig,j}(q)$, it is likely that $R_{sig,i}(q)$ covers a smaller neighborhood of q than $R_{sig,j}(q)$ is, assuming that the densities of points in $R_{sig,i}(q)$ and $R_{sig,j}(q)$ are not particularly different.

(F_3) **Average Distance from Query.** If the average distance between q and a point in $R_{sig,i}(q)$ is shorter than that of $R_{sig,j}(q)$, it is likely that $R_{sig,i}(q)$ is smaller than $R_{sig,j}(q)$.

(F_4) **Maximum Distance from Query.** If the maximum distance between q and a point in $R_{sig,i}(q)$ is shorter than that of $R_{sig,j}(q)$, it is likely that either $R_{sig,i}(q)$ is smaller than $R_{sig,j}(q)$, or q is located closer to the center of $R_{sig,i}(q)$ than to the center of $R_{sig,j}(q)$. Notice that there are some points in $R_{sig,j}(q)$ whose distances from q are greater than the distance between q and any point in $R_{sig,i}(q)$.

While F_1 and F_2 can be computed efficiently using techniques such as bucket hashing[1], calculating F_3 and F_4 is computationally very expensive because they are query-specific. In S2LSH, we approximate F_3 and F_4 using intermediate results of distance calculations performed for previous queries. Therefore, S2LSH can compute approximate values, F_3' and F_4', only when it performs k-NN search of multiple queries. Accordingly, we define two effectiveness measures, E' and E'', separately, and use E'' only if multiple queries are given.

$$E'(R_{sig,i}(q), q) = \begin{cases} 0 & \text{if } F_2(R_{sig,i}(q)) = 1 \\ \frac{F_1(R_{sig,i}(q))}{F_2(R_{sig,i}(q))-1} & \text{otherwise} \end{cases}$$

$$E''(R_{sig,i}(q), q) = \frac{1}{F_3'(R_{sig,i}(q), q) + F_4'(R_{sig,i}(q), q)}$$

For a given query q, S2LSH selects a fixed number of candidates from highly ranked signature regions of q among L signature regions of q from the signature pool. Currently, the number of candidates is determined by considering both k and the time budget.

4. EXPERIMENTS

Experimental Settings. (a) **Dataset:** We use 7 datasets containing different numbers of points and represented with various dimensions as shown in Table 1. They include audio data, images, and textual data with various feature extraction methods. (b) **Baselines:** The three baseline approaches are Brute-force, E2LSH [7, 2], and C2LSH [4]. To our best knowledge, C2LSH is the most recent and efficient LSH scheme for k-NN search. However, we include E2LSH as a baseline since we observed while comparing many existing LSH approaches that E2LSH outperforms C2LSH with careful parameter tuning. We applied various optimization techniques to enhance the performance of the three baselines for fair comparison. (c) **Accuracy Measure:** We use the fraction of correct k-NN points($k = 10$) as a measure of k-NN approximation accuracy. The average k-NN search time we report in this section is the average of 1000 queries. (d) **Effectiveness Measure:** For most of the experiments in this section, we use E' only since we execute each query seperately. For the experiments with multiple queries shown in Figure 4, we use both E' and E''.

Dataset	Num points	Num dim.	Feature Description
Corel	300,000	14	Image dataset
NUS-WIDE (CH)	200,000	64	Color histogram from Flickr images
Audio	50,000	192	Marsyas music dataset
NUS-WIDE (BoW)	100,000	500	Bag of words based on SIFT
Shape	25,000	544	Shape benchmark
MNIST	60,000	784	Handwritten digits
GIST1M	100,000	960	Image dataset

Table 1: Summary on various datasets.

Impact of Dataset. Table 2 shows the performance comparison results of S2LSH and the three baselines. We measured the average k-NN search time in 7 datasets listed in Table 1. S2LSH is shown to generate more accurate k-NN search results with less average execution time in all the

[1] `http://www.mit.edu/~andoni/LSH/`

7 datasets. This means that we can use S2LSH in various types of datasets.

Dataset	Brute-force	E2LSH	C2LSH	S2LSH
Corel	74ms (1.00)	6ms (0.96)	66ms (0.85)	**2ms (0.97)**
NUS-WIDE (CH)	120ms (1.00)	9ms (0.91)	47ms (0.82)	**4ms (0.92)**
Audio	75ms (1.00)	9ms (0.89)	16ms (0.87)	**8ms (0.92)**
NUS-WIDE (BoW)	384ms (1.00)	169ms (0.88)	187ms (0.90)	**103ms (0.91)**
Shape	97ms (1.00)	11ms (0.90)	11ms (0.90)	**10ms (0.93)**
MNIST	346ms (1.00)	61ms (0.92)	32ms (0.81)	**21ms (0.94)**
GIST1M	726ms (1.00)	162ms (0.92)	134ms (0.82)	**75ms (0.92)**

Table 2: The average k-NN search time per query and the corresponding approximation accuracy.

Impact of Underlying Hash Function. To show that the superiority of S2LSH is not limited to a particular hash function, we experimented with two different hash functions, Spherical Hashing [6] and random hyperplane [1]. We chose them since Spherical Hashing is data-dependent and based on Euclidean distance while random hyperplane does not consider the original data distribution and it uses the cosine distance. As shown in Figure 2 and Figure 3, S2LSH consistently shows the best performance regardless of the type of underlying hash functions.

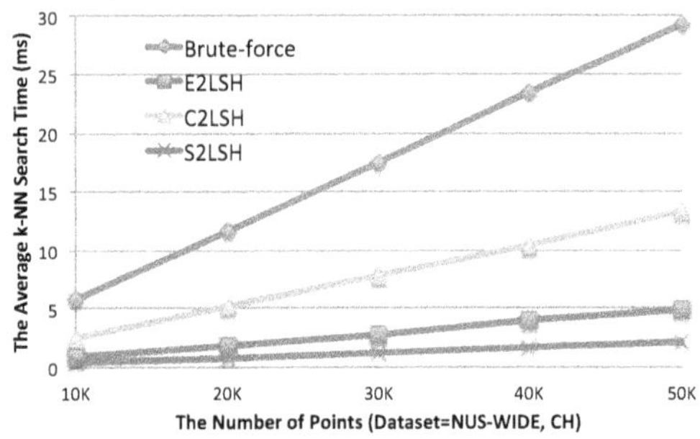

Figure 2: Performance comparison using Spherical Hashing as underlying hash function.

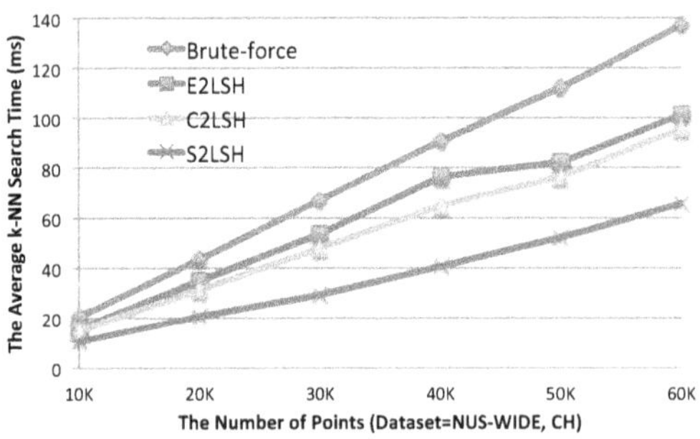

Figure 3: Performance comparison using random hyperplane as underlying hash function.

Impact of E''. In the experiment in Figure 4, we used all the points in a given dataset as queries and performed k-NN search for each query point. Since multiple queries are given, S2LSH can efficiently approximate F_3 and F_4 using the results of distance calculations performed for previous queries. We increased the number of queries from 10K to 50K and measured the total elapsed time. It is shown that by using E'' along with E', the performance of S2LSH can be further improved. Also, the gap between the total search time of S2LSH and those of the baselines grows rapidly as the number of queries increases.

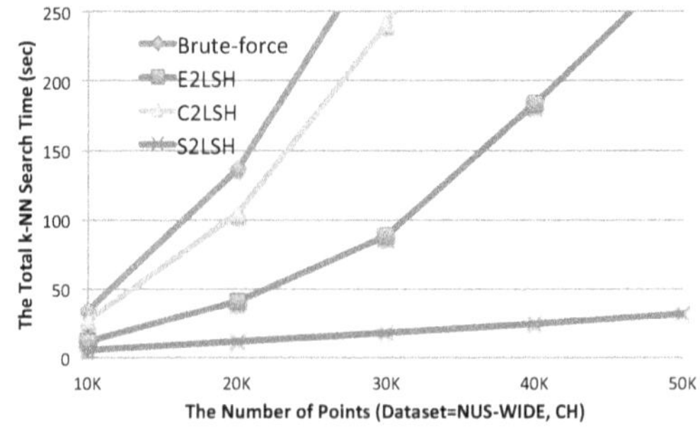

Figure 4: Performance comparison with multiple query points (Spherical Hashing is used).

5. CONCLUSION

We proposed a novel LSH scheme for k-NN approximate search, called *S2LSH*. In S2LSH, we first generate a highly diversified signature pool for a given dataset. Then, for a given query, we rank signature regions of the query using the effectiveness measures, and select points in highly ranked signature regions as k-NN candidates of the query. Experiments show that S2LSH consistently outperforms baseline approaches in various datasets, with different underlying hash functions, and when executing with multiple queries.

6. ACKNOWLEDGEMENTS

This work was supported by the National Research Foundation of Korea (NRF) grant funded by the Korea Government (MSIP) (No.2015R1A2A2A04005646).

7. REFERENCES

[1] M. S. Charikar. Similarity estimation techniques from rounding algorithms. In *STOC*, pages 380–388. ACM, 2002.

[2] M. Datar, N. Immorlica, P. Indyk, and V. S. Mirrokni. Locality-sensitive hashing scheme based on p-stable distributions. In *SOCG*, pages 253–262. ACM, 2004.

[3] J. Davidson, B. Liebald, J. Liu, P. Nandy, T. Van Vleet, U. Gargi, S. Gupta, Y. He, M. Lambert, B. Livingston, et al. The youtube video recommendation system. In *RecSys*, pages 293–296. ACM, 2010.

[4] J. Gan, J. Feng, Q. Fang, and W. Ng. Locality-sensitive hashing scheme based on dynamic collision counting. In *SIGMOD*, pages 541–552. ACM, 2012.

[5] A. Gionis, P. Indyk, R. Motwani, et al. Similarity search in high dimensions via hashing. In *VLDB*, volume 99, pages 518–529, 1999.

[6] J.-P. Heo, Y. Lee, J. He, S.-F. Chang, and S.-E. Yoon. Spherical hashing. In *CVPR*, pages 2957–2964. IEEE, 2012.

[7] P. Indyk and R. Motwani. Approximate nearest neighbors: towards removing the curse of dimensionality. In *STOC*, pages 604–613. ACM, 1998.

[8] Y. Tao, K. Yi, C. Sheng, and P. Kalnis. Quality and efficiency in high dimensional nearest neighbor search. In *SIGMOD*, pages 563–576. ACM, 2009.

Core-Sets for Canonical Correlation Analysis

Saurabh Paul
Computer Science Department, Rensselaer Polytechnic Institute, NY, USA
saurabhpaul2006@gmail.com

ABSTRACT

Canonical Correlation Analysis (CCA) is a technique that finds how "similar" are the subspaces that are spanned by the columns of two different matrices $\mathbf{A} \in \mathbb{R}^{m \times n}$ and $\mathbf{B} \in \mathbb{R}^{m \times \ell}$. CCA measures similarity by means of the cosines of the so-called principal angles between the two subspaces. Those values are also known as canonical correlations of the matrix pair $(\mathbf{A}, \mathbf{B})$. In this work, we consider the over-constrained case where the number of rows is greater than the number of columns ($m > \max\{n, \ell\}$). We study the problem of constructing "core-sets" for CCA. A core-set is a subset of rows from $\mathbf{A}$ and the corresponding subset of rows from $\mathbf{B}$ - denoted by $\hat{\mathbf{A}}$ and $\hat{\mathbf{B}}$, respectively. A "good" core-set is a subset of rows such that the canonical correlations of the core-set $(\hat{\mathbf{A}}, \hat{\mathbf{B}})$ are "close" to the canonical correlations of the original matrix pair $(\mathbf{A}, \mathbf{B})$. There is a natural tradeoff between the core-set size and the approximation accuracy of a core-set. We present two algorithms namely, single-set spectral sparsification and leverage-score sampling, which find core-sets with additive-error guarantees to canonical correlations.

Categories and Subject Descriptors

G.3 [**Probability and Statistics**]: Correlation and regression analysis; G.1.0 [**Numerical Analysis**]: Numerical Algorithms

General Terms

Algorithms, Theory, Experimentation

Keywords

Canonical Correlation Analysis; Sampling; Dimension Reduction

1. INTRODUCTION

Canonical Correlation Analysis (CCA) [1] is an important technique in data mining, scientific computing, statistics, and machine learning. CCA has been used in many applications of data mining like dimensionality reduction, multi-view learning, learning of word embeddings.

Permission to make digital or hard copies of all or part of this work for personal or classroom use is granted without fee provided that copies are not made or distributed for profit or commercial advantage and that copies bear this notice and the full citation on the first page. Copyrights for components of this work owned by others than ACM must be honored. Abstracting with credit is permitted. To copy otherwise, or republish, to post on servers or to redistribute to lists, requires prior specific permission and/or a fee. Request permissions from Permissions@acm.org.
CIKM'15, October 19–23, 2015, Melbourne, Australia.
© 2015 ACM. ISBN 978-1-4503-3794-6/15/10 ...$15.00.
DOI: http://dx.doi.org/10.1145/2806416.2806618.

DEFINITION 1. *Let $\mathbf{A} \in \mathbb{R}^{m \times n}$ and $\mathbf{B} \in \mathbb{R}^{m \times \ell}$, and assume that $p = rank(\mathbf{A}) \geq rank(\mathbf{B}) = q$. The* canonical correlations *$\sigma_1(\mathbf{A},\mathbf{B}) \geq \sigma_2(\mathbf{A},\mathbf{B}) \geq \cdots \geq \sigma_q(\mathbf{A},\mathbf{B})$ of the matrix pair $(\mathbf{A},\mathbf{B})$ are defined recursively by the following formula ($i = 1, \ldots, q$):*

$$\sigma_i(\mathbf{A},\mathbf{B}) = \max_{\mathbf{x} \in \mathcal{A}_i, \mathbf{y} \in \mathcal{B}_i} \sigma(\mathbf{Ax},\mathbf{By}) =: \sigma(\mathbf{Ax}_i,\mathbf{By}_i),$$

where

- $\sigma(\mathbf{u},\mathbf{v}) = |\mathbf{u}^T\mathbf{v}| / (\|\mathbf{u}\|_2 \|\mathbf{v}\|_2)$,
- $\mathcal{A}_i = \{\mathbf{x} \in \mathbb{R}^n : \mathbf{Ax} \neq \mathbf{0}, \mathbf{Ax} \perp \{\mathbf{Ax}_1, \ldots, \mathbf{Ax}_{i-1}\}\}$,
- $\mathcal{B}_i = \{\mathbf{y} \in \mathbb{R}^\ell : \mathbf{By} \neq \mathbf{0}, \mathbf{By} \perp \{\mathbf{By}_1, \ldots, \mathbf{By}_{i-1}\}\}$.

The m-dimensional unit vectors ($i = 1 : q$)

$$\mathbf{Ax}_i / \|\mathbf{Ax}_i\|_2, \quad and \quad \mathbf{By}_i / \|\mathbf{By}_i\|_2,$$

are called the canonical *or* principal vectors. *The vectors*

$$\mathbf{w}_i = \mathbf{x}_i / \|\mathbf{Ax}_i\|_2, \quad and \quad \mathbf{p}_i = \mathbf{y}_i / \|\mathbf{By}_i\|_2,$$

are called canonical weights *(or* projection vectors*). Here, $\mathbf{x}_i / \|\mathbf{Ax}_i\|_2 \in \mathbb{R}^n$ and $\mathbf{y}_i / \|\mathbf{By}_i\|_2 \in \mathbb{R}^\ell$, for all $i = 1 : q$. (The canonical weights/vectors are* not *uniquely defined.)*

The following classical result from Golub and Zha [2] indicates a deterministic polynomial-time CCA algorithm.

THEOREM 1. *[2] Let $\mathbf{A} \in \mathbb{R}^{m \times n}$ and $\mathbf{B} \in \mathbb{R}^{m \times \ell}$ with $p = rank(\mathbf{A}) \geq rank(\mathbf{B}) = q$. Let $\mathbf{A} = \mathbf{U_A \Sigma_A V_A^T}$ be the thin SVD of $\mathbf{A}$ with $\mathbf{U_A} \in \mathbb{R}^{m \times p}$, $\mathbf{\Sigma_A} \in \mathbb{R}^{p \times p}$, and $\mathbf{V_A} \in \mathbb{R}^{n \times p}$. Let $\mathbf{B} = \mathbf{U_B \Sigma_B V_B^T}$ be the thin SVD of $\mathbf{B}$ with $\mathbf{U_B} \in \mathbb{R}^{m \times q}$, $\mathbf{\Sigma_B} \in \mathbb{R}^{q \times q}$, and $\mathbf{V_B} \in \mathbb{R}^{\ell \times q}$. Let $\mathbf{U_A^T U_B} = \mathbf{U \Sigma V}^T$ be the full SVD of $\mathbf{U_A^T U_B} \in \mathbb{R}^{p \times q}$ with $\mathbf{U} \in \mathbb{R}^{p \times q}$, $\mathbf{\Sigma} \in \mathbb{R}^{q \times q}$, and $\mathbf{V} \in \mathbb{R}^{q \times q}$. Then, for $i \in [q] : \sigma_i(\mathbf{A},\mathbf{B}) = \mathbf{\Sigma}_{ii}$. The canonical weights are given by the columns of $\mathbf{V_A \Sigma_A^{-1} U} \in \mathbb{R}^{n \times q}$ (for $\mathbf{A}$) and $\mathbf{V_B \Sigma_B^{-1} V} \in \mathbb{R}^{\ell \times q}$ (for $\mathbf{B}$).*

In this work, we are interested in constructing "core-sets" for CCA. A core-set is a subset of (rescaled) rows from $\mathbf{A}$ and the corresponding subset of (rescaled) rows from $\mathbf{B}$ - denoted by $\hat{\mathbf{A}}$ and $\hat{\mathbf{B}}$, respectively. The canonical correlations and the canonical weights of a "good" core-set $(\hat{\mathbf{A}}, \hat{\mathbf{B}})$ are "close" to the canonical correlations and canonical weights of the original matrix pair $(\mathbf{A},\mathbf{B})$. Core-sets are important because they identify the most influential rows of the matrix pair $(\mathbf{A},\mathbf{B})$ with respect to CCA.

Notation. $\mathbf{A}, \mathbf{B}, \ldots$ denote matrices and $\boldsymbol{\alpha}, \mathbf{b}, \ldots$ denote column vectors; $\mathbf{e}_i$ is the standard basis, whose dimensionality will be clear from the context; $\mathbf{I}_m$ is the $m \times m$ identity matrix, and $\mathbf{0}_{m \times n}$ is the $m \times n$ all-zeros matrix. $\mathcal{R}(.)$ denotes the column space of its argument matrix. We make use of the Singular Value Decomposition (SVD) of a matrix $\mathbf{A} \in \mathbb{R}^{m \times n}$ of rank $\rho \leq \min\{m, n\} = \alpha$ and we distinguish between the "thin" and the "full" SVD of $\mathbf{A}$. The thin SVD of $\mathbf{A}$ is $\mathbf{A} = \mathbf{U}\boldsymbol{\Sigma}\mathbf{V}^T$, where $\mathbf{U} \in \mathbb{R}^{m \times \rho}$ is an orthogonal matrix containing the left singular vectors of $\mathbf{A}$, $\boldsymbol{\Sigma} \in \mathbb{R}^{\rho \times \rho}$ is a diagonal matrix containing only the positive singular values $\sigma_1 \geq \sigma_2 \geq \ldots \sigma_\rho > 0$, and $\mathbf{V} \in \mathbb{R}^{n \times \rho}$ is an orthogonal matrix containing the right singular vectors of $\mathbf{A}$. The full SVD of $\mathbf{A}$ is $\mathbf{A} = \mathbf{U}\boldsymbol{\Sigma}\mathbf{V}^T$, where $\mathbf{U} \in \mathbb{R}^{m \times \alpha}$ is an orthogonal matrix containing the left singular vectors of $\mathbf{A}$, $\boldsymbol{\Sigma} \in \mathbb{R}^{\alpha \times \alpha}$ is a diagonal matrix containing the singular values $\sigma_1 \geq \sigma_2 \geq \ldots \sigma_\alpha \geq 0$, and $\mathbf{V} \in \mathbb{R}^{n \times \alpha}$ is an orthogonal matrix containing the right singular vectors of $\mathbf{A}$.

We use $i:j$ to denote the set $i, ..., j$, and $[m] = 1:m$. We denote by $[\mathbf{A}; \mathbf{B}]$ the matrix obtained by concatenating the columns of $\mathbf{B}$ next to the columns of $\mathbf{A}$. Given a subset of indices $T \subseteq [m]$, the corresponding "sampling" matrix $\mathbf{S}$ is the $|T| \times m$ matrix obtained by discarding from $\mathbf{I}_m$ the rows whose index is not in T. Note that $\mathbf{SA}$ is the matrix obtained by keeping only the rows in $\mathbf{A}$ whose index appears in T and $\mathbf{DSA}$ is the matrix obtained by keeping only the rows in $\mathbf{A}$ whose index appears in T and then rescaling those rows by the corresponding elements of a square diagonal matrix $\mathbf{D}$. We call $\mathbf{D}$ a "rescaling" matrix.

Contributions. We present a deterministic and a randomized algorithm to construct core-sets of sizes $r = O(p\varepsilon^{-2})$ and $r = O\left(\frac{p}{\varepsilon^2} \log\left(\frac{p}{\varepsilon^2\sqrt{\delta}}\right)\right)$ respectively, where ε is a user specified accuracy parameter with $1/2 > \varepsilon > 0$ and δ is a failure probability. We use single-set spectral sparsification and leverage-score sampling as the deterministic and randomized algorithms respectively for core-set construction. We prove that the canonical correlations and canonical weights of the core-set are an additive ε approximation far from the canonical correlations and canonical weights of the input matrix pair $(\mathbf{A}, \mathbf{B})$.

Related work. The work more closely related to ours is that of Avron et al., [3], who also provided a core-set construction (randomized) algorithm for CCA. Unfortunately, the approximation bound of their algorithm is weak and it is only useful for matrices with low "coherence". Their method used linear combination of data-points, whereas we select pure data-points for approximate core-set construction.

DEFINITION 2. *Given a matrix $\mathbf{A}$ with m rows and rank p, the* coherence *of $\mathbf{A}$ is defined as* $\mu(\mathbf{A}) = \max_{i \in [m]} \left\|\mathbf{e}_i^\top \mathbf{U}_\mathbf{A}\right\|_2^2$, *where $\mathbf{e}_i$ is the i-th standard basis (column) vector of $\mathbb{R}^m$, and $\mathbf{U}_\mathbf{A} \in \mathbb{R}^{m \times p}$ contains the left singular vectors of $\mathbf{A}$ from the thin SVD of $\mathbf{A}$.*

The coherence of a matrix is a measure of how close a basis is to sharing a vector with a canonical basis. Note that the coherence of $\mathbf{A}$ is a property of the column space of $\mathbf{A}$, and does not depend on particular choice of basis (e.g. the basis described by the columns of $\mathbf{A}$). Therefore, if $\mathcal{R}(\mathbf{A}) = \mathcal{R}(\mathbf{B})$ then $\mu(\mathbf{A}) = \mu(\mathbf{B})$. Furthermore, it is easy to verify that if $\mathcal{R}(\mathbf{A}) \subseteq \mathcal{R}(\mathbf{B})$, then, $\mu(\mathbf{A}) \leq \mu(\mathbf{B})$. We also mention that for every matrix $\mathbf{A}$ with m rows: $\text{rank}(\mathbf{A})/m \leq \mu(\mathbf{A}) \leq 1$.

THEOREM 2. *[3] Suppose $\mathbf{A} \in \mathbb{R}^{m \times n}$ $(m \geq n)$ has rank p and $\mathbf{B} \in \mathbb{R}^{m \times \ell}$ $(m \geq \ell)$ has rank $q \leq p$. Let $0 < \varepsilon < 1/2$ be an accuracy parameter and $0 < \delta < 1$ be a failure probability parameter. Let $\omega = \text{rank}([\mathbf{A}; \mathbf{B}]) \leq p + q$. Let r be an integer such that $54\varepsilon^{-2} m\mu([\mathbf{A}; \mathbf{B}]) \ln(12\omega/\delta) \leq r \leq m$. Let T be a random subset of $[m]$ of cardinality r, drawn from a uniform distribution over such subsets, and let $\mathbf{S} \in \mathbb{R}^{r \times m}$ be the sampling matrix corresponding to T rescaled by $\sqrt{m/r}$. Denote $\hat{\mathbf{A}} = \mathbf{SA} \in \mathbb{R}^{r \times n}$ and $\hat{\mathbf{B}} = \mathbf{SB} \in \mathbb{R}^{r \times \ell}$.*

For $i = 1:q$, let $\sigma_i(\hat{\mathbf{A}}, \hat{\mathbf{B}})$ be the canonical correlations of $(\hat{\mathbf{A}}, \hat{\mathbf{B}})$, and $\hat{\mathbf{w}}_i = \hat{\mathbf{x}}_i / \left\|\hat{\mathbf{A}}\hat{\mathbf{x}}_i\right\|_2 \in \mathbb{R}^n$ and $\hat{\mathbf{p}}_i = \hat{\mathbf{y}}_i / \left\|\hat{\mathbf{B}}\hat{\mathbf{y}}_i\right\|_2 \in \mathbb{R}^\ell$ be the canonical weights (or projection vectors) of $(\hat{\mathbf{A}}, \hat{\mathbf{B}})$. Also, $\hat{\mathbf{x}}_i \in \mathbb{R}^n$ and $\hat{\mathbf{y}}_i \in \mathbb{R}^\ell$ are some vectors chosen as in Definition 1, but for the pair $(\hat{\mathbf{A}}, \hat{\mathbf{B}})$. Then, w.p. $1 - \delta$ all the following hold simultaneously:

1. *(Approximation of Canonical Correlations) For every $i = 1, 2, \ldots, q$: $|\sigma_i(\mathbf{A}, \mathbf{B}) - \sigma_i(\hat{\mathbf{A}}, \hat{\mathbf{B}})| \leq \varepsilon + 2\varepsilon^2/9$.*
2. *(Approximate Orthonormal Bases) The vectors $\{\mathbf{A}\hat{\mathbf{w}}_i\}_{i \in [q]} \in \mathbb{R}^m$ form an approximately orthonormal basis. That is, for any $c \in [q]$, $\frac{1}{1+\varepsilon/3} \leq \|\mathbf{A}\hat{\mathbf{w}}_c\|_2^2 \leq \frac{1}{1-\varepsilon/3}$, and for any $i \neq j$, $|\langle \mathbf{A}\hat{\mathbf{w}}_i, \mathbf{A}\hat{\mathbf{w}}_j \rangle| \leq \frac{\varepsilon}{3-\varepsilon}$. In particular, $\|\mathbf{W}^T\mathbf{A}^T\mathbf{A}\mathbf{W} - \mathbf{I}_q\|_2 \leq \frac{2\varepsilon q}{3}$ where $\mathbf{W} = [\hat{\mathbf{w}}_1, \ldots, \hat{\mathbf{w}}_q]$. Similarly, for the set of $\{\mathbf{B}\hat{\mathbf{p}}_i\}_{i \in [q]} \in \mathbb{R}^m$.*
3. *(Approximate Correlation) For every $i = 1, 2, \ldots, q$:*

$$\frac{\sigma_i(\mathbf{A}, \mathbf{B})}{1 + \varepsilon/3} - 2\varepsilon \leq \sigma(\mathbf{A}\hat{\mathbf{w}}_i, \mathbf{B}\hat{\mathbf{p}}_i) \leq \frac{\sigma_i(\mathbf{A}, \mathbf{B})}{1 - \varepsilon/3} + 2\varepsilon.$$

2. SAMPLING TECHNIQUES

To sample a subset of rows from the matrix pair $(\mathbf{A}, \mathbf{B})$, we use the single-set spectral sparsification algorithm (BSS, in short) of Batson et al. [4] presented as Algorithm 1 and leverage-score sampling [5]. Below, we present the description and qualitative results of the algorithms when they are used to sample a subset of rows from a tall-and-skinny matrix with orthonormal columns.

Algorithm 1: Single-set Spectral Sparsification
Input: $\mathbf{U} = [\mathbf{u}_1, \mathbf{u}_2, ...\mathbf{u}_m]^T \in \mathbb{R}^{m \times d}$ with $\mathbf{u}_i \in \mathbb{R}^d$ and $r > d$.
Output: Matrices $\mathbf{S} \in \mathbb{R}^{r \times m}, \mathbf{D} \in \mathbb{R}^{r \times r}$.
1. Initialize $\mathbf{A}_0 = \mathbf{0}_{d \times d}$, $\mathbf{S} = \mathbf{0}_{r \times m}$, $\mathbf{D} = \mathbf{0}_{r \times r}$.
2. Set constants $\delta_L = 1$ and $\delta_U = \left(1 + \sqrt{\ell/r}\right) / \left(1 - \sqrt{\ell/r}\right)$.
3. **for** $\tau = 0$ to $r - 1$ **do**

- Let $L_\tau = \tau - \sqrt{r\ell}$; $U_\tau = \delta_U(\tau + \sqrt{\ell r})$.
- Pick index $i \in \{1, 2, ..m\}$ and $t_\tau > 0$, such that

$$\mathcal{U}(\mathbf{u}_i, \delta_U, \mathbf{A}_\tau, U_\tau) \leq \mathcal{L}(\mathbf{u}_i, \delta_L, \mathbf{A}_\tau, L_\tau),$$

where, $\mathcal{U}(\mathbf{u}, \delta_U, \mathbf{A}, U) =$

$$\frac{\mathbf{u}^T\left((U + \delta_U)\mathbf{I}_\ell - \mathbf{A}\right)^{-2}\mathbf{u}}{\hat{\Phi}(U, \mathbf{A}) - \hat{\Phi}(U + \delta_U, \mathbf{A})} + \mathbf{u}^T\left((U + \delta_U)\mathbf{I}_\ell - \mathbf{A}\right)^{-1}\mathbf{u},$$

$\mathcal{L}(\mathbf{u}, \delta_L, \mathbf{A}, L) =$

$$\frac{\mathbf{u}^T\left(\mathbf{A} - (L + \delta_L)\mathbf{I}_\ell\right)^{-2}\mathbf{u}}{\Phi(L + \delta_L, \mathbf{A}) - \Phi(L, \mathbf{A})} - \mathbf{u}^T\left(\mathbf{A} - (L + \delta_L)\mathbf{I}_\ell\right)^{-1}\mathbf{u},$$

$\Phi(L, \mathbf{A}) = \sum_{i=1}^{\ell} \frac{1}{\lambda_i - L}$ and $\hat{\Phi}(U, \mathbf{A}) = \sum_{i=1}^{\ell} \frac{1}{U - \lambda_i}$.

- Let $t_\tau^{-1} = \frac{1}{2}\left(\mathcal{U}\left(\mathbf{u}_i, \delta_U, \mathbf{A}_\tau, U_\tau\right) + \mathcal{L}\left(\mathbf{u}_i, \delta_L, \mathbf{A}_\tau, L_\tau\right)\right)$
- Update $\mathbf{A}_{\tau+1} = \mathbf{A}_\tau + t_\tau \mathbf{u}_i \mathbf{u}_i^T$; set $\mathbf{S}_{\tau+1,i_\tau} = 1$ and $\mathbf{D}_{\tau+1,\tau+1} = 1/\sqrt{t_\tau}$.

4. **end for**
5. Multiply all the weights in $\mathbf{D}$ by $\sqrt{r^{-1}\left(1-\sqrt{(\ell/r)}\right)}$.
6. Return $\mathbf{S}$ and $\mathbf{D}$.

LEMMA 1. *(BSS Sampling [4]) Given $\mathbf{U} \in \mathbb{R}^{m\times d}$ with $m > d$ satisfying $\mathbf{U}^T\mathbf{U} = \mathbf{I}_d$ and sampling parameter $r > d$, there exists a deterministic algorithm to construct sampling and rescaling matrices $\mathbf{S} \in \mathbb{R}^{r\times m}$ and $\mathbf{D} \in \mathbb{R}^{r\times r}$ such that for all $i = 1 : d$ and $\varepsilon = 3\sqrt{d/r}$, it is: $\sqrt{1-\varepsilon} \le \sigma_i(\mathbf{DSU}) \le \sqrt{1+\varepsilon}$. The running time of the algorithm is $O(md^2r)$.*

We will also use a generalization of Lemma 1.The proof of this lemma (Lemma 2) can be found in page 49 of [6]. A similar lemma can be shown for leverage-score sampling.

LEMMA 2. *[6] Given $\mathbf{A} \in \mathbb{R}^{m\times d}$ of rank p with $m > d$ and sampling parameter $r > p$, there exists a deterministic algorithm to construct sampling and rescaling matrices $\mathbf{S} \in \mathbb{R}^{r\times m}$ and $\mathbf{D} \in \mathbb{R}^{r\times r}$ such that for $\varepsilon = 3\sqrt{p/r}$ and $\mathbf{R} = \mathbf{DS}$, it is: $\left\|\mathbf{A}^T\mathbf{R}^T\mathbf{R}\mathbf{A} - \mathbf{A}^T\mathbf{A}\right\|_2 \le \varepsilon \|\mathbf{A}\|_2^2$. The running time of the algorithm is $O(md^2r)$. The algorithm in this lemma applies the algorithm of the previous lemma on the matrix $\mathbf{U_A} \in \mathbb{R}^{m\times p}$ from the thin SVD of $\mathbf{A}$.*

2.0.1 Leverage-Score Sampling

Let $\mathbf{U}$ be the top-d left singular vectors of the data matrix $\mathbf{X} \in \mathbb{R}^{m\times d}$. A carefully chosen probability distribution of the form $p_i = \frac{\|\mathbf{U}_i\|_2^2}{d}$ for $i = 1,..m$, i.e. proportional to the squared Euclidean norms of the rows of the left-singular vectors is constructed. Select r rows of $\mathbf{U}$ in i.i.d trials and re-scale the rows with $1/\sqrt{p_i}$. The time complexity is dominated by the time to compute the SVD of $\mathbf{X}$.

LEMMA 3. *(Leverage-score Sampling [5]) Let $\mathbf{U} \in \mathbb{R}^{m\times d}$ have orthonormal columns with $m > k$ and $\mathbf{U}^T\mathbf{U} = \mathbf{I}_k$. Let $0 \le \beta \le 1$, $0 < \delta < 1$, and $4kln(2k\delta)/\beta \le r \le n$. Let $\mathbf{S} \in \mathbb{R}^{r\times m}$ and $\mathbf{D} \in \mathbb{R}^{r\times r}$ be the sampling and re-scaling matrices. Then for all $i = 1, \cdots, k$, w.p. at least $(1-\delta)$, for $\epsilon = \sqrt{\frac{4kln(2k/\delta)}{r\beta}}$, $\sqrt{1-\epsilon} \le \sigma_i(\mathbf{DSU}) \le \sqrt{1+\epsilon}$.*

3. MAIN RESULT

Consider the following algorithm to construct a core-set for the CCA of a matrix pair using BSS. A similar algorithm can be shown by using leverage-score sampling. Inputs are $\mathbf{A} \in \mathbb{R}^{m\times n}$ of rank p, $\mathbf{B} \in \mathbb{R}^{m\times \ell}$ of rank $q \le p$, and accuracy parameter $0 < \varepsilon < 1/2$. We further assume that $m \ge p + q$.

1. $\mathbf{C} = [\mathbf{U_A}; \mathbf{U_B}] \in \mathbb{R}^{m\times(p+q)}$. Here, $\mathbf{U_A} \in \mathbb{R}^{m\times p}$ and $\mathbf{U_B} \in \mathbb{R}^{m\times q}$ are the left singular vectors of $\mathbf{A}$ and $\mathbf{B}$ from the thin SVD of $\mathbf{A}$ and $\mathbf{B}$, respectively.
2. Let $\mathbf{U_C} \in \mathbb{R}^{m\times\omega}$ be the left singular vectors of $\mathbf{C}$ from the thin SVD of $\mathbf{C}$. Let $\omega = \text{rank}(\mathbf{C}) \le p + q$.
3. Let $\mathbf{U}_T = [\mathbf{U_A}; \mathbf{U_B}; \mathbf{U_C}] \in \mathbb{R}^{m\times(p+q+\omega)}$ and notice that $\text{rank}(\mathbf{U}_T) = \omega \le p + q \le 2p$.
4. Let $\mathbf{U} \in \mathbb{R}^{m\times\omega}$ be the left singular vectors of $\mathbf{U}_T$ from a thin SVD of $\mathbf{U}_T$.
5. Choose $r = \lceil 6561 \cdot \omega/\varepsilon^2 \rceil$ rows of $\mathbf{U}$ with the algorithm of Lemma 1 and construct sampling and rescaling matrices $\mathbf{S} \in \mathbb{R}^{r\times m}$ and $\mathbf{D} \in \mathbb{R}^{r\times r}$. For simplicity, we use $\mathbf{R} = \mathbf{DS}$.
6. $\hat{\mathbf{A}} \leftarrow \mathbf{RA} \in \mathbb{R}^{r\times p}$, $\hat{\mathbf{B}} \leftarrow \mathbf{RB} \in \mathbb{R}^{r\times q}$.

Next, we give our quality-of-approximation result for the core-set $(\hat{\mathbf{A}}, \hat{\mathbf{B}})$ in the above algorithm using BSS. Note that the core-set size using BSS-sampling is $r = O(p\varepsilon^{-2})$. We can show similar results for leverage-score sampling.

THEOREM 3. *For $i = 1 : q$, let $\sigma_i(\hat{\mathbf{A}}, \hat{\mathbf{B}})$ be the canonical correlations of $(\hat{\mathbf{A}}, \hat{\mathbf{B}})$, and $\hat{\mathbf{w}}_i = \hat{\mathbf{x}}_i / \left\|\hat{\mathbf{A}}\hat{\mathbf{x}}_i\right\|_2 \in \mathbb{R}^n$ and $\hat{\mathbf{p}}_i = \hat{\mathbf{y}}_i / \left\|\hat{\mathbf{B}}\hat{\mathbf{y}}_i\right\|_2 \in \mathbb{R}^\ell$ be the canonical weights (or projection vectors) of $(\hat{\mathbf{A}}, \hat{\mathbf{B}})$. Also, $\hat{\mathbf{x}}_i \in \mathbb{R}^n$ and $\hat{\mathbf{y}}_i \in \mathbb{R}^\ell$ are some vectors chosen as in Definition 1, but for the pair $(\hat{\mathbf{A}}, \hat{\mathbf{B}})$. Then, all three statements (1), (2), (3) of Theorem 2 hold simultaneously.*

3.1 Proof of Theorem 3

We first prove two intermediate results.

LEMMA 4. *Let $\mathbf{A} \in \mathbb{R}^{m\times n}$ and $\mathbf{S}_1 \in \mathbb{R}^{r_1\times m}$ and $\mathbf{S}_2 \in \mathbb{R}^{r_2\times n}$ be sampling matrices. Then, $\left\|\mathbf{S}_1\mathbf{A}\mathbf{S}_2^T\right\|_2 \le \|\mathbf{A}\|_2$.*

PROOF. $\left\|\mathbf{S}_1\mathbf{A}\mathbf{S}_2^T\right\|_2 \le \|\mathbf{S}_1\|_2 \|\mathbf{A}\|_2 \left\|\mathbf{S}_2^T\right\|_2 \le \|\mathbf{A}\|_2$. □

LEMMA 5. *Consider the algorithm in the previous section. Then, all three hold simultaneously,*

- *For $r \in [p]$, $\sqrt{1-\varepsilon/3} \le \sigma_r(\mathbf{RU_A}) \le \sqrt{1+\varepsilon/3}$.*
- *For $k \in [q]$, $\sqrt{1-\varepsilon/3} \le \sigma_k(\mathbf{RU_B}) \le \sqrt{1+\varepsilon/3}$.*
- *For $h \in [r]$, $\sqrt{1-\varepsilon/3} \le \sigma_h(\mathbf{RU_C}) \le \sqrt{1+\varepsilon/3}$.*

PROOF. Lemma 2 gives $\left\|\mathbf{U}_T^T\mathbf{R}^T\mathbf{R}\mathbf{U}_T - \mathbf{U}_T^T\mathbf{U}_T\right\|_2 \le (\varepsilon/27)\|\mathbf{U}_T\|_2^2$. Also, $\|\mathbf{U}_T\|_2 = \|[\mathbf{U_A}; \mathbf{U_B}; \mathbf{U_C}]\|_2 = \|[\mathbf{U_A}; \mathbf{0}_{m\times q}; \mathbf{0}_{m\times\omega}] + [\mathbf{0}_{m\times p}; \mathbf{U_B}; \mathbf{0}_{m\times\omega}] + \mathbf{Z}\|_2 \le 3$. The last inequality follows since, $\mathbf{U_A}, \mathbf{U_B}, \mathbf{U_C}$ are unitary matrices. In the above, $\mathbf{Z} = [\mathbf{0}_{m\times p}; \mathbf{0}_{m\times q}; \mathbf{U_C}]$. So far, we have proved $\left\|\mathbf{U}_T^T\mathbf{R}^T\mathbf{R}\mathbf{U}_T - \mathbf{U}_T^T\mathbf{U}_T\right\|_2 \le (\varepsilon/3)$. Next,

$$\mathbf{U}_T^T\mathbf{U}_T = \begin{bmatrix} \mathbf{U_A^TU_A} & \mathbf{U_A^TU_B} & \mathbf{U_A^TU_C} \\ \mathbf{U_B^TU_A} & \mathbf{U_B^TU_B} & \mathbf{U_B^TU_C} \\ \mathbf{U_C^TU_A} & \mathbf{U_C^TU_B} & \mathbf{U_C^TU_C} \end{bmatrix} = \begin{bmatrix} \mathbf{I}_p & \mathbf{U_A^TU_B} & \mathbf{U_A^TU_C} \\ \mathbf{U_B^TU_A} & \mathbf{I}_q & \mathbf{U_B^TU_C} \\ \mathbf{U_C^TU_A} & \mathbf{U_C^TU_B} & \mathbf{I}_\omega \end{bmatrix},$$

$$\mathbf{U}_T^T\mathbf{R}^T\mathbf{R}\mathbf{U}_T = \begin{bmatrix} \mathbf{U_A^TR^TRU_A} & \mathbf{U_A^TR^TRU_B} & \mathbf{U_A^TR^TRU_C} \\ \mathbf{U_B^TR^TRU_A} & \mathbf{U_B^TR^TRU_B} & \mathbf{U_B^TR^TRU_C} \\ \mathbf{U_C^TR^TRU_A} & \mathbf{U_C^TR^TRU_B} & \mathbf{U_C^TR^TRU_C} \end{bmatrix},$$

where, for notational convenience we used $\mathbf{R} = \mathbf{DS}$. The diagonal block matrices of $\mathbf{U}_T^T\mathbf{R}^T\mathbf{R}\mathbf{U}_T - \mathbf{U}_T^T\mathbf{U}_T$ are $\mathbf{U_A^TR^TRU_A} - \mathbf{I}_p$, $\mathbf{U_B^TR^TRU_B} - \mathbf{I}_q$ and $\mathbf{U_C^TR^TRU_C} - \mathbf{I}_\omega$. From Lemma 4 we have $\left\|\mathbf{U_A^TR^TRU_A} - \mathbf{I}_p\right\|_2 \le \varepsilon/3$, $\left\|\mathbf{U_B^TR^TRU_B} - \mathbf{I}_q\right\|_2 \le \varepsilon/3$, $\left\|\mathbf{U_C^TR^TRU_C} - \mathbf{I}_\omega\right\|_2 \le \varepsilon/3$. The result in the lemma follows by appropriate use of Weyl's inequality [1]. □

[1]Let $\mathbf{X}, \mathbf{Y} \in \mathbb{R}^{m\times n}$. Then, for all $i = 1, \ldots, \min(m, n)$: $|\sigma_i(\mathbf{X}) - \sigma_i(\mathbf{Y})| \le \|\mathbf{X} - \mathbf{Y}\|_2$.

We also use the following "structural" result for dimensionality reduction in Canonical Correlation Analysis.

THEOREM 4. *(CCA dimension reduction [3]) Let* $\mathbf{A} \in \mathbb{R}^{m \times n}$ $(m \geq n)$ *have rank p and* $\mathbf{B} \in \mathbb{R}^{m \times \ell}$ $(m \geq \ell)$ *have rank* $q \leq p$. *Let* $0 < \varepsilon < 1/2$ *be an accuracy parameter. Let* $\mathbf{A} = \mathbf{U_A \Sigma_A V_A^T}$, *with* $\mathbf{U_A} \in \mathbb{R}^{m \times p}$, $\mathbf{\Sigma_A} \in \mathbb{R}^{p \times p}$, *and* $\mathbf{V_A^T} \in \mathbb{R}^{p \times n}$ *be the thin SVD of* $\mathbf{A}$. *Let* $\mathbf{B} = \mathbf{U_B \Sigma_B V_B^T}$, *with* $\mathbf{U_B} \in \mathbb{R}^{m \times q}$, $\mathbf{\Sigma_B} \in \mathbb{R}^{q \times q}$, *and* $\mathbf{V_B^T} \in \mathbb{R}^{q \times n}$ *be the thin SVD of* $\mathbf{B}$. *Let* $\mathbf{C} := [\mathbf{U_A}; \mathbf{U_B}] \in \mathbb{R}^{m \times (p+q)}$. *Let* $\mathbf{C} = \mathbf{U_C \Sigma_C V_C^T}$, *with* $\mathbf{U_C} \in \mathbb{R}^{m \times \omega}$, $\mathbf{\Sigma_C} \in \mathbb{R}^{\omega \times \omega}$, *and* $\mathbf{V_C^T} \in \mathbb{R}^{\omega \times n}$ *be the thin SVD of* $\mathbf{C}$ *with* $\omega = rank(\mathbf{C}) \geq rank(\mathbf{B}) \geq rank(\mathbf{A})$. *Assume the following relations hold for some matrix* $\mathbf{R} \in \mathbb{R}^{r \times m}$ $(r \geq \max\{n, \ell\})$:

1. *For every* $r \in [p]$: $\sqrt{1 - \varepsilon/3} \leq \sigma_r(\mathbf{RU_A}) \leq \sqrt{1 + \varepsilon/3}$.
2. *For every* $k \in [q]$: $\sqrt{1 - \varepsilon/3} \leq \sigma_k(\mathbf{RU_B}) \leq \sqrt{1 + \varepsilon/3}$.
3. *For every* $h \in [\omega]$: $\sqrt{1 - \varepsilon/3} \leq \sigma_h(\mathbf{RU_C}) \leq \sqrt{1 + \varepsilon/3}$.

Denote $\hat{\mathbf{A}} = \mathbf{RA} \in \mathbb{R}^{r \times n}$ *and* $\hat{\mathbf{B}} = \mathbf{RB} \in \mathbb{R}^{r \times \ell}$. *For* $i = 1 : q$, *let* $\sigma_i(\hat{\mathbf{A}}, \hat{\mathbf{B}})$ *be the canonical correlations of* $(\hat{\mathbf{A}}, \hat{\mathbf{B}})$, *and* $\hat{\mathbf{w}}_i = \hat{\mathbf{x}}_i / \left\|\hat{\mathbf{A}}\hat{\mathbf{x}}_i\right\|_2 \in \mathbb{R}^n$ *and* $\hat{\mathbf{p}}_i = \hat{\mathbf{y}}_i / \left\|\hat{\mathbf{B}}\hat{\mathbf{y}}_i\right\|_2 \in \mathbb{R}^\ell$ *be the canonical weights (or projection vectors) of* $(\hat{\mathbf{A}}, \hat{\mathbf{B}})$. *Also,* $\hat{\mathbf{x}}_i \in \mathbb{R}^n$ *and* $\hat{\mathbf{y}}_i \in \mathbb{R}^\ell$ *are some vectors chosen as in Definition 1, but for the pair* $(\hat{\mathbf{A}}, \hat{\mathbf{B}})$. *Then, all three statements* (1), (2), (3) *of Theorem 2 hold simultaneously.*

The proof of Theorem 3 follows by using the three conditions of Lemma 5 into Theorem 4.

4. EXPERIMENTAL RESULTS

We performed experiments on synthetic data on an intel-i7 desktop with 8GB RAM in MATLAB environment. We compared the canonical correlation coefficients of the full-data with leverage-score sampling, single-set spectral sparsification and uniform sampling. Since, leverage-score sampling (uniform sampling) is a randomized algorithm, we repeat the experiments ten times to get around the randomness and choose the result from the best run.

We generate a pair of tall-and-thin matrices $\mathbf{A}$ and $\mathbf{B}$,

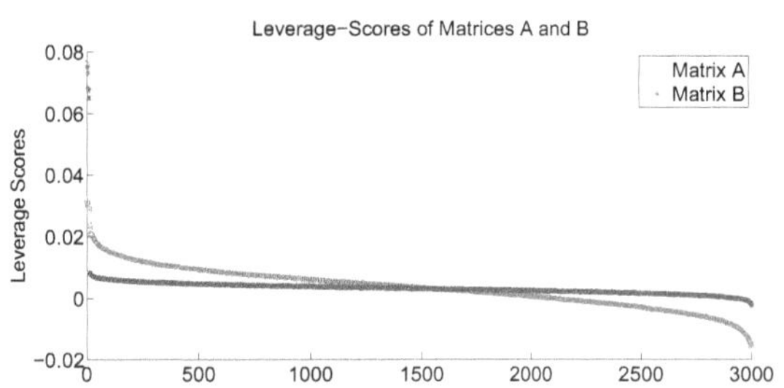

Figure 1: Plots of Leverage-scores of Synthetic Data.

(of size m-by-n, where m=3000 and n=10) with specific leverage-scores using [7]. By construction, the first 10 leverage scores of $\mathbf{A}$ are generated by $b1 + (a1 - b1) * rand(10, 1)$, where $a1 = 10, b1 = 9$ and the next 2990 leverage-scores are generated by $b2 + (a2 - b2) * randn(2990, 1)$, where $a2 = 3, b2 = 1$, and rand(m,n) and randn(m,n) are the Matlab functions generating mn i.i.d entries from the standard uniform distribution and standard normal distribution respectively. The first 10 leverage-scores are high, while the next batch of leverage-scores are low, as seen in Fig 1. The leverage-scores for matrix $\mathbf{B}$ were generated similarly with the values of $a1, b1, a2, b2$ set to 10, 8, 0.4, 0.6 respectively. The number of rows to be sampled r, was set to $(2n + 1)$ and $4n + 2$. BSS and leverage-score sampling select the rows with "high leverage-scores", while uniform sampling picks up the rows with low leverage-scores. Table 1 shows the mean and standard deviation of the errors of approximate canonical correlations with that of full-data for the three methods. Approximate canonical correlations using BSS and Leverage-score are almost identical to that of exact canonical correlations and are much better than uniform sampling.

Table 1: Mean and standard deviation (in parenthesis) of errors of canonical correlations for different sampling methods.

	BSS	Leverage-score	Uniform
r=2n+1	0.000(0.000)	0.1319(0.2933)	0.3858(0.3340)
r=4n+2	-0.000(0.000)	0.000(0.000)	0.5694(0.2855)

5. CONCLUSION

We present two provably accurate dimension reduction methods for CCA which work well empirically. BSS and Leverage-score sampling are becoming popular and have been used for core-set selection for ordinary least squares [8], feature selection for linear SVM [9] and regularized least squares classifier [10]. A possible future direction would be to include real-world scenarios where such core-sets may be useful.

Acknowledgements. The author thanks Prof. Petros Drineas of Rensselaer Polytechnic Institute and Dr. Christos Boutsidis of Yahoo! Labs for fruitful discussions which resulted in this work. The author was supported by IIS-1302231 and BigData-1447283.

6. REFERENCES

[1] H. Hotelling. Relations between two sets of variates. *Biometrika*, pages 321–377, 1936.
[2] G. H. Golub and H. Zha. *The canonical correlations of matrix pairs and their numerical computation.* Springer, 1995.
[3] H. Avron, C. Boutsidis, S. Toledo, and A. Zouzias. Efficient dimensionality reduction for canonical correlation analysis. *SIAM J. Scientific Computing*, 36(5), 2014.
[4] J.D. Batson, D.A. Spielman, and N. Srivastava. Twice-ramanujan sparsifiers. In *Proceedings of the 41st annual ACM STOC*, pages 255–262, 2009.
[5] M. Rudelson and R. Vershynin. Sampling from large matrices: An approach through geometric functional analysis. *J. ACM*, 54(4), 2007.
[6] C. Boutsidis. *Topics in Matrix Sampling Algorithms.* PhD thesis, Rensselaer Polytechnic Institute, 2011.
[7] I. C. F. Ipsen and T. Wentworth. The effect of coherence on sampling from matrices with orthonormal columns, and preconditioned least squares problems. *SIAM J. Matrix Analysis Applications*, 35(4):1490–1520, 2014.
[8] C. Boutsidis, P. Drineas, and M. Magdon-Ismail. Near-optimal coresets for least-squares regression. *IEEE Trans. on Information Theory*, 59(10):6880–6892, 2013.
[9] S. Paul, M. Magdon-Ismail, and P. Drineas. Feature selection for linear svm with provable guarantees. In *Proc of 18th AISTATS*, pages 735–743. JMLR W&CP 38, 2015.
[10] S. Paul and P. Drineas. Deterministic feature selection for regularized least squares classification. In *Proc. of ECML-PKDD*, volume 8725 of *LNCS*, pages 533–548, 2014.

DeepCamera: A Unified Framework for Recognizing Places-of-Interest based on Deep ConvNets

Pai Peng Hongxiang Chen Lidan Shou Ke Chen Gang Chen Chang Xu
Zhejiang University, Hangzhou, China
{pengpai_sh, hxchen, should, chenk, cg, Xc0903}@zju.edu.cn

ABSTRACT

In this work, we present a novel project called DeepCamera(DC) for recognizing places-of-interest(POI) with smartphones. Our framework is based on deep convolutional neural networks(ConvNets) which are currently state-of-the-art solutions to vision recognition tasks such as our mission. We propose a novel ConvNet by introducing a new layer called "spatial layer" which captures spatial knowledge from a geographic view. As a result, both spatial and visual knowledge contribute to generating a hybrid probability distribution over all possible POI candidates. Furthermore, we compress multiple trained deep ConvNets into one single shallow net called "shNet" which achieves competitive performance with ensemble methods. Our preliminary experiments conducted on real-world dataset have shown promising POI recognition results.

Categories and Subject Descriptors

H.2.8 [**Database Applications**]: Image Database

Keywords

places-of-interest; deep learning; image recognition

1. INTRODUCTION

The KPCB annual Internet Trends report(2014)[3] states that the global smartphone user base has hit 1.5 billion and all internet-connected citizens share over 1.8 billion photos every day via image-sharing social media platforms(e.g. Flickr and Facebook). Such large amounts of images have been a rich treasure to be explored, making a more intelligent and convenient life for human beings.

When a tourist is visiting a scenic spot for the first time, the fastest way to know the history of places-of-interest(POI) in front of him is using his accompanied smartphone to take a picture toward that POI. Then a pop-up of place name is expected to display as well as its related further detailed information. Our recent work called *DeepCamera*(DC) describes a technical framework to meet the demand of such scenario. The aim of DC is developing a system based on deep neural networks for recognizing outdoor POIs with the help of rich sensors embedded in smartphones.

Our solution relies on two assumptions: (1) a POI database which records the POI names and their exact geo-locations, (2) an image database which maps image IDs to their semantic POIs. These two assumptions do seem reasonable with availability of gazetteer such as [2] and numerous photos shared on the web. Then our goal is to identify the target POI for a query photo with camera geometries in smartphones, also known as *field-of-view*(FOV for short). A typical FOV includes four parameters: the GPS location, the angles of view, the maximum visible distance, and the direction of the smartphone camera.

Deep *Convolutional Neural Networks*(ConvNets) have shown powerful abilities to deal with vision recognition tasks since it cut a figure in ImageNet 2012[5] as the champion team's solution. The idea behind ConvNet is a layer-wise model which mimics human visual system and brain structure. Its major contribution is concluded as mapping low level raw pixels into high level semantic object categories via bottom-up layers. Different from handcrafted features based model such as bag-of-visual-words(BOW)[9], ConvNet automatically learns progressive features in different layers in the same way as we human beings see the world.

In spite of strong discriminative power of ConvNet, it still would be at loss what to do when images are too similar in visual content. For example, temples in China and Japan share high degree of outdoor appearance similarites. As a result, the cell in the probability distribution generated by ConvNet would be quite close in Chinese and Japanese temples categories. Then, it comes very naturally that the smartphone locations would help to eliminate such ambiguities. The FOV geometries can further restrict the POI candidates within a small portion of entire POIs, filtering out most POIs which are unlikely to be captured by camera(e.g. ones which are behind or too far away from current location).

Interestingly, recent work *KC*[6, 7] is similar to ours with the same goal of recognizing POIs. However, KC represents images as BOW, which means that local features have to be extracted previously. Moreover, they adopt sparse coding to compute visual similarities which is known to be computationally expensive. We propose a novel model which equips ConvNet with geographic features by adding a new layer called "spatial layer" in ordinary ConvNet. Such layer includes a spatial probability distribution over all POIs based on FOV parameters from a geographic view. Thus, both spatial and visual knowledge contribute to generating a hybrid

Permission to make digital or hard copies of all or part of this work for personal or classroom use is granted without fee provided that copies are not made or distributed for profit or commercial advantage and that copies bear this notice and the full citation on the first page. Copyrights for components of this work owned by others than ACM must be honored. Abstracting with credit is permitted. To copy otherwise, or republish, to post on servers or to redistribute to lists, requires prior specific permission and/or a fee. Request permissions from Permissions@acm.org.
CIKM'15, October 19–23, 2015, Melbourne, Australia.
© 2015 ACM. ISBN 978-1-4503-3794-6/15/10 ...$15.00.
DOI: http://dx.doi.org/10.1145/2806416.2806620.

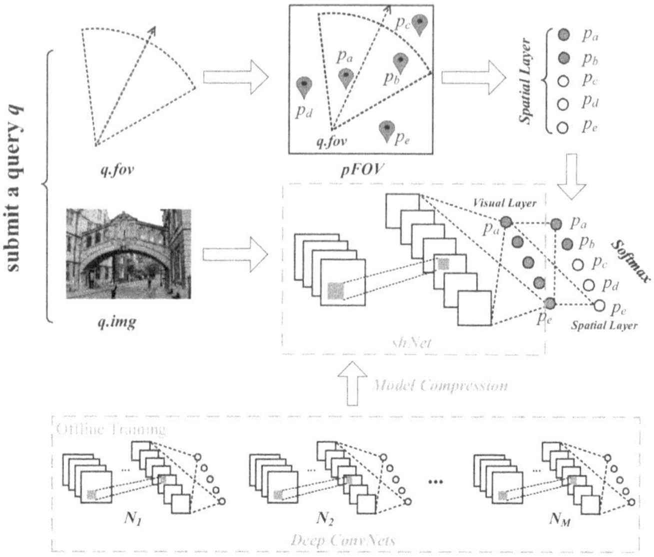

Figure 1: A toy example of DeepCamera framework. When a query q is issued, $q.fov$ and $q.img$ is processed in parallel. A shallow net called shNet compressed by multiple trained deep ConvNets(Section 2.2) will give a visual probability distribution for a given $q.img$(Section 2.1). The pFOV model filters out some unlikely POIs(p_c, p_d, p_e in our case) and outputs a spatial probability distribution which will be plugged into shNet(Section 2.3).

probability distribution over all possible POI candidates. One common way to boost performance of deep learning model is training multiple models by varying model parameters such as learning rate or different initializations and combine these pretrained models by ensemble methods such as bagging. However, such methods are not applicable to our mission since these ensemble methods usually decrease error variance by sacrificing online query efficiency while POI identification is expected to be done in real-time. Inspired by [4], we compress those pretrained deep models into one single shallow net called *shNet* which achieves competitive performance with ensemble methods.

Summary of contributions:

- We present a simple and effective framework for recognizing POIs in smartphones;
- We propose a novel ConvNet by adding a "spatial layer", thus equiping ordinary ConvNet with geographic features;
- We compress multiple deep ConvNets into one single shallow net with competitive performance in order to meet the demand of real-time;
- Experiments on real-world dataset has shown our model achieves as high as 97% accuracy for POI recognition.

2. DEEPCAMERA FRAMEWORK

We shall start by a definition of mathematical notation for DeepCamera. Suppose that we already have two databases: (1) a POI database P, where each POI $p \in P$ has geo-location attribute *p.loc*; (2) an image database S, where each image $s \in S$ has two attributes: a geo-location *s.loc* and a POI tag *s.poi* for its geographic and semantic label. A query q consists of two parts, namely the query image $q.img$ as the visual part and the query FOV $q.fov$ as the spatial part. We show a toy example of query processing in Figure 1.

We dive into the details of our DC framework in the remaining section as follows. *Deep ConvNet Model* outputs a visual probability distribution over all POIs. Then we train a shallow net via *Model Compression* in order to simultaneously increase accuracy and efficiency. Finally, we plug in the *Spatial Layer* which captures a geographic probability based on a query FOV.

2.1 Deep ConvNet Model

In this subsection, we describe our deep ConvNet model in two parts, namely the *Network Architecture*(detailed in Section 2.1.1) and *Network Training*(detailed in Section 2.1.2).

2.1.1 Network Architecture

We summarized 3 similar deep network in Table 1. The receptive fields in convolution layer are all set to 3×3 since deep model with small kernels has two advantages [8]: (1) makes the final decision function more descriminative; (2) descreases the number of parameters. The input size of our ConvNet is fixed as $3 \times 128 \times 128$(3 channels for RGB) subtracted from the mean RGB value of training set. The convolution stride is fixed to 1 pixel and the padding is also 1 pixel so that the output size is preserved after convolution operation.

All together, we add 5 MaxPooling layers as a downsampling technique among the stack of convolutional layers. The MaxPooling window is 2×2, with stride 2. Three fully-connected(FC) layers are stacked on top of convolutional layers. The first two FC layers have 1024 neurons with a Dropout[10] probability 0.5 and the last one's size depends on the number of POIs. The non-linear transformation we use is Rectified Linear Unit(ReLU)[5] after each convolution layer.

2.1.2 Network Training

The network training procedure is optimized by mini-batch gradient descent with RMSProp[1] which gains popularity very recently. The mini-batch size is set to 128. In addition to Dropout layers, we also introduce a L_2 weight decay as regularization(the penalty coefficient is 0.001). The initialization of learning rate is set 0.01 and it is decreased by multiplying 0.98 for every other 10 epochs until it reaches 0.0001. The data augmentation strategy is cropping rescaled images for each epoch iteration and then conduct randomly horizontal flipping and contrast(between 0.8 to 1.2).

2.2 Model Compression

A simple but effective way to boost a machine learning algorithm is to train many models previously and then combine these models to obtain a single model with higher accuracy. Such combination is called *ensemble methods*. However, the increasing accuracy is gained at the expense of efficiency since it will compute multiple models. Thus, we are motivated to obtain a shallow net(which we call *shNet*) but still with competitive performance. Next, we will briefly introduce two simple ensemble methods in Section 2.2.1 and describe how to train the shNet in Section 2.2.2.

2.2.1 Ensemble Methods

Simple Averaging Suppose we have already trained n models M_1, M_2, ..., M_n and there are m POIs(or classes) in total and N validation images. Then for a given query image

Table 1: Deep ConvNet Architecture(ReLU is not shown, XXX represents the number of POIs).

ConvNet Name	ConvNet Architecture
N_1(9 layers)	Input → Conv3-64 → MaxPool → Conv3-128 → MaxPool → Conv3-256 → Conv3-256 → MaxPool → Conv3-512 → MaxPool → Conv3-512 → MaxPool → FC-1024 → FC-1024 → FC-XXX → Softmax
N_2(11 layers)	Input → Conv3-64 → MaxPool → Conv3-128 → MaxPool → Conv3-256 → Conv3-256 → MaxPool → Conv3-512 → **Conv3-512** → MaxPool → Conv3-512 → **Conv3-512** → MaxPool → FC-1024 → FC-1024 → FC-XXX → Softmax
N_3(13 layers)	Input → Conv3-64 → **Conv3-64** → MaxPool → Conv3-128 → **Conv3-128** → MaxPool → Conv3-256 → Conv3-256 → MaxPool → Conv3-512 → **Conv3-512** → MaxPool → Conv3-512 → **Conv3-512** → MaxPool → FC-1024 → FC-1024 → FC-XXX → Softmax

q and a model M_i, let $\mathbf{P}(q = p_j; M_i)$ denote the probability that the query image q is predicted as POI $p_j (j = 1, 2, ..., m)$ under the model M_i. Then the simple averaging ensemble is:

$$\mathbf{P}(q = p_j; M_1, ..., M_n) = \frac{1}{n} \sum_{i=1}^{n} \mathbf{P}(q = p_j; M_i) \quad (1)$$

Weighted Averaging The simple averaging method consider each model as equal importance. However, models with high accuracy may be assigned with high votes which leads to a weighted averaging method. Assume α_i is the accuracy of model M_i on validation dataset, then the weighted averaging ensemble is:

$$\mathbf{P}(q = p_j; M_1, ..., M_n) = \sum_{i=1}^{n} \frac{\alpha_i}{\sum_{i=1}^{n} \alpha_i} \mathbf{P}(q = p_j; M_i) \quad (2)$$

2.2.2 *shNet Training*

After we have obtained an ensembled deep model M using methods in Section 2.2.1, we would like to train a shallow net shNet which mimics M. More concretely, shNet is trained to fit the *function* that learned by M. Note that such function is so complex that it cannot be learned by a shallow model on the original labels. Hence, we have to learn the function with the help of intermediate deep model first and then train another shallow model to mimic such function.

The last layer in M is a Softmax normalization to produce a probability distribution over different POIs. However, it is not reasonable to directly train the shNet on these probabilities since they are sometimes too difficult to be learned by cross-entropy loss function[4]. Thus the shNet is trained on *logits* which are values before the Softmax transformation. Training in the logit space will be much easier for shNet to capture the relationships between different POIs than probability space. For example, consider three POI probabilities output by M after Softmax [$2e{-}9$, $4e{-}5$, 0.9999]. It can be seen that the third POI dominate the probability space, hence, the information hidden in the first two POIs will not be captured if we train shNet on these probabilities, e.g. although the second POI is unlikely to be the target but it is still more likely than the first POI which may indicate that the last two POIs share similarities to some extent. The corresponding logit values are [10, 20, 30], which mitigates the serious bias in probability space, making shNet easier to learn.

The last important thing to note is that cross-entropy is not any longer applicable for training shNet as cost function since it will only focus on the true label's cell. Thus, we formulate the learning process as a L_2 loss regression problem in the logit space as detailed in [4].

Figure 2: Example of query photos in two dataset.

2.3 Spatial Layer

In work [6], it has been proposed a *probabilistic FOV model*(pFOV) which can estimate the likelihood of some POI being captured by a smartphone camera. The idea behind is to leverage the uncertainty of the phone's GPS location and build up a gaussian-based model to capture such uncertainty. In our case, we will obtain a geo-spatial probability distribution over different POIs via pFOV model which forms our "spatial layer". We call the last layer after Softmax in shNet "visual layer" since it represents probabilities in the visual space. Then we plug a new "spatial layer" on top of the "visual layer". The weight matrix $\mathbf{W}$ between these two layers is:

$$\mathbf{W} = \beta \cdot \mathbf{\Sigma}(1, 1, ..., 1) \quad (3)$$

where β is a weighted preference for spatial phase and $\mathbf{\Sigma}$ is a diagonal matrix with all ones in the diagonal. β is a hyper-parameter which should be tuned in validation set.

3. EXPERIMENTAL RESULTS

3.1 Dataset Description

We conduct our experiments on two different dataset, namely *Singapore 151K*(S) and *NewYork 296K*(N).

Singapore 151K Singapore 151K is provided by [6] which contains 151,193 geotagged images with 2,256 distinct POIs. They also collect a query set consisting of 680 smartphone captured photos(with the ground truth POIs) and each photo is associated with FOV parameters.

NewYork 296K In total, 296,156 geotagged images associated with 1,512 different POIs are downloaded from Flickr. We get the POI list in NewYork region from [2] and use these POI names as query keywords via Flickr API. Unlike Singapore 151K, we were not able collect an extra query set acquired by smartphones. We select 500 images as query photos, which do not contain camera direction obviously. In such case, we slightly modify equation 1 in [6] by remov-

Table 2: Results of Different Models

Model	Acc(S)	Acc(N)	Time(S)	Time(N)
KC[6]: Spatial($\lambda = 1$)	48%	-	-	-
KC: Visual($\lambda = 0$)	77%	-	-	-
KC: Spatial+Visual($\lambda = 0.5$)	92%	-	0.68s	-
N_1	85.4%	78.2%	0.0030s	0.0017s
N_2	87.5%	82.7%	0.0041s	0.0026s
N_3	88.3%	83.1%	0.0048s	0.0035s
Averaged Ensembles(AE)	89.0%	84.3%	0.0962s	0.0645s
Weighted Ensembles(WE)	91.2%	85.8%	0.1138s	0.0769s
WE+SpatialLayer	**97.0%**	**91.1%**	0.1619s	0.1084s
shNet	88.4%	81.2%	**0.0013s**	**0.0011s**
shNet+SpatialLayer	95.3%	88.8%	0.0494s	0.0326s

ing the first item, i.e. the probability distribution now only depends on the distance d.

3.2 Performance Results

We summarize the performance results of different models in Table 2. Note that these results are averaged over all query set. Experiments are conducted on a Linux Server with 64GB memory and GPU mode is NVIDIA-TITAN X.

The first three models(as our baseline) and results are reported in KC[6] in the case of query box = 0.6 km, which performs best when cross validated. Our best single model of deep ConvNet N_1, N_2, N_3 acquires 85%, 87%, 88% recognition accuracy in Singapore dataset, all exceeding the pure visual phase in KC. In order to obtain averaged and weighted ensembles, we vary the ConvNet with different initialization, learning rate, gradient descent algorithm(such as normal SGD, Momentum and AdaGrad). The weighted ensembles perform better than simple averaging as expected, rise to 91%. The shNet architecture is as suggested in [4], a 3-layer network with one pooling layer. For the sake of saving space, we only report the best shNet which possesses roughly 32M parameters. Note that such best shNet accuracy is still lower than ensembles since shNet is a model which attempts to *approximate* the function learned by ensembles. Nevertheless, it considerably reduces online query time compared with ensembles. Finally, we combine spatial layer into ensembles and shNet. As a result, it increases recognition accuracy significantly due to geo-spatial remediation embedded in pFOV model. Overall, our shNet+SpatialLayer increases recognition accuracy and query response time is $\times 13$ faster than [6]. Same conclusions can be drawn from New York dataset.

3.3 ConvNet Visualization

Due to limited space, we plot the weights in the first layer learned by network N_1 for Singapore dataset in Figure 3(b) and NewYork dataset in Figure 3(e). It can be seen that there are 64 weights, which corresponds to the number of feature maps in the first convolutional layer, with kernel size 3×3. We also show 2 query sample images and their 64 activations in the first layer in Figure 3. Note that with 1 pixel padding, each activation output size keeps the same as input.

4. CONCLUSION

We have presented a novel framework DeepCamera for recognizing places-of-interest with smartphones. Our framework is based on Convolutional Neural Networks. In order to respond user queries in real-time, we compressed multiple

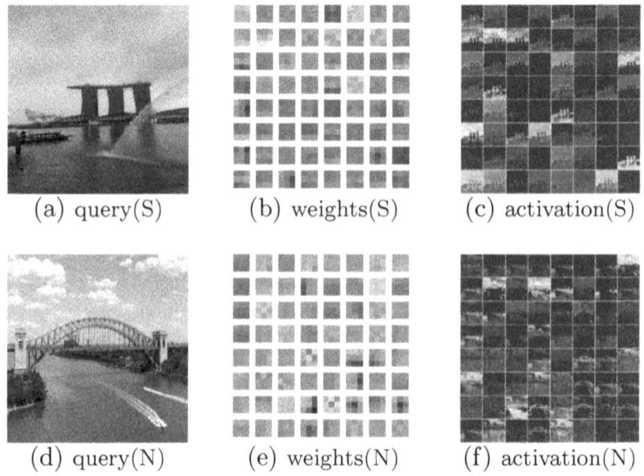

Figure 3: Visualizing deep ConvNet N_1.

trained ConvNets into one single model shNet which proves to achieve competative performance with ensemble methods. A spatial layer is stacked on top of shNet to combine the geographic features. Our framework is evaluated on real-world dataset and beats the baseline.

Acknowledgments

The work is supported by the National Key Basic Research Program of China (GrantNo. 2015CB352400), National High Technology Research Development Program of China (GrantNo. 2013AA040601), and the National Science Foundation of China (GrantNo. 61170034).

5. REFERENCES

[1] http://www.cs.toronto.edu/~tijmen/csc321/slides/.

[2] http://www.geonames.org/.

[3] http://www.kpcb.com/internet-trends.

[4] L. J. Ba and R. Caurana. Do deep nets really need to be deep? *CoRR*, abs/1312.6184, 2013.

[5] A. Krizhevsky, I. Sutskever, and G. E. Hinton. Imagenet classification with deep convolutional neural networks. In *NIPS*, pages 1097–1105. 2012.

[6] P. Peng, L. Shou, K. Chen, G. Chen, and S. Wu. The knowing camera: Recognizing places-of-interest in smartphone photos. In *SIGIR*, pages 969–972, 2013.

[7] P. Peng, L. Shou, K. Chen, G. Chen, and S. Wu. The knowing camera 2: recognizing and annotating places-of-interest in smartphone photos. In *SIGIR*, pages 707–716, 2014.

[8] K. Simonyan and A. Zisserman. Very deep convolutional networks for large-scale image recognition. *CoRR*, abs/1409.1556, 2014.

[9] J. Sivic and A. Zisserman. Video google: A text retrieval approach to object matching in videos. In *ICCV*, pages 1470–1477, 2003.

[10] N. Srivastava, G. Hinton, A. Krizhevsky, I. Sutskever, and R. Salakhutdinov. Dropout: A simple way to prevent neural networks from overfitting. *JLMR*, 15:1929–1958, 2014.

Structured Sparse Regression for Recommender Systems

Mingjie Qian[†], Liangjie Hong[§], Yue Shi[§], Suju Rajan[§]
† Department of Computer Science, University of Illinois at Urbana-Champaign, IL, USA
§ Personalization Sciences, Yahoo Labs, CA, USA
mqian2@illinois.edu, {liangjie,yueshi,suju}@yahoo-inc.com

ABSTRACT

Feature-based collaborative filtering models, such as state-of-the-art factorization machines and regression-based latent factor models, rarely consider features' structural information, ignoring the heterogeneity of inter-type and intra-type relationships. Naïvely treating all feature pairs equally would potentially deteriorate the overall recommendation performance. In addition, human prior knowledge and other hierarchical or graphical structures are often available for some features, e.g., the country-state-city hierarchy for geographic features and the topical taxonomy for article features. It is a challenge to utilize the prior knowledge to further boost performance of state-of-the-art models. In this paper we employ rich features from both user and item sides to enhance latent factors learnt from interaction data, uncovering hidden structures from features' relationships and learning sparse pairwise and tree structural connections among features. Our framework borrows the modeling strengh from both structural sparsity modeling and latent factor models. Experiments on a real-world large-scale recommendation data set demonstrated that the proposed model outperforms several strong state-of-the-art baselines.

Categories and Subject Descriptors

H.3.5 [**Information Storage and Retrieval**]: Online Information Services

Keywords

Structured Sparse Regression, Structured Sparse Feature Graph Learning, Hierarchical Sparse Coding, Structured Sparse Coding, Feature-based Collaborative Filtering

1. INTRODUCTION

Feature based latent factor models have received increasing attention in recent years due to its capability to effectively solve the cold-start problem. There have been many feature based collaborative filtering (CF) models proposed recently, which can be grouped into two categories. The first type of models includes all variants of latent factor models (LFM) which have been proven as an effective approach to personalization and recommender systems. The core of LFM is to learn user-specific and item-specific features from user-item interactions and utilize these features for future predictions/recommendations. State-of-the-art LFM exploits low-rank latent spaces of users and features and treats latent factors that are learnt from user-item historical data as features. This type of models has gained significant successes in a number of applications, including the Netflix competition. The second category is the factorization machine (FM), which explicitly learns the mapping function from features to rating score circumventing the dependency on user/item latent factors as in the latent factor models, resulting in an effective model for the cold start problem [9].

Although these feature-based CF models have been shown to be effective, they do not utilize the feature structure information. For example, conventional latent factor models (e.g., matrix factorization or tensor factorization models) like RLFM [1, 2] learn mapping functions from user/item features to user/item latent vectors assuming the features have a flat first-order structure. Later, [10] showed that this kind of mapping can be extended to any non-linear models. Although the formalism is flexible, it leaves too much room for practitioners to choose which non-linear model to use for a particular application. Also, it is hard to incorporate human prior knowledge on the feature structure into the framework, unless through careful feature engineering, and the proposed inference algorithm is difficult to use in large-scale settings. Similar to RLFM, Gantner et al. [4] proposed a model to explicitly learn the mapping function from features to latent factors, resulting in an effective model for the cold start problem. But it still makes the flat first-order feature structure assumption. In the other line of work, Rendle et al. [9] proposed a more compact model called factorization machine FM. Basically FM is a second-order regression model which directly maps the user-item-event concatenated features to rating score by learning the implicit mapping functions from features to latent factors, resulting in an effective model for the cold start problem. However, the issue of encoding structural human prior information still boils down to sophisticated feature engineering and it's not clear how to incorporate the heterogenous feature structures into model training to enhance the rating prediction performance. Though FM considers the second-order feature structure, it simply uses all the feature pairs for prediction. Quite

Permission to make digital or hard copies of all or part of this work for personal or classroom use is granted without fee provided that copies are not made or distributed for profit or commercial advantage and that copies bear this notice and the full citation on the first page. Copyrights for components of this work owned by others than ACM must be honored. Abstracting with credit is permitted. To copy otherwise, or republish, to post on servers or to redistribute to lists, requires prior specific permission and/or a fee. Request permissions from Permissions@acm.org.
CIKM'15, October 19–23, 2015, Melbourne, VIC, Australia
Copyright 2015 ACM 978-1-4503-3794-6/15/10 ...$15.00.
DOI: http://dx.doi.org/10.1145/2806416.2806641.

a lot of work in sparse coding area have shown that many signals tend to have a sparse representation from basic components in nature, and a sparse model often outperforms a dense model and also has the variable selection effect. Inspired by this, a sparse model that uses an appropriate subset of feature pairs might have a better performance.

In practices, human prior knowledge or explicit structure information about these features is also sometimes available. For example, the topical categories on news articles may naturally be organized into hierarchies or graphs. Another good example would be demographical information about users, especially their geo-locations that are aligned with countries, states and cities, defined in real-world geo-political settings. These prior knowledge and structures are invaluable information for better user understanding and profiling and eventually better recommendation results. However, it is not straightforward to encode this kind of structural prior knowledge into state-of-the-art recommendation models like RLFM and FM. One approach might be to construct features capturing these structures and embed them into regression models. But the interplay between an optimal way to construct such features and train a better regression model based on these features to map to latent features becomes non-trivial in this case. Some previous work has been proposed to impose structural information on latent variable models, which are not necessarily directed graphical models. For instance, He et al. [5] proposed a general learning framework which induces sparsity on the undirected graphical model imposed on the vector of latent factors. Although the paper shares a similar idea with our framework, their work cannot handle heterogeneous types of features and complex dependencies. Also, it is hard to link their work to state-of-the-art LFM used in CF settings. Along the line of undirected graphical models, Min et al. [8] proposed sparse high-order Boltzmann machines, aiming to capture dependencies between latent variables. Again, it is not obvious to plug the model into state-of-the-art CF approaches.

In this paper, we propose a structured sparse second-order regression model with structural prior knowledge in a principled way. The notion of types of features is introduced such that different types of features would have different structures (e.g., topical categories versus geographical locations). We consider two kinds of structures. For inter-typed features (which are of different kinds), the model is able to learn sparse relationships between different types of features (e.g., age and gender). For intra-typed features (which are in the same kind) that have a hierarchy (tree), e.g., we have the country-state-city hierarchical tree for the geo-location feature terms, the model learns a sparse hierarchical structure on the tree such that if a parent feature edge (or interchangeably a feature pair) is selected, then all its descendant edges should be selected as well, and if a parent edge is removed then all its descendant edges should be removed too.

2. STRUCTURED SPARSE REGRESSION

We model the rating score of an event by a user on an item by a second-order polynomial regression

$$\hat{y} = b + \langle \mathbf{w}, \mathbf{x} \rangle + \sum_{i=1}^{p} \sum_{j=i+1}^{p} \alpha_{ij} x[i] x[j], \qquad (1)$$

where b is the global bias for all events, $\mathbf{w}$ is the first-order weights, and p is the feature size. $\mathbf{x}$ is the concatenated feature vector for the user-item-event triplet as is used in FM. Apparently, we directly use a pair-wise weight factor α_{ij} for each feature pair (or edge) (i, j) rather than the inner product of latent factors $\mathbf{v}_i$ and $\mathbf{v}_j$ in FM because it would be easier to learn the structures by imposing structured sparsity-inducing norm regularization, otherwise we would need to minimize the approximation error to push $\alpha_{ij} \approx \langle \mathbf{v}_i, \mathbf{v}_j \rangle$ for any activated feature pair (i, j). Actually the feature size is relatively small w.r.t. the data size which is usually the case for practical large-scale machine learning problems, thus the complexity of $O(p^2)$ should not be the bottleneck.

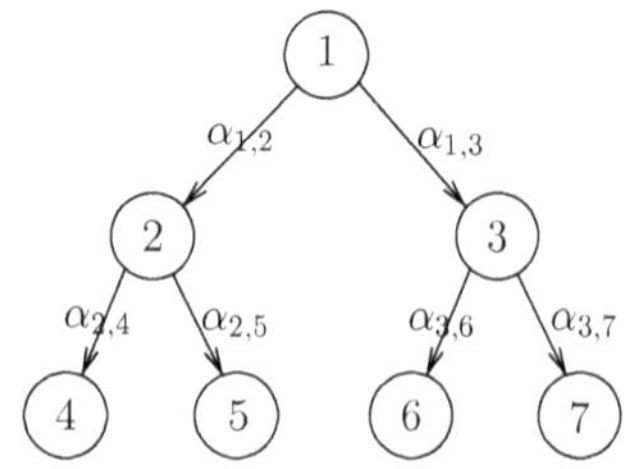

Figure 1: An illustration of hierarchy for features of the same type. Each node corresponds to a feature node, and each edge a feature pair.

2.1 Structured Sparse Priors with Heterogeneous Features

As we discussed before, heterogeneous feature types exist for the user-item-event triplet. For users, it is comparatively easy to obtain certain prior structures for some types of features (e.g., geographical locations), while it is not straightforward for other types (e.g., age and gender).

We partition the features into different types (groups). Let T denote the number of feature types for users and $\mathcal{G} = \{g_1, g_2, \ldots, g_T\}$ the non-overlapping grouping of feature indices, i.e., partition of feature indices by feature types. g_t is the set of feature indices for feature type t. Denote p_t the number of features in feature type t, so that we have $g_t = \left\{\sum_{s=1}^{t-1} p_s + 1, \sum_{s=1}^{t-1} p_s + 2, \ldots, \sum_{s=1}^{t-1} p_s + p_t\right\}$ and $\sum_{s=1}^{T} p_s = p$. If we differentiate different types of features, the second-order term in Equation 1 can be further expanded as

$$\underbrace{\sum_{t=1}^{T} \sum_{t'=t+1}^{T} \sum_{k \in g_t} \sum_{k' \in g_{t'}} \alpha_{kk'} \mathbf{x}[k] \mathbf{x}[k']}_{\text{Inter-type Edges}} + \underbrace{\sum_{t=1}^{T} \sum_{\substack{k,k' \in g_t \\ k \neq k'}} \alpha_{kk'} \mathbf{x}[k] \mathbf{x}[k']}_{\text{Intra-type Edges}}.$$

As we partition features into different types, edges of the whole pair-wise feature graph are divided into two parts as well: inter-type edges and intra-type edges. Intra-type edges are initialized from prior knowledge if we have prior hierarchies while inter-type edges are learned. Figure 1 gives an example of the hierarchy for features of one type.

We impose a sparse prior on all inter-typed feature edges, whereas in order to learn sparse hierarchical structure on certain intra-typed feature edges (e.g., geo features), we cast the problem into a hierarchical sparse coding problem by using structured sparsity-inducing norms as regularization [11, 6]. The hierarchical sparsity-inducing regularization has a desirable property that if one edge is included then all its ancestor edges should all be included as well. Equivalently, if one edge is removed from the tree, then all its descendant edges should all be removed too. We can also view the edge hierarchy as pre-ordering of edges, i.e., the parent edge has to be pre-ordered before its child edges. For intra-type edges with hierarchy, we use tree-structured set of groups defined as follows [6].

Definition 1. A set of edge groups $\mathcal{G} \triangleq \{g\}_{g\in\mathcal{G}}$ is said to be tree-structured in $\{1,\ldots,|\mathcal{E}|\}$ if $\bigcup_{g\in\mathcal{G}} g = \{1,\ldots,|\mathcal{E}|\}$ and if for all $g,h \in \mathcal{G}, (g\cap h \neq \emptyset) \Rightarrow (g \subseteq h \ or\ h \subseteq g)$, where $\mathcal{E}$ is the set of intra hierarchical feature graph edges. For such a set of groups, there exists a (non-unique) total order relation $\preceq$ such that:

$$g \preceq h \Rightarrow \{g \subseteq h \text{ or } g \cap h = \emptyset\}.$$

We can also say that the tree-structured set of groups consists of all the subtrees. As we can see from the definition, we can expand this tree-structured set of groups by adding inter edge and self-edge groups, where each inter edge and self-edge forms a singleton edge group, without affecting the total order relation since they are non-overlapping sets of singleton groups isolated from the tree-structured set of groups. We thus propose to use a mixed singleton and tree-structured sparsity-inducing norm $\mathcal{T}(\boldsymbol{\alpha})$ imposed on the whole feature graph edge weight vector $\boldsymbol{\alpha}$ which is defined as $\mathcal{T}(\boldsymbol{\alpha}) \triangleq \sum_{g\in\mathcal{G}} \left\|\boldsymbol{\alpha}_{|g}\right\|_2$, where $\boldsymbol{\alpha}_{|g}$ is the vector composed of elements of $\boldsymbol{\alpha}$ for indices in edge group g.

2.2 Optimization Problem

Adding the standard l_2-norm regularization on b and $\mathbf{w}$, we want to minimized the regularized risk on all N events

$$\min \frac{1}{N}\sum_{n=1}^{N}\|y_n - \hat{y}_n\|^2 + \lambda \sum_{\theta\in\{b,w_i\}} \theta^2 + \nu\mathcal{T}(\alpha), \quad (2)$$

where λ and ν are positive real number parameters for regularization. b and w_i can be updated by alternating least-squares (ALS) optimization by

$$\theta^* = \frac{\theta \sum_{n=1}^{N} h_\theta^2(\mathbf{x}_n) + \sum_{n=1}^{N} h_\theta(\mathbf{x}_n)\, e_n}{\sum_{n=1}^{N} h_\theta^2(\mathbf{x}_n) + N\lambda}, \quad (3)$$

where $e_n = y_n - \hat{y}_n$ is the training error of the nth event, and

$$h_\theta(\mathbf{x}) = \frac{\partial \hat{y}(\mathbf{x})}{\partial \theta} = \begin{cases} 1, & \text{if } \theta \text{ is } b \\ x[i], & \text{if } \theta \text{ is } w_i \end{cases}.$$

We apply proximal gradient descent to update $\alpha_{|g}$ for each group g in a block coordinate descent strategy where the key step is to compute the proximal mapping w.r.t. l_2-norm

$$\alpha_{|g}{}^{k} = \mathrm{Prox}_{\frac{N\nu}{L}\|\cdot\|_2}\left(\alpha_{|g}{}^{k-1} - \frac{1}{L}\nabla_{\alpha_{|g}} f\left(\alpha_{|g}{}^{k-1}\right)\right),$$

where $f(\alpha_{|g}) = \frac{1}{N}\sum_{n=1}^{N}\|\hat{y}_n - y_n\|^2$, and L is the lipschitz constant for f. To speed up the algorithm, we need to estimate L to avoid line search. By applying Gersgorin theorem, it can be proved that $L = 2\left\|\sum_{n=1}^{N} h_{\alpha_{|g}}(\mathbf{x}_n)\, h_{\alpha_{|g}}(\mathbf{x}_n)^T\right\|_\infty$. Note that e_n should be updated accordingly each time b, $\mathbf{w}$, and $\alpha_{|g}$ are updated to guarantee the correctness of the algorithm. The final algorithm has an $O(Np^2)$ time complexity and an $O(p^2 + N\bar{z})$ space complexity where $\bar{z}$ is the average number of non-zero elements for all event feature vectors.

3. EXPERIMENTS

Dataset: We use Yahoo's homepage stream data as a running example of our experiments. A dataset from a sample of traffic of users from six international sites, including United Kingdom, France, Italy, Germany, Spain and Ireland of Yahoo homepage streams is collected. The dataset contains users' interactions, clicks and views, on articles shown in the stream section from May 1st, 2014 to May 16th, 2014. We group users by time periods and construct sessions of all items a user consumed in a particular time period (e.g., months, day, hour and etc.). Mimicking real settings of online systems, events from May 1st to May 9th are used to build the training set, and the remaining events are used to build the test set. The training set has 4.75M events based on the interaction between between 37,668 users and 30,260 news items. The test set has 4.46M events based on the interaction between between 45,422 users and 25,569 news items.

Features: The critical part of our proposed framework, with other feature-based `CF` is to utilize different types of user and item features. Therefore, in addition to the user interaction data, the dataset also includes the user-side features and item-side features. The user-side feature set consists of three components:

- **Gender**: Categorical, no prior structure, three dimensional (e.g., male, female and unknown).
- **Age**: Categorical, no prior structure, ten dimensional age groups.
- **Geographical areas**: Categorical, a tree-like prior structure, including countries, states and cities. which yields 6744-dimension user-side features. Note that not all features have prior structures. The item-side feature set consists:
- **Content publisher**: Categorical, no prior structure.
- **Topical categories**: Multi-valued (e.g., one article could fall into multiple categories), a directed acyclic graph (DAG) prior structure.

which results in 1347-dimension item-side features. Finally, each event is associated with one item-specific feature denoted as **Freshness**, which measures the lifetime of the item. Summarizing, the dataset has 8,092-dimension explicit features for all events, the average number of non-zero features for each event is 8.682.

Evaluation Method and Metrics: In addition to evaluating how well we can fit the data by measuring Rooted-Mean-Squared-Error (`RMSE`), we also evaluate the proposed methods in terms of ranking metrics. We use Mean-Average-Precision (`MAP`), Mean-Reciprocal-Rank (`MRR`) and Precision@10 (`P@10`) as main evaluation metrics.

Baselines: We compare our model, denoted as `STSR` with three standard baseline methods:

- `ZeroMean`: A model uses zero vectors as the as priors for user/item latent factors. This includes all classic `LFM` models like [7].
- `RLFM`: A model uses linear regression output as priors for user/item latent factors. This includes models like [1, 3].
- `FM`: A model directly maps features to ratings by a

Table 1: **Average performance with standard deviation shown in parentheses. (* represents '0.000', i.e., *14 = 0.00014).**

Overall performance				
Method	RMSE	MAP	MRR	P@10
ZeroMean	.757(*00)	.122(*16)	.149(*20)	.038(*04)
RLFM	.339(*07)	.157(*74)	.196(*99)	.052(*31)
FM	.329(*00)	.167(*00)	.207(*00)	.053(*00)
STSR	.329(*00)	.175(*14)	.218(*15)	.058(*05)
Cold-start performance				
Method	RMSE	MAP	MRR	P@10
ZeroMean	.961(*13)	.129(*03)	.147(*03)	.037(*02)
RLFM	.339(*03)	.166(*73)	.194(*83)	.050(*23)
FM	.329(*00)	.176(*00)	.205(*00)	.052(*00)
STSR	.329(*00)	.185(*18)	.218(*22)	.057(*06)

second-order regression model with latent feature factorization [9].

Setting: We do grid search for all parameters of all models and report the best average performance in 5 runs. For ZeroMean and RLFM, we do grid search for σ^2, σ_u^2, and σ_v^2 in $\{10^{-2}, 10^{-1}, \ldots, 10^2\}$, and latent space dimensionality K in $\{5, 10, 20, 50\}$. For FM, we do grid search for the regularization parameter λ in $\{10^{-4}, 10^{-3}, 10^{-2}, 10^{-1}\}$ and latent space dimensionality K in $\{4, 8, 16, 32\}$. For STSR, we search λ in $\{10^{-4}, 10^{-3}, 10^{-2}, 10^{-1}\}$ and ν in $\{10^{-9}, 10^{-7}, 10^{-5}, 10^{-3}, 10^{-1}\}$.

3.1 Experimental Results

We run each model for 5 times from different initialization and average the metrics from multiple runs. The comparison result is shown in Table 1. From the table we see that STSR outperforms other models in all ranking metrics significantly. As expected, ZeroMean does poorly in all ranking metrics, which validates the statement made in previous studies that it does not handle cold-start problems. RLFM does significantly better than ZeroMean, implying that features are critical to address cold-start problems and better user/item factors might be learned by utilizing features. FM performs significantly better than RLFM which is consistent with the statement in literature. Finally, STSR learns sparse relationships among features and only the links that are truly contributing to the performance will be enabled through structured sparse coding. Thus, the sparse structure learned from STSR turns out making a difference in terms of ranking metrics.

Parameter Analysis: We investigate how different sets of parameters impacting the performance in Figure 2. The optimal parameters are $\lambda = 0.001$, $\nu = 10^{-5}$. The figure shows that STSR is not very sensitive to ν with wide ranges, the metrics only differ in ten-thousandths place. STSR is mildly sensitive to λ when λ is relatively small, but larger λ does badly hurt the ranking performance. In practice, one can use a validation set (with gold standard) to tune the parameters by grid search.

4. CONCLUSIONS

We proposed a structured sparse regression model that is able to learn heterogeneous sparse structure on the user/item features. We developed an efficient learning algorithm that scales linearly to the number of events. Experiments on a large-scale news recommendation dataset have demonstrated the superior performance of our model compared to the state-of- the-art alternatives, especially for the cold start users, for whom the structure of features turns out to be critical information for the recommendation quality.

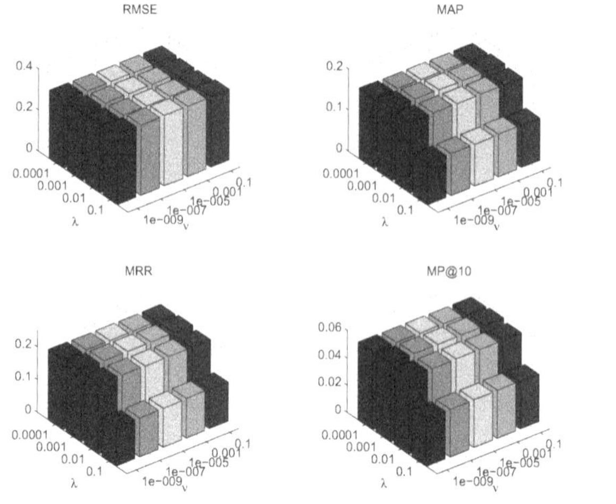

Figure 2: Average metrics in 5 runs with different λ and ν for STSR

5. REFERENCES

[1] D. Agarwal and B.-C. Chen. Regression-based latent factor models. In *Proceedings of KDD*, pages 19–28. ACM, 2009.

[2] D. Agarwal and B.-C. Chen. fLDA: matrix factorization through latent Dirichlet allocation. In *Proceedings of WSDM*, pages 91–100. ACM, 2010.

[3] T. Chen, W. Zhang, Q. Lu, K. Chen, Z. Zheng, and Y. Yu. SVDFeature: A toolkit for feature-based collaborative filtering. *The Journal of Machine Learning Research*, 13(1):3619–3622, Dec. 2012.

[4] Z. Gantner, L. Drumond, C. Freudenthaler, S. Rendle, and L. Schmidt-Thieme. Learning attribute-to-feature mappings for cold-start recommendations. In *Proceedings of the 2010 IEEE International Conference on Data Mining*, ICDM '10, pages 176–185, 2010.

[5] Y. He, Y. Qi, K. Kavukcuoglu, and H. Park. Learning the dependency structure of latent factors. In *Advances in Neural Information Processing Systems 25*, pages 2375–2383. 2012.

[6] R. Jenatton, J. Mairal, G. Obozinski, and F. Bach. Proximal methods for hierarchical sparse coding. *The Journal of Machine Learning Research*, 12:2297–2334, 2011.

[7] Y. Koren, R. Bell, and C. Volinsky. Matrix factorization techniques for recommender systems. *Computer*, 42(8):30–37, Aug. 2009.

[8] M. R. Min, X. Ning, C. Cheng, and M. Gerstein. Interpretable sparse high-order boltzmann machines. In *AISTATS*, pages 614–622, 2014.

[9] S. Rendle. Factorization machines with libfm. *ACM Transactions on Intelligent Systems and Technology*, 3(3):57:1–57:22, May 2012.

[10] L. Zhang, D. Agarwal, and B.-C. Chen. Generalizing matrix factorization through flexible regression priors. In *Proceedings of RecSys*, pages 13–20. ACM, 2011.

[11] P. Zhao, G. Rocha, and B. Yu. The composite absolute penalties family for grouped and hierarchical variable selection. *The Annals of Statistics*, pages 3468–3497, 2009.

Analyzing Document Intensive Business Processes Using Ontology

Suman Roychoudhury
TCS Research
54B Hadapsar Industrial Estate
Pune, 411013, India
suman.roychoudhury@tcs.com

Vinay Kulkarni
TCS Research
54B Hadapsar Industrial Estate
Pune, 411013, India
vinay.vkulkarni@tcs.com

Nikhil Bellarykar
TCS Research
54B Hadapsar Industrial Estate
Pune, 411013, India
nikhil.bellarykar@tcs.com

ABSTRACT

Knowledge is manifested in an enterprise in various forms ranging from unstructured operational data, to structured information like programs, as well as relational data stored in databases to semi-structured information stored in XML files. This information embodies the core of an enterprise knowledge base and analyzing the knowledge base can result in intelligent decision making. In order to realize this goal we begin with representing and analyzing unstructured knowledge present in an enterprise. In particular, this paper presents a real life example of a document intensive business process (International Trade) and attempts to model and analyze the process in a formal way. Typically, the information contained in a document intensive business process is of operational nature and requires extensive manual verification, which is both time consuming and error prone. Therefore, this research aims to eliminate such exhaustive manual verification by constructing a knowledge base in the form of ontology and apply suitable rule based reasoners to automate the verification process.

Categories and Subject Descriptors

I.2.4 [**Knowledge Representation Formalisms and Methods**] - Representation languages D.2.2 [**Design Tools and Techniques**] - Decision tables I.2.6 [**Learning**] - Concept learning, Knowledge acquisition I.2.7 [**Natural Language Processing**] - Language models, Language parsing and understanding

General Terms

Algorithms, Management, Documentation, Design, Experimentation, Human Factors, Languages, Verification.

Keywords

Knowledge representation, semantic rules, natural language processing, machine learning, international trade, letter of credit.

Permission to make digital or hard copies of all or part of this work for personal or classroom use is granted without fee provided that copies are not made or distributed for profit or commercial advantage and that copies bear this notice and the full citation on the first page. Copyrights for components of this work owned by others than ACM must be honored. Abstracting with credit is permitted. To copy otherwise, or republish, to post on servers or to redistribute to lists, requires prior specific permission and/or a fee. Request permissions from Permissions@acm.org.

CIKM'15, October 19-23, 2015, Melbourne, VIC, Australia
© 2015 ACM. ISBN 978-1-4503-3794-6/15/10…$15.00
DOI: http://dx.doi.org/10.1145/2806416.2806638

1. INTRODUCTION

Documents form the core of many business processes in an organization. Typically they contain several pieces of information that may have a structured format but generally having unstructured data as contents. The data contained in these documents are governed by rules as laid out in the operational manual of these business processes or in certain key documents that are themselves part of the business process. In other words, these documents contain information that has a syntactic structure as well as a behavior whose semantics is governed by the underlying operations. Since these documents needs to manually verified, it takes a considerable effort and time to validate the contents of these documents against the presumed rules as determined by the core operations. Moreover human validation and verification is subjected to unavoidable errors. This was precisely one of the prime challenges that were posed to us – (the R&D team) in our organization, which runs several business process services for major global enterprises operating in different verticals like financial, healthcare, consumer durables, retail etc. We were given a tour of one of the key business process services for a global financial bank – the precise area being *International Trade,* which generally draws a significant share of GDP for any country. It is a critical business process and rich in documents. It requires intense validation and verification by humans and cost of error is enormous. Our objective was to evaluate the document intensive nature of such processes and reduce manual intervention wherever possible. Therefore, in this short paper, we lay down our experience in describing the problem, the challenges and solutions that can be offered so as to enable intelligent document verification-as-a-service (dVaaS). The rest of the paper is outlined as follows. Section 2 describes the case and challenges with respect to document verification in general and in particular to International Trade. Section 3 describes our line of attack in the light of the identified challenges before we conclude in Section 4.

2. CASE DESCRIPTION AND CHALLENGES

International trade is a process of buying goods across countries or continents involving buyers and sellers. Although, at first the process seems simple, yet it involves considerable risks for both buyer and seller especially with regards to how a payment would be made during purchasing of goods across international borders. For example, the buyers run the risk of paying upfront without receiving the goods whereas the seller runs the risk of shipping the goods without receiving full payment. Therefore, to avoid this unusual situation, intermediate banks becomes a mediator between the buyer and seller and a financial instrument called Letter-of-Credit plays a key role in providing assurance to both

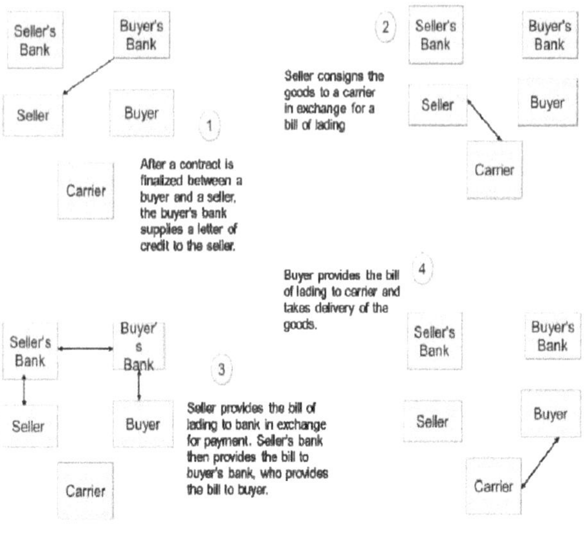

Figure 1. Letter of credit process steps

buyer and seller regarding fulfillment of goods and payment. Fig. 1 describes how international trade works. In step 1, after a contract is finalized between a buyer and seller, the buyer's bank supplies a letter of credit to the seller. In step 2, the seller dispatches the goods to a carrier in exchange of a Bill-of-Lading. In step 3, the seller provides the Bill-of-Lading and other key documents like Commercial Invoice, Inspection Certificate, Certificate-of-Origin, Packing List etc., to the seller's bank in exchange of payment from the buyer's bank. This is the key labor intensive step that requires extensive manual verification, which we would like to eliminate.

Now we list out some of the key challenges that need to be addressed so as to provide a solution to the problem.

Challenge 1 – There needs to be a way to formally represent the knowledge captured in a set of documents for a given business process. The representation should be such that it is machine processable and computable, i.e., it must be able to represent the syntactic nature of the data contained in these documents as well as the behavior in the form of semantic rules that are present in the certain operational documents (like Letter-of-Credit) and other mandatory codes enforced upon by the business process.

Challenge 2 – There needs to be a way to mine or retrieve the information available in natural language text in these documents. Standard techniques for named entity extraction and relationship extraction exists that generally uses supervised learning methods to improve the accuracy of extracted information [1]. The current state-of-the art with respect to entity and relationship extraction is accurate to the extent of 90% - 77% respectively. However, the type of information that is extracted generally tends to answer a different set of questions, which is rather explicit in the unstructured document and syntactic in nature. The kind of information we seek tend to be more semantic in nature, i.e., we would like to extract the behavior in terms of rules from the set of operational documents and then validate them against individual instances.

Both the challenges are linked, i.e., one needs to know the class of rules and how the knowledge is represented before any standard information retrieval techniques can be applied. Moreover, because of the difference in abstraction in the nature of information extracted and the rule language required to automate

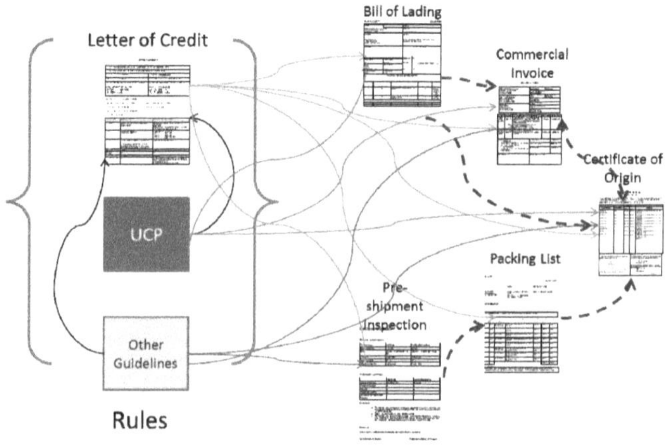

Figure 2. Documents involved in LoC process

the verification, a third challenge may arise which will require suitable translators to bridge the abstraction gap. Nevertheless, we would first need to address Challenge 1 before we take a deeper investigation dive towards resolving Challenge 2. Although in this paper, we describe the document verification problem in terms of International trade, the core idea is common to many other document intensive processes that require manual verification like Mortgage Processing, Medical Reporting, Financial Auditing etc.

3. ONTOLGY FOR INTERNATIONAL TRADE

In order to represent the domain concepts and knowledge with respect to International Trade, we firstly categorize the documents by their type. Classically, the entire document verification process as shown in Fig. 2, is governed by the Letter-of-Credit (LoC) that identifies the key stakeholders involved (e.g., Banks, Buyer, Seller, Carrier, Items or goods), the rules and regulations to follow along with what steps to resort to when an exception

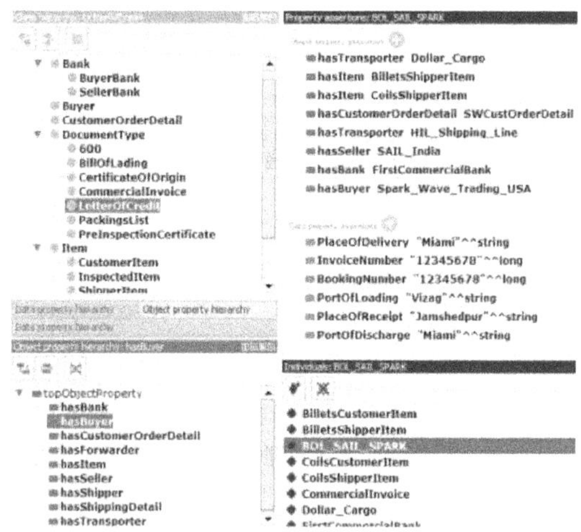

Figure 3. Ontology for International Trade

occurs. LoC varies from one transaction to another. Additionally there are other fixed guidelines and uniform customs code and practice (UCP 600) [2] that governs any transaction that takes place between the buyer and seller. In order to receive payment in lieu of shipment of goods, the seller produces a set of documents to the receiving bank. These documents are Bill-of-Lading, Commercial Invoice, Certificate of Origin, Packing List and Pre-shipment inspection document among others. The bank needs to verify these documents against the terms and conditions as laid out in the LoC and UCP 600 (as laid out by the solid lines in Fig.

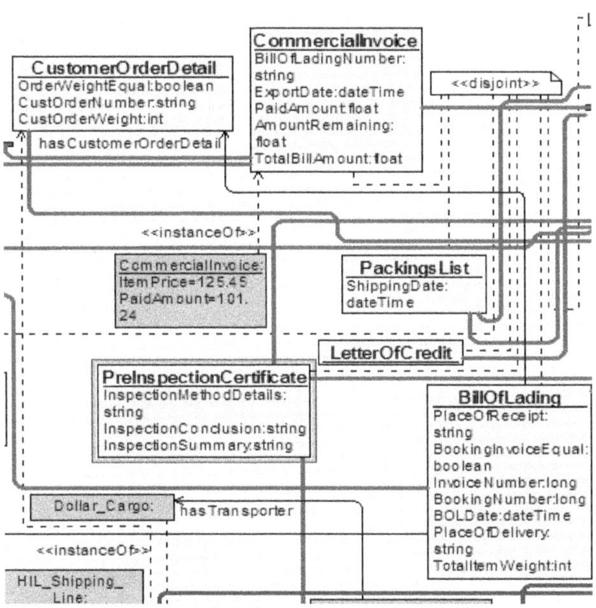

Figure 4. Metamodel and its instances for LoC Process

2). In addition to the above rules, there are internal validation rules that endorse the internal sanctity of these operational documents. These are shown by dotted arrows.

Fig. 3 shows the ontology for the entire set of documents that essentially captures the key concepts of International Trade. Some of the key entities in this ontology are Banks, Buyer, Seller, Transporter, Ordered Item, Customer Invoice, Shipping Detail, Customer Order Detail etc. Entities have typed properties that are either object types (e.g., *hasBank*) or data types (*hasName*). A subset of the metamodel and specific instances of documents (e.g., commercial invoice) for the International Trade domain is shown in Fig 4.

As mentioned earlier, the documents contain rules in natural language text that needs to be formally captured for automated reasoning. Table 1 shows a subset of 57 SWRL (semantic web rule language) rules [3] that we have manually constructed from the original textual description (see 2nd column of Table 1) present in the LoC and UCP 600 documents. Each rule has an antecedent and a consequent and has an abstract syntax similar to Horn-like rules.

So far we have been only able to address Challenge 1, which was critical to solve before attempting Challenge 2. To solve Challenge 2, we propose an overall architecture as described in Figs. 5 and 6 that enables the *dVaas* platform. Fig. 5 shows the more generic architecture than can be used by any document verification process. The architecture shows that there are generally two types of documents – a) principal documents that are instance specific and b) general guidelines, standard operating procedures that are instance independent. Both a) and b) contains rules, however, only rules contained in a) needs to be automatically extracted (machine learning techniques) whereas those in b) can be manually encoded as this is a one-time activity. Supporting or instance specific documents are then validated against the extracted rules (e.g., 3rd column of Table 1) by the processing engine. Although we do not describe in further details the internal steps, standard techniques such as parsing of natural language text to infer the grammatical units and then extracting binary relationship among entities in the text using ontology based scope expansion/restriction is used. However a major challenge is to extract appropriate class concepts necessary for assembling the rule bodies of SWRL rules.

Fig. 6 shows the specific architecture with respect to the given case study (i.e., International Trade). In the architecture, the fixed set of rules (as those present in UCP [2]) are manually encoded (one-time activity) and variable set of rules from LoC require natural language processing and machine learning techniques [1] for automated extraction. We believe that since there will be an abstraction gap between the named entities and relationship so extracted from the natural language text of LoC, a *semantic bridge* must be built as part of the extraction engine of Fig 6 to translate the named entities and corresponding relationship to a form closer to the rules domain (3rd column of Table 1). The semantic bridge infers information in terms of the key actors of a rule, its underlying objective, and what events it can raise to meet its desired goal. For example, for rule 1 in Table 1, the key actors are *BillOfLading*, *BookingNumber* and *InvoiceNumber*, its objective (consequent) is to verify whether booking and invoice number is equal (*BookingInvoiceEqual*), and it must raise an event called *equal to verify this objective*. Thus the semantic

Table 1. Translating textual rules to formal definition

	Textual description of the rule in LoC or UCP 600	Formal representation of the rule in SWRL
1.	Invoice number and the booking number mentioned in the Bill of Lading should match with each other.	*BillOfLading(?p), InvoiceNumber(?p, ?r), BookingNumber(?p, ?q), equal(?q, ?r) -> BookingInvoiceEqual(?p, true)*
2.	Description of the item in the Bill Of lading and the Commercial invoice should match with each other.	*BillOfLading(?p), equal(?r, ?s), ItemDescriptionBOL(?p, ?r), ItemDescriptionInvoice(?q, ?s), CommercialInvoice(?q) -> DescriptionConsistent(?p, true)*
3.	If the bill of lading indicates a place of receipt or taking in charge different from the port of loading, the on board notation must also include the port of loading stipulated in the Credit and the name of the vessel on which the goods have been loaded, even if they have been loaded on the vessel named in the bill of lading.	*1) BillOfLading(?p), PortOfLoading(?p, ?q), PlaceOfReceipt(?p, ?r), DifferentFrom (?q, ?r) -> placesEqual(?p, false)* *2) BillOfLading(?p), placesEqual(?p, false), LetterOfCredit(?q), PortOfLoading(?q, ?r), PlaceOfReceipt(?q, ?s), PortOfLoading(?p, ?t), PlaceOfReceipt(?p, ?u), equal(?r, ?u), equal(?t, ?s) -> ConditionalPlaceMentioned(?q, true)*
4.	If the item description is similar to the detrimental description given in UCP 600 document, don't approve the item.	*BillOfLading(?p), ItemDescriptionBOL(?p, ?q), 600(?r), DetrimentalDescription(?r,?s), containsIgnoreCase(?q, ?s) ->Approve(?p, false)*
5.	If partial shipments are prohibited, the invoice covers the complete shipment as required by the L/C or is within the 5% tolerance allowed by the UCP,	*LetterOfCredit(?p), tp2(?p, ?r), BillOfLading(?s), partialshipments(?p,false), TotalItemWeight(?s, ?t), greaterThanOrEqual(?r, ?t) -> WeightDiffincompleteShipmentOkay(?p, true)*

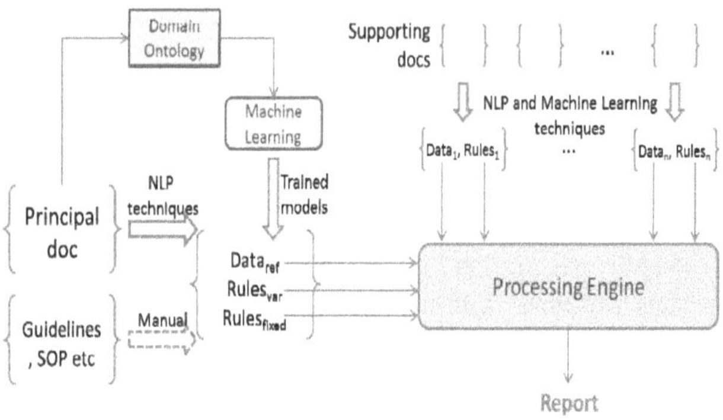

Figure 5. Generic architecture of document verification process

bridge helps to bridge the class concepts necessary to assemble the rule bodies. Just like behavior is extracted in the form of rules by the extraction engine, the model instances or individuals' needs to be extracted from the operational documents (see Fig. 6). A contextual parser is used verify the individual instances against the stored knowledge base (ontology) and finally both the rules and instances are fed into an ontology based processing/knowledge engine for formal verification.

An associated challenge in providing an automated solution towards *dVaaS* concerns with semantic equivalence of texts. Typically there are declarative statements present in multiple

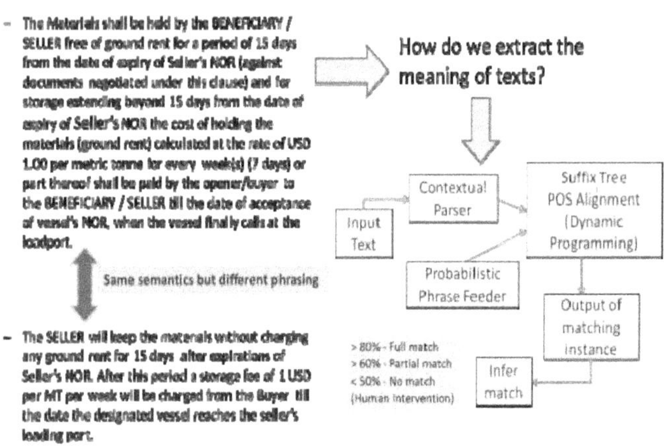

Figure 7. Semantic Equivalence in Text

documents that have different phrasings but same meaning. An example is shown in Fig. 7. In such cases, we propose to apply contextual probabilistic based semantic matching techniques so as to establish equivalence relationship between similar looking texts [4]. A contextual parser along with a probabilistic phrase feeder tries to establish relationship among subject and similarity analysis (text alignment) is carried out using suffix trees and dynamic programing techniques. Anything that matches below 50% is considered a no match and requires further manual intervention whereas anything that matches above 80% is considered a comprehensive match. Automatic semantic role labeling [5] is another useful technique that will be explored in the light of the above challenge.

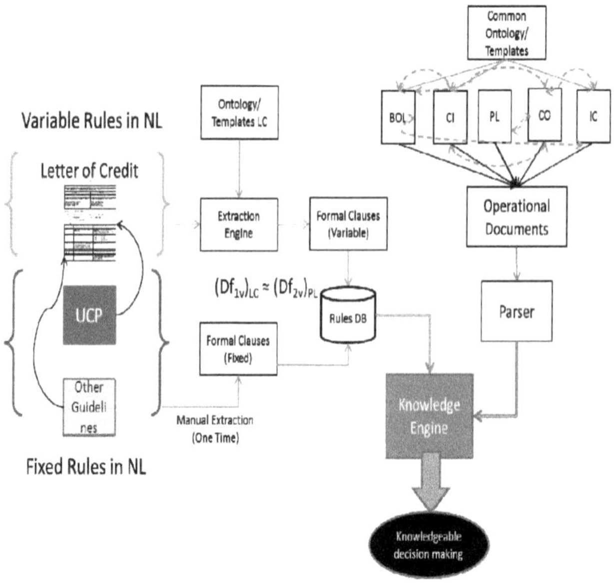

Figure 6. Specific architecture with respect to LoC

4. CONCLUSION AND FUTURE ROADMAP

This visionary short paper presents our initial line of attack towards analyzing document intensive business processes. The ideas presented are mainly focused on addressing Challenge 1 i.e., to create a suitable knowledge representation using ontology for a real life example from the financial domain - International Trade (LoC). However, the concepts developed are not just restricted to LoC but applicable to any other document intensive business processes. In addition, the operational behavior or semantics of the domain is captured using a rule language – SWRL. To address Challenge 2, we have proposed an architecture that uses supervised machine learning techniques with a core focus on semantic extraction of relationships to construct rules from natural language text. The idea presented in this paper is only a stepping stone towards realizing our broader vision of fully automated intelligent document verification (*dVaaS)* platform, which is largely unexplored within the scientific community.

5. REFERENCES

[1] Aggarwal, C. C., and Zhai, C., 2012. *Mining text data*, Springer, ISBN: 978-1-4614-3222-7.

[2] Rodrigo, T. , 2011. *UCP 500 to 600: a forward movement*. J. eLaw, Murdoch University, 18(2), pp. 1-21.

[3] Hassanpour, S., O'Connor, M. J., and Das, A. K., 2011. A framework for the automatic extraction of rules from online text. In *Proc. of the 5th Int. Symp. on Rules*, Barcelona, Spain, pp. 266-280.

[4] Hassanpour, S., O'Connor, M. J., and Das, A. K., 2013. A semantic-based method for extracting concept definitions from scientific publications: evaluation in the Autism Phenotype domain. *J. of Biomedical Semantics,* 4:14.

[5] Gildea, D., and Jurafsky, D., 2000. Automatic Labeling of Semantic Roles. In *Proc. of the 38th Annual Conference of the Association for Computational Linguistics (ACL-00)*, Hong Kong, pp. 512–520.

Transductive Domain Adaptation with Affinity Learning

Le Shu
Computer and Information Sciences
Temple University
1925 N. 12 St. Philadelphia, PA
le.shu@temple.edu

Longin Jan Latecki
Computer and Information Sciences
Temple University
1925 N. 12 St. Philadelphia, PA
latecki@temple.edu

ABSTRACT

We study the problem of domain adaptation, which aims to adapt the classifiers trained on a labeled source domain to an unlabeled target domain. We propose a novel method to solve domain adaptation task in a transductive setting. The proposed method bridges the distribution gap between source domain and target domain through affinity learning. It exploits the existence of a subset of data points in target domain which distribute similarly to the data points in the source domain. These data points act as the bridge that facilitates the data similarities propagation across domains. We also propose to control the relative importance of intra- and inter- domain similarities to boost the similarity propagation. In our approach, we first construct the similarity matrix which encodes both the intra- and inter- domain similarities. We then learn the true similarities among data points in joint manifold using graph diffusion. We demonstrate that with improved similarities between source and target data, spectral embedding provides a better data representation, which boosts the prediction accuracy. The effectiveness of our method is validated on standard benchmark datasets for visual object recognition (multi-category).

Categories and Subject Descriptors

H.4 [**Information Systems Applications**]: Miscellaneous; D.2.8 [**Software Engineering**]: Metrics—*complexity measures, performance measures*

Keywords

Domain Adaptation, Affinity Learning

1. INTRODUCTION

In recent years, domain adaptation has gained significant attention in many areas of applied machine learning, including bioinformatics, speech and language processing, computer vision etc. In these practical problems, given that the instances in the training and testing domains may be drawn from different distributions, traditional learning method can not achieve good performance on the new domain. Domain adaptation algorithms are therefore designed to bridge the distribution gap between training (source) data and testing (target) data. Domain adaptation methods seek to eliminate the difference between source and target distributions.

In this paper, we propose a transductive method to explicitly improve intra- and inter- domain similarities. Our contribution is two-fold: first, we perform affinity learning via graph diffusion to bridge the distribution gap of source and target domain. The key idea is to exploit the existence of a subset of data points in the target domain which distributes similarly to the data points in the source domain. We denote this subset of data points as Bridge Points (BP). Through graph diffusion, we propagate the similarities between BP and other data points in the target domain, as well as the similarities between BP and data points in the source domain. Affinity learning is able to give robust pairwise similarities of data points, since all paths between all pairs of data points are considered. In this way, affinity learning can bridge distribution gap of source and target domain. As our experimental results clearly demonstrate, our assumption that part of the target data is similar to part of the source data is often satisfied by real world data sets. Figure 1 illustrates our motivation. Our second contribution is to adjust the intra- and inter- domain similarities. The intuition is that data points in the same domain are often more similar to each other than to those in different domain. In graph diffusion process, this makes the similarity propagation from data points in source domain to data points in target domain ineffective. Therefore, the proposed adjustment of the intra- and inter- domain similarities is a key step in making the affinity propagation successful. We balance the intra- and inter- domain edges by picking equal number of nearest neighbors in source and target domain for each data point and also re-weight intra- and inter- domain edges.

In summary, given the similarity matrix of source and target data, the procedure of our framework includes the following key steps: 1) Similarity Adjustment: re-weight intra- and inter- domain similarities. 2) Affinity Learning: iteratively learn similarities in joint geometric structure via Tensor Product Graph Diffusion (TPGD)[18]. 3) Spectral Embedding: apply spectral embedding on diffusion matrix to get a low-dimensional representation. In this paper, we use Tensor Product Graph Diffusion(TPGD) [18] to capture the joint manifold structure for the source and target domain. As demonstrated in [18], TPGD can robustly discover

Permission to make digital or hard copies of all or part of this work for personal or classroom use is granted without fee provided that copies are not made or distributed for profit or commercial advantage and that copies bear this notice and the full citation on the first page. Copyrights for components of this work owned by others than ACM must be honored. Abstracting with credit is permitted. To copy otherwise, or republish, to post on servers or to redistribute to lists, requires prior specific permission and/or a fee. Request permissions from Permissions@acm.org.
CIKM '15, October 19-23, 2015, Melbourne, VIC, Australia
©2015 ACM ISBN 978-1-4503-3794-6/15/10$15.00
DOI: http://dx.doi.org/10.1145/2806416.2806643.

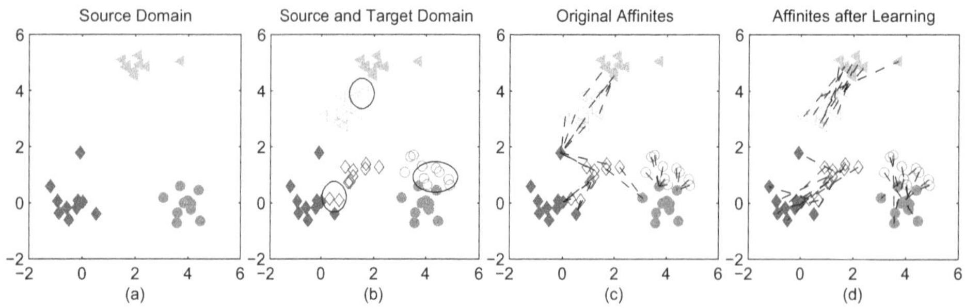

Figure 1: Schematic illustration of utilizing affinity learning for unsupervised domain adaptation. (a) Data points in source domain. Each color represents one class. (b) Data points in source and target domains. Solid shapes represent the data points in the source domain, hollow shapes represent the data points in the target domain. Black circles mark the Bridge Points, which is subset of data instances in the target domain and have similar distribution as data instances in the source domain. (c) The lines connect points in the target domain to their nearest neighbors in the source domain with the original similarities. (d) The lines connect points in the target domain to their nearest neighbors in the source domain after the affinity learning.

the true, underlying manifold structure in image retrieval. We utilize TPGD to learn joint geometric structure in the context of domain adaptation when training and testing are drawn from different distributions.

The rest of the paper is organized as follows. We first give a brief review of related works in Section 2. In Section 3, we describe the proposed affinity learning for domain adaptation task. In particular, we describe how to construct the transition probability matrix with similarity adjustment. We also show how to perform graph diffusion on a tensor product graph to obtain robust similarities. In Section 4, we present our experimental results on benchmark datasets and compare it to several state-of-the-art methods. Finally, we come to the conclusion is in Section 5.

2. RELATED WORK

Domain adaptation has been extensively studied in many research areas [13, 8, 2, 19]. Domain adaptation can be categorized into three types. The first type are self-labeling approaches, which include self-training [14] and co-training [2]. The second type of algorithms proposes to weight or select training instances to minimize the discrepancy distance [7, 9]. Our work belongs to the third type, which aims at finding "good" feature representations to minimize domain divergence and classification error, such as [1, 5, 12]. In particular, for object recognition application in computer vision, many works have been proposed to learn new feature representation, such as [11, 16, 4]. Compared to existing approaches, our method focus on affinity learning to bridge the distribution gap between source and target domain.

While our work share some common components compared to graph-based semi-supervised method, such as [20] where graph is used to propagate labels, the key difference is that we aim to solve the domain adaptation problem and our goal is to use affinity learning to improve the noisy pairwise similarities due to domain shift. That motivates us to reweight the inter- and intra- domain edges, and use spectral embedding to obtain the low dimensional domain-invariant data representation.

There are also several works attempting to solve transfer learning in a transductive setting [15, 10, 3]. They apply label propagation to zero-shot and few-shot learning based on attribute graph or semantic graph. [17] exploits the mixture distribution to refine the classification labels. These work did not try to improve pair-wise similarities.

3. PROPOSED APPROACH

We assume that our data originate from two domains, Source (S) and Target (T). Source data $D_S = \{(x_S^1, y_S^1), (x_S^2, y_S^2), \cdots, (x_S^{N_S}, y_S^{N_S})\}$ is fully labeled, each pair (x_S^i, y_S^i) lies in $R^d \times y$ space. The source data are sampled from some distribution $P_S(X, Y)$. The target data has equal dimension d as the source data but is sampled from a different distribution $P_T(X, Y)$. We denote the target data as $D_T = \{(x_T^1, ?), (x_T^2, ?), \cdots, (x_T^{N_T}, ?)\}$, whose labels are unknown. Given D_S and D_T, our goal is to infer the class labels of data points in D_T.

In the rest of this section, we first describe how to construct the transition matrix P for source and target data jointly. We then iteratively learn the joint geometric structure and capture true similarities among data points in source and target domain. After we get the diffusion matrix, we compute the Laplacian graph and solve the smallest K eigenvectors to obtain a new feature representation of data points in source domain and target domain. After that, any classification approach can be adopted to predict labels for target data. In this work, we choose SVM classifier with linear kernel.

3.1 Cross-domain Graph Construction

The goal of this section is to construct the transition matrix of a graph G whose nodes consist of data points in both source and target domain. We use P_{SS} and P_{TT} to denote the transition probability matrices of data points in the source and target domains respectively. P_{ST} and P_{TS} denote the transition probability matrix of data points across domains. We construct the overall transition matrix as follows:

$$P = \begin{bmatrix} \beta P_{SS} & (1-\beta)P_{ST} \\ (1-\beta)P_{TS} & \beta P_{TT} \end{bmatrix} \quad (1)$$

where β controls the relative importance of the intra- and the inter- domain transition probabilities and $\beta \in [0, 1]$. Empirically, β can be set by solving $\frac{\beta}{1-\beta} = \frac{2N_S N_T}{N_S^2 + N_T^2}$, which calibrates the average inter- and intra- domain edge weights to be close.

P_{SS} and P_{TT} are row-wise normalized similarity matrices which are computed as:

$$P_{SS} = D_{SS}^{-1} A_{SS} \quad P_{TT} = D_{TT}^{-1} A_{TT} \quad (2)$$

where A_{SS} is the similarity matrix of data points in source domain and A_{TT} encodes the similarities between data points in target domain. D_{SS} and D_{TT} are the diagonal matrices of the row sums of A_{SS} and A_{TT}.

To compute A_{SS}, we take advantage of the available labels of source data, and define "closeness" in a supervised manner, i.e., nodes i and j are connected if x_i and x_j share the same label. The similarity matrix A_{SS} is defined as follows:

$$A_{SS}(i,j) = \begin{cases} \frac{x_S^j \cdot x_S^i}{\|x_S^j\| \cdot \|x_S^i\|} & \text{if } x_S^i \text{ and } x_S^j \text{ share the same label} \\ & \text{and } x_S^i \in N_p(x_S^j) \text{ or } x_S^j \in N_p(x_S^i) \\ 0 & \text{otherwise.} \end{cases}, \quad (3)$$

Here, we use N_p to denote the p nearest neighbors. In the source domain, the label information is embedded into the similarity matrix. While we compute the similarity matrix A_{SS} with the cosine similarity measure, other similarity measures may also be applicable.

To compute A_{TT}, since the labels of target data are not available, we define "closeness" in an unsupervised manner, i.e., nodes i and j are connected if i is among p nearest neighbors of j or j is among p nearest neighbors of i. Formally, we have:

$$A_{TT}(i,j) = \begin{cases} \frac{x_T^j \cdot x_T^i}{\|x_T^j\| \cdot \|x_T^i\|} & \text{if } x_T^i \in N_p(x_T^j) \text{ or } x_T^j \in N_p(x_T^i) \\ 0 & \text{otherwise.} \end{cases}, \quad (4)$$

where $N_p(x_T^i)$ is the set of p nearest neighbors of x_T^i.

Similarly cross-domain transition probability matrices P_{ST} and P_{TS} are computed as follows:

$$P_{ST} = D_{ST}^{-1} A_{ST} \quad P_{TS} = D_{TS}^{-1} A_{TS} \quad (5)$$

where A_{ST} denotes the cross-domain similarities. D_{ST} and D_{TS} are the diagonal matrices of the row sums of A_{ST} and A_{TS}. A_{ST} is computed as follows:

$$A_{ST}(i,j) = \begin{cases} \frac{x_S^i \cdot x_T^j}{\|x_S^i\| \cdot \|x_T^j\|} & \text{if } x_S^i \in N_p(x_T^j) \text{ or } x_T^j \in N_p(x_S^i) \\ 0 & \text{otherwise.} \end{cases}, \quad (6)$$

To summarize, we introduce two major differences in the transition matrix construction process which are tailored for unsupervised domain adaptation task: First, we add supervised information to the similarity matrix A_{SS} to remove noisy entries in A_{SS}. Second, we control the relative importance of intra-domain and inter-domain transition probabilities. When building KNN connected graph, we balance the intra- and inter- domain edges by picking equal number of nearest neighbors in source and target domain for each data point. We also perform a reweighting on the intra- and inter-domain similarities. As demonstrated by our experiments in Section 4.1, these two steps greatly boost the performance of affinity learning which results in a better data representation, and therefore a higher prediction accuracy.

3.2 Diffusion Process on Tensor Product Graph

In this section we review tensor product graph diffusion process introduced in [18]. Given the edge (transition probability matrix) P, we define $Q^{(1)} = P$ and

$$Q^{(t+1)} = P\, Q^{(t)}\, P^T + I, \quad (7)$$

where I is the identity matrix. We iterate (7) until convergence. Let us denote the limit matrix by $Q^* = \lim_{t\to\infty} Q^{(t)}$. A closed form expression for Q^* is as follows:

$$\lim_{t\to\infty} Q^{(t)} = Q^* = P^* = \text{vec}^{-1}(\sum_{i=0}^{t} \mathbb{P}^i)\ \text{vec}(I)). \quad (8)$$

The proof of the convergence of (7) and closed form equation can be found in [18], where $\mathbb{P}$ is the tensor product of P with itself. Since $Q^* = P^*$, we obtain that the iterative algorithm on Q defined by (7) yields the same similarities as the TPG diffusion process on $\mathbb{P}$ for a sufficient number of iterations.

4. EMPIRICAL STUDY

In this section, we present our experimental results on visual object recognition tasks. We set K and p in our method through cross-validation based on classification error of data samples in source domains. We first compare to the baseline approach and evaluate the performance gain at each step and give detailed analysis. This provides clear insight about the merits of the proposed method. Our results on benchmark datasets are also favorable when compared to several state-of-the-art domain adaptation methods.

We perform experiments using 4 object recognition datasets, which includes: Amazon, Webcam, DSLR. These three datasets are first introduced in [16]. Additionally, we use Caltech-256 in [6] as the fourth dataset to further evaluate the proposed methods. Each dataset is treated as a domain and 10 common object categories are extracted. We downloaded the processed datasets with SURF features from [5]. We conduct each experiment using every pair of source and target dataset. We report the recognition accuracy on every pair of source and target dataset.

4.1 Performance Analysis

As the baseline approach, we adopt the original features and train a linear SVM model on source domain. To illustrate the significance of performance gain using affinity learning to facilitate domain adaptation, we study four variants of our method. In the first variant, we apply spectral embedding directly to the original similarity matrix. In the second variant, we add intra- and inter- domain similarities reweighting before applying spectral embedding. In the third variant, we apply graph diffusion to the original similarity matrix before applying spectral embedding. In the final variant, we put all components together which is the proposed approach.

We compare the recognition accuracy of the baseline approach and the 4 variants in Tabel 1. We can see that low-dimensional feature representation obtained by spectral embedding can preserve most of the information for each dataset, whose accuracy is comparable to the baseline, but with no improvement. If we adjust intra- and inter- domain similarities and apply spectral embedding, the average recognition accuracy improves 7.5% compared to that of the baseline. If we apply affinity learning and spectral embedding together, the average recognition accuracy improves 4.6% compared to that of the baseline. If we combine adjusting intra- and inter- domain similarities and affinity learning through graph diffusion, the performance improves 10.0% compared to that of the baseline method. Overall, these results demonstrate that adjusting intra- and inter-domain similarities can facilitate the affinity learning, and affinity learning can provide more reliable affinities for data points in joint manifold.

Table 1: Recognition Accuracy on 8 pairs of datasets, where: C : Caltech, A : Amazon, W : Webcam, D : DSLR. SE: spectral embedding; SA: similarity adjustment; TPGD: tensor product graph diffusion; Our Method = SA+TPGD+SE.

%	A-D	A-W	D-A	D-W	W-A	W-C	C-D	C-W	Average
Baseline	40.8	41.7	32.3	73.6	34.1	29.9	42.0	40.7	41.9
SE	40.1	40.7	34.4	66.4	35.7	28.7	47.1	43.7	42.1
SA + SE	45.8	44.4	41.1	89.5	38.7	35.0	52.8	49.1	49.6
TPGD + SE	43.9	41.0	34.8	74.9	**39.8**	35.2	54.1	48.5	46.5
Our Method	**50.3**	**49.0**	**40.5**	**92.2**	39.7	**36.8**	**55.4**	**52.9**	**52.1**

Table 2: Recognition Accuracy on 8 pairs of datasets, where C : Caltech, A : Amazon, W : Webcam, D : DSLR.

%	A-D	A-W	D-A	D-W	W-A	W-C	C-D	C-W
Baseline	40.8	41.7	32.3	73.6	34.1	29.9	42.0	40.7
TCA[12]	36.3	27.8	28.7	82.0	24.2	22.5	45.2	32.5
KMM[7]	42.7	42.4	36.0	83.0	31.9	29.0	53.5	45.8
GFK[5]	42.7	40.7	36.2	76.3	31.8	30.9	43.3	44.7
LandMark[4]	47.1	46.1	33.4	78.0	**40.2**	35.4	**57.3**	49.5
Our Method	**50.3**	**49.0**	**40.5**	**92.2**	39.7	**36.8**	55.4	**52.9**

4.2 Comparison with State-of-the-art Methods

We compare the proposed method to several state-of-the-art methods: KMM [7], TCA [12], GFK [5], LandMark [4]. Table 2 summarizes accuracy of object recognition on 8 pairs of source and target domains obtained from the four datasets. For the compared methods, most results are quoted from [4], except for D-A and D-W which we generated using the code downloaded from authors' websites. The average recognition accuracy of our method improves 3.7% when compared to that of the second best method 'LandMark'. Our method performs the best on 6 out of 8 pairs of domains.

5. CONCLUSIONS

We propose a novel transductive domain adaptation method. Empirical results clearly demonstrate that it outperforms state-of-the-art methods.

6. ACKNOWLEDGMENTS

This work was in part supported by NSF under Grants OIA-1027897 and IIS-1302164.

7. REFERENCES

[1] John Blitzer, Ryan T. McDonald, and Fernando Pereira. Domain adaptation with structural correspondence learning. In *EMNLP*, 2006.

[2] Minmin Chen, Kilian Q. Weinberger, and John Blitzer. Co-training for domain adaptation. In *NIPS*, pages 2456–2464, 2011.

[3] Yanwei Fu, Timothy M. Hospedales, Tao Xiang, Zhen-Yong Fu, and Shaogang Gong. Transductive multi-view embedding for zero-shot recognition and annotation. In *ECCV*, pages 584–599, 2014.

[4] Boqing Gong, Kristen Grauman, and Fei Sha. Connecting the dots with landmarks: Discriminatively learning domain-invariant features for unsupervised domain adaptation. In *ICML*, pages 222–230, 2013.

[5] Boqing Gong, Yuan Shi, Fei Sha, and Kristen Grauman. Geodesic flow kernel for unsupervised domain adaptation. In *CVPR*, pages 2066–2073, 2012.

[6] G. Griffin, A. Holub, and P. Perona. Caltech-256 object category dataset. Technical Report 7694, California Institute of Technology, 2007.

[7] Jiayuan Huang, Alexander J. Smola, Arthur Gretton, Karsten M. Borgwardt, and Bernhard Schölkopf. Correcting sample selection bias by unlabeled data. In *NIPS*, pages 601–608, 2006.

[8] Hal Daumé III. Frustratingly easy domain adaptation. In *ACL*, 2007.

[9] Jing Jiang and ChengXiang Zhai. Instance weighting for domain adaptation in nlp. In *ACL*, 2007.

[10] Yu-Gang Jiang, Jun Wang, Shih-Fu Chang, and Chong-Wah Ngo. Domain adaptive semantic diffusion for large scale context-based video annotation. In *ICCV*, pages 1420–1427, 2009.

[11] Brian Kulis, Kate Saenko, and Trevor Darrell. What you saw is not what you get: Domain adaptation using asymmetric kernel transforms. In *CVPR*, 2011.

[12] Sinno Jialin Pan, Ivor W. Tsang, James T. Kwok, and Qiang Yang. Domain adaptation via transfer component analysis. In *IJCAI*, pages 1187–1192, 2009.

[13] Sinno Jialin Pan and Qiang Yang. A survey on transfer learning. *IEEE Trans. Knowl. Data Eng.*, 22(10):1345–1359, 2010.

[14] Rajat Raina, Alexis Battle, Honglak Lee, Benjamin Packer, and Andrew Y. Ng. Self-taught learning: transfer learning from unlabeled data. In *ICML*, 2007.

[15] Marcus Rohrbach, Sandra Ebert, and Bernt Schiele. Transfer learning in a transductive setting. In *NIPS*, pages 46–54, 2013.

[16] Kate Saenko, Brian Kulis, Mario Fritz, and Trevor Darrell. Adapting visual category models to new domains. In *ECCV*, 2010.

[17] Dikan Xing, Wenyuan Dai, Gui-Rong Xue, and Yong Yu. Bridged refinement for transfer learning. In *PKDD*, pages 324–335, 2007.

[18] Xingwei Yang, Lakshman Prasad, and Longin Jan Latecki. Affinity learning with diffusion on tensor product graph. *IEEE Trans. Pattern Anal. Mach. Intell.*, 35(1):28–38, 2013.

[19] Chao Zhang, Lei Zhang, Wei Fan, and Jieping Ye. Generalization bounds for representative domain adaptation. *CoRR*, abs/1401.0376, 2014.

[20] Xiaojin Zhu, Zoubin Ghahramani, and John D. Lafferty. Semi-supervised learning using gaussian fields and harmonic functions. In *ICML*, 2003.

Update Summarization using Semi-Supervised Learning Based on Hellinger Distance

Dingding Wang
Department of Computer & Electrical Engineering and Computer Science
Florida Atlantic University
777 Glades Road
Boca Raton, FL 33431
wangd@fau.edu

Sahar Sohangir
Department of Computer & Electrical Engineering and Computer Science
Florida Atlantic University
777 Glades Road
Boca Raton, FL 33431
ssohangir2014@fau.edu

Tao Li
School of Computing and Information Sciences
Florida International University
11200 SW 8 Street
Miami, FL 33199
taoli@cs.fiu.edu

ABSTRACT

Update summarization aims to generate brief summaries of recent documents to capture new information different from earlier documents. In this paper, we propose a new method to generate the sentence similarity graph using a novel similarity measure based on Helliger distance and apply semi-supervised learning on the sentence graph to select the sentences with maximum consistency and minimum redundancy to form the summaries. We use TAC 2011 data to evaluate our proposed method and compare it with existing baselines. The experimental results show the effectiveness of our proposed method.

Categories and Subject Descriptors

H.3.3 [**Information Storage and Retrieval**]: Information Search and Retrieval

Keywords

Update Summarization; Semi-Supervised Learning; Hellinger Distance

1. INTRODUCTION

Popular online publishers and social media users produce huge amount of text data every day, so it is critical to extract the most important and up-to-date information to help users quickly understand these documents. Thus update document summarization has been receiving more and more attention, which aims to generate a query-relevant summary of multiple articles, under the assumption that the user has already read the earlier articles. Update summarization provides a useful way to make users stay in the know of developing and evolving events. For example, in the event of the spread of the Ebola virus in 2014, the earlier articles reported the Ebola outbreak in West Africa, then there was news about the infected cases found in Europe and the US, and later reports showed that no new cases was diagnosed in the US after December 2014. In this event, since people highly concerned about the development of disease control, a timely updated event summary will help people understand the situation quickly and conveniently.

The problem of update summarization was introduced in Document Understanding Conference (DUC) by National Institute of Standards and Technology (NIST) in 2007 and was a main task of the summarization track in Text Analysis Conference (TAC) through 2008 $\sim$ 2011. Given a topic q, it is required to summarize a set of document B under the assumption that the reader has already read and summarized an earlier set of documents A. Both the summaries of document sets A and B should focus on the given topic and the summary of B must be the least redundant with the summary of A.

The existing research on update summarization mainly focuses on query-relevant sentence ranking, graph optimization, and model-based analysis using cosine similarity [12]. For example, Boudin et al. [1] used Maximal Marginal Relevance (MMR) to rank the sentences and selected the top-ranked sentences to form the summaries. Delort et al. [2] proposed a topic model to identify the novelty in the document collection. Shen et al. [11] applied a minimum dominating set approximation to find the most important sentences on the sentence similarity graph. Wan [15] proposed a co-ranking algorithm to solve the problem. Li et al. [6] proposed a complex three-level hierarchical dirichlet process model to select sentences. Wang et al. [16] proposed an incremental hierarchical clustering based summarization approach to update summaries in real time.

In this paper, we propose a new similarity measure which is based on Hellinger distance to better capture the sentence relationships than the Euclidean distance based cosine similarity. We apply the MMR strategy to generate the summary for the earlier document set, and then propose a label propagation approach using the Green's function to determine the sentence importance in the later document set. The redundancy in the update summary is also eliminated in the final selection procedures. In the experiments, we use TAC 2011 dataset to evaluate the proposed method and compare the results with existing update summarization systems.

Permission to make digital or hard copies of all or part of this work for personal or classroom use is granted without fee provided that copies are not made or distributed for profit or commercial advantage and that copies bear this notice and the full citation on the first page. Copyrights for components of this work owned by others than ACM must be honored. Abstracting with credit is permitted. To copy otherwise, or republish, to post on servers or to redistribute to lists, requires prior specific permission and/or a fee. Request permissions from Permissions@acm.org.
CIKM'15, October 19–23, 2015, Melbourne, Australia.
© 2015 ACM. ISBN 978-1-4503-3794-6/15/10 ...$15.00.
DOI: http://dx.doi.org/10.1145/2806416.2806628.

2. THE PROPOSED METHODOLOGIES

2.1 Hellinger Distance Based Similarity Calculation

In IR, each document is represented by a nonnegative vector: $x = (x_1, x_2, \ldots, x_m)^T$ where x_t relates to the frequency of term t in the document and m is the size of the vocabulary. Because x is nonnegative, we may review them as probability and normalize each document to $\sum_{i=1}^m x_i = 1$.

One of the most widely used similarities between two documents x and y is the cosine similarity, which can be directly derived from Euclidean distance as follows. Assuming each document is normalized to 1 in L_2 norm: $\sum_{i=1}^m x_i^2 = 1$. The Euclidean distance between x and y is

$$d_{\text{Euclid}}(x, y) = \Big[\sum_i (x_i - y_i)^2\Big]^{\frac{1}{2}} = \Big[2 - 2\sum_i x_i y_i\Big]^{\frac{1}{2}} \quad (1)$$

The constant 2 here is unimportant. From Eq.(1), the Euclidean distance corresponds directly to the cosine similarity in Eq.(2).

$$\cos(x, y) = \frac{\sum_{i=1}^m x_i y_i}{\sqrt{\sum_{i=1}^m x_i^2}\sqrt{\sum_{i=1}^m y_i^2}}. \quad (2)$$

Since the word-document associations are nonnegative, it is expected that they are better treated with probabilistic approaches. However Euclidean distance is generally not a good metric for dealing with probabilities. Thus in this paper, we propose a new similarity, the square-root cosine (sqrt-cos) similarity, based on Hellinger distance which is more appropriate for solving IR problems such as measuring query relevance.

The hellinger distance between probabilities x and y is defined as follows.

$$H(x, y) = \Big[\sum_i^m (\sqrt{x}_i - \sqrt{y}_i)^2\Big]^{\frac{1}{2}} = \Big[2 - 2\sum_i^m \sqrt{x_i y_i}\Big]^{\frac{1}{2}}, \quad (3)$$

since $\sum_i x_i = 1$ and $\sum_i y_i = 1$.

Hellinger distance has two important properties which makes it a better distance measure in IR tasks. (a.) It is a metric because it is symmetric and satisfies triangle inequality:

$$H(x, y) = H(y, x), \; H(x, z) \leq H(x, y) + H(y, z).$$

(b.) Helinger distance relates closely to the widely used KL divergence (also called information gain, or relative entropy)

$$\text{KL}(x, y) = \sum_i^m x_i \log\frac{x_i}{y_i} \quad (4)$$

They are special cases of the α-distance between two probability distributions [4, 9]

$$D_\alpha(x, y) = \frac{1}{\alpha(1-\alpha)}\sum_{i=1}^m \Big[x_i^\alpha y_i^{1-\alpha} - \alpha x_i + (\alpha - 1) y_i\Big] \quad (5)$$

Helinger distance is a special case at $\alpha = 1/2$:

$$H(x, y) = \sqrt{\frac{1}{2} D_{\frac{1}{2}}(x, y)}.$$

while the KL divergence is the case at

$$D_1(x, y) \;=\; \lim_{\alpha \to 1} D_\alpha(x, y) = \text{KL}(x, y),$$

$$D_0(x, y) \;=\; \lim_{\alpha \to 0} D_\alpha(x, y) = \text{KL}(y, x). \quad (6)$$

Therefore, Hellinger distance can be viewed as the symmetric middle point of KL divergence.

Assuming each document is normalized to 1 in L_1 norm: $\sum_{i=1}^m x_i = 1$, the Hellinger distance leads naturally to the SqrtCos similarty in Eq.(7).

$$\text{SqrtCos}(x, y) = \frac{\sum_{i=1}^m \sqrt{x_i y_i}}{(\sum_{i=1}^m x_i)(\sum_{i=1}^m y_i)}. \quad (7)$$

In recent research, there is a trend in IR is to use binary weighting instead of the traditional term frequency (**tf_idf**). We point out that Hellinger distance and SqrtCos similarity bridge between these two (extreme) situations. For example, if the frequency of word A is 4 and the frequency of word B is 1, in **tf_idf** weighting their relative importance is 4:1. In binary weighting, their relative importance is 1:1. In Hellinger distance, their relative importance is $\sqrt{4} : 1$. Therefore, Hellinger distance can be alternatively viewed as a compromise between tf_idf and binary weighting.

In order to utilize the advantages of Hellinger distance as discussed above, in this paper we use SqrtCos to calculate the pairwise sentence similarity to generate summaries for both the earlier document set A and the later coming set B.

2.2 Generating the Query-Relevant Summary for Document Set A using revised MMR

In order to summarize document set A, we revise Maximal Marginal Relevance (MMR) which has been successfully applied in query-relevant multi-document summarization systems in the following two ways: (1) The proposed SqrtCos similarity based on Hellinger distance will be used as the similarity measure. (2) The average similarity is used to determine the redundancy between a candidate sentence and the selected sentences. We use the average similarity instead of the maximum similarity in the original MMR for document summarization because we prefer to exclude sentences which are similar to more than one sentences in the selected sentence set.

Thus the respective incremental algorithm optimizes the following condition:

$$\max_{x_j \in A - S_{m-1}} [SqrtCos(x_j; q) - \frac{1}{m-1}\sum_{x_i \in S_{m-1}} SqrtCos(x_j; x_i)], \quad (8)$$

where S_{m-1} is current selected sentence set containing $m-1$ sentences, x_i is a sentence in S, and x_j is the candidate for the $m-th$ sentence to be selected.

2.3 Generating Update Summaries for Document Set B

Once we have the selected sentences from document set A, we can construct a sentence graph based on the pair wise SqrtCos similarities among sentences in A and B as shown in Figure 1. The sentences from A are labeled as 1 to represent sentences in the summary of A and 0 to represent sentences not selected. The question marks represents the sentence labels to be assigned in document set B. Once the sentence graph is constructed, the sentence selection problem can be treated as a label propagation from labeled data (i.e., sentences in A) to unlabeled data (i.e., sentences in B). In its simplest form, label propagation is like a random walk on

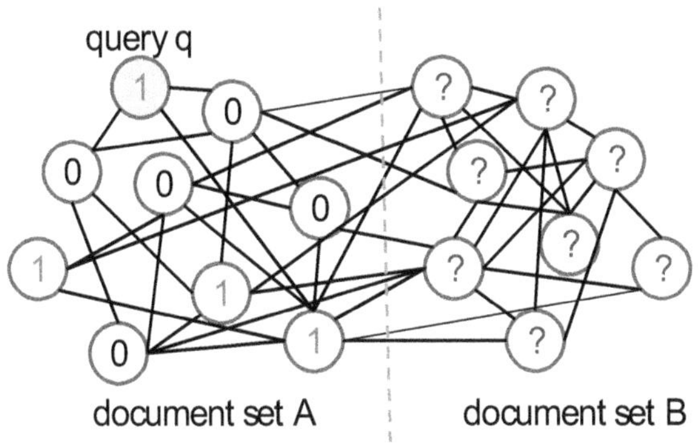

Figure 1: Label Propagation on Sentence Similarity Graph.

a graph [14]. There are different approaches to solve label propagation problems including using the diffusion kernel [5, 13], the harmonic nature of the diffusive function, etc. In this paper, in order to keep the coherency and consistency of the generated summaries, we emphasize the global and coherent nature of label propagation and apply the Green's function of the Laplace operator to solve the problem [3, 10].

2.3.1 Label Propagation using Green's Function

Given a graph with edge weights W, the *combinatorial Laplacian* is defined to be $L = D - W$, where D is the diagonal matrix consisting of the row sums of W; i.e., $D = \text{diag}(W\mathbf{e})$, $\mathbf{e} = (1 \cdots 1)^T$. Green's function for a generic graph is defined as the inverse of $L = D - W$. We construct Green's function using eigenvectors of L:

$$L\mathbf{v}_k = \lambda_k \mathbf{v}_k, \ \mathbf{v}_p^T \mathbf{v}_q = \delta_{pq}, \tag{9}$$

where $\mathbf{v}_1, \ldots, \mathbf{v}_n$ are the eigenvectors of L, $\lambda_1, \ldots, \lambda_n$ the eigenvalues of L, such that $0 = \lambda_1 \leq \lambda_2 \leq \cdots \leq \lambda_n$ and such that the inner product of $\mathbf{v}_i$ and $\mathbf{v}_j$ is 1 if $i = j$ and 0 otherwise. We assume the graph is connected (otherwise we deal with each connected component one at a time). The first eigenvector is a constant vector $\mathbf{v}_1 = \mathbf{e}/\sqrt{n}$ whose associated eigenvalue is 1. After discarding this zero-mode, Green's function is defined as the positive definite part of L

$$G^{(1)} = L_+^{-1} = \frac{1}{(D-W)_+} = \sum_{i=2}^{n} \frac{\mathbf{v}_i \mathbf{v}_i^T}{\lambda_i}. \tag{10}$$

Note that Green's function can also be defined on the generalized eigenvectors of the Laplacian matrix:

$$L\mathbf{u}_k = \zeta_k D\mathbf{u}_k, \ \mathbf{u}_p^T D\mathbf{u}_q = \mathbf{z}_p^T \mathbf{z}_q = \delta_{pq}. \tag{11}$$

where $0 = \zeta_1 \leq \zeta_2 \leq \cdots \leq \zeta_n$ are the eigenvalues and the zero-mode is again the first eigenvector $\mathbf{u}_1 = \mathbf{e}/\sqrt{n}$. Then we have

$$G^{(2)} = \frac{1}{(D-W)_+} = \sum_{k=2}^{n} \frac{\mathbf{u}_k \mathbf{u}_k^T}{\zeta_k}. \tag{12}$$

2.3.2 Sentence Selection Procedures

In our sentence graph, edge weights W represent the pairwise SqrtCos similarities among topic q, sentences in document sets A and B. The sentence selection problem is illustrated in Figure 1. Let y_0 represent the partial labels obtained from document set A, we compute the complete labels as the linear influence propagation:

$$y = Gy_0, \tag{13}$$

where G is the Green's function built from the constructed sentence graph.

Once we obtain the sentence labels, we only keep the sentences with label "1" in document set B which indicates the sentences are relevant to the given topic and contents in the earlier document set. If the total length of the sentences labeled to be "1" is longer than the required summary length, we will eliminate sentences which are most similar to the sentences in the summary of A and least similar to the sentences in B and the given query.

3. EXPERIMENTS

3.1 Data Set

In the experiments, we use TAC 2011 update summarization dataset for evaluating our method and comparing it with existing methods. In this dataset, there are 44 topics and for each topic there are 10 newswire articles in both document set A and B (representing the earlier collection of documents and the later documents respectively). A list of aspects for each topic is given and the task requires to generate a 100-word summary for both document set A and B. When generating the summary for document set B, the assumption is that the user has already read the earlier articles. Summaries generated by human labelers are provided in this task for evaluation.

3.2 Evaluation Measures

In the evaluation, we will compare the results by different methods with the human created summaries using Rouge toolkit (version 1.5.5) [7]. it is widely applied by Document Understanding Conference(DUC) and TAC for document summarization performance evaluation. It measures the quality of a summary by counting the unit overlaps between the candidate summary and a set of reference summaries. Several automatic evaluation methods are implemented in ROUGE, such as ROUGE-N, ROUGE-L, ROUGE-W and ROUGE-SU. ROUGE-N is an n-gram recall ROUGE-L uses the longest common subsequence (LCS) statistics, while ROUGE-W is based on weighted LCS and ROUGE-SU is based on skip-bigram plus unigram. Intuitively, the higher the ROUGE scores, the more similar the two summaries.

3.3 Baselines

In the experiments, we use the following widely used update summarization methods as the baselines.

- Lead: The method selects the leading sentences in the documents to form the summary until its length reaches the required length.

- Centroid: The method applies the MEAD algorithm [8] to extract sentences according to the following three parameters: centroid value, positional value, and first sentence overlap. Both Lead and Centroid are standard methods provided by NIST.

- MMR: The method uses MMR like criterion to select sentences and at the same time reduce the redundancy among the selected sentences [1].
- CoRank: The method proposes a co-ranking process to rank sentences based on predefined update and consistency scores [15].
- DomSet: The method uses minimum dominating set to select sentences [11].

3.4 Experimental Results

Table 1 shows the Rouge scores of our method and the baseline methods using TAC 2011 data.

Methods	Rouge-1	Rouge-2	Rouge-SU
Lead	0.294	0.057	0.094
Centroid	0.283	0.059	0.091
MMR	0.347	0.075	0.115
CoRank	0.368	0.088	0.127
DomSet	0.359	0.083	0.120
Our Method	0.373	0.091	0.136

Table 1: Update summarization performance comparison on TAC 2011 data using ROUGE evaluation methods.

From the results, we have the following observations. (1) The original MMR outperforms the baselines with straightforward strategies such as Lead and Centroid. It is because MMR maximizes the relevance of the selected sentences with the topic and also reduces the redundancy among the sentences. (2) More advanced ranking methods like CoRank and graph-based methods like DomSet outperform MMR because they either take into consideration the consistency or utilize the overall relationships among sentences. (3) Our proposed method has the best results and significantly outperforms the original MMR because we use the Hellinger distance based similarity measure which deals with probabilities better. We also use label propagation with Green's function into the update summary generation so that the advantages of semi-supervised learning methods can be applied directly.

4. CONCLUSION AND FUTURE WORK

In this paper, we propose a new update summarization method which first uses a similarity measure based on Helliger distance to capture the semantics among documents and then applies a semi-supervised method using label propagation with Green's function to generate the update summaries. Experiments on TAC 2011 data show the effectiveness of the proposed method. In this paper, we just use the given topic description as a single query to find related contents in the documents, and the learning problem is a binary classification problem. In the future, we can further detect the aspects in the topics and transfer the problem into multi-class semi-supervised learning problems to obtain more accurate results for better coverage and consistency.

Acknowledgement

The work is partially supported by National Science Foundation under grant CNS-1126619, IIS-1213026, and CNS-1461926.

5. REFERENCES

[1] F. Boudin, M. El-Beze, and J. Torres-Moreno. The lia update summarization systems at tac 2008. In *Proceedings of TAC 2008*, 2008.

[2] J.-Y. Delort and E. Alfonseca. Dualsum: A topic-model based approach for update summarization. In *Proceedings of the 13th Conference of the European Chapter of the Association for Computational Linguistics*, EACL '12, pages 214–223, 2012.

[3] C. Ding, H. D. Simon, R. Jin, and T. Li. A learning framework using green's function and kernel regularization with application to recommender system. In *Proceedings of ACM SIGKDD 2007*, pages 260–269, ACM.

[4] A. O. Hero, B. Ma, O. Michel, and J. Gorman. Alpha divergence for classification, indexing and retrieval. Technical report, University of Michigan, 2001.

[5] R. I. Kondor and J. Lafferty. Diffusion kernels on graphs and other discrete structures. In *In Proceedings of the ICML*, pages 315–322, 2002.

[6] J. Li, S. Li, X. Wang, Y. Tian, and B. Chang. Update summarization using a multi-level hierarchical dirichlet process model. In *Proceedings of COLING 2012*, pages 1603–1618, 2012.

[7] C.-Y. Lin and E. Hovy. From single to multi-document summarization: A prototype system and its evaluation. In *Proceedings of ACL*, 2002.

[8] D. Radev, H. Jing, M. Stys, and D. Tam. Centroid-based summarization of multiple documents. *Information Processing and Management*, pages 919–938, 2004.

[9] A. Renyi. On measures of entropy and information. *Proc. Fourth Berkeley Symp. Math. Stat. and Probability*, 1960.

[10] B. Shao, D. Wang, T. Li, and M. Ogihara. Music recommendation based on acoustic features and user access patterns. *Trans. Audio, Speech and Lang. Proc.*, 17(8):1602–1611, 2009.

[11] C. Shen and T. Li. Multi-document summarization via the minimum dominating set. In *Proceedings of the 23rd International Conference on Computational Linguistics (Coling 2010)*, pages 984–992, 2010.

[12] A. Singhal. Modern information retrieval: A brief overview. *Bulletin of the IEEE Computer Society Technical Committee on Data Engineering*, page 24(4): 35ÍC43, 2001.

[13] A. J. Smola and R. Kondor. Kernels and regularization on graphs. *Learning Theory and Kernel Machines Lecture Notes in Computer Science*, pages 144–158, 2003.

[14] M. Szummer and T. Jaakkola. Partially labeled classification with markov random walks. In *Proceedings of NIPS*, pages 945–952, 2001.

[15] X. Wan. Update summarization based on co-ranking with constraints. In *Proceedings of COLING 2012: Posters*, pages 1291–1300, 2012.

[16] D. Wang and T. Li. Document update summarization using incremental hierarchical clustering. In *Proceedings of the 19th ACM International Conference on Information and Knowledge Management*, CIKM '10, pages 279–288, 2010.

Multi-view Clustering via Structured Low-rank Representation

Dong Wang, Qiyue Yin, Ran He, Liang Wang, Tieniu Tan
Center for Research on Intelligent Perception and Computing (CRIPAC)
Institute of Automation, Chinese Academy of Sciences
{dwang, qyyin, rhe, wangliang, tnt} @nlpr.ia.ac.cn

ABSTRACT

In this paper, we present a novel solution to multi-view clustering through a structured low-rank representation. When assuming similar samples can be linearly reconstructed by each other, the resulting representational matrix reflects the cluster structure and should ideally be block diagonal. We first impose low-rank constraint on the representational matrix to encourage better grouping effect. Then representational matrices under different views are allowed to communicate with each other and share their mutual cluster structure information. We develop an effective algorithm inspired by iterative re-weighted least squares for solving our formulation. During the optimization process, the intermediate representational matrix from one view serves as a cluster structure constraint for that from another view. Such mutual structural constraint fine-tunes the cluster structures from both views and makes them more and more agreeable. Extensive empirical study manifests the superiority and efficacy of the proposed method.

Categories and Subject Descriptors

H.3 [**Information search and retrieval**]: Clustering

General Terms

Algorithms; Design; Experimentation

Keywords

Multi-view clustering; multi-modal learning; structure regularizer

1. INTRODUCTION

Multi-view clustering concerns the problem of partitioning data points into a series of subsets in an unsupervised way given their feature representations under different views. Here in the context of this paper, a view simply refers to one feature modality of the data rather than the physical view angle such as front-view versus side-view face images [23]. In many applications, the data points being processed are collected from multiple sources and thus have different view-specific attributes. For instance, in image classification an image can be either represented using the traditional hand-crafted feature like SIFT or automatically learned feature obtained from deep learning techniques [7]. Even though the information from any view is somehow sufficient for the clustering task, taking advantage of the complementary information across views is beneficial and can better facilitate the clustering process in most cases.

In the literature, a spectrum of methods are proposed to seek better clustering results by capturing the view complementarity. Among them, one line of research is to directly unify the multi-view information in the clustering process. For instance, in [15] a co-training flavored spectral clustering algorithm was proposed to encourage the clustering agreement between views. Another one is [16] which attempted to regularize on the eigenvectors of view-specific graph laplacians and achieve consistent clusters across views. Another line of research is to first learn a latent representation for multi-view data and then perform clustering on such representation to learn the partition. A notable one is [19] which employed matrix factorization to discover a common latent structure shared by all views and give rise to compatible clustering results. Besides, CCA based multi-view clustering methods also fall into this category [9] [5]. Yet another line of research is by fusing the clustering results obtained from individual views toward a consensus [8] [13].

Different from the aforementioned methods, we tackle the multi-view clustering problem from the perspective of structured low-rank representation. Similar to [24] [21], for each view we also assume similar samples can be used to linearly reconstruct each other. The resulting representational matrix reflects the cluster structure which should be ideally block diagonal. As in [18] [17], low-rankness is a nice property favored by many subspace clustering algorithms due to its better grouping effect. So the key idea of our method is on one hand to impose a low-rank constraint on such representational matrix to let similar samples stay together. On the other hand, since the ideal clustering result should be unanimous irrespective of views, the representational matrix derived from each view is further asked to conform with one another as much as possible through a mutual structure constraint.

Concretely, when alternatively optimizing the objective with respect to one of the representational matrices once at a time while keeping the others fixed, our method actually solves a low-rank linear regression problem. And it happens to enforce that the to-be-determined representational matrix for another view should refer to that fixed intermediate grouping structure. Over time the complementary information among different views is communicated and shared. The grouping structure for one view derived from the previous step helps rectify and fine-tune the to-be-decided grouping structure for a different view in the current step.

In summary, the contributions of this paper are the following:

Permission to make digital or hard copies of all or part of this work for personal or classroom use is granted without fee provided that copies are not made or distributed for profit or commercial advantage and that copies bear this notice and the full citation on the first page. To copy otherwise, to republish, to post on servers or to redistribute to lists, requires prior specific permission and/or a fee.
CIKM'15 October 19 - 23, 2015, Melbourne, VIC, Australia
Copyright is held by the owner/author(s). Publication rights licensed to ACM.
ACM 978-1-4503-3794-6/15/10 ...$15.00.
DOI: http://dx.doi.org/10.1145/2806416.2806629.

• We propose a novel multi-view clustering method based on structured low-rank representation. Such a joint regularization framework explicitly minimizes the grouping differences across views and gives rise to better clustering performance.

• We develop an effective algorithm inspired by iterative reweighted least squares for solving our formulation. And extensive experimental results on benchmark datasets validate the usefulness of our method.

2. PROPOSED MODEL AND SOLUTION

In our model, under each view similar data points are used to linearly reconstruct each other. Given the data matrix $X_v \in \mathbb{R}^{d_v \times n}$ and reconstruction coefficient matrix $Z_v \in \mathbb{R}^{n \times n}$ where v denotes one of the two views A and B, d_v is the feature dimension of view v and n is the number of data points, our proposed method is formulated as follows.

$$\min_{Z_A, Z_B} \sum_{v \in \{A,B\}} (\frac{1}{2}||X_v - X_v Z_v||_F^2 + \lambda ||Z_v||_*) + \frac{\beta}{2}||Z_A - Z_B||_F^2 \tag{1}$$

As in [24] [21], (1) is called a structured low-rank representation since when fixing Z_B, the cluster structure from view A is contrained to agree with a latent cluster structure from view B or vice versa. The first term in this objective is the linear reconstruction term and in particular we seek a lowest rank representation by imposing a trace norm regularizer on Z_v. By virtue of the grouping effect of such a low-rank constraint, the underlying intrinsic cluster structure can be unveiled.

Apart from pursuing better clustering structure for any single view, our model also favors a consistent cluster membership across views. In multi-view clustering, it is usually anticipated that a data point should be assigned to the same cluster irrespective of views. To this end, the last term in our objective is designed to minimize the difference of cluster structures from different views. When treating the candidate samples used to reconstruct the target sample as a dictionary, Z_A and Z_B are the view-specific representational responses on the dictionary, which indicates the sample affinity and cluster structure.

λ and β are the hyper-parameters that control the tradeoff between corresponding terms.

Note that our model can be easily generalized to more than three views by summing the reconstruction and cluster difference terms over all views. Given the space limit and for simplicity, in this section we base our introduction on a two-view scenario.

When it comes to solving the proposed objective, it is not easy to optimize (1) directly given the existence of a trace norm regularizer. So we reformulate our objective by following a well established variational formulation for trace norm [6] [14], in which the statement below holds true for the representational matrix Z_A (Similar for Z_B)

$$\begin{aligned} ||Z_A||_* &= \frac{1}{2} \inf_{S_A \succcurlyeq 0} tr(Z_A^T S_A^{-1} Z_A) + tr(S_A) \\ &= \frac{1}{2} \inf_{S_A \succcurlyeq 0} \sum_{i=1}^{n} Z_{Ai}^T S_A^{-1} Z_{Ai} + tr(S_A) \end{aligned} \tag{2}$$

where the infimum is obtained for $S_A = (Z_A Z_A^T)^{1/2}$. Z_{Ai} is the i-th column of matrix Z_A. Here S_A can be seen as an intermediate variable during the optimization procedure.

In the outer loop of our algorithm, we alternatively solve for one of the representational matrix Z_A or Z_B while keeping the other one fixed. In light of the results from (2), when we optimize the objective with respect to Z_A in a column-wise fashion, (1) can be simplified into the following:

$$\begin{aligned} \min_{Z_{Ai}} \inf_{S_A \succcurlyeq 0} & \sum_{i=1}^{n} ||X_{Ai} - X_A Z_{Ai}||_2^2 + \lambda Z_{Ai}^T S_A^{-1} Z_{Ai} \\ & + \beta(Z_{Ai}^T Z_{Ai} - 2 Z_{Ai}^T Z_{Bi}) + \lambda tr(S_A) \end{aligned} \tag{3}$$

The above objective is jointly convex in (Z_{Ai}, S_A). And we solve it in the inner loop of our algorithm. In order to optimize this objective function by alternating the minimization over (Z_{Ai}, S_A), we need to add a term $\lambda \mu_A tr(S_A^{-1})$ which ensures S_A is invertible and thus the infimum can be attained [6] [14]. Here μ_A is a small scaler. And S_A is then given by:

$$S_A = (Z_A Z_A^T + \mu_A I)^{1/2} \tag{4}$$

When S_A is given, (3) becomes an iterative re-weighted least squares problem whose solution is the following:

$$Z_{Ai} = (X_A^T X_A + \beta I + \lambda S_A^{-1})^{-1} (X_A^T X_{Ai} + \beta Z_{Bi}) \tag{5}$$

Similarly, when we solve for Z_B while fixing Z_A, based on the same optimization strategy S_B is given by

$$S_B = (Z_B Z_B^T + \mu_B I)^{1/2} \tag{6}$$

and then we obtain the solution for each column of the representational matrix Z_B as follows:

$$Z_{Bi} = (X_B^T X_B + \beta I + \lambda S_B^{-1})^{-1} (X_B^T X_{Bi} + \beta Z_{Ai}) \tag{7}$$

When optimizing our method following the procedure as shown in Algorithm 1, empirically it can quickly converge after five to ten iterations. And one of the advantages for solving the objective in a column-wise fashion is that we can select a few nearest neighbors to approximately reconstruct a target sample. This makes sense because Z should ideally be block diagonal which implies that candidate samples less similar to the target play insignificant roles in the reconstruction. In such case we update Eqn.(4)-(7) only using smaller data matrices or representational matrices whose entries are extracted from the nearest neighbor positions in the original large matrices. This strategy alleviates the burden of high computational cost due to the large number of samples in the databases. The most time-consuming part is computing (4) and (6) which involves Singular Value Decomposition (SVD) [12]. If we use k nearest neighbors ($k \ll n$) for the linear reconstruction, we only need to decomposite multiple much smaller $k \times k$ matrices rather than the original large $n \times n$ matrix, which reduces the complexity from $O(n^3)$ to $O(nk^2)$. Another advantage is that it is convenient to develop a paralleled solution which may further speed up the algorithm. Once Z_A and Z_B are obtained, we average them by letting $Z = (|Z_A| + |Z_B|)/2$. Then a spectral clustering algorithm like [20] is applied on Z to achieve the final clustering results.

3. EXPERIMENTAL RESULTS

In this section, we test our method on widely used benchmark databases and compare with a series of baselines in order to validate the usefulness of the proposed model.

3.1 Databases

UCI Handwritten Digit dataset [1] consists of features of handwritten digits (0–9). The dataset is represented in terms of six features and contains 2000 samples with 200 in each category. Similar

Algorithm 1 Multi-view clustering via structured low-rank representation (MVCSL)

Input:
Data matrices X_A and X_B, parameters λ and β. Initial guesses Z_A, Z_B, number of clusters c, number of nearest neighbors k for reconstruction and $\mu_A = \mu_B = 10^{-5}$

```
while not converged do
    // Solve Z_A with Z_B fixed
    for i = 1 : n do
        Update S_A using Equation (4);
        Update Z_Ai using Equation (5) ;
    end for
    // Solve Z_B with Z_A fixed
    for i = 1 : n do
        Update S_B using Equation (6);
        Update Z_Bi using Equation (7);
    end for
end while
```

Output: Z_A, Z_B and final clustering results

to [16], we select the 76 Fourier coefficients of the character shapes and the 216 profile correlations as two views of the original dataset.

Movies617 dataset [3] consists of 617 movies with 17 labels extracted from IMDb. The two views are the 1878 keywords and the 1398 actors with a keyword used for at least 2 movies and an actor appeared in at least 3 movies.

Animal dataset [2] consists of 30475 images of 50 animals with six pre-extracted features for each image. Three kinds of features, namely PyramidHOG (PHOG), colorSIFT and SURF, are chosen as three views. We select the first ten categories with each including randomly chosen 50 samples as a subset for evaluation.

Pascal VOC 2007 dataset [4] consists of 20 categories with a total of 9,963 images. We use the Color feature and Bow feature as two-view visual representation. Furthermore, those images with multiple categories are removed, thus leaving 5,649 images for e-valuation.

NUS WIDE dataset [11] consists of 269,648 images of 81 categories collected from Flickr. In our experiments, We select 500 images from each of the five classes with the most number of images for evaluation. Six types of low level features are given and we use color correlogram and wavelet texture as two-view representations for multi-view clustering.

3.2 Experimental settings

We extensively compare our method with many representative baselines including 1) *S_Spectral*: Use spectral clustering in [20] to cluster each view's data and select the best clustering result. 2) *S_LowRank*: Use only single-view low-rank representation to construct the affinity matrix and then apply spectral clustering in [20] to cluster the dataset. We also report the best clustering results. 3) *Combined*: Concatenate features from two views and apply low-rank representation without the mutual structural constraint on the combined feature to perform clustering. 4) *PairwiseSC, Centroid-SC*: [16] Two objectives for co-regularizing the eigenvectors of all views' Laplacian matrices. 5) *Co_Training*: [15] Alternately modify one view's graph structure using the other view's information. 6) *Multi_NMF*: [19] A multi-view non-negative matrix factorization method to group the multi-view data. Note that this method is not applicable on NUS dataset since it requires all non-negative input features. 7) *Multi_SS*: [22] A structure sparsity based multi-view clustering and feature learning framework. The parameters in these methods are carefully selected to achieve their best results.

Whenever K-means is involved, it is run 20 times with random initialization. To speedup the optimization process, during the linear reconstruction we select 100 nearest neighbors of a sample point for its reconstruction. To measure the clustering results, we use accuracy (ACC) and normalized mutual information (NMI). Readers can refer to [10] for more details about such measures. Both mean and standard deviation are reported.

3.3 Experimental results and analysis

It can be seen from Table 1 and 2 that our proposed method (MVCSL) consistently outperforms other baselines using both measures. First of all, comparing with single-view methods like either $S\_Spectral$ or $S\_LowRank$, our method always has an upper hand, which evidences the necessity of utilizing the complementary information among different views and exploring intrinsic group structure. Second, a naive concatenation of features from multiple views as the baseline $Combined$ does is somehow ineffective. However our method explicitly asks the view-specific cluster structure, which is manifested in the representational matrices arising from the data reconstruction, to agree with each other as much as possible. Therefore the additional complementary information across views is shared and thus more accurate clustering results can be obtained. Besides, our method also beats other baselines by a considerable margin. The baseline $Multi\_SS$ puts the data from all views together and explores its global structure. It enforces the sparsity between views while somehow neglecting the intrinsic structure for any individual view. But this is where our low-rank constraint imposed on each view stands out. Our method takes into account both the intra-view partition and inter-view association, which proves that such structured low-rank framework is quite helpful in the multi-view clustering problem.

As mentioned previously, our method can be extended to scenarios involving three or more views, The superior results of our method on the three-view Animal dataset proves full well that the proposed method is also workable beyond two views.

When selecting the parameters λ and β, we empirically grid-search in the interval [0.001, 10]. And their influences on the clustering performance are shown in Figure 1 and 2. By pairing proper λ and β, it is not difficult to get satisfactory results. Given the s-pace limit, only results on the Movies617 dataset are reported and similar trends can be observed on the other datasets as well.

4. CONCLUSION

We have proposed a novel multi-view clustering method through a structured low-rank representation. On one hand, with the help of better grouping effect of a low-rank regularizer, similar data points are assigned together with higher accuracy. On the other hand, a mutual structure constraint is imposed to achieve consistent cluster memberships across views. The view-specific representational matrices resulting from the data reconstruction alternatively serve as the structural reference for one another. The experimental results demonstrate the effectiveness of our proposed method.

5. ACKNOWLEDGEMENTS

This work is jointly supported by National Basic Research Program of China (No.2012CB316300) and National Science Foundation of China (No.61175003, No.61135002 and No.61403390).

6. REFERENCES

[1] http://archive.ics.uci.edu/ml/datasets/Multiple+Features.
[2] http://attributes.kyb.tuebingen.mpg.de/.
[3] http://membres-lig.imag.fr/grimal/data.html.

ACC(%)	Digits	Movies617	VOC	Animal	NUS
S_Spectral	66.37(4.44)	25.70(1.13)	15.64(0.43)	27.21(1.50)	33.85(0.18)
S_LowRank	66.53(5.31)	30.02(1.05)	17.09(0.41)	31.71(1.88)	34.74(0.02)
Combined	71.83(6.19)	32.93(1.53)	13.98(0.37)	32.51(1.00)	30.28(0.14)
PairwiseSC	80.82(6.30)	27.89(1.64)	11.93(0.14)	31.65(1.59)	33.07(0.14)
CentroidSC	82.77(7.14)	28.57(1.17)	13.98(0.39)	31.06(2.02)	34.80(0.99)
Co_Training	80.22(6.84)	30.74(1.28)	14.84(0.33)	30.35(1.48)	35.15(1.03)
Multi_NMF	69.24(6.28)	26.99(1.19)	12.57(0.23)	30.56(1.02)	N/A
Multi_SS	72.45(4.10)	29.60(1.10)	12.47(0.26)	32.11(1.86)	32.39(0.05)
MVCSL	**85.10(4.89)**	**33.51(1.13)**	**17.16(0.68)**	**32.61(1.34)**	**36.33(0.04)**

Table 1: Clustering results in terms of accuracy on five benchmark databases.

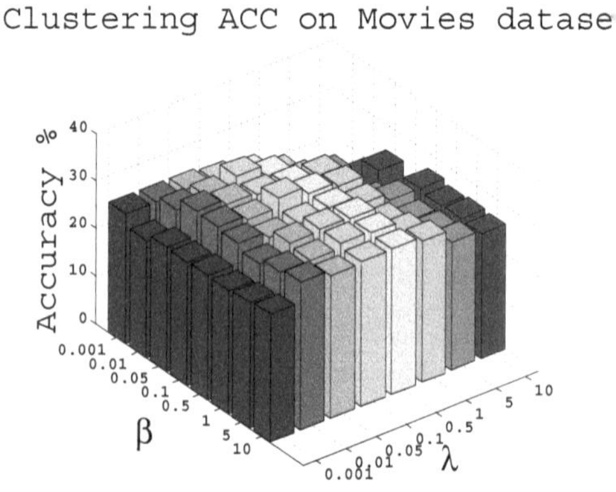

Figure 1: Accuracy vs. parameters λ and β on the Movies617 database

NMI(%)	Digits	Movies617	VOC	Animal	NUS
S_Spectral	62.30(1.85)	25.47(0.85)	9.34(0.19)	15.70(0.65)	6.64(0.15)
S_LowRank	69.79(1.81)	30.15(0.80)	7.05(0.18)	18.42(1.10)	7.68(0.01)
Combined	70.92(2.03)	32.11(0.89)	9.33(0.30)	20.09(0.58)	5.14(0.27)
PairwiseSC	75.84(2.37)	28.04(0.73)	6.07(0.12)	19.90(1.51)	6.87(0.01)
CentroidSC	76.76(2.58)	28.02(0.72)	9.50(0.28)	18.50(1.48)	7.84(0.26)
Co_Training	75.90(2.27)	30.74(1.28)	9.88(0.21)	18.98(0.73)	8.51(0.16)
Multi_NMF	65.05(2.30)	27.45(0.55)	6.40(0.19)	18.77(0.71)	N/A
Multi_SS	74.55(2.49)	30.09(1.32)	6.76(0.11)	21.25(1.76)	5.63(0.02)
MVCSL	**79.95(1.58)**	**34.79(0.92)**	**10.31(0.21)**	**22.11(0.83)**	**8.60(0.01)**

Table 2: Clustering results in terms of NMI on five benchmark databases.

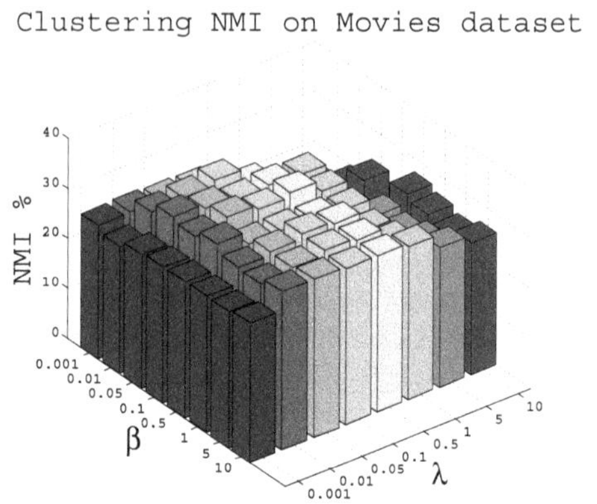

Figure 2: NMI vs. parameters λ and β on the Movies617 database

[4] http://pascallin.ecs.soton.ac.uk/challenges/VOC/voc2007/.

[5] U. Ahsan and I. Essa. Clustering social event images using kernel canonical correlation analysis. In *IEEE Conference on CVPR Workshops*, pages 814–819, 2014.

[6] A. Argyriou, T. Evgeniou, and M. Pontil. Multi-task feature learning. In *NIPS*, 2007.

[7] Y. Bengio, A. C. Courville, and P. Vincent. Representation learning: A review and new perspectives. *IEEE Transactions on Pattern Analysis and Machine Intelligence*, 35:1798–1828, 2013.

[8] E. Bruno and S. Marchand-Maillet. Multiview clustering: A late fusion approach using latent models. *In ACM Conference on Research and Development in Information Retrieval*, pages 736–737, 2009.

[9] K. Chaudhuri, S. M. Kakade, K. Livescu, and K. Sridharan. Multi-view clustering via canonical correlation analysis. *In International Conference on Machine Learning*, pages 129–136, 2009.

[10] W.-Y. Chen, Y. Song, H. Bai, C.-J. Lin, and E. Y. Chang. Parallel spectral clustering in distributed systems. *IEEE Transactions on Pattern Analysis and Machine Intelligence*, 33(3):568–586, 2011.

[11] T.-S. Chua, J. Tang, R. Hong, H. Li, Z. Luo, and Y.-T. Zheng. Nus-wide: A real-world web image database from national university of singapore. In *ACM Conference on Image and Video Retrieval*, 2009.

[12] E. Grave, G. Obozinski, and F. Bach. Trace lasso: a trace norm regularization for correlated designs. In *NIPS*, pages 2187–2195, 2011.

[13] D. Greene and P. Cunningham. A matrix factorization approach for integrating multiple data views. *In European Conference on Machine Learning and Knowledge Discovery in Databases*, pages 423–438, 2009.

[14] Y. Guo. Convex subspace representation learning from multi-view data. In *AAAI*, 2013.

[15] A. Kumar and H. D. Iii. A co-training approach for multi-view spectral clustering. *In International Conference on Machine Learning*, pages 393–400, 2011.

[16] A. Kumar, P. Rai, and H. D. Iii. Co-regularized multiview spectral clustering. *In Neural Information Processing Systems*, pages 1413–1421, 2011.

[17] G. Liu, Z. Lin, S. Yan, J. Sun, Y. Yu, and Y. Ma. Robust recovery of subspace structures by low-rank representation. *IEEE Transactions on Pattern Analysis and Machine Intelligence*, 35(1):171–184, 2013.

[18] G. Liu, Z. Lin, and Y. Yu. Robust subspace segmentation by low-rank representation. *In International Conference on Machine Learning*, pages 663–670, 2010.

[19] J. Liu, C. Wang, J. Gao, and J. Han. Multi-view clustering via joint nonnegative matrix factorization. *In SIAM International Conference Data Mining*, pages 252–260, 2013.

[20] J. Shi and J. Malik. Normalized cuts and image segmentation. *IEEE Transactions on Pattern Analysis and Machine Intelligence*, 22(8):888–905, 2000.

[21] W. Tang, R. Liu, Z. Su, and J. Zhang. Structure-constrained low-rank representation. *IEEE Transactions on Neural Networks and Learning Systems*, 2014.

[22] H. Wang, F. Nie, and H. Huang. Multi-view clustering and feature learning via structured sparsity. *In International Conference on Machine Learning*, pages 352–360, 2013.

[23] C. Xu, D. Tao, and C. Xu. A survey on multi-view learning. *arXiv preprint arXiv:1304.5634*, 2013.

[24] Y. Zhang, Z. Jiang, and L. S. Davis. Learning structured low-rank representations for image classification. *In Computer Vision and Pattern Recognition*, pages 676–683, 2013.

Partially Labeled Data Tuple Can Optimize Multivariate Performance Measures

Jim Jing-Yan Wang
Computational Bioscience Research Center,
King Abdullah University of Science and
Technology, Thuwal 23955-6900, Saudi Arabia
jimjywang@gmail.com

Xin Gao*
Computational Bioscience Research Center,
King Abdullah University of Science and
Technology, Thuwal 23955-6900, Saudi Arabia
xin.gao@kaust.edu.sa
* Corresponding author

ABSTRACT

Multivariate performance measure optimization refers to learning predictive models such that a desired complex performance measure can be optimized over a training set, such as the F1 score. Up to now, all the existing multivariate performance measure optimization methods are limited to a completely labeled data tuple, i.e., the label tuple is complete. However, in real-world applications, sometimes it is difficult to obtain a complete label tuple. In this paper, we show that the multivariate performance measures can also be optimized by learning from partially labeled data tuple, when the label tuple is incomplete. We introduce a slack label tuple to represent the sought complete true label tuple, and learn it jointly with a hyper predictor, so that it can be consistent to the known labels, prediction results, and is smooth in the neighborhood. We develop an iterative learning algorithm to learn the slack label tuple and the hyper predictor. Its advantage over state-of-the-art multivariate performance measure optimization methods is shown by experiments on benchmark data sets.

Categories and Subject Descriptors

I.2.6 [**ARTIFICIAL INTELLIGENCE**]: Learning

General Terms

Algorithm

Keywords

Multivariate performance measures; Partially labeled data; Slack label tuple

1. INTRODUCTION

When solving machine learning problems, we often learn a predictive model from a training set, and then use it to predict the class labels of some testing data points. To evaluate the prediction results, various multivariate performance measures can be employed to compare the predicted labels against the ground truth labels. For example, prediction accuracy (ACC), area under the receiver operating characteristic curve (AUC), the F1 score, and recall precision break even point (PRBEP) are popular multivariate performance measures in various applications [3, 6]. However, while those multivariate performance measures are used to evaluate the prediction results, they are ignored when the predictive model is learned from the training set. During the training procedure, traditional learning methods usually employ a simple loss function to compare the true label of a training point against its corresponding predicted label. Minimizing such loss functions cannot guarantee that a desired multivariate performance can be optimized directly.

Recently, some works were proposed to learn predictive models so that a desired multivariate performance can be optimized directly. For example, Joachims [3] proposed a support vector method for optimizing multivariate performance measures by approximating a complex multivariate loss function as its upper bound, and using a cutting-plane algrithm. Zhang et al. [8] proposed a novel smoothing strategy for multivariate performance measure by using Nesterov's accelerated gradient method. Li et al. [4] proposed to adapt an existing classifier to optimize a desired multivariate performance measure, by adding an adaptation function to the existing classifier. Mao and Tsang [5] proposed a joint features selection and classifier learning method for multivariate performance optimization by using a two-layer cutting plane algorithm . These works minimize a loss function corresponding to the desired multivariate performance to learn the predictive model. This loss function is a function of a data tuple of the training data points, and a label tuple of the corresponding labels.

A very basic assumption behind these methods is that all the labels of the data points of the data tuple are available. This assumption, however, does not always hold in real-world applications. In many applications, we only have a partially labeled data tuple, i.e., only the labels of a few data points in the training data tuple are available, while the labels of the remaining data points are missing. Up to now, there is no work proposed to learning predictive models from partially labeled data tuple. In this paper, we show that multivariate performance can also be optimized by learning a predictive model from a partially labeled data tuple. We propose a novel method to optimize a multivariate performance measure by using a partially labeled data tuple. A slack label tuple

Permission to make digital or hard copies of all or part of this work for personal or classroom use is granted without fee provided that copies are not made or distributed for profit or commercial advantage and that copies bear this notice and the full citation on the first page. Copyrights for components of this work owned by others than ACM must be honored. Abstracting with credit is permitted. To copy otherwise, or republish, to post on servers or to redistribute to lists, requires prior specific permission and/or a fee. Request permissions from Permissions@acm.org.
CIKM'15, October 19–23, 2015, Melbourne, Australia.
© 2015 ACM. ISBN 978-1-4503-3794-6/15/10$15.00.
DOI: http://dx.doi.org/10.1145/2806416.2806630

is introduced to represent the desired complete true label tuple, and it is learned jointly with a hyper predictor. The labels of slack label tuple are imposed to be consistent with the known labels, the prediction results, and smoothness over neighborhood. To learn the hyper predictor, we minimize a multivariate loss function to compare the slack label tuple against the prediction results of the hyper predictor. The learning problem is modeled by a unified minimization problem, and solved using an iterative algorithm.

This paper is organized as follows: in Section 2, we describe the proposed method, in Section 3, the method is evaluated experimentally, and in Section 4, the paper is concluded.

2. PROPOSED METHOD

2.1 Problem formulation

We assume we have a data tuple of n data points, denoted as $\overline{\mathbf{x}} = (\mathbf{x}_1, \cdots, \mathbf{x}_n)$, where $\mathbf{x}_i \in \mathbb{R}^d$ is the d-dimensional feature vector of the i-th data point, and a corresponding label tuple $\overline{y} = (y_1, \cdots, y_n)$, where $y_i \in \{+1, -1\}$ is the the binary class label of the i-th data point. However, the label tuple is incomplete, and only the first $l < n$ labels $y_1, \cdots, y_l$ are known, while the remaining labels are missing. To predict the label tuple of the data tuple, we design a hyper predictor as follow,

$$\overline{y}^* = \underset{\overline{y}' \in \{+1,-1\}^n}{\arg\max} \sum_{i=1}^{n} \mathbf{w}^\top \mathbf{x}_i y_i', \tag{1}$$

where $\overline{y}^* = (y_1^*, \cdots, y_n^*) \in \{+1, -1\}^n$ is the predicted label tuple, and $\mathbf{w} \in \mathbb{R}^d$ is the predictor parameter. To measure the perdition results, traditional multivariate performance optimization methods use a complex multivariate loss function to compare $\overline{y}^*$ against $\overline{y}$, $\Delta(\overline{y}^*, \overline{y})$, and minimize it to learn the predictor parameter, $\mathbf{w}$. However, since $\overline{y}$ itself is incomplete, we cannot optimize $\Delta(\overline{y}^*, \overline{y})$ directly anymore. To solve this problem, we propose a slack label tuple $\overline{z} = (z_1, \cdots, z_n) \in \{+1, -1\}^n$ to represent the true label tuple, and learn $\overline{z}$ and $\mathbf{w}$ simultaneously. To this end, we formulate the learning problem as the following constrained minimization problem,

$$\begin{aligned} &\min_{\mathbf{w}, \overline{z}} \left\{ \frac{1}{2}\|\mathbf{w}\|^2 + C_1 \Delta(\overline{y}^*, \overline{z}) + C_2 \sum_{i=1}^{n} \left\| z_i - \sum_{j:\mathbf{x}_j \in \mathcal{N}_i} \omega_{ij} z_j \right\|_2^2 \right\}, \\ &s.t.\ \overline{z} \in \{+1, -1\}^n,\ and\ z_i = y_i, \forall\ i = 1, \cdots, l. \end{aligned} \tag{2}$$

In this formulation, the first term $\frac{1}{2}\|\mathbf{w}\|^2$ is minimized to reduce the complexity of the predictor. The second term $\Delta(\overline{y}^*, \overline{z})$ is minimized to optimize the loss function corresponding to a sought multivariate performance measure. The last term is proposed to seek the smoothness of slack labels over each neighborhood. $\mathcal{N}_i$ is the neighborhood of $\mathbf{x}_i$, and ω_{ij} is the weight of $\mathbf{x}_j$ for reconstruction of $\mathbf{x}_i$, and it is obtained by solving the following constrained quadratic program problem,

$$\begin{aligned} &\min_{\omega_{ij}|j:\mathbf{x}_j \in \mathcal{N}_i} \left\| \mathbf{x}_i - \sum_{j:\mathbf{x}_j \in \mathcal{N}_i} \omega_{ij} \mathbf{x}_j \right\|_2^2 \\ &s.t. \sum_{\mathbf{x}_j \in \mathcal{N}_i} \omega_{ij} = 1,\ and\ \omega_{ij} \geq 0, \forall\ j : \mathbf{x}_j \in \mathcal{N}_i. \end{aligned} \tag{3}$$

The constraint $z_i = y_i, \forall\ i = 1, \cdots, l$, is to guarantee the slack labels of the first data points are consistent to their known labels.

Because $\Delta(\overline{y}^*, \overline{z})$ is usually complex, and sometimes does not have a close form, it is difficult to minimize (2) directly. We seek the upper bound of $\Delta(\overline{y}^*, \overline{z})$ and minimize it instead. According to (1), we have

$$\begin{aligned} &\sum_{i=1}^{n} \mathbf{w}^\top \mathbf{x}_i z_i \leq \sum_{i=1}^{n} \mathbf{w}^\top \mathbf{x}_i y_i^*, \forall \overline{z} \in \{+1, -1\}^n, \\ &\Rightarrow 0 \leq \sum_{i=1}^{n} \mathbf{w}^\top \mathbf{x}_i (y_i^* - z_i), \\ &\Rightarrow \Delta(\overline{y}^*, \overline{z}) \leq \sum_{i=1}^{n} \mathbf{w}^\top \mathbf{x}_i (y_i^* - z_i) + \Delta(\overline{y}^*, \overline{z}) \\ &\leq \max_{\overline{y}''' \in \{+1,-1\}^n} \left(\sum_{i=1}^{n} \mathbf{w}^\top \mathbf{x}_i (y_i''' - z_i) + \Delta(\overline{y}''', \overline{z}) \right) \\ &= \sum_{i=1}^{n} \mathbf{w}^\top \mathbf{x}_i (y_i'' - z_i) + \Delta(\overline{y}'', \overline{z}), \end{aligned} \tag{4}$$

where $\overline{y}'' = (y_1'', \cdots, y_n'') \in \{+1, -1\}^n$ is a label tuple to replace $\overline{y}^*$ to seek the upper bound of $\Delta(\overline{y}^*, \overline{z})$,

$$\overline{y}'' = \underset{\overline{y}''' \in \{+1,-1\}^n}{\arg\max} \left(\sum_{i=1}^{n} \mathbf{w}^\top \mathbf{x}_i (y_i''' - z_i) + \Delta(\overline{y}''', \overline{z}) \right). \tag{5}$$

By replacing $\Delta(\overline{y}^*, \overline{z})$ in (2) by its upper bound in (4), we have the following constrained minimization problem,

$$\begin{aligned} &\min_{\mathbf{w}, \overline{z}} \left\{ \frac{1}{2}\|\mathbf{w}\|^2 + C_1 \left(\sum_{i=1}^{n} \mathbf{w}^\top \mathbf{x}_i (y_i'' - z_i) + \Delta(\overline{y}'', \overline{z}) \right) \right. \\ &\left. + C_2 \sum_{i=1}^{n} \left\| z_i - \sum_{\mathbf{x}_j \in \mathcal{N}_i} \omega_{ij} z_j \right\|_2^2 \right\}, \\ &s.t.\ \overline{z} \in \{+1, -1\}^n,\ and\ z_i = y_i, \forall\ i = 1, \cdots, l. \end{aligned} \tag{6}$$

2.2 Optimization

The problem in (6) is difficult to optimize directly. Thus we use an alternate optimization strategy to solve this problem in an iterative algorithm. Noting $\overline{y}''$ in (5) is also a function of $\mathbf{w}$ and $\overline{z}$, and each iteration we first update it by fixing $\mathbf{w}$ and $\overline{z}$ as in the previous solution. Then one of $\mathbf{w}$ and $\overline{z}$ is updated in turn while the other one is fixed.

2.2.1 Updating $\mathbf{w}$

To update $\mathbf{w}$, we fix $\overline{y}''$ and $\overline{z}$, and remove the terms irrelevant to $\mathbf{w}$, and obtain the following minimization problem,

$$\min_{\mathbf{w}} \left\{ g(\mathbf{w}) = \frac{1}{2}\|\mathbf{w}\|^2 + C_1 \left(\sum_{i=1}^{n} \mathbf{w}^\top \mathbf{x}_i (y_i'' - z_i) \right) \right\}. \tag{7}$$

We use a gradient descent method to minimize this problem,

$$\mathbf{w}^{new} = \mathbf{w}^{old} - \eta \nabla g(\mathbf{w})|_{\mathbf{w}=\mathbf{w}^{old}}, \tag{8}$$

where $\nabla g(\mathbf{w}) = \mathbf{w} + C_1 \sum_{i=1}^{n} \mathbf{x}_i (y_i'' - z_i)$ is the gradient function, and η is the gradient step.

2.2.2 *Updating $\bar{z}$*

To update $\bar{z}$, we fix $\mathbf{w}$ and $\bar{y}''$, remove the terms irrelevant to $\bar{z}$, and obtain the following problem,

$$\begin{aligned}
\min_{\bar{z}} &\left\{ C_1 \left(\sum_{i=1}^{n} \mathbf{w}^\top \mathbf{x}_i (y_i'' - z_i) + \Delta(\bar{y}'', \bar{z}) \right) \right. \\
&\left. + C_2 \sum_{i=1}^{n} \left\| z_i - \sum_{\mathbf{x}_j \in \mathcal{N}_i} \omega_{ij} z_j \right\|_2^2 \right\}, \\
&s.t.\ \bar{z} \in \{+1, -1\}^n,\ and\ z_i = y_i, \forall\ i = 1, \cdots, l.
\end{aligned} \tag{9}$$

In this problem, since the first l labels of $\bar{z}$ is constrained to be identical to the known labels, we only need to consider the remaining $n - l$ labels, $z_{l+1}, \cdots, z_n$. We solve this problem by fixing $z_1, \cdots, z_l$, and performing a local search in the space of $(z_{l+1}, \cdots, z_n)$.

2.3 Iterative algorithm

Based on the optimization results, we develop an iterative algorithm to learn $\mathbf{w}$ and $\bar{z}$. The developed algorithm, named as OPLD, is described in Algorithm 1.

Algorithm 1 Iterative algorithm to Optimize multivariate performance measure from Partially Labeled Data tuple (O-PLD).

Input: Data tuple $\bar{\mathbf{x}}$, and labels of its first l data points, $y_1, \cdots, y_n$;
Input: Tradeoff parameters C_1 and C_2;
Input: Iteration number T.
Initialize $\mathbf{w}_0$ and $\bar{z}_0$;
for $t = 1, \cdots, T$ **do**
  Update $\bar{y}_t''$ according to (5) by fixing $\mathbf{w}_{t-1}$ and $\bar{z}_{t-1}$;
  Update $\mathbf{w}_t$ according to (8) by fixing $\bar{y}_t''$ and $\bar{z}_{t-1}$;
  Update $\bar{z}_t$ according to (9) by fixing $\mathbf{w}_t$ and $\bar{y}_t''$.
end for
Output: Output the learned $\mathbf{w}_T$ and $\bar{z}_T$.

3. EXPERIMENTS

In this section, we test the proposed algorithm on optimization of various multivariate performance measures.

3.1 Data sets

The following data sets were used in our experiments,

- **Splice**: The task of this data set is to classify two classes of splice junctions in a DNA sequence [7]. There are 3,190 data points in this data set, and the number of features of each data point is 61.
- **Reuters**: This data set is the Reuters-21578 collection [2]. In this experiment, we target on a binary classification problem on this data set. The money-fx documents are defined as positive data points, while the others documents are defined as negative data points. The number of data points in this data set is 11,069, and the number of features is 8,315.
- **Mitfaces**: This data set is a training set constructed for the face detection problem, and it is from CBCL at MIT [1]. The number of data points in this data set is 6,997, and the number of features is 361.

3.2 Experiment protocol

To conduct the experiments, we first randomly split the entire data set in to a training set and a test set. To do this, we randomly select 50% of the data points as the training data points, and left the remaining 50% data points as the test data points. The training set was used to train the hyper predictor to optimize a given multivariate performance measure, and then the predictor was used to classify the data points in the test set, and the prediction results are evaluated by the corresponding multivariate performance measure. We randomly select about 30% training data points as labeled data points, while left the remaining training data points as unlabeled data points. The tradeoff parameters are optimized over the training set by using cross validation. This procedure of random split is repeated ten times to avoid bias of each split.

3.3 Experimental results

3.3.1 *Comparison to state-of-the-art multivariate performance optimization methods*

We compare the proposed method against several state-of-the-art multivariate performance optimization methods, including support vector machine for performance optimization (SVM^{perf}) [3], smoothing for multivariate scores (SM-S) [8], classifier adaptation for performance optimization (CAPO) [4], and feature selection for multivariate performance measure (FS_{multi}) [5]. Please note that the compared methods can only use the labeled training data points while ignoring the unlabeled data points. The boxplots of ten trails of experiments of optimization of ACC, F1 score, PRBEP, and AUC are given in Figure 1. From this figure, we can see that the proposed algorithm outperforms the compared methods significantly over all data sets. This is not surprising because it is the only algorithm that explores the entire training set and learns from the tuple with incomplete label tuple.

3.3.2 *Sensitivity to parameters*

There are two tradeoff parameters, C_1 and C_2, in the proposed method, and we show the curves of optimized PRBEP against different values of C_1 and C_2 over Mitfaces data set in Figure 2. From this figure, we can see the performance is stable to both these two parameters. The performance is improved slightly when the values are larger.

3.3.3 *Running time*

Table 1: Running times of compared methods (in seconds).

Methods	ACC	F1	PRBEP	AUC
OPLD	130.48	141.08	152.97	155.56
FS_{multi}	86.77	88.30	90.06	87.62
CAPO	87.65	88.17	90.07	91.94
SMS	56.49	55.24	54.72	55.62
SVM^{perf}	65.91	64.45	69.16	68.25

We also compare the running time of different methods on optimization of various multivariate performance measures over the Splice data set. The running time is shown in Table 1. We can see that the proposed method consumes the most

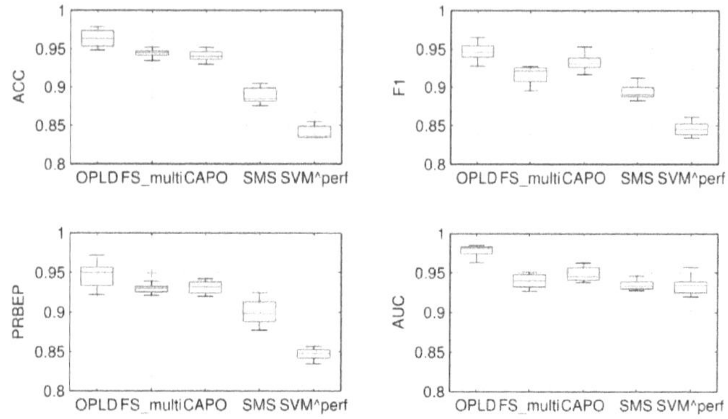

(a) Splice

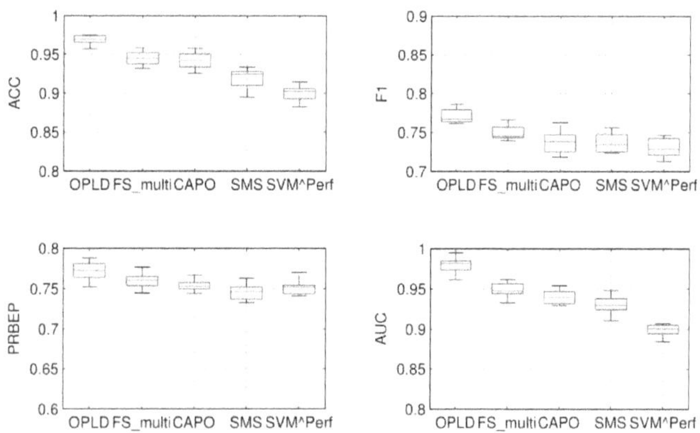

(b) Reuters

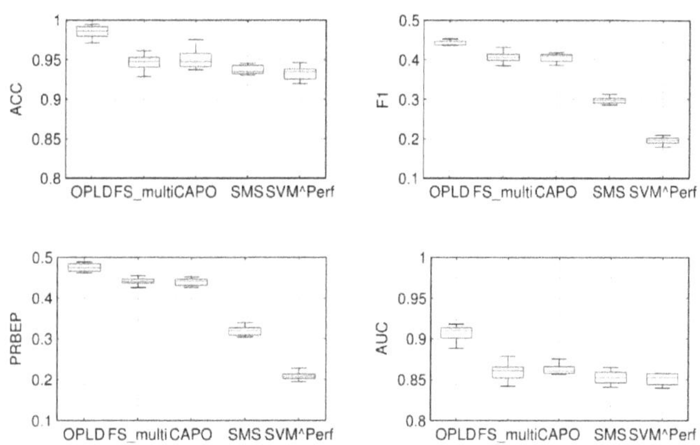

(c) Mitfaces

Figure 1: Boxplots of variouse multivariate performance measures of ten trails of experiments.

training time for optimizations of different performance measures. This is not surprising, since the compared algorithms can only explore a limited number of labeled data points, while our algorithm utilizes the entire training set of both labeled and unlabeled data points.

4. CONCLUSION

In this paper, we show that partially labeled data tuple can also be used to learn predictive models to optimize a complex multivariate performance measure. We develop an effective algorithm to optimize multivariate performance measures from partially labeled data tuple, by introducing a slack complete label tuple, and updating it jointly with the hyper predictor parameters. Experimental results show its significant advantage over existing multivariate performance measure optimization methods which only utilise the labeled data points.

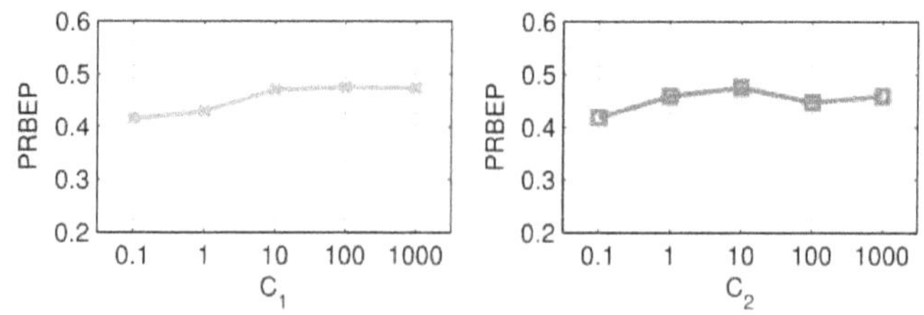

Figure 2: Sensitivity curves of parameters C_1 and C_2.

Acknowledgements

Research reported in this publication was supported by competitive research funding from King Abdullah University of Science and Technology (KAUST), Saudi Arabia.

5. REFERENCES

[1] M. Alvira and R. Rifkin. An empirical comparison of snow and svms for face detection. Technical Report 2001-004, MIT, 2001.

[2] F. Debole and F. Sebastiani. An analysis of the relative hardness of reuters-21578 subsets. *Journal of the American Society for Information Science and Technology*, 56(6):584–596, 2005.

[3] T. Joachims. A support vector method for multivariate performance measures. In *Proceedings of the 22nd International Conference on Machine Learning*, pages 377–384, 2005.

[4] N. Li, I. W. Tsang, and Z.-H. Zhou. Efficient optimization of performance measures by classifier adaptation. *Pattern Analysis and Machine Intelligence, IEEE Transactions on*, 35(6):1370–1382, 2013.

[5] Q. Mao and I. W.-H. Tsang. A feature selection method for multivariate performance measures. *Pattern Analysis and Machine Intelligence, IEEE Transactions on*, 35(9):2051–2063, 2013.

[6] G. Markovits, A. Shtok, O. Kurland, and D. Carmel. Predicting query performance for fusion-based retrieval. In *21st ACM International Conference on Information and Knowledge Management, CIKM 2012*, pages 813–822, 2012.

[7] M. O. Noordewier, G. G. Towell, and J. W. Shavlik. Training knowledge-based neural networks to recognize genes. In *Advances in Neural Information Processing Systems*, pages 530–536, 1991.

[8] X. Zhang, A. Saha, and S. Vishwanathan. Smoothing multivariate performance measures. *The Journal of Machine Learning Research*, 13(1):3623–3680, 2012.

Modeling Infinite Topics on Social Behavior Data with Spatio-temporal Dependence

Peng Wang
Institute of Inform. Eng., CAS
& Alibaba Group
xingxuan.wp@alibaba-inc.com

Peng Zhang
QCIS, University of Technology Sydney
Peng.Zhang@uts.edu.au

Chuan Zhou
Institute of Information Engineering, CAS
zhouchuan@iie.ac.cn

Zhao Li
Alibaba Group
lizhao.lz@alibaba-inc.com

Guo Li
Institute of Information Engineering, CAS
guoli@iie.ac.cn

ABSTRACT

The problem of modeling topics on user behavior data in social networks has been widely studied in social marketing and social emotion analysis, where latent topic models are commonly used as the solutions. The user behavior data are highly related in time and space, which demands new latent topic models that consider both temporal and spatial distances. However, existing topic models either fail to model these two factors simultaneously, or cannot handle the high order dependence among user behaviors. In this paper we present a new nonparametric Bayesian model *Time and Space Dependent Chinese Restaurant Processes* (TSD-CRP for short). TSD-CRP can auto-select the number of topics and model high-order temporal and spatial dependence behind user behavior data. Empirical results on real-world data sets demonstrate the effectiveness of the proposed method.

Keywords

Topic models, social networks, nonparametric Bayesian models, temporal and spatial dependence

1. INTRODUCTION

Topic modeling plays an important role in social network applications, such as social marketing, user behavior modeling, and emotion analysis [1, 2, 3]. In this paper, we study a challenging problem of modeling time and space dependent user behavior data in social networks.

Latent topic models are widely used in modeling user behavior data in social network [1, 2]. The basic assumption behind these models is that a user's behavior is determined by a set of latent variables. By learning the latent variables, we can learn user behavior patterns. To date, existing latent topic models mainly consider text content extracted from behavior data. However, in reality, user behavior data in social networks are highly correlated *w.r.t.* time and space.

- **Temporal dependence.** First, user behavior data tend to be consistent due to the *action inertia*. Second, behaviors of a group of users tend to be correlated, i.e., users may discuss some topic at a certain period of time due to *global event*, e.g, the *World Cup.*
- **Spatial dependence.** The spatial dependence can be conducted through both online and offline relations. First, user behaviors tend to be correlated to the friends in social network due to *social influence* [3]. Second, topics of social users at the same location are likely to be correlated. For example, people in *Louvre Museum* tend to tweet about the *art.*

The temporal and spatial factors inspire us to model user behavior data beyond just text data in social networks. Although recent work on topic models such as the regression based latent factor models [1] consider both temporal and spatial factors, these models are not designed to handle long distance/term dependence. However, long distance/term dependence is common for users [1].

To model the spatio-temporal topic in social networks, we present a new Bayesian nonparametric model *Time and Space Dependent Chinese Restaurant Processes (TSD-CRP for short)* that can auto-select a proper number of topics. As TSD-CRP combines both spatial and temporal distances into a unified distance measure, where the temporal-spatial distance serves as a prior knowledge of two behavior records belonging to the same topic. So it can naturally model high order of dependence. Empirical results on real-world data sets demonstrate the effectiveness of the TSD-CRP.

2. RELATED WORK

To model time-dependent topics, a line of topic models have been proposed to extend the original LDA on temporal data [2, 4, 5]. However, these works were constructed un-

[1]From the perspective of time, some topics may merge periodically with long intervals. From the perspective of space, some users (especially celebrities) may influence users with indirect relations.

Permission to make digital or hard copies of all or part of this work for personal or classroom use is granted without fee provided that copies are not made or distributed for profit or commercial advantage and that copies bear this notice and the full citation on the first page. Copyrights for components of this work owned by others than ACM must be honored. Abstracting with credit is permitted. To copy otherwise, or republish, to post on servers or to redistribute to lists, requires prior specific permission and/or a fee. Request permissions from Permissions@acm.org.

CIKM'15, October 19–23, 2015, Melbourne, Australia.

© 2015 ACM. ISBN 978-1-4503-3794-6/15/10 ...$15.00.

DOI: http://dx.doi.org/10.1145/2806416.2806635.

der a strict Markov assumption and thus require to set the number of topics in advance. However, the topic number cannot be predefined and high-order dependence between user behavior records need to be considered. To model space dependent topics, existing work [3, 6] uses various types of regularization terms to enable users falling in the same space cluster to be classified together. However, the regularization terms are restricted to neighbors due to the expensive time cost and many parameters to tune. In fact, user behavior records from high-order neighbors are also correlated. Recently, a number of work combines both temporal and spatial factors in a single model [1, 7]. However, most of these models directly combine the previous mentioned technologies for modeling temporal and spatial dependence. With temporal and spatial factors involved, these models would become drastically complex.

Based on the above observations, we proposed a novel TSD-CRP model to address this problem. Our model differs from existing temporal and spatial topics models in that our model describe long term-distance dependence through a unified temporal-spatial distance measurement, and our model can auto-select proper number of topics based on data at hand.

3. TIME AND SPACE DEPENDENT CRP

We first briefly introduce the problem setting. The behavior data of user u at time t location l is denoted as $x = (w, u, t, l)$, where w is the text content determined by both the latent topic z and the parameter of the topic ϕ_z, i.e., $w \sim F(\phi_z)$.

Our goal is to discover the time and space dependent latent topics under the observed user behavior data. We wish to have solutions with two properties. First, behavior data assigned to the same topic are concentrated with respect to both time and space. Second, the number of topics are auto-selected.

As a generative model, we first introduce the generative process of TSD-CRP, then we present the method to measure the temporal and spatial distance between user behavior data records.

3.1 The Generative Procedure of TSD-CRP

In TSD-CRP, data records are generated sequentially. For each record i, a link c_i is generated from i to one of its previous records. The probability of $c_i = j$ is determined by the distance $d_{i,j}$ between i and j. A record can also link to itself (e.g., a new topic is created) with a probability proportional to a scaling parameter α. The topic assignment can be derived from these links, i.e., two data records share the same topic if they are mutually reachable, as depicted in Figure 1. Once the topic assignments are determined, the observed content are generated based on the parameters of the topics. The general procedure of TSD-CRP is summarized in Eq. (1).

$$p(c_i = j|D, f, \alpha) \propto \begin{cases} f(d_{i,j}) & j \neq i \\ \alpha & j = i \end{cases} \qquad (1)$$

$$\phi_k \sim H, \quad w_i \sim F(\phi_{z(c)_i})$$

where α is the scaling factor, d_{ij} is a distance between customer i and j, $f(\cdot)$ is the decay function which mediates how distance affects the probability of customer assignments, H is the base measure of topics, ϕ_k is the parameter of the topic, and $z(c)$ is the topic assignments inferred from $c_{1:i}$.

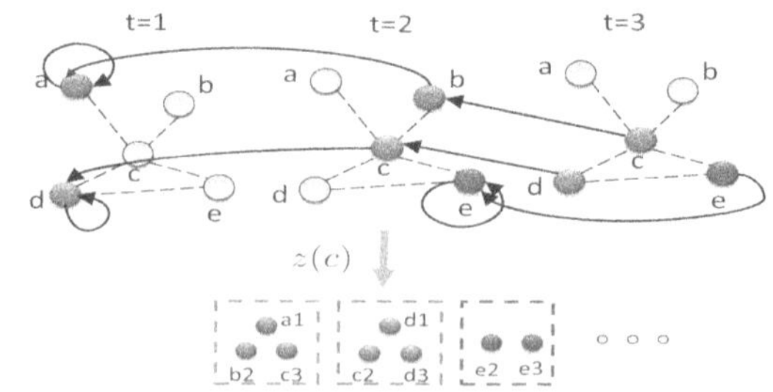

Figure 1: Top: an illustration of the data assignments of TSD-CRP in a social network with five users. The color of the circles indicates the latent topics of user behavior data (gray circles indicate the absence). Each arrow denotes a data assignment. Bottom: The corresponding topic assignments of user behavior data.

3.2 Temporal and Spatial Dependence

Based on the generation procedure of TSD-CRP, the dependence between records are determined by the distance $d_{i,j}$ and the decay function $f(\cdot)$. Then, two problems need to be settled:

- How to define the unified distance measurement when both temporal and spatial information are considered;
- How to define the decay function which determine how dependence decays over distance.

Behavior distance measure. The temporal distance of behavior data is measured by their time difference. As behavior data records are obtained sequentially, a record only depends on previous records. So we have the following definition,

Definition 1. ***Temporal distance*** *$T_{i,j}$ for user behavior data $x_i = (u_i, t_i, l_i, w_i)$ and $x_j = (u_j, t_j, l_j, w_j)$ can be measured as*

$$T_{i,j} = \begin{cases} t_i - t_j & if\ t_i > t_j \\ \infty & if\ t_i \leq t_j \end{cases} \qquad (2)$$

We consider both online and offline distances to measure the spatial distance between behavior data records. The online distance can be measured by the number of hops of the shortest path from u_i to u_j, which is denoted by $\tau^{on}_{u_i,u_j}$. If u_j is unreachable from u_i, $\tau^{on}_{u_i,u_j} = \infty$. For the off-line distance, we assume that if two users are at the same location, i.e., $l_i = l_j$, the off-line distance is defined as $\tau^{off}_{u_i,u_j} = 1$, otherwise $\tau^{off}_{u_i,u_j} = \infty$. Note that we do not use the Euclidean distance between users, as it is hard to calculate and often bring noise [7]. To sum up, we have the following definition.

Definition 2. ***The spatial distance*** *$S_{i,j}$ between $x_i = (u_i, t_i, l_i, w_i)$ and $x_j = (u_j, t_j, l_j, w_j)$ is defined as*

$$S_{i,j} = \frac{\tau^{on}_{u_i,u_j} \tau^{off}_{u_i,u_j}}{\tau^{on}_{u_i,u_j} + \tau^{off}_{u_i,u_j}} \qquad (3)$$

where $\tau^{on}_{u_i,u_j}$ denotes the distance of the shortest path between u_i to u_j. $\tau^{off}_{u_i,u_j} = 1$ if locations $l_i = l_j$; otherwise $\tau^{off}_{u_i,u_j} = \infty$.

Algorithm 1 Fully Bayesian TSD-CRP.

Input: A social network $G = \{U, E\}$, Time span T;
Hyper parameters $\{k_\lambda, \theta_\lambda, H, \alpha\}$.
Output: User behavior data records X.

```
Initialization as λ ~ Gamma(k_λ, θ_λ), i ← 0, X = ∅;
for t = 0 : T, u ∈ U do
  if u is active in t then
    i ← i + 1;
    Calculate {d_{i,j} | j = 0 : i − 1} with Eqs.(2 3 4);
    Generate c_i as in Eq.(1);
    if c_i = i then
      Assign to a new cluster, φ_new ~ H, z_i ← i;
    else
      Assign to an existing cluster, z_i ← z_{c_i};
    end if
    Generate content, w_i ~ F(φ_{z_i});
    Append x_i = {u, t, l_i = ∅, w_i} to X;
  end if
end for
return X
```

Intuitively, influential time span of a behavior data record decays rapidly along the social connections, so we use a non-linear combination of $S_{i,j}$ and $T_{i,j}$ to define the unified distance measure between behavior records.

Definition 3. ***The temporal-spatial distance*** *$d_{i,j}$ between $x_i = (u_i, t_i, l_i, w_i)$ and $x_j = (u_j, t_j, l_j, w_j)$ is defined as*

$$d_{i,j} = T_{i,j} e^{S_{i,j}} \tag{4}$$

Decay function. The decay function $f(d_{i,j})$ defines the relationship between the probability of $c_i = j$ and the distance $d_{i,j}$. Intuitively, the shorter the distance is, the more likely that the two behavior data records are assigned to the same topic. To model a high-order dependence, we set $f(d_{i,j}) > 0$ even for large $d_{i,j}$. So we use the exponential decay function with parameter λ, i.e, $f(d) = e^{-\lambda d}$.

Determining the parameter λ is difficult. We add a prior distribution to λ and make TSD-CRP to be a fully Bayesian model. So the parameter λ will be inferred from the data. As λ is limited to be positive, we use the Gamma prior for λ with vague parameters $(k_\lambda, \theta_\lambda)$,

$$\lambda \sim Gamma(k_\lambda, \theta_\lambda) \tag{5}$$

The generation procedure of the fully Bayesian TSD-CRP is summarized in Algorithm 1.

4. MODEL LEARNING

Model learning is to compute the posterior distribution of the latent variables, i.e., the customer assignments $c_{1:N}$, the global parameters λ conditioned on the observed user behavior data $x_{1:N}$, the hyper-parameters $\{k_\lambda, \theta_\lambda, H, \alpha\}$ and the behavior distance matrix $D = \{d_{i,j} | i, j = 1 : N\}$. As the posterior of $p(c_{1:N}, \lambda | x_{1:N}, D, \alpha, k_\lambda, \theta_\lambda, H)$ is not tractable in direct evaluation, we use Expectation-Maximization (EM) algorithm. In the E-step, we estimate the expectation of customer assignments $c_{1:N}$ with λ fixed. In the M-step, we maximize the expectation of data likelihood *w.r.t.* λ.

E-step. In the E-step, we use Gibbs sampling to iteratively sample c_i with the remaining data links c_{-i} fixed,

$$p(c_i | c_{-i}, x_{1:N}, D, \alpha, \lambda, H) \propto p(c_i | D, \alpha, \lambda) p(x_{1:N} | z(c_{1:N}), H). \tag{6}$$

The first term is the prior given in Eq.(1). The second term describes the likelihood of observations which can be decomposed as follows:

$$p(x_{1:N} | z(c_{1:N}), H) = \prod_{k=1}^{K(c_{1:N})} p(x_{z(c_{1:N})=k} | z(c_{1:N}), H). \tag{7}$$

where $K(c_{1:N})$ is the total number of topics derived from $c_{1:N}$.

Sampling from Eq. (6) takes two stages. First, we remove the customer assignment c_i from the current configuration. Second, we consider the probability of each possible value of c_i and how it changes the likelihood term by moving from $p(x_{1:N} | z(c_{-i}), H)$ to $p(x_{1:N} | z(c_{1:N}), H)$. So c_i can be sampled with Eq. (8),

$$p(c_i | c_{-i}, x_{1:N}, D, \alpha, \lambda) \propto \begin{cases} p(c_i | D, \alpha, \lambda) R(x, z, H) & \text{if } c_i \text{ joins } l \text{ and } m; \\ p(c_i | D, \alpha, \lambda) & \text{otherwise,} \end{cases} \tag{8}$$

where $R(x, z, H) = \frac{p(x_{z(c_{1:N})=k} | H)}{p(x_{z(c_{1:N})=l} | H) p(x_{z(c_{1:N})=m} | H)}$.

M-step. In the M-step, we update λ by maximizing the expectation of the data likelihood, which is equivalent to finding its posterior with $c_{1:N}$ fixed.

$$\begin{aligned} p(\lambda | c_{1:N}, k_\lambda, \theta_\lambda) &\propto L(\lambda | c_{1:N}) \times Gamma(\lambda | k_\lambda, \theta_\lambda) \\ &\propto \lambda^{k_\lambda + N - 1} exp(-\lambda(1/\theta_\lambda + \Upsilon(c_{1:N}))). \end{aligned} \tag{9}$$

where $\Upsilon(c_{1:N}) = \sum_i d_{i,c_i}$ for all i with $c_i \neq i$. So λ is updated by Eq.(10):

$$\lambda_{new} = \frac{k_\lambda + n}{1/\theta_\lambda + \Upsilon(c_{1:N})} \tag{10}$$

The inference procedure iterates the E-step and M-step until convergence.

Time Complexity. At each iteration, the E-step needs to sample customer assignment of all behavior data $c_{1:N}$. For each c_i, the complexity is determined by the sample space $S = |i \cup \{j | f_\lambda(d_{i,j}) > \epsilon\}|$. The volume S is assumed to be a const value for a given data set. So the time cost of the E-step is $O(NS)$. The M-step needs to update the global parameter, whose time cost is $O(N)$. Thus, the time complexity of one iteration of the EM procedure is $O(NS)$.

5. EXPERIMENTS

5.1 Experimental Settings

Data sets. The statistics of the data sets are summarized in Table 1. We mainly use location in user profile to calculate spatial distance between records.

Benchmarks. We compare TSD-CRP with CRP [8] , Recurrent CRP (RCRP) [2], Dynamic Topic Models (DTM) [4], and Topic-link LDA (TL-LDA) [6][2].

Measures. TSD-CRP defines a probability distribution over unseen data. Models that give higher probability to the unseen records better capture the topic distributions. We randomly select 5% records in the data set as the test

[2]Some previously mentioned user behavior models, such as [1, 7], belong to collaborative filtering models, which cannot model user topics.

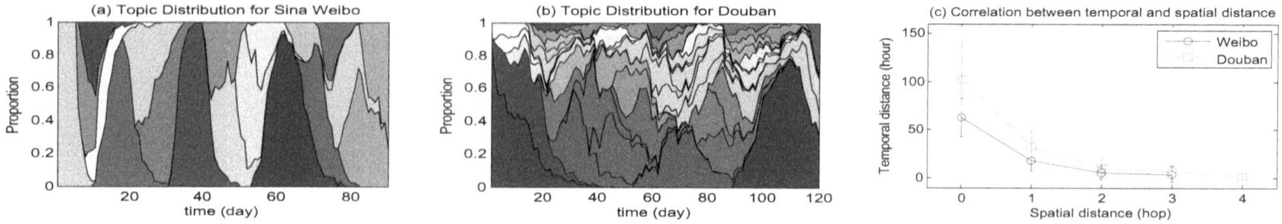

Figure 2: (a)(b)The topic distribution over time. (c) Correlation between temporal and spatial distances.

Table 1: Data statistics

Datasets	# Users	# links	# Behaviors	Time span
Weibo[3]	14K	344K	1.81M	3 months
Douban[4]	10K	189K	0.87M	4 months

Table 2: Comparisons *w.r.t.* log-likelihood ($\times 10^7$).

	TSD-CRP	CRP	RCRP	DTM	TL-LDA
Weibo	**-14.92**	-15.22	-15.08	-15.62	-15.42
Douban	**-4.474**	-4.629	-4.504	-4.781	-4.843

data to calculate the likelihood, and use the rest of the data as training set.

5.2 Results

Comparisons *w.r.t.* log-likelihood. In this test, we compare the results on behavior data records *w.r.t.* the log likelihood. The results are given in Table 2. We can observe the following results. First, TDS-CRP outperforms other methods in the data sets, which demonstrates that temporal and spatial information can help improve model accuracy. Second, parametric Bayesian models, e.g., DTM and TL-LDA, performs worse than nonparametric Bayesian models. This is because nonparametric models can auto-select the number of topics and thus more robust on the user behavior data in social networks.

Exploring temporal dependences. The topics recovered by TDS-CRP are concentrated in the temporal dimension. We visualize the temporal dependence by plotting the topic distribution over time in Figure 2 (a,b). As the total number of topics is huge, we only plot the top-20 topics. We observe that topics are highly concentrated *w.r.t.* time. The result is more obvious on the data set Weibo than on Douban. Moreover, TSD-CRP can model periodic topics which cannot be modeled by previous methods.

Correlation between spatial and temporal dependences. We also test the relationship between the temporal and spatial distances for records falling into the same topic. The results are depicted in Figure 2(c). We can observe that the closer the spatial distance the larger time span two records are correlated.

6. CONCLUSIONS

In this paper, we study a challenging problem of modeling time and space dependent user behavior data in social networks. We present a new Bayesian nonparametric model, TSD-CRP, to model the *temporal* and *spatial* factors hidden behind user behavior data. We briefly summarize our contributions as follows: 1) As a nonparametric Bayesian model, TSD-CRP can auto-select the number of topics; 2) TSD-CRP can handle high-order dependence among user behaviors; 3) TSD-CRP uses a unified measure to describe spatial and temporal distances without using any complicated regularization terms that have many parameters; 4) In experiments, we validate that TSD-CRP outperforms the state-of-the-art social behavior topic models on real-world data sets.

[3]`http:\\www.weibo.com`, the twitter-like SN in China.
[4]`http:\\www.douban.com`.

7. ACKNOWLEDGMENTS

This work was supported by the NSFC (No. 61370025), and the Strategic Leading Science and Technology Projects of CAS (No.XDA06030200), 973 project (No. 2013CB329605) and Australia ARC Discovery Project (DP140102206). C. Zhou is corresponding author.

8. REFERENCES

[1] D. Agarwal and B.-C. Chen. Regression-based latent factor models. In *Proceedings of the 15th ACM SIGKDD international conference on Knowledge discovery and data mining*, pages 19–28. ACM, 2009.
[2] A. Ahmed and E. P. Xing. Dynamic non-parametric mixture models and the recurrent chinese restaurant process: with applications to evolutionary clustering. In *SDM*, pages 219–230. SIAM, 2008.
[3] A. Anagnostopoulos, R. Kumar, and M. Mahdian. Influence and correlation in social networks. In *Proceedings of the 14th ACM SIGKDD international conference on Knowledge discovery and data mining*, pages 7–15. ACM, 2008.
[4] D. M. Blei and J. D. Lafferty. Dynamic topic models. In *Proceedings of the 23rd international conference on Machine learning*, pages 113–120. ACM, 2006.
[5] N. Du, M. Farajtabar, A. Ahmed, A. Smola, and L. Song. Dirichlet-hawkes processes with applications to clustering continuous-time document streams. In *Proceedings of 21st KDD*, 2015.
[6] Y. Liu, A. Niculescu-Mizil, and W. Gryc. Topic-link lda: joint models of topic and author community. In *proceedings of the 26th annual international conference on machine learning*, pages 665–672. ACM, 2009.
[7] Z. Lu, D. Agarwal, and I. S. Dhillon. A spatio-temporal approach to collaborative filtering. In *Proceedings of the third ACM conference on Recommender systems*, pages 13–20. ACM, 2009.
[8] J. Pitman. Exchangeable and partially exchangeable random partitions. *Probability Theory and Related Fields*, 102(2):145–158, 1995.

ASEM: Mining Aspects and Sentiment of Events from Microblog

Ruhui Wang
SPCCTA, School of Electronics and Computer Engineering, Peking University
aloe_wrh@sz.pku.edu.cn

Weijing Huang
Key Laboratory of High Confidence Software Technologies(Ministry of Education), EECS PKU
huangwaleking@gmail.com

Wei Chen*
Key Laboratory of High Confidence Software Technologies(Ministry of Education), EECS PKU
pekingchenwei@pku.edu.cn

Tengjiao Wang
Key Laboratory of High Confidence Software Technologies(Ministry of Education), EECS PKU
tjwang@pku.edu.cn

Kai Lei
SPCCTA, School of Electronics and Computer Engineering, Peking University
leik@pkusz.edu.cn

ABSTRACT

Microblogs contain the most up-to-date and abundant opinion information on current events. Aspect-based opinion mining is a good way to get a comprehensive summarization of events. The most popular aspect based opinion mining models are used in the field of product and service. However, existing models are not suitable for event mining. In this paper we propose a novel probabilistic generative model (ASEM) to simultaneously discover aspects and the specified opinions. ASEM incorporate a sequence labeling model(CRF) into a generative topic model. Additionally, we adopt a set of features for separating aspects and sentiments. Moreover, we novelly present a continuously learning model. It can utilize the knowledge of one event to learn another, and get a better performance. We use five real world events to do experiment. The experimental results show that ASEM extracts aspects and sentiments well, and ASEM outperforms other state-of-art models and the intuitive two-step method.

Categories and Subject Descriptors

H.3.3 [**Information Search and Retrieval**]: Text Mining

Keywords

Topic Model; Aspect Extraction; Aspect-Specific Sentiment Analysis; Event Extraction

*Corresponding author.

Permission to make digital or hard copies of all or part of this work for personal or classroom use is granted without fee provided that copies are not made or distributed for profit or commercial advantage and that copies bear this notice and the full citation on the first page. Copyrights for components of this work owned by others than ACM must be honored. Abstracting with credit is permitted. To copy otherwise, or republish, to post on servers or to redistribute to lists, requires prior specific permission and/or a fee. Request permissions from Permissions@acm.org.
CIKM'15, October 19–23, 2015, Melbourne, Australia.
© 2015 ACM. ISBN 978-1-4503-3794-6/15/10 ...$15.00.
DOI: http://dx.doi.org/10.1145/2806416.2806622.

1. INTRODUCTION

Aspect-based opinion mining has been an active research area in natural language processing and Web mining in recent years. Many works have been proposed to do the summarization of products and services. Meanwhile, it is also very important to extract aspects and sentiments in events. For example, in the event of "Occupy Wall Street", demonstrators held multifarious signs and the contents of the appeal are varied. How to understand the reasons of the demonstration is a very important issue. In this paper we figure out this problem by extracting aspects and the specified sentiments in events. In our work, event aspect means the most commonly discussed topics in event. The aspect-specific sentiment represents the social emotions toward the aspects. Consider the following tweet of Twitter "Republicans very concerned about human rights abuses". In this tweet, "republicans" and "human rights" are two aspects, and the respective specified sentiments are "concerned" and " abuses".

An intuitive method to solve this problem is dividing it into two steps. Firstly, extract aspects in events with aspect extraction or clustering methods. Secondly, analyse the sentiment distribution of these aspects. However, extracting aspects and opinion words simultaneously can enhance the performance both of them.

Many works have been proposed to identify aspect and sentiment words in the field of products or services. Many of them use frequent itemset mining[1][4] to extract aspects. The main limitation of these methods is that they do not group related aspects together.

Some researchers use topic models to identify aspect-specific opinion words in the field of product. However, these existing models are not suitable for event mining for the following two reasons. Firstly, microblogs are more noisy and diversified, and the aspects of events are not constant while the aspects of products are relatively constant. As a result supervised learning models, weaken supervised models and models with seeds, such as [6][9], cannot be used in event extraction. On the other hand, many researchers use LDA as a purely unsupervised model[3][8]. However, Lin and He[5] suggested that fully unsupervised topic models are unable to identify opinion words well. Secondly, the count of sentiment words is far less than aspect words in events. And the previous models has not consider this factor.

In this paper, we propose an unsupervised probabilistic generative model (ASEM), which can simultaneously extract aspects and aspect-specific opinion words of events. And it can group related aspects together. A novelty of ASEM is the integration of CRF model with the LDA model. We use a general dataset[1] to train the CRF model only once. We use the CRF model to label the latent aspects, and input its result to ASEM as an important feature. Moreover, we observed that the distribution of aspect and sentiment words is consistent with the distribution of POS tags. So we introduce POS tags as features to help separate aspect and sentiment words. So that our model is not only unsupervised, but also can separate aspect and sentiment words very well.

What's more, we discover an important feature of event. That events of the same type may have many aspects in common. For example, there are over 40% words of "CIA" event show in "NYPD" event too, not including stop words. With this observation, we propose a novel model to keep learning between events. We use five real data sets of hot events to do experiment, and the result verifies our assumption.

2. THE PROPOSED MODEL

2.1 ASEM Model

ASEM is an extension of LDA which can jointly extract aspects and sentiment words. Follow [2][7] we give two assumptions:(1) There are K aspects in a given collection of microblogs from one event, and microblogs are mixture of topics. (2) Each word is assigned to a single aspect.

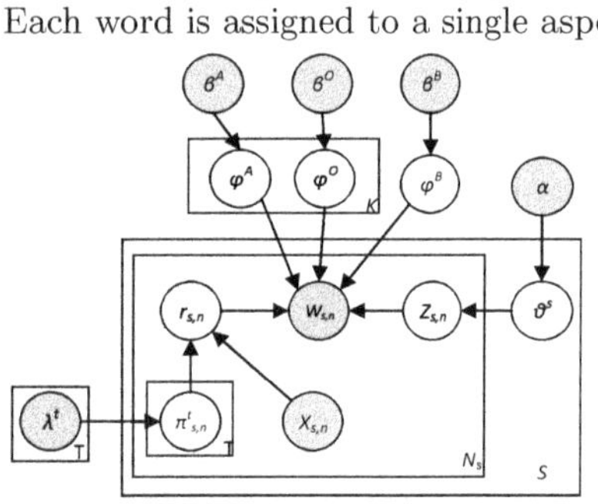

Figure 1: ASEM Model

2.1.1 *Generative Process*

The graphical representation of ASEM is shown in Fig.1. Let V be the vocabulary size, S be the number of microblogs, N_s be the number of words in one microblog s and K denote the number of topics. In each topic, there are both aspects and the aspect-specific sentiments. For word distributions, we set three multinomial from three different Dirichlet prior : a background model φ^B with parameter β^B, K aspect models $\varphi^A_{k=1\cdots K}$ with parameter β^A, and K sentiment models $\varphi^O_{k=1\cdots K}$ with parameter β^O. Then for each microblog s, we draw a topic distribution $\theta^s \sim Dir(\alpha)$.

For each word w in microblog s, we draw an aspect assignment $z_{s,n} \sim Multi(\theta^s)$. We further introduce a switch variable $r_{s,n} \in \{B, A, O\}$ for the nth word $w_{s,n}$ to indicates whether it is a background, aspect or sentiment word. $\pi^t_{s,n}$ denotes the distribution of aspects and sentiments in microblogs. Let T denote the number of different types of word. In our model there are five types in total, one is CRF labeled words and the other four are syntactic roles: *nouns*, *adjectives*, *verbs*, *others*. Some sentiment words are mislabeled in CRF, so in our model, the type of adjectives and verbs are prior to CRF labeled type. We use $X_{s,n}$ as features, which is the POS tag of current word. We only use the single POS tag as feature, not including the contextual words and POS tags as in [9]. It is because that tweet is much more irregular with bad spellings or abbreviation. After data cleaning many words are deleted, and the structures of sentences are broken. We cannot use the dependence between words, as a compromise we use the POS tag independently as features.

2.1.2 *Inference*

We use Gibbs Sampling to inference the model. Due to the space limit, we leave out the derivation details and only show the sampling formulas. The sampling formula of latent variables z and r are follow:

$$p(z_{s,n}=k, r_{s,n}=A|z_{\neg s,n}, r_{\neg s,n}, x, \alpha, \beta^A, \beta^B, \beta^O, \lambda) \propto \frac{\beta^A_v + C^A_{k,v}}{\sum_{v=1}^{V}(\beta^A_v + C^A_{k,v})} \cdot \frac{\alpha_k + C_{s,k}}{\sum_{k=1}^{K}(\alpha_k + C_{s,k})} \cdot \frac{\lambda^t_A}{\lambda^t_A + \lambda^t_B + \lambda^t_O} \quad (1)$$

$$p(z_{s,n}=k, r_{s,n}=O|z_{\neg s,n}, r_{\neg s,n}, x, \alpha, \beta^A, \beta^B, \beta^O, \lambda) \propto \frac{\beta^O_v + C^O_{k,v}}{\sum_{v=1}^{V}(\beta^O_v + C^O_{k,v})} \cdot \frac{\alpha_k + C_{s,k}}{\sum_{k=1}^{K}(\alpha_k + C_{s,k})} \cdot \frac{\lambda^t_O}{\lambda^t_A + \lambda^t_B + \lambda^t_O} \quad (2)$$

$$p(r_{s,n}=B|r_{\neg s,n}, x, \alpha, \beta^A, \beta^B, \beta^O, \lambda) \propto \frac{\beta^B_v + C^B_v}{\sum_{v=1}^{V}(\beta^B_v + C^B_v)} \cdot \frac{\lambda^t_B}{\lambda^t_A + \lambda^t_B + \lambda^t_O} \quad (3)$$

where $C_{s,k}$ is the number of words assigned to topic k in sentence s. $C^A_{k,v}$ is the number of times that word v is assigned to topic k as an aspect, $C^O_{k,v}$ is the number of times that word v is assigned to topic k as a sentiment word, and C^B_v is the number of times that word v is assigned to be a background word. $_{\neg s,n}$ denotes counts excluding sentence s. t represents the type of word v, it is equal to $X_{s,n}$.

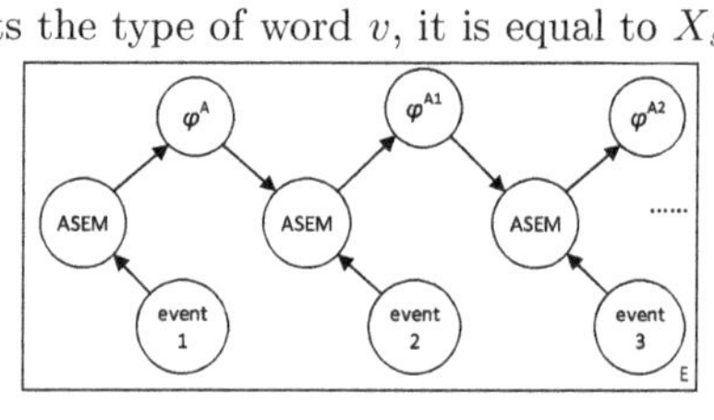

Figure 2: Continuous Learning Model

2.2 Continuous Learning Model

We observed that aspects of two events from the same type may have similarities. For example, CIA and NYPD are two political events, and *obama* is an aspect in both of them. So we propose an continuous learning model, which can keep learning from events in the same kind.

The learning process is show in Fig.2. E is the group of events, all of them belong to a same kind, such as: *political events*, *sports events*, *entertainment events*. φ^A is the

[1]http://www.cnts.ua.ac.be/conll2000/chunking/

Table 1: Some statistics of the data sets

Dataset	CIA	Cuba	NYPD	Bengals	Rajon
Tweets	30722	341041	400000	289913	101886
Tokens	254808	2942419	3519923	2137976	1018952

Table 2: The setting of λ

	r _ a	n n	er	a j	er
λ_A	400	400	20	20	200
λ_O	40	20	400	400	200
λ_B	1	200	20	20	400
λ'_A	400	400	400	20	400
λ'_O	40	400	400	400	400
λ'_B	1	400	400	20	400

aspect model in ASEM. Firstly, we use ASEM to learn the *event*1, save its aspect model φ^A. Then we use the φ^A to initialize our model to learn *event*2. And then the same way to learn *event*3 and so on.

By utilizing the result of previous event, our model can usually have a better performance. Empirical evaluation on real world data sets shows that continuous learning have a better performance than single event.

3. EXPERIMENTAL SETUP

To evaluate our model we use two kinds of real-world events: *political events* and *sports events*. We crawl al-l data sets from Twitter with it's *Search API* [2]. We set parameter q to species the key word to retrieve tweets. The *Search API* provides *max_id* and *since_id* parameter, so that we can get tweets continuously.

We crawl five hot events occured from December 2014 to January 2015.(1)*CIA event*: U.S. Senate released it-s report on the CIA's use of "harsh interrogation" tactic-s against prisoners. (2)*Cuba event*: Obama and Castro announced to reestablish diplomatic relations. (3)*NYPD event*: A gunman shot dead two police officers in New York. (4)*Bengals event*: The Cincinnati Bengals win the Pittsburgh Steelers.(5)*Rajon event*: Rajon Rondo full highlights vs Lakers. Detail statistics are shown in Table 1.

After data preprocessing, we use CRF++[3] model to label latent aspects by identifying our own features, including: *Token*, *POS* and *Named Entity*. To quantitatively evaluate our model, we randomly select 200 tweets from Cuba and Bengals event separately. We label each word to background, aspect and sentiment word.

For our hybrid model, we run 500 iterations of Gibbs sampling. We set K to be 20 and the Dirichlet priors α as 0.01. Following [9], we fixed $\beta_A = \beta_O = \beta_B = 0.01$. We set up the value of λ by cross validation with an optimal group of values which is shown in the first three rows of Table 2.

4. EXPERIMENTS

4.1 Qualitative Results

In Table 3 we show the sample results identified by ASEM model. Due to space limit, we only show three aspects of the Cuba and NYPD event. For each aspect we list top 10 aspect words and the related sentiment words. We can see that generally aspects and sentiment words are separated, and opinion words correspond to aspects very well. For example, "torture" is an aspect in "Human Rights" and the specific sentiment words are "worst", "awkward". In topic "relations" of Cuba, "relations" and "rapprochement" are related aspects. Correspondingly the sentiment words are "good", "diplomatic" and "free".

[2]http://apiwiki.twitter.com/

[3]http://crfpp.googlecode.com/svn/trunk/doc/index.html ?source=navbar

Table 3: Example Aspects and Sentiments Extracted by ASEM

Cuba		NYPD	
Human Rights		Pray	
aspect	sentiment	aspect	sentiment
rights	defending	officers	killed
torture	worst	families	sad
human	called	prayers	slain
republicans	abuses	today	pray
obama	complaining	family	mourn
moment	awkward	brooklyn	bless
decade	warned	brothers	tragically
sin	cuban	sons	fallen
deal	bashing	thoughts	heartbreaking
dungeon	concerned	mourning	entire
Relation		Victim	
aspect	sentiment	aspect	sentiment
relations	major	officer	married
obama	visit	officers	rip
embargo	diplomatic	ramos	fatal
travel	improved	liu	murdered
propaganda	good	son	killed
rapprochement	long	veteran	white
americans	change	rafael	racist
usa	free	wenjian	slain
cancun	united	blasio	responsible
american	restore	brooklyn	shooting
President		Peaceful Protest	
aspect	sentiment	aspect	sentiment
president	communist	cops	racist
castro	hope	eric	arrest
obama	finish	garner	condemn
thaw	visit	protesters	controversial
castros	happy	murder	resign
raul	hails	brown	resigndeblasio
south	bring	people	strongly
bahamas	respect	death	urge
obamas	normalize	michael	peaceful
authorities	affirms	police	shit

4.2 Evaluation of Results

We use manually annotated data sets of Cuba and Benjals event to do experiment. Precision(P), Recall(R) and the $F1$ value to be the metrics. ASEM is a probabilistic model, we run 10 times for each experiment, and list the average P and R in Table 4. Our standard result named ASEM.

To evaluate the advantage of using CRF labeled data, we remove the CRF labeled data from ASEM. The result is shown in Table 4 named as ASEM_NC. We can see that without CRF labeling, the average $F1$ has dropped about fifteen percentage points, and $F1$ of sentiment have no influence. Which is consistent with our expectation, as the CRF labeled data are latent aspects which affect aspects only.

In order to prove the importance of POS tag features, we do contrast experiments ASEM_NB. We weaken the influence of POS tags by setting up λ with the value ofλ'_A, λ'_O , λ'_B in Table 2. We can see that both the performance of aspect and sentiment extraction have a big decline.

Moreover, we choose ME-LDA [9] as the compared method. ME-LDA can also extract both aspects and aspect-specific opinion words. We follow this paper and use six features: $\{w_{i-1}, w_i, w_{i+1}, POS_{i-1}, POS_i, POS_{i+1}\}$. Also we use our annotated tweets to train the model. The results are demon-

Table 4: Aspect-specific Sentiment Extraction Performance

Da a e	**M**			**M_NC**			**M_N**			**M _ D**			**Tw e**		
	P	R	F1	P	R	F1	P	R	F1	P	R	F1	P	R	F1
Cuba/Asp	83.0	88.0		79.5	60.2	68.5	78.7	61.7	69.2	60.2	85.0	70.5	69.0	93.1	79.2
Cuba/Senti	56.9	78.2	**9**	57.1	77.8		49.2	65.7	56.3	46.3	35.2	40.0	48.1	71.9	57.7
Ben/Asp	85.5	88.0		83.9	64.7	73.1	83.8	65.4	73.5	58.7	83.4	68.9	63.1	96.5	76.2
Ben/Senti	57.2	79.9		57.6	79.1		47.5	57.1	51.9	43.5	32.8	37.4	52.8	67.4	59.2

strated in column ME_LDA of Table 4. It can be seen that our model has a higher P and R value than ME_LDA, especially in the sentiment extraction.

In addition, we compare our model with two step methods. CRF Labeling is a famous method to extract aspects. We use CRF++ to extract aspects. Then use POS tags and a sentiment word dictionary to extract sentiment words. The results are demonstrated in column TwoStep of Table 4.

4.3 Continuous Learning Results

In this section, we prove the continuous learning character of our model. We have three *political* events: CIA, Cuba and NYPD, and two Sport events: Bengals and Rajon. Firstly we learn the CIA event and then use its φ_A to initialize NYPD event, and save the combined φ_A of these two events as φ'_A. Cuba/S represents the single Cuba event, while Cuba/L means the Cuba event with φ'_A initialization. As parameter φ_A is mostly influence the extraction of aspects, we just list the metrics of aspects in Table 5.

We can see that with the knowledge of previous event, our model can have a better performance with 2.5% improvement. The promotion of sport event is tiny, because Rajon is about basketball and Bengals is about football. The words they shared is 16% of Bengals, while the shared words of the three political events is 38% of Cuba.

Moreover, we compare the model labeled data with our manual annotations. We find many aspect words that do not discovered in Cuba/S, were discovered in the Cuba/L. For example, in tweet "agriculture big appetite cuba trade honolulu", "honolulu" was labeled as background in Cuba/S while it is labeled as aspects in Cuba/L. What's more, in NYPD event "honolulu" is an aspect discovered by our model. Which is the reason why our model can have a better performance in the continuous learning model.

Table 5: Continuous Learning Results

Da a e	P	R	F1
Cuba/S	83.0	88.0	85.4
Cuba/L	84.2	92.1	88.0
Bengals/S	85.5	88.0	86.7
Bengals/L	86.7	89.5	88.0

5. CONCLUSION

In this paper, we propose a topic model (ASEM), which can simultaneously extract aspects and aspect-specific opinion words of events. With the utilization of CRF model to do pre-extraction, we could leverage syntactic features to help extract aspect better. In addition, we introduce the POS tags as features to separate the aspect and sentiment words. We evaluate our model in five real world events, and compare it against an existing approach. The experiments give promising results. Most importantly, we propose a continuously learning model which can utilize the knowledge of one event to learn another. And the continuously learning model have a better performance than single event extraction.

Timeliness is a very important information in events. In the future, we plan to add time information into our model, so that we can identify the development trend of events.

6. ACKNOWLEDGEMENTS

This research is supported by the Natural Science Foundation of China (Grant No. 61300003), Specialized Research Fund for the Doctoral Program of Higher Education(Grant No. 20130001120001) and Ministry of Education & China Mobile Joint Research Fund Program (MCM20130361).

7. REFERENCES

[1] S. Blair-Goldensohn, K. Hannan, R. McDonald, T. Neylon, G. A. Reis, and J. Reynar. Building a sentiment summarizer for local service reviews. In *WWW Workshop on NLP in the Information Explosion Era*, volume 14, 2008.

[2] D. M. Blei, A. Y. Ng, and M. I. Jordan. Latent dirichlet allocation. *the Journal of machine Learning research*, 3:993–1022, 2003.

[3] S. Brody and N. Elhadad. An unsupervised aspect-sentiment model for online reviews. In *Human Language Technologies: The 2010 Annual Conference of the North American Chapter of the Association for Computational Linguistics*, pages 804–812. Association for Computational Linguistics, 2010.

[4] M. Hu and B. Liu. Mining and summarizing customer reviews. In *Proceedings of the tenth ACM SIGKDD international conference on Knowledge discovery and data mining*, pages 168–177. ACM, 2004.

[5] C. Lin and Y. He. Joint sentiment/topic model for sentiment analysis. In *Proceedings of the 18th ACM conference on Information and knowledge management*, pages 375–384. ACM, 2009.

[6] A. Mukherjee and B. Liu. Aspect extraction through semi-supervised modeling. In *Proceedings of the 50th Annual Meeting of the Association for Computational Linguistics: Long Papers-Volume 1*, pages 339–348. Association for Computational Linguistics, 2012.

[7] M. Steyvers and T. Griffiths. Probabilistic topic models. *Handbook of latent semantic analysis*, 427(7):424–440, 2007.

[8] I. Titov and R. T. McDonald. A joint model of text and aspect ratings for sentiment summarization. In *ACL*, volume 8, pages 308–316. Citeseer, 2008.

[9] W. X. Zhao, J. Jiang, H. Yan, and X. Li. Jointly modeling aspects and opinions with a maxent-lda hybrid. In *Proceedings of the 2010 Conference on Empirical Methods in Natural Language Processing*, pages 56–65. Association for Computational Linguistics, 2010.

Enhanced Word Embeddings from a Hierarchical Neural Language Model

Xun Wang, Katsuhito Sudoh and Masaaki Nagata
NTT Communication Science Laboratories, Kyoto, 619-0237, Japan
wang.xun, sudoh.katsuhito, nagata.masaaki@lab.ntt.co.jp

ABSTRACT

This paper proposes a neural language model to capture the interaction of text units of different levels, i.e.., documents, paragraphs, sentences, words in an hierarchical structure. At each paralleled level, the model incorporates Markov property while each higher-level unit hierarchically influences its containing units. Such an architecture enables the learned word embeddings to encode both global and local information. We evaluate the learned word embeddings and experiments demonstrate the effectiveness of our model.

Categories and Subject Descriptors

H.3.1 [**Information Storage and Retrieval**]: Content Analysis and Indexing abstracting methods; I.2.7 [**Computing Methodologies**]: Artificial Intelligence Natural Language Processing

General Terms

Algorithms; Experimentation

Keywords

neural network; hierarchical model; distributed representations; word embeddings

1. INTRODUCTION

Word embeddings represent words using real-valued, abstract and condensed vectors. There are two main families for learning embeddings for words: The first family leverages document-level word-occurrence statistics, such as LDA [Blei et al., 2003], GloVe [JeffreyPennington and Manning, 2014], or matrix factorization based approaches (e.g., LSA and SVD) given the intuition that co-occurrent words are relevant. Those global co-occurrence statistics based models neglect word order information about how local meanings are formed by neighboring words. The second category corresponds to local context window approaches (e.g.,[Bengio et al., 2006, Collobert and Weston, 2008, Mikolov et al., 2013a]). The downside of such models is that they poorly harness the global information at document, paragraph or sentence level. Some attempts try to bridge the gap between the two families: [Huang et al., 2012] proposes a document-level vector leveraged from tf-idf into local learning process and *paragraph vector* [Le and Mikolov, 2014] makes word prediction with the help of the leveraged document/paragraph/sentence level information. [Li et al., 2015b] explores hierarchical autoencoder for paragraph and document representations. Their efforts prove useful for learning sentence, paragraph and document representations. But they do not consider using the relations between different levels to improve the word embeddings which are the basis of all. Towards better word embeddings, we consider the intrinsic structure of text about how units are arranged to form meaningful context:

(1) **Horizontally**: as we look at discourse theory in early days (Mann and Thompson (1988)), in a coherent text, not only words, but clauses, sentences, and larger multi-clause groupings are tightly connected. Text units take their respective roles and interact with units at the same level (token-to-token, sentence-to-sentence and paragraph to paragraph) semantically, syntactically, and logically.

(2) **Vertically**: Words form the meanings of sentences; sentences form paragraphs, and then paragraphs form documents, which organizes the arrangements into a tree structure vertically.

The importance of tree structures in sentence, paragraph and document representation has been revealed by previous research [Socher et al., 2013, Li et al., 2014, Li et al., 2015a]. Here we show how they can be used to improve the word embeddings. The proposed model captures the two aforementioned aspects of meanings in a unified embedding learning framework which holds promise to bridge the gap between the co-occurrence based and prediction based embedding learning frameworks. Horizontally, we model each level of units based on the Markovian manner, where neighbouring unites are correlated based on the similar assumption we make in language model. Vertically, each unit (e.g., sentence) exerts its impact on its containing lower-level text units (e.g., words). Unlike [Huang et al., 2012] where document-level information is harshly incorporated, the proposed approach gently incorporates the order information at paragraph level and sentence level, and therefore preserves the semantic integrity of the contexts.

The adopted type of architecture arranges all text units in a unified structure, where influence of one unit is propagated to others (the siblings and children), naturally bridging the gap of and taking the merits from the aforementioned two learning families. To note, our approach is inspired by paragraph vector model [Le and Mikolov, 2014] where models paragraph and tokens within it in a two-level hierarchy where words are predicted given neighbours and its resided paragraph.

The proposed architecture is ultimately grounded on the lowest level of the hierarchical structure, words, by predicting the current token, where the embeddings for neighboring tokens, and higher levels text units are simultaneously updated. The proposed algo-

Permission to make digital or hard copies of all or part of this work for personal or classroom use is granted without fee provided that copies are not made or distributed for profit or commercial advantage and that copies bear this notice and the full citation on the first page. Copyrights for components of this work owned by others than ACM must be honored. Abstracting with credit is permitted. To copy otherwise, or republish, to post on servers or to redistribute to lists, requires prior specific permission and/or a fee. Request permissions from Permissions@acm.org.
CIKM'15, October 19–23, 2015, Melbourne, Australia.
© 2015 ACM. ISBN 978-1-4503-3794-6/15/10 ...$15.00.
DOI: http://dx.doi.org/10.1145/2806416.2806637.

rithm is a general one and can be adjusted to currently prevailed frameworks, e.g., skip-grammar models, CBOW, recurrent neural models [Mikolov et al., 2010]. The system can be optimized by standard strategies taken in embedding learning literature, either through standard softmax, or others like hierarchical softmax, NCE or negative sampling.

Note that the proposed algorithm ends up with distributed representations for documents, sentences and words, which could be used as input for different applications for different levels of units. But here we just keep the word embeddings for the proposed model has not been optimized regarding to upper level text units. For these large text units, it is still not clear how their meanings are made up from their containing words. Though several composition based neural network models [Tai et al., 2015, Zaremba and Sutskever, 2014, Socher et al., 2013] have been proposed and proved useful in a range of tasks, none of them manage to achieve the expected level of performance as word embedding models do.

We evaluate the learning frameworks on word analogy and word similarity tasks, two basic tasks for word embedding evaluation. Experimental results demonstrate that by harnessing the hierarchical structure of documents, we obtain better performances.

2. MODEL

Document D is comprised of a sequence of paragraphs $D = \{P_1, P_2, .., P_{N_D}\}$, paragraph P is comprised of a sequence of sentences $P = \{S_1, S_2, ...S_{N_P}\}$ and sentence S is comprised of a sequence of words $S = \{w_1, w_2, ..., w_{N_S}\}$, where N_D, N_P and N_S respectively denote the number of correspondent children in the document, paragraph and sentence. Each level text unit D, P, S, w is associated with a K dimensional embedding e_D, e_P, e_S and e_w. All text units are therefore arranged in into a tree hierarchy with $L = 4$ levels. Let η denote any node in the tree, where η could be document, paragraph, sentence or word with embedding e_η. $parent(\eta)$, $sibling(\eta)$ and $kid(\eta)$ respectively denote the parent, siblings and kids of η.

2.1 Revisit Distributed Neural Language Models

We first revisit the general neural learning framework for word embedding widely adopted in existing research.

Consider a sequence of word tokens $\{w_1, w_2, ..., w_N\}$. The conditional probability of current word is given by:

$$\begin{aligned} &p(w_n|w_{n-1}, ..., w_{n-k}, w_{n+1}, .., w_{n+k}) = \\ &f(e_n|g(e_{n-1}, ..., e_{n-k}, e_{n+1}, .., e_{n+k}), \Theta) \end{aligned} \tag{1}$$

where Θ denotes the parameter space involved in the probability function $f()$. $g()$ denotes the operation performed on neighboring vectors. Many different types of $g()$ have been explored such as averaging neighboring embeddings (CBOW) [Mikolov et al., 2013a], getting the dot product between w_n and each of its neighbors (skip-grams) [Mikolov et al., 2013a], concatenating neighboring vectors and projecting the concatenating into a low-dimensional space (e.g., [Collobert et al., 2011, Vaswani et al., 2013]), or convolving the preceding words using a recurrent network [Mikolov et al., 2011].

Commonly used forms of $f()$ include predicting current word using a softmax function or contrastive sampling. Many alternatives have been proposed for easy training, such as hierarchical softmax [Mikolov et al., 2013b] and Noise-contrastive Estimation [Vaswani et al., 2013, Mnih and Teh, 2012].

2.2 Joint Embedding Training from Hierarchical Structure

Our model take advantages of the hierarchitecture of text.

- Horizontally, we incorporate Markov property at each level of the tree structure.

- Vertically, kid embeddings are influenced by their parent nodes.

The model extends standard embedding learning framework by subsequently predicting embedding of every node η along the tree structure given its parent and siblings:

$$\begin{aligned} &p(\eta|parent(\eta), sibling(\eta)) \\ &\quad = f(e_\eta|g(e_{parent(\eta)}, \{e_{\eta', \eta' \in Sibling(\eta)}\}, \Theta) \end{aligned} \tag{2}$$

Thus, the probability of the whole document is given by:

$$\begin{aligned} &p(D|\Theta, e_D, \{e_P\}, \{e_S\}, \{e_w\}) \\ &= \prod_{\eta \in Tree} f(e_\eta|g(e_{parent(\eta)}, \{e_{\eta', \eta' \in Sibling(\eta)}\}, \Theta) \end{aligned} \tag{3}$$

As can be seen, for two words that do not reside in the same sentence, they will still distantly interact with each other as the influence is propagated up to the containing sentence embedding, paragraph embedding and document embedding, and then down to the other word. Therefore, the proposed model can to some extent capture global level statistics without losing the advantages of local neural composition.

On the other hand, based on the Markov property along each level of the trees, the meanings of adjacent text units interact with each other and preserves the integrity of meanings at each level, potentially leading to better representations at lower levels. Eventually these merits will be further propagated to word level prediction, leading to better word level embeddings.

For illustration purpose, we assume $g()$ takes the form the concatenation of sibling embeddings and parent embedding. $f(\cdot)$ takes the form of sigmoid function at sentence/paragraph level and softmax at word level. Let P denote the the paragraph that sentence S_i resides in, and S denotes the sentence that word w_i resides in, we have:

$$\begin{aligned} &p(e_{S_i}|\cdot) = \sigma(e_{S_i} \cdot g(e_P, e_{S_{i-1}}, ..., e_{S_{i-N}})] \\ &p(e_{w_i}|\cdot) = \frac{\exp(e_{w_i} \cdot g(e_S, e_{w_{i-1}}, ..., e_{w_{i-N}}))}{\sum_w \exp(e_w \cdot g(e_S, e_{w_{i-1}}, ..., e_{w_{i-N}}))} \end{aligned} \tag{4}$$

where $\sigma(\cdot)$ denotes sigmoid function.

Parameters Θ and embeddings are estimated by making MLE estimation:

$$\begin{aligned} &[\Theta, e_D, \{e_P\}, \{e_S\}, \{e_w\}] = \\ &\underset{\Theta', e'_D, e'_P, e'_S, e'_w}{\text{argmax}} \prod_D p(D|\Theta', e'_D, \{e'_P\}, \{e'_S\}, \{e'_w\}) \end{aligned} \tag{5}$$

2.3 Details of Implementation

Parameters Θ and word embeddings are to be estimated from the training corpus. Meanwhile we also estimate embeddings of document, paragraph and sentence given containing words and the correspondent embeddings. MLE estimation is implemented as is the same with previous work. A similar strategy can be found in [Le and Mikolov, 2014]. The estimated embeddings can be used as feature for downstream applications.

Model	WS-353	RG	MC	SCWS	RW
Skp-Grammar	68.7	78.1	71.5	58.1	37.2
Paragraph Vector	69.2	77.8	72.9	58.0	39.6
Joint Learning	71.2	78.6	73.8	57.9	41.7
CBOW	61.7	77.8	64.5	57.2	33.8
Paragraph Vector	62.4	79.1	65.8	56.9	34.2
Joint Learning	64.2	79.2	66.4	57.2	37.1
Concatenation	70.1	76.0	72.3	54.6	35.2
Paragraph Vector	70.0	77.1	72.5	57.2	37.9
Joint Learning	71.7	77.5	74.8	57.0	39.4
GloVe	68.6	77.5	77.2	52.7	39.2

Table 1: Spearman correlation results on word similarity tasks. Dimensionality of vectors are set to 300. All reported results are based on embeddings trained from the same Wiki2014 dataset. For each subset, Paragraph Vector and Joint Learning use the same $f(\cdot)$ and $g(\cdot)$ as the model at the top.

Model	Accuracy
Skp-Grammar	0.691
Paragraph-Vector	0.690
Joint Learning	0.714
CBOW	0.657
Paragraph-Vector	0.662
Joint Learning	0.678
Concatenation	0.702
Paragraph-Vector	0.706
Joint Learning	0.718
GloVe	0.716

Table 2: Results on word analogy task. Models are trained on the same Wiki2014 corpus. Skip-Grammar and CBOW are trained on Word2Vec.

We employ three forms of operational functions.
(1) Skip-grammar model [Mikolov et al., 2013a]:

$$f(e_\eta | g(e_{parent(\eta)}, \{e_{\eta', \eta' \in Sibling(\eta)}\}, \Theta) = \sigma(e_\eta \cdot e_{parent(\eta)}) \prod_{\eta' \in Sibling(\eta)} \sigma(e_\eta \cdot e_{\eta'}) \quad (6)$$

(2) CBOW like model [Mikolov et al., 2013a] which first averages the embeddings of parent and siblings and dot products with current node embedding:

$$\begin{aligned} & f(e_\eta | g(e_{parent(\eta)}, \{e_{\eta', \eta' \in Sibling(\eta)}\}, \Theta) \\ & = \sigma(e_\eta \cdot g(e_{parent(\eta)}, \{e_{\eta', \eta' \in Sibling(\eta)}\})) \\ & g(e_{parent(\eta)}, \{e_{\eta', \eta' \in Sibling(\eta)}\}) = \\ & \frac{1}{1 + |Sibling(\eta)|}(e_{parent(\eta)} + \sum_{\eta' \in Sibling(\eta)} e_{\eta'}) \end{aligned} \quad (7)$$

(3) Concatenation model which can takes sequence order information by first concatenating embeddings of parent and siblings and then projects the concatenated vector sharing same dimensionality with current node embedding:

$$\begin{aligned} & g(e_{parent(\eta)}, \{e_{\eta', \eta' \in Sibling(\eta)}\}) = \\ & tanh(W \cdot [e_S, e_{w_{i-1}}, ..., e_{w_{i-N}}]) \end{aligned} \quad (8)$$

where $[\cdot]$ denotes the concatenation of its containing vectors and W denotes the $(1 + N) \times K$ dimensional convolutional matrix. For concatenation approach, we use a dropout [Hinton et al., 2012, Srivastava, 2013] rate of 0.5.

The initialization of embeddings for sentences, paragraphs and sentences are conducted by averaging embeddings for its containing tokens using tf-idf, similar as in [Huang et al., 2012].

3. EXPERIMENTAL RESULTS

Word Similarity Evalution.

Word embeddings are evaluated in terms of standard word similarity measures to see whether taking account text hierarchy can improve those measures. We train our models using Wikipedia2014 dataset. We adopt a hierarchical softmax function for word prediction. The window size is set to 11.

We employ standard ontology evaluation metrics include Tofel-353 [Finkelstein et al., 2001], MC [Miller and Charles, 1991], RG [Rubenstein and Goodenough, 1965], SCWS [Huang et al., 2012], and RW [Luong et al., 2013]. Each dataset is comprised of pairs of words with gold-standard human annotations, indicating the similarity score between the pair of words. For example, "book, paper, 7.46" denotes the similarity score for word pair (book, paper) is 7.46. Standardly, we adopt cosine similarity. Spearmans rank correlation coefficient is then obtained between this score and human judgement.

Baselines include Skip-Grammar, CBOW, Concatenation paragraph vector [Le and Mikolov, 2014]. Experimental results are illustrated in Table 1. As can be seen, by considering the hierarchical structure of text units, better performance can be and have been achieved.

Word Analogy Task.

Word analogy evaluation aims at answering questions like "a is to b as c is to what". Question types include semantic ones like 'Beijing is to China like London to what" (captial) or syntactic ones like "dance to dancing as fly to what" (tense). The dataset is introduced in [Mikolov et al., 2013a] and contains 8,869 semantic questions and 10,675 syntactic questions. We follow the protocols described in [Mikolov et al., 2013c, JeffreyPennington and Manning, 2014] that to answer questions "a is to b as c is to what", we do the simple math by computing $E_b - E_a + E_c$, where E denotes the embedding for current word, and find the word d with closest representation based on cosine similarity.

Performances regarding different models are illustrated in Table 2. Similar phenomenon are observed as word similarity tasks where better performances are observed when text structure are considered. The proposed model gives better performances than previous models for word embeddings. Comparing with previous models, we consider both the local and global information.

The sole aim of this paper is to use text structure to improve word embeddings. We do generate embeddings for sentences, paragraphs and documents. But we cannot expect them to produce satisfying performances for a range of tasks without further improvements, which is our future work.

4. CONCLUSION

We present a hierarchical neural network model for word embeddings learning. Experiments verify the effectiveness of the learned word embeddings. As stated above, the learning of large text unit embeddings remains a problem. In the future we will explore new architectures to learn powerful embeddings for sentences, paragraphs and documents.

5. REFERENCES

[Bengio et al., 2006] Bengio, Y., Schwenk, H., Senécal, J.-S., Morin, F., and Gauvain, J.-L. (2006). Neural probabilistic language models. In *Innovations in Machine Learning*, pages 137–186. Springer.

[Blei et al., 2003] Blei, D. M., Ng, A. Y., and Jordan, M. I. (2003). Latent dirichlet allocation. *the Journal of machine Learning research*, 3:993–1022.

[Collobert and Weston, 2008] Collobert, R. and Weston, J. (2008). A unified architecture for natural language processing: Deep neural networks with multitask learning. In *Proceedings of the 25th international conference on Machine learning*, pages 160–167. ACM.

[Collobert et al., 2011] Collobert, R., Weston, J., Bottou, L., Karlen, M., Kavukcuoglu, K., and Kuksa, P. (2011). Natural language processing (almost) from scratch. *The Journal of Machine Learning Research*, 12:2493–2537.

[Finkelstein et al., 2001] Finkelstein, L., Gabrilovich, E., Matias, Y., Rivlin, E., Solan, Z., Wolfman, G., and Ruppin, E. (2001). Placing search in context: The concept revisited. In *Proceedings of the 10th international conference on World Wide Web*, pages 406–414. ACM.

[Hinton et al., 2012] Hinton, G. E., Srivastava, N., Krizhevsky, A., Sutskever, I., and Salakhutdinov, R. R. (2012). Improving neural networks by preventing co-adaptation of feature detectors. *arXiv preprint arXiv:1207.0580.*

[Huang et al., 2012] Huang, E. H., Socher, R., Manning, C. D., and Ng, A. Y. (2012). Improving word representations via global context and multiple word prototypes. In *Proceedings of the 50th Annual Meeting of the Association for Computational Linguistics: Long Papers-Volume 1*, pages 873–882. Association for Computational Linguistics.

[JeffreyPennington and Manning, 2014] JeffreyPennington, R. and Manning, C. (2014). Glove: Global vectors for word representation.

[Le and Mikolov, 2014] Le, Q. V. and Mikolov, T. (2014). Distributed representations of sentences and documents. *arXiv preprint arXiv:1405.4053.*

[Li et al., 2015a] Li, J., Jurafsky, D., and Hovy, E. (2015a). When are tree structures necessary for deep learning of representations? *arXiv preprint arXiv:1503.00185.*

[Li et al., 2014] Li, J., Li, R., and Hovy, E. (2014). Recursive deep models for discourse parsing.

[Li et al., 2015b] Li, J., Luong, M.-T., and Jurafsky, D. (2015b). A hierarchical neural autoencoder for paragraphs and documents. *arXiv preprint arXiv:1506.01057.*

[Luong et al., 2013] Luong, M.-T., Socher, R., and Manning, C. (2013). Better word representations with recursive neural networks for morphology. *CoNLL-2013*, 104.

[Mikolov et al., 2013a] Mikolov, T., Chen, K., Corrado, G., and Dean, J. (2013a). Efficient estimation of word representations in vector space. *arXiv preprint arXiv:1301.3781.*

[Mikolov et al., 2010] Mikolov, T., Karafiát, M., Burget, L., Cernockỳ, J., and Khudanpur, S. (2010). Recurrent neural network based language model. In *INTERSPEECH*, pages 1045–1048.

[Mikolov et al., 2011] Mikolov, T., Kombrink, S., Deoras, A., Burget, L., and Cernocky, J. (2011). Rnnlm-recurrent neural network language modeling toolkit. In *Proc. of the 2011 ASRU Workshop*, pages 196–201.

[Mikolov et al., 2013b] Mikolov, T., Sutskever, I., Chen, K., Corrado, G. S., and Dean, J. (2013b). Distributed representations of words and phrases and their compositionality. In *Advances in Neural Information Processing Systems*, pages 3111–3119.

[Mikolov et al., 2013c] Mikolov, T., Yih, W.-t., and Zweig, G. (2013c). Linguistic regularities in continuous space word representations. In *HLT-NAACL*, pages 746–751. Citeseer.

[Miller and Charles, 1991] Miller, G. A. and Charles, W. G. (1991). Contextual correlates of semantic similarity. *Language and cognitive processes*, 6(1):1–28.

[Mnih and Teh, 2012] Mnih, A. and Teh, Y. W. (2012). A fast and simple algorithm for training neural probabilistic language models. *arXiv preprint arXiv:1206.6426.*

[Rubenstein and Goodenough, 1965] Rubenstein, H. and Goodenough, J. B. (1965). Contextual correlates of synonymy. *Communications of the ACM*, 8(10):627–633.

[Socher et al., 2013] Socher, R., Perelygin, A., Wu, J. Y., Chuang, J., Manning, C. D., Ng, A. Y., and Potts, C. (2013). Recursive deep models for semantic compositionality over a sentiment treebank. In *Proceedings of EMNLP*.

[Srivastava, 2013] Srivastava, N. (2013). *Improving neural networks with dropout*. PhD thesis, University of Toronto.

[Tai et al., 2015] Tai, K. S., Socher, R., and Manning, C. D. (2015). Improved semantic representations from tree-structured long short-term memory networks. *arXiv preprint arXiv:1503.00075.*

[Vaswani et al., 2013] Vaswani, A., Zhao, Y., Fossum, V., and Chiang, D. (2013). Decoding with large-scale neural language models improves translation. In *EMNLP*, pages 1387–1392. Citeseer.

[Zaremba and Sutskever, 2014] Zaremba, W. and Sutskever, I. (2014). Learning to execute. *arXiv preprint arXiv:1410.4615.*

Improving Label Quality in Crowdsourcing Using Noise Correction

Jing Zhang
School of Computer Science and Engineering, Nanjing University of Science and Technology, China
jingzhang.cs@gmail.com

Victor S. Sheng
Department of Computer Science, University of Central Arkansas, U.S.A.
ssheng@uca.edu

Jian Wu
School of Computer Science and Technology, Soochow University, China
jianwu@suda.edu.cn

Xiaoqin Fu
Department of Computer Science, University of Central Arkansas, U.S.A.
xfu1@uca.edu

Xindong Wu
School of Computer Science and Information Engineering, Hefei University of Technology, China
xwu@hfut.edu.cn

ABSTRACT

This paper proposes a novel framework that introduces noise correction techniques to further improve label quality after ground truth inference in crowdsourcing. In the framework, an adaptive voting noise correction algorithm (AVNC) is proposed to identify and correct the most likely noises with the help of estimated qualities of labelers provided by the ground truth inference. The experimental results on two real-world datasets show that (1) the framework can improve label quality regardless of inference algorithms, especially under the circumstance that each example has a few noisy labels; and (2) since the algorithm AVNC considers both the number of and the probability of potential noises, it outperforms a baseline noise correction algorithm.

Categories and Subject Descriptors

H.2.8 [**Database Applications**]: Data Mining

Keywords

crowdsourcing; noise correction; label quality; inference

1. INTRODUCTION

Crowdsourcing systems provide a convenient way to collect labels for data at a low cost. To conquer the issue of low label quality, it is usual to obtain multiple labels from different labelers for the same object. A previous study [9] showed that the integrated label quality can be improved by simply using a straightforward ground truth inference algorithm. Recently, a great number of studies [1] [3] [8] [12] focused on improving the performance of ground truth inference. Although some studies [1] [12] proposed complicated models to describe different aspects of labeling, including the expertise, dedication of labelers and the difficulties of instances. However, no empirical study has proved that the performance of some algorithms is definitely superior to that of others on real-world datasets. This indicates that it is difficult to improve the integrated label quality remarkably only by proposing new inference algorithms.

This paper investigates a completely new direction of improving the label quality. We propose a novel framework that introduces noise correction techniques to further improve the label quality after a ground truth inference. Obviously, crowdsourced data after inference still have mislabeled instances, i.e., label noises. It would be promising to use noise handling techniques to identify and correct the label noises. The principle behind is that human intelligence is not always superior to machine intelligence under some circumstances, especially when labelers are not experts. For example, in the text classification tasks conducted by Shinsel et al [10], although each instance obtained six labels from different labelers, the overall integrated accuracy is still less than 94%, which is inferior to the accuracy predicted by an SVM classifier (≥ 99%) [5]. Thus, a potential high quality learning model may have a great opportunity to improve label quality. In order to accurately identify and correct the noises, the paper also proposes a novel adaptive voting noise correction algorithm (AVNC), which can collaborate with any inference algorithm. The experimental results show that a state-of-the-art noise correction approach can improve the integrated label quality, and the proposed algorithm AVNC performs much better.

2. FRAMEWORK

Figure 1 illustrates the proposed framework. In the framework, a dataset with multiple noisy (repeated) labels is first processed by a ground truth inference algorithm to form an *inferred* dataset D^I, where each instance has an integrated label. The instances whose integrated labels do not match their ground truths are noises. Since the ground truth of each instance is unknown, we have to estimate the probability of an instance being a noise. Based on the estimated probability, we can identify potential noises and filter them out. After filtering, the inferred dataset will be separated into a *noise* dataset and a *cleansed* dataset. The noise dataset will be further corrected. After correction, the updated noise dataset will be merged with the cleansed dataset to form an *enhanced* dataset D^E. Note that the enhanced dataset contains the same instances as the original dataset does, but the labels of some instances are updated. We expect that the label quality of the enhanced dataset is improved. In order to accurately estimate the probability of an instance being a noise, we take advantage of the information yielded from the inference stage to supervise noise identification. Here, three issues need to be further discussed.

Permission to make digital or hard copies of all or part of this work for personal or classroom use is granted without fee provided that copies are not made or distributed for profit or commercial advantage and that copies bear this notice and the full citation on the first page. Copyrights for components of this work owned by others than ACM must be honored. Abstracting with credit is permitted. To copy otherwise, or republish, to post on servers or to redistribute to lists, requires prior specific permission and/or a fee. Request permissions from Permissions@acm.org.

CIKM'15, October 19-23, 2015, Melbourne, VIC, Australia
© 2015 ACM. ISBN 978-1-4503-3794-6/15/10…$15.00
DOI: http://dx.doi.org/10.1145/2806416.2806627

The information generated by inference algorithms and used in noise filtering. Different inference algorithms model different aspects of crowdsourcing systems. Whitehill et al. [12] estimates labeler expertise and instance difficulties. Raykar et al. [8] estimates labelers' preferences to positive and negative instances. Bi et al. [1] estimates labeler expertise, dedication and instance difficulties. Estimated variables can provide information for noise filtering. Each specific algorithm is worthwhile to investigate a specific approach of using its information to supervise noise filtering. This paper only utilizes the off-the-shelf inference algorithms and their most common information—estimated labels of instances and estimated labeling qualities of labelers—to guard noise identification and filtering. We will demonstrate that this general information can improve the labeling quality.

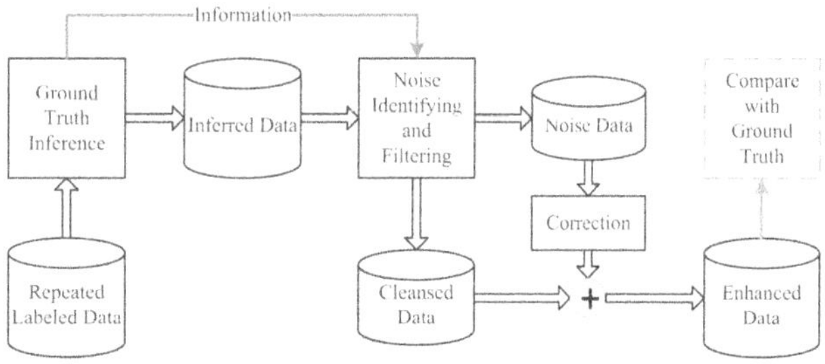

Figure 1 A framework of integrating noise handling techniques into crowdsourcing to improve label quality

The noise correction techniques. Many noise handling techniques have been proposed in the past two decades. A previous survey [6] reviewed filtering methods and pointed out that most of them cannot achieve a high performance even for binary classification. Correcting noises is a straightforward idea. However, the survey concluded that simply removing mislabeled instances is more efficient than trying to correct them. Thus, compared with noise filtering, literatures on noise correction are scarce. Alternatively, there is another way to train a learning model by directly using cleansed data after noise filtering, without attempting to correct any noise. Indeed, if our dataset has a great number of instances, we can only use the cleansed data to train a good model. However, this prerequisite does not always hold in crowdsourcing. A dataset obtained from crowdsourcing systems is not free, although it is much cheaper than hiring domain experts to complete the tasks. Furthermore, using crowdsourcing is not always to train a learning model. In some cases, we are only intent on obtaining a high quality dataset. That is why inference algorithms are so important in crowdsourcing. Overall, this paper focuses on label quality. We try to identify and correct noisy labels.

The number of labels for each instance. Labeling cost is one of the core issues in crowdsourcing. Sheng et al. [9] shows that when increasing the number of labels for each instance, the label quality improves. Some earlier study [9] used about 10 labels for each instance. However, in recent study [4], the average number of labels for each instance is from 3 to 6. Therefore, we expect our approach can improve the performance under different numbers of labels for each instance.

3. ADAPTIVE VOTING NOISE CORRECTION ALGORITHM

Our adaptive voting noise correction algorithm includes two steps: filtering and correction. Classification Filtering [7] is a general classical model prediction-based filtering algorithm. But it faces the risk of removing too many instances. Brodley and Friedl [2] introduced an algorithm using ensemble classifiers to address this issue. Our filtering step is also based on ensemble learning. To accurately identify noises, our approach answers two key questions that have not been addressed in traditional filtering algorithms [2] [7]. (1) *How many mislabeled instances should be filtered out?* (2) *Which noises have a higher priority to be filtered out, i.e. how to rank noises?*

3.1 Number of Noises Filtered Out

The information generated by an inference algorithm provides some hints to solve this problem. For an instance i, an inference algorithm assigns it an estimated label y_i (suppose the true label is y_i). The label that a labeler j provides the instance i is denoted by $l_i^{(j)}$, where $l_i^{(j)} \in \{-1,0,1\}$, -1, 1 and 0 represent negative, positive and null (i.e. labelers do not provided labels) respectively, for binary cases. We define the quality of the labeler j as:

$$p_j = \sum_{i=1}^{I} \mathbf{I}(l_i^{(j)} = y_i) \Big/ \sum_{i=1}^{I} | l_i^{(j)} | \quad (1)$$

where I is the total number of instances and $\mathbf{I}(\bullet$ is an indicator function that returns 1 if the test condition holds. Given the total number of labelers J, the average labeling quality of labelers is $\bar{p} = \sum_{j=1}^{J} p_j \big/ J$, where p_j is the labeling quality of a labeler j. Obtaining N labels from different labelers for each instance. The qualities of the labelers follow a uniform distribution with a mean quality $\bar{p}$. Then, the integrated labeling quality q is:

$$q = \Pr(y = y) = \sum_{i=1}^{\lfloor N/2 \rfloor} \binom{N}{i} \bar{p}^{N-i} (1 - \bar{p})^i \quad (2)$$

This is an ideal status with the highest integrated label quality. Thus, we can estimate the lower boundary of the number of noises after inference as:

$$\alpha = (1 - q) \cdot I \quad (3)$$

In reality, not all labelers have the same labeling quality $\bar{p}$. At the worst case, getting another label from a different labeler does not make any contribution to the improvement of the integrated label quality. Under this circumstance, we can estimate the upper boundary of the number of noises as:

$$\beta = (1 - \bar{p}) \cdot I \quad (4)$$

Although both α and β are not derived from any specific characteristic of an inference algorithm, they can be easily calculated by all inference algorithms.

Our algorithm is based on the voting of M classifiers. Supposed there are θ instances with at least $\lfloor M/2 \rfloor$ classifiers that predict them as noises, our algorithm uses the following equation to calculate the number of possible noises (denoted by N_r).

$$N_r = \max\{\alpha, \min\{\beta, \theta\}\} \quad (5)$$

How to determine θ will be further discussed in Section 3.3.

3.2 Rank of Noises

we introduce an auxiliary data structure $B^{(i)}$ for each instance i. B contains two fields c and e. $B_c^{(i)}$ counts the times that the predicted labels from M classifiers do not match the integrated label of the instance i. For an instance i, classifier m predicts it to be negative and positive with the probabilities $c_{-1}^{(m)}$ and $c_1^{(m)}$ respectively, and then $B_e^{(i)}$ is defined as the sum of all entropies:

$$B_e^{(i)} = -\sum_{m=1}^{M} (c_{-1}^{(m)} \log c_{-1}^{(m)} + c_1^{(m)} \log c_1^{(m)}) \quad (6)$$

We define a measure to rank each instance i based on these two fields as follows:

$$r^{(i)} = B_c^{(i)} + (1 - B_e^{(i)} \Big/ \sum_{i'=1}^{I} B_e^{i'}) \quad (7)$$

We sort instances in the descending order of $r^{(i)}$. The larger $r^{(i)}$, the more likely an instance might be a noise. Sorting with respect to Eq. 7 is a two layer sorting. Instances with the same value of B_c (the integer part of Eq. 7 is a primary key) are grouped together. For *M* classifiers, there are totally *M+1* groups. A larger B_c means that most classifiers predict this instance as a noise. Within the same group, the instances are further sorted according to the fraction part of Eq. 7 (i.e., the fraction part of Eq. 7 is a secondary key), which means that the smaller the entropy B_e of an instance, the more certainly the *M* classifiers predict it as a noise.

3.3 Pseudo Code of AVNC

AVNC takes the dataset after a ground truth inference D^I as an input. It first performs *M* rounds of K-fold cross-validation to predict the label of each instance. In each round *m*, we put all instances whose predicted labels match their inferred labels into a high quality set ($HQSet^{(m)}$) (lines 1-5). $HQSet^{(m)}$ will be used to build a model for noise correction in line 11. After *M* rounds of K-fold cross validation, AVNC sorts all instances in the descending order of $r^{(i)}$ (line 6). Based on this sorted list, we define θ as the number of instances whose $B_c^{(i)} \ge \lceil M/2 \rceil$ (line 7). At this point, the algorithm can determine the number of instances to be treated as noises by Eq.5 (line 8). After it separates D^I into a noise dataset and a cleansed dataset (line 9), it turns into the noise correction step. AVNC uses the *M HQSets* to build *M* models to predict the label for each instance in the noise dataset (lines 10-12). Since we believe that *HQSet* contains almost correct labeled instances, the model quality would be high enough to make a correct prediction. After each instance in the noise dataset is updated using the predicted label from the *M* classifiers, AVNC emerges the updated noise dataset into the cleansed set to form an updated high quality dataset D^E (lines 13-14).

In algorithm AVNC, note that when we make a correction for an instance *i* in the noise dataset, the instance *i* could be an instance in some high quality datasets *HQSets*. To avoid training a model to make prediction for its training instance, we remove this instance from all high quality datasets if they contain this instance before building models from them. This is shown in line 11. The notation $HQSet^{(m)}_{\setminus\{i\}}$ means the high quality dataset $HQSet^{(m)}$ does not contain the instance *i*.

Algorithm Adaptive Voting Noise Correction (AVNC)

Input: inferred dataset D^I, α, β, *K*, *M*
Output: enhanced dataset D^E

1. **for** *m = 1* **to** *M*
2. Shuffle the dataset D^I and use K-fold cross-validation to predict the label of each instance.
3. **for each** instance *i* in D^I
4. **if** predicted label ≠ inferred label
5. **then** $B_c^{(i)}$ += *1* **else** *add i* to $HQSet^{(m)}$
6. Sort all instances in the descending order of $r^{(i)}$ by Eq. 7
7. Calculate θ as the number of instances with $B_c^{(i)} \ge \lceil M/2 \rceil$
8. Calculate N_r using Eq. 5
9. The first N_r instances in D^I form the noise dataset *NoiseSet* and the rest ones form the cleansed dataset *CleansedSet*.
10. **for each** instance *i* in *NoiseSet*
11. Use $HQSet^{(m)}_{\setminus\{i\}}, 1 \le m \le M$ to create *M* models
12. Use these *M* models to predict the label of instance *i* and use majority voting to determine its final estimated label.
13. Combine *CleansedSet* and *NoiseSet* together to form the enhanced dataset D^E.
14. **return** D^E

4. EXPERIMENT

4.1 Two Real-World Datasets

In order to investigate the performance of our proposed framework and the algorithm AVNC in real-world environments, we use two datasets *adult600* and *eastpolitics800* respectively derived from the *adult* and the *20newsgroups* datasets in UCI machine learning repository to collect repeated labels from Amazon Mechanical Turk (MTurk). The two datasets have their ground true labels for all instances. We need the ground truths to validate whether the inferred labels or the corrected labels match them. The *adult600* dataset includes 600 instances, which is about "to predict whether a person's annual income exceeds $50K based on the census data in 1994." We randomly extracted 300 positive (≥ $50K) and 300 negative (< $50K) instances from *adult* and created the human intelligence tasks (HITs) on MTurk. Each HIT is completed by 10 different workers. It has 67 workers providing 6000 labels for this dataset. The *eastpolitics800* dataset includes 400 documents randomly extracted from those belonging to the class *talk.politics.mideast* as positive, and the other 400 ones randomly extracted from those belonging to the classes *soc.religion.christian*, *talk.politics.guns*, *talk.politics.misc* and *talk.religion.misc* as negative. Likewise, each task is completed by 10 different workers. It has 121 workers providing 8000 labels.

4.2 Experimental Setup

First, we will illustrate that the proposed framework can collaborate with different inference algorithms. Therefore, four inference algorithms MV, GLAD [12], RY [8], and ZC [3] are used in the experiments. For comparison, we introduce a baseline algorithm BC, which uses a voting filtering in [2] as its noise filtering, and then use a self-training semi-supervised algorithm in [11] for its noise correction. Both AVNC and BC are based on ensemble learning (*M* classifiers) with the K-fold cross-validation inside. In the experiments, we let *K = 10* and *M* = 5.

We are intent to investigate the performance under different numbers of labels for each instance. Supposed the experiment is for the situation that each instance has *n* ($1 \le n \le 10$) labels, the procedure is as follows. We first randomly choose *n* labels from the 10 noisy labels collected from MTurk for each instance in the dataset to form a new dataset *D*. Then, we run different ground truth inference algorithms on *D*. After an inference algorithm has done, we correct noises either using AVNC or BC. Thus, three comparable results on the label quality (in *accuracy*) will be obtained (1) only by (ground truth) inference, (2) by inference and BC, and (3) by inference and AVNC. For each *n*, we run experiment 10 times, the mean value of the integrated label quality in *accuracy* is reported. Both AVNC and BC need to build learning models. For *adult600*, the models are built with SMO in WEKA. For *eastpolitics800*, we remove stop words and the words with fewer than six characters in all documents. We use a text mining tool GATE (https://gate.ac.uk) to generate *bag-of-word* features. The models are built with SVM.

4.3 Results and Discussions

Figure 2 shows the experimental results on the *adult600* dataset. We have the following observations. (1) As the increasing of the number of labels for each instance, the data quality increases after inference. However, when the number of labels is greater than six, the increment is limited. The performance differences among four inference algorithms are not significant. RY is the best, which is only 1% or 2% (absolute value) higher than the others. (2)

Regardless of which inference algorithm is used, the noise correction algorithms (both BC and AVNC) can improve the label quality. This indicates that using noise handling to improve the inferred label quality is feasible. (3) The proposed AVNC obviously outperforms the baseline algorithm BC. Especially when the number of labels for each instance is less than six, the improvement is significant. The average absolute improvement is greater than 8% and even 13% at maximum extent.

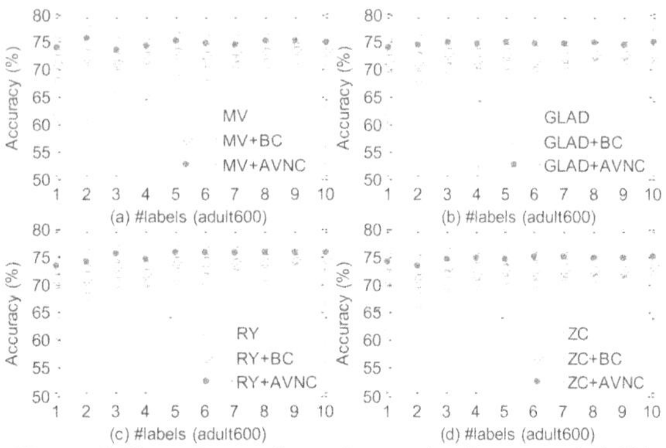

Figure 2 Experimental results on the dataset *adult600*

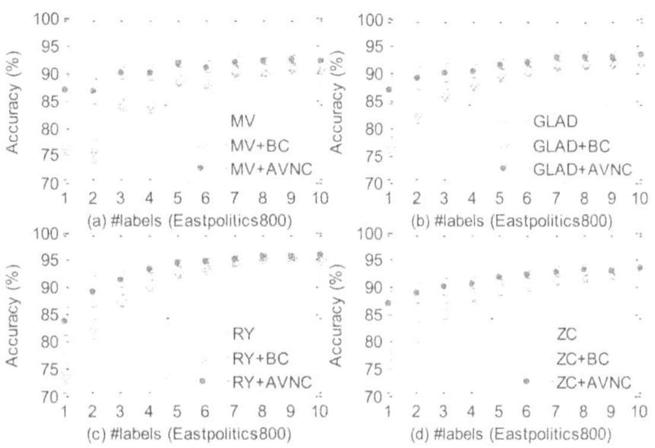

Figure 3 Experimental results on the dataset *eastpolitics800*

Figure 3 shows the results on the dataset *eastpolitics800*. Most observations are consistent with those on *adult600*. Again, our AVNC has the best performance. However, the performance of BC is statistically worse than inference without correction according to a two-tailed student's t-test in Table 1.

Table 1 Student's T-Test (*win/tie/loss, p-value=0.05*)

Infer	*Adult600*			*Eastpolitics800*		
	A vs. O	A vs. B	B vs. O	A vs. O	A vs. B	B vs. O
MV	10/0/0	10/0/0	10/0/0	10/0/0	10/0/0	0/3/7
GLAD	10/0/0	10/0/0	10/0/0	10/0/0	10/0/0	0/2/8
RY	10/0/0	10/0/0	10/0/0	7/3/0	10/0/0	0/2/8
ZC	10/0/0	10/0/0	10/0/0	10/0/0	10/0/0	0/0/10

A: AVNC, **B**: Baseline Correction, **O:** Only inference

From above real-world evaluation, we can draw the following conclusions. (1) It is feasible to introduce noise handling techniques to improve the data quality in crowdsourcing. The proposed framework can make improvement regardless of the inference algorithm used. (2) Especially, the proposed AVNC can significantly improve the label quality to a very high level when each instance has a few labels (e.g., ≤ 6), which means at least a half of budget will be saved. (3) Compared with BC, our proposed AVNC algorithm is significantly better, because the off-the-shelf noise handling algorithms do not take advantage of the output information of ground truth inference.

5. CONCLUSION

This paper proposed a novel framework to introduce noisy handling techniques for data quality improvement in crowdsourcing as well as a novel noise correction algorithm AVNC. The proposed approach takes advantage of the estimated labeling qualities to guide noise filtering and correction regardless of which inference algorithm is used. Evaluations on two real-world datasets together with four different inference algorithms demonstrated that the proposed framework and the proposed algorithm AVNC effectively improved the data quality and outperformed the state-of-the-art approach.

6. ACKNOWLEDGMENTS

This research has been supported by the Program for Changjiang Scholars and Innovative Research Team in University of the Ministry of Education, China, under grant IRT13059, the National 973 Program of China under grant 2013CB329604, the National Natural Science Foundation of China under grants 61229301, 61402311, the start-up funding of Nanjing University of Science and Technology, and the U.S. National Science Foundation under grant IIS-1115417.

7. REFERENCES

[1] Bi, W., Wang, L., Kwok, J. T., and Tu, Z. 2014. Learning to predict from crowdsourced data. In *UAI*.

[2] Brodley C. E. and Friedl, M. A. 1999. Identifying mislabeled training data. *J. Artificial Intelligence Research* 11, 131-167.

[3] Demartini, G., Difallah, D. E., and Cudré-Mauroux, P. 2012. ZenCrowd: Leveraging probabilistic reasoning and crowdsourcing techniques for large-scale entity linking. In *WWW*, 469-478.

[4] Fang, M., Yin, J., and Tao, D. 2014. Active learning for crowdsourcing using knowledge transfer. In *AAAI*, 1809-1815.

[5] Frank, E. and Bouckaert, R. R. 2006. Naive bayes for text classification with unbalanced classes. In *PKDD*, 503-510.

[6] Frénay , B and Verleysen, M. 2014. Classification in the presence of label noise: a survey. *IEEE Trans. Neural Networks and Learning Systems*, 25(5), 845-869.

[7] Gamberger, D., Lavrac, N., and Groselj, C. 1999. Experiments with noise filtering in a medical domain. In *ICML*, 143-151.

[8] Raykar, V. C., Yu, S., Zhao, L. H., Florin, C., Valadez, G. H., Bogoni, L., and Moy, L. 2010. Learning from Crowds. *J. Machine Learning Research* 11, 1297-1322.

[9] Sheng, V. S., Provost, F. and Ipeirotis, P. 2008. Get another label? Improving data quality and data mining using multiple, noisy labeler. In *ACM SIGKDD*, 614-662.

[10] Shinsel, A., Kulesza, T., Burnett, M., Curran, W., Groce, A., Stumpf, S., and Wong, W. K. 2011. Mini-crowdsourcing end-user assessment of intelligent assistants: A cost-benefit study. In *VL/HCC*, 47-54.

[11] Triguero, I., Sáez, J. A., Luengo, J., García, S., and Herrera, F. 2014. On the characterization of noise filters for self-training semi-supervised in nearest neighbor classification. *Neurocomputing*, 132, 30-41.

[12] Whitehill, J., Ruvolo, P., Wu, T., Bergsma, J., and Movellan, J. 2009. Whose vote should count more: optimal integration of labels from labelers of unknown expertise. In *NIPS*, 2035-2043.

Improving Collaborative Filtering via Hidden Structured Constraint

Qing Zhang, Houfeng Wang*
Key Laboratory of Computational Linguistics (Peking University) Ministry of Education, China
zqicl@pku.edu.cn, wanghf@pku.edu.cn

ABSTRACT

Matrix factorization models, as one of the most powerful Collaborative Filtering approaches, have greatly advanced the recommendation tasks. However, few of them are able to explicitly consider structured constraint for modeling user interests. To solve this problem, we propose a novel matrix factorization model with adaptive graph regularization framework, which can automatically discover latent user communities jointly with learning latent user representations, to enhance the discriminative power for recommendation. Experiments on real-world datasets demonstrate the effectiveness of the proposed method.

Categories and Subject Descriptors

H.3.3 [**Information Search and Retrieval**]: Information filtering

General Terms

Algorithms, Design, Experimentation

Keywords

Collaborative Filtering, Structured Constraint, Recommendation

1. INTRODUCTION

Recommender systems play an important role in our daily life, especially in this era of Big Data, which help users to find the information that they are rarely aware but really interested in. With the ability to make recommendations without clear content descriptions of items, Collaborative Filtering (CF) algorithms have been widely applied in various recommender systems. As one of the most powerful CF approaches, Matrix Factorization (MF) models have become popular and achieves the state-of-the-art performance [11]. However, MF approaches have also encountered some problems. Consider music recommendation as example. Different users may have different preferences on music genres, and they can be divided into different communities according to their interests. Therefore, an ideal recommendation system should take this structured property into consideration. To achieve this goal, most existing methods are mainly based on side information, such as social network and item content. In fact, a more fundamental solution is also needed. Recently, directly exploiting structured property for learning matrix factorization has gained much attention [10, 9]. Along this novel direction, we focus on how to incorporate structured prior into matrix factorization models for improving CF performance.

There are two main approaches for explicitly exploiting structured property for recommendation tasks. The first one is from permutation view, based on graph partitioning theories. Typically, [10] first transforms a sparse rating matrix into a bordered block-diagonal structure, and then uses the extracted denser submatrices for rating prediction separately. However, it is a pipeline framework which is independent of specific matrix factorization models. Though it can be used as a black box efficiently, this transforming process may not incorporate task specific information. The second one is from feature selection view, based on the regularization techniques [4]. In this category, [9] considers multiple user interests, and factorizes the rating matrices into latent factor spaces for each with group sparsity regularization. This approach assumes users' interests are determined by different sets of factors, and then could use a subset of the latent factors. The limitation is that the subgroups need to be pre-partitioned. In fact, how to find a reasonable partition is also a problem, which might propagate errors by the inappropriate grouping, into subsequent learning process.

Different from the above approaches, in this paper, we seek to enhance the performance of matrix factorization models through proposing an adaptive graph regularization on latent users, which is learnt automatically from data. The motivation behind the idea is to improve the discriminative power of latent user representations. It is achieved by incorporating structured prior, such that the points within the same communities become more similar, and those within different communities become less similar, in the latent factor space. Therefore, the proposed method can take structured property into consideration jointly with the recommendation task oriented objective, and can benefit from community induced discriminative power with the ability of automatically grouping without pre-partition.

2. PROBLEM FORMULATION

As shown in Definition 1, our goal is to predict the missing values in R, by computing the predicted values $r_{ij} = u_i^T v_j$. Although matrix factorization models also have a nice probabilistic interpretation with Gaussian noise [6], in this paper, we mainly focus on how to exploit structured constraint from algebra view.

DEFINITION 1 (MATRIX FACTORIZATION MODELS). *Given a sparse rating matrix $R = [r_{ij}]$, where the observed r_{ij} denotes*

---

*Corresponding author

Permission to make digital or hard copies of all or part of this work for personal or classroom use is granted without fee provided that copies are not made or distributed for profit or commercial advantage and that copies bear this notice and the full citation on the first page. Copyrights for components of this work owned by others than ACM must be honored. Abstracting with credit is permitted. To copy otherwise, or republish, to post on servers or to redistribute to lists, requires prior specific permission and/or a fee. Request permissions from Permissions@acm.org.
CIKM'15, October 19–23, 2015, Melbourne, Australia.
© 2015 ACM. ISBN 978-1-4503-3794-6/15/10 ...$15.00.
DOI: http://dx.doi.org/10.1145/2806416.2806623.

the rating of user i on item j, matrix factorization models aim to factorize $R = UV^T$, where U and V are low rank matrices with rows as latent users u_i^T and latent items v_j^T respectively.

To consider structured influence on modeling user preference, the most popular way is to incorporate side information, such as social network [5] and topic structure of item content [1]. This structured information has proven to be useful for building more accurate recommendation models. For the above approaches, the underlying assumption is that additional auxiliary resources with high quality are available in advance besides user rating information. In contrast, we consider a more fundamental case, only using rating matrix without side information. It could be easily extended to the scenarios of the above modeling approaches.

2.1 Laplacian Constraint for Block-diagonality

In this section, we introduce the recently proposed structured constraint [2], i.e., Laplacian constraint, to recommendation tasks, for explicitly capturing the latent user community structures while learning matrix factorization. The motivation could also be roughly explained from overlapping denoising perspective. As a toy example, a middle-school student buys a T-shirt and a pencil. A worker buys a T-shirt and a hammer. The hammer may be recommended to the student due to the overlapping T-shirt. Such noisy overlapping pattern often accounts for the fundamental reason why CF performance is highly sensitive to data in practice, which is seldom addressed explicitly in previous work. To consider this issue, we propose to constrain the overlapping patterns within different latent communities, as hidden structured constraint on global overlapping patterns for CF. In the following, we first show the definition of Laplacian matrix, and then present its connection with the structure of the affinity matrix.

DEFINITION 2 (LAPLACIAN MATIRX). *Consider an affinity matrix $W \in \mathbb{R}^{n \times n}$ of n samples with weights $W(i,i')$. The Laplacian matrix $L_W \in \mathbb{R}^{n \times n}$ is defined as: $L_W = D - W$, where $D = diag(d_1, ..., d_n)$ and $d_n = \Sigma_{i'} W(i,i')$. The normalized version is defined as $L_{W_{sys}} = D^{-\frac{1}{2}} L_W D^{-\frac{1}{2}}$.*

The following well known theorem relates the rank of the Laplacian matrix to the number of blocks in W.

THEOREM 1 ([7]). *Let W be an affinity matrix. The multiplicity k of the eigenvalue 0 of the corresponding Laplacian $L_{W_{sys}}$, equals the number of connected components (blocks) in W.*

Based on the above theorem, we can enforce a general square matrix to be k-block-diagonal to represent different latent communities. For the hidden graph constructed by latent users u_j, we construct an affinity matrix $W(j, j')$ using Gaussian kernel. Then we can define a set of k-block-diagonal matrix (k-BDMS) as the constraint term for optimization in Eq. (2),

$$\mathcal{K} = \{W | rank(L_{W_{sys}}) = n - k, \quad W(i,i') = w_{ii'} = exp(-\frac{\|u_i - u_{i'}\|_2^2}{\sigma^2})\}, \tag{1}$$

where $\|.\|_2^2$ denotes the $\ell 2$ norm, and σ^2 denotes the deviation. Ideally, the degree of overlapping constraint is expected to be flexibly controlled, which is considered in the proposed framework.

2.2 Adaptive Graph Regularization Framework

To incorporate the structured constraint, the straightforward applying Laplacian constraint on reconstructed rating matrix is not suitable, because this may violate the Nearly Isometric Property (NIP) as mentioned in [11] to undermine the performance. In addition, we expect to flexibly control the overlapping constraint. Therefore, we propose an adaptive hidden graph regularization framework, which is similar to [5], but our graph used for regularization is learnt automatically with block-diagonal prior, rather than a pre-defined one based on side information. We can automatically discover latent user communities jointly with learning latent user representations, to enhance the discriminative power. To achieve the goal, we have the following optimization objective:

$$\begin{aligned} \min_{U,V,W,S} \frac{1}{2} \sum_{i,j} c_{ij}(r_{ij} - u_i v_j^T)^2 + \frac{\lambda_W}{2} \sum_{i,i'} c_{w_{ii'}}(w_{ii'} - u_i s_{i'}^T)^2 \\ + \frac{\lambda_U}{2}\|U\|_F^2 + \frac{\lambda_V}{2}\|V\|_F^2 + \frac{\lambda_S}{2}\|S\|_F^2 \\ s.t. \; W \in \mathcal{K} \end{aligned} \tag{2}$$

where $\|\cdot\|_F$ is the Frobenius norm. In Eq.(2), the first term ensures that latent users U and items V can well approximate the observed ratings, where c_{ij} is a confidence parameter [8] for rating r_{ij}, $a > b$. If c_{ij} is large, we trust r_{ij} more, $c_{ij} = \begin{cases} a, r_{ij} = 1 \\ b, r_{ij} = 0. \end{cases}$ The second term in Eq. (2) is the graph regularization term, where $c_{w_{ii'}}$ is the confidence parameter for modeling $w_{ii'} = exp(-\frac{\|u_i - u_{i'}\|_2^2}{\sigma^2})$ $\in W$ that measures the similarity between latent users. The similarity weight $w_{ii'}$ in hidden graph W is automatically learnt from data with Laplacian constraint, i.e., $rank(L_{W_{sys}}) = n - k$ for pursuing k-block-diagonal structure as discussed in Section 2.1. This constraint $W \in \mathcal{K}$ in Eq. (1) is imposed on the Laplacian matrix of latent users through Gaussian kernel. Thus it can be directly optimized jointly with latent user representations, and then can improve their discriminative power. The remaining terms are used to avoid over-fitting, the parameters λ_U, λ_v and λ_S control the strength of each regularization term respectively. It is noted that the degree of overlapping constraint can not only be controlled by the parameter λ_W but also the number of latent groups flexibly.

2.3 Optimization with Structured Constraint

We employ an alternating optimization method to solve the problem, by updating U, V, S, W iteratively and alternatingly.

2.3.1 Learning U, V, S

The following update rules are obtained by setting the derivative of L with respect to u_i, v_j , and s_k to zero.

$$u_i = (\lambda_U I + V^{\mathrm{T}} D_{c_i} V + S^{\mathrm{T}} D_{w_i} S)^{-1} \cdot (V^{\mathrm{T}} D_{c_i} R_i + S^{\mathrm{T}} D_{w_i} W_i) \tag{3}$$

$$v_j = (\lambda_V I + U^{\mathrm{T}} D_{c_j} U)^{-1} \cdot (U^{\mathrm{T}} D_{c_j} R_j) \tag{4}$$

$$s_{i'} = (\lambda_S I + U^{\mathrm{T}} D_{w_{i'}} U)^{-1} \cdot (U^{\mathrm{T}} D_{w_{i'}} W_{i'}) \tag{5}$$

where I is an identity matrix of the same dimension as that of latent space. S is a matrix with rows as social factor-specific latent feature vectors for the learnt hidden graph W. R_i is a column vector with rating values $[r_{i1}, \ldots, r_{iJ}]^{\mathrm{T}}$. Similarly, $R_j = [r_{1j}, \ldots, r_{I_N j}]^{\mathrm{T}}$. For the hidden graph W, $W_i = [w_{i1}, \ldots, w_{iI_N}]^{\mathrm{T}}$ and $W_{i'} = [w_{1i'}, \ldots, w_{I_N i'}]^{\mathrm{T}}$, I_N and J are the total number of users and items respectively. D_{c_i} is a diagonal matrix with values $diag(c_{i1}, \ldots, c_{iJ})$ and $D_{c_j} = diag(c_{1j}, \ldots, c_{I_N j})$. D_{w_i}, and $D_{w_{i'}}$ are similarly defined with diagonal elements $c_{w_{i,.}}$ and $c_{w_{.,i'}}$ respectively. In addition, $c_{w_{ii'}}$ is the confidence parameters for $w_{ii'}$. The high confidence value a is set to the learnt user relations within the same communities, and the low confidence value b is set to those within different communities, where $a > b > 0$.

2.3.2 *Learning Hidden Graph Matrix, W*

After learning U, V, S, we can obtain the hidden graph W_O using Gaussian kernel as shown in Eq. (1). However, this variable matrix W_O may move out of the hidden structured constraint set, and no longer guarantees a k-block-diagonal structure. Thus, we need to project it back to the k-BDMS constraint set. The projection essentially finds a matrix W in $\mathcal{K}$ as defined in Eq. (1) which is closest to W_O in terms of the Euclidean distance. The involved optimization problem can be explicitly written as follows via Augmented Lagrangian Multiplier (ALM) method:

$$\min_{W,\tilde{Z}} \frac{1}{2}\|W - W_O\|_F^2 - \langle J, L_{W_{sys}}\rangle + \frac{\beta}{2}\|\tilde{Z} - L_{W_{sys}}\|_F^2 \\ s.t.\ rank(\tilde{Z}) = n - k \tag{6}$$

where J is the Lagrangian multiplier and β is an increasing weight parameter for the term of enforcing the auxiliary variable $\tilde{Z} = L_{W_{sys}}$. Thus the two constraints are decoupled and we can alternatively optimize W and $\tilde{Z}$. The solution to Eq. (6) is similar to that in [2], and we omit it here due to limited space. The difference is that our W is constructed from latent user representations using Gaussian kernel, with normalized Laplacian constraint.

Algorithm 1: Optimization Algorithm for HGMF

Input: Number of latent factors k, a sparse rating matrix R, standard deviation σ of Gaussian kernel, parameters λ_U, λ_V, λ_S and λ_W, confidence parameters a, b.
Output: U,V,S,W.

```
while t < T do
    Update each u_i^t with Eq. (3);
    Update each v_j^t with Eq. (4);
    Update each s_{i'}^t with Eq. (5);
    Update W^t by solving the problem in (6);
    t = t + 1;
end while
Return U, V, S, W;
```

2.3.3 *Implementation Details*

The naive calculation of $V^{\mathrm{T}}D_{c_i}V$, $S^{\mathrm{T}}D_{w_i}\ S$, $U^{\mathrm{T}}D_{c_j}U$ and $U^{\mathrm{T}}D_{w_{i'}}U$, requires time $O(K^2N_{user})$ or $O(K^2N_{item})$, where K is dimension of the latent space. Inspired by [3], e.g., we can rewrite $V^{\mathrm{T}}D_{c_i}V = V^{\mathrm{T}}(D_{c_i} - bI)V + bV^{\mathrm{T}}V$, where I is the corresponding identity matrix. Then we can pre-compute $bV^{\mathrm{T}}V$. Since $D_{c_i} - bI$ has only $\overline{N}_{user}$ non-zeros where $\overline{N}_{user} \ll N_{user}$, this sparsity can significantly speed up computation [5].

3. EXPERIMENTS

The experiments were conducted on two public real-world datasets[1]: LastFM and Delicious,with binary ratings, as shown in Table 1.

3.1 Experimental Setups

3.1.1 *Baselines and Settings*

- **PMF**: This method, described in [6], is a well-known matrix factorization method for CF, only using interactive rating information.

[1]Data available at http://grouplens.org/datasets/hetrec-2011/

Dataset	#User	#Item	Sparsity	#Ratings	#Avg. R
LastFM	1892	18745	0.28%	92834	49
Delicious	1867	69223	0.08%	104799	56

Table 1: Datasets Statistics. R denotes #rated per user.

Dataset	PMF	PMF-LMF	GSMF	GSMF-K	HGMF
LastFM	0.5761	0.5646	0.5923	0.5701	**0.5512**
Delicious	0.9084	0.8623	1.1321	0.8812	**0.8313**

Table 2: Model Comparison for RMSE.

- **PMF-LMF**: This method first uses LMF described in [10] to acquire submatrices as groups and then for each one performs PMF.
- **GSMF**: This method, described in [9], factorizes the rating matrices for multiple interests with group sparsity regularization. (without pre-partition)
- **GSMF-K**: The same GSMF method, described in [9]. GSMF-K denotes using k-means to partition the item set into k groups for GSMF.
- **HGMF**: Our model is described in this paper with Augmented Lagrangian Multiplier for learning hidden graph.

For easier comparison with previous proposed methods, we use Root Mean Square Error (RMSE) to measure the prediction accuracy in this work. For N rating-prediction pairs, i.e., the predicted r_i and true $\widehat{r}_i$, $RMSE = \sqrt{\sum_{i=1}^{N} \frac{(r_i - \widehat{r}_i)^2}{N}}$. We use Recall to measure top-k performance, $Recall@k = \frac{\#relevant\ in\ top-k\ list}{\#total\ relevant}$.

The experimental setting is as follows. Following [5, 9], we randomly select 90% of the data for training and the rest for testing. The random selection was carried out 5 times independently, and we report the average results. For all datasets, we set kernel $\sigma = 50$; $a = 1$, $b = 0.01$ in PMF and HGMF; $\alpha = 1$, $\beta = 0.1$, $\lambda = 0.01$ and $K_{pre} = 200$ in GSMF-K. The max iteration number is 200, and the number of latent factors $k = 200$. For two different datasets, **LastFM**: $\lambda_V = 0.1$ in PMF. $\widehat{\rho} = 0.005$ in LMF. $\lambda_U = 0.1$, $\lambda_V = 100$ in GSMF and HGMF. **Delicious**: $\lambda_U = 0.01$, $\lambda_V = 0.1$ in PMF, GSMF and HGMF. $\widehat{\rho} = 0.0016$ in LMF. The remaining parameters vary for our evaluation.

3.2 Results and Analysis

3.2.1 *Performance Comparison*

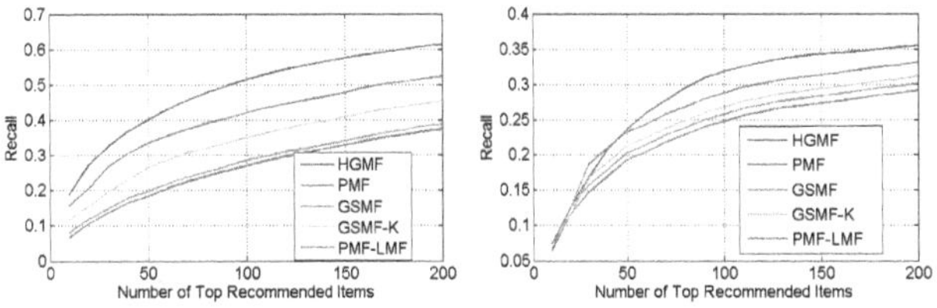

(a) LastFM (b) Delicious

Figure 1: Model Comparison for Recall.

Table 2 shows that, on the extremely sparse dataset, Delicious, our method can achieve considerable improvement compared PMF and other structured aware modeling approaches. This could be explained that in extremely sparse case, the common ratings for users are not sufficiently overlap such that the collaborative modeling fails due to the lack of co-occurrence pattern information. Therefore, considering structured property is important for modeling users, which can make the points within the same communi-

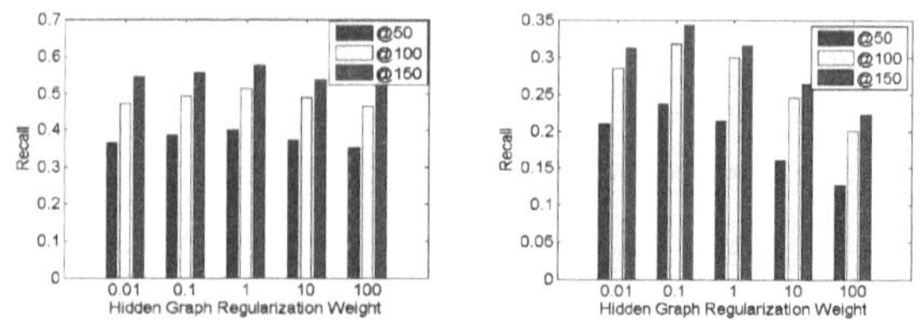

(a) LastFM (b) Delicious

Figure 2: Impact of Hidden Graph Weight.

λ_W	**0.01**	**0.1**	**1**	**10**	**100**
LastFM	0.5709	0.5612	**0.5565**	0.5712	0.7213
Delicious	0.8574	**0.8474**	0.8974	0.9415	1.1306

Table 3: Impact of Hidden Graph Weight (k=200).

ties more similar to distinguish dissimilar patterns. Although PMF-LMF, GSMF and GSMF-K take the structured property into consideration from different perspectives, the results of these methods still perform worse than our method. This could be explained that PMF-LMF is a pipeline approach which may not well extract subdenser matrices without task objective, especially when original data is not relatively dense enough. In contrast, our HGMF explores overlapping constraint in the more denser latent subspace. GSMF is limited to the pre-partitioned groups without adaptive grouping for task objective. Moreover, Figure 1 further validates the effectiveness of the proposed method in terms of Top-N performance.

3.2.2 *Impact of Hidden Graph Weight* λ_W

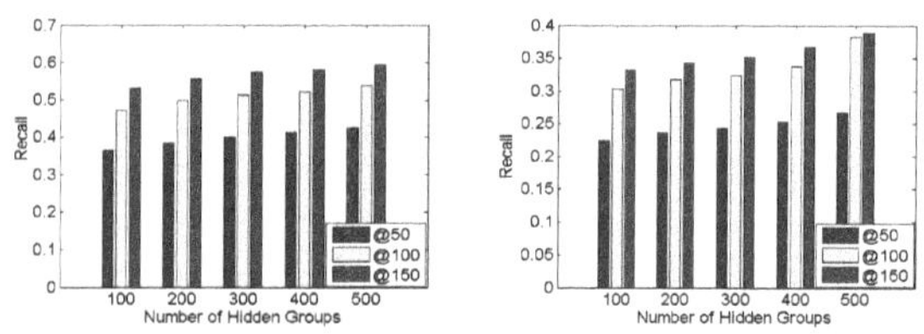

(a) LastFM (b) Delicious

Figure 3: Impact of the Number of Hidden Groups.

The parameter λ_W is introduced to control the contribution from hidden graph regularization for CF. Therefore, we investigate how our algorithm HGMF is influenced by the graph weight parameter. We vary the value of λ_W as $\{0.01, 0.1\ , 1, 10, 100\}$. Table 3 and Figure 2 show that in general, with the increase of λ_W, the performance in different datasets shows similar patterns: first increasing, reaching its highest value and then decreasing, obviously for Delicious. In particular, for the extremely sparse dataset, Delicious, lower value suggests good performance. For other more denser datasets, relatively higher value will improve the evaluation results. It could be explained that in the extremely sparse case, each latent user may rely on more latent neighbours. Thus, if we restrict its group membership tightly, the performance will decrease. For denser case, the rating matrix may introduces more noisy patterns. Thus, the larger regularization will separate the latent user from the noisy relevant users in the different latent communities.

3.2.3 *Impact of the Number of Hidden Groups*

Different from traditional regularization approaches, our method can naturally bridge different latent spaces with different dimensions, within the proposed adaptive hidden graph regularization framework. Therefore, we further investigate how our algorithm

#hidden group$k$	**100**	**200**	**300**	**400**	**500**
LastFM	0.5665	0.5565	0.5413	0.5395	0.5335
Delicious	0.8522	0.8474	0.8319	0.8205	0.8234

Table 4: Impact of the Number of Hidden Groups.

HGMF is influenced by the number of hidden groups (k in Eq. (6)), i.e., the approximate dimension of the learnt hidden graph space. It is noted that the dimension of latent factor space is 200. We vary the value of the number of hidden groups as $\{100, 200, 300, 400, 500\}$. Table 4 and Figure 3 show that fixing the optimal parameter λ_W, setting larger number of hidden groups will achieve better results in terms of RMSE and Recall. Empirically, we find this parameter is dependent on the parameter λ_W. Thus we can first fix this parameter and then change λ_W, or vise versa. Both cases can achieve the similar results. Intuitively, fixing λ_W, slightly enlarging the number of hidden groups will narrow the range of visible neighbours. It will make the learnt latent user representation more discriminative.

4. CONCLUSION

In this paper, we proposed a novel solution to explicitly exploiting structured property for collaborative filtering, without relying on side information. It could be seen as a principled way of constraining the potentially noisy overlapping patterns locally, while learning the global matrix factorization. This method benefits from the community induced discriminative power for recommendation, jointly with the ability of automatically grouping without prepartition. Experiments on two real-world datasets exhibit the promising performance, compared with some state-of-the-art methods.

5. ACKNOWLEDGMENTS

Our work is supported by National High Technology Research and Development Program of China (863 Program) (No.2015AA015402), National Natural Science Foundation (No.61433015 and No.61370117) and Major National Social Science Fund of China (No.12&ZD227).

6. REFERENCES

[1] D. Agarwal and B. Chen. flda: matrix factorization through latent dirichlet allocation. In *Proceedings of the WSDM*, pages 91–100, 2010.

[2] J. Feng, Z. Lin, H. Xu, and S. Yan. Robust subspace segmentation with block-diagonal prior. In *CVPR*, pages 3818–3825, 2014.

[3] Y. Hu, Y. Koren, and C. Volinsky. Collaborative filtering for implicit feedback datasets. In *ICDM*, pages 263–272, 2008.

[4] F. Nie, H. Huang, X. Cai, and C. H. Q. Ding. Efficient and robust feature selection via joint l21-norms minimization. In *Proceedings of NIPS*, pages 1813–1821, 2010.

[5] S. Purushotham and Y. Liu. Collaborative topic regression with social matrix factorization for recommendation systems. In *Proceedings of ICML*, 2012.

[6] R. Salakhutdinov and A. Mnih. Probabilistic matrix factorization. In *Proceedings of NIPS*, pages 1257–1264, 2007.

[7] U. von Luxburg. A tutorial on spectral clustering. *Statistics and Computing*, 17(4):395–416, 2007.

[8] C. Wang and D. M. Blei. Collaborative topic modeling for recommending scientific articles. In *Proceedings of KDD*, pages 448–456, 2011.

[9] T. Yuan, J. Cheng, X. Zhang, S. Qiu, and H. Lu. Recommendation by mining multiple user behaviors with group sparsity. In *Proceedings of AAAI*, pages 222–228, 2014.

[10] Y. Zhang, M. Zhang, Y. Liu, S. Ma, and S. Feng. Localized matrix factorization for recommendation based on matrix block diagonal forms. In *Proceedings of WWW*, pages 1511–1520, 2013.

[11] Y. Zhang, M. Zhang, Y. Zhang, Y. Liu, and S. Ma. Understanding the sparsity: Augmented matrix factorization with sampled constraints on unobservables. In *Proceedings of CIKM*, pages 1189–1198, 2014.

DOLAP 2015 Workshop Summary

Carlos Garcia-Alvarado
Pivotal Software Inc.
Palo Alto, CA 94304, USA

Carlos Ordonez
University of Houston
Houston, TX 77204, USA

Il-Yeol Song
Drexel University
Philadelphia, PA, USA

ABSTRACT

The ACM DOLAP workshop presents research that bridges data warehousing, On-Line Analytical Processing (OLAP), and other large-scale data processing platforms. The program has four interesting sessions on data warehouse design, database modeling, query processing, and text processing, as well as an invited paper on Big Data Database Design.

Categories and Subject Descriptors

H.2 [**General**]: [Database Management]

General Terms

Algorithms, Design, Performance, Theory

Keywords

Data Warehousing; OLAP

1. INTRODUCTION

Data warehousing is considered a mature technology to which almost every major organization has some effort dedicated. One such effort corresponds to On-Line Analytical Processing (OLAP), which comes to summarizations, cube aggregations, and exploratory queries. However, the establishment of large heterogeneous data repositories, also called "Data Lakes", and the adoption of cloud computing have triggered the development of a new generation of large-scale data processing platforms (e.g. Hadoop environment). Systems on these platforms have to reconsider the entire foundation of data warehouses (e.g. relational model and database design) to guarantee the required scalability and performance. Furthermore, a large variety of specialized tools has also to be taken into account to build solutions that coexist in this shared environment. In DOLAP 2015, we tackle some of these challenges and observe an increasing variety of data warehouses.

Permission to make digital or hard copies of part or all of this work for personal or classroom use is granted without fee provided that copies are not made or distributed for profit or commercial advantage and that copies bear this notice and the full citation on the first page. Copyrights for third-party components of this work must be honored. For all other uses, contact the Owner/Author.
Copyright is held by the owner/author(s).
CIKM'15, October 19–23, 2015, Melbourne, VIC, Australia.
ACM 978-1-4503-3794-6/15/10.
http://dx.doi.org/10.1145/2806416.2806876.

DOLAP 2015 includes 8 long papers and 4 short papers, accepted out of 31 submissions, grouped into four sessions: data warehouse design, database modeling, query processing, and text processing. The topics are diverse, including multidimensional design, query processing, ontology construction, semantic data warehouses, text databases, cloud computing, energy consumption optimization, stream data, join algorithms, metadata management, ETL, array databases, and conceptual modeling, among others. The program also includes a peer-reviewed invited paper that focuses on Big Data Design by presenting the challenges associated with processing data in the "Data Lake". The invited paper talk is given by a recognized researcher from the DBMS Design community, sharing his experiences and latest investigation on data modeling for big data.

2. PAPER SUMMARY

Session 1 presents research on data warehouse design. In [7], the authors introduce a programmable Semantic ETL (SETL) framework for creating semantic data warehouses. The framework defines a target ontology based on the domain of interest, extracts data from multiple heterogeneous data sources, transforms the source data into RDF triples, loads the data into a triple store, and publishes the data on the Web as linked data. The work in [10] presents a conceptual model, Semantic Warehouse of Trajectories (SWOT), which combines a semantic trajectory data warehouse with geometrical features. The SWOT data model is the result of a consensual schema representing spatio-temporal aspects enriched with an interpretation schema (hierarchical) featuring the contextual semantic characteristics of the trajectory (e.g. type of transportation, activity, and points of interest). The authors also provide a modeling CASE tool called SWOTCASE to support the proposed model. Paper [8] revisits physical design to consider energy consumption. As such, the authors propose a methodology called Eco-DMW in the context of materialized views. This work is based on a power consumption cost model that is implemented in conjunction with PostgreSQL's cost model in order to predict query power consumption. Furthermore, the authors developed a genetic algorithm to solve the multi-objective optimization problem that results of selecting a set of views constrained by a power consumption upper bound. The outcome of the methodology is a set of views that provide the best performance within certain power consumption limits.

Session 2 includes research on Database Modeling. Especially on topics that represent emerging areas for database design. An area that has been increasing attention in the database community is that of Array Databases. In [6], the authors explore a proposal for augmenting the standard relational database language (SQL) with multidimensional array capabilities (ASQL). In particular, the authors present a comprehensive definition of ASQL with its unifying array and set integration. This proposal should lead to new challenges in conceptual modeling for array data warehouses. Likewise, our invited paper focuses on the impact of the big data wave on database design. Therefore, this paper summarizes the challenges of database design in the past, present, and future. The paper in [1] presents an overview of the evolution of the data warehouse design given the challenges of big data. These difficulties include the different storage formats, data locality (or lack thereof), denormalization, data distribution and partitioning, among others. Finally, the paper defends the idea that database management systems are migrating into polyglot systems compounded by several NoSQL tools that leave the existing modeling tool set (e.g. UML, normalization theory) useless in this context. The author concludes the paper by presenting some open questions and research opportunities.

Session 3 focuses on OLAP query processing. In [12], the authors tackle the problem of finding an efficient join algorithm for stream data. Therefore, the authors propose two algorithms, Trie join and Bitrie join, to perform semi-stream similarity join between stream data and disk relational data. Their framework evaluates efficiency and effectiveness of the proposal by showing near real-time results. Similarly, the authors in [3] propose an efficient algorithm (roNNJ) to compute the nearest neighbor join with grouping attributes and selection predicates. The proposed algorithm is not impacted by redundant fetches and index false hits since is evaluated as a new physical operator with a similar set of states to those of the traditional Sort Merge Join operator (implemented in PostgreSQL). roNNJ computes the results in a single scan of the input relations as the result of a roNNJ query tree that is not dependent on the physical organization of the fact table. Finally, the authors prove that their approach has an upper bound complexity of $n \log n$. In addition to improved join algorithms for speeding up query processing, the decision on the type of hardware deployment to run the analytical workload is crucial to achieve the target performance and cost. In [5], the authors propose the SpotADAPT framework to choose the optimal cloud deployment in systems such as Amazon Web Services (AWS). Their algorithm is based on executing only a sample of the dataset on a subset of the AWS instance types. Then the algorithm will select the best deployment given the provided time and cost models. The algorithm allows the user to select between the fastest or the cheapest deployment by a particular date.

Session 4 presents research on Text Processing. In particular, the increase of semi-structured and unstructured data warehouses has led to multiple proposals involving keyword search processing with the semantic web using OLAP techniques. In [2], the authors present GoOLAP, a system developed to identify patterns of analytical tasks in workloads of text databases by leveraging the user's search expectations to provide results. In order to identify these patterns, the proposal provides a supervised classification model (semi-supervised for classification of rare queries) to evaluate the common tasks. The authors in [9] present a visualization tool to maximize recall during keyword searches. The efficiency of the tool relies on point and aggregate views that are maintained with a set of metrics and greedy algorithms. The work in [11], the authors propose data warehousing integration techniques by employing semi-automatic ontology construction to create a target schema "on-the-fly". In order to do so, the authors provide techniques for ontology extraction, matching, and merging. The result of this work is a prototype whose output can be used as a preprocessing step for Quarry, a data integration system. Similar work on unstructured data is explored in [4], where the authors arrange micro-blogs in a hierarchical structure of concepts. In other words, the authors integrate time-aware fuzzy formal concept analysis with OLAP. The major contribution of this paper is the aggregation of measures by considering primarily the temporal dimension and computing the target cube using the remaining dimensions. The proposed approach is exemplified with a real use case.

3. REFERENCES

[1] A. Abello. Big data design. In *Proc. ACM DOLAP Workshop*, 2015.

[2] S. Arnold, A. Löser, and T. Kilias. Resolving common analytical tasks in text databases. In *Proc. ACM DOLAP Workshop*, 2015.

[3] F. Cafagna, M. Böhlen, and A. Bracher. Nearest neighbour join with groups and predicates. In *Proc. ACM DOLAP Workshop*, 2015.

[4] A. Cuzzocrea, C. Maio, G. Fenza, V. Loia, and M. Parente. OLAP analysis of multidimensional tweet streams for supporting advanced analytics. In *Proc. ACM DOLAP Workshop*, 2015.

[5] D. Kaulakiene, C. Thomsen, T. Pedersen, U. Çetintemel, and T. Kraska. SpotADAPT: Spot-Aware (re-)Deployment of Analytical Processing Tasks on Amazon EC2. In *Proc. ACM DOLAP Workshop*, 2015.

[6] D. Misev and P. Baumann. Homogenizing data and metadata retrieval in scientific applications. In *Proc. ACM DOLAP Workshop*, 2015.

[7] R. Nath, K. Hose, and T. Pedersen. Towards a programmable semantic extract-transform-load framework for semantic data warehouses. In *Proc. ACM DOLAP Workshop*, 2015.

[8] A. Roukh, L. Bellatreche, A. Boukorca, and S. Bouarar. Eco-DMW: Eco-design methodology for data warehouses. In *Proc. ACM DOLAP Workshop*, 2015.

[9] M. Sifer, Y. Watanobe, and S. Bhalla. Efficient visualisation of the relative distribution of keyword search results in a corpus data cube. In *Proc. ACM DOLAP Workshop*, 2015.

[10] M. Silva, V. Times, J. Macêdo, and C. Renso. SWOT: A conceptual data warehouse model for semantic trajectories. In *Proc. ACM DOLAP Workshop*, 2015.

[11] R. Touma, O. Romero, and P. Jovanovic. Supporting data integration tasks with semi-automatic ontology construction. In *Proc. ACM DOLAP Workshop*, 2015.

[12] G. Weber, M. Naeem, C. Lutteroth, and H. Gao. S3j: A parallel semi-stream similarity join. In *Proc. ACM DOLAP Workshop*, 2015.

DTMBIO 2015: International Workshop on Data and Text Mining in Biomedical Informatics

Min Song
Department of Library and Information Science
Yonsei University
Korea
min.song@yonsei.ac.kr

Doheon Lee
Department of Bio and Brain Engineering
KAIST
Korea
dhlee@kaist.ac.kr

Karin Verspoor
Department of Computing and Information Systems
Health and Biomedical Info. Centre
The University of Melbourne
karin.verspoor@unimelb.edu.au

ABSTRACT

Held each year in conjunction with one of the largest data management conferences, CIKM, the Ninth ACM International Workshop on Data and Text Mining in Biomedical Informatics (DTMBIO'15) is organized to bring together researchers interested in development and application of cutting-edge data management and analysis methods with a specific focus on applications in biology and medicine. The purpose of DTMBIO is to foster discussions regarding the state-of-the-art applications of data and text mining on biomedical research problems. DTMBIO'15 will help scientists understand emerging trends and opportunities in the evolving area of informatics related techniques and problems in the context of biomedical research.

Categories and Subject Descriptors

J.3 [**Life and Medical Sciences**]: Medical information systems

General Terms

Life and Medical Sciences, Bioinformatics, Health informatics, Data mining, Natural Language Processing, Algorithms, Experimentation.

Keywords

ACM proceedings, DTMBIO, biomedical text mining

1. INTRODUCTION

With the advent of high-throughput technologies and electronic biomedical data collection, biomedical researchers need to effectively manipulate data to yield research answers. The rapid development of medical and health informatics techniques is tightly coupled with developments within several fields in computer science, including data and text mining, information retrieval, information extraction and database management systems, among others. A fundamental topic of research within medical and healthcare informatics is how to make effective use of the tremendous amount of biological and biomedical data to improve the understanding of biological systems. Such data include, but are not limited to, gene and protein sequences, gene expression profiles from microarray experiments, protein-protein interactions from proteomic studies, genetic variants identified in genomic studies, clinical data such as might be collected in an electronic medical record, and information from the literature and other textual resources ranging from radiology reports and clinical narratives to social media. The need to extract, understand, integrate, and make use of information embedded in such heterogeneous data automatically effectively drives the current research in medical and health informatics. Acquiring the most useful information from this complex data and interpreting them in light of all the relevant prior knowledge remains a challenging task. The aim of the 2015 workshop is to bring together researchers in the areas of data and text mining for biomedicine, who are interested in integrating and analyzing heterogeneous, structured and unstructured data.

The call for papers attracted 16 paper submissions and 8 poster submissions, mostly from Korea and Australia, with one paper originating in the UK. Each regular paper went through a rigorous double-blinded peer review by at least 3 members of the Program Committee. Based on the referee reports, the papers were ranked according to their reviews. The program committee accepted 7 papers which will be invited to a supplement issue of BMC Decision Making and Medical Informatics and 4 papers accepted for the workshop proceedings, of which only 1 is finally included. The papers, as well as the poster abstracts, cover a variety of topics, including relation extraction and knowledge discovery from the published biomedical literature, predictive methods for a number of different molecular interactions and biological characteristics, and issues relating to biomedical data integrity, including data duplication and anonymization. We hope that these proceedings will serve as a valuable reference for researchers and developers who are interested in applying data and text mining in biomedical applications.

Permission to make digital or hard copies of part or all of this work for personal or classroom use is granted without fee provided that copies are not made or distributed for profit or commercial advantage and that copies bear this notice and the full citation on the first page. Copyrights for third-party components of this work must be honored. For all other uses, contact the Owner/Author.
Copyright is held by the owner/author(s).

CIKM'15, October 19-23, 2015, Melbourne, VIC, Australia
ACM 978-1-4503-3794-6/15/10.
http://dx.doi.org/10.1145/2806416.2806880

2. SUMMARY

Accepted papers cover various research problems in biomedical informatics. Lin et al. [1] introduce a new privacy-preserving model for spontaneous reporting systems (SRSs) that collects adverse drug events reports. Their results indicate that the SRSs records have characteristics that differ from regular healthcare records such as rare events, multiple individual records, and multi-valued sensitive attributes. Kim et al. [2] propose a new prognostic marker to predict castration-resistant prostate cancer (CRPC) that is derived from the longitudinal biomarker, prostate specific antigen (PSA). Keum et al. [3] introduce a pipeline for predicting the compound-target interaction of natural products, using sequence similarity of the target and structural similarity of the compound based on bipartite matching. Jung [4] proposes a method to compute the dissimilarity between two gene expression samples based on features that represent pathway activity patterns. Preiss and Stevenson [5] examine the contribution of word-sense-disambiguation toward narrowing down literature-based discovery. Verspoor et al. [6] evaluate the performance of the extended PKDE4J, a relation extraction system, on the Variome corpus. Joe and Nam [7] propose a method to find individual genes which associate with worse survival rate in breast cancer samples in four different data sets. Chen et al. [8] evaluate the reproducibility on a different dataset of an algorithm developed for identifying duplicate records in biological databases.

3. CONCLUSION

This workshop continues the line of DTMBIO workshops organized in conjunction with CIKM in 2006, and 2008-2014. We invite researchers and practitioners from a variety of backgrounds such as computer science, information system, information science, bioinformatics, medical informatics, and medical sciences. The main objective of the workshop will be to strengthen the cooperation within the growing community in biomedical data and text mining research, allowing lively exchange of ideas and fostering of new collaborations.

4. REFERENCES

[1] Lin, W-Y and Duen-Chuan Yang, D-C. 2015. Privacy Preserving Data Anonymization of Spontaneous ADE Reporting System Dataset. In *DTMBIO 15*.

[2] Kim, Y., Park, Y.H., Lee, J.Y, Choi, I.Y. and Yu, H.J. 2015. Discovery of Prostate Specific Antigen Pattern to Predict Castration Resistant Prostate Cancer of Androgen Deprivation Therapy. In *DTMBIO 15*.

[3] Keum, J.S., Yoo, S.Y., and Nam, H.J. 2015. Prediction of Compound-Target Interactions of Natural Products Using Large-scale Drug and Protein Information. In *DTMBIO 15*.

[4] Jung, S.W. 2015. In-silico Interaction-Resolution Pathway Activity Quantification and Application to Identifying Cancer Subtypes. In *DTMBIO 15*.

[5] Preiss, J. and Stevenson, M. 2015. The Effect of Word Sense Disambiguation Accuracy on Literature Based Discovery. In *DTMBIO 15*.

[6] Verspoor, K., Heo, G.E., Kang, K.Y. and Song, M. 2015. Extraction of fine-grained semantic relations for the Human Variome. In *DTMBIO 15*.

[7] Joe, S.B. and Nam, H.J. 2015. Prognostic Factor Analysis for Breast Cancer Using Gene Expression Profiles. In *DTMBIO 15*.

[8] Chen, Q., Zobel, J., and Verspoor, K. 2015. Evaluation of a machine learning duplicate detection method for bioinformatics. In *DTMBIO 15*.

ECol 2015: First international workshop on the Evaluation on Collaborative Information Seeking and Retrieval

Leif Azzopardi[1], Jeremy Pickens[2], Tetsuya Sakai[3], Laure Soulier[4], Lynda Tamine[4]
[1] School of Computing Science, University of Glasgow - UK
[2] Catalyst Repository Systems - USA
[3] Waseda University - Japan
[4] Université de Toulouse UPS IRIT - France
[1] Leif.Azzopardi@glasgow.ac.uk, [2] jpickens@catalystsecure.com,
[3] tetsuyasakai@acm.org, [4] {soulier,tamine}@irit.fr

ABSTRACT

Collaborative Information Seeking/Retrieval (CIS/CIR) has given rise to several challenges in terms of search behavior analysis, retrieval model formalization as well as interface design. However, the major issue of evaluation in CIS/CIR is still underexplored. The goal of this workshop is to investigate the evaluation challenges in CIS/CIR with the hope of building standardized evaluation frameworks, methodologies, and task specifications that would foster and grow the research area (in a collaborative fashion).

Categories and Subject Descriptors

H.3.3 [**INFORMATION STORAGE AND RETRIEVAL**]: Information Search and Retrieval - *Clustering, Retrieval models, Search process*

General Terms

Collaborative Information Retrieval

Keywords

Collaborative information retrieval; collaborative information seeking; evaluation

1. INTRODUCTION

The paradigm of CIS/CIR refers to methodologies and technologies that support collective-knowledge sharing within a work team in order to solve a shared complex problem [2, 3]. One main challenge in CIS/CIR is to satisfy the mutual beneficial goals of both individual users and the collaborative group while maintaining a reasonable level of cognitive effort [7]. Evaluating CIS/CIR is challenging, as there are a variety of confounding factors such as the multi-user context, the exploratory aspect of the search through multi-session search activities, the multiplicity of relevance factors, the individual vs. collective value of relevance, the search interfaces supporting the collaborative interactions. In previous work, CIS/CIR evaluation relies on simulation-based protocols [1, 4, 10], user or log-based studies [6, 8, 9] and metrics leveraging the individual vs. collaborative dimensions of search effectiveness [7]. The most common evaluation strategy is to undertake both qualitative and quantitative evaluation according to the search tasks characteristics and evaluation objectives such as cognitive effort, usability, and individual vs. collective effectiveness. However, to date and to our knowledge, although substantial research advances in the evaluation of plenty information retrieval and seeking tasks have been achieved through international evaluation campaigns such as TREC, CLEF and NTCIR [5], no standardization effort has been achieved for the evaluation of CIS/CIR. We believe therein that there is an important need to investigate the evaluation challenge in CIS/CIR with the hope of building standardized evaluation frameworks that would foster the research area. Accordingly, our workshop, called ECol 2015[1], focuses on the following research questions without being exhaustive:

- What are the relevant factors for evaluating CIS/CIR scenarios, and what are the appropriate evaluation protocols?
- What are the properties of current evaluation metrics in CIS/CIR, and to what extent these properties are adequate to measure the benefice vs. cost of collaboration?
- How to leverage between individual relevance and collective relevance within the evaluation of a CIS/CIR setting, and how to measure the satisfaction of mutual beneficial goals surrounding individual and collective relevance?
- Should the collaborative interfaces be evaluated similarly to usual search interfaces?
- How to design standard evaluation framework for CIS/CIR?

2. SCOPE

Both theoretical and practical research papers are welcome from both research and industrial communities addressing the main conference topic, but will also consider

Permission to make digital or hard copies of part or all of this work for personal or classroom use is granted without fee provided that copies are not made or distributed for profit or commercial advantage and that copies bear this notice and the full citation on the first page. Copyrights for third-party components of this work must be honored. For all other uses, contact the Owner/Author.
Copyright is held by the owner/author(s).
CIKM'15, October 19–23, 2015, Melbourne, VIC, Australia.
ACM 978-1-4503-3794-6/15/10.
http://dx.doi.org/10.1145/2806416.2806881.

[1] http://irit.fr/ECol2015/

related aspects including models, methods, techniques and examples of CIS/CIR in theory and in practice. Original and unpublished papers are welcome on any aspects including (non exhaustive list):

- CIS/CIR evaluation framework design and implementation
- System-based vs. user-based evaluation approaches for CIS/CIR
- Simulation vs. log-studies vs. user-studies for collaborative search
- Novel or extended traditional evaluation measures, test collections, methodologies of operational evaluation.
- Models and methods of and for CIS/CIR
- Impact of the collaborative session temporal synchronicity on the evaluation
- Evaluation of domain application-oriented CIS/CIR: exploratory search, travel planning, education project, legal and medical domain...
- Evaluation of specific collaborative tasks (search, sense-making, intent understanding...)
- Studies on collective relevance judging
- Studies of collaborative behavior applicable to evaluation
- Evaluation of single vs. collaborative search session
- Connections to related research in contextual and interactive information seeking and retrieval
- Evaluation Concerns and Issues: Reliability, Repeatability, Reproducibility, Replicability
- Proposed evaluation tasks and collections for CIS/CIR

3. WORKSHOP FORMAT

We propose a half-day workshop organized as follows:

- One (1) keynote given by Chirag Shah. This keynote is expected to give a general background and launch discussions around some issues dealing with evaluation in CIS/CIR.

- Four (4) oral presentations given by authors of accepted papers.

- Short talks (1-2 minutes per group) could be performed in order to present to the whole participants the discussion achievement and outline some future research directions.

4. PROGRAM COMMITTEE

Luanne Freund, University of British Columbia
Martin Halvey, University of Strathclyde, UK
Gilles Hubert, Universtity of Toulouse, FRANCE
Hideo Joho, University of Tsukuba, JAPAN
Diane Kelly, University of North Carolina, USA
Ryan Kelly, University of Bath, UK
Jian-Yun Nie, University of Montreal, CANADA
Mark Sanderson, RMIT University, AUSTRALIA
Chirag Shah, Rutgers University, USA
Ian Soboroff, NIST, USA
Elaine Toms, University of Sheffield, UK
Takehiro Yamamoto, Kyoto University, JAPAN

5. ORGANIZERS

Leif Azzopardi, School of Computing Science at the University of Glasgow - UK
Jeremy Pickens, Catalyst Repository Systems - USA
Tetsuya Sakai, Waseda University - Japan
Laure Soulier, Université de Toulouse UPS IRIT - France
Lynda Tamine, Université de Toulouse UPS IRIT - France

6. ACKNOWLEDGMENTS

We thank ELIAS fundation for their grant #5907. We also thank the authors for their contributions and our programme committee members for their timely reviews.

7. REFERENCES

[1] C. Foley and A. F. Smeaton. Synchronous collaborative information retrieval: Techniques and evaluation. In *Springer ECIR*, pages 42–53, 2009.

[2] J. Foster. Collaborative information seeking and retrieval. *Annual Review of Information Science and Technology*, 40(1), 2006.

[3] P. Hansen and K. Järvelin. Collaborative information retrieval in an information-intensive domain. *Inf. Process. Manage.*, 41(5):1101–1119, 2005.

[4] H. Joho, D. Hannah, and J. M. Jose. Revisiting ir techniques for collaborative search strategies. In *Springer ECIR*, pages 66–77, 2009.

[5] N. Kando, T. Kato, T. Sakai, D. W. Oard, and M. Sanderson. Preface from NTCIR-11 general chairs. In *Proceedings of the 11th NTCIR Conference on Evaluation of Information Access Technologies, NTCIR-11, National Center of Sciences, Tokyo, Japan, December 9-12, 2014*, 2014.

[6] J. Pickens, G. Golovchinsky, C. Shah, P. Qvarfordt, and M. Back. Algorithmic mediation for collaborative exploratory search. In *ACM SIGIR*, pages 315–322, 2008.

[7] C. Shah and R. González-Ibáñez. Evaluating the synergic effect of collaboration in information seeking. In *ACM SIGIR*, pages 913–922, 2011.

[8] C. Shah, J. Pickens, and G. Golovchinsky. Role-based results redistribution for collaborative information retrieval. *Inf. Process. Manage.*, 46(6):773–781, 2010.

[9] L. Soulier, C. Shah, and L. Tamine. User-driven system-mediated collaborative information retrieval. In *SIGIR*, pages 485–494, 2014.

[10] L. Soulier, L. Tamine, and W. Bahsoun. On domain expertise-based roles in collaborative information retrieval. *Inf. Process. Manage.*, 2014, to appear.

Eighth Workshop on Exploiting Semantic Annotations in Information Retrieval (ESAIR'15)

CIKM 2015 Workshop

Krisztian Balog
University of Stavanger
Norway
krisztian.balog@uis.no

Jeffrey Dalton
Google Research
jeffdalton@google.com

Antoine Doucet
University of La Rochelle
L3i Laboratory
France
antoine.doucet@univ-lr.fr

Yusra Ibrahim
Max Planck Institute for Informatics
Saarbrücken, Germany
yibrahim@mpi-inf.mpg.de

ABSTRACT

The amount of structured content published on the Web has been growing rapidly, making it possible to address increasingly complex information access tasks. Recent years have witnessed the emergence of large scale human-curated knowledge bases as well as a growing array of techniques that identify or extract information automatically from unstructured and semi-structured sources. The ESAIR workshop series aims to advance the general research agenda on the problem of creating and exploiting semantic annotations. The eighth edition of ESAIR sets its focus on applications. We dedicate a special "annotations in action" track to demonstrations that showcase innovative prototype systems, in addition to the regular research and position paper contributions. The workshop also features invited talks from leaders in the field. The desired outcome of ESAIR'15 is a roadmap and research agenda that guides academic efforts and aligns them with industrial directions and developments.

Categories and Subject Descriptors

H.3 [**Information Storage and Retrieval**]: H.3.1 Content Analysis and Indexing; H.3.3 Information Search and Retrieval; H.3.4 Systems and Software

Keywords

Semantic annotations; knowledge bases; complex search tasks

Permission to make digital or hard copies of part or all of this work for personal or classroom use is granted without fee provided that copies are not made or distributed for profit or commercial advantage and that copies bear this notice and the full citation on the first page. Copyrights for third-party components of this work must be honored. For all other uses, contact the Owner/Author(s). Copyright is held by the owner/author(s).
CIKM'15, October 19–23, 2015, Melbourne, Australia.
ACM 978-1-4503-3794-6/15/10.
DOI: http://dx.doi.org/10.1145/2806416.2806879.

1. OVERVIEW

Over the recent years, major search engines have redesigned their search results to accommodate semantic information, including rich search results and direct question answering. Recently, web search engines all developed large-scale entity databases, including Google's Knowledge Graph, Yahoo!'s Web Of Objects, and Bing's Satori. At the heart of these efforts is large-scale semantic annotation of both queries and documents.

The goal of the ESAIR workshop series is to create a forum for researchers interested in the application of semantic annotations for information access tasks. By semantic annotations we refer to linguistic annotations (such as named entities, semantic classes or roles, etc.) as well as user annotations (such as micro-formats, RDF, tags, etc.). ESAIR'15 continues, with a renewed group of organizers, on the path set by the previous edition(s) of the workshop: clarifying the exact role of semantic annotations in supporting complex search tasks.

Annotations come in a variety of flavors (named entities, temporal information, geo-positional markers, semantic roles, sentiment, etc.) and there is a growing repertoire of tools and techniques available for extracting these annotations automatically from text. The question then presents itself: what, if anything, is missing? We seek to answer this question by focusing on applications that are rooted in specific, real-world use cases. To further sharpen this application-oriented focus, the workshop features a dedicated "annotations in action" track for presenting innovative prototype systems. A Best Demonstration Award, sponsored by Google, is presented to the participant(s) with the most outstanding demo at the workshop.

2. PROGRAMME AND ORGANIZATION

The workshop called for regular papers (4+ pages), position papers (2+1 pages), and demo papers (4 papers), which were each reviewed by at least 3 members of the program committee. The committee was keen on selecting papers that introduce novel ideas and will stimulate discussion in the workshop. The accepted contributions cover a wide spectrum of topics related to semantic annotations and information retrieval, including: healthcare, automatic translation, semantic search, question answering, knowledge profiling, topic modeling, contextual enrichment, named entity disambiguation, temporal tagging, and semantic annotation of video content. Out of the 19 submissions, the committee accepted a total of 10 papers (5 regular, 2 position, and 3 demo papers) to be presented at the workshop. In addition to the regular paper presentations and demonstration session, the programme includes invited talks by experts in the field, which will focus on the uprising challenges in semantic information access and retrieval. The workshop is intended to be highly interactive where everyone contributes and is planned to inspire the attendees to think "outside the box." Thus, the workshop will include focused discussion sessions at which researchers with similar interests can showcase their ideas and concerns. A final wrap-up session will conclude the event with the objective to formulate critical insights into the potential of semantic annotations, the barriers to success, and specific steps to take this research forward. We continue with the tradition of earlier ESAIR editions and organize a social event for further, more informal discussions among workshop participants and other CIKM attendees.

The list of accepted contributions, corresponding resources (slides, links, etc.), and all other outcomes of the workshop are available at `http://esair.org`.

Acknowledgments

The workshop is generously supported by Google, Inc. Google sponsors the Best Demonstration Award and the social event.

LSDS-IR'15: 2015 Workshop on Large-Scale and Distributed Systems for Information Retrieval

Ismail Sengor Altingovde
Middle East Technical University (METU)
Ankara, Turkey
altingovde@ceng.metu.edu.tr

B. Barla Cambazoglu
Yahoo Labs
Barcelona, Spain
barla@yahoo-inc.com

Nicola Tonellotto
ISTI-CNR
Pisa, Italy
nicola.tonellotto@isti.cnr.it

ABSTRACT

The growth of the Web and other Big Data sources lead to important performance problems for large-scale and distributed information retrieval systems. The scalability and efficiency of such information retrieval systems have an impact on their effectiveness, eventually affecting the experience of their users and monetization as well. The LSDS-IR'15 workshop will provide space for researchers to discuss the existing performance problems in the context of large-scale and distributed information retrieval systems and define new research directions in the modern Big Data era. The workshop expects to bring together information retrieval practitioners from the industry, as well as academic researchers concerned with any aspect of large-scale and distributed information retrieval systems.

Categories and Subject Descriptors

H.3.3 [**Information Storage and Retrieval**]: Information Search and Retrieval

Keywords

Web search; large-scale information retrieval; distributed information retrieval; efficiency; performance

1. OBJECTIVES

The scalability and efficiency of large-scale and distributed information retrieval systems are known to have an impact on their effectiveness. Consequently, performance-related issues continue to be important in the context of real-life information retrieval systems. Even within research laboratory settings, the size of the standard datasets are becoming exceedingly large (e.g., ClueWeb12: 1 billion documents, 27 TB uncompressed), requiring efficient and often distributed architectures to facilitate large-scale experimentation.

Traditionally, web-scale search engines employ large and highly replicated systems, operating on computer clusters in one or few data centers. Coping with the increasing number of user requests and indexable pages requires adding more resources. However, data centers cannot grow indefinitely. Scalability problems in information retrieval have to be addressed in the near future, and new distributed applications are likely to drive the way in which people use the Web. Distributed information retrieval is the point in which these two directions converge.

The LSDS-IR workshop series provides space for researchers to discuss the above-mentioned problems and define new directions for the work on large-scale and distributed information retrieval in the modern Big Data era. LSDS-IR plays an important role in the information retrieval community as a venue where early work addressing the workshop's topics can be discussed and matured. Finally, as the scale and type of data being search continues to grow as part of the modern Big Data era, efficient yet effective retrieval can only become more important in addressing information needs in corpora too large to be structured.

As in the previous years, the LSDS-IR'15 workshop aims to bring together both information retrieval practitioners from the industry, as well as academic researchers concerned with efficient and distributed information retrieval systems. The workshop also welcomes contributions that propose different ways of leveraging diversity and multiplicity of resources available in distributed systems. The main goal of the workshop is to attract people from industry and academia to present and discuss ideas, problems, and results in the efficiency of large scale and distributed information retrieval systems. In LSDS-IR'15, we expect a participation of around 15 people, including two invited speakers.

2. PAST EDITIONS

The LSDS-IR'15 workshop continues the efforts of the following workshops organized in the past:

- P2PIR (collocated with SIGIR'05, CIKM'06, and CIKM'07).
- HDIR (collocated with SIGIR'08).
- LSDS-IR (collocated with SIGIR'07, CIKM'08, SIGIR'09, SIGIR'10, CIKM'11, WSDM'13, WSDM'14).

The recent LSDS-IR workshops hosted several well-known keynote speakers, such as Ricardo Baeza-Yates (Yahoo Labs), Abdur Chowdury (Twitter), K. Selcuk Candan (Arizona State University), Aristides Gionis (Aalto University), Marcus Fontoura (Google), Sebastiano Vigna (Universita degli Studi di Milano), Torsten Suel (NYU), and Ching-Yung Lin (IBM TJ Watson).

Permission to make digital or hard copies of part or all of this work for personal or classroom use is granted without fee provided that copies are not made or distributed for profit or commercial advantage and that copies bear this notice and the full citation on the first page. Copyrights for third-party components of this work must be honored. For all other uses, contact the Owner/Author(s). Copyright is held by the owner/author(s).
CIKM'15, October 19–23, 2015, Melbourne, Australia.
ACM 978-1-4503-3794-6/15/10.
DOI: http://dx.doi.org/10.1145/2806416.2806877.

3. SCOPE

The topics that are of interest to the workshop are as follows:

- Distributed information retrieval applications
- Applications of cloud computing to information retrieval
- Big Data techniques for information retrieval applications
- Information retrieval on large-scale web archives
- Large-scale multimedia information retrieval
- Collection selection and result merging in federated information retrieval
- Multi-site and peer-to-peer web search
- Energy-aware processing techniques for information retrieval
- Information retrieval algorithms on novel computing architectures
- Distributed web crawling
- Inverted index partitioning and replication models
- Inverted index compression
- Retrieval models for distributed information retrieval
- Efficient and scalable distributed query processing
- Learning to rank efficiently
- Caching in information retrieval systems
- Standards and benchmarks for distributed information retrieval
- Studies on the impact of search efficiency on user experience

4. REVIEW PROCESS

The workshop program includes two types of contributions in the ACM double column format: original technical contributions (6 pages) and short position papers (4 pages). Position papers are important for the success of the workshop as a way of promoting discussions upon controversial and intriguing ideas. Submitted papers undergo a peer review process, coordinated by the organizers. Each paper is reviewed by at least three reviewers. The submission and reviewing processes are handled using the EasyChair conference management system.

5. FORMAT

The workshop is structured as a full-day workshop. It will consist of several short and full paper presentations. Each accepted contribution will be presented, allowing approximately 25 minutes for long papers (plus 10 minutes for questions) and 20 minutes for short papers (plus 10 minutes for questions). There will be two invited talks, which will be given by Simon Jonassen (Cxense) and Egemen Tanin (University of Melbourne). The invited talk durations are 45 minutes (plus 15 minutes for questions).

6. PROGRAM COMMITTEE

The LSDS-IR'15 program committee has a good mix of researchers from the academia and the industry:

- Xiao Bai (Yahoo Labs)
- Fidel Cacheda (University of A Coruña)
- Ruey-Cheng Chen (RMIT University)
- Shane Culpepper (RMIT University)
- Shuai Ding (Google)
- Veronica Gil Costa (National University of San Luis)
- Simon Jonassen (Cxense)
- Rifat Ozcan (Turgut Ozal University)
- Raffaele Perego (ISTI-CNR)
- Shaolei Ren (Florida International University)
- Fabrizio Silvestri (Yahoo Labs)
- Torsten Suel (New York University)
- Jiancong Tong (Baidu)
- Christos Tryfonopoulos (University of Peloponnese)
- Rossano Venturini (University of Pisa)

7. WORKSHOP ORGANIZERS

Ismail Sengor Altingovde recently served as a PC member in SIGIR (2011, 2014 and 2015), WSDM (2013, 2014), ECIR (2012, 2013, 2014, 2015), and CIKM (2013), as well as the previous editions of LSDS-IR in 2010 and 2011, and he co-chaired LSDS-IR in 2013 and 2014. He published papers in prestigious journals, including ACM TODS, TOIS, TWEB, JASIST, IEEE Intelligent Systems, Inf. Syst. and IP&M, as well as top-tier conferences including SIGIR, WWW, and CIKM, mostly on efficiency related topics such as crawling, caching, index pruning and query processing for Web search engines.

B. Barla Cambazoglu was a co-organizer of the LSDS-IR'10, LSDS-IR'11, and LSDS-IR'14 workshops. He was also the proceedings chair for WSDM'09 and the poster and proceedings chairs for ECIR'12. He served as an area chair in SIGIR'13 and SIGIR'14. He regularly serves in the program committees of SIGIR, WWW, and KDD conferences. He has papers published in prestigious journals including IEEE TPDS, JPDC, JASIST, ACM TWEB, Inf. Syst., IP&M as well as top-tier conferences including SIGIR, CIKM, WSDM, WWW, and KDD, mainly in the areas of information retrieval and web search.

Nicola Tonellotto is a co-organizer of the LSDS-IR'13 and LSDS-IR'14 workshops. Previously, he served as a PC member and reviewer in several HPC and IR conferences. Nicola has published papers on efficiency topics in information retrieval in prestigious journals and conferences such as ACM TOIS, SIGIR, ECIR, ICTIR, WSDM. Nicola has contributed to the development of several open source software packages, such as the Terrier information retrieval platform.

NWSearch 2015 - International Workshop on Novel Web Search Interfaces and Systems

Davood Rafiei
Department of Computing Science
University of Alberta
Edmonton, Canada
drafiei@ualberta.ca

Katsumi Tanaka
Department of Social Informatics
Kyoto University
Kyoto, Japan
tanaka@dl.kuis.kyoto-u.ac.jp

ABSTRACT
Held for the first time in conjunction with the ACM International Conference on Information and Knowledge Management (CIKM), NWSearch 2015 aims to bring together researchers, developers and practitioners who are interested in pushing the search boundary on the Web and exploring more novel forms of searches, interfaces, task formulations, and result organizations and presentations. In particular, the workshop seeks to identify some of the problems and challenges facing the development of such tools and interfaces and to flourish new ideas and findings that can shape or influence future research directions and developments. The workshop organizers solicited contributions that would fall within the large spectrum of human-computer interaction in one extreme and system production and development in the other extreme.

Categories and Subject Descriptors
H.3.3 [**Information Systems**]: Information Retrieval; H.3.0 [**Information Systems**]: World Wide Web

Gen2806416.2806882s
Algorithms; Design; Human Factors; Experimentation

1. INTRODUCTION
The World Wide Web offers one of the largest and most diverse collection of documents, and this provides both challenges and opportunities in searching and mining the collection. The traditional method of searching the collection has been through using some keyword queries, browsing top few answers (referred to as "10 blue links") and sometimes navigating the links. While this simple interface is effective and serves many general needs, it is very primitive in expressing more complex tasks and search scenarios. For example, too many searches require more than one query, and once the relevant documents are found, not much else is done on those documents. The aim of this workshop is to bring together researchers, developers and practitioners who are interested in pushing the search boundary on the Web and exploring more novel forms of searches, interfaces, task formulations, and result organizations and presentations.

The workshop provides a forum for discussions on a line of research that falls in the intersection of Web search, information retrieval, database queries and human computer interaction; however it differs from more traditional forums such as SIGIR, HCI and SIGMOD and more recent ones such as CHIIR that may focus on one or two of the aforementioned areas.

2. KEYNOTES
The workshop includes two invited keynotes on topics that are very closely related to the the topic of this workshop. One keynote is given by Marti Hearst from the University of California at Berkeley; her talk is on "*Still haven't found what I'm looking for: suggestions for next generation search user interfaces*" where she explores how people engagement changes over different devices and how this should affect search interfaces. Another keynote is given by Mark Sanderson from RMIT University in Melbourne on "*Hands and eyes free search*". Mark explores the area of spoken queries and search results.

3. PAPER SUMMARY
All submitted papers went through a rigorous peer review by at least three members of the program committee members. Based on the referee reports, the PC chairs selected four papers to be included in the program. Here is a summary of the accepted papers.

In a paper by Trippas, Spina, Sanderson and Cavedon [3], the authors present a spoken conversational search system with the aim of offering an effective and efficient interactive information retrieval over a speech-only channel. Speech-based systems have had more public exposures lately with systems such as Siri and Google Now running on millions of mobile phones and handsets. This paper, in particular, focuses on result presentation where the result should be presented at a volume and pace that can be comprehended by users; unlike a text presentation where the result is rather static and can be read or browsed multiple times, the problem is more challenging when the presented result is transient and there is not much trace of the message that can be referred to later. The authors evaluate the impact of the length of spoken summaries on the effectiveness of

Permission to make digital or hard copies of part or all of this work for personal or classroom use is granted without fee provided that copies are not made or distributed for profit or commercial advantage and that copies bear this notice and the full citation on the first page. Copyrights for third-party components of this work must be honored. For all other uses, contact the Owner/Author(s). Copyright is held by the owner/author(s).
CIKM'15, October 19–23, 2015, Melbourne, Australia.
ACM 978-1-4503-3794-6/15/10.
DOI: http://dx.doi.org/10.1145/2806416.2806882

the search; they also report a break-down of the results for single-faceted and multi-faceted searches.

A paper by Gkirtzou, Papastefanatos and Dalamagas [1] studies keyword search on RDF data and the problem of mapping keyword searches to SPARQL queries. The authors report a summary of their previous work on the subject, and the steps of breaking down the problem into (1) finding a set of matches for each keyword in the RDF graph, (2) enumerating the cartesian product of the matching sets, (3) generating what is referred to as *augmented summary graph*, and (4) mapping augmented summary graphs to query graphs. The augmented summary graph represents an aggregated summary of the matching RDF data as well as the graph entries for matched elements. A query pattern graph is derived based on the shortest paths between the matched elements. The authors discuss an evaluation scheme and some findings on the effectiveness of their mappings.

Zhao, Meng, Wang and Li [4] present a method that uses encyclopedic data to provide a query understanding. The authors highlight some of the shortcomings of named entity recognizers (such as Standard NER) when applied to short texts such as queries, hence the need for mapping queries to entities in an encyclopedia or a knowledge base to understand the query semantics. The authors present a method to map keyphrases in queries to relevant entities in a knowledge base. From the entities matching a query and the categories of those entities, the authors try to build a topic model of the query. The paper uses LDA topic model in particular and report experiments on a set of queries from Sougou World Wide Web competition and a comparison with alternative methods.

Finally, Liska, Sojka and Ruzicka [2] present their work on combining text and formula queries in mathematical information retrieval. The authors report their experiments on various query relaxation strategies for queries that include both formulas matching mathematical expressions and text matching the surrounding natural language text. The query relaxation assumes a conjunction semantics and explores splitting the queries into more intermediate expressions by dropping some pieces, evaluating those expressions and merging the results. The evaluation is done based on the NTCIR-11 Math-2 Task collection and the relevance judgements provided by the organizers.

4. CONCLUSIONS

The workshop aims to provide a focus group for those who are interested in exploring novel Web search interfaces and systems and opportunities for further research and collaborations. A similar but more local workshop was organized in Japan in August 2015 by Makoto Kato from Kyoto University, Yiqun Liu from Tsinghua University and the organizers of NWSearch 2015. The organizers hope that they can continue running this workshop in future years, in conjunction with relevant venues such as the CIKM and the World Wide Web Conferences.

References

[1] K. Gkirtzou, G. Papastefanatos, and T. Dalamagas. RDF keyword search based on keywords-to-sparql translation. In *Proc. of NWSearch Workshop*, 2015.

[2] M. Liska, P. Sojka, and M. Ruzicka. Combining text and formula queries in math information retrieval: Evaluation of query results merging strategies. In *Proc. of NWSearch Workshop*, 2015.

[3] J. R. Trippas, D. Spina, M. Sanderson, and L. Cavedon. Towards a spoken conversational search system. In *Proc. of NWSearch Workshop*, 2015.

[4] K. Zhao, X. Meng, Z. Wang, and H. Li. Using encyclopedic knowledge to understand queries. In *Proc. of NWSearch Workshop*, 2015.

PIKM 2015: The 8th ACM Workshop for Ph.D. Students in Information and Knowledge Management

In conjunction with the 24th ACM Conference on Information and Knowledge Management (CIKM 2015), October 19th, 2015, Melbourne, Australia

Mouna Kacimi
Free University of
Bozen-Bolzano, Italy
Mouna.Kacimi@unibz.it

Nicoleta Preda*
Versailles University
Versailles, France
preda@prism.uvsq

Maya Ramanath
Indian Institute of Technology
– Delhi, New Delhi, India
ramanath@cse.iitd.ac.in

ABSTRACT

The PIKM workshop offers Ph.D. students the opportunity to bring their work to an international and interdisciplinary research community, and create a network of young researchers to exchange and develop new and promising ideas. Similar to the CIKM, the PIKM workshop covers a wide range of topics in the areas of databases, information retrieval and knowledge management.

Categories and Subject Descriptors

H.2.0 [**Information Systems**]: Database Management; H.2.8 [**Information Systems**]: Database Management-Database Applications—*Data Mining*; H.3.3 [**Information Systems**]: Information Storage and Retrieval-Information Search and Retrieval

General Terms

Algorithms, Design, Experimentation, Performance, Theory

Keywords

CIKM; PIKM; doctoral consortium; Ph.D. forum; dissertations; database systems; information retrieval; knowledge management; interdisciplinary work; data mining

1. INTRODUCTION

PIKM is the Ph.D. workshop of the CIKM conference. PIKM aims at giving Ph.D students the opportunity to present their work to a wide audience, receive stimulating feedback from reviewers as well as the general CIKM audience, and facilitate interactions among PhD students. The research community also benefits from this workshop: it is a forum for the discussion of fresh new ideas from young scholars.

The PIKM workshop covers topics in all areas of the general CIKM conference. This includes database query processing, semantic search, and data mining. PIKM is a well established workshop. This is the eight time the workshop is being held, after successful workshops in 2007 [13, 14], 2008 [10, 12], 2010 [9, 8], 2011 [7], 2012 [15, 6], 2013 [11], and 2014 [16] at CIKM conferences. The workshop is one of the few Ph.D. workshops in conferences to target the three tracks of databases, information retrieval and knowledge management with some emphasis on inter-disciplinary research across these tracks as well.

To offer students valuable feedback for their submissions, we formed our program committee with experts from academia and industry, including both fresh graduates and senior researchers, thereby allowing for different viewpoints on the submissions. The program committee members are from various countries across the globe, including Austria, Australia, Canada, Denmark, France, Germany, Lebanon, India, Ireland, Israel, Italy, and the United States. They have provided tough, but detailed and constructive reviews of papers submitted to the workshop, thus providing the students with useful feedback. We sincerely thank them for their efforts.

PIKM 2015 is organised as a full day workshop with four sessions including the keynote talk. This year, there were 16 submissions from 11 countries. We have selected 5 papers [1, 2, 3, 4, 5]. The selected papers address problems from three research areas: databases, knowledge management, and data mining.

2. HIGHLIGHTS OF PIKM2015

Keynote Speaker. Dr. Gerard de Melo from Tsinghua University, Beijing, China. Gerard will share his insights on "Why Researchers are Managers".

Career Development Session This year, the program will include a career development session consisting in a mentoring presentation from an experienced researcher. This session will be led by Prof. Justin Zobel from the University of Melbourne, Australia.

Best Paper Award. Based on the reviews of the program committee, two papers [1, 3] were selected as candi-

*Nicoleta Preda's work is supported in part by the research project ALODIS (PEPS FASCIDO 2015 - CNRS).

Permission to make digital or hard copies of part or all of this work for personal or classroom use is granted without fee provided that copies are not made or distributed for profit or commercial advantage and that copies bear this notice and the full citation on the first page. Copyrights for third-party components of this work must be honored. For all other uses, contact the Owner/Author(s). Copyright is held by the owner/author(s).

CIKM'15, October 19–23, 2015, Melbourne, Australia.
ACM 978-1-4503-3794-6/15/10.
DOI: http://dx.doi.org/10.1145/2806416.2806873.

dates for the best paper award. The winner will be selected based on the oral presentation given at the workshop.

Best Reviewer Award. The program committee worked very hard to provide thoughtful reviews in a very short amount of time. Among the many excellent PC members, we would particularly like to recognize the outstanding efforts of Shady Elbassuoni, Fabian Suchanek and Martin Theobald and award the best reviewer award to Shady Elbassuoni.

We plan to write a review article that summarizes the proceedings of PIKM 2015. Such articles have been published in SIGIR Forum [14], SIGKDD Explorations [12], and SIGMOD Record [8, 6] for previous PIKM workshops.

3. ACKNOWLEDGMENTS

We would like to thank our program committee members for the effort of completing the reviews in a very short period of time. This year's program committee consisted of the following members:
Shady Elbassuoni American University of Beirut, Lebanon
Roxana Horincar Télécom ParisTech, France
Katja Hose Aalborg University, Denmark
Georgiana Ifrim University College Dublin, Ireland
Gjergji Kasneci SCHUFA, Germany
Rajasekar Krishnamurty IBM Almaden, USA
Claudio Luchesse CNR, Italy
Yelena Mejova Qatar Computing Research Institute, Qatar
Sebastian Michel University of Kaiserslautern, Germany
Abhishek Mukherji Samsung Research, USA
Anisoara Nica SAP AG, Canada
Nicola Orio University of Padova, Italy
Josiane Xavier Parreira SIEMENS AG, Austria
Michal Shmueli-Scheuer IBM Haifa Research Lab, Israel
Fabian M. Suchanek Télécom ParisTech, France
Joe Tekli Lebanese American University, Lebanon
Martin Theobald Ulm University, Germany

We are also grateful to CIKM 2015 organizers for their support and help and to the CIKM workshop chairs Shane Culpepper and Chee Yong Chan for their suggestions and advice.

4. REFERENCES

[1] S. Gandhi and T. Oates and A. Boedihardjo and C. Chen and J. Lin and P. Senin and S. Frankenstein and X. Wang. A Generative Model for Time Series Discretization Based on Multiple Normal Distributions. *In PIKM '15*, 2015.

[2] S. Rathee and M. Kaul and A. Kashyap. R-Apriori : An Efficient Apriori Based Algorithm on Spark. *In PIKM '15*, 2015.

[3] J. Huang and M. Peng and H. Wang. Topic Detection for Large Scale of Microblog Stream with High Utility Pattern Clustering. *In PIKM '15*, 2015.

[4] W. Labbadi and J. Akaichi. Efficient Top-k Query Answering Through its Top-N Rewritings Using Views *In PIKM '15*, 2015.

[5] R. Chitta and A. K. Jain and R. Jin. Sparse Kernel Clustering of Massive High-Dimensional Data Sets with Large Number of Clusters *In PIKM '15*, 2015.

[6] M. Kacimi, F. M. Suchanek, and A. S. Varde. Databases, information retrieval and knowledge management: exploring paths and crossing bridges. *SIGMOD Record*, 42(3):71–74, 2013.

[7] A. Nica and F. M. Suchanek. PIKM 2011: the 4th ACM workshop for Ph.D. students in information and knowledge management. In *Proceedings of the CIKM 2011*, pages 2633–2634, 2011.

[8] A. Nica, F. M. Suchanek, and A. S. Varde. Emerging multidisciplinary research across database management systems. *SIGMOD Record*, 39(3), 2010.

[9] A. Nica and A. S. Varde, editors. *Proceedings of PIKM 2010, Toronto, Ontario, Canada, October 30, 2010*. ACM, 2010.

[10] P. Roy and A. S. Varde, editors. *Proceedings of the Second Ph.D. Workshop in CIKM, PIKM 2008, Napa Valley, California, USA, October 30, 2008*. ACM, 2008.

[11] F. M. Suchanek and A. Nica. PIKM 2013: The 6th ACM workshop for Ph.D. students in information and knowledge management. In *Proceedings of CIKM 2013*, pages 2561–2562, New York, NY, USA, 2013. ACM.

[12] A. S. Varde. Challenging research issues in data mining, databases and information retrieval. *SIGKDD Explorations*, 11(1):49–52, 2009.

[13] A. S. Varde and J. Pei, editors. *Proceedings of the First Ph.D. Workshop in CIKM, PIKM 2007, Sixteenth ACM Conference on Information and Knowledge Management, CIKM 2007, Lisbon, Portugal, November 9, 2007*. ACM, 2007.

[14] A. S. Varde and J. Pei. Advances in information and knowledge management. *SIGIR Forum*, 42(1):29–35, 2008.

[15] A. S. Varde and F. M. Suchanek. PIKM 2012: 5th ACM workshop for phd students in information and knowledge management. In *21st ACM International Conference on Information and Knowledge Management, CIKM'12, Maui, HI, USA, October 29 - November 02, 2012*, pages 2776–2777, 2012.

[16] G. de Melo and M. Kacimi and A. S. Varde PIKM 2014: The 7th ACM Workshop for Ph.D. Students in Information and Knowledge Management. In *23rd ACM International Conference on Conference on Information and Knowledge Management, CIKM 2014, Shanghai, China, November 3-7*, pages 2098–2099, 2014.

TM 2015 – Topic Models: Post-Processing and Applications Workshop

Nikolaos Aletras, Jey Han Lau, Timothy Baldwin, Mark Stevenson
University College London; King's College London; The University of Melbourne; University of Sheffield
nikos.aletras@gmail.com; jeyhan.lau@gmail.com; tb@ldwin.net; mark.stevenson@sheffield.ac.uk

ABSTRACT

The main objective of the workshop is to bring together researchers who are interested in applications of topic models and improving their output. Our goal is to create a broad platform for researchers to share ideas that could improve the usability and interpretation of topic models. We expect this will promote topic model applications in other research areas, making their use more effective.

Categories and Subject Descriptors

I.7 [**Computing Methodologies**]: Document And Text Processing

Keywords

Topic Model, Topic Modeling, Topic Coherence, Topic Evaluation, Topic Similarity, Topic Model Applications

1. INTRODUCTION

Topic modelling is a popular tool for modelling document collections and has seen applications in a variety of domains, from medical science to digital humanities. Topic models provide an effective means of extracting topics from large document collections and have the advantage that they require no supervision or document labels. While topic models can be trained automatically, judicious processing of their output is often required in applications where human users interact directly with the topics generated by a model. For example, the raw output from topic models can be difficult to interpret and consequently labels (manually assigned or automatically generated) are often added to increase readability; visualisation of the relationship between documents and topics is not intuitively obvious and its design requires thoughtful consideration. In addition, topics can contain unrelated words which may make the navigation of the document collection difficult; a typical approach to tackle this is to filter out low quality topics by computing topic coherence. This workshop aims to bring together a wide range of tools and methodologies used in post-processing the output of topic models, with the goal of improving their usability and interpretation within user applications.

Permission to make digital or hard copies of part or all of this work for personal or classroom use is granted without fee provided that copies are not made or distributed for profit or commercial advantage and that copies bear this notice and the full citation on the first page. Copyrights for third-party components of this work must be honored. For all other uses, contact the Owner/Author(s). Copyright is held by the owner/author(s).
CIKM'15, October 19–23, 2015, Melbourne, Australia.
ACM 978-1-4503-3794-6/15/10.
DOI: http://dx.doi.org/10.1145/2806416.2806875.

2. TOPICS OF INTEREST

- Topic coherence
- Extrinsic topic models evaluation
- Topic representation (generation of topic labels)
- Topic similarity
- Applications of topic models
- Visualisation of document collections with topic models (topic browsers)
- Multimodal topic models
- Data sets for evaluating topic qualities, including coherence, labels and similarity

3. ORGANISERS

- Nikolaos Aletras (University College London)
- Jey Han Lau (King's College London)
- Timothy Baldwin (The University of Melbourne)
- Mark Stevenson (University of Sheffield)

UCUI'15: The 1st International Workshop on Understanding the City with Urban Informatics

Yashar Moshfeghi, Iadh Ounis, Craig Macdonald, Joemon M. Jose, Peter Triantafillou, Mark Livingston and Piyushimita Thakuriah
University of Glasgow Glasgow, UK
{Yashar.Moshfeghi, Iadh.Ounis, Craig.Macdonald, Joemon.Jose, Peter.Triantafillou, Mark.Livingston, Piyushimita.Thakuriah}@glasgow.ac.uk

ABSTRACT

Urban Informatics aims to exploit the large quantities of information produced by modern cities in order to gain insights into how they function. These insights lay the foundation for improving the lives of citizens, by improving the efficacy and efficiency of public services, and satisfying complex information needs arising within this context. The goal of the workshop is to provide a multidisciplinary forum which brings together researchers in Big Data (BD), Information Retrieval (IR), Data Mining, and Urban Studies, to explore novel solutions to the numerous theoretical, practical and ethical challenges arising in this context. These include difficulties in collecting city data, creating data management infrastructures, and providing new effective and efficient information access techniques to as many users as possible in the context of a smart city. To foster the development of new BD and IR approaches in Urban Informatics, the workshop makes available a representative dataset of city data, including Internet-based visual (Flickr) and textual (Tweets and News) media collections. The workshop provides enormous opportunities for data scientists who wish to understand the complexities of working with city data, conduct innovative research within Urban Informatics, and build a long-term community in this emerging research area.

Categories and Subject Descriptors

H.3.3 [**Information Systems**]: INFORMATION STORAGE AND RETRIEVAL—*Information Search and Retrieval*; H.0 [**Information Systems**]: GENERAL

Keywords

Big Data, Information Retrieval, Urban Informatics, Social Sciences

1. INTRODUCTION

The proposed UCUI workshop aims to exploit the multidisciplinary nature of the CIKM conference by fostering interaction between (i) social scientists addressing topics such as urban studies and transportation planning (ii) data scientists and researchers in Data Mining, IR and/or BD working on new approaches and applications for Urban Informatics, and (iii) urban practitioners, such as smart city data SMEs or representatives of local authorities or cities. The workshop focuses on understanding urban systems, and discussing related techniques, methods and tools. We sought papers that clearly create, or utilise, such novel sources of information for urban and regional analysis.

The expected outcomes of the UCUI workshop are manyfold. In addition to generating discussion and ideas on the emerging subject of Urban Informatics, we expect that the UCUI workshop aids the construction of a long-term community in the subject of Urban Informatics and create a research roadmap for it. This roadmap is written as a report in the SIGIR forum. In addition, depending on how the "Urban Informatics Data Challenge" (see below) progresses, the intention is to submit a new task based on this to a campaign such as TREC or CLEF.

Urban Informatics Data Challenge: As part of the workshop, we are providing access to newly published datasets relating to the iMCD project of the University of Glasgow's Urban Big Data Centre. This represents a unique opportunity to facilitate the comparison of approaches across a number of heterogeneous datasets, which were simultaneously collected over a fixed period of time, from various resources, including the Internet-based visual (Flickr) and textual (Twitter and News) media collections. Authors may submit papers that use either one or many of these datasets, potentially supplemented by their own datasets. Using the provided datasets, we set up a challenge to do a "Post-hoc Event Detection" task. The task is to predict the events that are occurring in Glasgow city within a testing period. An adequate period of training data, immediately prior to the testing period, for this city was provided. The workshop organisers choose the best papers for presentation during the workshop.

2. WORKSHOP THEME AND TOPICS

The UCUI workshop focuses on four different themes within the areas of Information Retrieval and/or Big Data, as follows:

1. Theoretical, experimental, and/or methodological developments which advance the state-of-the-art in Information Retrieval and/or Big Data management for Urban Informatics;

Permission to make digital or hard copies of all or part of this work for personal or classroom use is granted without fee provided that copies are not made or distributed for profit or commercial advantage and that copies bear this notice and the full citation on the first page. Copyrights for components of this work owned by others than ACM must be honored. Abstracting with credit is permitted. To copy otherwise, or republish, to post on servers or to redistribute to lists, requires prior specific permission and/or a fee. Request permissions from Permissions@acm.org.
CIKM'15, October 19–23, 2015, Melbourne, Australia.
© 2015 ACM.
ISBN 978-1-4503-3794-6/15/10 ...$15.00.
DOI: http://dx.doi.org/10.1145/2806416.2806878

2. Novel applications of Big Data and/or Information Retrieval approaches in Urban Informatics;
3. Experiences and use cases for Big Data and/or Information Retrieval approaches in Urban Informatics; and
4. Challenges in evaluating Urban Informatics tasks and applications.

With these themes in mind, the workshop solicits high-quality original research papers in topics which include, but are not limited to:

- New theory and models for urban Information Retrieval and Big Data computing
- Ultra-high efficiency compression, coding and transmission for urban data
- System architectures, scalability and efficiency
- Personalization, recommendation and filtering of urban data
- Deep learning and cloud computing for Urban Informatics
- Information extraction, knowledge representation, and reasoning over urban data
- Information Retrieval access techniques for Urban Informatics
- Use of social media in Urban Informatics
- Spatial, temporal, and graph data mining for Urban Informatics
- Filtering, time-sensitive and real-time search
- Novel applications of Information Retrieval and Big Data approaches in Urban Informatics (e.g., healthcare, energy, transportation, safety, crime, search and retail)
- Interaction, access, and visualization of urban data
- User-based evaluation, crowdsourcing-based evaluation, click models, interaction models in Urban Informatics
- Ethics, privacy and security in Urban Informatics

2.1 Participation and Selection Process

The UCUI workshop is a one-day workshop. We welcomed two types of submissions: technical and position papers, published in the ACM DL, and not exceeding 6 pages for technical papers and 4 pages for position papers (including references and figures).

The workshop program consists of two invited keynotes and six accepted papers. All accepted papers were original and previously unpublished. They went through a double-blind review process. Each submitted paper was peer-reviewed by at least three programme committee members. The workshop organisers then examined the reviews and made final paper selections for the workshop. Authors of accepted papers were invited to present their papers at the workshop.

In addition, the workshop program includes a session on an Urban Informatics Data Challenge task where the accepted participant papers were presented as posters. The participant papers were not peer-reviewed, and are only published on the workshop website.

3. ORGANISERS' BACKGROUND

The relevant experience of the organising committee is as follows:

- Yashar Moshfeghi has near 30 peer reviewed research publications, including several publications in top-tier conferences e.g. SIGIR, WWW, and CIKM. He has served as a PC member in various IR and BD conferences including SIGIR, ECIR, CIKM, KDD, Middleware, and EDBT. He also served as a local organizer in various local and international conferences.
- Craig Macdonald has co-organised a number of well-attended workshops at major IR conferences, e.g. ECIR, WSDM and CIKM. He was workshop chair and chair-at-large for CIKM 2011, and has served on the programme committees of all major IR conferences. His research interests encapsulate expert search, learning-to-rank, as well as information access within Smart cities. He is a co-investigator of the Urban Big Data Centre at the University of Glasgow.
- Iadh Ounis has authored over 150 refereed publications on a wide range of topics, including: large-scale Information Retrieval; social media search; Big Data analytics and information access within smart cities. He has been a track coordinator at TREC Blog and Microblog tracks. He was a co-chair of ESSIR 2007, the general chair of ECIR 2008, and a general co-chair of CIKM 2011. He recently co-chaired the OSIR 2012 and iASC 2014 workshops.
- Joemon M. Jose has published over 150 journal and conference articles on a wide range of topics, including interactive Information Retrieval, multimedia search, and social media search. He has organised a number of IR-related events like ICMR 2014, ECDL 2010, as well as workshops at previous SIGIR conferences, and IR Fest in Glasgow 2005. He has been senior PC member of the SIGIR, CIKM, and ECIR conferences.
- Peter Triantafillou has published over 100 papers in the research areas including Big Data Management, Cloud Infrastructures and Computing, Distributed Databases, Information Retrieval, and Social Networks/Systems. He has served in the Technical Program Committees of 100 international conferences, and has been the PC Chair or Vice-chair in several prestigious conferences.
- Mark Livingston is a social scientist with around 40 peer reviewed research publications both in public health and urban studies. His research interests are in understanding neighbourhoods and neighbourhood dynamics, which impact active travel and pedestrian accidents. He is currently the project manager of the iMCD project of the Glasgow Urban Big Data Centre.
- Piyushimita (Vonu) Thakuriah is a Professor of Urban Studies at the University of Glasgow. She is currently the Director of the Glasgow Urban Big Data Centre. Vonu's research interests are in smart transportation and the effective use of Big Data for urban planning, policy and business innovations. She has played a leadership role in the areas of Computational Transportation Science.

4. ACKNOWLEDGMENTS

We would like to thank all authors who submitted contributions and the program committee members for their excellent work to review the papers. We are also very grateful for the invited keynote speakers for their presentations in the workshop.

Author Index

www.ingramcontent.com/pod-product-compliance
Ingram Content Group UK Ltd.
Pitfield, Milton Keynes, MK11 3LW, UK
UKHW051418290926
15471UKWH00009B/1662

9 781450 341172